THE COMMON LAW LIBRARY

PROFESSIONAL NEGLIGENCE

OTHER TITLES IN THE COMMON LAW LIBRARY

Chitty on Contracts
Clerk & Lindsell on Torts
Chitty & Jacob's Queen's Bench Forms
Bullen & Leake & Jacob's Precedents of Pleadings
Charlesworth & Percy on Negligence
Bowstead on Agency
McGregor on Damages
Phipson on Evidence
Benjamin's Sale of Goods

AUSTRALIA
Law Book Co.
Sydney

CANADA and USA
Carswell
Toronto

HONG KONG
Sweet and Maxwell Asia

NEW ZEALAND
Brookers
Wellington

SINGAPORE and MALAYSIA
Sweet and Maxwell Asia
Singapore and Kuala Lumpur

THE COMMON LAW LIBRARY

JACKSON & POWELL

ON

PROFESSIONAL NEGLIGENCE

FIFTH EDITION

LONDON
SWEET & MAXWELL
2002

First edition (1982)
Second edition (1987)
Second impression (1988)
Third edition (1992)
Second impression (1994)
Fourth edition (1997)
Fifth edition (2002)

Published in 2002 by
Sweet & Maxwell Limited
100 Avenue Road, London NW3 3PF
Computerset by Interactive Sciences Ltd, Gloucester
Printed and bound in England by
Clays Ltd, St Ives plc

A catalogue record for this book is available from the British Library

No natural forests were destroyed to
make this product; only farmed timber
was used and replanted.

ISBN 0–421–82600–2

ISBN 0-421-82600-2

9 780421 826007 >

PREFACE

This fifth edition is the first without Rupert Jackson in either of his former capacities as co-author and general editor. This follows his elevation to the High Court bench in 1998. Happily he remains in the capacity of consultant editor. The present edition, no less than previous editions, still reflects his inspiration and contribution over the years, without which even the first edition would not have appeared. His achievement continues to spur on his successors. A vale and thanks also to Iain Hughes Q.C. who was an editor of the third and fourth editions.

Professional negligence remains an expanding domain. This is a product of many factors. Predominant is the pervasive role of professionals in a services dominated economy. Also featuring large is the blame culture of our age. Professionals are perceived as having deep pockets, if not broad shoulders. A perennial problem for the courts is to devise an appropriate polity which does not impose impossibly burdensome and uninsurable potential liability and yet which satisfies public perceptions of fairness.

The classification "professional negligence" invites association with the tort of negligence, as also does the ubiquitous duty of care and skill. Conventionally, pleading and reasoning intone the *Bolam* test and liability deduced from a factual inquiry into whether the defendant failed to exercise the care and skill of a paragon of virtue, the competent like professional. This approach has tended to nurture a tort culture centred on a hindsight perception of reasonableness. The tort genie has perhaps too long escaped as to enable rebottling, however much some developments may now be rued, such as concurrent liability in contract and tort. Moreover, the tort mist sometimes provides comforting envelopment for debatable rationale in apparently deserving cases.

Nevertheless contract rather than tort provides the framework for resolving the vast majority of claims against professionals. Analysis follows the conventional course of first ascertaining the nature of the bargain as reflected in express and implied terms. Tort needs only to be considered to the extent necessary to overcome perceived obstacles arising from the contractual analysis. The latter's advantage is its focus on ascertaining contractual intention and purpose. Too often these factors are obscured when viewed through a hindsight prism of reasonableness. Too often also does concentration on the duty of care and skill obscure the difference between the required standard of performance and the required scope of performance, yet ascertainment of scope may be the key determinant of not only liability but also the extent of loss.

Statutes and statutory context continue to feature often in claims against professionals. The impact is greatest in the case of statutes imposing regulatory regimes. The panoply of devices designed to raise standards may include statutory causes of action triggered by incompetence or worse. Statutory context may be decisive in shaping or denying an alleged duty at common law.

As in other fields, the law relating to fiduciary duties, confidence and human rights arises for increasing frequent consideration in relation to professionals.

[vii]

Over the last five years since the last edition of this book no single case merits mention in the Preface aside from *Hall v. Simons* which (at long last and predictably) consigned advocates' immunity from the realm of Arcadia to the realm of Atlantis.

This edition, like the last two, is very much a "chambers" endeavour. It is invidious to highlight individuals, but the roles of Mark Cannon and Hugh Evans have been as significant as the general editors in bringing this edition to fruition. Fiona Sinclair continues as editor from the fourth edition and we welcome to the "team" of editors Christopher Gibson Q.C., David Halpern, Leigh-Ann Mulcahy, Graeme McPherson, Paul Sutherland and Ben Elkington, as well as Anneliese Day, Sian Mirchandani, Amanda Savage and Scott Allen.

The division of labour has been as follows. The book has been divided into two Parts, the first dealing with General Principles and the second with Specific Professions. Part I, now comprising seven chapters, is a much expanded version of chapter 1 originally written and edited in previous editions by Rupert Jackson. Chapter 1 (the Nature of Professions) has been edited by John Powell. Chapter 2 (Duties and Obligations) has been edited by Mark Cannon assisted by Graham Chapman on the new section on confidentiality. Mark Cannon also edited Chapters 3 (Remedies), 4 (Contribution between Defendants) and 5 (Defences), assisted by Amanda Savage. Chapter 6 (Litigation) has been edited by Hugh Evans and Fiona Sinclair. Chapter 7 (Human Rights and Professionals) is an entirely new chapter written by Leigh-Ann Mulcahy assisted by Anneliese Day.

Chapter 8 (Construction Professionals) was originally written by John Powell and also edited by him in the second edition, edited by Roger Stewart in the third and fourth editions and by Fiona Sinclair in this edition. Chapter 9 (Surveyors) was originally written by John Powell and also edited by him in the second edition, edited by Iain Hughes in the third and fourth editions and by Roger Stewart in this edition. Chapters 10 (Solicitors) and 11 (Barristers) were originally written by Rupert Jackson and also edited by him in the second edition. Both chapters have in subsequent editions, including this edition, been edited by Hugh Evans. Chapter 12 (Medical Practitioners) was originally written by Rupert Jackson and edited by him in the second and third editions, edited by Fiona Sinclair in the fourth edition and edited in this edition by Christopher Gibson, assisted by Sian Mirchandani. Chapter 13 (Financial Practitioners) is an entirely new chapter written by John Powell together with Graeme McPherson. We thank Professor Eva Lomnicka for her advice and many suggestions in relation to this chapter. Chapter 14 (Insurance Brokers) was originally written by Rupert Jackson and also edited by him in the second edition, edited by Mark Cannon in the third and fourth editions and by Ben Elkington in the present edition. Chapter 15 (Accountants and Auditors) was originally written by John Powell and edited by him in the second, third and fourth editions. The present edition has been edited by David Halpern together with John Powell. Chapter 16 (Members and managing agents at Lloyds) was written by Mark Cannon for the fourth edition and edited by Ben Elkington in the present edition. Chapter 17 (Information Technology Professionals) is an entirely new chapter written by Paul Sutherland, assisted by Scott Allen. Chapter 17 (Patent Agents) is also an entirely new chapter, written by Hugh Evans.

We two retain overall editorial responsibility for the whole book.

The law is stated as of September 30, 2001, although it has been possible to incorporate mention of some later cases. However, Chapter 13 (Financial Practitioners) has been written on the basis that the Financial Services and Markets Act 2000 is generally in force, which it is not at present but which it is expected to be with effect from December 1, 2001.

We are grateful to the staff at Sweet & Maxwell for their efficiency and care in dealing with this edition. Our thanks also to Mark O'Callaghan who assisted with research.

JOHN L. POWELL
ROGER STEWART

4 NEW SQUARE,
LINCOLN'S INN,
LONDON WC2A 3RJ
OCTOBER 31, 2001

CONTENTS

	PAGE
Preface	vii
Table of Principal Works Referred to	xxvii
Table of Cases	xxxi
Table of Statutes	cliii
Table of Statutory Instruments	clxv
Tables of CPRs	clxix
Table of Abbreviations	clxxiii

	PARA.
1. THE NATURE OF PROFESSIONS	
1. General	1–001
2. Judicial discussion	1–002
3. The focus of this book	1–004
2. DUTIES AND OBLIGATIONS	
1. Professional Liability	2–001
(a) Positive Duties	2–001
(b) Restrictions and Inhibitions	2–005
2. Contractual Liability	2–007
3. Tortious Liability	2–013
(a) The tort of negligence	2–013
(b) Theoretical basis for the duty of care	2–022
(i) Lord Atkin's approach	2–022
(ii) *Hedley Byrne*	2–024
(iii) The inclusive approach	2–026
(iv) The threefold test	2–030
(v) The exclusive approach	2–036
(vi) Extensions of *Hedley Byrne*	2–045
(vii) The co-existence of different approaches	2–050
(viii) Commonwealth approaches to duty of care issues	2–054
(ix) Analysis	2–066
(c) Particular situations	2–079
(i) Public and local authorities: duty of care and statute	2–079
(ii) Directors and employees	2–087
(iii) Sub-agents and sub-contractors	2–094
(iv) Immunity	2–097
(d) Concurrent Liability, Contracts and Tortious Duties of Care	2–100
(e) Liability to Third Parties	2–109
4. The standard of skill and care	2–116

CONTENTS

(a) The meaning of reasonable skill and care — 2–116
(b) Relevance of defendant's qualifications and experience — 2–118
(c) Formulation of the standard — 2–120
(d) Organisation offering professional services — 2–121
(e) Undertaking work of other professions — 2–122
(f) New techniques — 2–123
(g) Changes in the standard required — 2–124
5. Fiduciary obligations — 2–125
(a) The nature of fiduciary obligations — 2–125
(b) Dealing with the principal — 2–134
(c) Unauthorised profits and diversion of opportunities — 2–141
(d) Undue influence — 2–142
(i) The classes of undue influence — 2–142
(ii) Rebutting the presumption — 2–146
6. Confidentiality — 2–147
(a) Introduction — 2–147
(b) Origins of the duty of confidence — 2–148
(c) Elements of the cause of action — 2–156
(d) The continuing duty to former clients — 2–164

3. REMEDIES
1. Damages — 3–001
2. Loss of remuneration — 3–006
3. Equitable remedies — 3–009
(a) Rescission — 3–009
(b) Equitable Compensation — 3–012
(i) Compensation for loss caused by breach of fiduciary obligation — 3–012
(ii) Equitable compensation for breach of confidence — 3–015
(c) Account of profits — 3–017
(d) Injunction — 3–018
4. Interest — 3–019
(a) Interest under the Supreme Court Act 1981 — 3–019
(b) Interest under the Civil Procedure Rules — 3–023
(c) Interest in Equity — 3–024

4. CONTRIBUTION BETWEEN DEFENDANTS
1. Introduction — 4–001
2. Entitlement to contribution — 4–002
3. Liability of the person claiming contribution — 4–003
(a) Basis of liability — 4–006
(b) Meaning of "the same damage" — 4–007
4. The Claim — 4–010
(a) Matters which cannot be raised in defence to a claim — 4–010
(b) Matters which can be raised in defence to a claim — 4–011
(c) Basis of assessment of contribution — 4–012
(d) Time for bringing a claim for contribution — 4–015

5. DEFENCES
1. Exclusion or restriction of liability — 5–001
(a) The Statutory Framework — 5–003

(b) Exclusion of Liability to Third Parties   5–007
2. Limitation in Contract and Tort   5–010
  (a) The Limitation Period   5–010
  (b) Date when cause of action in contract accrues   5–014
  (c) Date when cause of action in Tort accrues   5–016
        (i) Claims against architects and engineers   5–017
       (ii) Claims against surveyors   5–035
      (iii) Claims against solicitors   5–037
       (iv) Claims against insurance brokers   5–046
        (v) Claims against financial advisers   5–048
  (d) Effect of the Latent Damage Act 1986   5–049
  (e) Special rules re Personal Injury and Death   5–056
        (i) Primary limitation periods   5–056
       (ii) Discretionary exclusion of time limit   5–064
  (f) Fraud of concealment   5–069
3. Limitation in Equity   5–079
  (a) Express application of the Limitation Act 1980   5–081
  (b) Application of the Limitation Act 1980 by Analogy   5–088
  (c) Where there is no analogy or correspondence   5–096
4. Other equitable defences: Laches and Acquiescence   5–098
  (a) Laches   5–099
        (i) Unreasonable delay   5–103
       (ii) Prejudice to the defendant or third party   5–106
      (iii) Relationship between Laches and the Limitation Act
             1980   5–108
  (b) Acquiescence   5–109
5. Contributory negligence   5–113
  (a) Contributory negligence and contract   5–115
  (b) Application to professional negligence   5–117
  (c) Methods by which plaintiffs might seek to circumvent a
       plea of contributory negligence   5–119
  (d) Attribution   5–120

6. LITIGATION
  1. Group actions   6–001
    (a) General   6–001
    (b) Professional negligence   6–002
    (c) Procedure   6–003
    (d) Costs   6–005
  2. Expert evidence   6–006
    (a) The functions of the expert witness   6–006
    (b) Cases where expert evidence is not required   6–008
    (c) The Civil Procedure Rules   6–012
    (d) Relevance and admissibility of expert evidence   6–013
          (i) The appropriate discipline   6–014
         (ii) The appropriate questions   6–015
        (iii) Appropriate qualifications and experience   6–016
         (iv) Impartiality   6–017
    (e) The single joint expert   6–019

7. HUMAN RIGHTS AND PROFESSIONALS
  1. Introduction   7–001
  2. Relevant Convention rights   7–004
    (a) Article 6   7–005
    (b) Article 8   7–013
    (c) Article 1 of Protocol No. 1   7–014
  3. Negligence and duty of care   7–019
    (a) *Z. v. United Kingdom*   7–021
    (b) Interlocutory striking out   7–023
    (c) Switch from Article 6(1) to article 13   7–024
    (d) Tort or Convention?   7–026
    (e) Claims not governed by the HRA   7–028
  4. Immunities   7–030
  5. Lawyers   7–031
    (a) Wasted costs orders   7–032
    (b) Lawyer/client confidentiality and the Convention   7–033
  6. Medical practitioners   7–036
    (a) Introduction   7–036
    (b) Relevant Articles in relation to Medical Practitioners   7–038
      (i) Article 2   7–039
      (ii) Article 3   7–042
      (iii) Article 6   7–043
      (iv) Article 8   7–044
      (v) Article 9   7–045
      (vi) Article 12   7–046
  7. Particular Issues arising under the HRA in relation to Medical
    Practitioners   7–047
    (a) Clinical negligence and the *Bolam* test   7–047
    (b) Right to treatment   7–050
    (c) Withdrawal of treatment   7–055
    (d) Consent to treatment   7–059
    (e) Right of access to confidential information   7–060
    (f) Disclosure of confidential information   7–061
    (g) Disclosure of medical records and confidentiality   7–062
    (h) Patients' complaints procedures   7–064
  8. Professional disciplinary proceedings   7–065

8. CONSTRUCTION PROFESSIONALS
  1. Introduction   8–001
    (a) The construction professions   8–001
    (b) Claims against construction professionals   8–007
    (c) Forms of building contract   8–010
      (i) The "traditional" building contract   8–011
      (ii) The "design and build" or "turnkey" contract   8–014
      (iii) Management contracts   8–016
  2. Duties   8–017
    (a) Duties to client   8–017
      (i) Contractual duties   8–017
      (ii) Duties independent of contract   8–037
    (b) Duties to third parties   8–062
      (i) The definition of the type of loss   8–068

      (ii) Recovery by third parties in respect of personal
           injury and damage to "other property"   8–078
     (iii) The general exclusionary rule adopted in England
          with regard to the recovery of economic loss   8–084
     (iv) The English exceptions to the general exclusionary
          rule   8–088
      (v) The position in Canada   8–110
     (vi) The position in Australia   8–117
    (vii) The position in New Zealand   8–120
   (viii) The position in other jurisdictions   8–122
     (ix) Problems of scope of duty   8–123
  (c) Other torts   8–130
  (d) The standard of care and skill   8–131
      (i) The ordinary competent and skilled practitioner   8–131
     (ii) General practice and knowledge as evidence of the
         standard   8–142
    (iii) Expert evidence   8–149
    (iv) Res ipsa loquitur   8–154
     (v) Codes of practice and legislation   8–156
    (vi) Knowledge of the law   8–160
   (vii) Not every error is negligence   8–163
  (viii) The specialist practitioner   8–166
    (ix) Special steps and warranty of reasonable fitness   8–168
     (x) Reliance upon specialists and delegation to them   8–175
 3. Liability for breach of duty   8–180
  (a) Examination of site   8–181
  (b) Cost estimates and budgets   8–191
  (c) Compliance with legislation, planning and building
     Control requirements and codes of practice   8–198
  (d) Design and specification   8–201
  (e) Preparation of bills of quantities   8–129
  (f) Selection of contractor and the tender process   8–220
  (g) Advice on choice and terms of a building contract   8–223
  (h) Administration of the building contract   8–226
  (i) Supervision or inspection of the works   8–236
  (j) Certification   8–250
  (k) Specialist survey   8–257
  (l) Investigation of defects   8–260
  (m) The construction professional as an expert witness   8–261
 4. Damages   8–262
  (a) The scope of the duty   8–263
  (b) Remoteness   8–267
      (i) Causation   8–268
     (ii) Foreseeability   8–278
  (c) The measure of damages   8–283
  (d) Heads of damage   8–287
      (i) Costs of rectification   8–288
     (ii) Diminution in value   8–298
    (iii) Wasted expenditure   8–300
    (iv) Excess expenditure   8–301
     (v) Underpayment   8–302

    (vi) Consequential losses   8–303
    (vii) Liability to third parties   8–305
    (vii) Personal injuries   8–306
    (ix) Inconvenience, distress and loss of amenity   8–307
  (e) Mitigation of loss   8–311
  (f) Abatement of fees   8–314
5. Shared responsibility   8–315
  (a) Apportionment of liability   8–315
  (b) Contributory negligence   8–328

9. SURVEYORS
1. General   9–007
  (a) Bases of liability   9–007
  (b) Duties to client   9–019
    (i) Contractual duties   9–019
    (ii) Duties independent of contract   9–032
  (c) Duties to third parties   9–033
    (i) General principles   9–033
    (ii) Knowledge of reliance   9–039
    (iii) Duty of mortgagee's valuer to purchaser   9–043
  (d) The standard of care and skill   9–052
    (i) Reasonable standard   9–052
    (ii) General practice and knowledge as evidence of the standard   9–054
    (iii) Not every error is negligence   9–058
    (iv) The relevance of "the bracket"   9–059
    (v) Onus of proof   9–062
  (e) Limitation of liability   9–063
  (f) Mutual valuer   9–074
2. Liability for breach of duty   9–075
  (a) Failing to carry out instructions   9–077
  (b) Insufficient knowledge or experience   9–079
  (c) Failing to inspect properly   9–082
    (i) Failing to inspect particular parts   9–083
    (ii) Failing to uncover and open up   9–084
    (iii) Failing to observe   9–090
    (iv) Limited survey   9–097
    (v) Failing to recognise   9–099
  (d) Failing to make sufficient inquiries   9–100
  (e) Failing to make proper appraisal   9–104
  (f) Inadequate report   9–107
3. Damages   9–110
  (a) Has the Claimant sustained the loss claimed?   9–112
  (b) Is the loss claimed within the scope of the Defendant's duty?   9–113
  (c) Remoteness   9–119
    (i) Causation   9–120
    (ii) Foreseeability   9–125
  (d) Measure of damages   9–128
    (i) Negligent survey or valuation for a purchaser who completes a purchase   9–130

(ii) Negligent survey or valuation for a purchaser who
withdraws from purchase before completion — 9–149
(iii) Negligent survey or valuation for lender — 9–150
(iv) Overvaluation for vendor — 9–175
(v) Undervaluation for vendor — 9–176
(vi) Other work — 9–178
(vii) Inconvenience and discomfort — 9–181
(viii) Incidental expenses — 9–190

10. SOLICITORS
  1. General — 10–001
  (a) Duties to the client — 10–004
      (i) Contractual duties — 10–004
      (ii) Tortious duties — 10–013
      (iii) Fiduciary duties — 10–016
      (iv) Trust duties — 10–034
  (b) Duties to third parties — 10–040
      (i) General — 10–040
      (ii) Liability to beneficiaries without reliance — 10–047
      (iii) Duty of care to the other side — 10–055
      (iv) Solicitors liability on undertakings — 10–065
      (v) Other liabilities — 10–075
  (c) The standard of skill and care — 10–077
      (i) The standard of reasonableness — 10–077
      (ii) General practice as evidence of reasonable skill and
           care — 10–084
      (iii) The specialist solicitor and the inexperienced
            solicitor — 10–093
      (iv) Mitigating factors — 10–096
      (v) Aggravating factors — 10–098
      (vi) General observations — 10–104
  (d) Specific defences to a claim for breach of duty — 10–106
      (i) Immunity — 10–106
      (ii) Abuse of process — 10–108
      (iii) Acting on counsel's advice — 10–116
      (iv) Acting on client's instructions — 10–123
  (e) Solicitor's liability for costs — 10–125
  (f) Exclusion or restriction of liability by contract — 10–141
  (g) Practice and procedure — 10–142
      (i) Expert evidence — 10–143
      (ii) Privilege — 10–144
  2. Liability for breach of duty — 10–146
  (a) General — 10–146
  (b) Giving wrong advice — 10–151
  (c) Failing to give advice — 10–154
  (d) Misconduct of litigation — 10–175
  (e) Misconduct of non-contentious business — 10–192
      (i) Conveyancing — 10–193
      (ii) The investment of money and claims by lenders — 10–206
      (iii) Wills — 10–218
  3. Damages — 10–225

(a) Breach of fiduciary duty and breach of trust   10–226
(b) Remoteness   10–233
    (i) Causation   10–234
    (ii) Foreseeability   10–240
    (iii) The scope of the duty   10–244
(c) Measure of damages   10–249
    (i) Date of assessment   10–250
    (ii) Credit for benefits   10–252
    (iii) Evaluation of a chance   10–256
(d) Heads of damage   10–263
    (i) Loss of opportunity to acquire or renew an interest in property   10–264
    (ii) Difference in value of property   10–268
    (iii) Loss of opportunity to bring proceedings   10–277
    (iv) Loss of opportunity to defend proceedings   10–293
    (v) Losses on loans secured by mortgage   10–294
    (vi) Loss of some other financial advantage   10–297
    (vii) Liability to third parties   10–301
    (viii) Criminal liability   10–303
    (xi) Wasted expenditure   10–304
    (x) Incidental expenses   10–309
    (xi) Physical injury, inconvenience and distress   10–310
(a) Mitigation of damage   10–316
4. Apportionment of liability   10–323
(a) Contributory negligence   10–323
(b) Apportionment of liability   10–328

11. BARRISTERS
1. General   11–001
(a) The function of a barrister   11–001
(b) Duties to clients   11–004
(c) Duties to third parties   11–006
(d) The Standard of Skill   11–008
(e) Immunity   11–009
(f) Abuse of process   11–025
(g) Liability for costs   11–026
2. Liability for breach of duty   11–036
3. Damages   11–052

12. MEDICAL PRACTITIONERS
1. General   12–001
(a) Duties to patient   12–005
    (i) Contractual duties   12–005
    (ii) Statutory duties   12–011
    (iii) Common law duty of care   12–015
(b) Duties to third parties   12–031
(c) The standard of skill and care   12–067
(d) General and approved practice   12–090
    (i) Acting in accordance with general and approved practice   12–092
    (ii) Departing from general and approved practice   12–106

(e) Expert evidence   12–111
(f) *Res ipsa loquitur*   12–117
(g) Consent to treatment   12–124
    (i) Limits to consent   12–126
    (ii) Voluntary consent   12–128
    (iii) Informed consent   12–130
    (iv) Capacity to consent   12–135
(h) Allied professions   12–149
(i) Hospitals and health authorities   12–152
(j) Apportionment of liability   12–164
(k) Lord Woolf's reforms   12–166
2. Liability for breach of duty   12–167
(a) Failing to prevent illness   12–169
(b) Failing to attend or examine a patient   12–172
(c) Wrong diagnosis   12–177
(d) Error in the course of treatment   12–186
(e) Failure of communication between hospitals or medical practitioners   12–197
(f) Failing to explain treatment or warn   12–201
(g) Mishandling of mentally disturbed patients   12–233
3. Damages   12–241
(a) Remoteness   12–242
    (i) Causation   12–243
    (ii) Foreseeability   12–282
(b) Measure of damages   12–287
    (i) Damages for personal injury   12–287
    (ii) Aggravated damages   12–288
    (iii) Damages in wrongful birth and conception claims   12–289
    (iv) Impact of the Human Rights Act 1998   12–301
    (v) Claims by unwanted disabled child   12–302
    (vi) Negligent report   12–303
    (vii) Scope of liability for economic loss   12–304

13. FINANCIAL PRACTITIONERS
1. General   13–001
(a) Scope   13–001
(b) Scheme   13–002
(c) The financial sector   13–003
(d) Regulation   13–006
(e) The 1986 Act   13–010
(f) FSMA   13–011
    (i) General   13–011
    (ii) The FSA   13–012
    (iii) The general prohibition   13–013
    (iv) The financial promotion restriction   13–015
    (v) Authorised persons   13–017
    (vi) Approved persons   13–019
    (vii) Exempt persons   13–020
    (viii) Members of professions   13–021
(g) European aspects   13–023
(h) The continuing relevance of the common law   13–024

2. Duties and liabilities 13–026
   (a) Sources 13–026
   (b) Relevant approach 13–027
   (c) Application of the FSMA regime 13–028
       (i) Regulation activities 13–029
       (ii) Financial promotion 13–031
       (iii) Investment 13–033
       (iv) Nature of the services 13–035
       (v) Status of provider of financial services 13–036
       (vi) Status of recipient of financial services 13–037
   (d) Duties and liabilities under the FSMA 13–038
   (e) Regulatory rules and the FSA Handbook 13–039
       (i) General 13–039
       (ii) The principles for businesses 13–044
       (iii) Statements of Principle and Code of Practice for
             Approved Persons 13–045
       (iv) The "Conduct of Business" sourcebook ("COB") 13–046
   (f) FSMA imposed regulatory liabilities 13–069
       (i) Liabilities related to lack of authorisation 13–070
       (ii) Liabilities related to authorised persons 13–073
       (iii) Liabilities related to EEA firms 13–079
       (iv) Liabilities related to official listing of securities . 13–080
   (g) Other statutory liabilities 13–083
       (i) Liability related to unlisted securities 13–084
       (ii) The Misrepresentation Act 1967 13–085
   (h) Contractual duties 13–089
       (i) Relevant contracts 13–089
       (ii) Regulatory requirements as to terms of business and
            customer agreements 13–09
       (iii) Incorporation of regulatory duties in contract 13–091
       (iv) Duty of care and skill 13–092
       (v) Appointed representatives 13–095
   (i) Tort based duties 13–099
   (j) Fiduciary duties 13–115
3. Breach of duty 13–117
   (a) General 13–117
   (b) Misleading promotion 13–118
4. Defences and relief 13–131
   (a) General 13–131
   (b) Limited immunity of regulators from liability in
       damages 13–132
   (c) Restriction of liability by contract 13–133
   (d) Statutory relief 13–135
5. Remedies including damages 13–136
   (a) General 13–136
   (b) Remedies available to regulators 13–137
       (i) Grounds for application to court 13–138
       (ii) Persons against whom orders available 13–141
       (iii) Orders available 13–143
       (iv) The FSA's extra-judicial power to require
            restitution 13–148

      (v) The FSA Enforcement manual   13–149
  (c) Remedies available to private litigants   13–150
      (i) Rescission of contract induced by
         misrepresentation   13–151
      (ii) Recovery of money or property paid under
         agreements made by or through unauthorised
         persons   13–152
      (iii) Damages or compensation   13–157
  6. Shared responsibility   13–167
  (a) Contributory negligence   13–167
  (b) Contribution   13–168
  7. The process of resolving claims   13–169
  (a) Ombudsman   13–170
  (b) Compensation scheme   13–190
  (c) Parallel proceedings   13–205

14. INSURANCE BROKERS
  1. General   14–001
  (a) Duties to client   14–010
      (i) Contractual duties   14–010
      (ii) Duties independent of contract   14–014
  (b) Duties to third parties   14–017
      (i) Duties to insurers   14–018
      (ii) Duties to other third parties   14–025
  (c) The standard of skill and care   14–032
  2. Liability for breach of duty   14–036
  (a) Failing to effect insurance   14–038
  (b) Effecting insurance, but not on the terms specified by the
      client   14–043
  (c) Effecting insurance which does not meet the client's
      requirements   14–046
  (d) Failing to exercise discretion reasonably   14–057
  (e) Failing to act with reasonable speed   14–059
  (f) Failing to disclose material facts to the insurers   14–060
  (g) Making a misrepresentation to the insurers   14–069
  (h) Failing to keep the client properly informed as to the
      existence or terms of cover   14–074
  (i) Failing to give proper advice   14–081
  3. Damages   14–086
  (a) Remoteness   14–087
  (b) Causation   14–088
      (i) Intervening error or omission of the claimant   14–089
      (ii) Where the claimant would not have been insured in
         any event   14–097
      (iii) Where the required insurance would not have been
         granted if the full facts had been known   14–109
  (c) Foreseeability   14–113
      (i) Measure of damages   14–114
      (ii) Contributory negligence   14–126

15. ACCOUNTANTS AND AUDITORS

  1. Introduction   15–001
  2. Duties   15–008
    (a) The statutory context   15–009
       (i) Companies legislation: the company audit   15–010
      (ii) Regulatory statutes relating to the financial sector   15–025
     (iii) Whistle-blowing   15–030
    (b) Duties to client   15–031
       (i) Contractual duties   15–031
      (ii) Duty in tort   15–037
     (iii) Fiduciary duties   15–038
    (c) Duties to third parties   15–045
       (i) Overview   15–045
      (ii) *Caparo*   15–053
     (iii) Factors which may be relevant   15–062
     (iv) Categories of advisee   15–073
      (v) Policy considerations: duplication of remedies   15–087
     (vi) The Contracts (Rights Against Third Parties) Act 1999   15–088
     (vii) The Human Rights Act 1998   15–089
    (d) The standard of skill and care   15–090
       (i) General   15–090
      (ii) Auditing   15–093
    (e) Limitation of liability   15–100
  3. Liability for breach of duty   15–102
    (a) Auditing   15–102
       (i) Planning, control and recording   15–103
     (iii) Accounting and internal control systems   15–106
     (iii) Evidence   15–108
     (iv) Reporting   15–113
    (b) Other breaches of duty   15–117
  4. Damages   15–120
    (a) Remoteness   15–121
       (i) Causation   15–121
      (ii) Foreseeability   15–131
    (b) Measure of damages   15–132
    (c) Heads of damage   15–135
       (i) Lost investment or advance   15–136
      (ii) Overpayment   15–137
     (iii) Moneys wrongly paid out   15–138
     (iv) Defalcations by director or employee   15–139
      (v) Costs of fresh audit and investigations   15–140
     (vi) Avoidance of double recovery   15–141
     (vii) Tax advice and returns   15–143
    (viii) Late notices and returns   15–144
     (ix) Negligent advice   15–145
    (d) Contributory negligence and contribution   15–146
    (e) Failure to mitigate   15–152
    (f) Statutory relief   15–153

16. MEMBERS AND MANAGING AGENTS AT LLOYD'S
  1. General   16–001
    (a) Lloyd's of London   16–001
      (i) The old regime   16–004
      (ii) The current regime   16–006
      (iii) Regulation   16–007
      (iv) The LMX spiral in the 1980s   16–009
    (b) Duties to client   16–010
      (i) Contractual duties   16–010
      (ii) Duties independent of contract   16–012
      (iii) Fiduciary duties   16–015
    (c) Duties to third parties   16–016
  2. The standard of care   16–020
  3. Liability for breach of duty   16–023
    (a) Members' agent—failure to advise adequately as to syndicate participation   16–025
    (b) Managing agent—failure to plan properly   16–030
    (c) Managing agent—unjustified departure from plan   16–037
    (d) Managing agent—failure to obtain adequate reinsurance   16–038
      (i) Deciding what reinsurance cover to seek   16–039
      (ii) Choosing the reinsurer   16–046
      (iii) Maintaining commercial viability   16–050
      (iv) Obtaining valid reinsurance   16–052
    (e) Managing agent—negligent underwriting of individual risks   16–053
    (f) Managing agent—inadequate supervision of active underwriter   16–057
    (g) Managing agent—negligent in relation to reinsurance to close   16–058
  4. Damages   16–060
    (a) Remoteness   16–061
    (b) Causation   16–062
    (c) Foreseeability   16–071
    (d) Measure of damages   16–072
      (i) Members' agents—consequences of failure to advise adequately as to syndicate participation   16–073
      (ii) Losses caused by negligent underwriting   16–077

17. INFORMATION TECHNOLOGY PROFESSIONALS
  1. General   17–001
    (a) Standard software   17–002
    (b) Bespoke and modified standard software   17–004
    (c) The nature of software   17–005
    (d) Software as goods   17–007
    (e) Services or goods?   17–008
    (f) Nature of the service   17–010
    (g) Implied warranties at common law   17–013
  2. Duties   17–014
    (a) Duties to client   17–014
      (i) Bespoke software   17–014
      (ii) Modified standard software   17–023

(iii) Communication of client's purpose 17–031
(iv) Implementation and testing 17–036
(v) The importance of co-operation between the parties 17–038
(vi) Duties of support 17–044
(vii) Staff training 17–023
(viii) User's operation manual 17–046
(ix) Implied terms of reasonable skill and care 17–047
(x) Common law duty of care 17–051
(xi) Supply of standard/modified standard software: consultant or supplier? 17–052
(xii) Negligent misstatements 17–055
(xiii) Collateral contract 17–056
(xiv) Advice on computer systems 17–057
(xv) Grant of quiet possession: "time-bombs" 17–059
(b) Duties other than to client 17–061
(i) Common law liability to third parties 17–061
(ii) The Consumer Protection Act 1987 17–072
(iii) "Safety-critical" information 17–078
3. Standard of care and breach 17–079
(a) Standard of care 17–079
i. Contracts for services 17–079
ii. Contracts for sale/supply of goods 17–082
(b) "Bugs" and "bedding in"—inevitable defects and software 17–085
(c) The time when the obligation of fitness for purposes arises 17–090
(d) The time when the obligation ceases 17–092
(e) "State of the art" defence 17–094
4. Causation 17–095
5. Remedies 17–098
(a) Contract 17–099
(b) Repudiation: when possible? 17–100
(c) Acceptance: when deemed? 17–101
(d) Time of the essence? 17–102
(e) "Reliance loss" and "expectation loss": election necessary? 17–106
(f) *Quantum*: difficulties in calculation 17–112
(g) Tort 17–116
6. Exclusion and limitation of liability 17–118
7. Duty to mitigate 17–124
8. Contributory negligence 17–126
9. Limitation 17–131

18. PATENT AGENTS AND TRADE MARK ATTORNEYS
1. General 18–001
(a) The function of a patent agent 18–001
(b) The function of a trade mark attorney 18–006
(c) Duties to clients 18–008
(d) Duties to third parties 18–009
(e) The standard of skill 18–010

CONTENTS

    (f) Immunity   18–012

    (g) Liability for costs   18–013

    (h) Privilege   18–014

  2. Liability for breach of duty   18–015

  3. Damages   18–020

PAGE

Index   1237

TABLE OF PRINCIPAL WORKS REFERRED TO

Anderson, A.J., Bickford-Smith, S., Palmer, N.E., Redmond-Cooper, R., *Emden's Construction Law* (8th ed., revised 1990 with updates) Cited as *Emden*

Aronson, M. and Whitmore, H., *Public Torts and Contracts* (Law Book Co. Ltd, Australia, 1982)

Atiyah, P.S., *The Rise and Fall of Freedom of Contracts* (Clarendon Press, 1979)

Bar of England and Wales, *Code of Conduct* (6th ed.)

Bean, *Fiduciary Obligations and Joint Ventures* (Clarendon Press, Oxford, 1995)

Billins, Roger, *Solicitors' Duties and Liabilities* (Sweet & Maxwell 1999)

Birks, P, *The Fiduciary Relationship=Doctor and Patients: Wrongs and Remedies in the Twenty-First Century*(1996)

Bowstead. See Reynolds, FMB

Burrows, *Solving the Problem of Concurrent Liability: Understanding the Law of Obligations* (Hart Publishing, 1998)

Charlesworth & Percy. See Percy, Judge R.A.

Chitty. See Guest, A.G.

Clarke, M.A., *The Law of Insurance Contracts* (2nd ed., Lloyd's of London Press, 1994)

Clerk & Lindsell. *See* Dias, R.W.M.

Cooke, Lord, *The Rights of Spring: The Law of Obligations, Essays in Celebration of John Fleming* (editors Cane and Stapleton) (Clarendon Press, 1998)

Copinger & James on Copyright

Cross, Sir Rupert, *Precedent in English Law* (3rd ed., Oxford University Press, 1977)

Dahrendorf, R, *Defence of the English Professions, Journal of the Royal Society of Medicine, Vol.77, p.178* (March 1984)

Day, *Multi-Party Actions* (LAG 1995)

Denning, The Right Hon. Lord, *The Discipline of Law* (Butterworths, 1979)

Devlin, *The Judge and Case Law: The Judge* (1979)

Dias, R.W.M. (general editor), *Clerk & Lindsell on Torts* (18th ed., Sweet & Maxwell, 1995) Cited as *Clerk & Lindsell*

Dingwall and Lewis (editors) *The Sociology of the Professions* (Macmillan, 1983)

Durkheim, E, *Professional Ethics and Civil Morals* (Greenwood Press, 1983)

Emden. See Anderson, AJ

Encyclopaedia of Information Technology Law

Evans H, *Lawyer's Liabilities* (2nd ed)/1st ed

Finn, Professor, *Commercial Aspects of Trusts and Fiduciary Obligations* (McKendrick editor)

Finn, *Fiduciary Obligations* (The Law Book Company Ltd, Australia, 1977)
Flenley and Leech *Solicitor's Negligence* (Butterworths 1999)

Giesen, D., *Comparative legal developments: Decision-Making and Problems of Incompetence* (Grubb, A, 1994)
Goff & Jones, *The Law of Restitution* (5th Ed. 1998)
Gower, L.C.B, Professor, *Review of Investor Protection* (Cmnd 9125)
Guest, AG (general editor), *Chitty on Contracts* (Sweet & Maxwell 28th ed.) Cited as *Chitty*
Guide to the Professional Conduct of Solicitors. See Law Society, *Guide to the Professional Conduct of Solicitors* (8th ed. 1999)
Gurry, *Breach of Confidence* (Claredon Press, Oxford, 1984) *Gurry*

Halsbury's Laws of England (4th ed., Butterworths)
Hart, H.L.A. and Honore, T., *Causation in the Law* (2nd Ed., Clarendon Press, 1985)
Hodges, *Multi-Party Actions* (Oxford 2001)
Hodgin, R.W. *Insurance Intermediaries: Law and Regulation* (looseleaf, Lloyd's of London Press)
Hollander & Salzedo, *Conflict of Interest & Chinese Walls* (Sweet & Maxwell, 2000)
Holmes, OW, *The Common Law* (Little, Brown & Co., 1881)
Holyoak & Allen, *Civil Liability for Defective Premises* (1982)
Howard, M.N., Crane, P., Hochberg, D.A. (editors), *Phipson on Evidence* (Sweet & Maxwell 15th ed.)
Hudson. See Wallace, I.N. Duncan.
Hudson, AA, *Building, Engineering and Shipbuilding Contracts* (4th ed. 1914, Sweet & Maxwell) Cited as *Hudson's Building Contracts*
Hudson's Building Contracts. See Hudson, AA

Johnson, T.J., *Professions and Power* (Macmillan, 1972)

Keating. May, Sir Anthony
Kemp, DA, McI (general editor) The Quantum of Damages (Looseleaf, Sweet & Maxwell) Cited *Kemp & Kemp*
Kemp & Kemp. See Kemp, DA, McI
Kennedy, Professor I and Grubb, A., *Medical Law* (1998 ed., Butterworths) Cited as *Kennedy and Grubb*
Kennedy and Grubb. See Kennedy, Professor I
Kerly's Law of Trade Marks and Tradenames (13th ed 2001)
Kiln, Robert, *Reinsurance in Practice* (3rd ed., Witherby & Co., 1991)

Law Society, *Guide to the Professional Conduct of Solicitors* (8th ed. 1999)
Lester & Pannick's *Human Rights Law & Practice* (Butterworths)
Likierman, Professor Andrew, *Professional Liability. Report of the Study Teams* (HMSO, 1989)
Lindley & Banks on Partnership (1995)
Lloyd's *Information Technology Law* (2nd ed)
Lomnicka, E.Z. and Powell, J.L., *Encyclopedia of Financial Services Law* (looseleaf, Sweet & Maxwell)

McGee, A., *Limitation Periods* (Sweet & Maxwell, 3rd ed., 1998)
MacGillvray and Parkington. See Parkington, M.
McGregor. See McGregor, H,
McGregor, H., *McGregor on Damages* (Sweet & Maxwell 16th ed.) Cited
  McGregor
McKendrick (editor) *Commercial Aspects of Trust and Fiduciary Obligations*
  (Clarendon Press, Oxford, 1992)
Mann, Professor F.A., *The Legal Aspect of Money* (4th ed., Oxford University
  Press, 1982)
Markesinis, Auby, Coester-Waltjen and Deakin. *Tortious Liabiluity of Statutory
  Bodies,* (Hart Publishing, Oxford and Portland, Oregon, 1999)
Martin, C.R.A., *Law Relating to Medical Practice* (Pitman Medical Publishing
  Co. Ltd)
May, Sir Anthony, Williamson, A and Uff, J., *Keating on Building Contracts* (7th
  ed) Cited as *Keating*
Meagher, Gummow & Lehane, *Equity, Doctrine and Remedies* (3rd Ed., Butter-
  worths, 1992)
Morse, G. (principal editor), *Palmer's Company Law* (looseleaf, Sweet & Max-
  well 25ed.). Cited as *Palmer*
Mulcahy, L. (editor) *Human Rights & Civil Practice* (Sweet & Maxwell:
  2001)
Mulcahy's *Human Rights and Civil Practice. See* Mulcahy, L.

Palmer. See Morse, G.
Parkington, M. (general editor), *MacGillivray and Parkington on Insurance Law*
  (9th ed., Sweet & Maxwell)
Percy, Judge R.A. and Walton, C., *Charlesworth & Percy on Negligence* (9th ed.,
  Sweet & Maxwell, 1996) Cited as *Charlesworth & Percy*
Phipson on Evidence. See Howard, M.N.
Pollock on Tort (13th ed.)
Powell, J.L., *Issues and Offers of Company Securities: The Stock Exchange
  Markets-The New Regimes* (Sweet & Maxwell 1988)
Powell, *Professional and client: the duty of care: Wrongs and Remedies in the
  Twenty-first Century* ((editor Birks) Clarendon Press (1996))
Power, M.J. and Harris, N.H., *Medical Negligence* (Butterworths, 1999) Cited as
  Powers and Harris
Powers and Harris. See Power M J.

Reed: *Computer Law* (3rd Ed)
Reynolds, FMB, *Bowstead on Agency* (16th ed., Sweet & Maxwell, 1995) Cited
  as *Bowstead*
Rose, F.D., *Consensus ad Idem* (Sweet & Maxwell, 1996)
Rowland, D. & Macdonald, E. *Information Technology Law* (2nd ed Butter-
  worths)

Salzedo, *Conflict of Interest and Chinese Walls* (Sweet & Maxwell 2000)
Silverman, F, *The Law Society's Conveyancing Handbook*
Simpson, *Professional Negligence and Liability*
Snell, *Equity* (13/30th ed., Sweet & Maxwell, 2000)
Spry, *Equitable Remedies* (5th ed, Sweet & Maxwell, 1997)
Stroud's Judicial Dictionary (6th ed)

Tawney, RH *The Acquisitive Society* (Harvester Press 1982)
Terrell, *Law of Patents* (15th edn. 2000)
Toulson & Phipps, *Confidentiality* (Sweet & Maxwell 2nd 1996) Cited as *Toulson & Phipps*
Treitel, *Contract* (10th ed.)

Wade, *Administrative Law* (6th ed.)
Wallace. I.N. Duncan, *Hudson's Building and Engineering Contracts* (11th ed) Cited as *Hudson*
Williams, Granville, *Joint Torts and Contributory Negligence* (Stevens & Sons, 1951)
Woolf, Lord, *Access to Justice* (HMSO, 1996, July 1996)
Wright, Lord, *The Study of Law* (1938) 54 L.Q.R. 185
Wurtzburg and Mills, *Building Society Law* (Looseleaf, Stevens & Sons)

Zander, *Legal Services for the Community* (MT Smith 1978)

TABLE OF CASES

PARA.

115 Place Co-op. Housing Assn. v. Burke (1994) 116 D.L.R. (4th) 657, CA (BC) 10–72

33246 B.C. Ltd v. 0909 Management Inc. (2000) 80 B.C.L.R. (3d) 299, CA (BC) 10–230

347671 B.C. Ltd v. Blaikie (2001) 2 C.C.L.T. (3d) 290, Sup Ct (BC) 10–61

789538 Ontario Ltd v. Gambin Associates (1999) 27 R.P.R. (3d) 210 10–332

A (A Minor), Re (1988) 10 Fam.L. 339; *The Times*, February 25 1988, CA 10–121

A (Children) (Conjoined Twins: Medical Treatment) (No.1), Re; *sub nom.* A (Children) (Conjoined Twins: Surgical Separation), Re [2001] Fam. 147; [2001] 2 W.L.R. 480; [2000] 4 All E.R. 961; [2001] 1 F.L.R. 1; [2000] 3 F.C.R. 577; [2000] H.R.L.R. 721; [2001] U.K.H.R.R. 1; 9 B.H.R.C. 261; [2000] Lloyd's Rep. Med. 425; (2001) 57 B.M.L.R. 1; [2001] Crim. L.R. 400; [2001] Fam. Law 18; (2000) 150 N.L.J. 1453; *The Times*, October 10, 2000; *The Independent*, October 3, 2000, CA 7–41

A (Mental Patient: Sterilisation), Re; *sub nom.* A (Medical Treatment: Male Sterilisation), Re; R-B (A Patient) v. Official Solicitor; RB (Male Patient: Sterilisation), Re [2000] 1 F.L.R. 549; [2000] 1 F.C.R. 193; [2000] Lloyd's Rep. Med. 87; (2000) 53 B.M.L.R. 66; [2000] Fam. Law 242; (2000) 97(2) L.S.G. 30; *The Times*, March 15, 2000, CA 12–142, 12–144

A (Minors) (Conjoined Twins: Separation). *See* A (Children) (Conjoined Twins: Medical Treatment) (No.1), Re.

A v. C (No.1); *sub nom.* A & B v. C, D, E, F, G and H (No.1) [1981] Q.B. 956 (Note); [1981] 2 W.L.R. 629; [1980] 2 All E.R. 347; [1980] 2 Lloyd's Rep. 200, QBD (Comm Ct) 13–146

—— v. National Blood Authority; *sub nom.* Hepatitis C Litigation, Re [2001] 3 All E.R. 289; [2001] Lloyd's Rep. Med. 187; *The Times*, April 4, 2001; *The Daily Telegraph*, April 3, 2001, QBD 6–01, 12–14, 12–226

AB v. South West Water Services Ltd; Gibbons v. South West Water Services Ltd [1993] Q.B. 507; [1993] 2 W.L.R. 507; [1993] 1 All E.R. 609; [1993] Env. L.R. 266; [1993] P.I.Q.R. P167; (1993) 143 N.L.J. 235; [1992] N.P.C. 146; *The Times*, November 26, 1992; *The Independent*, November 18, 1992, CA 12–288

—— v. Tameside and Glossop H.A. [1997] 8 Med.L.R. 91; (1997) 35 B.M.L.R. 79; [1997] P.N.L.R. 140; (1996) 15 Tr. L.R. 78; (1996) 93(44) L.S.G. 30; *The Times*, November 27, 1996, CA 12–22, 12–116, 12–158, 12–159

AB Marintrans v. Comet Shipping Co. Ltd; Shinjitsu Maru No.5, The [1985] 1 W.L.R. 1270; [1985] 3 All E.R. 442; [1985] 1 Lloyd's Rep. 568; (1986) 83 L.S.G. 43, QBD (Comm Ct) 5–115

ABB Power Construction Ltd v. Norwest Holst Engineering Ltd (2000) 2 T.C.L.R. 831; (2001) 17 Const. L.J. 246, QBD (T&CC) 8–340

ABB Zantingh Ltd v. Zedal Building Services Ltd [2001] B.L.R. 66; [2001] E.G.C.S. 9, QBD (T&CC) 8–340

ADT v. Binder Hamlyn [1996] B.C.C. 808, QBD 15–63, 15–65, 15–72, 15–77, 15–79, 15–92, 15–110, 15–112

AGC (Advances) Ltd v. R Lowe Lippman Figdor & Franck (1990) 4 A.C.S.R. 337, Sup Ct (Vic) 15–82, 15–136

A.H.A. v. X [2001] 2 F.C.R. 634; [2001] Lloyd's Rep. Med. 349; *The Independent*, June 25, 2001 (C.S), Fam Div 7–63

PARA.

AJ Bekhor & Co. Ltd v. Bilton [1981] Q.B. 923; [1981] 2 W.L.R. 601; [1981] 2 All E.R. 565; [1981] 1 Lloyd's Rep. 491; [1981] Com. L.R. 50; 125 S.J. 203, CA 13–146

A&J Fabrications (Batley) Ltd v. Grant Thornton (A Firm) (No.2) [2000] B.P.I.R. 1; [1999] Lloyd's Rep. P.N. 863; [1999] P.N.L.R. 811; (1999) 96(31) L.S.G. 41; (1999) 143 S.J.L.B. 213; *The Times*, August 5, 1999, Ch D 10–43

AMF International v. Magnet Bowling [1968] 1 W.L.R. 1028; [1968] 2 All E.R. 789; 66 L.G.R. 706; (1968) 112 S.J. 522, QBD 8–14, 8–131, 8–249, 8–250, 8–279

AM&S Europe v. Commission of the European Communities. *See* Australian Mining & Smelting Europe Ltd v. Commission of the European Communities (Case 155/79).

AS James Pty Ltd v. CB Duncan [1970] V.R. 705 5–115

AWA Ltd v. Daniels t/a Deloitte Haskins & Sells; *sub nom.* Daniels v. Anderson (1992) 7 A.C.S.R. 759, on appeal (1995) 16 A.C.S.R. 607 .... 15–111, 15–112, 15–153

Aaron's Reefs v. Twiss [1896] A.C. 273, HL (UK-Irl) 13–118

Abacus Cities Ltd, Re [1987] 1 W.W.R. 755, QB (Alberta) 10–61

Abbas v. Kenney [1996] 7 Med.L.R. 47; (1996) 31 B.M.L.R. 157, QBD 12–183

Abbey National Mortgages plc v. Key Surveyors Nationwide Ltd [1996] 1 W.L.R. 1534; [1996] 3 All E.R. 184; 80 B.L.R. 52; 53 Con. L.R. 93; [1996] P.N.L.R. 120; [1996] 2 E.G.L.R. 99; [1996] 33 E.G. 88; [1996] E.G.C.S. 23; [1996] N.P.C. 14; (1996) 72 P. & C.R. D1, CA 9–06, 9–102

Abbey National plc v. Clive Travers & Co. [1999] Lloyd's Rep. P.N. 753; [1999] P.N.L.R. 819, CA 10–145

—— v. David Prosser & Co. [2001] P.N.L.R. 15, Ch D 10–145

—— v. Solicitors Indemnity Fund Ltd [1997] P.N.L.R. 306, QBD 10–39

Abbott v. Strong [1998] 2 B.C.L.C. 420; *The Times*, July 9, 1998, Ch D 15–71

Aberdeen Railway Co. v. Blaikie Brothers (1854) 1 Macq. 461 2–135

Aberdeen Town Council v. Aberdeen University (1877) 2 App.Cas. 544 .... 2–140, 3–09

Abrams v. Abrams and Woodford & Ackroyd [1997] C.L.Y. 384, DR (Winchester) 10–62

Abraxas Computer Services Ltd v. Rabin Leacock Lipman [2000] E.G.C.S. 70; [2000] N.P.C. 63, QBD 10–259, 10–265, 10–273

Absolute Rentals Ltd v. Glencor Enterprises Ltd [2000] C.I.L.L. 1637 8–343

Ackbar v. CF Green & Co. Ltd [1975] Q.B. 582; [1975] 2 W.L.R. 773; [1975] 2 All E.R. 65; [1975] 1 Lloyd's Rep. 673; 119 S.J. 219, QBD 5–13

Ackers v. Wigan Health Authority [1991] 2 Med.L.R. 232 [1983] 2 All E.R. 245 12–80

Acmanne v. Belium (1983) 40 D.R. 251 7–59

Acrecrest Ltd v. WS Hattrell & Partners [1983] Q.B. 260, CA; affirming (1979) 252 E.G. 1107; [1980] J.P.L. 172 .... 8–191, 8–281

Acton v. Graham Pearce & Co. [1997] 3 All E.R. 909, Ch D 10–106, 10–110, 10–113, 10–181, 10–260, 10–280

Adams v. Rhymney Valley D.C. (2001) 33 H.L.R. 41; (2001) 3 L.G.L.R. 9; [2000] Lloyd's Rep. P.N. 777; [2001] P.N.L.R. 4; [2000] 3 E.G.L.R. 25; [2000] 39 E.G. 144; [2000] E.G.C.S. 94; (2000) 150 N.L.J. 1231; [2000] N.P.C. 83; *The Times*, August 11, 2000; *The Independent*, October 23, 2000 (C.S), CA 8–150, 8–151, 8–210

Adams Holden & Pearson v. Trent R.H.A. (1989) 47 B.L.R. 34; 47 B.L.R. 39, CA 8–28

Adams-Eden Furniture Ltd v. Kansa General International Insurance Co. (1996) 113 Man.R.(2d) 142, CA (Manitoba) 14–19, 14–24

Adamson, Ex p. (1878) 8 Ch.D. 807 3–11

PARA.

Addis v. Gramophone Co. Ltd [1909] A.C. 488; [1908–10] aaler 1; 78 L.J.K.B.
1122; 101 L.T. 466, HL 8–292, 9–181

Advent Systems Ltd v. Unisys Corp., 925 F 2d 670, CA (US) 17–07

Agneessens v. Belgium (App. No.12164/86) (1988) 58 D.R. 63 7–16

Aiken v. Stewart Wrightson Members Agency Ltd [1996] 2 Lloyd's Rep. 577,
CA; affirming [1995] 1 W.L.R. 1281; [1995] 3 All E.R. 449; [1995] 2
Lloyd's Rep. 618; *The Times*, March 8, 1995, QBD (Comm Ct) 2–51, 2–106,
8–59, 14–61, 14–65, 16–12, 16–17, 16–52, 16–70, 16–80

Aikmac Holdings Ltd v. Loewen (1993) 86 Man.R. (2d) 56, QBD (Manitoba) 10–286

Airedale NHS Trust v. Bland [1993] A.C. 789; [1993] 2 W.L.R. 316; [1993] 1 All
E.R. 821; [1993] 1 F.L.R. 1026; [1994] 1 F.C.R. 485; [1993] 4 Med.L.R. 39;
[1993] Fam. Law 473; (1993) 143 N.L.J. 199; *The Times*, February 5, 1993;
The Independent, February 5, 1993; *The Guardian*, February 5, 1993, HL 12–09,
12–69, 12–99, 12–139, 12–145

Aït-Mouhoub v. France (2000) 30 E.H.R.R. 382; [1998] H.R.C.D. 976, ECHR 7–07

Akedian Co. Ltd v. Royal Insurance Australia Ltd (1999) 1 V.R. 80, Sup Ct
(Vic) 14–60, 14–64, 14–65, 14–69, 14–117, 14–121

Albert, Prince v. Strange (1849) 1 De.G & Sm. 652; (1849) 1 Mac. & G. 25 2–148,
2–150

Alberta Workers' Compensation Board v. Riggins (1993) 95 D.L.R. (4th) 532,
CA (New Brunswick) 10–286

Albrighton v. Royal Prince Alfred Hospital [1979] 2 N.S.W.L.R. 165, Sup Ct
(NSW) 12–90

—— v. Royal Prince Alfred Hospital [1980] 2 N.S.W.L.R. 542 12–205

Alcoa Minerals of Jamaica Inc. v. Broderick [2000] 3 W.L.R. 23; [2000] B.L.R.
279; (2000) 2 T.C.L.R. 850; [2000] Env. L.R. 734; (2000) 144 S.J.L.B. 182;
The Times, March 22, 2000, PC (Jam) 8–284, 8–295, 8–315, 14–121

Alcock v. Chief Constable of South Yorkshire; *sub nom.* Jones v. Wright; Penk v.
Wright; Jones v. Chief Constable of South Yorkshire; Copoc v. Chief
Constable of South Yorkshire [1992] 1 A.C. 310; [1991] 3 W.L.R. 1057;
[1991] 4 All E.R. 907; [1992] P.I.Q.R. P1; (1992) 89(3) L.S.G. 34; (1991)
141 N.L.J. 166; (1992) 136 S.J.L.B. 9; *The Times*, November 29, 1991; *The
Independent*, November 29, 1991; *The Guardian*, December 11, 1991, HL 2–75,
12–34, 12–35, 12–36

Aldrich v. Norwich Union Life Insurance Co. Ltd (formerly Norwich Union Life
Insurance Society); Norwich Union Life Insurance Society v. Qureshi;
Norwich Union Life Insurance Co. Ltd v. Qureshi [1999] 2 All E.R. (Comm)
707· CA; affirming [1998] C.L.C. 1605; [1999] Lloyd's Rep. I.R. 263, QBD
(Comm Ct) 13–119

—— v. Norwich Union Life Insurance Co. Ltd [1998] C.L.C. 1621; [1999]
Lloyd's Rep. I.R. 276, Ch D 13–119

Alexander v. Cambridge Credit Corp. Ltd (1985) 10 A.C.L.R. 42 15–121

—— v. Cambridge Credit Corp. Ltd (1987) 9 N.S.W.L.R. 310 15–123

—— v. Mercouris [1979] 1 W.L.R. 1270; [1979] 3 All E.R. 305; (1979) 252 E.G.
911; 123 S.J. 604, CA 8–45

Alexander Turnbull & Co. Ltd v. Cruickshank and Fairweather (1905) 22 R.P.C.
521, IH 18–20, 18–23

Alfred James Dunbar v. A&B Painters Ltd and Economic Insurance Co. Ltd and
Whitehouse & Co. [1986] 2 Lloyd's Rep. 38, CA; affirming [1985] 2
Lloyd's Rep. 616, QBD 14–14, 14–72, 14–90, 14–106, 14–112

Alfred McAlpine & Son (Pty) Ltd v. Transvaal Provincial Administration [1974]
(3) S.A.L.R. 506 8–14

Ali v. Courtaulds Textiles Ltd [1999] Lloyd's Rep. Med. 301; (2000) 52
B.M.L.R. 129; *The Times*, May 28, 1999, CA 5–58

PARA.

Al Kandari v. JR Brown & Co. [1988] Q.B. 665; [1988] 2 W.L.R. 671; [1988] 1
All E.R. 833; [1988] Fam. Law 382; (1988) 85(14) L.S.G. 50; (1988) 138
N.L.J. 62; (1988) 132 S.J. 462, CA 10–62, 10–63, 10–74

All Lift Consultants Ltd v. Adam Crane Service (1980) Ltd (1988) 88 A.R. 208,
QBD (Alberta) 14–46

Allan v. Greater Glasgow Health Board, 1998 S.L.T. 580; (1993) 17 B.M.L.R.
135, OH 12–230, 12–289

Allan Jacobbson v. Sweden (No.2) (App. No.16970/90), February 19, 1998 7–06

Allcard v. Skinner (1887) L.R. 36 Ch.D. 145, CA 2–143, 2–144, 2–145, 5–97, 5–105,
5–106

Allen v. Allen (1968) 112 S.J. 965, DC 10–183

——— v. Bloomsbury H.A. [1993] 1 All E.R. 651; [1992] P.I.Q.R. Q50; [1992] 3
Med.L.R. 257, QBD 12–289, 12–292

——— v. Bone (1841) 4 Beav. 493; 49 E.R. 429 10–176

——— v. Clark (1863) 7 L.T. 781 .... 10–193, 10–301

——— v. Ellis & Co. [1990] 1 E.G.L.R. 170; [1990] 11 E.G. 78 .... 9–108, 9–186

——— v. Gulf Oil Refining Ltd [1981] A.C. 1001; [1981] 2 W.L.R. 188; [1981] 1
All E.R. 353; [1981] J.P.L. 353; 125 S.J. 101, HL 2–81

——— v. Sir Alfred McAlpine & Sons Ltd; Bostic v. Bermondsey & Southwark
Group Hospital Management Committee; Sternberg v. Hammond [1968] 2
Q.B. 229; [1968] 2 W.L.R. 366; [1968] 1 All E.R. 543; 112 S.J. 49; 112 S.J.
72, CA 10–187

——— v. Unigate Dairies Ltd. See Ridehalgh v. Horsefield.

Alliance & Leicester Building Society v. Chopra [1994] N.P.C. 52, CA 10–174

——— v. Edgestop Ltd; Alliance & Leicester Building Society v. Dhanoa; Alliance
& Leicester Building Society v. Samra [1999] Lloyd's Rep. P.N. 868, Ch
D 10–35, 10–229, 10–327

——— v. Edgestop Ltd (Application for Leave); Alliance & Leicester Building
Society v. Dhanoa; Alliance & Leicester Building Society v. Samra; Mercan-
tile Credit Co. Ltd v. Lancaster; Alliance & Leicester Building Society v.
Hamptons, Transcript LTA 94/5856/B, CA; affirming [1993] 1 W.L.R. 1462;
[1994] 2 All E.R. 38; [1994] 2 E.G.L.R. 229; [1993] E.G.C.S. 93; [1993]
N.P.C. 79, Ch D 5–118, 9–10, 13–100

——— v. J&E Shepherd [1995] G.W.D. 11–608, OH 9–06, 9–93, 9–108

Allied Finance and Investment Ltd v. Haddow & Co. [1983] N.Z.L.R. 22 10–57

Allied Maples Group Ltd v. Simmons & Simmons [1995] 1 W.L.R. 1602; [1995]
4 All E.R. 907; [1996] C.L.C. 153; 46 Con. L.R. 134; [1955–95] P.N.L.R.
701; (1995) 145 N.L.J. 1646; [1995] N.P.C. 83, CA 3–05, 8–287, 8–288, 9–176,
10–258, 10–259, 10–260, 10–261, 11–55, 12–256, 12–257, 12–260,
12–272, 13–160, 14–112, 15–87, 15–133, 15–134, 18–20, 18–21

Allied Trust Bank Ltd v. Edward Symmons & Partners [1994] 22 E.G. 116;
[1993] E.G.C.S. 163; [1993] N.P.C. 134; [1994] 1 E.G.L.R. 165, QBD 9–22,
9–58

Allin v. City and Hackney H.A. [1996] 7 Med.L.R. 167, CC 12–22

Allison v. Clayhills [1904–07] All E.R. 500; (1908) 97 L.T. 709 ...... 2–131, 2–144, 10–17

——— v. Rayner (1827) 7B. & C. 441; 1 Man. & Ry.K.B. 241; 6 L.J.O.S.K.B. 85;
108 E.R. 788 10–165

Al Nakib Investments (Jersey) Ltd v. Longcroft [1990] 1 W.L.R. 1390; [1990] 3
All E.R. 321; [1991] B.C.L.C. 7; [1990] B.C.C. 517; (1990) 87(42) L.S.G.
37; (1990) 140 N.L.J. 741; *The Times*, May 4, 1990; *The Independent*, May
10, 1990; *Financial Times*, May 18, 1990, Ch D 13–81, 13–108, 15–78

Al-Sabah v. Ali; *sub nom.* Al-Sabah v. Al Hawaz; Al-Sabah v. Brickwood,
Transcript A3/1999/0374, A3/1999/0375, CA; reversing [1999] E.G.C.S.
11; (1999) 96(5) L.S.G. 38; *The Independent*, January 27, 1999, Ch D 10–92

PARA.

Al Saudi Banque v. Clarke Pixley (A Firm) [1990] Ch. 313; [1990] 2 W.L.R. 344; [1989] 3 All E.R. 361; (1989) 5 B.C.C. 822; [1990] B.C.L.C. 46; [1989] P.C.C. 442; [1989] Fin. L.R. 353; (1990) 87(10) L.S.G. 36; (1989) 139 N.L.J. 1341; *The Times*, August 4, 1989; *The Independent*, August 25, 1989; *Financial Times*, August 8, 1989; *The Daily Telegraph*, August 14, 1989, Ch D 15–69, 15–82, 15–136

Amerena v. Barling (1995) 69 P. & C.R. 252; [1993] E.G.C.S. 111; [1993] N.P.C. 90, CA; reversing [1993] E.G.C.S. 28, QBD 10–250, 10–269, 10–275

Amersfort Ltd v. Kelly Nichols & Blayney [1996] E.G.C.S. 156, Ch D 10–160

Anderson v. Elsworth (1861) 3 Giff. 154; 30 L.J.Ch. 922; 4 L.T. 822; 7 Jur.(N.S.) 1047; 9 W.R. 888; 66 E.R. 363 10–166

—— v. Forth Valley Health Board, 1998 S.L.T. 588; 1998 S.C.L.R. 97; (1998) 44 B.M.L.R. 108; 1998 Rep. L.R. 3; 1997 G.W.D. 39–2016, OH 12–289

Andrew v. Kounnis Freeman [1999] 2 B.C.L.C. 641; [2000] Lloyd's Rep. P.N. 263, CA 15–47, 15–51, 15–67, 15–84

Andrew Master Hones Ltd v. Cruickshank and Fairweather [1981] R.P.C. 389, CA [1979] F.S.R. 268; [1980] R.P.C. 16, Ch D 2–118, 18–10, 18–17, 18–20

Andrews v. Hawley (1857) 26 L.J. Ex. 323 10–121

—— v. Mowbray (1805–07) Wils.Ex. 71 .... 2–134, 2–136

—— v. Schooling [1991] 1 W.L.R. 783; [1991] 3 All E.R. 723; 53 B.L.R. 68; 26 Con. L.R. 33; (1991) 23 H.L.R. 316; (1991) 135 S.J. 446; *The Times*, March 21, 1991, CA 8–44, 8–47

Aneco Reinsurance Underwriting Ltd (In Liquidation) v. Johnson & Higgins Ltd [2000] 1 All E.R. (Comm) 129; [1999] C.L.C. 1918; [2000] Lloyd's Rep. I.R. 12; [2000] Lloyd's Rep. P.N. 1; [2000] P.N.L.R. 152, CA; affirming in part [1998] 1 Lloyd's Rep. 565; *The Times*, November 14, 1997, QBD (Comm Ct) 3–03, 10–236, 14–61, 14–68, 14–71, 14–110, 14–120, 14–128

Anglia Commercial Properties v. South Bedfordshire D.C. (1984) 1 Const. L.J. 39, OH 8–181, 8–190

Anglia Hastings & Thanet Building Society v. House & Son [1955–95] P.N.L.R. 209, QBD 9–10, 10–207, 10–331

Anglia Television Ltd v. Reed [1972] 1 Q.B. 60; [1971] 3 W.L.R. 528; [1971] 3 All E.R. 690; 115 S.J. 723, CA 10–305, 17–105, 17–106, 17–108

Anglo African Merchants Ltd v. Bayley; Exmouth Clothing Co. Ltd v. Bayley [1970] 1 Q.B. 311; [1969] 2 W.L.R. 686; [1969] 2 All E.R. 421; [1969] 1 Lloyd's Rep. 268; 113 S.J. 281, QBD (Comm Ct) 14–03

Anglo Group plc v. Winther Browne & Co. Ltd; *sub nom.* Winther Brown & Co. Ltd v. Anglo Group plc, 72 Con. L.R. 118; [2000] I.T.C.L.R. 559; [2000] Masons C.L.R. 13; (2000) 144 S.J.L.B. 197, QBD (T&CC) 6–14, 8–155, 17–38, 17–40, 17–41, 17–42, 17–127

Anns v. Merton L.B.C.; *sub nom.* Anns v. Walcroft Property Co. Ltd [1978] A.C. 728; [1977] 2 W.L.R. 1024; [1977] 2 All E.R. 492; 75 L.G.R. 555; (1977) 243 E.G. 523; (1988) 4 Const. L.J. 100; [1977] J.P.L. 514; (1987) 84 L.S.G. 319; (1987) 137 N.L.J. 794; 121 S.J. 377, HL 2–18, 2–27, 2–29, 2–30, 2–35, 2–38, 2–39, 2–43, 2–52, 2–54, 2–60, 2–66, 2–84, 5–19, 8–71, 8–72, 8–73, 8–74, 8–88, 8–89, 8–94, 8–95, 8–112, 8–113, 8–116, 8–119, 8–124, 10–42, 10–47, 10–58, 15–48

Anthony v. Wright (Investments: Auditing) [1995] B.C.C. 768; [1995] 1 B.C.L.C. 236; *The Independent*, September 27, 1994, Ch D 15–86

Antonelli v. Allen [2001] Lloyd's Rep. P.N. 487, Ch D 10–147

—— v. Wade Gery Farr, *The Times*, December 29, 1992, QBD 11–33

Antoniades v. United Kingdom (1990) 64 D.R. 232 7–30

Apatu v. Peach Prescott & Jamieson [1985] 1 N.Z.L.R. 50 .... 10–100, 10–261, 10–322

Appleby v. Walsall H.A. [1999] Lloyd's Rep. Med. 154, QBD 5–58

Applegate v. Moss; *sub nom.* Archer v. Moss [1971] 1 Q.B. 406; [1971] 2 W.L.R. 541; [1971] 1 All E.R. 747; 3 B.L.R. 1; (1970) 114 S.J. 971, CA 5–70

PARA.

Appleton v. Garrett [1996] P.I.Q.R. P1; [1997] 8 Med.L.R. 75; (1997) 34
   B.M.L.R. 23, QBD 12–124, 12–133, 12–288
Appo v. Barker [1981] 50 F.L.R. 198, Sup Ct (Northern Territory) 10–282
Aquaculture Corp. v. New Zealand Green Mussel Co. Ltd [1990] 3 N.Z.L.R. 299,
   at 301 per Cooke P. 2–154
Arab Bank plc v. John D Wood (Commercial) Ltd; Arab Bank plc v. Browne
   [2000] 1 W.L.R. 857; [2000] Lloyd's Rep. I.R. 471; [2000] Lloyd's Rep.
   P.N. 173; [1999] E.G.C.S. 133; (1999) 96(47) L.S.G. 30; (2000) 144 S.J.L.B.
   6; [1999] N.P.C. 134; The Times, November 25, 1999, CA 9–53, 9–57, 9–59,
                                 9–61, 9–97, 9–105, 9–121, 9–122, 9–160, 9–172
Arbiter Group plc v. Gill Jennings & Every [2001] R.P.C. 4; [2000] Lloyd's Rep.
   P.N. 669; [2000] P.N.L.R. 680, CA 10–88, 10–148, 18–19
Arbuthnott v. Feltrim Underwriting Agencies Ltd [1995] C.L.C. 437, QBD
   (Comm Ct) 16–30, 16–31, 16–33, 16–34, 16–37, 16–40, 16–41, 16–42, 16–44,
                           16–45, 16–51, 16–55, 16–57, 16–71, 16–78, 16–81
—— v. Feltrim Underwriting Agencies Ltd (No.2) [1995] C.L.C. 1150, QBD
   (Comm Ct) 16–78, 16–79
—— v. Feltrim Underwriting Agencies Ltd (In Liquidation) (No.3) [1996] C.L.C.
   714, QBD (Comm Ct) 16–78, 16–79
Archer v. Hickmotts (Evidence) [1997] P.N.L.R. 318, CC 6–08, 10–142
Arenson v. Arenson. See Arenson v. Casson Beckman Rutley & Co.
—— v. Casson Beckman Rutley & Co.; sub nom. Arenson v. Arenson [1977]
   A.C. 405; [1975] 3 W.L.R. 815; [1975] 3 All E.R. 901; [1976] 1 Lloyd's
   Rep. 179; 119 S.J. 810, HL 5–04, 2–97, 8–106, 8–253, 9–04, 15–117
Argento v. Italy (1999) 28 E.H.R.R. 719, ECHR 7–06
Argyll, Duchess of v. Beuselinck [1972] 2 Lloyd's Rep 172, Ch D 2–116, 2–118,
                              10–83, 10–93, 10–149, 10–162, 14–33
Argyll, Margaret Duchess of v. Duke of Argyll [1967] Ch. 302; [1965] 2 W.L.R.
   790; [1965] 1 All E.R. 611, Ch D 2–154
Arklow Investments Ltd v. Maclean [2000] 1 W.L.R. 594; (2000) 144 S.J.L.B. 81,
   PC (NZ) 2–129, 2–154, 2–156
Armagas Ltd v. Mundogas SA; Ocean Frost, The [1986] A.C. 717; [1986] 2
   W.L.R. 1063; [1986] 2 All E.R. 385; [1986] 2 Lloyd's Rep. 109; (1986) 83
   L.S.G. 2002; (1986) 130 S.J. 430, HL 13–104
Armitage v. Brewer and Knott (1932) 77 Acct.L.R. 28 .... 15–31, 15–94, 15–139
—— v. Palmer (1960) 175 E.G. 315, CA 8–165, 8–192
—— v. Paynter Construction Ltd [1999] 2 N.Z.L.R 535 .... 2–132, 10–24
Armstrong v. Jones (1869) 4 C.P.D. 6; cited in Hudson's Building Contracts (4th
   ed., 1914), Vol. 2, p.6; Hudson (10th ed., 1970) 8–133, 8–253, 8–290
Arndt v. Smith [1996] 7 Med.L.R. 108, CA (BC); reversing [1996] 7 Med.L.R.
   35, Sup Ct (BC) 5–13, 12–29, 12–54, 12–55, 12–203, 12–231, 12–264, 12–269
Arthur E Green & Co. v. Central Advance and Discount Corporation Ltd (1920)
   63 Acct.L.R. 1 15–112
Arthur JS Hall & Co. v. Simons; sub nom. Harris v. Scholfield Roberts & Hall;
   Barratt v. Ansell (t/a as Woolf Seddon); Barratt v. Woolf Seddon; Cockbone
   v. Atkinson Dacre & Slack; Harris v. Scholfield Roberts & Hill [2000] 3
   W.L.R. 543; [2000] 3 All E.R. 673; [2000] B.L.R. 407; [2000] E.C.C. 487;
   [2000] 2 F.L.R. 545; [2000] 2 F.C.R. 673; [2001] P.N.L.R. 6; [2000] Fam.
   Law 806; [2000] E.G.C.S. 99; (2000) 97(32) L.S.G. 38; (2000) 150 N.L.J.
   1147; (2000) 144 S.J.L.B. 238; [2000] N.P.C. 87; The Times, July 21, 2000;
   The Independent, July 25, 2000, HL 2–77, 2–97, 7–30, 7–31, 9–04, 10–107,
                     10–108, 10–109, 10–110, 10–111, 10–112, 11–08, 11–09, 11–14,
                                 11–15, 11–25, 11–40, 11–51, 11–55, 18–12
Arthur Young & Co. v. WA Chip & Pulp Co. Pty Ltd. See WA Chip & Pulp Co.
   Pty. Ltd v. Arthur Young & Co.

PARA.

Ashcroft v. Mersey R.H.A. [1985] 2 All E.R. 96, CA; affirming [1983] 2 All E.R. 245, QBD 12–80, 12–193

Ashingdane v. United Kingdom; Series A, No.93;(1985) 7 E.H.R.R. 528, ECHR 7–07

Ashton v. Philip Conway Thomas & Co. (1939) B.W.C.C. 246 10–277

—— v. Wainwright [1936] 1 All E.R. 805; 154 L.T. 399; 80 S.J. 346; 100 J.P. 195; 52 T.L.R. 372; 34 L.G.Rev. 193 .... 10–156, 10–303

Aslan v. Clintons (1984) 134 N.L.J. 584 10–166

Associated Provincial Picture Houses Ltd v. Wednesbury Corp. [1948] 1 K.B. 223; [1947] 2 All E.R. 680; 63 T.L.R. 623; 112 J.P. 55; 45 L.G.R. 635; [1948] L.J.R. 190; 177 L.T. 641; 92 S.J. 26, CA 2–84

Association X v. United Kingdom (1978) 14 D.R. 31 7–50

Assured Advances Ltd v. Ashbee & Co. [1994] E.G.C.S. 169, QBD 9–61

Astley v. Austrust Ltd [1999] Lloyd's Rep. P.N. 758; (1999) 161 A.L.R. 155, HC (Bar) 5–113, 5–115, 10–15, 10–324

Ata v. American Express Bank Ltd, *The Times*, June 26, 1998, CA 13–116, 13–129, 13–134, 13–159, 13–160

Atkins v. Atkins [1993] E.G.C.S. 54, Ch D 10–199

Atkins (GW) Ltd v. Scott (1991) 7 Const. L.J. 215, CA 8–292

Atlas Ceiling & Partition Co. Ltd v. Crowngate Estates (Cheltenham) Ltd, Transcript HT–00–32, QBD (T&CC) 8–340

Att.-Gen. v. Blake [2001] 1 A.C. 268; [2000] 3 W.L.R. 625; [2000] 4 All E.R. 385; [2000] 2 All E.R. (Comm) 487; [2001] I.R.L.R. 36; [2000] E.M.L.R. 949; (2000) 23(12) I.P.D. 23098; (2000) 97(32) L.S.G. 37; (2000) 150 N.L.J. 1230; (2000) 144 S.J.L.B. 242; *The Times*, August 3, 2000; *The Independent*, November 6, 2000 (C.S), HL; affirming [1998] Ch. 439; [1998] 2 W.L.R. 805; [1998] 1 All E.R. 833; [1998] E.M.L.R. 309; (1998) 95(4) L.S.G. 33; (1998) 148 N.L.J. 15; (1998) 142 S.J.L.B. 35; *The Times*, December 22, 1997; *The Independent*, December 19, 1997, CA 2–125, 2–133, 2–154, 2–164, 3–01

—— v. Clarendon (1810) 17 Ves.Jun. 491 2–135

—— v. Dudley (1915) C.Coop. 146 2–135

—— v. Emerson (1889) 24 Q.B.D. 56, CA 10–67

—— v. Guardian Newspapers Ltd (No.1); *sub nom.* Spycatcher: Guardian/ Observer Discharge; Attorney General v. Observer Ltd; Attorney General v. Times Newspapers [1987] 1 W.L.R. 1248; [1987] 3 All E.R. 316; [1989] 2 F.S.R. 81; (1987) 84 L.S.G. 2689; (1987) 137 N.L.J. 785; (1987) 131 S.J. 1122, HL 2–151

—— v. Guardian Newspapers Ltd (No.2); Attorney General v. Observer Ltd (No.2); Attorney General v. Times Newspapers Ltd (No.2) [1990] 1 A.C. 109; [1988] 3 W.L.R. 776; [1988] 3 All E.R. 545; [1989] 2 F.S.R. 181; (1988) 85(42) L.S.G. 45; (1988) 138 N.L.J. 296; (1988) 132 S.J. 1496; *The Times*, October 14, 1988; *The Independent*, October 14, 1988, HL 2–147, 2–150, 2–154, 2–156, 2–160, 2–162, 3–11, 3–17, 13–166

Att.-Gen. of Hong Kong v. Reid [1994] 1 A.C. 324; [1993] 3 W.L.R. 1143; [1994] 1 All E.R. 1; (1993) 143 N.L.J. 1569; (1993) 137 S.J.L.B. 251; [1993] N.P.C. 144; *The Times*, November 12, 1993; *The Independent*, November 24, 1993, PC (NZ) 10–22

Attard v. Samson, 98 E.G. 121; 116 N.L.J. 640; (1966) 110 S.J. 249; *The Times*, March 23, 1966 .... 10–100, 10–322, 10–165

Atwell v. Michael Perry & Co.; *sub nom.* Atwell v. Perry & Co. [1998] 4 All E.R. 65; [1998] P.N.L.R. 709; *The Times*, July 27, 1998, Ch D 11–14

Atzori v. Dr Chan King Pan [1999] 3 H.K.L.R.D. 77 12–196

Aubrey Jacobus & Partners v. Gerrard, June 1981, unreported 8–198, 8–199, 8–221, 8–232

PARA.

Auburn Municipal Council v. ARC Engineering Pty Ltd [1973] 1 N.S.W.L.R.
513 .... 8–291, 8–294

Auckland Area Health Authority v. Att.-Gen. [1993] 1 N.Z.L.R. 235, HC
(NZ) 12–145

Aurum Investments Ltd v. Avonforce Ltd (In Liquidation) [2001] Lloyd's Rep.
P.N. 285; (2001) 17 Const. L.J. 145, QBD (T&CC) 8–14, 8–251, 8–325

Austcan Investments Pty. Ltd v. Sun Alliance Insurance Ltd (1992) 57 S.A.S.R.
343 .... 14–43, 14–80

Austin Hall Building Ltd v. Buckland Securities Ltd [2001] B.L.R. 272, QBD
(T&CC) 8–342

Australia v. John Fairfax & Sons Ltd (1980) 147 C.L.R. 39, HC (Aus) 2–154

Australia and New Zealand Banking Group Ltd v. Cattan, august 2, 2001,
unreported, QBD (Comm Ct) 13–120, 13–125, 13–127, 13–134, 13–159

Australian Mining & Smelting Europe Ltd v. Commission of the European
Communities; sub nom. AM&S Europe v. Commission of the European
Communities (Case 155/79) [1983] Q.B. 878; [1983] 3 W.L.R. 17; [1983] 1
All E.R. 705; [1982] E.C.R. 1575; [1982] 2 C.M.L.R. 264; [1982] F.S.R.
474; (1983) 127 S.J. 410; The Times, May 20, 1982, ECJ 7–34

Austrust Pty Ltd v. Astley (1993) 60 S.A.S.R. 354, Sup Ct (Aus) 10–165

Auto Concrete Curb Ltd v. South Nation River Conservation Authority [1993] 3
S.C.R. 201, Sup Ct (Ont) 8–117

Auty v. National Coal Board [1985] 1 W.L.R. 784; [1985] 1 All E.R. 930; (1985)
82 L.S.G. 1782; (1985) 129 S.J. 249; The Times, April 3, 1984, CA 3–20

Avco Financial Services v. Holstein (1980) 109 D.L.R. (3d) 129 9–100

Avon Insurance plc v. Swire Fraser Ltd [2000] 1 All E.R. (Comm) 573; [2000]
C.L.C. 665; [2000] Lloyd's Rep. I.R. 535, QBD (Comm Ct) 13–87

Avonale Blouse Co. Ltd v. Williamson & Geo. Town (1947–48) 81 Ll. L. Rep.
492, KBD 14–38, 14–42

Axa Equity & Law v. Goldsack & Freeman [1994] 1 E.G.L.R. 175; [1994] 23
E.G. 130; [1994] E.G.C.S. 34, QBD 9–58

Aylwin v. Aylwin [1902] P. 203; 71 L.JU.P. 130; 87 L.T. 142, PDAD 10–219, 10–220

B (A Minor) (Wardship: Sterilisation), Re [1988] A.C. 199; [1987] 2 W.L.R.
1213; [1987] 2 All E.R. 206; [1987] 2 F.L.R. 314; 86 L.G.R. 417; [1987]
Fam. Law 419; (1987) 151 L.G. Rev. 650; (1987) 84 L.S.G. 1410; (1987)
137 N.L.J. 432; (1987) 131 S.J. 625, HL 12–142, 12–144

B (A Child) v. Leeds H.A. [2001] EWCA Civ 51, CA 12–125

B v. B (Wasted Costs: Abuse of Process) [2001] 1 F.L.R. 843, Fam Div 10–131,
10–132, 10–332, 11–28, 11–31

—— v. Croydon H.A.; sub nom. LB v. Croydon H.A. [1995] Fam. 133; [1995]
2 W.L.R. 294; [1995] 1 All E.R. 683; [1995] 1 F.L.R. 470; [1995] 1 F.C.R.
662; [1995] P.I.Q.R. P145; [1995] Fam. Law 244; (1994) 144 N.L.J. 1696;
The Times, December 1, 1994; The Independent, November 30, 1994,
CA 12–136, 12–140, 12–140

—— v. United Kingdom (App. No.10615/83) (1984) 38 D.R. 213 7–32

BBL v. Eagle Star Insurance Co. Ltd. See Banque Bruxelles Lambert S.A. v.
Eagle Star Insurance Co. Ltd.

BC Rail Ltd v. Canadian Pacific Consulting Services Ltd (1990) 47 B.C.L.R. 49,
CA (BC) 8–173

BCCI v. Price Waterhouse (No.2). See Bank of Credit and Commerce International (Overseas) Ltd (In Liquidation) v. Price Waterhouse (No.2).

BDG Roof Bond Ltd (In Liquidation) v. Douglas [2000] 1 B.C.L.C. 401; [2000]
B.C.C. 770; [2000] Lloyd's Rep. P.N. 273; [2000] P.N.L.R. 397, Ch D 10–05,
10–60

PARA.

BFG Bank AG v. Brown & Mumford Ltd [1997] P.N.L.R. 202; [1996] E.G.C.S.
169; [1996] N.P.C. 153, CA 9–107
B Johnson & Co. (Builders) Ltd, Re [1955] Ch. 634; [1955] 3 W.L.R. 269; [1955]
2 All E.R. 775; 99 S.J. 490, CA 15–24
BL Holdings Ltd v. Roberts J Wood & Partners, 12 B.L.R. 1, CA; reversing 10
B.L.R. 48; [1978] J.P.L. 833; 122 S.J. 525; *The Times*, July 21, 1978,
QBD 8–133, 8–163, 8–200
BNP Mortgages Ltd v. Barton Cook & Sams [1996] 1 E.G.L.R. 239; (1997) 13
Const. L.J. 118, QBD 9–61
Babcock Energy Ltd v. Lodge Sturtervant Ltd (1994) 41 Con.L.R. 45 8–306
Babury Ltd v. London Industrial plc (1989) 189 N.L.J. 1596; *The Times*, October
20, 1989, QBD 10–126
Backwell v. AAA [1997] 1 V.R. 182 12–288
Bacon v. Howard Kennedy (A Firm) [1999] P.N.L.R. 1; (2000) 1 W.T.L.R. 169,
Ch D 5–45, 10–51, 10–259
Badgley v. Dickinson (1886) 13 A.R. 494 8–253
Bagot v. Stevens Scanlon & Co. Ltd [1966] 1 Q.B. 197; [1964] 3 W.L.R. 1162;
[1964] 3 All E.R. 577; [1964] 2 Lloyd's Rep. 353; 2 B.L.R. 67; 108 S.J. 604,
QBD 2–100, 5–14, 8–50, 8–52
Bahai v. Rashidian; *sub nom.* Ali-Sheikh Bahai v. Rashidian [1985] 1 W.L.R.
1337; [1985] 3 All E.R. 385; (1985) 82 L.S.G. 2162; (1985) 135 N.L.J.
1033; (1985) 129 S.J. 777; *The Times*, October 9, 1985, CA 10–133
—— v. Rashidian (No.2), *The Times*, June 11 1986 10–132
Baikie v. Chandless (1811) 3 Camp. 17; 170 E.R. 12291, NP 10–77
Bailey v. Abraham (1849) 14 L.T.(O.S.) 219 10–207
—— v. Bullock [1950] 2 All E.R. 1167; 66 T.L.R. (Pt. 2) 791; [1950] W.N. 482;
94 S.J. 689, KBD 9–187, 10–311, 10–309
—— v. Gallagher [1996] 2 I.L.R.M. 433, Sup Ct (Irl) 12–235
Bailey (E) & Co. v. Balholm Securities [1973] 2 Lloyd's Rep. 404, QBD (Comm
Ct) 13–160
Baker v. Carter (1935) 1 Y.& C.Ex. 25 2–135
—— v. Kaye [1997] I.R.L.R. 219; (1998) 39 B.M.L.R. 12; *The Times*, December
13, 1996, QBD 12–25, 12–64
—— v. Ollard & Bentley (1982)126 S.J. 593, CA 5–38
—— v. Turville (2001) 38 R.P.R. (3d) 155, CA (Ontario) 10–196
—— v. Willoughby [1970] A.C. 467; [1970] 2 W.L.R. 50; [1969] 3 All E.R.
1528; 7 K.I.R. 457; 114 S.J. 15, HL 10–234, 12–246
Balabel v. Air India [1988] Ch. 317; [1988] 2 W.L.R. 1036; [1988] 2 All E.R.
246; (1988) 138 N.L.J. 85; (1988) 132 S.J. 699, CA 10–1
Balamoan v. Holden & Co. (1999) 149 N.L.J. 898; *The Independent*, June 15,
1999, CA 10–94, 10–95, 10–181
Balcomb v. Wards Construction (Medway) Ltd, Pethybridge v. Wards Construc-
tion (Medway) Ltd (1981) 259 E.G. 765 .... 8–173, 8–191
Baldwin v. Chalker (1984) 48 Nfld. & P.E.I.R; 142 A.P.R. 86, CA
(Newfoundland) 10–15
Balfour Beatty Construction (Scotland) Ltd v. Scottish Power (1994) 71 B.L.R.
20; 1994 S.L.T. 807; *The Times*, March 23, 1994, HL 8–280, 8–282
Ball v. Banner; Neill Clerk (A Firm) v. Healey & Baker, Transcript
A3/2000/0246, CA; reversing [2000] Lloyd's Rep. P.N. 569; [2000]
E.G.C.S. 36; (2000) 97(12) L.S.G. 45, Ch D 4–07, 9–10, 9–15, 9–36, 9–116,
9–174, 13–119
Baloch v. Leonard & Kalin [1996] E.G.C.S. 181, QBD 10–316
Banco Exterior Internacional v. Mann [1995] 1 All E.R. 936; [1995] 1 F.L.R. 602;
[1995] 2 F.C.R. 282; (1995) 27 H.L.R. 329; (1995) 145 N.L.J. 179; [1994]
N.P.C. 150; *The Times*, December 19, 1994; *The Independent*, December 8,
1994, CA 2–146

PARA.

Bancroft v. Harrogate H.A. [1997] 8 Med.L.R. 398, QBD 12–22, 12–223
Bank fur Handel und Effekten v. Davidson (1975) 55 D.L.R. (3d) 303 13–130
Bank of Credit and Commerce International (Overseas) Ltd (In Liquidation) v.
    Price Waterhouse (No.2) [1998] Lloyd's Rep. Bank. 85; [1998] B.C.C. 617;
    [1998] E.C.C. 410; [1998] P.N.L.R. 564; (1998) 95(15) L.S.G. 32; (1998)
    142 S.J.L.B. 86; The Times, March 4, 1998, CA 2–41, 2–53, 2–73, 15–47, 15–48,
                        15–49, 15–63, 15–66, 15–70, 15–71, 15–72, 15–80, 15–126
Bank of East Asia Ltd v. Shepherd & Wedderburn, WS, 1995 S.C. 255; 1995
    S.L.T. 1074; 1995 S.C.L.R. 598, Ex Div 10–217
Bank of East Asia v. Tsien Wui Marble Factory Ltd [2000] 1 H.K.L.R.D. 268 5–16,
                        5–20, 5–24, 5–25, 5–27, 5–28, 8–79, 8–124
Bank of New South Wales v. Rogers (1941) 65 C.L.R. 42 2–145
Bank of New Zealand v. New Zealand Guardian Trust Co. Ltd [1999] 1 N.Z.L.R.
    664 9–117
Bank of Nova Scotia v. Hellenic Mutual War Risk Association (Bermuda) Ltd;
    Good Luck, The (No.2) [1992] 1 A.C. 233; [1991] 2 W.L.R. 1279; [1991] 3
    All E.R. 1; [1991] 2 Lloyd's Rep. 191; (1991) 141 N.L.J. 779; The Times,
    May 17, 1991; The Independent, May 31, 1991; Financial Times, May 21,
    1991, HL; reversing [1990] 1 Q.B. 818; [1990] 2 W.L.R. 547; [1989] 3 All
    E.R. 628; [1989] 2 Lloyd's Rep. 238; (1990) 87(10) L.S.G. 34; The Times,
    April 20, 1989, CA 2–104, 14–19, 14–60
Banks v. Reid (1977) 81 D.L.R. (3d) 730, CA (Ontario) 11–24
—— v. Woodhall Duckham Ltd (No.2); sub nom. Stathams (Wasted Costs
    Order), Re [1997] P.I.Q.R. P464, CA 10–138
Bannerman Brydone Folster & Co. v. Murray [1972] N.Z.L.R. 411 10–82
Banque Bruxelles Lambert S.A. v. Eagle Star Insurance Co. Ltd. Also see South
    Australia Asset Management Corp. v. York Montague Ltd.
Banque Financiere de la Cite S.A. (formerly Banque Keyser Ullmann SA) v.
    Westgate Insurance Co. (formerly Hodge General & Mercantile Co. Ltd);
    sub nom. Banque Keyser Ullmann S.A. v. Skandia (U.K.) Insurance Co.;
    Skandia (U.K.) Insurance Co. v. Chemical Bank; Skandia (U.K.) Insurance
    Co. v. Credit Lyonnais Bank Nederland NV [1991] 2 A.C. 249; [1990] 3
    W.L.R. 364; [1990] 2 All E.R. 947; [1990] 2 Lloyd's Rep. 377; (1990)
    87(35) L.S.G. 36; (1990) 140 N.L.J. 1074; (1990) 134 S.J. 1265, HL;
    affirming [1990] 1 Q.B. 665; [1989] 3 W.L.R. 25; [1989] 2 All E.R. 952;
    [1988] 2 Lloyd's Rep. 513; [1989] Fin. L.R. 1; (1989) 133 S.J. 817; The
    Times, August 24, 1988; The Independent, August 19, 1988; Financial
    Times, August 12, 1988, CA 2–104, 14–19, 14–60
Banque Keyser Ullmann S.A. v. Skandia (U.K.) Insurance Co. See Banque
    Financiere de la Cite S.A. (formerly Banque Keyser Ullmann S.A.) v.
    Westgate Insurance Co. (formerly Hodge General & Mercantile Co. Ltd).
Barclays Bank plc v. Fairclough Building Ltd (No.1) [1995] Q.B. 214; [1994] 3
    W.L.R. 1057; [1995] 1 All E.R. 289; 68 B.L.R. 1; 38 Con. L.R. 86; (1995)
    11 Const. L.J. 35; [1995] E.G.C.S. 10; (1994) 91(25) L.S.G. 30; (1994) 138
    S.J.L.B. 118; The Times, May 11, 1994, CA 2–04, 5–115, 5–118, 14–130
—— v. Fairclough Building Ltd (No.2); Carne (Structural Repair) Co. Ltd v.
    Trendleway Ltd (1995) 76 B.L.R. 1; 44 Con. L.R. 35; [1995] I.R.L.R. 605;
    [1995] P.I.Q.R. P152; The Times, February 15, 1995; The Independent,
    February 20, 1995 (C.S.), CA 8–60
—— v. Lougher (1996) 1 Con.L.R. 75, QBD (OR) 10–74
—— v. O'Brien [1994] 1 A.C. 180; [1993] 3 W.L.R. 786; [1993] 4 All E.R. 417;
    [1994] 1 F.L.R. 1; [1994] 1 F.C.R. 357; (1994) 26 H.L.R. 75; (1994) 13 Tr.
    L.R. 165; [1994] C.C.L.R. 94; [1994] Fam. Law 78; [1993] E.G.C.S. 169;
    (1993) 143 N.L.J. 1511; (1993) 137 S.J.L.B. 240; [1993] N.P.C. 135; The
    Times, October 22, 1993; The Independent, October 22, 1993, HL 2–142,
                                                        10–205, 12–28

PARA.

Barclays Bank plc v. Taylor; Trustee Savings Bank of Wales and Border Counties
v. Taylor [1989] 1 W.L.R. 1066; [1989] 3 All E.R. 563; [1989] Fin. L.R. 304;
(1990) 87(4) L.S.G. 66; (1989) 133 S.J. 1372, CA 2–161
—— v. Weeks Legg & Dean; *sub nom.* Barclays Bank plc v. Dean; Barclays Bank
plc v. Layton Lougher & Co.; Mohamed v. Fahiya; Barclays Bank plc v. NE
Hopkin John & Co. [1999] Q.B. 309; [1998] 3 W.L.R. 656; [1998] 3 All
E.R. 213; [1998] P.N.L.R. 729; (1999) 77 P. & C.R. 320; [1998] 3 E.G.L.R.
103; [1998] 40 E.G. 182; (1998) 95(25) L.S.G. 33; (1998) 95(21) L.S.G. 38;
(1998) 142 S.J.L.B. 180; [1998] N.P.C. 89; (1998) 76 P. & C.R. D27; *The
Times,* June 15, 1998; *The Independent,* June 3, 1998, CA 2–10, 10–10, 10–68
Barclay-White v. Guillaume & Sons [1996] E.G.C.S. 123, QBD 10–271
Barings plc (In Administration) v. Coopers & Lybrand [1997] B.C.C. 498; [1997]
1 B.C.L.C. 427; [1997] E.C.C. 372; [1997] I.L.Pr. 576; [1997] P.N.L.R. 179;
The Times, December 6, 1996; *The Independent,* January 13, 1997 (C.S.),
CA 15–80, 15–87
Barings plc (In Liquidation) v. Coopers & Lybrand (No.2); Barings Futures
(Singapore) Pte Ltd (In Liquidation) v. Mattar (No.2) [2001] Lloyd's Rep.
Bank. 85; [2001] Lloyd's Rep. P.N. 379; [2001] P.N.L.R. 22; (2001) 98(13)
L.S.G. 40; *The Times,* March 7, 2001; *The Daily Telegraph,* February 27,
2001, Ch D 6–09
Barking & Dagenham L.B.C. v. Terrapin Construction Ltd [2000] B.L.R. 479; 74
Con. L.R. 100, CA 8–255
Barnes v. Addy (1873–74) L.R. 9 Ch. App. 244; (1874) 22 W.R. 505; (1874) 43
L.J. Ch. 513; (1874) 30 L.T. 4, CA 10–38
—— v. Crabtree, *The Times,* November 1, 2, 1955 12–19
—— v. Hay (1988) 12 N.S.W.L.R. 337; [1988] Aus. Torts Reports 67, 558,
CA 10–238, 10–317
Barnett v. Chelsea and Kensington Hospital Management Committee [1969] 1
Q.B. 428; [1968] 2 W.L.R. 422; [1968] 1 All E.R. 1068; 111 S.J. 912,
QBD 12–16, 12–17, 12–173, 12–245, 12–251
Baron v. Hartford Fire Insurance Co. [1998] 1 H.K.L.R.D. 411, CFI (HK) 14–31
Barrett v. Enfield L.B.C. [1999] 3 W.L.R. 79; [1999] 3 All E.R. 193; [1999] 2
F.L.R. 426; [1999] 2 F.C.R. 434; (1999) 1 L.G.L.R. 829; [1999] B.L.G.R.
473; (1999) 11 Admin. L.R. 839; [1999] Ed. C.R. 833; (1999) 2 C.C.L. Rep.
203; [1999] P.I.Q.R. P272; (1999) 49 B.M.L.R. 1; [1999] Fam. Law 622;
(1999) 96(28) L.S.G. 27; (1999) 143 S.J.L.B. 183; *The Times,* June 18, 1999,
HL; reversing [1998] Q.B. 367; [1997] 3 W.L.R. 628; [1997] 3 All E.R. 171;
[1997] 2 F.L.R. 167; [1997] 3 F.C.R. 145; (1998) 10 Admin. L.R. 230;
(1997) 37 B.M.L.R. 16; [1997] Fam. Law 534; *The Times,* April 22, 1997,
CA 2–77, 2–84, 2–85, 12–57, 12–60, 12–84, 12–238
—— v. Reynolds (1998) 20 R.P.R. (3d) 14 10–24
—— v. Reynolds (1998) 170 N.S.R. (2d) 201, CA (Nova Scotia) 10–25
—— v. Swindon Hospital Management Committee (1973) (cited in Legal Proceedings Against Doctors and Health Authorities (Taliscourt Publications,
1980), p. 10 12–80
Barrister (Wasted Costs Order) (No.1 of 1991), Re; *sub nom.* H (A Barrister), Ex
p.[1993] Q.B. 293; [1992] 3 W.L.R. 662; [1992] 3 All E.R. 429; (1992) 95
Cr. App. R. 288; (1992) 142 N.L.J. 636; (1992) 136 S.J.L.B. 147; *The Times,*
May 6, 1992; *The Independent,* April 23, 1992; *The Guardian,* May 6, 1992,
CA 10–129, 11–27
Barrister (Wasted Costs Order) (No.4 of 1992), Re, *The Times,* March 15, 1994;
The Independent, March 15, 1994, CA 11–33, 11–34
Barrister (Wasted Costs Order) (No.9 of 1999), Re (2000) 16 P.N. 122; (2000)
97(26) L.S.G. 36; *The Times,* April 18, 2000, CA (Crim Div) 11–08, 11–35,
11–40

PARA.

Barron v. Fitzgerald (1840) 6 Bing.N.C. 201; 8 Scott 460; 9 L.J.C.P. 154; 4 Jur.
88; 133 E.R. 79 14–43

Barrymore (Michael) v. News Group Newspapers Ltd [1997] F.S.R. 600, Ch
D 2–156

Bartlett v. Barclays Bank Trust Co. Ltd (No.2) [1980] Ch. 515; [1980] 2 W.L.R.
430; [1980] 2 All E.R. 92; 124 S.J. 221, Ch D 10–34

Barton v. Stuart Hepburn & Co. [1926] E.G.D. 206 .... 9–107, 9–134

Bartter v. Gambril (1932) 76 S.J. 868 .... 10–161, 10–249

Basildon D.C. v. JE Lesser (Properties) Ltd [1985] Q.B. 839; [1984] 3 W.L.R.
812; [1985] 1 All E.R. 20; 8 Con. L.R. 89; (1984) 1 Const. L.J. 57; (1984)
81 L.S.G. 1437; (1984) 134 N.L.J. 330, QBD 5–115

Batchelor v. Pattison and Mackersy (1876) 3 R. 914; 13 S.C.L.R. 589, 1 Div 11–10

Bateman v. Owen White [1996] 1 P.N.L.R. 1, CA 10–106

Bates, Ex p., L.R. 4 Ch. 577 18–16

Bates v. Robert Barrow Ltd; Ansell v. Robert Barrow Ltd [1995] 1 Lloyd's Rep.
680; The Times, February 9, 1995, QBD (Comm Ct) 14–35, 14–58, 14–113

Batten v. Wedgwood Coal & Iron Co. (No.2) (1886) L.R. 31 Ch. D. 346; (1884)
28 Ch.D. 317; 54 L.J.Ch. 686; 52 L.T. 212; 33 W.R. 303, Ch D 10–46

Battersby v. Tottman (1984) 35 S.A.S.R. 577, upheld on appeal (1985) 37
S.A.S.R. 542 .... 12–81, 12–95, 12–191, 12–205

Baumgartner v. Baumgartner (1995) 122 D.L.R. (4th) 543, CA (BC) 10–31

Baxall Securities Ltd v. Sheard Walshaw Partnership [2001] C.L.C. 188; [2001]
B.L.R. 36; (2001) 3 T.C.L.R. 8; 74 Con. L.R. 116; [2001] Lloyd's Rep. P.N.
85; [2001] P.N.L.R. 9; (2001) 17 Const. L.J. 150; The Daily Telegraph,
November 14, 2000, QBD (T&CC) 8–84, 8–85, 8–181, 8–209, 8–278

Baxter v. FW Gapp & Co. Ltd; Baxter v. Gapp [1939] 2 K.B. 271; [1939] 2 All
E.R. 752, CA 9–52, 9–81, 9–100, 9–151, 9–152, 9–158

Bayer v. Balkin (1995) 31 A.T.R. 295 10–207

Bayliss v. Blagg (1954) 1 B.M.J. 709 12–185

Beach Petroleum NL v. Kennedy [1999] N.S.W.C.A. 408; [1999] 48 N.S.W.L.R.
1, CA (NSW) 2–131, 10–230

Beale v. Kyte [1907] 1 Ch. 564, Ch D 5–105

—— v. South Devon Ry Co. Ltd (1864) 3 H. & C. 337; (1861–73) All E.R. 972;
11 L.T. 184; 12 W.R. 1115; 159 E.R. 560, Ex Ch 10–77

Bean v. Wade (1885) 2 T.L.R. 157, CA 5–14, 10–05, 10–13

Beaton v. Nationwide Anglia Building Society (formerly Nationwide Building
Society) [1991] 2 E.G.L.R. 145; [1991] 38 E.G. 218; The Times, October 8,
1990, DC 9–68

Beattie v. Furness-Houlder Insurance (Northern) Ltd 1976 S.L.T. (Notes) 60,
OH 14–107

Beaumont v. Humberts (A Firm) [1990] 2 E.G.L.R. 166; [1990] 49 E.G. 46; The
Times, July 17, 1990, CA 9–50, 9–61, 9–104

Becker v. Medd (1897) 13 T.L.R. 313, CA 14–126

Beckmat Holdings Ltd v. Tassou (1982) 18 Alta. L.R. (2d) 300, CA (Alberta) 10–156

Begusic v. Clark, Wilson & Co. (1992) 92 D.L.R. (4th) 273, Sup Ct (BC) 10–6

Behrens v. Smith (1997) 153 Sask. R. 294 .... 12–131, 12–02

Behrooz Siasati v. Bottoms & Webb (a firm) [1997] N.P.C. 20 [1997] E.G.C.S.
22, QBD 10–199

Belcher Food Products Ltd v. Miller & Black, 1999 S.L.T. 142; 1998 G.W.D.
16–775, OH 8–255

Bell v. Lever Bros Ltd; sub nom. Lever Bros Ltd v. Bell [1932] A.C. 161, HL 10–164

—— v. Peter Browne & Co. [1990] 2 Q.B. 495; [1990] 3 W.L.R. 510; [1990] 3
All E.R. 124; (1990) 140 N.L.J. 701, CA 2–09, 2–103, 5–14, 5–45, 10–12, 10–13

—— v. Strathairn & Blair (1954) 104 L.J. 618 .... 10–83, 10–152

PARA.

Bell v. Tinmouth (1988) 53 D.L.R. (4th) 731, CA (BC) 14–70

Bell Hotels (1935) v. Motion (1952) 159 E.G. 496; [1952] C.P.L. 403 .... 9–100, 9–110

Bellefield Computer Services Ltd v. E Turner & Sons Ltd; Unigate (U.K.) Ltd v.
E Turner & Sons Ltd [2000] B.L.R. 97; (2000) 2 T.C.L.R. 759; [2000]
N.P.C. 9, CA 8–62, 8–83, 8–95

Bell's Indenture, Re; *sub nom.* Bell v. Hickley [1980] 1 W.L.R. 1217; [1980] 3
All E.R. 425; 123 S.J. 322, Ch D 10–147, 10–207

Belmont Finance Corp. Ltd v. Williams Furniture Ltd [1979] Ch. 250; [1978] 3
W.L.R. 712; [1979] 1 All E.R. 118; 122 S.J. 743, CA 15–151

Beloff (Nora) v. Pressdram Ltd [1973] 1 All E.R. 241; [1973] F.S.R. 33; [1973]
R.P.C. 765; *The Times*, October 19, 1972, Ch D 2–160

Belous v. Willetts [1970] V.R. 45 5–115

Belvedere Motors Ltd v. King [1981] 2 E.G.L.R. 131; (1981) 260 E.G. 813 9–74

Benarr v. Kettering H.A. (1988) 138 N.L.J. 179 12–289

Beningfield v. Baxter (1886) 12 App.Cas. 167 .... 2–135, 3–09

Bennett, Ex p. (1805) 10 Ves.Jun. 381 .... 2–138, 2–140, 3–09

Bennett v. Greenland Houchen & Co. [1998] P.N.L.R. 458, CA 5–13, 10–312

Bentley v. Bristol and Weston H.A. (No.2) [1991] 3 Med.L.R. 1, QBD 12–186

—— v. Gaisford [1997] Q.B. 627; [1997] 2 W.L.R. 401; [1997] 1 All E.R. 842;
(1996) 146 N.L.J. 1615; *The Times*, November 4, 1996; *The Independent*,
October 31, 1996, CA 10–65, 10–72

Bere v. Slades, 25 Con. L.R. 1; [1989] 46 E.G. 100; (1990) 6 Const. L.J. 30 9–85

Beresforde v. Chesterfield B.C. [1989] 2 E.G.L.R. 149; [1989] 39 E.G. 176;
(1990) 10 Tr. L.R. 6, CA 9–31

Berg Sons & Co. v. Mervyn Hampton Adams [1993] B.C.L.C. 1045; [1992]
B.C.C. 661; *Financial Times*, July 10, 1992 .... 15–11, 15–70, 15–74, 15–126,
15–127

Bergen v. Sturgeon General Hospital (1984) 28 C.C.L.T. 155, QBD (Alberta) 12–184,
12–199

Berlevy v. Blyth Dutton (a firm) [1997] E.G.C.S. 133, CA 10–155

Bernasconi v. Nicholas Bennett & Co. [2000] B.C.C. 921; [2000] B.P.I.R. 8;
[2000] Lloyd's Rep. P.N. 285; [1999] N.P.C. 132, Ch D 10–236, 11–53

Berriman v. Rose Thomson Young (Underwriting) Ltd [1996] L.R.L.R. 426;
[1996] C.L.C. 1283; [1996] 5 Re. L.R. 121; Lloyd's List, August 1, 1996
(I.D.), QBD (Comm Ct) 16–25, 16–27, 16–31, 16–32, 16–33, 16–34, 16–40,
16–43, 16–46, 16–47, 16–49, 16–57, 16–69, 16–78

Berry v. Calderdale H.A. [1998] Lloyd's Rep. Med. 179, CA 5–65

Berwick v. Wickens Holdings Ltd, October 1, 2000, unreported 8–81, 8–261

Beta Computers (Europe) Ltd v. Adobe Systems (Europe) Ltd 1996 S.L.T. 604;
[1996] C.L.C. 821; [1997–98] Info. T.L.R. 73; [1996] F.S.R. 367; [1998]
Masons C.L.R. Rep. 104, OH 17–02, 17–21, 17–22

Bevan Investments Ltd v. Blackhall & Struthers (No.2) 11 B.L.R. 78; [1978] 2
N.Z.L.R. 97, CA (NZ) [1973] 2 N.Z.L.R. 45 ...... 8–52, 8–123, 8–159, 8–207, 8–283,
8–285, 8–290, 8–291, 8–294, 8–302, 8–305, 8–315

Bigg v. Howard Son & Gooch [1990] 1 E.G.L.R. 173; 32 Con. L.R. 39; [1990]
12 E.G. 111 .... 9–110, 9–140, 9–183, 9–189, 9–190

Biggar v. McLeod [1978] 2 N.Z.L.R. 9, CA 11–14

Biggin & Co. Ltd v. Permanite Ltd [1951] 2 K.B. 314; [1951] 2 All E.R. 191;
[1951] 2 T.L.R. 159; 95 S.J. 414, CA 8–327

Bijeau v. Pelletier and the Co-operators General Insurance Co. (1996) 176
N.B.R.(2d) 241, CA (New Brunswick) 14–75

PARA.

Birmingham Corp. v. West Midland Baptist (Trust) Association Inc. ; *sub nom.* West Midland Baptist (Trust) Association Inc. v. Birmingham Corp. [1970] A.C. 874; [1969] 3 W.L.R. 389; [1969] 3 All E.R. 172; (1969) 133 J.P. 524; 67 L.G.R. 571; (1969) 20 P. & C.R. 1052; 113 S.J. 606, HL; affirming [1968] 2 Q.B. 188; [1968] 2 W.L.R. 535; [1968] 1 All E.R. 205; (1968) 132 J.P. 127; (1968) 19 P. & C.R. 9; 111 S.J. 851; *The Times,* October 30, 1967, CA 9–56, 9–176

Birmingham Midshires Building Society v. Infields (A Firm) 66 Con. L.R. 20; [1999] Lloyd's Rep. P.N. 874; [1999] E.G.C.S. 77, QBD (T&CC) 5–55

—— v. Wretham, 63 Con. L.R. 93; [1999] Lloyd's Rep. P.N. 133; [1999] P.N.L.R. 685; [1999] 1 E.G.L.R. 69; [1999] 07 E.G. 138; [1998] E.G.C.S. 176, QBD (T&CC) 5–54

Birmingham Midshires Mortgage Services Ltd v. Ansell [1998] P.N.L.R. 237, Ch D 10–145

—— v. David Parry & Co.; *sub nom.* Hypo-Mortgage Services Ltd v. David Parry & Co. [1997] E.G.C.S. 150; [1997] N.P.C. 153, CA; affirming, 51 Con. L.R. 1; [1996] P.N.L.R. 494; [1996] E.G.C.S. 39, Ch D 10–09, 10–212, 10–325

—— v. Phillips [1998] P.N.L.R. 468, QBD 10–294

Birse Construction Ltd v. Haiste Ltd [1996] 1 W.L.R. 675; [1996] 2 All E.R. 1; [1996] C.L.C. 577; 76 B.L.R. 31; 47 Con. L.R. 162; [1996] P.N.L.R. 8; (1996) 93(2) L.S.G. 29; (1996) 140 S.J.L.B. 25; *The Times,* December 12, 1995, CA 4–07, 8–319

Birtchnell v. Equity Trustees, Executors and Agency Co. Ltd (1929) 42 C.L.R. 384 2–131

Bishop v. Watson, Watson and Scoles (1972) 224 E.G. 1881 9–99

Bittlestone v. Keegan Williams [1997] E.G.C.S. 8, [1997] N.P.C. 3, Ch D 10–199

Black King Shipping Corp. v. Massie; Litsion Pride, The [1985] 1 Lloyd's Rep. 437; (1984) 134 N.L.J. 887, QBD (Comm Ct) 14–37

Blackburn Low & Co. v. Vigors (1887) L.R. 12 App. Cas. 531; 57 L.J.Q.B. 114; 87 L.T. 730; 36 W.R. 449; 3 T.L.R. 837; 6 Asp.M.C.C. 216, HL 14–41

Blackham v. Heythorpe (1917) 23 C.L.R. 156 2–139

Blackwell v. Barroile Pty. Ltd (1994) 123 A.L.R. 81 10–41

Blaenau Gwent B.C. v. Robinson Jones Design Partnership Ltd, 53 Con. L.R. 31, QBD (OR) 8–296

Blair v. Alderney Consultants (1998) 168 N.S.R.(2d) 287, Sup Ct (Nova Scotia) 8–113, 8–190

—— v. Assets Co. Ltd [1896] A.C. 409; 12 T.L.R. 409, HL 10–152

Bliss v. South East Thames R.H.A. [1987] I.C.R. 700; [1985] I.R.L.R. 308, CA 10–313, 10–314

Block Brothers Industries Ltd v. Westland Insurance Centre Ltd (1993) 84 B.C.L.R.(2d) 319 14–39

Blood v. Cotton [1943] N.I.L.R. 68, CA (Irl) 10–192

Bloor Construction (U.K.) Ltd v. Bowmer & Kirkland (London) Ltd [2000] B.L.R. 314; (2000) 2 T.C.L.R. 914, QBD (T&CC) 8–341

Bloor Italian Gifts Ltd v. Dixon (2000) 48 O.R. (3d) 760, CA (Ontario) 15–101, 15–103, 15–143, 15–146

Blundell, Re; *sub nom.* Blundell v. Blundell (1889) L.R. 40 Ch. D. 370; [1886–90] All E.R. 837; 57 L.J.Ch. 730; 58 L.T. 933; 36 wr 779; 4 T.L.R. 506, Ch D 10–37

Blyth v. Bloomsbury H.A. [1993] 4 Med.L.R. 151, CA 12–213, 12–221, 12–225

—— v. Fladgate; Morgan v. Blyth; Smith v. Blyth [1891] 1 Ch. 337; 60 L.J.Ch. 66; 63 L.T. 546; 39 wr 422; 7 T.L.R. 29, Ch D 10–05, 10–36, 10–207

Board of Governors of the Hospitals for Sick Children v. McLaughlin & Harvey plc (1987) 19 Con.L.R. 25 .... 8–297, 8–298, 8–313

PARA.

Boardman v. Phipps; *sub nom.* Phipps v. Boardman [1967] 2 A.C. 46; [1966] 3
W.L.R. 1009; [1966] 3 All E.R. 721; 110 S.J. 853, HL 2–141, 2–151, 10–21,
17–05
Bogg v. Raper, *The Times*, April 22, 1998, CA 10–20
Bolam v. Friern Hospital Management Committee [1957] 1 W.L.R. 582; [1957]
2 All E.R. 118; [1955–95] P.N.L.R. 7; 101 S.J. 357, QBD 2–03, 2–116, 6–08,
7–47, 7–48, 8–145, 8–147, 8–148, 8–150, 8–151, 9–06, 9–24,
9–102, 9–105, 10–90, 12–68, 12–69, 12–93, 12–142, 12–158,
12–159, 12–176, 12–190, 12–191, 12–202, 12–205, 12–207,
12–208, 12–209, 12–210, 12–211, 12–212, 12–213, 12–215,
12–219, 12–229, 12–231, 12–234, 12–237, 12–262, 12–263,
12–271, 12–272
Boland v. Yates Property Corporation Pty. Ltd. (2000) 167 A.L.R. 575, HC
(Aus) 11–24, 11–39
Bolitho (Deceased) v. City and Hackney H.A. [1998] A.C. 232; [1997] 3 W.L.R.
1151; [1997] 4 All E.R. 771; [1998] P.I.Q.R. P10; [1998] Lloyd's Rep. Med.
26; (1998) 39 B.M.L.R. 1; [1998] P.N.L.R. 1; (1997) 94(47) L.S.G. 30;
(1997) 141 S.J.L.B. 238; *The Times*, November 27, 1997, HL; affirming
[1993] P.I.Q.R. P334; [1993] 4 Med.L.R. 381, CA 2–117, 6–08, 8–147, 10–88,
12–68, 12–71, 12–86, 12–98, 12–99, 12–100, 12–101, 12–159,
12–213, 12–271, 12–272, 12–273
Bolkiah v. KPMG; *sub nom.* HRH Prince Jefri Bolkiah v. KPMG [1999] 2 A.C.
222; [1999] 2 W.L.R. 215; [1999] 1 B.C.L.C. 1; [1999] P.N.L.R. 220; (1999)
149 N.L.J. 16; (1999) 143 S.J.L.B. 35; *The Times*, April 20, 1999; *The
Independent*, January 12, 1999, HL 2–132, 2–162, 2–165, 10–27, 10–28, 10–30,
10–31, 15–41, 15–42, 15–44, 15–43
Bolton v. Jameson & Mackay [1989] S.L.T. 222, 1 Div 10–62
—— v. New Zealand Insurance Co. Ltd [1995] 1 N.Z.L.R. 224 ..... 14–60, 14–66, 14–113,
14–121, 14–123, 14–131
—— v. Puley [1983] 2 E.G.L.R. 138; (1983) 267 E.G. 1161; (1983) 133 N.L.J.
558 .... 9–94, 9–131, 9–140, 9–184
Boncristiano v. Lohmann [1998] 4 V.R. 82, CA (Vic) 8–311
Bond v. Livingstone [2001] P.N.L.R. 30, QBD 10–82, 10–119
Bonnington Castings Ltd v. Wardlaw; *sub nom.* Wardlaw v. Bonnington Castings
Ltd [1956] A.C. 613; [1956] 2 W.L.R. 707; [1956] 1 All E.R. 615; 1956 S.C.
(H.L.) 26; 1956 S.L.T. 135; 54 L.G.R. 153; 100 S.J. 207, HL 8–273, 12–243
Boobyer v. David Holman & Co. Ltd (No.2) [1993] 1 Lloyd's Rep. 96, QBD
(Comm Ct) 16–10
Boorman v. Brown. *See* Brown v. Boorman.
Booth v. Davey (1988) 138 N.L.J. 104, CA 10–166
Boros v. Bodnar, Wanhella and Courtney [1988] 6 W.W.R. 645 10–98
Bos v. Brauer (1992) 3 Alta.L.R. (3d) 318 14–23
Bossee v. Clavette (1984) 56 N.B.R. (2d) 375, CA (New Brunswick) 10–261
Boudreau v. Benaiah (2000) 182 D.L.R. (4th) 569, CA (Ontario) 10–315
Boulting v. Association of Cinematograph Television and Allied Technicians
[1963] 2 Q.B. 606; [1963] 2 W.L.R. 529; [1963] 1 All E.R. 716; 107 S.J.
133, CA 2–140, 10–101
Bourgoin S.A. v. Ministry of Agriculture, Fisheries and Food [1986] Q.B. 716;
[1985] 3 W.L.R. 1027; [1985] 3 All E.R. 585; [1986] 1 C.M.L.R. 267;
(1985) 82 L.S.G. 3435; *The Times*, August 3, 1985, CA 13–132
Bourne v. McEvoy Timber Preservation Ltd [1976] 1 E.G.L.R. 100; (1975) 237
E.G. 496 .... 9–39, 9–140
—— v. Swan & Edgar Ltd; *sub nom.* Bourne's Trade Marks [1903] 1 Ch. 211,
Ch D 5–106
Bousfield v. Creswell (1810) 2 Camp. 545 14–37

PARA.

Bouygues U.K. Ltd v. Dahl-Jensen U.K. Ltd [2001] 1 All E.R. (Comm) 1041;
[2001] C.L.C. 927; [2000] B.L.R. 522; (2001) 3 T.C.L.R. 2; 73 Con. L.R.
135; (2000) 97(35) L.S.G. 36; *The Times*, August 17, 2000, CA; affirming
[2000] B.L.R. 49; (2000) 2 T.C.L.R. 308; 70 Con. L.R. 41; *The Independent*,
February 7, 2000 (C.S.), QBD (T&CC) 8–338
Bova v. Spring [1994] 5 Med.L.R. 120, QBD 12–77, 12–184, 12–185
Bow Valley Husky (Bermuda) Ltd v. Saint John Shipbuilding Ltd (1997) 153
D.L.R. (4th) 385 2–60
Bowdage v. Harold Michelmore & Co., 183 E.G. 233; (1962) 106 S.J. 512 10–169
Bowen v. Paramount Builders (Hamilton) Ltd [1977] 1 N.Z.L.R. 394 2–77
Bowles v. Johnson [1988] 4 W.W.R. 242, QB (Manitoba) 10–61, 10–324
Bown v. Gould & Swayne [1996] P.N.L.R. 130; [1996] N.P.C. 5, CA 2–116, 6–06,
6–08, 10–142, 10–194
Boyce v. Rendells (1983) 268 E.G. 268 10–165
Boyd Knight v. Purdue [1999] N.Z.L.R. 278, CA (NZ) 3–02, 15–28, 15–78, 15–126,
15–127
Bracey v. Carter (1840) 12 Ald. & El. 373; 113 E.R. 853 10–307
Bradburn v. Great Western Railway (1874–75) L.R. 10 Ex. 1; [1874–80] aaler
195; 44 L.J.Ex. 9; 31 L.T. 464; 23 W.R. 48 16–74
Bragg v. Oceanus Mutual Underwriting Association (Bermuda) Ltd; Ulster
Marine Insurance Co. Ltd v. Oceanus Mutual Underwriting Association
(Bermuda) Ltd [1982] 2 Lloyd's Rep. 132; [1982] Com. L.R. 165, CA 10–108
Braid v. WL Highway & Sons (1964) 191 E.G. 433 ..... 10–235, 10–249, 10–274, 10–276,
10–301
Brain v. Mador (1985) 32 C.C.L.T. 157 12–95
Bramelid and Malmstrom v. Sweden (App. Nos 8588 & 8589/79) (1983) 5
E.H.R.R. 249, Eur Comm HR 7–16
Brandeis (Brokers) Ltd v. Herbert Black, May 25, 2001, unreported 13–89, 13–91,
13–116, 13–128, 13–166
Brandeis Goldschmidt & Co. Ltd v. Western Transport Ltd [1981] Q.B. 864;
[1981] 3 W.L.R. 181; [1982] 1 All E.R. 28; [1981] F.S.R. 481; 125 S.J. 395,
CA 9–153
Brantford, City of v. Kemp and Wallace-Carruthers & Associates Ltd (1960) 23
D.L.R. (2d) 640, CA; (1959) 21 D.L.R. (2d) 670, HC (Ontario) 8–116, 8–188,
8–212, 8–290, 8–294
Braun Estate v. Vaughan (1997) 124 Man. R. (2d) 1 .... 12–195, 12–199
Bray v. Stuart A West & Co. [1989] N.L.J.R. 753 .... 10–69, 10–71
Brazier v. Ministry of Defence [1965] 1 Lloyd's Rep. 26, QBD 12–80, 12–122,
12–192
Breen v. Williams (1996) 138 A.L.R. 259; (1996) 186 C.L.R. 71 ..... 2–125, 2–175, 2–131,
12–29
Brenner v. Gregory (1972) 30 D.L.R. (3d) 672, HC (Ontario) 10–203
Brickenden v. London Loan & Saving [1934] 3 D.L.R. 465, PC 3–13, 10–228, 10–230
Brickfield Properties v. Newton; Rosebell Holdings v. Newton [1971] 1 W.L.R.
862; [1971] 3 All E.R. 328; 115 S.J. 307, CA 5–15, 8–29, 8–30
Briffett v. Gander & District Hospital Board (1996) 29 C.C.L.T. (2d) 251, CA
(Newfoundland) 12–112
Briggs v. Pitt-Payne [1999] Lloyd's Rep. Med. 1; (1999) 46 B.M.L.R. 132, ...5–58CA
Brinsden v. Williams [1894] 3 Ch.D. 185; 38 S.J. 603; 63 L.J.Ch. 713; 71 L.T.
177; 42 W.R. 700; 10 T.L.R. 571; 8 R. 574, Ch D 10–100, 10–207
Briody v. St Helens and Knowsley A.H.A. (Claim for Damages and Costs) [2001]
EWCA Civ 1010, CA; affirming [2000] 2 F.C.R. 13; [2000] P.I.Q.R. Q165;
[2000] Lloyd's Rep. Med. 127; (2000) 53 B.M.L.R. 108; (2000) 97(5)
L.S.G. 33; (2000) 144 S.J.L.B. 57; *The Times*, March 1, 2000
—— v. St Helens and Knowsley A.H.A. [1999] Lloyd's Rep. Med. 185, CA 5–58

PARA.

Bristol and West Building Society v. A Kramer & Co. [1995] N.P.C. 14; *The Times*, February 6, 1995; *The Independent*, January 26, 1995, Ch D 5–118, 10–08, 10–327

—— v. Aitken Nairn WS, 2000 S.L.T. 763; 2000 S.C.L.R. 47; 1999 G.W.D. 26–1258, 2 Div 10–217

—— v. Baden Barnes Groves & Co. [2000] Lloyd's Rep. P.N. 788, Ch D 10–217

—— v. Christie [1996] E.G.C.S. 53, QBD 10–331

—— v. Daniels & Co. [1997] P.N.L.R. 323, Ch D 10–229

—— v. Fancy & Jackson [1997] 4 All E.R. 582; [1997] N.P.C. 109, Ch D 10–04, 10–09, 10–24, 10–75, 10–206, 10–209, 10–211, 10–213, 10–214, 10–215, 10–296, 10–319, 10–326

—— v. May May & Merrimans (No.2) [1998] 1 W.L.R. 336; [1997] 3 All E.R. 206; [1997] N.P.C. 31, Ch D 10–229, 10–252

—— v. Mothew (t/a Stapley & Co.); *sub nom.* Mothew v. Bristol and West Building Society [1998] Ch. 1; [1997] 2 W.L.R. 436; [1996] 4 All E.R. 698; [1997] P.N.L.R. 11; (1998) 75 P. & C.R. 241; [1996] E.G.C.S. 136; (1996) 146 N.L.J. 1273; (1996) 140 S.J.L.B. 206; [1996] N.P.C. 126; *The Times*, August 2, 1996, CA 2–05, 2–125, 2–127, 2–128, 2–129, 2–132, 3–13, 5–91, 8–63, 9–121, 10–16, 10–23, 10–24, 10–35, 10–102, 10–206, 10–229, 10–295, 12–28, 13–115, 14–36, 15–39, 15–122

—— v. Rollo Steven & Bond, 1998 S.L.T. 9; 1997 G.W.D. 22–1096, OH 10–295

British American Tobacco Co. Ltd v. Netherlands; Series A, No.331–A; (1996) 21 E.H.R.R. 409; *The Times*, December 11, 1995, ECHR 7–06

British Citizens Assurance Co. v. L Woolland & Co. (1921) 8 Ll. L. Rep. 89, KBD 14–14, 14–43, 14–89, 14–114

British Columbia Hydro & Power Authority v. BG Checo [1993] 1 S.C.R. 12, Sup Ct (Can) 8–51

—— v. ND Lea & Associates (1992) 69 B.C.L.R. (2d) 309, Sup Ct (Can) 8–113

British Columbia Ltd v. HBT Agra Ltd (1994) 120 D.L.R. (4th) 726, CA (BC) 8–118

British Columbia v. RBO (1995) 6 B.C.L.R. (3d) 59 8–113

British Fermentation Products Ltd v. Compair Reavell Ltd [1999] 2 All E.R. (Comm) 389; [1999] B.L.R. 352; (2000) 2 T.C.L.R. 704; 66 Con. L.R. 1, QBD (T&CC) 8–22

British Mutual Investment Co. v. Cobbold (1874–75) L.R. 19 Eq. 627, Ct of Chancery 10–207, 10–225

British Racing Drivers Club Ltd v. Hextall Erskine & Co. [1996] 3 All E.R. 667; [1997] 1 B.C.L.C. 182; [1996] B.C.C. 727; [1996] P.N.L.R. 523, Ch D 10–239, 10–308, 10–324

British Sugar plc v. NEI Power Projects Ltd, 87 B.L.R. 42; [1997–98] Info. T.L.R. 353; [1998] I.T.C.L.R. 125; (1998) 14 Const. L.J. 365, CA 8–305

British Telecommunications plc v. James Thomson & Sons (Engineers) Ltd [1999] 1 W.L.R. 9; [1999] 2 All E.R. 241; 1999 S.C. (H.L.) 9; 1999 S.L.T. 224; 1999 S.C.L.R. 126; [1999] B.L.R. 35; (1999) 1 T.C.L.R. 1; 61 Con. L.R. 1; [1999] 1 Lloyd's Rep. I.R. 105; [1999] Lloyd's Rep. I.R. 105; (1999) 96(4) L.S.G. 40; (1999) 143 S.J.L.B. 28; [1998] N.P.C. 161; 1999 G.W.D. 1–47; *The Times*, December 11, 1998, HL 2–51, 8–128

Broadley v. Guy Clapham & Co. [1994] 4 All E.R. 439; [1993] 4 Med.L.R. 328; *The Times*, July 6, 1993; *The Independent*, September 9, 1993, CA 5–58

Broadmoor Special Hospital Authority v. R; *sub nom.* Broadmoor Special H.A. v. R [2000] Q.B. 775; [2000] 1 W.L.R. 1590; [2000] 2 All E.R. 727; [2000] E.M.L.R. 245; [2000] Lloyd's Rep. Med. 65; (2000) 52 B.M.L.R. 137; (2000) 97(3) L.S.G. 36; (2000) 144 S.J.L.B. 48; *The Times*, February 9, 2000; *The Independent*, January 25, 2000, CA 12–49

Broadoak Properties Ltd v. Young & White [1989] 1 E.G.L.R. 263 .... 9–140, 9–144, 9–191

PARA.

Brocklehurst (Deceased), Re Estate of; *sub nom.* Hall v. Roberts; Estate of Sir
Philip Lee Brocklehurst (Deceased), Re [1978] Ch. 14; [1977] 3 W.L.R. 96;
[1978] 1 All E.R. 767; 121 S.J. 633, CA 2–145
Brocklesby v. Armitage & Guest [2001] 1 All E.R. 172; [1999] Lloyd's Rep. P.N.
888; [2000] P.N.L.R. 33; [2001] 1 E.G.L.R. 67; [2001] 14 E.G. 150 .... 5–74, 5–75,
5–76, 5–77, 9–09
Bromley L.B.C. v. A Ellis (Luff & Sons, Third Party) [1971] 1 Lloyd's Rep. 97;
(1970) 114 S.J. 906, CA 14–03, 14–14, 14–31, 14–59, 14–77, 14–114
——— v. Rush & Tompkins Ltd, 35 B.L.R. 94; (1985) 1 Const. L.J. 374; [1985]
C.I.L.L. 179, QBD 5–22
Brooks v. Alker (1975) 60 D.L.R. (3d) 577 2–144
——— v. Homes Office (1999) 48 B.M.L.R. 109 .... 12–70, 12–78
Brown v. Bennett [1999] 1 B.C.L.C. 649; [1999] B.C.C. 525, CA 10–38
——— v. Boorman; *sub nom.* Borman v. Brown (1844) 11 Cl. & Fin. 1; 8 E.R.
1003, HL; affirming (1842) 3 Q.B. 511; 2 Gale & Dav. 793; 11 L.J.Ex. 437;
114 E.R. 603 .... 2–100, 10–13
——— v. British Columbia (Minister of Transportation and Highways) (1994) 112
D.L.R. (4th) 1 2–84
——— v. Cuff Roberts [1996] C.L.Y. 4499, CA 10–268
——— v. Gilbert-Scott (1992) 35 Con.L.R. 120 .... 8–238, 8–242, 8–244
——— v. Guardian Royal Exchange Assurance plc [1994] 2 Lloyd's Rep. 325;
(1994) 91(9) L.S.G. 40; (1994) 138 S.J.L.B. 35; [1994] N.P.C. 8; *The Times,*
January 27, 1994; *The Independent,* February 11, 1994, CA 10–145
——— v. Howard (1820) 2 Brod. & B. 73; 4 Moore C.P. 508; 129 E.R. 885 5–14
——— v. Inland Revenue Commissioners [1965] A.C. 244; [1964] 3 W.L.R. 511;
[1964] 3 All E.R. 119; 1964 S.C. (H.L.) 180; 1964 S.L.T. 302; 42 T.C. 42;
43 A.T.C. 244; [1964] T.R. 269; 108 S.J. 636, HL 10–20
——— v. KMR Services Ltd; Sword Daniels v. Pitel [1995] 4 All E.R. 598; [1995]
2 Lloyd's Rep. 513; *The Times,* July 26, 1995; *The Independent,* September
13, 1995; Lloyd's List, October 3, 1995 (I.D.), CA; affirming [1994] 4 All
E.R. 385; *The Independent,* April 19, 1994; *The Guardian,* April 22, 1994,
QBD 8–282, 16–10, 16–20, 16–25, 16–26, 16–27, 16–28, 16–64, 16–65, 16–66,
16–71, 16–73, 16–74, 16–75
——— v. Lewisham and North Southwark H.A. [1999] Lloyd's Rep. Med. 110;
(1999) 48 B.M.L.R. 96, CA 12–18, 12–244, 12–273, 12–282
——— v. Raphael [1958] Ch. 636; [1958] 2 W.L.R. 647; [1958] 2 All E.R. 79; 102
S.J. 269, CA 13–86
——— v. Tolley (1874) 31 L.T. 485; 39 J.P. 214 10–192
——— v. University of Alberta Hospital [1997] 145 D.L.R. (4th) 63, CA
(Alberta) 12–73, 12–75, 12–199, 12–260
Browne v. Guys & Lewisham NHS Trust [1997] 8 Med.L.R. 132, CC (Central
London) 12–121, 12–122
Brownie Wills v. Shrimpton [1988] 2 N.Z.L.R. 321 2–112
Brownie Wills (A Firm) v. Shrimpton [1999] Lloyd's Rep. P.N. 39; [1999]
P.N.L.R. 552, CA (NZ) 10–43
Bruschett v. Cowan [1991] 2 Med.L.R. 271, CA (Newfoundland) 12–127, 12–276
Brushett v. Cowan (1990) 3 C.C.L.T. (2d) 195 5–114
Bryan v. Maloney, 74 B.L.R. 35; 51 Con. L.R. 29; (1995) 11 Const. L.J. 274, HC
(Aus) 2–63, 2–64, 8–78, 8–119, 8–120
Bryant v. Busk (1827) 4 Russ 1; 38 E.R. 705 10–197
——— v. Goodrich (1966) 110 S.J. 108, CA 10–153, 10–267
Buckland v. Mackesy; Buckland v. Watts, 208 E.G. 969; 118 N.L.J. 1009; (1968)
112 S.J. 841; *The Times,* October 17, 1968, CA 9–78, 9–110, 9–149, 10–203
——— v. Watts. See Buckland v. Mackesy.
Buckley v. Lane Herdman & Co. [1977] C.L.Y.B. 3143 .... 10–301, 10–309, 10–311,
10–313

PARA.

Buckley v. National Union of General and Municipal Workers [1967] 3 All E.R.
767; 4 K.I.R. 277; 112 S.J. 292, Assizes (Manchester) 10–282
—— v. United Kingdom (1997) 23 E.H.R.R. 101; [1997] 2 P.L.R. 10; [1996]
J.P.L. 1018; *The Times*, October 9, 1996; *The Independent*, October 10,
1996, ECHR 7–48
Bucknam v. Kostuick (1983) 3 D.L.R. (4th) 99, HC (Ontario) 12–204
Budrewicz v. Stojanowski (1998) 41 O.R. (3d) 78, HC (Ontario) 10–43
Buerckert v. Mattison [1997] 1 W.W.R. 430, QB (Saskatchewan) 10–286
Bull v. Devon A.H.A. [1993] 4 Med.L.R. 117, CA 12–121, 12–158, 12–160, 12–200
Bullock v. Lloyds Bank Ltd [1955] Ch. 317; [1955] 2 W.L.R. 1; [1954] 3 All E.R.
726; 99 S.J. 28, Ch D 2–144
Bulmer v. Gilman (1842) 4 Man. & G. 108; 3 Scott N.R. 781; 11 L.J.C.P. 174;
6 Jur. 761; 134 E.R. 45 10–96
Burdick v. Garrick (1870) L.R. 5 Ch. App. 233; 39 L.J.Ch. 368; 18 W.R. 387,
CA 5–90, 5–93, 10–20
Burgess v. Newcastle H.A. [1992] 3 Med.L.R. 224, QBD 12–93
Burgoine v. Taylor (1878) 9 Ch.D. 1; 47 L.J.Ch. 542; 38 L.T. 438; 26 W.R. 568,
CA 10–183
Burns v. Furby (1885) 4 N.Z.L.R. S.C. 110 8–253
Burrell Hayward & Budd v. Chris Carnell and David Green, February 20, 1992,
unreported 8–06, 8–225
Burton v. Burton [1980] Ch. 240 13–142
—— v. Islington H.A.; *sub nom.* B v. Islington H.A.; De Martell v. Merton and
Sutton H.A. (No.1) [1993] Q.B. 204; [1992] 3 W.L.R. 637; [1992] 3 All E.R.
833; [1992] 2 F.L.R. 184; [1992] 2 F.C.R. 845; [1992] P.I.Q.R. P269; [1993]
4 Med.L.R. 8; (1992) 89(17) L.S.G. 51; (1992) 142 N.L.J. 565; (1992) 136
S.J.L.B. 104; *The Times*, March 25, 1992; *The Independent*, April 8, 1992;
The Guardian, May 20, 1992, CA 12–55
Butler v. Knight (1867) L.R. 2 Ex 109; 36 L.J.Ex. 66; 15 L.T. 621; 15 W.R.
407 .... 10–189, 10–292
Byrne v. Hall Pain & Foster [1999] 1 W.L.R. 1849; [1999] 2 All E.R. 400; 68
Con. L.R. 110; [1999] Lloyd's Rep. P.N. 147; [1999] P.N.L.R. 565; [1999]
1 E.G.L.R. 73; [1999] 12 E.G. 165; (1999) 15 Const. L.J. 388; [1998]
E.G.C.S. 182; (1999) 96(5) L.S.G. 37; (1999) 143 S.J.L.B. 36; [1998] N.P.C.
164; *The Times*, January 8, 1999, CA 5–35, 9–09

C, Re (1908) 53 S.J. 119, DC 10–68
C, Re, March 5, 1997, unreported 12–141
C (A Child) (HIV Testing), Re; *sub nom.* C (A Minor) (HIV Test), Re [1999] 2
F.L.R. 1004CA [2000] Fam. 48; [2000] 2 W.L.R. 270; [1999] 3 F.C.R. 289;
(1999) 50 B.M.L.R. 283; *The Times*, September 14, 1999, Fam Div 12–148
C (A Minor) (Medical Treatment), Re; *sub nom.* C (A Minor) (Withdrawal of
Lifesaving Treatment), Re [1998] 1 F.L.R. 384; [1998] 1 F.C.R. 1; [1998]
Lloyd's Rep. Med. 1; (1998) 40 B.M.L.R. 31; [1998] Fam. Law 135; *The
Independent*, December 11, 1997, Fam Div 12–148
C (A Minor) (Medical Treatment: Court's Jurisdiction), Re; *sub nom.* C (A
Minor) (Detention for Medical Treatment), Re [1997] 2 F.L.R. 180; [1997]
3 F.C.R. 49; [1997] Fam. Law 474; (1997) 94(13) L.S.G. 29; (1997) 141
S.J.L.B. 72; *The Times*, March 21, 1997; *The Independent*, March 20, 1997,
Fam Div 12–148
C (Adult: Refusal of Medical Treatment), Re [1994] 1 W.L.R. 290; [1994] 1 All
E.R. 819; [1994] 1 F.L.R. 31; [1994] 2 F.C.R. 151, Fam Div 12–136, 12–140,
12–141
C v. A Health Authority, November 3, 1998, unreported, QBD 12–176, 12–272,
12–277

PARA.

C v. C (Wasted Costs Order) 3140[1994] 2 F.L.R. 34; [1994] 2 F.C.R. 1012;
[1994] Fam. Law, Fam Div 10–135
—— v. Mirror Group Newspapers; *sub nom.* Clare v. Mirror Group Newspapers
(1986) Ltd [1997] 1 W.L.R. 131; [1996] 4 All E.R. 511; [1996] E.M.L.R.
518; [1996] 2 F.L.R. 532; [1997] 1 F.C.R. 556; [1996] Fam. Law 671; (1996)
146 N.L.J. 1093; *The Times,* July 15, 1996; *The Independent,* July 19, 1996,
CA 5–72
CBS Songs Ltd v. Amstrad Consumer Electronics plc (No.1) [1988] A.C. 1013;
[1988] 2 W.L.R. 1191; [1988] 2 All E.R. 484; [1988] 2 F.T.L.R. 168; [1988]
R.P.C. 567; (1988) 132 S.J. 789; *The Times,* May 13, 1988; *The Independent,*
May 17, 1988 (C.S.); *Financial Times,* May 18, 1988; *The Guardian,* May
19, 1988, HL 15–50
CIL Securities v. Briant Champion Long [1993] 42 E.G. 281; [1993] E.G.C.S.
22 9–179
CJD Group B v. Medical Research Council. *See* Group B Plaintiffs v. Medical
Research Council.
CW Dixey & Sons Ltd v. Parsons (1964) 192 E.G. 197, QBD 10–98, 10–165
Cade v. Cade (1998) 71 S.A.S.R. 571, Full Ct (Aus) 10–154
Cady v. Hanson (1989) 51 D.L.R. (4th) 139, CA (BC) 10–160
Caldeira v. Gray [1936] 1 All E.R. 540; 80 S.J. 243, PC 12–192
Calderbank v. Calderbank [1976] Fam. 93; [1975] 3 W.L.R. 586; [1975] 3 All
E.R. 333; (1975) 5 Fam. Law 190; 119 S.J. 490, CA 10–283
Calico Printers Assn. v. Barclays Bank Ltd (1931) 145 L.T. 151 2–94
Callaghan (t/a Stage 3 Discotheque) v. Thompson [2000] C.L.C. 360; [2000]
Lloyd's Rep. I.R. 125, QBD (Comm Ct) 14–03, 14–09
Callander v. Oelrichs (1838) 5 Bing.N.C. 58; 1 Arn. 401; 6 Scott 761; 8 L.J.C.P.
25; 4 L.T. 341; 2 Jur. 967; 132 E.R. 1026 .... 14–38, 14–74
Calne Gas Co. v. Curtis (1918) 59 Acct.L.R. 17 .... 15–90, 15–95
Caltex Oil (Australia) Pty v. Dredge Willemstad, The (1976) 136 C.L.R. 529;
(1977) 51 A.L.J.R. 270, HC (Aus) 2–65
Calver v. Westwood Veterinary Group [2001] P.I.Q.R. P11; [2001] Lloyd's Rep.
Med. 20; (2001) 58 B.M.L.R. 194; [2001] Lloyd's Rep. P.N. 102, CA 12–105
Cambridge Credit Corp. Ltd v. Hutcheson (1985) 9 A.C.L.R. 545; 9 A.C.L.R.
669 15–121
—— v. Hutcheson (No.1) (1983) 8 A.C.L.R. 123 15–121
—— v. Hutcheson (No.2) (1983) 8 A.C.L.R. 513 15–121
—— v. Hutcheson (No.3) (1983) 8 A.C.L.R. 526 15–121
Cameron Publications Ltd v. Piers, Conrod & Allen (1986) 35 B.L.R. 32, Sup Ct
(Nova Scotia) 15–110
Campbell and Fell v. United Kingdom; Series A, No.80; (1985) 7 E.H.R.R. 165,
ECHR 7–08
Campbell v. Clason (1838) 1 Dunlop 270; (1840) 2 Dunlop 1113, Ct Sess 10–294
—— v. Edwards [1976] 1 W.L.R. 403; [1976] 1 All E.R. 785; [1976] 1 Lloyd's
Rep. 522; 119 S.J. 845, CA 9–62, 9–74
—— v. Rickards (1833) 5 B. & Ad. 840; 2 Nev. & M.K.B. 542; 2 L.J.K.B. 206;
110 E.R. 1001 14–60
—— v. United Kingdom; Series A, No.233A; (1993) 15 E.H.R.R. 137; *The
Times,* April 1, 1992; *The Independent,* April 16, 1992; *The Guardian,* April
2, 1992, ECHR 7–33
—— v. Walker (1800) 5 Ves.Jun. 678 2–135
Canada Southern Petroleum v. Amoco Canada Petroleum Co. (1997) 144 D.L.R.
(4th) 30, CA (Alberta) 10–31
Canada Trustco Mortgage Company v. Barlet & Richardes and Gates (1996) 28
O.R. 768, CA (Ontario) 10–228
Canadian General Insurance Company v. Lacey, Stoyles Insurance Services Ltd
(1985) 56 Nfld. & P.E.I.R. 125, DC (Newfoundland) 14–23

PARA.

Canadian Land Reclaiming and Colonizing Co., Coventry and Dixon's Case, Re
  (1880) 14 Ch.D. 660, 670 15–24
Canadian National Railway Co. v. Norsk Pacific Steamship Co.; Jervis Crown,
  The (1992) 91 D.L.R. (4th) 289 .... 2–43, 2–59, 8–77, 8–112, 8–113
Canadian Pacific Railway Co. v. Aikins, MacAulay & Thorvaldson (1998) 157
  D.L.R. (4th) 473, CA (Maniba) 10–31
Canadian Woodmen of the World v. Hooper [1933] 1 D.L.R. 168 .... 15–116, 15–121
Canberra Formwork Pty Ltd v. Civil & Civic Ltd (1982) 41 A.C.T.R. 1 8–81
Cancer Research Campaign v. Ernest Brown & Co. [1997] S.T.C. 1425; [1998]
  P.N.L.R. 592, Ch D 10–45, 10–49, 10–221, 10–260
Candler v. Crane Christmas & Co. [1951] 2 K.B. 164; [1951] 1 All E.R. 426;
  [1951] 1 T.L.R. 371; 95 S.J. 171, CA 2–25, 2–70, 2–110, 3–02, 9–20, 9–41, 9–47,
                                               9–48, 12–57, 15–53, 15–54, 15–136
Candlewood Navigation Corp. v. Mitsui Osk Lines; Mineral Transporter, The
  andIbaraki Maru, The [1986] A.C. 1; [1985] 3 W.L.R. 381; [1985] 2 All E.R.
  935; [1985] 2 Lloyd's Rep. 303; (1985) 82 L.S.G. 2912; (1985) 135 N.L.J.
  677; (1985) 129 S.J. 506, PC (Aus) 2–29
Cane v. Allen (1814) 2 Dow 289 .... 2–131, 2–134
Cann v. Willson (1888) L.R. 39 Ch. D. 39; 32 S.J. 542; 57 L.J.Ch. 1034; 59 L.T.
  723; 37 W.R. 23; 4 T.L.R. 588, Ch D 9–33, 9–34, 9–48
Canson Enterprises Ltd v. Boughton & Co. (1992) 85 D.L.R. (4th) 129, Sup Ct
  (Can) 3–11, 3–13, 10–230, 10–327
—— v. Boughton & Co. [1996] 1 W.W.R. 412, CA (BC) 10–25, 10–230
Canterbury v. Spence, 464 F. 2d 772 (D.C. Cir. 1972) 12–130, 12–211
Cantwell v. Petersen (1983) 139 D.L.R. (3d) 466 .... 9–83, 9–91
Caparo Industries plc v. Dickman [1990] 2 A.C. 605; [1990] 2 W.L.R. 358;
  [1990] 1 All E.R. 568; [1990] B.C.L.C. 273; [1990] B.C.C. 164; [1990]
  E.C.C. 313; [1955–95] P.N.L.R. 523; (1990) 87(12) L.S.G. 42; (1990) 140
  N.L.J. 248; (1990) 134 S.J. 494; The Times, February 12, 1990; The Inde-
  pendent, February 16, 1990; Financial Times, February 13, 1990; The
  Guardian, February 15, 1990; The Daily Telegraph, February 15, 1990, HL
  [1989] Q.B. 653; [1989] 2 W.L.R. 316; [1989] 1 All E.R. 798; [1989]
  B.C.L.C. 154; (1989) 5 B.C.C. 105; [1989] P.C.C. 125; (1988) 138 N.L.J.
  289; (1989) 133 S.J. 221; The Times, August 8, 1988; The Independent,
  August 10, 1988; Financial Times, August 5, 1988; The Daily Telegraph,
  August 26, 1988, CA 2–18, 2–31, 2–37, 2–42, 2–43, 2–47, 2–69, 2–75, 2–79,
                              2–103, 2–110, 2–113, 7–19, 7–23, 8–70, 8–121, 10–40, 10–48,
                              9–35, 9–49, 9–113, 12–46, 12–289, 12–290, 12–295, 13–111,
                              15–11, 15–36, 15–45, 15–48, 15–49, 15–50, 15–52, 15–53,
                              15–56, 15–60, 15–61, 15–65, 15–69, 15–70, 15–74, 15–76,
                              15–77, 15–78, 15–82, 15–83, 15–125, 15–141, 16–18, 17–51,
                              17–65, 17–66, 17–70
Cape Breton Ltd, Re (1885) 29 Ch.D. 795 3–10
Capital and Counties plc v. Hampshire C.C.; John Munroe (Acrylics) Ltd v.
  London Fire and Civil Defence Authority; Church of Jesus Christ of Latter
  Day Saints (Great Britain) v. West Yorkshire Fire and Civil Defence Author-
  ity; Digital Equipment Co. Ltd v. Hampshire C.C. [1997] Q.B. 1004; [1997]
  3 W.L.R. 331; [1997] 2 All E.R. 865; [1997] 2 Lloyd's Rep. 161; (1997) 147
  N.L.J. 599; (1997) 141 S.J.L.B. 92; The Times, March 20, 1997; The
  Independent, April 10, 1997, CA .... 2–77, 2–83, 2–99, >12–15, 12–19, 12–21,
                                            12–66
Cardin v. City of Montreal (1961) 29 D.L.R. (2d) 492 .... 12–80, 12–83
Cardy & Co. v. Taylor and Roberts, 38 Con. L.R. 79; [1994] E.G.C.S. 46; [1994]
  N.P.C. 30 .... 8–144, 8–184, 8–279, 8–307
Carindale Country Club Estate Pty. Ltd v. Astill (1993) 115 A.L.R. 112 10–31

PARA.

Carl Zeiss Stiftung v. Herbert Smith & Co. (No.2) [1969] 2 Ch. 276; [1969] 2
W.L.R. 427; [1969] 2 All E.R. 367; [1969] F.S.R. 40; [1969] R.P.C. 316; 112
S.J. 1021; *The Times*, December 11, 1968, CA 10–37
Carlton v. Fulchers [1997] P.N.L.R. 33, CA 10–12, 10–185
Carosella v. Ginos and Gilbert Pty. (1981) 27 S.A.S.R. 515 .... 8–217, 8–325
Carr v. Inland Revenue Commissioners [1944] 2 All E.R. 163; 171 L.T. 177,
CA 1–08
Carradine Properties Ltd v. DJ Freeman & Co. [1999] Lloyd's Rep. P.N. 483;
[1955–95] P.N.L.R. 219; (1989) 5 Const. L.J. 267; *The Times*, February 19,
1982, CA 5–114, 8–136, 10–141, 10–142, 10–162, 10–170
Carr-Glynn v. Frearsons [1999] Ch. 326; [1999] 2 W.L.R. 1046; [1998] 4 All E.R.
225; [1999] 1 F.L.R. 8; [1998] 3 F.C.R. 487; [1999] P.N.L.R. 13; [1998]
Fam. Law 739; [1998] E.G.C.S. 128; (1998) 148 N.L.J. 1487; [1998] N.P.C.
136, CA 10–48, 10–52, 10–221, 15–74
Carruthers v. Hodgson (1896) 100 L.T.J. 395 10–192
Carter (t/a New Chapel Developments) v. TG Baynes & Sons [1998] E.G.C.S.
109, Ch D 10–247, 10–273
Cartledge v. E Jopling & Sons Ltd [1963] A.C. 758; [1963] 2 W.L.R. 210; [1963]
1 All E.R. 341; [1963] 1 Lloyd's Rep. 1; 107 S.J. 73, HL 5–16, 5–19, 5–22, 5–31
Carver v. Hammersmith and Queen Charlotte's H.A., February 25, 2000, unre-
ported, QBD 12–231, 12–277
Carvin v. Dunham Brindley & Linn [1997] E.G.C.S. 90, CA 10–199
Casey v. Hugh James Jones & Jenkins [1999] Lloyd's Rep. P.N. 115, QBD 10–191,
10–284
—— v. Provan (1984) 11 D.L.R. (4th) 708, HC (Ontario) 12–203, 12–264
Cassey v. Morrison (1993) 15 O.R. (3d) 223, CA (Ontario) 10–25
Cassidy v. Ministry of Health [1951] 2 K.B. 343; [1951] 1 All E.R. 574; [1951]
1 T.L.R. 539; (1952) 96 S.J. 253; 95 S.J. 253, CA 12–121, 12–153, 12–155
Castell v. De Greef (1994) (4) S.A. 408 12–207
Cataford v. Moreau (1981) 114 D.L.R. (3d) 585 12–289
Cates v. Indermaur (1858) 1 F. & F. 259, NP 10–116, 10–180
Cavan v. Wilcox (1973) 44 D.L.R. (3d) 42 12–120
Cavanagh v. Bristol & Weston H.A. [1992] 3 Med.L.R. 49, QBD 12–175
—— v. Ulster Weaving Co. [1960] A.C. 145; [1959] 3 W.L.R. 262; [1959] 2 All
E.R. 745; [1959] 2 Lloyd's Rep. 165; 103 S.J. 581, HL 12–94
Cave v. Robinson Jarvis & Rolf (A Firm); *sub nom.* Robinson Jarvis and Rolf (A
Firm) v. Cave [2001] EWCA Civ 245; [2001] C.P. Rep. 66; [2001] Lloyd's
Rep. P.N. 290; [2001] P.N.L.R. 23; (2001) 17 Const. L.J. 262; [2001]
E.G.C.S. 28; [2001] N.P.C. 36; *The Independent*, April 9, 2001 (C.S), CA 5–74,
5–77, 5–78
Cavendish Funding Ltd v. Henry Spencer & Sons Ltd [1998] P.N.L.R. 122;
[1998] 1 E.G.L.R. 104; [1998] 06 E.G. 146; [1997] E.G.C.S. 146; [1997]
N.P.C. 150, CA 9–121, 9–171, 9–172
Cedar Transport Group v. First Wyvern Property Trustees Co.; *sub nom.* Cedar
Transport v. Wyvern (1982) 258 E.G. 1077 .... 8–167, 8–253, 8–254
Cee Bee Marine Ltd v. Lombard Insurance Co. Ltd [1990] 2 N.Z.L.R. 1, CA
(NZ) 14–46, 14–104, 14–105, 14–111, 14–112, 14–112, 14–124
Cemp Properties (U.K.) Ltd v. Dentsply Research & Development Corp. [1989]
2 E.G.L.R. 205; [1989] 35 E.G. 99, Ch D 10–56, 10–270, 10–302
—— v. Dentsply Research & Development Corp. (No.2) [1991] 2 E.G.L.R. 197;
[1991] 34 E.G. 62, CA 6–14, 9–06
Central Trust Co. v. Rafuse (1986) 31 D.L.R. (4th) 481, Sup Ct (Can) 8–51, 8–52,
10–15, 10–81, 10–82, 10–143, 10–323
—— v. Rafuse (1993) 95 D.L.R. (4th) 269, CA (Alberta) 10–323
Century Homes Pty Ltd (in liquidation), Re (1984) 73 F.L.R. 462, Fed Ct
(Aus) 10–21

PARA.

Chamberlain v. Boodle & King [1982] 1 W.L.R. 1443; [1982] 3 All E.R. 188; 125 S.J. 257; *The Times*, April 1, 1981, CA 5–03, 10–140

Chambers v. Goldthorpe; Restell v. Nye [1901] 1 Q.B. 624; 45 S.J. 325; [1900–03] All E.R. 969; 70 L.J.K.B. 482; 84 L.T. 444; 49 W.R. 401; 17 T.L.R. 304, CA 8–14, 8–253

Champion v. Rigby (1830) 1 Russ. & M. 539 .... 2–137, 2–139

Channon v. Lindley Johnstone (A Firm) [2000] 2 F.L.R. 734; [2000] Fam. Law 712, QBD 10–109, 10–181

Chaplin v. Hicks [1911] 1 K.B. 786, CA 12–251, 17–112

Chapman v. Rix [1994] 5 Med.L.R. 2, HL 12–198

—— v. Van Toll; Van Toll v. Chapman (1857) 8 E. & B. 396; 27 L.J.Q.B. 1; 30 L.T.O.S. 116; 8 Jur.(N.S.) 1126; W.R. 17; 120 E.R. 148 10–175

—— v. Walton (1833) 10 Bing. 57; 3 Moo. & S. 389; [1824–34] All E.R. 384; 2 L.J.C.P. 910; 131 E.R. 826 .... 14–32, 14–57

Chappel v. Hart [1999] Lloyd's Rep. Med. 223, HC (Aus) 12–257, 12–261, 12–266, 12–267, 12–268

Chappell v. Cooper; *sub nom.* Player v. Bruguiere [1980] 1 W.L.R. 958; [1980] 2 All E.R. 463; 124 S.J. 544, CA 5–65

Charette v. Provenzano (1978) 7 C.C.L.R. 23, HC (Ontario) 10–271

Chariot Inns Ltd v. Assicurazioni Generali S.p.a. [1981] I.R. 199 14–65

Charles v. Altin (1854) 15 C.B. 46 14–124

—— v. Hugh James Jones & Jenkins [2000] 1 W.L.R. 1278; [2000] 1 All E.R. 289; [2001] P.I.Q.R. P1; [2000] Lloyd's Rep. P.N. 207; *The Times*, December 22, 1999, CA 10–283, 10–288

Chasney v. Anderson [1950] 4 D.L.R. 223, Sup Ct (Can) 12–95, 12–194

Chatterton v. Gerson [1981] Q.B. 432; [1980] 3 W.L.R. 1003; [1981] 1 All E.R. 257; 124 S.J. 885, QBD 12–127, 12–131, 12–202, 12–208, 12–232, 12–262, 12–263

Chelmsford D.C. v. TJ Evers Ltd, 25 B.L.R. 99; (1984) 1 Const. L.J. 65, QBD 5–15, 8–33

Chelsea Building Society v. Goddard & Smith [1996] E.G.C.S. 157, QBD 10–332

Chennells v. Bruce (1939) 55 T.L.R. 422 2–144

Cherekwayo v. Grafton (1993) 84 Man.R. (2d) 81 12–195

Cherry v. Borsman (1992) 94 D.L.R. (4th) 487, CA (BC) 12–55

Cherry Ltd v. Allied Insurance Brokers Ltd [1978] 1 Lloyd's Rep. 274, QBD 14–14, 14–15, 14–31

Chesham Properties Ltd v. Bucknall Austin Management Services Ltd, 82 B.L.R. 92; 53 Con. L.R. 22, QBD (OR) 5–15, 8–28, 8–36, 8–38, 8–63

Chester v. Afshar, December 21, 2000, unreported, QBD 12–263

Chief Constable of North Yorkshire v. Audsley [2000] Lloyd's Rep. P.N. 675, QBD 10–132, 11–28, 11–30

Chilton v. Blair (1914) 8 B.W.C.C. 1, CA 10–69

Chin Keow v. Government of Malaysia [1967] 1 W.L.R. 813; 111 S.J. 333, PC 12–68, 12–72, 12–106

Chin Sin Motor Works v. Arosa Development Sdn Bhd [1992] 1 M.L.J. 23 8–99

China Light & Power Company Limited v. Michael Ford [1996] 1 H.K.L.R. 57, CA 11–05

Chissell v. Poole Hospital NHS Trust [1998] Lloyd's Rep. Med. 357, CC (Bournemouth) 12–176

Chong v. Scott Collins & Co. (1954) 164 E.G. 662 .... 9–92, 9–110

Choukalos v. Smith Lyons (1994) 97 B.C.L.R. (2d) 122 10–31

Chown v. Parrott; *sub nom.* Choun v. Parrott (1863) 14 C.B. (N.S.) 74; 2 New.Rep. 127; 32 L.J.C.P. 197; 9 Jur.(N.S.) 1290; 11 W.R. 668; 8 L.T. 391 10–189

Christensen v. Scott [1996] 1 N.Z.L.R. 273 10–42

PARA.

Christiani and Nielsen Ltd v. Lowry Centre Development Co. Ltd, unreported, June 29, 2000 .... 8–339, 8–340

Christie v. Wilson; *sub nom.* Wilson v. Christie [1998] 1 W.L.R. 1694; [1999] 1 All E.R. 545; [1998] P.N.L.R. 748; (1998) 95(30) L.S.G. 25; (1998) 142 S.J.L.B. 205; *The Times*, July 6, 1998; *The Independent*, June 22, 1998 (C.S.), CA 10–33

Christofi v. Barclays Bank plc [2000] 1 W.L.R. 937; [1999] 4 All E.R. 437; [1999] 2 All E.R. (Comm) 417; [1999] Lloyd's Rep. Bank. 469; [2000] 1 F.L.R. 163; [1999] B.P.I.R. 855; [2000] Fam. Law 161; (1999) 96(29) L.S.G. 29; *The Times*, July 1, 1999, CA 2–156

Christopher Moran Holdings Ltd v. Carden & Godfrey (A Firm), 73 Con. L.R. 28, QBD (T&CC) 8–167, 8–203, 8–204

Chubey v. Ahsan (1977) 71 D.L.R. (3d) 550 .... 12–80, 12–193

Cia de Seguros Imperio v. Heath (REBX) Ltd (formerly CE Heath & Co. (America) Ltd); *sub nom.* Companhia de Seguros Imperio v. Heath (REBX) Ltd [2001] 1 W.L.R. 112; [2000] 2 All E.R. (Comm) 787; [2000] C.L.C. 1543; [2001] Lloyd's Rep. I.R. 109; [2000] Lloyd's Rep. P.N. 795; *The Times*, September 26, 2000; *The Independent*, October 23, 2000 (C.S), CA; affirming [1999] 1 All E.R. (Comm) 750; [1999] C.L.C. 997; [1999] Lloyd's Rep. I.R. 571; [1999] Lloyd's Rep. P.N. 571; *The Independent*, May 3, 1999 (C.S.), QBD (Comm Ct) 2–127, 5–79, 5–92

Citadel Management Inc. v. Equal Ltd; *sub nom.* Citadel Management Inc. v. Thompson [1999] 1 F.L.R. 21; [1998] Fam. Law 738; (1998) 95(36) L.S.G. 32; (1998) 142 S.J.L.B. 253; *The Times*, September 25, 1998, CA 10–72

Citibank Savings Ltd v. Nicholson (1997) 70 S.A.S.R. 206 10–167

Citicorp Australia Ltd v. O'Brien (1996) 40 N.S.W.L.R. 398, CA (NSW) 10–203

City Equitable Fire Insurance Co. Ltd, Re [1925] Ch. 407; [1924] All E.R. Rep. 485, CA 15–24, 15–33, 15–90, 15–95, 15–96, 15–98, 15–100, 15–110, 15–112, 15–121

Clarence Construction Ltd v. Lavallee (1980) 111 D.L.R. (3d) 582; (1982) 132 D.L.R. (3d) 153, CA (BC) 10–25, 10–61, 10–100, 10–166

Clarion Ltd v. National Provident Institution [2000] 1 W.L.R. 1888; [2000] 2 All E.R. 265, Ch D 13–91

Clark, Re (1851) 1 De G.M. & G. 43; affirming (1851) 13 Beav. 173; 51 E.R. 67 10–116

Clark, Re; Clark v. Moore, Moores (Chemists) Ltd (1920) 150 L.T.Jo. 94 2–140

Clark v. Clark (No.2) [1991] 1 F.L.R. 179; [1990] F.C.R. 953; [1991] Fam. Law 58; (1991) 141 N.L.J. 206 .... 10–119, 10–132

—— v. Kirby Smith [1964] Ch. 506; [1964] 3 W.L.R. 239; [1964] 2 All E.R. 835; [1964] 2 Lloyd's Rep. 172; 108 S.J. 462, Ch D 10–13, 10–237, 10–265

—— v. MacLennan [1983] 1 All E.R. 416, QBD 12–86, 12–106, 12–247, 12–254

—— v. Woor [1965] 1 W.L.R. 650; [1965] 2 All E.R. 353; 109 S.J. 251, QBD 5–70

Clark Boyce v. Mouat [1994] 1 A.C. 428; [1993] 3 W.L.R. 1021; [1993] 4 All E.R. 268; (1993) 143 N.L.J. 1440; (1993) 137 S.J.L.B. 231; [1993] N.P.C. 128; *The Times*, October 7, 1993; *The Independent*, October 12, 1993, PC (NZ) 2–128, 2–133, 8–63, 9–20, 10–25, 10–101, 10–160

Clarke v. Adams (1950) 94 S.J. 599 .... 12–97, 12–222

—— v. Bruce Lance & Co. [1988] 1 W.L.R. 881; [1988] 1 All E.R. 364; (1988) 85(2) L.S.G. 37; (1987) 137 N.L.J. 1064; (1987) 131 S.J. 1698; (1988) 7 Tr. L. 200, CA 10–51, 10–52, 10–53

—— v. Couchman (1885) 20 L.J. 318 10–307

—— v. Hurst (1992) 4 S.A. 630 12–145

—— v. Marlborough Fine Art (London) Ltd, *The Times*, July 5, 2001, Ch D 5–88, 5–97

—— v. Milford (1987) 38 D.L.R. (4th) 139, CA (Nova Scotia) 10–304

—— v. Worboys, *The Times*, March 18, 1952, CA 12–120

PARA.

Clarke Poje and Kenney (1989) 38 B.C.L.R. (2d) 110, CA (BC) 10–143, 10–261
Clay v. AJ Crump & Sons Ltd [1964] 1 Q.B. 533; [1963] 3 W.L.R. 866; [1963]
  3 All E.R. 687; 4 B.L.R. 80; 107 S.J. 664, CA 5–03, 8–80, 8–251, 8–277, 8–308
Clayton v. Kearsey (1935) 79 S.J. 180, KBD 10–185, 10–277
—— v. Woodman & Son (Builders) Ltd; Woodman & Son (Builders) Ltd v.
  Charles E Ware & Son [1962] 2 Q.B. 533; [1962] 1 W.L.R. 585; [1962] 2
  All E.R. 33; 4 B.L.R. 65; 106 S.J. 242, CA; reversing [1961] 3 W.L.R. 987;
  [1961] 3 All E.R. 249; 105 S.J. 889, QBD 8–14, 8–129, 8–248, 8–250
Clemence v. Clarke (1880) cited in Hudson's Building Contracts (4th ed.), Vol.
  2, p. 54 8–241
Cliarlariello v. Schacter (1991) 76 D.L.R. (4th) 449, Sup Ct (Can) 12–127, 12–204
Clinton v. Regina District Health Board and Gellner (1998) 171 Sask. R. 44, QBD
  (Saskatchewan) 12–240, 12–273
Clunis v. Camden and Islington H.A. [1998] Q.B. 978; [1998] 2 W.L.R. 902;
  [1998] 3 All E.R. 180; (1997–98) 1 C.C.L. Rep. 215; (1998) 40 B.M.L.R.
  181; [1998] P.N.L.R. 262; (1998) 95(2) L.S.G. 23; (1998) 142 S.J.L.B. 38;
  The Times, December 10, 1997; *The Independent*, December 9, 1997,
  CA 12–238
Coad v. Cornwall and Isles of Scilly H.A. [1997] 1 W.L.R. 189; [1997] P.I.Q.R.
  P92; [1997] 8 Med.L.R. 154; (1997) 33 B.M.L.R. 168; (1996) 93(27) L.S.G.
  28; (1996) 140 S.J.L.B. 168; *The Times*, July 30, 1996, CA 5–65
Coban v. Allen [1997] 8 Med.L.R. 316; *The Times*, October 14, 1996, CA 5–57
Cochrane v. Graham & Sibbald, 1987 S.C. 63; 1987 S.L.T. 622, 2 Div 9–192
Cock Russell & Co. v. Bray Gibb & Co. Ltd (1920) 3 Ll.L.Rep. 71, KBD (Comm
  Ct) 14–59
Cockerell v. Cholmeley (1830) 1 Russ. & M. 418 5–105
Coco v. AN Clark (Engineers) Ltd [1968] F.S.R. 415; [1969] R.P.C. 41, Ch D 2–148,
  2–155, 2–156, 2–162
Coffin v. MacBeath (1990) 81 Nfld. & P.E.I.R. 333, CA (Newfoundland) 10–277
Cohen v. Selby; *sub nom.* Simmon Box (Diamonds) Ltd, Re [2001] 1 B.C.L.C.
  176, CA 15–24
Coldman v. Hill [1919] 1 K.B. 443; 63 S.J. 166; [1918–19] All E.R. Rep. 434; 88
  L.J.K.B. 491; 120 L.T. 412; 35 T.L.R. 146, CA 9–120
Coles v. Reading and District Hospital Management Committee (1963) 107 S.J.
  115; *The Times*, January 30, 1963 12–197
—— v. Sir Frederick Young (Insurances) Ltd (1929) 33 Ll.L.Rep. 83 14–85
—— v. Trescothick (1804) 9 Ves.Jun. 234 2–138
Collard v. Saunders (1972) 221 E.G. 797 .... 9–91, 9–131, 9–140, 9–142, 9–191, 10–268
Collicutt, Re, 128 N.S.R.(2d); 359 A.P.R. 81 10–219
Collin Hotels v. Surtees [1988] 1 W.W.E. 272, CA (Saskatchewan) 10–294
Collins v. Brebner [2000] Lloyd's Rep. P.N. 587, CA 10–231
—— v. Hertfordshire C.C. [1947] K.B. 598; [1947] 1 All E.R. 633; 63 T.L.R.
  317; 111 J.P. 272; [1947] L.J.R. 789; 176 L.T. 456, KBD 12–153, 12–155,
  12–192
Colmer v. Merrett, Son & Street (1914) 50 Acct.L.R. 21 .... 15–112, 15–136
Columbus Co. Ltd v. Clowes [1903] 1 K.B. 244; 72 L.J.K.B. 330; 51 W.R. 366,
  KBD 8–50, 8–184, 8–314, 8–316
Comber v. Anderson (1808) 1 Camp. 523 14–57
Commerce Capital v. Berk (1989) 5 R.P.R. (2d) 177, CA (Ontario) 10–228
Commercial Bridging plc v. Nelsons [1998] C.L.Y. 4018, Ch D 10–166
Commercial Financial Services Ltd v. McBeth & Co., 1988 S.L.T. 528; 1988
  S.C.L.R. 248, OH 9–71
Commissioners of Inland Revenue v. Maxse [1919] 2 K.B. 647; 88 L.J.K.B. 752;
  63 S.J. 429; 120 L.T. 680; 35 T.L.R. 348; 12 Tax.Cas. 56, CA 1–07
Commonwealth Bank of Australia v. Smith (1992) 111 A.L.R. 687; (1992) 102
  A.L.R. 453, Fed Ct (Aus) 10–100, 10–228

PARA.

Commonwealth Insurance Co. v. Groupe Sprinks S.A. [1983] 1 Lloyd's Rep. 67,
QBD (Comm Ct) 14–70
Communications Groups Inc. v. Warner Communications, Misc. 2d 17–07
Compania Financiera Soleada S.A. v. Hamoor Tanker Corp. Inc.; Borag, The
[1981] 1 W.L.R. 274; [1981] 1 All E.R. 856; [1981] 1 Lloyd's Rep. 483;
[1981] Com. L.R. 29; 125 S.J. 185, CA 8–298
Company (No.000022 of 1993), Re [1993] B.C.C. 726 10–135
Company (No.006798 of [1996] 1 W.L.R. 491; [1996] 2 All E.R. 417; [1996] 2
B.C.L.C. 48; [1996] B.C.C. 395; 49 Con. L.R. 39, Ch D 10–135
Company's Application, Re [1989] Ch. 477; [1989] 3 W.L.R. 265; [1989] 2 All
E.R. 248; [1989] B.C.L.C. 462; [1989] I.C.R. 449; [1989] I.R.L.R. 477;
[1989] Fin. L.R. 345; (1989) 139 N.L.J. 542; (1989) 133 S.J. 917, Ch D 2–160
Computastaff Ltd v. Ingledew Brown Bennison and Garrett [1983] 2 E.G.L.R.
150; (1983) 268 E.G. 906; (1983) 133 N.L.J. 598 ...... 9–10, 10–194, 10–301, 10–331
Comyn Ching Ltd v. Linkirk Hardware Ltd, April 1997, unreported, QBD 17–53
Confederation Life v. Shepherd, McKenzie (1992) 29 R.P.R. (2d) 271, HC
(Ontario) 10–25, 10–93
Conn v. Munday (1955) 166 E.G. 465 .... 9–83, 9–91, 9–110
Connell v. Odlum [1993] 2 N.Z.L.R. 257 10–58
Connolly-Martin v. Davis; sub nom. Connolly-Martin v. D [1999] Lloyd's Rep.
P.N. 790; [1999] P.N.L.R. 826; (1999) 96(23) L.S.G. 35; The Times, June 8,
1999; The Independent, June 18, 1999, CA 11–07
Connor & Labrum v. Regoczi-Ritzman; sub nom. Connor v. Ritzman [1995]
E.G.C.S. 98; [1995] N.P.C. 97; (1995) 70 P. & C.R. D41, Ch D 10–239, 10–272
Conry v. Simpson [1983] 3 All E.R. 369, CA 5–65
Considine v. Camp Hill Hospital (1982) 133 D.L.R. (3d) 11, Sup Ct (Nova
Scotia) 12–119, 12–203, 12–264
Consultants Group International v. John Worman Ltd (1985) 9 Con. L.R. 46 8–17,
8–174, 8–175
Consumers Glass Co. Ltd v. Foundation Co. of Canada (1985) 20 D.L.R. (4th)
126, CA (Ont) 10–15
Container Transport International Inc. v. Oceanus Mutual Underwriting Associa-
tion (Bermuda) Ltd (No.1) [1984] 1 Lloyd's Rep. 476, CA 14–61
Convent Hospital v. Eberlin & Partners, May 1, 1984, unreported 8–236
Conway v. Crowe Kelsey & Partners (1994) 39 Con. L.R. 1, QBD (OR) 8–51
——— v. Home Securities Ltd (1996) 108 Man.R. (2d) 58 14–54
Cook v. Bowen (1997) 39 B.C.L.R. (3d) 12 8–113
——— v. Collingridge (1823) Jacob 607 2–135
——— v. Deeks [1916] 1 A.C. 554, PC (Can) 2–141
——— v. Power (1992) R.P.R. (2d) 207, Sup Ct (Newfoundland) 10–332
——— v. S. See Cook v. Swinfen.
——— v. Swinfen; sub nom. Cook v. S [1967] 1 W.L.R. 457; [1967] 1 All E.R. 299;
(1966) 110 S.J. 964, CA; reversing in part [1966] 1 W.L.R. 635; [1966] 1 All
E.R. 248; 109 S.J. 972; The Times, December 3, 1965; The Guardian,
December 3, 1965, QBD 9–126, 10–13, 10–121, 10–238, 10–243, 10–293,
10–312
Coolee Ltd v. Wing Heath & Co. (1930) 38 Ll. L. Rep. 157; (1930) 47 T.L.R. 78,
KBD 14–14, 14–63
Coolgardie Goldfields Ltd, Re; sub nom. Cannon Son & Morten, Re [1900] 1 Ch.
475, Ch D 10–67, 10–69
Coomber, Re; sub nom. Coomber v. Coomber [1911] 1 Ch. 723, CA 2–129
Cooper v. Hobart (2000) 184 D.L.R. (4th) 287, CA (BC) 2–86
——— v. Stephenson (1852) Cox M. & H. 627; (1852) 21 L.J. Q.B. 292; 19
L.T.(O.S.) 155; 16 Jur. 424 10–207

PARA.

Cooperative Retail Services Ltd v. Taylor Young Partnership Ltd; Cooperative
Retail Services Ltd v. Hoare Lea & Partners; Cooperative Retail Services
Ltd v. Carillion Construction Ltd (formerly Tarmac Construction (Contracts)
Ltd); Cooperative Retail Services Ltd v. East Midlands Electricity Electrical
Installations Services Ltd (t/a Hall Electrical) (In Liquidation) [2000] 2 All
E.R. 865; [2000] B.L.R. 461; (2001) 3 T.C.L.R. 4; 74 Con. L.R. 12; [2001]
Lloyd's Rep. I.R. 122; (2000) 16 Const. L.J. 347; *The Independent*, October
2, 2000 (C.S); *The Independent*, July 14, 2000, CA 8–128, 8–322
Copeland v. Smith; *sub nom.* Copeland v. Smith & Goodwin [2000] 1 W.L.R.
1371; [2000] 1 All E.R. 457; [2000] C.P. Rep. 14; (1999) 143 S.J.L.B. 276;
The Times, October 20, 1999, CA 11–37
Coppen v. Impey [1916] C.P.D. 309 12–69
Copthorne Hotel (Newcastle) Ltd v. Arup Associates (No.1), 58 Con. L.R. 105;
(1996) 12 Const. L.J. 402, QBD (OR) 8–156, 8–165, 8–197, 8–267, 8–271
Corbett v. Bond Pearce (A Firm) [2001] EWCA Civ 531; [2001] Lloyd's Rep.
P.N. 501; (2001) 2 W.T.L.R. 419; [2001] 3 All E.R. 769; (2001) 151 N.L.J.
609, CA 10–48, 10–52, 10–248
Corbin v. Penfold Metallising Co. Ltd [2000] Lloyd's Rep. Med. 247; (2000)
97(17) L.S.G. 35; (2000) 144 S.J.L.B. 203; *The Times*, May 2, 2000, CA 5–58,
5–60, 5–68
Corder v. Banks, *The Times*, April 9, 1960 12–175
Corfield v. DS Bosher & Co. [1992] 1 E.G.L.R. 163; [1992] 04 E.G. 127 9–179,
10–184, 10–285
—— v. Grant, 59 B.L.R. 102; 29 Con. L.R. 58; [1992] E.G.C.S. 36, QBD 8–231,
8–240, 8–242
Corisand Investments Ltd v. Druce & Co. [1978] 2 E.G.L.R. 86; (1978) 248 E.G.
315 .... 9–34, 9–53, 9–54, 9–62, 9–75, 9–105, 9–106, 9–110, 9–127, 9–152, 9–153,
9–163
Cork Mutual Benefit Terminable Society v. Atkins Chirnside & Co. (1905) 45
Acct.L.R. 13 15–110
Corley v. North West Herefordshire H.A. [1997] 8 Med.L.R. 45, QBD 12–111
Cosgrove v. Pattison [2001] C.P. Rep. 68; [2001] C.P.L.R. 177; [2001] T.L.R.
113; *The Times*, February 13, 2001, Ch D 6–16
Costa v. Georghiou (1985) 1 .P.N. 201 .... 5–38, 10–13
Costiga v. Rzicka (1984) 33 Alta. L.R. (2d) 21 10–12
Cosyns v. Smith (1983) 146 D.L.R. (3d) 622, CA (Ontario) 14–38, 14–126
Cottingham v. Attey Bower & Jones [2000] Lloyd's Rep. P.N. 591; [2000]
P.N.L.R. 557; [2000] E.G.C.S. 48; (2000) 97(19) L.S.G. 43; [2000] N.P.C.
37; *The Times*, April 19, 2000, Ch D 10–194, 10–245, 10–319
Cotton v. Heyl [1930] 1 Ch. 510; [1930] All E.R. Rep. 375; 99 L.J.Ch. 289; 143
L.T. 16, Ch D 10–73
—— v. Wallis [1955] 1 W.L.R. 1168; [1955] 3 All E.R. 373; 99 S.J. 779, CA 8–167,
8–241
Coughlin v. Kuntz [1990] 2 W.W.R. 737, CA (BC) 12–109
Coulthard v. Disco Mix Club Ltd [2000] 1 W.L.R. 707; [1999] 2 All E.R. 457;
[1999] E.M.L.R. 434; [1999] F.S.R. 900; *The Times*, March 25, 1999; *The
Independent*, March 8, 1999 (C.S.), Ch D 5–88, 5–91, 5–97
—— v. Neville Russell [1998] 1 B.C.L.C. 143; [1998] B.C.C. 359; [1998]
P.N.L.R. 276; *The Times*, December 18, 1997, CA 15–18, 15–51, 15–81
Countrywide Banking Corporation Ltd v. Kingston [1990] 1 N.Z.L.R. 629 10–66
County Natwest v. Pinsent & Co. [1994] 3 Bank. L.R. 4, QBD 10–207
County Personnel (Employment Agency) Ltd v. Alan R Pulver & Co. [1987] 1
W.L.R. 916; [1987] 1 All E.R. 289; [1986] 2 E.G.L.R. 246; (1987) 84 L.S.G.
1409; (1986) 136 N.L.J. 1138; (1987) 131 S.J. 474; *The Times*, October 29,
1986, CA 3–01, 9–140, 9–142, 9–146, 9–158, 9–179, 9–191, 10–07, 10–154,
10–166, 10–172, 10–249, 10–250, 10–269, 10–272

PARA.

Cox v. Leech (1857) 1 C.B.(N.S.) 617; 26 L.J.C.P. 125; 28 L.T.(O.S.) 370; 3
Jur.(N.S.) 442; 5 W.R. 1990; 140 E.R. 254 .... 10–175, 10–307
—— v. Pemberton Holmes [1993] 6 W.W.R. 603 CA (BC) 10–16
—— v. Saskatoon [1942] 1 D.L.R. 74 12–120
Coyle v. Ray F. Fredericks Insurance Ltd (1984) 64 N.S.R. (2d) and 143 A.P.R.
93, Sup Ct (Nova Scotia) 14–43, 14–115
Coyne v. Wigan H.A. [1991] 2 Med.L.R. 301, QBD 12–119
Craig (Deceased), Re; *sub nom.* Meneces v. Middleton; Craig, Re [1971] Ch. 95;
[1970] 2 W.L.R. 1219; [1970] 2 All E.R. 390; 114 S.J. 171, Ch D 2–145
Craig v. Troy (1997) 16 W.A.R. 96, Sup Ct (Aus) 15–82, 15–119, 15–130, 15–146
—— v. Watson (1845) 8 Beav. 427; 50 E.R. 167 10–207
Craneheath Securities Ltd v. York Montague Ltd [2001] Lloyd's Rep. P.N. 348;
[1996] 1 E.G.L.R. 130; [1996] 07 E.G. 141; [1995] E.G.C.S. 113; [1995]
N.P.C. 104, CA; affirming [1994] 21 E.G. 124; [1993] E.G.C.S. 213; [1994]
1 E.G.L.R. 159, Ch D 9–23, 9–58, 9–60, 9–61, 9–103, 9–105
Crawford v. Board of Governors of Charing Cross Hospital, *The Times*, Decem-
ber 8, 1953, CA 12–74
Creation Records Ltd v. News Group Newspapers Ltd [1997] E.M.L.R. 444;
(1997) 16 Tr. L.R. 544; (1997) 20(7) I.P.D. 20070; (1997) 94(21) L.S.G. 32;
(1997) 141 S.J.L.B. 107; *The Times*, April 29, 1997, Ch D 2–156
Credit Lyonnais Bank Nederland NV v. Burch [1997] 1 All E.R. 144; [1996] 5
Bank. L.R. 233; [1997] C.L.C. 95; [1997] 1 F.L.R. 11; [1997] 2 F.C.R. 1;
(1997) 29 H.L.R. 513; (1997) 74 P. & C.R. 384; [1997] Fam. Law 168;
(1996) 93(32) L.S.G. 33; (1996) 146 N.L.J. 1421; (1996) 140 S.J.L.B. 158;
[1996] N.P.C. 99; *The Times*, July 1, 1996; *The Independent*, June 27, 1996,
CA 2–146
Creech v. Mayorcas (1966) 198 E.G. 1091, Ch D 10–105, 10–146, 10–198, 10–276
Crestar Ltd v. Carr, 37 B.L.R. 113; [1987] 2 F.T.L.R. 135; (1987) 3 Const. L.J.
286; (1987) 84 L.S.G. 1966; (1987) 131 S.J. 1154, CA 8–255
Cretanor Maritime Co. Ltd v. Irish Marine Management Ltd; Cretan Harmony,
The [1978] 1 W.L.R. 966; [1978] 3 All E.R. 164; [1978] 1 Lloyd's Rep. 425;
122 S.J. 298, CA 13–146
Creutzfeldt-Jakob Litigation Group B v. Medical Research Council and Secretary
of State for Health. *See* Group B Plaintiffs v. Medical Research Council.
Crichton v. Hastings (1973) 29 D.L.R. (3d) 692 12–222
Crimdon, The [1900] P. 171; 69 L.J.P. 103; 82 L.T. 660; 48 W.R. 623; 16 T.L.R.
403, PDAD 10–67
Crimmins v. Stevedoring Industry Finance Committee [1999] H.C.A. 59 .... 2–65, 2–69
Crits v. Sylvester (1956) 1 D.L.R. (2d) 502, affirmed (1956) 5 D.L.R. (2d) 601,
Sup Ct (Can) 12–75
Crivon v. Barnet Group Hospital Management Committee, *The Times*, November
19, 1958, CA 12–183
Cross v. David Martin & Mortimer [1989] 1 E.G.L.R. 154 ...... 9–90, 9–92, 9–108, 9–140,
9–185, 9–189, 9–190, 9–191
Crosse & Crosse v. Lloyds Bank plc [2001] EWCA Civ 366; [2001] P.N.L.R. 34;
[2001] N.P.C. 59, CA 5–50, 5–55, 10–296
Crossley v. Crowther (1851) 9 Hare 384; 21 L.J.Ch. 565; 18 L.T.(O.S.) 181; 68
E.R. 556 10–6
Crossman v. Stewart (1977) 5 C.C.L.T. 45 12–276
—— v. Ward Bracewell & Co. (1989) 6 P.N. 103 .... 10–41, 10–154, 10–314
Crown Estate Commissioners v. John Mowlem & Co. Ltd, 70 B.L.R. 1; 40 Con.
L.R. 36; (1994) 10 Const. L.J. 311, CA 8–255
Cuff v. London and County Land and Building Co. Ltd [1912] 1 Ch. 440; 81
L.J.Ch. 426; 106 L.T. 285; 28 T.L.R. 218; 19 Mans. 166, CA 15–21
Cullen v. Eaton-Smith, November 4, 1993, unreported 10–109

PARA.

Cullinane v. British Rema Manufacturing Co. Ltd [1954] 1 Q.B. 292; [1953] 3
W.L.R. 923; [1953] 2 All E.R. 1257; 97 S.J. 811, CA 10–305, 17–109
Cummings v. Croydon Health Authority, March 24, 1998, unreported, QBD 12–173
Curran v. Docherty [1995] S.L.T. 716, OH 10–312
—— v. Northern Ireland Coownership Housing Association Ltd [1987] A.C. 718;
[1987] 2 W.L.R. 1043; [1987] 2 All E.R. 13; 38 B.L.R. 1; (1987) 19 H.L.R.
318; (1987) 84 L.S.G. 1574; (1987) 131 S.J. 506, HL (NI); reversing [1986]
8 N.I.J.B. 1, CA (NI) 9–31
Currie v. Inland Revenue Commissioners; Durant v. Inland Revenue Commis-
sioners [1921] 2 K.B. 332; 90 L.J.K.B. 499; 125 L.T. 371; 12 Tax. 257,
CA 1–07
Customs and Excise Commissioners v. Hedon Alpha [1981] Q.B. 818; [1981] 2
W.L.R. 791; [1981] 2 All E.R. 697; 125 S.J. 273, CA 13–135, 15–153
Cyr v. Pelletier (1991) 116 N.B.R. (2d) 137, CA (New Brunswick) 10–185
Czarnikow Ltd v. Koufos. See Koufos v. C Czarnikow Ltd; Heron II, The.

D, Re. See D (Adult: Medical Treatment), Re.
D (Adult: Medical Treatment), Re [1998] 1 F.L.R. 411; [1998] 1 F.C.R. 498;
(1997) 38 B.M.L.R. 1; [1997] Fam. Law 787, Fam Div 12–146
D (Medical Treatment: Mentally Disabled Patient), Re; sub nom. D (Medical
Treatment: Consent), Re [1998] 2 F.L.R. 22; [1998] 2 F.C.R. 178; (1998) 41
B.M.L.R. 81; [1998] Fam. Law 324; (1997) 94(48) L.S.G. 30; (1998) 142
S.J.L.B. 30; The Times, January 14, 1998, Fam Div 12–146
D v. A & Co. [1900] 1 Ch. 484; 69 L.J.Ch. 382; 82 L.T. 47; 48 W.R. 429, Ch
D 10–66
—— v. D (1962) 106 S.J. 959, Div Ct 10–192
—— v. Dr Ahmed, March 26, 1998, unreported, QBD 12–174, 12–273
—— v. United Kingdom (1997) 24 E.H.R.R. 423; 2 B.H.R.C. 273; (1998) 42
B.M.L.R. 149; The Times, May 12, 1997, ECHR 7–55
D (A Child) v. Walker; sub nom. Walker v. D (A Child) [2000] 1 W.L.R. 1382;
[2000] C.P.L.R. 462; [2001] H.R.L.R. 1; [2000] U.K.H.R.R. 648; [2000]
P.I.Q.R. P193; (2000) 97(22) L.S.G. 44; The Times, May 17, 2000; The
Independent, June 12, 2000 (C.S), CA 6–16, 7–31
D&F Estates Ltd v. Church Commissioners for England [1989] A.C. 177; [1988]
3 W.L.R. 368; [1988] 2 All E.R. 992; 41 B.L.R. 1; 15 Con. L.R. 35; [1988]
2 E.G.L.R. 213; (1988) 4 Const. L.J. 100; (1988) 85(33) L.S.G. 46; (1988)
138 N.L.J. 210; (1988) 132 S.J. 1092, HL 2–28, 2–39, 2–62, 2–77, 8–59, 8–73,
8–86, 8–87, 8–88, 8–91, 8–96, 8–98, 17–69
DCT v. Levick (2000) 168 A.L.R. 383, Fed Ct (Aus) 10–135
DNB Mortgages Ltd v. Bullock & Lees [2000] Lloyd's Rep. P.N. 290; [2000]
P.N.L.R. 427; [2000] 1 E.G.L.R. 92; [2000] 17 E.G. 168; [2000] E.G.C.S.
16; The Times, March 24, 2000; The Independent, March 20, 2000 (C.S.),
CA 5–36, 9–165
DSL Group Ltd v. Unisys International Services Ltd (No.1), 41 Con. L.R. 33,
QBD (OR) 8–327
—— v. Unisys International Services Ltd (No.2) [1995] Masons C.L.R. Rep. 5,
QBD 17–51, 17–55
DW Moore v. Ferrier [1988] 1 W.L.R. 267; [1988] 1 All E.R. 400; (1988) 132 S.J.
227, CA 2–103, 5–40, 10–13
Dace v. Redland Aggregates Ltd [1997] E.G.C.S. 123, Ch D 10–119, 11–31
Dairy Containers Ltd v. NZI Bank Ltd, [1995] 2 N.Z.L.R. 30 ..... 15–31, 15–91, 15–96,
15–101, 15–105, 15–107, 15–109, 15–146, 15–148, 15–150
Daisley v. BS Hall & Co. (1972) 225 E.G. 1553 .... 9–54, 9–55, 9–93, 9–99, 9–108, 9–141
Dale v. Munthali (1978) 78 D.L.R. (3d) 588 12–185
Dalgleish v. Bromley Corp. (1953) 162 E.G. 623 ; [1953] C.P.L. 411 ..... 8–190, 8–302

PARA.

Dallinga v. Sun Alliance Insurance Co. (1993) 10 Alta.L.R. (3d) 59 14–53
Damodaran s/o Raman v. Choe Kuan Him [1980] A.C. 497; [1979] 3 W.L.R. 383;
 123 S.J. 537, PC (Mal) 10–70
Dangar's Trusts, Re (1889) 41 Ch.D. 178; 58 L.J.Ch. 315; 60 L.J. 491; 37 W.R.
 651; 5 T.L.R. 266 10–46
Dangerfield v. David [1911] 17 W.L.R. 249 12–68
Daniels v. Anderson (1995) 16 A.C.S.R. 607, Sup Ct (NWS) (1992) 7 A.C.S.R.
 759 .... 5–114, 5–115, 15–03, 15–107, 15–116, 15–133, 15–146, 15–148, 15–149
—— v. Walker. *See* D (A Child) v. Walker.
Danns v. Department of Health [1998] P.I.Q.R. P226, CA; affirming [1996]
 P.I.Q.R. P69, QBD 12–160
Dareway Properties Ltd v. Glovers [1998] C.L.Y. 4025, QBD 10–316
Dark v. Boock [1991] 1 N.Z.L.R. 496 10–173
Darker v. Chief Constable of the West Midlands; *sub nom.* Docker (Deceased) v.
 Chief Constable of the West Midlands [2001] 1 A.C. 435; [2000] 3 W.L.R.
 747; [2000] 4 All E.R. 193; (2000) 97(32) L.S.G. 38; (2000) 150 N.L.J.
 1421; (2000) 144 S.J.L.B. 243; *The Times*, August 1, 2000; *The Independ-
 ent*, November 6, 2000 (C.S), HL 2–97
Darley v. Shale [1993] 4 Med.L.R. 161, Sup Ct (NSW) 12–81, 12–188
Darlington B.C. v. Waring & Gillow (Holdings) Ltd [1988] 2 E.G.L.R. 159;
 [1988] 45 E.G. 102, DC 9–74
Darlington Building Society v. O'Rourke James Scourfield & McCarthy [1999]
 Lloyd's Rep. P.N. 33; [1999] P.N.L.R. 365; *The Times*, November 20, 1998,
 CA 10–145, 10–217
Das v. Ganju [1999] P.I.Q.R. P260; [1999] Lloyd's Rep. Med. 198; (1999) 96(19)
 L.S.G. 28; (1999) 143 S.J.L.B. 129; *The Times*, May 4, 1999, CA 5–58, 5–68,
 12–289
Da Sousa v. Minister of State for Immigration, Local Government and Ethnic
 Affairs (1993) 114 A.L.R. 708, Fed Ct (Aus) 10–135
Dauntly v. Hyde (1841) 6 Jur. 133 10–183
Davca Building Supplies Ltd v. Wedgewood Insurance Ltd and Clarke (1992) 99
 Nfld. & P.E.I.R. 203 14–54
Davey v. Woolley, Hames, Dale & Dingwall (1982) 133 D.L.R. (3d) 647, CA
 (Ontario) 10–25
Davies v. Davies [2000] 1 F.L.R. 39; [1999] 3 F.C.R. 745; [2000] Fam. Law 23,
 CA 10–29
—— v. Hood (1903) 88 L.T. 19; 19 T.L.R. 158 10–13
—— v. Lock (1844) 3 L.T.(O.S.) 125 10–13
—— v. Parry (Idris) (1988) 20 H.L.R. 452; [1988] 21 E.G. 74; [1988] 20 E.G.
 92 9–69
—— v. Taylor (No.1) [1974] A.C. 207; [1972] 3 W.L.R. 801; [1972] 3 All E.R.
 836; 116 S.J. 864, HL 12–257, 12–260
Davies (Joseph Owen) v. Eli Lilly & Co. (No.1) [1987] 1 W.L.R. 1136; [1987] 3
 All E.R. 94; [1987] 2 F.T.L.R. 154; (1987) 84 L.S.G. 2042; (1987) 137
 N.L.J. 1183, CA 6–05
—— v. Eli Lilly & Co. (No.3), *The Times*, January 16, 1988; *The Independent*,
 January 15, 1988; *The Guardian*, January 15, 1988, QBD 10–103
Davies, Ward & Beck v. Baker and McKenzie (1998) 164 D.L.R. (4th) 423, CA
 (Ontario) 10–31
Davis v. Barking, Havering and Brentwood H.A. [1993] 4 Med.L.R. 85, QBD 12–125,
 12–127, 12–131
—— v. Jacobs [1999] Lloyd's Rep. Med. 72; (2000) 51 B.M.L.R. 42, CA 5–58
—— v. Radcliffe [1990] 1 W.L.R. 821; [1990] 2 All E.R. 536; [1990] B.C.C. 472;
 [1990] B.C.L.C. 647; (1990) 87(19) L.S.G. 43; (1990) 134 S.J. 1078, PC
 (IoM) 2–30, 2–86, 13–114, 15–50
—— v. Sprott & Sons (1960) 177 E.G. 9 9–32

PARA.

Davy v. Mead [1987] 2 N.Z.L.R. 443 5–115

Davy-Chiesman v. Davy-Chiesman [1984] Fam. 48; [1984] 2 W.L.R. 291; [1984]
1 All E.R. 321; (1984) 81 L.S.G. 44; (1983) 127 S.J. 805; *The Times*,
November 21, 1983, CA 10–117, 10–179

Day v. Cook [2001] EWCA Civ 592; [2001] Lloyd's Rep. P.N. 551, CA;
reversing in part [2000] P.N.L.R. 178, QBD (Merc Ct) 10–18, 10–300

—— v. Mead [1987] 2 N.Z.L.R. 443, CA (NZ) 10–19, 10–327

De Bussche v. Alt (1878) 8 Ch.D. 286 .... 2–135, 3–10, 14–13

De Freitas v. O'Brien and Connelly. *See* Defreitas v. O'Brien.

De Freville v. Dill (1927) 96 L.J.K.B. 1056 .... 12–84, 12–239

De Jong, Baljet and Van den Brink v. Netherlands; Series A, No.77; (1986) 8
E.H.R.R. 20, ECHR 13–26

De la Giroday v. Brough (1997) 33 C.L.R. (3d) 171 12–260

De Martell v. Merton and Sutton H.A. (Liability Issue) (No.2) [1995] 6 Med.L.R.
234, QBD 12–245

De Meza & Stuart v. Apple van Straten Shena & Stone [1975] 1 Lloyd's Rep.
498, CA; affirming [1974] 1 Lloyd's Rep. 508, QBD 5–114, 5–115, 15–146

De Roufigny v. Peale (1811) 3 Taunt 484; 128 E.R. 192 10–183

Dean v. Allin & Watts [2001] EWCA Civ 758; (2001) 145 S.J.L.B. 157; *The
Times*, June 28, 2001, CA 10–05, 10–57, 10–60, 10–82

Debtor (No.1594 of 1992), Re, *The Times*, December 18 1992, Ch D 10–9

Deeny v. Gooda Walker Ltd (No.1) [1996] L.R.L.R. 183; *The Times*, October 7,
1994; *The Independent*, October 5, 1994, QBD 2–116, 14–43, 16–06, 16–09,
16–20, 16–30, 16–31, 16–32, 16–33, 16–34, 16–35, 16–40, 16–41,
16–43, 16–48, 16–49, 16–50, 16–55, 16–56, 16–57, 16–67,
16–68, 16–72, 16–78, 16–79, 16–81, 16–82

—— v. Gooda Walker Ltd (No.2); Albert v. Gooda Walker Ltd; Brownrigg v.
Gooda Walker Ltd [1996] 1 W.L.R. 426; [1996] 1 All E.R. 933; [1996]
L.R.L.R. 109; [1996] S.T.C. 299; [1996] 5 Re. L.R. 43; (1996) 93(15) L.S.G.
32; (1996) 146 N.L.J. 369; (1996) 140 S.J.L.B. 92; *The Times*, March 8,
1996, HL 16–76

Deerness v. John R Keeble & Son (Brantham) Ltd [1983] 2 Lloyd's Rep. 260;
[1983] Com. L.R. 221; (1983) 133 N.L.J. 641; *The Times*, October 18, 1982,
HL 5–65

Defreitas v. O'Brien; *sub nom.* De Freitas v. O'Brien; Defreitas v. Connelly
[1995] P.I.Q.R. P281; [1995] 6 Med.L.R. 108; [1955–95] P.N.L.R. 680; *The
Times*, February 16, 1995; *The Independent*, April 3, 1995 (C.S.), CA 12–100,
12–196

Delaney v. Southmead H.A. [1995] 6 Med.L.R. 355, CA 12–119, 12–121, 12–123

Deloitte Haskins & Sells v. National Mutual Life Nominees [1993] A.C. 774;
[1993] 3 W.L.R. 347; [1993] 2 All E.R. 1015; [1993] B.C.L.C. 1174; (1993)
143 N.L.J. 883; (1993) 137 S.J.L.B. 152, PC (NZ) 15–27, 15–86

Demarco v. Ungaro (1979) 95 D.L.R. (3d) 385, HC (Ontario) 11–24

Demerara Bauxite Co. Ltd v. Hubbard [1923] A.C. 673, PC (WI) 2–138, 2–139, 10–18

Dendaas v. Yackel (1980) 109 D.L.R. (3d) 455, Sup Ct (BC) 12–229

Dennis v. Symons and Harris [1937] E.G.D. 56 .... 8–201, 8–214

Denny v. Budgen (1955) 166 E.G. 433 .... 9–88, 9–91, 9–134

Dent v. Davis Blank Furniss [2001] Lloyd's Rep. P.N. 534, Ch D 10–275

Denton v. Donner (1856) 23 Beav. 285 2–139

Department of Health & Community Services v. JWB and SMB (1992) 66
A.L.J.R. 300, HC (Aus) 12–142

Department of National Heritage v. Steensen Varming Mulcahy (1998) 60 Con.
L.R. 33, QBD (OR) 8–35, 8–145, 8–216, 8–265, 8–270, 8–293

PARA.

Department of the Environment v. Thomas Bates & Sons Ltd [1991] 1 A.C. 499;
[1990] 3 W.L.R. 457; [1990] 2 All E.R. 943; 50 B.L.R. 61; 21 Con. L.R. 54;
[1990] 46 E.G. 115; (1990) 134 S.J. 1077; *The Times*, July 27, 1990, HL 8–61,
8–62, 8–75, 8–86
Derry v. Ministry of Defence (1999) 11 Admin. L.R. 758; [1999] P.I.Q.R. P204;
(1999) 49 B.M.L.R. 62; (1999) 96(16) L.S.G. 36; *The Times*, March 30,
1999, CA 12–14
—— v. Peek; *sub nom.* Peek v. Derry (1889) L.R. 14 App. Cas. 337; [1886–90]
All E.R. 1; 58 L.J.Ch. 864; 61 L.T. 265; 54 J.P. 148; 38 W.R. 33; (1889) 5
T.L.R. 625; 1 Meg. 282, HL; reversing (1887) 37 Ch.D. 541; 57 L.J.Ch. 347;
59 L.T. 78; 36 W.R. 899; 4 T.L.R. 84, CA 9–33
Desmond v. Boyles [1985] I.R. 449, HC 10–200
Dettman v. Metropolitan & Provincial Bank Ltd (1863) 1 H. & M. 641 2–144
Devine v. Jefferys [2001] Lloyd's Rep. P.N. 301; [2001] P.N.L.R. 16; [2001]
P.N.L.R. 407, QBD (Merc Ct) 9–148
Deyong v. Weeks (1984) 33 Alta. L.R. (2d) 338, CA (Alberta) 10–143
Di Ciacca v. Archbald Sharp & Sons [1994] S.L.T. 421, OH 10–268
Diack v. Bardsley (1983) 25 C.C.L.T. 159, Sup Ct (BC); and (1984) 31 C.C.L.T.
308, CA (BC) 12–203, 12–264
Diamond v. Ranger Unicity Insurance Brokers Ltd (1997) 119 Man.R. (2d) 99 14–82
Dickinson v. James Alexander & Co. (1990) 6 P.N. 205 .... 10–178, 10–190, 10–283,
10–312, 10–313, 10–319, 10–322
Dickson & Co. v. Devitt (1916) 86 L.J.K.B. 315; 32 T.L.R. 547; 21 Com.Cas.
291 .... 14–11, 14–36, 14–43, 14–89, 14–94, 14–127
Diennet v. France; Series A, No.315–B; (1996) 21 E.H.R.R. 554, ECHR 7–65

Digby Brown & Co. v. Lyall [1995] S.L.T. 932, OH 10–68
Dillon v. Le Roux [1994] 6 W.W.R. 280, CA (BC) 12–78, 12–185
Dimond v. Lovell [2000] 2 W.L.R. 1121; [2000] 2 All E.R. 897; [2000] R.T.R.
243; [2000] C.C.L.R. 57; 2000 Rep. L.R. 62; (2000) 97(22) L.S.G. 47;
(2000) 150 N.L.J. 740; *The Times*, May 12, 2000; *The Independent*, May 17,
2000, HL 13–165
Dimond Manufacturing Co. Ltd v. Hamilton [1969] N.Z.L.R. 609, CA (NZ) 15–78,
15–97, 15–137, 15–153
Director General of Fair Trading v. First National Bank plc [2000] Q.B. 672;
[2000] 2 W.L.R. 1353; [2000] 2 All E.R. 759; [2000] 1 All E.R. (Comm)
371; [2000] Lloyd's Rep. Bank. 130; [2000] C.C.L.R. 31; (2000) 97(7)
L.S.G. 39; *The Times*, March 14, 2000, CA 8–24
Discain Project Services Ltd v. Opecprime Development Ltd (Application for
Summary Judgment) [2000] B.L.R. 402, QBD (T&CC) 8–341
District of Surrey v. Carroll-Hatch and Associates Ltd (1979) 10 D.L.R. (3d)
218 .... 8–116, 8–187, 8–188
Dixey & Sons v. Parsons (1964) 192 E.G. 197 14–49
Dixon v. Hovill (1828) 4 Bing. 665; 5 C.1 Moo. & P. 656; 6 L.J.C.P.(O.S.) 155;
130 E.R. 925 .... 14–44, 14–57
D'Jan of London, Re; *sub nom.* Copp v. D'Jan [1993] B.C.C. 646; [1994] 1
B.C.L.C. 561, Ch D (Companies Ct) 13–135, 15–24, 15–153
Djemal v. Bexley H.A. [1995] 6 Med.L.R. 269, QBD 12–77, 12–180, 12–185
Dobbie v. Medway H.A. [1994] 1 W.L.R. 1234; [1994] 4 All E.R. 450; [1994]
P.I.Q.R. P353; [1994] 5 Med.L.R. 160; (1994) 144 N.L.J. 828; *The Times*,
May 18, 1994; *The Independent*, June 6, 1994 (C.S.), CA 5–59, 5–65
Dodd Properties (Kent) Ltd v. Canterbury City Council [1980] 1 W.L.R. 433;
[1980] 1 All E.R. 928; 13 B.L.R. 45; (1979) 253 E.G. 1335; (1980) 124 S.J.
84, CA 3–01, 8–285, 8–295, 8–315, 9–128, 9–136, 9–137, 9–185, 10–249,
10–217, 13–161, 14–114, 15–132
Dogma Properties Ltd v. Gale (1984) 136 N.L.J. 453, DC 10–193

PARA.

Doiron v. Cassie Populaire D'Inkerman Ltee (1985) 17 D.L.R. 660, CA (New Brunswick) 10–286, 10–324

Dolman v. Penrose (1983) 34 S.A.S.R. 481, Sup Ct (Aus) 10–283, 10–285

Domb v. Isoz [1980] Ch. 548; [1980] 2 W.L.R. 565; [1980] 1 All E.R. 942; (1980) 40 P. & C.R. 516; (1979) 123 S.J. 838; *The Times*, December 5, 1979, CA 10–202

Dombo Beheer BV v. Netherlands; Series A, No.274–A; (1994) 18 E.H.R.R. 213, ECHR 7–11, 7–67

Dominion Freeholders Ltd v. Aird (1966) 67 S.R. (N.S.W.) 150 .... 15–94, 15–147

Donaldson v. Beckett (1774) 2 Brown 129 2–72

—— v. Haldane & Haldane (1840) 7 C. & F. 762; Mews' Dig. Xiii 1411, S.C. 1 Robin. 226, HL 10–207, 10–294

Donellan v. Watson (1990) 21 N.S.W.L.R. 335, CA (NSW) 11–14

Donmez v. Barnes [1996] E.G.C.S. 129, QBD 10–166

Donoghue v. Stevenson; *sub nom.* McAlister v. Stevenson [1932] A.C. 562; 1932 S.C. (H.L.) 31; 1932 S.L.T. 317; [1932] W.N. 139, HL 2–18, 2–19, 2–21, 2–22, 2–26, 2–27, 2–66, 2–67, 2–72, 2–102, 8–80, 8–85, 8–87, 8–95, 8–91, 8–94, 9–32, 12–45, 15–48, 17–63, 17–67, 17–69

Donovan v. Cork County Council [1967] I.R. 173 10–89

—— v. Gwentoys Ltd [1990] 1 W.L.R. 472; [1990] 1 All E.R. 1018; (1990) 87(15) L.S.G. 40; (1990) 134 S.J. 910; *The Times*, March 23, 1990; *The Independent*, March 23, 1990; *The Guardian*, March 28, 1990, HL 5–67, 10–186

Dooby v. Watson (1888) 39 Ch.D. 178; 57 L.J.Ch. 865; 58 L.T. 943; 36 W.R. 764; 4 T.L.R. 584 .... 10–01, 10–207

Doran v. Delaney [1996] 1 I.R.L.M. 490 .... 10–59, 10–195, 10–268

Dorey & Dorey v. Romney (1982) 51 N.S.R. (2d); 102 A.P.R. 53, Sup Ct (Nova Scotia) 10–297

Dorsch v. City of Weyburn (1986) 23 D.L.R. (4th) 379 10–61

Dorset Yacht Co. v. Home Office. *See* Home Office v. Dorset Yacht Co. Ltd.

Dotesio v. Biss (No.2) (1912) 56 S.J. 736, CA 10–69

Doughty v. General Dental Council [1988] A.C. 164; [1987] 3 W.L.R. 769; [1987] 3 All E.R. 843; (1987) 84 L.S.G. 2767; (1987) 131 S.J. 1357, PC (UK) 12–04

—— v. North Staffordshire H.A. [1992] 3 Med.L.R. 81, QBD 12–196

Douglas v. Hello! Ltd [2001] 2 W.L.R. 992; [2001] 2 All E.R. 289; [2001] E.M.L.R. 9; [2001] 1 F.L.R. 982; [2001] H.R.L.R. 26; [2001] U.K.H.R.R. 223; 9 B.H.R.C. 543; [2001] F.S.R. 40; *The Times*, January 16, 2001; *The Daily Telegraph*, January 9, 2001, CA .... 72–147, 2–154, 2–156, –02

—— v. Stuart Wyse Ogilvie Estates Ltd; *sub nom.* Douglas v. Ogilvie, 2001 S.L.T. 689; 2000 G.W.D. 25–953, OH 10–241, 10–268

Doundoulakis v. Sdrinis & Co. [1989] V.R. 781, Sup Ct (Vic) 5–43

Dove v. Banhams Patent Locks Ltd [1983] 1 W.L.R. 1436; [1983] 2 All E.R. 833; (1983) 133 N.L.J. 538; (1983) 127 S.J. 748, QBD 5–20

Dowdie v. Camberwell H.A. [1997] 8 Med.L.R. 368, QBD 12–84, 12–188, 12–190

Downes v. Glazebrook (1817) 3 Mer. 200 .... 2–135, 2–134

Downs v. Chappell; Downs v. Stephenson Smart [1997] 1 W.L.R. 426; [1996] 3 All E.R. 344; [1996] C.L.C. 1492, CA 10–234, 15–79, 15–122

Downsview Nominees Ltd v. First City Corp. Ltd (No.1); *sub nom.* First City Corp. Ltd v. Downsview Nominees Ltd (No.1) [1993] A.C. 295; [1993] 2 W.L.R. 86; [1993] 3 All E.R. 626; [1993] B.C.C. 46; [1994] 2 B.C.L.C. 49; (1992) 89(45) L.S.G. 26; (1992) 136 S.J.L.B. 324; *The Times*, December 15, 1992; *The Independent*, December 14, 1992 (C.S.), PC (NZ) 2–127, 15–50

Dowson & Mason v. Potter [1986] 1 W.L.R. 1419; [1986] 2 All E.R. 418; (1986) 83 L.S.G. 3429; (1986) 130 S.J. 841, CA 2–152

Drake v. Pontefract H.A. [1998] Lloyd's Rep. Med. 425, QBD 12–180, 12–237

Drinnan v. CW Ingram & Sons, 1967 S.L.T. 205, OH 9–32, 9–83, 9–126, 9–187

PARA.

Driscoll-Varley v. Parkside H.A. [1991] 2 Med.L.R. 346, QBD 5–58
Driver v. William Willett (Contractors), Ltd [1969] 1 All E.R. 665, Assizes
   (Sussex) 8–81, 8–272, 8–308
Dryden v. Surrey County Council [1936] 2 All E.R. 535; (1936) 80 S.J. 656 12–149,
   12–194
Du Bosky & Partners v. Shearwater Property Holdings, 61 B.L.R. 64, CA 3–07
Dubai Aluminium Co. Ltd v. Salaam; Dubai Aluminium Co. Ltd v. Amhurst;
   Dubai Aluminium Co. Ltd v. Amhurst Brown Martin & Nicholson [2001]
   Q.B. 113; [2000] 3 W.L.R. 910; [2000] 2 Lloyd's Rep. 168; [2000] Lloyd's
   Rep. P.N. 497; [2000] P.N.L.R. 578; *The Times*, April 21, 2000, CA 4–05, 4–11,
   4–14, 10–147
Dube v. Dionne (1998) 201 N.B.R. (2d) 387, CA (New Brunswick) 10–62
Dueck v. Manitoba Mennonite Mutual Insurance Co. (1993) 83 Man.R.(2d)
   291 14–74
Duke Group Ltd v. Pilmer (1999) 31 A.C.S.R. 213, Sup Ct (Aus) (1994) 27
   A.C.S.R. 1 .... 15–37, 15–74, 15–86, 15–94, 15–112, 15–121, 15–122, 15–126,
   15–128, 15–129, 15–130, 15–131, 15–146, 15–151
Dunbar v. A&B Painters Ltd. *See* Alfred James Dunbar v. A&B Painters Ltd and
   Economic Insurance Co. Ltd and Whitehouse & Co.
—— v. Tredenick (1813) 2 Ball & Beatty 304 2–137
Duncan v. Cuelenaere [1987] 2 W.W.R. 379, Q.B. (Saskatchenwan) 10–124
—— v. Gumleys, 1987 S.L.T. 729; [1987] 2 E.G.L.R. 263, 2 Div 9–128, 9–130, 9–131
Duncan Investments Ltd v. Underwoods [1998] P.N.L.R. 754; [1998] E.G.C.S.
   98; [1998] N.P.C. 102, CA; reversing [1997] P.N.L.R. 521, Ch D 9–13, 9–40
Dunlop v. Woollahra Municipal Council [1982] A.C. 158; [1981] 2 W.L.R. 693;
   [1981] 1 All E.R. 1202; 125 S.J. 199, PC (Aus) 10–96
Dunn v. Fairs, Blissard Barnes & Stowe (1961) 105 S.J. 932 .... 10–96, 10–169
—— v. Hallen (1861) 2 F. & F. 642 10–183
Dunne v. National Maternity Hospital [1989] I.R. 109 12–95
Duomatic Ltd, Re [1969] 2 Ch. 365; [1969] 2 W.L.R. 114; [1969] 1 All E.R. 161;
   112 S.J. 922, Ch D 13–135, 15–74, 15–153
Durrant v. Burke [1993] 4 Med.L.R. 258, QBD 12–174
Dutfield v. Gilbert H Stephens and Sons [1988] 18 Fam. Law 473 10–123
Dutton v. Bognor Regis Urban D.C. [1972] 1 Q.B. 373; [1972] 2 W.L.R. 299;
   [1972] 1 All E.R. 462; [1972] 1 Lloyd's Rep. 227; 3 B.L.R. 11; 70 L.G.R.
   57; (1971) 116 S.J. 16; *The Times*, December 18, 1971, CA 2–39, 8–70, 8–73,
   8–77
Dwyer v. Roderick (1983) 80 L.S.G. 3003; (1982) 132 N.L.J. 176; (1983) 127
   S.J. 806, CA 12–165

E (A Minor) (Wardship: Medical Treatment), Re [1993] 1 F.L.R. 386; [1994] 5
   Med.L.R. 73, Fam Div 12–148
E v. Australian Red Cross Society (1991) 105 A.L.R. 53, CA (Aus) [1991] 2
   Med.L.R. 303 12–12
Eagle Star Insurance Co. Ltd v. Gale & Power (1955) 166 E.G. 37; [1955] J.P.L.
   679 .... 9–30, 9–128, 9–163, 9–164
—— v. National Westminster Finance Australia Ltd (1985) 58 A.L.R. 165 14–38,
   14–110, 14–124
Eames London Estates Ltd v. North Hertfordshire D.C.,18 B.L.R. 50; (1981) 259
   E.G. 491, QBD 8–186, 8–205
Earl v. Wilhelm (2000) 183 D.L.R. (4th) 45, CA (Saskatchewan) 10–54, 10–218,
   10–221, 10–324
Early v. Newham H.A. [1994] 5 Med.L.R. 214, QBD 12–113, 12–158, 12–159,
   12–188

PARA.

East Ham Corp. v. Bernard Sunley & Sons [1966] A.C. 406; [1965] 3 W.L.R. 1096; [1965] 3 All E.R. 619; [1965] 2 Lloyd's Rep. 425; 64 L.G.R. 43; 109 S.J. 874, HL 8–18, 8–131, 8–165, 8–167, 8–241, 8–255, 8–295, 8–300, 8–317

Eastgate Group Ltd v. Lindsey Morden Group Inc., March 22, 2001, unreported 15–147

Eckersley v. Binnie (1988) 18 Con. L.R. 1; [1955–95] P.N.L.R. 348, CA 2–116, 5–13, 5–15, 8–31, 8–81, 8–82, 8–133, 8–139, 8–207, 8–210, 8–281, 8–308

Edgar v. Lamont, 1914 S.C. 277 12–14

Edgeworth Construction Ltd v. ND Lea & Associates Ltd; Edgeworth Construction Ltd v. Walji [1993] 3 S.C.R. 206; 66 B.L.R. 56; (1993) 107 D.L.R. (4th) 169, Sup Ct (Can); reversing in part 54 B.L.R. 11, CA (BC) 2–61, 2–89, 8–116, 9–14

Editions Périscope v. France; Series A, No.234–B; (1992) 14 E.H.R.R. 597, ECHR 7–06, 7–32

Edler v. Greenwich and Deptford Hospital Management Committee, *The Times*, March 7, 1953 .... 12–174, 12–178

Edward Wong Finance Co. Ltd v. Johnson Stokes & Master [1984] A.C. 296; [1984] 2 W.L.R. 1; (1983) 80 L.S.G. 3163; (1983) 127 S.J. 784, PC (HK) 2–03, 10–85, 10–88, 10–148, 10–200, 12–94, 13–92, 18–19

Edwards Karawacki Smith & Co. Pty. Ltd v. Jacka Nominees Pty Ltd (1994) 15 A.C.S.R. 503 .... 15–86, 15–127

Edwards v. Meyrick (1842) 2 Hare 60 .... 2–131, 2–138

Egedebo v. Windermere District Hospital (1993) 78 B.C.L.R. (2d) 63 12–245

Ekkebus v. Lauinger (1990) 73 O.R. (2d) 743, HC 10–243

Elanay Contracts Ltd v. Vestry [2001] B.L.R. 33; (2001) 3 T.C.L.R. 6, QBD (T&CC) 8–342

Elcano Acceptance Ltd v. Richmond, Richmond, Stambler & Mills (1989) 68 O.R. (2d) 165, HC (Ontario) 10–82

—— v. Richmond, Richmond, Stambler & Mills (1985) 31 C.C.L.T. 201, HC (Ontario) 10–93, 10–97

Electra Private Equity Partners v. KPMG Peat Marwick [2000] B.C.C. 368; [2001] 1 B.C.L.C. 589; [1999] Lloyd's Rep. P.N. 670; [2000] P.N.L.R. 247, CA 2–78, 15–69, 15–79, 15–82

Eley v. King & Chasemore (A Firm) [1989] 22 E.G. 109; (1987) 139 N.L.J. 791, CA 9–92

Elguzouli-Daf v. Commissioner of Police of the Metropolis; McBrearty v. Ministry of Defence [1995] Q.B. 335; [1995] 2 W.L.R. 173; [1995] 1 All E.R. 833; (1995) 7 Admin. L.R. 421; (1995) 145 N.L.J. 151; *The Times*, November 23, 1994, CA 10–64

—— v. Crown Prosecution Service. *See* Elguzouli-Daf v. Commissioner of Police of the Metropolis.

Elkington v. Holland (1842) 9 M. & W. 659; (1842) 1 Dowl.(N.S.) 643; 11 L.J.Ex. 273; 6 Jur. 374 .... 10–96, 10–192

Elland Developments Ltd v. Smith [1995] E.G.C.S. 141 10–168

Elliott v. Bickerstaff (1999) 48 N.S.W.L.R. 214. CA (NSW) 12–121, 12–194

Ellis v. Sampson (1927) 71 S.J. 621 10–104

—— v. Wallsend District Hospital [1990] 2 Med.L.R. 103, CA (NSW) 12–264

Ellison v. L [1998] 1 N.Z.L.R 416 12–288

Elton John v. Price Waterhouse [2001] EWHC Ch 438 .... 15–19, 15–34, 15–86

Emeh v. Kensington and Chelsea and Westminster A.H.A. [1985] Q.B. 1012; [1985] 2 W.L.R. 233; [1984] 3 All E.R. 1044; (1984) 81 L.S.G. 2856; (1984) 128 S.J. 705, CA 12–274, 12–279, 12–280, 12–289, 12–292, 12–293, 12–297

Emmanuel v. DBS Management plc [1999] Lloyd's Rep. P.N. 593, Ch D 13–97, 13–104, 13–112

Employers Corporate Investments Pty Ltd v. Cameron (1977) 3 A.C.L.R. 120 15–147

PARA.

Empress Assurance Corporation Ltd v. CT Bowring & Co. Ltd (1905) 11
Com.Cas. 107 .... 14–18, 14–24
Endhill Pty Ltd v. Grasso Searles & Romano [1993] 2 Qd.R. 136 10–264
Engel v. Janzen (1990) 65 D.L.R. (4th) 760, CA (BC) 14–81
——— v. Netherlands (No.1); Series A, No.22; (1979–80) 1 E.H.R.R. 647,
ECHR 7–08
English Exporters (London) Ltd v. Eldonwall Ltd [1973] Ch. 415; [1973] 2
W.L.R. 435; [1973] 1 All E.R. 726; (1973) 25 P. & C.R. 379; 117 S.J. 224,
Ch D 9–102
Enlayde Ltd v. Roberts [1917] 1 Ch. 109; 86 L.J.Ch. 149; 115 L.T. 901; 33 T.L.R.
52; 61 S.J. 86, Ch D 14–44
Enola Apts. Ltd v. Young (1979) 30 R.P.R. 94, Sup Ct 10–207
Environment Agency (formerly National Rivers Authority) v. Empress Car Co.
(Abertillery) Ltd; *sub nom.* Empress Car Co. (Abertillery) Ltd v. National
Rivers Authority [1999] 2 A.C. 22; [1998] 2 W.L.R. 350; [1998] 1 All E.R.
481; [1998] Env. L.R. 396; [1988] E.H.L.R. 3; [1998] E.G.C.S. 16; (1998)
95(8) L.S.G. 32; (1998) 148 N.L.J. 206; (1998) 142 S.J.L.B. 69; [1998]
N.P.C. 16; *The Times*, February 9, 1998, HL 15–125
Equitable Debenture Assets Corp. v. Moss (William) Group Ltd (1984) 11 Con.
L.R. 1; (1984) 1 Const. L.J. 131, QBD (OR) 8–33, 8–102, 8–177, 8–216, 8–218,
8–223, 8–323
——— v. Moss (William) Group Ltd, 11 Con. L.R. 1; (1984) 1 Const. L.J. 131,
QBD (OR) 5–15
Equiticorp v. Hawkins [1991] 3 N.Z.L.R. 700 10–38
Erlanger v. New Sombrero Phosphate Company (1878) 3 App.Cas. 1218 ..... 2–135, 3–09,
3–10, 5–100
Ernst & Whinney v. Willard Engineering (Dagenham) Ltd, 40 B.L.R. 67; 13 Con.
L.R. 57; (1987) 3 Const. L.J. 292, QBD (OR) 8–94
Esanda Finance Corporation Ltd v. Peat Marwick Hungerfords (1997) 71
A.L.J.R. 448;(1997) 188 C.L.R. 241, HC (Aus) 9–49, 15–69, 15–83
Esso Petroleum Co. Ltd v. Mardon [1976] Q.B. 801; [1976] 2 W.L.R. 583; [1976]
2 All E.R. 5; [1976] 2 Lloyd's Rep. 305; [1976] 2 E.G.L.R. 29; 2 B.L.R. 82;
120 S.J. 131, CA 2–100, 2–116, 9–175, 10–13, 17–56
Esterhuizen v. Allied Dunbar Assurance plc [1998] 2 F.L.R. 668; [1998] Fam.
Law 527; *The Times*, June 10, 1998, QBD 10–222
Estill v. Cowling Swift & Kitchin; Bean v. Cowling Swift & Kitchin [2000]
Lloyd's Rep. P.N. 378; (2000) 1 W.T.L.R. 417, Ch D 10–42, 10–119, 11–06,
11–08, 11–46
Etam plc v. Baker Almond (A Firm) [2001] E.G.C.S. 21, Ch D 9–10, 9–97
Etridge v. Pritchard Englefield [1999] Lloyd's Rep. P.N. 702; [1999] P.N.L.R.
839, CA 10–205, 10–234
Etter and Hart v. Commercial Union Assur. Co. (1998) 166 N.S.R. (2d) 299, CA
(Nova Scotia) 14–56
Eurodynamic Systems plc v. General Automation Ltd September 6, 1988, unre-
ported, QBD 17–16, 17–36, 17–85
Europe Mortgage Co. Ltd v. GA Property Services Ltd [1999] Lloyd's Rep. P.N.
709; [1999] 3 E.G.L.R. 53; [1999] 50 E.G. 77, QBD 9–116
European Partners in Capital (Epic) Holdings BV v. Goddard & Smith [1992] 41
E.G. 118; [1992] 2 E.G.L.R. 155, CA 9–06
Evans v. Duncombe (1831) 1 Cr. &. J. 372; 1 Tyr. 283; 9 L.J.(O.S.) Ex. 82 10–69
——— v. Liverpool Corp. [1906] 1 K.B. 160; 74 L.J.K.B. 742; 21 T.L.R. 588; 69
J.P. 263; 3 L.G.R. 868, KBD 12–43, 12–152, 12–170
Eve, Re (1986) 31 D.L.R. (4th) 1, Sup Ct (Can) 12–142

PARA.

Everett v. Griffiths (No.1) [1921] 1 A.C. 631; 90 L.J.K.B. 737; 125 L.T. 230; 85
J.P. 149; 65 S.J. 395; 37 T.L.R. 481; 19 L.G.Rev. 283, HL; affirming [1920]
3 K.B. 163; 89 L.J.K.B. 429; 125 L.T. 230; 37 T.L.R. 481; 85 J.P. 149; 65
S.J. 395; 19 L.G.Rev. 283, CA 2–113, 12–239
—— v. Hogg, Robinson & Gardner Mountain (Insurance) [1973] 2 Lloyd's Rep.
217, QBD (Comm Ct) 14–69, 14–102, 14–107
Everingham v. Ontario (1992) 88 D.L.R. (4th) 755, Div Ct (Ontario) 10–31
Excess Life Insurance Co. Ltd v. Fireman's Insurance Co. of Newark New Jersey
[1982] 2 Lloyd's Rep. 599, QBD (Comm Ct) 14–03
Eyre v. Measday [1986] 1 All E.R. 488; (1986) 136 N.L.J. 91, CA 12–07, 12–10,
12–230
Ezekiel v. Lehrer [2001] Lloyd's Rep. P.N. 401; [2001] P.N.L.R. 33; (2001)
98(20) L.S.G. 42; (2001) 145 S.J.L.B. 109; The Times, April 4, 2001, Ch D 5–72,
5–74
—— v. McDade [1995] 2 E.G.L.R. 107; [1995] 47 E.G. 150; [1994] E.G.C.S.
194, CA 9–144, 9–189

F (In Utero), Re [1988] Fam. 122; [1988] 2 W.L.R. 1288; [1988] 2 All E.R. 193;
[1988] 2 F.L.R. 307; [1988] F.C.R. 529; [1988] Fam. Law 337; (1988) 152
J.P.N. 538; (1988) 138 N.L.J. 37; (1989) 133 S.J. 1088; (1988) 132 S.J. 820,
CA 7–41
F (Mental Patient: Sterilisation), Re. See F v. West Berkshire H.A.; sub nom. F
(Mental Patient: Sterilisation), Re.
F v. R (1983) 33 S.A.S.R. 189, Sup Ct (Aus) 8–151, 12–69, 12–95, 12–205, 12–229
—— v. West Berkshire H.A.; sub nom. F (Mental Patient: Sterilisation), Re
[1990] 2 A.C. 1; [1989] 2 W.L.R. 1025; [1989] 2 All E.R. 545; [1989] 2
F.L.R. 376; (1989) 139 N.L.J. 789; (1989) 133 S.J. 785, HL 12–69, 12–124,
12–137, 12–138, 12–142, 12–144
F&G Reynolds (Whitchurch) Ltd v. Joseph, The Times, November 6, 1992 10–97
FC, Re [1888] W.N. 77 10–73
FG Minter Ltd v. Welsh Health Technical Services Organisation, 13 B.L.R. 1,
CA; reversing 11 B.L.R. 1, QBD 8–106
FG Whitley & Sons Ltd v. Thomas Bickerton [1993] 1 E.G.L.R. 139; [1993] 07
E.G. 100; [1992] E.G.C.S. 25 9–09
FNCB Ltd (formerly First National Commercial Bank plc) v. Barnet Devanney
(Harrow) Ltd (formerly Barnet Devanney & Co. Ltd); sub nom. FNCB Ltd
v. Barnet Devanney & Co. Ltd [1999] 2 All E.R. (Comm) 233; [1999]
Lloyd's Rep. P.N. 908; [2000] P.N.L.R. 248; (1999) 96(28) L.S.G. 28; The
Times, September 28, 1999; The Independent, July 19,1999 (C.S.), CA 14–48,
14–117, 14–125
FSA v. Lukka, April 23, 1999, unreported, Ch D 13–145
FW Cook Ltd v. Shimizu (U.K.) Ltd [2000] B.L.R. 199, QBD (T&CC) 8–340
Fairline Shipping Corp. v. Adamson [1975] Q.B. 180; [1974] 2 W.L.R. 824;
[1974] 2 All E.R. 967; [1974] 1 Lloyd's Rep. 133; (1973) 118 S.J. 406,
QBD 2–90
Fairthorne, Re (1846) 3 Dow. & L. 548; 1 N.P.C. 391; 1 Saund. & C. 40; 15
L.J.Q.B. 131; 6 L.T.(O.S.) 377; 10 Jur. 287 10–66
Fairweather v. Asden Securities (1979) 13 B.L.R. 40, DC 8–255
Faithfull v. Kesteven (1910) 103 L.T. 56, CA 10–77, 10–153
—— v. Wiltshire Health Authority, March 29, 2000, unreported, QBD 12–232
Fallows v. Randle [1997] 8 Med.L.R. 160, CA 12–119
Fangrove Pty Ltd v. Tod Group Holdings Pty Ltd [1999] 2 Qd. R. 236, CA
(Queensland) 8–119
Fanhaven Pty. Ltd v. Bain Dawes Northern Pty. Ltd [1982] 2 N.S.W.L.R. 57 14–34,
14–35, 14–67, 14–84

PARA.

Faragher v. Gerber [1994] E.G.C.S. 122, QBD 10–193

Farley v. Skinner [2001] UKHL 49 .... 3–01, 3–16

—— v. Skinner (No.2), 73 Con. L.R. 70; [2000] Lloyd's Rep. P.N. 516; [2000]
P.N.L.R. 441; [2000] 2 E.G.L.R. 125; [2000] E.G.C.S. 52; (2000) 97(15)
L.S.G. 41; [2000] N.P.C. 40; *The Times*, April 14, 2000, CA 9–77, 9–101, 9–181

Farmer v. Turner & Son (1899) 15 T.L.R. 522, QBD 10–104

Farrar v. Farrars Ltd (1888) 40 Ch.D. 395; 58 L.J.Ch. 185; 60 L.T. 121; 37 W.R.
196; 5 T.L.R. 164, CA 10–19

Farrell v. Merton Sutton & Wandsworth H.A., July, 31, unreported 12–40, 12–293,
12–299

Farrer v. Copley Singletons [1998] P.N.L.R. 22; (1998) 76 P. & C.R. 169; [1997]
N.P.C. 113, CA 10–124, 10–155, 10–165

Farrington v. Rowe, McBride & Partners [1985] 1 N.Z.L.R. 83, CA (NZ) 10–228

Farthing v. North East Essex H.A. [1998] Lloyd's Rep. Med. 37, CA 5–66

Fashion Brokers Ltd v. Clarke Hayes [2000] Lloyd's Rep. P.N. 398; [2000]
P.N.L.R. 473, CA 10–194

Fasken v. Campbell Godfrey v. Seven-Up Canada Inc. (2000) 182 D.L.R. (4th)
315, affirming (1997) 142 D.L.R. (4th) 456, HC (Ontario) 10–324

Fastrack Contractors Ltd v. Morrison Construction Ltd [2000] B.L.R. 168; 75
Con. L.R. 33; (2000) 16 Const. L.J. 273, QBD (T&CC) 8–339, 8–340

Fayed v. United Kingdom; Series A, No.294–B; (1994) 18 E.H.R.R. 393; *The
Times*, October 11, 1994; *The Independent*, October 6, 1994; *The Guardian*,
September 26, 1994, ECHR 7–06, 7–07, 7–30, 7–66, 13–25

Feist v. Gordon [1991] 2 Med.L.R. 376, CA (Alta) 12–120

Fell v. Brown (1791) Peake 131 11–10

Fenech v. East London and City H.A. [2000] Lloyd's Rep. Med. 35; [2000]
P.N.L.R. 205, CA 5–58

Fennon v. Anthony Hodari & Co. [2001] Lloyd's Rep. P.N. 183, CA 5–55

Ferguson v. Hamilton Civic Hospitals (1983) 144 D.L.R. (3d) 214, HC (Ontario)
(1985) 18 D.L.R. (4th) 638, CA (Ontario) 12–203, 12–264

—— v. Lewis (1879) 14 L.J. 700 .... 10–149, 10–307

Ferris v. Rusnak (1984) 9 D.L.R. (4th) 183, QB (Alberta) 10–25, 10–100, 10–102,
10–262

Fidgeon v. Carroll (1956) 168 E.G. 557 .... 9–91, 9–140

Fidias Consulting Engineering Ltd v. Thymaras [1985] 1 W.W.R. 752 8–316

Filipovic v. Upshall (2000) 33 R.P.R. (3d) 178 10–5

Filmlab Systems International Ltd v. Pennington [1995] 1 W.L.R. 673; [1994] 4
All E.R. 673; (1993) 143 N.L.J. 1405; *The Times*, July 9, 1993, Ch D 10–132,
10–237, 11–28, 11–30

Finance for Mortgages Ltd v. Farley & Co. [1998] P.N.L.R. 145; [1996] E.G.C.S.
35; [1996] N.P.C. 19, QBD 5–55

Financeamerica Realty Limited v. Gillies (1983) 40 Nfld. & P.E.I.R. 169, CA
(Newfoundland) 10–207

Finers v. Miro [1991] 1 W.L.R. 35; [1991] 1 All E.R. 182; (1990) 140 N.L.J.
1387; (1990) 134 S.J. 1039; *The Independent*, September 19, 1990, CA,
CA 10–32

Fine's Flowers Ltd v. General Accident Assurance Co. of Canada (1978) 81
D.L.R. (3d) 139 .... 14–12, 14–14, 14–36, 14–74, 14–81

Finlay v. Murtagh [1979] I.R. 249, Sup Ct (Irl) 10–15

Finlayson v. Armidale City Council (1994) 123 A.L.R. 155, Fed Ct (Aus) 8–120

Finley v. Connell Associates (Application to Strike Out) [1999] Lloyd's Rep. P.N.
895; (1999) 96(26) L.S.G. 27; *The Times*, June 23, 1999, QBD 10–115

Firestone Canada Inc. v. American Home Assurance Co. (1989) 67 O.R. (2d)
471 .... 14–14, 14–50, 14–126

PARA.

Firman v. Ellis; Ince v. Rogers; Down v. Harvey; Pheasant v. Smith (Tyres) [1978] Q.B. 886; [1978] 3 W.L.R. 1; [1978] 2 All E.R. 851; 122 S.J. 147, CA 5–65
First Interstate Bank of California v. Cohen Arnold & Co. [1996] 5 Bank. L.R. 150; [1996] C.L.C. 174; [1996] P.N.L.R. 17; [1995] E.G.C.S. 188; (1996) 140 S.J.L.B. 12; *The Times*, December 11, 1995, CA 15–133, 15–134
First National Commercial Bank plc v. Andrew S Taylor (Commercial) Ltd [1997] P.N.L.R. 37; [1995] E.G.C.S. 200, QBD 9–172
—— v. Humberts [1995] 2 All E.R. 673; [1996] 5 Bank. L.R. 177; 73 B.L.R. 90; [1995] 1 E.G.L.R. 142; [1995] 14 E.G. 140; (1995) 11 Const. L.J. 227; [1995] E.G.C.S. 1; [1995] N.P.C. 1; *The Times*, January 27, 1995; *The Independent*, February 14, 1995, CA 5–36
—— v. Loxleys [1997] P.N.L.R. 211; [1996] E.G.C.S. 174; (1996) 93(43) L.S.G. 26; (1997) 141 S.J.L.B. 6; [1996] N.P.C. 158; *The Times*, November 14, 1996, CA 10–57
Fish v. Kapur [1948] 2 All E.R. 176; 64 T.L.R. 328, KBD 12–16, 12–119, 12–149, 12–245
—— v. Kelly (1864) 17 C.B.(N.S.) 194; 142 R.R. 315 10–40
—— v. Wilcox [1994] 5 Med.L.R. 230; *The Times*, March 4, 1993, CA 12–289
Fisher v. Knibbe (1992) 3 Ala. L.R. (3d) 97 10–278
—— v. Knowles [1982] 1 E.G.L.R. 154; (1982) 262 E.G. 1083 .... 9–19, 9–77, 9–82, 9–140
—— v. Ruislip-Northwood Urban D.C. [1954] K.B. 584, CA 2–84
Fitzgerald v. Lane [1989] A.C. 328; [1988] 3 W.L.R. 356; [1988] 2 All E.R. 961; [1990] R.T.R. 133; (1988) 85(32) L.S.G. 44; (1988) 138 N.L.J. 209; (1988) 132 S.J. 1064, HL 4–14, 15–148
Fitzpatrick v. Batger & Co. [1967] 1 W.L.R. 706; [1967] 2 All E.R. 657; 111 S.J. 276, CA, CA 10–187
Flandro v. Mitha (1992) 93 D.L.R. (4th) 222, Sup Ct (BC) 10–166
Flannagan v. Mate [1876] 2 Vict.L.R. 157 .... 8–199, 8–316
Fleming v. Securities Commission [1995] 2 N.Z.L.R. 514 2–55
Flemington Properties Pty Ltd v. Raine & Horne Commercial Pty Ltd (1998) 155 A.L.R. 345 9–109
Fletcher v. Bench (1973) 4 B.M.J. 117 .... 12–119, 12–149
—— v. Manitoba Public Insurance Co. (1990) 74 D.L.R. (4th) 636 .... 14–12, 14–81
Fletcher & Son v. Jubb, Booth & Helliwell [1920] 1 K.B. 275 .... 10–80, 10–81, 10–185
Fleury v. Woolgar [1996] 37 Alta. L.R. (3d) 346 .... 12–76, 12–185
Flexible Packaging (Pinetown) (Pty) Ltd. v. Marianhill Mission Institute (2000) (1) S.A. 141 8–61
Florida Hotels Pty Ltd v. Mayo (1965) 113 C.L.R. 588 ..... 8–80, 8–146, 8–243, 8–250, 8–307
Flower & Hart (a firm) v. White Industries (QLD) Pty Ltd *See* White Industries (QLD) Pty Ltd v. Flower & Hart (a firm).
Flower Bowl (a firm) v. Hodges Menswear Ltd., *The Times* June 14 1988, CA 10–187
Floyd v. Nangle (1747) 3 Atk. 568 10–146
Flying Colours Film Co. v. Assicurazioni Generali SpA [1993] 2 Lloyd's Rep. 184, CA 14–11
Fogg v. Gaulter (1960) 110 L.J. 718 15–36
Fomento (Sterling Area) v. Selsdon Fountain Pen Co. [1958] 1 W.L.R. 45; [1958] 1 All E.R. 11; [1958] R.P.C. 8; 102 S.J. 51, HL 15–96, 15–11, 15–112
Fomin v. Oswell (1813) 3 Camp. 357 .... 14–49, 14–99
Fontaine v. Loewen Estate (1997) 156 D.L.R. (4th) 181, Sup Ct (Can) 8–156
Forbes v. Wandsworth H.A. [1997] Q.B. 402; [1996] 3 W.L.R. 1108; [1996] 4 All E.R. 881; [1996] 7 Med.L.R. 175; (1997) 36 B.M.L.R. 1; (1996) 93(15) L.S.G. 32; (1996) 146 N.L.J. 477; (1996) 140 S.J.L.B. 85; *The Times*, March 21, 1996, CA 5–61, 5–62, 5–65

PARA.

Forbouys v. Gadhavi [1993] N.P.C. 122 10–172
Ford Motor Co. Ltd v. HLM Design Ltd, 1997 S.L.T. 837, OH 8–279
Ford v. White & Co. [1964] 1 W.L.R. 885; [1964] 2 All E.R. 755; 108 S.J. 542,
    Ch D 9–130, 9–131, 9–135, 9–136, 10–368
Fordgate Wandsworth Ltd v. Bernard Neville & Co. [1999] E.G.C.S. 98, Ch D 10–152
Foreman v. O'Driscoll & Partners [2000] Lloyd's Rep. P.N. 720, QBD 5–74, 5–77
Forsikringsaktieselskapet Vesta v. Butcher [1989] A.C. 852; [1989] 2 W.L.R.
    290; [1989] 1 All E.R. 402; [1989] 1 Lloyd's Rep. 331; [1989] Fin. L.R.
    223; (1989) 133 S.J. 184, HL; affirming [1988] 3 W.L.R. 565; [1988] 2 All
    E.R. 43; [1988] 1 Lloyd's Rep. 19; [1988] 1 F.T.L.R. 78; [1988] Fin. L.R.
    67; (1988) 4 Const. L.J. 75; (1988) 85(31) L.S.G. 33; (1988) 132 S.J. 1181,
    CA; affirming [1986] 2 All E.R. 488; [1986] 2 Lloyd's Rep. 179, QBD
    (Comm Ct) 2–103, 5–115, 5–116, 8–330, 14–14, 14–59, 14–92, 14–126, 14–128,
                                                                          17–126
Forster v. Outred & Co. [1982] 1 W.L.R. 86; [1982] 2 All E.R. 753; 125 S.J. 309,
    CA 2–103, 5–37, 5–38, 5–40, 5–41, 5–42, 10–13
Foshan Hua Da Industrial Co. v. Johnson, Stokes & Master (a firm) [1999]
    H.K.L.R.D. 418 10–165
Foster, Re; sub nom. Foster v. Crusts (1986) 2 P.N. 193; [1986] B.C.L.C. 307 10–42
Foster v. Crusts [1986] B.C.L.C. 307 10–42
Four Solicitors, Ex p. Incorporated Law Society, Re [1901] 1 Q.B. 187, QBD 10–22
Fowell v. National Coal Board, The Times, May 28, 1986, CA 5–61
Fowkes v. Duthie [1991] 1 All E.R. 337; (1991) 141 N.L.J. 130; The Times,
    January 11, 1991; The Independent, December 21, 1990, QBD 10–188
Fowler v. Wyatt (1857) 24 Beav. 232 2–145
Fox v. Everingham (1983) 50 A.L.R. 3371 .... 10–100, 10–166
—— v. Glasgow & South Western Hospitals Board, 1955 S.L.T. 337, OH 12–153
—— v. Mackreth (1788) 2 Bro.C.C. 400, 2 Cox 320, affirmed (1791) 4 Bro.P.C.
    258 3–10
—— v. Morrish, Grant and Co. [1918] T.L.R. 126 .... 15–31, 15–112, 15–139
—— v. Riverside Health Trust; sub nom. Riverside Mental Health NHS Trust v.
    Fox [1994] 1 F.L.R. 614; [1994] 2 F.C.R. 577; (1994) 6 Admin. L.R. 250;
    [1995] 6 Med. L.R. 181; [1994] Fam. Law 321; The Times, October 28,
    1993; The Independent, November 15, 1993 (C.S.), CA 12–140
Foxley v. United Kingdom (App. No.3327/96) (2001) 31 E.H.R.R. 25; 8
    B.H.R.C. 571; The Times, July 4, 2000, ECHR 7–34
Fozal v. Gofur, The Times July 9, 1993 CA 11–26
Francis v. Francis and Dickerson [1956] P. 87; [1955] 3 W.L.R. 973; [1955] 3 All
    E.R. 836; 99 S.J. 891, PDAD 10–116
Francome v. Mirror Group Newspapers Ltd [1984] 1 W.L.R. 892; [1984] 2 All
    E.R. 408; (1984) 81 L.S.G. 2225; (1984) 128 S.J. 484, CA 2–160
Frank H Wright (Constructions), Ltd v. Frodoor Ltd [1967] 1 W.L.R. 506; [1967]
    1 All E.R. 433; 111 S.J. 210, QBD 15–112
Frank v. Seifert Sedley & Co., 191 E.G. 29; (1964) 108 S.J. 523 .... 10–192, 10–237
Frankland v. Cole (1832) 2 Cr. & J. 590; S.C. 1 L.J.Ex. 189 10–175
Frankston and Hastings Corp. v. Cohen (1960) 102 C.L.R. 607 ...... 15–95, 15–98, 15–112
Franses v. Barnett (1956) 168 E.G. 425 9–98
Fraser Park South Estates Ltd v. Lang Michener Lawrence & Shaw [2001] 3
    C.C.L.T. (3d) 270, CA (BC) 10–261
Fraser v. BN Furman (Productions) Ltd [1967] 1 W.L.R. 898; [1967] 3 All E.R.
    57; [1967] 2 Lloyd's Rep. 1; 2 K.I.R. 483; (1967) 111 S.J. 471, CA 14–103,
                                                                  14–104, 14–105, 14–106
—— v. Vancouver General Hospital [1951] 3 W.W.R. (N.S.) 337, affirmed [1952]
    3 D.L.R. 785, Sup Ct (Can) 12–78
Fraser Valley Mushroom Growers' Co-operative Association v. MacNaughton &
    Ward Ltd (1982) 37 B.C.L.R. 20, Sup Ct (BC) 14–59

PARA.

Frawley v. Neill [2000] C.P. Rep. 20; (1999) 96(12) L.S.G. 33; (1999) 143
S.J.L.B. 98; *The Times*, April 5, 1999, CA 5–101
Fray v. Voules (1859) 1 E. & E. 839 .... 10–121, 10–123, 10–189
Fredette v. Wiebe (1986) 29 D.L.R. (4th) 534, Sup Ct (BC) 5–114, 12–281
Freeman v. Home Office [1984] Q.B. 524; [1984] 2 W.L.R. 802; [1984] 1 All
E.R. 1036; (1984) 81 L.S.G. 1045; (1984) 128 S.J. 298, CA 12–124, 12–128
—— v. Marshall & Co. (1966) 200 E.G. 777 .... 9–52, 9–91, 9–131, 9–140, 9–191
—— v. Sutter [1996] 4 W.W.R. 748 12–54
Freeman & Lockyer v. Buckhurst Park Properties (Mangal) Ltd [1964] 2 Q.B.
480; [1964] 2 W.L.R. 618; [1964] 1 All E.R. 630; 108 S.J. 96, CA 13–98
Frenchay Healthcare NHS Trust v. S [1994] 1 W.L.R. 601; [1994] 2 All E.R. 403;
[1994] 1 F.L.R. 485; [1994] 3 F.C.R. 121; [1994] P.I.Q.R. P118; [1994] Fam.
Law 320; (1994) 144 N.L.J. 268; *The Times*, January 19, 1994, CA 12–146
Freudiana Holdings Ltd, Re, *The Times*, December 4 1995, CA 10–132, 10–133,
11–28
Friend v. Young [1897] 2 Ch. 421, Ch D 5–93
Friends Provident Life Office v. Hillier Parker May & Rowden [1997] Q.B. 85;
[1996] 2 W.L.R. 123; [1995] 4 All E.R. 260; (1996) 71 P. & C.R. 286;
[1995] E.G.C.S. 64; [1995] N.P.C. 63; *The Times*, April 15, 1995, CA 4–06
Frost v. Chief Constable of South Yorkshire; White v. Chief Constable of South
Yorkshire; Duncan v. British Coal Corp. [1999] 2 A.C. 455; [1998] 3 W.L.R.
1509; [1999] 1 All E.R. 1; [1999] I.C.R. 216; [1999] I.R.L.R. 110; (1999) 45
B.M.L.R. 1; (1999) 96(2) L.S.G. 28; (1998) 148 N.L.J. 1844; (1999) 143
S.J.L.B. 51; *The Times*, December 4, 1998; *The Independent*, December 9,
1998, HL 2–71, 2–75, 2–77, 12–34, 12–301
—— v. Moody Homes Ltd; *sub nom.* Hoskisson v. Donald Moody; Hoskisson v.
Moody Homes Ltd, 46 B.L.R. 81; 31 Con. L.R. 54; (1990) 6 Const. L.J. 43;
(1989) 5 Const. L.J. 205, QBD (OR) 8–298
Fryer v. Bunney [1982] 2 E.G.L.R. 130; (1982) 263 E.G. 158 .... 9–58, 9–190
—— v. Royal Institution of Chartered Surveyors; *sub nom.* Royal Institution of
Chartered Surveyors v. Wiseman Marshall [2000] Lloyd's Rep. P.N. 534;
[2000] P.N.L.R. 649; *The Times*, May 16, 2000, CA 10–132, 10–133, 11–28,
11–30
Furber v. Kratter, *The Times*, July 21, 1988; *The Independent*, August 9, 1988;
The Guardian, September 8, 1988 .... 12–233, 12–235
Fussell v. Beddard (1942) 2 B.M.J. 411 12–80

G (A Child) v. Kingsmill (No.2) [2001] EWCA Civ 934, CA 10–190, 11–45, 11–54
G (Children) (Care Proceedings: Wasted Costs), Re; *sub nom.* G, S and M
(Children) (Wasted Costs), Re; G, S and H (Care Proceedings: Wasted
Costs), Re [2000] Fam. 104; [2000] 2 W.L.R. 1007; [1999] 4 All E.R. 371;
[2000] 1 F.L.R. 52; [1999] 3 F.C.R. 303; [2000] Fam. Law 24, Fam Div 10–132,
11–35
G v. International Christian Mission Inc. (1995) 125 D.L.R. (4th) 712, CA (Nova
Scotia) 10–31
G&K Ladenbau (U.K.) Ltd v. Crawley & de Reya [1978] 1 W.L.R. 266; [1978]
1 All E.R. 682, QBD 2–03, 10–90, 10–197, 10–242, 10–297
GF (Medical Treatment), Re; *sub nom.* G (Termination of Pregnancy), Re; GF (A
Patient), Re [1992] 1 F.L.R. 293; [1991] F.C.R. 786; [1993] 4 Med.L.R. 77;
[1992] Fam. Law 63; (1991) 155 L.G. Rev. 951; *The Times*, January 31,
1991, Fam Div 12–144
GKN Keller Canada Ltd v. Hartford Fire Insurance Co. (1983) 27 C.C.L.T. 61,
HC (Ontario) 14–46
GM v. MM: The Director-General, Department of Family Services and Aborigi-
nal and Island Affairs (1994) F.L.C. 668 12–142

PARA.

GP&P Ltd v. Bulcraig & Davies (1986) 2 E.G.L.R. 148 .... 9–10, 10–234, 10–253,
10–272, 10–305

GUS Property Management Ltd v. Littlewoods Mail Order Stores Ltd, 1982
S.L.T. 533 9–112

GUS Property Management v. Littlewoods Mail Order Stores Ltd; *sub nom.* J
Dykes Ltd v. Littlewoods Mail Order Stores Ltd, 1982 S.C. (H.L.) 157, HL;
reversing 1982 S.L.T. 50, OH 8–153

Gable House Estates Ltd v. Halpern Partnership (1995) 48 Con. L.R. 1, QBD
(OR) 8–62, 8–189, 8–194, 8–267, 8–271

Gafford v. Graham (1999) 77 P. & C.R. 73; [1999] 3 E.G.L.R. 75; [1999] 41 E.G.
159; (1999) 96(40) L.S.G. 44; (1998) 95(21) L.S.G. 36; (1998) 142 S.J.L.B.
155; [1998] N.P.C. 66; *The Times*, May 1, 1998, CA 5–104, 5–111

Gagnon v. Stortini [1974] 4 O.R. (2d) 270 12–149

Gail Taylor v. Shropshire Area H.A. (No.2) [2000] Lloyd's Rep. Med. 96,
QBD 12–292, 12–293, 12–294

Gainers Inc. v. Pocklington (1995) 125 D.L.R. (4th) 50, CA (Alberta) 10–31

Gala v. Preston (1991) 172 C.L.R. 243 2–63

Galambos v. Kindrachuk Enterprises Ltd (1988) 63 Sask.R. 229, QBD
(Saskatchewan) 14–42

Gallant v. Fialkov (1989) 69 O.R. (2d) 297 .... 12–186, 12–248

Galloway v. Hanley (1956) 1 B.M.J. 580 .... 12–80, 12–192

Galoo Ltd v. Bright Grahame Murray [1994] 1 W.L.R. 1360; [1994] 1 All E.R.
16; [1994] B.C.C. 319; *The Times*, January 14, 1994, CA 8–270, 10–236, 15–123,
15–124, 15–138, 16–66, 18–22

Ganger v. St Paul's Hospital (1997) 40 B.C.L.R. 116, CA (BC) 12–240

Garamella v. New York Medical College [1999] Lloyd's Rep. Med. 343, US
Ct 12–49

Gardiner v. Mounfield [1990] 1 Med.L.R. 205 12–178

Gardner v. Marsh & Parsons [1997] 1 W.L.R. 489; [1997] 3 All E.R. 871; [1997]
P.N.L.R. 362; (1998) 75 P. & C.R. 319; [1997] 1 E.G.L.R. 111; [1997] 15
E.G. 137; [1996] E.G.C.S. 186; (1996) 93(46) L.S.G. 28; (1996) 140
S.J.L.B. 262; [1996] N.P.C. 162; *The Times*, December 2, 1996, CA 9–141,
9–144, 9–148, 10–255, 10–175

Garland v. Ralph Pay and Ransom [1984] 2 E.G.L.R. 147; (1984) 271 E.G.
106 9–176

Garrant v. Moskal [1985] 6 W.W.R. 31, CA (Saskatchewan) 10–62

Gart & Hodge v. Frame Son & Co. (1839) 6 C. & F. 193 10–301

Gartside v. Sheffield, Young & Ellis [1983] N.Z.L.R. 37, CA (NZ) 10–49

Gascoine v. Ian Sheridan & Co. [1994] 5 Med.L.R. 437, QBD 10–280, 11–54, 12–74

Gaskin v. United Kingdom; Series A, No.160; [1990] 1 F.L.R. 167; (1990) 12
E.H.R.R. 36; *The Times*, August 28, 1989, ECHR 7–60

Gathergood v. Blundell [1992] 3 N.Z.L.R. 643, CA 10–38

Gaughan v. Bedfordshire H.A. [1997] 8 Med.L.R. 182, QBD 12–149, 12–188

Gaunt v. Gold Star Insurance Co. Ltd [1991] 2 N.Z.L.R. 341 14–123

Gauntlett v. Northampton H.A. (1990) 6 P.N. 107 12–237

Gautrin v. France (1999) 28 E.H.R.R. 196; [1998] H.R.C.D. 555, ECHR 7–32, 7–65,
7–66, 7–67

Gebhard v. Consiglio dell'Ordine degli Avvocati e Procuratori di Milano (Case
C–55/94) [1996] All E.R. (E.C.) 189; [1995] E.C.R. I–4165; [1996] 1
C.M.L.R. 603; [1996] C.E.C. 175; *The Times*, December 13, 1995, ECJ 10–2

Geddis v. Proprietors of Bann Reservoir (1878) 3 App.Cas. 430 2–81

Gee, Re (1845) 10 Jur. 694 10–66

General Accident Fire & Life Assurance Corp. Ltd v. JH Minet & Co. Ltd (1942)
74 Ll.L.Rep. 1 .... 14–89, 14–93, 14–94, 14–114, 14–127

PARA.

General Accident Fire & Life Assurance Corp. Ltd v. Peter William Tanter; Zephyr, The [1985] 2 Lloyd's Rep. 529, CA; reversing [1984] 1 W.L.R. 100; [1984] 1 All E.R. 35; [1984] 1 Lloyd's Rep. 58; (1984) 134 N.L.J. 35; (1983) 127 S.J. 733, QBD (Comm Ct) 14–18, 14–20, 14–24, 14–40

General Mediterranean Holdings S.A. v. Patel [2000] 1 W.L.R. 272; [1999] 3 All E.R. 673; [1999] C.P.L.R. 425; [1999] 2 Costs L.R. 10; [2000] H.R.L.R. 54; [2000] U.K.H.R.R. 273; [1999] Lloyd's Rep. P.N. 919; [1999] P.N.L.R. 852; (1999) 149 N.L.J. 1145; [1999] N.P.C. 98; The Times, August 12, 1999, QBD (Comm Ct) 7–35

General Mediterranean Holdings v. Patel [1999] 3 All E.R. 673 10–131

Geoffrey Silver & Drake v. Baines; sub nom. Silver (Geoffrey) & Drake (A Firm) v. Baines (Thomas Anthony) (t/a Wetherfield Baines & Baines (A Firm)) [1971] 1 Q.B. 396; [1971] 2 W.L.R. 187; [1971] 1 All E.R. 473; (1970) 114 S.J. 865, CA 10–68, 10–70, 10–73

George Barkes (London) Ltd v. LFC (1988) Ltd (t/a LFC Insurance Group) [2000] P.N.L.R. 21, CC (Central London) 14–79, 14–98, 14–124

George Buchanan v. Newington Property Centre, 1992 S.C.L.R. 583, Sh Ct (Lothian) 9–189

George Fischer Holdings Ltd v. Multi Design Consultants Ltd; George Fischer Holdings Ltd v. Davis Langdon & Everest, 61 Con. L.R. 85; The Independent, May 4, 1998 (C.S.), QBD (OR) 8–97, 8–216, 8–243, 8–256, 8–290, 8–301

George Hawkins v. Chrysler (U.K.) Ltd and Burne Associates, 38 B.L.R. 36, CA 8–173, 8–175, 8–214, 8–215

George Mitchell (Chesterhall) Ltd v. Finney Lock Seeds Ltd [1983] 2 A.C. 803; [1983] 3 W.L.R. 163; [1983] 2 All E.R. 737; [1983] 2 Lloyd's Rep. 272; [1983] Com. L.R. 209, HL 5–04

George Parke v. The Fenton Gretton Partnership [2001] C.I.L.L. 1712 8–337

Georgiadis v. Greece (1997) 24 E.H.R.R. 606, ECHR 7–67

Gerber v. Pines (1935) 79 S.J. 13 .... 12–80, 12–192, 12–221

German v. Major (1985) 20 D.L.R. (4th) 703, CA (Alberta) 10–62

Gertrude, The [1927] W.N. 265; 138 L.T. 239; 44 T.L.R. 1; 17 Asp.M.L.C. 343 10–69

Giannarelli v. Wraith (1988) 91 A.L.R.417, HC (Aus) 11–24

Gibbons v. Nelsons (A Firm) [2000] Lloyd's Rep. P.N. 603; [2000] P.N.L.R. 734; (2000) 1 W.T.L.R. 453; (2000) 97(19) L.S.G. 44; The Times, April 21, 2000, Ch D 10–50

Gibbs v. Daniel (1862) 4 Giff. 1 10–18

Gibraltar General Insurance Company v. L.E. Yingst Co. Ltd (1990) 89 Sask. R. 93, QBD (Saskatchewan) 14–23, 14–58, 14–99

Gibson Lea Retail Interiors Ltd v. Makro Self Service Wholesalers Ltd, unreported, July 24, 2001 8–340

Gibson v. Jeyes (1801) 6 Ves. Jun. 266; 31 E.R. 1044 .... 2–137, 10–18

Gilbert v. Cooper (1848) 17 L.J. Ch. 265; 11 L.T.(O.S.) 169 10–69

—— v. Shanahan [1998] 3 N.Z.L.R. 528 .... 5–39, 10–162, 10–230, 10–324

Gilbride v. Sincock (1955) 166 E.G. 129 .... 8–214, 8–290

Giles v. Rhind, July 24, 2001, unreported 15–142

Gill v. Lougher (1830) 1 Cr. & J. 170; 1 Tyr. 121; 9 L.J.Ex.(O.S.) 24; 35 R.R. 697 .... 10–175, 10–307

Gillick v. West Norfolk and Wisbech A.H.A. [1986] A.C. 112; [1985] 3 W.L.R. 830; [1985] 3 All E.R. 402; [1986] Crim. L.R. 113; (1985) 82 L.S.G. 3531; (1985) 135 N.L.J. 1055; (1985) 129 S.J. 738, HLx8>12–148

Giradet v. Crease & Company (1987) 11 B.C.L.R. (2d) 361 2–127

Girard v. Royal Columbian Hospital (1976) 66 D.L.R. (3d) 676, Sup Ct (BC) 12–119

Giurelli v. Girgis (1980) 24 S.A.S.R. 264, Sup Ct (Aus) 12–180

Gladwell v. Steggall (1839) 5 Bing.(N.C.) 733; 8 Scott 60; 8 L.J.C.P. 361; 3 Jur. 535; 53 R.R. 257 12–15

PARA.

Glantz v. Polikoff & Co. [1993] N.P.C. 145, QBD 10–35

Glasgow Assurance Corp. v. William Symondson & Co. (1911) 104 L.T. 254; 27
    T.L.R. 245; 11 Asp.M.L.C. 583; 16 Com.Cas. 109 .... 14–18, 14–24

Glasgow, University of v. William Whitfield; *sub nom.* University Court of the
    University of Glasgow v. William Whitfield and John Laing (Construction)
    Ltd; University of Glasgow v. John Laing (Construction) Ltd (1988) 42
    B.L.R. 66; (1989) 5 Const. L.J. 73, QBD 5–15, 5–22, 8–35, 8–36, 8–38

Glass v. Cambridge H.A. [1995] 6 Med.L.R. 91 12–122

Glencot Development and Design Co. Ltd v. Ben Barrett & Son (Contractors) Ltd
    [2001] B.L.R. 207; (2001) 3 T.C.L.R. 11, QBD (T&CC) 8–341

Glennon v. Commissioner for Taxation of the Commonwealth of Australia (1972)
    127 C.L.R. 503 2–135

Glicksman v. Redbridge H.A., 2000 WL 1084378; June 29, 2000, unreported 12–105,
    12–113

Gloucestershire H.A. v. MA Torpy & Partners Ltd (t/a Torpy & Partners) (No.1)
    (1997) 55 Con. L.R. 124, QBD (OR) 8–62, 8–137, 8–169, 8–215

Godefroy v. Dalton (1830) 6 Bing 460; 4 Moo. & P. 149; 8 L.J.C.P.(O.S.) 79; 31
    R.R. 467 .... 10–77, 10–80, 10–121, 10–180

—— v. Jay (1831) 7 Bing. 413; 5 Moo. & P. 284; 9 L.J.C.P.(O.S.) 122 ..... 10–186, 10–293

Gold v. Essex C.C. [1942] 2 K.B. 293; [1942] 2 All E.R. 237; 167 L.T. 166; 58
    T.L.R. 357; 40 L.G.R. 249, CA 12–185

—— v. Haringey H.A. [1988] Q.B. 481; [1987] 3 W.L.R. 649; [1987] 2 All E.R.
    888; [1988] 1 F.L.R. 55; [1987] Fam. Law 417; (1987) 84 L.S.G. 1812;
    (1987) 137 N.L.J. 541, CA 6–08, 8–147, 12–69, 12–96, 12–153, 12–213, 12–229,
    12–289

—— v. Mincoff Science & Gold [2001] Lloyd's Rep. P.N. 423; (2001) 98(3)
    L.S.G. 44; [2001] N.P.C. 6, Ch D 5–77, 10–164

Gold Star Insurance Co. Ltd v. Gaunt [1998] 3 N.Z.L.R. 80, CA (NZ) 14–03, 14–60,
    14–123

Goldcorp Exchange Ltd (In Receivership), Re; *sub nom.* Kensington v. Unrepre-
    sented Non-Allocated Claimants; Goldcorp Finance Ltd, Re [1995] 1 A.C.
    74; [1994] 3 W.L.R. 199; [1994] 2 All E.R. 806; [1994] 2 B.C.L.C. 578;
    (1994) 13 Tr. L.R. 434; (1994) 91(24) L.S.G. 46; (1994) 144 N.L.J. 792;
    (1994) 138 S.J.L.B. 127; *The Times*, June 2, 1994, PC (NZ) 2–129, 2–130, 15–38

Golder v. United Kingdom; Series A, No.18; (1979–80) 1 E.H.R.R. 524,
    ECHR 7–10

Goldman v. Abbott [1989] 48 E.G. 151; (1989) 139 S.J. 828, CA 10–69, 10–74

Goldsworthy v. Brickell [1987] Ch. 378; [1987] 2 W.L.R. 133; [1987] 1 All E.R.
    853; (1987) 84 L.S.G. 654; (1987) 131 S.J. 102, CA 2–145, 5–98

Gomer v. Pitt & Scott (1922) 12 Ll.L.Rep. 115 14–81

Gonda v. Kerbel (1982) 24 C.C.L.T. 222, Sup Ct (Ontario) 12–189, 12–204

Goodall v. Simpson, March 6, 1991, OH 9–70

Goode v. Nash (1979) 21 S.A.S.R. 419, 423, Sup Ct (Aus) 12–15, 12–189

Gooderham v. Bank of Novia Scotia [2000] 47 O.R. 3d 554, Sup Ct (Can) 14–109

Goodwill v. British Pregnancy Advisory Service [1996] 1 W.L.R. 1397; [1996] 2
    All E.R. 161; [1996] 2 F.L.R. 55; [1996] 2 F.C.R. 680; [1996] P.I.Q.R. P197;
    [1996] 7 Med.L.R. 129; (1996) 31 B.M.L.R. 83; (1996) 93(5) L.S.G. 31;
    (1996) 146 N.L.J. 173; (1996) 140 S.J.L.B. 37; *The Times*, January 29, 1996;
    The Independent, January 19, 1996, CA 2–42, 12–24, 12–46, 12–47, 12–48,
    12–54

Goody v. Baring [1956] 1 W.L.R. 448; [1956] 2 All E.R. 11; 100 S.J. 320, Ch
    D 10–100, 10–160, 10–174

Goorkani v. Tayside Health Board, 1991 S.L.T. 94, OH 12–191, 12–225

Gordon v. JB Wheatley & Co.; *sub nom.* Gordon v. Wheatley & Co. [2000]
    Lloyd's Rep. P.N. 605; [2000] P.N.L.R. 755; (2000) 97(24) L.S.G. 40; *The
    Times*, June 6, 2000, CA 5–40, 5–43, 13–10

PARA.

Gordon v. Miller (1838) 1 D. (Ct of Sess.) 832 8–253
—— v. Wilson, 1992 S.L.T. 849; [1992] 3 Med.L.R. 401, OH 12–94, 12–96
Gordon Shaw Concrete Products Ltd v. Design Collaborative Ltd (1985) 35
    C.C.L.T. 100, CA (Nova Scotia) 8–193, 8–199, 8–316
Gore Mutual Insurance Company v. Barton (1979) 12 B.C.L.R. 261 14–23
Gorham v. British Telecommunications plc [2000] 1 W.L.R. 2129; [2000] 4 All
    E.R. 867; [2001] Lloyd's Rep. I.R. 531; [2000] Lloyd's Rep. P.N. 897;
    [2001] P.N.L.R. 2; [2000] Pens. L.R. 293; (2000) 97(38) L.S.G. 44; (2000)
    144 S.J.L.B. 251; The Times, August 16, 2000, CA 2–114, 10–53, 13–109,
                                              13–111, 13–159, 13–167, 14–02, 14–26
Gorrie v. Nielsen [1989] 2 W.W.R. 437, CA (Alberta) 10–196
Gouzenko v. Harris (1977) 72 D.L.R. (3d) 293, HC (Ontario) 10–187, 10–282
Gover v. State of South Australia and Perriam (1985) 39 S.A.S.R. 543, Sup Ct
    (Aus) 12–74, 12–265
Governors of Board of Hospitals for Sick Children v. McLaughlin & Harvey
    (1987) Con.L.R. 25 .... 8–214, 8–219
Governors of the Peabody Donation Fund v. Sir Lindsay Parkinson & Co. Ltd
    [1985] A.C. 210; [1984] 3 W.L.R. 953; [1984] 3 All E.R. 529; 28 B.L.R. 1;
    83 L.G.R. 1; [1984] C.I.L.L. 128; (1984) 81 L.S.G. 3179; (1984) 128 S.J.
    753, HL 2–28, 2–75, 2–76, 12–289
Gowten v. Wolverhampton H.A. [1994] 5 Med.L.R. 432, QBD 12–230
Grabber Industrial Products Central Ltd v. Stewart & Co. (2000) 185 D.L.R. (4th)
    303, CA (BC) 10–31
Graham v. Persyko (1984) 30 C.C.L.T. 84, 96, HC (Ontario) 12–282
—— v. Persyko (1986) 27 D.L.R. (4th) 699, CA (Ontario) 12–191
Grainary Restaurant Ltd v. American Home Insurance Co. (1987) 81 N.B.R. (2d)
    151; 205 A.P.R. 151, CA (New Brunswick) 14–77
Gran Gelato Ltd v. Richcliff (Group) Ltd [1992] Ch. 560; [1992] 2 W.L.R. 867;
    [1992] 1 All E.R. 865; [1992] 1 E.G.L.R. 297; [1991] E.G.C.S. 136; (1992)
    142 N.L.J. 51; The Times, December 19, 1991; The Independent, December
    18, 1991, Ch D 10–56, 10–57, 10–59, 13–88
Granville Savings & Mortgage Corp. v. Slevin (1994) 108 D.L.R. (4th) 383, Sup
    Ct (1992) 93 D.L.R. (4th) 268, CA (Maniba) 10–61
Grare v. France (1993) 15 E.H.R.R. C.D. 100 7–59
Gray v. Buss Murton (A Firm) [1999] P.N.L.R. 882 .... 10–06, 10–219
—— v. Richards Butler (Supervision of Execution) (2000) 1 W.T.L.R. 143, Ch
    D 10–222
—— v. TP Bennett & Son (1987) 43 B.L.R. 63 8–15
Graybriar Industries Ltd v. Davis & Co. (1992) 46 B.C.L.R. (2d) 164, affd 72
    B.C.L.R. (2d) 190, CA (BC) 10–165, 10–199, 10–261
Great Luxembourg Railway Company v. Magnay (No.2) (1858) 23 Beav. 586 3–10
Greater Nottingham Cooperative Society v. Cementation Piling and Foundations
    Ltd [1989] Q.B. 71; [1988] 3 W.L.R. 396; [1988] 2 All E.R. 971; 41 B.L.R.
    43; (1988) 4 Const. L.J. 216; (1988) 138 N.L.J. 112; (1988) 132 S.J. 754,
    CA 2–104, 8–59
Greaves & Co. (Contractors) Ltd v. Baynham Meikle & Partners [1975] 1 W.L.R.
    1095; [1975] 3 All E.R. 99; [1975] 2 Lloyd's Rep. 325; 4 B.L.R. 56; 119 S.J.
    372, CA; affirming [1974] 1 W.L.R. 1261; [1974] 3 All E.R. 666; [1975] 1
    Lloyd's Rep. 31; 118 S.J. 595, QBD 2–02, 2–11, 8–17, 8–133, 8–146, 8–170,
                                                      8–171, 8–173
Green v. Berry [2001] 1 Qd.R. 605, CA (Queensland) 10–290
—— v. Collyer-Bristow [1999] Lloyd's Rep. P.N. 798; [1999] N.P.C. 56, QBD 10–82,
                                     10–94, 10–119, 11–08, 11–37
—— v. Cunningham John & Co. (1995) 46 Con.L.R. 62, CA 10–282
—— v. Dixon (1837) 1 Jur. 137 10–207
—— v. Hancocks (A Firm) [2001] Lloyd's Rep. P.N. 212, CA 10–119, 11–38

PARA.

Green v. Ipswich B.C. [1988] 1 E.G.L.R. 239 9–10
—— v. Turner [1999] P.N.L.R. 28, Ch D 10–246
Greenfield v. Irwin (A Firm); *sub nom.* Greenfield v. Flather [2001] EWCA Civ
    113; [2001] 1 W.L.R. 1279; [2001] 1 F.L.R. 899; [2001] P.I.Q.R. Q7; [2001]
    Lloyd's Rep. Med. 143; (2001) 59 B.M.L.R. 43; *The Times*, February 6,
    2001, CA 7–44, 12–289, 12–291, 12–301
—— v. Secretary of State for the Home Department. *See* R. (on the application
    of Greenfield) v. Secretary of State for the Home Department.
Gregg & Co. v. Gardner [1897] 2 I.R. 122 10–180
Gregory v. Pembrokeshire H.A. [1989] 1 Med.L.R. 81 .... 12–231, 12–277
—— v. Shepherds (A Firm) [2000] Lloyd's Rep. P.N. 724; [2000] P.N.L.R. 769;
    (2001) 81 P. & C.R. 10; [2000] 3 E.G.L.R. 49; [2000] 50 E.G. 100; [2000]
    E.G.C.S. 78; (2000) 97(28) L.S.G. 32; (2000) 97(26) L.S.G. 39; [2000]
    N.P.C. 69; *The Times*, June 28, 2000, CA 10–146, 10–200, 10–275, 10–317
—— v. Tarlo (1964) S.J. 219; *The Times*, March 6, 1964 .... 10–185, 10–279
Gresley v. Mousley (1858) 4 De G. & J. 78 2–137
Gretton & Starkey (trading as Open Systems Design) v. British Millerain Co. Ltd,
    July 29, 1998, unreported 17–14, 17–26, 17–27, 17–30, 17–32, 17–41
Grey (HA), Re [1892] 2 Q.B. 440; 61 L.J.Q.B. 795; 57 J.P. 246; 41 W.R. 3; 8
    T.L.R. 694, CA 10–69
Grey v. Webster (1984) 14 D.L.R. (4th) 706 (New Brunswick) 12–10, 12–119
Griffiths v. Dawson & Co. [1993] 2 F.L.R. 315; [1993] 2 F.C.R. 515; [1993] Fam.
    Law 476; *The Times*, April 5, 1993 10–178
—— v. Evans [1953] 1 W.L.R. 1424; [1953] 2 All E.R. 1364; 97 S.J. 812, CA 10–06,
    10–160, 10–162
—— v. Fleming [1909] 1 K.B. 805, CA 10–300
Grima v. MacMillan (1972) 27 D.L.R. (3d) 666, CA (Ontario) 10–176
Groom v. Crocker [1939] 1 K.B. 194; (1938) 60 Ll. L. Rep. 393, CA 2–100, 10–04,
    10–05, 10–13, 10–103, 10–123, 10–156, 10–313
—— v. Selby [2001] Lloyd's Rep. Med. 39, QBD 12–300, 12–301
Grossman v. Steward (1977) 5 C.C.L.T. 45, Sup Ct (BC) 5–114
Grosvenor (Mayfair) Estates Ltd v. Raja, *The Times* November
2nd 1990, CA 10–55
Group B Plaintiffs v. Medical Research Council; *sub nom.* Creutzfeldt-Jakob
    Disease Litigation (No.5), Re; CJD Litigation (No.5), Re [2000] Lloyd's
    Rep. Med. 161; (2000) 54 B.M.L.R. 92; (1998) 41 B.M.L.R. 157, QBD 12–23,
    12–110, 12–283
Grove v. Jackman and Masters (1950) 155 E.G. 182 .... 9–88, 9–91, 9–134, 9–191
Grovedeck Ltd v. Capital Demolition Ltd [2000] B.L.R. 181; (2000) 2 T.C.L.R.
    689; *The Independent*, May 8, 2000 (C.S.), QBD (T&CC) 8–340
Grupo Torras S.A. v. Al Sabah (No.5); *sub nom.* Al-Sabah v. Grupo Torras SA;
    Bonafonte v. Grupo Torras S.A. [2001] Lloyd's Rep. Bank. 36; [2001]
    C.L.C. 221; [2001] Lloyd's Rep. P.N. 117, CA 10–39
Guardian Insurance Co. v. Sharp [1941] 2 D.L.R. 417 .... 15–106, 15–107, 15–112,
    15–121
Guerra v. Italy (1998) 26 E.H.R.R. 357; 4 B.H.R.C. 63; [1998] H.R.C.D. 277,
    ECHR 7–44
Guest v. Smythe (1870) L.R. 5 Ch.App. 551 2–136
Guild (Claims) Ltd v. Eversheds [2000] Lloyd's Rep. P.N. 910; *The Times*,
    August 16, 2000, Ch D 10–246
Gunn-Russo v. Nugent Care Society; *sub nom.* R. (on the application of Gunn-
    Russo) v. Nugent Care Society [2001] EWHC Admin 566; (2001) 151 N.L.J.
    1250, QBD (Admin Ct) 7–60
Gunns v. Par Insurance Brokers [1997] 1 Lloyd's Rep. 173, QBD 14–67, 14–90,
    14–102
Gupta v. General Medical Committee, July 25, 2001, unreported, QBD 7–67

PARA.

Gurd v. A Cobden Soar & Son (1951) 157 E.G. 415 .... 9–34, 9–93, 9–134

Gwembe Valley Development Co. Ltd v. Koshy [1998] 2 B.C.L.C. 613, Ch D 5–90

H (A Patient), Re; *sub nom.* H (Adult: Incompetent), Re [1998] 2 F.L.R. 36; [1998] 3 F.C.R. 174; (1997) 38 B.M.L.R. 11; [1998] Fam. Law 460, Fam Div 12–146

H (Mental Patient: Diagnosis Consent), Re [1993] 1 F.L.R. 29; [1992] 2 F.C.R. 707; [1993] 4 Med.L.R. 91; [1993] Fam. Law 131; *The Times*, July 17, 1992, Fam Div 12–144

H (Minors) (Abduction: Acquiescence), Re. *See* H v. H (Child Abduction: Acquiescence).

H v. H (Child Abduction: Acquiescence); *sub nom.* H (Minors) (Abduction: Acquiescence), Re [1998] A.C. 72; [1997] 2 W.L.R. 563; [1997] 2 All E.R. 225; [1997] 1 F.L.R. 872; [1997] 2 F.C.R. 257; [1997] Fam. Law 468; *The Times*, April 17, 1997; *The Independent*, April 15, 1997, HL 5–103

—— v. Norway (1992) 73 D.R. 155 7–41

—— v. Royal Alexandra Hospital for Children [1990] 1 Med.L.R. 297, Sup Ct (NSW) 12–205, 12–226, 12–265

H Parsons (Livestock) Ltd v. Uttley Ingham & Co. Ltd [1978] Q.B. 791; [1977] 3 W.L.R. 990; [1978] 1 All E.R. 525; [1977] 2 Lloyd's Rep. 522; 121 S.J. 811, CA 8–282

HE Kane Agencies Ltd v. Coopers & Lybrand (1983) 23 C.C.L.T. 233, (1985) 17 D.L.R. (4th) 695 15–146

HF Pension Trustees Ltd v. Ellison [1999] Lloyd's Rep. P.N. 489; [1999] P.N.L.R. 894; [1999] O.P.L.R. 67; (1999) 96(8) L.S.G. 30; *The Times*, March 5, 1999, Ch D 5–54, 10–147

HG&R Nominees Pty. Ltd v. Fava [1997] 2 V.R. 366, Sup Ct (Vic) 10–5

HIH Casualty and General Insurance Ltd v. Chase Manhattan Bank; Chase Manhattan Bank v. HIH Casualty and General Insurance Ltd [2001] EWCA Civ 1250, CA; reversing in part [2001] 1 All E.R. (Comm) 719; [2001] 1 Lloyd's Rep. 30; [2001] C.L.C. 48; [2001] Lloyd's Rep. I.R. 191; *The Times*, September 19, 2000, QBD (Comm Ct) 14–18, 14–19

HIT Finance v. Lewis and Tucker [1993] 2 E.G.L.R. 231 .... 9–112, 9–171

HIT Finance Ltd v. Cohen Arnold & Co. [2000] Lloyd's Rep. P.N. 125, CA; reversing [1998] 1 E.G.L.R. 140, QBD 15–79, 15–90, 15–126

HIV Haemophiliac Litigation, Re [1996] P.I.Q.R. P220; (1998) 41 B.M.L.R. 171; [1996] P.N.L.R. 290; (1990) 140 N.L.J. 1349; *The Independent*, October 2, 1990; *The Guardian*, September 28, 1990; *The Daily Telegraph*, October 11, 1990, CA 6–01, 12–160, 12–171

HW Nevill (Sunblest) Ltd v. William Press & Sons Ltd; *sub nom.* HW Nevill (Sunblest) Ltd v. Wilhaum Press & Sons, 20 B.L.R. 78, QBD 8–255

Haag v. Marshall (1989) 1 C.C.L.T. (2d) 99 10–234

Haberstich v. McCormick & Nicholson (Negligence), 1975 S.C. 1; 1975 S.L.T. 181, 1 Div 10–268

Habib Bank Ltd v. Habib Bank AG [1981] 1 W.L.R. 1265; [1981] 2 All E.R. 650; [1982] R.P.C. 1; 125 S.J. 512, CA 5–104, 5–111

Hacker v. Thomas Deal & Co. [1991] 2 E.G.L.R. 161; [1991] 44 E.G. 173 ..... 9–24, 9–85, 9–86, 9–91, 9–93

Hadley v. Baxendale (1854) 9 Ex. 341; 23 L.T.(N.S.) 69; 2 C.L.R. 517; 23 L.J.Ex. 179; 8 Jur. 358; 2 W.R. 302, Ex Ct 8–280, 8–283, 8–305, 9–127, 10–294, 17–111

Haig v. Bamford (1976) 72 D.L.R. (3d) 66, Sup Ct (Can) 15–31, 15–77

—— v. Bamford [1977] 1 S.C.R. 466 8–116

Haigh v. Wright Hassall & Co. [1994] E.G.C.S. 54, CA 10–171, 10–199

Haines v. Bellisimo (1978) 82 D.L.R. (3d) 215 12–240

PARA.

Hajgato v. London Health Association (1982) 36 O.R. (2d) 669, affirmed (1983)
44 O.R. (2d) 264 .... 12–122, 12–193, 12–204, 12–264
Hale v. Guildarch [1999] P.N.L.R. 44, QBD 2–49, 2–88, 13–113
Halewood International Ltd v. Addleshaw Booth & Co. [2000] Lloyd's Rep. P.N.
298; [2000] P.N.L.R. 788, Ch D 2–166, 10–30, 15–44
Halford v. Brookes (No.1) [1991] 1 W.L.R. 428; [1991] 3 All E.R. 559; *The
Times*, November 28, 1990; *The Independent*, November 27, 1990; *The
Guardian*, November 28, 1990, CA 5–65
Halifax Building Society v. Edell [1992] Ch. 436; [1992] 3 W.L.R. 136; [1992]
3 All E.R. 389; [1993] E.C.C. 462; [1992] 1 E.G.L.R. 195; [1992] 18 E.G.
151; (1993) 12 Tr. L.R. 117; [1992] E.G.C.S. 33; [1992] N.P.C. 38; *The
Times*, March 11, 1992, Ch D 9–18
—— v. Richard Grosse & Co. [1997] E.G.C.S. 111, QBD 10–295
—— v. Urquart-Dykes & Lord [1997] R.P.C. 55; [2000] Lloyd's Rep. P.N. 318,
Ch D 18–16, 18–17, 18–18, 18–21, 18–22
Halifax Mortgage Services Ltd (formerly BNP Mortgages Ltd) v. Stepsky [1996]
Ch. 207; [1996] 2 W.L.R. 230; [1996] 2 All E.R. 277; [1996] 1 F.L.R. 620;
[1996] 2 F.C.R. 97; (1996) 28 H.L.R. 522; [1996] Fam. Law 279; (1996)
93(1) L.S.G. 21; (1996) 140 S.J.L.B. 9; [1995] N.P.C. 184; *The Times*,
December 1, 1995, CA 10–102, 10–199
Halifax Mortgage Services Ltd v. S&S (A Firm) [1998] P.N.L.R. 616, QBD 10–212
Halifax plc v. Gould & Swayne [1999] P.N.L.R. 184; [1998] 3 E.G.L.R. 177;
[1998] E.G.C.S. 127; [1998] N.P.C. 128, CA 10–318
—— v. Ringrose & Co. [2000] Lloyd's Rep. P.N. 309; [2000] P.N.L.R. 483;
(2000) 150 N.L.J. 58; [1999] N.P.C. 157, QBD 5–55, 5–72, 5–73, 5–74, 10–210
Halkyard v. Mathew [1999] 67 Alta. L.R. (3d) 174, QBD (Alberta) 12–133, 12–204
Hall v. Foong (1995) 65 S.A.S.R. 281, Full Court, (Aus) 10–152, 10–257
—— v. Hallett (1784) 1 Cox 134 3–10
—— v. Lees [1904] 2 K.B. 602; 73 L.J.K.B. 819; 91 L.T. 20; 20 T.L.R. 678; 53
W.R. 17, KBD 12–152
—— v. Meyrick [1957] 2 Q.B. 455; [1957] 3 W.L.R. 273; [1957] 2 All E.R. 722;
101 S.J. 574, CA 10–161, 10–162, 10–220
—— v. Semple (1862) 3 F. & F. 337; 130 R.R. 843 12–239
—— v. Simons. *See* Arthur JS Hall & Co. v. Simons.
Hallam-Eames v. Merrett Syndicates Ltd [1996] 5 Re. L.R. 110; [1996] 7
Med.L.R. 122; [2001] Lloyd's Rep. P.N. 178; [1955–95] P.N.L.R. 672; *The
Times*, January 25, 1995; *The Independent*, January 25, 1995, CA 5–54
Hallatt v. North West Anglia Health Authority [1998] Lloyds Rep Med 197 12–273
Hallmark Financel Insurance Brokers Ltd v. Fraser & Beatty (1991) 1 O.R. (3d)
641, HC (Ontario) 10–170
Hambro v. Burnand [1904] 2 K.B. 10, CA 13–103
Hamilton v. Birmingham Regional Hospital Board [1969] 2 B.M.J. 456 12–124
—— v. Fife Health Board 1993 S.C. 309; 1993 S.L.T. 624; 1993 S.C.L.R. 408;
[1993] 4 Med.L.R. 201, Ex Div 12–55
Hamlin v. Edwin Evans (A Firm) 80 B.L.R. 85; 52 Con. L.R. 106; (1997) 29
H.L.R. 414; [1996] P.N.L.R. 398; [1996] 2 E.G.L.R. 106; [1996] 47 E.G.
141; [1996] E.G.C.S. 120; (1996) 93(27) L.S.G. 29; (1996) 140 S.J.L.B.
167; [1996] N.P.C. 110; *The Times*, July 15, 1996; *The Independent*, July 24,
1996, CA 5–50, 5–54
Hammersmith Hospitals NHS Trust v. Troup Bywaters & Anders [2001] EWCA
Civ 793, CA; affirming [2000] Env. L.R. 343, QBD (T&CC) 8–169, 8–215
Hammond v. West Lancashire H.A. [1998] Lloyd's Rep. Med. 146; (1998) 95(14)
L.S.G. 23; *The Times*, March 5, 1998, CA 5–66
Hanave Pt Ltd v. Lfot Pt Ltd (2000) 168 A.L.R. 318; (2000) 27 R.P.R. (3d) 210,
Fed Ct (Aus) 10–05, 10–199, 10–332
Hancke v. Hooper (1835) 7 C. & P. 81 .... 12–68, 12–152

PARA.

Hancock v. BW Brazier (Anerley) Ltd [1966] 1 W.L.R. 1317; [1966] 2 All E.R. 901, CA 2–04
—— v. Tucker [1999] Lloyd's Rep. P.N. 814, QBD 8–192, 8–202, 8–265, 8–268
Hanflex Pty Ltd v. N.S. Hope & Associates [1990] 2 Qd.R. 218, Full Ct (Queensland) 10–234
Hanif v. Middleweeks (A Firm) [2000] Lloyd's Rep. P.N. 920, CA 10–278, 15–134
Hanson v. Lorenz and Jones [1987] 1 F.T.L.R. 23; (1986) 136 N.L.J. 1088, CA 10–18
Hants County Business Development Centre Ltd v. Poole (1999) 172 N.S.R. (2d) 393 10–45
Hardman v. Amin [2000] Lloyd's Rep. Med. 498; (2001) 59 B.M.L.R. 58; [2001] P.N.L.R. 11, QBD 12–292, 12–300, 12–301
Hardware Services Pty. Ltd v. Primac Association Ltd (1988) 1 Qd.R. 393, Sup Ct (Queensland) 10–61
Hardy v. Wamsley-Lewis (1967) 203 E.G. 1039 ...... 9–58, 9–91, 9–108, 9–131, 9–132, 9–139, 9–140, 9–191
Hardy Employees' Credit Union Ltd v. Moll Chadwick & Co. [1980] Qd.R. 362 15–112
Harley v. McDonald [1999] 3 N.Z.L.R. 545, CA (NZ) 10–118
—— v. McDonald; *sub nom.* Harley v. McDonald Glasgow Harley; Harley v. Glasgow Harley; Glasgow Harley (A Firm) v. McDonald [2001] UKPC 18; [2001] 2 W.L.R. 1749; [2001] Lloyd's Rep. P.N. 584; *The Times*, May 15, 2001, PC (NZ) 10–126, 10–132, 11–29
Harman v. United Kingdom (App. No.10038/82) (1984) 38 D.R. 53 7–08
Harmer v. Cornelius (1858) 5 C.B.(N.S.) 236 2–02

Harnett v. Fisher [1927] A.C. 573; 96 L.J.K.B. 856; 135 L.J. 602; 43 T.L.R. 567; 71 S.J. 470, HL 12–239
Harrild v. Ministry of Defence [2001] Lloyd's Rep. Med. 117, QBD 5–58
Harrington v. Binns (1863) 3 F. & F. 942 .... 10–185, 10–292
Harris v. Carruthers (1902) 2 N.S.W.S.R. 100, CA 10–192
—— v. Nantes & Wylde; *sub nom.* Harris v. Nantes & Wilde [1997] E.C.C. 570; [1997] N.P.C. 7, CA 10–44
—— v. Treemenheere (1808) 15 Ves.Jun. 34 2–137
—— v. Wyre Forest D.C. [1988] Q.B. 835; [1988] 2 W.L.R. 1173; [1988] 1 All E.R. 691; (1988) 20 H.L.R. 278; [1988] 05 E.G. 57; (1988) 85(7) L.S.G. 40; (1988) 138 N.L.J. 15; (1988) 132 S.J. 91; (1988) 7 Tr. L. 170, CA 2–30, 2–85, 2–92, 9–27
—— v. Wyre Forest D.C. *Also See* Smith v. Eric S Bush; Harris v. Wyre Forest D.C.
Harris (John) Partnership v. Groveworld Ltd 75 Con. L.R. 7; [1999] P.N.L.R. 697, QBD (T&CC) 8–192, 8–314
Harrison v. Bloom Camillin (No.1), *The Independent*, June 28, 1999 (C.S.), Ch D 15–134
—— v. Bloom Camillin (No.2) [2000] Lloyd's Rep. P.N. 89; [2001] P.N.L.R. 7; (1999) 96(45) L.S.G. 32; *The Times*, November 12, 1999, Ch D 15–134
—— v. Bloom Camillin (Preliminary Issues) [2000] C.P. Rep. 83, Ch D 10–281, 10–284, 10–285, 10–287, 10–289
Harry Jagdev & Co. (Wasted Costs Order) (No.2 of 1999), Re; *sub nom.* Harry Jagdev & Co, Re; Firm of Solicitors (Wasted Costs Order) (No.2 of 1999), Re (1999) 96(33) L.S.G. 32; *The Times*, August 12, 1999; *The Independent*, November 1, 1999 (C.S.), CA (Crim Div) 10–133, 10–134
Hart v. Chappell [1994] 5 Med.L.R. 365, Sup Ct (NSW) [1999] Lloyd's Rep. Med. 223, HC (Aus) 12–207
Hart & Hodge v. Framce, Son & Co. (1839) 6 C. & F. 193, HL; Mews' Dig. Xiii 1467; S.C. Macl. And R. 595; 3 Jur. 547; 7 Scots R.R. 241 10–238

PARA.

Hartle v. Laceys (A Firm) [1999] Lloyd's Rep. P.N. 315; (2000) 16 Const. L.J. 44,
CA 8–268, 10–259, 10–276, 10–314
Hartley v. Birmingham City Council [1992] 1 W.L.R. 968; [1992] 2 All E.R. 213;
The Independent, August 16, 1991, CA 5–67
Harvest Trucking Co. Ltd v. Davis (t/a PB Davis Insurance Services) [1991] 2
Lloyd's Rep. 638; (1991) 135 S.J.L.B. 443; *The Times*, March 20, 1991,
QBD 14–04, 14–32, 14–76, 14–79, 14–115
Harvey Credit Union Ltd v. GH Ward & Partners (1981) 15 B.L.R. 307 15–147
Haseldine v. Daw & Son Ltd [1941] 2 K.B. 343; 111 L.J.K.B. 45; 165 L.T. 185;
58 T.L.R. 1; [1941] 3 All E.R. 156, CA 5–07
Haslam & Hier-Evans, Re [1902] 1 Ch. 765; 46 S.J. 381; 71 L.J.Ch. 374; 86 L.T.
663; 50 W.R. 444; 18 T.L.R. 461, CA 10–22
Hastingwood Property Ltd v. Saunders Bearman Anselm [1991] Ch. 114; [1990]
3 W.L.R. 623; (1990) 140 N.L.J. 817; (1990) 134 S.J. 1153, Ch D 10–65
Hatch v. Lewis (1861) 2F. & F. 467; (1861) 7 H. & N. 367; S.C. 31 L.J.Ex. 26;
7 Jur.(N.S.) 1085; 10 W.R. 58; 5 L.T. 254 10–182
Hatcher v. Black, *The Times*, July 2, 1954 .... 12–68, 12–217
Haughian v. Paine (1987) 37 D.L.R. (4th) 624, CA (Saskatchewan) 12–203, 12–264
Havenledge Ltd v. Graeme John & Partners [2001] Lloyd's Rep. P.N. 223; [2001]
P.N.L.R. 17; [2001] N.P.C. 9, CA; reversing [2000] Lloyd's Rep. P.N. 614;
[2000] P.N.L.R. 804, QBD 5–26, 5–43
Hawkins v. Clayton (1988) 164 C.L.R. 539; 78 A.L.R. 69, HC (Aus) 10–15, 10–45,
10–223
—— v. Harwood (1849) 4 Ex. 503; S.C. 7 D. & L. 181; 19 L.J.Ex. 33 10–183
Hay v. Grampian Health Board [1995] 6 Med.L.R. 28 .... 12–121, 12–236
Hayes v. Dowding [1996] P.N.L.R. 578, Ch D 10–144
—— v. James & Charles Dodd (A Firm) [1990] 2 All E.R. 815; (1988) 138 N.L.J.
259, CA 8–311, 10–241, 10–242, 10–249, 10–255, 10–269, 10–272, 10–314,
10–315, 10–317, 14–123
—— v. James & Charles Dodd (A Firm) [1990] 2 All E.R. 815; (1988) 138 N.L.J.
259, CA 9–158, 9–183
Hayne v. Rhodes (1846) 8 Q.B. 342; S.C. 15 L.J.Q.B. 137; 10 Jur. 71 10–207
Hayward v. Edinburgh Royal Infirmary Board of Management; MacDonald v.
Glasgow Western Hospitals Board of Management, 1954 S.C. 453; 1954
S.L.T. 226, 1 Div 12–153
Haywood v. Roadknight [1927] V.L.R. 512 2–138
Head v. Gould [1898] 2 Ch. 250; 67 L.J.Ch. 480; 78 L.J. 739; 46 W.R. 597; 14
T.L.R. 444; 42 S.J. 553, Ch D 10–226
Heafield v. Crane, *The Times*, July 31, 1937 12–170
Heathcote v. David Marks & Co. [1996] 1 E.G.L.R. 123; [1996] 03 E.G. 128,
QBD 5–50, 9–10
Heatley v. William H Brown Ltd [1992] 1 E.G.L.R. 289; [1991] E.G.C.S. 115 3–21,
9–92, 9–108, 9–144, 9–189
Heaven v. Pender (t/a West India Graving Dock Co.) (1882–83) L.R. 11 Q.B.D.
503, CA 2–19, 8–87, 9–33
Hedley Byrne & Co. Ltd v. Heller & Partners Ltd [1964] A.C. 465; [1963] 3
W.L.R. 101; [1963] 2 All E.R. 575; [1963] 1 Lloyd's Rep. 485; 107 S.J. 454,
HL 2–18, 2–21, 2–23, 2–24, 2–27, 2–38, 2–42, 2–43, 2–45, 2–46, 2–47, 2–48,
2–49, 2–50, 2–55, 2–61, 2–64, 2–67, 2–69, 2–71, 2–74, 2–77, 2–78,
2–85, 2–103, 2–105, 2–110, 2–126, 5–07, 5–24, 5–25, 8–50,
8–51, 8–60, 8–61, 8–62, 8–69, 8–90, 8–98, 8–99, 8–101, 8–102,
8–104, 8–105, 8–106, 8–110, 8–111, 8–116, 8–118, 8–221, 9–13,
9–34, 9–41, 9–48, 10–40, 10–48, 12–24, 12–46, 12–294, 12–297,
14–15, 14–18, 14–20, 14–24, 14–31, 15–53, 15–54, 15–55,
17–51, 17–55

PARA.

Heil v. Rankin; Rees v. Mabco (102) Ltd; Schofield v. Saunders & Taylor Ltd; Ramsay v. Rivers; Kent v. Griffiths; W (A Child) v. Northern General Hospital NHS Trust; Annable v. Southern Derbyshire H.A.; Connolly v. Tasker [2001] Q.B. 272; [2000] 2 W.L.R. 1173; [2000] 3 All E.R. 138; [2000] I.R.L.R. 334; [2000] P.I.Q.R. Q187; [2000] Lloyd's Rep. Med. 203; (2000) 97(14) L.S.G. 41; (2000) 150 N.L.J. 464; (2000) 144 S.J.L.B. 157; *The Times*, March 24, 2000; *The Independent*, March 28, 2000, CA 12–246

Helicopter Equipment Ltd v. Marine Insurance Co. Ltd [1986] 1 N.Z.L.R. 448 .... 14–03, 14–60

Helle v. Finland (1998) 26 E.H.R.R. 159; [1998] H.R.C.D. 186, ECHR 7–67

Hellewell v. Chief Constable of Derbyshire [1995] 1 W.L.R. 804; [1995] 4 All E.R. 473; (1995) 92(7) L.S.G. 35; (1995) 139 S.J.L.B. 49; *The Times*, January 13, 1995, QBD 2–156

Hellings v. Parker Breslin Estates [1995] 2 E.G.L.R. 99; [1995] 29 E.G. 119; [1994] E.G.C.S. 128, Ch D 9–78

Hemmens v. Wilson Browne (A Firm) [1995] Ch. 223; [1994] 2 W.L.R. 323; [1993] 4 All E.R. 826; [1994] 2 F.L.R. 101; [1994] Fam. Law 669; (1993) 90(45) L.S.G. 45; *The Times*, June 30, 1993, Ch D 10–53

Henderson v. Hagblom [2000] 7 W.W.R. 357, QB (Saskatchewan) 10–182

—— v. Henderson (1843) 3 Hare 100 10–115

—— v. Merrett Syndicates Ltd; Hallam-Eames v. Merrett Syndicates Ltd; Hughes v. Merrett Syndicates Ltd; Arbuthnott v. Fagan and Feltrim Underwriting Agencies; Deeny v. Gooda Walker Ltd [1995] 2 A.C. 145; [1994] 3 W.L.R. 761; [1994] 3 All E.R. 506; [1994] 2 Lloyd's Rep. 468; (1994) 144 N.L.J. 1204; *The Times*, July 26, 1994; *The Independent*, August 3, 1994, HL; affirming ; *The Times*, December 30, 1993; *The Independent*, December 14, 1993, CA; affirming [1994] 2 Lloyd's Rep. 193; *The Times*, October 20, 1993, QBD (Comm Ct) 2–05, 2–42, 2–47, 2–94, 2–105, 2–127,8–50, 8–51, 8–54, 8–60, 8–62, 8–98, 8–111, 8–116, 8–123, 9–07, 9–32, 9–35, 9–113, 10–14, 10–16, 10–40, 12–24, 12–58, 13–106, 13–115, 14–20, 14–36, 15–48, 16–04, 16–05, 16–06, 16–10, 16–11, 16–12, 16–13, 16–14, 16–15, 16–20, 16–54, 17–51, 18–8

—— v. Merrett Syndicates Ltd (No.2) [1997] L.R.L.R. 265; [1996] 5 Re. L.R. 279; [1996] P.N.L.R. 32, QBD (Comm Ct) 2–116, 5–119, 15–146, 16–20, 16–58, 16–59

—— v. Temple Pier Co. Ltd [1998] 1 W.L.R. 1540; [1998] 3 All E.R. 324; [1999] P.I.Q.R. P61; (1998) 95(20) L.S.G. 35; (1998) 142 S.J.L.B. 156; *The Times*, May 2, 1998; *The Independent*, April 29, 1998, CA 5–51

Hendy v. Milton Keynes H.A. (No.2) [1992] 3 Med.L.R. 119, QBD 12–193

Henley v. Cloke & Sons [1991] 2 E.G.L.R. 141; [1991] 37 E.G. 145 9–69

Henry Ansbacher & Co. Ltd v. Binks Stern [1998] Lloyd's Rep. Bank. 1; [1998] P.N.L.R. 221; (1997) 94(27) L.S.G. 22; (1997) 141 S.J.L.B. 151; *The Times*, June 26, 1997, CA 10–76

Henry Squire, Cash Chemist Ltd v. Ball Baker & Co. (also Mead v. Ball Baker & Co) (1912) 106 L.T. 197 .... 15–90, 15–91, 15–112

Hepworth v. Kerr [1995] 6 Med.L.R. 139, QBD 5–56, 5–61, 12–106, 12–109, 12–113, 12–284

Hercules Managements Ltd v. Ernst & Young [1997] 146 D.L.R. (4th) 577 .... 2–69, 15–48

Heron II, The. *See* Koufos v. C Czarnikow Ltd; Heron II, The.

Herschel Engineering Ltd v. Breen Property Ltd [2000] B.L.R. 272; (2000) 2 T.C.L.R. 473; 70 Con. L.R. 1; (2000) 16 Const. L.J. 366; *The Times*, May 10, 2000, QBD (T&CC) 8–336, 8–343

Herschtal v. Stewart & Ardern Ltd [1940] 1 K.B. 155; 84 S.J. 79; [1939] 4 All E.R. 123; 109 L.J.K.B. 155; L.T. 331; 56 T.L.R. 48; 45 Com.Cas. 63, KBD 12–45

PARA.

Heskell v. Continental Express Ltd [1950] 1 All E.R. 1033; (1949–50) 83 Ll. L.
Rep. 438; [1950] W.N. 210; 94 S.J. 339, KBD 8–274
Hesse v. Briant (1856) 4 De G.M. & G. 623 2–140
Hewett v. Alf Brown's Transport Ltd; Hewett v. Brown & Mason Ltd; Hewett v.
Wimpey Construction (U.K.) Ltd [1992] I.C.R. 530, CA; affirming [1991]
I.C.R. 471 8–48
Heywood v. Roadknight [1927] V.L.R. 512 2–140
—— v. Wellers (A Firm) [1976] Q.B. 446; [1976] 2 W.L.R. 101; [1976] 1 All
E.R. 300; [1976] 2 Lloyd's Rep. 88; (1975) 120 S.J. 9, CA 3–07, 3–08, 8–309,
9–120, 10–13, 10–146, 10–175, 10–262, 10–307, 10–312, 10–313
Hicks v. Sallitt (1853) 3 De G.M & G. 783 5–91
Higgins v. Hatch & Fielding [1996] 1 E.G.L.R. 133; [1996] 10 E.G. 162; [1995]
E.G.C.S. 105, CA 5–54, 9–10
—— v. North West Metropolitan Hospital Board and Bach [1954] 1 W.L.R. 411;
[1954] 1 All E.R. 414; 98 S.J. 147, QBD 12–153
Hill v. Chief Constable of West Yorkshire [1989] A.C. 53; [1988] 2 W.L.R. 1049;
[1988] 2 All E.R. 238; 152 L.G.R. 709; (1988) 152 L.G. Rev. 709; (1988)
85(20) L.S.G. 34; (1988) 138 N.L.J. 126; (1988) 132 S.J. 700, HL 2–75, 2–84,
2–98, 7–19, 7–23, 12–49
—— v. Debenham, Tewson and Chinnocks [1955–95] P.N.L.R. 44; (1958) 171
E.G. 835, QBD (OR) 9–53, 9–58, 9–62, 9–83, 9–87, 9–88, 9–91, 9–92, 9–96,
9–107, 9–108, 9–110, 9–131, 9–140, 9–191
—— v. Featherstonlaugh (1831) 7 Bing. 570; 5 Moo. & P. 541; 131 E.R. 200 10–307
—— v. Finney (1865) 4 F & F. 616 .... 10–149, 10–293
—— v. Harris [1965] 2 Q.B. 601; [1965] 2 W.L.R. 1331; [1965] 2 All E.R. 358;
109 S.J. 333, CA 10–193
—— v. Rose [1990] V.R. 129 3–11
—— v. Van Erp (1995–97) 188 C.L.R. 159 .... 2–42, 2–64, 2–65
—— v. Van Erp (1997) 71 A.L.J.R. 487, 188 C.L.R. 159 10–54
Hill Samuel Bank Ltd v. Frederick Brand Partnership, 45 Con. L.R. 141; (1994)
10 Const. L.J. 72, QBD 8–271
Hilliard, Ex p.; Smith, Re (1845) 2 Dowl. & L. 919; 1 N.P.C. 185; 14 L.J.Q.B.
225; S.L.T.(O.S.) 58, 59; 9 Jur. 664 10–69
Hillman v. Black [1996] 67 S.A.S.R. 490, Sup Ct (Aus) 12–66
Hills v. Potter (Note) [1984] 1 W.L.R. 641; [1983] 3 All E.R. 716; (1984) 128 S.J.
224, QBD 5–69, 12–96, 12–131, 12–209, 12–232
Hillyer v. Governors of St Bartholomew's Hospital [1909] 2 K.B. 820 ..... 12–152, 12–153
Hilton Canada v. SNC Lavalin (1999) 176 N.S.R. (2d) 155 .... 8–142, 8–261
Hind v. York H.A. [1998] P.I.Q.R. P235; [1997] 8 Med.L.R. 377, QBD 5–58
Hindson v. Weatherill (1854) 5 De G.M. & G. 301; " Eq.Rep. 733; 23 L.J.Ch.
820; 23 L.T.(O.S.) 149; 18 Jur. 499; 2 W.R. 507; 43 E.R. 886 10–17
Hines v. Willans [1997] C.L.Y. 3368 .... 10–12, 10–23
Hinfey v. Salford H.A. [1993] 4 Med.L.R. 143, QBD 12–155, 12–188
Hingorani v. Blower [1976] 1 E.G.L.R. 104; (1975) 238 E.G. 883 .... 9–34, 9–39, 9–95,
9–131, 9–132, 9–140
Hipkins v. Jack Cotton Partnership [1989] 2 E.G.L.R. 157; [1989] 45 E.G. 163 9–85,
9–93, 9–140, 9–141, 9–143, 9–189
Hiron v. Pynford South Ltd [1992] 2 E.G.L.R. 138; 60 B.L.R. 78; 35 Con. L.R.
71; [1992] 28 E.G. 112 9–07
Hirst v. Etherington [1999] Lloyd's Rep. P.N. 938; (1999) 96(31) L.S.G. 42;
(1999) 149 N.L.J. 1110; The Times, July 21, 1999; The Independent, October
4, 1999, CA 10–66
Hoadley v. Edwards [2001] E.G.C.S. 46, Ch D 9–96, 9–131, 9–141, 9–189
—— v. Edwards, March 28, 2001, unreported 8–301
Hobson v. Munkley (1977) 74 D.L.R. (3d) 408 12–119
Hoby v. Built (1832) B. & D. 350; 1 L.J.K.B. 121; 110 E.R. 131 10–191

PARA.

Hocking v. Bell [1948] W.N. 21 12–194

Hodge v. Clifford Cowling & Co. [1990] 2 E.G.L.R. 89; [1990] 46 E.G. 120,
    CA 10–265

Hodgkinson v. Simms (1994) 97 B.C.L.R. (2d) 1, Sup Ct (Can) 15–39, 15–40

Hodgson v. Imperial Tobacco Ltd (No.1) [1998] 1 W.L.R. 1056; [1998] 2 All E.R.
    673; [1998] 1 Costs L.R. 14; [1999] P.I.Q.R. Q1; (1998) 41 B.M.L.R. 1;
    (1998) 95(15) L.S.G. 31; (1998) 148 N.L.J. 241; (1998) 142 S.J.L.B. 93; *The
    Times*, February 13, 1998; *The Independent*, February 17, 1998, CA 10–135

Hoffman v. Meyer [1956] (2) S.A.L.R. 752. 8–253

Holbeck Hall Hotel Ltd (aka Dawntime Ltd) v. Scarborough B.C. (No.1); Scar-
    borough B.C. v. Geotechnical Engineering (Northern) Ltd, 57 Con. L.R.
    113; [1997] 2 E.G.L.R. 213; [1997] N.P.C. 141; *The Times*, October 15,
    1997; *The Independent*, October 13, 1997 (C.S.), QBD (OR) 8–260, 8–271

Holden v. Holden & Pearson (1910) 102 L.T. 398; 26 T.L.R. 307; 54 S.J. 328,
    DC 10–183

Holden & Co. v. CPS; Steele Ford & Newton (A Firm) v. CPS; McGoldrick &
    Co. v. CPS; Robin Murray & Co. v. CPS; Bradburys (A Firm) v. CPS [1990]
    2 Q.B. 261; [1990] 2 W.L.R. 1137; [1990] 1 All E.R. 368; (1990) 90 Cr.
    App. R. 385; (1990) 87(10) L.S.G. 35; (1990) 134 S.J. 197, CA 10–181

Holder v. Holder [1968] Ch. 353; [1968] 2 W.L.R. 237; [1968] 1 All E.R. 665;
    112 S.J. 17, CA 2–136, 5–105

Holgate v. Lancashire Mental Hospitals Board [1937] 4 All E.R. 19, Assizes
    (Liverpool) 12–49

Holland v. The Devitt & Moore Nautical College Ltd, *The Times*, March 4,
    1960 .... 10–108, 12–187

Holland Hannen & Cubitts (Northern) Ltd v. Welsh Health Technical Services
    Organisation, 35 B.L.R. 1; 7 Con. L.R. 1; [1985] C.I.L.L. 217, CA 8–161, 8–165,
    8–217, 8–328, 8–329

Hollis v. Birch (1993) 81 B.C.L.R. (2d) 1, CA (BC) 12–264

Holman v. Loynes (1852) 4 De G.M. & G. 270 2–139

Holmes v. Board of Hospital Trustees of City of London (1978) 81 D.L.R. (3d)
    67 12–120

—— v. H Kennard & Son (1985) 49 P. & C.R. 202; (1985) 82 L.S.G. 363; (1984)
    128 S.J. 854, CA 10–193, 10–194

—— v. National Benzole Co. (1965) 109 S.J. 971; *The Times*, November 30,
    1965 10–165

Holt v. Payne Skillington (1984) 77 B.L.R. 51; 49 Con. L.R. 99; [1996] P.N.L.R.
    179; [1995] E.G.C.S. 201; (1996) 93(2) L.S.G. 29; (1996) 140 S.J.L.B. 30;
    [1995] N.P.C. 202; *The Times*, December 22, 1995, CA 2–107, 8–58, 9–32,
    17–51

Holy Monasteries v. Greece; Series A, No.301–A; (1995) 20 E.H.R.R. 1,
    ECHR 7–17

Home Office v. Dorset Yacht Co. Ltd [1970] A.C. 1004; [1970] 2 W.L.R. 1140;
    [1970] 2 All E.R. 294; [1970] 1 Lloyd's Rep. 453; 114 S.J. 375, HL;
    affirming [1969] 2 Q.B. 412; [1969] 2 W.L.R. 1008; [1969] 2 All E.R. 564;
    113 S.J. 227, CA 2–18, 2–21, 2–26, 2–27, 2–38, 2–71, 2–72, 2–77, 2–84, 2–86,
    12–49, 12–51, 12–52

Homes by Jayman Ltd v. Kellam Berg (1998) 54 Alt. L.R. 272, CA (1995) 29
    Alta. L.R. (3d) 1 .... 8–161, 8–330

Hongkong Bank of Canada v. Phillips [1998] 2 W.W.R. 606, QB (Maniba) 10–25

Hooberman v. Salter Rex [1985] 1 E.G.L.R. 144; (1985) 274 E.G. 151; [1984]
    C.I.L.L. 128 .... 9–56, 9–91,9–92, 9–131, 9–140, 9–142

Hood v. National Farmers Union [1994] 01 E.G. 109; [1993] E.G.C.S. 96, CA 10–184

—— v. Shaw (1960) 176 E.G. 1291 .... 9–96, 9–107, 9–140, 9–191

—— v. West End Motor Car Packing Co. [1917] 2 K.B. 38, CA 14–40

PARA.

Hooper v. Fynmores (A Firm) (2001) 98(26) L.S.G. 45; (2001) 145 S.J.L.B. 156;
  The Times, July 19, 2001, Ch D 10–223
—— v. Young [1998] Lloyd's Rep. Med. 61, CA 12–121, 12–122
Hopewell Project Management Ltd v. Ewbank Preece Ltd [1998] 1 Lloyd's Rep.
  448, QBD 8–128
Hopkins v. Mackenzie [1995] P.I.Q.R. P43; [1995] 6 Med.L.R. 26; [2001]
  Lloyd's Rep. P.N. 600; (1994) 91(45) L.S.G. 38; (1994) 138 S.J.L.B. 222;
  The Times, November 3, 1994; *The Independent,* October 27, 1994, CA 5–43
Hopp v. Lepp (1980) 112 D.L.R. (3d) 67 .... 12–201, 12–202, 12–203, 12–209
Horbury v. Craig Hall & Rutley (1991) 7 P.N. 206; (1991) E.G.C.S. 81; (1996)
  C.I.L.L. 1173 .... 5–35, 5–50, 9–09
Hordern v. Hordern [1910] A.C. 465, PC (Aus) 2–136
Hornal v. Neuberger Products [1957] 1 Q.B. 247; [1956] 3 W.L.R. 1034; [1956]
  3 All E.R. 970; 100 S.J. 915, CA 13–101
Horner v. WD Irwin & Sons Ltd [1972] N.I.L.R. 202 10–62
Hornsby v. Clark Kenneth Leventhal [1998] P.N.L.R. 635, CA 13–112
Horsefall v. Haywards (A Firm); *sub nom.* Horsfall v. Haywards (A Firm) [1999]
  1 F.L.R. 1182; [1999] Lloyd's Rep. P.N. 332; [1999] P.N.L.R. 583; (2000)
  1 W.T.L.R. 29; [1999] Fam. Law 383; (1999) 96(10) L.S.G. 31; (1999) 143
  S.J.L.B. 66; [1999] N.P.C. 25; *The Times,* March 11, 1999, CA 10–320
Hosier & Dickinson v. P&M Kaye. *See* P&M Kaye Ltd v. Hosier & Dickinson
  Ltd; *sub nom.* Hosier & Dickinson v. P&M Kaye.
Hospital Products Ltd v. United States Surgical Corp. (1984) 156 C.L.R. 41 2–128,
                                                                              2–130, 2–132
Hossack v. Ministry of Defence, April 18, 2000, unreported, CA 12–247
Hotson v. East Berkshire H.A.; *sub nom.* Hotson v. Fitzgerald [1987] A.C. 750;
  [1987] 3 W.L.R. 232; [1987] 2 All E.R. 909; [1955–95] P.N.L.R. 330; (1987)
  84 L.S.G. 2365; (1987) 131 S.J. 975, HL 3–05, 9–128, 10–259, 12–05, 12–252,
                          12–253, 12–254, 12–255, 12–257, 12–258, 12–260, 14–112
Houghton & Co. v. Nothard Lowe & Wills. *See* JC Houghton & Co. v. Nothard
  Lowe & Wills Ltd.
Houghton v. Fayers [2000] Lloyd's Rep. Bank. 145; [2000] 1 B.C.L.C. 511; *The
  Times,* February 9, 2000, CA 10–37
Housecroft v. Burnett [1986] 1 All E.R. 332; (1985) 135 N.L.J. 728, CA 12–299,
                                                                                     12–300
Housing Loan Corp. plc v. William H Brown Ltd [1999] Lloyd's Rep. P.N. 185,
  CA 9–116, 9–121, 9–169, 9–170, 9–171
Hovenden v. Lord Annesley (1806) 2 Sch. & L. 607 .... 5–90, 5–91, 5–93
How v. Earl Winterton [1896] 2 Ch. 626, CA 5–90
Howael Ventures (1984) Inc. v. Arthur Anderson & Co. [1996] 7 W.W.R. 383 15–127
Howard v. Horne & Sons, 16 Con. L.R. 55; [1990] 1 E.G.L.R. 272, QBD 9–131
—— v. Wessex R.H.A. [1994] 5 Med.L.R. 57, QBD 12–122
Howarth v. Adey [1996] 2 V.R. 535, CA (Vic) 12–55
Howell v. Young (1826) 5 B. & C. 259; 8 D. & R. 14; 4 L.J.K.B.(O.S.) 160; 2 Car.
  & P. 238 .... 5–14, 10–13
Howkins & Harrison v. Tyler [2001] Lloyd's Rep. P.N. 1; [2001] P.N.L.R. 27;
  [2000] E.G.C.S. 91; [2000] P.N.L.R. 623; *The Times,* August 8, 2000, CA 4–06,
                                                               4–09, 9–173, 10–332
Howlett, Re; *sub nom.* Howlett v. Howlett [1949] Ch. 767; [1949] 2 All E.R. 490;
  65 T.L.R. 569; [1949] L.J.R. 1632; 93 S.J. 632, Ch D 5–105
Hucks v. Cole (1968) 112 S.J. 483; [1993] 4 Med.L.R. 393 .... 12–72, 12–75, 12–76,
                                                             12–98, 12–100, 12–186
Hudson Turner Furs Ltd v. American Insurance Co. (1964) 43 D.L.R. (2d) 323,
  HC (Ontario), appeal dismissed (1965) 48 D.L.R. (2d) 508 14–72
Huegenin v. Baseley (1807) 14. Ves.Jun. 273 2–146
Hughes, Ex p. (1802) 6 Ves.Jun. 617 3–09

PARA.

Hughes v. Cooper [1998] 41 B.C.L.R. 109 12–275
—— v. Kingston upon Hull City Council [1999] Q.B. 1193; [1999] 2 W.L.R.
1229; [1999] 2 All E.R. 49; [1999] Env. L.R. 579; (1999) 31 H.L.R. 779;
(1998) 95(44) L.S.G. 36; (1999) 143 S.J.L.B. 54; *The Times*, December 9,
1998; *The Independent*, November 16, 1998 (C.S.), QBD 10–92
—— v. Lloyds Bank plc (Administrators of the Estate of Mukherjee) [1998]
P.I.Q.R. P98, CA 12–24, 12–303
—— v. Lord Advocate (1963) [1963] A.C. 837; [1963] 2 W.L.R. 779; [1963] 1
All E.R. 705; 1963 S.C. 31; 1963 S.C. (H.L.) 31; 1963 S.L.T. 150; (1963)
107 S.J. 232, HL 12–282
—— v. Waltham Forest H.A. [1991] 2 Med.L.R. 155; *The Times*, November 9,
1990, CA 12–93
Hulse v. Wilson (1953) 2 B.M.J. 890 12–179
Humphrey v. Bowers (1929) 45 T.L.R. 297 2–113
Hunt v. Brandie (1998) 38 O.R. (3d) 154, CA (Ontario) 14–19
—— v. Luck [1902] 1 Ch. 428, CA 10–160
—— v. National Health Service Litigation Authority [2000] WL 1480071,
QBD 12–272
Hunter v. Atkins (1832–4) 3 My. & Cr. 113 2–145
—— v. Chief Constable of the West Midlands; McIlkenny v. Chief Constable of
the West Midlands; Walker v. Chief Constable of the West Midlands; Power
v. Chief Constable of Lancashire [1982] A.C. 529; [1981] 3 W.L.R. 906;
[1981] 3 All E.R. 727; 125 S.J. 829; *The Times*, November 26, 1981, HL 7–30,
10–108, 10–113
—— v. Hanley; *sub nom.* Galloway (or Hunter) v. Hanley, 1955 S.C. 200; 1955
S.L.T. 213; [1955–95] P.N.L.R. 1, 1 Div 2–116, 12–106
—— v. Hunter [2001] 4 W.W.R. 28, CA (Maniba) 10–126
—— v. J&E Shepherd, 1992 S.L.T. 1095; Scotsman, April 10, 1991, OH 9–126,
9–191
Hurlingham Estates Ltd v. Wilde & Partners [1997] 1 Lloyd's Rep. 525; [1997]
S.T.C. 627; [1997] B.T.C. 240; (1997) 147 N.L.J. 453; *The Times*, January
3, 1997; *The Independent*, February 17, 1997 (C.S.), Ch D 10–06, 10–94
Hurrell v. Bullard (1863) 3 F. & F. 445 .... 14–32, 14–57
Husky Oil v. Saint John Shipbuilding (1997) 153 D.L.R. 385, Sup Ct (Can) 8–114
Hussain v. Cuddy Woods & Cochrane (A Firm) [2001] Lloyd's Rep. P.N. 134,
CA 11–44
Hussey v. Eels [1990] 2 Q.B. 227; [1990] 2 W.L.R. 234; [1990] 1 All E.R. 449;
[1990] 19 E.G. 77; (1990) 140 N.L.J. 53, CA 10–255
Hutchinson v. Harris (1978) 10 B.L.R. 19, CA 3–07, 3–08, 8–222, 8–275, 8–305,
8–310, 8–316
Hutton v. East Dyfed H.A. [1998] Lloyd's Rep. Med. 335, QBD 12–182
Huxford v. Stoy Hayward & Co. (1989) 5 B.C.C. 421 .... 10–42, 15–82
Hyde v. Tameside Area H.A. (1986) 2 P.N. 26; *The Times*, April 16, 1981, CA 12–237

IBA v. EMI and BICC. *See* Independent Broadcasting Authority v. EMI Electron-
ics Ltd.
ICS Ltd v. West Bromwich Building Society. *See* Investors Compensation
Scheme Ltd v. West Bromwich Building Society (No.2).
IM Properties plc v. Cape & Dalgleish [1999] Q.B. 297; [1998] 3 W.L.R. 457;
[1998] 3 All E.R. 203; (1998) 95(31) L.S.G. 34; (1998) 95(24) L.S.G. 34;
(1998) 148 N.L.J. 906; (1998) 142 S.J.L.B. 174; *The Times*, May 28, 1998,
CA 3–19
Ibbotson v. Shippey (1879) 23 S.J. 388 10–177
Icarom (formerly Insurance Corp. of Ireland) v. Peek Puckle International [1992]
2 Lloyd's Rep. 600, QBD (Comm Ct) 14–59

PARA.

Ikumene Singapore Pte Ltd v. Leon Chee Leng [1993] 3 S.L.R. 24, CA (Sing) 15–82
Imeson v. Lister (1920) L.T.Jo. 446 2–140
Immobiliare Saffi v. Italy (2000) 30 E.H.R.R. 756; 7 B.H.R.C. 256, ECHR 7–16
Imperial College of Science and Technology v. Norman & Dawbarn (A Firm), 8
    Con. L.R. 107; (1986) 2 Const. L.J. 280 .... 5–25, 8–240
Inche Noriah v. Shaik Allie bin Omar [1929] A.C. 127; [1928] All E.R. Rep. 189;
    98 ljpc 1; 140 L.T. 121; 45 T.L.R. 1, PC (Sing) 2–145, 2–146, 10–17
Income Trust Co. v. Watson (1984) 26 B.L.R. 228, HC (Ontario) 10–165, 10–234
Indata Equipment Supplies Ltd (t/a Autofleet) v. ACL Ltd (1997) [1998] 1
    B.C.L.C. 412; [1998] F.S.R. 248; (1997) 141 S.J.L.B. 216; The Times,
    August 14, 1997, CA 2–154
Independent Broadcasting Authority v. EMI Electronics Ltd; sub nom. IBA v.
    EMI Electronics Ltd and BICC Construction Ltd (1980) 14 B.L.R. 1;
    [1955–95] P.N.L.R. 179, HL 2–12, 2–123, 8–20, 8–99, 8–116, 8–140, 8–160,
                                           8–167, 8–172, 8–207, 8–273, 8–281, 17–94
Inder Lynch Devoy & Co. v. Surbritsky [1979] 1 N.Z.L.R. 87 10–235
Infantino v. MacLean [2001] 3 All E.R. 802; The Times, July 20, 2001; The
    Independent, July 30, 2001 (C.S), QBD 10–201
Ingles v. City of Toronto (2000) 183 D.L.R. (4th) 193 2–62

—— v. Tutkaluk Constructions Ltd; sub nom. Ingles v. City of Toronto [2000] 1
    S.C.R. 298; (2000) 183 D.L.R. (4th) 193, Sup Ct (Can) 8–115
Initial Services v. Putterill [1968] 1 Q.B. 396; [1967] 3 W.L.R. 1032; [1967] 3 All
    E.R. 145; 2 K.I.R. 863; 111 S.J. 541, CA 2–160
Inter-Leisure Ltd v. Lamberts [1997] N.P.C. 49, QBD 10–259
International Laboratories Ltd v. Dewar (1933) 3 D.L.R. 665, CA (Manitoba) 15–31,
                                    15–96, 15–97, 15–107, 15–115
Introvigne v. Commonwealth of Australia (1980) 32 A.L.R. 251, Fed Ct (Aus) 8–81,
                                           8–130, 8–141
Invercargill City Council v. Hamlin [1996] A.C. 624; [1996] 2 W.L.R. 367;
    [1996] 1 All E.R. 756; 78 B.L.R. 78; 50 Con. L.R. 105; (1996) 146 N.L.J.
    246; (1996) 140 S.J.L.B. 86; The Times, February 15, 1996, PC (NZ) 2–56, 2–57,
                         5–26, 5–27, 5–30, 5–31, 5–32, 8–69, 8–79, 8–88, 8–123
Investments Ltd v. Winn (1972) 223 E.G. 2334 10–159
Investors Compensation Scheme Ltd v. West Bromwich Building Society (No.1);
    Investors Compensation Scheme Ltd v. Hopkin & Sons; Alford v. West
    Bromwich Building Society; Armitage v. West Bromwich Building Society
    [1998] 1 W.L.R. 896; [1998] 1 All E.R. 98; [1998] 1 B.C.L.C. 531; [1997]
    C.L.C. 1243; [1997] P.N.L.R. 541; (1997) 147 N.L.J. 989; The Times, June
    24, 1997, HL 15–36
—— v. West Bromwich Building Society (No.2) [1999] Lloyd's Rep. P.N. 496,
    Ch D 6–02, 10–163, 13–86, 13–106, 13–125, 13–198
Investors in Industry Commercial Properties Ltd v. South Bedfordshire D.C.;
    [1986] Q.B. 1034; [1986] 2 W.L.R. 937; [1986] 1 All E.R. 787; 32 B.L.R.
    1; 5 Con. L.R. 1; [1986] 1 E.G.L.R. 252; (1986) 2 Const. L.J. 108; (1986)
    83 L.S.G. 441; (1986) 136 N.L.J. 118; (1986) 130 S.J. 71, CA 6–11, 8–138,
                                   8–153, 8–181, 8–190, 9–06, 9–55
Ireland v. Livingston (1872) L.R. 5 H.L. 395; 41 L.J.Q.B. 401; 27 L.J. 79; 1
    Asp.M.L.C. 389 14–44
Ireson v. Pearman (1825) 3 B. & C. 799; 5 D. & R. 687; 27 R.R. 490; 3
    L.J.K.B.(O.S.) 119; 107 E.R. 930 .... 10–99, 10–121
Irish Nationwide B.S. v. Malone (1999) I.L.T.243, Sup Ct (Irl) 14–59
Irish Woollen Co. Ltd v. Tyson (1900) 27 Acct.L.R. 13, CA (Irl) 15–94, 15–106,
                                            15–112
Iron Trades Mutual Insurance Co. Ltd v. JK Buckenham Ltd [1990] 1 All E.R.
    808; [1989] 2 Lloyd's Rep. 85, QBD (Comm Ct) 5–46, 5–47, 5–53

PARA.

Irving v. Morrison (1877) 27 U.C.C.P. 242 .... 8–253, 8–303
Islamic Republic of Iran Shipping Lines v. Denby [1987] 1 Lloyd's Rep. 367;
    [1987] 1 F.T.L.R. 30; (1986) 136 N.L.J. 1162, QBD (Comm Ct) 10–22, 10–226
Islander Trucking Ltd (In Liquidation) Ltd v. Robinson & Gardner Mountain
    (Marine) Ltd [1990] 1 All E.R. 826, QBD (Comm Ct) 5–46, 5–47
Izzard v. Field Palmer [2000] 1 E.G.L.R. 177, CA 9–108

J (A Minor) (Child in Care) (Medical Treatment), Re [1993] Fam. 15; [1992] 3
    W.L.R. 507; [1992] 4 All E.R. 614; [1992] 2 F.L.R. 165; [1992] 2 F.C.R.
    753; [1993] 4 Med.L.R. 21; [1992] Fam. Law 541; (1992) 136 S.J.L.B. 207;
    The Times, June 12, 1992; *The Independent*, June 11, 1992; *The Guardian*,
    June 17, 1992, CA 12–148
JC Houghton & Co. v. Nothard Lowe & Wills Ltd [1928] A.C. 1; (1927–28) 29
    Ll. L. Rep. 63, HL; affirming [1927] 1 K.B. 246; (1926) 25 Ll. L. Rep. 469,
    CA 13–104
JD Williams & Co. Ltd v. Michael Hyde & Associates Ltd; *sub nom.* Michael
    Hyde & Associates Ltd v. JD Williams & Co. Ltd [2001] B.L.R. 99; (2001)
    3 T.C.L.R. 1; [2000] Lloyd's Rep. P.N. 823; [2001] P.N.L.R. 8; [2000]
    N.P.C. 78; *The Times*, August 4, 2000, CA 6–08, 8–133, 8–147, 8–148, 8–149,
                                                            8–150, 8–215
J Dykes Ltd v. Littlewoods Mail Order Stores Ltd. *See* GUS Property Manage-
    ment v. Littlewoods Mail Order Stores Ltd.
JEB Fasteners Ltd v. Marks Bloom & Co. [1983] 1 All E.R. 583, CA; affirming
    [1981] 3 All E.R. 289; [1982] Com. L.R. 226, QBD 15–69, 15–70, 15–121
J Jarvis & Sons Ltd v. Castle Wharf Developments Ltd; J Jarvis & Sons Ltd v.
    Gleeds Management Services Ltd; J Jarvis & Sons Ltd v. Franklin Ellis
    Architects Ltd; Castle Wharf Developments Ltd v. J Jarvis & Sons Ltd
    [2001] EWCA Civ 19; [2001] Lloyd's Rep. P.N. 308; [2001] N.P.C. 15; *The
    Times*, February 28, 2001, CA 8–105, 8–110, 8–135, 8–136, 8–279
J Sainsbury plc v. Broadway Malyan, 61 Con. L.R. 31; [1999] P.N.L.R. 286, QBD
    (OR) 4–13, 8–34, 8–164, 8–165, 8–288, 8–325, 8–326, 8–327
JW Bollom & Co. Ltd v. Byas Mosley & Co. Ltd [1999] Lloyd's Rep.P.N. 598 14–55,
                           14–79, 14–102, 14–108, 14–117, 14–124, 14–130
Jacks v. Bell (1828) 3 C. & P. 316; 172 E.R. 437 10–165
—— v. Davis (1983) 141 D.L.R. (3d) 355, CA (BC) 10–25
Jackson v. Horizon Holidays Ltd [1975] 1 W.L.R. 1468; [1975] 3 All E.R. 92;
    119 S.J. 759, CA 8–309, 10–313
Jacobs v. Great Yarmouth and Waveney H.A. [1995] 6 Med.L.R. 192, CA 12–80,
                                              12–119, 12–123
—— v. Morton & Partners (1994) 72 B.L.R. 92, QBD 8–92, 8–93
Jacobus Marler Estates Ltd v. Marler (1913) 85 L.J.P.C. 167n 3–10
Jagwar Holdings Ltd v. Julian (1992) 6 N.Z.C.L.C. 68,041 15–153
Jalmoon Pty Ltd v. Bow [1997] 2 Qd.R. 62, CA (Queensland) 10–229
James, Ex p. (1803) 8 Ves.Jun. 337 .... 2–135, 2–137, 2–138
James v. Dunlop (1931) 1 B.M.J. 730 12–194
—— v. Evans; *sub nom.* Evans v. James (Administratrix of Hopkin's Estate)
    [2001] C.P. Rep. 36; [2000] 3 E.G.L.R. 1; [2000] 42 E.G. 173; [2000]
    E.G.C.S. 95; [2000] N.P.C. 85; (2000) 80 P. & C.R. D39; *The Times*, August
    2, 2000, CA 10–75
—— v. London Borough of Havering (1992) 15 B.M.L.R. 1, CA 12–235
James McNaughton Paper Group Ltd v. Hicks Anderson & Co. [1991] 2 Q.B.
    113; [1991] 2 W.L.R. 641; [1991] 1 All E.R. 134; [1991] B.C.L.C. 235;
    [1990] B.C.C. 891; [1991] E.C.C. 186; [1955–95] P.N.L.R. 574; (1990) 140
    N.L.J. 1311; *The Independent*, September 11, 1990, CA 2–70, 2–73, 2–75,
                           15–49, 15–62, 15–63, 15–70, 15–72, 15–78, 15–79

PARA.

Jameson v. Central Electricity Generating Board (No.1) [2000] 1 A.C. 455;
[1999] 2 W.L.R. 141; [1999] 1 All E.R. 193; [1999] 1 Lloyd's Rep. 573;
[1999] P.I.Q.R. Q81; (1999) 96(5) L.S.G. 37; (1999) 143 S.J.L.B. 29; *The
Times*, December 17, 1998, HL; reversing [1998] Q.B. 323; [1997] 3 W.L.R.
151; [1997] 4 All E.R. 38; [1997] P.I.Q.R. Q89; (1997) 141 S.J.L.B. 55; *The
Times*, February 25, 1997, CA 4–10

—— v. Simon (1899) 1 F. (Ct of Sess.) 1211; 7 slt 133; 36 S.L.R. 883 .... 8–146, 8–240

Jamieson, Austin & Mitchell Ltd v. Battrum [1934] 1 W.W.R. 324, Sup Ct
(Alberta) 15–31, 15–112

Jarvis, Re; *sub nom.* Edge v. Jarvis [1958] 1 W.L.R. 815; [1958] 2 All E.R. 336;
102 S.J. 546, Ch D 5–106

Jarvis v. Moy Davies Smith Vandervell & Co. [1936] 1 K.B. 399; 105 L.J.K.B.
309; 154 L.T. 365, CA 2–100

—— v. Swans Tours Ltd [1973] Q.B. 233; [1972] 3 W.L.R. 954; [1973] 1 All
E.R. 71; 116 S.J. 822, CA 8–309, 10–313

—— v. T Richards & Co. (1980) 124 S.J. 793 10–264

Jayman Ltd v. Kellam Berg (1998) 54 Alta. L.R. (3d) 272), CA (Alberta) (1995)
29 Alta. L.R. (3d) 1 8–242

Jefford v. Gee [1970] 2 Q.B. 130; [1970] 2 W.L.R. 702; [1970] 1 All E.R. 1202;
[1970] 1 Lloyd's Rep. 107; 114 S.J. 206, CA 3–22

Jeffreys v. Boosey (1854) 4 H.L.C. 814 2–151

Jefri Bolkiah, Prince v. KPMG. *See* Bolkiah v. KPMG.

Jenkins v. Betham (1855) 15 C.B. 167; 3 C.L.R. 373; 24 L.J.C.P. 94; 100 R.R.
297; 1 Jur.(N.S.) 237; 3 W.R. 283; 139 E.R. 384 .... 9–56, 9–104

—— v. Public Curator (1953) 90 C.L.R. 113 2–145

Jenmain Builders Ltd v. Steed & Steed [2000] Lloyd's Rep. P.N. 549; [2000]
P.N.L.R. 616; (2000) 97(13) L.S.G. 45, CA 10–158, 10–248

Jensen v. MacGregor (1992) 93 D.L.R. (4th) 68, Sup Ct (BC) 10–62

Jewo Ferrous BV v. Lewis Moore (A Firm) [2001] Lloyd's Rep. P.N. 6; [2001]
P.N.L.R. 12; *The Times*, November 30, 2000, CA 10–4

Jindi (Nominees) Ltd v. Dutney (1993) 26 A.T.R. 206 15–143

Jobling v. Associated Dairies [1982] A.C. 794; [1981] 3 W.L.R. 155; [1981] 2 All
E.R. 752; 125 S.J. 481, HL 10–234, 12–246

John Barker Construction Ltd v. London Portman Hotel Ltd, 83 B.L.R. 31; 50
Con. L.R. 43; (1996) 12 Const. L.J. 277, QBD (OR) 8–235

John Fox (A Firm) v. Bannister King & Rigbeys [1988] Q.B. 925; [1987] 3
W.L.R. 480; [1987] 1 All E.R. 737; (1987) 84 L.S.G. 2692; (1987) 137
N.L.J. 122; (1987) 131 S.J. 1063, CA 10–65, 10–68, 10–69, 10–72, 10–73

John Fulton and Co. Ltd, Re [1932] N.I. 35 15–114

John Holland Construction and Engineering Ltd v. Majorca Products (2000)
Const.L.J. 114, Sup Ct (Vic) 8–110, 8–121, 8–132, 8–258

John Mowlem & Co. plc v. Eagle Star Insurance Co. Ltd (No.1), 62 B.L.R. 126;
33 Con. L.R. 131, QBD (OR) 8–132

John Pfeiffer Pty Ltd v. Canny (1981) 148 C.L.R. 218 8–70

Johns v. Kelly [1986] 1 Lloyd's Rep. 468, QBD (Comm Ct) 14–09, 14–37

Johnson v. Agnew [1980] A.C. 367; [1979] 2 W.L.R. 487; [1979] 1 All E.R. 883;
(1979) 38 P. & C.R. 424; (1979) 251 E.G. 1167; 123 S.J. 217, HL 3–01

—— v. Bingley [1997] P.N.L.R. 392; [1995] N.P.C. 27; *The Times*, February 28,
1995, QBD 10–92, 10–203

—— v. Buttress (1936) 56 C.L.R. 113 2–145

—— v. Chief Constable of Surrey, *The Times*, November 23, 1992, CA 5–72

PARA.

Johnson v. Gore Wood & Co.; *sub nom.* Johnson v. Gore Woods & Co. [2001] 2
W.L.R. 72; [2001] 1 All E.R. 481; [2001] C.P.L.R. 49; [2001] 1 B.C.L.C.
313; [2001] P.N.L.R. 18; (2001) 98(1) L.S.G. 24; (2001) 98(8) L.S.G. 46;
(2000) 150 N.L.J. 1889; (2001) 145 S.J.L.B. 29; *The Times*, December 22,
2000; *The Independent*, February 7, 2001 (C.S), HL 10–115, 10–300, 10–315,
15–87, 15–141
—— v. Perez (1989) 82 A.L.R. 587 .... 10–278, 10–283, 10–287
Johnston v. Leslie & Goodwin Financial Services Ltd [1995] L.R.L.R. 472 14–37
Johnstone v. Thorburn (1901) 3 F. 497 10–207
Joliffe v. Charles Coleman & Co. (1964) 219 E.G. 1608 .... 10–265, 10–316
Jonas & Erickson Software v. Fitz-Wright Co. Ltd, October 5, 1990, Sup Ct
(BC) 17–52, 17–53
Jonathan Wren & Co. Ltd v. Microdec plc [1999] 65 Con. L.R. 157, QBD
(T&CC) 17–24, 17–26, 17–35
Jones v. Department of Employment [1989] Q.B. 1; [1988] 2 W.L.R. 493; [1988]
1 All E.R. 725; (1988) 85(4) L.S.G. 35; (1987) 137 N.L.J. 1182; (1988) 132
S.J. 128, CA 13–114, 15–50
—— v. GD Searle & Co. [1979] 1 W.L.R. 101; [1978] 3 All E.R. 654; 122 S.J.
435, CA 5–64
—— v. Jones [1970] 2 Q.B. 576; [1970] 3 W.L.R. 20; [1970] 3 All E.R. 47; 114
S.J. 374, CA 10–188
—— v. Manchester Corp.; Ryan v. Fildes [1952] 2 Q.B. 852; [1952] 2 All E.R.
125; [1952] 1 T.L.R. 1589; 116 J.P. 412, CA 12–17, 12–155, 12–164, 12–185
—— v. Sherwood Computer Services plc [1992] 1 W.L.R. 277; [1992] 2 All E.R.
170; *The Times*, December 14, 1989, CA 15–117
—— v. Stones [1999] 1 W.L.R. 1739; (1999) 78 P. & C.R. 293; [1999] 3 E.G.L.R.
81; [1999] 42 E.G. 135; (1999) 96(22) L.S.G. 34; *The Times*, June 3, 1999,
CA 5–104, 5–111
Jonesco v. Evening Standard Co. Ltd [1932] 2 K.B. 340, CA 10–73
Joyal v. Starreveld [1996] 37 Alta. L.R. 19 .... 12–232, 12–248, 12–264, 12–274
Joyce v. Merton, Sutton and Wandsworth H.A. [1996] P.I.Q.R. P121; [1996] 7
Med.L.R. 1, CA 12–80, 12–99, 12–111, 12–272, 12–175
Judge v. Huntingdon H.A. [1995] 5 Med.L.R. 223, QBD 12–176, 12–181, 12–184,
12–255, 12–257
Junior Books Ltd v. Veitchi Co. Ltd [1983] 1 A.C. 520; [1982] 3 W.L.R. 477;
[1982] 3 All E.R. 201; 1982 S.C. (H.L.) 244; 1982 S.L.T. 492; [1982] Com.
L.R. 221; 21 B.L.R. 66; (1982) 79 L.S.G. 1413; 126 S.J. 538, HL 8–87, 8–88,
8–102, 8–123
Junor v. McNicol, *The Times*, March 26, 1959, HL 12–77
Just v. British Columbia (1989) 64 D.L.R. (4th) 689 2–84

K v. P [1993] Ch. 140; [1992] 3 W.L.R. 1015; [1993] 1 All E.R. 521, Ch D 4–06
Kadaja v. CAA (1995) 23 O.R. (3d) 275, General Division (Ontario) 14–12, 14–46
Kaliszewska v. J Clague & Partners (1984) 5 Con. L.R. 62; (1984) Const. L.J.
137; [1984] C.I.L.L. 131 .... 8–159, 8–191, 8–214, 8–296
Kalkinis v. Allstate Insurance Company of Canada (1998) 41 O.R. (3d) 528, CA
(Ontario) 14–12, 14–54, 14–82
Kamahap Enterprises Ltd v. Chu's Central Market (1990) 64 D.L.R. (4th) 167,
CA (BC) 10–61
Kamloops, City of v. Nielson (1984) 10 D.L.R. (4th) 641 ...... 2–43, 2–58, 2–60, 8–112,
8–115
Kapfunde v. Abbey National plc [1998] E.C.C. 440; [1999] I.C.R. 1; [1998]
I.R.L.R. 583; [1999] Lloyd's Rep. Med. 48; (1999) 46 B.M.L.R. 176; *The
Times*, April 6, 1998; *The Independent*, April 1, 1998, CA 2–85, 2–113, 12–25,
12–57, 12–64, 12–65, 12–305

PARA.

Kapur v. Marshall (1978) 85 D.L.R. (3d) 566, HC (Ontario) 12–80

Karpenko v. Paroian, Courey, Cohen & Houston (1981) 117 D.L.R. (3d) 383, HC
(Ontario) 11–43

Kaufmann v. Credit Lyonnais Bank (1995) 7 Admin. L.R. 669; [1995] C.L.C.
300; *The Times*, February 1, 1995, Ch D 13–206

Kavanagh, Re; *sub nom.* Bankrupt, Ex p. v. Abrahamson (1964) 108 S.J. 320 12–174

Kay's Tutor v. Ayrshire and Arran Health Board [1987] 2 All E.R. 417; 1987 S.C.
(H.L.) 145; 1987 S.L.T. 577, HL 12–186, 12–245

KB (Adult) (Mental Patient: Medical Treatment), Re (1994) 19 B.M.L.R. 144;
[1994] 2 F.C.R. 1051 12–140

Kealey v. Berezowski [1996] 136 D.L.R. (4th) 708 12–289

Keech v. Sandford (1726) Cas. t. K. 61 2–141

Keefe v. Marks (1989) 16 N.S.W.L.R. 713, CA 11–14, 11–24

Keep Point Development Ltd v. Chan Chi Yim [2000] 3 H.K.L.R.D. 166 10–199

Keete v. King [1938] E.G.D. 65 .... 8–214, 8–221, 8–316

Kehoe v. Louth [1992] I.L.R.M. 282, Sup Ct 10–268

Kelley v. Corston [1998] Q.B. 686; [1998] 3 W.L.R. 246; [1997] 4 All E.R. 466;
[1998] E.C.C. 141; [1998] 1 F.L.R. 986; [1998] 1 F.C.R. 554; [1998]
P.N.L.R. 37; [1998] Fam. Law 399; (1997) 94(32) L.S.G. 28; (1997) 147
N.L.J. 1276; (1997) 141 S.J.L.B. 206; [1997] N.P.C. 111; *The Times*, August
20, 1997, CA 10–106, 11–14

Kelly v. Bastible [1997] 8 Med.L.R. 15; (1997) 36 B.M.L.R. 51; [1997] P.N.L.R.
227; (1997) 94(2) L.S.G. 24; (1997) 141 S.J.L.B. 5; *The Times*, November
15, 1996; *The Independent*, December 10, 1996, CA 5–65

—— v. Cooper [1993] A.C. 205; [1992] 3 W.L.R. 936; [1994] 1 B.C.L.C. 395;
[1992] E.G.C.S. 119; (1992) 136 S.J.L.B. 303; [1992] N.P.C. 134; *The
Times*, November 5, 1992, PC (Ber) 2–132, 13–115, 14–15

—— v. Finbarr J Crowley [1985] I.R. 212 .... 10–202, 10–268

—— v. London Transport Executive [1982] 1 W.L.R. 1055; [1982] 2 All E.R.
842; 126 S.J. 262, CA 11–26

—— v. Lundgard (1996) 40 Alta.L.R (3d) 234 .... 12–24, 12–274, 12–303

Kemp v. Burt (1833) 4 B. & Ad. 424; 1 N. & M. 262; 2 L.J.K.B. 69; 38 R.R. 278;
110 E.R. 515 10–116

Kenburgh Investments (Northern) Ltd (In Liquidation) v. David Yablon Minton
(A Firm); *sub nom.* David Yablon Minton (A Firm) v. Kenburgh Investments
(Northern) Ltd (In Liquidation) [2000] C.P.L.R. 551; [2001] B.P.I.R. 64;
[2000] Lloyd's Rep. P.N. 736; (2000) 97(29) L.S.G. 46; *The Times*, July 11,
2000, CA 4–10

Kendall Wilson Securities Ltd v. Barraclough [1986] N.Z.L.R. 576, CA (NZ) 9–171,
10–330

Kennedy (BJ) Agency (1984) Ltd v. Kilgour Bell Ins. (1999) 139 Man.R.(2d)
276, QBD (Manitoba) 14–55, 14–98

Kennedy v. Brown (1863) 13 C.B.(N.S.) 677; 1 New.Rep. 275; 32 L.J.C.P. 137;
7 L.T. 626; 9 Jur.(N.S.) 119; 11 W.R. 284; 143 E.R. 268 11–04

—— v. KB Van Emden & Co.; *sub nom.* Kennedy v. Emden; Jordan v. Gershon
Young Finer & Green; Burdge v. Jacobs Kane & Blok [1996] P.N.L.R. 409;
(1997) 74 P. & C.R. 19; [1997] 2 E.G.L.R. 137; [1997] 44 E.G. 201; (1996)
93(16) L.S.G. 31; (1996) 140 S.J.L.B. 99; [1996] N.P.C. 56; *The Times*,
April 5, 1996, CA 10–251, 10–275

—— v. Steinberg; *sub nom.* Rowan v. Steinberg, 1998 S.C. 379; 1997 S.L.T.
1204; 1997 S.C.L.R. 595; [1997] 8 Med. L.R. 30; 1997 Rep. L.R. 5; 1997
G.W.D. 7–287, OH 12–72, 12–191

Kenney v. Hall, Pain and Foster [1976] 2 E.G.L.R. 29; (1976) 239 E.G. 355 9–20,
9–52, 9–80, 9–100, 9–123, 9–135, 9–139, 9–175

Kenny v. Lockwood [1932] 1 D.L.R. 507 12–201

PARA.

Kenny & Good v. MGICA [2000] Lloyd's Rep. P.N. 25, HC (Aus) 3–02, 5–36, 9–117,
9–127, 9–160
Kenny & Reynolds Ltd v. Pyper [1964] E.G.D. 419 8–227
Kensington and Chelsea and Westminster A.H.A. v. Wettern Composites [1985]
1 All E.R. 346; 31 B.L.R. 57; (1984) 1 Con.L.R. 114; (1984) 134 N.L.J. 887,
DC 5–20, 5–25, 8–15, 8–58, 8–133, 8–139, 8–242, 8–244, 8–247, 8–330
Kent v. Griffiths (No.3) [2001] Q.B. 36; [2000] 2 W.L.R. 1158; [2000] 2 All E.R.
474; [2000] P.I.Q.R. P57; [2000] Lloyd's Rep. Med. 109; (2000) 97(7)
L.S.G. 41; (2000) 150 N.L.J. 195; (2000) 144 S.J.L.B. 106; *The Times*,
February 10, 2000; *The Independent*, February 9, 2000, CA 2–84, 12–20, 12–31
Kenyon v. Bell, 1953 S.C. 125; 1952 S.L.T. (Notes) 78, OH 12–251
Kenyon-Brown v. Desmond Banks & Co. (Undue Influence) [2000] Lloyd's Rep.
Bank. 80; [2000] Lloyd's Rep. P.N. 338; [2000] P.N.L.R. 266; (1999) 149
N.L.J. 1832; [1999] N.P.C. 140, CA 10–160, 10–205
Ker v. John H. Allan & Sons, 1949 S.L.T. (Notes) 20, OH 9–20, 9–82, 9–88, 9–91,
9–98
Kerly, Son & Verden, Re [1901] 1 Ch. 467; 45 S.J. 206; [1900–03] All E.R. Rep.
858; 70 L.J.Ch. 189; 83 L.T. 699; 49 W.R. 211; 17 T.L.R. 189, CA 10–67, 10–69,
10–71, 10–73
Kerridge v. James Abbott & Partners [1992] 2 E.G.L.R. 162 9–91
Kershaw v. Whelan [1996] 1 W.L.R. 358; [1996] 2 All E.R. 404; *The Times*,
December 20, 1995, QBD 10–144
—— v. Whelan (No.2) (1997) 141 S.J.L.B. 37; *The Times*, February 10, 1997,
QBD 5–91
Ketteman v. Hansel Properties Ltd [1987] A.C. 189; [1987] 2 W.L.R. 312; [1988]
1 All E.R. 38; 36 B.L.R. 1; [1987] 1 F.T.L.R. 284; 85 L.G.R. 409; [1987] 1
E.G.L.R. 237; (1987) 84 L.S.G. 657; (1987) 137 N.L.J. 100; (1987) 131 S.J.
134, HL; affirming [1984] 1 W.L.R. 1274; [1985] 1 All E.R. 352; 27 B.L.R.
1; (1985) 49 P. & C.R. 257; (1984) 271 E.G. 1099; [1984] C.I.L.L. 109;
(1984) 81 L.S.G. 3018; (1984) 128 S.J. 800, CA 5–20, 10–188
Kienzle v. Stringer (1981) 35 O.R. (2d) 85, CA (Ontario) 10–274, 10–276
Killick v. PricewaterhouseCoopers (a firm) [2001] P.N.L.R. 1 10–53
—— v. PricewaterhouseCoopers (No.1) [2001] 1 B.C.L.C. 65; [2001] Lloyd's
Rep. P.N. 17; [2001] P.N.L.R. 1; (2001) 2 W.T.L.R. 699, Ch D 15–74, 15–101
Kilroy v. Kilroy [1997] P.N.L.R. 66, CA 10–134
Kines Estate v. Lychuk (1998) 123 Man L.R. (2nd) 151 12–51
King v. Hawkins & Co., *The Times*, January 28, 1982 .... 10–240, 10–271, 10–317
—— v. Sullivan Insurance Inc. (1993) 109 Nfld. & P.E.I.R. 227 14–75
—— v. Victor Parsons & Co. [1973] 1 W.L.R. 29; [1973] 1 All E.R. 206; [1973]
1 Lloyd's Rep. 189; 116 S.J. 901, CA 5–70
King (or Fiehl) v. Chambers & Newman (Insurance Brokers) Ltd [1963] 2
Lloyd's Rep. 130, QBD 14–45, 14–79
Kingston Cotton Mill Co. Ltd (No.2), Re [1896] 2 Ch. 279, CA 15–24, 15–90, 15–95,
15–96, 15–110, 15–112, 15–131
Kinsella v. Russell Kinsella Pty. Limited [1986] 5 A.C.L.C. 215, CA (Aus) 15–74
Kirkham v. Chief Constable of Greater Manchester; *sub nom.* Kirkham v. Ander-
ton [1990] 2 Q.B. 283; [1990] 2 W.L.R. 987; [1990] 3 All E.R. 246; (1990)
140 N.L.J. 209; (1990) 134 S.J. 758; *The Independent*, February 10, 1989,
CA 12–237
Kitchen v. McMullin (1989) 50 C.C.L.T. 215, CA (New Brunswick) 12–203, 12–264
—— v. McMullin [1990] 1 Med.L.R. 352 12–226
—— v. Royal Air Force Association [1958] 1 W.L.R. 563; [1958] 2 All E.R. 241;
[1955–95] P.N.L.R. 18; 102 S.J. 363, CA 5–70, 10–262, 10–277, 10–278,
10–279, 10–282, 11–54
Kite v. Malycha (1998) 71 S.A.S.R. 325, Sup Ct (Aus) 12–75, 12–176, 12–275

PARA.

Kitechnology BV v. Unicor GmbH Plastmaschinen [1994] I.L.Pr. 568; [1995]
F.S.R. 765, CA 2–152
Kitney v. Jones Lang Wootton [1988] 1 E.G.L.R. 145 9–09
Klass v. Germany; Series A, No.28; (1979–80) 2 E.H.R.R. 214, ECHR 7–24
Kleinwort Benson Ltd v. De Montenegro [1994] N.P.C. 46 10–139
—— v. Sandwell B.C. See Westdeutsche Landesbank Girozentrale v. Islington
L.B.C.
Klingson v. Ramsay [1985] 5 W.W.R. 411, Sup Ct (BC) 10–61, 10–324
Knaggs v. JA Westaway & Sons (1996) 40 N.S.W.L.R. 476, CA 10–126
Knapp v. Ecclesiastical Insurance Group plc [1998] Lloyd's Rep. I.R. 390; [1998]
P.N.L.R. 172; The Times, November 17, 1997, CA 5–43, 5–47
Knight v. Bowyer (1858) 2 De G.F & J. 421 5–104
—— v. Bradley, May 13, 1998, unreported, QBD 12–188, 12–195
—— v. Home Office [1990] 3 All E.R. 237; (1990) 140 N.L.J. 210, QBD 12–155
—— v. West Kent H.A. [1998] Lloyd's Rep. Med. 18; (1998) 40 B.M.L.R. 61,
CA 12–190
Knightley v. Johns [1982] 1 W.L.R. 349; [1982] 1 All E.R. 851; [1982] R.T.R.
182; 126 S.J. 101, CA 8–270
Knott v. Bolton (1978) 10 B.L.R. 19 .... 8–311, 8–312
—— v. Bolton (1995) 11 Const. L.J. 315 9–181
Knox v. Gye (1872) L.R. 5 H.L. 656, HL (UK-Irl) 5–90, 5–91, 5–93, 5–94
—— v. Till [2000] Lloyd's Rep. P.N. 49; [2000] P.N.L.R. 67, CA (NZ) 10–51, 10–219
Koerber v. Trustees of Kitchener-Waterloo Hospital (1987) 62 O.R. (2d) 613 12–68,
12–69, 12–73, 12–75, 12–84
Kolan v. Solicitor (1969) 7 D.L.R. (3d) 481 aff'd. (1970) 11 D.L.R. (3d) 672, CA
(Ontario) 10–197
Koracvich v. Ortho Pharmaceuticals (Canada) Ltd (1995) 25 C.C.L.T. (2d) 295,
CA (BC) 12–54
Korz v. St. Pierre (1988) 43 D.L.R. (4th) 528, CA (Ontario) 10–18
Koseck v. Germany (1987) 9 E.H.R.R. 328 7–06
Kotowich v. Petursson [1994] 4 W.W.R. 669, CA (Manitoba) 10–197
Koufos v. C Czarnikow Ltd; Heron II, The; sub nom. C Czarnikow Ltd v. Koufos;
Heron II, The [1969] 1 A.C. 350; [1967] 3 W.L.R. 1491; [1967] 3 All E.R.
686; [1967] 2 Lloyd's Rep. 457; 111 S.J. 848, HL 8–280, 10–240, 10–251
Kralj v. McGrath and St Theresa's Hospital [1986] 1 All E.R. 54; (1985) 135
N.L.J. 913, QBD 12–22, 12–282, 12–288
Krambousanos v. Jedda (1996) 142 A.L.R. 604 .... 10–45, 10–205
Krcmár v. Czech Republic (App. No.35376/97); (2001) 31 E.H.R.R. 41,
ECHR 7–06
Kripps v. Touche Ross & Co. (1997) 33 B.C.L.R. (3d) 254, CA (BC) 15–16, 15–66,
15–91
Kueper v. McMullin (1986) 30 D.L.R. (4th) 408, CA (New Brunswick) 12–246
Kutilin v. Auerbach (1989) 34 B.C.L.R. (2d) 23 .... 10–68, 10–72
Kvaerner Construction (Regions) Ltd v. Kirkpatrick & Partners Consulting Engi-
neers Ltd (1999) S.C. 291 8–266
Kwak v. Odishaw [1985] 2 W.W.R. 222, CA (BC) 10–61
Kwik Fit Insurance Services Ltd v. Bull Information Systems Ltd, Transcript HT
99–178, June 23, 2000, QBD (T&CC) 17–107, 17–111
Kyle v. P&J Stormonth Darling [1994] S.L.T. 191, IH 10–278
Kyriacou v. Kogarah Municipal Council (1995) 88 L.G.E.R.A. 110, Sup Ct
(NSW) 10–268, 10–328

PARA.

L (Children) (Care Proceedings: Cohabiting Solicitors), Re [2001] 1 W.L.R. 100;
[2000] 2 F.L.R. 887; [2000] 3 F.C.R. 71; [2000] Fam. Law 810; (2000)
97(40) L.S.G. 42; (2000) 144 S.J.L.B. 238; *The Times*, July 27, 2000, Fam
Div 10–33
L (Medical Treatment: Gillick Competence), Re; *sub nom.* L (A Minor), Re
[1998] 2 F.L.R. 810; [1999] 2 F.C.R. 524; (2000) 51 B.M.L.R. 137; [1998]
Fam. Law 591, Fam Div 12–148
L v. Hesley Hall Ltd [2001] UKHL 22; [2001] 2 W.L.R. 1311; [2001] 2 All E.R.
769; [2001] I.C.R. 665; [2001] I.R.L.R. 472; [2001] 2 F.L.R. 307; [2001] 2
F.C.R. 97; [2001] E.L.R. 422; (2001) 98(24) L.S.G. 45; (2001) 151 N.L.J.
728; (2001) 145 S.J.L.B. 126; [2001] N.P.C. 89; *The Times*, May 10, 2001;
The Independent, June 11, 2001 (C.S); *The Daily Telegraph*, May 8, 2001,
HL 2–85
—— v. Robinson [2000] 3 N.Z.L.R. 499 12–288
LAC Minerals Ltd v. International Corona Resources Ltd (1989) 61 D.L.R. (4th)
14, ... 2–127, 2–128, 2–154
—— v. International Corona Resources Ltd [1990] F.S.R. 441, Sup Ct (Can) 13–115
LB Martin Construction Ltd. v. Gaglardi (1978) 91 D.L.R. (3d) 393, Sup Ct
(BC) 14–104
LCB v. United Kingdom (1999) 27 E.H.R.R. 212; 4 B.H.R.C. 447; [1998]
H.R.C.D. 628; *The Times*, June 15, 1998, ECHR 7–41
Laboratories Ltd v. Dewar (1933) 3 D.L.R. 665 15–90
Labreche Estate v. Harasymiw (1992) 89 D.L.R. (4th) 95 .... 14–59, 14–129
Lacey, Ex p. (1802) 6 Ves.Jun. 625 .... 2–134, 2–135, 2–137, 2–138
Lacroix v. Dominique (1999) 141 Man. R. (2nd) 1 12–225
Lagunas Nitrate Company v. Lagunas Syndicate [1899] 2 Ch. 392, CA 2–134
Laidler v. Elliott (1825) 3 B. & C. 738; 107 E.R. 907 10–96
Lake v. Bushby [1949] 2 All E.R. 964; [1950] W.N. 28; 94 S.J. 82, KBD 10–100,
10–158, 10–268
Laker Airways Inc. v. FLS Aerospace Ltd [2000] 1 W.L.R. 113; [1999] 2 Lloyd's
Rep. 45; [1999] C.L.C. 1124; *The Times*, May 21, 1999; *The Independent*,
May 24, 1999 (C.S.), QBD (Comm Ct) 10–33, 11–05
Lalese Enterprises Inc. v. Arete Technologies Inc., 59 C.P.R. 3d 438, Sup Ct
(BC) 17–14
Lampitt v. Poole B.C. [1991] 2 Q.B. 545; [1990] 3 W.L.R. 179; [1990] 2 All E.R.
887; 49 B.L.R. 82, CA 4–01
Lamshed v. Lamshed (1963) 37 A.L.J.R. 301; (1963) 109 C.L.R. 440 5–106
Lancashire Loans Ltd v. Black [1934] 1 K.B. 380; [1933] All E.R. Rep. 201; 103
L.J.K.B. 129; 150 L.T. 304, CA 2–144, 10–17
Landall v. Dennis Faulkner & Alsop [1994] 5 Med.L.R. 268, QBD 10–106, 11–14,
12–24
Landau v. Werner (1961) 105 S.J. 1008, CA; affirming (1961) 105 S.J. 257 2–123,
12–107, 12–233
Langdon v. Godfrey (1865) 4 F. & F. 445; 176 E.R. 639 10–207
Langley v. Campbell, *The Times*, November 6, 1975 .... 12–75, 12–185
—— v. North West Water Authority [1991] 1 W.L.R. 697; [1991] 3 All E.R. 610;
The Times, April 9, 1991; *The Daily Telegraph*, April 18, 1991, CA 10–175
Lanphier v. Phipo (1838) 8 C. & P. 475; 173 E.R. 581 .... 2–02, 12–67
Lapierre v. Young (1981) 117 D.L.R. (3d) 643, HC (Ontario) 10–25, 10–100, 10–149
Larche v. Ontario (1990) 75 D.L.R. (4th) 377, CA (Ont) 8–134, 12–240
Larussa-Chigi v. CS First Boston Ltd [1998] C.L.C. 277, QBD (Comm Ct) 13–34,
13–91
Laskin v. Bache & Co. Ltd (1972) 23 D.L.R. (3d) 385 13–130
Last v. Post (1952) 1 9 E.G. 240; [1952] C.P.L. 255 .... 9–55, 9–92, 9–110, 9–134
Launder, Re; Launder v. Richards (1908) 98 L.T. 554 10–73
Lavanchy v. Leverson (1859) 1 F. & F. 615; 175 E.R. 876 10–188

PARA.

Lavelle v. Hammersmith and Queen Charlotte's Special Health Authority, January 16, 1998, unreported, CA 12–189, 12–193
Law v. Cunningham & Co. (A Firm) [1993] E.G.C.S. 126 10–169
Law Estate v. Simice (1994) 21 C.C.L.T. (2d) 228 affirmed (1996) 27 C.C.L.T. (2d) 127, CA (BC) 12–200, 12–276
—— v. Simice [1995] 4 W.W.R. 672, CA (BC) 12–275
Law Hospital NHS Trust v. Lord Advocate, 1996 S.C.L.R. 491 12–146
Law Society v. KPMG Peat Marwick; sub nom. R. v. KPMG Peat Marwick McLintock [2000] 1 W.L.R. 1921; [2000] 4 All E.R. 540; [2000] Lloyd's Rep. P.N. 929; [2000] P.N.L.R. 831; (2000) 97(30) L.S.G. 40; (2000) 150 N.L.J. 1017; The Times, July 6, 2000; The Independent, July 5, 2000, CA; affirming [2000] 1 All E.R. 515; [2000] E.C.C. 456; [2000] Lloyd's Rep. P.N. 219; [2000] P.N.L.R. 364; (1999) 96(44) L.S.G. 40; (1999) 149 N.L.J. 1698; (1999) 143 S.J.L.B. 269; The Times, November 3, 1999; The Independent, December 13, 1999 (C.S.), Ch D 15–26, 15–48, 15–85, 15–87, 15–127, 15–131
Law Wan-lan v. Well-Built Development Co. Ltd [1988] 2 H.K.L.R. 435, CA (HK) 10–61
Lawrence v. Hampton & Sons (1964) 190 E.G. 107 .... 9–58, 9–93, 9–140
—— v. Potts (1834) 6 Car. & P. 428; 172 E.R. 1306 10–191
Lawrence & Co. [1998] C.L.Y. 1016, CA 10–128
Lawrie v. Gentry Developments Inc. (1990) 72 O.R. (2d) 512, HC (Ontario) 10–324
Lawson v. Laferriere (1991) 78 D.L.R. (4th) 609, Sup Ct (Can) 12–259, 12–260
Layden v. Cope (1984) 28 C.C.L.T. 140, QBD (Nova Scotia) 12–184
Layton v. Westcott (1993) 6 Alta.L.R. 91, QBD (Nova Scotia) 12–264
Layzell v. Smith Morton & Long [1992] 1 E.G.L.R. 169; [1992] 13 E.G. 118 10–266
Le Brasseur and Oakley, Re; sub nom. L & O, Re [1896] 2 Ch. 487; 65 L.J.Ch. 763; 74 L.T. 717; 45 W.R. 87; 40 S.J. 637, CA 11–10
Le Compte v. Belgium; Van Leuven v. Belgium; De Meyere v. Belgium; Series A, No.43; [1982] E.C.C. 240; (1982) 4 E.H.R.R. 1, ECHR 7–327–65, 7–66, 7–67,
Le Lievre v. Gould [1893] 1 Q.B. 491; 62 L.J.Q.B. 353; 68 L.T. 626; 41 W.R. 468; 57 J.P. 484, CA 9–32, 9–33, 9–41, 14–18, 14–24
Le Page v. Kingston and Richmond H.A. [1997] 8 Med.L.R. 229, QBD 12–83, 12–187, 12–272
Leach v. Crossley, 30 B.L.R. 95; 8 Con. L.R. 7, CA 8–201, 8–219
Leander v. Sweden; Series A, No.116; (1987) 9 E.H.R.R. 433; The Times, April 25, 1987, ECHR 7–24
Leathley v. John Fowler & Co. [1946] K.B. 579, CA 3–10
Lee v. Bateman, The Times, October 31, 1893 8–246
—— v. Dixon (1863) 3 F. & F. 744; 130 R.R. 901; 176 E.R. 341 .... 10–124, 10–175
—— v. O'Farrell (1988) 43 C.C.L.T. 269 12–195
—— v. Sankey (1873) L.R. 15 Eq. 204; 27 L.T. 809; 21 W.R. 286 10–37
—— v. South West Thames R.H.A. [1985] 1 W.L.R. 845; [1985] 2 All E.R. 385; (1985) 82 L.S.G. 2015; (1985) 135 N.L.J. 438; (1985) 128 S.J. 333, CA 12–221
—— v. Thompson (1990) 6 P.N. 91, CA 2–103, 10–12, 10–13
—— v. Walker (1872) L.R. 7 C.P. 121 .... 14–35, 18–16
Leeds & Holbeck Building Society v. Alex Morison & Co. (No.2), 2001 S.C.L.R. 41; [2001] P.N.L.R. 13; 2000 G.W.D. 30–1194, OH 10–215, 10–295
Leeds and Holbeck Building Society v. Arthur & Cole [2001] Lloyd's rep. P.N. 649, QBD 5–74, 5–91, 5–92
Leeds Estate, Building and Investment Co. v. Shepherd (1887) 36 Ch.D. 787 .... 15–110, 15–112, 15–138
Leeds Permanent Building Society v. Walker Fraser & Steele, 1995 S.L.T. (Sh Ct) 72, Sh Ct (Glasgow) 9–168

PARA.

Lees v. English and Partners [1977] E.G.D. 566; [1977] 1 E.G.L.R. 65 .... 9–108, 9–131, 9–140

—— v. Nuttall (1834) 2 My. & K. 891 2–141

Legal & General Mortgage Services Ltd v. HPC Professional Services [1997] P.N.L.R. 567, QBD 9–60, 9–105

Legge v. Young [1949] E.G.D. 186 9–134

Lehmann v. McArthur (1867–68) L.R. 3 Ch. App. 496, CA in Chancery 5–103

Leicester Guardians v. Trollope (1911) 75 J.P. 196 .... 8–15, 8–246

Leigh and Sillivan Ltd v. Aliakmon Shipping Co. Ltd; Aliakmon, The [1986] A.C. 785; [1986] 2 W.L.R. 902; [1986] 2 All E.R. 145; [1986] 2 Lloyd's Rep. 1; (1986) 136 N.L.J. 415; (1986) 130 S.J. 357, HL 2–29, 17–117

Leigh v. Unsworth (1972) 230 E.G. 501 .... 9–32, 9–53, 9–58, 9–92, 9–93

—— v. William Hill & Son (1956) 168 E.G. 396 .... 9–91, 9–98

Leon Engineering & Construction Co. Ltd (In Liquidation) v. Ka Duk Investment Co. Ltd 47 B.L.R. 139; (1989) 5 Const. L.J. 288, HC (HK) 8–109

Levy v. Spyers (1856) 1 F. & F. 3; 175 E.R. 599 10–98

Lewis v. Collard (1853) 14 C.B. 208; 2 C.L.R. 1345; 23 L.J.C.P. 32; 22 L.T.(O.S.) 135; 139 E.R. 86; 2 W.R. 105 10–77

—— v. Knight (1832) 1 Dowl. 261 10–69

—— v. Samuel (1846) 8 Q.B. 685; 1 N.P.C. 424; 15 L.J.Q. 218; 10 Jur. 429; 7 L.T.(O.S.) 60; 115 E.R. 1031 10–307

—— v. Tressider Andrews Associates Pty. Ltd [1987] 2 Qd.R. 533 .... 14–34, 14–35, 14–58, 14–74, 14–81, 14–124

Lewisham Investment Partnership Ltd v. Morgan [1997] 2 E.G.L.R. 150; [1997] 51 E.G. 75; [1997] N.P.C. 155; The Times, November 25, 1997, Ch D 9–52

Leyland Shipping Co. Ltd v. Norwich Union Fire Insurance Society Ltd [1918] A.C. 350, HL 8–274

Lidl Properties v. Clarke Bond Partnership [1998] Env. L.R. 662, QBD (OR) 8–100

Liesbosch, The; sub nom. Owner of Dredger Liesbosch v. Owners of SS Edison; Liesbosch Dredger v. SS Edison [1933] A.C. 449; [1933] All E.R. Rep. 144; (1933) 45 Ll. L. Rep. 123, HL 8–298, 9–185, 14–121

Life Assurance Corporation v. Tanter; Zephyr, The. See General Accident Fire and Life Assurance Corp. Ltd v. Peter William Tanter; Zephyr, The.

Liff v. Peasley [1980] 1 W.L.R. 781; [1980] 1 All E.R. 623; 124 S.J. 360, CA 5–65

Liles v. Terry [1895] Q.B. 679; 40 S.J. 53; [1895–99] All E.R. Rep. 1018; 65 L.J.Q.B. 34; 73 L.T. 428; 44 W.R. 116; 12 T.L.R. 26, CA 2–144, 10–17

Lillicrap v. Nalder & Son [1993] 1 W.L.R. 94; [1993] 1 All E.R. 724, CA 10–144

Lillicrap, Wassenaar and Partners v. Pilkington Brothers (S.A.) (Pty) Ltd [1985] 1 S.A.L.R. 475 8–124

Lindsay v. Mid-Western Health Board [1993] I.L.R.M. 550, Sup Ct (Irl) 12–123

Lindsay Petroleum Co. v. Hurd; Lindsay Petroleum Co. v. Farewell; Lindsay Petroleum Co. v. Kemp (1873–74) L.R. 5 P.C. 221, PC (Can) 5–99, 5–105

Linque Pollard v. Hugh Crockard, January 22, 1997 12–

Linsley v. Kirstiuk (1986) 28 D.L.R. (4th) 495, Sup Ct (BC) 10–45

Linsley, Re; sub nom. Cattley v. West [1904] 2 Ch. 785; 73 L.J.Ch. 841; 53 W.R. 172; 48 S.J. 606, Ch D 10–226

Lion Laboratories Ltd v. Evans [1985] Q.B. 526; [1984] 3 W.L.R. 539; [1984] 2 All E.R. 417; (1984) 81 L.S.G. 1233; (1984) 81 L.S.G. 2000; (1984) 128 S.J. 533, CA 2–160

Lion Nathan Ltd v. CC Bottlers Ltd [1996] 1 W.L.R. 1438; [1996] 2 B.C.L.C. 371; (1996) 93(24) L.S.G. 26; (1996) 140 S.J.L.B. 174; The Times, May 16, 1996, PC 9–59

PARA.

Lipkin Gorman v. Karpnale Ltd [1991] 2 A.C. 548, HL; reversing [1989] 1
W.L.R. 1340; [1992] 4 All E.R. 409; [1989] B.C.L.C. 756; [1989] Fin. L.R.
137; (1990) 87(4) L.S.G. 40; (1989) 139 N.L.J. 76; (1990) 134 S.J. 234; *The
Times*, November 19, 1988; *The Independent*, October 17, 1988 (C.S.);
Financial Times, October 19, 1988; *The Daily Telegraph*, October 28, 1988,
CA; reversing [1987] 1 W.L.R. 987; [1992] 4 All E.R. 331; [1987] B.C.L.C.
159; [1986] F.L.R. 271; (1986) 136 N.L.J. 659; (1987) 131 S.J. 940,
QBD 5–115
Lipschitz v. Wolpert and Abrahams [1977] 2 S.A.L.R. 732 15–24
Lister v. Hesley Hall Ltd. *See* L v. Hesley Hall Ltd.
—— v. Lister (1802) 6 Ves.Jun. 631 2–135
Litsion Pride, The. *See* Black King Shipping Corp. v. Massie; Litsion Pride,
The
Little Hayes Nursing Home, Ltd v. Marshall (1993) 66 P. & C.R. 90; [1993]
E.G.C.S. 32; [1993] N.P.C. 29, Ch D 9–74
Liverpool and Wigan Supply Association Ltd, Re [1907] Acct.L.R. 4 .... 15–24, 15–112
Liverpool Roman Catholic Archdiocesan Trustees Inc. v. Goldberg (No.1) [2001]
1 All E.R. 182; [2000] Lloyd's Rep. P.N. 836; [2001] P.N.L.R. 19; *The
Times*, July 18, 2000, Ch D 5–74, 5–77
—— v. Goldberg (No.2) [2001] Lloyd's Rep. P.N. 518; (2001) 98(17) L.S.G. 38;
The Times, March 9, 2001, Ch D 6–09, 10–142
Livingstone v. Frasso [1997] C.L.Y. 604 10–132
—— v. Rawyards Coal Co. (1880) 5 App.Cas. 25, H.L.(Sc.); 42 L.T. 334; 44 J.P.
392; 28 W.R. 357; Court of Sess.Cas. (4th) vi, 922; xvi Scotch Law Rep.
530 .... 8–285, 9–128, 9–152, 10–249, 13–161, 14–114, 15–132
Lloyd v. Coote & Ball [1915] 1 K.B. 242, KBD 2–144
—— v. Grace Smith & Co. [1912] A.C. 716, HL 15–150
—— v. Popely [2001] 1 C.L. 77 13–152
Lloyd Cheyham & Co. v. Littlejohn & Co. [1987] B.C.L.C. 303; [1986] P.C.C.
389 .... 15–15, 15–91
Lloyds Bank Ltd, Re; *sub nom.* Bomze v. Bomze; Lederman v. Bomze [1931] 1
Ch. 289, Ch D 2–142
Lloyds Bank plc v. Burd Pearse [2001] Lloyd's Rep. P.N. 452, CA; reversing
[2000] P.N.L.R. 71; [1999] E.G.C.S. 99, Ch D 5–42, 5–55
—— v. Crosse & Crosse. *See* Crosse & Crosse v. Lloyds Bank plc.
—— v. Parker Bullen [2000] Lloyd's Rep. P.N. 51; [1999] E.G.C.S. 107; [1999]
N.P.C. 99, Ch D 10–199, 10–259, 10–325
Lloyd's Litigation, The. *See* Henderson v. Merrett Syndicates Ltd.
Locabail (U.K.) Ltd v. Bayfield Properties Ltd (Leave to Appeal); Locabail
(U.K.) Ltd v. Waldorf Investment Corp. (Leave to Appeal); Timmins v.
Gormley; Williams v. Inspector of Taxes; R. v. Bristol Betting and Gaming
Licensing Committee, ex p. O'Callaghan [2000] Q.B. 451; [2000] 2 W.L.R.
870; [2000] 1 All E.R. 65; [2000] I.R.L.R. 96; [2000] H.R.L.R. 290; [2000]
U.K.H.R.R. 300; 7 B.H.R.C. 583; (1999) 149 N.L.J. 1793; [1999] N.P.C.
143; *The Times*, November 19, 1999; *The Independent*, November 23, 1999,
CA 10–33, 11–05
Lock v. Scantlebury, *The Times*, July 25, 1963 .... 12–119, 12–149, 12–178
Locke v. Camberwell H.A. [1991] 2 Med.L.R. 249, CA; reversing (1990) 140
N.L.J. 205; *The Times*, December 11, 1989; *The Independent*, January 29,
1990 (C.S.), QBD 10–94, 10–118, 10–119, 10–121, 11–49
Logan v. Uttlesford D.C. (1984) 134 N.L.J. 500; *The Times*, February 21,
1984 4–10
Logical Computer Ltd v. Euro Carparks Ltd, June 19, 2001, unreported, QBD 17–112,
17–128
Lomond Assured Properties Ltd v. McGrigor Donald, 2000 S.L.T. 797; 1999
S.C.L.R. 568; 1999 G.W.D. 11–512, OH 8–306, 10–255, 10–309

PARA.

London and General Bank (No.2), Re [1895] 2 Ch. 673; 64 L.J.Ch. 866; 73 L.T.
304; 44 W.R. 80; 11 T.L.R. 573; 39 S.J. 706; 2 Mans. 555; 12 R. 520, CA 15–24,
15–94, 15–95, 15–110, 15–112, 15–114, 15–115, 15–116, 15–130,
15–138
London and General Bank, Re [1895] 2 Ch. 166; 11 T.L.R. 374, CA 15–24
London and South of England Building Society v. Stone [1983] 1 W.L.R. 1242;
[1983] 3 All E.R. 105; (1983) 267 E.G. 69; (1983) 80 L.S.G. 3048; (1983)
127 S.J. 446, CA 9–152, 9–164
London Congregational Union Inc. v. Hariss & Harriss [1988] 1 All E.R. 15; 35
B.L.R. 58; 8 Con. L.R. 52; [1986] 2 E.G.L.R. 155; (1986) 280 E.G. 1342;
(1987) 3 Const. L.J. 37, CA; reversing in part [1985] 1 All E.R. 335; (1984)
1 Const. L.J. 54; [1984] C.I.L.L. 85, QBD 2–103, 5–20, 5–21, 5–25, 8–214,
8–283, 8–290, 8–295, 8–315
London Drugs Ltd v. Kuehne & Nagel International Ltd (1992) 97 D.L.R. (4th)
261 2–89
London Hospital, Trustees of v. TP Bennett (1987) 13 Con.L.R. 22 .... 8–167, 8–245,
8–246, 8–277
London Oil Storage Co. Ltd v. Seear, Hasluck & Co. (1904) 31 Acct.L.R. 1 15–112,
15–121
London School Board v. Northcroft, Son and Neighbour (1889) cited in Hudson's
Building Contracts (4th ed.), Vol. 2, p. 147 .... 8–166, 8–221
London Underground v. Kenchinton Ford plc (1998) 63 Con.L.R. 1 8–220
London, Chatham and Dover Railway Co. v. South Eastern Railway Co. [1893]
A.C. 429 3–22
Long v. Orsi (1836) 18 C.B. 610; 26 L.J.C.P. 127; 27 L.T.(O.S.) 158; 139 E.R.
1509 10–176
Longmeid v. Holliday (1851) 6 Ex. 761; 20 L.J.Ex. 430; 155 E.R. 752 2–102
Lonrho plc v. Fayed (No.2) [1992] 1 W.L.R. 1; [1991] 4 All E.R. 961; The
Guardian, April 16, 1991, Ch D 13–87
—— v. Tebbit [1992] 4 All E.R. 280; [1993] B.C.L.C. 96; [1992] B.C.C. 779;
The Times, June 10, 1992; The Independent, June 9, 1992; The Guardian,
June 24, 1992, CA 13–114
Loosemore v. Financial Concepts (A Firm) [2001] Lloyd's Rep. P.N. 235, QBD
(Merc Ct) 5–77, 13–92, 13–123
López Ostra v. Spain; Series A, No.303–C; (1995) 20 E.H.R.R. 277, ECHR 7–44
Losner v. Michael Cohen & Co. (1975) 119 S.J. 340, CA 10–106, 10–176
Love v. Mack (1905) 92 L.T. 345 .... 9–32, 9–103
Loveday v. Renton [1990] 1 Med.L.R. 117; The Times, March 31, 1988; The
Guardian, April 2, 1988, QBD 6–01, 12–111
Lowns v. Woods (1996) Aust. Tort Reports 63,151, CA (NSW) 12–19, 12–31, 12–79
Lowry v. Guildford (1832) 5 C. & P. 234; 172 E.R. 953 10–183
—— v. Woodroffe, Buchanan and Coulter (1950) 156 E.G. 375 .... 9–91, 9–134
Lowther v. Lowther (1806) 13 Ves.Jun. 95 2–138
Lubenham Fidelities and Investment Co. Ltd v. South Pembrokeshire D.C. (1986)
6 Con.L.R. 85, CA 8–107, 8–132, 8–270
Lucky Venture Holdings v. Hogue (1988) 56 Man.R. (2d) 172, CA
(Manitoba) 10–62
Luddy's Trustee v. Peard (1886) 33 Ch.D. 500 3–09
Luff v. Lord (1864) 34 Beav. 220 2–134
Lunghi v. Sinclair [1966] W.A.R. 172 2–139
Luscombe v. Roberts and Pascho (1962) 106 S.J. 373 15–127
Luxmoore-May v. Messenger May Baverstock [1990] 1 W.L.R. 1009; [1990] 1
All E.R. 1067; [1990] E.C.C. 516; [1990] 07 E.G. 61; (1990) 140 N.L.J. 89,
CA 1–09, 2–114, 9–58
Lybert v. Warrington Health Authority [1996] 7 Med.L.R. 71, C.A 12–158, 12–223,
12–230, 12–232, 12–279

PARA.

Lynne v. Gordon Doctors & Walton (1991) 135 S.J.L.B. 29; *The Times*, June 17,
1991 10–299
Lyon v. Home (1868) L.R. 6 Eq. 655 2–143
Lyons v. JW Bentley Ltd (1944) 77 Ll.L.R. 335 14–67

M (A Minor) v. Newham London Borough Council. *See* X (Minors) v. Bed-
fordshire C.C.; M (A Minor) v. Newham L.B.C.; E (A Minor) v. Dorset
C.C.; Christmas v. Hampshire C.C. (Duty of Care); Keating v. Bromley
L.B.C.
MB (Caesarean Section), Re; *sub nom.* L (Patient: Non-Consensual Treatment),
Re; L (An Adult: Non-Consensual Treatment), Re; MB (Medical Treat-
ment), Re [1997] 2 F.L.R. 426; [1997] 2 F.C.R. 541; [1997] 8 Med. L.R.
217; (1997) 38 B.M.L.R. 175; [1997] Fam. Law 542; (1997) 147 N.L.J. 600;
The Times, April 18, 1997; *The Independent*, April 8, 1997, CA 12–136, 12–139,
12–141
MC Strata Title Plan No. 1075 v. RSP Architects & Planners & Engineers [1996]
1 S.L.R. 113 8–124
MS v. Sweden (1999) 28 E.H.R.R. 313; 3 B.H.R.C. 248; (1999) 45 B.M.L.R. 133,
ECHR 7–62, 7–63
MacCulloch v. McInnes, Cooper & Robertson (2001) 178 N.S.R. (2d) 324, CA
(Nova Scotia) 10–82
MacCullough v. Corbett (1982) 133 D.L.R. (3d) 43, CA (Nova) 10–25
MacDonald Estate (1994) 95 Man. R. (2d) 123, CA (Maniba) 10–18
MacDonald Estate v. Martin (1999) 77 D.L.R. (4th) 249 2–166
MacDonald v. Board of Management for Glasgow Western Hospitals. *See* Hayward v. Edinburgh Royal Infirmary Board of Management.
—— v. Charlie Cook Insurance Inc. (1985) 55 Nfld. & P.E.I.R. 248; 162 A.P.R.
248, Sup Ct (Prince Edward Island) 14–42
—— v. Lockhart (1981) 118 D.L.R. (3d) 397, CA (Nova Scotia) 10–226
—— v. Martin [1990] 3 S.C.R. 1235 10–31
—— v. Ross (1983) 24 C.C.L.T. 242, 247, Sup Ct (Nova Scotia) 12–193
—— v. York County Hospital (1973) 1 O.R. (2d) 653, CA (Ontario) 12–185
MacDonell v. M. & M. Developments Ltd (1998) 175 N.S.R. (2d) 89, Sup Ct
(1998) 157 D.L.R. (4th) 240, (Nova Scotia) 10–16, 10–324
MacDougall v. MacDougall's Executors; *sub nom.* MacDougall v. Clydesdale
Bank Trustees, 1994 S.L.T. 1178; 1993 S.C.L.R. 832, OH 10–54
Macey v. Debenham, Tewson & Chinnocks [1993] 1 E.G.L.R. 149; [1993] 12
E.G. 127 .... 9–62, 9–104
Machin v. Adams, 84 B.L.R. 79; 59 Con. L.R. 14; [1998] E.C.C. 75; [1997]
E.G.C.S. 74; [1997] N.P.C. 73, CA 8–100
Mackenzie Patten & Co. v. British Olivetti Ltd, January 11, 1984, unreported,
QBD 17–56
MacKenzie v. Hall & Co. (1951) 157 E.G. 492 .... 9–53, 9–62, 9–91
—— v. MacKenzie (1998) 162 D.L.R. (4th) 674, CA (Nova Scotia) 10–221
Mackenzie v. Middleton, Ross & Arnot, 1983 S.L.T. 286, 1 Div 10–285
MacKenzie v. Royal Bank of Canada [1934] A.C. 468, PC (Can) 2–142
Mackie v. Wilde [1998] 2 I.R. 570, HC (Irish) 10–6
MacMahon v. James Doran & Co. [2001] P.N.L.R. 857, QB (NI) 10–236, 10–248
Macmillan v. AW Knott Becker Scott Ltd; Abrahams v. Macmillan [1990] 1
Lloyd's Rep. 98, QBD (Comm Ct) 2–90, 14–04, 14–14, 14–28
Macob Civil Engineering Ltd v. Morrison Construction Ltd [1999] C.L.C. 739;
[1999] B.L.R. 93; (1999) 1 T.C.L.R. 113; 64 Con. L.R. 1; [1999] 3 E.G.L.R.
7; [1999] 37 E.G. 173; (1999) 15 Const. L.J. 300; (1999) 96(10) L.S.G. 28;
The Times, March 11, 1999; *The Independent*, March 1, 1999 (C.S.), QBD
(T&CC) 8–337, 8–341

PARA.

MacPhail v. Desrosiers (1998) 166 N.S.R. (2d) 81, (1998) 170 N.S.R. (2d) 145, CA (Nova Scotia) 12–51, 12–117

Macpherson & Kelley v. Kevin J Prunty & Associates [1983] 1 V.R. 573, Sup Ct (Vic) 8–53, 10–329

MacQuarie Bank Ltd v. Myer [1994] 1 V.R. 350, App Div 10–26

MacWilliam v. Jeffrey (1993) 127 N.B.R. (2d) 113 12–245

Madley v. Cousins Coombe & Mustoe [1997] E.G.C.S. 63, QBD 10–5

Madole v. State Farm Mutual Automobile Insurance Co. (1995) 32 Alta.L.R. (3d) 265 14–54

Maes Finance Ltd v. AL Phillips, *The Times*, March 25, 1997, Ch D 10212, 10–323

Maguire v. Makaronis (1996–97) 188 C.L.R. 449, HC (Aus) 3–09

—— v. Makaronis (1997) 144 A.L.R. 729; [1996] 188 C.L.R. 449, HC (Aus) 2–129, 3–13, 10–228

Mahmood v. Siggins [1996] 7 Med.L.R. 76, QBD 12–233, 12–236

Mahon v. Osborne [1939] 2 K.B. 14; 83 S.J. 134; [1939] 1 All E.R. 335; 108 L.J.K.B. 567; 160 L.T. 329, CA 2–02, 12–68, 12–81, 12–90, 12–120, 12–166, 12–194

Mahoney v. Purnell [1996] 3 All E.R. 61; [1997] 1 F.L.R. 612; [1997] Fam. Law 169, QBD 10–101, 10–250

Maillet and Pothier v. Haliburton & Comeau (1983) 55 N.S.R. (2d); 114 A.P.R. 311, Sup Ct (Nova Scotia) 10–190

Mainwaring v. Goldtech Investments Ltd, *The Times*, February 19, 1991 10–135

Mainz v. Dodd (James and Charles), 122 S.J. 645; *The Times*, July 21, 1978 10–187

Major v. Buchanan (1975) 9 O.R. (2d) 491, HC (Ontario) 10–165

—— v. Wilcox, February 4, 1999, unreported, CA 12–176, 12–222

Male v. Hopmans (1967) 64 D.L.R. (2d) 105, CA (Ontario) 12–215

Malette v. Shulman [1991] 2 Med.L.R. 162, CA (Ont) 12–138

Mallesons Stephen Jacques v. Trenorth Ltd [1999] 1 V.R. 727, CA (Vic) 10–237

Mallette v. Hagarty (1994) 19 Alta.L.R. (2d) 201, HC (Alberta) 12–204

Mallough v. Barber (1815) 4 Camp. 150 14–58

Maloco v. Littlewoods Organisation Ltd; *sub nom.* ined Casesmith v. Littlewoods Organisation Ltd [1987] A.C. 241; [1987] 2 W.L.R. 480; [1987] 1 All E.R. 710; 1987 S.C. (H.L.) 37; 1987 S.L.T. 425; 1987 S.C.L.R. 489; (1987) 84 L.S.G. 905; (1987) 137 N.L.J. 149; (1987) 131 S.J. 226, HL 2–86, 8–245

Malone v. Commissioner of Police of the Metropolis (No.2) [1979] Ch. 344; [1979] 2 W.L.R. 700; [1979] 2 All E.R. 620; (1979) 69 Cr. App. R. 168; 123 S.J. 303, Ch D 3–15

Malyon v. Lawrence Messer and Co.; *sub nom.* Malyon v. Lawrance, Messer & Co. [1968] 2 Lloyd's Rep. 539; (1968) 112 S.J. 623, QBD 10–243, 10–279, 10–298, 10–312

Mander v. Commercial Union Assurance Co. plc; Mander v. Prudential Assurance Co. Ltd; Mander v. Gyngell Dobinson Gregory Co. Ltd [1998] Lloyd's Rep. I.R. 93, QBD (Comm Ct) 14–39, 14–61, 14–118

Manley v. Palache (1895) 73 L.T. 98; 11 R. 566, PC 10–182

Mann v. Chetty & Patel [2001] C.P. Rep. 24; [2001] Lloyd's Rep. P.N. 38, CA 6–09

Manning v. Wilkin (1848) 12 L.T. (O.S.) 249, NP 10–116

Manor Electronics v. Dickson (1990) 140 N.L.J. 590; *The Times*, February 8, 1990; *The Independent*, February 19, 1990 (C.S.), Ch D 10–120

Manortarn Ltd v. Rose & Bird [1995] E.G.C.S. 142, QBD 10–323

Mansouri v. Bloomsbury Health Authority, *The Times*, July 20, 1987 10–187

Manufacturers' Mutual Insurance Ltd v. John H Boardman Insurance Brokers Pty. Ltd (1994) 68 A.L.J.R. 385 14–03

Manzanilla Ltd v. Corton Property and Investments Ltd (No.2) [1997] 3 F.C.R. 389; *The Times*, August 4, 1997, CA 10–132, 10–133

Mara v. Browne [1896] 1 Ch. 199; 40 S.J. 131; 65 L.J.Ch. 225; 73 L.T. 638; 44 W.R. 330; 12 T.L.R. 111, CA 10–36

PARA.

Marbel Developments Ltd v. Pirani (1994) 18 C.C.L.T. (2d) 229, Sup Ct (BC) 10–94,
10–324

Marc Rich & Co. AG v. Bishop Rock Marine Co. Ltd; Nicholas H, The [1996]
A.C. 211; [1995] 3 W.L.R. 227; [1995] 3 All E.R. 307; [1995] 2 Lloyd's
Rep. 299; [1996] E.C.C. 120; (1995) 145 N.L.J. 1033; (1995) 139 S.J.L.B.
165; *The Times*, July 7, 1995; *The Independent*, August 18, 1995; Lloyd's
List July 19, 1995 (I.D.), HL 2–50, 2–51, 2–67, 2–76, 2–113, 8–80, 10–40

Marcic v. Thames Water Utilities Ltd (Preliminary Issues) [2001] 3 All E.R. 698;
[2001] N.P.C. 95; [2001] E.H.L.R. Dig. 6; *The Independent*, July 9, 2001
(C.S), QBD (T&CC) 7–02

Marder v. Sautelle & Hicks [1988] 2 E.G.L.R. 187; [1988] 41 E.G. 87, CA 9–148

Mariola Marine Corp. v. Lloyd's Register of Shipping; Morning Watch, The
[1990] 1 Lloyd's Rep. 547; [1991] E.C.C. 103, QBD (Comm Ct) 2–113, 9–47

Markal Investments Ltd v. Morley Shafron Agencies Ltd (1990) 67 D.L.R. (4th)
422, CA (BC) 44 D.L.R. (4th) 745 .... 14–38, 14–112

Markes v. Coodes [1997] P.N.L.R. 252, QBD 5–54

Market Wizard Systems (U.K.) Ltd, Re [1998] 2 B.C.L.C. 282; [1998–99] Info
T.L.R. 19; [1998] I.T.C.L.R. 171; [1999] Masons C.L.R. 1; (1998) 95(33)
L.S.G. 34; (1998) 142 S.J.L.B. 229; *The Times*, July 31, 1998, Ch D
(Companies Ct) 13–119

Marriott v. West Midlands Health Authority [1999] Lloyd's Rep. Med. 23, CA 12–78,
12–104, 12–179

Marsden v. Bateman [1993] 4 Med.L.R. 181, QBD 12–245

Marshall v. Curry (1933) 3 D.L.R. 260 .... 12–126, 12–138

—— v. Lindsey County Court [1935] 1 K.B. 516, affirmed [1937] A.C. 97 12–90,
12–152, 12–170, 12–222

Martel Building Ltd v. Canada [2000] 2 S.C.R. 860 8–114

—— v. Queen, The (2000) 193 D.L.R. (4th) 1 .... 2–58, 2–71

Martin v. Bell Ingram, 1986 S.C. 208; 1986 S.L.T. 575, 2 Div 9–57, 9–70, 9–140,
9–191

—— v. Britannia Life Ltd [2000] Lloyd's Rep. P.N. 412, Ch D 5–48, 13–98, 13–122

—— v. Goldfarb (1999) 41 O.R. (3d) 161 .... 10–115, 10–300, 10–314

Martin Boston & Co. v. Roberts [1996] P.N.L.R. 45; [1995] N.P.C. 28; *The Times*,
March 17, 1995, CA 10–78, 10–104, 10–178, 10–258

Mason v. Forgi (1984) 31 C.C.L.R. 66, Sup Ct (Nova Scotia) (1986) 38 C.C.L.T.
171, CA (New Brunswick) 12–203

Mathew v. Maughold Life Assurance Co. Ltd (1987) 3 P.N. 98, CA 10–41, 10–142,
10–32, 11–06, 11–08, 11–47

Matlock Green Garage Ltd v. Potter Brooke-Taylor & Wildgoose (A Firm) [2000]
Lloyd's Rep. P.N. 935 .... 10–241, 10–265, 10–316

Matrix Securities Ltd v. Theodore Goddard [1998] S.T.C. 1; [1998] P.N.L.R. 290;
[1997] B.T.C. 578; (1997) 147 N.L.J. 1847, Ch D 10–94, 10–118, 11–08, 11–42

Matthew Hall Ortech Ltd v. Tarmac Roadstone Ltd, 87 B.L.R. 96, QBD (OR) 8–255

Matthews v. East Suffolk Health Authority, February 25, 2000, unreported,
CA 12–273

Matto v. Rodney Broom Associates [1994] E.G.C.S. 48; [1994] N.P.C. 40, CA 9–58,
9–93, 9–98, 9–144

May v. Woollcombe Beer & Watts [1999] P.N.L.R. 283; [1998] 3 E.G.L.R. 94;
[1998] 51 E.G. 88, QBD (Merc Ct) 6–08, 10–142

Maydew v. Forrester (1814) 5 Taunt. 615; 128 E.R. 831 .... 14–60, 14–115

Maymac Environmental Services Ltd v. Faraday Building Services Ltd (2000) 75
Con.L.R. 101 8–339

Maynard v. West Midlands R.H.A.; *sub nom.* Maynard v. West Midlands Area
Health Authority [1984] 1 W.L.R. 634; [1985] 1 All E.R. 635; (1984) 81
L.S.G. 1926; (1983) 133 N.L.J. 641; (1984) 128 S.J. 317; *The Times*, May
9, 1983, HL 2–03, 6–08, 12–68, 12–69, 12–71, 12–75, 12–94, 12–183

PARA.

McAllister v. Lewisham and North Southwark Health Authority [1994] 5
Med.L.R. 343 .... 12–113, 12–223
McBride's Ltd v. Rooke and Thomas [1941] 4 D.L.R. 45 .... 15–31, 15–97, 15–107,
15–112, 15–131, 15–139
McCafferty v. Merton Sutton & Wandsworth H.A. [1997] 8 Med L.R. 387,
QBD 12–188
McCandless v. General Medical Council [1996] 1 W.L.R. 167; [1996] 7 Med.
L.R. 379; (1996) 30 B.M.L.R. 53; (1996) 93(5) L.S.G. 31; (1996) 140
S.J.L.B. 28; The Times, December 12, 1995, PC (U.K.) 12–04
McCann v. Western Farmers Mutual Insurance Co. (1978) 87 D.L.R. (3d) 135 14–12,
14–46
McCormack v. Redpath Brown & Co. Ltd, The Times, March 24, 1961 12–178
McCullagh v. Lane Fox and Partners Ltd, 49 Con. L.R. 124; [1996] P.N.L.R. 205;
[1996] 1 E.G.L.R. 35; [1996] 18 E.G. 104; [1995] E.G.C.S. 195; [1995]
N.P.C. 203; The Times, December 22, 1995, CA; affirming 38 Con. L.R. 14;
[1995] E.C.C. 157; [1994] 08 E.G. 118; [1994] E.G.C.S. 2; (1994) 138
S.J.L.B. 54; [1994] N.P.C. 4; The Times, January 25, 1994, QBD 5–07, 5–09,
9–10, 9–13, 9–28, 9–64, 9–67, 9–108, 10–57
McDonald v. Martin [1990] 3 S.C.R. 1235 10–31
McElroy Milne v. Commercial Electronics Ltd [1993] 1 N.Z.L.R. 39 .... 10–251, 10–261
McFadyen v. Harvie [1942] 4 D.L.R. 647 12–120
McFarlane v. Tayside Health Board; sub nom. Macfarlane v. Tayside Health
Board [2000] 2 A.C. 59; [1999] 3 W.L.R. 1301; [1999] 4 All E.R. 961; 2000
S.C. (H.L.) 1; 2000 S.L.T. 154; 2000 S.C.L.R. 105; [2000] 1 F.C.R. 102;
[2000] P.I.Q.R. Q101; [2000] Lloyd's Rep. Med. 1; (2000) 52 B.M.L.R. 1;
(1999) 149 N.L.J. 1868; 1999 G.W.D. 39–1888; The Times, November 26,
1999; The Independent, December 3, 1999, HL 2–71, 5–13, 12–07, 12–280,
12–289, 12–290, 12–291, 12–292, 12–293, 12–294, 12–295,
12–297, 12–298, 12–299, 12–300, 12–301, 12–304
—— v. Wilkinson; Hegarty v. EE Caledonia Ltd [1997] 2 Lloyd's Rep. 259;
[1997] P.N.L.R. 578; The Times, February 13, 1997; The Independent,
February 18, 1997, CA; reversing [1996] 1 Lloyd's Rep. 406, QBD 2–116,
10–282, 11–08, 11–14, 11–50
McFeeley v. United Kingdom (App. No.8317/78) (1981) 3 E.H.R.R. 161, Eur
Comm HR 7–08
McGhee v. National Coal Board [1973] 1 W.L.R. 1; [1972] 3 All E.R. 1008; 1973
S.C. (H.L.) 37; 1973 S.L.T. 14; 13 K.I.R. 471; 116 S.J. 967, HL 8–273, 12–237,
12–247, 12–248
McGonigle v. Hutton [1995] 6 B.N.I.L. 68 9–124
McGrath v. Kiely & Powell [1965] I.R. 497 .... 12–24, 12–303
McIlgorm v. Bell Lamb & Joynson [2001] P.N.L.R. 28, QBD 11–44
McInerney v. MacDonald (1992) 93 D.L.R. (4th) 415 12–29
McIntyre & Co. v. FJ Krutwig (1922) 10 Ll.L.R. 430 14–45
McIntyre v. Herring Son & Daw; Johnson v. Herring Son & Daw [1988] 1
E.G.L.R. 231, DC 9–61, 9–101, 9–104
McKaskell v. Benseman [1989] 3 N.Z.L.R. 75 3–11
McKay v. Essex A.H.A. [1982] Q.B. 1166; [1982] 2 W.L.R. 890; [1982] 2 All
E.R. 771; 126 S.J. 261, CA 12–55, 12–280, 12–302
McKenzie v. McDonald [1927] V.L.R. 134 .... 2–136, 3–10, 3–11
—— v. Potts (1997) 50 Con.L.R. 40 8–328
McLaren Maycroft & Co. v. Fletcher Development Co. Ltd [1973] 2 N.Z.L.R.
100, CA (NZ) 8–52
McLean v. Weir (1977) 3 C.C.L.T. 87, 101, Sup Ct (BC) 6–06, 12–73, 12–111
McLeish v. Amoo-Gottfried & Co. [1994] 10 P.N. 102 10–315
McLellan v. Fletcher (1987) 3 P.N. 202; (1987) 137 N.L.J. 593; The Times, June
3, 1987 .... 10–299, 10–323

PARA.

McLelland v. Greater Glasgow Health Board, 2001 S.L.T. 446, Ex Div; affirming
in part 1998 S.C. 305; 1999 S.L.T. 543; 1998 S.C.L.R. 1081; 1999 Rep. L.R.
1; 1998 G.W.D. 34–1754; *The Times*, October 14, 1998, OH 12–289, 12–293,
12–298

McLennan v. Newcastle H.A. (1992) 3 Med. L.R. 215, QBD 12–230

McLoughlin v. O'Brian [1983] 1 A.C. 410; [1982] 2 W.L.R. 982; [1982] 2 All
E.R. 298; [1982] R.T.R. 209; (1982) 79 L.S.G. 922; 126 S.J. 347, HL 12–33

McManus Developments Ltd v. Barbridge Properties Ltd and Blandy & Blandy
[1996] P.N.L.R. 431; [1992] N.P.C. 49, CA 10–195, 11–08, 11–40

McMaster v. Byrne [1952] W.N. 239; 96 S.J. 325; [1952] 1 All E.R. 1362, PC 10–19

McMorran's Cordova Bay Ltd v. Harman (1979) 106 D.L.R. 495, CA (BC) 10–256

McMullen v. Caren Farrell [1993] I.R.L.R. 123 .... 10–125, 10–142

McMurray v. Spicer (1867–68) L.R. 5 Eq. 527, Ct of Chancery 5–103

McNamara v. Martin Mears & Co. (1983) 126 S.J. 69 .... 10–190, 10–283, 10–285

McNealy v. Pennine Insurance Co. [1978] 2 Lloyd's Rep. 18; [1978] R.T.R. 285;
122 S.J. 229, CA 14–03, 14–51, 14–66

McNicol v. Insurance Unlimited (Calgary) Ltd (1992) 5 Alta.L.R. (3d) 158 14–43

—— v. Sportsman's Book Stores [1930] MaG. C.C. 116 2–156

McPhail's Equipment Co. v. 'Roxanne III' (1994) 93 B.C.L.R. (2d) 73, Sup Ct
(BC).; affirmed on appeal at (1995) 2 B.C.L.R.(3d) 393) 10–61

McPherson v. Watt (1877–78) L.R. 3 App. Cas. 254, HL 10–19

Meadows v. Meadows (1853) 16 Beav. 401; 51 E.R. 833 10–166

Mean v. Thomas [1998] E.G.C.S. 2; (1998) 95(5) L.S.G. 30, QBD 10–155

Medcalf v. Mardell [2001] P.N.L.R. 372, CA 11–32, 13–101

Medforth v. Blake [2000] Ch. 86; [1999] 3 W.L.R. 922; [1999] 3 All E.R. 97;
[1999] B.C.C. 771; [1999] 2 B.C.L.C. 221; [1999] B.P.I.R. 712; [1999]
Lloyd's Rep. P.N. 844; [1999] P.N.L.R. 920; [1999] 2 E.G.L.R. 75; [1999]
29 E.G. 119; [1999] E.G.C.S. 81; (1999) 96(24) L.S.G. 39; (1999) 149
N.L.J. 929; *The Times*, June 22, 1999; *The Independent*, June 24, 1999,
CA 2–127

Meerkin & Apel v. Rossett Pty. Ltd [1998] 4 V.R. 54, Sup Ct (Vic) 10–5

Melanson v. Cochrane Sargent, Nicholson & Paterson (1968) 68 N.B.R. (2d) 370,
CA (New Brunswick) 10–278, 10–282

Melik & Co. v. Norwich Union Fire Insurance Society and Kemp [1980] 1
Lloyd's Rep. 523, QBD 14–85

Meloche v. Hotel Dieu Grace Hospital (1999) 179 D.L.R. (4th) 77 CA
(Ontario) 12–105, 12–248

Melrose v. Davidson & Robertson, 1993 S.C. 288; 1993 S.L.T. 611; 1993
S.C.L.R. 365, 1 Div 9–72

Melton Medes v. Securities and Investments Board [1995] Ch. 137; [1995] 2
W.L.R. 247; [1995] 3 All E.R. 880; *The Times*, July 27, 1994; *The Independent*, August 8, 1994 (C.S.), Ch D 13–132

Melton v. Walker & Stanger (1981) 125 S.J. 861 5–38

Memery Crystal v. O'Higgins [1998] E.C.C. 299; [1997] 7 C.L. 457, QBD 10–57

Merc Property Ltd, Re [1999] 2 B.C.L.C. 286; *The Times*, May 19, 1999; *The
Independent*, May 3, 1999 (C.S.), Ch D 10–132

Mercantile Building Society v. JW Mitchell Dodds & Co. [1993] N.P.C. 99,
CA 10–195

Mercantile Credit Co. Ltd v. Fenwick; Mercantile Credit Co. Ltd v. Speechly
Bircham [1999] 2 F.L.R. 110; [1999] Lloyd's Rep. P.N. 408; [1999] Fam.
Law 453; [1999] E.G.C.S. 22; (1999) 96(10) L.S.G. 30; (1999) 143 S.J.L.B.
74; *The Times*, February 23, 1999, CA 2–10, 10–10

Mercer v. King (1859) 1 F. & F. 490, NP 10–182

Meredith v. Macfarlane (1915) 9 O.W.N. 160 8–165

PARA.

Meridian Global Funds Management Asia Ltd v. Securities Commission [1995]
2 A.C. 500; [1995] 3 W.L.R. 413; [1995] 3 All E.R. 918; [1995] B.C.C. 942;
[1995] 2 B.C.L.C. 116; (1995) 92(28) L.S.G. 39; (1995) 139 S.J.L.B. 152;
The Times, June 29, 1995, PC (NZ) 15–151
Merivale Moore plc v. Strutt & Parker [1999] Lloyd's Rep. P.N. 734; [2000]
P.N.L.R. 498; [1999] 2 E.G.L.R. 171; [1999] E.G.C.S. 59; (1999) 96(19)
L.S.G. 27; [1999] N.P.C. 48; *The Times*, May 5, 1999, CA 9–06, 9–60, 9–61,
9–100, 9–105, 9–116
Merrett v. Babb [2001] EWCA Civ 214; [2001] 3 W.L.R. 1; [2001] Lloyd's Rep.
P.N. 468; [2001] P.N.L.R. 29; [2001] 1 E.G.L.R. 145; [2001] E.G.C.S. 24;
(2001) 98(13) L.S.G. 41; (2001) 145 S.J.L.B. 75; *The Times*, March 2, 2001;
The Independent, February 23, 2001, CA 2–69, 2–78, 2–92, 2–93, 9–14, 9–35,
9–47, 10–41, 13–113, 15–49
Merton L.B.C. v. Lowe (1981) 18 B.L.R. 130, CA 8–32, 8–180, 8–215
—— v. Stanley Hugh Leach Ltd, 32 B.L.R. 51; (1986) 2 Const. L.J. 189, Ch D 8–229,
8–230, 8–234
Messineo v. Beale (1978) 81 D.L.R. (3d) 713, CA (Ontario) 10–268
Meyer v. Gordon (1981) 17 C.C.L.T. 1, Sup Ct (BC) 12–180, 12–189
—— v. Rogers (1991) 78 D.L.R. (4th) 307, HC (Ontario) 12–264
Michael v. Ensoncraft Ltd [1990] E.G.C.S. 156 9–183
—— v. Hart [1901] 2 K.B. 161 13–159
Michael Hyde & Associates Ltd v. JD Williams & Co. Ltd. *See* JD Williams &
Co. Ltd v. Michael Hyde & Associates Ltd.
Michael Salliss & Co. Ltd v. Calil, 13 Con. L.R. 68; (1988) 4 Const. L.J. 125,
QBD (OR) 8–107, 8–109
Michaels v. Valentine (1923) 16 Ll.L.Rep. 244, Mayor's and City of London
Court 14–76
Mickle v. Salvation Army Grace Hospital (1998) 166 D.L.R. (4th) 743 12–231,
12–264
Micklefield v. SAC Technology Ltd [1990] 1 W.L.R. 1002; [1991] 1 All E.R. 275;
[1990] I.R.L.R. 218, Ch D 13–134
Micron Computer Systems Ltd v. Wang (U.K.) Ltd, May 9, 1990, unreported,
QBD 17–34, 17–87
Mid Kent Water plc v. Batchelor [1994] 1 E.G.L.R. 185; [1994] 07 E.G. 197;
[1993] E.G.C.S. 103 9–74
Middleton v. Steeds Hudson [1998] 1 F.L.R. 738; [1998] Fam. Law 322,
QBD 10–123, 10–174
Midland Bank plc v. Bardgrove Property Services Ltd, 60 B.L.R. 1, CA; affirm-
ing 24 Con. L.R. 98; [1991] 2 E.G.L.R. 283 8–103
—— v. Cameron Thom Peterkin & Duncans, 1988 S.L.T. 611; 1988 S.C.L.R.
209, OH 10–58, 10–207
—— v. Cox McQueen [1999] Lloyd's Rep. Bank. 78; [1999] 1 F.L.R. 1002;
[1999] Lloyd's Rep. P.N. 223; [1999] P.N.L.R. 593; [1999] Fam. Law 310;
[1999] E.G.C.S. 12; (1999) 96(6) L.S.G. 36; (1999) 149 N.L.J. 164; [1999]
N.P.C. 11; *The Times*, February 2, 1999; *The Independent*, January 29, 1999,
CA 2–10, 10–10, 10–11
Midland Bank Trust Co. Ltd v. Hett Stubbs & Kemp [1979] Ch. 384; [1978] 3
W.L.R. 167; [1978] 3 All E.R. 571; [1955–95] P.N.L.R. 95; 121 S.J. 830;
The Times, December 2, 1977, Ch D 2–08, 2–09, 2–100, 2–103, 2–116, 5–14,
5–45, 6–07, 6–08, 8–28, 8–36, 8–50, 8–51, 8–147, 9–32, 10–04,
10–07, 10–13, 10–12, 10–14, 10–78, 10–94, 10–94, 10–142,
10–162, 12–115, 13–106, 15–34
Midland Mortgage Corp. v. Jawl & Bundon (1999) 64 B.C.L.R. (3d) 1; (1999) 8
W.W.R. 535, CA (BC) 10–43, 10–207
Miles v. Judge (1997) 37 C.C.L.T. 160 12–78

PARA.

Miles v. Redbridge & Waltham Forest Health Authority February 18, 2000,
unreported, QBD 12–250
Miliangos v. George Frank (Textiles) Ltd (No.1) [1976] A.C. 443; [1975] 3
W.L.R. 758; [1975] 3 All E.R. 801; [1976] 1 Lloyd's Rep. 201; [1975] 2
C.M.L.R. 585; 119 S.J. 774, HL 10–250
Miller v. Cannon Hill Estates Ltd [1931] 2 K.B. 113; 75 S.J. 155; [1931] All E.R.
Rep. 93; 100 L.J.K.B. 740; 144 L.T. 567, KBD 2–04
—— v. Guardian Insurance Co. of Canada (1997) 149 D.L.R. (4th) 375; (1995)
127 D.L.R. (4th) 717 .... 14–12, 14–54, 14–89
—— v. James (1823) 8 Moore C.P. 208 10–69
Mills v. Haywood (1877) L.R. 6 Ch. D. 196, CA 5–103
Miloslavsky v. Aldington. See Tolstoy Miloslavsky v. Aldington.
Ministry of Defence v. Scott Wilson Kirkpatrick. See Scott Wilson Kirkpatrick &
Partners v. Ministry of Defence.
Minories Finance v. Arthur Young; Minories Finance v. Arthur Young (a firm)
and Bank of England [1989] 2 All E.R. 105; [1988] Fin. L.R. 345; The
Times, July 27, 1988; The Independent, July 20, 1988, QBD 13–114
Mint Security v. Blair, Miller (Thomas R) & Son (Home) and Darwin Clayton (E
C) and Co. [1982] 1 Lloyd's Rep. 188, QBD 14–14, 14–76, 14–110, 14–115
Minton v. Kenburhg Investments (Northern) Ltd (in Liquidation), The Times July
11 2000 10–115
Mirage Entertainment Corp. Ltd v. Arthur Young (1992) 6 N.Z.C.L.C. 68 15–146
Miro Properties Ltd v. J Trevor & Sons [1989] 1 E.G.L.R. 151; [1989] 08 E.G.
125, DC 9–140
Mirza v. Bhandal, The Independent, June 14, 1999 (C.S.), QBD 8–45, 8–46, 8–47
Mitchell v. Homfray (1881–82) L.R. 8 Q.B.D. 587, CA 2–144
Mitor Investments Pty. Ltd v. General Accident Fire and Life Assurance Corpora-
tion Ltd [1984] W.A.R. 365 .... 14–14, 14–46, 14–74
Mitzner v. Miller & Beazley Ltd (1993) 11 Alta.L.R. (3d) 108 14–46
M'Mackin v. Hibernian Bank [1905] 1 I.R. 296 2–144
M'Neill v. Millen & Co. Ltd [1907] 2 I.R. 328 14–81
Moage Ltd, Re (1998) 153 A.L.R. 711, Fed Ct (Aus) 10–23
Mobil Oil Hong Kong Ltd v. Hong Kong United Dockyards Ltd (The Hu Lien)
[1991] 1 Lloyd's Rep. 309 8–80
Modbury Triangle Shopping Centre Pty. Ltd v. Anzil [2000] H.C.A. 61 ...... 2–64, 2–86
Moffat v. Witelson (1980) 111 D.L.R. (3d) 712 .... 12–186, 12–254
Mondel v. Steel (1841) 8 M. & W. 858; 1 Dowl.(N.S.) 1; [1835–42] All E.R. Rep.
511; 10 L.J.Ex. 426; 151 E.R. 1288 .... 3–08, 8–316
Moneypenny v. Hartland (1826) 2 Car. & P. 378 .... 3–08, 8–185, 8–193, 8–316, 9–110
Montesquieu v. Sandys (1811) 18 Ves.Jun. 302 .... 2–131, 2–138
Montreal Tramways v. Leveille [1933] 4 D.L.R. 337, Sup Ct (Can) 12–55
Montriou v. Jefferys (1825) 2C. & P. 113; Ry. & M. 317; 172 E.R. 51, NP 10–81
Moody v. Cox & Hatt [1917] 2 Ch. 71; 61 S.J. 398; [1916–17] All E.R. Rep. 548;
86 L.J.Ch. 424; 116 L.T. 740, CA 2–137, 2–140, 10–17, 10–23, 10–100
Moore, Re (1881) 51 L.J.(N.S.) Ch. 72 2–140
Moore v. Castlegar & District Hospital (1996) 25 B.C.L.R. 12–245
—— v. Mourgue (1776) 2 Cowp. 479; 98 E.R. 2297 14–57
—— v. Worthing D.H.A. [1992] 3 Med. L.R. 431, QBD 12–80
—— v. Zerfahs [1999] Lloyd's Rep. P.N. 144, CA 14–12, 14–72
Moores v. Yakeley Associates Ltd, March 23, 2000, CA; affirming (2000) 2
T.C.L.R. 146; 62 Con. L.R. 76, QBD (T&CC) 8–23, 8–24
Moorgate Tobacco Co. Ltd v. Philip Morris Ltd (No.2) (1984) 156 C.L.R. 415 2–154,
2–156, 2–162
Morash v. Lockhart & Ritchie Ltd (1978) 95 D.L.R. (3d) 647 .... 5–114, 14–75, 14–129
Morera-Loftus v. Wray Castle Ltd [1999] Lloyd's Rep. Med. 159, QBD 12–150,
12–176

PARA.

Moresk Cleaners Ltd v. Hicks [1966] 2 Lloyd's Rep. 338; 4 B.L.R. 50; 116 N.L.J.
1546, Assizes (Cornwall) 8–165, 8–140, 8–143, 8–181, 8–187, 8–180, 8–290
Morgan v. Perry (1973) 229 E.G. 1737 ...... 9–95, 9–127, 9–131, 9–140, 9–142, 9–190,
9–191
Morgan Crucible Co. plc v. Hill Samuel Bank & Co. Ltd [1991] Ch. 295; [1991]
2 W.L.R. 655; [1991] 1 All E.R. 148; [1991] B.C.C. 82; [1991] B.C.L.C.
178; (1990) 140 N.L.J. 1605; *The Independent*, October 25, 1990, CA 2–75,
15–60, 15–74, 15–75
Morgan Grenfell & Co. Ltd v. Welwyn Hatfield D.C. [1995] 1 All E.R. 1; *The
Times*, June 1, 1993, QBD 13–29
Morgan Stanley UK Group v. Puglisi Cosentino [1998] C.L.C. 481, QBD (Comm
Ct) 13–124, 13–167
Morision v. Moat (1851) 9 Hare 241 .... 2–150, 2–154
Morley v. Loughnan [1893] 1 Ch. 736, Ch D 2–144
Morning Watch, The. *See* Mariola Marine Corp. v. Lloyd's Register of Shipping;
Morning Watch, The.
Morrell v. Morrell (1882) 7 P.D. 68; 51 L.J.C.P. 49; 46 L.T. 485 10–220
Morris v. Duke-Cohan & Co. (1975) 119 S.J. 826; *The Times*, November 22,
1975 10–301
—— v. Winsbury-White [1937] 4 All E.R. 494 .... 2–09, 12–08, 12–120
Morris, Re; *sub nom.* Lloyds Bank v. Peake [1971] P. 62; [1970] 2 W.L.R. 865;
[1970] 1 All E.R. 1057; (1969) 113 S.J. 923; *The Times*, November 11,
1969, PDAD 10–224
Morrison v. Forsyth [1995] 6 Med.L.R. 6 12–174
—— v. Patel (1988) 44 C.C.L.T. 264 12–93
Morse v. Barrett (Leeds) Ltd (1993) 9 Const.L.J. 158, Ch D 8–97
—— v. Royal (1806) 12 Ves.Jun. 355 2–134
Mortgage Corp. Ltd v. Mitchells Roberton, 1997 S.L.T. 1305; 1997 G.W.D.
19–901, OH 10–9
Mortgage Corp. plc v. Halifax (SW) Ltd (No.2) [1999] Lloyd's Rep. P.N. 159,
QBD 9–172, 10–294
—— v. Lambert & Co. [2000] Lloyd's Rep. Bank. 207; [2000] B.L.R. 265;
[2000] Lloyd's Rep. P.N. 624; [2000] P.N.L.R. 820; *The Times*, April 24,
2000, CA ; affirming [1999] Lloyd's Rep. P.N. 947; [1999] 3 E.G.L.R. 59;
[1999] 42 E.G. 138; [1999] E.G.C.S. 109; *The Times*, October 11, 1999, Ch
D 5–55, 9–09, 9–165
Mortgage Express Ltd v. Bowerman & Partners (No.1) [1996] 2 All E.R. 836;
[1996] E.C.C. 228; [1996] P.N.L.R. 62; [1996] 1 E.G.L.R. 126; [1996] 04
E.G. 126; [1995] E.G.C.S. 129; [1995] N.P.C. 129; *The Times*, August 1,
1995, CA 10–160, 10–206, 10–208, 10–209, 10–210, 10–211, 10–212
—— v. Dunsmore Reid & Smith, 1996 G.W.D. 40–2295, 1 Div 9–58
—— v. S Newman & Co. (No.2) [2000] Lloyd's Rep. P.N. 745, CA; reversing
[2000] P.N.L.R. 298; [1999] E.G.C.S. 123, Ch D 10–39, 10–210
Mortgage Funding Corp. plc v. Tisdall Nelson Nari & Co. [1998] P.N.L.R. 81,
QBD (OR) 10–210, 10–295
Morton v. Arbuckle (No.2) [1919] V.L.R. 487 15–38
—— v. Harper Grey Easton (1995) 8 B.C.L.R. (2d) 53, Sup Ct (BC) 10–174
Moss v. Heckingbottom (1958) 172 E.G. 207 .... 9–77, 9–82, 9–140
Mosvolds Rederi A/S v. Food Corp. of India; Damodar General TJ Park, The and
King Theras, The [1986] 2 Lloyd's Rep. 68, QBD (Comm Ct) 13–91
Motor Crown Petroleum Ltd v. SJ Berwin & Co.; *sub nom.* SJ Berwin & Co. v.
Motor Crown Petroleum Ltd [2000] Lloyd's Rep. P.N. 438; [2000] N.P.C.
26, CA 10–259
Mouat v. Clark Boyce [1992] 2 N.Z.L.R. 559, CA (NZ) 5–115, 10–15, 10–16, 10–324
Mounds View, City of v. Walijarva (1978) 263 N.W. (2d) 420, Sup Ct
(Minnesota) 17–12

PARA.

Mount Banking Corp. Ltd v. Brian Cooper & Co. [1992] 2 E.G.L.R. 142; [1992]
35 E.G. 123; [1992] N.P.C. 99 9–61
Mount v. Barker Austin [1998] P.N.L.R. 493, CA 10–262, 10–291, 15–134
Movitex Ltd v. Bulfield [1988] B.C.L.C. 104 .... 2–134, 2–140, 10–19
Mowbray v. Merryweather [1895] 2 Q.B. 640, CA 8–279
Moyes v. Lothian Health Board, 1990 S.L.T. 444, OH 12–213
Muirhead v. Industrial Tank Specialities Ltd; Muirhead v. ITT (U.K.) Ltd;
Muirhead v. Leroy Somer Electric Motors Ltd [1986] Q.B. 507; [1985] 3
W.L.R. 993; [1985] 3 All E.R. 705; [1986] E.C.C. 225; (1986) 83 L.S.G.
117; (1985) 135 N.L.J. 1106; (1985) 129 S.J. 855, CA 8–102
Mukheiber v. Raath (2000) 52 B.M.L.R. 1065, Sup Ct (SA) 12–289
Muldoon v. Mays of Lilliput Ltd [1993] 1 E.G.L.R. 43; [1993] 14 E.G. 100 9–52,
9–53, 9–62, 9–104
Muller v. Linsley & Mortimer [1996] P.N.L.R. 74; (1995) 92(3) L.S.G. 38; (1995)
139 S.J.L.B. 43; The Times, December 8, 1994, CA 10–144
Mullholland's Will Trusts, Re [1949] 1 All E.R. 46 2–136
Mullins v. Howell (1879) 11 Ch. D. 673 10–69
Munkenbeck & Marshall v. Kensington Hotel (1999) 15 Const. L.J. 231, QBD 8–4,
17–10
——— v. Regent Health & Fitness Club Ltd (No.2), 59 Con. L.R. 145, QBD
(OR) 8–159
Munro v. United Oxford Hospitals (1958) 1 B.M.J. 167 12–186
Murphy v. Brentwood D.C. [1991] 1 A.C. 398; [1990] 3 W.L.R. 414; [1990] 2 All
E.R. 908; [1990] 2 Lloyd's Rep. 467; 50 B.L.R. 1; 21 Con. L.R. 1; (1990)
22 H.L.R. 502; 89 L.G.R. 24; (1991) 3 Admin. L.R. 37; (1990) 6 Const. L.J.
304; (1990) 154 L.G. Rev. 1010; (1990) 87(30) L.S.G. 15; (1990) 134 S.J.
1076; The Times, July 27, 1990; The Independent, July 27, 1990, HL 2–18, 2–28,
2–39, 2–40, 2–42, 2–43, 2–46, 2–50, 2–52, 2–56, 2–59, 2–62, 2–66,
2–71, 2–77, 2–103, 5–19, 5–24, 5–26, 5–52, 8–51, 8–60, 8–61,
8–62, 8–69, 8–70, 8–74, 8–75, 8–80, 8–81, 8–84, 8–85, 8–86,
8–89, 8–93, 8–91, 8–94, 8–96, 8–97, 88–98, 8–102, 8–112,
8–115, 8–119, 8–120, 8–124, 8–125, 8–122, 8–123, 8–124,
8–205, 8–277, 8–325, 9–34, 9–37, 10–40, 10–42, 10–48, 12–289,
15–45, 15–50
——— v. Wirral Health Authority [1996] 7 Med.L.R. 99, QBD 12–113
Murray v. Lloyd [1989] 1 W.L.R. 1060; [1990] 2 All E.R. 92; (1989) 21 H.L.R.
525; [1990] 1 E.G.L.R. 274; (1989) 86(41) L.S.G. 36; (1989) 139 N.L.J.
938; (1989) 133 S.J. 1405; The Times, June 27,1989, Ch D 10–273
——— v. MacQuarie Bank Ltd (1992) 105 A.L.R. 612, Fed Ct (Aus) 10–31
——— v. McMurchy [1949] 2 D.L.R. 443 12–126
——— v. Yorkshire Fund Managers Ltd [1998] 1 W.L.R. 951; [1998] 2 All E.R.
1015; [1998] F.S.R. 372; (1998) 95(3) L.S.G. 24; (1998) 95(4) L.S.G. 33;
(1998) 142 S.J.L.B. 45; The Times, December 18, 1997, CA 2–155, 2–158
Murray Bourne Dyck v. FMA Farm Management Associates Ltd (1996) 3
W.W.R. 509 .... 15–91, 15–144
Mutual Life & Citizens Assurance Co. v. Evatt [1971] A.C. 793; [1971] 2 W.L.R.
23; [1971] 1 All E.R. 150; [1970] 2 Lloyd's Rep. 441; 114 S.J. 932; [1969]
1 Lloyd's Rep. 535; (1968) 42 A.L.J.R. 316; (1968) 122 C.L.R. 556; The
Times, November 17, 1970, HC (Aus) 9–38
Mutual Reinsurance Co. Ltd v. Peat Marwick Mitchell & Co.; sub nom. Mutual
Reinsurance Co. Ltd v. KPMG Peat Marwick [1997] 1 Lloyd's Rep. 253;
[1996] B.C.C. 1010; [1997] 1 B.C.L.C. 1; [1997] P.N.L.R. 75; The Times,
October 15, 1996, CA 15–24
Muzio v. North West Herts H.A. [1995] 6 Med. L.R. 184, QBD 12–192
Myers v. Elman; sub nom. Myers v. Rothfield [1940] A.C. 282, HL 10–126
——— v. Thompson & London Life Insurance Co. (1967) 63 D.L.R. (2d) 476 14–14

PARA.

N v. Agrawal; *sub nom.* N, Re [1999] Lloyd's Rep. Med. 257; [1999] P.N.L.R.
939; *The Times*, June 9, 1999, CA 12–66

—— v. Warrington H.A., March 9, 2000, unreported, CA 12–298

NHS Trust A v. M; NHS Trust B v. H [2001] Fam. 348; [2001] 2 W.L.R. 942;
[2001] 1 All E.R. 801; [2001] 2 F.L.R. 367; [2001] 1 F.C.R. 406; [2001]
H.R.L.R. 12; [2001] Lloyd's Rep. Med. 28; (2001) 58 B.M.L.R. 87; [2001]
Fam. Law 501; *The Times*, November 29, 2000; *The Daily Telegraph*,
October 31, 2000, Fam Div 7–58, 12–147

NM Rothschild & Sons Ltd v. Berenson; *sub nom.* Rothschild & Sons Ltd v.
Berenson [1997] N.P.C. 15, CA; reversing [1995] N.P.C. 107; (1995) 70 P.
& C.R. D45, Ch D 10–42

Nadeau v. Rice (1990) 109 N.B.R. (2d) 243, CA (New Brunswick) 10–103

Nadreph Ltd v. Willmett & Co.; *sub nom.* Nadreth v. Willmett & Co. [1978] 1
W.L.R. 1537; [1978] 1 All E.R. 746; 122 S.J. 744, Ch D 10–252

Naish v. Thorp Wright & Puxon [1998] C.L.Y. 4024 11–39

Napier, Lord and Ettrick v. RF Kershaw Ltd (No.1); Lord Napier and Ettrick v.
Hunter [1993] A.C. 713; [1993] 2 W.L.R. 42; [1993] 1 All E.R. 385; [1993]
1 Lloyd's Rep. 197; (1993) 137 S.J.L.B. 44; *The Times*, December 16, 1992;
The Independent, December 11, 1992, HL 16–74

Nash v. Eli Lilly & Co. [1993] 1 W.L.R. 782; [1993] 4 All E.R. 383; [1992] 3
Med.L.R. 353; *The Times*, October 7, 1992, CA 5–57, 5–61, 5–62, 5–65

—— v. Evens & Matta [1988] 1 E.G.L.R. 130; [1988] 04 E.G. 131 9–97

—— v. Phillips (1974) 232 E.G. 1219, Ch D 10–100, 10–158, 10–235, 10–258,
10–264

National Bank of Greece S.A. v. Pinios Shipping Co. (No.1); *sub nom.* Pinios
Shipping Co. v. National Bank of Greece S.A. [1990] 1 A.C. 637; [1989] 3
W.L.R. 1330; [1990] 1 All E.R. 78; [1990] 1 Lloyd's Rep. 225; [1988] 2
F.T.L.R. 9; [1988] Fin. L.R. 249; [1990] C.C.L.R. 18; (1990) 87(4) L.S.G.
33; (1989) 139 N.L.J. 1711; (1990) 134 S.J. 261; *The Times*, December 1,
1989; *The Independent*, December 6, 1989; *Financial Times*, December 5,
1989, HL 2–104

National Health Service Trust v. D [2000] 2 F.L.R. 677; [2000] 2 F.C.R. 577;
[2000] Lloyd's Rep. Med. 411; (2000) 55 B.M.L.R. 19; [2000] Fam. Law
803; *The Times*, July 19, 2000, Fam Div 7–41, 7–56

National Home Loans Corp. plc v. Giffen Couch & Archer (a firm) [1998] 1
W.L.R. 207 .... 10–206, 10–214, 10–211, 10–212

National Insurance and Guarantee Corporation v. Imperio Reinsurance Co. (U.K.)
Ltd [1999] Lloyd's Rep I.R. 249 .... 14–43, 14–53, 14–95, 14–127

National Justice Compania Naviera S.A. v. Prudential Assurance Co. Ltd; Ikarian
Reefer, The (No.1) [1995] 1 Lloyd's Rep. 455, CA; reversing [1993] 2
Lloyd's Rep. 68; [1993] F.S.R. 563; [1993] 37 E.G. 158; *The Times*, March
5, 1993, QBD (Comm Ct) 6–14, 9–06

National Mutual Life Association of Australasia Ltd v. Coffey & Partners Pty. Ltd
[1991] 1 Qd.R. 401, CA (Queensland) 8–120

National Mutual v. Sentry (1989) A.L.R. 539, Fed Ct (Aus) 10–31

National Oilwell (U.K.) Ltd v. Davy Offshore Ltd [1993] 2 Lloyd's Rep. 582,
QBD (Comm Ct) 8–128, 8–322

National Westminster Bank plc v. Morgan [1985] A.C. 686; [1985] 2 W.L.R. 588;
[1985] 1 All E.R. 821; [1985] F.L.R. 266; (1985) 17 H.L.R. 360; (1985) 82
L.S.G. 1485; (1985) 135 N.L.J. 254; (1985) 129 S.J. 205, HL 2–145

Nationwide Anglia Building Society v. Lewis [1998] Ch. 482; [1998] 2 W.L.R.
915; [1998] 3 All E.R. 143; *The Times*, March 6, 1998; *The Independent*,
March 9, 1998 (C.S.), CA 10–147

—— v. Various Solicitors (No.1) [1999] P.N.L.R. 52; (1998) 95(6) L.S.G. 24;
(1998) 148 N.L.J. 241; (1998) 142 S.J.L.B. 78; *The Times*, February 5, 1998,
Ch D 10–145

PARA.

Nationwide Building Society v. Archdeacons [1999] Lloyd's Rep. P.N. 549, Ch
D 10–209, 10–325
—— v. ATM Abdullah & Co. [1999] Lloyd's Rep. P.N. 616, Ch D 10–209, 10–215,
10–296, 10–326
—— v. Balmer Radmore [1999] Lloyd's Rep. P.N. 241; [1999] Lloyd's Rep. P.N.
558, Ch D 3–13, 10–24, 10–325
—— v. Goodwin Harte [1999] Lloyd's Rep. P.N. 338, Ch D 10–24, 10–214, 10–325
—— v. J. R. Jones [1999] Lloyd's Rep. P.N. 414 ...... 10–209,10–214, 10–296, 10–325
—— v. Littlestone & Cowan [1999] Lloyd's Rep. P.N. 625, Ch D 10–209, 10–216,
10–325
—— v. Richard Grosse & Co. [1999] Lloyd's Rep. P.N. 348, Ch D 10–24, 10–214,
10–325
—— v. Thimbleby & Co. [1999] Lloyd's Rep. P.N. 359; [1999] P.N.L.R. 733;
[1999] E.G.C.S. 34; [1999] N.P.C. 29; The Independent, March 15, 1999
(C.S.), Ch D 10–327, 13–100
—— v. Vanderpump & Sykes [1999] Lloyd's Rep. P.N. 422, Ch D 10–24, 10–209,
10–214, 10–325
—— v. Various Solicitors (No.3); Nationwide Building Society v. Singh &
Garland Wells; Nationwide Building Society v. Richard Grosse & Co.;
Nationwide Building Society v. Archdeacons; Nationwide Building Society
v. Waters & Co.; Nationwide Building Society v. JR Jones; Nationwide
Building Society v. Borm Reid & Co.; Nationwide Building Society v.
Adams Delmar; Nationwide Building Society v. Littlestone & Cowan;
Nationwide Building Society v. Goodwin Harte; Nationwide Building Society v. Vanderpump & Sykes; Nationwide Building Society v. ATM Abdullah
& Co.; Nationwide Building Society v. Balmer Radmore [1999] P.N.L.R.
606; [1999] E.G.C.S. 15; (1999) 96(9) L.S.G. 31; (1999) 143 S.J.L.B. 58;
[1999] N.P.C. 15; The Times, March 1, 1999, Ch D 10–24, 10–35, 10–206,
10–209, 10–212, 10–214, 10–215,, 10–216, 10–231, 10–296,
10–327
—— v. Various Solicitors (No.4) [1999] C.P.L.R. 606; [2000] Lloyd's Rep. P.N.
71; The Independent, October 25, 1999 (C.S.), Ch D 6–05
Nawoor v. Barking Havering and Brentwood H.A. [1998] Lloyd's Rep. Med.
313, QBD 12–72
Naylor v. Preston A.H.A.; Foster v. Merton and Sutton H.A.; Thomas v. North
West Surrey H.A.; Ikumelo v. Newham H.A. [1987] 1 W.L.R. 958; [1987]
2 All E.R. 353; (1987) 84 L.S.G. 1494; (1987) 137 N.L.J. 474; (1987) 131
S.J. 596, CA 12–221
Needler Financial Services v. Taber, The Times, August 9, 2001, Ch D 13–165
Neigel v. France [1997] E.H.R.L.R. 424 7–06
Neighbour v. Barker [1992] 40 E.G. 140; [1992] E.G.C.S. 85; [1992] N.P.C. 76,
CA 10–196
Neill v. Crown Prosecution Service; sub nom. Neill v. DPP (1997) 161 J.P. 153;
[1997] C.O.D. 171; (1997) 161 J.P.N. 110; The Times, January 8, 1997,
QBD 10–139
Neisner-Kratt Enterprises v. Building Design 2 (1988) 39 Business Law Reports
98 8–138
Nelson Guarantee Corp. Ltd v. Hodgson [1958] N.Z.L.R. 609 .... 5–114, 15–18, 15–31,
15–91, 15–148
Nelson v. Nelson [1997] 1 W.L.R. 233; [1997] 1 All E.R. 970; [1997] B.P.I.R.
702; [1997] P.N.L.R. 413; (1997) 94(2) L.S.G. 26; (1997) 147 N.L.J. 126;
(1997) 141 S.J.L.B. 30; The Times, January 8, 1997, CA 10–75
—— v. Rye and Cocteau Records Ltd [1996] 1 W.L.R. 1378; [1996] 2 All E.R.
186; [1996] E.M.L.R. 37; [1996] F.S.R. 313; The Times, December 5, 1995,
Ch D 5–88, 5–90, 5–91, 5–100
—— v. Spooner (1861) 2 F. & F. 613, NP 8–198

PARA.

Nemer v. Whitford (1983) 33 S.A.S.R. 208 8–316
Neodox Ltd v. Borough of Swindon Pendlebury (1958) 5 B.L.R. 34 .... 8–229, 8–230
Nestle v. Best [1996] P.N.L.R. 444, CA 10–109, 11–41
Nettleship v. Weston [1971] 2 Q.B. 691; [1971] 3 W.L.R. 370; [1971] 3 All E.R.
    581; [1971] R.T.R. 425; 115 S.J. 624, CA 2–118
Neumeister v. Austria (No.1); Series A, No.8; (1979–80) 1 E.H.R.R. 91,
    ECHR 7–11
Neushul v. Mellish & Harkavy, 203 E.G. 27; 117 N.L.J. 546; (1967) 111 S.J. 399,
    CA 10–01, 10–55, 10–102, 10–171
New Forty-Four Mines Ltd v. St. Paul Fire & Marine Insurance Co. (1987) 78
    A.R. 364, CA (Alberta) 14–46
New Hampshire Insurance Co. Ltd v. MGN Ltd (1996); Maxwell Communication
    Corp. plc (In Administration) v. New Hampshire Insurance Co. Ltd [1997]
    L.R.L.R. 24; [1996] C.L.C. 1728, CA 14–49, 14–117
New Islington and Hackney Housing Association Ltd v. Pollard Thomas and
    Edwards Ltd [2001] B.L.R. 74; [2001] Lloyd's Rep. P.N. 243; [2001]
    P.N.L.R. 20; (2001) 17 Const. L.J. 55, QBD (T&CC) 5–15, 5–21, 5–25, 5–26,
                                                                 5–27, 5–34, 5–55, 8–38
New Zealand Shipping Co. Ltd v. AM Satterthwaite & Co. Ltd; Eurymedon, The;
    sub nom. AM Satterthwaite & Co. Ltd v. New Zealand Shipping Co. Ltd
    [1975] A.C. 154; [1974] 2 W.L.R. 865; [1974] 1 All E.R. 1015; [1974] 1
    Lloyd's Rep. 534; 118 S.J. 387; [1971] 2 Lloyd's Rep. 399; [1972] N.Z.L.R.
    385, PC (NZ) 5–07
New Zealand Social Credit Political League Inc. v. O'Brien [1984] 1 N.Z.L.R.
    84, CA (NZ) 10–62
Newbury International Ltd v. Reliance National Insurance Co. (U.K.) and Tyser
    Special Risks [1994] 1 Lloyd's Rep. 83, QBD (Comm Ct) 14–61, 14–99
Newbury v. Bath D.H.A. (1998) 47 B.M.L.R. 138, QBD 12–92, 12–188, 12–195,
                                                         12–213, 12–254, 12–262, 12–263
Newcastle Building Society v. Paterson Robertson & Graham [2001] P.N.L.R.
    780, OH 10–295
Newell v. Goldenberg [1995] 6 Med. L.R. 371, QBD 12–100, 12–230, 12–279
Newen, Re; sub nom. Carruthers v. Newen [1903] 1 Ch. 812; 47 S.J. 300; 72
    L.J.Ch. 356; 88 L.T. 264; 51 W.R. 297; 19 T.L.R. 247, Ch D 10–189
Newham L.B.C. v. Taylor Woodrow (1982) 19 B.L.R. 99, CA 8–139
Newman v. Phillips Fox (1999) 21 W.A.R. 309, Sup Ct 10–31
Newsome v. Bennie S. Cohen & Son (Qld) Pty. Ltd [1941] Q.S.R. 270 14–43
Newton v. Newton's Model Laundry Ltd, The Times, November 3, 1959 12–178
Niagara Frontier Caterers Ltd. v. Continental Insurance Co. of Canada (1990) 74
    O.R. (2d) 191, HC (Ontario) 14–46
Nickolls v. Ministry of Health, The Times, February 4, 1955, CA 12–78
Nielsen v. Watson (1982) 125 D.L.R. 326, HC (Ontario) 10–194
Niemietz v. Germany; Series A, No.251B; (1993) 16 E.H.R.R. 97, ECHR 7–34
Nikolaou v. Papasavas Phillips & Co. (1989) 82 A.L.R. 617, HC (Aus) 10–278,
                                                                 10–283, 10–287
Nishimatsu-Costain-China Harbour Joint Venture v. Ip Kwan & Co. [2001]
    H.K.L.R.D. 84, CA (HK) 10–33, 10–103
Nitrigin Eireann Teoranta v. Inco Alloys Ltd [1992] 1 W.L.R. 498; [1992] 1 All
    E.R. 854; 60 B.L.R. 65; (1992) 89(3) L.S.G. 34; (1991) 141 N.L.J. 1518;
    [1991] N.P.C. 17; The Times, November 4, 1991; The Independent, Novem-
    ber 28, 1991, QBD 2–16, 5–16, 8–82, 8–102
Nocton v. Lord Ashburton [1914] A.C. 932; [1914–15] All E.R. Rep. 45,
    HL 2–100, 2–126, 2–172, 3–11, 5–94, 10–13, 10–18, 10–149, 10–226
Noel v. Lewis Holdings Ltd (1990) 44 B.C.L.R. (2d) 37, CA (BC) 10–191
Noranda Australia Ltd v. Lachlan Resources N.L. (1988) 13 N.S.W.L.R. 1 2–128
Norberg v. Wynrib (1992) 92 D.L.R. (4th) 449 .... 2–133, 12–29

PARA.

Nordic Holdings Ltd v. Mott MacDonald Ltd., July 27, 2001, unreported 8–138,
8–271, 8–293
Norfolk and Norwich Healthcare NHS Trust v. W [1996] 2 F.L.R. 613; [1997] 1
F.C.R. 269; (1997) 34 B.M.L.R. 16; [1997] Fam. Law 17, Fam Div 12–139,
12–141
North & South Trust Co. v. Berkeley; sub nom. Berkeley v. North & South Trust
Co. [1971] 1 W.L.R. 470; [1971] 1 All E.R. 980; [1970] 2 Lloyd's Rep. 467;
(1970) 115 S.J. 244, QBD (Comm Ct) 2–140, 14–03
North American Land & Timber Co. Ltd v. Watkins [1904] 2 Ch. 233, CA;
affirming [1904] 1 Ch. 242, Ch D 5–93
North Eastern Cooperative Society v. Newcastle Upon Tyne City Council [1987]
1 E.G.L.R. 142; (1987) 282 E.G. 1409 9–74
North West Metropolitan Regional Hospital Board v. TA Bickerton & Son; sub
nom. Bickerton & Son v. North West Metropolitan Regional Hospital Board
[1970] 1 W.L.R. 607, HL; affirming [1969] 1 All E.R. 977; 67 L.G.R. 83;
112 S.J. 922, CA 8–20
North West Water Authority v. Binnie [1990] 3 All E.R. 547; 30 Con. L.R. 136,
QBD 8–82
North Western Rail Co. v. Sharp; sub nom. London & North Western Rail Co. v.
Sharp (1854) 10 Exch. 451; 3 C.L.R. 52; 24 L.J.Exch. 44; 24 L.T.(O.S.) 82;
18 Jur. 964; 156 E.R. 514; 3 W.R. 12 10–192
Northern Developments (Cumbria) Ltd v. J&J Nichol [2000] B.L.R. 158; (2000)
2 T.C.L.R. 261, QBD (T&CC) 8–338
Northern Rock Building Society v. Archer; Archer v. Hickmotts [1999] Lloyd's
Rep. Bank. 32; (1999) 78 P. & C.R. 65; [1998] N.P.C. 132, CA 6–08, 10–142,
10–205
Northumberland Insurance Ltd v. Alexander (1984) 8 A.C.L.R. 882; (1988) 13
A.C.L.R. 170 15–121
Norton v. Relly (1764) 2 Eden 286 2–143
Norwest Refrigeration Services Pty. Ltd v. Bain Dawes (W.A.) Pty. Ltd (1984) 55
A.L.R. 509, HC (Aus) 14–74
Norwich City Council v. Harvey (Paul Clarke) [1989] 1 W.L.R. 828; [1989] 1 All
E.R. 1180; 45 B.L.R. 14; (1989) 5 Const. L.J. 154; (1989) 86(25) L.S.G. 45;
(1989) 139 N.L.J. 40; (1989) 133 S.J. 694; The Times, January 11, 1989; The
Independent, January 16, 1989 (C.S.); The Independent, January 6, 1989,
CA 8–128
Norwich Union Life Insurance Society v. Qureshi. See Aldrich v. Norwich Union
Life Insurance Co. Ltd (formerly Norwich Union Life Insurance Society).
Nottidge v. Prince (1860) 2 Giff. 246 2–143
Nottingham Community Housing Association Ltd v. Powerminster Ltd [2000]
B.L.R. 309; (2000) 2 T.C.L.R. 678; 75 Con. L.R. 65; (2000) 16 Const. L.J.
449, QBD (T&CC) 8–340
Nova Scotia Home for Coloured Children v. Avramovitch (1983) 58 N.S.R. (2d)
267 8–205
Nwabueze v. General Medical Council [2000] 1 W.L.R. 1760; (2000) 56
B.M.L.R. 106; The Times, April 11, 2000, PC (UK) 7–67
Nyckeln Finance Co. Ltd (In Administration) v. Edward Symmons & Partners
(No.2) [1999] Lloyd's Rep. P.N. 953, CA 9–102
Nyckeln Finance Co. Ltd v. Stumpbrook Continuation Ltd [1994] 33 E.G. 93;
[1994] 2 E.G.L.R. 143, QBD 9–172
Nye Saunders & Partners v. AE Bristow (1987) 37 B.L.R. 92, CA 8–145, 8–180,
8–195, 8–198, 8–199, 8–302, 8–316
Nykredit Mortgage Bank plc v. Edward Erdman Group Ltd. Also see South
Australia Asset Management Corp. v. York Montague Ltd.
—— v. Edward Erdman Group Ltd, October 1, 1993 unreported 9–112, 9–113, 9–159,
9–165

PARA.

Nykredit Mortgage Bank plc v. Edward Erdman Group Ltd [1996] 1 E.G.L.R.
119 9–53
—— v. Edward Erdman Group Ltd (No.2) [1997] 1 W.L.R. 1627; [1998] 1 All
E.R. 305; [1998] Lloyd's Rep. Bank. 39; [1998] C.L.C. 116; [1998] 1 Costs
L.R. 108; [1998] P.N.L.R. 197; [1998] 1 E.G.L.R. 99; [1998] 05 E.G. 150;
(1998) 95(1) L.S.G. 24; (1998) 142 S.J.L.B. 29; [1997] N.P.C. 165; (1998)
75 P. & C.R. D28; *The Times*, December 3, 1997, HL 3–04, 3–19, 5–36, 5–37,
5–41, 5–42, 5–47, 9–09, 9–21, 9–61, 9–115, 9–161, 9–162, 9–163,
9–165, 10–295

O (A Minor) (Costs: Liability of Legal Aid Board), Re; *sub nom.* O (A Minor)
(Legal Aid Costs), Re [1997] 1 F.L.R. 465; [1997] Fam. Law 242; *The
Times*, November 25, 1996, CA 10–133, 10–136
O (A Minor) (Medical Treatment), Re [1993] 2 F.L.R. 149; [1993] 1 F.C.R. 925;
[1993] 4 Med. L.R. 272; [1993] Fam. Law 454; (1993) 157 L.G. Rev. 165;
(1993) 137 S.J.L.B. 107; *The Times*, March 19, 1993, Fam Div 12–148
O&R Jewellers Ltd v. Terry [1999] Lloyd's Rep. I.R. 436, QBD 14–64, 14–111
Oakes v. Hopcroft [2000] Lloyd's Rep. Med. 394; (2000) 56 B.M.L.R. 136;
[2000] Lloyd's Rep. P.N. 946; *The Independent*, October 30, 2000 (C.S),
CA 5–13, 5–54
Oates v. Anthony Pittman & Co. [1998] P.N.L.R. 683; (1998) 76 P. & C.R. 490;
[1998] E.G.C.S. 82, CA 10–272, 10–269, 10–274
—— v. Harte Reade & Co. [1999] 1 F.L.R. 1221; [1999] P.I.Q.R. P120; [1999]
Lloyd's Rep. P.N. 215; [1999] P.N.L.R. 763; [1999] Fam. Law 383,
QBD 10–312
O'Bonswain v. Paradis [1994] 5 Med.L.R. 399, HC (Ontario) 12–127
O'Brien v. Hooker Homes (1993) A.S.C. 56–217, Sup Ct (NSW) 10–170, 10–199
—— v. Hughes-Gibb & Co. Ltd [1995] L.R.L.R. 90 .... 14–12, 14–54
O'Connor v. BDB Kirby & Co.; *sub nom.* O'Connor v. DBD Kirby & Co. [1972]
1 Q.B. 90; [1971] 2 W.L.R. 1233; [1971] 2 All E.R. 1415; [1971] 1 Lloyd's
Rep. 454; [1971] R.T.R. 440; 115 S.J. 267, CA 14–32, 14–72, 14–90, 14–91
—— v. First National [1991] I.R.L.M. 208 10–203
—— v. Foley [1905] 1 I.R. 1 2–144
O'Donovan v. Cork County Council [1967] I.R. 173, Sup Ct (Irl) 12–75, 12–95,
12–100
O'Driscoll v. Dudley H.A. [1998] Lloyd's Rep. Med. 210, CA 5–58
Official Assignee of Collier v. Creighton [1993] 2 N.Z.L.R. 534, CA (NZ) 10–21
Ogden & Co. Pty. Ltd v. Reliance Fire Sprinkler Co. Pty. Ltd [1975] 1 Lloyd's
Rep. 52, Sup Ct (Aus) 14–10, 14–14, 14–66, 14–73
Okafor v. Malcolm Slowe & Co. (1968) 207 E.G. 345 10–124
Oksuzoglu v. Kay [1998] 2 All E.R. 361; [1998] Lloyd's Rep. Med. 129; (1998)
42 B.M.L.R. 43; *The Times*, February 26, 1998, CA 12–245
Old Gate Estates Ltd v. Toplis and Harding and Russell [1939] 3 All E.R. 209 9–32,
9–102
Oldschool v. Gleeson (Construction) Ltd (1976) 4 B.L.R. 103, QBD 8–131, 8–249
Oliver v. McKenna & Co, *The Times*, December 20 1995, Ch D 10–109
Oliver, Derksen Arkin v. Fulmyk (1995) 126 D.L.R. (4th) 123, CA (Maniba) 10–31
Olley v. Marlborough Court Ltd [1949] 1 K.B. 532; [1949] 1 All E.R. 127; 65
T.L.R. 95; [1949] L.J.R. 360; 93 S.J. 40, CA 9–73
O'Malley-Williams v. The Board of Governors of the National Hospital for
Nervous Diseases (1975) 1 B.M.J. 635 .... 12–119, 12–213, 12–227
Omega Trust Co. Ltd v. Wright Son & Pepper (No.1) [1997] P.N.L.R. 424; (1998)
75 P. & C.R. 57; [1997] 1 E.G.L.R. 120; [1997] 18 E.G. 120; [1996] N.P.C.
189; (1997) 73 P. & C.R. D39, CA 5–07, 9–39, 9–63, 9–71

PARA.

Omega Trust Co. Ltd v. Wright Son & Pepper (No.2) [1998] P.N.L.R. 337,
 QBD 9–172, 10–211, 10–217, 10–325
Ontario Ltd v. Gambin Associates (1999) 29 R.P.R. (3d) 210, CA (Ontario) 10–268
Opat v. National Mutual Life Association of Australasia Ltd [1992] 1 V.R.
 283 8–120
O'Reilly v. Whittington Hospital NHS Trust, March 17, 2000, QBD 12–18, 12–244
Orchard v. South Eastern Electricity Board [1987] Q.B. 565; [1987] 2 W.L.R.
 102; [1987] 1 All E.R. 95; (1986) 130 S.J. 956, CA 10–131, 10–135, 10–179,
 11–07
Ormindale Holdings Ltd v. Ray, Wolfe, Connel, Lightbody & Reynolds (1981)
 116 D.L.R. (3d) 346; (1982) 135 D.L.R. (3d) 557, CA (BC) 10–96, 10–152
Osman v. J Ralph Moss [1970] 1 Lloyd's Rep. 313, CA 10–303, 14–14, 14–77, 14–81,
 14–122
—— v. United Kingdom [1999] 1 F.L.R. 193; (2000) 29 E.H.R.R. 245; 5
 B.H.R.C. 293; (1999) 1 L.G.L.R. 431; (1999) 11 Admin. L.R. 200; [1999]
 Crim. L.R. 82; [1998] H.R.C.D. 966; [1999] Fam. Law 86; (1999) 163 J.P.N.
 297; The Times, November 5, 1998, ECHR 7–06, 7–19, 7–20, 7–21, 7–23, 7–29,
 7–40, 7–52, 15–89
Ostby v. Bondar [1998] 61 Alta. L.R. 341, QBD (Alberta) 12–203, 12–232
Oswald v. Countrywide Surveyors Ltd [1994] E.G.C.S. 150 9–108
—— v. Countrywide Surveyors Ltd, 50 Con. L.R. 1; [1996] 2 E.G.L.R. 104;
 [1996] 37 E.G. 140; [1996] E.G.C.S. 100, CA 9–91
Otago Cheese Co. Ltd v. Nick Stoop Builders Ltd, May 1992, unreported 8–122
Otter v. Church, Adams, Tatham & Co. [1953] Ch. 280; [1953] 1 W.L.R. 156;
 [1953] 1 All E.R. 168; 97 S.J. 48, Ch D 10–151, 10–257, 10–264, 15–133
Ottley v. Gilbey (1845) 8 Beav. 602; 14 L.J.Ch. 177; 4 L.T.(O.S.) 411; 50 E.R.
 237 10–179
Outwing Construction Ltd v. H Randell & Son Ltd [1999] B.L.R. 156; 64 Con.
 L.R. 59; (1999) 15 Const. L.J. 308, QBD (T&CC) 8–337
Ouwens v. Ace Builders Pty. Ltd (1989) 52 S.A.S.R. 344, Sup Ct (Aus) 10–79
Overseas Tankship (U.K.) Ltd v. Miller Steamship Co. Pty Ltd; Wagon Mound,
 The (No.2); sub nom. Miller Steamship Co. Pty Ltd v. Overseas Tankship
 (U.K.) Ltd; RW Miller & Co. Pty Ltd v. Overseas Tankship (U.K.) Ltd
 [1967] 1 A.C. 617; [1966] 3 W.L.R. 498; [1966] 2 All E.R. 709; [1966] 1
 Lloyd's Rep. 657; 110 S.J. 447, PC (Aus) 8–210
Owen v. Fielding [1998] E.G.C.S. 110, Ch D 10–255, 10–268
Owners of Cargo Laden on Board the Albacruz v. Owners of the Albazero;
 Albacruz, The and Albazero, The; sub nom. Concord Petroleum Corp. v.
 Gosford Marine Panama S.A. [1977] A.C. 774; [1976] 3 W.L.R. 419; [1976]
 3 All E.R. 129; [1976] 2 Lloyd's Rep. 467; 120 S.J. 570, HL 16–72
Owners of Liesbosch Dredger v. Owners of Steamship Edison. See Liesbosch,
 The.
Oxford University (t/a Oxford University Press) v. John Stedman Design Group
 (1991) 7 Const. L.J. 102, QBD (OR) 11–43
Oxford University Fixed Assets Ltd v. Architects Design Partnership (1999) 64
 Con.L.R. 13 .... 8–255, 8–321
Oxford University Press v. John Stedman Design Group (1990) 34 Con.L.R. 1 8–324
Oxley v. Penwarden [2001] C.P.L.R. 1; [2001] Lloyd's Rep. Med. 347, CA 6–15

P (a Barrister) (Wasted Costs Order), Re, The Times, July 23 2001, CA 11–28
P v. St James and Seacroft University Hospital NHS Trust [2001] EWCA Civ
 560; [2001] 3 W.L.R. 376; [2001] 3 All E.R. 97; [2001] 2 F.L.R. 401; [2001]
 P.I.Q.R. Q12; [2001] Lloyd's Rep. Med. 309; (2001) 98(22) L.S.G. 35;
 (2001) 145 S.J.L.B. 118; The Times, April 24, 2001; The Daily Telegraph,
 April 17, 2001, CA 2–53, 5–13, 12–294

PARA.

P&M Kaye Ltd v. Hosier & Dickinson Ltd; *sub nom.* Hosier & Dickinson v. P&M Kaye [1972] 1 W.L.R. 146, HL; affirming [1970] 1 W.L.R. 1611; [1971] 1 All E.R. 301; 114 S.J. 929, CA 8–14, 8–253, 8–255

P&O Developments Ltd v. Guy's & St Thomas NHS Trust; Guy's & St Thomas NHS Trust v. P&O Developments Ltd [1999] B.L.R. 3; 62 Con. L.R. 38; (1999) 15 Const. L.J. 374, QBD (T&CC) 8–327

PCW (Underwriting Agencies) Ltd v. Dixon (PS) [1983] 2 All E.R. 697 (Note), CA; affirming [1983] 2 All E.R. 158; [1983] 2 Lloyd's Rep. 197, QBD 13–146

PCW Syndicates v. PCW Reinsurers [1996] 1 W.L.R. 1136; [1996] 1 All E.R. 774; [1996] 1 Lloyd's Rep. 241; *The Times*, October 10, 1995; *The Independent*, September 8, 1995; Lloyd's List, December 7, 1995 (I.D.), CA 14–19

PK Finans International (U.K.) v. Andrew Downs & Co. [1992] 1 E.G.L.R. 172; [1992] 24 E.G. 138

PS Refson & Co. Ltd v. Saggers; Exclusivity Horlogere Ltd v. Peoples Jewellers Ltd; Whittaker v. Jolley [1984] 1 W.L.R. 1025; [1984] 3 All E.R. 111; (1984) 81 L.S.G. 975; (1984) 128 S.J. 152, Ch D 10–68

Pacific Acceptance Corp. Ltd v. Forsyth [1970] 92 W.N. (N.S.W.) 29 .... 15–18, 15–33, 15–91, 15–92, 15–94, 15–95, 15–96, 15–97, 15–103, 15–105, 15–107, 15–110, 15–111, 15–112, 15–115, 15–147, 15–153

Pacific Associates v. Baxter [1990] 1 Q.B. 993; [1989] 3 W.L.R. 1150; [1989] 2 All E.R. 159; 44 B.L.R. 33; 16 Con. L.R. 90; (1989) 139 N.L.J. 41; (1989) 133 S.J. 123; *The Times*, December 28, 1988; *The Independent*, January 6, 1989, CA 2–61, 2–96, 8–105, 8–108, 8–109, 8–110, 8–121, 8–127, 8–258

Padhiar v. Patel [2001] Lloyd's Rep. P.N. 328, QBD 10–126, 10–134

Page v. A Solicitor (1971) 20 D.L.R. 532, CA (New Brunswick), aff'd 29 D.L.R. 386 10–286

—— v. Smith [1996] A.C. 155; [1995] 2 W.L.R. 644; [1995] 2 All E.R. 736; [1995] 2 Lloyd's Rep. 95; [1995] R.T.R. 210; [1995] P.I.Q.R. P329; (1995) 92(23) L.S.G. 33; (1995) 145 N.L.J. 723; (1995) 139 S.J.L.B. 173; *The Times*, May 12, 1995; *The Independent*, May 12, 1995; Lloyd's List, May 25, 1995 (I.D.), HL 12–22, 12–35, 12–283

Paimano v. Raiss; *sub nom.* Raiss v. Paimano; Palmano v. Raiss [2001] Lloyd's Rep. P.N. 341; [2001] P.N.L.R. 21; [2000] N.P.C. 101, QBD 12–24

Paine, Re (1912) 28 T.L.R. 201, Ch D 10–6

Painter v. Rae [1998] 127 Man. R. (2d) 133, QBD (Manitoba) 12–203, 12–264

Palacath Ltd v. Flanagan [1985] 2 All E.R. 161; [1985] 1 E.G.L.R. 86; (1985) 274 E.G. 143; (1985) 135 N.L.J. 364, QBD 2–97, 9–74

Palmer v. Durnford Ford [1992] Q.B. 483; [1992] 2 W.L.R. 407; [1992] 2 All E.R. 122; (1991) 141 N.L.J. 591; *The Times*, November 11, 1991, QBD 2–97, 10–109, 11–25

—— v. Tees H.A. (2000) 2 L.G.L.R. 69; [2000] P.I.Q.R. P1; [1999] Lloyd's Rep. Med. 351; [2000] P.N.L.R. 87; *The Times*, July 6, 1999, CA 12–37, 12–50, 12–52

Palmers Ltd v. ABB Power Construction Ltd [1999] B.L.R. 426; (2000) 2 T.C.L.R. 322; 68 Con. L.R. 52; *The Times*, October 6, 1999, QBD (T&CC) 8–339, 8–340

Pan Atlantic Insurance Co. Ltd v. Pine Top Insurance Co. Ltd [1995] 1 A.C. 501; [1994] 3 W.L.R. 677; [1994] 3 All E.R. 581; [1994] 2 Lloyd's Rep. 427; (1994) 91(36) L.S.G. 36; (1994) 144 N.L.J. 1203; (1994) 138 S.J.L.B. 182; *The Times*, July 27, 1994; *The Independent*, August 4, 1994, HL 14–61

Pangood Ltd v. Barclay Brown & Co. Ltd [1999] 1 All E.R. (Comm.) 460; [1999] Lloyd's Rep. I.R. 405; [1999] Lloyd's Rep. P.N. 237; [1999] P.N.L.R. 678, CA 14–13

—— v. Barclay Brown & Co. Ltd [1999] 1 All E.R. (Comm.) 460; [1999] Lloyd's Rep. I.R. 405; [1999] Lloyd's Rep. P.N. 237; [1999] P.N.L.R. 678, CA 2–96

Pankhurst v. Garner & Co. (1960) 25 D.L.R. (2d) 515 13–130

PARA.

Pantalone v. Alaouie (1989) 18 N.S.W.L.R. 119 8–300

Papachelas v. Greece (2000) 30 E.H.R.R. 923, ECHR 7–17

Papageorgious v. Seyl and Parkland Farm Power & Equipment Ltd (199) 45
  B.C.L.R. (2d) 319, CA (BC) 10–261

Papparis v. Charles Fulton & Co. Ltd [1981] I.R.L.R. 104 10–4

Paragon Finance plc v. Crangle & Co. [1999] E.G.C.S. 25, Ch D 10–210

—— v. Thakerar & Co.; Paragon Finance plc v. Thimbleby & Co. [1999] 1 All
  E.R. 400; (1998) 95(35) L.S.G. 36; (1998) 142 S.J.L.B. 243; *The Times*,
  August 7, 1998, CA 5–73, 5–84, 5–87, 5–88, 5–90, 5–91, 5–94, 5–95, 5–97,
  10–36, 10–229

Paragon Finance plc (formerly National Home Loans Corp. plc) v. Freshfields
  [1999] 1 W.L.R. 1183; [2000] C.P. Rep. 81; [1999] Lloyd's Rep. P.N. 446;
  (1999) 96(20) L.S.G. 40; (1999) 143 S.J.L.B. 136; [1999] N.P.C. 33; *The
  Times*, March 22, 1999; *The Independent*, March 16, 1999, CA 10–144

Park Hall School v. Overend [1987] 2 I.R. 1 .... 10–82, 10–165

Park v. Hammond (or Hammond) (1816) 6 Taunt. 495; (1816) 2 Marsh. 189; 4
  Camp. 344; 128 E.R. 1127 .... 14–35, 14–51

Parker v. Rolls (1854) 14 C.B. 691; 139 E.R. 284 .... 10–77, 10–192

Parkinson v. St James and Seacroft University Hospital NHS Trust. *See* P v. St
  James and Seacroft University Hospital NHS Trust.

—— v. West Cumberland Management Committee (1955) 1 B.M.J. 977 12–181

Parry v. Clwyd H.A. [1997] P.I.Q.R. P1; [1997] 8 Med.L.R. 243, QBD 5–58

—— v. North West H.A. [1994] 5 Med. L.R. 259, QBD 12–149, 12–181

Parry-Jones v. Law Society [1969] 1 Ch. 1; [1968] 2 W.L.R. 397; [1968] 1 All
  E.R. 177; 111 S.J. 910, CA 10–26, 10–32

Parsons v. Way and Waller (1952) 159 E.G. 524; [1952] C.P.L. 417 .... 9–92, 9–149

Partington, Re; Partington v. Allen (1887) 57 L.T. 654 .... 10–207, 10–226

Partington v. Wandsworth L.B.C. [1989] C.L.Y. 2563 12–49

Partridge v. Morris [1995] E.G.C.S. 158; [1995] C.I.L.L. 1095, QBD 8–223, 8–311

Pass, Re (1887) 35 W.R. 410, CA 10–67

Passannante v. Italy (1998) 26 E.H.R.R. C.D. 153 7–54

Patel v. Daybells (A Firm) [2001] P.N.L.R. 43 .... 10–88, 10–200, 10–275

—— v. Hooper & Jackson [1999] 1 W.L.R. 1792; [1999] 1 All E.R. 992; [1999]
  Lloyd's Rep. P.N. 1; [1998] E.G.C.S. 160; (1998) N.L.J. 1751; [1998] N.P.C.
  149; *The Times*, December 3, 1998; *The Independent*, November 18, 1998,
  CA 9–133, 9–147, 9–188, 9–189, 9–190, 9–191

Paterson v. Chadwick; *sub nom.* Paterson v. Northampton and District Hospital
  Management Committee [1974] 1 W.L.R. 890; [1974] 2 All E.R. 772; 118
  S.J. 169, QBD 5–13

Paton v. United Kingdom (App. No.8416/78) (1981) 3 E.H.R.R. 408, Eur Comm
  HR 7–41, 12–280

Pauling's Settlement Trusts, Re; *sub nom.* Younghusband v. Coutts & Co. (No.1)
  [1964] Ch. 303, CA; affirming in part [1962] 1 W.L.R. 86; [1961] 3 All E.R.
  713; 106 S.J. 135, Ch D 2–144, 5–105, 5–108

Pavey v. Ministry of Defence [1999] P.I.Q.R. P67; [1999] Lloyd's Rep. Med. 9;
  The Times, November 25, 1998; *The Independent*, November 25, 1998,
  CA 5–58

Payer v. Peerless Plating Rack Co. (1998) 37 O.R. (3d) 781, CA (Ontario) 14–12,
  14–81

Payne v. John Setchell Ltd, March 16, 2001, unreported, QBD (T&CC) 8–38, 8–46,
  8–61, 8–96, 8–101, 8–176

—— v. St Helier Group Hospital Management Committee [1952] C.L.Y. 2442 12–78,
  12–164

Peach v. Ian G Chalmers & Co., (1992) S.C.L.R. 423; [1992] 2 E.G.L.R. 135,
  OH 9–99

Peach Publishing Ltd v. Slater & Co. [1998] B.C.C. 139 .... 2–78, 15–63, 15–78, 15–79

PARA.

Peake v. Vernon & Thompson (1990) 49 B.C.L.R. (2d) 245, Sup Ct (BC) 10–61

Pearce v. United Bristol Healthcare NHS Trust [1999] E.C.C. 167; [1999]
P.I.Q.R. P53; (1999) 48 B.M.L.R. 118, CA 12–72, 12–207, 12–213, 12–217,
12–218, 12–220, 12–248, 12–263, 12–270

Pearless de Rougemont & Co. v. Pilbrow (No.2) [1999] 3 All E.R. 355; [1999]
2 Costs L.R. 109; [1999] 2 F.L.R. 139; (1999) 149 N.L.J. 441; (1999) 143
S.J.L.B. 114; *The Times*, March 25, 1999; *The Independent*, May 10, 1999
(C.S.), CA 10–8

Pearson v. Fryer, *The Times*, April 4, 2000, CA 8–156

—— v. Sanders Witherspoon (A Firm) [2000] Lloyd's Rep. P.N. 151; [2000]
P.N.L.R. 110; *The Independent*, December 6, 1999 (C.S.), CA 15–134

Pech v. Tilgals (1994) 28 A.T.R. 197 .... 15–37, 15–118, 15–143, 15–146

Peek v. Derry. *See* Derry v. Peek; *sub nom.* Peek v. Derry.

—— v. Gurney (1873) L.R. 6 H.L. 377, HL 15–77

Pegrum v. Fatharly (1996) 14 W.A.R. 92, CA (Aus) 10–05, 10–207

Pelky v. Hudson Bay Insurance Co. (1981) 35 O.R. (2d) 97, HC (Ontario) 10–179,
10–189, 10–190

Pellegrin v. France (2001) 31 E.H.R.R. 651, ECHR 7–06

Pendlebury's Ltd v. Ellis Green & Co. (1936) 80 Acct.L.R. 39 15–115

Penn v. Bristol and West Building Society; *sub nom.* Brill & Co. v. Penn [1997]
1 W.L.R. 1356, CA; affirming [1995] 2 F.L.R. 938; [1996] 2 F.C.R. 729;
[1996] Fam. Law 28; (1995) 92(27) L.S.G. 31; (1995) 139 S.J.L.B. 164; *The
Times*, June 19, 1995, Ch D 10–44, 10–53, 10–75, 10–92, 10–155

Penney v. East Kent H.A. [2000] Lloyd's Rep. Med. 41; (2000) 55 B.M.L.R. 63;
[2000] P.N.L.R. 323; (1999) 96(47) L.S.G. 32; (1999) 143 S.J.L.B. 269; *The
Times*, November 25, 1999; *The Independent*, November 24, 1999, CA 12–72,
12–116

Perini Corp. v. Commonwealth of Australia (1969) 12 B.L.R. 82, Sup Ct (NSW) 8–14,
8–233

Permanent Building Society v. Wheeler (1994) 14 A.C.S.R. 109 2–127

Permanent Trustee Australia Ltd v. Boulton [1994] 33 N.S.W.L.R. 735 10–143

Perre v. Apand Pty Ltd [1999] H.C.A. 36 2–72

Perrett v. Collins [1998] 2 Lloyd's Rep. 255; [1999] P.N.L.R. 77; *The Times*, June
23, 1998, CA 2–65, 2–67, 2–68, 2–69, 2–90, 2–91, 8–80

Perri v. Zaitman [1984] V.R. 314, Sup Ct 10–286

Perring v. Rebutter (1842) 2 M. & Rob. 429 11–10

Perruche case, November 17, 2000, Assemblée Plénierè 12–303

Perry v. Edwin Coe, *The Independent*, April 1 1994 10–155

—— v. Sidney Phillips & Son [1982] 1 W.L.R. 1297; [1982] 3 All E.R. 705; 22
B.L.R. 120; (1982) 263 E.G. 888; (1982) 79 L.S.G. 1175; 126 S.J. 626, CA;
reversing [1982] 1 All E.R. 1005; (1981) 260 E.G. 389, QBD 8–315, 9–92,
9–130, 9–131, 9–133, 9–136, 9–140, 9–184, 9–188, 9–189

—— v. Tendring D.C.; Thurbon v. Tendring D.C., 30 B.L.R. 118; 3 Con. L.R. 74;
[1985] 1 E.G.L.R. 260; (1984) 1 Const. L.J. 152; [1985] C.I.L.L. 145, QBD 5–23,
8–139, 9–10

Peter Pan Manufacturing Corp. v. Corsets Silhouette Ltd [1964] 1 W.L.R. 96;
[1963] 3 All E.R. 402; [1963] R.P.C. 45; 108 S.J. 97, Ch D 3–.1713–166

Peter Unruh Construction Company Ltd v. Kelly-Lucy & Cameron [1976] 4
W.W.R. 419, Sup Ct (Alberta) 14–46, 14–130

Petrofina (U.K.) Ltd v. Magnaload Ltd [1984] Q.B. 127; [1983] 3 W.L.R. 805;
[1983] 3 All E.R. 35; [1983] 2 Lloyd's Rep. 91; 25 B.L.R. 37; (1983) 80
L.S.G. 2677; (1983) 127 S.J. 729, QBD (Comm Ct) 8–128, 8–322

Peyman v. Lanjani [1985] Ch. 457; [1985] 2 W.L.R. 154; [1984] 3 All E.R. 703;
(1984) 48 P. & C.R. 398; (1985) 82 L.S.G. 43; (1984) 128 S.J. 853, CA 3–10,
10–196

Pfeiffer v. E&E Installations [1991] 1 E.G.L.R. 162; [1991] 22 E.G. 122, CA 8–260

PARA.

Phelps v. Hillingdon L.B.C.; *sub nom.* G (A Child), Re; Anderton v. Clwyd C.C.;
G (A Child) v. Bromley L.B.C.; Jarvis v. Hampshire C.C. [2000] 3 W.L.R.
776; [2000] 4 All E.R. 504; [2000] 3 F.C.R. 102; (2001) 3 L.G.L.R. 5;
[2000] B.L.G.R. 651; [2000] Ed. C.R. 700; [2000] E.L.R. 499; (2000) 3
C.C.L. Rep. 156; (2000) 56 B.M.L.R. 1; (2000) 150 N.L.J. 1198; (2000) 144
S.J.L.B. 241; *The Times,* July 28, 2000; *The Independent,* November 13,
2000 (C.S), HL 2–47, 2–69, 2–77, 2–82, 2–83, 2–84, 2–85, 12–27, 12–62,
12–238, 12–305
Philips v. Ward [1956] 1 W.L.R. 471; [1956] 1 All E.R. 874; 100 S.J. 317, CA 9–91,
9–127, 9–130, 9–131, 9–133, 9–134, 9–136, 9–137, 9–140, 9–141,
9–142 9–143, 9–145, 9–146, 9–147
Phillips v. Grampian Health Board [1991] 3 Med.L.R. 16 12–179
—— v. Millings (1871) 7 Ch.App. 244; 41 L.J.Ch. 211; 20 W.R. 129, LC 10–166
Phosgate Sewage Company v. Hartmount (1875) 5 Ch.D. 394 2–135
Photo Production Ltd v. Securicor Transport Ltd [1980] A.C. 827; [1980] 2
W.L.R. 283; [1980] 1 All E.R. 556; [1980] 1 Lloyd's Rep. 545; 124 S.J. 147,
HL 5–06
Pickett v. British Rail Engineering Ltd; *sub nom.* Ralph Henry Pickett
(Deceased), Re [1980] A.C. 136; [1978] 3 W.L.R. 955; [1979] 1 All E.R.
774; [1979] 1 Lloyd's Rep. 519; 122 S.J. 778, HL 9–188
Pickles v. Insurance Brokers Registration Council [1984] 1 W.L.R. 748; [1984] 1
All E.R. 1073; (1984) 81 L.S.G. 1205; 128 S.J. 365, DC 14–04
Pierre-Bloch v. France (1998) 26 E.H.R.R. 202; [1998] H.R.C.D. 14, ECHR 7–07
Pilkington v. Wood [1953] Ch. 770; [1953] 3 W.L.R. 522; [1953] 2 All E.R. 810;
97 S.J. 572, Ch D 10–158, 10–241, 10–318, 10–320, 15–152
Pimm v. Roper (1862) 2 F. & F. 783 .... 12–14, 12–303
Pine v. Solicitors Disciplinary Tribunal; *sub. nom.* In the Matter of a Solicitor,
January 11, 2001, unreported 7–65
Pinnock v. Wilkins & Sons, *The Times,* January 29, 1990, CA 3–22, 10–289
Piper v. Daybell Court-Cooper & Co. (1969) 210 E.G. 1047 ...... 10–158, 10–241, 10–268,
10–307, 10–311
Pippin v. Sheppard (1822) 11 Price 400147 E.R. 512 12–14
Pirelli General Cable Works Ltd v. Oscar Faber & Partners [1983] 2 A.C. 1;
[1983] 2 W.L.R. 6; [1983] 1 All E.R. 65; (1983) 265 E.G. 979; *The Times,*
December 11, 1982, HL 2–46, 2–103, 5–17, 5–18, 5–19, 5–20, 5–22, 5–24, 5–25,
5–26, 5–30, 5–31, 5–40, 8–51, 8–60, 8–79
Pisani v. Attorney-General of Gibraltar (1974) L.R. 5 P.C. 516 2–137
Pitman v. Francis (1884) Cab. & El. 355 10–160
Pitt v. Yalden (1767) 4 Burr. 2060 10–77
Pittman Estate v. Bain (1994) 112 D.L.R. (4th) 257 .... 12–06, 12–07, 12–12, 12–43,
12–54, 12–171
Place Co-operative Housing Association v. Burke, Tomchenko, Duprat (1994)
116 D.L.R. (4th) 657 10–65
Plant Construction plc v. Clive Adams Associates (No.2); *sub nom.* Plant Con-
struction Ltd v. JMH Construction Services Ltd [2000] B.L.R. 137; (2000)
2 T.C.L.R. 513; 69 Con. L.R. 106; *The Times,* March 1, 2000, CA 8–14, 8–251,
8–325
Plant v. Pearman (1872) 41 L.J.Q.B. 169; 26 L.T. 313; 20 W.R. 314 10–175
Platform Home Loans Ltd v. Oyston Shipways Ltd [2000] 2 A.C. 190; [1999] 2
W.L.R. 518; [1999] 1 All E.R. 833; [1999] C.L.C. 867; (1999) 1 T.C.L.R.
18; [1999] P.N.L.R. 469; [1999] 1 E.G.L.R. 77; [1999] 13 E.G. 119; [1999]
E.G.C.S. 26; (1999) 96(10) L.S.G. 31; (1999) 149 N.L.J. 283; (1999) 143
S.J.L.B. 65; [1999] N.P.C. 21; *The Times,* February 19, 1999; *The Independ-
ent,* March 5, 1999, HL 3–04, 5–117, 9–116, 9–166, 9–171, 9–174, 10–295,
10–325, 15–131, 15–146
Plowright v. Lambert (1885) 52 L.T. 646 2–139

PARA.

Polini v. Gray; Sturla v. Freccia (1880) 28 W.R. 360 10–69
Polishuk v. Hagarty (1983) 149 D.L.R. (3d) 65, upheld (1985) 14 D.L.R. (4th)
    446 .... 10–08, 10–234
Polkinghorne v. Holland (1934) 51 C.L.R. 143, HC (Aus) 10–147
Pollard v. Clayton (1855) 1 K. & J. 463 .... 5–103, 5–106
—— v. Crockard, January 22, 1997, unreported 12–72
Poolton v. Paci (1999) 21 R.P.R. (3d) 212 10–268
Port of Sheerness Ltd v. Brachers (1997) I.R.L.R. 214 .... 10–152, 10–285
Porter v. Prudential of America General Insur. Co. (1995) 146 N.S.R.(2d) 81, Sup
    Ct (Nova Scotia) 14–72, 14–90
Portland, Duke of v. Wood's Trustees, 1962 S.L.T. 321 9–191
Portman Building Society v. Bevan Ashford (A Firm) [2000] Lloyd's Rep. Bank.
    96; [2000] Lloyd's Rep. P.N. 354; [2000] P.N.L.R. 344; (2000) 80 P. & C.R.
    239; [2000] 1 E.G.L.R. 81; [2000] 07 E.G. 131; [2000] E.G.C.S. 2; (2000)
    79 P. & C.R. D25, CA 10–251, 10–252, 10–294, 10–296
—— v. Hamlyn Taylor Neck [1998] 4 All E.R. 202; [1998] P.N.L.R. 664; (1999)
    77 P. & C.R. 66; [1998] 2 E.G.L.R. 113; [1998] 31 E.G. 102, CA 10–232
—— v. Royal Insurance plc (t/a Fox & Sons) [1998] P.N.L.R. 672, CA 10–145
Poseidon Ltd v. Adelaide Petroleum N.L. (1994) 68 A.L.J.R. 313 10–261
Possfund Custodian Trustee Ltd v. Diamond; Parr v. Diamond [1996] 1 W.L.R.
    1351; [1006] 2 All E.R. 774; [1996] 2 B.C.L.C. 665; The Times, April 18,
    1996, Ch D 13–108, 15–77, 15–78
Potter v. London Transport Board (1965) 109 S.J. 233 10–177
Potts v. Sparrow (1836) 6 C. & P. 749; 172 E.R. 147, NP 10–116
Pountney v. Griffiths; sub nom. R. v. Bracknell Justices, ex p. Griffiths [1976]
    A.C. 314; [1975] 3 W.L.R. 140; [1975] 2 All E.R. 881; [1975] Crim. L.R.
    702; 119 S.J. 493, HL 12–235
Powell v. Boladz; sub nom. Powell v. Boldaz [1998] Lloyd's Rep. Med. 116;
    (1998) 39 B.M.L.R. 35, CA 12–42, 12–66
—— v. Guttman (1979) 89 D.L.R. (3d) 180 12–275
—— v. Powell [1900] 1 Ch. 243; 69 L.J.Ch. 164; 82 L.T. 84; 44 S.J. 134, Ch D 2–144,
    10–100, 10–123
—— v. United Kingdom. See William and Anita Powell v. United Kingdom.
—— v. United Kingdom; Rayner v. United kingdom; Series A, No.172; (1990)
    12 E.H.R.R. 355; The Times, February 22, 1990, ECHR 7–07
Poynter v. Hillingdon Health Authority (1997) 37 B.M.L.R. 192, QBD 12–75,
    12–213, 12–217, 12–218, 12–219, 12–220, 12–270
Pozzolanic Lytag Ltd v. Bryan Hobson Associates [1999] B.L.R. 267; (1999) 1
    T.C.L.R. 233; 63 Con. L.R. 81; [1999] Lloyd's Rep. P.N. 125; (1999) 15
    Const. L.J. 135; (1999) 143 S.J.L.B. 30; The Times, December 3, 1998, QBD
    (T&CC) 6–12, 8–154, 8–236
Predeth v. Castle Phillips Finance Co. [1986] 2 E.G.L.R. 144; (1986) 279 E.G.
    1355, CA 9–20, 9–24, 9–78
Prendergast v. Sam & Dee Ltd [1989] 1 Med.L.R. 36 .... 12–165, 12–275
Prentis Donegan & Partners Ltd v. Leeds & Leeds Co. Inc. [1998] 2 Lloyd's Rep.
    326; [1998] C.L.C. 1132, QBD (Comm Ct) 14–13
President of India v. La Pintada Compania Navigacion SA; La Pintada, The
    (No.1); sub nom. La Pintada Compania Navegacion S.A. v. President of
    India (No.1) [1985] A.C. 104; [1984] 3 W.L.R. 10; [1984] 2 All E.R. 773;
    [1984] 2 Lloyd's Rep. 9; [1984] C.I.L.L. 110; (1984) 81 L.S.G. 1999; (1984)
    128 S.J. 414, HL 14–121
Pressos Compania Naviera S.A. v. Belgium; Series A, No.332; (1996) 21
    E.H.R.R. 301, ECHR 7–06, 7–16
Preston v. Torfaen B.C., 65 B.L.R. 1; 36 Con. L.R. 48; [1955–95] P.N.L.R. 625;
    [1993] E.G.C.S. 137; [1993] N.P.C. 111; The Times, July 21, 1993; The
    Independent, September 24, 1993, CA 8–104, 9–37

PARA.

Pretty v. Fowke (1887) 3 T.L.R. 845 .... 10–207, 10–294
Prettys v. Michael Carter, July 31, 2001, unreported 5–74
Price v. Bullen (1825) 3 L.J.(O.S.) K.B. 39 10–183
—— v. Society of Lloyd's [2000] Lloyd's Rep. I.R. 453, QBD (Comm Ct) 16–02
Price Waterhouse v. BCCI Holdings (Luxembourg) S.A. [1992] B.C.L.C. 583;
    The Times, October 30, 1991; Financial Times, November 1, 1991, Ch D 2–160,
                                                                                    2–161
—— v. Kwan [2000] 3 N.Z.L.R. 39, CA 15–85, 15–86
Pride Valley Foods Ltd v. Hall & Partners (Contract Management) Ltd [2001]
    EWCA Civ 1001; 76 Con. L.R. 1; [2001] N.P.C. 103, CA; reversing in part
    (2000) 16 Const. L.J. 424; [2000] N.P.C. 55, QBD (T&CC) 6–12, 8–08, 8–153,
                                                        8–155, 8–219, 8–211, 8–271, 8–331
Pridham v. Nash (1986) 33 D.L.R. (4th) 304, HC (Ontario) 12–127
Priestly v. Stone (1888) 4 T.L.R. 730 8–221
Prior v. McNabb (1977) 78 D.L.R. (3d) 319, HC (Ontario) 10–185, 10–282
Private Bank & Trust Co. Ltd v. S (U.K.) Ltd (formerly Sallmans (U.K.) Ltd)
    [1994] 3 Bank. L.R. 33; (1994) 67 P. & C.R. 166; [1993] 09 E.G. 112;
    [1993] E.G.C.S. 12, QBD 9–61
Privest Properties Ltd v. Foundation Co. of Canada Ltd (1995) 128 D.L.R. (4th),
    Sup Ct (1997) 143 D.L.R. (4th) 635, CA (BC) 8–97, 8–139, 8–215
Professional Reprographic Services v. DPS Typecraft, February 15, 1993, unre-
    ported, CA 17–94
Project Consultancy Group v. Trustees of the Gray Trust [1999] B.L.R. 377;
    (2000) 2 T.C.L.R. 72; 65 Con. L.R. 146, QBD (T&CC) 8–340
Prout v. Crowley (1956) 1 B.M.J. 580 12–192
Pryke (John W) v. Gibbs Hartley Cooper Ltd; Excess Insurance Co. Ltd v. Gibbs
    Hartley Cooper Ltd [1991] 1 Lloyd's Rep. 602, QBD (Comm Ct) 2–78, 2–107,
                                        14–18, 14–19, 14–24, 14–34, 14–107, 14–128
Public Trustee v. Till [2001] 2 N.Z.L.R. 508 10–219
Pudney v. Union-Castle Mail Steamship Co. Ltd [1953] 1 Lloyd's Rep. 73,
    QBD 12–183, 12–189
Pullen v. Gutteridge Haskins & Davey Pty. Ltd [1993] 1 V.R. 27, Sup Ct
    (Victoria) 5–26, 8–37, 8–53, 8–141, 8–212, 8–262
Punford v. Gilberts Accountants [1999] E.C.C. 91; [1998] P.N.L.R. 763, CA 10–218,
                                                                                    15–145
Punjab National Bank v. De Boinville [1992] 1 W.L.R. 1138; [1992] 3 All E.R.
    104; [1992] 1 Lloyd's Rep. 7; [1992] E.C.C. 348; (1991) 141 N.L.J. 85; The
    Times, June 4, 1991; Financial Times, June 5, 1991, CA 2–40, 2–93, 9–14,
                                                10–57, 14–14, 14–27, 14–28, 16–18
Purves v. Landell (1845) 12 C. & F. 91; 8 E.R. 1332, HL 10–77, 10–105, 11–10
Pyrenees Shire Council v. Day [1998] H.C.A. 3; (1998) 192 C.L.R. 330 .... 2–64, 2–66,
                                                                                2–69, 8–121

Queen, The v. Bonython (1984) 38 S.A.S.R. 45 .... 6–13, 9–06
Quevillon v. Lamoureux (1975) 52 D.L.R. (3d) 476, CA (Quebec) 10–185
Quinby Enterprises Ltd (in liquidation) v. General Accident Fire and Life Assur-
    ance Corporation Public Ltd Co. [1995] 1 N.Z.L.R. 726 14–67
Quinn v. Burch Bros (Builders) Ltd [1966] 2 Q.B. 370; [1966] 2 W.L.R. 1017;
    [1966] 2 All E.R. 283; 1 K.I.R. 9; 110 S.J. 214, CA 5–115, 8–279

R (A Minor) (Medical Treatment), Re [1992] 2 F.L.R. 585 12–144
R (A Minor), Re, July 16, 1996, unreported, CA 12–158, 12–200
RB Burden Ltd v. Swansea Corp. [1957] 1 W.L.R. 1167; [1957] 3 All E.R. 243;
    55 L.G.R. 381; 101 S.J. 882, HL 8–14, 8–253, 8–254, 8–258

PARA.

RG Carter Ltd v. Edmund Nuttall Ltd, unreported, June 21, 2000 8–332
RL Polk & Co. (Great Britain) v. Hill (Edwin), 41 B.L.R. 84; [1988] 18 E.G.
71 5–23
R (L) v. Witherspoon [2000] 1 F.L.R. 82; [1999] 3 F.C.R. 202; [1999] Lloyd's
Rep. P.N. 401; [1999] P.N.L.R. 776; [2000] Fam. Law 19, CA 10–110, 10–248
RM Turton & Co. Ltd v. Kerslake & Partners [2000] Lloyd's Rep.P.N. 967, CA
(NZ) 8–111, 8–123
R&T Thew Ltd v. Reeves (No.2) [1982] Q.B. 1283; [1982] 3 W.L.R. 869; [1982]
3 All E.R. 1086; 126 S.J. 674, CA 10–80
RP Howard & Witchell v. Woodman Matthews & Co. [1983] B.C.L.C. 117;
[1983] Com. L.R. 100; (1983) 133 N.L.J. 598 ..... 10–42, 10–162, 10–168, 10–202
R. v. A (Wasted Costs Order); sub nom. R. v. Hickman & Rose; Hickman & Rose
(Wasted Costs Order) (No.10 of 1999), Re [2000] P.N.L.R. 628; The Times,
May 3, 2000, CA (Crim Div) 10–120, 10–136
—— v. Architects' Registration Tribunal, ex p. Jaggar [1945] 2 All E.R. 131 8–4
—— v. Basra (Wasted Costs Order); sub nom. Douglas Narayan & Partners v.
Khan [1998] P.N.L.R. 535, CA (Crim Div) 10–137
—— v. Bateman (1925) 94 L.J.K.B. 791; 41 T.L.R. 557; 133 L.T. 730; 89 J.P.
162; 69 S.J. 622; 19 Cr.App.R. 8 .... 12–68, 12–78
—— v. Blatt, The Times May 30 1996 11–05
—— v. Bournewood Community and Mental Health NHS Trust, ex p. L; sub
nom. L, Re [1999] 1 A.C. 458; [1998] 3 W.L.R. 107; [1998] 3 All E.R. 289;
[1998] 2 F.L.R. 550; [1998] 2 F.C.R. 501; (1997–98) 1 C.C.L. Rep. 390;
(1998) 44 B.M.L.R. 1; [1998] C.O.D. 312; [1998] Fam. Law 592; (1998)
95(29) L.S.G. 27; (1998) 148 N.L.J. 1014; (1998) 142 S.J.L.B. 195; The
Times, June 30, 1998; The Independent, June 30, 1998, HL 12–133, 12–135,
12–143
—— v. Bracknell JJ., ex p. Griffiths. See Pountney v. Griffiths.
—— v. Cambridge D.H.A., ex p. B (No.1) [1995] 1 W.L.R. 898; [1995] 2 All
E.R. 129; [1995] 1 F.L.R. 1056; [1995] 2 F.C.R. 485; [1995] 6 Med.L.R.
250; [1995] C.O.D. 407; [1995] Fam. Law 480; (1995) 145 N.L.J. 415; The
Times, March 15, 1995; The Independent, March 14, 1995, CA 7–51, 12–148,
12–160
—— v. Camden L.B.C., ex p. Martin [1997] 1 W.L.R. 359; [1997] 1 All E.R. 307;
[1997] 1 F.L.R. 950; [1997] 3 F.C.R. 659; (1997) 9 Admin. L.R. 134; [1997]
C.O.D. 107; [1997] Fam. Law 472; (1997) 161 J.P. Rep. 288; The Times,
November 11, 1996, QBD 10–128
—— v. Central Birmingham Health Authority, ex p. Walker (1987) 3 B.M.L.R.
32 12–160
—— v. Chance, ex p. Smith; R. v. Chance, ex p. Coopers & Lybrand [1995]
B.C.C. 1095; (1995) 7 Admin. L.R. 821; The Times, January 28, 1995,
QBD 13–205
—— v. Collins, ex p. Brady [2000] Lloyd's Rep. Med. 355; (2001) 58 B.M.L.R.
173, QBD 12–137
—— v. Cox and Railton (1884) 14 Q.B.D. 153; 49 J.P. 374; [1881–85] All E.R.
Rep. 68; 54 L.J.M.C. 41; 52 L.T. 25; 33 W.R. 396; 1 T.L.R. 181; 15
Cox.C.C. 611, CCR, CA 10–32
—— v. Croydon H.A. [1998] P.I.Q.R. Q26; [1998] Lloyd's Rep. Med. 44; (1998)
40 B.M.L.R. 40; The Times, December 13, 1997; The Independent, December 4, 1997, CA 12–26, 12–66, 12–185, 12–244, 12–282, 12–289, 12–304
—— v. Department of Health, ex p. Source Informatics Ltd (No.1) [2001] Q.B.
424; [2000] 2 W.L.R. 940; [2000] 1 All E.R. 786; [2000] Eu. L.R. 397;
[2001] F.S.R. 8; [2000] Lloyd's Rep. Med. 76; (2000) 52 B.M.L.R. 65;
[2000] C.O.D. 76; The Times, January 18, 2000; The Independent, February
21, 2000 (C.S.), CA 2–155, 2–158, 2–156

PARA.

R. v. Derby Magistrates Court, ex p. B [1996] A.C. 487; [1995] 3 W.L.R. 681; [1995] 4 All E.R. 526; [1996] 1 Cr. App. R. 385; (1995) 159 J.P. 785; [1996] 1 F.L.R. 513; [1996] Fam. Law 210; (1995) 159 J.P.N. 778; (1995) 145 N.L.J. 1575; [1995] 139 S.J.L.B. 219; *The Times*, October 25, 1995; *The Independent*, October 27, 1995, HL 7–35

—— v. General Medical Council, ex p. Kyros Nicolaides. *See* R. (on the application of Nicolaides) v. General Medical.

—— v. General Medical Council, ex p. Toth [2000] 1 W.L.R. 2209; [2000] Lloyd's Rep. Med. 368; (2000) 97(27) L.S.G. 39; *The Times*, June 29, 2000, QBD 7–67

—— v. Horsham D.C., ex p. Wenman [1995] 1 W.L.R. 680; [1994] 4 All E.R. 681; (1992) 24 H.L.R. 669; (1995) 7 Admin. L.R. 73; [1992] C.O.D. 427; (1995) 159 L.G. Rev. 365; (1993) 143 N.L.J. 1477; [1993] N.P.C. 129; *The Times*, October 21, 1993; *The Independent*, October 7, 1993, QBD 10–120, 11–30

—— v. Human Fertilisation and Embryology Authority, ex p. Blood; *sub nom.* R. v. Human Fertilisation and Embryology Authority, ex p. DB [1999] Fam. 151; [1997] 2 W.L.R. 807; [1997] 2 All E.R. 687; [1997] 2 C.M.L.R. 591; [1997] Eu. L.R. 370; [1997] 2 F.L.R. 742; [1997] 2 F.C.R. 501; (1997) 35 B.M.L.R. 1; [1997] C.O.D. 261; [1997] Fam. Law 401; (1997) 147 N.L.J. 253; *The Times*, February 7, 1997; *The Independent*, February 11, 1997, CA 7–45

—— v. Hutton [1978] N.I. 139 2–145

—— v. Immigration Appeal Tribunal, ex p. Gulbamer Gulsen [1997] C.O.D. 430, QBD 10–128

—— v. Institute of Chartered Accountants in England and Wales, ex p. Brindle [1994] B.C.C. 297; *The Times*, January 12, 1994, CA 13–205

—— v. Investors Compensation Scheme Ltd, ex p. Bowden [1996] A.C. 261; [1995] 3 W.L.R. 289; [1995] 3 All E.R. 605; [1995] 2 B.C.L.C. 342; (1995) 145 N.L.J. 1260; (1995) 139 S.J.L.B. 188; [1995] N.P.C. 126; *The Times*, July 18, 1995; *The Independent*, July 21, 1995, HL; reversing [1995] Q.B. 107; [1994] 3 W.L.R. 1045; [1995] 1 All E.R. 214; [1995] 1 B.C.L.C. 374; [1995] C.O.D. 12; *The Times*, June 30, 1994; *The Independent*, August 29, 1994 (C.S.), CA 13–162, 13–198, 13–199

—— v. Knutsford Crown Court, ex p. Middleweek [1992] C.O.D. 348; *The Times*, March 23, 1992, DC 10–132

—— v. Lambert (Steven); R. v. Ali (Mudassir Mohammed); R. v. Jordan (Shirley) [2001] UKHL 37; [2001] 3 W.L.R. 206; [2001] 3 All E.R. 577; (2001) 98(33) L.S.G. 29; (2001) 145 S.J.L.B. 174; *The Times*, July 6, 2001; *The Independent*, July 19, 2001; *The Daily Telegraph*, July 17, 2001, HL 7–13

—— v. Liverpool City Council, ex p. Horn [1997] P.N.L.R. 95, QBD 10–140

—— v. Liverpool City Council, ex p. May [1994] C.O.D. 144, QBD 10–139

—— v. Lord Chancellor, ex p. Lightfoot; *sub nom.* Lightfoot v. Lord Chancellor [2000] Q.B. 597; [2000] 2 W.L.R. 318; [1999] 4 All E.R. 583; [2000] B.C.C. 537; [2000] H.R.L.R. 33; [2000] B.P.I.R. 120; (1999) 96(31) L.S.G. 35; (1999) 149 N.L.J. 1285; *The Times*, August 18, 1999; *The Independent*, November 1, 1999 (C.S.), CA; affirming [1999] 2 W.L.R. 1126; [1998] 4 All E.R. 764; [1999] B.P.I.R. 118; [1999] C.O.D. 87; (1998) 148 N.L.J. 1230; [1998] N.P.C. 134, QBD 7–07

—— v. Luton Family Proceedings Court Justices ex p. R [1998] C.L.Y. 496, CA 11–28

—— v. M (Wasted Costs Order) [1996] 1 F.L.R. 750; [1997] 1 F.C.R. 42; [1996] Fam. Law 350; (1997) 161 J.P.N. 40, QBD 10–139

—— v. M (Wasted Costs Order); *sub nom.* Howells (Solicitors), Re [2000] P.N.L.R. 214, CA (Crim Div) 10–134

PARA.

R. v. Mid Glamorgan Family Health Services, ex p. Martin [1995] 1 W.L.R. 110;
[1995] 1 All E.R. 356; [1995] 1 F.L.R. 282; [1995] 2 F.C.R. 578; [1995]
P.I.Q.R. P103; [1994] 5 Med. L.R. 383; (1994) 91(38) L.S.G. 42; (1994) 138
S.J.L.B. 195; *The Times,* August 16, 1994; *The Independent,* September 7,
1994, CA 7–60, 12–09, 12–30, 12–221
—— v. North and East Devon H.A., ex p. Coughlan [2001] Q.B. 213; [2000] 2
W.L.R. 622; [2000] 3 All E.R. 850; (2000) 2 L.G.L.R. 1; [1999] B.L.G.R.
703; (1999) 2 C.C.L. Rep. 285; [1999] Lloyd's Rep. Med. 306; (2000) 51
B.M.L.R. 1; [1999] C.O.D. 340; (1999) 96(31) L.S.G. 39; (1999) 143
S.J.L.B. 213; *The Times,* July 20, 1999; *The Independent,* July 20, 1999,
CA 7–54, 12–161
—— v. North West Lancashire H.A., ex p. A; *sub nom.* North West Lancashire
H.A. v. A; R. v. North West Lancashire H.A., ex p. D; R. v. North West
Lancashire H.A., ex p. G [2000] 1 W.L.R. 977; [2000] 2 F.C.R. 525; (1999)
2 C.C.L. Rep. 419; [1999] Lloyd's Rep. Med. 399; (2000) 53 B.M.L.R. 148;
The Times, August 24, 1999; *The Independent,* October 5, 1999, CA 12–161
—— v. Oxfordshire C.C., ex p. Wallace; *sub nom.* R. v. Oxfordshire Education
Authority, ex p. W [1987] 2 F.L.R. 193; (1987) 151 L.G. Rev. 590; (1987)
137 N.L.J. 542, DC 10–120
—— v. Panel on Take-overs and Mergers, ex p. Fayed [1992] B.C.L.C. 938;
[1992] B.C.C. 524; (1993) 5 Admin. L.R. 337; *The Times,* April 15, 1992;
Financial Times, April 14, 1992, CA 13–205
—— v. Paul Wurth S.A. [2000] I.C.R. 860; *The Times,* March 29, 2000, CA
(Crim Div) 8–48
—— v. Personal Investment Authority Ombudsman Bureau Ltd, ex p. Johannes
Mooyer. *See* R. (on the application of Mooyer) v. Personal Investment
Authority Ombudsman Bureau Ltd.
—— v. Portsmouth Hospitals NHS Trust, ex p. Glass [1999] 2 F.L.R. 905; [1999]
3 F.C.R. 145; (1999) 11 Admin. L.R. 991; [1999] Lloyd's Rep. Med. 367;
(1999) 50 B.M.L.R. 269; [2000] C.O.D. 54; [1999] Fam. Law 696; (1999)
96(32) L.S.G. 31; (1999) 143 S.J.L.B. 220; *The Times,* July 26, 1999, CA 12–148
—— v. Qadi [2000] P.N.L.R. 137, CA (Crim Div) 10–140
—— v. Richardson (Diane) [1999] Q.B. 444; [1998] 3 W.L.R. 1292; [1998] 2 Cr.
App. R. 200; (1998) 43 B.M.L.R. 21; [1999] Crim. L.R. 62; (1998) 95(17)
L.S.G. 30; (1998) 142 S.J.L.B. 131; *The Times,* April 6, 1998; *The Independent,* April 3, 1998, CA (Crim Div) 12–133
—— v. Rodney (Roger) [1997] P.N.L.R. 489, CA 11–34
—— v. Runighian (1977) Crim.L.R. 361, Crown Ct (Warwick) 12–235
—— v. Secretary of State for Scotland [1999] 2 A.C. 512; [1999] 2 W.L.R. 28;
[1999] 1 All E.R. 481; 1999 S.C. (H.L.) 17; 1999 S.L.T. 279; 1999 S.C.L.R.
74; (1999) 96(4) L.S.G. 37; 1998 G.W.D. 40–2075; *The Times,* December 7,
1998; *The Independent,* December 8, 1998, HL 12–49
—— v. Secretary of State for Social Services, ex p. Hincks (1980) 1 B.M.L.R. 93,
C.A 12–160
—— v. Secretary of State for the Home Department ex p. Mahmood (Wasted
Costs Order) [1999] C.O.D. 119, QBD 10–140, 11–34
—— v. Secretary of State for the Home Department, ex p. Amnesty International,
February 15, 2000, unreported, DC 7–62
—— v. Secretary of State for the Home Office ex p. Begum [1995] C.O.D.
176 11–31
—— v. Secretary of State for the Home Office ex p. Wong (Tim Fat) [1995]
C.O.D. 331, QBD 10–132
—— v. Securities and Investments Board, ex p. Independent Financial Advisers
Association [1995] 2 B.C.L.C. 76; [1995] C.O.D. 240; *The Times,* May 18,
1995, QBD 13–12, 13–169

PARA.

R. v. Securities and Investments Board, ex p. Sun Life Assurance Society plc
[1996] 2 B.C.L.C. 150; [1996] C.L.C. 52; (1996) 8 Admin. L.R. 297; [1996]
C.O.D. 8; *The Times*, October 9, 1995; *The Independent*, October 5, 1995,
QBD 13–12, 13–169
—— v. Shacter (Norman) [1960] 2 Q.B. 252; [1960] 2 W.L.R. 258; [1960] 1 All
E.R. 61; (1960) 44 Cr. App. R. 42; 124 J.P. 108; 104 S.J. 90, CCA 15–24
—— v. Sheffield Health Authority (1994) 25 B.M.L.R. 1 12–160
—— v. Special Commissioners of Income Tax, ex p. Morgan Grenfell & Co. Ltd.
See R. (on the application of Morgan Grenfell & Co. Ltd) v. Special
Commissioner of Income Tax.
—— v. Tew (1752) Say. 50; 96 E.R. 800 10–183
—— v. United Kingdom Central Council for Nursing, Midwifery & Health
Visiting, ex p. Tehrani. *See* Tehrani v. United Kingdom Central Council for
Nursing Midwifery and Health Visiting.
—— v. Westminster London Borough, ex p. Geehan & Butler [1995] C.O.D. 204,
QBD 10–136
—— v. Whiteley (Nicholas Alan) (1991) 93 Cr. App. R. 25; (1991) 155 J.P. 917;
[1992] E.C.C. 485; [1993] F.S.R. 168; [1991] Crim. L.R. 436; (1991) 155
J.P.N. 378; (1991) 135 S.J. 249; *The Times*, February 6, 1991; *The Independent*, March 25, 1991 (C.S.); *The Daily Telegraph*, February 15, 1991, CA
(Crim Div) 17–21, 17–67, 17–112
—— v. Williscroft [1975] V.R. 292 2–69
R. (on the application of Carroll) v. Secretary of State for the Home Department;
sub nom. R. v. Secretary of State for the Home Department, ex p. Carroll; R.
(on the application of Greenfield) v. Secretary of State for the Home
Department; R. (on the application of Al-Hasan) v. Secretary of State for the
Home Department [2001] EWCA Civ 1224, CA; affirming [2001] EWHC
Admin 110; [2001] H.R.L.R. 34, QBD (Admin Ct) 7–08
R. (on the application of Greenfield) v. Secretary of State for the Home Department; *sub nom.* Greenfield v. Secretary of State for the Home Department
[2001] EWHC Admin 129; [2001] 1 W.L.R. 1731; [2001] H.R.L.R. 35; *The
Times*, March 6, 2001; *The Independent*, April 2, 2001 (C.S), QBD (Admin
Ct) 7–08
R. (on the application of Mooyer) v. Personal Investment Authority Ombudsman
Bureau Ltd [2001] EWHC Admin 247, QBD (Admin Ct) 13–182
R. (on the application of Morgan Grenfell & Co. Ltd) v. Special Commissioner
of Income Tax; *sub nom.* R. v. Inland Revenue Commissioners, ex p.
Morgan Grenfell & Co. Ltd; R. v. Special Commissioners of Income Tax, ex
p. Morgan Grenfell & Co. Ltd [2001] EWCA Civ 329, CA; affirming [2001]
1 All E.R. 535; [2000] S.T.C. 965; [2000] S.T.I. 1609; (2000) 97(48) L.S.G.
37; (2000) 150 N.L.J. 1717; *The Times*, November 22, 2000, QBD (Admin
Ct) 7–35
R. (on the application of Nicolaides) v. General Medical Council [2001] EWHC
Admin 625, QBD (Admin Ct) 7–67
Radcliffe v. Price (1902) 18 T.L.R. 466 2–144
Radford v. De Froberville [1977] 1 W.L.R. 1262; [1978] 1 All E.R. 33; 7 B.L.R.
35; (1978) 35 P. & C.R. 316; 121 S.J. 319, Ch D 3–01
Rae v. Meek (1889) 14 App. Cas. 558, HL 10–207
Raflatac Ltd v. Eade [1999] 1 Lloyd's Rep. 506; [1999] B.L.R. 261, QBD (Comm
Ct) 5–115, 8–55, 8–59, 8–276, 8–206
Rahman v. Arearose Ltd [2001] Q.B. 351; [2000] 3 W.L.R. 1184, CA 12–246, 12–274
Rainford House Ltd (In Administrative Receivership) v. Cadogan Ltd [2001]
C.I.L.L. 1709; [2001] N.P.C. 39, QBD (T&CC) 8–343
Raintree Ltd v. Holmes (1984) 134 N.L.J. 522 10–203
Raiss v. Paimano. *See* Paimano v. Raiss.
Rajdev v. Becketts [1989] 2 E.G.L.R. 144 .... 9–04, 9–74, 9–179

PARA.

Raji Abu Shkara v. Hillingdon H.A. [1997] 8 Med.L.R. 114, CA 12–185
Rakusen v. Ellis, Munday & Clark [1912] 1 Ch. 831; [1911–13] All E.R. Rep.
 813; 81 L.J.Ch. 409; 106 L.T. 556; 28 T.L.R. 326, CA 10–26
Rama v. Millar [1996] 1 N.Z.L.R. 257; [1996] C.L.C. 186, PC (NZ) 3–14, 3–24,
 10–231
Ramesh Kumar Kapur v. JW Francis & Co. [2000] Lloyd's Rep. I.R. 361; [1999]
 Lloyd's Rep. P.N. 834, CA 14–91
Rampling v. Haringey Health Authority, July 30, 1996, unreported 12–179, 12–184
Ramwade v. WJ Emson & Co. [1987] R.T.R. 72; (1986) 83 L.S.G. 2996; (1986)
 130 S.J. 804, CA 14–114, 14–121
Rance v. Mid-Downs H.A. [1991] 1 Q.B. 587; [1991] 2 W.L.R. 159; [1991] 1 All
 E.R. 801; [1990] 2 Med. L.R. 27; [1991] Fam. Law 24; (1990) 140 N.L.J.
 325, QBD 12–231, 12–278, 12–292
Rand v. East Dorset H.A. [2000] Lloyd's Rep. Med. 181; (2000) 56 B.M.L.R. 39,
 QBD 12–231, 12–285, 12–294, 12–297, 12–299, 12–300
Randall v. Errington (1805) 10 Ves.Jun. 423 .... 2–134, 2–135, 3–09
Random Ford Mercury Sales Ltd v. Noseworthy (1992) 95 D.L.R. (4th) 168 14–81
Rashid, Dr v. Jurusan Malaysia Consultants Ltd [1997] 3 M.L.J. 546 8–124
Ratcliffe v. Plymouth and Torbay H.A. [1998] P.I.Q.R. P170; [1998] Lloyd's Rep.
 Med. 162; (1998) 42 B.M.L.R. 64, CA 12–119, 12–123
Ratty v. Haringey H.A. [1994] 5 Med.L.R. 413, CA 12–183
Rawlings v. Rentokil Laboratories Ltd (1972) 223 E.G. 1947 9–191
Rayment v. HG Needham & Son (1953) 163 E.G. 4 .... 8–214, 9–34
Razzel v. Snowball [1954] 1 W.L.R. 1382; [1954] 3 All E.R. 429; 119 J.P. 23; 98
 S.J. 787, CA 12–153
Read v. Nerey Nominees Pty Ltd [1979] V.R. 47 5–115
Reading v. Attorney General; *sub nom.* Reading v. King, The; Reading's Petition
 of Right, Re [1951] A.C. 507; [1951] 1 All E.R. 617; [1951] 1 T.L.R. 480;
 95 S.J. 155, HL; affirming [1949] 2 K.B. 232; [1949] 2 All E.R. 68; 65
 T.L.R. 405, CA 2–141
Reardon v. Kings Mutual Insurance Co. (1981) 120 D.L.R. (3d) 196 14–74
Reaveley v. Safeway Stores plc [1998] P.N.L.R. 526, CA 10–120, 10–136
Reay v. British Nuclear Fuels plc; Hope v. British Nuclear Fuels plc [1994] Env.
 L.R. 320; [1994] P.I.Q.R. P171; [1994] 5 Med.L.R. 1; The Independent,
 November 22, 1993 (C.S.); The Guardian, October 15, 1993, QBD 6–01, 12–55
Recha and Klein v. Yeamans and Gere (1993) 135 N.B.R. (2d) 360, CA (New
 Brunswick) 10–19
Reddy v. Lachlan [2000] Lloyd's Rep. P.N. 858, CA 10–68
Redman v. Instant Nominees Pty Ltd [1987] W.A.R. 277 .... 10–286, 10–283
Redmond v. Densmore (1997) 153 Nfld & P.E.I.R. 181, CA (Newfoundland) 10–197
Reece v. Rigby (1821) 4 B. & Ald. 202; 106 E.R. 912 10–183
Reeman v. Department of Transport [1997] 2 Lloyd's Rep. 648; [1997] P.N.L.R.
 618, CA 2–41
Rees Hough Ltd v. Redland Reinforced Plastics Ltd (1984) 27 B.L.R. 136; (1984)
 Const. L.J. 67; [1984] C.I.L.L. 84; (1984) 134 N.L.J. 706, QBD 8–36
Rees v. Sinclair [1974] 1 N.Z.L.R. 180, CA 10–106, 11–13, 11–24
Reeve v. Palmer (1859) 5 C.B.(N.S.) 84; 28 L.J.C.P. 168; 5 Jur(N.S.) 916; 7 W.R.
 325; 141 E.R. 33, Ex Ch 10–192
Reeves v. Thrings & Long [1996] P.N.L.R. 265; [1993] E.G.C.S. 196; [1993]
 N.P.C. 159, CA 10–172, 10–250, 10–269
Refson & Co. v. Saggers. See PS Refson & Co. Ltd v. Saggers.
Regal (Hastings) Ltd v. Gulliver [1967] 2 A.C. 134 (Note); [1942] 1 All E.R. 378,
 HL 2–141, 3–17
Reggentin v. Beecholme Bakeries [1968] 2 Q.B. 276; (1967) 111 S.J. 216, CA 10–187
Regina, University of v. Pettick (1992) 77 D.L.R. (4th) 615 8–116

PARA.

Reibl v. Hughes (1980) 114 D.L.R. (3d) 1, Sup Ct (Can) 12–29, 12–69, 12–95,
12–124, 12–130, 12–131, 12–201, 12–202, 12–203, 12–208,
12–209, 12–264

Reid v. Secretary of State for Scotland. *See* R. v. Secretary of State for Scotland

Reilly v. Merseyside R.H.A. [1995] 6 Med. L.R. 246; *The Independent*, April 29,
1994, CA 12–37

Reisner v. Regents of the University of California (1995) 37 Cal.Rptr 2d 518 12–44,
12–47, 12–54

Rendel v. Edgelow (1909) 53 S.J. 237 10–169

Rentokil Pty Ltd v. Channon [1990] 19 N.S.W.L.R. 417, CA (NSW) 9–140

Republic International Ltd v. Fletcher Ramos, Unreported, August 30, 2000 9–91,
9–190, 9–191

Revelstoke Credit Union v. Miller (1984) 28 C.C.L.T. 17 .... 15–110, 15–139, 15–146

Rey v. Graham & Oldham (A Firm) [2000] B.P.I.R. 354, QBD 10–123, 10–259,
10–315

Reynolds, Ex p (1800) 5 Ves.Jun. 707 3–10

Reynolds v. Health First Medical Group [2000] Lloyd's Rep. Med. 240, CC
(Hitchin) 12–07

Rhodes v. Bate (1865) L.R. 1. Ch. 252; 13 L.T. 778; 12 Jur.(N.S.) 178; 14 W.R.
292 10–17

Ricci v. Masons [1993] 38 E.G. 154 .... 10–250, 10–265

Rich v. Pierpont (1862) 3 F. & F. 35 .... 12–16, 12–68

Richard Roberts Holdings Ltd v. Douglas Smith Stimson Partnership (No.2)
(1990) 46 B.L.R. 50; 22 Con. L.R. 69, QBD 8–143, 8–177, 8–215, 8–219, 8–297

Richards v. Cox [1943] 1 K.B. 139 ; (1942) 74 Ll. L. Rep. 23, CA 10–99

—— v. Revitt (1877–78) L.R. 7 Ch. D. 224, Ch D 5–112

Richardson v. Kitching [1995] 6 Med.L.R. 257, QBD 12–185, 12–245, 12–253

—— v. LRC Products Ltd [2000] P.I.Q.R. P164; [2000] Lloyd's Rep. Med. 280;
(2001) 59 B.M.L.R. 185, QBD 12–13, 12–276, 12–298

Riddell v. Porteous [1999] 1 N.Z.L.R. 1, CA (NZ) 8–123

Riddett v. D'Arcy (1960) 2 B.M.J. 1607 12–178

Ridehalgh v. Horsefield; Allen v. Unigate Dairies Ltd; Antonelli v. Wade Gery
Farr; Philex plc v. Golban; Roberts v. Coverite (Asphalters) Ltd; Watson v.
Watson (Wasted Costs Orders) [1994] Ch. 205; [1994] 3 W.L.R. 462; [1994]
3 All E.R. 848; [1994] B.C.C. 390; [1994] 2 F.L.R. 194; [1955–95] P.N.L.R.
636; [1994] Fam. Law 560; [1994] E.G.C.S. 15; (1994) 144 N.L.J. 231;
[1994] N.P.C. 7; *The Times*, January 28, 1994; *The Independent*, February 4,
1994, CA 10–82, 10–118, 10–120, 10–138, 10–129, 10–130, 10–131, 10–132,
10–133, 10–134, 10–135, 10–182, 11–08, 11–27, 11–30, 11–33,
11–40, 11–51

Ridley v. Tiplady (1855) 20 Beav. 44 10–183

Ridsdel, Re; *sub nom.* Ridsdel v. Rawlinson [1947] Ch. 597; [1947] 2 All E.R.
312; [1947] L.J.R. 1486; 91 S.J. 483, Ch D 15–112

Rieger v. Croft & Finlay (1992) 5 W.W.R. 700, Sup Ct (BC) 10–330

Ring, The [1931] P. 58 ; (1931) 39 Ll. L. Rep. 251, PDAD 10–71

Ritchie v. Chichester H.A. [1994] 5 Med.L.R. 187, QBD 12–106, 12–119, 12–192

Rivard v. Mutual Life Insurance Co. of Canada (1992) 9 O.R. (3d) 545, General
Division (Ontario) 14–70

Riverside Mental Health NHS Trust v. Fox. *See* Fox v. Riverside Health Trust.

Rivtow Marine Ltd v. Washington Iron Works [1974] S.C.R. 1189 8–77

Robb v. East London & City Health Authority, May 8, 1998, unreported 12–72,
12–191

Robbie v. Graham & Sibbald [1989] 2 E.G.L.R. 148; 1989 S.L.T. 870; 1989
S.C.L.R. 578, OH 9–72

Roberge v. Bolduc [1991] 1 S.C.R. 374, Sup Ct (Can) 10–89, 10–143

PARA.

Roberts v. Coverite. *See* Ridehalgh v. Horsefield.

—— v. Hopwood; *sub nom.* R. v. Roberts, ex p. Scurr; R. v. Roberts, ex p. Scurr [1925] A.C. 578, HL 15–112

—— v. J Hampson & Co. (A firm) [1990] 1 W.L.R. 94; [1989] 2 All E.R. 504; (1988) 20 H.L.R. 615; [1988] 37 E.G. 110; (1990) 87(4) L.S.G. 74; (1989) 133 S.J. 1234; [1988] 2 E.G.L.R. 181, QBD 9–34, 9–52, 9–57, 9–73, 9–84, 9–85, 9–91, 9–97, 9–131, 9–140, 9–189

—— v. JW Ward & Son (1982) 126 S.J. 120, CA 10–192

—— v. Plaisted [1989] 2 Lloyd's Rep. 341; *The Times*, July 19, 1989, CA 14–60

—— v. Winbow [1999] P.I.Q.R. P77; [1999] Lloyd's Rep. Med. 31; (1999) 49 B.M.L.R. 134; (1999) 96(4) L.S.G. 39; (1999) 143 S.J.L.B. 21; *The Times*, January 12, 1999, CA 5–58

Robertson v. Canadian Imperial Bank of Commerce [1994] 1 W.L.R. 1493; [1995] 1 All E.R. 824; [1995] E.C.C. 338; (1994) 91(41) L.S.G. 39; (1994) 138 S.J.L.B. 211; *The Times*, November 16, 1994, PC (StV) 2–161

—— v. Fleming (1861) 4 Macq. 167 .... 10–47, 10–54

—— v. Nottingham H.A.; *sub nom.* R (A Minor) (No.2), Re [1997] 8 Med. L.R. 1; (1997) 33 B.M.L.R. 178, CA 12–156, 12–157, 12–158, 12–200, 12–245, 12–249

Robins v. Meadows & Moran [1991] 2 E.G.L.R. 137; [1991] 29 E.G. 145; [1990] E.G.C.S. 157 10–174

Robinson v. Abbott (1894) 20 V.L.R. 346 2–137

—— v. Graves [1935] 1 K.B. 579, CA 17–10, 17–15

—— v. Jacklin [1996] 7 Med.L.R. 83, QBD 12–113

—— v. Post Office [1974] 1 W.L.R. 1176; [1974] 2 All E.R. 737; 16 K.I.R. 12; (1973) 117 S.J. 915, CA 12–16, 12–106, 12–245

—— v. Ridley (1821) 6 Madd. 2 3–09

—— v. Salford H.A. [1992] 3 Med.L.R. 270, QBD 12–289

Rochdale Healthcare NHS Trust v. C [1997] 1 F.C.R. 274, Fam Div 12–139

Roche v. Peilow [1986] I.L.R.M. 189, Sup Ct (Ireland) 10–89

—— v. Sherrington [1982] 1 W.L.R. 599; [1982] 2 All E.R. 426; 126 S.J. 312, Ch D 2–144

Roe v. Cullinane Turnbull Steele & Partners (No.2) [1985] 1 N.Z.L.R. 37 10–207

—— v. Ministry of Health; Woolley v. Ministry of Health [1954] 2 Q.B. 66; [1954] 2 W.L.R. 915; [1954] 2 All E.R. 131; 96 S.J. 319, CA 12–73, 12–84, 12–122, 12–286

—— v. Robert McGregor & Sons; Bills v. Roe [1968] 1 W.L.R. 925; [1968] 2 All E.R. 636; 112 S.J. 235, CA 10–180

Rogers v. Rosedimond Investments (Blakes Market) (1978) 247 E.G. 467, CA 9–102

—— v. Whitaker [1993] 4 Med.L.R. 79; (1992) 175 C.L.R. 479; [1992] A.L.M.D. 6993, HC (Aus) 12–29, 12–69, 12–75, 12–95, 12–206, 12–207, 12–213, 12–244, 12–265

Roker House Investments Ltd v. Saunders [1997] E.G.C.S. 137, Ch D 10–250

Roman Corp. Ltd v. Peat Marwick Thorne (No.1) (1992) 8 B.L.R. 43, Court of Justice, (Ontario) 15–35

Roman Corp. Ltd v. Peat Marwick Thorne (No.2) (1993) 12 B.L.R. (2d) 10, Court of Justice, (Ontario) 15–35

Ron Miller Realty Ltd v. Honeywell, Wotherspoon and Beedell (1992) 4 O.R. (3d) 492, HC (Ontario) 10–90

Rona v. Pearce (1953) 162 E.G. 380 .... 9–91, 9–107, 9–121

Ronaldson v. Drummond & Reid (1991) 8 Rettie 767, Ct Sess 10–294

Rondel v. Worsley; *sub nom.* Rondel v. W [1969] 1 A.C. 191; [1967] 3 W.L.R. 1666; [1967] 3 All E.R. 993; 111 S.J. 927; *The Times*, November 23, 1967, HL 10–104, 10–106, 10–181, 11–04, 11–05, 11–09, 11–10, 11–11, 11–13, 11–18, 11–40

PARA.

Rooks Rider v. JR Steel [1994] 1 W.L.R. 818 [1993] 4 All E.R. 716; (1993) 143
N.L.J. 1063; *The Times*, July 1, 1993, Ch D 10–69
Rose v. Mitton (1994) 111 D.L.R. (4th) 217, CA (Nova Scotia) 10–287
Rosetown v. Wilson Agencies Ltd (1989) 77 Sask.R. 42, QBD
(Saskatchewan) 14–54
Rosin v. MacPhail (1997) 142 D.L.R. (4th) 304, CA (BC) 10–31
Ross Harper & Murphy v. Banks, 2000 S.C. 500; 2000 S.L.T. 699; 2000 S.C.L.R.
736; [2000] Lloyd's Rep. P.N. 631; [2000] P.N.L.R. 631; *The Times*, May
30, 2000, OH 10–147
Ross v. Caunters [1980] Ch. 297; [1979] 3 W.L.R. 605; [1979] 3 All E.R. 580, Ch
D 2–28, 10–42, 10–47, 10–48, 10–49, 10–51, 10–53, 10–54, 10–223
—— v. Secretary of State for Scotland [1990] 1 Med.L.R. 235 12–160
Rothschild v. Berenson. *See* NM Rothschild & Sons Ltd v. Berenson.
Roussel v. Bertrand (1996) 183 N.B.R. (2d) 81, CA (New Brunswick) 10–228
Routestone Ltd v. Minories Finance Ltd; Routestone Ltd v. Bird [1997] B.C.C.
180; [1997] 1 E.G.L.R. 123; [1997] 21 E.G. 148; [1996] N.P.C. 83, Ch D 9–06,
9–52, 9–58
Rowan v. Steinberg. *See* Kennedy v. Steinberg.
Rowlands v. Collow [1992] 1 N.Z.L.R. 178 .... 8–52, 8–239, 8–254, 8–311
Rowling v. Takaro Properties Ltd [1988] A.C. 473; [1988] 2 W.L.R. 418; [1988]
1 All E.R. 163, PC (NZ) 2–77, 2–84, 13–114, 15–50
Roy v. Edmond Vienneau Assurance Ltee (1986) 67 N.B.R. (2d) 16; 172 A.P.R.
16, CA (New Brunswick) 14–75
Royal Bank of Canada v. Clark (1978) 88 D.L.R. (3d) 76, aff'd 105 C.L.R. (3d)
85, Sup Ct (Can) 10–255
Royal Bank of Scotland plc v. Etridge (No.2) [1998] 4 All E.R. 705; [1998] 2
F.L.R. 843; [1998] 3 F.C.R. 675; (1999) 31 H.L.R. 575; [1998] Fam. Law
665; (1998) 95(32) L.S.G. 31; (1998) 148 N.L.J. 1390; [1998] N.P.C. 130;
(1998) 76 P. & C.R. D39; *The Times*, August 17, 1998, CA 2–142, 2–145, 2–146,
10–04, 10–205
Royal Brompton Hospital NHS Trust v. Hammond (No.1) [1999] B.L.R. 162;
(2000) 2 T.C.L.R. 92; 66 Con. L.R. 42; (1999) 15 Const. L.J. 395; (1999)
149 N.L.J. 89;[2001] C.I.L.L. 1714; *The Independent*, January 25, 1999
(C.S.), QBD (T&CC) 6–08, 8–149, 8–155, 8–157, 8–165, 8–231, 8–235, 8–327
—— v. Hammond (No.2), 69 Con. L.R. 132, QBD (T&CC) 8–320
—— v. Hammond (No.3), 69 Con. L.R. 145; [2000] Lloyd's Rep. P.N. 643, CA;
affirming [1999] B.L.R. 385, QBD (T&CC) 4–08, 4–09, 8–307, 8–319
—— v. Hammond (No.4) [2000] B.L.R. 75; 69 Con. L.R. 170, QBD (T&CC) 8–20,
8–229
—— v. Hammond (No.7) [2001] C.I.L.L. 1714 .... 6–08, 6–13
Royal Brunei Airlines Sdn Bhd v. Tan; *sub nom.* Royal Brunei Airlines Sdn Bhd
v. Philip Tan Kok Ming [1995] 2 A.C. 378; [1995] 3 W.L.R. 64; [1995] 3 All
E.R. 97; [1995] B.C.C. 899; (1995) 92(27) L.S.G. 33; (1995) 145 N.L.J.
888; [1995] 139 S.J.L.B. 146; *The Times*, May 29, 1995; *The Independent*,
June 22, 1995, PC (Bru) 10–36, 10–38, 10–39
Royal Institution of Chartered Surveyors v. Wiseman Marshall. *See* Fryer v.
Royal Institution of Chartered Surveyors.
Rozanes v. Bowen (1928) 32 Ll.L.Rep. 98, CA 14–03
Rubicon Computer Systems Ltd v. United Paints Ltd (2000) 2 T.C.L.R. 453;
[2000] Masons C.L.R. 3, CA 17–59, 17–60
Ruiz Torija v. Spain; Series A, No.303–A; (1995) 19 E.H.R.R. 553, ECHR 7–67
Rumbelows v. AMK (1982) 19 B.L.R. 25, QBD 8–59, 8–125
Rumsey v. Owen white & Catlin (1978) 245 E.G. 225, CA 10–149, 10–297, 10–302
Ruparel v. Awan [2001] Lloyd's Rep. P.N. 258, Ch D 10–66
Russel v. Fraser (1981) 118 D.L.R. (3d) 733 10–219
Russell v. Fraser (1981) 118 D.L.R. (3d) 733, CA (BC) 10–220

PARA.

Russell v. Palmer (1767) 2 Wils. 325 10–185

Russell McVeagh McKenzie Bartleet & Co. v. Tower Corp. [1998] 3 N.Z.L.R.
641, CA (NZ) 10–31

Russell-Cooke Trust Co. v. Elliott, March 23, 2001, unreported 13–10

Ruxley Electronics and Construction Ltd v. Forsyth; Laddingford Enclosures Ltd
v. Forsyth [1996] A.C. 344; [1995] 3 W.L.R. 118; [1995] 3 All E.R. 268; 73
B.L.R. 1; 45 Con. L.R. 61; (1995) 14 Tr. L.R. 541; (1995) 11 Const. L.J.
381; [1995] E.G.C.S. 11; (1995) 145 N.L.J. 996; (1995) 139 S.J.L.B. 163;
The Times, July 3, 1995; *The Independent*, July 12, 1995, HL 3–01, 8–292,
8–293, 8–300, 8–311, 8–312, 10–313, 17–112

Ryan v. Public Trustee [2000] 1 N.Z.L.R. 700 10–219

Rylands v. Fletcher; *sub nom.* Fletcher v. Rylands (1868) L.R. 3 H.L. 330;
[1861–73] All E.R. Rep. 1; 37 L.J.Ex. 161; 19 L.T. 220; 33 J.P. 70, HL;
affirming (1866) L.R. 1 Exch. 265; 4 H. & C. 263; 35 L.J.Ex. 154; 14 L.T.
523; 30 J.P. 486; 12 Jur.(N.S.) 603; 14 W.R. 799, Ex Chamber 12–170

S (A Minor) (Consent to Medical Treatment), Re [1994] 2 F.L.R. 1065; [1995] 1
F.C.R. 604; [1995] Fam. Law 20, Fam Div 12–148

S (A Minor) v. North Birmingham H.A. (1998) 40 B.M.L.R. 103, CA 12–273

S (Adult Patient: Sterilisation: Patient's Best Interests), Re; *sub nom.* SL (Adult
Patient) (Sterilisation), Re; SL v. SL; SL (Adult Patient) (Medical Treatment), Re [2001] Fam. 15; [2000] 3 W.L.R. 1288; [2000] 2 F.L.R. 389;
[2000] 2 F.C.R. 452; [2000] Lloyd's Rep. Med. 339; (2000) 55 B.M.L.R.
105; [2000] Fam. Law 711; (2000) 97(24) L.S.G. 40; *The Times*, May 26,
2000, CA 12–142, 12–144, 12–145

S (Adult: Refusal of Treatment), Re [1993] Fam. 123; [1992] 3 W.L.R. 806;
[1992] 4 All E.R. 671; [1993] 1 F.L.R. 26; [1992] 2 F.C.R. 893; [1993] 4
Med. L.R. 28; [1993] Fam. Law 221; (1992) 142 N.L.J. 1450; (1992) 136
S.J.L.B. 299; *The Times*, October 16, 1992; *The Independent*, October 14,
1992, Fam Div 12–139

S v. M (Wasted Costs Order) [1998] 3 F.C.R. 665; *The Times*, March 26, 1998,
Ch D 11–28

SCM (United Kingdom) Ltd v. WJ Whittall & Son Ltd [1971] 1 Q.B. 337; [1970]
3 W.L.R. 694; [1970] 3 All E.R. 245; 114 S.J. 706, CA 2–27

SEC Chenery Corporation (1943) 318 U.S. 80 2–129

SG (Adult Mental Patient: Abortion), Re [1991] 2 F.L.R. 329; [1991] F.C.R. 753;
[1993] 4 Med. L.R. 75; [1991] Fam. Law 309, Fam Div 12–144

SL (Adult Patient) (Sterilisation), Re. *See* S (Adult Patient: Sterilisation: Patient's
Best Interests), Re.

Sa'ad v. Robinson [1989] 1 Med.L.R. 40 12–185

SAAMCO v. York Montague Ltd. *See* South Australia Asset Management Co.
Ltd v. York Montague Ltd.

Sabapathi v. Huntley [1938] 1 W.W.R. 317 12–185

Sabri-Tabrizi v. Lothian Health Board 1998 S.C. 373; 1998 S.L.T. 607; (1998) 43
B.M.L.R. 190; 1998 Rep. L.R. 37; 1998 G.W.D. 5–247, OH 12–274

Sadler v. Henry (1954) 1 B.M.J. 1331 12–179

Saffery v. Wray (1846) 7 L.T.(O.S.) 183 10–307

Saif Ali v. Sydney Mitchell & Co. [1980] A.C. 198; [1978] 3 W.L.R. 849; [1978]
3 All E.R. 1033; [1955–95] P.N.L.R. 151; 122 S.J. 761, HL 2–116, 9–58, 10–106,
11–08, 11–09, 11–10, 11–11, 11–12, 11–13, 11–40, 11–55

Saigol v. Cranley Mansion Ltd (No.2) (2000) 72 Con.L.R. 54, CA 8–300

PARA.

St Albans City and District Council v. International Computers Ltd [1996] 4 All
E.R. 481; [1997–98] Info. T.L.R. 58; [1997] F.S.R. 251; (1996) 15 Tr. L.R.
444; [1998] Masons C.L.R. Rep. 98; (1997) 20(2) I.P.D. 20020; *The Times*,
August 14, 1996, CA 5–04, 17–02, 17–05, 17–07, 17–08, 17–13, 17–18, 17–21,
17–28, 17–29, 17–30, 17–41, 17–50, 17–60, 17–64, 17–82, 17–84,
17–89, 17–94, 17–120, 17–121
St George's Healthcare NHS Trust v. S (Guidelines); R. v. Collins, ex p. S (No.2)
[1999] Fam. 26; (1997–98) 1 C.C.L. Rep. 578; [1998] Fam. Law 662; *The
Times*, August 3, 1998, CA 12–136, 12–139
—— v. S; R. v. Collins, ex p. S (No.1) [1998] 3 W.L.R. 936; [1998] 3 All E.R.
673; [1998] 2 F.L.R. 728; [1998] 2 F.C.R. 685; (1997–98) 1 C.C.L. Rep.
410; (1998) 44 B.M.L.R. 160; [1998] C.O.D. 396; [1998] Fam. Law 526;
(1998) 95(22) L.S.G. 29; (1998) 148 N.L.J. 693; (1998) 142 S.J.L.B. 164;
The Times, May 8, 1998; *The Independent*, May 12, 1998, CA 7–41
St Isidore Asphalte Ltee v. Luminex Signs Ltd (1996) 176 N.B.R.(2d) 135, QBD
(New Brunswick) 14–12, 14–53, 14–82
St Marylebone Property Co. Ltd v. Payne [1994] 2 E.G.L.R. 25; [1994] 45 E.G.
156, CC 9–28
Salgo v. Leland Stanford Jr. University Board of Trustees 154 Cal.App 2d 560;
317 P. 2d 170 (1957) 12–130
Salih v. Enfield A.H.A. [1991] 3 All E.R. 400; [1991] 2 Med. L.R. 235; *The
Independent*, March 26, 1991; *The Guardian*, May 2, 1991; *The Daily
Telegraph*, April 8, 1991, CA 12–289, 12–300
Salomon v. A Salomon & Co. [1897] A.C. 22, HL 2–89
Saltman Engineering Co. v. Campbell Engineering Co. (1948) [1963] 3 All E.R.
413 (Note); (1948) 65 R.P.C. 203, CA 2–156
Salvage Association v. CAP Financial Services Ltd [1995] F.S.R. 654, QBD 17–48,
17–50, 17–102, 17–106, 17–113, 17–119, 17–120, 17–122
Saminadhen v. Khan [1992] 1 All E.R. 963 (Note), CA 10–103
Sampson v. John Boddy Timber (1995) 145 N.L.J. 851; *The Independent*, May
17, 1995, CA 11–30
Samuels v. Davis [1943] K.B. 526; [1943] 2 All E.R. 3; 112 L.J.K.B. 561; 168
L.T. 296, CA 2–12, 8–172, 12–11, 12–149
San Sebastian Property v. Minister Administering the Environmental Planning
and Assessment Act 1979 (1986) 162 C.L.R. 340 8–120
Sanderson v. Walker (1807) 13 Ves.Jun. 60, ... 2–134
Sandown Hotels Ltd v. Phelps (1953) 167 E.G. 595 .... 8–243, 8–290
Sansom v. Metcalfe Hambleton & Co. 57 Con. L.R. 88; [1998] P.N.L.R. 542;
[1998] 2 E.G.L.R. 103; [1998] 26 E.G. 154; [1997] E.G.C.S. 185; (1998)
95(5) L.S.G. 28; (1998) 142 S.J.L.B. 45; [1997] N.P.C. 186; *The Times*,
December 29, 1997m, CA 6–06, 6–11, 8–153, 9–06, 9–52, 15–91
Saphena Computing Ltd v. Allied Collection Agencies Ltd [1995] F.S.R. 616,
CA 17–30, 17–31, 17–36, 17–37, 17–40, 17–92, 17–100
Sarginson Brothers v. Keith Moulton & Co. Ltd (1942) 73 Ll. L. Rep. 104,
Assizes (Birmingham) 9–56, 14–14, 14–35, 14–83
Sasea Finance Ltd (In Liquidation) v. KPMG (formerly KPMG Peat Marwick
McLintock) (No.2) [2000] 1 All E.R. 676; [2000] 1 B.C.L.C. 236; [2000]
B.C.C. 989; [2000] Lloyd's Rep. P.N. 227, CA; reversing [1999] B.C.C.
857; *The Times*, August 25, 1998, Ch D 15–41, 15–126, 15–138
Saumarez v. Medway and Gravesend Hospital Management Committee (1953) 2
B.M.J. 1109 .... 12–178, 12–254
Saunders and Collard v. Broadstairs Local Board (1890) cited in Hudson's
Building Contracts (4th ed., 1914), Vol. 2, p. 164 .... 8–196, 8–214, 8–221, 8–247,
8–303
Saunders v. Leeds Western H.A. [1993] 4 Med.L.R. 355; (1985) 129 S.J. 225,
QBD 12–119

PARA.

Savage v. Board of School Trustees [1951] 3 D.L.R. 39 .... 8–196, 8–197, 8–198

Saxby v. Morgan [1997] P.I.Q.R. P531; [1997] 8 Med.L.R. 293; (1997) 38
B.M.L.R. 126; *The Times*, May 2, 1997, CA 5–58, 12–289

Sayers v. Collyer (1885) L.R. 28 Ch. D. 103, CA 5–107

Scally v. Southern Health and Social Services Board [1992] 1 A.C. 294; [1991]
3 W.L.R. 778; [1991] 4 All E.R. 563; [1991] I.C.R. 771; [1991] I.R.L.R.
522; (1991) 141 N.L.J. 1482; (1991) 135 S.J. 172; *The Times*, October 24,
1991; *The Independent*, October 25, 1991; *Financial Times*, October 30,
1991; *The Guardian*, November 20, 1991, HL 2–104

Scarborough Building Society v. Howes Percival (1998) 76 P. & C.R. D4, CA 10–147

Scarborough Harbour Commission v. Robinson, Coulson Kirby & Co. (1934) 78
Acct.L.R. 65 15–112

Sceptre Resources Ltd v. Deloitte Haskins & Sells (1991) 83 Alta L.R. (2d) 157,
Sup CA (Alberta) 15–91

Schering Chemicals Ltd v. Falkman Ltd [1982] Q.B. 1; [1981] 2 W.L.R. 848;
[1981] 2 All E.R. 321; 125 S.J. 342, CA 10–26

Scholes v. Brook (1892) 64 L.T. 674; affirming (1891) 63 L.T. 837; 7 T.L.R.
214 9–32

Schroders Incorporated v. Hogan Systems Inc., 522 NYS 2d 404 17–07

Schuppan (A Bankrupt) (No.1), Re; *sub nom.* Bankrupt (No.400 of 1995), Re
[1996] 2 All E.R. 664; [1997] 1 B.C.L.C. 211; [1996] B.P.I.R. 486; *The
Times*, March 22, 1996, Ch D 10–27

Schweizer v. Central Hospital (1974) 53 D.L.R. (3d) 494 12–124

Scott v. Bloomsbury H.A. [1990] 1 Med.L.R. 214 12–112

—— v. London & St Katherine Docks (1865) 3 H. & C. 596 12–118

—— v. Wakefield A.H.A. [1997] 8 Med. L.R. 341, CA 12–111

Scott Group Ltd v. McFarlane [1978] 1 N.Z.L.R. 553 .... 15–78, 15–97, 15–137

Scott Wilson Kirkpatrick & Partners v. Ministry of Defence; Dean & Dyball
Construction Ltd v. Ministry of Defence [2000] B.L.R. 20; 73 Con. L.R. 52,
CA 8–134, 8–243, 8–247, 8–294, 8–299

Scudder v. Prothero & Prothero, 116 N.L.J. 612; (1966) 110 S.J. 248, QBD 10–181

Scuriaga v. Powell (1979) 123 S.J. 406 .... 5–58, 12–289, 12–293

Sea Harvest Corporation (Pty) Ltd v. Duncan Dock Cold Storage (Pty) Ltd, 2000
(1) S.A. 827, Sup Ct (SA) 8–282

Seager v. Copydex Ltd (No.1) [1967] 1 W.L.R. 923; [1967] 2 All E.R. 415; 2
K.I.R. 828; [1967] F.S.R. 211; [1967] R.P.C. 349; 111 S.J. 335, CA 2–152,
2–154, 2–156, 3–11

—— v. Copydex Ltd (No.2) [1969] 1 W.L.R. 809; [1969] 2 All E.R. 718; [1969]
F.S.R. 261; [1969] R.P.C. 250; 113 S.J. 281, CA 3–11, 3–15

Sealand of the Pacific v. Robert C. McHaffie Ltd (1974) 51 D.L.R. (3d) 702, CA
(BC) 2–89, 8–118, 8–203, 8–215

Seale v. Perry [1982] V.R. 193, Sup Ct (Vic) 10–54

Searle v. AR Hales & Co. Ltd; Hand v. AR Hales & Co. Ltd [1996] L.R.L.R. 68,
QBD 14–03

Searles v. Cann & Hallett [1999] P.N.L.R. 494, QBD 10–53, 10–60

Seavision Investment S.A. v. Evennett (Norman Thomas) and Clarkson Puckle;
Tiburon, The [1992] 2 Lloyd's Rep. 26; *The Times*, January 29, 1992; *The
Independent*, February 4, 1992, CA; affirming [1990] 2 Lloyd's Rep. 418,
QBD (Comm Ct) 14–11, 14–39, 14–122

Seaway Trust Co. v. Markle (1991) 7 C.C.L.T. (2d) 83, ... 10–61

Secretary of State for the Environment v. Essex Goodman & Suggitt [1986] 1
W.L.R. 1432; 32 B.L.R. 140; [1985] 2 E.G.L.R. 168; (1985) 275 E.G. 308;
(1985) 1 Const. L.J. 302; (1986) 83 L.S.G. 2755; (1986) 130 S.J. 574, QBD
(OR) 5–35, 9–09, 9–10

PARA.

Secretary of State for the Home Department v. Robb [1995] Fam. 127; [1995] 2
W.L.R. 722; [1995] 1 All E.R. 677; [1995] 1 F.L.R. 412; [1995] 1 F.C.R.
557; [1995] Fam. Law 185; (1994) 144 N.L.J. 1695; *The Times*, October 21,
1994; *The Independent*, October 10, 1994 (C.S.), Fam Div 12–137
Secretary of State for Trade and Industry v. Grant, September 15, 2000,
unreported 13–10, 13–119
Secretary, Department of Health and Community Services v. JWB (1992) 106
A.L.R. 385, 453, HC (Aus) 12–124
Securities and Investments Board v. Lloyd-Wright 1994] 1 B.C.L.C. 147; [1993]
4 All E.R. 134, Ch D 13–137
—— v. Pantell S.A. (No.1) [1990] Ch. 426; [1989] 3 W.L.R. 698; [1989] 2 All
E.R. 673; [1989] B.C.L.C. 590; (1989) 139 N.L.J. 754, Ch D 13–137, 13–142,
13–146
—— v. Pantell S.A. (No.2) [1993] Ch. 256; [1992] 3 W.L.R. 896; [1993] 1 All
E.R. 134; [1993] B.C.L.C. 146; (1992) 142 N.L.J. 931; (1992) 136 S.J.L.B.
198; [1992] N.P.C. 79; *The Times*, June 24, 1992; *The Independent*, June 30,
1992; *Financial Times*, July 2, 1992, CA 10–03, 10–76, 13–142, 13–145
—— v. Scandex Capital Management A/S [1998] 1 W.L.R. 712; [1998] 1 All
E.R. 514; (1998) 95(6) L.S.G. 24; (1998) 148 N.L.J. 85; (1998) 142 S.J.L.B.
63; *The Times*, December 20, 1997, CA 13–137, 13–142, 13–145
—— v. Vandersteen Associates NV [1991] B.C.L.C. 206 13–119
Seeward Mortgage Investment Corp. v. First Citizens Financial Corp. (1983) 45
B.C.L.R. 87 9–54
Segenhoe Ltd v. Akins (1990) 1 A.C.S.R. 691, Sup Ct (NSW) 15–138, 15–152
Selfe v. Ilford and District Hospital Management Committee (1970) 114 S.J. 935;
The Times, November 26, 1970; *The Guardian*, November 26, 1970 12–149,
12–236
Selvanathan v. General Medical Council [2001] Lloyd's Rep. Med. 1; (2001) 59
B.M.L.R. 95; *The Times*, October 26, 2000, PC (UK) 7–67
Semeniuk v. Cox [2000] 70 Alta. L.R. (3d) 30, QBD (Alberta) 12–203
Seney v. Crooks [1998] 166 D.L.R (4th) 337, CA (Alberta) 12–203, 12–204, 12–264,
12–275
Sergius v. Janax Design & Drafting (1992) 64 B.C.L.R. (2d) 176 8–93
Serre v. De Tilly (1975) 8 O.R. (2d) 490, HC (Ontario) 12–179
Sew Hoy & Sons Ltd v. Coopers & Lybrand [1996] 1 N.Z.L.R. 392, CA (NZ) 15–124
Seyfert v. Burnaby Hospital Society (1986) 27 D.L.R. (4th) 96 .... 12–181, 12–251
Seymour v. Seymour (1996) 40 N.S.W.L.R. 358 10–45
Shacklock v. Chas. Osenton, Lockwood & Co. (1964) 192 E.G. 819 9–62
Shade v. Compton Partnership [2000] Lloyd's Rep. P.N. 81; [2000] P.N.L.R. 218,
CA 10–312
Shah (Chandrakant Keshavlal) v. Singh (Gurdip) [1996] P.N.L.R. 83, QBD 10140
Shakoor (Administratrix of the Estate of Shakoor) v. Situ (t/a Eternal Health Co.)
[2001] 1 W.L.R. 410; [2000] 4 All E.R. 181; (2001) 57 B.M.L.R. 178; *The
Independent*, May 25, 2000, QBD 12–74, 12–76, 12–151, 12–225, 12–262
Shankie-Williams v. Heavey [1986] 2 E.G.L.R. 139; (1986) 279 E.G. 316, CA 9–40,
9–121
Sharp and Roarer Investments Ltd v. Sphere Drake Insurance; Moonacre, The
[1992] 2 Lloyd's Rep. 501, QBD (Comm Ct) 2–118, 14–33, 14–49, 14–52,
14–62, 14–69, 14–71, 14–81, 14–85, 14–124, 14–130
Sharpe, Re; *sub nom.* Masonic and General Life Assurance Co. v. Sharpe;
Bennett, Re [1892] 1 Ch. 154, CA 5–90
Sharpe v. Leicestershire H.A. [1994] C.L.Y. 1535 12–245
—— v. Southend H.A. [1997] 8 Med. L.R. 299; *The Times*, May 9, 1997,
QBD 12–112
Shaw v. Applegate [1977] 1 W.L.R. 970; [1978] 1 All E.R. 123; (1978) 35 P. &
C.R. 181; 121 S.J. 424, CA 5–106, 5–107, 5–110

PARA.

Shaw v. Arden (1832) 9 Bing. 287; 1 Dowl. 705; 2 Moo. & S. 341; 2 L.J.C.P. 1;
131 E.R. 623 10–307
—— v. Fraser Southwell [1999] Lloyd's Rep. P.N. 633, CA 10–275
—— v. Halifax (SW) Ltd [1994] 2 E.G.L.R. 95 .... 9–132, 9–190, 9–191
Sheldon v. RHM Outhwaite (Underwriting Agencies) Ltd [1996] A.C. 102;
[1995] 2 W.L.R. 570; [1995] 2 All E.R. 558; [1995] 2 Lloyd's Rep. 197;
(1995) 92(22) L.S.G. 41; (1995) 145 N.L.J. 687; (1995) 139 S.J.L.B. 119;
The Times, May 5, 1995; *The Independent*, May 9, 1995; Lloyd's List, May
24, 1995 (I.D.), HL 5–70, 5–71, 5–74, 5–77
Shelley Films Ltd v. Rex Features Ltd [1994] E.M.L.R. 134, Ch D 2–156
Shenkin v. DM Hall & Son, January 23, 1996, unreported 9–177
Shepherd Construction Ltd v. Mecright Ltd [2000] B.L.R. 489, QBD (T&CC) 8–340
Sherlock v. North Birmingham H.A. *See* S (A Minor) v. North Birmingham
H.A.
Sherman (Deceased), Re; *sub nom.* Walters (Deceased), Re; Trevenen v. Pearce
[1954] Ch. 653; [1954] 2 W.L.R. 903; [1954] 1 All E.R. 893; 98 S.J. 302, Ch
D 3–09
Sherson & Associates Pty Ltd v. Bailey [2000] N.S.W.C.A. 275, CA (NSW) 8–313
Sherwood and Casson Ltd v. Mackenzie, November 30, 1999, unreported 8–338
Shiells and Thorne v. Blackburne (1789) 1 H.Bl. 158; 2 R.R. 750 12–07
Shigeva v. Schafer (1984) 5 N.S.W.L.R. 502, HC 10–41, 10–95
Shilcock v. Passman (1836) 7 Car. & P. 289 .... 10–77, 10–188, 10–311
Shorrock v. Meggitt [1991] B.C.C. 471; *The Times*, June 4, 1991, CA 15–114
Short v. McCarthy (1820) 3 B. & Ald. 626; 100 E.R. 789 5–14
Short & Compton v. Brackett (1904) Acct.L.R. 8 15–110
Shortland v. Northland Health Limited [1998] N.Z.L.R. 433, CA (NZ) 12–146
Shui On Construction Co. Ltd v. Shui Kay Co. Ltd (1984–85) 1 Con.L.J. 305 8–107
Sidaway v. Board of Governors of the Bethlem Royal Hospital [1985] A.C. 871;
[1985] 2 W.L.R. 480; [1985] 1 All E.R. 643; (1985) 82 L.S.G. 1256; (1985)
135 N.L.J. 203; (1985) 129 S.J. 154, HL; affirming [1984] Q.B. 493; [1984]
2 W.L.R. 778; [1984] 1 All E.R. 1018; (1984) 81 L.S.G. 899; (1984) 128 S.J.
301, CA 12–09, 12–29, 12–30, 12–69, 12–71, 12–75, 12–94, 12–96, 12–102,
12–109, 12–124, 12–131, 12–135, 12–201, 12–207, 12–210,
12–212, 12–213, 12–217, 12–218, 12–219, 12–227, 12–229,
12–232
Siddell v. Smith Cooper & Partners; Follows v. Smith Cooper & Partners [1999]
Lloyd's Rep. P.N. 79; [1999] P.N.L.R. 511, CA 15–51, 15–67, 15–68, 15–69,
15–82
Silkstone and Haigh Moor Coal Company v. Edey [1900] 1 Ch. 16, Ch D 2–140
Silver v. Morris (1995) 139 N.S.R. (2d) 18, CA (Nova Scotia) 10–6
—— v. United Kingdom; Series A, No.161; (1983) 5 E.H.R.R. 347, ECHR 7–24,
7–33
Silver and Drake v. Baines. *See* Geoffrey Silver & Drake v. Baines.
Simaan General Contracting Co. v. Pilkington Glass Ltd [1988] Q.B. 758; [1988]
2 W.L.R. 761; [1988] 1 All E.R. 791; 40 B.L.R. 28; [1988] F.T.L.R. 469;
(1988) 138 N.L.J. 53; (1988) 132 S.J. 463, CA 2–94
Simmons v. Pennington & Son [1955] 1 W.L.R. 183; [1955] 1 All E.R. 240; 99
S.J. 146, CA 10–84, 10–201
Simonius Vischer & Co. v. Holt Thompson [1979] 2 N.S.W.L.R. 322 .... 5–114, 5–115,
15–36, 15–148
Simple Simon Catering v. JE Binstock Miller & Co. (1973) 228 E.G. 527; (1973)
117 S.J. 529, CA 9–130, 9–135, 9–136, 10–166, 10–274
Simpson v. Grove Tompkins & Co., 126 S.J. 347; *The Times*, May 17, 1982,
CA 10–264
—— v. Norwest Holst Southern Ltd [1980] 1 W.L.R. 968; [1980] 2 All E.R. 471;
124 S.J. 313, CA 5–65

PARA.

Sims v. Craig Bell & Bond [1991] 3 N.Z.L.R. 535, CA 10–18
Sinclair v. Bowden Son and Partners (1962) 183 E.G. 95 9–98
Sinclair-Jones v. Kay [1989] 1 W.L.R. 114; [1988] 2 All E.R. 611; (1988) 138
    N.L.J. 99; (1989) 133 S.J. 220, CA 10–188
Sincock v. Bangs (Reading) [1952] C.P.L. 562; (1952) 160 E.G. 134 .... 8–316, 9–91,
    9–98, 9–110, 9–134
Singer & Friedlander Ltd v. John D Wood & Co. [1955–95] P.N.L.R. 70; (1977)
    243 E.G. 212, QBD 9–20, 9–34, 9–44, 9–53, 9–56, 9–58, 9–60, 9–61, 9–62,
    9–75, 9–101, 9–104, 9–106, 9–107, 9–156
Sion v. Hampstead H.A. [1994] 5 Med. L.R. 170; [1994] J.P.I.L. 241; *The Times*,
    June 10, 1994, CA 12–39, 12–40
Siraj-Eldin v. Campbell Middleton Burness & Dickson [1989] S.L.T. 122, IH 10–278,
    10–282
Skandia Property (U.K.) Ltd v. Thames Water Utilities Ltd [1999] B.L.R. 338;
    The Times, September 7, 1999, CA 8–298, 8–299
Skelton v. Lewisham and North Southwark H.A. [1998] Lloyd's Rep. Med. 324,
    QBD 12–69, 12–73
Skimming v. Goldberg (1993) 6 W.W.R. 59, QB (Manitoba) 10–25
Skirzyk v. Crawford (1990) 64 Man.R. (2d) 220, QB (Manitoba); aff'd. June 11,
    1991 10–324
Skitt v. Khan [1997] 8 Med.L.R. 105, CA 5–58
Slater v. Baker (1767) 2 Wils.K.B. 359; 95 E.R. 860 12–201
—— v. Hoyle & Smith Ltd [1920] 2 K.B. 11; [1918–19] All E.R. Rep. 654; 90
    L.J.K.B. 401; 122 L.T. 611; 36 T.L.R. 132; 25 Com.Cas. 140, CA 9–148
Slater Wilmshurst v. Crown Group [1991] 1 N.Z.L.R. 344, HC 10–200
Slevin v. Southampton and South West Hampshire H.A. [1997] 8 Med.L.R. 175,
    QBD 5–58
Smith v. Anderson (1880) L.R. 15 Ch. D. 247, CA 13–29
—— v. Auckland Hospital Board [1964] N.Z.L.R. 241; [1965] N.Z.L.R. 191 12–216
—— v. Barking, Havering and Brentwood H.A. [1994] 5 Med.L.R. 285, QBD 12–263
—— v. Brighton and Lewes Hospital Management Committee, *The Times*, May
    2, 1958 .... 12–149, 12–192, 12–284
—— v. Carter, 1995 S.L.T. 295; 1994 S.C.L.R. 539, OH 9–38
—— v. Chadwick (1884) 9 App.Cas. 187 15–129
—— v. Cologan (1788) 2 T.R. 188n 14–38, 14–93
—— v. Eric S Bush; Harris v. Wyre Forest D.C. [1990] 1 A.C. 831; [1989] 2
    W.L.R. 790; [1989] 2 All E.R. 514; (1989) 21 H.L.R. 424; 87 L.G.R. 685;
    [1955–95] P.N.L.R. 467; [1989] 18 E.G. 99; [1989] 17 E.G. 68; (1990) 9 Tr.
    L.R. 1; (1989) 153 L.G. Rev. 984; (1989) 139 N.L.J. 576; (1989) 133 S.J.
    597, HL 2–18, 2–30, 2–47, 2–78, 2–92, 2–93, 2–103, 2–110, 2–116, 5–04, 5–07,
    5–08, 5–09, 9–14, 9–20, 9–27, 9–30, 9–31, 9–34, 9–35, 9–36, 9–37,
    9–39, 9–43, 9–45, 9–46, 9–47, 9–48, 9–49, 9–50, 9–51, 9–57,
    9–63, 9–64, 9–65, 9–67, 9–69, 9–70, 9–71, 9–72, 9–83, 9–84,
    9–85, 10–40, 14–28, 15–48, 15–59, 15–60
—— v. Kay (1859) 7 H.L.C. 750 2–144
—— v. Lascelles (1788) 2 T.R. 187 .... 14–38, 14–74
—— v. Leicestershire H.A.; *sub nom.* Smith v. Leicester H.A. [1998] Lloyd's
    Rep. Med. 77, CA 5–58
—— v. Lewisham Group Hospital Management Committee, (1955) 2 B.M.J. 64;
    The Times, June 21, 1955 12–186
—— v. Linskills [1996] 1 W.L.R. 763; [1996] 2 All E.R. 353; (1996) 146 N.L.J.
    209; (1996) 140 S.J.L.B. 49; *The Times*, February 7, 1996, CA 10–109
—— v. Littlewoods Organisation Ltd. *See* Maloco v. Littlewoods Organisation
    Ltd.
—— v. Mansi [1963] 1 W.L.R. 26; [1962] 3 All E.R. 857; 106 S.J. 876, CA 10–100
—— v. McInnis (1979) 91 D.L.R. (3d) 190 11–48

PARA.

Smith v. Price (1862) 2 F. & F. 748, NP 14–114

—— v. Salford H.A. [1994] 5 Med.L.R. 321, CA 12–186, 12–188, 12–193, 12–213,
12–216, 12–270

—— v. Sheard (1906) 34 Acct.L.R. 65 15–31

—— v. South Wales Switchgear Co. Ltd [1978] 1 W.L.R. 165; [1978] 1 All E.R.
18; 1978 S.C. (H.L.) 1; 1978 S.L.T. 21; 8 B.L.R. 1; 122 S.J. 61, HL 5–06

—— v. St Helier Group Hospital Management Committee, *The Times*, May 10,
1956 12–80

—— v. Tunbridge Wells Health Authority [1994] 5 Med.L.R. 334 ...... 12–101, 12–223

—— v. Wells (1993) 105 Nfld. & P.E.I.R. 351, CA (Newfoundland) 10–185

Smith (Caroline) v. National Health Service Litigation Authority [2001] Lloyd's
Rep. Med. 90, QBD 3–05, 12–257

Smith Kline & French Laboratories (Australia) Ltd v. Department of Community
Services (1990) A.L.R. 87 2–162

—— v. Secretary to the Department of Community Services and Health (1991)
99 A.L.R. 679, Fed Ct (Aus) 2–158

Smith New Court Securities Ltd v. Scrimegeour Vickers (Asset Management) Ltd
[1997] A.C. 254 10–250

—— v. Scrimgeour Vickers (Asset Management) Ltd; Smith New Court Securi-
ties Ltd v. Citibank NA [1997] A.C. 254; [1996] 3 W.L.R. 1051; [1996] 4
All E.R. 769; [1997] 1 B.C.L.C. 350; (1996) 93(46) L.S.G. 28; (1996) 146
N.L.J. 1722; (1997) 141 S.J.L.B. 5; *The Times*, November 22, 1996; *The
Independent*, November 27, 1996, HL 10–250, 13–88, 13–100, 15–122, 15–123

Smolinski v. Mitchell (1995) 10 B.C.L.R. (3d) 366, Sup Ct (BC) 10–51

Smyth v. Huey [1993] N.I. 236, QBD 10–315

Sneesby v. Goldings, 45 Con. L.R. 11; [1995] 2 E.G.L.R. 102; [1995] 36 E.G.
136; [1994] E.G.C.S. 201, CA 9–130, 9–144, 9–190

Snell v. Farrell (1990) 4 C.C.L.T. 229, Sup Ct (Can) 12–248

Snipper v. Enever Freeman & Co. [1991] 2 E.G.L.R. 270 10–251

Societe Anonyme D'Intermediaries Luxembourgeois v. Farex [1995] L.R.L.R.
116 14–21

Société Commerciale de Réassurance v. Eras International Ltd (formerly Eras
(UK)); *sub nom.* Eras EIL Actions, Re [1992] 2 All E.R. 82 (Note); [1992]
1 Lloyd's Rep. 570; *The Times*, November 28, 1991; *The Independent*,
January 27, 1992 (C.S.); *Financial Times*, November 29, 1991, CA 5–53

Society of Lloyd's v. Clementson (No.3) [1997] L.R.L.R. 175; [1996] C.L.C.
1590; [1997] E.C.C. 193; [1996] 5 Re. L.R. 215; *The Times*, May 14, 1996,
QBD (Comm Ct) 16–02, 16–05, 16–09

Sohal v. Brar [1999] 63 Alta. L.R. (3d) 280 .... 12–174, 12–260

Solicitor, Ex p.; Hales, Re [1907] 2 K.B. 539, Div Ct 10–65, 10–67

Solicitor, Ex p.; Incorporated Law Society, Re (1895) S.J. 219 10–165

Solicitors, Re (1916) 11 W.W.R. 529, CA (BC) 10–68

Solicitor, Re [1966] 1 W.L.R. 1604; [1966] 3 All E.R. 52, Ch D 10–67, 10–73

Solicitor, Re (1969) 113 S.J. 549, DC 10–73

Solicitor (Chinese Walls), Re [1999] P.N.L.R. 950, QBD (T&CC) 2–166, 10–28

Solicitor (Wasted Costs Order) (No.1 of 1994), Re; *sub nom.* Ronald A Prior &
Co. (Solicitors), Re [1996] 1 Cr. App. R. 248; [1996] 1 F.L.R. 40; [1996] 3
F.C.R. 365; [1996] Fam. Law 83; (1996) 160 J.P.N. 514; (1995) 92(28)
L.S.G. 40; (1995) 139 S.J.L.B. 157; *The Times*, June 27, 1995, CA (Crim
Div) 10–137

Solicitor (Wasted Costs Order), Re [1993] 2 F.L.R. 959; [1993] Fam. Law 627;
(1993) 137 S.J.L.B. 107; *The Times*, April 16, 1993, CA 10–140

Solicitors (1995 C. No.2433), Re [1997] Ch. 1; [1996] 3 W.L.R. 16; [1995] 3 All
E.R. 482; [1995] F.S.R. 783, Ch D 2–162, 2–167, 10–27

PARA.

Solicitors (A Firm), Re [1992] Q.B. 959; [1992] 2 W.L.R. 809; [1992] 1 All E.R.
353; (1991) 141 N.L.J. 746; (1991) 135 S.J.L.B. 125; *The Times*, June 20,
1991; *The Independent*, June 26, 1991, CA 2–162, 10–27
Solicitors (A Firm), Re [2000] 1 Lloyd's Rep. 31, QBD (Comm Ct) 2–166, 10–30
Somasundaram v. M Julius Melchior & Co. [1988] 1 W.L.R. 1394; [1989] 1 All
E.R. 129; (1988) 138 N.L.J. 253; (1988) 132 S.J. 1732, CA 10–106, 10–108,
10–109, 11–14, 11–25
Sonardyne Ltd v. Firth & Co. [1997] E.G.C.S. 84, QBD 10–166
South Australia Asset Management Corp. v. York Montague Ltd; United Bank of
Kuwait plc v. Prudential Property Services Ltd; Nykredit Mortgage Bank plc
v. Edward Erdman Group Ltd; Banque Bruxelles Lambert S.A. v. Eagle Star
Insurance Co. Ltd [1997] A.C. 191; [1996] 3 W.L.R. 87; [1996] 3 All E.R.
365; [1996] 5 Bank. L.R. 211; [1996] C.L.C. 1179; 80 B.L.R. 1; 50 Con.
L.R. 153; [1996] P.N.L.R. 455; [1996] 2 E.G.L.R. 93; [1996] 27 E.G. 125;
[1996] E.G.C.S. 107; (1996) 93(32) L.S.G. 33; (1996) 146 N.L.J. 956;
(1996) 140 S.J.L.B. 156; [1996] N.P.C. 100; *The Times*, June 24, 1996; *The
Independent*, July 2, 1996, HL; reversing in part [1995] Q.B. 375; [1995] 2
W.L.R. 607; [1995] 2 All E.R. 769, CA 3–02, 3–04, 3–13, 4–07, 5–36, 5–117,
8–265, 8–266, 8–267, 2–268, 8–285, 9–07, 9–08, 9–09, 9–10, 9–21,
9–59, 9–61, 9–81, 9–102, 9–104, 9–106, 9–112, 9–113, 9–116,
9–117, 9–121, 9–122, 9–128, 9–150, 9–151, 9–152, 9–156,
9–157, 9–160, 9–162, 9–166, 9–167, 9–172, 9–174, 10–206,
10–236, 10–244, 10–248, 10–250, 10–274, 10–287, 10–295,
10–296, 12–18, 12–244, 12–304, 13–100, 13–111, 13–158, 14–88,
14–110, 14–119, 14–120, 15–51, 15–59, 15–119, 15–122, 15–125,
15–126, 17–61, 17–116, 18–22
South Australia Asset Management Corporation v. York Montague Ltd, April 6,
1995, unreported 9–113, 9–159, 9–160
South Buckinghamshire NHS Trust v. R (A Patient) [1996] 7 Med. L.R. 401, Fam
Div 12–146
South Lakeland D.C. v. Curtins Consulting Engineers plc, May 23, 2000,
unreported 8–20, 8–209
South Pacific Manufacturing Co. Ltd v. New Zealand Security Consultants &
Investigations Ltd [1992] 2 N.Z.L.R. 282, CA (NZ) 2–54, 2–68, 2–71, 2–77,
8–122, 14–28
South West Water Services Ltd v. International Computers Ltd [1999] B.L.R.
420; [1998–99] Info. T.L.R. 154; [1999] I.T.C.L.R. 439; [2001] Lloyd's
Rep. P.N. 353; [1999] Masons C.L.R. 400, QBD (T&CC) 5–04, 17–102, 17–114,
17–123
Southcomb v. Bishop of Exeter (1847) 6 Ha. 213 5–103
Southern Water Authority v. Carey [1985] 2 All E.R. 1077, QBD 8–36
—— v. Lewis and Duvivier (No.1); *sub nom.* Southern Water Authority v.
Duvivier, 27 B.L.R. 111; (1984) 1 Const. L.J. 70; [1984] C.I.L.L. 90,
QBD 8–59
—— v. Lewis and Duvivier (No.2) (1984) 1 Const. L.J. 74, QBD (OR) 8–59, 8–125,
8–126, 8–128
SP Catterson & Sons Ltd, Re (1937) 81 Acct.L.R. 62 15–107
Spargo v. North Essex D.H.A. [1997] P.I.Q.R. P235; [1997] 8 Med.L.R. 125;
(1997) 37 B.M.L.R. 99; (1997) 94(15) L.S.G. 26; (1997) 141 S.J.L.B. 90;
The Times, March 21, 1997, CA 5–57, 5–60, 5–61
Sparham-Souter v. Town & Country Developments (Essex) Ltd [1976] Q.B. 858;
[1976] 2 W.L.R. 493; [1976] 2 All E.R. 65; 3 B.L.R. 70; 74 L.G.R. 355;
(1976) 241 E.G. 309; 120 S.J. 216, CA 5–19
Spartan Steel & Alloys Ltd v. Martin & Co. (Contractors) Ltd [1973] Q.B. 27;
[1972] 3 W.L.R. 502; [1972] 3 All E.R. 557; 14 K.I.R. 75; 116 S.J. 648,
CA 2–27

PARA.

Spector v. Ageda [1973] Ch. 30; [1971] 3 W.L.R. 498; [1971] 3 All E.R. 417; 22
P. & C.R. 1002; 115 S.J. 426, Ch D 10–19, 10–226
Spence v. Bell [1982] 6 W.W.R. 385, CA (Alberta) 10–79
Spencer, Re (1870) 39 L.J. Ch. 841; 21 L.T. 808; 18 W.R. 240, LC 10–177
Spencer-Ward v. Humberts [1995] 1 E.G.L.R. 123; [1995] 06 E.G. 148; [1994]
E.G.C.S. 129; [1994] N.P.C. 105, CA 5–54, 9–10
Spillane v. Wasserman (1992) 13 C.C.L.T. 267, HC (Ontario) 12–45
Spring v. Guardian Assurance plc [1995] 2 A.C. 296; [1994] 3 W.L.R. 354;
[1994] 3 All E.R. 129; [1994] I.C.R. 596; [1994] I.R.L.R. 460; (1994)
91(40) L.S.G. 36; (1994) 144 N.L.J. 971; (1994) 138 S.J.L.B. 183; *The*
Times, July 8, 1994; *The Independent*, July 12, 1994, HL 2–34, 2–45, 2–48, 8–98,
10–40, 12–63
—— v. Pride (1864) 4 De G.J. & S. 395 2–137
Spry v. Calman and Camberwell Health Authority, Unreported, April 6, 1998 12–189
Stacey v. Chiddy [1993] 4 Med.L.R. 216, Sup Ct (NSW) 12–174, 12–185
Stadel v. Albertson [1954] 2 D.L.R. 328 12–236
Stafford v. Conti Commodity Services Ltd [1981] 1 All E.R. 691; [1981] 1
Lloyd's Rep. 466; [1981] Com. L.R. 10, QBD (Comm Ct) 13–129
—— v. Stafford (1857) 1 De G. & J. 193 5–105
Stag Line Ltd v. Tyne Ship Repair Group Ltd; Zinnia, The [1984] 2 Lloyd's Rep.
211; (1985) 4 Tr. L. 33, QBD (Comm Ct) 8–36
Staines Warehousing Co. Ltd v. Montagu Executor & Trustee Co. Ltd [1987] 2
E.G.L.R. 130 9–74
Standard Chartered Bank v. Pakistan National Shipping Corp. (No.2); Standard
Chartered Bank v. Mehra [2000] 1 All E.R. (Comm) 1; [2000] 1 Lloyd's
Rep. 218; [2000] Lloyd's Rep. Bank. 40; [2000] C.L.C. 133; *The Times*,
March 15, 2000; *The Independent*, December 9, 1999, CA 2–91, 13–100
Stanford v. Roberts (1884) 26 Ch.D. 155 10–46
Stannard v. Ullithorne (1834) 10 Bing. 491 10–166
Stanton v. Callaghan [2000] Q.B. 75; [1999] 2 W.L.R. 745; [1998] 4 All E.R.
961; [1999] C.P.L.R. 31; [1999] B.L.R. 172; (1999) 1 T.C.L.R. 50; 62 Con.
L.R. 1; [1999] P.N.L.R. 116; [1998] 3 E.G.L.R. 165; [1999] 15 Const. L.J.
50; [1998] E.G.C.S. 115; (1998) 95(28) L.S.G. 32; (1998) 95(33) L.S.G. 33;
(1998) 148 N.L.J. 1355; (1998) 142 S.J.L.B. 220; [1998] N.P.C. 113; *The*
Times, July 25, 1998; *The Independent*, July 16, 1998, CA 2–97, 8–263, 12–24,
12–303
Stathams (Wasted Costs Order), Re. *See* Banks v. Woodhall Duckham Ltd
(No.2).
Steeds v. Peverel Management Services Ltd [2001] EWCA Civ. 419; *The Times*,
May 16, 2001; *The Daily Telegraph*, April 10, 2001, CA 5–68
Steele Ford & Newton v. Crown Prosecution Service (No.2); *sub nom.* Holden &
Co. v. Crown Prosecution Service (No.2); Bradburys v. Crown Prosecution
Service (No.2); Robin Murray & Co. v. Crown Prosecution Service (No.2);
McGoldrick & Co. v. Crown Prosecution Service (No.2) [1994] 1 A.C. 22;
[1993] 2 W.L.R. 934; [1993] 2 All E.R. 769; (1993) 97 Cr. App. R. 376;
[1994] C.O.D. 102; (1993) 143 N.L.J. 850; (1993) 137 S.J.L.B. 152; *The*
Times, May 28, 1993; *The Independent*, June 10, 1993, HL 10–128
Stefanyshyn v. Rubin (1996) 113 Man. R. (2d) 133 12–194
Steljes v. Ingram (1903) 19 T.L.R. 534 8–50
Stephens v. Avery [1988] Ch. 449; [1988] 2 W.L.R. 1280; [1988] 2 All E.R. 477;
[1988] F.S.R. 510; (1988) 85(25) L.S.G. 45; 132 S.J. 822; *The Times*,
February 27, 1988; *The Independent*, February 27, 1988, Ch D 2–156, 2–160
Stephenson Blake (Holdings) Ltd v. Streets Heaver Ltd [2001] Lloyd's Rep. P.N.
44; [1998] Masons C.L.R. Rep. 25, QBD (OR) 17–57, 17–104, 17–113, 17–125,
17–127
Stern and Sirotkin v. Oakfield Estates Ltd [1937] E.G.D. 70 .... 8–201, 8–214

PARA.

Stevens v. Bermondsey & Southwark Group Hospital Management Committee
(1963) 107 S.J. 478 .... 12–24, 12–274, 12–303
—— v. Gullis [2000] 1 All E.R. 527; [2001] C.P. Rep. 3; [1999] B.L.R. 394;
(2000) 2 T.C.L.R. 385; 73 Con. L.R. 42; [2000] P.N.L.R. 229; [1999] 3
E.G.L.R. 71; [1999] 44 E.G. 143; (2000) 16 Const. L.J. 68; *The Times*,
October 6, 1999; *The Independent*, October 14, 1999, CA 6–14, 8–155, 12–114
Stevenson v. Nationwide Building Society [1984] 2 E.G.L.R. 165; (1984) 272
E.G. 663; (1984) 1 Const. L.J. 239; (1985) 82 L.S.G. 36 .... 9–30, 9–64, 9–108
—— v. Rowand (1830) 2 Dow. & Co. 104; 4 Wils. & S. 177; 6 E.R. 668, HL 10–84,
10–98
—— v. Watson (1878–79) L.R. 4 C.P.D. 148; 48 L.J.C.P. 187; 27 L.T. 348; 20
W.R. 784, CPD 8–106
Stevenson Estate v. Siewert (2000) 86 Alta. L.R. (3d) 159, CA (Alta) 10–76
Steward v. Rapley [1989] 1 E.G.L.R. 159 .... 9–91, 9–128, 9–131, 9–140, 9–141, 9–145,
9–189
Stewart v. Canadian Broadcasting Association (1997) 150 D.L.R. (4th) 24, HC
(Ontario) 10–21, 11–05
—— v. H.A. Brechin & Co., 1959 S.C. 306; 1959 S.L.T. (Notes) 45, OH 9–82, 9–83,
9–90, 9–91, 9–107
—— v. Layton (1992) 111 A.L.R. 687, Fed Ct, General Division 10–25, 10–100,
10–228
—— v. Rundle [1940] 2 D.L.R. 503 2–145
Stewart Wrightson Group Ltd v. Crocker (1979) 124 S.J. 83; *The Times*, Decem-
ber 19, 1979, CA 10–104
Stijdom Park Extension 6 (PTY) Ltd v. Abcon [1998] 4 S.A.L.R. 844, Sup Ct
(SA) 8–249
Stinchcombe & Cooper Ltd v. Addison, Cooper, Jesson & Co. (1971) 115 S.J.
368 .... 10–156, 10–264
Stirling v. Poulgrain [1980] 2 N.Z.L.R. 402 10–202
Stobie v. Central Birmingham Health Authority (1994) 22 B.M.L.R. 135 12–230
Stockdale v. Nicholls [1993] 4 Med.L.R. 190, QBD 12–174, 12–179
Stockton v. Mason [1978] 2 Lloyd's Rep. 430; [1979] R.T.R. 130, CA 14–03
Stoffberg v. Elliott [1923] C.P.D. 148 12–124
Stokes v. Guest Keen & Nettlefold (Bolt & Nuts) Ltd [1968] 1 W.L.R. 1776; 5
K.I.R. 401; 112 S.J. 821, Assizes 12–83, 12–106, 12–169
—— v. Prance [1898] 1 Ch. 212; 42 S.J. 68; 67 L.J.Ch. 69; 77 L.T. 395; 46 W.R.
183 10–165
—— v. Trumper (1855) 3 W.R. 615, CA; (1855) 2 K. & J. 232; 25 L.T.(O.S.) 140;
3 W.R. 503; 69 E.R. 766 10–307
Storey v. Charles Church Developments Ltd; *sub nom.* Storey v. Charles Church
Developments plc (1995) 73 Con. L.R. 1; (1996) 12 Const. L.J. 206, QBD
(OR) 8–60, 8–62
—— v. Charles Church Developments plc (1995) 73 Con.L.R. 1 .... 8–159, 8–308
Stormont Main Working Men's Club v. J. Roscoe Milne Partnership (1988) 13
Con.L.R. 126 8–206
Stovin v. Wise and Norfolk C.C. [1996] A.C. 923; [1996] 3 W.L.R. 388; [1996]
3 All E.R. 801; [1996] R.T.R. 354; (1996) 93(35) L.S.G. 33; (1996) 146
N.L.J. 1185; (1996) 140 S.J.L.B. 201; *The Times*, July 26, 1996; *The
Independent*, July 31, 1996, HL 2–52, 2–69, 2–77, 2–84
Stovold v. Barlows [1996] C.L.C. 228; [1996] E.C.C. 101; [1996] P.N.L.R. 91;
[1995] E.G.C.S. 155; (1995) 92(40) L.S.G. 22; [1995] N.P.C. 154; (1996) 71
P. & C.R. D3; *The Times*, October 30, 1995, CA 8–287, 10–201, 10–259
Stoyles Insurance Services Ltd (1985) 56 Nfld. & P.E.I.R. 125, DC
(Newfoundland) 14–23

PARA.

Straddlers Groups A and C v. Secretary of State for Health ; *sub nom.* Creutzfeldt-
Jakob Disease Litigation (No.8), Re; CJD Litigation (No.8), Re (2000) 54
B.M.L.R. 104, QBD 12–254
Strangeways-Lesmere v. Clayton [1936] 2 K.B. 11; 80 S.J. 306; [1936] 1 All E.R.
484; 105 L.J.K.B. 385; 154 L.T. 463; 52 T.L.R. 374 .... 12–149, 12–152, 12–192
Strategic Minerals Corp. NL v. Basham (1997) 25 A.C.S.R. 470, Sup Ct 15–129
Strathford East Kilbride Ltd v. HLM Design Ltd, 1999 S.L.T. 121; 1997 S.C.L.R.
877; 1997 Rep. L.R. 112; 1997 G.W.D. 31–1554; *The Times*, December 1,
1997, OH 8–89
Stratton Ltd v. West, *Financial Times*, April 11, 1990, Ch D 10–198, 10–234
Stringer v. Peat Marwick Mitchell & Co. [2000] 1 N.Z.L.R. 450 15–85
Strong & Pearl v. S. Allison & Co. Ltd (1926) 25 Ll.L.Rep. 504 ...... 14–14, 14–47, 14–49,
14–81, 14–122
Stronghold Investments Ltd v. Renkema (1984) 7 D.L.R. (4th) 427, CA (BC) 10–154
Strongman (1945) v. Sincock [1955] 2 Q.B. 525; [1955] 3 W.L.R. 360; [1955] 3
All E.R. 90; 99 S.J. 540, CA 8–201
Strover v. Harrington [1988] Ch. 390; [1988] 2 W.L.R. 572; [1988] 1 All E.R.
769; (1988) 56 P. & C.R. 302; [1988] 09 E.G. 61; 132 S.J. 416, Ch D 9–24,
10–199
Stubbings v. United Kingdom [1997] 1 F.L.R. 105; [1997] 3 F.C.R. 157; (1997)
23 E.H.R.R. 213; 1 B.H.R.C. 316; [1997] Fam. Law 241; *The Times*,
October 24, 1996; *The Independent*, October 24, 1996, ECHR 7–10
—— v. Webb [1993] A.C. 498; [1993] 2 W.L.R. 120; [1993] 1 All E.R. 322;
[1993] 1 F.L.R. 714; [1993] P.I.Q.R. P86; [1993] Fam. Law 342; (1993) 137
S.J.L.B. 32; *The Times*, December 17, 1992; *The Independent*, January 19,
1993, HL 5–12
Sturla v. Freccia. *See* Polini v. Gray.
Sudesh Madan v. General Medical Council (Interim Suspension Order) [2001]
EWHC Admin 577, QBD (Admin Ct) 7–67
Sullivan v. Layton Lougher & Co. [1995] 2 E.G.L.R. 111; [1995] 49 E.G. 127,
CA 5–40, 9–10
—— v. West Yorkshire Passenger Transport Executive [1985] 2 All E.R. 134,
CA 6–10, 10–142
Summers v. Congreve Horner & Co. and Independent Insurance Co., 27 Con.
L.R. 53, CA; reversing [1991] 2 E.G.L.R. 139; [1991] 36 E.G. 160; [1991]
E.G.C.S. 80; [1991] N.P.C. 83; *The Times*, July 22, 1991; *The Independent*,
July 9, 1991 9–107
Summit Financial Group Ltd v. Slaughter & May (a firm), *The Times* April 5
1999, Ch D 10–148
Summit Property Ltd Pitmans (A Firm) [2001] Lloyd's Rep. P.N. 164; [2000]
N.P.C. 97, Ch D 10–11, 10–191
Sun Microsystems Inc.'s Trade Mark Application [2001] R.P.C. 461, TMR 18–13
Sunderland v. McGreavey [1987] I.R. 372 8–144
Surrey, District of v. Carroll-Hatch and Associates Ltd (1979) 101 D.L.R. (3d)
218, 222 8–14
Sushma Lal v. Secretary of State for the Home Department [1992] Imm. A.R.
303, CA 10–131
Sutcliffe v. Chippendale and Edmondson (1982) 18 B.L.R. 149, QBD 8–238, 8–240,
8–244, 8–252, 8–253, 8–254
—— v. Sayer [1987] 1 E.G.L.R. 155; (1987) 281 E.G. 1452, CA 9–57
—— v. Thackrah [1974] A.C. 727; [1974] 2 W.L.R. 295; [1974] 1 All E.R. 859;
[1974] 1 Lloyd's Rep. 318; 118 S.J. 148, HL 8–14, 8–106, 8–110, 8–165, 8–221,
8–229, 8–253, 8–254, 8–303, 9–04
Sutherland Shire Council v. Heyman [1955–95] P.N.L.R. 238; (1985) 60 A.L.R.
1; (1985) 59 A.L.J.R. 564; (1986) 2 Const. L.J. 161, HC (Aus) 2–28, 2–37, 2–38,
2–39, 2–63, 2–84, 8–53, 8–70, 8–119, 12–19, 14–27, 15–48

PARA.

Sutherland v. CR Maton & Son Ltd 3 B.L.R. 87; (1976) 240 E.G. 135; [1976]
J.P.L. 753; [1979] 2 E.G.L.R. 81, QBD 9–10
—— v. Public Trustee [1980] 2 N.Z.L.R. 536, Sup Ct 10–51, 10–54, 10–123, 10–220
Sutton v. Population Services Family Planning Programme Ltd, *The Times*,
November 7, 1981, CA 12–245, 12–260
Swannell v. Ellis (1823) 1 Bing. 347; 8 Moore C.P. 340; 2 L.J.(O.S.)C.P. 8; 130
E.R. 140 10–183
Swindle v. Harrison [1997] 4 All E.R. 705; [1997] P.N.L.R. 641; [1997] N.P.C.
50; *The Times*, April 17, 1997, CA 2–137, 3–09, 3–12, 10–18, 10–231, 10–234,
15–122
Swindon and Marlborough NHS Trust v. S, *The Guardian*, December 10,
1994 12–146
Swinfen v. Lord Chelmsford (1860) 5 H. & N. 890; 29 L.J.Ex. 382; 2 L.T. 406;
6 Jur.(N.S.) 1035; 8 W.R. 545; 157 E.R. 1436 11–10
Swingcastle Ltd v. Alastair Gibson (A Firm) [1991] 2 A.C. 223; [1991] 2 W.L.R.
1091; [1991] 2 All E.R. 353; [1955–95] P.N.L.R. 590; [1991] 17 E.G. 83;
[1991] C.C.L.R. 55; [1991] E.G.C.S. 46; (1991) 141 N.L.J. 563; (1991) 135
S.J. 542; *The Times*, April 19, 1991; *The Independent*, May 16, 1991;
Financial Times, April 24, 1991, HL 9–52, 9–81, 9–128, 9–151, 9–152, 9–153,
9–157, 9–160, 9–163, 10–294
Swinney v. Chief Constable of Northumbria (No.1) [1997] Q.B. 464; [1996] 3
W.L.R. 968; [1996] 3 All E.R. 449; [1996] P.N.L.R. 473; (1996) 146 N.L.J.
878; *The Times*, March 28, 1996, CA 3–11
Swyny v. Harland [1894] 1 QB 707; 38 S.J. 256; [1891–94] All E.R. Rep. 1260;
63 L.J.Q.B. 415; 70 L.T. 227; 42 W.R. 297; 10 T.L.R. 276; 9 r. 210, CA 10–67
Sykes v. Midland Bank Executor & Trustee Co. Ltd [1971] 1 Q.B. 113; [1970]
3 W.L.R. 273; [1970] 2 All E.R. 471; 114 S.J. 225, CA 8–271, 10–07, 10–105,
10–155, 10–166, 10–234, 10–257, 11–55, 12–269
Symes v. Nipper (1840) 12 Ald. & El. 377 10–307
Syrett (Pamela) v. Carr and Neave, 54 B.L.R. 121; [1990] 48 E.G. 118; (1990) 6
Const. L.J. 305[1990] 2 E.G.L.R. 161, QBD 9–91, 9–140, 9–142, 9–143, 9–189
Systems Team Plusmark Ltd v. Kingswood Fluid Power Group plc, Transcript
QBENI 95/1063/E, April 30, 1996, unreported, CA 17–43

T, Re; *sub nom.* T v. T [1988] Fam. 52; [1988] 2 W.L.R. 189; [1988] 1 All E.R.
613; [1988] 1 F.L.R. 400; [1988] Fam. Law 126; (1987) 84 L.S.G. 2456;
(1987) 131 S.J. 1286; *The Times*, July 11, 1987, Fam Div 12–142
T (A Minor) (Wardship: Medical Treatment), Re; *sub nom.* T (A Minor) (Liver
Transplant: Consent), Re; C (A Minor) (Medical Treatment: Refusal of
Parental Consent), Re [1997] 1 W.L.R. 242; [1997] 1 All E.R. 906; [1997]
1 F.L.R. 502; [1997] 2 F.C.R. 363; [1997] 8 Med. L.R. 166; (1997) 35
B.M.L.R. 63; (1996) 93(42) L.S.G. 28; (1996) 146 N.L.J. 1577; (1996) 140
S.J.L.B. 237; *The Times*, October 28, 1996; *The Independent*, October 29,
1996, CA 12–148
T (Adult: Refusal of Treatment), Re; *sub nom.* T (Consent to Medical Treatment)
(Adult Patient), Re [1993] Fam. 95; [1992] 3 W.L.R. 782; [1992] 4 All E.R.
649; [1992] 2 F.L.R. 458; [1992] 2 F.C.R. 861; [1992] 3 Med. L.R. 306;
[1993] Fam. Law 27; (1992) 142 N.L.J. 1125; *The Times*, August 21, 1992;
The Independent, July 31, 1992; *The Guardian*, August 5, 1992, CA 12–127,
12–129, 12–135
T v. T. *See* T, Re; *sub nom.* T v. T.
TA Bickerton & Son Ltd v. NW Metropolitan Regional Hospital Board. *See*
North West Metropolitan Regional Hospital Board v. TA Bickerton &
Son.

PARA.

T&A (Children) (Risk of Disclosure), Re; *sub nom.* T (Children) (Care Proceedings: Guardian ad Litem), Re [2000] 1 F.L.R. 859; [2000] 1 F.C.R. 659; [2000] Lloyd's Rep. P.N. 452; [2000] Fam. Law 398; (2000) 164 J.P.N. 426; (2000) 97(3) L.S.G. 37; (2000) 144 S.J.L.B. 49; *The Times*, February 1, 2000, CA 2–166, 2–167, 10–29

TL Creda Ltd v. Hay Fielding Ltd, October 30, 1984, unreported, CA 14–40

T O'Donoghue Ltd v. Harding [1988] 2 Lloyd's Rep. 281; *Financial Times*, July 27, 1988, QBD 14–85

TP & KM v. United Kingdom (App. No.28945/95) [2001] 2 F.L.R. 549; [2001] 2 F.C.R. 289; *The Times*, May 31, 2001, ECHR 7–20, 7–22

TSB Bank plc v. Robert Irving & Burns [2000] 2 All E.R. 826; [1999] Lloyd's Rep. P.N. 956; [2000] P.N.L.R. 384, CA 10–145

Tahir v. Haringey H.A. [1998] Lloyd's Rep. Med. 104, CA 12–249

Tai Hing Cotton Mill Ltd v. Liu Chong Hing Bank Ltd (No.1) [1986] A.C. 80; [1985] 3 W.L.R. 317; [1985] 2 All E.R. 947; [1985] 2 Lloyd's Rep. 313; [1986] F.L.R. 14; (1985) 82 L.S.G. 2995; (1985) 135 N.L.J. 680; (1985) 129 S.J. 503, PC (HK) 2–104, 10–13, 14–18

Tailleur v. Grande Prairie General & Auxiliary Hospital [2000] 74 Alta. L.R. (3d) 20, CA (Can) 12–195, 12–245

Tameside and Glossop Acute Services NHS Trust v. CH (A Patient) [1996] 1 F.L.R. 762; [1996] 1 F.C.R. 753; (1996) 31 B.M.L.R. 93; [1996] Fam. Law 353; *The Independent*, February 26, 1996 (C.S.), Fam Div 12–141

Tan v. East London and City H.A. [1999] Lloyd's Rep. Med. 389, CC (Chelmsford) 12–40

Tanna v. Tanna 190672, May 25, 2001, unreported, Ch D 5–106

Tarasoff v. Regents of University of California (1976) 551 P.2d 334 ...... 12–44, 12–49, 12–51

Target Holdings Ltd v. Redferns (No.1) [1996] A.C. 421; [1995] 3 W.L.R. 352; [1995] 3 All E.R. 785; (1995) 139 S.J.L.B. 195; [1995] N.P.C. 136; *The Times*, July 21, 1995; *The Independent*, August 10, 1995; *The Independent*, July 21, 1995, HL 3–13, 10–35, 10–206, 10–229

Targett v. Torfaen B.C. [1992] 3 All E.R. 27; (1992) 24 H.L.R. 164; [1992] P.I.Q.R. P125; [1992] 1 E.G.L.R. 274; [1991] E.G.C.S. 125; (1991) 141 N.L.J. 1698; [1991] N.P.C. 126, CA 8–81, 8–82, 8–85, 8–205, 8–227

Tate & Lyle Industries v. Greater London Council [1983] 2 A.C. 509, HL; reversing [1982] 1 W.L.R. 970, CA; reversing [1982] 1 W.L.R. 149; [1981] 3 All E.R. 716; 125 S.J. 865, QBD 8–306

Tate v. Hart [1999] Lloyd's Rep. P.N. 566; [1999] P.N.L.R. 787; *The Independent*, March 8, 1999 (C.S.), CA 10–133, 10–138

Taylor Fashions Ltd v. Liverpool Victoria Trustees Co. Ltd; Old & Campbell Ltd v. Liverpool Victoria Friendly Society [1982] Q.B. 133; [1981] 2 W.L.R. 576; [1981] 1 All E.R. 897; [1981] Com. L.R. 34; (1979) 251 E.G. 159, Ch D 5–111

Taylor v. Director of the Serious Fraud Office; *sub nom.* Taylor v. Serious Fraud Office [1999] 2 A.C. 177; [1998] 3 W.L.R. 1040; [1998] 4 All E.R. 801; [1999] E.M.L.R. 1; *The Times*, November 4, 1998; *The Independent*, November 3, 1998, HL 2–97

—— v. Hall (1870) 4 I.R.C.L. 467 8–46

—— v. McGillivray (1993) 110 D.L.R. (4th) 64, QBD (New Brunswick) 12–29

—— v. Obee (1816) 3 Price 83 2–136

—— v. Ribby Hall Leisure Ltd [1998] 1 W.L.R. 400; [1997] 4 All E.R. 760; *The Times*, August 6, 1997, CA 10–69, 10–71

—— v. Rover Co. Ltd [1966] 1 W.L.R. 1491; [1966] 2 All E.R. 181, Assizes (Birmingham) 17–66

—— v. Shropshire H.A. (No.1) [1998] Lloyd's Rep. Med. 395, QBD 12–127, 12–232

PARA.

Taylor v. Shropshire H.A. (No.2) [2000] Lloyd's Rep. Med. 96, QBD 12–297, 12–299, 12–300

—— v. Somerset H.A. [1993] P.I.Q.R. P262; [1993] 4 Med. L.R. 34, QBD 12–38, 12–39

—— v. Warners, July 21, 1987, unreported 10–203

—— v. West Kent H.A. [1997] 8 Med.L.R. 251, QBD 12–184, 12–195, 12–200

—— v. Worcester and District H.A. [1991] 2 Med.L.R. 215, QBD 12–80

Teasdale v. Williams & Co. (1984) 269 E.G. 1040, CA 10–254, 10–265

Teh Khem On v. Yeoh [1995] 2 M.L.J. 663 8–124

Tehrani v. United Kingdom Central Council for Nursing Midwifery and Health Visiting, 2001 S.C. 581; 2001 S.L.T. 879; [2001] I.R.L.R. 208; 2001 G.W.D. 4–165, OH 7–66

Templer v. McLachlan (1806) 2 B. & P.(N.R.) 136 .... 8–316, 10–307

Tenenbaum v. Garrod [1988] 2 E.G.L.R. 178 .... 9–103, 9–121

Tennant Radiant Heat v. Warrington Development Corp. [1988] 1 E.G.L.R. 41; [1988] 11 E.G. 71; (1988) 4 Const. L.J. 321, CA 5–115

Tepko Pty Ltd v. Water Board [2001] H.C.A. 19; (2001) 75 A.L.J.R. 775 .... 2–112, 9–38

Ter Neuzen v. Korn (1995) 127 D.L.R. (4th) 577, Sup Ct (Can) 12–12, 12–74, 12–100, 12–104, 12–171

Tesco Stores Ltd v. Norman Hitchcox Partnership Ltd; Clark Care Group Ltd v. Norman Hitchcox Partnership Ltd; Maidstone Grove Ltd v. Norman Hitchcox Partnership Ltd (1997) 56 Con. L.R. 42, QBD (OR) 8–34, 8–84, 8–94, 8–103

Tew v. H.A. Whitburn & Son (1952) 159 E.G. 56 9–91

Texas Homecare Ltd v. Royal Bank of Canada Trust Co. (Jersey) Ltd [1996] C.L.C. 776 .... 14–11, 14–30, 14–46

Thake v. Maurice [1986] Q.B. 644; [1986] 2 W.L.R. 337; [1986] 1 All E.R. 479; (1986) 83 L.S.G. 123; (1986) 136 N.L.J. 92, CA 12–07, 12–10, 12–67, 12–86, 12–228, 12–232, 12–289, 12–292

Theodore Goddard v. Fletcher King Services Ltd [1997] 2 E.G.L.R. 131; [1997] 32 E.G. 90, QBD 9–10, 10–330

Theodorou v. Camden & Islington Health Authority, November 3, 1997, unreported 12–73

Theriault v. Assurance Levesque et autres (1995) 162 N.B.R.(2d) 365, QBD (New Brunswick) 14–79

Thomas v. Devonport Corporation [1900] 1 Q.B. 16; 63 J.P. 740; 16 T.L.R. 9; 69 L.J.Q.B. 51; 81 L.T. 427; 48 W.R. 89, CA 15–112

Thomas Cheshire & Co. v. Vaughan Bros & Co. [1920] 3 K.B. 240; (1920) 3 Ll. L. Rep. 213, CA 14–106

Thomas Gerrard & Son, Re [1968] Ch. 455; [1967] 3 W.L.R. 84; [1967] 2 All E.R. 525; 111 S.J. 329, Ch D 15–24, 15–92, 15–94, 15–98, 15–112, 15–130, 15–131, 15–138

Thomas Miller & Co. v. Richard Saunders and Partners [1989] 1 E.G.L.R. 267 .... 9–04, 9–120, 9–124

Thompson v. Blake-James; sub nom. Thomson v. James [1998] P.I.Q.R. P286; [1998] Lloyd's Rep. Med. 187; (1998) 41 B.M.L.R. 144, CA 12–66, 12–220, 12–224, 12–275, 12–284

—— v. Brown Construction Ltd (t/a George Albert Brown (Builders) & Co.); sub nom. Thompson v. Brown Construction (Ebbw Vale) Ltd [1981] 1 W.L.R. 744; [1981] 2 All E.R. 296; 125 S.J. 377, HL 5–64, 5–65, 5–67, 10–188

—— v. Clive Alexander & Partners, 59 B.L.R. 77; 28 Con. L.R. 49; [1955–95] P.N.L.R. 603; (1992) 8 Const. L.J. 199, QBD (OR) 8–45, 8–46

—— v. Fraser, The Times, 4th October 1985, CA 10–133

—— v. Howley [1977] 1 N.Z.L.R. 16 .... 10–189, 10–285

—— v. Schmidt (1891) 56 J.P. 212; (1891) 8 T.L.R. 120, CA 12–274

Thompson Estates v. Byrne (1993) 114 N.S.R. (2d) 395, CA (Nova Scotia) 12–120

PARA.

Thompson's Settlement, Re [1986] Ch. 99; [1985] 3 W.L.R. 486; [1985] 3 All
  E.R. 720; (1985) 129 S.J. 575, Ch D 2–134, 2–135, 2–136, 2–140
Thomson Snell & Passmore v. Rose [2000] P.N.L.R. 378, CA 10–176
Thorne v. Harris & Co. (1953) 163 E.G. 324 .... 9–88, 9–91, 9–134
—— v. Northern Group Hospital Management Committee (1963) 108 S.J. 115;
  The Times, June 6, 1964 .... 12–149, 12–164, 12–236, 12–237
Thornton v. Nicol [1992] 3 Med.L.R. 41, QBD 12–179
—— v. Shoe Lane Parking [1971] 2 Q.B. 163; [1971] 2 W.L.R. 585; [1971] 1 All
  E.R. 686; [1971] 1 Lloyd's Rep. 289; [1971] R.T.R. 79; (1970) 115 S.J. 75,
  CA 9–73
Thors v. Weekes (1990) 92 A.L.R. 131, Fed Ct (Aus) 10–61
Three Rivers D.C. v. Bank of England (No.3) [2000] 2 W.L.R. 1220; [2000] 3 All
  E.R. 1; [2000] Lloyd's Rep. Bank. 235; [2000] 3 C.M.L.R. 205; [2000] Eu.
  L.R. 583; (2000) 2 L.G.L.R. 769; (2000) 97(23) L.S.G. 41; *The Times*, May
  19, 2000, HL 2–80, 13–105, 13–132
Throwley Homes v. Sharratts [1998] N.P.C. 57, QBD 10–41
Tiffin Hldg. Ltd v. Millican, (1967) 60 D.L.R. (2d) 469, Sup Ct approving 49
  D.L.R. (2d) 216 10–79
Titanic Investments Ltd v. Macfarlanes [1997] N.P.C. 105, Ch D 10–166, 10–259
Tito v. Waddell (No.2); Tito v. Attorney General [1977] Ch. 106; [1977] 3 W.L.R.
  972; [1977] 2 W.L.R. 496; [1977] 3 All E.R. 129 (Note), Ch D 2–134
Toby Construction Products Ltd v. Computer Bar Sales Pty Ltd [1983] 2
  N.S.W.L.R. 48 .... 17–14, 17–15, 17–16, 17–63
Toikan International Insurance Broking Pty. Ltd v. Plasteel Windows Australia
  Pty. Ltd (1988) 15 N.S.W.L.R. 641, CA (NSW) 14–105
Tolstoy Miloslavsky v. Aldington [1996] 1 W.L.R. 736; [1996] 2 All E.R. 556;
  [1996] P.N.L.R. 335; (1996) 93(1) L.S.G. 22; (1996) 140 S.J.L.B. 26; *The
  Times*, December 27, 1995; *The Independent*, January 3, 1996, CA 10–119,
  10–135
Tomlinson v. Broadsmith [1896] 1 Q.B. 386; 40 S.J. 318; 12 T.L.R. 216; 65
  L.J.Q.B. 308; 74 L.T. 265; 44 W.R. 471, CA 10–155
Tonitto v. Bassal (1992) 28 N.S.W.L.R. 564, CA (NSW) 10–99
Toromont Industrial Holdings Ltd v. Thorne, Gunn, Helliwell and Christenson
  (1976) 73 D.L.R. (3d) 122, CA (Ontario) (1975) 62 D.L.R. (3d) 225 15–121,
  15–140
Toronto Industrial Leaseholds v. Posesorski (1995) 119 D.L.R. (4th) 193, CA
  (Ontario) 10–268, 10–269, 10–272
Town Investments Ltd v. Department of the Environment; *sub nom.* London
  County Freehold and Leasehold Properties v. Department of the Environ-
  ment; HEPC (Mayfair Properties) v. Department of the Environment [1978]
  A.C. 359; [1977] 2 W.L.R. 450; [1977] 1 All E.R. 813; (1977) 34 P. & C.R.
  48; 121 S.J. 203, HL 13–29
Townley v. Jones (1860) 8 C.B.(N.S.) 289; 29 L.J.C.P. 299; 6 Jur.(N.S.) 1159; 141
  E.R. 1177 10–183
Townsend (Builders) v. Cinema News & Property Management [1959] 1 W.L.R.
  119; [1959] 1 All E.R. 7; 123 J.P. 115; 57 L.G.R. 174; 103 S.J. 74; (1958)
  20 B.L.R. 118, CA 8–99, 8–201
Tozer Kemsley & Millbourn Holdings Ltd v. J Jarvis & Sons Ltd (1983) 4 Const.
  L.J. 24, QBD (OR) 5–21
Tracy v. Atkins (1979) 105 D.L.R. (3d) 632, CA (BC) 10–61
Trade Practices Commission v. CC (New South Wales) Pty. Ltd (1994) 125
  A.L.R. 94 .... 10–25, 10–100
Transport & Trading Co. Ltd v. Olivier & Co. Ltd (1925) 21 Ll.L.R. 379 14–38
Transportation Agency Ltd v. Jenkins (1972) 223 E.G. 1101 ..... 10–166, 10–302, 10–306,
  10–317

PARA.

Transvaal Lands Company v. New Belgium (Transvaal) Land and Development
    Company [1914] 2 Ch. 488 2–140
Trask v. Clark & Sons [1980] C.L.Y.B. 2588 .... 10–268, 10–311, 10–313
Tredget v. Bexley H.A. [1994] 5 Med.L.R. 178 12–40
Treloar v. Henderson [1968] N.Z.L.R. 1085, HC 10–318
Tremayne v. T Mortimer Burrows and Partners (1954) 165 E.G. 232 .... 9–91, 9–108,
                                                                                9–134, 9–191
Treml v. Ernest W Gibson & Partners [1955–95] P.N.L.R. 228; (1984) 272 E.G.
    68; (1984) 1 Const. L.J. 162; [1984] 2 E.G.L.R. 162, QBD 9–131, 9–140, 9–148,
                                                                                9–190, 9–191
Trend Publishing (H.K.) Limited v. Vivien Chan & Co. (a firm) [1996] 2
    H.K.L.R. 227, HC (HK) 10–57
Trevor Ivory Ltd v. Anderson [1992] 2 N.Z.L.R. 517, CA (ZA) 2–88
Trill v. Sacher (No.2), *The Times*, November 14, 1992, CA 10–138
Trizec Equities v. Ellis-Don Management Services Ltd (1998) 66 Alta.L.R. (3d)
    1 8–261
Trizec Properties Ltd v. Husky Oil Operations Ltd (1997) 148 D.L.R. (4th) 300,
    CA (Alberta) 10–31
Trust Co. of Australia v. Perpetual Trustees (1997) 42 N.S.W.L.R. 237 10–248
Trusted v. Clifford Chance (2000) 1 W.T.L.R. 1219 .... 10–50, 10–218
Trustee of the Property of Apfel (A Bankrupt) v. Annan Dexter & Co. (1926) 70
    Acct.L.R. 57 15–31
Trustee of the Property of Blue Band Navigation Co. Ltd v. Price Waterhouse &
    Co. (No.2) [1934] 3 D.L.R. 404, CA (BC) 15–112
Try Build Ltd v. Invicta Leisure (Tennis) Ltd (2000) 71 Con. L.R. 140, QBD
    (OR) 8–20, 8–140, 8–181, 8–208, 8–257, 8–268, 8–306
Tsimatakopoulos v. Hemmingway [1993] 4 S.A.L.R. 428 8–124
Tucker v. Allen & Co. (A Firm) [2001] P.N.L.R. 884, QBD 10–164
——— v. Tees H.A. [1995] 6 Med.L.R. 54, QBD 12–193
Tudor Jones v. Crowley Colosso Ltd [1996] 2 Lloyd's Rep. 619; Lloyd's List,
    August 1, 1996 (I.D.), QBD (Comm Ct) 14–48, 14–92, 14–127
Tunnel Refineries v. Bryan Donkin (1998) C.I.L.L. 1392 8–94
Turner Page Music Ltd v. Torres Design Associates (1997) C.I.L.L. 1263 ..... 3–08, 8–159,
                                                            8–290, 8–297, 8–303, 8–316
——— v. Torres Design Associates Ltd, *The Times*, August 7 1998, CA 10–132
Turner v. Garland and Christopher (1853) cited in *Hudson's Building Contracts*
    (4th ed., 1914) Vol. 2, p. 1 .... 8–167, 8–207
Turpin v. Bilton (1843) 5 Man. & G. 455; 6 Scott N.R. 477; 12 L.J.C.P. 167; 4
    L.T. 341; 7 Jur. 950; 134 E.R. 641 .... 14–40, 14–59
Twenty Two A Property Investments Ltd v. Simpson Curtis (A Firm) [2000]
    E.G.C.S. 140; [2000] N.P.C. 129, CA 10–9
Twidale v. Bradley [1990] 2Qd.R. 464 10–268
Twins Transport Ltd v. Patrick & Brocklehurst (t/a HV&C Patrick Estates
    Developers) (1983) 25 B.L.R. 65, QBD 8–59, 8–125
Twinsectra v. Francis John Yardley [2000] Lloyd's Rep. P.N. 239 .... 10–38, 10–68
Tyrer v. District Auditor of Monmouthshire (1973) 230 E.G. 973, DC 8–166, 8–221,
                                                                                8–224

UBAF Ltd v. European American Banking Corp.; Pacific Colocotronis, The
    [1984] Q.B. 713; [1984] 2 W.L.R. 508; [1984] 2 All E.R. 226; [1984] 1
    Lloyd's Rep. 258; (1984) 81 L.S.G. 429; (1984) 128 S.J. 243, CA 5–41, 5–70
UCB Bank plc v. David Pinder plc [1998] 2 E.G.L.R. 203, [1998] P.N.L.R. 398 9–168,
                                                                                9–172, 10–195
——— v. Hepherd Winstanley & Pugh [1999] Lloyd's Rep. P.N. 963; (1999)
    96(34) L.S.G. 34; *The Times*, August 25, 1999, CA 10–325

PARA.

UCB Corporate Services Ltd (formerly UCB Bank plc) v. Clyde & Co. [2000] 2
All E.R. (Comm) 257; [2000] Lloyd's Rep. P.N. 653; [2000] P.N.L.R. 841,
CA 10–10, 10–327
—— v. Halifax (SW) Ltd (In Liquidation) (Valuation) [2000] 1 E.G.L.R. 87;
[2000] 16 E.G. 137; [2000] E.G.C.S. 28, CA 9–106
UCB Home Loans Corp. Ltd v. Carr [2000] Lloyd's Rep. P.N. 754, QBD 5–73, 5–87
Udale v. Bloomsbury A.H.A. [1983] 1 W.L.R. 1098, QBD 12–289
Udall (t/a Udall Sheet Metal & Co) v. Capri Lighting Ltd; *sub nom.* Solicitor
(Richard Oxley Whiting), Re [1988] Q.B. 907; [1987] 3 W.L.R. 465; [1987]
3 All E.R. 262; (1987) 84 L.S.G. 1334; (1987) 137 N.L.J. 293; 131 S.J. 443,
CA 10–65, 10–68, 10–69, 10–70,10–72, 10–74
Ulster Bank Ltd v. Fisher & Fisher [1999] N.I. 68; [1999] P.N.L.R. 794, Ch D
(NI) 10–65, 10–115
Ultramares Corp. v. Touche (1931) 174 N.E. 441, CA (New York) 2–63, 2–71, 9–47,
15–45
Underwood, Son & Piper v. Lewis [1894] 2 Q.B. 306; 38 S.J. 479; [1891–94] All
E.R. Rep. 1203; 10 T.L.R. 465; 64 L.J.Q.B. 60; 70 L.T. 833; 42 W.R. 517;
9 R. 440, CA 3–07
Unioil International Pty Ltd v. Deloitte Touche Tohnasts [1997] 17 W.A.R. 98,
HC (Aus) 10–31, 10–228
United Bank of Kuwait plc v. Prudential Property Services Ltd [1994] 2 E.G.L.R.
100 .... 9–113, 9–158, 9–159, 9–160, 9–171
—— v. Sahib [1997] Ch. 107; [1996] 3 W.L.R. 372; [1996] 3 All E.R. 215;
[1996] 2 F.L.R. 666; (1997) 73 P. & C.R. 177; [1997] Fam. Law 17; [1996]
E.G.C.S. 19; [1996] N.P.C. 12; *The Times*, February 13, 1996, CA 10–82
United Bank of Kuwait v. Hammoud; City Trust Ltd v. Levy [1988] 1 W.L.R.
1051; [1988] 3 All E.R. 418; (1988) 138 N.L.J. 281; (1988) 132 S.J. 1388,
CA 10–66, 10–74, 10–146
United Co-Operatives v. Sun Alliance and London Assurance Co. [1987] 1
E.G.L.R. 126; (1987) 282 E.G. 91 9–74
United Marketing Co. v. Kara [1963] 1 W.L.R. 523; [1963] 2 All E.R. 553; [1963]
1 Lloyd's Rep. 331; 107 S.J. 312, PC (Ken) 14–40
United Mills Agencies Ltd v. Harvey Bray & Co. [1952] 1 All E.R. 225 (Note);
[1951] 2 Lloyd's Rep. 631; [1952] 1 T.L.R. 149; 96 S.J. 121, KBD 2–117, 14–34,
14–80
United Mining and Finance Corp. v. Becher [1911] 1 K.B. 840; CA; [1910] 2
K.B. 296; [1908–10] All E.R. Rep. 876; 79 L.J.K.B. 1006; 103 L.T. 65,
KBD 10–65, 10–67
Unity Insurance Brokers Pty Ltd. v. Rocco Pezzano Pty Ltd (1998) 154 A.L.R.
361 14–117
University of Manchester v. Hugh Wilson & Lewis Womersley (A Firm) (1984)
1 Const. L.J. 162; [1984] C.I.L.L. 126 .... 8–33, 8–131, 8–159, 8–140, 8–241, 8–247,
8–249, 8–254
Unruh Construction Company Ltd v. Kelly-Lucy & Cameron Adjusters Ltd
[1976] 4 W.W.R. 419, Sup Ct (Alberta) 14–
Uppal v. United Kingdom (No.1) (App. No.8244/78); (1981) 3 E.H.R.R. 391, Eur
Comm HR 7–06
Upstone v. GDW Carnegie & Co., 1978 S.L.T. (Sh. Ct.) 4, Sh Pr 9–130
Urbanski v. Patel (1978) 84 D.L.R. (3d) 650 12–32
Urry v. Bierer, *The Times*, July 15, 1955, CA 12–83, 12–194
Uxbridge Permanent Benefit Building Society v. Pickard [1939] 2 K.B. 248,
CA 10–146

Vale v. Van Oppen & Co. Ltd (1921) 37 T.L.R. 367; 6 Ll.L.Rep. 167 ..... 14–44, 14–57
Valerie Pratt v. George J Hill Associates (1987) 38 B.L.R. 25, CA 8–223

PARA.

Valness v. MacLowich (1998) 168 Sask.R. 45, CA (Saskatchewan) 10–278

Van Laun Ex p.; Chatterton, Re; *sub nom.* Van Laun, ex p. Pattullo [1907] 2 K.B.
23; 51 S.J. 344; [1904–07] All E.R. Rep. 157; 23 T.L.R. 384; 76 L.J.K.B.
644; 97 L.T. 69; 14 Mans. 91, CA 10–16

Van Marle v. Netherlands; Series A, No.101 (1986) 8 E.H.R.R. 483, ECHR 7–16

Van Mol v. Ashmore (1999) 168 D.L.R. (4th) 637, CA (BC) 12–132, 12–204

Van Soest v. Residual Health Management Unit [2000] 1 N.Z.L.R. 179 12–35

Vancouver General Hospital v. McDaniel (1935) 152 L.T.R. 56, PC 12–92, 12–170

Vaz-Oxlade v. Volkenstein (2000) 35 R.P.R. (3d) 165, CA (Ontario) 10–196

Veasey v. Millfeed Co. Ltd; *sub nom.* Veasey v. Pickering Kenyon; Millfeed Co.
Ltd v. Pickering Kenyon [1997] P.N.L.R. 100, CA 10–139, 10–260

Veljkovic v. Vrybergen [1985] V.R. 419 14–44

Velos Group Ltd v. Harbour Insurance Services Ltd [1997] 2 Lloyd's Rep. 461,
CC (Central London) 14–03, 14–09

Venables v. News Group Newspapers Ltd; Thompson v. News Group News-
papers Ltd [2001] 2 W.L.R. 1038; [2001] 1 All E.R. 908; [2001] E.M.L.R.
10; [2001] 1 F.L.R. 791; [2001] H.R.L.R. 19; [2001] U.K.H.R.R. 628; 9
B.H.R.C. 587; [2001] Fam. Law 258; (2001) 98(12) L.S.G. 41; (2001) 151
N.L.J. 57; (2001) 145 S.J.L.B. 43; *The Times*, January 16, 2001; *The
Independent*, January 17, 2001; *The Daily Telegraph*, January 16, 2001, Fam
Div 7–13

Verderame v. Commercial Union Assurance Co. plc [1992] B.C.L.C. 793; [2000]
Lloyd's Rep. P.N. 557; [1955–95] P.N.L.R. 612; *The Times*, April 2, 1992;
The Independent, May 25, 1992 (C.S), CA 10–42, 10–314, 14–29, 14–121,
14–123

Vermont Construction Inc. v. Beatson (1976) 67 D.L.R. (3rd) 95, Sup Ct (Can) 8–117,
8–138, 8–180

Vernon v. Bloomsbury H.A. [1995] 6 Med.L.R. 297, QBD 12–123, 12–191

Victoria Laundry (Windsor) v. Newman Industries [1949] 2 K.B. 528; [1949] 1
All E.R. 997; 65 T.L.R. 274; 93 S.J. 371, CA 9–125, 10–240, 12–282, 15–131

Videto v. Kennedy (1981) 17 C.C.L.T. 307, CA (Ontario) 12–204

Vienneau v. Arsenault (1982) 41 N.B.R. (2d) 82, CA (New Brunswick) 10–164

Viking Grain Storage Ltd v. TH White Installations Ltd, 33 B.L.R. 103; 3 Con.
L.R. 52; [1985] C.I.L.L. 206, QBD 8–17, 8–174

Vilvarajah v. United Kingdom; Series A, No.215; (1992) 14 E.H.R.R. 248; *The
Times*, November 12, 1991; *The Independent*, November 5, 1991; *The
Guardian*, November 6, 1991, ECHR 7–24

Virgin Management Ltd v. De Morgan Group plc [1996] E.G.C.S. 16; [1996]
N.P.C. 8, CA 10–170

—— v. Defendant Morgan Group plc, January 24, 1996, unreported 8–136

Voli v. Inglewood Shire Council [1963] A.L.R. 657; (1963) 56 Qd. R. 256; (1963)
110 C.L.R. 74 .... 8–53, 8–81, 8–130, 8–133, 8–138, 8–141, 8–204, 8–205, 8–277,
8–308

Voller v. Portsmouth Corporation (1947) 203 L.T.J. 264 .... 12–149, 12–193

Vyse v. Foster (1874) L.R. 7 H.L. 318 2–136

W (A Minor) (Medical Treatment: Court's Jurisdiction), Re; *sub nom.* J (A
Minor) (Consent to Medical Treatment), Re [1993] Fam. 64; [1992] 3
W.L.R. 758; [1992] 4 All E.R. 627; [1992] 3 Med. L.R. 317; (1992) 142
N.L.J. 1124; *The Times*, July 15, 1992; *The Independent*, July 14, 1992; *The
Guardian*, July 22, 1992, CA 12–136, 12–140, 12–148

W (An Adult: Mental Patient) (Sterilisation), Re, 993] 1 F.L.R. 381; [1993] 2
F.C.R. 187; [1993] Fam. Law 208 .... 12–142, 12–144

PARA.

W v. Egdell [1990] Ch. 359; [1990] 2 W.L.R. 471; [1990] 1 All E.R. 835; (1990) 87(12) L.S.G. 41; (1990) 134 S.J. 286; *The Independent*, November 10, 1989, CA 2–158, 2–160

—— v. Essex C.C.; *sub nom.* W1–6 v. Essex C.C. [2000] 2 W.L.R. 601; [2000] 2 All E.R. 237; [2000] 1 F.L.R. 657; [2000] 1 F.C.R. 568; [2000] B.L.G.R. 281; (2000) 53 B.M.L.R. 1; [2000] Fam. Law 476; (2000) 164 J.P.N. 464; (2000) 97(13) L.S.G. 44; (2000) 144 S.J.L.B. 147; *The Times*, March 17, 2000, HL 12–36, 12–41, 12–160

—— v. United Kingdom; Series A, No.121; (1988) 10 E.H.R.R. 29, ECHR 7–07

WA Chip & Pulp Co. Pty. Ltd v. Arthur Young & Co.; *sub nom.* Arthur Young & Co. v. WA Chip & Pulp Co. Pty Ltd (1988) 13 A.C.L.R. 283, Sup Ct (Aus) (1987) 12 A.C.L.R. 25 .... 15–110, 15–121

WE Acres Crabmeal Ltd v. Brien's Insurance Agency Ltd (1988) 90 N.B.R. (2d) 77; 228 A.P.R. 77, QBD (New Brunswick) 14–60

Wade v. Licardy (1993) 33 N.S.W.L.R. 1 10–65

Wagner v. International Railway Co. (1921) 232 N.Y. 1 2–

Wagon, The. *See* Overseas Tankship (U.K.) Ltd v. Miller Steamship Co. Pty Ltd; Wagon Mound, The.

Waine v. Kempster (1859) 1 F. & F. 695 10–124

Wales v. Wales (1967) 111 S.J. 946; *The Times*, November 29, 1967 10–312

Walker v. Boyle; *sub nom.* Boyle v. Walker [1982] 1 W.L.R. 495; [1982] 1 All E.R. 634; (1982) 44 P. & C.R. 20; (1982) 261 E.G. 1090; (1982) 79 L.S.G. 954; 125 S.J. 724, Ch D 10–167

—— v. Geo H Medlicott & Son [1999] 1 W.L.R. 727; [1999] 1 All E.R. 685; [1999] 1 F.L.R. 1095; [1999] Lloyd's Rep. P.N. 20; [1999] P.N.L.R. 531; [1999] Fam. Law 214; (1999) 96(1) L.S.G. 24; [1998] N.P.C.156; *The Times*, November 25, 1998, CA 10–320

—— v. Giffen Couch & Archer [1988] E.G.C.S. 64 10–268

—— v. Hall [1984] Fam. Law 21; (1983) 80 L.S.G. 2139; (1983) 127 S.J. 550, CA 10–203

—— v. Hungerfords (1987) 19 A.T.R. 745, Sup Ct (Aus) (1987) 44 S.A.S.R. 532 .... 15–143, 15–146

—— v. Stones [2001] 2 W.L.R. 623; [2000] 4 All E.R. 412; [2000] Lloyd's Rep. P.N. 864; (2000) 1 W.T.L.R. 975; (2000) 97(35) L.S.G. 36; *The Times*, September 26, 2000; *The Independent*, July 27, 2000, CA 10–39, 10–147

Walkin v. South Manchester H.A. [1995] 1 W.L.R. 1543; [1995] 4 All E.R. 132; [1996] 7 Med.L.R. 211; *The Times*, July 3, 1995, CA 5–13, 5–43, 5–44, 12–48, 12–289

Walkley v. Precision Forgings Ltd [1979] 1 W.L.R. 606; [1979] 2 All E.R. 548; 123 S.J. 548, HL 5–65

Wall v. Hegarty [1980] I.R.L.M. 124 10–54

—— v. Lefever [1998] 1 F.C.R. 605; *The Times*, August 1, 1997, CA 10–132, 10–133, 11–35

Waller v. AB (A firm) [2001] 2 C.L. 465, QBD 10–175

Wallersteiner v. Moir (No.2); *sub nom.* Moir v. Wallersteiner (No.2) [1975] Q.B. 373; [1975] Q.B. 508 (Note); [1975] 2 W.L.R. 389; [1975] 1 All E.R. 849; 119 S.J. 97, CA 3–24

Wallshire Ltd v. Aarons [1989] 1 E.G.L.R. 147; [1989] 2 E.G. 81, DC 9–74

Walpole v. Partridge & Wilson [1994] Q.B. 106; [1993] 3 W.L.R. 1093; [1994] 1 All E.R. 385; *The Times*, July 8, 1993; *The Independent*, September 23, 1993, CA 2–97, 10–109, 10–113, 11–25

Walter (D) & Co. Ltd v. Neville Eckley & Co. [1997] B.C.C. 331, Ch D 10–131

Wan v. McDonald (1992) 105 A.L.R. 473 10–100

Wapshot v. Davies Donovan & Co. [1996] 1 P.N.L.R. 361 .... 10–250, 10–268, 10–275, 10–311

Warboys v. Cartwright [1992] E.G.C.S. 110; [1992] N.P.C. 106 10–153

PARA.

Ward of court, In the matter of a [1995] 2 I.R.L.M. 401, Sup Ct (Irish) 12–146
Ward, Re; Simmons v. Rose, Weeks v. Ward (1862) 31 Beav. 1; 54 E.R. 1037 10–146
Wardley Australia Ltd v. Western Australia (1992) 66 A.L.J.R. 839; (1992) 109
    A.L.R. 247, HC (Aus) 5–38, 5–39, 10–13
Waribay Pty Ltd v. Minter Ellison [1991] 2 V.R. 391, App Div (Vic) 10–261
Warmingtons v. McMurray [1937] 1 All E.R. 562, CA 10–11
Warner v. Basildon Development Corp. (1991) 7 Const. L.J. 146, CA 8–42, 9–94
Warren v. Greig, The Lancet, February 9, 1935 12–83
—— v. Henry Sutton & Co. [1976] 2 Lloyd's Rep. 276, CA 14–69
—— v. Warren [1997] Q.B. 488; [1996] 3 W.L.R. 1129; [1996] 4 All E.R. 664;
    [1996] 2 F.L.R. 777; [1997] 1 F.C.R. 237; [1996] Fam. Law 720, CA 10–139
Waterkeyn v. Eagle Star & British Dominions Insurance Co. Ltd (1920) 4
    Ll.L.Rep. 178; 5 Ll.L.Rep. 42 14–45
Waters v. Maguire [1999] Lloyd's Rep. P.N. 855, QBD 10–182, 11–14, 11–42
—— v. Park, The Times, July 15, 1961 12–228
—— v. West Sussex H.A. [1995] 6 Med.L.R. 362, QBD 12–109
Watson v. British Boxing Board of Control Ltd [2001] 2 W.L.R. 1256; [2001]
    P.I.Q.R. P16; (2001) 98(12) L.S.G. 44; (2001) 145 S.J.L.B. 31; The Times,
    February 2, 2001; The Independent, January 11, 2001; The Daily Telegraph,
    January 16, 2001, CA 2–70, 2–91
—— v. Watson 10–120
Watts v. Assets Co. Ltd [1905] A.C. 317 5–106
—— v. Hyde (1846) 2 Coll. 368 10–166
—— v. Morrow [1991] 1 W.L.R. 1421; [1991] 4 All E.R. 937; 54 B.L.R. 86; 26
    Con. L.R. 98; (1991) 23 H.L.R. 608; [1991] 2 E.G.L.R. 152; [1991] 43 E.G.
    121; (1992) 8 Const. L.J. 73; [1991] E.G.C.S. 88; (1992) 89(14) L.S.G. 33;
    (1991) 141 N.L.J. 1331; [1991] N.P.C. 98; The Independent, August 20,
    1991; The Guardian, September 4, 1991, CA; reversing 24 Con. L.R. 125;
    [1991] 15 E.G. 113; [1991] 14 E.G. 111; The Independent, November 19,
    1990 (C.S.), QBD (OR) 3–22, 8–309, 8–311, 9–24, 9–85, 9–91, 9–92, 9–99,
                   9–128, 9–130, 9–131, 9–133, 9–140, 9–142, 9–145, 9–146, 9–147,
                    9–181, 9–182, 9–184, 9–188, 9–189, 9–190, 10–272, 10–314,
                                             10–315, 14–123
—— v. Public Trustee for Western Australia [1980] W.A.R. 97, Sup Ct (Aus) 10–54,
                                                 10–222
—— v. Savills [1998] E.G.C.S. 99; (1998) 95(25) L.S.G. 34, CA 9–62, 9–106
Waugh v. HB Clifford & Sons Ltd [1982] Ch. 374; [1982] 2 W.L.R. 679; [1982]
    1 All E.R. 1095, CA 10–189
Webster v. Chapman (1997) 155 D.L.R. (4th) 82, CA (Manitoba) 12–204, 12–222,
                                                  12–248
—— v. Cooper & Burnett [2000] Lloyd's Rep. P.N. 167; [2000] P.N.L.R. 240,
    CA 5–55
—— v. De Tastet (1797) 7 T.R. 157; 101 E.R. 908 14–106
Weedon v. Hindwood, Clarke & Esplin (1974) 234 E.G. 121 .... 9–56, 9–104, 9–176
Weir v. JM Hodge & Son, 1990 S.L.T. 266, OH x8>10–54
Welburn v. Mayberry (1971) 115 S.J. 468, CA 10–187
Weld-Blundell v. Stephens [1920] A.C. 956; 89 L.J.K.B. 705; 36 T.L.R. 640; 64
    S.J. 529, HL; affirming [1919] 1 K.B. 520, CA 15–36, 15–130
Weller & Co. v. Foot & Mouth Disease Research Institute [1966] 1 Q.B. 569;
    [1965] 3 W.L.R. 1082; [1965] 3 All E.R. 560; [1965] 2 Lloyd's Rep. 414;
    109 S.J. 702, QBD 2–27
Welsh v. Chief Constable of Merseyside [1993] 1 All E.R. 692, QBD 10–64, 10–106
Welton v. North Cornwall D.C. [1997] 1 W.L.R. 570; (1997) 161 J.P. 114; (1997)
    9 Admin. L.R. 45; [1997] P.N.L.R. 108; (1996) 93(34) L.S.G. 34; (1996)
    140 S.J.L.B. 186; The Times, July 19, 1996; The Independent, July 23, 1996,
    CA 2–53, 2–85

PARA.

Wenden v. Trikha (1991) 8 C.C.L.T. (2d), affirmed (1993) 14 C.C.L.T. (2d) 225,
CA (Alberta) 12–51
Wernikowski v. Kirkland, Murphy & Ain (2000) 181 D.L.R. (4th) 625, CA
(Ontario) 10–109
Wessex R.H.A. v. HLM Design (1994) C.I.L.L. 907 .... 8–51, 8–275
West Coast Finance Ltd v. Gunderson, Stokes, Walton and Co. (1974) 56 D.L.R.
(3d) 468, CA (BC) (1974) 44 D.L.R. (3d) 232 .... 15–121, 15–146
West Faulkner Associates v. Newham L.B.C. (1994) 71 B.L.R. 1; (1995) 11
Const. L.J. 157; [1994] E.G.C.S. 179; [1994] N.P.C. 142; *The Times*,
November 16, 1994; *The Independent*, December 19, 1994 (C.S.), CA 8–20,
8–162, 8–237, 8–303
West London Observer v. Parsons (1955) 166 E.G. 749, QBD 10–168
West Mercia Safetywear, Liquidator of v. Dodd; *sub nom.* West Mercia Safety-
wear (In Liquidation) v. Dodd (1988) 4 B.C.C. 30; [1988] B.C.L.C. 250;
[1988] P.C.C. 212, CA 15–74
West Midland Baptist (Trust) Association (Incorporated) v. Birmingham Corp.
See Birmingham Corp. v. West Midland Baptist (Trust) Association Inc.; *sub
nom.* West Midland Baptist (Trust) Association Inc. v. Birmingham Corp.
West Sussex Properties Ltd v. Chichester D.C., June 28, 2000, unreported 5–108
Westdeutsche Landesbank Girozentrale v. Islington L.B.C.; Kleinwort Benson
Ltd v. Sandwell B.C. [1996] A.C. 669, HL; reversing [1994] 1 W.L.R. 938;
[1994] 4 All E.R. 890; 92 L.G.R. 405; (1994) 158 L.G. Rev. 981; (1994)
91(8) L.S.G. 29; (1994) 138 S.J.L.B. 26; *The Times*, December 30, 1993;
The Independent, January 5, 1994, CA 5–108
Western Challenge Housing Assoication Ltd v. Percy Thomas Partnership (1995)
C.I.L.L. 1018 5–26
Western Counties Steam Bakeries & Milling Co, Re [1897] 1 Ch. 617; 41 S.J.
365; 13 T.L.R. 276; 45 W.R. 418, CA 15–24
Western Trust & Savings Ltd v. Clive Travers & Co. [1997] P.N.L.R. 295; (1998)
75 P. & C.R. 200, CA 10–319
——— v. Strutt & Parker [1999] P.N.L.R. 154; [1998] 3 E.G.L.R. 89; [1998] 44
E.G. 208; [1998] E.G.C.S. 121; [1998] N.P.C. 116; *The Times*, September
17, 1998, CA 9–21, 9–42
Westlake v. Bracknell D.C. (1987) 19 H.L.R. 375; [1987] 1 E.G.L.R. 161; (1987)
282 E.G. 868 9–09
——— v. JP Cave [1998] N.P.C. 3, QBD 10–317
Westmelton v. Archer [1982] V.R. 305 .... 2–144, 10–17
Westminster Road Construction & Engineering Co. Ltd, Re (1932) Acct.L.R.
38 .... 15–112, 15–138
Westway Homes v. Gore Wood & Co. [1991] N.P.C. 85; *The Times*, July 7, 1991,
CA 10–105, 10–314
Whale View Investments Ltd v. Kensland Realty Ltd [2000] 2 H.K.L.R.D.
261 10–97
Whalley v. Roberts & Roberts [1990] 1 E.G.L.R. 164; [1955–95] P.N.L.R. 506;
[1990] 06 E.G. 104, QBD 9–06, 9–20, 9–57, 9–85, 9–95
Whelton Sinclair (a firm) v. Hyland [1992] 2 E.G.L.R. 158; [1992] 41 E.G. 112,
CA 10–44
Whichote v. Lawrence (1798) 3 Ves.Jun. 740 2–135
White v. Jones [1995] 2 A.C. 207; [1995] 2 W.L.R. 187; [1995] 1 All E.R. 691;
[1995] 3 F.C.R. 51; (1995) 145 N.L.J. 251; (1995) 139 S.J.L.B. 83; [1995]
N.P.C. 31; *The Times*, February 17, 1995; *The Independent*, February 17,
1995, HL 2–18, 2–48, 2–64, 2–95, 2–114, 8–98, 10–40, 10–44, 10–45, 10–48,
10–49, 10–50, 10–53, 10–54, 10–57, 10–60, 10–218, 10–223,
12–58, 13–110, 14–20, 14–26, 15–48, 15–122, 15–128
——— v. Mead (1840) 2 Ir. Eq. Rep. 240 2–143
——— v. Turner (1981) 120 D.L.R. (3d) 269; (1983) 5 D.L.R. (4th) 282 12–186

PARA.

White v. Turner (1981) 31 O.R.(2d) 773 12–202
—— v. Westminster Hospital Board of Governors, *The Times*, October 26, 1961;
    The Guardian, October 26, 1961 .... 12–80, 12–193
White Industries (QLD) Pty Ltd v. Flower & Hart (a firm) (1999) 163 A.L.R. 744,
    Fed Ct (Aus) 10–126, 10–137
Whiteford v. Hunter [1950] W.N. 553; 94 S.J. 758, HL 12–74, 12–81, 12–92, 12–183
Whitehouse v. Jordan [1981] 1 W.L.R. 246; [1981] 1 All E.R. 267; 125 S.J. 167,
    HL 2–114, 8–165, 10–104, 12–68, 12–68, 12–75, 12–84, 12–86, 12–190
Whiteman v. Hawkins (1878) 4 C.P.D. 13; 43 J.P. 272; 39 L.T. 629; 27 W.R.
    262 10–317
Whiteoak v. Walker (1988) 4 B.C.C. 122 .... 15–90, 15–117
Whiteways Contractors (Sussex) Ltd v. Impresa Castelli Construction UK Ltd, 75
    Con. L.R. 92; (2000) 16 Const. L.J. 453, QBD (T&CC) 8–339
Whitfield v. North Durham H.A.; *sub nom.* Whitfield v. North Durham H.A.
    (Sued as Durham H.A.) [1995] P.I.Q.R. P361; [1995] 6 Med.L.R. 32, CA 5–68
Whittingham v. Crease & Co. (1978) 88 D.L.R. (3d) 353, Sup Ct (BC) 10–222
Whitty v. Lord Dillon (1860) 2 F. & F. 67 .... 9–104, 9–110
Wickstead v. Browne (1992) 30 N.S.W.L.R. 1 2–127
Widgery v. Tepper (1878) 38 L.T. 434 2–139
Wilcox v. Norberg & Wiggins Insurance Agencies Ltd [1979] 1 W.L.R. 414 14–14
Wilkens Nel Argitekte v. Stephenson [1987] 2 S.A.L.R. 628 8–193
Wilks v. Thingoe (Suffolk) Regional District Council (1954) 164 E.G. 86 8–232
Willerby Caravan Company Ltd v. Liddle, unreported, July 9, 1999, CA 8–214
William and Anita Powell v. United Kingdom (App. No.45305/99) [2000]
    E.H.R.L.R. 650 .... 7–40, 7–48, 7–52
William Hill Organisation v. Sunley & Sons (1982) 22 B.L.R. 1, CA 8–59
Williams v. Fitzmaurice (1858) H. & N. 844; 157 E.R. 709 8–43
—— v. Gibbs (1836) 5 Ad. & E. 208; 2 H. & W. 241; 6 N. & Mbk. 788; 11 E.R.
    1144 10–175
—— v. Johnson [1937] 4 All E.R. 34 2–144
—— v. Natural Life Health Foods Ltd [1998] 1 W.L.R. 830; [1998] 2 All E.R.
    577; [1998] B.C.C. 428; [1998] 1 B.C.L.C. 689; (1998) 17 Tr. L.R. 152;
    (1998) 95(21) L.S.G. 37; (1998) 148 N.L.J. 657; (1998) 142 S.J.L.B. 166;
    The Times, May 1, 1998, HL 2–47, 2–49, 2–78, 2–88, 2–89, 2–91, 2–93, 9–14,
                                                8–98, 10–40, 10–41
—— v. North Liverpool Hospital Management Committee, *The Times*, January
    17, 1959, CA 12–80, 12–192
—— v. Scott [1900] A.C. 499, PC (Aus) 2–135
—— v. State of New York (1955) 127 N.E. 2d 545 2–77
—— v. Williams (1881) 17 Ch.D. 437 10–37
—— v. Williams and Partridge (1910) 54 S.J. 506, CA 10–68, 10–69
Williams-Ashman v. Price & Williams [1942] 1 Ch. 219 10–37
Williamson v. East London and City H.A. [1998] Lloyd's Rep. Med. 6; (1998) 41
    B.M.L.R. 85, Ch D 12–125, 12–213
Willis v. Barron; *sub nom.* Barron v. Willis [1902] A.C. 271; [1900–03] 3 All E.R.
    Rep. 867; 71 L.J.Ch. 609; 86 L.T. 805; 18 T.L.R. 602, HL 2–144, 10–17
Willmott v. Barber (1881) L.R. 17 Ch. D. 772, CA; affirming in part (1880) L.R.
    15 Ch. D. 96, Ch D 5–105, 5–110
Wills v. Wood (1984) 81 L.S.G. 1211; (1984) 128 S.J. 222; *The Times*, March 24,
    1984, CA 10–102
Wilsher v. Essex A.H.A. [1988] A.C. 1074; [1988] 2 W.L.R. 557; [1988] 1 All
    E.R. 871; (1988) 138 N.L.J. 78; (1988) 132 S.J. 418, HL; affirming [1987]
    Q.B. 730; [1987] 2 W.L.R. 425; [1986] 3 All E.R. 801; (1986) 83 L.S.G.
    2661; (1986) 136 N.L.J. 1061; (1986) 130 S.J. 749; *The Times*, August 6,
    1986, CA 2–118, 2–121, 9–120, 10–234, 10–262, 12–77, 12–84, 12–155,
                            12–159, 12–243, 12–247, 12–248, 12–254, 14–112

PARA.

Wilson v. Baxter Payne & Lepper [1985] 1 E.G.L.R. 141; (1985) 273 E.G. 406 3–21,
9–131, 9–140

—— v. Bloomfield (1979) 123 S.J. 860, CA 10–56

—— v. Le Fevre Wood & Royle, 66 Con. L.R. 74; [1996] P.N.L.R. 107; *The
Independent*, October 12, 1995, CA 5–54

—— v. Rowswell (1970) 11 D.L.R. (3d) 737, Sup Ct (Can) 10–294

—— v. Tucker (1822) 3 Stark 154; D. & Ry. N.P. 30; 171 E.R. 805, NP 10–207,
10–294

—— v. Vancouver Hockey Club (1983) 5 D.L.R. (4th) 282 12–185

Wimpey Construction (U.K.) Ltd v. Poole (DV) [1984] 2 Lloyd's Rep. 499; 27
B.L.R. 58; (1984) 128 S.J. 969, QBD (Comm Ct) 8–133, 8–168

Winch v. Jones; Winch v. Hayward [1986] Q.B. 296; [1985] 3 W.L.R. 729; [1985]
3 All E.R. 97; (1985) 129 S.J. 669, CA 12–235

Winkworth v. Edward Baron Development Co. [1986] 1 W.L.R. 1512; [1987] 1
All E.R. 114; [1987] B.C.L.C. 193; [1987] 1 F.L.R. 525; [1987] 1 F.T.L.R.
176; (1987) 53 P. & C.R. 378; [1987] Fam. Law 166; (1987) 84 L.S.G. 340;
(1986) 130 S.J. 954, HL 15–74

Winnipeg Condominium Corporation v. Bird Construction Co. (1995) 121 D.L.R.
(4th) 193, Sup Ct (Can) 2–62, 8–77, 8–93, 8–113, 8–119

Winston Cooper v. Smith Llewelyn Partnership [2000] C.P.L.R. 52, CA; affirming [1999] P.N.L.R. 576, QBD 10–151

Winter v. Irish Life Assurance plc [1995] 2 Lloyd's Rep. 274; Lloyd's List, May
18, 1995 (I.D.), QBD 14–03

Winterbottom v. Wright (1852) 10 M. & W. 109; 11 L.J.Ex. 415; 152 E.R. 402 2–102

Wintle v. Nye (No.2); *sub nom.* Wells, In the Estate of [1959] 1 W.L.R. 284;
[1959] 1 All E.R. 552; *The Times*, December 19, 1958, HL 10–17

Wipfli v. Britten (1982) 28 C.C.L.T. 104, Sup Ct (BC), (1984) 13 D.L.R. (4th)
169 .... 12–179, 12–247

Wisbech R.D.C. v. Ward [1927] 2 K.B. 556; [1928] 2 K.B. 1; 91 J.P. 200; [1927]
All E.R. Rep. 486; 44 T.L.R. 62; 97 L.J.K.B. 56; 138 L.T. 308; 26 L.G.R. 10,
CA 8–253

Wiseman Lee (Solicitors) (Wasted Costs Order) (No.5 of 2000), Re; *sub nom.* R.
v. Wiseman Lee (Solicitors) [2001] EWCA Crim 707; (2001) 145 S.J.L.B.
119; *The Times*, April 5, 2001, CA (Crim Div) 10–132

Wiszniewski v. Central Manchester H.A.; *sub nom.* Wisniewski v. Central Manchester H.A. [1998] P.I.Q.R. P324; [1998] Lloyd's Rep. Med. 223, CA;
affirming [1996] 7 Med.L.R. 248, QBD 12–100, 12–173, 12–181, 12–272,
12–284

Wolverhampton M.B.C. v. DB (A Minor); *sub nom.* B (A Minor) (Treatment and
Secure Accommodation), Re; A M.B.C. v. DB [1997] 1 F.L.R. 767; [1997]
1 F.C.R. 618; (1997) 37 B.M.L.R. 172; [1997] Fam. Law 400; (1997) 161
J.P.N. 413, Fam Div 12–141

Wolverine Tube (Canada) Inc. v. Noranda Metal Industries Limited (1995) 26
O.R. 577 8–118

Wong v. 407527 Ontario Ltd (1999) 26 R.P.R. (3d) 262, CA (Ontario) 10–172,
10–196, 10–197, 10–200

Wood v. McVicar [1990] G.W.D. 37–2143 9–145

—— v. Thurston, *The Times*, May 25, 1951 12–178

Woodford & Ackroyd v. Burgess [2000] C.P. Rep. 79; [1999] Lloyd's Rep. P.N.
231; *The Times*, February 1, 1999; *The Independent*, February 1, 1999
(C.S.), CA 6–09, 10–142

Woodglen v. Owens (1999) 27 R.P.R. (3d) 237, CA (Ontario) 10–203

Woods v. Martins Bank [1959] 1 Q.B. 55; [1958] 1 W.L.R. 1018; [1958] 3 All
E.R. 166; 102 S.J. 655, Assizes (Leeds) 2–216

Woods Hardwick Ltd v. Chiltern Air Conditioning Ltd [2001] B.L.R. 23, QBD
(T&CC) 8–341

PARA.

Woodward v. Hutchins [1977] 1 W.L.R. 760; [1977] 2 All E.R. 751; 121 S.J. 409,
    CA 2–156

—— v. Wolferstans [1997] N.P.C. 51; *The Times*, April 8, 1997, Ch D 10–44, 10–160

Woolcott v. Excess Insurance Co. Ltd and Miles, Smith Anderson & Game Ltd
    (No.1) [1979] 1 Lloyd's Rep. 231, CA; reversing [1978] 1 Lloyd's Rep. 633,
    QBD 14–23

—— v. Excess Insurance Co. Ltd and Miles, Smith Anderson & Game Ltd (No.2)
    [1979] 2 Lloyd's Rep. 210, QBD 14–03, 14–23

Wooldridge v. Hicks (S) & Son, 162 E.G. 513; [1953] C.P.L. 700 .... 9–88, 9–91, 9–134

Woolgar v. Chief Constable of Sussex [2000] 1 W.L.R. 25; [1999] 3 All E.R. 604;
    (2000) 2 L.G.L.R. 340; [1999] Lloyd's Rep. Med. 335; (1999) 50 B.M.L.R.
    296; (1999) 96(23) L.S.G. 33; (1999) 149 N.L.J. 857; (1999) 143 S.J.L.B.
    195; *The Times*, May 28, 1999, CA 2–160

Woolwich Building Society v. Fineberg [1998] P.N.L.R. 216, CA 10–132, 10–137

Worboys v. Acme Investments Ltd, 4 B.L.R. 133; (1969) 210 E.G. 335; 119
    N.L.J. 322, CA 6–08, 8–147, 8–214

Worby v. Rosser [1999] Lloyd's Rep. P.N. 972; [2000] P.N.L.R. 140; (1999)
    96(24) L.S.G. 39; *The Times*, June 9, 1999, CA 10–48, 10–52

Workplace Technologies Ltd v. E Squared Ltd [2000] C.I.L.L. 1607 .... 8–338, 8–339

Worster v. City and Hackney H.A., *The Times*, June 22, 1987 12–10

Wraight v. Johnston (1858) 1 F. & F. 128, NP 10–189

Wright v. British Railways Board [1983] 2 A.C. 773; [1983] 3 W.L.R. 211;
    [1983] 2 All E.R. 698, HL 3–20

—— v. Carter [1903] 1 Ch. 27; [1900–03] All E.R. Rep. 706; 72 L.J.Ch. 138; 87
    L.T. 624; 51 W.R. 196; 19 T.L.R. 29, CA 2–144, 2–146, 10–17

—— v. Morgan [1926] A.C. 788, PC (NZ) 2–135, 2–137

Wroth v. Tyler [1974] Ch. 30; [1973] 2 W.L.R. 405; [1973] 1 All E.R. 897; 25 P.
    & C.R. 138; (1972) 117 S.J. 90, Ch D 5–103

Wynniatt-Husey v. RJ Bromley (Underwriting Agencies) plc [1996] L.R.L.R.
    310, QBD (Comm Ct) 16–10, 16–11, 16–14, 16–19, 16–20, 16–30, 16–31,
                16–32, 16–33, 16–34, 16–37, 16–40, 16–42, 16–50, 16–57, 16–68

Wynston v. MacDonald (1980) 105 D.L.R. (3d) 527, (1981) 119 D.L.R. (3d), CA
    (Ontario) 10–61

X (A Child) v. Woollcombe Yonge (A Firm) [2001] Lloyd's Rep. P.N. 274;
    (2001) 2 W.T.L.R. 301, Ch D 6–08, 10–223

X (HA) v. Y [1988] 2 All E.R. 648; [1988] R.P.C. 379; (1987) 137 N.L.J. 1062,
    QBD 2–160

X (Minors) v. Bedfordshire C.C.; M (A Minor) v. Newham L.B.C.; E (A Minor)
    v. Dorset C.C.; Christmas v. Hampshire C.C. (Duty of Care); Keating v.
    Bromley L.B.C. [1995] 2 A.C. 633; [1995] 3 W.L.R. 152; [1995] 3 All E.R.
    353; [1995] 2 F.L.R. 276; [1995] 3 F.C.R. 337; 94 L.G.R. 313; (1995) 7
    Admin. L.R. 705; [1995] Fam. Law 537; (1996) 160 L.G. Rev. 103; (1996)
    160 L.G. Rev. 123; (1995) 145 N.L.J. 993; *The Times*, June 30, 1995; *The
    Independent*, June 30, 1995, HL 2–41, 2–80, 2–81, 2–84, 2–85, 2–95, 2–113,
               12–22, 12–57, 12–60, 12–61, 12–63, 12–66, 12–84, 12–153,
                       12–155, 12–160, 12–239, 12–305

X and Y v. Pal (1991) 23 N.S.W.L.R. 26, [1992] 3 Med.L.R. 195, CA (NSW) 12–43,
                                    12–55, 12–171

X v. Denmark (App No.9974/82) (1983) D.R. 282 7–42

—— v. Germany (1985) 7 E.H.R.R. 152 7–59

—— v. Ireland (1974) 7 D.R. 78 7–50

—— v. United Kingdom (1978) 14 D.R. 31 7–40

PARA.

Y (Mental Patient: Bone Marrow Donation), Re; *sub nom.* Y (Mental Incapacity:
Bone Marrow Transplant), Re; Y (Adult Patient) (Transplant: Bone Mar-
row), Re [1997] Fam. 110; [1997] 2 W.L.R. 556; [1996] 2 F.L.R. 787; [1997]
2 F.C.R. 172; (1997) 35 B.M.L.R. 111; [1997] Fam. Law 91, Fam Div 12–142
Yager v. Fishman & Co. [1944] 1 All E.R. 552; (1944) 77 Ll. L. Rep. 268, CA 10–104,
10–168, 10–169
Yamada v. Mock (1996) 136 D.L.R. (4th) 124, HC (Ontario) 10–207
Yardley v. Coombes (1963) 107 S.J. 575 .... 10–185, 10–279
Yates Property Corporation v. Boland (1998) 157 A.L.R. 30; [1999] Lloyd's Rep.
PN 459, Fed Ct (Aus) 2–118
Yellow Submarine Deli Inc. v. A.G.F. Hospitality Associates Inc. [1998] 2
W.W.R. 701 10–76
Yeoman v. Ferries [1967] S.C. 255, OH 10–278
Yepremian v. Scarborough General Hospital (1980) 110 D.L.R. (3d) 513 12–275
Yerkey v. Jones (1938–9) 63 C.L.R. 649 2–142
Yianni v. Edwin Evans & Sons [1982] Q.B. 438; [1981] 3 W.L.R. 843; [1981] 3
All E.R. 592; (1981) 259 E.G. 969; 125 S.J. 694; *The Times*, July 29, 1981,
QBD 2–28, 9–10, 9–34, 9–43, 9–45, 9–47, 9–63
Ying Ho Co. Ltd v. Man Kwok Leung [2000] 3 H.K.L.R.D. 191 10–10
York Buildings Company v. Mackenzie (1795) 8 Bro.P.C. 42 3–09
Yorkshire Enterprises Ltd v. Robson Rhodes, June 17, 1998, unreported 15–77, 15–79,
15–126
Youell v. Bland Welch & Co. Ltd; Superhulls Cover, The (No.2) [1992] 2 Lloyd's
Rep. 127, CA; affirming [1990] 2 Lloyd's Rep. 423, QBD (Comm Ct) 14–11,
14–14, 14–21, 14–43, 14–50, 14–77, 14–79, 14–89, 14–92, 14–94,
14–110, 14–120, 14–126, 14–127
Young v. Blake (1887) *reported in Hudson's Building Contracts* (4th ed., 1914),
Vol. 2, p. 110 8–221
—— v. Purdy [1996] 2 F.L.R. 795; [1997] 1 F.C.R. 632; [1997] P.N.L.R. 130;
[1997] Fam. Law 93; *The Times*, November 7, 1995, CA 10–191, 10–236
—— v. Robson Rhodes (A Firm) [1999] 3 All E.R. 524; [1999] Lloyd's Rep. P.N.
641; *The Times*, May 11, 1999, Ch D 2–166, 15–44
—— v. Tomlinson [1979] 1 N.Z.L.R. 441 .... 8–143, 8–203, 8–311
—— v. Young [1993] 4 S.C.R. 3, Sup Ct (Can) 10–126
Younge v. Toynbee [1910] 1 K.B. 215 10–75
Yue Xiu Finance Co. Ltd v. Dermot Agnew (formerly trading as Deloitte Haskins
& Sells) [1996] 1 H.K.L.R. 137 .... 15–71, 15–77
Yuen Kun Yeu v. Att.-Gen. of Hong Kong [1988] A.C. 175 15–50
—— v. Attorney General of Hong Kong [1988] A.C. 175; [1987] 3 W.L.R. 776;
[1987] 2 All E.R. 705; [1987] F.L.R. 291; (1987) 84 L.S.G. 2049; (1987)
137 N.L.J. 566; (1987) 131 S.J. 1185, PC (HK) 13–114, 15–50
Yuill & Co. v. Robson [1908] 1 K.B. 270 14–44

Z v. Finland (1998) 25 E.H.R.R. 371; (1999) 45 B.M.L.R. 107, ECHR 7–61, 7–62
—— v. United Kingdom (App. No.29392/95) [2001] 2 F.C.R. 246; 10 B.H.R.C.
384; *The Times*, May 31, 2001, ECHR 15–89
—— v. United Kingdom (App. No.29392/95) [2001] 2 F.L.R. 612, ECHR [2000]
2 F.C.R. 245; (2000) 2 L.G.L.R. 212; *The Times*, May 31, 2001, Eur Comm
HR 7–02, 7–20, 7–21, 7–23
—— v. United Kingdom, 28 E.H.R.R. C.D. 65 12–57
Zakrzewski v. Chas Oldhams & Sons (1981) 260 E.G. 1125, QBD 10–250
Zanatta Installations Ltd v. Elite Insurance Co. (1994) 92 B.C.L.R.(2d) 374, CA
(BC) 14–23
Zealander v. Laing Homes Ltd (2000) 2 T.C.L.R. 724, QBD (T&CC) 8–25
Zimmer v. Ringrose (1981) 16 C.C.L.T. 51 CA (Alberta) 12–109

PARA.

Zubaida (t/a Elley's Enterprises) v. Hargreaves [2000] Lloyd's Rep. P.N. 771;
    [1955–95] P.N.L.R. 665; [1995] 1 E.G.L.R. 127; [1995] 09 E.G. 320, CA;
    affirming [1993] 43 E.G. 111, QBD 9–06, 9–102
Zulu Airwear Inc. v. Khanna Holdings Ltd (1998) 55 B.C.L.R. (3d) 136, Sup Ct
    (BC) 14–43
Zwebner v. Mortgage Corp. plc [1998] P.N.L.R. 769; [1998] E.G.C.S. 104, CA;
    reversing in part [1997] P.N.L.R. 504; [1997] N.P.C. 42, Ch D 2–10, 10–09,
    10–10, 10–75, 10–327

TABLE OF STATUTES

PARA.

Australia
1923 Sale of Goods Act 17–15
1936 Companies Act
s. 115 15–98
1937 Wrongs Act
s. 27A 5–115
1974 Trade Practices Act 17–15
1984 Insurance Contracts Act
s. 28 14–117

New Zealand
1947 Contributory Negligence
Act 5–115
1978 Matrimonial Property Act
s. 21 10–58
Securities Act
s. 50(2) 15–27

United Kingdom
1854 Common Law Procedure
Act (17 & 18 Vict.,
c.125)
s. 3 10–175
1858 Lord Cairns' Act 3–15
Medical Act (21 & 22
Vict., c.90) 12–01
1862 Companies Act (25 & 26
Vict., c.89)
s. 165 15–24
1875 Public Health Act (38 & 39
Vict., c.55) 12–152
1888 County Courts Act (55 &
52 Vict., c.43)
s. 116 8–50
1890 Lunacy Act (53 & 54 Vict.,
c.5)
s. 20 12–274
Partnership Act (c.39)
s. 5 10–147
s. 9 10–147
s. 10 .... 4–05, 10–147
s. 11 10–147
Companies (Winding-up)
Act (53 & 54 Vict.,
c.63)
s. 10 15–24
1893 Public Authorities Protection Act (56 & 57
Vict., c.61) 10–81

PARA.

1893 Sale of Goods Act (c.73)
s. 4 17–10
1906 Marine Insurance Act (6
Edw. 7, c.41)
s. 4 14–106
(2)(b) 14–106
s. 18(1) 14–61
s. 19 14–19
s. 20(4) 13–87
s. 24(1) 14–64
1907 Patents and Designs Act
(c.29)
s. 62 18–03
1908 Companies (Consolidation)
Act (8 Edw. 7, c.69)
s. 113 15–98
s. 215 15–24
1919 Acquisition of Land (Assessment of Compen-
sation) Act (9 & 10
Geo. 5, c.57)
s. 2, r. 5 9–176
1925 Trustee Act (15 & 16 Geo.
5, c.19)
s. 30(1) 5–87
s. 61 .... 13–135, 15–153
Law of Property Act (15 &
16 Geo. 5, c.20)
s. 40 ..... 10–119, 10–161, 11–37
Workmen's Compensation
Act (15 & 16 Geo. 5,
c.84) 10–277
1929 Companies Act (19 & 20
Geo. 5, c.23)
s. 276 15–24
Infant Life (Preservation)
Act (19 & 20 Geo. 5,
c.34)
s. 1 12–278
1930 London Building Act 8–43
s. 5 8–43
Third Parties (Rights
against Insurers) Act
(c.25) 13–194
1935 Law Reform (Married
Women and Tortfea-
sors) Act (25 & 26
Geo. 5, c.30) 4–01, 8–39,
8–56
s. 6 12–164

PARA.

1935 Law Reform (Married Women and Tortfeasors) Act—*cont.*
s. 6(1)(c) 4–01, 8–56
1936 Public Health Act (26 Geo. 5 & 1 Edw. 8, c.49) 10–71
1939 Limitation Act (2 & 3 Geo. 6, c.21) 5–89
s. 2(1) 5–13
s. 21(1) 12–153
s. 26 5–70
War Risks Insurance Act (2 & 3 Geo. 6, c.57) 14–83
1944 Education Act (c.31) 12–62
1945 Law Reform (Contributory Negligence) Act (8 & 9 Geo. 6, c.28) 5–115, 5–116, 9–11, 14–126, 14–127, 15–146, 15–149
s. 1 .... 5–115, 5–117
(1) 5–113, 9–11, 9–167, 9–168
s. 4 .... 5–115, 9–11
1946 National Health Service (9 & 10 Geo. 6, c.81) 12–153
1947 Crown Proceedings Act (c.44)
s. 10 12–14
1948 National Assistance Act (c.29) 12–161
Companies Act (11 & 12 Geo. 6, c.38)
s. 333 15–24
s. 448 .... 13–135, 15–153
1950 Arbitration Act (14 Geo. 6, c.27)
s. 21 5–115
1954 Occupiers' Liability Act 2–79
Landlord and Tenant Act (2 & 3 Eliz. 2, c.56) 10–151, 10–265, 10–330
Pt II 10–202, 10–265, 10–316, 10–330
s. 25 10–44
Pharmacy Act (c.61) 12–03
ss. 1–6 12–03
1957 Occupiers' Liability Act (c.5 & 6 Eliz. 2, c.31)
s. 2 8–250
1959 Mental Health Act (7 & 8 Eliz. 2, c.72)
s. 5 12–235

PARA.

1959 Mental Health Act—*cont.*
s. 141 12–235
(2) 12–235
1960 Professions Supplementary to Medicine Act (c.60)
ss. 2–7 12–03
1962 Building Societies Act (c.10 & 11 Eliz. 2, c.37) 9–43
s. 25(1) 9–29
s. 30 9–43
1963 Limitation Act (c.57) 5–16
1967 Misrepresentation Act (c.7) 13–24, 13–27, 13–85, 13–87, 13–119, 13–157
s. 2(1) 13–85, 13–88, 13–167
(2) 13–85, 13–119, 13–151
Matrimonial Homes Act (c.75) 10–194
Abortion Act (c.87) 7–41, 12–285
s. 1(1)(a)–(d) 12–278
s. 4 7–45
1969 Family Law Reform Act (c.46)
s. 1 5–10
s. 8(1) 12–148
1970 Administration of Justice Act (c.31)
s. 32(1) 5–13
1971 Dogs Act 10–176
Fire Precautions Act (c.40) 9–106
Criminal Damage Act (c.48) 17–67
s. 1 17–21
(1) 17–21
1972 Civil Evidence Act (c.30)
s. 3 9–06
Defective Premises Act (c.35) 2–57, 8–40, 8–41, 8–42, 8–86, 8–88, 8–278
s. 1 .... 8–44, 8–328, 9–12
(1) **8–41**, 8–45, 8–46, 8–66, 9–12
(5) 8–46
s. 2 8–42
s. 7(3) 8–66, 8–88
European Communities Act (c.68) 8–04, 13–119
s. 2(2) 13–23, 13–84, 15–29

PARA.

1973 Matrimonial Causes Act
(c.18)
s. 10 10–178
1974 Juries Act (c.23)
s. 9(1) 1–05
Sched. 1, Pt III 1–05
Health and Safety at Work
etc. Act (c.37)
s. 15 8–48
s. 47(2) 8–48
Insurance Companies Act
(c.49) 13–6
Solicitors Act (c.74) 10–03,
15–26
s. 1 10–01
s. 19 10–01
s. 20 10–01
s. 22 10–01
s. 23 10–01
s. 33 10–20
s. 37 10–03
s. 59(1) 5–03, 10–141
s. 60(5) 5–03
s. 65(2) 10–11
1975 Limitation Act (c.54) 5–16
1976 Congenital Disabilities
(Civil Liability) Act
(c.28) 12–55
s. 1 12–55
(4) 12–55
(5) 12–73, 12–106
s. 1A 12–55
Fatal Accidents Act
(c.30) 5–63
1977 Patents Act (c.37)
s. 1 18–08
s. 2 18–08
s. 15 18–17
s. 72 18–20
s. 102A 18–03
s. 103 18–14
Insurance Brokers (Regis-
tration) Act (c.46) 14–02,
14–04, 14–05
s. 1 14–04
s. 2 14–04
s. 3 14–04
s. 4 14–04
s. 10 .... 14–04, 14–60
s. 22 14–04
National Health Services
Act (c.49) 12–07, 12–21
12–139
s. 3 ..... 12–160, 12–162, 12–169
s. 8 12–162

PARA.

1977 National Health Services
Act—cont.
Sched. 5, para. 15 12–162
Unfair Contract Terms Act
(c.50) 2–30, 5–03, 5–05,
5–07, 5–53, 8–22, 8–23,
8–24, 9–27, 9–28, 9–46,
9–49, 9–63, 9–64, 9–65,
9–66, 9–71, 9–72, 9–73,
10–143, 13–134, 15–101,
17–119
Pt I 9–27
Pt II 9–27, 9–72
s. 1(1) 5–03, 5–53
(2) 13–134
ss. 2–4 13–134
s. 2 17–119
(1) 5–03, 8–22, 9–27
(2) 5–04, 9–27
s. 3 8–22
s. 11 .... 5–04, 17–119
(1) 5–04
(3) 5–04, 9–64, 9–68,
9–70
(5) 9–64
s. 15(1) 9–72
s. 16 9–72
s. 25(3)(d) 9–72
s. 29(1)(a) 13–134
s. 29(2) 13–134
s. 29(3) 13–134
Sched.
para. 1(1)(a) 13–134
(e) 13–134
1978 Civil Liability (Contribution) Act (c.47) 4–01,
4–07, 4–09, 8–21, 8–56,
8–318, 8–324, 8–331,
9–173, 10–328, 12–246,
13–168, 15–147
s. 1 .... 8–319, 8–322, 8–326
(1) 4–02, 4–03, 4–09,
8–318, 9–173
(2) 4–03
(3) 4–10
(4) 4–03, 4–04, 4–05,
4–11, 8–326
(5) 4–11
s. 2 4–12
(1) 4–12, 8–325
(2) 8–325
s. 3(3)(a) 4–12
(b) 4–12
(c) 4–12
s. 6(1) 4–06

PARA.

1979 Banking Act (c.37) 13–6
      Estate   Agents'   Act
         (c.38) 9–02
      s. 1(1) 9–02
         (2)(d) 9–02
      Sale of   Goods Act
         (c.54) 17–07, 17–13,
                         17–84, 17–99
      s. 12(2)(b) 17–59
      ss. 13–15 2–02
      s. 14 17–82
         (2) 17–14, **17–82**, 17–83
            (A) **17–82**
            (B) **17–82**
            (C) **17–82**
         (3) 17–14, 17–82, 17–83
         (6) 17–99
      s. 35 17–101
         (1) 17–93
      s. 61 17–07
1980 Limitation (Amendment)
      Act (c.24)
      s. 7 5–70
      Health Services Act (c.53)
      s. 1 12–162
      Limitation Act (c.58) 5–10,
                   5–16, 5–50, 5–67, 5–70,
                   5–79, 5–80, 5–82, 5–90,
                                        5–91
      s. 2 .... 5–89, 5–93
      s. 5 ..... 5–88, 5–89, 5–91, 5–93,
                                       5–108
      s. 8 .... 5–10, 8–64
      s. 10 4–15
      ss. 11–14 5–12
      s. 11 .... 5–12, 5–64, 10–82,
                      10–119, 12–48
         (1) 5–13, 12–289
         (4) 5–56
         (5) 5–56
      s. 12 5–64
         (1) 5–63
         (2) 5–63
      s. 14 .... 5–54, 5–61, 5–62
         (1) 5–56, 5–57
            (b) 5–58
            (c) 5–61
         (2) 5–56
         (3) 5–56, 5–61
         (4)(a) 5–16
      s. 14A 5–11, 5–29, 5–30,
                 5–45, 5–50, 5–51, 5–53, 5–54,
                 5–55, 5–74, 5–77, 8–46, 9–09,
                             9–10, 9–165
         (5) 5–50, 5–51

PARA.

1980 Limitation Act—*cont.*
      s. 14A(6) 5–50
         (7) 5–50, 9–10
         (8) 5–50
         (9) 5–50
         (10) 5–50
      s. 14B 5–51, 5–74, 5–77
         (2) 5–51
      s. 15 5–82
      s. 16 5–82
      s. 20(2) 5–82
         (4) 5–82
      s. 21 ..... 5–82, 5–83, 5–86, 5–88
         (1) 5–87
            (b) 5–90
      s. 22 5–82
      s. 28(1) 5–10
      s. 28A 5–51
      s. 31 .... 5–29, 5–30
      s. 32 .... 9–09, 5–70, 5–72, 5–74,
                                 5–76, 5–77
         (1) **5–70**, 5–73, 13–100
            (b) 5–50, 5–51, **5–70**,
                   5–71, 5–72, 5–74, 5–75
         (2) **5–70**, 5–74, 5–75,
                   5–76, 5–77, 5–78, 8–296
      s. 33 .... 4–08, 5–12, 5–66, 5–67,
                   5–69, 10–185, 10–321
         (1) 5–64
         (3) 5–64
            (a)–(e) 5–64
            (f) 5–64
      s. 36 .... 5–81, 5–84, 5–89, 5–90,
                   5–91, 5–92, 5–93, 5–108
         (2) 5–98
      s. 38(1) 5–13, 5–72
         (2) 5–10
         (3) 5–10
         (9) 5–72
1981 Supreme   Court   Act
         (c.54) 3–19
      s. 18(1)(f) 14–122
      s. 35A 3–19, 3–24
         (1) 3–19, 9–162
         (2) 3–20
      s. 51(6) 18–13
      Supreme Court Act (c.54)
      s. 51 10–127
         (9) 10–175
      Education Act (c.60) 12–62
1982 Lloyd's Act (c. xiv) 16–01,
                                        16–07
      Supply of Goods and Serv-
         ices Act (c.29) 8–27,
                   12–12, 17–83, 17–84

	PARA.
1982 Supply of Goods and Services Act—*cont.*	
s. 1	17–83
s. 4	12–11, 17–83
s. 12	18–12
s. 13 .... 2–07, 2–11, 8–27, 9–20, 10–77, 12–07, 13–92, 14–10, 16–10, 16–11, 17–49, 17–50, 18–10, 15–36	
s. 14(1)	8–28
(2)	8–28
s. 16	2–11
Insurance Companies Act (c.50)	13–6, 14–06
s. 2	13–30
s. 21A	15–30
Administration of Justice Act (c.53)	
s. 20	10–218
1983 Mental Health Act (c.20)	12–49, 12–57, 12–141, 12–142, 12–143, 12–233
Pt II	12–239
s. 2	12–139
s. 3	12–140
(3)	12–239
s. 63	12–140
s. 117	12–238
s. 118	12–234
(3)	12–234
(4)	12–234
s. 131	12–235
(1)	12–143, 12–233
s. 139	12–235
(1)	12–235
(2)	12–235
ss. 512–564	12–140
Medical Act (c.54)	12–01
s. 46	12–01
s. 47	12–01
s. 48	12–01
s. 49	12–01
Judgments Act (1 & 2 Vict., c.110)	
s. 17	3–22
1984 Occupiers' Liability Act (c.3)	2–79
Trade Marks (Amendment) Act (c.19)	
s. 12(3)	18–16
Dentist Act (c.24)	12–02
s. 15	12–02
s. 26	12–02
s. 38	12–02

	PARA.
1984 Building Act (c.55)	
s. 36(1)	10–194
(2)	10–194
(6)	10–194
Police and Criminal Evidence Act (c.60)	2–161
1985 Companies Act (c.6)	9–15, 15–9, 15–10, 15–12, 15–19, 15–81, 15–113
s. 67(1)	9–15
s. 151	15–81
s. 226	15–14
(2)	15–17
(3)	15–14, 15–15
(4)	15–17
(5)	15–17
s. 227	15–14
s. 235	15–34, 15–113
(1)	15–19
(2)	15–19
(3)	15–19
s. 236(1)	15–19
(4)	15–19
s. 237	15–20
(1)	15–20, 15–98, 15–113
(4A)	15–20
ss. 246–249	15–17
s. 247B(2)(b)	15–17
s. 248	15–20
s. 256	15–15
s. 310	5–03, 15–100
s. 320	10–239
s. 384(1)	15–12
(2)	15–12
s. 385(2)	15–12
s. 385A	15–12
s. 386	15–12
s. 387	15–12
s. 388A	15–12
(1)	15–21
(2)	15–21
(3)	15–21
(4)	15–21
(5)	15–21
s. 390	15–21
s. 390A	15–13
s. 390B	15–13
s. 391	15–22
(2)	15–22
s. 391A(1)	15–22
(3)–(6)	15–22
s. 392	15–23
(2)	15–23
(5)	15–23

PARA.

1985 Companies Act—*cont.*
s. 392(3)–(7) 15–23
(8) 15–23
s. 394 .... 15–22, 15–23
(3)–(7) 15–23
s. 394A 15–23
s. 631 15–24
s. 727 .... 13–135, 15–24,
15–120, 15–153
Sched. 4 .... 15–14, 15–15
para. 36A 15–15
Family Law (Scotland) Act
(c.37)
ss. 8–10 9–177
Administration of Justice
Act (c.61) 10–02
Insolvency Act (c.65)
s. 19 15–24
Housing Act (c.68)
Pt XVI 8–43
s. 575(1) 8–43
1986 Agriculture Holdings Act
(c.5)
s. 39 10–266
Latent Damage Act
(c.37) 5–16, 5–25, 5–27,
5–39, 5–49, 5–50, 5–52,
5–53, 5–76, 8–39, 8–46,
8–54, 9–10
s. 1 5–50
s. 2 5–52
(2) 5–50, 5–51
s. 3 .... 5–23, 5–52, 8–61
(1) **8–61**
(b) 5–51
(5) 5–51
(6) 5–51
s. 4(1)(a) 5–49
(b) 5–49
(3) 5–52
(4) 5–52
Insolvency Act (c.45)
s. 212 .... 10–115, 15–24,
15–120
s. 371 7–34
Building Societies Act
(c.53) 9–17, 9–43, 9–168,
13–6
s. 13 .... 2–92, 9–14
(1) 9–29
(c) 9–29
s. 62 .... 9–05, 9–150
s. 82 15–30
s. 83(1) 9–17
Sched. 12 9–18

PARA.

1986 Building Societies Act
—*cont.*
Pt II 9–17
para. 3 9–18
Financial Services Act
(c.60) 10–03, 10–206,
9–15, 13–1, 13–2, 13–6,
13–7, 13–9, 13–10, 13–11,
13–12, 13–14, 13–15,
13–17, 13–18, 13–19,
13–21, 13–22, 13–25,
13–28, 13–29, 13–32,
13–33, 13–38, 13–39,
13–40, 13–42, 13–44,
13–45, 13–46, 13–49,
13–55, 13–69, 13–71,
13–72, 13–75, 13–76,
13–77, 13–78, 13–79,
13–81, 13–85, 13–92,
13–95, 13–97, 13–98,
13–110, 13–112, 13–121,
13–124, 13–126, 13–127,
13–132, 13–137, 13–138,
13–140, 13–142, 13–145,
13–146, 13–147, 13–148,
13–157, 13–167, 13–170,
13–174, 13–190, 13–192,
14–06, 15–5, 15–7
Pt I 13–10
Chap. VI 13–10
Chap. VIII 13–10, 13–23
Pt IV 13–23, 13–81, 15–28,
15–29, 15–60
Pt V 13–12
Pt VII 13–12
Pt VIII 13–12
Pt XI 13–12
Pt XII 13–12
Pt XIII 13–12
Pt XIX 13–12
Pt XVII 13–12
Pt XVIII 13–12
Pt XX 13–12
Pt XXI 13–12
Pt XXII 13–12
Pt XXIII 13–12
Pt XXIV 13–12
Pt XXV 13–12
Pt XXVI 13–12
ss. 1–128C 13–10
s. 1 .... 13–28, 13–33
(1) 13–10, 13–29, 13–33
(2) 13–10, 13–30
(3) 13–14, 13–30
s. 2 13–33

PARA.

1986 Financial Services Act
—cont.

s. 3 .... 9–16, 13–10, 13–13,
13–28, 13–29, 13–96, 13–145
ss. 4–6 13–71
s. 4 13–10
s. 5 .... 13–10, 13–152, 14–08
   (1)(b) 13–152
   (6) 13–152, 13–153
s. 6 .... 9–16, 13–10, 13–137,
13–146
   (2) 13–142, 13–145
   (3) 13–145, 13–147
   (4) 13–145, 13–147
ss. 7–34 13–10
s. 7 13–10
ss. 15–21 13–21
s. 15 13–10
s. 25 13–10
ss. 35–46 13–20
ss. 36–41 13–20
s. 43 13–91
s. 44 .... 13–20, 13–95, 13–97,
13–98, 13–112
   (2) 13–96
   (6) 13–95, 13–97
   (7) 13–95, 13–97
s. 47 13–119
s. 47A 13–44
ss. 48–56 13–10
s. 51 13–10
s. 55 13–10
ss. 56–71 13–12
ss. 56–58 13–28
s. 56 .... 13–10, 13–15, 13–32,
13–72, 13–156
   (2) 13–15
s. 57 .... 13–10, 13–15, 13–32,
13–72, 13–119, 13–156
   (3) 13–15
s. 58 .... 13–10, 13–32
s. 61 ..... 13–10, 13–72, 13–137,
13–146, 14–06
   (1) 13–142, 13–145
   (3) 13–145, 13–147
   (4) 13–145, 13–147
s. 62 .... 2–79, 13–38, 13–76,
13–77, 13–110, 13–122, 13–123,
13–156, 13–167, 14–06
s. 62A 2–79, 13–10, 13–38,
13–76, 13–77, 13–110, 13–156,
13–167
s. 63 13–29
s. 75–95 .... 13–10, 13–23
s. 75(1) 13–34

PARA.

1986 Financial Services Act
—cont.

s. 79(3) 15–29
s. 90 15–29
s. 104–117 13–12
s. 109 15–30
s. 114 13–10
ss. 118–131 13–12
s. 132 .... 13–152, 14–58
   (6) 13–153
s. 135 15–30
ss. 142–157 15–28
s. 142(7) 15–29
s. 150 13–157
   (1) 9–15, 15–29
   (5) 13–81
s. 151 15–29
ss. 165–176 13–12
s. 166(1) 9–15
ss. 178–192 13–12
s. 179 .... 13–132, 13–206
s. 180 13–206
s. 187 .... 13–12, 13–132,
13–132
ss. 193–204 13–12
s. 207(1) 13–20
ss. 214–324 13–12
ss. 235–284 13–12
ss. 285–301 13–12
ss. 325–333 13–12
ss. 334–339 13–12
ss. 340–346 13–12
ss. 347–354 13–12
ss. 355–379 13–12
ss. 380–386 13–12
ss. 387–396 13–12
Sched. 1 13–30
Pt I 13–10, 13–30, 13–33
para. 1 13–33
para. 2 13–33
para. 3 13–33
para. 4 13–33
para. 5 13–33
para. 6 13–33
para. 7 13–33
para. 8 13–33
para. 9 13–33
para. 10 13–33
para. 11 13–33
Pt II 13–10, 13–28, 13–29,
13–30
para. 12 13–30
para. 13 13–30
para. 13A 13–30
para. 14 13–30

PARA.

1986 Financial Services Act
    —cont.
    para. 15 13–30
    para. 16 13–30
    para. 16A 13–30
    Pt III 13–10, 13–29, 13–30
    para. 17–23 13–30
    para. 18–22 13–30
    para. 19–23 13–30
    para. 22 13–30
    para. 24 13–30
    para. 24A 13–30
    para. 25A 13–30
    para. 25B 13–30
    Pt IV 13–30
    Pt V 13–30

1987 Banking Act (c.22) 13–6,
                    13–132, 13–137
    s. 3 13–30
    s. 5 13–33
    s. 37 2–161
    s. 39 2–160
    s. 47 15–30
    s. 48 13–137
    s. 49 13–137
    s. 93 13–137
    Crown   Proceedings
        (Armed Forces) Act
        (c.25) 12–14
    Criminal   Justice   Act
        (c.38)
    s. 2 2–160
    Consumer Protection Act
        (c.43) 12–12, 12–13,
                12–14, 12–226, 17–72,
                        17–74, 17–75
    s. 1(2) 17–73
    s. 3(1) 17–76
        (2) 17–76
    s. 4(1)(e) 17–77
    s. 45 17–73

1988 Income and Corporation
        Taxes Act (c.1)
    s. 113(2) 15–144
    Access to Medical Reports
        (c.28) 12–64
    Copyright, Designs and
        Patents Act (c.48)
    s. 274(1) 18–03
    s. 275 18–04
    s. 276 18–04
    s. 277 18–04

PARA.

1988 Copyright, Designs and
        Patents Act—cont.
    s. 280 18–14
    s. 292 18–03

1989 Law of Property (Miscella-
        neous Provisions) Act
        (c.34)
    s. 2 .... 10–82, 10–119, 11–37
    Companies Act (c.40) 7–21,
                13–10, 15–9, 15–10,
                            15–15
    Pt II 15–12
    ss. 24–54 15–12
    s. 24(1) 15–12
    s. 25 15–12
    s. 30 15–12
    s. 119 15–12
    s. 193 13–77
    Children Act (c.41) 12–153,
                            12–160
    Opticians Act (c.44)
    ss. 7–9 12–03

1990 National   Health   Service
        and Community Care
        Act (c.19) 12–87, 12–160
    s. 1 12–162
    s. 4 12–163
        (3) 12–163
    s. 5 12–163
    s. 21 12–87
    Access to Health Records
        Act (c.23) 12–30, 12–221
    Human   Fertilisation   and
        Embryology   Act
        (c.37)
    s. 37(1)–(3) 12–278
    s. 44 12–55
    Law Reform (Miscellane-
        ous Provisions) (Scot-
        land) Act (c.40)
    s. 68 9–71
        (6) 9–72
    Courts and Legal Services
        Act (c.41) 10–02, 10–175,
                11–01, 18–03, 18–13
    s. 4 .... 10–127, 11–26
    s. 27 .... 11–01, 18–03
    s. 28 18–03
    s. 34 10–02
    s. 35 10–02
    s. 58 10–135
    s. 61(1) 11–04
        (2) 11–04
    s. 62 .... 10–106, 11–17

PARA.

1991 Property Misdescriptions
Act (c.29) 9–13
s. 1(1) 9–13
(4) 9–13
(5) 9–13
s. 5(1) 9–13
Medical Qualifications
(Amendment) Act
(c.38) 12–01
1992 Nurse, Midwives and
Health Visitors Act
(c.16) 12–149
Medicinal Products: Pre-
scription by Nurses,
etc. Act (c.28) 12–149
Friendly Societies Act
(c.40)
s. 79 15–30
1993 Osteopaths Act (c.21)
ss. 2–4 12–03
s. 6 12–03
Criminal Justice Act
(c.36)
Pt V 13–138, 13–140
1994 Trade Marks Act (c.26)
s. 76 18–06
s. 82 .... 18–06, 18–07
s. 84 18–07
s. 87 18–14
Sale and Supply of Goods
Act (c.35) 2–04, 12–11,
17–28
1995 Health Authorities Act
(c.17) 12–162
s. 1 12–19
Pensions Act (c.26) 13–06
Civil Evidence Act
(c.38) 9–102
Medical (Professional Performance) Act
(c.51) 12–01
s. 4 12–01
1996 Arbitration Ac (c.23) 8–25,
8–338
s. 29 2–97
s. 42 8–337
s. 90 8–25
Housing Grants, Construc-
tion and Regeneration
Act (c.53) 8–264, 8–343
Pt II 8–11, 8–332
s. 104(1) 8–334
(2) 8–334
(e) 8–341
(6)(a) 8–334

PARA.

1996 Housing Grants, Construction and Regeneration
Act—cont.
s. 105 8–335
(2) 8–335
s. 107 8–334
(5) 8–334
s. 108 8–9
(1)–(4) 8–333
(1) 8–332
(3) 8–332
1997 Civil Procedure Act
(c.12) 10–131
Architects Act (c.22)
s. 20 8–4
Nurses, Midwives and
Health Visitors Act
(c.24) 12–149
ss. 7–9 12–03
Social Security (Recovery
of Benefits) Act
(c.27)
s. 1 10–290
1998 Public Interest Disclosure
Act (c.23) 2–160
Human Rights Act (c.42) 7–01,
7–02, 7–03, 7–25, 7–28,
7–29, 7–36, 7–37, 7–41,
7–49, 7–50, 8–342,
12–161, 12–301, 13–25,
15–89
s. 2 .... 7–01, 7–25
s. 3 7–01
s. 6 .... 7–01, 7–37, 7–39, 8–342,
13–189
(1) 8–342, 13–25,
13–132, 13–189
s. 7 .... 7–01, 7–49
(1) 7–25, 13–26
(a) 7–26, 7–28
s. 8 7–27
s. 18 7–02
s. 19 7–02
s. 20 7–02
s. 21(5) 7–02
s. 22(2) 7–02
(4) 7–25
1999 Access to Justice Act
(c.22)
s. 36 10–01
Contracts (Rights of Third
Parties) Act (c.31) 8–67,
15–88
s. 1 8–67
(1)(a) 8–67

PARA.

1999 Contracts (Rights of Third
       Parties) Act—*cont.*
         s. 1(1)(b) 8–67
             (2) 8–67
             (3) 8–67
             (5) 8–67
         s. 3(2) 8–67
             (3) 8–67
             (4) 8–67
         s. 10(2) 8–68
             (3) 8–68
2000 Financial   Services   and
       Markets Act (c.8) 10–03,
             10–206, 13–1, 13–2, 13–7,
                 13–9, 13–11, 13–12,
                 13–13, 13–14, 13–15,
                 13–17, 13–19, 13–20,
                 13–21, 13–25, 13–28,
                 13–31, 13–34, 13–38,
                 13–39, 13–41, 13–41,
                 13–42, 13–44, 13–50,
                 13–69, 13–71, 13–72,
                 13–74, 13–75, 13–76,
                 13–77, 13–79, 13–82,
                 13–85, 13–95, 13–97,
                 13–119, 13–120, 13–131,
                 13–132, 13–133, 13–137,
                 13–138, 13–139, 13–140,
                 13–146, 13–147, 13–148,
                 13–152, 13–156, 13–157,
                 13–167, 13–176, 13–192,
                 13–195, 13–203
                 14–02, 14–04, 14–05,
                 14–06, 14–36, 14–80,
                 15–05, 15–25, 15–30,
                 16–07
         Pt IV 13–12, 13–17, 13–18,
                 13–42, 13–74, 13–84
         Pt IX 13–12, 13–21, 13–25
         Pt VI 13–23, 13–76, 13–81,
                 15–29
         Pt VIII 13–25
         Pt X 13–12
         Pt XIII 13–79
         Pt XIX 16–07
         Pt XV 13–12, 13–78, 13–190
         Pt XVI 13–12, 13–169
         Pt XVI 13–12, 13–171
         Pt XVII 13–23
         Pt XX 13–21
         Pt XXII 15–5, 15–25
         Pt XXVI 13–25
         s. 1 13–132
             (3) 13–12, 13–25, 13–189
         s. 2 13–12

PARA.

2000 Financial   Services   and
       Markets Act—*cont.*
         s. 2(2) 13–12
             (3) 13–12
         ss. 3–6 13–12
         s. 19 .... 13–13, 13–29, 13–96,
                 14–08
         s. 20 13–156
         s. 21 .... 13–15, 13–31, 13–33,
                 13–34, 13–50
             (1) 13–50
             (3) 13–16
             (5) 13–16
             (8) 13–31
             (9) 13–33
             (10) 13–33
             (11) 13–33
             (14) 13–33
             (15) 13–32, 13–33
         s. 20 13–74
         s. 21 13–156
         s. 22 ..... 13–29, 13–33, 13–172,
                 14–07, 16–08
             (1) 13–34
             (4) 13–33
             (5) 13–33
         s. 23 .... 13–13, 13–71
             (2) 13–13
         s. 25 .... 13–15, 13–72
         ss. 26–28 14–08
         s. 26 13–152
             (1) 13–152
             (2) 13–153
             (3) 13–152
             (4) 13–152
         s. 27 13–152
             (1) 13–152
             (2) 13–153
             (3) 13–152
             (4) 13–152
         s. 28(2) 13–153
             (3) 13–153
             (4) 13–153
             (5) 13–153
             (6) 13–153
             (7) 13–153
             (8) 13–153
             (9) 13–152, 13–153
         s. 29 13–155
         s. 30 13–156
             (2) 13–156
             (3) 13–156
             (4) 13–156
             (8) 13–156
         s. 31 13–17

PARA.

2000 Financial Services and Markets Act—*cont.*

s. 37	13–10
s. 38	13–20
(2)	13–95
s. 39	13–20, 13–95, 13–97
(1)	13–95, 13–96
(3)	13–48, 13–95, 13–97
(4)	13–48, 13–95, 13–97
ss. 40–55	13–12, 13–18
s. 40(4)	13–17
s. 41	13–18
s. 42	13–18
(7)	13–18
s. 43	13–17
s. 48(4)	13–17
s. 51(3)	13–42
ss. 56–58	16–08
s. 56	13–21
(6)	13–75
(8)(b)	13–21
ss. 59–63	13–12, 13–19
s. 59(1)	13–75
(2)	13–75
s. 64	13–44, 13–45
(1)	13–42
(2)	13–42, 13–45
(8)	13–45
s. 66(2)(a)	13–45
s. 71	13–75, 13–156
ss. 72–103	13–12, 13–81, 15–29
s. 74	13–81
(4)	13–76
(5)	13–81
s. 79(2)	13–81
(3)	13–81
s. 84	13–82
s. 85	13–82, 13–156
s. 86(1)	15–29
s. 90	13–81, 13–157
(2)	13–81
(5)	15–29
(6)	13–81
(7)	13–81
s. 102	13–25, 13–132
s. 103(1)	13–84
(2)	13–81
ss. 118–131	13–25
s. 118	13–148
s. 119	13–42
s. 122(1)	13–42
ss. 132–137	13–12, 13–21, 13–25
ss. 138–177	13–12

PARA.

2000 Financial Services and Markets Act—*cont.*

s. 138	13–42, 13–44
s. 139	13–42
s. 140	13–42
s. 141	13–42
s. 142	13–42
s. 143	13–42, 13–76
s. 144	13–42
s. 145	13–15, 13–42, 13–44
s. 146	13–42, 13–44, 13–78
s. 147	13–42
s. 149	13–42, 13–76
s. 150	13–41, 13–43, 13–76, 13–77, 13–78, 13–119, 13–156, 13–167, 14–08, 14–46, 14–80, 16–08, 16–23
(2)	13–43, 13–44, 13–76
(3)	13–77
(4)(a)	13–76
(b)	13–76
(5)	13–77
s. 151(1)	13–78
(2)	13–78
s. 153	13–39
(1)	13–40
(2)	13–40, 13–78
(4)	13–78
(6)	13–78
s. 154	13–39, 13–78
s. 156	13–44
s. 157	13–42, 13–44
(1)	13–40
ss. 193–204	13–79
s. 202	13–79
ss. 212–224	13–12
s. 212(1)–(5)	13–190
s. 213(1)	13–190, 13–192
(2)	13–190
s. 216	13–203
s. 217	13–203
s. 219	13–193
s. 220	13–193
s. 221(2)	13–193
s. 222	13–132
(1)	13–204
s. 224	13–193
ss. 225–234	13–12, 13–170
s. 225(1)	13–170
s. 226	13–170
(2)	13–171
(b)	13–176, 13–177
(c)	13–176, 13–177
(3)(a)	13–171

PARA.

2000 Financial Services and
Markets Act—*cont.*
s. 226(4) 13–172
s. 227 .... 13–170, 13–173
  (2)(d) 13–177
  (3)(a) 13–171
  (6) 13–171
  (5) 13–184
s. 229(2)(a) 13–183
  (b) 13–183, 13–187
  (3) 13–183
  (4) 13–186, 13–187
  (8)(a) 13–187
  (b) 13–184
  (9) 13–184
s. 230(1) 13–187
  (3) 13–187
  (4) 13–187
s. 231(1) 13–180
s. 232(2) 13–180
s. 235(1) 13–34
s. 253 13–133
s. 285 13–20
s. 291 13–132
s. 314–324 16–07
s. 315(2) 13–196, 16–07
ss. 325–333 13–21
s. 325(1) 13–21
s. 325(3) 13–21
s. 326 13–21
s. 327 13–21
s. 328 13–21
s. 329 13–21
s. 330 13–21
s. 331 13–21
s. 332(1) 13–21
  (2) 13–21
  (5) 13–21
ss. 235–284 13–23
ss. 340–346 15–5
s. 342 15–30
s. 343 15–30
s. 344 15–30
s. 348 13–132
s. 380 .... 10–76, 13–137
  (1) 13–141, 13–144,
                          13–145
  (2) 13–141, 13–142,
                          13–145
  (3) 13–141, 13–142,
                          13–146
  (5) 13–145
  (6) 13–144
  (a) 13–137

PARA.

2000 Financial Services and
Markets Act—*cont.*
s. 381 .... 13–137, 13–142
  (1) 13–144
  (6) 13–145
s. 382 .... 10–76, 13–137,
                          13–145, 13–147
  (1) 13–141, 13–142
  (9) 13–137
s. 383 .... 13–137, 13–142,
                          13–145, 13–147
s. 384 13–148
  (1) 13–137
  (2) 13–137
s. 386 13–137
ss. 387–396 13–25
s. 387 13–21
s. 388 13–21
s. 401(1) 13–138
  (2)(a) 13–138
s. 402 13–140
  (1) 13–138
s. 412 13–29
s. 417(1) 13–13, 13–20,
  13–74, 13–75, 13–76, 13–77,
                          13–140, 13–148
s. 418 13–14
  (1)(a) 13–17
  (2)(b) 13–17
Sched. 1
para. 7 13–132
para. 8(8) 13–132
para. 19 .... 13–12, 13–25,
                          13–132
para. 19(2) 13–132
Sched. 2 .... 13–29, 13–32
Pt II 13–33
Sched. 3 .... 13–14, 13–17
Pt III 13–17
para. 16(2) 13–152
  (4) 13–155
para. 17(2) 13–152
Sched. 4 13–17
Sched. 6 13–18
Sched. 10 .... 13–81, 15–29
Sched. 17 .... 13–132, 13–167
para. 10 13–189
  (2) 13–189
para. 14 13–171
para. 16 13–184
para. 18 13–171
  (5) 13–189

TABLE OF STATUTORY INSTRUMENTS

PARA.

1961 Construction (General Provisions) Regulations 1580 reg. 50(2) 8–81

1973 House Building Standards (Approved Scheme etc) Order 1843 8–42

1975 House Building Standards (Approved Scheme etc) Order 1402 8–42

1977 House Building Standards (Approved Scheme etc) Order 642 8–42

1978 Insurance Brokers Registration Council (Code of Conduct) Approval Order 1394 14–04

1979 House Building Standards (Approved Scheme etc) Order 381 8–42

1980 Control of Lead at Work Regulations 1248 8–48

1982 Supply of Services (Exclusion of Implied Terms) Order 1771 18–12

1986 Criminal Cases (General) Regulations 1335 10–132

1988 Insurance Brokers Registration Council (Code of Business) Rules Approval Order 950 14–06

1990 Register of Patent Agents Rules 1457 18–4

Accounting Standards (Prescribed Body) Regulations 1667 15–14

1991 Building Regulations 2768 8–158

Companies Act 1985 (Disclosure of Remuneration for Non-Audit Work) Regulations 2128 15–13

Law Reform (Miscellaneous Provisions) (Scotland) Act 1990 (Commencement No. 3) Order 330 9–72

1991 Financial Services Act 1986 (Restriction of Right of Action) Regulations 489 .... 13–77, 14–07

1992 National Health Service (General Medical Services) Regulations 635 12–17

Sched. 2 12–169

Transfer of Functions (Financial Services) Order 1315 13–10

1993 Money Laundering Regulations 1933 13–140

1994 Auditors (Financial Services Act 1986) Rules 526 15–30

Building Regulations (Amendment) Regulations 1850 8–158

Construction (Design and Management) Regulations 3140 .... 8–40, 8–48, 8–158, 8–216

Insurance Brokers Registration Council (Code of Conduct) Approval Order 2569 14–04

Unfair Terms in Consumer Contracts Regulations 3159 .... 5–05, 8–25, 9–27, 15–101

1995 Financial Services Act 1986 (Investment advertisements) (Exemptions) (No 2) Order 1536 13–32

Public Offers of Securities Regulations 1537 .... 13–23, 13–84, 15–29

reg. 14 13–157

1996 Dental Qualifications (Recognition) Regulations 1496 12–02

Financial Services Act 1986 (Investment advertisements) (Exemptions) Order 1586 13–32

PARA.

1996   Financial Institutions (Prudential Supervision) Regulations 1669 15–30

1997   Financial Services Act 1986 (Investment advertisements) (Exemptions) Order 963 13–32

1998   Housing Grants, Construction and Regeneration Act (England and Wales) (Commencement No. 4) Order 650 8–333

  Human Rights Act 1998 (Commencement) Order 2882 7–02

  Scheme of Construction Contracts 649 8–333

1999   Public Offers of Securities (Amendment) Regulations 734 .... 13–23, 13–84

  Public Offers of Securities (Amendment) (No 2) Regulations 1146 .... 13–23, 13–84

  Unfair Terms in Consumer Contracts Regulations 2083 .... 5–05; 8–21, 8–24, 8–25; 15–101

    reg. 5(1) **5–05**; 8–24

    reg. 5(2) 8–24

    reg. 5(5), Sched. 2, para. 1 8–25

    reg. 5(5), Sched. 2, para. 1(q) 8–25

  Unfair Arbitration Agreements (Specified Amount) Order 2167 8–25

2000   Human Rights Act 1998 (Commencement No. 2) Order 1851 7–02

2001   Financial Services and Markets Act 2000 (Regulated Activities) Order 544 ...... 13–30, 13–32, 13–33, 13–36, 13–49, 13–96, 14–06

    part. II, chap. II, art. 4 13–30

    part. II, chap. II, arts 5–9 13–30

    part. II, chap. III, art. 4 13–30

PARA.

2001   Financial Services and Markets Act 2000 (Regulated Activities) Order 544—*cont.*

    part. II, chap. III, arts 10–13 13–30

    part. II, chap. IV, arts 4, 14–20 13–30

    part. II, chap. IV, art. 4 13–30

    part. II, chap. IV, arts 14–20 13–30

    part. II, chap. IV, art. 66 13–30

    part. II, chap. IV, arts 68–72 13–30

    part. II, chap. V, art. 4 13–30

    part. II, chap. V, arts 21–24 13–30

    part. II, chap. V, arts 67–72 13–30

    part. II, chap. VI, art. 4 13–30

    part. II, chap. VI, arts 25–36 13–30

    part. II, chap. VI, arts 67–72 13–30

    part. II, chap. VII, art. 4 13–30

    part. II, chap. VII, arts 37–39 13–30

    part. II, chap. VII, art. 66 13–30

    part. II, chap. VII, art. 68 13–30

    part. II, chap. VII, art. 69 13–30

    part. II, chap. VIII, art. 4 13–30

    part. II, chap. VIII, arts 40–44 13–30

    part. II, chap. VIII, arts 66–69 13–30

    part. II, chap. VIII, art. 71 13–30

    part. II, chap. IX, art. 4 13–30

    part. II, chap. IX, arts 45–50 13–30

    part. II, chap. IX, art. 66 13–30

    part. II, chap. IX, art. 69 13–30

PARA.

2001 Financial Services and
Markets Act 2000
(Regulated Activities)
Order 544—*cont.*
part. II, chap. X, art.
4 13–30
part. II, chap. X, art.
51 13–30
part. II, chap. XI, art.
4 13–30
part. II, chap. XI, art.
4(2) 13–30
part. II, chap. XI, art.
52 13–30
part. II, chap. XII, art.
4 13–30
part. II, chap. XII, arts
53–55 13–30
part. II, chap. XII, arts
67–70 13–30
part. II, chap. XII, art.
72 13–30
part. II, chap. XIII, art.
4 13–30
part. II, chap. XIII, arts
56–58 13–30
part. II, chap. XIV, art.
4 13–30
part. II, chap. XIV, art.
59 13–30
part. II, chap. XIV, art.
60 13–30
part. II, chap. XV, art.
4 13–30
part. II, chap. XV, arts
61–63 13–30
part. II, chap. XVI, arts
4 13–30
part. II, chap. XVI, arts
64 13–30
part. II, chap. XVI, arts
65 13–30
part. II, chap. XVI, arts
72 13–30
part. III, art. 74 13–33
part. III, art. 75 13–33
part. III, art. 76 13–33
part. III, art. 77 13–33
part. III, art. 78 13–33
part. III, art. 79 13–33
part. III, art. 80 13–33
part. III, art. 81 13–33
part. III, art. 82 13–33
part. III, art. 83 13–33
part. III, art. 84 13–33

PARA.

2001 Financial Services and
Markets Act 2000
(Regulated Activities)
Order 544—*cont.*
part. III, art. 85 13–33
part. III, art. 86 13–33
part. III, art. 87 13–33
part. III, art. 88 13–33
Financial Services and
Markets Act 2000 Ap-
pointed Representa-
tives) Regulations
1217 13–96
Financial Services and
Markets Act 2000
(Designated Profes-
sional Bodies) Order
1225 13–21
Financial Services and
Markets Act 2000 (Fi-
nancial Promotion)
Order 1335 .... 13–32, 13–33,
13–36, 13–50
art. 4 13–33
art. 7 13–51
art. 74 13–33
Sched. 1. para. 13 13–33
Sched. 1. para. 14 13–33
Sched. 1. para. 15 13–33
Sched. 1. para. 16 13–33
Sched. 1. para. 17 13–33
Sched. 1. para. 18 13–33
Sched. 1. para. 19 13–33
Sched. 1. para. 20 13–33
Sched. 1. para. 21 13–33
Sched. 1. para. 22 13–33
Sched. 1. para. 23 13–33
Sched. 1. para. 24 13–33
Sched. 1. para. 25 13–33
Sched. 1. para. 26 13–33
Sched. 1. para. 27 13–33
Financial Services and
Markets Act 2000
(Rights of Action)
Regulations 2256 reg.
3 .... 13–74, 13–77, 13–75,
13–79, 14–08, 16–08
reg. 4 13–74
reg. 5 13–75
reg. 6 13–77

PARA.

2001 Financial Services and
       Markets Act 2000
       (Rights of Action)
       Regulations—*cont.*
       reg. 7 13–79
Financial Services and
       Markets Act (Varia-
       tion of Threshold
       Conditions) Order
       2507 13–18
The Financial Services and
       Markets Act 2000
       (Appointed Represen-
       tatives) (Amendment)
       Regulations 2508 13–96

PARA.

2001 Financial Services and
       Markets Act 2000
       (Transitional Provi-
       sions) (Ombudsman
       Scheme and Com-
       plaints Scheme) Order
       2326 art. 1(1)(a) 13–171
       art. 2(1) 13–178
       art. 3(1) 13–178
       art. 4 13–178
       art. 5 13–178
       art. 6 13–178
       art. 7 13–178
       arts 8–10 13–178

TABLE OF CIVIL PROCEDURE RULES

PARA.

1998 Civil Procedure Rules (S.I.
    1998 No. 3132) 3–22, 6–1,
        7–02, 8–155, 9–102,
        10–73, 10–175, 10–188,
        12–114, 12–221
    r.1.1 8–9
    r.2.3 18–13
    r.3.4 12–16
    r.3.4(2)(a) 5–97
    r.6.9(1) 10–201
    Pt 7 8–339
    rr.19.10–19.15 6–3
    r.19.11(1) 6–3
    r.19.11(2) 6–3
    r.19.12 6–3
    r.19.13 6–3
    Pt 20 .... 8–318, 8–326
    Pt 24 .... 5–97, 8–9
    Pt 35 .... 6–10, 6–15
    r.35.1 6–10
    r.35.3 .... 6–15, 9–06
    r.35.4 .... 6–10, 10–142

PARA.

1998 Civil   Procedure   Rules
    —cont.
    r.35.5(1) 6–10
    r.35.5(2) 6–10
    r.35.7 6–16
    r.35.8 9–06
    r.35.8(1) 6–16
    r.35.8(2) 6–16
    r.35.8(5) 6–16
    r.35.10(1) 6–15
    r.35.10(2) 9–06
    Pt 36 3–23
    r.36.12(1) 3–23
    r.36.21 3–23
    Pt 48 6–5
    r.48.6A 6–5
    r.48.7 .... 10–127, 18–13
    r.48.7(3) 7–35, 10–131
    Pt 49 8–10
    Sched. 1, RSC 3–23
    Ord. 14A 9–71
    Ord. 62, r. 11 10–127
    Sched. 2, CCR 3–23

TABLE OF PRACTICE DIRECTIONS

PARA.

Pt 19 6–03
s. 2.1–3.9 6–03
para. 2.2 6–03
para. 6.5 6–03
para. 13 6–03
para. 14.1 6–03
para. 15 6–03
Pt 35
para. 1.1 6–14
s. 1.2–1.6 6–14
Pre-Action Protocol for Construction and Engineering Disputes 8–09
Practice Direction – Protocols
para. 1.1 8–09
para. 1.2 8–09
para. 1.3 8–09
para. 1.4 8–09
para. 2.1 8–09
para. 2.3(1) 8–09
para. 2.3(2) 8–09
para. 2.3(3) 8–09
para. 2.3(4) 8–09
para. 3 8–09
para. 4.1 8–09
para. 4.2 8–09
para. 4.3 8–09

PARA.

Practice Direction – Protocols
—cont.
para. 5 8–09
para. 5.2 8–09
Practice Note (Official Solicitor to the Supreme Court: Vegetative State) [1996] 4 All E.R. 766; [1996] 2 F.L.R. 375; [1996] 3 F.C.R. 606; (1997) 34 B.M.L.R. 20; [1996] Fam. Law 579; (1996) 146 N.L.J. 1585, Sup Ct 12–146
Practice Note (Official Solicitor: Sterlisation) [1993] 3 All E.R. 222; [1993] 2 F.L.R. 222; [1993] 4 Med.L.R. 302; *The Times*, June 22, 1993, Fam Div 12–144
Practice Statement (HL: Judicial Precedent); *sub nom.* Practice Note (HL: Judicial Precedent) [1966] 1 W.L.R. 1234; [1966] 2 Lloyd's Rep. 151; 110 S.J. 584, HL 2–18

United States of America
Uniform Commercial Code 17–07
Art. 2–105 17–07

TABLE OF ABBREVIATIONS

AAS = Australian Accounting Standard

A.B.L.R. = Australian Business Law Review

A.C. = Appeal Cases (Law Reports)

A.C.E. = Association of Consulting Engineers

A.C.T.R. = Australian Capital Territory Reports

AFBD = Association of Futures Brokers and Dealers

AG = Auditing Guideline

A.H.A = Area Health Authority

AIDS = Acquired Immune Deficiency Syndrome

AIM = Alternative Investment Market

A.J.A = Administration of Justice Act 1982

A.L.J. = Australian Law Journal

A.L.J.R. = Australian Law Journal Reports

A.L.R. = Australian Law Reports

APB = Auditing Practices Board

APER = statements of Principle and Code of Practice for Approved Persons

A.R. = Alberta Reports 1977–

A.R.I.C.S. = Professional Associate of the Royal Institute of Chartered Surveyors

A.S.B. = Accounting Standards Board

A.S.C. = Accounting Standards Committee

A.T.S. = anti-tetanus serum

AUTH = Authorisation

A.V.S.C. = Assets Valuation Standards Committee

Acct = Accountant

Acct = Accountancy

Ad.& E. = Adolphus and Ellis Reports

Affd = affirmed

All E.R. = All England Law Report

App.Cas. = Law Reports Appeal Cases 1875–1890

Atk. = Atkyn's Reports

Att.Gen. = Attorney-General

Aust. = Australia

B. & P. or Bos.& Pul. = Bosanquet and Puller's Reports

B. & P. or Bos.& Pul.(N.R.) = Bosanquet and Puller's New Reports

B.C.C. = British Company Law Cases

BCLC = Butterworths Company Law Cases

B.C.L.R. = British Columbia Law Reports

B.J.A.L. = British Journal of Administrative Law.

B.L.R. = Business Law Review

B.M.J. = British Medical Journal

Beav. = Beavan's Report

Bing. = Bingham's Reports

Bos. & Pul. (N.R.). See B. & P

Build.L.R. = Building Law Reports

Burr. = Burrow's Reports

c. = Chapter (of an Act of Parliament)

C. & F. or Cl. & Fin. = Clark and Finnelly's Reports

C. & P. or Car. & P. = Carrington and Payne's Report

CA = Court of Appeal

CAA = Civil Aviation Authority

C.A.C.A. = Chartered Association of Certified Accountants

C.B. (N.S.) or (O.S.) = Common Bench Reports (New Series) or (Old Series)

C.C.A. = Court of Criminal Appeal

CCAB = Consultative Committee of Accounting Bodies

C.C.L.T. = Canadian Cases on the Law of Torts 1976–

C.C.R. = County Court Rules

CDM Reg's = Construction (Design and Management) Regulations 1994

C.I.L.L. = Construction Industry Law Letter

C.I.M.A. = Chartered Institute of Management Accountants

C.I.P.F.A. = Chartered Institute of Public Finance and Accountancy

CIS = Collective Investment Schemes

C.J. = Lord Chief Justice

CJD = Cretzfelt-Jacob disease

C.J.Q. = Civil Justice Quarterly

C.L.C. = Current Law Consolidated

C.L.J. or Camb.L.J. = Cambridge Law Journal

C.L.R. = Commonwealth Law Reports

C.L.Y.B. = Current Law Year Book
C.M.L.R. = Common Market Law Reports
C.M.L.Rev. = Common Market Law Review
CNST = Clinical Negligence Scheme for Trusts
COAF = Complaints against the FSA
COB = Conduct of Business
C.O.D. = Crown Office Digest
COMP = Compensation
COND = Threshold Conditions
C.P. = Construction Practice
C.P.D. = Law Reports Common Pleas Division 1875–1880
C.P.L. = Current Property Law
C.P.R. = Civil procedure Rules
C.P.S. = Crown Prosecution Service
C.Q.S. = Chartered Quantity Surveyor
CRED = Credit Union
C.S.W. = Chartered Surveyor Weekly
CTG (trace of a babies heart/scan) = ???
Camp. = Campbell's Reports
Can. = Canada
Can.B.R. or Canadian B.R. = Canadian Bar Review
Can.Bar J. = Canadian Bar Journal
Car. & P. See C. & P.
Ch. = Chancery (Law Report)
Ch.D. = Chancery Division
Chit. = Chitty's Practice Reports
Cmnd. = Command Paper
Coll = Collyer's Report
Com.Cas. = Commercial Cases
Com.L.R. = Commercial Law Reports
Commercial Acct. = Commercial Accountant
Con.L.R. = Construction Law Report
Const.L.J. = Construction Law Journal
Conv. (or Conveyancer) (N.S.) = Conveyancer and Property Lawyer (New Service)
Cr. & J. = Crompton and Jervis's Reports
Cr.App.R. = Criminal Appeal Reports
Crim.L.J. = Criminal Law Journal

D. = Duxbury's Reports of the High Court of the South Africian Republic
D.C. = District Council
D.C. = Divisional Court
DCE Letters = Dear Chief Executive Letters
DEC = Decision making
DISP = Dispute resolution: Complaints
D.L.R. = Dominion Law Reports

DPB = designated professional body
D.P.P. = Director of Prosecution
DSDM = Dynamic Systems Development Method
DTI = Department of Trade and Industry
DVT = deep vein thrombosis
De G.M. & G. = De Gex, Macnaghten and Gordon's Reports
Div. Ct = Division Court
Dow. & Cl = Dow and Clark's Reports

E. & B. = Ellis and Blackburn's Reports
E. & E. = Ellis and Ellis's Reports
E.C. = European Community
E.C.T. = electro-convulsive therapy
E.E.C. = European Economic Community
E.G. = Estates Gazette
E.G.C.S. = Estates Gazette Case Summaries
E.G.D. = Estates Gazette Digest of Cases
E.G.L.R. = Estates Gazette Law Reports
E.H.R.L.R. = European Human Rights Law review
E.H.R.R. = European Human Rights Report
EMD = Emerging Market Debt
EMLR = Entertainment and Media Law Reports
ENF = Enforcement
E.N.T = ear, nose & throat
ERP = estimated restricted realisation price
East = East's Report
Ex.D. = Law Reports, Exchequer Division

F. = Sessions Cases, 5th series [Fraser] (Scotland)
F & F = Foster and Finlason's Reports
FCE = fibro-cartilaginous embolism
FIMBRA = Financial Intermediaries, Managers and Brokers Regulatory Organisation
FIT = The Fit and Proper Test for Approved Persons
FLR = Financial Law Report
F.L.R. = Federal Law Reports
F.L.R.or Fam.L.R. = Family Law Report
FOS = Financial Ombudsman Service
FPO = Financial Services and Markets Act 2000 (Financial Promotion) Order 2001
FRC = Financial Reporting Council

F.R.I.C.S. = Fellow of the Royal Institute of Chartered Surveyors

FRS's = Financial Reporting Standards

FSA = Financial Services Authority

FSA 1986 = Financial Services Act 1986

FSMA = Financial Services and Markets Act 2000

F.S.R. = Fleet Street Patent Law Report

FTLR = Financial Times Law Report

Fam. = Family Division (Law Reports)

Fam.Law = Family Law

GEN = General provisions

GISC = General Insurance Standards Council

GLO = Group Litigation Order

GTT = glucose tolerance test

G.W.D. = Green's Weekly Digest

Giff = Giffard's Reports

H. & C. = Hurlstone and Coltman's Reports

H. & N. = Hurlstone and Norman's Reports

H.A. = Health Authority

HBRV = House Buyer's Report and Valuation

HGH = Human Growth Hormone

H.I.V. = Human Immuno-Deficiency Virus

H.K.C.A. = Hong Kong Court of Appeal

HL = House of Lords

H.L.R. = Housing Law Reports

H.M.S.O. = Her Majesty's Stationery Office

HRA = Human Rights Act

Har.L.R. or Havard L.R. = Havard Law Review

IBNR = Incurred but not reported

IBRC = Insurance Brokers Registration Council

I.C.E. = Institute of Civil Engineers

I.C.L.Q. = International and Comparative Law Quarterly

I.C.R. = Industrial Cases Reports

I.E.E. = Institute of Electrical Engineers

I.L.J. = Industrial Law Journal

I.L.P. = International Legal Practitioner

I.L.R.M. = Irish Law Times Reports

I.L.T.R. = Irish Law Times Report

IMRO = Investment Management Regulatory Organisation

IOB = Insurance Ombudsman

IPRU = 5 Interim Prudential sourcebooks

I.Q.S. = Institute of Quantity Surveyors

I.R. or Ir.R. = Irish Reports (Eire)

I.R.L.R. = Industrial Relations Law Reports

ISA = Individual Savings Account

I.S.V.A. = Incorporated Society of Valuers and Auctioneers

I.T.L. or Ir.L.T. = Irish Law Times

I.T.R. = Industrial Tribunal Reports

Ir.Jur. = Irish Jurist

Ir.Jur.(N.S.) Irish Jurist (New Series)

Ir.Jur.Rep. = Irish Jurist Reports

I.Mech.E = Institute of Mechanical Engineers

I.Struct.E = Institute of Structural Engineers

J.P. = Justice of the Peace Reports

J.P.N. = Justice of the Peace Journal

K. & J. = Kay and Johnson's Reports

K.B. = King's Bench (Law Reports)

LAUTRO = Life Assurance and Unit Trust Regulatory Organisation

L.B.C. = London Borough Council

L.C. = Lord Chancellor

L.C.J. = or C.J. = Lord Chief Justice

L.G.R. = Local Government Reports

L.G.Rev. = Local Government Review

L.J. = Law Journal Newspapers

L.J. and L.JJ. = Lord Justice, Lords Justices

L.J.N.C.C.R. = Law Journal Newspaper County Court Reports

L.J.Q.B. = Law Journal Queen's Bench (N.S.) 1831–1946

L.J.R. = Law Journal Reports

LLD = Lloyd's

L.M.C.L.Q. = Lloyd's Maritime and Commercial Quarterly

LMX = London market excess of loss

L.P. = Reference to denote Lands Tribunal decisions (transcripts available from the Lands Tribunal)

L.Q.R. = Law Quarterly Review

L.R. = Land Report

L.R.Eq. = Law Reports, Equity Cases

L.R.Ex. = Law Report, Exchequer.

L.S. = Legal studies

L.S.Gaz. = Law Society Gazette

L.T. = Law Times
L.T.J. = Law Times Journal
L.T.R. = Law Times Reports
Lit. = Litigation
Ll.L.Rep. = Lloyd's List Reports (before 1951)
Ll.P.C. = Lloyd's Prize Cases
Lloyd's Rep. = Lloyd's List Reports (1951 onwards)

M. & Rob. = Maclean and Robinson's Scotch Appeals
M. & W. = Meeson & Welsby's Reports
MAR = Market Conduct
M.I.G.s = Mortgage Indemnity Guarantees
ML = Money Laundering
M.L.J. = Malayan Law Journal
M.L.R. = Modern Law Review
M.O.D. = Ministry of Defence
MORT = Mortgages
M.R. = Master of the Rolls
MV = market value
Macq = Macqueen's Scotch Appeals
Med.L.R. = Medical Law Reports
Med.Law Rev. = Medical Law Review

N.B.R. = New Brunswick Reports
N.H.B.C. = National House Builder Registration Council
N.H.S. = National Health Service
N.I. = Northern Ireland; Northern Ireland Reports
N.I.C.A. = Northern Ireland, Court of Appeal
N.I.J.B. = Northern Ireland Judgment Bulletin
N.I.L.Q. = Northern Ireland Legal Quarterly
N.I.L.R. = Northern Ireland Law Reports
N.S.R. = Nova Scotia Reports
N.S.W.C.A. = New South Wales Court of Appeal
N.S.W.L.R. = New South Wales Law Reports
N.W. = North Western Provinces High Court Reports
N.Z.L.R. = New Zealand Law Reports
N.Z.U.L.R. = New Zealand Universities Law Review
New L.J. = New Law Journal
Nfld & P.E.I.R. = Newfoundland & Prince Edward Islands Reports

OBO = Office of the Banking Ombudsman
OBSO = Office of the Building Society Ombudsman
OIO = Office of the Investment Ombudsman
OMV = open market value
O.R. = Ontario Reports
O.W.N. = Ontario Weekly Notes
Ord. = Order

P. = Probate, Divorce and Admiralty (Law Reports)
p. and pp. = page and pages
PC = Privy Council
PCC = Palmer's Company Cases
PERLS = principal exchange rate linked security
PIA = Personal Investment Authority
PIAOB = PIA Ombudsman Bureau
PIAS = Personal Insurance Arbitration Service
PML = probable maximum loss
P.N. = Professional Negligence
PPH = Primary Pulmonary Hypertension
PPI = policy proof of interest
PRIN = Principles of Businesses
PRINCE = Projects in Controlled Environments
PROF = Professional firm
PTSD = post traumatic stress disorder
PVS = persistent vegetative state
P.W = Price Waterhouse
para. = paragraph
Peake = Peake's Reports
Price = Prices Reports

Q.B. = Queens' Bench (Law Reports)
Q.B.D. = Queens' Bench Division
Q.C. = Queens Counsel
Q.L.R. = Queensland Law Reporter
Q.S. = Quarter Sessions
Q.S.R. = Queensland State Reports
Qd.R. = Queensland Reports

r. = rule
RAO = Financial Services and Markets Act 2000 (Regulated Activities) Order 2001
RCH's = recognised clearing houses
REC = Recognised Investment Exchanges an Recognised Clearing Houses
R.H.A. = Regional Health Authority

R.I.B.A. = Royal Institute of British Architects

R.I.C.S. = Royal Institution of Chartered Surveyors

RIE's = recognised investment exchanges

R.L.F. = retrolental fibroplasias

R.P.B. = recognised professional body

R.P.C. = Reports of Patent Design and Trade Mark Cases

R.P.R. = Real Property Reports (Canada)

RSB = recognised supervisory body

R.S.C. = Rules of the Supreme Court

RTA = Road Traffic Accident

reg. = regulation

Revd. = reversed

S. or Scot = Scotland

s. or ss. = section, sections (of an Act of Parliament)

S.A. = South Africa

S.A.L.J. = South Africa Law Journal

S.A.L.R. = South Africa Law Reports

SAR's = Rules Governing Substantial Acquisition of Shares

SAS = Statement of Auditing Standard

S.A.S.R. = South Australian State Reports

S.C. = Session Cases

S.C.(H.L.) = Session Cases (House of Lords)

S.C.(J.) = Session Cases (High Court of Justiciary)

SFA = Securities and Futures Authority

SFA CB = SFA Complaints Bureau and Arbitration Services

S.I. = Statutory Instrument

S.I.B. = Securities and Investments Board

S.J. = Solicitor Journal

S.L.G. = Scottish Law Gazette

S.L.R. = Scottish Law Reporter (Reports 1865–1925)

S.L.R. = Scottish Law Review (Sheriff Court Reports 1885–1963)

S.L.R. = Statute Law Revision

S.L.T. = Scots Law Times

S.L.T. (Notes) = Scots Law Times Notes of Recent Decisions

S.L.T. (Sh.Ct.) = Scots Law Times Sheriff Court Reports

S.N. = Sessions Notes

S.R.O. = self-regulating organisation

S.R.&.O. = Statutory Rules and Orders

SSADM = Structural Systems Analysis and Design Method

SSAP's = Statements of Standard Accounting Practice

S.T.I.A. = Short term Investment account

SUP = Supervision

SYSC = senior management arrangements, Systems and Controls

Sask.R. = Saskatchewan Reports

Sc.Jur.Scottish Jurist

Sched. = Schedule (to an Act of Parliament)

Stark = Starkie's Reports

TC = Training and Competence

TCC = Technology and Construction Court

TCHM = Traditional Chinese Herbal Medicine

T.L.R. = Times Law Report

TSA = The Securities Association

Taunt = Taunton's Reports

U.C.T.A. = Unfair Contract Terms Act

UKLA = UK Listing Authority

U.S = United States Supreme Courts Reports

V.C. = Vice Chancellor

V.L.R. = Victorian Report

V.R. = Victoria Reports

W.A.L.R. = West Australian Law Reports

W.A.R. = Western Australian Law Reports

W.L.R. = Weekly Law Reports

W.N. = Weekly Notes (Law Reports)

W.N.(N.S.W.) = Weekly Notes (New South Wales)

W.W.R. = Western Weekly Reports

Wils.K.B. = J. Wilson's Reports, King's Bench

XL = excess of loss reinsurance

CHAPTER 1

THE NATURE OF PROFESSIONS

		PARA.			PARA.
1.	General	1–01	3.	The focus of this book	1–04
2.	Judicial discussion	1–02			

1. GENERAL

A definition of "the professions" is pre-eminently a matter for social historians **1–001** or for sociologists rather than lawyers.[1] Generally speaking, however, the occupations which are regarded as professions have four characteristics:

(1) **The nature of the work:** The work done is skilled and specialised. A substantial part of the work is mental rather than manual. A period of theoretical and practical training is usually required before the work can be adequately performed.

(2) **The moral aspect:** Practitioners are usually committed, or expected to be committed, to certain moral principles, which go beyond the general duty of honesty.[2] They are expected to provide a high standard of service for its own sake. They are expected to be particularly concerned about the duty of confidentiality. They also, normally, owe a wider duty to the community, which may on occasions transcend the duty to a particular client or patient.[3]

(3) **Collective organisation:** Practitioners usually belong to a professional association, which regulates admission and seeks to uphold the standards of the profession. Such associations commonly set examinations to test competence and issue professional codes on matters of conduct and ethics.[4]

---

[1] A helpful collection of definitions of "profession" is to be found in App. 5 to the Monopolies Commission's Report on the Professions (October 1970). For a general introduction to the sociology of professions, see T. J. Johnson, *Professions and Power* (Macmillan, 1972).

[2] See, *e.g.* discussion of the professions in Tawney, *The Acquisitive Society* (Harvester Press, 1982) and Durkheim, *Professional Ethics and Civil Morals* (Greenwood Press, 1983).

[3] For example, a doctor's duty to prevent the spread of contagious diseases may outweigh his duty to a particular patient. An accountant, certifying the accounts of a firm of solicitors or auditing the accounts of a public company, may find himself obliged to act contrary to the immediate interests of his clients. Similarly, a barrister or solicitor is under a professional obligation to draw the court's attention to relevant authorities, even if they are adverse to his client's case. Architects have a responsibility for public safety and environmental considerations, which go beyond their immediate duty to the client. This public responsibility of professions is discussed by Sir Gordon Borrie in "The Professions—Expensive Monopolies or Guardians of the Public Interests?" (Fourth Hamptons Lecture given at the Society of Valuers and Auctioneers on November 14, 1983).

[4] Ralf Dahrendorf argues that the crucial distinction between professions in Britain and those on the European Continent is that in Britain the professions are self-governing and independent, whereas elsewhere in Europe they are regulated by the state. He points out that if any major profession is slack in the enforcement of its own standards, public confidence in all professions is undermined. On Dahrendorf's analysis, this would have far-reaching social consequences. Dahrendorf argues that the

(4) **Status:** Most professions have a high status in the community. Some of their privileges are conferred by Parliament.[5] Some are granted by common consent.

During the 20th century, an increasing number of occupations have been seeking and achieving "professional" status. This has led inevitably to some blurring of the features which traditionally distinguish the professions from other occupations.[6] Nevertheless, most of the "new" professions still tend to possess the characteristics listed above.[7]

2. JUDICIAL DISCUSSION

1–002   Judicial discussion about the nature of professions occurs principally in tax cases, where the issue is whether or not the tax-payer is carrying on a profession. In *IRC v. Maxse*,[8] Scrutton L.J. approached the matter in this way:

> "The next question is what is a 'profession'? I am very reluctant finally to propound a comprehensive definition. A set of facts not present to the mind of the judicial propounder, and not raised in the case before him, may immediately arise to confound his proposition. But it seems to me as at present advised that a 'profession' in the present use of language involves the idea of an occupation requiring either purely intellectual skill, or of manual skill controlled, as in painting and sculpture, or surgery, by the intellectual skill of the operator, as distinguished from an occupation which is substantially the production or sale or arrangements for the production or sale of commodities. The line of demarcation may vary from time to time. The word 'profession' used to be confined to the three learned professions, the Church, Medicine and Law. It has now, I think, a wider meaning."[9]

1–003   The matter arose again in *Carr v. IRC*,[10] in which the Court of Appeal upheld a finding that an optician was carrying on a profession. Du Parcq L.J. stated:

---

condition of the British professions is "an index of the state of liberty in this country". See Dahrendorf, "Defence of the English Professions", in (1984) *J. of the Royal Society of Medicine*, 178 (Vol. 77).

[5] For example, members of the medical and similar professions are entitled to be excused from jury service: Juries Act 1974, s.9(1) and Sched. 1, Pt III.

[6] Indeed, some sociologists argue that the traditional view of the professions (as set out in the first part of para. 1–001 above) is no longer valid: see Dingwall and Lewis (eds), *The Sociology of the Professions* (Macmillan, 1983).

[7] A leading article in *The Times*, January 5, 1980, discussing the recent expansion of the professions, summarised what the community expected of the professions in these terms:

> "For an occupation to become a profession in the commonly accepted sense of the word means more than for its practitioners to enjoy the privileges of controlling their own entry and regulating their own conduct. It means also that they must have specialised skills acquired by intellectual and practical training, that they have a high degree of detachment and integrity, and, above all, that they have a strong sense of responsibility and an exceptional commitment to the interests of their clients which transcends all other commitments."

The authors are grateful to *The Times* for permission to use this quotation.

[8] [1919] 1 K.B. 647.

[9] *ibid.* at 657. Scrutton L.J. elaborated on the meaning of "profession" two years later in *Currie v. IRC* [1921] 2 K.B. 332 at 343:

> "I myself am disposed to attach some importance in findings as to whether a profession is exercised or not to the fact that the particular man is a member of an organised professional body with a recognised standard of ability enforced before he can enter it and a recognised standard of conduct enforced while he is practising it."

[10] [1944] 2 All E.R. 163.

"It seems to me to be dangerous to try to define the word 'profession', as Scrutton L.J. realised . . . I think that everybody would agree that, before one can say that a man is carrying on a profession, one must see that he has some special skill or ability or some special qualifications derived from training or experience. Even then one has to be very careful, because there are many people whose work demands great skill and ability and long experience and many qualifications who would not be said by anybody to be carrying on a profession. Ultimately one has to ask this question: Would the ordinary man, the ordinary reasonable man . . . say now, in the time in which we live, of any particular occupation, that it is properly described as a profession? Times have changed. There are professions today which nobody would have considered to be professions in times past. Our forefathers restricted the professions to a very small number; the work of the surgeon used to be carried on by a barber, whom nobody would have considered a professional man. The profession of the chartered accountant has grown up in comparatively recent times, and other trades, or vocations . . . may in future years acquire the status of professions." [11]

3. THE FOCUS OF THIS BOOK

Fortunately, it is not necessary for the purpose of this book to attempt a **1–004** comprehensive definition of the professions. There is no serious dispute as to the professional status of many of the specific occupations discussed in the following chapters. The editors are conscious of other occupational groups (such as actuaries) which are equally regarded as professions, but which are not dealt with in this book. The choice which has been made is largely governed by the amount of litigation which each profession has generated. [12] The main focus is not upon particular occupational groups but rather upon principles applicable to professional liability generally, as illustrated in their application in respect of different occupational groups, some of which may be recognised as professions and others not (or not quite yet). What is apparent is the enduring nature of these principles and their ready adaptability to other occupations, including some which may be seen as "new professions", as illustrated in the cases of financial practitioners [13] and information technology professionals. [14]

---

[11] *ibid.* at 166E–167A.

[12] The principles which are discussed in the following chapters are, of course, equally applicable to the other professions: see, *e.g.* the reasoning of the Court of Appeal in *Luxmoore-May v. Messenger May Baverstock* [1990] 1 W.L.R. 1009 (concerning art auctioneers).

[13] See Chap. 13, below.

[14]. See Chap. 17, below.

Chapter 2

DUTIES AND OBLIGATIONS

PARA.

1. Professional Liability 2–01
   (a) Positive Duties 2–01
   (b) Restrictions and Inhibitions 2–05
2. Contractual Liability 2–07
3. Tortious Liability 2–13
   (a) The tort of negligence 2–13
   (b) Theoretical basis for the duty
       of care 2–22
       (i) Lord Atkin's approach .. 2–22
       (ii) *Hedley Byrne* 2–24
       (iii) The inclusive approach . 2–26
       (iv) The threefold test 2–30
       (v) The exclusive approach   2–36
       (vi) Extensions of *Hedley
            Byrne* 2–45
       (vii) The co-existence of
            different approaches 2–50
       (viii) Commonwealth
            approaches to duty of
            care issues 2–54
       (ix) Analysis 2–66
   (c) Particular situations 2–79
       (i) Public and local
            authorities: duty of care
            and statute 2–79
       (ii) Directors and
            employees 2–87
       (iii) Sub-agents and sub-
            contractors 2–94
       (iv) Immunity 2–97
   (d) Concurrent Liability, Contracts
       and Tortious Duties of Care 2–100
   (e) Liability to Third Parties 2–109
4. The standard of skill and care 2–116
   (a) The meaning of reasonable
       skill and care 2–116
   (b) Relevance of defendant's
       qualifications and experience .. 2–118
   (c) Formulation of the standard ... 2–120
   (d) Organisation offering
       professional services 2–121
   (e) Undertaking work of other
       professions 2–122
   (f) New techniques 2–123
   (g) Changes in the standard
       required 2–124
5. Fiduciary obligations 2–125
   (a) The nature of fiduciary
       obligations 2–125
   (b) Dealing with the principal 2–134
   (c) Unauthorised profits and
       diversion of opportunities 2–141
   (d) Undue influence 2–142
       (i) The classes of undue
            influence 2–142
       (ii) Rebutting the
            presumption 2–146
6. Confidentiality 2–147
   (a) Introduction 2–147
   (b) Origins of the duty of
       confidence 2–148
   (c) Elements of the cause of
       action 2–156
   (d) The continuing duty to former
       clients 2–164

1. PROFESSIONAL LIABILITY

(a) *Positive Duties*

Traditionally, the professions operate in spheres where success cannot be **2–001** achieved in every case. Very often success or failure depends upon factors beyond the professional person's control (such as the patient's stamina during a long operation or the credibility of a particular witness at trial). Even where the critical factors are within the professional person's control, he still cannot guarantee success. In matters of fine judgment or great complexity no human being can be right every time.

The problem which the courts have faced in devising the standard of perform- **2–002** ance which the law will require of professional persons is to find a standard which provides proper protection for the consumer, whilst allowing for the factors mentioned in the previous paragraph.[1] Broadly speaking, the solution which has been found is to require that professional persons should possess a certain minimum degree of competence and that they should exercise reasonable care in the discharge of their duties. At this level of generality, the approach of the courts (and, on occasions, the formulation of this approach) has hardly changed over the last 150 years. In *Lanphier v. Philpos*[2] (a medical negligence case tried in 1838), Tindal C.J. directed the jury in these terms:

> "Every person who enters into a learned profession undertakes to bring to the exercise of it a reasonable degree of care and skill. He does not undertake, if he is an attorney, that at all events you shall gain your case, nor does a surgeon undertake that he will perform a cure; nor does he undertake to use the highest possible degree of skill."

In *Greaves and Co. (Contractors) Ltd v. Baynham Meikle and Partners*[3] (a claim against consulting engineers decided in 1975), Lord Denning M.R. stated:

> "Apply this to the employment of a professional man. The law does not usually imply a warranty that he will achieve the desired result, but only a term that he will use reasonable care and skill. The surgeon does not warrant that he will cure the patient. Nor does the solicitor warrant that he will win the case."[4]

A professional person may owe this duty to exercise reasonable skill and care as a contractual obligation, in the tort of negligence or as a statutory duty, although in the case of statutory duty, a stricter duty may be prescribed so that there could be fault without want of skill and care.

2–003   The striking feature of the passages quoted in the previous paragraph (and of many similar pronouncements about professional liability)[5] is that they focus upon professions which are bound to have an appreciable failure rate. In practice, however, different professions enjoy varying degrees of success. It is not surprising if a litigating solicitor says that some of his clients lose their cases or if a doctor says that some of his patients do not recover. It is most surprising if an engineer says that some of the bridges which he designs fall down; or if a conveyancing solicitor says that some of his clients do not acquire good title to their properties. The expectations created by different professions or by different

---

[1] See, *e.g.* the judgment of Scott L.J. in *Mahon v. Osborne* [1939] 2 K.B. 14 at 16:
"The case is one of general importance because its facts illumine the principles which apply. It calls for close attention by reason of the double need, on the one hand, of enforcing a high standard of care in the surgeon against the grave danger of an overlooked swab, and, on the other, of protecting the surgeon from the risk of condemnation for actionable want of care where he has in reality been doing his best for his patient."

[2] (1838) 8 Car. & P. 475. See also the judgment of Willes J. in *Harmer v. Cornelius* (1858) 5 C.B.(N.S.) 236:
"*Spondes peritiam artis.* Thus, if an apothecary, a watchmaker, or an attorney be employed for reward, they each impliedly undertake to possess and exercise reasonable skill in their several arts. The public profession of an art is a representation and undertaking to all the world that the professor possesses the requisite ability and skill."

[3] [1975] 1 W.L.R. 1095.

[4] *ibid.* at 1100D. However, on the particular facts of that case, it was held that the consulting engineers had given a warranty that they would achieve a certain result.

[5] See, *e.g.* the well-known direction to the jury given by McNair J. in *Bolam v. Friern Hospital Management Committee* [1957] 1 W.L.R. 582. See Chap. 12, para. 12–69, below.

branches within the same profession vary. The reasonable expectation of consumers is bound to have some impact on the application of the general principle stated in the previous paragraph. This may explain the divergence of judicial approach between medical negligence cases (such as *Maynard v. West Midlands RHA*)[6] and cases concerning solicitors engaged in non-contentious work[7] (such as *G.K. Ladenbau v. Crawley & De Reya*[8] and *Edward Wong Finance Co. Ltd v. Johnson Stokes & Master*[9]). The cases concerning individual professions have tended to develop along their own separate lines. It is therefore convenient to consider each profession separately, as is done in Section 2 of this book. The one common feature of all professions, however, is that they are not generally held to warrant that they will achieve the results which their clients desire.

Thus the professional person as defendant enjoys a privileged position. Unlike the building contractor[10] or the shop-keeper,[11] he does not normally guarantee his product. However, his privileged position has been eroded in certain respects by developments in the law of contract and tort.[12] These are summarised in the following paragraphs and more specifically discussed in the chapters dealing with the individual professions in Section 2. **2–004**

(b) *Restrictions and Inhibitions*

As well as coming under a positive duty to exercise reasonable skill and care in the performance of his duties, a professional person may also find that, as a result of having undertaken those duties, he is prevented in law from acting in certain ways. While it is possible to describe these inhibitions in terms of positive duties, they are better considered as restrictions on a professional's conduct rather than as goals which he must attain. The obligations of a fiduciary are, in general, negative: for example a duty not to make a secret profit. In the same way a professional person will generally be under a duty not to reveal to third parties information given to him in confidence. Attempts are sometimes made to extend professional liability by pleading alternative claims based upon breach of a fiduciary duty to exercise reasonable skill and care. However, this approach was deprecated by Lord Browne-Wilkinson in *Henderson v. Merrett Syndicates Ltd*[13] and rejected decisively by the Court of Appeal in *Bristol and West Building Society v. Mothew*.[14] **2–005**

These restrictions on the conduct of a professional person fall into three categories: **2–006**

---

[6] [1984] 1 W.L.R. 634. See Chap. 12, para. 12–94, below.
[7] The policy considerations which underlie the apparently higher standard demanded of conveyancing solicitors were explored by Hoffmann L.J. in a lecture to the Professional Negligence Bar Association on October 14, 1992: "The reasonableness of lawyers' lapses" (1994) 10 P.N. 6. See also Evans, Chapter 1, above.
[8] [1978] 1 W.L.R. 266. See Chap. 10, para. 10–90, below.
[9] [1984] A.C. 296. See Chap. 10, paras 10–85 to 10–86, below.
[10] See, *e.g. Miller v. Cannon Hill Estates Ltd* [1931] 2 K.B. 113; *Hancock v. B. W. Brazier (Anerley) Ltd* [1966] 1 W.L.R. 1317; *Barclays Bank plc v Fairclough Building Ltd* [1995] Q.B. 214.
[11] See the Sale of Goods Act 1979, ss.13–15, as amended by the Sale and Supply of Goods Act 1994.
[12] For example, as a result of decisions on concurrent liability (discussed later in this chapter), in relation to limitation architects and engineers are in a substantially worse position than contractors and sub-contractors.
[13] [1995] 2 A.C. 145 at 204–206. See further (1995) 111 L.Q.R. 1, *per* Heydon.
[14] [1998] Ch. 1 at 16C–18F. Discussed further in para. 2–127 below.

(1) *Fiduciary obligations*: These are the varying restrictions imposed in equity on professional persons acting in a fiduciary capacity, having at their heart a core duty of undivided loyalty. The extent to which a professional person will be subject to such obligations will depend upon the extent to which the client is entitled to expect such undivided loyalty.

(2) *Undue influence*: A professional person who acquires (or is deemed to have acquired) a degree of ascendancy over a client is not permitted to abuse that client's confidence by using it to obtain some material advantage whether by gift or a transaction which favours the professional person.

(3) *Confidentiality*: A professional person is generally not permitted to reveal confidential information acquired from or on behalf of a client.

The first two are discussed in detail in paragraphs 2–125 to 2–146, below and the third in paragraphs 2–147 to 2–167, below. Where appropriate they are also considered in the context of particular professions in Section 2.

2. CONTRACTUAL LIABILITY

2–007   Historically, the law of contract is the principal means by which the courts have exercised control over the standard of performance of professional persons.[15] In most instances there is a contract between the professional person and his client, whereby the former agrees to render certain services and the latter agrees to pay a specified, alternatively a reasonable, fee. In such a contract there is generally implied by law a term that the professional person will exercise reasonable skill and care.[16]

2–008   As Oliver J. pointed out in *Midland Bank Trust Co. Ltd v. Hett, Stubbs & Kemp*,[17] the obligation to exercise reasonable skill and care is not the only contractual term which ought to be considered in a professional negligence action:

> "The classical formulation of the claim in this sort of case as 'damages for negligence and breach of professional duty' tends to be a mesmeric phrase. It concentrates attention on the implied obligation to devote to the client's business that reasonable care and skill to be expected from a normally competent and careful practitioner as if that obligation were not only a compendious, but also an exhaustive, definition of all the duties assumed under the contract created by the retainer and its acceptance. But, of course, it is not. A contract gives rise to a complex of rights and duties of which the duty to exercise reasonable care and skill is but one. If I employ a carpenter to supply and put

---

[15] See Atiyah, *The Rise and Fall of Freedom of Contract* (Clarendon Press, 1979), p. 416.
[16] This common law principle is now embodied in s.13 of the Supply of Goods and Services Act 1982.
[17] [1979] Ch. 384.

up a good quality oak shelf for me, the acceptance by him of that employment involves the assumption of a number of contractual duties. He must supply wood of an adequate quality and it must be oak. He must fix the shelf. And he must carry out the fashioning and fixing with the reasonable care and skill which I am entitled to expect of a skilled craftsman. If he fixes the brackets but fails to supply the shelf or if he supplies and fixes a shelf of unseasoned pine, my complaint against him is not that he has failed to exercise reasonable care and skill in carrying out the work but that he has failed to supply what was contracted for."[18]

The particular illustration chosen by Oliver J. in the above passage must be **2–009** used with caution, since the obligations of a carpenter to his employer are generally of a different nature to those owed by a professional person to his client.[19] Nevertheless, in every contract between a professional person and his client there will be express or implied terms defining the nature of the engagement. Thus if a surveyor is instructed to produce a report on certain property, there is an express or implied obligation to inspect it.[20] If a surgeon agrees with his patient to perform a particular operation, there may be an implied term that he will "give the necessary supervision thereafter until the discharge of the patient".[21] If a solicitor is instructed to effect the grant of an option, there are implied terms that he will draw up the option agreement and effect registration.[22] The importance of specific terms such as these is that (i) a professional person will be liable if he breaks them, quite irrespective of the amount of skill and care which he has exercised and (ii) the defence of contributory negligence is not available.[23]

Where a professional is retained on express terms the court may have to **2–010** construe those terms to determine whether they create absolute obligations or whether the professional merely promises to exercise reasonable skill and care in undertaking a specified task or to achieve a specified result. The recent decision of the Court of Appeal in *Midland Bank plc v. Cox McQueen*[24] provides helpful guidance as to how to approach such questions of construction. In that case solicitors were retained by a bank to obtain the signatures of a Mr and Mrs Duke to various documents and to explain the implications of a mortgage to them. Mr Duke introduced to the solicitors an imposter, telling them she was Mrs Duke. In an action against the solicitor the bank contended that the solicitors had undertaken an absolute duty to obtain Mrs Duke's signature. The Court of Appeal rejected that argument. Lord Woolf M.R. (with whom the other members of the Court agreed) said:

"If commercial institutions such as banks wish to impose an absolute liability on members of a profession they should do so in clear terms so that the solicitors can

---

[18] *ibid.* at 434E-H. See also Chap. 10, para. 10–07, below.
[19] See para. 2–04, above.
[20] See Chap. 9, para. 9–20, below.
[21] See *Morris v. Winsbury-White* [1937] 4 All E.R. 494 at 500C–D and Chap. 6, para. 6–03, below.
[22] See *Midland Bank Trust Co. Ltd v. Hett, Stubbs & Kemp* [1979] 1 Ch. 384 at 435B and Chap. 10, para. 10–07, below. See also Nicholls L.J.'s analysis of the solicitors' duties in *Bell v. Peter Browne and Co.* [1990] 2 Q.B. 495 at 500.
[23] See Chap. 5, para. 5–115, below.
[24] [1999] P.N.L.R. 593 and [1999] Lloyd's Rep. P.N. 223.

appreciate the extent of their obligation which they are accepting . . . Unless the language used is a retainer clearly has this consequence, the courts should not be ready to impose obligations on solicitors which even the most careful solicitor may not be able to meet."

This suggests that courts will be slow to construe professionals' retainers as giving rise to strict obligations, although it does not follow that in appropriate cases they will not do so.[25]

2–011   However, much of the professional person's work is not regulated by specific contractual terms such as these. Within the framework set by his instructions the professional person normally attempts to achieve a particular result (*e.g.* the solution of an engineering problem or the restoration of the patient to good health) or he renders a certain kind of service (*e.g.* financial advice or architectural design). In the absence of express terms[26] to the contrary effect, there is implied by law a term that the professional person will carry out these activities with reasonable skill and care.[27]

2–012   By way of exception to the general principles stated above, there are a small number of cases in which the professional person is simply required to achieve a specified result[28] and there is no need for a contractual term defining the skill and care which he must use. Engagements of this kind are the most onerous undertaken by professional persons. For example, where a dentist agrees to make a denture for his patient, his obligation is not to exercise reasonable skill and care (nor even exceptional skill and care) but to produce a denture which will be fit for its purpose.[29] An I.T. consultant may also owe the same standard in respect of computer software provided under a contract with a client.[30] In *IBA v. EMI and BICC*,[31] it was argued that contracts by architects or engineers to do design work fell into the same category. The point did not arise directly for decision in the House of Lords. However, Lord Scarman, founding himself on *Samuels v. Davis*[32] expressed the opinion *obiter* that "one who contracts to design an article for a purpose made known to him undertakes that the design is reasonably fit for the purpose".[33]

---

[25] See also *Mercantile Credit Company Ltd v. Fenwick* [1999] Lloyd's Rep. P.N. 408 and *Barclays Bank plc v. Weeks Legg & Dean (a firm)* [1999] Q.B. 309. A strict construction was placed on a solicitor's undertaking in *Zwebner v. The Mortgage Corp. Ltd* [1998] P.N.L.R. 769. See further Chap. 10, paras 10–09 and 10–10, below.

[26] Or implied terms arising from the particular circumstances of the retainer: *e.g. Greaves and Co. (Contractors) Ltd v. Baynham Meikle & Partners* [1975] 1 W.L.R. 1095, discussed in Chap. 8, paras 8–168 and 8–169, below.

[27] See ss.13 and 16 of the Supply of Goods and Services Act 1982.

[28] See, *e.g.* Chap. 10, para. 10–09 and Chap. 14, para. 14–11, below.

[29] *Samuels v. Davis* [1943] K.B. 526.

"It does not help to consider cases of an artist painting a picture or a sculptor making a bust, or to refer to cases of surgical operations in the ordinary sense. Clearly a dentist is in the same position as any other surgeon from the point of view of the law. If a dentist takes out a tooth or a surgeon removes an appendix, he is bound to take reasonable care and to show such skill as may be expected from a qualified practitioner. The case is entirely different, where a chattel is ultimately to be delivered."

[30] See Chap. 8, paras 8–168 to 8–174 and Chap. 17, paras 17–14 to 17–30, below.

[31] (1978) 11 Build.L.R. 29, CA; (1980) 14 Build.L.R. 1, HL.

[32] [1943] 1 K.B. 526.

[33] (1980) 14 Build.L.R. 48. See further at Chap. 8, para. 8–170, below.

3. Tortious Liability

(a) *The Tort of Negligence*

The tort of negligence[34] is complete when three conditions are satisfied: **2–013**

(1) the defendant owes a duty of care to the claimant;

(2) the defendant has acted or spoken in such a way as to break that duty of care; and

(3) the claimant has suffered relevant damage as a consequence of the breach.

The first condition. This is discussed below.[35] The essential questions to be   **2–014**
considered in every case are whether a duty of care existed and, if so, what was its scope.

The second condition. Once the existence and scope of the duty of care have   **2–015**
been established, the question of breach turns upon whether the defendant exercised the requisite degree of skill and care in the performance of his tortious duty.[36]

The third condition. The third condition is satisfied if the claimant suffers   **2–016**
damage within the scope of the defendant's duty.[37] Thus if the defendant's duty is only to protect the claimant against personal injury or physical damage, then that kind of damage (rather than pure financial loss) must be inflicted, in order to complete the tort of negligence.[38] Accordingly, the questions of duty and damage (the first and third conditions) are interrelated. In determining whether the defendant owed any relevant duty to the claimant, it is necessary to characterise the damage flowing from the breach of such duty. Once damage of the requisite character has been established, the subsequent inquiry is directed to quantum.[39]

Situations in which a duty of care exists. A owes a duty to exercise   **2–017**
reasonable care in relation to B in those situations where the courts have held (or Parliament has enacted) that a duty of care exists. Obvious examples are: where A is a car driver and B is anyone who might be injured by A's careless driving (*e.g.* another motorist, a cyclist, a pedestrian or a passenger); where A is the

---

[34] For a general discussion of the tort of negligence, which is beyond the scope of this book, see Charlesworth & Percy.
[35] See paras 2–17 to 2–78, below.
[36] See Section 4, below and the chapters in Section 2 on individual professions, especially on "Liability for Breach of Duty".
[37] See the discussion of minimum actionable damage in Stapleton, "The Gist of Negligence" in (1988) 104 L.Q.R. 213.
[38] *Nitrigin Eireann Teoranta v. Inco Alloys Ltd* [1992] 1 W.L.R. 498, *per* May J. is a good illustration of this. Damage to the pipes supplied by the defendant was economic loss in respect of which the defendant owed the claimant no duty of care. Only when damage was caused to other property nearly a year later was the plaintiff's cause of action in tort complete. See further Chap. 5, paras 5–16 to 5–48, below.
[39] See Chap. 3, paras 3–01 to 3–05, below and the sections on "Liability for Breach of Duty" in the chapters on individual professions.

occupier of premises and B is a visitor; where A is B's employer; or where A is a medical practitioner and B is his patient. However, obvious situations, whether covered by earlier decisions or an Act of Parliament, do not necessarily answer the question whether a particular duty of care is owed in a novel situation. In order to decide whether a duty of care is owed in a novel situation, some analogy or guiding principle must be derived from earlier authorities.

2–018   Over the last 80 years or so, a series of new situations have been considered by the House of Lords and either accepted as giving rise to a duty of care, or alternatively held not to do so. Important examples are:

(1) The manufacturer of a product owes a duty to take reasonable care to protect the ultimate consumer against personal injury.[40]

(2) A bank giving a reference on behalf of its customer to a third party owes a duty (in the absence of any effective disclaimer) to take reasonable care to protect the third party against financial loss.[41]

(3) Borstal officers, when allowing borstal boys to work on an island, have been held to owe a duty to the owners of nearby yachts to take reasonable care to prevent the boys escaping and causing damage to property.[42]

(4) A local authority exercising its supervisory functions in relation to the construction of dwelling-houses has been held to owe a duty to future owners and occupiers to protect them against the cost of repairing defects which would be liable to affect health or safety.[43] This decision was subsequently departed from by the House of Lords,[44] pursuant to the Practice Statement (Judicial Precedent) 1966.[45]

(5) A surveyor instructed by a building society to value a modest house for mortgage purposes, has been held to owe a duty to protect the prospective mortgagor against economic loss flowing from unreported defects.[46]

(6) Auditors of a public company have been held not to owe a duty of care to persons who might purchase shares (or to shareholders who might purchase more shares) in reliance upon the audited accounts.[47]

(7) Solicitors instructed to prepare a will have been held to owe a duty of care to the intended beneficiaries.[48]

2–019   Appellate decisions in the major "duty of care" cases have normally comprised two elements: first, there is a line of reasoning leading to the specific result; secondly, there is a more general discussion about the law of tort and duties of care, which is intended to justify (or to provide a theoretical basis for) the specific line of reasoning which has been adopted. The *ratio* of these

---

[40] *Donoghue v. Stevenson* [1932] A.C. 562.
[41] *Hedley Byrne and Co. Ltd v. Heller & Partners Ltd* [1964] A.C. 465.
[42] *Dorset Yacht Co. v. Home Office* [1970] A.C. 1004.
[43] *Anns v. Merton London Borough Council* [1978] A.C. 728.
[44] *Murphy v. Brentwood District Council* [1991] 1 A.C. 398.
[45] [1966] 1 W.L.R. 1234.
[46] *Smith v. Eric S. Bush* [1990] 1 A.C. 831.
[47] *Caparo Industries plc v. Dickman* [1990] 2 A.C. 605.
[48] *White v. Jones* [1995] 2 A.C. 207.

decisions is always to be found in the first element, namely the line of reasoning leading to the specific result. However, the other element (the general discussion) often attracts more attention from commentators and sometimes is treated almost as if it were the *ratio* of the case.[49] This is unfortunate, because the "theoretical discussion" element in these cases is not consistent and could hardly be expected to be so, in view of the broad jurisprudential problems with which it grapples. It is submitted that any attempt to rationalise the numerous appellate decisions on duty of care should begin by analysing those decisions into their two principal elements.

The line of reasoning leading to the specific result. This is dealt with in the chapters on individual professions in the sections dealing with duty of care.[50]   **2–020**

The theoretical discussion. The theoretical discussion which occurs in the major "duty of care" cases is referred to below.[51] It is part of the continuing quest by the courts to find some rational explanation for the conclusions to which they are driven in individual cases. Although (as previously stated) these passages are not part of the *rationes* of the cases in which they occur and, inevitably, they are not consistent and are not of universal application,[52] nevertheless they have assumed great importance in the development of the law of negligence and so to any general consideration of professional negligence (which is the business of this part of this chapter).   **2–021**

(b) *Theoretical Basis for the Duty of Care*[53]

(i) *Lord Atkin's approach*

In *Donoghue v. Stevenson*,[54] the House of Lords by a majority of 3:2 held that the manufacturer of ginger beer owed a duty of care to the ultimate consumer. The   **2–022**

---

[49] See the warning in Lord Atkin in *Donoghue v. Stevenson* [1932] A.C. 562, at 583–584: discussed at para.2–22, below.

" . . . in the branch of the law which deals with civil wrongs, dependent in England at any rate entirely upon the application by judges of general principles also formulated by judges, it is of particular importance to guard against the danger of stating propositions of law in wider terms than is necessary, lest essential factors be omitted in the wider survey and the inherent adaptability of English law be unduly restricted. For this reason it is very necessary in considering reported cases in the law of torts, that the actual decision alone should carry authority, proper weight, of course, being given to the dicta of the judges."

(See also *Heaven v. Pender* (1883) 11 Q.B.D. 503, where Cotton and Bowen L.JJ. declined to agree with Brett M.R. "in laying down unnecessarily the larger principle which he entertains".)

[50] See the sections headed "Duties to Third Parties" in the chapters on individual professions.

[51] See paras 2–22 to 2–78, below.

[52] In his speech in *Dorset Yacht Co. Ltd v. Home Office* [1970] A.C. 1004 at 1060D (discussed in para. 2–26, below), Lord Diplock said at 1060E of the well-known passage in Lord Atkin's speech in *Donoghue v. Stevenson* [1932] A.C. 562 (set out in para. 2–22, below):

"Used as a guide to characteristics which will be found to exist in conduct and relationships which give rise to a legal duty of care this aphorism marks a milestone in the modern development of the law of negligence. But misused as a universal, it is manifestly false."

(See also Lord Devlin in *Hedley Byrne and Co. Ltd v. Heller & Partners Ltd* [1964] A.C. 465 at 525.)

[53] This section focuses mainly on the principal House of Lords and Privy Council decisions on duty of care over the last 70 years. The varying approaches adopted in the major Commonwealth jurisdictions are also considered.

[54] [1932] A.C. 562.

majority (Lords Atkin, Thankerton and Macmillan) dealt principally with authorities concerning the liability of manufacturers and analogous cases. But also, in the general part of their speeches, they discussed whether there was some broad principle which underlay all cases where the law imposed a duty of care. The leading speech for the majority was given by Lord Atkin. He noted that the courts decide whether there is a duty of care in the specific cases, which come before them, and thus the law has been developed in respect of particular relationships: salesman and customer, landlord and tenant and so forth.[55] He continued:

> "And yet the duty which is common to all the cases where liability is established must logically be based upon some element common to the cases where it is found to exist. To seek a complete logical definition of the general principle is probably to go beyond the function of the judge, for the more general the definition the more likely it is to omit essentials or to introduce non-essentials.
>
> ... At present I content myself with pointing out that in English law there must be, and is, some general conception of relations giving rise to a duty of care, of which the particular cases found in the books are but instances. ... The rule that you are to love your neighbour becomes in law, you must not injure your neighbour; and the lawyer's question, Who is my neighbour? receives a restricted reply. You must take reasonable care to avoid acts or omissions which you can reasonably foresee would be likely to injure your neighbour. Who, then, in law is my neighbour? The answer seems to be—persons who are so closely and directly affected by my act that I ought reasonably to have them in contemplation as being so affected when I am directing my mind to the acts or omissions which are called in question."[56]

2–023   In the context of Lord Atkin's speech the phrase "injure your neighbour" means to cause some kind of physical or psychological harm to the plaintiff. If the soft drink in *Donoghue v. Stevenson* had been perfectly harmless but of lower nutritional value than advertised, Mrs Donoghue would have had no claim against the manufacturer for any financial loss which she might suffer.[57]

(ii) *Hedley Byrne*

2–024   Compared with the duty of care to prevent physical injury, the duty to prevent economic loss has caused the courts great problems, outside the obvious areas of economic loss consequent upon personal injury or damage to property. In *Hedley Byrne and Co. Ltd v. Heller & Partners Ltd*,[58] the plaintiffs suffered financial losses as a result of acting in reliance on favourable references given by the bankers of Easipower Ltd (which subsequently went into liquidation). The House of Lords held that the bankers owed no duty to the plaintiffs only because the references had been given "without responsibility". Thus the House of Lords recognised, in principle, that a person making a statement could owe a duty to the recipient (with whom he has no contract) to take reasonable care and that, in the event of breach, he could be liable for economic losses suffered by the recipient.

2–025   In the general part of their speeches the Law Lords discussed two interrelated problems, the extent of liability for words as opposed to deeds and the extent of liability for financial loss rather than (or not resulting from) physical injury. In

---

[55] *ibid.* at 579.
[56] *ibid.* at 580.
[57] For example, paying an excessive price for the drink; alternatively, purchasing additional ingredients to bring the drink up to the advertised nutritional value.
[58] [1964] A.C. 465.

general terms, all five Law Lords recognised that it would be unacceptable to impose liability on third parties for all financial losses foreseeably suffered as a result of negligent mis-statement. They saw as the principal mechanism for restricting such liability the nature of the relationship between the parties, rather than the nature of the loss.[59] Although different formulations were used, they emphasised the need for a special relationship. Lord Reid said that expressly or by implication from the circumstances, the defendant must have undertaken some responsibility to the plaintiff. Lord Devlin said that a duty to take care in respect of words arises when the relationship between the parties is contractual, fiduciary or "equivalent to contract", *i.e.* there would be a contract but for the lack of consideration.[60] Significantly, the House of Lords overruled *Candler v. Crane, Christmas and Co.*[61] and held that the law was correctly stated in the dissenting judgment of Denning L.J.

(iii) *The inclusive approach*

The *Dorset Yacht* **case.** In *Dorset Yacht Co. Ltd v. Home Office*,[62] the House **2–026** of Lords held, on a preliminary issue, that borstal officers supervising borstal boys staying on Brownsea Island, owed a duty to the owners of nearby yachts to take reasonable care to prevent the boys escaping and causing damage. In the general part[63] of his speech Lord Reid said:

" ... there has been a steady trend towards regarding the law of negligence as depending on principle so that, when a new point emerges, one should ask not whether it is covered by authority but whether recognised principles apply to it. *Donoghue v. Stevenson* may be regarded as a milestone, and the well-known passage in Lord Atkin's speech[64] should I think be regarded as a statement of principle. It is not to be treated as if it were a statutory definition. It will require qualification in new circumstances. But I think that the time has come when we can and should say that it ought to apply unless there is some justification or valid explanation for its exclusion. For example, causing economic loss is a different matter ... "

Anns v. Merton. the two-stage test. In *Anns v. Merton LBC*,[65] structural **2–027** movement occurred causing cracking in a block of flats in Wimbledon. The lessees of seven flats claimed damages against the local authority for the negligence of its employees in approving foundations of inadequate depth. The House of Lords held on a preliminary issue that in performing its supervisory functions the local authority owed a duty of care to future owners and occupiers of the flats. The principal speech was given by Lord Wilberforce, with whom Lords Diplock, Simon and Russell agreed. In the general part of his speech Lord Wilberforce said[66]:

"Through the trilogy of cases in this House—*Donoghue v. Stevenson* [1932] A.C. 562, *Hedley Byrne and Co. Ltd v. Heller & Partners Ltd* [1964] A.C. 465 and *Dorset Yacht*

---

[59] Lord Devlin protested that the distinction between pure financial loss and financial loss consequent upon physical injury was irrational: see *ibid.* at 517. See also *per* Lord Hodson at the bottom of 509, *ibid.*
[60] *ibid.* at 483, *per* Lord Reid and at 528–529, *per* Lord Devlin.
[61] [1951] 2 K.B. 164. See paras 2–110 to 2–113, below.
[62] [1970] A.C. 1004.
[63] *ibid.* at 1026–1027.
[64] See para. 2–22, above.
[65] [1978] A.C. 728.
[66] *ibid.* at 751G–752B.

Co. Ltd v. Home Office [1970] A.C. 1004—the position has now been reached that in order to establish that a duty of care arises in a particular situation, it is not necessary to bring the facts of that situation within those of previous situations in which a duty of care has been held to exist. Rather the question has to be approached in two stages. First, one has to ask whether, as between the alleged wrongdoers and the person who has suffered damage there is a sufficient relationship of proximity or neighbourhood such that, in the reasonable contemplation of the former, carelessness on his part may be likely to cause damage to the latter—in which case a prima facie duty of care arises. Secondly, if the first question is answered affirmatively, it is necessary to consider whether there are any considerations which ought to negative, or to reduce or limit the scope of the duty or the class of person to whom it is owed or the damages to which a breach of it may give rise: see *Dorset Yacht* case [1970] A.C. 1004 at 1027, *per* Lord Reid. Examples of this are *Hedley Byrne's* case [1964] A.C. 465 where the class of potential plaintiffs was reduced to those shown to have relied upon the correctness of statements made, and *Weller and Co. v. Foot and Mouth Disease Research Institute* [1966] 1 Q.B. 569; and (I cite these merely as illustrations, without discussion) cases about 'economic loss' where, a duty having been held to exist, the nature of the recoverable damages was limited: see *SCM (United Kingdom) Ltd v. W.J. Whittall & Son Ltd* [1971] 1 Q.B. 137 and *Spartan Steel & Alloys Ltd v. Martin and Co. (Contractors) Ltd* [1973] Q.B. 27."

2–028   **Subsequent use of the two-stage test.** This two-stage test gained wide currency and was used as the rationale of the decision in numerous novel situations where a duty of care was alleged.[67] The problem with this test was the undue weight which it attributed to foreseeability of damage, and the substantial extension of tortious liability which it appeared to presage. Indeed the Anns decision itself, which was justified by reference to this test, was the subject of strong criticism[68] and the High Court of Australia declined to follow it.[69] In England, the retreat began in 1984, with the decision of the House of Lords in *Governors of the Peabody Donation Fund v. Sir Lindsay Parkinson and Co. Ltd.*[70] In that case developers claimed damages against a local authority for permitting the developers' own contractor to depart from the approved drainage design. Lord Keith, with whom the other four Law Lords agreed, held that the local authority owed no relevant duty to the developers. In the general part of his speech he said:

"There has been a tendency in some recent cases to treat these passages [*i.e.* the passages set out above[71]] as being themselves of a definitive character. This is a temptation which should be resisted. The true question in each case is whether the particular defendant owed to the particular plaintiff a duty of care having the scope

---

[67] See, *e.g.* the reasoning in *Yianni v. Edwin Evans & Sons* [1982] Q.B. 438 and *Ross v. Caunters* [1980] Ch. 297 in relation to the liability of surveyors and solicitors respectively to third parties. Interestingly, despite the subsequent demise of the *Anns* two-stage test, the House of Lords has held that the results in both cases were correct. This illustrates the point made in paras 2–52 to 2–53, below.

[68] See, *e.g. D. & F. Estates Ltd v. Church Commissioners for England* [1989] A.C. 177; *Murphy v. Brentwood District Council* [1991] 1 A.C. 38; I. N. Duncan Wallace Q.C., "Negligence and Defective Buildings: Confusion Confounded?" in (1989) 105 L.Q.R. 46.

[69] *Shire of Sutherland v. Heyman* (1985) 60 A.L.R. 1. In a percipient article, I. N. Duncan Wallace Q.C. suggested that this case was a turning-point in the law of tort and that the higher judiciary both in England and the Commonwealth were beginning to apply the traditional principles more rigorously: see "The Shire of Sutherland Case in the High Court of Australia" in (1986) Int.Const.L.Rev., Vol. 3, Pt 2.

[70] [1985] A.C. 210.

[71] See paras 2–26 to 2–27, above.

which is contended for, and whether he was in breach of that duty with consequent loss to the plaintiff. A relationship of proximity in Lord Atkin's sense must exist before any duty of care can arise, but the scope of the duty must depend on all the circumstances of the case . . . So in determining whether or not a duty of care of particular scope was incumbent upon a defendant it is material to take into consideration whether it is just and reasonable that it should be so."[72]

In *Candlewood Navigation Corp. Ltd v. Mitsui OSK Lines Ltd*,[73] the Privy **2–029** Council emphasised the importance of limiting liability for economic loss, although they considered that this could be achieved within the *Anns* two-stage test.[74] In *Leigh and Sillivan Ltd v. Aliakmon Shipping Co. Ltd*,[75] buyers of goods, to whom risk but not property had passed, unsuccessfully claimed against the ship owners in respect of damage caused to the goods in transit. The reasoning leading to the specific decision was that the plaintiffs could not claim for loss of or damage to property unless they had either legal ownership or possessory title to the property at the time when the loss or damage occurred. The decision was given in a single speech by Lord Brandon, with whom the other four Law Lords agreed. In rejecting an argument based on the *Anns* two-stage test, Lord Brandon commented that it was not intended to provide a universally applicable test of the existence and scope of a duty of care in the law of negligence. In particular, it should not be adopted in situations where previously it has been repeatedly held that a duty of care does not exist.[76] This decision may have been the death knell of the *Anns* two-stage test. Once it is recognised that this is inconsistent with a substantial body of earlier duty of care cases, the test has little utility as a guide to the solution of future problems.

(iv) *The threefold test*

Once the shortcomings of the inclusive approach were recognised, the courts **2–030** moved towards a more neutral framework within which to consider the existence of a duty of care.[77] In *Smith v. Eric S. Bush*,[78] a surveyor instructed by a building society failed to spot a serious defect in a house (inadequate support for upstairs chimneys) and the building society granted a mortgage to the plaintiff. Both the mortgage application form and the report contained a disclaimer of liability for the accuracy of the report, but that disclaimer was ineffective by reason of the

---

[72] [1985] A.C. 210 at 240–241.

[73] [1986] A.C. 1.

[74] *ibid.* at 24H–25D.

[75] [1986] A.C. 785.

[76] *ibid.* at 815.

[77] For example in *Yuen Kun Yeu v. Att.-Gen. of Hong Kong* [1988] A.C. 175 proceedings by investors (who had suffered losses) against the Commissioner of Deposit-taking Companies in Hong Kong were dismissed as disclosing no reasonable cause of action. Lord Keith, delivering the judgment of the Privy Council, emphasised the importance of proximity as well as foreseeability in relation to the first stage of the *Anns* test (*ibid.* at 191–192). He also said that in future that test should not be regarded as in all circumstances a suitable guide to the existence of a duty of care. Factors which weighed heavily in the actual decision were the large number of potential plaintiffs (anyone who might invest in Hong Kong), the nature of the Commissioner's functions and his limited powers. See also *Davis v. Radcliffe* [1990] 1 W.L.R. 821, where the Privy Council reached a similar conclusion. See further para. 2–86, below.

[78] [1990] 1 A.C. 831. *Smith v. Eric S. Bush* and *Harris v. Wyre Forest District Council* were heard together. The reasoning in relation to both cases is important and should be considered together. These cases are discussed more fully in Chap. 9, paras 9–46 to 9–50, below.

Unfair Contract Terms Act 1977.[79] The House of Lords held that the surveyor, though instructed by the mortgagee, owed a duty to the prospective mortgagor to exercise reasonable care when inspecting and reporting. The line of reasoning leading to the specific result is set out in Chapter 9, below.[80] In the more general part of his speech Lord Griffiths (with whom Lord Keith and Lord Brandon agreed) stated:

> "In what circumstances should a duty of care be owed by the adviser to those who act upon his advice? I would answer—only if it is foreseeable that if the advice is negligent the recipient is likely to suffer damage, that there is a sufficiently proximate relationship between the parties and that it is just and reasonable to impose the liability."[81]

2–031 Shortly after the decisions discussed in the previous paragraph the House of Lords returned to the same issues in *Caparo Industries plc v. Dickman*.[82] The plaintiffs, having taken over a public limited company ("F"), alleged that the audited accounts on which they had relied were inaccurate and misleading. They brought proceedings against two directors of F for fraud and against the auditors for negligence in certifying that the accounts showed a true and fair view of F's position on the stated date. On a preliminary issue the House of Lords held that the auditors owed no duty to the plaintiffs, either as potential investors or as existing shareholders considering the purchase of further shares. Three principal speeches were delivered by Lord Bridge, Lord Oliver and Lord Jauncey.

2–032 In the general part of his speech Lord Bridge said that the quest for a single general principle to determine the existence and scope of the duty of care in any situation had failed. He continued:

> "What emerges [from the recent decisions] is that, in addition to the foreseeability of damage, necessary ingredients in any situation giving rise to a duty of care are that there should exist between the party owing the duty and the party to whom it is owed a relationship characterised by the law as one of 'proximity' or 'neighbourhood' and that the situation should be one in which the court considers it fair, just and reasonable that the law should impose a duty of a given scope upon the one party for the benefit of the other. But it is implicit in the passages referred to that the concepts of proximity and fairness embodied in these additional ingredients are not susceptible of any such precise definition as would be necessary to give them utility as practical tests, but amount in effect to little more than convenient labels to attach to the features of different specific situations which, on a detailed examination of all the circumstances, the law recognises pragmatically as giving rise to a duty of care of a given scope."[83]

Lord Bridge went on to say that the law now attached more significance to the traditional categorisations as guides to the existence and scope of the duty of care. He then focused on the authorities concerning negligent advice/economic loss ("this relatively narrow corner of the field"[84]) for the purpose of determining the instant case.

2–033 In the general part of his speech Lord Oliver expressed similar views. Having referred to the extensive financial losses which could foreseeably result from negligent statements, he continued:

---

[79] See Chap. 5, para. 5–08, below.
[80] See paras 9–46 to 9–50, below.
[81] [1990] 1 A.C. 831 at 864H–865A.
[82] [1990] 2 A.C. 605. Discussed in Chap. 15, paras 15–53 to 15–61, below.
[83] *ibid.* at 617–618.
[84] *ibid.* at 619E.

"Thus the postulate of a simple duty to avoid any harm that is, with hindsight, reasonably capable of being foreseen becomes untenable without the imposition of some intelligible limits to keep the law of negligence within the bounds of common sense and practicality. Those limits have been found by the requirement of what has been called a 'relationship of proximity' between plaintiff and defendant and by the imposition of a further requirement that the attachment of liability for harm which has occurred be 'just and reasonable'. But although the cases in which the courts have imposed or withheld liability are capable of an approximate categorisation, one looks in vain for some common denominator by which the existence of the essential relationship can be tested. Indeed it is difficult to resist a conclusion that what have been treated as three separate requirements are, at least in most cases, in fact merely facets of the same thing, for in some cases the degree of foreseeability is such that it is from that alone that the requisite proximity can be deduced, whilst in others the absence of that essential relationship can most rationally be attributed simply to the court's view that it would not be fair and reasonable to hold the defendant responsible. 'Proximity' is, no doubt, a convenient expression so long as it is realised that it is no more than a label which embraces not a definable concept but merely a description of circumstances from which, pragmatically, the courts conclude that a duty of care exists."[85]

The same threefold test was adopted by three members of the House of Lords in *Spring v. Guardian Assurance plc.*[86] In that case the plaintiff was frustrated in his efforts to set up in business selling insurance by an adverse reference from the defendants, his former employers. The trial judge held that the defendants had been negligent but not malicious in preparing the adverse reference. The Court of Appeal allowed an appeal by the defendants on the grounds that they owed no relevant duty of care to the plaintiff.[87] The House of Lords allowed the plaintiff's appeal by a majority of four to one. Out of that majority Lord Lowry,[88] Lord Slynn[89] and Lord Woolf[90] all approached the issues using the threefold test. 2–034

Summary. It appeared that following the demise of the *Anns* two-stage test ("the inclusive approach") a new framework emerged for considering, or at least for explaining, some of the major decisions on duty of care. This involved considering three questions: 2–035

(1) whether it was reasonably foreseeable that the plaintiff would suffer the kind of damage which occurred;

(2) whether there was sufficient proximity between the parties;

(3) whether it was just and reasonable that the defendant should owe a duty of care of the scope alleged.

(v) *The exclusive approach*

The perceived difficulty with the threefold approach set out in the previous paragraph is that questions (2) and (3) are so broad that it is frequently impossible 2–036

---

[85] *ibid.* at 633A–D.
[86] [1995] 2 A.C. 296. For a discussion of this decision see "The Right of Spring" by Lord Cooke in Cane and Stapleton (eds), *The Law of Obligations, Essays in Celebration of John Fleming* (Clarendon Press, 1998). Lord Cooke considers the decision in the context of the law of defamation and the law of employment.
[87] The Court of Appeal's decision was strongly criticised by Weir, "The case of the careless referee" in (1993) 52 C.L.J. 376.
[88] [1995] 2 A.C. 296 at 325–326.
[89] *ibid.* at 334–336.
[90] *ibid.* at 342.

to tell how they would be answered on the facts of any individual case. The questions are highly subjective. Furthermore, every new case must be approached from first principles.

2–037   Lord Oliver grappled with these problems in *Caparo Industries plc v. Dickman*[91] in the passage quoted in paragraph 2–33, above. He recognised that it was impossible to state "some general principle which will determine liability in an infinite variety of circumstances".[92] He went on to commend the incremental approach stated by Brennan J. in *Sutherland Shire Council v. Heyman*.[93]

2–038   **The incremental approach.** In *Sutherland Shire Council v. Heyman*, the High Court of Australia declined to hold a local authority liable to a subsequent house purchaser for negligent inspection of foundation works. In considering the proper approach to the duty of care question, Brennan J. stated:

> "Of course, if foreseeability of injury to another were the exhaustive criterion of a prima facie duty to act to prevent the occurrence of that injury, it would be essential to introduce some kind of restrictive qualification—perhaps a qualification of the kind stated in the second stage of the general proposition in *Anns*. I am unable to accept that approach. It is preferable, in my view, that the law should develop novel categories of negligence incrementally and by analogy with established categories, rather than by a massive extension of a prima facie duty of care restrained only by indefinable considerations which ought to negative, or to reduce or limit the scope of the duty or the class of person to whom it is owed."[94]

2–039   **Adoption of incremental approach by House of Lords.** In *Murphy v. Brentwood District Council*,[95] the plaintiff purchased a house which had been built with defective foundations, and claimed damages against the local authority for negligence in approval of the plans. The official referee awarded him £35,000, representing his loss on resale of the house in its defective condition. The decision was upheld by the Court of Appeal (on the basis of *Anns v. Merton LBC*[96]) but reversed by the House of Lords. An enlarged committee of seven Law Lords heard the appeal. They rejected both the general statement of principle in *Anns* (the two-stage test) and the specific decision in that case. Accordingly the House departed from its own previous decision in *Anns* pursuant to the Practice Statement (Judicial Precedent),[97] and overruled *Dutton v. Bognor Regis UDC*[98] and "all cases subsequent to *Anns* which were decided in reliance on it".[99] The

---

[91] [1990] 2 A.C. 605.
[92] *ibid.* at 633.
[93] (1984–1985) 157 C.L.R. 424.
[94] *ibid.* at 481. See also Lord Devlin in *Hedley Byrne and& Co. Ltd v. Heller & Partners Ltd* [1964] A.C. 465, at 536: "Is the relationship between the parties in this case such that it can be brought within a category giving rise to a special duty? As always in English law, the first step is such an inquiry is to see how far the authorities have gone, for new categories in the law do not spring into existence overnight." The second sentence in that passage was cited by Lord Diplock in *Dorset Yacht Co. Ltd. v. Home Office* [1970] A.C. 1004 at 1058F in the course of a rigorous analysis of the role of authority in the law of negligence.
[95] [1991] 1 A.C. 398.
[96] [1978] A.C. 728.
[97] [1966] 1 W.L.R. 1234.
[98] [1972] 1 Q.B. 373.
[99] [1991] 1 A.C. 398 at 472G in the speech of Lord Keith. In total five substantive speeches were delivered, but the speech of Lord Keith was the only one with which all members of the Committee expressed their agreement.

House of Lords held[1] that the correct manner to determine the existence and scope of the duty of care in novel situations was the incremental approach stated by Brennan J. in *Sutherland Shire Council v. Heyman*.[2] They went on to hold that the damage in *Anns* should be characterised as pure economic loss.[3] Recognition of a duty of care owed by local authorities and builders in respect of such loss would, in effect, introduce a "transmissible warranty of quality".[4] That would be inconsistent with existing authority and principle as to the scope of a duty of care owed by the manufacturers of chattels. The three-stage test was not invoked, although it was not disapproved.[5] *Anns* was disapproved because, on the analysis in *Murphy v. Brentwood D.C.* and the earlier related decision in *D. & F. Estates Ltd v. Church Commissioners for England*,[6] it introduced a wide-ranging novel category of duty of care which conflicted with established principle.

A decision in the aftermath of *Murphy* which illustrates the operation of the **2–040** incremental approach is *Punjab National Bank v. de Boinville*.[7] The facts of that case are set out in paragraph 14–28, below. The Court of Appeal held that it was a justifiable increment to hold that an insurance broker owed a duty of care to a person who he knew would become an assignee of the relevant insurance policy.

Relationship between the incremental approach and the threefold test. **2–041** The incremental approach did not supplant the threefold test discussed in paragraphs 2–30 to 2–35, above. It can be seen as providing guidance to the application of the threefold test and a warning of the potential danger of deciding whether a particular duty of care is owed simply by reference to general statements of principle.[8] It can also be analysed as providing an alternative approach which should lead to the same answer in any given case.[9]

Continued application of the threefold test. However the relationship **2–042** between it and the incremental approach is analysed, *Murphy* did not mark the demise of the threefold test. In *X (minors) v. Bedfordshire C.C.*,[10] the House of

---

[1] See *ibid.* at 461E-F, *per* Lord Keith.

[2] (1984–1985) 157 C.L.R. 424 at 481.

[3] See, *per* Lord Keith at 466, *per* Lord Bridge at 475–479, *per* Lord Oliver at 484 and *per* Lord Jauncey at 496–497.

[4] *ibid.*, *per* Lord Keith at 469B.

[5] Lord Oliver in particular continued to speak of the need to establish "proximity" in cases of economic loss, although recognising that it was 'an expression which persistently denies definition": *ibid.* at 487G.

[6] [1989] A.C. 177 discussed in Chap. 8, para. 8–071, below.

[7] [1992] 1 W.L.R. 1138.

[8] "The incremental approach also has been the subject of criticism but in the absence of some guiding principle of universal application this approach ensures that developments in the law will take place in measured steps": *Bank of Credit and Commerce International (Overseas) Ltd v. Price Waterhouse (No.2)* [1998] P.N.L.R. 564 at 586, *per* Sir Brian Neill. In *Reeman v. Department of Transport* [1997] P.N.L.R. 618, Phillips L.J., having said that the threefold test was the correct approach, said at 625A-C:

"When confronted with a novel situation the court does not, however, consider these matters in isolation. It does so by comparison with established categories of negligence to see whether the facts amount to no more than a small extension of a situation already covered by authority, or whether a finding of the existence of a duty of care would effect a significant extension of the law of negligence. Only in exceptional cases will the court accept that the interests of justice justify such an extension of the law."

[9] See para. 2–50, below.

[10] [1995] 2 A.C. 633; see also (1996) 112 L.Q.R. 134, *per* Cane.

Lords decided two groups of cases brought against local authorities, "the child care cases" and "the education cases". In the child care cases, the House of Lords struck out claims by children against local authorities for negligence in the exercise of their powers under the Children Act 1989 and preceding statutes. In the first case, five children claimed damages for the local authority's wrongful failure to take them into care. In the second case, a child claimed damages for wrongly being taken into care. In the education cases the House of Lords declined to strike out claims by pupils with special needs against a number of education authorities for negligence in the exercise of their powers under the Education Acts.[11] Lord Browne-Wilkinson (with whom Lord Jauncey, Lord Lane and Lord Ackner agreed) set out the general approach in the first part of his speech, before dealing with the individual cases. When Lord Browne-Wilkinson came to determine the duty of care question applying "the usual principles", he asked himself:

> "Was the damage to the plaintiff reasonably foreseeable? Was the relationship between the plaintiff and the defendant sufficiently proximate? Is it just and reasonable to impose a duty of care?"[12]

However, when considering whether it was fair, just and reasonable to impose a common law duty on the local authorities in the child care cases, Lord Browne-Wilkinson referred to the decision in *Caparo Industries Plc. v. Dickman*[13]:

> "that, in deciding whether to develop novel categories of negligence the court should proceed incrementally and by analogy with decided categories."[14]

Thus the two approaches co-exist.[15] The incremental approach may assist the court in determining the question of proximity or the "just and reasonable" question. The incremental approach may determine the answer in such a way that the court need not even consider the threefold test.[16] If existing authority provides an answer by way of analogy, then there is no (or less) need to consider the question on the basis of more general principle.[17]

2–043　　　　**Criticisms of incremental approach.** Whereas the *Anns* two-stage test had been criticised as unduly expansive, the incremental approach adopted by the

---

[11] This decision is considered further in paras 2–84 to 2–85, below.
[12] [1995] 2 A.C. 633 at 739A–B (see also 749D–E). Lord Jauncey (who re-affirmed the threefold test at 728E–F), Lord Lane and Lord Ackner agreed with Lord Browne-Wilkinson.
[13] [1990] 2 A.C. 605.
[14] [1995] 2 A.C. 633 at 751C (see also at 762C—the education cases).
[15] See also *Hill v. Van Erp* (1995–1997) 188 C.L.R. 159 (discussed in para. 2–64, below) at 178, *per* Dawson J. and at 190, *per* Toohey J. commenting on the lack of real difference between the approach based on proximity (discussed in paras 2–63 to 2–65, below) and the incremental approach.
[16] See, *e.g. Henderson v. Merrett Syndicates Ltd* [1995] 2 A.C. 145 at 181C-D. The plaintiffs succeeded on the incremental approach, *viz.* an extension of the *Hedley Byrne* principle, and Lord Goff did not consider it necessary to embark upon the threefold test. In *Goodwill v. British Pregnancy Advisory Service* [1996] 1 W.L.R. 1397 the plaintiff failed on the incremental approach and her claim was struck out. There was no separate consideration of the threefold test.
[17] This can be characterised as a justification of intellectual sloth or as an application of the doctrine of judicial precedent.

House of Lords in *Murphy* was seen by some commentators as too restrictive.[18] The view was expressed that the "new orthodoxy" was empty and would freeze the law of negligence at the stage it had then reached.[19] These criticisms were expressed in varying forms by the courts of Canada and New Zealand, who declined to adopt the incremental approach.[20] In giving the majority judgment in *Canadian National Railway Co. v. Norsk Pacific Steamship Co.*,[21] McLachlin J. stated:

> "They [the Canadian courts] will refuse to accept injustice merely for the sake of the doctrinal tidiness which is the motivating spirit of *Murphy*. This is in the best tradition of the law of negligence, the history of which exhibits a sturdy refusal to be confined by arbitrary forms and rules where justice indicates otherwise . . . "[22]

> "I consider that, from a doctrinal point of view, this court should continue on the course charted in *Kamloops* rather than reverting to the narrow exclusionary rule as the House of Lords did in *Murphy*."[23]

These criticisms were not entirely fair. Whilst in general terms the approach of **2–044** the courts to duty of care issues has been more conservative since the demise of *Anns*, the House of Lords is quite prepared to take substantial "incremental" steps in order to achieve a just result, even if not always adopting the incremental approach. This is most vividly demonstrated in the recent extensions of the *Hedley Byrne* principle.

(vi) *Extensions of Hedley Byrne*

In *Spring v. Guardian Assurance plc*[24] (discussed in paragraph 2–34, above), **2–045** Lord Goff reached his conclusion on a different basis to the majority. He concluded that the defendants were liable on the basis of the *Hedley Byrne* principle. He considered that the concept of "special skill" which featured in the reasoning in *Hedley Byrne* included "special knowledge". Thus an employer giving a reference about a former employee had the requisite special skill. Lord Goff also extended the concept of reliance to include the situation where a person trusts his former employer to give an accurate reference. This latter extension was a substantial leap. Two apparently cardinal features of the *Hedley Byrne* principle were (i) that the claimant had received the negligent statement and (ii) that the claimant had acted in the belief that the negligent statement was true. In the instant case Mr Spring did not satisfy either of those two conditions.

Application of Hedley Byrne to parties in contractual relationship. Once **2–046** the House of Lords in *Murphy* had characterised defects in buildings as pure economic loss, the question immediately arose whether previous claims against architects and engineers, brought in tort in order to defeat a limitation defence,

---

[18] The "pockets of case law" approach favoured by the House of Lords in *Caparo* and *Murphy* was strongly criticised by J. Stapleton in her article "Duty of care and economic loss: a wider agenda" in (1991) 107 L.Q.R. 249. She criticised the manner in which pockets were selected and the grouping of cases which resulted. She argued that "pocket analysis" should be abandoned and replaced by an agenda of policy concerns (at 284–286).
[19] D. Howarth, "Negligence after Murphy: time to rethink" in (1991) 50 C.L.J. 58.
[20] See paras 2–54 to 2–62, below.
[21] (1992) 91 D.L.R. (4th) 289.
[22] *ibid.* at 365.
[23] *ibid.* at 371.
[24] [1995] 2 A.C. 296.

were rightly decided. The pre-eminent case to which this question applied was *Pirelli General Cable Works Ltd v. Oscar Faber & Partners*.[25] In a passage of considerable importance to professional negligence Lord Keith said[26]:

> "It would seem that in a case such as *Pirelli*, where the tortious liability arose out of a contractual relationship with professional people, the duty extended to take reasonable care not to cause economic loss to the client by the advice given. The plaintiffs built the chimney as they did in reliance on that advice. The case would accordingly fall within the principle of *Hedley Byrne & Co. Ltd v. Heller & Partners Ltd*."[27]

2–047   This question arose for decision in *Henderson v. Merrett Syndicates Ltd*.[28] The names on a number of syndicates at Lloyd's brought actions against both their members' agents and managing agents in respect of massive losses which they had suffered. Saville J., the Court of Appeal and the House of Lords all held that, in addition to their various contractual duties, managing agents owed a duty of care in tort both to direct and indirect names to carry out their functions with reasonable skill and care. The principal speech was given by Lord Goff, with whom Lord Keith, Lord Mustill, Lord Nolan and Lord Browne-Wilkinson agreed. Lord Goff stated that the governing principle was that contained in *Hedley Byrne*. This established liability for words as well as deeds, and for pure economic loss as well as physical damage. The assumption of responsibility, although it had been criticised,[29] was "at least in cases such as the present" a crucial feature for establishing Hedley Byrne liability.[30] Towards the end of his discussion of general principle Lord Goff stated:

> "It follows that, once the case is identified as falling within the *Hedley Byrne* principle, there should be no need to embark upon any further enquiry whether it is 'fair, just and reasonable' to impose liability for economic loss—a point which is, I consider, of some importance in the present case."[31]

On that basis if a case can be brought within the *Hedley Byrne* principle by means of the incremental approach, it is not necessary to embark upon the threefold test discussed in paragraphs 2–30 to 2–35, above.

2–048   **The disappointed beneficiary.** A further extension of the Hedley Byrne principle occurred in *White v. Jones*.[32] In July 1986, the testator wrote to his

---

[25] [1983] 2 A.C. 1, discussed in Chap. 5, paras 5–17 to 5–34, below.
[26] *Murphy v. Brentwood District Council* [1991] 1 A.C. 398 at 466F-G.
[27] [1964] A.C. 465.
[28] [1995] 2 A.C. 145. Discussed in Chap. 16. Further discussed by Powell in "Professional and client: the duty of care", published in Birks (ed.), *Wrongs and Remedies in the Twenty-First Century* (Clarendon Press, 1996), pp. 58–61.
[29] *Smith v. Eric S. Bush* [1990] 1 A.C. 831 at 862B-F and 864H, *per* Lord Griffiths; *Caparo Industries plc v. Dickman* [1990] 2 A.C. 605 at 628G, *per* Lord Roskill. For more recent criticism, see *Phelps v. Hillingdon B.C.* [2000] 3 W.L.R. 776 at 791F, *per* Lord Slynn: "The phrase means simply that the law recognises that there is a duty of care. It is not so much that responsibility is assumed as that it recognised or imposed by law." References to recent academic criticism are listed in the speech of Lord Steyn in *Williams v. Natural Health Life Foods Ltd* [1998] 1 W.L.R. 830 at 837C-D.
[30] *Henderson v. Merrett* [1995] 2 A.C. 145 at 180–181.
[31] *ibid.* at 181.
[32] [1995] 2 A.C. 207. Discussed in Chap. 10, paras 10–48 to 10–50. Further discussed by Powell in "Professional and client: the duty of care", published in Birks (ed.), *Wrongs and Remedies in the Twenty-First Century*, (Clarendon Press, 1996) pp. 61–62 and by Murphy, "Expectation Losses, Negligent Omissions and the Tortious Duty of Care" in (1996) C.L.J. 43.

solicitors stating that he wished to make a new will leaving most of his estate to his daughters, who had been cut out of the existing will. The solicitors failed to give effect to these instructions before the testator died. By a bare majority the House of Lords held that the solicitors owed a duty of care to the daughters, the intended beneficiaries. The majority comprised Lord Goff, Lord Browne-Wilkinson and Lord Nolan. Both Lord Goff and Lord Browne-Wilkinson based their decision on an extension of *Hedley Byrne*. They considered that on a number of grounds justice required the solicitors to have a liability to intended beneficiaries, and that the *Hedley Byrne* principle afforded the proper means of overcoming the conceptual difficulties which would otherwise arise. They concluded that solicitors who undertook the task of preparing a will "assumed responsibility" for that task and so towards the intended beneficiaries. This decision involves a further substantial extension of the *Hedley Byrne* principle. The intended beneficiary, unlike the representee in *Hedley Byrne* or the employee in *Spring*, need have had no prior connection with, or even knowledge of, the testator's solicitors. The relevant conduct is not a statement but the performance of a task (preparing a will) or, as in *White v. Jones*, the omission to perform a task.

Practical application of the extended *Hedley Byrne* principle. In *Williams* 2–049
v. Natural Life Health Foods Ltd,[33] Lord Steyn (with whom Lord Goff, Lord Hoffmann, Lord Clyde and Lord Hutton agreed) described the extended *Hedley Byrne* principle as:

> "the rationalisation or technique adopted by English law to provide a remedy for the recovery of damages in respect of economic loss caused by the negligent performance of services."[34]

Once a case is identified as falling within that principle, then there is no need to consider whether it is "fair, just and reasonable" to impose liability.[35] In that case the director and principal shareholder of Natural Life Health Foods Ltd was sued for negligent advice which had been given by the company. The House of Lords, reversing the Court of Appeal, dismissed the claim, because the director (as opposed to the company) had not assumed responsibility to the claimants. Lord Steyn gave guidance as to the practical application of the extended *Hedley Byrne* principle.[36] The court must focus not on the state of mind of the defendant, but on communications between the claimant and the defendant. The claimant must show that he reasonably relied upon an assumption of responsibility by the defendant.[37]

(vii) *The co-Existence of different approaches*

Relationship of the extended *Hedley Byrne* principle with the threefold 2–050
test and the incremental approach. It is not entirely clear whether the decisions

---

[33] [1998] 1 W.L.R. 830. Discussed in Grantham and Rickett, "Directors' 'Tortious' Liability: Contract, Tort or Company Law?" in (1999) 62 M.L.R. 133.
[34] *ibid.* at 834F.
[35] *ibid.* at 834G.
[36] *ibid.* at 835–837.
[37] It is clear that claimants face a substantial hurdle in any case where they seek to hold personally liable in negligence the employee of a company providing professional services: see, *e.g. Hale v. Guildarch Ltd* [1999] P.N.L.R. 44 (claim in tort against employees of a limited company which gave financial advice dismissed). The position of directors and employees of limited liability companies is discussed in paras 2–87 to 2–93, below.

which involved the extended *Hedley Byrne* principle were putting that principle forward in place of the threefold test[38] and the incremental approach or as an alternative approach to be adopted in appropriate cases (and, if the latter, in which cases one approach should be applied rather than another). Nor was the relationship between the threefold test and the incremental approach spelt out in *Murphy v. Brentwood D.C.*[39] So long as extensions of the *Hedley Byrne* principle are legitimate and consistent with its underlying rationale, then there should be no conflict between them and decisions made by applying the threefold test or the incremental approach. The are simply different routes to the same conclusion and are based upon the same decisions and principles, however expressed in terms of general principle.

2–051   In *Marc Rich and Co. A.G. v. Bishop Rock Marine Co. Ltd,*[40] the House of Lords had to consider whether a classification society owed a duty of care to cargo owners when surveying a vessel. Such a claim had not been recognised in the English courts, nor in any foreign court. The damage suffered was physical damage, but the majority[41] held that the threefold test applied.[42] However, it was emphasised that the law developed incrementally in this area[43] and the possibility, on different facts, that direct contact between the classification society and cargo owners might have given rise to an assumption of responsibility by the former was recognised.[44] The majority concluded that on the facts pleaded no duty of care was owed because, even if there were sufficient proximity (which was not decided), it would not be fair just and reasonable to impose such a duty. They did not explain the relationship between the different approaches, but were able to use all of them without practical difficulty.[45]

2–052   **Three routes to the same destination.** In *Stovin v. Wise,*[46] a motorcyclist was injured in a collision with a car at a dangerous road junction. The car driver was held liable to the motorcyclist, but both at first instance and in the Court of Appeal recovered a 30 per cent contribution from the county council for failing to take steps to make the junction safer. The House of Lords by a bare majority allowed the council's appeal. The opinion of the majority was set out in the speech of Lord Hoffmann. After discussing the distinction between acts and omissions, he considered the decision in *Anns*, the House of Lords in *Murphy v. Brentwood D.C.* having left open the possibility that the council might have owed a duty of care in respect of physical injury. He said:

---

[38] In his dissenting speech in *Marc Rich & Co. A.G. v. Bishop Rock Marine Co. Ltd* [1996] A.C. 211 at 229H, Lord Lloyd described the decisions on the *Hedley Byrne* principles as "a parallel movement in the opposite direction" to that in which the House of Lords had moved when developing the threefold test. See also P. Cane "Contract, Tort and the Lloyd's Debacle" in F. D. Rose, (ed.), *Consensus ad Idem* Sweet and Maxwell, 1996), pp. 115–116.

[39] [1991] 1 A.C. 398. See para. 2–41, above.

[40] [1996] A.C. 211.

[41] *ibid.*, Lord Lloyd dissented. Lords Keith, Jauncey and Browne-Wilkinson agreed with Lord Steyn who gave the only reasoned speech of the majority.

[42] *ibid., per* Lord Steyn at 235D–236B. This was followed in *British Telecommunications plc v. James Thomson & Sons (Engineers) Ltd* [1999] 1 W.L.R. 9.

[43] [1996] A.C. 211 at 236B-C.

[44] *ibid.* at 237H–238A.

[45] In *Aiken v. Stewart Wrightson Members Agency Ltd* [1995] 1 W.L.R. 1281 (discussed in Chap. 16, paras 16–14 to 16–15) Potter J. applied the threefold test, but in doing so referred to assumption of responsibility when considering whether there was proximity and concluded that the duty of care was a "justifiable increment".

[46] [1996] A.C. 923; discussed by Harris in (1997) 113 L.Q.R. 398.

"Lord Wilberforce, who gave the leading speech, first stated the well-known two-stage test for the existence of a duty of care. This involves starting with the prima facie assumption that a duty of care exists if it is reasonably foreseeable that carelessness may cause damage and then asking whether there are any considerations which ought to 'negative, or to reduce or limit the scope of the duty or the class of person to whom it is owed or the damages to which a breach of it may give rise'. Subsequent decisions in this House and the Privy Council have preferred to approach the question the other way round, starting with situations in which a duty has been held to exist and then asking whether there are considerations of analogy, policy, fairness and justice for extending it to cover a new situation: see for example Lord Bridge of Harwich in *Caparo Industries plc v. Dickman* [1990] 2 A.C. 605 at 617–618. It can be said that, provided that the considerations of policy, etc., are properly analysed, it should not matter whether one starts from one end or the other."[47]

Lord Hoffmann then turned to the position of public authorities, which is discussed below.[48]

In *Bank of Credit and Commerce International (Overseas) Ltd. v. Price Waterhouse (No. 2)*,[49] Sir Brian Neill, with whom Brooke and Nourse L.JJ. agreed, suggested that it might be useful to look at a new set of facts by using each of the three approaches used and approved by the House of Lords and that: 2–053

"if the facts are properly analysed and the policy considerations are correctly evaluated the several approaches will yield the same result."[50]

This approach has found favour with the editors of *Clerk & Lindsell on Torts*[51] and was restated by a slightly differently constituted Court of Appeal in *Parkinson v. St James and Seacroft University Hospital NHS Trust*.[52]

(viii) *Commonwealth approaches to duty of care issues*

New Zealand. In *South Pacific Manufacturing Co. Ltd v. New Zealand Security Consultants and Investigations Ltd*[53] two actions were brought against the agents of insurers for alleged negligence in investigating fires. In the first case, the plaintiff was the creditor and principal shareholder of the insured who had lost property in the fire. In the second case, the plaintiff was the insured who had suffered losses as a result of the fire. In each case, the insurers, relying upon the investigations and report of their agents, had refused to pay out. The New Zealand Court of Appeal held that both actions should be struck out. In neither   2–054

---

[47] *ibid.* at 410–411. There is a useful discussion of the relationship between the *Anns* two-stage test and the threefold test in the dissenting speech of Lord Nicholls at 931H–932H.
[48] See para. 2–84, below.
[49] [1998] P.N.L.R. 564.
[50] *ibid.* at 586F.
[51] 18th edition, para. 7–95.
[52] [2001] 3 W.L.R. 376 at 382F ([2001] E.W.C.A. Civ. 530, para. 17), per Brooke L.J. with whom Hale L.J. and Sir Martin Nourse agreed.
   See also *Welton v. North Cornwall District Council* [1997] 1 W.L.R. 570 at 580E-F where Rose L.J., having remarked on the varying use of assumption of responsibility, the fair just and reasonable test and reliance on policy considerations said:
   "But I confess that I am unable to discern in the authorities any material difference attributable to that difference in language, either in the route charted or in the ultimate destination, when the existence of a duty of care is recognised or denied."
[53] [1992] 2 N.Z.L.R. 282.

case did the investigators for the insurers owe a duty of care to the plaintiff. All five judges favoured a modified version of the *Anns* two-stage test.

2–055   Cooke P. (with whom Hardie Boys J. agreed) formulated the correct approach in 15 propositions.[54] He began by stating (it is submitted quite correctly):

> "A broad two-stage approach or any other approach is only a framework, a more or less methodical way of tackling a problem. How it is formulated should not matter in the end. Ultimately the exercise can only be a balancing one and the important object is that all relevant factors be weighed. There is no escape from the truth that, whatever formula be used, the outcome in a grey area case has to be determined by judicial judgment. Formulae can help to organise thinking but they cannot provide answers."

The considerations which Cooke P. set out in the propositions which followed were familiar common law principles of equal validity both in England and New Zealand, although their application may vary according to the differing social conditions of the two countries. It is also fairly clear that the actual decision reached would have been the same in England, whether reached by reference to the threefold test, the incremental approach or by applying the extended *Hedley Byrne* principle, or some combination of them.[55]

2–056   In *Invercargill City Council v. Hamlin*,[56] the New Zealand Court of Appeal faced substantially the same issue as had confronted the House of Lords in *Murphy v. Brentwood D.C.*[57] In 1972, the plaintiff purchased a newly constructed house. The foundations were defective and gave rise to minor problems for the first 17 years. Then in 1989, the back door stuck badly and the plaintiff commissioned a report, which revealed the defective foundations. In 1990, the plaintiff commenced proceedings against the council for negligence by their building inspector in having approved the foundations in 1972. The New Zealand Court of Appeal held that the council was liable in negligence to the plaintiff.[58] In coming to the opposite decision from the House of Lords in *Murphy*, the court drew attention to the respects in which social factors, economic factors and the legislative framework prevailing in New Zealand differed from that in England. Cooke P. also commented at a more general level on the divergences between the Commonwealth jurisdictions.[59]

2–057   The Privy Council upheld the decision of the New Zealand Court of Appeal.[60] In delivering the opinion of the Privy Council Lord Lloyd stated that this branch

---

[54] *ibid.* at 294–299.
[55] The New Zealand Court of Appeal applied a broadly similar approach in *Fleming v. Securities Commission* [1995] 2 N.Z.L.R. 514, in which the Commission was held to owe no duty of care to investors who suffered loss. See the reasoning of Richardson J. (with whom most members of the court agreed) at 527–533.
[56] [1994] 3 N.Z.L.R. 513. Discussed by I. N. Duncan Wallace, "No Somersault after Murphy: New Zealand follows Canada" in (1995) 111 L.Q.R. 285.
[57] [1991] 1 A.C. 398.
[58] The limitation aspect is dealt with in para. 1–145, above.
[59] [1994] 3 N.Z.L.R. 513 at 523:
> "While the disharmony may be regrettable, it is inevitable now that the Commonwealth jurisdictions have gone on their own paths without taking English decisions as the invariable starting point. The ideal of a uniform common law has proved as unattainable as any ideal of a uniform civil law. It could not survive the independence of the United States; constitutional evolution in the Commonwealth has done the rest. What of course is both desirable and feasible, within the limits of judicial and professional time, is to take into account and learn from decisions in other jurisdictions."
[60] *Invercargill City Council v. Hamlin* [1996] A.C. 624. Discussed by I. N. Duncan Wallace, "No surprises in the Privy Council" in (1996) 112 L.Q.R. 369.

of the law of negligence was not suited to a single monolithic solution. He noted that in New Zealand community standards and expectations demanded the imposition of a duty of care on local authorities and builders alike to ensure compliance with local byelaws. He placed particular emphasis on the different statutory backgrounds in England and New Zealand. In particular, New Zealand had no legislation corresponding to our Defective Premises Act 1972. It can thus be seen that the application of broadly the same common law principles leads to opposing results in England and New Zealand.

Canada. In 1984, in *City of Kamloops v. Nielson*,[61] the Supreme Court of   **2–058**
Canada by a majority of 3:2 followed both the general approach and the actual decision of the House of Lords in *Anns*. It held a local authority liable in tort for failing to ensure compliance with building byelaws. In giving the majority judgment Wilson J. assessed an array of relevant factors (the distinction between acts and omissions, the area of local authorities' discretion, the nature of the loss, the floodgates argument and so forth) before concluding that a duty of care should be imposed. The Supreme Court of Canada continues to apply the *Anns* test.[62]

Following the change of tack by the House of Lords in *Murphy*, the Canadian   **2–059**
Supreme Court again had to consider whether or not to follow England. In *Canadian National Railway Co. v. Norsk Pacific Steamship Co. Ltd*,[63] the plaintiff railway company was the principal user, but not the owner of a bridge negligently damaged by the defendant. The plaintiff claimed its economic loss suffered through re-routing traffic while the bridge was being repaired. The Canadian Supreme Court by a majority of 4:3 held that the plaintiff was entitled to recover. The principal judgment for the majority was given by McLachlin J. with whom L'Heureux-Dube and Cory JJ. concurred. McLachlin J. defined the underlying problem as the search for a principled mechanism to limit liability for foreseeable economic loss flowing from negligence. She reviewed the different approaches adopted in the principal civil and common law jurisdictions. She rejected the House of Lords' approach in *Murphy* as unduly restrictive.[64]

McLachlin J. summarised the proper approach in these terms: **2–060**

"The matter may be put thus: before the law will impose liability there must be a connection between the defendant's conduct and plaintiff's loss which makes it just for the defendant to indemnify the plaintiff. In contract, the contractual relationship provides this link. In trust, it is the fiduciary obligation which establishes the necessary connection. In tort, the equivalent notion is proximity. Proximity may consist of various forms of closeness—physical, circumstantial, causal or assumed—which serve to identify the categories of case in which liability lies."[65]

After discussing the numerous disparate factors relevant to determining whether there is sufficient proximity, McLachlin J. continued:

---

[61] (1984) 10 D.L.R. (4th) 641.
[62] See, for example, *Martel Building Ltd v. The Queen* (2000) 193 D.L.R. (4th) 1: no duty of care owed by tenant to landlord to conduct negotiations for renewal of lease with reasonable skill and care. Perhaps surprisingly, the Court found that there was proximity, but that the existence of a duty of care was negated by ancillary policy factors which precluded the extension of the law of tort into commercial negotiations. This decision is discussed at (2001) 117 L.Q.R. 351: see Duncan Wallace Q.C., "Tender Call Obligations in Canada" (Duncan Wallace Q.C.).
[63] (1992) 91 D.L.R. (4th) 289.
[64] See para. 2–43, above.
[65] (1992) 91 D.L.R. (4th) 289 at 369.

"While proximity is critical to establishing the right to recover pure economic loss in tort, it does not always indicate liability. It is a necessary but not necessarily sufficient condition of liability. Recognising that proximity is itself concerned with policy, the approach adopted in *Kamloops* (parallelled by the second branch of *Anns*), requires the court to consider the purposes served by permitting recovery as well as whether there are any residual policy considerations which call for a limitation on liability. This permits courts to reject liability for pure economic loss where indicated by policy reasons not taken into account in the proximity analysis."[66]

2-061　　　In Canada, as in England, if a case falls within the *Hedley Byrne* principle, the court will impose a duty of care without any wider consideration of the policy factors. This is illustrated by *Edgeworth Construction Ltd v. N.D. Lea and Associates Ltd.*[67] The plaintiff successfully tendered to build a section of highway in British Columbia. The plaintiff lost money on the project, allegedly due to errors in the specifications and construction drawings. The construction contract excluded any liability on the part of the employer (the province) in respect of representations in the tender documents. The Canadian Supreme Court declined to strike out the plaintiff's claim against the engineering firm which had prepared the tender documents, including the specifications and construction drawings. The Court held that the claim fell directly within the *Hedley Byrne* principle. The defendants had provided information in the tender package for use by a definable group of persons. The plaintiff reasonably relied upon that information in preparing its bid. The contract between the plaintiff and the province, which protected the province from liability, was not inconsistent with a duty of care on the part of the engineers towards the plaintiffs. At a superficial level, it may be said that this decision is contrary to *Pacific Associates Inc. v. Baxter*,[68] decided by the English Court of Appeal. In reality, however, the appellate courts were applying the same legal principles in both cases, but the circumstances and contractual matrices were different.[69] The Court did, however, strike out the claim against individual engineers who had fixed their seals to the design documents.[70]

2-062　　　More recently, the Canadian Supreme Court has had to consider the question of tortious liability for defects in buildings. In *Winnipeg Condominium Corp. v. Bird Construction Co.*,[71] the defendant constructed an apartment building, which the plaintiff subsequently acquired. Defects in the cladding emerged, and in order to avoid accidents the plaintiff carried out remedial works at substantial cost. The

---

[66] *ibid.* at 371. The Canadian Supreme Court adopted a similar approach in *Bow Valley Husky (Bermuda) Ltd v. Saint John Shipbuilding Ltd* (1997) 153 D.L.R. (4th) 385. In that case the hirers of an oil rig suffered economic loss, as a result of a defective part which caused a fire on the rig. Their action in negligence against the manufacturers was dismissed. McLachlin J. (with whom La Forest J. agreed) held that a prima facie duty of care arose, but that this was negatived by policy considerations, in particular the problem of indeterminate liability: *ibid.* at 404–413. For discussion and analysis of this judgment see Feldthusen, "Dynamic change to maritime law—gracious retreat on relational economic loss", (1998) 6 Tort L.Rev. 164.
[67] (1993) 107 D.L.R. (4th) 169.
[68] [1990] 1 Q.B. 993; see further Chap. 8, para. 8–106.
[69] In the English case the plaintiff contractors had more extensive remedies available against the employers and on the facts there was no assumption of responsibility by the engineers towards the plaintiffs.
[70] This aspect of the decision is discussed further at para. 2–89, below.
[71] (1995) 121 D.L.R. (4th) 193.

Court declined to strike out the claim. In coming to this conclusion the Court declined to follow the specific decisions of the House of Lords in *D. & F. Estates Ltd v. Church Commissioners for England*[72] and *Murphy v. Brentwood D.C.*[73] The Court held that policy considerations militated in favour of imposing a duty of care. The classification of the claim as economic loss carried less weight than it would in England, especially since the building defect before rectification was a source of danger. In *Ingles v. City of Toronto*,[74] the Canadian Supreme Court held that a local authority which inspected a building's underpinnings owed a duty of care to the owner of the building, applying the *Anns* test.

Australia. As set out earlier, the incremental approach adopted by the House **2–063** of Lords in *Murphy* has its origins in Australia.[75] However, in the 1980s and 1990s, the Australian courts made more use of the concept of proximity as the vehicle for determining whether or not a duty of care exists.[76] Proximity might be established by precedent, namely if the parties stood in a relationship which was the subject of previous judicial decision. Absent any binding decision which is in point, a consideration of proximity enabled the court to assess and weigh all those factors which in England would be considered in applying the threefold test. This approach was exemplified in *Bryan v. Maloney*.[77] The defendant built a house with inadequate foundations on clay soil. The High Court of Australia held that the defendant was liable in negligence to a subsequent purchaser for the cost of remedial works. After a full review and weighing of the policy factors, the court held that sufficient proximity was established between the builder and the subsequent purchaser. The fact that the plaintiff's loss was economic did not justify denying recovery. In particular, recognition of a duty of care to avoid economic loss suffered by reason of defects to the house did not impose liability "in an indeterminate amount for an indeterminate time to an indeterminate class".[78] Nor did the imposition of such a duty unduly limit the builder's legitimate pursuit of his own economic advantage.[79]

In *Hill v. Van Erp*,[80] the High Court of Australia considered the vexed question **2–064** of whether a testator's solicitor owes a duty of care to the intended beneficiary. By a majority of 5 to 1 the Court held that the testator's solicitor does owe such a duty. Despite the mass of jurisprudence devoted to this topic throughout the common law world, the Court did not find its task an easy one. Brennan C.J., Gaudron and Gummow JJ. rejected the English route of expanding the *Hedley Byrne* principle to embrace the relationship between solicitor and intended

---

[72] [1989] A.C. 177; see further Chap. 8, para. 8–106.
[73] [1991] 1 A.C. 398.
[74] (2000) 183 D.L.R. (4th) 193.
[75] *Sutherland Shire Council v. Heyman* (1984–1985) 157 C.L.R. 424 at 481. See para. 2–38, above.
[76] Indeed the High Court of Australia came to treat "proximity" as the governing test for the existence and scope of a duty of care. The authorities are helpfully set out and analysed by Vaggelas, "Proximity, economic loss and the High Court of Australia" in (1997) 5 Tort L.Rev. 127.
[77] (1995) 182 C.L.R. 609, discussed by Duncan Wallace Q.C. (1997) 113 L.Q.R. 355. See also *Gala v. Preston* (1991) 172 C.L.R. 243.
[78] *ibid.* at 618 and 623, *per* Mason C.J., Deane J. and Gaudron J. quoting Cardozo C.J. in *Ultramares Corp. v. Touche* (1931) 174 N.E. 441 at 444.
[79] *ibid.* at 623–624, *per* Mason C.J., Deane J. and Gaudron J.
[80] (1995–1997) 188 C.L.R. 159.

beneficiary. The other two members of the majority, Dawson J. and Toohey J., considered that there were both assumption of responsibility and reliance in the more general sense. This case (like *White v. Jones* in England) also provided an opportunity for the highest appellate court to reappraise its approach to duty of care problems. The court recognised the limitations of "proximity" as an universal test for determining the existence and scope of a duty of care, but the majority (of the majority) were not prepared to abandon that approach. Dawson J. said:

> " . . . the requirement of proximity is at least a useful means of expressing the proposition that in the law of negligence reasonable foreseeability of harm may not be enough to establish a duty of care. Something more is required and it is described as proximity. Proximity in that sense expresses the result of a process of reasoning rather than the process itself, but it remains a useful term because it signifies that the process of reasoning must be undertaken. But to hope that proximity can describe a common element underlying all those categories of case in which a duty of care is recognised is to expect more of the term than it can provide."[81]

Toohey J. said that "the general conception [of proximity] must be taken as controlling the circumstances which might otherwise, by application of reasonable foreseeability alone, give rise to a duty of care".[82] Gaudron J. also found proximity a satisfactory analytical tool for resolving the duty of care problem. However, Brennan C.J. analysed all relevant factors without reference to proximity. Gummow J. found proximity to be of limited use; he noted Fleming's dismissal of proximity as "the currently fashionable touchstone of duty".[83] If "proximity" survived, it was not in good health.[84]

2–065   The marked decline in the fortunes of "proximity" as a useful test continued in the decision of the High Court of Australia in *Perre v. Apand Pty Ltd.*[85] The defendant sold potato seeds to a farmer in South Australia, who planted them. The resulting potato crop was infected with bacterial wilt. The plaintiffs were neighbouring farmers who were unable to export their crops to Western Australia, which banned the entry of potatoes grown within 20 miles of an outbreak of bacterial wilt. They suffered financial loss as a result. The loss suffered was accepted by the defendant to have been reasonably foreseeable and the defendant in fact knew that persons such as the plaintiffs would suffer such loss in the

---

[81] *ibid.* at 177–178.
[82] *ibid.* at 188.
[83] *ibid.* at 237.
[84] *ibid.* at 238 of the judgment of Kirby J. in *Pyrenees Shire Council v. Day* [1998] H.C.A. 3 (reported at (1998) 192 C.L.R. 330):

"Finally, in *Hill v. Van Erp*, four members of this Court recognised the limitations in the usefulness of the notion of proximity in determining individual claims to the existence of a duty of care enforceable at law. When to these voices is added the consistent criticism of "proximity" expressed for a decade by Brennan C.J., it is tolerably clear that proximity's reign in this Court, at least as a universal identifier of the existence of a duty of care at common law, has come to an end."

(The four members of the High Court of Australia in *Hill v. Van Erp* to whom Kirby J. was referring were Dawson J. at (1997) 188 C.L.R. 159 at 177–178, Toohey J. at 188–189, McHugh J. at 210–211 and Gummow J. at 237–239. As an example of the views of Brennan C.J. Kirby J. cited *Bryan v Maloney* (1995) 182 C.L.R. 609 at 653. Kirby J. explained what he meant in the passage quoted in *Modbury Triangle Shopping Centre Pty Ltd v. Anzil* [2000] H.C.A. 61 at para. 60. The decision in *Pyrenees* is discussed at (1998) 114 L.Q.R. 377, *per* Lunney).

[85] [1999] H.C.A. 36, reported in (1999) 164 A.L.R. 606.

circumstances. It was held that the defendant owed a duty of care to the plaintiffs in respect of their losses. In reaching that conclusion the seven members of the court addressed the question of the appropriate approach to novel cases. There was no unanimity of approach, however. McHugh J., who had long been sceptical as to the value of proximity as a guide,[86] said:

" . . . since the fall of proximity, the court has not made any authoritative statement as to what is to be the correct approach for determining the duty of care question. Perhaps none is possible. At all events, the differing views of the members of this court in the present case suggest that the search for a unifying element may be a long one."[87]

He went on to ask:

" . . . where does one find a conceptual framework that will promote predictability and continuity and at the same time facilitate change in the law when it is needed? I think that the existing legal materials already contain part of the answer. We have the established categories, a considerable body of case law and the useful concept of reasonably foreseeability. If a case falls outside an established category, but the defendant should reasonably have foreseen that its conduct would cause harm to the plaintiff, we have only to ask whether the reasons that called for or denied a duty in other (usually similar) cases require the imposition of a duty in the instant case. No doubt that may sometimes mean that, whether or not a duty is imposed at a particular time, will depend on the extent to which the case law has progressed to that time. But that is the way of the common law, the judges preferring to go 'from case to case, like the ancient Mediterranean mariners, hugging the coast from point to point, and avoiding the dangers of the open sea of system or science'.[88] It is not an approach that appeals to grand theorists who prefer to decide cases by general principles applicable to all cases. But in an area of law such as awarding damages for negligently inflicting economic loss, which is still developing and which has been recently cast aside from any unifying principle, there is no alternative to a cautious development of the law on a case by case basis."[89]

Gummow J. saw the absence of a "simple formula which can mask the necessity for examination of the particular facts" as a benefit, allowing the development of a coherent body of precedent against which the facts of particular cases can be judged, not by "the imposition of a fixed system of categories", but identifying relevant "salient features" and considering whether, allowing for the operation of appropriate "control mechanisms", the relationship gave rise to a duty of care.[90] Australia appears to have moved towards a combination of the incremental approach with a more explicit recognition of policy concerns.

---

[86] See his dissenting judgment in *Hill v. Van Erp* (1995–1997) 188 C.L.R. 159 at 210–211.
[87] [1999] H.C.A. 36 at 76; (1999) 164 A.L.R. 606 at 624. See also, *per* Gaudron J. at 614–615, *per* Kirby J. at 683–684 and, *per* Hayne J. at pages 697–698.
[88] Lord Wright, "The Study of Law", (1938) 54 L.Q.R. 185 at 196.
[89] (1999) 164 A.L.R. 606 at 629–630. See further McHugh J.'s judgment in *Crimmins v. Stevedoring Industry Finance Committee* [1999] H.C.A. 59 para. 78; reported in (1999) 167 A.L.R. 1 at 19–20.
[90] *ibid.* at 659–660. Gummow J.'s reference to "salient features" was taken from the judgment of Stephen J. in *Caltex Oil (Australia) Pty Ltd v. The Dredge Willemstad* (1976) 136 C.L.R. 529 at 576–577.

(ix) *Analysis*

2–066   **The problem.** If the only claims before the courts were in respect of personal injuries caused by swallowing snails lurking in opaque ginger beer bottles then the law would have been settled by *Donoghue v. Stevenson.*[91] There would be no need for the courts to search for principles upon which to base their decisions in novel situations. That is not the case. Novel claims come before the courts and have to be decided. However, the search for guiding principles or a useful test has not resulted in an answer which commands widespread acceptance.[92] Members of the House of Lords and Privy Council appear to proceed on different bases[93] and there is no unanimity between (or to an extent within) the major Commonwealth jurisdictions. This is not to say that the same result would not be reached in a particular case by the application of any of the different tests and approaches propounded in recent years by the House of Lords, nor in different Commonwealth jurisdictions, although, as the differing status of *Anns v. Merton LBC*[94] demonstrates, that would not always be the case.

2–067   **Limited role of statements of general principle.** It is submitted that the starting point should be to establish the purpose for which statements of general principle or of the appropriate test to be applied are made. That purpose is to try to provide guidance as to the approach to novel claims, based upon analysis of existing authority. The purpose is not to provide a test against which the body of existing authority should be tested for consistency or orthodoxy. Moreover, the need to resort to general principle should be limited. It is now nearly 70 years since the decision in *Donoghue v. Stevenson*[95] and 40 since *Hedley Byrne and Co. Ltd v. Heller & Partners Ltd.*[96] It should not be necessary and is not necessary to consider every claim in negligence from first principles. In many cases, indeed most, the existence of a duty of care is not in issue or falls to be decided by the application of what is a substantial body of existing authority.[97] The purpose of general tests or statements of principle should be to provide, or

---

[91] [1932] A.C. 562.
[92]   "The fundamental problem is that a single unifying principle for liability in negligence, easy to apply and predictable in outcome, has proved elusive. Differing theories hold the legal stage for a time. But then their defects and inadequacies are exposed. None has won permanent acceptance. The best that observers of this branch of the common law have been able to offer is the cautionary advice to study the cases in the hope of deriving guidance from analogies. However, in order to do this it is necessary to have some concept of the principle by which the analogy is to be discovered."
per Kirby J. in *Pyrenees Shire Council v. Day* [1998] H.C.A. 3 at 189 (reported in (1998) 192 C.L.R. 330).
[93] See, *e.g.* "The random element of their lordships' infallible judgments: an economic and comparative analysis of the tort of negligence from *Anns* to *Murphy*" by Markesinis and Deakin in (1992) 55 M.L.R. 619. It is pointed out that the House of Lords has considered "duty of care" issues on 12 occasions in the preceding 15 years. It is argued that the decisions show "an unsystematic and not fully thought-out series of shifts", and that inadequate consideration has been given to economic factors, foreign law and academic literature.
[94] [1978] A.C. 728.
[95] [1932] A.C. 562.
[96] [1964] A.C. 465.
[97] See for example *Perrett v. Collins* [1998] 2 Lloyd's Rep. 255, per Hobhouse L.J., at 263, col. 2, explaining that the decision of the Houses of Lords in *Marc Rich and Co. A.G. v. Bishop Rock Marine Co. Ltd* [1996] A.C. 211 (see para. 2–51, above) did not throw into doubt decided cases as to liability in negligence for personal injury and death.

at least to assist in the provision of, answers in truly novel situations, where there is no direct or closely analogous decision.

Role of authority. This suggests that the judicial decision making process 2–068 should not usually consist of a series of headings taken from statements of general principle or tests with two, three or more stages, but should begin with careful analysis of the facts relied upon as giving rise to the particular duty of care coupled with investigation of the existing authorities to see whether there is any direct or close authority which determines the answer.[98] This not only accords with the doctrine of precedent, but enables judges to reach consistent and predictable decisions. It also recognises the limits of general statements or tests as useful guides to the decision-making process as opposed to statements of the results of that process.[99]

Need for guiding principles. However, there is still a need to establish 2–069 guiding principles, not just because there should be some coherence and consistency between different decisions, but in order to afford guidance in truly novel situations.[1] This introduces an inevitable tension between the need to avoid formulations so short as to afford no practical guidance and the recitation of numerous principles to which different weight will be given by different judges

---

[98] "There is I suspect a danger here of the method of approach becoming more important than the objective. The objective is to ascertain whether it is appropriate that there be a duty of care in the particular case. So long as that objective is realised, I cannot think that it is of great moment whether it is attained by a two-stage test, an incremental approach, or some combination of the two. What matters is that there is an identification, an analysis and a weighing of all the competing considerations . . . "

(*South Pacific Manufacturing Co Ltd v. New Zealand Security Consultants and Investigations Ltd* [1992] 2 N.Z.L.R. 282, *per* Hardie Boys J., at 316 lines 12–18).

[99] See, *e.g.* the observations of Hobhouse L.J. in *Perrett v. Collins* [1998] 2 Lloyd's Rep. 255 at 258, col. 1, where he spoke of "the dangers of substituting for clear criteria, criteria which are incapable of precise definition and involve what can only be described as an element of subjective assessment by the Court: such ultimately subjective assessments tend inevitably to lead to uncertainty and anomaly which can be avoided by a more principled approach".

[1] See, *e.g. Perrett v. Collins* [1998] 2 Lloyd's Rep. 255 at 273, *per* Buxton L.J., col.1:

"For my part, if it were literally the case that considerations determining whether a duty exists in law do indeed collapse into a pragmatic decision whether there should be a duty in the particular circumstances, then I would see little role for an Appellate Court in elucidating that question. Deciding pragmatic issues, especially issues of fairness and reasonableness, would seem to be eminently a task for a first instance Judge, with which an Appellate Court will only interfere on very limited and special grounds, which do not include disagreement with the Judge's conclusion."

See also para. 240 of the judgment of Kirby J. in *Pyrenees Shire Council v. Day* [1998] H.C.A. 3 (reported in (1998) 192 C.L.R. 330):

"whatever the defects of the notions of 'foreseeability', 'proximity' and the imprecision of the policy evaluation inherent in measurement of 'fairness', 'justice' and 'reasonableness', some guidance must be given by the Court as to how the duty question is to be answered when it is contested in a particular case. Otherwise, confronted with a suggested new category, lawyers in their offices and courts in Australia would have no instruction for their task of reasoning by analogy from past categories. It would then be all too easy to declare that those categories are closed, leaving all future extensions to the unpredictable vagaries of specific legislation. This would amount to an abdication of the function of common law courts. Legislatures simply cannot anticipate the myriad of circumstances presenting with the assertion that a duty of care is, or is not, to be imposed by the common law. To perform the task of reasoning by analogy, accepting or rejecting new categories, the individual affected, the lawyer advising and the court deciding have a right to know at least the general approach which they should adopt in order to resolve the controversy." (footnotes omitted) in different cases.[2] The difficulty with the threefold test and with the extended *Hedley Byrne* principle, as with the test of "proximity" in Australia, is that they can amount to little more than statements that in law a particular duty of care exists or does not exist. They do not explain why that result is reached.[3] It is therefore not surprising that the different tests should lead to the same result,[4] although it may be easier to be led astray by one test than another.[5]

2–070   **The correct approach to existing authority.** The solution should lie in the correct analysis of existing authority. What needs to be deduced is not so much the result on the facts of the particular decision, but which were the important facts and why they were important. This has two results. First, an informed understanding of existing authority should allow most cases to be decided in accordance with that authority or by close analogy to it. Second, it should elicit more general principles to which recourse must be had in truly novel situations.[6] A good example of how this has been achieved in practice is to be found in decisions as to whether accountants owe duties of care to third parties for negligent misstatements (either in accounts or otherwise). Building on the dissenting judgment of Denning L.J. in *Candler v. Crane, Christmas and Co.*,[7] in *James McNaughton Group Ltd v. Hicks Anderson*,[8] the Court of Appeal identified

---

[2] See, *e.g. Crimmins v. Stevedoring Industry Finance Committee* [1999] H.C.A. 59 (reported in (1999) 167 A.L.R. 1, per McHugh J. at para. 77 (page 20):
"Since the demise of any unifying principle for the determination of the duty of care and the general acknowledgement of the importance of frank discussion of policy factors, the resolution of novel cases has increasingly been made by reference to a 'checklist' of policy factors (See Stapleton, 'Duty of Care Factors: a Selection from the Judicial Menus' in Cane and Stapleton (eds), *The Law of Obligations—Essays in Celebration of John Fleming* (1998), p. 59.) The result has been the proliferation of 'factors' that may indicate or negative the existence of a duty, but without a chain of reasoning linking these factors with the ultimate conclusion. Left unchecked, this approach becomes nothing more than the exercise of a discretion—like the process of sentencing, where the final result is determined by the individual 'judge's synthesis of all the various aspects' (*R. v. Williscroft* [1975] V.R. 292 at 300, *per* Adam and Crockett J.J.)."
[3] See, *e.g.* the passages from the speeches of Lord Bridge and Lord Oliver in *Caparo Industries plc v. Dickman* [1990] 2 A.C. 605 set out in paras 2–32 and 2–33, above as to the three-stage test. In *Phelps v. Hillingdon LBC* [2000] 3 W.L.R. 776, Lord Slynn said at 791 that "assumption of responsibility" means simply that the law recognises that there is a duty of care. It is not so much that responsibility is assumed as that it is recognised or imposed by the law. As May L.J. said in *Merrett v. Babb* [2001] E.W.C.A. Civ. 214, para. 41; [2001] 3 W.L.R. 3 at 18B:
"I also think that it is reaching for the moon—and not required by authority—to expect to accommodate every circumstance which may arise within a single short abstract formulation. The question in each case is whether the law recognises that there is a duty of care."
For criticism of the value of the "proximity" test in Australia see paras 2–64 and 2–65, above and *Hercules Managements Ltd v. Ernst & Young* (1997) 146 D.L.R. (4th) 577 at para. 23, *per* La Forest J.: " . . . the term 'proximity' itself is nothing more than a label expressing a result, judgment or conclusion; it does not, in and of itself, provide a principled basis on which to make a legal determination."
[4] See para. 2–52, above.
[5] See, *e.g.* Lord Hoffmann in *Stovin v. Wise* [1996] A.C. 923 at 949A-D (partly set out in para. 2–52, above).
[6] See, *e.g.* the judgment of Lord Philips M.R. in *Watson v. British Boxing Board of Control Ltd* [2001] 2 W.L.R. 1256. Faced with a novel claim, Lord Philips first identified the material facts, then analysed the authorities to deduce their underlying principles, and then applied those principles to the facts.
[7] [1951] 2 K.B. 164: see paras. 2–110 to 2–113, below.
[8] [1991] 2 Q.B. 113.

a number of factors which were likely to be relevant when deciding whether a duty of care was owed.[9] It is submitted that this level of analysis is more valuable than attempts to state principles which apply in all circumstances.[10]

The underlying principles. That is not to say that there are not underlying principles to the law of negligence. There are. They include the following: **2–071**

(1) A tortious duty of care is imposed by law on A in relation to B. A does not himself agree to the imposition of the duty, although it may result from his voluntary acts or agreement. A finding that A owes B a duty of care is therefore a legal conclusion drawn from the relevant facts.

(2) At the heart of liability for negligence is that A should reasonably have foreseen that carelessness on his part could result in damage to B or to a "relevant" class to which B belongs.[11] It does not follow that A owes a duty of care to B, but absent reasonable foreseeability of damage, he will not do so.

(3) While the careless infliction of reasonably foreseeable physical injury or of reasonably foreseeable damage to goods or other property requires to be justified if A is not to be required to compensate B for having inflicted it, that is not the case where the damage suffered does not involve personal injury or damage to goods or other property.[12]

(4) In the latter case (which covers both "pure economic loss"[13] and the failure to confer a benefit), the law of tort recognises both the difficulties in imposing a potentially wide liability on A[14] and that it may be entirely

---

[9] See Chap. 15, paras 15–062 to 15–070.

[10] However, if such an approach is to be adopted, it is important to guard against over-restrictive categorisation: see Stapleton, "Duty of care and economic loss: a wider agenda" in (1991) 107 L.Q.R. 249.

[11] If A is driving a car and the duty of care requires A to take care to avoid causing personal injury or death, then the "relevant" class would be other road users, passengers, pedestrians, etc. If A is making a statement, then the "relevant" class will not necessarily extend to all those whom A should reasonably foresee might act to their detriment in reliance on the statement. "Relevant" here is not definitive, but indicative of the need for further analysis.

[12] See, *e.g.*, *per* Lord Oliver in *Murphy v. Brentwood D.C.* [1991] 1 A.C. 398 at 487B-C:
"The infliction of physical injury to the person or property of another universally requires to be justified. The causing of economic loss does not. If it is to be categorised as wrongful it is necessary to find some factor beyond the mere occurrence of the loss and the fact that this occurrence could be foreseen."
But see the comment of Cooke P. in *South Pacific Manufacturing Co. Ltd v. New Zealand Security Consultants and Investigations Ltd* [1992] 2 N.Z.L.R. 282 and 296:
"The first concern of the law is naturally personal safety. Injury to the person is a kind of damage in a class of its own. Or at least most people would, I think, say so. On the other hand, a plaintiff awarded damages for harm to property is being compensated essentially for economic loss. It would be a crude system of law that drew a vital distinction for this purpose between tangible and intangible property interests"

[13] "Pure economic loss" now includes damage to a building or chattel caused by an inherent defect if A has supplied that building or chattel to B.

[14] See Cardozo C.J. in *Ultramares Corp. v. Touche* (1931) 174 N.E. 441 and in *Wagner v. International Railway Co.* (1921) 232 N.Y. 176.

legitimate and consistent with public policy for A to cause "pure economic loss"[15] or to fail to confer a benefit.

(5) Whatever the nature of the damage, a duty of care should be found where, and only where, it is reasonable for A to be liable to compensate B for having negligently caused the damage in question.[16]

It is not suggested that these underlying principles provide a mechanism for deciding whether a duty of care is owed in a novel situation. They do, however, provide some assistance in understanding decisions on particular facts and in identifying which facts were important.

2-072   The last of the underlying principles identified, namely that a duty of care should be imposed where it is reasonable for A to be liable to compensate B for having negligently caused the damage in question, can be criticised for being hopelessly vague and for inviting individual judges to decide particular cases according to their personal assessment of the reasonable outcome.[17] However, in this context reasonableness is not assessed by the judge solely on the basis of his own, personal criteria. Rather, existing authority is to be seen as representing "the cumulative experience of the judiciary of the actual consequences of lack of

---

[15] See, e.g. Lord Reid in *Dorset Yacht Co. Ltd v. Home Office* [1970] A.C. 1004 at 1027B:
"For example, causing economic loss is a different matter; for one thing, it is often caused by deliberate action. Competition involves traders being entitled to damage their rivals' interests by promoting their own, and there is a long chapter of the law determining in what circumstances owners of land can and in what circumstances they may not use their proprietary rights so as to injure their neighbours."
See also *Martel Building Ltd v. The Queen* (2000) 196 D.L.R. (4th) 1, paras 62–67 (discussed in para. 2–58, n. 62, above).
[16] See, e.g. Lord Reid in *Hedley Byrne and Co. Ltd v. Heller & Partners Ltd* [1964] A.C. 465 at 482 ("The law ought so far as possible to reflect the standards of the reasonable man. . . ").
In *Frost v. Chief Constable of South Yorkshire* [1999] 2 A.C. 455 at 495B, when considering whether to recognise a duty of care to protect from psychiatric harm in the absence of physical injury (an area of law in which the courts adopt a more restrictive approach akin to that adopted to cases of pure economic loss), Lord Steyn referred to "the man on the Underground". In *McFarlane v. Tayside Health Board* [2000] 2 A.C. 59 at 82B–C, Lord Steyn conducted a notional poll of commuters on the Underground when considering whether the parents of an unwanted but healthy child should recover damages for the cost of the child's upbringing.
[17] See, e.g. *Perre v. Apand Pty Ltd* [1999] H.C.A. 36 (reported in (1999) 164 A.L.R. 606 at para. 80 (p. 625), *per* McHugh J.:
"almost everyone would agree that courts should not impose a duty of care on a person unless it is fair, just and reasonable to do so. But attractive as concepts of fairness and justice may be in appellate courts, in law reform commissions, in the academy and among legislators, in many cases they are of little use, if they are of any use at all, to the practitioners and trial judges who must apply the law to concrete facts arising from real life activities. While the training and background of judges may lead them to agree as to what is fair or just in many cases, there are just as many cases where using such concepts as the criteria for duty would mean that "each judge would have a distinct tribunal in his own breast, the decisions of which would be as irregular and uncertain and various as the minds and tempers of mankind." *Donaldson v. Beckett* (1774) 2 Brown 129, *per* Lord Camden cited in "The Judge and Case Law" in Devlin, *The Judge* (1979) at 181. Lord Devlin was surely right when he said ("The Judge and Case Law" in Devlin, *The Judge* (1979) at 181):
"For a judge to decide fairly and convincingly every case that comes before him in the light only of his own sense of justice, he would have to be a superman. I doubt if there have ever been more than a handful of men on the bench who could do it, though doubtless there are slightly more who think that they could."

care in particular circumstances".[18] Reasonableness may underlie a decision that a manufacturer should owe a duty of care to a consumer who suffers personal injury as a result of a latent defect caused by the manufacturer's negligence,[19] and may be more explicitly stated as a factor in cases of negligent misstatement, where the reasonableness of the claimant's reliance will be relevant in determining whether he was owed a duty of care.[20]

Beyond such general statements, there is little to be gained in seeking to **2–073** enunciate universal principles which could provide practical assistance, for example, both in deciding whether a local authority owes a duty of care when assessing a child's educational needs and in deciding the extent to which an accountant who audits accounts or who makes a statement as to accounts (whether audited or management) at a meeting in the course of the takeover of his client company owes a duty of care. The situations are far removed from each other and the factors which emerge from the authorities have little in common.[21] Those factors, rather than a test of assumption of responsibility or the threefold test, provide the most useful and principled guidance when deciding whether a particular duty of care was owed.[22]

Nevertheless, the threefold test, the extended *Hedley Byrne* principle, based on **2–074** assumption of responsibility, and the incremental approach continue to be invoked and applied. It is therefore appropriate to say something about each.

The question of proximity. The concept of proximity is protean. In cases of **2–075** personal injury or damage to property, it may arise as a direct consequence of foreseeability of the harm.[23] In cases of pure economic loss, the purpose underlying the defendant's statements or actions is highly material in determining whether there was sufficient proximity. Indeed, this consideration was decisive in *Caparo Industries plc v. Dickman*,[24] in which the plaintiffs failed on proximity because the manner in which they used the accounts was not within the "purpose" for which those accounts had been prepared, having regard in particular to the statutory context. This consideration was also decisive in leading to the different results in *James McNaughton Paper Group Ltd v. Hicks Anderson and*

---

[18] *Per* Lord Diplock in *Dorset Yacht Co. Ltd v. Home Office* [1970] A.C. 1004 at 1058. Lord Diplock was discussing the judicial approach to questions of public policy when deciding whether a duty of care was owed, but the principle is the same.

[19] *Donoghue v. Stevenson* [1932] A.C. 562; see also para 2–22, above.

[20] See, *e.g.* Chap. 15, para. 15–70, below.

[21] In relation to local authorities see paras 2–75 to 2–85, below and in relation to accountants, see Chap. 15, paras 15–076 to 15–079.

[22] See, *e.g.* Sir Brian Neill in *Bank of Credit and Commerce International (Overseas) Ltd v. Price Waterhouse (No.2)* [1998] P.N.L.R. 564 at 5876D:

"The threefold test and the assumption of responsibility test indicate the criteria which have to be satisfied if liability is to attach. But the authorities also provide some guidance as to the factors which are to be taken into account in deciding whether these criteria are met."

His lordship then went on to list various factors (see also his judgment in *James McNaughton Paper Group Ltd v. Hicks Anderson* [1991] 2 Q.B. 113 at 125–127 discussed in Chap. 15, paras 15–002 to 15–072).

[23] However, if the claimant is one of a vast number of persons who are foreseeably at risk of personal injury/death, the claimant could still fail for lack of proximity (*Hill v. Chief Constable of West Yorkshire* [1989] A.C. 53) and special factors apply to claims for psychiatric injury or "nervous shock" (*Alcock v. Chief Constable of South Yorkshire Police* [1992] 1 A.C. 310 and *Frost v. Chief Constable of South Yorkshire Police* [1999] 2 A.C. 455).

[24] [1990] 2 A.C. 605. See Chap. 15, paras 15–053 to 15–061.

Co.[25] and *Morgan Crucible plc v. Hill Samuel and Co. Ltd.*[26] The underlying purpose of the defendant's functions is also relevant to the "just and reasonable" question,[27] discussed in the next paragraph. In terms of the development of the law of negligence, proximity served a useful purpose in focusing attention on the need to show more than foreseeability of loss and an absence of policy considerations if a duty of care, particularly in relation to pure economic loss, were to be found. However, as the Australian experience demonstrates,[28] the concept can be overworked.

2–76   **The "just and reasonable" question.** This was an important feature of the House of Lords decision in *Governors of the Peabody Donation Fund v. Sir Lindsay Parkinson and Co. Ltd*[29] and of many subsequent duty of care decisions,[30] in particular *Marc Rich and Co. A.G. v. Bishop Rock Marine Co. Ltd.*[31] When considering this question, it is submitted that judges are not bringing to bear purely personal or subjective opinions.[32] They are considering the application of established legal principles to the unique facts of individual cases (this is implicit in the word "just") as well as purely pragmatic considerations.

2–077   **Policy considerations in the context of "just and reasonable".** In this context, the role of the courts in policy matters falls to be considered. A cautious approach was advocated in decisions such as *D. & F. Estates Ltd v. Church Commissioners for England*[33] and *Murphy v. Brentwood D.C.*[34] However, the courts do have to reach decisions which involve policy factors.[35] They should not and, on occasions, do not shy away from doing so. On one view the law of negligence itself is based upon judicial assessment of "the demands of society for protection from the carelessness of others"[36] so that to an extent every decision

---

[25] [1991] 2 Q.B. 113. Discussed in Chap. 15, paras 15–062 to 15–070.
[26] [1991] Ch. 295. Discussed in Chap. 15, para. 15–76. Further authorities on this area are discussed in paras 15–76 to 15–79.
[27] *Peabody Donation Fund v. Sir Lindsay Parkinson and Co. Ltd* [1985] A.C. 210.
[28] See paras 2–63 to 2–65, above.
[29] [1985] A.C. 210.
[30] See, *e.g.* the cases discussed in paras 2–29 to 2–34, above.
[31] [1996] 1 A.C. 211, discussed in para. 2–51, above.
[32] See para. 2–72, above.
[33] [1989] A.C. 177. See the speech of Lord Bridge at 210E:
    " . . . it is again, in my opinion, a dangerous course for the common law to embark upon the adoption of novel policies which it sees as instruments of social justice but to which, unlike the legislature, it is unable to set carefully defined limitations."
[34] [1991] 1 A.C. 398. See the speech of Lord Oliver at 491F–492B:
    "But, in any event, like my noble and learned friends, I think that the achievement of beneficial social purposes by the creation of entirely new liabilities is a matter which properly falls within the province of the legislature . . . I do not, for my part, think that it is right for the courts not simply to expand existing principles but to create at large new principles in order to fulfil a social need in an area of consumer protection which has already been perceived by the legislature but for which, presumably advisedly, it has not thought it necessary to provide."
[35] "The test for the existence of a duty of care which looks to what the court considers is fair, just and reasonable is of a different order from the test of proximity or neighbourhood with its further ingredient of foreseeability. The test of fairness is a test which may principally involve considerations of policy.": *per* Lord Clyde in *Phelps v. Hillingdon LBC* [2000] 3 W.L.R. 776 at 808G.
[36] *Per* Lord Pearce in *Hedley Byrne and Co. Ltd v. Heller & Partners Ltd* [1964] A.C. 465 at 536. See also, *per* Lord Denning M.R. in *Dorset Yacht Co. Ltd v. Home Office* [1969] 2 Q.B. 412 at 426B:
    "It is, I think, at bottom a matter of public policy, which we as judges must resolve. This talk of 'duty' or 'no duty' is simply a way of limiting the range of liability for negligence."
    In his speech in the House of Lords in the *Dorset Yacht Co.* case, [1970] A.C. 1004, at 1058D,

involves questions of policy. For example, it was the House of Lords and not Parliament which removed an advocate's immunity from suit.[37] In doing so, they were assisted by knowledge that the absence of such immunity in Canada had not led to the dire consequences predicted by those who sought to uphold the existing position.[38] The experience of other jurisdictions and systems of law can assist when broad questions of policy arise.[39] The courts are less well equipped to consider questions such as the cost of insurance[40] or the possible inhibiting consequences of finding a duty of care on those found to owe it, although, such arguments have not always found favour.[41] However, there is a danger that when considering such questions they will fall back on speculation and their own, subjective views.[42] An important safeguard, more usually mentioned when a duty

---

Lord Diplock agreed with this passage from the judgment of Lord Denning and then went on to explain how this policy decision was to be made by reference to existing authority.

[37] *Arthur J. Hall and Co. v. Simons* [2000] 3 W.L.R. 543. "The judges created the immunity and the judges should say that the grounds for maintaining it no longer exist": *per* Lord Hoffmann at 576C.

[38] *ibid.* at 553C-E, *per* Lord Steyn and 566H–567C, *per* Lord Hoffmann.

[39] See, *e.g.* Markesinis, Auby, Coester-Waltjen and Deakin, *Tortious Liability of Statutory Bodies* (Hart Publishing, 1999).

[40] See, *e.g.* Lord Hoffmann in *Frost v. Chief Constable of South Yorkshire* [1999] 2 A.C. 455, at 510D, where he admitted that he was "not in a position to form a view one way or the other" on the likely volume of claims and consequent burden on insurers and public funds if the claim for psychiatric damage were allowed. However, see *per* Lord Steyn at 494E where he set out his fourth "objective policy consideration": "the imposition of liability for pure psychiatric harm in a wide range of situations *may* result in a burden of liability on defendants which *may* be disproportionate to tortious conduct involving perhaps momentary lapses of concentration, *e.g.* in a motor car accident" (emphasis added).

[41] See, *e.g.* Lord Reid in *Dorset Yacht Co. Ltd v. Home Office* [1970] A.C. 1004 at 1033B, where having cited the decision of the Court of Appeals of New York in *Williams v. State of New York* (1955) 127 N.E. (2d) 545 (where it was held that finding a duty of care would impact on the rehabilitative work done with prisoners), he said:

"It may be that the public servants of the State of New York are so apprehensive, easily dissuaded from doing their duty and intent on preserving public funds from costly claims that they could be influenced in that way. By my experience leads me to believe that Her Majesty's servants are made of sterner stuff."

See also *Barrett v. Enfield LBC* [1998] Q.B. 367 at 380A-C, *per* Evans L.J.:

"I would agree that what is said to be a 'policy' consideration, namely, that imposing a duty of care might lead to defensive conduct on the part of the person concerned and might require him to spend time or resources on keeping full records or otherwise providing for self-justification, if called upon to do so, should normally be a factor of little, if any, weight. If the conduct in question is of a kind which can be measured against the standards of the reasonable man, placed as the defendant was, then I do not see why the law in the public interest should not require those standards to be observed."

(Lord Slynn agreed with this when the case reached the House of Lords: [1999] 3 W.L.R. 79 at 94A.)

[42] For example, it is interesting to contrast the approach of Lord Hoffmann in *Arthur J. Hall and Co. v. Simons* [2000] 3 W.L.R. 543 at 563H–568B (where he rejected an argument based upon the anticipated effect on advocates of abolition of their immunity from suit in negligence) with his speech in *Stovin v. Wise* [1996] A.C. 923 at 958C:

"I think that it is important, before extending the duty of care owed by public authorities, to consider the cost to the community of the defensive measures which they are likely to take in order to avoid liability. It would not be surprising if one of the consequences of the *Anns* case and the spate of cases which followed was that local council inspectors tended to insist upon stronger foundations than were necessary."

In *Arthur J. Hall & Co.*, Lord Hoffmann had the benefit of Canadian experience and of the wasted costs jurisdiction in the English courts to guide him. In *Stovin v. Wise*, he and the other members of the House of Lords had no information as the likely consequences of a finding that a local authority owed a duty to exercise reasonable skill and care when deciding which dangerous junctions to render of care is found to be owed, is that liability will only be found if there is negligence and not just an error of judgment.[43] It is submitted that this is an important factor and that courts should, while avoiding leaps in the dark if at all possible, should bear in mind that to sound in damages, the error has to be such that no reasonably careful or reasonably competent defendant would have made it. The courts should be slow to accept unsupported assertions as to the deleterious consequences that would follow from finding that a duty of care was owed.[44]

2–078   **Assumption of responsibility and the extended *Hedley Byrne* principle.** In *Hedley Byrne and Co. Ltd v. Heller & Partners Ltd*[45] Lord Reid identified as the additional requirement which needed to be satisfied to give rise to a duty of care for a misstatement "that expressly or by implication from the circumstances the speaker or writer has undertaken some responsibility".[46] Whether someone has undertaken or assumed responsibility towards another in relation to a task or a statement can be a useful test when deciding whether he owed that other person a duty of care.[47] However, there are two difficulties. First, assumption of responsibility is of little use if the person making the statement or carrying out the task has expressly disclaimed liability in circumstances where that disclaimer is itself challenged as was the case in *Smith v. Eric S. Bush*.[48] References to *voluntary* assumption of responsibility tend "to import a degree of subjectivity".[49] Secondly, if the subjective, voluntary element is excised, so that the test is one of

---

safer. Markesinis, Auby, Coester-Waltjen and Deakin, *Tortious Liability of Statutory Bodies* (Hart Publishing, 1999), p. 79, postulate a "counter-hunch" to that made by Lord Hoffmann in *Stovin v. Wise*, namely that "the post-*Murphy* situation may be encouraging sloppy verification of building calculations" (See also (1) *South Pacific Manufacturing Co. Ltd v. New Zealand Security Consultants and Investigations Ltd* [1992] 2 N.Z.L.R. 282 at 312, lines 25–29: "And since the imposition of liability on local authorities effected by decisions such as *Bowen v. Paramount Builders (Hamilton) Ltd* [1977] 1 N.Z.L.R. 394, it is reasonable to assume there has been an improvement in their supervision of new house building. In my own trial experience I have heard statements by local body witnesses to that effect." (2) *Rowling v. Takaro Properties Ltd* [1988] A.C. 473 at 502D-E, where Lord Keith expressed a similar apprehension as that evinced by Lord Hoffmann in *Stovin v. Wise*.)

[43] See, *e.g. Dorset Yacht Co. Ltd v. Home Office, per* Lord Denning M.R. in the Court of Appeal [1969] 2 Q.B. 412 at 427B-H and, *per* Lord Reid in the House of Lords [1970] A.C. 1004 at 1032C-E ("I cannot believe that negligence or dereliction of duty is widespread among prison or Borstal officers"), *Arthur J. Hall and Co. v. Simons* [2000] 3 W.L.R. 543 at 554A-B, *per* Lord Steyn and *Phelps v. Hillingdon LBC* [2000] 3 W.L.R. 776 at 792B-E, *per* Lord Slynn and at 809B-G, *per* Lord Clyde.

[44] See, *e.g.,* the discussion of policy arguments advanced against a duty of care in *Capital and Counties Plc v. Hampshire C.C.* [1997] Q.B. 1004 at 1043D–1044F. The Court of Appeal had, however, found that there was no sufficient proximity, so that there was no duty of care.

[45] [1964] A.C. 465; see also paras 2–24 to 2–25, above.

[46] *ibid.* at 483. Lords Morris and Hodson considered that a duty would arise where a person with special skill or information "takes it upon himself" to give information or advice (*ibid.* at 502 and 514). Lord Devlin spoke of "a responsibility that is voluntarily accepted or undertaken" (*ibid.* at 529) and Lord Pearce of "persons holding themselves out in a calling or situation or profession [who] take on a task within that calling or situation or profession" (*ibid.* at 538).

[47] See, *e.g. Williams v. Natural Health Life Foods Ltd* [1998] 1 W.L.R. 830 (discussed in para. 2–49, above); *Al-Kandari v. J.R. Brown and Co.* [1988] Q.B. 665 (discussed in Chap. 10, para. 10–63) and *Pryke v. Gibbs Hartley Cooper Ltd* [1991] 1 Lloyd's Rep. 602 (discussed in Chap. 14, para. 14–24).

[48] [1990] 1 A.C. 831 (discussed in para. 2–30, above).

[49] *Merrett v. Babb* [2001] E.W.C.A. Civ. 214, para. 41; [2001] 3 W.L.R. 3 at 18A, *per* May L.J.

deemed assumption of responsibility, then as a test "assumption of responsibility" becomes little more than a statement that the law recognises a duty of care.[50] That is not to say that an objective assessment as to whether a defendant has undertaken responsibility to a claimant is not without value, for example, in the context of cases of negligent misstatement.[51] However, it is to recognise that in many cases in which a duty of care is found, the concept of assumption of responsibility affords little, if any, practical assistance in understanding why that conclusion is reached. As with proximity in the threefold test, assumption of responsibility can only be taken so far.

(c) *Particular situations*

(i) *Public and local authorities: duty of care and statute*

The tort of negligence and statute. Although the law of negligence is   2–079
essentially judge-made, statute is increasingly important. Statute has clarified or changed existing common law duties,[52] provided the context in which common law issues have to be decided,[53] created statutory duties actionable by those for whose protection the statutory duty was enacted[54] or those specified as being entitled to bring claims,[55] and has created powers and duties to be exercised by a variety of public bodies which may give rise to common law duties of care.[56] In recent years, the courts have had to grapple with a number of novel claims against public bodies or authorities in which it has been alleged that the body or authority was in breach of a tortious duty of care in relation to the exercise (or non-exercise) of its powers, duties or functions.

Lord Browne-Wilkinson's classification. In *X (minors) v. Bedfordshire*   2–080
C.C.[57] Lord Browne-Wilkinson identified four classes of claims:[58]

(1) Actions for breach of statutory duty *simpliciter* (*i.e.* irrespective of carelessness).

(2) Actions based solely on the careless performance of a statutory duty in the absence of any other common law right of action.

(3) Actions based on a common law duty of care arising either from the imposition of a statutory duty or from the performance of it.

---

[50] See para. 2–69, note 3, above.
[51] See, *e.g. Peach Publishing Ltd v. Slater and Co.* [1998] B.C.C. 139 at 146C, *per* Morritt L.J. and at 161E, *per* Nourse L.J. and *Electra Private Equity Partners v. KPMG Peat Marwick (a firm)* [1999] Lloyd's P.N. 670 at 682, *per* Auld L.J. These decisions are discussed in Chap. 15, para. 15–79.
[52] See, *e.g.* the Occupiers' Liability Act 1954 and the Occupiers' Liability Act 1984.
[53] See, *e.g. Caparo Industries plc v. Dickman* [1990] 2 A.C. 605, discussed in Chap. 15, para. 15–60).
[54] *Clerk and Lindsell on Torts*, (18th ed.), paras 11–09 to 11–40 and see para. 2–82, below.
[55] See, *e.g.* ss.62 and 62A of the Financial Services Act 1986 and s.150 of the Financial Services and Markets Act 2000.
[56] *Clerk and Lindsell on Torts* (18th ed.), Chap. 12 and see paras 2–83 to 2–84, below.
[57] [1995] 2 A.C. 633; see also para. 2–42 above.
[58] *ibid.* at 730H–731B.

(4) Misfeasance in public office, *i.e.* the failure to exercise, or the exercise of, statutory powers either with the intention to injure the claimant or in the knowledge that the conduct is unlawful.

In this section some brief consideration will be given to the first class and then the vexed question of the circumstances in which the existence or exercise of a statutory power or duty gives rise to a common law duty of care (the third class) will be addressed. The fourth class, misfeasance in public office, is beyond the scope of this book.[59] Before doing so, however, the second class needs to be explained.

2–081   **Careless exercise of a statutory duty.** Where Parliament has authorised an authority to carry out a particular act, the fact that carrying it out involves what would otherwise be a tortious act (*e.g.* nuisance) does not render the authority liable in damages: the authority has a complete defence to a claim—it is not wrongful to carry out an act which Parliament has authorised.[60] However, Parliament is not taken to have authorised the authority to carry out the act carelessly, so that if the authority has done the act carelessly, so as to cause damage, it has no defence based upon statutory authority. It follows that Lord Browne-Wilkinson's second class is concerned with the negation of a defence, rather than the recognition of a duty of care or other tortious claim.[61] The fact that a statutory power is exercised carelessly does not of itself give rise to a cause of action in tort. The claimant has to show that the circumstances were such that the person exercising the power owed him a duty of care when exercising it.[62]

2–082   **Breach of statutory duty *simpliciter* (Lord Browne-Wilkinson's first class).** Breach of statutory duty only gives rise to a private law cause of action if, on the true construction of the statute, the duty was imposed in order to protect a limited class of the public and Parliament intended to confer on members of that class a private right of action for breach of the duty.[63] Where there is an express provision in the statute, this principle is easy to apply.[64] It is more difficult to apply where there is no express provision. The most important factors in determining whether Parliament intended there to be a private right of action are:

(1) Whether the provision was designed to protect a limited class of individuals.

(2) Whether the statute provides for any other sanction for breach of the duty.

(3) Whether the claimant has alternative remedies.

---

[59] See *Clerk and Lindsell on Torts*, (18th ed), (paras 17–133 to 17–146) and *Three Rivers D.C. v. Governor and Company of the Bank of England (No.3)* [2000] 2 W.L.R. 1220.
[60] See, *e.g. Allen v. Gulf Oil Refining Ltd* [1981] A.C. 1001.
[61] See *X (minors) v. Bedfordshire C.C.* [1995] 2 A.C. 633 at 732C–733F, explaining *Geddis v. Proprietors of Bann Reservoir* (1878) 3 App.Cas. 430.
[62] *ibid.* at 734H–735A.
[63] *ibid.* at 731D–E.
[64] Examples are given in para. 11–09 of *Clerk and Lindsell on Torts*, (18th ed).

Of these, the first is the most important, with less weight being attached to the absence of other sanction or remedy. A broad analysis of the statute is required.[65] Analysis of the considerable body of authority as to the application of these factors is beyond the scope of this book.[66]

Common law duty of care arising either from the imposition of a statutory **2–083** **duty or from the performance of it.** The courts have not found an easy answer to the question when the imposition of a statutory duty or the performance of it should give rise to a common law duty of care. There is a reluctance to recognise the possibility of claims for negligent policy decisions, although there is also a recognition that the distinction between policy and operational questions is not always easy to make or useful in practice. The result has been a tendency to find that the natural persons through whom authorities discharge their statutory functions themselves owe common law duties of care, for breach of which their employees are vicariously liable. So, an education authority does not itself owe a common law duty to pupils to assess their educational needs, but the educational psychologist who makes the assessments is under a common law duty to them to carry out the assessments with reasonable skill and care.[67] In the same way, a fire authority owes no duty of care to property owners in its area, but if its employees attend a fire, they owe a common law duty of care to exercise reasonable skill and care not to create some new danger.[68]

The narrow scope for a common law duty of care. Recent decisions of the **2–084** House of Lords, particularly in *X (minors) v. Bedfordshire C.C.*[69] and *Stovin v. Wise*,[70] have established a number of formidable obstacles to a finding that a common law duty of care arises.[71] In considering whether a public body owes a duty of care when acting under a statute, the following questions need to be addressed:

(1) Did the statute impose a duty or confer a power or discretion?

(2) If the latter, then does the exercise of the power or discretion involve consideration of "policy" matters? If it does, then no duty of care will be owed because the courts will not begin to assess whether a particular

---

[65] *Phelps v. Hillingdon LBC* [2000] 3 W.L.R. 776 at 789E–H, *per* Lord Slynn.
[66] See *Clerk and Lindsell on Torts* (18th ed.), paras 11–10 to 11–34.
[67] *Phelps v. Hillingdon LBC* [2000] 3 W.L.R. 776.
[68] *Capital and Counties Plc v. Hampshire C.C.* [1997] Q.B. 1004.
[69] [1995] 2 A.C. 633.
[70] [1996] A.C. 923.
[71] For an excellent discussion of the underlying issues and a comparison of their treatment under U.S. and Commonwealth law, see Aronson and Whitmore, *Public Torts and Contracts* (Law Book Co. Ltd, Australia, 1982). More recent appellate decisions have been criticised and compared with the approaches adopted in French and German law in Markesinis, Auby, Coester-Waltjen and Deakin, *Tortious Liability of Statutory Bodies* (Hart Publishing, Oxford and Portland, Oregon, 1999). See also Craig, "Negligence in the Exercise of a Statutory Power" in (1978) 94 L.Q.R. 428; Bowman and Bailey, "Negligence in the Realms of Public Law—Positive Obligation to Rescue?" in [1984] P.L. 27; Bowman and Bailey, "The Policy/Operational Dichotomy—a Cuckoo in the Nest" in [1986] C.L.J. 430; Howarth, "Negligence after Murphy: Time to Rethink" in [1991] C.L.J. 58 at 94–95; Bailey and Bowman, "Public Authority Negligence Revisited" [2000] C.L.J. 85. This area of the law could be important in claims against health authorities if the defence of lack of resources is advanced: see Chap. 12, below. It is also relevant in the regulated financial services industry: see Chap. 13.

decision was negligent,[72] at least where the decision involved weighing of competing public interests.[73]

(3) If the decision whether to exercise the power or discretion did not involve "policy" matters, then only if the authority or body acted so unreasonably that its act or decision fell outside the scope of the power or discretion conferred by Parliament, could there be a breach of any duty of care.[74]

(4) In cases where there might be a duty of care (i.e. where the statute imposed a duty) or in which the exercise of a power or discretion did not involve "policy" matters and was so unreasonable as to fall outside the scope of the power or discretion, then, in deciding whether a duty of care

---

[72] In *Anns v. Merton LBC* [1978] A.C. 728 (see paras 2–27 and 2–39, above) the House of Lords concluded that in the operational sphere a public authority could owe a duty of care to persons affected by its acts or omissions. In the sphere of policy, a public authority's tortious liability would be much more limited, but it did not enjoy total immunity.

However, in *Rowling v. Takaro Properties Ltd* [1988] A.C. 473 at 501B-D, the Privy Council opined that it might be more helpful to identify a class of "policy or planning" decisions, such as "discretionary decisions on the allocation of scarce resources or the distribution of risks" which are simply not suitable for judicial resolution at all (strictly speaking this was *obiter* because it was held that the decision in issue was not negligent). The reason why such decisions are not suitable for judicial resolution may be because of a reluctance to become involved in political questions, or because it will be extremely difficult to show that such a decision was negligent: when that difficulty is considered together with the probable availability of public law remedy and the possible consequences on public administration, then policy factors dictate that no duty of care should be owed: *ibid.* at 502A–F.

This was taken further in *X (minors) v. Bedfordshire C.C.* [1995] 2 A.C. 633, where, at 737F–G Lord Browne-Wilkinson said if the matters relevant to the exercise of discretion included "policy" matters, which might be difficult to identify, then the court could not begin to assess them. Having noted the difference of approach in *Anns v. Merton LBC* [1978] A.C. 728 and *Rowling v. Takaro Properties Ltd* [1988] A.C. 473, Lord Browne-Wilkinson concluded that "a common law duty of care in relation to the taking of decisions involving policy matters cannot exist": [1995] A.C. 633 at 738H.

On the policy/operational distinction, see also *Barratt v. Enfield LBC* [1999] 3 W.L.R. 79 at 96H, *per* Lord Slynn and *Phelps v. Hillingdon LBC* [2000] 3 W.L.R. 776 at 810H–811B, *per* Lord Clyde.

[73] See the analysis of Lord Hutton in *Barratt v. Enfield LBC* [1999] 3 W.L.R. 79 at 103F–108H and *Phelps v. Hillingdon LBC* [2000] 3 W.L.R. 776 at 790C, *per* Lord Slynn. See also *Sutherland Shire Council v. Heyman* (1985) 157 C.L.R. 424 at 469, where Mason J. observed:

"[T]he dividing line between [policy and operational factors] will be observed if we recognize that a public authority is under no duty of care in relation to decisions which involve or are dictated by financial, economic, social or political factors or constraints. Thus budgetary allocations and the constraints which they entail in terms of allocation of resources cannot be made the subject of a duty of care. But it may be otherwise when the courts are called upon to apply a standard of care to action or inaction that is merely the product of administrative direction, expert or professional opinion, technical standards or general standards of reasonableness."

[74] In *X (minors) v. Bedfordshire C.C.* [1995] 2 A.C. 633 at 736A–737E, Lord Browne-Wilkinson considered the extent to which a decision involving the exercise of discretion might be justiciable in the law of negligence. If the decision was not so unreasonable as to fall outside the ambit provided by the statute (i.e. if it was not unreasonable in the *Associated Provincial Picture Houses Ltd v. Wednesbury Corp.* [1948] 1 K.B. 223 sense), then it was authorised by Parliament and so not actionable (this reflects Lord Browne-Wilkinson's second class: see para. 2–81 above). In *Barratt v. Enfield B.C.* [1999] 3 W.L.R. 79 at 95G–96E, Lord Slynn queried whether it was strictly necessary to show *Wednesbury* unreasonableness, but said that if the test were instead whether there had been "no real exercise of the discretion", then this was "very much the administrative law test". In the same case Lord Hutton observed at 111A–D that where the claim arose from the exercise of a power (as opposed to a decision whether to exercise it) then the common law concept of negligence was to be preferred to the public law concept of *Wednesbury* unreasonableness.

is owed in a particular case the courts apply normal principles,[75] but with particular regard to the statute which is the source of the duty, power or discretion.[76] In cases concerning the exercise of statutory powers, a duty of care could only arise in exceptional circumstances.[77]

(5) Finally, it should be borne in mind that once a decision has been taken to exercise a statutory power, then the exercise of it may give rise to circumstances in which the public body or authority owes a duty of care to the claimant.[78] In such cases, if a duty of care would be owed if the relevant acts were performed otherwise than in the exercise of a statutory power, a duty of care is not excluded because the acts were performed in the exercise of such a power.[79]

Vicarious liability. The fact that a public authority or body does not itself owe **2–085** a duty of care does not mean that the employees through whom it performs its functions do not themselves owe duties of care for breach of which their employer may be vicariously liable.[80] So, if an employee gives advice in circumstances akin to those in *Hedley Byrne and Co. Ltd v. Heller & Partners*

---

[75] In *X (minors) v. Bedfordshire C.C.* [1995] 2 A.C. 633 at 739A–D, when considering whether a common law duty of care arose in the operational sphere, Lord Browne-Wilkinson said that the usual principles in the threefold test should be applied, albeit that particular regard had to be had to the statutory framework: *ibid.* at 739A–D. Lord Browne-Wilkinson also attached significance to the fact that in the nearest analogies, *Hill v. Chief Constable of West Yorkshire* [1989] A.C. 53 and *Yuen Ken Yeu v. Att.-Gen. of Hong Kong* [1988] A.C. 175, no duty of care had been found: *ibid.* at 751C–G. The threefold test was also applied in *Barratt v. Enfield LBC* [1999] 3 W.L.R. 79 at 97F, *per* Lord Slynn.

Lord Nicholls provided a helpful summary of earlier authority as to proximity in his dissenting speech in *Stovin v. Wise* [1996] A.C. 923 at 937B–F.

[76] *Stovin v. Wise* [1996] A.C. 923 at 952F–953A. Lord Nicholls, who dissented as to the result, expressed the position in these terms at 935B–C:

"Public authorities operate within a statutory framework. Since the will of the legislature is paramount in this field, the common law should not impose a concurrent duty inconsistent with this framework. A common law duty must not be inconsistent with the performance by the authority of its statutory duties and powers in the manner intended by Parliament, or contrary in any other way to the presumed legislative intention."

[77] *Stovin v. Wise* [1996] A.C. 923. Giving the speech with which the majority agreed, Lord Hoffmann stated that the policy/operation distinction (which had first been formulated in *Anns*: see n. 72, above) was an inadequate tool. He considered that the Canadian cases (*Just v. British Columbia* (1989) 64 D.L.R. (4th) 689 and *Brown v. British Columbia (Minister of Transportation and Highways)* (1994) 112 D.L.R. (4th) 1) which proceeded on that basis were unsatisfactory. After reviewing the public authority line of cases and observing that the fact that Parliament had conferred a discretion rather than imposed a statutory duty indicated that Parliament had not intended to create a common law right of compensation, Lord Hoffmann concluded:

"In summary, therefore, I think that the minimum preconditions for basing a duty of care upon the existence of a statutory power, if it can be done at all, are, first, that it would in the circumstances have been irrational not to have exercised the power, so that there was in effect a public law duty to act, and secondly, that there are exceptional grounds for holding that the policy of the statute requires compensation to be paid to persons who suffer loss because the power was not exercised." [1996] A.C. 923 at 953D–E.

Lord Hoffmann went on to find that neither condition was satisfied in that case.

[78] *Barratt v. Enfield LBC* [1999] 3 W.L.R. 79 at 102D–103E, *per* Lord Hutton, citing *Fisher v. Ruislip-Northwood UDC* [1954] K.B. 584, *Dorset Yacht Co. Ltd v. Home Office* [1970] A.C. 1004 and *Sutherland Shire Council v. Heyman* (195) 157 C.L.R. 424. See, *e.g. Kent v. Griffiths* [2000] 2 W.L.R. 1158, CA: ambulance service, having accepted an emergency call, owed a duty of care (no question arose as to the adequacy or allocation of resources).

[79] *Phelps v. Hillingdon LBC* [2000] 3 W.L.R. 776 at 790E, *per* Lord Slynn.

[80] *Lister v. Hesley Hall Ltd* [2001] U.K.H.L. 22, reported in [2001] 2 W.L.R. 1311.

Ltd,[81] he will owe a duty of care and his employer will be vicariously liable for his negligence.[82] However, it will always be necessary to consider the employee's purpose in giving advice and whether it would tend to discourage the performance of the statutory duty being performed.[83] Thus in *X (minors) v. Bedfordshire C.C.*[84] claims in the child care cases based on breach of duties of care owed by social workers and psychiatrists were struck out because the individuals concerned were working for and reporting to their employer.[85] There was also obvious potential for conflict between parents and social services in such cases.[86] However, in the education cases, there was an arguable case that educational psychologists owed duties of care: in contrast to the child care cases, there was no conflict between their duty to their employer and a duty of care owed to the children referred to them.[87] The willingness of the courts to recognise vicarious liability provides a means of redress which their reluctance to find direct duties of care would otherwise deny. Although it might be thought that this consequence would weigh against finding vicarious liability, in fact it is the availability of redress by way of vicarious liability which makes it easier to find against direct liability.[88]

2–086   **Supervisors and regulators.** The banking and financial services fields are and have been subject to regulation and supervision in a number of common law jurisdictions for some time.[89] When a financial institution or bank fails, customers who suffer losses will often complain that the regulator failed them. Given that at least one of the purposes of the regulatory/supervisory systems is to provide protection to investors, it might be thought that the regulator would owe investors a duty of care in relation to the exercise of its powers and functions. However, such claims have not met with success. In *Yuen Kun Yeu v. Att.-Gen.*

---

[81] [1964] A.C. 465.

[82] *Welton v. North Cornwall D.C.* [1997] 1 W.L.R. 570: environmental health officer taking it upon himself to advise guest house owners as to works needed to comply with statutory requirements.

[83] *Harris v. Evans* [1998] 1 W.L.R. 1285: health and safety inspector reporting to local authorities did not owe a duty of care to the proprietors of the business about which he reported. His statements were made to the authorities to advise them and it would discourage proper reporting if the subjects of reports could bring claims for damages. The distinction between this case and *Welton* is narrow. It is for the defendant to establish that the imposition of a duty of care would have this effect and it will only be possible to do so in exceptional cases: *Phelps v. Hillingdon LBC* [2000] 3 W.L.R. 776 at 790G, *per* Lord Slynn.

[84] [1995] 2 A.C. 633: see para. 2–42, above.

[85] *ibid.* at 752D–753F, *per* Lord Browne-Wilkinson:
   "In my judgment in the present cases, the social workers and the psychiatrist did not, by accepting the instructions of the local authority, assume any duty of care to the plaintiff children. The professionals were employed or retained to advise the local authority in relation to the well-being of the plaintiffs but not to advise or treat the plaintiffs."
(See also *Kapfunde v. Abbey National Plc.* [1999] Lloyd's Rep. Med. 48, discussed in para. 2–113, below.)

[86] *Phelps v. Hillingdon LBC* [2000] 3 W.L.R. 776 at 811G–H, *per* Lord Clyde. There should be no potential for conflict between the interests of children and the interests of local authorities.

[87] *ibid.* at 764F–764B. Despite the misgivings expressed in *Barratt v. Enfield LBC* [1999] 3 W.L.R. 79 at 83E-H by Lord Browne-Wilkinson about this part of his speech, it was vindicated in *Phelps v. Hillingdon LBC* [2000] 3 W.L.R. 776.

[88] *Phelps v. Hillingdon LBC* [2000] 3 W.L.R. 776 at 8089A–C, *per* Lord Clyde. It is submitted, however, that the readiness to recognise vicarious liability undermines many of the "policy" considerations said to militate against direct liability. The recognition of duties of care owed by employees for advice given presents its own difficulties: see para. 2–93, below.

[89] See Chap. 13 for the position in the United Kingdom under the Financial Services and Markets Act 2000.

of Hong Kong[90] the plaintiffs were depositors in a registered deposit-taking company, which had been run fraudulently. They brought a claim against the Commissioner of Deposit-Taking Companies, established under an Ordinance whose purposes included "to make provision for the protection of persons who deposit money". The Privy Council struck out the claim. Having criticised the *Anns* test,[91] the Privy Council turned to the question whether there were sufficiently close and direct relations between the Commissioner and would-be depositors to give rise to a duty of care. While loss by would-be depositors was foreseeable, the Commissioner had to balance their interests with those of existing depositors (who might be prejudiced were he to exercise his power to remove the company from the register and so, in effect, put it out of business).[92] This did not suggest an intention by the legislature that the Commissioner should owe would-be depositors a duty of care. The Commissioner had no wider powers to control the day-to-day management of the company[93] and the plaintiffs were members of a very wide class of those inhabitants of Hong Kong who might deposit money with the company.[94] The failure of the claim in *Yuen Kun Yeu v. Att.-Gen. of Hong Kong*[95] and the striking out of the similar claim in the later decision of the Privy Council in *Davis v. Radcliffe*[96] provide a useful warning of the difficulties of establishing a duty of care where the statutory duty, power or function is for the general benefit of society or of a wide section of society.[97]

(ii) *Directors and employees*

Many professions are allowed to provide their services by way of limited liability **2–087**
companies, *e.g.*, architects, engineers, surveyors, valuers, insurance brokers and financial advisers. However, the actual work must be done by natural persons, either directors or other employees. Other professionals provide services through their employees, themselves often professionally qualified. In such cases there will be no contract between the client and the employee. In cases in which the limited company or other principal is solvent and insured the position of the directors or employees is rarely controversial. However, that is not always the case and it is not uncommon for a claimant to allege that a director or employee owed a duty of care in tort.

Limited liability companies. In *Williams v. Natural Life Health Foods Ltd*[98] **2–088**
advice as to taking a franchise of a health food shop was given by a limited company acting principally by its managing director, whose personal experience

---

[90] [1988] A.C. 175.
[91] See para. 2–30, n. 77, above.
[92] *cf. Davis v. Radcliffe* [1990] 1 W.L.R. 821 at 827A–D where the Privy Council held that the need to balance competing interests was also a factor weighing against the existence of a duty of care.
[93] *Dorset Yacht Co. Ltd v. Home Office* [1970] A.C. 1004 was distinguished on this ground. The degree of control exercised by a defendant over a third party usually has to be high for a defendant to owe a duty of care to prevent the third party causing loss and damage: see *Smith v. Leurs* (1945) 70 C.L.R. 256 and *Modbury Triangle Shopping Centre Pty Ltd v. Anzil* [2000] H.C.A. 61. See generally *Smith v. Littlewoods Organisation Ltd* [1987] A.C. 241 (particularly at 270–274).
[94] *cf. Davis v. Radcliffe* [1990] 1 W.L.R. 821, where the Finance Board of the Isle of Man was operating a licensing system "in the interests of the public as a whole" (at 827A).
[95] [1988] A.C. 175.
[96] [1990] 1 W.L.R. 821.
[97] See also *Cooper v. Hobart* (2000) 184 D.L.R. (4th) 287, British Columbia CA: claim against registrar appointed under Mortgage Brokers Act struck out.
[98] [1998] 1 W.L.R. 890.

was trumpeted in the company's brochure and who played a prominent part in producing detailed financial projections provided to the plaintiff. The plaintiff claimed that the managing director owed him a duty of care. The House of Lords reversed the decision of the trial judge and Court of Appeal that he did.[99] Lord Steyn, who gave the only reasoned speech, agreed with Sir Patrick Russell, who dissented in the Court of Appeal, that it was an inevitable feature of a one-man company that the managing director would be the person who was possessed of the qualities essential for the functioning of the company, but that this did not mean that the managing director assumed personal responsibility to the company's customers. Nor did the fact that the company's brochure placed great emphasis on the managing director's experience and expertise. He held that the managing director had not "crossed the line" and assumed personal responsibility.[1] Lord Steyn placed particular reliance on two judgments of La Forest J. in the Supreme Court of Canada.

2–089   **The Canadian cases.**[2] In the first, *London Drugs Ltd v. Kuehne & Nagel International Ltd*,[3] the plaintiff delivered a valuable transformer to the first defendant, a limited company, under a contract which limited the company's liability to $40. It was then damaged through the negligence of the company's employees. They were also sued. The majority held that the employees owed a duty of care, but that their liability was limited by the terms of the contract between their employer and the plaintiff. La Forest J. dissented on the question of duty. He said:[4]

> "In my view, where the plaintiff has suffered injury to his property pursuant to contractual relations with the company, he can be considered to have chosen to deal *with a company*."

> "A plaintiff who chooses to enter into a course of dealing with a limited liability company can, in most cases, be held to have voluntarily assumed the risk of the company being unable to satisfy a judgment in contract or for vicarious liability. That the customer takes this risk in matters of contract has been accepted since *Salomon v. A. Salomon and Co.* [1897] A.C. 22, HL. Now that many contractual claims are bought concurrently as tort claims, the customer should not be able to shift this risk to the employee by claiming in tort."

La Forest J. agreed with the other members of the Court in the second decision, *Edgeworth Construction Ltd v. N.D. Lea and Associates Ltd.*[5] That was a claim by a contractor who had entered a road building contract, the specifications and drawings for which had been prepared by a limited company of engineers. The contractor sued both the limited company and the individual engineers who affixed their seals to the drawings. The claim against the individuals was struck

---

[99] *ibid.* See also the decision of the New Zealand Court of Appeal in *Trevor Ivory Ltd v. Anderson* [1992] 2 N.Z.L.R. 517.

[1] See also *Hale v. Guildarch Ltd* [1999] P.N.L.R. 44.

[2] See also *Sealand of the Pacific v. Robert C. McHaffie Ltd* (1974) 51 D.L.R. (3d) 702 (British Columbia Court of Appeal: an architect employed by a limited company did not owe a personal duty of care to a third party with whom the company entered a contract).

[3] (1992) 97 D.L.R. (4th) 261.

[4] *ibid.* at 289d and 290h–291a.

[5] [1993] 3 S.C.R. 206.

out. In *Williams v. Natural Life Health Foods Ltd*,[6] Lord Steyn set out this passage from the judgment of La Forest J.:[7]

"The situation of the individual engineers is quite different. While they may, in one sense, have expected that persons in the position of the appellant would rely on their work, they would expect that the appellant would place reliance on their firm's pocketbook and not theirs for indemnification; see *London Drugs*, at 386–387. Looked at the other way, the appellant could not reasonably rely for indemnification on the individual engineers. It would have to show that it was relying on the particular expertise of an individual engineer without regard to the corporate character of the engineering firm. It would seem quite unrealistic, as my colleague observes, to hold that the mere presence of an individual engineer's seal was sufficient indication of personal reliance (or for that matter voluntary assumption of risk)."

In *Williams v. Natural Health Life Foods Ltd*,[8] Lord Steyn said that this reasoning was "instructive" and "consistent with English law".

Assumption of personal responsibility and reasonable reliance. The approach of La Forrest J. is instructive in a number of respects. First, in the explicit recognition that, usually, a person who agrees to deal with a limited company takes the risk that the company will prove to be insolvent. Analysis in terms of which party assumed a particular risk is or should be an important feature of the law of negligence. Second, in recognising that the relevant reliance had to be not on the individual director or employee's skill or ability, but on his pocket. Third, in approaching the question both from the perspective of the individual employees as well as from that of the plaintiffs—what was it reasonable for the defendant employees to assume in terms of their personal responsibility towards the plaintiffs?[9] It would be reasonable for them to assume that they would be personally liable if they had done something which, viewed objectively, indicated that they were assuming direct responsibility to the plaintiffs. In general, directors and employees should not be taken to have assumed personal responsibility, at least in cases of economic loss,[10] although there will be occasions on which they have done so.[11] 2–090

Employees of firms and individuals. Where the employer is not a limited liability company, then one element in the reasoning of La Forest J. is not present, at least in the same terms. There has been no assumption by the claimant of the risk of dealing with a limited liability company. However, it could be said a client who contracts with a firm or principal is generally to be taken to be relying on that firm or principal, rather than on its employees. While the fact that a defendant has or does not have insurance is not, apparently, a relevant consideration when considering whether to impose a duty of care,[12] the fact that the 2–091

---

[6] [1998] 1 W.L.R. 803 at 836H–837A.
[7] [1993] 3 S.C.R. 206 at 212.
[8] [1998] 1 W.L.R. 830 at 837B.
[9] *cf.* the approach of Evans J. in *MacMillan v. A.W. Knott Becker Scott Ltd* [1990 1 Lloyd's Rep. 98, discussed in Chap. 14, para. 14–28, below.
[10] In cases of personal injury, directors and employees have no special protection: see, *e.g.*, *Alder v. Dickson* [1955] 1 Q.B. 158, discussed by Hobhouse L.J. in *Perrett v. Collins* [1998] 2 Lloyd's Rep. 255.
[11] As in *Fairline Shipping Corp. v. Adamson* [1975] Q.B. 180.
[12] See, *e.g. Watson v. British Boxing Board of Control Ltd* [2001] 1 W.L.R. 1256 at 1282B, *per* Lord Philips M.R., agreeing with Buxton L.J. in *Perrett v. Collins* [1998] 2 Lloyd's Rep. 255 at 276–277.

client, employer and employee were proceeding (or objectively are to be taken to have been proceeding) on the basis that the employer and not the employee would have professional indemnity insurance would, on the approach of La Forest J., be a telling consideration against finding that the employee personally owed a duty of care, absent some further factor indicating personal responsibility.[13]

2–092   *Merrett v. Babb.* The position of an employed valuer who personally signs a mortgage valuation which his employer has been retained to provide was considered by the Court of Appeal in *Merrett v. Babb.*[14] The employer in that case was a firm, not a limited liability company. The mortgage valuation was signed by the defendant employee personally and contained the statement required by section 13 of the Building Societies Act 1986 that he was not disqualified from providing a valuation. It was not seen by the claimant, whose claim was based on *Smith v. Eric S. Bush.*[15] The majority[16] held that a duty of care was owed by the defendant employee, Mr Babb. His position was said to be indistinguishable from that of Mr Lee, the individual surveyor in *Harris v. Wyre Forest D.C.*, the case heard at the same time as *Smith v. Eric S. Bush.* Since Mr Lee had been held to owe a duty of care (for breach of which his local authority employer was vicariously liable), so did Mr Babb.

2–093   This decision illustrates the potential danger of finding that individual employees personally owe duties of care when discharging duties on behalf of their employers in cases where individual employees are not separately represented and the employer is solvent.[17] Those decisions are then found to have unintended consequences. *Merrett v. Babb*[18] is best explained as a decision on the special facts involved in cases such as *Smith v. Eric S. Bush.*[19] However, it should not be applied more generally and the conflict between it and *Williams v. Natural Health Life Foods Ltd*[20] should be resolved.[21]

(iii) *Sub-agents and sub-contractors*

2–094   Sometimes a professional will not discharge his obligations to his client personally or by an employee, but by sub-contracting with another professional. In such

---

[13] In *Standard Chartered Bank v. Pakistan National Shipping Corp.* [2000] 1 Lloyd's Rep. 218 the Court of Appeal applied the decision in *Williams v. Natural Health Life Foods Ltd* [1998] 1 W.L.R. 830 to a claim in deceit and held that a director who made false representations on a company's notepaper was not personally liable (although he might have been a joint tortfeasor with the company, which had committed deceit). This decision may take the protection of directors too far. It has little to do with the reasoning of La Forest J.

[14] [2001] E.W.C.A. Civ. 214, reported in [2001] 3 W.L.R. 1.

[15] [1990] 1 A.C. 831. See Chap. 9, paras 9–46 to 9–50, below.

[16] May L.J. and Wilson J. Aldous L.J. dissented.

[17] See, *e.g.* the decision of the Court of Appeal in *Punjab National Bank v. de Boinville* [1992] 1 W.L.R. 1138 (discussed in Chap. 14, para. 14–27) that insurance brokers employed by two limited companies themselves owed a duty of care to the plaintiff. This is hard to reconcile with *Williams v. Natural Health Life Foods Ltd* [1998] 1 W.L.R. 830. In *Punjab National Bank v. de Boinville* the individuals were not separately represented. See also the cases on the vicarious liability of public bodies and authorities discussed in para. 2–85, above and *Smith v. Eric S. Bush* [1990] 1 A.C. 831 itself.

[18] [2001] E.W.C.A. Civ. 214, reported in [2001] 3 W.L.R. 1.

[19] [1990] 1 A.C. 831. See *Williams v. Natural Health Life Foods Ltd* [1998] 1 W.L.R. 830 at 837D, *per* Lord Steyn and *Merrett v. Babb* [2001] E.W.C.A. Civ. 214, paras 23 and 40, *per* May L.J. and para. 58, *per* Wilson J.

[20] [1998] 1 W.L.R. 830.

[21] The House of Lords has refused leave to appeal in *Merrett v. Babb* [2001] 1 W.L.R. 1859.

cases the question can arise as to whether the sub-contractor/agent owes a duty of care in tort to the ultimate client. In considering the duties owed by sub-agents to the ultimate principal the editor of *Bowstead & Reynolds on Agency* says:

"The present position as to the rules of law affecting the sub-agent in England is not.. as firmly fixed as might appear."[22]

Older authority suggests that no duty of care is owed,[23] but must be treated with caution in the light of subsequent developments and in particular of the decision of the House of Lords in *Henderson v. Merrett Syndicates Ltd.*[24] The finding as to concurrent liability was merely part of the reasoning leading to the conclusion that a managing agent at Lloyd's owed a duty of care not only to direct names (with whom he had contracted), but also to indirect names, who had contracted with a members' agent who had in turn contracted with the managing agent.[25] The members' agents remained contractually liable to these indirect names for loss suffered as a result of any want of care on the part of the managing agent. The House of Lords allowed the indirect names to sue the managing agents for the same loss. In rejecting the argument on behalf of the managing agents that the parties had agreed to structure their relationships by a chain of contracts so as to exclude any duty of care on the part of managing agents to indirect names, Lord Goff gave this guidance for future cases:

"I wish however to add that I strongly suspect that the situation which arises in the present case is most unusual; and that in many cases in which a contractual chain comparable to that in the present case is constructed it may well prove to be inconsistent with an assumption of responsibility which has the effect of, so to speak, short circuiting the contractual structure so put in place by the parties. It cannot therefore be inferred from the present case that other sub-agents will be held directly liable to the agent's principal in tort."[26]

Lord Goff then went on to give the example of a subcontractor in a building contract who would not ordinarily be liable to the employer for economic loss.[27]

Lord Goff had approached the question by considering whether a duty of care **2–095** was owed without considering the impact of the contractual context and then, having concluded that, subject to consideration of the contractual context, a duty was owed, he found nothing in the contractual context to displace that conclusion. This was because the contractual and tortious duties were not materially different.[28] There was no conflict between the contractual and tortious duties.[29] "The Names were not seeking to impose on the managing agents any obligation beyond that which the retainer itself required to be performed."[30] The managing agents were writing insurance contracts on behalf of direct and indirect names

---

[22] *Bowstead & Reynolds on Agency* (16th ed.), para. 5–011.
[23] See, *e.g. Calico Printers Association v. Barclays Bank Ltd* (1931) 145 L.T. 151.
[24] [1995] 2 A.C. 145. See para. 2–47, above and, in relation to concurrent liability, para. 2–105, below.
[25] See Chap. 16, para. 16–08, below for an explanation of the relevant factual background.
[26] [1995] 2 A.C. 145 at 195G–H.
[27] Lord Goff approved the decision of the Court of Appeal in *Simaan General Contracting Co. v. Pilkington Glass Ltd (No.2)* [1988] Q.B. 758.
[28] [1995] 2 A.C. 145 at 195A.
[29] *X (Minors) v. Bedfordshire C.C.* [1995] 2 A.C. 633 at 739D, *per* Lord Browne-Wilkinson.
[30] *ibid.* at 753D.

and it was they who would suffer loss in the first instance should the managing agents be careless. As for other situations, the position has been summarised in these terms by Lord Browne-Wilkinson in *White v. Jones:*[31]

> " . . . the fact that the defendant assumed to act in the plaintiffs' affairs pursuant to a contract with a third party is not necessarily incompatible with the finding that, by so acting, the defendant also entered into a special relationship with the plaintiff . . . this factor should not lead to the conclusion that a duty of care will necessarily be found to exist even where there is a contractual chain of obligations designed by the parties to regulate their dealings."

2–096   **Competing considerations.** In deciding whether a duty of care is owed, the courts have to balance competing considerations. On the one hand, the sub-agent or contractor will be providing part of the service which the intermediate agent or contractor has promised to provide to the ultimate client. He will owe a contractual duty to exercise reasonable skill and care and a concurrent tortious duty. There should be little scope for conflict between those duties and a duty of care owed to the ultimate client. On the other hand, there is no direct contractual relationship and the parties have chosen to regulate their relations by a chain of contracts. The client has his remedy against the intermediate contractor or agent, who will in turn have recourse against the sub-contractor or agent should he fail to exercise reasonable skill and care.[32] Moreover the relations and dealings between two professional firms may not readily translate into a duty of care owed to the client of one firm.[33]

(iv) *Immunity*

2–097   By tradition certain professions enjoyed immunity from suit on the grounds of public interest. The development of the law of tort and a reappraisal of the public interest have led to the narrowing of such immunity. The immunity of advocates was first limited to work done in court and to a small category of pre-trial work and was then removed entirely.[34] The immunity of expert witnesses is now limited to work done in court and to related pre-trial work.[35] Architects are no longer immune from suit in respect or certificates negligently given.[36] Similarly, "mutual valuers" have lost their immunity.[37] There are suggestions in the

---

[31] [1995] 2 A.C. 207 at 274D–E.
[32] See, *e.g. Pacific Associates Inc. v. Baxter* [1990] 1 Q.B. 993 and "Duty of care: peripheral parties and alternative opportunities for deterrence" by Stapleton in (1995) 111 L.Q.R. 301.
[33] See, *e.g. Pangood Ltd v. Barclay Brown and Co. Ltd* [1999] Lloyd's Rep. I.R. 405, discussed in Chap. 14, para. 14–13.
[34] *Arthur J. Hall and Co. v. Simons* [2000] 3 W.L.R. 543. See Chap. 10 and 11, para. 10–111 and paras 11–15 to 11–23. Advocates should continue to enjoy the same immunity as others from any action brought against them on the ground that things said or done in proceedings were said or done maliciously or falsely: *Taylor v. Director of Public Prosecutions* [1999] 2 A.C. 177 and *Darker v. Chief Constable of West Midlands* [2000] 3 W.L.R. 747.
[35] *Palmer v. Durnford Ford* [1992] 1 Q.B. 483 at 488. Other aspects of the decision in *Palmer* (but not this aspect) were doubted by the Court of Appeal in *Walpole v. Partridge & Wilson* [1994] Q.B. 106 at 123–125. See further *Stanton v. Callaghan* [1999] P.N.L.R. 116: expert immune both in respect of his evidence at trial and in respect of the contents of a report prepared for exchange, but not for advice given as to the merits of his client's claim.
[36] See para. 2–129, below.
[37] See Chap. 9, para. 9–74, below; *Arenson v. Arenson* [1977] A.C. 405; *Palacath Ltd v. Flanagan* [1985] 2 All E.R. 161.

authorities that the surviving immunities may be further cut down, or even abolished, in the future.[38]

Certainly when new situations arise in which there is a case for immunity on grounds of public interest, there is now a tendency to deal with the matter under the rubric of duty of care. Thus in *Yuen Kun Yeu v. Att.-Gen. of Hong Kong*,[39] the Privy Council acknowledged that there was a case for giving the Commissioner of Deposit-Taking Companies immunity on the grounds of public policy, but they based their decision on the absence of any relevant duty of care. Likewise, in *Hill v. Chief Constable of West Yorkshire*,[40] Lord Keith (with whom Lords Brandon, Oliver and Goff agreed) considered that the police should be immune from claims of the kind made by Mrs Hill, on grounds similar to those justifying advocates' immunity. But he based his decision on the absence of any duty of care owed by the police to the deceased.   **2-098**

The concept of immunity as a device to protect the judicial process[41] serves a useful function. It is submitted that immunity should now be limited to the established categories. The question whether or not a new class of persons should be "immune" in respect of specified activities (e.g. the fire service in putting out fires) involves consideration of substantially the same factors as the "just and reasonable" question in the threefold test. It is unhelpful for the courts to consider (and indeed for advocates to argue) the same matters twice under different headings. The concept of immunity evolved before the courts had developed a satisfactory framework within which to assess all factors relevant to the existence and scope of a duty of care. Now that such a framework exists, the concept of immunity as a separate ground for denying liability in new situations which arise is otiose. Thus, the liability of fire brigades was extensively reviewed by the Court of Appeal in *Capital and Counties plc v. Hampshire C.C.*[42] The ratio of the decision that the fire brigade owed no tortious duty in respect of any failure to fight fires adequately was that there was no assumption of responsibility towards the property owners. It is submitted that the court was right to base its decision on the established tests for duty of care, rather than on immunity (which the fire brigades were claiming). The principles governing duty of care are now sufficiently developed that it is unnecessary to create new categories of immunity.   **2-099**

(d) *Concurrent Liability, Contracts and Tortious Duties of Care*

The question whether a professional person owes a duty of care in tort to his client, in addition to his contractual obligations, is one which exercised the courts   **2-100**

---

[38] In *Arenson v. Arenson* [1977] A.C. 405 Lord Kilbrandon stated that even arbitrators are not immune from suit (at 430–431). Lords Salmon and Fraser suggested that this may be the case, but expressed no firm opinion on the point (at 440D-E and 442D). But see now s.29 of the Arbitration Act 1996. See also *Darker v. Chief Constable of the West Midlands* [2000] 3 W.L.R. 747, where the House of Lords held that witness immunity in relation to evidence given or to be given in court proceedings did not extend to the earlier investigative process undertaken by the police.

[39] [1988] A.C. 175 at 198. See para. 2–86, above.

[40] [1989] A.C. 53 at 63–64.

[41] By freeing those involved from undue pressure and by preventing relitigation.

[42] [1997] Q.B. 1004.

intermittently throughout the last century and gave rise to conflicting authority.[43] The authorities relevant to each profession will be discussed in the chapters which follow. At the present stage, the topic is dealt with only at the level of generality.

(i) Competing considerations

2–101   The existence of a contract under which the client pays the professional person for his services can be said to militate in favour of imposing a tortious duty co-extensive with the contractual obligations. The relationship between the parties is a close one, and its objective is to confer a benefit (often an economic benefit) on the client. The client relies upon the professional person and the latter can readily foresee the kind of loss or damage which will ensue if he is careless. The professional person has chosen to contract with the client and so has assumed responsibility. There can be little doubt, but that if the professional were acting without charging, he would owe a duty of care in tort. On the other hand, it can be said that the existence of the contract militates against imposing a duty of care: the only practical result of imposing a concurrent duty of care is to give the client the benefit of an alternative limitation period.[44]

(ii) Authority

2–102   Whilst there has been strong judicial support for both sides of this debate, the weight of authority has supported concurrent liability. In *Donoghue v. Stevenson*[45] Lord Macmillan stated:

> " . . . there is the equally well-established doctrine that negligence apart from contract gives a right of action to the party injured by that negligence—and here I use the term negligence, of course, in its technical legal sense, implying a duty owed and neglected. The fact that there is a contractual relationship between the parties which may give rise to an action for breach of contract, does not exclude the co-existence of a right of action founded on negligence as between the same parties, independently of the contract, though arising out of the relationship in fact brought about by the contract. Of this the best illustration is the right of the injured railway passenger to sue the railway company either for breach of the contract of safe carriage or for negligence in carrying him."[46]

Lord Macmillan cited the 13th edition of *Pollock on Torts*, which suggested that two previous decisions[47] of the Court of Exchequer, said to support the contrary view, had been misunderstood.

---

[43] For cases in which it was held that a professional man's liability lay only in contract, see *e.g. Jarvis v. Moy, Davies, Smith, Vandervell and Co.* [1936] 1 K.B. 399 (stockbrokers); *Groom v. Crocker* [1939] 1 K.B. 194 (solicitors); *Bagot v. Stevens Scanlan and Co. Ltd* [1966] 1 Q.B. 197 (architects). For cases in which a concurrent duty of care was recognised, see *e.g. Boorman v. Brown* (1842) 3 Q.B. 511 and (1844) 11 Cl. & Fin. 1; *Nocton v. Lord Ashburton* [1914] A.C. 932 at 956, *per* Viscount Haldane L.C.; *Esso Petroleum Co. Ltd v. Mardon* [1976] Q.B. 801 at 819, *per* Lord Denning M.R.; *Midland Bank Trust Co. Ltd v. Hett, Stubbs & Kemp* [1979] Ch. 384.
[44] See Chap. 5, paras 5–16 to 5–55, below.
[45] [1932] A.C. 562.
[46] *ibid.* at 609–610.
[47] *Winterbottom v. Wright* (1852) 10 M. & W. 109; *Longmeid v. Holliday* (1851) 6 Ex. 761.

A number of more recent decisions concerning solicitors,[48] insurance bro- **2–103**
kers[49] and engineers/architects[50] either held or proceeded on the basis that there
was concurrent liability in contract and tort. Concurrent liability has been
accepted in principle, although it seldom arises in practice, in medical negligence
cases.[51] Furthermore, in several pre-1994 duty of care cases the House of Lords
indicated *obiter* the view that professional persons owe concurrent duties to their
clients in contract and tort. In *Smith v. Eric S. Bush*,[52] Lord Jauncey (with whom
Lords Keith and Brandon agreed), discussing the relationship between the defendant surveyors and the building society, said that the surveyors "not only entered
into contractual relations with the building society but also came under a duty in
tort to it to exercise reasonable care in carrying out their survey and preparing
their report."[53] In *Caparo Industries plc v. Dickman*,[54] Lord Bridge (with whom
Lords Roskill and Ackner agreed) began his discussion of the professional man's
liability to third parties from the premise that he owed a duty in tort to his own
client.[55] Finally in *Murphy v. Brentwood D.C.*[56] Lord Keith (with whom all other
Law Lords agreed) explained that the engineers' tortious liability to their clients
in *Pirelli* was based upon the *Hedley Byrne* principle.[57] Logically, this must be
correct. If "a relationship equivalent to contract" gives rise to a tortious duty to
protect against economic loss, as Lord Devlin maintained in *Hedley Byrne*,[58] *a
fortiori* a contractual relationship between the parties should have the same
result.

The principal recent authority upon which opponents of concurrent liability **2–104**
relied was the decision of the Privy Council in *Tai Hing Cotton Mill Ltd v. Liu
Chong Hing Bank Ltd*.[59] Lord Scarman, giving the opinion of the Judicial
Committee of the Privy Council, stated:

> "Their Lordships do not believe that there is anything to the advantage of the law's
> development in searching for a liability in tort where the parties are in a contractual
> relationship. This is particularly so in a commercial relationship. Though it is possible
> as a matter of legal semantics to conduct an analysis of the rights and duties inherent
> in some contractual relationships including that of banker and customer either as a
> matter of contract law when the question will be what, if any, terms are to be implied

---

[48] See, *e.g. Midland Bank Trust Co. Ltd v. Hett, Stubbs & Kemp* [1979] 1 Ch. 384; *Forster v. Outred
and Co.* [1982] 1 W.L.R. 86; *D. W. Moore and Co. Ltd v. Ferrier* [1988] 1 W.L.R. 267; *Bell v. Peter
Browne and Co.* [1990] 2 Q.B. 495. But see the caveat expressed by Lloyd L.J. in *Lee v. Thompson*
(1990) 6 P.N. 91.
[49] Set out in Chap. 14, para. 14–14, below. See in particular the decision of the Court of Appeal in
Forsikringsaktieselskapet Vesta v. Butcher [1989] A.C. 852 at 860B, *per* O'Connor L.J. and at
879E–F, *per* Sir Roger Ormrod.
[50] *Pirelli General Cable Works Ltd v. Oscar Faber & Partners* [1983] 2 A.C. 1; *London Congregational Union Inc. v. Harriss & Harriss* [1988] 1 All E.R. 15. See Chap. 8, paras 8–47 to 8–49,
below.
[51] See Chap. 12, paras 12–15 to 12–17, below.
[52] [1990] 1 A.C. 831. Discussed in para. 2–30, above.
[53] *ibid.* at 870E.
[54] [1990] 2 A.C. 605. Discussed in paras 2–31 to 2–33, above.
[55] *ibid.* at 619C: "In advising the client who employs him the professional man owes a duty to
exercise that standard of skill and care appropriate to his professional status and will be liable both
in contract and in tort for all losses which his client may suffer by reason of any breach of that
duty."
[56] [1991] 1 A.C. 398. Discussed in para. 2–39, above.
[57] See the passage from Lord Keith's speech quoted in para. 2–46, above.
[58] [1964] A.C. 464 at 528–529.
[59] [1986] A.C. 80.

or as a matter of tort law when the task will be to identify a duty arising from the proximity and character of the relationship between the parties, their Lordships believe it to be correct in principle and necessary for the avoidance of confusion in the law to adhere to the contractual analysis: on principle because it is a relationship in which the parties have, subject to a few exceptions, the right to determine their obligations to each other, and for the avoidance of confusion because different consequences do follow according to whether liability arises from contract or tort, e.g. in the limitation of action."[60]

The *Tai Hing* case was an appeal from Hong Kong and it concerned the relationship of banker and customer.[61] The professional negligence cases referred to earlier in this section were not expressly disapproved. Indeed in his careful choice of words in this passage, although Lord Scarman deprecated the introduction of tortious liability in a contractual situation, he stopped short of saying that there was no such liability. The other authority sometimes relied upon by opponents of concurrent liability was *Greater Nottingham Co-operative Society Ltd v. Cementation Piling and Foundations Ltd*,[62] but it is submitted that properly understood this case is authority for the proposition that a contract limits the scope of any tortious duties arising, not that it excludes such duties.

(iii) *Henderson v. Merrett*

2–105 The issue finally arose for decision by the House of Lords in *Henderson v. Merrett Syndicates Ltd.*[63] The facts are set out in paragraph 2–47, above. In the case of the direct names there was, of course, a contract between the plaintiffs and the managing agents. Lord Goff, with whom the other law lords agreed, considered that all the elements of a *Hedley Byrne* relationship were present. He recognised that there were two possible views about the effect of the contractual relationship: first, the view taken in France that the contract excludes a remedy in tort; secondly, the view taken in Germany that contractual and tortious claims may be concurrent. After a full analysis of the authorities and the literature, Lord Goff rejected the view that the existence of a contractual duty excluded any parallel duty in tort between the same parties.[64]

(iv) *The scope of the concurrent duty*

2–106 The tortious duty arises from the relationship between the parties and the function which the professional person/firm is performing. It is a duty to use

---

[60] *ibid.* at 107B–D. This passage was considered by the Court of Appeal in *Banque Keyser Ullmann SA v. Skandia (U.K.) Insurance Co. Ltd* [1990] 1 Q.B. 665 at 800: "Lord Scarman's opinion contains a valuable warning as to the consequences of an ever-expanding field of tort. It should not be part of the general function of the law of tort to fill in contractual gaps." The same passage was considered and applied by the House of Lords in *Scally v. Southern Health and Social Services Board* [1992] 1 A.C. 294 in the context of a contract of employment.

[61] Lord Scarman's point is more apposite in the commercial context than other contexts, as he himself said. In this regard, see the decisions of the Court of Appeal (both of which subsequently went to the House of Lords) in *National Bank of Greece SA v. Pinios Shipping Co. (No. 1)* [1990] 1 A.C. 637 and *Bank of Nova Scotia v. Hellenic Mutual War Risks Association (Bermuda) Ltd, The "Good Luck"* [1990] 1 Q.B. 818.

[62] [1989] Q.B. 71.

[63] [1995] 2 A.C. 145.

[64] The decision is supported by Burrows, "Solving the Problem of Concurrent Liability" in *Understanding the Law of Obligations* (Hart Publishing, 1998). The countervailing arguments are discussed by Powell: see "Professional and client: the duty of care", published in Birks (ed.), *Wrongs and Remedies in the Twenty-First Century* (Clarendon Press, 1996).

reasonable care in identified respects. Thus the tortious and contractual duties have different origins. Although concurrent, these duties are not necessarily co-extensive. Since the contract of retainer may impose obligations to achieve specific results[65] or may impose liability for sub-agents,[66] the concurrent duty of care imposed by the law of tort may fall short of, or be less onerous than, the contractual obligations of the retainer.

(v) *Can the concurrent duty in tort be more extensive than the contractual obligations?*

As a matter of principle, if the contract of retainer governs the whole of the parties' relationship, the answer should be no. If, however, the contract governs only part of the parties' dealings, in other aspects of the parties' mutual activities there may be a tortious duty of care but no parallel contractual obligation.[67] Examples might be: an architect instructed to design a project, who later gratuitously assists in marketing the building; an accountant retained to audit a company's accounts, who gives general management advice upon which the directors reasonably rely (perhaps because of the accountant's experience in that field of business). In any particular case, it will be important to establish whether the professional in effect undertook some further task or gave some advice beyond that which he had contracted to give.

2–107

(vi) *Further significance of the contract*

Absent some act or advice beyond the scope of his contract, it is in the contract between the professional and his client that the extent of his tortious duty will be found. His tortious duty of care will be no greater in scope than the implied contractual promise to exercise reasonable skill and care. Moreover, the contract can have greater significance: by defining what the professional is to do, it may explain the scope of his responsibility and the extent to which responsibility or risk is to rest with his client or is to be borne by others.

2–108

(e) *Liability to Third Parties*

The extent to which a professional person owes duties of care to persons other than his client has been the source of considerable litigation, as well as academic debate, over the last 40 years. A significant proportion of the major "duty of care" cases arises in the context of professional negligence. There appear to be three reasons for this. First, much of a professional man's work consists of supplying advice or information, errors in which can lead to (sometimes extensive) financial loss. The courts' reluctance to award damages for negligence causing economic loss is reduced (but not eliminated) when negligent advice was given in a professional context. Thus a number of borderline economic loss claims arise. Secondly, because of the standards which the professions are expected to uphold and the status which they still enjoy, it is commonplace for a third party to rely upon a professional man to perform his task skilfully and

2–109

---

[65] See paras 2–08 to 2–10, above.

[66] See, *e.g.* for example, the position of the members' agents in *Aiken v. Stewart Wrightson Members Agency Ltd* [1995] 1 W.L.R. 1281 at 1293–1305.

[67] *Pryke v. Gibbs Hartley Cooper Ltd* [1991] 1 Lloyd's Rep. 602, discussed in Chap. 14, para. 14–24, below; *Holt v. Payne Skillington* (1995) 77 B.L.R. 51 at 71–74.

impartially, even when the interests of the third party and the client are opposed. Third, professional persons are usually insured. They are therefore attractive targets. The widespread reliance upon the professions by society lies at the root of a legal problem, which is expressed in the plethora of third-party liability cases. If professional persons were liable to all who relied upon them to act skilfully, their liability would be unduly wide and oppressive. If professional men were liable only to their clients, this would be hopelessly out of step with the reasonable expectations of society.

(i) *Denning L.J.'s dissenting judgment*

2–110 Any general discussion of professional liability to third parties must start from the dissenting judgment of Denning L.J. in *Candler v. Crane, Christmas and Co.*[68] This had the distinction of being approved by the House of Lords in *Hedley Byrne & Co. Ltd v. Heller and Partners Ltd*[69] and in some of the more recent landmark cases it has been heavily relied upon by the House of Lords.[70] In *Candler v. Crane, Christmas and Co.*,[71] the plaintiff invested £2,000 in a company in reliance on the company's accounts. The company's accountants had given the plaintiff a copy of those accounts and discussed them with him. The accounts had been prepared negligently and the plaintiff lost the whole of his investment. The majority of the Court of Appeal (in a decision now overruled) held that the accountants owed no relevant duty to the plaintiff. In his dissenting judgment Denning L.J. said:

"Let me now be constructive and suggest the circumstances in which I say that a duty to use care in statement does exist apart from a contract in that behalf.

First, what persons are under such a duty? My answer is those persons such as accountants, surveyors, valuers and analysts, whose profession and occupation it is to examine books, accounts and other things, and to make reports on which people—other than their clients—rely in the ordinary course of business . . . [72]

Secondly, to whom do these professional people owe this duty? I will take accountants, but the same reasoning applies to the others. They owe the duty, of course, to their employer or client; and also I think to any third person to whom they themselves show the accounts, or to whom they know their employer is going to show the accounts, so as to induce him to invest money or take some other action on them. But I do not think the duty can be extended still further so as to include strangers of whom they have heard nothing and to whom their employer without their knowledge may choose to show their accounts. . . . The test of proximity in these cases is: did the accountants know that the accounts were required for submission to the plaintiff and use by him? . . . [73]

Thirdly, to what transactions does the duty of care extend? It extends, I think, only to those transactions for which the accountants knew their accounts were required. For instance, in the present case it extends to the original investment of £2,000 which the plaintiff made in reliance on the accounts, because the accountants knew that the accounts were required for his guidance in making that investment; but it does not extend to the subsequent £200 which he made after he had been two months with the

---

[68] [1951] 2 K.B. 164. Discussed in Chap. 15, paras 15–53 and 15–54, below.
[69] [1964] A.C. 465.
[70] See *Smith v. Eric S. Bush* [1990] 1 A.C. 831 at 844–845, *per* Lord Templeman and at 867–868, *per* Lord Jauncey and *Caparo Industries plc v. Dickman* [1990] 2 A.C. 605 at 621–623, *per* Lord Bridge and at 656–657, *per* Lord Jauncey.
[71] [1951] 2 K.B. 164.
[72] *ibid.* at 179.
[73] *ibid.* at 180–181.

company. This distinction, that the duty only extends to the very transaction in mind at the time, is implicit in the decided cases."[74]

(ii) *Analysis of Denning L.J.'s dissenting judgment*

What persons are under the duty? Denning L.J. explained that the reason 2-111
why professional men owed the duty was because their callings required particular knowledge and skill. They can, therefore, reasonably be expected to apply that knowledge and exercise that skill. Thus the level of performance required by the duty is not unreasonable or unduly burdensome. The special knowledge and skill of professional persons also go to whether it is reasonable for a third party to rely on them.[75]

To whom is the duty owed? The duty is owed to the client and to those third 2-112
parties with whom the professional person deals directly with a view to influencing their future conduct (*e.g.* by making an investment or loan). It also extends to third parties to whom the professional person knows his views will be conveyed by his client for the same purpose. This limits the class of those to whom the duty is owed. It recognises that there are limits to the extent to which it is reasonable to impose a duty of care on a professional person and so limits to the extent to which it is reasonable for a third party to rely on him. It is reasonable to impose liability (and for there to be reliance) where the advice or information is conveyed by the professional person himself or by his client in circumstances in which the former is to be taken as knowing that it will be conveyed and relied on.[76]

To what transactions does the duty of care extend? Denning L.J. limited the 2-113
duty to the specific transaction for which the professional knew that the advice or information was required. He emphasised that the purpose for which a professional man produces a report or information is of crucial importance, giving a number of examples which remain sound today:

(1) " . . . a doctor, who negligently certifies a man to be a lunatic when he is not, is liable to him, although there is no contract in the matter, because the doctor knows that his certificate is required for the very purpose of deciding whether the man should be detained or not; but an insurance company's doctor owes no duty to the insured person, because he makes his examination only for the purposes of the insurance company: see *Everett v. Griffiths* [1920] 3 K.B. 163 at 211 and 217."[77]

Over 40 years later, the Court of Appeal held that a doctor who was retained to examine the plaintiff for his potential employer owed no duty of care in tort.[78]

---

[74] *ibid.* at 182–183.
[75] Denning L.J. explained that professional persons "are not liable, of course, for casual remarks made in the course of conversation, nor for other statements made outside their work, or not made in their [professional] capacity" (*ibid.* at 180).
[76] See, *e.g.* the recent decision of the High Court of Australia in *Tepko Pty Ltd v. Water Board* [2001] H.C.A. 19 (reported in (2001) 75 A.L.J.R. 775), at para. 47 and the recent decision of the New Zealand Court of Appeal in *Brownie Wills v. Shrimpton* [1998] 2 N.Z.L.R. 321.
[77] *ibid.* at 183.
[78] *Kapfunde v. Abbey National Plc.* [1999] Lloyd's Rep. Med. 48. See further *X (minors) v. Bedfordshire C.C.* [1995] 2 A.C. 633 at 752D–753F, *per* Lord Browne-Wilkinson.

(2) "So also, a Lloyd's surveyor who, in surveying for classification purposes, negligently passes a mast as sound when it is not, is not liable to the owner for damage caused by it breaking, because the surveyor makes his survey only for the purpose of classifying the ship for the Yacht Register and not otherwise: *Humphrey v. Bowers* (1929) 45 T.L.R. 297."[79]

In *The "Morning Watch"*,[80] Phillips J. held that a classification society which prepared a special survey of a vessel owed no duty of care in tort to an intending purchaser: the survey was needed if the vessel was to be kept classed at Lloyd's and the purchaser was not intended to act on the result of the survey.[81]

(3) "Again, a scientist or expert (including a marine hydrographer) is not liable to his readers for careless statements in his published works. He publishes his work simply for the purpose of giving information, and not with any particular transaction in mind at all. But when a scientist or an expert makes an investigation and report for the very purpose of a particular transaction, then, in my opinion, he is under a duty of care in respect of that transaction."[82]

The decision of the House of Lords in *Caparo Industries plc v. Dickman*[83] reflected the courts' continuing concern to limit those who could bring claims against the maker of a widely published statement (in *Caparo* the auditors of company accounts). The purpose for which the relevant statement was made in *Caparo* was found in the statutory context and provided the answer as to who could bring a claim and for what loss.

(iii) *Intended beneficiaries*

2–114 Denning L.J. did not have in mind cases such as *White v. Jones*,[84] which has already been applied by analogy to the intended beneficiaries of pension and life assurance cover in *Gorham v. British Telecommunications Plc*.[85] There will be a limited number of cases in which the client engages the professional person to effect a transaction designed to benefit third parties in circumstances in which, by the time the failure to effect the transaction by reason of the professional person's breach of duty is discovered, the client is no longer in a position (as opposed to no longer willing) to effect the transaction. In those circumstances, the intended beneficiaries may be owed a duty of care by the professional person.

Particular professions

2–115 The above general principles apply to all professional persons. Cases concerning particular professions are considered in Section 2 below.

---

[79] [1951] 2 K.B. 164 at 183.
[80] [1990] 1 Lloyd's Rep. 547.
[81] See also *Marc Rich and Co. A.G. v. Bishop Rock Marine Co. Ltd* [1996] A.C. 211, discussed in para. 2–51, above.
[82] [1951] 2 K.B. 164 at 183.
[83] [1990] 2 A.C. 605. Discussed in Chap. 15, paras 15–53 to 15–61, below.
[84] [1995] 2 A.C. 207, discussed in para. 2–48, above.
[85] [2000] 1 W.L.R. 2129, CA.

4. THE STANDARD OF SKILL AND CARE

(a) *The meaning of reasonable skill and care*

In order to discharge the implied contractual obligation stated above[86] as well as the duty of care in tort,[87] the professional person must exercise reasonable skill and care. The cases abound with paraphrases of this term and explanations of what it means, and some of these are quoted in the chapters concerning individual professions.[88] No single formulation commands universal assent. It is common ground that the standard of skill and care must be determined by reference to members of the profession concerned, rather than the man on the Clapham omnibus. Where the authorities differ, however, is on the question whether the requisite standard is (a) that which members of the particular profession do in fact achieve ordinarily,[89] or (b) that which, in the opinion of the court, members of the profession ought to achieve.[90] The distinction is frequently blurred, for example, in definitions which refer to the standard attained by "reasonably competent" members of the profession.[91] These definitions, however, properly fall into the second category, since it is for the court to decide what is meant by "reasonably competent" members of the profession. They may or may not be equated with practitioners of average competence.[92]

---

[86] See para. 2–07, above.

[87] There is a suggestion by Megarry J. in *Argyll v. Beuselinck* [1972] 2 Lloyd's Rep. 172 at 183 that the implied contractual duty to exercise reasonable skill and care may, on occasions, impose a higher standard than the duty of care in tort. (See Chap. 10, para. 10–93, below.) The editors are unaware of any decision in which the claimant has succeeded in contract but failed in tort by reason of this distinction. For the opposite view, see *Esso Petroleum Co. Ltd v. Mardon* [1976] 1 Q.B. 801 at 820A–B.

[88] See in particular Chap. 12, para. 12–68, below. The definition of "negligent" and "non-negligent" mistakes is a matter which occurs with particular frequency in the medical cases.

[89] See, *e.g. Hunter v. Hanley* (1955) S.C. 200 at 204–205; *Bolam v. Friern Hospital Management Committee* [1957] 1 W.L.R. 582 at 586; *Andrew Master Hones Ltd v. Cruikshank & Fairweather* [1980] R.P.C. 16 at 18, *per* Graham J.; the finding of negligence was not challenged on appeal; *Whitehouse v. Jordan* [1981] 1 W.L.R. 246 at 257–258, *per* Lord Wilberforce; *Smith v. Eric S. Bush* [1990] 1 A.C. 831 at 851C–D; *Luxmoore-May v. Messenger May Baverstock* [1990] 1 W.L.R. 1009 at 1020. This is the view adopted in *Halsbury*:
"When a person has held himself out as being capable of attaining standards of skill either in relation to the public generally, for example by driving a car, or in relation to some person for whom he is performing a service, he is required to show the skill normally possessed by persons doing that work. Doctors and members of other professions and callings must, therefore, exercise the standard of skill which is usual in their profession or calling."
Halsbury's Laws of England (4th ed.), Vol. 34, para. 12 (reproduced by kind permission of Butterworths Ltd).

[90] See, *e.g. Midland Bank Trust Co. Ltd v. Hett, Stubbs & Kemp* [1979] 1 Ch. 384: "The extent of the legal duty in any given situation must, I think, be a question of law for the court" (*per* Oliver J. at 402C); *Bown v. Gould & Swayne* [1996] P.N.L.R. 130.

[91] See, *e.g. Saif Ali v. Sydney Mitchell and Co.* [1980] A.C. 198 at 218C–E and 220D–E, *per* Lord Diplock; *Whitehouse v. Jordan* [1981] 1 W.L.R. 246 at 263E–F, *per* Lord Fraser; *Eckersley v. Binnie and Partners* (1988) 18 Con.L.R. 1 at 79, *per* Bingham L.J. and *McFarlane v. Wilkinson* [1997] 2 Lloyd's Rep. 259 at 275, *per* Brooke L.J.

[92] The last part of this paragraph and the first part of the next paragraph were cited with approval by Phillips J. in *Deeny v. Gooda Walker* [1996] L.R.L.R. 183 at 207 and by Cresswell J. in *Henderson v. Merrett Syndicates Ltd (No. 2)* [1996] 1 P.N.L.R. 32 at 36.

2–117   It is submitted that of the two approaches discussed in the preceding paragraph, the second is correct.[93] Suppose a profession collectively adopts extremely lax standards in some aspect of its work. The court does not regard itself as bound by those standards and will not acquit practitioners of negligence simply because they have complied with those standards.[94] Thus, evidence as to general and approved practice, although of very considerable importance, is not automatically conclusive in every case. It was pointed out above[95] that there is a divergence in the approach of the courts towards the different professions. This divergence of approach is illustrated in the extent to which the courts are willing to override or disregard evidence of established practice within individual professions. This will be analysed and discussed in the chapters which follow on the individual professions. At the level of generality, however, there is now a perceptible trend on the part of the courts to question more closely the practices of the professions. This has been seen in the recent Lloyd's litigation, where the practices of part of the Lloyd's market have been closely scrutinised following the catastrophic losses suffered by many names.[96] This trend has also been seen in recent medical negligence cases, where the courts have made their own assessment of the reasonableness of certain clinical practices.[97]

(b) *Relevance of defendant's qualifications and experience*

2–118   Another problem[98] which arises in this context is whether the professional person should be judged by reference to (a) the standard of skill and care appropriate to a practitioner with his particular qualifications and experience or (b) the standard of skill and care appropriate to his profession generally. There is some support for the former approach to be found in the earlier medical negligence cases,[99] (*obiter*) in a decision of Megarry J. concerning a solicitor[1] and in one decision concerning insurance brokers.[2] However, the latter view is more generally

---

[93] The second approach was adopted by the House of Lords in *Bolitho v. City and Hackney H.A.* [1998] A.C. 232. At 241–242, Lord Browne-Wilkinson (with whom Lords Slynn, Nolan, Hoffmann and Clyde agreed) said: "The use of these adjectives—responsible, reasonable and respectable—all show that the court has to be satisfied that the exponents of the body of opinion relied upon can demonstrate that such opinion has a logical basis." Lord Browne-Wilkinson went on to say that it would very seldom be right for a judge to reach the conclusion that views genuinely held by a competent medical expert were unreasonable; and that the case before the House was not one of those rare cases. See further Chap. 12, paras 12–101 to 12–103, below.

[94] Conversely, if a profession adopts unduly high standards the practitioner is not necessarily negligent if he fails to comply with them: see, *e.g. United Mills Agencies Ltd v. Harvey Bray and Co.* [1951] 2 Lloyd's Rep. 631 at 643, col. 2.

[95] See para. 2–03, above.

[96] See Chap. 16.

[97] See Chap. 12, paras 12–94 to 12–100, below.

[98] This is part of a wider problem (which is outside the scope of this book), namely the extent to which the personal attributes of the defendant are relevant in determining whether he was negligent. Thus the learner driver is judged by the standard of a competent and experienced driver: see *Nettleship v. Weston* [1971] 2 Q.B. 691. But certain qualifications or disabilities cannot sensibly be disregarded (for example, the fact that the defendant only has one arm). There is a general discussion of this problem in *The Common Law* by O. W. Holmes (Little, Brown and Co., 1881), Lecture 3.

[99] See the first edition of this book, Chap. 6, para. 6–11.

[1] *Argyll v. Beuselinck* [1972] 2 Lloyd's Rep. 172 at 183, discussed in Chap. 10, para. 10–93, below. See also *Yates Property Corp. v. Boland* (1998) 157 A.L.R. 30 and [1999] Lloyd's Rep. P.N. 459, Federal Court of Australia.

[2] *Sharp and Roarer Investments Ltd v. Sphere Drake Insurance plc, The Moonacre* [1992] 2 Lloyd's Rep. 501, discussed in Chap. 14, para. 14–33, below.

adopted.[3] In *Andrew Master Hones Ltd v. Cruikshank & Fairweather*,[4] a case concerning patent agents in which this point was argued, Graham J. stated:

> "The degree of knowledge and care to be expected is thus seen to be that degree possessed by a notional duly qualified person practising that profession. The test is, therefore, if I may put it that way, an objective test referable to the notional member of the profession and not a subjective test referable to the particular professional man employed."[5]

It is submitted that neither the subjective approach nor the objective approach   **2-119**
is wholly satisfactory. As to the subjective approach, it is unrealistic and impracticable in each case (a) to formulate a standard by reference to the defendant's assumed capabilities, and then (b) to determine if he has achieved that particular standard. As to the objective approach, it seems equally unrealistic to demand identical standards of competence from persons who come from different ranks of the same profession (for example, junior hospital doctors and consultants, or leading and junior counsel). It is suggested that the correct approach (and that which is in practice adopted) is to judge the defendant by reference to the standard of skill and care appropriate to members of his profession,[6] who have the same status or formal position as the defendant. Where the defendant holds himself out as a specialist in a particular field, he should be judged by the standards appropriate to a specialist in that field, even if there is no formal recognition of his specialisation.[7]

(c) *Formulation of the standard*

It is therefore suggested that the standard of skill and care which a professional   **2-120**
person is required to exercise may be defined as follows: that degree of skill and care which is ordinarily exercised by reasonably competent members of the profession, who have the same rank[8] and profess the same specialisation (if any) as the defendant. If the standard is formulated in this way, it is fair to both parties. The professional person will not be held liable in the absence of personal fault on his part. The client is adequately protected, because it is normally actionable negligence if a professional person undertakes work beyond his competence.[9]

(d) *Organisation offering professional services*

Where the defendant is an organisation offering professional services (*e.g.* a firm   **2-121**
or a hospital) rather than an individual, different considerations arise. Such an organisation possesses the skills of specialists and generalists and of senior and junior staff. It should deploy such skills as necessary. Thus if, in a hospital, a houseman is required to do the work of a consultant, the standard by which his

---

[3] See, *e.g.* Chap. 8, para. 8–166, below, concerning architects; *Wilsher v. Essex AHA* [1987] Q.B. 730 concerning medical practitioners (discussed in Chap. 12, para. 12–77, below).
[4] [1980] R.P.C. 16. The case went to the Court of Appeal, but not on the issue of negligence.
[5] *ibid.* at 18.
[6] But see para. 2–121, below.
[7] See Chap. 10, para. 10–94 and Chap. 12, para. 12–75, below.
[8] The term "rank" is not entirely satisfactory. It is intended to describe the different levels within hierarchical professions such as medicine.
[9] See, *e.g.* Chap. 10, para. 10–98 and Chap. 12, para. 12–78, below.

services will be judged is the standard of the consultant.[10] In other words, an organisation is judged by the standard of skill and care appropriate to the professional staff who ought to have been undertaking the work in question.

(e) *Undertaking work of other professions*

2–122   Where a person strays across the boundaries of his own profession and undertakes work normally performed by some allied profession, it is submitted that he should be judged by the standard of skill and care applicable to members of the latter profession. Thus if a surveyor agrees to design and to supervise the construction of a building, he should be judged by the standard of a reasonably competent architect.[11]

(f) *New techniques*

2–123   One problem which commonly occurs in the scientific professions, such as medicine and engineering, is that posed by new techniques. At the general level, innovation and the development of new techniques is plainly desirable. In individual cases, however, where the new technique has failed, the defendant usually faces the allegation that he was negligent to depart from general and approved practice. Such cases are discussed later.[12] It is doubted that any general principle[13] can be formulated in respect of such cases, beyond that stated above.[14] However, important matters in determining whether the defendant exercised reasonable skill and care are: (a) whether there was any necessity to attempt a new technique in the instant case,[15] (b) whether the client was adequately informed of the risks involved, and (c) the amount and quality of the preliminary research carried out.

(g) *Changes in the standard required*

2–124   It follows from what has been said above that the standard of skill and care required by law of any given profession is not fixed for all time. Advances in knowledge may render certain courses of conduct "negligent", which were formerly quite acceptable.[16] Furthermore, quite independently of any advances in knowledge, there may be a general improvement in the standards of a particular profession. If so, the standard of the reasonably competent practitioner changes and mistakes which were formerly tolerable come to be regarded as negligent. In addition, the publication of written standards by a profession's governing body may itself bring about a raising or a changing of the quality of work which is required to constitute "reasonable skill and care". There is now a growing trend

---

[10] See *Wilsher v. Essex AHA* [1987] Q.B. 730 at 750–751, *per* Mustill L.J., with whom Glidewell L.J. agreed. This issue did not arise on the appeal to the House of Lords.
[11] See Chap. 9, below.
[12] See Chap. 8, para. 8–138 and Chap. 12, paras 12–109 and 12–110, below.
[13] The statement of the Court of Appeal in *Landau v. Werner* (1961) 105 S.J. 1008 that "success was the best justification for unusual and unestablished treatment" is of little assistance.
[14] See para. 2–119, above.
[15] There was such necessity in *IBA v. EMI and BICC* (1980) 14 Build.L.R. 1.
[16] See, *e.g.* Chap. 12, paras 12–73 to 12–74, below.

amongst professional bodies to publish written standards which reflect the best practices of the profession.[17]

5. FIDUCIARY OBLIGATIONS

(a) *The nature of fiduciary obligations*

The contractual obligations owed by a professional person are agreed by him in return for his clients' promise to pay for his services. In broad terms, the law imposes a tortious duty of care on him where a client or third party is reasonably relying upon his professional skill and knowledge or where his client has retained him to confer a benefit on others. Fiduciary obligations are of a different order. They are based upon the trust reposed by a client in his professional adviser, and in particular the trust that the professional will act solely in his client's interests and not in his own. This is sometimes described as a "duty of loyalty", but in effect it amounts to an inhibition: a professional should not put himself in a position in which his duty to act in his client's interests is in conflict with his own interests, let alone prefer his own interests to those of his client should there be a conflict.[18] The obligations which flow from this general prohibition are called fiduciary obligations. **2–125**

"Fiduciary duty of care". Before considering fiduciary obligations, it is necessary to identify those obligations which are not fiduciary. Fiduciary relationships played an important part in the development of the law of tort in the last century, particularly in the context of claims against professional and other advisers. In *Nocton v. Lord Ashburton*,[19] damages (by way of equitable compensation) were awarded for breach of fiduciary duty by a solicitor who gave bad advice which led a client to act in the interests of the solicitor rather than himself. Viscount Haldane L.C. held that the trial judge had been wrong to treat the claim as based upon deceit. "It was really an action based on the exclusive jurisdiction of a Court of Equity over a defendant in a fiduciary position in respect of matters which at law would also have given a right to damages for negligence."[20] Thereafter, until the decision in *Hedley Byrne & Co. Ltd v. Heller and Partners Ltd*,[21] the existence of a fiduciary relationship was seen as a means of enabling **2–126**

---

[17] See, *e.g.* surveyors (see Chap. 9, paras 9–23 to 9–25), solicitors (see Chap. 10, para. 10–91) and accountants (see Chap. 15, paras 15–93 to 15–96).

[18] See, *e.g.* the formulation by Millett L.J. in *Bristol & West Building Society v. Mothew* [1998] Ch. 1 at 18B–C:

"The distinguishing obligation of a fiduciary is the obligation of loyalty. The principal is entitled to the single-minded loyalty of his fiduciary. This core liability has several facets. A fiduciary must act in good faith; he must *not* make a profit out of his trust. he must *not* place himself in a position where his duty and his interest may conflict; he may *not* act for his own benefit or the benefit of a third person without the informed consent of his principal." (emphasis added)

See also *Att.-Gen. v. Blake* [1998] Ch. 439 at 455, where Lord Woolf M.R. giving the judgment of the Court of Appeal (himself and Millett and Mummery L.JJ.) said at 455E:

" . . . equity is proscriptive, not prescriptive: see *Breen v. Williams* (1996) 186 CLR 71. It tells the fiduciary what he must not do. It does not tell him what he ought to do."

[19] [1914] A.C. 932.

[20] *ibid.* at 957.

[21] [1964] A.C. 465, discussed in paras 2–24 to 2–25, above.

damages to be recovered for negligent advice.[22] In *Hedley Byrne* itself the House of Lords relied upon its earlier decision in *Nocton v. Lord Ashburton* and recognised that damages could be recovered if there were a "special relationship".

2–127   This led some to allege and, at least in Canada,[23] to hold that a professional who gave negligent advice would be liable not only in contract and tort, but also for breach of fiduciary duty. It is hard to see what purpose was served by adding a third cause of action, unless it was hoped to circumvent a limitation period which would defeat both the contractual and tortious claim.[24] It may be that this trend arose from a misconception that any breach of any duty by a fiduciary is a breach of fiduciary duty.[25] It is not.[26] It is now clear that there is no separate "fiduciary duty of care". Rather, the liability of a negligent fiduciary is "a paradigm of the general duty to act with care imposed by law on those who take it upon themselves to act for or advise others".[27] The duty to exercise skill and care may be owed by a fiduciary, but it is not a fiduciary duty: it is a tortious and, where appropriate, contractual duty.[28]

---

[22] See, *e.g.* the decision of Salmon J. in *Wood v. Martins Bank Ltd* [1959] 1 Q.B. 55.

[23] See, *e.g.* the authorities concerning doctors discussed in Chap. 12, para. 12–29, below. For an example of similar confusion see *Wickstead v. Browne* (1992) 30 N.S.W.L.R. 1. In *Breen v. Williams* (1996) 186 C.L.R. 71 several members of the High Court of Australia remarked upon the different approach of the Canadian courts to that adopted in Australia.

[24] As to which see *Cia de Seguros Imperio v. Heath (REBX) Ltd* [2001] 1 W.L.R. 112 discussed in Chap. 5, paras 5–93 to 5–95, below.

[25] See the judgment of Southin J. in *Giradet v. Crease and Co.* (1987) 11 B.C.L.R. (2d) 361 at 362:

"Counsel for the plaintiff spoke of this case in his opening as one of breach of fiduciary duty and negligence. It became clear during his opening that no breach of fiduciary duty is in issue. What is in issue is whether the defendant was negligent in advising on the settlement of a claim for personal injuries suffered in an accident. The word 'fiduciary' is flung around now as if it applied to all breaches of duty by solicitors, directors of companies and so forth. But 'fiduciary' comes from the Latin 'fiducia' meaning 'trust'. Thus, the adjective, 'fiduciary' means of or pertaining to a trustee or trusteeship. That a lawyer can commit a breach of the special duty of a trustee, *e.g.* by stealing his client's money, by entering into a contract with the client without full disclosure, by sending the client a bill claiming disbursements never made and so forth is clear. But to say that simple carelessness is giving advice is such a breach is a perversion of words. The obligation of a solicitor of care and skill is the same obligation of any person who undertakes for reward to carry out a task. One would not assert of an engineer or physician who had given bad advice and from whom common law damages were sought that he was guilty of a breach of fiduciary duty. Why should it be said of a solicitor?"

(This passage has been approved by La Forest J. in *LAC Minerals Ltd v. International Corona Resources Ltd* (1989) 61 D.L.R. (4th) 14, by Ipp J. in *Permanent Building Society v. Wheeler* (1994) 14 ACSR 109 and by Millett L.J. in *Bristol & West Building Society v. Mothew* [1998] Ch. 1.)

[26] See para. 2–128, below.

[27] *Henderson v. Merrett Syndicates Ltd.* [1995] 2 A.C. 145 at 205F, *per* Lord Browne-Wilkinson. See (1995) 111 L.Q.R. 1, *per* Heydon.

[28] *Bristol & West Building Society v. Mothew* [1998] Ch. 1 at 16C–18F, *per* Millett L.J., applying *Permanent Building Society (in liq) v. Wheeler* (1994) 14 A.C.S.R. 109 and *Nocton v. Lord Ashburton* [1914] A.C. 932 at 956, where Viscount Haldane L.C. said:

"My Lords, the solicitor contracts with his client to be skilful and careful. For failure to perform his obligation he may be made liable at law in contract or even in tort, for negligence in breach of a duty imposed on him. In the early history of the action of assumpsit this liability was indeed treated as one for tort. There was a time when in cases of liability for breach of a legal duty of this kind the Court of Chancery appears to have exercised a concurrent jurisdiction. That was not remarkable, having regard to the defective character of legal remedies in those days. But later on, after the action of assumpsit had become fully developed, I think it probable that a demurrer for want of equity would always have lain to a bill which did no more than seek to enforce a claim for damages for negligence against a solicitor."

Effect of fiduciary obligations on contractual and tortious duties. The fact   **2–128**
that a professional person is subject to fiduciary obligations and so may be called
a fiduciary, does not mean that all his duties to his client are fiduciary duties. His
contractual and tortious duties are still owed in contract and tort. They do not
become fiduciary duties because he is a fiduciary.[29] Nor is the scope of the
contractual or tortious duties enlarged because the professional person also owes
fiduciary duties,[30] even if in certain circumstances they might he said to require
him to advise his client.[31] The courts will not impose fiduciary obligations to
make good a failure by a party to a contract to obtain adequate protection of his
interests which could have been achieved by the inclusion of appropriate contractual provisions.[32]

The nature of fiduciary obligations. Fiduciary duties or obligations are a   **2–129**
difficult area of the law.[33] In essence they represent equity's attempt to regulate
the conduct of those whom it regards as bound to act in the interest of others
rather than for themselves.[34] Where one person (the principal) is to be taken as
trusting another (the fiduciary) to act in the principal's interests, equity will not
allow the fiduciary to act in his own interests or in those of a third party. The
obligation of the fiduciary is not to allow his own self interest to conflict with his
duty to act in the principal's interests. The extent of that duty will depend upon
the extent to which he is trusted[35] to act in the interests of the principal so that

---

There may also be an equitable duty on a mortgagee or receiver to exercise skill and care:
Downsview Nominees Ltd v. First City Corp. Ltd [1993] A.C. 295 and *Medforth v. Blake* [2000] Ch.
86. However, this is not a fiduciary duty.

[29] "The expression 'fiduciary duty' is properly confined to those duties which are peculiar to
fiduciaries and the breach of which attracts legal consequences differing from those consequent upon
the breach of other duties. Unless the expression is so limited it is lacking in practical utility. In this
sense it is obvious that not every breach of duty by a fiduciary is a breach of fiduciary duty." *per*
Millett L.J. in *Bristol & West Building Society v. Mothew* [1998] Ch. 1 at 16C–D. See also, *per* La
Forest J. in *LAC Minerals Ltd v. International Corona Resources Ltd* (1989) 61 D.L.R. (4th) 14 at 28.
In *Noranda Australia Ltd v. Lachlan Resources N.L.* (1988) 13 N.S.W.L.R. 1, the parties to a joint
venture provided in their contract that the "relationship of the parties shall be fiduciary in nature".
It was held that this did not mean that every term of the contract was also a fiduciary obligation: the
provision as to the fiduciary relationship only applied to terms relevant to the duty of each party to
act in the mutual interest of both.

[30] See *Clark Boyce v. Mouat* [1994] 1 A.C. 428, discussed in para. 2–133, below.

[31] If a professional person chooses to deal with his client in relation to property within the scope of
his fiduciary obligation of loyalty, then if he is to uphold the transaction he must show that he gave
certain advice: see para. 2–237, below. However, he owes no contractual or tortious duty to give that
advice: the consequence of a failure to give it is to expose him to a claim to have the transaction set
aside (or possibly for equitable compensation), not to a claim for damages in contract or tort.

[32] *Hospital Products Ltd v. United States Surgical Corp.* (1984) 156 C.L.R. 41 at 147, *per* Dawson
J.

[33] Finn, *Fiduciary Obligations* (The Law Book Company Ltd, Australia, 1977) remains the classic
text. See also McKendrick (ed.), *Commercial Aspects of Trusts and Fiduciary Obligations* (Clarendon
Press, Oxford, 1992) and Bean, *Fiduciary Obligations and Joint Ventures* (Clarendon Press, Oxford,
1995).

[34] "A fiduciary is someone who has undertaken to act for or on behalf of another in a particular matter
in circumstances which give rise to a relationship of trust and confidence." *per* Millett L.J. in *Bristol
& West Building Society v. Mothew* [1998] Ch. 1 at 18A, cited with approval by the Privy Council
in *Arklow Investments Ltd v. Maclean* [2000] 1 W.L.R. 594.

[35] The extent of the trust depends upon the application of principle to the particular facts: it is not just
a matter of the subjective intent of the principal.

it is not possible to postulate a series of fiduciary duties which apply to all fiduciaries.[36] Fletcher Moulton L.J. explained this in his much quoted judgment in *Re Coomber*[37]:

> "Fiduciary relations are of many different types; they extend from the relation of myself to an errand boy who is bound to bring back my change up to the most intimate and confidential relations which can possibly exist between one party and another where the one is wholly in the hands of the other because of his infinite trust in him. All these are cases of fiduciary relations, and the Courts have again and again, in cases where there has been a fiduciary relation, interfered and set aside acts which, between persons in a wholly independent position, would have been perfectly valid. Thereupon in some minds there arises the idea that if there is any fiduciary relation whatever any of these types of interference is warranted by it. They conclude that every kind of fiduciary relation justifies every kind of interference. Of course that it absurd. The nature of the fiduciary relation must be such that it justifies the interference."[38]

2-130   So, in each case it is important to establish the extent of the trust, for that will define the extent to which equity will intervene. The trust and confidence which gives rise to fiduciary obligations is not, or need not, be emotional. For example, a director owes fiduciary obligations to his company. In this sense it is to be contrasted with the confidence which is the basis for the equitable doctrine of undue influence.[39] It is based upon reliance, but not the same sort of reliance which may underlie a tortious duty of care.[40] Nor it is simply reliance on another party to a contract to perform his obligations under it.[41] Rather it is the fact that the principal so relies on the fiduciary as to leave the principal vulnerable to any

---

[36] Professor Finn proffered this definition of a fiduciary in his essay in McKendrick (ed.), *Commercial Aspects of Trusts and Fiduciary Obligation*:

"A person will be a fiduciary in his relationship with another when and in so far as that other is entitled to expect that he will act in that other's interests or (as in a partnership) in their joint interests, to the exclusion of his own several interest".

In its Report "Fiduciary Duties and Regulatory Rules" (Law Com. No. 236), the Law Commission gave the following definition:

"Broadly speaking, a fiduciary relationship is one in which a person undertakes to act on behalf of or for the benefit of another often as an intermediary with a discretion or power which affects the interests of the other who depends on a fiduciary for information and advice."

[37] [1911] 1 Ch. 723 at 728–729.

[38] In *Re Goldcorp Exchange Ltd* [1995] 1 A.C. 74, Lord Mustill, giving the opinion of the Privy Council, said at 98A–B:

"To describe someone as a fiduciary, without more, is meaningless. As Frankfurter J. said in *S.E.C. Chenery Corp.* (1943) 318 U.S. 80 at 885–86, cited in *Goff & Jones, The Law of Restitution* (4th ed., 1993), p. 644:

"To say that a man is a fiduciary only begins analysis; it gives direction to further inquiry. To whom is he a fiduciary? What obligations does he owe as a fiduciary? In what respect has he failed to discharge these obligations? And what are the consequences of his deviation from duty?'"

See also *Maguire v. Makaronis* (1997) 188 C.L.R. 449 at 464, where Brennan C.J. and Gaudron, McHugh and Gummow JJ. said:

" . . . to say that the appellants stood as fiduciaries to the respondents calls for the ascertainment of the particular obligations owed to the respondents and consideration of what acts and omissions amounted to failure to discharge those obligations."

[39] See para. 2–144, below.

[40] For example, an engineer asked to design foundations may be relied upon by the building owner, but the engineer will not owe any fiduciary obligations as to the adequacy of his design.

[41] *Re Goldcorp Exchange Ltd* [1995] 1 A.C. 74 at 98C–G.

disloyalty by the fiduciary and so reliant on his good faith.[42] It follows that a commercial relationship at arm's length, with both parties on an equal footing is unlikely to give rise to fiduciary obligations.[43]

The significance of the retainer. When considering the extent of a professional person's fiduciary obligations the scope and terms of any retainer (together with the scope of any tortious duty of care) need to be considered. In particular, it is necessary to ascertain what a professional person has been retained to do and the terms upon which he has agreed to do it in order to establish whether and to what extent he is in a position of trust.[44] If, for example, a professional person is retained to advise or act in relation to a particular piece of property, there is no fiduciary obligation preventing him from purchasing other property as to which he was not retained to advise.[45] So, a solicitor who was retained to act on a libel action can purchase from his client property unrelated to that action in the same way as a complete stranger could.[46] In every case, it is a question of determining what the subject matter of the professional's retainer was.[47] **2–131**

The terms of the retainer are also of importance. Equity will not impose a fiduciary obligation which is inconsistent with the terms agreed. So in *Kelly v. Cooper*[48] the Privy Council had to decide whether an estate agent owed a client, who instructed him on the sale of his house, a fiduciary duty not to act simultaneously for the owner of a neighbouring house, which might interest prospective purchasers of the client's house. The client argued that an agent owed his principal an undivided duty of loyalty, so that if the agent acted for the neighbour without the client's informed consent he would be in breach of contract and in **2–132**

---

[42] *Hospital Products Ltd v. United States Surgical Corp.* (1984) 156 C.L.R. 41 at 142, *per* Dawson J.:

"There is, however, the notion underlying all the cases of fiduciary obligation that inherent in the nature of the relationship itself is a position of disadvantage or vulnerability on the part of one of the parties which causes him to place reliance upon the other and requires the protection of equity acting upon the conscience of that other . . . From that springs the requirement that a person under a fiduciary obligation shall not put himself in a position where his interest and duty conflict or, if conflict is unavoidable, shall resolve it in favour of duty and shall not, except by special arrangement, make a profit out of his position."

[43] *ibid.* at 170, *per* Gibbs C.J.

[44] "Even in the case of a solicitor client relationship, long accepted as a status based fiduciary relationship, the duty is not derived from the status. As in all such cases, the duty is derived from what the solicitor undertakes, or is deemed to have undertaken, to do in the particular circumstances . . . Whether the relationship derives from retainer, less formal arrangement or self-appointment, it must be examined to see what duties are thereby imposed on the fiduciary and the scope and ambit of those duties.": New South Wales Court of Appeal in *Beach Petroleum NL v. Kennedy* [1999] N.S.W.C.A. 408 (reported (1999) 48 N.S.W.L.R. 1), paras 188 and 192 (pp. 45–46 of the report).

[45] *Montesquieu v. Sandys* (1811) 18 Ves.Jun. 302, *Cane v. Allen* (1814) 2 Dow 289 and *Edwards v. Meyrick* (1842) 2 Hare 60.

[46] *Alison v. Clayhills* (1907) 97 L.T. 709 at 712. A solicitor would still have to show that he was not exercising undue influence: see para. 2–144, below.

[47] In the context of the fiduciary obligations between partners, Dixon J. said in *Birtchnell v. Equity Trustees, Executors and Agency Co. Ltd* (1929) 42 C.L.R. 384 at 408:

"The subject matter over which the fiduciary obligations extend is determined by the character of the venture or undertaking for which the partnership exists; and this is to be ascertained, not merely from the express agreement of the parties, whether embodied in written instruments or not, but also from the course of dealing actually pursued by the firm."

In all cases where a fiduciary obligation is alleged it is necessary to identify the "subject matter" in this way: see *Breen v. Williams* (1996) 186 C.L.R. 71, para.14, *per* Brennan C.J.

[48] [1993] A.C. 205.

breach of fiduciary duty. Both claims failed. It is well known that estate agents act for many clients at the same time and that there may well be a conflict of interest between their various clients. Nevertheless, estate agents are regularly instructed on that basis. The Privy Council accordingly held that a term was to be implied into the estate agent's retainer that he would be entitled to act for other, competing clients. That left the claim for breach of fiduciary duty. The Privy Council approved a passage from the judgment of Mason J. in *Hospital Products Ltd v. United States Surgical Corp.*[49] and held that, since the contract allowed the estate agent to act for other clients whose interests might conflict with those of the plaintiff, he would not be in breach of any fiduciary duty by so acting. This reflected the general rule that a principal who gives his informed consent to a fiduciary acting also for someone else with a conflicting interest (or potentially conflicting interest), cannot complain that the principal faces a potential conflict between his duty to him and to his other client.[50]

2–133 The Privy Council came to a similar conclusion in *Clark Boyce v. Mouat.*[51] In that case solicitors acted both for a son, who was borrowing a sum of money, and for his mother, who was charging her house as security for the loan. They advised the mother to seek independent legal advice, but she declined to do so. In due course the son became bankrupt and the mother had to repay the loan. She sued the solicitors for breach of contract, negligence and breach of fiduciary duty. The Privy Council held that there was no reason why a solicitor should not act for two parties with competing interests so long as each had been advised of the conflict. Whether there was a conflict and, if there was, what its extent was depended upon what the solicitor was being retained to do for each party. Therefore, the crucial question was the extent of their retainer by the mother. The Privy Council upheld the trial judge's decision that the mother had not retained the solicitors to advise as to the wisdom of the proposed transaction. Their retainer required them to carry out the necessary conveyancing and to explain the legal consequences of the transaction. This had been done, so that the claims in contract and negligence failed. The Privy Council then rejected the claim, because, in the words of Lord Jauncey:

---

[49] (1984) 156 C.L.R. 41 at 97:
  "That contractual and fiduciary relationships may co-exist between the same parties has never been doubted. Indeed, the existence of a basic contractual relationship has in many situations provided a foundation for the erection of a fiduciary relationship. In these situations it is the contractual foundation which is all important because it is the contract that regulates the basic rights and liabilities of the parties. The fiduciary relationship, if it is to exist at all, must accommodate itself to the terms of the contract so that it is consistent with, and conforms to, them. The fiduciary relationship cannot be superimposed upon the contract in such a way as to alter the operation which the contract was intended to have according to its true construction."

[50] *Bristol & West Building Society v. Mothew* [1998] Ch. 1 at 18H–19B, *per* Millett L.J. The fiduciary must, however, act in good faith in the interests of each of his clients and, if an actual conflict of interest arises, then he may have to cease acting for one or possibly both clients: *ibid.* at 19D-H. See further the decision of the New Zealand Court of Appeal in *Armitage v. Paynter Construction Ltd* [1999] 2 N.Z.L.R. 534, where the solicitor's instructions to act for both parties to a joint venture did create a conflict when the solicitor became aware that one party was in financial difficulties. By paying joint venture money to that party he consciously preferred its interests to that of the other party. In *Bolkiah v. KPMG (a firm)* [1999] 2 A.C. 222 at 235A–C, Lord Millett said that companies which competed with each other were to be inferred to have consented to the same firm of auditors acting for them and for their competitors.

[51] [1994] 1 A.C. 428.

"A fiduciary duty concerns disclosure of material facts in a situation where the fiduciary has either a personal interest in the matter to which the facts are material or acts for another party who has such an interest. It cannot be prayed in aid to enlarge the scope of contractual duties."[52]

(b) Dealing with the principal

"Self-dealing" and "fair-dealing". There is a well-established distinction in the authorities between cases in which the fiduciary is himself the seller or buyer on behalf of the principal ("self-dealing") and cases where the role of the fiduciary is limited to advising or assisting in the transaction or some earlier involvement in the subject matter of the transaction ("fair dealing").[53] In cases of self-dealing, the transaction is usually said to be voidable without more at the instance of the principal. In cases of fair dealing, it is for the fiduciary to show that he took no advantage of his position in that he gave full value and made full disclosure to the principal. In fact, if a fiduciary who was "self-dealing" did give full value and make full disclosure to his principal, then the transaction would not be voidable—the principal would have given his full consent. In effect, it is open to a fiduciary to turn what would be a self-dealing case into a fair-dealing case,[54] although his close connection with the relevant property may make it more difficult for him to show that he has made full disclosure.[55]   **2–134**

Self-dealing. The prohibition on self-dealing is strict. The conflict between duty and interest is so great that a fiduciary is presumed not to have succeeded in ignoring his own interests[56] and the sale is voidable at the instance of the principal.[57] There is no need for the principal to show that the transaction was on   **2–135**

---

[52] *ibid.* at 437G. See also *Norberg v. Wynrib* (1992) 92 D.L.R. (4th) 449 at 481, *per* Sopinka J.:
"Fiduciary duties should not be superimposed on those common law duties simply to improve the nature or extent of the remedy."
In *Att.-Gen. v. Blake* [1998] Ch. 439 at 453D, Lord Woolf M.R., giving the judgment of the Court of Appeal (himself, Millett and Mummery L.JJ.) referred to this as a "salutary warning".
[53] The distinction was made in early cases such as *Ex parte Lacey* (1802) 6 Ves.Jun. 625, *Randall v. Errington* (1805) 10 Ves.Jun. 423, *Morse v. Royal* (1806) 12 Ves.Jun. 355 and *Cane v. Allen* (1814) 2 Dow. 289. In *Tito v. Waddell (No.2)* [1977] Ch. 106 at 241, Megarry V.-C. rejected an argument that there was only one rule (see also *Re Thompson's Settlement* [1986] Ch. 99 at 110–116, *per* Vinelott J.).
[54] *Ex parte Lacey* (1802) 6 Ves. Jun. 625; *Randall v. Errington* (1805) 10 Ves.Jun. 423, as explained by Megarry V.-C. in *Tito v. Waddell (No.2)* [1977] Ch. 106 at 242D, *Sanderson v. Walker* (1807) 13 Ves.Jun. 60, *Andrews v. Mowbray* (1805–07) Wils.Ex. 71 at 73; *Downes v. Grazebrook* (1817) 3 Mer. 200; *Luff v. Lord* (1864) 34 Beav. 220 at 227, *per* Romilly M.R., *Lagunas Nitrate Company v. Lagunas Syndicate* [1899] 2 Ch. 392 and *Movietex Ltd v. Bulfield* [1988] BCLC 104 at 118e–g, *per* Vinelott J.
[55] *Ex parte Lacey* (1802) 6 Ves.Jun. 625 at 626.
[56] *Cook v. Collingridge* (1823) Jacob 607 at 621, *per* Lord Eldon L.C.
[57] *Campbell v. Walker* (1800) 5 Ves.Jun. 678, *Ex parte Lacey* (1802) 6 Ves.Jun. 625, *Att.-Gen. v. Clarendon* (1810) 17 Ves.Jun. 491 at 500, *Downes v. Glazebrook* (1817) 3 Mer. 200, *Aberdeen Railway Co. v. Blaikie Brothers* (1854) 1 Macq. 461, *Phosgate Sewage Company v. Hartmount* (1875) 5 Ch.D. 394, *Erlanger v. New Sombrero Phosphate Company* (1878) 3 App.Cas. 1218, *Williams v. Scott* [1900] A.C. 499, *Wright v. Morgan* [1926] A.C. 788, *Glennon v. Commissioner for Taxation of the Commonwealth of Australia* (1972) 127 C.L.R. 503 and *Re Thompson's Settlement* [1986] Ch. 99.

unfavourable terms or that the fiduciary has made a profit.[58] While the rule might seem harsh, the usual remedy is to set aside the transaction on terms which reflect the consideration given by the fiduciary and any work or improvement he has carried out on the property concerned. It does not usually involve the payment of compensation by the fiduciary to the principal.[59]

2–136   **Fair dealing**. The fair dealing rule is also based on a conflict between duty and interest. It will apply where the fiduciary has a sufficient duty to act in the interests of the principal in respect of a transaction that he will not be permitted to advance his own interest unless he obtains the informed consent of the principal and gives full value. In considering what role a person must have in order to be subject to this fiduciary obligation, the approach of Dixon J. in *McKenzie v. McDonald*[60] is instructive:

> "Did the defendant occupy such a position of confidence towards the plaintiff as to bring him within the equitable requirements of full disclosure and open dealing? In my opinion he did. He assumed the function of advising and assisting a woman in a difficult situation in the acquisition of a residence by means of the disposal or pledging of her property. He was necessarily furnished with an intimate knowledge of her financial position, her obligations, and family needs. He proceeded to advise her upon the wisdom and practicability of raising money by mortgage, and acted for her in an effort to do so. He undertook the sale of her farm, and acquired such information as he could in relation to it, and offered his counsel as to its condition and the price she had asked and in effect should ask."

This emphasises the need for there to be confidence and trust in a person, so as to render the principal vulnerable to an abuse of that trust.[61] Nineteenth-century authority suggests, for example, that it is enough to be a close friend of the principal consulted about a proposed sale,[62] but that a person whose role is confined to providing details of a proposed sale is not subject to the fair dealing rule.[63] In the same way, a person who occupies a fiduciary position is nevertheless permitted to exercise rights and options which were acquired before he did so: there is no abuse of trust or confidence in doing so.[64]

---

[58] *Ex parte* Lacey (1802) 6 Ves.Jun. 625 at 627, *per* Lord Eldon L.C., *Ex parte James* (1803) 8 Ves.Jun. 337 at 348, *per* Lord Eldon L.C., *Randall v. Errington* (1805) 10 Ves.Jun. 423 and *Att.-Gen. v. Dudley* (1915) C.Coop. 146. It is no defence that the fiduciary purchased the property at auction (*Whichote v. Lawrence* (1798) 3 Ves.Jun. 740, *Lister v. Lister* (1802) 6 Ves.Jun. 631, *Beningfield v. Baxter* (1886) 12 App.Cas. 167), nor that the price paid by the fiduciary was as good or better as could be obtained elsewhere (*Baker v. Carter* (1935) 1 Y.& C.Ex. 259, *De Bussche v. Alt* (1878) 8 Ch.D. 286). In short "it is no answer to a claim to set aside a transaction which infringes the self-dealing rule that the transaction was fair or even generous to the trust estate" (*Re Thompson's Settlement* [1986] Ch. 99 at 118B, *per* Vinelott J.).
[59] See Chap. 3, paras 3–09 and 3–10, below.
[60] [1927] V.L.R. 134 at 145.
[61] *cf. Holder v. Holder* [1968] Ch. 353, where a named executor performed some slight functions in that capacity and then purported to renounce his executorship and subsequently bought estate property at a fair price. The Court of Appeal declined to apply the self-dealing rule to him. He "had never acted as executor in a way which could be taken to amount to acceptance of a duty to act in the interests of the beneficiaries": *per* Vinelott J. in *Re Thompson's Settlement* [1986] Ch. 99 at 116C.
[62] *Taylor v. Obee* (1816) 3 Price 83.
[63] *Andrews v. Mowbray* (1805–07) Wils.Ex. 71 and *Guest v. Smythe* (1870) L.R. 5 Ch.App. 551.
[64] *Vyse v. Foster* (1874) L.R. 7 H.L. 318, *Hordern v. Hordern* [1910] A.C. 465 and *Re Mullholland's Will Trusts* [1949] 1 All E.R. 460.

Full advice and disclosure. In *Gibson v. Jeyes*,[65] Lord Eldon L.C. applied the   **2–137**
fair-dealing rule is these terms to a claim against an attorney who had sold an
annuity to a client he had been advising:

> "he might contract: but then he should have said, if he was to deal with her for this, she
> must get another attorney to advise her as to the value: or, if she would not, then out
> of that state of circumstances this clear duty results from the rule of this Court, and
> throws upon him the whole onus of the case; that, if he will mix with the character of
> attorney that of vendor, he shall, if the propriety of the contract comes in question,
> manifest, that he has given her all that reasonable advice against himself that he would
> have given her against a third person."[66]

The fiduciary must show not only that he disclosed all the relevant information
which he had, but that he had obtained all the information which he should have
done.[67] However, he is not obliged to give advice which he would not have given
had he had no personal interest in the transaction.[68] It is not enough for the
fiduciary simply to resign from his position: if he adopts that course, then he still
has to show that he disclosed all relevant information.[69]

Particular difficulties arise when the known value of property increases after it   **2–138**
is acquired by a fiduciary because of some subsequent discovery or event. The
fiduciary would have to show that he disclosed all that he knew[70] and if there
were suspicion that he might have known what was discovered later, then the
transaction would probably be set aside on the application of the principal.[71]
However, if the subsequent event was not anticipated, then the fact that it
increased the value of the property sold to the fiduciary does not render the sale
voidable.[72]

Full value. Full value will mean the current market value[73] on the basis of the   **2–139**
knowledge which the principal should have had. It may be at least as favourable
as what could have been obtained from a third party[74] and, if the fiduciary had

---

[65] (1801) 6 Ves.Jun. 266 at 278.

[66] See also *Harris v. Treemenheere* (1808) 15 Ves.Jun. 34, *Dunbar v. Tredenick* (1813) 2 Ball &
Beatty 304, *Champion v. Rigby* (1830) 1 Russ. & M. 539, *Gresley v. Mousley* (1859) 4 De G.& J. 78,
Pisani v. Att.-Gen. of Gibraltar (1874) L.R. 5 P.C. 516, *Robinson v. Abbott* (1894) 20 V.L.R. 346,
Moody v. Cox & Hatt [1917] 2 Ch. 71 and *Swindle v. Harrison* [1997] 4 All E.R. 705.

[67] *Gresley v. Mousley* (1858) 4 De G. & J. 78.

[68] *Pisani v. Att.-Gen. of Gibraltar* (1974) L.R. 5 P.C. 516 at 537–538.

[69] *Ex parte Lacey* (1802) 6 Ves.Jun. 625 at 626, *Ex parte James* (1803) 8 Ves.Jun. 337 at 348, *Spring
v. Pride* (1864) 4 De G.J. & S. 395 and *Wright v. Morgan* [1926] A.C. 788.

[70] *Haywood v. Roadknight* [1927] V.L.R. 512.

[71] See *Ex parte Lacey* (1802) 6 Ves.Jun. 625 at 627, *Ex parte James* (1803) 8 Ves.Jun. 337 at 349,
Coles v. Trescothick (1804) 9 Ves.Jun. 234 at 248 and *Ex parte Bennett* (1805) 10 Ves.Jun. 391, where
Lord Eldon L.C. discusses the approach to be adopted in a case where land was sold to a fiduciary
and valuable mineral deposits were later found. See also *Lowther v. Lowther* (1806) 13 Ves.Jun. 95,
where Lord Erskine L.C. appears to have thought that if the defendant had acted as agent on the sale
of a painting subsequently found to be a Titian, then the sale would be set aside.

[72] *Montesquieu v. Sandys* (1811) 18 Ves.Jun. 302 (value of reversionary interest increased dramat-
ically when the healthy incumbent died and the successor appointed was aged 60) and *Demerara
Bauxite Co. Ltd v. Hubbard* [1924] A.C. 673. *Edwards v. Meyrick* (1842) 2 Hare 60 is a borderline
case.

[73] *Demerara Bauxite Co. Ltd v. Hubbard* [1926] A.C. 673.

[74] *Denton v. Donner* (1856) 23 Beav. 285, *Plowright v. Lambert* (1885) 52 L.T. 646 and *Lunghi v.
Sinclair* [1966] W.A.R. 172.

an advisory role, on terms which the fiduciary would have advised the principal to accept from a third party.[75]

2–140   **The fiduciary's interest.** The fiduciary will have an interest in any transaction to which he personally is a party. Equity looks at the substance rather than the form of a transaction, so that if a party to the transaction is a limited company which is no more than the fiduciary's *alter ego*, the transaction will be subject to the rule.[76] A share holding which is not so small that it can be disregarded is sufficient to bring the rule into effect.[77] If the other party is the fiduciary's partner or a firm in which he is a partner the rule applies.[78] The fact that a fiduciary was acting for a third party who was a party to the transaction is sufficient, for the fiduciary has divided loyalties.[79] It is always worth bearing in mind the dictum of Upjohn L.J. in *Boulting v. Association of Cinematograph, Television and Allied Technicians*[80]:

> "A broad rule like this[81] must be applied with common sense and with an appreciation of the sort of circumstances in which over the last 200 years and more it has been applied and thrived. It must be applied realistically to a state of affairs which discloses a real conflict of duty and interest and not to some theoretical conflict."

(c) *Unauthorised profits and diversion of opportunities*

2–141   While acting in the interests of his principal a fiduciary may be able to further his own interests by profiting from his fiduciary position or by diverting to himself opportunities which properly belong to his principal. The classic case of the latter is *Keech v. Sandford*,[82] where a trustee of a lease took the reversion personally, having failed to obtain a renewal for the trust, and was held to hold it on trust for the beneficiary. In the same way, a fiduciary whose role is to negotiate for a purchase on behalf of his principal cannot purchase for himself.[83] Nor can he exploit confidential information which he learns in his fiduciary capacity for his own benefit.[84] Again, it is important to establish the extent of the subject matter of the fiduciary obligation. In relation to bribes and secret commissions the courts have been willing to stretch the definition of fiduciary to provide a remedy.[85]

---

[75] *Champion v. Rigby* (1830) 1 Russ. & M. 539, *Holman v. Loynes* (1852) 4 De G.M. & G. 270 and *Widgery v. Tepper* (1878) 38 L.T. 434; *cf. Blackham v. Heythorpe* (1917) 23 C.L.R. 156.

[76] *Silkstone and Haigh Moor Coal Co. v. Edey* [1900] 1 Ch. 167, where the company was "a mere trustee" for the fiduciary.

[77] *Transvaal Lands Co. v. New Belgium (Transvaal) Land and Development Co.* [1914] 2 Ch. 488, *Re Clark; Clark v. Moore, Moores (Chemists) Ltd* (1920) 150 L.T.Jo. 94 and *Movietex Ltd v. Bulfield* [1988] BCLC 104 at 122e–g.

[78] *Re Moore* (1881) 51 L.J. (N.S.) Ch. 72 and *Re Thompson's Settlement* [1986] Ch. 99.

[79] *Ex parte Bennett* (1805) 10 Ves.Jun. 381, *Hesse v. Briant* (1856) 4 De G.M. & G. 623, *Moody v. Cox & Hatt* [1917] 2 Ch. 71, *Imeson v. Lister* (1920) L.T.Jo. 446 and *Heywood v. Roadknight* [1927] V.L.R. 512; *cf. North and South Trust Co. v. Berkeley* [1971] 1 W.L.R. 470 at 484H–485A, *per* Donaldson J.

[80] [1964] 2 Q.B. 606 at 637–638.

[81] Upjohn L.J. was considering the rule that a fiduciary should not allow his personal interest to conflict with his duty.

[82] (1726) Cas. t. K. 61; *cf. Aberdeen Town Council v. Aberdeen University* (1877) 2 App.Cas. 544.

[83] *Lees v. Nuttall* (1834) 2 My. & K. 891 and *Cook v. Deeks* [1916] 1 A.C. 554.

[84] *Boardman v. Phipps* [1967] 2 A.C. 46 and *Regal (Hastings) Ltd v. Gulliver* [1967] 2 A.C. 134 (note). This may overlap with a claim for breach of confidence: see paras 2–147 to 2–162, below.

[85] *Reading. v. Att.-Gen.* [1951] A.C. 507 affirming [1949] 2 K.B. 232: ex-sergeant using uniform to assist smuggling operation.

(d) *Undue influence*[85a]

(i) *The classes of undue influence*

Gifts, deeds and other transactions may be set aside if procured by the undue 2–142
influence of one person over another. In recent years cases have been divided into
two classes, with the second class itself sub-divided into two.[86] Class 1 concerns
cases of actual undue influence. Class 2 concerns cases where the existing
relationship between the parties is such that there is a presumption that by reason
of the trust and confidence placed in him one exerts influence over the other. The
first sub-division of class 2 (class 2A) is of relationships which are automatically
assumed to give rise to undue influence. The second sub-division (class 2B) is
cases where it is shown that one party to a relationship placed such trust and
confidence in the other party that a presumption of undue influence may arise.
That is relatively easy to establish between spouses.[87] There is some uncertainty
as to whether in class 2 cases the person seeking to set aside the transaction must
show that it was manifestly disadvantageous.[88]

Class 1: Actual undue influence. Cases of actual undue influence are rela- 2–143
tively infrequent and turn upon their own special facts. In the leading case of
Allcard v. Skinner[89] Lindley L.J. referred to four earlier decisions as instances of
actual undue influence. One was a case where coercion was shown[90] and the
others were cases involving charlatans.[91]

Class 2A: Relationships which are presumed to give rise to undue influ- 2–144
ence. Class 2A relationships include doctor and patient,[92] solicitor and client,[93]
parent and child,[94] guardian and ward[95] and religious adviser and disciple.[96] They
are all relationships in which one party is likely to trust and be influenced by the
other. They are essentially personal relationships. The trust and confidence

---

[85a] This section should be read subject to the decision of the House of Lords in *Royal Bank of Scotland v. Etridge* [2001] UKHL 44.

[86] *Royal Bank of Scotland Plc v. Etridge (No.2)* [1998] 4 All E.R. 705 at 711f–j, *per* Stuart-Smith L.J. giving the judgment of the Court of Appeal (himself, Millett and Morritt L.JJ.).

[87] *Barclays Bank Plc v. O'Brien* [1994] 1 A.C. 180 at 190C–191B, *per* Lord Browne-Wilkinson. See also *Re Lloyds Bank Ltd, Bomze v. Bomze* [1931] 1 Ch. 289 at 302, *per* Maugham J., *Mackenzie v. Royal Bank of Canada* [1934] A.C. 468 at 475, *per* Lord Atkin and *Yerkey v. Jones* (1938–9) 63 C.L.R. 649 at 659, *per* Latham J. and at 675 and at 677, *per* Dixon J.

[88] See *Royal Bank of Scotland Plc v. Etridge (No.2)* [1998] 4 All E.R. 705 at 713d–g.

[89] (1887) 36 Ch.D. 145 at 181.

[90] *White v. Mead* (1840) 2 Ir. Eq. Rep. 240.

[91] *Norton v. Relly* (1764) 2 Eden 286, *Nottidge v. Prince* (1860) 2 Giff. 246 and *Lyon v. Home* (1868) L.R. 6 Eq. 655.

[92] See, *e.g. Mitchell v. Homfray* (1881) 8 Q.B.D. 587, *Radcliffe v. Price* (1902) 18 T.L.R. 466, *Williams v. Johnson* [1937] 4 All E.R. 34 and *Brooks v. Alker* (1975) 60 D.L.R. (3d) 577.

[93] See, *e.g. Liles v. Terry* [1895] Q.B. 679, *Wills v. Barron* [1902] A.C. 271, *Wright v. Carter* [1903] 1 Ch. 27, *Allison v. Clayhills* (1907) 97 L.T. 709 and *Lloyd v. Coote & Ball* [1915] 1 K.B. 242.

[94] See, *e.g. Powell v. Powell* [1900] 1 Ch. 243, *O'Connor v. Foley* [1905] 1 I.R. 1, *M'Mackin v. Hibernian Bank* [1905] 1 I.R. 296, *Lancashire Loans Ltd v. Black* [1934] 1 K.B. 380, *Bullock v. Lloyds Bank Ltd* [1955] 1 Ch. 817 and *Re Pauling's Settlement Trusts* [1964] Ch. 303. The presumption weakens and eventually disappears as the child is emancipated by age, marriage and living away from the parent.

[95] See, *e.g. Smith v. Kay* (1859) 7 H.L.C. 750 and *Dettman v. Metropolitan and Provincial Bank Ltd* (1863) 1 H. & M. 641.

[96] See, *e.g. Allcard v. Skinner* (1887) 36 Ch.D. 145, *Morley v. Loughnan* [1893] 1 Ch. 736, *Chennells v. Bruce* (1939) 55 T.L.R. 422 and *Roche v. Sherrington* [1982] 2 All E.R. 426.

involved is different from that which characterises fiduciary relationships, for example the relationship between a commercial principal and his agent or between a limited company and its directors.[97] It is therefore not surprising that a solicitor who enters a transaction with a corporate client may find it relatively easy to show that the client was acting of its own free will and so uphold the transaction.[98]

2–145   **Class 2B: Relationships which are shown to involve the necessary trust and confidence.** There is a deliberate reluctance to define the circumstances in which one person will be found on the facts to be in such a relationship to another as to be able to influence him, because the courts will not fetter their powers to prevent victimisation.[99] Nevertheless, it is possible to analyse the decided cases so as to discover what has led to a finding that one person was in a position to influence another. The class 2A relationships indicate that the relationship will usually be intimate and personal. In *Yerkey v. Jones,*[1] Dixon J. said that examination of the relations which were presumed to give influence showed that not only did they give one party "an opportunity of obtaining ascendancy or confidence and of abusing it" but also that "in none of those relations is it natural to expect the one party to give property to the other". In *Re Brockehurst's Estate,*[2] Bridge L.J. found three characteristics of those relationships presumed to give one party influence over the other: a duty to advise, a position of actual or potential dominance and the existence of trust and confidence. He suggested that the first two were the most useful. In *Goldsworthy v. Brickell,*[3] Nourse L.J. said:

> "In all of these relationships . . . the principle is the same. It is that the degree of trust and confidence is such that the party in whom it is reposed, either because he is or has become an adviser of the other or because he has been entrusted with the management of his affairs or everyday needs or for some other reason, is in a position to influence him into effecting the transaction of which complaint is later made."

So, undue influence is often found where an old person is looked after by someone else,[4] but where a reasonable degree of independence is retained, influence will not be found.[5] In the same way, a woman in her fifties was found to be under the influence of her uncle because she relied on him completely in

---

[97] There is an overlap between fiduciary relationships and relationships giving rise to a presumption of undue influence (*e.g.* solicitor and client). However, they involve different types of unconscionable conduct.

[98] As in *Westmelton v. Archer* [1982] V.R. 305.

[99] *Hunter v. Atkins* (1832–4) 3 My. & Cr. 113 at 140–141, *per* Lord Brougham L.C., *Allcard v. Skinner* (1887) 36 Ch.D. 145 at 183, *per* Lindley L.J. and *National Westminster Bank Plc v. Morgan* [1985] A.C. 686, at 709, *per* Lord Scarman.
"Just as the degree of unfairness in the transaction may vary widely, so may the nature of the relationship between the parties. The capacity of one person to influence another varies with the degree of trust and confidence reposed by that other in him. In some relationships the capacity for influence may be slight; in others it may be overwhelming." *Royal Bank of Scotland Plc v. Etridge (No.2)* [1998] 4 All E.R. 705 at 713h–714a.

[1] (1938–1939) 63 C.L.R. 649 at 675.

[2] [1978] Ch. 14 at 41.

[3] [1987] Ch. 378 at 401D.

[4] See, *e.g. Inche Noriah v. Sheik Allie Bin Omar* [1929] A.C. 127, *Johnson v. Buttress* (1936) 56 C.L.R. 113, *Stewart v. Rundle* [1940] 2 D.L.R. 503, *Re Craig, Meneces v. Middleton* [1971] Ch. 95 and *Goldsworthy v. Brickell* [1987] Ch. 378.

[5] *Jenkins v. Public Curator* (1953) 90 C.L.R. 113, *Re Brockehurst's Estate* [1978] Ch. 14 and *R. v. Hutton* [1978] N.I. 139.

business matters and always followed his advice.[6] On the other hand, strong evidence will be needed to show that one businessman had influence over another.[7] Professional relationships which are commercial in character are unlikely to give rise to influence, whereas those which are more intimate and personal may well do so.

(ii) *Rebutting the presumption*

In order to rebut the presumption, the person seeking to uphold the transaction **2–146** has to show that either the other party was acting free from his influence or that he was placed in an equivalent position by the receipt of independent legal advice.[8] The problem is not lack of understanding, but lack of independence.[9] It follows, that if independent legal advice is to be relied upon, then it is not enough that the nature of the transaction is explained. The advisor must be competent and properly informed.[10] He should consider whether the transaction should be entered at all and, if so, whether on the proposed or different terms. The advisor should evaluate the risks involved.[11] However, if the person seeking to uphold the advice knows that the other party has received independent legal advice, he is not without more on notice that it was inadequate.[12]

6. CONFIDENTIALITY[13]

(a) *Introduction*

A duty of confidence arises when confidential information comes to the know- **2–147** ledge of a person in circumstances where he has notice, or is held to have agreed, that the information is confidential, with the effect that it would be just in all the circumstances that he should be precluded from disclosing the information to others.[14] Although not intended to be a definitive statement when it was given, this proposition provides a useful starting point for the consideration of this area of predominantly judge-made law that reflects the willingness of judges to afford

---

[6] *Bank of New South Wales v. Rogers* (1941) 65 C.L.R. 42.

[7] *Fowler v. Wyatt* (1857) 24 Beav. 232 at 236–237, *per* Romilly M.R.

[8] *Royal Bank of Scotland Plc v. Etridge (No.2)* [1998] 4 All E.R. 705 at 714c–d and *Inche Noriah v. Sheik Allie Bin Omar* [1929] A.C. 127.

[9] *Banco Exterior Internacional v. Mann* [1985] 1 All E.R. 936 at 946, *per* Hobhouse L.J. As Lord Eldon L.C. said in *Huegenin v. Baseley* (1807) 14. Ves.Jun. 273 at 300: "The question is not whether she knew what she was doing, had done, or proposed to do, but how the intention was produced."

[10] *Wright v. Carter* [1903] 1 Ch. 27.

[11] *Royal Bank of Scotland Plc v. Etridge (No.2)* [1998] 4 All E.R. 705 at 715b–717c.

[12] *ibid.* at 721a–722j. However, the transaction may be so outrageous that the person seeking to uphold it will be on notice that the advice was not adequate, for, had it been adequate, the other party would not have proceeded: *Credit Lyonnais Bank Nederland N.V. v. Burch* [1997] 1 All E.R. 144, CA.

[13] See generally Toulson and Phipps, *Confidentiality* (Sweet and Maxwell, 1996) ("Toulson & Phipps"). Gurry, *Breach of Confidence* (Clarendon Press, Oxford, 1984) ("Gurry") is also useful, if rather dated. Meagher, Gummow and Lehane, *Equity, Doctrines and Remedies* (3rd ed., Butterworths, 1992) provide a helpful analysis in Chap. 41. Confidentiality may overlap with a developing civil right to privacy: see, *e.g. Douglas v. Hello! Ltd* [2001] 2 W.L.R. 992, CA. The latter is not discussed in this section, the existing law of confidentiality being of more general application to professional persons. However, as the law of privacy develops it may well impact on professionals such as doctors, insurance brokers and solicitors.

[14] *Att.-Gen. v. Guardian Newspapers (No.2)* [1990] 1 A.C. 109 at 281B, *per* Lord Goff.

protection to people from being taken advantage of by those to whom they have entrusted confidential information.[15] It is a subject of particular importance to the professional and, indeed, the obligation to keep matters confidential is one of the defining features of a professional relationship.[16]

(b) *Origins of the duty of confidence*

2–148   **Prince Albert v. Strange.** A duty of confidence and a remedy for its breach has long been recognised by English law.[17] The jurisdiction is most often thought to be equitable in nature but until the foundation stone of the modern law was laid in *Prince Albert v. Strange*[18] there was no general right of relief in respect of the misuse (threatened or actual) of confidential information.[19] In *Prince Albert v. Strange* the plaintiff obtained an injunction restraining the defendant from publishing a catalogue containing a collection of private etchings made by Queen Victoria and Prince Albert. The collection was to be published by the defendant in a catalogue that described the etchings, announced an exhibition of them and included a false statement to the effect that the catalogue had royal consent. The defendant had obtained copies of the etchings from an employee of a printer who had received plates of the etchings in order to make copies for the Queen. The plaintiff sought an injunction to prevent publication of the catalogue on two grounds. The first was that publication would infringe the plaintiff's proprietary rights in the etchings. The second was that the contents of the catalogue had been derived from a breach of trust and thus that the plaintiff was entitled to an injunction on the basis of knowing receipt. The plaintiff was successful on both arguments both at first instance and on appeal. On appeal, while asserting that its facts brought it squarely within the existing law,[20] Lord Cottenham L.C. stated that "this case by no means depends solely upon the question of property, for a breach of trust, confidence, or contract, would of itself entitle the Plaintiff to an injunction".[21]

2–149   The defendant argued that there was no infringement of the plaintiff's proprietary rights in the etchings by mere descriptions of them appearing in the catalogue. Further, he denied on affidavit having any reason to suspect that the etchings had been obtained by unlawful means. It has been suggested that these submissions, directed as they were to the two principle strands of the plaintiff's case had some force.[22] It is for this reason that it might be thought that the case went some way in establishing a more general (equitable) jurisdiction for obtaining a remedy of a threatened or actual breach of confidence.

2–150   **Theoretical bases for the jurisdiction after *Prince Albert v. Strange*.**[23] Lord Cottenham's list of grounds upon which the injunction in the Prince Albert case

---

[15] *ibid.* at 267H, *per* Lord Griffiths.

[16] See Chap. 1, para. 1–01.

[17] The jurisdiction was described as "ancient" by Megarry J. in *Coco v. A. N. Clark (Engineers) Ltd* [1969] R.P.C. at 46. See Chap. I of Toulson and Phipps, *op.cit.*, for an historical review of the jurisdiction.

[18] (1849) 1 De.G & Sm. 652; (1849) 1 Mac. & G. 25.

[19] A comprehensive summary of the older cases can be found in Toulson and Phipps, *op.cit.*, at paras 1–01 to 1–05 inclusive.

[20] The established categories of liability being infringement of proprietary rights, breach of contract, breach of trust by the defendant and knowing receipt.

[21] (1849) 1 Mac. & G. 25 at 43.

[22] See Toulson and Phipps, *op.cit.*, at para. 1–07.

[23] A detailed examination of this subject is beyond the scope of this work but reference should be made to the helpful analysis in Toulson and Phipps, *op.cit.*, Chap. II.

may have been granted has been used to broaden the jurisdiction. Nevertheless, a coherent theoretical justification for this extension was lacking with its existence being more assumed than explained:

> "In some cases it has been referred to as property, in others contract, and in others again, it has been treated as founded upon trust or confidence, meaning, as I conceive, that the Court fastens the obligation on the conscience of the party ... but whatever grounds the jurisdiction is founded, the authorities leave no doubt as to the exercise of it."[24]

Nevertheless, the basis upon which the courts act is not merely a matter of academic interest. It goes to the practical question of the remedies available, in particular to the questions whether the courts can award damages or equitable compensation and, if so, on what basis. Lord Cottenham mentioned three possibilities: property, contract or some trust-like obligation that binds the recipient's conscience. In the *Spycatcher* case,[25] at least one member of the House of Lords deliberately avoided the "fundamental" question of whether or not, contract apart, the duty arose out of some obligation of conscience arising from the circumstances of the receipt of the information or whether confidential information was itself property.[26]

A Proprietary Right? This last question has led to a sharp division of opinion. **2–151**
This is most obviously demonstrated by the decision of the House of Lords in *Boardman v. Phipps*.[27] In that case purchasers of shares in a company made a profit by reason of their special position in relation to a trust which owned a substantial holding in the company. At the date they acquired their shares both purchasers were agents of the trustees and were able to obtain information about the company by reason of their position. One of the purchasers was the solicitor to the trustees. Neither purchaser reported these matters to the trustees. The House of Lords held by a majority of 3 to 2 that the purchasers were liable to account for the profits made, subject to an allowance for the value of their work. In the course of their speeches differing views were expressed as to whether information was or could be property. A majority (but not the same majority as that which concurred in the actual result) expressed doubts as to whether information could strictly be property.[28] Their views accord with much earlier authority that there was no property in a set of ideas.[29]

---

[24] *Morision v. Moat* (1851) 9 Hare 241 at 255, *per* Turner V.-C.
[25] *Att.-Gen. v. Guardian Newspapers Ltd (No.2)* [1990] 1 A.C. 109.
[26] *ibid.* at 281, *per* Lord Goff.
[27] [1967] 2 A.C. 46.
[28] Viscount Dilhorne (dissenting) thought that "some information and knowledge can be properly regarded as property", but that the information in question was not "to be regarded as property of the trust in the same way as shares held by the trust" (*ibid.* at 89–90). Lord Cohen said that "Information is, of course, not property in the strict sense of that word" (*ibid.* at 102). Lord Upjohn (dissenting) was of the opinion that "information is not property at all" (*ibid.* at 127). Lord Hodson dissented "from the view that information is of its nature something which is not properly to be described as property" (*ibid.* at 107). Finally, Lord Guest thought that the information acquired "became trust property" (*ibid.* at 115). It is submitted that there is little to be gained from debating this point, which was not the point of difference between the majority and the minority.
[29] *Jeffreys v. Boosey* (1854) 4 H.L.C. 814. See also *Bowstead and Reynolds on Agency* (16th ed.), para. 6–076. In *Att.-Gen. v. Guardian Newspapers Ltd* [1987] 1 W.L.R. 1248 at 1264D-F, Browne-Wilkinson V.-C. accepted that information "is not property in any sense", but still preferred an analysis based on "the traditional terms of equitable rights over property".

2–152 Nevertheless, the notion that confidential information may have the character—or at least some of the characteristics—of property persisted. Thus in *Seager v. Copydex Ltd (No. 2)*,[30] the Court of Appeal ordered damages for the misuse of confidential information to be assessed by reference to the market value of the information and, further, that once the damages had been paid the right to use the information in question would belong to the defendants. This approach was adopted by analogy with the assessment of damages for conversion. As has been pointed out,[31] the difficulty with this approach is that ordinarily liability for breach of confidence is founded upon conduct that binds the conscience, whereas the liability to pay damages for conversion may exist where the defendant is unaware of the true ownership of the property. Further, there is recent authority to the effect that claims for breach of confidence "do not arise in tort"[32] and so it would appear that this line of argument has now withered on the vine.[33] Nevertheless, aspects of such claims remain similar to claims in tort and it is important to bear tortious concepts in mind when considering this jurisdiction.

2–153 **Contract.** Here the position is more straight-forward. Particular contractual relationships, of which many professional relationships are good examples, give rise to express or implied terms imposing duties of confidence. In such circumstances, an award of damages for breach of the duty is not problematic. However, given that many claims for breach of confidence will not have a basis in contract, if the justification for the extra-contractual jurisdiction is not to be found in concepts of property (be it equitable or tort-based), a theoretical basis for the award of damages in equity must be found.

2–154 **A free-standing equitable duty.** The most coherent justification for the existence of an equitable duty of confidence and a jurisdiction to provide a remedy for its breach would seem to lie in the notion that the recipient of confidential information has his conscience bound in such a way that breach of his duty should properly be actionable. Here, the conceptual analysis is obviously similar to that employed in the case of fiduciary obligations.[34] The focus is on the relationship between the parties, the knowledge and conscience of one of them

---

[30] [1969] 1 W.L.R. 809.
[31] By Toulson and Phipps, at para. 2–16.
[32] *Kitechnology BV v. Unicor GmbH* [1995] F.S.R. 765.
[33] But see Goff and Jones, *The Law of Restitution* (5th ed.), p. 762, where it is suggested that there may be concurrent liability for a breach of confidence in contract and tort and the court may act on the assumption that the information was the property of the confider which the recipient had converted. In *Dowson and Mason Ltd v. Potter* [1986] 1 W.L.R. 1419, damages were assessed on the basis that confidential information was property. However, this was because of the terms of a consent order.
[34] Indeed, it is sometimes described as a fiduciary obligation: see *Att.-Gen. v. Blake* [1998] Ch. 439 at 454F. However, as Henry J. observed when giving the opinion of the Privy Council in *Arklow Investments Ltd v. Maclean* [2000] 1 W.L.R. 1, at 600F-G, little is gained by attaching this label. What matters is whether in the particular circumstances equity requires that information be kept confidential. The better view is that, while a fiduciary may well find himself obliged to maintain the confidentiality of information, "Where . . . the essence of the complaint is misuse of confidential information, the appropriate cause of action in favour of the party aggrieved is breach of confidence and not breach of fiduciary duty" (*per* Sopinka J. in *LAC Minerals Ltd v. International Corona Resources Ltd* (1989) 61 D.L.R. (4th) 14, cited by Otton L.J. in *Indata Equipment Supplies Ltd v. ACL Ltd* [1998] 1 BCLC 412 at 419h–420a).

and the type of duty imposed is in the nature of an inhibition rather than a requirement (as in the case of a tortious duty of care) to meet a required standard of conduct. This approach is not without support from the authorities. Thus in *Fraser v. Evans*,[35] Lord Denning M.R. commented:

> "The jurisdiction is based not so much on property or on contract as on the duty to be of good faith. No person is permitted to divulge to the world information which he had received in confidence, unless he had just cause or excuse for doing so."[36]

This approach has also been adopted in other jurisdictions such as Australia **2–155** where it has been said that the rational basis for the general equitable jurisdiction "lies in the notion of an obligation of conscience arising from the circumstances in or through which the information was communicated or obtained".[37] Quite apart from its conceptual lucidity, such an approach has the advantage of providing a clear justification for an award of damages (or equitable compensation) for breach of confidence. Other attempts have been made to justify the availability of this remedy for breach of what would appear to be an exclusively equitable duty, but these have largely been unpersuasive.[38] However, the recognition of a free-standing equitable duty of confidence and a corresponding jurisdiction to provide a full range of remedies, including damages (or equitable compensation properly so-called), for its breach appears consistent with developments in the analogous area of the law of fiduciary obligations.[39] The question remains as to whether this free-standing equitable jurisdiction simply augments the existing bases for the recognition of a duty of confidence, or whether it is of itself the single basis upon which the jurisdiction as a whole may be explained. In New Zealand the jurisdiction is seen as deriving historically from equity, but it has been suggested that its origins are of less relevance than its existence: the courts will now award damages for breach of a duty of confidence.[40] Again, in Canada, there is support for the view that an action for breach of confidence is now to be regarded as *sui generis* with a wide variety of available remedies.[41] In

---

[35] [1969] 1 QB 349 at 361.

[36] See also, *e.g. Morison v. Moat* (1851) 9 Hare 241 and *Seager v. Copydex Ltd* [1967] 1 W.L.R. 923 at 931F, *per* Lord Denning M.R.:

"The law on this subject does not depend on any implied contact. It depends on the broad principle of equity that he who has received information in confidence shall not take unfair advantage of it. He must not make use of it to the prejudice of him who gave it without obtaining his consent."

See also *Att.-Gen. v. Guardian Newspapers Ltd (No.2)* [1990] 1 A.C. 109 at 215G–H, *per* Bingham L.J.

[37] *Moorgate Tobacco Co. Ltd v. Philip Morris Ltd (No.2)* (1984) 156 C.L.R. 415 at 438, *per* Deane J., High Court of Australia.

[38] See, *e.g.* the suggestion by Lord Goff that damages are available by reason of a "beneficent interpretation" of Lord Cairns' Act in *Att.-Gen. v. Guardian Newspapers (No.2)* [1990] 1 A.C. 109 at 286D–E and the alternative justification for the award of damages in *Seager v. Copydex Ltd* [1967] 1 W.L.R. 923 on the basis of a quantum meruit in Goff and Jones, *The Law of Restitution* (5th ed., 1998), p. 760.

[39] See Chap. 3, paras 3–15 and 3–16, below.

[40] *Aquaculture Corp. v. New Zealand Green Mussel Co. Ltd* [1990] 3 N.Z.L.R. 299 at 301, *per* Cooke P.

[41] *LAC Minerals Ltd v. International Corona Resources Ltd* (1989) 61 D.L.R. (4th) 14, *per* Sopinka J. The remedies available included an award of damages and the imposition of a constructive trust.

Australia the existence of an independent equitable jurisdiction has been recognised for some time.[42] The latter is the preferable view.[43] There is a coherent justification for an independent equitable jurisdiction, namely that the recipient of information which he knows or should know is confidential, should maintain that confidentiality. To bring all cases of breach or threatened breach of confidence within other categories such as claims for abuse of property or breach of a fiduciary obligation would or might involve stretching those categories beyond their proper limits. To exclude claims which did not fall within the proper limits of such categories would be to deny a remedy where one should be given.[44] It is with this independent duty of confidence that the rest of this section is concerned.

(c) *Elements of the cause of action*

2–156   A claim for breach of confidence may be established if three essential requirements are met:

(1) the information that forms the subject matter of the action must be confidential;

(2) it must have been imparted by the confider to the recipient in circumstances which justify the imposition of a duty of confidence; and

(3) the recipient must have used or disclosed the information without the authority or consent of the confider, possibly to the detriment of the confider.[45]

2–157   **Confidentiality of the information.** The information which it is alleged is the subject of a duty of confidence must display a "necessary quality of confidence about it".[46] It must not be something which is public property and public

---

[42] *Moorgate Tobacco Co. Ltd v. Philip Morris Ltd (No.2)* (1984) 156 C.L.R. 415 at 437–438, *per* Deane J:

"It is unnecessary, for the purposes of the present appeal, to attempt to define the precise scope of the equitable jurisdiction to grant relief against an actual or threatened abuse of confidential information not involving any tort or any breach of some express or implied contractual provision, some wider fiduciary duty or some copyright or trade mark right. A general equitable jurisdiction to grant such relief has long been asserted and should, in my view, now be accepted: see *Commonwealth of Australia v. John Fairfax & Sons Ltd* (1980) 147 C.L.R. 39 at 50–52. Like most heads of exclusive equitable jurisdiction, its rational basis does not lie in proprietary right. It lies in the notion of an obligation of conscience arising from the circumstances in or through which the information was communicated or obtained."

This was approved by Scott J. and Bingham L.J. in *Att.-Gen. v. Guardian Newspapers (No.2)* [1990] 1 A.C. 109 at 147H and 216B. For subsequent development of the law in Australia see Toulson and Phipps, para. 2–23.

[43] Lord Keith recognised "an independent equitable principle of confidence" in *Att.-Gen. v. Guardian Newspapers Ltd (No.2)* [1990] 1 A.C. 109 at 255E. See also *Duchess of Argyll v. Duke of Argyll* [1967] Ch. 302 at 318–322, *per* Ungoed-Thomas J. and *Douglas v. Hello! Ltd* [2001] 2 W.L.R. 992 at 1024B-E, *per* Sedley L.J.

[44] See also Toulson and Phipps, at para. 2–24.

[45] See *Coco v. A.N. Clark (Engineers) Ltd* [1969] R.P.C. 41 at 47, *per* Megarry J. described by Simon Brown L.J. in *R. v. Department of Health, ex p. Source Informatics Ltd* [2000] 2 W.L.R. 904 at 946C as the "conventional starting point for considering the nature and scope of the duty of confidentiality". See also *Murray v. Yorkshire Fund Managers Ltd* [1998] 1 W.L.R. 951 at 956G–H, *per* Nourse L.J.

[46] *Saltman Engineering Co. Ltd v. Campbell Engineering Co. Ltd* (1948) 65 R.P.C. 203 at 215, *per* Lord Greene M.R.

knowledge.[47] Nevertheless, it is possible for confidential information to be comprised of information that is in the public domain. What is essential, at least in a commercial context, is that the confider has used his brain in compiling that information or using it in a particular way and has produced a result that can only be achieved by another person if that same exercise is performed.[48] It must have "the basic attribute of inaccessibility".[49] So taking unauthorised photographs of a confidential event could amount to a breach of confidence.[50] Information can lose its confidential quality with time.[51] A duty of confidence will not apply to mere trivia or useless information.[52] It is important to identify what information is at issue: for example, it is one thing to disclose the identities of patients who are prescribed various drugs, but another just to disclose information as to which doctors prescribed which drugs, while not revealing the identities of their patients.[53]

Circumstances in which the information is imparted. The information must   **2–158** be confided in the sense that the recipient knows or should know that he should keep it confidential. This will largely be a question of fact in any particular case. In the case of a professional person to whom information is imparted by a client, it will not usually be hard to show.

---

[47] *Seager v. Copydex Ltd* [1967] 1 W.L.R. 923 at 931G, *per* Lord Denning M.R. ("public knowledge") and *Woodward v. Hutchins* [1977] 1 W.L.R. 760 at 764D, *per* Lord Denning M.R. ("in the public domain"). Information "in the public domain" has been described as meaning "no more than that the information is so generally accessible that, in all the circumstances, it cannot be regarded as confidential": *per* Lord Goff in *Att.-Gen. v. Guardian Newspapers (No.2)* [1990] 1 A.C. 109 at 282C–D. See also *Christofi v. Barclays Bank Plc* [2000] 1 W.L.R. 937, CA (no breach of confidentiality by plaintiff's bank in advising trustee in bankruptcy of plaintiff's husband that a caution the trustee had registered had been warned off the register—the trustee should have been advised of this anyway).

[48] *Saltman Engineering Co. Ltd v. Campbell Engineering Co. Ltd* (1948) 65 R.P.C. 203 at 215, *per* Lord Greene M.R.

[49] *Att.-Gen. v. Guardian Newspapers Ltd (No.2)* [1990] 1 A.C. 109 at 215B, *per* Bingham L.J. referring to Gurry, at p.70. See also *Douglas v. Hello! Ltd* [2001] 1 W.L.R. 992 (photos of celebrity wedding) and Toulson and Phipps, at para. 3–09.

[50] *Douglas v. Hello! Ltd* [2001] 2 W.L.R. 992 at 1012A–B, *per* Brooke L.J. and at 1035E–G, *per* Keene L.J. See also *Shelley Films Ltd v. Rex Features* Ltd [1994] E.M.L.R. 134, *Hellewell v. Chief Constable of Derbyshire* [1995] 1 W.L.R. 804, at 807H and *Creation Records Ltd v. News Group Newspapers Ltd* [1997] E.M.L.R. 444.

[51] See, *e.g. Att.-Gen. v. Guardian Newspapers Ltd (No.2)* [1990] 1 A.C. 109 at 215C–E, *per* Bingham L.J., giving the example of the planned date for D-Day, which was highly confidential before the landings, but became known to the world at large within a few days. See also *Arklow Investments Ltd v. Maclean* [2000] 1 W.L.R. 594 at 600H. However, a person who has received the information while it was confidential will not be allowed to obtain advantage from his early receipt when it ceases to be confidential: *Coco v. A.N. Clark (Engineers) Ltd* [1969] R.P.C. 41 at 47 referring to *Seager v. Copydex Ltd* [1967] 1 W.L.R. 923.

[52] See, *e.g.* Lord Goff in *Att.-Gen. v. Guardian Newspapers (No.2)* [1990] 1 A.C. 109 at 282D. The information has to be significant to the confider in that it is important to him to maintain its confidentiality (see *Moorgate Tobacco Co. Ltd v. Philip Morris Ltd (No.2)* (1984) 156 C.L.R. 414 at 438, *per* Deane J.). It follows that details of someone's private life are not "trivia": *Stephens v. Avery* [1988] Ch. 499 and *Barrymore v. News Group Newspapers Ltd* [1997] F.S.R. 600. For an example of confidential information which was also useless, see *McNicol v. Sportsman's Book Stores* [1930] MaG. C.C. 116, where Maugham J. refused to restrain a threatened breach of confidence as to a "perfectly useless" betting system based on the age of the moon (see *Att.-Gen. v. Guardian Newspapers (No.2)* [1990] 1 A.C. 109 at 149C–D, *per* Scott J.).

[53] *R. v. Department of Health, ex p. Source Informatics Ltd* [2000] 2 W.L.R. 904, CA.

2-159   **Misuse.** The third requirement for liability for breach of a duty of confidence is that the confidential information has been or is threatened to be misused by the recipient. Misuse will usually involve unauthorised disclosure of the information to a third party, but need not do so.[54] The recipient will have been given the information so that he can use it for some purpose or purposes. To be actionable the use must involve taking some improper use of the information.[55] So, while it may be possible to misuse only part of the information confided,[56] if that part of the information can be used so as to preserve the confidential interest in it which the recipient is bound to protect, then there will be no misuse.[57] So, in a case concerning use of confidential information which had been given to pharmacists Simon Browne L.J. said:

> "To my mind the one clear and consistent theme emerging from all these authorities is this: the confidant is placed under a duty of good faith to the confider and the touchstone by which to judge the scope of his duty and whether or not it has been fulfilled or breached is his own conscience, no more and no less. One asks, therefore, on the facts of this case: would a reasonable pharmacist's conscience be troubled by the proposed use to be made of patients' prescriptions? Would he think that by entering [the applicants'] scheme he was breaking his customers' confidence, making unconscientious use of the information they provide?"[58]

2-160   **Justified use.** The protection afforded by equity is against misuse of confidential information. The conscience of the pharmacist in Simon Brown L.J.'s test would not be troubled if disclosure, although unauthorised, were in the public interest or required by law. While these aspects of the law of confidentiality can be treated as defences, they are better seen as examples of unauthorised use, which is not a misuse.[59]

2-161   **Disclosure justified in the public interest.** Where it is said by a defendant that his unauthorised disclosure was required in the public interest, the court has to weigh two competing interests: the public interest in maintaining confidence

---

[54] For example, using confidential information to compete against the confider's commercial interests.

[55] *Smith Kline and French Laboratories (Australia) Ltd v. Secretary to the Department of Community Services and Health* (1991) 99 A.L.R. 679 at 691–692, (Federal Court of Australia). In *Murray v. Yorkshire Fund Managers Ltd* [1998] 1 W.L.R. 951, CA, the plaintiff was one of a group of six people who had come together to produce a confidential business plan for the takeover of a company. He provided a copy to a third party so the third party could consider whether to invest. The third party then approached the other members of the group and proceeded with them, but without the plaintiff. He had not been provided with the confidential plan to approach the others, but it involved no breach of confidence in discussing it with them—they knew its contents already. Nor, given the loose relationship between the plaintiff and the other members of the group, had there been any misuse of the information.

[56] See Gurry, p. 258.

[57] *R. v. Department of Health, ex p. Source Informatics Ltd* [2000] 2 W.L.R. 904: pharmacists providing details of drugs prescribed by doctors not in breach of duty of confidentiality to the patients, because the information had been anonymised; *cf. W v. Edgell* [1990] Ch. 359 at 417, where Bingham L.J. suggested that a psychiatrist could discuss an individual case in an article or in memoirs or in gossiping with friends if he took appropriate steps to conceal the identity of his patient.

[58] *ibid.* at 952E–F.

[59] See, *e.g. Att.-Gen. v. Guardian Newspapers Ltd (No.2)* [1990] 1 A.C. 109 at 282E–F, where Lord Goff treated the possibility that public interest might favour disclosure as a limiting principle to the broad general principle. Other limiting principles were that the information must still be confidential and must not be useless or trivial.

against a countervailing public interest favouring disclosure.[60] The latter extends to all matters of which disclosure is required in the public interest, and not just to information relating to a crime or fraud.[61] However, publication to the world at large or to the media may not be justified, while more limited publication may be.[62] So, in *Francombe v. Mirror Group Newspapers*,[63] publication in a national newspaper of information obtained in breach of confidence by illegal wire tapping was not justified, whereas in *Lion Laboratories Ltd v. Evans*,[64] employees of a company which made intoximeters were justified in informing another national newspaper that the intoximeters were unreliable.[65] A useful example of this balancing exercise in the context of auditors is *Price Waterhouse v. BCCI Holdings (Luxembourg) SA*.[66] Price Waterhouse ("PW") acted as auditors to the BCCI group of companies. The firm also performed a variety of other functions including reporting to an internal committee of BCCI on problem loans made by that bank. PW were also required to report to BCCI's solicitors in order that they could advise BCCI. After the financial collapse of BCCI the Serious Fraud Office and the Bank of England served a number of notices on PW demanding the production of documents under section 2 of the Criminal Justice Act 1987 and section 39 of the Banking Act 1987. PW wished to co-operate with these demands and sought declarations that the information sought was not protected by either legal professional privilege or a duty of confidence. Having found that the information was not subject to legal professional privilege and that even if it was, section 39 of the Banking Act 1987 could nevertheless require its disclosure, Millett J. turned to consider the issue of confidence. He found that the public interest in the effective regulation and supervision of authorised banking institutions outweighed the public interest in maintaining the confidence in the information.[67]

Disclosure required by law. It is no misuse of confidential information to disclose if it that disclosure is required by law. So, for example, disclosure of   **2–162**

---

[60] See, *e.g. Att.-Gen. v. Guardian Newspapers Ltd (No.2)* [1990] 1 A.C. 109 at 282E-F, *per* Lord Goff.

[61] *ibid.* at 282G–H, *per* Lord Goff, citing *Beloff v. Pressdram Ltd* [1973] 1 All E.R. 241 at 260F, *per* Ungoed-Thomas J. and *Lion Laboratories Ltd v. Evans* [1985] Q.B. 526 at 550C, *per* Griffiths L.J. (see also the judgment of Bingham L.J. in [1990] 1 A.C. 109 at 222A–E and that of Scott J. at 159H–161A which are to like effect); *cf.* the Public Interest Disclosure Act 1998, which applies to disclosure by employees.

[62] "The disclosure must, I should think, be to one who has a proper interest to receive the information. Thus it would be proper to disclose a crime to the police; or a breach of the Restrictive Trade Practices Act to the registrar. There may be cases where the misdeed is of such a character that the public interest may demand, or at least excuse, publication on a broader field, even to the press.": *Initial Services Ltd v. Putterill* [1968] 1 Q.B. 396 at 405–406, *per* Lord Denning M.R. (see further *Att.-Gen. v. Guardian Newspapers Ltd (No.2)* [1990] 1 A.C. 109 at 282E–F and 222E–H, *per* Bingham L.J.)

[63] [1984] 1 W.L.R. 893, CA.

[64] [1985] Q.B. 526, CA.

[65] Other examples include *Stephens v. Avery* [1988] Ch. 499, *X. v. Y.* [1988] 2 All E.R. 648 and *Woolgar v. Chief Constable of Sussex Police* [2000] 1 W.L.R. 25.

[66] [1992] BCLC 583, *per* Millett J.

[67] See also *W v. Edgell* [1990] Ch. 359, *per* Scott J., CA (disclosure of psychiatric report to mental health review tribunal justified and overrode the duty of confidence owed by a doctor to his patient) and *Re a Company's Application* [1989] Ch. 477, *per* Scott J. (disclosure to FIMBRA and the Inland Revenue by former employee of FIMBRA member of member's alleged breaches of FIMBRA rules and tax irregularities permitted). These cases are discussed in Toulson and Phipps, at paras 6–12 to 6–20.

confidential and even privileged documents may be required by statute.[68] Confidential documents may have to be disclosed in litigation.[69]

2–163   **Detriment.** It is sometimes suggested that a claimant must also establish that he has suffered or will suffer detriment as a result of a breach of confidence.[70] There are powerful arguments that he need not.[71] In any event, the answer will lie in the nature of the confidential interest which the recipient is bound to preserve and in the remedy being sought. For example, where the confidential information concerns the claimant's health or personal life, a claim for an injunction to restrain unauthorised disclosure could be allowed even though the claimant might not be able to show that he would suffer financial detriment were the information to be publicised. However, once the information had been made public then, unless there were a claim for an account of profits, he would have no obvious remedy unless he could show actual damage.[72] There is a danger in this area of descending into semantics.[73]

(d) *The continuing duty to former clients*[74]

2–164   **A Continuing Duty.** A distinctive feature of a duty of confidence is that it is a continuing duty that survives the termination of the professional-client relation-

---

[68] See, *e.g. Price Waterhouse v. BCCI Holdings (Luxembourg) SA* [1992] BCLC 583, where Millett J. held that s.37 of the Banking Act 1987 empowered the Bank of England to require production of privileged, confidential documents.

[69] See, *e.g. Robertson v. Canadian Imperial Bank of Commerce* [1994] 1 W.L.R. 1493, PC. See also *Barclays Bank Plc (trading as Barclaycard) v. Taylor* [1989] 1 W.L.R. 1066, CA (banks not in breach of contractual duty of confidentiality in complying with and not challenging access orders under Police and Criminal Evidence Act 1989). See also Chap. 10, para. 10–32, below.

[70] See, *e.g. Att.-Gen. v. Guardian Newspapers Ltd (No.2)* [1990] 1 A.C. 109 at 270F, *per* Lord Griffiths. On this topic generally see Toulson and Phipps, 6–01 to 6–04.

[71] See, *e.g.* the judgment of Gummow J. in *Smith Kline and French Laboratories (Australia) Ltd v. Department of Community Services* (1990) A.L.R. 87 at 126:
   "The basis of the equitable jurisdiction to protect obligations of confidence lies, as the present case illustrates, in an obligation of conscience arising from the circumstances in or through which the information, the subject of the obligation, was communicated or obtained: *Moorgate Tobacco Co. Limited v Philip Morris Limited (No. 2)* (1984) 156 C.L.R. 414 at 438. The obligation of conscience is to respect the confidence, not merely to refrain from causing detriment to the plaintiff. The plaintiff comes to equity to vindicate his right to observance of the obligation, not necessarily to recover loss or to restrain infliction of apprehended loss. To look into a related field, when has equity said that the only breaches of trust to be restrained are those that would prove detrimental to the beneficiaries?"
   Once it is appreciated that to be confidential the information must be of significance to the claimant, the need to show detriment would appear to be superfluous or readily fulfilled.

[72] *Att.-Gen. v. Guardian Newspapers Ltd (No.2)* [1990] 1 A.C. 109 at 255H–256A, *per* Lord Keith, who was not of the view that detriment should have to be shown.

[73] *ibid.* at 281H–282B, *per* Lord Goff:
   "I would also, like Megarry J. in *Coco v. A.N. Clark (Engineers) Ltd* [1969] R.P.C. 41 at 48, wish to keep open the question whether detriment to the plaintiff is an essential ingredient of an action for breach of confidence. Obviously, detriment or potential detriment to the plaintiff will nearly always form part of his case: but this may not always be necessary . . . In the present case the point is immaterial, since it is established that in cases of Government secrets the Crown has to establish not only that the information is confidential, but also that publication would be to its 'detriment' in the sense that the public interest requires that it should not be published. That the word 'detriment' should be extended so far as to include such a case perhaps indicates that everything depends upon how wide a meaning can be given to the word "detriment" in this context."

[74] See generally Hollander and Salzedo, *Conflicts of Interest and Chinese Walls* (Sweet and Maxwell, 2000).

ship so that the professional will be obliged to preserve the confidentiality of information imparted during the course of the retainer after that retainer has come to an end.[75] In many cases (*e.g.* medical records) this will not create any difficulty. However, there are circumstances in which the continuing duty of confidentiality owed to a former client might conflict with duties owed to a different client. Absent the informed consent of the former client, the professional person or firm will be prevented from acting for the second client unless there is no risk of disclosure.[76] In this context "no risk", means that there is no real risk, as opposed to a merely fanciful risk. The risk need not be substantial, at least in cases where questions of legal professional privilege arise.[77]

The basis upon which the court acts is not to prevent a conflict between duty to one client and duty to another: there is no fiduciary duty to advance the interests of a former client.[78] Rather it is to protect and preserve the confidentiality in information which has been imparted during the course of the retainer or other professional relationship.

Bolkiah v. KPMG (a firm). The law in this area has been authoritatively stated **2–165** by Lord Millett in *Bolkiah v. KPMG (a firm).*[79] The defendant firm of chartered accountants were the auditors of an investment agency established to hold and manage various assets of the government of Brunei. The plaintiff was a member of the royal family of Brunei and chairman of the agency. In 1996, he instructed the firm to provide forensic accountancy and litigation support services in relation to litigation concerning his financial affairs. In the course of this work the firm was given access to highly confidential information concerning the plaintiff's assets. The litigation was settled in 1998 and the firm then undertook no further work for the plaintiff. In 1998, the plaintiff was removed from his position as chairman of the agency and the government of Brunei began an investigation into the activities of the agency during the period when the plaintiff had been its chairman. As part of this investigation the agency retained the firm to investigate the whereabouts of certain assets which it was suspected had been misappropriated by the plaintiff. The firm took steps to try to protect the plaintiff's confidentiality by erecting "Chinese Walls" between those who had worked on the plaintiff's litigation and those who were to undertake the investigative work for the agency. The plaintiff commenced an action for breach of confidence and sought an injunction restraining the firm from acting for the agency.

The information obtained by the firm during the course of its retainer by the **2–166** plaintiff was clearly confidential, he had not consented to its disclosure and it was of obvious relevance to the investigation that the agency now wished the firm to carry out. The House of Lords was not convinced that the proposed Chinese Walls would be sufficiently strong to avoid a risk of information passing through

---

[75] *Bolkiah v. KPMG* [1999] 2 A.C. 222 at 235D, *per* Lord Millett.
[76] Particular problems arise where the professional firm owes a duty to a new client to divulge confidential information imparted by a former client. In such circumstances, unless the new client agrees to release the firm from that duty, it may well be impossible for the firm to act: *Re A Firm of Solicitors* [1992] Q.B. 959 and *Re A Firm of Solicitors* [1997] Ch. 1.
[77] *Bolkiah v. KPMG (a firm)* [1999] 2 A.C. 222 at 237B, *per* Lord Millett. See also *Re A Firm of Solicitors* [1997] Ch. 1 at 9, *per* Lightman J.
[78] *ibid.* at 235C–D, *per* Lord Millett. See also *Att.-Gen. v. Blake* [1998] Ch. 439 at 453H, CA:
  "We do not recognise the concept of a fiduciary obligation which continues notwithstanding the determination of the particular relationship which gives rise to it. Equity does not demand a duty of undivided loyalty from a former employee to his former employer. . . "
[79] [1999] 2 A.C. 222.

them. While there was no rule of law that such measures were ineffective, the assumption was that information would move within a firm. The firm had to show by clear and convincing evidence that effective measures had been taken to ensure that no disclosure would occur.[80] Lord Millett recognised the importance of Chinese walls, for example in the City of London and in the Core Conduct of Business Rules published by the Financial Services Authority. However, he was not satisfied that *ad hoc* measures such as those proposed by the defendant firm would be sufficiently effective, not least because the proposed Chinese wall would be within a single department and office, between colleagues who were accustomed to working with each other.[81]

2–167   **Factors to consider.** Factors to consider. In order to justify the court's intervention there must be a non-fanciful risk that confidential information will leak to the new client. It will be important in any case to consider the nature of the information in question and its relevance to the new client's affairs. It may also be relevant to consider whether the information is still remembered by those to whom it was imparted.[82] When considering these matters, it must be borne in mind that there has to be a real risk, but, at least in cases involving legal professional privilege, the risk need not be substantial.

---

[80] *ibid.* at 237H–238A. Lord Millett adapted a dictum of Sopinka J. in *MacDonald Estate v. Martin* (1999) 77 D.L.R. (4th) 249 at 269 that the court should grant an injunction "unless satisfied on the basis of clear and convincing evidence that all reasonable measures have been taken to ensure that no disclosure will occur". However, Lord Millett's formulation replaced "all reasonable" with "effective".

[81] Lord Millett also referred to the Law Commission, Consultation Paper on Fiduciary Duties and Regulatory Rules (1992) (Law. Com. No. 124) which described Chinese walls as normally involving some combination of (i) physical separation of the various departments so as to insulate them from each other (often extending to separate dining arrangements, etc.); (ii) an educational programme, normally recurring, to emphasise the importance of not improperly or inadvertently imparting confidential information; (iii) strict and detailed procedures for dealing with a breach of a Chinese wall and the maintenance of proper records when it occurred; (iv) monitoring by compliance officers of the effectiveness of the wall; (v) disciplinary sanctions for breach of it. He did not appar to doubt that such a wall would be effective. For a case where a Chinese wall was held to be sufficient between those members of firm A, who had acted for the plaintiff as experts in relation to a claim against firm B, when firm A and firm B merged, see *Young v. Robson Rhodes (a firm)* [1999] 3 All E.R. 524, *per* Laddie J. See also *Re a firm of Solicitors* [1999] P.N.L.R. 950, *In the matter of T & A (Children)* [2000] Lloyd's Rep. P.N. 452, *Halewood International Ltd v. Addleshaw Booth and Co.* [2000] P.N.L.R. 788 and *Re a firm of Solicitors* [2000] 1 Lloyd's Rep. 31 discussed in Chap. 10, paras 10–28 to 10–30, below.

[82] "Confidential information passing between solicitor and client and otherwise acquired by a solicitor on behalf of his client may, like any other confidential information communicated to anyone else, subsequently cease to be confidential. Confidential documents and information may become common knowledge or at least known to an opponent in the course of a trial. Some information may be memorable and some eminently forgettable. Common sense requires recognition that not all confidential information acquired by a solicitor will remain in the mind of the solicitor or be susceptible of being triggered as a recollection after the lapse of a period of time. For the purpose of the law imposing constraints upon solicitors acting against the interests of former clients, the law is concerned with the protection of information which (a) was originally communicated in confidence, (b) at the date of the later proposed retainer is still confidential and may reasonably be considered remembered or capable, on the memory being triggered, of being recalled and (c) relevant to the subject matter of the subsequent proposed retainer.": *Re A Firm of Solicitors* [1997] Ch. 1 at 9G–10A, *per* Lightman J.

See also *In the matter of T & A (Children)* [2000] Lloyd's Rep. P.N. 452 (no reason to suppose that a solicitor remembered details of a client's personal circumstances imparted 13 years earlier and no reason to suppose that information imparted more recently to a firm of solicitors' criminal department, even if recollected, would filter through to another department during the relevant period of a few days).

CHAPTER 3

REMEDIES

	PARA.			PARA.
1. DAMAGES	3–01	(c)	Account of Profits	3–17
(a) Banque Bruxelles		(d)	Injunction	3–18
Lambert SA v. Eagle Star		4.	INTEREST	
Insurance Co	3–02	(a)	Interest under the	
(b) Allocation at risk	3–03		Supreme Court Act 1981 .	3–19
(c) Subsequent			(i) General	3–19
developments	3–04		(ii) Medical negligence:	
(d) Assessing damages on a			claims for personal	
hypothetical basis	3–05		injuries	3–20
2. LOSS OF REMUNER-			(iii) Damages for	
ATION	3–06		inconvenience and	
3. EQUITABLE REMEDIES	3–06		discomfort	3–21
(a) Rescission	3–09		(iv) Interest on damages	
(b) Equitable Compensation			for pecuniary losses	
(i) Compensation for			in solicitors' and	
loss caused by			surveyor's	
breach of fiduciary			negligence actions ...	3–22
obligation	3–12	(b)	Interest under the Civil	
(ii) Equitable			Procedure Rules	3–23
compensation for		(c)	Interest in Equity	3–24
breach of confi-				
dence	3–15			

1. DAMAGES

The principal object of an award of damages is to put the claimant[1] in the position **3–01** he would have occupied if the breach of duty had not occurred, so far as money can do this and subject to the rules as to remoteness and mitigation of damage.[2] There are no general principles which apply to damages for professional negligence (as opposed to damages for negligence or breach of contract generally). The damage which professionals inflict, when things go wrong, covers the whole spectrum from personal injury through damage to property and economic loss. The most that can be said at the general level is that within individual professions

---

[1] The term "claimant" will be used in this Chapter to describe the client or patient. The term "defendant" will be used for the professional man. Often the roles are the other way round in practice, as when the professional sues for fees owed and the client counterclaims for professional negligence.

[2] In *Attorney-General v. Blake* [2000] 3 W.L.R. 625 the House of Lords, by a majority of four to one, recognised that in exceptional cases a defendant in breach of contract could be ordered to account to the claimant for the profits made from his breach. Such cases will be extremely rare. For circumstances in which the court will make an award for non-pecuniary damage other than personal injury see *Farley v. Skinner* [2001] UKHL 49, [2001] 3 W.L.R. 899.

or clusters of professions certain kinds of loss or damage commonly recur and these have given rise to particular rules.[3] See, for example, the solicitors' negligence cases in which the claimant loses his opportunity to bring proceedings[4] or the surveyors' negligence cases where the claimant purchases a property with defects of which he was unaware.[5] A general discussion of the law of damages is beyond the scope of this book. In the chapters relating to individual professions, an attempt will be made to show how the general principles governing damages are commonly applied to claims against the individual professions.[6]

3–02   *Banque Bruxelles Lambert SA v. Eagle Star Insurance Co. Ltd.* In *Banque Bruxelles Lambert SA v. Eagle Star Insurance Co. Ltd*[7] the House of Lords introduced a new factor into the assessment of damages. The facts and the reasoning of the decision are set out and analysed in Chapter 9.[8] Although the group of cases before the House of Lords concerned surveyors, the decision plainly affects recoverability of damage across the whole field of professional negligence. Before considering questions of remoteness or causation, it is necessary to determine the scope of the duty which was breached. Where the negligence lies in what the defendant said (as opposed to what he did), it is first necessary to characterise the negligent statement as "advice" or "information". In cases of advice, the defendant will be responsible for all the foreseeable loss which is a consequence of the claimant having acted on that advice[8a]. In cases of negligent information (on which the claimant has acted) the defendant is only responsible "for all the foreseeable consequences of the information being wrong". In practice,[9] this generally means that one takes the damages which would be recoverable on a "restitution" basis and then excludes those losses which the claimant would have suffered even if the negligent information had been correct. This further narrows the scope of potential liability: in *Candler v. Crane, Christmas & Co.*[10] Denning L.J. suggested that a professional person would only be liable to a third party in respect of losses incurred on the transaction for which he knew his views were required. The effect of *Banque*

---

[3] Strictly speaking, these may not be "rules" at all. It may simply be that the courts, in applying the general principle of restitutio to similar factual situations, inevitably adopt similar methods of assessment. See *Radford v. De Froberville* [1977] 1 W.L.R. 1262, at 1268–1271; *Johnson v. Agnew* [1980] A.C. 367; *Dodds Properties (Kent) v. Canterbury City Council* [1980] 1 W.L.R. 433; *County Personnel Ltd v. Alan R. Pulver & Co.* [1987] 1 W.L.R. 916; *Ruxley Electronics and Construction Ltd v. Forsyth* [1996] 1 A.C. 344. Jane Stapleton's article "The normal expectancies measure in tort damages" (1997) 113 L.Q.R. 257 provides an interesting review of the topic. On Stapleton's analysis the "normal expectancies" measure (rather than the "entitled result" measure) applies in most professional negligence actions. This is so whether the defendant has inflicted injury or merely failed to secure a benefit, and whether the claim is formulated in contract or in tort.

[4] Chap. 10, paras 10–277 to 10–292.

[5] Chap. 9, paras 9–130 to 9–148.

[6] See the sections of the Chapters concerning individual professions titled "Damages".

[7] [1997] A.C. 191. See (1997) 113 L.Q.R. 1 and (1999) 115 L.Q.R. 527 (Stapleton) and (2001) 17 Professional Negligence, 146 (Evans).

[8] See Chap. 9, paras 9–113 to 9–116

[8a] See, *e.g. Aneco Reinsurance Underwriting Ltd v. Johnson & Higgins* [2001] UKHL 51.

[9] We say "in practice", because the House of Lords rejected the "cap" as the theoretical basis of their decision.

[10] [1951] 2 K.B. 164: see Chapter 2, paras 2–110 to 2–113.

Bruxelles Lambert SA v. Eagle Star Insurance Co. Ltd,[11] at least in cases of "information", is to restrict the liability of the defendant to the specific consequences of the information which he provided being inaccurate. It matters not that the claimant can show that he would not have entered the transaction had he been given non-negligent information.

Allocation of risk. The same result could have been achieved by considering **3–03** the allocation of risk between the lender and the valuer.[12] The valuer takes the risk that his valuation negligently misstates the current value of the property. The lender takes the risks that the borrower will be unable to meet his obligations and that the value of his security will fall (and/or the amount outstanding on the loan will rise) so that, on the assumption that the valuer has given a non-negligent valuation, he will be out of pocket. The lender will often have insured against that eventuality. On that analysis, a decision that a negligent valuer should pay all the losses suffered as a result of entering the loan transaction would transfer loss which was at the lender's risk (or at the risk of his insurers) to the valuer (and, in most cases, to his insurers).[13]

Subsequent developments. Following its decision in *Banque Bruxelles Lam-* **3–04** *bert SA v. Eagle Star Insurance Co. Ltd,*[14] the House of Lords has had to resolve related issues as to interest on damages[15] and contributory negligence.[16]

Assessing damages on a hypothetical basis. A common feature of pro- **3–05** fessional negligence litigation is that the court must determine what course events would have taken if the defendant had properly discharged his professional duty. If given competent treatment, would the patient have recovered? If given competent advice, would the client have taken the lease? If proceedings had been started within the limitation period (or had not been dismissed for want of prosecution), what damages would the claimant have recovered? If the broker had obtained suitable insurance cover, would the insurers have paid out in the events which subsequently occurred? Although these topics will be dealt with individually in the subsequent chapters, the general principle[17] is this:

---

[11] [1997] A.C. 191. In *Kenny & Good Pty. Ltd v. MGICA (1992) Ltd* [2000] Lloyd's Rep. PN 25 (1999) 163 A.L.R. 611 the High Court of Australia declined to follow the House of Lords' decision. The New Zealand Court of Appeal referred to it with apparent approval in *Boyd Knight v. Purdue* [1999] 2 N.Z.L.R. 278.
[12] See "Damages: The judiciary at sea?" by Powell, (2001) 17 Professional Negligence 206. See also Chapter 2, para. 2–90.
[13] *Aneco Reinsurance Underwriting (In Liquidation) Ltd. v. Johnson and Higgins Ltd* [2001] UKHL 51 provides a useful illustration. The plaintiffs were reinsurers whose claim against the retrocessionaires failed because of negligence by the defendant brokers. The total risk reinsured was U.S.$30 million of which U.S.$10 million was subject to retrocession cover. The plaintiffs would not have reinsured the risk at all had the brokers not been in negligent (cover would not have been available in practice had full disclosure been made). The Court of Appeal increased damages to U.S.$30 million (Aldous L.J. dissenting), even though the plaintiffs had taken the risk of a claim of U.S.$20 million without retrocession cover. The House of Lords dismissed the appeal (Lord Millett dissenting) because the defendants had been under a duty to advise, not just to provide information. The claimant had not taken the risk of proceeding on negligent advice.
[14] [1997] A.C. 191.
[15] *Nykredit Mortgage Bank Plc v. Edward Edrman Group Ltd (No.2)* [1997] 1 W.L.R. 1627 (see Chapter 9).
[16] *Platform Home Loans Ltd v. Oyston Shipways Ltd* [2000] 2 A.C. 190 (see Chapter 5, para. 5–117).
[17] See *Allied Maples Group Ltd v. Simmons & Simmons* [1995] 1 W.L.R. 1602.

(i) Where the question is what the claimant would have done, if the defendant had given competent advice or had otherwise acted competently, this is determined by the court on the balance of probabilities. Damages are then assessed on that hypothesis without any discount to reflect the possibility that the claimant might have acted differently.

(ii) Where the question is what some third party would have done, if the defendant had performed competently, damages are assessed on a "loss of a chance" basis. The court must consider what are the chances that the insurers would have paid out; or that the "other side" would have yielded; or that the judge in the original action would have found for the claimant on liability; and so forth. The damages must then reflect the value of this chance which has been lost.

(iii) The medical cases[18] fall into a different category. It is generally a question of past fact whether the claimant's condition was amenable to treatment at the time of the negligent diagnosis or treatment. The court must determine this question on the balance of probabilities (like any other question of past fact) and then award damages on that basis.[19]

2. Loss of Remuneration

3–06 A further question which commonly arises is whether a finding of negligence disentitles the professional person to his fees. If the fees have been paid, the client will probably seek to recover them. If they have not been paid, there will often be a counterclaim for the amount owing. In spite of the frequency with which this question arises, the courts have not been entirely consistent in their approach to it: see, for example, the surveyors' cases mentioned below.[20]

3–07 The first matter to consider in every case is the nature of the contract between the parties. A solicitor's retainer to bring or defend an action is usually an entire contract.[21] An agreement with an architect to provide the normal services as defined in the R.I.B.A. conditions of engagement is not entire, but severable into stages.[22] In a contract of the latter kind there can be no dispute as to the defendant's entitlement to be paid for those stages of the work which have been properly carried out.[23] The crucial questions are:

(a) In the case of an entire contract, what remuneration can be recovered where the defendant was negligent? and

---

[18] Sub-para. (iii) refers to the negligent diagnosis and negligent treatment cases. The negligent advice cases (where the patient contends that properly advised, he would not have undergone the treatment) fall within sub-para. (i), above.

[19] *Hotson v. East Berkshire A.H.A.* [1987] A.C. 750. See also Chap. 12, paras 12–271 to 12–273, which indicates a different approach to hypothetical questions in the medical context. However, see *Smith v. National Health Service Litigation Authority* [2001] Lloyd's Rep. Med. 90 where Andrew Smith J. held that *Allied Maples Ltd v. Simmons & Simmons (a firm)* [1995] 1 W.L.R. 1602 applied to a claim for damages for failure to undertake an examination which might, but might not, have revealed an existing condition, leading to earlier treatment.

[20] See Chap. 9, para. 9–110.

[21] *Underwood, Son & Piper v. Lewis* [1894] 2 Q.B. 306; *Heywood v. Wellers* [1976] Q.B. 446 at 458.

[22] *Hutchinson v. Harris* (1978) 10 Build.L.R. 19.

[23] The same principle applies to quantity surveyors: *Du Bosky & Partners v. Shearwater Property Holdings plc* (1992) 61 B.L.R. 64.

(b) In the case of a severable contract, what remuneration can be recovered for that part or stage of the work which was negligently performed?

This topic is discussed in the chapters on individual professions.[24] The approach which is adopted in most cases, and which, it is submitted, is correct, is that where the defendant's negligence renders his services valueless, he is not entitled to recover (or to retain) any remuneration for the work in question.[25] In any other case, where the defendant has substantially (albeit negligently) performed the work, he is entitled to be paid the normal remuneration and the client must rely upon his remedy in damages.[26] A more difficult question is whether there is an intermediate band of cases in which the defendant's entitlement to fees is neither wholly extinguished by his negligence nor wholly preserved. In *Mondel v. Steel*[27] (which concerned a shipbuilder's claim for the balance of the price of a ship) it was held that there could be an abatement of the price to reflect "how much less the subject matter of the action was worth, by reason of the breach of contract". In *Hutchinson v. Harris*[28] the Court of Appeal expressed doubt whether the principle of *Mondel v. Steel* could ever be applied to contracts for professional services. It is submitted that this doubt is well founded. Once it is established that the professional person has substantially performed his task and that his services were of some value to the client, an award of damages (if properly computed) should afford sufficient compensation to the client.

3–08

3. EQUITABLE REMEDIES[29]

(a) *Rescission*

Rescission of the impugned transaction is the usual remedy for breach of fiduciary duty in dealings between principal and fiduciary[30] or undue influence.[31] Rescission involves setting aside the transaction so as to place each

3–09

---

[24] See Chap. 8, para. 8–314 (architects), Chap. 9, para. 9–110 (surveyors), and Chap. 10, para. 10–307 (solicitors).

[25] *e.g. Heywood v. Wellers* [1976] Q.B. 446.

[26] See, *e.g. Moneypenny v. Hartland* (1824) 1 Car. & P. 352; (1826) 2 Car. & P. 378: " . . . unless that negligence or want of skill has been to an extent that has rendered the work useless to the defendants, they must pay him, and seek their remedy in a cross action. For if it were not so, a man, by a small error, might deprive himself of his whole remuneration" (*per* Best C.J.). Furthermore an award of damages coupled with a remission of liability for fees would often result in the client receiving double compensation; see *Hutchinson v. Harris* (1978) 10 Build.L.R. 19, at 32 (*per* Stephenson L.J.) and at 46 (*per* Waller L.J.).

[27] (1841) 8 M. & W. 858.

[28] (1978) 10 Build.L.R. 19, at 31. In *Turner Page Music Ltd v. Torres Design Associates Ltd.* [1997] C.I.L.L. 1263 the official referee distinguished *Hutchinson v. Harris* on the grounds that in the instant case the contract between the parties was not an entire contract. He ordered an abatement of the professional fees due to the defendants, to reflect the fact that they had failed to produce a bill of quantities.

[29] A full discussion of equitable remedies is beyond the scope of this book. See Spry, *Equitable Remedies* (5th ed., 1997, Sweet & Maxwell), Snell's Equity (30th ed., 2000, Sweet & Maxwell) and Meagher, Gummow & Lehane, *Equity, Doctrines and Remedies*, (3rd ed., 1992, Butterworths). Remedies such as specific performance and rectification are not considered at all, since they are rarely sought in claims against professional persons.

[30] See Chapter 2, paras 2–134 to 2–140.

[31] If a guarantee or other security has been given under undue influence, then the usual remedy is an order that the document be delivered up and cancelled.

party in the position in which he would have been had it not been entered.[32] Where a contract is avoided at the instance of a claimant, he must himself do equity by restoring the benefit he received under the contract and by giving an allowance for any capital expenditure by the defendant which has enhanced the value of any property or other asset which had been transferred to the defendant under the impugned transaction.[33] If he has received money under the impugned transaction, it must be returned with interest.[34] So, where the transaction is a loan by a fiduciary to his principal by way of mortgage, the principal must repay the principal with interest.[35] The defendant must also account for any profits or other benefits derived from the subject property.[36]

3–10   Rescission will not be ordered where, even by making all possible allowances, it would not be possible to undo the transaction.[37] So, where third parties have acquired the relevant property or interests in it for value and without notice, rescission will not be possible.[38] However, if the property has been sold on by the defendant at a profit, then he will be liable to account for that profit.[39] Particular problems arise in cases in which the claimant has rendered rescission impossible by selling on the subject property. If he has done so with knowledge of his right to rescind, then he has no good reason to complain.[40] If he has done so in ignorance, then he may have no remedy, although he may be able to claim equitable compensation.[41] A claim to rescission is also lost if the claimant has affirmed the transaction with knowledge of the relevant facts and of his right to seek rescission.[42]

---

[32] It is therefore very different from a common law award of damages for breach of contract or negligence, which seeks only to place the claimant in the position which he would have been had there been no breach of contract or duty.

[33] *York Buildings Company v. Mackenzie* (1795) 8 Bro.P.C. 42; *Ex parte Hughes* (1802) 6 Ves.Jun. 617; *Ex parte Bennett* (1805) 10 Ves.Jun. 381; *Robinson v. Ridley* (1821) 6 Madd. 2; *Luddy's Trustee v. Peard* (1886) 33 Ch.D. 500; and *Beningfield v. Baxter* (1886) 12 App.Cas. 167.
   If the fiduciary has diminished the value of the estate, then that is taken into account to: see, for example, *Sidny v. Ranger* (1841) 12 Sim. 118 (fiduciary had cut down timber on estate).

[34] *York Buildings Company v. Mackenzie* (1795) 8 Bro.P.C. 42; *Luddy's Trustee v. Peard* (1886) 33 Ch.D. 500; and *Re Sherman* [1954] Ch. 658.

[35] *Maguire v. Makaronis* (1996–97) 188 C.L.R. 449 (High Court of Australia). But see *Swindle v. Harrison* [1997] 4 All E.R. 707 (CA), discussed in paras 3–12 to 3–13, below, for a possible alternative remedy.

[36] *York Buildings Company v. Mackenzie* (1795) 8 Bro.P.C. 42; *Randall v. Errington* (1805) 10 Ves.Jun. 423; *Aberdeen Town Council v. Aberdeen University* (1877) 2 App.Cas. 544; *Erlanger v. New Sombrero Phosphate Co.* (1878) 3 App.Cas. 1218; *Beningfield v. Baxter* (1886) 12 App.Cas. 167; and *Re Sherman* [1954] Ch. 658.

[37] *Erlanger v. New Sombrero Phosphate Co.* (1878) 3 App.Cas. 1218.

[38] *McKenzie v. McDonald* [1927] V.L.R. 134.

[39] *Hall v. Hallett* (1784) 1 Cox 134; *Fox v. Mackreth* (1788) 2 Bro.C.C. 400, 2 Cox 320, affirmed (1791) 4 Bro.P.C. 258; *Ex parte Reynolds* (1800) 5 Ves.Jun. 707; and *De Bussche v. Alt* (1878) 8 Ch.D. 286.

[40] See, for example, *Great Luxembourg Railway Company v. Magnay (No. 2)* (1858) 23 Beav. 586 and *Re Cape Breton Ltd* (1885) 29 Ch.D. 795.

[41] *Re Cape Breton Ltd* (1885) 29 Ch.D. 795 at 805 *per* Cotton L.J. and 811 *per* Fry L.J.; *Jacobus Marler Estates Ltd v. Marler* (1913) 85 L.J.P.C. 167n.

[42] *Peyman v. Lanjani* [1985] Ch. 457 (C.A.), applying *Leathley v. John Fowler & Co. Ltd* [1946] K.B. 579 (C.A.).

(b) *Equitable compensation*

(i) *Compensation for loss caused by breach of fiduciary obligation*

The usual remedies for breach of fiduciary duty are rescission of the transaction **3–11** in which the fiduciary had an undisclosed interest or an account of the fiduciary's secret profits. In his speech in *Nocton v. Lord Ashburton*[43] Viscount Haldane L.C. explained that in appropriate cases equitable compensation akin to damages had been awarded by equity against a fiduciary. This element of his speech was not immediately developed. Although an award of damages is not usually regarded as a remedy for breach of an equitable obligation,[44] there has been a recognition in the English authorities that damages may be awarded for breach of an equitable duty of confidence.[45] More recently, courts in Australia, New Zealand and Canada have taken the lead in awarding compensation for damage suffered as a result of breach of fiduciary duty.[46]

The remedy is now recognised in English law for breaches of fiduciary **3–12** obligation. In *Swindle v. Harrison*[47] the Court of Appeal had to consider to what extent proof of a causal link between a breach of fiduciary duty and loss should be established if compensation or damages were to be awarded. The existence of the remedy of compensation or damages appears to have been accepted. Mr Swindle was a solicitor. Mrs Harrison wished to mortgage her house to acquire a restaurant business for her son to run. Part of the money was to be raised by a loan from a brewery. That loan had not been agreed when Mrs Harrison exchanged contracts for the restaurant and paid a deposit of £44,000, despite warnings from her solicitor as to the risk to which she was exposing herself. The date for completion approached, but the brewery declined to make the loan. Mrs Harrison and her son were unable to borrow the money needed from their bank. Mr Swindle offered to advance the money needed at five per cent over base and for an arrangement fee of £1,000. The terms offered were reasonable and Mrs Harrison accepted them. Mr Swindle did not reveal that his firm would receive half the arrangement fee itself, paying the balance to its bank, and that he was borrowing the money at two and a half per cent over base and so, if Mrs Harrison made the payments due, would make a modest profit. Mrs Harrison was able to complete, but the restaurant was not a success. She lost her home and any equity in the restaurant. Mr Swindle brought proceedings to enforce the charge. Mrs Harrison counterclaimed for damages for negligence and breach of fiduciary duty, alleging that Mr Swindle was in breach of duty in failing to reveal the profit he would be making. She claimed her entire loss on the venture.

The claim in negligence was bound to fail because Mrs Harrison was unable **3–13** to show that, had Mr Swindle informed her of the profit he would be making, she would not have proceeded. That left her claim for breach of fiduciary duty. There had clearly been a breach of fiduciary duty, albeit not serious. The usual remedy

---

[43] [1914] A.C. 932. See also *McKenzie v. McDonald* [1927] V.R. 134 (Dixon AJ).

[44] See, for example, *Ex parte Adamson* (1878) 8 Ch.D. 807, at 819 *per* James and Baggallay L.JJ.

[45] *Swinney v. Chief Constable of Northumbria Police Force* [1997] Q.B. 464, applying a dictum of Lord Goff in *Attorney-General v. Guardian Newspapers (No. 2)* [1990] 1 A.C. 109 and *Seager v. Copydex Ltd* [1967] 1 W.L.R. 923 and [1969] 1 W.L.R. 809.

[46] See, for example, the authorities cited by Professor Finn at page 40 of *Commercial Aspects of Trusts and Fiduciary Obligations* (McKendrick ed), which include *Hill v. Rose* [1990] VR 129, *McKaskell v. Benseman* [1989] 3 N.Z.L.R. 75 and *Canson Enterprises Ltd v. Boughton & Co.* (1991) 85 D.L.R. (4th) 129.

[47] [1997] 4 All E.R. 707.

would have been rescission of the loan, so that Mrs Harrison would have had to repay the principal sum borrowed together with interest either at a rate assessed by the Court or at the contractual rate.[48] That remedy was of little use to Mrs Harrison. She claimed her entire loss on the restaurant business, relying on a dictum of Lord Thankerton in *Brickenden v. London Loan & Savings Co.*[49] The argument failed. Evans L.J. rejected it on the basis that considerations of causation applied to claims for compensation for non-fraudulent breaches of fiduciary duty, following *Bristol & West Building Society v. Mothew.*[50] Staughton L.J.'s analysis was more subtle. He distinguished between the traditional remedies for a breach of fiduciary duty involving non-disclosure by the fiduciary of his interest in the transaction (which rendered it voidable at the election of the beneficiary, so that, as stated by Lord Thankerton in *Brickenden*, considerations as to the causative effect of non-disclosure did not arise) and a claim for damages for breach of fiduciary duty. As to the latter, Staughton L.J. held that it was necessary to satisfy the test of common law if damages were to be recovered. Mrs Harrison failed to satisfy that test, so her claim failed. Mummery L.J., the third member of the Court, expressly recognised the availability of equitable compensation as a remedy for breach of fiduciary duty. Having observed that common law considerations of remoteness and foreseeability were generally irrelevant to restitutionary remedies for breach of trust or fiduciary duty, he held that:

> "Although equitable compensation, whether awarded in lieu of rescission or specific restitution or whether simply awarded as monetary compensation, is not damages, it is still necessary for Mrs Harrison to show that the loss suffered has been caused by the relevant breach of fiduciary duty. Liability is not unlimited. There is no equitable by-pass of the need to establish causation."[51]

He went on to apply the decision of the House of Lords in *Banque Bruxelles Lambert S.A. v. Eagle Star Insurance Co. Ltd.*[52] and to hold that Mrs Harrison's loss arose not from any want of information about the loan from her solicitors, but from her purchase of the restaurant.

3–14   Thus, in claims for compensation for loss caused by breach of a fiduciary obligation, the claimant will have to establish causation, *i.e.* that he would have acted differently had the fiduciary complied with his obligations.[53] In assessing

---

[48] *Maguire v. Makaronis* (1996–97) 188 C.L.R. 449 (High Court of Australia).
[49] [1934] 3 D.L.R. 465, at 469: "When a party, holding a fiduciary relationship, commits a breach of his duty by non-disclosure of material facts, which his constituent is entitled to know in connection with the transaction, he cannot be heard to maintain that disclosure would not have altered the decision to proceed with the transaction, because the constituent's action would be solely determined by some other fact, such as the valuation by another party of the property proposed to be mortgaged. Once the court has determined that the non-disclosed facts were material, speculation as to what course the constituent, on disclosure, would have taken is not relevant." This is discussed as part of a wider analysis of causation in relation to equitable remedies in the judgments of Brennan C.J. and Gaudron, McHugh and Gummow JJ. in *Maguire v. Makaronis* (1996–97) 188 C.L.R. 449 at 467–474. See also (1994) 110 L.Q.R. 238 (Heydon). In *Nationwide Building Society v. Balmer Radmore (a firm)* [1999] Lloyd's Rep. P.N. 241, Blackburne J., having explained the factual background to the decision in *Brickenden*, said at 274: "It may be therefore that, although couched in entirely general terms, it is appropriate to approach Lord Thankerton's remarks with caution and avoid elevating what he said in the context of that case into a statement of inflexible principle."
[50] [1998] Ch. 1 (C.A.).
[51] [1997] 4 All E.R. 707 at 733h.
[52] [1997] 1 A.C. 191.
[53] See also *Rama v. Millar* [1996] 1 N.Z.L.R. 257, where, giving the opinion of the Privy Council, Lord Nicholls said at 260–261: "This is not a case of a claim that a fiduciary should account for an unauthorised profit. The claim is for the amount of loss Mr Millar is said to have sustained by Mr

compensation, the courts are trying to compensate for the consequences of the breach of the fiduciary obligation and in doing so they apply common sense views as to what loss resulted from the breach and so falls to be compensated.[54]

(ii) *Equitable compensation for breach of confidence*[55]

There is jurisdiction under Lord Cairns' Act 1858 to award damages in lieu of an injunction. This has been used to justify awards of damages for breach of confidence. However, it could not justify an award of damages where a grant of an injunction would not be ordered—most obviously when the confidential information had already been disclosed.[56] The English courts have awarded damages for breach of confidence.[57]   **3–15**

Once it is appreciated that there is an equitable obligation of confidence,[58] then the availability of equitable compensation in appropriate cases resolves this problem. Such compensation should be awarded for actual loss and damage, but there is no reason in principle why it should not compensate the claimant for distress and inconvenience.[59]   **3–16**

(c) *Account of profits*

An account of profits is the appropriate remedy where a fiduciary has made an unauthorised profit by breaching his fiduciary obligations[60] or where profit has been made from a breach of confidence.[61]   **3–17**

(d) *Injunction*

An injunction—both interim and final—can be used to restrain a breach or threatened breach of confidence. In such cases it is essential that the injunction   **3–18**

Rama's breach of fiduciary duty. This calls for consideration of what would have happened if Mr Rama had fulfilled his fiduciary duties and kept Mr Millar informed." In *Nationwide Building Society v. Balmer Radmore (a firm)* [1999] Lloyd's Rep. P.N. 241, Blackburne J., having reviewed the authorities, including a passage from the speech of Lord Browne-Wilkinson in *Target Holdings Ltd v. Redferns* [1996] A.C. 421 at 432E–H, said at 278: "That broad statement encourages me to think that where, as in the cases before me, what is at issue is the consequence of a misrepresentation or non-disclosure made by the fiduciary which has caused the beneficiary to authorise the application of his monies in a particular way, the only sensible approach to the question of compensation for the consequences of the misrepresentation or non-disclosure is to consider what would have happened if there had been no misrepresentation or the appropriate disclosure had been made."

[54] *Canson Enterprises Ltd v. Boughton & Co.* (1991) 85 D.L.R. (4th) 129 at 163, *per* McLachlin J. approved by the House of Lords in *Target Holdings Ltd v. Redferns (a firm)* [1996] A.C. 421 at 439A.

[55] See Toulson & Phipps, *Confidentiality* (Sweet & Maxwell, 1996) paras 10–09 to 10–13.

[56] *Malone v. Metropolitan Police Commissioner* [1979] Ch. 344, at 360A–C, *per* Megarry V.-C.

[57] *Seager v. Copydex Ltd. (No.2)* [1969] 1 W.L.R. 809. Damages were awarded on the basis of the value of the information, after which the information would belong to the defendant. Meagher, Gummow & Lehane, *Equity, Doctrines and Remedies*, (3rd ed., 1992, Butterworths) are scathing about this decision: see paras [4118] and [4127].

[58] See Chapter 2, para. 2–154.

[59] *cf. Farley v. Skinner* [2001] UKHL 49, reported at [2001] 3 W.L.R. 899.

[60] See, for example, *Regal (Hastings) Ltd v. Gulliver* [1967] 2 A.C. 134n, *per* Lord Russell of Killowen at 149F.

[61] *Peter Pan Manufacturing Corporation v. Corsets Silhouette Ltd* [1963] R.P.C. 45 (claim was made both in equity and in contract); *Attorney-General v. Guardian Newspapers Ltd* [1990] 1 A.C. 109.

be unambiguous and that it extend only to information which is truly confidential.[62]

4. Interest

(a) Interest under the Supreme Court Act 1981

(i) General

3–19 The court has a discretion to award simple interest on any damages awarded to a claimant and will generally do so.[63] The discretion extends to both the rate of interest awarded and the period for which it should run, commencing with the date when the cause of action arose and ending with the date of the judgment.[64] In the purely commercial context (*i.e.* most claims against insurance brokers, auditors, underwriting agents, etc.) commercial rates of interest are awarded and no further discussion is called for here.

(ii) Medical negligence: claims for personal injuries

3–20 In respect of damages for personal injuries the rules as to interest are clear and well settled. In brief, interest must be awarded unless the court is satisfied that there are special reasons to the contrary.[65] Interest is normally awarded on special damages at half the appropriate rate from the date of accident until trial. The appropriate rate is the Special Account Rate (formerly the Short Term Investment Rate). The details of this rate, together with much other useful information, are conveniently set out in "Facts and Figures", an annual publication by the Professional Negligence Bar Association. No interest is awarded on damages for future loss of earnings or earning capacity. Interest on general damages for pain, suffering and loss of amenities should be awarded at the rate of two per cent per annum from the date of service of the writ until the date of trial.[66]

(iii) Damages for inconvenience and discomfort

3–21 In respect of general damages for inconvenience and discomfort, interest at two per cent will generally[67] be awarded from the date of the inconvenience to trial,

---

[62] See Toulson & Phipps, *Confidentiality* (1996, Sweet & Maxwell) paras 10–01 to 10–02.

[63] Section 35A of the Supreme Court Act 1981 empowers the court to award interest on sums paid before judgment. However, this power does not extend to sums recovered by the claimant before the commencement of proceedings: see *I.M. Properties plc v. Cape & Dalgleish* [1999] Q.B. 297. In that case the claimants claimed against their auditors losses flowing from negligent audits. They had recovered part of the losses from their former chief executive before issuing the writ. The Court of Appeal held that no interest could be awarded in respect of that part of the loss.

[64] Section 35A(1) of the Supreme Court Act 1981. In *Nykredit Mortgage Bank plc v. Edward Erdman Group Ltd* [1997] 1 W.L.R. 1627 the House of Lords rejected the (ingenious) argument that there was a distinction between the date when a cause of action accrued and the date when it "arose" within the meaning of section 35A of the Supreme Court Act 1981: see 1638B.

[65] Section 35A(2) of the Supreme Court Act 1981.

[66] *Wright v. British Railways Board* [1983] 2 A.C. 773 and see the analysis by Purchas L.J. in *Auty v. National Coal Board* [1985] 1 W.L.R. 784 at 809.

[67] Such interest was awarded in *Heatley v. William H. Brown Ltd* [1992] 1 E.G.L.R. 289, 297. Occasionally such interest has not been awarded, but no reasons have been given: *Wilson v. Baxter Payne & Lepper* [1985] 1 E.G.L.R. 141.

applying the principles applicable to the award of interest on general damages in personal injury actions.

(iv) *Interest on damages for pecuniary losses in solicitors' and surveyors' negligence actions*

Interest is awarded to compensate the claimant for being deprived of his damages **3–22** for a period of time, not as compensation for the damage done to him[68] or as a punishment for the defendant. For this reason the nature of the transaction giving rise to the claim will be material to the choice of the rate of interest. A commercial transaction will more readily attract a commercial rate of interest than a domestic house purchase. The decisions of the Court of Appeal in *Pinnock v. Wilkins & Sons*[69] and *Watts v. Morrow*[70] establish that the court may take the rate applicable to judgments by section 17 of Judgments Act 1838. However, that is only an option and should not be applied without considering whether some other, more flexible rate is more appropriate.[71]

(b) *Interest under the Civil Procedure Rules*

Part 36 of the Civil Procedure Rules concerns offers to settle and payments into **3–23** court. Unlike the Rules of the Supreme Court and the County Court Rules which they replaced, the Civil Procedure Rules enable claimants to make offers to settle their claims. If the offer is made more than 21 days before the start of the trial, a defendant has 21 days to accept the claimant's offer without needing the court's permission, but may only accept it after that with the court's permission.[72] Rule 36.21 applies where a claimant obtains a judgment against a defendant which is more advantageous than the proposals contained in his offer. In such circumstances the court may award interest on the whole or part of any sum of money (excluding interest) awarded to the claimant at a rate of up to 10 per cent above the base rate for some or all of the period from the latest date on which the defendant could have accepted the offer without needing the permission of the court.

(c) *Interest in Equity*

Equity has its own independent jurisdiction to award interest.[73] It has the power **3–24** to award compound interest if appropriate. Equity's purpose in cases against delinquent fiduciaries is not to punish them, but to ensure that they have made no

---

[68] *per* Lord Herschell L.C. in *London, Chatham and Dover Railway Co. v. South Eastern Railway Co.* [1893] A.C. 429 at 437. And see the dicta of Lord Denning M.R. in *Jefford v. Gee* [1970] 2 Q.B. 130 at 146.

[69] *The Times*, January 29, 1990.

[70] [1991] 1 W.L.R. 1421.

[71] For a detailed critique of these decisions see paras 1–182 to 1–188 of the fourth edition of this work.

[72] CPR, Rule 36.12(1).

[73] *Wallersteiner v. Moir (No. 2)* [1975] Q.B. 373 (C.A.); *Rama v. Millar* [1996] 1 N.Z.L.R. 257 (P.C.).

profit from abuse of their position.[74] Therefore, compound interest will only be awarded if either the defendant has himself received compound interest or should have done so. Otherwise, equity is likely to adopt a similar approach in deciding which is the appropriate rate as that adopted under section 35A of the Supreme Court Act 1981.

---

[74] *Wallersteiner v. Moir (No. 2)* [1975] Q.B. 373 at 388B–D *per* Lord Denning M.R, at 397C–F and 406D–E *per* Scarman L.J. The earlier authorities are set out in this decision.

Chapter 4

CONTRIBUTION BETWEEN DEFENDANTS

	PARA.		PARA.
1. Introduction	4–01	(a) Matters which cannot be raised in defence to a claim	4–10
2. Entitlement to contribution	4–02	(b) Matters which can be raised in defence to a claim	4–11
3. Liability of the person claiming contribution	4–03	(c) Basis of assessment of contribution	4–12
(a) Basis of liability	4–06	(d) Time for bringing a claim for contribution	4–15
(b) Meaning of "the same damage"	4–07		
4. The Claim	4–10		

1. INTRODUCTION

Where the claimant's injury or loss was caused by the breach of duty of more **4–01** than one person, contribution proceedings are often instituted between the parties alleged to be responsible. Earlier editions of this book have discussed the Law Reform (Married Women and Tortfeasors) Act 1935, the Civil Liability (Contribution) Act 1978 and the somewhat complicated interrelationship between the two Acts. The time has now passed, however, when any proceedings are likely to be brought under the 1935 Act.[1] For discussion of that Act and the transitional provisions, see the second and third editions of this book and the Court of Appeal's decision in *Lampitt v. Poole B.C. (Taylor, Third Party).*[2] This chapter is concerned with the Civil Liability (Contribution) Act 1978.[3]

2. ENTITLEMENT TO CONTRIBUTION

Section 1(1) of the Civil Liability (Contribution) Act 1978 provides that, subject **4–02** to the qualifications thereafter set out, "any person liable in respect of any damage suffered by another person may recover contribution from any other person liable in respect of the same damage (whether jointly with him or otherwise)".

3. LIABILITY OF THE PERSON CLAIMING CONTRIBUTION

Section 1(1) gives a right to claim contribution to "any person liable". In practice **4–03** contribution claims are often made between co-defendants who are both denying

---

[1] Such proceedings might be brought if the limitation period had been suspended, because the claimant was under a disability or because of fraud or deliberate concealment by the defendant.

[2] [1991] 2 Q.B. 545.

[3] The Act was passed following the Law Commission's Report on Contribution (Law Com. No. 79) and replaces s.6(1)(c) of the Law Reform (Married Women and Tortfeasors) Act 1935. For a comprehensive review of the working of the Act, see C. Mitchell, "The Civil Liability (Contribution) Act 1978" in [1997] R.L.R. 27.

liability and against whom no finding of liability has been made. There is no difficulty in those circumstances, because their respective liability to the claimant will be determined at the trial of the claimant's action against them. However, there are two respects in which the requirement of liability is qualified. First, the fact that by the time the claim for contribution is made the person making it has acquired a defence of limitation which bars the remedy, but not the right,[4] provides no defence.[5] This is sensible, because if a claim were made against a defendant at the end of the applicable limitation period, he might otherwise be unable to claim contribution.[6] Secondly, if the person claiming contribution has made or agreed to make any payment in bona fide settlement or compromise of a claim, then he is entitled to claim contribution "without regard to whether or not he himself is or ever was liable in respect of the damage, provided, however, that he would have been liable assuming the factual basis of the claim against him could be established".[7] Two issues arise in relation to this provision: (i) what is the "factual basis" of the claim and (ii) for the purposes of assessing contribution, is the settling party to be deemed to have been liable on that basis, or is it for the party against whom contribution is sought to establish that he was.[8]

4–04   Most issues in most claims are issues of fact. However, there will also be issues of law or of mixed fact and law, or of pure law. Where, for example, there is an issue as to whether a duty of care in tort was owed in particular circumstances, that is a question of law, not of fact. The effect of section 1(4) is that the party claiming contribution must show that, had the factual basis of the claim against him been proved, then any issues of law as to his liability would have been resolved against him. For example, if a claim were brought against an accountant for allegedly making a representation to a third party as to his client company's accounts, then it would not matter that the accountant denied making the statement: that was an allegation of fact. However, it would be open to the party against whom contribution was claimed to argue that in the circumstances alleged, no duty of care was imposed as a matter of law.

4–05   The question of what a party who had settled a claim had to prove in order to claim a contribution arose in *Dubai Aluminium Co. Ltd v. Salaam*.[9] In that case the original claim had been brought against a number of defendants, including a firm of solicitors, one of whose partners was alleged to have knowingly participated in a major fraud. The other partners reached a settlement with the claimant on terms that the allegations against them and against the allegedly fraudulent partner were withdrawn. They then claimed a contribution against other defendants (but not against their partner). One issue was whether that partner had been acting in the ordinary course of the business of the firm so as to render his partners vicariously liable for his wrongful acts.[10] Counsel and the Court of Appeal proceeded on the basis that this was a question of fact.[11] The Court of Appeal held that, if he had acted as had been alleged by the claimant, then the allegedly fraudulent partner had not done so in the ordinary course of the

---

[4] Most limitation periods bar the remedy, but not the right. Of those relevant to claims against professional persons, s.14B is the only one which bars the right. The others bar the remedy.
[5] Civil Liability (Contribution) Act 1978, s.1(2).
[6] See para. 4–15, below, for the time for bringing a claim for contribution.
[7] Civil Liability (Contribution) Act 1978, s.1(4).
[8] The second issue is addressed in para. 4–12, below.
[9] [2001] Q.B. 113, CA.
[10] Partnership Act 1890, s.10.
[11] [2001] Q.B. 113 at 142B, *per* Aldous L.J.

business of the firm and so held that the other partners had no right to claim a contribution.[12] This decision may be doubted because, if the question of what constituted the ordinary course of the firm's business was a question of fact, then that fact was to be taken as alleged by the claimant before the claim was settled and not as found by the judge or Court of Appeal. That the claimant's factual allegations might not be correct (or established) is expressly recognised in section 1(4).

(a) *Basis of liability*

Section 6(1) provides: **4–06**

> "A person is liable in respect of any damage for the purposes of this Act if the person who suffered it (or anyone representing his estate or dependents) is entitled to recover compensation from him in respect of that damage (whatever the legal basis of his liability, whether tort, breach of contract, breach of trust or otherwise)."

This is widely drafted and has been so interpreted. It enables a claim for contribution to be made between defendants where the claimant has a claim against one for professional negligence and against another for restitution in respect of the same matter.[13] It is not certain whether it extends to a claim in debt.[14]

(b) *Meaning of "the same damage"*

While contribution may be claimed on the basis of the widest possible range of   **4–07** liabilities, both the person claiming and the person from whom contribution is claimed must be liable to the same person in respect of the same damage.[15] This problem was considered by the Court of Appeal in *Birse Construction Ltd v. Haiste*.[16] Birse contracted with Anglian Water to design and construct a reservoir. Birse engaged Haiste, consulting engineers, to assist in preparing their tender and designing the reservoir. N, an employee of Anglian, administered the project as engineer. Following completion, defects emerged. Birse settled Anglian's claim against it by constructing a new reservoir at its own expense. Birse brought

---

[12] *ibid.* at 132H–134E, *per* Evans L.J. and at 142A–144C, *per* Aldous L.J.: Turner J. agreed with both on this aspect of the decision.

[13] *Friends Provident Life Office v. Hillier Parker May & Rowden* [1997] Q.B. 85, CA. Auld L.J., with whom Saville and Rose L.JJ. agreed, recited s.6(1) and said at 103A–C:

> "It is difficult to imagine a broader formulation of an entitlement to contribution. It clearly spans a variety of causes of action, forms of damage in the sense of loss of some sort, and remedies, the last of which are gathered together under the umbrella of 'compensation'. The Act was clearly intended to be given a wide interpretation, as Ferris J. observed in *K. v. P. (J., Third Party)* [1993] Ch. 140 at 148, holding that illegality was arguably not a defence to a claim under the Act of 1978."

[14] *Howkins & Harrison v. Taylor* [2001] Lloyd's Rep. P.N. 1, CA.

[15] In the light of the decision of the House of Lords in *Banque Bruxelles Lambert SA v. Eagle Star Insurance Co. Ltd* [1997] A.C. 191 (see Chap. 3, para. 3–02, above), it is now possible for one party to be liable only for some of the damage suffered. This does not prevent another party responsible for the whole damage from claiming contribution: *Ball v. Banner* [2000] Lloyd's Rep. P.N. 569, *per* Hart J. See also *Rahman v. Areanose Ltd* [2000] 3 W.L.R. 1184 (CA).

[16] [1996] 1 W.L.R. 675.

proceedings against Haiste for negligence. Haiste brought contribution proceedings against N under the Civil Liability (Contribution) Act 1978. The Court of Appeal held that the contribution proceedings should be struck out. The ground of the decision was that the damage allegedly caused by N to Anglian was not "the same damage" as the damage allegedly caused by Haiste to Birse. Sir John May stated:

> "The Act is in my opinion concerned with the relatively simple sharing of existing liability. I would be surprised if against this background the Act created potentially complicated and some might say tortuous legal relationships."[17]

Roch L.J. summarised his reasoning and conclusion:

> "The damage suffered by Anglian in this case was the physical defects in the reservoir. The damage suffered by Birse was the financial loss of having to construct a second reservoir for Anglian. Anglian and Birse did not suffer the same damage."[18]

4–08   In the same way, where a claimant suffers personal injuries and his claim against the person who negligently caused them is not issued in time, he may have a claim against his former solicitor. His claim against the solicitor is clearly related to the original claim, but it is not for the same damage. The damage in the original claim was the personal injuries themselves. The damage in the second claim is the loss of the chance to bring the original claim (or the reduced value of that claim if he has to rely on section 33 of the Limitation Act 1980).[19] This example was given by Stuart-Smith L.J. in his judgment in *Royal Brompton Hospital National Health Service Trust v. Hammond.*[20] In that case the claimant sought damages against the architect for negligently granting the contractor extensions of time. The architect sought to claim a contribution from the contractor. The Court of Appeal held that the claim against the architect was for damage in the sense of impairment of the claimant's rights against the contractor. That was not the same damage as the claimant's claim against the contractor to have the extensions of time set aside. The position would be different if the claim against the architect were for negligent supervision or inspection of the contractor's work. In that case both would be liable for the defective work and so liable for the same damage.

4–09   The same reasoning was applied by the Court of Appeal in *Howkins & Harrison v. Tyler.*[21] In that case the claimant was a firm of valuers which had compromised a claim against it by a building society. The claim had been for allegedly negligent overvaluation of a property taken as security for a loan to the defendants. Having settled the building society's claim, the firm brought an action for contribution. The claim failed on a preliminary issue as to whether the firm and the defendants had been liable for the same damage. Scott V.-C., with whom Aldous and Sedley L.JJ. agreed, proposed this test:

> "Suppose that A and B are the two parties who are said each to be liable to C in respect of 'the same damage' that has been suffered by C. So C must have a right of action of some sort against A and a right of action of some sort against B. There are two

---

[17] *ibid.* at 680C.
[18] *ibid.* at 682F.
[19] As to which see Chap. 5, paras 5–64 to 5–69, below.
[20] [2000] Lloyd's Rep. P.N. 643 at 647.
[21] [2001] Lloyd's Rep. P.N. 1.

questions that should then be asked. If A pays C a sum of money in satisfaction, or on account, of A's liability to C, will that sum operate to reduce or extinguish, depending upon the amount, B's liability to C? Secondly, if B pays C a sum of money in satisfaction or on account of B's liability to C, would that operate to reduce or extinguish A's liability to C? It seems to me that unless both of those questions can be given an affirmative answer, the case is not one to which the 1978 Act can be applied. If the payment by A or B to C does not *pro tanto* relieve the other of his obligations to C, there cannot, it seems to me, possibly be a case for contending that the non-paying party, whose liability to C remains un-reduced, will also have an obligation under section 1(1) to contribute to the payment made by the paying party."[22]

Applying that test to the facts, payment by the valuers to the building society did not reduce the debt secured on the property.[23] Scott V.-C.'s test is helpful and the other Court of Appeal cases are consistent with it.[24]

4. THE CLAIM

(a) *Matters which cannot be raised in defence to a claim*

It is no defence to a claim for contribution that had the original claimant brought   **4-10**
the claim he would have faced a good limitation defence, unless that defence barred the right and not the remedy.[25] It would also appear that it is no defence that the person from whom contribution is sought has reached a settlement with the original claimant.[26]

(b) *Matters which can be raised in defence to a claim*

Judgments given in any part of the United Kingdom between the original   **4-11**
claimant and the person from whom contribution is claimed are conclusive as to any issue determined in the latter's favour.[27] So, if there has been a judgment on liability in his favour, there is no right to claim contribution, even if the party seeking contribution disagrees with that result.

---

[22] *ibid.* at 4. See also *Eastgate Group Ltd v. Lindsey Morden Group Inc* [2001] EWCA Civ 1446.
[23] Scott V.-C. then considered to what extent the valuers might have a claim were the building society subsequently to recover the full debt or by joining the building society to a claim for the debt. Such claims, however, would be matters of subrogation and restitution and had nothing to do with the Civil Liability (Contribution) Act 1978: *ibid.* at 5.
[24] For example, in *Royal Brompton Hospital National Health Service Trust v. Hammond* [2000] Lloyd's Rep. P.N. 643, the claim against the architect might be reduced *pro tanto* by the payment of money by the contractor, but not vice versa.
[25] Civil Liability (Contribution) Act 1978, s.1(3). See para. 4–03, n. 4, above.
[26] See *Kenburgh Investments (Northern) Ltd (in liquidation) v. Minton* [2000] Lloyd's Rep. P.N. 736 at 743, CA and *Logan v. Uttlesford D.C.* (1986) 136 New L.J. 541 and the decision of the Court of Appeal in *Jameson v. Central Electricity Generating Board* [1998] Q.B. 323. However, the settlement may have extinguished the original claimant's right to make any further claim, so that the person seeking contribution was not liable to him: see *Jameson v. Central Electricity Generating Board* [2001] 1 A.C. 455, HL (reversing the decision of the Court of Appeal on this ground).
[27] Civil Liability (Contribution) Act 1978, s.1(5).

(c) *Basis of assessment of contribution*

4–12 The principles of apportionment are set out in section 2 of the Civil Liability (Contribution) Act 1978. Section 2(1) provides that "the amount of the contribution recoverable from any person shall be such as may be found by the court to be just and equitable having regard to the extent of that person's responsibility for the damage in question". It is for the person seeking contribution to prove that the person from whom contribution is sought would have been liable to the original claimant and the basis of his responsibility for the relevant damage. The question arises whether, in a case in which the person claiming contribution settled the claim against him,[28] his liability is to be assumed or has to be proved by the person against whom contribution is sought if he wishes contribution to be assessed on the basis that the other was also responsible. The decision of the Court of Appeal in *Dubai Aluminium Co. Ltd v. Salaam*[29] proceeds on the basis that liability is to be assumed and does not have to be proved by the person against whom contribution is sought. However, it might be said that section 1(4) envisages a claim by someone who denies that he was liable to the original claimant on the facts, but claims that he nevertheless made a bona fide settlement.[30] This provision would serve little purpose if the assessment of contribution proceeds on the basis that he is deemed to have been liable.

4–13 The person against whom contribution is claimed can rely upon any defence of contributory negligence which he would have had against the original claimant[31] and on any limitation on his liability under statute or under any agreement made before the damage occurred.[32] Contribution can only be claimed to the extent that the party from whom it is claimed would in fact have been liable and not by reference to settlement of an overstated claim.[33]

4–14 Where the client suffers loss or injury as a result of the negligence of two or more of his professional advisers, the apportionment of liability between them is governed by the same general principles as apply to any other wrongdoers. The court should have regard both to the culpability of the various parties and to the extent to which each party's conduct "caused" the damage in question.[34] Questions of apportionment arise most commonly in the building professions and these are discussed in Chapter 8.[35] Apportionment of liability for medical accidents is discussed in Chapter 12.[36] Apportionment of liability between successive solicitors or between solicitors and members of other professions is discussed in Chapter 10.[37] The question of apportionment between defendants should be considered separately from the assessment of contributory negligence as between the claimant and all defendants.[38]

---

[28] See paras 4–03 to 4–05, above.
[29] [2001] Q.B. 113, CA.
[30] See para. 4–03, above.
[31] Civil Liability (Contribution) Act 1978, s.2(3)(b) and (c).
[32] *ibid.*, s.3(3)(a).
[33] *J. Sainsbury plc v. Broadway Malyan* [1999] P.N.L.R. 286, *per* Judge Lloyd Q.C.
[34] Where one partner was culpable and his "innocent" partners seek a contribution, they are to be treated as culpable when seeking contribution: *Dubai Aluminium Co. Ltd v. Salaam* [2001] Q.B. 113, CA.
[35] See Chap. 8, paras 8–315 to 8–317, below.
[36] See Chap. 12, paras 12–164 to 12–165, below.
[37] See Chap. 10, paras 10–328 to 10–332, below.
[38] *Fitzgerald v. Lane* [1989] A.C. 328.

(d) *Time for bringing a claim for contribution*

Section 10 of the Limitation Act 1980 provides that a claim for contribution **4–15**
within two years of a judgment or arbitration award against him in favour of the
original claimant or of the date of any agreement to make a payment in settlement
of a claim against him.

CHAPTER 5

DEFENCES

	PARA.		PARA.
1. Exclusion or restriction of liability .	5–01	3. Limitation in Equity	5–79
(a) The Statutory Framework	5–03	(a) Express application of the	
(b) Exclusion of Liability to Third		Limitation Act 1980	5–81
Parties	5–07	(b) Application of the Limitation	
2. Limitation in Contract and Tort	5–10	Act 1980 by Analogy	5–88
(a) The Limitation Period	5–10	(c) Where there is no analogy or	
(b) Date when cause of action in		correspondence	5–96
contract accrues	5–14	4. Other equitable defences: Laches	
(c) Date when cause of action in		and Acquiescence	5–98
Tort accrues	5–16	(a) Laches	5–99
(i) Claims against architects		(i) Unreasonable delay	5–103
and engineers	5–17	(ii) Prejudice to the	
(ii) Claims against surveyors	5–35	defendant or third party	5–106
(iii) Claims against solicitors	5–37	(iii) Relationship between	
(iv) Claims against insurance		Laches and the	
brokers	5–46	Limitation Act 1980	5–108
(v) Claims against financial		(b) Acquiescence	5–109
advisers	5–48	5. Contributory negligence	5–113
(d) Effect of the Latent Damage		(a) Contributory negligence and	
Act 1986	5–49	contract	5–115
(e) Special rules re Personal Injury		(b) Application to professional	
and Death	5–56	negligence	5–117
(i) Primary limitation		(c) Methods by which plaintiffs	
periods	5–56	might seek to circumvent a	
(ii) Discretionary exclusion		plea of contributory	
of time limit	5–64	negligence	5–119
(f) Fraud or concealment	5–69	(d) Attribution	5–120

1. EXCLUSION OR RESTRICTION OF LIABILITY

Traditionally, professional persons have not normally sought to exclude or restrict their liability to clients or patients for breach of duty. In evidence to the Royal Commission on Legal Services, the Law Society argued that it was "one of the marks of a fully developed profession" that they should not do so.[1] Attempts to exclude liability to third parties are more common, for example by means of a paragraph at the end of a report stating that no liability is accepted to anyone other than the client.

5–001

As a result of mounting concern about the incidence and effect of professional negligence litigation, this whole question was reviewed in 1988–1989. The

5–002

---

[1] Quoted in para. 23.39 of the Royal Commission's Report, Cmnd. 7648 (1979). The Royal Commission was not persuaded by this view and recommended that an enquiry should be set up to review the question of limiting liability for all professions: see para. 23.30 of the Report. In 1987, the Law Society Council decided that there was "no objection as a matter of conduct" to solicitors seeking to limit liability to their level of insurance cover: see the Council statement published in the *Law Society's Gazette* May 27, (1987), p. 1545.

Secretary of State for Trade and Industry appointed three study teams to look into the problems of auditors, surveyors and the construction industry professions. Their reports together with the report of the Steering Group, chaired by Professor Likierman, were published in April 1989.[2] These established that there had been a significant increase in the number and size of professional negligence claims in the 1980s, unrelated to any discernible increase in negligence; that professional indemnity premiums had increased proportionately (despite cyclical fluctuations due to changes in the insurance market); that increased costs were being passed on to the clients and that professionals were becoming more cautious to the detriment of their clients. Possible solutions, including contractual limitations of liability, were discussed. In a later consultation paper,[3] the Common Law Team of the Law Commission, whilst opposing the principle of proportionate liability, recognised "the very real problems faced by many professional defendants in obtaining affordable insurance".[4] They considered that professional persons ought to be able to limit their liability and that they were entitled to greater certainty in this regard.

> "It seems unsatisfactory to tell the professional who structures his liability and insurance position with great care that the reasonableness of carefully drafted clauses on which he will rely will be assessed on a 'case by case' basis."[5]

(a) *The Statutory Framework*

5–003   Any provision in a "contentious business agreement"[6] with a solicitor purporting to exclude liability for negligence or breach of duty is void.[7] In the case of auditors engaged by a company to carry out a statutory audit, any provision in their contract of engagement[8] purporting to exempt them from liability for negligence or breach of duty is also void.[9] The statute of most general application, however, is the Unfair Contract Terms Act 1977. Section 2(1) provides that a person cannot "by reference to any contract term or to a notice given to persons generally or to particular persons exclude or restrict his liability for death or personal injury resulting from negligence". The term "negligence" embraces both the tort of negligence and breach of any contractual obligation to exercise reasonable skill or care.[10] The profession principally affected by section 2(1) is, of course, the medical profession. Since the damage resulting from medical negligence is almost always some form of personal injury,[11] doctors are effectively prevented from excluding or restricting liability for negligence. Other

---

[2] See "Professional Liability: Report of the Study Teams", Chairman: Professor Andrew Likierman (HMSO, 1989).

[3] "Feasibility Investigation of Joint and Several Liability", (HMSO, 1996).

[4] *ibid.*, para. 5.1.

[5] *ibid.*, para. 5.18.

[6] Defined in the Solicitors Act 1974, s.59(1). See also *Chamberlain v. Boodle & King* [1982] 1 W.L.R. 1443.

[7] *ibid.*, s.60(5). There is no similar provision affecting agreements for non-contentious business, but see the Law Society Statement "Limitation of Liability by Contract" (7th ed., 1996), discussed in Chap. 10, para. 10–141, below.

[8] Or in the articles of the company.

[9] Companies Act 1985, s.310. See further Chap. 15, para. 15–100, below. The Auditors' Study Team recommended that this provision should be amended to allow the limitation of liability to a reasonable level. See the Likierman Report, *op. cit.*

[10] Unfair Contract Terms Act 1977, s.1(1).

[11] See Chap. 12, para. 12–287, below.

professions affected to a lesser extent are architects and engineers, whose negligence could on occasion lead to personal injury.[12]

Negligence which results in damage other than personal injury or death is dealt **5–004** with in section 2(2). A person cannot exclude or restrict liability for such negligence by reference to a contract term or notice, except in so far as that term or notice satisfies "the requirement of reasonableness". The test of "reasonableness" is explained in section 11.[13] In the case of a contract term, the court must consider whether it was a fair and reasonable one having regard to the circumstances in the actual or constructive knowledge of the parties at the time the contract was made.[14] In the case of a notice, the court must consider whether it would be fair and reasonable to allow reliance on it, having regard to all the circumstances when the alleged liability arose.[15] It is thought that it would generally be unreasonable for a professional person to exclude liability altogether for negligence *vis-à-vis* his client.[16] There can, of course, be no objection to a term limiting the task which a professional person undertakes[17] (for example, a surveyor may be instructed to report only on major structural defects). However, once the task has been defined, it would seem contrary to the principles for which the professions stand[18] if they could then contract out of liability. Notices or contractual terms which merely seek to limit a professional person's liability to a specified sum may fall into a different category, although they are subject to the requirement of reasonableness.[19] Section 11(4) of the Act provides that where a person seeks to restrict his liability in this way, the court shall have regard in particular to (a) the resources which he could expect to be available to him for the purpose of meeting the liability; and (b) how far it was open to him to cover

---

[12] See, *e.g. Clay v. A.J. Crump & Sons Ltd* [1964] 1 Q.B. 533.

[13] The operation of s.11 is briefly discussed by the House of Lords in *George Mitchell (Chesterhall) Ltd v. Finney Lock Seeds Ltd* [1983] 2 A.C. 803 at 815–816. J. Adams and R. Brownsword review the earlier authorities in "The Unfair Contract Terms Act: A Decade of Discretion" in (1988) 104 L.Q.R. 94. They criticise the *George Mitchell* decision as having given rise to undue uncertainty. For a general discussion of the "reasonableness" test, see Chitty, paras 14–081 to 14–094.

[14] Unfair Contract Terms Act 1977, s.11(1).

[15] *ibid.*, s.11(3). The distinction between subss. (1) and (3) is of considerable importance in the context of professional negligence. Where there is no contract between the parties the court can have regard to the nature and quality of the defendant's negligent conduct, when deciding whether the disclaimer satisfies the "reasonableness" test. Where there is a contract, the court can only take account of the actual negligence in the instant case as being an example of the kind of negligence for which the contract purports to exclude liability. Thus the relevance of the defendant's actual conduct is much diminished.

[16] See the reasoning of the House of Lords in *Smith v. Eric S. Bush* [1990] 1 A.C. 831, where a disclaimer of liability towards a party one stage removed from the client was held to be unreasonable.

[17] See, *e.g.* Chap. 9, paras 9–73, 9–97 and 9–98, below.

[18] But see *Arenson v. Arenson* [1977] A.C. 405 at 431, where Lord Kilbrandon expressed the view that if arbitrators were not immune from liability in negligence, it would be entirely reasonable for them to exclude such liability:

"I am afraid I cannot go along with my noble and learned friend, Lord Salmon, when he suggests that such insistence would be damaging to a man's professional reputation. I think he would be saying something like this: I will accept your reference. I shall take every care and give you the whole benefit of my skills. But probably one of you will be dissatisfied with my award. I decline absolutely to accept the risk of having to defend a negligence suit, even though I be confident that I have not been negligent. I have no ambition, nor can I afford, to be a successful defendant, even in a leading case."

[19] See, *e.g.*, *St Albans City and District Council v. International Computers Ltd* [1996] 4 All E.R. 481, CA and *South West Water Services Ltd v. International Computers Ltd* [2001] Lloyd's Rep. P.N. 353, *per* (Judge Toulmin Q.C.) cases concerning the supply of computers.

himself by insurance. Professional persons commonly practise individually or in small firms. The damages resulting from professional negligence (particularly in the realm of financial advice or the design of buildings) may be far beyond the means of the practitioner or firm which is liable. If insurance were taken out to cover the full potential liability of such practitioners (and if insurers or reinsurers were willing to provide such cover), the effect could be to inflate their fees to an unacceptable level. It may be therefore that if a professional firm takes out the maximum insurance cover which is available (or which is reasonable in the circumstances), and then seeks to restrict its liability to that sum, such restriction would satisfy the requirement of reasonableness.[20]

5–005 **Effect of the E.C. Directive.** In 1993, the E.C. Directive on Unfair Terms in Consumer Contracts was adopted[21] under Article 100a of the E.C. Treaty. This has now been implemented in England and Wales by the Unfair Terms in Consumer Contracts Regulations 1999.[22] The regulations apply to any contract between a seller or supplier and a consumer. A professional person or firm is, of course, a "supplier" of professional services. A "consumer" is any natural person acting outside his trade, business or profession. The regulations apply to all terms of the contract which have not been individually negotiated, and any terms which were negotiated if an overall assessment indicates that they are in fact a pre-formulated standard contract. The operative provision is in regulation 8, which provides that any "unfair term" in a contract with a consumer shall not be binding on the consumer. The definition of "unfair term" is in regulation 5(1), namely:

"A contractual term which has not been individually negotiated shall be regarded as unfair, if, contrary to the requirement of good faith, it causes a significant imbalance in the parties' rights and obligations under the contract, to the detriment of the consumer."

The 1999 Regulations apply to all kinds of contract terms, and are not limited to exemption clauses. In practice, it seems unlikely that any clause limiting the liability of a professional, which satisfies the requirement of reasonableness under the Unfair Contract Terms Act 1977, would be held to be "unfair" under the 1994 Regulations.[23]

5–006 Quite apart from the statutory restraints mentioned above, if the professional man is to exclude or restrict his liability for negligence, he must ensure that:

(1) if a contractual term is relied upon, it is expressly incorporated into the contract of engagement[24];

(2) if a notice is relied upon, it was drawn to the client's attention; and

---

[20] See *Smith v. Eric S. Bush* [1990] 1 A.C. 831 at 859, *per* Lord Griffiths. See also paras 5.18–5.19 of "Feasibility investigation of joint and several liability" by the Common Law Team of the Law Commission (HMSO, 1996).
[21] Directive 93/13. Discussed in Chitty, paras 15–004 to 15–007.
[22] Replacing the Unfair Terms in Consumer Contracts Regulations 1994, which continue to apply to contracts made between July 1, 1995 and the coming into force of the 1999 Regulations.
[23] See Chitty, para. 15–050.
[24] As to which, see Chitty, Chaps 12 and 14 .

(3) in either case, the wording used is sufficiently clear to apply to negligence.[25]

(b) *Exclusion of Liability to Third Parties*

The exclusion of liability to third parties presents special problems. In the ordinary way, by reason of the doctrine of privity of contract, an exemption clause contained in the professional person's contract of engagement will not be binding upon third parties.[26] Thus an architect cannot avoid liability to future purchasers of a building which he designs, by reference to an exemption clause contained in his original contract of engagement.[27] However, the professional person may in some cases be able to avoid undertaking any duty to third parties in the first place, by means of a suitably worded disclaimer.[28] Thus in *Hedley Byrne and Co. Ltd v. Heller and Partners Ltd*,[29] it was held that, since the defendant bankers stipulated that their references were given "without responsibility", they did not undertake any duty to the plaintiffs. "A man cannot be said voluntarily to be undertaking a responsibility if at the very moment when he is said to be accepting it he declares that in fact he is not" (*per* Lord Devlin).[30] This aspect of *Hedley Byrne* (which was in fact the ratio of the decision) has been less fully explored than the general part of the speeches concerning duty of care. However, the principle was applied in *McCullagh v. Lane Fox and Partners*.[31] In that case the purchaser of a house claimed damages against the vendor's agents for negligently mis-stating the size of the garden. The Court of Appeal held that the disclaimer in the agents' particulars (which satisfied the requirement of reasonableness under the Unfair Contract Terms Act 1977) negatived any assumption of responsibility by the agents to the purchaser.[32] Thus the first question to consider in every case is whether the defendant has incurred a duty

5–007

---

[25] As to which, see Chitty, Chap. 14, particularly at paras 14–010 to 14–012. By far the safest way of excluding or restricting liability for negligence is to use the word "negligence" or some synonym for it. See, generally *Smith v. South Wales Switchgear Co. Ltd* [1978] 1 W.L.R. 165 and *Photo Production Ltd v. Securicor Transport Ltd* [1980] A.C. 827.

[26] *Haseldine v. Daw & Son* [1941] 2 K.B. 343 illustrates the general principle. The position would be otherwise if the client contracted as agent for the third party: *New Zealand Shipping Co. Ltd v. A. M. Satterthwaite and Co. Ltd* [1975] A.C. 154.

[27] However, the terms of the contract of engagement may still be relevant in determining whether the third parties have a claim in negligence: see Chap. 8, paras 8–106 and 8–128, below.

[28] The question whether the Unfair Contract Terms Act 1977 applies to such a disclaimer is discussed by K. M. Stanton, "Disclaiming Tort Liability: The Unfair Contract Terms Act 1977" in (1985) 1 P.N. 132.

[29] [1964] A.C. 465, discussed in Chap. 2, paras 2–24 to 2–25, above.

[30] *ibid.* at 533. See also at 493, *per* Lord Reid, at 504, *per* Lord Morris, at 511, *per* Lord Hodson and at 540, *per* Lord Pearce.

[31] [1996] 1 E.G.L.R. 35.

[32] The same principle was applied in *Omega Trust Co. Ltd v. Wright Son and Pepper* [1997] 1 E.G.L.R. 120. The defendant surveyors prepared a report for lender clients which contained the following disclaimer:

"This report shall be for private and confidential use of the clients for whom the report is undertaken and should not be reproduced in whole or in part or relied upon by third parties for any use whatsoever without the express written authority of the surveyors."

The Court of Appeal held that this disclaimer satisfied the test of reasonableness under the Unfair Contract Terms Act 1977; and that it prevented any duty of care arising to lenders who were not the clients, but who relied upon the report.

of care to the third party,[33] and in relation to that the existence of a disclaimer or attempted disclaimer is relevant but not decisive.[34]

5–008 **Exclusion clauses in mortgage applications.** The effect of disclaimers on third party liability has been considered extensively in the context of mortgage applications. This topic is dealt with in Chapter 9, below.[35] The principal authority is the decision of the House of Lords in *Smith v. Eric S. Bush* and *Harris v. Wyre Forest D.C.*[36] It is clear from the facts of *Smith* and *Harris* that there were strong grounds in both cases for holding that the disclaimers were not fair and reasonable. The House of Lords' decision was closely tied to the facts of those cases, and may have been otherwise if the property were an expensive one, where the purchaser might be expected to commission his own survey report.[37]

5–009 **General comment.** There are powerful policy arguments for restricting professional liability within sensible bounds, as was shown by the Likierman Report.[38] It is submitted that in situations where the third party has not paid for the services, it may well be reasonable for a professional person to exclude liability altogether (especially in a commercial context, which the *Smith* and *Harris* cases were not).[39] Furthermore in any case where third party liability is likely to be substantial, it ought to be "fair and reasonable" to limit such liability to the amount of insurance cover sensibly available.

2. LIMITATION IN CONTRACT AND TORT

(a) *The Limitation Period*

5–010 Under the Limitation Act 1980 claims founded on tort[40] or simple contract[41] are barred after the expiration of six years from the date on which the cause of action accrues. In the case of persons under a disability (defined as infants or persons of unsound mind)[42] "the action may be brought at any time before the expiration of six years from the date when he ceased to be under a disability or died

---

[33] As to which see Chap. 2, paras 2–109 to 2–115, above.

[34] See *Smith v. Eric S. Bush* [1990] 1 A.C. 831.

[35] See Chap. 9, paras 9–64 to 9–70, below.

[36] [1990] 1 A.C. 831.

[37] *ibid.* at 859G-H, *per* Lord Griffiths.

[38] See para. 5–02, above.

[39] However, in *McCullagh v. Lane Fox and Partners* [1996] 1 E.G.L.R. 35 at 46 it was held reasonable to exclude liability to third parties for misstatement in the context of a house sale.

[40] Limitation Act 1980, s.2. For a general discussion of limitation of actions in tort, see A. McGee, *Limitation Periods* (Sweet and Maxwell, 3rd ed., 1998) and Clerk and Lindsell, Chap. 33. For an overview of limitation of actions in general and proposals for reform, see the Law Commission Report on Limitation of Actions (Law Com. 270). This book is concerned only with limitation in the context of professional negligence.

[41] *ibid.*, s.5. For a general discussion of limitation of actions in contract, see A. McGee, *Limitation Periods, op. cit.*, Chitty, Chap. 29 and the Law Commission Report on Limitation of Actions. Claims based on a specialty (*i.e.* a contract under seal) have a limitation period of 12 years: Limitation Act 1980, s.8.

[42] *ibid.*, s.38(2). An "infant" is a person under 18: see Family Law Reform Act 1969, s.1. For the definition of "unsound mind", see Limitation Act 1980, s.38(2) and (3).

(whichever first occurred)".[43] The limitation period is also extended in cases of fraud, concealment or mistake.[44]

Latent damage. In cases of latent damage other than personal injuries, an alternative limitation period for claims in negligence is available to the plaintiff, namely three years from the "starting date" as defined in section 14A of the Limitation Act 1980.[45]   **5–011**

Personal injuries and death. Claims in respect of personal injuries or death are subject to a time limit of three years and are governed by special rules.[46] These special rules determine the date upon which time begins to run[47] and confer a discretion on the court to disapply the time limit.[48]   **5–012**

Characterising the claim. It is clearly important at the outset to determine whether the damages claimed are "in respect of personal injuries",[49] in order to establish what the limitation period is and whether there is discretion to extend it. Obviously most, but not all, claims against medical practitioners fall into this category. In *Walkin v. South Manchester H.A*,[50] the Court of Appeal held that a mother's claim for a failed sterilisation operation was a claim for damages "in respect of personal injuries". Although the losses for which she claimed were economic, the unwanted pregnancy was an "impairment" and thus fell within the definition of "personal injuries" in section 38(1) of the Limitation Act 1980. The Court left open whether a claim by a man for a failed vasectomy, leading to the unwanted pregnancy of his partner, would also be classified as a claim for personal injuries.[51] Somewhat different considerations may arise if a medical practitioner fails to diagnose an incurable defect in an unborn child, so that the child is born rather than aborted.[52] In this scenario (unlike the failed sterilisation cases) the pregnancy is a desired state of affairs at the time and the claim should only be for the costs of rearing a disabled child.[53] It may be appropriate to distinguish *Walkin* on this basis. In the same way, if a medical practitioner negligently fails to diagnose the true extent of the condition of a claimant who is pursuing a claim for personal injuries, a claim for damages against him will not be for personal injuries, but for financial loss.[54] Turning to other professions,   **5–013**

---

[43] *ibid.*, s.28(1).

[44] See paras 5–70 to 5–78, below.

[45] See paras 5–49 to 5–55, below.

[46] Limitation Act 1980, ss.11–14 and 33. Section 11 of the Limitation Act 1980 does not apply to actions for trespass to the person, even where the consequence is personal injury. Accordingly, the limitation period for such claims is six years, and the court has no discretion to extend that period: *Stubbings v. Webb* [1993] A.C. 498.

[47] See paras 5–56 to 5–63, below.

[48] See paras 5–64 to 5–69, below.

[49] Limitation Act 1980, s.11(1).

[50] [1995] 1 W.L.R. 1543.

[51] As to which see *McFarlane v. Tayside Health Board* [2000] 2 A.C. 59 and *Parkinson v. St James and Seacroft University Hospital NHS Trust* [2001] EWCA Civ 530 (reported at [2001] 3 W.L.R. 376), particularly at paras 56–73, *per* Hale L.J.

[52] As to which see Chap. 12, paras 12–277, 12–292 and 12–295, below.

[53] See also *Arndt v. Smith* (1996) 7 Med. L.R. 108: the British Columbia Supreme Court held that claims by the parents of a disabled child (who would have been aborted in the event of competent ante-natal advice) were claims for economic loss and thus subject to a six-year limitation period.

[54] See *Oakes v. Hopcroft* [2000] Lloyd's Rep. P.N. 946, CA, where this was common ground.

sometimes claims are made against architects and engineers in respect of personal injury (for example following the Abbeystead disaster).[55] But where a solicitor errs in the prosecution of litigation, with the result that his client fails to recover damages for personal injuries, it is submitted that the client's claim against the solicitor should not be characterised as one "in respect of personal injuries". His claim is one for pure financial loss, namely the value of the chose in action which he has lost. Thus section 11 of the Limitation Act 1980 would not apply to such a professional negligence action and the limitation period would be six years.[56] In *Bennett v. Greenland Houchen and Co.*[57] the plaintiff sued his former solicitors for allegedly mishandling earlier litigation, with the result that he became clinically depressed. The Court of Appeal held that this was an action in respect of personal injuries:

> "In asking, 'what is this case all about?' the obvious conclusion here must be that it does include a claim for personal injury. Consequently the action should have been brought within the three year period."[58]

(b) *Date when Cause of Action in Contract Accrues*

5–014   In claims for breach of contract the cause of action accrues when the breach occurs, whether or not damage is suffered at that time.[59] Thus where the professional person does something contrary to the express or implied terms of his retainer, time begins to run (at least for the contractual claim) on the date of that act. Where the professional person omits to do something which is required by his retainer, it is less easy to identify when his breach of contract occurred.[60] In *Midland Bank Trust Co. Ltd v. Hett, Stubbs & Kemp*,[61] Oliver J. held that the solicitors' obligation to register the option continued until the date when effective registration became impossible, and that an action for breach of contract against the solicitors could be begun up to six years from the date when the obligation lapsed.[62] The question of a solicitor's continuing duty was considered by the

---

[55] *Eckersley v. Binnie and Partners* (1988) 18 Con.L.R. 1.

[56] This view is supported by *Ackbar v. C. F. Green and Co. Ltd* [1975] Q.B. 582, a claim against insurance brokers for failing to obtain passenger liability insurance as instructed. The plaintiff was subsequently injured when travelling as a passenger in his lorry. Croom-Johnson J. held that the proviso to s.2(1) of the Limitation Act 1939 (as amended) did not apply and that the limitation period was six years. He observed that the same principles would apply to claims against solicitors for failing to issue proceedings in time or for allowing proceedings to be dismissed for want of prosecution: *ibid.* at 586C. But *cf. Paterson v. Chadwick* [1974] 1 W.L.R. 890: the words "a claim in respect of personal injuries" are construed differently in s.32(1) of the Administration of Justice Act 1970 (discovery against third parties).

[57] [1998] P.N.L.R. 458.

[58] *ibid.* at 465, *per* Otton L.J. It is possible that the claim for personal injuries was too remote to sound in damages.

[59] Thus claims against solicitors were held to be statute-barred in *Short v. McCarthy* (1820) 3 B. & Ald. 626; *Brown v. Howard* (1820) 2 Brod. & B. 73; *Howell v. Young* (1826) 5 B. & C. 259. In *Bagot v. Stevens Scanlan and Co. Ltd* [1966] 1 Q.B. 197 a claim against architects was held to be statute-barred. In so far as these cases decided that there is no concurrent liability in tort, they are no longer good law: see Chap. 2, paras 2–100 to 2–108, above.

[60] This issue is discussed by Evans, "Negligent Omissions by Solicitors and Limitation" in (1991) 7 P.N. 50.

[61] [1979] Ch. 384. For the facts see Chap. 10, para. 10–07, below.

[62] *Bean v. Wade* (1885) 2 T.L.R. 157, which appears to be to the contrary effect, was distinguished with some difficulty. For a detailed analysis of this decision, see *Midland Bank v. Hett, Stubbs & Kemp* [1979] 1 Ch. 384 at 435–438.

Court of Appeal in *Bell v. Peter Browne & Co.*[63] In that case the plaintiff transferred his former matrimonial home to his wife in 1978, on the under-standing that whenever it was sold he would receive one-sixth of the proceeds. The solicitors who were acting for him failed to protect his interest by a declaration of trust or mortgage or by entering a caution on the land register. In 1986, the former wife sold the matrimonial home and spent the proceeds. The plaintiff started proceedings against the solicitors in 1987. The Court of Appeal held that the contractual claim accrued in 1978 and was therefore statute-barred. The fact that the solicitors could have remedied their breach at any time before the wife sold the house did not mean that there was a continuing breach of contract right up to 1986.[64] The Court of Appeal ostensibly distinguished *Midland Bank Trust Co. Ltd v. Hett, Stubbs & Kemp*,[65] but the distinctions drawn were so fine that the authority of *Midland Bank* on this particular issue has been substantially weakened.

An architect, who is engaged to design and supervise the construction of a **5–015** building, is sometimes said to be under a continuing duty to keep his design under review during the construction period.[66] Such a duty generally continues until practical completion. Indeed, in *University of Glasgow v. William Whit-field*,[67] Judge Bowsher Q.C. (rejecting the architects' limitation defence) held that the duty continued beyond practical completion.[68] An engineer has been held to be under a similar continuing duty.[69] The nature of any continuing duty was considered by Dyson J. in *New Islington and Hackney Housing Association Ltd v. Pollard Thomas & Edwards Ltd.*[70] He suggested that an architect would not be under a duty to review the design of foundations unless there was some particular reason for him to do so. He rejected the suggestion that absent some such reason any breach of duty in relation to design was a continuing breach. This accords with common sense and is to be welcomed.

(c) *Date when Cause of Action in Tort Accrues*

In claims based on the tort of negligence the cause of action accrues when the **5–016** claimant suffers actionable damage.[71] This may be when the breach of duty

---

[63] [1990] 2 Q.B. 495.

[64] See, *per* Nicholls L.J. at 500–501 and, *per* Beldam L.J. at 509.

[65] [1979] Ch. 384.

[66] *Brickfield Properties Ltd v. Newton* [1971] 1 W.L.R. 862 at 873F, *per* Sachs L.J.; *Equitable Debenture Assets Corp. Ltd v. William Moss Group Ltd* (1984) 2 Con.L.R. 1 at 24, *per* Judge Newey Q.C.

[67] (1988) 42 B.L.R. 66. Distinguished in *Chesham Properties Ltd v. Bucknall Austin Project Management Services Ltd* (1996) C.I.L.L. 1189.

[68] *ibid.* at 78. In *New Islington and Hackney Housing Association Ltd v. Pollard Thomas & Edwards Ltd* [2001] P.N.L.R. 515, Dyson J. suggested at 522 that this decision was "heavily coloured by the special facts of the case" and that Judge Bowsher Q.C. was not "stating a general principle". See also the *obiter* discussion about duties continuing after practical completion in the dissenting judgment of Bingham L.J. in *Eckersley v. Binnie and Partners* (1988) 18 Con.L.R. 1 at 146–147.

[69] *Chelmsford D.C. v. T.J. Evers* (1983) 25 Build.L.R. 99 at 106, *per* Judge Smout Q.C.

[70] [2001] P.N.L.R. 515.

[71] The damage must be "beyond what can be regarded as negligible": *Cartledge v. E. Jopling & Sons Ltd* [1963] A.C. 758 at 772, *per* Lord Reid. It must be "real damage as distinct from purely minimal damage" (*per* Lord Evershed at 774). See further, *Bank of East Asia v. Tsien Wui Marble Factory Ltd and others* [2000] H.K.L.R.D. 268, below. If the claimant suffers damage which is irrecoverable in law, that does not start the limitation period running: *Nitrigin Eireann Teoranta v. Inco Alloys Ltd* [1992] 1 W.L.R. 498, (May J).

occurs or it may be at some later date (for example, when the client acts in reliance on negligent advice). Where the claimant is unaware that he has suffered damage until many years after the event, the basic limitation period would effectively prevent him from obtaining any remedy. Parliament has intervened a number of times to relieve the injustice which this causes. The Limitation Acts 1963 and 1975 introduced special provisions for the protection of plaintiffs in personal injury actions.[72] The Latent Damage Act 1986 provided an alternative limitation period in cases of latent damage not involving personal injuries.[73] But none of this legislation has dispensed with the need to consider when, on basic common law principles, the cause of action in negligence accrued. For example, in a case of latent damage a plaintiff who does not begin proceedings within three years of the "starting date" is still entitled to do so within six years of the accrual of his cause of action.[74]

(i) Claims against architects and engineers

5–017   *Pirelli.* The leading case is *Pirelli General Cable Works Ltd v. Oscar Faber and Partners,*[75] hereafter referred to as *Pirelli. Pirelli* was decided on December 9, 1982 and substantially changed what was previously thought to be the law.[76] All cases on this topic decided before December 9, 1982 must, therefore, be treated with caution. In *Pirelli*, the principal speech was given by Lord Fraser.[77] Lords Bridge, Brandon and Templeman expressed agreement with that speech and made no further comment. Lord Scarman also expressed agreement with that speech, but added a brief comment deploring the current state of the law and looking forward to future legislation on latent damage.

5–018   **Facts of *Pirelli.*** The brief facts of *Pirelli* were as follows: the plaintiffs engaged the defendants, a firm of consulting engineers, to advise on and design an addition to their factory premises, which included a chimney. The chimney was constructed in June and July 1969. An unsuitable material (Lytag) was used in its construction. By April 1970, cracks developed at the top of the chimney. The plaintiffs could not have discovered the damage with reasonable diligence before October 1972. They did not in fact discover the damage until November 1977. The writ was issued in October 1978. The House of Lords rejected the argument that the cause of action accrued when the damage to the chimney became discoverable (October 1972). The House of Lords held that the cause of action accrued in the spring of 1970 when damage, in the form of cracks near the top of the chimney, must have come into existence.[78] Therefore, the plaintiff's claim was statute-barred.

5–019   **House of Lords reasoning in *Pirelli.*** Lord Fraser, who made the only substantive speech,[79] reasoned as follows:

---

[72] These are now consolidated in the Limitation Act 1980 and are dealt with in paras 5–56 to 5–69, below.
[73] Dealt with in paras 5–49 to 5–55, below.
[74] Limitation Act 1980, s.14(4)(a).
[75] [1983] 2 A.C. 1. Discussed by K. M. Stanton, "Limitation of Actions in Professional Negligence Cases" in (1983) 99 L.Q.R. 175.
[76] See the first edition of this book, para. 1–48.
[77] Summarised at para. 5–19, below.
[78] [1983] 2 A.C. 1 at 19D.
[79] See para. 5–17, above.

(1) In *Cartledge v. E. Jopling & Sons Ltd*,[80] the House of Lords held that a cause of action for personal injury accrues when the injury occurs, not when it is capable of being discovered by the claimant.[81]

(2) The principle of *Cartledge v. E. Jopling & Sons Ltd*[82] is applicable to cases of damage to property as well as to personal injury claims.[83]

(3) The fact that the owners of damaged property suffer no financial loss unless and until the damage is discovered is irrelevant. They "have a damaged article when, but for the defendant's negligence, they would have had a sound one".[84]

(4) There is a distinction between a defect in property and damage to that property.

"Unless the defect is very gross, it may never lead to any damage at all to the building. It would be analogous to a predisposition or natural weakness in the human body which may never develop into disease or injury. The plaintiff's cause of action will not accrue until damage occurs, which will commonly consist of cracks coming into existence as a result of the defect even though the cracks or the defect may be undiscovered and undiscoverable. There may perhaps be cases where the defect is so gross that the building is doomed from the start, and where the owner's cause of action will accrue as soon as it is built, but it seems unlikely that such a defect would not be discovered within the limitation period. Such cases, if they exist, would be exceptional."[85]

(5) The reasoning of the Court of Appeal in *Sparham-Souter v. Town and Country Developments (Essex) Ltd*[86] on the limitation issue was incorrect. The reference to that decision by the House of Lords in *Anns v. Merton LBC*[87] did not amount to approval of the whole decision.[88]

(6) (*Obiter*) The duty of the builder and the local authority[89] is owed to owners of the property as a class; "if time runs against one owner, it also runs against all his successors in title".[90]

(7) (*Obiter*) There is probably no analogy between the negligent design of the chimney in the present case and cases of negligent advice by a solicitor.

"It seems to me that, except perhaps where the advice of an architect or consulting engineer leads to the erection of a building which is so defective as to be doomed from the start, the cause of action accrues only when physical damage occurs to the building."[91]

---

[80] [1963] A.C. 758.
[81] [1983] 2 A.C. 1 at 13.
[82] [1963] A.C. 758.
[83] [1983] 2 A.C. 1 at 14.
[84] *ibid.* at 16D.
[85] *ibid.* at 16F–H.
[86] [1976] Q.B. 858.
[87] [1978] A.C. 728 at 760.
[88] [1983] 2 A.C. 1 at 15–18.
[89] And by implication the duty of the designer, although Lord Fraser did not expressly say this. But this *obiter* passage must now be read subject to *Murphy v. Brentwood D.C.* [1991] 1 A.C. 398.
[90] *ibid.* at 18B–E.
[91] *ibid.* at 18G–H.

5–020   **"Doomed from the start".** The decision in *Pirelli* opened up a number of matters for debate. One frequently discussed question was when it could be said that a building was "doomed from the start", with the result that time began to run upon practical completion. A number of enterprising defendants contended that the defects alleged against them were so serious as to fall within this category. Such arguments usually failed. In a series of cases (principally official referee cases) the courts held that Lord Fraser's comments on buildings which were "doomed from the start" were of very limited application. In *Dove v. Banhams Patent Locks Ltd*,[92] Hodgson J. held that an inadequate security gate installed by burglary prevention specialists was not doomed from the start. The plaintiffs' cause of action did not accrue until a burglar broke the gate down some 12 years later. In *London Congregational Union Inc. v. Harriss and Harriss*,[93] Judge Newey Q.C. rejected the argument that a church and hall were doomed from the start merely because design errors had created the likelihood of flooding. The cause of action accrued when the first flooding occurred. Judge Newey's decision on this issue was upheld by the Court of Appeal.[94] A similar approach was adopted in *Kensington and Chelsea and Westminster Area Health Authority v. Wettern Composites*.[95] Stone mullions were inadequately fixed to the external walls of a hospital extension. Judge Smout Q.C. rejected the argument that the building or part of the building was doomed from the start. The cause of action accrued when the mullions moved. In *Ketteman v. Hansel Properties Ltd*,[96] the Court of Appeal treated Lord Fraser's references in *Pirelli* to buildings "doomed from the start" as being of very limited application, and their decision was upheld by the House of Lords.[97] The House of Lords held that a building was not "doomed from the start" merely because it had a latent defect which would inevitably result in damage in due course.[98]

5–021   A case,[99] however, where the "doomed from the start" argument succeeded was *Tozer Kemsley & Millburn (Holdings) Ltd v. J. Jarvis & Sons Ltd.*[1] The claim concerned an allegedly defective air conditioning plant. Judge Stabb Q.C. held, obiter, that on the basis of the plaintiff's allegations, the cause of action accrued when the plant was installed. The fact that the defects manifested themselves subsequently with increasing severity was irrelevant.[2] A similar result was reached in the more recent decision of Dyson J. in *New Islington and Hackney*

---

[92] [1983] 1 W.L.R. 1436.
[93] [1985] 1 All E.R. 335.
[94] [1988] 1 All E.R. 15.
[95] [1985] 1 All E.R. 346.
[96] [1984] 1 W.L.R. 1274 at 1288–1289.
[97] [1987] A.C. 189.
[98] This issue was considered by Litton L.J. in *Bank of East Asia v. Tsien Wui Marble Factory Ltd and others* [2000] H.K.L.R.D. 268. His comments are strictly *obiter* because the court below had found as a fact that the defective cladding, which formed the subject matter of the dispute, was not doomed from the start. Litton P.J. noted that it would be a rare case where a defect which was so profound as to render a building "bound to fail" did not give rise to physical damage within six years. He rejected the notion that a cause of action could accrue prior to the occurrence of quantifiable physical damage. Implicit in this is a rejection of the argument that a different accrual date applies where a building is "doomed from the start". See further paras 5–28 to 5–34, below.
[99] For two further examples (one of which is doubted), see A. McGee, *Limitation Periods, op. cit.*, pp. 64–66.
[1] (1983) 4 Con.L.R. 24.
[2] *ibid.* at 30–32. See also *London Congregational Union Inc. v. Harriss and Harriss* [1988] 1 All E.R. 15 at 23G *per* Ralph Gibson L.J.

Housing Association v. Pollard Thomas & Edwards Ltd.[3] In cases in which the defect to the property is self-contained in that it does not cause damage to any other part, the latest date (if knowledge or discoverability of the defect is not the test) on which damage occurs is practical completion of the building.

Degree of damage required. A separate problem[4] arising from *Pirelli* is what   **5–022** degree of damage to the building must occur in order for the cause of action to accrue (assuming that physical damage to the building is the relevant damage). This question has arisen since *Pirelli* a number of times. In *Bromley LBC v. Rush & Tompkins Ltd*,[5] a case concerning alleged defects in reinforced concrete, Judge Stabb Q.C. held that depassivation and the commencement of corrosion of the steel reinforcement did not constitute "relevant and significant damage". However, the occurrence of hairline cracking of the concrete, caused by the progress of corrosion of the steel reinforcement, did constitute relevant and significant damage. Therefore the cause of action accrued when the hairline cracking occurred.[6] In *University of Glasgow v. William Whitfield*,[7] Judge Bowsher Q.C. held that condensation alone was not damage; the cause of action in tort only accrued when the condensation caused structural damage to the building.

Successive owners. Separate problems arise from that part of Lord Fraser's   **5–023** speech which is summarised in sub-paragraph (6) above.[8] The notion that time may run against a future owner of damaged property before he has acquired any interest in the property is curious in theory and bizarre in practice.[9] As Judge Newey Q.C. pointed out in *Perry v. Tendring D.C.*,[10] if the second owner is to sue, the first owner must assign his cause of action to him. On the hypothesis that all parties are unaware of the damage, this is an unlikely event, at least at the time of sale. Moreover, the first owner, having incurred no remedial costs and having sold at market price, has suffered no loss. It is therefore arguable that the assignee (the subsequent owner who actually suffers loss) can recover nothing. These problems have now been resolved by section 3 of the Latent Damage Act 1986.[11]

Effect of *Murphy* on *Pirelli*. The most important question to consider in   **5–024** relation to Pirelli is the impact of *Murphy v. Brentwood D.C.*[12] As stated earlier,[13] the House of Lords in that case held that defects in buildings should be characterised as economic loss. Lord Keith, with whom all other law lords agreed, explained *Pirelli* as a case of reliance on negligent advice falling within the

---

[3] [2001] P.N.L.R. 515.
[4] For general guidance, see *Cartledge v. E. Jopling & Sons Ltd* [1963] A.C. 758.
[5] (1985) 4 Con.L.R. 44.
[6] *ibid.* at 52–53.
[7] (1988) 42 Build. L.R. 66 at 76.
[8] See para. 5–19, above.
[9] The problem is discussed by G. Robertson, "Defective Premises and Subsequent Purchasers" in (1983) 99 L.Q.R. 559 and J. Holyoak, "Limitation Periods in Economic Loss" in (1984) 128 S.J. 234.
[10] (1984) 30 Build. L.R. 118 at 142–143. See also *R. L. Polk and Co. (Great Britain) Ltd v. Edwin Hill and Partners* (1988) 41 Build.L.R. 84.
[11] See below.
[12] [1991] 1 A.C. 398.
[13] See Chap. 2, para. 2–39, above.

Hedley Byrne principle. As to the accrual of the cause of action, Lord Keith said:

> "The defendants there had in relation to the design been in contractual relations with the plaintiffs, but it was common ground that a claim in contract was time-barred. If the plaintiffs had happened to discover the defect before any damage had occurred there would seem to be no good reason for holding that they would not have had a cause of action in tort at that stage, without having to wait until some damage had occurred. They would have suffered economic loss through having a defective chimney upon which they required to expend money for the purpose of removing the defect. It would seem that in a case such as *Pirelli*, where the tortious liability arose out of a contractual relationship with professional people, the duty extended to take reasonable care not to cause economic loss to the client by the advice given. The plaintiffs built the chimney as they did in reliance on that advice. The case would accordingly fall within the principle of *Hedley Byrne v. Heller and Partners Limited.*"[14]

5–025   Thus *Pirelli* is a case in which economic loss was recoverable. It is arguable that the effect of this analysis is to push back the accrual of the cause of action in such a case, to an earlier date than has previously been assumed—namely the date when the claimant acted in reliance on the negligent design.[15] If this analysis is correct, then the decisions in *London Congregational Union v. Harriss and Harriss*[16] and *Kensington and Chelsea and Westminster Area Health Authority v. Wettern Composites*[17] have been impliedly overruled. Furthermore, this analysis would create some consistency between the architect/engineer cases discussed in this section and the solicitor/insurance broker cases discussed below.[18] This approach would not appear to work injustice, since Parliament has made adequate provision for cases where defects are concealed by the Latent Damage Act 1986.[19]

5–026   An alternative view which has been canvassed by some commentators is that the reconciliation of *Murphy* and *Pirelli* requires the substitution of the date of discoverability for the date of occurrence of physical damage, as the date when

---

[14] *ibid.* at 466F. This view was accepted by Ching P.J. in *Bank of East Asia* [2000] 1 H.K.L.R.D. 268 at 339E. Litton P.J. was critical of this "re-classification" of *Pirelli* as a case of economic loss. See further paras 5–28 to 5–34, below and Mullany, "Limitation of actions—where are we now?" in [1993] L.M.C.L.Q. 34.

[15] See in this respect the judgment of Judge Smout in *Imperial College of Science and Technology v. Norman & Dawbarn* (1986) 8 Con.L.R. 107 at 125 where, although the judge held following *Pirelli* that a cause of action in respect of design against a firm of architects did not arise until actual damage had occurred, he also held that any damage flowing from a failure to warn as to a limited design life must have accrued when the client acted on the architect's design recommendations. See also *New Islington and Hackney Housing Association Ltd v. Pollard Thomas & Edwards Ltd* [2001] P.N.L.R. 515 at 529, *per* Dyson J.: "If as Lord Keith said, *Pirelli* falls within the principle of *Hedley Byrne & Heller and Partners* [1964] A.C. 465 and is an economic loss case, then it is difficult to see why the cause of action in *Pirelli* did not accrue when the plaintiffs relied on the advice of the engineers by instructing them to proceed with the construction of the chimney." However, Dyson J. held that he was bound to follow *Pirelli* and hold that knowledge or discoverability of the defect was not the relevant test.

[16] [1985] 1 All E.R. 335 and [1988] 1 All E.R. 15, discussed in para. 5–20, above.

[17] [1985] 1 All E.R. 346, discussed in para. 5–20, above.

[18] See paras 5–37 to 5–47, below.

[19] See paras 5–49 to 5–55, below. See *New Islington and Hackney Housing Association Ltd v. Pollard Thomas & Edwards Ltd* [2001] P.N.L.R. 515 at 529, *per* Dyson J. But see *Bank of East Asia v. Tsien Wui Marble Factory and others* [2000] 1 H.K.L.R.D. 268 and, in particular, *per* Ching P.J. at 341–343, *per* Bokhary P.J at 358A and, *per* Lord Nicholls at 363B (this decision is discussed further in paras 5–28 to 5–34, below).

"damage" is suffered for the purposes of determining when the cause of action in negligence accrues. In other words, it is said that the start date has become later rather than earlier.[20] This view was rejected at first instance in *Western Challenge Housing Association Ltd v. Percy Thomas Partnership*.[21] However, in the context of New Zealand law it was considered more favourably by the Privy Council in *Invercargill City Council v. Hamlin*.[22] The facts of *Invercargill* and the relevant dates are set out in Chapter 2, paragraph 2–56, above. The Privy Council upheld the decision of the New Zealand Court of Appeal that Mr Hamlin's cause of action accrued in 1989, when the defective foundations first became reasonably discoverable and were in fact discovered. The Privy Council referred to some of the criticisms which have been expressed of Pirelli and concluded:

> "Once it is appreciated that the loss in respect of which the plaintiff in the present case is suing is loss to his pocket, and not for physical damage to the house or foundations, then most, if not all the difficulties surrounding the limitation question fall away. The plaintiff's loss occurs when the market value of the house is depreciated by reason of the defective foundations, and not before. If he resells the house at full value before the defect is discovered, he has suffered no loss. Thus in the common case the occurrence of the loss and the discovery of the loss will coincide."[23]

The Privy Council left open the question whether *Pirelli* should still be regarded as good law in England, although it was not such in New Zealand.[24]

If the *Invercargill* analysis is adopted as part of English law, then in respect of claims against architects and engineers the reforms introduced by the Latent Damage Act 1986[25] will be largely otiose.[26] However, in *New Islington and Hackney Housing Association Ltd v. Pollard Thomas & Edwards Ltd*,[26a] Dyson J. held that the claimant housing association suffered loss and damage in relation to inadequate sound-proofing at practical completion of the building at the latest. **5–027**

Bank of East Asia. The above contrasting approaches views have recently been considered by the Hong Kong Court of Final Appeal in *Bank of East Asia Ltd v. Tsien Wui Marble Factory Ltd and others*.[27] The claim in *Bank of East Asia* concerned the granite cladding of a tower block being built for the plaintiff. **5–028**

---

[20] See Mullany, "Limitation of actions and latent damage" in (1991) 54 M.L.R. 216 at 227–228; McKendrick,"*Pirelli* re-examined" in (1991) 11 Journal of Legal Studies 326 at 335–336; Mullany, "Limitation of actions—where are we now?" in [1993] L.M.C.L.Q. 34 at 43. In *Pullen v. Gutteridge Haskins & Davey Pty Ltd* [1993] 1 V.R. 27, the Appeal Division of the Supreme Court of Victoria declined to follow *Pirelli*, holding that damage occurred only when the latent defect became known or manifest.

[21] (1995) C.I.L.L. 1018.

[22] [1996] A.C. 624.

[23] *ibid.* at 648C-D.

[24] *ibid.* at 649C. In *Havenledge Ltd v. Graeme John and Partners (a firm)* [2001] P.N.L.R. 419, CA, Sir Antony Evans said at 424 that *Pirelli* remained binding as an authoritative statement of English law. In *New Islington and Hackney Housing Association Ltd v. Pollard Thomas & Edwards Ltd* [2001] P.N.L.R. 515 at 529 Dyson J. held that he was bound to follow *Pirelli* and that "the knowledge test has not been applied in English law".

[25] See paras 5–49 to 5–55, below.

[26] The statutory provisions in respect of latent damage had a considerable influence on the majority of the Hong Kong Court of Final Appeal in *Bank of East Asia Ltd v. Tsien Wui Marble Factory Ltd and others* [2000] 1 H.K.L.R.D. 268, discussed in paras 5–28 to 5–34, below.

[26a] [2001] P.N.L.R. 515.

[27] [2000] 1 H.K.L.R.D. 268. See (2001) 117 L.Q.R. 20 (Limitation and Latent Damage in Hong Kong: Mullany)

Palmer and Turner were the architects and engineers. The cladding was completed in March 1982, the building as a whole in July 1983. The cladding failed. Proceedings were issued against Palmer and Turner in 1996. Palmer and Turner admitted negligence but argued that the claim was time barred; more than six years having elapsed since the occurrence of damage and the accrual of the cause of action.[28]

5–029   Latent damage provisions mirroring those in section 14A of the Limitation Act 1980[29] were introduced into the Limitation Ordinance in 1991 by section 31. However, the plaintiff could not avail itself of section 31 if the action had already become statute barred by the date on which they came into force, July 31, 1991. The central issue for the Court was therefore when the cause of action accrued. By a majority of 3:2 the Court of Final Appeal held that the limitation period had expired before the issue of proceedings. All five judges gave reasons for their decision. Substantive judgments were delivered by Litton P.J. and Ching P.J. in the majority and by Bokhary P.J. in the minority; Nazareth N.P.J. delivered a short judgment agreeing with the majority and Lord Nicholls N.P.J. delivered a short dissenting judgment agreeing with Bokhary P.J. The parties agreed that the loss to the plaintiff should properly be characterised as economic loss. All members of the Court agreed, except for Litton P.J. who favoured a return to the "common sense" view that the loss suffered was both economic and physical. It was not right to "unhook" the physical element.

5–030   **When was damage first suffered?** The majority endorsed the approach of the House of Lords in *Pirelli* and rejected the alternative approach of the Privy Council in *Invercargill City Council v. Hamlin*.[30] The majority were considerably influenced by the fact that the approach adopted in *Invercargill* was not reconcilable with the statutory scheme in Hong Kong. There was no equivalent of section 31 (or section 14A) in New Zealand, such provision was unnecessary because the law in New Zealand had developed along different lines from that in England. Of the discoverability test, Ching P.J. said "the discovery of damage is self-evidently not the occurrence of damage".[31]

5–031   Some variance of views is apparent between the judgments of Litton P.J. and Ching P.J. Litton P.J. concluded that the cause of action accrued in 1985 when, on the evidence, physical damage in a "real and substantial sense" first occurred.[32] Ching P.J. accepted that the loss under consideration in this case was economic. In the absence of proof as to when such economic loss occurred, the court "may, if not must, take the date of the occurrence of the physical damage as being the date of the economic loss".[33]

5–032   **The views of the minority.** The minority fully endorsed the approach of the Privy Council in *Invercargill City Council v. Hamlin*.[34] Bokhary P.J. expressed

---

[28] The contractual action against both parties was clearly time barred. The sub-contractor did not admit negligence and sought unsuccessfully to argue that it had relied on independent contractors.
[29] See paras 5–49 to 5–55, below.
[30] [1996] A.C. 624.
[31] [2000] 1 H.K.L.R.D. 268 at 319C.
[32] *ibid.* at 301D–F, 303F–H and 310B. In following *Pirelli* and rejecting *Invercargill*, Litton P.J. placed great reliance on the judgment of Lord Reid in *Cartledge and others v. Jopling (E.) & Sons Ltd* [1963] A.C. 758 at 772. Litton L.J. said: "it cannot be the policy of the legislature to encourage speculative law-suits".
[33] *ibid.* at 344C.
[34] [1996] A.C. 624.

the view that the approach could not sensibly be confined to New Zealand: "Either it is convincing or it is not".[35] The approach of the Privy Council in *Invercargill* recognised that economic loss in building defects cases occurred when the market value of the building was diminished. This was the only manner in which the term "economic loss" had substance and real meaning.[36] So far as he statutory position was concerned, Bokhary P.J. rejected the notion that, merely because legislation had been passed to give relief against an unjust judicial decision, the legislature was to be taken to have set that judicial decision in stone.[37]

Lord Nicholls emphasised that physical damage to the building and financial **5–033** loss to its owner were not necessarily linked. Financial loss might be suffered before any physical damage occurred. "To make the accrual of the cause of action dependent on the presence or absence of physical damage to a building is to ignore the realities of defectively designed or defectively constructed building works."[38] He also agreed with Bokhary P.J. that the statutory provisions should not be taken to freeze the common law in effect at the time of its enactment.[39] Lord Nicholls considered that there were two possibilities for the date of accrual of the action: the first was when the plaintiffs accepted and paid for the building. At that date it acquired something which, because of the defect, was inherently less valuable. The second alternative was when the defect became patent. Until then, the market value of the building was undiminished. In Lord Nicholls' view, "despite powerful arguments to the contrary, the preponderance of high authority now supports the view that, as regards latent defects in buildings, the second possibility is to be preferred".[40]

Uncertainty. The present state of the law in this area cannot be regarded as **5–034** satisfactory. The difference of view between the appellate courts and their members who have had to grapple with this issue indicates its difficulty. The "discoverability" test is attractive in that it goes to the market value of the building. It is, however, an ignorant market and the claimant will not have sold the building before the defect is in fact discovered—otherwise he would not be a claimant. The alternative, that loss is suffered when an inherently less valuable building is constructed, threatens to revive "doomed from the start" arguments.[41]

(ii) *Claims against surveyors*

Claims by purchasers. Where a person purchases property in reliance on a **5–035** survey report which fails to disclose material defects, the courts have repeatedly held that the measure of damages is the difference between the price paid and the value of the property as it ought to have been described.[42] Quite consistently with this approach, Judge Hawser Q.C. held in *Secretary of State for the Environment*

---

[35] [2000] 1 H.K.L.R.D. 268 at 356D.
[36] *ibid.* at 356F–G.
[37] *ibid.* at 358H.
[38] *ibid.* at 362E–F.
[39] *ibid.* at 363J.
[40] *ibid.* at 363B.
[41] See generally *New Islington and Hackney Housing Association Ltd v. Pollard Thomas & Edwards Ltd* [2001] P.N.L.R. 515, *per* Dyson J.
[42] See Chap. 9, paras 9–130 to 9–148, below.

v. Essex Goodman & Suggitt[43] that the cause of action accrued when the plaintiffs acted in reliance upon the survey report (and became irrevocably committed to lease the property in question). In the case of a house purchaser, the cause of action would normally accrue when contracts are exchanged. This approach was adopted in *Horbury v. Craig Hall & Rutley*.[44] In *Byrne v. Hall Pain & Foster*,[45] the plaintiffs exchanged contracts to purchase the lease of a flat on July 8, 1988. They completed the purchase on July 22, 1988. They issued their writ against the allegedly negligent surveyors on July 18, 1994. The Court of Appeal held that the cause of action accrued on exchange of contracts rather than completion, and accordingly that the claim was statute barred.

5–036 **Mortgagees.** Where a mortgagee lends money upon inadequate security as a consequence of a negligent valuation, he generally suffers loss when he makes or agrees to make the loan. The cause of action, therefore, should accrue on that date and not on the date when the borrower defaults. Different considerations arise, however, in marginal cases where the value of the mortgaged property, although lower than stated in the negligent valuation, equals or exceeds the sum lent. In that situation the Court of Appeal has held that the plaintiff does not suffer loss, and the cause of action in tort does not accrue, until such time as the indebtedness exceeds the value of the security.[46] The approach of the Court of Appeal in *First National Commercial Bank* was approved by the House of Lords in *Nykredit Mortgage Bank plc v. Edward Erdman Group Ltd*[47] (which was the sequel to its decision in *Banque Bruxelles Lambert SA v. Eagle Star Insurance Co. Ltd*[48]). The House of Lords held that the lender's cause of action in tort against a negligent valuer accrues on the date when the value of the security plus the value of the borrower's covenant is less than the amount owed by the borrower.[49] In *Kenny and Good Pty. Ltd v. MGICA (1992) Ltd*,[50] the High Court of Australia held that loss occurs when it is reasonably ascertainable that sale of the mortgaged property will result in a loss.

(iii) *Claims against solicitors*[51]

5–037 **Where client incurs an obligation.** In *Forster v. Outred & Co.*,[52] the plaintiff signed a mortgage deed charging her property to H, as security for a loan by H to her son. She claimed that she had done so as the result of the defendant

---

[43] [1986] 1 W.L.R. 1432.

[44] [1991] C.I.L.L. 692: cause of action accrued when plaintiff exchanged contracts to purchase.

[45] [1999] 1 W.L.R. 1849, CA Simon Brown L.J. cited para. 1–146 of the previous edition of this work at 1853C–E.

[46] *First National Commercial Bank plc v. Humberts* [1995] 2 All E.R. 673. It was, however, a material fact in this case that the commitment fee paid by the borrower covered the plaintiff's initial costs of making the advance: *ibid.* at 676–677.

[47] [1997] 1 W.L.R. 1627.

[48] [1997] A.C. 191.

[49] This decision was applied in *DNB Mortgages Ltd v. Bullock & Lees (a firm)* [2000] P.N.L.R. 427, where the Court of Appeal grappled with the questions as to how the value of the mortgagor's covenant was to be valued and how to value the mortgaged property over a period of falling prices.

[50] [2000] Lloyd's Rep. P.N. 25 and (1999) 163 A.L.R. 611, *per* Gaudron J.; McHugh J. stated that this would be, at the earliest, when the mortgagor defaulted.

[51] See also Evans, *op. cit.*, Chap. 10.

[52] [1982] 1 W.L.R. 86. Approved by the House of Lords in *Nykredit Mortgage Bank plc v. Edward Erdman Group Ltd* [1997] 1 W.L.R. 1627.

solicitors' negligence. The Court of Appeal held, on an interlocutory appeal, that the plaintiff's loss accrued when she signed the mortgage deed and not at a later date when the demand for payment was made under the deed. Accordingly the plaintiff's claim[53] was statute-barred. Stephenson L.J., who gave the leading judgment, said:

> " . . . the plaintiff has suffered actual damage through the negligence of her solicitors by entering into the mortgage deed, the effect of which has been to encumber her interest in her freehold estate with this legal charge and subject her to a liability which may, according to matters completely outside her control, mature into financial loss—as indeed it did. It seems to me that the plaintiff did suffer actual damage in those ways; and subject to that liability and with that encumbrance on the mortgage property was then entitled to claim damages."[54]

Dunn L.J. gave a short concurring judgment, in which he said:

> "I would hold that in cases of financial or economic loss the damage crystallises and the cause of action is complete at the date when the plaintiff, in reliance on negligent advice, acts to his detriment."[55]

The same approach was adopted by the Court of Appeal in *Baker v. Ollard &* **5–038** *Bentley*[56] and *Costa v. Georghiou*[57] and by Nourse J. in *Melton v. Walker & Stanger*.[58] This line of authority was reviewed in some detail by the High Court of Australia in *Wardley Australia Ltd v. Western Australia*.[59] The plaintiff in that case gave an indemnity in 1987 in reliance on representations made by the defendants. In 1989, the plaintiff was called upon to make payment pursuant to the indemnity. In 1991, the plaintiff sought to amend its statement of claim by adding a statutory claim (for which there was a three year limitation period) to the effect that it had been induced to give the indemnity by the defendant's misleading representations. The High Court held that the plaintiff suffered loss when it was called upon to pay, not when it entered into the indemnity agreement. Therefore the amendment was made within the limitation period and should not be struck out. Four of the seven members of the Court gave a single judgment to the following effect: where P enters into a contract which exposes him to a contingent liability, he does not suffer damage until the contingency is fulfilled. If *Forster v. Outred & Co.*[60] and the other English cases contradict this principle, then they ought not to be followed in Australia. It is unreasonable to expect P to commence proceedings before the contingency is fulfilled. Moreover, if damages are assessed on a contingency basis, they might not be adequate.

---

[53] Under the second writ. The first action was struck out for want of prosecution.

[54] *ibid.* at 98D–E.

[55] *ibid.* at 99F.

[56] (1982) 126 S.J. 593: alleged cause of action accrued on date when property conveyed to plaintiff, not at later date when problems arose.

[57] (1984) 1 P.N. 201: cause of action accrued when plaintiff entered into sub-underlease with defective rent review clause, not nine years later when the rent review clause was intended to operate.

[58] (1981) 125 S.J. 861: alleged cause of action accrued when plaintiff executed agreement drafted by defendant solicitors, not at later date when High Court held that agreement did not have effect intended by plaintiff.

[59] (1992) 109 A.L.R. 247.

[60] [1982] 1 W.L.R. 86.

5–039   The New Zealand Court of Appeal has recently considered *Wardley* and stated the provisional view that "the Australian approach is in general terms preferable to the English".[61] In that case the claimant claimed damages for negligent lack of advice, as a result of which the claimant guaranteed the performance of certain obligations under a lease. The Court held that, since the guarantee imposed present liabilities rather than contingent liabilities, the claimant's cause of action accrued when he signed the guarantee and accordingly his claim in negligence was statute barred.

5–040   **Where client acquires less valuable rights than intended.** If a solicitor's negligence diminishes the value of rights acquired by the client, actionable damage normally occurs at the time of acquisition of those rights rather than at the moment when they are exercised. This is illustrated by the decision of the Court of Appeal in *D.W. Moore and Co. Ltd v. Ferrier*.[62] In 1971, the plaintiff insurance brokers engaged solicitors to draft a contract between themselves and F, who was to become an employee/director. The contract contained a restrictive covenant. In 1975, the parties entered into a further agreement drafted by the solicitors, containing a restrictive covenant in similar terms. In 1980, F ceased to be employed by the plaintiffs and started to compete with them. It emerged that the restrictive covenant did not provide the protection which had been expected. The plaintiffs started proceedings in May 1985, but it was held on a preliminary issue that their claim was statute-barred. The Court of Appeal held that *Forster v. Outred and Co.*[63] was not inconsistent with *Pirelli* and was still good law. They further held that a valid restrictive covenant was a thing of value, and therefore the plaintiffs must have suffered some loss (capable of quantification) both in 1971 and in 1975. Therefore the plaintiffs' causes of action against the solicitors had accrued in 1971 and 1975. The same principle was applied by the Court of Appeal in *Lee v. Thompson*,[64] *Sullivan v. Layton Lougher and Co.*[65] and *Gordon v. J.B. Wheatley and Co. (a firm)*.[66]

5–041   The Court of Appeal appears to have adopted a somewhat different approach in an earlier decision, *UBAF Ltd v. European American Banking Corp.*[67] The plaintiffs claimed that in December 1974 they had agreed to participate in two loans to shipping companies in reliance on incorrect information supplied by the defendants, and that in March 1976 the shipping companies had defaulted. The writ was issued in December 1981. The Court of Appeal declined to strike out the action on the grounds that it was statute-barred. Ackner L.J., giving the judgment of the Court, said:

---

[61] *Gilbert v. Shanahan* [1998] 3 N.Z.L.R. 528 at 542. New Zealand has no equivalent of the Latent Damage Act 1986.
[62] [1988] 1 W.L.R. 267.
[63] [1982] 1 W.L.R. 267.
[64] (1990) 6 P.N. 91: claim against solicitor for failing to obtain good title to house; cause of action accrued at time of purchase (1975) not when the problem came to light (1984).
[65] [1995] 2 E.G.L.R. 111: defendant solicitors acted for plaintiff in the purchase of a 63-year lease of premises; it was alleged that the solicitors failed to explain circumstances which would make subsequent enfranchisement more expensive; held that the plaintiff suffered "damage" on the date of purchase (because the leasehold interest was less valuable than he was entitled to expect) and not when he became entitled to leasehold enfranchisement; claim statute barred.
[66] [2000] Lloyd's Rep. P.N. 605: claimant operated a private mortgage scheme; defendant solicitors failed to advise of impact of Financial Services Act 1986, exposing him to claims; held that loss was suffered when individual clients entered transactions which were vulnerable under that Act.
[67] [1984] Q.B. 713. This was not a case involving solicitors: but the same principles were involved. The court distinguished *Forster & Outred and Co.* [1982] 1 W.L.R. 86.

"The defendants successfully contended before Leggatt J. that the accrual of the cause of action occurred when the plaintiffs parted with their money and acquired instead claims for repayment of money lent against borrowers, whose ability to repay was, contrary to the alleged representations, a matter of considerable doubt. Again, there is a short answer to this question—it depends upon the facts as found at the trial. The plaintiffs do not assert that they are entitled to damages to be measured by the difference in the value of the chose in action which they acquired by making this loan as compared with the value it would have had if the representations had been accurate, as in a claim for a breach of warranty. Their case is that, if they had known the respects in which the representations were inaccurate, they would not have entered into the contract. Accordingly, it is argued by the defendants that, at the very moment of entering into that contract, the plaintiffs must have suffered damage. In our judgment, this bare proposition is not self-evident. The plaintiffs are suing in tort—the tort of negligence. To establish a cause of action they must establish not only a breach of duty, but that that breach of duty occasioned them damage. This is axiomatic. It is possible, although it may be improbable, that, at the date when the plaintiffs advanced their money, the value of the chose in action which they then acquired was, in fact, not less than the sum which the plaintiffs lent, or indeed even exceeded it."[68]

This was, in effect, a striking out application, rather than a trial of the limitation issue. It may have limited impact on the solicitor cases.[69]

The line of cases following *Forster v. Outred and Co.* was reviewed by the **5–042** House of Lords in *Nykredit Mortgage Bank plc v. Edward Erdman Group Ltd*.[70] It follows from *Nykredit* that a cause of action by a mortgage lender against a solicitor will only accrue in tort when the value of the security (*i.e.* the mortgaged property and the borrower's covenant) is less than the amount owed.[71]

Previous action dismissed for want of prosecution. In *Hopkins v. Mac-* **5–043** *Kenzie*,[72] as a result, allegedly, of negligence by the defendant solicitor, the plaintiff's claim against a hospital for medical negligence had been dismissed for want of prosecution. The Court of Appeal held that the cause of action in tort against the solicitor accrued when the original claim was actually dismissed, and not at any earlier date. The Court rejected the submission that the cause of action accrued when the solicitor's delay was such that the original claim would inevitably be dismissed. The advantage of this approach is that the date when the cause of action accrues can be identified with certainty. On the other hand, if the original action is excessively stale before it is dismissed, the client has long since ceased to have a chose in action of any value. Suppose the original action "goes to sleep" but is not struck out. There must come a time when the claimant's cause of action accrues against his own solicitors, so that he can commence proceedings. If he does not commence proceedings then, the limitation period should

---

[68] *ibid.* at 725. This reasoning is criticised by K. M. Stanton, "Reforming Limitations of Actions" in (1986) 2 P.N. 75.

[69] See Evans, *op. cit.*, pp. 179–180. The decision may be consistent with *Nykredit Mortgage Bank plc v. Edward Erdman Group Ltd* [1997] 1 W.L.R. 1627, since it was possible that at trial the plaintiffs would show that they were not under-secured until within six years of the issue of proceedings.

[70] [1997] 1 W.L.R. 1627. See para. 5–36, above.

[71] *Lloyds Bank plc v. Burd Pearse* [2000] P.N.L.R. 71, *per* Evans-Lombe J. (failure to advise on restrictive covenants which reduced value of claimant bank's security. Held that it was for the defendant to prove that loss had been suffered more than six years before the issue of proceedings in accordance with *Nykredit Mortgage Bank plc v. Edward Erdman Group Ltd* and that the defendant had failed to do so).

[72] (1995) 6 Med.L.R. 26. Discussed in Evans, *op. cit.*, pp. 186–188.

start to run against him.[73] It is therefore submitted that *Hopkins v. MacKenzie* does not lay down an universal principle,[74] and that each "dismissal for want of prosecution" claim should be decided on its own facts. The way that the plaintiff chooses to frame his pleadings should not determine the limitation issue.[75]

5–044   **Where the client purchases a property.** Usually, time will run from the date of exchange of contracts in the same way that it does in cases involving surveyors.[76] However, solicitors may be in breach of duty in failing to advise that the property, although worth what the client is paying for it, is unsuitable for his intended purposes. In such a case no loss is suffered when the property is purchased,[77] Rather it is suffered when the claimant expends money to further his purpose, such expenditure being abortive and so recoverable as damages.[78]

5–045   **Omissions capable of being remedied.** The final problem to consider is analogous to that referred to above.[79] When does the cause of action accrue in tort in respect of breaches which are capable of being remedied? So long as the matter can be put right, it may be thought that the client has suffered no loss. Indeed this was the view taken by Oliver J. in *Midland Bank Trust Co. Ltd v. Hett, Stubbs and Kemp*.[80] He held that the plaintiff did not suffer actual damage until August 1967, when the property was conveyed and the option was defeated. However, in *Bell v. Peter Browne and Co.*[81] the Court of Appeal held that the plaintiff suffered damage in 1978 and that his cause of action in tort accrued then.[82] In essence, if the plaintiff's legal or equitable rights were diminished in value, then he suffered damage, despite the fact that it would have been possible to restore their value in the unlikely event that anyone had turned his mind to the matter. Similar considerations apply in claims by disappointed beneficiaries under *White v. Jones*.[83] On one view, loss is suffered when the will is not made (or not properly made) in their favour, so depriving them of a saleable expectancy. On the other, it is only on the death of the solicitor's client that the earlier failure becomes incapable of remedy. In *Bacon v. Howard Kennedy (a firm)*,[84] Judge Bromley Q.C., sitting as a judge of the High Court, held that the latter analysis was correct. In many such cases (but not in *Bacon*) the disappointed beneficiaries will be able to rely on section 14A of the Limitation Act 1980.[85]

---

[73] *cf. Doundalikis v. Anthony Sdrinis and Co.* [1989] V.R. 781.

[74] Indeed, it is not easy to reconcile with other authorities: see *Knapp v. Ecclesiastical Insurance Group Plc* [1998] P.N.L.R. 172 at 187D, *per* Hobhouse L.J. (See also (1) *Gordon v. J. B. Wheatley and Co. (a firm)* [2000] Lloyd's Rep. P.N. 605 at 610, where Kennedy L..J. said that *Hopkins v. Mackenzie* was "of limited assistance because, as all three judges made clear, so much turned on the precise nature of the plaintiff's cause of action in that case"; (2) *Havenledge Ltd v. Graeme John and Partners (a firm)* [2001] P.N.L.R. 419 at 435, where Pill L..J. said that the decision "does not establish a general principle".)

[75] *cf. Walkin v. South Manchester H.A.* [1995] 1 W.L.R. 1543 at 1551C–H, *per* Auld L.J. The question is when the claimant first suffered actionable damage and not when he claims that he did.

[76] See para. 5–35, above.

[77] Unless the costs of the purchase constitute damage because the claimant will need to sell and move to suitable premises.

[78] *Havenledge Ltd v. Graeme John and Partners (a firm)* [2001] P.N.L.R. 419, CA.

[79] See para. 5–14, above.

[80] [1979] Ch. 384. For the facts of this case, see Chap. 10, para. 10–07, below.

[81] [1990] 2 Q.B. 495. For the facts see para. 5–14, above.

[82] See the reasoning of Nicholls L.J. at 502–503 and of Beldam L.J. at 509–510, *ibid.*

[83] [1995] 2 A.C. 207, discussed in Chap. 10, paras 10–48 to 10–50.

[84] [1998] P.N.L.R. 1.

[85] See paras 5–49 to 5–55, below.

(iv) Claims against insurance brokers

A similar approach has been adopted in claims against insurance brokers. *Iron* **5–046**
Trades Mutual Insurance Co. Ltd v. J.K. Buckenham Ltd[86] involved a claim
against brokers for obtaining reinsurance contracts which proved to be voidable.
Kenneth Rokison Q.C. held, on a striking out application, that the cause of action
in tort accrued when the reinsurance contracts were executed, not when the
reinsurers sought to avoid them. In *Islander Trucking Ltd v. Hogg Robinson and
Gardner Mountain (Marine) Ltd*,[87] brokers arranged "goods in transit" insurance
for the plaintiff in 1980. In 1985, the insurers avoided the policy for alleged non-
disclosure and misrepresentation. Evans J. held, on a summons relating to joinder
of parties, that the cause of action in tort accrued when the insurance contract was
made, not when the insurers avoided.

The Court of Appeal approved both *Iron Trades Mutual* and *Islander Trucking* **5–047**
in *Knapp v. Ecclesiastical Insurance Group plc.*[88] The Court held that if an
insurance broker negligently procured a voidable insurance policy, the cause of
action against the broker accrued when the policy incepted, not on the date of
avoidance by the insurers. Ten days later the House of Lords came to the same
conclusion in *Nykredit Mortgage Bank plc v. Edward Erdman Group Ltd.*[89] In
Compannia de Seguros Imperio v. Heath (REBX) Ltd,[90] Langley J. held that the
cause of action against a broker for wrongly committing an insurer to fronting a
risk under a binding authority arose when the insurer was committed the risk and
so was exposed to a greater liability or potential liability.[91]

(v) Claims against financial advisers

Consistently with the approach to claims against surveyors, solicitors and insur- **5–048**
ance brokers, a client of a financial adviser will suffer loss and damage when he
makes an investment or otherwise acts to his detriment in reliance upon negligent
advice.[92]

(d) Effect of the Latent Damage Act 1986

This Act is based upon the recommendations made by the Law Reform Commit- **5–049**
tee in its 24th Report,[93] published in November 1984. The Act deals with latent
damage not including personal injuries.[94] Its main objects are to protect claimants

---

[86] [1990] 1 All E.R. 808. Discussed by K. M. Stanton, "Limitation of Actions: Latent Damage and
the Insurance Broker" in (1989) 1 P.N. 158.
[87] [1990] 1 All E.R. 826.
[88] [1998] P.N.L.R. 172.
[89] [1997] 1 W.L.R. 1627 at 1634C.
[90] [1999] Lloyd's Rep. 571.
[91] However, insurers do not necessarily suffer loss when they insure a risk: their aim is to make a
profit from the premiums received.
[92] *Martin v. Britannia Life Ltd* [2000] Lloyd's Rep. P.N. 412, *per* Jonathan Parker J. (damage suffered
when inappropriate policies were issued to the claimant and the claimant made payments associated
with them).
[93] Cmnd. 9390 (1984).
[94] The Act came into force on September 18, 1986. It does not affect any actions commenced before
that date: s.4(1)(b). Nor does it enable actions to be brought which had become statute-barred before
that date: s.4(1)(a).

who, for good reason, are unaware that they have a cause of action for a number of years, and at the same time to protect defendants against unduly stale claims.[95]

5–050   The Act provides[96] for a new section (section 14A) to be inserted into the Limitation Act 1980, which provides, in effect, two alternative periods of limitation in cases of latent damage.[97] The claimant may either bring his claim within six years from the date on which the cause of action accrued or within three years from the "starting date". The "starting date" is defined as follows:

> "The earliest date on which the plaintiff or any person in whom the cause of action was vested before him first had both the knowledge required for bringing an action for damages in respect of the relevant damage and a right to bring such an action."[98]

The knowledge referred to in this passage means knowledge both:

> "(a) of the material facts about the damage in respect of which damages are claimed; and
>
> (b) of the other facts relevant to the current action mentioned in subsection (8) below."[99]

The phrase "material facts about the damage" means such facts as would lead a reasonable person to consider the damage sufficiently serious to justify instituting proceedings.[1] The "other facts" referred to in (b) above are:

> "(a) that the damage was attributable in whole or in part to the act or omission which is alleged to constitute negligence; and
>
> (b) the identity of the defendant; and
>
> (c) if it is alleged that the act or omission was that of a person other than the defendant, the identity of that person and the additional facts supporting the bringing of an action against the defendant."[2]

However, knowledge that the particular acts or omissions did or did not, as a matter of law, involve negligence is irrelevant.[3] For the purposes of these provisions a person is deemed to know matters which he ought reasonably to have observed or ascertained or (in appropriate circumstances) learnt from

---

[95] For a fuller account of the thinking which led up to the Act, see the Law Reform Committee's 24th Report.

[96] Latent Damage Act 1986, s.1.

[97] It should be noted, however, that s.14A of the Limitation Act 1980 does not apply in cases of deliberate concealment by the defendant. In such cases the plaintiff can still rely upon s.32(1)(b) of the Limitation Act 1980, which is more favourable to him. (See s.2(2) of the Latent Damage Act 1986.)

[98] Limitation Act 1980, s.14A(5).

[99] *ibid.*, s.14A(6).

[1] *ibid.*, s.14A(7).

[2] *ibid.*, s.14A(8).

[3] *ibid.*, s.14A(9).

experts.[4] Where different heads of damage occurred at different times, a claimant cannot circumvent these provisions by abandoning heads of damage which are inconvenient to his case on limitation.[5]

The 15-year long stop. The Act also provides for a long stop, as recom-   5–051
mended by the Law Reform Committee.[6] A new section (section 14B) is inserted into the Limitation Act 1980,[7] which prevents an action for damages for negligence being brought:

" . . . after the expiration of fifteen years from the date (or, if more than one, from the last of the dates) on which there occurred any act or omission—

(a) which is alleged to constitute negligence; and
(b) to which the damage in respect of which damages are claimed is alleged to be attributable (in whole or in part)."

This provision overrides section 14A. It bars the commencement of proceedings 15 years after the breach of duty, even if the plaintiff remains unaware of his cause of action throughout the 15-year period, and even if the cause of action does not accrue during that period.[8] However, the long stop does not operate in cases to which section 32(1)(b) of the Limitation Act 1980 applies (postponement of limitation period in cases of deliberate concealment).[9]

Miscellaneous provisions. The Latent Damage Act 1986 makes consequential   5–052
provisions in respect of persons under a disability.[10] The Act also makes special provision for successive owners of property which is affected by latent damage.[11] Section 3 provides that a fresh cause of action shall accrue to the subsequent owner upon his acquisition of the property; but that for limitation purposes the cause of action shall be deemed to have accrued on the date when a cause of action accrued to his predecessor in title. This overcomes the problem discussed above.[12] Furthermore, even if the subsequent owner acquires the property more than six years after the cause of action accrued, he still has three years[13] from the

---

[4] For the full provision as to constructive knowledge see *ibid.*, s.14A(10). The plaintiff is also fixed with the knowledge of his solicitors: *Heathcote v. David Marks and Co.* [1996] 1 E.G.L.R. 123 (but see *Lloyds Bank Plc v. Crosse & Crosse (a firm)* [2001] P.N.L.R. 830, CA for the significance of the scope of the solicitors' retainer).
[5] *Horbury v. Craig Hall & Rutley* [1991] C.I.L.L. 692; approved by the Court of Appeal in *Hamlin v. Edwin Evans* (1996) C.I.L.L. 1173. Dugdale discusses the decision in *Horbury* in "Latent damage: the application of the discoverability principle to survey reports" (1991) 7 P.N. 193. Dugdale argues that *Horbury* illustrates some of the flaws in the Latent Damage Act 1986 and that the Act is in urgent need of revision.
[6] See paras 4–10 to 4–14 of their 24th report.
[7] By s.1 of the Latent Damage Act 1986.
[8] Limitation Act 1980, s.14B(2).
[9] Latent Damage Act 1986, s.2(2).
[10] Latent Damage Act 1986, s.2, which inserts s.28A into the Limitation Act 1980.
[11] This provision only applies to damage which was latent when the property was transferred from one owner to his successor: see subss. 3(1)(b), (5) and (6) of the Latent Damage Act 1986.
[12] See para. 5–23, above.
[13] Subject to the long stop: see s.14B of the Limitation Act 1980.

"starting date"[14] in which to bring proceedings.[15] However, in view of the House of Lords' decision in *Murphy v. Brentwood D.C.*,[16] these provisions may be more of academic interest than of practical importance.

5-053   **Meaning of "negligence".** One important question[17] of construction arises in respect of the Act as a whole. Does the word "negligence" mean the tort of negligence? Or does it also include the breach of a contractual duty to exercise reasonable skill and care? In the Unfair Contract Terms Act 1977 the word "negligence" is used in the wider sense, and is so defined in section 1(1). There is no definition of the word "negligence" in the Latent Damage Act 1986. There is little doubt that the draughtsman of the Act intended to use the word "negligence" in the narrow sense, meaning the tort of negligence.[18] It is so used in the Law Reform Committee's 24th Report on which the Act is based.[19] In *Société Commerciale de Réassurance v. ERAS (International) Ltd*,[20] the Court of Appeal held, with regret, that section 14A of the Limitation Act 1980 applied only to actions for the tort of negligence. It did not apply to claims framed in contract.

5-054   **Date of knowledge.** The language of section 14A echoes that of section 14.[21] Accordingly the authorities on the construction of section 14 are valuable by way of analogy.[22] However, more recent authority has accumulated on the application of section 14A itself.[23] Section 14A does not require the claimant to know that he has a possible cause of action. What it does require is that he must know the material facts founding that cause of action.[24] If the time comes when the claimant expresses a clear view that the defendant is responsible for the mishap, it is difficult for him thereafter to deny that he had sufficient "knowledge" to

---

[14] As defined in s.14A(5) of the Limitation Act 1980.

[15] Section 3 of the Latent Damage Act 1986 is subject to special transitional provisions: Latent Damage Act 1986, subss. 4(3) and (4). In brief, the section only applies where the claimant acquired his interest in the damaged property after September 18, 1986. The alternative limitation period (three years from the "starting date") is not available where the original cause of action accrued before September 18, 1986. The object of these provisions appears to be that the defendant should not be deprived of any limitation defence which accrued before the Act came into force. (This is the objective of all transitional provisions in s.4. But the achievement of this object is rather more complex in the case of s.3. The transitional provisions affecting s.3 did not appear in the Latent Damage Bill, as originally published. They were added during the Bill's passage through Parliament.)

[16] [1991] 1 A.C. 398.

[17] This question is discussed by K. M. Stanton, "Reforming Limitations of Actions" in (1986) 2 P.N. 75. This article was written shortly after the Latent Damage Bill was first published.

[18] Since this view has now been judicially confirmed, no lengthy justification is offered. However, the editors' arguments in support of this view can be found in para. 1–124 of the third edition of this book.

[19] See, *e.g.* 24th Report, para. 2.1, third sentence and n. 3.

[20] [1992] 2 All E.R. 82. See also the decision of Mr K. Rokison Q.C. in *Iron Trades Mutual Insurance Co. Ltd v. J. K. Buckenham Ltd* [1990] 1 All E.R. 808 at 821–823; discussed by N. J. Mullany, "Reform of the Law of Latent Damage" in (1991) 54 M.L.R. 349 at 359–360.

[21] See paras 5–56 to 5–62, below.

[22] See *Spencer-Ward v. Humberts* [1995] 1 E.G.L.R. 123 at 125; *Hallam-Eames v. Merrett Syndicates Ltd* [1995] 7 Med.L.R. 122 at 125.

[23] In relation to surveyors, see Chap. 9, para. 9–09, below.

[24] *Higgins v. Hatch & Fielding* [1996] 1 E.G.L.R. 133. Knowledge of facts founding a different cause of action from that sued on will not cause time to run in respect of the latter claim: *Birmingham Midshires Building Society v. Wretham* [1999] P.N.L.R. 685 at 692D—693A citing *Hamlin v. Edwin Evans* [1996] P.N.L.R. 398, CA.

trigger section 14A. The mere fact that the claimant would need expert evidence to confirm his view before launching proceedings does not alter the situation.[25] In *Hallam-Eames v. Merrett*,[26] the Court of Appeal considered what degree of knowledge the Lloyd's names on a long tail syndicate must have in order to trigger section 14A in respect of their claims against the managing agents and the auditors. The court gave a single judgment. It stated that the act or omission of which the claimant must have knowledge "must be that which is causally relevant for the purposes of an allegation of negligence". The court applied section 14A to the facts of the *Merrett* litigation as follows:

"What, on these principles, are the facts which constitute the negligence of which the Names complain? It would in our view be incomplete to say that it was the writing of the run off reinsurance policies or the RITCs or the certification of the syndicate accounts. These facts in themselves do not amount to acts of which the Names would even prima facie be entitled to complain. It is necessary to add the allegation that the run off policies and the RITCs exposed the Names to potentially huge liabilities and that the certified accounts attributed values to IBNRs, none of which were in fact capable of reasonable quantification."[27]

In applying section 14A the courts have been ready to fix claimants with **5-055** knowledge which they should have acquired. In *Finance for Mortgages Ltd v. Farley and Co.*[28] the plaintiff lenders claimed damages against surveyors for allegedly negligent valuation. Kay J. held that the plaintiffs ought to have commenced possession proceedings against the borrowers at a much earlier date and ought to have procured a valuation of the property within about six weeks from obtaining possession. The plaintiffs were fixed with constructive knowledge of the value of the property as from that time, and accordingly their claim was statute barred.[29] In the same way, in *Webster v. Cooper & Burnett*[30] the claimant

---

[25] *Spencer-Ward v. Humberts* [1995] 1 E.G.L.R. 123; *Wilson v. Le Fevre Wood & Royle* [1996] P.N.L.R. 107.

[26] [1995] 7 Med.L.R. 122.

[27] ibid. at 126. See also *Oakes v. Hopcroft* [2000] Lloyd's Rep. P.N. 946, CA. Hoffmann L.J.'s approach in *Hallam-Eames* was followed in *Markes v. Coodes* [1997] P.N.L.R. 252 (solicitor's negligence). In *H.F. Pensions Trustees Ltd. v. Ellison* [1999] P.N.L.R. 489, Jonathan Parker J. held that knowledge by the plaintiff pension trustee that money had been paid away in reliance on the solicitor defendant's advice was sufficient for section 14A and that it was not necessary for the claimant to know either (i) that the payment was unlawful or (ii) that the advice was negligent so that a claim for losses incurred (by way of irrecoverable payments made to the Inland Revenue and costs of earlier litigation) was statute-barred. *Sed quaere*. The case compromised before an appeal was heard.

[28] [1998] P.N.L.R. 145.

[29] A similar approach was adopted in *Birmingham Midshires Building Society v. Infields* [1999] Lloyd's Rep. P.N. 874, *per* Judge Bowsher Q.C. The defendant solicitor acted for the borrower and claimant lender. The defendant knew that the borrower planned to let the flat in contravention of the written mortgage terms, but did not notify the claimant of this fact. The claimant lender sued the defendant, who raised a limitation defence. The claimant argued that it was entitled to rely on section 14A. Although the claimant lender's arrears department had the requisite knowledge more than three years prior to issue of the writ, the claimant argued that such knowledge had not been passed on to the legal department. Judge Bowsher held that, if true, it was a matter for criticism of the claimants, who should have had a system in place to ensure important information was passed on. However, the judge found as a fact that the legal department must have had sight of the relevant correspondence which revealed the reasons for the borrower's default. See also *Halifax Plc v. Ringrose and Co. (a firm)* [2000] Lloyd's Rep. P.N. 309, *per* Bell J. (claim by lenders against solicitors) and *New Islington and Hackney Housing Association Ltd v. Pollard Thomas & Edwards Ltd* [2001] P.N.L.R. 515, *per* Dyson J. (claim by housing association against architects).

[30] [2000] P.N.L.R. 240, CA.

had failed to read carefully a statement sent to her 8 years before she issued proceedings. Had she done so, she would have realised that her house had been charged to secure her husband's business debts (her claim being that her solicitors had failed to advise her of the effect of the charge). She was fixed with the knowledge which she should have acquired and her claim was statute-barred.[31] However, the question will always be whether the claimant should reasonably have acquired the relevant knowledge. So, in *The Mortgage Corp. v. Lambert and Co. (a firm)*[32] the claimant lender had received reports from a debt collection agency indicating a current value of the property well below that reported by the defendant surveyor a year or so earlier. While that might have led the lender to query the original valuation, a reasonable lender would not necessarily have obtained a retrospective valuation at that stage, or more than three years before the issue of proceedings. It followed that the lender could rely on section 14A.[33] In cases in which the claimant has had the benefit of expert or professional advice, it is important to bear in mind the scope of the instructions given.[34]

(e) *Special Rules re Personal Injury and Death*

(i) *Primary limitation periods*

5-056   **Personal injuries.** Where the claimant claims damages for negligence, nuisance or breach of duty in respect of personal injuries,[35] the limitation period (which is only three years) begins on the date when the cause of action accrued or on "the date of knowledge", if later.[36] If the injured person dies before the expiry of three years, the limitation period begins on the date of death or on "the date of the personal representative's knowledge" if later.[37] The "date of knowledge" is defined in section 14(1) of the Limitation Act 1980 as the date on which the claimant or his personal representative first knew:

"(a) that the injury in question was significant[38]; and

(b) that the injury was attributable in whole or in part to the act or omission which is alleged to constitute negligence, nuisance or breach of duty; and

(c) the identity of the defendant; and

(d) if it is alleged that the act or omission was that of a person other than the defendant, the identity of that person and the additional facts supporting the bringing of an action against the defendant."

---

[31] See also *Fennon v. Anthony Hodari and Co. (a firm)* [2001] Lloyd's Rep. P.N. 183, CA: client knew that her damage was attributable to a failure to tell her the nature and effect of the document she had signed and it did not matter that she was not aware that the failure was negligent.
[32] [2000] P.N.L.R. 820.
[33] See also the approach of Evans-Lombe J. in *Lloyds Bank plc v. Burd Pearse* [2000] P.N.L.R. 71 (for the facts see para. 5–42, n. 71, above), at 81D-F (claimant bank had no reason to check the documents of title when it had no reason to suppose that it security was inadequate; the bank was not to be fixed with constructive knowledge of facts which its solicitors might have learnt, but did not).
[34] *Lloyds Bank Plc v. Crosse & Crosse (a firm)* [2001] E.W.C.A. Civ. 366 (reported at [2001] P.N.L.R. 830, CA: solicitors retained at later date by claimant on relatively narrow basis).
[35] As to which, see para. 5–13, above.
[36] Limitation Act 1980, s.11(4).
[37] *ibid.* s.11(5).
[38] "Significant" is defined in s.14(2).

Knowledge that any acts or omissions did or did not, as a matter of law, involve negligence is irrelevant.[39] For the purpose of section 14(1) a person is deemed to know matters which he ought reasonably to have observed or ascertained or (in appropriate circumstances) learnt from experts.[40]

Nash v. Eli Lilly and Co. The Court of Appeal considered in detail the   5–057
construction and application of section 14(1) in *Nash v. Eli Lilly and Co.*[41] The court proceeded on the basis that "knowledge" in section 14(1):

> "is a condition of mind which imports a degree of certainty and that the degree of certainty which is appropriate for this purpose is that which, for the particular plaintiff, may reasonably be regarded as sufficient to justify embarking upon the preliminaries to the making of a claim for compensation such as the taking of legal or other advice."[42]

The court discussed the difference between knowledge and belief. If a claimant held a firm belief that his injury was attributable to[43] an act or omission by the defendant, but he thought it necessary to obtain reassurance or confirmation by experts, then he would not be regarded as having "knowledge" until his enquiries were (or ought to have been) completed.[44]

Application to medical negligence.[45] In the context of medical negligence   5–058
actions, the most important part of the definition of "date of knowledge" is subparagraph (b). The claimant is often aware that his medical treatment has not been wholly successful. This in itself does not necessarily indicate that there has been any mishap. If the claimant is not alerted to the relevant act or omission until he consults another doctor or specialist, that may well be that date when time begins to run.[46] In *Broadley v. Guy Clapham and Co.*,[47] however, it must

---

[39] See the last part of s.14(1).

[40] For the full provision as to constructive knowledge, see s.14(3). Where the plaintiff instructs an expert who fails to ascertain the material facts, and erroneously advises that there is no claim, the plaintiff is not expected to be unduly sceptical; nor is he thereby fixed with constructive knowledge: *Hepworth v. Kerr* (1995) 6 Med.L.R. 139.

[41] [1993] 1 W.L.R. 782. Applied in *Coban v. Allen* [1997] 8 Med.L.R. 316.

[42] *ibid.* at 792C–D.

[43] The meaning of "attributable" was discussed in *Nash v. Eli Lilly and Co.* [1993] 1 W.L.R. 782 at 797–799 and in *Spargo v. North Essex District Health Authority* [1997] 8 Med.L.R. 125 at 130.

[44] *ibid.* at 795. Constructive knowledge is discussed below.

[45] For other cases illustrating the principles in this section see: *Skitt v. Khan* [1997] 8 Med.L.R. 104; *Parry v. Clwyd H.A.* [1997] 8 Med.L.R. 243; *Slevin v. Southampton and S.W. Hampshire H.A.* [1997] 8 Med.L.R. 175; *Saxby v. Morgan* [1997] 8 Med.L.R. 293; *Hind v. York H.A.* [1997] 8 Med.L.R. 377; *Smith v. Leicester H.A.* [1998] Lloyd's Rep. Med. 77; *Bates v. Leicester H.A.* [1998] Lloyd's Rep. Med. 93; *O'Driscoll v. Dudley H.A.* [1998] Lloyd's Rep. Med. 211; *Briggs v. Pitt-Payne & Lias* [1999] Lloyd's Rep. Med. 1; *Pavey v. Ministry of Defence* [1999] Lloyd's Rep. Med. 9; *Roberts v. Winbow* [1999] Lloyd's Rep. Med. 31; *Davis v. Jacobs & Camden Islington H.A.* [1999] Lloyd's Rep. Med. 72; *Appleby v. Walshall H.A.* [1999] Lloyd's Rep. Med. 154; *Briody v. St. Helen's and Knowsley A.H.A.* [1999] Lloyd's Rep. Med. 185; *Das v. Ganju* [1999] Lloyd's Rep. Med. 198; *Ali v. Courthaulds Textiles Ltd.* [1999] Lloyd's Rep. Med. 301; *French v. East London and City H.A.* [2000] Lloyd's Rep. Med. 35; *Corbin v. Penfold Metallising Company Ltd* [2000] Lloyd's Rep. Med. 246 and *Harrild v. Ministry of Defence, Robert Jones, Agnes Hunt and others* [2001] Lloyd's Rep. Med. 117. For a detailed and comprehensive review of this aspect of limitation, see R. James, "The Limitation Period in Medical Negligence Claims" in (1998) Med.L.R. 62.

[46] As in *Scuriaga v. Powell* (1979) 123 S.J. 406; *Driscoll-Varley v. Parkside H.A.* (1991) 2 Med.L.R. 346; *Davis v. City & Hackney H.A.* (1989) 2 Med.L.R. 366 and *Harrild v. Ministry of Defence, Robert Jones, Agnes Hunt and others* [2001] Lloyd's Rep. Med. 117.

[47] [1994] 4 All E.R. 439.

have been obvious to the plaintiff, even without the benefit of expert advice, that there was something significantly wrong and she was thereby fixed with knowledge. Hoffmann L.J. summarised the approach in this way:

> "Section 14(1)(b) requires that one should look at the way the plaintiff puts his case, distill what he is complaining about and ask whether he had, in broad terms, knowledge of the facts on which that complaint is based."[48]

5–059   The crucial question is when the claimant became aware, or constructively aware, that the injury was attributable to the defendant's act or omission. The claimant need not be alerted to the question of negligence. In *Dobbie v. Medway H.A.*,[49] the plaintiff's breast was removed unnecessarily during an operation in 1973. Shortly after the operation the plaintiff learnt that the removal was unnecessary, in that the lump in her breast (the original cause for concern) was benign. Even though the plaintiff was unaware of any possible negligence until many years later, the Court of Appeal held that the plaintiff had the requisite knowledge, and that time had begun to run, in 1973. All that the plaintiff needed to know was that she had suffered significant harm (namely the removal of a breast) and that this was due to the act or omission of the health authority.

5–060   Similar reasoning was adopted in *Spargo v. North Essex District Health Authority*.[50] The Court of Appeal held that a claimant would not have the requisite knowledge "if she thinks she knows that her condition is capable of being attributed to the act or omission alleged to constitute negligence, but she is not sure about this and would and would need to check with an expert before she could properly be said to know that it was".[51] However, where the claimant was "clear in her mind" that there was a connection between an alleged misdiagnosis and her injury, there was no need for the court to go further and inquire whether a rational person would be willing to say that the claimant knew there was a possible causal connection between her suffering and the omission she had identified without first going to a doctor to seek confirmation.[52]

5–061   Pursuant to section 14(3), a person is deemed to know matters which he ought reasonably to have observed or ascertained or (in appropriate circumstances) learnt from experts. The burden of proof of showing want of reasonable action is on the defendant.[53] Where the claimant instructs an expert who fails to ascertain the material facts, and erroneously advises that there is no claim, the claimant is not expected to be unduly sceptical; nor is he thereby fixed with constructive knowledge.[54] However, if prior to seeking such advice the claimant has a sufficiently firm belief that his or her injury is attributable to the defendant's negligence to amount to knowledge, time begins to run then.[55] While it has been

---

[48] *ibid.* at 448.

[49] [1994] 1 W.L.R. 1234.

[50] [1997] 8 Med. L.R. 125.

[51] *ibid.* at 130, *per* Brooke L.J. Brooke L.J. laid down four principles concerning the application of section 14(1) at pages 129–130 of the judgment. The Court of Appeal in *Corbin v. Penfold Metallising Co. Ltd* [2000] Lloyd's Rep. Med 247 at 249(12) held that the principles laid down by Brooke L.J. were "not merely guidelines but authoritative statements of how section 14 should be interpreted".

[52] *ibid.* at 131.

[53] *Nash v. Eli Lilly and Co.* [1993] 1 W.L.R. 782 and *Forbes v. Wandsworth Health Authority* (1996) 7 Med. L.R. 175.

[54] *Hepworth v. Kerr* (1995) 6 Med.L.R. 139.

[55] See *Spargo v. North Essex District Health Authority* [1997] 8 Med L.R.. 125, discussed at para. 5–60, above.

suggested that for this purpose a solicitor is not treated as being an "expert"[56], in *Henderson v. Temple Pier Co.*[57] the Court of Appeal held that, for the purposes of section 14, the claimant was fixed with constructive knowledge of facts which her solicitors ought to have ascertained.[58]

These principles were applied in *Forbes v. Wandsworth Health Authority.*[59] **5–062** The plaintiff had two operations on his leg, which was subsequently amputated. Nine years later he consulted a solicitor, who obtained an expert report. This indicated that the leg could have been saved but for a negligent delay in carrying out the second operation. On the basis of this expert evidence, the claimant began his action. The Court of Appeal held by a majority that the plaintiff was fixed with constructive knowledge from about 12 to 18 months following the operation. The court reasoned as follows: if medical treatment does not have the desired result, the patient is not to know whether "it is just one of those things" or whether there has been negligence. If he might want to claim, he should obtain expert advice reasonably promptly. He cannot sit back for years, then obtain an expert report and commence proceedings in reliance on section 14. In this case, a reasonable man would have taken advice within 12–18 months of the operation.[60]

Death. The limitation period for claims under the Fatal Accidents Act 1976 **5–063** (which is three years) begins to run on the date of death or the "date of knowledge"[61] of the person for whose benefit the claim is brought.[62]

(ii) *Discretionary exclusion of time limit*

The statutory discretion. In the case of actions in respect of personal injuries **5–064** or death,[63] the court has discretion under section 33(1) of the Limitation Act 1980 to disapply the time limits,

"having regard to the degree to which:

(a) the provisions of section 11 or 12 of this Act prejudice the plaintiff or any person whom he represents; and

(b) any decision of the court under this subsection would prejudice the defendant or any person whom he represents."

---

[56] *Fowell v. National Coal Board*, The Times, May 28, 1986.
[57] [1998] 1 W.L.R. 1540.
[58] *ibid.* at 1545D–E, *per* Bracewell J.:
"Even if the solicitor is to be regarded as an appropriate expert, the facts were ascertainable by him without the use of legal expertise. The proviso (section 14(1)(c)) is not intended to give an extended period of limitation to a person whose solicitor acts dilatorily in acquiring information which is obtainable without particular expertise."
[59] [1997] Q.B. 402.
[60] *ibid.* at 412, *per* Stuart-Smith L.J. Both Stuart-Smith and Evans L.JJ. held that the test was wholly objective, dicta in *Nash v. Eli Lilly and Co.* [1993] 1 W.L.R. 782 at 799H, to the effect that the objective test should be qualified by reference to the claimant's character and intelligence were doubted. Roch L.J., whilst expressing some difficulty with the qualification set out in *Nash v. Eli Lilly and Co.*, regarded himself as bound by that qualification.
[61] As to which, see paras. 5–54 and 5–56, above.
[62] Limitation Act 1980, s.12(2). It is a precondition that the deceased died before the expiry of the period when he could maintain an action in respect of the injury: see s.12(1). There may be different limitation periods for different dependants.
[63] As to which, see para. 5–13, above.

Section 33(3) provides that in acting under the section the court shall have regard to all the circumstances of the case, including a number of matters which are specifically set out.[64]

5–065   **Manner in which the discretion is exercised.** This provision first appeared in the Limitation Act 1975. It has generated a great deal of case law, principally arising from road traffic accidents or accidents at work. Broadly speaking, it is a precondition for success that the claimant has suffered some prejudice by reason of the existence of the limitation period. Thus if he has previously issued a writ, which was in time but has lapsed, he cannot have suffered such prejudice and the court will not normally disapply the time limit.[65] Once this hurdle has been crossed, however, the court does have a discretion[66] to be exercised generally (in accordance with the statutory criteria) and not on the basis that the time limits should only be disapplied in exceptional cases.[67] If the claimant's substantive case is weak, that factor weighs against the exercise of the discretion in his favour.[68] Furthermore, the sheer length of the delay between the mishap and the issue of proceedings may be a powerful factor against disapplying the time limit.[69] The discretion should not be exercised in a different way in large group actions from the way in which it is exercised in ordinary cases.[70] In exercising its discretion the court may have regard to the insurance position of any other defendants against whom the claimant has begun proceedings in time.[71]

5–066   The following points should be noted in considering prejudice to the defendant:

(1) It is not correct to say that the defendant is not prejudiced, simply because he is insured. The defendant and his insurer should be treated as a composite unit.[72]

(2) Where the factual evidence depends upon surviving medical records rather than the recollection of witnesses, it may be more difficult for the

---

[64] Limitation Act 1980, s.33(3)(a)–(e). For a discussion of the six matters set out therein see the speech of Lord Diplock in *Thompson v. Brown* [1981] 1 W.L.R. 744 at 751–752. For the purposes of sub-para. (f) the plaintiff may, in appropriate cases, be required to answer interrogatories as to the general nature of any medical, legal or other expert advice which he has received: *Jones v. G. D. Searle and Co.* [1979] 1 W.L.R. 101.

[65] *Walkley v. Precision Forgings* [1979] 1 W.L.R. 606; *Deerness v. John R. Keeble & Son (Brantham) Ltd* [1983] 2 Lloyd's Rep. 260.

[66] The Court of Appeal is generally reluctant to interfere with the judge's exercise of this discretion: see *Conry v. Simpson* [1983] 3 All E.R. 369.

[67] *Firman v. Ellis* [1978] Q.B. 886; as explained by Ormrod L.J. in *Chappell v. Cooper* [1980] 1 W.L.R. 958 at 967G–H; *Simpson v. Norwest Holst (Southern)* [1980] 1 W.L.R. 968 at 976E–G; *Thompson v. Brown* [1981] 1 W.L.R. 744 at 751–752; *Halford v. Brookes* [1991] 1 W.L.R. 428.

[68] *Nash v. Eli Lilly and Co.* [1993] 1 W.L.R. 782 at 807–808; *Forbes v. Wandsworth Health Authority* [1997] Q.B. 402.

[69] See, *e.g. Dobbie v. Medway H.A.* [1994] 1 W.L.R. 1234. In considering the length of, and the reasons for, the delay "on the part of the plaintiff", the test is subjective rather than objective. The court must have regard to the claimant's actual state of mind, rather than to what a reasonable person would think or do in the claimant's position: *Coad v. Cornwall H.A.* [1997] 1 W.L.R. 189. Delay after the claimant has consulted solicitors may be particularly relevant to the exercise of the court's discretion, particularly in the absence of any explanation of such delay: *e.g. Berry v. Calderdale H.A.* [1998] Lloyd's Rep. Med. 179.

[70] *Nash v. Eli Lilly and Co.* [1993] 1 W.L.R. 782 at 810.

[71] *Liff v. Peasley* [1980] 1 W.L.R. 781 at 788–789.

[72] *Kelly v. Bastible* [1997] 8 Med.L.R. 15.

defendant to show sufficient prejudice flowing from delay for the purpose of section 33.[73]

(3) Even where medical records have been lost, the defendant may still be unable to show prejudice, as in *Hammond v. West Lancashire Health Authority*.[74]

Relevance of fault on the part of the claimant's legal advisers. The fact that   5–067
the plaintiff would have a claim against his own solicitors, in the event that no
direction is made under section 33, has been held to be a highly relevant
consideration.[75] However, even in cases where "if the action were not allowed to
proceed the plaintiff would have a cast-iron case against his solicitor in which the
measure of damages will be no less than those that he would be able to recover
against the defendant if the action were allowed to proceed", this factor is not
conclusive. The claimant may still, quite reasonably, prefer to sue the original
tortfeasor rather than his own solicitors.[76]

Moreover, generally any failings by the claimant's solicitor will not be attrib-   5–068
uted to the claimant. This emerges from three recent decisions of the Court of
Appeal. The first of these is *Das v. Ganju*.[77] Sir Christopher Staughton, giving the
leading judgment of the Court of Appeal, quoted from the earlier decision of
Whitfield v. North Durham Health Authority[78] and said: "If that passage means
that as a matter of law anything done by the lawyers must be visited on the client,
it cannot in my view be reconciled with other authority . . . that other authority is
Thompson v. Brown". Buxton L.J. held that the availability of a remedy against
solicitors only arose as a factor where it was established that otherwise the
claimant should be permitted to proceed. Buxton L.J. expressly reserved his view
as to whether such alternative remedy might ever be relevant except where the
claimant's case against his solicitors was unanswerable. *Das v. Ganju* was
followed in *Corbin v. Penfolds Metallising Co. Ltd*.[79] The trial judge has attributed delay on the part of the claimant's solicitors to the claimant. Buxton L.J.
said that, unless, as a matter of law a claimant was bound by and bore responsibility for his solicitor's actions, such attribution was not right. On the evidence,
the claimant had done what any man his position might have been expected to
have done, namely gone to apparently efficient and responsible solicitors and left
them to get on with it. He was not persuaded that each case should be considered
on its own facts, holding that the court was speaking more generally and saying

---

[73] See, *e.g. Farthing v. N.E. Essex H.A.* [1998] Lloyd's Rep. Med. 37.
[74] [1998] Lloyd's Rep. Med. 146. In that case X-rays had been destroyed with the result that there was
no evidence to refute the conclusions which the hospital had drawn from those X-rays.
[75] *Thompson v. Brown* [1981] 1 W.L.R. 744 at 752–753; *Donovan v. Gwentoys Ltd* [1990] 1 W.L.R.
472; *Ramsden v. Lee* [1992] 2 All E.R. 204. For further discussion, see J. Steiner, "Solicitors'
Liability and the Limitation Act 1980—Tipping the Scales" (1990) 6 P.N. 183, where it is argued that
courts should refrain from prejudging the outcome of subsequent solicitors' negligence litigation.
[76] *Thompson v. Brown* [1981] 1 W.L.R. 744 at 750. See also *Hartley v. Birmingham D.C.* [1992] 1
W.L.R. 968. In the latter case the writ in a personal injuries action was issued one day late owing to
the negligence of the plaintiff's solicitors. An important factor in the Court of Appeal's decision to
disapply the time limit was the prejudice which the plaintiff would suffer, if suing her own solicitor
rather than the original tortfeasor. The new defendant, *i.e.* the plaintiff's own solicitor, would know
much more about the weak points of her case than the original defendant: see, *per* Parker L.J. at
980D–E and, *per* Leggatt L.J. at 983D–E.
[77] [1999] Lloyd's Rep. Med. 198.
[78] [1995] 6 Med. L.R. 32 at 35.
[79] [2000] Lloyd's Rep. Med. 247.

that there was certainly no rule of law to visit the faults of the lawyers on the claimant.[80] Finally, in *Steeds v. Peverel Management Services*,[81] Sir Christopher Slade (giving the judgment of the Court of Appeal) concluded that the above authorities demonstrated that fault on the part of the claimant's solicitors was not to be attributed to the claimant personally. This was not to say, however, that the existence of a claim by the claimant against the solicitors was irrelevant—it was a factor in weighing the prejudice suffered by the claimant if the discretion under section 33 were not exercised.

5–069   **The relevance of section 33 to professional negligence litigation.** The principal relevance of section 33 of the Limitation Act 1980 to professional negligence is therefore twofold. First, it will sometimes enable solicitors who have failed to issue a writ in time to escape the consequences of their own negligence. In such a situation it is not uncommon for the solicitors' insurers to finance the claimant's application under section 33.[82] Secondly, it will sometimes enable patients (or their personal representatives) to begin medical negligence actions after the expiry of the normal limitation period.[83] In such cases the court will apply the same general principles in exercising its discretion as were discussed in the previous paragraphs. However, the fact that the action is one for professional negligence may be an additional factor in the defendant's favour.

(f) *Fraud or Concealment*

5–070   Section 32(1) of the Limitation Act 1980 provides that where:

"(a) the action is based upon the fraud of the defendant; or

(b) any fact relevant to the plaintiff's right of action has been deliberately concealed from him by the defendant[84] the period of limitation shall not begin to run until the plaintiff has discovered the fraud [or] concealment . . . or could with reasonable diligence have discovered it."[85]

Section 32(2) provides:

"For the purposes of subsection (1) above, deliberate ommission of a breach of duty in circumstances in which it is unlikely to be discovered for some time amounts to deliberate concealment of the facts involved in that breach of duty."

This form of wording appeared for the first time in section 7 of the 1980 Limitation (Amendment) Act, amending section 26 of the 1939 Act.[86] Section 7 was based on (although not identical to) the recommendations of the Law Reform

---

[80] *ibid.* at para. 26.
[81] [2001] E.W.C.A. Civ. 419, March 30, 2001.
[82] See Chap. 10, para. 10–333, below.
[83] See, *e.g. Hills v. Potter* [1984] 1 W.L.R. 641 at 653–654.
[84] The plaintiff is entitled to rely on s.32(1)(b), even where he is making a claim for fraud: see *UBAF Ltd v. European American Banking Corp.* [1984] Q.B. 713 at 727.
[85] The parts relating to mistakes have been omitted from the quotation, as they are not specifically relevant to professional negligence actions.
[86] Consolidated by the Limitation Act 1980.

Committee in its 21st Report.[87] The Law Reform Committee reviewed cases in which the then section 26 had been considered[88] and concluded that the provision should be reformulated so as to incorporate the feature of unconscionability but to "reproduce in a more intelligible form the construction placed on that section by the courts".[89]

Effect of deliberate concealment some time after breach. In *Sheldon v. RHM Outhwaite (Underwriting Agencies) Ltd*,[90] the House of Lords held by a bare majority that section 32(1)(b) operates to postpone the start of the limitation period even where the deliberate concealment occurs some time after accrual of the cause of action. When time starts to run again, the claimant will have the full limitation period, not just the balance that was left at the time of the deliberate concealment.   **5–071**

"Any fact relevant to the right of action." The claimant may only invoke section 32(1)(b) where the defendant has concealed "any fact relevant to the right of action". "Action" is defined broadly in section 38(1) of the Act. By virtue of section 38(9) references in section 32 to a right of action include references to a cause of action. The meaning of "any fact relevant to the right of action" was considered by the Court of Appeal in *Johnstone v. The Chief Constable of Surrey*.[91] The court applied a "statement of claim" test; a fact is only relevant for the purposes of section 32 (1) (b) if it is one which has to be pleaded in order to constitute the cause of action. "Any fact" means that if one relevant fact is deliberately concealed, then the provision will apply and, if more than one relevant fact is concealed, then time will only begin to run when all of them have been discovered (or could have been discovered with reasonable diligence).[92]   **5–072**

When time runs again. Under section 32(1), time begins to run when the plaintiff discovers the fraud or concealment or could, with reasonable diligence, have discovered it. The claimant bears the burden of proving that the fraud or concealment could not have been discovered with reasonable diligence.[93] Guidance as to the test of reasonable diligence is to be found in the judgment of Millett L.J. in *Paragon Finance plc v. D. B. Thackerar*[94]:   **5–073**

---

[87] Final Report on Limitation of Actions, Cmnd. 6923 (1977). Note that the Committee deliberately did not make any reference to the likelihood of the defendant's act remaining undiscoverable for a substantial period, or at all. See para. 2.25 of the 21st Report.

[88] *Kitchen v. Royal Air Force Association* [1958] 1 W.L.R. 563; *Clark v. Woor* [1965] 1 W.L.R. 650; *Applegate v. Moss* [1971] 1 Q.B. 406; *King v. Victor Parsons and Co.* [1973] 1 W.L.R. 29.

[89] See the Final Report, para. 2.22. Given the nature of the 1980 Act, however, pre–1980 legislation and authorities should not be relied on in construing s.32, unless there is ambiguity in the wording: see the speeches of Lords Keith and Browne-Wilkinson and in *Sheldon v. RHM Outhwaite (Underwriting Agencies) Ltd* [1996] A.C. 102 at 140E and 144E–G respectively, *cf., per* Lord Lloyd at 146D.

[90] [1996] 1 A.C. 102.

[91] *The Times*, November 23, 1992, CA (Civil Division) Transcript No. 961 of 1992. See further *C v. Mirror Group Newspapers Ltd* [1997] 1 W.L.R. 131.

[92] *Halifax plc v. Ringrose and Co. (A Firm)* [2000] P.N.L.R. 483 at 494A–B, *per* Bell J. Cited in *Ezekiel v. Lehrer* [2001] P.N.L.R. 812, *per* Evans-Lombe J.

[93] *Paragon Finance plc v. D.B. Thakerar* [1999] 1 All E.R. 400. See also *Halifax plc v. Ringrose and Co.(a firm)* [2000] P.N.L.R. 492, *per* Bell J. at 493E.

[94] [1999] 1 All E.R. 400, at 418d.

"the question is not whether the claimant **should** have discovered the fraud sooner but whether they **could** with reasonable diligence have done so. The burden of proof is on them. They must establish that they **could not** have discovered the fraud without exceptional measures which they could not reasonably be expected to take . . . in the course of argument May L.J. observed that the test was how a person carrying on a business of the relevant kind would act if he had adequate but not unlimited staff and resources and were motivated by reasonable but not excessive sense of urgency. I respectfully agree."[95]

5–074 In *Liverpool Roman Catholic Archdiocese Trustees Inc. v. Goldberg*,[96] Laddie J. concluded that breach of duty, as opposed to the relevant facts, must have been discovered or discoverable with reasonable diligence by the claimant in order to start time running:

"Section 32(2) . . . deems intentional commission of a breach of duty which is unlikely to be discovered in the same way as if it were deliberate concealment of the facts which are necessary to maintain the action for breach of duty. Thus even if all the facts are known to the claimant, the intentional commission of the breach of duty in circumstances where the breach is unlikely to be discovered, results in the creation of a legal fiction, namely that the facts are unknown."[97]

5–075 **Section 32(2): "Deliberate commission of a breach of duty'.'** In *Brocklesby v. Armitage and Guest*,[98] hereafter referred to as *Brocklesby,* the Court of Appeal

---

[95] See also *UCB Home Loans Corp. Ltd v. Carr* [2000] Lloyd's Rep. P.N. 754, *per* Crane J. for an application of this to a claim against solicitors.

[96] [2001] P.N.L.R. 503. This case extended *Brocklesby v. Armitage and Guest* [2000] P.N.L.R. 33, discussed in paras 5–75 and 5–76, below.

[97] *ibid.* at 191C–D. Laddie J. held that this conclusion was reinforced by s.32(2)—the word "it" in "deliberate commission of duty in circumstances in which it is unlikely to be discovered" referred back to the breach of duty. It is the breach of duty which must be concealed. The same opinion was expressed by Jonathan Parker L.J. in *Cave v. Robinson Jarvis and Rolf* [2001] P.N.L.R. 573 at 589. However, His Honour Judge Playford Q.C. expressed strong disagreement with this "legal fiction theory" in *Prettys v. Michael Carter* July 31, 2001 (unreported):

"With respect and regret I cannot agree with the legal fiction theory as proposed by Laddie J. in [*Goldberg*] . . . In my respectful view, this theory:
    (a) cannot accommodate the views of the House of Lords in *Sheldon v. RHM Outhwaite (Underwriting Agencies) Ltd* [1996] 1 A.C. 102. It does not seems to me possible to distinguish this authority by setting it in context; the context was section 32, and while the House was considering section 32(1)(b) rather than section 32(2), the latter merely explains or expands the former and is part of a consistent whole;
    (b) deprives section 14A and probably section 14 and section 14B of any effect. While I can understand Sedley L.J.'s observation in *Cave v. Robinson Jarvis & Rolf* (a case in which the House of Lords has given unconditional leave to appeal): 'This may as readily been an unintended consequence' I think it unlikely that so many years of litigation in this most fertile of fields proceeded on the basis that the true effect of section 32 was overlooked;
    (c) it ignores the express provision that 'the period of limitation shall not begin to run until the plaintiff has discovered the concealment or could with reasonable diligence have discovered it'. . . . If facts that are known are deemed to be unknown, there is little, if any scope for actual discovery of the 'concealment' and it is hard to imagine what scope there can be for reasonable diligence. In fact the legal fiction results in an indefinite postponement of the period of limitation, with no clear indication as to when it begins . . . it seems to me that the legal fiction theory bids fair to abolish the concept of limitation, in so far as it applies to case of negligence or breach of contract . . . . For my part I would follow the principles set out in *Foreman v. O'Driscoll* [2000] Lloyd's Rep. 720 at 722 , decided after *Brocklesby*".

See also *Halifax plc v. Ringrose and Co. (a firm)* [2000] P.N.L.R. 483 at 493E , cited in *Leeds and Holbeck Building Society v. Arthur and Cole* [2001] Lloyd's Rep. P.N. 649, and *Ezekiel v. Lehrer* [2001] P.N.L.R. 812 at paras 31 and 33.

[98] [2000] P.N.L.R. 33.

considered the meaning of "deliberate concealment" in section 32(1)(b), as expanded by section 32(2). In that case the claimant purchased property from a company in which he was a shareholder, with the aid of a building society loan. In 1989, the company agreed to repurchase the property in consideration of a release of the claimant's liability to the building society. The defendant solicitors acted in this repurchase transaction. The claimant vacated the property and the company took over the mortgage repayments. In November 1990, the company went into liquidation and ceased making repayments. In 1992, the building society sought to recover the payment arrears, at which point the claimant discovered that the transfer to the company and the release from the claimant's obligations to the building society had not been effected. The action by the building society was compromised in February 1996. The claimant issued proceedings against the defendant solicitors in June 1997. The defendant pleaded that the action was time barred. The claimant argued that sections 32(1)(b) and 32(2) applied, so that time did not begin to run until mid-1992 when he discovered that the transaction had not been completed. The Court of Appeal considered the meaning of sections 32(1)(b) and 32(2). Morritt L.J. held that it was sufficient that the defendant intentionally and deliberately does something which is a breach of duty (in circumstances such that it would not be discovered for some time). The defendant did not have to know that his act or omission amounted to a breach of duty:

"the conclusion I reach is that it is not necessary for the purpose of extending the limitation period pursuant to section 32(1)(b) to demonstrate that the fact relevant to the claimant's right of action has been deliberately concealed in any sense greater than that the commission of the act was deliberate in the sense of being intentional and that the act or omission, as the case may be, did involve a breach of duty whether or not the actor appreciated that legal consequence."[99]

The result of this decision is that nearly every breach of duty by a professional **5–076** man will fall within section 32 of the Limitation Act 1980. Only breaches which are either (i) so obvious that the client will appreciate that they are breaches of duty at the time they are committed or (ii) which involve no deliberate act (for example, forgetting to issue legal proceedings in time) will be subject to the usual rules. It is hard to understand why Parliament would have intended such a result. Nor is it clear what purpose was served by the enactment of the Latent Damage Act 1986 if *Brocklesby* is correctly decided. It is submitted that the alternative construction of section 32(2), namely that the defendant must consciously be breaching his duty, rather than just deliberately doing something which he is unaware constitutes a breach of his duty, is to be preferred.

Subsequent decisions. *Brocklesby* was followed at first instance in *Liverpool* **5–077** *Roman Catholic Archdiocese Trustees Inc. v. Goldberg,*[1] *Gold v. Mincoff Science and Gold*[2] and *Loosemore v. Financial Concepts (a firm).*[3] The Court of Appeal was invited to reconsider its decision in *Brocklesby* in *Cave v. Robinson Jarvis & Rolf.*[4] The defendant, who had lost at first instance, submitted that the words

---

[99] *ibid.* at 42G.
[1] [2001] P.N.L.R. 503, *per* Laddie J.
[2] [2000] All E.R. (D.) 2412.
[3] [2001] Lloyd's Rep. P.N. 235.
[4] [2001] P.N.L.R. 573.

in section 32(2) should be taken at face value: "deliberate" was used consciously to connote intention or awareness and not mere negligence or inadvertence; "breach of duty" was not shorthand for an act or omission amounting to breach of duty. The defendant further submitted that the *Brocklesby* interpretation of section 32(2) led to overlap and/or inconsistency with the latent damage provisions in sections 14A and 14B. The Court of Appeal held that, whilst there was considerable force in the defendant's submissions, *Brocklesby* was not "manifestly wrong" and as such it was bound by its previous decision. Jonathan Parker L.J., in particular, expressed concern about the decision in *Brocklesby*:

> " ... in particular, I find the reasoning and the decision difficult to reconcile with the observations of Lords Browne-Wilkinson and Lord Nicholls in *Sheldon v. Outhwaite* to the effect that section 32 is concerned with unconscionability and impropriety. At page 145H, for example, Lord Browne-Wilkinson refers to the 'underlying rationale of the section', *i.e.* section 32, as being that the defendants should not be 'entitled to benefit from their own unconscionable behavior by deliberately concealing the facts relevant to the plaintiff's cause of action'. Yet if *Brocklesby* is right, a wholly innocent act or omission may suffice to deprive a defendant of a limitation defence. I am also concerned that the effect of the decision in *Brocklesby* as I understand it is to render the word deliberate in section 32(2) more or less otiose."[5]

This decision, unlike *Brocklesby*, is going to the House of Lords.[6]

5–078   **Section 32(2): "Circumstances in which it is unlikely to be discovered for some time".** The "it" referred to here must be the deliberate commission of a breach of duty.[7] There is no case law concerning at what point in time the unlikelihood must exist, the degree of unlikelihood required or what period constitutes "some time". It is suggested that the unlikelihood must exist at the time of the breach, that it has to be significant (*i.e.* not fanciful), and that "some time" must mean a material time in the context of the period of limitation.

3. LIMITATION IN EQUITY

5–079   The application of the Limitation Act 1980 to claims for equitable relief is somewhat complex. The applicable principles have been developed over a considerable period of time and many of the relevant cases on the subject were decided in the 19th century.[8] However, this area of law has been subjected to scrutiny in several recent cases in the Court of Appeal and the High Court. Those

---

[5] [2001] P.N.L.R. 573 at 589.

[6] *Brocklesby* was also considered in *Foreman v. O'Driscoll* [2000] Lloyd's Rep. P.N. 722, *per* Nigel Baker Q.C., sitting as a Deputy Judge of the High Court.

[7] But see *Cave v. Robinson Jarvis & Rolf* [2001] P.N.L.R. 573 at 589, *per* Jonathan Parker L.J.: "In my judgment, the word 'it' in section 32(2) plainly refers (on the *Brocklesby* basis) to the fact that the deliberate act (or omission) was a breach of duty". Jonathan Parker L.J. was rejecting an argument based on the assumption that *Brocklesby* was correctly decided. It is submitted that the construction which he put forward is strained and further illustrates the unsatisfactory result in *Brocklesby*.

[8] A matter about which two members of the Court of Appeal in *Cia de Seguros Imperio v. Heath (REBX) Ltd* [2001] 1 W.L.R. 112 expressed dissatisfaction: see para. 5–95, below.

judgments contain discussion of the previous authorities and the relevant principles, and provide the focus of this section. [9]

For present purposes, the application of the Limitation Act 1980 to claims for equitable relief can be divided into two categories: (1) express application or (2) application by analogy. Each will be considered in turn.

Before considering those two above categories, a third category deserves brief **5–080** mention. This is where equity acts "in obedience" to the statute. Equity is said to act "in obedience" in cases where a legal right sought to be enforced in equity is time barred under the Act. The authorities do not consistently make the distinction between cases where equity acts in obedience, and cases where it acts by analogy. The distinction is also ignored in section 36 of the 1980 Act (below), which should be construed broadly so as to encompass both categories.[10]

(a) *Express application of the Limitation Act 1980*

The 1980 Act contains express provisions in respect of the following equitable **5–081** claims:

(1) Actions in respect of trust property.[11]

(2) Actions claiming personal estate of a deceased person.[12]

(3) Actions to recover land.[13]

(4) Actions to redeem mortgaged land.[14]

The first of these is the most important in the context of claims against **5–082** professionals. As will be seen, attempts by claimants to rely on section 21 against professional defendants have not met with success. Section 21 provides as follows:

"Time limit for actions in respect of trust property

    (1) No period of limitation prescribed by this Act shall apply to an action by a beneficiary under a trust, being an action—

        (a) in respect of any fraud or fraudulent breach of trust to which the trustee was a party or privy; or
        (b) to recover from the trustee trust property or the proceeds of trust property in the possession of the trustee, or previously received by the trustee and converted to his use . . .

---

[9] For a fuller discussion of limitation in the context of claims for equitable relief, see: Spry, *Equitable Remedies* (5th ed., Sweet and Maxwell, 1997), pp. 244–245 and 416–427; Snell *Equity* (13th ed., Sweet and Maxwell, 2000), paras 3–16—3–18 and 13–20 and the Law Commission Report on Limitation of Actions (Law Com. 270), paras 2.39–2.47 and 2.52–2.66 (and proposals for reform at paras 4.94–4.137 and 4.158–4.196). The equitable doctrines of laches and acquiescence are discussed separately, at paras 5–98 to 5–112, below.
[10] See Spry *Equitable Remedies, op. cit.,* pp. 417– 418. The authorities discussed below concern the application of the Act by analogy.
[11] Limitation Act 1980, s.21.
[12] *ibid.,* s.22.
[13] *ibid.,* ss.15, 20(2) and 20(4).
[14] *ibid.,* s.16.

(3) Subject to the preceding provisions of this section, an action by a beneficiary to recover trust property or in respect of any breach of trust, not being an action for which a period of limitation is prescribed by any other provision of this Act, shall not be brought after the expiration of six years from the date on which the cause of action accrued."

This provision clearly applies to an action based upon a fraudulent breach of trust or to recover trust property or its proceeds from a trustee. In recent years, there have been attempts to extend its effect to other claims.

5–083   Section 21 was considered by the Court of Appeal in *Paragon Finance plc v. D.B. Thakerar and Co. (a firm)*.[15] In two cases conjoined on appeal, the defendant solicitors acted for the plaintiff mortgage lender and for a number of borrowers in relation to the purchase and mortgage of several flats. The defendants were alleged to have known that the borrowers were sub-purchasers buying at prices significantly higher than the prices paid by the sub-vendor to the vendor, but to have failed to inform the plaintiff of this fact. The borrowers defaulted on the mortgages and the security proved to be of substantially less value than the sums advanced by the plaintiff. The plaintiff brought claims for breach of contract, negligence and breach of fiduciary duty, and, after expiry of six years from the last transaction, sought to amend their claim to allege fraud, conspiracy to defraud, fraudulent breach of trust and intentional breach of fiduciary duty.[16] The plaintiffs submitted that no period of limitation applied to the claims for fraudulent breach of trust and intentional breach of fiduciary duty.

5–084   Millett L.J., delivering the judgment of the Court of Appeal, distinguished two categories of constructive trusteeship. The first category covers cases where the defendant, although not expressly appointed as a trustee, assumes the duties of a trustee by a lawful transaction which is independent of, and precedes the breach of trust. The second category covers those cases where the trust obligation arises as a direct consequence of the unlawful transaction impeached by the claimant. The constructive trustee in the first category is a "real" trustee. His possession of the trust property is affected from the outset by the trust and confidence by means of which he obtained it. The "constructive trustee" in the second category is not in fact a trustee at all, although he may be liable to account as if he were. The constructive trust is a remedial mechanism by which equity gives relief for fraud.[17] Millett L.J. observed:

> " . . . any principled system of limitation should be based on the cause of action and not the remedy. There is a case for treating fraudulent breach of trust differently from other frauds, but only if what is involved really is a breach of trust. There is no case for distinguishing between an action for damages for fraud at common law and its counterpart in equity based on the same facts merely because equity employs the formula of constructive trust to justify the exercise of the equitable jurisdiction."[18]

5–085 Millett L.J. held that the defendants were fiduciaries and held the plaintiffs' money on a resulting trust for them pending completion. However, the plaintiffs could not establish and did not rely on a breach of this trust. They alleged that the money which was obtained from them was obtained by fraud, and sought to

---

[15] [1999] 1 All E.R. 400.
[16] The application of s.36 of the Limitation Act 1980 to the proposed amendment to allege intentional breach of fiduciary duty is discussed at paras 5–84 to 5–86, below.
[17] [1999] 1 All E.R. 400 at 408j–409f.
[18] *ibid.* at 414a–b.

raise a constructive trust in their favour in its place. The constructive trust was thus of the second type and section 21 of the Limitation Act 1980 did not apply. It followed that the defendants had an arguable limitation defence of which they should not be deprived by amendment.[19]

Millett L.J.'s twofold categorisation of constructive trusts was applied in *UCB* **5–086** *Home Loans v. Carr*.[20] The claimant lender brought proceedings for damages and/or equitable compensation for deceit, breach of trust, breach of contract and/ or negligence against the defendant firm of solicitors in connection with two residential mortgage transactions in which the defendant had acted for the claimant. At trial of the preliminary issue on limitation Crane J. followed *Paragon Finance plc v. D.B. Thakerar and Co. (a firm)*[21] and held that a constructive trust of the second kind did not fall within section 21 so that the claim in relation to it was time barred, because the claimants had failed to bring themselves with section 32 of the Limitation Act 1980.[22] However, he concluded that the claimants could, in principle, rely on the first type of constructive trust given the terms of the solicitors' retainer. That claim for fraudulent breach of trust, if proved, would not subject to a limitation period by reason of section 21(1) of the Limitation Act 1980.[23]

The analysis in *Paragon Finance plc v. D. B. Thakerar and Co. (a firm)*[24] was **5–087** also applied in *Coulthard v. Disco Mix Club Ltd*.[25] The claimant sued the defendants in respect of various agency and management agreements allegedly entered into for the commercial exploitation of dance mixes prepared and recorded by the claimant. The claimant's principal complaint involved allegations of under-accounting. That allegation formed the basis of claims for breach of duty to account, fraudulent breach of contract, breach of fiduciary duty and dishonest breach of fiduciary duty. The claimant also claimed that two of the defendants were liable to account as constructive trustees. Jules Sher Q.C., sitting as a Deputy High Court judge, cited passages of Millett L.J.'s judgment in *Paragon Finance plc v. D. B. Thakerar and Co. (a firm)*[26] and continued:

"What the *Paragon Finance* case makes clear is that the critical boundary in these cases lies between those cases where the defendant is a true trustee (be it of an express trust or a constructive trust) and those where he is not. In the *Nelson v. Rye*[27] relationship, which is the same in this respect as Mr Coulthard's and Mr Prince [the third defendant]'s relationship, the relationship is not that of trustee and beneficiary. The touchstone of a true trusteeship is trust property . . . at no stage in Mr Coulthard's pleading or evidence is an asset or fund identified as an asset or fund which is or should have been held in a trustee capacity. This is why the dispute attracts the application of the six year limit under section 5 of the Act, directly or by analogy. Had there been a true trust

---

[19] *ibid.* at 409g–h and 414e–g.
[20] [2000] Lloyd's Rep. P.N. 754.
[21] [1999] 1 All E.R. 400.
[22] See paras 5–70 to 5–78, above.
[23] *UCB Home Loans v. Carr* [2000] Lloyd's Rep. P.N. 754. at 768–769. Crane J. stated that the evidence relating to the possible breach of trust of either kind had not been fully presented to him and as such, he could only express his views on the matter. Further, s.30(1) of the Trustee Act 1925 might prevent the claimants from establishing breach of trust against the defendants for the default of their employee in the absence of wilful default on their part, such default not being alleged.
[24] [1999] 1 All E.R. 400.
[25] [2000] 1 W.L.R. 707. See also *Clarke v. Marlborough Fine Art (London) Ltd* (unreported, May 15, 2001, *per* Patten J.)
[26] [1999] 1 All E.R. 400.
[27] [1996] 1 W.L.R. 1378, *per* Laddie J. See para 5–90, below.

of property alleged, the relevant section would have been section 21; and to the extent to which there was fraud, or a receipt by the trustee and conversion to his use, there would not have been any limitation defence."[28]

In the circumstances, the constructive trust which arose was merely remedial and section 21 did not apply.

(b) Application of the Limitation Act 1980 by Analogy

5–088   The relevant provision of the Limitation Act 1980 is section 36, which provides as follows:

> *"Equitable jurisdiction and remedies*
>
>   (1) The following time limits under this Act, that is to say—
>
>   (a) the time limit under section 2 for actions founded on tort
>   (b) the time limit under section 5 for actions founded on simple contract . . .
>   shall not apply to any claim for specific performance of a contract or for an injunction or for other equitable relief, except in so far as any such time limit may be applied by the court by analogy in like manner as the corresponding time limit under any enactment repealed by the Limitation Act 1939 was applied before 1 July 1940.
>
>   (2) Nothing in this Act shall affect any equitable jurisdiction to refuse relief on the ground of acquiescence or otherwise."

5–089   The application of section 36 to claims for breach of fiduciary duty was considered in *Paragon Finance plc v. D. B. Thakerar and Co. (a firm).*[29] The plaintiffs argued that a claim for account in respect of a breach of fiduciary duty was outside the scope of the 1980 Act, relying on *Nelson v. Rye.*[30] Millett L.J. held that *Nelson v. Rye* was wrongly decided,[31] and, in any case irrelevant.[32] Millett L.J. stated:

> " the law on this subject has been settled for more than a hundred years. An action for an account brought by a principal against his agent is barred by the statutes of limitation unless the agent is a trustee of the money which he received: see *Burdick v. Garrick*

[28] [2000] 1 W.L.R. 707 at 732A–D.

[29] [1999] 1 All E.R. 400.

[30] [1996] 1 W.L.R. 1378, *per* Laddie J. The defendant, in his capacity as the plaintiff musician's business manager, collected the plaintiff's fees and royalties and accounted to him annually for his net income, after deduction of his own commission. After the relationship ended, the plaintiff claimed an account. Laddie J. recognised that the defendant's liability to account was contractual, but held that this was irrelevant because the plaintiff had chosen to sue for breach of fiduciary duty, rather than for breach of contract. The defendant's failure to account was either a breach of fiduciary duty, which fell outside the 1980 Act, or was a breach of constructive trust, which fell within s.21(1)(b) of the Act.

[31] It would appear to follow that the decision of Harman J. in *Gwembe Valley Development Co. Ltd v. Koshy* [1998] 2 B.C.L.C. 613 is wrong in so far as it follows *Nelson v. Rye*.

[32] In Millett L.J.'s judgment, *Nelson v. Rye* was not on point because in that case the defendant's liability arose from his receipt of money in circumstances which made him an accounting party. In the *Paragon Finance* case, unless and until the underlying transactions were set aside, the defendants had duly accounted for the money advanced by the plaintiffs. The plaintiffs did not claim an account on the basis that the receipt of the money by the defendants made them accounting parties. Rather, they claimed equitable compensation for breach of fiduciary duty and sought all necessary accounts to enable that compensation to be quantified: see [1999] 1 All E.R. 400 at 416g–h.

(1870) L.R. 5 Ch. App. 233, *Knox v. Gye* (1872) L.R. 5 H.L. 656 and *Re Sharpe, Re Bennett, Mason and General Life Assurance Co. v. Sharpe* [1892] 1 Ch. 154. A claim for an account in equity, absent any trust, has no equitable element; it is based on legal, not equitable rights: see *How v. Earl Winterton* [1896] 2 Ch. 626 at 693, *per* Lindley L.J. Where the agent's liability to account was contractual, equity acted in obedience to the statute: see *Hovenden v. Lord Annesley* (1806) 2 Sch. & Lef. 607 at 631, *per* Lord Resedale. Where, as in *Knox v. Gye*, there was no contractual relationship between the parties, so that the liability was exclusively equitable, the court acted by analogy with the statute. Its power to do so is implicitly preserved by section 36 of the 1980 Act . . . Accordingly the defendant's liability to account for more than six years before the issue of the writ depended on whether he was, not merely a fiduciary (for every agent owes fiduciary duties to his principal), but a trustee, that is to say whether he owed fiduciary duties in relation to the money."[33]

Further explanation as to the application of section 36 was provided by Jules **5–090** Sher Q.C., sitting as a Deputy High Court Judge in *Coulthard v. Disco Mix Club Ltd and another.*[34] He held that most of the claims for breach of fiduciary duty were in reality claims for simple breach of the contractual duty to account, not breaches of fiduciary duty. As such, the claim was governed by section 5 of the Act: "The Act of 1980 cannot be side-stepped by describing [the claims for breach of contract] as claims in breach of fiduciary duty".[35] In so far as the pleaded claims were in reality claims for breach of fiduciary duty—such as the claim that the "deliberately and dishonestly" withheld money due to the claimant—the question was whether the Act would be applied by analogy. The judge cited this passage from *Knox v. Gye*[36]:

" . . . For where the remedy in equity is correspondent to the remedy at law, and the latter is subject to a limit in point of time by the Statute of Limitations, a court of equity acts by analogy to the statute and imposes on the remedy it affords the same limitation. This is the meaning of the common phrase, that a court of equity acts by analogy to the Statute of Limitations, the meaning being, that where the suit in equity corresponds with an action at law which is included in the words of the statute, a court of equity adopts the enactment of the statute as its own rule or procedure. But if any proceedings in equity be included in the words of the statute, there a court of equity, like a court of law, acts in obedience to the statute . . . where the court of equity frames its remedy on the basis of the common law and supplements the common law by extending the remedy to parties who cannot have an action at common law, there the court of equity acts in analogy to the statute, that is, it adopts the statute as the rule of procedure regulating the remedy it affords."[37]

He then said: **5–091**

"Two things emerge from these passages. First, where the court of equity was simply exercising a concurrent jurisdiction giving the same relief as was available in a court of law the statute of limitation would be applied. But secondly, even if the relief afforded by equity was wider than that available at law the court of equity would apply the

---

[33] [1999] 1 All E.R. 400 at 415h–j. Millett L.J. doubted that the defendant in *Nelson v. Rye* was a trustee of the money, since he was not obliged to keep the trust property separate from his own and apply it exclusively for the benefit of the plaintiff beneficiary. As such, he was not a (true) constructive trustee.

[34] [2000] 1 W.L.R. 707.

[35] *ibid.* at 728B–G, relying on the classification of fiduciary duties proposed by Millett L.J. in *Bristol and West Building Society v. Mothew* [1998] Ch. 1 at 18.

[36] (1872) L.R. 5 H.L. 656.

[37] *ibid.* at 674–675.

statute by analogy where there was "correspondence" between the remedies available at law or in equity.

Now, in my judgment, the true breaches of fiduciary duty—*i.e.* the allegations of deliberate and dishonest under-accounting, are based on the same factual allegations as the common law claims of fraud. The breaches of fiduciary duty are thus no more than the equitable counterparts of the claims at common law. The court of equity, in granting relief for such breaches would be exercising a concurrent jurisdiction with that of the common law . . .

[Counsel for the plaintiff] argues that the court of equity will apply the statute by analogy only where the equitable remedy is being sought in support of a legal right or the court of equity is being asked to apply a purely legal right, and he cites passages from *Hicks v. Sallitt* (1853) 3 De G.M & G. 783 and *Hovenden v. Lord Anersley* (1806) 2 Sch. & Lef. 697. I have no doubt that the principles of application by analogy to the statute (or, in obedience to the statute, as the Lord Chancellor preferred to describe it in its application to the facts of Hovenden's case) are quite apposite in the situations envisaged by [counsel for the plaintiff]. But, in my judgment, they have a much wider scope than that: one could scarcely imagine a more correspondent set of remedies as damages for fraudulent breach of contract and equitable compensation for breach of fiduciary duty in relation to the same factual situation, namely the deliberate withholding of money due by a manager to his artist. It would have been a blot on our jurisprudence if those self same facts gave rise to a time bar in the common law courts but none in the courts of equity."[38]

5–092   The application of section 36 of the Limitation Act 1980 arose in a very different context in *Cia de Seguros Imperio v. Heath (REBX) Ltd.*[39] The claimant, an insurance and re-insurance company, brought proceedings against the defendant brokers, in respect of the latter's operation of various binding authorities. The claimant sought damages for breach of contract, negligence and breach of fiduciary duty in respect of various agreements, and for negligent misstatements, negligent misrepresentation and collateral warranty in respect of certain documents. At trial of the preliminary issue of limitation, Langley J. held that all the claims were time barred.[40] The defendant appealed in respect of the time limit in respect of fiduciary duty. The Court of Appeal upheld Langley J.'s judgment.[41]

5–093   Waller L.J., with whom Sir Christopher Staughton and Clarke L.J. agreed, accepted the claimant's submission that the claim included breaches of fiduciary duty independent from causes of action in contract or tort, so that sections 2 and 5 of the Limitation Act 1980 were not directly applicable. The question, then, was whether, by section 36, sections 2 and 5 were to be applied by analogy. In his judgment, in applying section 36, the court was not looking to see whether a

---

[38] [2000] 1 W.L.R. 707, at 730A–E. The judgment of Ebsworth J. in *Kershaw v. Wheelan (No. 2), The Times,* February 10, 1997 might have assisted the plaintiff but was based on *Nelson v. Rye* [1996] 2 All E.R. 186, which had been disapproved in *Paragon Finance plc v. D.B. Thakerar and Co. (a firm)* [1999] 2 All E.R. 400. The approach in *Coulthard* was adopted by Morland J. in *Leeds and Holbeck Building Society v. Arthur and Cole* [2001] Lloyd's Rep. P.N. 649 (claim for breach of fiduciary duty against a solicitor).

[39] [2001] 1 W.L.R. 112. Followed in *Leeds and Holbeck Building Society v. Arthur and Cole* [2001] Lloyd's Rep. P.N. 649.

[40] [1999] Lloyd's Rep. I.R. 571. Langley J.'s judgment contains detailed consideration of the authorities and the arguments raised by counsel on both sides. For discussion of the first instance decision and, in particular, Langley J.'s implied acceptance of an exception to the principle that the statute of limitations applied by analogy to claims for breach of fiduciary duty, where the fiduciary validly received or held property for the person to whom he owes the duty, see McGee, "Fiduciary Duties and Limitation Periods" in [2001] 20 C.J.Q. 171.

[41] [2001] 1 W.L.R. 112.

limitation period had actually been applied to a dishonest breach of fiduciary duty by analogy before July 1, 1940, but rather asking whether it would have been applied had the issue arisen. The court must act "in a like manner" to a court sitting prior to July 1, 1940.[42] Waller L.J. held that the principles set out in relevant passages from *Knox v. Gye*[43] and Spry's *Equitable Remedies*,[44] combined with authorities cited by the defendant,[45] supported the submission that equity would have taken the view that it should apply the statute by analogy to a claim for damages or compensation for dishonest breach of fiduciary duty:

> " . . . what is alleged against the defendants as giving rise to a dishonest breach of duty are precisely those facts which are relied on for alleging breach of contract and tort. It is true that there is an extra allegation of "intention" but that does not detract from the fact that the essential factual allegations are the same. Furthermore the claim is one for 'damages'. The prayer for relief has now been amended with out leave to add a claim for 'equitable relief' but the reality of the claim is that it is one for damages, the assessment of which would be no different whether the claim was maintained as a breach of contract or continued simply as a dishonest breach of fiduciary duty claim."[46]

Counsel for the claimant had argued that the line to be drawn between those **5–094** cases where equity applied the statute of limitation by analogy and those where it did not was defined by the question whether equity was acting in its "exclusive" jurisdiction or its "concurrent" jurisdiction. He relied on the speech of Viscount Haldane L.C. in *Nocton v. Lord Ashburton*[47] and the judgment of Millet L.J. in *Paragon Finance plc v. D. B. Thakerar and Co. (a firm)*. Waller L.J. disagreed with both submissions. So far as *Nocton v. Lord Asburburton* was concerned, the claimant was faced with the difficulty, as expressed by Langley J., that limitation was not in issue in that case, and, further, that *Knox v. Gye*[48] was not cited. So far as *Paragon Finance* was concerned, Waller L.J. stated:

> "In my view, it is fundamentally to misunderstand the judgment of Millett L.J. to suggest that he would have approved the view that a claim for *damages* brought against a fiduciary, even alleging a dishonest breach of that duty, would be free from limitation. In my view, his treatment of *Nelson v. Rye* demonstrates that point and demonstrates beyond peradventure that the question whether equity was exercising its exclusive as opposed to its concurrent jurisdiction does *not* supply the definitive answer as to whether equity applied the statute by analogy."[49]

Waller L.J. cited a passage from Millett L.J.'s judgment in *Paragon Finance* **5–095** *plc v. D. B. Thakerar and Co. (a firm)*[50] and concluded: "This made it clear that, even where equity was acting in its exclusive jurisdiction, the statute was applied by analogy".[51] Sir Christopher Staughton and Clarke L J., agreeing with Waller

---

[42] [2001] 1 W.L.R. 112 at 120A.
[43] (1872) L.R. 5 H.L. 656 at 674.
[44] 5th ed., Sweet and Maxwell, 1997, pp. 419–420.
[45] *Hovenden v. Lord Annesley* (1806) 2 Sch. & Lef. 607, *Burdick v. Garrick* (1870) L.R. 5 Ch. App. 233, *Friend v. Young* [1897] 2 Ch. 421 and *North American Land and Timber Co. Ltd v. Watkins* [1904] 1 Ch. 242.
[46] [2001] 1 W.L.R. 112 at 121D–E.
[47] [1914] A.C. 932 at 958.
[48] (1872) L.R. 5 H.L. 656.
[49] [2001] 1 W.L.R. 112 at 122B–D.
[50] [1999] 1 All E.R 400 at 415–416.
[51] [2001] 1 W.L.R. 112 at 122D–G.

L.J., noted that it was not obvious why it was still necessary to have special rules for specific performance, or an injunction, or other equitable relief. If a distinction, for limitation purposes, still had to be drawn, it was to be hoped that a revised statute would enact with some precise where that distinction should be drawn, rather than leaving it to "research into cases decided long ago".[52]

(c) *Where There is no Analogy or Correspondence*

5–096   It follows from the above that, whether equity is acting in its exclusive or auxiliary jurisdiction, statutory limitation periods will be applied by analogy where equity gives the same relief as was available at law, or where there is "correspondence" between the remedies available at law or in equity. Where there is no such equivalent or correspondent legal remedy, no analogy can be drawn so that, in the absence of an express statutory provision, the claim will not be subject to a limitation period.[53]

5–097   A claim to set aside a transaction on the grounds of undue influence would fall within this exception. The matter was considered, albeit indirectly, in *Clarke v. Marlborough Fine Art (London) Ltd and another.*[54] The case concerned a claim by the executor of the estate of Francis Bacon in respect of various agreements between Francis Bacon and the defendants. The particulars of claim alleged breach of fiduciary duty, breach of duty to account under an agency agreement, and undue influence. The defendants argued that each of the claims based on breach of fiduciary duty and undue influence were time barred.[55] So far as the former was concerned, they relied on *Coulthard v. Disco Mix Club Ltd*[56] and *Paragon Finance plc v. D. B. Thakerar and Co. (a firm)*[57] and argued that the constructive trusts pleaded were remedial and the claims for breach of fiduciary duty underlying them were time barred. Patten J. was not satisfied that the claim was one which clearly fell into the remedial category, although the claims were difficult, and preferred to leave the question to trial. So far as the claim in undue influence was concerned, he said:

> "I am very far from satisfied that a Court of Equity would ever have barred a claim in undue influence by analogy with the statute. No case has been found in which this was done and in *Coulthard* Mr Sher Q.C. seems to have accepted (see page 725G) that the only available defences would be laches and acquiescence.[58] Further confirmation of this can be found in *Allcard v. Skinner* (1887) 36 Ch. D 145 at 174 and 186. I am not

---

[52] *ibid.* at 124.
[53] The doctrines of laches and acquiescence may apply on the facts: see paras 5–98 to 5–112, below.
[54] May 15, 2001, Unreported, *per* Patten J.
[55] The limitation point was one of several arguments raised by the defendants in support of their application to strike out the claim under CPR, r. 3.4(2)(a) and obtain summary judgment under Part 24 of the CPR.
[56] [2000] 1 W.L.R. 707; see para. 5–91, above.
[57] [1999] 1 All E.R. 400; see paras 5–84 to 5–87, above.
[58] Jules Sher Q.C. stated at follows: "Mr Coulthard claims in the alternative to set aside [the agreement] . . . on the grounds of undue influence and abuse of confidence. I see considerable problems ahead in terms of laches and acquiescence in this claim for equitable relief . . . " [2000] 1 W.L.R. 707 at 725G.

therefore prepared to strike out these claims on the basis that they are time barred."[59]

This reasoning would apply to other equitable claims which had no correspondence or analogy with those for which a period of limitation is specified in the Limitation Act 1980.

4. OTHER EQUITABLE DEFENCES: LACHES AND ACQUIESCENCE[60]

The equitable defences of laches and acquiescence are expressly preserved by   **5–098**
section 36(2) of the Limitation Act 1980.[61] The doctrine of laches concerns unreasonable delay on the part of the claimant in the commencement or prosecution of proceedings which, in all the circumstances, renders it inequitable to grant the equitable relief sought. The defence of acquiescence arises where the claimant assents or "lies by" in respect of the acts of another, and it is unjust in all the circumstances to grant the relief sought. This will be satisfied where, for example, the claimant has expressly or impliedly represented that he will not rely on his rights.[62] Both are doctrines of equity and apply to claims for equitable relief. Where a period of limitation is prescribed by statute, then equity will not reduce the period which Parliament has stipulated.[63]

(a) *Laches*

The classic statement of the defence is to be found in *Lindsay Petroleum Co. v.*   **5–099**
Hurd[64]:

> "Now the doctrine of laches in the courts of equity is not an arbitrary or technical doctrine. Where it would be practically unjust to give a remedy, either because the party has, by his conduct, done that which might fairly be regarded as a waiver of it, or where

---

[59] In *Allcard v. Skinner* (1887) 36 Ch. D 145, A sought to recover property transferred to S, on the grounds of undue influence. At 174, Cotton L.J. said:
"The Defendant has not pleaded the Statute of Limitations, and I do not suggest that she could successfully have done so. In cases where the fact of undue influence depends on the result of conflicting evidence, delay must be important, but it cannot be disputed that the plaintiff was in a state which necessarily subjected here to a powerful influence . . . ."
Cotton L.J. then considered the application of the defence of laches. Lindley L.J. said, at 186:
"More than six years had elapsed between the time when the plaintiff left the sisterhood and the commencement of the present action. The action is not one of those to which the state of limitation in terms applied, nor is that statute pleaded. But this action very closely resembles an action for money had and received where laches and acquiescence are relied upon . . . "
[60] See, in general, Spry, *Equitable Remedies* (5th ed., Sweet and Maxwell, 1997), pp. 225–237 and 431–438; Snell, *Equity* (13th ed., Sweet and Maxwell, 2000) paras 3–19 and 45–24; Meagher, Gummow and Lehane, *Equity: Doctrines and Remedies* (3rd ed., Butterworths, 1992) and Law Commission, *Limitation of Actions*, (Consultation Paper No. 151), paras 9.12 to 9.20 and Law Commission Report on Limitation of Actions (Law Com. 270), paras 2.97–2.99.
[61] See para. 5–89, above.
[62] The terms laches and acquiescence are used interchangeably and without consistency in the authorities and the textbooks. The interrelationship between laches, acquiescence and estoppel and the scope of each is a matter of academic debate, full exploration of which is beyond the scope of this work (see the comments of Nourse L.J. in the Court of Appeal in *Goldsworthy v. Brickell* [1987] Ch. 378 at 410A–D.)
[63] But see para. 5–108, below.
[64] (1874) L.R. 5 P.C. 221.

by his conduct or neglect he has, though perhaps not waiving that remedy, yet put the other party in a situation in which it would not be reasonable to place him if the remedy were afterwards to be asserted, in either of these cases lapse of time and delay are most material. But in every case, if an argument against relief, which otherwise would be just, is founded upon mere delay, that delay of course not amounting to bar by statute of limitations, the validity of that defence must be tried upon principles substantially equitable. Two circumstances, always important in such cases, are length of delay and the nature of the acts done during the interval, which might affect either party and cause a balance of justice or injustice in taking the one course or the other, so far as relates to the remedy."[65]

So, mere passage of time is not the only factor, as in limitation. Equity considers the claimant's acts as well to see whether it would now be equitable to allow him the relief sought.

5–100   The above passage was cited by Lord Blackburn in *Erlanger v. New Sombrero Phosphate Co.*,[66] who continued:

"I have looked in vain for any authority which gives a more distinct and definite rule that this; and, I think from the nature of the inquiry, it must always be a question of more or less, depending on the degree of diligence which might reasonably be required, and degree of change which has occurred, whether the balance of justice or injustice is in favour of granting the remedy or withholding it. The determination of such a question must largely depend on the turn of mind of those who have to decide, and must therefore be subject to uncertainty; but that, I think, is inherent in the nature of the inquiry."[67]

The flexibility of the defence was stressed more recently by Laddie J. in *Nelson v. Rye*[68]:

"It can be misleading to approach the equitable defence of laches and acquiescence as if they consisted of a series of precisely defined hurdles which a litigant must struggle before the defence is made out . . . these defences are not technical or arbitrary. The courts have indicated over the years some of the factors which must be taken into consideration in deciding whether the defence runs. Those factors include the period of delay, the extent to which the defendant's position has been prejudiced by the delay and the extent to which that prejudice was caused by the actions of the plaintiff. I accept that mere delay alone will almost never suffice, but the court has to look at all the circumstances, including in particular those factors set out above, and then decide whether the balance of justice or injustice is in favour of granting the remedy or withholding it. If substantial prejudice will be suffered by the defendant, it is not necessary for the defendant to prove that it was caused by the delay. On the other hand, the plaintiff's knowledge that the delay will cause such prejudice is a factor to be taken into account."[69]

5–101   In *Frawley v. Neil*,[70] Aldous L.J., whilst recognising that previous authorities might be relevant to the question whether it would be conscionable to uncon-scionable for the relief to be granted, emphasised that the modern approach does not require an inquiry into whether the circumstances of a particular case can be

---

[65] *ibid.* at 239–40, *per* Lord Selbourne L.C.
[66] (1878) 3 App. Cas. 1218.
[67] *ibid.* at 1279.
[68] [1996] 1 W.L.R. 1378 (but see para. 5–90, above).
[69] *ibid.* at 1392.
[70] *The Times*, April 5, 1999 (transcript CHANF 97/1573/3).

fitted within the confines of a preconceived formula derived from earlier cases. Rather, the court should adopt a broad approach, to ascertain whether it would in all the circumstances be unconscionable for a party to be permitted to assert his beneficial right.

It follows that it is neither possible nor desirable to formulate a precise test or list of factors necessary for the defence to be satisfied. However, the authorities do provide some useful guidance as to what is meant by delay and the circumstances in which such delay might render the remedy unconscionable.[71] These will be discussed below.   **5–102**

(i) Unreasonable Delay

Length of delay. Whether the claimant's delay is unreasonable depends on all the circumstances of the case. Delay which might otherwise be unreasonable might be reasonable depending upon the defendant's conduct or whether the parties are in negotiations.[72] However, mere protest by the claimant, where, following negotiations, the defendant continues to act in contravention of the claimant's rights will not justify delay.[73] It should be remembered that the crucial question is whether the delay is such as to render grant of the relief equitable. As such, even a short delay may trigger the defence, if the defendant has been prejudiced as a result.[74]   **5–103**

It has been suggested that where relief is sought in the exclusive jurisdiction of the court, as opposed to its auxiliary or concurrent jurisdiction, a longer delay might be required before the defence of laches operates. This is because the claimant has no remedies at law, and denial of equitable relief is, in effect, a denial of his rights altogether.[75] However, there are contrary observations in *Habib Bank Ltd. v. Habib Bank A.G. Zurich*[76] in which counsel for the plaintiffs sought to make such a distinction. Faced with arguments as to whether the plaintiff was asserting a legal or an equitable right, Oliver L.J., with whom Watkins and Stephenson L.JJ. agreed, stated: **5–104**

"I have to confess that I detect in myself, despite the erudition displayed by both counsel, a strong predilection for the view that such distinctions are both archaic and arcane and that in the year 1980 they have but little significance for anyone but a legal historian. For myself, I believe that the law as it has developed over the past 20 years has now evolved a far broader approach to the problem than that suggested by Mr Aldous and one which is in no way dependent upon the historical accident of whether

---

[71] The principles derived from the authorities are also relevant to the defence of acquiescence, discussed in paras 5–109 to 5–112, below.

[72] *Southcomb v. Bishop of Exeter* (1847) 6 Ha. 213, followed in *McMurray v. Spicer* (1868) L.R. 5 Eq. 527 at 537. See also *Re H. (Abduction: Acquiescence)* [1998] A.C. 72 at 88–89, HL(E).

[73] *Lehmann v. McArthur* (1868) L.R. 3 Ch. 496.

[74] See, *e.g.* in an example rather removed from claims against professionals, where the claimant seeks specific performance of a contract the subject matter of which is of a fluctuating value, the claimant would be required to act more expeditiously than otherwise might be the case. See *Mills v. Haywood* (1877) 6 Ch. D. 196, *Pollard v. Clayton* (1855) 1 K. & J. 463 and *Wroth v. Tyler* [1974] Ch. 30 at 53.

[75] See Spry, *op. cit.*, p. 437, citing as an example *Knight v. Bowyer* (1858) 2 De G.F & J. 421.

[76] [1981] 1 W.L.R. 1265, albeit in the context of acquiescence—the defences are so similar that the same must be said of laches.

any particular right was first recognised by the common law or was invented by the Court of Chancery."[77]

5–105   **Time from which delay judged.** Prima facie, the time from which the claimant's delay is judged is the time at which he became aware of the facts giving rise to a right to claim the equitable relief in question. In *Lindsay Petroleum Co. v. Hurd*,[78] it was said: "In order that the remedy should be lost by laches or delay, it is, if not universally, at all events ordinarily . . . necessary that there should be sufficient knowledge of the facts constituting the title to relief."[79] The extent of knowledge required depends on the circumstances of the case and the remedy claimed.[80] It is clear that time will not begin to "run" where the claimant is under undue influence.[81]

(ii) *Prejudice to the defendant or a third party*

5–106   There are several bases on which it might be held that the claimant's delay has resulted in prejudice to the defendant or a third party, such that the remedy should not be granted.[82] Examples are:

(1) Where the defendant loses access to documentary evidence which affects his ability to defend himself, or the lapse of time renders it difficult for the defendant to recall material facts.[83]

(2) Where dispositions are made by the defendant or a third party and it would be unjust in all the circumstances to disturb them.[84]

(3) Where the defendant expends money or incurs and additional liability, or has let pass opportunities to mitigate his position.[85]

(4) Where, by delaying, the claimant has placed the defendant under unfair suspense or gained an unfair advantage.[86]

5–107   Where the defence is made out the claimant is not necessarily deprived of a remedy altogether. For example, the claimant who seeks an injunction may be

---

[77] *ibid.* at 1284–1285. The dicta was subsequently followed by the Court of Appeal in *Gafford v. Graham* (1999) 77 P. & C.R. 73 and *Jones and another v. Stones* [1999] 1 W.L.R. 1793 at 1744.
[78] (1874) L.R. 5 P.C. 221.
[79] *ibid.* at 241.
[80] See *Holder v. Holder* [1968] Ch. 353 at 369 (approved on this point on appeal at 383), approving *Re Pauling's Settlement* [1962] 1 W.L.R. 86 at 108. Examples of cases in which it has been held that that knowledge of the relevant facts gives rise to a presumption of knowledge of the right to an equitable remedy are: *Stafford v. Stafford* (1857) 1 De. G. & J. 193 at 202 and *Allcard v. Skinner* (1887) 36 Ch. D. 145 at 188, *per* Lindley L.J. Authorities to the contrary are: *Cockerell v. Cholmeley* (1830) 1 Russ. & M. 418 at 425, *Wilmott v. Barber* (1880) 15 Ch. D. 96 at 105, *Re Howlett* [1949] Ch. 676 at 775.
[81] *Allcard v. Skinner* (1887) 36 Ch. D 145; *Beale v. Kyte* [1907] 1 Ch. 564.
[82] See, generally Spry, *op. cit.*, pp. 230–235 and 434–438.
[83] *Bourne v. Swan & Edgar* [1903] 1 Ch. 211 at 219 and *Watts v. Assets Co. Ltd* [1905] A.C. 317 at 333. See also *Tanna and another v. Tanna and another* (unreported, May 25, 2001).
[84] Whether or not they were made for value.
[85] See *Shaw v. Applegate* [1977] 1 W.L.R. 970, *Fysh v. Page* (1956) 96 C.L.R. 233.
[86] See *Allcard v. Skinner* (1887) 36 Ch. D 145, *Lamshed v. Lamshed* (1963) 109 C.L.R. 440 at 453 and *Pollard v. Clayton* (1855) 1 K. & J. 462 (where the price of the subject matter of the contract was fluctuating). Delay will be particularly relevant where the claim is to a business; the claimant is not permitted to wait and see if the business prospers: *Re Jarvis* [1958] 1 W.L.R. 815.

granted a limited injunction, or conditions may be imposed to ensure the defendant is not prejudiced. Alternatively, damages in lieu of the injunction may be obtained.[87]

(iii) *Relationship between Laches and The Limitation Act 1980*

It was held in *Re Pauling's Settlement*[88] that, there being an express statutory **5–108** provision providing a limitation period in respect of the claim, there was no room for the equitable doctrine of laches.[89] On the other hand, in *Kleinwort Benson Ltd v. Sandwell B.C.*,[90] Hobhouse J. noted that it was common ground between the parties that (in so far as section 5 of the Limitation Act 1980 applied) a six-year limitation period should be applied by analogy under section 36 of the Act, and there remained jurisdiction to refuse relief on the grounds of laches.[91]

(b) *Acquiescence*

As mentioned above, there is considerable overlap between the defences of **5–109** laches and acquiescence. The principles underlying laches set out at paras 5–099 to 5–107, above apply equally to the defence of acquiescence, and will not be repeated. However, several authorities concerned specifically with the defence of acquiescence deserve mention. These are discussed below.

A leading case in this area is *Shaw v. Applegate*.[92] The plaintiff sought to **5–110** enforce a covenant entered into in 1967 not to use his land as an "amusement arcade". Breaches of the covenant had occurred since 1971. The claimant brought injunction proceedings in 1973 but did not apply for an interlocutory injunction. The trial occurred in 1976. In the meantime, the defendant had continued to carry on his business. Buckley L.J. considered that it was unnecessary for the defendant to establish each of the five elements of the defence set out by Fry J. in *Willmott v. Barber*.[93] In his judgment, the test to be applied was whether upon the facts of the case it would be dishonest or unconscionable for the plaintiff to rely on his rights.[94]

A similar approach was adopted in *Habib Bank Ltd v. Habib Bank A.G.* **5–111** *Zurich*[95]:

---

[87] *Sayers v. Collyer* (1884) 28 Ch. D 103 at 110, *Shaw v. Applegate* [1977] 1 W.L.R. 970 at 978–979 and 981.

[88] [1961] 1 W.L.R. 86.

[89] *ibid.* at 115, *per* Wilberforce J. (approved by the Court of Appeal in [1964] Ch. 303 at 353).

[90] [1994] All E.R. 890.

[91] *ibid.* at 943d–e. See also *West Sussex Properties Ltd v. Chichester D.C.* (ureported, June 28, 2000) at para. 32. Presumably, the same remarks apply to the defence of acquiescence.

[92] [1977] 1 W.L.R. 970.

[93] (1880) 15 Ch. D 105 at 106. The five elements were: (1) the defendant must have made a mistake as to his legal rights; (2) the defendant must have expended some money or must have done some act (not necessarily upon the claimant's land) on the faith of his mistaken belief; (3) the claimant must know of the existence of his own right which is inconsistent with the right claimed by the defendant; (4) the claimant must know of the defendant's mistaken belief of his rights; (5) the claimant must have encouraged the defendant in his expenditure of money or in the other acts which he has done, either directly or by abstaining from asserting his legal right.

[94] *ibid.* at 978. The judge held that it was not dishonest or unconscionable for the claimant to seek to enforce his rights, since he had been in doubt as to his legal rights. However, the defendant had been lulled into a false sense of security, so that the appropriate remedy was damages in lieu of an injunction.

[95] [1981] 1 W.L.R. 1265.

"[The defence] requires a very much broader approach which is directed rather than ascertaining whether, in particular individual circumstances, it would be unconscionable for a party to be permitted to deny that which, knowingly or unknowingly, he has allowed or encouraged another to assume to his detriment, than to inquiring whether the circumstances can be fitted within the confines of some preconceived formula . . . ."[96]

This was said by the Court of Appeal in the recent decision in *Jones v. Stones* to encapsulate the law.[97] So far as previous authorities were concerned, they assisted in showing was acts could be relevant in deciding whether it would be unconscionable to allow a party to proceed upon a particular basis, but did not lay down principles which had to be met and applied in every case. At the heart of estoppel or acquiescence lay an encouragement or allowance of a party to believe something to his detriment.

5–112   Finally, it should be noted that the fact that the claimant has acquiesced in a small and limited breach does not preclude him for all time from complaining about wider and more important breaches: see *Richards v. Revitt*.[98]

5. CONTRIBUTORY NEGLIGENCE

5–113   Where a person suffers damage "as a result partly of his own fault and partly of the fault of any other person or persons . . . the damages recoverable in respect thereof shall be reduced to such extent as the court thinks just and equitable having regard to the claimant's share in the responsibility for the damage".[99] In the context of professional negligence a successful plea of contributory negligence by the defendant is less common than in other areas of negligence. This is because the parties often do not stand on an equal footing (as they do in, say, claims arising from road traffic accidents). If the defendant makes a mistake, it may be difficult to say that the client was negligent not to spot it or correct its effect, unless the client is expected to be wiser than his own professional advisers.[1]

---

[96] *ibid.* at 128 *per* Oliver L.J., with whom Watkins and Stephenson L.JJ. agreed. See also *Taylors Fashions Ltd v. Liverpool Trustees Co.* [1982] Q.B. 133 at 155.

[97] [1999] 1 W.L.R. 1739 at 1744H, *per* Aldous L.J. Aldous L.J. also approved dicta to the effect that the modern approach should not depend upon the historical accident of whether any particular right existed at common law or was invented by the Court of Chancery. See also *Gafford v. Graham* (1999) 77 P. & C.R. 73 and para. 5–104, above.

[98] (1877) 7 Ch.D 22 4 at 226.

[99] Law Reform (Contributory Negligence) Act 1945, s.1(1). For a general discussion of contributory negligence, see G. Williams, *Joint Torts and Contributory Negligence* (Stevens & Sons, 1951), Pt Two and Charlesworth & Percy, paras 3–04 to 3–67. For an analysis of the three principal types of case in which contributory negligence arises, see N. Gravells, "Three Heads of Contributory Negligence" in (1977) 93 L.Q.R. 581.

[1] It is sometimes argued on behalf of a claimant that there can be no contributory negligence because it was the duty of the defendant to protect him from the very damage which he suffered. This argument was recently rejected by the High Court of Australia in *Astley v. Austrust Ltd* (1999) 161 A.L.R. 155; [1999] Lloyd's Rep. P.N. 758. The Court stated that, while in some circumstances a claimant might be able to have relied upon the defendant to perform his duty and so not be held to have been contributorily negligent, there is no absolute rule. The question is always whether the claimant took reasonable care and while the role and duty of the defendant are relevant factors, they will not always be determinative.

There are, of course, exceptions to the very general statements made in the   **5-114**
previous paragraph. First, the claimant may be particularly well placed to spot or
correct the defendant's mistake.[2] Secondly, the claimant may do something quite
separate which aggravates the consequences of the defendant's breach of duty.
For example, a lender having received a negligently high valuation of the
proposed security, may proceed to make a loan which would in any event be
imprudent[3]; a patient may take larger doses than instructed of a drug which it was
negligent of his doctor to prescribe.[4] In *De Meza v. Apple*,[5] the plaintiffs, a firm
of solicitors, engaged the defendants, a firm of auditors, to complete some
consequential loss insurance certificates. The defendants made certain mistakes
which Brabin J. held amounted to breaches of duty, and as a result the plaintiffs
were under-insured when a fire occurred at one of their offices. However, Brabin
J. considered that the plaintiffs themselves had also been negligent in regard to
their insurance. He apportioned responsibility 70 per cent to the defendants and
30 per cent to the plaintiffs. Where a relevant fact is not communicated by the
client to his professional advisers, the question commonly arises whether the
client was negligent to withhold it or the defendant was negligent not to elicit it.
If the client is an experienced businessman, the court is more likely to treat his
omission as amounting at least to contributory negligence.[6]

(a) *Contributory negligence and contract*

One important question, until relatively recently the subject of conflicting Eng-   **5-115**
lish authority and still the subject of a divergence between the English and
Australian courts, is whether the defence of contributory negligence is available
when the plaintiff's claim is brought in contract alone.[7] If the defendant is in
breach of an implied contractual duty to exercise reasonable care, does this
amount to "fault" within section 1 of the Act?[8] Paull J. in *Quinn v. Burch Bros
(Builders) Ltd*[9] and Brabin J. in *De Meza v. Apple*[10] held that it did, but in each
case the Court of Appeal found it unnecessary to decide the point. The Supreme

---

[2] Thus in claims against auditors for failing to detect defalcations by company employees, it is quite
often argued that the directors were similarly negligent. See, *e.g. Nelson Guarantee Corp. Ltd v.
Hodgson* [1958] N.Z.L.R. 609 at 619–620; *Simonius Vischer and Co. v. Holt and Thompson* [1979]
2 N.S.W.L.R. 322; *Daniels v. Anderson* (1995) 16 A.C.S.R. 607. *Morash v. Lockhart & Ritchie Ltd*
(1979) 95 D.L.R. (3rd) 647, the plaintiff was 75 per cent contributorily negligent for failing to keep
himself informed about his insurance cover for a long period.
[3] See chap. 9, paras. 9–166 to 9–172, below.
[4] See also *Grossman v. Stewart* (1977) 5 C.C.L.T. 45, British Columbia Supreme Court: defendant
prescribed drug for plaintiff's skin disorder, without warning her that there were risks involved in the
prolonged use of the drug. The plaintiff continued to use the drug for a long period after defendant
had stopped prescribing it. Damages were reduced by two-thirds for contributory negligence. See also
Fredette v. Wiebe (1986) 29 D.L.R. (4th) 534 and *Brushett v. Cowan* (1990) 3 C.C.L.T. (2d) 195.
[5] [1974] 1 Lloyd's Rep. 508. The issue of contributory negligence did not arise on appeal: [1975] 1
Lloyd's Rep. 498.
[6] See, *e.g. Carradine Properties Ltd v. D. J. Freeman and Co.* (1989) 5 Const. L.J. 267, discussed
in Chap. 10, below.
[7] The seminal academic discussion of this question is G. Williams, *Joint Torts and Contributory
Negligence, op. cit.*, Chap. 8. Williams argues forcefully that the Act ought to, and does, apply to
actions for breach of contract: see pp. 214–222.
[8] The word "fault" is defined in s.4 as meaning "negligence, breach of statutory duty or other act
or omission which gives rise to a liability in tort or would, apart from this Act, give rise to the defence
of contributory negligence".
[9] [1966] 2 Q.B. 370.
[10] [1974] 1 Lloyd's Rep. 508, QBD; [1975] 1 Lloyd's Rep. 498, CA.

Court of Victoria, construing a statute which closely followed the English Act, came to the opposite conclusion.[11] In *Basildon D.C. v. J. E. Lesser Properties Ltd*,[12] Judge Newey Q.C., after considering a number of English and Commonwealth authorities, concluded that in a claim for breach of contract apportionment of liability under the Law Reform (Contributory Negligence) Act 1945 was not permissible. This conclusion was based upon the fact that before the passing of the Act contributory negligence by the plaintiff was a complete defence to actions in tort, but not to actions in contract. Neill L.J. came to the same conclusion in *A.B. Marintrans v. Comet Shipping*[13] (an appeal from arbitrators to the Queen's Bench Division by way of a special case stated pursuant to section 21 of the Arbitration Act 1950). Neill L.J. commented that his conclusions as to the construction of the Act may well lead to unsatisfactory results in some cases. Plaintiffs would be able to avoid the apportionment provisions by suing in contract, even when a claim in tort would be equally appropriate or more appropriate. The next decision on the point was that of Hobhouse J. in *Forsikringsaktieselskapet Vesta v. Butcher*.[14] Hobhouse J. declined to follow the reasoning of Judge Newey in *Basildon D.C. v. J. E. Lesser Properties Ltd*[15] and Neill L.J. in *A. B. Marintrans v. Comet Shipping*.[16] Instead, he divided the cases where the problem arises into three categories:

"(1) Where the defendant's liability arises from some contractual provision which does not depend on negligence on the part of the defendant.

(2) Where the defendant's liability arises from a contractual obligation which is expressed in terms of taking care (or its equivalent) but does not correspond to a common law duty to take care which would exist in the given case independently of contract.

(3) Where the defendant's liability in contract is the same as his liability in the tort of negligence independently of the existence of any contract."

5–116   Hobhouse J. held that the case before him fell into category (3) and that in such a case liability could be apportioned under the Act, except where this was expressly prohibited by some term of the contract between the parties. The Court of Appeal (one of whose members, significantly, was Neill L.J.) upheld Hobhouse J.'s conclusion and the reasoning on which it was based.[17] This analysis was applied by Alliott J. in *Lipkin Gorman v. Karpnale Ltd*[18] and upheld by the Court of Appeal.[19] In *Tennant Radiant Heat Ltd v. Warrington Development*

---

[11] *Belous v. Willetts* [1970] V.R. 45; *A. S. James Pty Ltd v. C. B. Duncan* [1970] V.R. 705; *Read v. Nerey Nominees Pty Ltd* [1979] V.R. 47. The point was considered, but not decided, by the New South Wales Court of Appeal in *Simonius Vischer and Co. v. Holt & Thompson* [1979] 2 N.S.W.L.R. 322. For a discussion of the earlier Australian cases, see J. Swanton, "Contributory Negligence as a Defence to Actions for Breach of Contract" in 55 A.L.J. 278. Swanton argues that the defence of contributory negligence ought to be available whether the action is framed in contract or tort. See now *Daniels v. Anderson* (1995) 16 A.C.S.R. 607.
[12] [1985] 1 Q.B. 839.
[13] [1985] 1 W.L.R. 1270.
[14] [1986] 2 All E.R. 488.
[15] [1985] 1 Q.B. 839.
[16] [1985] 1 W.L.R. 1270.
[17] [1989] A.C. 852. See the judgment of O'Connor L.J. at 860–867 and Neill L.J. at 875 and Sir Roger Ormrod at 879. This issue did not arise on the subsequent appeal by the reinsurers to the House of Lords.
[18] [1987] 1 W.L.R. 987 at 997.
[19] [1989] 1 W.L.R. 1340 at 1360.

Corp.,[20] the Court of Appeal held that contributory negligence had no application in the context of a claim for breach of a repairing covenant. This decision is consistent with *Forsikringsaktieselskapet Vesta*, since such a claim would fall into category (1).[21] The Court of Appeal applied the same analysis in *Barclays Bank plc v. Fairclough Building Ltd.*[22] The New Zealand Court of Appeal considered these questions *obiter* in *Mouat v. Clarke Boyce*[23] in relation to the New Zealand Contributory Negligence Act 1947. It favoured the approach adopted by the English Court of Appeal.[24] However, the High Court of Australia has declined to follow Hobhouse J. and the Court of Appeal, holding in *Astley v. Austrust Ltd*[25] that section 27A of the South Australian Wrongs Act 1937 (which is to similar effect as section 1 of the Law Reform (Contributory Negligence) Act 1945) did not allow the court to reduce damages for breach of a contractual duty which was concurrent with the tortious duty of care owed by a solicitor. In view of the importance of the issues involved and the division of judicial opinion to which they have given rise, the matter cannot be regarded as finally resolved until it has been considered by the House of Lords.

(b) *Application to professional negligence*

The debate as to the applicability of the Law Reform (Contributory Negligence) Act 1945 to actions for breach of contract is of considerable importance in the context of professional negligence. In the great majority of such cases the client has concurrent claims against his professional adviser both in contract and tort.[26] It would seem both unjust and illogical if the client is able to escape the consequences of his own negligence by suing in contract alone. In the ordinary way professional negligence cases fall into category (3), as defined by Hobhouse J. in *Forsikringsaktieselskapet Vesta v. Butcher.*[27] As the law now stands, therefore, in most professional negligence actions, whether the claimant chooses to sue in contract or tort or both, the defence of contributory negligence is available.

5–117

The decision of the House of Lords in *Banque Bruxelles Lambert SA v. Eagle Star Insurance Co. Ltd*[28] identifies a two-stage inquiry which will be appropriate

5–118

---

[20] [1988] 1 E.G.L.R. 41.

[21] This case was decided six weeks after the Court of Appeal's decision in *Forsikringsaktieselskapet Vesta* and it appears that only a brief report of the earlier decision was available.

[22] [1995] Q.B. 214. Since the defendant was in breach of a strict contractual duty, this was a category (1) case and the defence of contributory negligence was held not to be available. For an example of a category (2) case where a defence of contributory negligence was not available see *Raflatac v. Eade* [1999] 1 Lloyd's Rep. 506, *per* Colman J. (defendant contractor owed contractual duty to exercise reasonable skill and care, but no duty of care in tort to avoid economic loss).

[23] [1992] 2 N.Z.L.R. 559.

[24] See the judgment of Cooke P. at 564, *ibid.* Although the underlying decision on liability has now been reversed (see [1994] 1 A.C. 428), this separate judgment on contributory negligence was not considered by the Privy Council. The New Zealand Court of Appeal had earlier held that contributory negligence applied to a claim for breach of fiduciary duty: *Davy v. Mead* [1987] 2 N.Z.L.R. 443.

[25] [1999] H.C.A. 6, reported at (1999) 161 A.L.R. 155 and [1999] Lloyd's Rep. 758 This decision is discussed by Blom, "Contributory Negligence and Contract—A Canadian view of *Astley v. Austrust Ltd*" in [2000] Tort Law Rev. 70. As he explains, the Canadian statutory provisions are different, antedating the Law Reform (Contributory Negligence) Act 1945, although different Provinces have different provisions.

[26] See Chap. 2, paras 2–100 to 2–108, above.

[27] [1986] 2 All E.R. 488 and [1989] A.C. 852.

[28] [1997] A.C. 191: see Chap. 3, para. 3–02, above.

in many professional negligence actions: (i) What is the overall damage which P has suffered as a result of acting on D's report? (ii) Which part of that loss is recoverable in damages against D? The interaction between this approach to damages and section 1 of the Law Reform (Contributory Negligence) Act 1945 gave rise to disagreement between first instance judges. This has now been resolved by the House of Lords in *Platform Home Loans Ltd v. Oyston Shipways Ltd.*[29] "Damage" for the purpose of section 1 means the overall loss, not merely that part for which the defendant is liable on *Banque Bruxelles Lambert* principles. In cases where the whole of the overall damage is recoverable in damages against the defendant (subject to contributory negligence), there is no difficulty. However, where only part of the overall loss is recoverable in damages, then it is not just and equitable to reduce the damages twice, once to take account of the *Banque Bruxelles Lambert* decision and then again for contributory negligence: the total amount of damage should be reduced and then damages awarded at whichever is the lower of that figure and the damages recoverable on *Banque Bruxelles Lambert* principles. The same principles apply in respect of any profession whose function it is to produce reports.

(c) *Methods by which plaintiffs might seek to circumvent a plea of contributory negligence*

5–119 The plea of contributory negligence is not available in answer to a claim for deceit.[30] Thus where the facts warrant pleading deceit, as opposed to mere negligence, the defence of contributory negligence can be pre-empted by this means. However, before proceeding to plead and prove a claim for deceit, the claimant's advisers should consider the possible impact upon the defendant's insurance arrangements. An alternative possible method of forestalling the defence of contributory negligence would be to base the claim upon some specific term in the retainer which does not require the use of reasonable care.[31] The Court of Appeal stated in *Barclays Bank plc v. Fairclough Building Ltd*[32] that it was "at least arguable" that contributory negligence could be defeated by proving a failure to possess the requisite skill, as opposed to a failure to exercise that skill. This passage is *obiter* and, it may be thought, the reasoning is not attractive. The gravamen of the claim is that the defendant did not deploy reasonable skill and care in performing his task. Whether the defendant lacked the requisite abilities or simply did not bother to use them is at one remove from the real complaint. It is part of the background. Nor is the distinction easy to draw in practice. Suppose the defendant had part of the requisite skill and could have acquired the rest by consulting a reference book from his shelf? It may be thought undesirable that plaintiffs should avoid the consequences of their own negligence by means of such rarified distinctions.

---

[29] [2000] 2 A.C. 190. Discussed by Dugdale, "Contributory Negligence applied to Economic Loss: *Platform Home Loans* and *Fancy & Jackson*" in (1999) 62 M.L.R. 281 and by Stapleton, "Risk Taking by Commercial Lenders" in (1999) 115 L.Q.R. 527.

[30] *Alliance and Leicester Building Society v. Edgestop Ltd* [1993] 1 W.L.R. 1462.

[31] *Bristol and West Building Society v. Kramer and Co.*, The Times, February 6, 1995, but see Chap. 2, para. 2–10, above.

[32] [1995] Q.B. 214 at 222–223.

(d) Attribution[33]

Where two professionals have been negligent, the question may arise whether 5–120 either can establish contributory negligence on the basis that the other's mistakes should be "imputed" to the client. Whilst for certain purposes the conduct of an agent is treated as that of the principal, such an argument is unattractive in this context. Proportionate liability is not part of English law and has recently been rejected by the Law Commission.[34] It should not be introduced by this circuitous means. The appropriate course for a defendant is to sue the agent for contribution. In *Henderson v. Merrett Syndicates Ltd (No. 2)*,[35] Cresswell J. rejected a contention by the defendant auditors that the negligence of the managing agents should be "attributed" to the plaintiff names and thus constitute contributory negligence. Whilst this decision was based upon the "unusual and complex structure of Lloyd's", it may perhaps be followed on a more general basis.[36]

---

[33] This question has arisen in the context of claims against auditors and is discussed in Chap. 15, paras 15–146 to 15–151.

[34] See para. 5–02, above.

[35] [1996] P.N.L.R. 32.

[36] The question of attribution in the context of contributory negligence is discussed in depth by A. Bartlett Q.C., "Attribution of contributory negligence: agents, company directors and fraudsters" in (1998) 114 L.Q.R. 460. Bartlett supports the "both ways" test, *viz.*:

"The fault of the connected person should be attributed to the plaintiff as contributory negligence where—and only where—the relationship between them is such that the plaintiff would in principle be liable to a third party because of errors of the connected person."

Bartlett argues (a) that the actual results of most reported cases can be reconciled with this test and (b) that this approach can be justified on policy grounds. He is accordingly critical of the sparse reasoning which supports the decision in *Henderson v. Merrett Syndicates Ltd (No. 2)* [1996] P.N.L.R. 32.

CHAPTER 6

LITIGATION

	PARA.			PARA.
1. Group actions	6–001	(d) Relevance and admissibility of expert evidence		6–013
(a) General	6–001	(i) The appropriate discipline		6–014
(b) Professional negligence	6–002			
(c) Procedure	6–003	(ii) The appropriate questions		6–015
(d) Costs	6–005			
2. Expert evidence	6–006	(iii) Appropriate qualifications and experience		6–016
(a) The functions of the expert witness	6–006			
		(iv) Impartiality		6–017
(b) Cases where expert evidence is not required	6–008	(e) The single joint expert		6–019
(c) The Civil Procedure Rules	6–012			

1. GROUP ACTIONS

(a) *General*

Group actions, also known as multi-party actions, and as class actions in other jurisdictions, concern the litigation of a number of claims having some similarity, usually the same claimant or defendants and similar legal and factual issues, which are administered together by the same judge. There has been an upsurge in group actions during the 1980s and 1990s. They may cover a large variety of types of claims, including actions against employers for personal injury,[1] litigation alleging cancer from industrial plants,[2] transport disaster claims,[3] claims for environmental nuisance,[4] perhaps most well known of all a number of pharmaceutical product liability claims,[5] other product liability actions,[6] claims against arms of the state for negligence causing personal injury,[7] and financial loss by

6–001

---

[1] The British Coal Vibration White Finger Litigation and the Respiratory Disease Litigation, which mostly resulted in success for the claimants.

[2] The Sellafield childhood leukemia cases, which failed on causation in *Reay and Hope v. British Nuclear Fuels PLC* (1994) 5 Med L.R. 1; *B & D v. X Co.*

[3] See, *e.g.* the *Herald of Free Enterprise* disaster of 1987 (where three arbitrators set landmark awards for post-traumatic stress disorder), the Hillsborough football stadium disaster of 1989.

[4] The Docklands Nuisance actions (some of which settled, some of which were withdrawn).

[5] The Pertussis Vaccine Litigation (see *Loveday v. Renton* [1990] 1 M.L.R. 117, where the case effectively ended with failure by the plaintiffs on a preliminary issue on causation); the Opren Litigation (where proceedings were discontinued); the Myodil Litigation (where a core cohort achieved settlements), the large and expensively unsuccessful Benzodiazepene Litigation; the Norplant Litigation (where legal aid was withdrawn shortly before trial) and the Hepatitis C Litigation where the claimants succeeded at trial (reported as *A v. National Blood Authority* [2001] 3 All E.R. 289). In many of these cases, causation has been the key issue on which the claimants failed.

[6] See, *e.g.* the Tobacco Litigation, which ended in failure for the claimants following a preliminary issue on limitation.

[7] The HIV Haemophilac Litigation, which was settled following a preliminary hearing in the Court of Appeal (reported at [1996] P.N.L.R. 290); the Cretzfeldt Jakob Disease Litigation, where the claimants succeeded in establishing liability (reported at [1996] 7 Med. L.R. 309).

investors from alleged negligent misstatements in prospectuses.[8] There have also been a number of professional negligence group actions, which will be briefly considered below. As a result of all this litigation, there has been a great deal of experience in how to manage and litigate group actions. Some of it is reflected in reported decisions and in the new provisions for group actions in the Civil Procedure Rules ("CPR"), but much of it is necessarily of a more informal kind which is best found in the leading books on the subject.[9]

(b) *Professional negligence*

6–002   A number of group actions have arisen in the field of professional negligence. The most prominent are as follows. The massive losses suffered by names at Lloyd's in the late 1980s and early 1990s have given rise to a number of group actions against members' agents, managing agents and underwriters.[10] The fall in the property market at about the same time led to many actions by lenders against the solicitors and surveyors they had retained, and there have been two multi-party actions against solicitors brought by two of the building societies.[11] Home Income Plans, a scheme to raise income on the strength of mortgages which caused clients loss, led to unsuccessful litigation by the assignee of the investors against many firms of solicitors.[12] Several of the pharmaceutical group actions involve subsidiary allegations of clinical negligence,[13] and there have been clinical negligence group actions.[14]

(c) *Procedure*

6–003   CPR, Pt 19, rr. 10–15, and the accompanying Practice Direction, are concerned with group litigation. No similar body of rules existed before 2000. A court can make a Group Litigation Order, or "GLO", where there are or are likely to be a number of claims giving rise to GLO issues.[15] A GLO must[16] contain directions about the establishment of a register,[17] specify the GLO issues to identify the claims, and specify a management court. Judgments or orders in one claim are generally binding on other claims.[18] Directions may be given[19] varying the GLO

---

[8] The Lockton Litigation.

[9] See Hodges, *Multi-Party Actions* (Oxford, 2001) and Day, *Multi-Party Actions* (LAG, 1995). While the latter was written long before the new Civil Procedure Rules, it still provides valuable insights, and it includes helpful pleadings and orders in the appendices.

[10] See Chap. 16, below.

[11] The Bristol and West Building Society and the Nationwide Building Society. See further Chap. 10, para. 10–206 *et seq.*

[12] *Investors Compensation Scheme Ltd v. West Bromwich Building Society* [1999] Lloyd's Rep. P.N. 496; see further Chap. 10, para. 10–163.

[13] See, *e.g.* the HIV Haemophiliac Litigation and the Hepatitis Litigation.

[14] See, *e.g.* the cervical screening cases brought against East Kent Health Authority.

[15] CPR, r. 19.11(1). No guidance is given as to how the court should exercise the discretion. The Practice Direction at paras 2.1–3.9 sets out a number of preliminary steps which must be undertaken before applying for a GLO, the information required for making an application, and which Judges must approve any order.

[16] CPR, r. 19.11(2).

[17] While para. 6.5 of the Practice Direction envisages that this will normally be kept by the court, it may well be more convenient for a lead solicitor to do so.

[18] CPR, r. 19.12.

[19] CPR, r. 19.13.

issues, providing for tests claims to proceed,[20] appointing lead solicitors,[21] specifying what is to be included in a statement of case,[22] and providing for a cut-of date for joining the litigation and for publicising the GLO.[23] Co-ordinated litigation may be carried out outside the framework of GLOs in appropriate cases, for instance by the use of representative actions.

The new rules only lay down, and can only lay down, a very broad framework, **6–004** as the circumstances of potential group actions can be very diverse. A fundamental issue in many cases is likely to be whether the group action should progress by deciding generic issues without investigating any or many individual cases first, or whether individual cases should be properly pleaded and scrutinised before deciding on which generic issues should be tried.[24] In general, a high degree of co-operation is required between the lawyers for the opposing sides,[25] and judges have had to be active and interventionist in these type of actions long before the Woolf reforms.

(d) *Costs*

CPR, r. 48.6A provides special rules where a court has made a GLO. The two **6–005** fundamental rules are that any order for common costs against group litigants imposes several liability only for an equal proportion of those costs, and that the paying party will generally be liable to the receiving party for the individual costs of his claim and an equal proportion of the common costs. These rules reflect the general practice which had already developed in a number of cases.[26] The costs of test cases are generally generic costs. It is common in practice for claimants joining a group action to become immediately responsible for an equal proportion of generic costs.

2. EXPERT EVIDENCE

(a) *The functions of the expert witness*

In the context of liability issues in professional negligence actions, the expert **6–006** witness commonly performs two functions. First, he sets out and explains the relevant technical matters, *e.g.* the relevant principles of engineering and how they were applied to the building project in question, or the principles of valuation and how they were applied in the defendant surveyor's valuation or report. To this extent, the expert witness is performing a didactic role: he is

---

[20] See also para. 15 of the Practice Direction.
[21] This is a necessary provision of last resort. Selection of a lead solicitor in almost always voluntary, and para. 2.2 of the Practice Direction assists in this process.
[22] There is often provision for "Master pleadings", and para. 14.1 of the Practice Direction envisages that "Group Particulars of Claim" may be provided.
[23] See also para. 13 of the Practice Direction.
[24] See Hodges, *op. cit.*, pp. 15–18.
[25] For instance, in the selection of test cases. In general, it will be in the interests of all parties for the test cases to include as many contentious issues as reasonably possible, and to include both strong and weak cases, so that judgment in those test cases will provide the maximum assistance in settling the remaining cases.
[26] See, *e.g. Davies (Joseph Owen) v. Eli Lilly and Co.* [1987] 1 W.L.R. 1136, CA; *Nationwide Building Society v. Various Solicitors (No. 4)* [2000] Lloyd's Rep. P.N. 70.

explaining the technical aspects of the case in language comprehensible to laymen. Expert evidence of this sort may be largely or wholly uncontroversial. For example, the expert witnesses in a clinical negligence case may agree that the claimant's condition is the result of an adverse reaction to a new drug administered by the defendant. The court must understand and resolve any conflicts between expert evidence of this sort before it can consider the question of negligence. Where there is a dispute on questions of technical fact, the court may prefer the theory advanced by one expert witness over that advanced by another, but it will not assume technical expertise: it will not substitute a third theory of its own where that theory is not supported by the evidence of any of the expert witnesses.[27]

6–007   The second function of the expert witness is to assist the court in deciding whether the acts or omissions of the defendant constituted negligence. He will recount the current state of knowledge at the material time and the standards ordinarily observed in his profession, including any relevant general and approved practice or differing schools of thought. Expert evidence that a reasonably competent member of the defendant's profession would not have committed the act or omission in question is generally necessary before the court will find that he was negligent. Thus in *Sansom v. Metcalfe Hambleton and Co.*[28] Butler-Sloss L.J. said[29]:

> " . . . a court should be slow to find a professionally qualified man guilty of a breach of his duty of skill and care towards a client (or third party) without evidence from those within the same profession as to the standard expected on the facts of the case and the failure of the professionally qualified man to measure up to that standard."

(b) *Cases where expert evidence is not required*

6–008   In two categories of cases, supportive expert evidence is not necessary for a finding of negligence. The first category is solicitors' negligence cases. Expert evidence is rarely admitted upon the question whether a solicitor has discharged his duty of skill and care. The rationale appears to be that the courts themselves possess the necessary professional expertise to decide the question. In *Midland Bank v. Hett, Stubbs & Kemp*,[30] Oliver J. criticised the practice of calling solicitors to give evidence as to what they would have done in a particular

---

[27] In the clinical negligence case *McLean v. Weir* (1977) 3 C.C.L.T. 87 in the British Columbia Supreme Court, Gould J. summarised the position in a manner which, it is submitted, is equally applicable in England (at 101):
> "It is true that the court may accept in whole or in part or reject in whole or in part the evidence of any witness on the respective grounds of credibility or plausibility, or a combination of both. But in technical matters, unlike in lay matters within the traditional intellectual competence of the court, it cannot substitute its own medical opinion for that of qualified experts. The court has no status whatsoever to come to a medical conclusion contrary to unanimous medical evidence before it even if it wanted to, which is not the situation in this case. If the medical evidence is equivocal, the court may elect which of the theories advanced it accepts. If only two medical theories are advanced, the court may elect between the two or reject them both; it cannot adopt a third theory of its own, no matter how plausible such might be to the court."

[28] [1998] P.N.L.R. 542. The defendant surveyor's appeal from a finding that he had negligently conducted a survey was allowed on the basis that the only relevant expert evidence called by the plaintiff had been from a structural engineer.

[29] *ibid.* at 549.

[30] [1979] Ch. 384 at 402.

situation and doubted that such evidence was admissible.[31] This dictum was approved and applied by the Court of Appeal in *Bown v. Gould & Swayne*,[32] in which the Court upheld an order disallowing the evidence of a conveyancing expert in a solicitors' negligence action. Millett L.J. commented that if a judge needed assistance with regard to conveyancing practice, the proper way was to cite the relevant textbooks.[33]

The second category of cases where a finding of negligence may be made notwithstanding expert evidence in support of the defendant's conduct or the lack of evidence critical of it are those cases in which the *Bolam* test does not apply. Three types of case make up this category[34]:

(1) Cases in which the court considers that there is no logical basis for the **6–009** body of opinion in accordance with which the defendant acted. In *Bolitho v. City and Hackney Health Authority*,[35] a clinical negligence case, Lord Browne-Wilkinson said[36]:

" . . . the Court is not bound to hold that a defendant doctor escapes liability for negligent treatment or diagnosis just because he leads evidence from a number of medical experts who are genuinely of the opinion that the defendant's treatment or diagnosis accorded with sound medical practice. In the *Bolam* case itself, McNair J. [1957] 1 W.L.R. 583, 587 stated that the defendant had to have acted in accordance with the practice accepted as proper by a '*responsible* body of medical men'. Later, at 588, he referred to 'a standard of practice recognised a proper by a competent *reasonable* body of opinion'. Again, in the passage which I have cited from *Maynard*'s case, Lord Scarman refers to a 'respectable' body of professional opinion. The use of these adjectives—responsible, reasonable and respectable—all show that the court has to be satisfied that the exponents of the body of opinion relied upon can demonstrate that such opinion has a logical basis."

He concluded[37]:

" . . . if, in a rare case, it can be demonstrated that the professional opinion is not capable of withstanding logical analysis, the judge is entitled to hold that the body of opinion is not reasonable or responsible."

(2) Cases in which the expert evidence called by the defendant is in reality **6–010** no more than the personal opinion of an expert witness as to what he would have done in the position of the defendant. Such evidence does not establish that the defendant's conduct was in line with a responsible *body*

---

[31] *ibid.* This passage is quoted in full and discussed further in Chap. 10, para. 10–142, below.
[32] [1996] 1 P.N.L.R. 130.
[33] See *May v. Woollcombe Beer & Watts* [1999] P.N.L.R. 283: expert evidence held admissible in relation to conveyancing matters where there was no answer provided by textbooks; *Archer v. Hickmotts* [1997] P.N.L.R. 318: expert evidence concerning advice which should have been given in relation to a mortgage to secure a loan which the client was taking to assist her brother setting up his solicitor's practice was admitted, as the court had no familiarity with the matters in question and there were no text books which could assist (the judgment was reversed on appeal but without mention of expert evidence: see *sub nom. Northern Rock Building Society v. Archer* (1998) 78 P.& C.R. 65).
[34] See *Michael Hyde and Associates Ltd v. J.D. Williams and Co. Ltd* [2001] P.N.L.R. 233, CA.
[35] [1998] A.C. 232, HL.
[36] *ibid.* at 241.
[37] *ibid.* at 243. See, for further discussion of this case and for cases where the court has rejected expert evidence which was held not to withstand critical evaluation on this basis, Chap. 12, paras 12–101 to 12–105, below.

of opinion or with a recognised *practice* within his profession. In *Midland Bank Trust Co. Ltd v. Hett Stubbs & Kemp*,[38] a solicitors' negligence case, Oliver J. said[39]:

> "Clearly, if there is some practice in a profession, some accepted standard of conduct which is laid down by a professional institute or sanctioned by common usage, evidence of that can and ought to be received. But evidence which really amounts to no more than an expression of opinion by a particular practitioner of what he thinks that he would have done had he been placed, hypothetically and without the benefit of hindsight, in the position of the defendants, is of little assistance to the court . . . "

It is thought that this does not prevent the court receiving assistance from expert witnesses in cases where there is no general and approved practice or specific school of thought by reference to which the defendant's conduct can either be justified or condemned as negligent. In such cases, the court may still be assisted by the evidence of an expert witness as to how, in his experience and opinion, an ordinarily competent member of his profession would have acted in the position of the defendant. This may be quite different to the manner in which he personally would have acted.

6–011   (3) Cases in which it is not necessary to apply any particular professional expertise in order to decide whether the defendant has failed to exercise the skill and care expected of an ordinary member of his profession. For example, in the architect's negligence case of *Worboys v. Acme Investments Ltd*[40] Sachs L.J. recognised that there were cases where an omission on a plan was so glaring as to require no evidence of general practice and instanced a house without provision for a staircase. In the architect's negligence case of *Royal Brompton Hospital NHS Trust v. Hammond (No. 7)*,[41] Judge Seymour Q.C. put it this way[42]:

> " . . . if I am satisfied on the evidence that an obvious mistake was made which would not have been made by any careful person of whatever profession, or, indeed, of none, then I can find that the person who made that mistake was negligent. What I cannot do, as it seems to me, is to substitute my own view for that of a professional person of the appropriate discipline on any matter in respect of which any special skill, training or expertise is required to make an informed assessment."

In *Michael Hyde and Associates Ltd v. J.D. Williams and Co. Ltd*,[43] also an architect's negligence case, the Court of Appeal held that the trial judge had been entitled to conclude that, on the facts of that case, the

---

[38] [1979] Ch. 384.
[39] *ibid.* at 402. This passage was approved by the Court of Appeal in *Bown v. Gould & Swayne* [1996] P.N.L.R. 130 and in the architect's negligence case of *Michael Hyde and Associates Ltd v. J.D. Williams and Co. Ltd* [2001] P.N.L.R. 233 and was applied in the solicitors' negligence case of *X v. Wollcombe Yonge* [2001] Lloyd's Rep. P.N. 274.
[40] (1969) 210 E.G. 335, CA. See also the clinical negligence case of *Gold v. Haringey Health Authority* [1988] 1 Q.B. 481 at 490, *per* Lloyd L.J.:
"If the giving of contraceptive advice required no special skill, then I could see an argument that the *Bolam* test should not apply."
[41] [2001] C.I.L.L. 1714. See further Chap. 8, para. 8–149, below.
[42] *ibid.* at 1715.
[43] [2001] P.N.L.R 233, CA. See further Chap. 8, para. 8–148, below.

exercise of judgment involved in deciding whether the defendant was negligent did not of itself require any special architectural skills. He did not have to "get under the skin of a different profession" in order to assess whether or not the defendants had failed to use reasonable skill and care and, accordingly, was entitled to make a finding of negligence in face of expert evidence which supported the defendant's conduct.[44]

(c) *The Civil Procedure Rules*

Lord Woolf's final report on the civil justice system, published in July 1996,[45] **6–012** heralded a new and restrictive approach to expert evidence which has been embodied in England and Wales in Part 35 of the Civil Procedure Rules. Under CPR, r. 35.4, no party may call an expert witness without the court's permission. The principle which guides the court in deciding whether or not to permit expert evidence is set out in CPR, r. 35.1: expert evidence is to be restricted to that which is reasonably required to resolve the proceedings. Thus the use of expert evidence is now wholly subject to the control of the court and the court is encouraged to exercise its powers to decide that no expert evidence shall be called upon a particular issue, that a single expert shall be jointly instructed by the parties[46] or that expert evidence shall be adduced in writing only.[47] For example, in the solicitors' negligence case of *Mann v. Chetty & Patel*,[48] the Court of Appeal held that expert evidence would be permitted on only one of the quantum issues which arose in the case, whereas the claimant sought to adduce expert evidence on three such issues. The Court of Appeal stated that, in deciding whether to allow expert evidence, the court had to make a judgment on at least three matters:

(i) how cogent the proposed expert evidence would be ("cogency");

(ii) how helpful that evidence would be in resolving any of the issues in the case ("usefulness"); and

(iii) how much the evidence would cost and the relationship between that cost and the sums at stake ("proportionality").

(d) *Relevance and admissibility of expert evidence*

The modern approach to expert evidence encourages the court to be vigilant in **6–013** its scrutiny of expert evidence, both before and at trial. If permission has been

---

[44] *ibid.* at para. 27. Ward L.J. also observed (at para. 26) that the judge would also have been entitled to disapply the *Bolam* test on the basis that the case fell into the second category:
"He may well have been able to discount the evidence on that basis for I find little to suggest that there were two recognised but contrary views of an accepted practice governing the decision in question. As I read the evidence the experts were doing no more than putting themselves forward as reasonably competent architects and then saying what they would have done in the circumstances in which Mr Warrington found himself."
[45] *Access to Justice* (HMSO, 1996).
[46] See paras 6–019 to 6–020, below.
[47] CPR, r. 35.5(1) provides that expert evidence shall be given in a written report unless the court directs otherwise. In fast-track cases (those worth less than £15,000) experts will not be permitted to give oral evidence unless that is necessary in the interests of justice: CPR, r. 35.5(2).
[48] [2001] Lloyd's Rep. P.N. 38, CA. See also the accountants' negligence case of *Barings plc (In Liquidation) v. Coopers & Lybrand* [2001] Lloyd's Rep. P.N. 379.

given to call expert evidence, objection may be made to its admissibility and this should be done as soon as possible. It is no longer necessary to make such objection to the trial judge only,[49] nor is it desirable to leave such a challenge until trial.

(i) *The appropriate discipline*

6–014 Particular care is required in the instructing of expert witnesses and the presentation of their evidence. The first question must be whether the task undertaken by the defendant was one within his own proper and usual professional sphere. If it was not, there may be a question whether he should be judged not according to the practice of his own profession but rather according to the professional practice of the specialism in which he purported to operate.[50] If so, an expert of that discipline should be instructed.

(ii) *The appropriate questions*

6–015 Secondly, it is important that the evidence of an expert witness is confined to matters which are relevant to the issues before the court. In *Pozzolanic Lytag Ltd v. Bryan Hobson Associates*,[51] Dyson J. stated that the expert witnesses should have confined themselves to the question whether there was a common practice in the engineering profession as to what engineers who are engaged as project managers do in relation to the insurance obligations of building contractors. Instead, they considered numerous other issues including contributory negligence, which was a matter for the court. He warned[52]:

> "Prolix expert reports directed to issue with which they should not be concerned merely add to the expense of litigation. Everything possible should be done to discourage this. In appropriate cases, this will include making special orders for costs."

(iii) *Appropriate qualifications and experience*

6–016 Thirdly, the expert witness must be properly qualified to provide an opinion upon the issues to be determined. The court will consider "whether the witness has acquired by study or experience sufficient knowledge of the subject to render his

---

[49] The position used to be more complicated. Where it was disputed whether expert evidence was admissible, the master or judge in chambers was not entitled to rule on the admissibility of such evidence, see *Sullivan v. West Yorkshire Passenger Transport Executive* [1985] 2 All E.R. 134, CA. However, in *Woodford & Ackroyd v. Burgess* [1999] Lloyd's Rep. P.N. 231, the Court of Appeal held that a judge who was not the trial judge could rule on admissibility under the inherent jurisdiction. See also *Liverpool Roman Catholic Archdiocese Trustees Incorporated v. Goldberg (No. 2)* [2001] Lloyd's Rep. P.N. 518, where Neuberger J. set out in six steps the proper approach to an application to exclude expert evidence on the grounds that it was inadmissible.

[50] See, *e.g. Investors in Industry Commercial Properties v. South Bedfordshire D.C.* [1986] 1 All E.R. 787 and *Sansom v. Metcalfe Hambleton and Co.* [1998] P.N.L.R. 542, discussed further at Chap. 8, para. 8–151, below.

[51] [1999] B.L.R. 267.

[52] *ibid.* at 275. See also *Pride Valley Food Ltd v. Hall and Partners (Contract Management) Ltd* (2000) 76 Con.L.R. 1, where Judge Toulmin C.M.G., Q.C. concluded that the claimant's expert evidence provided little or no assistance. Amongst other criticisms, he pointed out that the report was overlong, included opinions on matters of fact and law which were questions for decision by the court and included expressions of opinion as to what the expert himself would have done in the defendant's position. The Court of Appeal did not comment on this passage: [2001] E.W.C.A. Civ. 1001; 2001 76 Con.L.R. 1 at 36). See further Chap. 8, para. 8–155, below.

opinion of value in resolving the issues before the court".[53] In *Royal Brompton Hospital NHS Trust v. Hammond (No. 7)*.[54] Judge Seymour Q.C. rejected the evidence of the claimant's expert architect in its entirety. He warned that, if experts are to give useful evidence, they must be given sufficient time to master the relevant documents. Further, they should avoid making assumptions (or accepting instructions to make assumptions) the accuracy of which is central to the questions which they are to address.[55] Finally, they should make sure that they have contemporary knowledge of practice in their own profession. The evidence from the claimant's expert architect was found wanting in each of these respects. The latter point serves to remind that an expert who has a working knowledge of contemporary practice in the relevant profession may often be more credible than an expert, however highly qualified, who has not practised for many years.

(iv) *Impartiality*

Fourthly, the evidence of an expert witness must be independent and impartial.   **6–017** CPR, r. 35.3 provides expressly that the duty of an expert to assist the court overrides any obligation to the party from whom he receives his instructions or by whom he is paid. The expert's report must be addressed to the court and not to his instructing party.[56] It is counter-productive to instruct a "hired gun", *i.e.* an expert whose evidence is biased towards the instructing party and who will seek to advocate his instructing party's case.[57] In *Anglo Group plc v. Winther Brown and Co. Ltd*,[58] Judge Toulmin C.M.G., Q.C. disregarded the evidence of two expert witnesses who had failed to act independently of their instructing parties. The judge also restated and extended the guidelines as to the duties and responsibilities of expert witnesses in civil cases which were set out by Cresswell J. in *National Justice Compania Naviera SA v. Prudential Assurance Co. Ltd (The Ikarian Reefer)*[59] so as to reflect the principles enshrined in the Civil Procedure Rules and emphasise the need for an expert witness to be impartial:

> "1. An expert witness should at all stages in the procedure, on the basis of the evidence as he understands it, provide independent assistance to the court and the parties by way of objective unbiased opinion in relation to matters within his expertise. This applies as much to the initial meetings of experts as to evidence at trial. An expert witness should never assume the role of an advocate.
>
> 2. The expert's evidence should normally be confined to technical matters on which the court will be assisted by receiving an explanation, or to evidence of common

---

[53] *The Queen v. Bonython* (1984) 38 S.A.S.R. 45 at 46, *per* King C.J.
[54] [2001] C.I.L.L. 1714. For the facts, see para. 8–149, below.
[55] See also the *Commercial Court Guide*, para. H2.12: an expert should state the assumptions upon which his opinion is based, and if a stated assumption is, in the opinion of the expert, unreasonable or unlikely, he should state that clearly.
[56] CPR, Pt 35, Practice Direction 1.1.
[57] In the valuer's negligence case of *Cemp Properties (U.K.) Ltd v. Dentsply Research and Development Corp.* [1991] 2 E.G.L.R. 197 at 200, the Court of Appeal commented that:
"It is a sad feature of modern litigation that expert witnesses, particularly in valuation cases, instead of giving evidence of their actual views as to the true position, enter into the arena and, as advocates, put forward the maximum or minimum figures as best suited to their side's interests. If experts do this, they must not be surprised if their views carry little weight with the judge. In this case, such evidence rightly led the judge to reject the expert evidence on both sides."
One of the main objectives of CPR, Pt 35 is to eliminate partisan expert evidence.
[58] Unreported, March 1, 2000.
[59] [1993] 2 Lloyd's Rep. 68 at 81.

professional practice. The expert witness should not give evidence or opinions as to what the expert himself would have done in similar circumstances or otherwise seek to usurp the role of the judge.

3. He should co-operate with the expert of the other party or parties in attempting to narrow the technical issues in dispute at the earliest possible stage of the procedure and to eliminate or place in context any peripheral issues. He should co-operate with the other expert(s) in attending without prejudice meetings as necessary and in seeking to find areas of agreement and to define precisely areas of disagreement to be set out in the joint statement of experts ordered by the court.

4. The expert evidence presented to the court should be, and be seen to be, the independent product of the expert uninfluenced as to form or content by the exigencies of the litigation.

5. An expert witness should state the facts or assumptions upon which his opinion is based. He should not omit to consider material facts which could detract from his concluded opinion.

6. An expert witness should make it clear when a particular question or issue falls outside his expertise.

7. Where an expert is of the opinion that his conclusions are based on inadequate factual information he should say so explicitly.

8. An expert should be ready to reconsider his opinion, and if appropriate, to change his mind when he has received new information or has considered the opinion of the other expert. He should do so at the earliest opportunity."

6–018   In *Stevens v. Gullis*,[60] the defendant's expert building surveyor had failed in his duty to act impartially and had also failed to comply with the requirements of the Civil Procedure Rules in relation to his report[61] and to a joint memorandum of matters agreed with the claimant's expert. The value which the court places upon the impartiality of expert evidence is demonstrated by the Court of Appeal's decision to uphold an order debarring the defendant from calling his expert, notwithstanding that both claimant and defendant had invited the court to accept his evidence.

(e) *The single joint expert*

6–019   A notable innovation introduced by the Civil Procedure Rules is the court's power, at any stage in an action, to direct that expert evidence on a particular issue shall be given by a single joint expert.[62] Either party is entitled to give the joint expert instructions but such instructions must be copied to the other party.[63] The parties are jointly and severally liable for the joint expert's fees and expenses unless the court directs otherwise.[64] In professional negligence cases, the use of single joint experts will commonly be restricted to issues which allow little scope for disagreement, such as matters of scientific or technical fact and/or quantum, rather than to issues of breach of duty which require the court to consider the range of professional practice. *The Queen's Bench Guide*[65] supports this approach:

---

[60] [2000] 1 All E.R. 527.
[61] CPR, r. 35.10(1) imposes requirements as to the contents of an expert's report, which are set out in CPR, Pt 35, Practice Direction, paras 1.2–1.6.
[62] CPR, r. 35.7.
[63] CPR, r. 35.8(1) and (2).
[64] CPR, r. 35.8(5).
[65] Para. 7.9.5.

"In very many cases it is possible for the question of expert evidence to be dealt with by a single expert. Single experts are, for example, often appropriate to deal with questions of quantum in cases where primary issues are as to liability. Likewise, where expert evidence is required in order to acquaint the court with matters of expert fact, as opposed to opinion, a single expert will usually be appropriate. There remain, however, a body of cases where liability will turn upon expert opinion evidence and where it will be appropriate for the parties to instruct their own experts. For example, in cases where the issue for determination is as to whether a party acted in accordance with proper professional standards, it will often be of value to the court to hear opinions of more than one expert as to the proper standard in order that the court becomes acquainted with the range of views existing upon the question and in order that the evidence can be tested in cross-examination."

In *Oxley v. Penwarden*,[66] the Court of Appeal confirmed that the Civil Proce- **6–020** dure Rules do not provide a presumption that a single joint expert will be instructed in every case. It permitted the parties in a complex clinical negligence case to instruct separate experts on the issue of causation, as to which there were two schools of thought in the medical profession.

It may happen that one party will be dissatisfied with the report of a single joint expert when it is produced and will wish to apply for permission to instruct another expert with a view to deciding whether there are aspects of the single joint expert's report which he should challenge. In *Daniels v. Walker*,[67] the Court of Appeal held that such permission might be granted where the dissatisfied party's reasons were not fanciful, especially where (as was the case in *Daniels*) the parties had initially agreed to instruct a single joint expert and the sum at stake was substantial. The question whether the dissatisfied party might go further and call his own expert at trial was considered in *Cosgrove v. Pattison*.[68] In that case, which involved a boundary dispute, Neuberger J. allowed a party to call evidence from a second expert when that party alleged that the single joint expert might be biased. He provided the following, non-exhaustive list of factors which would be relevant upon any application to call a second expert: the nature of the dispute, the number of issues to which the expert evidence was relevant, the reasons for requiring another expert's report, the amount of money at stake, the effect of allowing a further expert witness upon the conduct of the trial, the delay that calling a further expert would cause, any other special features and the overall justice to the parties in the context of the litigation.

---

[66] [2001] Lloyd's Rep. P.N. 347, CA.
[67] [2000] 1 W.L.R. 1382.
[68] [2001] T.L.R. 113.

CHAPTER 7

HUMAN RIGHTS AND PROFESSIONALS

	PARA.		PARA.
1. Introduction	7–01	(ii) Article 3	7–42
2. Relevant Convention rights	7–04	(iii) Article 6	7–43
(a) Article 6	7–05	(iv) Article 8	7–44
(b) Article 8	7–13	(v) Article 9	7–45
(c) Article 1 of Protocol No. 1	7–14	(vi) Article 12	7–46
3. Negligence and duty of care	7–19	7. Particular issues arising under the	
(a) Z. v. United Kingdom	7–21	HRA in relation to Medical	
(b) Interlocutory striking out	7–23	Practitioners	7–47
(c) Switch from Article 6(1) to		(a) Clinical negligence and the	
Article 13	7–24	*Bolam* test	7–47
(d) Tort or Convention?	7–26	(b) Right to treatment	7–50
(e) Claims not governed by the		(c) Withdrawal of treatment	7–55
HRA	7–28	(d) Consent to treatment	7–59
4. Immunities	7–30	(e) Right of access to confidential	
5. Lawyers	7–31	information	7–60
(a) Wasted costs orders	7–32	(f) Disclosure of confidential	
(b) Lawyer/client confidentiality		information	7–61
and the Convention	7–33	(g) Disclosure of medical records	
6. Medical practitioners	7–36	and confidentiality	7–62
(a) Introduction	7–36	(h) Patients' complaints	
(b) Relevant Articles in relation to		procedures	7–64
Medical Practitioners	7–38	8. Professional disciplinary	
(i) Article 2	7–39	proceedings	7–65

1. INTRODUCTION

The Human Rights Act 1998 ("HRA") was passed to give "further effect" to the   **7–001**
European Convention for the Protection of Human Rights and Fundamental
Freedoms 1950 ("the Convention") in domestic law. The Act has done this by
four key methods:

(1) by section 6 of the HRA, it has created a new statutory tort, making it
unlawful for a "public authority" to act incompatibly with the Convention. A "Public authority" is defined to include courts and tribunals and
any person or body who exercises a "public function". The court's duty
arising from section 6 means that the Convention has effect on both the
common law and equity;

(2) by section 7 of the HRA, it empowers a "victim"[1] of a violation of
Convention rights to bring proceedings against a "public authority"

---

[1] HRA, s.7(7). The test is the same as under Article 34 of the Convention. An individual only has
standing if he is actually and directly affected by the act or omission which is the subject of the
complaint, although he may also be a victim if he could potentially be affected by the act or omission:
Dudgeon v. United Kingdom [1982] 4 E.H.R.R. 149.

guilty of such a violation or raise the violation in any legal proceedings;

(3) by section 3 of the HRA, it has created a strong interpretive obligation on judges and administrative decision-makers to construe all past and future legislation compatibly with the Convention, "so far as it is possible to do so"; and

(4) by section 2 of the HRA, it has placed a duty on courts to "take into account" Strasbourg jurisprudence whenever a Convention issue arises.

7–002   The HRA came into force on October 2, 2000.[1a] The impact on civil law to date has been appreciable as the following examples highlight:

(1) On occasion, an action will now succeed before domestic courts using the HRA when it would have failed under pre-existing domestic law (*e.g. Marcic v. Thames Water Utilities*,[2] a claim arising out of serious and repeated flooding of the claimant's premises with foul water due to the failure to effect remedial drainage work where a claim under the HRA for a continuing failure to act after October 2, 2000 succeeded where a claim based on nuisance or breach of statutory duty would fail).

(2) The impetus of Article 8 (the right to respect for private life) has led the domestic courts to begin to develop a substantive law of privacy in *Douglas v. Hello!*[3]

(3) The Civil Procedure Rules ("CPR") and rules of evidence are in turn being measured against the benchmark of the Convention for compatibility.

(4) The approach of the European Court of Human Rights ("the European Court") in *Z v. United Kingdom*[4] may provide an added incentive to litigants to frame tortious claims based on pre-October 2000 acts or omissions additionally as a breach of a Convention right so that if they do not succeed before the English courts, they can argue for a remedy in Strasbourg based on breach of the State's obligation to provide an effective remedy before a national authority for the alleged Convention violation under Article 13.

7–003   The primary effect of the HRA is in relation to issues of procedure and in relation to substantive legal areas such as tort, administrative law and equity. As a general rule, it has limited application to contract law. This chapter seeks to provide an introduction to the interaction between the HRA and professional liability. It is based on Chapter 17—"Professional Liability and Negligence" of

---

[1a] The Human Rights Act 1998 (Commencement No. 2) Order 2000 (S.I. 2000 No. 1851) (c.47)—apart from s.18 (appointment of judges), s.20 (powers of ministers to make orders under the HRA) and s.21(5) (substitution of other sentences for the death penalty) which came into force on the passing of the Act on November 9, 1998: s.22(2) of the HRA; and s.19 (statements of compatibility) which came into force on November 24, 1998; see the Human Rights Act 1998 (Commencement) Order 1998 (S.I. 1998, No. 2882) (c.71).

[2] *The Independent*, July 9, 2001, H.H.J. Havery Q.C.

[3] [2000] 2 W.L.R. 817, CA.

[4] Application No. 29392/95, unreported, May 10, 2001.

L. Mulcahy (ed.), *Human Rights and Civil Practice* (Sweet & Maxwell 2001). Reference should be made to that text for a fuller discussion of the HRA and its ramifications both for professional liability and for its implications on civil procedure and evidence.[5]

2. RELEVANT CONVENTION RIGHTS

The Articles of the Convention that are of principal relevance to professional liability are:　　　　　　　　　　　　　　　　　　　　　　　　　　　　**7–004**

- Article 6: the right to a fair trial;

- Article 8: the right to respect for private and family life, home and correspondence; and

- Article 1 of Protocol No. 1: the right to peaceful enjoyment of possessions.

(a) *Article 6*

Article 6 states:　　　　　　　　　　　　　　　　　　　　　　　　　　**7–005**

"(1) In the determination of his civil rights and obligations or of any criminal charge against him, everyone is entitled to a fair and public hearing within a reasonable time by an independent and impartial tribunal established by law. Judgment shall be pronounced publicly but the press and public may be excluded from all or part of the trial in the interests of morals, public order or national security in a democratic society, where the interests of juveniles or the protection of private life of the parties so require, or to the extent strictly necessary in the opinion of the court in special circumstances where publicity would prejudice the interests of justice.

(2) Everyone charged with a criminal offence shall be presumed innocent until proved guilty according to law.

(3) Everyone charged with a criminal offence has the following minimum rights:
　　(a) to be informed promptly, in a language which he understands and in detail, of the nature and cause of the accusation against him;
　　(b) to have adequate time and facilities for the preparation of his defence;
　　(c) to defend himself in person or through legal assistance of his own choosing or, if he has not sufficient means to pay for legal assistance, to be given it free when the interests of justice so require;
　　(d) to examine or have examined witnesses against him and to obtain the attendance and examination of witnesses on his behalf under the same conditions as witnesses against him; and
　　(e) to have the free assistance of an interpreter if he cannot understand or speak the language used in court."

Article 6 concerns the "determination" of "civil rights and obligations" or of　**7–006**
a "criminal charge". These expressions have autonomous meanings within

---

[5] L. Mulcahy (ed.), *Human Rights and Civil Practice* (Sweet and Maxwell, 2001), Chap. 10— "The Civil Procedure Rules" and Chap. 11— "Evidence".

European human rights law.[6] The classification of proceedings in domestic law as civil will not necessarily be determinative. The European Court has adopted an incremental approach to the definition of "civil rights and obligations". They include issues arising in contract, tort,[7] commercial law, insurance law, real and personal property, intellectual property,[8] restitution,[9] planning,[10] education, family law and succession. Preliminary investigative procedures, such as a DTI investigation, are not determinative of a civil right.[11] Pure "public" law rights are not generally regarded as "civil rights", *e.g.* the entry and removal of immigrants.[12] Matters concerning public employment may be regarded as "public rights".[13] Further, proceedings regarding political rights are not within Article 6(1).[14] The European Court has focused on identification of a pecuniary right or interest in determining whether a right was a "civil" right: *Editions Périscope v. France.*[15]

7–007   The requirement for a "determination" means that there must be a dispute (in the French text, a *contestation*) concerning the civil right or obligation in question. Preliminary issues, issues of liability or quantum and issues solely as to costs all fall within the definition. Proceedings are not determinative of a civil right or obligation if they merely constitute a preliminary investigative stage[16] or form part of an administrative process.[17] The requirement that there be a dispute over a civil right in order to bring Article 6(1) into play has been construed to cover not only disputes concerning the scope of a right but also its very existence under domestic law.[18] In *Aït-Mouhoub v. France,*[19] in determining the applicability of Article 6(1), the court asked itself whether there was a dispute over a "civil right" which could be "said, at least on arguable grounds to be recognised under domestic law" and whether the proceedings were "directly decisive" of that right. Article 6(1) "does not in itself guarantee any particular content for the "rights and obligations" in the substantive law of the Contracting States". A civil right or obligation only attracts Article 6(1) when it is "recognised" by national law: *Powell and Rayner v. United Kingdom,*[20] though it is not always easy to

---

[6] L. Mulcahy, *op. cit.,* paras 3.55 *et seq.*

[7] A pending negligence claim is a possession within the meaning of Art. 1 of Protocol No. 1 (*Pressos Compania SA v. Belgium* (1996) 21 E.H.R.R. 301) and will therefore attract Art. 6. See also *Osman v. United Kingdom* (2000) 29 E.H.R.R. 245.

[8] *British American Tobacco Co. Ltd v. Netherlands* (1996) 21 E.H.R.R. 409.

[9] *Krcmár v. Czech Republic,* Application No. 35376/97 March 3, 2000, European Court.

[10] *Allan Jacobbson v. Sweden (No. 2),* Application No. 16970/90, Judgment of February 19, 1998 at para. 39.

[11] *Fayed v. United Kingdom* (1994) 18 E.H.R.R. 393.

[12] *Uppal v. United Kingdom* (1981) 3 E.H.R.R. 391.

[13] *Koseck v. Germany* (1987) 9 E.H.R.R. 328; *Neigel v. France* [1997] E.H.R.L.R. 424; *Argento v. Italy* (1999) 28 E.H.R.R. 719. See now *Pellegrin v. France* (2001) 31 E.H.R.R. 651 in which the European Court has reviewed the law in this area and narrowed the employment disputes excluded from the scope of Art. 6(1) to those which are raised by public servants whose duties typify the specific activities of the public service insofar as they are designed to safeguard the general interests of the State and of other public authorities (*e.g.* the armed forces or police).

[14] *Pierre-Bloch v. France* (1998) 26 E.H.R.R. 202.

[15] (1992) 14 E.H.R.R. 597, para. 40.

[16] *Fayed v. United Kingdom* (1994) 18 E.H.R.R. 393.

[17] *R. v. Lord Chancellor, ex p. Lightfoot* [2000] 2 W.L.R. 318, CA; [1999] 2 W.L.R. 1126, *per* Laws J.

[18] *Ashingdane v. United Kingdom* (1985) 7 E.H.R.R. 528.

[19] (2000) 30 E.H.R.R. 382.

[20] (1990) 12 E.H.R.R. 355. See also *W v. United Kingdom* (1988) 10 E.H.R.R. 29.

distinguish between procedural and substantive limitations: *Fayed v. United Kingdom*.[21]

Proceedings may be designated as a "criminal charge" irrespective of the **7–008** domestic law designation by reference to three criteria formulated by the European Court in *Engel v. Netherlands*[22]:

(1) the classification in domestic law;

(2) the nature of the offence or conduct in question; and

(3) the severity of any possible penalty.

If a domestic court can impose imprisonment, this will generally be sufficient to define the proceedings as "criminal" unless the "nature, duration or manner of execution of the imprisonment" is not "appreciably detrimental".[23] So, for instance, prison disciplinary proceedings[24] and contempt proceedings[25] have been held to be criminal proceedings for the purpose of Article 6, notwithstanding their domestic designation.

Article 6(1), which applies to both civil and criminal proceedings, encom- **7–009** passes various express and implied rights. The express rights are:

(1) the right to a fair hearing;

(2) the right to a public hearing except to the extent that (a) it is strictly necessary where publicity would prejudice the interests of justice or in the interests of (b) morals (c) public order (d) national security (e) juveniles or (f) the protection of the private life of the parties;

(3) the right to a hearing within a reasonable time;

(4) the right to an independent and impartial tribunal established by law; and

(5) public judgment.

The right of access to a court, which has been implied into Article 6[26] is of **7–010** general importance in relation to any restrictions on the liability of potential defendants. This right is not absolute but is qualified. However, any restriction must be justified in that:

(a) it must have a legitimate aim;

(b) it must not impair the very essence of the right; and

(c) the restriction must be proportionate to the aim to be achieved.[27]

---

[21] (1994) 18 E.H.R.R. 393, para. 67.
[22] *Engel v. Netherlands* (1979) 1 E.H.R.R. 647.
[23] *ibid.*, para. 82.
[24] *Campbell & Fell v. United Kingdom* (1985) 7 E.H.R.R. 165; *cf. McFeeley v. United Kingdom* (1981) 3 E.H.R.R. 161. See also *Greenfield v. Secretary of State for the Home Department, The Times,* March 6, 2001, Div. Ct.; *R. v. Carroll and another, ex p. Secretary of State for the Home Department,* unreported, February 16, 2001, Admin. Ct. (adjudications relating to prisoners not legal proceedings but disciplinary proceedings).
[25] *Harman v. United Kingdom* (1984) 38 D.R. 53; Application No. 10038/82.
[26] See *Golder v. United Kingdom* (1979) 1 E.H.R.R. 524.
[27] *Stubbings v. United Kingdom* (1997) 23 E.H.R.R. 213.

7–011   Other implied rights are the right to equality of arms, which means that each party must be afforded a reasonable opportunity to present his case (including his evidence) under conditions which do not place him at a substantial disadvantage *vis-à-vis* his opponent,[28] and the right to effective participation in a hearing.

7–012   Article 6(1) is applicable to all proceedings including actions between private parties and is therefore of particular relevance to the professional liability context, which will often involve purely private parties. In addition to the rights set out above, a defendant to a criminal charge also enjoys the following additional rights:

(a) the right against self-incrimination implied into Article 6(1);

(b) the presumption of innocence set out in Article 6(2); and

(c) the specific procedural guarantees set out in Article 6(3) including the right to know the nature of the charge against him, the right to have sufficient time and facilities to adequately prepare a defence and the right to legal aid where the interests of justice so require.

(b) *Article 8*

7–013   Article 8 states:

> "(1) Everyone has the right to respect for his private and family life, his home and his correspondence.
>
> (2) There shall be no interference by a public authority with the exercise of this right except such as is in accordance with the law and is necessary in a democratic society in the interests of national security, public safety or the economic well-being of the country, for the prevention of disorder or crime, for the protection of health or morals, or for the protection of the rights and freedoms of others."

Article 8(1) provides a right to respect for private and family life, home and correspondence. The right to private life provided by this section is a qualified right and is subject to restrictions justified by reference to Article 8(2), *e.g.* national security, the economic well-being of the country and the protection of the rights and freedoms of others. Any derogation from the right must also be "in accordance with the law", which means that it must have a positive legal basis and must be "necessary in a democratic society" which means that the interference must (i) have a pressing social aim and (ii) be proportionate to the aim to be achieved. It is important to note that Article 8 has "vertical effect" in that it restrains infringements of privacy by a public authority. It does not, prima facie, apply between individuals (so-called "horizontal effect"). However, since the court is a public body, it can be argued that it should ensure that there are no unwarranted interferences with the interests protected by Article 8, even by private bodies.[29] It is clear that some judges are already taking this line[30] though the full degree of the HRA's horizontal effect is not yet apparent.

---

[28] *Dombo Beheer B.V. v. Netherlands* (1994) 18 E.H.R.R. 213, para. 33. See also *Neumeister v. Austria* (1979) 1 E.H.R.R. 91.

[29] See L. Mulcahy, *op. cit.*, paras 5.15 *et seq.*

[30] *R. v. Lambert* [2001] 3 W.L.R. 206, para. 114; *Venables v. Newsgroup Newspapers Ltd* [2001] 2 W.L.R. 1038, QBD, para. 27.

(c) *Article 1 of Protocol No. 1*

Article 1 of Protocol No. 1 to the Convention states: 7–014

"Every natural or legal person is entitled to the peaceful enjoyment of his possessions. No one shall be deprived of his possessions except in the public interest and subject to the conditions provided for by law and by the general principles of international law.

The preceding provisions shall not, however, in any way impair the right of a State to enforce such laws as it deems necessary to control the use of property in accordance with the general interest or to secure the payment of taxes or other contributions or penalties."

Article 1 of Protocol No. 1 encompasses three principles: 7–015

(1) the right to peaceful enjoyment of possessions;

(2) the right not to be deprived of possessions except in the public interest and in accordance with the law; and

(3) the State's right to exercise control over possessions in accordance with the general interest or to secure the payment of taxes, etc.

Article 1 of Protocol No. 1 protects economic rights. Possessions include all   7–016
movable and immovable property, contractual rights including leases, orders for possession of property,[31] judgment debts,[32] shares,[33] goodwill[34] and even a claim for compensation in tort.[35] Both natural and legal persons are expressly conferred with rights under this Article.

The European Court has shown a tendency to assimilate the assessment of all   7–017
interferences with the peaceful enjoyment of possessions under a single test of fair balance: any interference must not place a disproportionate burden on the individual owner or result in discriminatory treatment. It has in general seen the availability of an effective remedy and the provision of compensation[36] as a necessary element in preserving a fair balance, whether the interference involves the deprivation of property or the control of its use. In relation to compensation, Article 1 of Protocol No. 1 requires payment of an amount reasonably related to the value of the property, but does not guarantee a right to full compensation in all circumstances.[37]

Other Articles of the Convention which are relevant to clinical negligence such   7–018
as Article 2 (the right to life) are discussed at paragraph 7–038, below.

3. NEGLIGENCE AND DUTY OF CARE

In 1998, the European Court gave what was perceived to be a landmark judgment   7–019
in *Osman v. United Kingdom*.[38] The case concerned a claim brought against the

---

[31] *Immobiliare Saffi v. Italy* (2000) 30 E.H.R.R. 756.
[32] *Agneessens v. Belgium* (1988) 58 D.R. 63, Application No. 12164/86.
[33] *Bramelid and Malmstrom v. Sweden* (1982) 5 E.H.R.R. 249.
[34] *Van Marle v. Netherlands* (1986) 8 E.H.R.R. 483.
[35] *Pressos Compania Naviera SA v. Belgium* (1996) 21 E.H.R.R. 301.
[36] See, *e.g. Holy Monasteries v. Greece* (1995) 20 E.H.R.R. 1.
[37] *Papachelas v. Greece* (2000) 30 E.H.R.R. 923, para. 48 (legitimate objectives of "public interest" may call for less than reimbursement of full market value).
[38] (2000) 29 E.H.R.R. 245.

police arising out of the failure to protect a child, Ahmet Osman, from the threatening and obsessive attentions of a teacher culminating in serious injury to Ahmet and the death of his father. The Court of Appeal struck out the claim applying the rule formulated by the House of Lords in *Hill v. Chief Constable of the West Yorkshire Police*[39] that it was not fair, just and reasonable for the police to owe a duty to an individual member of the public in relation to the investigation and suppression of crime. The European Court of Human Rights held that to strike out a claim based on the failure of a claimant to establish a duty of care where the court had held that it was not fair, just and reasonable to impose such a duty[40] in that class of case was a disproportionate restriction on the claimant's right of access to a court and violated Article 6 of the Convention. The Court held that the approach created a blanket "immunity" for the police in relation to their primary function.

7–020   The application of Article 6 as formulated in *Osman* undoubtedly hindered the use of striking out, a very important tactical weapon in professional negligence cases, for a couple of years. The European Court subsequently resiled from this position in *Z v. United Kingdom*[41] and *T.P. & K.M. v. United Kingdom*[42] (both complaints to Strasbourg arising out of the child abuse cases in *X (Minors) v. Bedfordshire County Council*[43]) conceding that the striking out of the cases where domestic courts held that it was not fair, just and reasonable to impose a duty of care was a matter of substantive law and did not violate Article 6(1). However, the Court found a violation of Article 13 of the Convention (the right to an effective remedy before a national authority). This is itself likely to impact on striking out and possibly also on substantive law.

(a) *Z v. United Kingdom*

7–021   The applicants in *Z* were four siblings. Over a period of four-and-a-half years, serious concerns were raised about the health and well-being of the applicants, including reports that some of the children were stealing food from school bins, that they were kept in filthy rooms or had physical bruising. Ultimately, the children were placed in emergency foster care after their mother threatened to batter them if they were not taken into care. The Official Solicitor commenced proceedings on behalf of the applicants against the local authority, claiming damages for negligence on the basis that the authority, through its child protection staff including psychiatrists and social workers, failed to have proper regard for the children's welfare and to take effective steps to protect them. The applicants' claims were struck out in proceedings culminating in the House of Lords. Lord Browne-Wilkinson, who gave the leading judgment, stated that public policy considerations were such that local authorities should not be held liable in negligence in respect of the exercise of their statutory duties safeguarding the welfare of children under the Children Act 1989. The applicants made a complaint to the European Commission of Human Rights in Strasbourg.

---

[39] [1989] A.C. 53, HL.
[40] This is the third limb of the three-limb test for the existence of a duty of care established in *Caparo Industries plc v. Dickman* [1990] 2 A.C. 605, HL, the first two being reasonable foreseeability of loss or damage and proximity between the claimant and defendant.
[41] Application No. 29392/95, May 10, 2001; *The Times*, May 31, 2001.
[42] Application No. 28945/95, May 10, 2001; *The Times*, May 31, 2001.
[43] [1995] 2 A.C. 633, HL.

The Commission applied the principles established in *Osman* to the facts of *Z* and held that there had been a breach of the right of access to court in Article 6 and a breach of Article 3 (the prohibition on inhuman or degrading treatment). The case was then referred to the European Court.[43a] In its judgment,[44] the Court also found a violation of Article 3, agreeing with the Commission that the failure to provide the applicants with appropriate protection against serious, long-term neglect and abuse breached the prohibition on inhuman and degrading treatment.[45] In relation to Article 6(1) and the claimed violation of the right of access to a court, the Court considered Article 6(1) to be applicable to the case on the grounds that there was a serious and genuine dispute about the existence of the right asserted by the applicants under the domestic law of negligence, as shown by the grant of legal aid to the applicants and permission to appeal to the House of Lords. However, it did not consider Article 6(1) to have been violated. The Court expressly resiled from *Osman*, stating that it considered its reasoning in that judgment to have been based on an understanding of the law of negligence which had to be reviewed. It accepted the Government's argument that the inability of the applicants to sue the local authority flowed not from an "immunity" but from the applicable principles governing the substantive right of action in domestic law.[46] Accordingly, the Court appeared to have effectively accepted that *Osman* was decided *per incuriam* although it did not expressly overrule the decision. However, the Court having found that there was no violation of Article 6(1), went on to hold that there was a violation of Article 13 (the right to an effective remedy before a national authority for breach of a Convention right)[47] and awarded damages by way of just satisfaction for breach of the applicants' rights under Article 3.

The European Court's decision in *T.P. & K.M. v. United Kingdom*[48] was to the   **7–022**
same effect as *Z* though it involved a primary breach of a different Article, namely Article 8. The European Court found that the failure by the local authority to submit promptly the question of disclosure of a video interview and its transcript for determination in care proceedings deprived the applicants of an adequate involvement in the decision-making process and violated the right to respect for family life in Article 8 of the Convention.[49] It also found a violation of Article 13 because the applicants did not have the possibility of obtaining an enforceable award of compensation for the damage suffered due to the breach of Article 8.[50] The implications of *Z* and *T.P. & K.M.* are now considered.

(b) *Interlocutory striking out*

In light of *Z*, there is almost certainly now no restraint on domestic courts   **7–023**
imposed by Article 6(1) in relation to striking out claims based on a failure to establish a duty of care because it is not fair, just and reasonable to impose one. The European Court has accepted that this constitutes a matter of substantive domestic law and that Article 6(1) is not violated in principle. However, in *Z*, the

---

[43a] (1999) 28 E.H.R.R. CD 65; [2000] 2 F.C.R. 245, Eur. Comm. H.R.
[44] Application No. 29392/95, May 10, 2001; *The Times*, May 31, 2001.
[45] *ibid.*, para. 75.
[46] Application No. 29392/95, May 10, 2001; *The Times*, May 31, 2001, para. 100.
[47] *ibid.*, para. 111.
[48] Application No. 28945/95, May 10, 2001; *The Times*, May 31, 2001.
[49] *ibid.*, para. 82.
[50] *ibid.*, para. 110.

Court did not expressly overrule *Osman*. Accordingly, it is not wholly clear whether *Osman* survives but is now confined to its own facts (and perhaps therefore continues to apply in relation to public interest immunity on the part of the police arising from the decision of *Hill v. Chief Constable of West Yorkshire*[51]) or whether *Osman* has been impliedly overruled. It is suggested that the domestic courts will probably adopt the latter position. However, there is still scope for an *Osman* argument if a decision concerns more than one aspect of the exercise of local authorities' powers and duties such that it can be said to amount to an arbitrary removal of the courts' jurisdiction to determine a whole range of civil claims.[52]

(c) *Switch from Article 6(1) to Article 13*

7-024   Article 13 guarantees an "effective remedy before a national authority" to everyone who claims that his rights and freedoms under the Convention have been violated,[53] so long as that claim is arguable in terms of the Convention.[54] Unlike Article 6(1) which applies to protect the right of access to a court in relation to *any* civil right or obligation which is merely arguable in domestic law, the right to an effective remedy under Article 13 is limited to providing an effective remedy for an "arguable" breach of another Convention right. Accordingly, Article 13 is parasitic upon establishing the arguability of another Convention right. It is therefore weaker in the protection given to a complainant than Article 6. Article 13 requires that where an individual considers himself to have been prejudiced by a measure allegedly in breach of the Convention, he should have a remedy before a national authority in order to have the claim decided and, if appropriate, to obtain redress.[55] The authority referred to in Article 13 does not need to be a judicial authority[56] and Article 13 does not require any particular remedy.[57] The aggregate of the possible channels of redress in the national legal system may be taken into account.[58]

7-025   Article 6(1) is incorporated into domestic law through the HRA whilst Article 13 is not. Accordingly, on the face of it, the courts will not be in breach of their obligation under section 6 of the HRA to act compatibly with Convention rights if they fail to provide an effective remedy pursuant to Article 13. However, before the European Court, the State (in the "person" of the U.K. Government) can be liable for its collective failure (including by its courts) to provide an effective remedy before a national authority for an individual to argue that his Convention rights have been violated. Since courts do have a duty under section 2 of the HRA to take into account Strasbourg case law, including that relating to Article 13,[59] this may influence courts in favour of allowing a claim to proceed

---

[51] [1989] A.C. 53, HL.
[52] *Z v. United Kingdom*, Application No. 29392/95, May 10, 2001; *The Times*, May 31, 2001, para. 98.
[53] *Klass v. Germany* (1980) 2 E.H.R.R. 214, para. 64.
[54] *Boyle and Rice v. United Kingdom* (1988) 10 E.H.R.R. 425, para. 52.
[55] *Klass v. Germany* (1980) 2 E.H.R.R. 214, para. 64; *Leander v. Sweden* (1987) 9 E.H.R.R. 433, para. 77(a).
[56] *Leander v. Sweden* (1987) 9 E.H.R.R. 433, para. 77(b).
[57] *Vilvarajah v. United Kingdom* (1992) 14 E.H.R.R. 248, para. 122.
[58] *Silver v. United Kingdom* (1983) 5 E.H.R.R. 347, paras 113(c) and 118; *Leander v. Sweden* (1987) 9 E.H.R.R. 433, para. 77(c).
[59] See H.L. Deb., November 18, 1997, col. 476 (L. Chancellor).

to a full hearing on the merits as a matter of existing domestic law in order to avoid the State subsequently being found by the European Court to be in breach of Article 13 for having struck out the claim. The Court recognised in *Z* that a claimant who wishes to complain of a breach of his Convention rights does post-HRA have an effective remedy for Article 13 purposes through the claim mechanism in section 7(1) of the HRA. However, the operation of the limitation provision in section 22(4) of the HRA means that a claim can only be brought under section 7(1)(a) if the act or omission occurs on or after the date of the HRA coming into force, *i.e.* October 2, 2000. This gives rise to a potential inconsistency in treatment between claims based on acts or omissions which occurred prior to October 2, 2000 where no HRA claim will lie, and those based on acts or omissions following that date, where a claimant can bring a claim under the HRA based on the same set of facts and circumstances. This inconsistency may also influence the willingness of the courts to countenance claims in tort in order to avoid divergence of treatment in similar cases solely related to the date the cause of action arose.

(d) *Tort or Convention?*

One likely result of *Z* is that in circumstances where a cause of action in tort is not clearly established as a matter of domestic law, claims are now more likely to be framed as claims under section 7(1)(a) of the HRA either independently of or, more probably in addition to, a tortious claim. Examples include the following: **7–026**

    (1) actions against the police arising out of death or serious injury—Article 2 (right to life);

    (2) clinical negligence—Article 2 (right to life);

    (3) claims based on failures in child protection against psychiatrists, social workers and local authorities—Article 3 (prohibition on torture inhuman or degrading treatment), or if less serious, Article 8 (right to respect for private life); and

    (4) claims against educational psychologists based on failure to diagnose dyslexia or other special needs—Article 8 (right to respect for private life) or possibly, Article 2 of Protocol No. 1 (right to education).

Framing a claim under the HRA instead of or in addition to a claim in tort has the following implications: **7–027**

    (1) a one-year limitation period applies rather than the usual limitation periods in tort[60];

    (2) there may be a potential difference in level of damages awarded. Domestic courts are obliged by section 8 of the HRA to award damages on same principles as the European Court, whose awards have generally been low[61];

---

[60] L. Mulcahy, *op. cit.*, para. 8.26.
[61] *ibid.*, paras 9.18 *et seq.*

(3) under certain Convention Articles (*e.g.* Articles 8 and 10), once an interference is established by the claimant or admitted by the defendant, the burden of proof is then on the defendant to justify his conduct. This amounts to an effective reversal of the traditional burden of proof in civil claims[62]; and

(4) the evidential requirements in a Convention claim may be different. Evidence of social statistics, government policy and the existence of other remedies may be required, in contrast to traditional common law claims.[63]

(e) *Claims not governed by the HRA*

7–028 In the case of claims arising out of acts and omissions which took place prior to October 2, 2000, where no section 7(1)(a) of the HRA claim lies, the issue arises as to what the courts will now do in relation to applications to strike out tortious claims that come before them which also raise arguable violations of Convention rights. It is possible that there will be an indirect effect arising from the Court's finding in *Z* of a violation of Article 13. If a claim based on an act or omission which pre-dates the coming into force of the HRA can be:

(1) framed as an arguable breach of a substantive Convention right; and

(2) there is no adequate alternative extra-judicial remedy

this may lead to reluctance on the part of domestic courts to strike out a claim brought in tort because this will encourage the claimant who has been shut out to take his case immediately to Strasbourg. Such a claimant is likely to succeed in Strasbourg in showing a violation of Article 13 if he can make out an arguable breach of a substantive Convention right and show that he has been denied the opportunity to argue that right and, if appropriate, to obtain redress before a national authority.

7–029 The influence of *Z* and the hitherto less well-known Article 13 may mean that, despite the fact that *Osman*, read in the light of *Z*, no longer outlaws the striking out of cases for failure to establish a duty of care on public policy grounds because it is contrary to Article 6(1), there are still Convention constraints on the striking out of claims and the expansionist trend to substantive tortious liability in novel areas of the law may nevertheless continue. It is also likely that *Z* will provide an impetus for the future development of claims under the HRA and in tort in parallel with each other.

4. IMMUNITIES

7–030 European human rights law does not look favourably on immunities from suit. In *Fayed v. United Kingdom*,[64] the European Court held that it would not be

---

[62] *ibid.*, para. 4.50.
[63] *ibid.*, para. 8.62.
[64] (1994) 18 E.H.R.R. 393.

consistent with the rule of law or the basic principle of access to a court underlying Article 6(1) if a state could:

> "without restraint or control by the Convention enforcement bodies, remove from the jurisdiction of the courts a whole range of civil claims or confer immunities from civil liability on large groups or categories of persons".[65]

Had it survived *Arthur J.S. Hall v. Simons*,[66] advocates' immunity may potentially have infringed Article 6. In this context, there remains scope for Article 6 arguments in relation to the *Hunter v. Chief Constable of the West Midlands Police*[67] principle that it is an abuse of process for a person to bring a civil action by way of a collateral attack on a final decision of a court if that principle is extended beyond narrow limits. Further, there are possible Convention arguments in relation to the outstanding issue of whether the abolition of advocates' immunity has prospective or retrospective effect.[68] Any extension to the current immunities of arbitrators, experts or witnesses could also arguably contravene Article 6.[69]

5. LAWYERS

The HRA is likely to raise new lawyers' liability issues where lawyers have **7-031** failed to consider or raise HRA points or where wasted costs orders are made for the raising of what a judge regards as unnecessary arguments,[70] possibly including unnecessary human rights arguments.[71] Two areas of relevance to lawyers' liabilities—the wasted costs jurisdiction and legal professional privilege—are now considered.

(a) *Wasted costs orders*

The applicability of Article 6(1) to the wasted costs jurisdiction is not wholly **7-032** clear. In *B v. United Kingdom*,[72] the European Commission stated that the making of a wasted costs order in that case against a solicitor who had failed to arrange legal representation in a criminal case did not involve the determination of "civil rights and obligations" but concerned the administration of justice and that Article 6(1) was not applicable. However, the European Court has not yet considered the applicability of Article 6(1) to the wasted costs jurisdiction and its general approach to Article 6(1) would suggest that it might well consider it to

---

[65] *ibid.*, para. 65.
[66] [2000] 3 W.L.R. 543, HL.
[67] [1982] A.C. 539, HL.
[68] Whilst a claimant might argue in favour of retrospective effect using Art. 6(1), a defendant might argue that such a course would infringe his legitimate expectation contrary to Art. 6(1) or Art. 1 of Protocol No. 1 (though even where an individual has a legitimate expectation that a certain state of affairs will prevail, Art. 1 of Protocol No. 1 does not necessarily protect such an expectation from the retrospective effect of a judicial decision: *Antoniades v. United Kingdom* (1990) 64 D.R. 232).
[69] See further L. Mulcahy, *op. cit.*, paras 17.41 *et seq.*
[70] *Arthur J.S. Hall v. Simons* [2000] 3 W.L.R. 543, at 589B–C, *per* L. Hope, HL (the power of the judge to make a wasted costs order in a criminal case in regard to advancing what the judge may regard as unnecessary arguments may breach the HRA).
[71] See, *e.g. Daniels v. Walker, Practice Note* [2000] 1 W.L.R. 1382 at 1386H–1387C.
[72] (1984) 38 D.R. 213, Application No. 10615/83.

be applicable. The formulation by the European Court of the "identification of a pecuniary right or interest" test for deciding whether a procedure is determinative of civil rights or obligations in *Editions Périscope v. France*[73] (which postdates *B v. United Kingdom*) might now be argued to encompass a wasted costs application. Where considerations of impropriety are in issue, it is likely that Article 6(1) is engaged in light of the settled view of the European Court that professional disciplinary proceedings regulating the right to practice a profession concern the determination of civil rights and must conform to Article 6(1): *Le Compte v. Belgium*.[74] If Article 6(1) applies on the ground that a wasted costs application does determine the respondent's civil rights and obligations, the procedure will attract the express and implied rights set out at paragraphs 7–09 and 7–011, above.

(b) *Lawyer/client confidentiality and the Convention*

7–033   The European Court has recognised under Article 8 the principle of the right to respect for communications between a person and his lawyer (this being important for the furtherance of a person's rights under Article 6): *Silver v. United Kingdom*.[75] The issue has principally arisen in the context of control over prisoners' correspondence by prison authorities. In *Campbell v. United Kingdom*,[76] the Court stated:

> "It is clearly in the general interest that any person who wishes to consult a lawyer should be free to do so under conditions which favour full and uninhibited discussion. It is for this reason that the lawyer-client relationship is, in principle, privileged.
> . . . the Court sees no reason to distinguish between the different categories of correspondence with lawyers which, whatever their purpose, concern matters of a private and confidential character. In principle, such letters are privileged under Article 8. This means that the prison authorities may open a letter from a lawyer to a prisoner when they have reasonable cause to believe that it contains an illicit enclosure which the normal means of detection have failed to disclose. The letter should, however, only be opened and should not be read. Suitable guarantees preventing the reading of the letter should be provided, *e.g.* opening the letter in the presence of the prisoner. The reading of a prisoner's mail to and from a lawyer, on the other hand, should only be permitted in exceptional circumstances when the authorities have reasonable cause to believe that the privilege is being abused in that the contents of the letter endanger prison security or the safety of others or are otherwise of a criminal nature."

7–034   In *Niemietz v. Germany*,[77] police searched a lawyer's offices looking for information to reveal the identity and possible whereabouts of a person who was the subject of a criminal investigation. The European Court held that the search violated Article 8, recognising that activities of a professional character could fall within the concept of private life and correspondence in Article 8. It recognised that where a lawyer was involved, an encroachment on professional secrecy might have repercussions on the proper administration of justice and the rights guaranteed by Article 6. In *Foxley v. United Kingdom*,[78] the European Court

---

[73] (1992) 14 E.H.R.R. 597.
[74] (1982) 4 E.H.R.R. 1. See also *Gautrin v. France* (1999) 28 E.H.R.R. 196.
[75] (1983) 5 E.H.R.R. 347.
[76] (1993) 15 E.H.R.R. 137.
[77] (1993) 16 E.H.R.R. 97.
[78] Application No. 33274/96, June 20, 2000; *The Times*, July 4, 2000.

found a violation of Article 8 when the applicant's trustee in bankruptcy, to whom the applicant's post was being redirected by order under section 371 of the Insolvency Act 1986, had opened and made copies of correspondence addressed to the applicant from his legal advisers. Lawyer/client confidentiality is also protected by E.C. law, which is another legal source of fundamental rights protection: Case 155/79 *A.M. & S. Europe Ltd v. Commission of the European Communities.*[79]

In the United Kingdom, the common law recognises the right to legal confi- **7–035** dentiality which arises between a person and their legal adviser as a matter of substantive law, not just procedure (except that the recognition is not afforded where the client is trying to use the relationship to commit a crime or for some unlawful purpose). Legal confidentiality is regarded as a right of great constitutional importance because it is seen as necessary bulwark of a person's right of access to justice whether as a claimant or as a defendant: *R. v. Derby Magistrates' Court, ex p.B.*[80] The general protection given to legal confidentiality in English law, through both the common law doctrine of legal professional privilege and the equitable doctrine of confidence, is likely to satisfy, and arguably go beyond, the requirements of Article 8.[81] The protection of legal professional privilege in domestic law is so strong that it will not be abrogated even where it may be relevant to the defence of a defendant charged with murder in a criminal trial.[82] However, the interrelationship between legal confidentiality and the right to a fair trial may need to be further scrutinised in light of the Convention, especially since Article 8(2) permits of an interference with Article 8(1) rights in the interests of the "the protection of the rights and freedoms of others" including the right to a fair trial under Article 6. The Rules Committee attempted to make a limited though unsuccessful inroad into privilege through the legislative route. However, in *General Mediterranean Holdings v. Patel,*[83] Toulson J. held that CPR, r. 48.7(3) (subsequently revoked), which permitted the court to order disclosure of privileged documents to the court and/or to the other party in the context of a wasted costs application against solicitors, was *ultra vires* to the extent that it cut down the substantive right to legal confidentiality. He had regard to the "high value which the [Strasbourg] court accorded to legal confidentiality" in coming to his decision.

6. MEDICAL PRACTITIONERS

(a) *Introduction*

Just as the implementation of the HRA has received significant media coverage, **7–036** so have cases involving medical practitioners attracted increasing publicity. Patients have become increasingly aware of their "rights" in relation to those who treat them and expectations of medical care and treatment have increased. As advances in science have brought benefits, there are also increasing legal and

---

[79] [1983] Q.B. 878.
[80] [1996] A.C. 487, HL.
[81] See, *e.g. R. v. Special Commissioners, ex p. Morgan Grenfell and Co.*, November 8, 2000, Admin. Ct.
[82] *R. v. Derby Magistrates' Court, ex p. B* [1996] A.C. 487, HL.
[83] [1999] 3 All E.R. 673.

moral difficulties as to how such technology should be applied. It is perhaps in this area of professional liability that the HRA is likely to have the most immediate impact.

7–037 A distinction in the Act's application may need to be drawn between the public and the private sectors. National Health Service ("NHS") patients being treated by general practitioners, health authorities and trusts can expect them as public authorities to act compatibility with Convention rights in relation to the provision of health care services. Individual rights of action under the HRA will also lie against the Department of Health in appropriate circumstances. However, the position of private patients is less clear. Whilst it would appear that Parliamentary intention was that those who treated patients privately would not be "public authorities" for the purpose of the HRA,[84] the position is less clear where, for example, NHS Trusts contract the treatment of patients out to private clinics. It would seem undesirable for a two-tier health care system to develop depending on the capacity in which a patient was being treated. It may well be that the courts will use their ability to interpret rights and duties in a manner which is compatible with Convention rights in such a way as to prevent such a situation arising. It seems unlikely that individual healthcare professionals, as opposed to their employing organisations, will be regarded as falling within the definition of "public authority".

(b) *Relevant Articles in relation to Medical Practitioners*

7–038 Medical issues encompass a fairly wide range of Convention articles, namely:

- Article 2: the right to life;
- Article 3: the right not to be subject to inhuman and degrading treatment;
- Article 6: the right to a fair trial, including proceedings before the General Medical Council and the General Dental Council[85];
- Article 8: the right to respect for private and family life;
- Article 9: the right to respect to freedom of thought, conscience and religion;
- Article 12: the right to marry and found a family; and
- Article 14: the prohibition of discrimination in relation to Convention rights.

(i) *Article 2*

7–039 Article 2 concerns the protection by law of human life. The right is absolute and, with one limited exception,[86] cannot be subject to derogation. The Article

---

[84] H.L. Deb., November 24, 1997, col. 811 (Lord Chancellor stated that doctors would be public authorities within the meaning of s.6 of the HRA in relation to their NHS practice but not their private practice). See further L. Mulcahy, *op. cit.*, chap. 8 and para. 8.17.
[85] See at paras 7–066 *et seq.*, below.
[86] The only derogation permitted by Art. 15 is in respect of deaths resulting from lawful acts of war.

imposes two duties on the State (and through section 6 of the HRA, on health authorities, NHS Trusts and the Department of Health):

(1) not to take a person's life save in the limited circumstances set out in Article 2(2)[87]; and

(2) to take reasonable measures to protect life.

The Article imposes both a negative obligation to refrain from depriving **7–040** someone of their life and a positive duty to take reasonable measures to protect life: *X v. United Kingdom.*[88] It also includes a duty on the State to take preventative operational measures to protect an individual whose life is at risk from the criminal acts of another individual: *Osman v. United Kingdom.*[89] Recognised as one of the most fundamental of all human rights, this article is likely to play a significant role in medical law issues. Despite the reference to "life", Article 2 is not restricted to cases where actual loss of life occurs. It is sufficient if loss of life is one possible consequence of the conduct complained of.[90]

Examples of the potential application of Article 2. Article 2 might be **7–041** invoked in the following situations[91]:

(a) *Abortion*: Prior to the HRA, the position in English law was that an unborn child had no existence separate from its mother and could be aborted under the terms of the Abortion Act 1967.[92] In *Paton v. United Kingdom,*[93] the Commission held that a foetus had no absolute right to life as the term "everyone" in Article 2 generally only applied post-natally but it left open the question whether the foetus did have some right to life (for example, if it was able to live independently of its mother). In *H v. Norway,*[94] the Commission held that the abortion of a foetus for social reasons was not contrary to Article 2 where there was "a difficult situation of life" in relation to the mother. These decisions, which allow a wide margin of appreciation in relation to the right to life, were relied on by one member of the Court of Appeal in the case of the conjoined twins in *Re A (Minors) (Conjoined Twins: Separation).*[95] Ward L.J. stated that Article 2 was subject to an implied limitation that justified the balancing approach taken

---

[87] Art. 2 expressly provides that deprivation of life shall not be regarded as inflicted in contravention of the Article when it results from the use of force which is no more than absolutely necessary: (a) in defence of any person from unlawful violence; (b) in order to effect a lawful arrest or to prevent the escape of a person lawfully detained; or (c) in action lawfully taken for the purpose of quelling a riot or insurrection.

[88] (1978) 14 D.R. 31.

[89] (2000) 29 E.H.R.R. 245.

[90] Reaffirmed by the European Court of Human Rights in *William and Anita Powell v. United Kingdom* [2000] E.H.R.L.R. 650 at 654; Application No. 45305/99, May 4, 2000.

[91] For more extensive treatment of these subjects, please see L. Mulcahy, *op. cit.*, paras 17.69–17.90.

[92] *Re F (in utero)* [1988] Fam. 122, CA; *St George's Healthcare NHS Trust v. S* [1998] 3 W.L.R. 936 at 957A.

[93] (1980) 3 E.H.R.R. 408.

[94] (1992) 73 D.R. 155.

[95] [2001] 2 W.L.R. 480; [2000] Lloyd's Rep. Med. 425, CA.

by the Court in allowing the twins to be separated despite the fact that this would cause certain death to one of the twins.[96]

(b) *Euthanasia*: Article 2 confers a right to life but not a right to die. Neither the Commission nor the Court has yet given a substantive ruling on the issue of euthanasia and again a wide margin of appreciation would seem applicable. The national court's duty to respect the sanctity of human life and the refusal to sanction a course of conduct aimed at terminating life or accelerating death was recently affirmed at first instance in *A National Health Service Trust v. D.*[97] See also *R. v. Director of Public Prosecutions, ex p. Dianne Pretty*[97a] in which the Divisional Court held that whilst the Convention might permit a state to allow assisted suicide, it did not require the state to allow it. Articles 2 and 3 of the Convention were said to be aimed at the protection and preservation of life and the dignity of death, not at protecting a person's right to procure his own death.

(c) *Withdrawal of treatment*: This is dealt with at paragraphs 7–055 *et seq.*, below;

(d) *Right to information on life-threatening risks*: Article 2 has been applied in the health and environmental contexts to life-threatening hazards in so far as these hazards may be attributed to the State.[98] Applying analogous principles, the HRA ought to be considered by medical authorities when deciding how to deal with potential life-threatening health risks and particularly in relation to the provision of advice or information relating to those risks.

(ii) *Article 3*

7–042   The right not to be subjected to inhuman or degrading treatment may be invoked in relation to issues of forced treatment or the maintenance of life by artificial support. It will often conflict with the right to life, but may nonetheless be relied upon as a basis for complaint. Article 3 will also apply to issues arising in relation to the refusal of treatment and experimental treatment.[99] The courts will have to grapple with whether the patient's definition of inhuman or degrading treatment, or that of the medical profession, should prevail.

(iii) *Article 6*[1]

7–043   Article 6 is perhaps the most important article as far as clinical negligence generally and tribunal procedure is concerned. It will also be possible for medical

---

[96] Walker L.J. and Brooke L.J. preferred to base their decision on the fact that the doctor's purpose in performing the operation was to save life, even if the extinction of another life was a virtual certainty and therefore this was not intentional killing. The word "intentionally" in Art. 2 was said to apply only where the purpose of the prohibited action was death (consistent with existing domestic law on this subject). The Court's consideration of the human rights aspects of the appeal is extremely brief.

[97] [2000] 2 F.L.R. 677; [2000] Lloyd's Rep. Med. 411; *The Times*, July 19, 2000, *per* Cazalet J.

[97a] *The Times*, October 23, 2001, DC.

[98] *LCB v. United Kingdom* (1999) 27 E.H.R.R. 212. See further L. Mulcahy, *op. cit.*, paras 17.85–17.87 and paras 19.70 *et seq.*

[99] The European Commission has held that experimental medical treatment may amount to inhuman treatment, if not torture, in the absence of consent: *X v. Denmark* (1983) D.R. 282; Application No. 9974/82. For further discussion of this issue see L. Mulcahy, *op. cit.*, para. 17.83.

[1] For an introduction to Art. 6 please see paras 7–005 *et seq.*, above and for a fuller treatment, please see L. Mulcahy, *op. cit.*, Chap. 3.

practitioners (and other healthcare professionals) to invoke Article 6 to protect their rights in disciplinary proceedings before their regulatory bodies. Even prior to the coming into force of the HRA, regulatory bodies were changing certain procedures in order to ensure compatibility with the Convention. Article 6 in the disciplinary context is dealt with at paragraphs 7–065 *et seq.*, below.

(iv) *Article 8*

The right to respect for private and family life affects a wider range of issues than might at first be thought including, for example, consent to treatment,[2] the right to information on life-threatening risks,[3] the confidentiality of medical records,[4] a patient's right of access to medical records[5] or disclosure of the fact that a person has HIV or AIDS.[6] It might also be arguable that the right to respect for private life in Article 8 supports an entitlement to abortion, an issue which has yet to be ruled upon by the European Court. However, in *Greenfield v. Irwin and others*,[7] Lord Justice Buxton indicated (albeit *obiter*[8]) that the claimant was highly unlikely to be able to rely on Article 8 in order to allow her to claim damages for loss of employment caused by reason of a negligent failure to diagnose a pregnancy. The court drew attention to the fact that states were permitted a wide margin of appreciation in relation to Article 8.

7–044

(v) *Article 9*

The right to freedom of thought, conscience and belief may be invoked in relation to issues of refusal of treatment. It may also be relevant where a medical practitioner holds a conscientious objection to abortion and the extent to which they may lawfully object to having any association whatsoever with an abortion procedure.[9]

7–045

(vi) *Article 12*

The right to marry and found a family may be relevant to issues of who is entitled to receive fertility treatment on the NHS.[10]

7–046

7. PARTICULAR ISSUES ARISING UNDER THE HRA IN RELATION TO MEDICAL PRACTITIONERS

(a) *Clinical negligence and the* Bolam *test*

It is suggested by some practitioners that Article 2 may provide a means for challenging the long established *Bolam* test and the court's adherence to the

7–047

---

[2] See para. 7–059, below.
[3] *Guerra v. Italy* (1998) 26 E.H.R.R.357; *López Ostra v. Spain* (1995) 20 E.H.R.R. 277.
[4] See paras 7–062 to 7–063, below.
[5] See para. 7–060, below.
[6] See L. Mulcahy, *op. cit.*, para. 17.88
[7] [2001] 1 W.L.R. 1279
[8] By reason of the fact that the HRA was not in force at the time of the original judgment.
[9] See further Leonard Hammer, "Abortion Objection in the United Kingdom Within the Framework of the European Convention on Human Rights and Fundamental Freedoms" in [1999] E.H.R.L.R. 564 at 575, who argues that s.4 of the Abortion Act 1967 does not provide sufficient protection for abortion objectors.
[10] See, *e.g. R. v. Human Fertilisation and Embryology Authority, ex p. Blood* [1999] Fam. 151; [1997] 2 All E.R. 687 and para. 7–053, below.

"respectable body of medical opinion" approach.[11] The argument put forward is that the *Bolam* test is inconsistent with the right to life unless the domestic courts construe the requirement to take reasonable care as equivalent to the requirement to make adequate provision for medical care. If the care provided is negligent then, by definition, it will not have been adequate. However, the converse may not apply and care that is inadequate is not necessarily negligent. It is suggested that Article 2 may do away with the need to establish negligence at all if a health authority fails to show that it has made adequate provision for medical care in circumstances where the life of the patient was at risk.

7–048   It is also suggested that Article 2 might be used to argue in the context of clinical negligence claims that death or injury could have been avoided if a more senior doctor had been made available to carry out the operation or provide the necessary care or treatment.[12] This could raise the *Bolam* standard from the reasonably competent "doctor" to, for example, the reasonably competent "consultant". The willingness of the courts to accept such changes to the principles for establishing liability in clinical negligence cases remains to be seen. In the light of the decision in *Powell v. United Kingdom*,[13] defendants to clinical negligence claims are likely to argue that once the healthcare system itself is found to be adequate, the behaviour of individual professionals within that system does not fall within the jurisdiction of Article 2. Support for this proposition may also be derived from the European Commission's decision in *Buckley v. United Kingdom*,[14] where the administration of drugs in circumstances leading to a patient's death did not disclose grounds for negligence in domestic law, thereby resulting in the Commission finding that the complaint under Article 2 was "manifestly ill-founded". However, in the *Powell* case,[15] the Court did state that the procedural obligation under Article 2:

> "extends to the need for an effective independent system for establishing the cause of death of an individual under the care and responsibility of health professionals and any liability on the part of the latter".

7–049   Whilst it is uncertain whether the HRA will cause the traditional principles of negligence in the medical context to be modified, Article 2 will undoubtedly provoke a re-evaluation of the policy considerations underlying the courts' review of professional judgments. Further, the ability to bring a direct action against a public authority for breach of Article 2 under section 7 of the HRA potentially creates a new and additional cause of action against health authorities or NHS Trusts which may develop on the basis of different principles to the tort of negligence.

(b) *Right to treatment*

7–050   There is scope for arguing under the HRA that health authorities and NHS Trusts are obliged to make adequate provision for medical care in all cases where the right to life of the patient in question would otherwise be endangered. The question was raised in *X v. Ireland*,[16] but the Commission held that it was

---

[11] See further Philip Havers Q.C. in Powers and Harris (eds), *Medical Law* (Butterworths, 1999).
[12] *ibid.*
[13] [2000] E.H.R.L.R. 650.
[14] (1997) 23 E.H.R.R. 101.
[15] [2000] E.H.R.L.R. 650.
[16] (1974) 7 D.R. 78.

unnecessary to determine this issue because the applicant had in fact received treatment and her life had not been endangered. In *Association X v. United Kingdom*,[17] it was held that the State must take adequate and appropriate steps to protect life and that this might raise issues with respect to the adequacy of medical care. The case concerned the steps taken by the state to reduce the risks to life by introducing a vaccination programme for children. On the facts before it, the Commission found no evidence to suggest that the vaccinations had been administered poorly or that proper steps had not been taken to minimise any risks.

The European Court has allowed Contracting States an almost unfettered **7–051** discretion in relation to the allocation of resources pursuant to the doctrine of the margin of appreciation.[18] Prior to the implementation of the HRA, domestic courts also showed a marked reluctance to become involved in decisions in this area. For example, in *R. v. Cambridge Health Authority, ex p. B*,[19] the Health Authority decided not to give a particular treatment to a young female patient suffering from leukaemia on the basis that it might only have a 20 per cent chance of success and therefore it was not in her best interests and scarce resources should not be allocated to it. The Court of Appeal upheld the Health Authority's decision stating that this was an area in which the Court could not make a judgment as to how a limited budget was best allocated to the maximum advantage of the maximum number of patients.[20]

It might at first appear that such an approach would no longer be consistent **7–052** with the Convention. The right to life is an absolute right to which, in theory, lack of financial resources to provide the care in question provides no defence. However, the European Court stated in *Osman v. United Kingdom*,[21] albeit in the context of the obligations on the police to take positive steps to protect life, that the Article 2 obligation must be interpreted in a way which "does not impose an impossible or disproportionate burden on the authorities".[22] Further, in *Powell v. United Kingdom*,[23] the Court stated that whilst Article 2 required the State to take appropriate steps to safeguard the lives of those within its jurisdiction, where the State made adequate provision for securing high professional standards among health professionals and the protection of patients' lives, matters such as errors of judgment or negligent co-ordination among health professional were insufficient to call a Contracting State to account from the standpoint of its obligations under Article 2. The HRA, however, allows courts to look at both the decision making process and the merits of the decision. Thus, resource allocation decisions will have to become more transparent.[24]

Blanket bans on treatment may be challenged as being incompatible with the **7–053** Convention. For example, a blanket ban on the basis of age may arguably contravene Articles 3, 8 and 14. If the ban related to resuscitation, it might also

---

[17] (1978) 14 D.R. 31.
[18] On the doctrine of margin of appreciation, see further L. Mulcahy, *op. cit.*, Chap. 4 and paras 4.22 *et seq.*
[19] [1995] 1 W.L.R. 898.
[20] *ibid.* at 906, *per* Sir Thomas Bingham M.R. See also James and Longley, "Judicial Review and Tragic Choices" in [1995] P.L. 367 and O'Sullivan, "The Allocation of Scarce Resources and the right to life under the ECHR" in [1998] P.L. 389.
[21] (2000) 29 E.H.R.R. 245.
[22] *ibid.*, para. 116.
[23] [2000] E.H.R.L.R. 650.
[24] Lord Irvine of Lairg, "The Development of Human Rights in Britain under an Incorporated Convention on Human Rights" in [1998] P.L. 221 at 224.

breach Article 2. A decision not to fund fertility treatment could potentially violate Articles 8 and 12.[25]

7–054   Hospital waiting lists may also be challenged if the facts merit it. In *Passannante v. Italy*,[26] the Commission held that excessive delay by a public authority in providing a medical service to which a patient is entitled, and the fact that such delay has (or is likely to have) a serious impact on the patient's health could amount to an interference with the right to respect for private life under Article 8(1). In *R. v. North and East Devon Health Authority, ex p. Coughlan*,[27] the Court of Appeal held that the decision of the health authority to close an NHS home in which the applicant was a resident constituted a breach of Article 8. Although Article 8(2) permits justification for an interference with the right to respect for private life on the ground of resources, such derogation would have to be applied without discrimination "on any ground" pursuant to Article 14.

(c) *Withdrawal of treatment*

7–055 As stated above, Article 2 provides for a right to live. It does not state that there is a duty to live. Equally, there is no right to die. This area is further complicated by the potential incapacity of patients to make clear their own wishes by reason of their medical condition. In *D v. United Kingdom*,[28] the European Court emphasised the importance of dying with dignity, although it declined to rule on the Article 2 contentions.

7–056   In *A National Health Service Trust v. D*,[29] a 19-month-old child suffered from a severe, chronic and worsening lung disease which meant that his life expectancy was very short. The paediatricians involved in his care were firmly of the opinion that it would not be in the child's best interest to be readmitted to intensive care to undergo further resuscitation involving artificial ventilation. His parents were totally opposed to any such inaction but the paediatrician they instructed for the purpose of the hearing expressed the same opinion as the doctors in charge of their child's care. Cazalet J. agreed with the expressed medical opinion as to what was in the child's best interests in granting a declaration that treatment to prolong the child's life would not be required. Such a declaration was held not to infringe Article 2 because the decision was in the child's best interests. Article 3 was relied upon to support the principle that a person had a right to die with dignity. The judge set out four general principles to be used as a framework in such cases:

7–057   (1) the court's paramount consideration is the best interests of the child and this involves a careful consideration of the views of the parents. However, those views cannot override the court's views of the child's best interests;

---

[25] See further L. Mulcahy, *op. cit.*, paras 17.89 to 17.90.
[26] (1998) 26 E.H.R.R. C.D. 153.
[27] [2000] 2 W.L.R. 622; [1999] C.O.D. 340, CA. Contrast *Frank Cowl v. Plymouth City Council* [2001] E.W.H.C. Admin. 734 (September 14, 2001) in which Scott Baker J. held that the consultation process carried out by a local authority prior to closing a residential care home for the elderly was adequate and not in breach of the Convention.
[28] (1997) 24 E.H.R.R. 423.
[29] [2000] 2 F.L.R. 677; [2000] Lloyd's Rep. Med. 411; *The Times*, July 19, 2000, *per* Cazalet J.

(2) the court's respect for the sanctity of human life imposes a strong obligation to take all steps capable of preserving life, save in exceptional circumstances;

(3) there is no question of approving a course of action aimed at terminating life or accelerating death; and

(4) it is well established that a court will not direct a doctor to provide treatment which he or she is unwilling to give and which is against clinical judgment.

In *NHS Trust A v. M; NHS Trust B v. H*,[30] Dame Butler-Sloss held that a   **7–058** decision to cease treatment in a patient's best interests was not an intentional deprivation of life contrary to Article 2, which imported a deliberate act, not an omission. In relation to the State's positive obligation under Article 2 to take adequate and appropriate steps to safeguard life, where a responsible clinical decision was made to withhold treatment that was not in the patient's best interests, and that accorded with a respectable body of medical opinion, the State's positive obligation was discharged.

(d) *Consent to treatment*

When the courts are asked to consider the issue of the extent of a doctor's duty   **7–059** to warn the patient of the risks and complications of a procedure, this Article may be sought to be relied upon in support of a doctrine of "informed consent" based on a patient's right to know, in place of the doctor-based duty which is currently favoured by the English courts. Consent can, however, be overridden in certain circumstances. For example, in *Acmanne v. Belgium*,[31] the applicant's challenge to compulsory tuberculosis screening failed. It was held that although there was interference with private life, it was justified in order to protect health.[32]

(e) *Right of access to confidential information*

In principle, Article 8 may confer a right of access by a person to personal or   **7–060** confidential information. For example, in *Gaskin v. United Kingdom*,[33] the Strasbourg Court upheld Gaskin's argument that his rights under Article 8 had been breached by the refusal of the local authority to disclose documents relating to his upbringing in care.[34] This has implications for the domestic common law

---

[30] [2001] 2 W.L.R. 942; [2001] 1 All E.R. 801; [2001] Lloyd's Rep. Med. 28, *The Times*, November 29, 2000, Dame Elizabeth Butler-Sloss P.
[31] (1983) 40 D.R. 251.
[32] See also *Grare v. France* (1993) 15 E.H.R.R. C.D. 100 (even if treatment regime of a voluntary patient in a psychiatric hospital which had unpleasant side effects could be said to be an invasion of the applicant's private life, it was justified by need) and *X v. Germany* (1985) 7 E.H.R.R. 152 (force feeding detainees on hunger strike).
[33] (1990) 12 E.H.R.R. 36.
[34] See also *Gunn-Russo v. Nugent Care Society and Secretary of State for Health* [2001] E.W.H.C. Admin., July 20, 2001 (the disclosure of adoption records by a voluntary adoption agency required a balancing exercise to be conducted between disclosure and confidentiality. Domestic law in this field was held to be compatible with the Convention).

position that a former patient had no right of access to records at common law in *R. v. Mid-Glamorgan Family Health Services, ex p. Martin.*[35]

(f) *Disclosure of confidential information*

7–061   Equally, the disclosure of confidential information may breach Article 8. In *Z v. Finland,*[36] a reference in a published judgment to an applicant's full name which led to the disclosure of her HIV status breached her right to a private life.

(g) *Disclosure of medical records and confidentiality*

7–062   The European Court of Human Rights has confirmed that a patient's medical records are included in Article 8. In *MS v. Sweden,*[37] the applicant claimed she had suffered a back injury as a result of a fall at work with the consequence that she was unable to return to work. She therefore made a claim against the Social Insurance Office. However, she was a long-term sufferer from spondylolisthesis, which can cause chronic back pain. Without her consent, the Social Insurance Office obtained her medical records from the clinic that had treated her back injury and rejected her claim for compensation the basis that they showed her injuries had not been caused at work. The records revealed that the applicant had had an abortion after the alleged injury at work but the abortion records related the abortion to serious back problems suffered during an earlier pregnancy and not a work-related injury. Importantly, the Court held that the applicant had not waived her rights by commencing the action and that:

> "The protection of personal data not least medical data is of fundamental importance to a person's enjoyment of his or her right to respect for private and family life . . . "

However, on the facts, it was held that whilst there was an interference with the applicant's rights, Article 8(2) was satisfied because there was a proportionate and legitimate aim in the information being sought, namely the protection of the economic well-being of the country by reason of the allocation of public funds. It may be harder to impose a duty of confidentiality on a large Health Trust where files are passed from one department to another and viewed by doctors, nurses, secretaries and administrators alike.[38]

7–063   In *A Health Authority v. X and others,*[39] Munby J. applied the principles set out in *Z v. Finland*[40] and *MS v. Sweden*[41] in holding that there was a compelling public interest requiring the disclosure of medical records by a health authority investigating allegations that medical practitioners had breached their terms of service. However, he also emphasised that such disclosure was an interference with a patient's rights under Article 8 and could only be justified where there

---

[35] [1995] 1 W.L.R. 110; [1995] 1 All E.R. 356, CA.
[36] (1998) 25 E.H.R.R. 371.
[37] (1999) 28 E.H.R.R. 313. See also *Z v. Finland* (1998) 25 E.H.R.R. 371.
[38] In relation to disclosure of medical reports, see also *R. v. Secretary of State for the Home Department, ex p. Amnesty International,* unreported, February 15, 2000, DC (fairness required that medical reports on Senator Pinochet should be disclosed to the four states which had requested sight of them).
[39] *The Independent,* June 25, 2001, *per* Munby J.
[40] (1997) 25 E.H.R.R. 371.
[41] (1997) 28 E.H.R.R. 313.

were effective and adequate safeguards against abuse. The following safeguards were said to be typically required:

(1) the maintenance of the confidentiality of the documents themselves;

(2) the minimum public disclosure of any information derived from the documents; and

(3) the protection of the patient's anonymity.

It was also emphasised that it was the duty of every public body, including the court, to ensure that that confidentiality was preserved and that there were effective and adequate safeguards against abuse before authorising the transfer of medical records from one doctor to a public body or from one public body to another. In *Cornelius v. De Taranto*,[41a] Morland J. found a breach of the duty of confidentiality when a consultant forensic psychiatrist disclosed a medico-legal report to a third party without the client's express consent and awarded damages of £3,750 for the breach.[41b] The judge rejected an argument that the only remedy should be nominal damages, stating that it would be a hollow protection of the right to respect for private and family life in Article 8 of the Convention if nominal damages were the only remedy for disclosure of details in breach of that right.[41c]

(h) *Patient's complaints procedures*

On applications for disclosure of documents created pursuant to patients' com- **7–064** plaints procedures, Article 8 may have to be considered, both in relation to the rights of the patient and the rights of those being investigated.

8. PROFESSIONAL DISCIPLINARY PROCEEDINGS

Professional disciplinary proceedings will amount to the determination of civil **7–065** rights and obligations for the purpose of Article 6(1) if the private right of the professional to practice his profession is actually or potentially interfered with.[42] In *Gautrin v. France*,[43] the European Court confirmed that Article 6(1) applies to hearings before medical and dental disciplinary bodies where these affect the professional's right to continue to practise his profession. This confirmed the position set out in several earlier cases including *Diennet v. France*,[44] in which it was held that the French Medical Disciplinary Council fell within the Article.[45] The European Court has left open the question whether professional disciplinary proceedings amount to the determination of a criminal charge, an issue which

---

[41a] (2001) E.M.L.R. 329.
[41b] *ibid.*, para. 66.
[41c] The Court of Appeal did not disturb the judge's decision on this point on appeal [2001] E.W.C.A. Civ. 1511 (October 10, 2001).[42] *Le Compte, Van Leuven and De Meyere v. Belgium* (1982) 4 E.H.R.R. 1, paras 47–49.
[43] (1999) 23 E.H.R.R. 196.
[44] (1996) 21 E.H.R.R. 554.
[45] See also *König v. Germany* (1980) 2 E.H.R.R. 170 and *Albert and Le Compte v. Belgium* (1983) 5 E.H.R.R. 533.

became superfluous following the finding that there was a determination of civil rights and obligations.[46] If they were to constitute determination of a criminal charge, they would additionally attract the application of Article 6(2) which enshrines the presumption of innocence, and Article 6(3) which gives a number of specific additional guarantees to those subjected to criminal charges.[46a]

7–066   It follows that any disciplinary tribunal which can interfere with a practitioner's ability to practice will in general have to itself comply with the requirements of Article 6. However, any defect in procedure may be saved if there is a full appeal to, or review by, an Article 6 compliant court or tribunal with jurisdiction to rectify factual errors or to examine whether the sanction is proportionate to the fault or which can remedy any incompatibility below.[47] In practice, appeals from professional disciplinary tribunals tend only to examine whether the body made an error of law, whether by breaching the duty of fairness or otherwise. There is not usually a full review on the merits. A limited power of appeal may be sufficient for the purposes of meeting the Article 6 requirement to provide a fair hearing in some cases though not in others. Accordingly, there is increasing pressure for the disciplinary proceedings to themselves embody the procedural protections required by Article 6 (and other procedural safeguards).[48] Professional bodies with power to suspend or debar professionals from practice are therefore being subjected to greater procedural scrutiny in light of the HRA. These include:

(1) the respective disciplinary tribunals of the Law Society and the Bar Council;

(2) the disciplinary tribunal of the Institute of Chartered Accountants; and

(3) the Professional Conduct Committee and Health Committee of the General Medical Council and the General Dental Council and the equivalent bodies for other medical practitioners such nurses, midwives, health visitors and physiotherapists.[49]

Procedural guarantees

7–067   In general, a professional disciplinary tribunal will be required to satisfy at least the following requirements to comply with Article 6(1) in conjunction with domestic law principles of natural justice[50]:

---

[46] *Le Compte, Van Leuven and De Meyere v. Belgium* (1982) 4 E.H.R.R. 1, para. 53. The Divisional Court in *Pine v. Solicitors Disciplinary Tribunal; sub. nom. In the Matter of a Solicitor*, unreported, January 11, 2001, held that proceedings before the Solicitors Tribunal relating to failure to maintain proper accounts and permitting misleading information to be delivered to the Law Society were not the determination of a criminal charge. This finding was not challenged on a subsequent appeal to the Court of Appeal [2001] E.W.C.A. Civ. 1574 (October 25, 2001).

[46a] See para. 7–012, above.

[47] *Le Compte, Van Leuven and De Meyere v. Belgium* (1982) 4 E.H.R.R. 1, para. 51; *Gautrin v. France* (1999) 28 E.H.R.R. 196, para. 57; *R. v. United Kingdom Central Council for Nursing, Midwifery and Health Visiting, ex p. Tehrani* [2001] I.R.L.R. 208.

[48] See further L. Mulcahy, *op. cit.*, paras 20.29–20.30.

[49] On the European Court's analysis, it seems unlikely that proceedings which do not have direct power to interfere with a practitioner's right to practise will be subject to Art. 6: see *Fayed v. United Kingdom* (1994) 18 E.H.R.R. 393.

[50] See further L. Mulcahy, *op. cit.*, paras 17.106 *et seq.* and Chap. 20—"Civil Disciplinary Proceedings".

(a) the tribunal must be independent and impartial: *Gautrin v. France.*[51] The European Court has upheld complaints based not just on actual independence or bias but on its mere appearance[52];

(b) equality of arms must be maintained: the right to a fair hearing means that all parties must have a reasonable opportunity of presenting their respective cases under conditions that do not place them at a substantial disadvantage *vis-à-vis* their opponents[53];

(c) there should be sufficient disclosure of documents to meet the requirement of fairness: the right to a fair hearing may require that documents which form the basis of a complaint or defence should be provided to the complainant or the professional. It might be necessary to impose conditions on disclosure (*e.g.* confidentiality) in order to maintain fairness to another party's rights: *R. v. General Medical Council, ex p. Toth*[54];

(d) parties should be able to comment upon advice of legal advisers and assessors: where a disciplinary tribunal is assisted by a legal adviser or assessor fairness requires that the parties are afforded an opportunity to comment on that advice and the committee should have an opportunity to consider their comments before making their determination: *Nwabuaze v. General Medical Council*[55];

(e) the hearing should generally be in public: Article 6(1) requires that professional disciplinary proceedings are held in public, unless the limited exceptions set out in the Article apply.[56] Where matters of professional secrecy or protection of the private life of a professional or his patient or client are concerned, this may justify sitting in camera.[57] Where the professional waives his right to a public hearing expressly or tacitly, the conduct of disciplinary proceedings in private does not contravene the Convention[58];

(f) reasons should be given: an Article 6 compliant disciplinary tribunal also has to give reasons for its decision.[59] The extent to which reasons need to be given is as yet unclear[60]; and

---

[51] (1999) 28 E.H.R.R. 196.
[52] *ibid.* In *R. v. General Medical Council, ex p. Kyros Nicolaides* [2001] E.W.H.C. 625, July 27, 2001, Sir Richard Tucker held that the Professional Conduct Committee of the GMC was not biased or in breach of Art. 6 when it gave a decision concerning the conduct of a professional during a previous disciplinary hearing before the GMC.
[53] See *Dombo Beheer v. Netherlands* (1994) 18 E.H.R.R. 213.
[54] [2000] 1 W.L.R. 2129.
[55] [2000] 1 W.L.R. 1760.
[56] *Gautrin v. France* (1999) 28 E.H.R.R. 196, para. 42.
[57] *Le Compte, Van Leuven and De Meyere v. Belgium* (1982) 4 E.H.R.R. 1, para. 59.
[58] *ibid.*
[59] See *Ruiz Torija v. Spain* (1995) 19 E.H.R.R. 553; *Georgiadis v. Greece* (1997) 24 E.H.R.R. 606; *Helle v. Finland* (1998) 26 E.H.R.R. 159.
[60] In *Selvanathan v. General Medical Council, The Times*, October 26, 2000, the Privy Council referred to the new obligation on the General Medical Council to give reasons and Lord Hope indicated that a general explanation would be required identifying the reasons for the finding made; and the reasons for the imposition, or non-imposition of a penalty.

(g) there should be a procedure to challenge a proposed interim suspension: a professional should be warned about the possibility of interim suspensions pending the substantive disciplinary hearing and should have an opportunity to make representations and if necessary, call witnesses: *Gupta v. The General Medical Council.*[61]

---

[61] Unreported, July 25, 2001. See also *Sudesh Madan v. The General Medical Council* [2001] E.W.H.C. Admin. 577.

CHAPTER 8

CONSTRUCTION PROFESSIONALS

PARA.

1. Introduction
   (a) The construction professions .. 8–001
   (b) Claims against construction
       professionals 8–007
   (c) Forms of building contract 8–010
       (i) The "traditional"
           building contract 8–011
       (ii) The "design and build"
            or "turnkey" contract 8–014
       (iii) Management contracts .. 8–016
2. Duties
   (a) Duties to client
       (i) Contractual duties 8–017
       (ii) Duties independent of
            contract 8–037
   (b) Duties to third parties 8–062
       (i) The definition of the type
           of loss 8–068
       (ii) Recovery by third parties
            in respect of personal
            injury and damage to
            "other property" 8–078
       (iii) The general exclusionary
             rule adopted in England
             with regard to the
             recovery of economic
             loss 8–084
       (iv) The English exceptions
            to the general
            exclusionary rule 8–088
       (v) The position in Canada . 8–110
       (vi) The position in
            Australia 8–117
       (vii) The position in New
             Zealand 8–120
       (viii) The position in other
              jurisdictions 8–122
       (ix) Problems of scope of
            duty 8–123
   (c) Other torts 8–130
   (d) The standard of care and skill
       (i) The ordinary competent
           and skilled practitioner . 8–131
       (ii) General practice and
            knowledge as evidence
            of the standard 8–142
       (iii) Expert evidence 8–149
       (iv) *Res ipsa loquitur* 8–154
       (v) Codes of practice and
           legislation 8–156

PARA.

       (vi) Knowledge of the law ... 8–160
       (vii) Not every error is
             negligence 8–163
       (viii) The specialist
              practitioner 8–166
       (ix) Special steps and
            warranty of reasonable
            fitness 8–168
       (x) Reliance upon specialists
           and delegation to them . 8–175
3. Liability for breach of duty 8–180
   (a) Examination of site 8–181
   (b) Cost estimates and budgets 8–191
   (c) Compliance with legislation,
       planning and building control
       requirements and codes of
       practice 8–198
   (d) Design and specification 8–201
   (e) Preparation of bills of
       quantities 8–219
   (f) Selection of contractor and the
       tender process 8–220
   (g) Advice on choice and terms of
       a building contract 8–223
   (h) Administration of the building
       contract 8–226
   (i) Supervision or inspection of
       the works 8–236
   (j) Certification 8–250
   (k) Specialist survey 8–257
   (l) Investigation of defects 8–260
   (m) The construction professional
       as an expert witness 8–261
4. Damages 8–262
   (a) The scope of the duty 8–263
   (b) Remoteness 8–267
       (i) Causation 8–268
       (ii) Foreseeability 8–278
   (c) The measure of damages 8–283
   (d) Heads of damage 8–287
       (i) Costs of rectification 8–288
       (ii) Diminution in value 8–298
       (iii) Wasted expenditure 8–300
       (iv) Excess expenditure 8–301
       (v) Underpayment 8–302
       (vi) Consequential losses 8–303
       (vii) Liability to third parties 8–305
       (viii) Personal injuries 8–306
       (ix) Inconvenience, distress
            and loss of amenity 8–307

[209]

	PARA.			PARA.
(e) Mitigation of loss	8–311		(a) Apportionment of liability	8–315
(f) Abatement of fees	8–314		(b) Contributory negligence	8–328
5. Shared responsibility			6. Adjudication	8–330

1. INTRODUCTION

(a) *The construction professionals*

8–001 The professions which are the subject of this chapter are those concerned with building and engineering works: principally architects, engineers and quantity surveyors. Given the variety of modern contractual arrangements, building methods and titles, it is sometimes difficult both to identify the professional man and to distinguish him from a building contractor. The chapter includes consideration of tasks traditionally undertaken by professional men under an obligation to exercise reasonable skill and care even although such tasks (for example, design) may in fact be undertaken by a building contractor. Since the subject of this book is professional negligence, this chapter is limited to discussing such claims and only brief consideration will be given to other types of claim against construction professionals. For further discussion and fuller treatment of the required qualifications, professional bodies and terms and conditions of engagement of construction professionals, reference should be made to the relevant sections in the standard textbooks on building law generally.[1] In considering the liability of construction professionals for professional negligence, it will be necessary briefly to consider other types of case and in particular the liability in tort of builders and local authorities. Recent decisions in England and in other Commonwealth jurisdictions concerning builders and local authorities have immense importance for construction professionals, but the ambit of such decisions remains uncertain.[2]

8–002 **Architects.** An "architect" is: "one who possesses, with due regard to aesthetic as well as practical considerations, adequate skill and knowledge to enable him (i) to originate, (ii) to design and plan, (iii) to arrange for and supervise the erection of such buildings or other works calling for skill in design and planning as he might, in the course of his business, reasonably be asked to carry out or in respect of which he offers his services as a specialist."[3] Subject to certain qualifications, statute restricts practising or carrying on business under any name, style or title containing the word "architect" to persons registered by the

---

[1] See Hudson's *Building and Engineering Contracts* (11th ed.), chap. 2; Keating's *Building Contracts* (7th ed.), chap. 13; and Emden's *Construction Law* (8th ed., revised 1990 with later updates), Division IV, chap. 6.

[2] See further paras 8–062 to 8–129, below.

[3] This is the definition adopted and acted upon by the Tribunal of Appeal from the Architects' Registration Council and cited by the Divisional Court in *R. v. Architects' Registration Tribunal, ex p. Jaggar* [1945] 2 All E.R. 131, 134. The use of the word "supervise" may now be open to question. In the then current edition of the RIBA Conditions, clause B provided "The Architect shall give such periodical supervision and inspection as may be necessary to ensure that the works are being executed in general accordance with the contract." In all editions of the Conditions from 1971 onwards, the obligation to supervise has been replaced with an obligation to carry out periodic inspections. See further, para. 8–236, below.

Architects' Registration Board.[4] Architects are currently the only construction professionals who are subject to a statutory requirement of registration. The Board, through the Registrar of Architects, admits applicants to registration who it is satisfied fulfil the requisite qualifications. The usual qualification is that the applicant has passed an examination in architecture recognised by the Board. Architects also belong to one of the professional bodies, chief among which is the Royal Institute of British Architects (RIBA). Both the Architects' Registration Board and the RIBA prescribe codes of conduct.[5]

Engineers. "Engineer" is a term descriptive of a much wider range of occupations and professions than those the subject of this chapter.[6] No precise definition of the term is available. The term is applied here to a person who in a contract for engineering works performs functions analogous to those of an architect under a "traditional" building contract[7] or a person who is employed in connection with a building or engineering project for more specialist skills than those usually possessed by an architect, for example a civil, structural, mechanical or electrical engineer. There is an increasingly wide range of specialist engineers and consequently a wide range of qualifications and professional bodies. The most important professional body for civil engineers is the Institution of Civil Engineers (ICE).[8] Membership of the Institution entitles a person to describe himself as a Chartered Civil Engineer.[9] Other important professional bodies include the Institution of Structural Engineers (I.Struct.E),[10] the Institution of Mechanical Engineers (I.Mech.E)[11] and the Institution of Electrical Engineers (IEE).[12]   **8–003**

Quantity surveyors. The duties of a quantity surveyor were judicially described in the nineteenth century as "taking out in detail the measurements and quantities from plans prepared by an architect, for the purpose of enabling   **8–004**

---

[4] See the Architects Act 1997, s.20. The 1997 Act consolidated earlier legislation including orders made under the European Communities Act 1972. In *Munkenbeck and Marshall v. Kensington Hotel* (1999) 15 Const. L.J. 231, the defendant argued that he was not obliged to pay fees as he had contracted for the services of registered architects. The court rejected this as, on a true analysis of the contract, the defendant had contracted only for the services of architecturally qualified personnel.

[5] Copies of the current codes of conduct and further information are available on the website of the Architects' Registration Board at www.arb.org.uk and on the RIBA website at www.architecture.com.

[6] In his 1994 Presidential Address to the Institution of Civil Engineers, Dr Edmund Hambly described the range of activities undertaken by civil engineers as follows: "Civil engineers manage the conception, innovation, promotion, design, construction, operation, maintenance and eventual removal of the amenities of modern civilisation. These amenities range from water supply to offshore energy, transport systems to buildings, land reclamation to municipal services and industrial production to environmental improvement."

[7] As provided for in the ICE Conditions of Contract.

[8] Further information is available on the ICE's website at www.ice.org.uk.

[9] See Hudson, *op. cit.* pp. 248–249.

[10] Further information is available on the Institution of Structural Engineers' website at www.istructe.org.uk. Historically, structural engineers had a particular expertise in the use and properties of reinforced concrete.

[11] Further information is available at the Institution of Mechanical Engineers' website at www.imeche.org.uk.

[12] Further information is available at the Institution of Electrical Engineers' website at www.iee.org.uk.

builders to calculate the amounts for which they would execute the plans."[13] This description is rather anachronistic, as a quantity surveyor's duties today commonly extend to the preparation of estimates, bills of quantities and schedules for pricing by contractors together with negotiation with contractors and the valuation of work done for the purpose of interim and final certificates issued by the architect. Although often perceived as the professional man most closely concerned with controlling cost on the part of the client, it has been pointed out that a quantity surveyor's powers in this regard are strictly limited. As a quantity surveyor neither designs the works, nor issues variation instructions nor assesses extensions of time,

> "all that a quantity surveyor can do is (a) to check that tenders of contractors or subcontractors are reasonably priced before he recommends acceptance; (b) to measure work executed accurately; (c) exercise vigilance in the valuation of variations or the checking of the valuation of variations submitted to him by the contractor; (d) make a fair assessment of any additional sums which may be due to a contractor as a result of extension of time, acceleration instructions and so forth."[14]

In the wider context of the construction industry, however, quantity surveyors are commonly recognised as possessing an expertise in construction economics beyond that of other construction professionals. They are used extensively as claims consultants in connection with contractual disputes between building owners and building contractors. Qualifications or registration are not prescribed by law for practice, but quantity surveyors commonly belong to the Royal Institution of Chartered Surveyors (RICS).[15] Practical training and examination are today the usual prerequisites to admission to membership of the RICS, which prescribes a code of conduct for its members.

8–005   **Building surveyors.** Surveyors who qualify within the building surveying division of the RICS are known as building surveyors. They commonly undertake work traditionally performed by architects, such as the design and inspection of construction works, but have a particular expertise in the interpretation and application of the Building Regulations, which are designed to preserve the safety of people using new or refurbished buildings.

8–006   **Project managers.** When a construction project is particularly large or complex, the owner may appoint a project manager to act as his representative. There is, as yet, no recognised professional body for project managers in the United Kingdom, although the RICS has a Project Management Forum and both the RIBA and the Association of Consulting Engineers (ACE) publish standard forms of contract for the appointment of a project manager.[16] The obligations of

---

[13] *Taylor v. Hall* (1870) 4 I.R.C.L. 467, *per* Morris J. at 476.
[14] *per* Mr Recorder Jackson Q.C. in *Burrell Hayward & Budd v. Chris Carnell and David Green*, unreported, February 20, 1992 (counterclaim by a firm of architects against a firm of quantity surveyors for alleged negligence in failing to control costs and failing to keep the architects properly informed of the likely costs of the project was dismissed).
[15] Further information is available on the RICS website at www.rics.org.uk.
[16] The RIBA Form of Appointment as a Project Manager (PM/99); the ACE Conditions of Engagement, 1995—Agreement E for use where a Consulting Engineer is engaged as a Project Manager.

a project manager will depend upon the particular terms of his engagement but will commonly include many of the functions traditionally performed by an architect or engineer who is acting for the employer.[17]

(b) *Claims against construction professionals*

The Pre-Action Protocol. Anyone who is contemplating making a claim for 8–007 professional negligence against a construction professional must bear in mind the Pre-Action Protocol for Construction and Engineering Disputes. The protocol was published in September 2000 and came into force on October 2, 2000. It was originally drafted for use in cases destined for the Technology and Construction Court, but has been approved for use in all courts.[18] It applies to "all construction and engineering disputes (including professional negligence claims against architects, engineers and quantity surveyors)".[19] It is thought that the reference to architects, engineers and quantity surveyors is not exclusive, so that claims for professional negligence against other construction professionals, such as building surveyors or project managers, should be treated as subject to the protocol. The objectives of the protocol are (i) to encourage the exchange of early and full information about the prospective legal claim, (ii) to enable parties to avoid litigation by agreeing a settlement of the claim before commencement of proceedings and (iii) to support the efficient management of proceedings where litigation cannot be avoided.[20] The protocol provides for a detailed letter of claim,[21] a detailed response (including any counterclaim)[22] and a detailed response to any counterclaim, followed by one or more without prejudice meetings between the parties[23] at which they shall seek to identify the main

---

[17] It follows that care must be taken to see that an expert witness in a claim against a project manager has the appropriate qualification(s). See *Pride Valley Foods Ltd v. Hall & Partners (Contract Management) Ltd* (2001) 76 Con. L.R. 1, 24, "There is an initial difficulty in accepting expert opinion evidence in relation to the duties of project managers. There is no chartered or professional institution of project managers nor a recognisable profession of project managers. In so far as it may be appropriate to accept expert evidence, the nature of the evidence that might be acceptable will depend on what the project manager has agreed to do. In some cases the project manager will be the architect who will design the project and then, acting as project manager, supervise the contractor and the sub-contractors in carrying out the work. ... At the other end of the scale the project manager will supervise the work of the contractor and sub-contractors and ensure that the work is carried out in conformity with the design drawings. In these circumstances the project manager will have no design function even to the extent of providing an outline specification." *Per* H.H. Judge Toulmin C.M.G., Q.C. The Court of Appeal did not comment on this part of the judgment: [2001] E.W.C.A. Civ. 1001, (2001) 76 Con.L.R. 1, 36.
[18] Pursuant to para. 1.1 of the Civil Procedure Rules Practice Direction—Protocols.
[19] Protocol, para. 1.1.The protocol does not apply to certain types of claim, which are described in para. 1.2. Those exceptions include a claim in which an application for summary judgment under Part 24 of the Civil Procedure Rules will be made and a claim to enforce the decision of an adjudicator to whom a dispute has been referred under s.108 of the Housing Grants, Construction and Regeneration Act 1996.
[20] Protocol, para. 1.3; Practice Direction—Protocols, para. 1.4.
[21] Protocol, para.3.
[22] Protocol, para. 4.3. The detailed letter of response will be preceded by an acknowledgement (para. 4.1). A detailed response is not required if the defendant raises objection to the court's jurisdiction, requires the matter to go to arbitration or contends that he is not the correct defendant (para. 4.2).
[23] Protocol, para. 5.

issues in their dispute, to identify the root cause of disagreement in respect of each issue, consider whether and how the dispute might be resolved without the need for litigation and, if litigation is unavoidable, what steps should be taken to see that it is conducted in accordance with the overriding objective defined in Part 1.1 of the Civil Procedure Rules.[24] If proceedings are then commenced, the court will be able to treat the standards set in the protocol as the normal reasonable approach to pre-action conduct.[25] This is significant, because the court will take into account compliance or non-compliance with the protocol when giving directions for the management of subsequent proceedings and when making costs orders.[26] In particular, a party which fails to comply may be ordered to pay all or part of the other party's costs of later proceedings, which may be on the indemnity basis.[27] A successful claimant who has failed to comply with the protocol may recover interest for a shorter period or at a lower rate than he otherwise would; conversely, an unsuccessful defendant who did not comply may be ordered to pay interest at a higher rate.[28]

8–008 **The Technology and Construction Court.** Many cases which include claims of professional negligence against construction professionals are brought in the Technology and Construction Court (TCC), which is a division of the High Court of Justice and used to be known as the Official Referees Court. Proceedings in the TCC are specialist proceedings governed by Part 49 of the Civil Procedure Rules. Accordingly, the Civil Procedure Rules apply to proceedings in the TCC only subject to the provisions of Practice Direction—Technology and Construction Court. The Practice Direction also includes Forms to be used in drafting orders made at case management conferences and pre-trial reviews in the TCC and are designed to take into account the special nature of the issues in TCC cases, which are typically both complex and technical.

8–009 **Adjudication.** Part II of the Housing Grants, Construction and Regeneration Act 1996 introduced a form of mandatory dispute resolution known as "adjudication". A claim for damages for professional negligence against a construction professional may be referred to adjudication in certain circumstances. The decision of an adjudicator is binding upon the parties, and will be enforced by the court, pending any formal legal or arbitral proceedings which are taken in order to obtain a final decision on the same dispute. The important subject of adjudication is considered more fully in a later section of this chapter.[29]

(c) *Forms of building contract*

8–010 Before embarking on a discussion of professional negligence liability in the context of the construction professions, it is important to outline the usual

---

[24] Protocol, para. 5.2.
[25] Protocol, para. 1.4.
[26] CPR Practice Direction—Protocols, para. 2.1.
[27] CPR Practice Direction—Protocols, para. 2.3(1) and (2).
[28] CPR Practice Direction—Protocols, para. 2.3(3) and (4).
[29] See paras 8–330 to 8–341, below.

position of each in relation to other persons involved in a construction project. This position will depend upon the type of contractual arrangement used. Most building projects will use one of three types of contractual arrangement: (a) a "traditional" building contract; (b) a "design and build" or "turnkey" contract; or (c) a "management" contract.

(i) *The "traditional"building contract*

In the traditional form of building contract,[30] there will be a contract between the **8–011** employer and the building contractor and a separate contract between the employer and the architect (and/or other professional consultants). The price payable for the building works may be fixed either by reference to works identified on drawings or specifications (in which event the contractor will generally be obliged to carry out all such work for a fixed sum) or for works quantified in a bill of quantities (in which event the contractor will generally be entitled to be paid additional moneys in the event that the actual quantities exceed those identified in the contractual documents).[31] The basic principle is that the employer, through his professional consultants, provides the design and the contractor builds to that design. Thus, subject to variations or other events leading to a change in the contract price, the employer under a traditional building contract should know at the outset of a project both its likely final costs and the precise nature and scope of the building project.

At the initial stages, where the architect's services will mainly be of an **8–012** advisory nature, he is unlikely to be the employer's agent.[32] But on being instructed to act as architect in relation to a building project and to proceed with the works, for many purposes he becomes the employer's agent.[33] His general function will be to act on behalf of the employer and to protect his interests.[34] It was formerly held that in relation to the issue of certificates, or at least the final certificate, the architect ceased to be the employer's agent and became an arbitrator or quasi-arbitrator,[35] but this is no longer the law.[36] A specialist engineer or quantity surveyor may be employed pursuant to a contract with the employer only, with the main contractor or sub-contractor only, or with the architect only. As a result of the growth in multi-disciplinary practices, a single firm may be able to provide to an employer the skills of architects, specialist

---

[30] The JCT Standard Form of Building Contract 1998 edition With Quantities or Without Quantities is a good example. Further information about the various standard form building contracts published by the Joint Contracts Tribunal Limited is available on its website at www.jctltd.co.uk.

[31] Hudson, *op. cit.*, pp. 415–416.

[32] Hudson, *op. cit.*, p. 269.

[33] See, *e.g. Chambers v. Goldthorpe* [1901] 1 K.B. 624, CA at 634; *R. B. Burden Ltd v. Swansea Corporation* [1957] 1 W.L.R. 1167, CA at 1172; *Clayton v. Woodman & Son (Builders) Ltd* [1962] 2 Q.B. 533, 539; *A.M.F. International Ltd v. Magnet Bowling Ltd* [1968] 1 W.L.R. 1028, 1046; *Hosier & Dickinson Ltd v. P. & M. Kaye Ltd* [1970] 1 W.L.R. 1611, CA at 1615. For an example of a case where an architect was held not to be the employer's agent see *District of Surrey v. Carroll-Hatch and Associates Ltd* (1979) 101 D.L.R. (3d) 218, 222.

[34] See, *e.g. R. B. Burden Ltd v. Swansea Corporation* [1957] 1 W.L.R. 1167, CA at 1172. When he issues certificates for payment, however, "he stands apart from the owner (*i.e.* employer) and enjoys to some extent an independent authority of his own", *per* Lord Radcliffe, *ibid.* at 1172. See para. 8–251, below for status of architect in issuing certificates.

[35] *e.g. Chambers v. Goldthorpe* [1901] 1 Q.B. 624.

[36] See *Sutcliffe v. Thackrah* [1974] A.C. 727 and generally on this issue para. 8–251, below.

engineers and quantity surveyors. Except in quite unusual circumstances, however, an architect in private practice remains an independent contractor.[37] He is not generally the agent of the contractor.[38] In general, a contractor will be responsible both for his own method of working and for the design of necessary temporary works.[39]

8–013 In larger traditional building projects the employer may appoint a clerk of works. Although employed pursuant to a contract with the employer his status and function in relation to other parties in a building project may be difficult to analyse legally. His powers and duties are frequently set out in the contract between the employer and the contractor,[40] but only to a limited extent is he likely to be the employer's agent. As between the architect and the clerk of works the general division of function is that the latter is to attend to matters of detail.[41] The clerk of works is not the representative of the architect unless he is the architect's employee.[42]

(ii) The "design and build" or "turnkey" contract

8–014 In the "traditional" form of building contract, the architect plays a central role not just in design but also in contract administration as the leader of the

---

[37] *A.M.F. International Ltd v. Magnet Bowling Ltd* [1968] 1 W.L.R. 1028, 1045; also *Clayton v. Woodman & Son (Builders) Ltd* [1962] 2 Q.B. 533, 539. In the latter case (reversed, although not on the instant point, on appeal) Salmon J. stated unequivocally: " . . . an architect is clearly an independent contractor. The building owner has no control over the manner in which the architect does his work." This statement requires qualification. As observed by Lord Reid in *Sutcliffe v. Thackrah* [1974] A.C. 727, 737 the architect in many matters is bound to act on the employer's instructions, whether he agrees with them or not. In this regard see the Australian case of *Perini Corporation v. Commonwealth of Australia* (1969) 12 B.L.R. 82: held that there was an implied term in the contract between the plaintiff contractor and defendant employer that the latter would ensure that the Director of Works (an employee of the defendants but discharging the functions of an architect) did his duty as certifier; cf. the South African case of *Alfred McAlpine & Son (Pty) Ltd v. Transvaal Provincial Administration* [1974] (3) S.A.L.R. 506 (no implied term in contract between contractor and employer that engineer would introduce variations "at reasonable times").

[38] *Hosier & Dickinson Ltd v. P. & M. Kaye Ltd* [1970] 1 W.L.R. 1611, CA at 1615.

[39] See *Plant Construction Ltd v. Clive Adams Associates and JMH Construction Services Ltd* [2000] B.L.R. 137, CA; *Aurum Investments Ltd v. Avonforce Ltd* [2001] Lloyd's Rep. P.N. 285.

[40] See the various forms of the JCT Standard Form of Building Contract 1998 ed., cl. 12 (derived from the 1963 Form, cl. 10). The RIBA and the Institute of Clerks of Works have co-operated to produce the *Clerk of Works' Manual* (1994, 3rd ed.) which describes the position and duties of the clerk of works when the JCT Standard Form is used. The manual is obtainable from RIBA Publications Ltd, 56–64 Leonard St., London EC2A 4LT and at www.ribabookshop.com.

[41] See *Leicester Guardians v. Trollope* (1911) 75 J.P. 197 and *Gray v. T. P. Bennett & Son* (1987) 43 B.L.R. 63 where, at 78, the clerk of works was described as "the eyes and ears of the architect" (architects and engineers not liable for defective construction of brickwork to nurses' home which the contractor had deliberately concealed—see further para. 8–243, below).

[42] *East Ham Corporation v. Bernard Sunley & Sons Ltd* [1966] A.C. 406, 443. Note *Kensington and Chelsea and Westminster A.H.A. v. Wettern Composites Ltd* (1984) 1 Con.L.R. 114, 139: employer held vicariously liable for the negligence of the clerk of works. In *Gray v. T. P. Bennett & Son* (1987) 43 B.L.R. 63 the architects refused to employ the clerk of works unless given an indemnity by the plaintiff, which the plaintiff was not prepared to provide. The clerk of works thus remained the employee of the plaintiff but was held not negligent on the facts in failing to spot deliberatively destructive workmanship by the contractor. See further paras 8–244 and 8–245, below. Note that the "engineer's representative" under the ICE Conditions of Contract 1999 (7th ed.), cl. 2(3), although performing similar tasks to a clerk of works, is in a different contractual position and is responsible to the engineer.

professional team.[43] In large modern building projects this role can be criticised as outdated.[44] The increasingly specialised nature of such matters as structural and services design means that the architect may have little to contribute to the most important aspects of buildings. Moreover it is likely to be the contractor rather than the architect to whom the employer will have to look to ensure that the project is effectively co-ordinated and controlled so as to be produced on time and at the right price.

There are many forms of contract[45] in which the employer employs a con- **8–015** tractor both to design and construct a building. Such contracts may have both advantages and disadvantages for the employer. In the absence of express provision, the contractor will be required to produce works fit for their intended purpose.[46] It will generally not be possible, as often occurs in a traditional contract, for a designer to blame the contractor for defective workmanship and for the contractor to respond with allegations of defective design. However, in providing the design, a contractor is likely to seek to minimise the cost of a design in a way which may be unnecessary for an independent professional man. If the employer's right to a building which is reasonably fit for its purpose is replaced by an obligation merely to exercise reasonable care and skill in design,[47] an employer is likely to have substantially less protection in respect of the quality of the design than he would have under a traditional contract. Although consultants may be retained by the employer directly (particularly to provide a check on the design carried out by the contractor), the main designers are likely to be retained by the contractor with the result that disputes concerning alleged pro-

---

[43] In an article "*Anns* beyond repair" (1991) 107 L.Q.R. 228, I. N. Duncan Wallace Q.C. criticises some professional institutions for asserting a "captain of the ship status" and failing to correct "the serious judicial and public misunderstanding and exaggeration of the effectiveness and degree of supervision, or of day-to-day control over methods of working, which can be afforded either in practice or contractually by a supervising architect or engineer."

[44] In a paper "Supervision: an architect's view" for the Society of Construction Law on April 5, 1988 (see the Society's website at www.scl.org.uk), Francis Goodall suggests that an architect is a designer, who may have little skill or talent for the supervision and inspection role assigned to him: "Supervision, inspection, are things for a manager, the man who can sieve sand and organize the wrought iron gate or the fountain, once someone with other, dare I say more creative, talents than his has designed it in the first place."

[45] Such contracts are given a variety of different names such as "turnkey", "design and build" or "package deal". Many are major contractors' own standard forms but others, such as the JCT Standard Form of Building Contract with Contractor's Design (1998) and the ICE Design and Construct Conditions of Contract (1992, revised 1998), are provided by industry bodies. The names are not always helpful in ascertaining the precise obligations undertaken: see the article by I. N. Duncan Wallace Q.C., "Contracts for industrial plant projects" (1984) 1 I.C.L.R. 322 and Hudson, *op. cit.*, at pp. 426 to 431.

[46] See *e.g. Viking Grain Storage Ltd v. T. H. White Installations Ltd* (1986) 33 B.L.R. 103 (held to be an implied term that completed works would be reasonably fit for their purpose as a grain drying and storage installation where the defendant contractor had offered to carry out a package deal of design, execution and management). See further the cases of *Greaves & Co. (Contractors) Ltd v. Baynham Meikle & Partners* [1974] 1 W.L.R. 1261 and *Consultants Group International v. John Worman Ltd* (1985) 9 Con.L.R. 46, discussed further at paras 8–168 to 8–174 below, which both concerned the extent of liability of design sub-contractors in situations where their immediate employers had undertaken an obligation to provide works reasonably fit for their purpose to the ultimate employer.

[47] As, for example, in the JCT Standard Form With Contractor's Design (1998) which, by clause 2.5, restricts the contractor's liability in respect of design to that of an independent designer under a separate contract with the employer.

fessional negligence are likely to be between the contractor and one or more professional men.[48]

(iii) *Management contracts*

8–016   Many large building projects now involve a "management" contractor. Although the JCT in the United Kingdom has, since 1987, published a standard form of management contract together with associated works contracts,[49] many different forms of management contract are found. Typically, the management contractor is paid the actual cost of the works, plus a fee. The construction works are carried out by separate "works" or "trade" contractors. Typically, the management contractor enters into the works or trade contracts with the works or trade contractors. Sometimes, the works contracts are made directly with the employer (in which case, the management contractor is often known as the "construction manager"). Although each works contract may be for a fixed price, it is very unlikely that there will be an overall fixed price at the commencement of the works as all of the packages will not then have been let. In the absence of some form of bonus agreement whereby the management contractor is rewarded for achieving reductions in price, there is no direct financial incentive for the management contractor to achieve economies. Further there may be considerable scope for claims by one works contractor that he has been disrupted by the activities of another. Whereas in a traditional contract it is the main contractor who has the financial incentive to sort such disputes out, in a management contract, such disputes may well fall for the account of the employer.[50] In most management contracts, professional consultants will still be employed by the employer but their precise role, particularly in the supervision of works, is likely to be substantially affected by the presence and powers of the management contractor.

2. Duties

(a) *Duties to client*

(i) *Contractual duties*

8–017   **Express terms.** As in the case of other professions the primary basis for the duties of a construction professional in a particular case is the contract pursuant to which he is engaged. More commonly than with other professions, construction professionals are engaged pursuant to written contracts in standard form.[51]

---

[48] For an example see *Consultants Group International v. John Worman Ltd* (1987) 9 Con.L.R. 46 (specialist architects found to owe design obligations to contractor which were co-extensive with those owed by contractor to client with the result that architects owed an obligation to design building so that it was fit for its purpose) discussed at para.8–172, below.

[49] Now the JCT Standard Form of Management Contract 1998, known as MC 98, with standard Works Contract Conditions (WKS/1–3).

[50] For powerful criticism of most management contracts see Hudson, *op. cit.* pp. 431–435.

[51] By para. 2.1 of its Code of Professional Conduct (1997) the RIBA requires that a member undertake "when making an engagement, whether by an agreement for professional services, by a contract of employment or by a contract for the supply of services and goods, to state whether or not professional indemnity insurance is held and to have defined beyond reasonable doubt and recorded the terms of the engagement including the scope of the service, the allocation of responsibilities and any limitation of liability, the method of calculation or [*sic*] remuneration and the provision for termination and adjudication."

In the case of architects, those most frequently used are published in standard form by the RIBA[52] whilst the most common forms for engineers are the ACE Conditions of Engagement Agreements.[53] A standard form is also produced by the RICS for quantity surveying services but this appears to be in less common general use.[54] Whether oral or written the contract will need to be carefully scrutinised in a professional negligence claim in order to determine the nature and extent of the engagement undertaken. For example an architect engaged by an employer may have been engaged for only some or all of the following duties: advising, examining the site, preparing designs, drawings and plans, supervising the works and certifying their value for the purpose of the payment provisions of the building contract.[55] For example, in *Tesco v. Norman Hitchcox Partnership*,[56] Judge Lewis Q.C. considered the terms of the defendant architects' engagement and held that they had undertaken an obligation to design the works, but no obligation to supervise their construction.

Although a construction professional's duties are defined by the terms of his **8–018** contract (and any concurrent duty of care or fiduciary duty), it will often be necessary to look beyond the terms of that contract in order to ascertain what precisely is required by way of discharge of those duties. This necessity arises from the fact that a building project involves a whole matrix of relationships where each party's individual responsibilities can only be evaluated in the light of the responsibilities assumed by others. Thus in ascertaining the scope of an architect's express contractual duties under a retainer made in connection with a "traditional" building contract it may be necessary to examine closely the terms of the contract between the employer and the main contractor[57] or whether

---

[52] Until 1982, the RIBA issued various editions of their Conditions of Engagement. In 1982, the Conditions were superseded by a document entitled "Architect's Appointment" (and known as the "Blue Book") which was intended to be used for ordinary building works and another entitled "Architect's Appointment Small Works" for use with smaller works. In 1990 the RIBA issued the RIBA Architect's Appointment Historic Buildings: Repairs and Conservation Works for use with such works. In 1992, the "Architects Appointment" document was superseded by the RIBA Standard Form of Agreement for the Appointment of an Architect, which is now in its 1999 edition and is known as SFA/99. In 1992 the RIBA also issued the Standard Form of Agreement for the Appointment of an Architect for Design and Build in two different forms according to whether the Architect was to work for the employer or the contractor. The current editions are obtainable from RIBA Publications Ltd (see n. 40 above) and many of the above documents are conveniently reprinted in *Emden*, Division X.

[53] A total of nine agreements are published by the ACE according to the role being undertaken by the Engineer. All were originally published in 1995, superceding eight forms which had been published in 1981. The current editions with amendments are obtainable from the ACE at 12 Caxton St, London SW1H 0QL or at www.acenet.co.uk and are conveniently reprinted in *Emden*, Division Z.

[54] The RICS "Form of Agreement, Terms and Conditions for the Appointment of a Quantity Surveyor", obtainable from RICS Bookshop, 12 Great George St, London SW1P 3AD and also reprinted in *Emden*, Volume 5, Tab Y.

[55] For the list of architect's duties drawn up by Hudson (an architect as well as a lawyer) for architects in the United Kingdom when retained by the employer, see Hudson, *op.cit.* pp. 266–267.

[56] (1997) 56 Con. L.R 42.

[57] For examples, see : *T. A. Bickerton & Son Ltd v. N.W. Metropolitan Hospital Board* [1969] 1 All E.R. 977, CA (having regard to the terms of the main building contract which required the architect to issue instructions in regard to the expenditure of prime cost, it was the duty of the architects to issue such instructions whenever necessary); *West Faulkner Associates v. London Borough of Newham* (1994) 71 B.L.R. 1, CA (architects in breach of duty to clients in failing to issue notice under the main building contract to contractor as a prelude to determination); *Royal Brompton Hospital NHS Trust v. Hammond (No. 4)* [2000] B.L.R. 75 (mechanical and electrical engineers' obligation to use reasonable skill and care to see that co-ordination drawings were provided in time to allow the building contractor to meet the contract programme was not diluted or altered by provisions in the building contract which required the contractor to co-ordinate drawings); *South Lakeland District*

special responsibility for design or materials has been undertaken direct to the employer by specialist engineers or sub-contractors.[58]

8–019   **Limitation of liability.** The standard conditions of engagement published by the professional bodies for use in retaining construction professionals include terms which are designed to allow the professional to limit his liability for breach of those conditions in various ways. For example, the RIBA Standard Form of Agreement for the Appointment of an Architect (SFA/99) includes:

(a) a clause which imposes a contractual limitation period for the bringing of a claim against the architect (by action or arbitration) which may be shorter than the statutory limitation period[59];

(b) a clause which limits the architect's liability for loss and damage to a specified sum[60]; and

(c) a clause which limits the architect's liability to that sum which he would be liable to pay assuming that there had been an apportionment of liability similar to that permitted by the Civil Liability (Contribution) Act 1978 between the architect and other parties liable in respect of the same damage (such as contractors and other consultants) and that such other parties had already satisfied their liability to the claimant.[61]

It can readily be seen that such provisions claim significant benefits for the architect if sued by his employer; the latter clause, in particular, places upon the employer the risk that other parties who might be liable to the employer will become insolvent and so unable to contribute to the employer's loss. Such terms may be open to challenge under the Unfair Contract Terms Act 1977 and/or the Unfair Terms in Consumer Contracts Regulations 1999.

8–020   In broad terms, section 3 of the Unfair Contract Terms Act 1977 provides that a contract term which seeks to exclude or restrict liability for negligence is unenforceable unless the term satisfies the statutory test of reasonableness.[62] The prohibition applies only where one party deals as a consumer or on the other's written standard terms of business. Unless the client is a home-owner or otherwise retains the construction professional outside the course of any business, so that he is a consumer, the question will become whether the incorporation of standard conditions of engagement into the construction professional's retainer means that the contract is made on the architect's written standard terms of

---

Council v. Curtins Consulting Engineers plc, unreported, May 23, 2000, H.H. Judge Thornton Q.C., (argument by engineers who designed multi-storey car park that they owed no duty in respect of structural elements supplied by a specialist supplier was rejected; the engineers owed a duty to specify performance standards for those elements and to check the specialist supplier's design calculations); *Try Build Ltd v. Invicta Leisure Tennis Ltd* (2000) 71 Con.L.R. 141 (argument by engineers that they were entitled to leave elements of the design to the specialist supplier was rejected; the engineers ought to have specified those elements or at least made clear in their specification that design of those elements was left to the specialist supplier).

[58] See *I.B.A. v. E.M.I. and B.I.C.C.* (1980) 14 B.L.R. 1 (for the facts, see para. 8–097, below).

[59] Condition 7.2.

[60] Condition 7.3.1.

[61] Condition 7.3.2.

[62] See generally chap. 5, paras 5–03—5–04. By s.2(1), any term or non-contractual notice which seeks to exclude or restrict liability for death or personal injury is void, but the standard forms under discussion contain no such terms.

business. That question arose in *British Fermentation Products Ltd v. Compair Reavell Ltd.*[63] The defendants contracted to supply and install a centrifugal air compressor at the claimants' premises. The contract was made on the Institution of Mechanical Engineers Model Form contract (1975 ed.) with 1978 amendments, which included an exclusion clause. The defendants sought to rely on that clause and the claimants argued that it was unreasonable under the Unfair Contract Terms Act 1977. Judge Bowsher Q.C. held that the Act did not apply since, although the contract terms were written standard terms of business, they were not shown to have been the defendants' written standard terms of business. He commented that, for the Act to apply to model forms drafted by an outside body, there must be proof that the model form is invariably or at least usually used by the party in question; it must be shown that either by practice or by express statement a party has adopted a model form as his standard terms of business.[64]

Assuming that the Act can be shown to apply, the question whether the term **8–021** challenged will survive the statutory test of reasonableness will depend upon the facts in each case. In *Moores v. Yakeley,*[65] the defendant architect contracted to provide his services in connection with the construction of a new bungalow for the plaintiff. The contract was made on the 1992 edition of the RIBA Standard Form of Agreement for the Appointment of an Architect (SFA/92), which provided that the defendant's liability for loss and damage caused by breach of the Agreement would be limited to £250,000. Since the plaintiff was a consumer, it was common ground that the statutory test of reasonableness under the Unfair Contract Terms Act 1977 applied. Dyson J. held that the term satisfied that test. Relevant factors were that the sum referred to was based on the defendant's reasonable assessment of the likely total construction cost of the bungalow, that the sum was over ten times the defendant's anticipated fee for the project and that the plaintiff was in a stronger bargaining position than the defendant (there was a severe recession in the building industry at the time, the plaintiff's financial resources were far in excess of the defendant's and the plaintiff had solicitors to protect his interest in negotiations with the defendant). The Court of Appeal upheld the judge's decision[66] for the reasons which he gave.

The protection afforded to consumers by the Unfair Contract Terms Act 1977 **8–022** is supplemented by the Unfair Terms in Consumer Contracts Regulations 1999,[67] which implement into English law the E.C. Council's Directive on Unfair Terms in Consumer Contracts.[68] The Regulations apply only to terms in contracts made by consumers who are natural persons, so that a company cannot rely upon the Regulations. There is as yet no authority upon the application of the Regulations

---

[63] [1999] B.L.R. 352.
[64] *ibid.* at 361.
[65] (1998) 62 Con.L.R. 76.
[66] Unreported, March 23, 2000.
[67] Revoking and replacing the Unfair Terms in Consumer Contracts Regulations 1994, which came into force on July 1, 1995. Detailed consideration of the Regulations is outside the scope of this work and the reader is referred to *Chitty on Contracts* (28th ed.), paras 15–004 to 15–076.
[68] European Directive (93/13). For consideration of the test of unfairness under the 1994 Regulations, which is substantially the same under the 1999 Regulations, see *Director General of Fair Trading v. First National Bank plc* [2000] 2 W.L.R. 1353, CA and commentaries at (2000) 116 L.Q.R. 557 and [2000] C.L.J. 242. For general discussion of the Regulations, see Macdonald, E., "The Emperor's old clauses: misleading terms and the unfair terms in consumer contracts regulations" [1999] C.L.J. 413.

to the standard terms of engagement published by the construction-related professional bodies, but two potential areas of dispute are clear. First, the Regulations apply only where a term has not been "individually negotiated".[69] Terms in standard form conditions of engagement, such as the financial limitation clause which was considered in *Moores v. Yakeley*,[70] are typically published in a form which allows the parties to choose and insert the figure or period of time which is to form the limitation in question. It will be a question of fact in each case whether such a term was individually negotiated, but the extent to which the consumer has been able to influence the figure or period of time inserted, and thereby, the substance of the term, will always be a relevant consideration.[71]

8–023   The second likely area of challenge arises because the standard conditions used for the engagement of construction professionals commonly include a clause requiring that disputes arising under the engagement be referred to arbitration. This may be to the detriment of the consumer, particularly where he has claims against both professional and contractor in respect of the same loss. Unless all parties consent, he would be required to bring separate proceedings against each defendant (*i.e.* by separate arbitrations with the professional and the contractor or by arbitration with the professional and legal proceedings against the contractor) which will inevitably increase his costs of securing compensation. The Arbitration Act 1996 provides, by sections 89–91, that a term which constitutes an arbitration agreement with a consumer[72] is unfair for the purposes of the Unfair Terms in Consumer Contracts Regulations so far as it relates to a claim for a pecuniary remedy which does not exceed £5,000.[73] A clause requiring a claim in excess of that sum to be referred to arbitration, unless individually negotiated, will be open to challenge under the Regulations in the normal way. The Regulations contain a "grey list" of terms which, subject to the facts of any particular case, may be regarded as unfair.[74] A challenge to an arbitration agreement in standard conditions of engagement is likely to be assisted by the fact that the "grey list" includes any term which has the object or effect of "excluding or hindering the consumer's right to take legal action or exercise any other legal remedy, particularly by requiring the consumer to take disputes exclusively to arbitration not covered by legal provisions".[75] In *Zealander & Zealander v. Laing Homes Ltd*,[76] a case decided under the 1994 Regulations, Judge Havery Q.C. held that an arbitration agreement contained in the National House Builders Council's "Buildmark" guarantee was unfair and unenforceable.

8–024   **Implied terms.** As the employer's agent the construction professional will owe to his principal all the usual duties of an agent. In particular he will owe his principal contractual duties to serve him with reasonable care, skill and diligence

---

[69] reg. 5(1).

[70] (1998) 62 Con.L.R (Dyson J.); unreported, March 23, 2000, CA.

[71] reg. 5(2) provides that "a term shall always be regarded as not having been individually negotiated where it has been drafted in advance and the consumer has therefore not been able to influence the substance of the term."

[72] Which, for these purposes, includes a legal person such as a company as well as a natural person: Arbitration Act 1996, s.90.

[73] The sum in question is prescribed by order, currently the Unfair Arbitration Agreements (Specified Amount) Order 1999 (S.I. 1999 No.2167) (effective January 1,2000).

[74] reg. 5(5), Sched. 2, para. 1.

[75] *ibid.*, para. 1(q).

[76] [2000] T.C.L.R. 724.

and also to serve him faithfully. He will also as agent have authority to bind his principal. As a corollary of that authority, he must not exceed it and if he does he may incur personal liability to third parties for breach of warranty of authority. Treatment of a construction professional's authority as agent is, however, outside the scope of this book and reference should be made to the standard building law textbooks.[77]

The contractual duty to serve his client with reasonable care and skill will, **8–025** however, arise irrespective of whether the nature of the engagement is such as to make the construction professional the client's agent and irrespective of whether standard form conditions of engagement are used. The Supply of Goods and Services Act 1982 provides that such a duty is implied in a contract for the supply of a service where the supplier is acting in the course of a business.[78] This duty is further discussed below, together with the circumstances in which a construction professional may be under the more onerous contractual duty to ensure that his design is reasonably fit for its required purpose.[79]

The duty to exercise reasonable care and skill is frequently pleaded as if it **8–026** were a comprehensive or exhaustive definition of all the duties of a construction professional to his client. It is not.[80] Other duties may properly be implied as terms of the relevant contract. In the circumstances stated in section 14(1) of the Supply of Goods and Services Act 1982[81] there will be an implied term that the supplier will carry out the required service within a reasonable time. What is a reasonable time is a question of fact.[82] Whether other terms should be implied will be decided through application of the usual common law rules for implication of terms.[83]

The scope of contractual duties. A further unusual feature of contracts for the **8–027** services of construction professionals, when compared to those of other professionals, is that the building projects in connection with which they are retained may continue for many months or, often, years. The question may then arise, particularly in the context of limitation, whether the construction professional has a duty to revisit or review the services which he has provided at an earlier stage

---

[77] See Hudson, *op. cit.*, pp. 269–281; Keating, *op. cit.*, pp. 379–387.

[78] Supply of Goods and Services Act 1982, s.13.

[79] See paras 8–131 and 8–168 to 8–174.

[80] Note the passage quoted in chap. 10, para. 10–007 from Oliver J.'s judgment in the solicitor's negligence case, *Midland Bank Trust Co. Ltd v. Hett, Stubbs & Kemp* [1979] Ch. 384, 435.

[81] The circumstances are where "the time for the service to be carried out is not fixed by the contract, left to be fixed in a manner agreed by the contract or determined by the course of dealing between the parties".

[82] Supply of Goods and Services Act 1982, s.14(2).

[83] *e.g.* in *Adams Holden & Pearson v. Trent R.H.A.* (1989) 47 B.L.R. 34, the Court of Appeal rejected an attempt by architects to imply a term as to extra payment for extra services into a contract under seal so as to take advantage of the resulting 12-year limitation period on the grounds that the term sought to be implied was not necessary to fill an obvious omission in the express terms of the contract. In *Chesham Properties Ltd v. Bucknall Austin Project Management Services* (1996) 82 B.L.R. 92 Judge Hicks Q.C. gave detailed consideration to the question whether there were to be implied into the contracts of engagements of architects, engineers, quantity surveyors and project managers terms that they should report on the actual or possible deficiencies of themselves or their fellow professionals. Having considered the detailed terms of each engagement, he found: (a) that the project managers were obliged to report on the deficiencies of others (but not themselves); (b) that the architects were obliged to report on the deficiencies of the engineer and quantity surveyor but not the project manager (who was employed long after the architect and could not, accordingly, have been in the contemplation of the parties at the time of the contract); and (c) that the engineers and quantity surveyors had no duty to report on their own deficiencies or on those of fellow professionals.

of the project. A prominent example of this is the question whether a designer is under a continuing obligation to review his design. Although it will be necessary to look at the circumstances of each engagement, it is clear law that a designer who also supervises or inspects work will generally be obliged to review his design up until that design has been included in the work. In *Brickfield Properties Ltd v. Newton*[84] Sachs L.J. said: "The architect is under a continuing duty to check that his design will work in practice and to correct any errors which may emerge. It savours of the ridiculous for the architect to be able to say ' . . . true my design was faulty, but of course, I saw to it that the contractors followed it faithfully. . . . ' ".[85]

8–028   After *Brickfield*, there were several decisions holding that a designer owes a continuing duty to review his design. It remained unclear, however, whether the duty requires proactive conduct by the designer (whereby he takes positive steps to see that his design was and remains appropriate), or merely reactive conduct (whereby he is under an obligation to reconsider the appropriateness of his design only if and when some potential defect in the design comes to his notice). The duration of the duty also remained unclear: in particular, whether it extended beyond the date of practical completion of the works designed.

8–029   Common sense suggests that a duty to take proactive steps to review a design after it has been built will be rare. In his dissenting judgment in *Eckersley v. Binnie & Partners*[86] Bingham L.J. said *obiter*[87]:

> "It has never, to my knowledge, been held that a professional man who advises on a tax scheme or on draft trading conditions, is thereafter bound to advise his client if, within a period of years, the statutory provisions or the relevant authorities change. Nor has it ever to my knowledge been suggested that a retired practitioner is bound, during his retirement, to keep in touch with developments in his profession in this way. These would be novel and burdensome obligations. On the other hand, counsel for the plaintiffs was able to advance persuasive examples, involving dangers to life and health, where some response by a professional man might well be called for. What is plain is that if any such duty at all is to be imposed, the nature, scope and limits of such a duty require to be very carefully and cautiously defined. The development of the law on this point, if it ever occurs, will be gradual and analogical."

8–030   In *London Borough of Merton v. Lowe*,[88] the defendant architects were retained to design and supervise the construction of an indoor swimming pool. Part of their design called for suspended ceilings rendered with a coat of Pyrok, a proprietary material. After practical completion but before the final certificate had been issued, cracks were discovered in the ceilings. The architects required the contractor to remedy those defects, but did not consider whether the use of Pyrok was an inappropriate design. Judge Stabb Q.C. held that the architects were in breach of duty in failing to do so. He said[89]:

> "I am now satisfied that the architect's duty of design is a continuing one, and it seems to me that the subsequent discovery of a defect in the design, initially and justifiably thought to have been suitable, reactivated or revived the architect's duty in relation to

---

[84] [1971] 1 W.L.R. 862.
[85] *ibid.* at 873.
[86] (1988) 18 Con.L.R. 1. For outline facts of the case see para. 8–79, below.
[87] *ibid.* at 146. Neither of the other Lords Justices considered this point in view of their findings.
[88] (1981) 18 B.L.R.130, CA.
[89] This passage from the unreported judgment of Judge Stabb Q.C. is quoted at (1981) 18 B.L.R. 130, 133.

design and imposed upon them the duty to take such steps as were necessary to correct the results of that initially defective design."

The Court of Appeal upheld Judge Stabb's decision on this point. This case appears to support a purely reactive duty to review design.

In *Chelmsford District Council v. T.J. Evers*[90] Judge Smout Q.C. said that in the **8–031** absence of provision to the contrary there must be an obligation upon an engineer who contracts to design and supervise the execution of his design, to review his design "as necessary" until the works are completed and expressed the view[91] that the engineer's duty to review his design continued until the works were completed. However, this judgment was given in the context of the defendant engineers' attempt to resist joinder in the action on limitation grounds. It is not possible to tell, from the limited report of the facts of the case, just how the learned judge intended to qualify the duty to review by his use of the words "as necessary". Judge Newey Q.C. in one case[92] held that the defendant architects (who were engaged to design and inspect the works) owed a duty until practical completion to check their initial design as work proceeded and to correct it if necessary. The architects were in breach of that duty in failing properly to investigate leaks in the curtain walling which they had designed which occurred before practical completion.[93] It is not clear, therefore, that this case is authority for a proactive duty to review.

In *Tesco v. Norman Hitchcox Partnership*,[94] Judge Lewis Q.C. stated that he **8–032** was in no doubt that where an architect designed a building and administered the building contract, the architect had a continuing duty to his client in contract and in tort to see that the design of the building was appropriate up to the time of completion. That duty required the architect to remedy defects in his design if such defects came to his attention before completion of the works.[95] In *J Sainsbury plc v. Broadway Malyan*[96] Judge Lloyd Q.C. said[97]:

> " . . . an architect is under a continuing duty as regards design. That duty does not require an architect (or engineer or other professional person) to keep previous work under constant review or to report a mistake hat has been discovered, except where third parties may be affected, since the client's interests are protected by the law relating to concealment, but it does come into play when an architect has occasion to look again at the design, eg. where there is evidence of a possible deficiency or where, as here, the design itself is to be modified. BM's decision not to adopt its original design for the wet fish area ought to have caused it to look again at it and advise Sainsbury that the 1984 design was wrong."

---

[90] (1983) 25 B.L.R. 99, 106. See also *Edelman v. Boehm* (1964) *South Australia Law Society Judgment Notices, per* Lord Chief Justice Napier (quoted in *Chelmsford D.C. v. Evers, ibid.* at 106).

[91] *ibid.* at 106.

[92] *Equitable Debenture Assets Corporation Ltd v. William Moss Group Ltd* (1984) 2 Con.L.R. 1, 24.

[93] In *Victoria University of Manchester v. Hugh Wilson* (1984) 2 Con.L.R. 43 (contractors liable in respect of defective fixing of tiles although design of such tiles by architects also defective), the same judge held (at 73) that the defendant architects' duty to review and amend their design lasted until completion. In that case he added that on the facts he did not have to decide whether the duty lasted longer.

[94] (1997) 56 Con. L.R 42.

[95] *ibid.* at 170.

[96] [1999] P.N.L.R. 286.

[97] *ibid.* at 311A-B.

Both decisions, therefore, suggested that the continuing duty to review design is reactive: it arises only if the designer is asked to conduct a review or some event occurs which would cause a reasonably competent designer to look again at his design.

8–033   Two decisions of Judge Bowsher Q.C. might be thought to suggest a proactive duty to review design which also continues beyond practical completion. In *University of Glasgow v. William Whitfield,*[98] where continuing problems with water ingress were experienced at the date of practical completion, Judge Bowsher Q.C. said *obiter* that an architect's duty to design extended beyond practical completion until the building was in fact "complete". In *Department of National Heritage v. Steensen Varming Mulcahy,*[99] Judge Bowsher Q.C. held that mechanical engineers were under a continuing duty to keep their design under review to see whether in fact it was and remained appropriate as construction progressed; it was not open to a designer, he said, to defend an allegation of negligent design by claiming that the design was executed with reasonable care and skill at the outset but became inappropriate by reason of external factors over which the designer had no control.

8–034   It is difficult to reconcile these suggestions of a proactive continuing duty to review design with authority to the effect that, in the absence of an express term or express instructions to investigate and report upon the causes of defects, there will be no implied obligation upon a professional man to report to a client upon his own deficiencies. In *Chesham Properties Ltd v. Bucknall Austin Project Management Services Ltd,*[1] Judge Hicks Q.C. in finding that no such duty was owed stated,

> "The duty sought to be pleaded here—to advise, warn or inform of their own actual or potential deficiencies in performance—is more specific, more directly contrary to the architects' own interests, and therefore less likely to arise by construction or implication than the duty postulated by Judge Bowsher in *Glasgow University v. Whitfield* to reveal 'what he knows of the design defects as possible causes of the problem'."

8–035   The position is plainly different if the professional man accepts express instructions to investigate and report upon defects, thereby accepting a new obligation to review his original design. This occurred in the Australian case of *Pullen v. Gutteridge.*[2] The Victorian Court of Appeal found that the defendant engineers were liable for the negligent design of a swimming pool complex and found that the claim in respect of that design was not statute barred. However the court also found that the engineers were at fault in not reporting properly on the cause of the defects which were subsequently discovered when instructed to do so:

---

[98] (1988) 42 B.L.R. 66, 78.

[99] (1998) 60 Con. L.R. 33 at 89.

[1] (1996) 82 B.L.R. 92. See also *Midland Bank Trust Co. Ltd v. Hett, Stubbs & Kemp* [1979] 1 Ch. 384 *per* Oliver J. at 403B: "It is not seriously arguable that a solicitor who or whose firm has acted negligently comes under a continuing duty to take care to remind himself of the negligence of which, ex hypothesi, he is unaware"; *Rees Hough Ltd v. Redland Reinforced Plastics Ltd* (1984) 27 B.L.R. 136 at 149 (manufacturers and sellers of pipes not obliged to warn that they had been unable to design to the contractual specification); *Southern Water Authority v. Carey* [1985] 2 All E.R. 1077 (sub-contractors on sewage project not obliged to warn main contractor or engineer of defects in sub-contract works); cf. *Stag Line v. Tyne Shiprepair Group Ltd* [1984] 2 Lloyd's Rep. 211 (implied duty on ship-repairer to inform ship-owner of the use of potentially hazardous lining material contrary to specification when ship-repairer became aware of the same).

[2] [1993] 1 V.R. 27, Victoria CA.

"Had the respondent acted with reasonable care when asked to investigate and report to the appellant, its investigations would have had two consequences. In the first place, it would have come to realise, or at the very least to entertain a strong suspicion, that its own design of the sub-structure was seriously deficient and that the deficiency was responsible for many of the defects that had emerged and were emerging. In the second place, it would have communicated this realisation or suspicion to its client."[3]

The English authorities referred to above (with the apparent exception of **8–036** *Chesham Properties Ltd v. Bucknall Austin Project Management Services Ltd*[4]) were considered by Dyson J. in *New Islington Health Authority v. Pollard Thomas & Edwards*.[5] The defendant architects were engaged to design and supervise the construction of flats for the claimant, under two building contracts. After practical completion but before issue of the final certificates under the building contracts, the claimant received complaints from its tenants that sound-proofing in the properties was poor. It asked the architects for details of their design for sound insulation of the flats and whether that design complied with the Building Regulations. The architects provided the information requested but took no steps to review their design for the sound insulation. The claimant argued that the architects owed a continuing duty to check and review their design until the end of their retainer, which was marked by the issue of the final certificates. Dyson J. rejected that submission. He held, first, that a designer who also supervised or inspected work would generally be obliged to review that design up until the design had been included in the work. If his design was for part of the works only, his duty would extend only until that part had been built. Secondly, the duty to review design will arise only if the designer has good reason to reconsider his original design. Giving as an example an architect who designs and supervises the construction of the foundations of a building only, Dyson J. said[6]:

"In my view, in the absence of an express term or express instructions, he is not under a duty specifically to review the design of the foundations, unless something occurs to make it reasonably necessary, or at least prudent, for a reasonably competent architect to do so. For example, a specific duty might arise if, before completion, the inadequacy of the foundations causes the building to show signs of distress; or if the architect reads an article which shows that the materials that he has specified for the foundations are not fit for their purpose; or if he learns from some other source that the design is dangerous. In such circumstances, I am in no doubt that the architect would be under a duty to review the design, and, if necessary, issue variation instructions to the contractor to remedy the problem. But in the absence of some reason such as this, I do not think that an architect who has designed and supervised the construction of foundations is thereafter under an obligation to review his design."

Thirdly, Dyson J held that an architect who, as in *New Islington Health Authority*, had been engaged on the RIBA Standard Conditions of Engagement to design and supervise the construction of the entire works would owe a duty to review his design up until practical completion. Thereafter, the architect was not entitled to issue variation instructions to the building contractor and the terms of his own engagement imposed no express or implied duty to review his design. If

---

[3] *ibid.* at 86.
[4] (1996) 82 B.L.R. 92.
[5] [2001] P.N.L.R. 515. The reasoning deployed in this case was foreshadowed in A. Nissen, "The duty to review a design—is it real or artificial?" (1997) 13 Con. L.J. 221.
[6] *ibid.* para. 16.

the employer asks the architect to investigate a potential design defect after practical completion, the architect is entitled to refuse or to say that he will do so only if paid an additional fee, since the work of investigating the effectiveness of his original design is not part of his original contract of engagement.[7] Finally, Dyson J. held that whenever the duty to review arises, it is limited in scope to a reactive duty[8]:

> "In my judgment, the duty does not require the architect to review any particular aspect of the design that he has already completed unless he has good reason for so doing. What is a good reason must be determined objectively, and the standard is set by reference to what a reasonably competent architect would do in the circumstances."

It was held that the claimant's request for information about the defendants' design for sound insulation was not sufficient to activate the defendants' duty to review their design: it was merely a request for information and not a request that the defendant investigate the noise insulation problem at the flats.

(ii) Duties independent of contract

8–037   Duties may be imposed by law on a construction professional towards his client as well as towards the rest of the world. The statutory duties which are imposed are reasonably clear. The nature and extent of duties imposed by common law are less clear. The principal practical importance of tortious claims is that contractual claims in respect of latent defects against construction professionals are often statute-barred before the defects in respect of which complaint is made are discovered. The Latent Damage Act 1986 provides considerable relief to a claimant making such claims if he is able to bring his claim in negligence. The Act has no application to contractual claims.[9]

8–038   **Duties imposed by statute.** Two pieces of legislation significantly affect the duties which construction professionals owe to their clients: the Defective Premises Act 1972 and the Construction (Design and Management) Regulations 1994.

---

[7] On that basis, Dyson J. distinguished the decision of Judge Bowsher Q.C. in *University of Glasgow v. William Whitfield* (see para. 8–033 above): on the facts of that case, the architect's failure to review his design had been in breach of a duty imposed by a fresh retainer created by the employer's request that the architect investigate problems of water ingress at the building after practical completion. It remains difficult, however, to reconcile Dyson J.'s view of the scope of the duty with that of Judge Bowsher Q.C., who clearly had in mind a proactive duty which existed before the defects arose and before the employer's request was made. At (1988) 42 B.L.R. 66, 78, he said, "Equally, I take the view that where, as here, an architect has had drawn to his attention that damage has resulted from a design which he knew or ought to have known was bad from the start, he has a particular duty to his client to disclose what he had been under a continuing duty to reveal, namely what he knows of the design defects as possible causes of the problem."

[8] *ibid.* para. 20. See, to similar effect, *Payne v. John Setchell Ltd*, unreported, March 16, 2001, *per* Judge Lloyd Q.C. at para. 21: "It is now in my view well established that a designer's duty of care only requires a reconsideration of the design if the designer becomes aware or should have been aware of the need to reconsider the design." For the facts of that case, see para. 8–059 below.

[9] See chap. 5, paras 5–49—5–55. The existence of tortious liability will also affect a claim for contribution under the Law Reform (Married Women and Tortfeasors) Act 1935 although any such claims are now likely to be very rare as the Act applies only to cases where the relevant damage occurred or the relevant obligations were assumed before January 1, 1979. In practice the 1935 Act is now only likely to be of importance where the operation of the limitation period is suspended by reason of the fact that a claimant is an infant or patient. For discussion of the 1935 Act, see chap. 1 of the 3rd ed. paras 1–77 to 1–79.

The Defective Premises Act 1972. Section 1(1) of the Defective Premises Act   8–039
1972[10] provides:

"(1) A person taking on work for or in connection with the provision of a dwelling
(whether the dwelling is provided by the erection or by the conversion or enlargement
of a building) owes a duty—

(a) if the dwelling is provided to the order of any person, to that person; and
(b) without prejudice to paragraph (a) above, to every person who acquires an
interest (whether legal or equitable) in the dwelling; to see that the work which
he takes on is done in a workmanlike or, as the case may be, professional manner,
with proper materials and so that as regards that work the dwelling will be fit for
habitation when completed."

Section 2 of the Act states that provided certain requirements are fulfilled no   8–040
action shall be brought under section 1 where rights in respect of defects are
conferred by an "approved scheme". At present there are no such approved
schemes.[11] Until March 31, 1979, the main approved scheme was the 10–year
protection scheme of the National House-Builders Registration Council which
covered the vast majority of new houses constructed in this country and thus
provided an enormous restriction on the practical operation of section 1.[12]

The duty set out in section 1 applies only to work taken on after the com-   8–041
mencement date of the Act, which was January 1, 1974. Furthermore, the Act
applies only to "dwellings". The term is not defined in the Act. In a different
context, it has been held to mean a buildings used or intended to be used as
residences by one or more families, and provided with all necessary parts and
appliances, such as floors, windows, staircases, etc.[13] Modern statutory definitions of the term include "any house, flat or other unit designed or adapted for
living in".[14] A "dwelling-house" was defined in the London Building Act 1930
as "a building used or constructed or adapted to be used wholly or principally for
human habitation".[15]

Section 1 of the Act applies to the failure to carry out necessary remedial work   8–042
as well as to the carrying out of work badly. In *Andrews v. Schooling and
Others*,[16] the purchasers of a leasehold flat claimed damages against the freehold

---

[10] The Act does not apply in Scotland or Northern Ireland.
[11] The House Building Standards (Approved Scheme etc.) Orders 1973, 1975 and 1977 (S.I. 1973 No.
7 1843, S.I. 1975 No. 1402 and S.I. 1977 No. 642) were replaced by the House Building Standards
(Approved Scheme etc.) Order 1979 (S.I. 1979 No. 381) which did not apply to the NHBC scheme
due to changes in the NHBC scheme. This was resolved following a little known agreement between
the Secretary of State and the NHBC. Through most of the 1980s it was widely thought that the
NHBC scheme was an excluded scheme. Thus in *Warner v. Basildon Corporation* (1991) 7 Const.
L.J. 146, CA, Ralph Gibson L.J. said: "About 97 per cent of houses constructed in any year are built
under the NHBC Scheme approved under section 2 of the Defective Premises Act 1972 and, in
consequence, the section 1 remedy is excluded." For further discussion of this matter see I. N.
Duncan Wallace Q.C., "*Anns* beyond repair" (1991) 107 L.Q.R. 228, 242.
[12] For criticism of this restriction and other comments on the operation of the Act see J. R. Spencer,
"The Defective Premises Act 1972—defective law and defective law reform" [1974] C.L.J. 307
[13] See *Halsbury's Laws*, Vol. 4(2) (4th ed., reissue), para. 335 n. 53 and para. 375 referring to the
decision in *Williams v. Fitzmaurice* (1858) H. & N. 844, 157 E.R. 709, where the court held that a
contract to provide a house fit for occupation included provision of the floor boards.
[14] Housing Act 1985, Part XVI, s.575(1), in the context of assistance available to the purchasers of
defective dwellings originally built by public authorities.
[15] London Building Act 1930, s.5. For numerous further definitions and statements as to the meaning
of "dwelling" and "dwelling-house" see *Stroud's Judicial Dictionary* (6th ed.).
[16] [1991] 1 W.L.R. 783.

owners and developers from whom the flat was purchased on the basis that the cellar was unfit for habitation through damp. The defendants had carried out no work to the cellar, but were held liable under section 1 of the Act for failing to do so.

8–043   There is a question of construction as to whether section 1(1) of the Act imposes three separate duties to carry out work (a) in a workmanlike or professional manner, (b) with proper materials and (c) so that the dwelling will be fit for habitation when completed or whether there is a single duty and the requirement of fitness for habitation is a measure of the standard required in the performance of that duty. In *Thompson v. Clive Alexander & Partners*[17] Judge Lewis Q.C. considered this matter and held the latter construction to be correct. He based his reasoning first on statements by members of the Court of Appeal in *Alexander v. Mercouris*[18] and secondly on his view that the plain intention of the Act was only to see that dwellings were built in such a way as to ensure that they were fit for habitation on completion. The decision is somewhat difficult to reconcile both with the words of the statute and with observations by Buckley and Goff L.JJ. in *Alexander v. Mercouris* that a cause of action would arise during the course of construction once bad workmanship had taken place (although it appears to have been implicit that the bad workmanship would be such as to render the dwelling unfit for habitation if and when the dwelling was completed). If correct, the decision imposes a significant limit on the scope of the Act, since failure to carry out work in a workmanlike or professional manner or with proper materials will not amount to a breach of the duty imposed by section 1(1) if the dwelling is nevertheless fit for habitation.

8–044   Subsection 1(5) provides that any cause of action under the section shall be deemed for limitation purposes to have accrued at the time when the dwelling was completed. As the general limitation period is six years, this may provide a slightly longer period than in contract especially if a professional undertakes only the design of a dwelling. However, in *Payne v. John Setchell Ltd*,[19] Judge Lloyd Q.C. held that a claim under the Defective Premises Act does not amount to an "action for damages for negligence" within the meaning of section 14A of the Limitation Act 1980 (introduced by the Latent Damage Act 1986). Accordingly, a claimant under the Act does not have the benefit of an extension of time of three years from the date of knowledge subject to the long-stop of 15 years. This result would in any event follow from the construction of section 1(1) adopted in *Thompson v. Clive Alexander & Partners*[20]: a duty to ensure that a dwelling is fit for habitation goes beyond a duty to exercise reasonable skill and care.

8–045   A dwelling will be unfit for habitation when completed notwithstanding that a defect is latent rather than patent. In *Andrews v. Schooling*,[21] Balcombe L.J. said:

---

[17] (1992) 28 Con.L.R. 49. In *Mirza v. Bhandal*, unreported, April 27, 1999, Latham J. proceeded as if the former construction were correct, so that there would be no breach of the duty imposed by s.1(1) if the dwelling was in fact fit for habitation. It is not clear, however, whether Latham J. had heard argument on the point.

[18] [1979] 1 W.L.R. 1270.

[19] Unreported, March 16, 2001, approving the view adopted in the 4th edition of this work. For the facts, see para. 8–059 below.

[20] (1992) 28 Con.L.R. 49. In *Mirza v. Bhandal*, unreported, April 27, 1999, Latham J. proceeded as if the former construction were correct, so that there would be no breach of the duty imposed by s.1(1) if the dwelling was in fact fit for habitation. It is not clear, however, whether Latham J. had heard argument on the point.

[21] [1991] 1 W.L.R. 783, CA at 790.

"If, when the work is completed, the dwelling is without some essential attribute—*e.g.* a roof or a damp course—it may well be unfit for human habitation even though the problems resulting from the lack of that attribute have not then become patent. A house without a roof is unfit for habitation even though it does not rain until some months after the house has been completed."

This approach was followed in *Mirza v. Bhandal*.[22] In that case, it was argued that a dwelling was fit for habitation at the time of its completion since its inadequate foundations had not by then brought about its collapse, although they were expected to do so within fifteen years thereafter unless underpinned. Latham J. rejected that argument:

"The dwelling, when completed, carried with it the seeds of its destruction. It seems to me that such a dwelling cannot properly be described as fit for habitation. . . . Although the effects of defective foundations are not as immediately dramatic as the lack of a roof, it seems to me that the principle remains the same. The inadequacy of the foundations was inevitably going to produce a situation in which the house would collapse. I do not consider that a house with foundations as inadequate as that can be described as fit for habitation when completed."

The Construction (Design and Management) Regulations 1994. In addition to statutory duties which provide a directly enforceable civil remedy, there are also statutory obligations which impose extensive obligations upon professional men which do not give rise to direct civil rights but are nonetheless likely to be of importance in civil proceedings. Thus regulation 13 of the Construction (Design and Management) Regulations 1994[23] imposes obligations upon a designer: **8-046**

(a) not to prepare a design for any project unless he has taken reasonable steps to ensure that a client is aware of the (extensive) duties to which the client is subject by reason of the regulations;

(b) (subject to a requirement of reasonable practicality) to ensure that any design that he prepares[24] and which he is aware will be used for the purposes of construction work includes among the design consideration adequate regard to the need:

  (i) to avoid foreseeable risks to the health and safety of any person at work carrying out construction work or cleaning work in or on the structure at any time, or of any person who may be affected by the work of such a person at work;

  (ii) to combat at source risks to the health and safety of any person at work carrying out construction work or cleaning work in or on the structure at any time or of any person who may be affected by the work of such a person at work; and

---

[22] Unreported, April 27, 1999.
[23] S.I. 1994 No. 3140, made under s.15 of the Health and Safety at Work etc. Act 1974 which came into force on March 31, 1995.
[24] For discussion of the meaning of "prepares a design" in the context of a criminal prosecution under the CDM Regulations, see *R. v. Paul Wirth SA* [2000] I.C.R. 860, CA (a design and build contractor which approved a latch design prepared by its specialist sub-contractor did not prepare the design of the latch for the purposes of reg. 13(2)(a)).

(iii) to give priority to measures which will protect all persons at work who may carry out construction work or cleaning work at any time and all persons who may be affected by the work of such persons at work over measures which only protect each person carrying out such work;

(c) (subject to a requirement of reasonable practicality) to ensure that the design includes adequate information about any aspect of the project or structure or materials which might affect the health or safety of any person at work carrying out construction work or cleaning work in or on the structure at any time or of any person who may be affected by the work of such a person at work; and

(d) to co-operate with the planning supervisor (who is responsible for the preparation of a health and safety plan) and with any other designer to enable each of them to comply with the requirements and prohibitions placed upon them in relation to the project.

Although regulation 21 expressly states that a breach of the majority of the Regulations shall not confer a right of action in civil proceedings, which would otherwise be given by section 47(2) of the Health and Safety at Work etc. Act 1974, it is likely that a court would find that a breach of the regulations amounted to a breach of a common law duty of care.[25]

8–047 **Duties imposed at common law.** Claims made against construction professionals in tort by their clients will generally be for economic loss. Until recently there was a very real debate as to whether the existence of a contract precluded the existence of a concurrent duty of care.[26] In England and Canada it has now been decided that the mere existence of a contract will not exclude a concurrent duty of care although the parties will (subject to statutory limitations) be able to restrict such a duty if they wish to do so. Although the position is less well established, it appears likely that courts in Australia and New Zealand would take the same view.

8–048 In *Henderson v. Merrett Syndicates Ltd,*[27] the House of Lords conducted an extensive analysis of previous English and Commonwealth authorities before concluding that under the *Hedley Byrne* principle, the plaintiffs who were direct Names at Lloyds of London were owed a duty of care in tort as well as in contract by the managing agents. Lord Goff gave the leading speech. He praised and substantially adopted the analysis of Oliver J. in *Midland Bank Trust Co. v. Hett, Stubbs & Kemp*[28] and expressly considered[29] *Bagot v. Stevens Scanlan & Co.*

---

[25] See *Hewett v. Alf Brown's Transport Ltd* [1991] I.C.R. 471 where the court accepted a submission that requirements of the Control of Lead at Work Regulations 1980 (S.I. 1980 No. 1248) were equivalent to the common law requirements in dismissing a claim against an employer in respect of an employee's exposure to lead. See also J. Barber, "Potential side-effects of the CDM Regulations" (1997) 13 Const. L.J. 95.
[26] See chap. 2, paras 2–100—2–106.
[27] [1995] 2 A.C. 145.
[28] [1979] Ch. 384. See further chap. 10, para. 10–013, below.
[29] *ibid.* at 185.

Ltd,[30] in which Diplock L.J., sitting at first instance on the trial of a preliminary
issue as to whether the action was barred by limitation, held that an architect
employed under a contract with the employer to supervise the laying of a
drainage system owed him a duty in contract only and not in tort. In reaching this
decision, Diplock L.J. had felt compelled to recognise that a different conclusion
might be reached "where the law in the old days recognised either something in
the nature of a status like a public calling (such as common carrier, common
innkeeper, or a bailor and bailee) or the status of master and servant".[31] Having
pointed out that it was also necessary to add claims against doctors and dentists
to the list, Lord Goff stated that he found it startling "that, in the second half of
the 20th century, a problem of considerable practical importance should fall to be
solved by reference to such an outmoded form of categorisation as this". Later,
Lord Goff stated[32]:

> "Attempts have been made to explain how doctors and dentists may be concurrently
> liable in tort while other professional men may not be so liable, on the basis that the
> former cause physical damage whereas the latter cause pure economic loss (see the
> discussion by Christine French in (1981–84) 5 Otago L.R. 236, 280–281). But this
> explanation is not acceptable, if only because some professional men, such as archi-
> tects, may also be responsible for physical damage. As a matter of principle, it is
> difficult to see why concurrent remedies in tort and contract, if available against the
> medical profession, should not also be available against members of other professions,
> whatever form the relevant damage may take."

The rationale for the concurrent duty of care in tort was provided by the
Hedley Byrne principle[33]:

> "However, at least in cases such as the present . . . there seems to be no reason why
> recourse should not be had to the concept, which appears after all to have been adopted,
> in one form or another, by all of their Lordships in *Hedley Byrne* . . . . In addition, the
> concept provides its own explanation why there is no problem in cases of this kind
> about liability for pure economic loss; for if a person assumes responsibility to another
> in respect of certain services, there is no reason why he should not be liable in damages
> for that other in respect of economic loss which flows from the negligent performance
> of those services. It follows that, once the case is identified as falling within the *Hedley
> Byrne* principle, there should be no need to embark upon any further enquiry whether
> it is 'fair, just and reasonable' to impose liability for economic loss . . . The concept
> indicates too that in some circumstances, for example where the undertaking to furnish
> the relevant service is given on an informal occasion, there may be no assumption of
> responsibility; and likewise that an assumption of responsibility may be negatived by an
> appropriate disclaimer."

His conclusion[34] was that:

---

[30] [1966] 1 Q.B. 197. See also to the same effect *Steljes v. Ingram* (1903) 19 T.L.R. 534: claim against
architect for negligent supervision held to be an action "founded on contract" within the meaning of
s.116 of the County Courts Act 1888, so that the claimant was only entitled to county court costs. If
the claim had been founded on tort, costs on the High Court scale would have been awarded. Earlier
in the same year in *Columbus Co. v. Clowes* [1903] 1 K.B. 244, a claim against an architect for
negligent survey of a site, Wright J. (at 248) left open the issue whether the action was one of contract
or of tort.
[31] *ibid.* at 204–205.
[32] *ibid.* at 190.
[33] *ibid.* at 181. See chap. 2, paras 2–24—2–25.
[34] *ibid.* at 194–195.

" . . . the common law is not antipathetic to concurrent liability, and that there is no sound basis for a rule which automatically restricts the claimant to either a tortious or a contractual remedy. The result may be untidy; but, given that the tortious duty is imposed by the general law, and the contractual duty is attributable to the will of the parties, I do not find it objectionable that the claimant may be entitled to take advantage of the remedy which is most advantageous to him, subject only to ascertaining whether the tortious duty is so inconsistent with the applicable contract that, in accordance with ordinary principle, the parties must be taken to have agreed that the tortious remedy is to be limited or excluded."

8–049   Even before *Henderson*, there were many architects' negligence cases pleaded in contract and in tort where the availability of the concurrent remedy was not questioned.[35] An example of a leading case where it was assumed that a duty lay in tort as well as contract was *Pirelli General Cable Works Ltd v. Oscar Faber & Partners*.[36] The plaintiff building owners sued the defendant consulting engineers for the negligent design of a chimney extension. The claim was initially in contract and in tort for the costs of rectification of a chimney which had cracked but the plaintiffs conceded that the contractual claim was time-barred. In *Murphy v. Brentwood District Council*,[37] Lord Keith, with whom all the other law lords agreed, explained *Pirelli* as a case in which tortious liability arose out of a contractual relationship as a consequence of the *Hedley Byrne* principle,[38] thus presaging the result in *Henderson*. As was pointed out in *Henderson*,[39] the Supreme Court of Canada had already reached a similar decision in the solicitors' case of *Central Trust Co. v. Rafuse*,[40] where Le Dain J., giving the leading judgment also paid tribute to Oliver J.'s judgment in *Midland Bank* and stated[41]:

"A concurrent or alternative liability in tort will not be admitted if its effect would be to permit the plaintiff to circumvent or escape a contractual exclusion or limitation of liability for the act or omission that would constitute the tort. Subject to this qualification, where concurrent liability in tort and contract exists the plaintiff has the right to assert the cause of action that appears to be the most advantageous to him in respect of any particular legal consequence."

This decision is entirely consistent with the later decision of the Supreme Court of Canada in *British Columbia Hydro & Power Authority v. BG Checo*[42] where the Court held that an employer was liable to a building contractor in tort for a negligent misstatement contained in tender documents. The court held that the contractor's right to sue in tort existed unless expressly precluded by the contract, which it was not.

---

[35] See n. 70 to para. 2–21 of the 3rd edition of this work for examples of such cases. In two first instance decisions, *Wessex R.H.A. v. HLM Design* (1994) C.I.L.L. 907 and *Conway v. Crown Kelsey* (1994) 39 Con.L.R. 1, official referees had held that architects and engineers owed duties of care in tort concurrent to those which had been accepted in contract.
[36] [1983] 2 A.C. 1.
[37] [1991] 1 A.C. 398.
[38] *ibid.* at 466F.
[39] [1995] 2 A.C. 145 at 191.
[40] (1986) 31 D.L.R. (4th) 481. See further chap. 10, para. 10–015, below.
[41] *ibid.* at 522.
[42] [1993] 1 S.C.R. 12.

Bagot was originally followed in the New Zealand architect's case of *Bevan* **8–050**
Investments Ltd v. Blackhall and Struthers (No. 2)[43] and in *McLaren Maycroft &*
Co. v. Fletcher Development Co. Ltd[44] the New Zealand Court of Appeal held
that a claim for negligence in the performance of professional services was a
claim in contract and contract only. However, in *Rowlands v. Collow*[45] Thomas
J. felt able to find an engineer to be concurrently liable for the design of a
driveway in contract and in tort and refused to follow the decision of the New
Zealand Court of Appeal. The judge did so on the basis of decisions in other
Commonwealth jurisdictions and, in particular, *Central Trust Company v. Rafuse*.
He stated:

> "There is no doubt that the decisions and literature are overwhelmingly in favour of
> concurrent liability. I venture to suggest that this preponderance of support for con-
> current liability reflects the merits of the competing arguments. The issue is now
> virtually incontestable; a person who has performed professional services may be held
> liable concurrently in contract and in negligence unless the terms of the contract
> preclude the tortious liability."

It appears that a similar position prevails in Australia. In *Pullen v. Gutteridge*[46] **8–051**
the Court of Appeal of Victoria rejected a submission that an architect did not
owe a duty of care to his client in respect of economic losses. The court
summarised the position in Australia as follows[47]:

> " . . . ever since *Voli v. Inglewood Shire Council* (1963) 110 C.L.R. 74 it has been clear
> that an architect or engineer may be liable to his client in tort as well as in contract. We
> refer also to *Macpherson & Kelley v. Kevin J. Prunty & Associates* [1983] 1 V.R. 573,
> especially at 580, *per* Lush J., where it is said that the view is no longer tenable that
> concurrent liability in tort exists only where some physical injury or damage is likely
> to result. Moreover, it is apparent that the matter of 'reliance', which will often be
> important in determining the existence of relevant proximity, need not be pleaded or
> proved where there is a relationship of a professional man and his client. A duty of care
> is implicit in such a relationship, as is perhaps reliance itself: *Sutherland Shire Council
> v. Heyman* (1984–1985) 157 C.L.R. 424 at 497 and 502 *per* Deane J. It is, in any event,
> manifest beyond argument that the appellant, as a client, in fact relied on the respondent
> as the designer of the centre."

The importance of concurrent liability. The main practical reason for the **8–052**
debate as to the existence of concurrent liability arises from the different treatment accorded to contractual and tortious claims. As a tortious claim requires
damage, it may accrue later and the Latent Damage Act 1986, which extends the
limitation period to three years from the "date of knowledge" as defined (up to
a maximum "long-stop" period of 15 years), applies only to claims in negligence. Some commentators have criticised the apparent influence of procedure
on substantive law. Thus I.N. Duncan Wallace Q.C., in an article prior to *Henderson*,[48] stated:

---

[43] [1973] 2 N.Z.L.R. 45 at first instance. The appeal reported in [1978] 2 N.Z.L.R. 97 related to
quantum of damages only. The facts are set out in n. 89 to para. 8–121, below.
[44] [1973] 2 N.Z.L.R. 100.
[45] [1992] 1 N.Z.L.R. 178.
[46] [1993] 1 V.R. 27.
[47] *ibid.* at 39–40.
[48] "Anns beyond repair" (1991) 107 L.Q.R. 228, 247.

"These rather complicated concepts of concurrent liability, relatively recently developed throughout the Commonwealth countries over the past 20 years, appear to have been principally dictated by the need of defendants to secure the benefit of statutory limitation, contribution or apportionment remedies not then currently available in contract, rather than on any substantive principle. By contrast the current climate in the House of Lords seems disposed, many may think wisely, to restore and affirm the important distinctions between tort and contract. This would be facilitated, it is suggested, by eliminating the artificial pressures arising from purely procedural differences of remedy. The extension of the Act of 1986 to liability in contract (or, to the exact contrary, repealing the 1986 Act altogether), therefore would reduce the artificial arguments and litigation arising from questions of concurrent liability, as well as provide a means of doing justice to contractual plaintiffs."[49]

Such calls were decisively rejected. In *Henderson*, Lord Goff stated[50]:

"I think it is desirable to stress at this stage that the question of concurrent liability is by no means only of academic significance. Practical issues, which can be of great importance to the parties, are at stake. Foremost among these is perhaps the question of limitation of actions. If concurrent liability in tort is not recognised, a claimant may find his claim barred at a time when he is unaware of its existence. This must moreover be a real possibility in the case of claims against professional men, such as solicitors or architects, since the consequences of their negligence may well not come to light until long after the lapse of six years from the date when the relevant breach of contract occurred. Moreover the benefits of the Latent Damage Act 1986, under which the time of the accrual of the cause of action may be postponed until after the plaintiff has the relevant knowledge, are limited to actions in tortious negligence. This leads to the startling possibility that a client who has had the benefit of gratuitous advice from his solicitor may in this respect be better off than a client who has paid a fee. Other practical problems arise, for example, from the absence of a right to contribution between negligent contract-breakers; from the rules as to remoteness of damage, which are less restricted in tort than they are in contract; and from the availability of the opportunity to obtain leave to serve proceedings out of the jurisdiction. It can of course be argued that the principle established in respect of concurrent liability in contract and tort should not be tailored to mitigate the adventitious effects of rules of law such as these, and that one way of solving such problems would no doubt be to rephrase such incidental rules as have to remain in terms of the nature of the harm suffered rather than the nature of the liability asserted (see Tony Weir, XI Int.Encycl.Comp.L. ch.12, para. 72). But this is perhaps crying for the moon; and with the law in its present form, practical considerations of this kind cannot sensibly be ignored."

8–053   If a claimant pleads his claim in tort as well as in contract, the defendant may raise a defence of contributory negligence.[51] Although it is probable that the defence will also be available in an action brought in contract alone, the matter has yet to reach the House of Lords.[52]

---

[49] For consideration of how best to protect sufferers from latent damage see "Limitation of actions and latent damage—an Australian perspective" (1991) 54 M.L.R. 216 and N. J. Mullany, "Reform of the law of latent damage" (1991) 54 M.L.R. 349.

[50] *ibid.* at 185.

[51] Conversely, to the extent that a concurrent duty of care in tort is narrower than contractual duties, there will be no defence of contributory negligence. See, for example, *Raflatac Ltd v. Eade* [1999] B.L.R. 261, discussed at para. 8–057 below. Contributory negligence is discussed in relation to the construction professions at paras 8–328 to 8–330, below.

[52] See the discussion at chap. 5, paras 5–115—5–116.

The right to claim contribution under the Law Reform (Married Women and **8–054** Tortfeasors) Act 1935[53] only arises as between tortfeasors. It does not apply as between a tortfeasor and a contract breaker or between two contract breakers. Thus for contribution to be recoverable under the 1935 Act by an architect, engineer or quantity surveyor from another tortfeasor (*e.g.* a contractor or sub-contractor), or vice versa, each must have been liable to the client in tort in respect of the same damage. Nevertheless, the importance of the 1935 Act is receding fast with time so that it is now likely to be relevant only if a limitation defence is, for some reason, disapplied with respect to a claimant. The Act was repealed with effect from the coming into force of the Civil Liability (Contribution) Act 1978 on January 1, 1979. Rights of contribution under the 1978 Act are not limited to claims between tortfeasors.[54]

The scope of the concurrent duty in tort. The question, "what does the **8–055** concurrent duty of care in tort require?" begs the response, "duty of care in doing what?" That response focuses the inquiry on what was agreed to be done, *i.e.* the contract. Moreover the touchstone of implication is necessity not reasonableness. Recognition of this principle prompts caution against patching over perceived holes in the matrix of contractual duties as between parties to a building project with duties of care in tort and against construing the duty to exercise reasonable care and skill as a duty to do that which is reasonable. Normally, however, the contractual relationship between a construction professional and his client will establish sufficient proximity, assumption of responsibility and reliance to found a coterminous duty of care in tort. The construction professional will owe a duty to his client in tort to exercise reasonable skill and care in providing the services which he contracted to provide.

It will be rare that a concurrent duty of care in tort will require the taking of **8–056** steps extending beyond those required to discharge the duties expressed or implied in the contract, including in particular the duty to exercise reasonable care and skill. However, should the professional contracting party provide advice or services which are outside the ambit of his retainer, he may be held to have owed a duty of care in tort in respect of such advice or services which is necessarily wider in scope than his contractual duties. One such case was *Kensington and Chelsea and Westminster A.H.A. v. Wettern Composites Ltd.*[55] The defendant structural engineers' contractual duties included the checking of drawings for the adequacy of fixings to cladding but not, as held by the judge, the supervision of the installation of the fixings. Defects in the installation of the fixings were observed by the engineers. Judge Smout Q.C. held that although there was no contractual duty requiring the engineers to follow up their observations, their duty of care to the plaintiff client in tort did require them to do so. They were not, however, in breach of the duty as they had notified the architects.

The contract may go further than defining the duties undertaken. It may **8–057** contain terms qualifying, limiting or even excluding any concurrent duty of care in tort. Such express terms are rare in contracts with professional men (as distinct

---

[53] s.6(1)(c).
[54] Rights of contribution under the 1978 Act are discussed in chap. 4. See also paras 8–315 to 8–327 below.
[55] (1984) 1 Con.L.R. 114. For an example involving surveyors, see *Holt v. Payne Skillington* (1995) 77 B.L.R. 51.

from contracts with building contractors, sub-contractors or suppliers).[56] It may often be the case, however, that a professional man has a defence to an action in tort which is not available to him in contract. If a professional engages a sub-consultant to perform part of his tasks, he will owe no duty of care in tort to his client in relation to that work unless he owed a duty to carry out that work which was a non-delegable duty for the purposes of the law of tort.[57] The principle is illustrated by the decision of Colman J. in *Raflatac Ltd v. Eade*.[58] The defendant main contractor agreed to carry out certain works for the plaintiff building owner, including the replacement of a sprinkler system. With the plaintiff's agreement, the defendant sub-contracted the replacement of a sprinkler system to a specialist sub-contractor. The sub-contractor carried out the work negligently. The plaintiff alleged breach of the main contractor's concurrent duty of care in tort. It was held that the main contractor owed to the plaintiff a contractual duty to exercise care and skill in the conduct of the entire works, including the replacement of the sprinkler system, but did not owe a parallel duty of care in tort in respect of the replacement of the sprinkler system. Since the plaintiff and the main contractor had agreed that this part of the works would be sub-contracted out, the main contractor did not assume responsibility to the plaintiff for the skill and care with which it was carried out.

8–058   There is currently a conflict of authority at first instance as to whether the concurrent duty of care in tort owed by a construction professional to his client is limited to a duty to avoid causing personal injury or damage to other property of his client, or extends to taking care to avoid economic loss. In *Storey v. Charles Church Developments Ltd*,[59] the defendant designed and built a house for the plaintiff. Structural faults appeared as a result of defective design of the foundations. The plaintiff claimed damages for breach of the defendant's concurrent duty of care in tort. It was common ground that the plaintiff's loss was economic loss. Judge Hicks Q.C. held that the defendant did owe a duty of care in respect of such loss. In accordance with the reasoning of the House of Lords in *Henderson*, the judge applied the *Hedley Byrne* principle to the question of the defendant's concurrent duty. He held that, by reason of its contract with the plaintiff, the defendant had assumed a responsibility to him to exercise reasonable skill and care in designing the house and the plaintiff had relied upon him to do so. That assumption of responsibility and concomitant reliance occurred because of the relationship created by the contract between the parties and the resulting duty of care in tort was not limited by the terms of the contract. It followed that the defendant's duty in tort was a duty to avoid causing economic

---

[56] *e.g. Rumbelows Ltd v. A.M.K.* (1980) 19 B.L.R. 25; *William Hill Organisation Ltd v. Bernard Sunley and Sons Ltd* (1982) 22 B.L.R. 1, CA; *Twins Transport Ltd v. Patrick and Brocklehurst* (1983) 25 B.L.R. 65; *Southern Water Authority v. Lewis and Duvivier* (No. 1) (1984) 1 Con.L.R. 40 and (No. 2) (1984) 1 Con.L.R. 50; *Greater Nottingham Co-operative Society Ltd v. Cementation Piling and Foundations Ltd* [1989] Q.B. 71.

[57] *D. & F. Estates Ltd v. Church Commissioners for England* [1989] A.C. 177, 208 *per* Lord Bridge; *Aiken v. Stewart Wrightson Members Agency Ltd.* [1995] 1 W.L.R. 1281 (member's agents at Lloyd's did not owe a duty of care in tort to the Names with whom they had contracts in respect of work delegated to managing agents, who had no contracts with the Names). For a discussion of non-delegable duties in tort, see *Clerk & Lindsell on Tort* (18th ed.), paras 5–48—5–61.

[58] [1999] B.L.R. 261.

[59] (1995) 73 Con.L.R. 1. For discussion of this and other decisions, see Ndekugri I., "Concurrent liability in contract and tort in the construction industry" (2000) 16 Const.L.J. 13.

loss to his client.[60] It was argued that a builder can never be liable in tort for economic loss, in reliance upon the decision of the House of Lords in *Murphy v. Brentwood District Council*.[61] Judge Hicks dismissed that argument. *Murphy* was distinguishable on the facts, particularly since there was no contract between the parties in *Murphy*. Furthermore, Lord Keith in *Murphy*[62] had referred with approval to the decision in *Pirelli General Cable Works Ltd v. Oscar Faber and Partners*[63] in which it was assumed that a designer owed a concurrent duty in tort to avoid causing economic loss to his client.[64]

In *Payne v. John Setchell Ltd*,[65] Judge Lloyd Q.C. declined to follow the **8–059** decision in *Storey*. In that case, the claimants were the purchasers of cottages which had been built for a Mrs Wright. Mrs Wright had engaged the defendant civil and structural engineer to assist in the construction of the cottages. The defendant had designed raft foundations for the cottages, inspected the construction of those foundations and certified that they were satisfactorily constructed and suitable for support of the cottages. The claimants alleged that raft foundations were an inappropriate design and had caused structural problems which required remedial work. The claimants argued that, until Mrs Wright sold the cottages to them, she had had a cause of action against the defendant for breach of his concurrent duty of care in tort in designing the foundations and certifying their suitability. It was common ground that if Mrs Wright had had such a cause of action, the claimants would have acquired an identical cause of action upon their acquisition of the cottages, under section 3 of the Latent Damage Act 1986.[66] The judge regarded the decisions of the House of Lords in *Murphy* and, to the like effect, in *Department of the Environment v. Thomas Bates & Son*[67] as establishing that[68]:

"as a matter of policy, any person undertaking work or services in the course of a construction process is ordinarily liable only for physical injury or for property damage other than to the building itself but is not liable for other losses—ie economic loss. If any liability for such economic loss is to arise it must be for other reasons, *e.g.* as a result of advice or statements made upon which reliance is placed in circumstances

---

[60] See, to similar effect *Barclays Bank plc v. Fairclough Building Ltd (No.2)* (1995) 76 B.L.R. L.R. 1 (a sub-sub-contractor owed a duty of care in tort to the sub-contractor in performing the sub-sub-contract works; duty not limited to physical damage).
[61] [1991] 1 A.C.398; discussed further at para. 8–072 below.
[62] *ibid.* at 466.
[63] [1983] 2 A.C. 1.
[64] See para. 8–049 above.
[65] Unreported, March 16, 2001. The position would appear to be similar in South Africa: *Kohler Flexible Packaging (Pinetown) (Pty) Ltd v. Marianhill Mission Institute* (2000) (1) S.A. 141.
[66] s.3(1) states:
   "Subject to the following provisions of this section, where—
   (a) a cause of action ('the original cause of action') has accrued to any person in respect of any negligence to which damage to any property in which he has an interest is attributable (in whole or in part); and
   (b) another person acquires an interest in that property after the date on which the original cause of action accrued but before the material facts about the damage have become known to any person who, at the time when he first has knowledge of those facts, has any interest in the property;
   a fresh cause of action in respect of that negligence shall accrue to that other person on the date on which he acquires his interest in the property."
[67] [1991] 1 A.C. 499; discussed further at para. 8–073 below.
[68] Unreported, March 16, 2001, at para. 30.

which create a relationship where there is in law to be an assumption of the responsibility for loss—*i.e.* within the principle of *Hedley Byrne v. Heller* . . . . In my judgment a designer is not liable in negligence to the client or to a subsequent purchaser for the cost of putting right a flaw in a design that the designer has produced that has not caused physical injury or damage, just as a contractor is not liable."

Accordingly, the judge held that the defendant did not owe to his client, Mrs Wright, any duty of care in tort to avoid causing economic loss. Since the claimants had suffered economic loss only (the cost of remedial works to cure the defects in the cottages' foundations), they acquired no useful cause of action upon acquisition of the cottages under section 3 of the Latent Damages Act 1986.

8–060   It is respectfully submitted that Judge Lloyd's analysis of the decisions in *Murphy* and *D.O.E v. Bates* is entirely correct so far as concerns the scope of duty of care owed by the builder or designer of a property to a person with whom he has no contract, but not in relation to the scope of the duty in tort owed by such person *to his client*. That duty was not the subject of discussion in those cases. Furthermore, it is very difficult to reconcile the judge's approach with the words of Lord Goff in *Henderson*, explaining that the concurrent duty of care in tort is a *Hedley Byrne* duty, which encompasses economic loss[69]:

"However, at least in cases such as the present . . . there seems to be no reason why recourse should not be had to the concept, which appears after all to have been adopted, in one form or another, by all of their Lordships in *Hedley Byrne* . . . . In addition, the concept provides its own explanation why there is no problem in cases of this kind about liability for pure economic loss; for if a person assumes responsibility to another in respect of certain services, there is no reason why he should not be liable in damages for that other in respect of economic loss which flows from the negligent performance of those services. It follows that, once the case is identified as falling within the *Hedley Byrne* principle, there should be no need to embark upon any further enquiry whether it is "fair, just and reasonable" to impose liability for economic loss . . . ."

Pending appellate consideration of the scope of the concurrent duty of care in tort owed by a construction professional to his client, it is thought that the view adopted by Judge Hicks Q.C. in *Storey* is the better view.

8–061   **Fiduciary duties.** Although the vast majority of claims against construction professionals are brought either in contract or in the tort of negligence, other claims are sometimes made which overlap with those discussed in this book. As set out above,[70] a construction professional may act as agent for his client and have the power to alter the client's legal relationships. As a consequence, when acting in such capacity, he is likely to owe fiduciary duties to his client. However such fiduciary duties will not enlarge the scope of contractual duties. In *Chesham Properties Ltd v. Bucknall Austin Project Management Services Ltd*[71] the plaintiff sought to make out a case that the defendant project managers, architects,

---

[69] [1995] 2 A.C. 146 at 181. See also *Bellefield Computer Services Ltd v. E. Turner & Sons Ltd* [2000] B.L.R. 97, where Schiemann L.J. (at 102) clearly regarded a designer's concurrent duty of care in tort as a duty to avoid causing economic loss; see also *Gable House Estates Ltd v. The Halpern Partnership* (1995) 48 Con.L.R. 1, 106 *per* Judge Lewis Q.C. and *Gloucestershire Health Authority v. Torpy* (1997) 55 Con.L.R. 124, 135 per Judge Bowsher Q.C.

[70] See para. 8–012. For a general discussion of fiduciary obligations owed by professionals, see chap. 2, paras 2–125—2–146.

[71] (1996) 82 Build. L.R. 92.

engineers and quantity surveyors owed fiduciary duties to warn their employer client of their own actual or potential deficiencies in performance and/or those of their fellow professionals. In finding that no such fiduciary duty was owed, Judge Hicks Q.C. adopted the statement of the Privy Council in the solicitors' case of *Clarke Boyce v. Mouat*[72]:

> "A fiduciary duty concerns disclosure of material facts in a situation where the fiduciary has either a personal interest in the matter to which the facts are material or acts for another party who has such an interest. It cannot be prayed in aid to enlarge the scope of contractual duties."

(b) *Duties to Third Parties*

Collateral warranties. A construction professional may undertake express contractual duties to a person other than his immediate client. For example, a building owner who contracts with a design and build contractor may wish to make sure that he will have a remedy for defective design in the event that the contractor becomes insolvent. If the contractor has sub-contracted the design work to an architect, the employer may require the architect to sign a collateral warranty. In consideration for the employer awarding the main contract to the contractor, who is the architect's client, or for nominal consideration, the architect undertakes an obligation to the employer to use reasonable skill and care in performing the work sub-contracted to him.[73] Sometimes, such a document is executed under seal, when it may be known as a "duty of care deed". In that case, not only will the employer be entitled to bring an action for any breach of duty in respect of design against a party which is likely to have the benefit of professional indemnity insurance, but he will also have 12 years within which to bring such an action.[74] The liability of the construction professional to such a third party will then be governed by ordinary contractual rules. **8–062**

Just as an architect, engineer or quantity surveyor may have duties imposed upon him towards his client by operation either of statute or of common law so he may have duties imposed towards third parties. **8–063**

Duties imposed by statute. In England and Wales,[75] the major relevant statutory duty in relation to dwellings is the Defective Premises Act 1972. Section 1(1) of that Act is set out and discussed above.[76] As is apparent from the **8–064**

---

[72] [1994] 1 A.C. 428 at 437G. Any claim for breach of fiduciary duty brought now would need to take into account the decision of the Court of Appeal in *Bristol & West Building Society v. Mothew* [1998] Ch. 1 that a breach of fiduciary duty requires intentional misconduct and is not made out where the conduct complained of is consistent with mere oversight; the latter gives rise to a claim for breach of contract or negligence only.

[73] The British Property Federation has published two Forms of Agreement for Collateral Warranties after consultation with RIBA, ACE, RICS and the insurance industry. One form (referred to as "CoWa/F"), is for use where the warranty is given to a funding institution; the other ("CoWa/P&T") is for use with a purchaser or tenant. Each form contains an undertaking by the professional in these terms: "The Firm warrants that it has exercised and will continue to exercise reasonable skill [and care] [care and diligence] in the performance of its duties to the Client under the Agreement . . .".

[74] The limitation period for an action brought on a contract under seal is 12 years: Limitation Act 1980, s.8.

[75] By s.7(3) the Act does not apply to Scotland or Northern Ireland.

[76] See paras. 8–039 to 8–045, above.

words of the section, any duty is owed to "every person who acquires an interest (whether legal or equitable) in the dwelling."

8–065   **The Contracts (Rights of Third Parties) Act 1999.** Strictly speaking, this Act[77] does not impose duties on construction professionals. Rather, it creates an exception to the doctrine of privity of contract so as to enable a third party to acquire rights under a contract if that is what the parties to the contract intended. However, because construction professionals operate in circumstances in which their services may well be regarded as conferring a benefit on parties other than their immediate client, the Act is of potential importance in any consideration of the liability of construction professionals. Detailed consideration of the Act is outside the scope of this work and only the principal provisions are outlined below.[78] Section 1 of the Act gives a third party a right to enforce a term of a contract if the contract expressly provides that he may[79] or if the relevant term purports to confer a benefit on him.[80] The third party will have such a right unless, on a true construction of the contract, the parties to it did not intend the term to be enforceable by the third party.[81] The third party must be expressly identified in the contract by name, class or description, but he does not need to have existed at the date when the contract was made.[82] He is entitled to the same remedies for breach of contract as would be available if he were a party to the contract, *i.e.* he can recover his own loss.[83] Defences available to the promisor[84] include defences and set-off which the promisor would have had against the other contracting party if that party had sought to enforce the term,[85] and also any defence or counterclaim which the promisor would have had against the third party if the third party had been a party to the contract.[86] Thus, if the promisor was induced to enter the contract by the third party's misrepresentation, he could set up this defence in the third party's claim even although it would not have been available had the promisee brought the claim.

8–066   The Act came into force on November 11, 1999. It applies only to contracts entered into on or after May 11, 2000, unless expressly incorporated into a contract made before that date.[87] Its effect upon claims against construction professionals is not yet widely apparent. It is likely that employers and other third parties who are in a position to do so will continue to require collateral warranties from construction professionals engaged by others, so as to avoid the potentially

---

[77] The Act substantially implements "Privity of Contract: Contracts for the Benefit of Third Parties", Law Commission Report No. 242 (Cm. 3329, 1996).

[78] For detailed consideration, see *Chitty on Contracts* (28th ed.), paras 19–075 to 19–102; C. MacMillan., "A birthday present for Lord Denning: The Contracts (Rights of Third Parties) Act 1999" (2000) 63 M.L.R. 721; T. Roe, "Contractual intention under section 1(1)(b) and 1(2) of the Contracts (Rights of Third Parties) Act 1999" (2000) 63 M.L.R. 887; N. Andrews, "Strangers to justice no longer: the reversal of the privity rule under the Contracts (Rights of Third Parties) Act 1999" [2001] C.L.J. 353; A. Burrows, "The Contracts (Rights of Third Parties) Act 1999 and its implications for commercial contracts", a lecture given to the Society of Construction Law on May 23, 2000.

[79] s.1(1)(a).

[80] s.1(1)(b).

[81] s.1(2).

[82] s.1(3).

[83] s.1(5).

[84] *i.e.* the contracting party which bears the burden of performing the relevant term.

[85] s.3(2) and (3).

[86] s.3(4).

[87] s.10(2) and (3).

difficult questions of contractual construction which may arise upon a claim under the Act. Moreover, it is to be anticipated that, in future, construction professionals will take care to see that the operation of the Act is expressly excluded from their professional appointments.[88]

Duties imposed at common law. The general principles upon which the **8–067** courts act in seeking to decide whether a duty of care should be imposed at common law are discussed in chapter 2 above.[89] Although it is submitted that courts throughout the Commonwealth have regard to the same principles, there has been a considerable divergence in the results in similar factual situations. This divergence has been most marked when considering whether a subsequent purchaser can recover damages for economic loss (generally the cost of repair of a defective building) from a person involved in the original building operation. In England and Wales, the House of Lords has expressed considerable reluctance to allow such claims.[90] Unless the House of Lords once again departs from its previous decisions, it is likely that a subsequent purchaser will only be able to claim damages for economic loss if he can rely upon the *Hedley Byrne*[91] principle. Although the courts of Canada, Australia and New Zealand (including the Privy Council on a New Zealand appeal[92]) have discussed (and differed upon) the precise importance and significance of economic loss, none have limited claims for economic loss to the same extent as the House of Lords has done. The differing approaches taken throughout the Commonwealth render a unified discussion of this area both unsatisfactory and, potentially, misleading. Accordingly, this part of the work is organised in the following way:

(i) The definition of the type of loss. In view of the differing approaches taken in respect of different types of loss and different categorisations of such loss, it is important to define the type of loss which is sought to be recovered.

(ii) Recovery by third parties in respect of personal injury and damage to "other property". This area presents little difference of approach between the various Commonwealth jurisdictions.

(iii) The general exclusionary rule adopted in England with regard to the recovery of economic loss. This section considers the basic English rule as set out in *Murphy v. Brentwood District Council.*[93]

(iv) The English exceptions to the general exclusionary rule. This section discusses the possibility of escaping the general exclusionary rule by one of the three exceptions contemplated in *Murphy*: the complex structure theory; the prevention of damage to third party property; and the application of the *Hedley Byrne* principle.

(v) The position in Canada.

---

[88] The RIBA Standard Form of Agreement for the Appointment of an Architect (SFA/99) expressly excludes the operation of the Act: cl. 7.6.
[89] See chap. 2, paras 2–22—2–78 and 2–109—2–115.
[90] See paras 8–084 to 8–086, below.
[91] See paras 8–096 to 8–109, below.
[92] *Invercargill City Council v. Hamlin* [1996] A.C. 624. See further paras 8–077 and 8–121, below.
[93] [1991] 1 A.C. 398, HL.

(vi) The position in Australia.

(vii) The position in New Zealand.

(viii) The position in other jurisdictions.

(ix) Problems of scope of duty. This section discusses the problem of defining the scope of duty in the absence of a contract.

(i) *The definition of the type of loss*

8–068 In *Sutherland Shire Council v. Heyman*[94] Brennan J., in a passage which has been substantially approved in the House of Lords[95] and which it is submitted accurately summarises the common law as applied in England, stated:

> "Liability in tort is for damage done, not for damage merely foreseeable or threatened or imminent. . . . The corollary is that a postulated duty of care must be stated in reference to the kind of damage that a plaintiff has suffered and in reference to the plaintiff or a class of which the plaintiff is a member. I venture to repeat what I said in *John Pfeiffer Pty Ltd v. Canny*[96]: 'His duty of care is a thing written on the wind unless damage is caused by the breach of that duty; there is no actionable negligence unless duty, breach and consequential damage coincide. . . . For the purposes of determining liability in a given case, each element can be defined only in terms of the others.' It is impermissible to postulate a duty of care to avoid one kind of damage—say, personal injury—and, finding the defendant guilty of failing to discharge that duty, to hold him liable for the damage actually suffered that is of another and independent kind—say, economic loss. Not only may the respective duties differ in what is required to discharge them: the duties may be owed to different persons or classes of person. That is not to say that a plaintiff who suffers damages of some kind will succeed or fail in an action to recover damages according to his classification of the damage he suffered. The question is always whether the defendant was under a duty to avoid or prevent that damage, but the actual nature of the damage suffered is relevant to the existence and extent of any duty to avoid or prevent it."

8–069 The above passage is a clear reaffirmation of the importance of classifying the type of damage which had been blurred in *Dutton v. Bognor Regis Urban District Council*[97] and *Anns v. Merton L.B.C.*[98] In *Dutton* the Court of Appeal held that a local authority which negligently inspected the foundations of a house built on an old rubbish tip was liable to a subsequent purchaser of the house for the costs of strengthening the foundations so that there was no danger to health and safety and for a (presumably continuing) diminution in value. In a famous dictum,[99] Lord Denning said:

> "The damage done here was not solely economic loss. It was physical damage to the house. If [counsel for the defendant's] submission were right, it would mean that if the inspector negligently passes the house as properly built and it collapses and injures a person, the council are liable: but if the owner discovers the defect in time to repair

---

[94] (1984–1985) 157 C.L.R. 425: local authority held not liable to the subsequent purchasers of a house for structural defects caused by inadequate footings. Although all members of the High Court of Australia were agreed as to the result, only a bare majority held that there was no duty of care.
[95] See *Caparo Industries plc v. Dickman* [1990] 2 A.C. 605, *per* Lord Oliver at 651, *per* Lord Bridge at 627; *Murphy v. Brentwood District Council* [1991] A.C. 398 *per* Lord Keith at 464B.
[96] (1981) 148 C.L.R. 218, 241–242.
[97] [1972] 1 Q.B. 373.
[98] [1978] A.C. 728.
[99] [1972] 1 Q.B. 373, 396.

it—and he does repair it—the council are not liable. That is an impossible distinction. They are liable in either case."

In *Anns v. Merton LBC*[1] a local council was sued for the costs of remedying **8–070** defects in a block of flats caused by movement of the foundations and consequential losses by seven lessees of the flats by reason of having negligently approved or inspected the foundations. At first instance and in the Court of Appeal, the only issue was whether the claims were statute-barred. In the House of Lords, the council was granted leave to challenge the existence of a duty of care. The House of Lords held that the council would be liable for the negligence of its inspector in inspecting the foundations and that such a duty was not statute-barred as it arose only when there was a present or imminent danger to the health of the persons occupying it. Lord Wilberforce (with whom three other Law Lords agreed) accepted that the position of a local authority should be no worse than that of a builder.[2] Later in his judgment he said[3]:

"In my opinion [the damages recoverable] may also include damage to the dwelling house itself.... To allow recovery for such damage to the house follows, in my opinion, from normal principle. If classification is required, the relevant damage is in my opinion material, physical damage, and what is recoverable is the amount of expenditure necessary to restore the dwelling to a condition in which it is no longer a danger to the health or safety of persons occupying and possibly (depending on the circumstances) expenses arising from necessary displacement."

The decisions in *Dutton* and *Anns* have now been respectively overruled and **8–071** departed from. In *D. & F. Estates Ltd v. Church Commissioners for England*,[4] the plaintiff lessees of a flat sued the main contractors who had built the plaintiffs' flat for the cost of remedying defective plasterwork originally installed by subcontractors together with associated consequential costs. The House of Lords held *inter alia* that the loss sustained in renewing the plasterwork amounted to irrecoverable pure economic loss, ie. either the cost of repairing the defects or the diminution in the value of the property as a result of the defects. Both Lord Bridge[5] and Lord Oliver[6] were clear that the plasterwork had caused no significant damage to any other relevant property. Both, however, left open the question whether individual items of a "complex structure" such as a house could be treated separately with the result that the defective construction of one part of the house, such as the foundations, which gave rise to damage to another part, such as the walls, could be said to give rise to damage which was not pure economic loss.[7]

In *Murphy v. Brentwood District Council*[8] Mr Murphy, a subsequent purchaser **8–072** of a house, sued a local authority for having negligently passed plans with the result that the foundations cracked and extensive damage was caused to the walls and pipes of the house. The judge held that the damage was such as to cause an imminent danger to Mr Murphy's health and safety. Mr Murphy's claim was for

---

[1] [1978] A.C. 728.
[2] *ibid.* at 758.
[3] *ibid.* at 759G.
[4] [1989] 1 A.C. 177.
[5] *ibid.* at 207.
[6] *ibid.* at 214E.
[7] See *per* Lord Bridge at 207 and *per* Lord Oliver at 212. See further paras 8–089 to 8–094, below.
[8] [1991] 1 A.C. 398.

£35,000, being the reduction in the price which he obtained on a sale of the house in its defective condition. £35,000 was less than the cost of repair would have been. The House of Lords unanimously departed from *Anns*, holding that where a defect in a house was discovered before any injury to person or health or damage to property other than the defective house itself had occurred, no action lay against a local authority. The question whether a local authority owed a duty in respect of injury to persons[9] or "other" property[10] was expressly left open, as was the question whether the builder of defective premises could be held responsible for the cost necessarily incurred by a building owner in protecting himself from potential liability to third parties in respect of personal injury.[11] Lord Keith (with whom all the other law lords agreed) stated[12]:

> "In my opinion it must now be recognised that, although the damage in *Anns* was characterised as physical damage by Lord Wilberforce, it was purely economic loss."[13]

8–073   In *Department of the Environment v. Thomas Bates and Son Ltd*,[14] the defendant builders who built an office complex were sued by under-lessees of part of the complex in respect of the cost of strengthening the pillars of a building so as to allow it to carry its design load. The House of Lords applied their decision in *Murphy* in finding that the loss suffered by the plaintiffs was purely economic and thus irrecoverable against the builders.

8–074   Although they have been unwilling to accept that the categorisation is as important as the House of Lords has deemed it to be, the Supreme Court of Canada, the High Court of Australia and the Privy Council (on a New Zealand appeal) have all made it clear that they accept that the House of Lords was correct to categorise loss claimed by a subsequent purchaser in respect of defects in a structure as economic loss.

8–075   In *Canadian National Railway Co. v. Norsk Pacific Steamship Co. (The Jervis Crown)*,[15] the Canadian Supreme Court found a barge operator who negligently damaged a bridge liable for economic losses incurred by the operator of a railway which had the right to use, but did not own, the bridge. McLachlin J., with whom two of the other members of the majority agreed, defined the underlying problem as the search for a principled mechanism to limit liability for foreseeable economic loss flowing from negligence. In *Winnipeg Condominium Corporation v. Bird Construction Co.*,[16] the defendant constructed an apartment building which the plaintiff acquired as a subsequent owner. Following the collapse of part of the stone cladding, the plaintiff replaced all of the cladding in order to avoid further accidents and sought to claim the costs from the original main contractor, cladding sub-contractor and architect. The Supreme Court of Canada refused to strike out the claim. La Forest J. (with whom all the other judges agreed) stated[17]:

---

[9] *per* Lord MacKay at 457H.
[10] *per* Lord Keith at 463H.
[11] *per* Lord Bridge at 475H and *per* Lord Oliver at 489C; discussed further at para. 8–095, below.
[12] *ibid.* at 466H.
[13] See also *per* Lord Oliver at 484A.
[14] [1991] 1 A.C. 499.
[15] (1992) 91 D.L.R. (4th) 289.
[16] (1995) 74 B.L.R. 1, (1995) 121 D.L.R. (4th) 193.
[17] *ibid.* at 10.

"Traditionally, the courts have characterised the costs incurred by a plaintiff in repairing a defective chattel or building as "economic loss" on the grounds that costs of those repairs do not arise from injury to property apart from the defective chattel or building itself; see *Rivtow Marine Ltd v. Washington Iron Works* [1974] S.C.R. 1189, at page 1207. For my part, I would find it more congenial to deal directly with the policy considerations underlying that classification as was done in an analogous situation in *Dutton v. Bognor Regis Urban District Council* [1972] 1 Q.B. 373, CA, *per* Lord Denning M.R. (at pages 396–398), and Sachs L.J. (at pages 403–404). However, I am content to deal with the issues in the terms in which the arguments were formulated. Adopting this traditional characterisation as a convenient starting point for my analysis, I observe that the losses claimed by the Condominium Corporation fall quite clearly under the category of economic loss."

In *Bryan v. Maloney,*[18] the majority of the High Court of Australia found the defendant builder liable to a subsequent purchaser for having negligently constructed a house with foundations that were inadequate to withstand seasonal changes in the clay soil. The case proceeded upon the basis that only economic loss was being claimed. Mason C.J., giving the judgment of the majority, stated: **8–076**

"Whilst the relationship between Mr Bryan and Mrs Manion with respect to physical injury to Mrs Manion's person or property must be distinguished from the relationship between them with respect to mere economic loss, the significance of such a distinction varies according to the particular type of economic loss which is involved in the relevant category of case. Here, the distinction is between ordinary physical damage to a house by some external cause and mere economic loss in the form of diminution in value of a house when the adequacy of its footings first becomes manifest by consequent damage to its fabric. Obviously that distinction, which has only recently attained general acceptance . . . , is an essentially technical one . . . ".[19]

In *Invercargill City Council v. Hamlin,*[20] the Privy Council considered a New Zealand case where the plaintiff employed a builder to construct his house in accordance with plans which had been approved by the local authority. The local authority also conducted inspections of the building works. When cracks appeared in the property, the plaintiff sued the local authority for negligence, and two linked questions arose: (a) whether a duty of care was owed by the authority to the plaintiff; and (b) when such a cause of action arose. In upholding the decision of the New Zealand Court of Appeal, the Privy Council found that, in New Zealand, local authorities did owe a duty to the plaintiff and that the limitation period did not begin to run until the defects could, with reasonable diligence, have been discovered.[21] In respect of the second question, Lord Lloyd, who delivered the advice to Her Majesty, made it clear that the plaintiff's claim was for economic loss and not physical damage: **8–077**

"Once it is appreciated that the loss in respect of which the plaintiff in the present case is suing is loss to his pocket, and not for physical damage to the house or foundations, then most, if not all the difficulties surrounding the limitation question fall away. The plaintiff's loss occurs when the market value of the house is depreciated by reason of the defective foundations and not before. If he resells the house at full value before the

---

[18] (1995) 74 B.L.R. 35.
[19] *ibid.* at 46H.
[20] [1996] A.C. 624.
[21] Thus finding that the decision of the House of Lords in *Pirelli General Cable Works Ltd v. Oscar Faber* [1983] 2 A.C. 1 was not good law in New Zealand.

defect is discovered, he has suffered no loss. Thus in the common case the occurrence of the loss and the discovery of the loss will coincide."[22]

(ii) *Recovery by third parties in respect of personal injury and damage to "other property"*

8–078   **Personal injury.** It has long been held that architects and other construction professionals owe a duty of care not to cause personal injury to those whom they could reasonably foresee might be injured as a result of their negligence.[23] Thus in *Clay v. A.J. Crump & Sons Ltd*[24] the employer requested demolition contractors to leave a wall standing as protection against intruders. The architect promised the employer to look into the matter and inquired of the demolition contractors whether it was safe to leave the wall standing. They replied that it was, relying on the advice of a foreman. Subsequently the architect visited the site but never inspected the wall, which was left standing in a dangerous condition. When the building contractors came on site their managing director cursorily examined the wall but failed to appreciate its condition. The wall collapsed, injuring the plaintiff, a labourer employed by the building contractors. The Court of Appeal held that the architect, demolition contractors and building contractors owed a duty of care and were liable to the plaintiff. Responsibility was apportioned 42 per cent to the architect, 38 per cent to the demolition contractors and 20 per cent to the building contractors. The case was argued and resolved upon a general level, the main issues being whether the plaintiff was within the contemplation of the architect and whether the examination by building contractors absolved the architect from his duty to the plaintiff. The court reached its result as a result of the application of the principles in *Donoghue v. Stevenson*.[25] Ormerod L.J. stated[26]:

"The architect, by reason of his contractual arrangement with the building owner, was charged with the duty of preparing the necessary plans and making arrangements for the manner in which the work should be done. This involved taking precautions or giving instructions for them to be taken so that the work could be done with safety. It must have been in the contemplation of the architect that builders would go on the site as the whole object of the work was to erect buildings there. It would seem impossible to

---

[22] *ibid.* at 384A. Following the transfer of sovereignty, the Hong Kong Court of Final Appeal held in *Bank of East Asia v. Tsien Wui Marble Factory Ltd* [2000] 1 H.K.L.R.D. 268 that the claim by a purchaser of a building with defective granite cladding to recover the cost of remedial works in tort from the sub-contractor who had negligently installed the cladding and the architects who had negligently designed the building was statute-barred. A majority in the Court held, preferring the English authorities on limitation to other Commonwealth authorities, that the loss was economic. Dissenting on the question of when the purchaser's cause of action accrued, Lord Nicholls of Birkenhead followed the reasoning in *Invercargill* and held that the plaintiff's cause of action accrued when the defects became reasonably discoverable.
[23] See, for example, *Murphy v. Brentwood District Council* [1991] 1 A.C. 398 at 487 *per* Lord Oliver and *Mobil Oil Hong Kong Ltd v. Hong Kong United Dockyards Ltd (The Hu Lien)* [1991] 1 Lloyd's Rep. 309 at 329 *per* Lord Brandon. However, in *Marc Rich & Co v. Bishop Rock Marine Co Ltd* [1996] 1 A.C. 211, a House of Lords' majority held that "whatever the nature of the harm sustained . . . it is necessary to consider the matter not only by inquiring about foreseeability but also by considering the nature of the relationship between the parties; and to be satisfied that in all the circumstances it is fair just and reasonable to impose a duty of care." (*per* Lord Steyn at 235.) It appears, therefore, that the test to be applied to determine the existence of a duty in tort to avoid causing physical harm is more demanding than has hitherto been thought.
[24] [1964] 1 Q.B. 533, CA.
[25] [1932] A.C. 562, HL.
[26] *ibid.* at 557.

contend that the plaintiff would not be affected by the decisions and plans drawn up by the architect."[27]

The decision in *Clay* was considered by the Court of Appeal in *Perrett v. Collins*,[28] where the defendants had certified as airworthy an aircraft which later crashed and injured the plaintiff, a passenger. The submission that the defendants owed no duty of care to the plaintiff was rejected. Hobhouse L.J. said[29]:

" . . . it has never been a requirement of the law of the tort of negligence that there be a particular antecedent relationship between the defendant and the plaintiff other than one that the plaintiff belongs to a class which the defendant contemplates or should contemplate would be affected by his conduct. Nor has it been a requirement that the defendant should inflict the injury upon the plaintiff. . . . In cases of personal injury, it suffices that the activity of the defendant has given rise to the situation which has caused the injury to the plaintiff. Where the defendant is involved in an activity which, if he is not careful, will create a foreseeable risk of personal injury to others, the defendant owes a duty of care to those others to act reasonably having regard to the existence of that risk. . . .

and, later[30]:

"Where the plaintiff belongs to a class which either is or ought to be within the contemplation of the defendant and the defendant by reason of his involvement in an activity which gives him a measure of control over and responsibility for a situation which, if dangerous, will be liable to injure the plaintiff, the defendant is liable if as a result of his unreasonable lack of care he causes a situation to exist which does in fact cause the plaintiff injury."

There are relatively few cases concerning design defects which have caused **8–079** physical injuries to persons after completion of the works. Provided that injury is foreseeable, personal injuries caused by such defects will give rise to an actionable duty of care. In *Eckersley v. Binnie & Partners*,[31] the defendants were consulting engineers who had been employed by a water authority to design and supervise the construction of a water tunnel and associated valve house. They were found liable in negligence to 31 plaintiffs who were, or were representatives of, members of a visiting party who were injured or killed in an explosion at the valve house caused by the ignition of methane gas. Neither at first instance nor on appeal was there any dispute that the consulting engineers owed a duty of care, although there was considerable dispute as to whether the presence of methane gas was reasonably foreseeable.[32] In *Targett v. Torfaen Borough Council*[33] the Court of Appeal held that a local authority that had designed and built a council house was liable to a tenant who had been injured as a result of the negligent failure to provide a handrail or adequate lighting, notwithstanding the plaintiff's knowledge of the defects that had caused his injuries. The Court

---

[27] See also *Florida Hotels Pty Ltd v. Mayo* (1965) 113 C.L.R. 588. The majority of the High Court of Australia held that an architect owed a duty of care in supervising building works to an injured labourer employed by the employer who engaged no main contractor but employed his own tradesmen and labourers. This case is discussed further at paras 8–241 and 8–248, below.
[28] [1998] 2 Lloyd's Rep. 255.
[29] *ibid.* at 261.
[30] *ibid.* at 262.
[31] (1988) 18 Con.L.R. 1.
[32] As to which see paras 8–208 and 8–279, below.
[33] [1992] 3 All E.R. 27.

refused to accede to the defendant's argument that the effect of *Murphy v. Brentwood District Council*[34] was that the local authority was not liable for injuries caused by patent defects. Both Leggatt L.J.[35] and Sir Donald Nicholls V.-C.[36] emphasised that the essential question was whether it was reasonable for a plaintiff to avoid a danger once he was aware of the same. On the facts of the case a weekly tenant was in no position to remedy the dangerous situation and the council was therefore liable, although a deduction of 25 per cent was appropriate for the plaintiff's contributory negligence in failing to look where he was going.[37] In *Berwick v. Wickens Holdings Ltd*,[38] injury was caused many years after completion of the defective building. The claimant's husband was an employee of a building contractor (John Lay) which was engaged to refurbish a 25-year old building. He was killed when the building collapsed. The building was originally constructed by another contractor (Wickens), which had added two floors to an existing single-storey building. The claimant sued Wickens, John Lay and the structural engineer retained by John Lay to assess the structural stability of the building. The expert witnesses who gave evidence at trial agreed that the method of construction adopted by Wickens was "so remote from acceptable building practice as to be beyond reasonable expectation." The judge held that Wickens was in breach of its duty of care to the claimant's husband, but that neither John Lay nor the structural engineers were liable. Wickens had created a building which was at risk of collapse in the event of any interference with its structure, but with no outward signs that this was so: the building was a trap and the collapse was caused by the trap being sprung in a way which was foreseeable by Wickens. John Lay and its structural engineers also owed a duty of care to avoid causing personal injury to the claimant's husband, but neither was in breach of that duty.[39] John Lay was entitled to rely upon the structural engineers' advice as to the safety of the building and the engineers had carried out proper investigations before giving that advice. The collapse of the building was not foreseeable upon the information reasonably available to them.

8–080   **Damage to other property.** Although it might be possible for the law to impose a duty of care only in respect of personal injuries, it is generally accepted that a construction professional will owe a duty not to cause physical damage to

---

[34] [1991] 1 A.C. 398.

[35] [1992] 3 All E.R. 27, 36.

[36] *ibid.* at 37.

[37] For further examples of cases where a duty of care to avoid personal injury has been held to exist in respect of building professionals see: *Driver v. William Willett (Contractors) Ltd* [1969] 1 All E.R. 665 (engineers employed by building contractors as consulting safety and inspecting engineers held to owe a duty of care to the plaintiff, a labourer employed by the contractors, who was injured by the collapse of a scaffold board from a hoist. The contractors were also held liable and responsibility was apportioned in the ratio of 40 per cent to the contractors and 60 per cent to the engineers); *Canberra Formwork Pty Ltd v. Civil & Civic Ltd* (1982) 41 A.C.T.R. 1 (site engineer employed by a building contractor liable for the death of a workman for failing to take reasonable steps to prevent the use of a dangerous formwork box on site); *Voli v. Inglewood Shire Council* [1963] A.L.R. 657 (defendant architect liable to plaintiff injured by collapse of a stage in a public hall designed by the architect)— see further para. 8–128, below; *cf. Introvigne v. Commonwealth of Australia* (1980) 32 A.L.R. 251 (defendant architect not liable to plaintiff schoolboy who had swung on a flagpole designed by the architect, as there was no duty to guard against schoolboy abuses).

[38] Unreported, October 1, 2000, Bell J.

[39] Bell J. further held that there was no material difference between John Lay's duty at common law and its statutory duty under reg. 50(2) of the Construction (General Provisions) Regulations 1961, which was also subject to the requirement that harm be foreseeable.

property other than that in respect of which he is engaged. Thus in *North West Water Authority v. Binnie & Partners*,[40] there was no argument that the defendant engineers who had been found liable for the personal injury caused to the plaintiffs in *Eckersley v. Binnie & Partners*[41] owed a different duty to the water authority in respect of damage suffered to its property. Drake J. found that there was no practical difference between the issues that the defendant wished to raise in the second case from those that it had raised in the first case. In *Nitrigin Eireann Teoranta v. Inco Alloys Ltd*,[42] May J., on the hearing of preliminary issues, found that no cause of action had arisen when a pipe supplied by specialist pipe-makers to a building owner cracked and was repaired as the cost of repair amounted to irrecoverable economic loss. However he found the pipe-makers liable for the losses caused by a subsequent explosion when the pipe cracked again a year later causing damage to the surrounding plant, on the basis that such damage amounted to damage to other property and was recoverable. His finding was based on the assumption that it was reasonable for the plaintiff not to discover (and thus repair) the cause of cracking when it first occurred. In the light of *Targett*,[43] this finding appears correct. However the judge's further statement, *obiter*,[44] that even if the plaintiff ought reasonably to have diagnosed the cause of the cracking on the first occasion, this would not have affected the accrual of a cause of action on the second, is inconsistent with the reasoning in *Targett*.

In *Bellefield Computer Services Ltd v. E. Turner & Sons Ltd*,[45] the subsequent **8–081** purchaser of a diary processing plant claimed damages in tort against the builder of the plant for damage caused when fire spread from the storage area of the plant to the remainder. The storage area was designed to be separated from the rest of the plant by an internal fire-stop compartment wall. The builder had failed to construct the wall to full height, with the result that fire was able to pass over the top of the wall. On a trial of preliminary issues, Bell J. held that the builder owed a duty of care to the claimant in respect of damage to his plant, equipment, stock and other chattels in the areas of the building outside the storage area under the principle discussed in this section: damage to those items was a foreseeable result of the builder's failure properly to construct the wall and they were property distinct from the building itself. He held that no duty of care was owed in relation to damage to the fabric of the building outside the storage area, and losses consequential upon such damage. The Court of Appeal upheld the trial judge's decision on all points. The claimant argued that the damage caused to the fabric of the building outside the storage area was physical damage rather than economic loss, because the defective wall itself did not cause any damage in the way that defective foundations cause cracking in the structures which they support. The wall merely created a situation in which the fire was able to cause more damage than it otherwise would. The Court of Appeal rejected this argument, approving this statement from the judgment of Bell J.[46]:

" . . . there is no conceptual or qualitative difference (and certainly none which I feel able to formulate) between the case of defective foundations which fail to cope with

---

[40] (1989) 30 Con.L.R. 136.
[41] (1988) 18 Con.L.R. 1. See para. 8–079 above.
[42] [1992] 1 W.L.R. 498. See also McGee, A., "Back to Pirelli" (1992) 108 L.Q.R. 364, where this decision is discussed.
[43] See para. 8–079 above.
[44] *ibid.* at 506.
[45] [2000] B.L.R 97, C.A., and see further para. 8–093 below.
[46] *ibid.* at 108.

shrinkage or heave in the subsoil and to support the building, resulting in cracked walls and pipes, and the case of a defective roof which fails to cope with and to keep out water, and the case of the defective fire stop wall which fails to cope with and to contain fire which goes on to injure other parts of the building. If the resulting injury to the fabric of the building itself is to be seen as purely economic loss in the first two of those cases, it must, in my view, be seen as economic loss in the third."

The Court also rejected as artificial the claimant's argument that the parts of the dairy which were separated from the storage area by the defective wall should be regarded as "other property" because those parts were put to different uses.

8–082   The House of Lords held in *Murphy v. Brentwood District Council*[47] that a builder owes a duty of care in tort to a subsequent occupier of a property which he has built to avoid causing personal injury or damage to other property of the occupier. The question whether a construction professional owes the same duty to a subsequent occupier arose for decision in *Baxall Securities Ltd v. Sheard Walshaw Partnership*.[48] The defendants were architects who had been engaged by a developer for the design and construction of a warehouse. The claimant was a lessee of the warehouse and used it to store electrical goods. Due to the inability of the siphonic roof drainage system to cope with rainfall, rainwater flooded through the roof of the warehouse on two occasions, damaging the claimant's goods. The claimant sued in tort, alleging that the defendants had negligently failed to see that adequate overflows were installed and to design a roof drainage system which was able to cope with the rainfall levels which ought to have been anticipated. The defendants argued that they owed no duty of care in tort to the claimant because it was a subsequent occupier. Alternatively, they argued that any such duty was negatived in relation to the lack of overflows because the claimant ought reasonably to have discovered that defect before taking the lease.

8–083   The judge considered the reasoning in *Donoghue v. Stevenson* and in *Murphy*. He held that since, following *Murphy*, a builder owes a duty of care to avoid physical damage to a subsequent occupier in appropriate circumstances, there was no reason why an architect should not owe the same duty in appropriate circumstances. However, the reasoning deployed in *Donoghue v. Stevenson* and in *Murphy* meant that there would be no duty where there was a reasonable possibility of inspection by the subsequent occupier.[49] In that case, there would not be a sufficiently proximate relationship between the parties to justify the imposition of a duty; alternatively, it would not be just, fair and reasonable to impose a duty. The claimant did have a reasonable opportunity to inspect the building before entering the lease; it would be normal for a prospective tenant to have the building inspected by a surveyor and that is what the claimant had done. It was irrelevant that the claimant's surveyor did not discover the defects. Accordingly, the judge held, the defendants owed no duty to the claimant in respect of the lack of overflows. That was a defect which the claimant's surveyor ought to have discovered and it was not fair, just or reasonable that the defendants' liability should depend upon the assiduity of the claimant's advisers.

---

[47] [1991] 1 A.C. 398.

[48] [2001] P.N.L.R. 256. Such a duty had been held to exist by Judge Lewis Q.C. in *Tesco v. Norman Hitchcox Partnership* (1998) 56 Con. L.R. 42, but the judge preferred to consider the matter afresh and from first principles.

[49] *ibid.* at 275–276, quoting the speech of Lord Atkin in *Donoghue v. Stevenson* at 580–582, and at 280–281, quoting the speech of Lord Keith in *Murphy* at 464.

However, the defendants did owe a duty in respect of damage attributable to the use of an inadequate design rainfall rate because neither the claimant nor its surveyor could reasonably have been expected to discover that the drainage system was under-designed in that way. This decision is an important reminder that the *Donoghue v. Stevenson* duty to avoid causing physical harm is subject to the "intermediate examination" exception which is commonly discussed in relation to the liability of a manufacturer to a consumer for a dangerously defective product, but less commonly seen in building cases. Since it will be reasonable to expect that most subsequent occupiers of buildings will carry out some form of inspection before taking up occupation, the exception is likely to prove important in the defence of claims against construction professionals for negligently causing physical harm.[50] A duty of care is owed in respect of latent defects, only.

(iii) *The general exclusionary rule adopted in England with regard to the recovery of economic loss*

The core of the modern English exclusionary rule concerning the recovery of **8–084** economic loss is to be found in three decisions of the House of Lords: *D. & F. Estates Ltd v. Church Commissioners for England*,[51] *Murphy v. Brentwood District Council*[52] and *Department of the Environment v. Thomas Bates and Son*.[53] The three decisions rely on three main arguments: (a) that the recovery of "pure" economic loss goes beyond existing decisions based upon the *Donoghue v. Stevenson*[54] principle; (b) that there are policy reasons for not allowing such an extension; and (c) that the courts should not intervene in an area where Parliament has legislated (by the Defective Premises Act 1972).

The first two arguments were foreshadowed in the dissenting speech of Lord **8–085** Brandon in *Junior Books Ltd v. Veitchi Co. Ltd*[55]:

"My Lords, it appears to me clear beyond doubt that, there being no contractual relationship between the respondents and the appellants in the present case, the foundation, and the only foundation, for the existence of a duty of care owed by the defenders to the pursuers, is the principle laid down in the decision of your Lordships' House in *Donoghue v. Stevenson* [1932] A.C. 562. The actual decision in that case related only to the duty owed by a manufacturer of goods to their ultimate user or consumer, and can be summarised in this way: a person who manufactures goods which he intends to be used or consumed by others, is under a duty to exercise such reasonable care in their manufacture as to ensure that they can be used or consumed in the manner intended without causing physical damage to persons or their property. While that was the actual decision in *Donoghue v. Stevenson*, it was based on a much wider principle embodied in passages in the speech of Lord Atkin, which have been quoted so often that I do not find it necessary to quote them again here. Put shortly, that wider principle is that, when a person can or ought to appreciate that a careless act or omission on his part may result in physical injury to other persons or their property, he owes a duty to all such persons to exercise reasonable care to avoid such careless act or omission. It is, however, of

---

[50] But, as was recognised in *Baxall*, there are cases in which an occupier who discovers a defect is unable to rectify the defect or move from the property; in such cases, that person is not deprived of a remedy: *Targett v. Torfaen Borough Council* [1992] 3 All E.R. 27, discussed at para. 8–079 above.

[51] [1989] A.C. 177.

[52] [1991] 1 A.C. 398

[53] [1991] 1 A.C. 490. The facts of each of the cases are set out in paras 8–071 to 8–073, above.

[54] [1932] A.C.562, HL.

[55] [1983] 1 A.C. 520 at 549 and 550–551.

fundamental importance to observe that the duty of care laid down in *Donoghue v. Stevenson* was based on the existence of a danger of physical injury to persons or their property. That this is so, is clear from the observations made by Lord Atkin at pp. 581–582 with regard to the statements of law of Brett M.R. in *Heaven v. Pender* (1883) 11 Q.B.D. 503, 509. It has further, until the present case, never been doubted, so far as I know, that the relevant property for the purpose of the wider principle on which the decision in *Donoghue v. Stevenson* was based, was property other than the very property which gave rise to the danger of physical damage concerned. . . .

. . . There are two important considerations which ought to limit the scope of the duty of care which it is common ground was owed by the appellants to the respondents on the assumed facts of the present case. The first consideration is that, in *Donoghue v. Stevenson* itself and in all the numerous cases in which the principle of that decision has been applied to different but analogous factual situations, it has always been either stated expressly, or taken for granted, that an essential ingredient in the cause of action relied on was the existence of danger, or the threat of danger of physical damage to persons or their property, excluding for this purpose the very piece of property from the defective condition of which such danger, or threat of danger, arises. To dispense with that essential ingredient in a cause of action of the kind concerned in the present case would, in my view, involve a radical departure from long-established authority. The second consideration is that there is no sound policy reason for substituting the wider scope of the duty of care put forward for the respondents for the more restricted scope of such duty put forward by the appellants. The effect of accepting the respondents' contention with regard to the scope of the duty of care involved would be, in substance, to create, as between two persons who are not in any contractual relationship with each other, obligations of one of those two persons to the other which are only really appropriate as between persons who do have such a relationship between them. In the case of a manufacturer or distributor of goods, the position would be that he warranted to the ultimate user or consumer of such goods that they were as well designed, as merchantable and as fit for their contemplated purpose as the exercise of reasonable care could make them. In the case of sub-contractors such as those concerned in the present case, the position would be that they warranted to the building owner that the flooring, when laid, would be as well designed, as free from defects of any kind and as fit for its contemplated purpose as the exercise of reasonable care could make it. In my view, the imposition of warranties of this kind on one person in favour of another, when there is no contractual relationship between them, is contrary to any sound policy requirement. It is, I think, just worthwhile to consider the difficulties which would arise if the wider scope of the duty of care put forward by the respondents were accepted. In any case where complaint was made by an ultimate consumer that a product made by some persons with whom he himself had no contract was defective, by what standard or standards of quality would the question of defectiveness fall to be decided? In the case of goods bought from a retailer, it could hardly be the standard prescribed by the contract between the retailer and the wholesaler, or between the wholesaler and the distributor, or between the distributor and the manufacturer, for the terms of such contracts would not even be known to the ultimate buyer. In the case of sub-contractors such as the appellants in the present case, it could hardly be the standard prescribed by the contract between the sub-contractors and the main contractors, for, although the building owner probably be aware of those terms, he could not, since he was not a party to such contract, rely on any standard or standards prescribed in it. It follows that the question by what standard or standards alleged defects in a product complained of by its ultimate user or consumer are to be judged remains entirely at large and cannot be given any just or satisfactory answer."

Lord Brandon's speech received express approval in *D. & F. Estates* from Lord Bridge,[56] with whom all of the other law lords agreed, and from Lord

---

[56] [1989] A.C. 177 at 202.

Oliver[57] who gave the only other substantive speech. The general rule, therefore, is that a local authority, a contractor and a construction professional do not owe a duty of care in tort to avoid causing pure economic loss to persons with whom they have no contract.

The importance of the Defective Premises Act 1972 and the preceding Law **8–086** Commission Report in setting out and limiting the scope of duties owed to subsequent purchasers was emphasised by Lord Bridge in *D. & F. Estates*,[58] and by all five law lords who gave substantive speeches in *Murphy*.[59] Lord Mackay[60] considered that there were two options open to the House of Lords: either the overruling of *Anns* or a removal of the qualifications in *Anns* (*i.e.* that a cause of action should only arise when a defect became dangerous and should not be available when the defect was discovered). In deciding which of the options should be taken, he made express reference to the Defective Premises Act before deciding that it would not be a proper exercise of the judicial function to create a large new area of common law liability.[61] In the light of: (a) the fact that the Defective Premises Act does not apply to Scotland or Northern Ireland[62]; and (b) the subsequent decision of the Privy Council in *Invercargill v. Hamlin*[63] to the effect that the New Zealand courts were justified in finding that, in the absence of an equivalent statute to the Defective Premises Act, social conditions required the imposition of extensive common law duties of the sort contemplated by Lord Mackay, there was created the intriguing possibility of the House of Lords deciding on a Scottish or Northern Irish appeal, that the law of Scotland or Northern Ireland should be the same as that of New Zealand rather than England.[64]

In Scotland, at least, that possibility has not materialised. In *Strathford East* **8–087** *Kilbride Ltd v. HLM Design Ltd*,[65] Lord MacLean in the Outer House of the Court of Session held that architects employed by a landlord owed no duty to the tenants to avoid causing them economic loss in the absence of any assumption of responsibility by the architect to the tenants. He thus followed *Murphy* in preference to numerous Commonwealth decisions which had continued to follow *Anns* and had declined to adopt *Murphy*.[66]

(iv) *The English exceptions to the general exclusionary rule*

Unless the House of Lords decides once again to depart from its own previous **8–088** decisions, there are three situations, contemplated by the House of Lords, in which claimants may seek to recover "pure" economic loss against construction

---

[57] *ibid.* at 215.

[58] *ibid.* at 208.

[59] [1991] 1 A.C. 398 *per* Lord Mackay at 457, Lord Keith at 472, Lord Bridge at 480, Lord Oliver at 491 and Lord Jauncey at 498.

[60] *ibid.* at 457.

[61] It is arguable, however, that the limitations on the availability of a remedy under the Defective Premises Act 1972 (see paras. 8–039 to 8–045 above) are such that reliance upon this statute as providing a remedy for third parties in all cases where a remedy might be thought appropriate is unjustified.

[62] See s.7(3) of the Act.

[63] [1996] A.C. 624. See further para. 8–121, below.

[64] See also the note "A prophet not rejected in his own land" by J. M. Thompson in (1994) 110 L.Q.R. 361 and the cases there cited. Thompson points out that *Junior Books* is followed in Scotland and is not treated as lacking authority in the way that it is in England.

[65] 1997 S.C.L.R. 877.

[66] The Commonwealth decisions are discussed further at paras 8–110 to 8–121 below.

professionals with whom they have no contract: (i) the application of the "complex structure theory"; (ii) expenditure necessary to avoid liability to third parties; and (iii) the application of the *Hedley Byrne* or reliance principle.

8–089   **The complex structure theory.** The complex structure theory was first raised in *D. & F. Estates* by Lords Bridge[67] and Oliver.[68] Lord Bridge stated:

> "However, I can see that it may well be arguable that in the case of complex structures, as indeed possibly in the case of complex chattels, one element of the structure should be regarded for the purpose of the application of the principles under discussion as distinct from another element, so that damage to one part of the structure caused by a hidden defect in another part may qualify to be treated as damage to 'other property', and whether the argument should prevail may depend on the circumstances of the case."

The theory was discussed again in *Murphy*. Lord Oliver[69] contented himself with making it clear that he had not put forward the theory with any enthusiasm. Each of the other law lords plainly thought that the theory might apply in the future although they gave differing examples of such application. Lord Keith said[70]:

> "Lord Bridge . . . suggested that in the case of a complex structure such as a building one element of the structure might be regarded for *Donoghue v. Stevenson* purposes as distinct from another element, so that damage to one part of the structure caused by a hidden defect in another part might qualify to be treated as damage to 'other property'. I think that it would be unrealistic to take this view as regards a building the whole of which had been erected and equipped by the same contractor. In that situation the whole package provided by the contractor would, in my opinion, fall to be regarded as one unit rendered unsound as such by a defect in the particular part. On the other hand, where, for example, the electric wiring had been installed by a sub-contractor and due to a defect caused by lack of care a fire occurred which destroyed the building, it might not be stretching ordinary principles too far to hold the electrical sub-contractor liable for the damage."

Lord Bridge said[71]:

> "A critical distinction must be drawn here between some part of a complex structure which is said to be a 'danger' only because it does not perform its proper function in sustaining the other parts and some distinct item incorporated in the structure which positively malfunctions so as to inflict positive damage on the structure in which it is incorporated. Thus, if a defective central heating boiler explodes and damages a house or a defective electrical installation malfunctions and sets the house on fire, I see no reason to doubt that the owner of the house, if he can prove that the damage was due to the negligence of the boiler manufacturer in the one case or the electrical contractor in the other, can recover damages in tort on *Donoghue v. Stevenson* principles. But the position of the law is entirely different where by reason of the inadequacy of the foundations of the building to support the weight of the superstructure, differential settlement and consequential cracking appears. . . . "

---

[67] [1989] A.C. 177 at 207.
[68] *ibid.* at 213.
[69] [1991] 1 A.C. 398 at 484D.
[70] *ibid.* at 470H.
[71] *ibid.* at 478E.

Lord Jauncey said[72]:

"It seems to me that the only context for the complex structure theory in the case of a building would be where one integral component of the structure was built by a separate contractor and where a defect in such a component had caused damage to other parts of the structure, *e.g.* a steel frame erected by a specialist contractor which failed to give adequate support to floors or walls. Defects in such ancillary equipment as central heating boilers or electrical installations would be subject to the normal *Donoghue v. Stevenson* principles if such defects gave rise to damage to other parts of the building."

The complex structure theory was applied in *Jacobs v. Morton & Partners*.[73] **8–090** The judge applied what he termed "the complex structure exception" in finding, on the hearing of preliminary issues, that defendant engineers retained by house owners to design and supervise remedial foundation works owed a duty of care to subsequent purchasers not to cause damage to the house itself. The judge emphasised that the scope of the complex structure exception was limited. In deciding whether it could be applied in a particular case, he considered that four considerations were relevant:

(a) whether the item in question was constructed by someone other than the main contractor responsible for the main building works;

(b) whether the item in question had retained its separate identity or had been merged with the remainder of the building;

(c) whether the item positively inflicted damage on the building or simply failed to perform its function; and

(d) whether the item was constructed at a different time from the remainder of the building.

It is difficult to find a policy justification for the existence of the complex **8–091** structure theory or exception. Thus it would appear that the cost of repairing damage to a building caused by the explosion of a boiler would be treated as recoverable physical damage against a heating engineer engaged solely in relation to the installation of a boiler one month after the construction of a house but as irrecoverable economic loss against an engineer engaged in relation to the construction of the whole of the house. Such a distinction can surely not be justified, as it would mean that the greater the responsibility undertaken, the smaller the subsequent liability and vice versa.[74] In *Sergius v. Janax Design & Drafting*,[75] the purchaser of a property claimed that the geotechnical engineer who had advised the vendor of the property upon the ground conditions was

---

[72] *ibid.* at 497C.
[73] (1994) 72 B.L.R. 92.
[74] See also the criticism of *Jacobs* by the editors of the *Building Law Reports* in the commentary to the report where they suggest that the decision must be treated with care as (a) it is by no means certain that the complex structure theory survived reconsideration by Lord Bridge in *Murphy*; (b) the complex structure theory has not received favourable comments; and (c) the exception has been criticised in the light of experience in Germany in an article by John Fleming, "Property damage— economic loss: a comparative view" (1989) 105 L.Q.R. 508.
[75] (1992) 64 B.C.L.R. (2d) 176. The case was decided before the decision of the Canadian Supreme Court in *Winnipeg Condominium Corporation v. Bird Construction Co.* (see para. 8–111, below) which held that pure economic loss was recoverable in tort in Canada.

liable for damage to the property, relying on the complex structure theory. Newbury J. at first instance in British Columbia rejected the theory. He said[76]:

> "Although not without its attractions, this argument overlooks the fact that those cases denying recovery for pure economic loss are concerned not so much with the nature of the damage as with the fact that the plaintiff is seeking to recover the cost of repairing a defective product which has been supplied or sold by a person against whom the plaintiff has no warranty in contract. The law's reluctance to create contract-like warranties in favour of such a plaintiff, rather than any distinction in principle based on the type of damage per se, is at the heart of the rule against recovery."

8–092   There is now a considerable body of English case law which suggests that the complex structure theory is not a viable route to recovery in respect of pure economic loss. In *Ernst & Whinney v. Willard Engineering (Dagenham) Ltd*,[77] a case decided before *Murphy*, the plaintiff assignees of the lease of an office building discovered defective air conditioning ductwork. They sued in negligence two sub-contractors who had originally installed the ductwork together with the consulting mechanical and electrical engineers. On the hearing of a preliminary issue, the judge held that no duty of care was owed by the engineers or the sub-contractors. His judgment paid deference to the then existing authority of *Anns* and the primary basis for it was that it would be neither just nor reasonable to impose liability on the defendants. However, he was also asked to find whether the defects alleged amounted to physical damage. He said[78]:

> "In my view, the answer is 'No.' I cannot think that a defect in a constituent part of a building can be regarded as constituting physical damage to the building of which it forms part. I find it even more difficult to accede to the notion that the purchaser of a building comprising such a defect can make such an assertion in respect of the building he bought."

In *Warner v. Basildon Development Corp.*,[79] a decision given the day before the decision in *Murphy*, the purchaser of a house sought to rely on the complex structure theory in his claim in tort against the contractor responsible for building the foundations of the house. The Court of Appeal held that it was not open to it to adopt the theory of complex structures (or complex chattels) as an adjunct to the principle of *Donoghue v. Stevenson* as applied to building operations, since the theory formed no part of the principles set out in *D.&F. Estates*.[80] In *Tesco v. Norman Hitchcox Partnership*,[81] Judge Esyr Lewis Q.C. rejected an attempt to apply the complex structure theory in respect of a supermarket so as to allow recovery for damage to the supermarket as a result of the defective design of the fire inhibition structures within the building. In *Tunnel Refineries v. Bryan Donkin*,[82] Mr Recorder Susman Q.C. accepted a submission that he was bound by the decision of the Court of Appeal in *Warner* to find that there was no room for the complex structure theory in English law.

---

[76] *ibid.* at 198.
[77] (1987) 40 B.L.R. 67.
[78] *ibid.* at 81.
[79] (1991) 7 Const. L.J. 146.
[80] [1989] 1 A.C. 177 and see para. 8–084 above.
[81] (1997) 56 Con.L.R. 42.
[82] (1998) C.I.L.L. 1392.

The Court of Appeal considered a submission based upon the complex struc- **8–093**
ture theory again in *Bellefield Computer Services Ltd v. E. Turner & Sons Ltd.*[83]
The claimant argued that it was entitled to recover for damage caused to parts of
the dairy other than the storage area which was bounded by the inadequately
constructed fire-stop wall because those parts of the building were put to different
uses from the storage area. The argument was rejected and the decision of Bell
J. at first instance was upheld, albeit without comment upon the status of the
complex structure theory as such. Schiemann L.J. pointed out that it was unrealistic to regard parts of the diary as separate properties just because different parts
were put to different uses: the dairy was constructed as one unit, marketed as a
unit, bought for use as a unit and used by the claimant as a unit.[84]

In *Payne v. John Setchell Ltd*,[85] having considered the speeches of the various **8–094**
members of the House of Lords in *D.&F. Estates* and *Murphy*, the judge held that
the complex structure theory was no longer tenable. That case concerned two
cottages which were built off the same foundation slab. The defendant was
responsible for the design of the foundations. Each of the claimants was a
subsequent purchaser of one of the cottages. They argued that, because the
foundations were inadequate, each of the cottages constituted a danger to the
adjacent cottage. They claimed an indemnity against their liabilities to each other
to make their respective properties safe. They sought to rely upon the complex
structure theory, arguing that the foundation slab and each of the cottages were
"other property" so far as the other cottage was concerned. The judge rejected
the complex structure theory and the argument. He held that in applying the
concept of "other property", it was necessary to be realistic. It would be
completely unrealistic to treat the part of the foundation slab under one cottage
as if it were separate from the part under the other cottage.[86]

Expenditure necessary to avoid liability to third parties. In *Murphy*, Lord **8–095**
Bridge suggested a possible exceptional case whereby economic loss might be
recoverable[87]:

> "... if a building stands so close to the boundary of the building owner's land that after
> discovery of the dangerous defect it remains a potential source of injury to person or
> property on the neighbouring land or on the highway, the building owner ought, in
> principle, to be entitled to recover in tort from the negligent builder the cost of obviating
> the danger, whether by repair or demolition, so far as that cost is necessarily incurred
> in order to protect himself from potential liability to third parties."

Lord Oliver[88] (with whom Lord Ackner agreed, whilst also agreeing with Lord
Bridge) expressly deferred consideration of whether such a qualification existed
whilst expressing his doubt as to its basis. If Lord Bridge is correct it would seem
that the owner of a house in the centre of a city may be able to claim the cost of
repairing the house so as to prevent it collapsing into a busy highway whilst the
owner of an identical property set in its own land will not be able to recover. The

---

[83] [2000] B.L.R 97, CA. For the facts, see para. 8–081 above. For discussion, see the commentary by
I. N. Duncan Wallace Q.C., "*Donoghue v. Stevenson* and "complex structure": *Anns* revisted?" [2000]
116 L.Q.R. 530.
[84] *ibid.* at 100.
[85] Unreported, March 16, 2001. For the facts, see para. 8–059 above.
[86] *ibid.* at para. 39.
[87] [1991] 1 A.C. at 475F.
[88] *ibid.* at 489C.

exception was applied in *Morse v. Barrett (Leeds) Ltd.*[89] The plaintiffs, who were largely subsequent purchasers of houses, joined together to re-build an old wall which had been rendered dangerous by the action of the defendant, the original builder of the houses. The judge found that the claim fell squarely within Lord Bridge's suggested qualification.[90] However in *George Fischer Holding Ltd v. Multi Design Consultants Ltd*,[91] Judge Hicks Q.C. refused to follow *Morse*. Having found that a design sub-contractor owed a collateral contractual duty to the plaintiff, the judge went on to consider what would have been the position had he been wrong. In that case, he considered the costs of averting a danger to the public would not have been recoverable as the statements of Lords Bridge and Oliver amounted only to minority dicta and were contrary to the decision of the majority in *Murphy*.

8–096   **The Hedley Byrne or reliance principle.** Both Lord Oliver in *D. & F. Estates*[92] and Lords Bridge and Keith in *Murphy*[93] drew attention to the possibility of economic loss being recoverable by reason of the application of the application of the decision of the House of Lords in *Hedley Byrne v. Heller & Partners*.[94] Although that decision is typically associated with the giving of information or advice, Lord Goff in *Henderson* made clear that it extends to a broad range of circumstances in which "special skill" is exercised[95]:

> "[T]he facts of *Hedley Byrne* itself . . . show that the concept of a 'special skill' must be understood broadly. . . . [T]hough *Hedley Byrne* was concerned with the provision of information and advice, the example given by Lord Devlin of the relationship between solicitor and client . . . show[s] that the principle extends beyond the provision of advice and information to include the performance of other services."

The last decade of the twentieth century saw a considerable extension to the ambit of the *Hedley Byrne* principle in other areas of the law,[96] and recent decisions suggest that it is by this route that liability of construction professionals to persons other than their clients will be found to the greatest extent in the future in England.

8–097   There is, of course, no reason in principle why a construction professional should not incur liability by a straight application of the decision in *Hedley Byrne*, namely where he makes a statement to a person who is entitled to and does rely on such statement. In *Townsend (Builders) Ltd v. Cinema News and*

---

[89] (1993) 9 Const.L.J. 158, Ch.D.

[90] In an article, "Has construction law been taken to the wreckers?" (1991) 65 A.L.J. 270, 274, P. Gerber and R. Jackson point out that although a person may be obliged, if he is not to be liable in nuisance, to remedy a mischief on his own land once he is aware of the same, it does not follow that he is entitled to recover the cost of remedy from the author of the mischief. *Cf. Privest Properties Ltd v. Foundation Co. of Canada Ltd* (1995) 128 D.L.R. (4th) 577 where Drost J. in the British Columbia Supreme Court found that the defendant architects would have been liable to the plaintiff owners of a building for the cost of removing negligently installed asbestos products but for his finding that the products did not constitute a danger to the health and safety of the occupants of the building. The British Columbia Court of Appeal dismissed the plaintiff's appeal: (1997) 143 D.L.R. (4th) 635.

[91] (1998) 61 Con. L.R. 85 at 109–111.

[92] [1989] A.C. 177 at 213.

[93] [1991] 1 A.C. 398 at 465 and 481.

[94] [1964] A.C. 465.

[95] [1995] 2 A.C. 145 at 178–181.

[96] See chap. 2, paras 2–45—2–49 and particularly the cases of *Spring v. Guardian Assurance plc* [1995] 2 A.C. 296, *Henderson v. Merrett Syndicates Ltd* [1995] 2 A.C. 145, *White v. Jones* [1995] 2 A.C. 207 and *Williams v. Natural Life Health Foods Ltd* [1998] 1 W.L.R. 830.

Property Management[97] an architect wrote to the building contractors that he would be responsible for serving all notices required by building by-laws. The Court of Appeal held that he was under a duty to the contractors to serve such notices and liable in tort for damages caused by late service. Although the case was decided before *Hedley Byrne*, it is submitted that it was decided in accordance with the principles later set out by the House of Lords.[98] Similarly the concession made in the House of Lords in *I.B.A. v. E.M.I. and B.I.C.C.*[99] is explicable on the basis of a direct application of *Hedley Byrne*. The plaintiff employers (I.B.A.) engaged the first defendants (E.M.I.) as main contractors for the design, construction and erection of a television mast and E.M.I. in turn engaged the second defendants (B.I.C.C.) as sub-contractors for design, construction and erection of the mast. There was no contract between I.B.A. and B.I.C.C. but it was conceded by the latter that they owed a duty of care to I.B.A., possibly because B.I.C.C. gave I.B.A. a direct assurance, in response to a specific request, that the mast would not oscillate dangerously. The assurance proved false and the mast collapsed. The House of Lords held that B.I.C.C. were negligent in the design of the mast and consequently in giving the assurance and were accordingly directly liable to I.B.A. O'Connor J. and the Court of Appeal both held that the assurance by B.I.C.C. amounted to a contractual warranty but this finding was unanimously rejected by the House of Lords.[1]

Similarly, in *Machin v. Adams*,[2] an architect was asked by his clients, who **8-098** were in the process of selling their house to the plaintiff for use as a care home, to write a letter setting out the then state of alteration and refurbishment works at the house together with the amount of time necessary to complete the same. The defendant knew that the letter was to be shown to persons other than his clients, probably including the purchaser of the house. The Court of Appeal found that the defendant would have owed a duty of care to the plaintiff in respect of the letter but for the fact that he understood that he would be required to return on completion of the works in order to certify the same before the completion of the sale. Because of this understanding the Court of Appeal found that the defendant could not have anticipated that the plaintiff would take some irrevocable step based upon the letter. In *Lidl Properties v. Clarke Bond Partnership*,[3] the plaintiff claimed that it had purchased a site for the development of a supermarket in reliance upon advice given to it by the defendant engineers as to the level of ground contamination at the site and the likely cost of decontamination. At the time, the defendants were retained by developers who intended to purchase the site, decontaminate it and sell it on to the plaintiff. Even although the defendants' advice was given gratuitously, at a hastily arranged *ad hoc* meeting, Judge Wilcox held that the defendants owed a duty of care in respect of that advice. They were giving advice within the scope of their expertise and experience to a party who would foreseeably rely upon it for the purposes of making an offer to purchase the site. Accordingly, the defendants had assumed

---

[97] (1958) 20 B.L.R. 118. The late Donald Keating Q.C. questioned whether this case was still good law at (1992) 8 Const.L.R. 405, 406.
[98] See also the decision of Lin Beng Choon J. in the Malaysian High Court in *Chin Sin Motor Works v. Arosa Development Sdn Bhd* [1992] 1 M.L.J. 23 (architects employed by developer liable for negligent misstatements in certificates relied on by the plaintiff purchaser and financier).
[99] (1980) 14 B.L.R. 1, H.L.; (1979) 11 B.L.R. 29, CA.
[1] *ibid.* at 22–24, 32, 41.
[2] (1997) 84 B.L.R. 79.
[3] [1998] Env. L.R. 622.

responsibility to the plaintiff to advise with reasonable care and skill. The extent of their duty was limited, however, by the purpose of the meeting, which had been called in order that the plaintiff might form a view as to the likely cost of the defendants' proposed decontamination scheme. The defendants did not owe a duty to give an *ad hoc* risk assessment or a comprehensive presentation of the history and investigation of the site. In the event, the claim was dismissed because the defendants were not in breach of their duty and the plaintiff had not in fact relied upon the defendants' advice.

8–099   The *Hedley Byrne* duty found in *Payne v. John Setchell Ltd*[4] was also limited, but in time. The claimants were the subsequent purchasers of cottages. The defendant civil and structural engineer had been engaged by the vendor of the cottages to assist in their construction. The defendant had designed raft foundations for the cottages, inspected the construction of those foundations and certified that they were satisfactorily constructed and suitable for support of the cottages. The claimants alleged that they had purchased the cottages in reliance upon the defendant's certificates. On a trial of preliminary issues, Judge Lloyd Q.C. observed that the purpose of providing the certificates was to furnish the vendor with a document which could be used to satisfy a prospective purchaser that the foundations had been soundly built to a satisfactory design, even although N.H.B.C. cover was not available. The defendant intended that his certificates would be seen and relied upon by subsequent purchasers and it followed that he owed such purchasers a duty to take care that the statements made in or to be inferred from the certificates were reliable. The certificates were to be regarded as statements that the design of the foundations had been prepared with reasonable care.[5] The judge added, *obiter*, that the defendant's duty was not unlimited in time. Since, for all practical purposes, the certificates were to be treated as tantamount to N.H.B.C. cover, it was foreseeable only that they would be regarded as valid for a period of 10 years from completion of the building works.

8–100   Greater difficulties can be expected to occur in deciding the situations in which construction professionals owe duties to persons other than their clients to prevent economic loss because such persons are entitled to rely upon the professionals or are in a sufficiently close relationship that a duty of care should be imposed, even although no misleading communication is made by a professional to the claimant. In *Junior Books Ltd v. Veitchi Co. Ltd*,[6] nominated flooring subcontractors were found liable to a building owner for the costs of remedying a defective floor which they had laid. In *Murphy*, Lord Bridge stated[7]:

> "There may, of course, be situations where, even in the absence of contract, there is a special relationship of proximity between builder and building owner which is sufficiently akin to contract to introduce the element of reliance so that the scope of the duty of care owed by the building to the owner is wide enough to embrace purely economic loss. The decision in *Junior Books Ltd v. Veitchi Co. Ltd* can, I believe, only be understood on this basis."[8]

---

[4] Unreported, March 16, 2001.
[5] *ibid.* at para. 46.
[6] [1983] 2 A.C. 520.
[7] [1991] 1 A.C. at 481D.
[8] See also *per* Lord Keith at 466G.

As has been pointed out on many occasions,[9] such an explanation for the decision in *Junior Books* is very difficult to justify. The building owner in *Junior Books* chose to enter into a single contract with a main contractor, presumably relying on the competence and financial solvency of that contractor. The use of nominated sub-contractors is (or was) generally thought to give the owner some of the benefits of choice of sub-contractor without the burdens of a direct contract. It is difficult to see why the law should decide to provide further benefits to the owner.[10]

In *Midland Bank v. Bardgrove Property Services Ltd*[11] the plaintiff land **8–101** owner's action against developers and builders of adjoining land together with two firms of consulting engineers employed in relation to the temporary and permanent works respectively was unsuccessful. The plaintiff alleged that excavation by the defendants had led to a loss of stability and risk of future movement which had caused it to expend money on shoring works on its own land. The claim was brought against all defendants in negligence and against the builder and developer for interference with a natural right of support. At the trial of preliminary issues Judge Thayne Forbes Q.C. held, *inter alia*, that the developer was entitled to carry out the excavations on its own land with the result that it did not owe a duty of care and the other defendants could owe no wider duty than that of the developer. He also held that the plaintiff's claim was for economic loss which was irrecoverable in negligence in the absence of a "special relationship".[12] He found that no such special relationship existed.

Duties of care to subsequent purchasers. An attempt to apply the wider **8–102** *Hedley Byrne* principle was denied by the Court of Appeal in *Preston v. Torfaen Borough Council*.[13] The plaintiffs were the first purchasers from a local authority of a house which had been built on an in-filled quarry. The defendants were the engineers who had carried out the site investigation for the local authority. It was accepted, for the purposes of a preliminary issue: (1) that the defendants had held themselves out as experts to give specific advice for a specific purpose; (2) that they must have known that the local authority would rely on that advice as it in

---

[9] See, *e.g.* per Robert Goff L.J. in *Muirhead v. Industrial Tank Specialities Ltd* [1986] Q.B. 507, 528. In *Nitrigin Eireann Teoranta v. Inco Alloys Ltd* [1992] 1 W.L.R. 498, 505, May J. stated that it would be intellectually dishonest to distinguish that case from *Junior Books* and did not do so. The judge simply declined to apply *Junior Books* on the basis that it was unique and depended in some (unspecified) way on *Hedley Byrne*.

[10] See also the pre-*Murphy* decision of *Equitable Debenture Assets Corporation Ltd v. William Moss Group Ltd* (1984) 2 Con.L.R. 1, where the question arose whether curtain walling consultants, Winmart, engaged not by the plaintiff employer but by the employer's architects, Morgan, owed a duty of care to the employer. Judge Newey Q.C. answered the question affirmatively but emphasised the circumscribed nature of the duty: "The duties which Winmart owed had to be performed within the scope of their employment by Morgan. They would and I think did on occasions draw attention to the need for further work to be done to avoid risks, but they could not officiously advise or inspect when not asked to do so. They would therefore only be blamed if they failed to perform correctly what their instructions allowed them to do." On the facts Winmart were held not liable.

[11] (1990) 24 Con.L.R. 98. The plaintiff's appeal (which concerned the action against the landowner alone) was dismissed and is reported at 60 B.L.R. 1.

[12] *ibid.* at 115. See also *Tesco v. Norman Hitchcox Partnership* (1997) 56 Con. L.R. 42 where H.H.J. Esyr Lewis Q.C. found that the defendant architects had not assumed a responsibility to the plaintiff to carry out any inspections wider than those which it was actually obliged to carry out pursuant to its contract with the plaintiff. He further found that the detailed contractual relationships entered into by the parties showed that the plaintiff did not rely on the architects carrying out any such wider inspections.

[13] [1993] C.I.L.L. 864.

fact did; (3) that the local authority had power to sell the house; and (4) that the defendants must have known that whoever occupied the house at the time that the defects became manifest would inevitably suffer economic loss as a result of any negligent advice. In the absence of any form of negligent misstatement by the defendants to the plaintiffs, the Court of Appeal found that the above facts were not sufficient to ground liability in negligence. Sir Michael Fox pointed out that a builder would not have been liable to the plaintiff and did not consider that there was any reason for the defendants to be placed in any different position.

8–103   **Duties of care to contractors.** It may be that the English courts will, in the future, be prepared to use the *Hedley Byrne* principle to permit claims to be made by contractors against construction professionals engaged by the employer in respect of either negligent certificates or tender information.[14] Although there is a decision of the Court of Appeal[15] which suggests that it will be rare for such a duty to be owed, a more recent decision in the same court[16] confirms that there is no reason in principle why such a duty may not be found in appropriate circumstances.

8–104   In the nineteenth-century case of *Stevenson v. Watson*[17] a building contractor claimed that an architect owed him a duty to exercise due care and skill in ascertaining sums due to him for building work and that the architect was in breach of that duty in certifying as payable by the employer a sum much lower than that properly due. The court expressed much sympathy for the claim[18] but felt constrained by previous authorities to hold that in carrying out his certifying functions the architect was in the position of an arbitrator and was immune from action in the absence of fraud or collusion with the employer. In *Sutcliffe v. Thackrah*[19] however, the House of Lords held that an architect did not, in the absence of specific agreement, act as arbitrator between the employer and the contractor and was not immune from an action in negligence at the suit of the employer for over-certification. The question whether in the same circumstances the architect might owe a duty to the contractor was expressly left undecided.[20] In *Arenson v. Arenson*[21] Lord Salmon expressed the view that the architect in *Sutcliffe v. Thackrah* owed the contractor a duty to use reasonable care in issuing his certificates "arising out of their proximity" and referred to *Hedley Byrne* in support.[22]

---

[14] See the Canadian cases discussed at paras 8–110 to 8–116, below.
[15] *Pacific Associates Inc. v. Baxter* [1990] 1 Q.B. 993 discussed at para. 8–106, below
[16] *J. Jarvis & Sons Ltd v. Castle Wharf Developments Ltd* [2001] E.W.C.A. Civ.19, [2001] Lloyd's Rep. P.N. 308 discussed at para. 8–108 below.
[17] (1879) 4 C.P.D. 148.
[18] *ibid.* at 156.
[19] [1974] A.C. 727.
[20] *ibid.* at 736, *per* Lord Reid.
[21] [1977] A.C. 405, 438.
[22] Similarly in *F. G. Minter Ltd v. Welsh Health Technical Services Organisation* (1979) 11 B.L.R. 1, the contractor and sub-contractor were respectively entitled to be reimbursed for certain direct loss and expense caused by variations and delay in issuing instructions. There were a number of variations and the progress of works was affected by lack of necessary instructions. Claims for consequent direct loss and expense were made and ultimately paid with the exception of claims for finance charges and for being kept out of moneys for the periods between the occurrence and certification of the direct loss and expense. Parker J. rejected the latter claims in an action by the contractor against the employer but expressed the view, *obiter*, at 13 that the charges "might give rise to a claim against the architect".

The only reported English case[23] of a successful claim in tort by a contractor **8–105** against an architect, engineer or quantity surveyor for late or under-certification is *Michael Salliss & Co. Ltd v. Calil and William F. Newman & Associates.*[24] The plaintiff contractor was employed by the first defendants in respect of refurbishment works under the JCT 1963 Private Form of Contract. The second defendants were the architects and quantity surveyors under the contract. At the hearing of preliminary issues, Judge Fox-Andrews Q.C. held[25]:

> "If the architect unfairly promotes the building employer's interest by low certification or merely fails properly to exercise reasonable care and skill in his certification it is reasonable that the contractor should not only have the right as against the owner to have the certificate reviewed in arbitration but also should have the right to recover damages against the unfair architect."

The leading case on the existence of a duty of care owed by construction **8–106** professionals to a contractor after building works have begun is *Pacific Associates Inc. v. Baxter.*[26] The plaintiff contractors had been engaged in extensive dredging and reclamation work in the Persian Gulf for the ruler of Dubai. Conditions of the contract provided that in the event of encountering unforeseeable obstructions, the plaintiff was, after certification by the defendant engineers, entitled to payment for costs. Another condition provided for arbitration of disputes between the Ruler and the plaintiffs whilst General Condition 86 provided:

> "Neither . . . the engineer nor any of his staff, nor the engineer's representative shall be in any way personally liable for the acts or obligations under the contract, or answerable for any default or omission on the part of the employer in the observance or performance of any of the acts, matters or things which are herein contained."

Following a certification dispute, the plaintiff commenced arbitration proceedings against the Ruler which were settled on payment of £10 million. The plaintiffs then issued proceedings against the defendants seeking a further £45 million claiming that the losses had been caused by the defendants' negligent certification. The judge decided on the hearing of a preliminary issue that the loss claimed could not be recoverable and struck the claim out. This decision was upheld by the Court of Appeal. Purchas, Gibson and Russell L.JJ.[27] all made it clear that they regarded both the presence of the arbitration clause, whereby the contractor was entitled to challenge the engineer's decision in proceedings against the employer, and the disclaimer as fatal to the imposition of a duty of care.

---

[23] But note *Lubenham Fidelities and Investment Co. Ltd v. South Pembrokeshire D.C.* (1986) 6 Con.L.R. 85, CA in which the Court of Appeal heard an appeal from Judge Newey who had decided at first instance that such a duty existed. There was no argument upon the point in the Court of Appeal and the court was not therefore required to consider whether a duty in fact existed. Also note the Hong Kong case of *Shui On Construction Co. Ltd v. Shui Kay Co. Ltd* (1984–85) 1 Con.L.J. 305 in which Hunter J. refused to strike out allegations in a statement of claim that the defendant architects owed to the plaintiff main contractors a duty of care in the performance of mainly administration functions and also a duty to act fairly and impartially.

[24] (1987) 13 Con.L.R. 68.

[25] *ibid.* at 78.

[26] [1990] 1 Q.B. 993. For discussion, see Trottman, T., *"Pacific Associates v. Baxter*: time for re-consideration?" (1999) 15 Const.L.J. 449.

[27] At 1022–1024, 1031–1034 and 1037–1039, respectively.

8–107   Although not expressly overruled, it is now accordingly doubtful whether *Salliss* is good law. Purchas L.J. stated specifically[28] that a question mark must reside over the decision. More importantly there would appear to be no reason to attribute less importance to an arbitration clause in the JCT 1963 Standard Form than to that in the *Pacific Associates* case. *Pacific Associates* was followed in the Hong Kong case of *Leon Engineering & Construction Co. Ltd v. Ka Duk Investment Co. Ltd*[29] where Bokhary J. refused leave to the plaintiff building contractors to join architects as defendants to an action on the ground that they owed a duty to give proper, timely and impartial consideration to the plaintiffs' claims under the building contract. The basis of the decision was that there was adequate machinery under the contract between the employer and the contractor to enforce the contractor's rights. There may, however, be exceptional cases where a case can be brought in the absence both of a disclaimer and a valid and effective arbitration clause or other method of challenging a decision by an architect or engineer. It may be possible to circumvent the restrictions imposed by the Court of Appeal's decision by alleging alternative causes of action providing, of course, that the appropriate factual basis exists.[30]

8–108   The cases discussed above involved unsuccessful attempts to argue that a construction professional acting for the employer owes a duty to the contractor in the administration of the building contract.[31] The situation is different before the contractor has committed himself to build the works by entering the building contract. In *J. Jarvis & Sons Ltd v. Castle Wharf Developments Ltd*,[32] the defendant was the developer of a office and leisure complex on flagship site in Nottingham. It engaged project managers (GMS) to act on its behalf in seeking tenders for the design and construction of the works. The claimant contractor was invited to tender. It proposed a scheme which differed from the developer's scheme. Following discussions between the contractor and GMS, at which certain modifications to the contractor's proposed scheme were agreed, the developer sent to the claimant a letter stating its intention to enter a design and build contract with the claimant. The claimant then commenced work on site. Some months later, the local planning authority informed the claimant that the scheme which it was building was not in accordance with the planning permission which had been issued to the developer and threatened enforcement proceedings. The claimant alleged that it had begun work in reliance upon negligent misstatements made to it by GMS to the effect that the claimant's proposed scheme, modified as discussed, would be in line with the existing planning permission. GMS argued that it owed no duty of care to the claimant, relying upon *Pacific Associates v. Baxter*. The Court of Appeal held that, although generally a professional acting for a principal which had entered or was about to enter a contract would not owe a duty of care in tort to the other party to the contract, there was no reason in principle why a construction professional retained by an employer could not owe a *Hedley Byrne* duty of care in relation

---

[28] *ibid.* at 1020C.
[29] (1990) 47 B.L.R. 139. See further the Canadian cases discussed at paras 8–110 to 8–116, below.
[30] See para. 8–130, below.
[31] A similar claim failed for similar reasons in *John Holland Construction Engineering Ltd v. Majorca Products* (2000) 16 Const.L.J. 114, Supreme Court of Victoria. In that case, Byrne J. went further and held that the employer's architects did not owe a duty in tort to the contractor to act fairly and impartially in the administration of the building contract. It is submitted that this does not represent the position in English law: see *Sutcliffe v. Thakrah* [1974] A.C. 727, HL.
[32] [2001] E.W.C.A. Civ. 19, [2001] Lloyd's Rep. P.N. 308.

to statements made to a contractor and upon which the contractor relied in tendering for the building contract.[33] At that stage, there was no contract between the contractor and the employer which might negate such a duty by providing the contractor with alternative remedies; indeed, on the facts of this case, a building contract was never concluded. In the event, although the court was not persuaded that the claimant had proved the statements which it attributed to GMS, it was not necessary to decide whether GMS owed a duty of care to the claimant. It was clear that the claimant had not relied upon the statements which it alleged and, therefore, the claim failed on causation.[34]

The decision in *R.M. Turton & Co Ltd v. Kerslake & Partners*[35] was not cited in *Jarvis v. Castle Wharf* but it is submitted that the dissenting judgment of Thomas J. in the New Zealand Court of Appeal in that case provides powerful reasoning in support of the existence of a *Hedley Byrne* duty of care owed by a construction professional to a tendering contractor. The defendants were mechanical services engineers retained by a health authority's architects for the construction of a new hospital. They prepared a mechanical services specification for use in the tender process which specified the installation of particular heat pumps with a required minimum output. The plaintiff's tender was accepted. Following installation of the heating system, it was discovered that the pumps specified by the defendants were not capable of producing the required output. The plaintiff carried out remedial work pursuant to its obligations under the building contract and sought to recover the cost from the defendants as damages for negligence. A majority in the New Zealand Court of Appeal (Henry and Keith JJ.) held that the defendants owed no duty of care to the contractor. Such a duty would be inconsistent with the contractual arrangements made between the parties concerned; in particular, the plaintiff had a claim in contract against its specialist sub-contractor, which had installed the pumps, and the sub-contractor in turn had a claim against the manufacturer of the pumps, which had claimed in its literature that the pumps had the required output. In those circumstances, it was not fair, just and reasonable to impose a duty of care upon the defendants. Thomas J. dissenting, regarded considerations of fairness, justice and reasonableness irrelevant in deciding whether a *Hedley Byrne* duty existed. If the requirements for a *Hedley Byrne* duty (assumption of responsibility for the provision of special skill and concomitant reliance) are satisfied, a duty of care exists. The contractual arrangements between the parties are relevant only to the question whether those requirements are met on the facts of the particular case.[36] As Thomas J. appreciated, the approach which he favoured and the approach which the majority adopted contain all of the same factual elements and ought to produce the same answer on the facts of any given case. That they did not do so in *Turton v. Kerslake* was probably the result of differing approaches to the practicalities of the situation in which a tendering contractor finds itself. In particular, Thomas J. pointed out that the contractual arrangements ignored the possibility of insolvencies, which are a fact of life and would render the contractor's remedies in contract worthless. The majority view was that, precisely because insolvencies are a fact of life, the parties must be taken to have considered their possible

8–109

---

[33] *ibid.* at para. 53 in the judgment of the court, which was given by Peter Gibson L.J.
[34] See para. 8–277 below.
[35] [2000] Lloyd's Rep. P.N. 967, New Zealand Court of Appeal.
[36] This analysis is in line with the statement of Lord Goff in *Henderson* which is quoted at para. 8–060 above, and upon which Thomas J. relied.

impact when making their contractual arrangements. Thomas J. also pointed out the comparative advantages of the defendant engineers and the tendering contractor. The tender period is typically too short to allow the contractor and its prospective sub-contractors to carry out a full analysis and investigation into the accuracy of the specification. The employer's engineers, by contrast, are likely to have had a much longer time to prepare the specification and, moreover, are likely to have better access to relevant information that the contractor. Furthermore, the fiercely competitive nature of the tendering process means that contractors cannot reasonably be expected to price for possible defects in the specification since they would thereby jeopardise their chances of obtaining the building contract. In those circumstances, Thomas J. held that the defendants had assumed responsibility to the contractor for the accuracy of statements made in the specification and it was reasonable for the contractor to rely upon the same, so that a *Hedley Byrne* duty of care arose. It is submitted that Thomas J.'s insight into the commercial realities of the typical tender process provides compelling reasons why, on appropriate facts, a construction professional acting for the employer should owe a duty of care to a tendering contractor for loss caused by careless misstatements in the tender documents.

(v) *The position in Canada*[37]

8–110   In Canada, the Supreme Court has refused to follow the decision in *Murphy*. Although the Court has emphasised that the categorisation of the loss does not determine the existence of a duty, it has accepted the need to find some acceptable control mechanism in cases involving the recovery of economic loss by third parties. In *Canadian National Railway v. Norsk Pacific Steamship Co.*[38] McLachlin J. with whom two of the other members of the majority agreed, stated that she considered that the previous Canadian Supreme Court decision in *City of Kamloops v. Nielson*[39] was to be preferred to *Murphy*. She considered that the crucial issues were proximity and the question whether there were any residual policy considerations calling for a limitation on liability.[40]

> "A consideration of proximity requires that the court review all of the factors connecting the negligent act with the loss; this includes not only the relationship between the parties but all forms of proximity—physical, circumstantial, causal or assumed indicators of closeness. While it is impossible to define comprehensively what will satisfy the requirements of proximity or directness, provision may be found as types of relationships or situations are defined in which the necessary closeness between negligence and loss exists."[41]

---

[37] For further discussion of the cases mentioned in this section, see the articles by Nicholas Rafferty: "Tortious liability for purely economic loss" (1993) 9 P.N. 87, "Liability of builders to subsequent purchasers for construction defects" (1995) 1 P.N. 84, "Pure economic loss in the Supreme Court—again" (1997) 13 P.N. 42, "Recent professional negligence decisions from the Supreme Court of Canada" (1998) 14 P.N. 67 and "Pure economic loss in the Supreme Court of Canada—the final word?" (1999) 15 P.N. 13.

[38] (1992) 91 D.L.R. (4th) 289. For facts see para. 8–075, above

[39] (1984) 10 D.L.R. (4th) 641.

[40] *i.e.* the two-stage test formulated by Lord Wilberforce in *Anns v. Merton LBC* [1978] A.C. 728: see para. 8–070 above.

[41] (1992) 91 D.L.R. (4th) at 371.

The leading case is, however, *Winnipeg Condominium Corporation v. Bird* **8–111**
Construction Co.[42] La Forest J. (with whom all the other judges agreed) stated
that he was in favour of allowing the possibility of tortious recovery by a building
owner in respect of the cost of repairing dangerous defects from the original
builder of the apartment building for what seemed to him to be compelling policy
considerations. His reasoning was as follows: (a) there was no universal principle
governing the recovery of economic loss: whether economic loss was recoverable had to be considered in the light of the particular situation in which
economic loss was sought to be recovered and the policy considerations applicable to that situation[43]; (b) the structure in question was not merely shoddy but
dangerous[44]; (c) as a matter of policy "a person who participates in the construction of a large and permanent structure which, if negligently constructed, has the
capacity to cause serious damage to other persons and property in the community,
should be held to a reasonable standard of care"[45]; (d) the fact that defendant had
negotiated a separate contract with the original owner of the building did not
prevent a separate duty being owed to subsequent purchasers[46]; (e) it was
reasonably foreseeable to contractors that if they designed or constructed a
building negligently with latent defects, subsequent purchasers might suffer
personal injury or damage to other property when those defects manifested
themselves[47]; (f) the reasonable likelihood that a defect in a building would cause
injury to its inhabitants is sufficient to ground a contractor's duty in tort to
subsequent purchasers for the cost of repairing that defect if that defect is
discovered prior to any injury and if it poses a real and substantial danger to the
inhabitants of the building[48]; (g) allowing recovery in tort for the cost of repair
of dangerous defects serves an important preventative function by encouraging
socially responsible behaviour; (h) there was no risk of indeterminate liability
because the potential class of claimants was limited to the very class for whom
the building was constructed, namely the inhabitants[49]; (i) there was no risk of
liability being found in an indeterminate amount because the amount of the
liability will always be limited by the reasonable cost of repairing the dangerous

---

[42] (1995) 1221 D.L.R. (4th) 193. For facts see para. 8–075, above. In *Cook v. Bowen* (1997) 39
B.C.L.R. (3d) 12, Owen-Flood J. followed Bird in finding that an engineer who negligently designed
a sewage system for a developer so as to create a health risk owed a duty of care to a subsequent
purchaser. In *Blair v. Alderney Consultants* (1998) 168 N.S.R.(2d) 287, Hamilton J. in the Supreme
Court of Nova Scotia, found an engineer, who had negligently designed a storm water drainage
system for a developer, liable to a builder who bought a plot of land with the intention of selling it
on. The builder, who himself built the property in breach of the building code, claimed that flooding
at the property led to a delay in selling the property and a diminution in its value. The judge does not
appear to have considered the relevant Canadian authorities (particularly *Bird*) but simply decided
that the loss was, in principle, recoverable on the basis of *Anns*. Although he found the builder liable
for 50 per cent of his losses (as a result of his own breaches of the building code), it is submitted that
this decision is difficult to reconcile with either principle or authority. No danger to health was alleged
(the only flooding was to the basement of the property) and the case was not put upon the basis of
recovering works necessary to avert such a danger. Moreover the builder was able to inspect the
sewer system and should have taken it into account when deciding how much he should pay for
purchasing the land.
[43] *ibid.* at 10C.
[44] *ibid.* at 10F.
[45] *ibid.* at 14D.
[46] *ibid.* at 16I.
[47] *ibid.* at 23F.
[48] *ibid.* at 24D.
[49] *ibid.* at 31D.

defect in the building and restoring the building to a non-dangerous state[50]; (j) there was little risk of liability for an indeterminate period of time as the contractor would only be liable for the cost of repair during the useful life of the building[51]; and (k) that there was no justification for applying the maxim caveat emptor as the subsequent purchaser was often in a poor position to find latent defects.[52] La Forest J. made it clear that he drew no distinction between a builder and anyone else who was negligent in the planning or construction of a building[53] and expressly left open the question whether a claim should be allowed against negligent builders or professionals in respect of non-dangerous defects in a building.[54] Although the decisions of the Supreme Court have not been free from criticism in Canada,[55] there does appear to be a coherent policy justification for the stance of the court.[56]

8–112   La Forest and McLachlin JJ. were in the minority in the Supreme Court of Canada for part of their decision in *Husky Oil v. Saint John Shipbuilding*.[57] In that case, the court was obliged to consider again the extent to which economic loss was recoverable as well as the impact of contractual obligations on tortious duties. The plaintiffs were two oil companies ("A" and "B") which had decided to drill off the east coast of Canada together with an offshore company ("C") which had been incorporated so as to contract for the construction of an oil rig and later own the rig. A and B agreed to hire the rig from C. A fire occurred on the rig due to (a) the fact that an important electrical safety device was not installed and (b) that a highly flammable material "Thermaclad" was used in a specialist system installed at C's specific request. A and B claimed against the defendant rig-builder the hire payments they were obliged to pay to C during the time that the rig was out of operation and C claimed the cost of repairs and lost revenues. The majority of the Supreme Court (La Forest and McLachlin JJ. dissenting) held that the contractual obligations between C and the defendant negated the tortious obligation which would otherwise have existed on the

---

[50] *ibid.* at 30G.
[51] *ibid.* at 30I.
[52] *ibid.* at 32H.
[53] *ibid.* at 14C.
[54] *ibid.* at 26I. He pointed out that such claims were permitted in Quebec.
[55] See *British Columbia Hydro & Power Authority v. N. D. Lea & Associates* (1992) 69 B.C.L.R. (2d) 309 where Newbury J. pointed out that it was difficult to produce a single principle from the diverse judgments in *Norsk Pacific*. In an article in the *Canadian Bar Review*, "Economic loss and the Supreme Court of Canada: an economic critique of *Norsk Steamship* and *Bird Construction*", Feldthusen and Palmer assert that the Supreme Court's analysis of the policy which permitted recovery is misplaced. They argue that in *Bird* the risk had already been allocated by sophisticated commercial parties whilst in *Norsk Pacific*, the plaintiff was better placed to insure against potential loss than was the defendant particularly as potential plaintiffs were virtually unlimited.
[56] See "No somersault after *Murphy*: New Zealand follows Canada" by I. N. Duncan Wallace Q.C. in (1995) 111 L.Q.R. at 285. See also *British Columbia v. R.B.O.* (1995) 6 B.C.L.R. (3d) 59 where Preston J. imposed a duty of care to a housing co-operative on an engineer who acted as a sub-contractor to an architect who contracted with the co-operative to design a housing project. The basis of this decision was that the engineer knew that his design drawings would be relied on by the co-operative. However he refused to impose a duty of care towards the government commission which funded the project as the engineer did not know that the commission would rely on his design drawings and had insufficient information to assess the risk of reliance.
[57] (1997) 153 D.L.R. 385. For commentaries, see I. N. Duncan Wallace Q.C., "Contractual relational loss in Canada" [1998] 114 L.Q.R. 371 and Raffety, N., "Pure economic loss in the Supreme Court of Canada—the final word?" (1999) 15 P.N. 13. See also *Martel Building Ltd v. Canada* [2000] 2 S.C.R. 860 (a party to a negotiation for the renewal of a lease did not owe a duty of care to the other party in its conduct of the negotiations or a subsequent tender process).

defendant to warn C of the risks associated with the use of Thermaclad. The Court unanimously held that A and B were not entitled to recover the loss suffered as a result of damage to the property of a third party—termed "contractual relational economic loss". McLachlin J., who gave the leading judgment, reiterated that it was necessary to apply a two-stage test: the first step was to consider whether the relationship of neighbourhood or proximity necessary to found a prima facie duty of care was present the second was to consider whether the policy concerns that usually preclude recovery of contractual relational economic loss, such as indeterminacy, were over-ridden. She concluded that A and B surmounted the first hurdle as the defendant knew of the existence of the plaintiffs and knew or ought to have known that they would lose money if the rig were shut down. However any such duty was negatived by policy and in particular the problem of indeterminate liability to persons who could claim to be in the same or similar position as A and B such as other investors in the project.

More recently, the Supreme Court of Canada has considered the question **8–113** which arose in *Murphy* upon similar facts. The claim in *Ingles v. Tutkaluk Construction Ltd*[58] was brought by a homeowner against the contractor which had agreed to lower the basement of his house and against the Corporation of the City of Toronto. The City's building inspectors had carried out a partial inspection of the works, but had accepted the contractor's assurance that underpinning which it had installed had been carried out in accordance with the City's requirements. That was not the case. Applying the two-stage test developed in *Anns* and adopted in *City of Kamloops v. Nielsen*, the Supreme Court held that the City owed to the claimant a duty of care at common law to avoid the economic loss represented by the contractor's inherently defective building works.

The Canadian courts have also applied an approach similar to Lord Wilber- **8–114** force's two-stage test for a duty of care in *Anns*[59] to claims which are capable of justification in England under the *Hedley Byrne* principle.[60] In *Edgeworth Construction v. N.D. Lea & Associates Ltd*[61] the Supreme Court held that a contractor which relied on tender documents prepared by engineers for the employer in order to put forward a price could sue the engineers for economic losses sustained as a result of negligent errors in such documents. This was so even though there was an express term in the contract between the employer and the contractor that any representations in the tender documents were furnished merely for information and did not amount to warranties. McLachlin J. (with whom five of the other six judges concurred) took the view that the errors amounted to negligent misrepresentations which the engineers knew would be

---

[58] [2000] 1 S.C.R. 298; (2000) 183 D.L.R. (4th) 193 *sub nom. Ingles v. City of Toronto*.

[59] [1978] A.C. 728; see para. 8–070 above. In *Henderson v. Merrett Syndicates Ltd* [1995] 2 A.C. 145, Lord Goff stated that the *Hedley Byrne* principle comprehended policy considerations, so that it would not be necessary to consider matters of policy in a case which fell within the principle: see para. 8–060 above.

[60] Scrutiny of the facts may reveal a contractual relationship between the employer and "third party" who is sought to be made liable under the Hedley Byrne principle: see *City of Brantford v. Kemp and Wallace-Carruthers & Associates Ltd* (1960) 23 D.L.R. (2d) 640, Ontario CA, the facts of which are described at para. 8–186, below; cf. *I.B.A. v. E.M.I. and B.I.C.C.* (1978) 11 B.L.R. 29, CA; (1980) 14 B.L.R. 1, HL, the facts of which are set out at para. 8–097, above. The Court of Appeal's finding that B.I.C.C.'s assurance amounted to a contractual warranty to I.B.A. was reversed by the House of Lords.

[61] (1993) 107 D.L.R. (4th) 169 overturning the decision of the Court of Appeal of British Columbia reported at (1991) 54 B.L.R. 16.

likely to be relied on by the contractor and were in fact relied upon. The claim fell within the principle set out in *Hedley Byrne* and the subsequent decision of the Supreme Court of Canada in *Haig v. Bamford*.[62] She considered the only real question to be whether the terms of the contract between the contractor and the employer negated the duty of care which would otherwise have been held to have arisen. It was held that the contract did not provide the engineers with protection (a) because it did not purport to do so; and (b) because the engineers could have taken alternative measures to protect themselves by, for example, putting a disclaimer on its design documents. McLachlin J. did not consider that there were any policy considerations militating against the imposition of a duty of care: she pointed out that it made greater practical sense for the pre-tender engineering work to be done by one firm rather than have all tenderers checking such work.[63] In the earlier case of *University of Regina v. Pettick*,[64] the Saskatchewan Court of Appeal considered a claim, brought solely in negligence by a university against defendant architects and engineers for defects in a gymnasium which they had designed. The Court categorised the claim as being one for economic losses and rejected the claim against the architects on the grounds that they had fulfilled their obligations by ensuring that reasonably competent engineers were appointed. However, by a majority, the Court found the engineers to be liable. A proximate relationship was created as a result of a call by the university for testing which the engineers undertook to provide. The case was decided expressly in reliance on the decision in *Hedley Byrne*.[65]

8-115   By contrast in *Auto Concrete Curb Ltd v. South Nation River Conservation Authority*[66] the Supreme Court overruled the Ontario Court of Appeal which had held that an engineer was liable to a contractor for negligence in the pre-engineering stage of a tender process for a contract for dredging a river.[67] The trial judge had made findings of fact: (a) that two alternative methods of performing the contract would have been within the contemplation of a reasonably competent engineer who was preparing tender documents; (b) that a reasonably competent engineer would have made inquiries of statutory authorities having jurisdiction in relation to the project and included relevant information in the tender documents (such inquiries would have revealed the need for additional permits for one of the methods); (c) that the engineer knew or ought to have known that the contractor and other bidders would rely on the information contained in the tender documents and the failure to include relevant information constituted a negligent misrepresentation; (d) that the need to obtain permits was

---

[62] [1977] 1 S.C.R. 466.

[63] See also *District of Surrey v. Carroll-Hatch and Associates Ltd* (1979) 101 D.L.R. (3d) 218, British Columbia CA. Structural engineers engaged by an architect were held to owe a duty of care to the employer despite the absence of a contract between the employer and them. The engineers were held guilty of negligent misrepresentation first by implying in a letter to the employer that an adequate soils investigation had been done and secondly by certifying to the employer that the design work performed by them complied with the Canadian National Building Code. Both representations were incorrect. It is unclear whether the representations formed the basis of the finding that the engineers were negligent in failing to warn the employer of the need for a deep soils report and of the risk in proceeding with the construction without such report. Although the engineers had warned the architect of the need for the report, the architect was not the agent of the employer for this purpose. The engineers should have warned the employer directly. The architect was similarly held liable in negligence, including negligent misrepresentation. He was further held liable in contract.

[64] (1992) 77 D.L.R. (4th) 615.

[65] See especially 655–657 *per* Sherstobitoff J.A.

[66] [1993] 3 S.C.R. 201.

[67] (1992) 89 D.L.R. (4th) 393.

not one that was made known or was reasonably foreseeable from the bid documents; and (e) that it was not reasonable to expect the contractor within a two-week period for tender to canvass and make enquiries when the engineer had had some four months to make appropriate enquiries. The Supreme Court held that it was no part of the function of the engineer to advise the contractor as to his method of work. Accordingly the engineer was under no duty to proffer such advice.[68] The decision would, presumably, have been different if the engineer had taken it upon himself to give misleading advice.

No *Hedley Byrne* duty will be imposed in respect of reports or advice provided **8–116** for persons other than the claimant unless the defendant is, at least, aware that his report or advice would be so used. Thus in *British Columbia Ltd v. HBT Agra Ltd*,[69] the British Columbia Court of Appeal found that the defendant engineer, who had prepared a report for the owner of land which stated that the land was "essentially free of risk of subsidence associated with abandoned mines", did not owe a duty to a subsequent owner of part of the land who relied on the report as the defendant was not aware that his report would be supplied to the plaintiff or to persons in the position of the plaintiff. Similarly an express disclaimer will be effective in Canada (as in England) to prevent a duty of care arising. In *Wolverine Tube (Canada) Inc. v. Noranda Metal Industries Limited*,[70] the defendant prepared environmental reports for an industrial client under a contract which provided that the reports were not be used outside the client's organisation without the defendant's permission. Each of the reports contained a clear disclaimer of liability to third parties. The client delivered reports prepared by the plaintiff to a third party who was contemplating purchasing three sites. The third party then acquired the sites which it alleged were contaminated and sued the defendants. The Ontario Court of Appeal struck out the action on the grounds that the disclaimer and the terms of the contract with the client were such as to prevent a duty of care from arising.[71]

(vi) *The position in Australia*

By refusing to follow *Anns*, the High Court of Australia had been taken in **8–117** England as having re-emphasised the traditional limitations on the recovery of

---

[68] See also *Vermont Construction Inc. v. Beatson* (1976) 67 D.L.R. (3rd) 95 where the Supreme Court of Canada, by a majority, rejected a claim in tort by a contractor against an architect for loss caused by delay occasioned by defective plans. Although arising from the civil law jurisdiction of Quebec, the common law position was extensively analysed.

[69] (1994) 120 D.L.R. (4th) 726.

[70] (1995) 26 O.R. 577.

[71] See also *Sealand of the Pacific v. Robert C. McHaffie Ltd* (1974) 51 D.L.R. (3d) 702, where the plaintiff employer sued the defendant naval architects and their employee, Mr McHaffie. The British Columbia Court of Appeal rejected the claim against both the employer and the employee for negligent misrepresentation. At 706, *per* Seaton J.A.:

"Here Mr McHaffie did not undertake to apply his skill for the assistance of Sealand. He did exercise, or fail to exercise, his skill as an employee of McHaffie Ltd in the carrying out of its contractual duty to Sealand. Further, while Sealand may have chosen to consult McHaffie Ltd because it had the benefit of Mr McHaffie's services as an employee, it was with McHaffie Ltd that Sealand made a contract and it was upon the skill of McHaffie Ltd that it relied."

The claim against McHaffie Ltd failed on the basis that "the duty and liability ought to be discovered in the contract" but the company was held liable for breach of contract in failing to consider and make inquiries about the suitability of a product which proved unsuitable for the required construction, on an underwater aquarium.

economic loss in tort.[72] It is now apparent that this view is too simplistic. *In Sutherland Shire Council v. Heyman*,[73] the High Court held that in the ordinary situation of the negligent approval of building plans, there was not a sufficient relationship of proximity between a local authority and a plaintiff to enable a duty of care to be imposed. However in *Bryan v. Maloney*,[74] the High Court of Australia held, by a majority of four to one, that a professional builder owed a duty of care to a subsequent purchaser in respect of financial loss caused by a failure to construct the house with proper footings. It is notable that it was not alleged that the foundations caused a danger to the subsequent purchaser with the result that the decision goes significantly further than that of the Supreme Court of Canada in *Winnipeg*. Four factors were held to give rise to a sufficient degree of proximity to found a duty of care: (a) the house was a permanent structure which was intended to be used indefinitely; (b) it was obviously foreseeable that the negligent construction of the footings was likely to cause economic loss to a subsequent purchaser; (c) a subsequent purchaser would have less opportunity to inspect the footings than the first purchaser to whom the builder plainly owed a duty of care; and (d) in the absence of competing or intervening negligence or some other causative event, the causal proximity between negligence on the part of the builder and subsequent economic loss was the same regardless of whether the loss was suffered by the first or a subsequent purchaser.[75] Brennan J. (who dissented) expressly approved the decision in *Winnipeg* to the effect that economic loss to remedy dangerous defects in a property should be recoverable.[76] Thus all of the members of the High Court would have been prepared to allow a greater degree of recovery than contemplated by the House of Lords in *Murphy*.

8–118   *Bryan v. Maloney* emphasised the re-emergence of "proximity" as a useful tool in Australia for seeking to establish when the law will impose a duty of care. In *San Sebastian Property v. Minister Administering the Environmental Planning and Assessment Act 1979*,[77] Gibbs C.J., Mason, Wilson and Dawson JJ. stated:

> "The relationship of proximity is an integral constituent of the duty of care concept. We refer to that relationship in its broader sense, namely, as embracing a general limitation upon the test of reasonable foreseeability, this being the sense in which it has been discussed and applied in recent judgments of this court . . . The notion of proximity,

---

[72] See the passage from the judgment of Brennan J. quoted in para. 8–068, above.
[73] (1984–1985) 157 C.L.R. 424.
[74] (1995) 74 B.L.R. 35. See I. N. Duncan Wallace Q.C., "*Murphy* rejected: the *Bryan v. Maloney* landmark" (1995) 3 Tort L.R. 231 and "The *Murphy* saga in Australia: *Bryan* in difficulties?" (1997) 113 L.Q.R. 355.
[75] The article by Sir Robin Cooke, "An impossible distinction" (1991) 107 L.Q.R. 46 was referred to by Mason C.J. in his consideration of the policy considerations which made the imposition of a duty of care desirable. In *Fangrove Pty Ltd v. Tod Group Holdings Pty Ltd* [1999] 2 Qd. R. 236, the Queensland Court of Appeal distinguished *Bryan v. Maloney* in deciding that an architect who designed a dangerous parapet on a commercial building was not liable to the subsequent owner of the building when it collapsed and damaged the building itself. The Court drew attention to the facts that the premises were commercial and that a purchaser could ordinarily be expected to undertake a survey before purchasing the premises (see at 242) when the defect would have been apparent. There was, accordingly, no basis for asserting that the architect assumed responsibility to the plaintiff. The Court expressly disclaimed any suggestion that the dangerous nature of the defect meant that the costs of repairing the building became recoverable.
[76] (1994) 74 Build. L.R. 35 at 71–72.
[77] (1986) 162 C.L.R. 340 at 355.

because it limits the loss that would otherwise be recoverable if foreseeability were used as an exclusive criterion of the duty of care, is of vital importance when the plaintiff's claim is for pure economic loss. When the economic loss results from negligent misstatement, the element of reliance plays a prominent part in the ascertainment of a relationship of proximity between the plaintiff and the defendant, and therefore in the ascertainment of the duty of care. But when the economic loss results from a negligent act or omission outside the realm of negligent misstatement, the element of reliance may not be present. It is in this sphere that the absence of reliance as a factor creates an additional difficulty in deciding whether a sufficient relationship of proximity exists to enable the plaintiff to recover economic loss."[78]

The High Court of Australia returned to the question of recovery in tort for economic loss in *Pyrenees Shire Council v. Day*.[79] A local authority was held liable (by a majority) to tenants of a building and (unanimously) to the freeholders when a defectively constructed fireplace caused the building to burn down. A building inspector had seen the fireplace and warned the tenants (but not the freeholders) against its use but had not exercised statutory powers to require its alteration or repair. In finding the council liable to both tenants and freeholders. Kirby J. declined to regard proximity as the general principle underlying and limiting the existence of a duty of care in tort. He adopted,[80] instead, a three-stage test: **8–119**

"1. Was it reasonably foreseeable to the alleged wrongdoer that particular conduct or an omission on its part would be likely to cause harm to the person who has suffered damage or a person in the same position?

2. Does there exist between the alleged wrongdoers and such person a relationship characterised by the law as one of 'proximity' or 'neighbourhood'?

3. If so, is it fair, just and reasonable that the law should impose a duty of given scope upon the alleged wrongdoer for the benefit of such person?"

---

[78] Three decisions of the lower courts illustrate the flexible approach adopted in seeking to establish whether sufficient proximity exists. In *National Mutual Life Association of Australasia Ltd v. Coffey & Partners Pty Ltd* [1991] 1 Qd.R. 401, the Queensland Court of Appeal refused to strike out a claim by subsequent purchasers of a property for the cost of repairing cracks in the foundations against engineers instructed by the original owner and builder of the property on the basis that there was a serious question as to whether the subsequent purchaser had placed reliance on the original engineers. In *Opat v. National Mutual Life Association of Australasia Ltd* [1992] 1 V.R. 283, Southwell J. at first instance in Victoria on the hearing of a preliminary issue, held that a builder could, in certain circumstances be liable for economic losses to future purchasers who were unidentified by name. However, he held that it would be necessary to plead and prove reliance by such purchasers in order to establish the necessary proximity for a duty of care to arise. In *Finlayson v. Armidale City Council* (1994) 123 A.L.R. 155, Burchett J. at first instance in the Federal Court of Australia, found the defendant council liable for negligently re-zoning contaminated land as residential land and subsequently granting a development application. The judge considered that the actions of the council created a hazard and that, having created such a hazard, it was the council's duty to take reasonable care to avoid the threatened injury. He also considered that a duty of care could be imposed as there was sufficient reliance on the basis that where a public authority was in a better position than an individual to assess and avoid a danger, an individual who suffered damage as a result of the authority's negligence could be said to have relied upon the authority.

[79] (1998) 192 C.L.R. 330. For commentary, see Lunney, M., "Don't play with matches" [1998] 114 L.Q.R. 377.

[80] *ibid.* at para. 244.

As Kirby J. recognised, this was the test adopted by the House of Lords in *Caparo v. Dickman*,[81] suggesting that the approach to novel duty of care situations in Australia is moving closer to that deployed by the courts of England and Wales.[82]

(vii) *The position in New Zealand*

8–120   The courts in New Zealand have consistently refused to follow either the principles set out in *Murphy* or the actual result in the case. In *South Pacific Manufacturing Co. Ltd v. New Zealand Security Consultants & Investigations Ltd*,[83] the New Zealand Court of Appeal stated that negligence law in New Zealand had not changed as a result of the decision. In *Otago Cheese Co. Ltd v. Nick Stoop Builders Ltd*[84] (a claim against a local authority for economic loss) Fraser J. stated:

> "The existence and general nature of the duty which arises in this sort of case is now well established . . . this district council was under a duty to take reasonable care: (1) in deciding whether the plans complied with the byelaws or were deficient in some respect; (2) in deciding whether and when to exercise its power to inspect; and (3) in carrying out any such inspection."

8–121   In *Invercargill City Council v. Hamlin*,[85] the Privy Council upheld the New Zealand Court of Appeal which had held that it was settled law in New Zealand that councils were liable to house owners and subsequent owners for defects caused or contributed to by building inspectors' negligence. The five member Court of Appeal pointed out differences between New Zealand and English law which might justify a difference in approach including: (a) most people owned homes built for them by small scale builders; (b) there had been extensive government support for low cost housing; (c) it had not been the practice for reports by engineers and surveyors to be commissioned on house purchases; and (d) standard byelaws considered comfort and standards of workmanship. It is doubted whether the last is, in truth, a distinction as the Building Regulations in the United Kingdom also deal with such matters. Cooke P., who had written an influential article in a non-judicial capacity[86] which was critical of the decision in *Murphy*, pointed out that the House of Lords had accepted[87] that a tortious duty to take reasonable care to avoid causing economic loss could arise from an assumption of responsibility, whether by contract or otherwise. He also pointed out that the New Zealand courts had not had to consider a case such as *Junior*

---

[81] [1990] 2 A.C. 605. In "Duty of care in Australia: is the fog lifting" (1998) 72 A.L.J. 871, Dr Katter suggests that the three-stage test is now becoming conventional in Australia. In his article, "Pure economic loss in the High Court of Australia: reinventing the square wheel" [2000] Tort L.Rev. 33, Bruce Feldthusen examines and criticises the development of this area of the law in Australia.

[82] See also *John Holland Construction and Engineering Ltd v. Majorca Products* (2000) 16 Const.L.J. 114, in which Byrne J. in the Supreme Court of Victoria applied considerations similar to those deployed by the English Court of Appeal in *Pacific Associates v. Baxter* (see para. 8–106 above) in deciding that construction professionals engaged by an employer to administer the building contract did not owe a duty of care to avoid causing economic loss to the contractor.

[83] [1992] 2 N.Z.L.R. 282 (claims by assured for negligence against professional fire investigators employed by insurer struck out for disclosing no reasonable cause of action).

[84] Unreported (Dunedin, CP 180/89, May 1992).

[85] [1996] A.C. 624, P.C.; [1994] 3 N.Z.L.R. 513, New Zealand CA.

[86] "An impossible distinction" (1991) 107 L.Q.R. 46.

[87] In *Henderson v. Merrett Syndicates Ltd* [1995] 2 A.C. 145.

Books[88] where it might be said that in a case of industrial construction, the parties had so structured their relationships as to avoid giving rise to an assumption of responsibility and, thus, a duty of care.[89] The Privy Council recognised that New Zealand judges were better able to interpret conditions in New Zealand than they were. Given the upheavals in England as compared with the comparative uniformity of approach in New Zealand, the Privy Council had no difficulty in adopting the reasoning of the New Zealand Court of Appeal.

(viii) *The position in other jurisdictions*

A similar position to that in England and Wales has been adopted by the Hong **8–122** Kong Court of Final Appeal following the transfer of sovereignty in *Bank of East Asia v. Tsien Wui Marble Factory Ltd.*[90] However the courts in Singapore and Malaysia have now indicated their preference for the decisions of other Commonwealth countries rather than that of the House of Lords in *Murphy*. In *MC Strata Title Plan No. 1272 v. Ocean Front Pte Ltd*[91] and *MC Strata Title Plan No. 1075 v. RSP Architects & Planners & Engineers*,[92] the Singapore Court of Appeal declined to follow *Murphy*, holding that the management corporation of a residential condominium could sue the developers and the developer's architects for pure economic loss arising from the faulty construction of the common parts of the building. In the Malaysian case of *Dr Rashid v. Jurusan Malaysia Consultants Ltd*,[93] James Foong J. refused to follow *Murphy* although it would

---

[88] [1983] 1 A.C. 520

[89] Cooke P. may have overlooked the first instance decision in *Bevan Investments Ltd v. Blackhall and Struthers (No. 2)* [1973] 2 N.Z.L.R. 97, where the plaintiff employer contracted with the first defendant architect for the design and construction of a leisure centre. The architect engaged the second defendant structural engineer to advise on structural aspects of the design. There was no contract between the employer and the engineer although the former was fully aware of the latter's involvement. The design provided for the construction of squash courts above a skating rink some 60 feet wide, and for the lift slab method of construction. The judge found that the engineer accepted responsibility for the safety and adequacy of the design from the structural viewpoint. During the course of construction but before any engineering aspects of the design had been put to the test, the engineer emigrated to Australia and was replaced by another engineer. Construction to the original design was subsequently abandoned when after several unsuccessful attempts it proved impossible to lift the first floor slab into position. It was contended for the engineer that he was a mere deputy of the architect and that the employer was limited to a claim in contract against the latter. This argument was rejected by Beattie J. who, applying Lord Atkin's neighbour principle, held that the engineer owed a duty of care to the employer. He was held to have been in breach of that duty and negligent in failing to provide a safe and adequate design and also in failing to provide proper details and specifications to the engineer who replaced him. In *Riddell v. Porteous* [1999] 1 N.Z.L.R. 1, the Court of Appeal of New Zealand made it clear that a plaintiff suing a local authority in respect of negligent inspections of building work did not have to be a current owner in order to succeed. In that case the plaintiffs had sold their house to a third party to whom they were found liable for breach of contract in respect of defects in a wooden "deck". They were able to pass on the extent of their liability to both the builder who had negligently constructed the deck and the council who had negligently inspected it. See also *R.M. Turton & Co Ltd v. Kerslake & Partners* [2000] Lloyd's Rep.P.N. 967, New Zealand CA, discussed at para. 8–109 above.

[90] [1998] 2 H.K.L.R.D. 373. See n. 22 to para. 8–077 above and, for further discussion, see R. Glofcheski, "The law of limitations as applied to latent building defects" (2000) 16 Const.L.J. 379 and N. J. Mullaney, "Limitation and Latent Damage in Hong Kong" (2001) 117 L.Q.R. 21.

[91] [1996] 1 S.L.R. 113.

[92] [1999] 2 S.L.R. 449.

[93] [1997] 3 M.L.J. 546. The decision has been welcomed by Grace Xavier in an article at [1988] 3 M.L.J. xxvi where the author provides a review of other relevant Malaysian decisions. The decision in *Murphy* has been followed in Malaysia: *Teh Khem On v. Yeoh* [1995] 2 M.L.J. 663 (claim by purchaser against architects and engineers employed by vendor builder in respect of defective foundations dismissed).

appear that, in England, the plaintiffs' claim against the defendant engineers would have succeeded in contract. In the South African case of *Lillicrap, Wassenaar and Partners v. Pilkington Brothers (S.A.) (Pty) Ltd*,[94] engineers initially engaged by the employer but subsequently engaged as sub-contractors were held not to owe a duty of care to the employer. The court by a majority considered it undesirable to extend the Aquilian action under South African law (similar to negligence in English law) to the duties subsisting between the parties to a contract for professional services. After referring to Lord Wilberforce's two-stage test to a duty of care in *Anns v. Merton LBC* Grosskopf A.J.A., in a passage which may ironically now reflect English law, stated:

> "South African law approaches the matter in a more cautious way ... and does not extend the scope of the Aquilian action to new situations unless there are positive policy considerations which favour such an extension."

However in *Tsimatakopoulos v. Hemmingway*,[95] Foxcroft J., in the Cape Provincial Division, refused to follow *Murphy* and found the defendant engineer who had designed a retaining wall to owe a duty to a subsequent purchaser to avoid economic loss.

(ix) *Problems of scope of duty*

8–123   Given the absence of a contract, there may be difficulties in assessing the scope of a construction professional's duty of care to third persons and in particular the extent to which such a duty may be limited by the terms of the professional's contract with his own client. This is an area where there is likely to be a difference in attitude according to whether the loss sought to be recovered is physical injury (where the contract is likely to be relevant only to the ambit of the task that the professional was undertaking) or economic loss (where the terms of the contract may be relevant in assessing whether a duty of care will arise, at all, to a third party). The varying importance of the existence or terms of a contract between a professional and his client in the assessment of whether or not a duty of care should be imposed to prevent economic loss is apparent from the discussion of the difference in Commonwealth decisions above.[96]

8–124   An English example of the importance of contractual terms in deciding whether a duty to avoid causing economic loss exists is provided by *Southern Water Authority v. Lewis & Duvivier*.[97] Under the terms of a main contract between a building employer (A) of whom the plaintiff was the successor under statute, and a main contractor (B), the latter's liability in respect of defects was limited as from the issue of "taking-over certificates". Such certificates were issued. Upon discovery of defects the plaintiff sued sub-contractors engaged by B to carry out the works. The question whether in view of the issue of taking-

---

[94] [1985] 1 S.A.L.R. 475, partially reported in (1984–85) 1 Const.L.J. 211.

[95] [1993] 4 S.A.L.R. 428.

[96] See paras 8–096 to 8–121 above. See also *Rumbelows Ltd v. A.M.K.* (1980) 19 B.L.R. 25 (specialist pipework sub-contractors' duty in tort to building owner was not limited by a clause in the sub-contract limiting their liability to the replacement of defective materials); *Twins Transport Ltd v. Patrick and Brocklehurst* (1983) 25 B.L.R. 65 (main contractor's duty in tort to the building owner was not limited by the terms of the contractor's contract with the developer). Note that these cases, as well as *Southern Water Authority v. Lewis & Duvivier*, were decided before the decision in *Murphy v. Brentwood District Council*: it is doubtful whether the sub-contractors would be held to owe a duty in tort on the same facts today.

[97] (1984) 27 B.L.R. 111.

over certificates duties of care were owed by two sub-contractors to the plaintiff was tried as a preliminary point of law and answered in the negative. Judge Smout Q.C. observed[98]:

> "The contractual setting may not necessarily be overriding, but is relevant in the consideration of the scope of the duty in tort for it indicates the extent of the liability which the plaintiffs' predecessors wished to impose. To put it more crudely . . . the contractual setting defines the area of risk which the plaintiffs' predecessors chose to accept and for which they may or may not have sought insurance."

8–125 Similarly, in *Pacific Associates Inc. v. Baxter*,[99] it was held that engineers engaged by the building owner did not owe a duty in tort to the main contractor in respect of payment certificates issued by them because the building contract provided (a) that the main contractor was entitled to challenge the engineers' certificates in arbitral proceedings against the employer and (b) that the engineers were not to be held personally liable for their conduct in administering the contract. Purchas L.J. said[1]:

> " . . . where the parties have come together against a contractual structure which provides for compensation in the event of failure of one of the parties involved, the court will be slow to superimpose an added duty of care beyond that which was in the contemplation of the parties at the time that they came together."

8–126 As foreseen by Judge Smout Q.C. in *Southern Water Authority v. Lewis & Duvivier*,[2] insurance clauses in building contracts have proved particularly important in determining the existence and scope of duties of care owed in tort to third parties, at least where the duty is alleged to have been owed by a sub-contractor responsible for causing physical damage to property. In *Norwich City Council v. Harvey*,[3] the Court of Appeal dismissed a claim by a building owner against a roofing sub-contractor for damages for negligently caused fire damage. Both the owner and the sub-contractor had contracted with the main contractor on the basis that the owner had assumed, and would insure against, the risk of damage by fire. In those circumstances, it was not fair, just or reasonable to impose a duty of care in tort to avoid such damage upon the sub-contractor. On similar facts, but different contract terms, the sub-contractor was held to owe a duty in tort to avoid causing damage to the property of the building owner in *British Telecommunications plc v. Thomson Ltd.*[4] The House of Lords on a Scottish appeal held that the provisions of the main building contract reinforced rather than undermined the existence of a duty of care owed by a domestic sub-contractor to the owner. The insuring obligations set out in the main building contract provided that the owner, the main contractor and nominated sub-contractors were to be joint insureds under a policy of insurance to be maintained by the owner in respect of fire damage. One assured cannot sue a co-assured for a loss in respect of which the co-assured is entitled to the benefit of the same

---

[98] *ibid.* at 124.
[99] [1990] 1 Q.B. 993. For the facts, see para. 8–106 above.
[1] *ibid.* at 1010.
[2] (1984) 27 B.L.R. 111; see para. 8–124 above.
[3] [1989] 1 W.L.R. 828.
[4] [1999] 1 W.L.R. 9, HL.

insurance.[5] As a domestic sub-contractor, the defendant was outside the class of persons *vis-à-vis* whom the owner had assumed the risk of fire. Accordingly, he could not rely upon the contract terms so as to avoid liability to the building owner for negligently caused fire damage. The defendant engineers in *Hopewell Project Management Ltd v. Ewbank Preece Ltd*[6] argued that they were joint insureds with the employer under two policies of insurance taken out in accordance with the provisions of the building contract and that, therefore, they could not be held liable on a subrogated claim brought by insurers in the name of the employer. The argument failed. The parties insured under the policies included "contractors and sub-contractors". Mr Recorder Jackson Q.C. held that the engineers were not insured under the policies. He observed that it is not normal practice to describe a professional firm as a contractor or sub-contractor, even although that firm enters into contracts with its clients.[7] Similarly, it is unusual for contracts made by construction professionals to contain insurance provisions such as those considered in the *Norwich City Council* and *British Telecommunications* cases.[8] In the light of those decisions, it would certainly be prudent for an architect or engineer engaged by a design and build contractor to make sure that, if the building contract provides that the employer shall insure against (and thereby assume the risk of) physical damage to the property, such provision is replicated or incorporated in his own contract.

8–127   An illustration of a personal injuries case where the architect's contract was relevant to the scope of his duties in tort is *Clayton v. Woodman & Son (Builders) Ltd*.[9] In that case a building project entailed incorporation of an old gable and the cutting of a groove along its base in order to take the concrete floor of a new lift motor house. During a site inspection by the architect the plaintiff, an experienced bricklayer and an employee of the building contractors, suggested to him that owing to the difficulty of incorporating the gable it would be better to pull it down. The architect rejected the suggestion, having satisfied himself that the gable could be safely incorporated. The specification required the retention of the gable and the provision of necessary shoring by the contractors. The groove was cut but the gable collapsed, injuring the plaintiff. At first instance Salmon J. held the contractors negligent and in breach of statutory duty in failing to shore and strut the gable. He further held that given their "exceptionally close relationship" the architect owed a duty to the plaintiff to take reasonable care for his safety and that he was in breach of that duty since he had in effect instructed the plaintiff to cut the groove. The Court of Appeal took a different view and held that the architect did not owe a duty in the circumstances. The architect had not given any direct instructions to the plaintiff but, given his decision that the gable could be safely incorporated, had taken the right decision in the interests of the employer to adhere to the specification. The manner of executing the groove was within the province of the contractors and it was the manner of execution adopted, namely without shores or struts, which had caused the injury. If, in contrast, the architect had directed the plaintiff as to how the groove was to be cut he would have been

---

[5] *Petrofina (UK) Ltd v. Magnaload Ltd* [1984] QB 127; *National Oil Wells (UK) Ltd v. Davy Off-Shore Ltd* [1993] 2 Lloyd's Rep. 582. See also *Co-operative Retail Services Ltd v. Taylor Young Partnership* (2000) 74 Con.L.R. 12, discussed further at para. 8–320, below.
[6] [1998] 2 Lloyd's Rep. 448.
[7] *ibid.* at 455.
[8] Although such contracts do commonly impose upon the professional an obligation to maintain professional indemnity insurance.
[9] [1962] 1 W.L.R. 585, CA, reversing Salmon J. at first instance, [1962] 2 Q.B. 533.

stepping outside his own province. Moreover, if he had so directed when he knew or ought to have known that it would have been done in a dangerous manner, a duty might have been imposed upon him.[10]

Windeyer J. summarised the position in relation to personal injury actions in **8–128** *Voli v. Inglewood Shire Council*[11]:

> " . . . neither the terms of the architect's engagement, nor the terms of the building contract, can operate to discharge the architect from a duty of care to persons who are strangers to those contracts. Nor can they directly determine what he must do to satisfy his duty to such persons. That duty is cast upon him by law, not because he made a contract, but because he entered upon the work. Nevertheless his contract with the building owner is not an irrelevant circumstance. It determines what was the task upon which he entered. If, for example, it was a design for a stage to bear only some specified weight, he would not be liable for the consequence of someone thereafter negligently permitting a greater weight to be put upon it."[12]

The facts of *Voli* were that the plaintiff was injured by the collapse of a stage in a public hall designed by the defendant architect. The plaintiff was held to owe a duty of care so to design the platform as to make it safe for any burden reasonably to be expected. The specified joists supporting the stage were not strong enough to bear such a burden and the architect was consequently liable in negligence to the plaintiff. In *Introvigne v. Commonwealth of Australia*[13] the issue of injury to a third party through misuse of an article designed by an architect was considered. The plaintiff schoolboy was swinging from the halyard of a flagpole in the school quadrangle when the truck fastened to the top of the pole collapsed and injured him. In an action against the architects, *inter alios*, the court recognised that an abuse of a particular article in a particular way might be so notorious as to make such abuse reasonably foreseeable.[14] On the facts, however, it was held that the architects when designing the flagpole were not under a duty of care to guard against schoolboy abuses.

The extent of a duty of care to a contractor in respect of design and supervision **8–129** causing loss to adjoining property was considered *obiter* by Judge Stabb Q.C., in *Oldschool v. Gleeson (Construction) Ltd.*[15] While abjuring the view that the relationship of consulting engineer and contractor did not admit a duty of care owed by the former to the latter, he continued:

> " . . . it seems abundantly plain that the duty of care of an architect or of a consulting engineer in no way extends into the area of how the work is carried out. Not only has he no duty to instruct the builder how to do the work or what safety precautions to take but he has no right to do so, nor is he under any duty to the builder to detect faults during the progress of the work. The architect, in that respect, may be in breach of his duty to his client, the building owner, but this does not excuse the builder for faulty work. I take the view that the duty of care which an architect or a consulting engineer owes to a third party is limited by the assumption that the contractor who creates the work acts at all material times as a competent contractor. The contractor cannot seek to pass blame for incompetent work on to the consulting engineer on the grounds that he failed to prevent it. . . . But if . . . the design was so faulty that the competent contractor

---

[10] *ibid.* at 592 *per* Donovan L.J. and at 595 *per* Pearson L.J.
[11] [1963] A.L.R. 657.
[12] *ibid.* at 662.
[13] (1980) 32 A.L.R. 251, Federal Court of Australia.
[14] *ibid.* at 273.
[15] (1976) 4 B.L.R. 103: consulting engineers held not negligent on the facts.

in the course of executing the works could not have avoided the resulting damage, then on principle it seems to me that the consulting engineer responsible for that design should bear the loss."[16]

(c) *Other torts*

8-130   Although there is scarce authority in this area, there is no reason why, on appropriate facts, a construction professional who undertakes an appointment as contract administrator should not be held liable to the building contractor or the employer for the torts of inducing breach of contract or wrongful interference with contract. Claims are most likely to be made by a contractor which is disappointed with the way in which a contract administrator has exercised his certification function. An illustration is provided by *Lubenham Fidelities & Investment Co. Ltd v. South Pembrokeshire District Council*.[17] The plaintiff contractor claimed damages against the defendant architect and contract administrator for financial loss alleged to have been caused by the architect's interim payment certificates. There was an issue as to the correct interpretation of terms of the building contract which provided for the deduction of liquidated damages payable by the contractor from sums certified by the architect as payable to the contractor. The Court of Appeal held that, although the architect's interpretation of those provisions was incorrect, so that excessive sums had been deducted as against the contractor, the architect was not liable for wrongful interference with the building contract (or for procuring a breach of contract by the employer). The architect had applied his erroneous interpretation in good faith, albeit negligently, and had not intended deliberately to misapply the provisions of the contract so as to deprive the plaintiff of its entitlements. It was recognised that the architect would have been exposed to such liability had he deliberately misapplied the provisions of the building contract in issuing his certificates with the intention of depriving the contractor of the larger sums to which it would otherwise be entitled.[18]

(d) *The Standard of Care and Skill*

(i) *The ordinary competent and skilled practitioner*

8-131   As in the case of other professions the standard generally required of an architect in discharging his duties is the reasonable skill, care and diligence of an ordinary competent and skilled architect. The standard is more fully expressed by Windeyer J. in the Australian case of *Voli v. Inglewood Shire Council*[19] as follows:

---

[16] *ibid.* at 131. See also *A.M.F. International Ltd v. Magnet Bowling Ltd* [1968] 1 W.L.R. 1028, 1053, *per* Mocatta J.; *East Ham Corporation v. Bernard Sunley & Sons Ltd* [1966] A.C. 406, 444, 449. In *Victoria University of Manchester v. Hugh Wilson* (1984) 2 Con.L.R. 43 Judge Newey Q.C. expressed the view, *obiter*, that the words of Judge Stabb Q.C. in *Oldschool* must now be regarded as too widely expressed. However, it is suggested that Judge Newey's criticism is itself now out of line with modern authority.

[17] (1986) 6 Con.L.R. 85.

[18] *ibid.* at 114. See, to similar effect: *John Mowlem v. Eagle Star* (1992) 62 B.L.R. 126; *John Holland Construction and Engineering Ltd v. Majorca Products* (2000) Const.L.J. 114, Supreme Court of Victoria.

[19] [1963] A.L.R. 657

"An architect undertaking any work in the way of his profession accepts the ordinary liabilities of any man who follows a skilled calling. He is bound to exercise due care, skill and diligence. He is not required to have an extraordinary degree of skill or the highest professional attainments. But he must bring to the task he undertakes the competence and skill that is usual among architects practising their profession. And he must use due care. If he fails in these matters and the person who employed him thereby suffers damage, he is liable to that person. This liability can be said to arise either from a breach of his contract or in tort."[20]

The standard may be similarly expressed for engineers,[21] quantity surveyors and other construction professionals. In *Eckersley v. Binnie & Partners*,[22] Bingham L.J. who dissented on the result but not, it is submitted, on the standard to be applied said:

" . . . a professional man should command the corpus of knowledge which forms part of the professional equipment of the ordinary member of his profession. He should not lag behind other ordinarily assiduous and intelligent members of his profession in knowledge of new advances, discoveries and developments in his field. He should be alert to the hazards and risks inherent in any professional task he undertakes to the extent that other ordinarily competent members of the profession would be alert. He must bring to any professional task he undertakes no less expertise, skill and care than other ordinarily competent members would bring but need bring no more. The standard is that of the reasonable average. The law does not require of a professional man that he be a paragon combining the qualities of polymath and prophet."[23]

What is required to fulfil the standard will vary according to the facts and **8–132** circumstances of each case. Thus in *Larche v. Ontario*,[24] the Ontario Court of Appeal upheld the trial judge's rejection of a claim that architects were liable to a patient at a psychiatric hospital who was injured when he fell from the roof as a result of alleged negligence in the design of a railing. The Court[25] upheld the judge's finding that "what was designed was reasonable and represented the discharge of the architects' duty to design a barrier which met an acceptable security standard in the particular location it was constructed at this type of psychiatric facility".[26] An English illustration is provided by the decision at first instance in *Ministry of Defence v. Scott Wilson Kirkpatrick*.[27] The third defendants were structural engineers. They were engaged by the Ministry of Defence

---

[20] *ibid.* at 661. See also, *e.g. Armstrong v. Jones* (1869) cited in *Hudson's Building Contracts* (4th ed., 1914), vol. 2, at p. 6, 7, *per* Baron Fitzgerald; *B.L. Holdings Ltd v. Robert J. Wood & Partners* (1978) 10 B.L.R. 48, 80; *Kensington and Chelsea and Westminster A.H.A. v. Wettern Composites* (1984) 1 Con.L.R. 114, 131.

[21] *e.g. Greaves & Co. (Contractors) Ltd v. Baynham Meikle & Partners* [1975] 1 W.L.R. 1095, CA, 1101, *per* Lord Denning M.R.; *Wimpey Construction U.K. Ltd v. Poole* [1984] 2 Lloyd's Rep. 499, 505 *et seq.*, *per* Webster J. (this case is discussed further at para. 8–166, below in relation to the specialist practitioner).

[22] (1988) 18 Con.L.R. 1. For the facts see para. 8–079, above and for further discussion on the question of foreseeability see para. 8–279, below.

[23] *ibid.* at 80. This passage was quoted with approval by the Court of Appeal in *Michael Hyde & Associates Ltd v. J.D. Williams & Co. Ltd* [2001] P.N.L.R. 233, para. 24 *per* Ward L.J. (with whom Sedley and Nourse L.JJ. agreed). For further discussion of this case, see para. 8–146 below.

[24] (1990) 75 D.L.R. (4th) 377.

[25] *ibid.* at 380.

[26] See further chap. 12, para. 12–240.

[27] Unreported, July 1997, Mr Recorder Coles Q.C. The dismissal of the claim against the third defendants was not the subject of the appeal at [2000] B.L.R. 20. The decision is discussed further at para. 8–241 below.

to design a scheme of works for the repair and refurbishment of a wooden shipbuilding slip at its Plymouth dockyard. The original slip was a large wooden structure which had been built in the early seventeenth century using the same methods as were then used to build ships. The roof timbers had been attached to the main structure using cast iron nails which varied in length from 8 inches to 12 inches. The engineers' design for repair of the roof included the replacement of rotten timbers with sound wood and the instruction that such new timbers be "well fixed as existing", *i.e.* that nails of similar length and strength as the original nails should be used. The repair works were not carried out for some years, by which time the engineers' involvement had ceased. Later, during bad weather, the roof of the slip was lifted off the main structure by wind and came to rest in a nearby playing field. The Ministry of Defence alleged that the third defendants had been negligent in designing the repairs on a "like-for-like" basis and that they ought to have followed modern codes of practice which would have required the use of steel angles, straps and bolts to fix the roof timbers to the main structure. The claim failed. The judge held that the engineers' design was appropriate since the original building had remained intact for nearly 200 years, proving the adequacy of nails of the type originally used. Furthermore, the principles of design which were appropriate in new buildings were not necessarily appropriate in the repair of older buildings; in particular, the slip was of considerable historic and architectural significance and the engineers were right to seek to replicate the original method of construction in the repairs which they designed.

8-133   The qualifications and experience of his client may also influence what is required of the professional man in discharge of his duties. The claim against the architects in *J. Jarvis & Sons Ltd v. Castle Wharf Developments Ltd*[28] provides an example. The first defendant was the developer of an office and leisure complex on a flagship site in Nottingham. The third defendants were architects who, initially, were engaged by the developer to obtain planning permission for the development. The claimant contractor was invited to tender for the detailed design and construction of the development. It proposed a scheme which differed from the developer's scheme. Following discussions between the contractor and the developer's project manager at which certain modifications to the contractor's proposed scheme were agreed, the developer sent to the contractor a letter stating its intention to enter a design and build contract with the contractor. The architects were not involved in the tender process or in the discussions with the contractor. The architects' contract with the developer was then novated to the contractor and the contractor began work on site. Some months later, the local planning authority informed the claimant that the scheme which it was building was not in accordance with the planning permission which had been issued to the developer and threatened enforcement proceedings. The contractor alleged that, until then, it had believed that its proposed scheme, modified as discussed with the developer's project manager, would be in line with the existing planning permission. It claimed that the architects should have advised it of the true planning position at the outset of their novated engagement and, in failing to do so, were in breach of their duty of care in contract and in tort. The claim succeeded at first instance but the architects' appeal was upheld.

---

[28] [2001] E.W.C.A. Civ. 19, [2001] Lloyd's Rep. P.N. 308. For discussion of the claim against the project managers, see para. 8–108 above; for discussion of the findings on causation, see para. 8–277 below.

The Court of Appeal accepted the architects' submission that, in the absence **8–134** of any express or implied request for advice, a professional has a duty to offer unsolicited advice only when his reasonable perception of his client's skill and experience suggests that his client needs such advice. The following words of Donaldson L.J. in the solicitors' case of *Carradine Properties Ltd v. D.J. Freeman &Co.*[29] applied equally to architects:

> "A solicitor's duty to his client is to exercise all reasonable skill and care in and about his client's business. In deciding what he should do and what advice he should tender the scope of his retainer is undoubtedly important, but it is not decisive. If a solicitor is instructed to prepare all the documentation needed for the sale or purchase of a house, it is no part of his duty to pursue a claim by the client for unfair dismissal. But if he finds unusual covenants or planning restrictions, it may indeed be his duty to warn of the risks and dangers of buying the house at all, notwithstanding that the client has made up his mind and is not seeking advice about that. I say only that this *may* be his duty because the precise scope of that duty will depend inter alia upon the extent to which the client appears to need advice. An inexperienced client will need and will be entitled to expect the solicitor to take a much broader view of the scope of his retainer and of his duties than will be the case with an experienced client."

The claimant in *Jarvis*, the Court held, was a design and build contractor which had taken on a major development. The architects were entitled to suppose that the claimant had informed itself of and understood the planning position. Furthermore, the architects did not know that the claimant in fact had a limited and erroneous understanding of the position and the claimant failed to establish that the architects were put on inquiry as to the accuracy of the claimant's understanding. In those circumstances, the architects' duty to exercise reasonable care and skill did not require them to volunteer advice to the claimant as to the planning position.

However, once it is established that a professional man owes a duty to provide **8–135** advice or services to his client, the fact that his client has special skills in the same area does not reduce the standard of care which is required in order to discharge that duty. In *Gloucestershire Health Authority v. Torpy,*[30] the defendant mechanical services engineers argued that the fact that their client was experienced and knowledgeable in the area of incinerator technology meant that their obligations to him were reduced. Judge Bowsher Q.C. rejected that argument, saying[31]: "I cannot see how it can possibly be right to suggest that, for example, conveyancing counsel should accept from a solicitor engaged to convey his house a lower than usual standard of care."

The starting point for any consideration of what must be done to discharge his **8–136** duty to exercise reasonable care and skill is the professional man's contract.[32] In

---

[29] (1982) [1999] Lloyd's Rep. P.N. 483, 487. This passage was also approved by the Court of Appeal in the solicitors' case *Virgin Management Ltd v. Defendant Morgan Group plc*, unreported, January 24, 1996.

[30] (1997) 55 Con.L.R. 124.

[31] *ibid.* at 146.

[32] See *Investors in Industry Commercial Properties v. South Bedfordshire D.C.; Ellison & Partners and Hamilton Associates (Third Parties)* [1986] 1 All E.R. 787, CA at 806F; *Nordic Holdings Ltd v. Mott MacDonald Ltd*, unreported, July 27, 2001 *per* Judge Seymour Q.C. at para. 82. See also *Neisner-Kratt Enterprises v. Building Design 2* (1988) 39 *Business Law Reports* 98 where the Saskatchewan Court of Queen's Bench examined closely the inspection provisions in the Royal Architectural Institute of Canada's standard form agreement (similar to the RIBA agreement), before concluding no breach had occurred.

a claim against a construction professional it may also be relevant to look not only at the terms of the contracts between the professional and the employer but also at the terms of other contracts to which the professional is not party, such as a building contract in which he is named as contract administrator.[33]

8–137   The relevant standard is that of competent practitioners prevailing at the time when the particular professional services are performed,[34] as distinct from the perhaps higher standard of competent practitioners prevailing at the time of the trial.

8–138   On the other hand, what is required to fulfil the standard is not static and will vary as circumstances change. In particular the standard will reflect the need for the construction professions to keep pace with new skills and technology.[35] It will apply even if the architect embarks on a novel design as illustrated by *I.B.A. v. E.M.I. and B.I.C.C.*[36] In that case the design of the cylindrical television mast by the sub-contractors B.I.C.C. was at and beyond the frontiers of professional knowledge. The House of Lords nevertheless held that they were in breach of their duty to exercise reasonable skill and care in the design of the mast. The relation of the required standard to the novel design was considered by Lord Edmund-Davies:

> "Judgment on hindsight has to be avoided. . . . Justice requires that we seek to put ourselves in the position of B.I.C.C. when first confronted by their daunting task, lacking all empirical knowledge and adequate expert advice in dealing with the many problems awaiting solution. But those very handicaps created a clear duty to identify and to think through such problems, including those of static and dynamic stresses, so that dimensions of the venture into the unknown could be adequately assessed and the ultimate decision as to its practicability arrived at."[37]

The exercise of reasonable skill and care may even require the abandonment of a project:

> "The project may be alluring. But the risks of injury to those engaged in it, or others, or to both, may be so manifest and substantial, and their elimination may be so difficult to ensure with reasonable certainty that the only proper course is to abandon the project altogether. Learned Counsel for B.I.C.C. appeared to regard such a defeatist outcome as unthinkable. Yet circumstances can and have at times arisen in which it is plain commonsense, and any other decision foolhardy. The law requires even pioneers to be prudent."[38]

---

[33] See *Vermont Construction Inc. v. Beatson* (1976) 67 D.L.R. (3d) 95, 103 and *Voli v. Inglewood Shire Council* [1963] A.L.R. 657, 662, discussed at para. 8–128, above.

[34] *e.g. Newham LBC v. Taylor Woodrow* (1982) 19 B.L.R. 99, CA at 128; *Kensington and Chelsea and Westminster A.H.A. v. Wettern Composites* (1984) 1 Con.L.R. 114, 131; *Perry v. Tendring District Council* (1984) 3 Con.L.R. 75, 97 ("On the totality of the evidence I must . . . conclude that at the material time [1965] the competent engineer would not have known of long-term heave"); *Eckersley v. Binnie & Partners* (1988) 18 Con.L.R. 1, *per* Bingham L.J. at 80; *Privest Properties Ltd v. Foundation Co. of Canada Ltd* (1995) 128 D.L.R. (4th) 577 upheld at (1997) 143 D.L.R. (4th) 635 (architects should have known in early 1970s that a specified product contained asbestos).

[35] See *Moresk Cleaners Ltd v. Hicks* [1966] 2 Lloyd's Rep. 338, 343.

[36] (1980) 14 B.L.R. 1, HL For facts see para. 8–097, above.

[37] *ibid.* at 31.

[38] *ibid.* at 28.

Similarly, in *Victoria University of Manchester v. Wilson*,[39] Judge Newey Q.C. said[40]:

> "For architects to use untried, or relatively untried, materials or techniques cannot in itself be wrong, as otherwise the construction industry can never make any progress. I think, however, that architects who are venturing into the untried or little tried would be wise to warn their clients specifically of what they are doing and to obtain their express approval."

Where a design involves an element of risk as compared to an available **8–139** alternative, the exercise of reasonable care and skill may require an architect or engineer to inform the employer of the element of risk and the superior safety of the alternative design. For example, in *Pullen v.Gutteridge*,[41] the Court of Appeal of Victoria held that engineers were liable for failing to warn their employer of the risks attaching to their foundation design for a swimming pool complex and for failing to advise upon possible alternative designs. On the other hand, judged by the standard of reasonable care, an architect will generally not be liable for misuse of a structure designed by him. Thus the architect who designed the flagpole in *Introvigne v. Commonwealth of Australia*[42] was not liable to the plaintiff schoolboy who sustained injury as a result of swinging from its halyard. The court considered that to ask the architect at the design stage to assume that ordinary precautions would not be taken, such as padlocking the halyard to the pole and reasonable supervision of the pupils by the teachers, would have imposed too heavy a duty upon the architects. Again in *Voli v. Inglewood Shire Council*[43] the architect who designed the stage would not have been liable for a collapse caused by someone permitting a greater weight to be placed upon it than it was designed to bear. Nevertheless, as recognised by the court in *Introvigne*,[44] the duty to take reasonable care might impose liability upon an architect in the case of abuse of an article designed by him if the abuse were so notorious as to be reasonably foreseeable.

It will be no answer to a claim for professional negligence that the practitioner **8–140** had insufficient time to undertake a competent job unless the professional has pointed out the inevitable risks caused by a lack of time and the client has consented to taking such a risk. However if a professional is asked to undertake a task quickly, the time available (which is known to both parties) may affect the court's assessment of the scope of the defendant's retainer. Thus in *Hilton Canada v. SNC Lavalin*,[45] engineers were asked to undertake a survey of a hotel within one and a half days of the proposed purchase. Scanlan J. stated that it was not a defence for the engineers to state that they did not have sufficient time to perform the task as, were that the case, they should either have refused the retainer or pointed out the risks clearly to their client. However, he did take the

---

[39] (1984) 2 Con.L.R. 43.
[40] *ibid.* at 74. See also *Try Build Ltd v. Invicta Leisure Tennis Ltd* (2000) 71 Con.L.R. 141 (engineers held in breach of duty for failing to advise their client, a design and build contractor, upon the need for tests to establish that the novel features of a sports hall roof construction had been developed successfully by the specialist supplier).
[41] [1993] 1 V.R. 27.
[42] (1980) 32 A.L.R. 251. For facts see para. 8–128, above.
[43] [1963] A.L.R. 657 at 662 *per* Windeyer J. For the facts, see para. 8–128, above.
[44] (1980) 32 A.L.R. 251, 273.
[45] (1999) 176 N.S.R. (2d) 155. See further para. 8–257 below.

known time-scale into account in determining the extent of the inspection which the engineers were obliged to undertake.

8–141 A practitioner may not have the particular knowledge or expertise required by his client. In that event the exercise of reasonable care and skill may require the practitioner to inform the client accordingly and either to decline acceptance of instructions or to seek himself, or advise the client to seek, specialist advice and assistance.[46] The importance of an architect expressly informing his client as to the limits of his own knowledge or as to the need for further specialist advice is shown by the decision of Judge Newey Q.C. in *Richard Roberts Holdings Ltd v. Douglas Smith Stimson Partnership and Others*[47] where architects were retained in relation to alterations to a dyeworks. The architects had enjoyed a long-standing relationship with the plaintiffs as a result of friendship between the managing director of the plaintiffs and a partner in the architects. No consulting engineer specialising in dyeworks was engaged on the project although one had been engaged on a previous similar project. In initially preparing their drawings, the architects assumed that an effluent tank would be lined with stainless steel. The employer was concerned by the anticipated cost of £35,000 for the lining and requested that cheaper alternatives be sought. Eventually an alternative lining was designed and installed for £3,240 by a specialist contractor with whom the employer contracted direct. Upon the failure of the lining, the plaintiff sued both the sub-contractor for defective design and the architect, alleging breach of contract in recommending or permitting the alternative method of lining the tank. The sub-contractor took no part in the trial. The architects were found liable notwithstanding that they neither charged nor recovered fees in respect of the lining of the effluent tank. The judge found[48]:

> "In my view the architects were employed by [the plaintiffs] to act as architects for the creation of the Hinckley Dyeworks. They were not responsible for equipment . . . which [the plaintiffs'] staff would design and fix for themselves, but their position was not as it had been at Loughborough, in that they were to design the effluent cooling tanks and also the mixing room floor. The lining was I think an integral part of the tank. The architects did not know about linings, but part of their expertise as architects was to be able to collect information about materials of which they lacked knowledge and/or experience and to form a view about them. If the architects felt that they could not form a reliable judgment about a lining for the tank, they should have informed [the plaintiffs] of that fact and advised them to take other advice, possibly from a chemist."

(i) *General practice and knowledge as evidence of the standard*

8–142 The knowledge required of an architect, engineer or quantity surveyor will generally be judged by the standard of the ordinary competent practitioner in the profession concerned.[49] If a man is unqualified but holds himself out as possessing a skill, he will be judged by the standards of a reasonably competent qualified person. Thus in *Cardy v. Taylor*,[50] an unqualified person practising as an architect was judged by the standards of a reasonably competent architect. If a practitioner

---

[46] See *Moresk Cleaners Ltd v. Hicks* [1966] 2 Lloyd's Rep. 338, 343; see also *Young v. Tomlinson* [1979] 2 N.Z.L.R. 441, 458.
[47] (1988) 46 B.L.R. 50.
[48] *ibid.* at 66.
[49] See chap. 2, paras. 2–116—2–124.
[50] (1994) 38 Con.L.R. 79.

carries out tasks usually carried out by the members of another profession, he will be judged by the standards of that other profession. In the Irish case *Sunderland v. McGreavey*[51] an architect was engaged by the plaintiffs to carry out a visual inspection of property which they were considering purchasing and to prepare a report. Lardner J. stated[52] that the duty of the architect was to "inspect the building with the eye of a competent architect and to draw the inferences which such an architect would draw from what he sees." In so far as the architect was carrying out a task normally undertaken by a surveyor, it is submitted that this was inaccurate; the architect should have been judged by the standard of a reasonably competent surveyor.

8–143 The standard of reasonable care and skill is usually established by reference to the general practice of the construction profession concerned. In *Nye Saunders and Partners v. Alan E. Bristow*[53] Stephen Brown L.J. expressly applied the test in *Bolam v. Friern Hospital Management Committee*[54] to decide whether an architect had fulfilled the required standard:

> "Where there is a conflict as to whether he has discharged that duty, the courts approach the matter upon the basis of considering whether there was evidence that at the time a responsible body of architects would have taken the view that the way in which the subject of enquiry had carried out his duties was an appropriate way of carrying out the duty, and would not hold him guilty of negligence merely because there was a body of competent professional opinion which held that he was at fault."

8–144 Although evidence of general practice may materially assist a court, it is not decisive of what is required to discharge the standard of reasonable care. That is for the court to decide having regard to the circumstances of the particular case.[55]

8–145 Furthermore, the *Bolam* test will not be applied to determine whether a professional is in breach of a duty to exercise reasonable skill and care in every case in which such an allegation is made. There are three categories of case in which the court is entitled not to apply the *Bolam* test and, therefore, to make a finding of negligence notwithstanding expert evidence that a body of professional opinion supports the course which the defendant took.

   (i) Cases in which the court considers that there is no logical basis for the body of opinion in accordance with which the defendant acted. In *Bolitho v. City & Hackney Health Authority*,[56] a medical negligence case, Lord Browne-Wilkinson said[57]:

---

[51] [1987] I.R. 372
[52] *ibid.* at 385.
[53] (1987) 37 B.L.R. 92, 103 (for the facts see para. 8–193 below). This dictum was cited by H.H.J. Bowsher Q.C. in *Department of National Heritage v. Steensen Varming Mulcahy* (1998) 60 Con. L.R. 33 at 84.
[54] [1957] 1 W.L.R. 582 discussed at chap. 12, para. 12–69, below. This is in fact the second part of the *Bolam* test. The first part states merely that the performance of a skilled professional will be judged by reference to the care and skill practised by the ordinary member of his profession.
[55] See *Florida Hotels Pty Ltd v. Mayo* (1965) 113 C.L.R. 588 at 593 *per* Barwick C.J. and 601 *per* Windeyer J.; *Jameson v. Simon* (1899) 1 F. 1211, Ct of Sess. at 1222 *per* Lord Trayner; *Greaves & Co. (Contractors) Ltd v. Baynham Meikle & Partners* [1975] 1 W.L.R. 1095, CA, discussed at para. 8–168, below.
[56] [1998] A.C. 232, HL.
[57] *ibid.* at 241.

"the Court is not bound to hold that a defendant doctor escapes liability for negligent treatment or diagnosis just because he leads evidence from a number of medical experts who are genuinely of the opinion that the defendant's treatment or diagnosis accorded with sound medical practice. In the *Bolam* case itself, McNair J. [1957] 1 W.L.R. 583, 587 stated that the defendant had to have acted in accordance with the practice accepted as proper by a '*responsible* body of medical men'. Later, at p.588, he referred to 'a standard of practice recognised a proper by a competent *reasonable* body of opinion.' Again, in the passage which I have cited from *Maynard's case*, Lord Scarman refers to a 'respectable' body of professional opinion. The use of these adjectives—responsible, reasonable and respectable—all show that the court has to be satisfied that the exponents of the body of opinion relied upon can demonstrate that such opinion has a logical basis."

He concluded[58]:

"if, in a rare case, it can be demonstrated that the professional opinion is not capable of withstanding logical analysis, the judge is entitled to hold that the body of opinion is not reasonable or responsible."

(ii) Cases in which the expert evidence called by the defendant is in reality no more than the personal opinion of an expert witness as to what he would have done in the position of the defendant. Such evidence does not establish that the defendant's conduct was in line with a responsible *body* of opinion or with a recognised *practice* within his profession. In *Midland Bank Trust Co. Ltd v. Hett Stubbs & Kemp*,[59] a solicitors' negligence case, Oliver J. said[60]:

"Clearly, if there is some practice in a profession, some accepted standard of conduct which is laid down by a professional institute or sanctioned by common usage, evidence of that can and ought to be received. But evidence which really amounts to no more than an expression of opinion by a particular practitioner of what he thinks that he would have done had he been placed, hypothetically and without the benefit of hindsight, in the position of the defendants, is of little assistance to the court . . . ."

(iii) Cases in which it is not necessary to apply any particular expertise in, for example, the field of architectural practice, in order to decide whether the defendant has failed to exercise the skill and care expected of an ordinary member of his profession. For example, in *Worboys v. Acme Investments Ltd*[61] Sachs L.J. recognised that there were cases where an omission on a plan was so glaring as to require no evidence of general practice and instanced a house without provision for a staircase.

---

[58] *ibid.* at 243.

[59] [1979] Ch. 384.

[60] *ibid.* at 402. This passage was quoted with approval in the architects' case *Michael Hyde & Associates Ltd v. J.D. Williams & Co. Ltd* [2001] P.N.L.R 233, para 26 *per* Ward L.J. (with whom Sedley and Nourse L.JJ. agreed): see para. 8–146, below. In this category of case, it would perhaps be more accurate to say that the initial criteria for application of the *Bolam* test are not met rather than that the test is disapplied.

[61] (1969) 210 E.G. 335, CA. See also the medical negligence case of *Gold v. Haringey Health Authority* [1988] 1 Q.B. 481, 490 *per* Lloyd L.J. : "If the giving of contraceptive advice required no special skill, then I could see an argument that the *Bolam* test should not apply."

Those three categories of case in which the *Bolam* test will not be applied were **8–146** recognised by the Court of Appeal in *Michael Hyde & Associated Ltd v. J.D. Williams & Co. Ltd*,[62] holding that the instant case fell into the third category. The trial judge found that the defendant architects were negligent in failing to investigate the seriousness of a risk of discoloration of stored textiles caused by a gas heating system. This finding was made despite evidence from experts who confirmed that they would have done no more than the defendants did. The judge held that the defendants failed to apply reasonable care when they failed to realise that the system supplier's refusal to remove a disclaimer of liability for discoloration of materials suggested that the risk might be more serious than the supplier's salesman would admit. The judge declined to apply the *Bolam* test, saying: "These factors in my judgment are not peculiar to architectural or engineering practice. It was a matter of weighing risks against benefits . . . ." The Court of Appeal dismissed the claimant's appeal. Ward L.J. (with whom Sedley and Nourse L.JJ. agreed) held that the judge was entitled to come to the conclusion that the exercise of judgment involved in deciding whether further investigation of the risk of discoloration was required did not of itself require any special architectural skills. He did not have to "get under the skin of a different profession" in order to assess whether or not the defendants had failed to use reasonable skill and care.[63]

In *Royal Brompton Hospital NHS Trust v. Hammond (No. 7)*,[64] Judge Seymour **8–147** Q.C. considered the analysis in *Michael Hyde v. Williams* and summarised the principles applying in the third category of cases thus:

> "if I am satisfied on the evidence that an obvious mistake was made which would not have been made by any careful person of whatever profession, or, indeed, of none, then I can find that the person who made that mistake was negligent. What I cannot do, as it seems to me, is to substitute my own view for that of a professional person of the appropriate discipline on any matter in respect of which any special skill, training or expertise is required to make an informed assessment."[65]

In that case, the claimant alleged that its architects had been negligent in granting unwarranted extensions of time to the contractor which was engaged in building a new hospital for the claimant. Having rejected as unhelpful the evidence of the claimant's expert architect, the judge held that he could find the architects negligent only if he was satisfied that they had made an error which no one applying reasonable common sense would have made. On the facts, and without the assistance of supportive expert evidence, the majority of the claimant's allegations of breach failed. The case illustrates the importance of the

---

[62] [2001] P.N.L.R 233, CA.
[63] *ibid.* at para. 27. Ward L.J. also observed (at para. 26) that the judge would also have been entitled to disapply the *Bolam* test on the basis that the case fell into the second category: "He may well have been able to discount the evidence on that basis for I find little to suggest that there were two recognised but contrary views of an accepted practice governing the decision in question. As I read the evidence the experts were doing no more than putting themselves forward as reasonably competent architects and then saying what they would have done in the circumstances in which Mr Warrington found himself."
[64] [2001] C.I.L.L. 1714.
[65] *ibid.* at 1715.

correct application and presentation of expert evidence in professional negligence cases.[66]

8–148　　　It might have been thought that the issue of breach of duty in *Adams v. Rhymney Valley District Council*[67] could have been decided without the application of any particular professional skill, but the Court of Appeal reached a different view. The defendant local authority installed window locks with removable keys in housing occupied by the claimants. The keys to the windows were kept out of reach of the claimants' three children. In a house fire, the family were unable to reach the keys in order to use the bedroom windows as a means of escape, and the three children perished as a result. The claimants alleged that the defendant was negligent and in breach of statutory duty in failing to install push-button locks, which could have been readily opened in an emergency. The locks had been chosen by the defendant's housing department, which had not consulted the local fire or police services and had not considered the relative merits of different types of lock design. Sir Christopher Staughton identified[68] the key issue as:

> "whether the *Bolam* test still applies, although the particular defendant did not in fact have the qualifications of a professional in the relevant field of activity, and although he did not go through the process of reasoning which a qualified professional could consider before making a choice."

The majority in the Court of Appeal held that the test did apply and that, in the light of expert evidence to the effect that a reasonably competent window designer could have chosen a lock with removable keys in preference to the push-button type, the defendant was not in breach of its duty of care to the claimants. In his dissenting judgment Sedley L.J. held that the *Bolam* test was not appropriate to determine whether a defendant has failed to exercise reasonable skill and care in a case where the defendant has not exercised, and has not purported to exercise, any special skill. In other words, to have one's performance measured by reference to the *Bolam* test is a privilege reserved to those who have considered and reflected upon the alternative courses available and made a conscious choice between them.[69] It is submitted that this is an impracticably stringent requirement for the application of the test, since many reasonably careful and competent professionals properly practice in accordance with the manner which they have been taught rather than from first principles. It was expressly rejected by Sir Christopher Staughton[70]:

> "Seeing that, upon the hypothesis which is inherent in the problem, a respectable body of professionals have been and are in favour of each course, I do not see that the defendant is required to go through the same thought process in order to deserve the support of those who favour the course which he chooses. The consultant who naturally chooses one method out of long experience is as much entitled to rely on the *Bolam* doctrine as one who sits down in his chair and goes through the whole process of choice again."

---

[66] See further paras 8–149 to 8–153, below.
[67] [2001] P.N.L.R 68.
[68] *ibid.* at para 42.
[69] See, to similar effect, the judgment of the same judge in *Michael Hyde & Associates Ltd v. J.D. Williams & Co. Ltd* [2001] P.N.L.R 233, para. 46.
[70] [2001] P.N.L.R 68 at para. 43.

However, it remains difficult to see why the defendants in *Adams* should have enjoyed the benefit of the *Bolam* test. As demonstrated by the reasoning set out in the judgment of Sedley L.J., the relative merits of locks with removable keys and push-button locks for use in local authority housing for families were capable of being assessed without the exercise of any particular professional expertise, as a matter of reasonable common sense. As such, the case arguably fell into the third category of cases identified in *Michael Hyde v. Williams* as not requiring the application of the *Bolam* test.[71]

(iii) *Expert evidence*

The decision as to the standard of skill and care required of a defendant professional is ultimately a matter for the court, and not for the profession in the form of expert witnesses. In *F. v. R.*,[72] King C.J. put it this way: **8–149**

> "The ultimate question, however, is not whether the defendant's conduct accords with the practices of his profession or some part of it, but whether it confirms to the standard of reasonable care demanded by the law. That is a question for the court and the duty of deciding it cannot be delegated to any profession or group in the community."

However, in most cases in which construction professionals are alleged to have fallen below the required standard of skill and care, the court will be assisted by expert evidence as to either or both: **8–150**

   (i) matters of scientific or technical fact. To this extent, the expert's function is merely didactic, in that he explains the technical aspects of the case in terms comprehensible to the layperson. Expert evidence of this sort may be largely or wholly uncontroversial;

   (ii) the standards ordinarily observed in his profession, including the existence of schools of thought, bodies of opinion or of recognised practices within the profession.

Indeed, save in those (relatively rare) cases in which the issue of breach of duty can properly be decided as a matter of ordinary common sense,[73] expert evidence that the reasonably competent professional would not have committed the act or omission complained of will be essential for a finding of breach of duty.

Care is required in the selection and presentation of expert evidence. In the first place, evidence will be admitted only from a member of the profession to which the defendant belongs.[74] In *Investors in Industry Commercial Properties v. South Bedfordshire D.C.*[75] the Court of Appeal held that there was no sustainable **8–151**

---

[71] See paras 8–145 to 8–146, above. In her article "Something 'old', something 'new', something 'borrowed' ... The continued evolution of *Bolam*" (2001) 17 P.N. 75, Paula de Prez criticises the application of the *Bolam* test in *Adams* and comments that it is distasteful for negligence litigation to be successfully defended on the basis of coincidence rather than competence.

[72] (1983) S.A.S.R. 189, 194, Supreme Court of South Australia. See further C. Leong, and P. Chan, "Architects' design duties: a shift from *Bolam's* to the objective test" (1999) 15 P.N. 3.

[73] See paras 8–145 to 8–146 above.

[74] Or, where the defendant was providing services normally provided by members of another profession, from a member of that profession: see para. 8–142 above.

[75] [1986] 1 All E.R. 787. For the facts, see para. 8–188 below.

claim against architects, primarily because there was no relevant evidence from other architects as to standards in the profession. Slade L.J. said[76]:

> "Expert evidence from suitably qualified professional persons is, in our judgment, admissible to show what competent architects in the position of Hamiltons could reasonably have been expected to know and do in their position at the relevant time. Indeed, in our judgment, there could be no question of the Court condemning them for professional negligence . . . unless there were appropriate expert evidence to support the allegation that their conduct fell below the standard which might reasonably be expected of an ordinarily competent architect . . . . The expert evidence before the judge consisted of evidence from three engineers and one architect, Mr Foster. The questions put to the engineers and answered by them included questions relating to the nature and extent of the professional duties owed by Hamiltons to Anglia. However, we think that little reliance can be placed on their answers to these particular questions, which related to a profession other than their own."

The only expert architect, Mr Foster, was called by the defendants. In the face of his evidence, the Court held that the plaintiff had not established that the architects were in breach of duty. The claim in *Sansom v. Metcalfe Hambleton & Co.*[77] arose out of a building surveyor's failure to draw his client's attention to crack in the wall of the property. The trial judge found the defendant to have been negligent and in so doing accepted the evidence of the claimant's expert structural engineer in preference to that of the defendant's expert building surveyor. The Court of Appeal held that this finding was not supported by relevant and admissible evidence. Butler-Sloss L.J. said[78]:

> "a court should be slow to find a professionally qualified man guilty of a breach of his duty of skill and care towards a client (or third party) without evidence from those within the same profession as to the standard expected on the facts of the case and the failure of the professionally qualified man to measure up to that standard."

8–152 Secondly, it is important that the evidence of an expert witness is confined to matters which are relevant to the issues before the court and upon which the witness is properly qualified to comment. In *Pozzolanic Lytag Ltd v. Bryan Hobson Associates*[79] the defendant engineers were engaged in connection with the construction of a storage dome for pulverised fuel ash. The services which they agreed to provide included project management in relation to the contract for construction of the dome, which was awarded to a design and build contractor. The dome collapsed due to design defects. It transpired that the contractor

---

[76] *ibid.* at 808–809.
[77] [1998] P.N.L.R. 542.
[78] *ibid.* at 549. Note also the Scottish case of *J. Dykes Ltd v. Littlewoods Mail Order Stores Ltd*, 1982 S.L.T. 50 (action against firm of consulting engineers dismissed after allegations of breach of duty against the firm were held to be irrelevant in that the pursuers did not link the alleged duties to the standard of ordinary professional competence of consultant engineers) and *Pride Valley Foods Ltd v. Hall & Partners (Contract Management) Ltd* (2000) 76 Con.L.R. 1, 24 (there being no established profession of project manager, care was needed to select expert witnesses who were able to give useful evidence as to the standard of care to be applied in the discharge of a project manager's duty of care: see the passage from the judgment of Judge Toulmin C.M.G., Q.C. which is quoted at n. 17 to para. 8–006 above) (the Court of Appeal did not comment on this passage: [2001] E.W.C.A. Civ. 1001, [2001] 76 Con.L.R.1, 36).
[79] [1999] B.L.R. 267.

was insolvent and uninsured. The claimant alleged that the defendants were in breach of duty as project managers in that they had failed to see that the contractor had taken out indemnity insurance against claims for design defects, as required by the building contract. Dyson J. stated that the expert witnesses should have confined themselves to the question whether there was a common practice in the engineering profession as to what engineers, who are engaged as project managers, do in relation to the insurance obligations of contractors. Instead, they considered numerous other issues including contributory negligence, which was a matter for the court. He warned[80]:

> "Prolix expert reports directed to issue with which they should not be concerned merely add to the expense of litigation. Everything possible should be done to discourage this. In appropriate cases, this will include making special orders for costs."

In *Pride Valley Food Ltd v. Hall and Partners (Contract Management) Ltd*,[81] **8–153** the claimant sought to adduce the expert evidence of an architect in support of its claim against the defendant project manager. Judge Toulmin C.M.G., Q.C. concluded that the evidence provided little or no assistance. Amongst other criticisms,[82] he pointed out that the report was overlong, included opinions on matters of fact and law which were questions for decision by the court and included expressions of opinion as to what the expert himself would have done in the defendant's position. In *Royal Brompton Hospital NHS Trust v. Hammond (No. 7)*,[83] the evidence of the claimant's expert architect was rejected in its entirety by the trial judge. Judge Seymour Q.C. warned that, if experts are to give useful evidence, they must be given sufficient time to master the relevant documents. In a typical construction case, the volume of documentation which an expert will need to digest may be very large. Further, experts should avoid making assumptions (or accepting instructions to make assumptions) the accuracy of which is central to the questions which they are to address.[84] Finally, experts should make sure that they have contemporary knowledge of practice in their own profession. The claimant's expert architect's evidence was found wanting in each of these respects. The more restrictive attitude of modern courts towards expert evidence was confirmed when the Court of Appeal upheld an order debarring the defendant from calling his expert building surveyor in *Stevens v. Gullis*.[85] The expert had failed in his duty to act impartially and had also to comply with the requirements of the Civil Procedure Rules in relation to his report and a joint memorandum of matters agreed with the claimant's expert.

---

[80] *ibid.* at 275.
[81] (2001) 76 Con.L.R. 1; the claimant's appeal on causation succeeded ([2001] E.W.C.A. 1001, (2001) 76 Con.L.R. 1,36).
[82] See the passage quoted at n. 17 to para. 8–006 above on the need for care in selecting an expert to give evidence on a claim against a project manager.
[83] [2001] C.I.L.L. 1714. For the facts, see para. 8–147 above. See also *Anglo Group plc v. Winther Brown & Co. Ltd*, unreported, March 1, 2000, Judge Toulmin C.M.G., Q.C. (evidence of defendant's computer systems expert disregarded for failure to comply with duty of impartiality).
[84] See also the Commercial Court Guide, para. H2.12: an expert should state the assumptions upon which his opinion is based, and if a stated assumption is, in the opinion of the expert, unreasonable or unlikely, he should state that clearly.
[85] [2000] 1 All E.R. 527.

(iv) *Res ipsa loquitur*

8–154   It follows from the considerations set out above that it will be very rarely that there is room for the application of the maxim *res ipsa loquitur*[86] in a professional negligence action against a construction professional. The failure of a building or the issue of a certificate for the wrong amount will very rarely be sufficient, of itself, to demonstrate that there has been a failure to take reasonable care on the part of a construction professional. In *Copthorne Hotel (Newcastle) Ltd v. Arup Associates*,[87] Judge Hicks Q.C. found that the plaintiff had failed to make out a case of negligent estimation in respect of piling costs where the defendants had estimated a figure of £425,000 against an out-turn cost of £975,000. No evidence had been led as to what figure the defendants should have used for pile diameter, which was an essential element in arriving at a price. The judge said:

> "I hope and believe that I am not over-simplifying if I record the impression that the plaintiff's main hope was that I would be persuaded to find in their favour simply by the size of the gap, absolutely and proportionately, between the cost estimate and the successful tender.
> The gap was indeed enormous. It astonished and appalled the parties at the time, and it astonishes me. I do not see, however, how that alone can carry the plaintiff home. There is no plea or argument that the maxim 'res ipsa loquitur' applies. Culpable underestimation is of course one obvious explanation of such a discrepancy, but far from the only one . . . ."

8–155   It will be particularly important to adduce cogent evidence of a failure to exercise reasonable care where the task performed by the construction professional requires the application of skill and judgment to complex facts. In *Royal Brompton Hospital NHS Trust v. Hammond (No. 7)*[88] the complaint was that architects had granted extensions of time to the building contractor which were too lengthy. The project, the construction of a new hospital, was large and complex. In considering claims for extensions of time, the architects were required to calculate the effect of various delaying factors upon the programme for the works so as to arrive at a revised contractual completion date. Expert evidence adduced on the question of contract programming was to the effect that the accuracy with which works can be re-programmed depends upon the quality of the information available. Judge Seymour Q.C. said[89]:

> "All of this does, of course, emphasise the vital point that the duty of a professional man, generally stated, is not to be right, but to be careful. While, unless in a particular case the professional man is actually wrong, the fact that he has not been careful will probably not cause his client any loss, the fact that he is in the event proved to be wrong is not, in itself, any evidence that he has been negligent. His conduct has to be judged having regard to the information available to him, or which ought to have been

---

[86] The doctrine has been abandoned in Canada: *Fontaine v. Loewen Estate* (1997) 156 D.L.R. (4th) 181, Supreme Court of Canada. See also *Pearson v. Fryer, The Times*, April 4, 2000, in which Roch L.J. said of the maxim: "It troubles me that we still tend to fall into the habit of talking about maxims or doctrines which go under labels in Latin whose meaning does not express a defined principle, and which those for whose benefit [they exist] will probably not understand."
[87] (1996) 58 Con. L.R. 105.
[88] [2001] C.I.L.L. 1714. For the facts, see para. 8–146 above.
[89] *ibid.* at 1717.

available to him, at the time that he gave his advice or made his decision or did whatever else it is that he did."

(v) *Codes of practice and legislation*

A feature of the construction professions is the large number of codes of practice **8–156** and published standards relating to the manner of construction. Moreover, the manner of construction is extensively regulated by statutory regulations both in the United Kingdom[90] and in the Commonwealth. The purpose of such codes, standards and regulations is to provide for standards of safety and good building practice. Since they broadly reflect good practice, the question frequently arises as to whether non-compliance with relevant codes or regulations is indicative of negligence. Claims against construction professionals are frequently based on alleged breach of a duty to take reasonable care to ensure that the design was in accordance with the requirements of building regulations or byelaws. The premise behind such formulations of the duty is that non-compliance is indicative of negligence. In the case of specific requirements such formulations need qualification to provide for forms of construction which, although they do not comply with the regulations, may be wholly consistent with their broad purpose, in particular safety. Many regulations, however, are sufficiently broad to allow wide flexibility of form of construction.

The effect of non-compliance with codes of practice was extensively con- **8–157** sidered in relation to a claim against an engineer for negligent design by Beattie J. in *Bevan Investments Ltd v. Blackhall and Struthers (No. 2)*.[91] He took the view that:

> "Bearing in mind the function of codes, a design which departs substantially from them is prima facie a faulty design, unless it can be demonstrated that it conforms to accepted engineering practice by rational analysis. If I am correct in this appreciation, and if on the evidence it is established that the design in several material respects fails to comply with the relevant codes, then [the defendant engineer] and his experts must show that the design is capable of rational analysis and is adequate and safe. I do not go so far as to say however that the mere circumstance that a client is unaware that the designer is working outside a code can of itself categorise a designer's actions as negligent."[92]

Expert evidence was given in the same case that rigid application of codes would stifle a number of progressive advances. Beattie J. nevertheless commended the view that experimental proposals should have the encouragement or actual approval of the client and would need to embody sound engineering design and practice. This view was followed in *Kaliszewska v. John Clague & Partners*[93] where the defendant architect was found to have been negligent in his design of foundations for a bungalow, having failed:

---

[90] See the Building Regulations 1991 which came into force on June 1, 1992 (as now amended by the Building Regulations (Amendment) Regulations 1994) and the Construction (Design and Management) Regulations 1994 discussed in para. 8–46, above.

[91] [1973] 2 N.Z.L.R. 45. For the facts see n.89 to para. 8–121, above.

[92] *ibid.* at 65–66. Also note *Victoria University of Manchester v. Hugh Wilson* (1984) 2 Con.L.R. 43, 74 *per* Judge Newey Q.C.: "CP 212 and other literature were not binding on the architects in the sense that they were obliged to follow their recommendations precisely, but they should certainly have taken them into account and disregarded them only if they had good scientific reasons for so doing."

[93] (1984) 5 Con.L.R. 62.

" . . . to call evidence or to show by rational analysis that although the defendant's design did not comply with the current Codes of Practice and did not appear to be within the mainstream of knowledge, it was nevertheless as a result of local conditions adequate."[94]

8–158 A professional is not, however, entitled slavishly to follow the provisions of a code of practice without considering its precise relevance to the project in hand. In *I.B.A. v. E.M.I. and B.I.C.C.*,[95] Lord Fraser said[96]:

"I have reached the firm conclusion that B.I.C.C. failed in their duty of care when they applied the code of practice that had been found appropriate for lattice masts to the new cylindrical mast at Emley Moor without noticing that the reason for disregarding ice on the stays was not applicable to a cylindrical mast. They were therefore negligent in their design."

8–159 Similarly in *Holland Hannen and Cubitts (Northern) Ltd v. Welsh Health Technical Services Organisation*,[97] Robert Goff L.J. said[98]:

"The structural engineer will therefore simply consider the profile of the floor as such; and ask himself the question whether there is a significant risk that the floor, with that profile, in the building in question, may be unacceptable. In considering that question he cannot simply rely on the codes of practice. It is plain from the evidence that the code of practice is no more than a guide for use by professional men, who have to exercise their own expertise; this must moreover be especially true in a case such as the present, where the design was a novel one, omitting as it did a finishing screed. Practice alone can, I consider, provide of itself no reliable guide where, as here, a novel design concept is being used."

A Canadian decision to the same effect is *Homes by Jayman v. Kellam Berg*.[99] The Alberta Court of Appeal pointed out that compliance with regulations or any statutory law, whist relevant in setting the standard of care, could not be a complete defence to an allegation of negligence. The court found that although

---

[94] *ibid.* at 77. In *Turner Page Music Ltd v. Torres Design Associates* (1997) C.I.L.L. 1263, Judge Hicks Q.C. found that the defendant architects were negligent in failing to provide adequate means of escape for a refurbished theatre, with the result that Building Regulations approval was refused. He rejected the defendants' submission that refusal of Building Regulations approval was a routine experience which did not reflect upon the designer. In *Munkenbeck & Marshall v. Regent Health and Fitness Club Ltd (No. 2)* (1997) 59 Con. L.R. 145, Judge Rich Q.C., accepted a submission that where plans were submitted to a local authority which were not in accordance with "an approved document" relating to the provision of adequate fire escapes and recognised by s.7 of the Building Act 1984, it was for the architects who had submitted the plans to demonstrate that the plans would nonetheless be acceptable under the Building Regulations. See also *Storey v. Charles Church Developments plc* (1995) 73 Con.L.R. 1, where designers of a house were held negligent for failing to take proper account of the Building Regulations, British Standards and other published guidance in designing for a site upon which there were various mature trees.
[95] (1980) 14 B.L.R. 1, HL For facts see para. 8–097, above.
[96] *ibid.* at 36–37.
[97] (1985) 35 Build. L.R. 1. For facts see para. 8–215 below.
[98] *ibid.* at 25; Goff L.J. dissented as to whether the engineers were obliged to consider the aesthetic importance of the floor and consequently the other members of the court did not regard the engineer as bound to ask himself the question which Goff L.J. poses. Nonetheless it is submitted that his words are relevant and apposite to questions which a professional man is obliged to ask.
[99] (1997) 54 Alta. L.R. (3d) 272.

septic tanks designed by an engineer complied with the relevant codes they were nonetheless too small.

(vi) *Knowledge of the law*

The knowledge of law required of an architect was considered by Gibson J. at **8–160** first instance in *B. L. Holdings Ltd v. Robert J. Wood and Partners.*[1] It was conceded in that case that when an architect agrees to act in some field of activity commonly carried on by architects, in which a knowledge and understanding of certain principles of law are required, and if the work is to be done properly and the client's interest protected, the architect must have a sufficient knowledge of those principles of law in order reasonably to protect his client from danger and loss. The judge added that in many particular cases a professional man engaging in such work would have, and display, a sufficient knowledge of the relevant principles of law by knowing, and by advising his client, that he knows little or nothing of them, and by refusing to incur expense on behalf of his client or to expose him to risk of financial loss, until his client had obtained legal advice or decided to act upon his own judgment.[2] This passage was approved by the Court of Appeal in *West Faulkner Associates v. London Borough of Newham*[3] where the Court was considering whether the mistaken construction of a standard form clause in a building contract was one which a reasonably competent architect could have held. The Court held that it was not and Brown L.J. (with whom the other members of the Court agreed) went on: "At the very least [the architect] should have realised that the clause might fall to be construed differently . . . and in those circumstances should either himself have sought, or asked his client to seek, legal advice specifically upon the point."[4]

In the *B. L. Holdings* case the defendant architects agreed to act for the **8–161** plaintiff clients in the obtaining of planning permission for an office building. They thereby, in the judge's view, took upon themselves the obligation of knowing enough of the principles of law relating to office development control to be able to advise their clients adequately and reasonably to protect them from damage and loss. The defendants were wrongly advised by an officer of the local planning authority that certain areas were to be excluded in calculating the area of a building for the purpose of determining whether the limit was exceeded beyond which an office development permit was required. Acting on that advice the architects designed a building which exceeded those limits. Planning permission was granted and the building was erected. On subsequent discovery of the need for a permit and that the planning permission was accordingly void, the plaintiffs were unable to let the building for some three years until the permit limits were raised. Notwithstanding the misleading advice of the local planning officer, Gibson J. held that the architects were in breach of their relevant obligation and accordingly liable in failing to warn their clients of the danger of the planning application being of no effect in law. The Court of Appeal,[5] although not disapproving Gibson J.'s statements of principle, reversed the decision and absolved the architects of liability on the facts. One passage in Gibson J.'s judgment was particularly referred to in reversing his decision: "I

---

[1] (1978) 10 B.L.R. 48.
[2] *ibid.* at 70.
[3] (1994) 71 B.L.R. 1 at 15.
[4] *ibid.* at 18H.
[5] (1979) 12 B.L.R. 1.

think that not a few architects engaged in this work would have been misled exactly as [the particular architect concerned] was and I think that he might well have been followed in error by some lawyers."[6] The decision of the Court of Appeal can thus be viewed as a rare example of the errors of other members of the profession being invoked to absolve the defendant architects of negligence.

8–162   Building regulations and byelaws provide the context in which designers are most commonly required to consider matters of law. Here, also, the construction professional will discharge his duty of care unless no reasonably competent and careful member of his profession would have interpreted the relevant provisions in the way that he has. In *J. Sainsbury plc v. Broadway Malyan*,[7] consulting engineers were retained by architects acting in connection with the design and construction of a superstore. The design included a compartment wall separating the sales area of the store from the service area. The architects' design provided for one side only of the wall above roof girder level to be fire-resistant. When a fire spread from the service area to the sales area, the store owner claimed damages against the architects for defective design of the compartment wall. The architects compromised the store owner's action and claimed contribution from the engineers, alleging that they ought to have appreciated and warned that the roof girder was part of the compartment wall and therefore subject to the fire-resistance requirements of the Building Regulations. Judge Lloyd Q.C. held that, on the correct construction of the relevant Building Regulations, the girder was not an "element of structure" which required fire protection but that, if he was wrong about that, the engineers would not have been negligent had they failed to appreciate that the girder was an "element of structure" within the meaning of the Regulations. He said[8]:

> "The interpretation of the Building Regulations is ultimately a question of law, but it is relevant to consider how they strike the non-lawyers, such as engineers, for whom they are intended and who have to understand and apply them. It does not of course follow that if the correct meaning is not recognised by such a reasonably competent person then that person is negligent. The degree to which such a person is expected to be familiar with the meaning and operation of [the] Regulations is a separate issue."

(vii) *Not every error is negligence*

8–163   The standard of reasonable care and skill is not a standard of perfection. It does not make an architect, for example, the insurer[9] or guarantor[10] that work has been properly done. It is not sufficient to prove an error in order to show that there has been a failure to exercise reasonable care and skill. Actual negligence must be

---

[6] (1978) 10 B.L.R. 48, 77, and see (1979) 12 B.L.R. 1, CA at 16, *per* Browne L.J., and at 18 *per* Lawton L.J.
[7] [1999] P.N.L.R. 286.
[8] *ibid.* at 302–303.
[9] See *Moresk Cleaners Ltd v. Hicks* [1966] 2 Lloyd's Rep 338, 342 *per* Judge Sir Walker Carter O.R.
[10] See *East Ham Corporation v. Bernard Sunley & Sons Ltd* [1966] A.C. 406, 427 *per* Viscount Dilhorne. See also the Canadian case of *Meredith v. Macfarlane* (1915) 9 O.W.N. 160: microscopic perfection of an architect's work is not required.

proven.[11] Similarly an error of judgment or wrong opinion is not necessarily negligent.[12]

Moreover trivial or few errors may not necessarily be negligent. Thus in **8–164** *London School Board v. Northcroft, Son and Neighbour*[13] as a result of two errors by a clerk employed by the defendant quantity surveyors, builders were overpaid two sums of £118 and £15 15s. on buildings to the value of £12,000. The judge rejected the plaintiff employer's claim that the clerk was negligent in making the two errors. A stricter view was taken in another quantity surveyor's case, *Tyrer v. District Auditor of Monmouthshire*.[14] In that case in one particular contract the quantity surveyor had made a simple mathematical error in issuing an interim certificate. Lord Widgery C.J. conceded that this was an error which could happen at any time, "but the obligation was on the appellant to ensure that adequate checks were made".[15] The quantity surveyor was, however, held on the facts to have been "negligent over and over again". It may well be that if there had only been the one error in the interim certificate and if it had involved a small sum, a different view might have been taken. Clearly the more and the greater in consequence the errors, the more difficult it will be to resist a finding of negligence, if only because there will be a strong suggestion of a fault in the system adopted by the quantity surveyor to produce his valuations.

In the case of errors in supervision (or inspection) the question frequently **8–165** arises whether the error pertains to a matter of detail or not. Thus where what is required of an architect is reasonable examination of the building works, it is recognised that some defects and insufficiencies might escape his notice.[16] Where an employer directly employs a clerk of works and also engages an architect, examining matters of detail are for the former leaving the latter to attend to more important matters.[17] Moreover, a certain degree of tolerance must be allowed for in determining the quality of work supervised, although this does not entail giving an architect a general dispensing power.[18] In a mid-nineteenth

---

[11] See *Sutcliffe v. Thackrah* [1974] A.C. 727, 760 *per* Lord Salmon: "It by no means follows that a professional valuation was negligently given because it turns out to have been wholly wrong. Nor does the fact that an architect's certificate was given for the wrong amount of itself prove negligence against the architect." See also Robert Goff L.J.'s judgment in *Holland Hannen and Cubitts (Northern) Ltd v. Welsh Health Technical Services Organisation* (1985) 35 B.L.R. 1, 22 where he states: "The true answer must be to recognise that his obligation is only to exercise due care and skill, though, where he is held to have been negligent, to identify precisely the negligence to which he is held guilty." Goff L.J.'s dissent on one aspect of the case is not thought to affect this. See further para. 8–215, below. See also *Copthorne Hotel (Newcastle) Ltd v. Arup Associates*, (1996) 12 Const. L.J. 402 where Judge Hicks Q.C. found that an enormous difference between a predicted piling price and the tender price was insufficient, of itself, to establish that the prediction had been negligent; and the extract from the judgment of Judge Seymour Q.C. in *Royal Brompton Hospital NHS Trust v. Hammond (No. 7)* [2001] C.I.L.L. 1714 which is quoted at para. 8–155 above.

[12] See *Armitage v. Palmer* (1960) 175 E.G. 315, CA *per* Harman L.J.; *East Ham Corporation v. Bernard Sunley & Sons Ltd* [1966] A.C. 406, 443 *per* Lord Upjohn; *J. Sainsbury plc v. Broadway Malyan* [1999] P.N.L.R. 286, 300 *per* Judge Lloyd Q.C. The qualification "not necessarily negligent" is important: see the medical negligence case of *Whitehouse v. Jordan* [1981] 1 W.L.R. 246, 257–258, 263 and 268.

[13] (1889) cited in *Hudson's Building Contracts* (4th ed.), Vol. 2, p. 147.

[14] (1973) 230 E.G. 973.

[15] *ibid.* at 974.

[16] See *East Ham Corporation v. Bernard Sunley & Sons Ltd* [1966] A.C. 406 especially at 427. Also see *Cedar Transport Group Ltd v. First Wyvern Property Trustees Co. Ltd* (1981) 258 E.G. 1077.

[17] See para. 8–244, below. Somewhat anomalously in *London Hospital Trustees v. T. P. Bennett & Son* (1987) 13 Con.L.R. 22 Judge Stabb Q.C. said (at 28) that, although a clerk of works was the employee of the building owner, "in fact he was also the eyes and ears of the architect".

[18] See *Cotton v. Wallis* [1955] 1 W.L.R. 1168, CA at 1176 and 1177.

century case Erle J. expressed the view: "if you employ [an architect] about a novel thing, about which he has had little experience, if it has not had the test of experience, failure may be consistent with skill. The history of all great improvements show failure of those who embark in them."[19] While it is correct in principle to state that failure may be consistent with skill, Erle J.'s view seems generally reflective of a less safety-conscious age than the present. A reflection of modern standards in relation to a novel design, particularly where there are safety implications, is found in Lord Edmund-Davies's speech in *I.B.A. v. E.M.I. and B.I.C.C.*[20] It must be recognised, however, that it is unrealistic to expect standards of perfection in construction works. The case of *Christopher Moran Holdings Ltd v. Carden & Godfrey*[21] concerned the reconstruction of a historic building on the site of Thomas More's garden in Chelsea, London, at a total cost of "many millions of pounds".[22] In response to its architect's claim for unpaid fees, the building owner counterclaimed damages for negligence in four respects. One of the complaints was that there was inadequate headroom on the stairs leading to a tower room looking over the River Thames. Judge Wilcox found, on the facts, that the problem was not the result of breach of duty on the part of the architects, but he also noted that the defect could be repaired at a cost of £450.75 and remarked[23]:

> "Looked at in its proper context, this is a minor complaint. It is easy of resolution and is typical of the minor matters that crop up in complex schemes such as this and does not necessarily connote negligence on anyone's part."

(viii) *The specialist practitioner*

8–166 When the client deliberately obtains and pays for an architect, engineer or quantity surveyor of especially high skills, is the required standard not the conventional standard of the ordinary competent and skilled practitioner but some higher standard? This question was answered negatively in the case of engineers by Webster J. in *Wimpey Construction U.K. Ltd v. Poole.*[24] In that case the plaintiff company was alleged to have been negligent in the design of a new quay wall at Southampton. The design had been carried out by the company's engineering department which employed some most experienced designers and at least one designer of exceptionally high qualifications. Applying the conventional test the judge held that the company had not been negligent in that design. The judge nevertheless accepted that it was the duty of a professional man to exercise reasonable care in light of his actual knowledge and that the question whether he had exercised reasonable care could not be answered by reference to a lesser degree of knowledge than in fact he had, on the grounds that the ordinarily competent practitioner would only have that lesser degree of knowledge.[25]

8–167 Moreover, where a practitioner holds himself out as a specialist in a well recognised speciality practised by some but not all within a wider profession,

---

[19] *Turner v. Garland and Christopher* (1853) cited in *Hudson's Building Contracts* (4th ed., 1914) Vol. 2, p. 1.
[20] (1980) 14 B.L.R. 1, 18: see para. 8–097, above.
[21] (1999) 73 Con.L.R. 28.
[22] *ibid.* at 30.
[23] *ibid.* at 40.
[24] [1984] 2 Lloyd's Rep. 499, 506.
[25] *ibid.* at 506–507.

such as geotechnical engineers within the engineering profession, the relevant standard is that of the ordinary competent and skilled practitioner in that special-ity.[26] In *Gloucestershire Health Authority v. Torpy*,[27] the defendant engineers were engaged in connection with the design and specification of new incinerators for a hospital. The incinerators installed failed to meet performance requirements and were unsuitable. Judge Bowsher Q.C. drew a distinction between specialist engineers (who were to be judged by the standards appropriate to such special-ists) and general practice engineers with experience of a particular specialism (who were to be judged by the standard of such general practitioners). The defendants were mechanical and engineering building services engineers who claimed to have extensive experience in incinerator technology. The judge rejected the argument that, on that account, the defendants were to be judged by the standard of specialists. They were general practitioners with experience in a particular field, rather than specialists in that field, and were to be judged by reference to the care and skill exercised by ordinary mechanical and engineering building services engineers.

(ix) *Special steps and warranty of reasonable fitness*

While generally in the course of his ordinary employment a construction pro- **8–168** fessional is under no higher duty than the duty to use reasonable care and skill, the circumstances of a particular case may require special steps to be taken in order to fulfil that duty. In *Greaves & Co. (Contractors) Ltd v. Baynham Meikle & Partners*[28] the plaintiff contractors were required to design and build a warehouse for the storage of heavy oil drums. They sub-contracted the structural design of the warehouse to the defendant engineers. It was made known to the engineers that the first floor had to take the weight of loaded fork-lift trucks. After the warehouse was built the first floor began to crack owing to vibration caused by the movement of the trucks. It was held that the engineers had not designed the floor with sufficient strength to withstand the vibration. Further, the engineers had misconstrued a warning of vibration in the type of construction used in the relevant code of practice. Kilner-Brown J. at first instance, confronted with evidence indicating a divergence of view as to what a competent engineer would have done and a strong body of opinion that the defendant engineers had not failed, held that the engineers were not in breach of their duty to exercise reasonable care and skill. But on the facts he held that the engineers owed a higher duty and that they were in breach of that duty. The Court of Appeal,[29] although upholding the judge's decision, reversed him on this point. It held that there was no such higher duty on professional men and that what the judge meant was that in the circumstances of the case, special steps were required to discharge the duty to exercise reasonable care and skill and that those steps had not been taken.

---

[26] See further chap. 10, para. 10–093.
[27] (1997) 55 Con.L.R. 124. On very similar facts, Judge Toulmin C.M.G., Q.C., in *Hammersmith Hospitals NHS Trust v. Troup Bywaters & Anders* [2000] Env. L.R. 343 held that the defendants were to be judged by the standard of ordinarily competent building services engineers and not as if they were experts in combustion, incineration or waste handling technology. On the facts in that case, the engineers were not in breach of duty: affirmed on appeal ([2001] E.W.C.A. Civ.793, unreported, May 25, 2001).
[28] [1974] 1 W.L.R. 1261.
[29] [1975] 1 W.L.R. 1095.

8–169   It was held in *Greaves* that the defendant engineers were in breach of an implied term in their contract with the contractors that their design would be reasonably fit for the purpose, namely for use of loaded fork-lift trucks. The judges in the Court of Appeal were at pains to emphasise that the term was implied in the particular circumstances of the case and that they were not deciding the question whether an architect or an engineer employed to design a house or a bridge impliedly warranted that his design would be fit for the purpose.[30] Lord Denning M.R. mooted that that question might have to be answered some day as a matter of law.

8–170   This question was subsequently considered in *I.B.A. v. E.M.I. and B.I.C.C.*[31] It was argued for the sub-contractors, B.I.C.C., who had designed the television mast, that since design was normally a function for a professional man they should be under no higher duty than that generally applicable to such a man namely a duty to exercise reasonable care and skill according to the accepted standards of his profession. The argument was rejected by the Court of Appeal on two grounds.[32] First, the issue of the extent of the contractors' and sub-contractors' obligations in relation to design had to be determined in the ultimate analysis by reference to the interpretation of the contract concerned. There was no good reason for not importing into the contract between I.B.A., the employer, and E.M.I., the main contractor, and between E.M.I. and B.I.C.C., an obligation as to reasonable fitness for the purpose or for importing a different obligation in relation to design from the obligation which plainly existed in relation to materials. Secondly, there was a good commercial reason in favour of such an obligation. Contracts such as the one concerned should be interpreted so that ultimate liability, if something went wrong, should rest where it properly belonged. The Court of Appeal's decision on the point is the more striking in view of its decision that B.I.C.C. were not liable in negligence. On appeal the House of Lords[33] held that B.I.C.C. were negligent and most of their lordships, therefore, did not consider it necessary to decide the issue of the extent of the contractual obligation as to design. The issue was, however, considered *obiter* by Lord Scarman.[34] He saw no reason why one who in the course of his business contracted to design, supply and erect a television aerial mast was not under an obligation to ensure that it was reasonably fit for the purpose for which he knew it was intended to be used. He did not accept that the design obligation of the supplier of an article was to be equated with the obligation of a professional man in the practice of his profession. In support of his view he relied upon the Court of Appeal's decision in *Samuels v. Davis*.[35] In that case it was held that, where a dentist undertook for reward to make a denture for a patient, it was an implied term of the contract that the denture would be reasonably fit for its intended purpose. The fact of the article being supplied, as well as being designed, was invoked both by the Court of Appeal in the latter case and by Lord Scarman in *I.B.A.* as the crucial distinction justifying the higher duty to ensure that the design

---

[30] *ibid.* at 1100, 1102 and 1103.
[31] (1980) 14 B.L.R. 1, HL. For the facts see para. 8–097, above.
[32] (1978) 11 B.L.R. 29, 49–52.
[33] (1980) 14 B.L.R. 1.
[34] *ibid.* at 47. Viscount Dilhorne added (*ibid.* at 26) however that he "would have been surprised" had not E.M.I. and B.I.C.C. undertaken an obligation to supply a mast "reasonably fit for its intended purpose".
[35] [1943] K.B. 526.

was reasonably fit for the purpose, as opposed to the duty to take reasonable care and skill in the design.[36]

Both *Greaves* and Lord Scarman's dictum were considered in *George Hawkins* **8–171** *v. Chrysler (U.K.)*[37] where engineers were engaged to design showers to be installed at a foundry. An employee slipped and sued the foundry owners, who in turn brought third-party proceedings against the engineers. The judge at first instance found that the engineers were not in breach of their duty to exercise reasonable care but were in breach of an implied warranty to provide "as safe a floor as was practicable in the expertise of the profession to provide a safe floor for these men in these conditions".[38] The Court of Appeal dismissed the foundry owners' appeal on the negligence issue but upheld the engineer's appeal on the warranty. On the evidence there were no grounds upon which a warranty going beyond an engineer's normal obligation to exercise reasonable skill and care should be founded and there was no basis for the implication of such a warranty in law.[39]

In *Consultants Group International v. John Worman Ltd*[40] the plaintiffs (CGI) **8–172** provided specialist architectural and consultancy services under an agreement with the defendant contractors ("the CGI agreement") in connection with the refurbishment of an abattoir by the defendant under a contract with the abattoir owner, Turner ("the Turner agreement"). Provided that the design and construction of the abattoir fulfilled certain criteria, Turner was entitled automatically to a domestic United Kingdom grant and was entitled to be considered for a further E.C. grant. When CGI sued the defendant for fees, the defendant counterclaimed for alleged breaches of the CGI agreement. Preliminary issues were ordered to decide *inter alia* whether: (a) it was a term of the Turner agreement that the works and/or designs would be fit for their purpose; (b) whether it was a term of the CGI agreement that CGI would carry out their works so that the completed project would be fit for its purpose; and (c) whether CGI would be liable to the defendants if the designs and specifications of CGI were not such as to comply with the design requirements entitling Turner to be considered for an E.C. grant. Judge Davies Q.C. held that, in the context of the case, "fitness for purpose" really meant that works should be designed and executed to the standards demanded by United Kingdom and E.C. requirements for grant aid[41] with the result that issues (b) and (c) fell to be considered together. He then held that on a true construction

---

[36] Lord Scarman's final formulation of the circumstances giving rise to the higher duty seems, in isolation, not to reflect this distinction: "In the absence of any term (express or to be implied) negativing the obligation, one who contracts to design an article for a purpose made known to him undertakes that the design is reasonably fit for the purpose" (1980) 14 B.L.R. 1, 48. From the context, however, it is clear that he contemplates both design and supply of the article by its designer.

[37] (1986) 38 B.L.R. 36.

[38] Which was not, in fact, the warranty pleaded. The pleaded warranty was that the material used for the floor would be fit for use in a wet shower room.

[39] See *per* Fox L.J. at 49–51, *per* Dillon L.J. at 53–54 and *per* Neill L.J. at 54–56. See also *Balcomb v. Wards Construction (Medway) Ltd* (1980) 259 E.G. 765, where Sir Douglas Frank Q.C., sitting as a High Court judge, rejected an argument that a warranty, apparently as to the reasonable fitness of foundation specifications provided by engineers, was to be implied in a contract between developers and the engineers. In *B.C. Rail Ltd v. Canadian Pacific Consulting Services Ltd* (1990) 47 B.C.L.R. 49 the British Columbia Court of Appeal found there to be an implied warranty of fitness for purpose in a contract where the defendant engineers had agreed to design and install an overhead contact system for a railway line. The warranty was found to be both reasonable and necessary on a proper construction of the contract.

[40] (1985) 9 Con.L.R. 46.

[41] *ibid.* at 49.

of the contract documents it was an express term of the Turner contract that the works should be fit for this purpose and further held that if he was wrong, such a term would have been implied.[42] The judge found that the defendants had made it clear to CGI that they had no experience of abattoir work and would be dependent on CGI's experience and expertise[43] and that CGI were the "prime movers in the project from start to finish".[44] As a result he found that it was also an express, alternatively an implied, term of the CGI agreement that the works would be so designed by CGI that the completed project would be fit for its purpose.[45]

8–173   It is submitted that the approach both of the Court of Appeal in *Hawkins* and of Judge Davies Q.C. in *Consultants Group International* in undertaking an analysis of the relationship between the designer and his client is correct. There will be no absolute answer as to whether one who designs but does not supply an article or build a structure is under a duty to ensure that it is reasonably fit for its intended purpose, but such a duty will not be implied by law. It will therefore arise either on a true construction of the parties' agreement or as an implication from the common intention of the parties.

8–174   Similarly, in the absence of special circumstances, a construction professional who designs a structure, inspects its construction and issues a certificate to that effect will not normally be taken thereby to have warranted or represented that the structure is fit for its purpose. In *Payne v. John Setchell Ltd*,[46] the defendant engineer was responsible for the design of foundations for cottages which were later purchased by the claimants. The claimants alleged that they relied in making their purchases upon certificates issued by the defendant which stated that he was satisfied that the foundations had been constructed in accordance with his design and were suitable for support of dwellings. Judge Lloyd Q.C. rejected the claimant's contention that the defendant had thereby certified that the foundations were fit for their purpose. The judge pointed out that a certificate has to be construed in the light of the obligations pursuant to which it has been issued. He said[47]:

> "The claimants' case in respect of the third retainer—for the certificate—was that the defendant had certified the fitness of the foundation for its purpose. In my judgment the defendant did not undertake to issue such certificate nor is the certificate to be read as certifying the foundations' fitness for purpose. . . . A certificate expresses the judgment, opinion or skill of the person issuing it, usually, but not always, in relation to a matter called for by a construction contract (where the certifier is sometimes also acting in a quasi-arbitral capacity). . . . It is not normally a warranty nor is it to be read as tantamount to a warranty, particularly if issued by a professional person, although it may amount to a warranty. If issued by a contractor who has undertaken full and complete performance of the contract it may be taken as its formal confirmation that it has duly fulfilled all the obligations undertaken under the contract which will probably include obligations of an absolute nature. To that extent it might be or be equivalent to a warranty especially if given to or intended for a third party. The other contracting party will not normally need such a document as it will have its rights under the contract. A professional person however does not normally undertake obligations of an

---

[42] The judge had little difficulty with this, having already decided in *Viking Grain Storage Ltd v. T.H. White Installations Ltd* (1985) 3 Con.L.R. 53 that a term of fitness for purpose was to be implied into a contract for the design and construction of a grain drying and storage installation.
[43] *ibid.* at 34.
[44] *ibid.* at 59.
[45] *ibid.* at 60.
[46] Unreported, March 16, 2001. For the facts, see para. 8–059 above.
[47] *ibid.* at para. 20.

absolute nature but only undertakes to exercise reasonable professional skill and care in performance of the relevant service or in the production of the product. Thus the certificate of 20 October 1988, particularly since it refers to the two visits to the site, can only be read as an expression of the opinion of the defendant that as the result of such inspections the defendant had reasonable grounds for believing that the construction of the foundation had been satisfactorily carried out to its design and, by implication, that there were no circumstances known to the defendant as a result of those inspections which cast doubt on the defendant's original judgment in the production of that design."

(x) *Reliance upon specialists and delegation to them*

Modern developments in materials and technologies in the construction industry **8–175** have been so numerous and so rapid as to exceed the ability of even the most talented and assiduous professional men to master them all. Architects and others must of necessity seek the assistance of specialists when they reach the limits of their knowledge.[48] This consideration raises the question whether it is a defence to a construction professional alleged to have been negligent in the performance of a task which he agreed to perform to show (a) that he relied upon the advice or work of specialists or even delegated the performance of the task to them, and (b) that such reliance or delegation was reasonable. The question is the more acute given that a construction professional in some circumstances may be negligent in not seeking specialist assistance. Much as sympathy for his dilemma may favour an affirmative answer to the question, at least upon initial impression, there is the countervailing consideration that such an answer may leave the client without remedy either against the construction professional or the specialist in the absence of a direct agreement between the client and the specialist.

The question admits of no general answer. In principle and authorities apart, it **8–176** is submitted that the question should be approached as follows. First, the concept of reliance in this context needs to be defined. At one extreme, a construction professional may wholly rely upon specialists effectively to the extent of complete delegation. At the other extreme the professional may only rely on specialists to the extent that in the formulation of his design he takes account of articles by them in professional journals or detailed product specifications reflecting specialist research. The key distinction is between: (a) the case where a professional relies upon specialist assistance to a point that on any objective assessment it must be recognised that the relevant task is performed by the specialists and not the professional; and (b) the case where, despite reliance upon specialists, an objective assessment results in the conclusion that the task is still essentially performed by the professional. In making the distinction a crucial criterion, albeit not the only one, is the extent to which the professional exercises an independent judgment. But the distinction is ultimately one of degree. It is only reliance of the kind in case (a) which is the subject of the question. Where the reliance is of the kind in case (b), the question does not arise since the performance was that of the professional and not specialists.

---

[48] *Equitable Debenture Assets Corp. Ltd v. William Moss Group Ltd* (1984) 2 Con.L.R. 1, 25 *per* Judge Newey Q.C. The same judge in *Richard Roberts Holdings Ltd v. Douglas Smith Stimson Partnership and Others* (1988) 46 B.L.R. 50, 66 said: "If the architects felt that they could not form a reliable judgment about a lining for the tank, they should have informed Holdings of that fact and advised them to take other advice, possibly from a chemist." For the facts and further discussion of this case see para. 8–141, above.

8–177   In answering the question, the starting point is the construction professional's contract. If he agreed to perform the relevant task personally, reasonable reliance upon specialists would not be a defence; in such a case the relevant breach of duty would, logically, not be failure to choose competent specialists but incompetence by the construction professional himself. On the other hand, the contract may expressly or by implication permit reliance upon specialists or the client may otherwise permit it. In that case, reasonable reliance upon specialists will provide a defence in appropriate circumstances. In the same case, however, the construction professional may be shown to have been in breach of his duty in not initially choosing specialists of appropriate competence or in not properly reviewing the specialists' advice or other work, and thus not discovering errors which a member of his profession of ordinary competence ought to have discovered upon such review. Nevertheless, it is submitted that the client's permission and the professional's consequent power to rely upon or to delegate to specialists cannot be derived, without more specific provision in the professional's contract, from his duty to exercise reasonable care and skill nor from the standard applicable to that duty, being that of the ordinary competent member of his profession.

8–178   The authorities are not entirely consistent as to the answer to the question. In *Moresk Cleaners Ltd v. Hicks*[49] it was held that it was not the ordinary practice of the profession for an architect to delegate his work on design and then to seek to disown responsibility for it.[50] The defendant architect was held negligent in the design of the reinforced concrete frame to a building; the architect had delegated that part of the building's design to a structural engineer.[51] *Moresk* is to be contrasted with *Merton LBC v. Lowe*[52] where the defendant architect was appointed in 1964 under then existing RIBA Conditions of Engagement to design and supervise the construction of a swimming pool. His design included suspended ceilings surfaced with a proprietary product called Pyrok supplied by Pyrok Ltd. That company was nominated as the sub-contractor for the purpose of plastering the ceilings. In the event the ceiling surfacing failed and had to be replaced. The cause was an imbalance of the mix of the undercoats and the Pyrok

---

[49] [1966] 2 Lloyd's Rep. 338.

[50] See also in this respect the decision of the Court of Appeal in *Nye Saunders and Partners v. Alan E. Bristow* (1987) 37 B.L.R. 92. The facts are set out at para. 8–193, below. The court rejected the contention that an architect was entitled too rely wholly on the fact that he had referred a request for a cost estimate to a quantity surveyor. At 107 Stephen Brown L.J. said:

"Of course it was a very sensible and prudent step for Mr Nye to take to consult a quantity surveyor who is an expert in computing costs. But in my judgment he cannot avoid responsibility for the fact that he did not draw the attention of his client to the fact that inflation was not taken into account. The duty rested fairly and squarely upon Mr Nye and it cannot be avoided by, as it were, seeking to move the responsibility onto Mr Parker."

[51] Note also the judgment of Judge Sir Walker Carter O.R. at 343:

"If the [architect] was not able, because this form of reinforced concrete was a comparatively new form of construction to design it himself, he had three courses open to him. One was to say, 'This is not my field.' The second was to go to his client, the building owner, and say, 'This reinforced concrete is out of my line. I would like you to employ a structural engineer to deal with this aspect of the matter.' Or he can, while retaining responsibility for the design, himself seek the advice and assistance of a structural engineer, paying for his service out of his own pocket but having at any rate the satisfaction of knowing that if he acts upon that advice and it turns out to be wrong, the person whom he employed to give the advice will owe the same duty to him as he, the architect, owes to the building owners."

On the subject of delegation of design functions by architects to engineers or other specialists, see Hudson (*op. cit.*), pp. 302–307.

[52] Unreported at first instance, but reported on appeal at (1981) 18 B.L.R. 130.

finishing coat. Pyrok Ltd alone knew the constituents of that coat. Two facts are important. First, it was accepted that mix was part of the design of the specialist sub-contractor's product. Secondly, the judge found that that element of the design formed part of the detailed design for which the architect was responsible. Nevertheless he was held not negligent in originally accepting and approving Pyrok Ltd's specification for the ceiling.[53] At first instance Judge Stabb Q.C. held that the architect was entitled (a) to assume that the specification which did not specify the mix, provided for the same proper mix as specified in an earlier quotation by Pyrok Ltd, and (b) to rely on Pyrok Ltd to apply a proper mix. On appeal this finding was upheld, but apparently on the basis, as expressed by Waller L.J., that the original decision to employ Pyrok Ltd was reasonable in view of its successful work done elsewhere. *Moresk* was distinguished on the ground that in that case the architect "had virtually handed over to another the whole task of design" and "could not escape responsibility for the work which he was supposed to do by handing it over to another".[54] *Merton LBC v. Lowe* thus appears to provide an affirmative answer to the question posed above,[55] at least where the relevant reliance by the architect relates to a limited aspect of his design responsiblity. It is inconsistent, however, with the approach adumbrated above[56] and also with that of the judge in *Moresk*.

The particular RIBA Conditions incorporated in the architect's contract in **8–179** *Merton London Borough Council v. Lowe* did not contain the specific provisions relating to specialist sub-contractors and suppliers contained in more recent editions. They provide that the architect may recommend that the specialist sub-contractors and suppliers should design and execute any part of the work and that while he will be responsible for the direction and integration of their design and for general inspection of their work, he will not be responsible for the detailed design or performance of the work entrusted to them.[57] There is a similar specific provision relating to consultants. This provides that the architect will advise on the need for independent consultants, and will be responsible for the direction and integration of their work but not for the detailed design, inspection and performance of the work entrusted to them.[58] The effect of this and related provisions were considered by the Court of Appeal in *Investors in Industry*

---

[53] The architect was nevertheless held negligent on another ground: in failing to carry out a proper investigation after cracking in the ceilings had developed. See para. 8–030 above.

[54] (1981) 18 B.L.R. 130 at 148, CA. Note also Pigeon J.'s majority judgment in the Canadian case of *Vermont Construction Inc. v. Beatson* (1976) 67 D.L.R. (3d) 95. In holding that a party charged with negligence could "clear his feet" if he shows that he acted in accordance with general and approved practice, he found (at 103) that the defendant architects had acted in accordance with the practice of architects generally in relying on engineers to make stress calculations for the structures for which they prepared plans. Accordingly he absolved the architects of negligence in not checking the engineers' calculations even though they could have done so.

[55] See para. 8–175.

[56] See paras 8–176 to 8–177.

[57] RIBA 1971 Conditions of Engagement with 1975, 1976 and 1979 amendments, cl. 1.40; RIBA Architect's Appointment 1982 with 1982, 1987 and 1988 amendments, cl. 3.8; RIBA Standard Form of Agreement for the Appointment of an Architect (1992), cl. 4.2.5 and, to similar effect, RIBA Standard Form of Agreement for the Appointment of an Architect (1999), cl. 3.12. See also n. 52 to para. 8–017, above. Similar provisions are found in the various form of the ACE Conditions of Engagement for engineers.

[58] *ibid.*, cl. 1.22, cl. 3.6, cl. 4.1.7 and cl. 3.11. Similar provisions are found in the various forms of the ACE Conditions of Engagement for engineers.

Commercial Properties v. South Bedfordshire District Council; Ellison & Part-ners and Hamilton Associates (Third Parties)[59]:

> "Whether or not in any given instance these conditions apply, it must generally be the duty of an architect to exercise reasonable care in the work he is engaged to perform. However, clauses 1.20, 1.22 and 1.23 of the RIBA conditions, in our judgment, clearly contemplate that, where a particular part of the work involved in a building contract involves specialist knowledge or skill beyond that which an architect of ordinary competence may reasonably be expected to possess, the architect is at liberty to recommend to his client that a reputable independent consultant, who appears to have the relevant specialist knowledge or skill, shall be appointed by the client to perform this task. If following such a recommendation a consultant with these qualifications is appointed, the architect will normally carry no legal responsibility for the work to be done by the expert which is beyond the capability of an architect of ordinary competence; in relation to the work allotted to the expert, the architect's legal responsibility will normally be confined to directing and co-ordinating the expert's work in the whole. However, this is subject to one important qualification. If any danger or problem arises in connection with the work allotted to the expert, of which an architect of ordinary competence reasonably ought to be aware and reasonably could be expected to warn the client, despite the employment of the expert, and despite what the expert says or does about it, it is in our judgment the duty of the architect to warn the client. In such a contingency he is not entitled to rely blindly on the expert, with no mind of his own, on matters which must or should have been apparent to him."[60]

Two points should be noted. Under the relevant RIBA Conditions the archi-tect's responsibility is excluded only where the client follows his recommenda-tion or advice as to the use of specialist sub-contractors and suppliers or consultants. Secondly, the propositions of law in the quoted passage deal only with the position where the architect's advice as to the use of consultants is followed by the client.

3. LIABILITY FOR BREACH OF DUTY

8–180 This part of the chapter considers breach of duty by an architect, engineer or quantity surveyor which consists of:

(i) breach of the implied contractual duty to exercise reasonable care and skill[61];

---

[59] [1986] 1 All E.R. 787, CA. This case is reported at first instance *sub nom. Anglia Commercial Properties Ltd v. South Bedfordshire D.C.* (1984) 2 Con.L.R. 99. The relevant facts so far as they related to the architects are stated at para. 8–188, below.

[60] *ibid.* at 807–808. Construction professionals were found negligent in failing to check and warn of deficiencies in the designs prepared by specialist sub-contractors in *Try Build Ltd v. Invicta Leisure Tennis Ltd* (2000) 71 Con.L.R. 141 (engineers failed to appreciate that novel features of a design for a sports hall roof developed by a specialist supplier had not been successfully developed and were inadequate) and *Baxall Securities Ltd v. Sheard Walshaw Partnership* [2001] P.N.L.R 256 (architects failed to specify and check the design rainfall rate to be used in the design by a specialist sub-contractor of a roof drainage system. Judge Bowsher Q.C. pointed out that the sub-contractor would naturally adopt a low rate in order to reduce his tender price and increase his chance of securing the sub-contract; that was a matter against which the architects should have protected their client by specifying the appropriate rate in the tender documentation).

[61] See paras 8–017 to 8–036, above

(ii) breach of any duty of care owed to the client independently of his contractual duties[62]; and

(iii) breach of any duty of care owed to a third party.[63]

These breaches will be jointly described as negligence. Instances in which the relevant professions have been or may be liable for breach of duty are discussed below under 12 heads generally descriptive of the tasks commonly undertaken by them. Those tasks are considered broadly in the order in which they are likely to be performed over the course of a building project. Finally, the question of breach of duty by a construction professional acting as an expert witness for the purpose of litigation is discussed.

(a) *Examination of site*

A construction professional, typically an architect or engineer, who is charged   **8–181**
with the design of a building or other structure will owe a duty to satisfy himself that the chosen site is suitable for the proposed works. This may involve him in one or more of the following activities:

(i) measuring the site;

(ii) ascertaining the nature and properties of the ground below the site;

(iii) considering the likely effects of the proposed works on the ground conditions;

(iv) considering the effects of non-physical constraints on building, such as planning requirements.

The work of other consultants or contractors may overlap with the architect or engineer's work in respect of each activity: in those cases, it will be necessary to consider the extent to which the architect or engineer is entitled to rely upon information provided by such persons.

Measuring the site. The site must be neither too small nor too large for the   **8–182**
building to be erected upon it. Liability for failure to appreciate that the site and the proposed works are not compatible in this way has arisen in cases where the architect or engineer has attempted a "short-cut", relying upon inaccurate information provided by others rather than carrying out or organising his own measured survey. Thus in *Columbus Co. v. Clowes*[64] an architect was held negligent in failing to survey and measure a site himself, assuming instead that information provided by a person who was not authorised by the building owner to provide such information was correct. In consequence he had drawn plans and specifications on the basis of dimensions smaller than the actual dimensions of the site. The consequences of a similar error were more serious in *Cardy v. Taylor*[65] because the site proved too small for the proposed works. The architects relied upon plans supplied by their client (the building contractor) or by the

---

[62] See paras 8–037 to 8–061, above.
[63] See paras 8–062 to 8–129, above.
[64] [1903] 1 K.B. 244.
[65] (1994) 38 Con.L.R. 79.

building owner which lacked dimensions, were inconsistent and were of uncertain authorship. When the inaccuracies were discovered, the building had to be redesigned and a fresh application for planning permission made. The architects were found liable for the resulting loss on the basis that no competent architect would present an application for planning permission without accurate site information. Judge Bowsher Q.C. pointed out that, whilst it might be acceptable for an architect to rely upon survey information provided by a contractor which accepted responsibility for its accuracy, the architects were not in that position and should have taken their own measurements of the site.

8–183   **Ground investigations.** An architect or engineer who designs a building should take reasonable care to see that there is adequate information, from his own investigations or from those of a specialist consultant or contractor, as to the sub-soil conditions. It is particularly important to bear in mind that conditions below ground may vary between different areas of the site. In *Moneypenny v. Hartland*[66] an engineer relied upon the results of a site investigation which revealed that the proposed site for the foundations of a planned bridge was founded on rock. The engineer then changed the location of the foundations to an area which was not covered by the site investigation. In consequence he grossly underestimated the cost of construction because the underlying ground there turned out to be clay, which was unable to support the foundations. The engineer was held negligent in failing to carry out his own investigation into ground conditions at the location which he chose for the foundations.

8–184   The nature of a site may require extensive tests and examinations, both during and after excavations. This will be particularly important where the nature of the ground is poor or presents special difficulties for the proposed building, for example, if there is made ground (*i.e.* non-natural, man-made ground). Thus in *Eames London Estates Ltd v. North Hertfordshire District Council*[67] an industrial building was constructed on made ground. The foundations proved inadequate with the result that extensive repairs and possible rebuilding was required. The architect entrusted with the design of the building including the foundations had made no examination of the soil. Although knowing that it was made ground, he thought that it was an old railway embankment. Judge Edgar Fay Q.C. held that the architect should have satisfied himself about the land's bearing capacity,[68] and that he could not shed his responsibility for foundations by ascertaining what would "get by the local authority", as he appeared to have done. He was held negligent in two respects: first, in specifying the loading for piers without any attempt to ascertain for himself whether the ground was suitable for the loading, and secondly in putting aside a query as to the adequacy of the depth of excavations for foundations properly raised by a practical man on the spot.[69]

8–185   Often ascertainment of the ground conditions at a site will be beyond the expertise of an architect or engineer. In such a case the exercise of due care may require the architect to advise the employer accordingly and either to engage

---

[66] (1824) 1 Car. & P. 351 (first instance); (1826) 2 Car. & P. 378.
[67] (1980) 259 E.G. 491.
[68] The judge observed that "the 25 in. Ordnance Survey maps are part of the furnishings of local architects' offices" and that a glance at the relevant map would have shown that the railway had crossed only part of the site: *ibid.* at 495.
[69] *ibid.* at 495.

himself or to advise the employer to engage specialists to carry out the requested ground investigation.[70] As the cases discussed in the following paragraphs demonstrate, he may nevertheless retain a responsibility to consider carefully the value of the information provided by specialists and to advise as to its limitations.

In the Canadian case of *District of Surrey v. Carroll-Hatch and Associates* **8–186** *Ltd*,[71] an engineer engaged by architects to inspect trial pits was held negligent for failing to warn that the information available from the pits was inadequate to establish the load-bearing capacity of the ground. In *City of Brantford v. Kemp and Wallace-Carruthers & Associates Ltd*,[72] the site for a new fire hall and police station consisted of an old rubbish tip. The safer design entailed supporting the whole building on piles. The riskier but cheaper design, which the defendant engineers adopted, was a "floor on earth" method which entailed supporting the main walls on piles but placing partition walls on floors laid on granular fill and suspended from the main walls. Proper examination of the site would have demonstrated the need for the safer design but the engineers had not carried out such examination either before or during excavations. They were held liable in negligence for the subsequent failure of the internal walls and floors. The Ontario Court of Appeal also held that in the circumstances of the case it was not enough for the defendant engineers to rely on the result of percussion tests made by a soil testing firm, knowing the limitations of sampling tests of any kind on ground of this sort.

The need for construction professionals making preliminary investigations into **8–187** the nature of a site to give clear warnings as to any risks or inaccuracies in their results is also illustrated by *Gable House Estates v. The Halpern Partnership*.[73] The defendant architects advised that the redevelopment of a building would result in useable office space of between 35,056 and 34,163 square feet, depending upon which of four schemes was adopted. It was found that the actual area was only 31,769 square feet. The judge found that it would not have been possible for the architects to have forecasted the useable office space to an accuracy of 500 square feet. In those circumstances, the architects did not discharge their duty simply by qualifying their estimates with the words "All areas approximate". That was an insufficient warning of errors of up to 500 square feet.[74]

Similarly in *Investors in Industry Commercial Properties v. South Bedford-* **8–188** *shire District Council; Ellison & Partners and Hamilton Associates (Third Parties)*[75] the plaintiff developer engaged a firm of architects to design and act as architects in relation to the construction of four warehouses on a site known to be infilled land, formerly the site of a large swimming pool. The architect's contract incorporated the then RIBA Conditions of Engagement including the

---

[70] See, for example, *District of Surrey v. Carroll-Hatch and Associates Ltd* (1979) 10 D.L.R. (3d) 218, considered at para. 8–186 below. Also see the passage from *Moresk Cleaners Ltd v. Hicks* [1966] 2 Lloyd's Rep. 338, 343 set out in n. 51 under para. 8–178, above.

[71] (1979) 10 D.L.R. (3d) 218, British Columbia CA.

[72] (1960) 23 D.L.R. (2d) 641, Ontario CA.

[73] (1995) 48 Con.L.R. 1.

[74] For further discussion of this case see para. 8–192, below.

[75] [1986] 1 All E.R. 787, CA. This case is reported at first instance *sub nom. Anglia Commercial Properties Ltd v. South Bedfordshire D.C.* (1984) 2 Con.L.R. 99.

particular clause, clause 1.22, discussed above.[76] Upon the architect's recommendation a firm of structural engineers was engaged by the plaintiff to design and supervise the construction of the foundations. At first instance, the engineers were held to have been at fault in failing to see that a proper site investigation had been carried out. Only "quite useless" trial holes had been dug, when the only possible way of investigating the particular ground was by means of bore holes and subsequent laboratory analysis of the undisturbed samples.[77] The claim against the architects in respect of the foundations, however, failed. Judge Sir William Stabb Q.C. held that the architects were entitled to rely upon the engineers' judgment as to what foundations were suitable and that the architects had properly met the risk presented by the nature of the ground by seeing that consulting engineers were appointed to deal with it.[78] The Court of Appeal affirmed the judge's finding on the point, also holding that, in the circumstances, clause 1.22 read together with other relevant RIBA Conditions defined and limited the scope of the architects' contractual duty to the plaintiff employer in respect of the foundations.[79]

8–189   **The effect of the proposed works.** In some cases, it will be necessary for the designer to take into account the likely effect on ground conditions of the proposed works themselves. For example, the drought of 1976 gave rise to a number of cases which explored the effect of the removal of trees from sites founded on London clay. In *Acrecrest Ltd v. W.S. Hattrell & Partners*,[80] architects were held negligent in giving insufficient regard to the removal of trees from a site for development. Water which would have been absorbed by the trees was absorbed by the ground, giving rise to swelling or "heave" of the clay, and damage to the new building.[81] In *Kaliszewska v. John Clague & Partners*,[82] an architect designing foundations for a new bungalow who failed to appreciate the significance of removal of trees from a site based on London clay was found negligent. He had failed to address the problem in any methodical way or to use the current knowledge in his profession which was available to him.[83]

8–190   **Non-physical constraints.** Even in the absence of instructions so to do, the exercise of reasonable care may require an architect to make reasonable enquiries

---

[76] See para. 8–179.

[77] (1984) 2 Con.L.R. 99, 100–101.

[78] *ibid.* at 103.

[79] [1986] 1 All E.R. 787, CA at 807. Note also the passage from the judgment quoted at para. 8–179, above. For further examples of failure to examine site properly, see *Blair v. Alderney Consultants* (1998) 168 N.S.R. (2d) 287 (engineer employed by developer to design storm drainage for a development was negligent in not having gone onto adjoining Crown land a short distance from the development itself. Had he done so, he would have seen a drain outlet which was not shown either on aerial plans or plans from the Department of Transportation. The engineer's argument that it was unreasonable to expect him to walk between adjoining developments and that he was entitled to rely on the plans was rejected on the basis that access was, in this case, possible and experience showed that the plans often contained errors); *Dalgliesh v. Bromley Corporation* (1953) 162 E.G. 623 (architects negligently failed to warn that the slope of the site was such that the development would be uneconomical as a result of the need for expensive levelling works).

[80] (1979) 252 E.G. 1107 (first instance), [1983] Q.B. 260, CA.

[81] Engineers were held liable on similar facts in *Balcomb v. Wards Construction (Medway) Ltd* (1980) 259 E.G. 765.

[82] (1984) 5 Con.L.R. 62.

[83] *ibid.* at 77.

concerning the rights of neighbours, for example, about easements[84] and restrictive covenants, or planning restrictions,[85] lest they be infringed by subsequent building. The circumstances of each case will usually require detailed examination in order to establish whether the duty to make such enquiries was undertaken by the architect or by other agents of the employer, for example, his solicitors,[86] or even by the employer himself. Where he has not carried out such enquiries, the prudent course for an architect is to warn his client that he has not done so.

(b) *Cost estimates and budgets*

Before embarking on a building project a client will commonly ask an architect, **8-191** engineer or quantity surveyor for an estimate of the cost. Although in giving the estimate precision is not required, reasonable care and skill must be exercised. In *Moneypenny v. Hartland*[87] the employer refused to pay the engineer's fees since the actual cost of a project greatly exceeded the engineer's estimate. Best C.J., holding that the engineer was not entitled to be paid for his work, stated:

> "it is not a trifling deviation from an estimate that is to prevent a party recovering. But if a surveyor delivers an estimate, greatly below the sum at which a work can be done, and thereby induces a private person to undertake what he would not otherwise do, then I think he is not entitled to recover."[88]

In *Gordon Shaw Concrete Products Ltd v. Design Collaborative Ltd*,[89] the Nova Scotia Court of Appeal found there to have been a total failure of consideration as well as negligence when the defendant architects were instructed to undertake a preliminary study to see if a house could be constructed for $60,000 and, if it was feasible, to provide final drawings and specifications. The preliminary design report estimated a building cost of $60,144 but when final drawings and estimates were submitted it transpired that the design could not be implemented for less than $100,000. The plaintiffs sought the return of all money paid on account. Macdonald J.A. said:

---

[84] See *Armitage v. Palmer* (1959) 173 E.G. 91 *per* Lloyd Jacob J.: "If by reason of the manner in which an architect sited a building it infringed an easement enjoyed by a neighbouring owner of which the architect had actual or constructive notice, he had not exercised reasonable skill and care." On the facts, which concerned a neighbour's allegation that his right of light had been infringed, the architect was held not negligent.

[85] The primary restriction imposed by planning legislation is that the owner of the land must consent to the proposed development. In *John Harris Partnership v. Groveworld Ltd* [1999] P.N.L.R. 697, architects failed to notice that part of the proposed site was owned not by their client but by the local authority. They were liable for increased costs incurred in obtaining a revised planning permission. See also *Hancock v. Tucker* [1999] Lloyd's Rep. P.N. 814, where it was alleged that architects' conduct of a planning application had caused unnecessary delays on obtaining permission. On the facts, they were not negligent: see further para. 8-200 below.

[86] See chap. 10, para. 10-199, below.

[87] (1826) 2 Car. & P. 378. See also para. 8-183, above.

[88] *ibid.* at 381.

[89] (1985) 35 C.C.L.T. 100. See also the South African case of *Wilkens Nel Argitekte v. Stephenson* [1987] 2 S.A.L.R. 628 in which the Orange Free State Provincial Court of Appeal held that architects, who accepted instructions containing a specific requirement that the final cost of the project was in no circumstances to exceed the estimated cost of R100,000, were not entitled to fees for drawing up plans when it became clear that the cost of the project built in accordance with those plans would be substantially higher than the estimated cost.

"The appellant was under a duty to submit an estimate of construction costs that was reasonably close to the ultimate cost and if there was a wide discrepancy between the two then to satisfactorily explain the reason for the discrepancy. There was here no reasonable or satisfactory explanation of the great discrepancy between the estimated and ultimate construction figure."

It is doubted whether the finding of a total failure of consideration can be justified. Nonetheless, it would appear that on the facts of the case the finding of a breach of duty which led to damages equalling all amounts paid beyond those necessary to secure a competent preliminary estimate led to substantially the same result.

8–192   One of the principal reasons for instructing a construction professional to provide an estimate of likely construction costs is that the client wishes to know and plan for the total expenditure which he faces if he proceeds with the project in question. Accordingly, it is important that the professional should advise his client in clear terms as to any matters which he has not taken into account in his estimate but which might affect the actual final cost and any factors which he has included but which may change during over the life of the project. It may also be appropriate to indicate the level of accuracy to which his estimate has been prepared. A good example of the last consideration is provided by the decision of Judge Lewis Q.C. in *Gable House Estates v. The Halpern Partnership*.[90] The defendant architects provided a preliminary cost plan and elemental specification showing a cost for the works of £5.8 million and useable office space of 33,928 square feet. It was found that the actual area was only 31,769 square feet. The judge found that the architects could not have estimated the area to an accuracy of more than 500 square feet. However, they knew that the amount of the lettable square feet, rather than its quality, was of great importance to the plaintiff. In those circumstances, the formula "All areas approximate" was an insufficient warning of the possibility that the stated square footage could not be achieved.

8–193   The decision of the Court of Appeal in *Nye Saunders and Partners v. Alan E. Bristow*[91] illustrates the importance of clear warnings as to matters which may cause the final cost to differ from the estimated cost. The facts were that the plaintiff architects were retained by the defendant, a well-known businessman, in 1973 to prepare and submit a planning application for the renovation of his mansion. The defendant informed the plaintiffs that he had about £250,000 to spend and asked the plaintiffs to provide a written estimate of the likely cost of the works. The plaintiffs consulted a quantity surveyor and wrote to the defendant enclosing a schedule of costs amounting to some £238,000. Neither the schedule nor the architects' covering letter mentioned the effect of likely increases in inflation: in fact, it was wholly based on then current prices. Mr Bristow assumed that inflation had been taken into account. Following the grant of planning permission the plaintiffs were engaged in March 1974 to proceed with the scheme. At a meeting in September of the same year, an up-to-date statement showed likely costs to completion of £440,000, including a figure for inflation during the 18 months' contract period. Mr Bristow thereupon cancelled the project and refused to pay the plaintiffs' fees on the grounds that their services had been valueless. The plaintiffs sued for their fees. The claim was

---

[90] (1995) 48 Con.L.R. 1.
[91] (1987) 37 Build. L.R. 92.

defended upon the basis that had a proper estimate been provided Mr Bristow would not have commenced the project. The defence succeeded and the plaintiff's appeal was rejected. It was held that the plaintiffs did not avoid liability to Mr Bristow for the costs advice given by passing the preparation of that advice to a quantity surveyor, since the plaintiffs retained a responsibility to warn Mr Bristow that inflation had not been taken into account.[92] The plaintiffs were also found negligent at first instance for failing to warn that the estimate included no sum for contingencies.

Saunders is consistent with the Canadian case of *Savage v. Board of School* **8–194** *Trustees*[93] where it was held that an architect had failed to exercise reasonable care and skill in providing an estimate of $110,000 for building a school. The lowest tender received was $157,000. The court asserted that if an architect furnished an estimate as part of his contract, it must at his peril be reasonably near the ultimate cost, and that where any deficiency appeared on its face to be unreasonable, the burden rested upon the architect to show how it arose and that he was not at fault. Much of the discrepancy was explained by inadequate checking and rechecking of the estimate. The main defence that the events happened in a period of rising prices was rejected on the facts, including on the ground that the trend in prices was known to the architect and should have been allowed for in his estimates.

It is submitted that *Savage* was incorrect to the extent that the court found that **8–195** the burden was upon the defendant to explain a discrepancy in his estimate. Subsequent events should not, as a matter of principle, cause the burden of proof to shift. Thus a finding of negligence should not follow merely from the fact that the final cost is very significantly higher than a construction professional's estimate. In *Copthorne Hotel (Newcastle) Ltd v. Arup Associates*,[94] Judge Hicks Q.C. found that the plaintiff had failed to make out a case of negligent estimation in respect of piling costs where the defendants had estimated a figure of £425,000 against an out-turn cost of £975,000. No evidence had been led as to what figure the defendants should have used for pile diameter which was an essential element in arriving at a price. The judge said:

> "I hope and believe that I am not over-simplifying if I record the impression that the plaintiff's main hope was that I would be persuaded to find in their favour simply by the size of the gap, absolutely and proportionately, between the cost estimate and the successful tender.
>
> The gap was indeed enormous. It astonished and appalled the parties at the time, and it astonishes me. I do not see, however, how that alone can carry the plaintiff home. There is no plea or argument that the maxim 'res ipsa loquitur' applies. Culpable under-estimation is of course one obvious explanation of such a discrepancy, but far from the only one . . . ."

Subject to the question of burden of proof, however, it is submitted that both **8–196** *Saunders* and *Savage* were correctly decided. Although the construction professional is in no better position than anybody else to foretell the rate of future

---

[92] See the passage from the judgment of Slade L.J. quoted at para. 8–151 above.
[93] [1951] 3 D.L.R. 39.
[94] (1996) 58 Con. L.R. 105.

general inflation, he should know more about the effect of inflation on the building industry in the short term so that, for example, he should know when the next wage increase is expected and what is the current trend in costs of materials. Moreover he and he alone knows to what extent, if at all, he has taken inflation into account. However, if he bases his estimate on current building costs and makes it plain that he has done so,[95] that ought to be sufficient.[96] Ultimately, the issue whether an estimate is so wrong as to be negligent and the issue whether the estimated figure should take account of future inflation are questions of fact dependent on the particular circumstances of each case. Much will turn upon the terms of the quantity surveyor's or architect's contract of engagement. If he agrees to estimate the ultimate cost of the project then the estimate which he provides will be judged on this basis.[97]

8-197   If an architect, engineer or quantity surveyor knows that his client has a financial limit for a building project, the duty to exercise reasonable care requires that he consider whether the limit is likely to be exceeded and warn the client accordingly. Thus in the Australian case of *Flannagan v. Mate*[98] an architect's claim for fees failed in circumstances where he was told by the client that his limit was £4,000 yet the project could not be completed for anything like that sum and was abandoned. Even if a costs limit is not specified an architect should plan works capable of being carried out at a reasonable cost having regard to their scope and function.[99]

---

[95] The estimate should indicate whether (i) it is based on building costs as at that date, or (ii) it represents the anticipated tender figure (which will presumably be received some months or even years in the future), or (iii) it represents the total anticipated costs of construction (which will presumably be very much more than the tender figure unless a fixed price contract is proposed). If (i), the estimator should indicate those matters which may affect the tender and/or final price.

[96] It is submitted that the view taken by Judge Stabb Q.C., O.R., in the unreported case of *Aubrey Jacobus and Partners v. Gerrard*, June 1981 is also compatible with *Saunders* and *Savage*. In that case architects with the assistance of quantity surveyors provided an estimate in June 1979 of £365,000 for building a house with a swimming pool. The lowest tender received in November 1979 was approximately £417,000. Since this tender assumed a "fluctuating" contract, the ultimate cost of the building would have been very much higher. The client did not proceed to construction and contended that the estimate was negligently given. The judge rejected the argument that the estimate should have represented the ultimate cost of the project and that it should have taken account of cost increases over the period to completion of the works: "In my judgment the quantity surveyor's duty is to estimate the cost at current rates but to make it plain that the estimate is given on that basis and that increased costs are excluded. If then he is asked to estimate the extent of the likely increases, he can do it with such qualifications as he wishes to add, but I do not consider he is under any duty to volunteer it." He considered that the same applied to the architects.

[97] Note Cockburn C.J.'s direction to the jury in *Nelson v. Spooner* (1861) 2 F. & F. 613, a case of an architect's claim for fees in circumstances where the lowest tender substantially exceeded his estimate: "There are three questions for you–(1) Whether it was an express condition that the works shown in the revised plan should be capable of being executed for the estimated sum? If not, then (2) Whether there is an implied condition in such cases, that the work shall be capable of being done for a sum reasonably near to the estimated sum? If so, then (3) Do you think that the plaintiff's estimate was so reasonably sufficient, as that the defendants ought to have employed him?"

[98] [1876] 2 Vict. L.R. 157. Also note *Aubrey Jacobus & Partners v. Gerrard*, unreported, June 1981, *per* Judge Stabb Q.C.: " . . . it is submitted the quantity surveyor had to advise the client if the financial limit was likely to be exceeded. If the quantity surveyor knows that there is a financial limit and he knows it is likely to be exceeded, I think it is his duty to advise the client, that no such limit has been set in this case." See also *Nye Saunders v. Alan E. Bristow* (1987) 37 B.L.R. 92 discussed at para. 8–193, above and *Gordon Shaw Concrete Products Ltd v. Design Collaborative Ltd* (1985) 35 C.C.L.T. 100 discussed at para. 8–191, above.

[99] See Hudson, *op. cit.* at 325.

(iii) *Compliance with legislation, planning and building control requirements and codes of practice*

This subject, including the important case of *B.L. Holdings Ltd v. Robert J. Wood & Partners*[1] is more fully considered above.[2] Generally a member of the construction professions is not expected to have a detailed knowledge of the law but rather such knowledge as is expected of the reasonably competent practitioner. If he lacks sufficient knowledge, or considers that there is a specific point upon which his client should be advised but upon which he is not qualified to advise, he should warn his client to consult a specialist.   **8–198**

An architect or engineer engaged to design a building is expected to be familiar with planning and building control requirements and, usually, will be responsible for ensuring compliance with them. In *Strongman v. Sincock*[3] it was conceded that it was "the universal practice" for the architect and not the builder to obtain licences then required for certain building work. In *Townsends (Builders) Ltd v. Cinema News Property Management*[4] an architect was held liable in negligence to building contractors for late service of notices required by building bylaws because he had undertaken to be responsible for serving such notices. Whether an architect is responsible for ensuring compliance with such requirements, however, ultimately depends on the facts of each case and in particular the scope of his instructions.[5]   **8–199**

It will normally be prudent for an architect or engineer who is instructed to make an application for planning permission or building regulations approval to liaise informally with the relevant officers of the local authority before submitting any application. In this way, he is able to tailor his design to the authority's requirements, conserving time and cost. The plaintiff in *Hancock v. Tucker*[6] engaged the defendant architects to seek planning permission for his intended conversion of a hotel to residential flats. Over the following year, in the course of their informal discussions with the local planning authority, the architects proposed four different schemes, as they sought to take into account the planners' comments. By the time that planning permission was achieved, the value of the property had fallen significantly. The plaintiff alleged that the architects had wasted time, and should have either persisted with their initial scheme or sought permission at an early stage for the scheme which was ultimately passed by the planners. Toulson J. dismissed the claim. He approved the architects' decision to seek, through informal liaison with the planners, the scheme which was most likely to be permitted before submitting any formal application. He said[7]:   **8–200**

---

[1] (1978) 10 B.L.R. 48 (first instance); (1979) 12 B.L.R. 1, CA.
[2] See paras 8–156 to 8–162, above.
[3] [1955] 2 Q.B. 525, CA.
[4] See (1958) 20 B.L.R. 118.
[5] See para. 8–190, above in relation to inquiries concerning rights of neighbours and planning restrictions. Also note the briefly reported cases of *Stern and Sirotkin v. Oakfield Estates Ltd* [1937] E.G.D. 70 (term of contract with architects that plans should be such as to comply with and satisfy the local authority. Plans held defective and architects held liable in several respects); *Dennis v. Symons and Harris* [1937] E.G.D. 56 (plaintiff alleged that plans did not comply with byelaws. Architects held negligent in not allowing enough airspace at back of building. It is unclear from the report whether this negligence comprised failure to ensure plans complied with byelaws); and *Leach v. Crossley* (1984) 8 Con.L.R. 7, CA (engineer failed to use a revised Code of Practice when asked the maximum weight of a particular material allowable on a roof: see para. 8–217, below, where this case is more fully discussed).
[6] [1999] P.N.L.R. 814.
[7] *ibid.* at 821–822.

"I am not satisfied that the strategy adopted by Mr Tucker in relation to the original form of application and the subsequent amendments were such as no reasonably competent architect would have adopted in the circumstances. On the contrary, it seems to me that he took a rational and understandable approach in response to the various suggestions and objections raised by the planning authority and the highway authority."

(d) Design and specification

8–201   One of the primary functions of an architect (or, in the case of an engineering contract, an engineer) is design, including the preparation of plans, drawings, specifications, the selection of materials and proprietary products and advice as to suitable specialist contractors. Whilst the standard commonly applicable in designing is that of reasonable care, particular circumstances may require special steps to be taken in order to fulfil that standard and there may even be a duty to ensure that the design is reasonably fit for its intended purpose.[8] An architect or engineer who has agreed to design a structure may not escape liability for a negligent design on the ground that he delegated the design to another person unless by the terms of his contract delegation is permitted and his liability for the delegated design is excluded or limited.[9] If a design is outside his expertise the proper course is for him to inform his client accordingly and either himself to engage, or to advise the employer to engage, a person with the required expertise.[10] In the New Zealand case of *Young v. Tomlinson*[11] architects were held negligent in the design of a wall which was defective "owing to the architects having moved a little out of their specialised field." They were also held negligent in not having sought the advice of structural engineers for the design.[12]

8–202   **Approvals.** The approval of defective plans or drawings by the employer will not absolve the architect from liability in circumstances in which the employer is relying on him to avoid defects, unless the employer has given his approval with full knowledge of the defects.[13] Where the client is a layperson, even a layperson who has experience of building matters, merely copying plans to him will not be sufficient to apprise him of a defect or material change in design.[14] It is submitted that the position will be different where the client is a developer or design and

---

[8] See paras 8–168 to 8–174, above. Note also *Sealand of the Pacific v. Robert C. McHaffie Ltd* (1974) 51 D.L.R. (3d) 702: naval architects held on the facts to have agreed to make enquiries as to the suitability of certain concrete for an aquarium beyond talking to the suppliers and looking at a pamphlet concerning the use of the concrete in a different manner from that intended.

[9] See paras 8–175 to 8–179, above.

[10] *ibid.*

[11] [1979] 2 N.Z.L.R. 441.

[12] Compare *Christopher Moran Holdings Ltd v. Carden & Godfrey* (1999) 73 Con.L.R. 28, where architects who advised their client that the provision of mechanical and electrical services for a swimming pool was outside their expertise and that he should retain specialist consultants were held to have discharged their duty.

[13] Note in this regard *Voli v. Inglewood Shire Council* [1963] A.L.R. 657, 663–664.

[14] See *Christopher Moran Holdings Ltd v. Carden & Godfrey* (1999) 73 Con.L.R. 28, where Judge Wilcox held that architects were in breach of duty in failing to explain to their client the nature of a revision to their design, the reasons for it and the options open to him in respect of it.

build contractor which maintains its own in-house design expertise and is sent the plans for the purpose of checking and approving them.

Architects and engineers commonly seek to defend their designs against criticism by relying on approvals granted by building control and other authorities. This defence typically fails. In *Eames London Estates Ltd v. North Hertfordshire District Council*[15] an industrial building was constructed on made ground. The foundations proved inadequate because the architect entrusted with the design of the building including the foundations had made no investigation of ground conditions. Judge Edgar Fay Q.C. held that the architect should have satisfied himself about the land's bearing capacity and that he could not shed his responsibility for foundations by ascertaining what would "get by the local authority", as he appeared to have done. The Commonwealth authorities are to the same effect. In *Voli v. Inglewood Shire Council*,[16] the defendant architects designed a stage which collapsed because the joists supporting it were insufficiently strong. The High Court of Australia held that it was no defence for the architects to point to the fact that their design had been passed by the Public Works Department. Similarly, in *Nova Scotia Home for Coloured Children v. Avramovitch*,[17] where a sewage disposal system failed because the ground conditions at site were unsuitable, Rogers J. rejected the designer's defence based on approvals and advice given by the Provincial Department of Health. In *Voli*, Windeyer J. conceded that the fact that plans were approved by a public authority might in some cases, although not on the facts of that particular case, be relevant in considering whether or not an architect was in fact negligent. In the common situation of an architect's or engineer's negligent design having been approved by a local authority building inspector, it is submitted that such approval will be treated by the courts as irrelevant to the issue of the architect's or engineer's liability. *Murphy v. Brentwood District Council*[18] makes it clear that, in England, in the usual exercise of its statutory powers a local authority owes no duty to anyone to protect them against economic loss. Such responsibility will rest solely with the architect or engineer who is employed to draw up the plans.[19]

8–203

Compliance with the client's brief. The designer should take reasonable care to provide a design which meets his client's requirements. If the client expresses his instructions in terms which leave the designer in doubt as to what the client's purpose is, the designer has a duty to seek clarification so as to ascertain what is the purpose he is instructed to achieve. Judge Bowsher Q.C. made this point in *Stormont Main Working Men's Club v. J. Roscoe Milne Partnership*.[20] In that case, the plaintiff complained that an extension to the club which had been designed by the defendant architects was defective because the position of pillars meant that the space around the snooker tables was less than that required for national competitions. The judge found, on the facts, that the plaintiff had not

8–204

---

[15] (1980) 259 E.G. 491. See para. 8–184, above.
[16] [1963] A.L.R. 657.
[17] (1983) 58 N.S.R. (2d) 267.
[18] [1991] 1 A.C. 398. For discussion of this case see para. 8–082, above.
[19] In *Targett v. Torfaen Borough Council* [1992] 3 All E.R. 27, the Court of Appeal emphasised that the essential question, in deciding whether a tortfeasor was liable for personal injuries caused by a defect of which the plaintiff had knowledge, was whether it was reasonable for the plaintiff to avoid the danger given the knowledge. See further para. 8–079, above.
[20] (1988) 13 Con.L.R. 126, 133.

intended to create facilities for playing competition snooker and had given no instructions to that effect. The architects reasonably understood that their client's purpose in instructing them was to get planning permission for an extension allowing whatever improvement to the games facilities was practicable and were not negligent in designing the same.

8–205   **Novel designs.** Especially where a design is experimental or in need of amplification as the construction progresses, an architect is under a continuing duty to consider whether his design will work in practice and to correct any errors which may emerge.[21] In the case of a novel design, failure may be consistent with the exercise of reasonable care and skill. In *Turner v. Garland and Christopher*,[22] Erle J. directed the jury:

> "You should bear in mind that if the building is of an ordinary description, in which he [the architect] has an abundance of experience, and it proved a failure, this is evidence of a want of skill and attention. But if out of ordinary course, and you employ him about a novel thing, about which he has little experience, if it has not had the test of experience, failure may be consistent with skill. The history of all great improvements shows failure of those who embark in them; this may account for the defect of the roof."

But, particularly where the failure of a novel design may present danger and a threat to safety, it will be incumbent on the designer to show that his design, albeit novel, is capable of rational analysis and to anticipate, and to provide for, all possible causes of failure.[23] Prudence may even justify the abandonment of a design.[24]

8–206   Where specialist suppliers or sub-contractors are involved in the development of a novel design, the construction professional must avoid the temptation to assume that any failure of the design will not result in a finding of liability against him. It will be in the short-term interests of suppliers or sub-contractors to under-specify so as to keep their prices low and increase their prospects of obtaining the work. The construction professional should take care to protect his client against loss resulting from inadequate design or specification by others. In *Try Build Ltd v. Invicta Leisure Tennis Ltd*,[25] structural and civil engineers were engaged by a building owner in connection with the design and construction of two tennis halls. The claimant was the design and build contractor, to whom the engineers' contract was novated. The claimant contracted with a specialist sub-contractor for the design, supply and construction of the roofs of the halls. The design was novel: each roof comprised four inflated foil cushions held in place by a rope

---

[21] For discussion of the nature and scope of the designer's duty to review his design, see paras 8–123 to 8–129, above.

[22] (1853) cited in *Hudson's Building Contracts* (4th ed.), Vol. 2, p. 1 (architect employed to plan and superintend buildings incorporating new patent concrete roofs absolved of want of competent skill despite failure of roofs).

[23] See *Eckersley v. Binnie* (1988) 18 Con.L.R. 1, discussed further at para. 8–208 below.

[24] See *I.B.A. v. E.M.I. and B.I.C.C.* (1980) 14 B.L.R. 1, 14 discussed in para. 8–097, above and *Bevan Investments Ltd v. Blackhall and Struthers (No. 2)* [1973] 2 N.Z.L.R. 45, 65–66 discussed in n. 89 to para. 8–121, above.

[25] (2000) 1 Con.L.R. 141.

edge detail. The roofs leaked. Having carried out remedial works pursuant to its obligations under the building contract, the claimant sought damages from the engineers in respect of its losses. It was common ground that the causes of the leakage were (a) tearing of the foil at the edge details because the foil was too thin and (b) faulty design of the waterproofing details. Judge Bowsher Q.C. held that both matters were the result of breach of duty on the part of the engineers. They should have specified the conditions in which the roofs were required to be watertight and the required thickness of the edge foils. The judge rejected the engineers' arguments that those were matters which they were entitled to leave to the specialist contractor, and held that even if they were, the engineers should have advised their clients that this was what they were doing. Furthermore, the engineers should have advised on the need for tests to establish that the novel features of the design had been successfully developed by the sub-contractor. Had they done so, such tests would have revealed that the edge foils were too thin. The engineers' evidence that they had trusted in the expertise of the specialist sub-contractor was no answer: "Engineers who are engaged to supervise and check the work of others are not paid to trust those others blindly, though the degree of trust or lack of it may affect the depth of enquiries made."[26]

8–207 Judge Bowsher Q.C. applied the same principles in *Baxall Securities Ltd v. Sheard Walshaw Partnership*.[27] The defendant architects were held to have been negligent in failing to specify which of the rainfall rates identified in the relevant British Standard was to be assumed by a specialist sub-contractor in its design of a roof drainage system. They ought to have appreciated that, left to its own devices, the sub-contractor would be tempted to design on the basis of the lowest (and therefore the cheapest) rainfall rate. The foreseeable use of the property was such that this was not the appropriate rate.

Assessment of risk. A designer must take reasonable care to assess and cater **8–208** in his design for all those risks which he can reasonably foresee. In *Eckersley v. Binnie*,[28] the defendant engineers were found negligent and thus responsible for the Abbeystead disaster in which 16 people died and others were injured. As the judge at first instance held,[29] the central issue in the case was whether the accumulation of methane in the tunnel and valve house in sufficient quantities to cause the explosion ought reasonably to have been foreseen at the design stage. A majority in the Court of Appeal held that it ought.[30] Russell L.J. identified[31] the risks which a careful designer would not ignore by reference to the speech of

---

[26] *ibid.* at 169.

[27] [2001] P.N.L.R. 256. For the facts, see para. 8–082, above. See also *South Lakeland District Council v. Curtins Consulting Engineers plc*, unreported, May 23, 2000, Judge Thornton Q.C. (engineers were negligent in failing to specify performance standards for car park slabs to be supplied by a specialist sub-contractor and to check the sub-contractor's design calculations).

[28] (1988) 18 Con.L.R. 1. For the facts, see para. 8–079 above. See also *Adams v. Rhymney Valley District Council* [2001] P.N.L.R. 68, CA (design of window locking systems for local authority housing held not negligent although the choice of design led to fatalities when the windows could not be used as means of escape during a house fire).

[29] *ibid.* at 4.

[30] Although Bingham L.J.'s dissenting judgment (especially at 84–114) appears to provide a coherent and convincing argument to the effect that it was not foreseeable at the time of the design to a reasonably competent engineer.

[31] *ibid.* at 52.

Lord Reid in *The Wagon Mound*,[32] where, dealing with remote risks, Lord Reid said:

> "It does not follow that, no matter what the circumstances may be, it is justifiable to neglect a risk of such a small magnitude. A reasonable man would only neglect such a risk if he had a valid reason for doing so: eg. that it would involve considerable expense to eliminate the risk. He would weigh the risk against the difficulty of eliminating it. . . . a person must be regarded as negligent if he does not take steps to eliminate a risk which he knows or ought to know is a real risk and not a mere possibility which would never influence the mind of a reasonable man."

8–209   Similarly, in *Pride Valley Foods Ltd v. Hall & Partners (Contract Management) Ltd*,[33] it was held that project managers engaged for the design and construction of a bread-making factory had negligently failed to warn the client that the expanded polystyrene panels which he wished to use in order to keep costs down were highly combustible and, if ignited, would lead to a rapid spread of fire through the factory. The defendants' case was that they had indeed given such advice in the course of several conversations with their client, but it was found on the facts that they had not. The case illustrates the value of written confirmation of important advice to the client as to the risks of a design; had the defendants in *Pride Valley Foods* adopted that course, the issues in the case would have been considerably narrower.

8–210   In the Canadian case of *City of Brantford v. Kemp and Wallace-Carruthers & Associates Ltd*[34] it was held that where one design involved an element of risk compared with another, an engineer was under a duty to inform the employer of the element of risk and the superior safety of the alternative design. In that case the site for a new fire hall and police station consisted of an old rubbish tip. The safer design entailed supporting the whole building on piles. The riskier but cheaper design adopted was a "floor on earth" method which entailed supporting the main walls on piles but placing partition walls on floors laid on granular fill and suspended from the main walls. Proper examination of the site would have demonstrated the need for the safer design but the engineers had not carried out such examination either before or during excavations. They were held liable in negligence for the subsequent failure of the internal walls and floors. The Court of Appeal of Victoria followed *City of Brantford* in *Pullen v. Gutteridge*[35] in finding that engineers who had designed a swimming pool complex were negligent in not having warned the employer about the risks involved in their design and for not having suggested possible alternatives. The complex was constructed in an area with complex ground conditions and the court also found the engineers to be liable for not having taken into account experience at another, relatively nearby, site where long-term settlement had been experienced. It was held that either the engineers should have carried out further investigations to see whether similar settlement was likely or the complex should have been designed on the assumption that such settlement would be experienced.[36]

---

[32] [1967] A.C. 617 at 642.
[33] (2001) 76 Con.L.R. 1 (first instance). The Court of Appeal upheld the judge's finding on breach of duty, but remitted the case for retrial on the issue of causation: [2001] E.W.C.A. Civ. 1001, (2001) 76 Con.L.R. 1,36.
[34] (1960) 23 D.L.R. (2d) 641.
[35] [1993] 1 V.R. 27.
[36] *ibid.* at 48.

Published standards. In preparing a design the provisions of relevant build-   **8–211**
ing regulations and bye laws will need to be observed. Codes of practice should
be considered and departed from only with the most careful consideration of the
consequences. This topic is more fully considered above.[37]

Level of detail. A difficult question is the degree of detail required to be   **8–212**
included in plans, drawings and specifications.[38] Some omissions may be clearly
negligent.[39] Generally, however, the degree of detail required will depend upon
the facts of each case, in particular the nature of the architect's instructions and
the documents concerned. There will be wide differences of detail and even
accuracy required as between a preliminary design plan, a plan submitted for
planning permission and a working drawing. Owing to these varying circumstances many reported cases concerning negligence in design provide scant
indication as to a court's approach on other albeit superficially similar facts.[40]

Choice of materials. Choice of materials is an essential part of design.   **8–213**
Usually materials will be so familiar as to require no inquiry as to their suitability. In the case of untried or novel materials, whether used alone or in
conjunction with established materials, the exercise of reasonable care may

---

[37] See paras 8–156 to 8–162 and 8–198 to 8–200, above.

[38] Note *Keete v. King* [1938] E.G.D. 65. A collapse of a wall demonstrated the defectiveness of the
bill of quantities in failing to provide for shoring. MacNaghten J. considered this to amount to a
"grave omission" and held the architect who prepared the bill liable to the employer. The architect
owed a duty to prepare plans which were sufficient for the purpose of erecting the building.

[39] Note Sachs L.J.'s example of a design of a house without a staircase in *Worboys v. Acme
Investments Ltd* (1969) 210 E.G. 335, CA. Also see paras 8–142 to 8–148, above concerning the
importance of evidence of general practice.

[40] *Saunders and Collard v. Broadstairs Local Board* (1890) cited in *Hudson's Building Contracts* (4th
ed., 1914), Vol. 2, p. 164 (engineers instructed to design and supervise construction of sewerage
scheme negligent in failing; (i) to prepare plans showing properly works to be executed, (ii) to specify
adequate mix of concrete, (iii) to allow for proper ventilation); *Dennis v. Symons and Harris* [1937]
E.G.D. 56 (architect negligent in failing to allow enough airspace at back of building); *Stern and
Sirotkin v. Oakfield Estates Ltd* [1937] E.G.D. 70 (negligence counterclaim against architects comprising many items, some failing some succeeding, including one for failing to allow sufficient
headway in staircases); *Rayment v. H.G. Needham and Son* (1953) 163 E.G. 4 (architect instructed to
plan for rebuilding of war damaged property alleged to have been negligent in failing to make proper
provision for ventilation in cellar. Held not negligent; restoring cellar to same condition as before
seemed to comply with what a reasonable architect might have done at the time. Employer's appeal,
reported at (1953) 163 E.G. 542, dismissed); *Gilbridge v. Sincock* (1955) 166 E.G. 129 (drawing error
in roof structure by architect's assistant resulting in major alteration in size of bedrooms contrary to
approved plan: architect held negligent); *Worboys v. Acme Investments Ltd* (1969) 210 E.G. 215
(negligence conceded by architect in respect of improper siting of two houses on site plan; negligence
claim for making no provision for downstairs lavatories failed in absence of professional evidence of
failure to exercise due care); *London Congregational Union Inc. v. Harriss and Harriss* [1985] 1 All
E.R. 335 (negligent design of drainage systems: an appeal on the issue of limitation was upheld in
part at [1988] 1 All E.R. 15); *Kaliszewska v. John Clague & Partners* (1984) 5 Con.L.R. 62 (negligent
design of foundations); *George Hawkins v. Chrysler (U.K.)* (1986) 38 B.L.R. 36 (judge's finding that
third party engineers not liable for negligent design of showers at work-place upheld on appeal);
Governors of Board of Hospitals for Sick Children v. McLaughlin & Harvey (1987) Con.L.R. 25
(engineers who modified pile design were negligent in that the pile caps were (i) staggered for no
reason, (ii) too thin and (iii) did not comply with well-known "rule of thumb" as to their depth);
Willerby Caravan Company Ltd v. Liddle, unreported, July 9, 1999, CA (architect and surveyor held
not negligent upon failure of drainage system designed by him; the cause of failure was the
sequencing of the works, which was not his responsibility).

require an architect or engineer to make proper enquiries as to their suitability.[41] The same applies to the choice of proprietary products or systems: a construction professional may be required to make extensive enquiries as to the design assumptions adopted by the specialist supplier in developing such product or system. Thus, in *Michael Hyde & Associated Ltd v. J.D. Williams & Co. Ltd*,[42] the defendant architects were found negligent in accepting the assurances of a gas heating system salesman that the risk of discoloration of stored textiles by the system was minimal. When discoloration to materials stored by their client did occur, it was held that the defendants should have appreciated that the supplier's refusal to withdraw its disclaimer of liability for discoloration suggested that the risk was a serious one, notwithstanding the salesman's denials, and made enquiries of the supplier's technical department. The cases of *Gloucestershire Health Authority v. Torpy*[43] and *Hammersmith Hospitals NHS Trust v. Troup Bywaters & Anders*[44] both concerned complaints that building services engineers had negligently failed to make adequate investigations into the suitability and capacity of proprietary incinerator systems before advising that they be installed in hospitals. In the *Gloucestershire Health Authority* case, the engineers were found negligently to have failed to appreciate that the incinerators did not have the required output, because they had failed to investigate their capacity before advising the employer to accept the supplier's tender. In the *Hammersmith Hospitals* case, it was held that the engineers were not negligent, primarily because there was expert evidence that a reasonably competent building services engineer in 1991 would have accepted the manufacturer's data without independent verification and because the engineers were aware that the client would be required to accept the incinerators only if they passed post-installation performance tests.

8-214   **Buildability.** Two aspects of design which a designer should bear in mind are "buildability" and "supervisability". The Construction (Design and Management) Regulations 1994 require a designer to ensure that his design is safely buildable.[45] Further, as Judge Newey Q.C said in *Equitable Debenture Assets Corp. Ltd v. William Moss Group Ltd*[46]:

> "I think that if implementation of part of a design requires work to be carried out on site, the designer should ensure that the work can be performed by those likely to be employed to do it, in the conditions which can be foreseen, by the exercise of the care and skill ordinarily to be expected by them. If the work would demand exceptional skill, and particularly if it would have to be performed partly from scaffolding and often in

---

[41] See *Sealand of the Pacific v. Robert C. McHaffie* (1974) 51 D.L.R. (3d) 702 and also discussed in n. 71 to para. 8–116, above. Note also the facts of *Merton LBC v. Lowe* (1981) 18 B.L.R. 130, CA discussed at para. 8–178, above; *Richard Roberts Holdings Ltd v. Douglas Smith Stimson Partnership* (1988) 46 B.L.R. 50 (architects negligent in failing adequately to investigate linings of effluent tanks: see para. 8–141, above; and *Privest Properties v. Foundation Co. of Canada* (1995) 128 D.L.R. (4th) 577 upheld at (1997) 143 D.L.R. (4th) 635 (architects who specified product should have been aware that it contained asbestos before specification); *George Hawkins v. Chrysler (U.K.)* (1986) 38 B.L.R. 36 (engineers who selected shower room tiles after careful consideration of product data sheets and trade brochures and consultation with specialist flooring firm was held not negligent even although tiles turned out to be slippery).
[42] [2001] P.N.L.R 233, CA.
[43] (1997) 55 Con.L.R. 124.
[44] [2000] Env.L.R. 343, affirmed on appeal ([2001] E.W.C.A. 793, unreported, May 25, 2001).
[45] The regulations are discussed at para. 8–046, above.
[46] (1984) 2 Con.L.R. 1,21 (architects held negligent in various respects in relation to the design of curtain walling which was subject to extensive leaking).

windy conditions, then the design will lack what the experts in evidence described as 'buildability'. Similarly, I think that if a design requires work to be carried out on-site in such a way that those whose duty it is to supervise it and/or check that it has been done will encounter great difficulty in doing so, then the design will again be defective. It may perhaps be described as lacking 'supervisability'."

In *Department of National Heritage v. Steenson Varming Mulcahy*,[47] Judge Bowsher Q.C. cited Judge Newey's dictum with approval, pointing out[48]:

" . . . the words 'those likely to be employed to do [the work]' used by Judge Newey are important and are to be related to the differing facts of each case. It is not to be assumed in every case that the work is to be done by the 'ordinary' tradesman, in this case 'the ordinary electrician' . . . The designer is entitled to look at the facts of the project on which he is engaged and consider what is the standard of workmanship required by the employer and agreed by the contractor to be provided to do the particular work."

On the facts of that case, the judge rejected a contention that there was such widespread installation of defective cabling on the British Library project as to give rise to an inference that the design was at fault. Further, he held that the defendant engineers were entitled to expect that their design, which specified a high standard of finish, would be executed by a contractor which was able to meet that high standard. The roof design chosen by the defendants in *George Fischer Holding Ltd v. Multi Design Consultants Ltd*[49] for a warehouse was found to have been negligent because of, apparently, its lack of buildability. The design required the roof slopes to be clad using panels which were not continuous from eaves to ridge, but comprised a series of panels laid end to end and joined by "end laps". The design required perfect construction of the end lap joints if the roof was to be watertight. That was an unrealistic expectation. The use of end lap joints could and should have been avoided altogether.

Integration of design. It will often be the case that a designer instructed to **8–215** design only a part of a building will need to take account of the design of other parts. Thus in the South Australian case of *Carosella v. Ginos and Gilbert*[50] engineers were held negligent in recommending foundations designed without regard to the nature of the superstructure. However it appears from the decision of the majority in the Court of Appeal in *Holland Hannen & Cubitts (Northern) Ltd v. Welsh Health Technical Services Organisation*[51] that designers will not generally be required to consider their design from a point of view which goes beyond the extent of their own discipline. In that case CED were nominated sub-contractors to the plaintiff main contractors in respect of the design and supply of concrete floors for a hospital. AMP were engineers employed by CED who advised on the structural aspects of the floors. The original design was such that the profile of the floors would comply with CP116 but there was a subsequent change, made without reference to AMP, so that the floors were required to comply with CP204. The main contractors experienced difficulties in erecting partitions and a survey discovered that the floors complied with CP116 but not

---

[47] (1998) 60 Con.L.R. 33.
[48] *ibid.* at 85.
[49] (1998) 61 Con. L.R. 85.
[50] (1981) 27 S.A.S.R. 515.
[51] (1985) 35 B.L.R. 1.

CP204. It was apparent upon a visual inspection that the floors were not completely level, although there would have been no difficulty in pushing trolleys over the floors. The architects sought to condemn the floors and a delay resulted. The main contractors then sued both the employer and CED for loss and expense occasioned by the delay, whereupon CED brought in AMP. The Court of Appeal was agreed that AMP's obligation was to exercise the reasonable skill and care of ordinarily competent engineers but were divided as to the result of the application of this test. Lawton L.J. said[52]:

> "It would not be part of their function to visualise what the floors would look like when the final finishes had been applied. The appearance of the floors would be for the architect to visualize."

Dillon L.J. agreed[53]:

> "As I see it, however, matters of visual appearance or aesthetic effect are matters for the architect and are not within the province of the structural engineer. It is for the structural engineer to work out what the deflections of a floor will be; it is for the architect to decide whether a floor with those deflections will be visually or aesthetically satisfactory when the finishes chosen by the architect have been applied."

Robert Goff L.J. disagreed, taking the view[54] that the engineer was under a duty to ask himself the question "whether there is a significant risk that the floor, with that profile, in the building in question, may be unacceptable." He would have held that, as CED were effectively lay clients of AMP, they were under:

> "a duty to draw to the attention of their clients any matter within their expertise which might result in a significant risk of the structure being unacceptable to the building owner or his architect, and I can see no reason why this should exclude a risk that an aspect of the configuration of the structure might render it visually unacceptable."[55]

It is submitted that, whilst a designer may have no duty to consider his design from the point of view of a discipline which is not his own, he ought to take care to see that his design is compatible with the design of the remainder.

8–216   **Co-ordination of design.** As modern buildings have become more sophisticated, there has been an increasing use of specialist suppliers, sub-contractors and consultants. As the parties involved in a building project proliferate, the employer's desire for a single point of professional contact increases. The result is that a construction professional in general practice may find himself appointed "lead consultant", with responsibility for co-ordinating the work of numerous specialists who have greater expertise in their respective areas than he does. The duty to co-ordinate elements of the overall design which have been prepared by others can be an onerous duty. In *Equitable Debenture Assets Corp. Ltd v.*

---

[52] *ibid.* at 11. In their article "Are architects and engineers responsible for buildability in design?" (2000) 16 Const.L.J. 3, Philip Harris and Jonathan Leach argue that buildability is the sole province of the building contractor. It is submitted that the better view is that both the construction professional charged with design and the building contractor have a responsibility in relation to buildability; the extent of their respective responsibilities will depend on the facts in each case.

[53] *ibid.* at 31.

[54] *ibid.* at 25.

[55] *ibid.* at 26.

William Moss Group Ltd,[56] the defendant architects properly sought the assistance of specialist walling consultants, but failed properly to co-ordinate their work. They failed, amongst other things, to ask the consultants to make inquiries about the curtain walling sub-contractor, to enlist the consultants' help in checking and approving the sub-contractor's tender, to take steps to bring about co-operation between the contractor and the consultants in the preparation of working drawings and to involve the consultants fully in the supervision and inspection of the curtain walling installation.[57]

Client-instructed change to design. A designer will often be found to have **8–217** particularly onerous obligations if he is asked to review his design in order to overcome a specific obstacle. Thus in *Leach v. Crossley*,[58] the defendant engineers were engaged to produce engineering plans for the construction of a warehouse with a car park on its roof. A perfectly satisfactory initial design was prepared for the structural support of the car park assuming the use of a lightweight waterproofing material supplied by a particular company. Through no fault of the defendants, it was discovered that the material would not be satisfactory and an alternative would have to be used. The defendants were asked for the maximum weight that the car deck could carry so that possible alternatives could be investigated. Instead of re-doing the calculations, the defendants simply gave the figure for the weight of material allowed for in the design. They were held to have been negligent and liable to the plaintiffs when another light material which was within this weight failed on the basis that the roof could, in fact, have carried a heavier material.[59]

Over-design. Occasionally, the complaint will be that a designer has taken **8–218** excessive precautions in his design. One such case was *London Underground v. Kenchington Ford plc*.[60] The defendant engineers were engaged to design the station concourse slab for one of the new stations on the Jubilee Line extension. London Underground alleged that reasonably competent engineers would have designed a thinner, and therefore cheaper, slab than that which the defendants designed. Judge Wilcox dismissed the claim. There was expert evidence of a respectable school of thought in the structural engineering profession which would have adopted the defendants' approach.

---

[56] (1984) 2 Con.L.R. 1,21 (architects held negligent in various respects in relation to the design of curtain walling which was subject to extensive leaking).

[57] Where specialists are used to supply and install proprietary systems, there is a particular temptation for the generalist construction professional to neglect his duty by placing too much reliance upon the assumed expertise of those specialists: see the cases discussed at paras 8–205 and 8–213, above.

[58] (1984) 8 Con.L.R. 7. See, further, paras 8–123 to 8–129, above.

[59] See also *Richard Roberts Holdings Ltd v. Douglas Smith Stimson Partnership and Others* (1988) 46 B.L.R. 50 (architects held to have been negligent in design of effluent tank lining where original satisfactory lining rejected by client on grounds of cost); *Governors of Board of Hospitals for Sick Children v. McLaughlin & Harvey* (1987) 19 Con.L.R. 25 (engineers found negligent in respect of pile design which had been revised in order to save money where original design would have been satisfactory); *Pride Valley Foods Ltd v. Hall & Partners (Contract Management) Ltd* (2001) 76 Con.L.R. 1 (first instance), [2001] E.W.C.A. Civ. 1001, (2001) 76 Con.L.R. 1,36, CA (project managers held negligent in failing to warn the client that his chosen materials were highly combustible and if ignited would allow rapid spread of fire throughout the factory).

[60] (1998) 63 Con.L.R. 1.

(e) *Preparation of bills of quantities*

8–219 It is usually the function of a quantity surveyor to prepare bills of quantities. But when the task is undertaken by an architect or engineer he will be under the same duty as that required of a quantity surveyor, namely to take reasonable care and skill. Quantities are commonly prepared by reference to standard methods of measurements, with which a quantity surveyor is expected to be familiar. As demonstrated by *London School Board v. Northcroft, Son and Neighbour*,[61] minor errors may be insufficient to establish negligence in the preparation of quantities. Conversely, the greater the errors, whether in number or consequence, the more difficult it will be to resist a finding of negligence.[62] A quantity surveyor should take care to ensure that the quantities are reasonably sufficient and not excessive.[63] In practice a quantity surveyor often operates through the architect to whom he reports matters for onward transmission to the client if necessary. The quantity surveyor should take reasonable care to procure that the information is transmitted to the client, since he is under a direct obligation to him, although normally the quantity surveyor can assume that the architect will pass it on.[64] In addition to his duties to the client employer, a quantity surveyor may owe a *Hedley Byrne* duty to a contractor in respect of the preparation of bills of quantities included in tender documentation.[65]

(f) *Selection of contractor and the tender process*

8–220 A construction professional engaged by a building owner may be required to advise as to the means by which a contractor for the works should be selected. Unless the works require the unique skills of a particular contractor, or there is some particular urgency which makes a tender process impracticable, a construction professional should normally advise his client to select a contractor through a process of competitive tender rather than enter negotiations for a contract with a single contractor. In *Hutchinson v. Harris*,[66] an architect was held negligent in failing to put the work of converting a house out to competitive tender.

---

[61] (1889) *Hudson's Building Contracts* (4th ed., 1914), Vol. 2, p. 149.

[62] See generally para. 8–164, above including reference to the quantity surveyor case of *Tyrer v. District Auditor of Monmouthshire* (1973) 230 E.G. 973.

[63] Note *Keete v. King* [1938] E.G.D. 65. For facts see n. 38 to para. 8–212, above; note also *Saunders and Collard v. Broadstairs Local Board* (1890) reported in *Hudson's Building Contracts* (4th ed.), Vol. 2, p. 164; also note *Tyrer v. District Auditor of Monmouthshire* (1973) 230 E.G. 973 (quantity surveyor approved excessive quantities and prices in some contracts with builders when it was his duty not to accept rates he must have known to be ridiculously high: held negligent).

[64] *Aubrey Jacobus and Partners v. Gerrard*, unreported, June 1981, *per* Judge Stabb Q.C. For brief facts see n. 96 to para. 8–196, above.

[65] See generally paras 8–062 to 8–129 above on the subject of duty of care to third parties and in particular paras 8–103 to 8–109 concerning duties owed to contractors. In two late 19th century cases, claims by contractors against quantity surveyors arising from deficient quantities failed. In *Young v. Blake* (1887) reported in *Hudson's Building Contracts* (4th ed., 1914), Vol. 2, p. 110 the claim (against architects who were also quantity surveyors) was rejected on the ground that in being given power to measure the works and adjust the quantities, the architects were put in a quasi-judicial position and could not be sued for negligence or breach of warranty. Following *Sutcliffe v. Thackrah* [1974] A.C. 727 the particular ground of rejection no longer represents good law. In *Priestly v. Stone* (1888) 4 T.L.R. 730 the claim was rejected on the ground that there was no privity of contract between the builder and the quantity surveyor.

[66] 1977 (unreported), a decision of Judge Edgar Fay Q.C. at first instance. The appeal in the case is reported in (1978) 10 B.L.R. 19, from which the decision at first instance is apparent. An application by the architect for leave to cross-appeal out of time was refused.

A construction professional acting for a building owner or developer will **8–221** commonly be required by his terms of engagement to advise as to the list of contractors who are to be invited to tender and to appraise the tenders received. In each case, the exercise of reasonable care and skill may require him to make reasonable inquiries as to the solvency and capabilities of contractors, including nominated sub-contractors. An example is *Equitable Debenture Assets Corp. Ltd v. William Moss Group Ltd*,[67] where Judge Newey Q.C. held that architects were negligent in failing to make inquiries into the experience and capabilities of the nominated subcontractor which designed, supplied and installed what turned out to be defective curtain walling. Inquiries should have been made both before the subcontractor was invited to tender and after its tender had been submitted, in order properly to appraise that tender. In *Valerie Pratt v. George J. Hill Associates*,[68] architects were held to be in breach of their duty to recommend suitable reliable builders and guilty of negligent misrepresentation in describing as "very reliable" a builder who was, in fact, wholly unreliable. In *Partridge v. Morris*,[69] Judge Hicks Q.C. held that an architect who advised a lay client as to the acceptability of building tenderers should have checked their financial position. This they could and should have done by making enquiries of building merchants, obtaining bank references, obtaining trade credit references, making inquiries of other architects, arranging a company search or asking the contractor to provide its audited accounts for examination.

Further, the construction professional should take care, when examining the **8–222** amounts of quotations or tenders, not to advise the acceptance of rates which are unreasonable in the circumstances. In *Tyrer v. District Auditor of Monmouthshire*,[70] the quantity surveyor was found to have been in breach of duty when he approved quantities and prices in contracts with a contractor when he must have known that they were based on rates which were "ridiculously high".

(g) *Advice on choice and terms of a building contract*

A construction professional's engagement to advise upon choice of contractors **8–223** will commonly carry with it the obligation, whether express or implied, to consider the choice and terms of the contract between the employer and the contractor. There are many standard forms of building and engineering contract[71] and different forms will be appropriate for different types and sizes of project. In some cases, a contract drafted specifically for the project in hand will be appropriate. The exercise of reasonable care and skill may require the construction professional to advise the employer to reject a particular form of contract or a particular term if disadvantageous to the employer's interests.[72] Given the large

---

[67] (1984) 2 Con.L.R. 1 (architects held negligent in various respects in relation to the design of curtain walling which was subject to extensive leaking) at 26.

[68] Unreported; a decision of Recorder Barry Green Q.C. at first instance. The appeal is at (1987) 38 B.L.R. 25 where the only issue is as to damages but the issues at first instance are reasonably apparent.

[69] [1995] C.I.L.L. 1095.

[70] (1973) 230 E.G. 973

[71] Most of the standard forms in common use are reprinted in *Emden*, Vols 2–5.

[72] See the unreported decision in *Burrell Hayward & Budd v. Chris Carnell and David Green*, February 20, 1992, where a deputy official referee found that both the plaintiff quantity surveyors and the defendant architects were partially responsible for the use of an inappropriate building contract by the architect's clients; this had no causal effect, however, as the terms of the building contract were, in practice, ignored.

number of different standard forms which now exist and the multitude of decisions as to what particular provisions of the contract mean, it may be prudent for the architect either to seek himself or to advise his client to seek legal advice as to the meaning or effect of a particular term in a contract.[73] He should certainly do so if he is in real doubt as to the correct construction of an important term. It has been suggested that a construction professional may incur liability in negligence for recommending without modification (or proper explanation) one of the standard forms in general use in the United Kingdom,[74] but a professional should be cautious about recommending amendments to standard terms and, if in doubt as to the legal consequences of any proposed amendment, should take legal advice or recommend that the client does so.

8–224   If nominated sub-contractors or suppliers are to be used, the construction professional should normally advise the employer to refuse to nominate a particular sub-contractor unless that sub-contractor is prepared to guarantee or warrant directly to the employer the quality or fitness of his work and materials.

8–225   A building contract will normally comprise conditions of contract, contract drawings, a specification and a bill of quantities. Where professionals of different disciplines are involved in the preparation of the various constituent parts of the contract, care must be taken to see that they are consistent with each other. The drawings, specification and bill of quantities should together provide the contractor with a full and clear description of the work to be done. An architect may incur liability in negligence as well as for excess of authority if through failure to scrutinise contract documents he allows his client to enter into a contract for building works different from those which the client required him to provide for in specifications.[75]

(h) *Administration of the building contract*

8–226   Particularly when engaged in respect of a larger building project, a construction professional will commonly be responsible for performing a number of tasks which may collectively be described as administration of the main building contract. All the standard forms of building and engineering contracts provide for a named architect[76] or engineer.[77] The building contract gives certain powers and duties to that person to regulate the mutual rights and obligations of the employer and the building contractor. His tasks will include inspecting the works, issuing payment certificates, issuing orders for variation of the contract works, making decisions on the contractor's claims for extensions of time or for payment for delay and disruption, instructing the removal of defective work, determining the date of practical completion and loss and expense, and approving work to make

---

[73] See para. 8–160, above.

[74] Hudson, *op. cit.*, pp. 331–341.

[75] See *Kenny & Reynolds Ltd v. Pyper* [1964] E.G.D. 419 (error by architect in not deleting from specifications a percentage sum for a central heating system after decision to exclude the item, held to be inexcusable and negligent. On the facts the claim against the architect failed since the client was taken to have signed the building contract in the knowledge of the architect's error).

[76] See, for example, JCT Standard Form of Building Contract (1998 ed.), Art. 3A. The term is used where the person appointed is a registered architect. If he is not, then the same functions are performed by a "Contract Administrator" who is named in Art. 3B. The latter term replaces "Supervising Officer" in the 1980 edition of this standard form contract.

[77] See, for example, the ICE Conditions of Contract (1999 ed.).

good defects. The important functions of inspection and certification are considered in detail in the following sections of this chapter.[78]

Issuing instructions and information. Generally an architect should issue   **8–227** instructions and information required for the execution of works within a reasonable time. In *Neodox Ltd v. Borough of Swindon Pendlebury*,[79] Diplock J. held that there was no implied term in a civil engineering contract which required the employer, by his engineer, to provide information and instructions necessary for the execution of the works in sufficient time to enable the contractor to complete the works on time. He drew attention to the fact that the contract (like most building contracts) did not contemplate that the contractor would have all the required information before works commenced. Rather, it was anticipated that further information would be provided by the engineers during the course of the contract. There was therefore an implied term that necessary information and instructions would be given within a reasonable time. What amounts to a reasonable time will depend on the facts of each case, in particular the terms of the main building contract, but Diplock J. pointed out that reasonableness is not to be determined solely by reference to the interests of the contractor, but also by reference to the position of the engineer, his staff and the employer. Relevant factors would include the order in which the works are to be carried out, whether requests for particular information or instructions have been made by the contractor, whether the instructions relate to a variation to the works or to the original works and the time by which the contractor was required to complete the works.[80] Similarly, in *London Borough of Merton v. Stanley Hugh Leach Ltd*,[81] it was held that there was an implied term of the building contract (the JCT Standard Form of Building Contract, 1963 edition, July 1971 revision) that the architect would supply the contractor with accurate drawings and information during the course of the works. But for the fact that there were express terms in the building contract which required the architect to supply such instructions, drawings and information as were necessary for the contractor to complete its works in a regular and orderly manner and on time, it appears that such a term would have been implied.[82] Vinelott J. explained the position of the architect in the contractual relationship between employer and contractor[83]:

"under the standard conditions the architect acts as the servant or agent of the building owner in supplying the contractor with the necessary drawings, instructions, levels and the like and in supervising the progress of the work and in ensuring that it is properly carried out. He will of course normally though not invariably have been responsible for the design of the work. To the extent that the architect performs these duties the building owner contracts with the contractor that the architect will perform them with reasonable diligence and with reasonable skill and care. The contract also confers on the

---

[78] See paras 8–236 to 8–249 and 8–250 to 8–256 below.
[79] (1958) 5 B.L.R. 34.
[80] *ibid.* at 41–42. See also *Royal Brompton Hospital NHS Trust v. Hammond (No. 4)* [2000] B.L.R. 75, where Judge Hicks Q.C. held that consulting mechanical and electrical engineers had an obligation to use reasonable care and skill to see that their co-ordination drawings were provided in time to enable contractor to prepare his installation drawings and thus to carry out and complete the works in accordance with the contract programme. Provisions in the building contract which required the contractor to co-ordinate drawings did not dilute or alter the engineers' responsibility.
[81] (1985) 32 B.L.R. 51.
[82] *ibid.* at 81–83.
[83] *ibid.* at 78–79.

architect discretionary powers which he must exercise with due regard to the interests of the contractor and the building owner. The building owner does not undertake that the architect will exercise his discretionary powers reasonably; he undertakes that although the architect may be engaged or employed by him he will leave him free to exercise his discretion fairly and without improper interference by him . . . . [T]o the extent that the architect exercises these discretions his duty is to act fairly; 'the building owner and the contractor make their contract on the understanding that in all such matters the architect will act in a fair and unbiased manner and it must therefore be implicit in the owner's contract with the architect that he shall not only exercise due care and skill but also reach such decisions fairly, holding the balance between his client and the contractor' (see *Sutcliffe v. Thackrah* [1974] A.C. 727 *per* Lord Reid at p. 737)."

8–228   Implied terms such as those found in *Neodox* and in *Merton v. Leach* describe what the contract administrator has to do, as the employer's agent, to meet the employer's obligations to the contractor. Normally, the contractor's preferred remedy for late issue of information or instructions will be a claim against the employer under the building contract for an extension of time for completion or for payment in respect of delay and disruption, rather than a claim against the contract administrator in tort.[84] However, the contract administrator may be liable to indemnify the employer as his principal if his breach of duty puts the employer in breach of the building contract, renders him liable to the contractor for additional payments or causes him to incur costs by entitling the contractor to extensions of time.

8–229   On a complex or large project, the duties of a contract administrator may be onerous and require the exercise of good organisational and management skills. In *Corfield v. Grant*[85] Judge Bowsher Q.C. found an architect to be in breach of duty by reason of his failure properly to control a building project. The judge was particularly critical of the architect's failure to appoint and direct a suitably skilled and experienced assistant in a situation where the architect knew that speed was of the essence and it was necessary to organise a large number of matters at the same time. The judge found the architect to be responsible for the resultant "inadequately controlled muddle". In *The Royal Brompton Hospital NHS Trust v. Hammond (No. 1)*,[86] the Trust's predecessor had engaged Taylor Woodrow as main building contractor to carry out extensive building work at a hospital. The Trust settled Taylor Woodrow's claim for extra payments under the building contract and then claimed the costs of the settlement as damages against the various defendants, who had been the Trust's architects, engineers and project managers for the works. One of the Trust's allegations was that Taylor Woodrow had suffered loss and expense, which the Trust had been obliged under the building contract to pay, as a result of the "sheer number" of variation orders and instructions issued by the professional team during the course of the works. Judge Hicks Q.C. refused to strike out the allegation as bad in law, but made clear that it would require careful particularisation and proof.

8–230   Before ordering work additional to that agreed in the building contract, it will be both prudent and necessary in most cases to seek the express authority of the

---

[84] See paras 8–103 to 8–109 for discussion of the difficulties facing a claim in tort.
[85] (1992) 29 Con.L.R. 58.
[86] [1999] B.L.R. 162.

employer to do so. In *Wilks v. Thingoe (Suffolk) Regional District Council*[87] an architect was held negligent in having embarked on a course of extravagant expenditure without his employers' authority.

Applications for extensions of time and for extra payment. A construction   8–231
professional acting as contract administrator should take care in acceding to contractor's claims for extra payment and extensions of time. Any extensions granted and payments awarded should be reasonable and justified according to the terms of the main building contract. The contract administrator's duty in relation to applications for extensions of time was considered by the Supreme Court of New South Wales in *Perini Corporation v. Commonwealth of Australia*.[88] In that case, the building contract provided that the power to grant extensions of time lay with an official of the defendant, called the director of works. It was held that the director of works had a discretion whether to grant an extension of time, but was bound to give his decision on any application for an extension within a reasonable time; in the circumstances, that meant that he should give a decision as soon as his investigation into the facts was completed. Macfarlan J. said[89]:

"The measurement of a reasonable time in any particular case is always a matter of fact. Plainly the director must not delay, nor may he procrastinate, and in my opinion he is not entitled simply to defer a decision. On the other hand he is, in my opinion, and this follows from his obligation to give his own personal decision on the point, necessarily obliged to have available for that consideration such time as is necessary to enable him to investigate the facts which are relevant to making it. When that investigation is complete I am of the opinion that his decision should then be made."

The building contract in *London Borough of Merton v. Stanley Hugh Leach*   8–232
Ltd[90] provided that, if it became apparent that the progress of the works was delayed, the contractor should give written notice of the delay to the architect and the architect, if of the opinion that the works had been or were likely to be delayed, should grant an extension of time for completion.[91] The question arose whether the architect should grant an extension of time in the absence of written notice from the contractor. Vinelott J. held that the contract required the architect to estimate delay and, if appropriate, grant an extension of time, if he became aware of any event which was likely to cause delay and would entitle the contractor to an extension of time, regardless of whether he had received notice of delay from the contractor. The architect was not entitled to ignore events which were likely to cause delay to the works beyond the contractual completion

---

[87] (1954) 164 E.G. 86. Note as regards a quantity surveyor the unreported case of *Aubrey Jacobus & Partners v. Gerrard* (1981), the brief facts of which are given at n. 96 to para. 8–196, above, *per* Judge Stabb Q.C.: " . . . it is suggested that the quantity surveyor was under a duty to monitor or control the costs and advise the client. I am satisfied that no such duty exists. The architect is the team leader: he is primarily responsible for design and for the cost of it. If called upon, the quantity surveyor is there to provide information as to cost but not in my view to monitor or control it by carrying out checks at regular intervals as was suggested."

[88] (1969) 12 B.L.R. 82.

[89] *ibid.* at 102.

[90] (1985) 32 B.L.R. 51.

[91] The JCT Standard Form of Building Contract, 1963 ed., July 1971 revision, cl. 23. Care should be taken in applying the decision in cases concerning different contracts. Some contracts stipulate that the provision of notice by the contractor is a condition precedent to the contractor's entitlement to an extension of time.

date just because the contractor was not aware of the likely delay. However, if delay was reasonably apparent to the contractor but he failed to give written notice of it to the architect, that was a breach of contract by the contractor and could be taken into account by the architect in considering an extension of time.[92] It may be, for example, that the delay could have been reduced had the architect been given earlier notice of it; in that case, it may be appropriate to grant a shorter extension of time so that the contractor does not benefit from his breach of contract.

8–233   An architect is obliged to act fairly, lawfully, rationally and logically in considering an extension of time. In *John Barker Construction Ltd v. London Portman Hotel Ltd*,[93] Mr Recorder Toulson Q.C. held that the architect had failed to meet that standard. He had not carried out a logical analysis in a methodical manner of the impact which the delaying events had or were likely to have on the contractor's planned programme. He had made an impressionistic, rather than a calculated, assessment of the delay. He misapplied the provisions of the building contract and, where he allowed an extension of time, the allowances which he made bore no logical or reasonable relation to the delay in fact caused. The analysis required in order to assess the impact of delaying events upon the contractual completion date can be complex and the accuracy of the assessment will depend upon the quality of the information which is available to the architect, as the court recognised in *The Royal Brompton Hospital NHS Trust v. Hammond (No. 7)*.[94] Judge Seymour Q.C. heard evidence from an expert in construction programming, a Mr Gibson, and observed[95]:

> "Because the construction of a modern building, other than one of the most basic type, involves the carrying out of a series of operations, some of which, possibly, can be undertaken at the same time as some of the others, but many of which can only be carried out in a sequence, it may well not be immediately obvious which operations impact upon which other operations. In order to make an assessment of whether a particular occurrence has affected the ultimate completion of the work, rather than just a particular operation it is desirable to consider what operations, at the time the event with which one is concerned happens, are critical to the forward progress of the work as a whole. . . . the establishment of the critical path of a particular construction project can itself be a difficult task if one does not know how the contractor planned the job. Not only that, but the critical path may well change during the course of the works, and almost certainly will do if the progress of the works is affected by some unforeseen event. Mr Gibson frankly accepted that the various different methods of making an assessment of the impact of unforeseen occurrences upon the progress of construction works are likely to produce different results, perhaps dramatically different results. He also accepted that the accuracy of any of the methods in common use critically depends upon the quality of the information upon which the assessment exercise was based. All of this does, of course, emphasise the vital point that the duty of a professional man, generally stated, is not to be right, but to be careful. While, unless in a particular case the professional man is actually wrong, the fact that he has not been careful will probably not cause his client any loss, the fact that he is in the event proved to be wrong is not, in itself, any evidence that he has been negligent. His conduct has to be judged having regard to the information available to him, or which ought to have been

---

[92] (1985) 32 B.L.R. 51, 89–90.
[93] (1996) 83 B.L.R. 31.
[94] [2001] C.I.L.L. 1714.
[95] *ibid.* at 1716–1717. On the facts, only one of the employer's allegations of negligent grant of an unwarranted extension of time by the architect succeeded.

available to him, at the time he gave his advice or made his decision or did whatever else it is that he did."

Insurance and performance bonds. Building contracts commonly contain **8–234** provisions designed to preserve the employer's prospect of recovering losses if a defaulting contractor goes into liquidation. For example, the contractor may be required to provide a performance bond. Or he may be obliged to put in place insurance cover against his liabilities to the employer. Where such provisions are found, a construction professional acting for the employer should take care to see that his client's position is protected in the manner contemplated by the contract. The main action in *Convent Hospital v. Eberlin & Partners*[96] came about because the contractor had become insolvent without providing the performance bond required under the building contract. The employers alleged that their architect had been negligent in failing to see that a suitable bond was in force when the building contract was executed. Summary judgment was given for the employers. In *Pozzolanic Lytag Ltd v. Bryan Hobson Associates*,[97] the defendant engineers were appointed project managers in relation to the design and construction of storage facilities for pulverised fuel ash. Part of the works designed by the contractor collapsed due to design deficiencies. Although, under the building contract, the contractors should have been insured in respect of liability for such a collapse, they were not. Dyson J. held that the engineers, as project managers, were responsible for ensuring that insurance was in place and were liable to the plaintiff accordingly. He held that the fact that the project managers lacked the expertise necessary to assess the adequacy of the insurance arrangements which the contractor did have in place did not relieve them of their responsibility. He said[98]:

> "If a project manager does not have the expertise to advise his client as to the adequacy of the insurance arrangements proposed by the contractor, he has a choice. He may obtain expert advice from an insurance broker or lawyer. Questions may arise as to who has to pay for this. Alternatively, he may inform the client that expert advice is required, and seek to persuade the client to obtain it. What he cannot do is simply act as a 'postbox' and send the evidence of the proposed arrangements to the client without comment."

Notices of non-performance. Some standard form contracts contain provi- **8–235** sions allowing the contract administrator, on behalf of the employer, to issue notices warning a recalcitrant contractor of the consequences of poor performance.[99] The decision to issue such a notice should be the result of careful consideration. If a notice is negligently issued, the contractor may well incur loss

---

[96] Unreported, May 1, 1984. The facts of the main action are apparent from the first instance ((1989) 14 Con.L.R. 1) and Court of Appeal ((1989) 23 Con.L.R. 112) reports of the architects' third party proceedings against the contractors' managing director for fraudulently and/or negligently misrepresenting the position. For discussion of performance bonds in connection with certification, see para. 8–234 below.

[97] [1999] B.L.R. 267.

[98] *ibid.* at 272.

[99] See, for example, the JCT Standard Form of Building Contract (1998 ed.), cl. 27 (continuation of the specified default for 14 days after receipt of the notice entitles the employer to give notice to terminate the contractor's employment) and the ICE Conditions of Contract (7th ed. 1999), cl. 46(1) (if the rate of progress of the works is too slow to ensure completion by the contractual completion date, for any reason which does not entitle the contractor to an extension of time, the engineer may issue a notice to effect and the contractor must take steps to accelerate his progress).

and expense which he is entitled to recover from the employer and which the employer, in turn, will be able to recover from the contract administrator. On the other hand, a failure to act decisively to deal with a contractor's incompetence can also result in liability on the part of the contract administrator, as happened in *West Faulkner Associates v. London Borough of Newham*.[1] The defendant architects were engaged by a local authority to act as architect in respect of the refurbishment of a large number of flats which was being carried out by the contractor pursuant to JCT Standard Form of Building Contract, 1963 edition, 1977 revision. As a result of the contractor's inability properly to programme and supervise the works, the contractual completion date was substantially exceeded. Although Judge Newey Q.C. had sympathy for the architects, he found them to have been negligent in failing to serve a notice under clause 25(1)(b) of the contract stating that the contractor was failing to proceed regularly and diligently with the works (which notice would have led to the local authority being able to terminate the contractor's employment if its performance did improve). The judge said[2]:

> "The architects were without authoritative guidance as to the meaning of 'regularly and diligently'. They thought that provided [the contractor] had men and materials on site and were doing some work within the contractual period they were proceeding regularly and diligently. They did not seek to confirm this belief by consulting more experienced architects than themselves, taking legal advice or urging the council to take legal advice and communicate it to them . . .
>
> I think that if [the contractor's] failures had been less glaringly obvious the architects might have been justified in not serving a notice upon them—at least until they had obtained reliable guidance. Since however, [the contractor's] failures were so very extreme, I think that the architects should have realised that [the contractor] could not possibly be proceeding regularly and diligently and have given a notice to them. I feel sure that the ordinary competent architect would have taken that course . . . This was not a marginal case."

The Court of Appeal dismissed the appeal against the judge's decision. Brown L.J., with whom the other members of the Court agreed, held that a reasonably competent architect, who was required to have "a general knowledge of the law as applied to the most important clauses . . . of standard forms of building contract", could not have misconstrued the clause in the way that the defendant did. At the very least, he should have realised that it could be construed differently and either himself have taken legal advice or advised his client so to do.

(i) Supervision or inspection of the works

8–236   **Supervision or inspection?** Early forms of the RIBA Conditions of Engagement for the Appointment of an Architect provided that the architect was required to perform "periodical supervision" of the works.[3] Successive versions

---

[1] (1994) 71 B.L.R. 1, CA and (1992) 31 Con.L.R. 105, first instance.
[2] *ibid.* at 140.
[3] See, for example, Condition B of the 1962 Revision of the Conditions of Engagement, which was the clause under consideration in *Sutcliffe v. Chippendale and Edmondson* (1982) 18 B.L.R. 149: see para. 8–238, below.

of the RIBA Conditions have sought progressively to restrict the nature and scope of the architect's function in this respect. Thus the 1992 edition of the Standard Form of Agreement for the Appointment of an Architect referred, instead, to an obligation to carry out periodic inspections,[4] whereas the 1999 edition provides merely that the architect shall "make visits to the works in connection with [his] design"[5] and shall advise the client, where appropriate, that site inspectors should be appointed.[6] Such attempts by express terms to reduce the burden of the architect's obligation to consider the quality of the works as they progress are a reflection of the fact that claims against construction professionals in respect of defective works are very common.[7]

It is submitted that the difference between "supervision" and "inspection" is   **8–237**
not merely academic. In *Rowlands v. Collow*[8] Thomas J. drew a distinction between an engineer's obligation to "supervise" a building contract which involved "detailed and continuous direction" and an obligation to provide observation by way of oversight which required an engineer to carry out such inspections as were necessary to confirm that a design was being interpreted correctly and to ascertain that the works were being carried out in accordance with the contract documents.[9] A client who believes that his architect is supervising the building contractor will naturally consider that the architect has a greater responsibility if the works are defective than the client who understands that his architect is not on site for all or most of the time, but is carrying out inspections which are limited in number, duration and frequency. Accordingly, although the reported cases seldom reflect an understanding that a construction professional was obliged to maintain a full-time presence on site, caution is required when considering the older authorities which address an obligation to "supervise" rather than to inspect. For convenience, however, the term "supervision" is used below to refer generally to the obligation of a construction professional to monitor the quality of construction works.

The scope of the duty to supervise. The employer is entitled to expect his   **8–238**
architect or engineer so to administer and supervise the work as to ensure, as far as is reasonably possible, that the quality of the work matches up to the standard contemplated by the building contract.[10] In practice, the professional charged with supervising the works is likely also to be the professional whose responsibility it is to carry out administration of the building contract, including the task of certifying that the interim and final payments are due to the contractor. The certification function may require the architect or engineer to carry out detailed and frequent inspections. The inter-relationship between the supervision and certification functions was recognised by Judge Stabb Q.C. in *Sutcliffe v. Chippendale and Edmondson*[11]:

---

[4] cl. 3.1.
[5] Work Stage K1 and cl. 2.8.
[6] cl. 2.5.
[7] It may not be coincidence that inspection of the works is typically not a well-remunerated part of a construction professional's engagement; but the level of fee will not dictate the standard of care required: see *Brown v. Gilbert-Scott* (1992) 35 Con.L.R. 120, 123 *per* Mr Recorder Coles Q.C.
[8] [1992] 1 N.Z.L.R. 178 at 197.
[9] It was held that the engineer in an informal contract concerning the provision of a driveway was under an obligation to inspect only, but was nonetheless in breach of the same.
[10] *Sutcliffe v. Chippendale and Edmondson* (1982) 18 B.L.R. 149, 162, *per* Judge Stabb Q.C.
[11] (1982) 18 B.L.R. 149.

"Plainly it is part of an architect's duty of supervision, as agent for his employer, to see that the work is properly executed, and therefore to my mind supervision and the issuing of interim certificates cannot be regarded as wholly separate and distinct functions. . . . in a well supervised contract an architect would not certify for work not properly executed."

Similarly, in the Scottish case of *Jameson v. Simon*,[12] "reasonable supervision" was defined by Lord Trayner in such supervision as would enable the architect to certify that the work had been executed according to the contract. This is not to say that an construction professional who certifies payment for work which is fact defective because, despite reasonable skill and care, he is unaware of the defects, is necessarily in breach of his duty to supervise. This is one possible reading of the following words of Judge Bowsher Q.C. in *Corfield v. Grant*[13]:

"What is adequate by way of supervision and other work is not in the end to be tested by the number of hours worked on site or elsewhere, but by asking whether it was enough. At some stages of some jobs exclusive attention may be required to the job in question (either in the office or on site): at other stages of the same job, or during most of the duration of other jobs, it will be quite sufficient to give attention to the job only from time to time. The proof of the pudding is in the eating. Was the attention given enough for this particular job?"

Unfortunately the report does not make it clear whether the judge was discussing a contract where the architect was, in truth, obliged to supervise or whether he merely had an inspection obligation. The passage set out above is unexceptionable in so far as it states that a reasonably competent architect will realise that he needs to vary his input according to the nature of the job for which he is retained and the stage such a job has reached. Nevertheless in so far as the judge suggests that an architect's performance should be judged by the result achieved, it is submitted that the passage goes too far.[14] An architect's duty is to exercise reasonable skill and care in seeking to achieve a particular result; he does not guarantee that a particular result will be achieved.

8–239   Reasonable examination of the works does not require the architect to go into every matter in detail.[15] It is recognised that some defects and insufficiencies may escape his notice.[16] Further, it by no means follows that in failing to discover a defect which a reasonable examination would have disclosed the architect is necessarily negligent. The omission may be explicable as no more than an error of judgment or a deliberately calculated risk which in all the circumstances of the case was reasonable and proper.[17] Similarly in assessing the standard of materials

---

[12] (1899) 1 F. (Ct of Sess.) 1211, 1222.

[13] (1992) 29 Con.L.R. 58, 58–59.

[14] Apart, of course, from those rare cases where the maxim *res ipsa loquitur* applies. This may be the explanation for the decision in *Imperial College of Science and Technology v. Norman & Dawbarn* (1986) 8 Con.L.R. 107, where Judge Smout Q.C. held that architects had been negligent in their supervision by reference to the fact that some 75% of cladding tiles had been inadequately buttered.

[15] *Clemence v. Clarke* (1880) cited in *Hudson's Building Contracts* (4th ed.), Vol. 2, p. 54 at 59, *per* Grove J.

[16] *East Ham Corporation v. Bernard Sunley & Sons Ltd* [1966] A.C. 406, 428, *per* Viscount Dilhorne. See also *Victoria University of Manchester v. Hugh Wilson* (1984) 2 Con.L.R. 43, 76: on the facts the architects were held negligent in their supervision of the fixing of tiles.

[17] *ibid.* at 443 *per* Lord Upjohn.

and workmanship especially of a house "built down to a price" a certain degree of tolerance must be allowed for, although this does not give an architect a general dispensing power.[18]

Inspections by reference to stages of the works. As Judge Bowsher Q.C.   **8–240** pointed out in *Corfield v. Grant*,[19] the frequency and duration of inspections should be tailored to the nature of the works going on at site from time to time. The inspecting professional will not avoid a finding of negligence if he fails to see defects in the works because he has not arranged to examine critical stages of the works. This is illustrated by the decision in *Jameson v. Simon*.[20] In that case the architect was held negligent in failing to inspect the bottoming of the cement floor of a house either before or at the time the floor was laid. The bottoming was subsequently found to consist of waste material and to be the cause of dry rot. Evidence was adduced that the architect had visited the site on average once a week and had given as much supervision and inspection as it was customary to give according to the practice of architects. But that practice was insufficient to absolve the architect for failure to inspect so important a part of the work. Lord Trayner said[21]:

> "It is contended that the architect cannot be constantly at the work, and this is obviously true. But he or someone representing him should undoubtedly see to the principal parts of the work before they are hid from view, and if need be I think he should require a contractor to give notice before an operation is to be done which will prevent his so inspecting an important part of the work as to be able to give his certificates upon knowledge, and not an assumption, as to how work hidden from view had been done."

The defender architect had directed the plasterer who was to put down the cement to proceed with his work without knowing whether the work to be covered up by it had been properly done or not. Similarly, in *Brown v. Gilbert-Scott*[22] Mr Recorder Coles Q.C. held that the architect was only obliged to inspect works. Nonetheless, the architect was found to be in breach of duty because he had failed to inspect the works at a critical time, namely, the laying of the damp proof membrane.[23]

The responsibility for notifying the contractor that certain parts of the works   **8–241** should not be covered up before they have been inspected lies with the inspecting professional. In the Australian case of *Florida Hotels Pty Ltd v. Mayo*[24] the

---

[18] *Cotton v. Wallis* [1955] 1 W.L.R. 1168, CA at 1175–1177.
[19] See the passage quoted at para. 8–238 above.
[20] (1899) 1 F. (Ct of Sess.) 1211, 1222.
[21] *ibid.* at 1219 (also note Lord Moncrieff at 1224). See also *Kensington and Westminster and Chelsea A.H.A. v. Wettern Composites* (1984) 1 Con.L.R. 114, 123 *per* Judge Smout Q.C. (architects negligent in failing to appreciate that much of the work of fixing mullions would be speedily covered up in the course of the works and as such called for closer supervision than would otherwise be the case).
[22] (1992) 35 Con.L.R. 120 (Note).
[23] See also the Alberta case *Homes by Jayman Ltd v. Kellam Berg* (1995) 29 Alta. L.R. (3d) 1, where engineers were held to be liable for breach of a duty to provide some level of inspection and supervision in respect of the provision of a new septic tank system for a condominium. On appeal ((1998) 54 Alta. L.R. (3d) 272), the Alberta Court of Appeal found that the engineers were also liable for negligently designing the septic tanks so that they were too small.
[24] (1965) 113 C.L.R. 588.

building works included the construction of a hotel swimming pool. The employer did not engage a main contractor but employed his own tradesmen, labourers and foremen. He also engaged an architect pursuant to a contract whereby the latter agreed to: "give such periodical supervision and inspection as may be necessary to ensure that the works are being executed in general accordance with the contract; constant supervision does not form part of the duties undertaken by him." A labourer was injured by the collapse of concrete around the pool, following the removal of framework. The collapse was due to reinforcing mesh being laid longitudinally, not transversely, thereby reducing its strength. The mesh had been laid and the concrete had been poured between two visits of the architect. The labourer sued the employer, who sought contribution from the architect on the basis that he was in breach of his duty of care to the employer and also in breach of his contractual duty to the employer, in failing to supervise the works properly. Expert witnesses maintained that an architect should be present when concrete was poured and before this should satisfy himself that the formwork and reinforcing mesh were properly prepared. The architect was held in breach of his contractual duty to the employer in failing to make arrangements of a reliable nature to be informed before the concrete was poured and to give instructions that there was to be no covering up of the formwork and mesh before he inspected them. He was not entitled to rely on the contractor to give him notice of when the concrete was to be poured, even in circumstances where the contractor had given such notices in the past.[25] Similarly, in *George Fischer Holding Ltd v. Multi Design Consultants Ltd*,[26] Judge Hicks Q.C. found that employer's representatives (DLE) who failed to make any visits at all to the roof of a warehouse during its construction were "in gross breach of duty". He rejected their excuse that access was unsafe, on the basis that the representatives were entitled to require the contractor to provide safe access. He also rejected the defence that defective work would not have been detected even if inspections had taken place, because the work of making the joints would not necessarily or probably have been going on during visits, and if it were the workman would have taken untypical care while under the eye of the employer's representative:

"That defence fails at every level. As to missing the relevant phase of the operation, first, it is clear on the evidence that on visits of the frequency and length which Mr Gardiner says he carried out elsewhere on site, and even without any special attention to this point, the likelihood is that he would on many occasions have had the opportunity of seeing lap joints formed and sealed. Secondly, the formation of the joints was so obviously crucial that even if the overall frequency of visits was not increased special attention should have been paid to ensuring that they fully covered this aspect. But, thirdly, since this whole discussion predicates the acceptance by DLE of the very risky and inadvisable inclusion of lap joints in such shallow slopes, it was incumbent upon

---

[25] This decision may be justified in light of the expert evidence given and also of the employer having used his own labourers. Accordingly, he depended more on the architect than would have been reasonable if a main contractor had been engaged. Nevertheless, particularly on larger building projects, it seems unduly burdensome to expect an architect to carry out checks before, and be present during, the pouring of the concrete. Ultimately, however, the question is one for expert evidence of general practice relevant to a particular case.

[26] (1998) 61 Con. L.R. 85.

them to exercise the closest and most rigorous inspection and supervision of the process. The last point also disposes of the suggestion that workmen will 'put on a show' —either they cannot do that all the time, or if they do, that achieves the object anyway. Moreover it is any event part of the necessary skill of a competent inspecting officer to detect and make allowances for such behaviour."[27]

A part of the works which involves the repetition of the same small operation many times will not always be so critical as it was in that case, where the judge also held that a design which required perfect seals to be made between roof panels was a bad design.[28] In other cases, it may be sufficient for the inspecting professional to satisfy himself, by inspecting random examples, that the contractor's method of performing the operation is satisfactory. That was the situation in *Ministry of Defence v. Scott Wilson Kirkpatrick*,[29] where the second defendants were engineers engaged to act as superintending officers in relation to repair works at a dockyard slip. The roof of the slip was blown off during a storm because the contractor had not followed the method of fixing the roof timbers which was required by the building contract. The engineers were held to have been negligent in failing to satisfy themselves that the contractor was using a compliant method of fixing, although they were not required to check every one of the 350–odd joints (having inspected and improved the contractor's method, it would have been sufficient for the engineers to instruct the clerk of works that all of the connections should be formed in the same way). The connections in question were "at the heart of the contractual work".[30]

Confidence in the contractor. In *Sutcliffe v. Chippendale and Edmondson,*   **8-242**
Judge Stabb Q.C. linked the level of supervision required to the supervisor's understanding of the contractor's level of competence:

> "In think that the degree of supervision required of an architect must be governed to some extent by his confidence in the contractor. If and when something occurs which should indicate to him a lack of competence in the contractor, then, in the interests of his employer, the standard of his supervision should be higher."[31]

It is not necessarily the discovery of defective works which should put the supervising professional on notice that a particular contractor requires closer supervision. In *Kensington and Westminster and Chelsea A.H.A. v. Wettern Composites,*[32] Judge Smout Q.C. held[33] that a "lack of frankness" on the part of sub-contractors when defects were discovered was relevant to the level of supervision required, because it ought to have put the defendant architects "on

---

[27] *ibid.* at 126.
[28] See para. 8–214, above.
[29] Unreported, July 1997, Mr Recorder Coles Q.C. This point was not the subject of the appeal at [2000] B.L.R. 20.
[30] See also *Sandown Hotels Ltd v. Phelps* (1953) 167 E.G. 595 (architect engaged to take out specifications and supervise the repainting of a seaside hotel negligently failed to give sufficient attention to the preparation of woodwork, with the result that the paintwork flaked).
[31] *ibid.* at 162.
[32] (1984) 1 Con.L.R. 114.
[33] *ibid.* at 132.

their guard". Similarly, in *Brown v. Gilbert-Scott*[34] Mr Recorder Coles Q.C. accepted the submission that the architect should have taken into account the lack of relevant experience of the builder in deciding how often, and in how much detail, he would inspect the works.

8–243   **Defects intended by the contractor.** Whether a contractor's wrongdoing was accidental or deliberate may also affect the liability of the architect. In *London Hospital (Trustees) v. T. P. Bennett*[35] the defendant architects and engineers were held not to be in breach of duty to the plaintiff building owners where a building contractor's employees had deliberately planned to carry out hacking to concrete nibs. They knew that this was wrong in the absence of the professional team and the clerk of works. The contractual claim against the architects and engineers being statute-barred, the judge also held that if he was wrong, he would have found that there was no duty of care in tort to prevent third parties from causing damage and that the deliberate wrongdoing amounted to a *novus actus interveniens*.[36]

8–244   **The clerk of works.** In larger building projects where the employer employs a clerk of works as well as engaging an architect,[37] the usual division of functions is for the former to attend to matters of detail and for the latter to attend to more important matters. The issue then becomes what amounts to a matter of detail and what does not. In *Leicester Guardians v. Trollope*[38] an architect was held negligent in failing to supervise the laying of concrete. He had contended that it was for the clerk of works to supervise. Channel J. rejected the contention, considering that the laying of the concrete was a very important matter since a large area had to be covered. He continued:

> "if the architect had taken steps to see that the first block was all right, and had then told the clerk of works that the work in the others was to be carried out in the same way, I would have been inclined to hold that the architect had done his duty; but in fact he did nothing to see that the design was complied with. In my view this was not a matter of detail which could be left with the clerk of works."[39]

Similarly, in *Lee v. Bateman*[40] Cave J. directed the jury that the issue of whether certain beams in a fire-damaged building needed to be replaced was a matter for the architect and not the clerk of works.

8–245   Save where a clerk of works is employed by the architect, the architect will usually not be liable for negligence on the part of the clerk of works in carrying

---

[34] (1992) 35 Con.L.R. 120 (Note).
[35] (1987) 13 Con.L.R. 22.
[36] *ibid.* at 35, basing himself on the reasoning of Lord Goff in *Smith v. Littlewoods Organisation Ltd* [1987] A.C. 241.
[37] For the status of the clerk of works see para. 8–244, above.
[38] (1911) 75 J.P. 197.
[39] *ibid.* at 200; the architect was held negligent even assuming, as was alleged, the deviation from the design was attributed to the fraud of the clerk of works. The latter finding would not be correct if a case were brought in tort alone: see *London Hospital (Trustees of) v. T. P. Bennett* (1987) 13 Con.L.R. 22, discussed in para. 8–243, above.
[40] *The Times*, October 31, 1893.

out work within the clerk's sphere of function.[41] But the appointment of a clerk of works, whilst a factor to be taken into account, does not reduce the architect's liability to use reasonable skill and care to ensure compliance with design, as opposed to mere detail.[42] That view was noted by Mr Recorder Coles Q.C. in *Ministry of Defence v. Scott Wilson Kirkpatrick.*[43] There, the clerk of works was employed by the client but was substantially exercising powers delegated to him by the engineers retained to superintend the works. It was held that, insofar as the clerk of works was performing functions delegated to him by the engineers, the engineers remained liable for his acts and omissions. In *Saunders and Collard v. Broadstairs Local Board,*[44] moreover, it was held that engineers in the position of architects were negligent if they relied on the clerk of works since they knew him to be unreliable.

The contractor's method of working. That it is no part of an architect's usual **8–246** function to instruct the contractor as to the manner of performance of his work and the safety precautions to be taken has already been discussed.[45] This proposition is best illustrated by the case of *Clayton v. Woodman & Son (Builders) Ltd.*[46] Pearson L.J. considered the respective roles of builder and architect[47]:

> "It is quite plain, in my view, both as a general proposition and under the particular contract in this case, that the builder, as employer, has the responsibility at common law to provide a safe system of work . . . . It is important that that responsibility of the builder should not be overlaid or confused by any doubt as to where his province begins or some other person's province ends in that respect. The architect, on the other hand, is engaged as the agent of the owner for whom the building is being erected, and his function is to make sure that in the end, when the work has been completed, the owner will have a building properly constructed in accordance with the contract, plans, specification and drawings and any supplementary instructions which the architect may have given. The architect does not undertake (as I understand the position) to advise the builder as to what safety precautions should be taken or, in particular, as to how he should carry out his building operations. It is the function and the right of the builder to carry out his own building operations as he thinks fit, and, of course, in doing so, to comply with his obligations to the workman."

Moreover, in general, an architect owes no duty to a contractor to tell him **8–247** promptly during the course of construction, even as regards permanent work, where he is going wrong; he may, if he wishes, leave that to the final stages notwithstanding that the correction of a fault then may be much more costly to the builder than had his error been pointed out earlier[48] and notwithstanding that

---

[41] Note *Victoria University of Manchester v. Hugh Wilson* (1984) 2 Con.L.R. 43, 60, *per* Judge Newey Q.C.: "The architects should also have inspected the sub-contractors' work as it proceeded, but not as frequently as would the [clerk of works] since they were not permanently on the site and they were entitled to rely on [him] doing his work properly." On the facts, the architects were held negligent in their supervision of the fixing of tiles.
[42] *Kensington and Westminster and Chelsea A.H.A. v. Wettern Composites* (1984) 1 Con.L.R. 114, 133 *per* Judge Smout Q.C. See, further, para. 8–242, above.
[43] Unreported, July 1997, Mr Recorder Coles Q.C. The Court of Appeal held that it was unnecessary for it to express a view on this point: [2000] B.L.R. 20, 32.
[44] (1890) cited in *Hudson's Building Contracts* (4th ed., 1914), vol. 2, p. 164.
[45] See paras 8–127 to 8–128, above.
[46] [1962] 1 W.L.R. 585, CA reversing Salmon J. at first instance, [1962] 2 Q.B. 533. The case is discussed at para. 8–127, above.
[47] *ibid.* at 593.
[48] *per* Mocatta J. *in A.M.F. International Ltd v. Magnet Bowling Ltd* [1968] 1 W.L.R. 1028, 1052.

the architect in that respect may be in breach of his duty to the employer.[49] If, however, an architect is informed that the contractors are embarking on an "incredible act of folly" then as a matter of common sense he should intervene. Moreover, if he sees them not taking special precautions without which a risk of damage to property is likely to arise, he may be under a duty to his employer to warn them to take the precautions necessary.[50]

8–248   In the Australian case of *Florida Hotels Pty Ltd v. Mayo*[51] the employer did not engage a main contractor but employed his own workmen for the construction of a swimming pool. He also engaged an architect to: "give such periodical supervision and inspection as may be necessary to ensure that the works are being executed in general accordance with the contract; constant supervision does not form part of the duties undertaken by him." A labourer was injured by the collapse of concrete, due to inadequate reinforcement. The architect was held in breach of his contractual duty to the employer in failing to make arrangements of a reliable nature to be informed before the concrete was poured and to give instructions that there was to be no covering up of the reinforcement before he inspected it. The majority of the court also held that the architect owed a duty of care to the injured labourer and was in breach of it. This decision may be justified in light of the expert evidence given and also of the employer having used his own labourers. Accordingly he depended more on the architect than would have been reasonable if a main contractor had been engaged. A more difficult decision is *A.M.F. International Ltd v. Magnet Bowling Ltd.*[52] In that case the defendant employers, Magnet, engaged contractors, T, to build a bowling centre and also engaged the plaintiffs, A.M.F., to supply and install equipment for the bowling centre. Owing to lack of temporary precautions by T, the partially constructed building was flooded after heavy rain and A.M.F.'s equipment was damaged. In an action by A.M.F. against Magnet and T, Mocatta J. held them both to be in breach of the common duty of care imposed on them as occupiers of the building by section 2 of the Occupiers' Liability Act 1957 and liable to A.M.F. in the proportions of 40 and 60 per cent respectively. Magnet's breach consisted of the failure of the architect, their employee, either to check himself or to request the private architect engaged by Magnet to check that the building had been ready and safe to receive the valuable and sensitive property which Magnet were inviting A.M.F. to bring into the building. It is submitted that crucial to the decision were the facts that the equipment was valuable, that A.M.F. had a

---

[49] See *Oldschool v. Gleeson (Construction) Ltd* (1976) 4 B.L.R. 103, 131 quoted at para. 8–129, above. But cf. the differing views expressed by Judge Newey Q.C. in *Victoria University of Manchester v. Hugh Wilson* (1984) 2 Con.L.R. 43, 92: see n. 16 to para. 8–129, above.

[50] *Oldschool v. Gleeson (Construction) Ltd* (1976) 4 B.L.R. 103, 124–126. In *Stijdom Park Extension 6 (Pty) Ltd v. Abcon* [1998] 4 S.A.L.R. 844, the Supreme Court of Appeal of South Africa considered the circumstances in which an engineer might be called upon to intervene where a contractor wrongly constructed a steel reinforced slab. Howie J.A. stated at 855: "the engineer's contractual duty is to his client, not to the contractor. It is not even his duty to the contractor (although it might well be his duty to his client) to intervene if the latter appears to be going wrong unless it is apparent to him that the contractor does not know his business and is going to go wrong. In short, it is the contractor's decision how he carries out the construction work and he cannot pass the blame for defective work on to the engineer (or architect for that matter)." On the facts he rejected any suggestion that the engineer had been guilty of any "incredible act of folly" in the sense used in the text above.

[51] (1965) 113 C.L.R. 588, discussed at para. 8–241, above.

[52] [1968] 1 W.L.R. 1028.

contract with Magnet as opposed to being a mere sub-contractor and, in particular, that by that contract Magnet were themselves responsible for ensuring that the building was ready to accept delivery of the equipment.[53]

An architect may always undertake a duty to consider and advise upon the **8–249** need for precautions to be taken by a contractor as, for example, in the case of *Clay v. A. J. Crump & Sons Ltd.*[54] In that case, the architect was expressly requested by the employer to consider whether it was safe to leave standing a wall which subsequently collapsed. Similarly, interference by a professional in the contractor's method of working may result in liability if that interference results in injury or loss. In *Plant Construction Ltd v. Clive Adams Associates (No.1)*,[55] the claimant contracted with the Ford Motor Company to construct pits to take engine mount rigs at its research engineering centre. It sub-contracted the excavation of the pits to JMH. The excavation of one pit required the removal of part of the base of a stanchion which supported the roof of the centre. JMH was responsible under the sub-contract for the design of the necessary works of temporary support for the stanchion and roof. Ford's in-house engineer, Mr Furley, vetoed JMH's design and issued instructions dictating the manner of support. The engineer's design was inadequate and the roof collapsed. Judge Hicks Q.C. held that JMH owed a contractual duty of care to warn the claimant that the design was unsafe and had failed to discharge that duty.[56] However, he made a deduction of 80 per cent for contributory negligence on the part of the claimant which, through Mr Furley, was principally to blame for the adoption of an unsafe method of building temporary supports. The claimant's action against its independent consulting engineers had been settled, but the judge found that any reasonably competent engineer would have appreciated that Mr Furley's design was unsafe. Clearly, independent engineers who had interfered with the design of the temporary works as Mr Furley did would have been held liable to the claimant.

(j) *Certification*

The certification procedure. The standard forms of building and engineering **8–250** contracts provide that, on a monthly or other regular basis throughout the course of construction, the named architect or engineer must certify sums for payment

---

[53] The following passage at 1046 of Mocatta J.'s judgment is significant: "Accordingly, if [B, an employee of the private architects] was not consulted by [T] about flood precautions and never gave them his advice on the subject, there is considerable difficulty on the facts as I have so far stated them, and on the statements as to the functions of an architect in *Clayton v. Woodman & Sons (Builders) Ltd*, which I have cited, in blaming [B] for what occurred. Unless he was asked by Magnet for his advice as to the fitness of the building to receive A.M.F.'s timber, or to ensure its safety, I do not think, on the authority of *Clayton v. Woodman*, that I could hold him in law to blame for not warning Magnet to prevent A.M.F. coming in until the position had been secured and in not seeking to persuade [T] to do more than he did."

[54] [1964] 1 Q.B. 533, CA, discussed in para. 8–078, above.

[55] Unreported, September 3,1998, Judge Hicks Q.C. See also the appeal, which concerned the scope of the contractor's implied contractual duty to warn of an unsafe design ([2000] B.L.R. 137) and the subsequent decision of Judge Hicks Q.C. on causation ([2000] B.L.R. 205). This important decision of the Court of Appeal was applied by Dyson J. in *Aurum Investments Ltd v. Avonforce Ltd* [2001] Lloyd's Rep.P.N. 285.

[56] This finding was upheld on appeal ([2000] B.L.R. 205) but the Court of Appeal differed from the judge as to the scope of the duty and accordingly, remitted the issue of causation to him for retrial.

to the contractor. The contractor is entitled to be paid for work properly carried out. The architect or engineer therefore has an obligation to see that work has been executed in compliance with the contract before issuing a payment certificate. In addition, a quantity surveyor may be engaged to value the works for the purposes of the architect's or engineer's certificate. In that case, the role of the quantity surveyor is simply to assess the quantities of work carried out; the architect or engineer remains responsible for seeing that the work valued by the quantity surveyor has been properly carried out.[57] Payment certificates issued up to practical completion are referred to as "interim certificates"; at the end of the contract, a "final certificate" may be issued.

8–251   **Duty to client.** In issuing interim and final certificates the architect or engineer will generally not be immune from liability in negligence to the employer. In *Chambers v. Goldthorpe*[58] it was held by a majority of the Court of Appeal that in issuing a final certificate stating the amount due to the contractor, an architect occupied the position of an arbitrator or quasi-arbitrator and was immune from action by the employer for alleged negligence in over-certification. This position was said to follow from the fact that in issuing the certificate he had to act impartially towards the employer and the contractor and was no longer the former's agent. The immunity appears never to have been extended to an architect in issuing an interim certificate.[59] Moreover, the correctness of the decision was doubted.[60] Finally, the case was overruled by the House of Lords in *Sutcliffe v. Thackrah*.[61] In that case Judge Stabb Q.C. at first instance[62] held that architects were negligent in having over-certified sums in interim certificates as due to contractors who were turned off site and subsequently went into liquidation. The Court of Appeal[63] reversed his decision on the grounds that the architects were acting in an arbitral capacity but the House of Lords restored his decision. It was held that an architect did not enjoy an arbitrator's immunity unless certain indicia were met. These indicia were summarised by Lord Wheatley in a subsequent decision of the House of Lords, *Arenson v. Arenson*,[64] in which *Sutcliffe v. Thackrah* was applied to a case of auditors engaged to value shares:

> "The indicia are as follows: (a) there is a dispute or a difference between the parties which has been formulated in some way or another; (b) the dispute or difference has been remitted by the parties to the person to resolve in such a manner that he is called upon to exercise a judicial function; (c) where appropriate, the parties must have been

---

[57] *Sutcliffe v. Chippendale and Edmondson* (1982) 18 B.L.R. 149.
[58] [1901] 1 K.B. 624, CA Claims for negligent certification by employer against architects had succeeded or been recognised in the Scottish case of *Gordon v. Miller* (1838) 1 D. (Ct of Sess.) 832; the Irish case of *Armstrong v. Jones* (1869) 4 C.P.D. 6; the New Zealand case of *Burns v. Furby* (1885) 4 N.Z.L.R. S.C. 110, and the Canadian cases of *Irving v. Morrison* (1877) 27 U.C.C.P. 242 and *Badgley v. Dickinson* (1886) 13 A.R. 494.
[59] See *Wisbech R.D.C. v. Ward* [1927] 2 K.B. 556 at 565 *per* Sankey J., [1928] 2 K.B. 1, 23, *per* Atkin L.J. and *R. B. Burden Ltd v. Swansea Corporation* [1957] 1 W.L.R. 1167, 1172, *per* Lord Radcliffe.
[60] *Hosier & Dickinson Ltd v. P. & M. Kaye Ltd* [1970] 1 W.L.R. 1611, 1616, *per* Lord Denning M.R. *Chambers v. Goldthorpe* was not followed in the South African case of *Hoffman v. Meyer* [1956] (2) S.A.L.R. 752.
[61] [1974] A.C. 727.
[62] Reported *sub nom. Sutcliffe v. Chippendale and Edmondson* (1982) 18 B.L.R. 149.
[63] [1973] 1 W.L.R. 888.
[64] [1977] A.C. 405.

provided with an opportunity to present evidence and/or submissions in support of their respective claims in the dispute; and (d) the parties have agreed to accept his decision."[65]

In *Cedar Transport Group Ltd v. First Wyvern Property Trustees Co. Ltd*[66] a claim to immunity by architects in issuing a final certificate pursuant to the then current JCT Standard Form of Building Contract was rejected as the required indicia were not fulfilled. On the facts, however, the architects were absolved of negligence.

Interim certificates. The question of the degree of error likely to amount to negligence is more fully discussed above.[67] In *Sutcliffe v. Thackrah*,[68] Lord Salmon stated that the fact that an architect's certificate was given for the wrong amount did not of itself prove negligence against the architect. In the *Cedar Transport Group Ltd* case, £30 was claimed against the architects in respect of the contractor's failure to plaster a doorway. The judge rejected the claim, holding that it was *de minimis* and that in any event it could not amount to a failure to exercise such proper skill and judgment so as to constitute a breach of duty by the architects to the plaintiffs.[69] Clearly, however, in assessing amounts to be certified, an architect and any quantity surveyor engaged for the purpose must take care to ensure that claims for payment are reasonable and justified by the work done at the time, in quality and amount respectively.[70] The *locus classicus* in relation to the proper approach by an architect in issuing interim certificates remains the judgment of Judge Stabb Q.C. at first instance in *Sutcliffe v. Chippendale and Edmondson*.[71] Among the points made by the judge were the following. First, while any prolonged or detailed inspection or measurement at an interim stage is impracticable and not to be expected, more than a glance round is expected. Secondly, so long as the contractual basis of an interim certificate is the valuation of work properly executed, the architect should first satisfy himself as to the quality of the work, before requiring his employer by way of certificate to make payment for it. Thirdly, where a quantity surveyor is also engaged by the employer, the architect should keep him continually informed of any defective or improperly executed work observed so as to give him the opportunity of excluding it from interim valuations. Not to adopt this approach would entail the risk of the employer making excessive payments to the contractor which might prove irrecoverable, particularly in the event of the contractor's insolvency.[72]

8–252

---

[65] *ibid.* at 428.

[66] (1981) 258 E.G. 1077, 1080.

[67] See paras 8–163 to 8–165.

[68] [1974] A.C. 727, 760.

[69] (1981) 258 E.G. 1077, 1080.

[70] This may require careful liaison between the architect and the quantity surveyor. Thus in *Sutcliffe v. Thackrah* [1974] A.C. 727 the negligent overpayment on interim certificates was the result of one of the architects failing to pass on his knowledge of defects to quantity surveyors who assumed all the work was satisfactory. In *R.B. Burden v. Swansea Corporation* [1957] 1 W.L.R. 1167, it was held that the quantity surveyor had carried out his valuation improperly: he had been in too great a hurry and had omitted to make a visual valuation at site.

[71] (1982) 18 B.L.R. 149.

[72] *ibid.* at 165–166. See also *Victoria University of Manchester v. Hugh Wilson* (1984) 2 Con.L.R. 43, 78. In *Rowlands v. Collow* [1992] 1 N.Z.L.R. 178, 200 Thomas J. held that an engineer who certified the value of work done in an informal contract for the provision of a driveway accepted an obligation to inspect and assess the value of the work which had, in fact, been completed.

8-253   **Final certificates.** Although the obligations of an architect or engineer in issuing a final certificate do not differ materially from those which he owes in respect of interim certificates, the consequences of negligently issuing a final certificate are likely to be much more serious. This is because the final certificate may be held to be binding and conclusive as between the parties to the building contract. After issue of such a final certificate, an employer will have no remedy against the building contractor should defects become apparent in the building. Whether or not a final certificate is conclusive will depend upon the terms of the particular building contract, so that no general rule can be stated.[73] In *Crown Estates Commissioners v. John Mowlem & Co Ltd*,[74] the Court of Appeal held that a final certificate issued under clause 30.9 of the 1980 JCT Standard Form of Building Contract was conclusive evidence not merely in relation to those materials and workmanship which were expressly required by the contract to be to the reasonable satisfaction of the architect, but also in relation to any materials or workmanship where approval was inherently for the opinion of the architect. The decision has been criticised[75] and it led to an amendment (No.15) to the 1980 edition of the JCT Standard Form of Contract. The implications of the decision continue to be felt, however. Judge Lloyd Q.C. held in *Oxford University Fixed Assets Ltd v. Architects Design Partnership*[76] that an architect sued by his client in respect of defects in a building was not entitled to claim contribution from the building contractor pursuant to the Civil Liability (Contribution) Act 1978. A final certificate had been issued under clause 30.9 of the J.C.T. 1980 Standard Form of Building Contract. This was because the effect of the final certificate would have been to defeat any claim brought by the client directly with the result that no liability could be established against the contractor (by reason of section 1(6) of the 1978 Act). In *London Borough of Barking & Dagenham v. Terrapin Construction Ltd*,[77] the Court of Appeal followed the decision in *Crown Estates* in holding that the agreement of the contractor's final account issued under clause 30.8.1 of the JCT Standard Form of Building Contract with Contractor's Design (1981 edition) was conclusive evidence as to the quality and standard of all materials and workmanship which were inherently for approval by the architect, including compliance of the works with statutory requirements such as the Building Regulations. However, the Court rejected the defendant design and build contractor's argument that the certificate was also conclusive evidence that its design complied with the requirements of the contract. Thus an architect who negligently issues a final certificate which is conclusive evidence as to the quality and standards of materials and workmanship may find that he is unable to claim

---

[73] In addition to the cases mentioned in the text, see for further examples: *East Ham Corporation v. Bernard Sunley* [1966] A.C. 406, HL (RIBA Standard Form of Building Contract, 1950 revision); *P. & M.Kaye v. Hosier & Dickinson* [1972] 1 W.L.R. 146, HL (1963 JCT Standard Form of Building Contract); *Fairweather v. Asden Securities* (1979) 13 B.L.R. 40; *cf. H.W. Nevill (Sunblest) v. Wm Press & Son* (1981) 20 B.L.R. 78 (both cases concerning a pre–1976 version of 1963 JCT Standard Form of Building Contract); *Crestar v. Carr* (1987) 37 B.L.R. 113, CA (pre–1980 JCT Minor Works Contract); *Matthew Hall Ortech v. Tarmac Roadstone* (1997) 87 B.L.R. 96 (ICE Model Form of Conditions of Contract for Process Plants).
[74] (1994) 70 B.L.R. 1.
[75] See the commentary by I.N. Duncan Wallace Q.C. at (1995) 11 Const.L.J. 184; see also the Scottish case *Belcher Food Products Ltd v. Miller & Black* (1999) S.L.T. 142, a case concerning the 1963 JCT Standard Form of Building Contract, where Lord Gill distinguished *Crown Estates* and held that the final certificate was not conclusive evidence for all purposes of the standard and quality of the works.
[76] (1999) 64 Con. L.R. 13. For further discussion, see para. 8–319 below.
[77] [2000] B.L.R. 479, CA.

contribution from the contractor when defects appear; and an architect engaged by a design and build contractor will be vulnerable to a claim for contribution by the contractor if his design proves defective and the contractor is held liable to the employer.

Other certificates. The building contract may provide for the architect or **8–254** engineer to issue certificates which are not connected with valuation of the works. For example, the JCT Standard Forms provide for the issue of a certificate of practical completion. Normally, all but a small percentage of the contract price will become payable to the contractor upon issue of the certificate of practical completion. If the contractor then becomes insolvent and the certificate turns out to have been negligently issued, the employer is likely to seek redress from the architect or engineer. Furthermore, if a certificate of practical completion is issued before the works are in fact complete, when a certificate of non-completion should be issued instead, the employer will be unable to deduct liquidated damages from the sum payable to the contractor. An example is *George Fischer Holding Ltd v. Multi Design Consultants Ltd*,[78] where the issue of a certificate of practical completion by the employer's representatives was held to be premature in the light of "the host of items of incomplete or defective work" which remained.

Another kind of certificate was considered in *Try Build Ltd v. Invicta Leisure* **8–255** *Tennis Ltd*.[79] Structural and civil engineers were engaged by a building owner in connection with the design and construction of two tennis halls. The claimant was the design and build contractor, to whom the engineers' contract was novated. The claimant contracted with a specialist sub-contractor for the design, supply and construction of the roofs of the halls. The design was novel: each roof comprised four inflated foil cushions held in place by a rope edge detail. The roofs leaked. Having settled the employer's claim, the claimant sought damages from the engineers in respect of its losses. Judge Bowsher Q.C. found that the engineers had agreed with the claimant to issue a certificate in an agreed form which required them to have reviewed the sub-contractor's shop drawings and materials and inspected the components of the roof system at the sub-contractor's factory in Germany and on site. It was held that the engineers had signed the certificate when they knew that in doing so they were giving a certificate which was in part false and in part not supported by relevant investigations on their part. As such, the certificate was signed in breach of their duty to the claimant.

Duty to the contractor. Following the decision of the Court of Appeal in **8–256** *Pacific Associates Inc. v. Baxter*,[80] the circumstances in which it is now possible that a claim by a contractor against an architect for negligent certification could still succeed are discussed above.[81] A construction professional may certainly be held liable to his own client if default in carrying out his certification function puts the client in breach of the building contract. The employer warrants to the contractor that the certifier, as his agent, will perform his function fairly and impartially. If the certifier allows himself to be unduly influenced by the interests

---

[78] (1998) 61 Con.L.R. 85 at 132, 134–139.
[79] (2000) 71 Con.L.R. 141.
[80] [1990] 1 Q.B. 993.
[81] See paras 8–103 to 8–109.

of the employer, he will place the employer in breach of the building contract and render himself liable to the employer.[82]

(k) *Specialist survey*

8-257 Specialist engineers may be asked to inspect and report upon buildings with regard to their particular speciality. Thus, following widespread claims for subsidence, potential mortgagees and insurance companies often insist upon a property being inspected before purchase by a structural engineer if there is any indication of pre-existing movement. When carrying out such an inspection, the specialist will be judged by the standards of a reasonably competent specialist.

8-258 The reported cases reveal a number of examples. In *Pfeiffer v. E. & E. Installations*,[83] a surveyor had advised the plaintiffs who were considering buying a house to obtain specialist advice as the state of the gas-fired heating system, which was believed to be about 15 years old. As a result the plaintiffs approached the defendant heating engineers who inspected the system and pronounced it satisfactory. In fact, there were potentially dangerous cracks in the heat exchanger. The Court of Appeal, having established that it was common ground between the expert witnesses that an inspection for cracks should have been carried out by a heating engineer where a system was 15 years old, found that the defendants had been negligent.[84] In *Holbeck Hall Hotel Ltd v. Scarborough Borough Council*,[85] Judge Hicks Q.C. found that a specialist site investigation company was negligent in not making sufficiently specific or urgent recommendations for further investigations at a land-slip site. The case failed, however, on the issue of reliance.

8-259 Two Canadian cases and one recent English case illustrate that a survey will not, necessarily, reveal all defects even if competently carried out. In *Trizec Equities v. Ellis-Don Management Services Ltd*,[86] a claim against geotechnical engineers failed on the basis that the ground conditions encountered were unforeseen and unforeseeable with the result that the engineers had not acted negligently when designing the foundations of a substantial office complex. In *Hilton Canada v. S.N.C. Lavalin*,[87] the defendant engineers were engaged to carry out a "due diligence" survey of a hotel in which the plaintiff was contemplating taking an equity stake. The judge found that the extent of the engineers' obligations was to "determine if major defects were to be found and to assess the general condition of the building". He found that the engineers were not negligent in discovering that the steel structure of the hotel suffered from significant corrosion on the basis that there were no signs which should have alerted the engineers, undertaking a visual inspection, to the existence of the

---

[82] For a discussion of the circumstances in which the employer will be held to have interfered with or obstructed the due performance of the certifer's function, see *R.B.Burden Ltd v. Swansea Corporation* [1957] 1 W.L.R. 1167. See also *John Holland Construction and Engineering Ltd v. Majorca Products* (2000) Const.L.J. 114, Supreme Court of Victoria, where it was held on the facts that the certifying architects had not made their decisions with regard exclusively or predominantly to the interests of the employer.

[83] [1991] 1 E.G.L.R. 162.

[84] For further and much fuller discussion of negligent surveys and their consequences, see chap. 9.

[85] (1997) 57 Con.L.R. 113. For the appeal on a different point, see [2000] B.L.R. 109, CA. See further para. 8–269, below.

[86] (1998) 66 Alta. L.R. (3d) 1.

[87] (1999) 176 N.S.R. (2d) 155.

problem. In *Berwick v. Wickens Holdings Ltd*,[88] the claimant was the widow of a workman who was killed when the building upon which he was working collapsed. She brought a claim against the structural engineers who had been engaged by the building contractor to survey the building before refurbishment works commenced. It was held that the building was originally constructed in a manner "so remote from acceptable building practice as to be beyond reasonable expectation." Bell J. held that the engineers had carried out proper investigations before advising the contractor that the building was safe; the collapse of the building was not foreseeable upon the information reasonably available to them and accordingly they had not been negligent.

(l) *Investigation of defects*

It may sometimes be the case that a primary cause of action will be statute-barred **8–260** against designers but a claimant will allege that he should nonetheless be entitled to recover on the basis that the designers did not point out the deficiencies in their original design when instructed to consider defects which had arisen. This interesting question arose in *Pullen v. Gutteridge*[89] where the Court of Appeal of Victoria considered two actions against a firm of engineers. In the first action, the plaintiff alleged that the engineers had negligently designed a swimming pool complex. The engineers claimed that this action was statute-barred both in contract and in tort. The plaintiff accordingly commenced a second action alleging (1) that the engineers had failed to investigate defects properly during the limitation period; (2) that as a result of their negligence, the plaintiff had lost the opportunity of obtaining competent advice from other sources; and (3) that if they had obtained such advice, proceedings would have been commenced during the limitation period. The Court of Appeal found that the engineers were liable in the first action and that the defence of limitation failed, but nonetheless went on to consider the second action in case they were wrong in respect of their treatment of the first action. The Court's conclusion was expressed as follows[90]:

> "Had the respondent acted with reasonable care when asked to investigate and report to the appellant, its investigations would have had two consequences. In the first place, it would have come to realise, or at the very least to entertain a strong suspicion, that its own design of the sub-structure was seriously deficient and that the deficiency was responsible for many of the defects that had emerged and were emerging. In the second place, it would have communicated this realisation or suspicion to its client."

(m) *The construction professional as an expert witness*

Construction professionals of all disciplines may be called upon to provide expert **8–261** evidence for the purposes of building contract or professional negligence litigation (or arbitration). In *Stanton v. Callaghan*,[91] the defendant engineer had been engaged by the plaintiffs to provide expert evidence in their claim against their buildings insurers for subsidence at their property. He provided an expert report

---

[88] Unreported, October 1, 2000, Bell J. See further para. 8–079 above.
[89] [1993] 1 V.R. 27.
[90] *ibid.* at 86.
[91] [2000] Q.B. 75.

and signed a joint statement with the insurer's expert, which contained their agreed scheme of remedial work. The plaintiffs settled their action against the insurers and brought fresh proceedings against the engineer, alleging that the agreed remedial scheme was not feasible or sufficient and that it had negligently been proposed in his report and agreed with the insurer's expert. The engineer applied to strike out the action, arguing that he was immune from suit. In the Court of Appeal, Chadwick L.J. summarised[92] the pre-existing authority as showing:

> "(i) an expert witness who gives evidence at a trial is immune from suit in respect of anything which he says in court, and that immunity will extend to the contents of the report which he adopts as, or incorporates in, his evidence (ii) where an expert witness gives evidence at trial the immunity which he would enjoy in respect of that evidence is not to be circumvented by a suit based on the report itself and (iii) the immunity does not extend to protect an expert who has been retained to advise as to the merits of a party's claim in litigation from a suit by the party by whom he has been retained in respect of that advice, notwithstanding that it was in contemplation at the time when the advice was given that the expert would be a witness at the trial if that litigation were to proceed."

The Court held that the engineer was immune from suit, both in respect of the joint statement and in respect of his report. The immunity was justified by public policy and, in particular, the need to avoid the tension between a desire to assist the court and fear of the consequences of a departure from previous advice.

4. Damages

8–262   As in the case of other professions the usual remedy for breach of duty by an architect, engineer or quantity surveyor is an award of damages. This may be a provisional award, following from the decision of an adjudicator appointed under the Housing Grants, Construction and Regeneration Act 1996,[93] or it may be a final award made in legal or arbitral proceedings. The principles upon which damages are awarded in each case are identical.

(a) *The scope of the duty*

8–263   Following the decision of the House of Lords in *Banque Bruxelles Lambert SA v. Eagle Star Insurance Co. Ltd*[94] (*BBL*), it may be necessary in any case where damages are claimed for breach of contract or negligence to decide what for what kind of loss the claimant is entitled to compensation; in other words, to decide whether the loss claimed is within the scope of the duty breached.[95] This enquiry will go beyond that which is already necessary as to whether a duty of care will be imposed, at common law, in respect of economic loss as distinct from physical injury or damage to "other" property.[96] It follows, as Judge Bowsher Q.C. pointed

---

[92] *ibid.* at 100.
[93] Adjudication is discussed below at paras 8–330 to 8–341.
[94] [1997] A.C. 191.
[95] For full discussion of this case see chap. 9.
[96] See paras 8–078 to 8–083, above.

out in *Department of National Heritage v. Steensen Varming Mulcahy,*[97] that the damages claimed will affect the scope of the duty which it is necessary for a claimant to establish:

"The duty defines the relevant consequences. But the reverse is also true. If the Plaintiff by his pleading limits the relevant consequences, the limit on the consequences necessarily limits the number of relevant duties. In considering SVM's duties, it is important to remember what has been sometimes overlooked in this case, that because the damage claim is limited to loss arising out of damage to cables, the only relevant duties are duties to avoid the consequences of cable damage and loss of DNH arising from cable damage."

In *Hancock v. Tucker,*[98] Toulson J. put it this way:

" . . . in relation to the proper approach in law in respect of damages, the concepts of duty, causation and remoteness are connected, for if A's duty to B is defined in such a way as to exclude the relevant loss, B cannot claim that such loss has been caused by any breach of duty on the part of A. However, in some cases there may be no dispute about the scope of the duty and the real question is whether the loss should fairly and sensibly be regarded as a consequence of the breach or is too remote. Given that most events could be traced back to an almost infinite number of preceding events, it is a matter of judgment whether the connection between the wrongdoer's conduct and the plaintiff's loss is sufficiently close to make it fair to hold the wrongdoer responsible for the loss. In other cases the real argument may be as to the scope of the duty and, once that is established, there may be no room for serious argument over the causal connection between the breach of duty and the loss."

The decision in *BBL* also means that, in cases involving the giving of negligent **8–264** advice, it will be necessary to distinguish between a duty to provide information for the purpose of enabling another to decide upon a course of action and a duty to advise another as to what course of action to adopt.[99] In respect of the former duty, the House of Lords stated[1]:

"The measure of damages in an action for breach of duty to provide accurate information . . . is the loss attributable to the inaccuracy of the information which the plaintiff has suffered by reason of having entered into the transaction on the assumption that the information was correct. One therefore compares the loss he has actually suffered with what his position would have been if he had not entered into the transaction and asks what element of this loss is attributable to the inaccuracy of the information."

There are plainly some cases involving construction professionals providing **8–265** information where the decision in *BBL* is likely to be directly relevant: most

---

[97] (1998) 60 Con.L.R. 33 at 82.
[98] [1999] Lloyd's Rep. P.N. 814 at 822. For the facts, see para. 8–200, above.
[99] [1997] A.C. 191 at 216. See further chap. 9. *Cf. Kvaerner Construction (Regions) Ltd v. Kirkpatrick & Partners Consulting Engineers Ltd* (1999) S.C. 291, where a majority in the Scottish Court of Session held that a design and build contractor which had tendered on the basis of the defendant engineers' initial design work was entitled to recover from the engineers the extra cost to it of performing the building contract when the defendants' detailed design turned out to be more expensive than the initial design had suggested. Lord Marnoch, dissenting, preferred the defendant's argument (based on the passage quoted from *BBL)* that the claimant could recover its additional cost only if it could show that, if the defendants had provided the correct design information pre-tender, their tender price would have been increased by an amount equivalent to the additional costs and would have been accepted by the employer.
[1] *ibid.* at 97.

obviously providing a misleading cost estimate or providing misleading information to a client which forms part of the basis for his decision to proceed with a
project.[2] In such cases the loss recoverable will be restricted to the amount by
which the cost estimate was wrong or the information misleading. In *Gable
House v. The Halpern Partnership*[3] the official referee found (a) that the defendant architects had been negligent in their assessment of the nett lettable area of
a development; and (b) that, given competent advice, it was unlikely that the
plaintiff developers would have proceeded with the development. It appears that
the plaintiff's recoverable loss would now be restricted to the difference between
the value of the development with the advised lettable area and that with its
actual lettable area. Such a measure would be likely to be very much less than the
loss recoverable before the decision in *BBL,* which would have been likely to
have been taken to include all losses incurred in the development.

8–266   It is likely that some advice from building professionals can properly be
categorised as advice as to which course of action to adopt. In *Hancock v.
Tucker,*[4] the defendant architect was engaged to design and seek planning
permission for a scheme to convert his hotel into sheltered accommodation for
the elderly. He alleged that, as a result of the defendant's negligence, he would
have obtained planning permission for a suitable scheme two years earlier than
in fact he did. By that time, the value of the property had fallen. The claimant
sought to recover the difference between the values of the hotel with planning
permission at the date when planning permission was granted and the date when
it should have been granted. The defendant argued that this loss was caused by
a fall in the property market and was outside the scope of his duty. Toulson J.
held that there had been no breach of duty by the defendant, but said that if there
had, he would have found that loss caused by a fall in the market was within the
scope of his duty. The defendant had advised the claimant as to which course he
should take in the matter of seeking planning permission for the development of
the property, knowing that the purpose for which he was retained was to enable
the claimant to realise the maximum value of the property by selling it with the
best planning permission which he could obtain in the shortest time. It was
reasonably foreseeable that if the defendant was negligent, the claimant might
lose a marketing opportunity which it was his purpose to obtain. Accordingly, the
claimant would have recovered the loss claimed.[5] Further examples of advice as
to which course a client should adopt might include an architect advising that a
house should be situated in a particular position or an engineer advising that the

---

[2] See paras 8–191 to 8–197, above.
[3] (1995) 48 Con.L.R. 1. In *Copthorne Hotel (Newcastle) Ltd v. Arup Associates* (1996) 58 Con. L.R.
105, Judge Hicks Q.C. rejected an argument by the plaintiff that the effect of the decision in *BBL* was
to increase a defendant's liability for a mis-statement so that damages equivalent to the difference
between the amount of an estimate actually given and the amount of a competent estimate could be
recovered even if (as was the case) the plaintiff would have proceeded with the project in any
event.
[4] [1999] Lloyd's Rep. P.N. 814. For the facts, see para. 8–200, above. For another example of the
failure of an argument that the loss claimed was outside the scope of the defendant's duty, see *Try
Build Ltd v. Invicta Leisure Tennis Ltd* (2000) 71 Con.L.R. 141 (engineers' duty to certify the
adequacy of sub-contractor's roof design and materials was not limited to protecting the main
contractor against overpayment to the sub-contractor; the duty arose before the engineers' contract
was novated from the employer to the main contractor; had the engineers discharged their duty while
still engaged by the employer, the sub-contractor's design would not have been adopted and the loss
claimed would have been avoided); see further para. 8–255 above.
[5] *ibid.* at 824. See also the solicitors' case of *Hartle v. Laceys* [1999] Lloyd's Rep. P.N. 315, CA (for
the facts see chap. 10, para. 10–276).

way in which to cross a river was to use a tunnel. In such cases, as in *Hancock*, the decision in *BBL* is likely to be of limited assistance to the construction professional.

(b) *Remoteness*

It is trite law that although a breach of duty is established no loss and damage will   **8–267**
be recoverable if too remote. The claimant must establish that, broadly, the loss and damage were (a) caused by the relevant breach of duty[6] and (b) foreseeable.[7]

(i) *Causation*

A breach of duty may be so clearly the cause of loss, for example negligence in   **8–268**
design consisting of inadequate foundations, that causation is scarcely an issue. Nevertheless causation is essentially an issue of fact to be determined according to the particular circumstances of each case, and by the common sense of ordinary men rather than the logic of philosophers.[8] A finding as to causation in one case is, therefore, of limited guidance as to the appropriate finding as to causation in a different case even though the facts of each case may be similar.[9] Some general principles may be discerned, however.

Advice to the claimant. In cases where the breach of duty is a failure to advise   **8–269**
the claimant, he must establish on the balance of probabilities that, had the correct advice been given, he would have acted upon it.[10] The reported cases reveal many examples of the application of this rule. In *Gable House v. The Halpern Partnership*,[11] the judge found that the plaintiffs would not have commenced a development given proper advice from the defendants as to its nett lettable area even although the correct advice would still have given a development which fell within the plaintiff's investment criteria. An example going the other way is the case of *Copthorne Hotel (Newcastle) Ltd v. Arup Associates*,[12] where Judge Hicks Q.C. rejected a claim based upon an allegedly negligent cost estimate on the basis that, by the time of the estimate, the plaintiff was already

---

[6] As to which see paras 8–268 to 8–277, below.

[7] As to which see paras 8–278 to 8–282, below.

[8] *Knightley v. Johns* [1982] 1 W.L.R. 349, 367, *per* Stephenson L.J.; *Galoo v. Bright Grahame Murray* [1994] 1 W.L.R. 1360 *per* Glidewell L.J. at 1375A (discussed further in chap. 15, para. 15–123, below). In *Department of National Heritage v. Steensen Varming Mulcahy* (1998) 60 Con L.R. 33 at 102, Judge Bowsher Q.C. provided a helpful review of the authorities bearing upon questions of causation and stated: "The test is what an informed person in the building industry (not the man in the street) would take to be the cause without too much microscopic analysis but on a broad view. Where a loss has been occasioned by more than one cause, a plaintiff must show on the balance of probabilities that the breach complained of caused or materially contributed to the loss complained of."

[9] See, for example, the finding on the facts in *Lubenham Fidelities & Investment Co. Ltd v. South Pembrokeshire District Council* (1986) 6 Con.L.R. 85, CA. Following upon the issue by architects of interim certificates containing erroneous deductions, contractors suspended the execution of works and the employer eventually terminated the building contract. But both employer's and contractors' claims against the architects in respect of their losses failed. The necessary causal link between the architects' erroneous certificates and the losses consequent upon suspension of the works and termination of the building contract was not established.

[10] *Sykes v. Midland Bank* [1971] 1 Q.B. 113.

[11] (1995) 48 Con.L.R. For the facts, see para. 8–187, above.

[12] (1996) 58 Con.L.R. 105.

committed to the project and would have proceeded with it in any event.[13] Causation must be proved as a matter of fact. In *Holbeck Hall Hotel Ltd v. Scarborough B.C.*,[14] the defendant local authority faced a claim by hotel-owners for failing to take steps to stabilise the cliff upon which the hotel was sited, leading to its collapse. The local authority, in turn, sued the site investigation company which had investigated and reported upon earlier land-slips in the area. The authority's claim failed because there was no evidence that, had the company given definite and urgent warnings about the need for further investigation, such warnings would have been heeded. Judge Hicks Q.C. rejected the submission that it was possible to infer as a matter of law that the authority would have heeded such warnings; the issue was entirely one of fact.

8-270   **Advice to a third party.** A breach of duty may consist, however, in failure to order or advise another person to do a particular act and as a result of that other person's omission damage may be suffered. In order to establish that the damage was caused by the original breach of duty it is necessary to prove, on a balance of probabilities, that the other person would have complied with the order or advice given. Many breaches of duty in the context of supervision by an architect fall into this category. The point was expressly dealt with in *Driver v. William Willett (Contractors) Ltd.*[15] Having concluded that consultant safety engineers were in breach of their duty in failing to advise the contractors to have enclosed with wire mesh the hoist from which the plaintiff had fallen, Rees J. still had to go on to consider whether the plaintiff had established that, if the requisite advice had been given, the advice would have been accepted, the precautions taken and the accident prevented. He concluded that, on a balance of probabilities, the contractors would have implemented the advice and the accident would have been prevented.[16] The engineers were accordingly liable for the plaintiff's injuries.

8-271   **Concurrent causes.** In tort, if there are competing causes of the claimant's loss and he is responsible for none of them, he will recover in full if he establishes that the cause for which the construction professional is responsible materially contributed to his loss.[17] The decision in *I.B.A. v. E.M.I. and B.I.C.C.*[18]

---

[13] For further examples, see *Hill Samuel Bank Ltd v. Frederick Brand Partnership* (1993) 45 Con.L.R. 141 (claim against architects and engineers for recommending defective panels failed because the employer would have chosen to use those panels in any event); *Nordic Holdings Ltd v. Mott MacDonald Ltd*, unreported, July 27, 2001, Judge Seymour Q.C. (claim failed on causation because even if advised that a suspended warehouse floor would not crack whereas a fibre reinforced concrete slab floor would crack to a limited extent, the claimant would have "run the risk" of the latter because it was by far the less expensive option and minor cracking would not affect the claimant's use of the warehouse); *Pride Valley Foods Ltd v. Hall & Partners (Contract Management) Ltd* (2001) 76 Con.L.R. 1(first instance), [2001] E.W.C.A. Civ. 1001, (2001) 76 Con.L.R. 1, 36, CA (appeal against finding at first instance that employer would have insisted upon the use of cheaper panels in the construction of a factory even if warned by the defendant project managers that the panels were highly combustible was upheld; on the evidence, there was a low-cost method of complying with the defendants' advice; issue of causation remitted to the trial judge).
[14] (1997) 57 Con.L.R. 113 at 149. The appeal at [2000] 2 All E.R. 705 does not deal with this issue.
[15] [1969] 1 All E.R. 665.
[16] *ibid.* at 673. A case where the occurrence of loss depends upon the hypothetical actions of a third party may also be treated as a claim for a lost chance: see further para. 8-285 below.
[17] *Bonington Castings v. Wardlaw* [1956] A.C. 613, HL; *McGhee v. National Coal Board* [1972] 3 All E.R. 1008.
[18] (1980) 14 B.L.R. 1, 37, HL.

provides an illustration of this principle. The plaintiff employers (I.B.A.) engaged the first defendants (E.M.I.) as main contractors for the design, construction and erection of a television mast and E.M.I. in turn engaged the second defendants (B.I.C.C.) as sub-contractors for design, construction and erection of the mast. There was no contract between I.B.A. and B.I.C.C. but it was conceded by the latter that they owed a duty of care to I.B.A. The mast collapsed as a result of the combined operation of two causes: aerodynamic stress and asymmetric ice loading. B.I.C.C.'s design for the mast had provided for the former stress but, negligently, had made no provision for the latter. Although aerodynamic stress was by far the more important cause of the collapse, asymmetric ice loading had materially contributed to the collapse. B.I.C.C. was therefore liable in full for I.B.A.'s loss.

In contract, the position is less clear but there is authority for the following   **8–272** propositions:

(i) if a breach of contract is one of two causes of a loss, both causes co-operating and of approximately equal efficacy, the claimant can recover his loss in full on the basis that the breach materially contributed to the loss[19];

(ii) if one cause of a loss is the defendant's breach of contract and another cause is the contractual repsonsibility of the claimant, the claimant will recover if he can establish that the cause for which the defendant is responsible is the effective, dominant cause.[20]

The first situation is illustrated by those cases in which defective works may   **8–273** be attributed both to the contractor's poor workmanship and the architect failure properly to inspect the works. In *Hutchinson v. Harris*,[21] the architect argued that she was not liable for damages for negligent supervision of works, because the primary fault was that of the builder and the employer had not demonstrated that she was unable to recover damages from the builder. Judge Fay Q.C. rejected that argument:

" . . . where the duty of a contracting party is to supervise the work of another contracting party, it seems to me that there is a direct causal connection between the supervisor's negligent failure to prevent negligent work, and the damage represented by that negligent work. No doubt the builder is also liable. It is a case of concurrent breaches of contract producing the same damage. In my judgment the plaintiff has an action against both, although she cannot obtain damages twice over."[22]

Similarly, in *Wessex Regional Health Authority v. H.L.M. Design Ltd*, it was held that the employer had independent, concurrent and unlimited causes of action arising out of over-certification against the building contractor and the supervising architect. Accordingly, the settlement of the employer's claims against the contractor in an arbitration did not give the architect a defence to the employer's claim against him.

An example of the second situation would be a claim against a designer for   **8–274** delay in production of his design, where part of the reason for the delay was the

---

[19] *Heskell v. Continental Express Ltd* [1950] 1 All E.R. 1033 at 1048 *per* Devlin J.
[20] *Leyland Shipping v. Norwich Union* [1918] A.C. 350 at 370, HL.
[21] (1978) 10 B.L.R. 19, CA. The extract of the judgment at first instance, which was unaffected by the appeal, appears from the commentary at 22.
[22] (1995) 71 B.L.R. 32.

employer's late issue of instructions or necessary information. If, as a matter of fact, the designer's own delay was the dominant cause, the employer should recover in full; in certain circumstances, the employer's default may be recognised by a deduction for contributory negligence.[23]

8-275   **Intervening act of a third party.** The chain of causation may be broken by the act or omission of some third person. Thus in *London Hospital (Trustees) v. T. P. Bennett & Son*,[24] Judge Stabb held that if he had found the engineers or the architects to have been negligent in the performance of their supervisory functions, he would nonetheless have found that the contractor's employees' wrongdoing in hacking off concrete nibs amounted to a break in the chain of causation.[25] The familiar problem of whether the possibility of intermediate examination by a third person precluded the originally negligent person being liable for the plaintiff's damage or injury[26] was considered in the following two architect's negligence cases. In *Clay v. A. J. Crump & Sons Ltd*[27] both the defendant architect and demolition contractors argued that the building contractors had the last opportunity of examination of the safety of the site, that this broke the chain of causation and that accordingly they did not cause or contribute to the cause of the accident. The Court of Appeal rejected this argument, referring to a number of authorities on the subject of intermediate examination in the process. Upjohn L.J. posed the relevant question as: "Judged as a matter of fact: were the acts or omissions of the architect or the demolition contractors so remote that in the field of causation it can properly be said that they did not contribute to the accident?"[28] The answer was "No". Similarly in *Voli v. Inglewood Shire Council*[29] it was argued that the architect was exonerated from liability because before construction of the stage to his negligent design the plans and specifications had been submitted for approval to the state public works department and no objection had been made to the design and details of the stage. The examination by the department was said to be an intermediate examination breaking the chain of causation between the negligent design and the collapse of the stage causing injury to the plaintiff. The argument succeeded at first instance but failed on appeal when the architect was held liable. The approval of the public works department was required in order to obtain a state subsidy for the building and did not mean that the officers who examined the plans undertook to correct the architect's plans. Windeyer J. conceded that the fact that plans were approved by a public authority might in some cases, although not on the facts of the particular case, be relevant in considering whether or not an architect was in fact negligent. In the common situation of an architect's or engineer's negligent design having been approved by a local authority building inspector, it is submitted that such approval will be treated by the courts as irrelevant to the issue of the architect's or engineer's liability. *Murphy v. Brentwood District Council*[30] makes it clear that, in England, in the usual exercise of its statutory

---

[23] For an example, see *Raflatac v. Eade* [1999] B.L.R. 261. Contributory negligence is discussed at paras 8–328 to 8–330, below.
[24] (1987) 43 B.L.R. 63.
[25] *ibid.* at 87. For further discussion of this case see para. 8–243, above
[26] See McGregor, paras 153 to 175 (tort) and paras 236–246 (contract).
[27] [1964] 1 Q.B. 533, CA. For full facts see para. 8–078, above.
[28] *ibid.* at 569.
[29] [1963] A.L.R. 657. For facts see para. 8–128, above.
[30] [1991] 1 A.C. 398. For discussion of this case see para. 8–072, above.

powers a local authority owes no duty to anyone to protect them against economic loss. Such responsibility will rest solely with the architect or engineer who is employed to draw up the plans.[31]

It is submitted that a negligent survey or the lack of a survey before purchase **8–276** will be irrelevant to the issue of causation in a claim by a subsequent purchaser of a building against those concerned in its original construction, including the architect or an engineer.[32] Such claims are now likely to be rare, in England, given the limited circumstances in which a tortious duty not to cause economic loss is owed[33] but may arise either under the Defective Premises Act 1972[34] or as a result of the assignment of a contractual warranty. In the case of a claim under the Defective Premises Act, it is submitted that the courts would be unwilling to allow causation or contributory negligence to amount to a defence given Parliament's expressed desire to allow subsequent purchasers to claim in specific, limited, situations.

Intervening act of the claimant. In some cases, it will be the claimant's own **8–277** conduct which breaks the chain of causation.[35] In *A.M.F. International Ltd v. Magnet Bowling Ltd*,[36] Mocatta J., having apportioned liability to A.M.F. as between Magnet and T in the proportions of 40 and 60 per cent respectively, allowed Magnet to recover, to the extent of their liability to A.M.F., damages for breach of contract by T. Magnet's negligence *vis-à-vis* A.M.F. was irrelevant as an answer to their claim in contract against T on the authority of *Mowbray v. Merryweather*.[37] He was satisfied that on the facts it would not be proper to hold that Magnet's acts or omissions broke the chain of causation between the breaches of contract by T and the loss suffered by Magnet in the shape of their liability to A.M.F. In *J. Jarvis & Sons Ltd v. Castle Wharf Developments Ltd*,[38] the claimant design and build contractor suffered loss when it had to redesign a development which was halted by the local planning authority. The claimant alleged that it had believed that there was planning permission for the development in the form in which it had begun to build, and that this mistaken belief was the result of negligent misstatements made to it by the employer's project managers and by breaches of duty on the part of its own architects. On the facts, however, the claimant had not entered into any contract for the works and been provided with all of the relevant information regarding the planning position by the time that it commenced works on site. By its decision in those circumstances

---

[31] In *Targett v. Torfaen Borough Council* [1992] 3 All E.R. 27, the Court of Appeal emphasised that the essential question, in deciding whether a tortfeasor was liable for personal injuries caused by a defect of which the plaintiff had knowledge, was whether it was reasonable for the plaintiff to avoid the danger given the knowledge. See further para. 8–079, above.

[32] Although the foreseeable possibility of intermediate inspection by way of a survey may well negative the existence of any duty of care in tort: see, for an example, *Baxall Securities Ltd v. Sheard Walshaw Partnership* [2001] P.N.L.R 256, discussed at para. 8–082, above.

[33] See para. 8–102 , above.

[34] As to which see paras 8–039 to 8–045, above.

[35] *Quinn v. Burch Bros. (Builders)* [1966] 2 Q.B. 370, CA.

[36] [1968] 1 W.L.R. 1028, especially at 1060 (for facts see para. 8–248, above). In *Cardy v. Taylor* (1994) 38 Con.L.R. 79, Judge Bowsher Q.C. rejected an argument that a builder who failed to check that his architect had carried out a site survey was thereby negligent. The consequence was that the architect was obliged to indemnify the builder for the damages that the builder was obliged to pay to his client.

[37] [1895] 2 Q.B. 640.

[38] [2001] E.W.C.A. Civ. 19, [2001] Lloyd's Rep. P.N. 308. The project managers and architects were held not to have been in breach of any relevant duty: see paras 8–108 and 8–133 above.

to proceed with construction in advance of planning approval for its intended development, it had broken the chain of causation between any breach of duty by the construction professionals and its own loss.[39]

(ii) *Foreseeability*

8–278 In order to succeed, the claimant must establish not only that the damage was caused by the breach of duty of the architect, engineer or quantity surveyor, but also that it was foreseeable. If the claim is brought in contract, this means that the loss must either (a) arise naturally in the usual course of things from such a breach, or (b) have been in the contemplation of the parties at the time the contract was made as the probable result of the breach.[40] If the claim is brought in tort, it means that, at the time the breach of duty was committed, the damage (or at least the type of damage) was reasonably foreseeable as a consequence of the breach.[41]

8–279   The issue of foreseeability is frequently considered in the context of liability as opposed to damages, although relevant to both issues. For example, in *Eckersley v. Binnie & Partners*[42] the main issue both at first instance and on appeal was whether it was reasonably foreseeable to the defendant engineers that methane might gather in the valve house in quantities potentially dangerous to life and limb. Both the trial judge and the majority of the Court of Appeal considered that, on the facts, the engineers ought to have foreseen and guarded against the risk of methane. Similarly in *I.B.A. v. E.M.I. and B.I.C.C.*[43] in considering whether B.I.C.C. had been negligent the Court of Appeal regarded the crucial issue as whether B.I.C.C. should have foreseen the combination of causes which resulted in the collapse of the mast; namely, asymmetric ice loading on the stays and oscillation to the mast structure induced by an aerodynamic stress known as vortex shedding. O'Connor J. at first instance[44] held that the combination of causes was foreseeable and that B.I.C.C. was negligent. His finding was reversed by the Court of Appeal but restored by the House of Lords.[45]

---

[39] *ibid.* at 321–323 and 325–327. See also *Ford Motor Co. Ltd v. H.L.M. Design Ltd* 1997 S.L.T. 837, Court of Session, OH (application to strike out claim by employer against architects for negligent design of building on basis that, after discovering the defects, the employer had let the building to tenants but had voluntarily waived the tenant's repairing obligations so far as the defects were concerned. The application was dismissed; the employer could not be said to have suffered no loss merely because he could have avoided that loss by suing others).

[40] *Hadley v. Baxendale* (1854) 9 Exch. 341. In *Czarnikow Ltd v. Koufos* [1969] 1 A.C. 350 at 388 and in *Balfour Beatty Construction (Scotland) Ltd v. Scottish Power plc* (1994) 71 B.L.R. 20 at 26, the House of Lords has said that the test in relation to the second limb was whether the loss was likely to occur "with a very substantial degree of probability." For a full discussion of the requirement of foreseeability in contract, see *McGregor*, paras 247–274.

[41] For a full discussion of the requirement of foreseeability in tort, see *McGregor*, paras 192–209.

[42] (1988) 18 Con.L.R. 1.

[43] (1978) 11 B.L.R. 29, 99, CA.

[44] Unreported.

[45] (1980) 14 B.L.R. 1. For facts see para. 8–271, above. See also *Acrecrest Ltd v. W. S. Hattrell & Partners* (1979) 252 E.G. 1107 (at first instance) where one issue was whether the defendant architects should have foreseen, as they had not, the possibility of Dutch Elm Disease and that there would be "heave" damage in consequence. The unchallenged evidence was that such was the state of knowledge of architects at the relevant time that these matters were not reasonably foreseeable. If they had been the original and only cause of damage, the architects would not have been negligent nor liable for the damage which occurred by reason of those matters.

The type of loss. If it is foreseeable that breach of duty will cause the type of   **8–280**
loss which is in fact suffered, it is irrelevant that the neither the extent nor the
precise nature of the loss could have been foreseen.[46] Whether the foreseeable
loss was of the same type as the loss suffered will be a question of fact in each
case. Thus, in *Balfour Beatty Construction (Scotland) Ltd v. Scottish Power plc*,[47]
it was held that the demolition and reconstruction of an aqueduct was not a
foreseeable consequence of the interruption of the electricity supply to the
claimant's concrete batching plant. The electricity supplier did not know that the
claimant had contracted to build the aqueduct using continuous pouring of
concrete and so could not reasonably have foreseen the result of failure of the
power supply. Demolition of the aqueduct was a different type of loss from
wastage of concrete or site resources, which were foreseeable results of loss of
power. A further illustration is provided by the unusual facts of *Sea Harvest
Corporation (Pty) Ltd v. Duncan Dock Cold Storage (Pty) Ltd*.[48] The claimants
stored frozen fish in a cold store in the Table Bay harbour. The store and its
contents were destroyed when a distress flare, which had been fired in the
harbour as part of New Year celebrations, landed on the roof of the store and set
it alight. The roof of the store was non-combustible, but the fibreglass gutters
were not. The claimants alleged that the defendant had negligently failed to
install a sprinkler system at the store. It was common ground that such a system
would have extinguished or at least controlled the fire. A sprinkler system had
not been installed, upon the advice of consulting engineers who had designed the
store for the defendants. The Supreme Court of Appeal of South Africa held that
while the precise manner in which harm occurs need not be foreseeable, the
general manner of its occurrence must be foreseeable. The question was whether
the engineers ought reasonably to have foreseen the danger of fire emanating
from an external source on the roof of the building with sufficient intensity to
ignite the fibreglass gutters. The only conceivable such source was a flare. The
engineers were not aware of the practice of firing flares in the harbour to
celebrate New Year and a flare had never been known to cause a fire such as this,
since they were designed and required by regulation to burn out at 150 feet above
ground. It was held that the fire which occurred was not reasonably foreseeable.
It is thought that the same decision would have been reached by an English court
on the facts of that case.

Date for assessment of loss. In the New Zealand case of *Bevan Investments*   **8–281**
Ltd v. Blackhall and Struthers (No. 2)[49] the issue of foreseeability arose in the
context of consideration of the appropriate date for assessment of loss. There,
attempts to build a leisure centre to the original negligent design of the defendant
engineer were effectively abandoned in September 1969. It would have been
possible to have commenced completion of the building to a modified design in
October 1970. But owing to financial difficulties, disputes as to liability and
uncertainty as to the enforceability of any judgment obtained, the plaintiff
employer resolved that he could do nothing until his claims against the architect
engaged by him and the engineer engaged by the architect were settled or
adjudicated. Beattie J. at first instance held that the primary measure of damages

---

[46] *H. Parsons (Livestock) Ltd v. Uttley Ingham & Co Ltd* [1978] 3 Q.B. 791, CA, *Brown v. K.M.R.
Services Ltd* [1995] 2 Lloyd's Rep. 513, CA.
[47] (1994) 71 B.L.R. 20, HL.
[48] 2000 (1) S.A. 827.
[49] [1973] 2 N.Z.L.R. 45 (first instance) [1978] 2 N.Z.L.R. 97 (on appeal).

was essentially the costs of completing the building to the modified design and that such costs should be assessed as at the date of trial in May 1972. On appeal it was argued for the engineer that the appropriate date for assessment was October 1970 and that the delay between then and the date of trial, which had the effect of increasing the costs of completion, was not within the contemplation of the parties at the time when the engineer entered his contract of engagement with the architect. The argument was rejected. Richmond P. said:

> "If then [the engineer] had actually considered the likely effects of breaches of contract of the kind which occurred in the present case ought he reasonably to have had in contemplation, as 'a serious possibility' or 'a real danger' the possibility that a situation might develop which would make it commercially impossible for Bevan Investments to proceed with the completion of the building for reasons of the kind which were explained in evidence and which were accepted by Beattie J.? In my opinion [the engineer] ought to have done so. The particular design failure was of a kind unlikely to be discovered until an attempt was made to lift the first floor slab into place. At that stage Bevan Investments would be heavily involved financially with the contractors and very likely to be faced with difficult problems as between itself and the contractors. There would be a real danger of differences arising in matters of a technical nature and as to liability. In such circumstances there would be a real risk of difficulties also arising in relation to the availability of mortgage finance. Putting the matter more generally, there would be a real risk of a situation developing in which, even if Bevan Investments could by some means or other find the money to do so, it would simply not make sense, from a commercial point of view, to proceed with the work of completion until the complex difficulties facing Bevan Investments were resolved, if need be by litigation. I am therefore satisfied that in the circumstances of the present case [the engineer] should be regarded as having had in contemplation a real risk of serious delays over and beyond those likely to be caused merely by the need of Bevan Investments to secure the technical advice and modified plans necessary for it to let a contract for the completion of the building to a safe design."[50]

Richmond P. further saw no reason in principle why the engineer should not have had the contingency of the employers being unable to complete the work for the material reasons in contemplation as a sufficiently real danger to bring the case within the first rule in *Hadley v. Baxendale*.[51]

8–282 In *Alcoa Minerals of Jamaica Inc. v. Herbert Broderick*,[52] the Privy Council had to consider similar questions arising from a claim in tort. Mr Broderick owned a house which was damaged by pollutants emanating from Alcoa's alumina smelting plant. He could not afford the necessary repairs. At first instance, he recovered damages for nuisance which were measured as the cost of repairs at the time of trial. By that time, inflation and a fall in the value of the Jamaican dollar meant that the repair cost was significantly higher than at the date when the house was damaged. On appeal, Alcoa argued (a) that the recoverable cost of repair was that at the date of the breach, because that is the date in tort when damages should be assessed and (b) alternatively, that the recoverable cost of repair was that at the date when Mr Broderick ought reasonably to have carried out repairs. In deciding that date, his lack of funds

---

[50] [1978] 2 N.Z.L.R. 97, 118. See also as to the appropriate dates for assessment of damages *London Congregational Union Inc. v. Harriss and Harriss* [1985] 1 All E.R. 335 (at first instance). The appeal, at [1988] 1 All E.R. 15, did not deal with this point.
[51] (1854) 9 Ex. 341. See para. 8–278, above. For the relevant passage in Richmond P.'s judgment see [1978] 2 N.Z.L.R. 97, 117.
[52] [2000] B.L.R. 279.

should be ignored. The appeal was dismissed. It was held that the general rule that damages should be assessed at the date of the breach was subject to exceptions and should not be applied where it would cause injustice. Further, there was no absolute rule (in contract or in tort) that where a claimant does not have funds to repair damage at the date of the breach, his lack of funds was to be ignored in all cases when choosing a date for the assessment of damages. Here, it was "obviously foreseeable" by Alcoa that if a house of a person such as Mr Broderick were to be seriously damaged, he might not have the means to repair it and his ability to do so would depend on recovery of damages.[53]

(c) *The measure of damages*

Following the decision of the House of Lords in *Banque Bruxelles Lambert SA* **8–283** *v. Eagle Star Insurance Co. Ltd*[54] it is necessary to consider the type of loss which is recoverable before considering the measure of such loss. When the measure is considered, whether the claim is brought in contract or tort, the fundamental principle governing the measure of damages is that the claimant must be put so far as money can do it in the position he would have occupied if the construction professional had properly discharged his duty.[55] Broadly speaking, this can be achieved in one of two ways, depending upon the particular facts of the case: (i) by paying to the claimant the monetary equivalent of any benefits of which he has been deprived,[56] (ii) by indemnifying the claimant against any expenses or liability which he has incurred.[57]

Where as a result of the relevant breach of duty the claimant suffers non- **8–284** pecuniary loss, such as physical injury or inconvenience, then (subject to the rules as to remoteness) the claimant is entitled to general damages.[58]

Loss of a chance. In assessing damages, it will be necessary to consider what **8–285** would have happened if the architect, engineer or quantity surveyor had properly discharged his duty. There are two possible approaches to dealing with the issue. The first is to assess on a balance of probabilities what would have happened. The second is to assess damages by reference to the value of the chance of a particular hypothesis being fulfilled. In the light of the decision of the Court of Appeal in the solicitors' case of *Allied Maples Group Ltd v. Simmons & Simmons*,[59] it appears that, unless it is clear what would have happened, in a case where avoidance of the claimant's loss depends upon the hypothetical actions of a third party, damages should be assessed on the latter basis. For example, if an architect negligently failed to provide the correct information to the planning authority for the purposes of an application for planning permission which was in fact dismissed, the question will be: what was the chance that the authority

---

[53] *ibid.* at 286. This case is discussed further in relation to mitigation of loss at para. 8–313, below.
[54] [1997] A.C. 191. See further paras 8–263 to 8–266, above and chap. 9, below.
[55] See *Livingstone v. Rawyards Coal Co.* (1880) 5 App.Cas. 25, 39 and *Dodds Properties (Kent) v. Canterbury City Council* [1980] 1 W.L.R. 433, 451, 454, 456 (as to general principles), *Bevan Investments Ltd v. Blackhall & Struthers (No. 2)* [1978] 2 N.Z.L.R. 97.
[56] See the heads of damage discussed at paras 8–288 to 8–304, below.
[57] See the head of damage discussed at para. 8–305, below.
[58] See the head of damage discussed at paras 8–306 to 8–310, below.
[59] [1995] 1 W.L.R. 1602 followed in *Stovold v. Barlows* [1996] 1 P.N.L.R. 91. See further the discussion in chap. 10, paras 10–258 to 10–261.

would have granted permission had it been provided with the correct information? The claimant must prove on the balance of probabilities that it was a real and not a merely speculative chance; if he does that, the evaluation of the chance will be a matter for the quantification of damages. Normally, damages will be assessed as a percentage of the claimant's maximum possible recovery. By contrast, where the hypothetical outcome depends upon the action of the claimant, the claimant must prove, on the balance of probabilities, that he would have acted in such a way as to avoid the loss which he in fact suffered.[60] If he does that, then he will recover in full and no discount is made for the chance that he would not have acted in the relevant way.

8–266   The principles explained in *Allied Maples* were applied in *J Sainsbury plc v. Broadway Malyan*.[61] The plaintiff was the owner of a superstore in Chichester which was destroyed by a fire. The defendants were the architects who had designed the store. The plaintiff claimed the cost of reinstatement of the building on the basis that, had the defendants properly designed a compartment wall, the wall would have contained the fire for sufficient time to allow the fire brigade to prevent its spread. The architects settled the case against them on this basis, and then sought contribution from consulting engineers, EGP, who had been involved in the design. EGP argued that the settlement was not reasonable because the plaintiff's claim was, correctly analysed, a claim for the value of the lost chance that the fire brigade (a third party) would have contained the fire. Judge Lloyd Q.C. accepted this submission. He found on the facts that there was only a 35 per cent chance that the fire brigade would have contained the fire had the wall not been defective. The architects had unreasonably settled the main action at too high a figure because no discount had been given by the plaintiff for the 65 per cent chance that the fire would have spread out of control in any event.[62]

(d) *Heads of damage*

8–287   The losses which may result from breach of duty by architects and engineers and, to a much lesser extent, quantity surveyors cover a wide variety. Certain types of losses, however, are of common occurrence and are considered below. The discussion is not definitive of the type of loss for which liability may be incurred and ultimately the appropriate measure of loss and the types of loss depend upon the facts of each case. In particular much will depend upon the nature of any contractual term broken, the relationship of the claimant to the defendant and how far a building project has proceeded at the time the breach of duty is discovered.

(i) *Costs of rectification*

8–288   The costs of rectification will usually be the prime head of recoverable damage when a building suffers from defects which are consequent upon negligence by

---

[60] See, for example, para. 8–269, above.
[61] [1999] P.N.L.R. 286.
[62] *ibid.* at 325–326. The judge contrasted the case with a case where a storeowner wished to sell the store but found that its market value was reduced because of the defective wall: a claim for the diminution in value did not involve the hypothetical actions of a third party and so would not be a claim for loss of a chance.

an architect or engineer in examination of the site,[63] design[64] or supervision.[65] In a case[66] of negligent supervision by an architect resulting in a house not being built by the contractor in accordance with the building contract it was said:

" . . . the measure of damages could not by any possibility be what would be necessary to put the work in the condition required by the contract—that would be against the party who was paid for the performance of the work; but now the damages should be measured as to what loss the plaintiff has suffered by reason of the negligent performance of his duty of superintendence."[67]

Construed as a statement that the architect's duty of care is not to be equated with the builder's duty to carry out the work in the condition required by his contract, this is clearly correct. Further, the recoverable loss consequent upon negligent supervision may not be the costs of rectification. If, for example, it were shown that even given competent supervision the work would not have been carried out by the contractor in accordance with his contract then the recoverable loss would rather be the amount which the architect should have withheld, but did not withhold, on account of defective work in his interim or final certificates. For example, in *Turner Page Music Limited v. Torres Design Associates*,[68] Judge Hicks Q.C. found that the employer would not have wished defective work, which was negligently certified by the defendant architects, to have been remedied by the contractor due to pressure of time. As a result he found that the amount of the negligent over-certification was the proper measure of loss. If, on the other hand, it were shown that competent supervision would have resulted in the contractor's work being carried out in accordance with his contract (and it was reasonable for the employer to incur the costs necessary to rectify the defect), the costs of rectification would be the appropriate loss recoverable.

The need for care in identifying the loss suffered as a result of the breach of **8–289** duty in question is also demonstrated by the New Zealand case of *Bevan Investments Ltd v. Blackhall and Struthers (No. 2)*.[69] In that case, construction of a leisure centre to the original negligent design of the defendant engineer was

---

[63] *e.g. City of Brantford v. Kemp and Wallace-Carruthers & Associates Ltd* (1959) 21 D.L.R. (2d) 670, 683–684, Ontario High Court. The issue of damage was not subject of the appeal to the Ontario Court of Appeal reported at (1960) 23 D.L.R. (2d) 640. The facts of the case are given at para. 8–210, above.

[64] *e.g. Gilbride v. Sincock* (1955) 166 E.G. 129; *Moresk Cleaners Ltd v. Hicks* [1966] 2 Lloyd's Rep. 338 (damages agreed by reference to rectification cost). See also *Bevan Investments Ltd v. Blackhall and Struthers (No. 2)* [1978] 2 N.Z.L.R. 97; *London Congregational Union Inc. v. Harriss and Harriss* [1985] 1 All E.R. 335, 343–345 (first instance. Damages assessed by reference to rectification costs, but reduced on account of delay in bringing action to trial and of only one quotation for rectification works having been obtained. The appeal at [1988] 1 All E.R. 15 did not deal with this issue); *George Fischer Holding Ltd v. Multi Design Consultants Ltd* (1998) 61 Con.L.R. 85 (professional fees incurred by a plaintiff in working up a remedial scheme which was rejected by the court were also not recoverable as damages on the basis that, although incurred, they were part and parcel of the scheme which the court had found to be unnecessary; however, it was held that the fees were nonetheless recoverable as part of the costs of the litigation).

[65] See *Sandown Hotels Ltd v. Phelps* (1953) 167 E.G. 595. Costs of rectification as such were not awarded but rather the increased work of scheduled repainting because unsatisfactory supervised paintwork had to be burnt off as a whole.

[66] *Armstrong v. Jones* (1869), cited in *Hudson's Building Contracts* (4th ed., 1914), Vol. 2, p. 6 (Court of Exchequer (Ireland)).

[67] *ibid.* at 7, *per* Baron Fitzgerald.

[68] (1997) C.I.L.L. 1263.

[69] [1973] 2 N.Z.L.R. 45 (first instance).

abandoned, but completion to a modified design was possible and intended. Beattie J. held that the primary measure of damages was essentially the cost of completing the building to the modified design. On appeal[70] it was argued for the engineer that the appropriate measure of damages was the amount of wasted expenditure incurred by the plaintiff employer, namely the amount of his legal liability to the contractor less the salvage value of the partly completed structure (after duly taking into account incidental expenses). Particular reliance was placed on the *obiter dicta* of Hutley J.A. in the Australian case of *Auburn Municipal Council v. A.R.C. Engineering Pty Ltd*,[71] the essence of the argument being (1) that the engineer's duty was not to construct the building but to exercise reasonable care and skill in design and supervision, and (2) that consequent upon breach of the latter duty "the loss which the [plaintiff employer] experienced *qua* the [engineer] was not the loss of the building which it contracted to get, but the loss of its money in a futile enterprise."[72] There was no contractual nexus between the employer and the engineer but only between the employer and the architect (who was also a defendant) and between the architect and the engineer. For purposes of the argument, however, both architect and engineer were treated as one. The argument was rejected. Richmond P. said:

> "I can see no reason why the general rule that a plaintiff is entitled to be placed in the same position as he would have been in had the contract been performed should not provide the starting point in the case of an action for damages brought against an engineer for failing to carry out his implied contractual undertaking to use proper care and skill in the design and supervision of a building."[73]

He conceded that if it had appeared that proper care and skill by the engineer would have led to a situation where the owner would have completely abandoned all idea of building, then he would have agreed with Hutley J.A. that wasted expenditure was the appropriate measure of damages.

8–290   In considering whether to award the costs of rectification, it will always be relevant for the court to consider whether the costs of rectification are in proportion to the benefit to be obtained by such rectification. This is clear from the decision of the House of Lords in *Ruxley Electronics and Construction Ltd v. Forsyth*[74] where a contractor had, in breach of contract, constructed a private swimming pool to a depth of 6 feet rather than the required depth of 7 feet 6 inches. The trial judge had found as facts: (a) that the pool as constructed was perfectly safe to dive into; (b) that there was no evidence that the shortfall in depth decreased the value of the pool; and (c) the only practical method of achieving the required depth would be to demolish the pool and reconstruct it at a cost of £21,560. The judge further found that the cost of rectification was wholly disproportionate to the benefit to be gained by rectification and awarded damages for loss of amenity of £2,500. The Court of Appeal, by a majority, upheld the plaintiff's appeal against this award and awarded the costs of rectification but the House of Lords unanimously restored the decision of the trial judge.

---

[70] [1978] 2 N.Z.L.R. 97.
[71] [1973] 1 N.S.W.L.R. 513, New South Wales CA especially at 529 *et seq.* (on the facts, the measure of damages for negligent design of footings was held to be costs of rectification, namely, the cost of demolition plus costs of reconstruction estimated at the date the employers reasonably ought to have commenced reconstruction).
[72] *ibid.* at 535.
[73] [1978] 2 N.Z.L.R. 97, 108.
[74] [1996] 1 A.C. 344.

Before the House, the plaintiff sought to argue that damages for loss of amenity could not be awarded[75] and, as the plaintiff had undoubtedly suffered a real loss, he was entitled to the costs of rectification. The House of Lords declined to accept this proposition. As the defendant did not complain about the award of £2,500, there was no issue before it which required it to consider whether damages for loss of amenity were properly awarded.[76] Nevertheless even if damages for loss of amenity were not properly awarded, it did not follow that the plaintiff was entitled to the cost of reinstatement since it would be wholly unreasonable of him to incur those costs.[77] Similarly the House of Lords considered it irrelevant that (before the House) the plaintiff had offered an undertaking to use any damages for the purpose of rectifying the swimming pool. The plaintiff could not manufacture a loss where one did not exist.[78]

The House of Lords in *Ruxley* thus also confirmed the relevance of a claim-   **8–291** ant's intention or lack of intention to carry out repair works, when those works have not already been carried out by the time of trial. The use to which the claimant intends to put his damages is relevant to the question whether rectification would be reasonable, and therefore to the question of whether he has suffered a loss to that extent.[79] Thus in *Department of National Heritage v. Steensen Varming Mulcahy*,[80] project insurers brought a subrogated claim in the name of the Department of National Heritage against a firm of mechanical and electrical engineers who had provided the design and supervision for a part of the new National Library but were not themselves insured under the project insurance policy. The claim failed on liability but the judge found that even had liability been established he would have refused to permit recovery of the costs allegedly incurred in respect of remedying defective cables. The Department of National Heritage had publicly denied paying for any such remedial costs and the evidence suggested that the project insurers had paid for such works without reference to any obligation of the Department to reimburse the contractor. Similarly, in *Nordic Holdings Ltd v. Mott MacDonald Ltd*,[81] the claimant warehouse owner complained that its engineers had negligently failed to advise that a suspended floor rather than a fibre reinforced concrete slab floor should be built in two extensions to the warehouse. Judge Seymour Q.C. held that the engineers were not in breach of duty and that the claim would anyway have failed on causation,[82] but he also considered the measure of damages in case he was wrong on those points. The claim was for the wasted cost of laying fibre reinforced concrete floors in the extensions and the costs of demolishing those floors and constructing suspended floors in their place, as well as the costs of temporary works which had been carried out to repair cracks in the floors which were built. Judge Seymour Q.C. found that the claimant had no intention of demolishing the existing floors and building suspended floors. Accordingly, he held, the claimant

---

[75] By reason of the application of the decision in *Addis v. Gramophone Co. Ltd* [1909] A.C. 488.
[76] Although Lord Bridge (at 354), Lord Mustill (at 360–361) and Lord Lloyd (at 374) opined that such a loss was recoverable. Lord Keith agreed with Lords Mustill and Lloyd and the latter thought that the plaintiff was lucky to have received such a large award. Damages for loss of amenity on comparable facts had been awarded in *Atkins (G.W.) Ltd. v. Scott (1991)* 7 Const. L.J. 215, CA.
[77] See *per* Lord Lloyd at 374.
[78] See *per* Lord Lloyd at 373.
[79] For criticism of this approach, see B. Coote, "Contract damages, *Ruxley*, and the performance interest" [1997] C.L.J. 537.
[80] (1998) 60 Con. L.R. 33.
[81] Unreported, July 27, 2001.
[82] See n. 13 to para. 8–269, above.

had suffered no loss which was represented by the costs of that exercise and the costs of laying the original floors had not been wasted. The claimant was entitled to recover only the cost of the temporary repairs which it had carried out.

8–292   **Credit for cost of proper design.** Where rectification costs are claimed as damages for negligent design, it may be that the cost of the building built to a hypothetically proper design would have been higher than the actual cost of the building which was negligently designed. In such a case, the claimant must give credit for the amount by which the cost of construction of a proper design would have exceeded the actual cost, since he would have incurred that extra cost had the designer discharged his duty.[83] In *Ministry of Defence v. Scott Wilson Kirkpatrick*,[84] a contractor which had failed to secure the roof of a historic building in accordance with the building contract faced a claim from the Ministry for remedial works which were far more expensive than the original works would have been, even if performed in accordance with the contract. The contractors should have made critical connections between roof timbers using certain nails, but used much smaller nails instead. After the roof was blown off in a storm, the Ministry remade the connections using steel straps, saddles and bolts in accordance with a code of practice for the design of new buildings, rather than the large nails specified by the original contract. The Court of Appeal held that the cost of the steel components used by the Ministry was not recoverable as damages for the contractor's breach of contract. The relevant code of practice had not been incorporated into the original contract, so that the Ministry would have had to make additional payment for compliance with the code in any event.

8–293   **Date of assessment of repair costs.** The general rule for assessment of damages is the date when the cause of action arose, which in the case of breach of contract is the date of breach and in the case of the tort of negligence is the date when the damage was sustained. It is not, however, a universal rule, and a different date may be appropriate on the facts of a particular case.[85] In *Alcoa Minerals of Jamaica Inc. v. Herbert Broderick*,[86] the Privy Council confirmed that the rule should not be applied where it would result in injustice. Lord Slynn, who delivered the advice to Her Majesty, said[87]:

> "In a case where repairs have to be done at what is a heavy cost in relation to the plaintiff's financial position there may be stronger grounds for delaying the date of assessment that in a case where the plaintiff has undertaken a contractual obligation to

---

[83] See *Bevan Investments Ltd v. Blackhall and Struthers (No. 2)* [1973] N.Z.L.R. 45 (first instance), [1978] 2 N.Z.L.R. 97, New Zealand Court of Appeal. See also *City of Brantford v. Kemp and Wallace-Carruthers & Associates Ltd* (1959) 21 D.L.R. (2d) 670 (first instance; credit given for extra costs of piling systems which should have been used over actual cost of "floor on earth" type of flooring used) and *Auburn Municipal Council v. A.R.C. Engineering Pty Ltd* [1973] 1 N.S.W.L.R. 513 (similar credit).

[84] [2000] B.L.R. 20. For the facts, see para. 8–132 above.

[85] See *East Ham Corporation v. Bernard Sunley & Sons Ltd* [1966] A.C. 406 (held that damages for breaches of contract by a building contractor were to be assessed by reference to cost of remedial works not at or shortly after the date of the breaches in 1954 but at the date of necessary investigations and remedial works were carried out in 1960 and 1961). Also see *Dodds Properties (Kent) v. Canterbury City Council* [1980] 1 W.L.R. 433, CA and *London Congregational Union Inc. v. Harriss and Harriss* [1985] 1 All E.R. 335.

[86] [2000] B.L.R. 279. For the facts, see para. 8–282, above.

[87] *ibid.* at 283.

buy and pay for goods where he could go out into the market and buy the goods at or near the same price."

The Court also saw force in the statement that "failure by a wrongdoer to accept liability will in many cases be a crucial factor in justifying a plaintiff in postponing work of repair until final judgment."[88] The plaintiff in that case did not have the means to carry out the necessary works without an award of damages, and the defendant had maintained strongly that it was liable to pay none. He recovered his costs of repair as at the date of trial.

Damages for failure to review a design. None of the cases has dealt specifically with the question of whether the measure of damages for failing to correct a defective design will be the same as that for carrying out the defective design in the first place. The question would arise either where a professional was employed specifically to review another's design or where a claim in respect of the initial design was statute-barred but a claim in respect of reviewing it, was not. In the absence of concealment or an estoppel[89] such as to prevent a limitation defence from accruing, it is submitted that the contractual measure of damages for failing to review a design where a claim in respect of the original design obligations is statute-barred should be such as to put a claimant into the position that he would have been in if the design had been properly reviewed. Thus if the failure to review occurred immediately before practical completion, a claimant should be obliged to give credit for the (possibly substantial) costs which would have been incurred at that stage in correcting the design. **8–294**

Betterment. In *Richard Roberts Holdings Ltd v. Douglas Smith Stimson Partnership and Others*,[90] the question arose as to the circumstances in which a defendant professional may claim credit for "betterment", that is, when the claimant has re-built his building to a higher standard than that envisaged by the defendant's original design. Judge Newey Q.C. summarised the law as follows: **8–295**

"If the only practicable method of overcoming the consequences of a defendant's breach of contract is to build to a higher standard than the contract had required, the plaintiff may recover the cost of building to that higher standard. If, however, a plaintiff needing to carry out works because of a defendant's breach of contract, chooses to build to a higher standard than is strictly necessary, the courts will, unless the new works are

---

[88] *per* I. N. Duncan Wallace Q.C., "Costs of repairs: date for assessment", (1980) 96 L.Q.R. 341, 342–343.

[89] As to which see *Kaliszewska v. John Clague & Partners* (1986) 5 Con.L.R. 62 (architect who negligently designed bungalow outside limitation period not guilty of deliberate concealment within the meaning of s.32(2) of the Limitation Act 1980 but was estopped from alleging that cause of action did not accrue within six years of commencement of action because of post-completion representation that plaintiff had nothing to worry about). In *Blaenau Gwent B.C. v. Robinson Jones Design Partnership* 53 Con.L.R. 31 at 49–50, Judge Hicks Q.C. declined to follow the decision in *Kaliszewska* on the estoppel point on materially identical facts. He pointed out that where a defendant denies negligence but maintains a conditional plea that if, contrary to his primary case, he was negligent, the action is statute barred, it will be very difficult to assert that an earlier statement to the effect that he was not negligent can found an estoppel. The conditional case which is sought to be run at trial will be consistent with the original representation.

[90] (1988) 46 B.L.R. 50. For the facts, see para. 8–141, above.

so different as to break the chain of causation, award him the cost of the works less a credit to the defendant in respect of betterment."[91]

Whilst this summary of the law is unexceptionable, it does not mention any credit for the cost which would have been incurred by the plaintiff in building to a proper design in the first place. On the facts of *Richard Roberts*, where the original tank lining had cost only £3,240.52, it seems likely that a proper lining would, inevitably, have been more expensive at the time of installation and so a credit would have been appropriate.[92]

8–296 When a claimant has carried out remedial works before trial and seeks to recover the cost of those works, defendants very often produce expert evidence to support an assertion that the works were needlessly expensive and the claimant should, instead, have carried out an alternative cheaper scheme. It is submitted that the approach adopted by Judge Newey Q.C. in *Board of Governors of the Hospitals for Sick Children and Another v. McLaughlin and Harvey plc*[93] in considering this question is correct. In that case there had been a fierce debate before trial between the defendants' experts and the plaintiffs' expert as to the necessity for remedial works as a result of a defective pile design but the plaintiff had relied on its own expert's recommendations in carrying out remedial works before trial. In considering the law the judge stated:

"The plaintiff who carries out either repair or reinstatement of his property must act reasonably. He can only recover as damages the costs which the defendant ought reasonably to have foreseen that he would incur and the defendant would not have foreseen unreasonable expenditure. Reasonable costs do not, however, mean the minimum amount which, with hindsight, it could be held would have sufficed. When the nature of the repairs is such that the plaintiff can only make them with the assistance of expert advice the defendant should have foreseen that he would take such advice and be influenced by it . . . [94]

However reasonably the plaintiff acts, he can only recover in respect of loss actually caused by the defendant. If, therefore, part of a plaintiff's claim does not arise out of the defendant's wrong doing, but is due to some independent cause, the plaintiff cannot recover in respect of that part: *Owners of Liesbosch Dredger v. Owners of Steamship Edison*,[95] and *Compania Financiera "Soleada" SA v. Hamoor Tanker Corp. Inc., The Borag*.[96] The independent cause may take the form of an event which breaks, that is to say, brings to an end, a chain of causation from the defendant's breach of duty, so that the plaintiff cannot recover damages for any loss which he sustains after the event. The

---

[91] *ibid.* at 69. See also the same judge's judgment in *Board of Governors of the Hospitals for Sick Children and Another v. McLaughlin & Harvey plc* (1987) 19 Con.L.R. 25, 97–98. For consideration of some of the evidential difficulties which arise in connection with arguments on betterment in construction cases, see C. Ennis, "Credit for 'betterment' in quantum arguments" (2000) 16 Const.L.J. 31.

[92] See para. 8–292, above. In *Turner Page Music Limited v. Torres Design Associates* (1997) C.I.L.L. 1263, it was held that a competent designer would have provided additional and improved fire exits in his original design. As a result of a Building Regulations refusal, the additional and improved fire exits had to be provided by way of variation. The judge found that it was likely that the late addition of the fire exits had increased their cost by one third and awarded this sum as damages.

[93] (1987) 19 Con.L.R. 25.

[94] *ibid.* at 94.

[95] [1933] A.C. 449.

[96] [1981] 1 All E.R. 856, CA.

event may take the form of negligent advice upon which the plaintiff has acted. Another way of expressing the matter might be that the defendant could not reasonably have foreseen that the plaintiff would act on negligent advice. Advice which is not negligent will not by itself break the chain . . . If at the date of the trial no remedial works have been carried out by the plaintiff, then the court has in order to assess damages to decide what works should be done. The parties are entitled to put forward rival schemes and the court has to choose between them or variants of them . . . The assessment has to be made on the basis of what the plaintiff can reasonably do. Contrary to Mr Potter Q.C.'s submissions, in my view where works have been carried out, it is not for the court to consider *de novo* what should have been done and what costs should have been incurred either as a check upon the reasonableness of the plaintiff's actions or otherwise."[97]

The judge went on to find that the plaintiff's expert had not been negligent and that the plaintiff was entitled to recover the costs of remedial works carried out on his advice.[98]

It is, of course, possible that matters other than reliance on a negligent expert **8–297** could break the chain of causation. Thus if a claimant sought a guarantee from its professional advisers in relation to remedial works instead of the normal obligation to exercise reasonable skill and care, it is submitted that remedial works will have been caused not by a defendant's breach of duty but rather by a claimant's desire to have a greater degree of security in respect of the repaired building than that to which he had been entitled in respect of the original works. This was the case in *Ministry of Defence v. Scott Wilson Kirkpatrick*.[99] Between the date of the defective works carried out by the defendant contractor to the roof of the Ministry's building and the date when the roof was blown off in a storm, cladding to one side of the building was removed. The Ministry carried out remedial works after the storm and argued that it had reasonably relied upon professional advice as to the design of those works. The works were considerably more extensive and more expensive than the works required under the defendant's original contract. The Court of Appeal held that the relevant question was not whether the Ministry acted reasonably in following professional advice as to the appropriate remedial works. the removal of the cladding meant that circumstances had changed since the defendant's contract; at the time of the remedial works, the Ministry did not know whether, without the cladding, the original works would suffice even if properly performed. In those circumstances, it had acted reasonably, but the costs of so doing were not attributable to the defendant's breach of contract. Its damages were limited to the cost of carrying out remedial works to the standard specified in the defendant's contract.

---

[97] (1987) 19 Con.L.R. 25, 97.
[98] For a case where the same judge found that the plaintiff's expert engineer had been negligent and that the chain of causation was accordingly broken see *Frost and Another v. Moody Homes Limited and Others* (1989) 6 Const.L.J. 43. See also *Skandia Property (UK) v. Thames Water Utilities Ltd* [1999] B.L.R. 338, CA (claimant's expert's assumption that basement had been fully watertight before flooding was not reasonable; accordingly works to restore that level of waterproofing were not caused by the flood damage).
[99] [2000] B.L.R. 20. For the facts, see para. 8–133 above. See also *Skandia Property (UK) v. Thames Water Utilities Ltd* [1999] B.L.R. 338, CA (flooding to basement was not reasonably repaired by works to make the basement fully watertight. The basement had not been designed to be waterproof and the works were caused not by the damage caused by the defendant's neglect but by the claimant's desire to secure the basement against water ingress for the future).

(ii) *Diminution in value*

8–298   In certain cases it may be appropriate to award the diminution in value of land or property rather than the cost of repairing the same.[1] In *Pantalone v. Alaouie*[2] an engineer was found to be liable for the collapse of a building as a result of his negligence in failing to make clear to the owner of the adjoining property the precautions that would be required before undertaking excavations. Giles J. considered[3] that the essential question was whether it was reasonable to rebuild the building "judged in part by the advantages [to the plaintiffs] of rebuilding in relation to the additional cost to the defendants over the diminution in value."[4] Having decided, on the facts, that it would not be reasonable he therefore awarded diminution in value plus conveyancing costs (to reflect the fact that it was likely that the site would be sold and a replacement property purchased). Similarly, in *Saigol v. Cranley Mansion Ltd*,[5] negligent design and supervision by a building surveyor of works to the claimant's apartment led to the apartment being repossessed by her mortgagee. Although the costs of rectification were less than the diminution in the value of the apartment, the claimant was awarded the latter measure. The Court of Appeal held that the claimant, being out of possession, could not reasonably be expected to carry out remedial works. The appropriate measure of her loss was the diminution in the value of the apartment as a result of the need for rectification works. The costs of rectification were relevant only inasmuch as they might be taken into account by a valuer in deciding the market value of the apartment in its unrepaired state. It rejected the submission that the costs of rectification represented a ceiling on the amount which could be awarded for diminution in value.

8–299   In a few cases, it may be appropriate to award damages representing diminution in value as well as damages representing the costs of rectification. The effect of remedial works may not be to restore a property to the value which it would have had, all other things being equal, had the need for remedial works never existed. This is the result of purchasers being unwilling to purchase a property which has been associated with such remedial works and is known as "blight" or "stigma". It is commonly encountered in connection with works to repair subsidence damage.[6] The principle was approved by Judge Hicks Q.C. in *George Fischer Holding Ltd v. Multi Design Consultants Ltd*[7] in awarding damages for negligent over-certification:

> "In point of principle a plaintiff who carries out the best and most economical repair which can be devised to defective property but is left at the end with an asset for which purchasers in the market are not prepared to pay as much as for one which never had the defects has plainly lost both the money expended on the repair work and the residual difference in value."

---

[1] See the approval by Lord Cohen in *East Ham Corporation v. Bernard Sunley Ltd* [1966] A.C. 406, 434–435 of a statement in the then edition of *Hudson* to the effect that diminution of value of work done represented a possible measure of damages in an action against a building contractor.
[2] (1989) 18 N.S.W.L.R. 119.
[3] *ibid.* at 138.
[4] Thus anticipating the approach of the House of Lords in *Ruxley Electronics and Construction Ltd v. Forsyth*—see para. 8–290, above.
[5] (2000) 72 Con.L.R. 54, CA.
[6] See, for an example, *Hoadley v. Edwards* [2001] P.N.L.R. 41.
[7] (1998) 61 Con.L.R. 85 at 145.

(iii) *Wasted expenditure*

Wasted expenditure will be the appropriate measure of damages where, for **8–300** example, in reliance upon an architect's negligent design or underestimate of construction cost, an employer embarks upon construction of a building, incurring expenditure on contractors, but, on appreciating that the building cannot be completed except to a substantially modified design or at a price greatly in excess of the estimated cost, he decides to abort the whole project.[8] Clearly, recovery of wasted expenditure is subject to the employer's duty to mitigate his loss and credit should be given for the salvage value of the partly constructed building. In contrast if an architect gives a negligent underestimate of construction cost but the building is completed, the damages recoverable by the employer against the architect are likely to be nominal only, since he will have received a building to the value corresponding to the estimated construction cost and to the element of excess cost.

(iv) *Excess expenditure*

Excess expenditure will be the appropriate measure of damages where the **8–301** employer has overpaid the contractor in consequence of the architect or quantity surveyor having negligently issued certificates for amounts greater than those properly due to the contractor. The certified amounts may be excessive owing to overcertification of the quantity of work done by the contractor[9] or, as is more often the case, owing to insufficient deductions being made for defective work.[10] If the overpayment were made in consequence of overcertification in interim certificates, it may be difficult for the employer to demonstrate more than nominal loss, since, if the errors are discovered in time, appropriate adjustments may be made in subsequent interim certificates or the final certificate. There may be no such difficulty, however, if in the interim the contractor has become insolvent.[11] An example of the recovery of such expenditure is *West Faulkner Associates v. London Borough of Newham.*[12] Judge Newey Q.C. held that as a result of the architect's negligent failure to serve a notice under the building contract stating that the contractor was not proceeding regularly and diligently with the works, the employer lost the opportunity to be placed in a favourable contractual situation with regard to the contractor. As a result the employer was entitled to recover the additional costs charged by new, replacement, contractors, professional fees and certain other consequential losses which should not have been incurred.

---

[8] Damages for wasted expenditure would seem to have been awarded in *Dalgleish v. Bromley Corporation* (1953) 162 E.G. 623 but the matter is not clear from the brief report of the case. The fact that the refurbishment of the defendant's mansion would not have gone ahead was certainly the basis upon which the plaintiff's claim in *Nye Saunders v. Alan Bristow* (1987) 37 B.L.R. 92, CA failed; see para. 8–193, above. Note also the discussion of the *Bevan Investments Ltd* case at para. 8–289, above.

[9] *e.g. Irving v. Morrison* (1877) 27 U.C.C.P., 242 and *Saunders and Collard v. Broadstairs Local Board* (1890) cited in *Hudson's Building Contracts* (4th ed., 1914), Vol. 2, p. 164.

[10] Sutcliffe v. Thackrah [1974] A.C. 727.

[11] As in *Sutcliffe v. Thackrah, ibid.*

[12] (1992) 31 Con.L.R. 105. The appeal at (1994) 71 B.L.R. 1 dealt only with liability. A further example of a case where the court found that the proper measure of damages for negligent overcertification of defective work was the amount negligently over-certified is *Turner Page Music Limited v. Torres Design Associates* [1997] C.I.L.L. 1263.

(v) *Underpayment*

8–302   Where a construction professional is employed to advise a contractor as to the level of recovery to which he is entitled from an employer, any claim by the contractor against the professional would be for the amount underpaid by the employer as a result of negligent advice. Similarly in the event that a claim in tort by a contractor against an architect, engineer or quantity surveyor appointed by the employer for undercertification were successful,[13] the measure of damages would also be the element of underpayment. It might well be open to the architect, however, to contend on the facts that the contractor's claim should be reduced or extinguished on account of his contributory negligence in not challenging the amount of the certificate within any time limited for doing so.

(vi) *Consequential losses*

8–303   In addition to the primary measure of loss recoverable against an architect or engineer, certain consequential losses may be recoverable. Consequential loss has been defined as "loss and damage not directly and naturally resulting from the defendant's breach of contract".[14] In other words, it is loss which falls under the second limb of the test in *Hadley v. Baxendale*[15] and must have been in the reasonable contemplation of the parties at the time of making the contract as likely to result from the breach of contract with a very substantial degree of probability. For example, in addition to the cost of rectifying a house built to a negligent design, the cost to the occupiers of alternative accommodation during the period of rectification works may be recovered. Further, in the New Zealand case of *Bevan Investments Ltd v. Blackhall & Struthers (No. 2)*[16] a claim for loss of profits, consequent upon completion of the building of a leisure centre being delayed as a result of the defendant engineer's negligent design, was allowed. Claims for consequential losses, however, are more subject to successful resistance on grounds of remoteness or failure to mitigate than claims for other heads of loss.[17]

8–304   A head of consequential loss which is often claimed in cases concerning construction professionals is the cost of managerial time spent dealing with the consequences of the professional's breach of duty. In principle, such costs are recoverable in contract and in tort as expenditure which has been wasted as a result of the defendant's breach of duty.[18] In *Try Build Ltd v. Invicta Leisure Tennis Ltd*[19] Judge Bowsher Q.C. noted the typical evidential difficulties which attend claims for lost management time. The judge also pointed out the importance of distinguishing time spent by a claimant's employees in preparing claims

---

[13] See paras 8–103 to 8–109, above.

[14] *British Sugar plc v. N.E.I. Power Projects Ltd* (1997) 87 B.L.R. 42, CA.

[15] (1854) 9 Ex. 341. See para. 8–278, above.

[16] [1973] 2 N.Z.L.R. 45 (first instance); [1978] 2 N.Z.L.R. 97, CA. For facts and discussion of the case in the context of foreseeability, rectification costs and mitigation see paras 8–281, 8–289, above and para. 8–313, below.

[17] *e.g.* in *Hutchinson v. Harris* (1978) 10 B.L.R. 19, a case of negligent supervision by an architect, the employer's claim for loss of rental income was disallowed on the grounds that she had failed to take reasonable steps to mitigate her loss. On the evidence in the same case a claim for interest charges on a bank loan was also rejected.

[18] See *Tate and Lyle Food and Distribution Ltd v. Greater London Council* [1981] 3 All E.R. 716; *Babcock Energy Ltd v. Lodge Sturtevant Ltd* (1994) 41 Con.L.R. 45; *Lomond Assured Properties Ltd v. McGrigor Donald* (1999) S.L.T. 797 (Note).

[19] (2000) 71 Con.L.R. 141, 180–182. For the facts, see paras 8–206 and 8–255, above.

for litigation and time spent preparing practical solutions to the defects complained of; only the latter may be compensated in damages. Finally, the judge rejected the defendant engineers' argument that the claimant would have incurred the cost of its senior management in any event, so that no damages were recoverable, and awarded damages based upon the cost to the claimant of the relevant employees' time:

> "Where the time of a senior manager has been taken up by extra duties made necessary by the wrongdoing of a defendant, the employer... has lost the benefit of that individual's time which ought to have been devoted to his ordinary duties even (or perhaps especially) if the time lost was time which might have been spent looking out of the window thinking. The value of that time lost to the company may be enormous or small, but it can only be assessed by reason of the cost of the employee to the company."[20]

(vii) *Liability to third parties*

One consequence of an architect's negligence may be to expose the employer to liability to some third party.[21] For example, owing to his failure to make a proper site examination or to make proper enquiries, an architect draws plans showing inaccurate site dimensions with the consequence that a building erected to the plans encroaches upon a third party's land. If the third party recovers damages against the employer for trespass, the architect will be liable to indemnify the employer. Similarly if owing to an architect's negligent design or supervision[22] a third party is injured and recovers damages from the employer, the architect will be liable to indemnify the employer, irrespective of any claim in tort which the injured third party may have had against the architect. If the damage or injury to the third party is caused partly by the employer's default and partly by the architect's default, liability may be apportioned between the employer and the architect.[23]

8–305

(viii) *Personal injuries*

If in consequence of an architect's negligent design or supervision a person is injured[24] the measure of damages in a claim against the architect will be the usual measure for personal injuries. *Quantum* of damages for personal injuries is too vast a topic for this book and is more than adequately dealt with elsewhere.[25] In "disaster" situations where an architect or engineer's negligence caused or

8–306

---

[20] *ibid.* at 181–182. The same argument advanced by a defendant also failed in *Raflatac v. Eade* [1999] B.L.R. 261, 266.

[21] Thus in *Cardy v. Taylor* (1994) 38 Con.L.R. 79, the architect was found liable to indemnify the building contractor who employed him against losses which the contractor was obliged to pay to his client by reason of the architect's failure to carry out a site survey.

[22] *e.g. Florida Hotels Pty Ltd v. Mayo* (1965) 113 C.L.R. 588 (for facts see para. 8–241, above). *Royal Brompton Hospital NHS Trust v. Hammond* (2000) 69 Con.L.R. 145 is an example of a case where a client sues his professional advisers for impairing his prospects of achieving a favourable settlement with a contractor.

[23] See paras 8–315 to 8–327, below on shared responsibility.

[24] *e.g. Voli v. Inglewood Shire Council* (1963) 110 C.L.R. 74; *Clay v. A. J. Crump and Sons Ltd* [1964] 1 Q.B. 533, CA; *Driver v. William Willett (Contractors) Ltd* [1969] 1 All E.R. 665 (safety engineer). Note also *Storey v. Charles Church Developments plc* (1995) 73 Con.L.R. 1 (plaintiffs failed to recover damages for psychiatric illness caused by the consequences of the defendant's negligent foundation design).

[25] See Kemp and Kemp, *The Quantum of Damages* (Looseleaf, Sweet & Maxwell).

contributed to an explosion[26] or the collapse of a public building, such damages could, of course, be substantial. For discussion of procedural problems which arise in such matters with large numbers of claimants see above.[27]

(ix) *Inconvenience, distress and loss of amenity*

8–307   General damages for inconvenience and distress caused by the negligence of a construction professional may be recovered provided that either (i) a major or important part of the professional's engagement was to provide peace of mind, pleasure of freedom from discomfort[28] or (ii) the inconvenience is physical inconvenience caused by the defendant's breach and the distress is the direct result of that inconvenience.[29]

8–308   In *Hutchinson v. Harris*[30] the plaintiff employer claimed damages for frustration, vexation and distress against an architect "friend" who was held to have been negligent in failing to obtain competitive tenders, in supervising the conversion of a house into two maisonettes and a flat and in overcertifying payments to the builder. The claim was under three heads: first, the distress consequent upon continued litigation with the builder; secondly, the inconvenience of having to organise remedial work and thirdly, the aggravation suffered or to be suffered by tenants, aggravation which would rebound on the employer. The official referee refused to make any award in respect of those heads and the Court of Appeal, after an extensive review of cases in other contexts in which damages for distress and suchlike had been recovered, upheld his refusal. Stephenson L.J. said:

> "I am . . . clearly of the opinion that, in these days, we have reached a point where damages would have been properly awarded, as the judge thought, for any distress which had been caused to the plaintiff by her being kept out of her own house and home through having to do extensive repairs to it . . . . Here was a lady, no doubt wanting to do up these premises and convert them in order to obtain an income to support herself and her family but nevertheless embarking upon a commercial enterprise, converting these premises as a property owner, premises in which she had no intention of living herself but into which she intended to put tenants in order to draw rents from them. In those circumstances . . . the learned judge was quite right to hold that damages for distress and annoyance, under whichever of the heads now put by the plaintiff in this court, were not recoverable."[31]

8–309   In *Knott v. Bolton*,[32] the Court of Appeal held that an architect was not liable for damages for disappointment and distress to the plaintiffs who had employed him to build their house. It was alleged that the plaintiffs were distressed as a result of the failure to achieve a specified width for the staircase in their "dream home". There was no diminution in value occasioned by the narrowed staircase. Russell L.J. stated:

---

[26] As at Abbeystead; see *Eckersley v. Binnie & Partners* (1988) 18 Con.L.R. 1.
[27] See chap. 6.
[28] See, for example, the "holiday cases" of *Jarvis v. Swans Tours Ltd* [1973] Q.B. 233 and *Jackson v. Horizon Holidays Ltd* [1975] 1 W.L.R. 1468 and the solicitor's negligence case of *Heywood v. Wellers* [1976] Q.B. 446.
[29] See the surveyors' cases of *Watts v. Morrow* [1991] 1 W.L.R. 1421 and *Farley v. Skinner* [2001] UKHL 49, [2001] 3 W.L.R. 899, discussed at chap. 9, para. 9–099.
[30] (1978) 10 B.L.R. 19, CA.
[31] (1978) 10 B.L.R. 19, 37, see also Waller L.J. at 46 "[the plaintiff] had decided ... to invest money in property, and in doing so, in my view, she has to concern herself with this sort of problem as an inevitable incident of being a landlord".
[32] (1995) 1 Con.L.J. 375.

"Mr Cousins has endeavoured to persuade us that the true nature of the contract entered into by Mr Bolton in the instant case was to provide pleasure for Mr and Mrs Knott. I disagree. The true nature of the contract was that which an architect enters into in any situation where he is designing a home. The true nature of the contract was to design the home. It was not to provide for Mr and Mrs Knott, although that was a necessary ancillary of what Mr Bolton did."[33]

Knott v. Bolton was overruled by the House of Lords in *Farley v. Skinner*.[34] In a **8–310** case concerning a surveyor's negligent failure to report that a property was unlikely to be affected by aircraft noise, it was held that damages may be awarded for disappointment or distress caused by a breach of contract even although the sole object of the contract was not to provide peace of mind, freedom from distress or discomfort, comfort or pleasure. It is sufficient that the provision of an amenity is a major or important part of the contract. The House of Lords also considered, but did not overrule, other decisions of the Court of Appeal concerning solicitors[35] and surveyors[36] which were consistent with that in *Knott v. Bolton*. However, it remains likely that such damages will be modest.[37]

(e) *Mitigation of loss*

As in other classes of action, the claimant cannot recover damages in respect of **8–311** any loss which he ought reasonably to have avoided. The nature of the steps which he ought to have taken will depend on the facts of each case. In *Board of Governors of Hospitals for Sick Children*[38] Judge Newey Q.C. stated:

"The plaintiff has, whether as part of the requirement that he act reasonably or otherwise, a duty to mitigate his loss. This may require him if presented with two or more choices to choose the one which will keep his losses to the minimum. If he is

---

[33] See also *Partridge v. Morris* [1995] C.I.L.L. 1095 where Judge Hicks Q.C. similarly held that an architect was not employed to provide peace of mind to his client. However the plaintiff was entitled to modest damages for physical inconvenience and consequent distress.

[34] [2001] UKHL 49, [2001] 3 W.L.R. 899, discussed further at chap. 9, para. 9–182, below.

[35] *Hayes v. Dodd* [1990] 2 All E.R. 815. See further chap. 10, para. 10–272.

[36] *Watts v. Morrow* [1991] 1 W.L.R. 1421. See further chap. 9, para. 9–099.

[37] *Watts v. Morrow* [1991] 1 W.L.R. 1421, *Farley v. Skinner* [2001] UKHL 49, [2001] 3 W.L.R. 899. See further, chap. 9, para. 9–099. See also the New Zealand case of *Young v. Tomlinson* [1979] 1 N.Z.L.R. 441 where a house purchaser successfully sued the original owner, builder, council and architects in respect of various defects in the construction of a house. The judge, Quilliam J., recognised that in such a case general damage for frustration, discomfort, and inconvenience were awardable but added the significant caveat "such awards are not likely to be on a liberal basis unless, for example, it is shown that actual damage to health or the like has been involved" (at 462). He made a global assessment of such damages and apportioned part of it to the architect who was held liable only in respect of one wall subject to a design defect. See also the doubts expressed by Lord Lloyd in *Ruxley v. Forsyth* [1996] A.C. 344 at 374 as to the award of £2,500 in that case. For a useful summary of other cases concerning damages for distress and inconvenience see Franklin, K., "Damages for Heartache" (1988) 4 Const.L.J. 264 and (1992) 8 Const.L.J. 318. In *Boncristiano v. Lohmann* [1998] 4 V.R. 82, the Court of Appeal of Victoria rejected the principle that general damages representing compensation for physical inconvenience, anxiety or distress should be modest but stated that they should be "fair and reasonable". Nonetheless, the court refused to interfere with the judge's assessment of general damages of A$1,500 for the first plaintiff and A$250 for his wife, and pointed out that most awards under this head will, in fact, be low.

[38] (1987) 19 Con.L.R. 25 at 96. Compare *Sherson & Associates Pty Ltd v. Bailey* [2000] N.S.W.C.A. 275, New South Wales CA (plaintiff did not fail to mitigate his loss in taking no action to stabilise a defectively constructed wall on professional advice which did not suggest a risk of collapse).

incurring loss because he cannot use his property, his duty to mitigate may require him to repair it as quickly as possible, even if early repairs would cost more than later repairs would. The duty to mitigate may require the plaintiff to have regard to advice from third parties, or even from the defendant, or from the defendant's advisers."

8–312   It will often be the case that negligence by an architect or engineer leads to a client incurring additional professional fees in order to rectify or ameliorate an error. Such fees are, in principle, recoverable. Sometimes the original professional will be willing to rectify his own error for free but a client will wish to go elsewhere because he has lost confidence in his original adviser. The question then arises as to whether the client will be entitled to recover the additional fees paid to the replacement. It is submitted that unless the professional's breach has been such that, viewed objectively, the client is acting reasonably in taking the view that the professional may be incompetent, the failure to ask the original adviser to carry out the work will amount to a failure to mitigate. For example in *Columbus Co. Ltd v. Clowes*[39] Wright J. considered, *obiter*, that if the plaintiff employer were not to allow the defendant architect to make good at no extra charge the plans negligently prepared by him, but were to call in another architect who would probably insist on commencing the plans *de novo*, he would not be acting reasonably and would be incurring an unnecessary expense against the defendant. In *John Harris Partnership (a Firm) v. Groveworld Ltd*,[40] the defendant architects argued that fees paid to replacement professionals should be disallowed as they themselves would have been obliged to carry out the work for free. Although the judge held that they would have been so obliged, he also found that the architects would not, at the time, have accepted this. As a result, the result that the claim for fees was allowed.

8–313   The issue of mitigation of loss often arises where a claimant has not carried out necessary remedial works before trial but has waited to see whether he will recover the cost of the works as damages. If the cost of the works has increased between the date of breach and the date of trial, the defendant is likely to argue that the claimant has failed to mitigate his loss by carrying out the works earlier and therefore at lower cost. It appears that if a claimant can justify his delay on reasonable commercial grounds, the argument will fail. In the New Zealand case of *Bevan Investments Ltd v. Blackhall and Struthers (No. 2)*,[41] considered previously in the discussion of the issue of foreseeability,[42] it was held that the plaintiff employer had not failed to mitigate his loss by choosing to postpone commencement of completion of the leisure centre to a modified design, owing to financial constraints on the company.[43] In *Alcoa Minerals of Jamaica Inc. v. Herbert Broderick*,[44] where the claimant householder lacked the means to carry out remedial work before trial, the Privy Council identified the real question as whether his delay was an unreasonable failure to mitigate his loss. It held that it was not; given his circumstances, it was entirely reasonable for the claimant to

---

[39] [1903] 1 K.B. 244.
[40] [1999] P.N.L.R. 697.
[41] [1973] 2 N.Z.L.R. 45 (first instance) and [1978] 2 N.Z.L.R. 97, especially at 115–116.
[42] See also *London Congregational Union Inc. v. Harriss and Harriss* [1985] 1 All E.R. 335, 343–345.
[43] See the passage quoted at para. 8–281, above and, to similar effect, *Dodd Properties (Kent) Ltd v. Canterbury City Council* [1980] 1 W.L.R. 433, CA and *Perry v. Sidney Phillips* [1982] 1 W.L.R. 1927, CA.
[44] [2000] B.L.R. 279. For the facts, see para. 8–282, above.

wait until funds were made available to him by way of an award of damages in the action.

(f) *Abatement of fees*

A construction professional may be denied recovery of his fees if his breach of **8–314** duty is so serious as to be tantamount to non-performance.[45] In the more usual case, the normal course is to make an award of damages for the total of the loss sustained but to allow the recovery of fees.[46] In *Hutchinson v. Harris*,[47] however, in addition to recovering damages for negligent supervision the plaintiffs sought to resist the architect's claim for fees by invoking the defence adumbrated in *Mondel v. Steel*.[48] In that case, which concerned a claim by a shipbuilder for the price of a ship, Parke B. said that instead of claiming damages by way of set-off or counterclaim the defendant could:

> "defend himself by showing how much less the subject matter of the action was worth, by reason of the breach of contract; and to the extent that he obtains, or is capable of obtaining, an abatement of the price on that account, he must be considered as having received satisfaction for the breach of contract, and is precluded from recovering in another action to that extent; but no more."[49]

The defence failed in *Hutchinson v. Harris* on several grounds. First, the defence had not been pleaded or argued at first instance and no evidence had been adduced on the matter, as there should have been. Since the architect's contract, being on the basis of the RIBA Conditions of Engagement, was not an entire contract but a severable contract divided into several distinct stages, the architect's right to payment had to be considered and evidence had to be adduced in respect of each stage. Secondly, allowing the defence would have had the effect of permitting double recovery by the plaintiff since any element of abatement was included in the damages awarded. Thirdly, Stephenson L.J. considered that there was the greatest difficulty in applying the defence of abatement to a claim for professional services, certainly to such a claim made by the particular plaintiff. The subject matter of the builder's contract, *i.e.* conversion works, was quite distinct from that of the architect's contract, *i.e.* services including supervision. The fact that the work certified by the architect had not been done by the builder did not mean that the architect had not done the equivalent amount of her own work. He also observed that no case had been drawn to his attention, with

---

[45] *Moneypenny v. Hartland* (1826) 2 Car. & P. 378, 380–381, *per* Best C.J.: "Supposing negligence or want of skill to be sufficiently made out, unless that negligence or want of skill has been to an extent that has rendered the work useless to the defendants, they must pay him, and seek their remedy in a cross action. For if it were not so, a man by a small error might deprive himself of his whole remuneration ... " (for the facts see para. 8–183, above). See also *Flannagan v. Mate* [1876] 2 Vict.L.R. 157. An architect instructed to produce a design capable of being constructed within a specified cost is not necessarily to be deprived of his fees if he fails so to do: *Nemer v. Whitford* (1983) 33 S.A.S.R. 208, but *cf. Fidias Consulting Engineering Ltd v. Thymaras* [1985] 1 W.W.R. 752 and *Gordon Shaw Concrete Products Ltd v. Design Collaborative Ltd* (1985) 35 C.C.L.T. 100 discussed at para. 8–191, above. In *Keete v. King* [1938] E.G.D. 65 an architect was required to repay fees as well as pay damages. The precise basis for this double recovery is not apparent from the brief report.
[46] *e.g. Columbus Co. v. Clowes* [1903] 1 K.B. 244
[47] (1978) 10 B.L.R. 19.
[48] (1841) 8 M. & W. 858.
[49] *ibid.* at 872.

one possible exception,[50] in which a claim for professional services had been reduced or abated by the application of *Mondel v. Steel*. He also noted that Parke B. in the latter case stated that the defence of abatement "had not . . . extended to all cases of work and labour, as for instance, that of an attorney, *Templer v. M'Lachlen*,[51] unless no benefit whatever has been derived from it". In *Turner Page Music Limited v. Torres Design Associates Ltd*,[52] the defendant architects failed to produce a bill of quantities for the works although they had expressly agreed to do so. The contract was based upon the defendants' fee proposal, which divided their services into three phases. The provision of a bill of quantities was one item in Phase II. Judge Hicks Q.C. found that the price payable for the architects' services could be abated on the grounds of this failure. He distinguished *Hutchinson v. Harris*, apparently on the grounds that, on its true construction, the contract imposed a series of severable obligations upon the defendants. As such he found that the defendants were entitled to be paid their fee less an allowance for the work not done.

4. SHARED RESPONSIBILITY

(a) *Apportionment of liability*

8–315   A building project usually involves many participants with different functions and skills. Injury or damage to a claimant may be the product of breaches of duty by more than one participant. The courts are often unwilling to accept arguments from one negligent defendant that the negligence of another absolves them entirely. Thus in *East Ham Corporation v. Bernard Sunley & Sons Ltd*,[53] Lord Pearson, while conceding that the employers should be bound by the architect's examination or failure to examine the works in or after the defects liability period, continued:

> "On the other hand, it seems to me unreasonable, too favourable to the contractors, to let them shelter behind the architect's failure to detect faults in the course of his visits during the progress of the work. The architect's duty is to the employers and not to the contractors, and the extent of his obligation to make inspections and tests depend upon the contract with the employers and the arrangements made and the circumstances of the case. Prima facie the contractors should be and remain liable for their own breaches of contract, and should not have a general release from liability in respect of all breaches which the architect should have detected but failed to detect during the currency of that contract."[54]

8–316   While one participant (D1) may be liable to the claimant (C) for the whole of C's damage, D1 may seek indemnity or contribution from any other person (D2)

---

[50] *Sincock v. Bangs (Reading)* (1952) 160 E.G. 134.
[51] (1806) 2 Bos. & Pul.(N.R.) 936.
[52] (1997) C.I.L.L. 1263. See also *Nye Saunders and Partners v. Alan E. Bristow* (1987) 37 B.L.R. 92: in response to the architects' claim for fees, the defendant sought entire abatement of those fees by way of counterclaim. The claim was dismissed at first instance and on appeal, without suggesting any difficulty with abatement of professional fees but without reference to *Hutchinson v. Harris*.
[53] [1966] A.C. 406.
[54] *ibid.* at 449.

who is liable in respect of the same damage.[55] The right to indemnity or contribution may arise under a contract between D1 or D2. The Civil Liability (Contribution) Act 1978 provides a statutory right to contribution. Section 1(1) of the Act restricts recovery to where recovery can be made from another person "liable in respect of the same damage". The meaning of this phrase has been the subject of recent decisions in the Court of Appeal.

"The same damage". The decision of the Court of Appeal in *Birse Construc-* **8–317** *tion v. Haiste*[56] established that "the same damage" means damage suffered by the same person. In that case the plaintiff contractor (Birse) was awarded a contract by an employer (Anglia Water Authority) to design and construct a reservoir. The defendant (Haiste) was engaged by Birse to act as its consulting engineers in relation to the project. Anglia engaged one Newton to act as the "Engineer" under the building contract with Birse. The reservoir proved to be defective. Birse settled Anglia's claim against it and sought an indemnity in respect of the settlement from Haiste. Haiste, in turn, claimed contribution from Newton on the grounds that Newton was liable in respect of the "same damage" as Haiste were. The Court of Appeal found that the damage alleged against Haiste (*i.e.* Birse's loss in meeting Anglia's claim) was not the same damage as that in respect of which Newton could be held liable (*i.e.* Anglia's loss). The practical effect of the decision is significantly to restrict the ambit of the Act. Further, it is likely that ingenious methods may be attempted in order to circumvent its effect. For example, in the above case, Haiste might have alleged that Birse had failed to mitigate its own loss by claiming contribution directly from Newton, since both Birse and Newton could be held liable to Anglia for Anglia's loss.

The need for care in identifying whether damage is "the same" for the **8–318** purposes of a claim under the Act is also illustrated by the case of *Royal Brompton Hospital NHS Trust v. Hammond (No. 2)*.[57] The employer settled claims for delay made by the building contractor under the building contract and then claimed contribution from its professional advisers. The claim against the architects was that they had negligently granted extensions of time to the contractor and that, as a result, the employer had been obliged to pay substantial sums to the contractor for loss and expense and had been unable to deduct liquidated damages for delay in completion. The architect sought to bring contribution proceedings against the contractor. Judge Hicks Q.C. struck out the architects' claim on the grounds that the architects and the contractor were not liable to the employer in respect of the same damage. The damage suffered by the employer as a result of the contractor's default was delay in completion of the works; whereas the damage suffered by the employer as a result of the architects' alleged breaches was the weakening of its position in negotiating a financial settlement with the contractor in relation to that delay.

---

[55] The question of indemnity or contribution may arise not only as between defendants but also as between defendants and persons joined to the action as CPR Part 20 defendants (formerly known as "third parties").

[56] [1996] 1 W.L.R. 675. In *Royal Brompton Hospital v. Hammond* [1999] B.L.R. 385, Judge Hicks Q.C. held that where an employer sued its professional advisers for impairing its settlement prospects with a contractor, the sums paid to the contractor and the sums sought against the professionals were not "the same damage" for the purposes of s.1 of the Act. The practical effect of the decision was that the professionals were not able to join the contractors with whom the client had settled.

[57] (2000) 69 Con.L.R. 132, 133 (first instance), 156, CA.

8–319   **The effect of a final certificate.** An architect's claim for contribution against a building contractor failed for a different reason in *Oxford University Fixed Assets Ltd v. Architects Design Partnership*.[58] The defendant architect had been engaged to design and supervise the construction of a pharmacology unit at the University. Following completion of the works, they had issued a final certificate under clause 30.9 of the J.C.T. 1980 Standard Form of Building Contract. Defects in the works then emerged and the employer brought a claim against the architects. It was held that the architects were not entitled to claim contribution from the building contractor: as between the employer and the contractor, the final certificate was conclusive evidence that the standards and quality of workmanship and materials used by the contractor were in compliance with the building contract. According, the contractor would have been able to defeat any claim brought against him by the employer. It followed that the contractor was not a person liable in respect of the same damage as the architects.

8–320   **The effect of joint insurance.** A construction professional will face a similar difficulty in claiming contribution from a building contractor to an employer's claim where the employer and the building contractor are joint insureds under a policy of insurance which covers the damage of which the employer complains. In *Co-operative Retail Services v. Taylor Young Partnership*,[59] the defendants were architects and engineers who had been engaged by the claimant for the construction of its new headquarters in Rochdale. The main building contract provided that the main contractor (Wimpey) should take out a policy of insurance of the works in the joint names of the claimant, Wimpey and Wimpey's electrical sub-contractor (Hall). When the works were damaged by a fire, the claimant sued the architects and engineers. They, in turn, sought to claim contribution from Wimpey and Hall. For the purposes of a trial of preliminary issues, it was assumed that the fire was caused by breach of duty on the part of each of the architects, the engineers, Wimpey and Hall. Nevertheless, the difficulty which the professionals faced was in showing that Wimpey and Hall were persons liable to the claimant in respect of the fire damage. All three were joint insureds under the policy of insurance which paid out in respect of the fire damage. One co-insured cannot sue another for a loss in respect of which both are entitled to the benefit of the same insurance.[60] The professionals sought to avoid this difficulty by arguing that the question whether persons are liable in respect of the same damage for the purposes of section 1 of the 1978 Act is to be determined at the date when the damage occurs. At the date of the fire, no claim had yet been made under the insurance policy, so the claimant could then have recovered damages from Wimpey and Hall. The argument failed at first instance and on appeal. The Court of Appeal held that the relevant time for deciding whether persons are liable in respect of the same damage is the time when contribution is sought.[61] In any event, it was held, Wimpey and Hall had never been liable to the claimant. The rule which prohibits joint insureds from recovering against one another is not merely a procedural bar to a claim: it extinguishes liability which would otherwise have existed. This decision provides a further incentive to construction

---

[58] (1999) 64 Con.L.R. 13. For further discussion, see para. 8–253, above.
[59] (2000) 74 Con.L.R. 12 (first instance), (2000) 74 Con.L.R. 12, 29, CA.
[60] *Petrofina (UK) Ltd v. Magnaload Ltd* [1984] QB 127; *National Oil Wells (UK) Ltd v. Davy Off-Shore Ltd* [1993] 2 Lloyd's Rep.582. See para. 8–126 above.
[61] The Court did not distinguish between the date when contribution proceedings are brought and the date when judgment is given on the claim for contribution: that question remains for decision.

professionals to see that their contracts of engagement make provision for them to be jointly insured with the employer and contractor against physical damage to the works.

Distinct types of damage. It frequently happens in building cases that the   **8–321**
claimant sustains numerous types of damage, for each of which, only some defendants are liable. If C sustains two types of damage and D1, D2 and D3 are liable for the first type of damage but only D1 and D3 are liable for the second type of damage, then in contribution proceedings between D1, D2 and D3 separate apportionment must be made between (a) D1, D2 and D3 and (b) D1 and D3. For example, in *Equitable Debenture Assets Corp. Ltd v. William Moss Group Ltd,*[62] liability in negligence for the defective design of curtain walling and so for the cost of its replacement was apportioned 75 per cent to the specialist design sub-contractors and 25 per cent to the architects; whereas liability for negligence resulting in bad workmanship to the parapet walling and causing loss due to additional leaks was apportioned 80 per cent to the specialist sub-contractors, 5 per cent to the architects and 15 per cent to the main con-tractors.

Distinct causes of damage. Similarly if there are two distinct causes of   **8–322**
damage, it may be appropriate to come to an independent assessment as to responsibility for each head of damage even if the defendants are the same. In *Oxford University Press v. John Stedman Design Group,*[63] the plaintiff bought an action against its architects and main contractors for defects in the floor of a warehouse. The defects consisted of (i) cracks, (ii) surface crazing, and (iii) breakdown in the edges. The architects settled with the plaintiff and sought a contribution from the main contractors under the 1978 Act. Judge Lewis Q.C. apportioned responsibility in respect of the cracking 60 per cent to the architects and 40 per cent to the contractors; in respect of the crazing, he apportioned responsibility equally between the architects and the contractor and in respect of the damage to the edges, he apportioned responsibility wholly to the con-tractor.

Amount of contribution. Section 2(1) of the Act provides that the amount of   **8–323**
contribution recoverable by D1 from D2 is such as may be found by the court to be just and equitable having regard to the extent of D2's responsibility for the damage. Section 2(2) goes on to provide that the court has power to exempt D2 from liability to make contribution or to direct that the contribution to be recovered from D2 should amount to a complete indemnity. In assessing con-tribution, the court takes a broad approach, taking into account both the extent to which D1 and D2 caused damage to C and their relative culpability. It is thought that listing factors which might generally point to greater apportionment of responsibility to one type of person in a building operation as opposed to another is a process best avoided, since so much depends on the facts of each case. Obviously, in the case of a design error, the design team are likely to have the heavier apportionment than the building contractor (if he has any at all). On the other hand, in the case of a workmanship error the heavier apportionment is

---

[62] (1984) 2 Con.L.R. 1, 40.
[63] (1990) 34 Con.L.R. 1.

likely to be to the builder and not to persons supervising him.[64] As between construction professionals, the apportionment of responsibility for an error will depend upon the relative extent of their respective involvements and opportunities to avoid the error.[65]

8-324   **Settlement as damage.** Claims for contribution are often made by joining CPR Part 20 defendants in an action. If satisfied that the defendant (D) is liable in respect of the damage suffered by the claimant (C), and that the Part 20 defendant (T) could also have been held liable for C's damage, the court will apportion liability under the Act as between D and T at the same time as it gives judgment for C against D. In those circumstances, it is obviously not open to T to argue that he and D are not persons liable in respect of the same damage under section 1 of the Act. The position is different if D has settled C's claim before seeking contribution from T. Section 1(4) of the Act provides that D is entitled to contribution in that case if D "would have been liable [to C] assuming that the factual basis of the claim against him could be established." This allows T to argue that D never had a liability to C and so should not have settled C's claim, or that D's liability to C was worth less than D supposed so that D should have paid less in settlement than he did. T will then argue that he is liable to make no contribution, or that he is liable to make contribution to a lower sum than the sum which D paid in settlement of C's claim. An argument of this sort was made in *J. Sainsbury plc v. Broadway Malyan.*[66] The defendant architects, who had settled a claim for fire-damage caused by the negligent design of a wall at a super-store, claimed contribution from the employer's engineers for failing to point out a defect in the architects' design for a particular girder. The claim was rejected on its facts, but the judge considered the ambit of section 1 of the Act. He held that, where a settlement has been made, the party who seeks contribution must prove that the settlement was reasonable although he does not need to prove every ingredient of liability to do this. He went on to hold that the settlement concluded by the architects was unreasonable in two respects. First, the settlement was made on the basis that the architects were liable for the storeowner's entire loss. The loss alleged was the cost of reinstatement of all of the fire-damage, on the grounds that had the wall been properly designed, it would have contained the fire for sufficient time to allow the fire brigade to prevent its spread.

---

[64] But see para. 8–319, above. Note the Australian case of *Carosella v. Ginos and Gilbert Pty* (1981) 27 S.A.S.R. 515. The builder, the local authority, an engineering company and an engineer director of the company were sued and held liable. For the purpose of apportionment, the engineering company and the engineer director were treated as one and the apportionment made was 50% to the builder, 25% to the local authority and 25% to the engineering company and its director. The decision in *Murphy v. Brentwood District Council* [1991] 1 A.C. 398 would now mean that, in England, the local authority would not be liable. Accordingly apportionments made in cases where the law was thought to be different from now must be treated with some caution. As for the position where an architect relies upon specialists (*e.g.* an engineer) or delegates work to them, see paras 8–175 to 8–179, above. As to the responsibility of a professional when the contractor has a duty to warn of unsafe works, see *Plant Construction Ltd v. Clive Adams Associates and JMH Construction Services Ltd* [2000] B.L.R. 137, CA and *Aurum Investments Ltd v. Avonforce Ltd* [2001] Lloyd's Rep. P.N. 285.

[65] See, for an example, *J Sainsbury v. Broadway Malyan* (1988) 61 Con.L.R. 31, where Judge Lloyd Q.C. rejected a claim by negligent architects for a contribution from engineers who had failed to point out defective fire-protection on a particular girder. He held, however, that had the failure been made out, he would have found the engineers to be 12.5% to blame on the basis that the architects' failures were far more basic and widespread than the single failure by the engineers would have been.

[66] (1998) 61 Con.L.R. 31.

On its true analysis, however, this was a claim for the loss of the chance that the fire brigade would have been able to control the fire, and that chance was no higher than 35 per cent. Second, the settlement failed to include any discount for the storeowner's contributory negligence, which the judge assessed at 20 per cent. For both reasons, the sum paid by the architects in settlement was too high, and the engineers, if liable, would have been ordered to pay a contribution based on the lower sum which should have been paid.

There is a slight divergence of view at first instance as to whether the fact that **8–325** a settlement was entered into on legal advice is relevant to the question of whether that settlement is reasonable. Judge Hicks Q.C. (in *DSL Group v. Unisys International Services Ltd*[67]) and Judge Lloyd Q.C. (in *J Sainsbury plc v. Broadway Malyan*[68]) have taken the view that it is irrelevant whilst Judge Bowsher Q.C. (in *P. & O. Developments Ltd v. Guy's and St. Thomas' NHS Trust*[69]) has taken the view that the existence of such advice might go to the question of whether the settlement was reasonable one. It is clear that a claimant for contribution to a settlement must prove that the settlement was a reasonable one (rather than merely that it was reasonable of him to settle the claim).[70] In most cases, his follows from the fact that an unreasonable settlement will not be a foreseeable loss in most cases.

The discretion on apportionment. The Court of Appeal recognises that the **8–326** trial judge has a discretion as to apportionment with which it will not interfere unless he has misdirected himself.[71] Unless the trial judge has failed to apply the relevant tests under the Act or has exercised his discretion in an unreasonable manner, the prospects of a successful appeal against his apportionment are slender. So much was emphasised in *McKenzie v. Potts*.[72] Both a builder and an architect were found to be liable to a plaintiff under section 1 of the Defective Premises Act 1972, by reason of the use of defective backfill behind foundation walls. The builder was liable for the actual use of the materials and had misinformed the architects as to the nature of the materials. The architects were held liable for negligent supervision in that they had wrongly relied on the builder's assurance. The trial judge considered the relevant tests of causation (where he found each defendant to have been equally responsible) and relative culpability (where he found the builder to have been more responsible than the architect) in apportioning damages as to 60 per cent to the builder and 40 per cent to the architect. Although the Court of Appeal expressed sympathy for the architect, they refused to interfere with the exercise of the judge's discretion. Russell L.J. said[73]:

"I have to say that in my view other judges may have taken a more sympathetic view of the degree of culpability on the part of the architects, but, having acknowledged that to be the position, I cannot interfere with the apportionment as made by the judge. In

---

[67] (1994) 41 Con.L.R. 33 at 39–43.
[68] (1998) 61 Con.L.R. 31 at 64.
[69] (1998) 62 Con.L.R. 38 at 55.
[70] *Biggin v. Permanite* [1951] 2 K.B. 314, 326 *per* Singleton L.J.; *P. & O. Developments Ltd v. Guy's and St. Thomas' NHS Trust* (1998) 62 Con.L.R. 38; *Royal Brompton Hospital NHS Trust v. Hammond (No.1)* [1999] B.L.R. 162.
[71] *Holland Hannen and Cubitts (Northern) Ltd v. Welsh Health Technical Services Organisation* (1985) 35 B.L.R. 1, *per* Lawton L.J. at 18.
[72] (1997) 50 Con.L.R. 40, CA.
[73] *ibid.* at 42.

my view he was entitled to make it; it was within the spectrum of his discretion . . . ."

8-327   One case in which the Court of Appeal did feel able to exercise the discretion afresh is *Holland Hannen and Cubitts (Northern) Ltd v. Welsh Health Technical Services Organisation.*[74] The plaintiff building contractor sued both the employer and a nominated sub-contractor (CED) for losses occasioned by delay. Part of the delay was the responsibility of a design fault for which CED admitted liability and part of the delay was caused by a wrongful instruction which condemned the floors. The employer brought into the action both its architects (who had issued the wrongful instruction) and its engineers (WEP). CED brought in its own engineers (AMP). Judge Newey Q.C. held that responsibility for the delay should be apportioned two-thirds to the employer's architects and engineers (WEP) and one-third to CED. As between the design team, the judge took into account that the architects should have grappled with the problem at an earlier stage than they did and apportioned blame on an equal basis. He also found that AMP were liable to CED and should bear three-quarters of the sums for which CED were liable. The Court of Appeal by a majority reversed the finding that AMP were liable at all[75] and also found unanimously that the judge had erred in the exercise of his discretion in apportioning blame as between CED and the design team as he had not taken into account in that apportionment the architect's failure to grapple with the problem at an early stage.[76] The Court of Appeal therefore exercised its own discretion and re-apportioned blame two-thirds to the design team and one-third to CED.

(b) *Contributory negligence*

8-328   The question of apportionment of responsibility may also arise as between a plaintiff and a defendant if the latter successfully raises a defence of contributory negligence by the plaintiff.[77] Following the decision of the Court of Appeal in *Forsikringsaktieselskapet Vesta v. Butcher*[78] contributory negligence may be raised as a defence to certain contractual claims.[79]

---

[74] (1985) 35 B.L.R. 1.
[75] This is discussed at para. 8–215, above.
[76] *ibid. per* Lawton L.J. at 18, *per* Robert Goff L.J. at 28 and *per* Dillon L.J. at 33.
[77] Note *Kensington and Chelsea and Westminster A.H.A. v. Wettern Composites Ltd* (1984) 1 Con.L.R. 114, 135, *per* Judge Smout Q.C.: "I have reached the conclusion that the clerk of works' negligence whilst more than minimal is very much less than that of the architects. If I may adapt the military terminology, it was the negligence of the Chief Petty Officer as compared with that of the captain of the ship. I assess responsibility as to the clerk of works 20%, as to the architects 80%. By reason of the vicarious responsibility of the plaintiffs (for the clerk of works) I make a finding of contributory negligence of 20%". See also the decision of Preston J. in *Homes by Jayman Ltd v. Kellam Berg* (1995) 29 Alta. L.R. (3d) 1 where the judge found that errors of design by the engineer, together with errors of construction by a contractor and negligence by the plaintiff developer in failing to see that areas did not have traffic going over them were all partly responsible for the failure of a new septic tank system. He apportioned liability one third to each of the developer, engineer and contractor. On appeal, (1998) 54 Alta. L.R. (3d) 272, the Alberta Court of Appeal did not disturb the apportionment by the trial judge even though an additional design error by the engineer was found to have been made.
[78] [1989] A.C. 852.
[79] See chap. 4. See also A. Bartlett, "Attribution of contributory negligence: agents, company directors and fraudsters" (1998) 114 L.Q.R. 460.

It is important to distinguish the principles governing contributory negligence 8–329
and those which apply in the apportionment of liability between several wrongdoers.[80] In *Pride Valley Foods Ltd v Hall & Partners (Contract Management)
Ltd*,[81] project managers engaged by the claimant to design a bread-making
factory were held liable for negligently failing to advise him that the panels
which he wished to use to line the factory were highly combustible and would
allow rapid spread of fire throughout the factory if ignited. It was held that any
damages recoverable by the claimant for damage caused by a subsequent fire at
the factory should be reduced by 50 per cent for his contributory negligence in
failing to take reasonable steps to prevent a fire starting in the factory.[82] Sedley
L.J. considered[83] whether the issue of contributory negligence should be
approached in the same way as the issue of apportionment of liability between
defendants, and concluded that it should not. The main difference was that no
deduction for contributory negligence will be made where the harm caused by the
claimant's own negligence is wholly within the very risk which it was the
defendants' duty to guard him against:

" . . . the starting point of the two exercises is different. Contribution starts from a point
at which two or more defendants have been held to have contributed by their own fault
to the claimant's injury. The remaining task is then to measure their contributions by
gauging the relative causative potency of their respective faults and their comparative
blameworthiness. Contributory negligence, by contrast, starts from a point at which the
defendant alone has been held to have caused the claimant's injury by his fault. Not one
but three questions then arise. The first is whether the claimant too was materially at
fault. The second, if he was, is whether his fault lay within the very risk which it was
the defendant's duty to guard him against. It is only if his fault was not, or not wholly,
within the causative reach of the defendant's own neglect that the question of relative
culpability enters the picture. Here, no doubt, the similarities with the principles
applicable under the 1978 Act will be considerable; but here too it may be relevant that
the claimant's neglect was linked to the unfulfilled duty owed to him by the defendant."

In that case it was arguable that the claimant's neglect had such catastrophic
consequences only because of the defendants' breach of their duty to guard it
against precisely those consequences. For that reason, Sedley L.J. would have
deducted no more than one third of the claimant's damages for contributory
negligence but he, along with Brooke and Dyson L.JJ., declined to interfere with
the exercise of the trial judge's discretion on this point.

5. ADJUDICATION

Part II of the Housing Grants, Construction and Regeneration Act 1996, which 8–330
came into force on May 1, 1998,[84] introduced of new form of dispute resolution

---

[80] See paras 8–315 to 8–327.

[81] (2001) 76 Con.L.R. 1 (first instance), [2001] E.W.C.A. Civ. 1001, (2001) 76 Con.L.R. 1, 36,
CA.

[82] The judge at first instance held that the claimant's case failed on causation, since he failed to prove
that he would have accepted the advice which he should have been given by the defendants; the Court
of Appeal remitted the case to the judge for a further trial on causation, but dismissed an appeal
against his finding of 50% contributory negligence.

[83] (2001) 76 Con.L.R. 1, 59–60.

[84] Housing Grants, Construction and Regeneration Act (England and Wales) (Commencement No. 4)
Order 1998 (S.I. 1998 No.650).

which applies only to the construction industry. Under section 108(1) of the Act, a party to a construction contract has the right to refer any dispute arising under the contract to adjudication. When that right is exercised, the other party to the contract must submit to adjudication. The decision of the adjudicator is final and binding if the contract so provides, but otherwise is binding only until the dispute is finally determined by legal proceedings, by arbitration (if the contract contains an arbitration agreement or the parties otherwise agree to arbitration) or by settlement of the dispute.[85]

8–331　　Section 108(1)–(4) of the Act sets out a procedure for adjudication and requires that construction contracts include express terms which incorporate that procedure. In the absence of such express terms, a statutory scheme (the Scheme for Construction Contracts[86]) is implied into the contract.

8–332　　**Construction contracts.** The Act applies to all "construction contracts" made after May 1, 1998.[87] This term is very widely defined. Section 104(1) provides that a construction contract is an agreement with a person for carrying out "construction operations" or arranging for them to be carried out by others by way of sub-contract or otherwise, providing his own or other labour to carry them out. Most importantly for present purposes, section 104(2) includes within the definition any agreement for the provision of advisory services namely architectural, design, surveying, building, engineering, interior or exterior decoration and landscaping. It follows that most engagements of construction professionals made after May 1, 1998 will be construction contracts under the Act,[88] provided only that the project in connection with which the professional is retained is within the definition of "construction operations."

8–333　　**Construction operations.** This term is also widely defined,[89] so that it will apply to most construction and engineering contracts and to most related contracts for professional services. There are exceptions,[90] notable amongst which are pure supply contracts, extraction and drilling for minerals, oil or natural gas, activities concerned with sites occupied primarily with the nuclear, power, water, sewage, chemical, pharmaceutical, oil, gas, steel and food industries, the making, installation and repair of artistic works, concession agreements for private finance initiative projects and the off site construction of building components, materials, plant and machinery unless the contract is also for their installation.

8–334　　**The timetable.** The purpose of adjudication is to achieve early and swift resolution of disputes, albeit provisional resolution, so as to avoid construction projects being interrupted for long periods while disputing parties arbitrate or litigate their differences. To this end, the Act permits a notice of referral to be

---

[85] s.108(3). The parties by agreement can extend the scope of adjudication, but they cannot contract out of it: *R.G. Carter Ltd v. Edmund Nuttall Ltd*, unreported, June 21, 2000, Judge Thornton Q.C.

[86] S.I. 1998 No. 649.

[87] s.104(6)(a).

[88] The Act applies only to agreements in writing, but the definition of writing includes agreements which are merely evidenced in writing, where the agreement refers to a document or where there is merely an audio or visual record of the agreement: s.107. In particular, s.107(5) suggests that a purely oral agreement may be treated as in writing if reference is made to it in written submissions in adjudication, arbitral or judicial proceedings.

[89] See s.105.

[90] See s.105(2).

served at any time[91] and requires[92] a timetable which enables the adjudicator to be appointed and the dispute referred to him within seven days of such notice. Thereafter, the adjudicator must reach his decision within 28 days, although the parties can agree a longer period and the adjudicator can extend the time by 14 days with the agreement of the referring party. The adjudicator is entitled to take the initiative in ascertaining the facts and law which are relevant in deciding the dispute. It will be immediately apparent that while adjudication is likely to serve a useful purpose in dealing with relatively straightforward disputes which might otherwise cause severe disruption to a project, such as some disputes as to payment between the parties to a building contract, its suitability as a means of resolving complex building contract disputes and professional negligence claims is questionable. In practice, the client is able to spend many months preparing his claim, possibly with the assistance of independent experts, before serving a notice of referral upon the construction professional. The professional will then have something in the order of a fortnight to prepare and present his defence before the adjudicator makes his decision.

Enforcement of adjudicator's decisions. The court has power to enforce an   8–335
adjudicator's decision under section 42 of the Arbitration Act 1996.[93] The usual method of enforcement is by way of an order for summary judgment upon the application of the party in whose favour the decision was made, although where the decision requires a party to perform some obligation other than making a payment, a mandatory injunction will be available.

Challenging the adjudicator's decision. During the short time in which the   8–336
Act has been in force, there has accumulated a large body of case law dealing with the extent to which it is possible to resist the enforcement of an adjudicator decision. It is clear that the courts will enforce the decisions of adjudicators save where such decisions are made without jurisdiction In *Bouygues UK Ltd v. Dahl-Jensen UK Ltd*,[94] the adjudicator had made an obvious error in his calculations which meant that his decision was in favour of the claimant. It was common ground that, but for the error, the decision would have been in favour of the defendant. Nevertheless, the claimant obtained an order for summary judgment based on the decision. Dyson J., whose decision and reasoning were upheld by the Court of Appeal,[95] explained[96]:

> "the purpose of the scheme is to provide a speedy mechanism for settling disputes in construction contracts on a provisional interim basis, and requiring the decisions of adjudicators to be enforced pending final determination of disputes by arbitration, litigation or agreement, whether those decisions are wrong in point of law or fact.

---

[91] Note that adjudication provisions, like arbitration agreements, survive the determination of the contract: *A&D Maintenance and Construction Ltd v. Pagehurst Construction Services Ltd* (2000) 16 Const.L.J. 199. A reference to adjudication will be valid even after court proceedings have begun: *Herschel Engineering Ltd v. Breen Property Ltd* [2000] B.L.R. 272.
[92] s.104(2).
[93] *Macob Civil Engineering Ltd v. Morrison Construction Ltd* [1999] B.L.R. 93; *Outwing Construction Ltd v. H Randall & Son Ltd* [1999] B.L.R. 156. It will also create a debt which can be the subject of a statutory demand: *George Parke v. The Fenton Gretton Partnership* [2001] C.I.L.L. 1712.
[94] [2000] B.L.R. 49 (first instance).
[95] [2000] B.L.R. 522, CA.
[96] [2000] B.L.R. 49, 55.

Sometimes those mistakes will be glaringly obvious and disastrous in their consequences for the losing party. The victims of mistakes will usually be able to recoup their losses by subsequent arbitration or litigation, and possibly even by a subsequent adjudication. Sometimes, they will not be able to do so, where, for example, there is intervening insolvency, either of the victim or of the fortunate beneficiary of the mistake. . . . But in deciding whether the adjudicator has decided the wrong question rather than given a wrong answer to the right question, the court should bear in mind that the speedy nature of the adjudication process means that mistakes will inevitably occur, and, in my view, it should guard against characterising a mistaken answer to an issue that lies within the scope of the reference as an excess of jurisdiction."

In *Sherwood and Casson Ltd v. Mackenzie*,[97] Judge Thornton Q.C. summarised in five guidelines the approach which the court will take to enforcement of an adjudicator's decision:

(1) A decision of an adjudicator whose validity is challenged as to its factual or legal conclusions or as to procedural error remains a decision that is both enforceable and should be enforced.

(2) A decision that is erroneous, even if the error is disclosed by the reasons, will still not ordinarily be capable of being challenged and should, ordinarily, still be enforced.

(3) A decision may be challenged on the ground that the adjudicator was not empowered by the 1996 Act to make that decision, because there was no underlying construction contract between the parties or because he had gone outside his terms of reference.

(4) The adjudication is intended to be a speedy process in which mistakes will inevitably occur. Thus, the court should guard against characterising a mistaken answer to an issue, which is within an adjudicator's jurisdiction, as being an excess of jurisdiction. Furthermore, the court should give a fair, natural and sensible interpretation to the decision in the light of the disputes that are the subject of the reference.

(5) An issue as to whether a construction contract ever came into existence, which is one challenging the jurisdiction of the adjudicator, so long as it is reasonably and clearly raised, must be determine by the Court on the balance of probabilities with, if necessary, oral evidence.

8–337   **The adjudicator's jurisdiction.** An adjudicator does not have jurisdiction to decide his own jurisdiction, unless the parties confer that jurisdiction upon him.[98] In *Fastrack Contractors Ltd v. Morrison Construction Ltd*,[99] Judge Thornton Q.C. explained that there are four options available to a party who wishes to challenge the jurisdiction of an adjudicator:

---

[97] Unreported, November 30, 1999, applied by Judge Bowsher Q.C. in *Northern Developments (Cumbria) Ltd v. J. & J. Nichol* [2000] B.L.R. 158, 162–163. Note also that, in an appropriate case, the court will sever and enforce those parts of his decision which the adjudicator did have jurisdiction to make: *Workplace Technologies Ltd v. E Squared Ltd* [2000] C.I.L.L. 1607.
[98] *Palmers Ltd v. ABB Power Construction Ltd* [1999] B.L.R. 426; *Christiani and Nielsen Ltd v Lowry Centre Development Co Ltd*, unreported, June 29, 2000, Judge Thornton Q.C.; *Whiteways Contractors (Sussex) Ltd v. Impresa Castelli Construction UK Ltd* (2000) 75 Con.L.R. 92; *Maymac Environmental Services Ltd v Faraday Building Services Ltd* (2000) 75 Con.L.R. 101.
[99] [2000] B.L.R. 168, 178.

"If a party challenges the entire jurisdiction of the adjudicator...it has four options. Firstly, it can agree to widen the jurisdiction of the adjudicator so as to refer the dispute as to the adjudicator's jurisdiction to the same adjudicator. If the referring party agrees to that course, and the appointed adjudicator accepts the reference to him of this second dispute, the jurisdiction of the adjudicator could then be resolved as part of the reference. The challenging party could, secondly, refer the dispute as to jurisdiction to second adjudicator. This would not put a halt to the first adjudication, if that had already led to an appointment, since the adjudicator has a statutory duty, unless both parties agree otherwise, to decide the reference in a very short timescale. The challenging party could, thirdly, seek a declaration from the court that the proposed adjudication lacked jurisdiction. This option is of little utility unless the adjudicator has yet to be appointed or the parties agree to put the adjudication into abeyance pending the relatively speedy determination of the jurisdiction question by the court. The Technology and Construction Court can, for example, resolve questions of that kind within days of them being referred to it. Fourthly, the challenging party could reserve its position, participate in the adjudication and then challenge any attempt to enforce the adjudicator's decision on jurisdictional grounds."

The court will not grant an interim injunction restraining an adjudication[1]; if a party wishes to challenge the adjudicator's jurisdiction before he reaches his decision, it must take the third option described by Judge Thornton Q.C. and claim a declaration or a final injunction using the procedure in Part 7 of the Civil Procedure Rules.

Successful challenges to the jurisdiction of an adjudicator have been made on 8–338 the grounds that there was no dispute between the parties at the time of the notice of referral to adjudication[2]; that, in a case where the Scheme applied, the notice purported to refer more than one dispute for adjudication[3]; that the contract under which the dispute arose was not a construction contract within the meaning of the Act because it was not a contract for "construction operations"[4] or because it was concluded before May 1, 1998[5]; that the adjudicator's decision went beyond the bounds of the dispute referred to him.[6]

Natural justice. Where the statutory timetable for adjudication means that a 8–339 construction professional is unable properly to prepare and present his defence to a client's claim, he may be able to resist enforcement of the adjudicator's decision if he can show that this amounted to a serious a breach of the rules of

---

[1] *Workplace Technologies Ltd v. E Squared Ltd* [2000] C.I.L.L. 1607.

[2] *Fastrack Contractors Ltd v. Morrison Construction Ltd* [2000] B.L.R. 168; *Shepherd Construction Ltd v. Mecright Ltd* [2000] B.L.R. 489.

[3] *Fastrack Contractors Ltd v. Morrison Construction Ltd* [2000] B.L.R. 168; *Grovedeck Ltd v. Capital Demolition Ltd* [2000] B.L.R. 181.

[4] *ABB Power Construction Ltd v. Norwest Holst Engineering Ltd* (2001) 17 Const. L.J. 246, *Gibson Lea Retail Interiors Ltd v. Makro Self Service Wholesalers Ltd*, unreported, July 24, 2001; *cf. ABB Zantingh v. Zedal Building Services* [2001] B.L.R. 66, *Palmers Ltd v. ABB Power Construction* [1999] B.L.R. 426 and *Nottingham Community Housing Association Ltd v. Powerminster Ltd* [2000] B.L.R. 309.

[5] *The Project Consultancy Group v. The Trustees of the Gray Trust* [1999] B.L.R. 377, *cf. Atlas Ceiling and Partition Co Ltd v. Crowngate Estates (Cheltenham) Ltd*, unreported, February 18, 2000, Judge Thornton Q.C. and *Christiani and Nielsen Ltd v. Lowry Centre Development Co Ltd*, unreported, June 29, 2000, Judge Thornton Q.C..

[6] *FW Cook Ltd v. Shimizu (UK) Ltd* [2000] B.L.R. 199.

natural justice. Although mere procedural errors will not invalidate a decision,[7] conduct which seriously endangers the fair resolution of the dispute may well do so. In *Discain Project Services Ltd v. Opecprime Development Ltd*,[8] Judge Bowsher Q.C. declined to enforce a decision which had been reached after the adjudicator had discussed the substantive issues in the dispute during private telephone conversations with one of the parties, without recording the conversations or communicating their substance to the other party. It was held that this was a breach of the rules of natural justice, which require the adjudicator to be fair and impartial and avoid the appearance of bias. The judge warned, however, that only serious breaches of natural justice would prevent enforcement: "It would be quite wrong for parties to search around for breaches of the rules of natural justice. It is a question of fact and degree in each case, and in this case the adjudicator over-stretched the rules." In *Woods Hardwick Ltd v. Chiltern Air-Conditioning Ltd*,[9] architects referred their claim for unpaid fees to adjudication. Before giving a decision in favour of the architects, the adjudicator held discussions with third parties, including the RIBA and the local authority, without informing the client or allowing it the opportunity to comment on the information obtained. Judge Thornton Q.C. held that the adjudicator was in breach of his obligation to act impartially[10] and declined to enforce his decision. Similarly, in *Glencot Development and Design Company Ltd v. Ben Barrett & Son (Contractors) Ltd*,[11] an adjudicator's conduct in proceeding to a decision after he had become involved in without prejudice negotiations between the parties was held to invalidate his decision. The circumstances would lead a fair-minded and informed observer to conclude that there was a real possibility or danger that the adjudicator was biased.

8–340   **The Human Rights Act 1998.** Section 6 of the Human Rights Act 1998[12] provides that it is unlawful for a public authority to act in a manner which is incompatible with the European Convention on Human Rights. Article 6(1) of the Convention established the right to fair administration of justice states:

> "In the determination of his civil rights and obligations . . . everyone is entitled to a fair and public hearing within a reasonable time by an independent and impartial tribunal established by law. Judgment shall be pronounced publicly . . . ."

Both the short timetable prescribed by statute for the adjudication process and the fact that adjudication is not a public process have been relied upon in attempts to challenge the adjudication process as incompatible with Article 6 of the Convention. Two such attempts have failed at first instance. In *Elanay Contracts Ltd v. The Vestry*,[13] a decision made before the Human Rights Act 1998 came into

---

[7] *Macob Civil Engineering Ltd v. Morrison Construction Ltd* [1999] B.L.R. 93.Note that the adjudicator has a limited power to correct accidental omissions and errors in his decision, and doing so will not invalidate the decision: *Bloor Construction (UK) Ltd v. Bowmer & Kirkland (London) Ltd* [2000] B.L.R. 315.

[8] [2000] B.L.R. 402 (*ex tempore* reasons for granting permission to defend) and [2001] B.L.R. 285 (trial and full reasons).

[9] [2001] B.L.R. 23.

[10] s.104(2)(e) of the 1996 Act. The adjudicator was also in breach of para. 19 of the Scheme, which requires him to communicate information which he has obtained to both parties.

[11] [2001] B.L.R. 202.

[12] For further discussion as to the impact of the Human Rights Act 1998 upon claims for professional negligence, see chap. 7.

[13] [2001] B.L.R. 33.

force on October 1, 2000, Judge Havery Q.C. held that Article 6 of the Convention does not apply to an adjudicator's award or to proceedings before an adjudicator. The basis for his decision was that although adjudication is a determination of civil rights or obligations, it is not a final determination. By the time of the decision in *Austin Hall Building Ltd v Buckland Securities Ltd*,[14] the 1998 Act had come into force. The defendant to an application for summary judgment to enforce an adjudicator's decision argued that the whole system of adjudication established by the Housing Grants, Construction and Regeneration Act 1996 was incompatible with Article 6(1) of the Convention. Judge Bowsher Q.C. held that neither the 1998 Act nor the Convention applied to adjudication, although he described the question as "finely balanced".[15] The principal reason for the judge's decision was that an adjudicator is not a public authority.[16] He further held that, even if the Act and Convention applied, there was no breach of the requirement for a public hearing. In the first place, it was open to either party to ask the adjudicator to sit in public. A failure to make such a request amounted to waiver of the right. Furthermore, it was necessary to look at the entire adjudication process, including enforcement of the adjudicator's decision by way of court proceedings, to see whether Article 6 was breached. Since the court dealing with enforcement of the decision would normally sit in public, there was no breach of Article 6.

Impecuniosity. The enforcement of an adjudicator's decision might work   **8–341** substantial injustice if, between enforcement and a subsequent reversal of the decision in arbitral or legal proceedings, the enforcing party falls into financial difficulty and is unable to repay the sum awarded by the adjudicator. In *Herschel Engineering Ltd v. Breen Property Ltd*,[17] Dyson J. stated that in certain circumstances he might be prepared to order that enforcement of an adjudicator's decision would be stayed if such evidence were available. In *Absolute Rentals Ltd v. Glencor Enterprises Ltd*,[18] by contrast, Judge Wilcox refused a stay on grounds of impecuniosity, stating that a stay for that reason would frustrate the purpose of the legislation. In that case, however, there was insufficient evidence to enable the judge to find that the successful party was impecunious. In *Rainford House Ltd (in Administrative Receivership) v. Cadogan Ltd*,[19] Judge Seymour Q.C. held that the policy of the 1996 Act was not to transfer the risk of insolvency from one party to a dispute to the other. The Act merely addressed the question of which of two solvent parties should hold the monies in dispute pending final resolution of the dispute. If there was objective evidence of a substantial risk that money paid would be irretrievably lost, such a payment should not be required by way of enforcement of an adjudicator's decision. In that case, where the successful party was in administrative receivership, the judge ordered that the sum in dispute should be paid into court by the unsuccessful party pending final resolution of the dispute.

---

[14] [2001] B.L.R. 272.
[15] *ibid.* at 280.
[16] See s.6(1) of the 1998 Act.
[17] [2000] B.L.R. 272.
[18] [2000] C.I.L.L. 1637.
[19] [2001] C.I.L.L. 1709.

CHAPTER 9

SURVEYORS

PARA.
1. General
 (a) Bases of liability 9–001
 (b) Duties to client 9–019
  (i) Contractual duties 9–019
  (ii) Duties independent of
   contract 9–032
 (c) Duties to third parties 9–033
  (i) General principles 9–033
  (ii) Knowledge of reliance .. 9–039
  (iii) Duty of mortgagee's
   valuer to purchaser 9–043
 (d) The standard of care and
  skill 9–052
  (i) Reasonable standard 9–052
  (ii) General practice and
   knowledge as evidence
   of the standard 9–054
  (iii) Not every error is
   negligence 9–058
  (iv) The relevance of "the
   bracket" 9–059
  (v) Onus of proof 9–062
 (e) Limitation of liability 9–064
 (f) Mutual valuer 9–074
2. Liability for breach of duty 9–075
 (a) Failing to carry out
  instructions 9–077
 (b) Insufficient knowledge or
  experience 9–079
 (c) Failing to inspect properly 9–082
  (i) Failing to inspect
   particular parts 9–083
  (ii) Failing to uncover and
   open up 9–084
  (iii) Failing to observe 9–090
  (iv) Limited survey 9–097

PARA.
  (v) Failing to recognise 9–099
 d) Failing to make sufficient
  inquiries 9–100
 (e) Failing to make proper
  appraisal 9–104
 (f) Inadequate report 9–107
3. Damages 9–110
 (a) Has the Claimant sustained the
  loss claimed? 9–112
 (b) Is the loss claimed within the
  scope of the Defendant's
  duty 9–113
 (c) Remoteness 9–119
  (i) Causation 9–120
  (ii) Foreseeability 9–125
 (d) Measure of damages 9–128
  (i) Negligent survey or
   valuation for a purchaser
   who completes a
   purchase 9–130
  (ii) Negligent survey or
   valuation for a purchaser
   who withdraws from
   purchase before
   completion 9–149
  (iii) Negligent survey or
   valuation for lender 9–150
  (iv) Overvaluation for
   vendor 9–175
  (v) Undervaluation for
   vendor 9–176
  (vi) Other work 9–178
  (vii) Inconvenience and
   discomfort 9–181
  (viii) Incidental expenses 9–190

1. GENERAL

The general function of surveyors is to advise and act on behalf of clients in **9–001** matters concerned with land, buildings and chattels. This description is so broad as to be virtually meaningless. It is, consequently, usually more useful to define a surveyor's job by reference to the particular task that he is carrying out than by reference to his own description. Although many surveyors are still general practitioners, sub-specialisms have developed and continue to develop. Many of the activities carried out by such specialists are close to, and sometimes overlap with, activities which are carried out by other professions, so that a building surveyor may carry out tasks which might otherwise be undertaken by an architect or structural engineer, whilst a minerals surveyor will require a substantial body of geotechnical knowledge of the sort familiar to a geotechnical engineer. The core activity of most (although not all) surveyors, and that which has generated the most considerable body of recent litigation, is the valuation of land and interests in land.

9–002 There is no statutory regulation of qualification and practice as a surveyor.[1] The profession is subject to self-regulation in respect of these matters by the main professional organisation, the Royal Institution of Chartered Surveyors (RICS), which amalgamated with the Incorporated Society of Valuers and Auctioneers (ISVA) in July 2000. A candidate for membership of the RICS must choose a specialisation, and therefore division of the profession, at an early stage. The professional and practical requirements of the various divisions of the RICS vary to such an extent that it has not been thought desirable to devise a single Assessment of Professional Competence to cover membership of the RICS as a whole. There are therefore different tests, each of which reflects the needs of the particular area of specialisation.[2]

9–003 **Chartered surveyors.** There is a variety of routes to becoming a chartered surveyor, but all involve graduating from an approved degree or diploma course. In addition, all candidates must complete the appropriate Assessment of Professional Competence. This test takes the form of a minimum period of two years' experience with an approved firm of chartered surveyors, the submission by the candidate of a written summary of that experience and the solution to a practical task, relevant to their chosen specialisation, to be given at a formal interview.[3] Upon qualification a chartered surveyor becomes a professional associate of the RICS and may describe himself as a chartered surveyor, and use the initials ARICS[4] A chartered surveyor elected to the class of Fellow[5] may use the initials FRICS[6] A firm whose partners consist of Fellows and Professional Associates may use, in conjunction with its title, the designation "Chartered Surveyors".[7]

9–004 **Functions of surveyors.** Their specific activities may be categorised under the seven divisions of the RICS:

(a) commercial/residential[8];

---

[1] Estate agency work, defined as "the introduction, in the course of business, of prospective vendors and purchasers of an interest in land and activities designed to ensure the disposal or acquisition of that interest" is regulated by the Estate Agents' Act 1979. The Act does not apply to "things done . . . in the course of carrying out any survey or valuation pursuant to a contract which is distinct from that under which [estate agency work] is done" (see subss. 1(1) and 1(2)(d)).

[2] See for example the Guide and Rules to the Assessment of Professional Competence for Building Surveyors, RICS September 1998.

[3] Full details are provided in the appropriate Guide and Rules, published by RICS, and available from the Education and Membership Department, RICS, Surveyor Court, Westwood Way, Coventry CV4 8JE.

[4] RICS byelaw 13(1)(b).

[5] The requirements for election are set out in RICS byelaw 6. The election to the status of Fellow is a recognition of achievement and status within the profession.

[6] RICS byelaw 13(1)(a).

[7] RICS byelaw 13(2). Either all the partners must be Fellows or Professional Associates, or at least three-quarters of the partners must hold such designations. There are further detailed provisions in the byelaw.

[8] Sometimes referred to as "General Practice". This division includes those members who will often undertake inspections for mortgage valuations and house and flat buyers' reports.

(b) quantity surveying;

(c) building surveying;

(d) rural property;

(e) planning and development;

(f) land and hydrographic surveying;

(g) minerals surveying.

The descriptions of the divisions illustrates the extent to which surveyors operate in fields often more associated with other professions. In addition to the examples set out above,[9] a planning and development surveyor will often be instructed to appear as an advocate at a planning enquiry, rather than a solicitor or counsel. Similarly, surveyors are frequently retained to act in rent review arbitrations, rather than solicitors.[10] Most reported professional negligence cases against surveyors concern their activities of inspection and valuation and this chapter principally deals with those activities. Quantity surveying and supervision of construction works are considered in Chapter 8. Where surveyors act in planning enquiries and other contentious proceedings their conduct will be governed by principles similar to those that apply to solicitors acting in similar proceedings.[11] Surveyors frequently act as arbitrators (or "mutual valuers") in the context of rent reviews or agreements for the sale of property at market value.[12]

Two divisions of the RICS contain the overwhelming majority of the member-   **9–005** ship, those being commercial/residential and quantity surveying. The building surveying division is relatively small.[13] It is important to note that whilst inspection and valuation may be carried out by the same person in respect of relatively modest residential properties, they are really separate tasks involving the use of different skills. The assessment of defects, their importance and proper method of repair is a task for which a building surveyor should be suitably qualified and experienced. It is only because of the possible effect on value of significant defects and the requirement by lenders for accurate valuations that the public have become accustomed to an "ordinary" surveyor inspecting their house for defects rather than merely valuing it on the assumption that is free from significant defects. This tendency may have been reinforced by the search by lending institutions for cheap "surveys" on behalf of their clients and the willingness of valuers to undertake onerous tasks for very modest fees[14] whilst seeking to rely, usually unsuccessfully, on exemption clauses.

The division of tasks is relevant to the competence of expert witnesses in actions involving the professional competence of surveyors. A chartered building

---

[9] See para. 9–001.

[10] See for example, *Thomas Miller & Co. v. Richard Saunders and Partners* [1989] 1 E.G.L.R. 267 (where an analogy was drawn in argument between the position of counsel advising on evidence and a surveyor considering what evidence to submit to an arbitrator), and *Rajdev v. Becketts* [1989] 2 E.G.L.R. 144, para. 9–179 below.

[11] See chap. 10.

[12] A surveyor acting as an arbitrator (as distinct from an expert) will be immune from suit on the basis of judicial immunity. However he will not be immune on any other basis: see *Hall v Simons* [2000] 3 W.L.R. 543, *Sutcliffe v. Thackrah* [1974] A.C. 727 and *Arenson v Arenson* [1977] A.C. 405. See further paras 8–251 above and 11–015 below.

[13] In 1996, only 11%.

[14] Note the obligation imposed on building societies by s.62 of the Building Societies Act 1986.

surveyor is likely to have spent a considerable part of his professional life performing detailed examinations of different kinds buildings and their defects. A chartered surveyor qualified in, for example, the commercial/residential division of the RICS, is unlikely to have anything like the same degree of experience of defects, although he may have inspected many houses. Conversely a building surveyor is unlikely to be experienced in the valuation of property. For substantial properties a valuation is likely to be subject to a detailed survey carried out by a specialist building surveyor.

9–006   **Surveyors as expert witnesses.** An expert's evidence is founded on his training and experience. The court will consider "whether the witness has acquired by study or experience sufficient knowledge of the subject to render his opinion of value in resolving the issues before the court."[15] In England the Court rules now expressly provide that the duty of an expert to assist the court overrides any obligation to the party from whom he receives instructions[16] and that an expert report must contain a statement that the expert understands his duty to the court.[17] Guidance as to the duties and responsibilities of expert witnesses in civil cases was given by Cresswell J. in *National Justice Compania Naviera SA v. Prudential Assurance Co. Ltd.*[18] This was generally approved by the Court of Appeal subject to the qualification that an experienced expert, when assessing the significance of certain evidence, is entitled to weigh the probabilities and this may involve making use of the skills of other experts or drawing on his more general knowledge.[19] Surveyors acting as expert witnesses must take care to try to put themselves in the position in which the defendant surveyor found himself. The use of hindsight when making criticisms is likely to devalue an expert's evidence.[20] The court has power under CPR 35.8 to appoint a court valuation expert, and will do so in an appropriate case whether the parties agree or not.[21] The separation of the RICS into seven divisions, each representing a distinct area of practice, each with its own training and assessment syllabus, means that care needs to be taken before describing or accepting without enquiry a chartered surveyor as an expert for the purpose of a surveying or valuation case. Given the multiplicity of tasks which a surveyor can undertake, it is suggested that two questions need to be considered: (a) Was the task which the defendant undertook one within his own proper and usual professional sphere? If not, there may be a question as to whether he should be judged not according to the practice of his

---

[15] *per* King C.J. in *The Queen v. Bonython* (1984) 38 S.A.S.R. 45, 46. In *European Partners in Capital (EPIC) Holdings BV v. Goddard & Smith* [1992] 2 E.G.L.R. 155 the Court of Appeal held: "Issues of professional opinion, which must be chosen between if liability in negligence is to be established, will not as a general rule be issues suitable to be resolved on a summary judgment application." (Scott L.J. at 157E.)

[16] CPR 35.3.

[17] CPR 35.10(2).

[18] [1993] 2 Lloyd's Rep. 68, 81.

[19] [1995] 1 Lloyd's Rep. 455, 496. In *Cemp Properties (U.K.) Ltd v. Dentsply Research & Development Corporation* [1991] 2 E.G.L.R. 197, 200 the Court of Appeal commented. "It is a sad feature of modern litigation that expert witnesses, particularly in valuation cases, instead of giving evidence of their actual views as to the true position, enter into the arena and, as advocates, put forward the maximum or minimum figures as best suited to their side's interests. If experts do this, they must not be surprised if their views carry little weight with the judge. In this case, such evidence rightly led the judge to reject the expert evidence on both sides."

[20] See, *e.g.*, the Scottish case of *Alliance & Leicester Building Society v. J. & E. Shepherd* [1995] G.W.D. 11–608, OH, Lord MacLean. For the facts of the case see para. 9–108, n. 75.

[21] *Abbey National v Key Surveyors Nationwide Ltd* [1996] 1 W.L.R. 1534.

own usual profession but rather according to the professional practice of the specialism in which he purported to operate.[22] (b) If so, did the defendant act in accordance with practices which are regarded as acceptable by a respectable body of opinion in his profession?[23] Where a task is carried out by a professional man who is properly qualified to undertake the task, it will usually be necessary for there to be evidence from an expert of the same discipline to the effect that the defendant fell below the reasonable standard of his profession, before the court will be prepared to find him negligent.[24] Thus in *Sansom v. Metcalfe Hambleton & Co.*,[25] the Court of Appeal allowed an appeal by the defendant surveyor against a finding that he had negligently conducted a survey on the basis that the only relevant evidence called by the plaintiff had been from a structural engineer.[26] Butler-Sloss L.J., giving the judgment of the Court, stated:

> "In my judgment, it is clear ... that a court should be slow to find a professionally qualified man guilty of a breach of his duty of skill and care towards a client (or third party), without evidence from those within the same profession as to the standard expected on the facts of the case and the failure of the professionally qualified man to measure up to that standard. It is not an absolute rule ... but, less it is an obvious case, in the absence of the relevant expert evidence the claim will not be proved."[27]

(a) *Bases of liability*[28]

In England it is now settled law that surveyors may incur liability to their clients **9–007** for negligent valuations or reports both in contract and in tort.[29] If the appropriate

---

[22] See further para. 8–142 above and para. 10–094 below.

[23] See *Zubaida v. Hargreaves* [1995] 1 E.G.L.R. 127 *per* Hoffmann L.J. at 128A-B applying the well-known passage in *Bolam v. Friern Hospital Management Committee* [1957] 1 W.L.R. 582 at 587 and *Merivale Moore PLC v. Strutt & Parker* [2000] P.N.L.R. 498 *per* Buxton L.J. at 515C-E.

[24] In *Routestone Ltd v. Minories Finance Ltd* [1997] 1 E.G.L.R. 123, 127B Jacob J. held that the effect of the Civil Evidence Act 1972, s.3 was to make admissible the opinion of an expert on the question of whether or not a party had been negligent. He continued: "What really matters in most cases is the reasons given for the opinion. As a practical matter a well constructed expert's report containing opinion evidence sets out the opinion and the reasons for it. If the reasons stand up the opinion does, if not, not."

[25] [1998] P.N.L.R. 542.

[26] Similarly in *Whalley v. Roberts & Roberts* [1990] 1 E.G.L.R. 164, Auld J., when considering whether or not there had been a breach by the defendant surveyors of their duty of care heard evidence from two surveyors as well as an architect and a civil engineer. On the question of liability, he held that it was only the evidence of the surveyors to which he should pay attention. See also the architects case of *Investors in Industry v. South Bedfordshire District Council* [1986] 1All E.R. 787 *per* Slade L.J. at 808 to 809 where the judge stated that little reliance was to be placed on the answers of three engineers as to the duties of an architect. See further para. 8–151 above.

[27] At 549B. In *Merivale Moore PLC v. Strutt & Parker* [2000] P.N.L.R. 498 at 517A, Buxton L.J. stated that he was not prepared to hold that the adduction of expert evidence as to the "bracket" within which a competent valuation might be provided was necessary in every case: "As at present advised, I think that it is still open to the judge in a suitable case to hold that the valuation is so far removed from what was the true value of the property that it must be regarded as a valuation that was outside the limits open to a competent valuer, without specific professional evidence as to what those limits were."

[28] Where compensation is sought the RICS has established an arbitration scheme as an alternative to litigation between its members and their clients. It is intended to be inexpensive, swift and independent of the profession. The arbitration is conducted in writing and is administered independently from the RICS by the Chartered Institute of Arbitrators, 12 Bloomsbury Square, London WC1A 2LP.

[29] See para. 9–032 below. Following the decision of the House of Lords in *Henderson v. Merrett* [1995] 2 A.C. 145, cases such as *Hiron v. Pynford South Ltd* [1992] 2 E.G.L.R. 138 where Judge Newey Q.C. held that the fourth Defendant building surveyors did not owe a concurrent duty of care in tort to that owed in contract are not good law.

conditions are met, they may also incur liability to third parties in tort.[30] A surveyor who dishonestly puts forward a mortgage valuation or any other statement which causes loss will render himself liable to an action in deceit. Given the prevalence of mortgage frauds in the late 1980s and early 1990s together with the advantages of an action in deceit so far as foreseeability,[31] contributory negligence[32] and (possibly) the effect of the decision in *BBL*,[33] there has, recently, been a substantial increase in the number of fraud claims brought against surveyors in England. It is also conceivable that the act or omission complained of will give rise to liability under other torts,[34] but the claim so far as based on tort will usually be for common law negligence including negligent misrepresentation.

9–008   An unsettled question is as to the full implications of the decision of the House of Lords in *BBL v. Eagle Star*.[35] Lord Hoffman stated the *scope* of a valuer's duty (and therefore the kind of damages arising) was to be deduced, in tort from the purpose of the rule imposing the duty. In the case of an implied contractual duty, the nature and extent of the liability was to be defined by the term which the law implied. This appears to go beyond a traditional analysis of contracts where the court first deduces the extent of a party's obligations (whether by reference to express or implied terms) and then considers the damages which flow (by reference to considerations of causation, remoteness and foreseeability). A new area of consideration is thus introduced. It is, as yet, unclear whether the decision is limited to the particular factual situation in which it arose (*i.e.* a valuation for a mortgage lender) or has much wider and more general application.[36]

9–009   **Limitation.** Although a cause of action in negligence will have a different measure of loss from a cause of action in contract, in surveyors' negligence actions it is unlikely that there will be any practical difference in the result.[37] There may however be significant differences in the limitation period where it may well be beneficial to be able to sue in negligence as well as for breach of contract as (a) the primary limitation period will often start to run later and (b) the relief provided by section 14A of the Limitation Act 1980 whereby an action may be commenced within three years of the "date of knowledge"[38] is available only for actions in negligence.[39] The first of these differences is illustrated by the decision of the Court of Appeal in *Byrne v. Hall Pain & Foster*,[40] where the writ had been issued more than six years after the exchange of contracts, but less than six years after completion of the purchase. It followed that any contractual claim was statute barred as having occurred more than six years after any breach of contract. The question was thus as to whether the claimant had suffered loss so

---

[30] See para. 9–032 below.
[31] See para. 9–125 below.
[32] See para. 9–011 below.
[33] [1997] A.C. 191; see para. 9–155 below.
[34] Such as breach of confidence, trespass etc.
[35] [1997] A.C. 191.
[36] See generally paras 9–113 and 9–155 below.
[37] The decision of the House of Lords in *BBL v. Eagle Star* [1997] A.C. 191 at 212D proceeds upon this basis.
[38] Provided that it is within 15 years of the act of negligence.
[39] The Law Commission has recently recommended a uniform limitation period for actions not involving personal injuries with a single 10 year long-stop. S.32 of the Limitation Act, dealing with deliberate concealment, applies to actions both in contract and in tort.
[40] [1999] P.N.L.R. 565.

as to complete the cause of action in negligence. The Court unanimously held that on exchange the purchaser acquired an interest in the property, there arose an immediate obligation to insure the same, and the seller acquired rights of action against the purchaser. On exchange the purchaser accordingly suffered loss and the cause of action was complete. The appeal was dismissed and the action was struck out as statute barred.[41] The second difference has been the subject of several reported cases, of which a recent example is *Mortgage Corporation v. Lambert*[42] where, on the assumed facts, an advance had been made following a negligent valuation on June 25, 1990. The borrowers defaulted almost immediately and an order for possession was obtained in May 1991. The borrowers made repeated partial payments and promises to repay arrears with the result that the order was postponed and the lender was unable to sell the property until August 1996. The writ was issued on October 15, 1996. The primary question for the Court was, accordingly, whether the "date of knowledge" had occurred prior to October 15, 1993.[43] Prior to that date there had been several reports from debt-collectors which had put the estimated value of the property at substantially below the amount of the original valuation but there had been no retrospective valuation. Although Chadwick L.J. (with whom the other members of the Court agreed) considered that a prudent lender might well have been put on enquiry as to the validity of the original valuation, he considered the real question to be whether it was reasonable for a lender to obtain a retrospective valuation prior to October 15, 1993. On that issue there was no evidence. The Court considered that a lender would be behaving reasonably if (with almost three years to go until the expiry of the primary period and with the benefit of an order for possession) it had decided to wait until it had obtained possession before obtaining a retrospective valuation.[44]

Liability may also be concurrent with that of other professional persons. The **9-010** depth of the recession in the early 1990s caused a very considerable volume of

---

[41] The only point which caused the Court any difficulty was a passage in the speech of Lord Nicholls in *Nykredit v. Edward Erdman* [1997] 1 W.L.R. 1627 at 1630 where it appeared to be suggested that the cause of action accrued in tort at the time of completion of the purchase. Simon Brown L.J. held, however, that Lord Nicholls had not, in that case, intended to draw a distinction between exchange and completion. In *Secretary of State for the Environment v. Essex Goodman & Suggitt* [1986] 1 W.L.R. 1432, (Judge Hawser Q.C.) and *Horbury v. Craig Hall & Rutley* [1991] C.I.L.L. 692, (Judge Bowsher Q.C.). Official referees had previously determined that causes of action by house purchasers against surveyors in tort accrued on exchange of contracts (albeit, as was pointed out in *Byrne* at 568, the cases were of limited authorative value as the main issues were different: in *Essex Goodman* whether a cause of action accrued when damage occurred and in *Horbury* whether s.14A of the Limitation Act 1980 applied). See also *Kitney v. Jones Lang Wootton* [1988] 1 E.G.L.R. 145 (cause of action in respect of organising repair works necessary in order to fulfill a covenant for repair accrued when the stipulated period for the works to be done expired rather than when the Court subsequently held that the works had not been carried out) and *Westlake v. Bracknell District Council* [1987] 1 E.G.L.R. 161 (primary limitation period had expired at time of purchase but deliberate concealment and estoppel found on basis of verbal reassurances by the surveyor on a later visit). The question of whether, on the facts, the cause of action in tort accrued after the cause of action in contract was also debated in *F. G. Whitley & Sons Ltd v. Thomas Bickerton* [1993] 1 E.G.L.R. 139.

[42] [2000] P.N.L.R. 820.

[43] The Court found it unnecessary to consider an alternative argument that no loss had been sustained prior to October 15, 1990.

[44] In *Horbury v. Craig Hall & Rutley* (1991) 7 P.N. 206, (1991) E.G.C.S. 81 the plaintiff purchased a property in November 1980 relying on the defendant's survey report. In March 1984 the plaintiff was told by a builder that certain chimney breasts were unsupported and dangerous and she paid £132 for repair work. In July 1985 the plaintiff discovered dry rot in the floors. In February 1988 the plaintiff issued a writ claiming damages in tort for the consequences of a negligent survey. The judge

claims by lenders against both valuers and solicitors who had been retained prior to the making of the relevant loans where it was necessary to consider the respective liabilities of each. In such cases, subject to the application of the decision in *BBL*,[45] the allegations of negligence will usually be distinct, although the damage claimed will be the same. In other cases, the allegations of negligence will, themselves, overlap. Thus in *Theodore Goddard v. Fletcher King Services Ltd*,[46] a managing surveyor who failed to notice the deletion and omission of an upwards-only rent review provision in two leases was held to be 20 per cent liable for the damages paid by the solicitor who was instructed to prepare the leases, and who was held to have a continuing obligation to consider and check the content of both leases. Although the surveyor was not under a duty to read the entire lease, he should have noticed these deletions and omissions, because he was aware that the provisions were vital to his client.[47]

9–011   **Contributory negligence.** A negligent surveyor has the same right as any other defendant to defend an action against him by alleging that the plaintiff was negligent, and that such negligence caused, or contributed to, any loss proved. Contributory negligence does not involve breach of duty owed by a plaintiff to a defendant, but the failure by the plaintiff to use reasonable care to protect his own interests.[48] This topic is generally discussed in chapter 4 and below at paragraph 9–166 in relation to claims by lenders. However, a valuer personally or vicariously liable to the plaintiff for deceit is not entitled, either at common law or by reason of sections 1(1) and 4 of the Law Reform (Contributory

---

held that the defendants had been negligent in failing to observe the unsupported flues, and in failing to warn the plaintiff of the risk of rot affecting the floors. However the plaintiff's claim was statute barred. The three-year discoverability period under the Limitation Act 1980, s.14A, ran from the date when the plaintiff first had knowledge of the material facts concerning the damage in respect of which damages were claimed. The damage was the purchase of the property in November 1980 in reliance on a negligent survey report. The plaintiff acquired the relevant knowledge in March 1984 when she was told of the unsupported flues. This was more than three years before the writ was issued. The judge held that the facts known in March 1984 were such as to meet the requirements of s.14A(7). In *Heathcote v. David Marks & Co.* [1996] 1 E.G.L.R. 123, Buckley J. held that the plaintiffs' claim was statute barred, and their knowledge for the purpose of the Limitation Act 1980, s.14A included that of their solicitor, who had received a copy of the survey report in question more than three years prior to the expiry of the limitation period. See also *Spencer-Ward v. Humberts* [1995] 1 E.G.L.R. 123, CA, *Sullivan v. Layton Lougher & Co.* [1995] 2 E.G.L.R. 111, CA, and *Higgins v. Hatch & Fielding* [1996] 1 E.G.L.R. 133, CA, *Etam v. Baker Almond* [2001] E.G.C.S. 21, where in each case the plaintiffs' claim was held by the Court to be statute barred. For a discussion on the effect of the Latent Damage Act 1986 on surveyors reports and valuations, see T. Dugdale, "Latent damage: the application of the discoverability principle to survey reports" (1991) 7 P.N. 193.
[45] [1997] A.C.191, as to which see para. 9–174 below.
[46] [1997] 2 E.G.L.R. 131.
[47] Examples of other cases include: *Anglia Hastings & Thanet B.S. v. House & Son* [1981] 2 E.G.L.R. 17; *Computastaff Ltd v. Ingledew Brown Bennison and Garrett* [1983] 2 E.G.L.R. 150; *Secretary of State for the Environment v. Essex Goodman and Suggitt* [1986] 1 W.L.R. 1432; *G.P. & P. Ltd v. Bulcraig & Davis [1988]* 1 E.G.L.R. 138; *Green v. Ipswich Borough Council* [1988] 1 E.G.L.R. 239; *Banque Bruxelles Lambert SA v. Eagle Star Insurance Co. Ltd* [1994] 2 E.G.L.R. 108, Phillips J.; *McCullagh v. Lane Fox & Partners Ltd* [1996] 1 E.G.L.R. 35; *Ball v. Banner* [2000] Lloyd's L.R. P.N. 569 (although the liability of the property advisers was overturned on appeal).
[48] For example, the effect of a purchaser's failure to obtain a structural survey was considered by Cobb J. in *Sutherland v. C.R. Maton & Son* [1979] 2 E.G.L.R. 81 who held that the failure neither broke the chain of causation nor constituted negligence on the part of the plaintiff. In *Yianni v. Edwin Evans & Sons* [1982] Q.B. 438 Park J. had no doubt that such a failure could constitute contributory negligence. In *Perry v. Tendring District Council* [1995] 1 E.G.L.R. 260, Judge Newey Q.C. noted that whether or not such a failure was negligent would depend on the facts.

Negligence) Act 1945, to plead by way of defence that the plaintiff was guilty of contributory negligence.[49]

Defective Premises Act 1972. Since January 1, 1974, section 1 of the Defective Premises Act 1972 has imposed on a person taking on work for or in connection with the provision of a dwelling a duty to see that the work which he takes on is done in a workmanlike, or as the case may be, professional manner, with proper materials and so that as regards that work the dwelling will be fit for habitation when completed. The duty is owed to the person to whose order the dwelling is provided and to every person who acquires an interest in the dwelling.[50] A surveyor carrying out a survey or valuation of a dwelling would not ordinarily be regarded as "taking on work in connection with the provision of a dwelling", and so it is submitted has no liability in respect of such work under this Act.[51]

9–012

Liability in respect of statements about property matters. The Property Misdescriptions Act 1991[52] provides that where a statement that is false or misleading to a material degree is made about property matters in the course of estate agency business, the person by whom the business is carried on shall be guilty of an offence.[53] The commission of an offence under this Act does not of itself render any associated contract void or unenforceable.[54] Limitation periods for the commencement of a prosecution under the Act are three years from the date of the commission of the offence, or one year from the date of discovery of the offence by the prosecutor.[55] Civil liability for misdescriptions may also be founded in common law on the basis of *Hedley Byrne*.[56] In *Duncan Investments Ltd v. Underwoods*,[57] the Court of Appeal upheld the finding of liability against

9–013

---

[49] See *Alliance & Leicester Building Society and others v. Edgestop Ltd and others* [1993] 1 W.L.R. 1462. The plaintiffs were the victims of a mortgage fraud, one of the actors being a valuer, at the time an employee of Hamptons Residential, and subsequently convicted of offences of dishonesty involving the material valuations. Hamptons applied to amend their defence to allege that the plaintiffs were guilty of contributory negligence in failing to discover that the valuer was acting outside the scope of his employment, in failing to detect the dishonest nature of the applications for a mortgage, and in failing to act as a prudent lender in respect of the processing of the mortgage applications. Mummery J. held that prior to the 1945 Act, the contributory negligence of a plaintiff suing in deceit could not be pleaded as a defence (1474F) and that the position had not been changed by the 1945 Act (1477D). In a further decision in the same action, [1994] 2 E.G.L.R. 229, Mummery J. concluded that whilst the valuer had not been acting within the scope of his actual authority in valuing the properties, he had been acting within his ostensible authority, that the plaintiffs had not had notice of his want of authority when they relied upon the valuations and that Hamptons were, therefore, vicariously liable for the valuer's deceit.

[50] Defective Premises Act 1972, s.1(1). See further para 8–039 above.

[51] For further analysis see Holyoak and Allen, *Civil Liability for Defective Premises* (1982), chap. 4, and M. F. James, "The Defective Premises Act and 'fitness for habitation'" (1993) 9 P.N. 144.

[52] The Act received the Royal Assent on June 27, 1991 and came into force on that date. The Property Misdescriptions (Specified Matters) Order was made on November 11, 1992, and came into force on April 4, 1993. The Schedule to the Order sets out the specified matters for the purposes of s.1(1). For commentary on this Act, see D. W. Oughton, "The Property Misdescriptions Act 1991" (1992) 8 P.N. 59; G. Stephenson, "The regulation of estate agency" (1992) 8 P.N. 2; A. Reed, "Professional negligence and property sales" (1995) 2 P.N. 42; and S. Nield "Whose agent anyway?—estate agents' relationship with the buyer" (1995) 2 P.N. 49.

[53] Property Misdescriptions Act 1991, ss.1(1) and (5).

[54] *ibid.*, s.1(4).

[55] *ibid.*, s.5(1).

[56] [1964] A.C. 465.

[57] [1998] P.N.L.R. 754

the defendant estate agents who gave an oral estimate of the possible re-sale values of certain properties to an officer of the plaintiff property company during an inspection. The defendants' disclaimers were not effective, as they were limited to statements made on behalf of the vendors and the defendant had not been advising on behalf of the vendors. The defendants had advised the plaintiff knowing that the advice would be relied upon and that it was unlikely that the plaintiff would seek other independent advice. By contrast, in *McCullagh v. Lane Fox & Partners Ltd*,[58] the Court of Appeal held that a written disclaimer was effective to prevent liability from arising for both written and oral misstatements. But for the disclaimer ("all statements contained in these particulars as to this property are made without responsibility . . . ") the defendant estate agents would have been liable to the plaintiff purchaser for an overpayment of £75,000.[59] There was no basis for saying that it would be unfair to the plaintiff to allow the agents to rely upon the disclaimer, nor that it would be unreasonable. When considering whether in general an estate agent, like a solicitor, does not himself owe a duty of care to the purchaser, Nourse L.J. commented:

"the very function of an estate agent . . . is prone to take him out of the general and bring him under a particular duty to a prospective purchaser . . . an estate agent is well advised not to act for a vendor in a house sale without appropriate disclaimers, to which the attention of prospective purchasers is drawn".

9–014 **Liability of individuals.** In common with other professions, surveyors used to practice mainly as partners. However many chartered surveyors now practise in companies rather than in partnerships. The question therefore arises as to when an individual, who is not a partner, will incur personal liability—either as an employee or as a director of a company. As any relevant contract will not be with the individual, any liability will be tortious. In *Merrett v. Babb*,[60] the Court of Appeal held, by a majority, that Mr Babb, an individual surveyor employed by a partnership, had a personal liability to a residential mortgagor as a result of having signed a mortgage valuation pursuant to section 13 of the Building Societies Act 1986. In reliance principally on the decisions of the House of Lords in *Smith v. Bush* and *Harris v. Wyre Forest District Council*,[61] May L.J. held that it was unnecessary for there to be any personal dealings between an employee and a claimant in order for a duty of care to be imposed. He stated that it was irrelevant that Mr Babb was not insured and pointed out that in *Harris*, the House of Lords had imposed a duty of care on the employee of the local authority (although no distinction was drawn between the employee and his employer, the local authority in that case). In his dissenting judgment, Aldous L.J. relied on the decision in *Williams v. Natural Life*,[62] where the House of Lords had considered the circumstances in which a duty of care would be imposed on a director of a limited company in addition to that imposed on the company. He pointed out that there was required not only to be a relationship between the claimant and the

[58] [1996] 1 E.G.L.R. 35.
[59] At first instance, [1994] 1 E.G.L.R. 35, Colman J. had held that a vendor's estate agent owed a duty of care at common law to a purchaser of a property in respect of the oral misstatement but that the plaintiff had failed to prove that he had paid in excess of the market value for the property with the result that his claim was dismissed. For a commentary on the first instance case see Mullan, "An 'undes res'" (1994) 3 P.N. 92.
[60] [2001] Lloyd's L.Rep. P.N. 468.
[61] [1990] 1 A.C. 831
[62] [1998] 1 W.L.R. 830

principal but also between the claimant and the employee. Notwithstanding the personal signature of Mr Babb, he considered that no such relationship could be made out on the facts. It is submitted that the reasoning of Aldous L.J. is to be preferred to that of the majority. It is the economic entities which carry out (and benefit from) the provision of professional services which should bear responsibility for negligence acts or omissions. In the absence of fraud there appears no reason to impose a personal liability upon employees simply because they are the individuals through whom the services have been provided. If such duties are imposed, employees will be well advised to procure separate professional indemnity cover (so as to avoid the risk that their employers fail to take out or maintain appropriate insurance). Such insurance represents an extra and (largely) unnecessary cost. Aldous L.J.'s dissenting judgment is, moreover, consistent with the decision in *Edgeworth Construction v. Lea and Associates Ltd*[63] where the Canadian Supreme Court refused to impose a personal duty of care on engineers who had signed certificates. Although the decision in *Merrett* is binding on its own facts on English courts below the House of Lords, it is submitted that it is dangerous to assume that it will be necessarily be followed in all circumstances where a surveyor, acting either as a director or employee carries out all or the majority of professional work on behalf of a client. The heavy reliance of the majority on *Smith v. Bush* might permit a court to distinguish, for example, a case where the valuation was a commercial one carried out for a corporate client.[64] Whether valuers act as directors, partners or employees, there will be certain direct professional obligations imposed on them by the RICS.[65]

Liability in connection with company particulars. The Financial Services   **9–015** Act 1986 provides that a valuer may be held liable in respect of any false or misleading statement for which he is responsible in any listing particulars,[66] in respect of any untrue or misleading statement in a prospectus,[67] and, by the Companies Act 1985, in respect of any untrue statement in a prospectus.[68] In *Ball v. Banner*,[69] the Court of Appeal had to consider the liability of the defendant surveyors (described as property advisors) for a statement which was attributed to them in the prospectus of an Enterprise Zone Property Unit Trust (which was an unregulated investment under the Financial Services Act). Hart J. had found at first instance[70] that the statement in question, which related to the letting prospects of the property, had two possible meanings, one of which amounted to a statement which no competent surveyor could have made. He construed the statement to have the negligent meaning but the Court of Appeal held that the

---

[63] [1993] 3 S.C.R. 206—see further para 8–114 above.
[64] In *Punjab National Bank v. de Boinville* [1992] 1 W.L.R., 1138, the Court of Appeal held that insurance brokwers employed by a company providing professional services, and who were "entrusted with the whole or nearly the whole of the task which their employers undertook" owed a personal duty of care. In the light of *Williams v. Natural Life*, this is almost certainly too simplistic.
[65] See RICS reg. 10 made in connection with byelaw 19, as amended July 10, 1995.
[66] Financial Services Act 1986, s.150(1).
[67] *ibid.*, s.166(1).
[68] Companies Act 1985, s.67(1).
[69] Unreported, July 2000, Court of Appeal.
[70] The first instance judgment is reported at [2000] Lloyd's L.Rep. P.N. 569.

statement bore the other, reasonable, meaning. The liability of a valuer in respect of statements in prospectus bears similarities to that of an accountant, and the matter is discussed in detail below.[71]

9–016 **Liability in connection with a contravention of section 19 of the Financial Services and Markets Act 2000.** Valuers have a potential liability under this part of the Financial Services Act.[72]

9–017 **Liability under the building societies ombudsman scheme.** An existing borrower from a building society, who, when seeking a further advance relies to his detriment on a negligent valuation or survey prepared by a surveyor employed by the building society, may be able to invoke the ombudsman procedure as an inexpensive alternative to litigation. Section 83(1) of the Building Societies Act 1986 confers on an individual the right as against a building society to have any complaint concerning action taken by the society in relation to certain matters investigated under a scheme recognised by the Building Societies Commission. On June 5, 1987 a building societies ombudsman scheme was recognised by the Commission. The ombudsman's duties include the obligation to investigate any complaint received by him from an individual if:

(a) the complaint relates to action taken in the United Kingdom by a building society, and

(b) in relation to the grant or refusal to grant a borrowing member other or further advances secured on the same or different land, provided that the grounds of complaint are that

(c) the action complained of constitutes in relation to the complainant, in the case of a participating society, a breach of its obligations under the Building Societies Act 1986, its rules or any other contract, or unfair treatment or maladministration.[73]

9–018 Schedule 12 of the Act omitted any reference to surveys and valuations of land, therefore the only relevant matter of complaint is that part of paragraph 3 of Part II of Schedule 12 to the Act which refers to the grant or refusal to grant further advances to a borrowing member. The complainant must therefore have been an existing borrower at the time of the grant or refusal. Further, because the complaint must be about the acts or omissions of the society, the ombudsman has no jurisdiction to investigate complaints relating to valuations made by a non-employee surveyor. In *Halifax Building Society v. Edell*[74] Morritt J. held that the preparation, by surveyors directly employed by the plaintiff societies, of basic

---

[71] See Chap. 15, para. 15–029; note the extent to which the relevant legislation is in force at the time of writing. See *The Encyclopaedia of Financial Services*, edited by Professor E. Lomnicka and J. L. Powell Q.C. (Sweet & Maxwell).
[72] Financial Services Act 1986, s.6. For further discussion see chap. 13, para. 13–013.
[73] See cll. 14, 17 and 18 of the scheme, and Sched. 12, Part II of the Building Societies Act 1986. Details of the scheme were amended with effect from July 1, 1994.
[74] [1992] Ch. 436.

valuations, house buyers' reports and valuations, and structural surveys in connection with applications for further advances were all part of the society's process of administration. If negligently prepared, such work could amount to maladministration within Schedule 12 to the 1986 Act, and that accordingly, the ombudsman had jurisdiction to investigate and determine the borrower's complaints.[75]

(b) *Duties to client*

(i) *Contractual duties*

The primary basis of a surveyor's duties to his client is the contract of engagement between himself and his client. The contract may be written or oral or inferred from the conduct of the parties. By Practice Statement 2,[76] the RICS now requires a valuer to agree or confirm in writing his instructions *before* issuing his report. The instructions must deal, at a minimum with a total of 15 matters including the purpose of the valuation; the subject of the valuation; the basis or bases of valuation; so far as practicable assumptions to be made; the date of the valuation; limits of liability to parties other than the client; the nature of information provided and the fee or basis thereof.[77] If he fails to do so and there is any subsequent dispute as to the terms of his instructions, he may be at a serious disadvantage.[78]   **9–019**

A surveyor's duties will vary according to the circumstances of each case and in particular the purpose for which he is asked to report upon a particular property.[79] His express duties will primarily depend upon the instructions given,[80] for example, to carry out a structural survey or valuation of a named property.[81] He will invariably be under the implied, if not an express, duty to   **9–020**

---

[75] The ombudsman scheme is dealt with more fully in Wurtzburg and Mills, *Building Society Law* (looseleaf, Stevens & Sons), chap. 15.3 and Appendix D.

[76] For the application of RICS practice statements, see para. 9–022 below.

[77] Practice Statement 2, RICS Appraisal and Valuation Manual with Amendments 1–12 (effective from March 1, 2000). The professional obligations imposed as to the confirmation of instructions have become more extensive during the 1990s both as to extent and as to timing.

[78] See *Fisher v. Knowles* [1982] 1 E.G.L.R. 154 and para. 9–077, below. Note that *Fisher v. Knowles* was decided at a time when the very extensive Practice Statement 2 as to the content of instructions was not available from the RICS.

[79] See *Ker v. John H. Allan & Sons* 1949 S.L.T. (Notes) 20, *per* Lord Birnam; and note the caution expressed in *Singer and Friedlander Ltd v. John D. Wood & Co.* [1977] 2 E.G.L.R. 84, 85 by Watkins J.:

   "Whatever conclusion is reached, it must be without consideration for the purpose for which it is required. By this I mean that a valuation must reflect the honest opinion of the valuer of the true market value of the land at the relevant time, no matter why or by whom it is required, be it by merchant bank, land developer or prospective builder. So the expression, for example, 'for loan purposes' used in a letter setting out a valuation should be descriptive only of the reason why the valuation is required and not as an indication that were the valuation required for some other purpose a different value would be provided by the valuer to he who seeks the valuation. It might however be an indication that the valuer, knowing the borrowing of money was behind the valuation, acted with even more care than usual to try to be as accurate as possible."

RICS Practice Statement 3 now deals specifically with the Purposes of Valuations and seeks to provide that valuations for particular purposes have to provided on specified bases.

[80] See para. 9–031, below for the problems of construction of instructions.

[81] See *Predeth v. Castle Phillips Finance Co. Ltd* [1986] 2 E.G.L.R. 144 and para. 9–078, below.

exercise reasonable care and skill,[82] in both the work which results in the report, and the report itself.[83] In addition, certain specific duties may be implied. Thus a surveyor engaged to carry out a structural survey has been held to be under an implied duty to inspect the property so far as is reasonably practicable, whereas a surveyor carrying out a mortgage inspection and valuation may confine himself to a careful visual examination of the property.[84] It is submitted that a valuer is not under an implied duty to proffer unsought advice on the wisdom of entering into a property transaction in which he has been retained for a clearly defined and limited purpose.[85]

9–021   **The ambit of the decision in BBL.** As set out below,[86] in *BBL v. Eagle Star,*[87] the House of Lords limited the damages recoverable by a lender who had made a loan in reliance on a negligent valuation so that no greater loss of principal could be recovered than the difference between the negligent valuation and a correct valuation at the time of the loan. It did so by restricting the kind of loss for which a lender could recover for breach of an implied term to exercise reasonable skill and care by reference to the reasonable expectations of lender and borrower. It thus appears possible that lenders (or other claimants) may seek to circumvent the effects of *BBL* by carefully worded express terms which, for example, expressly imposed liability for all damages incurred by a lender, including responsibility for subsequent fall in the property market, on a negligent valuer.[88] In the absence of such express terms, the scope of a valuer's duty, and thus the damages recoverable, will be the same whether a claim is made for

---

[82] *e.g. Kenney v. Hall, Pain and Foster* [1976] 2 E.G.L.R. 29, 33. Surveyors' negligence cases are commonly determined only by reference to whether the surveyor failed to exercise reasonable care and skill. The word "negligence" is frequently used to indicate not only the specific tort but also breach of the implied contractual duty to exercise reasonable care and skill. Such a term is implied by the Supply of Goods and Services Act 1982, s.13.

[83] *per* Denning L.J. in *Candler v. Crane, Christmas & Co.* [1951] 2 K.B. 164, 179.

[84] Commenting about the level of expertise required of this class of service, Lord Griffiths in *Smith v. Bush* [1990] 1 A.C. 831, 858 said:

"It is only defects which are observable by a careful visual examination that have to be taken into account and I cannot see that it places any unreasonable burden on the valuer to require him to accept responsibility for the fairly elementary degree of skill and care involved in observing, following-up and reporting on such defects. Surely it is work at the lower end of the surveyor's field of professional expertise."

In *Whalley v. Roberts & Roberts* [1990] 1 E.G.L.R. 164, Auld J. stated:

"The defendants were not instructed to undertake a structural survey or a survey of the detail called for in the standard form of the Royal Institution of Chartered Surveyors House Buyers' Report and Valuation inspection. They were instructed to inspect and to provide a mortgage valuation report. It is common ground that this involved them in making a brief and reasonably careful visual inspection to enable them, in the terms of the bank report form, to provide a valuation and general guide as to the condition of the property. I am satisfied on the evidence before me that this would not normally involve the use of a spirit-level unless the lack of level in the property became evident on a visual inspection so as to call for further investigation."

[85] See the reasoning in *Clark Boyce v. Mouat* [1994] 1 A.C. 428, a solicitor's negligence case, considered at chap. 10, paras 10–015 to 10–016.

[86] See para. 9–160 below.

[87] [1997] A.C. 191.

[88] In one of the cases considered in the *BBL* appeals, *Nykredit Mortgage Services Ltd v. Edward Erdman*, the House of Lords rejected an argument by the lender that it was misled not merely by the final valuation figure but by errors in the detailed valuation report which had been produced pursuant to a detailed letter of engagement. Lord Hoffman did not consider, as a matter of construction, that the lender was entitled to place separate reliance on the information provided. See further para. 9–113 below.

breach of a common law duty of care or for breach of the ordinary implied term to exercise reasonable care and skill.[89]

RICS Practice Statements. Until December 31, 1995 chartered surveyors   9–022
were under a professional duty to comply with all practice statements published by the RICS.[90] These were published from time to time by the Assets Valuation Standards Committee of the RICS. This committee sought to ensure uniform methods of valuing fixed assets by chartered surveyors on behalf of client companies. As such valuations are often reproduced in the form of company accounts and prospectuses, consistency of method was important, to avoid the public being misled. These practice statements and guidance notes did not apply to valuations of domestic houses, or valuations for mortgages or loans secured on commercial property.[91] The position after December 31, 1995 is set out below.

RICS Appraisal and Valuation Manual. With effect from December 31,   9–023
1995 the RICS's Statement of Asset Valuation Practice and Guidance notes ("the Red Book") and its manual of Valuation Guidance notes ("the White Book") were withdrawn in respect of valuations undertaken after that date. The replacement of these works with the Appraisal and Valuation Manual[92] was intended to avoid confusion and to provide the profession, clients and the courts with authoritative guidance as to the assembly, interpretation and reporting of information relevant to the practice of valuation. A conscious decision was made by the RICS to prescribe minimum standards in respect of valuations over a much wider range of services than those to which the Red Book had applied. The manual contains Practice Statements in section one,[93] and compliance with these remains mandatory.[94] Section two contains Guidance Notes[95] providing assistance on good valuation practice. Although compliance with the latter is not

---

[89] Thus if the valuer in *Western Trust & Savings Ltd v. Strutt & Parker* [1999] P.N.L.R. 154 had been retained by the bank rather than merely owing it a duty of care at common law, the decision as to the scope of his duty is likely to have been the same—see further para. 9–042 below.

[90] RICS byelaw 24(11), in force February 11, 1991, byelaw 19(7) and associated Conduct Regulation.

[91] See AVSC reg. 25, agreed by RICS General Council July 9, 1990 and the notes thereto. The application of Guidance Notes was considered in *Allied Trust Bank Ltd v. Edward Symmons & Partners* [1994] 1 E.G.L.R. 165.

[92] The manual is now published by RICS Business Services Ltd and is available both in a looseleaf format and on disk from RICS Books, Surveyor Court, Westwood Way, Coventry CV4 8JE. In the five years since publication of the Manual in October 1995, it has been subject to 12 series of amendments, with the result that it is important, when considering the professional obligations of a surveyor at a particular moment, to ascertain the precise state of the Manual.

[93] There are currently 22 Practice Statements. The first seven apply to all valuations to which the Manual applies whilst the remaining 15 apply when a valuer is carrying out particular tasks such as the "Valuation and Appraisal of Commercial Land and Buildings for Secured Lending and Disposal Purposes" (Practice Statement 8) or the "Valuation of Mineral-Bearing Land and other Wasting Assets" (Practice Statement 22).

[94] The scope of the Practice Statements is set out in Practice Statement 1. Where valuations are carried out of properties outside the United Kingdom and/or are provided in accordance with European or International Standards and Practice, the valuer must either follow the general principles of the Practice Statements so far as possible or may choose to follow guidance published by the European Group of Valuers' Associations, the International Valuation Standards Committee or the relevant requirements/ guidance of any professional body recognised by the government of the country in which the valuation is to be reported. However in the latter case, the valuer is still obliged to comply with the Practice Statements to the extent that the alternative guidance is silent on matters addressed by the Manual.

[95] There are currently 20.

mandatory, the RICS warns that a departure should be made only for good reason.[96] The principal aims of the Appraisal and Valuation Manual were expressed to be as follows:

(a) to encourage valuers carefully to establish and understand at the outset their clients' needs and requirements, and to satisfy themselves that they are equipped to meet them to a satisfactory standard;

(b) to promote the consistent use of bases and assumptions upon which valuations are provided and the selection on each occasion of the basis which will meet the clients' proper needs;

(c) help valuers to achieve high standards of professional competence in the preparation of valuations and appraisals;

(d) promote the provision of unambiguous and readily comprehensible valuation and appraisal reports which provide the advice and information their readers need and should have;

(e) ensure that published references to valuations include clear, accurate and sufficient information which is not misleading.

Practice Statement 3 sets out the purposes of valuations and their bases, and includes a comprehensive table of purposes, properties and bases. The Appraisal and Valuation Manual now endorses the use of "estimated realisation price" (ERP) and "estimated restricted realisation price" as a basis of valuation in several common circumstances. These are bases of valuation that look forward in time to an assumed date of sale. They are based on market value (MV), or open market value (OMV) which must also be provided, save where the valuation is provided on a standard form supplied by the client.[97] Although the valuer must specifically and rationally discuss market trends the final figure is of necessity, speculative, and it is open to the instructing source to disagree with some or all of the assumptions made.[98] Valuations prepared on an ERP basis will be harder to challenge as negligent, and although the OMV figure which forms the basis of the new valuation can still be challenged, the instructing source may not have placed any reliance on the OMV.

Separate professional guidance[99] is published in respect of the preparation of building surveys of residential property.

9–024   These documents, and other professional information published by the RICS, have a threefold importance. First, by their authorship and the type of surveyor to whom each publication is directed, the RICS implies that a chartered building surveyor is more competent to undertake building surveys. This has implications

---

[96] In the introduction to the Appraisal and Valuation Manual, the RICS warns that "when an allegation of professional negligence is made against a surveyor, the court is likely to take account of any relevant practice statement published by the RICS in deciding whether or not the surveyor has acted with reasonable competence. Failure to comply with practice statements is likely to be adjudged negligent". Surveyors are not required to follow the advice and recommendations contained in the Guidance Notes, but many firms assert in their reports that they have done so, see for example *Craneheath Securities Ltd v. York Montague Ltd* [1994] 1 E.G.L.R. 159, Jacob J.; [1996] 1 E.G.L.R. 130, CA.

[97] See RICS Practice Statement 4.5 for title and definition of this basis.

[98] See RICS Practice Statements 4.5 and 4.6.

[99] *Building Surveys of Residential Property: A Guidance Note* published by RICS July 1996 and operative from October 1996.

for those without such a qualification who nevertheless carry out such surveys. They should be judged according to the standard of the reasonably competent chartered building surveyor, whatever their training and experience. Secondly, any surveyor who materially departs from the good practice set out in the notes appropriate to the type of inspection undertaken, will be at risk in a professional negligence action, a point made in the introduction to the Guidance Notes by the RICS. Unless such a departure can be justified,[1] expert evidence that the notes represent general and approved practice within the profession[2] is likely to lead to a finding of negligence.[3] Thirdly, the various services offered by surveyors have been classified and standard conditions of engagement have been prepared. The public is now offered an ascending level of service on defined terms. The existence of such a structure means that a surveyor who neglects to make plain to his client the precise nature of the service to be undertaken is doubly at risk. The surveyor will forfeit any protection the standard conditions of engagement may offer, and he may be held by the court to have in fact contracted to carry out a greater level of service than either he intended or his fee warrants.

The existence of the professional obligation of compliance with the Practice **9–025** Statements, together with the publication by the RICS of the various Guidance Notes and manuals discussed show that a body of guidance has been developed for surveyors the breach of which is intended to have the same force and effect in a professional negligence action as breach of the Financial Reporting Standards and Statements of Standard Accounting Practice would have in actions against accountants.[4]

Surveyors' standard conditions of engagement. To be incorporated into the **9–026** surveyor's contract of retainer, any standard conditions of engagement[5] must be made known to the client and agreed upon at the time when instructions are received. If they are not there is a real risk that they will be of no contractual effect.[6] These rules of construction of a contract pose special difficulties for a

---

[1] As it was in *Hacker v. Thomas Deal & Co.* [1991] 2 E.G.L.R. 161, where the surveyor did not carry a mirror when carrying out a building survey: "He is criticised for that by [counsel for the plaintiff], because that is one of the pieces of equipment that it is suggested in the literature put out by the Institute that every surveyor should consider carrying. But the passage that was read out says that this will depend upon the preferences of the individual surveyor." The judge held that it would not be right to hold the surveyor negligent in failing to carry a mirror simply because there was an opportunity to use it, unless he had been put upon inquiry. The facts of the case are set out at para. 9–086, below.

[2] See *Bolam v. Friern Hospital Management Committee* [1957] 1 W.L.R. 582.

[3] RICS guidance notes on the meaning of "open market value" and "forced sale value" were considered by the Court of Appeal in *Predeth v. Castle Phillips Finance Co. Ltd* [1986] 2 E.G.L.R. 144. In *Watts v. Morrow* [1991] 1 E.G.L.R. 150, it was held at first instance that the surveyor's departures from the RICS Practice Note on Structural Surveys of Residential Property made it more difficult for him to come to the right answer and contributed to his failure to come to the right answer. An appeal on the issue of liability was not pursued. In *Strover v. Harrington* [1988] Ch. 390 the absence of evidence that the defendant surveyors had acted contrary to accepted good professional practice was fatal to the plaintiff's claim. In *P.K. Finians International (U.K.) Ltd v. Andrew Downs & Co. Ltd* [1992] 1 E.G.L.R. 172 an allegation that the defendant valuer should not have made oral enquiries of the planning authorities was held unsustainable in view of the terms of guidance note 6 of the RICS Guidance Notes on the Valuation of Assets. The deputy judge also commented, *ibid.* at 174K, that "these guidance notes are not to be regarded as a statute . . . mere failure to comply with the guidance notes does not constitute negligence".

[4] For accountants, see chap. 15, para. 15–015.

[5] Or such other conditions as the surveyor may wish to adopt.

[6] Save possibly as a warning notice.

profession where time is frequently short, instructions are often received by telephone and a course of dealing between the parties is unlikely in the domestic context. This should be less of a problem where the surveyor is retained in respect of a survey or valuation of commercial property. It is commonplace for the fee to be agreed in advance and in such circumstances the surveyor has sufficient opportunity to make known and secure the incorporation into his contract of retainer suitable conditions of engagement.

9–027   **Unfair Contract Terms Act 1977.** Even if such standard conditions of engagement are incorporated into the contract, the surveyor's contract of engagement will be subject to the Unfair Contract Terms Act 1977 and the Unfair Terms in Consumer Contracts Regulations 1994.[7] By virtue of the provisions contained in Part I of the Act which extends to England and Wales and to Northern Ireland[8] a surveyor cannot by reference to any contract term or to any notice given to persons generally or to particular persons exclude or restrict his liability for death or personal injury resulting from negligence.[9] In the case of other loss or damage, a surveyor cannot by reference to any contract term or to any notice exclude or restrict his liability for negligence[10] except in so far as the term or notice satisfies the requirement of reasonableness. The Regulations provide that any "unfair term" shall not be binding on the consumer. It is submitted that any clause which satisfies the requirement of reasonableness under the Act, will not at the same time be held to be an "unfair term" within the meaning of the Regulations. The House of Lords considered the Act, its application to work undertaken by surveyors and valuers of domestic property, and the issue of reasonableness in *Smith v. Eric S. Bush.*[11]

9–028   The Court of Appeal considered an attempt by a plaintiff to avoid a written disclaimer in particulars issued by estate agents in *McCullagh v. Lane Fox & Partners Ltd.*[12] The defendants, both orally and in their particulars, described a property to a prospective purchaser as having grounds of "nearly one acre" and "0.92 acre". The plaintiff told them he was going to demolish the property and rebuild on the site, and would not be obtaining his own survey. The plaintiff exchanged contracts to buy the property for £875,000, after which he discovered the true area of the grounds to be 0.48 acre. He sued, claiming he had overpaid for the property.[13] The Court of Appeal rejected the plaintiff's attempts to strike down the disclaimer by reliance on the Unfair Contract Terms Act 1977. Observing that it was for the defendants to establish that it was fair and reasonable that

---

[7] For discussions of this Act and the case of *Stewart Gill Ltd v. Horatio Myer & Co. Ltd* [1992] Q.B. 600, see Peel, "Making more use of the Unfair Contract Terms Act 1977" (1993) 56 M.L.R. 98, and Brown and Chandler, "Unreasonableness and the Unfair Contract Terms Act" (1993) 109 L.Q.R. 41.

[8] Similar but not identical provisions are contained in Part II of the Act, which extends to Scotland only. See para. 9–072, below.

[9] s.2(1).

[10] A clause or notice that seeks to exclude a duty of care is subject to the provisions of the Unfair Contract Terms Act 1977 just as much as a clause or notice that attempts to exclude liability. See *Smith v. Eric S. Bush*; *Harris v. Wyre Forest District Council* [1990] 1 A.C. 831, *per* Lord Templeman at 848, Lord Griffiths at 856, and Lord Jauncey at 873, reversing the Court of Appeal on this point (*Harris v. Wyre Forest District Council* [1988] Q.B. 835).

[11] s.2(2). *Smith v. Eric S. Bush* [1990] 1 A.C. 831, see para. 9–065, below.

[12] [1996] 1 E.G.L.R. 35. This case is also discussed at paras 9–012 and 9–067.

[13] [1994] 1 E.G.L.R. 48, Colman J. The plaintiff failed; the judge held that although a duty of care was owed, the plaintiff had in fact bought the property for its true worth and had suffered no loss.

they should be allowed to rely upon the disclaimer, Hobhouse L.J.[14] noted that by his own observations at the time, the plaintiff put himself forward as a sophisticated and experienced member of the public, that he had had ample opportunity to read the particulars and was aware that it would contain a disclaimer, that he had ample opportunity to regulate his conduct in the light of the disclaimer and could have obtained an independent check on the area of the grounds. The plaintiff further had legal advice and representation, and enjoyed complete freedom of contract to negotiate as he chose. Hobhouse L.J. concluded that there was no basis for saying that it would be unfair to the claimant to allow the defendants to rely upon the disclaimer, nor that it would be unreasonable.[15] That reasoning may be contrasted with the case of *St Marylebone Property Co. Ltd v. Payne*,[16] where a property for sale by auction was illustrated by a misleading photograph, which indicated the property to be of greater extent than in fact was owned by the vendor. Despite the claimant company being directed by a very experienced valuer and property dealer, who well knew the auctioneer's standard conditions, it was held not to be reasonable in the circumstances of an auction sale for the defendant vendor to rely upon them, as the particulars were dominated by the misleading photograph, upon which it was to be expected an investment purchaser would rely.

Building societies. Most purchases of private dwellings are now made with the aid of an advance from a building society, bank, or centralised lender, secured by way of mortgage on the purchased property. In the case of a building society every director of the society is under a statutory duty to satisfy himself that arrangements are made for assessing the adequacy of the security to be taken in respect of advances to be made by the society.[17] The required arrangements as stated in the statute[18] include the provision of a written report as to the value of any freehold or leasehold estate comprised in the security and as to any factors likely to affect its value. The report must be provided by a "person who is competent to value, and is not disqualified under this section from making a report on, the land in question".[19] A report from an employee of a building society may in certain circumstances render the society liable to an investigation by the building societies ombudsman.[20] Although banks (and other commercial lenders) are not subject to the same direct statutory duties as building societies, they are subject to supervision and adopt similar standards as a matter of practice. Lenders may also be required to obtain valuations in order to satisfy their own insurers. In the case of loans above a certain percentage of equity (usually in the region of 75 per cent) lenders often obtain Mortgage Indemnity Guarantees (referred to as "MIGs") to insure themselves against the risk of default by

9–029

---

[14] [1996] 1 E.G.L.R. 35 at 46. The other members of the Court agreed with this part of the judgment of Hobhouse L.J.
[15] The Court went further. Even though the plaintiff had not read the disclaimer, since the plaintiff expected the particulars to contain a disclaimer it would "be unreasonable and unfair to the defendants to allow him to claim against the defendants as if there had been no such disclaimer". *ibid.*, at 46.
[16] [1994] 2 E.G.L.R. 25.
[17] The Building Societies Act 1986, s.13(1), with effect from January 1, 1987. Before that date a broadly similar obligation was imposed by the Building Societies Act 1962, s.25(1).
[18] Building Societies Act 1986, s.13(1)(c).
[19] *ibid.* The valuer need no longer be "prudent" or "experienced".
[20] See para. 9–017, above.

borrowers. There will be conditions attached to the MIGs which will almost invariably require the obtaining of valuations.[21]

9–030 **Surveys for lenders.** To the above ends building societies and other lenders engage surveyors to inspect and report upon properties the subject of applications for mortgage advances. Some lenders employ their "in house" surveyors for the purpose. Formerly building societies generally did not show the surveyor's report to the applicant for an advance.[22] Now they invariably do show it[23] and the surveyor is generally instructed on the basis that the applicant will see his report. Lenders usually offer to their prospective borrowers a structured range of survey services. The range usually consists of:

(a) a mortgage inspection and valuation;

(b) a house or flat buyer's report and valuation;

(c) a building survey, formerly known as a full structural survey, with valuation.[24]

The depth of the inspection and the detail of the report vary proportionally with the fee charged. Attempts are invariably made to draw to the attention of the prospective borrowers the nature and scope of the service being offered, and in particular to make clear the limited nature of the basic service, the mortgage inspection and valuation. Such explanations and conditions of engagement are usually set out not only in leaflets describing the survey services offered but also in mortgage application forms[25] and the surveyor's report itself.

9–031 The effect of these limitations will depend upon the wording of the particular documents and the facts in each case. Frequently, however, the effect of the documents is that two separate agreements are made. The first is an agreement between the building society and the prospective borrower whereby in consideration of the appropriate fee, the building society agrees:

(a) to instruct a surveyor to inspect the relevant property and to provide the required report on it;

(b) to provide a copy of the report to the applicant; and

(c) on the basis of the information contained in the mortgage application form, the surveyor's report and such further information as may be sought, to consider whether or not to offer the requested advance secured by mortgage on the property.

The second agreement is between the building society and the surveyor whereby in consideration for payment of the appropriate fee, the latter agrees to inspect the property and to provide a report to be shown to both the society and the

---

[21] For further discussion of MIGs in the context of reliance, see para. 9–122 below.

[22] Note the criticism of this practice as long ago as 1956 by Devlin J. in *Eagle Star Insurance Co. Ltd v. Gale and Power* (1955) 166 E.G. 37.

[23] As in, for example, *Stevenson v. Nationwide Buiding Society* [1984] 2 E.G.L.R. 165. See para. 9–064, below.

[24] Although it will be rare for such a survey to be carried out by a building surveyor as a building surveyor will not usually hold himself out as competent to provide a valuation.

[25] As was the case in *Smith v. Eric S. Bush* [1990] 1 A.C. 831.

applicant. In such a situation there may be no contractual nexus between the applicant and the surveyor. Accordingly, the applicant will be limited to making any claim against the surveyor in tort.[26] Where an independent surveyor has been instructed by the lender, the prospective borrower will generally have no remedy against the society in respect of a negligent report, unless the original choice of surveyor can in some way be challenged.[27]

(ii) *Duties independent of contract*

The fact that there exists a contract between a surveyor and his client does not preclude the surveyor being under a concurrent duty of care to his client[28] apart from contract.[29] Indeed, following the decision of the House of Lords in *Henderson v. Merrett*,[30] there will usually be imposed a tortious duty where a contractual duty of care exists although the tortious duty will not necessarily be co-extensive with all of the obligations assumed by contract. The existence of such a concurrent duty was expressly recognised by Lord Jauncey in *Smith v. Eric S. Bush*[31]:   **9–032**

> "the building society instructed the [surveyors] who, by accepting these instructions, not only entered into contractual relations with the building society but also came under a duty in tort to it to exercise reasonable care in carrying out their survey and preparing their report. To that extent they were in no different position to that of any other professional person who has accepted instructions to act on behalf of a client".

In *Holt and Another v. Payne Skillington and De Groot Collis*[32] certain advice was given to the plaintiffs by an employee of the second defendant surveyors as to the application of planning laws. This advice was outside the terms of the surveyors contract of retainer. The Court of Appeal referred to *Midland Bank Trust Co. Ltd v. Hett Stubbs & Kemp*[33] and held that it was well settled law that where there is a contract under which a party assumes contractual duties, a

---

[26] See para. 9–033, below.
[27] See the dicta by Lord Griffiths in *Smith v. Bush* [1990] 1 A.C. 831, 865:
"I do not accept the view of the Court of Appeal in *Curran v. Northern Ireland Co-ownership Housing Association Ltd* [1986] 8 N.I.J.B. 1, that a mortgagee who accepts a fee to obtain a valuation of a small house owes no duty of care to the mortgagor in the selection of the valuer to whom he entrusts the work. In my opinion, the mortagee in such a case, knowing that the mortgagor will rely upon the valuation, owes a duty to the mortgagor to take reasonable care to employ a reasonably competent valuer. Provided he does this the mortgagee will not be held liable for the negligence of the independent valuer who acts as an independent contractor."
In *Beresforde v. Chesterfield Borough Council* [1989] 2 E.G.L.R. 149, the defendant building society delivered under their own name an independent valuer's report to the plaintiffs. The plaintiffs claimed that the building society had therefore adopted the report as their own but the claim against the building society was struck out by the judge. Whilst expressing considerable doubt as to whether the claim could succeed ("very formidable difficulties indeed in any such claim achieving success" *per* Parker L.J. at 151) the Court of Appeal allowed the plaintiffs' appeal on the ground that the plaintiffs' claims were not so plainly unarguable that they ought to be stopped forthwith.
[28] See the discussion on concurrent liability in contract and tort in Chap. 2, paras 2–100 *et seq.*
[29] See *Leigh v. Unsworth* (1972) 230 E.G. 501, and the dicta of Judge Everett at 501, set out under n. 89, para. 9–024 of the third edition of this work, and the Scottish case of *Drinnan v. C. W. Ingram & Sons*, 1967 S.L.T. 205 and the dicta of Lord Milligan at 207, set out under n. 22, para. 9–009 of the second edition of this work.
[30] [1995] 2 A.C. 145.
[31] [1990] 1 A.C. 831, 870.
[32] [1996] P.N.L.R. 179.
[33] [1979] Ch. 384.

concurrent duty of care can also exist in tort. Furthermore, in the absence of a contractual term which precluded or restricted the duty of care in tort, it was open to the court to find that the duty of care in tort was wider than the concurrent duties in contract. The trial judge was therefore entitled to hold that a duty of care in tort was owed by the surveyors in respect of the advice as to the planning position. However, on the facts the plaintiffs had failed to prove an unequivocal representation upon which they had relied.[34]

(c) Duties to third parties

(i) General principles

9–033   **The traditional view.** It was formerly the prevailing view that a surveyor could only incur liability for professional negligence in contract and hence only to his client unless he were guilty of fraud.[35] Exceptionally for the period, in *Cann v. Willson*[36] the defendant valuers were held liable to a third party. Instructed by the mortgagor, they had sent their valuation to the plaintiff mortgagee's solicitors. On later being informed by the solicitors that the valuation was required for mortgage purposes, the valuers confirmed their figure. Acting on the valuation, the plaintiff lent on mortgage and suffered loss upon the mortgagor's default, the amount realised on sale of the property being less than the valuation figure. Chitty J. held the valuers liable on two grounds. First, that they owed a duty of care to the mortgagees and had negligently failed to discharge it.[37] Secondly, that their statement as to the value was made recklessly and without reasonable ground for believing it to be true.[38] *Cann v. Willson* was overruled, however, in *Le Lievre v. Gould*[39] in which the Court of Appeal reasserted the formerly prevailing view.[40]

9–034   **Effect of Hedley Byrne.** In *Hedley Byrne & Co. Ltd v. Heller and Partners Ltd*[41] the House of Lords took the view that *Cann v. Willson* was rightly

---

[34] See also para. 2–107 above.

[35] See *Scholes v. Brook* (1891) 63 L.T. 837, (1892) 64 L.T. 674; *Le Lievre v. Gould* [1893] 1 Q.B. 491, CA; *Love v. Mack* (1905) 92 L.T. 345; *Davis v. Sprott & Sons* (1960) 177 E.G. 9 (claim in negligence by mortgagors against estate agents in respect of a report and valuation of a bungalow as a security for a mortgage prepared by the latter upon the instructions of prospective mortgagees. Action dismissed upon estate agents' summons to strike out, on the ground that the statement of claim disclosed no reasonable cause of action against them. *Per* Pennycuick J.: " ... it seemed that the statement of claim contained no allegation of a contractual relation between the plaintiffs and the second defendants. If there was no such relation there could be no liability in damages for breach of duty". Leave to appeal was granted but apparently not pursued). An attempt to extend the doctrine in *Donoghue v. Stevenson* [1932] A.C. 562 to valuers was made *in Old Gate Estates Ltd v. Toplis and Harding and Russell* [1939] 3 All E.R. 209 (claim in negligence by company against valuers instructed by its promoters in respect of their excessive valuation of property known by the valuers to be used for the purpose of the company. Wrottesley J. dismissed the claim on the ground that the doctrine in *Donoghue v. Stevenson* was confined to negligence resulting in danger to life, limb or health and accordingly did not extend to the facts of the case).

[36] (1888) 39 Ch.D. 39.

[37] *ibid.* at 43, following *Heaven v. Pender* (1883) 11 Q.B.D. 503.

[38] *ibid.* at 44, following the Court of Appeal's decision in *Peek v. Derry* (1887) 37 Ch.D. 541. The latter case had not at the time proceeded to the House of Lords.

[39] [1893] 1 Q.B. 491, CA.

[40] Following the House of Lords' decision in *Derry v. Peek* (1889) 14 App.Cas. 337 overruling the Court of Appeal's decision in *Peek v. Derry*, above.

[41] [1964] A.C. 465.

decided.[42] Since *Hedley Byrne*[43] it is well established that in certain circumstances a surveyor owes a duty of care and may incur liability in negligence to a third party.[44] It is rare that a surveyor's negligence leads to direct physical injury and claims against surveyors are, accordingly, usually for economic loss. Given the restrictive attitude adopted by English law to the recovery of pure economic loss as exemplified by the decision in *Murphy v. Brentwood District Council*,[45] the courts have had to consider the circumstances in which recovery of such loss will be permitted.

The range of third persons who may be affected by a surveyor's default is **9–035** wide. For example, in the context of a property transaction the range may include the vendor and purchaser, mortgagor and mortgagee, and possibly subsequent purchasers.[46] However, the surveyor will not be under a duty of care to any person unless the circumstances are such as to give rise to a duty of care. The theoretical basis of valuers liability for economic loss was considered by May L.J. in *Merrett v. Babb*[47] when he pointed out the dangers and difficulties in seeking a single, universally applicable, test:

"During the last twenty years or more, intense and repeated attempts have been made to refine a comprehensive test, shortly expressed, to define circumstances in which a person owes a duty of care to another, breach of which causing loss will give rise to a claim for damages. If the damage is physical damage directly inflicted, there is rarely a problem. If the damage is what has been characterised as foreseeable economic loss, there may be a problem—the more so if what causes the loss is the giving of advice or the providing of information. In such cases especially—but, I think, in every case—reliance is an intrinsically necessary ingredient which appears in every formulation of a test. Beyond that, two strands of consideration emerged. These may for convenience be called the *Caparo* strand and the *Henderson* strand. The *Caparo* strand asks whether, in addition to foreseeability, there is a sufficient relationship of proximity and whether the imposition of a duty of care is fair, just and reasonable. The *Henderson* strand asks whether the defendant is to be taken to have assumed responsibility to the claimant to guard against the loss for which damages are claimed. The difficulty with the *Caparo* strand is that it sometimes seen as being unhelpfully vague. The difficulty with the *Henderson* strand is that it was originally expressed in terms of '*voluntary* assumption of responsibility' which tended to import a degree of subjectivity. *Henderson* itself put paid to that and, as Lord Slynn said in *Phelps*, '[assumption of responsibility] means simply that the law recognises that there is a duty of care. It is not so much that responsibility is assumed but that it is recognised or imposed by the law'. Thus the *Caparo* strand and the *Henderson* strand in reality merge. In my view, it is very often a helpful guide in particular cases to ask whether the defendant is to be taken to have

---

[42] *ibid.* at 489, 502, 535. The case was also approved by the House of Lords in *Smith v. Bush* [1990] 1 A.C. 831.

[43] Even prior to 1964 it was common for professional negligence claims by a client against a surveyor instructed by him to proceed in both negligence and contract, *e.g. Gurd v. A. Cobden Soar & Son* (1951) 157 E.G. 415; *Rayment v. Needham* (1953) 163 E.G. 4.

[44] *e.g. Hingorani v. Blower* [1976] 1 E.G.L.R. 104 especially at 106 (surveyor); *Singer and Friedlander Ltd v. John D. Wood & Co.* [1977] 2 E.G.L.R. 84 especially at 85; *Corisand Investments Ltd v. Druce & Co.* [1978] 2 E.G.L.R. 86; *Yianni v. Edwin Evans & Sons* [1982] Q.B. 438; *Roberts v. J. Hampson & Co.* [1988] 2 E.G.L.R. 181; *Smith v. Bush* [1990] 1 A.C. 831.

[45] [1991] 1 A.C. 398. for a full analysis and discussion see Chap. 12 and Chap. 8, paras 8–084 *et seq.*

[46] Note that the possibility of a surveyor being under a duty to such a person was expressly excluded by Lord Griffiths in *Smith v. Bush* [1990] 1 A.C. 831, 865.

[47] [2001] Lloyd's L.Rep. P.N. 468 at para. 41. For the facts and criticism of the actual decision where by an individual employed surveyor who signed a valuation for a building society was found to owe a duty of care to the purchaser, see para. 9–014 above.

assumed responsbility to the claimant to guard against the loss for which damages are claimed. But I also think that it is reaching for the moon—and not required by authority—to expect to accommodate every circumstance which may arise within a single short abstract formulation. The question in each case is whether the law recognises that there is a duty of care."

9–036   Given that no single factor leads to the imposition of a duty of care in a novel situation, the most helpful guidance is to be obtained by considering those circumstances in which duties of care have been imposed. The Courts have had no difficulty in accepting the existence of a duty where a valuer expressly and voluntarily assumes a duty to a particular group of people.[48] Greater difficulties occur when no such responsibility is voluntarily assumed. The leading English decision extending the liability of valuers is *Smith v. Bush*[49] where the House of Lords held that valuers employed by lenders to value modest residential properties owed a duty to individual borrowers. Lord Templeman (who together with Lords Griffiths and Jauncey gave a speech with which the other members of the House agreed) upheld the submission that it was unnecessary, in order for liability to be founded for there to be a *voluntary* assumption of responsibility by the valuer to the claimant—in fact a valuer would be likely to do everything that he could to avoid to avoid such responsibility. The real question was as to whether the law would impose such liability.[50] He stated:

> "I agree that by obtaining and disclosing a valuation, a mortgagee does not assume responsibility to the purchaser for that valuation. But in my opinion the valuer assumes responsibility to both mortgagee and purchaser by agreeing to carry out a valuation for mortgage purposes knowing that the valuation fee has bee paid by the purchaser and knowing that the valuation will probably be relied on by the purchaser in order to decide whether or not to enter into a contract to purchaser the house."[51]

9–037   Aside from cases of concurrent contractual and tortious liability, cases where liability has been voluntarily assumed and the situation (exemplified by *Smith v. Bush*) where a valuation is provided to a lender and relied on by a purchaser of a modest dwelling, the Courts have been cautious in imposing duties of care to third parties to prevent economic loss. An attempt to impose a duty was made in *Preston v. Torfaen Borough Council* and another.[52] The plaintiff purchased a house on an estate built by the defendant council over, allegedly, an infilled quarry. The defendant engineers had provided the council with a report on soil conditions and, it was alleged, negligently failed to identify the nature of the site. The action against the council was abandoned after the decision in *Murphy*, but that against the engineers was pursued to the Court of Appeal on a preliminary issue as to whether the engineers owed a duty of care to the plaintiff. The Court of Appeal held that no duty was owed. The engineers were no more proximate to the plaintiff than the builders, who could not be sued by reason of *Murphy*. The duty owed by the engineers to the council could not be extended to the plaintiff; as a potential purchaser he was an unidentified member of a class, and further, a

---

[48] The existence of a duty of care to investors on behalf of a firm of surveyors was conceded in respect of statements in a prospectus which were expressly attributed to the surveyors in *Ball v. Banner* [2000] Lloyd's L.Rep. P.N. 568 but the Judge refused to impose liability for other, non-attributed, statements.

[49] [1990] 1 A.C. 831.

[50] See further para. 9–047 below.

[51] *ibid.* at 847C.

[52] 65 Build. L.R. 1.

class that would not ask to see the report before purchase. These principles will apply to reports prepared in similar circumstances by surveyors.[53]

The High Court of Australia has recently considered whether liability should **9–038** be imposed upon a statutory water authority for negligently providing a "ball-park" figure to a developer for incurring the cost of bringing water to the developer's land.[54] By a majority of four to three, the Court decided that liability should not be imposed. Both the majority and the minority relied upon Barwick C.J.'s formulation in *Mutual life and Citizens Assurance Co. Ltd v. Evatt*[55]:

> "the speaker must realise or the circumstances be such that he ought to have realised that the recipient intends to act upon the information or advice in respect of his property or of himself in connetion with some matter of business or serious consequence . . . . The circumstances must be such that it is reasonable in all the circumstances for the recipient to seek, or to accept, and to rely upon the utterance of the speaker. The nature of the subject matter, the occasion of the interchange, and the identity and relative position of the parties as regards knowledge actual or potential and relevant capacity to form or exercise judgment will all be included in the factors which will determine the reasonableness of the acceptance of, and of the reliance by the recipient upon, the words of the speaker".

The fact that, despite reliance on the same test, the majority differed from the minority in deciding whether reliance was reasonable in the circumstances of the case shows how difficult it can be to predict whether a duty of care will be imposed in a particular novel factual situation. The same difficulty was displayed in the Scottish case of *Smith v. Carter*,[56] where Lord McCluskey held on a procedure roll debate that the pursuer, who was the co-purchaser of a property, was entitled to argue at trial that the defender valuer, who was unaware of her existence, nevertheless owed her a duty of care. Lord McCluskey held:

> "I am not prepared to affirm as a matter of general law that, in all circumstances, a surveyor who is instructed by an individual to carry out an inspection of property which that individual is considering buying owes no duty in the preparation and submission of his report of the inspection to any person who may join with the prospective purchaser in effecting the purchase. It cannot be uncommon for one person such as a relative or a friend who has some relevant experience in the property market to be acting as the undisclosed agent for another or as the spokesperson for a group interested in a possible property transaction."[57]

(ii) *Knowledge of reliance*

A duty of care will be more difficult to establish where it is claimed that the **9–039** surveyor ought to have known, although he did not actually know, that reliance would be placed on his advice by a third party.[58] As a matter of practice,

---

[53] For further commentary on this case, see chap. 8, para. 8–102.
[54] *Tepko Pty Ltd v. Water Board* (2001) 75 ALJR 775 commented on by Dr Katter, " 'Ball park' figures and the ambit of duty of care for negligent misstatement" at 75 A.L.J. 427.
[55] (1968) 122 C.L.R. 556 at 569–572.
[56] 1995 S.L.T. 295.
[57] *ibid.* at 297.
[58] See *Hingorani v. Blower* [1976] 1 E.G.L.R. 104. The surveyor instructed to carry out structural survey by National House Owners' Association in turn so instructed by purchaser. Held: the surveyor owed a duty of care to the purchaser. It is unclear from the report whether the surveyor knew that the particular purchaser would place reliance upon his advice. He did know, however, that his advice was for the purpose of house purchase. The decision is explicable on the ground that the surveyor ought to have known that the purchaser would rely upon his advice.

surveyors and valuers will often include express disclaimers seeking to prevent third parties from relying on their report. Although these disclaimers will not be effective in a *Smith v. Bush* context, they have been held to be effective in a commercial context.[59] An example of a duty being held to exist where the surveyor did not know that his report would be relied upon is *Bourne v. McEvoy Timber Preservation Ltd.*[60] The defendant timber rot specialists were instructed by the vendors of a house to report on fungal infestation and to estimate for its eradication upon the basis that if their estimate was accepted they had the job and were paid for it, but if not, they had nothing. The defendants inspected the house and provided a report and an estimate. There was no evidence that the claimant purchaser was ever shown the defendants' report but he, with the vendors' agreement, instructed and paid the defendants to carry out the work in the estimate. After completing the work the defendants provided a guarantee in which the plaintiff was named as client. Prior to the claimant instructing them to do the work, however, the defendants did not know of his existence or that he would see and rely upon their report. They did know that their report was connected with the proposed sale of the house. There was a later outbreak of dry rot in an area in which no dry rot had been reported. The defendants contended that in carrying out their inspection and report they did not owe a duty of care to the plaintiff since there was no "duty situation". Bristow J. rejected the defendants' contention:

> "I have to test whether there was sufficient proximity between the plaintiff and the defendants to give rise to a duty situation by asking myself the question: at the time the defendants made their inspection and reported to [the sellers] their principals, did they know, or ought they to have known, that the purchaser of the house might well be affected in the decisions which he took by the contents of their report? In my judgment the answer to that question on the evidence in this case must be 'yes'. The defendants knew the house was being 'tarted up' for sale. The defendants knew their report might go to the mortgagees. The fact that it might go to mortgagees meant that their findings must affect the value people would put on the house. What was the right value to put on the house must affect the . . . sellers, the mortgagees (if any), and most probably the third person concerned in the sale transaction, the buyer. The defendants regarded the buyer as the beneficiary of their work if they got the job. [The sellers] would fill in the buyer's name on the 20 year guarantee of their work, and the defendants would honour the guarantee in the hands of the occupiers from time to time of the house".[61]

On the facts, however, the defendants were held not negligent.

9–040   Similarly in *Shankie-Williams v. Heavey*[62] the defendant dry rot specialist was instructed to inspect a ground floor flat by its vendor. He provided a report stating that he had found no evidence of dry rot at the time of his inspection. He nevertheless gave certain timbers a precautionary spray of fungicide and guaranteed these timbers against recurrence of dry rot infestation for 30 years. Soon after the vendor sold not only the ground floor flat but also the first floor flat above. Dry rot appeared two years later in both flats and the defendant was sued in negligence by each purchaser. The Court of Appeal held that the defendant

---

[59] See *Omega Trust Co. Ltd v. Wright Son & Pepper* [1997] P.N.L.R. 425 and further at para. 9–071 below.
[60] [1976] 1 E.G.L.R. 100.
[61] *ibid.* at 101.
[62] [1986] 2 E.G.L.R. 139, CA.

owed a duty of care to the purchasers of the ground floor flat because the defendant knew that the vendor wanted a report or guarantee from him which he could show to prospective purchasers of the ground floor flat. However, it was held that he did not owe a duty of care to the purchaser of the first floor flat, since his instructions, report and guarantee related to the ground floor flat only.[63] Although in breach of his duty of care to the purchasers of the ground floor flat, the Court of Appeal held that the defendant was not liable to them. There was no evidence that those purchasers had seen the defendant's report and accordingly there was no causal connection shown between the defendant's breach of duty and the damage sustained by them.[64]

Where the surveyor neither knows nor ought to know that reliance is to be   **9–041** placed upon his advice by a third party, no duty of care will arise. In *Le Lievre v. Gould*[65] the claimant mortgagee agreed to advance to a builder sums secured by the mortgage of land the subject of building works. The instalments were quantified by reference to progress certificates provided by the mortgagee's surveyor. The defendant, a surveyor employed by the builder, was unaware of the agreement between the builder and the plaintiff mortgagee and his certificates were addressed to the builder. His certificates were communicated, apparently without his authority, by the builder to the mortgagee, who relied on them in advancing the mortgage instalments. It was held that the surveyor owed no duty of care to the mortgagee. The actual *ratio decidendi* was that there could be no duty in the absence of a contract between the mortgagee and the surveyor. While that *ratio* cannot survive *Hedley Byrne & Co. Ltd v. Heller and Partners Ltd*,[66] four of their Lordships in that case were inclined to support the actual decision in *Le Lievre v. Gould*.[67] Lord Reid in particular took the view that it would be difficult to establish the prerequisite degree of proximity to give rise to a duty of care on the facts of the case.[68]

A question which sometimes arises is as to whether a lender's reliance on a   **9–042** valuation is unreasonable so as to preclude him from recovering any loss. A range of possible results are possible in such a case: a court may decide that the

---

[63] *ibid.* at 141. May L.J. said:
"In my judgment, on the facts as I have outlined them, there was an insufficient nexus between the appellant and the intending purchaser of a lease of the first-floor flat (the third plaintiff). I ask myself, in the circumstances of this case, where is one to stop in this inquiry? If the appellant owed to the third plaintiff a duty of care when reporting on the ground-floor flat, to be occupied by the first and second plaintiffs, did he owe a similar duty to any intending purchaser of the second-floor flat? . . . I think not. If, contrary, to that view, the answer has to be in the affirmative then I pose the question: 'What about an adjoining occupier?' Supposing that this was a company converting not one house but a row of five houses in the street. Did [the defendant] in those circumstances, asked to inspect and report only upon the ground-floor flat [of one house], owe any duty to intending lessees of flats in the yet to be converted adjoining premises . . . ? Again, I think not."
[64] See also *Duncan Investments v. Underwoods* [1997] P.N.L.R. 521 where the defendant estate agents gave an oral estimate of possible re-sale values to the plaintiff knowing that the advice was likely to be relied upon and that it was unlikely that independent advice would be sought. The imposition of a duty of care was upheld on appeal.
[65] [1893] 1 Q.B. 491.
[66] [1964] A.C. 465.
[67] *ibid.* at 488 (Lord Reid), at 507 (Lord Hodson) at 519 (Lord Devlin) and at 535 (Lord Pearce). Lord Morris at 499 thought it unnecessary to consider the point.
[68] *ibid.* at 488. Lord Hodson at 507 and Lord Pearce at 535 preferred the justification of the decision given by Denning L.J. in *Candler v. Crane, Christmas & Co.* [1951] 2 K.B. 164, namely that the plaintiff mortgagees not only had the opportunity but had stipulated for inspection by their own surveyor.

particular transaction was outside the contemplation of the valuer so that no duty arises (or that the kind of damage suffered was beyond the scope of his duty); or that there was no causal link between the negligence and the loss suffered; or that the lender was guilty of contributory negligence or that the full loss should be recovered. In *Western Trust v Strutt & Parker*,[69] the question as to whether the lender was entitled to rely on a valuation arose in three different ways. A lender had agreed to provide a total loan of £1m. in three tranches in order to enable farm buildings to be converted into a holiday cottages complex—the first of £500,000 and the next two of £250,000. The security taken was over 14 of the 15 properties and excluded the largest property. In addition, three of the charged properties were built slightly beyond the charged land. The valuer was instructed by the developer to provide a valuation on all of the properties after the first two tranches had been made. He negligently provided a valuation of the entire holiday complex on the basis that it would provide permanent accommodation (for which there was no planning permission). The lender then not only provided the third tranche of the loan but also advanced two further loans of £500,000 and £150,000 ("the swimming pool loans") in order to build a swimming pool, sauna and café without, however, making any provision for the moneys to be advanced as the same were built. The questions arose (a) as to whether the lender was entitled to recover the first two tranches on the basis that had a competent valuation been provided, the lender would have sought to recover the same; (b) whether the lender could recover the third tranche given that the property valued (the whole complex) was different from that charged; and (c) whether the lender could recover the swimming pool loans. The Court of Appeal upheld the judge's decision that only the third tranche loan could be recovered, albeit with a reduction of 20 per cent for contributory negligence.[70] Both the first two tranches and the swimming pool loans were beyond the scope of the duty owed by the valuer. On the evidence, there was no reason for the valuer to suppose that his valuation was required in relation to the first two tranches.[71] So far as the swimming pool loans were concerned, the interval (some seven months) between the valuation and the further loans, together with the fact that there was no reason for the valuer to suppose that loans would be required other than immediately to complete the development, were sufficient to take them beyond the valuer's duty. In relation to the third tranche, Lord Woolf accepted[72] that if the difference between the property which a valuer valued and the property relied on by the lender was of sufficient significance, it would mean that the lender had ventured beyond the scope of duty owed by the valuer. In deciding whether this was the case, he stated:

> "A useful working test would be to ask what would be a reasonable response of a valuer to the question can the valuation still be relied on notwithstanding the difference between the property he valued and the property which was actually the subject matter of the valuation. If, for example, the valuation was of a number of identical properties but the loan was made in relation to only some of the properties, you would expect the reasonable valuer to respond that the difference did not matter because the value of the

---

[69] [1999] P.N.L.R. 154.

[70] Lord Woolf M.R. stated at 168 that he regarded the lender as being fortunate in only being held 20% to blame for the third tranche—see further para. 9–172 below.

[71] See at 168—although Lord Woolf made it clear that even if his conclusion as to duty was different, he would have rejected the suggestion that the lender could have improved its position as to the first two tranches.

[72] At 165.

lesser number of properties could be deduced by dividing the value given so as to reflect the reduction in the number of properties. If, however, no such calculation would be possible becaues the property being valued and the property which was the subject of the loan were significantly different, you would expect the response of the reasonable valuer to be otherwise."[73]

(iii) *Duty of mortgagee's valuer to purchaser*

The prime example of the imposition of a duty of care by the English courts in   **9–043** favour of third parties in this field has occurred in relation to valuation reports commissioned by lenders. The existence of such a duty was first recognised in the case of *Yianni v. Edwin Evans*,[74] confirmed in *Smith v. Bush*.[75] In *Yianni*, the claimants applied to a building society for a mortgage advance of £12,000, to purchase a house for £15,000. They paid the building society a valuation fee and the society instructed the defendant surveyors to value it. The surveyors' valuation was £15,000 and they reported that the house was suitable security for an advance of £12,000. In reliance on the report the society offered a mortgage advance of £12,000 to the plaintiffs. Together with the offer form the society sent the plaintiffs a notice stating that the making of an advance would not imply any warranty that the purchase price was reasonable.[76] A similar warning had been contained in the original application form for an advance completed by the plaintiffs. Moreover both the application form and an explanatory booklet accompanying the society's offer form stated that applicants who wished a survey for their own information and protection should instruct their own surveyor. The explanatory booklet further stated that the report of the valuer was confidential to the building society. The claimants decided not to instruct their own surveyor, choosing rather to rely on the fact of the building society making them an offer of a mortgage advance as indicative that the house was worth at least that amount. The plaintiffs discovered within 12 months of its purchase that the house was subject to severe structural damage. The cost of repairs was estimated at £18,000. In their claim against the defendants the claimants contended that:

(a) the defendants' statement to the building society that the house was suitable security for a loan of £12,000 meant that the house was worth at least £12,000;

(b) the statement was negligent;

(c) the defendants ought reasonably to have contemplated that the statement would be passed on by the building society to the plaintiffs;

---

[73] *ibid.* at 165–166.
[74] [1982] Q.B. 438.
[75] [1990] 1 A.C. 831. See para. 9–046, below.
[76] s.30 of the Building Societies Act 1962 provided "where a building society makes to a member an advance for the purpose of it being used in defraying the purchase price of freehold or leasehold estate, the society shall be deemed to warrant to the member that the purchase price is reasonable, unless, before any contract requiring a member to repay the advance is entered into, the society gives to the member a notice in writing in the prescribed form stating that the making of the advance implies no such warranty". The section and the whole of the Building Societies Act 1962 was repealed by the Building Societies Act 1986, the majority of which came into operation on January 1, 1987.

(d) the defendants knew or ought to have known that the claimants would rely upon it and would be inclined to buy the house and mortgage it to the building society; and

(e) the claimants did so and in consequence suffered damage.

The defendants accepted that their valuation was negligent but denied liability to the claimants, on the ground that they did not owe them a duty of care. Park J. held that the defendants did owe them a duty of care. He rejected arguments by the defendants, founded upon the statutory notice and the building society's literature, that the claimants' reliance on the valuation was unforeseeable and that the claimants had been contributory negligent in not obtaining an independent surveyor's report:

> "It was plainly a house at the lower end of the property market. The applicant for a loan would therefore almost certainly be a person of modest means who, for one reason or another, would not be expected to obtain an independent valuation, and who would be certain to rely, as the plaintiffs in fact did, on the defendants' valuation as communicated to him in the building society's offer. I am sure that the defendants knew that their valuation would be passed on to the plaintiffs and that the defendants knew that the plaintiffs would rely upon it when they decided to accept the society's offer."[77]

9–044   Park J. would appear to have been influenced in his conclusion by evidence adduced to the effect that only between 10 and 15 per cent of mortgage applicants to building societies had their own independent survey carried out. Although in accord with the expectations of consumer organisations, this decision represents a landmark in the extension of a surveyor's duty of care to third parties. Such a duty was held to exist despite the disclaimer of any implied warranty as to the reasonableness of the purchase price and the fact that the plaintiffs did not see (and were not intended to see) the report.[78]

9–045   **The impact of *Yianni*.** This decision had a considerable impact on those concerned with the domestic housing market.[79] One lender[80] considered the implications of *Yianni* and introduced a scheme whereby prospective borrowers were offered a choice between a valuation without liability on the valuer and a report which accepted that the valuer was under a duty to exercise reasonable skill and care. Such a report cost at least £100 more than a valuation for a house worth £20,000. Noting that the report did not involve any more work for the valuer, Lord Templeman in *Smith v. Bush*[81] was scathing about the scheme, its cost and the attempt to exclude liability for negligence:

> "On a million houses, this would represent increases of income to be divided between valuers, insurers and building societies of about £150m. It is hardly surprising that few

---

[77] [1982] 1 Q.B. 438, 456.
[78] In the reverse situation of a surveyor instructed by a mortgagor but told that reliance would be placed upon his advice by a mortgagee, a duty of care to the latter has been recognised: see *Singer & Friedlander Ltd v. John D. Wood & Co.* [1977] 2 E.G.L.R. 84.
[79] Concern about the consequences of this case for the surveying profession in part led to the establishment of a fact finding study team, under the chairmanship of Professor Andrew Likierman, which considered the practice of surveying. The report, *Professional Liability*, was published in 1989 by HMSO. For a commentary on the report see M. F. James, "Surveyors and the Likierman Report" (1990) 3 P.N. 119.
[80] The Abbey National Building Society.
[81] [1990] 1 A.C. 831.

purchasers have chosen the report instead of the valuation. Any increase in fees, alleged to be justified by the decision of this House in these appeals, will no doubt be monitored by the appropriate authorities. It is open to Parliament to provide that members of all professions or members of one profession providing services in the normal course of the exercise of their profession for reward shall be entitled to exclude or limit their liability for failure to exercise reasonable skill and care. In the absence of any such provision valuers are not, in my opinion, entitled to rely on a general exclusion of the common law duty of care owed to purchasers of houses by valuers to exercise reasonable skill and care in valuing houses for mortgage purposes."[82]

It is notable that such criticism was made shortly before the decline in property values at the end of the 1980s and beginning of the 1990s had become manifest. Given the modest fees charged for mortgage valuations and the extent of liability attaching to the same, it must be doubted that the criticism was fair. The standard conditions of engagement prepared by RICS now accept a duty of care to the prospective purchaser, whatever the level of service offered.

Smith v. Bush. The House of Lords *in Smith v. Bush; Harris v. Wyre Forest* **9–046** *District Council*[83] considered both the question of the duty of care to third parties and the application of the reasonableness test under the Unfair Contract Terms Act 1977.[84] The latter issue is considered below.[85] The facts of these cases are as follows. In *Smith v. Bush*, the claimant was sent a copy of the defendant surveyor's valuation report by the building society. The report stated that no essential repairs were necessary. The mortgage application form and report contained a disclaimer of liability for the accuracy of the report and a recommendation to the effect that the claimant should obtain independent advice. The claimant nevertheless relied on the report and bought the modest property. The chimneys were in fact defective. The claimant claimed damages from the surveyor who, *inter alia*, relied upon the disclaimer. In *Harris v. Wyre Forest District Council* the claimants purchased a small terraced house with a 95 per cent mortgage from the defendant council. They paid the valuation fee and signed the standard mortgage application which stated that the valuation was confidential, intended solely for the council and that no responsibility was accepted for the value or condition of the property. The claimants did not see the report but accepted the mortgage offered. Three years later they attempted to sell the house but a survey revealed structural defects in the property to the extent that it was uninhabitable and unsaleable.

In deciding that the valuer[86] owed a duty of care to the purchasers in each case, **9–047** the House of Lords expressly approved the decision of Park J. in *Yianni v. Edwin Evans & Sons*.[87] Lord Templeman concluded that "the duty of care which the

---

[82] *ibid.* at 853.

[83] [1990] 1 A.C. 831. Save where the different facts of the two cases require, the case is referred to as *Smith v. Bush*.

[84] For further commentary on the case, see M. F. James, "Negligence in mortgage valuations" (1989) 3 P.N. 73, and *ibid.*, "Surveyor's liability after *Smith v. Bush*" (1991) 3 P.N. 142.

[85] See para. 9–065.

[86] In *Smith v. Bush*, the valuer, in *Harris v. Wyre Forest D.C.*, the council, who, it was accepted, were vicariously liable for the acts and omissions of their employed valuer. In *Merrett v. Babb* [2001] Lloyds L.R.P.N. 468, the question arose as to whether an employed valuer (as distinct from his employer) owed a duty of care to a prospective purchaser. In deciding that such a duty was owed, May L.J. placed heavy reliance on the fact that the House of Lords had considered the professional status of the employed valuer in *Harris* to be important. See further para. 9–014 above.

[87] [1982] Q.B. 438, and see para. 9–043, above.

valuer owes to the building society is exactly the same as the duty of care which he owes to the purchaser"[88] and based his decision on his analysis of the relationship between the valuer and the purchaser as "akin to contract". Lord Templeman stated[89]: "The valuer knows that the consideration which he receives derives from the purchaser and is passed on by the mortgagee, and the valuer also knows that the valuation will determine whether or not the purchaser buys the house."

Lord Griffiths did not think that voluntary assumption of responsibility was a helpful or realistic test for liability.[90] He answered the question, "in what circumstances should a duty of care be owed by the adviser to those who act upon his advice?" as follows:

"only if it is foreseeable that if the advice is negligent the recipient is likely to suffer damage, that there is a sufficiently proximate relationship between the parties and that it is just and reasonable to impose the liability. In the case of a surveyor valuing a small house for a building society or local authority, the application of these three criteria leads to the conclusion that he owes a duty of care to the purchaser. If the valuation is negligent and is relied upon damage in the form of economic loss to the purchaser is obviously foreseeable. The necessary proximity arises from the surveyor's knowledge that the overwhelming probability is that the purchaser will rely upon his valuation, the evidence was that surveyors knew that approximately 90 per cent of purchasers did so and the fact that the surveyor only obtains the work because the purchaser is willing to pay his fee. It is just and reasonable that the duty should be imposed for the advice is given in a professional as opposed to a social context and liability for breach of the duty will be limited both as to its extent and amount. The extent of the liability is limited to the purchaser of the house—I would not extend it to subsequent purchasers. The amount of the liability cannot be very great because it relates to a modest house. There is no question here of creating a liability of indeterminate amount to an indeterminate class.[91] I would certainly wish to stress that in cases where the advice has not been given for the specific purpose of the recipient acting upon it, it should only be in cases where the adviser knows that there is a high degree of probability that some other identifiable person will act upon the advice that a duty of care should be imposed. It would impose an intolerable burden upon those who give advice in a professional or commercial context if they were to owe a duty not only to those to whom they give the advice but to any other person who might choose to act upon it".[92]

9–048 Lord Jauncey considered that in three of the cases discussed, the existence of direct contact between the negligent provider of information, and the plaintiff or his agent was important.[93] The fact that such contact was absent in the case of *Smith v. Bush* was noted by Lord Jauncey when he formulated his test, but on the facts, did not lead to a different result:

---

[88] [1990] 1 A.C. 831, at 851.

[89] *ibid.* at 846.

[90] *ibid.* at 862 and with less force, at 864.

[91] See the well-known dicta of Cardozo C.J. in *Ultramares Corporation v. Touche* (1931) 174 N.E. 441, quoted by Denning L.J. in *Candler v. Crane, Christmas & Co.* [1951] 2 K.B. 164, 183. The risk of creating such a liability led Phillips J. to reject the submission that Lloyd's Register of Shipping owed a duty of care to those foreseeably liable to suffer economic loss in consequence of reliance on an alleged negligent Classification Society survey of a ship. See *The Morning Watch* [1990] 1 Lloyd's Rep. 547, 560.

[92] [1990] 1 A.C. 831, at 865.

[93] *ibid.* at 870, 871. The cases Lord Jauncey referred to were *Cann v. Willson* (1888) 39 Ch.D. 39, *Candler v. Crane, Christmas & Co.* [1951] 2 K.B. 164, *and Hedley Byrne & Co. Ltd v. Heller & Partners Ltd* [1964] A.C. 465.

"I prefer to approach the matter by asking whether the facts disclose that the appellants in inspecting and reporting must, but for the disclaimers, by reason of the proximate relationship between them, be deemed to have assumed responsibility towards Mrs Smith as well as to the building society who instructed them.

There can only be an affirmative answer to this question. The four critical facts are that the appellants knew from the outset: (1) that the report would be shown to Mrs Smith; (2) that Mrs Smith would probably rely on the valuation contained therein in deciding whether to buy the house without obtaining an independent valuation; (3) that if, in those circumstances, the valuation was, having regard to the actual condition of the house, excessive, Mrs Smith would be likely to suffer loss; and (4) that she had paid to the building society a sum to defray the appellants' fee."[94]

Later, in *Caparo Industries plc v. Dickman*,[95] Lord Oliver stressed the impor- **9–049**
tance of the fact that the valuer knew that his valuation was likely to be relied on by the purchaser:

"[*Smith* and *Harris*] do not, I think, justify any broader proposition than that already set out, save that they make it clear that the absence of a positive intention that the advice shall be acted upon by anyone other than the immediate recipient—indeed an expressed intention that it shall not be acted upon by anyone else—cannot prevail against actual or presumed knowledge that it is likely to be relied upon in a particular transaction."[96]

In deciding that the knowledge of likely reliance should prevail against the valuers desire that the valuation should not be relied upon, the reasoning resolves to a simple question of policy.[97] Such considerations were expressly recognised by Lord Griffiths:

"It must, however, be remembered that this is a decision in respect of a dwelling house of modest value in which it is widely recognised by surveyors that purchasers are in fact relying on their care and skill. It will obviously be of general application in broadly similar circumstances. But I expressly reserve my position in respect of valuations of quite different types of property for mortgage purposes, such as industrial property, large blocks of flats or very expensive houses."[98]

Smith v. Bush did not decide the extent to which a duty of care would be found **9–050**
to exist in unusual or expensive properties. *Beaumont v. Humberts*[99] arose out of a valuation for reinstatement purposes of an unusual Grade II listed property in Dorset. The defendant valuers were instructed by the mortgagees and the plaintiff

---

[94] *ibid.* at 871E.
[95] [1990] 2 A.C. 605. See Chap. 15, para. 15–056. No duty of care was owed by the auditors of a public company to potential investors.
[96] *ibid.* at 638–639. See also the statement by Brennan C.J. in *Esanda Finance Corp. Ltd v. Peat Marwick Hungerfords* (1997) 188 C.L.R. 241 at 251–253 where he stressed the importance of the knowledge that the claimant was likely to rely on the negligent mis-statement and para. 15–083 below.
[97] For, it is submitted, the reasons adopted by the House of Lords when considering whether it was reasonable for the valuer to exclude his duty. See para. 9–065, below.
[98] *ibid.* at 859G. Such considerations were also relevant as to the application of the Unfair Contract Terms Act—as to which see paras 9–065 above and 9–073 below.
[99] [1990] 2 E.G.L.R. 166. Note that the purchaser was far removed from the archetypal purchaser of *Smith v. Bush, per* Staughton L.J.: "Mr Beaumont is an intelligent and sophisticated businessman and not a humble purchaser of a house of modest value . . . ."

was the mortgagor. By a majority[1] the Court of Appeal held that the necessary degree of proximity between the valuer and the mortgagor had been established and a duty of care existed. The principal facts relied upon by the Court of Appeal in coming to that conclusion were that the valuer had earlier carried out a full structural survey of the property (but not a valuation) for the plaintiff, and the plaintiff had suggested to the mortgagees that they employ the valuer to obtain the reinstatement value that he would in any event have to pay for.

9–051 An unintended consequence of the decision in *Smith v. Bush* is that a valuer may be exposed to double jeopardy in respect of the same negligent valuation. In factual circumstances similar to those which obtained in *Smith v. Bush* the valuer will owe a contractual duty to the lender, and a duty of care at common law to the borrower. An overvaluation caused by a negligent failure to observe defects may result in the borrower suing the valuer. Having recovered damages the borrower may not carry out repairs but instead may dissipate the fruits of the action. If there is a subsequent default by the borrower, the lender has a right to claim its loss from the valuer. The valuer cannot defeat such a claim on the basis that it has already met the claim by the borrower. The parties, the cause of action and the measure of damage would all be different.[2]

(d) *The standard of care and skill*

(i) *Reasonable standard*

9–052 In common with other professional persons and in the absence of an express term to the contrary, the standard required of a surveyor is that of the ordinary skilled man exercising the same skill as himself. He is variously described in the cases as the "reasonably skilled", "competent", "prudent" or "average" surveyor.[3] It will not be lower for a surveyor with no professional qualifications[4] or with limited experience whether generally[5] or of property in a particular area.[6] Nor will it make any difference that no fee[7] or a lower fee is charged or intended to

---

[1] Taylor and Dillon L.JJ., Staughton L.J. dissenting. In fact Staughton and Dillon L.J. disagreed on every main issue, and Taylor L.J. did not agree on all issues with either.

[2] To reduce the risk of such a situation arising a potentially negligent valuer might wish to involve the lender at an appropriate stage in any action brought by the borrower.

[3] This passage in the third edition (1992) was cited with approval by the court in *Muldoon v. Mays of Lilliput Ltd* [1993] 1 E.G.L.R. 43, 45. This paragraph in the fourth edition (1997) was also approved by the Court of Appeal in *Sansom v. Metcalfe Hambleton & Co.* [1998] 2 E.G.L.R. 103 and by the court in *Lewisham Investment Partnership Ltd v. Morgan* [1997] 2 E.G.L.R. 150. See generally on this topic *Tomlinson*, p. 37.

[4] See *Freeman v. Marshall & Co.* (1966) 200 E.G. 777, *per* Lawton J., 777: "[The defendant surveyor] had . . . had no organised course of training as a surveyor and had never passed any professional examination in surveying. He was a member of the Valuers Institution through election, not examination . . . In fairness to him, he claimed only to have a working knowledge of structures from the point of view of buying and selling, but if he held himself out in practice as a surveyor he must be deemed to have the skills of a surveyor and be adjudged upon them."

[5] See *Kenney v. Hall, Pain and Foster* [1976] 2 E.G.L.R. 29.

[6] See (on this point) *Baxter v. F. W. Gapp & Co. Ltd* [1938] 4 All E.R. 457 (first instance); [1939] 2 K.B. 752, CA especially passage from Goddard L.J.'s judgment at [1938] 4 All E.R. 459 quoted at para. 9–081, below. This case has been overruled on the issue of the calculation of interest by *Swingcastle Ltd v. Gibson* [1991] 2 A.C. 223.

[7] See *Kenney v. Hall, Pain and Foster* [1976] 2 E.G.L.R. 29, a negligent valuation case, *per* Goff J. at 33: "the defendants are right to concede that they owe such a duty of care to the plaintiff. It makes no difference whether or not they intended to charge a fee for their services. In point of law they could have done so, because whenever a professional man renders services to another at his request he is, in the absence of a contrary intention, entitled to charge for those services".

be charged for the services rendered. Thus in *Roberts v. J. Hampson & Co.*[8] Ian
Kennedy J. stated:

> "In my judgment, it must be accepted that where a surveyor undertakes a Scheme 1
> valuation it is understood that he is making a limited appraisal only. It is however, an
> appraisal by a skilled professional man. It is inherent in any standard fee work that some
> cases will colloquially be 'winners' and others 'losers' from the professional man's
> point of view. The fact that in an individual case he may need to spend two or three
> times as long as he would have expected, or as the fee structure would have contem-
> plated, is something that he must accept. His duty to take reasonable care in providing
> a valuation remains the root of his obligation."[9]

The *standard* therefore remains constant irrespective both of the nature of the
engagement and whether a claim is made in contract or tort. It is sometimes
contended that when a limited task is required, for example, a "quick survey",
the standard is lower. It is submitted that the contention is misconceived, as the
dicta by Ian Kennedy J. in *Roberts v. J. Hampson & Co.* illustrates. The point was
also succinctly made by Lord Cameron in the Scottish case, *Stewart v. H.A.
Brechin & Co.*[10]:

> "The first question is what was the contract; because until that is decided, the extent of
> the defenders' obligation to the pursuer cannot be determined. Whatever the extent of
> that obligation, the measure of the defenders' duty in its discharge is the same, namely,
> to display and apply reasonable care and a reasonable standard of professional compe-
> tence in doing the work they were employed to do, provided that the work fell within
> the proper scope of their professional activities."[11]

As is apparent from Lord Cameron's dictum, it does not follow from the fact that
the standard of care remains the same, that the scope and extent of the surveyor's
instructions will be irrelevant to the result achieved.[12]

The *standard* is not relaxed if the required task is carried out in unusual   **9–053**
circumstances, for example a valuation in a market showing signs of deep
depression or of unusual buoyancy or volatility.[13] Whether the standard was

---

[8] [1990] 1 W.L.R. 94.
[9] *ibid.* at 101. In *Routestone Ltd v. Minories Finance Ltd* [1997] 1 E.G.L.R. 123 at 126K, Jacob J.
described the standard of care of an estate agent as follows:
"The relevant legal standard was not in dispute. [The claimant] had to show that the advice given
by [the defendants] was more than erroneous—it had to amount to an error of the sort that would
not have been made by a reasonably competent estate agent professing himself to have the standard
and type of skill that [the defendants] held themselves out as having, and acting with ordinary
care . . . "
[10] [1959] S.C. 306.
[11] *ibid.* at 307.
[12] See further para. 9–057 below.
[13] See *Nykredit Mortgage Bank plc v. Edward Erdman Group Ltd* [1996] 1 E.G.L.R. 119 at 122, *per*
Peter Gibson L.J.: "it is plain on the evidence that it is wrong to take speculations about the future
movement of interest rates into account on a valuation, both in relation to demand and in relation to
developer's costs" *and Singer & Friedlander Ltd v. John D. Wood & Co.* [1977] 2 E.G.L.R. 84 at 86,
per Watkins J.: "The unusual circumstances of his task impose upon [a valuer] a greater test of his
skill and bid him to exercise stricter discipline in the making of assumptions without which he is
unable to perform his task, and I think he must beware of lapsing into carelessness or over-confidence
when the market is riding high. The more unusual be the nature of the problem, for no matter what
reason, the greater the need for circumspection."

complied with in a particular case, however, must be determined having regard to the circumstances and knowledge current at the time when the surveyor was required to carry out his instructions. The court must be careful "not to be wise after the event".[14] Genuinely unforeseeable events occurring after the valuation date must be disregarded whether they are adverse or beneficial to the surveyor's opinion of value. Thus in *Arab Bank v. John D Wood Commercial*,[15] the Court of Appeal criticised the trial Judge for "the use of inadmissible hindsight" in relying on an unusual renegotiation of rent which had occurred after the date of the first opinion of value in order to justify the overall valuation produced. Yet guarding against hindsight may be difficult where a long time has elapsed[16] between the allegedly negligent act and trial or where the state of knowledge at a particular time[17] is in issue.[18]

(ii) *General practice and knowledge as evidence of the standard*

9–054   What is required to fulfil the standard of care and skill in a particular case is usually determined by reference to the general practice of surveyors carrying out similar work. Thus what ought to be done is usually determined by asking what the "average"[19] or "ordinary competent"[20] surveyor would have done. While it remains open to a court to reject a general practice as not achieving the required standard, there has yet to be a precedent where a court has done so in the context of surveyors. Gibson J.'s decision in *Corisand Investments Ltd v. Druce & Co.*[21] that the defendants were negligent in not allowing for the speculative element in the property market in making their valuation, was criticised by some in the profession as going beyond general practice. The judge was nevertheless careful to reach his decision by reference to what an "ordinary competent valuer"[22] would have done. In his view, it would have included allowing for the speculative element.

---

[14] *Hill v. Debenham, Tewson and Chinnocks* (1958) 171 E.G. 835, *per* Judge Carter Q.C.
[15] [2000] Lloyd's L.Rep. P.N. 173 at 186.
[16] Note *Leigh v. Unsworth* (1972) 230 E.G. 501, where some seven-and-a-half years had elapsed. The delay may sometimes favour the defendant surveyor: *see MacKenzie v. Hall & Co.* (1951) 157 E.G. 492, a Scottish Court of Session case, the pursuers' claim against the defendant surveyors failed, effectively on this ground. *Per* Lord Mackintosh: "the onus of proof which lay upon the pursuer of an action for professional negligence was a heavy one, and in this case that onus was made still heavier by the pursuers' long delay in bringing the action".
[17] Note the unsuccessful attempt in *Corisand Investments Ltd v. Druce & Co.* [1978] 2 E.G.L.R. 86 especially at 90 to establish that the defendant valuers were negligent in not anticipating or suspecting the impending collapse of the property market when carrying out a valuation in September 1973.
[18] This passage in the third edition (1992) was cited with approval by the court in *Muldoon v. Mays of Lilliput Ltd* [1993] 1 E.G.L.R. 43, 46.
[19] *e.g. Daisley v. B. S. Hall & Co.* (1972) 225 E.G. 1553, *per* Bristow J. at 1555: "The duty of a practitioner of any professional skill which he undertakes to perform . . . is to see the things that the average skilled professional in the field would see, draw from what he sees the conclusions that the average skilled professional would draw, and take the action that the average skilled professional would take."
[20] *Corisand Investments Ltd v. Druce & Co.* [1978] 2 E.G.L.R. 86, 89. Note the Canadian case of *Seeward Mortgage Investment Corp. v. First Citizens Financial Corp.* (1983) 45 B.C.L.R. 87, 100, *per* Hamilton L.J.S.C.: "He could not expect from an appraiser the standard of inspection that would have been required of a professional engineer."
[21] [1978] 2 E.G.L.R. 86.
[22] *ibid.* at 92, 97.

The knowledge required of a surveyor is likewise described by reference to a   **9–055**
norm such as the "ordinary competent surveyor"[23] or "averaged skilled professional" as in *Daisley v. B.S. Hall & Co.*[24] In the latter case Bristow J. accepted
expert evidence that the risk to buildings on shrinkable clay subsoil adjacent to
poplar trees was notorious and was one of the subjects which was included in a
surveyor's education. The defendant surveyor who did not recognise the trees as
poplars was held negligent in failing, inter alia, to warn of the risk. In contrast in
Last v. Post,[25] Lloyd Jacob J. held that the defendant surveyor was not negligent
in not recognising disintegration of roof tiles through efflorescence: "As the
character of the phenomenon was so rare it would not be right to apply as the
standard of a competent surveyor the detection of a phenomenon."[26]

Duty to keep up to date. The average skilled surveyor is, however, required   **9–056**
to take reasonable steps to acquaint himself with changes and new developments
affecting his skill. From 1991 the RICS required its members to demonstrate a
commitment to their professional development, and now members of the Institution have an obligation to attend training and other events that are approved as
part of the Continuing Professional Development scheme. In *Hooberman v.
Salter Rex*[27] a surveyor failed to take proper account of warnings in professional
journals as to the lack of ventilation in flat roofs.[28] Judge Smout Q.C. stated: "I
am satisfied that in the light of knowledge in the construction industry and
amongst surveyors in 1977 it was generally appreciated that flat roofs were
vulnerable, that their construction had to be viewed with caution . . . and that a
competent surveyor should have appreciated at that time that they reflected a
serious potential danger."[29]

For the same reasons, a valuer must not only be familiar with the value of land
throughout the country in a general way, but must inform himself adequately of
market trends and be sensitive to them with particular regard for the locality in
which the land he values lies.[30] Moreover, a surveyor must keep himself reasonably acquainted with the law and changes in the law so far as his skill is affected.
Two cases illustrate this. In *Jenkins v. Betham*[31] the defendant surveyors and
valuers were alleged to have negligently valued ecclesiastical property. Parke B.
left to the jury the question whether the defendants supplied that ordinary degree
of skill and care which could reasonably be expected from country surveyors and
valuers. The jury found they did. The Court of Common Pleas ordered a new
trial. Jervis C.J. stated:

> "the defendants could not be expected to supply minute and accurate knowledge of the
> law; but we think that under the circumstances, they might properly be required to know

---

[23] See *Investors in Industry Commercial Properties v. South Bedfordshire District Council; Ellison & Partners and Hamilton Associates (Third Parties)* [1986] 1 All E.R. 787, *per* Slade L.J. at 808 to 809.
[24] (1972) 225 E.G. 1553.
[25] (1952) 159 E.G. 240. The defendant was nevertheless held negligent in failing to observe the deposit from the roof on the flooring and in failing consequently to warn the plaintiff of the condition of the roof.
[26] *ibid.* at 240.
[27] [1985] 1 E.G.L.R. 144.
[28] *ibid.* at 146.
[29] *ibid.* at 146.
[30] *per* Watkins J. in *Singer & Friedlander Ltd v. John D. Wood & Co.* [1977] 2 E.G.L.R. 84, 85.
[31] (1855) 15 C.B. 167.

the general rules applicable to the valuation of ecclesiastical property, and the broad distinction which exists between the cases of an incoming and outgoing tenant and incoming and outgoing incumbent".[32]

Similarly in *Weedon v. Hindwood Clarke and Esplin*[33] a valuer instructed in 1968 to negotiate with the district valuer the amount of compensation for land compulsorily acquired was held negligent either in not being aware of the change in the basis of valuation of such land brought about by the case of *West Midland Baptist (Trust) Association (Incorporated) v. Birmingham Corporation*[34] or because, being aware of it, he did not apply it as he should have. The Court of Appeal's decision in the *West Midland* case preceded the instructions and the House of Lords decision was pronounced in August 1979 preceding agreement on a figure between the defendant valuer and the district valuer in December 1969. Where, however, a surveyor is asked to advise on a matter of law it is submitted that the required standard of skill and care expected of him should be approached in the same way as by Hallet J. in *Sarginson Bros v. Keith Moulton & Co.*,[35] where he referred to "the steps which a reasonably prudent person would clearly have deemed necessary before that answer could be given with reasonable safety".

9–057   **Extent of duty determined by type of service offered.** As the different types of service offered by surveyors become more defined, so there is a growing body of case law on whether particular steps are or are not required for a particular service. Although the *standard* of care will not vary according to the instructions received, the extent of the surveyor's duty may well do so. This was expressly recognised by the Court of Appeal in *Arab Bank v. John D. Wood Commercial*[36] where a lender had lent £17.1m to a single purpose company to purchase an industrial estate in Darlington. It had received a valuation of £22m from one valuer (JDW) and had asked a second valuer (WGS) not to carry out its own valuation but only to review that of JDW. Having done so, WGS initially advised that a figure of £19m. was appropriate and then revised the figure to £20.6m. The judge found that WGS were not obliged to conduct a full investigation and appraisal of the property as they would have had to do if instructed to carry out a free-standing open market valuation. The Court of Appeal approved a passage in the judge's judgment[37] in which he indicated that the consequence of the limited nature of WGS's instructions was that they would benefit from a greater margin of error than would have been appropriate to JDW.

Similarly, commenting on mortgage inspections and valuations, Lord Griffiths in *Smith v. Bush*[38] said:

"It is only defects which are observable by a careful visual examination that have to be taken into account and I cannot see that it places any unreasonable burden on the valuer to require him to accept responsibility for the fairly elementary degree of skill and care involved in observing, following-up and reporting on such defects. Surely it is work at the lower end of the surveyor's field of professional expertise."

---

[32] *ibid.* at 393.
[33] (1974) 234 E.G. 121.
[34] [1968] 2 Q.B. 188, CA; [1970] A.C. 874, HL.
[35] (1942) 73 Ll.L.Rep. 104.
[36] [2000] Lloyd's L.Rep. P.N. 173.
[37] *ibid.* at 180 *per* Mance L.J.
[38] [1990] 1 A.C. 831, 858.

Lord Templeman, in the same case[39] also commented on the standard of expertise required for such work: "The valuer is and, in my opinion, must be a professional person, typically a chartered surveyor in general practice, who, by training and experience and exercising reasonable skill and care, will recognise defects and be able to assess value." In *Whalley v. Roberts & Roberts*,[40] Auld J. stated:

> "The defendants were not instructed to undertake a structural survey or a survey of the detail called for in the standard form of the Royal Institution of Chartered Surveyors House Buyers' Report and Valuation inspection. They were instructed to inspect and to provide a mortgage valuation report. It is common ground that this involved them in making a brief and reasonably careful visual inspection to enable them, in the terms of the bank report form, to provide a valuation and general guide as to the condition of the property. I am satisfied on the evidence before me that this would not normally involve the use of a spirit-level unless the lack of level in the property became evident on a visual inspection so as to call for further inspection."

In *Roberts v. J. Hampson & Co.*[41] Ian Kennedy J. described a building society valuation as follows:

> "It is a valuation and not a survey, but any valuation is necessarily governed by condition. The inspection is, of necessity, a limited one. Both the expert surveyors . . . agreed that with a house of this size they would allow about half an hour for their inspection on site. That time does not admit of moving furniture, or of lifting carpets, expecially where they are nailed down."

The Court of Appeal in *Sutcliffe v. Sayer*[42] considered a valuation prepared by an estate agent, and Butler-Sloss L.J. commented: "I do not consider that there is any duty upon a valuer to warn a purchaser as to the difficulty of resale . . . I can find no breach of the general duty of care to take proper steps to do the best that he can as a valuer and not as a qualified surveyor."[43]

(iii) *Not every error is negligence*

The standard of reasonable care and skill allows for a margin of differing opinion and even a degree of error. As Buxton L.J. stated: "It has frequently been observed that the process of valuation does not admit of precise conclusions, and thus that the conclusions of competent and careful valuers may differ, perhaps by a substantial margin, without one of them being negligent . . . ."[44] It is not enough to prove that the surveyor gave the wrong advice or that where there is room for two views he took the wrong view.[45] In *Luxmoore-May v. Messenger May Baverstock*[46] Slade L.J. considered that problem in the context of the standard of care owed by a firm of provincial fine art auctioneers and valuers:

9–058

---

[39] *ibid.* at 850.
[40] [1990] 1 E.G.L.R. 164, 168.
[41] [1990] 1 W.L.R. 94, 101.
[42] [1987] 1 E.G.L.R. 155.
[43] *ibid.* at 156. Contrast this case with the Scottish decision *of Martin v. Bell-Ingram*, 1986 S.L.T. 575 (Second Division) where, on appeal, it was held (at 583) that a surveyor carrying out a mortgage valuation for a building society owes a duty to the mortgagor not only to identify those defects which affect the value of the property but also those which materially would affect the decision whether or not to purchase.
[44] In *Merivale Moore v. Strutt & Parker* [2000] P.N.L.R. 498 at 515.
[45] *per* Judge Carter Q.C., in *Hill v. Debenham, Tewson and Chinnocks* (1958) 171 E.G. 835, 835.
[46] [1990] 1 W.L.R. 1009.

"The valuation of pictures of which the artist is unknown, pre-eminently involves an exercise of opinion and judgment, most particularly in deciding whether an attribution to any particular artist should be made. Since it is not an exact science, the judgment in the very nature of things may be fallible, and may turn out to be wrong. Accordingly, provided that the valuer has done his job honestly and with due diligence, I think that the court should be cautious before convicting him of professional negligence merely because he has failed to be the first to spot a 'sleeper' or the potentiality of a 'sleeper': see and compare the observations of Lord Wilberforce in relation to barristers in *Saif Ali v. Sydney Mitchell & Co.* [1980] A.C. 198, 214F–245G."[47]

The point was also well made by Judge Everett Q.C. in *Leigh v. Unsworth*[48] in which it was claimed that the surveyor was negligent in failing to observe signs of serious settlement in carrying out a structural survey:

"The carrying out of a survey and the reporting to a client involves observation, deduction and the exercise of professional skill and judgment. The mere fact that one professional man might suffer from an excessive caution does not mean that another man, exercising his judgment to the best of his skill and ability and taking perhaps a somewhat more optimistic view, is guilty of a departure from the appropriate standard of professional care and skill."[49]

The same point was made by Watkins J. in *Singer & Friedlander Ltd v. John D. Wood & Co.*[50] in respect of a valuation:

"The valuation of land by trained, competent and careful professional men is a task which rarely, if ever, admits of precise conclusion. Often beyond certain well-founded facts so many imponderables confront the valuer that he is obliged to proceed on the basis of assumptions. Therefore, he cannot be faulted for achieving a result which does not admit of some degree of error. Thus two able and experienced men, each confronted with the same task might come to different conclusions without any one being justified in saying that either of them lacked competence and reasonable care, still less integrity in doing his work."[51]

In *Craneheath Securities v. York Montague Ltd*[52] the Court of Appeal rejected the plaintiff's argument that if a sufficient number of errors in the defendants' valuation could be identified, the court should infer without direct evidence that the valuation figure itself was negligently wrong. Balcombe L.J. said:

"I reject [counsel's] submission, that if we were satisfied that there were a sufficient number of errors in the way [the valuer] has carried out his valuation we should in the circumstances of this case infer that his final result was wrong. Valuation is not a

---

[47] *ibid.* at 1020. See chap. 11, para.11–006, for a discussion of the duty of care owed by barristers.
[48] (1972) 230 E.G. 501.
[49] *ibid.* at 649.
[50] [1977] 2 E.G.L.R. 84.
[51] *ibid.* at 86. See also to the same *effect Craneheath Securities Ltd v. York Montague Ltd* [1994] 1 E.G.L.R. 159, Jacob J.; [1996] 1 E.G.L.R. 130, CA; *Allied Trust Bank Ltd v. Edward Symmons & Partners* [1994] 1 E.G.L.R. 165; *Axa Equity & Law Home Loans Ltd v. Goldsack Freeman* [1994] 1 E.G.L.R. 175; *Mortgage Express Ltd v. Dunsmore, Reid and Smith* [1996] G.W.D. 10–590 (the lenders sued in two actions heard together in respect of valuations of two properties, succeeding in one case, but failing to prove that the other valuation was outside an acceptable degree of variation and had been negligently carried out).
[52] [1996] 1 E.G.L.R. 130.

science, it is an art, and the instinctive 'feel' for the market of an experienced valuer is not something which can be ignored."[53]

In *Matto v. Rodney Broom Associates*[54] the Court of Appeal commented that:

"if a surveyor fails to appreciate the extent of past damage, or to carry out the investigations which proper care and skill required, he will, in the absence of very special circumstances, commit no breach of duty in giving advice which is right and consistent with his having exercised proper care and skill. A professional man is entitled to be lucky".[55]

(iv) *The relevance of "the bracket"*

Because competent valuers may legitimately differ from each other in providing   **9–059** competent valuations, a question which commonly arises is whether a valuer may be liable if he carelessly makes a material error in coming to his valuation but nonetheless produces a final figure which can be justified by a competent assessment. Thus it may be possible to show that a valuer failed to take account of a specific characteristic of the property which every competent valuer should have taken into account and that, had the characteristic been considered, the valuer's own final figure would have been altered although other valuers could nevertheless have justifiably arrived at the original figure. It is suggested that the answer to this question depends upon the nature of the instructions which the valuer has received. If his only material obligation is to produce a competent final valuation figure then it does not matter how he arrives at it. If, however, the valuer's obligations extend beyond the production of a final figure, the answer may be different. This analysis is supported by a dictum of Mance L.J. in *Arab Bank v. John D. Wood*[56] in which he referred to the Privy Council decision in *Lion Nathan Ltd v. C-C Bottlers Ltd*,[57] a case concerning the measure of damages in respect of a profit forecast which sellers of shares warranted to have been calculated on a proper basis and Lord Hoffman gave an example which suggested that a small but discrete error in double-counting might lead through directly to an award of damages:

"Where, as in the present case, criticism is addressed to factors such as rental value and yield which bear proportionately on the ultimately assigned value, the issues of the permissible range and of negligence are on any view inseparably linked. The value

---

[53] *ibid.* at 132. See also *Hardy v. Wamsley-Lewis* (1967) 203 E.G. 1039, where the defendant surveyed a house and overlooked a piece of skirting with waviness characteristic of dry rot. Paull J. stated at 1041 that if the matter had remained there and there had been nothing else at all, he would have required argument as to whether one failure actually constituted negligence on the part of a professional man; *Lawrence v. Hampton & Sons* (1964) 190 E.G. 107, *per* Mocatta J. at 111: "I have not overlooked [counsel's] argument that a competent surveyor may, without negligence, fail to notice a crack in a building"; *Fryer & another v. Bunney & another* [1982] 2 E.G.L.R. 130, *per* Judge Newey Q.C. at 134: "The mere fact that a surveyor misses something in the course of a survey does not necessarily make him negligent."
[54] [1994] 2 E.G.L.R. 163 at 168.
[55] In *Routestone Ltd v. Minories Finance Ltd* [1997] 1 E.G.L.R. 123, Jacob J. held that the fact that another estate agent would have marketed a property subject to a power of sale differently did not indicate negligence on the part of the defendant agents.
[56] [2000] P.N.L.R. 173 at 181.
[57] [1996] 1 W.L.R. 1438.

estimated results from the estimated rental values and yields. Where there is some discrete error, like that postulated in *Lion Nathan*, it may be appropriate to examine more closely the nature of the valuer's engagement. Is it simply to produce and end result and to do so within the range of 'reasonable foreseeable deviation'? Or may be to exercise reasonable skill and care in the circumstances (including whatever instructiosn may have been given) both in forming and in expressing an opinion on value? In the *SAAMCO* case, when it was before this court under the name of *Banque Bruxelles Lambert SA v. Eagle Star Insurance Co. Ltd* [1995] Q.B. 375, the judgment given by Sir Thomas Bingham M.R. (as he then was) at pages 403H–404G lends some support to the latter analysis. On that basis, if as a result of clearly identifiable negligence, a valuer arrives at a figure lower than he would otherwise have put forward, the line of reasoning indicated in *Lion Nathan* might still be applicable, although the end figure could not itself be said to fall outside the margin of legitimate valuation by valuers generally."

9-060   As is apparent from the above dictum, the English courts have ordinarily held that it is a necessary condition for liability, at least in the case of errors in the assessment of rentals or yields, that the final result should be outside "the bracket". This first became apparent from the decision of Watkins J. in *Singer & Friedlander Ltd v. John D. Wood & Co.*[58] where he stated:

"Pinpoint accuracy in the result is not, therefore, to be expected by he who requests the valuation. There is, as I have said, a permissible margin of error, the 'bracket' as I have called it. What can properly be expected from a competent valuer using reasonable care and skill is that his valuation falls within this bracket."

In *Craneheath Securities v. York Montague*,[59] the Court of Appeal dismissed an appeal where the claimant sought to infer a negligent final valuation figure from a number of alleged discrete errors. It was made clear that it was a necessary precondition to liability that it could be shown that the final valuation figure was wrong. The matter was considered by Buxton L.J. in *Merivale Moore v. Strutt & Parker*[60] where he stated that it was a necessary condition for liability that a valuation should fall outside the permissible bracket. He adopted as helpful an observation of Judge Langan Q.C. in *Legal & General Mortgage Services v. HPC Professional Services*[61] that once it is shown that the valuation falls outside the bracket:

"the plaintiff will by that stage have discharged an evidential burden. It will be for the defendant to show that, notwithstanding that the valuation is outside the range within which careful and competent valuers may reasonably differ, he nonetheless exercised the degree of care and skill which was appropriate in the circumstances".

He went on to make the points (a) that if a valuer did adopt an unprofessional practice or approach, then that might be taken into account in considering whether his valuation contained an unacceptable degree of error; and (b) that

---

[58] [1977] 2 E.G.L.R. 84 at 86.
[59] [2001] Lloyd's L.Rep. P.N. 348 *per* Balcombe L.J. at 350.
[60] [2000] P.N.L.R. 498 at 515 to 517.
[61] [1997] P.N.L.R. 567 at 574F.

where a valuation was shown to be outside the acceptable limit, that might be a strong indication that negligence had, in fact, occurred.

The extent of the bracket. The margin of error approach is not a principle of 9–061 law. It is an evidential approach to assist in the resolution of questions of primary liability. By itself, evidence as to the conclusion reached by a valuer does not prove that the valuer failed to exercise reasonable care and skill in coming to that conclusion, unless the doctrine of *res ipsa loquitur* applies. The duty on the valuer is to exercise reasonable skill and care. If the valuer did so then the fact that the result of the exercise of reasonable skill and care fell outside the "bracket" may be rebuttable evidence of negligence but does not of itself determine the issue of primary liability. Many properties do not have a single "true" value, and whilst the margin of error approach may be a convenient shorthand in many cases, it should not be applied without adequate consideration of the basic principles of negligence liability.The extent of permissible error will be determined by the judge having regard to the evidence. Plainly it will be much easier to value a property if it has itself been recently sold in the open market or if a number of closely comparable properties have recently been sold than will be the case if the property is unique or has very unusual characteristics. In *Merivale Moore v. Strutt & Parker*,[62] Buxton L.J. stated:

> "the 'bracket' is not be determined in a mechanistic way, divorced from the facts of the instance case. We were shown a list of figures giving either the bracket determined, or the percentage divergence from the true figure found nonetheless not to have been negligent, in a series of recent cases. I did not find that of assistance, save as a graphic reminder that it is not enough simply to shown that the valuation was different from the true value".

As a matter of practice, "the bracket" has usually been determined to lie in the range 10 to 20 per cent either side of a mean figure.[63] Judges have sometimes commented that expert evidence has suggested a closer correlation between competent valuations than they would suppose. In *Beaumont v. Humberts*,[64] a

---

[62] [2000] P.N.L.R. 499 at 517.
[63] According to expert evidence in *Singer & Friedlander v. John D. Wood* [1977] 2 E.G.L.R. 84, the permissible margin was 10% either side of "the right figure" but in exceptional circumstances it could be extended to about 15% either way. In *Private Bank & Trust Co. Ltd v. S. (U.K.) Ltd* [1993] 1 E.G.L.R. 144 the court concluded that on the evidence the defendant's valuations lay within a permissible margin of error of 15% either side of his valuation bracket. In *Banque Bruxelles Lambert SA v. Lewis & Tucker Ltd and others* [1994] 2 E.G.L.R. 108, the evidence before Phillips J. was that when valuations are based on comparables, one competent valuation may differ from another by as much as 20%. See at 118C. In *B.N.P. Mortgages Ltd v. Barton Cook & Sams* [1996] 1 E.G.L.R. 239, the evidence proved an acceptable range for the property in question to be 15%. In *Assured Advances Ltd v. Ashbee & Co.* [1994] E.G.C.S. 169, the valuers were approached by brokers and not the lender, and asked for a "quick £50 valuation". The court considered the proper approach was "to find a central accurate valuation and to establish a percentage above and below it which was the non-negligent zone. Anything outside that zone would be prima facie a negligent valuation". There was however no adequate evidence of the proper valuation, so the action failed. In *Arab Bank v. John D. Wood Commercial* [2000] Lloyd's L.Rep. P.N. 173 at 195, Mance L.J. plainly considered that a "bracket" of 20% above a correct figure was at the outer limits of a permissible range even for a "franking valuation"—see further para. 9–057 above.
[64] [1990] 2 E.G.L.R. 166. See para. 9–050 above.

case involving an alleged negligent valuation for reinstatement purposes, Staughton L.J. commented when dealing with the issue of breach of duty: "It is accepted that a surveyor or valuer may be wrong by a margin of 10 per cent either way without being negligent. (That in itself seems, in my uninstructed opinion, a high standard to impose; but it is, as I have said, accepted.)"[65] Similarly, in *Nykredit Mortgage Bank plc v. Edward Erdman Group Ltd*[66] the same Lord Justice commented:

> "There was evidence, which the judge accepted, that careful and skilled valuers did not inevitably arrive at precisely the same answer. If a given figure is taken as the true value, the range within which a valuer could arrive at some different amount without negligence was plus or minus 15 per cent. In the light of the sensitivity of the calculation I do not find that at all surprising."

If the property being valued is unique or unusual, then the use of a bracket may become inappropriate. Jacob J. commented in *Craneheath Securities Ltd v. York Montague Ltd*[67]:

> "The margin of error approach may well make sense when the property being valued has a number of good comparables (*e.g.* houses on an estate, forestry or farmland). Then one can in effect take an 'average' as the 'right' figure and look at the deviation from it ... But, as I say, the approach depends on evidence. I had no evidence before me which would begin to support a permissible 'margin of error' for a property such as Kingsdown."

It will, nevertheless be open to a judge to find that a valuation fell outside the permissible bracket even without express expert evidence as to the extent of the bracket in a particular case.[68]

(v) *Onus of proof*

9–062 The onus of proof rests "fairly and squarely" upon the plaintiff in an action for professional negligence against a surveyor.[69] It is not enough to prove that he was wrong. Negligence must be distinctly proved.[70] It may even be difficult to prove he was wrong by showing that the defendant's valuation was significantly higher

---

[65] *ibid.* at 169. See *McIntyre v. Herring Son & Daw* [1988] 1 E.G.L.R. 231, where Mr E.A. Machin Q.C., sitting as a deputy High Court judge, accepted at 233 that: "The widths of such brackets reflected only the evidence in that particular case and that there is no proposition of law that in valuation cases a valuer is not negligent if his valuation falls within such a bracket. The permissible width of the bracket must be a matter to be decided upon the evidence of any particular case." In *Mount Banking Corporation Ltd v. Brian Cooper & Co.* [1992] 2 E.G.L.R. 142, 144 dicta to the same effect appear. The deputy judge at 145K considered the proper approach to be: "assess here whether [the valuer's] approach was proper and what a competent approach could properly have resulted in. If [the valuer's] end result was within a modest margin of that figure, then he is not to be adjudged negligent".

[66] [1996] 1 E.G.L.R. 119 at 120. The defendants carried out a residual land valuation, acknowledged to be sensitive to the variables used in its calculation. The method was not criticised, but certain of the variables were.

[67] [1994] 1 E.G.L.R. 159 at 162. His decision was upheld on appeal: [2001] Lloyd's L.Rep. P.N. 348.

[68] See *per* Buxton L.J. in *Merivale Moore v. Strutt & Parker* [2000] P.N.L.R. 498 at 517.

[69] *Hill v. Debenham, Tewson and Chinnocks* (1958) 171 E.G. 835, 835

[70] See *Singer & Friedlander Ltd v. John D. Wood & Co.* [1977] 2 E.G.L.R. 84, 93.

or lower than another surveyor's valuation[71] or the price actually achieved[72] or that his estimate of individual items making up the calculation was on the high side.[73] It must be shown that his valuation and calculations were such that they could not have been arrived at by the exercise of reasonable care and skill.[74] Although it is sometimes stated that the onus of proof in a professional negligence action is a heavy one,[75] the standard is no more than that applicable to civil actions generally, namely proof on a balance of probabilities.[76]

(e) *Limitation of liability*

Surveyors reports and valuations may seek to limit liability in two ways—either by way of general limitations on the extent of liability owed to particular persons or groups or by clauses seeking to set out and limit the scope of particular services. The latter type of clause is discussed below.[77]   **9–063**

After *Yianni v. Edwin Evans and Sons*[78] it became common to find terms seeking to limit a surveyor's liability generally and, in particular, when a report was sought through a building society upon an application for a mortgage advance. The decision of the House of Lords in *Smith v. Eric S. Bush*[79] to the effect that such terms will be regarded as unreasonable within the meaning of the Unfair Contract Terms Act 1977 has neutered the practical effect of such clauses, at least so far as modestly priced domestic properties are concerned. The Courts have, however, upheld such clauses in the case of expensive or unusual properties and are generally willing to uphold appropriate clauses in a commercial context, as is shown by the decision in *Omega Trust Co. v. Wright Son & Pepper.*[80]

Residential property. *Stevenson v. Nationwide Building Society*[81] was the first reported English case illustrating the effect of disclaimer clauses contained in a mortgage application form in respect of a valuation carried out upon the society's   **9–064**

---

[71] *per* Geoffrey Lane L.J. in *Campbell v. Edwards* [1976] 1 W.L.R. 403, 408: "There is nothing to suggest that the valuer here did not take into consideration all the matters which he should have taken into consideration; and where the only basis of criticism is that another valuer has subsequently produced a valuation a third of the original one it does not afford, in my view, any ground for saying that Chesterton's valuation must have been or may have been wrong".

[72] Note Gibson J. in *Corisand Investments Ltd v. Druce & Co.* [1978] 2 E.G.L.R. 86 considered on the facts of that case that "the usefulness of comparing the valuation figure with the eventually realised sale price for the purpose of critical consideration of those valuation figures, is either non existent or extremely limited."

[73] See *Shacklock v. Chas. Osenton, Lockwood & Co.* (1964) 192 E.G. 819. The plaintiff sought to show that defendant valuer was negligent, particularly his approach of estimating a maximum figure and making deductions for various items. *Per* Mocatta J. at 821: "I do not think that [the defendant's] valuation can be faulted legally so as to show that he was professionally negligent . . . merely by going through these items and criticising them meticulously and suggesting that they are on the high side."

[74] The paragraph to this point in the fourth edition was stated to accurately state the law by Stuart-Smith L.J., with whom Mummery L.J. agreed in *Watts v. Savills*, CA June 16, 1998, para. 38.

[75] *MacKenzie v. Hall & Co.* (1951) 157 E.G. 492.

[76] This paragraph in the third edition (1992) was cited with approval *in Macey v. Debenham, Tewson & Chinnocks* [1993] 1 E.G.L.R. 149, 151M, and cited by the court in *Muldoon v. Mays of Lilliput Ltd* [1993] 1 E.G.L.R. 43, 45M.

[77] See para. 9–073, below.

[78] [1982] Q.B. 438. See para. 9–041, above.

[79] [1990] 1 A.C. 831.

[80] [1997] P.N.L.R. 425—see further para. 9–071, below.

[81] [1984] 2 E.G.L.R. 165.

instructions but intended to be shown to the mortgage advance applicant. The claimant, who was an estate agent, sought an advance of £42,750 from the defendant building society. The defendant instructed a valuer employed by it to report upon the property. A copy of his report was provided to the claimant. The claimant was granted the requested advance and purchased the property. A month later part of the floor collapsed. The property had a number of structural defects which the valuer had not observed. The judge[82] held that the valuer had failed to exercise reasonable care and skill and that the society would have been vicariously liable for the valuer if liable. Nevertheless in view of two clauses contained in the mortgage application form completed by the plaintiff, the claim failed. The first of these clauses stated that the inspection carried out by the society's valuer was not a structural survey and there might be defects which such a survey would reveal. The second clause contained the words that the report "was intended solely for the consideration of the society in determining what advance (if any) may be made on the security". The judge considered these words significant as indicating the limited purpose of the report. This was also made clear by the first clause. Nevertheless if those words had stood alone he would not have absolved the defendant from liability given the unusual nature of the building which demanded a careful inspection of its underside. The remaining words of the clause, however, were crucial: "no responsibility is implied or accepted by the society or its valuer for either the value or condition of the property by reason of such inspection and report". The judge stated that the words were unambiguous and free from doubt and it was accepted that, subject to the Unfair Contract Terms Act 1977, they constituted a valid disclaimer. It was further accepted as between the parties that the disclaimer was not a contract term but was rather a "notice (not being a notice having contractual effect)".[83] The relevant question was whether the notice satisfied the criterion of reasonableness under the Act, being that "it should be fair and reasonable to allow reliance on it, having regard to all the circumstances obtaining when the liability arose or (but for the notice) would have arisen".[84] The judge, having noted that the onus of showing that the disclaimer is fair and reasonable was on the defendants and that the test was subjective, considered section 11(5) of the Act:

> "When I bear in mind that the person affected by the disclaimer is someone well familiar with such disclaimers and with the possibility of obtaining a survey, and also familiar with the difference between a building society valuation and a survey and their different costs, it seems to me perfectly reasonable to allow the building society, in effect, to say to him that if he chooses the cheaper alternative he must accept that the society will not be responsible for the content to him."[85]

It is submitted that there were two crucial facts that distinguished this case. First, the claimant was an estate agent, a professional working in the precise area where his complaint lay. Secondly, the property was not a modest house at the lower end of the market. The claimant was buying a relatively expensive property, comprising two shops, a maisonette and a flat. There was to some extent an element of commercial dealing about the transaction. This case was cited to the House of

---

[82] Mr J. Wilmers Q.C. sitting as a deputy High Court judge.
[83] Unfair Contract Terms Act 1977, s.11(3).
[84] *ibid.*
[85] [1984] 2 E.G.L.R. 165, 170.

Lords in *Smith v. Bush*[86] but not referred to in any of the speeches. On its own facts *Stevenson v. Nationwide Building Society* can stand with *Smith v. Bush*, particularly given the decision of the Court of Appeal in *McCullagh v. Lane Fox & Partners.*[87]

The House of Lords considered in *Smith v. Bush*[88] the application of the Unfair **9–065** Contract Terms Act 1977 to mortgage valuations.[89] Their Lordships concluded that the Unfair Contract Terms Act 1977 applied to clauses or notices that sought to exclude a duty, as well as to clauses or notices that sought to exclude liability. Counsel for the valuers sought to argue that it was fair and reasonable for a valuer to rely on an exclusion clause. Lord Templeman summarised the argument as follows[90]:

> "(a) the exclusion clause is clear and understandable and reiterated and is forcefully drawn to the attention of the purchaser;
>
> (b) the purchaser's solicitors should reinforce the warning and urge the purchaser to appreciate that he cannot rely on a mortgage valuation and should obtain and pay for his own survey;
>
> (c) if valuers cannot disclaim liability they will be faced by more claims from purchasers some of which will be unmeritorious but difficult and expensive to resist;
>
> (d) a valuer will become more cautious, take more time and produce more gloomy reports[91] which will make house transactions more difficult;
>
> (e) if a duty of care cannot be disclaimed the cost of negligence insurance for valuers and therefore the cost of valuation fees to the public will be increased."

It was also argued that there was no contract between a valuer and a purchaser, that so far as the purchaser was concerned, the valuation was gratuitous,[92] and the valuer should not be forced to accept a liability he was unwilling to under-take.

None of these arguments were accepted by the House of Lords. Lord Temple- **9–066** man stated[93]:

> "All these submissions are inconsistent with the ambit and thrust of the Act of 1977. The valuer is a professional man who offers his services for reward. He is paid for those services. The valuer knows that 90 per cent of purchasers in fact rely on a mortgage valuation and do not commission their own survey. There is great pressure on a purchaser to rely on the mortgage valuation. Many purchasers cannot afford a second valuation. If a purchaser obtains a second valuation the sale may go off and then both

---

[86] [1990] 1 A.C. 831.
[87] [1996] 1 E.G.L.R. 35. For the facts and discussion see para. 9–013 above.
[88] [1990] 1 A.C. 831.
[89] For the facts of this case see para. 9–046, above.
[90] *ibid.* at 851.
[91] This may allude to an area of tension within the practice of many surveyors carrying out surveys and valuations of domestic property. Referrals from estate agents who have no such professional capability can be important to a practice. If a surveyor, through fear of litigation produces (non-negligent) reports that err on the side of gloom, a prospective sale may be lost, with it the estate agent's commission, and as a consequence a source of work for the surveyor may disappear.
[92] Although the purchaser had of course paid for the valuation, through the building society or local authority.
[93] [1990] 1 A.C. 831, at 852.

valuation fees will be wasted. Moreover, he knows that mortgagees, such as building societies and the council . . . are trustworthy and that they appoint careful and competent valuers and he trusts the professional man so appointed. Finally the valuer knows full well that failure on his part to exercise reasonable skill and care may be disastrous to the purchaser."

Lord Griffiths agreed that it would not be fair and reasonable for the surveyor to be permitted to exclude liability in the circumstances of the case.[94] He commented that it was impossible to draw up a complete list of the factors to be taken into account when a court has to decide whether an exclusion clause is fair and reasonable.[95] Lord Griffiths considered that the following matters should, in his view, always be considered:

(a) Were the parties of equal bargaining power?[96]

(b) Would it have been reasonably practicable to obtain the advice from an alternative source, taking into account considerations such as cost and time?[97]

(c) How difficult is the task being undertaken for which liability is being excluded?[98]

(d) What are the practical consequences of the decision on the question of reasonableness?[99]

(e) And, in the particular circumstances of the case, the question who employed the surveyor and paid his fees was material.[1]

9–067   It is important to emphasise that both *Smith v. Bush* and *Harris v. Wyre Forest District Council* dealt with domestic property purchases at the least expensive end of the market.[2] The decision of the Court of Appeal to permit the defendants to rely upon their exclusion clause in *McCullagh v. Lane Fox & Partners*[3] where the property was worth £800,000, illustrates the point made by the House of Lords.

---

[94] *ibid.* at 859.

[95] *ibid.* at 858.

[96] Lord Griffiths contrasted the case with the position resulting from a one-off retainer between parties of equal bargaining power.

[97] Lord Griffiths noted the financial pressure many first-time buyers are under, and the strain that making them buy the same advice twice would cause.

[98] Lord Griffiths applied this to the sums of money potentially at stake and the ability of the parties to bear the loss involved, which in turn raised the question of insurance. He noted that all surveyors are obliged to carry indemnity insurance, and that had to be compared to the financial catastrophe for the purchaser.

[99] Lord Griffiths applied this to the sums of money potentially at stake and the ability of the parties to bear the loss involved, which in turn raised the question of insurance. He noted that all surveyors are obliged to carry indemnity insurance, and that had to be compared to the financial catastrophe for the purchaser.

[1] Lord Griffiths noted, at 859, that it had not been argued that had the purchaser employed and paid the surveyor directly, it would still have been reasonable for the surveyor to exclude his liability. He considered "the present situation is not far removed from that of a direct contract between the surveyor and the purchaser".

[2] See the comments by Lord Templeman at 854, Lord Griffiths at 859, and Lord Jauncey at 874. See further para. 9–049 above.

[3] [1996] 1 E.G.L.R. 35. For the facts and discussion see paras 9–013 and 9–028, above.

Beaton v. Nationwide Building Society[4] was another case involving the valua- **9–068**
tion of a modest property. A disclaimer notice within the meaning of section
11(3) of the 1977 Act was set out on the mortgage application form, the offer of
advance and the copy of the valuation report provided to the claimants. The
notices that the plaintiffs accepted they had read included:

> "No responsibility is implied or accepted by the Society or its valuer for either the value
> or condition of the property by reason of the inspection and report. The Society does not
> undertake to give advice as to the value or condition of the property and accepts no
> liability for any such advice that may be given. The inspection carried out by the
> Society's valuer was not a structural survey and there may be defects which such a
> survey would reveal."

It was submitted that there were two specific matters which made it fair and
reasonable for the defendant to rely upon the disclaimers. First, the plaintiffs
were advised by their own solicitors to have a structural survey carried out and
made a positive decision not to have such a survey. The judge[5] noted that the
statistics showed that only 10 to 15 per cent of all purchasers of modest dwelling
houses trouble to obtain their own valuation and survey. The conduct of the
plaintiffs in not having a structural survey was thus to be anticipated. Further, the
report of the surveyor went much further than simply approving the application
for a mortgage at a stated valuation. The terms of the report stressed that certain
matters should be brought to the attention of the applicants, some of those
matters adversely affected the property and required remedial work, others,
including the critical question of structural movement, were positively reassuring. The judge held that the very terms of the report made it unfair and
unreasonable to permit the defendant to rely on disclaimers on this ground. The
second ground relied on by the defendant was that the plaintiff had been told by
the estate agent that the property had been partially underpinned. The judge
considered that if he had concluded as a fact that the agent had made it plain to
the plaintiff that there was cause for anxiety about the underpinning work, there
would be force in the defendant's submission, but he did not so find. The judge
therefore concluded that it would not be fair and reasonable to allow the
defendant to rely on the disclaimers.

In *Davies v. Idris Parry*[6] the valuer sought to rely upon a blanket exclusion of **9–069**
all liability for negligence in respect of a mortgage inspection and valuation. The
surveyor was unable to escape liability for his negligence in failing to draw
attention to major defects in the foundations of the property, defects that should
have been reasonably apparent during his visual inspection. The property was at
the lower end of the housing market and the surveyor knew that the plaintiff was
likely to rely upon the valuation. McNeill J. held that such an exclusion notice
was unreasonable.[7]

---

[4] [1991] 2 E.G.L.R. 145.
[5] Mr Neil Butterfield Q.C. (as he then was) sitting as a deputy High Court judge.
[6] [1988] 1 E.G.L.R. 147.
[7] See also *Henley v. Cloke & Sons* [1991] 2 E.G.L.R. 141, Judge Thayne-Forbes Q.C.: "The property
is a detached house with four bedrooms, which had been built in the 1930s . . . It is, and was then,
an attractive house, with central heating, garaging for two cars and a decent sized garden. It is situated
in a pleasant residential area of Maidstone. It was being offered for sale at a price of £78,000." This
was in 1984. However, after considering *Smith v. Bush*, counsel for the valuers (who prepared a
mortgage inspection and valuation), did not attempt to rely upon the disclaimers, or to argue that the
same were reasonable within the meaning of the 1977 Act.

9–070   The burden of proof is on the defendant to establish that in all the circumstances it is fair and reasonable that he should be allowed to rely upon his disclaimer of liability,[8] and the surveyor or lender will have to prove that any notices relied upon were brought to the attention of the plaintiff in time.[9]

9–071   **Commercial property.** In *Omega Trust Co. Ltd v. Wright Son & Pepper*[10] the defendant valuer provided a borrower with valuations of three commercial retail properties in central London. The valuation contained a disclaimer:

> "This report shall be for private and confidential use of the clients for whom the report is undertaken and should not be reproduced in whole or in part or relied upon by third parties for any use whatsoever without the express written authority of [the surveyors]."

The borrower applied to Omega for a loan of £350,000, and the valuer retyped a copy of its valuation to Omega. Unknown to the valuer, Omega could not lend all that the borrower had requested, and so applied to its associate company, Banque Finindus, for £200,000 of the total and supported this request with a copy of the valuation addressed to Omega. After completion of the loan the borrower went into liquidation and the properties proved worthless. The valuers applied under RSC Order 14A for a ruling as to whether they owed a duty of care to Banque Finindus. The Court of Appeal held that as Banque Finindus was a separate legal entity of which the valuers were ignorant, that bank could not be regarded as a "client" within the meaning of the disclaimer. The only client was Omega. The Court of Appeal considered that the disclaimer satisfied the requirement of reasonableness under the Unfair Contract Terms Act 1977, relying on the commercial setting of the transaction, rather than the domestic situation in *Smith v. Bush*. Henry L.J. said[11]:

> "The point that Lord Griffiths was making was that in a transaction involving a lot of money in a commercial context, both parties are well able to look after themselves, and it is not necessary to have any statutory protection for them. It is this point which, in my judgment, distinguishes this commercial case from those purchases of domestic houses with which other cases have dealt."

The Court of Appeal discussed the matters that would need to be considered: that the burden of proof to sustain the exemption clause was on the valuer, that the parties were of equal bargaining power, that it was reasonably practical for Banque Finindus to have obtained its own valuation from the valuer and within a reasonable timescale. Henry L.J. concluded[12]:

---

[8] s.11(3) of the 1977 Act, and see *Smith v. Bush, per* Lord Griffiths at 858.
[9] See *Goodall v. Simpson* (1991) Outer House Cases, March 6, 1991, Court of Session (unreported), and *Martin v. Bell-Ingram*, 1986 S.L.T. 575 where it was held that the surveyors could not rely upon a disclaimer of liability, as no disclaimer had been communicated to the prospective purchasers when the surveyors had communicated the terms of their report to the building society by telephone, and the same had been transmit onwards to the prospective purchasers or their solicitors. The terms of the disclaimer were not communicated to the prospective purchasers until after they had concluded their bargain to purchase the property.
[10] [1997] P.N.L.R. 425, CA.
[11] *ibid.* at 429D.
[12] *ibid.* at 430G.

"It seems to me that this professional valuer, valuing expensive properties in a commercial context, was entitled to know who his client was and to whom his duty was owed. He was entitled, it seems to me, to refuse to assume liability to any unknown lender, indeed I would go further and say that he is entitled to refuse to assume liability to any known lender to whom he had not agreed. He was entitled to increase the fee (or would have been) as a term of permitting the second lender to rely on the valuation because, as I have said, potentially it can be more expensive to be sued by two lenders rather than one. And if the second lender was not prepared to pay what is asked, it seems to me that the valuer would have been entitled to refuse to assume that liability to the bank, and the 1977 Act would not have required the contract to be rewritten."

Having found a valid and subsisting disclaimer, the Court of Appeal declined to rule on the question of whether a duty of care was owed by the valuers to Banque Finindus. The claim by Banque Finindus against the valuer was accordingly struck out.[13]

Scotland. The application of *Smith v. Bush* to Scotland was restricted prior to **9–072** April 1, 1991. The Unfair Contract Terms Act 1977, as it applied to Scotland, differed from the provisions that applied to England and Wales in that by section 15(1) the provisions in the Act preventing a party relying on an exclusion or restriction of liability clause applied only to contracts,[14] and by section 25(3)(d) any reference to excluding or restricting liability included only notices "having contractual effect". Where, therefore, a notice excluding liability had no contractual effect,[15] and where the same was clear and unambiguous, a court was obliged to give effect to it.[16] Section 68 of the Law Reform (Miscellaneous

---

[13] The extent to which a valuer may rely on a disclaimer in a commercial context was also considered in the Scottish case of *Commercial Financial Services Ltd v. McBeth & Co.* [1988] S.C.L.R. 248.. The valuation report was not addressed to the pursuer lender, but to the borrower, which passed it on to the lender. The report contained the following disclaimer: "In accordance with our standard practice, we must state that this valuation is for the use only of the parties to whom it is addressed and no responsibility is accepted to any third party for the whole or any part of its contents." Lord Mayfield held that the lender's claim in negligence was irrelevant in that the terms of the "clear" disclaimer were such as to negative any claim in negligence. Further, the claim based on breach of contract was also irrelevant in that the document upon which the lenders relied when making the loan and which was claimed to be the contract with the valuers, was clearly addressed to the borrower, and that even if the lender had instructed the valuers to produce a report, the actual report they relied on was that addressed to the borrowers. The action was dismissed.

[14] And not therefore to notices.

[15] As for example, a notice on a mortgage inspection and valuation report, prepared by a surveyor for a mortgagee pursuant to a contract of retainer, and subsequently provided by the mortgagee to the borrower. There is no contract between the surveyor and the borrower. See *Robbie v. Graham & Sibbald* [1989] 2 E.G.L.R. 148.

[16] *Robbie v. Graham & Sibbald* [1989] 2 E.G.L.R. 148, where Lord Weir was unable to apply the reasoning in *Smith v. Bush* [1990] 1 A.C. 831 as the disclaimer in the survey report obtained by a building society, and disclosed to the pursuers, was of no contractual effect. The action was dismissed. Lord Weir commented, at 149: "In reaching this conclusion I recognise that the pursuers may well feel a sense of injustice in that they are unable to take advantage of the Unfair Contract Terms Act 1977 as they would have been able to in England, with the possibility of succeeding in their action against the defenders. I am compelled, however, to apply the statutory law applicable to Scotland although I obtain no satisfaction in doing so in this particular case." Contrast *with Melrose v. Davidson & Robertson*, [1993] S.C. 288 where Lord Morton of Shuna construed an exclusion clause as a term of the contract between the purchasers and the building society, thereby allowing s.16 of the Unfair Contract Terms Act 1977 to exclude the effect of the clause. S.68 of the Law Reform (Miscellaneous Provisions) (Scotland) Act 1990 did not apply to the case. On a reclaiming motion, the First Division of the Inner House declined to interfere with the findings of Lord Morton; *ibid.*, 292.

Provisions) (Scotland) Act 1990, amended Part II of the Unfair Contract Terms Act 1977 to bring non-contractual notices within the statutory restrictions. Scots law was thereby made equivalent to English law after *Smith v. Bush*, as discussed in paragraph 9–065, above. The amendments were not retrospective and will only apply to liability for loss and damage suffered after April 1, 1991 when the section came into force.[17]

9–073   **Clauses defining extent of service performed.** A distinction must be drawn, however, between those clauses that attempt to exclude or restrict liability in negligence to the client and/or third parties, and those clauses which attempt to define more clearly the nature and extent of the service performed. It is usual, for example, even for structural survey reports to include a standard clause to the effect that no responsibility can be accepted in respect of defects in inaccessible or uninspected parts of the property.[18] Unless agreed to before or at the time of the relevant contract, such a clause would not be incorporated as a contractual term.[19] Nevertheless such a clause operates as a warning[20] and may prevent the plaintiff from establishing breach of the duty to exercise reasonable care and skill or reliance on the report in relation to inaccessible or uninspected parts. Much will depend upon the proper construction of the clause. A simple disclaimer of responsibility in relation to uninspected parts will not absolve the surveyor from liability for defects therein if a careful surveyor would have suspected their existence from signs in inspected parts and would have given a warning or advised further investigations.[21] Moreover, a clause seeking to exclude or limit liability, whether amounting to a contractual term or only to a notice not having contractual effect, will be subject to the Unfair Contract Terms Act 1977.[22]

(f) *Mutual valuer*

9–074   Frequently an agreement provides that in the event of a dispute between the parties as to valuation or assessment of rent of a property, they should be bound by the decision of a valuer jointly instructed by them or appointed on their behalf by a mutually selected third person.[23] The appointment must be made in accordance with the terms of the agreement. If it is not, any award will not be

---

[17] See s.68(6) and Law Reform (Miscellaneous Provisions) (Scotland) Act 1990 (Commencement No. 3) Order 1991 (S.I. 1991 No. 330).

[18] It is often a condition of a surveyor's professional indemnity insurance policy that his reports should contain such a clause. The Standard Conditions of Engagement prepared by the RICS for Home Buyers' Survey and Valuation contain such a clause, as do Model Conditions of Engagement for Building Surveys of Residential Property.

[19] See, *e.g. Olley v. Marlborough Court Ltd* [1949] 1 K.B. 532 and *Thornton v. Shoe Lane Parking Ltd* [1971] 2 Q.B. 163.

[20] See para. 9–097, below.

[21] See *Roberts v. J. Hampson & Co.* [1988] 2 E.G.L.R. 181, also at [1990] 1 W.L.R. 94 (abbreviated), discussed at para. 9–084, below.

[22] As discussed above, para. 9–065. For a commentary on the Act see K.M. Stanton, "Disclaiming tort liability: the Unfair Contract Terms Act 1977" (1985) 4 P.N. 132.

[23] For example, the President of RICS. Where a rent review clause provides for such an appointment, the President of RICS owes no duty to the parties to such a clause to refrain from making an appointment where proceedings are contemplated. The President "should not be a pawn in tactical moves between the parties". *See United Co-operatives Ltd v. Sun Alliance & London Assurance Co. Ltd* [1987] 1 E.G.L.R. 126. For a case where the Court of Appeal discussed the formalities of applying to the President of RICS for an appointment, see *Staines Warehousing Co. Ltd v. Montagu Executor & Trustee Co. Ltd* [1987] 2 E.G.L.R. 130.

binding.[24] If the decision is honestly made the parties will be bound thereby even though the valuation or assessment is so high or so low as to be negligent.[25] In the latter events, however, the aggrieved party may pursue a professional negligence action for his loss against the valuer,[26] unless the valuer is entitled to immunity as an arbitrator or possibly a quasi-arbitrator.[27]

2. LIABILITY FOR BREACH OF DUTY

A surveyor's breaches of duty may take one of four forms: **9–075**

(i) breach of a specific contractual duty;

(ii) breach of the implied contractual duty to exercise reasonable skill and care;

(iii) breach of the duty of skill and care owed by the surveyor to his client independently of the contract of engagement;

(iv) breach of the same duty as in (iii) but owed to a third party.

The word "negligence" is frequently used in surveyors' negligence cases as in other contexts to denote a default involving failure to exercise reasonable skill and care irrespective of whether the cause of action is contract or tort, and will be so used below. In a particular case, however, the negligent default will properly be analysed as one or more of the breaches of duty described in (i), (ii), (iii) and (iv). The default constituting the breach of duty in (i) need not necessarily involve negligence, but almost invariably it will and then it may also be characterised as such. Instances of default are categorised below under five heads, as follows:

---

[24] In *Darlington Borough Council v. Waring & Gillow (Holdings) Ltd* [1988] 2 E.G.L.R. 159, the appointment of an independent valuer was held not to have been carried out in accordance with the terms of the lease, the award was therefore not binding and the current rent continued.

[25] *Campbell v. Edwards* [1976] 1 W.L.R. 403, CA. For an extreme example see *Rajdev v. Becketts* [1989] 2 E.G.L.R. 144 where the independent valuer fixed the rent substantially above the proper open market rent. The increased rent had to be paid and the tenant sued his surveyors for failing to apply and operate the rent review provisions. See para. 9–179, below. Where valuers appointed by each party are unable to agree a valuation because of differences as to the proper approach, the court may be prepared to make declarations as to the factors to be taken into account. See *Little Hayes Nursing Home Ltd v. Marshall* [1993] E.G.C.S. 32 (valuation of property on the exercise of an option), and *Mid Kent Water plc v. Batchelor and others* [1994] 1 E.G.L.R. 185.

[26] *Campbell v. Edwards* [1976] 1 W.L.R. 403, 408, *per* Lord Denning, M.R. Note *Belvedere Motors Ltd v. King* [1981] 2 E.G.L.R. 131 (claim by landlords against the valuer appointed as an expert, not an arbitrator, to determine the rent under a rent review clause; the valuer was held not negligent). In *Wallshire Ltd v. Aarons* [1989] 1 E.G.L.R. 147, a claim against an independent surveyor, appointed by the President of RICS, and acting as an expert; held, on the facts, the valuer was not negligent.

[27] *Palacath Ltd v. Flanagan* [1985] 2 All E.R. 161: preliminary issue as to whether the surveyor appointed under a rent review clause was by the terms of the lease appointed as an arbitrator or quasi-arbitrator; it was held that he was not so appointed; he was appointed as an expert and was therefore not immune in respect of the landlord's claim against him for alleged negligence. See *also North Eastern Co-operative Society Ltd v. Newcastle upon Tyne City Council* [1987] 1 E.G.L.R. 142, where Scott J. held that on the facts it was intended that the independent surveyor should act as expert if appointed (as he was) by agreement between the parties, but that he should act as arbitrator if appointed, in default of agreement, by the President of RICS.

  (i) failing to carry out instructions;

  (ii) insufficient knowledge or experience;

  (iii) failing to inspect properly:

     (a) failing to inspect particular parts,
     (b) failing to uncover and open up,
     (c) failing to observe,
     (d) limited survey,
     (e) failing to recognise;

  (iv) failing to make sufficient inquiries;

  (v) inadequate report.

They are formulated primarily in the light of the broad steps required of a surveyor in carrying out a structural survey and/or a valuation. Nevertheless it must be emphasised that whether and, if so, to what extent each step has to be taken will vary according to the nature of the engagement and the circumstances of each case. For example, more will be required of a surveyor by way of inspection and examination of the property when instructed to carry out a building or structural survey as opposed to a domestic valuation. A commercial valuation, however, will usually require more beyond inspection of the subject property, as described by Watkins J. in *Singer and Friedlander Ltd v. John D. Wood and Co.*,[28] a case of negligent valuation of development land:

> "there is no diversion of opinion, save as to some details, about what in valuation is a general and approved practice between the valuers who have given evidence. . . . It consists of four fairly distinct stages of activity, namely, firstly, the sometimes tedious and laborious but vital approach work; secondly, analysing the information thereby gained, and so be enabled by the exercise of experience and judgment to accept facts and make assumptions; thirdly, applying the detailed discount method with comparables or some other justified by the circumstances as an alternative, or as a check, to the findings, and thereby produce the valuation; and fourthly informing the client of it".[29]

9–076 Owing to varying circumstances, it is dangerous to regard specific decisions as providing precedents. The facts of each case must be closely scrutinised and reported decisions regarded as providing indications at most as to the court's likely approach in similar situations. Individual cases are considered below under the appropriate heading for the primary default or one of the primary defaults. Several cases could be considered under a number of different headings. Moreover one default may lead to another, for example, a failure to observe may lead to a failure to report and to warn. Finally, the categories themselves do not cover the whole range of defaults for which a surveyor may incur liability but they include the majority of acts and omissions likely to arise in the course of a surveyor's work within the scope of this chapter.

---

[28] [1977] 2 E.G.L.R. 84
[29] *ibid.* at 217. Note also the "matters of principle and of fact" listed by Gibson J. in *Corisand Investments Ltd v. Druce & Co.* [1978] 2 E.G.L.R. 86, 89 to which an "ordinary competent valuer" in valuing property such as the hotel in that case should have regard. *Cf.* Lord Cameron's caution in the final sentence of the passage quoted at para. 9–082, below.

(a) *Failing to carry out instructions*

Whilst many breaches considered under other heads may be characterised as a **9–077** failure to carry out instructions, under this head are included cases where the surveyor has either failed completely to carry out his instructions or done something different. Extreme cases would be those of a surveyor instructed to survey a particular house either not inspecting it or inspecting the wrong property. More usual are cases where the surveyor carries out a more limited service than that for which he was engaged. Very often the crucial issue in such cases is one of fact, namely, what were the surveyors' instructions? In *Fisher v. Knowles*[30] the parties were in dispute both as to the nature of the terms of the surveyor's employment and how he was instructed. The judge, concluding that what the defendant was being instructed to do was something more than a bare valuation and less than a structural survey, held the defendant negligent. In *Moss v. Heckingbottom*[31] the defendant architect contended that his only instructions were to prepare plans. Barry J., however, preferred the evidence of the plaintiff that the defendant was instructed to make a structural survey of the house and outbuildings and to test and survey all services and equipment. He held the defendant in breach of contract in failing to do so and consequently in not discovering defects.[32] An example of a case where a surveyor would not have been found liable but for the specific terms of his instructions is *Farley v Skinner*[33] where the surveyor was specifically instructed to check that that there was no problem with aircraft noise at a house situated some 15 miles from Gatwick airport. Having accepted the claimant's account of the disputed instructions, the judge found that although there was no problem apparent at the time of his visit to the property, the surveyor should have made specific enquiries of the Civil Aviation Authority, in which event he would have ascertained that the house was close to a "stack" of aircraft used between 6 and 8 a.m. and between 5.30 and 7 p.m.

Failure to carry out instructions may result from misinterpretation or inade-   **9–078** quate enquiry of the client. This error may arise where the instructions are unspecific or ambiguous. In *Buckland v. Watts*[34] the evidence was that the plaintiff instructed the defendant, a chartered surveyor, to survey a house and prepare some plans. The defendant took his instructions to mean a measured survey only. Although the county court judge held the instructions to imply a measured survey, the Court of Appeal reversed his decision and held the defendant negligent in failing to carry out his instructions, and consequently in not discovering a variety of defects. *Per* Salmon L.J.: "If a prospective buyer of a house goes to a chartered surveyor and says, 'I want a survey and plans' that

---

[30] [1982] 1 E.G.L.R. 154.

[31] (1958) 172 E.G. 207.

[32] *ibid.* at 207, *per* Barry J.: "a structural survey entailed something more than the casual inspection of the building which had taken place when he and his assistant were preparing the plans. He might not have thought it necessary to draw attention to such defects as furniture beetle, loose frames and the like, which one would expect to find in any 200–year-old house. The truth was, however, that these were the type of defects to which attention should be drawn after a reasonably careful survey".

[33] [2000] P.N.L.R. 441. The reference is to the Court of Appeal report, which concerned the question of damages but from which the Judge's findings, against, which there was no appeal, are apparent (although Stuart-Smith L.J. hinted at 445 that he might have been prepared to entertain an appeal on liability). See also para. 9–181 below in relation to the recovery of damages.

[34] (1968) 208 E.G. 969.

ought to convey to any sensible surveyor that what the client wants to know is what is the structural condition of the house, and he also wants some plans of the house."[35]

Similarly in *Hellings v. Parker Breslin Estate*[36] the plaintiffs instructed the defendant letting agents to let a flat, making it plain that it was very important that they be able to recover possession at the end of the term granted. The plaintiffs intended to sell the flat for redevelopment purposes. The defendants failed to enquire as to their clients' intentions and to warn the plaintiffs in plain terms that they could not recover possession under a Case 11 letting unless they required the flat as their residence. This failure to determine their clients' precise requirements and intentions was held to be in breach of duty. In *Predeth v. Castle Phillips Finance Co. Ltd*,[37] the instructions were specific but the client, a finance company, argued that there was an overriding duty on the valuer to provide a true market value. The Court of Appeal rejected this argument. The defendant valuers having been instructed by the plaintiff finance company by letter to provide a "crash sale valuation", they owed no duty to advise the company on the true market value of the property. Fox L.J. stated: "He was given a particular task to do. It seems to me that he did it."

(b) *Insufficient knowledge or experience*

9–079 A person engaging a surveyor is entitled to expect that he is sufficiently knowledgeable and experienced to undertake the task required. If the surveyor lacks those qualifications and cannot make up for them, for example by making enquiries, he should refuse the engagement. The RICS Professional Indemnity Collective Policy imposes restrictions on those who may undertake surveys and valuations. If such work is carried out by an unqualified person, having less than five years experience, such work must be supervised or the prior consent of insurers obtained. What constitutes insufficient knowledge has already been considered.[38] Insufficient experience is illustrated by two further cases.

9–080 In *Kenney v. Hall, Pain and Foster*[39] the plaintiff was advised as to the value and reasonable asking price of a house by a property negotiator employed by the defendants. Both valuation and price were grossly excessive. Prior to giving his advice the negotiator had very limited experience. He had no formal qualifications and had only six months' experience working with estate agents in New Zealand and three months' experience working with the defendant. Goff J. held the defendant liable:

"In my judgment, at the material time [the negotiator] lacked the skill which could reasonably have been expected of a person in his position, to give the valuation. Furthermore, in failing to refer the matter properly back to the office for their opinion, he failed to exercise reasonable care in making the valuation. Lastly, having regard to

---

[35] *ibid.* at 973. Although the basis of liability seems to have been negligence (whether the tort or breach of the implied term to use reasonable care and skill) the defendant could equally have been held in breach of the specific express term to carry out a structural survey. The latter creates an absolute duty and there can be no question of whether the defendant exercised reasonable care and skill in interpreting his instructions.

[36] [1995] 2 E.G.L.R. 99.

[37] [1986] 2 E.G.L.R. 144.

[38] See para. 9–052, above.

[39] [1976] 2 E.G.L.R. 29; for further facts see para. 9–123, below.

the nature of the plaintiff's request for a written opinion, he was entitled to assume that the valuation . . . had been the subject of full and informal consideration by a partner or responsible employee of the defendant, and I am satisfied that it was not."[40]

In *Baxter v. F. W. Gapp & Co. Ltd*[41] the defendant valuer was experienced 9–081 generally but not in the value of properties in the locality of the bungalow, the subject of his advice. Goddard L.J. sitting at first instance stated:

"His duty was, first of all, to use reasonable care in coming to the valuation which he was employed to make and he must be taken to have held himself out as possessing the experience and skill required to value the particular property. If he did not know enough about the property market, or the value of the property at the place where the property was situate, he ought to have taken steps to inform himself of the values of the properties there, or of any circumstances which might affect the property. It would be no defence, for instance, to say: I made this valuation, but the reason why my valuation has proved incorrect, if it has proved incorrect, is that I was not a person, as you know, who practised in that locality."[42]

The Court of Appeal affirmed the decision.[43]

(c) *Failing to inspect properly*

This is the most common cause of complaint against surveyors. The complaints 9–082 may be sub-divided into more specific criticisms such as failure to inspect particular areas, failure to uncover or open up parts and failure to observe or to recognise. The latter are adopted as sub-headings below, together with a specific sub-category for the problem of the limited survey. The caution[44] concerning the varying nature of each case and not regarding any as establishing a precedent is particularly appropriate in the case of failure to inspect. That caution together with what generally is required by way of inspection on a visual survey is perhaps best expressed in a Scottish case, *Stewart v. H.A. Brechin & Co.*[45] by Lord Cameron:

" . . . all that the defenders were under contract to do was to make such valuation of the property and to carry out such visual inspection as was reasonably practicable in the circumstances, reporting anything of significance to their client if such should be found. 'Anything of significance' in this context, in my opinion, means anything so material as would or might influence a reasonable man in fixing a price to be offered by him for the subjects, or anything which to the skilled eye of a surveyor would be an indication of possible and material defect structural or otherwise in the property, such as would, or might reasonably, be expected to affect its value to a prospective purchaser or cause him to reconsider an intention to make an offer for it. As was put by Lord President Cooper in the briefly reported case of *Ker v. Allan*[46] ' . . . in conducting such an inspection a professional man should have a keen eye for anything showing or even

---

[40] *ibid.* at 34.
[41] [1938] 4 All E.R. 457.
[42] *ibid.* at 459; see also du Parcq L.J. on appeal, [1939] 2 K.B. 752.
[43] [1939] 2 K.B. 271. The House of Lords in *Swingcastle Ltd v. Gibson* [1991] 2 A.C. 223 overruled the case on the issue of calculation of interest. The House of Lords in *Banque Bruxelles Lambert SA v. Eagle Star Insurance Co. Ltd* [1997] A.C. 191 concluded that on its facts, the decision to award the plaintiff the entire loss was correct.
[44] See para. 9–075, above.
[45] (1959) S.C. 306.
[46] 1949 S.L.T. 20.

raising a suspicion of, any material defect (including dry rot), but he need not, and usually cannot, conduct an exhaustive search—least of all in a furnished and occupied dwelling house for possible latent defects of which there is no overt symptom, and the existence of which he has no reason to suspect. . . . ' In such circumstances it is obviously difficult and probably impracticable as well as undesirable to attempt to lay down in specific terms and categories what must be looked at or looked for when a surveyor proceeds to value a house, or the extent to which failure to examine any particular part or parts should be regarded as at least presumptive evidence of failure to exercise the due measure of professional care".[47]

(i) *Failing to inspect particular parts*

9–083 A building or structural survey entails more than a casual inspection of a property.[48] In carrying out such a survey a surveyor is expected to inspect all visible parts. In *Hill v. Debenham, Tewson and Chinnocks*[49] the defendant surveyor was instructed to survey and report on an old cottage which the plaintiff intended to buy and renovate. He was held negligent, *inter alia*, in giving no warning in respect of the rafters which had gone and the battens which needed renewing. The official referee concluded that the defendants' surveyor should in the circumstances have climbed up a ladder to a valley between two roofs and looked through gaps in missing tiles or, failing that, to warn that he did not know what the state of the rafters and battens would be. In *Stewart v. H. A. Brechin & Co.*[50] the defendant surveyor failed to inspect the roofspaces of an eighteenth century mansion house and outbuildings and thus failed to discover extensive woodworm infestation. In *Conn v. Munday*[51] the surveyor was held negligent apparently[52] in failing, *inter alia*, to discover in the course of his survey woodworm in the cellar of a house. He gave evidence that he did not know there was a cellar. A surveyor may also be expected to inspect other areas in so far as they may affect the structure of the property. Thus in the Scottish case of *Drinnan v. C.W. Ingram & Sons*[53] Lord Milligan stated that he could not see how a surveyor

---

[47] [1959] S.C. 306, 308. Note also *Fisher v. Knowles* [1982] 1 E.G.L.R. 154, *per* Sir Douglas Frank Q.C., sitting as a deputy High Court judge, at 154:
"The word 'defect' is a word having a number of connotations. Defects may be something which is inherent in the type and age of a building. For example, an Elizabethan cottage is likely to have the defect of having low ceilings, a defect both in the ordinary sense and in the statutory sense. To some people, though, that would be considered to be an enhancement. There are defects of some kind in every home. There are creaking floorboards, gaps between the wainscot and the floor. There are cracks in the ceilings. One would be very lucky indeed to buy even a new house, let alone a 25-year-old house as this one was without finding some cracks in the ceiling. It seems that in approaching this matter in the instant case I should have regard to those defects which were of such a nature as a prudent person would have put right and which would have been apparent to the defendant exercising the ordinary skill of an ordinary competent chartered surveyor, and taking into account the type and age of the property."

[48] *per* Barry J. in *Moss v. Heckingbottom* (1958) 172 E.G. 207. See the detailed guidance now provided by the RICS in "Building Surveys of Residential Property: A Guidance Note" (RICS, 1996, and earlier editions).

[49] (1958) 171 E.G. 835.

[50] (1959) S.C. 306.

[51] (1955) 166 E.G. 465. See also the Canadian case *Cantwell v. Petersen* (1983) 139 D.L.R. (3d) 466 (failing to inspect crawlspace beneath the house and thus to discover dry rot and insect infestation).

[52] The case is only briefly reported.

[53] [1967] S.L.T. 205.

required to supply an estimate of the value of a top flat could do so without having at least some regard to the structure of the building as a whole.[54]

(ii) *Failing to uncover and open up*

This is usually the substantive complaint where the surveyor has failed to **9–084** discover defects which at the time of his inspection were concealed, for example, under carpets, floorboards or in a wall. In determining liability, much will depend upon the nature of the instructions, the presence of suspicious signs in visible parts and the practicality of uncovering and opening up. Liability on this ground was established in *Roberts v. J. Hampson & Co.*[55] The claimants purchased a property relying on a mortgage valuation provided by the defendant surveyor. The report drew attention to some dampness in the external walls and a certain amount of dry rot in the skirting board of a bedroom, the valuer recommended that a timber specialist be engaged to eradicate the rot. No retention was recommended. In fact the property was subject to a serious infestation of dry rot that manifested itself a few months after the plaintiffs moved in. In a passage subsequently quoted by Lord Templeman with approval,[56] Ian Kennedy J. discussed the question of moving furniture and lifting carpets when the surveyor is instructed to carry out a mortgage valuation:

> "the position that the law adopts is simple. If a surveyor misses a defect because its signs are hidden, that is a risk that his client must accept. But if there is specific ground for suspicion and the trail of suspicion leads behind furniture or under carpets, the surveyor must take reasonable steps to follow the trail until he has all the information which it is reasonable for him to have before making his valuation".[57]

The principle underlying the striking phrase, "follow the trail of suspicion", **9–085** although not new, having been endorsed by the House of Lords in *Smith v. Bush*, has been applied in terms in a number of other cases. This obligation on the surveyor has also been described[58] as being "a diagnostic interpretation of a visual inspection". It is "judging what you cannot see by what you can see".[59] Other cases in which this principle has been applied include *Bere v. Slades*,[60] where certain walls of a property were of unconventional and defective construction. The plaintiffs conceded that this defect was not directly discoverable during

---

[54] *ibid.* at 208. He continued: "It may be that in the absence of precise instructions to do so a surveyor is not bound to make a meticulous examination of the fabric of a whole tenement but I should be surprised if it is not the normal practice to have regard to anything clearly visible in the structure of the building." The facts were that shortly after the defenders' report and in reliance upon it the pursuer purchased a tenement flat. Six months later the pursuer was informed by the city engineer that the whole tenement was in a dangerous condition and had to be demolished. The issue of liability was not decided, only preliminary issues being before the court.

[55] [1988] 2 E.G.L.R. 181. The case was described as one of "general application" by Lord Templeman in *Smith v. Bush* [1990] 1 A.C. 831, 850.

[56] In *Smith v. Bush, op. cit.* at 851.

[57] [1988] 2 E.G.L.R. 181, at 185.

[58] By a Mr Anderson, a surveyor, whilst giving evidence in *Hacker v. Thomas Deal & Co.* [1991] 2 E.G.L.R. 161.

[59] *Hacker v. Thomas Deal & Co.*, see previous note.

[60] [1989] 2 E.G.L.R. 160.

a mortgage valuation. They complained however, that the valuer, when carrying out his inspection, had failed to follow up a number of other defects, either by declining to value or to refer for greater inspection. The judge agreed that the duty to follow a trail of suspicion existed but held on the facts that the nature of the defects was not such as to give rise to such an obligation. He held that the valuer had prepared "a thoroughly competent report, carefully done and, I would add, masterly succinct".[61] In *Hipkins v. Jack Cotton Partnership*[62] a surveyor failed to observe cracking and patching in the rendering of a wall. The cracks were the manifestation of a structural defect in the foundations of the property that made underpinning necessary. It was held that a reasonably competent surveyor would have seen the cracks and asked himself why they were there. Scott Baker J. said: "These were clues that he should not have missed. These clues led at least to the query that the building was unsound, yet he missed them."[63] In *Whalley v. Roberts & Roberts*[64] the failure by a surveyor carrying out a mortgage valuation to detect that the house had been built out of level was, on the facts, and applying the test in *Roberts v. J. Hampson & Co.*, held to be not negligent.

9–086   *Hacker v. Thomas Deal & Co.*[65] involved a building survey of a substantial and expensive[66] property in Belgravia for an American investment banker. A virulent attack of dry rot was discovered by the defendant surveyors. The claimant alleged in his statement of claim that there were a number of matters that indicated a particular risk of dry rot and the consequential need for careful inspection. These were the age and character of the building, the existence of a sauna compartment underneath the area where the outbreak was found, and the surveyors' failure to observe and inspect inside a small trap in the roof of the sauna, and the traces of damp noted in the report. Added by amendment were the significance of the existence of the sauna, the plunge pool and jacuzzi area, inherent dampness of the basement, and the likelihood of condensation in the area around the sauna, plunge pool and jacuzzi area. Judge Fawcus held that the age and character of the building were readily apparent to the surveyor and that he knew precisely what sort of building he was dealing with. The judge criticised the amendments as afterthoughts: " . . . an example of *ex post facto* rationalisation of a conclusion that he [the claimant's expert witness] has already come to. If he did not think that the plunge pool and jacuzzi area and the likelihood of condensation were significant, one asks oneself why he did not mention it in the first place". The crucial question was whether the surveyor should have seen the small trap in the roof of the sauna and looked through, where he might have been able to see fruiting bodies of dry rot. Noting that the sauna was a prefabricated, self contained unit, the judge came to "the firm conclusion that he is not to be criticised for not seeing it", accepting the evidence of an expert surveyor that: " . . . although one is acting as a detective one does not start going into all the little crevices in the hopes of finding something unless there is some telltale sign

---

[61] *ibid.* at 163.
[62] [1989] 2 E.G.L.R. 157. This case has been overruled on the issue of measure of loss by the Court of Appeal's decision in *Watts v. Morrow* [1991] 1 W.L.R. 1421. See para. 9–141, below.
[63] [1989] 2 E.G.L.R. 157, 159.
[64] [1990] 1 E.G.L.R. 164.
[65] [1991] 2 E.G.L.R. 161.
[66] Purchased by the claimant for £1,625,000.

which indicates that it would be advisable to do so". The judge held that the claimant's claim failed.

Liability on the ground of failing to inspect particular parts was established in **9–087** *Hill v. Debenham, Tewson and Chinnocks*[67] where the defendant surveyor reported: "Flooring on first floor appears to be in fair condition although we could only judge from superficial examination." In fact there was a second layer of floorboards underneath, riddled with woodworm. The official referee took the view that having found beetle in the woodwork and wet rot on the ground floor, any competent surveyor would have lifted one or two floorboards on the first floor. "I find that the general and proved practice of the profession is to take up floorboards when you are put on inquiry, if such course is practicable." In fact it was "eminently practicable" to take up the boards, since the cottage was unoccupied and little more than a shell at the time of the inspection. He continued: "Even if I am wrong as to this, it is plainly the duty to warn if he does not look, and no warning was given as to what might be found when the floorboards were lifted."[68]

Liability on this ground may be more difficult to establish where uncovering **9–088** and opening up are not feasible, as may be the case where the premises are occupied and the floors have fitted carpets.[69] A more limited view of a surveyor's duty in such circumstances was taken in the briefly reported Scottish case of *Ker v. John H. Allan & Son.*[70] The defender surveyors were instructed by a prospective purchaser, the pursuer, to inspect a property and report verbally upon it the same day. This they did although the house was furnished and occupied and the time available before making the verbal report was very short. The pursuer failed to establish that the defenders were negligent in not looking under the floorboards. Lord Birnam accepted the evidence that the presence of dry rot ought always to be present in the mind of a surveyor and that he should always be on the lookout for any evidence that might to his skilled mind be suggestive of dry rot. He was nevertheless "unable to accept the view that in such circumstances his duty requires him in the absence of any suspicious circumstances to cause carpets and linoleum to be lifted and to go underneath floors and make a detailed examination of every hidden corner of a building".[71] On appeal to the Court of Session[72] the decision was affirmed. The Lord President, while expressly confining his attention to the facts of the case, added that the surveyors were not under a specific duty to inform the purchaser that they had not explored beneath the floors and in the hidden corners and concealed places. Similarly in *Thorne v. Harris & Co.*[73] the surveyor was unable to make a complete survey at the time the bungalow was furnished. He probed and looked around for rot but he could not examine under the floorboards. He was held not negligent in not discovering dry rot caused apparently by dampness spreading to the joists along sleeper plates attached to the outside wall and affecting the floorboards. By

---

[67] (1958) 171 E.G. 835.

[68] *ibid.* at 837.

[69] As indeed recognised by the Official Referee in *Hill v. Debenham, Tewson and Chinnocks, ibid.* at 837.

[70] [1949] S.L.T.(Notes) 20, OH.

[71] *ibid.* In any event it was not proved that dry rot would have been visible if the defenders had looked beneath the floor.

[72] Briefly summarised in (1949) 154 E.G. 473.

[73] (1953) 163 E.G. 324.

contrast in *Grove v. Jackman and Masters*[74] the defendant surveyors were held negligent. The presence of dry rot, caused by the sleeper walls not being honeycombed, could not have been discovered without taking up floorboards which was not possible at the time of survey since the vendors were still in, occupation. Lord Goddard C.J. concluded that there were indications which should have warned a competent and careful surveyor of the presence of dry rot. That being so, the defendants should have either arranged or advised the plaintiff to arrange for floorboards to be taken up and more thorough investigation made.[75]

9–089   Whether occupied or unoccupied, there are limits on the necessity to uncover or open up. Thus in *Bishop v. Watson, Watson and Scoles*,[76] McKenna J. said:

> "An architect like Mr Scoles who has agreed to make a visual survey is under no obligation to uncover those parts of the building where the flashings or damp proof courses should be found to see if they are there and, if they are, whether they are adequate. If he sees anything which would give a reasonably skilled person grounds to suspect that they are missing or inadequate he must draw his client's attention to the matter, but evidence that the building is of cavity construction is not itself ground for suspecting that the safeguards essential to that mode of construction have been omitted or botched."[77]

In that case the defendant was instructed to carry out a visual inspection and report upon a newly-built flat. Certain windows were covered on the inside with moisture but he concluded that the likely cause was condensation, not dampness. It later transpired, however, that the flat was subject to penetrating dampness through the cavity walls caused apparently by the absence of flashings and of a damp proof course to a horizontal concrete ring beam and vertical concrete columns respectively bridging the cavity walls. The defendant was held not negligent in failing to ascertain those facts and to observe what the plaintiff claimed were signs of defective construction or design.

(iii) *Failing to observe*

9–090   Even though a surveyor may inspect all parts of a property and even uncover some, he may be insufficiently observant. This may be due to a failure to carry out a sufficiently detailed examination, or over-familiarity with the property, or type of property, bringing with it a sense of false security. Consequently he may

---

[74] (1950) 155 E.G. 182.

[75] The surveyor reported that the bungalow was "soundly constructed on good modern principles of building", but Lord Goddard concluded that it was "as bad a piece of 'jerry building' as could be found in that district". In *Wooldridge v. Stanley Hicks & Son* (1953) 162 E.G. 513 the defendant surveyors were held negligent although detailed examination of a guest house was not possible since all the rooms were occupied and furnished. Expert evidence established that there were probably signs of dry rot which the defendants should have discovered. In *Denny v. Budgen* (1955) 166 E.G. 433 the surveyor was held negligent in not discovering woodworm in the floor. The defendant argued that he was protected by the fact that he said in his report that the floors were for the most part covered by linoleum, thus precluding examination. Pearce J., however, concluded that that indicated that some examination was possible.

[76] (1972) 224 E.G. 1881.

[77] *ibid.* at 1886.

fail to notice matters of significance.[78] In *Cross v. David Martin and Mortimer*,[79] a surveyor whom Phillips J. described as having taken "a lot of care" over an HBRV[80] survey, failed to notice and consider the significance of a hump in the hall floor. Together with certain other indicators, the hump should have alerted the surveyor to the possibility of subsidence. The fact that the defendant firm had inspected the property on the occasion of its previous sale may have lulled the surveyor into a false sense of security.[81] The surveyor was held negligent.

Dry rot and woodworm. Failure to discover dry rot, woodworm, or similar   **9–091** infestation is the source of many claims against surveyors. In carrying out a survey particular regard should be paid to areas of suspicion.[82] In *Oswald v. Countrywide Surveyors Ltd*[83] a surveyor was held negligent in failing expressly to warn of an infestation of death watch beetle, a warning of "woodworm" being held insufficient. In *Lowry v. Woodruffe, Buchanan and Coulter*[84] a surveyor was held negligent in failing to discover dry rot in an area of suspicion, a wooden framework above the front door. Further, he should look out for signs characteristic of certain defects such as dry rot waviness or ribbiness in the skirtings. One or two errors of observation might, however, be insufficient to establish negligence.[85] Thus in *Tew v. W. M. Whitburn & Son*[86] Parker J. considered failure to observe "ribbiness" of skirting boards "very slender evidence" on which to hold a professional man guilty of negligence and in *Hacker v. Thomas Deal & Co.*[87] a failure to observe a small trap door in the roof of a sauna, through which the fruiting bodies of dry rot might have been observed, was held not to be negligent. Similarly in *Hardy v. Wamsley-Lewis*[88] if the defendant surveyor had only failed to observe dry rot waviness in the skirting board between the front door and the staircase, Paull J. would have required argument as to whether one failure constituted negligence. But the defendant also discovered on a door post an indication that there had been dry rot although he concluded it was dormant. That being the case Paull J. was of the view that he ought to have "meticulously examined every bit of wood he could see, to see if there were signs of it spreading at all".[89] The evidence established that there were signs of active dry rot which the defendant ought to have seen despite the house being furnished and he was held negligent in failing to discover it.[90]

Defects in roof. Errors of observation are often alleged in respect of less   **9–092** accessible and visible areas of a property, particularly the roof and roofspace.

---

[78] Note the definition of "anything of significance" in this context by Lord Cameron in *Stewart v. H.A. Brechin & Co.* [1959] S.C. 306, 308: see para. 9–082, above.

[79] [1989] 1 E.G.L.R. 154.

[80] House Buyer's Report and Valuation. Phillips J.'s abbreviation.

[81] [1989] 1 E.G.L.R. 154, 158.

[82] This was a criticism made of the chartered surveyor in *Hacker v. Thomas Deal & Co.* [1991] 2 E.G.L.R. 161. See para. 9–086.

[83] [1996] 2 E.G.L.R. 104.

[84] (1950) 156 E.G. 375.

[85] See para. 9–058, above.

[86] (1952) 159 E.G. 56.

[87] [1991] 2 E.G.L.R. 161. See para. 9–086, above.

[88] (1967) 203 E.G. 1039.

[89] *ibid.* at 1041.

[90] Surveyors were also held liable for not discovering dry rot and similar infestation in the following cases: *Legge v. Young* [1949] E.G.D. 186 (dry rot in woodwork); *Grove v. Jackman and Masters* (1950) 155 E.G. 182 (dry rot in floors and joists); *Sincock v. Bangs (Reading)* [1952] C.P.L. 562 (dry

Thus in *Parsons v. Way and Waller Ltd*[91] the defendant surveyors' employee was held negligent in not properly examining the roof. Rafters were not properly tied at their feet, with the result that the roof was spreading towards the rear and thrusting against the back wall. Moreover, the wall plate which held the rafters had receded and projected over the brickwork, as was plainly visible inside and outside the house. Similarly in *Last v. Post*,[92] although the defendant surveyor genuinely and honestly thought he was paying adequate attention to everything visible and examined the roof from inside and then outside with binoculars, he failed to observe a considerable amount of deposit from tiles disintegrating through efflorescence. Although acquitted of not recognising that "rare phenomenon", he was held negligent in describing the roof as "soundly constructed" in his report, which no doubt he would not have done if he had observed the deposit. In *Eley v. King & Chasemore*[93] it was alleged that the chartered surveyor who carried out a structural survey of a property was negligent in failing to report on defects to the roof structure, including an absence of ventilation. The fact that the surveyor had failed to climb on to the roof was criticised by the claimant, but neither the trial judge nor the Court of Appeal agreed. The surveyor had inspected the roof space from inside the house, and the exterior of the roof from ground level. In the absence of any sign of defect, that degree of inspection and observation was held sufficient to discharge the surveyor's duty. That finding may be contrasted with the decision in *Heatley v. William H. Brown Ltd*[94] where the surveyor retained to provide a structural survey was unable to gain access to the roof voids and discussed with the plaintiffs the absence of such access. The report warned that parts of the property had fallen into disrepair. Despite the conversation, and the incorporation into the retainer of the defendants' written conditions of engagement which included reference to the limitations in a report where parts of the property were unexposed or inaccessible, the defendants were

---

rot and woodworm); *Wooldridge v. Stanley Hicks & Son* (1953) 162 E.G. 513 (dry rot in bedroom); *Tremayne v. T. Mortimer Burrows and Partners* (1954) 165 E.G. 232 (dry rot in shutters and window frames); *Denny v. Budgen* (1955) 166 E.G. 433 (woodworm in floors); *Conn v. Munday* (1955) 166 E.G. 465 (woodworm in cellar and dampness); *Leigh v. William Hill & Son* (1956) 168 E.G. 396 (woodworm); *Fidgeon v. Carroll* (1956) 168 E.G. 557 (woodworm in rafters, floors, shed and lavatory); *Philips v. Ward* [1956] 1 W.L.R. 471 (death watch beetle); *Hill v. Debenham, Tewson and Chinnocks* (1958) 171 E.G. 835 (woodworm in floorboards); *Stewart v. H.A. Brechin & Co.* [1959] S.C. 306 (woodworm in roof space); *Freeman v. Marshall & Co.* (1966) 200 E.G. 777 (rising damp, wet and dry rot); *Collard v. Saunders* (1972) 221 E.G. 797 (death watch beetle); *Cantwell v. Petersen* (1983) 139 D.L.R. (3d) 466 (dry rot and insect infestation); *Hooberman v. Salter Rex* [1985] 1 E.G.L.R. 144 (dry rot); *Roberts v. J. Hampson & Co.* [1988] 2 E.G.L.R. 181 (dry rot); *Steward v. Rapley* [1989] 1 E.G.L.R. 159 (dry rot); *Syrett v. Carr & Neave* [1990] 2 E.G.L.R. 161 (death watch beetle, note Court of Appeal considered case wrongly decided on measure of loss, see *Watts v. Morrow* [1991] 1 W.L.R. 1421); *Oswald v. Countrywide Surveyors Ltd* [1996] 2 E.G.L.R. 104 (death watch beetle); *Republic International Ltd v. Fletcher Ramos*, unreported, August 30, 2000, H.H.J. Havery Q.C. (dry rot). Surveyors were held not liable in the following cases: *Ker v. John H. Allan & Sons* 1949 S.L.T.(Notes) 20 (dry rot in floors); *MacKenzie v. R. & W. Hall* (1951) 157 E.G. 492 (dry rot); *Tew v. H.A. Whitburn & Son* (1952) 159 E.G. 56 (wet rot in woodwork); *Rona v. Pearce* (1953) 162 E.G. 380 (woodworm); *Thorne v. Harris & Co.* (1953) 163 E.G. 324; *Hacker v. Thomas Deal & Co.* [1991] 2 E.G.L.R. 161, see para. 9–086, above; *Kerridge v. James Abbott & Partners* [1992] 2 E.G.L.R. 162 (dry rot and timber decay).
[91] (1952) 159 E.G. 524.
[92] (1952) 159 E.G. 240.
[93] [1989] 1 E.G.L.R. 181.
[94] [1992] 1 E.G.L.R. 289 (official referee).

held to have provided a negligent report, in that further examinations and investigations ought to have been advised. A subsequent inspection, after the claimants had purchased the property and provided access to the roof voids, was also held to have been negligent.[95]

Subsidence and cracking. In carrying out a survey a surveyor must be particularly sensitive to signs of structural defects such as subsidence. This will require not only careful observation but also skilled inference, for example in evaluating a bulge or crack.[96] An example is *Matto v. Rodney Broom Associates*.[97] The Court of Appeal, reversing the trial judge, held the defendant surveyor liable for failing to warn the plaintiff in sufficient terms of a risk in the future of further subsidence, even though the property had been stable for many years. Liability was found despite "the basic skill and experience of the defendant" not having been proved to be lacking. Ralph Gibson L.J. commented[98]:

9–093

> "A buyer, unless he says otherwise, is not concerned only with structural damage likely to occur while he is, in the immediate future, living in the house but also with structural damage which is likely to occur at a more remote date of which the impact upon him will result . . . from the effect of that apparent likelihood of structural damage upon his ability to sell the house."

Moreover, this is an area where the distinction between a reasonable (although in retrospect mistaken) opinion on the one hand and negligence on the other is critical. Where a claim is made, in the absence of satisfactory contemporaneous evidence of facts other than the defendant surveyor's, much will depend upon expert evidence as to what should have been observed. Inevitably the problem of distinguishing accurate reconstruction from the revelation of hindsight is acute.[99] Accurate reconstruction will be more difficult the longer the period between the allegedly negligent inspection and trial as demonstrated by *Leigh v. Unsworth*[1] where it amounted to over seven-and-a-half years. In that case it was claimed that the defendant surveyor was negligent in failing to detect indications of serious settlement subsequent to the usual initial settlement common in newly built houses. It was held there were only indications of the latter and the defendant was

---

[95] Other cases illustrating negligent observation of the roof space include *Lowry v. Woodroffe, Buchanan and Coulter* (1950) 156 E.G. 375 (defective roofing and guttering); *Chong v. Scott Collins & Co.* (1954) 164 E.G. 662 (reporting that the roof had been repaired in a good and workmanlike manner when this was not the case); *Hill v. Debenham, Tewson and Chinnocks* (1958) 171 E.G. 835 (rafters gone and battens needing renewal); *Leigh v. Unsworth* (1972) 230 E.G. 501 (no vertical hangers and stating that there was fibreglass insulation when there was none); *Perry v. Sidney Phillips & Son* [1982] 1 All E.R. 1005 (first instance, leaky roof); *Hooberman v. Salter Rex* [1985] 1 E.G.L.R. 144 (defects in flat roof and lack of ventilation in void); *Cross v. David Martin & Mortimer* [1989] 1 E.G.L.R. 154 (loft conversion inadequate); *Watts v. Morrow* [1991] 1 E.G.L.R. 150 (first instance, defective roof covering).
[96] See *Hipkins v. Jack Cotton Partnership* [1989] 2 E.G.L.R. 157, where the surveyor negligently failed to observe cracks that were evidence of settlement.
[97] [1994] 2 E.G.L.R. 163.
[98] *ibid.* at 168.
[99] This was a criticism made of the claimants' experts in *Hacker v. Thomas Deal & Co.* [1991] 2 E.G.L.R. 161 (see para. 9–086, above), and again in *Alliance & Leicester Building Society v. J. & E. Shepherd* [1995] G.W.D. 11–608 (see para. 9–108, n. 75, below).
[1] (1972) 230 E.G. 501.

held not liable in respect of the settlement.[2] In *Lawrence v. Hampton & Sons*[3] in contrast the defendants were held negligent in failing to observe cracks and in failing to advise that underpinning was required and that there was a risk of even more underpinning being necessary.

9–094   The latter case also illustrates that a careful survey may require examination of matters extrinsic to the buildings themselves, such as the carrying out of further inquiries and advising the instruction of specialists. Thus also in *Daisley v. B. S. Hall & Co.*[4] Bristow J. stated that:

> "a surveyor who finds a house under 10 years old built as close to a row of poplars as High Trees was, where two of those trees had been felled for no apparent reason other than to reduce the risk of root damage, is under a duty to ascertain by effective means the nature of the subsoil whether or not he finds evidence of settlement of the house which may be due to subsoil shrinkage".[5]

9–095   **Camouflaged defects.** A careful surveyor should be suspicious of recent redecoration or repairs as they may have been deliberately carried out to conceal defects, particularly structural defects. O'Connor J. expressed this warning in *Hingorani v. Blower*,[6] where the vendor had "faked up" the house and redecorated it from "top to tail" internally and filled in a large external crack. The defendant surveyor was held negligent in failing to observe tell-tale signs of structural defects, in particular the filled-in external crack which was apparent. The same point was made in *Morgan v. Perry*[7] where what had been done by the vendor by way of repointing, in-filling and over-papering had the same effect as "a deliberate cover-up job". The defendant surveyor gave "a completely clean bill of health" to a house which two years later structural engineers advised should be demolished owing to subsidence. The house was built upon a steep slope and was slipping. The defendant was held negligent in failing to observe clear signs of subsidence. These included the "known potential dangers of a steeply sloping site" and repairs to the adjacent highway due to causes other than traffic. Examination of the latter would have led the surveyor to enquire of the local highway authority. Not all camouflaged defects can reasonably be exposed during an inspection. Much will depend on the existence or otherwise of other pointers to there being a hidden defect. In *Whalley v. Roberts & Roberts*[8] a construction defect that caused the property to have been built out of level had been deliberately camouflaged, both inside and outside the house. That fact with others[9] contributed to the judge's finding that the defendant surveyor, who had carried out a mortgage valuation, was not negligent in having failed to observe the defect.

---

[2] In *Hipkins v. Jack Cotton Partnership, ibid.*, the period between the date of the report and the trial was also some seven and a half years. This did not prevent the learned judge making findings that at the time of the inspection, a crack in the rendering had probably been patched up but was still visible and that a vine growing up the wall was not then of such a height as to obscure the crack.

[3] (1964) 190 E.G. 107. See also *Gurd v. A. Cobden Soar and Son* (1951) 157 E.G. 415 (defective drains and subsidence).

[4] (1972) 225 E.G. 1553. Note also *Bolton v. Puley* (1983) 267 E.G. 1161 (defective boundary wall).

[5] *ibid.* at 1555.

[6] [1976] 1 E.G.L.R. 104.

[7] (1973) 229 E.G. 1737.

[8] [1990] 1 E.G.L.R. 164.

[9] These were: (a) it was unusual for a building to be constructed out of level in that way; (b) such lack of level was usually associated with movement cracks; there were no such signs; (c) detection of the slope by sight or feel in such a property was not easy; (d) the effort to camouflage the lack of

Total of unnoticed defects. While failure to observe some defects may not **9–096**
amount to negligence,[10] the more numerous the material defects overlooked, the
more difficult it will be to resist a finding of negligence. In *Hill v. Debenham,
Tewson and Chinnocks*[11] the defendants were instructed to carry out a structural
survey of a dilapidated cottage which the plaintiff wished to purchase and
reinstate[12] into a habitable condition. The defendants were further required to
prepare plans and estimate the cost of reinstatement and structural alterations
based on the plans. They were held negligent in five respects. First, they failed
to notice the absence of a damp-proof course and advise the plaintiff to install
one since the cottage was subject to extensive damp. Secondly, they failed to
observe that the rafters and battens were defective and needed replacement.
Thirdly, they failed to lift floorboards and observe that a second layer of
floorboards underneath was riddled with worm. Fourthly, although the estimate
only purported to be rough and provisional, it was even by that standard
"fantastically optimistic and most misleading". Fifthly, they failed to warn the
plaintiff that decoration should be postponed until damp had been effectively
dealt with. Similarly in *Hood v. Shaw*[13] the defendant surveyor was held negligent in providing a report "very, very short of what one had the right to expect
from a qualified surveyor".[14] It contained errors of commission and omission. He
stated that he had not seen any sign of bulging or fractures and that the brickwork
and pointing, window frames and surrounds were in good order. In fact the
opposite was proved to be the case. Further, he failed to observe the installation
of a solid floor underneath the suspended floor, indicative of previous damp or
other defect.[15]

(iv) *Limited survey*

The particular nature of an engagement may require a less extensive inspection **9–097**
of a property than would ordinarily be the case. For example, a surveyor may be
engaged to ascertain a reasonable asking price for a property by a vendor, or its
value as security by a prospective mortgagee. In such circumstances the more
limited nature of the inspection is an important factor to take into account in
determining whether a surveyor has been negligent in overlooking a particular

---

true level; (e) the plaintiff, an experienced joiner, had failed to notice the defect when he first moved
in; and (f) the previous owner had lived in the property for some eight years without becoming aware
of the slope.
[10] See para. 9–058, above.
[11] (1958) 171 E.G. 835.
[12] *ibid.* at 837, *per* Judge Carter Q.C.:
"I should like to pause and consider the nature of the advice which should be given to a client who
is contemplating buying a house and converting it into living accommodation. What does he want
to know? The first thing in my view he wants to know is: 'Is the fabric of this house good enough
to justify the expense of conversion?' Any competent surveyor should realise that is the crucial
question about which he is called upon to advise. Houses have a life and the cheaper the conversion
the shorter the life. Before a surveyor advises spending money on conversion he should satisfy
himself that the fabric of the house is good enough to justify the spending of money on conversion."
[13] (1960) 176 E.G. 1291.
[14] *ibid.* at 1291, *per* Paull J.
[15] See also *Hoadley v. Edwards* [2001] E.G.C.S. where the surveyor was held liable for failing to
bring five significant defects relating to the condition of the plumbing, the windows and the wall ties
to the attention of the claimants.

defect.[16] The court may also permit a valuer a wider margin of error in relation to a valuation than would other wise have been the case. Thus in *Arab Bank v. John D. Wood Commercial Ltd*,[17] a valuer was instructed to comment upon another valuation produced of a substantial industrial estate. The judge held that the valuer was not only entitled to rely on the factual matters contained in that report (for example as to floor areas which had been over-stated) but indicated that he considered that the appropriate margin of error was higher than that applicable for the original valuer.[18] Whether the limited instructions will be sufficient to preclude a finding of negligence will depend upon the circumstances of each case, in particular the precise nature of the instructions and of the mistake made by the valuer.[19]

9–098 The problem has arisen in cases where a surveyor has agreed to carry out a limited, but ill-defined, survey, frequently for a reduced fee. In *Matto v. Rodney Broom Associates*[20] the Court of Appeal expressed sympathy for the defendant surveyor when finding him negligent, after delivering "a short report intended to serve his client swiftly and effectively and without a screen of qualification for his own protection", which nevertheless failed adequately to warn of the risk and possible expense of further subsidence.

As the majority of prospective purchasers choose one of the standard services now offered by surveyors, where the ambit of the inspection is known in advance, such survey cases are becoming unusual. The need for such standardised and defined services is illustrated by *Sincock v. Bangs (Reading)*,[21] where a surveyor gave a prospective purchaser client the choice of a "detailed survey" or a "general opinion" of a farm. The client elected the latter. Following the inspection and later purchase, the client discovered settlement in one corner of the house, dry rot and woodworm necessitating costly repairs. The client sued the surveyor and recovered damages. Barry J. concluded that it was the surveyor's duty to "warn the [client] of any defects which might have a material effect on the value of the property". He conceded that at the initial survey the surveyor had neither the time nor opportunity for carrying out a detailed examination of the structure. He nevertheless concluded that "making all allowances for the circumstances" the surveyor was negligent. Similarly in *Sinclair v. Bowden Son and Partners*[22] the surveyor was asked to do a survey quickly but not a full structural survey. He spent an hour-and-a-half at the property on a Saturday and at the

---

[16] See *Nash v. Evens & Matta* [1988] 1 E.G.L.R. 130 (mortgage valuation, surveyor did not report wall tie failure. Held, by Ewbank J., that surveyors fulfilled their duty on the basis of the limited inspection he was asked to make).

[17] [2000] Lloyd's L.Rep. P.N. 173.

[18] The Court of Appeal did not criticise this approach of the judge but did find that, even on the Judge's findings and following his approach, the second valuer had been negligent.

[19] See also the discussion of *Roberts v. J. Hampson & Co.* [1988] 2 E.G.L.R. 181, and *Smith v. Bush* [1990] 1 A.C. 831, at para. 9–057, above. In *Etam v. Baker Almond* [2001] E.G.C.S. 21, the valuers were required to provide a letter of comfort to a shopping chain which had decided to buy a store in Truro. The judge found that the claimants were looking for reassurance that they were not paying a "daft price". In that context the advice given was not unreasonable.

[20] [1994] 2 E.G.L.R. 163.

[21] (1952) C.P.L. 562.

[22] (1962) 183 E.G. 95. See also *Leigh v. William Hill and Son* (1956) 168 E.G. 396 (surveyor engaged by prospective purchaser to inspect and advise on the value of a house held negligent in failing to discover woodworm. The decision was affirmed on appeal when Singleton L.J. commented: "I have great sympathy with him. It was a valuation which had to be done fairly quickly and it may be that the inspection was not as complete as it might otherwise have been").

prospective purchaser's request sent him his report over the weekend. He charged seven guineas, rather than his 38 guinea fee for a full structural survey. Although he was doing "a rush job he did not want to do", Stephenson J. held him negligent in failing to observe the significance of new air bricks and thus discover wet rot and weevil. In *Franses v. Barnett*[23] a purchaser required and was charged less for a limited report for the primary purpose of discovering dry rot. The claimant failed, in view of the limited instructions, to establish negligence on the part of surveyors who had not discovered serious defects to the property exterior.

(v) *Failing to recognise*

Although a surveyor may carry out a comprehensive inspection and be suffi-   **9–099**
ciently observant, he may incur liability through failing to recognise a particular defect. The failure may be due to lack of knowledge on his part or mistaken attribution of the symptoms of the defect to another cause. In *Bryan Peach v. Iain G. Chalmers & Co.*[24] a surveyor preparing a valuation and report misunderstood and misdescribed the construction of the house, which was of the Dorran-type construction. The property was valued as if it were of traditional construction. There was a risk, never explained to the purchasers, that the bolts holding together the pre-cast concrete panels could corrode, requiring expensive repairs. As a consequence the property could prove difficult to sell, as lending institutions would be reluctant to lend on the security of the same. The pursuers overpaid by £9,000 and this sum was awarded. Lack of knowledge explains the failure to recognise in *Daisley v. B. S. Hall & Co.*[25] and *Last v. Post.*[26] In *Freeman v. Marshall*[27] the surveyor wrongly attributed to condensation what in fact was rising damp. He was held negligent in doing so. Alternatively, the surveyor may correctly diagnose the defects and their causes, but err in his assessment of their significance. In *Watts v. Morrow,*[28] where the chartered building surveyor's reassuring and detailed description of the roof was held to be negligent even though he correctly identified the principal defects, it was held by the official referee that the surveyor failed to recognise that the roof needed a comprehensive and expensive overhaul. As the first two cases demonstrate, the importance of expert evidence to establish the standard of a reasonably skilled surveyor is usually greater in cases of alleged failure to recognise than in cases of other inspection failure. Cases of failure to recognise, particularly when due to an error in attribution,[29] may involve differing views between experts as to the reasonable interpretation of particular symptoms at a certain time. Consequently, negligence may be more difficult to establish than in cases of other inspection failures.

---

[23] (1956) 168 E.G. 425. See also the Scottish case of *Ker v. John Allan & Son* 1949 S.L.T.(Notes) 20, and para. 9–088, above. The short notice and time for the inspection may have been important factors contributing to the successful defence.

[24] (1992) S.C.L.R. 423, [1992] 2 E.G.L.R. 135, OH, Lord Caplan.

[25] (1972) 225 E.G. 1553; see para. 9–055, above.

[26] (1952) 159 E.G. 240; see para. 9–055, above.

[27] (1966) 200 E.G. 777. *cf. Bishop v. Watson, Watson and Scoles* (1972) 224 E.G. 1881 (see para. 9–089 above).

[28] [1991] 1 E.G.L.R. 150 at first instance, reversed on appeal on the issue of measure of loss, [1991] 1 W.L.R. 1421, CA.

[29] *e.g.* disputes over interpretation of cracks in subsidence claims.

(d) *Failing to make sufficient inquiries*

9–100 Apart from inspecting a property, a surveyor may need to make a number of enquiries in order to carry out his instructions. A recent example is provided by the facts of *Western Trust v. Strutt & Parker*[30] where a valuer was found liable for negligently valuing a holiday complex on the basis that it formed permanent accommodation. Had he made enquiries of the local authority, he could and should have discovered the true position. As *Baxter v. F. W. Gapp & Co. Ltd*[31] and *Kenney v. Hall, Pain and Foster*[32] illustrate, if a surveyor is insufficiently aware of local market values, he should take steps to ascertain them. It may be necessary to carry out research and to make enquiries of local agents or a specific class of prospective vendors or purchasers. Thus in *Bell Hotels (1935) Ltd v. Motion*[33] the defendants, instructed to make an approximate valuation of the last free house in Melton Mowbray, were held negligent in failing to advise the plaintiffs that a brewery would be interested in buying. On the basis of the defendants' advice the plaintiffs sold the house to a buyer who almost immediately resold it at a considerable profit to a brewery. Although in the judgment the relevant default is described as failure to advise, clearly the effective default was failure to make sufficient enquiries of breweries themselves.

9–101 The more complex the task, the more detailed and painstaking the enquiries required of the surveyor. Authoritative guidance as to the appropriate methodology may be found in the appropriate Standards and Guidance Notes published by the RICS[34] and reference to the edition in force at the material time should always be made. A catalogue of factors and activities to be considered and undertaken at the stage of enquiry in carrying out a valuation is also set out in Watkins J.'s judgment in *Singer & Friedlander Ltd v. John D. Wood & Co.*[35] In that case the defendants were requested to value a site intended for development

---

[30] [1999] P.N.L.R. 154—see further para. 9–042 above.
[31] [1938] 4 All E.R. 457 (first instance); [1939] 2 K.B. 752, CA; see para. 9–081, above.
[32] [1976] 2 E.G.L.R. 29; for facts, see para. 9–080, above. See also the Canadian case, *Avco Financial Services v. Holstein* (1980) 109 D.L.R. (3d) 128.
[33] (1952) 159 E.G. 496.
[34] See paras 9–022 *et seq.*, above.
[35] [1977] 2 E.G.L.R. 84, 86:
   "The factors and activities which a competent valuer will consider and undertake in valuing land cannot be composed in such a way as to indicate an unvarying approach to every problem which confronts him. But a collection of them from which he will choose at will in a given circumstance must include the following:
   (a) The kind of development of the land to be undertaken.
   (b) The existence, if any, of planning permission in outline or in detail as to a part or the whole of the land. And if permission be for the building of houses, the situation and acreage of part of the land excluded from planning permission because, for example, of a tree preservation order, the need for schools and the layout of roads and other things. Furthermore, the number of houses permitted or likely to be permitted to be built by the planning authority is a relevant, indeed a vital factor.
   (c) The history of the land, including its use, changes in ownership and the most recent buying prices, planning applications and permissions, the implementation or otherwise of existing planning permissions, the reason for the failure, if it be the fact that a planning permission had not been implemented.
   (d) The position of the land in relation to surrounding countryside, villages and towns and places of employment; the quality of access to it, the attractiveness or otherwise of its situation.
   (e) The situation obtaining about the provision of services for example, electricity, sewage and other drainage and water.
   (f) The presence, if it be so, of any unusual difficulties confronting development which will

for the purpose of enabling the plaintiff finance houses to estimate the amount which they could advance to developers on a first mortgage of the site. The defendants were held negligent in valuing the site at £2,200,000. Three years later it was only worth £600,000. The primary ground for the finding of negligence was that the defendants had merely carried out "a hurried paper exercise" founded upon very little of the information that proper observance of the first of the four stages into which Watkins J. analysed the task of valuing land[36] would have provided. That stage consisted of "the sometimes tedious and laborious but vital approach work" consisting of inspecting the site, several enquiries and much research. The site had no comparable and a "dismal development record". Nevertheless the defendants were found to have only cursorily inspected it and ignored its imperfect characteristics and to have failed to make proper enquiries of the county planning authority.[37] It may also be necessary to carry out additional enquiries if unusual instructions are given.[38]

The professional use of hearsay information. To what extent may a surveyor, in carrying out a valuation, rely upon information gathered and provided by others without checking it? The answer will depend upon the nature of the information, the reputation of the person or body supplying it, and the ordinary practice of the profession. Of necessity, much useful information to a surveyor will be hearsay, for example comparable values provided by local estate agents, and specimen rental values published in the specialist press. Quite apart from the relaxations provided by the Civil Evidence Act 1995, it is not necessary for evidence of the value of comparable properties to be strictly proved by first-hand evidence where the evidence establishes that competent valuers make valuations on the basis of market intelligence which is hearsay. In a ruling in *Banque Bruxelles Lambert SA v. Lewis & Tucker Ltd and others*,[39] Phillips J. distinguished *English Exporters (London) Ltd v. Eldonwall Ltd*[40] which itself had been   **9–102**

---

tend to increase the cost of it to an extent which affects the value of the land. A visit to the site must surely find a prominent place among physical activities to be undertaken.

(g) The demand in the immediate localities for houses of the kind likely to be built, with special regard to the situation of places of employment and increases to be expected in demand for labour. This will involve, inevitably, acquiring knowledge of other building developments recently finished or still in progress, especially having regard to rate of disposal, dens ity and sale price of the houses disposed of. In this way the existence, if any, of local comparables, a valuable factor, can be discovered.

(h) Consultation with senior officers of the local planning authority is almost always regarded as an indispensable aid, likewise a knowledge of the approval planning policy for the local area; a study of the approved town or county map may prove rewarding.

(i) Whether ascertaining from the client if there have been other previous valuations of the land, and to what effect, should be undertaken is probably questionable because a valuer's mind should not be exposed to the possibilities of affectation by the opinion of others.

(j) If he is a man whose usual professional activities do not bring him regularly into the locality, or what is more important has never done so, he will obviously need to be especially careful in collecting as much relevant local knowledge as he can, possibly by consulting valuers who work regularly in the area.

(k) The availability of a labour force which can carry out the prospective development."

[36] *ibid.* at 217 and set out at para. 9–076 above.

[37] Guidance as to the proper approach of surveyors instructed in respect of rating valuations was given in *McIntyre v. Herring Son and Daw* [1988] 1 E.G.L.R. 231.

[38] An example is provided by the facts of *Farley v. Skinner* [2000] P.N.L.R. 441 where specific instructions were given to check that a house did not suffer from aircraft noise and the judge held that this required a check with the Civil Aviation Authority at Gatwick (the relevant local airport).

[39] (*No. 1*), unreported, February 26, 1993.

[40] [1973] 1 Ch. 415.

approved by the Court of Appeal in *Rogers v. Rosedimond Investments (Blakes Market) Ltd.*[41] These cases concerned the use of comparable evidence for the purposes of rent reviews. Phillips J. concluded:

> "One would of course normally expect the actual value of a property, *i.e.* the value that it would actually realise on the market, to tally with the opinion of competent valuers as to its value. But the questions what is the actual value and what opinion would a competent valuer form of the actual value are two different questions and it is the latter with which I am concerned. *English Exporters* and *Rogers v. Rosedimond* were concerned with the former question and I do not consider that the principles pronounced in those cases are applicable in this."[42]

In *Abbey National Mortgages plc v. Key Surveyors Nationwide Ltd*[43] the Court of Appeal, approving the approach and reasoning of Phillips J., held that an expert valuer was not confined to giving evidence based on comparables of which he had direct first-hand knowledge; having made careful and appropriate inquiries, the valuer was fully entitled to rely on what appeared to him to be reliable information. Direct first-hand knowledge was not required.[44]

9–103   A surveyor should be wary of relying on information from a person whose interests conflict with those of his client. Unless specifically instructed to rely on it, such information should be independently checked if possible. In *Old Gate Estates Ltd v. Toplis and Harding and Russell*[45] it was alleged that the surveyor instructed to value a property to be conveyed to the claimant company was negligent in not inquiring into figures as to its rents and outgoings provided by two directors of the company who were also sellers of the property. Since in calculating the figures the rates had been grossly understated the valuation was excessive. The defendants conceded that in an ordinary valuation it would be negligent for a valuer to value a property without himself collecting the material such as rent and outgoings upon which the valuation was made. In the circumstances and particularly in view of the suppliers of the information being an accountant and surveyor respectively and hence competent to ascertain it, the defendants denied that they were negligent. In the event the issue was not resolved, the defendants escaping liability on other grounds. In *Love v. Mack*[46] a valuer instructed to value a mineral water factory was apparently "taken in and

---

[41] [1978] 2 E.G.L.R. 48.

[42] The principle discussed by Phillips J. was considered and applied *in Zubaida v. Hargreaves* [1993] 2 E.G.L.R. 170. The defendant valuer, appointed as an independent expert to determine the rent of a restaurant on a rent review, acted in accordance with a practice accepted as proper by competent, respected, and professional opinion, in using as comparables rents of similar shop units. An appeal was dismissed; see [1995] 1 E.G.L.R. 127. The Court of Appeal noted that the defendant's use of certain comparables was supported by a respectable body of professional opinion (see 128B), applied the test in *Bolam v. Friern Hospital Management Committee* [1957] 1 W.L.R. 582 and dismissed the appeal.

[43] [1996] 3 All E.R. 183, 189.

[44] In *Nyckeln Finance v. Edward Symmons & Partners* [1999] Lloyd's L.Rep. P.N. 953, a case before the introduction of the Civil Procedure Rules and the Civil Evidence Act 1998, the Court of Appeal considered a case where the defendant wished to adduce evidence of a number of contemporaneous valuations of the subject property itself. The claimant was not prepared to concede that the valuations were themselves competent and objected to the valuers being called, on the basis that the defendant would benefit from a greater number of experts than it was permitted to call. The Court considered that the defendant should have leave to call the original valuers, as their evidence was too potentially important to be excluded.

[45] [1939] 3 All E.R. 209

[46] (1905) 92 L.T. 345

defrauded" by the mortgagor, who exaggerated the takings of the licensed houses. It was alleged that he was negligent in not checking the takings book and brewers' and distillers' invoices. Kekewich J., however, concluded that such checks were more than what was required by the necessities of the case and that "a man is not liable to an action because he is defrauded".[47] In *Craneheath Securities v. York Montague*,[48] one of the respects in which it was alleged that the defendant surveyors were negligent was in relying on an estimate of turnover for a restaurant provided by directors of a vendor for the purposes of a valuation for the funders of a purchaser. The valuer made clear that he had not seen any audited accounts and the allegation was rejected on the basis that the claimant could not show that the estimate was, in fact, incorrect.

(e) *Failing to make a proper appraisal*

A survey will usually entail no more than inspection and observation and reporting the results to the client. A valuation or a development brief,[49] however, will require detailed appraisal of the results of inspection and other enquiries before the client can be advised properly. Appraisal may, depending upon the property and the complexity of the assignment, be an extensive task. Apart from a detailed analysis of information obtained it may involve construction of terms in documents of title, consideration of statutory and planning requirements, calculation of periodic incomes and outgoings and investment returns. Any recent market history of the property will also have to be researched and considered. Where a property has recently been sold a valuer who gives an open market valuation without considering the implications of that recent sale is likely to be, in the absence of express instructions from the lender, negligent.[50] In arriving at a valuation figure a surveyor will be expected to apply a proper method of valuation and often check it by another method.[51] Moreover, it is a

9–104

---

[47] *ibid.* at 350. In *Tenenbaum v. Garrod* [1988] 2 E.G.L.R. 178, a case described as "strange" by Mustill L.J. in the Court of Appeal, an estate agent who provided a "valuation" of certain factory buildings was held not liable to the plaintiff as the "valuation" had never been intended as a genuine independent valuation of the property, rather that it was a mere negotiating weapon for the plaintiff to use, who had not relied on it and who only sought to blame the defendant when his plan to purchase the property at undervalue failed.
[48] [2001] Lloyd's L.Rep. P.N. 348.
[49] *i.e.* instructions to assess the development potential of a site. It may also include instructions to plan and supervise the development. See article by J. Ratcliffe (1979) 251 E.G. 1260.
[50] See *Banque Bruxelles Lambert SA v. Eagle Star Insurance Co. Ltd* [1994] 2 E.G.L.R. 108, at 118, *per* Phillips J.
[51] 4 See *Singer & Friedlander Ltd v. John D. Wood & Co.* [1977] 2 E.G.L.R. 84, *per* Watkins J. The relevant passage is set out in para. 9–101, n. 35, above. For examples of negligence in applying a wrong method of valuation see *Jenkins v. Betham* (1855) 15 C.B. 167; *Whitty v. Lord Dillon* (1860) 2 F. & F. 67; *Weedon v. Hindwood, Clarke and Esplin* (1974) 234 E.G. 121; *McIntyre v. Herring Son & Daw* [1988] 1 E.G.L.R. 231; *Beaumont v. Humberts* [1990] 2 E.G.L.R. 166. Cases in which the claimant's claim failed include: *Muldoon v. Mays of Lilliput Ltd* [1993] 1 E.G.L.R. 43, and *Macey v. Debenham, Tewson & Chinnocks* [1993] 1 E.G.L.R. 149 where the claimant, a solicitor, retained the defendant valuers to advise in respect of the proposed purchase for investment of certain freehold property. The advice given was to purchase the property; such advice included an analysis of yields. The claimant's claim failed, he having failed to prove that the valuer's report, and the calculations and deductions on which it was based, were such as could not have been arrived at if he had shown reasonable skill and care.

task that requires not only knowledge, skill and care but also careful judgment.

9-105 The fact that a valuer makes a material and negligent error in reaching his figure will not usually establish liability where the total valuation figure was itself not negligently high, as defined by the principle expressed in *Bolam v. Friern Hospital Management Committee*.[52] In *Mount Banking Corporation Ltd v. Brian Cooper & Co.*[53] the court rejected a submission by the plaintiff that provided it proved negligent errors in a valuer's calculation, it was entitled to recover even though the final valuation was within acceptable limits. The deputy judge rejected the argument that *Corisand Investments Ltd v. Druce & Co.*[54] was authority for such a proposition, and held[55]: "If the valuation that has been reached cannot be impeached as a total, then, however erroneous the method or its application by which the valuation has been reached, no loss has been sustained because, within the Bolam principle, it was a proper valuation." The Court of Appeal reviewed the authorities and considered the proper approach to adopt for "margin of error" cases in *Merivale Moore PLC v. Strutt & Parker*.[56] Buxton L.J. made four points. First, the "bracket" is not to be determined in a mechanistic way, divorced from the facts of the particular case. Secondly, if it is proved that in reaching the valuation, the valuer adopted an unprofessional practice or approach then that fact may be taken into account in considering whether the valuation contained an unacceptable degree of error. Thirdly, where it is shown that the valuation is outside the acceptable limit that may be a strong indication that the valuer has been negligent. However, the question still remains whether the valuer has been negligent in accordance with the principle expressed in *Bolam*: "To find that his valuation fell outside the 'bracket' is, as held by this Court in *Craneheath* and also, I consider, by the House of Lords in *Banque Lambert*, a necessary condition of liability, but it cannot in itself be sufficient." Fourthly, the adduction of expert valuation evidence is not a necessary precondition to a finding of negligence on the part of a valuer.

> "I think that it is still open to the judge in a suitable case to hold that the valuation is so far removed from what was the true value of the property that it must be regarded as a valuation that was outside the limits open to a competent valuer, without specific professional evidence being given of what those limits were."

Buxton L.J. commented however, that such evidence "plainly made the task of the trial judge much easier".

It should, however, be noted that the above approach is only likely to be appropriate if the only relevant obligation of a valuer is to produce a figure which a competent valuer could have produced. Thus in *Arab Bank v. John D. Wood Commercial Ltd*,[57] Mance L.J., after a full review of the authorities contemplated that a valuer could be liable for a discrete error (such as a failure to take account

---

[52] [1957] 1 W.L.R. 582.
[53] [1992] 2 E.G.L.R. 142. See also *Legal & General Mortgage Services Ltd v. HPC Professional Services* [1997] P.N.L.R. 567 where *Mount Banking* was followed. For a discussion on "the bracket" approach to valuation see J. Murdoch, "The margin of error approach to negligence in valuations" (1997) 3 P.N. 31.
[54] [1978] 2 E.G.L.R. 86.
[55] [1992] 2 E.G.L.R. 142, 145D.
[56] [1999] Lloyd's Rep. P.N. 734 at 744. See further para. 9–061 above.
[57] [2000] Lloyd's L.Rep. P.N. 173.

of asbestos) which would have affected his final figure.[58] In that case, the Court of Appeal considered that as the relevant valuation was more than 20 per cent different from the correct valuation, the valuer had an evidential burden to overcome to show that he had not been negligent which burden had not been discharged.[59]

Proper appraisal may be particularly difficult in a property "boom" but as Phillips J. stated in *Banque Bruxelles Lambert SA v. Eagle Star Insurance Co. Ltd*,[60] when a property market is booming it is inevitable that the current market price will be affected by the entry into the market of property speculators hoping to make capital gains. No discount falls to be made from the open market valuation for that reason. The consequences of an earlier property market "boom" are illustrated by *Corisand Investments Ltd v. Druce & Co.*[61] The defendant valuers were instructed to value a portfolio of properties including a hotel for the purpose of raising further finance secured upon a second mortgage. The plaintiffs were willing to lend up to 70 per cent of the valuation and they advanced a total of £60,000. Shortly after, there was a collapse in the property market, the borrower defaulted, the first mortgagees appointed a receiver and the properties were sold, including the hotel, for a total of £125,250. There remained nothing on sale to satisfy the second mortgage debt of £60,000. The plaintiffs sued the defendants, alleging that their valuation of the hotel was so excessive as to have been negligent. Gibson J. held that the defendants were negligent in three respects. First, the valuation reflected an estimate of the hotel's expenses which was excessively low. Secondly, while the defendants were not negligent in not anticipating or suspecting the impending collapse of the property market, they were negligent in not excluding from their valuation or identifying for the plaintiffs' guidance the speculative content (put at 20 per cent) in the estimated open market price, characteristic of a price "boom".[62] This finding followed from the judge's view that it was the duty of the defendants in preparing a valuation for mortgage purposes to exclude from their valuation any apparent content which might well not be available for sale by the mortgagee when he attempted to realise his security.[63] Thirdly, the defendants failed to allow in their valuation for expenditure necessary to put the hotel into the condition required by the Fire Precautions Act 1971:

"it was in my judgment the duty of a valuer preparing a valuation for mortgage purposes to make appropriate allowances for any significant defect or problem[64] in respect of which the purchasers in the market would calculate that they would have to

---

[58] At 181. See further para. 9–059 above for a full discussion of the margin of error.

[59] *ibid.* at 194–195.

[60] [1994] 2 E.G.L.R. 108 at 117.

[61] [1978] 2 E.G.L.R. 86.

[62] Phillips J. pointed out in *Banque Bruxelles Lambert SA v. Eagle Star Insurance Co. Ltd* [1994] 2 E.G.L.R. 108 at 117, that the basis of valuation being described by Gibson J. is a forced sale valuation, and that his comments should not be applied to an open market valuation. It does not, however, necessarily follow that a "forced sale" value (*i.e.* one within a limited period of time) will be lower than an open market value. For an example of a case where it was found that it was reasonable for there to be no discount in respect of a sale within 90 days to a mortgagee in possession, see *UCB Corporate Services Ltd v. Halifax (SW) Ltd and another* [2000] 1 E.G.L.R. 87.

[63] *cf.* Watkins J. in *Singer & Friedlander Ltd v. John D. Wood & Co.* [1977] 2 E.G.L.R. 84, 85.

[64] *e.g.* the "dismal development record" of the site in *Singer & Friedlander Ltd v. John D. Wood & Co.* [1977] 2 E.G.L.R. 84 (see para. 9–101, above).

spend money before being able to operate the hotel to make the estimated net income".[65]

Allowing reductions of 20 per cent for the speculative content and £8,000 for fire precaution works, the judge concluded that the hotel valuation was excessive by £63,000.[66]

In *Watts v. Savills*,[67] the valuer was held negligent at first instance for his failure to value on the basis that the land had significant development potential. This decision was reversed on appeal, it being held that whether land had development potential (and therefore a greatly enhanced value) was a question of opinion, and not fact. A valuer could therefore be mistaken without being negligent. It was only if no reasonably competent valuer, acting with reasonable skill and care, could have formed the view that the land had no development potential, that the defendant valuer could be held liable.

(f) *Inadequate report*

9–107 The nature of the report required will vary according to a surveyor's instructions. An oral report may only have been requested, although a written report is usually required and is always desirable. A written report is a vital document in surveyors' negligence cases not merely for its contents but also because it is indicative of what was done or not done by the surveyor.[68] For example, errors of omission or commission in a report are commonly the consequences of earlier errors in inspecting. The detail required will vary according to the instructions and circumstances in each case. A building or structural survey report will usually be much more detailed than a valuation report. Where pro-forma or approved report forms are used there is less opportunity for omission or misunderstanding as to the extent of the inspection. Even in the case of a valuation, much more may be required than simple quotation of a figure. For example, Watkins J. in *Singer & Friedlander Ltd v. John D. Wood & Co.*[69] stated that "a bank, although interested mainly in a figure or valuation is entitled to be made aware by the valuer of the whole of the circumstances of the planning history of the site, including his firm's previous acquaintance with it".[70] In the case of a building or structural survey the report should set out the facts and in particular state matters of significance and warn of material defects so as to enable a proper decision to be made.[71] In order to avoid a misleading impression certain general

---

[65] [1978] 2 E.G.L.R. 86, 99.

[66] Further cases arising out of valuations prepared during a distended property market are discussed at para. 9–150.

[67] Unreported, June 26, 1998, CA.

[68] Note *Barton v. Stuart Hepburn & Co.* [1926] E.G.D. 206. Rowlatt J. expressed the view that surveyors instructed to carry out a valuation should state in their report that they had not conducted a detailed inspection or thorough survey if that be the case.

[69] [1977] 2 E.G.L.R. 84.

[70] *ibid.* at 93.

[71] In *Summers v. Congreve Horner & Co.* [1991] 2 E.G.L.R. 139, Judge Fox-Andrews Q.C. held that there were four elements to a structural survey: the preparation for a visual inspection, the visual inspection, an evaluation of what had been seen at the inspection and the written report. The case went to the Court of Appeal on the issue of insurance cover, [1992] 2 E.G.L.R. 152. Note Lord Cameron's definition of "anything of significance" in *Stewart v. H.A. Brechin & Co.* 1959 S.C. 306, 308. The relevant passage is set out in para. 9–082, above. A surveyor abiding by the relevant Guidance Notes issued by the RICS should be able to demonstrate compliance with approved and general practice.

words may need to be avoided.[72] Moreover, if a surveyor cannot ascertain any fact he should say that he was unable to do so and, therefore, unable to express any opinion on it.[73]

Failure to warn.[74] Failure to warn is the subject of numerous surveyors'   **9–108** negligence cases and is frequently expressed to be the relevant default although the effective default may be an antecedent failure to inspect or to observe.[75] Certain defects call for a specific warning, for example, dry rot[76] and death watch beetle.[77] Further, the warning given must be sufficient. Thus, for example, Bristow J. in *Daisley v. B. S. Hall & Co.*[78] in considering the risk of settlement owing to shrinkable clay stated: "If circumstances are such that the risk is high, clearly [the surveyor] should warn his client not to go on with the purchase. If circumstances are such that the risk is very small it must, in my judgment, be his duty to say so."[79] In *Cross v. David Martin and Mortimer*[80] a surveyor carrying out an inspection for a RICS House Buyer's Report and Valuation correctly observed and briefly reported on the method of construction of a loft conversion. He was, however, held negligent[81] in failing to comment in his report more fully on the possible consequences of the conversion, namely that the original design concept of the roof had been violated, that the effect of what had been done could only be calculated with difficulty and that the roof space might not be capable of bearing the live loading imposed by a habitable room. The report should have expressly warned the plaintiffs that unless the conversion had received building regulation approval, it would not be safe to use the loft for anything other than

---

[72] *e.g.* in *Hood v. Shaw* (1960) 176 E.G. 1291 the defendant surveyor's description of the structure of a house as "sound and substantial" was criticised by Paull J. See also *BFG Bank AG v. Brown & Mumford Ltd* [1997] P.N.L.R. 202 where the Court of Appeal held that negligent valuers could only escape liability on their arguments that a letter was not a valuation and that the plaintiff should not have relied upon it if the plaintiff's interpretation of the same was unreasonable: "the question is whether an ordinary person to whom the letter was addressed could reasonably have thought that the extent of the risk being referred to was that there was no more than a 5 per cent risk of planning permission being refused" *per* Scott V.-C. at 208F.

[73] See *Rona v. Pearce* (1953) 162 E.G. 380, *per* Hilbery J.; also see *Hill v. Debenham, Tewson and Chinnocks* (1958) 171 EG 835, 837, *per* Judge Carter Q.C. "But applying the standard of the profession I entertain no doubt that the practice of the profession is 'If you do not look, you must warn.'"

[74] Despite the superficial attraction, there is no analogy between the cases discussed in this paragraph and the extensive jurisprudence on "failure to warn" in the context of medical negligence. See chap. 12, para. 12–201 *et seq.* None of the justifications for failing to warn of known risks of medical treatment applies in the context of advice about real property.

[75] See *Hill v. Debenham, Tewson and Chinnocks* (*ibid.*) for several instances of failure to warn; also *Lees v. English and Partners* [1977] E.G.D. 566 (failure to warn of bad "tie" between old and new brickwork); *Allen v. Ellis & Co.* [1990] 1 E.G.L.R. 170 (failure to warn of defective garage roof); *Alliance & Leicester Building Society v. J. & E. Shepherd* [1995] G.W.D. 11–608, OH, Lord MacLean (complaint of failure to warn of risk of flooding on the property from the nearby River Tay and Inchewan Burn, held, the plaintiff had not established that at the date of the survey no reasonably competent surveyor would have failed to appreciate that the property was at risk of flooding).

[76] See, *e.g. Hardy v. Wamsley-Lewis* (1967) 203 E.G. 1039. Paull J. there stated (at 1043) that it was clearly the surveyor's duty to report that what he found there had been dry rot, irrespective of its being dormant or not; also *Tremayne v. T. Mortimer Burrows and Partners* (1954) 165 E.G. 232.

[77] See *Oswald v. Countrywide Surveyors Ltd* [1994] E.G.C.S. 150, an infestation of woodworm had been reported, but the failure to specify an active infestation by death watch beetle, which caused considerably more damage than woodworm, was held to be negligent.

[78] (1972) 225 E.G. 1553.

[79] *ibid.* at 1555.

[80] [1989] 1 E.G.L.R. 154.

[81] *ibid.* at 158.

light storage. Similarly in *Izzard v. Field Palmer*,[82] a mortgage valuer who (correctly) observed that a former Ministry of Defence property was built using the Jesperson system, was found liable for failing to point out the defects in such a system or the effect that such a construction had on mortgage value. Frequently, survey reports contain standard clauses to the effect that no responsibility can be accepted in respect of defects in inaccessible or uninspected parts of the property.[83] This may be construed as a general warning and is often pleaded to rebut liability for undiscovered defects. In deciding such a clause's efficacy, much will depend upon its particular terms and the particular defects overlooked.[84] Such a clause is unlikely to help the surveyor if he both should and could have examined in an uninspected part where an existing material defect is subsequently discovered, as happened in *Heatley v. William H. Brown Ltd*.[85]

9–109   A valuer will not generally be liable to warn his client against the risk that others might reach a different, incorrect, valuation. This proposition is illustrated by the facts of the Australian case, *Flemington Properties Pty Ltd v. Raine & Horne Commercial Pty Ltd*.[86] The valuer had been retained to provide an opinion as to the "unimproved" value of some land in accordance with a New South Wales statute. The claimant had then purchased the land in reliance on the valuation whereupon the Valuer General wrongly valued the land at lower than the "worse case" scenario provided by the valuer. The Full Court of the Federal Court of Australia held that the valuer was not under a duty to guard against the risk of a misapplication of the statute. Tamberlin J. stated[87]:

> "The suggestion that [the valuer] ought to have warned the applicant that an incorrect, one lot basis of valuation might be used, cannot be accepted. The retainer should not be construed to require a determination of a figure on a basis contrary to the provisions of the Act or to warn that such an approach might be followed. A 'worst case' assessment calls for an assessment based on the application of proper valuation principles, having due regard to the correct interpretation of the Act. The possibility that a valuation might be arrived at, which is based on principles or provisions outside or foreign to the requirements of the Act, is contrary to the role of the valuer. If it were otherwise it would be extremely difficult, if not impossible, to give any satisfactory valuation advice. The task of the valuer, in this case was to apply the correct principles as required by the Act.
>
> In other words, a valuer cannot reasonably be under a duty to provide to a client a valuation by way of warning, which presupposes that the land will be valued on an erroneous basis. In the present case, of course, the position is that the valuation was made on what has been found to be a correct basis. The possibility that it might have been made on another basis which is erroneous is irrelevant. There is no breach of the retainer or negligence in carrying out a valuation on correct principles and warning a client as to the lower range valuations arrived at by the application of correct principles in accordance with the Act."

---

[82] [2000] 1 E.G.L.R. 76.
[83] See para. 9–073, above.
[84] See the discussion of exclusion clauses at paras 9–063 *et seq.*, above. The cases of *Stevenson v. Nationwide Building Society* [1990] 1 A.C. 831 and *McCullagh v. Lane Fox & Partners* [1996] 1 E.G.L.R. 35 are particularly relevant.
[85] [1992] 1 E.G.L.R. 289. See para. 9–092, above.
[86] (1998) 155 A.L.R. 345.
[87] At 346.

3. DAMAGES

An award of damages will usually be the only remedy for breach of duty by a **9–110**
surveyor. In certain circumstances a surveyor may be deprived of his fees.
Reported cases, however, do not reveal a consistent approach to the issue of
whether a negligent surveyor should be so deprived. In some cases recovery of
fees has been allowed[88] presumably on the basis that such fees would have been
incurred even if proper advice had been given. In other cases despite a damages
award for the extent of the loss sustained, fees have not been recovered[89] and
even been ordered to be repaid.[90] The preferable approach is to allow recovery
of fees where damages for the loss are awarded unless the surveyor's advice was
so wrong as properly to be described as worthless.[91]

Once a breach of contract or act of negligence has been established, the **9–111**
following questions may arise as to the recoverability of damage:

(a) Has the claimant sustained the loss claimed?[92]

(b) Is the loss claimed within the scope of the Defendant's duty?[93]

(c) Are the damages claimed too remote?[94]

(d) What is the correct measure of damages?[95]

(a) *Has the claimant sustained the loss claimed?*

A primary requirement for the recovery of damages is that the claimant should **9–112**
be able to establish that it has suffered the loss claimed or is to be taken as having
suffered such loss. A court will, in appropriate circumstances, be prepared to
disregard an artificial loss. Thus in *H.I.T. Finance Ltd v. Lewis & Tucker Ltd.*[96]
the claimant was unable to recover contractual interest which it had had to pay
to its two parents in order to make a loan following a negligent valuation from
the defendants. The claimant had only one executive officer, whose salary was
paid by a parent company. It had no other staff, no separate offices, no capital and
any residual profits were passed to its parents. The claimant was unable to
borrow funds to support its lending activities on the open market but was

---

[88] *Last v. Post* (1952) 1 9 E.G. 240; the claim for fees was admitted in *Bell Hotels (1935) Ltd v. Motion* (1952) 159 E.G. 496; *Conn v. Munday* (1955) 166 E.G. 465; *Corisand Investments Ltd v. Druce & Co.* [1978] 2 E.G.L.R. 86.
[89] *Sincock v. Bangs (Reading)* [1952] C.P.L. 562; *Hill v. Debenham, Tewson and Chinnocks* (1958) 171 E.G. 835; *Buckland v. Watts* (1968) 208 E.G. 969. In the first and third cases fees for other work were recovered. In *Whitty v. Lord Dillon* (1860) 2 F. & F. 67 the defence of *non indebitatus* succeeded against a claim for fees in respect of advice held to have been negligent.
[90] *Chong v. Scott Collins & Co.* (1954) 164 E.G. 662; *Hoadley v. Edwards* [2001] E.G.C.S. 46.
[91] See *Hill v. Debenham, Tewson and Chinnocks* (1958) 171 E.G. 835, 839, and the passages there quoted from Cockburn C.J.'s judgment in *Whitty v. Lord Dillon* (1860) 2 F. & F. 67 and from Best C.J.'s judgment in *Moneypenny v. Hartland* (1826) 2 C. & P. 378. In *Bigg v. Howard Son & Gooch* [1990] 1 E.G.L.R. 173 the plaintiff conceded that the defendant surveyors were entitled to set off against the plaintiff's damages the sum counterclaimed for fees.
[92] See para. 9–112 below.
[93] See para. 9–113 below.
[94] See para. 9–119 below.
[95] See para. 9–128 below.
[96] [1993] 2 E.G.L.R. 231.

constrained to borrow from its parent companies. Wright J. held that the claimant had no independence of operation, it was simply a financial arm of its two parents. Examining the underlying realities, the judge concluded that it was the parents who, in truth, provided the money for the loan, through the instrument of the claimant and that it was these two companies, rather than the claimant, which had suffered the loss that flowed from the negligence of the defendant. There was no evidence before the judge as to how the parent companies had financed the money that they passed to the claimant for onward loan. Nor was there any evidence showing how such money, if not lent to the claimant, would have been profitably employed. The judge felt able to take notice of the fact that both parent companies were, or were owned by major public limited companies and that surplus funds would be put to the best available use. The judge awarded one per cent over clearing bank base rate simple interest on the fluctuating balance due for the period since the loan was made.[97]

(b) *Is the loss claimed within the scope of the defendant's duty?*

9–113   In England, this question may arise as a result of the decision of the House of Lords in *BBL v. Eagle Star*.[98] The cases arose in the context of losses claimed by lenders who had made secured loans on the basis of negligent valuations of real property which had subsequently fallen in value. Although the actual decision applies directly only to such cases, the potential application of the principle is much greater. The Court of Appeal had described as "the necessary point of departure" the well-known and well-established principle that where an injury was to be compensated by damages, the damages should be as nearly as possible the sum which would put the plaintiff in the position in which he would have been if he had not been injured. The House of Lords disagreed, holding that it was first necessary to decide for what kind of loss the plaintiff was entitled to compensation. Lord Hoffmann noted the following points:

1.   The valuer was required by contract to provide an estimate of the price which the property might reasonably be expected to fetch if sold on the open market at the date of the valuation.

2.   The estimate of the price was information that was to form part of the material on which the lender was to decide whether, and if so how much,

---

[97] See also *G.U.S. Property Management Ltd v. Littlewoods Mail Order Stores Ltd*, 1982 S.L.T. 533 on the question of arm's-length transactions. In *Nykredit Mortgage Bank plc v. Edward Erdman Group Ltd*, October 1, 1993 (unreported), Judge Byrt Q.C. awarded the claimant interest at its borrowing rate on the money market, it being agreed that such a rate precisely reflected the loss suffered by the claimant. The rate varied between 0.25 to 0.4 over LIBOR from time to time and was calculated as simple interest on the capital sum lent, £2.45 m., from the date of the advance, giving credit for receipts of capital by way of reduction in the capital sum. Subsequent appeals did not touch on this point: Court of Appeal, damages: [1995] Q.B. 375, Court of Appeal, liability: [1996] 1 E.G.L.R. 119, and House of Lords, damages: [1997] A.C. 191.

[98] [1997] A.C. 191, Lord Goff, Lord Jauncey, Lord Slynn, Lord Nicholls, Lord Hoffmann. Only one reasoned speech was delivered, by Lord Hoffmann. The cases heard together for this appeal were *South Australia Asset Management Corporation v. York Montague Ltd*, (unreported) April 6, 1995, May J.; *United Bank of Kuwait plc v. Prudential Property Services Ltd* [1994] 2 E.G.L.R. 100, Gage J., [1995] Q.B. 375, CA.; *Nykredit Mortgage Services Ltd v. Edward Erdman Group Ltd*, Judge Byrt Q.C. sitting as a judge of the Queen's Bench Division, unreported, October 1, 1993. An appeal on liability in the latter case was heard subsequent to the appeal on damages: [1996] 1 E.G.L.R. 119, CA. See also para. 9–115 below.

to lend to the borrower. The valuation informs the lender of what the security is likely to be worth (at current values) if it has to be sold, and enables the lender to decide upon the appropriate loan to valuation cushion. This cushion is intended to cover contingencies such as a fall in the property market and non-negligent differences between the valuation and the actual market value.

3. Although the valuer knows that if he overvalues the property, the cushion will be reduced, he is not privy to the other considerations that the lender will take into account, such as the strength of the borrower's covenant, the value of other security to be offered, and the profitability of the proposed loan.

4. Because the valuer knows that the valuation is likely to be a very important element in the decisions to be made by the lender, the law implies a term into the contract of reasonable care and skill. The relationship between the parties also gives rise to a concurrent duty in tort,[99] the scope of the duty of care being the same as in contract.

5. A lender who sues a valuer, whether in contract or tort, must prove not only that the duty was owed, but that it was a duty in respect of the kind of loss which the lender has suffered.[1]

6. The scope of a valuer's duty is to be deduced in tort from the purpose of the rule imposing the duty. In the case of an implied contractual duty, the nature and extent of the liability is defined by the term which the law implies. The scope of the duty is that which the law regards as best giving effect to the express obligations assumed by the valuer, neither cutting them down so that the lender obtains less than he was reasonably entitled to expect, nor extending them so as to impose on the valuer a liability greater than he could reasonably have thought he was undertaking.

Lord Hoffman enunciated an apparently general principle, that a person under **9–114** a duty to take reasonable care to provide information on which someone else will decide upon a course of action is, if negligent, not generally regarded as responsible for all the consequences which flow from the course of action. He is responsible only for the consequences of the information being wrong. He made an apparently important distinction between a duty to provide information for the purpose of enabling another to decide upon a course of action, and a duty to advise another as to what course of action to adopt. In the former case, the informant must use reasonable skill and care to ensure that the information provided is correct. If it is not, and the informant is negligent, he will be responsible for all the reasonably foreseeable consequences of the information being wrong. In the latter case, the advisor must take reasonable care to consider all the potential consequences of that course of action, and if the advice is

---

[99] *Henderson v. Merrett Syndicates Ltd* [1995] 2 A.C. 145, HL.
[1] For this proposition, Lord Hoffmann relied upon *Caparo Industries plc v. Dickman* [1990] 2 A.C. 605, HL. See Chap. 15, para. 15–053 for discussion on this case. In *Caparo Industries plc* the House of Lords considered the duty in tort owed by auditors to shareholders. There was no contract between the parties, hence the need to consider the purposes of the audit. In the *Banque Bruxelles Lambert SA* cases, all the lenders, whether those who appeared in the Court of Appeal, or in the House of Lords, sued in contract as well as tort. It is not easy to transplant an analysis formulated for a tort only action to a case where the parties have regulated their position by contract.

negligent, the advisor will be responsible for all the reasonably foreseeable loss which is a consequence of that course of action being taken. The work ordinarily carried out by surveyors and valuers will, in the absence of express agreement, almost always fall into the category of providers of information.

9–115   In *Nykredit v. Edward Erdman (No. 2)*,[2] Lord Hoffman emphasised that the limitation on the damages recoverable by the lender arose not from any principle relating to causation or the measure of damages but rather from a limitation on the extent of the duty itself. He stated:

> "The principle approved by the House was that the valuer owes no duty of care othte lender in respect of his entering into the transaction as such and the it is therefore insufficient, for the purpose of establishing liability on the part of the valuer, to prove that the lender is worse off thane he would have been if he had not lent the money at all. What he must show is that he is worse off as a lender than he would have been if the security had been worth what the valuer said . . .
>
> It is important to emphasise that this is a consequence of the limited way in which the House defined the valuer's duty of care and has nothing to do with questions of causation or any limit or 'cap' imposed upon damages which would otherwise be recoverable. It was accepted that the whole loss suffered by reason of the fall in the property market was, as a matter of causation, properly attributable to the lender having entered into the transaction and that, but for the negligent valuation, he would not have done so. It was not suggested that the possibility of a fall in the market was unforeseeable or that there was any other factor which negatived the causal connection between lending and losing the money."[3]

9–116   Since *BBL*, the tendency in England has been to apply it as a form of special rule applicable so as to limit damages in the case of valuations or other information provided for lenders.[4] There has not been a case where it has been found that a valuer has advised as to the course of action which a lender should adopt rather than merely providing information. Similarly there has been no case where it has been found that the foreseeable consequences of information being wrong extended beyond the amount of damage which would have been sustained had the information been correct.[5] In *Platform Home Loans Ltd v. Oyston Shipways*,[6] Lord Cooke, in his dissenting judgment, hinted that he would have been prepared to consider an argument that the decision in *BBL* should be overturned.[7] Lord Hobhouse, giving one of the two speeches of the majority stated "The [BBL] principle is essentially a legal rule which is applied in a robust way without the need for fine tuning or a detailed investigation of causation."[8] He went on to point out that the novelty in Lord Hoffman's approach lay in applying principles

---

[2] [1997] 1 W.L.R. 1627.

[3] *ibid.* at 1638.

[4] For the application of the principle to solicitors see paras. 10–244 to 10–248 below. In *Aneco v. Johnson*, H.L., October 18, 2001, the majority of the House of Lords held that the important question was to determine the extent of a professionals instructions. That matter was simply a question of fact.

[5] For an example of a case where such a submission was rejected, see *Ball v. Banner* [2000] Lloyd's L.Rep. P.N. 569 at 582 to 583 *per* Hart J., where it was found that damages recoverable by investors on the basis of statements attributed to a property advisor in an Enterprise Zone prospectus were limited to the difference between the value of the investment if the statements had been correct and the value on the basis of the incorrect statement. The decision that the property advisor was liable was overturned on a different basis on appeal.

[6] [2000] 2 A.C. 190—see further para. 9–166 below.

[7] *ibid.* at 198D–E.

[8] *ibid.* at 207G.

which had previously been thought to apply to kinds of damage to its quantification.[9] In *Western Trust v. Strutt & Parker*,[10] the Court of Appeal rejected an argument that because a valuer had not valued precisely the same property as that on which a lender had lent, it was clear that the loan was outside the scope of his duty. Although Lord Woolf M.R. accepted that if the difference between the property which the valuer had valued and that relied upon by the lender for the purposes of making the loan was of sufficient significance, the proposition would be correct, that was not the case on the facts. An example of the application of the principles in *BBL* beyond its immediate factual context is provided by *Europe Mortgage Co Ltd v. GA Property Services Ltd*[11] where a valuer provided a negligent valuation of a large country house. But for the valuation, the lender would not have entered into the transaction at all. Some six years later the claimant disposed of its interest in the loan at a discount to a subsidiary whilst retaining its interest in any claim against the valuer. At that time, had there been a default, the claimant would have been able to repossess the property and satisfy its security. Moore-Bick J. upheld the defendant's contention that the scope of its duty extended only to a loss represented by a shortfall in the value of the property and consequently dismissed the claim.[12]

Even when applied to lending cases, the reasoning in *BBL* has received far **9–117** from universal approval.[13] In *Kenny & Good v. MGICA*,[14] the High Court of Australia had to consider a case where a valuer was required to provide an assessment of a development. The report expressly acknowledged that MGICA, the provider of a mortgage indemnity guarantee, might use and rely on the report. In addition to providing a valuation, the report stated that the property was "suitable security for investment of trust funds to the extent of 65% of our valuation for a term of 3–5 years". The property was valued at $5.35m. as it stood and at $5.5m. on completion, whereas the true value was between $3.9m. and $4m. On sale under two years after valuation, the property fetched only $2.65m. The five members of the High Court unanimously decided that MGICA was entitled to recover the entirety of its loss, although the reasoning of the four different judgments differed. Guadron J. rejected the approach taken by Lord Hoffman altogether. He regarded the critical question as being whether any part of the loss would have been avoided if the original valuation had been correct.[15] As he regarded the valuation as being the decisive consideration in MGICA's decision to insure the loan[16] and there was no suggestion that any loss would

---

[9] *ibid.* at 209G.
[10] [1999] P.N.L.R. 154 at 165.
[11] (1999) E.G.L.R. 77.
[12] In *Housing Loan Corporation v. William H. Brown* [1999] Lloyd's L.Rep. P.N. 185, the Court of Appeal held that a judge would have been entitled to find that a lender's loss occasioned as a result of making a loan based upon what it believed to be forced sale valuations of a property would have been beyond the scope of the valuer's duty given that the valuations were, in fact, given on an open market basis. The Court of Appeal upheld the judge's conclusion that the plaintiff had failed to establish reliance. See further para. 9–121 below.
[13] See *e.g.* Jane Stapleton, "Negligent valuers and falls in the property market" (1997) 113 L.Q.R. 1; Hugh Evans, "The scope of the duty revisited" (2001) 17 P.N. 146. It has been followed in New Zealand—see *Bank of New Zealand v. New Zealand Guardian Trust Co. Ltd* [1999] 1 N.Z.L.R. 664 at 682–683.
[14] (1999) 163 A.L.R. 611.
[15] *ibid.* at 620.
[16] *ibid.* at 619.

have been recoverable had the valuation been correct, the whole loss was recoverable. McHugh J. regarded the question as turning upon the proper construction of the contract between the valuer and the claimant or, in the case of a claim for negligent mis-statement, on the proper interpretation and ambit of the statement. In the ordinary case he regarded the valuer as being liable "only for such losses as a reasonable person would regard as flowing naturally from the negligent valuation or which are of a kind that should have been within the valuer's contemplation".[17]

Later he stated:

> "In the case of money lent on a valuation, the damages are confined to the difference between what was lent and what would have been lent on the true value of the property together with such expenses and other losses that were sufficiently likely to result from the breach of duty or that they were within the reasonable contemplation of the parties to the contract or arrangement. In either case, losses do not include the consequences of subsequent market declines."[18]

The reason why losses would not ordinarily include subsequent market declines was in McHugh J's view that insofar as a possible decline in market values was reasonably foreseeable, such a decline would already be factored into the true value of the property at the date of valuation whilst insofar as the decline was not reasonably foreseeable it was to be regarded as being outside the contemplation of the parties to the valuation arrangements.[19] In *Kenny* itself, however, McHugh J. took the view that the extent of the valuer's liability did extend to the whole of the loss—essentially because the statements made by the valuer related not merely to the value of the property but to the safety of the investment proposed.[20] Gummow J. agreed with the essence of McHugh J.'s reasoning whilst drawing a further distinction arising from the fact that MGICA's loss could not have occurred any earlier than when the mortgagor defaulted.[21] Kirby and Callinan JJ. had no difficulty in finding that, on the particular facts in *Kenny*, the whole loss would be recoverable as having been "foreshadowed in plain terms by the language of the instructions to the appellant which made clear the purpose for which the valuation was being procured"[22] but did not consider it necessary to formulate "general principles for the determination of the quantification of damages generally in cases of negligent valuations of property".[23]

9–118   The position in Australia therefore appears to be as follows:

(a) there is no question of there being any special rule whether of contract or tort applicable to the negligent valuation of property;

(b) where a valuer makes statements not merely as to the value of property but as to the wisdom of making a loan or otherwise extends the scope of his

---

[17] *ibid.* at 623.
[18] *ibid.* at 623.
[19] *ibid.* at 627 to 629.
[20] *ibid.* at 630.
[21] *ibid.* at 636.
[22] *ibid.* at 645.
[23] *ibid.* at 644.

duty, he will be liable for losses occasioned by subsequent falls in the property market;

(c) it may be important to decide whether the lender would have sustained part of the loss even if the valuation had been correct (for example because he would have made a smaller loan)[24];

(d) where a valuer merely gives advice as to the value of a property but a lender would not have made any loan but for such advice, the position is unclear.[25]

(c) *Remoteness*

Recovery of damages is subject to the overriding requirement that the loss or damage for which compensation is sought is not too remote. Broadly this requirement demands that the loss or damage must have been (i) caused[26] by the breach of duty; and (ii) be reasonably foreseeable[27]; and (iii) that recovery is not precluded by considerations of public or social policy.[28] **9–119**

(i) *Causation*

It is for the plaintiff to plead and prove causation of loss, and the mere fact that negligence has been established does not debar the negligent defendant from contesting this issue.[29] The plaintiff must prove that a breach of duty[30] on the part of the surveyor was the cause of the loss complained of. If the breach was not the cause of any injury, a claim in contract would succeed to the extent of an award of nominal damages only. A claim in tort would in those circumstances fail completely, as damage is a necessary component of the cause of action. **9–120**

Reliance. The essence of a surveyor's tasks discussed in this chapter being the giving of advice, the question of causation in such cases often resolves itself primarily into a question of reliance. Was the particular loss or damage sustained in consequence of reliance upon the surveyor's advice? However, although, establishing that the damage was sustained in consequence of the negligent **9–121**

---

[24] Following Guadron J.'s reasoning.

[25] McHugh and Gummow JJ. considered that losses occasioned by subsequent falls in the value of the property would not be recoverable whilst Guadron J. suggests that they would be. Kirby and Callinan JJ. reserved their position The reasoning of McHugh J. and Gummow J. would tend to suggest that losses occasioned by the fall in the property market will not.

[26] As to which see para. 9–120, below.

[27] As to which see para. 9–125, below.

[28] For a statement of the general principles see *McGregor*, paras 136–231 (in relation to tort) and paras. 232–281 (in relation to contract).

[29] See *Thomas Miller & Co. v. Richard Saunders & Partners* [1989] 1 E.G.L.R. 267, where it was argued that negligence by surveyors having been found, causation had to be assumed. Reliance was placed on certain dicta of Lord Denning M.R. in *Heywood v. Wellers* [1976] Q.B. 446 at 459, and *Coldman v. Hill* [1919] 1 K.B. 443. The judge held that such cases were an exception to the general rule and that the instant case did not fall within such an exception. He then held that there was no causal link between the negligence and the loss and gave judgment for the defendants. The dicta in *Heywood v. Wellers* had in fact been disapproved by the House of Lords in *Wilsher v. Essex Area Health Authority* [1988] A.C. 1074, H.L. See Chap. 10, para. 10–262 and Chap. 12, para. 12–077.

[30] In contract or tort.

advice is a necessary part of establishing reliance, it is not sufficient.[31] In *BBL* at first instance[32] Phillips J. held that in order to establish reliance on a valuation, a lender had to do more than establish that, but for the valuation, it would not have made the loan. It had to establish that it believed the valuation to be correct. It is submitted that this approach is correct.[33] Therefore, where a person does not consider a valuation correct but would not have made a loan without it (because, for example, he needs the valuation to protect his own position), there will be no reliance. Thus, in *Tenenbaum v. Garrod*[34] the Court of Appeal upheld the finding of the trial judge that the plaintiff had not relied upon a "spoof" valuation, procured by the plaintiff from the defendant solely for use by him as part of a scheme to acquire property at undervalue.[35] Similarly if the claimant fundamentally misinterprets the valuation advice it has received such that, but for the misinterpretation, the claimant would not have acted as he did, there will be no reliance. This was the position in *Housing Loan Corporation v. William H. Brown*[36] where a tertiary lender was required by its own backers to make loans up to a maximum of 75 per cent of the lower of two forced sale values. In fact a loan was made on the basis of the defendants' negligent open market valuations. The judge fully accepted the plaintiff's evidence that it had, in fact, relied on the advice received but found that such reliance hinged on its misinterpretation of the valuation as being made on a forced sale basis. Hirst L.J. held that the question as to whether a mistake was sufficiently fundamental to destroy reliance was one of fact and degree[37] but that, on the facts, the Judge had been fully entitled to come to his conclusion.[38] In an appropriate case, a court will, however, be prepared to infer reliance even where there is no direct evidence of the same.[39]

---

[31] For examples of cases where it was not established that the loss or damage was sustained consequential upon the advice, see *Rona v. Pearce*, (1953) 162 E.G. 380, where Hilbery J. although satisfied that the defendant surveyor had failed to exercise proper diligence and care in making his survey, "could not believe . . . that the report was a factor which influenced [the plaintiff] in buying the bungalow". The surveyor therefore succeeded in defending the plaintiff's claim and he was further given judgment on his counterclaim for survey fees. Similarly, in *Shankie-Williams v. Heavey* [1986] 2 E.G.L.R. 139, CA the plaintiff purchasers' claim against the defendant dry rot specialist failed because there was no evidence that they had seen his report.

[32] [1994] 2 E.G.L.R. 108 at 125.

[33] In *Cavendish Funding v. Henry Spencer* [1998] P.N.L.R. 122, the Court of Appeal accepted the proposition, for the purposes of the appeal and did not find it necessary to consider an argument, based on the judgment of Millett L.J. in *Bristol and West Building Society v. Mothew* [1996] 4 All E.R. 698, that it was unnecessary for a lender to establish that it would not have made the loan of the valuation had been different provided that the lender had, in fact, relied on the valuation and that it had been causative of the loan.

[34] [1988] 2 E.G.L.R. 178.

[35] See n. 47 to para. 9–103, above.

[36] [1999] Lloyd's L.Rep. P.N. 185.

[37] *ibid.* at 193.

[38] For an example of a case where a similar submission was rejected see *Arab Bank v. John D. Wood* [2000] Lloyd's L.Rep. P.N. 173 at 195. The plaintiff's evidence had been that it had instructed the defendant valuers to carry out a full open market valuation. In fact only a check on another valuation had been requested. The plaintiff's evidence was, however, rejected with the result that there was no basis for the suggestion that it had misinterpreted the advice that it had received.

[39] For an extreme example of such a case see *Cavendish Funding v. Henry Spencer* [1998] P.N.L.R. 122 where the Court of Appeal refused to interfere with the judge's inference that a grossly negligent valuation had been a substantial cause of the making of a loan. This was so although there were two valuations in the case; the claimant appeared to have ignored the lower valuation; the loan was made in breach of the provisions of the claimant's lending manual and there appeared reasons to doubt (at the least) the competence of the relevant lending officer who was not called to give evidence. Aldous

Mortgage indemnity guarantees. Very often lenders will obtain "mortgage   **9–122** indemnity guarantees" from insurers or other financial institutions to protect themselves (at least in part) against the risk of default by a borrower. The question has therefore arisen as to the extent to which a lender has relied upon a valuation in making a loan with the benefit of such a guarantee. The question first arose at first instance in *BBL* where Phillips J. considered whether the lender relied upon the impugned valuation or a mortgage indemnity guarantee when lending the "top slice" of the loan.[40] Phillips J. considered the argument that the lender was not relying on the value of the security to justify lending the top slice fallacious, as it confused the question of whether the lender was relying on the valuation when deciding to lend the top slice of the loan and their motivation for so relying. The amount of the valuation was the factor which determined the amount that was lent, including the top slice of that amount. The reason why the lenders were prepared to run the risk of advancing more than 70 per cent of the valuation was the belief that this risk had been transferred to the insurers, but that did not mean that the lender was not relying on the valuation when deciding how much to lend. There was no break in the chain of causation that linked the valuations and the totality of the sums advanced by the lender. This reasoning was adopted by Mance L.J. when considering a similar submission in *Arab Bank v. John D. Wood*.[41] Mance L.J. pointed out that the valuation had permitted the negotiation of the mortgage indemnity policy which had, in turn, permitted the bank to lend the top slice of the loan which reinforced, rather than undermined, the alleged reliance.

Novus actus interveniens. The issue of causation may not be determined   **9–123** solely by reference to reliance. While recovery may be refused on the basis that the damage was not caused by reliance upon the negligent advice, the refusal may conversely be rationalised on the basis that the damage was attributable to another cause. The interplay of both bases is best illustrated in *Kenney v. Hall, Pain and Foster*.[42] The plaintiff was advised by the defendant estate agents and surveyors that his house was worth not less than £90,000 and that adjoining flats leased to a third party were worth £50,000. He was also advised that a reasonable asking price for the whole property, called Culverlands House, was £150,000. Acting on the advice the plaintiff offered the property for sale for £150,000 in July 1973 through the defendants. Despite informal advice from another estate agent that the asking price was a "big handicap" and advice "off the record" from his bank manager that the bank had valued the whole of Culverlands House at £100,000, in September 1973 the plaintiff committed himself to buy another property, Wickham Lodge, for £47,500. That sum was some £10,000 above the price he originally thought he could afford. In October 1973 he committed himself to buy a cottage and a plot of land adjacent to Wickham Lodge, for a further £16,000. From November 1973 to April 1974 the plaintiff accepted estimates for extensive improvements to Wickham Lodge and the cottage, that expenditure totalling over £30,000. Expenditure on both purchases and improvements was financed by a bank bridging loan since Culverlands House remained

---

L.J. nonetheless viewed the history of the loan as being consistent only with reliance and causation.
[40] [1994] 2 E.G.L.R. 108 at 127. The "top slice" of the loan was the difference between an advance of 70% of valuation, and the 90% actually lent.
[41] [2000] Lloyds L.Rep. P.N. 173 at 197.
[42] [1976] 2 E.G.L.R. 29.

unsold. A general decline in property prices intervened and it was ultimately sold in July 1974 for £60,000, of which £24,000 went to the leaseholder of the flats. The cottage was later sold for £14,000. At the date of the trial in 1976 Wickham Lodge was worth £57,000 but the plaintiff owed to the bank over £85,000 in respect of capital and interest, and to builders over £9,000.

9–124 Having held the defendants negligent, Goff J. dealt with four arguments on causation. First it was argued that the plaintiff's action in committing himself to buy Wickham Lodge before he had found a purchaser for Culverlands House was unreasonable. It amounted to a *novus actus interveniens* and the plaintiff could not hold the defendants liable for the consequences of his action. Goff J. rejected the argument, concluding that in the circumstances of a buoyant property market in September 1973 it was not unreasonable for the plaintiff to commit himself as he did in the light of the advice received from the defendants. Secondly, at the time he committed himself to buy Wickham Lodge the plaintiff was no longer acting in reliance on the defendants' advice but on his own assessment of the situation. He had been warned by another estate agent that the asking price was a big handicap and he suspected that the defendants' valuation was too high. Goff J., however, considered the plaintiff was still relying substantially on the defendants' advice in the sense that, even allowing for his suspecting their figure to be rather high, the valuation still made him feel that he could safely commit himself to buy Wickham Lodge, and spend some money upon improvements, and cover his commitments by a quick sale of Culverlands House by a dramatic reduction of 25 per cent in the asking price. Thirdly, it was argued that following the bank manager's informal advice as to the property's value, the causative effect of the defendants' valuation ceased and thereafter the plaintiff must have been relying exclusively on the bank's valuation. That argument was also rejected on the basis that the plaintiff was still acting in substantial reliance on the defendants' valuation. Fourthly, it was argued that while it was reasonable to take into account some expenditure on Wickham Lodge, nevertheless the actual expenditure on Wickham Lodge went beyond what was reasonable in the circumstances and was profligate. This argument partly succeeded, as £5,000 was disallowed in damages for economies which should reasonably have been made. This was justified by Goff J. on grounds of causation: "I conclude that a part of his expenditure was incurred not by reason of his reliance on the defendants' valuation, but by reason of his own under-estimate of the cost of repair and renovation."[43]

(ii) *Foreseeability*

9–125 A claimant must establish not only that the loss was caused by the surveyor's breach of duty, but also that the loss was foreseeable. For a claim in contract, this

---

[43] *ibid.* at 36. See also: *Thomas Miller & Co. v. Richard Saunders & Partners* [1989] 1 E.G.L.R. 267, where Rougier J., having found the defendant surveyors negligent in their handling of a rent review arbitration, concluded that such failure was not causative of the plaintiff's loss as the particular decision of the arbitrator constituted an intervening act, and *McGonigle v. Hutton* [1995] 6 B.N.I.L. 68 where Girvan J. considered it "strongly arguable" that the failure by the puchaser's solicitor properly to investigate a warning given by the defendant surveyor as to whether certain roof space works were in breach of building control regulations, was a *novus actus interveniens* upon which the plaintiff had relied.

means that, at the time the contract was made, the loss was "reasonably foreseeable as likely to result from the breach".[44] For a claim in tort, it means that at the time the breach of duty was committed, the loss was reasonably foreseeable as a consequence of the breach.[45]

Foreseeability of damage is often in issue in surveyors' negligence cases, although rarely in the context of compensation for loss. The apparent paradox is explained by the fact that the issue of foreseeability will often be relevant to liability and will be resolved by the determination on liability, hence making unnecessary further consideration of the issue in relation to damage. For example, the issue whether a surveyor should have anticipated a sudden outbreak of dry rot (because, for example, the conditions were ripe for such an outbreak) may be relevant to whether he was in breach of his duty to exercise reasonable care and skill. Foreseeability of damage was considered at length in the Scottish case of *Drinnan v. C. W. Ingram & Sons*.[46] The pursuer contended that as a result of the defenders' negligent survey she was forced to leave her condemned flat and consequently suffered injury to her health, namely hypertension. The defenders contended that such injury was unforeseeable and they sought to have the relevant averments by the pursuer dismissed as irrelevant. After reviewing a number of authorities, including *Cook v. Swinfen*,[47] Lord Milligan refused to accede to the defenders' application. The case established, however, no more than that the forseeability of such injury was arguable on the facts, since no final decision on the issue was made. In another Scottish case, *Hunter v. J. & E. Shepherd*,[48] Lord Osborne refused to strike out a claim for the costs of alternative accommodation for the children of the family. Whilst repairs were being carried out, they stayed with relatives, the plaintiff paying for their board and lodging. The judge held that for the costs of the children's accommodation to be recoverable, it was not necessary for the plaintiff to have been legally obliged to support them; instead it was a question of foreseeability, and in the circumstances it was reasonably foreseeable that the plaintiff would regard himself as responsible for their accommodation during the period of remedial work.[49]

9–126

An issue which has arisen is whether a valuer should have foreseen a large rise in property prices. The general approach of the courts has been to refuse to permit claimants to recover additional losses because of such alleged foreseeability. In one sense it is, of course, foreseeable that prices may rise or fall. However a valuation of property should take into account the market expectation of such rises (or falls). Thus McHugh J. pointed out in *Kenny & Good v. MGICA*[50]: "in so far as a decline in the market was reasonably foreseeable, it will already be factored into the assessment of the true value of the property as at the date of valuation. In so far as the market decline was not reasonably foreseeable, any loss arising from the decline must be regarded as outside the contemplation of the parties . . . and not recoverable in an action for negligence or breach of contract". The question of the foreseeability of a large rise in property prices

9–127

---

[44] *per* Asquith L.J. in *Victoria Laundry (Windsor) Ltd v. Newman Industries Ltd* [1949] 2 K.B. 528.
[45] See *McGregor*, paras 198–201.
[46] 1967 S.L.T. 205.
[47] [1967] 1 W.L.R. 457.
[48] 1992 S.L.T. 1095.
[49] See further at para. 9–191, below.
[50] 163 A.L.R. 611 at 627.

arose directly in *Morgan v. Perry*.[51] In that case as a result of the defendant's survey in 1968 the plaintiff bought a house held to be valueless owing to settlement. The defendant argued that *Philips v. Ward*[52] established only a prima facie rule for measuring damages, which should be displaced if its application to a particular case involved a departure from the fundamental principle in *Hadley v. Baxendale*[53] and other cases. The motive for the argument was that in late 1971 and throughout 1972 house prices rose at an unprecedented rate. Therefore damages assessed by reference to 1968 house values in accordance with the *Philips v. Ward* principle would have been much less than damages assessed by reference to house values in 1971, when the extent of the damage had been properly investigated and ascertained. The defendant's argument was rejected, Judge Kenneth Jones Q.C. considering himself bound by *Philips v. Ward*. The judge went on to say that, even accepting the argument, he did not consider that: "the parties could be held reasonably to have contemplated that the plaintiff's loss would continue beyond the point where he first fully discovered the damage he had suffered; inflated 1973 values were far beyond the parties' horizon of contemplation."[54]

(b) *Measure of damages*

9–128   Whether the claim is brought in contract or tort the fundamental principle governing the measure of damages is that the plaintiff must be put, so far as money can, in the position he would have occupied if the surveyor had properly discharged his duty.[55] Evaluating that hypothetical position can present great practical difficulties[56] especially where what would have happened is in doubt, disputed or depends on what a third party would have done. To solve the problem courts have generally resorted to one of two alternative approaches. The first is to assess on a balance of probabilities what would have happened.[57] The second is to assess damages by reference to the value of the chance of a particular hypothesis being fulfilled.[58] The problem frequently arises in the form of whether, but for the surveyor's negligent advice, a purchaser would have purchased a property at all or for a lower price or a lender would have lent nothing on the property or a lower sum. In surveyors' negligence cases the usual

---

[51] (1973) 229 E.G. 1737.
[52] [1956] 1 W.L.R. 471, CA. See further para. 9–134 below.
[53] (1854) 9 Ex. 341.
[54] (1973) 229 E.G. 1737, 1740. See also *Corisand Investments Ltd v. Druce and Co.* [1978] 2 E.G.L.R. 86 especially at 97: defendant valuers held not negligent in not anticipating or suspecting impending collapse of property market.
[55] See *Livingstone v. Rawyards Coal Co.* (1880) 5 App.Cas. 25, 39 and *Dodd Properties (Kent) Ltd v. Canterbury City Council* [1980] 1 W.L.R. 433, 454, 456 (as to general principles). As to surveyors, see, *e.g. Swingcastle v. Gibson* [1991] 2 A.C. 223 at 232 *per* Lord Lowry; *Watts v. Morrow* [1991] 1 W.L.R. 1421; and *Banque Bruxelles Lambert S.A. v. Eagle Star Insurance Co. Ltd* [1997] A.C. 191.
[56] See, for example, the comments of Purchas L.J. in *Steward v. Rapley* [1989] 1 E.G.L.R. 159, 162.
[57] See, for example, the medical case of *Hotson v. East Berkshire Area Health Authority* [1987] A.C. 750, and the other medical cases discussed in Chap. 12, para. 12–252, *et seq.*
[58] See the solicitor cases discussed in Chap. 10, para. 10–249, *et seq.*

approach[59] is for damages to be assessed by reference to what would, on the balance of probabilities, have happened.[60]

The damages recoverable for breach of duty by surveyors and associated **9–129** topics are discussed below under the following headings:

(i) Negligent survey or valuation for a purchaser who completes a purchase:

    (a) The usual measure.
    (b) Relevance of cost of repairs.
    (c) Costs of extrication.
    (d) Collateral benefit.

(ii) Negligent survey or valuation for a purchaser who withdraws from purchase before completion.

(iii) Negligent survey or valuation for lender:

    (a) Assessment of the total loss.
    (b) Assessment of the scope of duty.
    (c) Interest on damages.
    (d) Contributory negligence by lender.

(iv) Overvaluation for vendor.

(v) Undervaluation for vendor.

(vi) Other work.

(vii) Inconvenience and discomfort.

(viii) Incidental expenses.

(i) *Negligent survey or valuation for a purchaser who completes a purchase*

(a) **The usual measure.** Where a person has completed the purchase[61] of a **9–130** property in reliance upon a negligent survey or overvaluation of the property by a surveyor,[62] the proper measure of damages has generally been expressed as the difference between (i) the value of the property without the defect and (ii) its

---

[59] However, in *Eagle Star v. Gale and Power* (1955) 166 E.G. 37, Devlin J. awarded mortgagees damages of £100 against the defendant surveyor to indemnify them against the possibility of not being able to recover their money from the mortgagor.

[60] The evidential basis must be laid, even when valuing a hypothetical situation. In *Duncan v. Gumleys* [1987] 2 E.G.L.R. 263, a surveyor's negligence action, the Lord Ordinary was provided with no evidence as to the value of the property in its defective condition. He therefore arrived at a "reasonable estimate" of £30,000 and deducted that from the surveyor's negligent valuation of £60,000. The Inner House held that the Lord Ordinary was not entitled to reach such a decision in the absence of evidence justifying it. Lord Ross: "In a case like the present it is clearly for the pursuer to lay before the court some evidence upon which the court can decide, perhaps by inference from expert opinion, what the measure of damages should be."

[61] Where the purchaser has not completed a purchase, he may maintain a claim for wasted expenditure. See para. 9–149, below. Where a purchaser would not have bought a property and takes steps to extricate himself from the purchase, he may maintain a claim for the costs of extrication. See para. 9–146.

[62] Where the surveyor has not warranted the absence of any need for major or further repairs. No such warranty is expressed or, it is submitted, implied, in any of the conditions of engagement connected with standard services offered by surveyors to their clients. For the measure of damage where such a warranty has been given, see para. 9–178, below.

value with the defect as at the date of purchase.[63] In calculating this difference in recent years, the value without the defect has generally been described as the price paid. The negligent surveyor's figure for the value of the property may, however, be the appropriate figure when it is lower than the price in fact paid for the property. The value with the defect is the market value of the property as at the date of purchase in its true condition.[64] Although the phrase "difference in value" is now in common use as a description of the proper measure, difference in value can usually be more accurately described as the overpayment or the excess paid for the property purchased. The premise underlying the assertion of difference in value as the proper measure is that the purchaser's loss is properly to be characterised as overpayment and not unacquired value, *i.e.* a money loss, not a value loss. The purchased property never had a value corresponding to the element of overpayment. The two expressions may therefore be properly defined as follows. "Diminution in value" means the amount by which the value of the property has been diminished by the unreported defects. "Excess purchase price paid" means the difference between the purchase price actually paid and the purchase price which would reasonably have been paid, if the plaintiff had persisted in his purchase after receipt of a competent survey report. In different cases and even in different judgments in the same cases, including *Philips v. Ward*[65] and *Perry v. Sidney Phillips & Son*,[66] difference in value and its two components have been expressed differently. This is mainly the consequence of there being on the particular facts of most cases no need for a more exact description, as the two components may readily be recognised.

9–131 Descriptions given for both components of the measure have obviously been based on the particular facts of each case. In respect of the first component,[67] the price paid has usually been accepted to be the correct sum,[68] but the value of the property expressly stated in the negligent surveyor's report may on the facts be more appropriate,[69] or the value of the property to be deduced from the description in the negligent surveyor's report but in which the value is not stated,[70] or

---

[63] See *Watts v. Morrow* [1991] 1 W.L.R. 1421, and para. 9–143, below, and for further examples the succinct statement of the principle by the Lord Justice-Clerk in *Duncan v. Gumleys* [1987] 2 E.G.L.R. 263, 265, and by Hoffmann L.J. in *Sneesby and another v. Goldings* [1995] 2 E.G.L.R. 102, 105: "The formulation is the difference between its market value in good condition and its market value on the basis that the surveyor had made a proper report to the client."

[64] See *Philips v. Ward* [1956] 1 W.L.R. 471, CA, as explained in *Ford v. White & Co.* [1964] 1 W.L.R. 885 and *Simple Simon Catering Ltd v. Binstock Miller & Co.* (1973) 228 E.G. 527, 529, CA.; also *Perry v. Sidney Phillips & Son* [1982] 1 W.L.R. 1297, CA.; *Watts v. Morrow* [1991] 1 W.L.R. 1421. See also the Scottish cases of *Stewart v. H.A. Brechin & Co.* [1959] S.C. 306 and *Upstone v. G. D. W. Carnegie & Co.*, 1978 S.L.T.(Sh.Ct.) 4, 5.

[65] See para. 9–135, below.

[66] See para. 9–137, below.

[67] See para. 9–130, above.

[68] *Philips v. Ward* [1956] 1 W.L.R. 471, CA. Romer L.J.; *Perry v. Sidney Phillips & Son* [1982] 1 W.L.R. 1297, CA (all three judges); *Ford v. White & Co.* [1964] 1 W.L.R. 885; *Lees v. English and Partners* [1977] 1 E.G.L.R. 65; *Bolton v. Puley* [1983] 2 E.G.L.R. 138; *Treml v. Ernest W. Gibson and Partners* [1984] 2 E.G.L.R. 162; *Hooberman v. Salter Rex* [1985] 1 E.G.L.R. 144; *Roberts v. J. Hampson & Co.* [1988] 2 E.G.L.R. 181; *Steward v. Rapley* [1989] 1 E.G.L.R. 159; *Watts v. Morrow* [1991] 1 W.L.R. 1421.

[69] *Philips v. Ward* [1956] 1 W.L.R. 471, CA 476, Morris L.J.; *Wilson v. Baxter, Payne and Lepper* [1985] 1 E.G.L.R. 141.

[70] *Freeman v. Marshall* (1966) 200 E.G. 777, 779; *Hardy v. Wamsley-Lewis* (1967) 203 E.G. 1039, 1043; *Hingorani v. Blower* [1976] 1 E.G.L.R. 104.

the value of the property in its assumed good condition,[71] or the value of the house without the defect.[72] For the second component,[73] descriptions given have included the value of the property as it should have been described in a competent surveyor's report,[74] the market value of the property,[75] the value of the property in its actual condition,[76] the price which the particular purchaser would have been prepared to give,[77] its value with the defect,[78] and the price which the particular purchaser would have succeeded in negotiating with the particular vendor.[79]

The problem of accurately describing both components of the measure was **9–132** raised in acute form in *Shaw and another v. Halifax (SW) Ltd.*[80] For a trial of preliminary issues it was agreed that on June 20, 1988 the defendant valuers valued the property at £37,000, when due to unreported defects its value was in fact only £32,000, and that on August 11, 1988 the plaintiffs purchased the property for £42,000 when its actual value due to the defects was £37,000.[81] The plaintiffs argued that they had suffered a loss of £5,000, being the difference between the price paid for the property and its actual value at the date of purchase. The defendants argued that the plaintiff had in fact suffered no loss, because the measure was the difference between the value of the property without the defect at the date of purchase (£37,000, as reported in June 1988) and the value with the defect at the date of purchase (also £37,000). The defendants relied upon *Hardy v. Wamsley-Lewis*[82] and *Hingorani v. Blower*[83] in support of

---

[71] *Philips v. Ward* [1956] 1 W.L.R. 471, CA at 473 Denning L.J.; *Hoadley v. Edwards* [2001] E.G.C.S. 46.

[72] *Duncan v. Gumleys* [1987] 2 E.G.L.R. 263, 265.

[73] See para. 9–130, above.

[74] *Philips v. Ward* [1956] 1 W.L.R. 471, CA, 473, Denning L.J. and 476, Morris L.J.; *Lees v. English and Partner* [1977] 1 E.G.L.R. 65.

[75] *Perry v. Sidney Phillips & Son* [1982] 1 W.L.R. 1297, CA at 1304, Oliver L.J. and 1306, Kerr L.J.; *Ford v. White & Co.* [1964] 1 W.L.R. 885, 888; *Treml v. Ernest W. Gibson and Partners* [1984] 2 E.G.L.R. 162; *Hooberman v. Salter Rex* [1985] 1 E.G.L.R. 144.

[76] *Perry v. Sidney Phillips & Son* [1982] 1 W.L.R. 1297, CA, 1303 "the property which he actually got" (Oliver L.J.); *Hill v. Debenham, Tewson and Chinnocks* (1958) 171 E.G. 835, 839 "its value as it actually existed, namely as a bad shell"; *Hardy v. Wamsley-Lewis* (1967) 203 E.G. 1039, 1043 "the value of it in the condition in which it truly was"; *Collard v. Saunders* (1972) 221 E.G. 797 "its value in its actual bad condition"; *Morgan v. Perry* (1973) 229 E.G. 1737, 1740 "its value as [the property] in fact was"; *Hingorani v. Blower* [1976] 1 E.G.L.R. 104, 105 "the value of the house . . . as it really was"; *Bolton v. Puley* [1983] 2 E.G.L.R. 138, 143 "its value in its actual condition"; *Watts v. Morrow* [1991] 1 W.L.R. 1421 "the value of the house in its true condition".

[77] *Perry v. Sidney Phillips and Son* [1982] 1 W.L.R. 1297, CA, 1302, Lord Denning M.R. and *Bolton v. Puley* [1983] 2 E.G.L.R. 138, 142.

[78] *Duncan v. Gumleys* [1987] 2 E.G.L.R. 263, 265

[79] See *Howard v. Horne & Sons* [1990] 1 E.G.L.R. 272 where the plaintiffs purchased the property for what was agreed by the independent surveyors to be its true market value of £200,250. A competent report, however, would have enabled them to negotiate a further reduction with the vendors. The official referee therefore awarded the plaintiffs £1,500, being the further reduction in the purchase price that they could have, but were unable to secure (little more than one-half per cent). Although the judgment does not deal with the evidence of the surveyors on this point, the case is explicable on the basis of imprecise terminology and a difference in value that would generally be regarded as immaterial. If the property could have been purchased for £198,750 with the aid of a proper survey report, then that was the true market value. The plaintiffs therefore recovered the difference between the price they paid and the price they would have paid with a proper report.

[80] [1994] 2 E.G.L.R. 95.

[81] *ibid.*, 96C.

[82] (1967) 203 E.G. 1039.

[83] [1976] 1 E.G.L.R. 104.

their submissions. The judge held that the plaintiffs were entitled to the difference between "the market value of the property without the defects and its market value in the defective condition"[84] and noted that if the actual value of the property on August 11, 1988 was £37,000 then its value in an assumed condition without the defects was obviously higher. The problem was analysed as follows:

> "If the price paid of £42,000 was the price which would reasonably have been paid on that date in the open market at arm's length by a willing buyer to a willing seller for the property without the defects, the plaintiffs' loss is £5,000; that is the difference between £42,000 and £37,000. If the market value of the property on the basis that it did not have the defects on August 11, 1988 was less than £42,000 the plaintiffs' loss is such market value less £37,000. In paying £42,000 the plaintiffs in that situation have paid above the market value of the property; the excess which they have paid over and above the market value of the property plainly cannot be a liability of the defendants. If the market value of the property without the defects was more than £42,000, the loss remains £5,000."[85]

In the event the plaintiffs recovered £5,000, on the basis that the price paid of £42,000 did represent the market value as at August 11, 1988.

9–133   In earlier editions of this work it was stated:

> "In *Philips v. Ward*,[86] *Perry v. Sidney Phillips & Son*,[87] and *Watts v. Morrow*,[88] the Court of Appeal has stated and re-stated that diminution in value is the proper measure of damage in respect of a negligent survey of a house for a private purchaser. This rule applies whether or not the purchaser has carried out repairs, whether or not the purchaser has retained or sold the property, and whether or not, if properly advised, the purchaser would not have bought the property. Unless and until the matter is considered by the House of Lords, that measure of damage will apply to virtually all cases arising out of domestic house surveys and/or valuations for prospective purchasers."[89]

In *Patel v. Hooper & Jackson*[90] Nourse L.J. endorsed the above statement from the fourth edition as being a correct statement of the prima facie rule applicable to the purchase of residential property. The only exception appears to be where it can be said that the purchaser is entitled to the costs of extrication from a purchase.[91]

9–134   Prior to *Philips v. Ward*,[92] the measure of damages awarded in cases where a person had completed his purchase of a property in reliance upon a negligent survey or overvaluation was the cost of rectifying the defects unreported or

---

[84] [1994] 2 E.G.L.R. 95, 97.
[85] *ibid.*, 97M.
[86] [1956] 1 W.L.R. 471.
[87] [1982] 1 W.L.R. 1297.
[88] [1991] 1 W.L.R. 1421.
[89] An exception would be where the surveyor has given a warranty. The decision of the Court of Appeal in *Watts v. Morrow* [1991] 1 W.L.R. 1421 is discussed and criticised by T. Dugdale in "*Watts v. Morrow*: penalising the house purchaser" (1992) 8 P.N. 152.
[90] [1999] Lloyd's L.Rep. P.N. 1 at 7–8.
[91] This was the measure of damages allowed in the actual case—see further para. 9–146 below.
[92] [1956] 1 W.L.R. 471, CA.

misreported.[93] The official referee's decision[94] rejecting that measure was upheld by the Court of Appeal in *Philips v. Ward*. In 1952 the plaintiff purchased a manor house for £25,000, in reliance upon the defendant surveyor's negligent report. It was later found to be affected by death watch beetle and woodworm. In his report the surveyor estimated the value of the property as somewhere between £25,000 and £27,000. It was found that in 1952 the necessary repair work would cost £7,000 at prices then prevailing but that even if a purchaser knew of the defects, a fair price would have been £21,000. The plaintiff was awarded not £7,000 but £4,000 in damages, the difference between £25,000 and £21,000. The case was generally accepted as establishing two principles in respect of the measure of damages for a surveyor's breach of contract in such circumstances:

(i) the measure was the difference in value; and

(ii) the damages should be assessed as at the date when the damage occurred, that is 1952, not as at the date of trial in 1956.

Formulation of measure of damage. The difference in value was expressed   **9–135**
by the three judges in *Philips v. Ward* as follows. Denning L.J. described it as the difference between the value of the property in its assumed good condition and the value in the bad condition which should have been reported to the client.[95] Morris L.J. described it as the difference between the value of the property as it was described in the surveyor's report; and its value as it should have been described.[96] Romer L.J. did not precisely formulate the relevant difference but he would appear to have taken it as the difference between the price paid and the market price of the property taking into account the defects which the surveyor failed to disclose.[97] As observed by Pennycuick J. in *Ford v. White & Co.*,[98] a solicitor's negligence case, each judge in *Philips v. Ward* assumed or held the price paid to be equivalent to the value in assumed good condition (or as described in the defendant's report) and treated the two expressions as interchangeable. He further observed that the mind of each judge was not directed to the type of case where the purchaser had paid a price less than the value of the property in assumed good condition.[99] In Pennycuick J.'s view: "In the simple case of the purchase of property at a price in excess of the market value as a result of the wrong advice, the measure of damage must be the difference between (1)

---

[93] See *Grove v. Jackman and Masters* (1950) 155 E.G. 182; *Lowy v. Woodroffe, Buchanan and Coulter* (1950) 156 E.G. 375; *Last v. Post* (1952) 159 E.G. 240; *Wooldridge v. Stanley Hicks and Son* (1953) 162 E.G. 513. The cost of rectifying defects would appear also to have been adopted in the following cases although it is not clear from the brief reports: *Barton v. Stuart Hepburn & Co.* [1926] E.G.D. 206; *Legge v. Young* [1949] E.G.D. 186; *Gurd v. A. Cobden Soar and Son* (1951) 157 E.G. 415; *Sincock v. Bangs (Reading)* (1952) C.P.L. 562; *Thorne v. Harris and Co.* (1953) 163 E.G. 324; *Denny v. Budgen* (1955) 166 E.G. 433. In *Tremayne v. T. Mortimer Burrows and Partners* (1954) 165 E.G. 232, McNair J. awarded £800 damages "as the cost of remedying the state of affairs that was found, or as the difference in value of the premises". The alternative bases of the award is no doubt indicative of the debate as to the proper measure, which was shortly thereafter resolved in *Philips v. Ward* (above).
[94] Unreported.
[95] [1956] 1 W.L.R. 471, 473.
[96] *ibid.* at 476.
[97] *ibid.* at 477–478.
[98] [1964] 1 W.L.R. 885.
[99] *ibid.* at 891.

the market value of the property at the date of purchase, and (2) the price actually paid."[1]

He justified adopting the price paid as opposed to the higher value of the property in assumed good condition by taking a striking example: "A sees a picture on sale at £100. He consults an art expert who negligently advises him that the picture is an old master worth £50,000. A buys the picture, but cannot in fact find a purchaser willing to pay more than £5 for it. Is his measure of damage £95 or £49,995? I should have thought obviously the former."[2]

Pennycuick J.'s observations were endorsed by Lord Denning M.R. in *Simple Simon Catering Ltd v. Binstock Miller & Co.*,[3] another solicitor's negligence case. Quoting Pennycuick J.'s painting example Lord Denning continued: "An earlier case *Philips v. Ward* [1956] 1 W.L.R. 471, when properly understood, proceeded on a similar basis . . . In those cases it was the difference between the price actually paid for the property on the basis that the advice was good, and the price at which it would be bought as it was in fact."[4]

9–136   In *Perry v. Sidney Phillips and Son*,[5] the Court of Appeal confirmed the explanation of *Philips v. Ward* given in *Ford v. White & Co.* and the *Simple Simon Catering Ltd* cases. The plaintiff purchased a house in 1976 for £27,000 in reliance upon the defendant surveyors' report. In the report the value of the property was stated at £28,500. Subsequently the property was found to have a number of serious defects, including a leaking roof and a septic tank with an offensive odour. The defendants were held negligent in not properly inspecting and reporting upon the property. The correct method of assessing damages was tried as a preliminary issue. At first instance[6] the judge[7] held that difference in value was not the universal test in surveyors' negligence cases and that the proper measure of damages on the facts[8] was "the cost of repair of the defects which a proper inspection by a reasonably competent surveyor would have brought to light" assessed as at the date of his judgment.[9] The judge based his conclusion upon various passages from the Court of Appeal judgments in *Dodd Properties (Kent) Ltd v. Canterbury City Council*[10] relating to the primary compensatory principle of a damages award.[11] The deputy judge was also satisfied that if he had taken difference in value as the appropriate measure, he would have been entitled to consider the matter of assessment at the date of judgment,[12] again on the basis of the *Dodd Properties* case. By the time of the Court of Appeal hearing[13] and owing to financial difficulty, the plaintiff had sold the property for £43,000. Accordingly, before that court, the cost of repair was not defended as the appropriate measure of damages. Rather it was submitted on the plaintiff's behalf that the correct measure was the difference between (a) the value of the property

---

[1] *ibid.* at 888.
[2] *ibid.* at 888–889
[3] (1973) 228 E.G. 527, CA.
[4] ibid. at 529.
[5] [1982] 1 W.L.R. 1297, CA.
[6] Reported at [1982] 1 All E.R. 1005.
[7] Mr Patrick Bennett Q.C. sitting as a deputy judge of the High Court.
[8] Including a finding of fact that the plaintiff did not intend to sell the property.
[9] [1982] 1 All E.R. 1005, 1012, 1015.
[10] [1980] 1 W.L.R. 433, CA. Not a surveyor's negligence case, but a case where physical damage had been caused to the property. The measure of loss was therefore different.
[11] [1980] 1 W.L.R. 433, 456, *per* Donaldson L.J., at 454–455, *per* Browne L.J.
[12] *ibid.* at 1011.
[13] [1982] 1 W.L.R. 1297.

at the date of trial if it had been in the condition in which it should have been, on the basis of the defendant surveyors' report, and (b) its value at the same date in its defective condition. This was tantamount to saying that the surveyors warranted their description and valuation of the property when their duty was the more limited one to exercise reasonable skill and care. The submission was rejected. The Court of Appeal reasserted the previously prevailing view that the appropriate measure of damages was the difference in value established in *Philips v. Ward* as explained in *Ford v. White & Co.* The plaintiff was entitled to interest on the difference. It was also held that the plaintiff was entitled to general damages for vexation and inconvenience.[14]

Each of the judges described the same calculation of loss somewhat differ- **9–137** ently. All agreed that the price paid by the plaintiff for the property was one element in the calculation. The other element was variously described. The *Dodd Properties* case[15] was distinguished as inapplicable essentially on the basis that it was concerned with physical damage being caused to the plaintiff's property. That being the case, the appropriate measure of damages justified by the primary compensatory principle was the cost of repairs. Moreover in that case the question did arise as to the time for assessment of the cost of repair. In the case of a surveyor who does not cause defects but instead inadequately reports them, the measure of loss being the diminution in value, no question of a time for assessment other than the time of purchase arises.

Nature of the loss. It is submitted that this last point becomes more clear if the **9–138** relevant measure is described not as the diminution in value but as the overpayment or the excess price paid. The relevant measure is a money loss not a value loss. The purchaser paid too much rather than obtained too little value. The property negligently reported upon never had an element of value corresponding to the overpayment. As a money loss, no question arises of assessing that loss other than when the money was lost on purchase. So long as English law, like virtually all jurisdictions, adheres to the principle of compensation by way of the actual sum as distinct from revaluation,[16] a plaintiff's entitlement in 1997 to £50,000 lost in 1990 is to £50,000 plus interest thereon for the interim period and not to the monetary equivalent (adjusted according to whatever inflation index as may appear appropriate) in 1997 of £50,000 in 1990.

Where the price paid exceeds the value of the property given in the negligent **9–139** surveyor's report and valuation, that value and not the price paid may (although not invariably) be the appropriate figure, on the basis that the element of the overpayment comprising the difference between the price paid and the value described would not be attributable to the surveyor's default.[17] In *Hardy v. Wamsley-Lewis*[18] for example, the value of the house as described in the defendant's report and its actual value were respectively assessed at £4,300 and

---

[14] See para. 9–181, below.
[15] See para. 9–136, above.
[16] See generally Professor F.A. Mann, *The Legal Aspect of Money* (4th ed.).
[17] For a similar approach see Goff J.'s ground for not awarding the full expenditure on repairs in *Kenney v. Hall, Pain and Foster* [1976] 2 E.G.L.R. 29, 36, dealt with at paras 9–080, 9–100, 9–123, above.
[18] (1967) 203 E.G. 1039.

£3,500. The plaintiff had nevertheless purchased it for £4,600. He was awarded the difference between £4,300 and £3,500 in damages.[19]

9–140   **Other decisions.** Despite attempts[20] to distinguish the difference in value measure established in *Philips v. Ward*,[21] it has since generally been followed and applied in all English and Scottish reported cases of a claim against a surveyor by a purchaser who completed the purchase in reliance upon a negligent survey or over-valuation.[22] The failure of attempts to distinguish *Philips v. Ward* demonstrates the wide application of the measure of damages established by it. In *Lawrence v. Hampton & Sons*[23] it was argued that *Philips v. Ward* was distinguishable where there was evidence that if there had been a proper report on the house, the purchaser would not have bought it. Mocatta J., although satisfied that there was positive evidence to that effect, held that that was no ground for distinguishing the decision: "in that case[24] the possibility that the purchaser would not have bought the property was dealt with in each of the judgments".[25]

---

[19] The difference between £4,600 and £3,500 was not claimed. But it is submitted that that would not have been the appropriate measure because the element of the overpayment between £4,300 and £4,600 was attributable to the plaintiff's own action in overpaying. See also *Hingorani v. Blower* [1976] 1 E.G.L.R. 104; difference in value apparently calculated by reference to the value of the property in the condition described by the defendant surveyor, assessed at £6,750, not the price paid of £7,000, and *Morgan v. Perry* (1973) 229 E.G. 1737.

[20] Principally *Hipkins v. Jack Cotton Partnership* [1989] 2 E.G.L.R. 157; *Syrett v. Carr & Neave* [1990] 2 E.G.L.R. 161; and dicta by Staughton L.J. in *Steward v. Rapley* [1989] 1 E.G.L.R. 159, 164 to the effect that cost of repairs may be the appropriate measure on the hypothesis that the plaintiff may never have entered into the contract at all. This argument was finally rejected by the Court of Appeal in *Watts v. Morrow* [1991] 1 W.L.R. 1421.

[21] [1956] 1 W.L.R. 471, CA.

[22] See *Fidgeon v. Carroll* (1956) 168 E.G. 557, CA; *Hill v. Debenham, Tewson and Chinnocks* (1958) 171 E.G. 835; *Moss v. Heckingbottom* (1958) 172 E.G. 207; *Hood v. Shaw* (1960) 176 E.G. 1291; *Lawrence v. Hampton & Sons* (1964) 190 E.G. 107; *Freeman v. Marshall* (1966) 200 E.G. 777; *Hardy v. Wamsley-Lewis* (1967) 203 E.G. 1039; *Collard v. Saunders* (1972) 221 E.G. 797 (a solicitor's negligence case); *Morgan v. Perry* (1973) 229 E.G. 1737; *Bourne v. McEvoy Timber Preservation Ltd* [1976] 1 E.G.L.R. 100; *Hingorani v. Blower* [1976] 1 E.G.L.R. 104; *Lees v. English and Partners* [1977] 1 E.G.L.R. 65; *Fisher v. Knowles* [1982] 1 E.G.L.R. 154; *Perry v. Sidney Phillips & Son* [1982] 1 W.L.R. 1297, CA; *Bolton v. Puley* [1983] 2 E.G.L.R. 138; *Treml v. Ernest W. Gibson and Partners* [1984] 2 E.G.L.R. 162; *Wilson v. Baxter, Payne and Lepper* [1985] 1 E.G.L.R. 141; *Hooberman v. Salter Rex* [1985] 1 E.G.L.R. 144; *Martin v. Bell-Ingram*, 1986 S.L.T. 575, 583 (Second Division); *County Personnel v. Alan R. Pulver & Co.* [1987] 1 W.L.R. 916, 925F, *per* Bingham L.J.; *Roberts v. J. Hampson & Co.* [1988] 2 E.G.L.R. 181, Ian Kennedy J.; *Miro Properties Ltd v. J. Trevor & Sons* [1989] 1 E.G.L.R. 151, Mr Recorder Bernstein Q.C.; *Cross v. David Martin & Mortimer* [1989] 1 E.G.L.R. 154, Phillips J.; *Steward v. Rapley* [1989] 1 E.G.L.R. 159, CA; *Broadoak Properties Ltd v. Young & White* [1989] 1 E.G.L.R. 263 (Judge Fox-Andrews Q.C.: "I find that in the absence of special circumstances the rule ought to be invariable. There should be certainty in this branch of the law"); *Bigg v. Howard Son & Gooch* [1990] 1 E.G.L.R. 173, Judge Hicks Q.C.; *Rentokil Pty Ltd v. Channon* [1990] 19 NSWLR 417 (where the New South Wales Court of Appeal held that damages should be assessed on the basis of diminution in the value of the property but, on the special facts of the case, by a majority, assessed at the date of hearing).

[23] (1964) 190 E.G. 107.

[24] *i.e. Philips v. Ward.*

[25] *ibid.* at 113. See *Philips v. Ward* [1956] 1 W.L.R. 471, Denning L.J. at 473, Morris L.J. at 476, Romer L.J. at 477–478. Romer L.J. said: "On this hypothesis his ignorance of the defects may be said to have worsened his position to the extent of £4,000 for he parted with £25,000 and became the possessor of property worth only £21,000." See also *Hardy v. Wamsley-Lewis* (1967) 203 E.G. 1039, 1043, *per* Paull J: "[the parties] seem fairly clearly agreed, that if dry rot had been seen and reported the house would not have been bought. In those circumstances it seems to me that the proper measure of damage is the difference in value between the place as it was on the basis of the report and the value of it in the condition in which it truly was". In *Lees v. English and Partners* (1977) E.G.D. 566, the measure of the difference between the price paid and the value of the house in its actual condition

It was also argued that the Court of Appeal was influenced by the fact that had the plaintiff in *Philips v. Ward* recovered £7,000 he would have made a profit. The judge firmly rejected the argument[26]:

> "I do not think the existence of that possibility in *Philips v. Ward* and its absence here, enables me to disregard the principle as to the measure of damages there laid down, which appears to me to be a general application in this kind of case, and was so regarded by Paull J. in *Hood v. Shaw*." [27]

(b) Relevance of cost of repairs. Where an attempt has been made to displace   9–141
the difference in value measure, it has usually been in favour of the cost of repairs. Except as a consequential loss item,[28] and the cases of *Hipkins v. Jack Cotton Partnership*[29] and *Syrett v. Carr and Neave*,[30] both first instance decisions overruled by the Court of Appeal in *Watts v. Morrow*,[31] such cost has not been allowed as such and the difference in value measure has prevailed. Application of that measure is particularly noteworthy in cases where the cost of repairs was significantly less than the difference in value. *Daisley v. B. S. Hall & Co.*[32] provides a rare reported example of such a case.[33] Owing to the surveyor's negligent non-observance of soil shrinkage damage, the plaintiff paid in 1968 £1,750 more than the true value of a house. Three years later and before trial it was established that no more than £250 was required to rectify the damage and eliminate the risk of further damage. Nevertheless £1,750 was awarded in damages upon the express basis of *Philips v. Ward*.[34]

A more usual situation is for the cost of repairs to be significantly higher than   9–142
the difference in value assessed at the date of purchase owing to inflation, the state of the property market, or deterioration of the defect (*e.g.* subsidence or dry rot) between that date and the date of discovery of the defects. In such cases, the courts have equally awarded damages based upon difference in value at the time

---

was applied despite the vendor's contention that had his surveyor properly reported he would "not have touched the house with a barge pole". May J. commented: "the vendor might have been able to get the money from another purchaser when the remedial work had been done".

[26] (1964) 190 E.G. 107, 113.

[27] (1960) 176 E.G. 1291, 1293.

[28] See para. 9–190, below.

[29] [1989] 2 E.G.L.R. 157.

[30] [1990] 2 E.G.L.R. 161.

[31] See para. 9–143, below.

[32] (1972) 225 E.G. 1553. See next note for the argument advanced to distinguish *Philips v. Ward*.

[33] See also *Hoadley v. Edwards* [2001] E.G.C.S. 46 where it appears that unplanned expenditure of £12,500 was incurred by the claimants and that further expenditure of £6,800 was required to bring the house into the expected structural condition. The judge nonetheless awarded damages of £40,000 as representing the overpayment made by the claimants together with damages for physical inconvenience and discomfort.

[34] See *ibid.* at 1557, *per* Bristow J.:

> "[Counsel for the plaintiff] submits that since *Philips v. Ward* clearly establishes that Mr Daisley would not in any circumstances have been entitled to more than £1,750 however much it might have cost him to do the necessary repairs if the hazard did bite so he cannot be said to have suffered less than that damage merely because the hazard never bites at all, and that the proper time to look at the assessment of loss is at the time of breach. I am satisfied that [counsel's] contention is right. What is sauce for the goose is sauce for the gander and if Mr Daisley would never be entitled to recover more than £1,750 as *Philips v. Ward* appears to me clearly to establish, it must follow that he will never be entitled to recover less; therefore there must be judgment for the plaintiff for £1,750." Contrast with the views to the contrary, *obiter*, of Staughton L.J. *in Steward v. Rapley* [1989] 1 E.G.L.R. 159, 164. See also on this point *Gardner v. Marsh & Parsons* [1997] 1 W.L.R. 489, CA, para. 9–144, n. 44 below.

of purchase.[35] In *Watts v. Morrow*[36] a determined attempt was made in the Court of Appeal to displace difference in value as the proper measure of loss for this type of case. The plaintiffs had purchased a farmhouse for £177,500 relying on the defendant's negligent structural survey report. By the time that serious defects had been discovered, the plaintiffs had moved into the property and carried out repairs at a cost of £33,961. The unchallenged evidence of the plaintiff's expert valuer was that in October 1986, the date of the contract to purchase, the value of the house in its true condition was £162,500. The plaintiffs therefore paid for the property £15,000 more than it was worth in its true condition. At first instance, the plaintiff's claim for the cost of repairs as the proper measure of damage was upheld. The official referee directed himself by reference to the principles stated by Bingham L.J. in *County Personnel Ltd v. Alan R. Pulver*,[37] to the effect that the diminution in value rule is almost always appropriate where property is acquired following negligent advice by surveyors, but that it is not an invariable approach and should not be mechanistically applied in inappropriate cases. The official referee noted that the facts of *Watts v. Morrow* were broadly similar to those of *Syrett v. Carr and Neave*,[38] a case also decided by him. The official referee held that the plaintiffs had acted reasonably in deciding to repair the property rather than reselling the same, and concluded that the plaintiffs were entitled to recover damages assessed as the cost of repairs, £33,961.

9–143   In the Court of Appeal the plaintiffs argued that the principle in *Philips v. Ward*, in so far as it could be regarded as a prima facie rule for the measure of damages in a claim against a negligent surveyor, was applicable only in cases where it is clear that the plaintiffs would have bought the property in any event, even if it had been accurately described by the surveyor. Given that the judge had found that the plaintiffs had acted reasonably in carrying out the repairs it was

---

[35] See *e.g. Morgan v. Perry* (1973) 229 E.G. 1737 where the plaintiff purchased a house in 1968 for £10,200, which later transpired to be valueless owing to soil subsidence. Investigations were only completed in 1971 and the case was tried in 1973. The recommended solution was demolition of the house, draining of the site and rebuilding. Estimates of the cost were £16,600 in 1969, £18,675 in 1971 and £24,000 in 1973. Due to the rise in house prices, the value of the house in the condition reported by the defendant would have been £24,000 or £25,000 at the date of trial. The plaintiff did not contend for the cost of repair, but the difference in value assessed at the completion of investigations in 1971. Kenneth Jones J. considered himself bound by *Philips v. Ward* and held the proper measure was the "differential value" of the house in 1968, which was assessed as equal to its then whole value, £10,200. In *Collard v. Saunders* (1972) 221 E.G. 797, the plaintiff sought the cost of repairs on the ground that repairs had been delayed owing to lack of means and accordingly cost more. Mocatta J. considered the case indistinguishable from that in *Philips v. Ward* and assessed damages by reference to the difference in value. Similarly in *Hooberman v. Salter Rex* [1985] 1 E.G.L.R. 144, the plaintiff purchased a maisonette in 1977 for £28,300. Dry rot so built up as to necessitate remedial work in 1980–81 at a cost of £6,391. If the remedial work required in 1977 had been carried out it was estimated that its cost would only have been £1,748 and the development of dry rot would have been prevented. Judge Smout Q.C. awarded the plaintiff damages of £875 in respect of his first head of claim, the difference between £28,300 and the market value of the maisonette in 1977 in its then true condition. The judge considered that the principles expressed in those two cases precluded him from awarding the plaintiff anything in respect of the second head of claim, the increase in the cost of remedial work caused by the development of dry rot, £6,391, less the estimated cost of preventative repairs which could have been effected in 1977.
[36] [1991] 1 W.L.R. 1421.
[37] [1987] 1 W.L.R. 916, 925. A solicitor's negligence action.
[38] [1990] 2 E.G.L.R. 161.

suggested that the full cost of such repairs should be awarded. Ralph Gibson L.J.[39] rejected the plaintiffs' argument, stating:

"It was rightly acknowledged for the plaintiffs that proof that the plaintiff, properly advised, would not have bought the property does not by itself cause the diminution in value rule to be inapplicable. It was contended, however, that it becomes inapplicable if it is also proved that it is reasonable for the plaintiff to retain the property and to do the repairs. I cannot accept that submission because:

(i) the fact that it is reasonable for the plaintiff to retain the property and to do the repairs seems to me to be irrelevant to determination of the question whether recovery of the cost of repairs is justified in order to put the plaintiff in the position in which he would have been if the contract, i.e. the promise to make a careful report, had been performed. The position is no different from that in *Philips*: the plaintiff would either have refused to buy or he would have negotiated a reduced price. Recovery of the cost of repairs after having gone into possession: that is to say in effect the acquisition of the house at the price paid less the cost of repairs at the later date of doing those repairs, is not a position into which the plaintiff could have been put as a result of proper performance of the contract. Nor is that cost recoverable as damages for breach of any promise by the defendant because, as stated above, there was no promise that the plaintiff would not incur any such cost.

(ii) In the context of the contract proved in this case, I have difficulty in seeing when or by reference to what principle it would not be reasonable for the purchaser of a house to retain it and to do the repairs. He is free to do as he pleases. He can owe no duty to the surveyor to take any cheaper course. The measure of damages should depend, and in my view does depend, upon proof of the sum needed to put the plaintiff in the position in which he would have been if the contract was properly performed, and a reasonable decision by him to remain in the house and to repair it, upon discovery of the defects, cannot alter that primary sum which remains the amount by which he was caused to pay more than the value of the house in its true condition.

(iii) If the rule were as contended for by the plaintiffs, what limit, if any, could be put on the nature and extent of the repairs of which the plaintiff could recover the cost? [Counsel for the plaintiffs] asserted that the cost of repairs awarded in this case was no more than putting the house in the condition in which, on reading the report, they believed the house to be. That, however, contains no relevant standard of reasonableness because, again, the defendant did not warrant that description to be true. To argue that to award damages on that basis is not to enforce a warranty never given but merely to 'reflect the losses which the plaintiffs have incurred' seems to me to be a circular statement.

(iv) I have considered whether the reasonableness of the amount which a plaintiff might recover towards the cost of repairing unreported defects in excess of the diminution in value might be determined by reference to the amount which the plaintiff could recover if he sold the property: i.e. the diminution in value plus any other recoverable losses and expenses. Such a limit was not contended for by [counsel for the plaintiffs]. It has the apparent attraction of enabling a plaintiff who chooses to retain the property to recover as much as he would recover if he chose to sell it. It seems to me, however, to be impossible to hold that such is the law in the case of such a contract as was made in this case. The plaintiff must, I think, prove that the loss which he claims to have suffered was caused by the breach of duty proved and he cannot do that by

---

[39] With whom both the President and Bingham L.J. agreed, Bingham L.J. noted that there should be "sound, prima facie rules to be applied in the ordinary run of cases" and stated: "In the present field . . . the purchase of houses by private buyers in reliance on a negligent survey of structure or condition, *Philips v. Ward* [1956] 1 W.L.R. 471 has been generally thought to lay down and in my view did lay down a prima facie rule for measuring damages." There was nothing in the facts of the present case to take it outside the prima facie rule in *Philips v. Ward*.

proving what his loss would have been in circumstances which have not happened."[40]

Ralph Gibson L.J. also rejected an argument that the plaintiffs could recover the cost of repairs as damages caused by entering into a transaction in reliance on the bad advice of the surveyor. The surveyor did not warrant that no repairs beyond those described in the survey report would be required within some period of time. In the absence of such a warranty, there was no basis for awarding the cost of repairs. The Court of Appeal held that *Hipkins v. Jack Cotton Partnership*[41] and *Syrett v. Carr and Neave*[42] were both wrongly decided on the issue of measure of damage.[43]

9–144   The reaffirmation by the Court of Appeal that the diminution in value principle, as distinct from the cost of repairs, was the proper measure of damage in cases where a person completed the purchase of a domestic property in reliance upon a negligent survey or overvaluation by a surveyor has been followed in all subsequent cases.[44] It should however be noted that the cases discussed in this section have concerned the sale of domestic property. Even cases involving commercial property such as *Broadoak Properties Ltd v. Young & White*[45] concerned the sale of a freehold. There is nothing in any of the reported cases to suggest that the diminution in value principle must apply to all land transactions, however far removed factually from those under consideration in the leading cases. Commercial transactions can often involve three parties: the developer of a new (and therefore apparently defect-free) building which is selling the freehold; an investor, typically a pension fund or similar institution, that is purchasing the freehold; and the purchaser of a leasehold interest from the developer, where the developer, with the benefit of the leasehold purchaser's covenants, is able to sell the "package" to the freehold purchaser. Should a negligent survey fail to reveal defects in such a building, it is by no means certain that the only measure of the leasehold purchaser's damage must be the diminution in value.

9–145   The cost of repairs can moreover assume considerable importance as part of the relevant material for an independent valuer attempting to establish the proper market value of a house at the time of the purchase. This was the situation in *Steward v. Rapley*[46] where the plaintiffs' independent surveyor took the cost of repairs to a house badly affected by dry rot to be the measure of the fall in the market value. Purchas L.J. summarised the position:

---

[40] [1991] 1 W.L.R. 1421 at 1435H.

[41] [1989] 2 E.G.L.R. 157.

[42] [1990] 2 E.G.L.R. 161.

[43] In Hipkins, the award should have been £8,900 plus interest. Given the delay between the purchase of the property and the trial, the total award would in any event have approached the cost of repairs.

[44] Examples include: *Heatley v. William H. Brown Ltd* [1992] 1 E.G.L.R. 289, *Ezekiel v. McDade* [1995] 2 E.G.L.R. 107, CA, *Matto v. Rodney Broom Associates* [1994] 2 E.G.L.R. 163, CA, and *Sneesby v. Goldings* [1995] 2 E.G.L.R. 102, 105, CA. In *Gardner v. Marsh & Parsons* [1997] 1 W.L.R. 489, CA, surveyors negligently overlooked a serious structural defect. This was only discovered when the property was about to be sold, and the defect was later rectified at the landlord's expense. The plaintiffs recovered damages on the diminution in value basis at the date of their original purchase. The surveyors appealed, arguing that had the defect been discovered on the original purchase the landlord would have rectified the same and the purchasers therefore suffered no loss. By a majority the Court of Appeal dismissed the surveyors' appeal, holding the actions of the landlord *res inter alios acta* and therefore collateral to the surveyors' negligence.

[45] [1989] 1 E.G.L.R. 263.

[46] [1989] 1 E.G.L.R. 159, CA.

"What in fact [the independent surveyor] has done is to take the costs of remedy as a measure and indication of the drop in the market value. He has not, and indeed it would be no part of his function, to say in law that it is open to the plaintiffs to recover the cost of repair and redecoration because, as the law stands at the moment, that is specifically not the position. But as I understand the state of the law, there is no objection to a person who wishes to present a professional assessment of a market value from arriving at that market value by taking a value based on a good state of condition in the house and then deducting from it, either fully or appropriately discounted, the cost of putting it into an acceptable marketable condition."[47]

This approach, and the necessary limitation to it, was confirmed by Ralph Gibson L.J. in *Watts v. Morrow*[48]:

"The cost of doing repairs to put right defects negligently not reported may be relevant to the proof of the market price of the house in its true condition: *see Steward v. Rapley*[49]; and the cost of doing repairs and the diminution in value may be shown to be the same. If, however, the cost of repairs would exceed the diminution in value, then the ruling in *Philips*, where it is applicable, prohibits recovery of the excess because it would give to the plaintiff more than his loss. It would put the plaintiff in the position of recovering damages for breach of a warranty that the condition of the house was correctly described by the surveyor and, in the ordinary case as here, no such warranty has been given."

(c) Costs of extrication. One possible factual situation which was expressly 9–146
left open by the Court of Appeal in *Watts v. Morrow* was a case where a claimant purchased a property, discovered defects, and then took steps to extricate himself from the property. Ralph Gibson L.J. stated:

"It is clear, and it was not argued to the contrary, that the ruling in *Philips* may be applicable to the case where the buyer has, after purchase, extricated himself from the transaction by selling the property. In the absence of any point on mitigation, the buyer will recover the diminution in value together with costs and expenses thrown away in moving in and out and of resale: see Romer L.J. in *Philips*. I will not here try to state the nature or extent of any additional recoverable items of damage. The damages recoverable where the plaintiff extricates himself from the transaction by resale are not necessarily limited to the diminution in value plus expenses. The consequences of the negligent advice and of the plaintiff entering into the transaction into which he would not have entered if properly advised, may be such that the diminution in value rule is not applicable. An example is the case of *County Personnel v. Pulver* [1987] 1 W.L.R. 916, CA, a case of solicitors' negligence, where the plaintiff recovered the capital losses caused by entering into the transaction."[50]

Thus it would appear that a claimant who buys a property which he would not have bought had he been properly advised and discovers very serious defects which lead him to sell the property may be entitled to recover all the losses sustained by reason of entering into the transaction. It is possible to contemplate a situation where such losses would include the cost of repairs. Thus if very serious dry rot was discovered, a claimant might be advised that it would be impossible to sell the property unless at least some works of rectification were

---

[47] *ibid.* at 161. The cost of repairs was used as a cross-check against the diminution in value in the Scottish case of *Wood v. McVicar* [1990] G.W.D. 37–2143, Lord Morton of Shuna.
[48] [1991] 4 All E.R. 937, 950F.
[49] [1989] 1 E.G.L.R. 159, CA.
[50] [1991] 1 W.L.R. 1421 at 1435D.

carried out in which event the costs of such repairs could be properly recoverable as mitigating the costs incurred in extricating the claimant from the transaction.

9–147 In *Patel v. Hooper & Jackson*,[51] the Court of Appeal awarded damages based on the costs of extrication from the transaction. The plaintiffs had purchased a house for £95,000 in reliance on a House Buyer's Report and Valuation. Having completed the purchase they discovered serious structural defects and damp which required to be corrected at substantial cost before the house was habitable. The plaintiffs were unable to afford to carry out the repairs and attempted to sell the house whilst living in alternative rentend accommodation. The Court of Appeal permitted an award of damages consisting of £25,250 being the difference in value; the costs of living in alternative accommodation for the five-year period until it was found that they ought reasonably to have put the house up for auction including the costs of moving from one set of rented accommodation to another and an award of £2,000 to each of the plaintiffs by way of general damages. The Court of Appeal refused to allow an award of the actual mortgage payments made in respect of the house as the judge had found that, but for the defendant's negligence, the plaintiffs would have bought a sound house for an equivalent price to that which they paid. The courts have also expressly contemplated awarding limited sums representing emergenccy work. In *Sneesby v. Goldings*[52] the trial judge had awarded the plaintiffs not only damages representing the diminution in value, but also £2,434.76 which they paid to a builder to construct permanent support work. Hoffmann L.J., reviewed the submissions of counsel for the appellant:

> "The principle laid down in *Philips v. Ward*, and followed by this court in *Watts v. Morrow* [1991] 1 W.L.R. 1421, is that a plaintiff is not entitled to be paid the costs of repairs. There are cases in which plaintiffs have, in addition to the diminution in value, been awarded the cost of emergency work not affecting the value of the property, such as the cost of hiring the acrow props in this case . . . [the builders'] bill was for permanent work and that should not have been included. In my view that must be right. The work which they did was simply repair work, which is excluded by the principle in *Philips v. Ward*."[53]

9–148 **(d) Collateral benefit.** As the difference in value represents the correct measure of damages in almost all cases, the courts have had to consider when it will be appropriate to oblige a claimant to give credit for collateral benefits received as a result of a purchase based upon negligent advice. The test applied by the courts has been whether the benefit received flowed directly from the transaction into which the claimant entered. The courts have had some difficulty in applying this test. The position may be complicated by the fact that to the extent that such benefits are foreseeable, they are likely to be reflected in the purchase price whilst to the extent that they are not, they could be regarded as irrelevant windfalls. The general tendency has been to restrict the taking into account of such benefits. An example of the approach adopted is to be found in *Gardner v. Marsh & Parsons*.[54] The plaintiffs purchased a long lease of a maisonette in a newly converted building in reliance on a full structural survey

---

[51] [1999] Lloyd's L.Rep. P.N. 1.
[52] [1995] 2 E.G.L.R. 102, 105, CA.
[53] *ibid.* at 105.
[54] [1997] 3 All E.R. 871.

report. Under the terms of the lease the landlords were responsible for carrying out structural repairs. The defendant surveyors negligently failed to point out a serious structural defect which was discovered three years after purchase when the plaintiffs attempted, unsuccessfully, to sell the property. After two years of negotiations, the necessary remedial works were carried out by the landlord. The Court of Appeal, by a majority, upheld the judge's award of £29,000, being the difference in value between the value of the maisonette in its assumed good condition and the actual value of the lease. The Court unanimously rejected, on the facts, the contention that had the report not been negligent, the defect would have been remedied by the landlord prior to purchase. The majority (Hirst and Pill L.JJ.) also found that, particularly given the long delay, the remedying of the defect could not be said to have formed part of the same transaction as the purchase. It followed that although the defect had been remedied at no cost to the plaintiffs, the benefit was collateral and not to be taken into account.[55] Similarly in *Treml v. Ernest W. Gibson and Partners*[56] the plaintiff in reliance on the defendant surveyors' report purchased a house subsequently found to have serious defects. An issue arose as to whether credit should be given for a grant towards the cost of repair received by the plaintiff from the local authority. Popplewell J. held:

> "I am clearly of the view that the sum does not fall to be deducted. Firstly, because it is irrelevant to a claim where the difference in value is the measure of damage and, secondly, because, to use legal shorthand, it is a collateral benefit which does not have to be taken into account."[57]

In *Marder v. Sautelle and Hicks*[58] the defendant surveyors negligently failed to warn the plaintiffs that the house had been constructed with defective materials. They purchased for £33,000 and then spent £26,000 on improvements and extensions. No repair was possible. The only solution was to demolish the defective part of the house and rebuild. The value of the house was taken to be £33,000, the site value, less demolition costs, was £13,500 with the difference between those two values being £19,500. That was the sum awarded by the judge. After the trial, the plaintiffs sold the property for £70,000.[59] The defendants appealed out of time and argued in the Court of Appeal that the £70,000 ought to be taken into account. This argument failed. Staughton L.J. considered that there were four reasons why the price obtained for the property might be of no benefit to the defendants. First, changes in the planning climate may have persuaded purchasers to pay more in the hope of building two houses rather than one house when the existing property had been demolished. Secondly, the £70,000 was at least partly explained by the extensions built and financed by the plaintiffs. Thirdly, the increase was accounted for to some extent by inflation in the property market, at rates that would have exceeded the 12 per cent simple interest awarded by the judge. Fourthly, the new purchasers may simply have paid too much: "in other words, the plaintiffs obtained a windfall. That would be

---

[55] Peter Gibson L.J. would have found that the plaintiffs' actions in obliging the landlords to comply with their obligations under the lease represented reasonable acts of mitigation of the plaintiffs' damage. As the acts were successful, the benefits were to be taken into account in the assessment of damages.
[56] [1984] 2 E.G.L.R. 162.
[57] *ibid.* at 72.
[58] [1988] 2 E.G.L.R. 187, CA.
[59] This was done openly, due notice of the intention having been given to the defendants.

a collateral matter for which the defendants could claim no credit".[60] The appeal was dismissed.[61]

(ii) *Negligent survey or valuation for a purchaser who withdraws from purchase before completion*

9–149 Where after a negligent survey or valuation a purchaser enters a contract for the purchase of a property but before completion discovers the defects overlooked and consequently does not proceed to completion, the purchaser will, prima facie, be entitled to damages for all the loss and expense incurred in entering and withdrawing from the contract to purchase so far as is attributable to the surveyors' default. Thus in *Buckland v. Watts*[62] the purchaser recovered in damages from the surveyor the amount of the deposit forfeited to the vendor, solicitors' fees incurred after the date of the surveyor's report and surveyor's fees attributable to the negligent survey.[63] Likewise in *Parsons v. Way & Waller Ltd*[64] the purchaser recovered the amount of his lost deposit.

(iii) *Negligent survey or valuation for lender*

9–150 A money lender, for example a bank, building society,[65] or finance company, will usually require a valuation of a property for the purpose of deciding the sum, if any, it is prepared to advance secured by a mortgage thereon. Following the decision in *BBL v. Eagle Star*,[66] it will almost invariably be necessary to carry out two tasks in order properly to assess the damages payable following a negligent valuation for a lender:

(a) assess the total loss suffered by the lender in accordance with the principles understood to be applicable prior to the decision in *BBL*; and

(b) assess whether the damages payable fall, in their entirety, within the scope of the duty undertaken by the valuer.

9–151 **(a) Assessment of the total loss.** Prior to the decision in *BBL*, the courts had simply sought to place a lender in the position which it would have been in had a competent valuation been provided to it. This involved ascertaining the losses sustained by entering into a loan and comparing them with the losses (if any)

---

[60] *ibid.* at 189. The Lord Justice referred to the analysis of collateral benefits in the then edition of *McGregor*, para. 16, and to *Slater v. Hoyle & Smith Ltd* [1920] 2 K.B. 11, and concluded: "I appreciate that this doctrine of collateral credit may not always seem very just to defendants who have to pay damages, but it is both logic and law."

[61] For an example of a case where it appears that the judge did find that claimants had suffered no loss, see *Devine v. Jefferys* [2001] P.N.L.R. 407 where it appears that H.H.J. Jack Q.C. held that borrowers who had had their debt extinguished by their lender more than six years after purchase had not suffered any relevant loss. The reasoning in the decision is not entirely clear and appears to support a contrary result to that achieved.

[62] (1968) 208 E.G. 969.

[63] Recovery of such fees in damages is surprising since such fees would have been incurred even if the surveyor had not been negligent.

[64] (1952) 159 E.G. 524. He failed on grounds of remoteness to recover fees paid to a building society for a valuation for mortgage purposes: see para. 9–092 above.

[65] In the case of a building society, a valuation is required by statute—s.62 of the Building Societies Act 1986.

[66] [1997] A.C. 191. For discussion as to the effects of the decision in relation to a valuer's scope of duty generally, see para. 9–113 above.

which would have been incurred had a competent valuation been provided. After *BBL* it is still necessary to carry out this task as a lender's recoverable losses cannot, in any circumstances, exceed the losses incurred. In *Swingcastle Ltd v. Gibson*,[67] the House of Lords had made it clear that a valuer did not warrant the accuracy of his valuation with the result that any profits which the lender had hoped to make as a result of entering into the loan would, ordinarily, be irrelevant. In 1985 the plaintiff, a finance company agreed to lend £10,000 to borrowers on the basis of a valuation of their house at £18,000 by a surveyor. The valuation was negligent. The annual rate of interest under the mortgage was 36.51 per cent with a default rate of 45.619 per cent if the borrowers fell into arrears. In 1986 the borrowers fell into arrears and surrendered possession to the lenders. The house was sold in February 1987 for £12,000, leaving a shortfall if accrued contractual interest were taken into account. The lenders brought an action in negligence against the valuer seeking to recover a total of £9,297.56, including accrued interest under the mortgage at the default rate. The county court judge gave judgment for £7,136.41, having disallowed a claimed early redemption penalty that could not properly have been awarded on the facts. The Court of Appeal[68] considered itself bound by *Baxter v. F. W. Gapp & Co. Ltd*,[69] and dismissed the appeal on the ground that the valuer was liable for the total amount of the lender's loss, including any unpaid interest at a default rate stipulated in the mortgage, as well as the principal sum advanced.

On the appeal to the House of Lords, the finance company deciding neither to **9–152** appear nor to make representations.[70] The valuer's case throughout the proceedings was that the lenders' calculation of their loss was made on the wrong basis. The damages should have been assessed on the basis that the lenders were entitled to be placed in the position that they would have been in if they had received a competent report from the valuer and had consequently made no loan to the borrowers. On the facts, it was argued that the lenders' damages were to be calculated on the basis that they should:

(a) take credit for the payment of £10,000 to the borrowers, £401.35 to their estate agents and £983.25 to their solicitors, and

(b) give credit for £1,734 paid by the borrowers between February 1985 and April 1986, and for £12,000 received on the sale of the property.

In addition, the finance company had for two years (or for such shorter period as might be thought proper) been deprived of the use of the £10,000 which they would not have lent but for the negligent valuation. The only speech was given by Lord Lowry, who began[71] by citing Lord Blackburn's dictum in *Livingstone*

---

[67] [1991] 2 A.C. 223, HL.

[68] [1990] 1 W.L.R. 1223.

[69] [1939] 2 All E.R. 752, CA.

[70] A decision that did not find favour with their Lordships, [1991] 2 A.C. 223 at 239. The conduct of the lenders may have contributed to the final order that the case be remitted with a direction that judgment be entered for the valuers, despite the fact that liability had been admitted in the county court and, on the appeal to the Court of Appeal, the valuers had asked for the substitution of a small amount of damages which had been admitted to be due.

[71] *ibid.* 232D.

v. Rawyards Coal Co.[72] He then cited (a) *Clerk and Lindsell on Torts*[73] which supported the contention that a mortgagee who can establish that no advance would have been made is entitled to recover the difference between the sum advanced and the sum recovered on sale of the property, plus any consequential losses and expenses; and (b) *McGregor on Damages*[74] which argued that (i) claims against valuers by the purchasers of property are to be assessed on a different basis from claims by the mortgagees of property; (ii) the relevant sum to be deducted from the amount of the unrecovered loan is not the true value of the property, but the amount that would have been lent if the valuer had not been negligent; (iii) the loss of the money advanced may be increased by expenses and reduced by receipts. Lord Lowry concluded: "The approach of the valuer in this case and the analysis of Neill L.J., which I have reproduced above, seem to me to be correct."[75] That statement then appeared to be of general application to circumstances where a lender proved it would not have lent with the benefit of non-negligent advice from a valuer. The case of *Baxter v. F. W. Gapp & Co. Ltd*[76] was then overruled by the House of Lords on the issue of calculation of damages:

> "My Lords, *Baxter v. F. W. Gapp & Co. Ltd* [1939] 2 K.B. 271, is not an attractive precedent. For one thing, it does not clearly exemplify the proposition contended for by the lenders, even if that proposition can be teased out of it; secondly, the dispute was about all the plaintiff's consequential damage and the pecuniary effect of the difference in interest rates . . . was relatively insignificant; and, thirdly and most important, the approach, if carefully scrutinised, seems contrary to principle: the aggrieved party was entitled to be placed in the same position as if the wrong had not occurred, and not to receive from the wrongdoer compensation for lost interest at the rate which the borrower had contracted to observe."[77]

Lord Lowry then considered the case as advanced by the lenders:

> "My Lords, it is clear that the lenders ought to have presented their claim on the basis that, if the valuer had advised properly, they would not have lent the money. Where they went wrong was to claim, not only correctly that they had to spend all the money which they did, but incorrectly that the valuer by his negligence deprived them of the interest which they would have received from the borrowers if the borrowers had paid up. The security for the loan was the property but the lenders did not have a further security consisting of a guarantee by the valuer that the borrowers would pay everything, or indeed anything, that was due from them to the lenders at the date, whenever it occurred, on which the loan transaction terminated. The fallacy of the lenders' case is that they have been trying to obtain from the valuer compensation for the borrowers' failure and not the proper damages for the valuer's negligence."[78]

This passage, and in particular the first sentence, strongly suggests that the House of Lords accepted that a distinction was to be made between a "no transaction"

---

[72] (1880) 5 App. Cas. 25, at 39.
[73] (16th ed., 1989), para. 11–45, pp. 670–671.
[74] (15th ed., 1988), paras 1212–1218, pp. 749–753.
[75] [1991] 2 A.C. 223, 237A.
[76] [1939] 2 K.B. 271.
[77] [1991] 2 A.C. 223, at 236.
[78] *ibid.* at 238.

and a "successful transaction" case when assessing damages in a lender/valuer case.[79] Lord Lowry then applied the reasoning to the facts of the case:

"Taking the figures I have mentioned of £10,000,[80] £401.35[81] and £983.25[82] on one side and £12,000[83] and £1,734[84] on the other, the lenders are £2,349.40 in credit. Clause 9 of the mortgage agreement provided that the lenders could debit the mortgage account with 'all costs expenses and disbursements incurred directly or indirectly in relation thereto'. This no doubt explains the claim for £344.99, though not the claim for interest thereon of £129.31. But I find it impossible to say whether the whole or part of the £344.99 should be taken into account against the valuer or simply be treated as administrative expenses of the mortgage chargeable by agreement against the borrowers. In the absence of any evidence as to how the lenders financed the loan or evidence showing how the money, if not lent to the borrowers, could have been profitably employed, I consider that 12 per cent interest, which would correspond to the 9 per cent allowed by Gibson J. in *Corisand Investments Ltd v. Druce & Co.* (1978) 248 E.G. 315, is the proper rate at which to recompense the lenders for being deprived of their £10,000. The actual time was two years, which would yield a result of £2,400, but one may ask whether it was reasonable for the tortfeasor to bear the liability up to the date of sale in February 1987, possession of the property having been surrendered on 30 June 1986. Moreover, it is not clear how a calculation of damages would be affected by the incidence of tax or whether this is a case in which it would have been reasonable for the court to contemplate partial recovery by the lenders against the borrowers: see *London and South of England Building Society v. Stone* [1983] 1 W.L.R. 1242. It was for the lenders to furnish the evidence by which to prove their case on the correct basis."[85]

---

[79] A point made by the Court of Appeal in *Banque Bruxelles Lambert SA v. Eagle Star Insurance Co. Ltd* [1995] Q.B. 375, 412. The measure of loss in a "no-transaction" case is:
  (a) the difference between the advance and any capital recovered, whether by way of repayment by the borrower, or from the sale of the mortgaged property; plus
  (b) consequential expenses, for example incurred in repossession proceedings against the borrower; plus
  (c) interest at an appropriate rate to reflect the loss of use of the capital sum advanced, credit being given for any interest payments made by the borrower.
Note the comment by Lord Lowry in *Swingcastle Ltd v. Alastair Gibson* [1991] 2 A.C. 223, 237: "There is, as Neill L.J. perceived, no cut and dried solution to calculating the amount of damages in cases of this kind. It depends on the evidence." In a "transaction" case, that is where there has been a negligent survey or valuation for a lender who would have lent a lesser sum with a proper survey or valuation, an appropriate measure of loss in such cases is:
  (a) the difference between (i) the advance actually made less any capital recovered, whether by way of repayment by the borrower, or from the sale of the mortgaged property, and (ii) the lesser advance that would have been made, less any capital that would have been recovered in such circumstances; plus
  (b) any consequential expenses that would not have been incurred in any event; plus
  (c) interest at an appropriate rate to reflect the loss of use of the additional capital sum advanced, credit being given for any interest payments received by the lender on the additional capital.
[80] The original advance.
[81] The estate agent's charges.
[82] Solicitor's fees.
[83] The sum received on the sale of the property.
[84] Sums paid to the lenders by the borrowers in respect of capital and interest between February 1985 and April 1986. Note that no distinction was made between the two elements. Where larger sums are involved, substantial repayments of capital by the borrower may well have an effect on the interest calculation.
[85] *ibid.* at 239. For criticism of this decision, see Dugdale, "Causation and the professional's responsibility" (1991) 7 P.N. 78.

9–153 Lord Lowry calculated interest to reflect the loss of use of capital at 12 per cent.[86] In doing so the House of Lords followed the nine per cent awarded by Gibson J. in *Corisand Investments*. In neither case, however, did the lender adduce evidence of what it cost to finance the advance, and in the absence of such evidence a rate approximating to the Special Account rate[87] was selected. Lenders will generally have no difficulty in proving what they paid for their funds, for example, from the money market, and higher rates are likely to be awarded where such evidence is accepted. Even when the rates have been determined, the calculation of interest to reflect the loss of use of capital is likely to prove troublesome where the borrower has made payments of both capital and contractual interest. In some cases, the computerised records of the lender will permit an accurate calculation of interest to be made. In others, a broad brush approach will be necessary.[88]

9–154 There may be rare cases where the lender is able to prove that funds available to it for lending were limited, and that had it received a proper valuation it would not have lent to the borrower, but to a different and identified borrower who would have paid full contractual interest but whose demand for finance from the lender could not be satisfied. In such circumstances, there would be the evidential basis for an argument by the lender that contractual interest should be awarded to reflect the loss of use of such capital. Recovery would be subject to such loss being reasonably foreseeable. This possibility was alluded to by Lord Lowry in *Swingcastle*: "In the absence of any evidence as to how the lenders financed the loan or evidence showing how the money, if not lent to the borrowers, could have been profitably employed . . . ",[89] a reference to the analysis of Neill L.J. in the Court of Appeal[90] that he had cited with approval:

> "The lender could be awarded a sum equivalent to the amount he would have earned by way of interest on another loan if he had had the money available for this purpose. In my view, however, such an award should not be made in the absence of evidence that the money lent would have been used for another transaction. This evidence would have to be directed to proving an unsatisfied demand for loans and I anticipate that such evidence might seldom be forthcoming. Moreover, even if evidence of a lost transaction were available, I see no reason why the interest should be at the default rate rather than at the ordinary rate provided for in a standard contract for this type of business . . . "[91]

9–155 **(b) Assessment of the scope of the duty.** An apparent consequence of the way in which damages were assessed in *Swingcastle* was that valuers bore the risk of a fall in the property market, but conversely acquired an advantage when the property market was rising. In a falling market, the price achieved for a property disposed of by a mortgagee in possession will generally be lower, and consequently the difference between the sum advanced in reliance of the negligent valuation, and the recovery by way of disposal of the property will be greater than in a static market. In addition, it may take longer to sell property in such a market, and so the period over which interest is awarded to reflect the loss of use of capital may be longer. In a rising market, the consequences of a negligent

---

[86] *ibid.* at 239.
[87] Or its predecessor, the Short Term Investment Account rate.
[88] But note *Brandeis Goldschmidt & Co. Ltd v. Western Transport Ltd* [1981] Q.B. 864.
[89] [1991] 2 A.C. 223, at 239.
[90] [1990] 1 W.L.R. 1223, CA.
[91] Cited by Lord Lowry, [1991] 2 A.C. 223, at 230, approved at 237.

valuation will be mitigated, and even extinguished, as the rise in the market brings the value of the property up towards the negligent valuation. In such a market, the value of a claim can diminish to the point where there is little commercial benefit in commencing proceedings.

The United Kingdom property market experienced a prolonged period of **9–156** sustained growth in the latter part of the 1980s, with a variety of established and new lending institutions competing to lend funds to support dealing in property. This period of rapid increase in values was followed by a severe market depression in the early 1990s. Although property market fluctuations had been experienced before,[92] the degree to which the property market collapsed was exceptional and on this occasion (unlike the 1970s) the effect was not masked or mitigated by inflation. A consequence of the nature and extent of the collapse was that lenders sought to recover their very substantial property lending losses from allegedly negligent valuers and solicitors. They sought to avoid this consequence, and the case which finally determined the issue of who should bear such losses was *BBL v. Eagle Star*.[93] The practical effect of the decision was that valuers were not held to be responsible for losses occasioned by the fall in the property market. As set out above,[94] the House did this by finding that, in the ordinary case, the scope of the duty undertaken by a valuer, whether in contract or in tort, did not extend to losses occasioned by a subsequent fall in the property market. Lord Hoffmann, giving the sole speech, stated:

> "The calculation of loss must . . . involve comparing what the plaintiff has lost as a result of making the loan with what his position would have been if he had not made it. If for example the lender would have lost the same amount of money on some other transaction, then the valuer's negligence has caused him no loss. Likewise if he had substantially overvalued the property so that the lender stands to make a loss if he has to sell the security at current values, but a rise in the property market enables him to realise enough to pay off the whole loan, the lender has suffered no loss."[95]

In this passage it is made clear that whilst it is the lender that in the ordinary course must bear the burden of a fall in the property market, the valuer also takes the benefit of any rise in the property market. Such a rise will reduce or extinguish any recoverable damages. Lord Hoffmann justified this by confirming that if the market rises, it reduces or eliminates the loss which the lender would otherwise have suffered. However, if it falls, "it may result in more loss than is attributable to the valuer's error. There is no contradiction in the asymmetry".[96] That loss did not fall within the scope of the valuer's duty of care.

The distinction between the "no-transaction" and "successful transaction" **9–157** cases was declared to be "quite irrelevant to the scope of the duty of care" and "not based on any principle and should . . . be abandoned."[97] In either case, the negligent valuer is responsible for the loss suffered by the lender in consequence

---

[92] "In 1972 the plaintiffs, in common with other finance houses, were obliged to raise their limits. This was because much land development and speculation was then going on and inflation was running high. There was a great deal of money in hand; interest rates were low in the first part of the year. Finance houses, or some of them, so it was said, were almost falling over one another in their eagerness to lend it." *per* Watkins J., *in Singer & Friedlander Ltd v. John D. Wood & Co.* [1977] 2 E.G.L.R. 84.
[93] [1997] A.C. 191.
[94] See paras 9–113 *et seq.* above.
[95] [1997] A.C. 191 at 217G.
[96] *ibid.* at 218B.
[97] *ibid.* at 218C.

of having lent upon an inaccurate valuation. However, the House of Lords did not go so far as to say that the distinction was of no practical use. On the contrary, Lord Hoffmann conceded that the distinction had "a certain pragmatic truth" when it came to calculating the lender's loss. He conceded that, faced with a "no transaction" claim, the most likely alternative to be advanced by a negligent valuer was a "successful transaction" simply because of the difficulty in proving what else the lender would have done with the money. Despite Lord Hoffmann's injunction to abandon the distinction, it is a distinction that will naturally and necessarily arise from the evidence in most cases and will require a specific finding of fact to enable the calculation of damages to take place. In *South Australia Asset Management Corporation v. York Montague Ltd* the House of Lords dismissed the appeal, yet May J. had carried out a conventional "no transaction/successful transaction" analysis. The practicality of the distinction was adverted to by Lord Lowry in *Swingcastle Ltd v. Gibson*[98] and Lord Hoffmann did not criticise the earlier decision; on the contrary, he invoked it as an example of the distinction he was making between the measure of damages for a breach of duty and the measure for a breach of warranty.[99]

9–158   The House of Lords dealt briefly with a number of other cases and submissions. Apart from the question of interest, the decision in *Baxter v. F. W. Gapp & Co. Ltd*[1] to award the whole of the loss suffered by the lender did not on its facts offend against the above principle.[2] The principle of causation that a plaintiff's reasonable attempt to cope with the consequences of the defendant's breach of duty does not break the causal connection between the breach of duty and the ultimate loss was reaffirmed.[3] The "cushion" theory was rejected. This theory involved calculating what the lender would have lost if a loan, of the same proportion of the true value of the property as the actual loan bore to the reported value, had been made. This permitted the lender to claim some of the losses caused by a fall in the market but limited to the proportion represented by the "cushion". Lord Hoffmann commented "there seems no justification for deeming him, in the teeth of the evidence, to have been willing to lend the same proportion on a lower valuation".[4] In so saying, Lord Hoffmann once again indicated that evidence as to whether the case was "no transaction" or "successful transaction" would be necessary. Only such evidence could provide the answer to whether the lender would indeed have lent nothing with a competent valuation, that being "the teeth of the evidence" which would make a cushion calculation involving the assumption that a lesser but proportionate loan would have been made, absurd. An argument that the rights acquired by the lender should be valued at the date of the loan, and compared with the amount of the loan, was rejected. Although such a procedure would ignore subsequent market movements, it would also ignore all subsequent events. Except in cases where all the loss caused by the breach could properly be quantified at once, the calculation of damages was bound to be affected by the extent to which loss in the future had

---

[98] [1991] 2 A.C. 223, 238F, and see para. 9–152 above.
[99] [1997] A.C. 191 at 216G.
[1] [1938] 4 All E.R. 457, Goddard L.J.; [1939] 2 K.B. 752, CA.
[2] [1997] A.C. 191 at 217E.
[3] *ibid.* at 219A. Examples cited in support by Lord Hoffmann included *County Personnel (Employment Agency) Ltd v. Alan R. Pulver & Co.* [1987] 1 W.L.R. 916 and *Hayes v. James & Charles Dodd* [1990] 2 All E.R. 815. It was in the latter case that Staughton L.J. first described and named the distinction between "no transaction" and "successful transaction" cases.
[4] [1997] A.C. 191 at 219G.

to be estimated at the date of trial.[5] The House of Lords also rejected the argument that the damage falling within the scope of the duty should be limited to the excess over the highest non-negligent valuation, rather than the excess over the correct valuation. Lord Hoffmann said:

"In deciding whether or not [the valuer] has been negligent, the court must bear in mind that valuation is seldom an exact science and that within a band of figures valuers may differ without one of them being negligent. But once the valuer has been found to have been negligent, the loss for which he is responsible is that which has been caused by the valuation being wrong. For this purpose the court must form a view as to what a correct valuation would have been. This means the figure which it considers most likely that a reasonable valuer, using the information available at the relevant date, would have put forward as the amount which the property was most likely to fetch if sold upon the open market. While it is true that there would have been a range of figures which the reasonable valuer might have put forward, the figure most likely to have been put forward would have been the mean figure of that range. There is no basis for calculating damages upon the basis that it would have been a figure at one or other extreme of the range."[6]

The "cap" theory whereby the lender's damages were limited to the amount **9–159** of the overvaluation, was also rejected, but in so doing, Lord Hoffmann noted that in practice the application of the "cap" was generally likely to produce the same result as the requirement that loss should be a consequence of the valuation being wrong.[7] This was because the usual consequence would be that the lender had made an advance which was thought to be secured to a correspondingly greater extent. This is illustrated by the actual result in each of the three appeals before the House of Lords, where in each case the "cap" theory provides the same answer as that given by Lord Hoffmann.[8]

(i) *South Australia Asset Management Corporation v. York Montague Ltd.* The negligent valuation of a development site in 1990 was £15 m., and a loan of £11 m. was made to a joint venture partnership. The actual value of the property in 1990 was £5 m. In 1994 the property was sold for £2.477 m. May J. quantified the loss at £9,753,000 and deducted 25 per cent for contributory negligence. The consequence of valuation being negligently wrong was that the lenders had £10 m. less security than they thought. If the lenders had had this margin, they would have suffered no loss. So the whole loss of £9,753,000 (less 25 per cent) was within the scope of the valuer's duty. The appeal was accordingly dismissed.

---

[5] *ibid.* at 220G.

[6] *ibid.* at 221G. The argument rejected by the House of Lords had never received judicial support. For example, in *United Bank of Kuwait v. Prudential Property Services Ltd* [1994] 2 E.G.L.R. 100, the negligent valuer argued that the starting point for any assessment of damages was the difference between the highest non-negligent valuation and the defendant valuer's negligent valuation. Gage J. preferred the submission of the plaintiff that the starting point was the correct valuation, as found by the judge. The plaintiff had contracted to obtain from the defendant the correct valuation, not the highest non-negligent valuation.

[7] *ibid.* at 219H.

[8] *ibid.* at 222B. The three cases were *South Australia Asset Management Corporation v. York Montague Ltd*, May J., unreported April 6, 1995; *United Bank of Kuwait plc v. Prudential Property Services Ltd* [1994] 2 E.G.L.R. 100, Gage J., [1995] Q.B. 375, CA; *Nykredit Mortgage Services Ltd v. Edward Erdman Group Ltd*, Judge Byrt Q.C. sitting as a judge of the Queen's Bench Division, unreported, October 1, 1993. An appeal on liability in the latter case was heard subsequent to the appeal on damages: [1996] 1 E.G.L.R. 119, CA.

(ii) *United Bank of Kuwait plc v. Prudential Property Services Ltd.* The negligent valuation of the property in 1990 was £2.5 m., a loan of £1.75 m. was made. In fact, in 1990 the actual value of the property was between £1.8 m. and £1.85 m. In 1992 the property was sold for £950,000. Gage J. calculated the loss (including unpaid interest) at £1,309,000. Applying the principle that damages were to be limited to the consequences of the valuation being wrong, the lender had £700,000 or £650,000 less security than was thought. As this sum was less than the amount ordered by Gage J. the appeal was allowed, and the damages were reduced to the difference between the valuation and the correct value. In default of agreement as to what the correct value was, the case was remitted to Gage J. for decision on the basis of the facts called at trial. The important question of interest was not dealt with, and adjourned *sine die.*

(iii) *Nykredit Mortgage Services Ltd v. Edward Erdman Group Ltd.* The negligent valuation in 1990 was £3.5 m., and a loan of £2.45 m. was made. The actual value of the property in 1990 was £2 m. In 1993 the property was sold for £345,000. Judge Byrt Q.C. calculated the loss at £3,058,000. Submissions by the lender based on what would have happened if the valuer had provided accurate information was held not to be the basis of the valuer's liability.[9] The appeal was allowed. The damages were the difference between £3.5 m. and the true value at the date of the valuation of £2 m.: £1.5 m.

9–160   Although the House of Lords rejected the "cap" argument, in practice the following steps appear to be required when calculating damages in a case where a lender sues a valuer in respect of an admitted or proved negligent over-valuation:

1. Distinguish between a duty on a valuer to provide information for the purpose of enabling a lender to decide upon a course of action, and a duty to advise a lender as to what course of action should be taken. In the absence of express contractual terms most, if not all, negligent valuation cases will be classified as negligent information cases.[10] If the case is one of the provision of negligent information, the procedure below is appropriate, which will limit damages to the foreseeable consequences of the information being wrong. If the case is one of negligent advice, the procedure adopted by the Court of Appeal in *BBL*[11] is appropriate, and the defendant will be liable for all the foreseeable loss which is a consequence of the plaintiff having acted on such advice.

2. Calculate the lender's actual loss. This is a conventional *Swingcastle*-type calculation of capital outlay less capital receipts, and loss of use of capital less income receipts. It will include losses caused by any fall in the property market. This will produce a number of heads of damage, for

---

[9] *ibid.* at 222H.
[10] See the discussion at para. 9–117 above in relation to the approach of the High Court of Australia in *Kenny & Good v. MGICA* [1999] H.C.A. 25.
[11] [1995] Q.B. 375, and see the guidance in *Swingcastle Ltd v. Alastair Gibson* [1991] 2 A.C. 223. These conventional ("transaction" and "no transaction") calculations have been set out in para. 9–152 at n. 79.

example irrecoverable losses on the capital sum lent, loss of use of the capital, and costs and expenses of repossession.[12]

3. Calculate the lender's hypothetical loss. This is an assessment on the basis that the lender's claim is for breach of warranty, that is damages assessed on the basis that the information provided by the valuer was accurate. This determines the position the lender would have been in if the valuation had been accurate, rather than a negligent over-valuation, and the lender had acted upon the same by lending the sum in fact lent. This will also produce a number of heads of damage, which may or may not be the same as those resulting from the actual loss calculation.

4. Damages are then calculated by deducting from the actual losses those hypothetical losses which would have been incurred in the event that the negligent valuation had been correct. The remaining losses fall within the scope of the duty that was breached. They may fairly be described as consequences of the valuation being wrong.

In almost every case, the same result will be obtained simply by comparing the amount of the negligent overvaluation with the actual loss, calculated in the conventional manner. Where the overvaluation exceeds the actual loss, the actual loss is awarded. Where the actual loss exceeds the overvaluation, the award is, for practical purposes, "capped" at the amount of the overvaluation. This is illustrated by comparing the result in *South Australia Asset Management Corporation v. York Montague Ltd* with that in *United Bank of Kuwait plc v. Prudential Property Services Ltd*.[13] It is however important to bear in mind that the House of Lords has rejected the concept of a "cap", and that the calculation described above is a measure of damages. This has consequences for example, for interest, which is applied to measures of damages, but would not be applied subsequent to an arbitrary "cap" on the plaintiff's damages.

The above approach to the assessment of damages was confirmed by the **9–161** House of Lords in the subsequent case *Nykredit Mortgage Bank plc v. Edward Erdman Group Ltd (No. 2)*.[14] In that case the question was as to the date upon which interest should run[15] but the House of Lords also took the opportunity further to explain the substantive judgment delivered in the speech of Lord Hoffmann. Lord Nicholls went through the steps necessary to identify whether a lender had sustained "measurable, relevant loss":

"The first step . . . is to identify the relevant measure of loss. It is axiomatic that in assessing loss caused by the defendant's negligence the basic measure is the comparison between (a) what the plaintiff's position would have been if the defendant had fulfilled his duty of care and (b) the plaintiff's actual position. Frequently, but not always, the plaintiff would not have entered into the relevant transaction had the defendant fulfilled his duty of care and advised the plaintiff, for instance, of the true value of the property. When this is so, a professional negligence claim calls for a

---

[12] It is important to note that it will be the actual outlay made by the lender which will be important in this calculation. Monies retained by a lender (for example in "blocked" deposit accounts) will be left out of a calculation of loss—see *Arab Bank v. John D. Wood* [2000] Lloyd's L.Rep. P.N. 173 at 198.

[13] See para. 9–159, above.

[14] [1997] 1 W.L.R. 1627.

[15] As to which see para. 9–162 below.

comparison between the plaintiff's position had he not entered into the transaction in question and his position under the transaction. That is the basic comparison."[16]

Lord Nicholls illustrated the workings of this "basic comparison" in the context of a lender's action in respect of a negligent valuation:

"The basic comparison is between (a) the amount of money lent by the plaintiff, which he would still have had in the absence of the loan transaction, plus interest at a proper rate, and (b) the value of the rights acquired, namely the borrower's covenant and the true value of the overvalued property."

The reference to interest in this context is to interest representing the cost to the lender of the money advanced, which would be claimed as special damages. Lord Nicholls then emphasised that in accordance with the opinion of Lord Hoffmann in the substantive judgments in the case the valuer was liable for the adverse consequences, flowing from entering into the transaction, which were attributable to the deficiency in the valuation. If the "basic comparison" demonstrated a loss, then it was necessary to enquire further and see whether all or part of that loss was the consequence of the deficiency in the security. He answered this inquiry by showing that, in the ordinary case, the damages will be "capped" to the extent of the over-valuation:

"Typically, the answer to this further inquiry will correspond with the amount of the loss as shown by the basic comparison, for the lender would not have entered into the transaction had he been properly advised, but limited to the extent of the over-valuation."[17]

9–162   (c) **Interest on damages.** The issue in *Nykredit* was as to the date from which interest should be payable to a lender making a claim against a negligent valuer following *BBL*. Lord Nicholls noted that the Supreme Court Act 1981 s.35A(1) (as amended) provided for statutory interest on damages for all or part of the period between the date when the cause of action arose and the date of judgment. This raised the question of when the lender's cause of action . Following his analysis of the decision in *BBL*,[18] Lord Nicholls concluded that this was the point when "relevant, measurable loss" occurred. This would be when the cause of action accrued and would provide the date from when statutory interest should run. Given that the "basic comparison" required an evaluation of the difference between the money lent plus interest and the value of the rights acquired by the lender, Lord Nicholls acknowledged that the borrower's covenant had to be evaluated. Lord Nicholls realised that this enquiry might produce "evidential and practical difficulties" and that the quantification of the lender's loss would be less certain and less satisfactory for being carried out prior to the disposal of the security property. However, valuing the worth of the borrower's covenant was not expected to be "unduly troublesome" and some guidance was provided.[19] On the facts of the case the borrower's covenant was worthless, there was immediate default and the amount lent at all times exceeded the true value of the property. The cause of action therefore arose at the date of completion of the loan in March 1990 and by December 1990 the lender had suffered its full allowable loss of

---

[16] [1997] 1 W.L.R. 1627 at 1631D.
[17] *ibid.* at 1632A–B.
[18] See para. 9–161 above.
[19] *ibid.* at 1632C.

£1.4 m. Interest was awarded at the agreed rate of 0.4 per cent above LIBOR from December 1990. Lord Hoffmann pointed out[20] that the loss reached £1.4 m. by December 1990 because of the cost to the lender of the funds it had advanced to the borrower. The lender could not claim statutory interest from the date of the loan in March 1990 because such an award would be double recovery.

Mortgagor's covenants to repay. *Nykredit* emphasised the potential impor-   9–163
tance of a proper assessment of a borrower's covenant both to the date to which interest should run and to the date from which the primary limitation period should run in tort.[21] This issue had received only limited judicial attention prior to the decision in *Nykredit*. In *Swingcastle v. Gibson*, the mortgagors' covenants to repay the money borrowed had been worthless and therefore irrelevant to the final calculation.[22] In *Eagle Star Insurance Co. Ltd v. Gale and Power*,[23] the covenants had, however, proved significant. Relying on the defendant surveyors' negligent survey and valuation the plaintiffs advanced £3,015 to a purchaser on the security of a house and the personal covenants of himself and his wife. The purchaser further covenanted to reduce the mortgage by £1,500 to be received in the near future. Owing to subsidence the house was worth only £1,600. The plaintiffs claimed damages measured by the difference between the valuation given and the actual value and contended that the covenants were irrelevant as *res inter alios acta*. Devlin J. rejected the argument, holding that the transaction had to be looked at as a whole and that the security could not be separated from the personal covenants. He considered that the only method of assessing damages was to calculate what the plaintiffs would have obtained had they realised their security. Since the two main items of security, the value of the house, £1,600, and the covenant to repay the £1,500 together amounted to £3,100, quite apart from the personal covenants, the plaintiffs would not have lost their money. He nevertheless concluded that it was not a case for nominal damages since something like illness might intervene, and the plaintiffs were awarded £100 in damages to indemnify them against the possibility of not being able to recover their money from the mortgagor.

Devlin J.'s decision in the *Eagle Star* case may be contrasted with the Court   9–164
of Appeal's decision in *London and South of England Building Society v. Stone*.[24] In that case the plaintiff building society in reliance upon the defendant valuer's report advanced to borrowers £11,880 secured by way of mortgage on a house purchased by the latter for £14,880. The advance was repayable over 25 years and the legal charge contained covenants by the borrowers to repay the advance and to keep the property in repair. Subsequently the house was found to be in danger of collapse through subsidence. The borrowers could not afford to finance the necessary repairs themselves and looked to the plaintiff for assistance. The cost of repairs was originally estimated at £14,000. The plaintiff decided to proceed with repairs which eventually cost £29,000. The borrowers maintained payments under the legal charge throughout and after completion of the repairs sold the house for £26,500 and repaid the outstanding advance. Russell J. at first instance[25] held that the defendant had been negligent and awarded the plaintiff

---

[20] *ibid.* at 1637H.
[21] See para. 9–009 above.
[22] See, for another example, *Corisand Investments Ltd v. Druce & Co.* [1978] 2 E.G.L.R. 86.
[23] (1955) 166 E.G. 37.
[24] [1983] 1 W.L.R. 1242, CA.
[25] Reported in [1982] 1 E.G.L.R. 139.

damages of £8,880 assessed by: (a) taking the difference between £11,880, the sum advanced, and what would have been advanced given a competent valuation, namely nil, and (b) crediting against that difference the sum of £3,000 being his assessment of the value to the building society of the borrowers' personal covenants. The judge refused to award the full cost of repairs in damages on the basis that the society had acted unreasonably in spending so much on repairs. The plaintiff successfully appealed against the deduction of £3,000. But the Court of Appeal were divided on the issue. Both O'Connor and Stephenson L.JJ. held that the plaintiff was under no duty to mitigate its loss by seeking to enforce the borrowers' covenants. Stephenson L.J. said:

> "the valuer is not merely asking the court to take account of what has actually been paid to the lenders; he is requiring the lenders to have taken action in claiming payment from the borrowers; and it is one thing for a wrongdoer to claim the benefit of a benefit obtained by the wronged party under a contract with another; it is quite another thing—and, in my judgment, a far stronger thing—to claim the valuation of the chance of such a benefit which the wronged party has deliberately chosen not to take. In that case it seems to me the wrongdoer must show that the wronged party's reasoned choice to waive his contractual rights against the third party is unreasonable in the ordinary course of events in the particular field of commercial business and in all the circumstances (it may be something special) of the particular case." [26]

Sir Denys Buckley, dissenting, considered that the £3,000 was correctly deducted and endorsed the approach of Devlin J. in *Eagle Star Insurance Co. Ltd v. Gale and Power*[27] in taking into account the borrowers' personal covenants. O'Connor L.J. considered that the latter case was wrongly decided, but Stephenson L.J. expressed no view on the matter.

9–165   After *Nykredit*, the correct approach to the proper valuation of a borrower's covenant was considered in the context of a dispute as to limitation, by the Court of Appeal in *DnB Mortgages v. Bullock & Lees*.[28] In February 1990 the plaintiff had loaned £136,000 on the security of a house valued at £170,000 by the defendants. The borrowers continued to make mortage payments until January 1991, when they defaulted. The writ was issued in May 1996. The judge found that the value of the house in May 1990 (*i.e.* six years before the writ) was £130,000 whilst the mortgage debt had, by then, reached £140,080, with the result that the value of the borrowers' covenant was critical in deciding whether or not the lender had suffered loss within the limitation period. The judge had found (largely taking into account the subsequent default) that the value of the covenant was not, by May 1990, worth as much as £10,000 with the result that the claim was statute barred. This conclusion would not, however, have been been apparent at May 1990. Robert Walker L.J., giving the sole substantive judgment, commented that it was not entirely clear from the speeches in the House of Lords, how the borrowers' covenant was to be valued.[29] He stated that there was some degree of tension in *Nykredit*

---

[26] [1983] 1 W.L.R. 1242, 1262, Stephenson L.J. rejected the argument that the borrowers' obligation to repay was so collateral or remote as to be disregarded altogether in measuring the lender's loss, *ibid.* at 1261.
[27] (1955) 166 E.G. 37.
[28] [2000] Lloyd's L.Rep. P.N. 290.
[29] *ibid.* at 295, col. 1.

"between the approach of valuing the mortgagor's covenant as part of a bundle of rights comprised in a marketable security (and to be valued as the market would have valued it at the time, without hindsight) and the approach of valuing it on fundamentals (that is, on the objective evidence, available when the case is heard, of the true state of affairs at the valuation date) . . . In this case the two approaches might lead to different results. So far as they would lead to different results, I consider that the mortgagor's covenant had to be valued on the evidence available to the deputy judge, restricted though it was, as to the true facts".[30]

It is now clear that the value of a borrower's covenant will be taken into account in deciding whether a lender has suffered loss following a negligent valuation. I will sometimes be necessary for a court to consider carefully the true financial circumstances of a borrower (rather than how they appeared at the time). This may widen the scope of the relevant enquiry.[31–32]

(d) Contributory negligence by lender. Because the lender's recovery is 9–166 confined to the consequences of the incorrect valuation, two questions arose as to the proper relationship between the damages recoverable from a valuer and contributory negligence by a lender. The first was whether, given that the lender could not recover more than the consequences of the information as to value being wrong, it was possible to argue that matters unrelated to such a loss, for example, imprudent lending practices, should not be considered negligence that has contributed to the loss at all. The second was as to whether any deduction should be applied to the entire loss suffered by the lender or only to such damages as the valuer was found liable for. Following the decision of the House of Lords in *Platform Home Loans Ltd v. Oyston Shipways Ltd*,[33] the law appears to be that any negligence which contributes to the decision to lend can be considered to be contributory negligence but that any reduction will be applied to the lender's total loss. In that case, the defendants negligently valued a property for £1.5 m. in 1990, when its true value was £1 m. The overvaluation was therefore £500,000. The plaintiff lent the borrower £1.05 m. The property was sold in 1993 for £435,000. The plaintiff sought to recover their overall loss of £680,174 in damages from the valuers. Jacob J. held that the plaintiffs were responsible for £40,000 of their loss because of a failure to mitigate the same, and had been a total of 20 per cent contributorily negligent in two respects. First, in lending 70 per cent of a loan to value ratio on a loan over £1 m., and secondly for failing to require the borrower properly to complete the mortgage application form. After further argument, Jacob J. rejected the argument that the two forms of contributory negligence should be treated differently, because one impinged on the duty of the valuer to provide the correct valuation, whereas the other did not. The contributory negligence of 20 per cent was applied across the board and judgment for £489,398 plus interest was given. On appeal,[34] Morritt L.J. concluded that the lender's overall loss was suffered partly as a result of its own fault

---

[30] *ibid.* at 295, col. 1 to col. 2.
[31–32] For a post-*Nykredit* example of a case where a judge found that a borrower's covenant was worthless at the time of making a loan, see *Mortgage Corporation v. Lambert* [1999] Lloyd's L.Rep. P.N. 947. This conclusion was not challenged on the appeal, reported at [2000] P.N.L.R. 820, which considered s.14A of the Limitation Act 1980—see further para. 9–009, above.
[33] [2000] 2 A.C. 190.
[34] [1998] Ch. 466.

and partly as a result of the fault of the valuers. The claim against the valuers, although limited in accordance with *BBL* was nonetheless a claim "in respect of" the overall loss suffered by the lender for it was an element in or ingredient of that loss. On that basis, the court entitled to apportion the damages in respect of the claim by reference to the lender's share of responsibility for the overall loss. However, the Court of Appeal allowed the defendants' appeal and applied the 20 per cent deduction to the overvaluation of £500,000, rather than to the overall loss with the result that damages of £400,000 were awarded.

9–167   The House of Lords, by a majority of four to one, allowed the lender's appeal. Lord Hobhouse concluded[35] that the totality of the plaintiffs' loss was partly caused by the defendant's fault and therefore the case came within the scope of section 1(1) of the 1945 Act. The court then had to form a view as to what was just and reasonable having regard to the plaintiff's share in the responsibility for the damage and to reduce the plaintiffs' recoverable damages accordingly. Lord Hobhouse concluded that the reduction of 20 per cent should be applied to the total loss (by then adjusted to £611,748) to give a figure of £489,398. That sum was below the overvaluation of £500,000 and therefore in accordance with *BBL* it was not just and equitable to make any further reduction. The House of Lords concluded that to apply the percentage reduction to the amount of the overvaluation would give rise to "unacceptable results".[36] The House of Lords criticised the methodology adopted by the trial judge and the reasoning adopted by the Court of Appeal, stating that the latter had "in effect" applied the same deduction twice over.

9–168   **Evaluating a lender's negligence.** A potentially negligent valuer will usually wish to consider whether the lender can properly be criticised as imprudent. To succeed in a plea of contributory negligence,[37] the negligent valuer will have to prove that some lack of care on the part of the lender (in respect of the lender's business interests) caused or contributed to the loss, despite the negligent valuation. Such a plea, if successful, can result in a finding of contributory negligence, a lack of causation of loss or a concurrent cause of loss. In order to constitute contributory negligence, the lender's fault must be causative of the damage in respect of which the lender claims. Fault which is not causative of damage is

---

[35] [2000] 2 A.C. 190 211A.

[36] See *per* Lord Hobhouse at 211G and Lord Millett at 214H.

[37] The Law Reform (Contributory Negligence) Act 1945, s.1(1) provides: "Where any person suffers damage partly of his own fault and partly of the fault of any other person or persons, a claim in respect of that damage shall not be defeated by reason of the fault of the person suffering the damage, but the damages recoverable in respect thereof shall be reduced to such extent as the court thinks just and equitable having regard to the claimant's share in the responsibility for the damage . . . " In *UCB Bank plc v. David Pinder plc* [1998] 2 E.G.L.R. 203, [1998] P.N.L.R. 398, the defendant valuer was in voluntary liquidation and took no part in the trial. A defence alleging contributory negligence by the plaintiff lender had however been served. The plaintiff attended to prove its case and contended that no effect could be given to the defence of contributory negligence, in the absence of attendance by the valuer, irrespective of the state of the evidence. It was held that since the defence had been pleaded it must be resolved on the evidence, however all the evidence was tendered by the plaintiff, and the court was not under a duty to look at documents in the trial bundle which were not so tendered and were therefore not evidence of their contents. In the circumstances contributory negligence had not been established. For further discussion of the topic of contributory negligence see H. Evans, "Contributory negligence by lenders" (1998) 1 P.N. 42.

irrelevant for this purpose.[38] The question of what conduct constitutes imprudent lending will usually be a matter for expert evidence and must be related to the nature of the business carried on by the lender. Different considerations may apply to the lending practices of a building society to those of a secondary bank. For example the Building Societies Act 1986, unlike the Banking Acts, restricts the primary security of a building society to that of freehold or leasehold estate and imposes an obligation of prudence on building societies. A building society, unlike a bank, is regulated by the Building Societies Commission, which from time to time issues DCE letters[39] and Prudential Notes that it expects to be observed, and the auditor of a building society has a statutory obligation to report to the Commission in respect of compliance.[40]

In *Housing Loan Corporation v. William H. Brown*[41] the Court of Appeal re-stated, albeit *obiter*, the correct approach to be adopted when considering contributory negligence by a lender, in that case in respect of a non-status loan. The Court upheld the judge's conclusion that the lender had fundamentally misunderstood the nature of the valuations being provided to it with the result that there was no reliance.[42] However, it expressly considered the correct approach to contributory negligence in case the matter went further. Having found on the evidence instances of fault on the part of plaintiff which partly caused the damage suffered, the trial judge had to determine the causative potency of each particular factor, as well as its blameworthiness. On the facts, the Court of Appeal agreed with the trial judge that a 75 per cent reduction for contributory negligence would have been appropriate. **9–169**

An issue which often arises is as to the relevance of internal controls to the assessment of fault on the part of a lender. It is suggested that their relevance may be twofold: (a) in identifying precautions which will usually be sensible; and (b) as an evidential tool to help a court assess whether a lender has approached the making of a loan with care and common sense. Thus in *Housing Loan Corporation v. William H. Brown*,[43] Hirst L.J. approved a passage from Mantell J.'s judgment where he had found that the lender should have complied with its own manual so as to act on the lower of two valuations, as being correct: **9–170**

> "I fully accept that it is not necessarily negligent for an autonomous body to step outside self imposed controls. What matters is whether or not the controls were in place for a sensible purpose. I judge it to be a sensible precaution to act upon the lower of two valuations. It is a precaution which acknowledges the difficulty in making an accurate valuation of certain properties and it is intended to safeguard the interests of the lender. In my judgment, it was foolish in the extreme to ignore Mr Wagstaff's valuation."

---

[38] See for example the Scottish case of *Leeds Permanent Building Society v. Walker, Fraser & Steele*, 1995 S.L.T.(Sh.Ct.) 72, 77. The pursuers sued valuers in respect of an allegedly negligent over-valuation of a domestic property. The pursuers confined their claim to losses resulting from negligence on the part of the valuers, and excluded all losses resulting from a forced sale on repossession. The defenders pleaded contributory negligence in that the pursuer had failed to give adequate consideration to the financial circumstances of the borrowers. These were struck out by the sheriff on the ground that "the averments of fault attributed to the pursuers are not causative of the loss which the pursuers seek in this action".

[39] "Dear Chief Executive" letters, a method whereby matters of concern to the Building Societies Commission may be communicated to a building society relatively informally.

[40] See Wurtzburg and Mills, *Building Society Law* (looseleaf, Stevens & Sons), chapter 18.01.

[41] [1999] Lloyd's Rep. P.N. 185 at 198

[42] See para. 9–121 above.

[43] [1999] Lloyd's L.Rep. P.N. 185 at 199.

9–171   The argument that once there is reliance on a negligent valuation there can be no contributory negligence has been expressly rejected in a number of reported cases; is inconsistent with the decision in *Platform Home Loans v. Oyston*[44] and has received no significant judicial support.[45] A related question that has arisen is whether the lavishness of the security extinguishes the obligation to act as a prudent lender. The tendency of the courts has been to permit a lender a degree of latitude where there appears to be ample security whilst still reserving the right to find that a lender has acted imprudently. Thus in *Housing Loan Corporation v. William H. Brown*,[46] Hirst L.J. was not prepared to go so far as to characterise the very act of non-status lending as being imprudent whilst nonetheless finding that, in the circumstances of the instant case, caution was called for. Similarly in *Kendall Wilson Securities v. Barraclough*,[47] it was held that reasonable prudence in a solicitor lender advancing trust funds dictated an investigation into the affairs of the prospective borrower, rather than total reliance on the security. Contributory negligence in respect of this failure was assessed at one third. In *H.I.T. Finance v. Lewis & Tucker Ltd*[48] the negligent valuation was £2,200,000. The advance secured on the property was £1,540,000. Wright J. commented[49]:

> "The cushion apparently provided by the property, on the basis of the defendant's valuation was accordingly £660,000. In such circumstances, even if the borrowers turned out to be complete men of straw, the lenders were entitled to regard themselves as being more than adequately covered not merely in respect of the capital sum lent, but also any likely loss of interest, and indeed all the costs and expenses likely to be incurred in foreclosing upon and realising the security . . . it is very difficult to see how such a lender could properly be characterised as being imprudent."

However, the judge continued: "I am not suggesting that the prudent lender, merely because he has the comfort of more than adequate security, is entitled to shut his eyes to any obviously unsatisfactory characteristics of the proposed borrower", and gave as an example of a lender not acting prudently the making of a loan in circumstances where he had substantial reason for suspecting the honesty of the borrower.[50] In *Cavendish Funding v. Henry Spencer*,[51] the Court of Appeal allowed a deduction of 25 per cent where a lender had decided to lend on the basis of a higher rather than a lower valuation of a property. The Court made it plain that the reduction was limited because of the gross nature of the

---

[44] [2000] 2 A.C. 190.
[45] The argument was rejected in the following reported cases: *Kendall Wilson Securities v. Barraclough* [1986] 1 N.Z.L.R. 576, *P.K. Finans International (U.K.) Ltd v. Andrew Downs & Co. Ltd* [1992] 1 E.G.L.R. 172, *United Bank of Kuwait v. Prudential Property Services Ltd* [1994] 2 E.G.L.R. 100; and *Housing Loan Corporation v. William H. Brown* [1999] Lloyd's L.Rep. P.N. 185 at 198.
[46] [1999] Lloyd's L.Rep. P.N. 185 at 199.
[47] [1986] 1 N.Z.L.R. 576, NZCA.
[48] [1993] 2 E.G.L.R. 231, Wright J.
[49] *ibid.* at 235E.
[50] This general approach was followed by Gage J. in *United Bank of Kuwait v. Prudential Property Services Ltd* [1994] 2 E.G.L.R. 100 at 106.
> "It seems to me that it is important to bear in mind Mr Justice Wright's observation that the nature and extent of enquiries required may vary widely, and that an important factor will be the margin of safety provided by the security offered."
[51] [1998] P.N.L.R. 122.

original over-valuation and that, even if the valuer had been given the opportunity to reconsider, the over-valuation would still have been gross.[52]

The appropriate reduction for proved contributory negligence is, inevitably, a **9–172** matter which will vary from case to case. It is possible only to give examples of reductions which have been made by reference to the facts of particular cases. In general criticisms tend to fall under the following general heads: (a) lending too much as a proportion of valuation; (b) failing properly to consider a valuation; (c) failing to make sufficient enquiries as to the status of a borrower; (d) failing to ascertain the purposes for which the loan was required; (e) failing to pick up on warning signs apparent from the transaction. In *Arab Bank v. John D. Wood*,[53] the Court of Appeal considered that the trial judge should reassess the issue of contributory negligence in the light of the lender's successful appeal on primary liability. It considered that the judge should consider issues arising from the facts: (1) that proper consideration had not been given as to how the loan was to be serviced and repaid at the end of its relatively short term; and (2) that the lender had not looked below the "bottom line" at the note of caution being sounded as to the valuation. On the facts, the Court rejected a suggestion that the lender had been substantially at fault in failing to enquire as to the reasons for an apparent discrepancy between the purchase price and the valuation. Phillips J. in *BBL* at first instance[54] assessed contributory negligence by the bank at 30 per cent, on the grounds that the bank should have sought and obtained explanations for the substantial differences between the purchase prices of the properties and the reported values: "a prudent bank would have required a specific and convincing explanation for the disparity in each case before relying on the property as the sole source of repayment of a loan of 90 per cent of the valuation". In *Nyckeln Finance*

---

[52] *ibid.* at 134.

[53] [2000] Lloyd's L.Rep. P.N. 173 at 204–206.

[54] [1994] 2 E.G.L.R. 108 at 137. In *Cavendish Funding Ltd v. Henry Spenser & Sons Ltd* [1996] P.N.L.R. 554, the Court of Appeal held that the plaintiffs' failure to review two valuations of the proposed security property received from different valuers at the same time in the light of their differences was negligent, and reduced the damages by 25%. In *UCB Bank plc v. David Pinder plc* [1998] P.N.L.R. 398, the plaintiff lender was held one-third to blame, principally for failing properly to investigate the value of the borrower's covenants. In *The Mortgage Corporation v. Halifax (SW) Limited* [1999] Lloyd's Rep. P.N. 159 at 178 the plaintiff lender was held 20% to blame, for failing to make proper enquiries as to the borrower's ability to service a very large loan and as to whether there were arrears on any existing or previous mortgages. In *Omega Trust Co. Ltd and Banque Finindus v. Wright Son & Pepper and Another (No.2)* [1998] P.N.L.R. 337, Douglas Brown J. held that the failings of Omega were "extensive and take this case well outside the range of percentage contributory negligence arrived at in a number of recent cases . . . on the remarkable facts of this case I assess the responsibility of Omega for failing to protect its own interests at 70 per cent". The instances of Omega's failure included ignoring the obvious inadequacies of the valuation reports; failing to act on their knowledge of the borrowers' adverse financial history; failing to appreciate that a clearing bank had declined the loan proposal; failing to give even ordinary scrutiny to the borrower's accounts; disregarding the contents of an Infolink search which revealed county court judgments against the director of the borrower and 46 recent credit searches against the borrower; most seriously in failing to challenge the director of the borrower who had certified to Omega that there was no litigation outstanding or threatened against himself or the borrower when in fact as Omega knew from the Infolink search there were already three judgments in existence with two more pending; failing to verify the freehold property allegedly owned by the director of the borrower; and failing to obtain banking references. *In First National Commercial Bank plc v. Andrew S. Taylor Commercial Ltd* [1997] P.N.L.R. 37 the surveyor was held not negligent, but if negligence had been found, then the trial judge would have found contributory negligence by the plaintiff lender of 75 per cent in failing to make adequate enquiries of the borrower and the guarantor.

Company Ltd v. Stumpbrook Continuation Ltd[55] a commercial property was sold for £23.5 m. but after exchange of contracts was valued by Jackson-Stops & Staff at £30.5 m. The plaintiff finance company then lent £21 m. to the purchaser. The loan, although only 70 per cent of the valuation, was 90 per cent of the sale price. Judge Fawcus, sitting as a judge of the High Court, held the plaintiffs to be 20 per cent to blame for proceeding without satisfying themselves as to the reliability of the valuation. In *South Australian Asset Management Corporation v. York Montague Ltd*[56] May J. held the bank negligent in failing to reassess the risk classification of the proposed loan as rigorously as the bank's own procedures required, negligent in failing to insist upon direct instructions from the bank to the valuer, as the bank's lending policy required, and causing or permitting a muddle to develop as to the extent to which certain joint venture proposals did or might contribute to an open market valuation. Making a "broad common-sense judgment" of the bank's share in the responsibility for this damage, May J. deducted 25 per cent from the loss.

9–173　　　(e) **Joint responsibility.** Two practical questions which commonly arise in relation to claims against valuers by lenders are: (a) whether such a valuer is entitled to seek contribution from defaulting borrowers pursuant to the Civil Liability (Contribution) Act 1978; and (b) how damages should be apportioned as between a valuer and another defendant who has caused the making of the loan. The first issue was addressed by the Court of Appeal in *Howkins v. Tyler and Powell*,[57] where the Court decided that the lender's claims against the valuer and the borrower were not in respect of the same damage.

> "'The damage' for which the respondents are liable is that the [lender] has not been paid the sum of money contractually due. The damage for which the appellants were liable was the damage to the [lender] in lending money that the lender would not otherwise have lent. The respective formulations of the 'damage', it seems to me, carry the case outside the scope of section 1(1) of the 1978 Act."[58]

He went on to explain his reasoning as follows:

> " . . . it seems to me that a simple test should be applied to identify a claim capable of being one to which the 1978 act can apply. That test is this: Suppose that A and B are the two parties who are said to be liable to C in respect of 'the same damage' that has been suffered by C. So C must have a right of action of some sort against A and a right of action of some sort against B. There are two questions that should then be asked. If A pays C a sum of money in satisfaction, or on account, of A's liability to C, will that sum operate to reduce or extinguish, depending upon the amount, B's liability to C? Secondly, if B pays C a sum of money in satisfaction or on account of B's liability to C, would that operate to reduce or extinguish A's liability to C? It seems to me that

---

[55] [1994] 2 E.G.L.R. 143. Jackson-Stops & Staff ceased trading on October 31, 1992 and changed its name to Stumpbrook Continuation Ltd. The name "Jackson-Stops & Staff" was then assigned to others.

[56] [1995] 2 E.G.L.R. 219.

[57] [2001] P.N.L.R. 634. The Court of Appeal expressly left open an issue which had been inadequately pleaded as to whether the valuers were entitled to be subrogated to the lenders rights against the borrowers.

[58] *per* Sir Richard Scott V.-C. at 639.

unless both of those questions can be given an affirmative answer, the case is not one to which the 1978 Act can be applied".[59]

As the quantification of the claim for damages against the valuer should take into account the proper value of the borrower's covenant to repay, it could not be said that the above questions could be answered in the affirmative.

The second question was considered by Hart J. in *Ball v. Banner*[60] where **9–174** contribution was sought by the sponsors of an Enterprise Zone Property Trust from the property advisors to the issue in respect of allegedly negligent mis-statements attributed to the property advisors.[61] The sponsors accepted that they were liable in respect of all losses suffered by the investors whilst, following the reasoning in *BBL* the losses recoverable against the property advisors were limited to those which were attributable to the specific statements attributed to them. Hart J., following the approach of the House of Lords in *Platform Home Loans v. Oyston*[62] found that the property advisors were, nonetheless, liable in respect of the same damage as that in respect of which the sponsors were liable. He drew attention to some apparently surprising consequences of his reasoning[63] but nonetheless concluded that he was obliged to consider apportionment first before considering the application of the *BBL* "cap". The practical effect is that if a valuer and another defendant each cause a lender to make a loan of £1m. and are held to be equally responsible for the same, the result of contribution proceedings will be determined by the relationship between the extent of the valuer's over-valuation and his degree of responsibilty. Thus if the over-valuation is only of £250,000, that will be the limit of damages recoverable from him. If, on the other hand, the over-valuation is of £750,000, the recoverable damages will be £500,000.

(iv) *Overvaluation for vendor*

Damages where there has been a negligent overvaluation for a vendor were **9–175** considered in *Kenney v. Hall, Pain and Foster*,[64] the relevant facts of which are set out above.[65] Relying upon the defendants' overvaluation of his own house and expecting the proceeds of sale to cover him, the plaintiff vendor incurred expenditure on buying and improving two other properties greatly in excess of what he would have incurred if he had been properly advised. The proceeds proved insufficient and were considerably exceeded by the expenditure. The parties accepted that the measure of damages should be assessed on the principle stated by Lord Denning M.R. in *Esso Petroleum Co. Ltd v. Mardon*[66]: "You should look into the future so as to forecast what would have been likely to happen if he had never entered into this contract; and contrast it with his position as it is now as a result of entering into it." The practical problems inherent in deciding what would have happened were avoided by the parties agreeing that if properly advised the plaintiff would have purchased another house at a cheaper

---

[59] *ibid.* at 639–640.
[60] [2000] Lloyd's L.Rep. P.N. 569.
[61] An appeal on the issue of liability was allowed.
[62] [2000] 2 A.C. 190.
[63] [2000] Lloyd's L.Rep. P.N. 569 at 585.
[64] [1976] 2 E.G.L.R. 29.
[65] See para. 9–080.
[66] [1976] Q.B. 801.

price than the two actually purchased. Damages were thus arrived at by comparing the hypothetical with the actual situation.[67]

(v) *Undervaluation for vendor*

9–176 Where as a result of a negligent undervaluation property is sold at a price less than that which should have been achieved if proper advice had been given, the normal measure of damages is the difference between the price at which the property was sold and the price that should have been achieved.[68] Surveyors may also be liable in respect of a negligent failure to sell development property for its true worth, because advice to maximise the development potential, for example to obtain appropriate planning permission, had not been given. In such circumstances the plaintiff may recover damages in respect of a loss of profit which he might, but for the negligence of the surveyor, have made. The plaintiff does not need to prove that on balance the profit would have been made, but the lost chance of such profit has to be substantial, and more than a mere speculative possibility. This principle was applied by Blackburne J. in *Obagi v. Stanborough (Developments) Ltd*[69] where the plaintiff failed to prove that even if the defendants had used their best endeavours, their chances of obtaining the necessary planning permission were more than a speculative possibility. The judge therefore awarded the plaintiffs £5 in nominal damages in respect of the defendant's breach of contract. In *Weedon v. Hindwood, Clarke and Esplin*[70] the defendant valuers failed to take into account a change in the law.[71] In consequence they recommended to the plaintiff trustees for acceptance an amount lower than the actual amount due as compensation on compulsory purchase of the property concerned. Damages were awarded representing the difference between the value of the land, which under the statute would have been the price due from the acquiring authority, and the amount recommended for acceptance. In the last case the amount recommended for acceptance was the same as the price paid by the purchaser.

9–177 The measure of damages resulting from an alleged undervaluation of property in the context of divorce proceedings was discussed in the Scottish case *of*

---

[67] [1976] 2 E.G.L.R. 29, 35.
[68] Note *Garland v. Ralph Pay and Ransom* [1984] 2 E.G.L.R. 147 (an estate agent's case).
[69] *The Times*, December 15, 1993; (1993) E.G.C.S. 205. In *Allied Maples Group Ltd v. Simmons & Simmons* [1995] 1 W.L.R. 1602, CA, the question was whether, in order to succeed in an action for breach of duty where the plaintiff's loss depended upon what an independent third party would have done in a hypothetical situation, the plaintiff must prove: (a) on a balance of probability, or (b) that there was a realistic (and not merely speculative) chance, that the third party would have acted so as to avoid or reduce the plaintiff's loss. The Court of Appeal held that (b) was correct. Damages were to be decided by evaluating the chance, and that issue did not depend on a balance of probability. The plaintiff was not obliged to prove more than it had lost something of substance: *i.e.* a measurable chance of negotiating significantly better terms. The House of Lords refused leave to appeal. The practical effect of this decision is that (a) plaintiff must prove on the balance of probabilities that he would have acted differently with correct advice; and (b) plaintiff must then prove that there was a realistic (and not merely speculative) chance that the third party would have acted so as to avoid or reduce his loss, and not on the balance of probabilities. This means that a loss of only a 10% chance means the recovery of damages.
[70] (1974) 234 E.G. 121.
[71] See *West Midland Baptist (Trust) Association (Incorporated) v. Birmingham Corporation* [1968] 2 Q.B. 188, CA; [1970] A.C. 874, HL: relevant date for assessment under s.2, r. 5, of the Acquisition of Land (Assessment of Compensation) Act 1919 held to be the date on which the work of reinstatement might reasonably have been commenced and not, as previously thought, the date of the service of the notice to treat.

Shenkin v. D. M. Hall & Son.[72] The pursuer obtained a valuation from the defenders of certain property he owned, advising the valuers that their report was needed for the purposes of his divorce settlement, and CGT. The property was valued by them at £115,000 and subsequently, as part of an overall divorce settlement, the pursuer transferred the property outright to his wife. When the pursuer's liability to CGT was finally determined, he discovered that the property was in fact worth £174,000 at the date of the defenders' valuation. The pursuer claimed that if he had been aware of the true value of the property, he would not have transferred the same to his wife and would have incurred no liability to CGT, or as part of the overall divorce settlement, he would have retained £60,000 of assets elsewhere. The pursuer claimed the £60,000 from the defenders, who sought to defeat the claim prior to trial by arguing that the underlying assumption was that the same divorce settlement would have been reached had the property been valued at £174,000, and that such an assumption was prima facie erroneous, in any event under Scots law.[73] Lord Osborne rejected the argument, deciding that it was open to the pursuer to try and quantify his loss at trial on the basis that the same settlement would have been achieved, as a question of fact.

(vi) *Other work*

Breach of warranty. If the unlikely event that a surveyor expressly warrants   **9–178**
the accuracy of his valuation of property,[74] the measure of damage is the difference between the situation the lender is in, having relied upon the valuation, and the situation the lender would have been in, had the warranted valuation been true. In other words, the lender is to be put in as good a position against the valuer as he would have been in against the borrower had the property had the value warranted by the valuer at the time of the valuation. Thus property market movements subsequent to the warranted valuation may be taken into account in determining what position the lender would have been in at any particular time, for example when the mortgaged property was in fact sold. If a valuation is warranted, it may well have a profound effect on the quantum of damages recoverable from the surveyor.

Rent reviews. Surveyors are frequently instructed to act for their clients in   **9–179**
negotiations and arbitrations arising out of periodic rent reviews. There is no simple measure of damage, the factual circumstances being capable of considerable variation. In *County Personnel (Employment Agency) Ltd v. Alan R. Pulver & Co.*,[75] a solicitors' negligence action arising out of advice given in respect of an underlease with an unusual rent review clause, the Court of Appeal rejected the argument that the court was bound to apply the diminution in value rule, and instead held that on the facts, the costs of extrication from the situation in which the plaintiff company found itself as a consequence of the negligent advice were recoverable. In *Rajdev v. Becketts*[76] the defendant surveyors negligently failed to make representations on behalf of the plaintiff shopkeeper to an independent surveyor appointed by the president of the RICS to determine the rent of the

---

[72] Unreported, January 23, 1996, Lord Osborne.
[73] See Family Law (Scotland) Act 1985, ss.8–10.
[74] Such a situation is only likely to occur where a surveyor provides his valuation on a standard form of report provided by, for example, a finance company and the form contains an express warranty.
[75] [1987] 1 W.L.R. 916. For further analysis, see Chap. 10, para. 10–172.
[76] [1989] 2 E.G.L.R. 144

shop. During negotiations the landlord had proposed an annual rental of £7,000, the plaintiff £4,600. The independent surveyor fixed a rent of £9,250. At trial the judge held that the proper open market rent at the review date was £7,000, and that the difference in value between a lease with a rent of £9,250, and one with a rent of £7,000, was £8,100. This was the sum awarded to the plaintiff in damages, a claim for additional sums in respect of a reduction in the value of the business carried on at the shop being rejected as containing elements of double recovery.[77]

9–180   The complications that can arise from applying the *restitutio* principle to rent review cases is well illustrated by *Knight v. Lawrence*.[78] This involved a negligent failure by a receiver to serve trigger notices in respect of the rent reviews for a number of tenanted properties. When the properties came to be sold by the mortgagees the prices realised were less than they would have been had the rents been increased in accordance with the rent review provisions. The Vice-Chancellor said:

> "The starting point is to try to ascertain what would have been the sale price of the properties if on December 11, 1984, the rent reviews had properly taken place. That involves two stages. First, to find out at what the reviewed rents would properly have been agreed. Second, to find out, taking into account the higher rent payable as a result of such review, what increased price would have been obtainable for each of the properties."[79]

Having considered the expert evidence, and concluding that the properties would have achieved £35,000 more than they did, the Vice-Chancellor said:

> "But that is not the measure of loss recoverable by the plaintiffs. The damages have to be assessed on the basis that they are to be put back into the position they would have been in had the sale taken place on that basis, that is to say if there had been a total realisation of £275,300. It is at that stage that the real complications are capable of arising."[80]

The Vice-Chancellor then sought to identify precisely how the additional sum would have been utilised, in order to put the plaintiffs into the position they would have been in, but for the negligence of the defendant.[81] This analysis could not be completed without the making of further enquiries.

(vii) *Inconvenience and discomfort*

9–181   A contract breaker is not in general liable for any distress, frustration, anxiety, displeasure, vexation, tension or aggravation which his breach of contract may cause to the innocent party. In *Watts v. Morrow*,[82] Ralph Gibson L.J. stated: "As to the law, it is, in my judgment, clear that the plaintiffs were not entitled to

---

[77] The calculation of damages resulting from the negligent conduct of rent reviews was also considered in *Corfield v. D. S. Bosher & Co.* [1992] 1 E.G.L.R. 163 and *CIL Securities Ltd v. Briant Champion Long* [1993] 2 E.G.L.R. 164.
[78] [1991] 1 E.G.L.R. 143.
[79] *ibid.* at 147.
[80] *ibid.* at 148
[81] The position of the plaintiffs would have been radically different, because with the extra sum, a variety of debts could and would have been met, the discharge of which would have left the plaintiffs free of liability.
[82] [1991] 1 W.L.R. 1421, at 1440.

recover general damages for mental distress not caused by physical discomfort or inconvenience resulting from the breach of contract." This follows what has become known as the rule in *Addis v. Gramophone Co. Ltd*,[83] to the effect that damages for mental distress are not recoverable in contract. In *Farley v. Skinner (No. 2)*,[84] the House of Lords[85] relaxed the rule so as to permit a claimant, who had specifically requested a surveyor to check on possible aircraft noise at a house that he was considering purchasing, to recover damages for inconvenience and discomfort when he discovered that the house was underneath one of the holding stacks for Gatwick Airport. Stuart-Smith L.J. had summarised the general reasons for refusing to permit damages to be recoverable as follows:

> "it is a policy decision that the law does not give compensation for distress, frustration, anxiety, displeasure, vexation or aggravation. But the reasons are understandable. In an action for damages for personal injury, the claimant must prove either physical injury or a recognised psychiatric injury. Distress and annoyance will not do. In an action against a professional man for negligent advice or information the damage that is normally within the contemplation of the parties is financial loss. But if the unreported defects have to be made good while the purchaser is living in the house, it is readily foreseeable that for a relatively short time whilst that work is being done, great physical discomfort and inconvenience of living on a building site, without facilities and in cramped conditions will be experienced. The court can appreciate the physical conditions and award an appropriate sum. But annoyance, vexation, etc., is entirely subjective; moreover as this case illustrates , I find it difficult to see how it can be assessed. The claimant decided, for his own personal reasons, not to move house. So if he is to be awarded damages for annoyance, over what period is it to be assessed: It is not just for a relatively short period while physical defects to the property are made good . . . ."[86]

The majority had also rejected the suggestion that the contract was one which fell within the exceptional category of contracts to provide pleasure, relaxation or peace of mind. Following the decision in the architects case of *Knott v. Bolton*,[87] Stuart-Smith L.J. pointed out that the contract as a whole, as distinct from one relatively minor part of the overall instructions, could not be said to fall within such a category.[88]

This reasoning was rejected by the House of Lords. Lord Steyn held[89] that the case has to be approached on the basis that the instruction to investigate aircraft noise formed a major part of the contract. It was thus permissible to award modest damages to effect the express term of the contract. He also rejected an argument that by failing to move out of the property, the claimant had lost the right to claim the damages.[90]

9–182

---

[83] [1909] A.C. 488.

[84] House of Lords, October 11, 2001 overturning the decision of the Court of Appeal at [2000] P.N.L.R. 441

[85] A two judge Court had, initially, been convened which disagreed. Mummery and Stuart-Smith LJJ formed the majority when the Court re-convened, whilst Clarke L.J. dissented.

[86] *ibid.* at 449.

[87] (1995) 11 Const. L.J. 315—see para. 8–311 above.

[88] [2000] P.N.L.R. 441 at 451 and see also *per* Mummery L.J. at 456.

[89] At para. 18.

[90] At para. 26.

9–183   Where the interest of the plaintiff in the property is commercial, rather than domestic, no award of general damages will be made.[91] Moreover, where the inconvenience and discomfort consequent upon the necessary repairs has been taken into account in the valuation evidence presented to the court, it is likely that no further sum by way of general damages will be awarded,[92] to avoid double recovery.

9–184   The argument that damages for inconvenience should not be awarded was earlier expressly rejected by the Court of Appeal in *Perry v. Sidney Phillips & Son*.[93] That case might be thought to be authority for a wider ambit of claim, encompassing distress and anxiety even where there were no specific instructions to the surveyor.[94] In that case Lord Denning M.R. stated:

> "It seems to me that Mr Perry is entitled to damages for all the vexation, distress and worry which he has been caused by reason of the negligence of the surveyor. If a man buys a house—for his own occupation—on the surveyor's advice that it is sound—and then finds out that it is in a deplorable condition, it is reasonably foreseeable that he will be most upset. He may, as here, not have the money to repair it and this will upset him all the more. That too is reasonably foreseeable. All this anxiety, worry and distress may nowadays be the subject of compensation."[95]

It is, however, clear from the facts of the case,[96] and from the judgments of Oliver and Kerr L.JJ., that the general damages awarded in *Perry v. Sidney Phillips & Son* were in respect of the physical discomfort suffered by the plaintiff, and that the case is therefore in accordance with the general proposition set out above.[97] Oliver L.J. summarised this part of the plaintiff's claim as being for: " . . . vexation, that is the discomfort and so on suffered by the plaintiff as a result of having to live for a lengthy period in a defective house which for one reason or another was not repaired over the period between the acquisition by the plaintiff and the date of trial".[98]

     Kerr L.J. commented:

> "So far as the question of damages for vexation and inconvenience is concerned, it should be noted that the judge has awarded these not for the tension or frustration of a person who is involved in a legal dispute in which the other party refuses to meet its liabilities. If he had done so, it would have been wrong, because such aggravation is

---

[91] See the dicta of Staughton L.J. in *Hayes v. Dodd* [1990] 2 All E.R. 815. In *Michael v. Ensoncraft Ltd* [1990] E.G.C.S. 156, a claim against a negligent contractor by a landlord for damages for inconvenience in respect of damage to a house acquired for investment purposes, was rejected by the trial judge on the ground that the interest of the plaintiff in the premises was a commercial one.

[92] *Bigg v. Howard Son & Gooch* [1990] 1 E.G.L.R. 173, 1474

[93] [1982] 1 W.L.R. 1297

[94] The case has, indeed, been taken to be authority for such a proposition. For example in *Bolton v. Puley* [1982] 2 E.G.L.R. 138, an action in respect of a negligent survey that omitted reference to an unstable boundary wall, Talbot J. expressly relied on *Perry v. Sidney Phillips*, when awarding general damages of £500: "Finally there is the plaintiff's claim for damages for distress, vexation and worry resulting from the alarming cost he was advised was necessary to put the wall into a stable and safe condition. There had been the worry, for instance, of possible consequences to the public from a possible collapse of the wall. As pointed out in *Perry v. Sidney Phillips & Son*, the damages under this heading may not be very substantial . . . ".

[95] [1982] 1 W.L.R. 1297, 1302

[96] The plaintiff was obliged to live in the property which he could not afford to repair, with serious defects in the roof, which leaked, and offensive smells from the defective septic tank.

[97] See para. 9–181, above. This was the conclusion reached by Ralph Gibson L.J. in his analysis of *Perry v. Sidney Phillips & Son* in *Watts v. Morrow* [1991] 1 W.L.R. 1421, 1440.

[98] [1982] 1 W.L.R. 1297, 1304.

experienced by almost all litigants. He has awarded these damages because of the physical consequences of the breach which were all foreseeable at the time."[99]

Where properly made, a claim for general damages will not be reduced solely **9–185** because a less impecunious plaintiff could have mitigated or extinguished such physical discomfort by carrying out repairs. The defendant firm in *Perry v. Sidney Phillips & Son* argued, on the basis of *The Liesbosch*,[1] that the claim for general damages by the plaintiff was an attempt to recover additional damages as a result of his poverty, that ought not to succeed. Oliver L.J. held that a proper formulation of the test to be applied was: "Was it reasonable in all the circumstances for the plaintiff not to mitigate his damage by carrying out the repairs which were required?"[2] and concluded on the facts[3] that the plaintiff's decision was reasonable. Kerr L.J. agreed and went further, drawing attention to the waning force of the decision in *The Liesbosch*.[4] Where, however, it would have been reasonable to carry out repairs earlier, then such damages will be either reduced or extinguished. In *Cross v. David Martin and Mortimer*[5] Phillips J. refused the plaintiffs general damages in respect of the distress and inconvenience caused by the existence for four years of a hole in their hall floor, on the ground that steps to mitigate such inconvenience could have been taken earlier. The judge did, however, award damages to reflect the considerable inconvenience that would be caused when repairs were carried out.

Injury to health. General damages for injury to health were awarded *in Allen* **9–186** *v. Ellis & Co.*,[6] a professional negligence claim against a surveyor. The plaintiff obtained a structural survey that negligently described the garage as being in a satisfactory condition. In fact the roof of the garage was old, brittle, fragile and in need of replacement. About a year after moving into the property, the plaintiff climbed onto the garage roof to investigate the source of a leak. When he stepped onto the roof he fell through[7] and was injured. The plaintiff's case was that had the report properly described the roof he would either have had it replaced, or would not have attempted to climb on to it to investigate its condition. Garland J. considered the question of reliance and causation: "The negligence must operate to an extent which is beyond *de minimis*, but it need not be the only operative cause; it can be one among others, provided it is substantial. Remoteness is a matter of the requisite degree of foreseeability."[8] On the facts of the case, the judge found the defendants negligent:

---

[99] *ibid.* at 1307.
[1] [1933] A.C. 449.
[2] [1982] 1 W.L.R. 1297, 1305
[3] Oliver L.J. noted at 1305, that the defendants "were strenuously resisting any liability at all for the repairs, and denying that they were responsible", and also that the finding of fact by the trial judge, that the plaintiff's conduct had been reasonable, could not be challenged in the Court of Appeal.
[4] *ibid.* at 1307:
   "it seems to me that the authority of what Lord Wright said in *The Liesbosch* . . . is consistently being attenuated in more recent decisions of this court, in particular in *Dodd Properties (Kent) Ltd v. Canterbury City Council* [1980] 1 W.L.R. 433 and what was said there, at pp. 458–459 by Donaldson L.J. If it is reasonably foreseeable that the plaintiff may be unable to mitigate or remedy the consequences of the other party's breach as soon as he would have done if he had been provided with the necessary means to do so from the other party, then it seems to me that the principle of *The Liesbosch* . . . no longer applies in its full rigour".
[5] [1989] 1 E.G.L.R. 154.
[6] [1990] 1 E.G.L.R. 170. 73 *ibid.* at 172.
[7] Despite attempting to spread his weight with a piece of wood.
[8] *ibid.* at 172.

"'The garage . . . is in satisfactory condition' is more than a failure to inform; it is positive misinformation. If the roof had been accurately described . . . he would never have been in peril of suffering the injuries which he did, in fact, suffer. I take the view that there is a sufficient causal connection, and also a sufficient degree of deemed foresight in the defendants at the time when they were negligent, connecting their negligence with what in fact occurred. In the circumstances, I take the view that the damages for personal injuries are not too remote from that negligence."[9]

An allegation of contributory negligence was dismissed, the judge pointing out that the plaintiff was a layman when it came to buildings. Accordingly, agreed general damages of £8,000 were awarded to the plaintiff.

9–187 In the Scottish case of *Drinnan v. C. W. Ingram & Sons*[10] the defender surveyors failed in their attempt to dismiss as too remote the pursuer's claim for injury to health. The point was only considered as a preliminary issue and the pursuer's right to damages for such injury was not finally determined. Damages for personal injury were included in the award in *Collard v. Saunders*.[11] As a result of the defendant solicitor's advice, the plaintiff employed an unqualified surveyor. The defendant admitted liability. From the judgment it is clear that damages were considered as if the case were a surveyor's negligence case.

9–188 **Quantum of damages.** The *quantum* of awards of general damages for inconvenience and discomfort has been variously described as "not extravagant", "not excessive but modest",[12] "may not be very substantial",[13] "modest",[14] and "restrained".[15] Each case must be decided on its own facts, and there is no conventional award for such damages. The Court of Appeal has stated that the proper approach is to fix a modest sum for the amount of physical discomfort endured having regard to the period of time over which it was endured.[16] An examination of reported cases suggests a broad tariff within which most negligent domestic survey cases will fall. Awards that fall well outside the ordinary range will have to be capable of justification by reference to the facts of the case, or be liable to be set aside on appeal.[17]

9–189 Examples of such awards include: *Roberts v. J. Hampson & Co.*,[18] where a young engaged couple of modest means were awarded a total of £1,500 in respect of "extreme" and "particularly upsetting" disruption caused to them in having to move out of their home during repairs; *Cross v. David Martin and Mortimer*,[19] where the plaintiffs were each awarded £500 in respect of the "considerable inconvenience and dislocation" that would be caused to them by

---

[9] 1967 S.L.T. 205.
[10] (1972) 221 E.G. 797.
[11] *per* Barry J. in *Bailey v. Bullock* [1950] 2 All E.R. 1167, 1172.
[12] *per* Lord Denning M.R. in *Perry v. Sidney Phillips & Son* [1982] 1 W.L.R. 1297, 1303.
[13] *per* Oliver L.J., *ibid.* at 1305.
[14] *per* Ralph Gibson L.J. in *Watts v. Morrow* [1991] 1 W.L.R. 1421, 1443 and *per* Nourse L.J. approving the description of the judge at first instance in *Patel v. Hooper & Jackson* [1999] Lloyd's L.Rep. P.N. 1 at p. 10.
[15] *per* Bingham L.J., *ibid.* at 1445.
[16] *per* Ralph Gibson L.J. in *Watts v. Morrow, ibid.* at 1443. In *Farley v. Skinner*, Lord Steyn expressly accepted that awards should be modest and that the award of £10,000 in that case was "certainly high" (at para. 28).
[17] The Court of Appeal will apply the principles reiterated by the House of Lords in *Pickett v. British Rail Engineering Ltd* [1980] A.C. 136. See also the commentary in Kemp & Kemp, *The Quantum of Damages* (Sweet & Maxwell), Vol. 1, Chap. 19.
[18] [1989] 2 All E.R. 504. A full report is at [1988] 2 E.G.L.R. 181.
[19] [1989] 1 E.G.L.R. 154.

repairs to the defective ground floor; *Steward v. Rapley,*[20] where at first instance, each plaintiff was awarded £1,000 in respect of the inconvenience and disturbance caused by remedial works made necessary by an extensive outbreak of dry rot. The award was not challenged on appeal; *Bigg v. Howard Son and Gooch,*[21] where the plaintiffs were awarded a total of £1,600 in respect of the discomfort and inconvenience caused by the extensive works necessary to make their home structurally sound; *Hipkins v. Jack Cotton Partnership,*[22] where the plaintiffs were obliged to move out of their home during underpinning works, and were awarded damages for the "worry and inconvenience on the lines of *Perry v. Sidney Phillips & Sons.* The plaintiffs seek £1,000. I think that is on the high side and award £750"[23]; *Watts v. Morrow*[24] where the plaintiffs' weekend home required substantial works over a period of eight months to the roof, windows and walls. The trial judge awarded each plaintiff £4,000. Bingham L.J. stated that such an award "far exceeded a reasonable award for the injury shown to have been suffered". The Court of Appeal substituted £750 for each plaintiff.[25] In *George Buchanan v. Newington Property Centre,*[26] the pursuers were obliged to move into rented accommodation for some eight months whilst extensive dry rot was eradicated. The rented accommodation was in a tall block of council-owned flats where the general level of social amenity was considerably less than that to which the pursuers were accustomed. The second pursuer was frightened to remain in the rented accommodation whilst the first pursuer was at work, and so she travelled into central Edinburgh most days. She consulted her doctor. Both pursuers became irritable with one another. Sheriff Scott was satisfied that "the pursuers had a miserable time of it, over a period, as a result of Mr Quinn's breach of duty. Happily, they have recovered. I consider that proper awards of solatium are £800 for the first pursuer and £1,200 for the second pursuer". In *Heatley v. William H. Brown Ltd*[27] the plaintiffs, a couple with three young children, were compensated for two years of having to live in premises that became wholly unsuitable for family living because of warnings of danger. Financial pressures prevented the family from moving out. Safe access to the only bathroom facilities available involved leaving the house. This inconveience was made much worse when the children were unwell and could not be taken outside. Eventually a portaloo was purchased and placed in the inner hall. The health of the second plaintiff was adversely affected and family relationships generally became strained. The judge awarded the first plaintiff £1,500, the second plaintiff £3,000. In *Ezekiel v. McDade*[28] the plaintiff purchased a property built using the "Bison" system. The defendant surveyor negligently failed to identify a serious defect involving a concrete purlin. This and other defects were not discovered until after the plaintiff had been made redundant, and had been forced to offer the property for sale as he could not maintain the payments due

---

[20] [1989] 1 E.G.L.R. 159.
[21] [1990] 1 E.G.L.R. 173.
[22] [1989] 2 E.G.L.R. 157.
[23] *per* Scott Baker J. at 160.
[24] [1991] 1 W.L.R. 1421.
[25] Ralph Gibson L.J. commented at 1442: "the award was excessive even if the judge had directed himself correctly. It was very substantially more than the awards made in similar cases apart from the award by the same judge in *Syrett*". The latter is a reference to *Syrett v. Carr & Neave* [1990] 2 E.G.L.R. 161, where an appeal was settled before hearing.
[26] 1992 S.C.L.R. 583.
[27] [1992] 1 E.G.L.R. 289.
[28] [1995] 2 E.G.L.R. 107.

on his mortgage. The property remained unsold, the plaintiff and his family endured lengthy eviction proceedings, and after eviction were housed in unsatisfactory temporary accommodation for some 12 months, before being rehoused to a proper standard. The official referee awarded £6,000 general damages for inconvenience and distress.[29] The Court of Appeal reduced this sum to £4,000, Nourse L.J. commenting that "the judge proceeded in part on a wrong basis, in that he overlooked the fact that the first plaintiff's financial difficulties and falling into arrears with his payments under the mortgage started before the house was put on the market and not after it failed to sell". In *Patel v. Hooper & Jackson*,[30] the Court of Appeal upheld an award of £2,000 to each of the plaintiffs who had been obliged not to move into their new home and to endure a succession of moves to different sets of rented accommodation over a five year period.[31]

(viii) *Incidental expenses*

9–190   It has been the usual,[32] but not invariable,[33] practice of the courts to reimburse plaintiffs for the incidental expenses of taking reasonable action to deal with defects to the property, despite the fact that the measure of damage has not been the reasonable cost of carrying out such repairs. This has been described as "not perhaps entirely logical, but it is well established and seems [to me] not unreasonable".[34] The objection is that such expenses are an adjunct of the remedial works. If the latter are not recoverable, why the former? In *Patel v. Hooper & Jackson*,[35] the Court of Appeal permitted the recovery of the costs of alternative accommodation when allowing the claimants to recover on the basis of the "costs

---

[29] [1994] 1 E.G.L.R. 255.

[30] [2000] Lloyd's L.Rep. P.N. 1.

[31] See also *Hoadley v. Edwards* [2001] E.G.C.S. 46 where Evans-Lombe J. made an award of £5,000 to the claimants who had had to endure works of structural improvement which they had not anticipated. From the reported facts, this award appears to have been high.

[32] In *Morgan v. Perry* (1973) 229 E.G. 1737 the cost of investigating the defects was held recoverable. In *Fryer v. Bunney* [1982] 2 E.G.L.R. 130, the plaintiffs were awarded £500 compensation in respect of the shrinkage to carpets moved to permit works to eradicate damp to take place. In *Treml v. Ernest W. Gibson & Partners* [1984] 2 E.G.L.R. 162, it was agreed between the parties that the plaintiff was entitled to recover the cost of reasonable accommodation during the period whilst the repairs were carried out, together with the cost of the removal and storage of her furniture. The judge also allowed the plaintiff to recover the cost of shoring up the property pending repair, and additional interest paid as a result of the plaintiff having to increase his mortgage to pay for the repairs. These cases were followed in *Shaw v. Halifax (SW) Ltd* [1994] 2 E.G.L.R. 95, 99 where as part of a preliminary issue, the cost of items including storage of furniture, consulting engineers' report, and building surveyors' report were held to be recoverable, subject to proof that they did not form part of the repair costs. In *Republic International Trust Co. Ltd v. Fletcher Ramos*, unreported, August 30, 2000, H.H.J. Havery Q.C. awarded £4,000 by way of damages for loss of use whilst repairs were carried out to a property which would not have been purchased but for a negligent survey report.

[33] For example, Judge Hicks Q.C. in *Bigg v. Howard Son & Gooch* [1990] 1 E.G.L.R. 173, 175 refused to award the plaintiffs the cost of alternative accommodation during repairs, stating that such an award was consistent only with a claim where the cost of repair was recoverable as the primary head of damages, which was not the case. The learned judge concluded: " . . . no separate award of damages for the cost of accommodation during repair is appropriate in cases of this kind, alternatively that if such an award is ever appropriate it is not so when the likely need for and probable cost of vacating the premises during repair, as foreseeable by a purchaser buying at the relevant date with knowledge of the defects, has been taken into account in assessing what price he would have been prepared to pay".

[34] *per* Phillips J. in *Cross v. David Martin & Mortimer* [1989] 1 E.G.L.R. 154, 159. The judge awarded £2,500 in respect of incidental expenses such as the cost of alternative accommodation for the period of the repairs, the cost of removing furniture to storage and bringing it back.

[35] [1999] Lloyd's L.Rep. P.N.

of extrication".[36] The Court of Appeal has yet to rule on whether such damages are recoverable when damages are limited to the diminution in value[37] but an indication that such claims would be permitted was provided in *Sneesby v. Goldings*.[38]

In *Broadoak Properties Ltd v. Young and White*,[39] Judge Fox-Andrews Q.C. **9–191** decided as a preliminary issue, subject to liability, the basis upon which damages should be assessed:

> "if expenses were reasonably incurred in investigating the true state of the premises this will be a recoverable head of damage. If and in so far as moneys were spent, *e.g.* on the front wall in respect of temporary works (whether building or professional costs) to prevent a nuisance or danger, these will be recoverable. Reasonable management time expended in respect of such investigation and temporary works will likewise be recoverable."[40]

In the Scottish case of *Hunter v. J. & E. Shepherd*,[41] Lord Osborne refused to strike out a claim for the costs of alternative accommodation against a firm of surveyors on the ground that:

> "The courts were not bound by rigid rules in assessing what amounted to fair compensation (*Duke of Portland v. Wood's Trustees*, 1962 S.L.T. 321), and where damages were sought for the difference between the price paid and the true value of defective property, costs associated with remedying the defects might also be recoverable, notwithstanding that the costs of the remedial works themselves were not recoverable (*Martin v. Bell-Ingram*, 1986 S.L.T. 575 followed)."[42]

In the common situation of a negligent survey for a purchase of a property the purchaser has been held entitled to recover the following costs and losses incurred during the period of necessary repairs: the costs of alternative accommodation[43] and of furniture removal and storage[44]; loss of use of part of the property[45] and loss of rent.[46] In the same situation the purchaser has also been

---

[36] See further para. 9–147 above.
[37] The point was expressly left open by the Court of Appeal in *Watts v. Morrow* [1991] 1 W.L.R. 1421, Ralph Gibson L.J. commenting at 1441 that: "We do not have to decide whether, if the plaintiff has to rent other accommodation during the carrying out of repairs, such costs will be recoverable in the absence of any contractual warranty as to the existence of defects requiring repairs, and I would reserve my decision upon it."
[38] [1995] 2 E.G.L.R. 102, at 105K. See para. 9–147.
[39] [1989] 1 E.G.L.R. 263.
[40] *ibid.* at 267.
[41] March 28, 1991, OH, G.W.D. 17–1043.
[42] For an echo of this reasoning in a solicitor's negligence action see the judgment of Bingham L.J. in *County Personnel Ltd v. Alan R. Pulver & Co.* [1987] 1 W.L.R. 916, 925.
[43] *Hood v. Shaw* (1960) 176 E.G. 1291 (the argument that such costs were irrecoverable since the difference in value was the only damage, was rejected*); Collard v. Saunders* (1972) 221 E.G. 797. In *Grove v. Jackman and Masters* (1950) 155 E.G. 182 the costs of alternative accommodation were awarded additionally to the cost of repairs. *Treml v. Ernest W. Gibson and Partners* [1984] 2 E.G.L.R. 162; *Cross v. David Martin and Mortimer* [1989] 1 E.G.L.R. 154; *Hunter v. J. & E. Shepherd*, March 28, 1991, OH, G.W.D. 17–1043; *Shaw v. Halifax* (SW) Ltd [1994] 2 E.G.L.R. 95, 99; *Republic International Trust Co. Ltd v. Fletcher Ramos*, unreported August 30, 2000. See also *Patel v. Hooper & Jackson* [2000] Lloyd's L.Rep. P.N. 1 and para. 9–147 above.
[44] *Grove v. Jackman and Masters* (1950) 155 E.G. 182: *Hill v. Debenham, Tewson and Chinnocks* (1958) 171 E.G. 835; *Treml v. Ernest W. Gibson and Partners* [1984] 2 E.G.L.R. 162; *Cross v. David Martin and Mortimer* [1989] 1 E.G.L.R. 154.
[45] *Tremayne v. T. Mortimer Burrows and Partners* (1954) 165 E.G. 232; *Rawlings v. Rentokil Laboratories Ltd.* (1972) 223 E.G. 1947 (not strictly a surveyor's negligence case).
[46] *Freeman v. Marshall & Co.* (1966) 200 E.G. 777.

held entitled to recover the costs of emergency supports,[47] investigating the defects,[48] expenditure upon wasted decorations and plastering,[49] management time[50] and even the cost of a minor item of repair.[51] In *Philips v. Ward*[52] Romer L.J. added, *obiter*, that if on learning of the real condition of the house the plaintiff had decided to leave and resell, he would have been entitled to recover from the defendant, in addition to the £4,000 diminution in value, his costs and expenses of moving in and moving out and of the resale.[53] In *Hardy v. Wamsley-Lewis*[54] where the plaintiff did decide to leave and resell, solicitors' costs on re-sale were allowed, but not, surprisingly, solicitors' costs on purchase.[55]

9–192   In the Scottish case of *Cochrane v. Sibbald & Graham*[56] a number of less common incidental expenses were claimed. The pursuer was moving from Scone to Dundee, with contractual entry set for July 1982, and actual entry planned for September 1982. Dry rot was discovered in September 1982 and so actual entry had to be postponed until repairs had been completed, which was not until May 1983. The previous house had been retained as the family home and commuting costs between Scone and Dundee were claimed, and allowed. The pursuer had mitigated his loss (the costs of alternative accommodation, including removal costs) by commuting. In addition, the pursuer recovered bridging loan interest incurred because the previous house had to be withdrawn from the market.

9–193   In attempting to apply the principle of *restitutio* in surveyors' negligence actions, the courts have been less than scrupulous in differentiating between the different measures of damage in contract and tort claims. In most of the cases there is a mix of compensation for the loss of the bargain with the surveyor,[57] which results in an award of the overpayment in the purchase price, and an attempt to put the plaintiff into the position he would have been in had the negligence never occurred, which permits consequential expenses to be awarded. In surveyors' negligence cases the practical difference between the different measures of damage is usually insignificant and with concurrent liability being

---

[47] *Treml v. Ernest W. Gibson and Partners* [1984] 2 E.G.L.R. 162; *Broadoak Properties Ltd v. Young & White* [1989] 1 E.G.L.R. 263.

[48] *Morgan v. Perry* (1973) 229 E.G. 1737; *Broadoak Properties Ltd v. Young & White* [1989] 1 E.G.L.R. 263; *Shaw v. Halifax* (SW) Ltd [1994] 2 E.G.L.R. 95, 99.

[49] *Hill v. Debenham, Tewson and Chinnocks* (1958) 171 E.G. 835 (this expenditure was a result of the defendants' negligence in not warning the plaintiff to postpone decorations pending cure of damp).

[50] *Broadoak Properties Ltd v. Young & White* [1989] 1 E.G.L.R. 263.

[51] *Hardy v. Wamsley-Lewis* (1967) 203 E.G. 1039 (cost of sweeping up dry rot on floor and making it level again. The basis of recovery of this is not stated in the judgment. It may be justified as a reasonable measure to make the house habitable pending the resale, the plaintiff choosing the reasonable alternative of living in the property to seeking accommodation elsewhere during the same period).

[52] [1956] 1 W.L.R. 471, 478.

[53] In *Rawlings v. Rentokil Laboratories Ltd* (1972) 223 E.G. 1947, legal fees on abortive sales were allowed.

[54] (1967) 203 E.G. 1039.

[55] See *McGregor*, para. 1285:
    " ... it is however difficult to see the basis for this ... denial of recovery, for on the assumption that the plaintiff would not have bought the property had the defendant submitted a true report, then the cost of neither purchase nor resale would have been incurred by him. True, he had contemplated incurring costs in purchasing a house, but such costs will still have to be incurred by him in acquiring a substitute for the defective house now disposed of".

[56] 1987 S.L.T. 622.

[57] The breach of the implied term to exercise reasonable skill and care.

assumed in most cases, there has been no incentive to determine the point on appeal.

Unless and until the point is otherwise determined by an appellate court, it is **9–194** likely that courts of first instance will continue to permit plaintiffs to recover damages in respect of reasonable and foreseeable expenses incurred in order to ascertain the true condition of the property, and reasonable and foreseeable incidental expenses incurred whilst repairing the same, on the ground that such expenses have been caused by the surveyor's breach of contract. This has the merit of achieving consistency with the situation that would be adopted where a plaintiff, on discovering the true condition of the property, immediately re-sells in order to purchase an alternative property. In addition to recovering any overpayment in price, such a plaintiff should recover the reasonable costs of the purchase and re-sale, on the basis that the former represented the recovery of expenses rendered futile by the breach, the latter expenses caused by the breach.

CHAPTER 10

SOLICITORS

PARA.

1. General 10–001
   (a) Duties to the client 10–004
       (i) Contractual duties 10–004
       (ii) Tortious duties 10–013
       (iii) Fiduciary duties 10–016
       (iv) Trust duties 10–034
   (b) Duties to third parties 10–040
       (i) General 10–040
       (ii) Liability to benefici-
            aries without reliance 10–047
       (iii) Duty of care to the other
            side 10–055
       (iv) Solicitors liability on
            undertakings 10–065
       (v) Other liabilities 10–075
   (c) The standard of skill and care 10–077
       (i) The standard of
            reasonableness 10–077
       (ii) General practice as
            evidence of reasonable
            skill and care 10–084
       (iii) The specialist solicitor
            and the inexperienced
            solicitor 10–093
       (iv) Mitigating factors 10–096
       (v) Aggravating factors 10–098
       (vi) General observations 10–104
   (d) Specific defences to a claim for
       breach of duty 10–106
       (i) Immunity 10–106
       (ii) Abuse of process 10–108
       (iii) Acting on counsel's
            advice 10–116
       (iv) Acting on client's
            instructions 10–123
   (e) Solicitor's liability for costs 10–125
   (f) Exclusion or restriction of
       liability by contract 10–141
   (g) Practice and procedure 10–142
       (i) Expert evidence 10–142
       (ii) Privilege 10–144
2. Liability for breach of duty 10–146
   (a) General 10–146
   (b) Giving wrong advice 10–151
   (c) Failing to give advice 10–154

PARA.

   (d) Misconduct of litigation 10–175
   (e) Misconduct of non-contentious
       business 10–192
       (i) Conveyancing 10–193
       (ii) The investment of
            money and claims by
            lenders 10–206
       (iii) Wills 10–218
3. Damages 10–225
   (a) Breach of fiduciary duty and
       breach of trust 10–226
   (b) Remoteness 10–233
       (i) Causation 10–234
       (ii) Foreseeability 10–240
       (iii) The scope of the duty ...10–244
   (c) Measure of damages 10–249
       (i) Date of assessment 10–250
       (ii) Credit for benefits 10–252
       (iii) Evaluation of a chance .10–256
   (d) Heads of damage 10–263
       (i) Loss of opportunity to
            acquire or renew an
            interest in property 10–264
       (ii) Difference in value of
            property 10–268
       (iii) Loss of opportunity to
            bring proceedings 10–277
       (iv) Loss of opportunity to
            defend proceedings 10–293
       (v) Losses on loans secured
            by mortgage 10–294
       (vi) Loss of some other
            financial advantage 10–297
       (vii) Liability to third parties 10–301
       (viii) Criminal liability 10–303
       (ix) Wasted expenditure 10–304
       (x) Incidental expenses 10–309
       (xi) Physical injury,
            inconvenience and
            distress 10–310
   (e) Mitigation of damage 10–316
4. Apportionment of liability 10–323
   (a) Contributory negligence 10–323
   (b) Apportionment of liability 10–328

1. GENERAL

Function of solicitors. It is the function of a solicitor to give advice on legal   **10–001**
matters and to act on behalf of clients in transactions of a legal nature. In order

to practise, the solicitor must (a) have been admitted as a solicitor, (b) have his name on the roll and (c) have a current practising certificate.[1] Solicitors have the right to practise as such in the Supreme Court, the county courts and certain other courts,[2] to undertake advocacy in the courts,[3] to convey real property,[4] and to prepare papers for the grant of probate or of letters of administration.[5] The skills which they are expected to possess include, for example, expertise in negotiation, some business sense[6] and, sometimes, skill in the investment of moneys.[7] In practice, solicitors frequently advise clients or act for them upon matters which are not strictly "legal".[8]

10–002   **Other providers of legal services.** Solicitors no longer enjoy the monopoly on acting as a solicitor in the courts, conveyancing and probate which existed before the Courts and Legal Services Act 1990. Authorised bodies may undertake such work, although no such body yet exists, save that in conveyancing the Act set up the Authorised Conveyancing Practitioners Board,[9] and Licensed Conveyancers have been allowed to practise since the Administration of Justice Act 1985. Lawyers from the European Union have a right to practise anywhere in the Union, subject to certain conditions[10] and thus continental lawyers have a right to practise in England and Wales. Such cross-border practice is regulated by the Lawyers' Service Directive,[11] and the Establishment of Lawyers Directive,[12] and such practitioners should follow the CCBE Code of Conduct for Lawyers in the European Community.

10–003   **Regulation.** Solicitors are subject to the discipline of the Law Society, whose powers are derived from the Solicitors Act 1974.[13] The core regulations are the Solicitors' Practice Rules.[14] The Council of the Law Society through the Office of the Supervision of Solicitors is concerned with professional discipline. Solicitors who carry on investment business have been subject to the regime of the Financial Services Act 1986,[15] and since October 2001 have been subject to the Financial Services and Markets Act 2000.[16] All solicitors used to have to be

---

[1] Solicitors Act 1974, s.1.

[2] *ibid.*, ss. 19 and 20.

[3] See now the Access to Justice Act 1999, s. 36.

[4] Solicitors Act 1974, s.22.

[5] *ibid.*, s.23.

[6] *e.g. Neushul v. Mellish & Harkavy* (1967) 111 S.J. 399.

[7] *e.g. Dooby v. Watson* (1888) 39 Ch.D. 178 at 182–183.

[8] See Taylor L.J. in *Balabel v. Air-India* [1988] Ch. 317 at 331H–332A.

[9] Courts and Legal Services Act 1990, ss. 34 and 35.

[10] See *Gebhard v. Consiglio dell'Ordine degli Avvocati e Procuratori di Milano* [1996] All E.R. (E.C.) 189.

[11] 77/249/EEC.

[12] 98/5/E.C.

[13] s. 31.

[14] Reprinted in the Law Society's *Guide to the Professional Conduct of Solicitors* (8th ed., 1999).

[15] See further the Solicitors' Investment Business Rules 1990 and the Financial Services (Conduct of Business) Rules 1990, both of which are reprinted in the Law Society's *Guide to the Professional Conduct of Solicitors* (8th ed., 1999). Liabilities under the Act include the liability to pay compensation if knowingly concerned in contraventions under s. 6 of the Act, on which see *Securities and Investment Board v. Pantell* [1993] Ch. 256, CA. See also commentary by S. Fennell in (1992) 8 P.N. 157.

[16] See further the Solicitors' Financial Services (Scope) Rules 2001, the Solicitors' Financial Services (Conduct of Business) Rules 2001, and the Solicitors' Financial Services (Amendment) Rules 2001. The Law Society is a designated professional body under the new Act, and firms may carry out certain regulated actitivities without being regulated by the Financial Services Authority.

insured with the Solicitors' Indemnity Fund, which indemnified members for negligence. Since September 1, 2000 insurance has been provided commercially by insurers who comply with certain minimum terms, and solicitors may also insure through a managing general agency which builds on the the the expertise of the old Solicitors' Indemnity Fund and insures with one commercial insurer.[17] For a general discussion of the solicitors' profession and its regulation, reference should be made to *Cordery*, or *The Law Society Guide to the Professional Conduct of Solicitors*.[18]

(a) *Duties to client*

(i) *Contractual duties*

Formation of the retainer. The *fons et origo* of a solicitor's duties is the   **10–004** retainer (or contract of engagement) between himself and the client.[19] The retainer may be written, oral, or inferred from conduct. In the case of formal instructions by lenders, the retainer is generally accepted either expressly in a letter, or impliedly by sending back the report on title.[20] A solicitor engaged by a lender to give independent advice to a potential mortgagor will generally be the agent of that borrower, and not the lender: see *Royal Bank of Scotland v. Etridge (No. 2)*.[21] In some cases it may not be clear precisely who instructed the solicitor. In *Jewo Ferrous BV v. Lewis Moore (A Firm)*[22] the solicitor was instructed on behalf of a client who was to provide a charge, and who in fact also acted for the party in whose favour the charge was to be made. The solicitor reasonably understood his instructions to come from the provider of the charge only, and he was retained by that party alone.[23]

Implied retainer. In a situation where the parties act as if the relationship of   **10–005** solicitor and client existed, although there is no express agreement to that effect, the court will readily hold that there is an implied retainer to be inferred from the

---

[17] The powers of the Law Society to regulate solicitors' insurance, with the concurrence of the Master of the Rolls, are provided by s. 37 of the Solicitors Act 1974.

[18] The current edition is the eighth of 1999, with the ninth expected in 2002.

[19] 'The retainer when given puts into operation the normal terms of the contractual relationship, including in particular the duty of the solicitor to protect the client's interest and carry out his instructions in the matters to which the retainer relates, by all proper means. It is an incident of that duty that the solicitor shall consult with his client on all questions of doubt which do not fall within the express or implied discretion left him, and shall keep the client informed to such an extent as may be reasonably necessary according to the same criteria." *per* Scott L.J. in *Groom v. Crocker* [1939] 1 K.B. 194 at 222. See also *Midland Bank v. Hett, Stubbs & Kemp* [1979] Ch. 384 at 402H: "The extent of his duties depends upon the terms and limits of that retainer and any duty of care to be implied must be related to what he is instructed to do." *per* Oliver J. In *Papparis v. Charles Fulton & Co. Ltd* [1981] I.R.L.R. 104 the Employment Appeal Tribunal considered that a general retainer to advise and conduct proceedings did not come to an end at the first stage of advice and resume when instructions were given to commence proceedings. For a detailed treatment of the retainer, including retainer by different types of persons and the determination of the retainer, see Roger Billins, *Solicitors' Duties and Liabilities* (Sweet & Maxwell, 1999), chapter 1.

[20] See *Bristol & West Building Society v. Fancy & Jackson (a firm)* [1997] 4 All E.R. 582 at 604j–605b (*per* Chadwick J.)

[21] [1998] 4 All E.R. 705.

[22] [20001] P.N.L.R. 12, CA.

[23] The solicitor explained that the bill provided to the chargee in a form only appropriate to a client was an oversight.

parties' conduct.[24] However, the facts of each case must be closely examined, and two cases illustrate circumstances where no retainer was implied. In *Dean v. Allin & Watts (a Firm)*[25] the solicitor acting for the borrower gave an undertaking to hold the deeds of a flat which belonged to an associate of the borrower to the order of the claimant, who was the proposed lender. The solicitor gave no advice about the security, but did not suggest that the claimant should seek independent legal advice. The Court of Appeal held that there was no implied retainer. The objective consideration of all the circumstances had to be considered, and included matters such as whether the party was liable for the solicitors' fees, instructed the solicitors directly, whether there had been a contractual relationship in the past and if so whether there had been advice to obtain independent legal advice.[26] In *BDG Roof-Bond Ltd v. Douglas*[27] the defendant solicitors acted for a client who sold his 50 per cent shareholding in the claimant company to that company. It was held that the solicitors were not retained by the company, despite the facts that they had acted for the company in the past and their bill had been addressed to the company. No one from the company had instructed the solicitors, who acted for one of its directors on the opposite side of the transaction.

10–006   **The need for writing.**[28] Where the retainer is oral, the solicitor ought, for the benefit of both parties, to record the terms in a letter to his client at the outset. At the very least, the nature of the retainer should be recorded in an attendance note. If the solicitor neglects this precaution and later there is a dispute as to what he was instructed to do, the solicitor will begin at a disadvantage.[29] If a solicitor considers that the services he is performing for a client are only limited, this

---

[24] See *Bean v. Wade* [1885] 2 T.L.R. 157, CA; *Blyth v. Fladgate* [1891] 1 Ch. 337 esp. at 355, ChD; *Groom v. Crocker* [1939] 1 K.B. 194, CA. A retainer was readily implied from the borrower's solicitor acting for the lender in *Pegrum v. Fatharly* (1996) 14 W.A.R. 92, Western Australia CA, and where the company's legally qualified director reviewed the documentation prior to exchange, see *Hanave Pt Ltd v. Lfot Pt Ltd* (2000) 168 A.L.R. 318, Federal Court of Australia. *cf. Meerkin & Apel v. Rossett Pty Ltd* [1998] 4 V.R. 54, where the Supreme Court of Victoria, reversing the trial judge, held that no retainer should be implied when solicitors prepared leases for a developer who passed them on to the owner of the property who had his own solicitors.

[25] [2001] Lloyd's Rep. P.N. 605; [2001] E.W.C.A. Civ. 758. *cf. Madley v. Cousins Coombe & Mustoe* [1997] E.G.C.S. 63, QBD, where the defendant solicitors acted for B in the purchase of property where a charge was to be taken over other property owned by the plaintiff and B. By delivering the charge to B for execution, the defendant had offered to act for both of them, and by sending the charge back the plaintiff had accepted that offer and thus retained the defendants. In any event, a retainer could be implied from the parties' conduct and relationship because the defendant had not suggested that the plaintiff should have independent legal advice. In contrast, in *H.G. & R. Nominees Pty Ltd v. Fava* [1997] 2 V.R. 366, Sup Ct Victoria, no retainer was to be implied from the fact that the defendant solicitors purportedly witnessed the plaintiffs' signatures on a mortgage.

[26] To similar effect, the Ontario Court of Appeal considered that the usual indicia of a solicitor–client relationship were meetings between the parties, retainer agreements, correspondence, and bills for services, see *Filipovic v. Upshall* (2000) 33 R.P.R. (3d) 178.

[27][2000] P.N.L.R. 397. For the facts, see para. 10–060 below.

[28] A solicitor is obliged to give information about costs and other matters pursuant to the Solicitors' Practice Rules 1990, r. 15, and the relevant code states that it is good practice to record all such information in writing.

[29] See *Crossley v. Crowther* (1851) 9 Hare 384 and *Re Paine* (1912) 28 T.L.R. 201, Ch.D. "If the solicitor does not take the precaution of getting a written retainer, he . . . must take the consequences:" *per* Denning L.J. in *Griffiths v. Evans* [1953] 1 W.L.R. 1424 at 1428. In *Gray v. Buss Murton (A Firm)* [1999] P.N.L.R. 882 Rougier J. explained that the underlying basis of this rule was that it was the client who knows what he wants done, and the solicitor should ascertain the client's wishes accurately. In *Mackie v. Wilde* [1998] 2 I.R. 570, Irish H Ct, Morris J. commented on this principle that any practice requiring one party's evidence to be preferred to another was unconstitutional, and the solicitor's evidence was in fact preferred.

should be put in writing to avoid misunderstanding.[30] Similarly, it is prudent for a solicitor to record in writing the advice that he gives during the retainer.[31] Thus, as an example, a solicitor should record in an attendance note and write to the client if he was not going to to give tax advice in a commercial transaction, see *Hurlingham Estates Ltd v. Wilde & Partners.*[32] In that case, Lightman J. rejected the solicitor's evidence that he had agreed with the clients that he would not give tax advice, and he also stated that any such limitation would require the client's fully informed consent.[33]

The nature of the duties. The nature of a solicitor's contractual duties was **10–007** discussed in some detail by Oliver J. in *Midland Bank v. Hett, Stubbs & Kemp.*[34] The plaintiffs, as executors of Mr Green, claimed damages against the defendant solicitors for failing to register an option granted to Mr Green by his father on March 24, 1961. On August 17, 1967 the father conveyed the farm to his wife for £500 in order to defeat the option. Subsequently, the defendants sought to remedy their omission by registering the option, and Mr Green then purported to exercise it, but to no effect as the option was unregistered at the time the farm was conveyed by the father to the mother. Oliver J. analysed the contractual duties of the defendants in this way:

> "The classical formulation of the claim in this sort of case as 'damages for negligence and breach of professional duty' tends to be a mesmeric phrase. It concentrates attention on the implied obligation to devote to the client's business that reasonable care and skill to be expected from a normally competent and careful practitioner as if that obligation were not only a compendious, but also exhaustive, definition of all the duties assumed under the contract created by the retainer and its acceptance. But, of course, it is not. A contract gives rise to a complex of rights and duties of which the duty to exercise reasonable care and skill is but one.
> . . . If one were to seek to write out in longhand the obligations which Mr Stubbs senior assumed when he engaged to act in the matter of the grant of the option, they were (1) to draw and have completed a proper and enforceable option agreement which would bind the parties; (2) to take such steps as were necessary and practicable to ensure that it was binding on the land into whosoever hands it might come before any third party acquired a legal estate; and (3) to carry out his work with the skill and care which a normally competent practitioner would bring to it."[35]

Oliver J.'s analysis of the solicitor's contractual duties is not easy to apply in cases where the solicitor is retained to do something more complex than effect an option, for example to conduct a personal injuries action. Presumably the solicitor's specific duties include (1) issuing the claim form within the limitation period, (2) obtaining a medical report and (3) instructing counsel. Suppose, however, the solicitor fails to send a letter before action, or to take a proof from a material witness before he dies, or to carry out the steps suggested in counsel's

---

[30] *Begusic v. Clark, Wilson & Co.* (1992) 92 D.L.R. (4th) 273, British Columbia Sup Ct. However, in *Silver v. Morris* (1995) 139 N.S.R. (2d) 18, Nova Scotia CA, the defendant solicitor was retained by an experienced businesswoman in the sale of a business, in which he would be expected to give advice on tax implications. As he had orally made it clear to the plaintiff that he knew nothing about tax, it was held that the solicitor was not retained to give tax advice.
[31] See para. 10–174 below.
[32] [1997] 1 Lloyd's Rep. 525.
[33] *Quaere* whether this is correct.
[34] [1979] Ch. 384.
[35] [1979] Ch. 384 at 434E–F and 435A–B.

advice on evidence: is this a breach of the solicitor's specific duties or simply a breach of the general duty to exercise skill and care? If one attempts to "write out in longhand" all the duties assumed by a solicitor upon his retainer, the list in most cases is liable to run to considerable length, unless it is confined to the most basic steps involved in the particular business which the solicitor is undertaking. In practice, the solicitor's failure to carry out some necessary step is normally treated as a breach of the general duty to exercise skill and care rather than a breach of some specific duty implied in the retainer.[36] In most cases it is submitted that this is the correct approach, although the duty of skill and care implies a number of general obligations.[37]

10–008   **Express instructions.** In some cases there may be express instructions which the court will treat as express terms of the contract.[38] For example, in *Pilbrow v. Pearless De Rougemont & Co.*[39] there was an express term that the legal services were to be provided by a solicitor, and thus there was non-performance by the defendant firm when the work was handled competently by an employee who was not a solicitor, so that the solicitors were not able to obtain payment of their fees. Detailed express terms are common in retainers by lenders. An early example is *Bristol and West Building Society v. Kramer*[40] where the defendant solicitors accepted standard form instructions to act for the plaintiff mortgage lenders, which included a requirement to notify the proposed mortgagee of certain matters. They were in breach of that instruction, which was held to be an express term of their retainer.

10–009   **Construction of express duties.**[41] An insertion by solicitors into their contract with their client of a one-sided provision will be construed *contra proferentem.*[42] Express instructions by lending institutions and the undertakings they require have been examined by the courts.[43] In particular, in a number of cases the Court

---

[36] See, for example: *Sykes v. Midland Bank Executor and Trustee Co. Ltd* [1971] 1 Q.B. 113, CA, at 125H: failure to advise on lease; *County Personnel (Employment Agency) Ltd v. Alan R. Pulver & Co.* [1987] 1 W.L.R. 916, CA: failure to advise on unusual term in lease.

[37] See para. 10–079.

[38] This has particular importance in the context of contributory negligence, see para. 10–327.

[39] [1999] 3 All E.R. 355, CA.

[40] *The Times,* February 6, 1995. See Flenley and Leech, *Solicitors' Negligence* (Butterworths, 1999) at para. 6.4 for a suggestion that *Kramer* would not be followed in any case which is not on all fours with it, given subsequent authority, on which see the next two paragraphs. More unusually, in *Polishuk v. Hagarty* (1983) 149 D.L.R. (3d) 65, upheld on this point on appeal at (1985) 14 D.L.R. (4th) 446, solicitors accepted an undertaking in lieu of the discharge of a mortgage. It was no defence that they had fulfilled the standard of the ordinarily competent solicitor, as they had a contractual duty to complete the transaction according to the terms of the contract of purchase, which they were not able to vary without consent.

[41] For a different example of the construction of the retainer letter see *Twenty Two A Property Investments Ltd v. Simpson Curtis (A Firm)* [2000] E.G.C.S. 140, CA. The client had an interest in property where the sale by the owner had to be completed by a certain date. He instructed the defendant solicitors to make sure his interests were protected and instructed the solicitor to actively pursue to make sure that matters were progressing. As a result, the solicitor had a duty to keep himself informed at all times what the owner's solicitor was doing and proposed to do, and to exert pressure on him.

[42] *Re a Debtor (No. 1594 of 1992), The Times,* December 18, 1992, ChD.

[43] For examples of a purposive constructions of such instructions see *Birmingham Midshires Mortgage Services Ltd v. David Parry and Co.* [1996] P.N.L.R. 494, upheld by CA [1997] N.P.C. 153 and [1997] E.G.C.S. 150 ("no other mortgages" construed as meaning on the security property only); *Bristol & West Building Society v. Fancy & Jackson (a firm)* [1997] 4 All E.R. 582 (see the *Colin Bishop* case where a "back to back" sale was sufficiently close to a sub-sale to require reporting).

of Appeal has addressed the issue of whether such duties should be construed as absolute obligations, or as qualified by the implied duty to use reasonable care and skill.[44] Most have concluded that the duties are qualified, and it is likely to be a rare case where a court will impose an absolute obligation.[45] Exceptionally, a claim for breach of an undertaking succeeded regardless of whether the solicitors were at fault in *Zwebner v. The Mortgage Corporation Ltd.*[46] There, the solicitors' report on title undertook that all appropriate documents would be properly executed before completion of the mortgage transaction. This was construed as an absolute obligation to ensure (*inter alia*) that one of the borrower's signatures was genuine, when in fact it was a forgery. The Court of Appeal held that the defendant solicitors were strictly liable, although they also found them negligent.

However, in the other decisions, the obligations were not construed to be **10–010** absolute. In *Barclays Bank Plc v. Weeks Legg & Dean (a firm)*,[47] the Court of Appeal determined appeals in three cases involving solicitors acting for purchasers of land who gave undertakings to the plaintiff bank on the bank's standard form. In each case, the solicitor had undertaken that any sums received would be "applied solely for acquiring a good marketable title". The court held that the undertaking was not absolute, but imposed a qualified obligation to obtain what a reasonably competent solicitor acting with skill and care would accept as a good marketable title. The undertaking was construed so that the solicitors' obligations pursuant to it were in conformity with the qualified obligations to their own clients and their trust obligations to the bank. In *Midland Bank plc v. Cox McQueen*[48] the Court of Appeal followed the *Barclays Bank* case, and distinguished *Zwebner*. In that case the retainer was to obtain the signature of a customer's wife to a legal charge, rather than properly to execute the documents, with no undertaking being given, and it was interpreted by the Court of Appeal as merely an obligation to use reasonable care and skill. The previous two cases were followed in *UCB Corporate Services Ltd v. Clyde & Co (A Firm)*[49] where the Court of Appeal held that an obligation to obtain an enforceable guarantee required the solicitors to do all that could be reasonably expected to achieve the desired result. Any absolute obligation would have to be in clear and unequivocal terms. Finally, in *Mercantile Credit Company Ltd v. Fenwick*[50] the Court of Appeal similarly held, without referring to any previous authority, that if a lender wished to impose an absolute obligation on its solicitors it must do so in clear terms.[51] There, the solicitors' obligation to the lender with regard to guarantors for whom they did not act was to make enquiries to satisfy

---

[44] See also *The Mortgage Corporation v. Mitchells Robertson* [1997] S.L.T. 1305, OH: mortgage instructions using the words "must", "should" and "will" were held to be capable of creating an absolute obligation.

[45] But strict liability is also imposed for breach of a warranty of authority, see para. 10–075 below.

[46] [1998] P.N.L.R. 769.

[47] [1999] Q.B. 309.

[48] [1999] P.N.L.R. 593. This case, and not *Zwebner*, was followed by the Hong Kong Court of Appeal in *Ying Ho Co Ltd v. Man Kwok Leung* [2000] 3 H.K.L.R.D. 191, where an undertaking to send duly executed documents in a property transaction was held to be an obligation to use reasonable care to ensure that the documents were executed by the owner of the property.

[49] [2000] P.N.L.R. 841.

[50] [1999] Lloyd's Rep. P.N. 408.

[51] A point also made by Lord Woolf M.R. in *Midland Bank plc v. Cox McQueen* [1999] P.N.L.R. 593 at 603.

themselves that there would be no challenge to the security being taken, but they gave no warranty to that effect.

10–011   **Termination of the retainer.** A client can determine the retainer at will. In litigation, there is an entire contract, and the solicitor can only terminate the retainer upon reasonable notice and for good cause, unless there is an agreement to the contrary.[52] The same probably applies to non-contentious matters.[53]

10–012   **Continuing obligations.** The question of whether an obligation is a continuing one may be of particular importance in determining whether a cause of action is statute-barred. In *Midland Bank v. Hett, Stubbs & Kemp*[54] the defendant solicitors contended that any claim against them for failing to register the option was statute-barred. Oliver J. rejected this contention, and held that the obligation to take such steps as were necessary and practicable to ensure that the option agreement was binding on the land was a continuing one until August 17, 1967, when it became incapable of effective performance. Therefore the claim for breach of contract was not statute-barred, since proceedings had been begun within six years of that date.[55] The concept of a continuing obligation has been subject to criticism in two subsequent Court of Appeal cases.[56] However, in *Carlton v. Fulchers*[57] Waller L.J. considered that there could be a continuing obligation on the defendant solicitor to preserve the plaintiff's cause of action during the currency of the retainer.

(ii) *Tortious duties*[58]

10–013   **History.** Until 50 years ago it was generally thought that a negligent solicitor was liable to his client both in contract and in tort.[59] However, there were authorities to the effect that the solicitor's liability lay in contract alone[60] and the issue was far from clear. The point was ostensibly resolved by the Court of Appeal in *Groom v. Crocker*,[61] in which it was held that the solicitor owed no duty to the client beyond the contractual duties arising from his retainer. For the

---

[52] *Summit Property Ltd v. Pitmans (A Firm)* [2001] Lloyd's Rep. P.N. 164, Park J. An example of a good reason is non-payment of fees, see Solicitors Act 1974 s. 65(2). See further para. 10–191.
[53] See the Law Society's *Guide to the Professional Conduct of Solicitors* (8th ed., 1999), para. 12–12, which gives examples of what may amount to a good reason. There would be no entire contract where a solicitor aggrees to act generally for a person or in a variety of matters, see *Warmingtons v. McMurray* [1937] 1 All E.R. 562, CA.
[54] [1979] Ch. 384. For the facts see para. 10–007 above.
[55] The defence of limitation also failed on other grounds. See para. 10–013.
[56] *Lee v. Thompson* (1990) 6 P.N. 91 at 93; *Bell v. Peter Browne & Co.* [1990] 2 Q.B. 495, esp. at 514F-G, 521G and 525E-H; see also *Costiga v. Rzicka* (1984) 33 Alta. L.R. (2d) 21. There will be some continuing fiduciary duties. For instance, a solicitor's duty of confidentiality continues, and thus he will have an obligation to decline to accept instructions from a new client because he has acquired knowledge from a former client, on which see paras 10–026 *et seq.*
[57] [1997] P.N.L.R. 337, relying on passages in *Bell v. Peter Browne & Co* [1990] 2 Q.B. 495 at 501 and 512. For the facts see para. 10–185 below. See also *Hines v. Willans* [1997] C.L.Y. 3368, summarised at para. 10–023 below.
[58] See further chap. 2 paras 2–100 *et seq.*
[59] See, for example: *Boorman v. Brown* (1844) 11 Cl. & Fin. 1 at 44; *Davies v. Lock* (1844) 3 L.T. (o.s.) 125; *Davies v. Hood* (1903) 88 L.T. 19, KBD at 20; *Nocton v. Ashburton* [1914] A.C. 932 at 956.
[60] *Howell v. Young* (1826) 5B. & C. 259; *Bean v. Wade* (1885) 2 T.L.R. 157, CA.
[61] [1939] 1 K.B. 194.

next 37 years *Groom v. Crocker* was followed without question.[62] However, the debate was reopened by the statement of Lord Denning M.R. in *Esso Petroleum Co. Ltd v. Mardon*[63] that *Groom v. Crocker*[64] was wrongly decided. In *Midland Bank v. Hett Stubbs & Kemp*[65] Oliver J. reviewed the authorities in considerable detail and came to the conclusion that *Groom v. Crocker* was no longer good law and the defendant solicitors were liable in negligence (as well as contract) for failing to register the option.[66] In *Forster v. Outred & Co.*[67] the Court of Appeal (without hearing argument on the point) approved *Midland Bank v. Hett Stubbs & Kemp*.[68] The Privy Council in *Tai Hing Cotton Mill Ltd v. Liu Chong Hing Bank Ltd*[69] at least impliedly cast doubt upon the basis of the decision, and in *Lee v. Thompson*[70] Lloyd L.J. considered the matter ripe for review.

The current law. In *Henderson v. Merrett Syndicates Ltd*[71] the House of Lords **10–014** decided that a duty of care in tort was owed by Lloyd's managing agents to Names, and that the existence of the duty of care was not excluded by the relevant contractual regime. The Names were free to pursue their remedy in contract or in tort. Lord Goff agreed with the reasoning of Oliver J. in *Midland Bank Trust Co. Ltd v. Hett, Stubbs & Kemp*.[72] The decision resolves this issue, at least for cases of professional negligence.

The position in the Commonwealth. Elsewhere in the Commonwealth the **10–015** courts have now held that solicitors are liable to their clients both in contract and tort. In Canada the Supreme Court of Canada decided in *Central Trust Co. v. Rafuse*[73] that the law should allow concurrent liability, and this applied to solicitors as well as other professionals. In Australia, the High Court of Australia have also held that there is concurrent liability, see *Astley v. Austrust Limited*.[74] The New Zealand Court of Appeal recognised concurrent liability in *Mouat v.*

---

[62] See, for example, *Clarke v. Kirby-Smith* [1964] 1 Ch. 506, ChD; *Cooke v. Swinfen* [1967] 1 W.L.R. 457, CA; *Heywood v. Wellers* [1976] Q.B. 446, CA.
[63] [1976] Q.B. 801 at 819. He pointed out that cases of high authority, such as *Nocton v. Ashburton* [1914] A.C. 932, had not been cited in *Groom v. Crocker.*
[64] [1939] 1 K.B. 194.
[65] [1979] Ch. 384. For the facts see para. 10–007.
[66] He held that the cause of action accrued when the option was incapable of being exercised. This decision on the date of the accrual of the cause of action is probably wrong given later decisions such as *D.W.Moore & Co. Ltd v. Ferrier* [1988] 1 W.L.R. 267, CA; and *Bell v. Peter Browne & Co.* [1990] 2 Q.B. 495, CA; see further chap. 5 para. 5–14. The law in Australia is probably different: see *Wardley Australia Ltd v. Western Australia* (1992) 66 A.L.J.R. 839 and (1992) 109 A.L.R. 247, discussed in chap. 5 para. 5–38. The decision in *Hett Stubbs* on concurrent liability was criticised by J.M. Kaye,"The liability of solicitors in tort" (1984) 100 L.Q.R. 680.
[67] [1982] 1 W.L.R. 86. This decision was followed by the Court of Appeal in *Costa v. Georghiou* (1985) 1 .P.N. 201, *D.W.Moore & Co. Ltd v. Ferrier* [1988] 1 W.L.R. 267, and *Bell v. Peter Browne & Co.* [1990] 3 W.L.R. 510.
[68] [1979] Ch. 384.
[69] [1986] A.C. 80 at 117.
[70] (1990) 6 P.N. 91, at 93 col. 2.
[71] [1995] 2 A.C. 145. See chap. 2. para. 2–105.
[72] [1979] Ch 384; see [1995] 2 A.C. 145 at 181H–182A.
[73] (1987) 31 D.L.R. (4th) 481. For the facts of this case see para. 10–081 The same result had been reached in *Baldwin v. Chalker* (1984) 48 Nfld. & P.E.I.R and 142 A.P.R. 86, Nfld CA, and *Consumers Glass Co. Ltd v. Foundation Co. of Canada* (1985) 20 D.L.R. (4th) 126, Ontario CA.
[74] [1999] Lloyd's Rep. P.N. 758: while there was concurrent liability, the defendant's plea of contributory negligence succeeded only in tort and not contract; see further para. 10–324. See also the earlier case of *Hawkins v. Clayton* (1988) 164 C.L.R. 539, High Court of Australia.

Clark Boyce.[75] In Ireland the Supreme Court has held that a solicitor is liable to his client both in contract and tort: see *Finlay v. Murtagh.*[76]

(iii) *Fiduciary duties*[77]

10–016 **General.** In addition to the contractual duties arising from his retainer and the general duty to exercise skill and care, the solicitor owes fiduciary duties to his client. The relationship between a solicitor and his client has been described as "one of the most important fiduciary relations known to our law".[78] However, the limits of those duties must be recognised. In *Clark Boyce v. Mouat*[79] the Privy Council concluded:

> "A fiduciary duty concerns disclosure of material facts in a situation where the fiduciary either has a personal interest in the matter to which the facts are material, or acts for another party who has such an interest. It cannot be prayed in aid to enlarge the scope of contractual duties."

The seven fiduciary duties listed below are of particular relevance to solicitors.[80] An allegation of breach of fiduciary duty or breach of trust may in some circumstances greatly assist a claimant, due to the different principles of compensation in some but not all cases,[81] and the potentially different rules as to contributory negligence.[82] Indeed, the Court of Appeal in *Bristol & West Building Society v. Mothew*[83] considered that the term "fiduciary duty" should be limited to those duties peculiar to fiduciaries where breach attracts different legal consequences from the breach of other duties.

10–017 **(1) Undue influence.**[84] A client may be induced by the undue influence of a solicitor to make a gift to him. It is well established that the solicitor–client relationship gives rise to a presumption of undue influence.[85] It applies to other

---

[75] [1992] 2 N.Z.L.R. 559. The point was not considered by the Privy Council on appeal at [1994] 1 A.C. 428.

[76] [1979] I.R. 249 (claim against a solicitor for failing to issue proceedings within the limitation period).

[77] See also chap. 2 paras 2–125 *et seq.* For a more extensive treatment of this topic see H. Evans, *Lawyer's Liabilities* (2nd ed., 2002), chap. 3. All the cases in this section concern solicitors unless otherwise stated.

[78] *per* Cozens-Hardy M.R. in *Re Van Laun* [1907] 2 K.B. 23, at 29. However, the fiduciary relationship does not generally extend beyond the retainer, see *Cox v. Pemberton Holmes* [1993] 6 W.W.R. 603 British Columbia CA. The relationship of fiduciary and contractual duties was described by Lord Browne-Wilkinson in *Henderson v. Merrett Syndicates Ltd* [1995] 2 A.C. 145 at 206A-D, a case which did not concern solicitors. Note that the seven fiduciary duties set out are not exhaustive. Thus, for instance, in *MacDonell v. M.& M. Developments Ltd* (1998) 157 D.L.R. (4th) 240, Nova Scotia CA, a solicitor was in breach of his fiduciary duty in continuing to act generally for the plaintiff for two months after he had decided to assert his own title to lands ostensibly held by the plaintiff.

[79] [1994] 1 A.C. 428, 437F-G.

[80] This classification is to an extent one of convenience only. Categories (2) to (5) are all aspects of the same general principle.

[81] See further paras 10–226 to 10–231 below.

[82] See further para. 10–327 below.

[83] [1998] Ch. 1 at 16. For the facts see paras 10–023 and 10–295.

[84] Properly speaking, this is not a breach of fiduciary duty, but it is convenient and common to treat the issue under this head.

[85] See, *e.g. Liles v. Terry* [1895] Q.B. 679, CA (voluntary conveyance of property by client to solicitor declared void); *Wright v. Carter* [1903] 1 Ch. 27, CA (property donated in trust to solicitor by client declared void).

transactions as well as gifts.[86] The presumption applies to gifts to the solicitor's relations. Thus a gift to the solicitor's son was set aside by the House of Lords in *Willis v. Barron*,[87] where the defendant was the plaintiff's husband's solicitor rather than her own. In *Liles v. Terry*[88] the Court of Appeal set aside a gift to the solicitor's wife on the basis of the presumption of undue influence. The presumption will apply after the relationship of client and solicitor has ended.[89] The presumption of undue influence does not strictly apply in the case of gifts by will,[90] although a similar but less rigorous doctrine does exist in such cases.[91] It is possible to rebut the presumption of undue influence by showing that the client exercised free will.[92] Legal advice is helpful in dispelling the presumption but it is probably not essential,[93] although some cases involving solicitors suggest the contrary.[94]

(2) Personal dealings with clients. In the well-known case of *Nocton v.* **10–018** *Ashburton*[95] a solicitor was found liable for breach of fiduciary duty when he had a personal interest in the transaction his client was entering, and he also acted for borrowers who were the other party of the transaction. In *Swindle v. Harrison*[96] Mummery L.J explained that *Nocton v. Ashburton* decided that a solicitor stands in a fiduciary relationship with his client, and when entering into a financial transaction with his client he was under a fiduciary duty to disclose all relevant facts known to him; such liability did not depend on proof of deceit or negligence. A solicitor is not permitted to enter transactions with his client, in circumstances where he has a duty to act in the interests of his client, without proof that he has given a fair price and that he has disclosed all the information he has concerning the transaction.[97] This is sometimes relevant when a solicitor enters a joint venture with his client, which was permitted in *Hanson v. Lorenz & Jones*.[98] In *Day v. Cook*[99] the defendant solicitor presented a number of transactions to the plaintiff in which the solicitor had an interest. Although the

---

[86] *Wright v. Carter* [1903] 1 Ch. 27 at 50 per Vaughan Williams L.J. *cf. Moody v. Cox and Hatt* [1917] 2 Ch. 71 at 79–80 per Lord Cozens-Hardy M.R.
[87] [1902] A.C. 271.
[88] [1895] Q.B. 679.
[89] *Allison v. Clayhills* (1907) 97 L.T. 709 at 712 *per* Parker J.
[90] *Hindson v. Weatherill* (1854) 5 De G.M. & G. 301.
[91] See *Wintle v. Nye* [1959] 1 W.L.R. 284, HL.
[92] As an illustration, see *Westmelton v. Archer* [1982] V.R. 305 where a well-informed corporate client was not relying on any confidence or expectation of legal advice, and the presumption was easily dispelled.
[93] *Inche Noriah v. Omar* [1929] A.C. 127; *Lancashire Loan Ltd v. Black* [1934] 1 K.B. 380 at 412–413. These cases do not concern solicitors.
[94] *e.g. Rhodes v. Bate* (1865) L.R. 1. Ch. 252 at 257.
[95] [1914] A.C. 932. For the facts of the case, see para. 10–226 below.
[96] [1997] 4 All E.R. 705 at 732.
[97] *Demerera Bauxite v. Hubbard* [1923] A.C. 673, PC (solicitor failed to disclose a rival bid, and the transaction was unenforceable). Thus obtaining independent legal advice will not be sufficient if the solicitors fails to make a full disclosure to the new solicitor, see *Gibbs v. Daniel* (1862) 4 Giff 1. The information must be sufficient for the client to give informed consent, see *Sims v. Craig Bell & Bond* [1991] 3 N.Z.L.R. 535, CA. See also *Gibson v. Jeyes* (1801) 6 Ves. Jun. 266.
[98] [1987] 1 F.T.L.R. 23. It would appear that the Court of Appeal considered it sufficient if the transaction was fair, and the client fully aware of its nature and effect. The question of the solicitor disclosing material facts does not seem to have been relevant. For illustrations of the dangers of joint ventures, see *Korz v. St. Pierre* (1988) 43 D.L.R. (4th) 528, Ontario CA, and *MacDonald Estate* (1994) 95 Man. R. (2d) 123, Manitoba CA.
[99] [2000] P.N.L.R. 178, Bristol Mercantile Court. These findings were not appealed to the Court of Appeal, see [2001] P.N.L.R. 32; [2001] E.W.C.A. Civ. 592.

plaintiff was fully informed, the solicitor was in breach of fiduciary duty as the transactions were not fair, for the solicitor obtained an unjustified advantage in them.

10–019   The rule cannot be circumvented, for instance by purchasing property from the client in the name of the solicitor's brother when the solicitor is the real purchaser.[1] The rule may apply after the termination of the solicitor–client relationship, as in *McMaster v. Byrne*.[2] The client had consistently resorted to the solicitor for advice about the formation and promotion of several companies and in relation to his will. The Privy Council held that a continuing relationship of confidence had arisen, and thus the solicitor was bound to disclose all material facts when the client granted him an option in relation to one of his companies after the termination of the solicitor–client relationship. A strict view was taken in *Spector v. Ageda*,[3] where the solicitor made a loan to the client. Megarry J. considered that as a general rule a solicitor ought never to act for a person in a transaction to which he himself is a party with an adverse interest, even after the fullest disclosure to the client, although he conceded that there may possibly be exceptions to this rule. If the solicitor has a significant interest in a company which is entering a transaction with his client, he may have to show at least that the sale was fair and honest.[4]

10–020   **(3) Obtaining a personal benefit.** A solicitor may not use his client's property to obtain a personal benefit. In *Brown v. Inland Revenue Commissioners*[5] the solicitor possessed clients' money which was not worth investing individually, as it was in small sums or was required soon. He kept some of these moneys on deposit in the firm's name and retained the interest. It was not disputed that the solicitor should not make a profit out of the clients' money. However it was argued that he could keep the money by custom or by agreement, and the defendant relied on the approval by the Law Society of Scotland of the practice and on the difficulty of allocating to particular clients the interest earned. The House of Lords found against the solicitor. The custom, while common, was not universal or notorious, and there was insufficient evidence to found an implied term, despite the difficulty of accurately determining sums due.[6] However, in *Bogg v. Raper*[7] a solicitor who inserted a standard clause in a will, exonerating the executors and trustees, of which he was to be one, from potential liabilities, was entitled to rely on it as a trustee. The clause did not confer a benefit, but defined the extent of the potential liabilities, and there was no conflict of interest.

---

[1] As in *McPherson v. Watt* (1877) 3 A.C. 254.

[2] [1952] 1 All E.R. 1362. See also *Longstaff v. Birtles*, *The Times*, September 18, 2001, C.A., where it was stated that the solicitor must cause the client to obtain independent legal advice.

[3] [1973] Ch. 30, at 47G-H. The transaction was set aside.

[4] *Farrar v. Farrars Ltd* (1888) 40 Ch. D. 395 at 410 and 415; for an explanation of the case see *Movitex Ltd v. Bulfield* [1988] B.C.L.C. 104 at 122–123. See also *Day v. Mead* [1987] 2 N.Z.L.R. 443, NZCA Similarly, in *Recha and Klein v. Yeamans and Gere* (1993) 135 N.B.R. (2d) 360, New Brunswick CA, the defendant solicitor was in breach of fiduciary duty in failing to disclose to his clients who were purchasing a restaurant that he had given a personal guarantee in relation to it for the vendor.

[5] [1965] A.C. 244, HL Scot. See also *Burdick v. Garrick* (1870) L.R. 5 Ch. 233.

[6] Moneys held on account are now governed by s. 33 of the Solicitors Act 1974 and the Solicitors' Accounts Rules 1991.

[7] *The Times*, April 22 1998, CA.

(4) Using a fiduciary position to make a personal profit. A solicitor may not   **10–021**
make use of his fiduciary position to gain a benefit for himself. In *Boardman v.
Phipps*[8] the defendant, Mr Boardman, acted as the solicitor to a trust that had a
minority shareholding in a private company. The company was not performing
satisfactorily, and he was asked to investigate. In his capacity as representative of
the trust, Mr Boardman attended meetings and obtained information. As a result,
it was decided by the trustees that the best solution was to obtain a majority of
the shareholdings, but they did not wish to seek the court's authority to do this.
Mr Boardman therefore obtained shares in the company, with the approval of
only some of the trustees. As a result of obtaining control of the company, he
made a substantial profit, as did the trust from their shareholdings. A bare
majority of the House of Lords held that Mr Boardman should disgorge the
profits he had made to the beneficiaries. Exceptionally, Mr Boardman was
remunerated on a liberal scale for the work he had undertaken. The primary
reason for liability was that a fiduciary is not permitted to make a profit by reason
of the opportunity or knowledge gained in that position, save with consent. A
subsidiary reason was that there was a conflict between Mr Boardman's interest
and his duties to the trust.[9]

(5) Bribes and secret commissions. A fiduciary is not allowed to accept   **10–022**
bribes or secret commissions. In *Islamic Republic of Iran v. Denby*[10] the solicitor's client was the defendant in a shipping dispute. The other side paid the
solicitor a commission to obtain a prompt and satisfactory settlement, which was
described by the judge as a bribe, and the client was entitled to recover the sums
from him. The rule applies to secret commissions that are not bribes, such as an
introducing fee.[11] If the client expressly or impliedly accepts the payment's
existence, he cannot later recover it from the solicitor, which is what happened
in *Re Haslam v. Hier-Evans*.[12] Solicitors were retained to act for a client in the
purchase of a patent. They had a note from vendors offering them commission if
they found a purchaser, and the solicitors showed it to the client before the patent
was purchased by him. The Court of Appeal held that the client's executors were
not allowed to deduct the commission from the solicitors' bill.

(6) Accepting inconsistent engagements. The issue of acting for both parties   **10–023**
in a transaction arises in the common law context of breach of the duty of

---

[8] [1967] 2 A.C. 46. See also *Official Assignee of Collier v. Creighton* [1993] 2 N.Z.L.R. 534, NZCA,
where the solicitor failed to inform his client who was considering purchasing a house that he was
also still interested in purchasing it. For an unusual application of this principle, see *Stewart v.
Canadian Broadcasting Association* (1997) 150 D.L.R. (4th) 24, Ontario H Ct, summarised at chap.
11, para. 11–005.
[9] *cf. Re Century Homes Pty Ltd (in liquidation)* (1984) 73 F.L.R. 462, Federal Court of Australia: the
solicitor purchased company property with the consent and at the invitation of the company, and was
thus not in breach of fiduciary duty.
[10] [1987] 1 Lloyd's Rep. 367. Leggatt J. was constrained by authority to hold that the recovery of the
secret profit was a claim for money had and received, and no proprietary remedy was available.
However, in *Attorney-General for Hong Kong v. Reid* [1994] 1 A.C. 324, a public prosecutor accepted
bribes as an inducement to exploit his position to obstruct the prosecution of some criminals. The
Privy Council decided that the bribes were held on constructive trust, and thus could be traced into
New Zealand houses.
[11] As in *Re Four Solicitors* [1901] 1 Q.B. 187.
[12] [1902] 1 Ch. 765.

reasonable care and skill,[13] but it also arises as a breach of fiduciary duty.[14] Common examples where there may be potential conflicts of duty are acting for vendor and purchaser in a conveyancing transaction, and acting for lender and purchaser.[15] In the seminal case of *Bristol & West Building Society v. Mothew*[16] the defendant solicitor acted for the plaintiff lender and the borrower in a mortgage transaction, an extremely common occurrence. The borrower arranged for a second charge on his existing property to be transferred to the new one. Despite knowing about this, the solicitor failed to report it to the plaintiffs and misrepresented to them the fact that the borrowers had no other indebtedness. The Court of Appeal held that the subsequent receipt and misapplication of the lender's moneys was not a breach of trust, absent deliberate concealment or an intention to mislead, and the earlier misrepresentation did not change the position. Furthermore, the Court considered that the term "fiduciary duty" should be limited to those duties peculiar to fiduciaries where breach attracts different legal consequences from the breach of other duties, and used the concept of loyalty as an organising principle. Millett L.J. analysed the fiduciary obligations owed to two clients into four categories. First, the "double employment" rule prevented a solicitor acting for two clients whose interests may conflict, without obtaining informed consent.[17] Consent was implied in that case where the solicitor acted for lender and borrower. Secondly, there was a duty of good faith. There had to be an intention to further the interests of one client to the prejudice of the other for there to be a breach of this obligation, although the conduct would not have to be dishonest. Thirdly and relatedly, under the "no inhibition principle", a fiduciary must not be inhibited by his duties to one client from carrying out his duties to the other. Breach of this obligation also required intentional conduct. Finally, the "actual conflict" rule requires a solicitor not to be in a position where he cannot fulfil his obligations to one client without failing the other.

10–024   **Application of *Mothew*.** There have been a number of reported cases in which *Mothew* has been applied.[18] In *Bristol & West Building Society v. Fancy &*

---

[13] See paras 10–100 to 10–102.

[14] See *Moody v. Cox and Hatt* [1917] 2 Ch. 71, esp. at 79 and 81. A breach of duty was found in that case, and it was no defence to say that he owed a duty to his other client not to disclose relevant information. In *Hines v. Willans* [1997] C.L.Y. 3368 the defendant solicitors acted for W and her husband on the making of identical reciprocal wills in 1985, and for W in various transactions thereafter, including in July 1990. In that month, the husband instructed the solicitors to change his will, leaving nothing to W, which they did. The Court of Appeal held that the defendants were in breach of fiduciary duty to W, and as the evidence suggested that the husband would have changed his mind very soon afterwards, the court rejected the appeal against an award of substantial damages.

[15] Although there will generally be informed consent, see *Bristol & West Building Society v. Mothew* [1996] 4 All E.R. 698.

[16] [1998] Ch. 1. For a critical commentary see S. Elliott, "Fiduciary liability for client mortgage frauds" (1999) 13 Tru. L.I. 74, where it is argued that previous cases show that a solicitor's negligence is also a breach of fiduciary duty where it is aggravated by conflicting interest or an adverse fiduciary engagement. In *Re Moage Ltd* (1998) 153 A.L.R. 711 the Federal Court of Australia, following *Mothew*, held that it had to be pleaded that the solicitor had intentionally preferred the interests of one client over another.

[17] There may be some cases where even express consent may not be sufficient, see the Canadian cases referred to below.

[18] See also *Armitage v. Paynter Construction Ltd* [1999] 2 N.Z.L.R 535. A solicitor acted for two clients who were undertaking a joint venture. When he knew that one of the joint venturers was in financial difficulties, he paid to it moneys which were due to both clients. Following *Mothew*, the New Zealand Court of Appeal found that an actual conflict had arisen.

Jackson (a firm),[19] Chadwick J. held that one of the defendant firms in that litigation, Steggles Palmer, were in breach of fiduciary duty by failing to inform the plaintiff building society that they acted for the vendor, but that breach did not assist the plaintiff in obtaining compensation. The solicitors had also failed to inform the plaintiff of various important facts about the vendor and purchaser, but Chadwick J. held that it had not been pleaded or proved that there had been a deliberate suppression of that information, and there was no breach of fiduciary duty. Thus the defendants were in breach of the "double employment" rule, but not the "actual conflict" rule.[20] In the other "managed" action that tried a number of individual test cases, *Nationwide Building Society v. Balmer Radmore (a firm)*[21] the judge also had to apply *Mothew*. In *Nationwide Building Society v. Balmer Radmore*[22] itself, Blackburne J. held that the defendant solicitors did not know that the borrowers were living at a different address, that information which might suggest such a fact which was on the purchase file was unavailable, in any event they would not have to disclose it, and there was no deliberate withholding of information. There were, however, findings of breach of fiduciary duty in two of the Nationwide "managed cases". In *Nationwide Building Society v. Goodwin Harte*[23] the solicitor knew of other transactions concerning the security property, and in particular that there had been four 125-year leases granted, and he should not have returned an unqualified report on title or confirmed that the borrower would reside there personally. Knowledge of these other transactions pointed to fraud, and thus overrode the duty of confidentiality to the borrower. Blackburne J. was prepared to hold that the solicitor acted consciously, deliberately and in bad faith. In *Nationwide Building Society v. Richard Grosse & Co.*[24] the solicitor submitted a clear report on title without investigating title at all, which particularly influenced the judge in finding a breach of fiduciary duty, and there was also a direct payment of deposit moneys. In *Birmingham Midshires Building Society v. Infields*[25] the defendant solicitor admitted negligence for failing to inform the claimant that the proposed borrower lived abroad and intended to let the security property. The solicitor elected to give evidence (as in *Richard Grosse & Co.*, and unlike in *Goodwin Harte*). The judge was influenced by his explanations and demeanour, and held that he was a good and honest man who did not deliberately prefer the interests of the borrower above those of the lender and was not in breach of fiduciary duty.

Canadian cases. Relatively few cases of this nature are framed as breach of **10–025** fiduciary duty in this country, unlike Canada. If Canadian jurisprudence were

---

[19] [1997] 4 All E.R. 582. In another case in that litigation, *Read & Rogers*, the judge was unwilling to infer that the solicitor had been dishonest, rather than being guilty of honest oversight.
[20] For an example of an actual conflict, see *Barrett v. Reynolds* (1998) 20 R.P.R. (3d) 14, Nova Scotia CA, where the lawyer had agreed with the purchaser and vendor clients that he would withdraw if there was a conflict, but on learning that the bank's approval of financing was conditional on the purchasers' ability to sell their house, he did not withdraw and he was in breach of fiduciary duty in failing to inform the vendor of the facts.
[21] [1999] P.N.L.R. 606. This report provides the introductory and general findings. The court's conclusions on the facts of the individual cases are to be found in the Lloyd's Rep. P.N.
[22] [1999] Lloyd's Rep. P.N. 559. Nor was there breach of fiduciary duty in *Nationwide Building Society v. Vanderpump & Sykes* [1999] Lloyd's Rep. P.N. 422.
[23] [1999] Lloyd's Rep. P.N. 338.
[24] [1999] Lloyd's Rep. P.N. 348.
[25] [1999] Lloyd's Rep. P.N. 874, H.H. Judge Bowsher Q.C., sitting as a judge of the Technology and Construction Court.

followed in this country, it would provide some qualification to the rule in *Clark Boyce v. Mouat*[26] that a solicitor might continue to act despite a potential conflict, if both clients give informed consent to his acting. Thus it has been held in Canada that a solicitor should not act where the transaction is very complicated, and particularly where a partner of the solicitor has a personal interest in that transaction,[27] where the client is unsophisticated and clearly needs protection and independent advice,[28] or where the conflict is acute.[29] The breach of fiduciary duty in such cases will normally be a failure to disclose information to the client that the solicitor discovers in the course of the retainer. For example, in *Lapierre v. Young*[30] the solicitor acted for both sides in a mortgage transaction, and was in breach of fiduciary duty by failing to disclose to the unsophisticated lender that a recent sale was for a smaller sum than he was lending, that the mortgage was in arrears, and that the borrower would pay a higher rate of interest. It has been held that the mere failure to advise about the existence of material retainers before and after the retainer with the claimant may be a breach of fiduciary duty,[31] as will be a failure to inform the purchaser client about the vendor's secret profit when the solicitor acted in the previous sale,[32] and the failure to inform the purchaser client of the vendor's secret profit which he did not know about but should have.[33] In Canada, unlike in England, there may be a breach of fiduciary duty in failing to disclose information to his client although the solicitor has no other client and no personal interest in the transaction.[34]

10–026   **(7) Confidence.**[35] Solicitors owe a duty to their clients[36] to preserve confidences, both as a matter of an implied contractual term,[37] and as a fiduciary duty.[38] The courts will restrain solicitors from potentially breaching confidences, as was established in *Rakusen v. Ellis, Munday & Clark*.[39] The risk of breach of confidence is particularly acute when firms amalgamate, and the Law Society has

---

[26] [1994] 1 A.C. 428 at 435F–H. For the facts see para. 10–101 below.
[27] *Davey v. Woolley, Hames, Dale & Dingwall* (1982) 133 D.L.R. (3d) 647, Ontario CA.
[28] *Ferris v. Rusnak* (1984) 9 D.L.R. (4th) 183, Alberta QB.
[29] *Trade Practices Commission v. CC (New South Wales) Pty Ltd* (1994) 125 A.L.R. 94.
[30] (1981) 117 D.L.R. (3d) 643, Ontario HCt. See also *MacCullough v. Corbett* (1982) 133 D.L.R. (3d) 43, Nova Scotia CA; *Clarence Construction Ltd v. Lavallee* (1980) 111 D.L.R. (3d) 582 British Columbia Sup Ct; *Skimming v. Goldberg* (1993) 6 W.W.R. 59, Manitoba QB; *Stewart v. Layton* (1992) 111 A.L.R. 687, Foster J.; *Hongkong Bank of Canada v. Phillips* [1998] 2 W.W.R. 606, Manitoba QB; *Barrett v. Reynolds* (1998) 170 N.S.R. (2d) 201, Nova Scotia CA.
[31] *Confederation Life v. Shepherd, McKenzie* (1992) 29 R.P.R. (2d) 271, Ontario HCt.
[32] See *Jacks v. Davis* (1983) 141 D.L.R. (3d) 355, British Columbia CA. *Quaere* whether acting in the previous sale was material to the decision.
[33] *Canson Enterprises Ltd v. Boughton* [1996] 1 W.W.R. 412, British Columbia CA.
[34] See, *e.g. Cassey v. Morrison* (1993) 15 O.R. (3d) 223, Ontario CA, aff'm'g (1989) 67 O.R. (2d) 65.
[35] See also chap. 2 paras 2–147 to 2–167 and chap. 15 paras 15–41 to 15–44. See generally Toulson and Phipps, *Confidentiality*, (Sweet & Maxwell, 1996, 2nd ed. 2002), and Hollander and Salzedo, *Conflicts of Interest and Chinese Walls* (Sweet & Maxwell, 2000).
[36] There may be a duty to preserve a confidence for a person "as good as" a client, such as a director of a client company, but the relevant relationship must be proved, and it was not in *MacQuarie Bank Ltd v. Myer* [1994] 1 V.R. 350, App. Div.
[37] See *Parry-Jones v. Law Society* [1969] 1 Ch. 1 at 7A–B *per* Lord Denning.
[38] *e.g. Schering Chemicals Ltd v. Falkman Ltd* [1982] Q.B. 1 at 27–28, a case which did not concern solicitors.
[39] [1912] 1 Ch. 831.

issued guidance on conflict arising on the amalgamation of firms of solicitors.[40]

Bolkiah. The law has been considered in a number of cases in the last **10–027** decade,[41] and in particular it has been reviewed by the House of Lords in *Bolkiah v. KPMG.*[42] While the case concerned accountants, they were undertaking litigation services, and the position of a solicitor would be at least as onerous, as the information would be privileged as well as confidential. The claimant must prove (i) that the solicitor is in possession of information which is confidential (and which he has not consented to disclose) and (ii) that the information may be relevant to the new matter in which the interest of the other client may be adverse to his own. The burden of proof is not a heavy one, and there is no presumption in favour of either side. The knowledge of one partner is not to be imputed to his fellow partners. If the two criteria mentioned above are satisfied, then the court will intervene unless satisfied that there is no risk of disclosure, in relation to which the defendant has the evidential burden. The risk has to be a real one, and not merely fanciful or theoretical. The court may be satisfied by clear and convincing evidence that effective measures have been taken to ensure that no disclosure will occur, such as the imposition of "Chinese walls" as an established part of the organisational structure. In *Bolkiah* itself, the House of Lords considered that the "Chinese walls" which were erected by KPMG were inadequate, as they were ad hoc and they were erected in a single department where personnel were accustomed to work together.

An illustration. *Re a Firm of Solicitors*[43] is an illustration of an injunction **10–028** being granted against solicitors following the principles of *Bolkiah*. The applicant architects were involved in litigation brought by a claimant. That claimant retained B of firm X in that litigation. The architects had been involved in other litigation with some common features to the present one, in which they had instructed A of firm Y. A left firm Y and joined firm X. The Technology and Construction Court granted an injunction restraining firm X from continuing to act for the claimant. A had possession of relevant confidential information, some of which had already been passed to B, and there was a real risk of further inadvertent disclosure.

---

[40] See the Law Society's *Guide to the Professional Conduct of Solicitors* (8th ed., 1999), annex 15A.

[41] *In Re a Firm of Solicitors* [1992] 1 Q.B. 959 a large firm was restrained from acting against their former clients despite the fact that old documents were in store, a different team were acting for the new clients, and there were no discussions between the old and new teams. Yet a majority of the court considered that there was a risk of breach because the new team might have discussed the matter in ways that they had forgotten, but would be brought back by a chance remark, and Chinese walls might fail and would generally be insufficient. In another case, also called *Re a Firm of Solicitors* [1997] Ch. 1, Lighman J. explained that the relevant test was that there was no reasonable prospect of any conflict. In that case an injunction was refused. See also *Re Schuppan (a bankrupt)* [1996] 2 All E.R. 664, where Robert Walker J. refused an injunction.

[42] [1999] 2 A.C. 222. Note that the requirements of chapter 15 of the Law Society's *Guide to the Professional Conduct of Solicitors* (8th ed., 1999), are more onerous. For commentary see J. O'Sullivan: "Lawyers, conflicts of interest and Chinese walls" (2000) 16 P.N. 88, and Ter Kah Leng, "Protecting confidential client information" (2000) 16 P.N. 103.

[43] [1999] P.N.L.R. 950.

10–029   **No confidential information.** In some cases there is no confidential information to be imparted. In *T & A (Children)*[44] a local authority applied for care orders in respect of children, which were opposed by the father. He sought to prevent solicitors acting for the guardian *ad litem*, as the solicitor concerned had acted for him in 1986 on burglary and theft charges, and the firm had acted for him in a number of minor criminal matters in 1997. The Court of Appeal upheld the judge's finding that the solicitor was not in possession of any confidential information, and there was no risk of a perception of injustice. The solicitor had no recollection of the 1986 matter, and she had no involvement in the criminal department of the firm, where the partner who had acted for the father had no recollection of him. The Court held that the unique nature of child care proceedings and the role of the guardian did not justify a departure from the principles of *Bolkiah*.

10–030   **Adequate barriers.** In some cases there are sufficient barriers to prevent a risk of disclosure of confidential information.[45] In *Halewood International Ltd. v. Addleshaw Booth & Co.*[46] the claimant owned the trade mark "Lambrini", and had been involved in injunctive proceedings in relation to the use of the name "Lamfresco". The solicitor who acted for the claimant moved to the defendant firm, which commenced acting for Italian wine growers who sold Lambrusco wine and who contended that the claimant was guilty of passing off. Applying *Bolkiah*, Neuberger J. held that the solicitor had probably obtained confidential information in the Lamfresco litigation that might be relevant to the Lambrusco litigation, although most of the evidence was in the public domain. The Judge held that the defendant solicitors then had a heavy evidential burden to show that there was no real risk of disclosure. They had set up an information barrier, and as the size of their intellectual property department in Leeds was relatively small and only one solicitor had confidential information, such a system would be easier to police than in the *Bolkiah* case. However, the Judge thought that there was still a small risk of disclosure of confidential information as the solicitor worked in the same building as the Lambrusco litigation team. The defendant solicitors were prepared to undertake that the solicitor would work in a different building, and on that basis the Judge did not grant the injunction. Another illustration is *Re a Firm of Solicitors,*[47] where a P&I Club sought to restrain solicitors from acting for defendants in litigation for unpaid release calls, where the defence alleged (*inter alia*) that supplementary calls were likely to be more than 25 per cent of advance calls. The club was also suing its insurance brokers for recommending certain reinsurers who had turned out to be worthless, where the brokers alleged that the club's managers were negligent in failing to check out the insurers. This was referred to the club's E&O underwriters, for whom the solicitors also acted. The failure of the reinsurers was one of the reasons for the difference between estimated and actual calls. The link between the two matters was held to be tenuous, but the Court did draw the inference that some of the existing information imparted by the club to its E&O underwriter's solicitors might be relevant to the proceedings. However, there was compelling evidence

---

[44] [2000] Lloyd's Rep. P.N. 452. *cf. Davies v. Davies* [1999] 3 F.C.R. 745, CA, where a solicitor was disqualified from acting for the husband in divorce proceedings where the solicitor had been consulted by the wife six years earlier about problems in the marriage.
[45] *Quaere* whether the two cases discussed in this para. can be reconciled with *Bolkiah*.
[46] [2000] P.N.L.R. 788.
[47] [2000] 1 Lloyd's Rep. 31, Timothy Walker J.

that the solicitor's information barrier, which was in place already, would work. The two matters had always been handled in two different departments, which were physically separated, there was no mixing of work, there was limited social contact and separate documentary storage. The solicitors had established the heavy burden of showing that the risk of inadvertent disclosure of confidential information was no more than theoretical, and Timothy Walker J. did not grant any injunction.

Commonwealth cases. The position in the Commonwealth varies. In *MacDonald v. Martin*[48] the Supreme Court of Canada adopted a two-fold approach. First, could the solicitor rebut the inference that he had received confidential information, without revealing any such information?[49] Secondly, was there a risk of using that information to prejudice the client? The court left open the possibility of professional bodies adopting effective screening rules, which subsequently happened, and the presumption that confidential information would be imparted was first rebutted in *Choukalos v. Smith Lyons*[50] by undertakings and following the Law Society's guidelines for screening devices. In Australia the test is whether there is a real and sensible possibility of a breach of confidence,[51] and *Bolkiah* has recently been followed and applied.[52] In New Zealand the test used for granting injunctions to restrain breaches of confidence is similar to that found in *Bolkiah*, but there is in addition a balancing exercise that is undertaken.[53]   **10–031**

Overriding confidence. The duty of confidence may be overridden in some circumstances.[54] For example, confidential matters may have to be disclosed to the Law Society, which can insist on the inspection of books and documents to check that there is compliance with its accounting rules.[55] The duty may be   **10–032**

---

[48] [1990] 3 S.C.R. 1235, which was applied in *e.g.* the following appellate decisions: *Baumgartner v. Baumgartner* (1995) 122 D.L.R. (4th) 543, British Columbia CA; *Canada Southern Petroleum v. Amoco Canada Petroleum Co.* (1997) 144 D.L.R. (4th) 30, Alberta CA; *Canadian Pacific Railway Co. v. Aikins, MacAulay & Thorvaldson* (1998) 157 D.L.R. (4th) 473, Manitoba CA; *Davies, Ward & Beck v. Baker and McKenzie* (1998) 164 D.L.R. (4th) 423, Ontario CA; *Everingham v. Ontario* (1992) 88 D.L.R. (4th) 755, Ontario Div Ct; *G v. International Christian Mission Inc.* (1995) 125 D.L.R. (4th) 712, Nova Scotia CA; *Gainers Inc. v. Pocklington* (1995) 125 D.L.R. (4th) 50, Alberta CA; *Grabber Industrial Products Central Ltd v. Stewart & Co.* (2000) 185 D.L.R. (4th) 303, British Columbia CA (refusing to restrain a solicitor married to a partner in the plaintiff's solicitors); *Oliver, Derksen Arkin v. Fulmyk* (1995) 126 D.L.R. (4th) 123, Manitoba CA; *Rosin v. MacPhail* (1997) 142 D.L.R. (4th) 304, British Columbia CA; *Trizec Properties Ltd v. Husky Oil Operations Ltd* (1997) 148 D.L.R. (4th) 300, Alberta CA. There are a large number of further cases, for which see the Canadian Abridgement.
[49] *cf.* the approach in Australia where the complainant has to identify the confidential information, see *Carindale Country Club Estate Pty Ltd v. Astill* (1993) 115 A.L.R. 112, Drummond J. But *Unioil International Pty Ltd v. Deloitte Touche Tohmatsu* [1997] 17 W.A.R. 98, HCt, followed the *McDonald v. Martin* approach. For a helpful explanation of some aspects of the law, see C. Edmonds," Trusing lawyers with confidences" (1997–98) 17 *Australian Bar Review* 222.
[50] (1994) 97 B.C.L.R. (2d) 122.
[51] *National Mutual v. Sentry* (1989) A.L.R. 539 and *Murray v. MacQuarie Bank Ltd* (1992) 105 A.L.R. 612, both Federal Court of Australia.
[52] *Newman v. Phillips Fox* (1999) 21 W.A.R. 309, Sup Ct.
[53] *Russell McVeagh McKenzie Bartleet & Co. v. Tower Corporation* [1998] 3 N.Z.L.R. 641, NZCA.
[54] See generally the Law Society's *Guide to the Professional Conduct of Solicitors* (8th ed. 1999), chap. 16; Toulson and Phipps, *Confidentiality* (Sweet and Maxwell, 1996, 2nd ed., 2002).
[55] See *Parry-Jones v. Law Society* [1969] 1 Ch. 1, CA.

negated if the lawyer has strong evidence of suspected fraud on the part of the client, and if so he can apply to the court for directions.[56]

10-033   **Restraint in other circumstances.** Applications have been made to restrain lawyers from acting in rather different circumstances.[57] In *Re L (Minors) (Care proceedings: Solicitors)*[58] two solicitors acting in care proceedings for the claimant mother and the local authority were cohabiting. This could give rise to an apprehension of bias, and it was crucial in this regard that the solicitor acted for the local authority, which was an arm of the state, in care proceedings. The court declared that the local authority's solicitor would no longer act unless the conduct of the case was transferred to another solicitor. In *Christie v. Wilson*[59] a solicitor-advocate was not prevented from acting in a libel action for a plaintiff when he had previously advised that the offending article was not defamatory. The case was decided on the construction of the Law Society's Code for Advocacy 1993. In *Locabail (U.K.) Ltd v. Bayfield Properties Ltd*[60] the Court of Appeal gave guidance on when a judge should disqualify himself from hearing a case in circumstances where his former firm had acted for one of the parties.

(iv) *Trust duties*

10-034   **Express and implied trusts.** The subject of traditional express trusts is not considered in this work. A solicitor's liability powers and duties will be governed by the trust deed. As a professional trustee acting for remuneration, a solicitor may have a higher standard of cared than an unpaid trustee.[61] In conveyancing transactions, money received by the solicitor will normally be held under an implied trust, and will be subject to the Solicitors' Accounts Rules 1991.

10-035   **Trusts and lender claims.** Trust concepts have been used in litigation by mortgage lenders against their former solicitors in the hope that there might be more advantageous rules on causation and loss, and the cases are considered in more detail below under the heading of damages.[62] Such cases start from the uncontroversial principle that client moneys are held by solicitors on trust. The more difficult issue is to identify which breaches of instruction will result in a breach of trust. It would appear from *Target Holdings Ltd v. Redferns*[63] that although a solicitor is a trustee with no authority to part with the mortgage moneys before completion, if he negligently completes before he has obtained good title, that is a breach of retainer and not a breach of trust. In *Bristol and West Building Society v. Mothew*[64] it was argued that the lender's instructions to the

---

[56] *Finers v. Miro* [1991] 1 W.L.R. 35, CA. See also *R. v. Cox and Railton* (1884) 14 Q.B.D. 153, CA. The issue has arisen in a number of cases brought by lenders, on which see para. 10–217 below.
[57] For an illustration of another potential area of dispute where the insurer appoints solicitors to act for the insured but also denies liability, see *Nishimatsu-Costain-China Harbour Joint Venture v. Ip Kwan & Co* [2001] H.K.L.R.D. 84, HKCA.
[58] [2001] 1 W.L.R. 100, Wilson J.
[59] [1998] 1 W.L.R 1694.
[60] [2000] Q.B. 451. See also the earlier case of *Laker Airways Inc. v. FLS Aerospace Ltd and Burton* [1999] Lloyd's Rep. 45, Rix J.: a barrister can generally act as arbitrator in a case where counsel comes from his chambers.
[61] *Bartlett v. Barclays Bank Trust Co. Ltd (No. 1)* [1980] Ch. 515 at 534.
[62] See further paras 10–226 to 10–231 below and Tomlinson, pp. 32–35.
[63] [1996] A.C. 421 at 428 *per* Lord Browne-Wilkinson, with whom all their Lordships agreed.
[64] [1998] Ch. 1, applied in *Nationwide Building Society v. Balmer Radmore* [1999] P.N.L.R. 606.

solicitor made the solicitor's authority to complete the transaction conditional on complying with all his obligations to the lender, so that any breach of obligation would cause the payment of monies to be without authority and thus in breach of trust. Millett L.J. rejected this argument, and held that the instructions would have to be very clearly worded to lead to such an inconvenient result. The position is likely to be different and the solicitor's authority to release funds will be vitiated if he knows that the borrower has made fraudulent misrepresentations, but conceals this, see *Alliance & Leicester Building Society v. Edgestop*.[65] In the unusual case of *Glantz v. Polikoff & Co.*,[66] the plaintiff loaned moneys to a purchaser involved in a fraud. The money was paid to the purchaser's solicitor, who was unaware of the fraud, and who held the money on trust. While the solicitor owed no duty of care to the plaintiff, he was in breach of trust in paying the money away, given the suspicious circumstances of which he was aware.

Constructive trusts. A solicitor's liability as a constructive trustee was analysed by Millett L.J. in *Paragon Finance plc v. Thakerar & Co.*[67] He distinguished two classes of case. In the first the defendant was not expressly appointed a trustee, but he assumed the duties of a trustee in a lawful transaction. In the second, the trust obligation arose out of the unlawful transaction which was impeached by the claimant, and the constructive trust is nothing more than a formula for equitable relief. There are examples of the first class of case, where the solicitor takes it upon himself to act as a trustee where he is not one,[68] but the second class of case has received more attention.[69] The traditional classification of this class distinguishes between knowing receipt of trust property and knowing assistance in a breach of trust.[70] This must be read subject to the reformulation of the jurisdiction based on the touchstone of the defendant's dishonesty by the Privy Council in *Royal Brunei Airlines v. Tan*.[71] This avoids grades of knowledge and subjectivity.   **10–036**

Knowing receipt. Solicitors may be liable for knowing receipt of trust property only when they have sufficient knowledge of the breach of trust.[72] In *Re Blundell*,[73] solicitors were paid out of a trust estate for work they had done in administering it. It was held that an agent had no obligation to enquire how the trustee had administered the estate, and they were not liable as constructive trustees, as they had no actual knowledge of the breach.[74] While they knew that one trustee had purchased part of the trust property for himself in breach of trust, they did not have notice that the transaction was such as to preclude the trustee   **10–037**

---

[65] [1999] Lloyd's Rep. P.N. 868, Hoffman J. This 1991 case was approved but distinguished in *Target* [1996] A.C. 421 at 439.
[66] [1993] N.P.C. 145, QBD.
[67] [1999] 1 All E.R. 400 at 408–409.
[68] See *Mara v. Browne* [1896] 1 Ch. 199, and *Blyth v. Fladgate* [1891] 1 Ch. 337, where solicitors were held liable when they sold exchequer bills and reinvested the money badly on the direction of a sole trustee who had then died, but before the appointment of any new trustee.
[69] For a helpful commentary on recent cases see A. Stafford, "Solicitor's liability for knowing receipt and dishonest assistance in breach of trust" (2001) 17 P.N. 3.
[70] See generally L. Aiken "The solicitor as constructive trustee" (1993) 67 A.L.J. 4.
[71] [1995] 2 A.C. 378.
[72] Dishonesty is not required here, see *Houghton v. Fayers* [2000]1 B.C.L.C. 511 at 516h *per* Nourse L.J.
[73] (1888) 40 Ch. D. 370.
[74] *ibid.* at 383.

from resorting to the trust fund for payment of legal costs. A similar view was taken in *Carl Zeiss Stiftung v. Herbert Smith & Co.*[75] The plaintiff, East German Carl Zeiss Stiftung, alleged that its West German counterpart held all its assets on trust. The defendants acted for the West German foundation, and the plaintiffs claimed that fees and disbursements paid to them were held on constructive trust. The Court of Appeal considered that mere knowledge of a claim was insufficient and did not amount to notice of the trust, absent bad faith. The quality of knowledge required will depend on the circumstances, and personal benefit may be relevant. In *Williams v. Williams*[76] a solicitor acting on the instructions of the trustee misapplied moneys which were subject to a marriage settlement in the honest but mistaken belief there was in fact no settlement, and he was not liable, although it would have been different if he had "wilfully shut his eyes".[77]

10–038   **Knowing assistance.**[78] A solicitor may be liable as a constructive trustee in what used to be categorised as knowing assistance in a dishonest and fraudulent design. In *Barnes v. Addy*,[79] solicitors had advised against the appointment as trustee of the husband of the tenant for life, but prepared the necessary deeds and introduced him to a broker to sell stock. Despite their assistance in the design, they were not liable, as they had no knowledge of the dishonest intention to misappropriate trust funds. A more modern example is *Equiticorp v. Hawkins*,[80] where Hong Kong solicitors assisted by supplying 50 shelf companies in what were alleged to be transactions which were illegal under New Zealand company law, albeit that they did not involve any embezzlement. Far from there being any knowledge of any illegality, the solicitors inquired about the transactions from other solicitors who had instructed them and were assured about the probity of the transactions. They were entitled to rely on those assurances.

As has been stated above, the Privy Council have now made it clear that there is no requirement of a dishonest and fraudulent design, and that the touchstone of liability is dishonesty by the party assisting the trustee.[81] In *Twinsectra v. Francis John Yardley*[82] the Court of Appeal applied *Royal Brunei Airlines v. Tan* in a case against a solicitor. Moneys were paid by the claimant lender to a Mr Sims under an express purpose trust to be applied in the acquisition of property, most of which moneys were paid to the defendant solicitor without the imposition of any restriction, although the solicitor knew of the restriction. The Court of Appeal held that the solicitor dishonestly assisted in Mr Sims' breach of trust, when he acquiesced in a short-term advance of £34,000 for another venture, and also knowing receipt when he used other parts of the money for the payment of

---

[75] [1969] 2 Ch. 276.
[76] (1881) 17 Ch. D. 437. There appears to have been personal benefit, see p. 445. *cf. Lee v. Sankey* (1873) L.R. 15 Eq. 204, where solicitors employed to receive the proceeds of the testator's real estate paid over the money to one trustee without the receipt or authority of the other and outside their mandate, and were found liable. There was, however, no dishonesty.
[77] *ibid.* at 445. See also *Williams-Ashman v. Price & Williams* [1942] 1 Ch. 219.
[78] Note that it may be sufficient if there is dishonest assistance in a breach of fiduciary duty, see *Brown v. Bennett* [1999] 1 B.C.L.C. 649 CA.
[79] (1874) L.R. 9 Ch.App. 244.
[80] [1991] 3 N.Z.L.R. 700.
[81] *Royal Brunei Airlines v. Tan* [1995] 2 A.C. 378. *cf.* the position in New Zealand where in *Gathergood v. Blundell* [1992] 3 N.Z.L.R. 643 the Court of Appeal held that the crucial question in knowing receipt or knowing assistance, where the knowledge in question was the breach of a fiduciary duty by a third party was knowledge of material facts giving rise to the existence of the duty and breach.
[82] [2000] Lloyd's Rep. P.N. 239, currently on appeal to the House of Lords.

his fees and other uses which were not the anticipated acquisition of property. Such a deliberate or reckless disregard for others' rights indicated dishonesty.

Dishonesty. A number of recent cases have considered similar instances of   **10–039** alleged dishonesty, and they are not all easy to reconcile. In *Walker v. Stones*[83] the Court of Appeal held that a solicitor trustee who committed a breach of trust in the genuine belief that what he was doing was for the benefit of the beneficiaries, was nevertheless dishonest if his belief, by objective standards, was so unreasonable that no reasonable trustee could have thought that the breach was for the benefit of the beneficiaries. In *Gruppo Torras v. Al-Sabah*[84] the Court of Appeal upheld a judge's finding of dishonest assistance against a Spanish lawyer. The Court considered that judicial restatements or refinements of the principles set out in *Royal Brunei* should be seen in the context of the factual circumstances before the Court, and emphasised that the test was whether the defendant was acting as an honest person would in the circumstances, which was an objective test. If there was "blind eye" dishonesty, which was refraining from asking questions which an honest man would, the Court should make this clear.

(b) *Duties to third parties*

(i) *General*

The general law.[85] It was formerly the law that solicitors owed no duty of care   **10–040** to persons who were not their clients for negligent misstatements relied upon by them.[86] The law changed after the case of *Hedley Byrne & Co. Ltd v. Heller & Partners Ltd*, which established liability for negligent misstatement relied upon by the claimant.[87] There has been considerable uncertainty about what principles *Hedley Byrne* established, and the test to be applied for determining whether a duty of care is owed. The dominant approach recently has been the tripartite test developed in *Smith v. Bush*,[88] *Caparo v. Dickman*,[89] *Spring v. Guardian Assurance Plc*.[90] and *Marc Rich & Co. v. Bishop Rock Marine Co. Ltd*[91] of foreseeability, proximity and whether it is just and reasonable to impose a duty of care.

---

[83] [2000] 4 All E.R. 412, essentially repeating what was said in *Royal Brunei*. Other cases against solicitors dealing with the vexed issue of dishonesty include *Abbey National v. Solicitors' Indemnity Fund* [1997] P.N.L.R. 307 (where Steel J. held that a person acted dishonestly if his action was dishonest by the standards of ordinary decent people and he personally should have realised that this was the case; the case concerned the construction of the SIF rules), and *Mortgage Express v. Newman* [2000] P.N.L.R. 298 (where the Court of Appeal held that in cases of alleged dishonesty the judge should consider the mind of the solicitor, the understanding and practice of solicitors at the time, and the events which took place, and then decide whether according to the standards of right-thinking members of society the act or omission was incompetent or dishonest).
[84] [2001] Lloyd's Rep. P.N. 117.
[85] See generally chap. 2 paras 2–13 to 2–78.
[86] For instance, in *Fish v. Kelly* (1864) 17 C.B. (N.S.) 194 the plaintiff consulted his employer's attorney, the defendant, about his rights if he gave notice terminating his employment. The defendant gave incorrect advice. The plaintiff's subsequent claim for damages was dismissed on the grounds that (i) the plaintiff was not the defendant's client and (ii) the advice was given during a casual conversation. This decision has subsequently been explained on the basis of the second ground only, see *Hedley Byrne & Co. Ltd v. Heller & Partners Ltd* [1964] A.C. 456 at 510 and 539.
[87] [1964] A.C. 465.
[88] [1990] 1 A.C. 837 at 865A, *per* Lord Griffiths.
[89] [1990] 2 A.C. 605 at 617H–618B (Lord Bridge) and 633B–C (Lord Oliver).
[90] [1995] 2 A.C. 296 *per* Lords Keith, Slynn and Woolf.
[91] [1996] A.C. 211.

Side by side with this general test, the courts have adopted an incremental approach from decided cases in *Murphy v. Brentwood District Council.*[92] Following this approach, *Hedley Byrne* has been interpreted as imposing liability when there has been a voluntary assumption of responsibility, and this has been applied by all of the House of Lords in *Henderson v. Merrett Syndicates Ltd,*[93] a minority in *Spring v. Guardian Assurance Plc,*[94] a majority in the solicitor's negligence case of *White v. Jones,*[95] and and all their Lordships in *Williams v. Natural Life Ltd.*[96]

10–041   **Reliance without retainer.** In *Crossan v. Ward Bracewell & Co.*[97] the plaintiff was charged with reckless driving, and consulted the defendant solicitors. They advised him that he should defend himself, or instruct the defendants, in which he case he would have to pay £50 on account of costs. They did not mention the possibilities of legal aid or of the plaintiff's insurers paying his costs. The plaintiff did not retain the defendants, but represented himself and pleaded guilty. He failed to notify his insurers of the accident, and they repudiated liability. Kennedy J. found the defendants liable, and decided that once the defendants had elected to hold themselves out as qualified to assist the plaintiff as to how he could obtain funds to pay legal costs, they owed him a duty of care. Similarly, in *Throwley Homes v. Sharratts*[98] the defendant solicitors acted for the plaintiff in a conveyancing transaction without fee. While there was no contractual retainer, Gage J. held that the defendants owed the plaintiff a duty of care in tort. Although it has been suggested in Australia that a person employed by a firm who undertakes work for a client will generally owe the client a duty of care in tort,[99] that will not normally be the case in England.[1]

10–042   **Reliance by non-client establishing duty.** The special case of whether a duty of care is owed to parties on the other side of litigation or a transaction from the solicitor's client is discussed below. There are some cases where it has been held that a duty of care was owed to an associate of the client who relied on the solicitor. In *Blackwell v. Barroile Pty Ltd*[2] the Australian Federal Court of Appeal decided that a solicitor owed a duty of care to the client's trustee in bankruptcy as a result of the reliance by the trustee on the solicitor, which gave rise to a relationship of proximity. The solicitor had to inform the trustee properly in response to the trustee's request for information about the client's affairs. In *Re Foster*[3] it was held that the solicitors acting for a company also owed a duty of

---

[92] [1991] 1 A.C. 398.
[93] [1995] 2 A.C. 145.
[94] [1995] 2 A.C. 296 (Lords Goff and Lowry).
[95] [1995] 2 A.C. 207. This case is discussed below at para. 10–048.
[96] [1998] 1 W.L.R. 830.
[97] (1989) 5 P.N. 103. Similarly for *Mathew v. Maughold Life Assurance Co. Ltd* (1987) 3 P.N. 98, CA. It is submitted that *Crossnan* is still good law on either modern test.
[98] [1998] N.P.C. 57.
[99] *Shigeva v. Schafer* (1984) 5 N.S.W.L.R. 502, HCt.
[1] See *Williams v. Natural Life Health Foods Ltd* [1988] 1 W.L.R. 830, HL, but see *Merrett v. Babb* [2001] 3 W.L.R. 1, two cases that did not concern solicitors.
[2] (1994) 123 A.L.R. 81. To similar effect, see *Estill v. Cowling* [2000] Lloyd's Rep. P.N. 378, discussed at chap. 11, para. 11–006.
[3] (1986) 2 P.N. 193. Also reported *sub nom. Foster v. Crusts* [1986] B.C.L.C. 307.

care to the two directors and secretary who had guaranteed the company's debts, where the solicitors were alleged to have negligently failed to register a legal charge which secured the debts.[4] *Re Foster* was based on the two-part test for liability found in the speech of Lord Wilberforce in *Anns v. Merton LBC*,[5] which has now been decisively rejected by the House of Lords in *Murphy v. Brentwood District Council*.[6] On the facts of *Re Foster* it would not appear that there was a voluntary assumption of responsibility, and it must be questionable whether the case is correctly decided. However, in *Rothschild v. Berenson*[7] solicitors acting for a lender which was obtaining funds from a consortium of banks were held by the Court of Appeal to have assumed responsibility to those banks.

Reliance by non-client without duty. However, recent cases have found no   **10–043** duty of care in analogous circumstances.[8] In *A. & J. Fabrication (Batley) Ltd v. Grant Thornton*[9] a creditor of a company wished to sue the solicitors who acted for its liquidators for failing to issue proceedings against the directors of the company within the limitation period. Astill J. refused leave to add the solicitors as additional defendants to an action the creditor had brought against the liquidator because no duty of care was owed. There had been no direct dealings or correspondence between the creditor and the solicitors, and it had primarily relied on the liquidator. The mere knowledge that advice might be passed on to and relied by the creditor, who was the principal funder of the liquidator's proceedings, did not create a duty of care. In *Brownie Wills v. Shrimpton*[10] solicitors acted for a company which was obtaining an overdraft from a bank. The plaintiff was a director of the company who guaranteed the overdraft, and signed it in the defendants' offices. He sued the defendant solicitors for failing to explain the nature of the guarantee to him. The New Zealand Court of Appeal held that the solicitors owed no duty of care to the director. To found a duty of care there needed to be reliance, and the reliance had to be reasonable, which depended on the reliance being induced by the conduct of the defendants. In fact the solicitors were instructed by the bank to obtain the guarantee, but the plaintiff

---

[4] See also *R.P. Howard Ltd v. Woodman Matthews & Company* [1983] B.C.L.C. 117. The solicitor was acting for the company, and it was held to be the principal shareholder too. Staughton J. stated, *obiter*, that the solicitor owed a duty of care to the company's principal shareholder, basing his conclusion in the two-stage test found in *Anns*. For possible limits to this case see *Verderame v. Commercial Assurance Co. Ltd* [1992] B.C.L.C. 793 (an insurance broker's case, see chap. 14, para. 14–029), and *Huxford v. Stoy Hayward & Co.* (1989) 5 B.C.C. 421 (an accountant's case see chap. 15, para. 15–082). *Howard* was followed with apparent approval by the New Zealand Court of Appeal in *Christensen v. Scott* [1996] 1 N.Z.L.R. 273, who refused to strike out a claim by guarantors and shareholders of a company which retained solicitors in a particular transaction, although it was also alleged that the plantiffs had been and remained personal clients of the solicitors.
[5] [1978] A.C. 728. See *Ross v. Caunters* [1980] 1 Ch. 297 at 309D–310E.
[6] [1991] 1 A.C. 398.
[7] [1995] N.P.C. 107; E.G.C.S. 17.
[8] In *Budrewicz v. Stojanowski* (1998) 41 O.R. (3d) 78 the Ontario High Court held that there was no duty of care by a solicitor who acted for a client lending money on mortgage towards the plaintiff who supplied the money, as there was no direct contact between the parties, no reliance, and any reliance would not have been reasonable. In *Midland Mortgage Corp. v. Jawl & Bundon* (1999) 64 B.C.L.R. (3d) 1. the British Columbia Court of Appeal held that there was no duty to another lender where such a duty might conflict with the duty owed to the lender client.
[9] [1999] P.N.L.R. 811.
[10] [1999] P.N.L.R. 553.

knew nothing of that. The plaintiff assumed that the defendants, as the company's solicitors, would look after the interests of the directors, but that assumption was not reasonable.

10–044   **Liability without reliance.** A number of cases have found duties of care in circumstances where there was no reliance by the claimant. They may be justified on the tripartite test, or by extending the voluntary assumption of responsibility despite the absence of reliance, as was done in *White v. Jones*.[11] In *Whelton Sinclair (a Firm) v. Hyland*[12] the plaintiff solicitors had acted for the defendant tenant in the assignment of a lease of a shop to him. The solicitors received a letter from the landlord informing them that he had served on the tenant a notice, under section 25 of the Landlord and Tenant Act 1954, to determine the lease of the shop. The Court of Appeal decided that there had subsequently been a contract between the solicitors and the tenant. They concluded, *obiter*, that in the context of the previous instructions and the landlord's letter, and knowing that there was a strict time-limit on the matter, the solicitors owed the tenants a duty of care either to indicate that they were not going to act or to take immediate steps to ensure that the defendant's interests were safeguarded. In *Penn v. Bristol and West Building Society*[13] a husband instructed a solicitor to carry out the sale of a house that was owned by him and his wife, but the wife was ignorant of the transaction and did not instruct the defendant solicitor. The conveyance was achieved by the forgery of the husband. However, as the solicitors should have been aware that the house was owned by the husband and the wife, and failed to check that she had given instructions too, a duty of care in tort arose. The judge referred to the proximity of the relationship, but by relying on *White v. Jones*[14] he must have considered that there was a voluntary assumption of responsibility.

10–045   **Commonwealth cases on liability without reliance.** A number of Commonwealth cases have imposed a duty of care despite the absence of reliance.[15] In the first two cases the analogy with *White v. Jones* is a strong one. In *Linsley v. Kirstiuk*[16] solicitors retained by an estate to advise on its administration were

---

[11] [1995] 2 A.C. 296. Disappointed beneficiary cases are discussed in paras 10–047 *et seq*. See also the following two cases. In *Harris v. Nantes & Wilde* [1997] N.P.C. 7, the defendant solicitors acted for the wife in the conveyance of a legal estate of property jointly held with her husband into her sole name, assigning the beneficial interest to the husband. They did not inform him of the transaction. The wife was in fact defrauding her husband. The Court of Appeal declined to strike out an action by the husband against the wife's solicitors in part because it was arguable that they owed him a duty of care. In *Woodward v. Wolferstans (a Firm), The Times*, April 8, 1997; [1997] N.P.C. 51, the defendant solicitors were retained by the plaintiff's father in relation to the purchase of property where he was acting as guarantor. Despite the fact that she did not rely on them, it was held that they owed her a duty of care as they had assumed responsibility to her, although there was no breach.
[12] [1992] 2 E.G.L.R. 158.
[13] [1996] 2 F.C.R. 729.
[14] See para. 10–048.
[15] See also *Krambousanos v. Jedda* (1996) 142 A.L.R. 604. Solicitors were retained by the applicants' son to advise them in respect of a mortgage to be taken over their property to provide him with a loan. The Federal Court of Australia found that there was a sufficient degree of proximity to establish a duty of care as there was an assumption of responsibility by the solicitors, although there had been no reliance by the applicants. On the facts, there was no breach of duty.
[16] (1986) 28 D.L.R. (4th) 495, British Columbia Sup. Ct.

held to owe a duty of care to the beneficiaries. In *Hawkins v. Clayton*[17] the respondent solicitors prepared and kept the testator's will, which appointed the appellant sole executor and residual beneficiary, unknown to him. After the testator's death, the solicitors failed to locate the appellant for six years, as a result of which the estate suffered various losses. A majority of the High Court of Australia held that no term could be implied into the contract between the solicitors and testator that the solicitors would locate the executor or anyone else interested in the will when the testator died. However, a majority found that the solicitors owed a duty of care in tort to the executor, who stood in the place of the testator.[18] In *Seymour v. Seymour*[19] a solicitor was retained by his aunt to act in relation to property. He mistakenly acted on the basis that she owned the fee simple. The New South Wales Court of Appeal held that he owed a duty to the aunt's children who were the remaindermen, as they would be damaged by the negligence, they were related to him, and they had entrusted him with the conduct of various matters for them. In contrast, in *Hants County Business Development Centre Ltd v. Poole*[20] a guarantor attended the lender's solicitor's offices to sign a guarantee. The Nova Scotia Court of Appeal held that the solicitors owed the guarantor no duty even to inform him that he should seek independent legal advice, although he was a former client, as there was no reliance and no reasonable perception by the solicitors of any reliance.

Acting as an officer of the court. It has been established for over a century   **10–046** that a solicitor acting as an officer of the court may be liable to persons who are not his clients.[21] For example, in *Batten v. Wedgwood Coal & Iron Co.*[22] the plaintiff's solicitor, M, had the conduct of a sale that took place pursuant to the order of the court. M failed to invest the proceeds in accordance with the court's order, with the result that no interest was earned. The defendants in the action, who would have been entitled to the interest, recovered the amount of their loss from M.[23] Presumably also, where the sale of the disputed property takes place by agreement between the parties, rather than by order of the court, the solicitor who has conduct of that sale will be liable both to his own client and to the other party.

(ii) *Liability to beneficiaries without reliance*

History.[24] It used to be the law that no duty of care was owed by a solicitor   **10–047** to persons who were not his client, and this included cases where there had been no reliance by the third party, as exemplified in the Scottish House of Lords case

---

[17] (1988) 78 A.L.R. 69. This difficult case is explained by K. Nicholson, "The duty of care owed by a solicitor: recent developments—an Australian perspective" (1989) 5 P.N. 1, and J. Fleming, "Must a solicitor tell?" (1989) 105 L.Q.R. 15. It is not clear whether a similar conclusion would be reached in England.

[18] Similarly, in *Cancer Research Campaign v. Ernest Brown & Co.* [1998] P.N.L.R. 592. Harman J. held that the solicitors advising the executors owed a duty of care to the executor only, and not the beneficiary. For the facts, see para. 10–221 below.

[19] (1996) 40 N.S.W.L.R. 358.

[20] (1999) 172 N.S.R. (2d) 393.

[21] See *Stanford v. Roberts* (1884) 26 Ch.D. 155 at 160; *Re Dangar's Trusts* (1889) 41 Ch.D. 178.

[22] (1886) 31 Ch.D. 346.

[23] Pearson J.:'I do not agree with the contention that [the solicitor] is not liable except to his own client . . . He was acting as an officer of the Court, and in that character was liable to the Court for the due discharge of his duty."

[24] For a more detailed treatment see the 3rd. ed. of this work at paras 4–16 to 4–24.

of *Robertson v. Fleming*.[25] In *Ross v. Caunters*[26] a disappointed beneficiary sued the testator's solicitors for negligently failing to notice that one of the attesting witnesses was the plaintiff's husband, as a result of which she forfeited her benefit under the will. After a detailed review of the authorities, Sir Robert Megarry V.-C. found for the plaintiff. It was unclear for some time whether *Ross v. Caunters* was good law,[27] on the basis that it was wholly inconsistent with the House of Lords' decision in *Robertson v. Fleming*,[28] that its consequences may subvert the principle of privity of contract, and that Sir Robert Megarry V.-C. based the decision in part on the test in *Anns v. Merton LBC*,[29] which was overturned by the House of Lords in *Murphy v. Brentwood District Council*.[30]

10–048   **White v. Jones.**[31] In *White v. Jones*[32] the House of Lords upheld the result achieved in *Ross v. Caunters* by a bare majority. Following a family row, a Mr Barratt made a will that left nothing to his two children. He was soon reconciled with them, and wanted to change it. He therefore sent a letter to the defendant solicitors with instructions to draft a new will leaving £9,000 to each of the plaintiffs. The solicitors failed to have the will completed in the two months before the testator died. They made two appointments to see Mr Barratt, but did not keep them, and he died three days before a third one. Thus the relationship on the facts was less close than in *Ross v. Caunters*, as there had been no will, rather than a defective one. The principal issue, however, was whether a duty of care was owed in either case. In the leading judgment, Lord Goff considered the reasons of justice that supported the imposition of a duty of care, and in particular the fact that without such a duty the only person who has a valid claim has suffered no loss, and the only person who has suffered a loss has no valid claim.[33] He held that a remedy should be extended under the principle in *Hedley Byrne v. Heller*,[34] enlarging the solicitor's assumption of responsibility to include the beneficiaries. Lord Browne-Wilkinson considered that a remedy should be extended to them as there was a close analogy with existing categories of special relationship such as fiduciary relationships or those within the principle of *Hedley Byrne v. Heller*.[35] Lord Nolan considered that the claim satisfied the criteria laid down in *Caparo Industries Plc v. Dickman*[36] and *Murphy v. Brentwood District Council*,[37] but he also seemed to consider that there was an implicit assumption of responsibility.[38] It would appear, however, that only the reasoning

---

[25] (1861) 4 Macq. 167.

[26] [1980] 1 Ch. 297.

[27] The arguments are explored in H.L. Evans, "Is *Ross v. Caunters* good law?" (1991) 7 P.N. 137. See also J.L. Dwyer, "Solicitors' duties in tort to person other than their clients" (1994) Tort L.R. 29.

[28] (1861) 4 Macq. 167. See in particular J.M. Kaye, "The liability of solicitors in tort", 100 L.Q.R. 680.

[29] [1978] A.C. 728, see *Ross v. Caunters* [1980] 1 Ch 297 at 309D–310E.

[30] [1991] 1 A.C. 398.

[31] For commentaries on this important decision, see J.C. Brady "Solicitors' duty of care in the drafting of will" (1995) 46 N.I.L.Q. 434; J.L. Dwyer "A comedy of errors" [1996] Tort L.R. 77; H. Evans, *Lawyers' Liabilities* (2nd ed., 2002), Chap. 1; T. Weir, "A Damnosa Hereditas" (1995) 111 L.Q.R. 357.

[32] [1995] A.C. 207.

[33] See [1995] A.C. 207 at 259G–260G.

[34] [1964] A.C. 465.

[35] See [1995] A.C. 207 at 275D-F.

[36] [1990] 2 A.C. 605.

[37] [1991] 1 A.C. 398; see [1995] A.C. 207 at 292F-G.

[38] *ibid.* at 294A.

in Lord Goff's speech received the support of the majority in the House of Lords, and the Court of Appeal has subsequently relied on it as expressing the *ratio* of the case rather than the other majority speeches.[39]

The scope of the principle.[40] The extension in *White v. Jones* of the principle   **10–049** of the voluntary assumption of responsibility to include liability to disappointed beneficiaries makes its further application unclear. In relation to the specific liability to beneficiaries, Lord Goff considered that it should be worked out in future cases.[41] There is guidance now from earlier cases, from decisions since *White v. Jones*, and there are also a number of indications in *White v. Jones* itself about the likely scope of the principle. It is clear from the facts of *White v. Jones* that there does not have to be any prepared will for there to be a duty of care,[42] and thus on the facts there was a less close relationship than existed in *Ross v. Caunters*. It should be noted that the scope of the duty owed to the beneficiary will not be wider than that owed to the testator, see *Cancer Research Campaign v. Ernest Brown & Co.*[43]

Identity of the beneficiary. In *White v. Jones* Lord Goff considered that the   **10–050** ordinary case was one where the intended beneficiaries are a small class of identified people, although he did not rule out liability in more remote circumstances.[44] Lord Nolan considered that there was no difficulty imposing liability where the disappointed beneficiaries were members of the testator's family, but that more remote beneficiaries would not necessarily be deprived of a remedy.[45] In *Gibbons v. Nelsons*[46] Blackburne J. held that a duty of care was only owed to an unidentified intended beneficiary where the solicitor knew of the benefit that the testator wished to confer, and the class of persons he wished to benefit. In *Trusted v. Clifford Chance*[47] Jonathan Parker J. held that no duty of care was owed to a disappointed beneficiary until the testator had decided to confer the particular testamentary benefit which it is complained was lost on that person.

Conflict of interest. A conflict between the duty owed by the solicitor to the   **10–051** testator and that to the potential beneficiary will prevent any duty of care being

---

[39] See *Carr-Glynn v. Frearsons (A Firm)* [1999] Ch. 326 at 335D; *Worby v. Rosser* [2000] P.N.L.R. 140 at 149B; *Corbett v. Bond Pearce (A Firm)* [2001] 3 All E.R. 769 at 775; [2001] E.W.C.A. Civ. 531, para. 18.

[40] See also paras 10–044 and 10–045. See further H. Evans, *Lawyers' Liabilities* (2nd ed., 2002), chap. 1.

[41] [1995] A.C. 207 at 269G.

[42] See to similar effect *Gartside v. Sheffield, Young & Ellis* [1983] N.Z.L.R. 37, NZCA: a solicitor who is instructed to prepare a will for a client, owes a duty of care to a beneficiary under the proposed will to carry out his instructions with due diligence and within a reasonable time.

[43] [1998] P.N.L.R. 592, discussed at para. 10–221 below. The point is obvious from the formulation in *White v. Jones* itself. The *Cancer Research* case also held that the solicitor owed no duty to the beneficiaries following the testator's death.

[44] *ibid.* at 269G-H.

[45] *ibid.* at 294H–295B.

[46] [2000] P.N.L.R. 734. There was also insufficiently unequivocal evidence of the testator's intentions. For a commentary see A. Sprince, "Disappointed beneficiaries and disappearing principles" (2001) 17 P.N. 104.

[47] (2000) 1 W.T.L.R. 1219. It is submitted that the formulation of the decision was too restrictive, although the same result would have been reached on the wider basis that the testator had not yet decided what to do.

owed to the latter.[48] In *Clarke v. Bruce Lance*[49] the plaintiff was a beneficiary under the testator's will of part of the income from a service station, and on the death of the testator's wife of the capital as well. The defendants were retained by the testator to act for him to vary the lease, granting the lessor an option to purchase the service station within six months of the death of the last survivor of the testator and his wife. Plainly, the plaintiff stood to lose out from the transaction. The Court of Appeal distinguished *Ross v. Caunters* principally on the basis that none of the factors considered by Megarry V.-C. to be material were present. There were four distinguishing features: there was no reason for the solicitors to contemplate that the plaintiff was likely to be affected by the deed of variation of the lease; the transaction did not have the benefit of the plaintiff as its object; if there were liability in such a case it would extend to an indeterminate class of potential beneficiaries; and if there were a breach to the client, he could sue for it, so that there might be double recovery.[50] This issue of a conflict of duties has recurred in recent cases.[51] In *Bacon v. Howard Kennedy*[52] it was held that a duty of care was owed to the potential beneficiary, who did not in fact exert undue influence over the testator, as there was no conflict of interest. In *Knox v. Till*[53] residuary beneficiaries under a will had to fight a probate action to establish that two later wills were made when the testator lacked testamentary capacity. The New Zealand Court of Appeal struck out a case brought by them against the solicitor who acted for the testator in relation to the later wills, as there would be a conflict between any duty owed to the testator, which was to carry out his instructions, and any duty owed to the original beneficiaries.

10–052   **Double recovery.** If the estate can recover damages, then it is unlikely that a duty of care will be owed to the disappointed beneficiary, and if the disappointed beneficiary can recover then it is unlikely that the estate will be able to do so too. Three Court of Appeal decisions illustrate this principle. In the leading case of *Carr-Glynn v. Frearsons (a Firm)*[54] it was alleged that the defendant solicitors had failed to advise the testatrix about severing a joint tenancy in property that she jointly owned. Following *Clarke v. Bruce Lance*, Lloyd J. held that a solicitor owed no duty of care to an intended beneficiary under a will whose gift was rendered ineffective where the solicitor caused loss to the estate, as the solicitor would otherwise be liable to the personal representatives and the beneficiary for

---

[48] See also the New Zealand case of *Sutherland v. Public Trustees* [1980] 2 N.Z.L.R. 536. The testator had deliberately chosen not to name the plaintiffs in his will as beneficiaries. The basis of the plaintiffs' claim was that the Public Trustees (who in the preparation of wills owed the same duty as a solicitor in private practice) ought to have given certain advice which would have caused the testator to name the plaintiffs as residuary beneficiaries. Jeffries J. held that the defendant owed no duty of care to the plaintiffs.

[49] [1988] 1 W.L.R. 881.

[50] In "Solicitor's duty to intended legatees: *Clarke v. Bruce Lance & Co.*" (1988) 4 P.N. 129, David Goddard argues that the reasons given are compelling, with the exception of the third which is exaggerated.

[51] See also *Smolinski v. Mitchell* (1995) 10 B.C.L.R. (3d) 366, British Columbia Sup. Ct. Sigurdson J. held that no duty of care was owed to a potential beneficiary in somewhat unusual circumstances. The testator informed the defendant solicitor that she wished to leave everything to him and to her cousin. The defendant advised that she should obtain independent advice first, and a delay occurred during which she died. The solicitor owed no duty of care to the cousin because it would conflict with his duty to the client.

[52] [1999] P.N.L.R. 1.

[53] [2000] P.N.L.R. 67.

[54] [1999] Ch. 326.

an identical loss. The Court of Appeal reversed that decision, and held that a duty of care was owed. The disappointed beneficiary would have received no benefit from a successful claim by the estate, as she had no interest in the residuary estate, and thus she should be permitted a remedy. The Court doubted whether the estate could in fact recover any substantial damages if it brought an action although it had suffered a loss, as the damages would fall into residue. The Court also held that the duty to the beneficiary extended beyond the preparation of the will to the service of a notice of severance, without which the relevant provision in the will could not take effect, as on a proper analysis it was part of the will-making process.[55] In contrast, in *Worby v. Rosser*[56] the Court of Appeal held that no duty of care was owed to beneficiaries under an earlier will, as the loss claimed, which was the costs of a successful challenge to the subsequent will that were irrecoverable, could be claimed from the solicitors by the estate. Finally, in *Corbett v. Bond Pearce (a Firm)*[57] the defendant firm admitted negligence with regard to an invalid will. The validity of that will had been successfully challenged, and the defendants compensated the disappointed beneficiaries with the net value of the estate before deduction of the costs of the probate action. The estate then sued the defendants, but the Court of Appeal held that it had suffered no recoverable loss. The loss within the scope of the duty was that of those who would suffer as a result of the will being invalid, not the loss of the beneficiaries under an earlier valid will. Furthermore, there would effectively have been double recovery, which the Court was determined to avoid.

Application beyond wills and solicitors. It is noteworthy that in *Clarke v.*   **10–053**
Bruce Lance[58] the fact that the transaction that was under attack was the variation of a lease rather than the making of a will was not one of the features that the Court of Appeal considered distinguished the case from *Ross v. Caunters*. In *White v. Jones* in the Court of Appeal,[59] Sir Donald Nicholls V.-C. considered that the principle would apply to a case where the solicitor is instructed to carry through a transaction of gift to a third party during the client's lifetime. In *Hemmens v. Wilson Browne*[60] the settlor instructed the defendant solicitor to draft a document giving the plaintiff the right to call on the settlor to pay her a sum of money. The document gave the plaintiff no enforceable rights, but the solicitors owed no duty of care to the plaintiff, because the settlor was still alive and able to rectify the situation if he wanted to, which he did not. However, the judge considered[61] that if a settlor acts on the advice of his solicitor and executes an irrevocable deed of settlement benefiting X instead of the intended Y, the solicitor may owe a duty of care to Y. However, in *White v. Jones*, Lord Goff seemed to consider[62] that liability was confined to cases where a solicitor negligently drafted or failed to draft a will, and the testator had died, and Lord Browne-Wilkinson[63] also seemed to reject the extension of the principle to *inter vivos*

---

[55] Thus duties to the testator outside the will-making process could not be translated into duties to a disappointed beneficiary.
[56] [2000] P.N.L.R. 140.
[57] [2001] 3 All E.R. 769; [2001] E.W.C.A. Civ. 531.
[58] [1988] 1 W.L.R. 881.
[59] [1995] 2 A.C. 207 at 227A-B.
[60] [1995] Ch. 223, Ch D.
[61] *ibid.* at 333H.
[62] [1995] 2 A.C. 207 at 262–D-F and 268D.
[63] *ibid.* at 276D.

transactions. In *Esterhuizen v. Allied Dunbar Assurance plc*[64] Longmore J. held that the defendant company which provided a will-making service to the testator owed a duty of care to the disappointed plaintiff beneficiaries, although it was not a firm of solicitors.

10–054   **Other jurisdictions.** In Scotland, *Ross v. Caunters* was not followed by the Inner House of the Court of Session in *Weir v. J.M. Hodge & Son*,[65] but the Scottish courts are now bound to follow *White v. Jones*. In the Commonwealth, *Ross v. Caunters* and *White v. Jones* have generally been followed. Claims by disappointed beneficiaries have twice been considered by the New Zealand courts. In the first case, *Sutherland v. Public Trustees*, *Ross v. Caunters* was distinguished on the facts.[66] However, in *Gartside v. Sheffield, Young & Ellis*, on facts quite close to those in *Ross v. Caunters*, the Court of Appeal refused to strike out the case, and approved of the decision in *Ross v. Caunters*.[67] In Australia the position was more fluid. In *Watts v. Public Trustee*[68] the Supreme Court of Western Australia followed *Ross v. Caunters*, but in *Seale v. Perry*[69] the Supreme Court of Victoria declined to do so. In *Hill v. Van Erp*[70] a majority of the High Court of Australia held that a solicitor who had a will witnessed by a person she knew to be the husband of an intended beneficiary owed a duty of care to that beneficiary. The majority was influenced by the fact that the interests of the client and of the intended beneficiary were coincident. Although they considered that the notion of proximity was of limited use in the determination of particular disputes, they held that recovery could not be based upon any assumption of responsibility by the solicitor, which was the foundation of the decision of the House of Lords in *White v. Jones*.[71] *Ross v. Caunters* was followed in Ireland.[72] The decision in *White v. Jones* has been followed in Canada.[73]

(iii) *Duty of care to the other side*[74]

10–055   **General considerations.** Even if there would otherwise be a duty of care, additional problems arise where the claimant is the solicitor or client on the other side of a transaction or, to an even greater extent, on the other side in litigation.

---

[64] [1998] 2 F.L.R. 6. See also *Gorham v. British Telecommunications* [2000] 4 All E.R. 867 where the Court of Appeal held that an insurance company advising a customer on pension and life cover owed the customer's dependants a duty of care, applying *White v. Jones*. Other cases in which there was a successful reliance on *White v. Jones* include: *Penn v. Bristol and West Building Society* [1996] 2 F.C.R. 729, discussed at para. 10–044; *Searles v. Cann and Hallett (a Firm)* [1999] P.N.L.R. 494, discussed at para. 10–060, *Killick v. Pricewaterhousecoopers (a Firm)* [2001] P.N.L.R. 1, discussed at chap. 15 para. 15–075.

[65] [1990] S.L.T. 266. The Court decided that it was bound by *Robertson v. Fleming* (1861) 4 Macq. 167. The case was followed in *MacDougall v. MacDougall's Executors* [1994] S.L.T. 1178, OH.

[66] [1980] 2 N.Z.L.R. 536, H Ct, see para. 10–051 above.

[67] [1983] N.Z.L.R. 37. See para. 10–049 above for the facts of the case.

[68] [1980] W.A.R. 97.

[69] [1982] V.R. 193, Full Court.

[70] (1997) 71 A.L.J.R. 487, 188 C.L.R. 159.

[71] [1995] 2 A.C. 207. For further discussion of this case, see chap. 2 para. 2–048.

[72] *Wall v. Hegarty* [1980] I.R.L.M. 124, Barrington J.

[73] *Earl v. Wilhelm* (2000) 183 D.L.R. (4th) 45, Saskatchewan CA.

[74] For an attempt at a theoretical justification of the law, see H. Evans *Lawyers' Liabilities* (2nd ed., 2002), chap. 2.

Any duty of care owed to the claimant would be likely to conflict with the solicitor's duty to his own client, and implies that no duty will be owed to the other side. Much of a solicitor's work, both in contentious and non-contentious business, is adversarial in nature. It is the solicitor's duty to protect his own client's interests, where there is an actual or potential conflict with the interests of other parties.[75] There are two facts which may point in the opposite direction. First, solicitors are officers of the court and owe duties to the court, which may conflict with instructions from the client.[76] Second, they are expected to exercise professional restraint, when the advancement of their clients' interests would involve saying or doing something that is dishonest or disreputable.[77]

Non-contentious business. In the ordinary way (and consistent with the　**10–056** *caveat emptor* principle) a vendor's solicitor does not owe a duty of care to the purchaser, who can reasonably be expected to rely upon his own solicitor to investigate title and similar matters. The same result will apply for most non-contentious business. No duty will be owed even if the solicitors make mis-reprentations to the other side. The leading case is *Gran Gelato Ltd v. Richcliff Ltd*.[78] Gran Gelato purchased an underlease from Richcliff. Gran Gelato's solicitors sent enquiries before contract to the second defendants, who were Richcliff's solicitors, which included an enquiry as to whether there were any rights affecting the superior lease which might inhibit the enjoyment of the underlease. The second defendants mistakenly replied "Not to the lessor's knowledge." Richcliff was found liable for this misrepresentation, which Gran Gelato had relied upon to their loss, but not the second defendants. The Vice-Chancellor considered that:

> "in normal conveyancing transactions solicitors who are acting for a seller do not in general owe to the would-be buyer a duty of care when answering inquiries before contract or the like."[79]

The judge did not consider that it was a fair and reasonable reaction that there ought to be a remedy against the solicitor in such circumstances, and he was influenced by the fact that the buyer had a remedy against the seller. However, he was not impressed by the argument that to impose a duty of care on solicitors would expose them to conflicting duties to the client and to the other side.

---

[75] The solicitor's duty to protect his client's interests against those of a third party may exist even where the client wishes to benefit that third party: see, *e.g. Neushul v. Mellish & Harkavy* (1967) 111 S.J. 399, CA.

[76] *e.g. Grosvenor (Mayfair) Estates Ltd v. Raja, The Times* November 2, 1990, CA: where a client instruct his solicitors to take no action in respect of his appeal, the solicitors should come off the record or inform the court of that situation.

[77] See the Law Society's *Guide to the Professional Conduct of Solicitors* (8th ed., 1999), p. 346, para. 17.01.

[78] [1992] Ch. 560, Nicholls V.-C. For commentary, see P. Cane, "Negligent solicitor escapes liability" (1992) 109 L.Q.R. 539; S. Fennell, "Representations and statements by solicitors to third parties" (1992) 7 P.N. 25. In the earlier case of *Wilson v. Bloomfield* (1979) 123 S.J. 860 the Court of Appeal refused to strike out a claim by purchasers of property alleging that the vendor's solicitors owed a duty of care to them in answering the enquiries before contract.

[79] [1992] Ch. 560, 570C-D. See also the dictum of Morritt J. in *CEMP Properties (U.K.) Ltd v. Dentsply Research & Development Corporation* [1989] 2 E.G.L.R. 205, 207.

10–057   **Judicial comments on *Gran Gelato*.** The decision in *Gran Gelato* was referred to with approval by Lord Goff in *White v. Jones*.[80] However, the Court of Appeal in *McCullagh v. Lane Fox & Partners Ltd*[81] considered that the reasoning in *Gran Gelato* was inconsistent with *Punjab National Bank v. DeBoinville*[82] unless it was confined to a special rule applicable to solicitors in conveyancing transactions, and the court was not wholly confident in identifying why such cases should differ. In *First National Bank plc v. Loxleys*[83] the Court of Appeal refused to strike out a similar action against solicitors who negligently replied to standard enquires before contract, and despite the existence of a disclaimer. In *Dean v. Allin & Watts (a Firm)*[84] the Court of Appeal appeared to approve *Gran Gelato*.

10–058   **Exceptions to the general rule: reliance on solicitor's representations.** A duty may arise in some special circumstances where (a) the purchaser or his solicitor are intended to (and do) rely on information given by the vendor's solicitor and (b) such reliance is reasonable. Thus if a solicitor gives a formal report or certificate, which he intends some other person (whether or not his client) to rely upon, then he should owe a duty of care to that other person. This is illustrated by the New Zealand case of *Allied Finance and Investment Ltd v. Haddow & Co.*[85] The plaintiffs lent $25,000 to one Hill on the security of a yacht, which they understood that he was buying. In fact the yacht was bought by E. Ltd, a company owned and controlled by Hill. Before the transaction was entered into, Hill's solicitors (the defendants) sent a letter to the plaintiffs' solicitors stating: "we . . . certify that the Instrument by way of Security is fully binding on Roger Kenneth Hill . . . We certify, on behalf of our client, that there are no other charges whatsoever on the yacht . . . " This letter failed to disclose that Hill was not buying the yacht himself. The Court of Appeal, reversing the decision of Pritchard J., held that the defendant solicitors owed a duty of care to the plaintiffs in respect of the letter and that the letter was misleading and negligent. Cooke J. stated:

> "I agree with Pritchard J. that the relationship between two solicitors acting for their respective clients does not normally of itself impose a duty of care on one solicitor to the client of the other . . . But surely the result of established principles is different when on request a solicitor gives a certificate on which the other party must naturally be expected to act. That is a classic duty of care situation . . . "[86]

---

[80] [1995] 1 A.C. 207 at 256D. See also *Memery Crystal v. O'Higgins* [1997] 7 C.L. 457, QBD, where it was held that a solicitor acting for one party in a commercial transaction owed no duty to the other party; the fact that he was represented by his own lawyer meant that the court should be slow to impose a duty of care. In *Trend Publishing (H.K.) Ltd v. Vivien Chan & Co. (a Firm)* [1996] 2 H.K.L.R. 227, the High Court of Hong Kong followed *Gran Gelato* in deciding that the landlord's solicitor owed no duty of care to the tenant in drafting the tenancy agreement.

[81] [1996] 1 P.N.L.R. 205 at 226–234.

[82] [1992] 1 Lloyd's Rep. 7, CA.

[83] [1997] P.N.L.R. 21.

[84] [2001] Lloyd's Rep. P.N. 605; [2001] E.W.C.A. Civ. 758.

[85] [1983] N.Z.L.R. 22.

[86] *ibid.* at 24. Richardson J. (at 30–31) and McMullin J. (at 35–36) came to the same conclusion by applying the two-stage test formulated by Lord Wilberforce in *Anns v. Merton LBC* [1978] A.C. 729.

A similar result was reached on the different facts of *Connell v. Odlum*.[87] Under section 21 of the New Zealand Matrimonial Property Act 1978, people who had married or intended to marry could contract out of the provisions of the Act. This required a certificate signed by a solicitor, stating that he had explained the implications of the deed and given her independent legal advice. The defendant solicitor, Mr Connell, had signed such a certificate for Mrs Odlum. Six years later, Mrs Odlum succeeded in setting the deed aside on the basis that it had not been properly explained to her. The New Zealand Court of Appeal concluded that there was no conflict of interest between the duties owed by the solicitor to Mr and Mrs Odlum, and that Mr Connell owed a duty of care to Mr Odlum by signing such a certificate. The Court therefore refused to strike out Mr Odlum's action against the solicitor.

Similarly, in the Scottish case of *Midland Bank plc v. Cameron, Thom,*   **10–059**
Peterkin & Duncans[88] the defendant solicitors acted for an individual who wished to borrow money from the plaintiff bank. The solicitors wrote to the Bank setting out a statement of their client's affairs, which was inaccurate. They were held to owe no duty of care to the Bank on the pleaded facts. Lord Jauncey considered that four factors were relevant in determining whether a solicitor owed a duty of care:

> "(1) the solicitor must assume responsibility for the advice or information furnished to the third party; (2) the solicitor must let it be known to the third party expressly or impliedly that he claims, by reason of his calling, to have the requisite skill or knowledge to give the advice or furnish the information; (3) the third party must have relied upon that advice or information as matter for which the solicitor has assumed personal responsibility; and (4) the solicitor must have been aware that the third party was likely so to rely."[89]

Midland Bank plc v. Cameron, Thom, Peterkin & Duncans was relied upon by the Irish Supreme Court in *Doran v. Delaney*.[90] The solicitors responded to requisitions on title asking the standard questions about whether there were any boundary disputes or threatened litigation with the answer "vendor says no". It was held that a duty of care was owed. The solicitors knew that there had been a dispute, but they were told by their client that it had been resolved, when in fact it had not been. The solicitors were held to owe a duty of care because they knew of the dispute and that the plaintiffs would rely on the reply, and they assumed responsibility for the information given in reply being correct. The Court accepted that on many occasions there would be no assumption of responsibility because the answer would be a statement of professional opinion on which the purchaser's solicitors would form their own view, or because they would simply be transmitting information without any assumption of responsibility. It would appear that *Doran v. Delaney* is difficult to reconcile with *Gran Gelato v. Richcliffe*.

---

[87] [1993] 2 N.Z.L.R. 257.
[88] [1988] S.L.T. 611, Outer House of the Court of Session.
[89] *ibid.* at 616.
[90] [1998] 2 I.L.R.M. 1, on appeal from the High Court. For a commentary, see U. de Vries, "Clients' instructions and solicitors' responsibilities" (1998) 14 P.N. 210.

10–060   **Other exceptions to the general rule.** In *Searles v. Cann and Hallett (a Firm)*[91] a duty of care was owed applying a different test. The solicitor acted for a businessman who borrowed money from the plaintiffs on the security of their property, and he prepared a deed of assignment of insurance policies in favour of the plaintiffs, which referred to a non-existent legal charge. Applying *White v. Jones*,[92] the borrower would not suffer any loss from the solicitor's negligence, but the unrepresented plaintiffs would do so. The duty of care was only to carry out the terms of the agreement between the parties, and there was thus no conflict between the duties owed by the solicitor to the plaintiffs and to his client. While there was negligence in preparing a composite charge over the property, there was no loss as it was effectively worthless. Similarly a duty of care was held to be owed in *Dean v. Allin & Watts (a Firm)*.[93] The solicitor acting for the borrower gave an undertaking to hold the deeds of a flat which belonged to an associate of the borrower to the claimant's order. The form of security, which was ineffective, had not been agreed before the solicitor had been instructed. There was therefore a potential conflict between the duties of the solicitor to his client and to the claimant. The Court of Appeal held[94] that the court should be slow to find that the solicitor had assumed a duty of care where there was such a conflict, which would ordinarily be an improbable assumption. However a duty was owed in that case where the retainer was to take the necessary steps to provide effective security which was a necessary part of the transaction, the unsophisticated lender was known not to be instructing solicitors and would rely on the solicitors, there was no disclaimer of a duty, there was in fact an identity of interest in providing effective security, and in default only the lender would suffer loss. Contrast *BDG Roof-Bond Ltd. v. Douglas*[95] where no duty of care was held to be owed. The defendants were solicitors for a client who sold his 50 per cent shareholding in the claimant company to that company. The transaction was invalid, and after the company went into liquidation the liquidator sought to recover the £135,000 paid to the client from his solicitors. It was held that the solicitors were not retained by the company, and that they owed it no duty of care. Park J. observed that the general trend was a reluctance to find that a professional adviser owed a common law duty to someone who was not his own client. There was not a sufficiently proximate relationship between the parties, and it was not just and fair to impose a duty of care, as the company was on the opposite side of the transaction. Nor did the solicitors voluntarily assume responsibility to the company.

10–061   **Commonwealth cases.** Two Australian cases have come to the conclusion that a duty of care will generally not be owed to the other side in non-contentious business.[96] The decisions have been more mixed in Canada, some holding that

---

[91] [1999] P.N.L.R. 494, QBD.
[92] [1995] 2 A.C. 207.
[93] [2001] Lloyd's Rep. P.N. 605; [2001] E.W.C.A. Civ. 758.
[94] Applying the tripartite test, but also in the case of Lightman J. on the basis of an assumption of responsibility following *White v. Jones*.
[95] [2000] P.N.L.R. 397.
[96] *Hardware Services Pty Ltd v. Primac Association Ltd* (1988) 1 Qd.R. 393, Queensland Sup. Ct: the mere reliance of the lessee on the lessor's solicitor to register a lease did not create a duty of care, for the solicitors never wrote to the lessee or conducted themselves in a way to raise the expectation of any such duty; *Thors v. Weekes* (1990) 92 A.L.R. 131, Fed. Ct of Australia.

there is no duty of care,[97] and others holding that there is,[98] and the fact that the other party is not legally represented is a crucial although not determinative factor in whether a duty of care is owed. In Hong Kong it has been held that a solicitor acting for a bank when witnessing the signature of an illiterate old lady on an assignment owed her no duty to advise her even to seek independent legal advice.[99]

Litigation. The existence of a conflict between a duty to the other side and to the solicitor's own client is all too apparent in litigation, and the court will not generally impose a duty of care, see *Al-Kandari v. J.R.Brown & Co.*[1] This result

10–062

[97] *Re Abacus Cities Ltd* [1987] 1 W.W.R. 755, Alberta QB: solicitor acting for bank owes no duty of care to bank's debtor when advising bank; *Dorsch v. City of Weyburn* (1986) 23 D.L.R. (4th) 379, Saskatchewan CA: solicitor acting for city held to owe no duty of care to landowner in negotiations for purchase of land; *Kamahap Enterprises Ltd v. Chu's Central Market* (1990) 64 D.L.R. (4th) 167, British Columbia CA: solicitor acting for vendor held to owe no duty of care to purchaser; *Kwak v. Odishaw* [1985] 2 W.W.R. 222, British Columbia CA: solicitor acting for other side in contract did not owe duty of care to plaintiff who signed promissory note drawn up by solicitor; *McPhail's Equipment Co. v. "Roxanne III"* (1994) 93 B.C.L.R. (2d) 73, British Columbia Sup. Ct; affirmed on appeal at (1995) 2 B.C.L.R.(3d) 393): solicitor for the vendor owed no duty of care to the purchaser; *Seaway Trust Co. v. Markle* (1991) 7 C.C.L.T. (2d) 83, Ontario Court of Justice: even if a solicitor knows that the transaction in which his client participates is fraudulent, he owed no duty of disclosure to the other side; *Wynston v. MacDonald* (1980) 105 D.L.R. (3d) 527, affirmed on appeal (1981) 119 D.L.R. (3d) 256, Ontario CA: mortgagor's solicitor held to owe no duty of care to mortgagee for negligent misstatement.

[98] *347671 B.C. Ltd v. Blaikie* (2001) 2 C.C.L.T. (3d) 290. British Columbia Sup.Ct: duty owed where law firm provided information that production company had ability to give plaintiffs priority to recoup their investment from concert revenues, where plaintiffs informed law firm that they would not be hiring their own lawyers and would be relying on information from defendant; *Bowles v. Johnston* [1988] 4 W.W.R. 242, Manitoba QB: solicitor acting for vendor owed duty of care to unrepresented purchaser; *Clarence Construction Ltd v. Lavallee* (1981) 132 D.L.R. (3d) 153, British Columbia CA: solicitor for purchaser owed duty to tell unrepresented vendor of change in mortgage, where solicitor had undertaken work for vendor; *Klingspon v. Ramsay* [1985] 5 W.W.R. 411 British Columbia Sup. Ct: solicitor acting for company owed a duty of care to unrepresented plaintiff investing in company when he created misleading impression about solvency of company; *Peake v. Vernon & Thompson* (1990) 49 B.C.L.R. (2d) 245, British Columbia Sup. Ct: solicitor for mortgagee owed duty to mortgagee as it undertook to register the mortgage documents which it failed to do; *Tracy v. Atkins* (1979) 105 D.L.R. (3d) 632, British Columbia CA: purchaser's solicitor held to owe a duty of care to the unrepresented vendor, who was relying on the defendant in certain respects, and the solicitor undertook work which would normally be carried out by the vendor's solicitor. But in *Granville Savings & Mortgage Corp. v. Slevin* (1992) 93 D.L.R. (4th) 268, a majority of the Manitoba Court of Appeal held that a solicitor representing a mortgagor owes no duty of care to the plaintiff mortgagee, where such a party is either represented or has declined to be represented as was the case there. The Supreme Court of Canada ((1994) 108 D.L.R. (4th) 383) reversed the decision of the Court of Appeal on the grounds that the evidence showed that the mortgagee had retained the solicitor.

[99] *Law Wan-lan v. Well-Built Development Co. Ltd* [1988] 2 H.K.L.R. 435, HKCA.

[1] [1988] 1 Q.B. 665, discussed in the next paragraph. For an example of where a duty of care was not owed see *Abrams v. Abrams and Woodford & Ackroyd* [1997] C.L.Y. 3840, Gage J., where solicitors acting for the husband in the settlement of matrimonial proceedings had done nothing to step outside their role as solicitors for the husband, and owed no duty to the wife. *Al-Kandari* was relied upon in *Jensen v. MacGregor* (1992) 93 D.L.R. (4th) 68, British Columbia Sup. Ct, where the court struck out a claim by a husband that the advice of his wife's lawyers to her upon their separation had caused him damage.

has been reached in Scotland,[2] New Zealand,[3] and Canada.[4] Similarly, a solicitor acting for a judgment creditor will not owe a duty of care to the judgment debtor.[5]

10–063   **Exceptions to the general rule.** In *Al-Kandari v. J.R.Brown & Co.*[6] a duty of care was held to be owed to the opposite party in litigation in very unusual circumstances. The case concerned a custody battle between the plaintiff mother and her Kuwaiti husband over their children, where the solicitors acted for the husband. There was a real risk that the husband would attempt to take the children to Kuwait, although custody had been granted to the plaintiff. It was agreed by the parties that the husband's passport, on which the children were registered, would be retained by the defendants to the order of the court. To enable the children's name to be removed from the passport, it was released to the Kuwaiti embassy, which assured the solicitors' agents that it would not be given to the husband. The husband managed to obtain his passport from the embassy, and kidnapped the children. The defendant solicitors were held to owe a duty of care to the plaintiff, which they breached by not informing her that the passport had been released to the embassy. The Court of Appeal made it clear that a solicitor does not normally owe a duty to the client's opponent.[7] However, the defendants had voluntarily agreed to hold the passport to the order of the court, although it would not seem that it was material whether that agreement amounted to an undertaking or not,[8] and had therefore "stepped outside their role as solicitors for their client and accepted responsibilities towards both their client and the plaintiff."[9]

10–064   **Criminal cases.** A further exception was established in *Welsh v. Chief Constable of Merseyside.*[10] The plaintiff was on bail from a magistrate's court for two offences of theft. He was then sentenced in the Crown Court for other matters, and asked for the offences of the theft to be taken into consideration. It was alleged that the Crown Prosecution Service had failed to inform the magistrates' court that the offences had been taken into consideration, with the result that the unsuspecting plaintiff was arrested for failing to answer his bail. Tudor Evans J. refused the application to strike out the action against the Crown Prosecution

---

[2] In *Bolton v. Jameson & Mackay* [1989] S.L.T. 222, the Inner House of the Court of Session decided that a husband's solicitors owed no duty of care to the wife in divorce proceedings.

[3] In *New Zealand Social Credit Political League Inc. v. O'Brien* [1984] 1 N.Z.L.R. 84 the New Zealand Court of Appeal held that when drafting a pleading a solicitor did not owe a duty of care to the litigant on the other side.

[4] In *German v. Major* (1985) 20 D.L.R. (4th) 703 the Alberta Court of Appeal held that prosecuting counsel did not owe a duty of care to the accused. In *Garrant v. Moskal* [1985] 6 W.W.R. 31, the Saskatchewan Court of Appeal held that in divorce proceedings the husband's lawyer owed no duty of care to the wife. In *Lucky Venture Holdings v. Hogue* (1988) 56 Man.R. (2d) 172 the Manitoba Court of Appeal held that a solicitor acting for a defendant owed no duty of care to his co-defendant. A solicitor was held to owe no duty of care to the opposite party in *Dube v. Dionne* (1998) 201 N.B.R. (2d) 387, New Brunswick CA.

[5] *Horner v. W.D. Irwin & Sons Ltd* [1972] N.I.L.R. 202, Gibson J.: no duty owed with respect to action taken pursuant to a writ of *fieri facias*.

[6] [1988] 1 Q.B. 665.

[7] See *ibid.* at 672C (Lord Donaldson) and 7675F-H (Bingham L.J.).

[8] See at 576G (*per* Bingham L.J.). It would seem that Lord Donaldson M.R. held the same view, because he does not use the concept "undertaking" in his discussion of whether a duty was owed at 672 A–F.

[9] *ibid.* at 672D, *per* Lord Donaldson M.R. See also Bingham L.J. at 675H–676A.

[10] [1993] 1 All E.R. 692 (see particularly 702A–703F).

Service and held that a duty of care was owed by the prosecutor to the defendant. He considered that the position of a prosecutor in criminal cases is very different from a solicitor in civil litigation; thus, for instance, there was a duty to make available to the defence witnesses who can give material evidence but who the prosecution do not intend to call. However, in *Elguzouli-Daf v. Crown Prosecution Service*[11] the Court of Appeal considered that in general prosecutors owed no duty of care to defendants in criminal cases, because such a duty would have an inhibiting effect on the discharge of the prosecutor's central function of prosecuting crime. The Court of Appeal were careful to distinguish *Welsh*, because in that case there was assumed to be an assumption of responsibility by the CPS to the defendant.

(iv) *Solicitors' liability on undertakings*

General.[12] Courts have the power to enforce summarily undertakings given by solicitors. It is part of the general jurisdiction of the courts to control solicitors' obligations, which is not confined to any fixed classification.[13] The jurisdiction is not for the purpose of enforcing legal rights, but is to ensure honourable conduct on the part of the court's officers.[14] While it has been suggested that dishonourable conduct is required before the court will enforce an undertaking,[15] the better view is that this is not so and only misconduct is needed.[16] A failure to implement an undertaking is prima facie to be regarded as misconduct, unless a solicitor can give an explanation for it.[17] The general nature of the jurisdiction to enforce solicitors' undertakings is summarised by Balcombe L.J. in the leading modern authority of *Udall v. Capri Lighting Ltd.*[18] The summary jurisdiction to enforce solicitors' undertakings also exists in Canada,[19] Australia,[20] and New Zealand.[21] **10–065**

---

[11] [1995] Q.B. 335.
[12] See further *Halsbury's Laws* vol. 44, paras 255–257 (especially on pre-Judicature Act cases which are not generally included here); *Cordery* section F4; the Law Society's *Guide to the Professional Conduct of Solicitors* (8th ed., 1999), chap. 18; J.E. Adam, "Solicitors' undertakings—an analysis of legal and professional conduct aspects" (1990) 6 P.N. 58; H.L. Evans, "The unpredictability of undertakings" (1996) 12 P.N. 90; *ibid.*, *Lawyers' Liabilities*, (2nd ed., 2002), chap. 6.
[13] See *Hastingwood Property Ltd v. Saunders Bearman Anselm* [1991] 1 Ch. 114 at 125E–126B, *per* Edward Nugee Q.C., sitting as a deputy High Court judge.
[14] *John Fox v. Bannister King & Rigbeys* [1988] Q.B. 925 p. 928B, *per* Nicholls L.J. Thus a subsequent action on the same issues will not be an abuse of process, as the earlier application for compensation for breach of an undertaking is disciplinary in nature, see *Ulster Bank Ltd v. Fisher & Fisher* [1999] P.N.L.R. 794, Girvan J.
[15] *Re a Solicitor, ex parte Hales* [1907] 2 K.B. 539 at 545, Div. Ct.
[16] *United Mining and Finance Corpn. v. Becher* [1910] 2 K.B. 296, KBD; *Udall v. Capri Lighting Ltd* [1988] Q.B. 907 at 917E–F, *per* Balcombe L.J.
[17] *Udall v. Capri Lighting Ltd* [1988] Q.B. 907 at 917E–F, *per* Balcombe L.J. (*cf.* Kerr L.J. at 924A–B); and *John Fox v. Bannister King & Rigbeys* [1988] Q.B. 925 at 930E–G, *per* Nicholls L.J., with whom Sir John Donaldson M.R. agreed. But see *Bentley v. Gaisford, The Times*, November 4, 1996.
[18] [1988] Q.B. 907 at 916C–918D.
[19] *e.g. 115 Place Co-operative Housing Association v. Burke, Tomchenko, Duprat* (1994) 116 D.L.R. (4th) 657.
[20] *e.g. Wade v. Licardy* (1993) 33 N.S.W.L.R. 1, Bryson J.
[21] *e.g. Countrywide Banking Corporation Ltd v. Kingston* [1990] 1 N.Z.L.R. 629.

10–066   **Undertaking as solicitor.** It has been long established[22] that an undertaking must be given in the capacity of a solicitor if it is to be enforced.[23] In *Silver and Drake v. Baines*[24] a solicitor obtained advances of money for a client, and undertook to repay the principal sums with interest. The Court of Appeal held that such an undertaking was not given in his capacity of a solicitor. Lord Denning M.R. considered that undertakings in relation to money were normally given by a solicitor to pay money that he has in his hands on trust, or that he will apply money in a particular way when he receives it.[25] In *United Bank of Kuwait v. Hammoud*[26] an employed solicitor gave undertakings that moneys which were to come under his control which belonged or were owed to his clients would be transferred to the plaintiff, on the strength of which the plaintiff made a loan to the clients. The Court of Appeal held that the undertaking was given in the capacity of a solicitor, and that it bound the firm. The case is significant for three reasons. First, the tests for whether the undertaking was given in the capacity of a solicitor, whether it was made in the usual way of business of the firm so that the partners would be bound by an undertaking of another partner, and whether it was made with ostensible authority so that a firm would be bound by an undertaking of its employee, were all in effect the same.[27] Secondly, that question was to be answered, as it was in the case, with the assistance of expert evidence.[28] Thirdly and consequently, elderly decisions showing what is within the ordinary authority of a solicitor should be treated with caution.

10–067   **Examples of undertakings.** Some assistance may still be gained from decided cases of no great antiquity. Solicitors have been liable for giving undertakings in their capacity as solicitors in litigation in the following circumstances[29]: undertaking to enter an appearance in a proposed action and to give bail not exceeding the value of their client's ship and cargo in order to avoid its arrest[30]; to acknowledge service for a defendant[31]; to pay over funds given to the solicitor for a particular purpose[32]; to pay stamp duties and penalties in relation to documents used in evidence which were not stamped[33]; and as the solicitor of

---

[22] See *e.g. Re Gee* (1845) 10 Jur. 694; *Re Fairthorne* (1846) 3 Dow. & L. 548.

[23] An undertaking given in proceedings by solicitors who were a party to the proceedings will of course be enforced in the normal way, although the undertaking was not given quae solicitor, see for example *D. v. A. & Co.* [1900] 1 Ch. 484, Cozens-Hardy J.

[24] [1971] 1 Q.B. 396.

[25] *ibid.* at 402F–G. Similar observations were made by Staughton L.J. in *United Bank of Kuwait Ltd v. Hammoud* [1988] 1 W.L.R. 1051. Applying these observations, solicitors who gave an undertaking to pay sums of money, where there was no element of actual contemplated work or services in the capacity of a solicitor, did not give the undertaking as solicitors, see *Ruparel v. Awan* [2001] Lloyd's Rep. P.N. 258, ChD.

[26] [1988] 1 W.L.R. 1051.

[27] See particularly Staughton L.J. at 1063B–D. *Hammoud* was followed by the Court of Appeal in *Hirst v. Etherington* [1999] Lloyd's Rep P.N. 938. The promise to pay money to a third party in that case was not part of a solicitor's business, and the mistaken assurance by the solicitor giving such an undertaking that it was given in the normal course of business did not give him authority to bind his partners.

[28] *ibid.* at 1063F. See also Glidewell L.J. at 1059B–F.

[29] See also the facts of cases which are stated in this section, and the further cases cited in Halsbury, above.

[30] *The Crimdon* [1900] P. 171.

[31] *Re Kerly, Son and Verden* [1901] 1 Ch. 467.

[32] *Re a Solicitor, ex parte Hales* [1907] 2 K.B. 539, Div. Ct.

[33] *Re Coolgardie Goldfields Ltd* [1900] 1 Ch. 475, ChD.

successful defendants to repay costs if the plaintiff's appeal succeeds.[34] In non-contentious matters solicitors have been liable for undertakings to the other party to repay moneys handed to them on behalf of their clients if no new agreement could be reached[35]; to pay over moneys recovered in litigation[36]; and to a bank to hold leases to the order of the bank and to account for the proceeds when sold.[37] The Law Society has issued guidance on the form of undertakings for discharge of building society mortgages and for bridging finance.[38]

Construction of the undertaking. Where the existence or construction of an   **10–068** undertaking is in doubt, it will generally be construed in favour of its recipient. The critical question is how it would reasonably have been understood by the recipient in the circumstances he received it. Thus a letter reciting the solicitor's instructions " to confim to you that on completion of the sale . . . I am to remit £26,000 to you" was held to be an undertaking given a previous letter from the client to the solicitor and the recipient which instructed the solicitor to issue an undertaking to pay the moneys to the recipient.[39] An undertaking must be given by the solicitor personally and not merely on behalf of his client. This may not be obvious. In *Re C*[40] a solicitor undertook as follows: "in consideration of you, on behalf of your clients agreeing to the proceedings . . . being adjourned for one week . . . we on behalf of our clients undertake to apply [for various cross-summonses] and to pay to you on behalf of your clients whatever balance may be adjudged by the magistrate to be due to your clients." The Divisional Court held that this was a personal undertaking, otherwise it would mean nothing as the client would be liable by the order of the magistrate in any event. However, even an undertaking by a client may impose an enforceable duty on his solicitors to act when their client is relying on them to implement it.[41] An undertaking need not use the word "undertaking", as is illustrated by *John Fox v. Bannister King & Rigbeys*.[42] The plaintiff had acted as solicitors for Mr Watts, and was owed moneys by him. The defendants acted for Mr Watts in selling two properties, and in relation to some of the proceeds they informed the plaintiff: " . . . no doubt you and [Mr Watts] will sort out as to the £18,000 which is still in my account and which of course I shall retain until you have sorted everything out." The Court of Appeal held that this was an undertaking not to part with the £18,000. Furthermore an undertaking may be oral rather than in writing,[43] although it is

---

[34] *Swyny v. Harland* [1894] 1 Q.B. 707, CA; *Att.-Gen. v. Emerson* (1889) 24 Q.B.D. 56, CA.

[35] *United Mining and Finance Corpn. v. Becher* [1910] 2 K.B. 296, KBD.

[36] *Re Pass* (1887) 35 W.R. 410, CA.

[37] *Re A Solicitor* [1966] 1 W.L.R. 1604.

[38] The Law Society's *Guide to the Professional Conduct of Solicitors* (8th ed., 1999), annex 25C.

[39] See *Reddy v. Lachlan* [2000] Lloyd's Rep. P.N. 858, CA, which is authority for the propositions in the first two sentences of this paragraph.

[40] (1908) 53 S.J. 119. For another example see *Re Solicitors* (1916) 11 W.W.R. 529, British Columbia CA, where an undertaking "on behalf of our client" to execute an agreement and make payment was held to be an undertaking by the solicitor; *cf. Digby Brown & Co. v. Lyall* [1995] S.L.T. 932, OH, where such words were not so construed.

[41] As in *Refson & Co. v. Saggers* [1984] 1 W.L.R. 1025, Nourse J., although no action was taken against the solicitors in that case.

[42] [1988] Q.B. 925. Note that the undertaking there was to the solicitors. It is often a matter of construction whether the undertaking was given to the solicitor on the other side or his client. For an illustration of the latter see *Kutilin v. Auerbach* (1989) 34 B.C.L.R. (2d) 23; for the facts, see below.

[43] Nor need it be embodied in an order of the court even though it be given in the context of litigation, see *Williams v. Williams and Partridge* (1910) 54 Sol. Jo. 506, CA.

good practice for the recipient to confirm it in writing.[44] Solicitors' undertakings to lenders are generally not construed to impose absolute obligations.[45]

10–069 **Absolute nature of enforcement.** The courts are strict in their enforcement of undertakings, subject to the discretion referred to in the next paragraph. This may in part reflect the nature of the jurisdiction,[46] and also the fact that a solicitor is not obliged to give an undertaking.[47] Thus a court will enforce an undertaking even if it is made by mistake,[48] or the solicitor's authority is withdrawn or the client instructs the client not to perform it,[49] or the solicitor no longer acts for the client.[50] The solicitor will not be released from the undertaking save with the consent of its recipient.[51] It is irrelevant that the undertaking is given without the authority of the client, although if the recipient knows this then the Court's attitude to enforcing it may be affected.[52] A solicitor will not be able to rely on a defence of limitation,[53] or lack of consideration,[54] or the absence of writing with respect to a contract for land.[55] In contrast, the position with respect to illegality would appear to be exactly the same as in a common law action.[56] In

---

[44] *Udall v. Capri Lighting Ltd* [1988] Q.B. 907 at 919H–920A *per* Kerr L.J.

[45] See para. 10–09 and 10–10 above, and in particular *Barclays Bank Plc v. Weeks Legg & Dean (a Firm)* [1999] Q.B. 309. In that case, Millet L.J. observed that money, supplied pursuant to an undertaking to apply any sums received solely to acquire a good and marketable title, was held on trust to be applied only in accordance with the terms of the undertaking. In *Twinsectra v. Francis John Yardley* [2000] Lloyd's Rep. P.N. 239 at 254 col. 1. the Court of Appeal suggested that the observation should be applied more widely to money received by a solicitor from a third party to be held by him on express terms.

[46] See para. 10–065 above.

[47] See *Re Hilliard, ex parte Smith* (1845) 2 Dowl. & L. 919 and (less clearly) *Chilton v. Blair* (1914) 8 B.W.C.C. 1, CA; *cf.* the unusual case of *Sturla v. Freccia* (1880) 28 W.R. 360, where it would appear that the Court of Appeal ordered that an undertaking should be given.

[48] Thus in *Dotesio v. Biss (No. 2)* (1912) 56 Sol. Jo. 736 the Court of Appeal enforced an undertaking that a solicitor should repay moneys paid if an appeal should succeed, as it did, although by an unfortunate error the original order required that the moneys should be paid to the solicitor's client rather than to him. *Cf. Mullins v. Howell* (1879) 11 Ch. D. 673, where the court considered that it had a discretion whether to enforce an undertaking given by mistake; the undertaking was not made by a solicitor.

[49] As in *The Gertrude* [1927] W.N. 265, Hill J.: solicitors gave an undertaking to appear and put in bail in a collision action in rem. Their clients then said that they had never given any such instructions, and the solicitors immediately informed the other side. However, they were liable on their undertaking.

[50] As in *Williams v. Williams and Partridge* (1910) 54 Sol. Jo. 506, where the Court of Appeal held that the undertaking to notify the other side to custody proceedings of any change of address by their client continued although the latter shortly changed her solicitors.

[51] See *Re Coolgardie Goldfields Ltd* [1900] 1 Ch. 475. Even a virtual waiver may be sufficient, see *Miller v. James* (1823) 8 Moore C.P. 208.

[52] *John Fox v. Bannister King & Rigbeys* [1988] Q.B. 925 at 929A-B *per* Nicholls L.J.; *cf. The Gertrude* [1927] W.N. 265.

[53] *Bray v. Stuart A. West & Co.* [1989] N.L.J.R. 753; see para. 10–071 for the facts. The judge disapproved of the *obiter dictum* of Farwell J. in *Re Kerly, Son and Verden* [1901] 1 Ch. 467 (also apparently disapproved by Rigby L.J. at 477), it is submitted correctly, on the basis of *Re Grey* [1892] 2 Q.B. 440, a case concerning the summary jurisdiction over solicitors which was not concerned with undertakings. However, the court has a discretionary power to strike out the claim for delay, see *Taylor v. Ribby Hall Leisure Ltd* [1998] 1 W.L.R. 400 summarised in para. 10–071 below.

[54] This is implicit in *Goldman v. Abbott* [1989] 48 E.G. 51 at 80 col. 1. at F.; see para. 10–074 for the facts. The rule is long established, see *Re Hilliard, ex parte Smith* (1845) 2 Dowl. &. L. 919.

[55] *Udall v. Capri Lighting Ltd* [1988] Q.B. 907 at 912C–E *per* Balcombe L.J. The rule is of some antiquity, see *e.g. Evans v. Duncombe* (1831) 1 Cr. &. J. 372.

[56] Thus for instance, an illegal undertaking to give a bail bond to a sheriff was held to be void in *Lewis v. Knight* (1832) 1 Dowl. 261.

Rooks Rider v. Steel[57] the defendant solicitors gave an undertaking to the plaintiff solicitors to pay their proper fees and disbursements in connection with a loan agreement. Unknown to either solicitors, the plaintiff's client intended to use the loan agreement to obtain money fraudulently, although the loan was in fact not made. Knox J. applied the normal principle that in relation to an agreement tainted by illegality a third party is only affected if he has notice of the illegality, and the Judge held that the undertaking should be enforced.

Discretion. In tension with the absolute nature of the enforcement of under-   **10–070** takings described above, the courts do retain a discretion whether or not to enforce them. This provides a good reason for the old rule that the full facts must be before the court.[58] In *Udall v. Capri Lighting Ltd*[59] Balcombe L.J. considered that while the facts that the undertaking was for a third party to act, or that there was a defence to an action at law, would not preclude the summary enforcement of an undertaking, they would be factors which the court may take into account when exercising its discretion.[60] Similarly, Kerr L.J. stated that an undertaking that a third party will do or refrain from doing something may affect the manner in which the court exercises its power,[61] as may any difficulties with legal professional privilege.[62] However, he considered that an order for enforcement would normally be made as a matter of course.[63] The exercise of the court's discretion is illustrated by three cases, two of which are summarised in the next paragraph. In *Damodaran v. Choe Kuan Him*[64] a solicitor acting for a purchaser gave the vendor an undertaking to pay over the purchase moneys on registration of transfer. There was (ultimately successful) litigation by a claimant against the vendor claiming an interest in the land, so that a *lis pendens* was entered on the register, as the solicitor knew when giving the undertaking. The Privy Council held that neither the existence of the suit, nor the protection of the interests of the claimant, nor the possibility of the purchaser suing the vendor for breach of contract were valid grounds to exercise a discretion to order payment of the sums into court rather than to the vendor.

Effect of delay. Two cases concerned with the exercise of the discretion   **10–071** consider the issue of delay. In *Bray v. Stuart A. West & Co.*[65] the vendor's solicitors undertook to the purchasers of land to discharge all subsisting charges. On completion in 1979 they did not discharge a local land charge that related to expenditure under the Public Health Act 1936. The local authority demanded payment only in 1987. Warner J. held that there was no limitation defence to a summary motion to enforce an undertaking. However, the judge considered that lapse of time was a factor that the court should have regard to in the exercise of its discretion. In that case, the purchaser was blameless and the solicitors

---

[57] [1994] 1 W.L.R. 818.
[58] *Gilbert v. Cooper* (1848) 17 L.J. Ch. 265.
[59] [1988] Q.B. 907.
[60] *ibid.* at 917G.
[61] *ibid.* at 919D–E.
[62] *ibid.* at 924D–E.
[63] *ibid.* at 923F *per* Kerr L.J. The contrasting dicta by Megaw L.J. in *Silver and Drake v. Baines* [1971] 1 Q.B. 396 at 405B–E suggesting a general discretion whether to enforce summarily are probably only applicable in the context of difficulties of proof.
[64] [1980] A.C. 497.
[65] [1989] N.L.J.R. 753.

careless, and the judge made an order in favour of the purchaser.[66] Contrast *Taylor v. Ribby Hall Leisure Ltd*,[67] where the undertaking was given in June 1989 and the plaintiffs suspected a breach in March 1990 but did not apply to the court until May 1995. The judge struck out the claim because there was inordinate and inexcusable delay that had seriously prejudiced the solicitor, and because no damage flowed from the breach of undertaking. The Court of Appeal considered that there was a discretionary power to strike out proceedings for contempt or which involved the court's supervisory power, and while it was generally preferable to make submissions on the effect of delay at the substantive hearing rather than by applying to strike out the claim, the court did not interfere with the judge's exercise of his discretion.

10–072   **Impossibility and compensation.** If the solicitor's undertaking is no longer capable of being carried out, then the court has a discretion whether to compensate the recipient. In *Udall v. Capri Lighting Ltd*[68] the defendant's solicitors gave an undertaking during the course of litigation to the plaintiff's solicitors that the defendant's directors would provide security for its liabilities by creating second charges on their personal properties. It was established that the undertaking could not be performed. The Court of Appeal held that they would not make an order requiring performance of the undertaking, as no court will make an order in vain and disobedience would amount to contempt. However the court may exercise its discretion to order the solicitor to pay compensation, and the Court of Appeal in *Udall* remitted the case to the court below for it to investigate whether compensation should be ordered.[69] Where it is impossible to perform the undertaking, it would appear that the recipient will have to show that he has suffered loss.[70] Contrast *Citadel Management Inc. v. Thompson*[71] where the solicitor alleged that an undertaking to make certain payments became impossible because his clients were unable to put him in funds. The Court of Appeal

---

[66] *cf. The Ring* [1931] P. 58, Bateson J., where solicitors undertook to accept service of a writ. The delay in issuing the writ was irrelevant, although the delay was only nine months. In the similar case of *Re Kerly, Son and Verden* [1901] 1 Ch. 467 at 477, Stirling L.J. considered that a delay of 18 months should be taken into account, but was not sufficient to prevent enforcement.

[67] [1998] 1 W.L.R. 400.

[68] [1988] Q.B. 907. In *Bentley v. Gaisford, The Times*, November 4, 1996, a solicitor had unwittingly broken an undertaking preserving the previous solicitor's lien by photocopying documents. The Court of Appeal refused to order compensation as the conduct was not inexecusable and was insufficient to merit reproof.

[69] For a slightly different approach see *115 Place Co-op. Housing Assn. v. Burke* (1994) 116 D.L.R. (4th) 657, British Columbia CA, where the plaintiff paid the defendant solicitors moneys owing to their client on an undertaking to deposit those moneys in their own name in a trust company. The trust company mistakenly paid out the moneys to the client. The plaintiff obtained judgment against the client, which later ceased to exist. The solicitors and the trust company were ordered to recreate the fund. They were not entitled to become involved in the assessment of damages against the client, but they could contest whether there were deficiencies in the contract covered by the undertaking.

[70] *ibid.* at 918F-G. See also *John Fox v. Bannister King & Rigbeys* [1988] Q.B. 925 at 930C–D. Thus in *Kutilin v. Auerbach* (1989) 34 B.C.L.R. (2d) 23 the defendant solicitor who acted for the wife in divorce proceedings gave an undertaking to the plaintiff to pay him or his wife moneys on determination of the entitlement to them. The plaintiff became so entitled, but the defendant mistakenly paid most of the moneys to the plaintiff's former lawyer, who deducted his fee before remitting the balance to the plaintiff. The British Columbia Court of Appeal did not award compensation for the moneys his lawyer had deducted, as the payment had reduced a legitimate obligation of the plaintiff, although they awarded damages of £2,500 on account of the defendant having wrongly deducted £600 for his own bill.

[71] [1999] 1 F.L.R. 21.

held that the undertaking could be performed. As the solicitor had not informed the plaintiff of the fact that his performance was dependent on others, he could not rely on that dependence to excuse his non-compliance. The Court also held that if circumstances changed so that it was no longer possible to fulfil an undertaking, the solicitor had to notify the recipient immediately, or be bound to honour it.

Practice and procedure. Sir John Donaldson M.R. in *John Fox v. Bannister* **10–073**
King & Rigbeys reaffirmed that the summary character of the jurisdiction lay not in the burden or standard of proof, but in the procedure, which was by originating summons[72] or simple application in existing proceedings.[73] While it was not usual, the court held that in an appropriate case the court can resolve issues of fact with the assistance of oral evidence and cross-examination, and can order pleadings and discovery.[74] As a consequence of its summary nature, the court will only exercise its jurisdiction in a clear case, as the Court of Appeal made clear in *Silver and Drake v. Baines*.[75] The application should be entitled in the matter of the solicitor, rather than with the title of the action.[76] If the undertaking was made to the Court of Appeal, the application should be to that court.[77] An undertaking to a County Court can be enforced in that court by committal.[78] An application for committal will normally result in an order for enforcement rather than for committal.[79] If the undertaking does not provide a period within which the act is to be done, it may be necessary to apply to the court first for an order fixing a period to do so.[80] It is not necessary to prove service of the undertaking on the respondent before an application for committal.[81]

Methods of enforcement. There are three ways in which undertakings can be **10–074**
enforced.[82] First, the recipient may apply to the court to exercise its inherent supervisory jurisdiction, which has been considered above. Secondly, there can be an application to the Law Society for professional misconduct. The Law Society can require implementation of the undertaking, but it does not have the power to order compensation or specific performance.[83] Thirdly, the recipient may have an action at law, most obviously in contract. Of the cases which have been cited above, only *United Bank of Kuwait v. Hammoud*[84] and *Goldman v. Abbott*[85] concerned the enforcement of an undertaking by an ordinary action, and both addressed the question of consideration. It was apparent that there was little difficulty in finding consideration in *Hammoud*,[86] which is surely typical. In

---

[72] See *Re a Solicitor* (1969) 113 Sol. Jo. 549. In the Chancery Division it was by motion, see *Re F.C.* [1888] W.N. 77. Such procedures have been abolished by the Civil Procedure Rules 1999.
[73] [1988] 1 Q.B. 925 at 931H.
[74] *ibid.* at 930E–F (Nicholls L.J.) and 931H (Donaldson M.R.).
[75] [1971] 1 Q.B. 396 at 403B–C *per* Lord Denning M.R. and at 403A–E *per* Megaw L.J.
[76] According to the headnote of in *Re Kerly, Son and Verden* [1901] 1 Ch. 467.
[77] As in *Jonesco v. Evening Standard Co. Ltd* [1932] 2 K.B. 340.
[78] County Courts Act 1984 s. 142.
[79] *Re a Solicitor* [1966] 1 W.L.R. 1604.
[80] See *Cotton v. Heyl* [1930] 1 Ch. 510 (where the undertaking was not by a solicitor).
[81] *Re Launder* (1908) 98 L.T. 554 (where the undertaking was not by a solicitor).
[82] *Udall v. Capri Lighting Ltd* [1988] Q.B. 907 at 916C–E *per* Balcombe L.J.
[83] See the Law Society's *Guide to the Professional Conduct of Solicitors* (8th ed. 1999), para. 18.02.2.
[84] [1988] 1 W.L.R. 1051.
[85] [1989] 2 E.G.L.R. 78.
[86] *ibid.* at 1057G–H.

Goldman v. Abbott[87] the tenant's solicitors undertook to pay the landlord's costs in relation to a licence to assign. The licence to assign was not given, but on the construction of the correspondence the Court of Appeal held that the undertaking applied whether or not it was given. The Court found that there was consideration for the undertaking by the landlord's processing the application, but significantly it seemed to consider that no consideration was required in any event.[88] Even if consideration is needed but is absent, there may be a duty of care in tort.[89]

(v) *Other Liabilities*

10–075   **Breach of warranty of authority.** In *Penn v. Bristol & West Building Society*[90] a husband instructed a solicitor to carry out the sale of a house that was owned by him and his wife. She was ignorant of the transaction and did not instruct the defendant solicitor, although the solicitor mistakenly thought that he was acting for both husband and wife. The conveyance was in fact achieved by the forgery of the husband. As a result, the purchaser obtained no title to the property, and the building society which had loaned him money suffered loss. The Court of Appeal held that the solicitors were liable to the building society for breach of warranty of authority. In *Penn*, the solicitors did not act for the building society, which had its own lawyers. It has been suggested by Chadwick J. in *Bristol & West Building Society v. Fancy & Jackson (a Firm)*[91] that solicitors would also be liable for breach of warranty of authority if they acted for borrowers and lenders, but the Court of Appeal held in *Zwebner v. The Mortgage Corporation Ltd*[92] that the true position is that there is a duty to take any steps necessary to make up for the absence of such a warranty. Similarly, a solicitor acting for a client in litigation warrants that he has a client who bore the name of the party to the proceedings and that the client had authorised the proceedings, but not that the client was solvent or had a good cause of action.[93] A solicitor does not have actual or ostensible authority to to conclude a binding contract for the purchase of land, unless he is given special authority.[94] Any actual authority will end if the client ceases to have capacity, and as a result a solicitor may well be in breach of his warranty of authority.[95] A solicitor has ostensible authority to settle litigation.[96]

10–076   **Fraud and other liabilities.** A solicitor may be liable in fraud to nonclients as much as to clients, as for example in *Henry Ansbacher & Co Ltd v. Bins*.[97] A

---

[87] [1989] 2 E.G.L.R. 78.
[88] *ibid.* at 80 col. 1 at F. In *Barclays Bank plc v. Lougher* (1996) 1 Con.L.R. 75 His Honour Judge Hicks Q.C., sitting as an Official Referee, held that consideration was required in an action to enforce an undertaking. It was given in that case by the plaintiff bank providing facilities to the defendant solicitor's client for the purchase of land, in return for the solicitor's undertaking to deal with the purchase moneys in a particular way. This issue was not considered on appeal, see [1999] Q.B. 309.
[89] As in *Al-Kandari v. Brown* [1988] Q.B. 665; see para. 10–063 for the facts. The court did not have to address the question of whether the solicitor's holding of the husband's passport amounted to an undertaking.
[90] [1997] 1 W.L.R. 1356.
[91] [1997] 4 All E.R. 582 at 612F–613E.
[92] [1998] P.N.L.R. 769.
[93] See *Nelson v. Nelson* [1997] 1 W.L.R. 233, CA.
[94] *James v. Evans* [2000] 42 EG 183, CA.
[95] *Younge v. Toynbee* [1910] 1 K.B. 215; *James v. Evans* [2000] 42 EG 183, CA.
[96] See para. 10–186 below.
[97] [1998] P.N.L.R. 221, CA.

solicitor may be liable for other torts. In *Yellow Submarine Deli Inc. v. A.G.F. Hospitality Associates Inc.*[98] it was alleged that the defendant solicitors had interfered in their clients' contractual relations with the plaintiff. Twaddle J.A., giving the judgment of the Manitoba Court of Appeal, rejected the claim as the plaintiff had not proved that the defendants had the intent necessary to establish the tort. In *Stevenson Estate v. Siewert*[99] solicitors were held liable for conversion of a cheque, a strict liability tort, as the recipient to whom it was sent did not have capacity and it should have been sent to a trustee in any event. A solicitor may be liable to pay compensation under the financial regulations governing investment business, if knowingly concerned in contraventions under section 6 of the Financial Services Act 1987, on which see *Securities and Investment Board. v. Pantell.*[1] See now sections 380 and 382 of the Financial Services and Markets Act 2000.[2]

(c) *The standard of skill and care*

(i) *The standard of reasonableness*

Reasonable care and skill. The solicitor, in common with other professional men, is required to exercise reasonable care and skill.[3] At this level of generality, the law is unchanged since the nineteenth century.[4] However, lack of reasonable skill and care was then identified with "gross negligence" or *crassa negligentia*, and the courts tended to be more indulgent to practitioners in the degree of error which they allowed.[5] It is submitted that the nineteenth century authorities on the standard of skill and care to be expected of attorneys should now be treated with caution, save to the extent that the decisions or the statements of principle which they lay down have been approved more recently.[6]　　**10–077**

The reasonably competent solicitor. The question whether the defendant solicitor made a mistake in any given case is usually capable of a definite answer. The question whether a particular mistake was negligent is a matter upon which (in borderline cases) the mere citation of authority is unlikely to be decisive. The judge applies what he perceives to be the standard of "the reasonably competent solicitor", a creature as mythical as the man on the Clapham omnibus. In　　**10–078**

---

[98] [1998] 2 W.W.R. 701.
[99] (2000) 86 Alta. L.R. (3d) 159, Alta. CA.
[1] [1993] Ch 256, CA.
[2] There are a number of remedies apart from compensation. See further chap. 13 paras 13–136 to 13–206.
[3] s. 13, Supply of Goods and Services Act 1982. This provision simply restates the common law.
[4] See, for example, *Shilcock v. Passman* (1836) 7 Car. & P. 289: "the question for us to consider is, whether the defendant has used reasonable skill and reasonable care" *per* Alderson B.; *Beale v. South Devon Ry Co. Ltd* (1864) 3 H. & C. 337: Crompton J. defined gross negligence as "the failure to exercise reasonable care, skill and diligence." In *Parker v. Rolls* (1854) 14 C.B. 691 the judge's direction to the jury that an attorney was "bound to bring a fair and reasonable amount of care and skill to the performance of his professional duty" was approved.
[5] See, for example, *Pitt v. Yalden* (1767) 4 Burr. 2060; *Baikie v. Chandless* (1811) 3 Camp. 17; *Godefroy v. Dalton* (1830) 6 Bing. 460; *Purves v. Landell* (1845) 12 C. & F. 91; *Lewis v. Collard* (1853) 14 C.B. 208. The latest use of the test is *Faithfull v. Kesteven* (1910) 103 L.T. 56, CA. In "The reasonableness of lawyers' lapses" (1994) 10 P.N. 6, Lord Hoffmann argues that the main reason for the change has been the availability of liability insurance.
[6] Recent years have seen the appearance of increasingly strict standards of liability" (Report of the Royal Commission on Legal Services, Cmnd. 7648 (1979), para. 23.27).

Midland Bank v. Hett, Stubbs & Kemp[7] Oliver J. emphasised that a solicitor should not be judged by the standard of a "particularly meticulous and conscientious practitioner . . . The test is what the reasonably competent practitioner would do having regard to the standards normally adopted in his profession . . ."[8]

10–079   **Content of the duty.** The duty of care and skill can be expressed as a number of general obligations:

> "The obligations of a lawyer are, I think, the following: (1) To be skilful and careful; (2) To advise his client on all matters relevant to his retainer, so far as may be reasonably necessary; (3) To protect the interest of his client; (4) To carry out his instructions by all proper means; (5) To consult with his client on all questions of doubt which do not fall within the express or implied discretion left to him; (6) To keep his client informed to such an extent as may be reasonably necessary, according to the same criteria."[9]

The precise content of the duty of reasonable skill and care will depend on the circumstances of each case. In particular, the standard of care must be judged by the nature and scope of the retainer.[10] Thus many cases will turn on an examination of the retainer.[11] When the solicitor is dealing with an enquiry from a third party, rather than with a client, the content of the standard of care is likely to be very much more limited in scope.[12]

10–080   **Judgment.** A solicitor is not expected to be faultless in his judgment.[13] The following statement of principle by Tindal C.J. in *Godefroy v. Dalton*[14] was approved by Scrutton L.J. in *Fletcher & Son v. Jubb, Booth & Helliwell*[15]:

> "It would be extremely difficult to define the exact limit by which the skill and diligence which an attorney undertakes to furnish in the conduct of a cause is bounded; or to trace precisely the dividing line between that reasonable skill and diligence which appears to satisfy his undertaking, and that *crassa negligentia* or *lata culpa* mentioned in some of the cases, for which he is undoubtedly responsible. The cases, however, which have been cited and commented on at the bar, appear to establish, in general, that he is liable for the consequences of ignorance or non-observance of the rules of practice of this Court; for the want of care in the preparation of the cause for trial; or of the

---

[7] [1979] Ch. 384. For the facts, see para. 10–107.

[8] *ibid.* at 402–403. This dictum was approved by the Court of Appeal in *Martin Boston & Co. v. Roberts* [1996] 1 P.N.L.R. 45 at 50.

[9] *Tiffin Hldg Ltd v. Millican* 49 D.L.R. (2d) 216 *per* Riley J., approved by the Supreme Court of Canada (1967) 60 D.L.R. (2d) 469.

[10] See paras 10–004 to 10–010.

[11] *e.g. Spence v. Bell* [1982] 6 W.W.R. 385, Alberta CA: defendant solicitor's retainer was limited to preparing a lease according to specific instructions, and did not extend to preparing a lease which financial institutions would accept for the purposes of financing.

[12] Thus in *Ouwens v. Ace Builders Pty Ltd* (1989) 52 S.A.S.R. 344, Sup. Ct of South Australia *in banco*, a solicitor told the respondent company that W, to whom the company was selling a house, would benefit from her father's estate. The solicitor owed no duty to the company to warn it of the limited enquiries made and of the possibility that W might divert her inheritance to her children. The warning would have been necessary if the solicitor was the company's adviser.

[13] For example, in *R.&T. Thew Ltd v. Reeves (No. 2)* (Note) [1982] Q.B. 1283, an error made by an articled clerk in the wording of an application for legal aid was held by Lord Denning M.R. not to amount to negligence: see 1287D.

[14] (1830) 6 Bing. 460.

[15] [1920] 1 K.B. 275 at 280; see also Bankes L.J. at 279.

attendance thereon with his witnesses, and for the mismanagement of so much of the conduct of a cause as is usually and ordinarily allotted to his department of the profession. Whilst on the other hand, he is not answerable for error in judgment upon points of new occurrence, or of nice or doubtful construction, or of such as are usually entrusted to men in the higher branch of the profession of the law."[16]

Knowledge of the law.[17] The solicitor is not, and never has been, expected to possess encyclopedic knowledge: **10–081**

"No attorney is bound to know all the law; God forbid that it should be imagined that an attorney, or a counsel, or even a Judge is bound to know all the law; or that an attorney is to lose his fair recompense on account of an error, being such an error as a cautious man might fall into."[18]

Although a solicitor is not "bound to know all the law", he ought generally to know where and how to find out the law in so far as it affects matters within his field of practice. However, before the solicitor is held liable for failing to look a point up, circumstances must be shown which would have alerted the reasonably prudent solicitor to the point which ought to be researched. The last two sentences were cited with approval by the Supreme Court of Canada in *Central Trust Co. v. Rafuse*,[19] where it was stated that a solicitor "must have sufficient knowledge of the fundamental issues or principles of law applicable to the particular work he has undertaken to enable him to perceive the need to ascertain the law on the relevant points".[20]

Examples. In most cases, the solicitor's ignorance has been found to be negligent. In *Central Trust Co. v. Rafuse*[21] the defendant solicitors knew that a mortgage was being given to obtain a loan to assist in the purchase of the company's own shares. A solicitor should have known that the capacity of a company to borrow and give security may be limited by the Companies Acts, and he should have examined the relevant legislation to ascertain those limits.[22] In **10–082**

---

[16] (1830) 6 Bing. 460 at 467–468.
[17] See further paras 10–151 and 10–152.
[18] *Montriou v. Jefferys* (1825) 2C. & P. 113 at 116. See also *Fletcher & Son v. Jubb, Booth & Helliwell* [1920] 1 K.B. 275: "Now it is not the duty of a solicitor to know the contents of every statute of the realm. But there are some statutes which it is his duty to know; and in these days when the defendants in so many actions are public authorities the Public Authorities Protection Act, 1893, is one of those statutes." (*per* Scrutton L.J. at 281.)
[19] (1987) 31 D.L.R. (4th) 481.
[20] *ibid.* at 524.
[21] (1987) 31 D.L.R. (4th) 481, Sup. Ct Canada.
[22] See also: *Elcano Acceptance Ltd v. Richmond, Richmond, Stambler & Mills* (1989) 68 O.R. (2d) 165, Ontario HCt: solicitor failed to include an interest provision in promissory notes sufficient to satisfy the Interest Act; held negligent as any reasonably competent solicitor practising in commercial law in Canada should be aware of the relevant provisions. However, the Ontario Court of Appeal ((1991) 79 D.L.R. (4th) 154) found that the solicitor had been negligent because he had failed to follow his normal practice of inserting an interest provision, which was an isolated error. In *MacCulloch v. McInnes, Cooper & Robertson* (2001) 178 N.S.R. (2d) 324, Nova Scotia CA, the lawyer was found to be negligent in failing to advise the client executor that before she could purchase estate assets she had to disclose a previous agreement to sell the assets on to a third party for more than three times the price. The law was clear that this was a breach of fiduciary duty, and the solicitor was aware of the potential problem but failed to research the issue. *Park Hall School v. Overend* [1987] 2 I.R. 1, Irish HCt: a solicitor was expected to know that a "subject to contract" document might be a sufficient memorandum of writing to make enforceable an agreement for the sale of land.

Dean v. Allin & Watts (a Firm)[23] the Court of Appeal found solicitors liable for failing to know that there was a significant question mark whether section 2 of the Law of Property (Miscellaneous Provisions) Act 1989, whereby a disposition of an interest in land can only be made in writing, incorporating all the agreed terms in one document, applied to an equitable charge by way of deposit of title deeds.[24] An opposite result was reached in the New Zealand case of *Bannerman Brydone Folster & Co. v. Murray*.[25] Solicitors failed to appreciate that an option was a clog on the equity of redemption. The Court of Appeal in Wellington held that this failure was not negligent. Although the topic was dealt with in the textbooks on real property, the facts were not such as would have alerted "the average solicitor in New Zealand" to the need to refer to a text book on the point. Similarly, in the wasted costs case of *Ridehalgh v. Horsefield*[26] the first of the six appeals concerned solicitors who misunderstood some landlord and tenant law. The Court of Appeal found they were not negligent, as the legislation was complex, the textbooks they consulted did not give a clear answer, they could not afford to consult specialist counsel, the county court judge saw nothing wrong with their analysis, and their argument was not discarded by counsel on appeal.

10–083   **Hindsight.** In determining whether the solicitor has exercised reasonable skill and care, he should be judged in the light of the circumstances at the time.[27] His actions or advice may, with the benefit of hindsight, be shown to have been utterly wrong, "but hindsight is no touchstone of negligence."[28]

(ii) *General practice as evidence of reasonable skill and care*[29]

10–084   **The general rule.** Where the solicitor makes a mistake as a result of acting in accordance with the general practice of the profession, this will not normally be regarded as negligence. In *Simmons v. Pennington*,[30] for example, solicitors acting for a vendor answered a requisition as to breaches of restrictive covenant in standard form, but "by ill luck" (*per* Denning L.J.) the court subsequently held that the answer entitled the purchaser to rescind. The defendants were acquitted of negligence. Conversely, where a solicitor falls into error as a result of departing from the general practice, this will generally be negligent.[31]

---

[23] [2001] Lloyd's Rep. P.N. 605; [2001] E.W.C.A. Civ. 758. The textbooks were equivocal on the issue, and the issue was not decided until *United Bank of Kuwait v. Sahib* [1997] Ch. 107 which occurred after the first three of the loan transactions. For the facts, see para. 10–005 above. A similar finding of negligence where the lawyers did not know about s. 2 was made in *Green v. Collyer-Bristow* [1999] Lloyd's Rep. P.N. 798, in the context of matrimonial litigation, where two of the three main texts did not refer to the change. See further chap. 11 para. 11–037.

[24] For another illustration, see *Bond v. Livingstone* [2001] P.N.L.R. 30, QBD, where solicitors considered that the limitation period for personal injuries under a contract was six years rather than three. They were negligent as they overlooked s. 11 of the Limitation Act 1980, "a mistake of the most basic kind".

[25] [1972] N.Z.L.R. 411.

[26] [1994] Ch. 205 at 240–245.

[27] *Bell v. Strathairn & Blair* (1954) 104 L.J. 618.

[28] *per* Megarry J. in *Duchess of Argyll v. Beuselinck* [1972] 2 Lloyd's Rep. 172 at 185 col. 1.

[29] See further H. Evans, *'Lawyers' Liabilities'* (2nd ed., 2002), chap. 4.

[30] [1955] 1 W.L.R. 183.

[31] *e.g.* in *Stevenson v. Rowand* (1830) 2 Dow. & Co. 104 the defendant, who was instructed to prepare a heritable bond, failed to give the necessary notice. Whether this rendered the bond invalid was a difficult question, which gave rise to a difference of judicial opinion but was ultimately decided against the client. The House of Lords held that the defendant had been negligent because he had "thought proper to depart from the ordinary mode of preparing heritable securities" (see at. 119).

An exception. The relevance of the general practice of the profession to a **10–085**
charge of negligence was considered in detail in the Hong Kong case of *Edward*
Wong Finance Co. Ltd v. Johnson Stokes & Master.[32] The plaintiffs agreed to
lend $1,355,000 to the purchasers of part of a factory, to be secured by a
mortgage. The fifth defendants (the plaintiff's solicitors) handed over the money
to Y, the vendor's solicitor, in return for an undertaking that Y would arrange for
repayment of the existing mortgage on the property and that he would within 10
days forward an assignment of the property from the vendors to the purchasers.
Y then left Hong Kong with the money. The existing mortgage on the property
was not discharged and the plaintiff's intended charge over the property was
worthless. It was established in evidence that, in the vast majority of conveyancing transactions in Hong Kong, the solicitor for the purchaser or mortgagee
handed over the purchase price in return for an undertaking from the vendor's
solicitor to forward the necessary documents of title within a stated time. This
"Hong Kong style" completion enabled conveyancing transactions to be carried
out far more quickly than elsewhere (where the money and the documents of title
were handed over simultaneously). This was the first occasion on which such a
transaction had fallen through because the vendor's solicitor had defaulted on his
undertaking. The trial judge held that the solicitors were negligent in participating in a Hong Kong style completion, in view of the special circumstances of that
case: Y was a recently established one-man firm and large sums of money were
involved. The Hong Kong Court of Appeal by a majority reversed this decision.
The Privy Council allowed an appeal by the plaintiffs and held that the solicitors
were negligent.

The Privy Council's reasoning was as follows: They did not condemn the **10–086**
practice of Hong Kong style completions. These were well suited to conditions
in Hong Kong.[33] But it was foreseeable that the practice might result in loss,
namely the embezzlement of the purchase moneys by the recipient. The foreseeability of this risk was proved by the fact that it was foreseen by a sub-committee
of the Law Society of Hong Kong which had reported on conveyancing matters
in 1965. Precautions could be taken to guard against the risk of embezzlement,
without undermining the basic features of the Hong Kong style completion.[34]
"The risk inherent in the Hong Kong style of completion as operated in the
instant case being foreseeable, and readily avoidable, there can only be an
affirmative answer to the third question, whether the respondents were negligent
in not foreseeing and avoiding that risk."[35] The Privy Council only differed from
the trial judge in that the solicitors' liability did not depend upon the special
circumstances, which the judge had described as "warning bells".[36]

It appears that the "precautions" which the solicitors failed to take in this case **10–087**
were not normally taken by solicitors who participated in a Hong Kong style
completion. Thus the defendant solicitors were held liable, despite the fact that
they had complied in all material respects with the general practice of the
profession in Hong Kong. Such a conclusion is not easily reconciled with the fact
that the Privy Council did not condemn the general practice. This is an unusual
case, in that the general practice of the profession (a) involved obvious risks and

---

[32] [1984] A.C. 296. For an illuminating discussion of the policy reasons behind this decision see Lord
Justice Hoffmann, "The reasonableness of lawyers' lapses" (1994) 10 P.N. 6.
[33] *ibid.* at 306E.
[34] *ibid.* at 307H–308B.
[35] *ibid.* at 308G. See also the policy reasons mentioned at 307F–G.
[36] *ibid.* at 308G–H.

(b) did not take account of a report by the local Law Society that had drawn attention to such risks. It is submitted that it is only in relatively rare and extreme cases such as this that a solicitor, who complies with the general practice of the profession, will be held to have been negligent.

10–088   **Judicial treatment of *Wong.*** *Wong* was referred to with apparent approval by Lord Browne-Wilkinson in the medical negligence case of *Bolitho v. City & Hackney Health Authority.*[37] It was relied on by the claimant in *Arbiter Group plc v. Gill Jennings and Every (a Firm),*[38] where the defendant patent agents had delegated the task of searching for a U.S. patent to U.S. patent searchers. The Court of Appeal distinguished *Wong* on the basis that it did not involve the delegation of a task to a third party. The Court recognised that delegation had in-built risks, but considered that it was often appropriate to delegate a task. In *Patel v. Daybells (a Firm)*[39] a case on very similar facts to *Wong,* Gray J. recognised the force of criticisms of it but felt constrained to accept the principle it laid down. However, he distinguished *Wong* on the basis of the short time-frame in which completion took place, and the defendant solicitors were not found to be negligent.

10–089   **Unsafe common practice.** The courts are likely to be more ready to condemn an unsafe common practice. In *Roche v. Peilow*[40] a house purchase was to be effected by a building contract. The building company had charged the property to their bank, but the defendant solicitors had not made a search in the Companies' Offices. The company went into liquidation after a number of stage payments had been made. The Irish Supreme Court held that the solicitors were negligent. Although they had followed a general practice of failing to make any search before the granting of a lease, the inherent risks were well known to the solicitors. The court followed a dictum in *Donovan v. Cork County Council*[41]:

> "If there is a common practice which has inherent defects, which ought to be obvious to any person giving the matter due consideration, the fact that it is shown to have been widely and generally adopted over a period of time does not make the practice any less negligent. Neglect of duty does not cease by repetition to be neglect of duty."[42]

10–090   **Differing practices.** The situation which more commonly arises is that there are several different "practices of the profession" each of which is followed by a substantial number of respected and conscientious solicitors.[43] Applying the "*Bolam* principle",[44] a solicitor who complies with any one of the accepted practices ought to escape a finding of negligence. However, the court may be rather less reluctant to come to a different conclusion in this situation than in a case where the solicitor has complied with a practice of the profession which is

---

[37] [1998] A.C. 232 at 242–243.
[38] [2000] P.N.L.R. 680. For the facts, see para. 10–148 below.
[39] [2001] P.N.L.R. 43.
[40] [1986] I.L.R.M. 189, Irish Sup. Ct, on appeal from the High Ct.
[41] [1967] I.R. 173 at 193. That case concerned medical negligence.
[42] Similarly in the civil law case of *Roberge v. Bolduc* [1991] 1 S.C.R. 374 the Supreme Court of Canada held that a common professional practice must be reasonable, and the defendant notary was found negligent as the practice he followed was not.
[43] See, *e.g.* P.H. Kenny, "The conveyancing retainer—1" (1982) 126 S.J. 387.
[44] *Bolam v. Friern Hospital Management Committee* [1957] 1 W.L.R. 582 at 587. See chap. 12 para. 12–093.

universally adopted. This is illustrated by *G&K Ladenbau v. Crawley & De Reya*,[45] where the issue was whether the defendants were negligent in failing to make a search of the commons register whilst acting for the plaintiffs on the purchase of a plot of vacant land. Two conveyancing solicitors gave evidence on each side as to their practice in making commons searches. Both the solicitors called on behalf of the defendants stated that, in the particular circumstances of this case, it would not have been their practice to make a commons search. Mocatta J. acknowledged the conveyancing experience of both these witnesses (whom he described as "distinguished and plainly very able solicitors"), but nevertheless proceeded to hold that the defendants had been negligent. The Judge decided that it could not be said that "two equally well-established schools of practice had emerged" which it is submitted is not the correct test. In any event, it is not clear that the issue strictly arose in the case. All the experts agreed that they would have considered the possible danger, whereas it had not occurred to the defendant. There was a conflict between the experts as to whether they would have considered that anything needed to be done, whereas the defendant stated that if he had been alerted to the danger he would have made the requisite searches.[46]

The tendency to uniformity. In June 1985, in response to a recommendation **10–091** made by the Royal Commission on Legal Services,[47] the Law Society's Working Party on Professional Standards issued three written standards. Some of the material has been replaced by a new Practice Rule 15 dealing with client care and a Client Care Code, and they are now incorporated with modifications into the Law Society's *Guide to the Professional Conduct of Solicitors*.[48] The Law Society has issued a number of publications to assist solicitors in practice, the most important of which is probably the Law Society's *Conveyancing Handbook*, which is reissued annually. These various guides are likely to carry great weight with the courts (a) as evidence of the general practice of the profession and (b), in certain situations, as an indication of what specific steps a reasonably careful and competent solicitor would take. Although these various sources are generally intended to reflect the existing practices of the profession, they are also likely to lead to a greater uniformity of practice. Thus with the passage of time it may become increasingly difficult for a solicitor to justify conduct which falls short of that described in the guides. In conveyancing, the "National Protocol" is likely to have the same effect.[49]

An illustration: taking instructions.[50] In *Johnson v. Bingley Dyson &* **10–092** *Furey*[51] the Court held that the principles laid down in the Law Society's *Guide to the Professional Conduct of Solicitors* were not the law, and a court must consider whether failure to observe the *Guide* was negligent in the particular

---

[45] [1978] 1 W.L.R. 266. See also para. 10–242 for the facts.
[46] In *Ron Miller Realty Ltd v. Honeywell, Wotherspoon and Beedell* (1992) 4 O.R. (3d) 492, Ontario HCt, affirmed (1993) 16 O.R. (3d) 255, summary judgment was granted despite the fact that the defendants had filed an affidavit from an expert suggesting that the mistake made by the defendants would have been made by most lawyers.
[47] Cmnd. 7648 (1979), vol. I, para. 22.57.
[48] 8th ed., 1999.
[49] See further para. 10–204.
[50] Note that the requirements of the Solicitors' Practice Rules 1990 are made under statute, and thus have the force of statute, see *Hughes v. Kingston upon Hull City Council* [1999] 2 All E.R. 49.
[51] *The Times*, February 28, 1995, [1995] N.P.C. 27, QBD

case. However, the court condemned a common practice established by expert testimony that, in cut-price conveyancing, the lawyer does not see his client, because it preferred the more authoritative principle in the *Guide* that solicitors should see their clients. Similarly, in *Penn v. Bristol & West Building Society*[52] the defendant solicitors were in breach of their duty to the plaintiff in the sale of the house she owned with her husband, as they failed to obtain instructions from her. The judge relied on the duty set out in the *Guide*[53] that when instructions were received from a third party, in that case her husband, the solicitor should obtain written instructions.

(iii) *The specialist solicitor and the inexperienced solicitor*

10–093   **An early statement of the law.** The position of the specialist solicitor was discussed, *obiter*, by Megarry J. in *Duchess of Argyll v. Beuselinck*[54]:

> "No doubt the inexperienced solicitor is liable if he fails to attain the standard of a reasonably competent solicitor. But if the client employs a solicitor of high standing and great experience, will an action for negligence fail if it appears that the solicitor did not exercise the care and skill to be expected of him, though he did not fall below the standard of a reasonably competent solicitor? If the client engages an expert, and doubtless expects to pay commensurate fees, is he not entitled to expect something more than the standard of the reasonably competent? I am speaking not merely of those expert in a particular branch of the law, as contrasted with a general practitioner, but also of those of long experience and great skill as contrasted with those practising in the same field of the law but being of a more ordinary calibre and having less experience. The essence of the contract of retainer, it may be said, is that the client is retaining the particular solicitor or firm in question, and he is therefore entitled to expect from that solicitor or firm a standard of care and skill commensurate with the skill and experience which that solicitor or firm has. The uniform standard of care postulated for the world at large in tort hardly seems appropriate when the duty is not one imposed by the law of tort but arises from a contractual obligation existing between the client and the particular solicitor or firm in question."[55]

Insofar as it deals with the position of a solicitor specialising in a particular area of law, the passage quoted above has Canadian support.[56] It would be absurd if a large city firm with a substantial commercial practice were expected to know no more about the rules of international trade than the "average" solicitor in practice. However, it is respectfully submitted that, amongst solicitors practising in the same field of law, the proposed distinction between those "of long experience and great skill" and those "of a more ordinary calibre and having less experience" would be difficult to apply in practice. It would also be somewhat invidious. The judge would need to begin by assessing the "calibre" of the defendant solicitor, before deciding whether he was negligent. Where a profession is stratified (such as the medical profession)[57] it is easier for the court to

---

[52] [1997] P.N.L.R. 393, ChD. Similarly, in *Al-Sabah v. Ali* [1999] E.G.C.S. 11, Ferris J. relied on the *Guide* and held that a solicitor should see the client personally or obtain written confirmation from him, particularly in that case where the transaction was the sale of the purported client's flats to the agent from whom the solicitor obtained instructions.

[53] Now para. 12.05 of the 8th ed., 1999.

[54] [1972] 2 Lloyd's Rep. 172.

[55] *ibid.* at 183.

[56] *Elcano Acceptance Ltd v. Richmond, Richmond, Stambler & Mills* (1985) 31 C.C.L.T. 201 at 213, Ontario HCt, and *Confederation Life v. Shepherd, McKenzie* (1992) 29 R.P.R. (2d) 271 at 297.

[57] See chap. 12, para. 12–077.

exact different standards of skill and care from its members, according to their status and qualifications. In the case of solicitors, however, there is no formal distinction between those who possess great ability and experience and those who do not. Futhermore, if a complex matter comes before a solicitor with insufficient specialist experience, in appropriate cases he should surely refer it to a competent specialist, and if he does not he should be liable as if he did possess sufficient specialist knowledge.

Correct approach. It is suggested, therefore, that the correct approach is to **10–094** judge the defendant solicitor by the standard of "the reasonably competent practitioner"[58] specialising in whatever areas of law the defendant holds himself out as a specialist.[59] This approach is consistent with principle and with authority in other areas of professional negligence.[60] In *Matrix Securities Ltd v. Theodore Goddard*[61] Lloyd J. had to consider the conduct of a city firm giving tax advice. He held that they should be judged by the standard to be expected of a reasonably competent firm of solicitors with a specialist tax department. The fact that the defendants were established city solicitors who professed very high levels of skill and care did not increase this duty. He rejected a suggestion that in the context of obtaining clearance from the Inland Revenue of a tax avoidance scheme, the letter which they sent should have obtained a 100 per cent reliable result. Contrast *Balamoan v. Holden & Co.*,[62] where the defendant was a solicitor in a small country town instructed by a legally aided client in a comparatively small claim for nuisance. The Court of Appeal held that the courts should not apply too rigorous a standard of care in such circumstances, as the solicitor had to be anxious not to incur costs which could not be recovered from the other side. Great weight would therefore be placed on the judgment of a local circuit judge as to the standards reasonably to be required of local litigation solicitors.

Non-solicitors. The position of a legal executive, unqualified clerk or trainee **10–095** might be different, because his qualifications are different. It has been held in an Australian case that a managing clerk who was sued for negligence had a duty to exercise the care expected of a managing clerk, not the higher standard of care expected of a solicitor.[63] In contrast, in *Balamoan v. Holden & Co.*[64] it was held that a one-man firm could not expect a lower standard of

---

[58] See *Midland Bank v. Hett Stubbs & Kemp* [1979] Ch. 384 at 402–403.
[59] The sentence in the text was specifically adopted and applied by Douglas Brown J. in *Green v. Collyer-Bristow* [1999] Lloyd's Rep. P.N. 798. A very similar test was adopted in *Hurlingham Estates Ltd v. Wilde & Partners* [1997] 1 Lloyd's Rep. 525 by Lightman J. of a "reasonably competent conveyancer and commercial lawyer". The case concerned a commercial conveyance. It is consistent with the approach adopted in the earlier wasted costs case of *Locke v. Camberwell Health Authority* (1990) 140 N.L.J. 205 at 205 col. 3. Moreland J., in considering the position of a solicitor inexperienced in medical negligence litigation, stated: "He is not expected to have the specialised expertise of a partner in a firm specialising in medical negligence work . . . He is expected to have the competence and the skill to be expected of a solicitor engaged in litigation in general practice." (The case was reversed on appeal on further facts coming to light, but nothing was said about the law: [1991] 2 Med. L.R. 253.)
[60] See chap. 2 paras 2–116 to 2–124. *cf. Marbel Developments Ltd v. Pirani* (1994) 18 C.C.L.T. (2d) 229, where the British Columbia Supreme Court rejected the argument that there should be different standards applied to geographical areas or practising environments.
[61] [1998] P.N.L.R. 290
[62] [1999] N.L.J. Prac. 898.
[63] *Shigeva v. Schafer* (1984) 5 N.S.W.L.R. 502, HCt.
[64] [1999] N.L.J. Prac. 898.

care to be applied to it merely because it delegated the case to an unqualified member of staff, if the conduct of that person fell below the standard appropriate for a solicitor.[65]

(iv) *Mitigating factors*

10–096   **Non-negligent types of mistake.** Although every case turns on its own facts, certain types of mistake are less likely to be branded as negligent than others. The construction of documents, for example, is one of the most prolific sources of disagreement amongst lawyers. The fact that a solicitor erred in construing, or in advising on the construction of, a statute or document is unlikely to constitute negligence, so long as the construction which he favoured was a tenable one.[66] Again, where the solicitor is in a dilemma (which is not of his making) and is forced to choose between two or more evils, the court will be slow to castigate his actual decision as negligent.[67]

10–097   **Lack of time.** It is sometimes suggested that lack of time is a mitigating factor. Where the lack of time arises because of pressure of other work, this is plainly not the case. No professional man ought to undertake more work than he is able to do properly. Where the lack of time arises because the client requires work to be done at great speed or because the solicitor is dealing with an emergency, then it is submitted that these are factors which should be taken into account in the solicitor's favour when determining whether or not a particular error was negligent. However, this is not an argument which can be pressed too far.[68] If the

---

[65] Even if a lower standard of care is applied to unqualified staff, the same result may be reached in most cases. The less qualified person may be negligent in not seeking more expert advice, and the firm which employs him may be negligent in giving a less qualified person work which is too difficult for him, or in supervising him insufficiently.

[66] See, for example, *Laidler v. Elliott* (1825) 3 B. & C. 738 (incorrectly construing a rule of court, the meaning of which was obscure); *Elkington v. Holland* (1842) 9 M. & W. 659 (incorrectly construing "a doubtful Act of Parliament"); *Bulmer v. Gilman* (1842) 4 Man. & G. 108 (incorrectly construing an order of the House of Lords which was "doubtful in its terms"); *Dunlop v. Woollahra Municipal Council* [1982] A.C. 158, PC (construction of two clauses in a planning scheme); *Ormindale Holdings Ltd v. Ray, Wolfe, Connel, Lightbody & Reynolds* (1981) 116 D.L.R. (3d) 346 and (1982) 135 D.L.R. (3d) 557, British Columbia CA (construction of statute).

[67] He may, though, be able to apply to the court for directions or seek counsel's advice. This is illustrated by *Dunn v. Fairs, Blissard, Barnes & Stowe* (1961) 105 S.J. 932: the deceased, who was dying of cancer, instructed a member of the defendant solicitors to purchase an annuity on her behalf. The solicitor carried out her instructions, even though her limited life expectancy made the transaction unwise. Barry J. dismissed a subsequent claim for negligence by the administrator of her estate. "He had been placed in a dilemma, for he owed a duty to his client and was faced with having to proceed with the purchase or take action which would have led her to suspect that she was suffering from an incurable disease. The solicitor had considered the situation with great care and his Lordship was not satisfied that his decision to allow her to invest as she did could in any sense be regarded as negligent."

[68] Thus in *Whale View Investments Ltd v. Kensland Realty Ltd* [2000] 2 H.K.L.R.D. 261, HCt, a solicitor was negligent in failing to prepare mortgage documents properly when instructions were faxed on Saturday August 30, and the documents returned at 9.36 a.m. on Tuesday September 2. The solicitors were negligent, as there was sufficient time to prepare the documents carefully and rather earlier than they did.

solicitor is required to perform a difficult task in inadequate time, he should clearly warn the client of the risks which are involved. The mere requirement to carry out work promptly is not a licence to be negligent.[69] On the other hand, solicitors are not justified in providing a second-rate service to clients who were slow in paying their fees.[70]

(v) *Aggravating factors*

Creation of unnecessary risks. Where the solicitor creates, or incurs, unnec-   **10–098** essary risks,[71] he is likely to be held liable for any consequential loss, however carefully he may have handled those risks and however skilfully he may have calculated the prospects of success at the outset. "It is negligence where there are two ways of doing a thing, and one is clearly right, and the other is doubtful, to do it in the doubtful way."[72] In *C. W. Dixey & Sons Ltd v. Parsons*[73] the defendant solicitors acted for the plaintiffs in granting a sublease of premises. Clause 2(10) of the head lease provided that the premises should not be used as a medical or quasi-medical establishment. The sub-lease as drafted by the defendants allowed the sub-lessee to use the premises for the purposes of a psychologist's consulting room. The head landlords took the view that this use infringed clause 2(10) of the head-lease and brought forfeiture proceedings, which were compromised. Salmon L.J. (sitting as an additional judge of the Queen's Bench Division) held that the defendants were negligent, and would have been negligent even if the use in question did not infringe clause 2(10):

"In the present circumstances the solicitor owed a duty to his client to take reasonable care, not only to protect his client against committing a breach of the law but to protect him against a risk of being involved in litigation ... In preparing a lease, as in the present case, a solicitor was presented with what was an obvious danger. It would not do for him to say that in his view it was all right. There was an obvious danger that a different view might be taken. In the present circumstances the ordinary careful solicitor would have gone to see his clients and advised them not to sign."[74]

---

[69] In *Elcano Acceptance Ltd v. Richmond, Richmond, Stambler & Mills* (1985) 31 C.C.L.T. 201, Ontario HCt, Smith J. put the matter in this way at 213: "As a matter of policy, it seems to me that a Court should not lightly lower the requisite standard of care because the solicitor was rushed by his client. The solicitor's duty is, at a minimum, to tell the client very explicitly that certain dangers arise if, under the pressures of deadline, certain matters are not attended to, and, at a maximum, to withdraw from the relationship."

[70] See *F. & G. Reynolds (Whitchurch) Ltd v. Joseph, The Times*, November 6, 1992.

[71] As by departing from the normal practice: see *Stevenson v. Rowland* (1830) 2 Dow. & Cl. 104 at 119 and para. 10–084 above.

[72] *Levy v. Spyers* (1856) 1 F. & F. 3, at 5 note (a): the defendant attorney was engaged to recover a sum due upon a judgment debt from one P. P. had agreed to give bills of exchange in discharge of the judgment debt. The defendant sent notes to P. rather than bills. It was held that the defendant acted negligently, even though the notes might have been sufficient.

[73] (1964) 192 E.G. 197.

[74] See also *Boros v. Bodnar, Wanhella and Courtney* [1988] 6 W.W.R. 645, Saskatchewan QB: a solicitor delayed issuing proceedings against a hospital for wrongful dismissal until beyond the relevant limitation period of only one-year. He believed, as did most lawyers, that the one-year period only applied to negligence actions against hospitals, which view subsequently proved to be wrong. He was found to be negligent in not adopting a more cautious approach.

10–099   **Acting beyond competence.** A solicitor creates unnecessary risks where he takes it upon himself to act in matters beyond his competence, or to advise on points which ought to be referred to counsel. In such circumstances he acts "at his peril".[75] If he errs, he may be held liable in negligence notwithstanding that he has exercised his utmost skill and care. In *Richards v. Cox*,[76] for example, the plaintiff consulted the defendant solicitor about a road traffic accident in which she was injured. The defendant's clerk took the view that it was not worth suing her driver since he was uninsured. The Court of Appeal held that on a proper construction of the relevant insurance policy (which was extremely difficult to construe) the driver was insured. Accordingly, the plaintiff recovered against her solicitor the damages which she should have obtained from the driver. On the issue of negligence, which was not specifically argued on the appeal, Goddard L.J. stated:

> " . . . it seems to me that the only negligence which can be alleged against [the solicitor's clerk] is that he took on himself to decide a somewhat difficult question."[77]

If a situation is fraught with danger, particular care may be required. Thus in *Tonitto v. Bassal*[78] a solicitor was found to be negligent in failing to comply strictly with the requirements of an option agreement, because it is common for grantees to seek to avoid the exercise of the option on the ground that its terms had not been complied with.

10–100   **Acting for parties with opposed interests.** Solicitors are not infrequently asked to act for two parties to a transaction with conflicting, or potentially conflicting, interests.[79] This practice, especially the practice of acting for both parties to a sale of land,[80] has frequently been condemned by the courts.[81] A solicitor who puts himself in this position may suddenly find that his duties to the respective clients require him to take two different, and mutually inconsistent, courses of action. In this situation, despite the exercise of the utmost skill and care, the solicitor must incur liability in negligence to one or other of the

---

[75] *Ireson v. Pearman* (1825) 3 B. & C. 799: "Now although it may not be part of the duty of an attorney to know the legal operation of conveyances, yet it is his duty to take care not to draw wrong conclusions from the deeds laid before him, but to state the deeds to counsel whom he consults, or he must draw conclusions at his peril."

[76] [1943] 1 K.B. 139.

[77] *ibid.* at 143.

[78] (1992) 28 N.S.W.L.R. 564, NSWCA.

[79] For the rules of professional conduct as to when it is proper or improper to act for both parties see the Law Society's *Guide to the Professional Conduct of Solicitors*, (8th ed. 1999), chaps 15 and 25. There may also be a breach of fiduciary duty in such circumstances, see paras 10–023 to 10–025 above.

[80] The circumstances in which it is permissible for a solicitor to act for both parties to a conveyancing transaction are now specified in r. 6 of the Solicitors Practice Rules 1990.

[81] *e.g. Goody v. Baring* [1956] 1 W.L.R. 448, ChD; *Smith v. Mansi* [1963] 1 W.L.R. 26, described by Danckwerts L.J. at 30 as "a shocking example of the trouble and expense which can arise from the employment (under a mistaken idea of saving time and expense) by the two parties to a sale of a solicitor who is already the solicitor of one of the parties."

clients.[82] Such a situation arose in *Nash v. Phillips*.[83] Even where so extreme a situation does not arise, the solicitor may encounter considerable difficulties as a result of acting in a dual capacity. If he makes a mistake or omission to the detriment of either party, the court will more readily castigate the error as "negligent," since he ought not to have put himself in such a position in the first place.[84] The same considerations apply *a fortiori* where the conflict is between the client and the solicitor himself.[85]

Informed consent. The Privy Council qualified this general principle in *Clark Boyce v. Mouat*.[86] A solicitor may act for two parties whose interests may conflict providing that he had obtained the informed consent of both of them to his acting, which must be given in the knowledge that there is a conflict and that as a result the solicitor may be disabled from disclosing to each party the full knowledge he possesses or from giving some advice.[87] In that case, the plaintiff wished to assist her son by granting a mortgage over her home as security for loans to be made to him. The defendant solicitors acted for her and her son. They advised the plaintiff to obtain independent advice. She required no more than conveyancing and an explanation of the legal implications of the transaction. As she was in full command of her faculties and was aware of what she was doing, the defendant had no duty to give unsought advice. The requirement of informed consent may be onerous, depending on the circumstances, as is illustrated by *Mahoney v. Purnell*.[88] The defendant solicitors acted for the plaintiff and his son-in-law on the sale of their jointly owned hotel from the plaintiff to the son-in-law. The solicitor had realised that the proposed transaction was potentially disadvantageous to the plaintiff, and knew that he trusted his son-in-law and was likely to be influenced by him. May J. held that the solicitor had advised the plaintiff that

10–101

---

[82] "The case has been put of a solicitor acting for vendor and purchaser who knows of a flaw in the title by reason of his acting for the vendor, and who, if he discloses that flaw in the title, which he knows as acting for the vendor, may be liable to an action by his vendor, and who, if he does not disclose the flaw in the title, may be liable to an action by the purchaser for not doing his duty as solicitor for him. It will be his fault for mixing himself up with a transaction in which he has two entirely inconsistent interests, and solicitors who try to act for both vendors and purchasers must appreciate that they run a very serious risk of liability to one or the other owing to the duties and obligations which such curious relation puts upon them." *per* Scrutton L.J. in *Moody v. Cox* [1917] 2 Ch. 71 at 91 (a fiduciary case, see at 79); cited and adopted by Danckwerts J. in *Goody v. Baring* [1956] 1 W.L.R. at 450. The Federal Court of Australia expressed similar views in *Fox v. Everingham* (1983) 50 A.L.R. 3371, basing them on *Moody v. Cox* and *Goody v. Baring*, and also in *Commonwealth Bank of Australia v. Smith* (1992) 102 A.L.R. 453. See further *Wan v. McDonald* (1992) 105 A.L.R. 473, Burchett J.; *Stewart v. Layton* (1992) 111 A.L.R. 687, Foster J.; *Trade Practices Commission v. CC (New South Wales) Pty Ltd* (1994) 125 A.L.R. 94, Hill J.
[83] (1974) 232 E.G. 1219, ChD.
[84] *e.g. Lake v. Bushby* [1949] 1 All E.R. 964, KBD; *Attard v. Samson* (1966) 110 S.J. 249, QBD. See also *Powell v. Powell* [1900] 1 Ch. 243 at 246–247, ChD. But *cf. Brinsden v. Williams* [1894] 3 ChD. 185. Canadian cases in which a solicitor acting for both parties has been held liable to one of them include *Clarence Construction Ltd v. Lavallee* (1980) 111 D.L.R. (3d) 582, British Columbia CA; *Lapierre v. Young* (1981) 117 D.L.R. (3d) 643, Ontario HCt; *Ferris v. Rusnak* (1984) 9 D.L.R. (4th) 183, Alberta QB.
[85] *Apatu v. Peach Prescott & Jamieson* [1985] 1 N.Z.L.R. 50 at 64, Eichelbaum J. There would be a breach of fiduciary duty: see para. 10–018.
[86] [1994] 1 A.C. 428 at 435–436 (following Upjohn L.J. in *Boulting v. Association of Cinematograph Television and Allied Technicians* [1963] 2 Q.B. 606 at 636).
[87] For possible qualifications to this rule see paras 10–023 and 10–028 above. Further, the position is different when advising a client who is about to enter a transaction and who may be subject to undue influence, see para. 10–205 below.
[88] [1996] 3 All E.R. 61.

he ought to think about getting independent advice, but did not tell him he should, and did not advise the plaintiff about the conflict of interest in sufficiently clear and emphatic terms so that the plaintiff was enabled to give his informed consent.

10–102   **Borrower and lender.** Similar problems can arise when a solicitor acts for both borrower and lender.[89] This matter was briefly considered by the Court of Appeal in *Wills v. Wood*,[90] a case where solicitors acted in connection with a loan between two of their private clients. Sir John Donaldson M.R. said that if the terms of the loans were already agreed, there might well be no problem.[91]

> "But if either party were seeking advice or the solicitors were involved in the negotiation of the terms or either party might thereafter seek to say that sufficient was known to the solicitors to create a duty to advise, the solicitors were exposing themselves to the risk of criticism."

The commonest situation in which solicitors act for both lender and borrower is, of course, the domestic conveyance. Both the purchaser and the mortgagees who are lending part of the purchase price very often employ the same solicitor. In recent years this has given rise to difficulties in the voluminous litigation brought by lenders against solicitors, which is explored later.[92] The arrangement does on occasions infringe the guidelines proposed by the Master of the Rolls in *Wills v. Wood*.[93] The fact that the solicitor in this situation acts for both the building society and the purchaser does not constitute an "aggravating factor" when considering whether a particular act or omission amounts to negligence, because there will normally be informed consent to the arrangement, as has been made clear by Millett L.J. in the leading judgment in *Bristol & West Building Society v. Mothew*.[94] Furthermore, the lender will not be imputed with the knowledge of the solicitor who failed to inform it of the real intention of the borrower if such information was imparted before the retainer.[95]

10–103   **Other circumstances of conflict.** Potential conflict may arise in very different circumstances. Thus in multi-party litigation, the requirement of confidentiality to existing clients in finalising a settlement may prevent a solicitor from acting for a new client to whom there would be a duty to give all available information.[96] There may be a conflict between an insured and his insurer.[97] Where a solicitor acts for a motorcyclist and his passenger in relation to injuries sustained in a road traffic accident, if the driver of the other vehicle alleges that the motorcyclist was at fault, the solicitor is in breach of fiduciary duty unless he advises the client of the conflict and ceases to act.[98] In criminal law, a solicitor

---

[89] See, *e.g. Neushul v. Mellish and Harkavy* (1967) 111 S.J. 399, CA, in which a solicitor acted for a lender in respect of a loan to one of his former clients. By reason of his knowledge of the borrower's financial affairs he "had put himself in hopeless difficulties."
[90] *The Times*, March 24, 1984.
[91] For an even stricter view see *Ferris v. Rusnak* (1984) 9 D.L.R. (4th) 183 at 191, Alberta QB.
[92] See paras 10–206 *et seq.*
[93] *The Times*, March 24, 1984.
[94] [1998] 1 Ch. 1.
[95] *Halifax Mortgage Services Ltd v. Stepsky* [1996] Ch.D. 207, CA.
[96] See *Davies v. Eli Lilly, The Times*, January 16, 1988.
[97] *e.g. Groom v. Crocker* [1939] 1 K.B. 194, CA; see further para. 10–190; *Nishimatsu-Costain-China Harbour Joint Venture v. Ip Kwan & Co.* [2001] H.K.L.R.D. 84, HKCA.
[98] *Nadeau v. Rice* (1990) 109 N.B.R. (2d) 243, New Brunswick CA.

who has acted for a defendant after his retainer is terminated cannot then act for a co-defendant where there has been a cut-throat defence.[99]

(vi) *General observations*[1]

A serious matter. Elderly cases suggest that allegations of negligence against   **10–104**
a solicitor are a grave matter. A charge of negligence against a solicitor must be
distinctly proved.[2] The issue of negligence should be approached "with the
greatest care," even though the sum at stake may not be large.[3] Thus it is
normally advisable to call the claimant, and not merely to rely on the correspondence.[4] In *Stewart Wrightson Group Ltd v. Crocker*[5] Lord Denning M.R.
observed that an error of judgment by solicitors did not amount to negligence. He
added that, where there is delay in prosecuting a claim, negligence must be "most
clearly established". Solicitors "should not be harassed by claims for negligence
years after the event". In the analogous case of barrister's negligence, Lord Reid
in *Rondel v. Worsley* considered that "the onus of proving professional negligence over and above errors of judgment is a heavy one."[6]

No requirement of moral censure. On the other hand, as the courts are often   **10–105**
at pains to emphasise, not every mistake amounting to professional negligence is
deserving of moral censure. In *Creech v. Mayorcas*[7] Pennycuick J. held the
defendant liable "with some regret" for what he described as "an understandable
slip" by the defendant's clerk. In *Sykes v. Midland Bank Executor & Trustee Co.
Ltd*[8] a solicitor was held to have been negligent in failing to explain the effect of
a particular provision in a sub-lease. In affirming this decision, Salmon L.J.
observed.

> "The common law, of course, recognises no degrees of negligence, but I should like to
> say that, in my view, the degree of blame in the present case was slight. It was the sort
> of negligence many a competent professional man may have committed on some
> isolated occasion in the course of his career."[9]

The solicitor's state of mind is irrelevant, and it is his course of conduct which
must be judged.[10]

---

[99] *Saminadhen v. Khan* [1992] 1 All E.R. 963, CA.

[1] The observations in this para. presumably apply with equal force to all professions. They are
included in this chapter since each of the cases cited concerns solicitors. Given the now common
occurrence of professional negligence litigation, it may be doubted whether such observations carry
the same force as they once did.

[2] *Farmer v. Turner & Son* (1899) 15 T.L.R. 522, QBD.

[3] *per* Acton J. in *Ellis v. Sampson* (1927) 71 S.J. 621.

[4] *Yager v. Fishman & Co.* [1944] 1 All E.R. 552 at 554D–E (Scott L.J.) and 556F (Goddard
L.J.).

[5] (1979) 124 S.J. 83; *The Times*, December 19, 1979. Lord Denning based his comments, in part, on
his own judgment in *Whitehouse v. Jordan* given a few days previously. This must now be read
subject to the House of Lords' decision in *Whitehouse v. Jordan* [1981] 1 W.L.R. 246: see chap. 12,
para. 12–084.

[6] [1969] 1 A.C. 191 at 230F. This was approved in the case of solicitors by Simon Brown L.J. in
Martin Boston & Co. v. Roberts [1996] 1 P.N.L.R. 45 at 50D.

[7] (1966) 198 E.G. 1091.

[8] [1971] 1 Q.B. 113.

[9] *ibid.* at 126. These observations contrast markedly with the dicta in the 19th century cases referred
to in para. 10–077 (in particular, *Purves v. Landell*).

[10] *Westway Homes Ltd v. Gore Wood & Co, The Times*, July 9, 1991.

(d) *Specific defences to a claim for breach of duty*

(i) *Immunity*

10–106 **History of immunity.** When a solicitor acted as an advocate, it used to be the case that he enjoyed the same immunity against a claim for negligence as a barrister.[11] No action lay against him for negligence in respect of the manner in which he conducts the case in court.[12] This applied to an action brought by the other side in litigation.[13] If the solicitor instructed counsel, then it was unclear whether he could claim immunity. On one view, he was not acting as an advocate and could not claim immunity, even for acts which if done by a barrister would be immune.[14] On another view, there should be no such distinction.[15] The immunity extended to any pre-trial work which was "so intimately connected with the conduct of the cause in court that it can fairly be said to be a preliminary decision affecting the way that cause is to be conducted when it comes to a hearing",[16] such as advising on whether to plead guilty or not guilty to a criminal charge.[17] That test was expressly followed in the context of solicitor's immunity by the Court of Appeal in *Bateman v. Owen White*.[18]

10–107 **Present law.** The immunity of advocates has been abolished by the House of Lords in *Hall v. Simons*[19] While that case concerned an attempt to strike out three cases brought against solicitors for negligence, the House of Lords primarily considered the position of barristers, and solicitor advocates were held to be in no different position.

(b) *Abuse of process*[20]

10–108 **Three old leading cases.** If a solicitor's negligence leads to the conviction of his client, then the client may not be able to sue him because the action would be an abuse of process. Much of the reasoning in the earlier cases discussed here may not be consistent with the observations of the House of Lords in *Hall v. Simons*,[21] which held in summary that the principle of abuse of process would

---

[11] *Rondel v. Worsley* [1969] 1 A.C. 191 *per* Lords Reid (at 232C–F), Morris (243G–244A), Pearce (267F) and Upjohn (284D); *Saif Ali v. Sidney Mitchell & Co.* [1980] A.C. 198, *per* Lords Wilberforce (at 215G–H), Diplock (224A) and Salmon (232F–G); *Somasundaram v. M. Julius Melchior & Co.* [1988] 1 W.L.R. 1394, CA. See chap. 11 paras. 11–09 to 11–24 in relation to barrister's immunity. s. 62 of the Courts and Legal Services Act 1990 confirmed that solicitor advocates would be treated in the same way as barristers in this respect, whatever the common law determined that that was.
[12] *e.g. Losner v. Michael Cohen & Co.* (1975) 119 S.J. 340, CA.
[13] *Welsh v. Chief Constable of Merseyside* [1993] 1 All E.R. 692 at 700C, Tudor Evans J.
[14] *Somasundaram v. M. Julius Melchior & Co.* [1988] 1 W.L.R. 1394 at 1403E–H, CA; *Acton v. Graham Pearce & Co (a firm)* [1997] 3 All E.R. 908, Chadwick J.
[15] *Landall v. Dennis Faulkner & Alsop* [1994] 5 Med. L.R. 268, Holland J.; *Kelley v. Corston* [1998] Q.B. 686, Pill L.J.
[16] *per* McArthy P. in *Rees v. Sinclair* [1974] 1 N.Z.L.R. 180, CA, applied by the House of Lords in *Saif Ali v. Sidney Mitchell & Co.* [1980] A.C. 198. The House of Lords did not specifically discuss the extent of the immunity of a solicitor advocate.
[17] *Somasundaram v. M. Julius Melchior & Co.* [1988] 1 W.L.R. 1394 at 1403D, CA.
[18] [1996] 1 P.N.L.R. 1, CA.
[19] [2000] 3 W.L.R. 543. For a discussion of this important decision in relation to immunity see chap. 11 paras 11–15 to 11–23. Earlier law may be relevant for acts and omissions before the date of the decision of the House of Lords if it is not of retrospective effect.
[20] For a detailed discussion, see H. Evans, *'Lawyers' Liabilities'*, (2nd ed. 2002), chap. 5; and *ibid.* *"Hall v. Simons"* and abuse of process (2001) 17 P.N. 219.
[21] [2000] 3 W.L.R. 543.

generally apply and only apply to criminal cases where the claimant's conviction had not been quashed. As the House of Lords gave limited guidance on the application of the doctrine, reference to previous cases may well still be necessary. There are three earlier leading decisions of the Court of Appeal to consider. The doctrine of abuse of process was first established in relation to solicitor's negligence in *Somasundaram v. M. Julius Melchior & Co.*[22] The plaintiff pleaded guilty to a charge of unlawfully wounding his wife. On release from prison, he sued his former solicitors, alleging that he had been overpersuaded to change his story and plead guilty. The Court of Appeal struck out the claim on the ground that it was frivolous and vexatious on its facts. The Court also considered that the claim was an abuse of process because it was a collateral attack on the final decision of another court which the plaintiff had had a full opportunity of contesting. They relied on *Hunter v. Chief Constable of the West Midlands Police*,[23] where six men convicted of an IRA bombing claimed that their confessions had been beaten out of them by the police. The criminal trial judge ruled out their evidence on a *voire dire*, and their appeal against their subsequent conviction failed. While in prison they commenced proceedings against the police for the very same assaults, which was held by the House of Lords to be an abuse of process. In *Somasundaram* the Court of Appeal also considered that it made no difference whether the original case under attack was a criminal one or a civil one,[24] a conclusion which is no longer good law.

The second leading decision is *Walpole v. Partridge & Wilson*.[25] The plaintiff **10–109** was convicted for obstructing a veterinary officer in the execution of his duty, and he appealed unsuccessfully to the Crown Court. He retained the defendant solicitors to advise him on the merits of a further appeal. He later brought proceedings alleging that the solicitors had failed to lodge an appeal, despite counsel's advice that there were valid grounds for an appeal by way of case stated on a point of law. The Court of Appeal declined to strike out the claim, considering that the initiation of proceedings which challenged the final decision of a court would not necessarily be an abuse of process, although it may be. Ralph Gibson L.J. recognised four exceptions to the principle, although the Court accepted that the list was not necessarily complete.[26] First, where the challenged decision was obtained by fraud, collusion or perjury where there is sufficient fresh evidence to support the allegation.[27] Secondly, where there was sufficient fresh evidence which "entirely changes the character of the case".[28] Thirdly,

---

[22] [1988] 1 W.L.R. 1394.

[23] [1982] A.C. 529, HL.

[24] [1988] 1 W.L.R. 1394 at 1402E–1403B. *Quaere* how this can be reconciled with *e.g. Bragg v. Oceanus Mutual* [1982] 2 Lloyd's Rep. 132, CA. See *Phipson on Evidence* (15th ed), para. 33–62.

[25] [1994] Q.B. 106.

[26] Contrast the law in Canada. In *Wernikowski v. Kirkland, Murphy & Ain* (2000) 181 D.L.R. (4th) 625, the Ontario Court of Appeal held that the doctrine was far more restricted and did not include the fresh evidence or fraud exceptions, being limited to improper motives, cases where the lawyer's incompetence had been unsuccessfully litigated, and cases where the the plaintiff had exhausted all remedies in the criminal process.

[27] *ibid.* at 116E–F.

[28] *ibid.* at 116B–C, followed by Laddie J. in *Oliver v. McKenna & Co., The Times*, December 20, 1995. *cf. Cullen v. Eaton-Smith* (unreported), November 4, 1993, where the Court of Appeal appeared to decide that there was no abuse of process where it was alleged that the defendant solicitor failed to produce evidence at the first trial, and the exception was not confined to cases where the evidence could not have been available at trial. Without fresh evidence now being available, an action is liable to be struck out, see *Nestle v. Best* [1996] P.N.L.R. 444, CA.

where it was alleged that the solicitors failed to prosecute an appeal on an issue of law, as in *Walpole*.[29] And fourthly, in some circumstances, where there had been no decision on the merits such as where the claimant had submitted to judgment.[30] As a result of the fourth exception, the Court of Appeal therefore doubted *Palmer v. Durnford Ford*,[31] where the plaintiffs' claim had been abandoned by consent at trial, and the judge held that the claim for negligence against the defendant solicitors was an abuse of process. Despite Lord Hoffmann's suggestion in *Hall v. Simons* that Ralph Gibson L.J.'s judgment was "admirable"[32] and the result correct,[33] it may be doubtful whether the reasoning in the case is in fact consistent with *Hall v. Simons*. In the third leading case, *Smith v. Linskills (a Firm)*[34] the Court of Appeal held that the defendant had had a full opportunity of contesting his criminal trial where he was present throughout and could give instructions, even if criticism could be made of the defence. In considering the fresh evidence exception, the possibility of further alibi witnesses whose evidence was still not before the court did not entirely change the character of the case. Finally, the fact that he had now been released from prison did not prevent the action being a collateral attack, and his own motive was irrelevant.[35]

10–110   **Other cases.** A number of subsidiary decisions should be mentioned.[36] In *Acton v. Graham Pearce & Co. (a Firm)*[37] Chadwick J. allowed the plaintiff's action against his former solicitors where he had been convicted as a result of their negligence but had succeeded in overturning the conviction on appeal. In *R.(L.) v. Witherspoon*[38] solicitors negligently failed to issue applications to restore contact between their client and her child. The local council then successfully applied to terminate contact between the mother and child, the court being strongly influenced by the fact that the child had been living with prospective adopters for 14 months. The Court of Appeal held that the action against the solicitors was not a collateral attack on that decision, as the judge making the adoption order had to take account of the significant new factors which would not have been present a year earlier. It is submitted that the results reached in all of these cases are consistent with *Hall v. Simons*.[39]

10–111   *Hall v. Simons* **in the Court of Appeal.** In *Hall v. Simons*[40] the House of Lords had to consider three cases where solicitors sought to strike out actions on the grounds of immunity and abuse of process. In the first, the client counterclaimed against his solicitors for failing to advise properly about the liability of

---

[29] *ibid.* at 117B–D.
[30] *Ibid.* at 124E–F.
[31] [1992] 1 Q.B. 483.
[32] [2000] 3 W.L.R. 543 at 575B.
[33] *ibid.* 577G.
[34] [1996] 1 W.L.R. 763.
[35] In this regard, the facts are similar to *Somasundaram v. Melchior*, above This rejection of the "dominant purpose" test followed Gibson L.J. in *Walpole's Case* [1994] Q.B. 106 at 120.
[36] See also *Channon v. Lindley Johnstone* [2000] 2 F.L.R. 734, QBD., where the court refused to strike out allegations against a solicitor where he had failed to adduce essential evidence in relation to ancillary relief proceedings.
[37] [1997] 3 All E.R. 909. For the facts of the case, see para. 10–280.
[38] [1999] P.N.L.R. 776.
[39] [2000] 3 W.L.R. 543.
[40] *ibid.*

other parties and as to timeous settlement in a building case that was settled on the eve of trial by a consent order. In the second action, the plaintiff sued his solicitors for negligent advice on the valuation of the matrimonial home in ancillary relief proceedings that were settled by a consent order approved by the court. In the third case, solicitors advised by counsel advised the plaintiff to settle matrimonial ancillary relief proceedings in a compromise approved by the court on an incorrect basis. The Court of Appeal refused to strike out the three cases, and a fourth that was not appealed to the House of Lords. They held that the applicable principles in relation to abuse of process were as follows. If a claimant's claim against his former legal advisers were an abusive collateral challenge to an earlier judgment of the court, it would ordinarily be struck out. To determine whether there were such a challenge, the court must examine the nature and effect of the judgment, the basis of the claim against the legal advisers, and any grounds relied on to justify the collateral challenge. A criminal conviction would be accorded greatest weight, and an interlocutory judgment or approved consent order in a civil case would have the least weight. Later proceedings would normally be a collateral attack upon an approved consent order, unless the negligence alleged deprived the plaintiff of appreciating that better terms were available than those he obtained, or made him accept a significantly worse settlement than he should have had. A claimant would have to explain why steps were not taken to challenge the consent order.

***Hall v. Simons* in the House of Lords.** The House of Lords upheld the 10–112 conclusion of the Court of Appeal, but on very different grounds. Before considering the views of their Lordships, the relationship of the speeches should be noted. The leading speeches were given by Lords Steyn and Hoffmann, with whom Lords Browne-Wilkinson and Millett agreed, adding brief reasons of their own. Lords Hope, Hutton and Hobhouse agreed with the majority that immunity should be abolished for civil litigation, but disagreed in relation to criminal proceedings. In relation to abuse of process, the position of criminal and civil cases were treated very differently. Most members of the House of Lords who considered the matter expressed their conclusions in substantially the same terms.

Criminal cases. In relation to criminal cases, the doctrine of abusive collateral 10–113 attack was upheld, although it was recast in rather different form. The principle in *Hunter v. Chief Constable of the West Midlands*[41] will generally prevent a claimant bringing proceedings unless and until his conviction has been set aside. However, it is clear that this is the general rule, and the principle was in fact expressed in slightly wider terms:

> " . . . the court can strike out as an abuse of process the second action in which the plaintiff seeks to relitigate issues decided against him in earlier proceedings if such relitigation would be manifestly unfair to the defendant or would bring the administration of justice into disrepute."[42]

When the conviction has not been set aside, it would according to Lord Steyn be prima facie an abuse to bring civil proceedings,[43] and according to Lord Browne-

---

[41] [1982] A.C. 529.
[42] [2000] 3 W.L.R. 543 at 556H, *per* Lord Browne-Wilkinson, 574C, *per* Lord Hoffmann.
[43] *ibid.* at 551F.

Wilkinson it would only be in truly exceptional circumstances that such an action should be allowed.[44] Lord Hoffman, with whom Lord Hutton agreed on this issue,[45] held[46] that such an action would ordinarily be an abuse but "there may be exceptional cases in which the issue can be tried without a risk that the conflict of judgments would bring the administration of justice into disrepute". Lord Hope did not consider the issue directly, although he agreed that the *Hunter* principle provided that a collateral challenge to a subsising conviction would be struck out.[47] Lord Millett similarly held that such an action would ordinarily be struck out.[48] Finally, Lord Hobhouse's views were significantly different from the rest of the Court. He considered that the *Hunter* principle would rarely apply to a client suing his lawyer, as he could argue that his purpose was to recover compensation.[49] None of their Lordships indicated that there would ever be any impediment from the doctrine of abusive collateral attack to a defendant whose conviction had been quashed from suing his former lawyers. Although the following is not necessarily a complete list, it would appear that the abuse of process principle will not prevent relitigation in the following circumstances:

(1) Where the criminal conviction has been quashed. Lord Hoffmann made this clear, and he mentioned and approved *Acton v. Graham Pearce & Co (a Firm).*[50] The point is also expressly mentioned by Lords Steyn,[51] Browne-Wilkinson,[52] and Millett.[53]

(2) According to Lord Hoffmann, where there has been a failure to appeal on a point of law. His Lordship cited *Walpole v. Partridge & Wilson*[54] in this regard as such an exceptional case. Lord Hoffmann also seemed to suggest that the failure to take an obvious point of law in the Crown Court would equally be a case where there was no collateral challenge.[55]

(3) Following a suggestion made by Lord Hope[56] negligence causing delay or continued detention in custody, which may operate to the client's disadvantage irrespective of whether he is eventually acquitted or convicted.

10–114   **Civil cases.** In relation to civil proceedings, the position is a little less clear. The doctrine of abuse of process will play little part. According to Lord Steyn, the doctrines of *res judicata*, issue estoppel and abuse of process "as understood in private law" will generally be sufficient.[57] Presumably, these doctrines will

---

[44] *ibid.* at 557A–B.
[45] *ibid.* at 60A–B.
[46] *ibid.* at 577C–H.
[47] [2000] 3 W.L.R. 543 at 593H.
[48] *ibid.* 623G.
[49] *ibid.* 621H–622A.
[50] [1997] 3 All E.R. 909. See [2000] 3 W.L.R. 543 at 577G.
[51] 551G.
[52] 557B–C.
[53] 623F.
[54] [1994] Q.B. 106, see para 10–109 above.
[55] *ibid.* at 575C.
[56] *ibid.* at 593H–594A. The suggestion was made in the context of a discussion of why he considered that the abuse of process principle would not provide sufficient protection because it would allow such exceptions.
[57] *ibid.* at 552A (Lord Steyn).

rarely be an impediment on a client suing his lawyer. Lord Steyn held that the *Hunter* principle would rarely be needed, but "it should still guard against unforeseen gaps."[58] Lord Hoffmann seemed to hold that the *Hunter* principle had no application at all in civil cases,[59] and consistent with his reasoning *res judicata* and issue estoppel would apply, if they were relevant.[60] However, he did consider that the interests of the successful claimant in a libel action might prevent the unsuccessful defendant from suing his former lawyers, as such an action would be unfair to him and thus would be an abuse of the process of the court.[61] The views of the other five of their Lordships on this issue are likely to carry very much less weight. It was not clear to Lord Browne-Wilkinson how far the *Hunter* principle would apply. Lords Hope, Hutton and Millett did not expressly address the issue. Lord Hobhouse took a very narrow view of the applicability of the *Hunter* principle in any context, as we have already seen.

Other types of abuse of process. In some cases brought against solicitors, the **10–115** issue of abuse of process is relevant, but raises no special issues peculiar to solicitors, as the solicitors did not represent the claimant in the unsuccessful proceedings which it is alleged give rise to the abuse. The governing principles in such cases are generally to be derived from *Henderson v. Henderson.*[62] It was not an abuse of process to run inconsistent cases where in one action against a guarantor she was sued to judgment, and in a subsequent case against a solicitor it was alleged that the guarantee was invalid.[63] It was held not to be an abuse of process to raise issues in ordinary proceedings against a solicitor which had been litigated in an application for compensation for breach of an undertaking, as the earlier proceedings were disciplinary in nature.[64] In *Johnson v. Gore Wood & Co. (a Firm)*[65] the plaintiff's company sued the defendant solicitors, which action was settled, and then he sued the solicitors arising out of the same matters which were the subject of the original action. The House of Lords held that this was not an abuse of process. While there was a public interest in the finality of litigation and the defendant not being vexed twice for the same matter, the issue should be judged broadly on the merits taking account of all the public and private interests involved and the facts of the case. It was not necessary to identify an additional element such as a collateral attack on a previous decision or some dishonesty to found an abuse of process. In the case in question, the fact that the plaintiff had not undertaken the first action was not important, as he was identified with his company, nor did it matter that the first action culminated in a compromise rather than a judgment. However, the plaintiff had reasons which he regarded as compelling for deferring prosecuting his personal claim, and the defendants had not attempted to strike out the action which he brought over a long period of time.

---

[58] *ibid.* at 552A.

[59] *ibid.* at 577A–B.

[60] *ibid.* at 572D–573B.

[61] *ibid.* at 578A–C.

[62] (1843) 3 Hare 100.

[63] *Finley v. Connell Associates (A Firm)* [1999] Lloyd's Rep. P.N. 895, Richards J. Similarly, in *Minton v. Kenburhg Investments (Northern) Ltd (in Liquidation), The Times,* July 11, 2000, liquidators who sued directors under the summary remedy under section 212 of the Insolvency Act 1986 could then sue solicitors in relation to the same transaction.

[64] *Ulster Bank Ltd v. Fisher & Fisher* [1999] P.N.L.R. 794, Girvan J.

[65] [2001] 2 W.L.R. 72. For the analogous Canadian position, see *Martin v. Goldfarb* (1999) 41 O.R. (3d) 161.

(iii) *Acting on counsel's advice*

10–116   **History.** It has been long established that if a solicitor acts in accordance with the advice of counsel, whom he has properly instructed, then usually he will not be held liable in negligence, even if counsel's advice proves to be mistaken or misconceived.[66] Many of the authorities were decided in an era when there was a greater disparity between barristers and those by whom they were instructed. Nowadays the most able law students are not necessarily attracted to the bar. A barrister's training is no more rigorous or extensive than that of a solicitor. Many solicitors specialise in particular aspects of the law, or particular kinds of litigation, as much as, or more than, the barristers whom they instruct. It is not surprising that the law has changed to a degree.

10–117   **The development of the law.** The gradual shift in the relationship between the two branches of the legal profession is illustrated by the decision of the Court of Appeal in *Davy-Chiesman v. Davy-Chiesman*.[67] In that case a solicitor acted for the husband (who was legally aided) in proceedings for financial relief against the wife (who was not legally aided). He pressed on with those proceedings when it was obvious that they would fail, acting in reliance on counsel's advice. Nevertheless the solicitor was ordered pursuant to what was then Order 62, rule 8 to pay all the costs of both parties after the date when it was obvious that the application would fail. May L.J., who delivered the leading judgment, said that it was the ordinary rule "that save in exceptional circumstances a solicitor cannot be criticised where he acts on the advice of properly instructed counsel."[68] He then qualified the proposition in this way:

> "However, this does not operate so as to give a solicitor an immunity in every such case. A solicitor is highly trained and rightly expected to be experienced in his particular legal fields. He is under a duty at all times to exercise that degree of care, to both client and the court, that can be expected of a reasonably prudent solicitor. He is not entitled to rely blindly and with no mind of his own on counsel's views."[69]

10–118   **Summaries of the modern law.** The law has been helpfully summarised in two Court of Appeal decisions. In *Locke v. Camberwell Health Authority*[70] it was stated in these terms:

---

[66] *Kemp v. Burt* (1833) 4 B. & Ad. 424: attorneys acted on the advice of counsel and a special pleader in complex litigation concerning turnpike roads; *Potts v. Sparrow* (1836) 6 C. & P. 749: "Where there is reasonable doubt whether an instrument be illegal or not, and there is no want of ordinary care and knowledge, and the attorney consults those in whom he has confidence, and acts under their advice—I repeat, it strikes me it would be too much to say that he is to guarantee the result" (*per* Tindal C.J.); *Manning v. Wilkin* (1848) 12 L.T. (o.s.) 249: counsel erred both in the pleading and in advice; *Re Clark* (1851) 1 De G.M. & G. 43: the defence failed, since it was not accepted that counsel had given the advice alleged; *Cates v. Indermaur* (1858) 1 F. & F. 259: attorney failed to use certain documents in evidence on the advice of counsel; *Francis v. Francis & Dickerson* [1956] P. 87 at 96: " . . . as a general rule a solicitor acting on the advice of properly instructed counsel can hardly be said to be acting unreasonably—save perhaps in some very exceptional circumstances" (*per* Sachs J. on a review of a legal aid taxation).
[67] [1984] Fam 48.
[68] [1984] Fam. 48 at 63E.
[69] *ibid.*, at 64A.
[70] [1991] 2 Med.L.R. 249 at 254. In *Harley v. McDonald* [1999] 3 N.Z.L.R. 545 at 573 the New Zealand Court of Appeal helpfully stated: "ordinarily the advice of counsel will be a powerful factor upon which solicitors can rely, but only if the advice comes in properly reasoned form and the solicitor is satisfied, after appropriate consideration, that the advice is tenable." (The case was reversed by the Privy Council on appeal [2001] 2 W.L.R. 1749; [2001] U.K.P.C. 18.)

"(1) In general, a solicitor is entitled to rely upon the advice of counsel properly instructed.

(2) For a solicitor without specialist experience in a particular field to rely on counsel's advice is to make normal and proper use of the Bar.

(3) However, he must not do so blindly, but must exercise his own independent judgment. If he reasonably thinks counsel's advice is obviously or glaringly wrong, it is his duty to reject it."

In *Ridehalgh v. Horsefield*[71] the court amplified the last point:

"A solicitor does not abdicate his professional responsibility when he seek the advice of counsel. He must apply his mind to the advice received. But the more specialist the nature of the advice, the more reasonable is it likely to be for a solicitor to accept it and act on it."

Illustrations: no defence. In a number of cases, reliance on counsel has been **10–119** held to be no defence.[72] In *Clark v. Clark (No. 2)*[73] solicitors acting for a wife, who was legally aided, sequestered the husband's assets. The costs were ordered to be paid from them first, leaving little for the wife. On counsel's advice, they subsequently attempted to vary the order, so that the assets should be applied first to the arrears of maintenance owed to the wife. The solicitors were found to be in breach of their duty to the Legal Aid Board in so doing. The breach of duty was clear and thus their defence of relying on counsel failed.[74] In *Green v. Collyer-Bristow*[75] matrimonial counsel negligently advised the plaintiff that she should seek specific enforcement of an agreement with her former husband to transfer real property to her. Both counsel and the solicitors failed to notice section 2 of the Law of Property (Miscellaneous Provisions) Act 1989, which imposed more onerous requirements with respect to the need for such an agreement to be in writing than the repealed section 40 of the Law of Property Act 1925. Although two of the three standard textbooks did not refer to the change in the law, both the barrister and the solicitor were held to be liable, and the

---

[71] [1994] Ch. 205 at 237G. In *Matrix Securities Ltd v. Theodore Goddard* [1998] P.N.L.R. 290 Lloyd J. considered that when leading counsel had given considered advice to the client, a solicitor's duty was only to give separate advice if there was an important point on which he regarded counsel's advice as being seriously wrong. Neither solicitor nor counsel were negligent on the facts of that case, on which see chap. 11, para. 11–42.

[72] The defence was also rejected in *Miloslavsky v. Aldington* [1996] 1 W.L.R. 736, CA, discussed at para. 10–135, in *Dace v. Redland Aggregates Ltd* [1997] E.G.C.S. 123, see further chap. 11 para. 11–031, and on an application by the defendants for summary judgment in *Green v. Hancocks (a Firm)* [2001] Lloyd's Rep. P.N. 212, CA, where the high street solicitors were entitled to rely on counsel for specialist advice, but arguably not on the question of whether the claimant had *locus standi* to sue, on which doubts had been raised in correspondence by other solicitors so that the firm should have informed the client that there were doubts about counsel's advice.

[73] [1991] 1 F.L.R. 179 at 192, Booth J.

[74] Solicitors were similarly found liable to pay costs, despite relying on counsel, in *Locke v. Camberwell Health Authority* (1990) 140 N.L.J. 205; the decision was reversed by the Court of Appeal on further facts coming to light: [1991] 2 Med. L.R. 253.

[75] [1999] Lloyd's Rep. P.N. 798. For another illustration see *Bond v. Livingstone* [2001] P.N.L.R. 30, where solicitors considered that the limitation period for personal injuries under a contract was six years, when it was plainly three years pursuant to s. 11 of the Limitation Act 1980. The defence of relying on counsel failed as the defendants were personal injury solicitors and section 11 is a basic provision. The defence also failed in *Estill v. Cowling* [2000] Lloyd's Rep P.N. 378, where the solicitor should have given himself some general knowledge of inheritance tax, and thus been able to instruct counsel properly and spot that he had not advised on that issue. For the facts see chap. 11 para. 11–046.

solicitor could not absolve his responsibility by claiming to have relied on counsel.

10–120   **Illustrations: successful defence.** In contrast, in the following cases the defence of relying on counsel was successful.[76] In *Watson v. Watson*, one of the appeals in *Ridehalgh v. Horsefield*[77] solicitors acting for a wife in divorce proceedings rejected an eminently sensible suggestion to amend a consent order dealing with the devolution of property, but they were not negligent in so doing in part because they relied on matrimonial and trust counsel. In *Reaveley v. Safeway Stores plc*[78] solicitors failed to advise a plaintiff in personal injury litigation that he was highly likely to lose the £2,500 offered by the defendants as he would not obtain in damages more than the benefits recoverable by the Compensation Recovery Unit of £16,000. The solicitors relied on counsel properly instructed who credibly advised that the action should proceed, and the defendants' doubts about the plaintiff's special damages claim did not alter that conclusion.

10–121   **Further limits to the defence.** In any event, a solicitor may still be liable for breach of contract if he acts contrary to the client's instructions, since counsel's advice, however prudent, cannot override the client's express instructions.[79] The defence will not avail a solicitor who has failed properly to instruct counsel,[80] or who has instructed counsel where it should have been obvious that counsel was not competent,[81] nor will it avail a solicitor who goes to counsel on matters which are within the solicitor's own province.[82]

10–122   **The position of the client.** In the kind of case under discussion the position of the client was once unenviable: the solicitor was not liable because he had acted on counsel's advice and counsel had complete immunity on grounds of public interest. The client's position has now improved in both respects. The

---

[76] See also *R. v. A. (Wasted Costs Order)* [2000] P.N.L.R. 628, CA, where solicitors were entitled to rely on counsel in making a bail application alleging that custody time limits had expired, where an unreported case not referred to in any standard textbook made it clear that there were no such limits in the circumstances of the case. In *R. v. Horsham District Council* [1995] 1 W.L.R. 680 Brooke J. held that solicitors could rely on counsel experienced in judicial review proceedings

[77] [1994] Ch. 205 at 255–264. The decisions in *R. v. Oxfordshire County Council, ex parte Wallace* (1987) 137 N.L.J. 542 and *Manor Electronics v. Dickson, The Times,* February 8, 1990 are of limited assistance, as they were decided under the old Ord. 62 r. 11 wasted costs provisions, which required serious misconduct.

[78] [1998] P.N.L.R. 526, CA.

[79] *Fray v. Voules* (1859) 1 E. & E. 839. But the client cannot insist upon matters which are not within his province, such as the contents of pleadings; see para. 10–177.

[80] *Ireson v. Pearman* (1825) 3 B. & C. 799: failure to place all relevant documents before counsel; *Andrews v. Hawley* (1857) 26 L.J. Ex. 323; *Locke v. Camberwell Health Authority* (1990) 140 N.L.J. 205, Moreland J.; reversed on new facts coming to light by the Court of Appeal [1991] 2 Med L.R. 253, CA.

[81] *Re A (a Minor)* (1988) 10 Fam.L. 339; *The Times,* February 25, 1988, CA.

[82] *Godefroy v. Dalton* (1830) 6 Bing. 460 at 649: "We lay no stress upon the fact, that the attorney had consulted his counsel as to the sufficiency of the evidence; because, we think, his liability must depend upon the nature and description of the mistake or want of skill which has been shown; and he cannot shift from himself such responsibility by consulting another where the law would presume him to have the knowledge himself." (*Per* Tindal C.J.). See also *Cook v. S.* [1966] 1 W.L.R. 635, QBD, (discussed in chap. 11 para. 11–041) where counsel's erroneous advice exacerbated the consequences of solicitor's previous negligence. The solicitor was held liable for all the resulting loss.

defence of "reliance on counsel's advice" is now rather more limited. Furthermore, counsel no longer enjoys immunity from suit.[83]

(iv) *Acting on client's instructions*

Duty to obey client. The solicitor will be in breach of duty if he does not follow his client's instructions.[84] Indeed, it is in general[85] the client's privilege, if he so wishes, to mismanage his affairs. He is entitled to pursue litigation with little prospect of success,[86] to lend on insufficient security, or to enter an unwise bargain, if he so chooses. The solicitor has a duty to advise on the legal hazards of the transaction,[87] but no more: **10–123**

> "It was the duty of the solicitor to inform and advise, ensuring that the information and advice was understood by the client. It was not part of his duty of care to force his advice on the client."[88]

Relying on this dictum, in *Middleton v. Steeds Hudson*[89] Johnson J. held that the defendant solicitors were not negligent in their advice to the plaintiff with respect to the financial arrangements he proposed to make with his former wife. The defendants had advised that the arrangements were over-generous to the wife, and had discussed alternatives. The defendants had no duty to repeat the advice or ensure that the husband followed it. If the advice the solicitor gives is disregarded he must carry out the client's instructions or else determine the retainer if the circumstances justify him in doing so.[90]

Exceptions to rule. It is, therefore, a good defence to an action for negligence that the solicitor was acting on express instructions from the client.[91] The defence will fail, however, where the client's instructions were the result of inadequate advice by the solicitor.[92] Thus in *Morris v. Duke-Cohan & Co.*[93] solicitors were held liable for exchanging contracts on a purchase, despite express instructions from the clients, since the solicitors had failed to warn them of the risks. "A solicitor did not do his duty merely by reporting facts to clients and then seeking **10–124**

---

[83] See chap. 11 paras. 11–009 to 11–024.

[84] For an example of a solicitor being found to be negligent in failing to follow his client's instructions, see *Re Graham & Oldham (a Firm)* [2000] B.P.I.R. 354, McKinnon J.

[85] The position may be more complicated if there is an insurer is funding litigation; see *e.g. Groom v. Crocker* [1939] 2 All E.R. 397, CA. If there is a risk of undue influence from a third party who may benefit from a transaction, the solicitor may have to decline to act if his advice is not accepted: *Powell v. Powell* [1900] 1 Ch. 243, ChD.

[86] The client, and not the attorney, is the *dominus litis*": *per* Erle J. in *Fray v. Voules* (1859) 1 E. & E. 839, at 848. See further para. 10–179.

[87] As to which see para. 10–165.

[88] *Dutfield v. Gilbert H. Stephens and Sons* [1988] 18 Fam. Law 473, *per* Anthony Lincoln J.

[89] [1998] 1 F.L.R. 738.

[90] See, *e.g. Sutherland v. Public Trustee* [1980] 2 N.Z.L.R. 536 at 548, Sup. Ct.

[91] *Waine v. Kempster* (1859) 1 F. & F. 695: a solicitor, acting for the purchaser of a quantity of hay, omitted to make the usual enquiries, since the client stated that he had made the enquiries and the result was satisfactory; *Okafor v. Malcolm Slowe & Co.* (1968) 207 E.G. 345, QBD.: the client insisted on completing the purchase before the result of searches was received; *Duncan v. Cuelenaere* [1987] 2 W.W.R. 379, Saskatchewan QB: when a solicitor is given instructions about what has happened, he is entitled to rely on them.

[92] *e.g. Lee v. Dixon* (1863) 3 F. & F. 744: an attorney brought proceedings in the wrong court. The express instructions of the client was no defence, unless he had been properly advised of the consequences.

[93] (1975) 119 S.J. 826; *The Times*, November 22, 1975.

instructions" (*per* Caulfield J.). In the Irish case of *McMullen v. Farrell*[94] Barron J. stated:

"A solicitor cannot in my view fulfil his obligations to his client merely by carrying out what he is instructed to do. This is to ignore the essential element of any contract involving professional care or advice . . . In my view a solicitor when consulted has an obligation to consider not only what the client wishes him to do but also the legal implication of the facts which the client brings to his attention. If necessary, he must follow up these facts to ensure that he appreciates the real problem with which he is being asked to deal."

(e) *Solicitor's liability for costs*[95]

10–125   The courts have the power in certain circumstances to order a solicitor to pay to his client or to the litigant on the other side any costs which have been incurred by reason of the solicitor's misconduct. The exercise of this power may circumvent the need to bring a professional negligence action. The appropriate test, by reason of statutory amendment, is one of simple negligence.

10–126   **History.** Since at least the eighteenth century, the superior courts of record have exercised jurisdiction over the attorneys on the roll of that court. The nature of the jurisdiction was reviewed by the House of Lords in *Myers v. Elman*.[96] It is clear from all the speeches that something more serious was required than mere negligence. Lord Maugham required "a serious dereliction of duty",[97] Lord Atkin "gross negligence",[98] and Lord Wright considered that a "mere mistake or error of judgment is not generally sufficient, but a gross neglect or inaccuracy in a matter which it is a solicitor's duty to ascertain with accuracy may suffice."[99] While the inherent jurisdiction continues to exist after the statutory amendments discussed below, it is difficult to foresee many circumstances in which it will be used given the easier requirements of the new provisions.[1] An exception is the special rule that where a solicitor institutes proceedings on behalf of a company without authority, he will be ordered to pay the other side's costs even though he acted bona fide and without negligence.[2] Since 1960 there have existed parallel

---

[94] [1993] 1 I.R. 123 at 142–3.
[95] For a critical view of the jurisdiction, see H. Evans, "The wasted costs jurisdiction" (2001) 65 M.L.R. 51 and *ibid.*, *'Lawyers' Liabilities'* (2nd ed. 2002), chap. 7.
[96] [1940] A.C. 282. The inherent jurisdiction remains the basis for the wasted costs jurisdiction in much of the commonwealth, see: *Harley v. McDonald* [2001] 2 W.L.R. 1749 (P.C., a New Zealand appeal); *White Industries (QLD) Pty Ltd v. Flower & Hart (a firm)* (1999) 163 A.L.R. 744, Fed. Ct. Aust., Full Court, and *Knaggs v. JA Westaway & Sons* (1996) 40 N.S.W.L.R. 476, CA; *Young v. Young* [1993] 4 S.C.R. 3, Supreme Court of Canada; *Hunter v. Hunter* [2001] 4 W.W.R. 28, Manitoba CA.
[97] [1940] A.C. 282 at 292.
[98] *ibid.* at 304.
[99] *ibid.* at 319.
[1] See para. 10–129 below for an example.
[2] *Babury Ltd v. London Industrial P.L.C.* (1989) 139 N.L.J. 1596, QBD. However, the court may reduce the amount of costs payable where the defendants were in a position to know the status of the company, see *Padhiar v. Patel* [2001] Lloyd's Rep. P.N. 328, QBD. There is a further exception in relation to wasted costs orders against non-parties, see para. 10–128 below.

Rules of the Supreme Court which have regulated and modified the inherent jurisdiction, and which have been changed a number of times.[3]

The present rule. Section 4 of the Courts and Legal Services Act 1990, which **10–127** came into force on October 1, 1991, substituted for section 51 of the Supreme Court Act new provisions relating to costs which include the following:

'(6) In any proceedings mentioned in subsection (1),[4] the court may disallow or (as the case may be) order the legal or other representative concerned to meet, the whole of any wasted costs or such part of them as may be determined in accordance with rules of court.

(7) In subsection (6) 'wasted costs' means any costs incurred by a party—

as a result of any improper, unreasonable, or negligent act or omission on the part of any legal or other representative or any employee of such a representative; or

which, in the light of any such act or omission occurring after they were incurred, the court considers it is unreasonable to expect that party to pay."

Order 62 rule 11 of the Rules of the Supreme Court, which reflected this statutory provision, has now been replaced under the Civil Procedure Rules by CPR Part 48.7 and paragraphs 2.1–2.7 of the accompanying Practice Direction. There are similar provisions relating to the criminal courts.[5]

Parties. The Court of Appeal neither had under the old law nor has under the **10–128** new law any jurisdiction to order that the costs of solicitors' successful appeals against wasted costs order should be paid out of central funds, see *Steele Ford & Newton v. C.P.S.*[6] A wasted costs order cannot be made in favour of the Court, but only in favour of a party.[7] Furthermore, in *R v. Camden LBC, ex parte Martin*[8] Sedley J. held that a wasted costs order can only be made in favour of a party to the action, and thus cannot be made for the benefit of a local authority which chooses to appear at an ex parte application for leave to apply for judicial review. However, in *R. v. Immigration Appeal Tribunal, ex parte Gulbamer Gulsen*[9] Buxton J. concluded that although *ex parte Martin* was correct in relation to the statutory wasted costs jurisdiction, at common law a wasted costs order could be made in favour of a non-party, although he declined to do so in that instance.

Court of Appeal guidelines. In *Re a Barrister (Wasted Costs Order) (No. 1 of* **10–129** *1991)*[10] the Court of Appeal laid down six guidelines for use in criminal cases.

---

[3] For discussion of the old rules, see the third edition of this work at para. 4–81 and the supplements thereto, and for a detailed review of the law up to 1986, see the second edition of this book, paras. 4–59–4–63.

[4] That is, all proceedings in the civil division of the Court of Appeal, the High Court and any county court.

[5] The Courts and Legal Services Act 1990, ss. 111 and 112.

[6] *The Times*, May 28, 1993, HL.

[7] See *Lawrence & Co.* [1998] C.L.Y. 1016, CA.

[8] [1997] 1 W.L.R. 359.

[9] [1997] C.O.D. 430.

[10] [1993] Q.B. 293.

While the decision was made in the context of a wasted costs order against a barrister in relation to his actions in court, the guidelines apply to all legal representatives.[11] In the leading case of *Ridehalgh v. Horsefield*[12] the Court of Appeal gave detailed guidelines on wasted costs orders in civil litigation, which are summarised in the following paragraphs,[13] with illustrations of how the guidelines have been applied in subsequent cases. It is noteworthy that all the five appeals against wasted costs orders in *Ridehalgh* were successful, and the Court of Appeal did not make an order on the sixth case where the solicitors had been ordered to show cause why an order should not be made. The facts of five of the individual cases are summarised elsewhere.[14]

10–130 **The meaning of the tests.** The Court of Appeal in *Ridehalgh v. Horsefield*[15] considered the meaning of "improper", "unreasonable" and "negligent". "Improper" includes conduct that would be a serious breach of a substantial duty of professional conduct. "Unreasonable" describes conduct which is vexatious or designed to harass the other side; the acid test is whether the conduct permits of a reasonable explanation. "Negligence" should be understood in an untechnical way as failure to act with the competence reasonably to be expected of ordinary members of the profession.

10–131 **The position of the respondent lawyer.** The Court of Appeal in *Ridehalgh v. Horsefield*[16] stated that courts should bear in mind the peculiar vulnerability of legal representatives acting for the recipients of legal aid. Furthermore, the jurisdiction was not subject to the immunity of an advocate, which still existed at that time, although a court must make full allowance for the fact that an advocate in court has to make decisions quickly and under pressure. Where an applicant seeks a wasted costs order against the other side, full allowance has to be made for the respondent lawyers' inability to tell the whole story due to professional privilege.[17] The threat of proposed applications should not be used

---

[11] See further chap. 11 para. 11–027.
[12] [1994] Ch. 205.
[13] For the summary of where a solicitor can rely on counsel, see paras 10–116 to 10–122 above.
[14] See paras 10–082, 10–120, 10–137, 10–182 and chap. 11 para. 11–033.
[15] [1994] Ch. 205 at 232–233.
[16] [1994] Ch. 205 at 234G–237D.
[17] CPR Part 48.7(3) purportedly permits the court to direct that privileged documents may be disclosed. In *General Mediterranean Holdings v. Patel* [1999] 3 All E.R. 673 Toulson J. held that legal professional privilege was not a rule of evidence, but a fundamental principle of the substantive law, which could not be overridden save by express language or necessary implication, which he could not find in the Civil Procedure Act 1997. As a result, he struck out the new rule. For an illustration of the problems caused by privilege, see *Walter v. Neville Eckley* [1997] B.C.C. 331. The registrar made a wasted costs order despite the solicitors swearing that they had relied on Counsel's opinion, which was privileged. Sir Richard Scott V.-C. held that the registrar was wrong to make a costs order based on speculation that counsel's opinion would not have helped the solicitors. However, by the time of the appeal, privilege had been waived. The Judge held that the solicitors were entitled to rely on counsel's wrong opinions, but that further evidence had thereafter come to light which should have caused the solicitors to reconsider the decision to make a misconceived discovery application, and the wasted costs order was therefore affirmed on different grounds. In some cases the Court is able to come to a clear decision despite the absence of waiver of privilege by making assumptions in the lawyers' favour, see *e.g. B v. B (Wasted Costs: Abuse of Process)* [2000] 1 F.L.R. 843, discussed at chap. 11 para. 11–031.

as a means of intimidation, although it may not be objectionable to alert the other side to the possibility.[18]

Procedure. The Court of Appeal in *Ridehalgh v. Horsefield*[19] gave guidance   **10–132** on the practice and procedure to be adopted in wasted costs application. First, in the ordinary way, applications for wasted costs orders are best left until after the end of the trial.[20] Secondly, save in obvious cases, the court should be slow to initiate an enquiry as to whether a wasted costs order should be made, and should leave it to the aggrieved party.[21] Thirdly, any procedure should be fair, simple, and summary. The court must be astute to control what could become a new and costly form of satellite litigation.[22] Fourthly, legal representatives should be given an opportunity to show why an order should not be made, but only when an apparently strong prima facie case had been made against them.[23] Fifthly, the

---

[18] The court agreed at 237–238 with the disapproval of threats expressed in *Orchard v. South Eastern Electricity Board* [1987] Q.B. 565, CA. In *Sushma Lal v. Secretary of State for the Home Department* [1992] Imm. A.R. 303, the Court of Appeal distinguished *Orchard*. In an immigration case, the solicitor had failed to make full disclosure on an ex parte application for leave to move for judicial review. It was held that in the circumstances it was not improper for the Treasury Solicitor to indicate that an application would be made for the solicitor to pay the costs personally if the proceedings were pursued.

[19] [1994] Ch. 205 at 238–239.

[20] The court approved of the views of Aldous J. in *Flimlab Systems International Ltd v. Pennington* [1995] 1 W.L.R. 673. For an exceptional case where it was justified hearing the wasted costs application before the conclusion of the main action, see *B v. B (Wasted Costs: Abuse of Process)* [20001] 1 F.L.R. 843, summarised at chap. 11 para. 11–031. An application should be made timeously, or it may be refused: *Clark v. Clark (No. 2)* [1991] 1 F.L.R. 179 at 194, Booth J.

[21] In such a case the guidance of *R. v. Knutsford Crown Court, ex p. Middleweek, The Times*, March 23, 1992 is helpful. The Divisional Court stated that judges should seek the assistance of counsel upon their powers, and it was advisable to consider such matters and whether it was necessary to make an order at all. For an example of a judge-initiated wasted costs order see *Re G (Minors) (Care Proceedings: Wasted Costs)* [2000] Q.B. 104, summarised at chap. 11 para. 11–035.

[22] The effect of the summary nature of the wasted costs jurisdiction and the costs of an application have been considered in a number of cases. In *Re Freudiana Holdings Limited, The Times*, December 4, 1995 the Court of Appeal held that allegations involving full scale relitigation of the issues in the original trial and which involved dishonesty should not proceed. In *Manzanilla Ltd v. Corton Property and Investments Ltd* [1997] 3 F.C.R. 389 the Court of Appeal held that the jurisdiction was inappropriate where there needed to be a detailed investigation of the facts or dishonesty was alleged, as such matters were not capable of summary determination. In *Turner Page Music v. Torres Design Associates Ltd, The Times*, August 7, 1998, the Court of Appeal held that a wasted costs application was inappropriate if it would result in complex proceedings involving detailed investigations of fact. In *Wall v. Lefever* [1998] 1 F.C.R. 605 the Court of Appeal held that the wasted costs jurisdiction should not be used to generate substantial additional costs in satellite litigation which was as expensive and complex as the original litigation. In *Royal Institution of Chartered Surveyors v. Wiseman Marshall* [2000] P.N.L.R. 649 the Court of Appeal stated that it would rarely be appropriate to grant an adjournment to investigate whether the client was willing to waive privilege, as that would create complexity and delay. In the context of the inherent jurisdiction which exists in New Zealand, the Privy Council opined that allegations should be confined strictly to questions which are apt for summary disposal by the Court, see *Harley v. McDonald* [2001] 2 W.L.R. 1749; see further chap. 11, para. 11–029. For a further example of a case where more time was spent on the wasted costs hearing than the substantive proceedings, see *Re Merc Property Ltd, The Times*, May 19, 1999, ChD.; and for a case where the likely costs of the wasted costs hearing was disproportionate and was therefore not pursued see *Chief Constable of North Yorkshire v. Audsley* [2000] Lloyd's Rep. P.N. 675.

[23] In *Livingstone v. Frasso* [1997] C.L.Y. 604 a wasted costs order was quashed by the Court of Appeal when the solicitors were not given an opportunity to show why the order should not be made. In *Re Wiseman Lee (Solicitors) (Wasted Costs Order) (No. 5 of 2000), The Times*, April 5, 2001, the Court of Appeal quashed a wasted costs order where the solicitors were given an opportunity to make representations by a certain date but failed to do so, as the procedure did not comply with natural justice or the Costs in Criminal Cases (General) Regulations S.I. 1986 No 1335. In a straightforward

court had a discretion as to whether the legal representative should show cause, which should not be automatic, and the costs of the enquiry compared with the costs claimed will be relevant. The court also has a discretion at the final stage of the enquiry whether to make an order.[24]

10–133   Cases since *Ridehalgh* have given further guidance on the procedure to be adopted.[25] The amount of wasted costs must be specified in the order, and the order cannot later be amended by adding a figure at a later date, see *Re Harry Jagdev & Co.*[26] In cases concerning children where an order for costs is sought against the Legal Aid Board or under the wasted costs jurisdiction, the procedure to be adopted is set out in *Re O (Costs: Liability of Legal Aid Board)*[27]: in general the applications should be drawn to the Legal Aid Board's attention. Where the Legal Aid Board or Community Legal Services Commission will be the beneficiary of the wasted costs order, it is also desirable to refer to them before making an application.[28] An appeal lies without leave.[29] It should be noted that it is permissible to compromise a wasted costs application. In *Manzanilla Ltd v. Corton Property and Investments Ltd*[30] the Court of Appeal approved the practice of placing a succinct written statement before the court following settlement. This would deal with matters relevant to the reputations of the lawyers involved, which, as a result of the settlement, would not otherwise have been brought to the court's attention.

10–134   **Causation.**[31] The Court of Appeal in *Ridehalgh v. Horsefield*[32] stated that it was essential to demonstrate a causal link between the improper, unreasonable or

---

case with limited costs involved, there may not need to be a full investigation: see *Woolwich Building Society v. Fineberg* [1998] P.N.L.R. 216. It may not be necessary to have two separate hearings to establish a prima facie case and to show case where the former can be determined at the hearing of the application about which complaint is made, see *B v. B (Wasted costs: abuse of process)* [2001] 1 F.L.R. 843, Wall J. *Quaere* whether the party seeking the costs should open at the hearing, as was suggested under the previous rules in *Bahai v. Rashidian (No. 2), The Times*, June 11, 1986, Drake J.

[24] In *R v. Secretary of State for the Home Office, ex p. Wong* [1995] C.O.D. 331 the solicitor for an applicant for judicial review did not come off the record when legal aid was withdrawn and let the application go to sleep. That had caused wasted costs, as the Treasury Solicitor would otherwise have conceded the application much earlier. However, the solicitor was not made to pay the wasted costs, because if the solicitor had gone off the record, the point on which the case turned may never have come to light, and an injustice would have been done.

[25] An application should normally be determined by the trial judge: *Bahai v. Rashidian* [1985] 1 W.L.R. 1337, CA; *Re Freudiana Holdings Ltd The Times*, December 4, 1995, CA.

[26] *The Times*, August 12, 1999, CA.

[27] [1997] 1 F.L.R. 465, CA.

[28] See *Tate v. Hart* [1999] P.N.L.R. 787.

[29] *Thompson v. Fraser, The Times,* October 4, 1985, CA. While there is a right of appeal against an order made in a wasted costs application, it should be exercised with great care where the judge at first instance had heard the evidence and seen the witnesses, see *Wall v. Lefever* [1998] 1 F.C.R. 605, CA. Appeals against decisions as to whether there was a prima facie case will be even rarer, see *Royal Institution of Chartered Surveyors v. Wiseman Marshall* [2000] P.N.L.R. 649, CA.

[30] [1997] 3 F.C.R. 389.

[31] There may be a tension between the relevant statute and the practice direction as to costs incurred before the misconduct, such as a case of inordinate delay, on which see Simpson, *Professional Negligence and Liability*, para. 9.428. *Quaere* whether causation could be established in such cases. Costs for a period of delay of four years were awarded under the wasted costs jurisdiction in *Padhiar v. Patel* [2001] Lloyd's Rep. P.N. 328, QBD.

[32] [1994] Ch. 205 at 237E–F.

negligent conduct and the wasted costs.[33] The importance of demonstrating a causal link is shown by *Kilroy v. Kilroy*,[34] where the Court of Appeal allowed an appeal against a wasted costs order as the judge had not identified the conduct of the solicitors which was improper, unreasonable or negligent, and he had failed to identify the costs wasted by the conduct, although a detailed enquiry was not required. In that case, there had been great delay in the litigation, but it was clear that much of the costs would have been incurred in any event.

Hopeless litigation.[35] The Court of Appeal in *Ridehalgh v. Horsefield*[36] stated **10–135** that a legal representative has not acted improperly, unreasonably or negligently merely because he acted for a party who pursued a claim or defence which was plainly doomed to fail. However, he should not lend his assistance to proceedings which are an abuse of process.[37] A number of cases have concerned the bringing of hopeless proceedings or applications. In *Re a Company (No. 006798 of 1995)*[38] Chadwick J. held that a solicitor who swore an affidavit in support of a winding-up petition asserting a belief that the company was insolvent acted improperly if he did not hold that belief and unreasonably if there were no grounds upon which a competent solicitor could have reached that view. On the facts, the solicitor acted unreasonably as the amount owed was based on adjustments to an account made by the petitioner unilaterally and of which the company had no knowledge, and he was ordered to pay the wasted costs incurred by the company. In *Tolstoy-Miloslavsky v. Aldington*[39] the plaintiff, a bankrupt, sought to set aside a libel judgment obtained by the defendant, on the grounds of fraud. The original libel was that the defendant was a major war criminal who had arranged the massacre of 70,000 people. The plaintiff relied on new evidence which purported to show that the defendant had lied at trial about the date he left Austria in May 1945. The new action was struck out as an abuse of process, as the new evidence could not show that the defendant had committed perjury, the date of departure had never been a crucial issue, the new evidence was not

---

[33] See also *R. v. M. (Wasted Costs Order)* [2000] P.N.L.R. 2, where solicitors issued a witness summons in unfortunately wide terms. The Court of Appeal held that no costs had been wasted, as a hearing would have been necessary at some stage, and the judge in fact dealt with the substance of the matter at the hearing of the defective summons in any event. The amount of wasted costs must be specified in the order, and the order cannot later be amended by adding a figure at a later date, see *Re Harry Jagdev & Co, The Times*, August 12, 1999, CA.

[34] [1997] P.N.L.R. 67.

[35] See also the cases discussed at chap. 11 paras 11–029 to 11–032. For another example see *Da Sousa v. Minister of State for Immigration, Local Government and Ethnic Affairs* (1993) 114 A.L.R. 708, Federal Court of Australia, where a wasted costs order was made against solicitors who pursued a misconceived application for judicial review of a decision refusing entry permits for which the applicant could not possibly have qualified; the solicitors failed to give reasonable attention to the relevant law and facts, and exposed their clients to possible prejudice by being excluded from applying for an entry permit in some other category.

[36] [1994] Ch. 205 at 233F–234F.

[37] See the similar comments by Sir John Donaldson M.R. in the context of the previous wasted costs jurisdiction in *Orchard v. South Eastern Electricity Board* [1987] Q.B. 565 at 572 that it is not for lawyers to impose a pre-trial screen through which a litigant must pass before he can put his case to the court.

[38] [1996] 1 W.L.R. 491. Similarly, in *Re a Company (No. 0022 of 1993)* [1993] B.C.C. 726, Knox J. held solicitors liable for wasted costs after they should have realised that an attempt to wind up a company was inappropriate because it was clear that the debt was disputed.

[39] [1996] 1 W.L.R. 736. Similarly, in *DCT v. Levick* (2000) 168 A.L.R. 383 the Federal Court of Australia made a wasted costs order against laywers who advanced a case which was so hopeless that it had no real chance of success.

decisive even on that issue, and it had been available at the date of trial. The Court of Appeal made a wasted costs order against the solicitors as they held that it was unreasonable to commence an "utterly hopeless" case on the facts, which was also an abuse of process as being a collateral attack on the previous decision, when they were acting without fee,[40] given the other aggravating circumstances of that case which included the fact that the plaintiff had never paid any of the damages or costs in the original action. Solicitors have also been ordered to pay costs as a result of their unreasonableness in rejecting a *Calderbank* offer.[41]

10–136   However, solicitors were not liable for pursuing an action which proved wrong but was not manifestly inappropriate in *Re O (a minor) (Wasted Costs Application)*.[42] Nor were solicitors held liable in *R. v. Westminster LBC, ex parte Geehan & Butler*,[43] where on careful analysis the application was probably not even arguable, but the solicitors had been forced to act very quickly as their clients had spent the night before the application sleeping rough. Nor were solicitors negligent in *Reaveley v. Safeway Stores plc*[44] for pursuing an action when they failed to advise a plaintiff that he was highly likely to lose the £2,500 offered by the defendants, as he would not obtain in damages more than the benefits recoverable by the Compensation Recovery Unit of £16,000. The solicitors relied on counsel properly instructed who credibly advised that the action should proceed.

10–137   **Abuse of process.** Solicitors have also been ordered to pay wasted costs where the proceedings or application were for an improper purpose, an issue which is often closely allied to whether proceedings were hopeless. In *Flower & Hart (a Firm) v. White Industries (Qld) Pty Ltd*[45] a solicitor was ordered to pay wasted costs when his purpose in instituting proceedings was to gain a temporary bargaining position for his client and not to vindicate his client's rights, regardless of whether the cause of action was arguable or not. Similarly, in *Woolwich Building Society v. Fineberg*[46] the improper use of a hopeless appeal to play for time in resisting the execution of a warrant for possession justified a wasted costs order. In *R. v. Basra (Wasted Costs Order)*[47] the Court of Appeal upheld a wasted costs order made against solicitors in a criminal case who had issued a witness

---

[40] In the pre–*Ridehalgh* case of *Mainwaring v. Goldtech Investments Ltd, The Times*, February 19, 1991, it was accepted by the Court of Appeal that a wasted costs order could be made if solicitors conducted litigation in the knowledge that there was no real likelihood of their ever having their costs and expenses reimbursed by their client, although on the facts of the case no order was made. For further details of the case see the comment by S. Fennell at [1991] 7 P.N. 199. However, in *Hodgson v. Imperial Tobacco Ltd* [1998] 1 W.L.R. 1056 the Court of Appeal held that a legal adviser acting under a conditional fee agreement permitted under s. 58 of the Courts and Legal Services Act 1990 was no more at risk of being made personally liable for costs than if he did not act under such an agreement.
[41] *C v. C (Wasted Costs Order)* [1994] 2 F.L.R. 34, Ewbank J. Some of the blame, and thus some of the costs, were shared by their former clients.
[42] [1994] 2 F.L.R. 842 Connell J.
[43] [1995] C.O.D. 204, Dyson J.
[44] [1998] P.N.L.R. 526, CA. Similarly, in *R. v. A. (Wasted Costs Order)* [2000] P.N.L.R. 628, CA, no order was made against solicitors who pursued an application for release from custody in ignorance of an unreported case which showed that the application was hopeless and in reliance on the advice of counsel.
[45] (1999) 163 A.L.R. 744, Fed. Ct Aust., Full Court.
[46] [1998] P.N.L.R. 216, Peter Gibson L.J. refusing leave to appeal.
[47] [1998] P.N.L.R. 535 See also *Re a Solicitor (Wasted Costs Order)* [1996] 1 F.L.R. 40, CA, where a solicitor had to pay the wasted costs for issuing a witness summons for disclosure of documents in a criminal matter which was wholly speculative.

summons for the improper purpose of obtaining discovery or to obtain material for cross-examination.

Difficulties with public funding.[48] In *Roberts v. Coverite*[49] no wasted costs   **10–138**
order was made against solicitors acting for plaintiffs in litigation who sent notices of issue of legal aid to the court to pass on to the defendants. The defendants did not receive the notices, and as a result the case was not settled timeously and cheaply. It was not negligent to fail to notice that a sealed copy had not been returned as requested, or to rely on the court to pass on the notice. Compare *Re Stathams (Wasted Costs Order)*[50] where the Court of Appeal upheld a wasted costs order against solicitors who failed to inform the other side that their client's legal aid had been withdrawn. They had acted negligently and unreasonably, and caused the defendants to waste costs by attending a hearing of an application for an adjournment of the plaintiff's appeal. But in *Tate v. Hart*[51] the Court of Appeal held that there was no obligation to inform the other side of the discharge of the client's legal aid when the withdrawal was the subject of an appeal. The statutory code did not require notification in such circumstances, and the Court would be slow to add to a detailed statutory code of conduct.

Misuse of procedure. Procedural errors may often lead to wasted costs. In *R.*   **10–139**
v. M (Wasted Costs Order)[52] no wasted costs order was made against solicitors who applied for unjustifiably wide disclosure of documents in a rape case, because the practice of seeking only more restricted classes of documents was recent. Similarly, in *Warren v. Warren*[53] solicitors issued a summons to compel a district judge to give evidence about the terms of a disputed undertaking. The Court of Appeal determined that although the law had been undecided as to whether the district judge was compellable, in fact he was not. However, the solicitors could not be criticised for not appreciating that the judge was not compellable, it was not unreasonable to seek his attendance as he was in a position to give the best evidence about the terms of the undertaking, and in view also of the disproportionate conduct of both sides no wasted costs order was made. In *Neill v. Crown Prosecution Service*[54] the Divisional Court considered that it was not improper for a solicitor to proceed with an old-style committal in an indecent assault case where the client had told him that the complainant had said that the prosecution may not go ahead, and where the solicitor had agreed that oral evidence was not necessary in the committal when the complainant appeared to give evidence. In contrast, in three cases, wasted costs orders were made. In *Kleinwort Benson v. Montenegro*[55] solicitors had to pay the wasted costs personally when they failed to disclose to the Court in an application for a Mareva injunction that their client was in fact bankrupt. In *Veasey v. Millfeed Co.*

---

[48] In *Trill v. Sacher, The Times,* November 14, 1992, the Court of Appeal made no wasted costs order where the delay which wasted costs was caused by the slow action of the legal aid authorities and the delay in obtaining counsel's opinion.
[49] The third of the appeals in *Ridehalgh v. Horsefield* [1994] Ch. 205 at 247–250.
[50] [1997] P.I.Q.R. 494.
[51] [1999] P.N.L.R. 787.
[52] [1996] 1 F.L.R. 751, Scott Baker J.
[53] [1997] Q.B. 488.
[54] [1997] C.O.D. 171.
[55] [1994] N.P.C. 46.

Ltd[56] the solicitor knew that the plaintiff was no longer in partnership, but served proceedings in the name of the partnership and failed to correct the error. He was found to be guilty of incompetence, and ordered to pay the costs of unnecessary striking out proceedings which were brought on account of the misnomer. In *R. v. Liverpool City Council, ex parte May*[57] Laws J. made a wasted costs order against solicitors who issued proceedings to commit for breach of an undertaking without warning, where the breach was at most technical and did not justify the draconian steps proposed.

10–140   **Other errors.** The Court of Appeal considered the defendant solicitors to have acted negligently and unreasonably in *Shah v. Singh*.[58] The solicitors successfully applied immediately before trial of an action to come off the record as their bills had not been paid, but the plaintiffs were not granted an adjournment of the trial. The solicitor concerned failed to impress upon the clerk who attended at court that the plaintiffs had just received legal aid, which would have led to an adjournment.[59] In *R. v. Secretary of State for the Home Department, ex parte Mahmood*[60] Richards J. made a wasted costs order against a solicitor who instructed a barrister for a hearing who had a known court commitment in the afternoon, when there was an obvious risk that their case might not be heard in the morning. In *R. v. Qadi*[61] the Court of Appeal upheld a wasted costs order made against a solicitor's clerk who took instructions from his client in a corridor where he knew the jury were likely to pass, as a result of which the jury overheard the conversation and a re-trial was ordered. In *R v. Liverpool City Council, ex parte Horn*[62] Buxton J. made a wasted costs order when the solicitor had concealed the fraudulent conduct of his client.

(f) *Exclusion or restriction of liability by contract*[63]

10–141   In a contentious business agreement, any provision exempting the solicitor from liability for negligence or breach of duty is void.[64] In the Law Society Council Statement *Limitation of liability by contract*[65] it was considered accept-

---

[56] [1997] P.N.L.R. 100. The court assumed without deciding that causation should be judged on the balance of probabilities, see para. 10–260.
[57] [1994] C.O.D. 144.
[58] [1996] 1 P.N.L.R. 83.
[59] cf. *Re A Solicitor (Wasted Costs Order)* [1993] 2 F.L.R. 959. No order was made by the Court of Appeal for a solicitor's error of judgment in failing to warn the court or his opponent that he might have to seek at a late stage an adjournment of a hearing because of difficulties with the Legal Aid Board.
[60] [1999] C.O.D. 119.
[61] [2000] P.N.L.R. 137.
[62] [1997] P.N.L.R. 95.
[63] The general principles of whether liability can be excluded or restricted are discussed in chap. 5, paras 5–001 to 5–009.
[64] Solicitors Act 1974, s. 60(5). "Contentious business agreement" is defined in s. 59(1). See also *Chamberlain v. Boodle & King* [1982] 1 W.L.R. 1443.
[65] Published in the *Law Society Gazette* on May 27, 1987. The revised version is substantially reproduced in the Law Society's *Guide to the Professional Conduct of Solicitors* (8th ed. 1999), para. 12.11.

able to restrict liability to not below the minimum level of insurance cover of £1,000,000 per firm per claim. The Council recognised that this is subject to the general law, in particular the Unfair Contract Terms Act 1977. Any such restriction must be brought to the attention of the client and accepted by him, preferably in writing.

(g) *Practice and procedure*[66]

(i) *Expert evidence*

In ascertaining the general practice or practices of the profession, the court will, of course, have regard to the evidence of solicitors who are called as witnesses by one or other party. However, in *Midland Bank v. Hett, Stubbs & Kemp*,[67] Oliver J. criticised the practice of calling solicitors to give evidence as to what they would have done in a particular situation:

10–142

> "I must say that I doubt the value, or even the admissibility, of this sort of evidence, which seems to be becoming customary in cases of this type. The extent of the legal duty in any given situation must, I think, be a question of law for the court. Clearly, if there is some practice in a particular profession, some accepted standard of conduct which is laid down by a professional institute or sanctioned by common usage, evidence of that can and ought to be received. But evidence which really amounts to no more than an expression of opinion by a particular practitioner of what he thinks that he would have done had he been placed, hypothetically and without the benefit of hindsight, in the position of the defendants, is of little assistance to the court; whilst evidence of the witnesses' view of what, as a matter of law, the solicitor's duty was in the particular circumstances of the case is, I should have thought, inadmissible, for that is the very question which it is the court's function to decide."[68]

This dictum was approved by the Court of Appeal in *Bown v. Gould & Swayne*,[69] where the Court rejected an application to allow a conveyancing expert. Millett L.J. commented that if a judge needed assistance with regard to conveyancing practice, the proper way was to cite the relevant textbooks. In *May v. Woollcombe*

---

[66] This section is not a complete or comprehensive account of practice and procedure relating to solicitor's negligence cases, but merely highlights two important issues that sometimes arise.

[67] [1979] Ch. 384.

[68] *ibid.* at 402B–D. See also the very similar view of Lord Denning M.R. in *Carradine Properties Limited v. D.J. Freeman and Co.* [1999] Lloyd's Rep. P.N. 483 at 486 col. 2. It is submitted that a wider view might be taken of the function of a solicitor as expert witness. Whilst, of course, the extent of the solicitor's duty is ultimately a question for the court, surely this is a mixed question of fact and law. Even if there is no directly relevant "practice of the profession", the evidence of other practitioners as to what they do in similar cases (and why) is likely to be of benefit to the court. A knowledge of the working of a solicitor's office, particularly of those departments handling non-contentious business, cannot be automatically imputed to the judge (or to counsel). In any event, experts are often called to give their view of what should have been done, *e.g.* the views of two Queen's Counsel were considered as to whether a fellow barrister had emphasised an important point with sufficient urgency in *Mathew v. Maughold Life Assurance Co. Ltd* (1987) 3 P.N. 98 at 104, CA. Furthermore, in medical negligence cases it is not uncommon for an expert witness to give evidence of what he would have done in the particular situation under consideration: see chap. 12 paras 12–111 to 12–116.

[69] [1996] 1 P.N.L.R. 130.

Beer & Watts,[70] H.H. Judge Raymond Jack Q.C., sitting in the Bristol Mercantile Court, held that expert evidence was admissible in relation to conveyancing matters where there was no answer provided by textbooks. Under the Civil Procedure Rules no party may call an expert without the court's permission, see CPR rule 35.4.[71] If permission has been given to call an expert, objection may be made to its admissibility, but this should be done so as soon as possible, and if there is real doubt as to whether the evidence should be admitted it should be allowed.[72]

10–143   **Practice abroad.** In Ireland the practice is similar to England.[73] In the Australian case of *Permanent Trustee Australia Ltd v. Boulton*[74] Young J. considered that expert evidence was permitted as to "industry-wide" good practice and what was common amongst solicitor of good repute, and how long it would take ordinary competent solicitors to complete transactions, but not as to the expert's view of negligence, or what that witness would have done, or the time for reasonable notice. However, in Canada, expert evidence is frequently called in circumstances where it would not be permitted in England,[75] although some courts have restricted its use.[76]

(ii) *Privilege*

10–144   **Waiver of privilege.** Privilege and its waiver can raise some difficult issues in solicitor's negligence cases, which have been explored in three decisions of the Court of Appeal. In *Lillicrap v. Nalder*[77] the defendant solicitors acted for the plaintiff property developers, and admitted negligence for failing to advise their clients on rights of way in a transaction. The solicitors denied causation, and attempted to amend their defence to plead previous retainers in which their advice had been ignored by the plaintiff. The plaintiff claimed that such matters were privileged, although it was accepted that there was an implied waiver of

---

[70] [1999] P.N.L.R. 283 Similarly, in *Archer v. Hickmotts* [1997] P.N.L.R. 318, H.H. Judge Brunning in the Nottingham County Court admitted expert evidence concerning the advice which should have been given in relation to a mortgage to secure a loan which the client was taking to assist her brother setting up his solicitor's practice, as the court had no familiarity with the matters in question and there were no textbooks which could assist. His judgment at the end of the trial was reversed by the Court of Appeal who made no mention of expert evidence, see *Northern Rock Building Society v. Archer* (1998) 78 P.& C.R. 65.
[71] The position used to be more complicated. Where it was disputed whether expert evidence was admissible, the master or judge in chambers was not entitled to rule on the admissibility of such evidence, see *Sullivan v. West Yorkshire Passenger Transport Executive* [1985] 2 All E.R. 134, CA. However, in *Woodford & Ackroyd v. Burgess* [1999] Lloyd's Rep. P.N. 231 the Court of Appeal held that a judge who was not the trial judge could rule on admissibility under the inherent jurisdiction. Further, the Court of Appeal in *Bown* held that a judge on a pre-trial review was entitled to make such a ruling.
[72] See *Liverpool Roman Catholic Archdiocese Trustees Incorporated v. Goldberg (No. 2)* [2001] Lloyd's Rep. P.N. 518, Neuberger J.
[73] *McMullen v. Caren Farrell* [1993] I.R.L.R. 123 at 141, Barron J.
[74] [1994] 33 N.S.W.L.R. 735.
[75] See *e.g. Central Trust Co. v. Rafuse* (1987) 31 D.L.R. (4th) 481 and *Roberge v. Bolduc* [1991] 1 S.C.R. 374, both Supreme Court of Canada.
[76] See *e.g. Clarke v. Poje and Kenney* (1989) 38 B.C.L.R. (2d) 110, at 117, British Columbia CA: in the absence of a standard practice within the profession, expert evidence is not admissible; *Deyong v. Weeks* (1984) 33 Alta. L.R. (2d) 338, Alta. CA: expert evidence allowed on the standard of competence to be expected, but not as to what he would have done, and such evidence was of little value in an unusual transaction.
[77] [1993] 1 W.L.R. 94.

privilege in relation to the transaction in question by the plaintiff suing the solicitors. The Court of Appeal held that the waiver extended to matters which were relevant to an issue in the proceedings,[78] which included the previous retainers, and they allowed the amendments. In *Muller v. Linsley*[79] the plaintiff sued the defendant solicitors for negligence in the transfer of his shares which had resulted in litigation with other shareholders which was settled. The reasonableness of the settlement was in issue, and the Court of Appeal held that there should be discovery of without prejudice negotiations leading up to the settlement. The court held that the correspondence was not privileged as the public policy rule only applied to admissions. A majority also held that any privilege was waived in relation to all matters relevant to the issues raised by the plaintiffs in the action.[80] However, in *Paragon Finance plc v. Freshfields*[81] the Court of Appeal held that the implied waiver extended to the solicitor-client relationship, and not to communications to which the solicitor was not privy. Thus the plaintiff was not obliged to disclose communications with different solicitors whom they later instructed to pursue and settle a claim against a third party arising from the transactions over which the defendant solicitors were being sued.

Two clients. Where a solicitor has acted for two clients, such as a borrower **10–145** and lender on a mortgage transaction, the lender will not be entitled to see privileged communications between the solicitor and the borrower, unless the solicitor's advice and assistance is employed in the furtherance of an iniquity.[82] The solicitors should consult their client with regard to an application for disclosure of privileged documents.[83] On the obligations of lenders to provide discovery in relation to contributory negligence, see *Portman Building Society v. Royal Insurance plc*.[84] As to the extent of waiver of privilege between insured and insured, see *TSB Bank plc v. Robert Irving & Burns*,[85] where it was held by the Court of Appeal that privilege was waived up until the emergence of an actual rather than possible conflict of interest, and the notification by the solicitors to the

---

[78] In *Paragon Finance plc v. Freshfields* [1999] Lloyd's Rep. P.N. 446 the Court of Appeal made clear that the decision did not go further than holding that the implied waiver extended to earlier trantactions handled by the solicitors.

[79] [1996] 1 P.N.L.R. 74.

[80] In *Paragon Finance plc v. Freshfields* [1999] Lloyd's Rep. P.N. 446 at 447 col. 2 the Court of Appeal stated that the case concerned "without prejudice" privilege, and the Court derived no statement of principle relevant to the case from the views which were expressed on waiver.

[81] [1999] Lloyd's Rep. P.N. 446. The Court overruled *Kershaw v. Whelan* [1996] 1 W.L.R. 358, where it had been held that the implied waiver of privilege extended to advice received from other solicitors, and not just the defendants, which was material to the issues in the proceedings. The Court also overrulled *Hayes v. Dowding* [1996] 1 W.L.R. 578.

[82] *Abbey National plc v. Clive Travers & Co.* [1999] P.N.L.R. 819, CA, following *Nationwide Building Society v. Various Solicitors* [1999] P.N.L.R. 52, Blackburne J., and to similar effect *Birmingham Midshires Mortgage Services Ltd v. Ansell* [1998] P.N.L.R. 237, ChD, *Abbey National PLC v. David Prosser & Co. (a Firm)* [2001] P.N.L.R. 15, ChD. (where it was held that the fraud did not need to be pleaded), and *Darlington Building Society v. O'Rourke James Scourfield & McCarthy* [1999] P.N.L.R 365, CA, discussed further at para. 10–217 below. As to what is confidential, see para. 10–217, and *Nationwide Building Society v. Various Solicitors* [1999] P.N.L.R. 52.

[83] *Abbey National plc v. Clive Travers & Co.* [1999] P.N.L.R. 819.

[84] [1998] P.N.L.R. 672, CA.

[85] [2000] P.N.L.R. 384. See also *Brown v. Guardian Royal Exchange Assurance plc* [1994] 2 Lloyd's Rep. 325.

insured of the conflict, with sufficient time for the insured to decide whether to instruct separate solicitors.[86]

2. LIABILITY FOR BREACH OF DUTY

(a) *General*

10–146   **Vicarious responsibility for breaches.** A firm of solicitors is liable not only for breaches of duty committed by its own staff,[87] but probably also for breaches committed by other solicitors acting as their agents within the scope of their authority.[88] Similarly if a solicitor entrusts his practice to a locum while he is away from the office for any reason, he will be liable for any breaches which the locum may commit. A solicitor will not, however, be liable for the defaults of a foreign lawyer he has instructed, who was an independent expert in the same way as an expert witness or counsel would be.[89]

10–147   A solicitor's partners are vicariously liable for his wrongful acts or omissions acting in the ordinary course of businss of the firm or with the authority of his co-partners, see section 10 of the Partnership Act 1890.[90] In *Re Bell's Indenture*[91] Vinelott J. held that a solicitor had implied authority in the ordinary course of business to accept trust moneys, but not to accept office as a trustee. In *Dubai Aluminium Company Ltd v. Salaam*[92] the Court of Appeal held that "wrongful acts" in section 10 included equitable wrongs such as dishonest assistance in a breach of trust, as well as tortious liability. However, the partners were not liable as no one dealing with the wrongdoer could have thought that he acted with ostensible authority of the partnership in the alleged wrongful administration and planning of a fraudulent scheme. Furthermore, the Court of Appeal decided in *Walker v. Stones*[93] that breaches of trust committed by a solicitor trustee fell outside the ordinary business of a partnership and could not give rise to vicarious liability under section 10. Similarly, under section 11 of the Partnership Act 1890

---

[86] For a detailed treatment of disclosure and privilege, see chap. 12 of Flenley and Leech's *Solicitor's Negligence* (Butterworths, 1999).

[87] e.g. *Floyd v. Nangle* (1747) 3 Atk. 568; *Creech v. Mayorcas* (1966) 198 E.G. 1091, ChD.; *Heywood v. Wellers* [1976] Q.B. 446, CA. The ostensible authority of both a partner and an employed solicitor was considered in a number of cases and in particular *United Bank of Kuwait Ltd v. Hammoud* [1988] 1 W.L.R. 1051, CA, see further para. 10–66. The vicarious responsibility extends to the fraud of a managing clerk, see *Uxbridge Permanent Benefit Building Society v. Pickard* [1939] 2 K.B. 248.

[88] *Re Ward, Simmons v. Rose, Weeks v. Ward* (1862) 31 Beav. 1: solicitor held liable for negligent representations made by London agent.

[89] *Gregory v. Shepherds* [2000] P.N.L.R. 769, CA. The solicitors were found liable on other grounds, see para. 10–200 for the facts.

[90] See also ss. 5, 9 and 11. It may be possible for the firm to obtain their excess from the defaulting partner who is in breach of a term to take reasonable care, see *Ross Harper & Murphy v. Scott Banks* [2000] P.N.L.R. 631, Outer House of the Court of Sessions. The same probably applies in England and Wales, although nineteenth century cases suggest the need to establish gross negligence.

[91] [1980] 1 W.L.R. 1217. In *Polkinghorne v. Holland* (1934) 51 C.L.R. 143, the High Court of Australia held that advice on investments was in the ordinary course of a solicitor's business, so that the innocent partners were not liable, but advice on entering a guarantee was not. Despite the high authority of the decision, such old cases should be treated with some caution as the nature of a solicitor's ordinary business may change over time.

[92] [2000] Q.B. 113. The case is currently on appeal to the House of Lords. For an example of a fraudulent solicitor acting in the ordinary course of the firm's business, so that his partners were liable, see *Scarborough Building Society v. Howes Percival* (1998) 78 P.&C.R. D4.

[93] [2000] 4 All E.R. 412

the firm is liable where a partner receives money or property of another within the scope of his apparent authority and misapplies it, or the firm receives money or property in the course of business and a partner misapplies it. Merely accepting a draft to hold the money to the client's order without any instructions is not acting within the course of business of a solicitor nor is it within the scope of a partner's apparent authority.[94] Where two firms merge, regardless of the terms of the merger, partners in one firm could not be liable for the earlier acts of a partner in the other firm.[95] A defendant who is a "salaried partner", that is who is held held out as a partner but is in fact merely an employee of the firm, will only be liable for the firm's defaults if the claimant can prove he relied on the defendant holding himself out as a partner.[96]

Delegation and organisation. In *Arbiter Group plc v. Gill Jennings and Every* **10–148** *(a Firm)*[97] the claimants sought advice from the defendant patent agents as to whether their new kind of jukebox might infringe an existing U.S. patent. The patent agents instructed U.S. patent searchers to carry out a search to check this, who reported erroneously that the patent was not in force, which the defendants passed on to the claimant. Swinton Thomas L.J. held:

> "A professional man in appropriate circumstances is entitled to delegate tasks. Whether he is entitled to delegate a particular task will depend on the nature of the task. He is entitled to delegate some tasks to others but is not entitled to delegate others. It all depends on the nature of the task involved. If he does delegate he must delegate to a suitably qualified and experienced person."[98]

The court recognised that there was a risk that the person to whom the task is delegated may make a mistake, and the question to be considered was the degree of risk and whether it was appropriate that the delegator should take it. In that case, the defendants were entitled to delegate the search to U.S. patent searchers, and they were entitled to rely on the results and not carry out further inquiries themselves.[99] If the drafting of documents is split between different departments of a firm, there is a potential for mismatch, and it is essential for someone with sufficiently general legal experience to have overall responsibility for reviewing the whole document, see *Summit Financial Group Ltd v. Slaughter & May (a Firm)*.[1]

Classification of breaches. Broadly speaking, breach of duty by a solicitor **10–149** may take one of five forms:

  (i) Breach of a specific contractual duty.[2]

  (ii) Breach of the implied contractual duty to exercise reasonable skill and care.[3]

---

[94] *Antonelli v. Allen* [2001] Lloyd's Rep. P.N. 487, Neuberger J.
[95] *H.F. Pension Trustees Ltd v. Ellison* [1999] P.N.L.R. 894, Jonathan Parker J.
[96] *Nationwide Building Society v. Lewis* [1998] Ch. 482, CA.
[97] [2000] P.N.L.R. 680.
[98] *ibid.* at 686.
[99] The claimant further relied on *Edward Wong Finance Co. Ltd v. Johnson Stokes & Master* [1984] A.C. 296, which was distinguished, see para. 10–088 above.
[1] *The Times*, April 5, 1999.
[2] See paras 10–004 to 10–012.
[3] See paras 10–007 and 10–077.

(iii) Breach of the duty of care owed by the solicitor to the client independently of his contractual duties.[4]

(iv) Breach of the duty of care owed by the solicitor to some third party who is not his client.[5]

(v) Breach of fiduciary or trust duties.[6]

Negligence is not an essential element of liability under the first head, although it is unusual for such a breach to occur without negligence.[7] The second, third and fourth heads involve breaches of the same standard of skill and care[8] and hereafter will jointly be described as "negligence",[9] a use of the term commonly adopted by professional negligence litigators which is apt to mislead other lawyers who confine the term to the third and fourth heads. Breach of trust and even more fiduciary used to play a comparatively small part in actions against solicitors, but has recently become more important. Breach of fiduciary duty may entail negligence,[10] but this is not necessary in order to establish liability.

10–150   Instances in which it has been held that solicitors are, or may be, liable for breach of duty are discussed below under four heads. It is not suggested that this catalogue is exhaustive. The cases serve to illustrate how the principles stated above operate in practice and, in particular, what the courts consider to be the standard of skill and care which may reasonably be expected of solicitors.[11]

(b) *Giving wrong advice*

10–151   **On the law.**[12] Giving advice is one of the principal functions of solicitors. If the solicitor gives incorrect advice on a point of common occurrence, where the law is clear, then he will be liable in negligence.[13] For example, in *Otter v. Church Adams Tatham & Co.*[14] the defendant solicitors advised that when M attained 21 his interest in certain settled property would become absolute. Subsequently (when M attained 21) they advised that there was no urgency about

---

[4] See paras 10–013 to 10–015

[5] See paras 10–040 to 10–064.

[6] See paras 10–016 to 10–039.

[7] *Ferguson v. Lewis* (1879) 14 L.J. 700 is an example of such a case. The defendant solicitor agreed to represent the plaintiff at the magistrate's court, but failed to attend. The defendant was acquitted of (gross) negligence, but held liable for breach of contract. For more modern examples, see para. 10–008 to 10–010 above.

[8] In certain circumstances the contractual duty of skill and care may be higher than that imposed by the law of tort: see *Duchess of Argyll v. Beuselinck* [1972] 2 Lloyd's Rep. 172 at 183 (discussed in para. 10–093). It is theoretically possible, therefore, that a solicitor may be held liable to his client under head (ii) but escape liability under head (iii).

[9] The distinction between the second and third heads becomes important where a defence is raised under the Limitation Acts. The distinction may also be important when quantifying damages, in particular in relation to the test for foreseeability, as to which see section 3 of this chapter.

[10] As in *Nocton v. Ashburton* [1914] A.C. 932. If negligence had been pleaded, it would not have been necessary to pursue the claim for breach of fiduciary duty. See also *Lapierre v. Young* (1981) 117 D.L.R. (3d) 643, Ontario HCt.

[11] For a general discussion of the standard of skill and care, see paras 10–077 to 10–105.

[12] See further paras 10–081 to 10–083.

[13] *Hill v. Finney* (1865) 4F & F. 616: erroneous advice in divorce proceedings; *Rumsey v. Owen, White & Catlin* (1978) 245 E.G. 225, CA: advice based on a misunderstanding of the Landlord and Tenant Act 1954.

[14] [1953] Ch. 280.

effecting the transfer of the property to him. In fact, M only had an equitable interest in tail in the property. In order to perfect his title, he should have executed a disentailing assurance. He died on active service before this was done. The point of law was a straightforward one, and Upjohn J. held that the defendants were negligent in not making a proper enquiry. In *Winston Cooper v. Smith Llewellyn Partnership*[15] the defendant solicitors failed to advise their clients that the relevant limitation period was six years from the date of exchange of contracts, not completion. They had failed to distinguish the cause of actions in contract and tort, and had failed to look up the relevant case law. Curtis J. held that the solicitors were negligent.

If a solicitor errs in his advice on a matter where the law is difficult, then he **10–152** is not liable in negligence so long as the opinion that he expresses is a reasonable one.[16] In such a situation, however, the solicitor would be prudent to qualify his advice, by stating that the matter is in doubt. However, the contrary view was expressed by Lord Shand in *Blair v. Assets Company*[17]:

> "It was (the solicitors') duty to form their own opinion, and to advise the liquidators accordingly. But it was not their duty, nor according to their instructions, to reason out the matter with the liquidators, to say whether their opinion was given with confidence or hesitation or to quote their authorities."

Where it is obvious that the solicitor's advice is no more than an expression of opinion on a moot point, then, according to Canadian authority,[18] a solicitor is not liable for failing to state this expressly: "The lawyer's advice in matters of statutory interpretation can never be more than an opinion . . . He is not, I think, normally required to warn experienced business clients of the possibility that the opinion, although firmly held, may not in fact prevail."[19] Contrast *Port of Sheerness Ltd v. Brachers*[20] where the defendant solicitors advised their clients that dismissing dockers who refused to accept new terms would cause claims limited to redundancy payments. There were two competing schools of thought at the time as to whether such circumstances would have given rise to claims for redundancy or more costly claims for unfair dismissal. Buckley J. nevertheless found the defendant solicitors negligent for failing to mention the risk that the dismissals would be found to be unfair.

Practical advice. A solicitor is often called upon to give practical advice, in **10–153** which legal considerations are only one factor. In such a situation, a mere error

---

[15] [1999] P.N.L.R. 576.

[16] *Bell v. Strathairn & Blair* (1954) 104 L.J. 618 (Scottish case). In *Fordgate Wandsworth Ltd v. Bernard Neville & Co.* [1999] E.G.C.S. 98 the defendant solicitors were held by Lloyd J. not to be negligent in advising their client landlord that there had probably been a surrender of the lease by operation of law, and the client should accept it although it was not definite that there had been a surrender.

[17] [1896] A.C. 409 at 431; see also Lord Herschell at 426.

[18] *Ormindale Holdings Ltd v. Ray, Wolfe, Connel, Lightbody & Reynolds* (1981) 116 D.L.R. (3d) 346 and (1982) 135 D.L.R. (3d) 577, British Columbia CA.

[19] *ibid., per* Taylor J. at first instance. Taylor J.'s decision was upheld in all respects on appeal and this passage was specifically approved: see (1982) 135 D.L.R. (3d) 577 at 579. In *Hall v. Foong* (1995) 65 S.A.S.R. 281, the Full Court of South Australia held that the defendant solicitor was negligent in giving the client definite advice that a contract to purchase property was void, when he knew his advice was contrary to a recent appellate decision, and he was in receipt of a preliminary advice from counsel that the contract was probably not void but that the client may be entitled to rescind it.

[20] (1997) I.R.L.R. 214.

of judgment by the solicitor is less likely to amount to negligence.[21] Where, however, the solicitor advises a course of action that is plainly wrong, then he will be liable.[22] The more the advice is based on legal considerations, the more likely it is that an error will be found to be negligent. In *Worboys v. Cartwright*[23] the vendor of a farm which the solicitor's client had purchased was resisting giving a date for vacant possession. The solicitors nevertheless advised the client to proceed to sell his farm at auction. Morritt J. held that the solicitors were negligent in their advice, as they had failed to assess the time an action for specific performance would take to be heard and the difficulty of making a decree effective.

(c) *Failing to give advice*

10–154   **Incomplete advice.** If a solicitor fails to give advice which is specifically requested, that is a clear breach of contract and a clear breach of duty.[24] However, claims of this nature seldom arise because (unless the retainer is terminated), the client usually presses the solicitor until he receives the advice which he is seeking. Claims for failure to give advice more commonly arise where the solicitor fails to give advice, which it was his duty to proffer, whether or not specifically requested[25]; or where (unknown to the client) the advice given is incomplete. An example of a solicitor giving incomplete advice is *Crossnan v. Ward Bracewell & Co.*[26] The plaintiff was accused of reckless driving, and consulted a solicitor, who advised him that he could plead guilty unrepresented, or he could instruct the solicitor to act for him and pay £50 as a deposit against costs. The solicitor failed to inform the plaintiff that his insurance company would arrange and pay for his legal representation, and was held to be negligent. An allegation of failing to give advice that a particular course of action should be taken is often very closely related to an allegation of failing to take that action.[27]

10–155   **Who to advise.**[28] Where a solicitor is acting for a firm, it is generally sufficient if he conveys his advice to, and seeks instructions from, the particular partner

---

[21] *Faithfull v. Kesteven* (1910) 103 L.T. 56, CA.

[22] *e.g. Bryant v. Goodrich* (1966) 110 S.J. 108: wrongly advising a wife to leave the matrimonial home after the breakdown of her marriage.

[23] [1992] E.G.C.S. 110.

[24] If the matter is outside the solicitor's sphere of competence, he may, of course, quite properly refer the client to another solicitor or take counsel's opinion.

[25] *e.g. Stronghold Investments Ltd v. Renkema* (1984) 7 D.L.R. (4th) 427, British Columbia CA: solicitor for purchaser of business failed to advise his client of the formalities necessary to transfer the fire insurance policy. A fire occurred and the plaintiff was uninsured.

[26] (1989) 4 P.N. 103, Kennedy J. See also *Cade v. Cade* (1998) 71 S.A.S.R. 571, Full Court of South Australia, where solicitors gave advice in relation to the purchase of shares in a company by one of its directors and shareholders, who was their client, to the other. They negligently failed to read the articles of association of the company, which gave their client special rights which would probably have caused him to be able to purchase the shares at a lower value.

[27] *e.g. County Personnel Ltd v. Alan R Pulver & Co.* [1987] 1 W.L.R. 916, CA, considered at para. 10–272 below.

[28] Advice to an agent with full authority is sufficient. In *Mean v. Thomas* [1998] E.G.C.S. 2, QBD, the defendant solicitors were not liable to the plaintiff, an experienced builder, for failing to inform him of the existence of restrictive covenants over the land he intended to purchase at auction and develop. The defendants had informed the plaintiff's agent that it was his responsibility to satisfy himself that there was no obstruction to the proposed development.

who is handling the matter.[29] Where a solicitor is acting for husband and wife, instructions are likely to be necessary from both.[30] Similarly, when instructed by two married couples in the purchase of property, a solicitor should not take instructions from the husband of one of the couples only, unless the three remaining parties have given him actual or ostensible authority to do so.[31] Where a solicitor engaged to act on behalf of three joint clients acts on instructions from one to the detriment of the first, he will be in serious breach of duty.[32]

As to the progress of the cause or matter. The solicitor owes a duty to inform   **10–156** the client of the progress of the transaction which he is handling on the client's behalf. If he fails in this duty, the client may suffer unnecessary loss[33] or even be exposed to criminal liability.[34] In such circumstances there is unlikely to be any defence to an action for negligence. Apart from satisfying his legitimate curiosity, the client needs to know of material developments, in order to decide whether he should give further instructions to the solicitor or modify his existing instructions. Where appropriate, the solicitor should invite further instructions at the same time as informing the client of developments:

> "It is an incident of that duty[35] that the solicitor shall consult with his client in all questions of doubt which do not fall within the express or implied discretion left him, and shall keep the client informed to such an extent as may be reasonably necessary according to the same criteria."[36]

Thus in litigation a solicitor ought to inform his client of any offers of settlement made by the other party.[37] There may be some matters of pure procedure which do not need to be discussed with the client.[38]

Professional duty to inform. The duty to keep the client informed is now   **10–157** reflected in the Solicitors Practice Rules 1990, r. 15,[39] which requires solicitors

---

[29] *Tomlinson v. Broadsmith* [1896] 1 Q.B. 386, CA; *Sykes v. Midland Bank Executor & Trustee Co. Ltd* [1971] 1 Q.B. 113, CA; *Berlevy v. Blyth Dutton (a firm)* [1997] E.G.C.S. 133, CA.

[30] *Penn v. Bristol & West Building Society* [1996] 2 F.C.R. 729, see para. 10–044 above; *cf.* the outdated views expressed in *Morris v. Duke-Cohan & Co.* (1975) 119 S.J. 826; *The Times*, November 22, 1975: a solicitor should "not take instructions from a wife when a husband was also available". *per* Caulfield J.

[31] *Farrer v. Messrs Copley-Singleton* [1998] P.N.L.R. 22, where the Court of Appeal held the defendant solicitors liable for failing to obtain instructions.

[32] *Perry v. Edwin Coe, The Independent*, April 1, 1994, Harman J.

[33] As in *Stinchcombe & Cooper Ltd v. Addison, Cooper, Jesson & Co.* (1971) 115 S.J. 368. Solicitors acted for the purchasers of land from the local authority. The contract provided that the vendors could rescind if the purchasers did not start building on the land within 12 months. The solicitors failed to inform the clients of this when contracts were exchanged (and the 12 months started to run). This failure was held to be negligent.

[34] As in *Ashton v. Wainwright* [1936] 1 All E.R. 805. A solicitor acted for the officers of a club which was about to move premises. He applied to have the registration of the club transferred to the new premises, but the application was refused. He failed to communicate this to his clients, who proceeded with the move and were subsequently convicted for supplying drink at an unregistered club. The solicitor was held liable: " . . . in failing to inform the clients of the position so as to give them the chance, at any rate, of deciding whether they would risk a move, as I am satisfied they would not have done, he was clearly guilty of a breach of duty towards them", *per* Goddard J. at 809.

[35] *i.e.* the duty arising upon the solicitor's retainer.

[36] *per* Scott L.J. in *Groom v. Crocker* [1939] 1 K.B. 194 at 222.

[37] See para. 10–190.

[38] See *Beckmat Holdings Ltd v. Tassou* (1982) 18 Alta. L.R. (2d) 300, Alta. CA.

[39] See The Law Society's *Guide to the Professional Conduct of Solicitors* (8th ed., 1999), p. 27.

to give information about costs and other matters in accordance with the Client Care Code. The Code[40] which mostly concerns information about costs, also requires:

> "Every solicitor in private practice must ensure that the client ... is given a clear explanation of the issues raised in a matter and is properly informed about its progress (including the likely timescale)."

This is amplified in the Law Society's *Guide to the Professional Conduct of Solicitors*[41]:

> "The solicitor should keep clients informed of the progress of matters. This may often be assisted by sending to clients copies of letters. In particular, it is important to tell clients of the reason for any serious delay. Requests for information should be answered promptly."

10–158   **In respect of matters which come to the solicitor's notice.** In the ordinary course of business a solicitor is likely to accumulate a substantial amount of information, much of which is of no interest to the client. It is the solicitor's duty, however, to identify any matters which are or may be important to the client and to bring them to his notice. In acting for a purchaser, for example, a solicitor would be negligent if he failed to advise his client of the existence of a right of way over the property[42] or of a defect in title.[43] In *Lake v. Bushby*[44] the second defendant was instructed to act as solicitor for the plaintiff, after the plaintiff had contracted to purchase certain property. The solicitor discovered from a local search that there was no planning permission for a bungalow which stood upon the property, but he did not communicate this fact to the plaintiff. Pritchard J. held that the solicitor was in breach of duty. If a solicitor discovers that his clients are involved in a "contracts race", he ought to notify them promptly.[45]

10–159   The solicitor may reasonably decide not to burden his client with what appear to be pure legal technicalities. Provided that he takes care to explain the gist of any relevant information he has acquired or the results of his searches, that should be sufficient. In *Central Land Investments Ltd v. Winn*[46] a solicitor was acting for the purchasers of a shop. He explained to them the nature of the redevelopment which was being undertaken in the vicinity of the shop and he pointed out that pedestrian traffic would be impeded. However, he did not tell his clients about the terms of a closure order affecting a nearby road, because he did not think it relevant. Melford Stevenson J. was "not prepared to differ from this view" and accordingly dismissed the claim.

10–160   **In respect of matters which he is not asked to investigate or advise upon.** In the ordinary way a solicitor is not obliged to travel outside his instructions and make investigations which are not expressly or impliedly requested by the

---

[40] *ibid.*, p. 270, para. 7(a).
[41] *ibid.*, p. 274, para. 13.06.3.
[42] *Piper v. Daybell Court-Cooper & Co.* (1969) 210 E.G. 1047.
[43] *Pilkington v. Wood* [1953] Ch. 770 (negligence admitted), ChD.
[44] [1949] 2 All E.R. 964.
[45] *Nash v. Phillips* (1974) 232 *e.g.* 1219, ChD. For the professional obligations of a seller's solicitors in such circumstances, see r. 6A of the Solicitors' Practice Rules 1990, discussed *in Jenmain v. Steed* [2000] P.N.L.R. 616, CA.
[46] (1972) 223 E.G. 2334.

client.[47] In *Clark Boyce v. Mouat*[48] the Privy Council considered that where the client who was in full command of her faculties, and apparently aware of what she was doing, sought the assistance of a solicitor in the carrying out of a particular transaction, the solicitor is under no duty to go beyond those instructions by proffering unsought advice on the wisdom of the transaction.[49] However, it is not possible to lay down any hard and fast rule, and the following two cases show where the courts tend to draw the line. In *Griffiths v. Evans*[50] the plaintiff sustained an accident at work and thereafter received weekly payments from his employers under the Workmen's Compensation Acts. He subsequently consulted the defendant solicitor, because he feared a reduction of the weekly payments. The defendant advised the plaintiff in respect of his claim under the Workmen's Compensation Acts. He did not consider, or advise the plaintiff, whether he had a claim for damages at common law in respect of the accident. The Court of Appeal (Denning L.J. dissenting) held that the defendant was not negligent:

> "I have found the question of negligence a difficult one. I think that the defendant, being wise after the event, may well reproach himself for not having gone outside the question put to him and made enquiries as to the accident generally. The variety of matters with which a solicitor has to have some familiarity increases annually. The case may well be on the borderline, but I am not satisfied that the plaintiff has made out a case of negligence."[51]

In *Goody v. Baring*[52] the defendant was acting for the purchaser of a residential property, the first and second floors of which were let to tenants. He ascertained from the vendor what rents were being paid by the tenants. He did not go on to check what were the standard rents fixed under the Rent Restriction Acts. In fact these were lower than the actual rents, with the result that the tenants subsequently recovered from the purchaser the amount of their overpayments. Danckwerts J. held that the defendant was in breach of duty in failing to make proper enquiries about the standard rent and to give the plaintiff "plain and clear advice" in that regard.[53] The judge deduced from *Hunt v. Luck*[54] that in the case of a tenanted property the purchaser's solicitor owed a duty to inquire of the tenants the terms on which they occupied and (in a case where the Rent Restriction Acts

---

[47] See also Bingham L.J.'s views in *Mortgage Express Ltd v. Bowerman & Partners* [1996] 2 All E.R. 836 at 842, quoted at para. 10–208 below. See further, *e.g. Pitman v. Francis* (1884) Cab. & El. 355. In *Amersfort Ltd v. Kelly Nichols & Blayney* [1996] E.G.C.S. 156, ChD, the defendant solicitors answered the three questions asked of them, but had not been asked to review the plaintiffs' lease generally. They had no duty to bring to the clients' attention any unusual features of the lease beyond answering the three questions. In *Woodward v. Wolferstans (a firm), The Times*, April 8, 1997; [1997] N.P.C. 51, the defendant solicitors were retained by the plaintiff's father in relation to the purchase of property, where he was acting as guarantor. While they owed her a duty of care, there was no breach in failing to explain the details of the transaction to her, as the retainer from the father was simply to secure a good and marketable title.

[48] [1994] 1 A.C. 428, at 437D.

[49] This is consistent with the House of Lords decision in *Royal Bank of Scotland plc v. Etridge* (No. 2), October 17, 2001, on which see para. 10–205.

[50] [1953] 1 W.L.R. 1424.

[51] *Per* Somervell L.J. at 1427.

[52] [1956] 1 W.L.R. 448.

[53] *ibid.* at 453–454. An aggravating factor in this case was that the defendant was acting for both vendor and purchaser. See para. 10–100.

[54] [1902] 1 Ch. 428.

apply) to enquire whether the rents paid were the standard or recoverable rents of the property.[55]

10–161   Another problem (closely allied to that discussed in the previous paragraph) is to what extent a solicitor should proffer unasked advice where the advice would not entail any investigation or work on the solicitor's part. In *Hall v. Meyrick*[56] the plaintiff (then Mrs James, a widow) and a Mr Hall consulted the defendant solicitor in connection with their wish to make wills, by which each would leave everything to the other. They did not state that they would or might get married, although the plaintiff's son (who was present during the interview) made a jocular reference to marriage. The defendant did not advise them that the effect of marriage would be to revoke their wills, unless made in contemplation of marriage. The plaintiff and Mr Hall subsequently married, in ignorance of this rule, and when Mr Hall died he was intestate. Ashworth J. held that the defendant had been negligent. The Court of Appeal allowed the defendant's appeal on a point of pleading and their consideration of the point of principle was, therefore, *obiter*. Hodson L.J. observed that it is not a solicitor's duty in every case to draw the attention of clients who make wills to the effect of marriage on a will. However, this was "a very special and unusual case" and he considered that the judge's decision was supported by the evidence.[57] Ormrod L.J. stated that a solicitor was under a duty to advise about the effect of marriage on a will, if the client told him of his intention to marry or even, perhaps, if the client's intention came to his knowledge in a less direct way. Ormrod L.J. would have been reluctant to find negligence in this case.

10–162   **Statements of principle in this regard.** In *Carradine Properties Ltd v. D.J. Freeman & Co.*,[58] the plaintiffs engaged contractors to demolish a building in Clacton. The contractors damaged an adjoining property, thereby exposing the plaintiffs to liability. The plaintiffs instructed the defendant solicitors to make a claim against the contractors and, subsequently, to consider making a claim against the estate agents who had selected those contractors. The plaintiffs did not inform the defendants that they themselves had an insurance policy covering the incident and they did not ask the defendants to consider the plaintiffs' insurance position. The Court of Appeal held that the defendants were not negligent in failing to think of the point themselves and to proffer advice upon it. Lord Denning M.R. attached importance to the fact that the plaintiffs' managing director was very experienced in insurance matters. Donaldson L.J. said that the precise scope of the duty to advise would depend, *inter alia*, upon the extent to which the client appeared to need advice:

---

[55] *cf. Cady v. Hanson* (1989) 51 D.L.R. (4th) 139, British Columbia CA: solicitor acted for purchaser of property which turned out to have zoning problems; held that he had no reason to scrutinise the interim agreement for defects which might make it void, and thus he was not negligent in not advising the plaintiff that it might be void.

[56] [1957] 2 Q.B. 455. See also *Bartter v. Gambrill* (1932) 76 S.J. 868. The plaintiff agreed with S, an adjoining landowner, to exchange part of her garden for a portion of S's land. After the agreement was made, the defendant solicitor was instructed to carry out the conveyancing. Subsequently the plaintiff regretted the transaction. She alleged that the original agreement did not satisfy s. 40 of the Law of Property Act 1925 and that the defendant was negligent in failing so to advise her. Luxmoore J. dismissed the claim: " . . . a solicitor was not obliged to point out to the person instructing him that he was not legally bound to carry out his bargain."

[57] *ibid.* at 475–476.

[58] [1999] Lloyd's Rep. P.N. 483

"An inexperienced client will need and will be entitled to expect the solicitor to take a much broader view of the scope of his retainer and of his duties than will be the case with an experienced client."[59]

Oliver J. considered these questions in *Midland Bank v. Hett, Stubbs & Kemp*[60] and formulated the general principle in these terms:

" . . . the court must beware of imposing upon solicitors—or upon professional men in other spheres—duties which go beyond the scope of what they are requested and undertake to do. It may be that a particularly meticulous and conscientious practitioner would, in his client's general interest, take it upon himself to pursue a line of enquiry beyond the strict limits comprehended by his instructions. But that is not the test. The test is what the reasonably competent practitioner would do having regard to the standards normally adopted in his profession, and cases such as *Duchess of Argyll v. Beuselinck* [1972] 2 Lloyd's Rep. 172; *Griffiths v. Evans* [1953] 1 W.L.R. 1424 and *Hall v. Meyrick* [1957] 2 Q.B. 455 demonstrate that the duty is directly related to the confines of the retainer."[61]

This should be contrasted with the dictum of the Court of Appeal of New Zealand in *Gilbert v. Shanahan*, which it is submitted is consistent with the views of Oliver J.[62]:

"Solicitors' duties are govered by the scope of their retainer, but it would be unreasonable and artificial to define that scope by reference only to the client's express instructions. Matters which fairly and reasonably arise in the course of carrying out those instructions must be regarded as coming within the scope of the retainer."

A recent illustration. In *Investors Compensation Scheme Ltd v. West Bromwich Building Society*[63] a number of individuals had entered Home Income Plans, whereby they remortgaged their house and the proceeds were invested, supplying an income. The interest on the mortgage was generally not paid, but was added to the amount secured. Rising property prices were supposed to keep the amount owed within 40 or 50 per cent of the value of the property. The scheme did not succeed, and the individuals suffered heavy losses. In complex proceedings brought by investors and their assignees, Evans-Lombe J. considered the scope of the duties owed by the solicitors in such transactions. They were instructed by the lender to complete the mortgage transactions, and also by the investors. Most of the investors had taken out mortgages before, and therefore were not to be treated as ignorant or inexperienced. The solicitors were often justified in taking the view that the investors would be familiar with the usual provisions of a mortgage securing a loan on property. The solicitors plainly owed a duty to explain the unusual provisions whereby the interest was rolled-up, and the factors which might affect the performance of the scheme such as fluctuations in property prices and interest rates. They had no duty to advise on the merits of the

10–163

---

[59] [1999] Lloyd's Rep. P.N. 483 at 487 col. 2, and see Lord Denning's similar remarks at 486. The view was adopted in *R.P. Howard Ltd v. Woodman Matthews* [1983] B.C.L.C. 117 at 121–122, Staughton J.
[60] [1979] Ch. 384.
[61] *ibid.* at 402–403.
[62] [1988] 3 N.Z.L.R. 528. The solicitor, who was instructed in respect of a lease and guarantee, should have advised his client that he did not have any obligation to sign the guarantee, although the client had not expressly sought advice on the matter.
[63] [1999] Lloyd's Rep. P.N. 496.

transaction, or speculate as to how property prices and interests rates may vary in the future, as that was not part of their expertise, and the investors were advised by FIMBRA-registered financial advisers.

10–164   **As to the solicitor's own negligence.** In *Gold v. Mincoff Science & Gold (a Firm)*[64] Neuberger J. held that it would be a relatively exceptional case where a solicitor would have a duty to advise that he had been negligent on an earlier occasion, otherwise an onerous implied general retainer would be imposed on the solicitor. However, on the facts of that case the solicitors should have investigated the draft mortgages the client was going to enter, and they would have been led back to consider earlier mortgages he had entered and as a result they would have been obliged to advise the client that they had been negligent and he should seek separate legal advice. Neuberger J. relied on the solicitor's professional duty, where he discovers an action or omission which would justify a claim, to inform the client that he should seek independent legal advice.[65]

10–165   **The duty to warn against particular risks.** There is generally a duty to point out any hazards of the kind which should be obvious to the solicitor but which the client, as a layman, may not appreciate.[66] In *Boyce v. Rendells*[67] the Court of Appeal accepted the following as a general proposition:

> "if, in the course of taking instructions, a professional man like a land agent or a solicitor learns of facts which reveal to him as a professional man the existence of obvious risks, then he should do more than merely advise within the strict limits of his retainer. He should call attention to and advise upon the risks."[68]

By way of example, solicitors have been held negligent for: failing to warn a purchaser of property of the risks which he ran by moving in and carrying out works of repair before contracts were exchanged[69]; failing to advise clients of the dangers which they ran by exchanging contracts for the purchase of new property, before the prospective purchaser of their existing property had paid a deposit[70]; failing to warn the client of numerous risks involved in a conveyancing

---

[64] [2001] Lloyd's Rep. P.N. 423. For a similar case see *Tucker v. Allen & Co. (a Firm)* [2001] P.N.L.R. 884, QBD, where solicitors failed to notice that there was no practicable access to the property the claimants were purchasing in 1988, and when a dispute arose about a right of way four year's later they negligently failed to mention their own earlier default.

[65] This is now para. 29.09 in the Law Society's *Guide to the Professional Conduct of Solicitors* (8th ed., 1999). If there is a conflict of interest, then the solicitor is plainly bound not to continue to act. However the proposed legal duty to inform the client that the solicitor has been negligent may contradict *Bell v. Lever Bros.* [1932] A.C. 161, although in practice this is bound to emerge when the advice that they can no longer act or that the client should seek independent legal advice is given. In Canada there is such a duty, see *Vienneau v. Arsenault* (1982) 41 N.B.R. (2d) 82, New Brunswick CA.

[66] Contrast *Foshan Hua Da Industrial Co. v. Johnson, Stokes & Master (a Firm)* [1999] H.K.L.R.D. 418. The plaintiff retained the defendant solicitors to prepare the documentation in respect of a loan it intended to make for the development of land on the security of shares in a company. The defendants advised the plaintiff not to proceed with the loan until the share certificate was produced, and advised that a legal mortgage over the shares was preferable to an equitable one. The High Court of Hong Kong held that the defendants were not negligent in failing to alert their clients to the possibility that the shares had been pledged elsewhere, nor for failing to detail the additional powers of a legal mortgage.

[67] (1983) 268 E.G. 268.

[68] *ibid.* at 272, col. 2.

[69] *Attard v. Samson* (1966) 110 S.J. 249, QBD.

[70] *Morris v. Duke-Cohan & Co.* (1975) 119 S.J. 826; *The Times*, November 22, 1975, QBD.

transaction[71]; failing to warn a mortgagee of the risk of lending money when the mortgage could not be registered[72]; failing to warn the assignee of an insolvent debtor of the risk which he ran in costs from the continued prosecution of an action[73]; failing to warn trustees of circumstances which may render them personally liable for the loss of trust moneys[74]; failing to advise lessees of premises that the user permitted in the proposed sub-lease would (or at least might) infringe the head-lease[75]; and failing to warn the owner of a business of the risks of transferring the shares to an investor most of which were to be held on trust for the owner, with the owner being employed as manager. A solicitor instructed in a contentious matter ought always to consider the merits of his client's case. If he considers the proposed claim or defence to be hopeless, he should say so, whether or not he is asked to advise on the merits.[76]

Explanation of legal documents. One of the principal areas in which the client looks to his solicitor for guidance is in the explanation of legal documents. Normally, the client either signs such documents or permits them to be sent on his behalf in reliance upon the solicitor's advice. The solicitor owes a general duty to explain such documents to the client, or at least to ensure that he understands the material parts.[77] The solicitor's duty to explain legal documents is reflected in the Law Society's guidance[78]: **10–166**

---

[71] *Major v. Buchanan* (1975) 9 O.R. (2d) 491, Ontario HCt.; *Graybriar Industries Ltd v. Davis & Co.* (1992) 46 B.C.L.R. (2d) 164, British Columbia Sup.Ct.

[72] *Income Trust Co. v. Watson* (1984) 26 B.L.R. 228, Ontario HCt.

[73] *Allison v. Rayner* (1827) 7B. & C. 441.

[74] *Re A Solicitor, ex p. Incorporated Law Society* (1895) S.J. 219. This was not a professional negligence action but a review of disciplinary proceedings before the Law Society. However, the legal duties of a solicitor were considered by the court: "A solicitor, whatever may be his other duties towards his client, ought always to make his client distinctly acquainted with the legal effect of any step he may take . . . Where their clients are unacquainted with the law, solicitors should always be extremely careful to explain to them fully what their duty is." See also *Stokes v. Prance* [1898] 1 Ch. 212 at 223–225, Stirling J., as to the solicitor's duty when advising trustees who are lending trust funds, and *Austrust Pty Ltd v. Astley* (1993) 60 S.A.S.R. 354, South Australia Sup. Ct.

[75] *C.W. Dixey & Sons Ltd v. Parsons* (1964) 192 E.G. 197, QBD. See also the restaurant cases referred to in n.82, below. *Park Hall School v. Overend* [1987] 2 I.R. 1, Irish High Court, is a surprising contrast to the cases cited above. A solicitor acted for a school in the proposed sale of land. The land had previously been sold at auction, although the sale had not gone ahead. Given the uncertain state of the law, it was not clear whether there existed a binding contract with the original proposed purchaser. The solicitor was found not to be negligent when he failed to warn his client that it might be already liable to convey the property, given that the original proposed purchaser had given no suggestion that he would assert his possible rights.

[76] *Jacks v. Bell* (1828) 3 C. & P. 316; *Holmes v. National Benzole Co.* (1968) 109 S.J. 971: "A solicitor who, without any investigation of his client's claim, allowed or encouraged a client to pursue a claim which proper investigation would at an early stage have shown to be a hopeless one was in breach of duty to his client . . . " (*per* Lyell J.).

[77] *e.g. Watts v. Hyde* (1846) 2 Coll. 368 at 380–381; *Meadows v. Meadows* (1853) 16 Beav. 401; *Anderson v. Elsworth* (1861) 3 Giff. 154 at 169: an attorney had to explain all the difference between a will and a deed when the client wanted to leave property by deed. *Clarence Construction Ltd v. Lavallee* (1980) 111 D.L.R. (3d) 582 and (1982) 132 D.L.R. (3d) 153, British Columbia CA; *Booth v. Davey* (1988) 138 N.L.J. 104, CA; *Donmez v. Barnes* [1996] E.G.C.S. 129; *Titanic Investments v. McFarlanes* [1997] N.P.C. 105, ChD.: there is a duty to give a proper explanation of any documents requiring signature, and where document were not to be signed by the client to ensure there were instructions to accept them based on an adequate explanation of their contents; risks which would not be obvious to a layman should be draw to the client's attention.

[78] The Law Society's *Guide to the Professional Conduct of Solicitors* (8th ed., 1999), p. 274, para. 13.04 n. 5.

> "Solicitors should normally explain to clients the effect of important and relevant documents."

In the case of a will, a solicitor should take particular care to ensure that the client understands and agrees to its provisions.[79] With an experienced business client it may not be necessary to do this.[80] In particular, a solicitor should explain any unusual provisions[81] or any provisions of particular relevance to the client's proposed activities.[82] In *Sykes v. Midland Bank Executor & Trustee Co. Ltd*[83] the plaintiffs took an underlease of office premises. The effect of one provision in the underlease was that whereas the sub-lessor could not unreasonably withhold his consent to a change of user, the head-lessor could do so. The solicitors failed to explain this to the plaintiffs and it was held that they were thereby in breach of duty.

> "When a solicitor is asked to advise on a leasehold title it is, in my judgment, his duty to call his client's attention to clauses in an unusual form which may affect the interests of his client as he knows them."[84]

The Federal Court of Australia has formulated a solicitor's duty to explain legal documents in similar terms,[85] expressly relying upon *Sykes v. Midland Bank Executor and Trustee Co. Ltd.*[86]

10–167   There must of course be a sensible limit upon the solicitor's duty to explain legal documents. When any such document (even a familiar document in common use) is put under the microscope, it will be found to abound with ambiguities, generalities or potential problems. In *Walker v. Boyle*[87] Dillon J. rejected the contention that a solicitor acting for the purchaser of a house ought to advise his client of the implications of condition 17 of the National Conditions of Sale (19th edition). He put the matter in this way:

---

[79] See further para. 10–220.

[80] *Aslan v. Clintons* (1984) 134 N.L.J. 584, Leonard J.

[81] *Stannard v. Ullithorne* (1834) 10 Bing. 491: "An attorney . . . is bound to take care, that his client does not enter into any covenant or stipulation that may expose him to a greater degree of responsibility than is ordinarily attached to the business in hand, or, at all events, that he does not do so till the consequences have been explained to him", *per* Tindal C.J.; *Phillips v. Millings* (1871) 7 Ch.App. 244; see also *Flandro v. Mitha* (1992) 93 D.L.R. (4th) 222, British Columbia Sup. Ct, (conveyancing notary failed to draw unusual rent revision clause to the attention of the purchaser). Thus solicitors were liable for failing to explain to their client that a proposed lease had been changed so that tenant's improvements were to be taken into account at rent reviews, see *Sonardyne Ltd v. Firth & Co.* [1997] E.G.C.S. 84, QBD.

[82] *Transportation Agency Ltd v. Jenkins* (1972) 223 E.G. 1101, Kerr J.: clients proposed to use premises as a restaurant. Solicitor's clerk failed to point out that there was a covenant prohibiting cooking; *Simple Simon Catering Ltd v. Binstock Miller & Co.* (1973) 228 E.G. 527, CA: clients proposed to use premises as a restaurant. Solicitors failed to point out or explain a covenant whereby the landlords, or persons licensed by them, were permitted to share the use of the kitchen.

[83] [1971] 1 Q.B. 113, CA.

[84] *ibid.* at 124B *per* Harman L.J. This dictum was cited in *County Personnel Ltd v. Alan R. Pulver & Co.* [1987] 1 W.L.R. 916, CA, where the plaintiffs took an underlease which had an unusual rent review lease whereby the rent was increased at the same percentage as the headlease. The defendant solicitors were held negligent in failing to advise the plaintiffs of the risks they faced. See para. 10–272 for the full facts. In contrast, in *Commercial Bridging plc v. Nelsons* [1998] C.L.Y. 4018, ChD., the defendant solicitor was held to have no obligation to a sophisticated commercial client to explain a short and straightforward deed of priority of which it was aware.

[85] *Fox v. Everingham* (1983) 50 A.L.R. 337 at 341.

[86] [1971] 1 Q.B. 113.

[87] [1982] 1 W.L.R. 495.

"It is, of course, the duty of a solicitor to advise his client about any abnormal or unusual term in a contract, but I think it is perfectly normal and proper for a solicitor to use standard forms of conditions of sale such as the National Conditions of Sale. I do not think he is called on to go through the small print of those somewhat lengthy conditions with a toothcomb every time he is advising a purchaser to draw the purchaser's attention to every problem which on a careful reading of the conditions might in some circumstance or other conceivably arise. I cannot believe that purchasers of house property throughout the land would be overjoyed at having such lengthy explanations of the National Conditions of Sale ritually foisted upon them."[88]

Reminders. As a general rule, there is no duty on a solicitor to remind a client   **10–168** of advice once it has been given. In *Yager v. Fishman & Co.*[89] the plaintiff's company held a 21-year lease of premises, under which the plaintiff guaranteed the payment of rent. The lease could be terminated early if the company gave notice on or before December 24, 1940. In October 1940 the plaintiff asked his solicitors (the second defendants) whether he could get his liability under the guarantee postponed. The solicitors replied that there was no way he could get out of his liabilities "at present". They did not go on to remind him that by giving notice before December 24 he could determine the underlease, nor did they advise him that he should take this course. The question of termination had been specifically referred to in earlier correspondence, and the Court of Appeal held that the solicitors were not negligent in failing to remind the plaintiff of the date by which notice should be given:

" . . . the respondent's solicitors were not bound to supply deficiencies in their client's memory unless they were clearly requested to do so. I am by no means sure that Yager would have welcomed a bill of costs which included charges for reminding him unasked of dates which he might be assumed to have in mind."[90]

Similarly, in *Elland Developments Ltd v. Smith*[91] the defendant solicitors had advised a property development company before exchange of contracts about the risks involved in purchasing property with possessory title only, and the need to seek better evidence of title. Rattee J. held that they had no duty to repeat such advice after exchange of contracts. The rule is not an invariable one. In *R.P. Howard Ltd v. Woodman Matthews*[92] the defendant solicitors were instructed by the plaintiffs in relation to a business tenancy which was expiring. When first instructed in October 1975, the solicitors told their clients of the need to initiate an application to the county court to obtain a new tenancy under the provisions of the 1954 Landlord and Tenant Act Part II. Negotiations then took place between the solicitors and their client's landlord. Staughton J. found that the

---

[88] *ibid.* at 507H–508A. In *Citibank Savings Ltd v. Nicholson* (1997) 70 S.A.S.R. 206 Perry J. suggested that going through a guarantee clause by clause would be very misleading to a lay person, and a solicitor should give a clear account in summary of the salient features of the transaction.
[89] [1944] 1 All E.R. 552. See also *West London Observer v. Parsons* (1955) 166 E.G. 749, QBD. The defendant solicitors acted for lessees. The lease could be renewed if the lessees gave notice on March 25, 1953 and were not, on that date, in breach of covenant. The defendants explained the provisions for renewal both in a letter dated October 1950 and during an interview in April 1951. It was held that the defendants were not negligent in failing to repeat that advice in or shortly before March 1953.
[90] *Per* Du Parcq L.J. at 558.
[91] [1995] E.G.C.S. 141.
[92] [1983] B.C.L.C. 117.

solicitors were negligent in not reminding their client of the need to make the application to the court.

10–169   **Advice on matters of business.**[93] A solicitor is not a general adviser on matters of business (unless he specifically agrees to act in that capacity). Thus he is not generally under a duty to advise whether, legal considerations apart, the transaction which he is instructed to carry out is a prudent one.[94] In *Yager v. Fishman & Co.*[95] one of the allegations against the solicitors was that they were negligent in failing to advise the plaintiff that he ought to determine the lease rather than keep it in existence and try to find a suitable tenant. The Court of Appeal rejected this contention. Scott L.J. pointed out that the solicitors were not specifically asked to advise on this question, and continued:

> "To impose on a solicitor the legal responsibility of answering such a business question would require both unequivocal instructions and unqualified acceptance; for it is no part of a solicitor's normal duty to profess the skill and experience for giving such advice."[96]

Goddard L.J. expressed the same view,[97] although he attached more weight to the fact that the plaintiff was an experienced business man:

> "The nature and amount of advice which, in a matter of this sort, a solicitor would be expected to give to a person wholly unacquainted with business may differ very materially from what he would offer to an experienced business man, who would naturally decide for himself the course he thought it in his interest to take."[98]

10–170   A similar approach was adopted by the Court of Appeal in *Carradine Properties Ltd. v. D.J. Freeman & Co.*[99] Eveleigh L.J. rejected the contention that the defendant solicitors should have advised the plaintiffs to consider whether they were insured in respect of the damage which had occurred. He stated: "The management of the company was well known to the defendants and they cannot be expected to tell the management to do that which commonsense would have

---

[93] One common problem which, strictly, falls under this heading is whether the solicitor for a lender should advise on the adequacy of the security. This is discussed in paras 10–207 to 10–210. For a criticism of this analysis of the law, see Patten, "The solicitor's liability for failing to spot mortgage fraud" (1995) 11 P.N. 2.

[94] *e.g. Rendel v. Edgelow* (1909) 53 S.J. 237, Neville J.: solicitor acted for the purchaser of property intended as an investment. The purchaser subsequently alleged that the bargain was a bad one and the plaintiff was negligent in failing to advise against it. Claim dismissed. In *Bowdage v. Harold Michelmore & Co.* (1962) 106 S.J. 512 the plaintiff granted a six-month option to P to purchase a piece of land for £400, which was twice extended. Before the final expiry of the option the plaintiff received a much higher offer from a third party, which she was unable to accept since P then exercised the option. Melford Stevenson J. held that the solicitor had no duty to advise whether the transaction was a prudent or to recommend that she should consult an independent valuer. See also *Dunn v. Fairs, Blissard, Barnes & Stowe* (1961) 105 S.J. 932: a solicitor accepted instructions from a woman aged 77 and dying of cancer to purchase an annuity. She died before the first payment was due. Barry J. held that the solicitor was not negligent. But there were special circumstances, in that the client was unaware of her condition, and the solicitor had no wish to alarm her, see para. 10–096. For a useful summary of the law, see *Law v. Cunningham & Co. (a Firm)* [1993] E.G.C.S. 126.

[95] [1944] 1 All E.R. 552. The facts are set out in para. 10–168.

[96] *ibid.* at 555.

[97] *ibid.* at 557–558.

[98] *ibid.* at 556.

[99] [1999] Lloyd's Rep. P.N. 483. The facts are set out in para. 10–162 above.

told them to do as a simple matter of business."¹ Similarly, in *Virgin Management v. De Morgan* solicitors were instructed by Virgin to carry a sale and development agreement into effect. The Court of Appeal held that the solicitors had no duty to advise their clients to try to negotiate a better deal by getting the purchaser to agree to pay VAT or to warn the clients that they may have to pay VAT.²

An exception. *Neushul v. Mellish & Harkavy*³ is an example of a case in which **10–171** solicitors were held to be negligent for failing to give "business" advice. The plaintiff, a widow, proposed to lend a substantial sum of money to F, a confidence trickster. F told her that he was contemplating marrying her, but gave no firm commitment. The plaintiff consulted the defendant solicitors for assistance in raising the money which she proposed to lend to F. The solicitors had previously acted for F and had some knowledge of his financial affairs. The Court of Appeal, by a majority, held that the solicitors were negligent in failing adequately to warn her against making the loan:

" . . . a solicitor who was carrying out a transaction for a client was not justified in expressing no opinion when it was plain that the client was rushing into an unwise, not to say disastrous, adventure"

(*per* Danckwerts L.J.). The facts of this case are unusual. The decision is consistent with dicta in the subsequent Court of Appeal case of *Carradine Properties v. D.J. Freeman & Co.*,⁴ to the effect that the duty to advise is wider where the client is obviously inexperienced or in need of advice.

Difficulty of drawing a distinction. The distinction between legal and busi- **10–172** ness matters is a question of degree. Thus in *County Personnel Ltd v. Alan R. Pulver & Co.*⁵ the plaintiffs took an underlease which had an unusual rent review lease whereby the rent was increased at the same percentage as the headlease. The defendant solicitors were found to be negligent in failing to advise the plaintiffs of the risks they faced unless the initial rents were known, because the mesne lessor might, as happened, have no reason to hold out for as low a rent as possible, for his lease was cheaper than the underlease which was at a con-siderably inflated value. They should have advised that both rents should be ascertained, and that the market level of rents should be investigated. Bingham L.J. said:

---

¹ *ibid.* at 487.
² [1996] N.P.C. 8. For another example see *Hallmark Financel Insurance Brokers Ltd v. Fraser & Beatty* (1991) 1 O.R. (3d) 641, Ontario HCt.: a solicitor interpreted a letter of intent in a particular way when drafting an agreement. He could assume that his experienced business clients would check that their instructions were being discharged when reading the agreement.
³ (1967) 111 S.J. 399. Similarly, in *O'Brien v. Hooker Homes* (1993) A.S.C. 56–217, Sup. Ct NSW a solicitor who arranged finance for the purchase of property by simple clients owed a duty to spell out the workings of their interest obligations.
⁴ [1999] Lloyd's Rep. P.N. 483. For the facts of this case see paras 10–162 and 10–170 above. For a further example of the difference in the advice which should be given to experienced and inexperienced clients, see *Haigh v. Wright Hassall & Co.* [1994] E.G.C.S. 54. For the facts see para. 10–199.
⁵ [1987] 1 W.L.R. 916. See also comment by D.N. Clarke (1987) 3 P.N. 40.

"I cannot accept the distinction drawn between legal consequences and financial implications, because in this case the significance of the legal consequences lay in the financial implications."[6]

The case should be contrasted with *Reeves v. Thrings & Long*.[7] The plaintiff, who was a businessman, wished to purchase a hotel. His solicitors, the defendants, advised him that access to the hotel car park was by licence only, with no guarantee of renewal if and when the licence was brought to an end. A majority of the Court of Appeal considered that there was no duty on the solicitor to advise his client upon the commercial implications or risks of the access provisions. Unlike the clause in *County Personnel Ltd v. Alan R. Pulver & Co.*, the implications of this clause were obvious. Similarly, in *Forbouys v. Gadhavi*[8] the purchasers of property had considerable business experience. Their solicitors advised them about the date of the rent review. They were not negligent in preventing them taking the commercial risk to proceed with the purchase without knowledge of the figure under the rent review.

10–173   **Unequal transactions.** A solicitor may act for one party in circumstances where the other is unrepresented and the transaction is potentially to the disadvantage of the latter. Common examples are guarantees, purchases of council houses under the right to buy scheme which are assisted by relations, and gifts. If there are indications that the donor might lack capacity to understand the document she was signing, the solicitor may owe a duty to his client, and potentially to the donor, to ensure that there is a medical examination to ascertain whether there is sufficient capacity.[9]

10–174   **The importance of attendance notes and written communication.** However admirable and comprehensive the advice which a solicitor gives, it is of no benefit to his defence unless it can be proved what advice was given. The solicitor is unlikely to recall after a period of several years what advice he gave to his client on a routine matter. The best he can do is to describe his usual advice in the particular circumstances or to speculate as to what he "must" have said, which is unlikely to carry as much weight as the recollection of the plaintiff.[10] There is no substitute for a proper attendance note, recording the gist of the advice that was given. The lack of attendance notes has materially increased the number of successful claims that are brought against solicitors.[11] It is prudent to

---

[6] *ibid.* at 924A. Similarly, Laskin J.A. held that legal and business advice was intermingled on some transactions, such as advice on negotiating security for a warranty on the purchase of property, see *Wong v. 407527 Ontario Ltd* (1999) 26 R.P.R. (3d) 262, Ontario CA.

[7] [1996] 1 P.N.L.R. 265.

[8] [1993] N.P.C. 122.

[9] See *Dark v. Boock* [1991] 1 N.Z.L.R. 496 at 500 *per* Heron J. See also para. 10–219 below.

[10] See *e.g. Goody v. Baring* [1956] 1 W.L.R. 448 at 452, Danckwerts J. *cf.* the position with doctors: chap. 12, para. 12–232. For an illustration see *Alliance and Leicester Building Society v. Chopra* [1994] N.P.C. 52. The defendant solicitor claimed to have informed the plaintiff lender that the cash price being paid for shares in a hotel company was £2.6m. and not the £6m. that the proposed purchaser had told them, although there was no confirmatory letter or attendance note. It was argued that the evidence should be rejected as incredible, as the plaintiff would have immediately re-examined the proposed loan. A majority of the Court of Appeal granted unconditional leave to defend, as there were lurking doubts about whether the building society would have immediately reexamined the loan if so advised.

[11] See N. von Benzon, "Avoiding solicitor's negligence" *Law Society Gazette*, May 29, 1985, p. 1559. See also para. 10–006 on the advisability of a written retainer.

confirm advice and instructions in writing. The Law Society recommends that "Solicitors should consider whether it is appropriate to confirm in writing the advice given and the instructions received."[12]

In *Robins v. Meadows & Moran*[13] solicitors acted for lessors who wished to determine a lease. The documents were contradictory, so that it was not possible to ascertain with confidence the information necessary for a valid notice of determination. There was a dispute as to whether or not the solicitors were instructed not to contact the lessor's former solicitors to see whether there were any further documents that may clarify the position. The attendance note, which was very brief, did not record the instructions, and the judge found against the solicitors. The judge further considered, citing the Law Society recommendation quoted above, that it was appropriate to confirm the position in writing.[14]

(d) *Misconduct of litigation*

Procedure. The conduct of litigation is in part a matter of routine and in part   **10–175**
it is an art. By exceptional ingenuity or foresight the solicitor may secure advantages (sometimes decisive) for his client over the other party. The skilful use of a request for further information, or a timely application for specific disclosure, may bring the other party to its knees in civil litigation. Ingenious pre-trial research and preparation may lead to an acquittal (sometimes an unmeritorious acquittal) in criminal proceedings. However, the solicitor is not negligent if he fails to display exceptional ingenuity in matters of tactics or procedure.[15] What is required of a solicitor is reasonable competence and reasonable familiarity with the procedures of the courts in which he practises.[16] This requirement will include following local practice directions.[17] Thus in *Cox v. Leech*[18] an attorney was held negligent for commencing proceedings in the Lord Mayor's Court. The court did not have power to issue a commission for the examination of witnesses abroad, and it was obvious that such a commission would be necessary during the course of the action:

"If an attorney, with or without express directions from his client, takes out a writ and proceeds thereon in a court of special and peculiar jurisdiction, he is bound to acquaint himself with the machinery by which the practice of that court is regulated, and to see

---

[12] The Law Society's *Guide to the Professional Conduct of Solicitors* (8th ed. 1999), para. 13.06 n. 6.

[13] [1991] 29 E.G. 145, Judge Bates sitting as a judge of the High Court. See also *Middleton v. Steeds Hudson* [1998] 1 F.L.R. 738, where Johnson J. expected that advice which was disregarded would be recorded in an attendance note, and the absence of any written records was "cogent" evidence in support of the plaintiff. On the facts, the Judge did in fact accept the defendants' account.

[14] See also *Morton v. Harper Grey Easton* (1995) 8 B.C.L.R. (2d) 53, British Columbia Sup. Ct: if there is a conflict between the evidence of a lawyer and his client about the terms of retainer, the client's version is to be preferred unless the lawyer can shows that the agreement was in writing.

[15] *e.g. Chapman v. Van Toll, Van Toll v. Chapman* (1857) 8 E. & B. 396: an attorney did not consider the procedural advantages of making an application under s. 3 of the Common Law Procedure Act 1854. It was held that this would not necessarily have occurred to a reasonably competent attorney, and he was not negligent.

[16] *e.g. Frankland v. Cole* (1832) 2 Cr. & J. 590; *Heywood v. Wellers* [1976] Q.B. 446, CA.

[17] See *Langley v. North West Water Authority* [1991] 3 All E.R. 610, CA. A solicitor was ordered to pay costs wasted through his failure to obey a local practice direction that required that, in personal injury litigation, authority to inspect hospital records should be sent with the particulars of claim.

[18] (1857) 1 C.B. (N.S.) 617. See also *Williams v. Gibbs* (1836) 5 Ad. & E. 208; *Plant v. Pearman* (1872) 41 L.J.Q.B. 169 (failing to register *lis pendens*).

that it is adequate to the carrying out of the objects of the suit." (*Per* Cockburn C.J.)

A solicitor may well be negligent if he sues in the High Court in respect of a matter which clearly should have been litigated in the county court.[19] This is likely to involve the client in unnecessary delay and expense and, if successful, the client may be penalised in costs.[20] Given the flexibility introduced under the Civil Procedure Rules, and the powers of transfer between courts, this should rarely be an issue now.[21]

10–176   **Issuing proceedings.** Before issuing proceedings, the solicitor should obtain written instructions to commence them.[22] He should take care to identify the proper parties. In *Long v. Orsi*[23] an attorney was held negligent when he issued proceedings on five bills of exchange, without first examining them. When he subsequently obtained the bills, it emerged that he had issued proceedings in the wrong name. In *Losner v. Michael Cohen & Co.*[24] solicitors were held negligent for issuing proceedings under the Dogs Act 1971, without first checking who owned the dogs in question or correctly naming all the owners in the summonses. However, in *Grima v. MacMillan*[25] it was held not to be negligent to sue a defendant without checking first whether he was still alive. A solicitor has no general duty to verify the creditworthiness of a proposed defendant before commencing proceedings unless there are specific indications that something is wrong.[26]

10–177   **Statements of case.** A solicitor may be liable for errors in the statements of case, where he drafts them himself.[27] However, he is not obliged to put into his pleading everything which the client requests and, on occasions, it would be "very negligent" to do so.[28] A solicitor might also be liable if he failed to give the other party reasonable notice of any intended amendment to a statement of case.[29]

---

[19] *e.g. Gill v. Lougher* (1830) 1 Cr. & J. 170; *Lee v. Dixon* (1863) 3 F. & F. 744. It is submitted that the principle is unaltered by the changes introduced by the Courts and Legal Services Act 1990 which provide for a greater parallel jurisdiction between the county court and the High Court, and a larger measure of flexibility between them. Similarly, it will be negligent to issue proceedings in Austria when greater damages could be recovered in the United Kingdom without taking proper advice from Austrian lawyers and counsel first: see *Waller v. AB (a Firm)* [2001] 2 C.L. 465, QBD.

[20] See s. 51(9) of the Supreme Court Act 1984: where litigation should have been commenced in the county court, the recoverable costs can be reduced by up to 25%.

[21] But note that the amount at stake must be more than £15,000 if an action is to be commenced in the High Court, and a personal injury action must be commenced in the County Court unless worth more than £50,000. See the High Court and County Court Jurisdiction Order 1991, as amended.

[22] *Allen v. Bone* (1841) 4 Beav. 493. It is submitted that proper attendance notes may be sufficient. See further para. 10–174 above.

[23] (1836) 18 C.B. 610.

[24] (1975) 119 S.J. 340, CA.

[25] (1972) 27 D.L.R. (3d) 666, Ontario HCt.

[26] *Thomson Snell & Passmore v. Rose* [2000] P.N.L.R. 378, CA, where the defendant's counterclaim for negligence on such a ground was rejected.

[27] *e.g. Re Spencer* (1870) 39 L.J. Ch. 841 (erroneous statement in a petition).

[28] *Per* Field J. in *Ibbotson v. Shippey* (1879) 23 S.J. 388.

[29] See, *e.g. Potter v. London Transport Board* (1965) 109 S.J. 233: leave was granted to amend and the hearing was adjourned. The solicitors were ordered to pay the costs thrown away.

Pursuing obvious remedy. A solicitor may be liable if he fails to pursue an   **10–178**
obvious remedy available to his client. Thus in *Dickinson v James Alexander &*
Co.[30] the defendant solicitors were instructed to deal with the break-up of the
plaintiff's marriage. The defendants failed to use ouster proceedings to remove
the plaintiff's husband from the matrimonial home, although the children were
suffering and the application would have succeeded. The solicitors were found to
be negligent in this failure. In *Griffiths v. Dawson*[31] it was held that a solicitor
consulted by a wife in late middle age married for many years to a man in
pensionable employment being divorced against her will on the grounds of
separation was negligent if he failed to file an application under section 10 of the
Matrimonial Causes Act 1973, which would have the effect of delaying the
hearing of a decree absolute while the financial circumstances were investigated.
In *Martin Boston & Co. v. Roberts*[32] the defendant solicitors compromised a
security for costs application by accepting a guarantee from a director of the
company which was the plaintiff in the original litigation. At the successful
conclusion to the litigation, the company was insolvent, and the director's house
was subject to new charges which reduced the value of the equity to nil. A
majority of the Court of Appeal held that the defendant solicitors were negligent
because they did not insist on a caution on the director's property and they failed
to demand further security for the company's appeal.

Pursuing unmeritorious claims or defences. If a solicitor takes up or pursues   **10–179**
a hopeless case (at least without advising his client that it is hopeless) he is in
breach of duty.[33] However, the mere fact that a claim or a defence proves
unsuccessful does not imply that it was hopeless.[34] Furthermore:

> "it must never be forgotten that it is not for solicitors or counsel to impose a pre-trial
> screen through which a litigant must pass before he can put his complaint or defence
> before the court."[35]

The question whether a solicitor was negligent in allowing his client to bring or
defend proceedings must be determined by reference to the circumstances at the
material time: these include the instructions given by the client, the facts known
to the solicitor, the expert reports available and so forth. If counsel, properly
instructed, had advised that the proceedings should be brought or defended, this
is very strong evidence (but not conclusive in every case) that the solicitor was
not negligent.[36]

Evidence. Decisions on matters of evidence frequently involve a high degree   **10–180**
of judgment. Witnesses on the fringe of events or corroborative witnesses often

---

[30] (1990) 6 P.N. 205 at 206 col. 2, Douglas Brown J.

[31] *The Times*, April 5, 1993, Ewbank J.

[32] [1996] 1 P.N.L.R. 45.

[33] *Davy-Chiesman v. Davy-Chiesman* [1984] Fam. 48, CA. Where the client is legally aided, the Law Society too should be advised that the case is hopeless.

[34] *e.g. Pelky v. Hudson Bay Insurance Co.* (1981) 35 O.R. (2d) 97, Ontario HCt: solicitors' decision to run a defence of *volenti non fit injuria* (which failed) was an error of judgment, but not negligent.

[35] *Orchard v. South Eastern Electricity Board* [1987] 1 Q.B. 565 at 572E (*per* Sir John Donaldson M.R.). *cf. Ottley v. Gilbey* (1845) 8 Beav. 602, where it was said that the solicitor has a duty to prevent useless litigation.

[36] See paras 10–116 to 10–122.

turn out to do more harm than good (if, for example, they are shaken in cross-examination or their evidence conflicts with that given by the primary witnesses). Errors of judgment made by solicitors in this regard are unlikely to be held negligent.[37] If the solicitor is acting on the advice of counsel, he usually has a good defence,[38] and it will normally be negligent if he fails to follow the advice of counsel.[39] For example, in *Roe v. Robert McGregor and Sons Ltd*[40] the solicitors acted for contractors who erected a fence and were sued for negligence by plaintiffs who crashed into the fence. The Court of Appeal held that the solicitors were not at fault in failing to interview a passenger in the car who it was reasonable to suppose would be extremely unlikely to give evidence against his friend the driver and might himself bring an action.

10–181 It is negligent if a solicitor fails to take reasonable steps to trace potential witnesses,[41] or delays seeking evidence before the trail goes cold.[42] Thus in *Holden & Co. v. Crown Prosecution Service*, a defendant was charged with possessing a shotgun without a licence, but claimed that it belonged to his brother.[43] The solicitors were told that the brother had gone to ground, and made no attempt to contact him despite knowing his address. The brother did attend court after the jury had retired, and the trial judge ordered a new trial. The Court of Appeal upheld the trial judge's order that the solicitors pay the cost of the aborted trial. Solicitors were found to be negligent in *Acton v. Graham Pearce & Co. (a Firm)*.[44] They failed to obtain full statements from an employee's former employer, when told by their client that documents from the employee which were highly relevant to criminal charges brought against him were not genuine and that the employee had been dismissed. The defendant solicitors also failed to submit documents to a document analyser.

10–182 It is usually negligent if the solicitor fails to take proofs of evidence from witnesses who are likely to be called,[45] although a client's full manuscript notes may be a sufficient proof from her.[46] It may not be negligent if a solicitor fails to scrutinise all the evidence closely. For example, in *Allen v. Unigate Dairies Ltd*[47] one of the complaints was that the solicitors failed to inquire as to the significance of a line on a plan, which in fact represented a wall between their client and the noise which he claimed induced his hearing-loss, as a result of which the case collapsed at trial. In an application that the solicitors pay the costs

---

[37] *e.g. Godefroy v. Dalton* (1830) 6 Bing. 460 (applying the old test of *crassa negligentia*; see para. 10–077).

[38] *Cates v. Indermaur* (1858) 1 F. & F. 259. See also paras 10–116 to 10–122.

[39] See Johnson J. in *Gregg & Co. v. Gardner* [1897] 2 I.R. 122 at 126.

[40] (1968) 1 W.L.R. 925 at 930G–H and 934G–H, CA.

[41] *e.g. Scudder v. Prothero & Prothero* (1966) 110 S.J. 248, QBD. In *Rondel v. Worsley* [1969] A.C. 191 Lords Reid at 231A and Upjohn at 285A expressed the view that this case may have been decided wrongly on its facts.

[42] *Balamoan v. Holden & Co.* [1999] N.L.J. Prac 898.

[43] [1990] 2 Q.B. 261, at 273–4. The case involved the (old) liability for wasted costs jurisdiction, and thus the test applied by the Court of Appeal was a more stringent one than mere negligence (see para. 10–126).

[44] [1997] 3 All E.R. 909. For another example see *Channon v. Lindley Johnstone* [2000] 2 F.L.R. 734, QBD., where the Court refused to strike out allegations that the solicitors in ancillary relief proceedings failed to obtain evidence about the husband's income, indebtedness to the bank, or medical evidence as to whether diabetes would affect his earnings capacity.

[45] *Hatch v. Lewis* (1861) 2F. & F. 467; *cf. Manley v. Palache* (1895) 73 L.T. 98.

[46] *Waters v. Maguire* [1999] Lloyd's Rep. P.N. 855, where Garland J. struck out a case against a barrister, who had no solicitor and was working for the Free Representation Unit, and held she was not negligent in failing to take a more detailed proof as she had a full note from the claimant.

[47] The second appeal in *Ridehalgh v. Horsefield* [1994] Ch. 205 at 245–247.

personally, the Court of Appeal held that the solicitors were not negligent. Although it is generally a matter for counsel whether expert evidence should be called, the choice of expert is usually made by the solicitor.[48] He may be held negligent, if he instructs an expert whose qualifications or experience render him unsuited to the task: " . . . Undoubtedly an attorney employed to conduct an action is bound to use due and proper care in the employment of persons whose evidence is material to the cause, to prepare themselves to give such evidences."[49]

At the hearing. If the solicitor is acting as advocate, he is no longer immune   **10–183** from suit for negligence in respect of the manner in which he conducts the case.[50] He is liable for any failure to make proper arrangements for the hearing. Thus it is negligent if the solicitor fails to organise the attendance of witnesses.[51] In one old case[52] the attorney arranged for the attendance of a material witness, but did not physically check whether he had arrived. The attorney was held liable in that he "neglected to make any enquiries at the adjacent coffee houses."[53] Whether or not a witness should be *subpoenaed* is a matter of judgment. The solicitor might err in this regard, without being negligent.[54] In *Allen v. Allen*[55] a material witness attended the hearing but "disappeared before giving evidence". Sir Jocelyn Simon P. expressed the view that there was no lack of reasonable diligence by solicitors in failing to ask for an adjournment. If a solicitor fails to instruct counsel[56] (where it was intended to do so) or to attend the hearing, he is plainly in breach of duty.[57]

---

[48] For an example of whether expert evidence had to be sought, see *Henderson v. Hagblom* [2000] 7 W.W.R. 357., Saskatchewan QB, where lawyers were found not to be negligent when they failed to obtain expert evidence when they represented unsuccessful defendants in a claim for damages for fire caused by the negligent construction of a chimney. The lawyers had formed the impression that the client did not want to spend much money on the case whereas as experts were expensive, and there was credible factual evidence that the chimney had been properly constructed which was not accepted at trial.

[49] *Per* Martin B. in *Mercer v. King* (1859) 1 F. & F. 490. The attorney instructed a surveyor as expert witness, who became drunk and did not carry out the necessary measurements. There was some evidence that the attorney knew that the surveyor was addicted to drinking. Held that there was a sufficient case to go to the jury.

[50] See paras 10–106 to 10–108.

[51] *Dunn v. Hallen* (1861) 2 F. & F. 642.

[52] *Reece v. Rigby* (1821) 4 B. & Ald. 202.

[53] *ibid.*, *per* Abbot C.J.

[54] *Price v. Bullen* (1825) 3 L.J. (o.s.) K.B. 39. The position would be different if the witness was plainly reluctant to attend. See also *Dax v. Ward* (1816) 1 Stark. 409: the attorney wrote to a witness and reasonably expected that he would attend.

[55] (1968) 112 S.J. 965.

[56] *De Roufigny v. Peale* (1811) 3 Taunt. 484; *Hawkins v. Harwood* (1849) 4 Ex. 503. ("Instructing counsel" means instructing counsel properly, so as to enable him to discharge his duty. In this case "the brief . . . became mere waste paper.")

[57] *R. v. Tew* (1752) Say. 50: the attorney failed to instruct counsel or attend trial; as a result client was non-suited "and afterwards thrown into gaol"; *Townley v. Jones* (1860) 8 C.B. (N.S.) 289: the attorney failed to instruct counsel or attend trial, and was ordered to pay the costs; *Burgoine v. Taylor* (1878) 9 ChD. 1, CA: a solicitor was ignorant that the case had been transferred to another judge, and so watched the wrong list; he was ordered to pay costs; *Holden v. Holden & Pearson* (1910) 102 L.T. 398; *Ridley v. Tiplady* (1855) 20 Beav. 44 (failure to attend summons); *Swannell v. Ellis* (1823) 1 Bing. 347 (failure to attend arbitration). But compare *Lowry v. Guildford* (1832) 5 C. & P. 234, in which there was a reasonable excuse for the attorney's absence. As to the solicitor's duty to remain in court see *Dauntly v. Hyde* (1841) 6 Jur. 133.

10–184   **After the hearing.** If there is a distinct possibility of an appeal, solicitors who represent clients who have lost litigation should advise them about their rights of appeal, and about the time-limits for implementing any appeal. Thus in *Corfield v. D. S. Bosher & Co.*[58] solicitors negligently failed to advise their clients about an appeal from a rent review arbitration, when the client had requested a reasoned award which showed that he was unhappy with the way the proceedings were going. Similarly in *Hood v. National Farmers Union*[59] the National Farmers Union were negligent in failing to advise on judicial review in relation to a decision of a Dairy Produce Quota Tribunal.

10–185   **Delay in commencing proceedings.** If solicitors delay issuing proceedings for so long that the claim becomes statute-barred, it is hard to see how there can ever[60] be a defence to a claim in negligence.[61] In *Fletcher & Son v. Jubb, Booth & Helliwell*[62] it was successfully argued at first instance that the defendant solicitors were not negligent in failing to appreciate that the limitation period for actions against local authorities was six months. The decision was reversed by the Court of Appeal.[63] Contrast *Carlton v. Fulchers,*[64] where the plaintiff instructed the defendant solicitors more than three years after she was injured in a road traffic accident. The Court of Appeal held that the defendants were not negligent in failing to issue proceedings immediately, as the insurers with whom they were dealing corresponded on the basis that there would be a trial or settlement. Thus an application under section 33 of the Limitation Act 1980 to disapply the limitation period would not have assisted the client, as those delays would not be held against the client. However, when the insurers took the limitation point, the defendants were negligent in failing to advise the plaintiff of the possibility of an application under section 33.

10–186   **Delay in defending proceedings.** Similarly, if solicitors acting for a defendant delay so long before entering an appearance or serving a defence, so that judgment is entered in default, it is hard to see how they could ever escape liability.[65] A defence which is sometimes put forward is that the client was applying for legal aid (now Community Legal Services Funding) and the solicitor

---

[58] [1992] 1 E.G.L.R. 163, Judge Peter Crawford Q.C. sitting as a deputy High Court judge.
[59] [1994] 1 E.G.L.R. 109, CA.
[60] Unless the client refuses to give instructions or to put the solicitor in funds.
[61] *e.g. Clayton v. Kearsey* (1935) 79 S.J. 180, K.B.D.; *Yardley v. Coombes* (1963) 107 S.J. 575, Edmund Davies J.; *Gregory v. Tarlo* (1964) S.J. 219, McNair J.; *Quevillon v. Lamoureux* (1975) 52 D.L.R. (3d) 476, Quebec CA (error caused by solicitor's misapprehension of date of accident); *Cyr v. Pelletier* (1991) 116 N.B.R. (2d) 137, New Brunswick CA; *Smith v. Wells* (1993) 105 Nfld & P.E.I.R. 351, Newfoundland CA. As to the delay in issuing proceedings to enforce a judgment, see *Russell v. Palmer* (1767) 2 Wils. 325; *Harrington v. Binns* (1863) 3 F. & F. 942.
[62] [1920] 1 K.B. 275.
[63] "Now it is not the duty of a solicitor to know the contents of every statute of the realm. But there are some statutes which it is his duty to know; and in these days when the defendants in so many actions are public authorities the Public Authorities Protection Act, 1893, is one of those statutes." (*Per* Scrutton L.J. at 281.) A Canadian decision to the same effect is *Prior v. McNab* (1977) 78 D.L.R. (3d) 319. The Ontario High Court relied on, *inter alia*, Scrutton L.J.'s judgment in *Fletcher & Son v. Jubb, Booth & Helliwell*.
[64] [1997] P.N.L.R. 337.
[65] *e.g. Godefroy v. Jay* (1831) 7 Bing. 413.

was awaiting the outcome of that application before taking any steps. It is hard to see how this defence could succeed. The solicitor in such circumstances is likely to have a number of choices: he can apply for a certificate; he could ensure that a sufficient extension of time is granted by the claimant's solicitors or the court; or he could make it plain to the client that he will not act unless and until public funding is granted, and that in the meantime the client must act in person.[66]

Delay after the action has commenced. Once proceedings are under way, the claimant's solicitor has a duty to prosecute the action with reasonable diligence.[67] If, therefore, the action is struck out for failing to comply with time limits or want of prosecution, he will have no defence to an action for breach of duty,[68] unless the client has caused or consented to the delay.[69] It appears that delay by counsel does not afford the solicitor a defence. If counsel is dilatory, the solicitor should regularly chase him up,[70] and if no response is forthcoming withdraw his instructions and pass them to another counsel "for a more ready response".[71] In recent years delay in the conduct of personal injuries litigation (either before or after the issue of the writ or claim form) has given rise to a substantial proportion of solicitors' negligence claims.[72] **10–187**

Even where the solicitor's delay does not result in the loss of an action, he may still be liable for breach of duty.[73] Thus if an adjournment is sought at a late stage because of lack of preparation, the court may exercise its powers to disallow the solicitor's costs.[74] Even before the introduction of the Civil Procedure Rules, the attitude of the courts had become less tolerant towards delay; thus Lord Griffiths stated in a case concerning late amendment: **10–188**

---

[66] See the *obiter* remarks of the judge approved by Lord Griffiths in *Donovan v. Gwentoys Ltd* [1990] 1 W.L.R. 472 at 476A–D, HL.

[67] *The Flower Bowl (a firm) v. Hodges Menswear Ltd, The Times*, June 14, 1988, CA.

[68] *e.g. Fitzpatrick v. Batger & Co. Ltd* [1967] 1 W.L.R. 706, CA; *Reggentin v. Beecholme Bakeries Ltd* [1968] 2 Q.B. 276: "It follows, almost inevitably, that the solicitors for the plaintiff were at fault: and are liable . . . for negligence.", *per* Lord Denning M.R. at 278C; *Welburn v. Mayberry* (1971) 115 S.J. 468, CA.

[69] See *Allen v. Sir Alfred McAlpine & Sons Ltd* [1968] 2 Q.B. 229 at 256, *per* Diplock L.J. See also *Gouzenko v. Harris* (1977) 72 D.L.R. (3d) 293, Ontario HCt.: delay by the solicitors who first acted for plaintiff held not to be negligent.

[70] Thus in *Mansouri v. Bloomsbury Health Authority, The Times,* July 20, 1987 a writ was issued towards the end of the limitation period and the papers were sent to counsel for his advice. Dillon L.J. stated that "it was not satisfactory for the solicitors simply to send chasers to counsel once a month."

[71] *Mainz v. James and Charles Dodd, The Times*, July 21, 1978, Watkins J.

[72] See A. Bradford, "Solicitors' negligence and personal injury claims" *Law Society Gazette*, August 28, 1985, p. 2323.

[73] *Shilcock v. Passman* (1836) 7 C. & P. 289: an attorney was engaged to secure the discharge of a client who was imprisoned for debt. As a result of delays caused by the attorney the client's discharge was delayed by about two months. The attorney was held liable. *cf. Lavanchy v. Leverson* (1859) 1 F. & F. 615: an attorney was not liable for the delay in securing the discharge of debtor, because he believed negotiations were in progress. See also *Jones v. Jones* [1970] 2 Q.B. 576 at 585, Salmon L.J., and *Thompson v. Brown* [1981] 1 W.L.R. 744 at 750G–751A, *per* Cumming Bruce L.J.: a solicitor who delays issuing a writ for personal injuries, with the result that the client's right to interest is prejudiced, may be guilty of negligence.

[74] *Fowke v. Duthie* [1991] 1 All E.R. 337, Macpherson J. See also *Sinclair-Jones v. Kay* [1989] 1 W.L.R. 114, CA.

"We can no longer afford to show the same indulgence towards the negligent conduct of litigation as was perhaps possible in a more leisured age. There will be cases in which justice will be better served by allowing the consequences of the negligence of the lawyers to fall upon their own heads rather than by allowing an amendment at a very late stage of the proceedings."[75]

10–189   **Settlement: consulting the client.** The solicitor has ostensible authority to compromise litigation on the client's behalf and any compromise which he makes (provided it does not involve a matter "collateral to the action") will bind the client.[76] Some nineteenth century authorities suggest that if a solicitor enters a reasonable compromise, without any reference to the client, there is no breach of duty,[77] unless the client has specifically forbidden that compromise.[78] The question presumably depends upon the terms of the particular retainer. Nowadays the courts would probably be reluctant to imply a term that the solicitor could settle without reference to his client, if no such term had been expressly agreed. The solicitor would be unwise if he took such a course in reliance on the authorities referred to above: they appear to be in conflict with *Sill v. Thomas*[79]; and they are not in accord with the general duty to inform the client of the progress of his legal affairs.[80] There was some discussion of this subject (albeit *obiter*) in *Waugh v. H.B. Clifford & Sons Ltd.*[81] Brightman L.J. considered that the solicitor's implied authority to compromise an action (as between himself and his client) was narrower than the ostensible authority. He took the example of a defamation action in which the defendant's solicitor may agree to settle at a large figure, which would be within his ostensible authority but not within his implied authority. "In the light of the solicitor's knowledge of his client's cash position it might be quite unreasonable and indeed grossly negligent for the solicitor to commit his client to such a burden without first inquiring if it were acceptable."[82] In the New Zealand case of *Thompson v. Howley*[83] Somers J. decided that a solicitor is negligent unless he obtains the express instructions of his client to settle an action.

10–190   **Settlement: the merits.** A solicitor is bound to exercise reasonable care in the conduct of settlement negotiations and in advising on the merits of any settlement proposed. Such advice often entails weighing up imponderable factors, and a

---

[75] *Ketteman v. Hansel Properties* [1987] 1 A.C. 189 at 220F–G.

[76] See *Waugh v. H.B. Clifford & Sons Ltd* [1982] Ch. 374, CA. The court will not regard a matter as "collateral" unless it really is extraneous to the action: *ibid.* at 388D.

[77] *Wraight v. Johnston* (1858) 1 F. & F. 128; *Chown v. Parrott* (1863) 14 C.B. (N.S.) 74; *Re Newen* [1903] 1 Ch. 812.

[78] *Fray v. Voules* (1859) 1 E. & E. 839; *Butler v. Knight* (1867) L.R. 2 Ex. 109.

[79] (1839) 8 C. & P. 762; see also *Pelky v. Hudson Bay Insurance Co.* (1981) 35 O.R. (2d) 97, Ontario HCt: solicitors for defendants and defendants' insurers failed to communicate an offer to settle at the policy limit.

[80] See para. 10–156.

[81] [1982] Ch. 374. For discussion of this decision, see P. Kenny, "Authority to compromise" 126 S.J. 663.

[82] *ibid.* at 387 (the other members of the Court of Appeal agreed, at 383A and 390C). This passage marks a shift from the earlier cases referred to above. Communication between solicitor and client is much easier and quicker now than it was when those cases were decided. Even if the proposed settlement is comfortably within the client's means, it is surely reasonable to consult the client first.

[83] [1977] 1 N.Z.L.R. 16.

mere error of judgment is unlikely in practice to constitute negligence.[84] Solicitors have been held liable, however, for advising their client to settle at too low a figure, as a result of their failure to make proper enquiries.[85] Particular problems arise where the defendant is insured, but with inadequate cover, and the same solicitor represents both the defendant and his insurers. Conflicts of interest can easily arise (*e.g.* if the claimant offers to accept the full amount for which the defendant is insured). The solicitor must keep both clients informed of offers which are made.[86] It may be necessary for separate solicitors to advise the insured defendant in respect of the settlement negotiations.

Ceasing to act. As a matter of law,[87] and of professional conduct,[88] the solicitor can only determine the retainer for good reason and upon reasonable notice. The solicitor is entitled to insist upon being put in funds by his client, in order to meet disbursements. If, after proceedings have begun, the client refuses to put him in funds, the solicitor is entitled to refuse to continue acting.[89] He must give reasonable notice of his requirement for funds.[90] A solicitor is also entitled to withdraw from proceedings if, having reasonable and probable grounds for commencing the action, he later finds that it cannot be maintained.[91] A solicitor

10–191

---

[84] See the law in relation to barristers on this point, set out at chap. 11 paras 11–043 to 11–045. Note that in *Griffin v. Kingsmill* [2001] E.W.C.A. Civ. 934 the solicitors were held to be liable for undersettling the action as well as counsel, and they did not seek to defend themselves on the basis that they relied on counsel. For a more common example see *Maillet and Pothier v. Haliburton & Comeau* (1983) 55 N.S.R. (2d) and 114 A.P.R. 311, Nova Scotia Sup. Ct: the plaintiff in a personal injuries action was awarded $75,000 by the jury at trial. The defendants appealed and on her solicitor's advice she accepted $40,000 in settlement. Her subsequent action against the solicitor was dismissed. Burchell J. said that the issue was not "what the Court of Appeal would have done." It was "whether a reasonably competent solicitor could have been sufficiently uncertain about the outcome of the appeal to conclude that the settlement at $40,000 was advisable" (*ibid.* at 315). It is submitted that this approach is correct. It is not desirable that a plaintiff should be able, too readily, to accept what is an offer from the original defendant (thus escaping the hazards of the original litigation) and then "top it up" by making a claim against his solicitors.

[85] *McNamara v. Martin Mears & Co.* (1983) 126 S.J. 69: the solicitor for a wife in matrimonial proceedings proposed a figure of £15,000 in settlement of her financial claims and advised her to accept £12,000. The solicitor ought to have ascertained the total assets of the family. He should have proposed a figure of £24,000 and advised rejection of the £12,000. See also the similar case of *Dickinson v. James Alexander & Co.* (1990) P.N. 205, where the negligence was admitted on these issues.

[86] *Pelky v. Hudson Bay Insurance Co.* (1981) 35 O.R. (2d) 97, Ontario HCt. Solicitors failed to communicate an offer of settlement to insurers. Judgment was ultimately given for more than the insurance limit.

[87] *Summit Property Ltd v. Pitmans (a Firm)* [2001] Lloyd's Rep. P.N. 164, Park J. There, the solicitor withdrew because he was told to do so by a related party who was not his client, but was held to have no good reason to do so and also gave the client inadequate notice. However, no loss was caused. For another example of a wrongful summary termination see *Young v. Purdy* [1997] P.N.L.R. 130, where no loss was caused.

[88] See further the Law Society's *Guide to the Professional Conduct of Solicitors* (8th ed., 1999), principle 12.12.

[89] Solicitors Act 1974, s.65(2). The section imposes a number of conditions, including the need for reasonable notice of the requirement of funds and of the withdrawal from the retainer.

[90] In *Hoby v. Built* (1832) B. & D. 350 the attorney told his client, five days before the commencement of the assizes in which the client's case was to be heard, that he needed funds in order to instruct counsel. The client failed to make any payment and the attorney did not instruct counsel. It was held that the attorney was in breach of duty in not giving reasonable notice. In *Noel v. Lewis Holdings Ltd* (1990) 44 B.C.L.R. (2d) 37 the British Columbia CA held that there was an implied term of the retainer that the solicitor may withdraw upon reasonable notice on non-payment of the accounts due.

[91] *Lawrence v. Potts* (1834) 6 Car. & P. 428.

will be negligent if, after public funding has been withdrawn, he fails to advise the client of the consequences of withdrawal and what steps he could take, and he is also under a duty to consider making representations to restore the funding.[92]

(d) *Misconduct of non-contentious business*

10–192   The variety of non-contentious work undertaken by solicitors is so wide, that few generalisations about the solicitor's duty in such cases can usefully be offered, beyond that set out in the first part of this chapter.[93] If, however, the solicitor errs in carrying out a straightforward task of the kind customarily undertaken by the profession, he is unlikely to escape a finding of negligence.[94] He is also unlikely to escape liability if he causes the client loss through failing to maintain adequate office procedures.[95]

(i) *Conveyancing*[96]

10–193   **Protecting the client: customary searches.** A large part of a solicitor's activities are directed towards protecting the client against possible future hazards. This is particularly true in the realm of conveyancing. If a solicitor fails to protect his client by making the customary enquiries and searches then he is negligent[97]:

> "It is clear negligence if an attorney suffers himself to be misled by the apparent respectability of the vendor, and thereby neglects his obvious duty of making reasonable inquiries into his title."[98]

A purchaser's solicitor should ensure that the vendor can show a good legal title free from adverse interests.[99] Thus in *Faragher v. Gerber*[1] a solicitor was held liable for failing to make enquiries which would have elicited plans for a major

---

[92] *Casey v. Hugh James Jones & Jenkins* [1999] Lloyd's Rep. P.N. 115, Thomas J.

[93] See paras 10–077 to 10–105.

[94] *e.g. Parker v. Rolls* (1854) 14 C.B. 691: drawing up an agreement which was unenforceable, since it was not under seal; *Brown v. Tolley* (1874) 31 L.T. 485: failure to give proper notices of creditors' meetings; *Carruthers v. Hodgson* (1896) 100 L.T.J. 395: appointing an incompetent stockbroker to sell the plaintiff's stock; *Roberts v. J.W. Ward & Son* (1982) 126 S.J. 120, CA: error in exercising option; *Harris v. Carruthers* (1902) 2 N.S.W.S.R. 100, CA: failure to notice or properly understand material words in a deed). *cf. Elkington v. Holland* (1842) 1 Dowl. (N.S.) 643.

[95] *e.g. Reeve v. Palmer* (1859) 5 C.B. (N.S.) 84: attorney liable for loss of deeds, unless he proves that he exercised reasonable care; *North Western Rail Co. v. Sharp* (1854) 10 Exch. 451: attorney's duty to deliver up documents "in a reasonable state or order"; *D v. D* (1962) 106 S.J. 959, Div. Ct: solicitor's duty to make quite sure that he has the client's correct address. The fact that he receives no answer to letters should put him on enquiry; *Frank v. Seifert Sedley & Co.* (1964) 108 S.J. 523, Melford Stevenson J.: solicitors accidentally sent draft contract to the wrong party; *Blood v. Cotton* [1943] N.I.L.R. 68, Northern Ireland CA: duty to render true accurate and intelligible accounts.

[96] For an alternative analysis of the cases see H. Evans, *'Lawyers' Liabilities'*, (2nd ed., 2002), chap. 4.

[97] Thus, for instance, solicitors acting for the purchasers of a sub-lease should inspect the head lease, *Hill v. Harris* [1965] 2 Q.B. 601, CA.

[98] *per* Mellor J. in *Allen v. Clark* (1863) 7 L.T. 781. Thus the solicitors will be negligent if they hand over the purchase money before such searches are conducted, see para. 10–200 below.

[99] See *Dogma Properties Ltd v. Gale* (1984) 136 N.L.J. 453, Kilner Brown J.; *Holmes v. Kennard & Son* (1984) 128 S.J. 854, CA: solicitors for purchasers were held liable for failing to take reasonable steps to protect their clients in respect of rights which had been registered by the vendor's wife.

[1] [1994] E.G.C.S. 122, QBD.

new highway, despite a reply to a local search which advised checking with the London Docklands Development Corporation.

Proper confirmation. Some care needs to be taken with the searches and enquiries, and the replies received should be properly considered. Thus the plans should be closely scrutinised to ensure that the limits of the property accord with what is supposed to be conveyed.[2] Similarly, if the pre-contract enquiries stated that all consents had been obtained for major renovations, the solicitors should obtain copies of the consents either from the vendor or from another source such as the local authority.[3] If the purchaser's solicitors receive formal answers to enquiries from the vendor's solicitors which contradict information from the estate agent, further enquiry should be made.[4] In *Holmes v. Kennard & Son*[5] the defendant solicitors, who acted for the purchasers, discovered that the vendor's wife had registered a notice protecting her rights under the Matrimonial Homes Act 1967. The wife's solicitors sent to the defendants a form for withdrawing a caution and not one for cancelling a notice. After completion, the wife succeeded in her objection to the cancellation of the charge. The defendants were found to be negligent in accepting a document which dealt with a caution and not a notice, and which had been signed by a person disclosing no authority to cancel the notice. In *Fashion Brokers Ltd v. Clarke Hayes (a Firm)*[6] the defendant solicitors relied on confirmation by telephone from a planning officer of the local authority that the intended use of the property which their client was purchasing conformed with its planning consent. The Court of Appeal held that it was not reasonable to rely on such oral confirmation, and the solicitors should have obtained proper authentication before completion.[7]

10–194

Suspicious circumstances. There may be suspicious circumstances which should prompt further action. Thus in *McManus Developments Ltd v. Barbridge Properties Ltd*[8] the plaintiff developers purchased some property. Between contract and completion a fence at the edge of the property was moved by the adjoining tenants to what they claimed was its true position. The defendants, who were the developers' solicitors and were told what had happened, only asked for the fence to be put back. The disputed strip did not belong to the property, and

10–195

---

[2] *Nielsen v. Watson* (1982) 125 D.L.R. 326, Ontario HCt: the plan showed the garage and the driveway outside the limits of property to be conveyed; solicitors held negligent. There is, however, no duty to inspect the property in the absence of special instructions, see *Bown v. Gould & Swayne* [1996] P.N.L.R. 130 *per* Millett L.J.

[3] *Cottingham v. Attey Bower & Jones (a Firm)* [2000] P.N.L.R. 557, Rimer J. If they had known of the absence of consent, the solicitors should also have advised that although there could be no notice under s. 36(1) or (2) of the Building Act 1984, as the works were carried out eight years before, there was a risk of injection proceedings under s. 36(6), which had no 12-month time limit.

[4] *Computastaff Ltd v. Ingledew Brown Bennison & Garrett* (1983) 268 E.G. 906, at 911 col. 1, McNeill J.

[5] (1984) 128 S.J. 854, CA.

[6] [2000] P.N.L.R. 473.

[7] The decision was in the context of third party proceedings brought by the defendant solicitor against the local authority.

[8] [1996] P.N.L.R. 431. However, the solicitors were not negligent in failing to supply a copy of the Land Registry plan to their clients, as that would not have added anything to the sale particulars which they had already. Similarly, in *Doran v. Delaney* [1996] 1 I.R.L.M. 490 there was some doubt about the boundaries of the property, but the plaintiff's own solicitors negligently failed to have the boundaries staked out or to insist on the provision of an ordnance survey map in the contract which would show the boundaries. This part of the decision was not appealed to the Supreme Court (reported at [1998] 2 I.L.R.M. 1).

the developers had to buy it in order to proceed with their plans. The Court of Appeal decided that the intrusion should have set alarm bells ringing about whether there was an underlying problem, and the defendant solicitors should have taken further action. Similarly, in *Mercantile Building Society v. J.W. Mitchell Dodds & Co.*[9] the defendant solicitors acting on a remortgage obtained a land certificate, in which there were indications that should have put a conveyancer on enquiry that something might be amiss. They showed it to the borrower to check what he thought he owned, but they failed to confirm the plan with the client lender who could have compared it with their valuers' plan which would have shown a discrepancy, and were held to be negligent.

10–196   **Standard of care not absolute.** While the standard of care in conveyancing cases is high, it is not absolute, as is illustrated by *Neighbour v. Barker.*[10] The defendant solicitors had advised the plaintiff clients to have a survey before purchase, but the advice was not followed. The plaintiffs employed a surveyor after purchase, who informed the defendants that the property their clients had just purchased had structural defects. The solicitors advised the plaintiffs to complete the sale, because the consequences of not doing so could be financially disastrous, which advice was followed. In fact the vendors had made fraudulent misrepresentations, which would have enabled the plaintiffs to escape from the transaction. They alleged that the defendants should have advised delay to investigate whether the plaintiffs had any remedy. However, the Court of Appeal decided that the defendants were not liable, because there was no reason why the defendants should have thought that there was any possible escape from the transaction.[11]

10–197   **Remote contingencies.** A solicitor is not liable for failing to protect his client against a remote contingency.[12] The remoteness of the contingency is an impor-

---

[9] [1993] N.P.C. 99, CA. Contrast *U.C.B. Bank plc v. David J. Pinder plc* [1998] P.N.L.R. 398, QBD., where solicitors could not have deduced from the plan that a small but significant part of the security property was outside the principal title. In accordance with normal practice, they sought the confirmation of the valuers that the area on the plan corresponded exactly with the area valued, and were informed " . . . we can confirm that the area shaded would appear to correspond with the premises". The solicitors were found not to be negligent.

[10] (1992) 40 *e.g.* 140. See also *Gorrie v. Nielsen* [1989] 2 W.W.R. 437, Alberta CA. P owned W Ltd and M Ltd. W Ltd sold the lease of an aircraft hangar to M Ltd, but the assignment was not registered. P then sold his shares in W Ltd, which by then owned M Ltd, and secured the deferred part of the purchase price on the lease, with the mortgage executed by W Ltd. The purchaser defaulted, and an action under the mortgage was met with the defence that W Ltd did not have an interest in leasehold property. The failure to file a *caveat* against the title was held to be an error of judgment, and the defendant solicitor was found not to be negligent. Contrast *Peyman v. Lanjani* [1985] 1 Ch. 457, where the Court of Appeal upheld a finding of negligence that a solicitor failed to advise his client that he could rescind the contract as the title was voidable, when the solicitor had sufficient grounds to enquire whether there were facts justifying such advice.

[11] Similarly, there was no duty to advise a client to obtain security for a warranty from a shell company when the lawyer was instructed after the agreement had been signed, and the scope of the retainer was thus implicitly limited, see *Wong v. 407527 Ontario Ltd* (1999) 26 R.P.R. (3d) 262, followed in *Vaz-Oxlade v. Volkenstein* (2000) 35 R.P.R. (3d) 165 and *Baker v. Turville* (2001) 38 R.P.R. (3d) 155, all Ontario CA.

[12] *e.g. Bryant v. Busk* (1827) 4 Russ. 1: the title deeds of property were destroyed by fire between exchange and completion. Sir John Leach M.R. observed that the purchaser's solicitor (who had looked at the deeds before the fire) was not culpably negligent for failing to notice who the attesting witnesses were. At the time of inspecting the deeds the solicitor did not have a fire in contemplation. His purpose was to ascertain if the contents of the deeds corresponded with the statement of the abstract.

tant question. Thus in *G. & K. Ladenbau v. Crawley & De Reya*[13] solicitors acting for a purchaser of vacant land failed to discover that rights of common had been registered against it. Mocatta J. held that the solicitors were negligent in failing to search the commons register even though, at the material time, it had seemed most unlikely that there would be any entry. The judge conceded that there was room for discretion in whether or not to make such a search "for example to densely built up land".[14] In contrast, in *Kotowich v. Petursson*[15] a solicitor was held not liable for failing to check zoning (*i.e.* planning permission) where his client already had a binding contract. The plaintiff was bound to complete, although she alleged she might have been able to exercise damage control.

Other errors. A solicitor is negligent if he fails to register any registerable **10–198** interest in, or rights over, land which his client may have.[16] In *Creech v. Mayorcas*[17] a solicitor completed the purchase of the lease of a shop without obtaining the landlord's licence to assign and licence for change of user, or any undertaking from the vendor's solicitors to obtain such licences. Pennycuick J. described the omission (which was made by a legal executive) as an "understandable slip", but held that the solicitor was liable.

Communicating with the client. A solicitor should advise his client about **10–199** important matters that come to his notice, such as the existence of a right of way, or a defect in title, or the absence of planning permission, or the existence of a "contracts race".[18] He should warn his client about risks that the client may not appreciate,[19] such as the nature and effect of a restrictive covenant and the risks

---

[13] [1978] 1 W.L.R. 266. See also para. 10–090.

[14] *ibid.* at 289A. See also *Kolan v. Solicitor* (1969) 7 D.L.R. (3d) 481 aff'd. (1970) 11 D.L.R. (3d) 672, Ontario CA: solicitor negligent in not searching to see if the property was subject to a demolition order in the special circumstances of knowing that the property was old, having directed his mind to the possibility of the property being substandard.

[15] [1994] 4 W.W.R. 669, Manitoba Q.B. Similarly in *Wong v. 407527 Ontario Ltd* (2000) 179 D.L.R. (4th) 38 the plaintiff purchased a block of flats with a warranty from a shell company as to the rental income. The Ontario Court of Appeal held that the defendant lawyer was not negligent in failing to advise an attempt to obtain security for the warranty, because by the time he was instructed the agreement was already executed. In contrast, in *Redmond v. Densmore* (1997) 153 Nfld & P.E.I.R. 181, Newfoundland CA, the defendant solicitor was negligent and caused the plaintiff loss in failing to report to him on zoning, as the contract for the purchase of the property could be rescinded on the grounds of misrepresentation.

[16] *e.g. Midland Bank v. Hett Stubbs & Kemp* [1979] Ch. 384, Oliver J.: failure to register option; *Stratton Ltd v. Weston, Financial Times*, April 11, 1990, ChD: failure to register an equitable lease when a receiver was appointed over the landlord.

[17] (1966) 198 E.G. 1091.

[18] See para. 10–156. The client will be fixed with knowledge communicated by the other side to the solicitor: *Strover v. Harrington* [1988] 1 Ch. 390, ChD, but *cf. Halifax Mortgage Services Ltd v. Stepsky* [1996] ChD 207, CA, see para. 10–102.

[19] See para. 10–165. Thus in *O'Brien v. Hooker Homes* (1993) A.S.C. 56–217, Sup. Ct NSW, a solicitor who arranged finance for the purchase of property by simple clients owed a duty to spell out the workings of their interest obligations. In *Keep Point Development Ltd v. Chan Chi Yim* [2000] 3 H.K.L.R.D. 166 the solicitors were found liable for failing to explain to unsophisticated clients the unusual danger of selling their property for option agreements on land which was not registered. In *Carvin v. Dunham Brindley & Linn* [1997] E.G.C.S. 90, part of the garden of a house was used as a storm drain which had not been adopted, and the purchaser was initially granted only a licence over it. It was intended that the remaining land would be conveyed to the purchaser in due course when the position had been finalised. The Court of Appeal upheld the judge's decision that the solicitor was not in breach of his duty to the prospective purchaser, a successful man of business, as he had

attached to it,[20] or of the advisability of making inquiries about the financial standing of the tenants when the purchase agreement expressly provided that the vendor gave no warranty about the issue.[21] In *Lloyds Bank plc v. Parker Bullen (a Firm)*[22] a solicitor was found liable for failing to inform the lendor that the lease of the property prevented alienation. The solicitor should explain the effect of the conveyance, in particular any unusual or important provisions[23]:

> "A person who goes to a lawyer with respect to a land transaction is entitled to expect that lawyer to investigate the state of any title that is germane to the matter and to explain to the client exactly what it is that is portrayed by the state of the title."[24]

Thus in *Atkins v. Atkins*[25] the solicitors failed explain the real purpose of the transaction to the plaintiff, which was to raise money on her house for her son, and was held to be negligent. In contrast, in *Haigh v. Wright Hassall & Co.*[26] a solicitor exchanged contracts on being assured by his client that a deposit cheque would be available that afternoon. The solicitor was held not to be liable; he had no duty to question how secure was the availability of the deposit cheque. However, the answer might have been different if the client was wholly inexperienced.

10–200   **Handing over the purchase money.** In *Gregory v. Shepherds*[27] the claimant instructed the defendant solicitors in connection with the purchase of Spanish property. They were not liable for the defaults of Spanish lawyers whom they instructed. However, the Court of Appeal held that the solicitors were negligent for paying over the client's money to the foreign purchaser without first obtaining specific confirmation that the searches which the Spanish lawyers had been instructed to carry out had been satisfactorily completed and that it was in order to make the payment. In *Edward Wong Finance Co. Ltd v. Johnson Stokes & Master*[28] it was held that solicitors for a prospective mortgagee were negligent to hand over funds to the vendor's solicitor in return for an undertaking. Where the purchaser wishes a deposit to be held until completion, his solicitor must inform the vendor's solicitor that the deposit is to be held as stakeholder.[29]

---

explained the nature of the licence and the fact that the plaintiff would not immediately be acquiring the title to the whole property.
[20] *Bittlestone v. Keegan Williams* [1997] E.G.C.S. 8, [1997] N.P.C. 3, ChD, unless the solicitor could satisfy himself that it was plainly unenforceable.
[21] *Hanave Pt Ltd v. Lfot Pt Ltd* (2000) 168 A.L.R. 318, Federal Court of Australia.
[22] [2000] Lloyd's Rep. P.N. 51, Longmore J.
[23] See paras 10–166 to 10–167.
[24] *per* Thackray J. in *Graybriar Industries Ltd v. Davis & Co.* (1992) 46 B.C.L.R. (2d) 164, 181. British Columbia Sup. Ct. Similarly, in *Behrooz Siasati v. Bottoms & Webb (a Firm)* [1997] N.P.C. 20 [1997] E.G.C.S. 22, QBD, the solicitor had a duty to a foreign client with limited English to take all reasonable steps to explain, if necessary through an interpreter, the nature and scope of the obligations of the lease of old commercial property which he intended to take on, of the risks involved, and to take reasonable steps to ensure that the client understood the advice, which should generally be reduced to writing so the client could obtain a translation.
[25] [1993] E.G.C.S. 54, ChD.
[26] [1994] E.G.C.S. 54, CA.
[27] [2000] P.N.L.R. 769, CA.
[28] [1984] A.C. 296. Distinguished by Gray J. in *Patel v. Daybells (a Firm)* [2001] P.N.L.R. 43 on the grounds that the time-frame for completion was short. See paras. 10–85 to 10–88 above. The implications of *Wong* for conveyancing practice in England are discussed in B. George, "Can solicitors safely trust each other?" 128 S.J. 231.
[29] *Desmond v. Boyles* [1985] I.R. 449, HCt.

Acting for the vendor.[30] Where the solicitor is acting for a vendor, his   **10–201**
answers to enquiries before contract or requisitions on title are of the utmost
importance. If the answers are erroneous, the client may be exposed to liability
to the purchaser. In the ordinary way, any mistake by the solicitor in this respect
is likely to be regarded as negligent, unless there is some justification such as
incorrect instructions from the client. In *Simmons v. Pennington*,[31] however,
solicitors who gave the incorrect answer to a requisition escaped liability, since
they had acted in accordance with the general practice of conveyancers and could
not reasonably have foreseen the consequences of their answer. Clerical errors
may be negligent. In *Stovold v. Barlows*[32] the defendant solicitors were found to
be negligent for failing to check whether the purchaser's solicitors were on the
DX before sending the deeds in an urgent transaction. They sent them to a retailer
with a similar name.

Time limits. Many conveyancing transactions are carried out within strict time   **10–202**
limits. The most obvious example is the requirement under the Landlord and
Tenant Act 1954 Part II with respect to business tenancies, where there are the
strict time limits for serving notices to renew leases and for applying to the court
to renew the lease.[33] Time limits may be imposed by some third party (for
example, the party "on the other side" of the transaction or the client's bank).
They may be imposed by the circumstances of the client. Thus in many domestic
conveyances it is essential that the exchange of contracts on the sale and the
purchase should be synchronised and also that the completion of those two
transactions should be synchronised. A failure by the solicitor to carry out his
client's instructions in this regard will usually be both a breach of contract and
negligent. The solicitor's task in synchronising exchanges of contracts has been
made easier by the decision of the Court of Appeal in *Domb v. Isoz*,[34] in which
it was held that (subject to instructions to the contrary) a solicitor could achieve
an exchange of contracts by means of a telephone conversation. Buckley L.J.
stated that in view of the integrity and standing of solicitors, this procedure did
not involve an undesirable degree of risk.[35] Where a conveyancing transaction is
carried out as part of a legitimate scheme to reduce tax liability, this may impose
special time constraints. In the New Zealand case of *Stirling v. Poulgrain*[36] the
first plaintiff instructed the defendant solicitors to transfer two farms to a trust, in
order to reduce the estate duty payable on her death. The Inland Revenue agreed

---

[30] For an unusual case see *Slater Wilmshurst v. Crown Group* [1991] 1 N.Z.L.R. 344, HCt. The vendor
of commercial property asked its solicitor to check the legal description of land. The solicitor made
no check on the register, and so missed a right of pre-emption to buy the property. Solicitors were
found negligent as undisclosed encumbrances could have caused argument later.
[31] [1955] 1 W.L.R. 183, CA. See also para. 10–084.
[32] [1996] P.N.L.R. 91, CA. *cf. Infantino v. MacLean* [2001] 3 All E.R. 802, where in the context of
the court's power under CPR 6.9(1) to dispense with service of a claim form, Douglas Brown J.
considered it arguable or even doubtful that solicitors were negligent for using the wrong DX address
by reason of a computer error.
[33] In general the duty of a solicitor, when his client as tenant is served with a notice under Part II of
the Landlord and Tenant Act 1954 is clear. He must tell his client of the two time limits. He must also
take such steps as are sufficient, in all the circumstances of the case, to ensure that if either time limit
is allowed to expire without the appropriate step being taken, that is the fault of the client." *Per*
Staughton J. in *R.P.Howard Ltd v. Woodman Matthews and Co.* [1983] B.C.L.C. 117, at 121E.
[34] [1980] Ch. 548.
[35] *ibid.* at 558.
[36] [1980] 2 N.Z.L.R. 402.

a valuation for both farms, provided that the transfers were effected by a specified date. The transaction was not completed in time, with the result that the valuation was increased by $90,000. Mahon J. held that the solicitors were in breach of contract,[37] and this decision was upheld by the Court of Appeal.[38]

10–203   **Wider duties.** A solicitor's duties in conveyancing may extend more widely than to strictly conveyancing matters. Some duties will be obvious from the nature of the purchase. Thus if the client is purchasing a public house, then the solicitor will need to enquire as to the nature of the liquor license.[39] In *Raintree Ltd v. Holmes*[40] the defendant solicitors acted for the plaintiff company in the purchase of land, which carried planning permission. The business of the company was to buy development land to build houses, as the solicitors knew. They failed to ascertain the expiry date of the planning permission, which was between the date of the conveyance and the date of the intended start of building works, and were held to be in breach of duty. When acting for a purchaser of property, the solicitor should, if he has any reason to doubt the matter, enquire whether the client has made proper financial arrangements.[41] If the client needs a mortgage in order to complete, the solicitor ought at least to warn him of the risks involved if contracts are exchanged before the mortgage has been arranged.[42] A more difficult question is whether the solicitor is obliged to advise a house purchaser of the advantages of a structural survey. Certainly it is good practice to do so. It appears from *Buckland v. Mackesy*[43] that where the client is inexperienced and the property is not new, the failure to give such advice could amount to negligence. The position with respect to an ordinary survey remains to be determined.[44] In *Johnson v. Bingley Dyson & Furey*[45] Mr Ben Hytner Q.C. sitting as a deputy High Court judge held that although there was no general duty to advise a seller to obtain an independent valuation, there was one in the circumstances of that case, where the client was suffering from mental illness and her son was not in a position to give her sound advice on such matters. If a house is

---

[37] *ibid.* at 407.

[38] *ibid.* at 413.

[39] *Kelly v. Finbarr J. Crowley* [1985] I.R. 212, Murphy J.

[40] (1984) 134 N.L.J. 522, Hobhouse J. *cf. Woodglen v. Owens* (1999) 27 R.P.R. (3d) 237, Ontario CA, where the lawyer had no obligation to inform his developer client that the easement he obtained for him might not be sufficient if the "part lot" control provisions were imposed. The developer had other lawyers acting for him generally, and the defendant's retainer was limited.

[41] See further para. 10–199. However, in *Citicorp Australia Ltd v. O'Brien* (1996) 40 N.S.W.L.R. 398, the New South Wales Court of Appeal held that a solicitor acting for unsophisticated clients in the purchase of property owed no duty to inform them of their views of the financial prospects of the mortgage they were taking out. The solicitors had given a short explanation of terms of the loan and mortgage.

[42] *Buckland v. Mackesy* (1968) E.G. 969, CA. See also H.W. Wilkinson, "The solicitor's duty on exchange of contracts" *New Law Journal*, February 23, 1978.

[43] (1968) 208 E.G. 969. The claim against the solicitor failed in this case, since it was held that he had given sufficient advice to his client. See Salmon L.J. at 971.

[44] In *Brenner v. Gregory* (1972) 30 D.L.R. (3d) 672, Ontario HCt, a solicitor was not liable in not advising clients of the danger of purchasing property without any survey; expert evidence showed that it was not the local practice to do so. *cf. O'Connor v. First National* [1991] I.R.L.M. 208 where Lynch J. held the solicitor liable in such circumstances, having regard to established conveyancing practice.

[45] [1997] P.N.L.R. 393.

purchased in joint names, it may be negligent not to take steps to find out and declare the extent of the beneficial interests.[46]

The National Protocol. On March 21, 1990 the Law Society launched a **10–204** "National Protocol" for domestic conveyancing and an accompanying Council Statement. The Council states that the protocol is to be "preferred practice", and there should be full disclosure to the other side of the extent to which the protocol will be followed.[47] The Law Society has also published formulae for exchanging contracts, and a code for completion by post.[48] These steps are likely to lead to a greater degree of standardisation of conveyancing transactions, and to be relevant to the question of negligence. The Law Society has also issued guidance on a solicitor's duties with regard to potential mortgage frauds, and with regard to property fraud generally (the "Green Card").[49]

Mortgages and undue influence. Solicitors are often instructed to advise in **10–205** cases where there may be undue influence. The most typical example is a wife who is entering a mortgage of property to raise money from a bank for her husband's business affairs.[50] In *Royal Bank of Scotland plc v. Etridge (No. 2)*[51] the House of Lords gave important guidance as to what should happen in such circumstances in the future. The leading speech of Lord Nicholls must be read with care to see precisely what is required of banks and solicitors, and the following is only a summary. The bank is put on inquiry whenever a wife offers to stand surety for her husband's debts, even if the wife held shares or was a director, and the same would apply whenever any person in a non-commercial relationship offers to guarantee the debts of another. Banks are unwilling to assume the responsibility of advising the wife, and their practice is to refer the wife to an independent legal adviser. For previous cases, it would be sufficient if the bank obtained confirmation that the solicitor had brought home to the wife the risks she was running by standing surety. For the future the bank has to write to the wife asking her to nominate solicitors, explaining a number of matters. If an appropriate response is received directly from the wife, the bank must provide the solicitor with the financial information needed to advise the wife, including such matters as the purpose of the new facility, the current amount of the

---

[46] "The Courts might soon have to consider whether a solicitor who failed to do so was not guilty of negligence." *Per* Dillon L.J. in *Walker v. Hall* (1983) 127 S.J. 550. The solicitor will probably have to advise his clients properly on the merits of a joint tenancy and tenancy in common: *Taylor v. Warners*, unreported July 21, 1987, Warner J., commented upon by Crail, *Law Society Gazette*, June 29, 1988, 26.

[47] The protocol is reproduced in many books on conveyancing, including all editions of F. Silverman, *The Law Society's Conveyancing Handbook*.

[48] Both are reproduced in the Law Society's *Guide to the Professional Conduct of Solicitors* (8th ed. 1999), Annexes 25D and 25E.

[49] Reproduced in *ibid.*, Annexes 25F and 25G.

[50] For an earlier example see *Northern Rock Building Society v. Archer* (1998) 78 P.&C.R. 65, CA: Mrs Archer provided funds for her brother to set up a solicitor's practice on the security of her house, with the repayments to be made by her. She was to be principal borrower, and her brother the surety. Her solicitors explained to her the consequences of a mortgage, but negligently failed to advise her that she was being treated as the borrower, and that in the absence of a collateral arrangement with her brother which did not appear from the documents she did not even have the limited protection as surety. See also *Krambousanos v. Jedda* (1996) 142 A.L.R. 604: solicitors were retained by the applicants' son to advise them in respect of a mortgage to be taken over their property. The Federal Court of Australia found that there was no breach of duty in failing to advise on the propriety of the transaction, as the retainer was only to explain the nature and effect of the mortgage.

[51] October 17, 2001. At the time of writing this is only reported in *The Times* October 17, 2001.

indebtedness and the previous and proposed overdraft facility. In general, it is acceptable for the solicitor to also act for the husband and bank.[52] The solicitor should ensure that he has the financial information which the bank should have disclosed, and he should see the wife alone at a face to face meeting without the husband being present. The solicitor will typically have to advise[53] as a minimum (1) on the nature of the documents and the practical implications, such as losing her home and bankruptcy; (2) on the seriousness of the risks involved, including the terms of the facility, the fact that it may increase, and whether there are other assets to cover the business if it were to fail; (3) that the wife has a choice whether to enter the transaction; and (4) obtain instructions that she wishes to proceed, or whether she would prefer the solicitor, for instance, to negotiate with the bank on the terms of the transaction. While such advice is onerous, unlike the Court of Appeal the House of Lords did not consider that the solicitor's duty was generally to ensure that the wife was free from undue influence. While the new scheme is only prospective as regards the bank, it is not wholly clear whether the solicitor's duties in the past would be the same as those imposed on them for the future, but it would seem that the duty is the same but without the need to have obtained the financial information.[54]

(ii) *The investment of money and claims by lenders*[54a]

10–206   **Introduction.**[55] The property crash of the early 1990s caused serious losses to many mortgage lenders. As a result, there has been a large volume of litigation against the surveyors and solicitors that the lenders instructed, which have generated a substantial body of law. There are seven leading cases which should be particularly considered. There are two lengthy first instance decisions in "managed litigation" by two lenders against a number of solicitors, see *Bristol & West Building Society v. Fancy & Jackson (a Firm)*[56] and *Nationwide Building Society v. Balmer Radmore (a Firm)*.[57] These largely apply five appellate decisions: *Mortgage Express Ltd v. Bowerman*[58] and *National Home Loans Corp plc v. Giffen Couch & Archer (a Firm)*,[59] both concerned with the extent of the solicitors' common law duties to lenders; *Bristol & West Building Society v.*

---

[52] Note also the restrictions on acting for lenders and borrowers from 1st October 1999 in paragraph 6(3) of the Solicitor's Practice Rules 1990 as amended (and published in the Law Society's *Guide to the Professional Conduct of Solicitors*, 8th ed., 1999).

[53] See paragraph 65 of Lord Nicholls' speech.

[54] One of the cases in the *Etridge* appeals, *Kenyon-Brown v. Desmond Banks & Co.*, was an appeal by solicitors in relation to a claim brought by their former client. The House of Lords reversed the decision of the Court of Appeal and held that the solicitor had given proper advice, see the speech of Lord Scott at paras 373–375.

[54a] This subject is affected by the Financial Services Act 1986 and the Financial Services and Markets Act 2000, see para. 10–003 above.

[55] This topic is extensively treated in chap. 7 of Flenley and Leech's *Solicitor's Negligence* (Butterworths, 1999), and see in particular the helpful explanation of the roles of the lender and solicitor in mortgage transactions discussed at paras. 7.7 to 7.13.

[56] [1997] 4 All E.R. 582; see paras 10–24, 10–75, 10–209, 10–213, 10–215, 10–296 and 10–326. For an interesting discussion of this case, see A. Sprince, "The liability of solicitors to lenders on borrower default" (1998) 14 P.N. 3.

[57] [1999] P.N.L.R. 606, see paras 10–24, 10–209, 10–214, 10–216, 10–217, 10–296 and 10–327.

[58] [1996] 2 All E.R. 836, see para. 10–208.

[59] [1998] 1 W.L.R. 207, see para. 10–211.

Mothew,[60] where Millett L.J. analysed in particular the fiduciary obligations owed by the solicitors; *Target Holdings Ltd v. Redferns,*[61] where the House of Lords considered the question of breach of trust; and *Banque Bruxelles Lambert v. Eagle Star Insurance Co. Ltd,*[62] a surveyor's case concerned with the scope of a professional's duty. Reference should also be made to the sections in this chapter dealing with express terms and their construction,[63] fiduciary duties and claims for breach of trust,[64] damages for breach of fiduciary duty,[65] damages for losses on loans secured by mortgage,[66] and contributory negligence.[67] A crucial feature which should be mentioned at the outset is that, unlike the vast majority of areas of a solicitor's work, the terms of the solicitor's retainer is normally governed by detailed instructions from the lender, which differ from one lender to another. While there is some room for the implication of implied duties in addition to the written duties, the scope for such implication is quite limited.

History. Before considering the modern law, some old and commonwealth **10–207** cases will be briefly summarised in this paragraph. They are now of limited importance given the wealth of recent English authority on this subject, and may not be wholly reconcilable with it. A solicitor acting for a lender of money is negligent if he does not take reasonable steps to protect his client's position.[68] Most obviously, if the solicitor missed or ignored a mortgage on the security property he will be liable.[69] In *Wilson v. Tucker*[70] for example, the client proposed to lend money on the security of a legacy given under a will. The attorney failed to read the whole of the will (which contained a clause rendering

---

[60] [1998] Ch. 1, see paras 10–23, 10–35 and 10–295.
[61] [1996] 1 A.C. 421, see para. 10–229.
[62] [1997] 1 A.C.191, see paras 10–244 and 10–295.
[63] Paras 10–08 to 10–10.
[64] Paras 10–23 to 10–25 and 10–35 to 10–39.
[65] Paras 10–226 to 10–232.
[66] Paras 10–294 to 10–296.
[67] Paras 10–323 to 10–327.
[68] *Cooper v. Stephenson* (1852) 21 L.J. Q.B. 292: if the attorney of a proposed mortgagee has reason to suspect that the proposed mortgagor has been bankrupt or insolvent, he ought to make proper searches to ascertain if this is so; *British Mutual Investment Company v. Cobbold* (1875) L.R. 19 Eq. 6271: a solicitor failed to spot a defect in the borrower's title to the property to be mortgaged. The defendant conceded that he would have been liable but for procedural error by plaintiff; *Pretty v. Fowke* (1887) 3 T.L.R. 845: a solicitor was found to be liable for failing to make proper enquiries concerning the tenancy of a piece of land proposed as security for a loan; *Roe v. Cullinane Turnbull Steele & Partners (No. 2)* [1985] 1 N.Z.L.R. 37, Quillam J.: on a sale of land to a company without capital for payment which was mostly deferred, the vendor's solicitor was negligent in not obtaining personal guarantees when he knew that the security over the land was worth less than the debt; *County Natwest Ltd v. Pinsent & Co.* [1994] 4 Bank L.R. 4, Hobhouse J.: solicitors failed to point out mismatch between duration of insurance cover and loan facility. *Pegrum v. Fatharly;* (1996) 14 W.A.R. 92, Western Australia CA: if the solicitor has reason to suspect that the borrower may be insolvent or the securities are inadequate in value, he should advise his client; *Yamada v. Mock* (1996) 136 D.L.R. (4th) 124, Ontario HCt: solicitor found liable for failing to ask imposter for mortgagor to verify his identity (a claim which may be brought in England for breach of warranty of authority, see para. 10–075 above); *Midland Mortgage Corp. v. Jawl & Bundon* (1999) 8 W.W.R. 535, British Columbia CA: solicitors were not negligent in failing to advise a lender of the riskiness of a mortgage over a short term lease, as their only duty was to implement lender's agreement with developer. But *cf. Bailey v. Abraham* (1849) 14 L.T. (o.s.) 219: a material deed affecting the proposed security was not shown to the attorney.
[69] *Financeamerica Realty Ltd v. Gillies* (1983) 40 Nfld. & P.E.I.R. 169, Newfoundland CA.
[70] (1822) 3 Stark. 154.

the legacy void in these circumstances) and was held to be negligent.[71] In *Anglia Hastings & Thanet Building Society v. House & Son*[72] solicitors, acting both for the purchaser of property and for the building society, were held liable for failing to report to the building society certain matters which cast doubt on the reliability of the purchaser. The solicitor is not, in the ordinary way, expected to advise on the value of the proposed security.[73] This is a matter on which the client must make up his own mind or take other professional advice. In *Brinsden v. Williams*[74] a loan was made by one client to another. The solicitors acted for both parties. The security proved insufficient. North J. held that the solicitors were not liable. They "did not recommend the security at all, but merely acted as solicitors in respect of a security between two clients of theirs, the sufficiency of which the persons proposing to lend the money considered for themselves".[75] The solicitor's responsibility may be enlarged if he is specifically instructed to consider the adequacy of the security and he accepts such instructions.[76] If in the course of investigating the borrower's title to a proposed security, the solicitor happens to discover facts that suggest that the value is insufficient, then he ought to point this out, whatever the terms of his retainer. In *Scholes v. Brook*[77] the valuers acting for a mortgagee substantially over-valued the property to be mortgaged. The solicitors had cause to doubt the accuracy of the valuation when, on investigating, they noticed the prices which had previously been paid for the property. They did not draw this to the attention of the client, but pointed it out to the valuers, who adhered to their original valuation. Romer J. held that the solicitors were not negligent. They "did what they ought to have done in calling [the valuers'] attention to the discrepancies."[78] It was not their duty to notify the client as well. Where a solicitor is trustee, it is his duty to check the sufficiency of any security before lending trust funds.[79] Where the security is insufficient and the beneficiaries claim against the trustees, the solicitor trustee is primarily liable.[80] The

---

[71] "I am of the opinion, that by law it is the duty of an attorney not to content himself with a partial extract from a will, unless something pass between himself and his client which shows that it is unnecessary to consult the original." (*Per* Abbot C.J.)

[72] (1981) 260 E.G. 1128, Bingham J.

[73] *Hayne v. Rhodes* (1846) 8 Q.B. 342; the issue in this case was whether the attorney had been specifically instructed to advise on the value of the security;. *Rae v. Meek* (1889) 14 App. Cas. 558: trustees consulted a law agent on the question whether they could lend on unfinished buildings. He replied, correctly, that they could. Held that the law agent was not negligent in failing to advise that the security was insufficient (see at 569); *Midland Bank plc v. Cameron, Thom, Peterkin & Duncans* [1988] S.L.T. 611, Outer House of the Court of Session: instructions to solicitors to prepare a standard security does not import a duty to verify its value.

[74] [1894] 3 Ch.D. 185.

[75] *ibid.* at 191.

[76] *e.g. Green v. Dixon* (1837) 1 Jur. 137. See also *Donaldson v. Haldane* (1840) 7 C. & F. 762; *Langdon v. Godfrey* (1865) 4 F. & F. 445. See the analysis of Kekewich J. in *Dooby v. Watson* (1888) 39 Ch.D. 178, followed in Canada by the Ontario Supreme Court in *Enola Apts. Ltd v. Young* (1979) 30 R.P.R. 94.

[77] (1891) 63 L.T. 837.

[78] However, the judge found that the valuers were negligent. This decision was affirmed on appeal: 64 L.T. 674.

[79] It is different if he is merely solicitor to the trust, rather than a trustee: *Johnstone v. Thorburn* (1901) 3 F. 497, a Scottish case.

[80] *Re Partington, Partington v. Allen* (1887) 57 L.T. 654, Stirling J.; *Blyth v. Fladgate, Morgan v. Blyth, Smith v. Blyth* [1891] 1 Ch. 337, Stirling J. As to the position of the partners of a solicitor trustee, see *Re Bell's Indenture* [1980] 1 W.L.R. 1217, Vinelott J.

solicitor may constitute himself a trustee of money received from the client.[81] The solicitor may owe different duties as trustee and as solicitor.[82]

The *Bowerman* duty. In *Mortgage Express Ltd v. Bowerman & Partners*[83] the   **10–208**
defendant solicitor acted for a purchaser and a mortgagee. He became aware that the vendor was purchasing the property for £150,000 when he was selling it on for £220,000, and the valuation figure was £199,000. This should have caused the solicitor to consider that such information might cause the plaintiff lenders to doubt the correctness of the valuation they had obtained. The defendants were found to be negligent in failing to report these matters to the plaintiff lender and the Court of Appeal upheld the decision. Sir Thomas Bingham M.R. held[84]:

> "A client cannot expect a solicitor to undertake work he has not asked him to do and will not wish to pay him for such work. But if in the course of doing the work he is instructed to do the solicitor comes into possession of information which is not confidential and which is clearly of potential significance to the client, I think that the client would reasonably expect the solicitor to pass it on and feel understandably aggrieved if he did not . . . if in the course of investigating title a solicitor discovers facts which a reasonably competent solicitor would realise might have a material bearing on the valuation of the lender's security or some other ingredient of the lending decision, then it is his duty to point this out."

It should be noted that the information must not be confidential.[85] The judge suggested that the duty may be wider than matters relevant to the valuation of the security, although subsequent cases have placed limits on this duty.[86]

Application of this duty. The *Bowerman* duty has been considered in the two   **10–209**
"managed" lenders' cases. In *Bristol & West Building Society v. Fancy & Jackson (a Firm)*[87] Chadwick J. determined eight cases brought by the plaintiff lender against various solicitors which had acted for it on the mortgage of various properties owned by different purchasers. In most of the cases, the allegations of breach depended on the terms of the lender's instructions. However, in one of the four categories of breach that the judge considered, it was alleged that some of the defendants failed to inform the plaintiff that there was a subsale, although the instructions imposed no obligation on them to do so. The judge held that if the price differential between the two sales were sufficient to call into question the valuation, then it should be reported. He did not think that a discrepancy of

---

[81] As in *Craig v. Watson* (1845) 8 Beav. 427. The facts were somewhat unusual, in that the solicitor "solicited his employment", suggested a loan of £3,000 and produced to the client a valuation of the proposed security in support of his advice.

[82] See for example *Bayer v. Balkin* (1995) 31 A.T.R. 295, Cohen J.: a trust faced taxation difficulties. As a solicitor to the trust, the plaintiff had a duty to consider the law for the avoidance of tax. As trustee he had to consider what was the best interests of the trust as a whole. While the plaintiff negligently failed to advise on the transfer of a flat acting as solicitor, the failure to transfer the flat was the result of a decision as a trustee, and it was not beneficial to the trust as a whole to do so. The defendants' counterclaim therefore failed.

[83] [1996] 2 All E.R. 836. See commentary by M.P. Thompson, "Conflicts of interest" (1996) 60 Conv. 204.

[84] *ibid.* at 842D–F.

[85] See para. 10–217 below on confidential information and information obtained before the retainer.

[86] Compare the narrower formulation of the duty by Millett L.J. [1996] 2 All E.R. 836 at 845F, and see paras 10–211 and 10–212 below.

[87] [1997] 4 All E.R. 582.

10 per cent between September 1988 and October 1989 required reporting in *Steggles Palmer*, although the solicitors were found liable for other reasons. In *Colin Bishop* there was an express obligation to report subsales, and the judge held that there was no relevant distinction between a subsale and a "back to back" sale, and the solicitors were liable for failing to report the latter. In *Nationwide Building Society v. Balmer Radmore (a Firm)*[88] Blackburne J. tried 12 representative claims brought by the Nationwide against various firms of solicitors. He concluded that the *Bowerman* duty to report to the lender would be confined to matters that were within the scope of the lender's interest which the solicitor was engaged to serve, and that this depended on the terms of the retainer. It would ordinarily be an implied obligation of the solicitors to pass on information obtained in the course of investigating title or preparing for completion which might cause the lender to doubt the correctness of the valuation or the bona fides of the borrower, but he expressed no view on whether the duty extended to information affecting some other ingredient of the lending decision. The *Bowerman* duty would be implied unless inconsistent with the express terms of the engagement, and it would only apply to information obtaining during the retainer which was not confidential. Thus in relation to subsales and back to back sales, the solicitor is generally under a duty to report them to the lender where the prices were significantly different.[89] These principles were applied in a number of individual cases. For instance, in *Nationwide Building Society v. A.T.M. Abdullah*[90] the solicitor was negligent in failing to report the fact that the transaction was a subsale at £63,000 when the principal sale was for £56,000 in a falling market and despite the fact that the head sale was from a mortgagee in possession who might be thought to be giving a discount.

10–210   **Further illustrations of the *Bowerman* duty.** A number of further cases illustrate the *Bowerman* duty. In *Mortgage Funding Corporation v. Tisdall Nelson Nari & Co.*[91] the defendant solicitors were found to be negligent in failing to report the purchase price of £59,750 at which property had been purchased shortly before the remortgage funded by the plaintiff, which suggested that the plaintiff lender had an erroneous view of the valuation of the property of £98,500. Solicitors negligently failed to inform the lender of the substantial discrepancy in price on a subsale of £275,000 and £110,000, and the existence of shorthold tenancies, in *Mortgage Express Ltd v. Newman & Co.*[92] Contrast *Paragon Finance plc v. Crangle & Co.*[93] where the solicitor was not negligent in failing to report a subsale where there was no inflated purchase price. In *Halifax Plc v. Ringrose & Co (a Firm)*[94] Bell J. held that solicitors were negligent in failing to report back to back sales where the prices were £108,500 and £155,000, and in failing to report the possible non-payment of a deposit, but not the fact that

---

[88] [1999] P.N.L.R. 606 at 637C–D.
[89] *ibid.* at 652G.
[90] [1999] Lloyd's Rep. P.N. 616. In *Nationwide Building Society v. Archdeacons* [1999] Lloyd's Rep. P.N. 549 it was held to be negligent to fail to report that the transaction had been purchased a few weeks before for £45,000 when the sale on was for £59,000 in a stagnant market. The solicitor was liable in *Nationwide Building Society v. J. R. Jones* [1999] Lloyd's Rep. P.N. 414 for failing to inform the lender of back to back transactions with a 53% price uplift. See also the *Littlestone & Cowan* case summarised at para. 10–216 below. *cf.* the *Vanderpump* case summarised at para. 10–214 below.
[91] [1998] P.N.L.R. 81.
[92] [1996] P.N.L.R 603, Ch.D.
[93] [1999] E.G.C.S. 25, Ch.D.
[94] [2000] P.N.L.R. 483.

the borrower had given different addresses, nor that there was a charging order and an inference of a second mortgage on another property as the claimant had given no instructions in relation to the borrower's creditworthiness, a matter which will now be considered.

The borrower's financial status. A solicitor will generally not owe an **10–211** implied duty to report to a lender client information casting doubt on the borrower's ability to repay the loan. The leading case suggesting a restrictive interpretation of the solicitor's retainer in this regard is *National Home Loans Corp plc v. Giffen Couch & Archer (a Firm)*.[95] The defendant solicitors knew that there were significant arrears on the proposed borrowers' existing mortgage, and that they had been threatened with proceedings. The plaintiff's instructions were detailed but did not require any reporting on the state of account of any existing mortgage. The Court of Appeal held that the defendant solicitors were not negligent in failing to advise the plaintiff of the matters in question, which did not relate to title or the adequacy of the security over the property. Peter Gibson L.J. set out five relevant factors[96]: (1) the solicitor's primary function in accordance with his instructions was to acquire a valid and effective first mortgage and a good and marketable title; (2) the lender provided detailed printed instructions, so that there was limited room for implying further duties[97]; (3) the only instructions concerning the borrower's financial circumstances were to undertake a bankruptcy search and report on what that revealed; (4) the lender did not send the solicitor a copy of the borrower's application, where the borrowers lied about the arrears; and (5) the report on title required the solicitors to certify that they were not aware of any material changes in the circumstances of the borrowers, implying that the lender was satisfied about such circumstances up to the offer. *Mortgage Express Ltd v. Bowerman & Partners*[98] was distinguished.

Giffen Couch & Archer was followed in *Birmingham Midshire Mortgage* **10–212** *Services Ltd v. David Parry and Co*.[99] The solicitor acting for the mortgagee had no obligation to investigate the borrower's position in relation to mortgages of other property he might hold unless he had express instructions to do so, as it was no part of his duty to supply information about the borrower's financial position. There are a number of cases that might suggest a more extensive duty, most importantly *Mortgage Express v. Bowerman*.[1] In *Halifax Mortgage Services Ltd*

---

[95] [1998] 1 W.L.R. 207. In an earlier case, *Omega Trust Company Ltd v. Wright Son & Pepper (No. 2)* [1998] P.N.L.R. 337, Douglas Brown J. held that solicitors were negligent in representing that the borrower was up to date with his rent, and in failing to carry out a bankruptcy search, which would not normally be required, when they knew that the borrower's principal had been in dubious financial circumstances, albeit as a result of confidential information which they were not obliged to disclose.

[96] *ibid.* at 214A–G.

[97] See the similar comments of Chadwick J. in *Bristol and West Building Society v. Fancy & Jackson* [1997] 4 All E.R. 582 at 603G.

[98] [1996] 2 All E.R. 836.

[99] [1997] N.P.C. 153 and [1997] E.G.C.S. 150, CA. The case also concerned a general condition that the borrower intended to reside in the property. The solicitor had to bring the clause to the borrower's attention, and report if he knew that the borrower did not so intend, but he had no duty to check that the borrower had such an intention. It was followed in *Nationwide Building Society v. Balmer Radmore* [1999] Lloyd's Rep P.N. 558, where the solicitor did not know and did not in the circumstances have to infer that that the borrower was not resident at the property in a remortgage.

[1] [1996] 2 All E.R. 836, CA, see para. 10–208.

v. S. & S.[2] Judge Humphrey Lloyd Q.C. found it difficult to reconcile *Giffen Couch & Archer* with *Mortgage Express v. Bowerman*. He held that the scope of the duty was a matter of fact and degree, but that if a solicitor was obliged to discharge any general duty of care above the specific instructions of the plaintiff lender, then that would include reporting matters of potential significance to the lender. As a result, the Judge refused to strike out an allegation that the defendant solicitors should have reported the knowledge they acquired of the borrower's impecuniosity. However in *Maes Finance Ltd v. Sharp & Partners*[3] Judge Bowsher Q.C. held that in a case where there was no express instruction to report any doubts about the borrowers' ability to repay the loan, then no such duty would be implied, and the defendant solicitors were therefore not liable in failing to report such matters. He held that *Giffen Couch & Archer* and *Mortgage Express v. Bowerman* could be distinguished from each other on the basis that one related to the value of the personal covenant, and the other to the value of the security property. The Judge was influenced by the fact that the lender was primarily interested in the adequacy of the security, the solicitors had not been told what inquiries if any the lender had made about the borrowers' financial circumstances, and a court should be slow to impose a duty on a solicitor which may well lead to a conflict between his duties to lender and borrower clients.

10–213   **The purchase price, direct payments and fraud.** In one of the categories of cases considered by Chadwick J. in *Bristol & West Building Society v. Fancy & Jackson (a Firm)*[4] it was alleged that some of the defendants had failed to report direct payments of the deposit. The report on title in each case stated that the solicitor confirmed that the details of the transaction accorded with the offer of advance, which extended to the purchase price. A solicitor would therefore have to make the inquiries that a reasonably competent solicitor would make to satisfy himself that the stated purchase price was the true one. Where the purchase price passed through the hands of the solicitor, he was able to make such a confirmation. Where it did not, the solicitor should normally seek confirmation from the vendor's solicitor that all the moneys had been paid, although it would be sufficient if the vendor gave a receipt for the full purchase price, unless the solicitor should have realised that there may be a fraud. The Judge considered that the Law Society's "Green Card" on mortgage fraud, published in March 1991, which referred to a deposit paid direct as a sign of fraud, could not be applied retrospectively to the transactions before him which happened at an earlier date. Thus in *Fancy & Jackson* itself the vendor was willing to give a full receipt, and there was no breach. In contrast, there was a breach in *Steggles Palmer* where the evidence before the solicitor suggested that the direct deposit had never been paid, and in *Baileys Shaw & Gillett* where the scanty evidence of payment of the deposit was contradicted by a number of factors.

10–214   In *Nationwide Building Society v. Balmer Radmore (a Firm)*,[5] Blackburne J. unsurprisingly held that it would ordinarily be an implied obligation of the solicitors to pass on information doubting the bona fides of the borrower.[6] The judge considered two main issues about price to which the issue of fraud may be

---

[2] [1998] P.N.L.R. 616.
[3] (1999) 69 Con.L.R. 46.
[4] [1997] 4 All E.R. 582.
[5] [1999] P.N.L.R. 606.
[6] *ibid.* at 636C. This should not undermine the general principle in *Giffen Couch & Archer.*

relevant. First,[7] there was an express obligation in the Nationwide's instructions for the solicitors to report discrepancies, which would include anything which in effect was a variation in price. This was in any event no more than a reflection of a general obligation connected with the possibility of fraud, and it was also implied in the report on title that the solicitor had made enquiries to satisfy himself that the stated purchase price was the true one. A vendor discharging the purchaser's costs and expenses would effectively be agreeing a reduction in purchase price, whereas the supply of a structural survey may not be. These principles were applied in *Nationwide Building Society v. Vanderpump & Sykes*.[8] There were back to back sales at £120,000 and £138,000 when a valuation of £130,000 had been obtained by the lender. The solicitor was not in breach of duty by failing to report the first sale at £120,000. However, there were a number of other curious features about the transaction so that the solicitor was negligent in giving unqualified confirmation that the purchase price was £138,000. The second issue considered by Blackburne J. was direct payments.[9] The judge agreed with the approach in *Fancy & Jackson* towards direct payments by the purchaser to the vendor, with the gloss that it applied even in cases before the "Green Card" issued by the Law Society in March 1991 which warned that direct payments were a badge of mortgage fraud. In most cases the solicitor would seek an explanation from his client, and probably confirmation of the payment in a falling market. Thus the solicitor was liable in *Nationwide Building Society v. J. R. Jones*[10] for failing to inform the lender of a direct payment of 31 per cent of the alleged purchase price.

Other matters. The two last categories of cases considered by Chadwick J. in **10–215** *Bristol & West Building Society v. Fancy & Jackson (a firm)*[11] should be mentioned. First, it was alleged that some of the defendants failed to inform the plaintiff of the borrower's intention to act in breach of a special condition of the mortgage. As the solicitors' instructions required them to report any matter at variance with the offer of advance, the defendants were in breach if they failed to do so. In *Clearys* the solicitors failed to disclose the fact that the borrower intended to redeem the existing mortgage to his bank but to grant it a second charge. While there was not strictly a breach of the condition to redeem prior mortgages, the solicitors should have appreciated that the second charge may be material to its lending decision, and they were negligent.[12] Secondly, given the confirmation in the report on title that the solicitor had investigated the title to the security property and he considered it to be good and marketable,[13] it was beyond

---

[7] *ibid.* at 646D–648F. For example, *see Nationwide Building Society v. Goodwin Harte* [1999] Lloyd's Rep. P.N. 338, and *Nationwide Building Society v. Richard Grosse & Co.* [1999] Lloyd's Rep. P.N. 348 (where there was a large uplift in price and a direct deposit). In both cases there was also a breach of fiduciary duty, see para. 10–024 above.

[8] [1999] Lloyd's Rep. P.N. 422.

[9] [1999] P.N.L.R. 606 at 648G–652D.

[10] [1999] Lloyd's Rep. P.N. 414.

[11] [1997] 4 All E.R. 582.

[12] *cf. Leeds & Holbeck Building Society v. Alex Morison & Co. (No. 2)* [2001] P.N.L.R. 13, Outer House, where the defenders were not negligent in failing to report a prospective breach of mortgage condition in that the borrowers were seeking funds to use the property for business purposes.

[13] In *Nationwide Building Society v. Balmer Radmore (a Firm)* [1999] P.N.L.R. 606 at 654B–655F Blackburne J. held that to be satisfied with title the solicitor must have seen reasonably up to date office copy entries of the registered title showing that the vendor is the registered proprietor. For a case where there was a breach of this requirement see *Nationwide Building Society v. ATM Abdullah* [1999] Lloyd's Rep. P.N. 616.

argument that a solicitor could not proceed to completion unless he had an official search certificate disclosing no adverse entries. Thus the solicitors were negligent in *Fancy & Jackson* for such a breach, although as the search was obtained shortly after completion only nominal damages were awarded. However, there would be no breach of the representation in the report on title if a solicitor accepted from the borrower's solicitor a mortgage deed that appeared on its face to be properly executed when it was not, and the defendants in *Cooke & Borsay* were not liable on that ground. Where a solicitor acted for the borrowers too, Chadwick J. held that he warranted that he acted with their authority.[14]

10–216   **Communicating with the client.** In *Nationwide Building Society v. Balmer Radmore (a firm)*[15] Blackburne J. held that where a solicitor came across something he was obliged to report, he should do so in sufficiently clear and comprehensive terms to be understood by the receipient, and unless obvious he must explain what the reasons are for reporting the matter. Thus in *Nationwide Building Society v. Littlestone & Cowan*[16] the judge held that on a remortgage with a valuation of £152,000 it was not sufficient to state in a report on title that the purchase price was £120,000. The solicitor also needed to give the date of the purchase, which was just three weeks earlier, and explain that the information might cast doubt on the valuation. In *U.C.B. Bank plc v. Hepherd Winstanley & Pugh*[17] the defendants sought consent from the plaintiff to a third charge over the property with a limit to the priority of the plaintiff's charge of £20,000. The plaintiff consented to the third charge, but not specifically to the priority. The Court of Appeal found the defendants liable for failing to have this specifically confirmed, and failing to obtain instructions directly from head office contrary to the plaintiff's standing instructions.

10–217   **Confidential information and fraud.**[18] The first decision to qualify the extent of the implied obligation to report relevant matters was *Bristol & West Building Society v. Baden Barnes Groves & Co*,[19] where Chadwick J. held that only information acquired in the course of the retainer by the plaintiff had to be reported, and any wider duty would be oppressive and unrealistic. In *Darlington Building Society v. O'Rourke James Scourfield & McCarthy*[20] the Court of Appeal similarly decided that if the solicitor is acting for the lender and borrower in a transaction, and the borrower in another transaction, information obtained in the other transaction is confidential, and should not be disclosed, unless there is

---

[14] This may not be quite correct. See para. 10–075 above.
[15] [1999] P.N.L.R. 606 at 656B.
[16] [1999] Lloyd's Rep. P.N. 625.
[17] [1999] Lloyd's Rep. P.N. 963.
[18] See also para. 10–145. Compare the position in Scotland. In *Bank of East Asia v. Shepherd & Wedderburn* [1995] S.L.T. 1074, the Inner House of the Court of Sessions held that if a solicitor acting for a potential lender is already in possession of information which tends to show that the security is of significantly less value than he knows the potential lender thinks, then he must report the facts to the client. The duty would be no less incumbent on him if the solicitor was already acting for the potential borrower. However there was no general duty to deal with the value of the property or financial status of the borrower. The *Bank of East Asia* case was followed in *Bristol & West Building Society v. Aitken Nairn, W.S.* [2000] S.L.T. 762, Second Division.
[19] [2000] Lloyd's Rep. P.N. 788, decided in 1996.
[20] [1999] P.N.L.R. 365.

reason to believe that the information shows a serious crime such as fraud by the borrower. The issue was discussed in more detail in *Nationwide Building Society v. Balmer Radmore (a Firm)*.[21] Blackburne J. held that by naming his own solicitor to the lender, the borrower must be taken to have authorised him to disclose whatever was necessary to comply with the lender's instructions. If the solicitor was in any doubt, he should seek the borrower's permission, and if consent was withheld, he should cease to act. If there was a conflict and the solicitor continued to act, conscious that he was benefiting the borrower at the expense of the lender, he would be in breach of fiduciary duty. The obligation to disclose information to the lender covered information acquired while doing the work that the lender had instructed him to do, but not, for instance, information that he obtained as a result of earlier transactions which he had carried out for the borrower.[22] The one exception to this limited disclosure obligation was that any information from any source which suggested that the borrower was intending to defraud the lender should be disclosed.

(iii) *Wills*[23]

General. In view of the decision in *White v. Jones*[24] a solicitor who is negligent in relation to a will may face an action by the disappointed beneficiary.[25] It should be noted that for there to be a breach of duty to the beneficiary, there must also be a breach to the testator: see *Punford v. Gilberts Accountants (a Firm)*.[26] It has been decided in Canada that any contributory negligence of the testator is not to be attributed to the beneficiary.[27] However, there is in some circumstances an obligation on the claimant to mitigate his loss by proceedings to rectify the will.[28]   **10–218**

Taking instructions. When a lay client seeks advice in imprecise and non-legal terms, the solicitor should clarify the extent and nature of the advice sought.[29] A solicitor is generally only required to consider and advise upon the   **10–219**

---

[21] [1999] P.N.L.R. 606 at 640G–646B.

[22] In an earlier case, *Omega Trust Company Ltd v. Wright Son & Pepper (No. 2)* [1998] P.N.L.R. 337, Douglas Brown J. had held, following previous decisions, that solicitors acting for a lender had no duty to disclose information about the borrower's poor financial state which they had acquired before the commencement of their retainer and which was confidential.

[23] See further A. Borkowski, "Solicitor's negligence in the preparation of wills" (1986) 2 P.N. 151; C.N. von Benzon "Avoiding solicitors' negligence in probate and trust work" *Law Society Gazette*, January 29, 1986, p. 263; A. Norris, "A sense of direction" (2001) New.L.J. 932.

[24] [1995] 2 A.C. 207; see para. 10–048 above.

[25] However, it may be possible for the solicitor to avoid liability by procuring rectification of the will under s. 20 of the Administration of Justice Act 1982.

[26] [1998] P.N.L.R. 763, CA. An accountant advised in relation to a transfer of the testator's home to his wife, and did not advise that if he pre decease of his wife, the bequest of the house to the plaintiff would be ineffective. There was no breach to the testator, as the matter was obvious to him, and thus no breach to the plaintiff. See also *Trusted v. Clifford Chance* (2000) 1 W.T.L.R. 1219, Jonathan Parker J., as authority for this proposition.

[27] *Earl v. Wilhelm* (2000) 183 D.L.R. (4th) 45, Saskatchewan CA.

[28] See para. 10–320 below.

[29] See *Gray v. Buss Murton (a Firm)* [1999] P.N.L.R. 882, Rougier J., where the solicitors failed to ask the intentions of the testator in a home-made will that erroneously gave a life interest to a beneficiary, rather than an absolute interest.

issue of testamentary capacity when the circumstances are such as a to raise doubts in the mind of a reasonably competent practitioner.[30] However, the position may be different if instructions are received from a third party, such as a will-writing company. If instructions are received from a third party, the solicitor should obtain written instructions from the client that he or she wishes to act, and in any case of doubt the solicitor should see the client.[31] If instructions are given by an interested party, it may be the duty of the solicitor to satisfy himself thoroughly as to the testator's volition and capacity, and to make the necessary inquiries so that if called upon he can show that the testator fully appreciated the effect of what he was doing.[32] If there were any danger of lack of sufficient information, or doubt about capacity or undue influence, the solicitor should see the client.[33] It is advisable for a solicitor to prepare an attendance note when taking instructions, and to record any advice given.[34]

10–220   **Giving advice.** A solicitor may fail to advise the testator properly. He should take care to ensure that the client understands and agrees to the provisions of the will.[35] He may have to give advice on matters which he is not specifically asked to advise upon. Thus, if a solicitor knows that his client intends to marry in the near future, he should advise that the will is revoked on marriage unless expressly made in contemplation of marriage.[36] If a solicitor has given advice, and it is not accepted, he has no duty to persuade the testator to act differently. This is illustrated by the New Zealand case of *Sutherland v. Public Trustee*.[37] The testator intended to leave his estate to his wife. The Public Trustee, who was in the same position as a solicitor, suggested to the testator that if his wife predeceased him, he could make a gift over to his step-children. The testator rejected this option. It was held, *obiter*, that there was no breach in failing to persuade the testator to change his mind.

---

[30] See *Public Trustee v. Till* [2001] 2 N.Z.L.R. 508, Randerson J.; there were no such circumstances in that case. The New Zealand Court of Appeal have held in *Knox v. Till* [2000] P.N.L.R. 67 that there would be no duty to refuse to act if there were doubts about testamentary capacity, and in any event whether a testator has testamentary capacity is outside a solicitor's professional expertise. No duty was owed to the beneficiaries in that case because there was a conflict of interest. See also *Ryan v. Public Trustee* [2000] 1 N.Z.L.R. 700, where it was suggested that if there was doubt about capacity the will should be executed and the opinions on capacity recorded. *cf.* Re Collicutt 128 N.S.R. (2d) and 359 A.P.R. 81 where the the Nova Scotia Probate Court suggested that with a very decrepit client, the solicitors should enquire about their mental competence and about the provisions of any former will.

[31] See the Law Society's *Guide to the Professional Conduct of Solicitors* (8th ed., 1999) at para. 12.05. On the status of the Guide see para. 10–091 above.

[32] *Russel v. Fraser* (1981) 118 D.L.R. (3d) 733 at 746, B.C.L.C., and cases referred to there. *Aylwin v. Aylwin* [1902] P. 203 lends some indirect support to this proposition.

[33] See further the *Guide* at para 24.01.

[34] See C.N. von Benzon, "Avoiding solicitors' negligence in probate and trust work" *Law Society Gazette*, January 29, 1986 at 263, and para. 10–174 above.

[35] " . . . it seems most unusual not to do one or other of two things, *viz.* either to read over the whole of the document which the party is about to sign or go through it passage by passage, and say there is a clause to this effect and a clause to that effect and so on," *per* Hannen P. in *Morrell v. Morrell* (1882) 7 P.D. 68 at 72–73. See also *Aylwin v. Aylwin* [1902] P. 203, J. Turing, "The will making process" (1980) 124 S.J. 268 and *Russell v. Fraser* (1981) 118 D.L.R. (3d) 733 at 746, British Columbia CA.

[36] *Hall v. Meyrick* [1957] 2 All. E.R. 722, CA. For the facts see para. 10–161.

[37] [1980] 2 N.Z.L.R. 536, Jeffries J.

The scope of the duty. The scope of the instructions and duty must be   **10–221**
examined. In *Cancer Research Campaign v. Ernest Brown & Co.*,[38] charities
which were to benefit under the will of P claimed that the defendants were
negligent in failing to advise P of the possibility of executing a deed of variation
of the will of her brother N, under which she had inherited a substantial estate,
and which deed would have substantially decreased the amount of inheritance tax
payable. Harman J. held that the solicitors owed no duty to either the testator or
the beneficiaries to advise on possible tax avoidance, the scope of their retainer
being only to settle the will. In contrast, in *Earl v. Wilhelm*[39] it was held that a
solicitor should inquire into the client's circumstances, and in the special circumstances of that case enquiries should have been made with the testator's accountant. If this were done it would have been found that the land the testator intended
to leave to the plaintiff beneficiaries belonged to his company. Similarly, in
MacKenzie v. MacKenzie[40] the Nova Scotia Court of Appeal found the defendant
solicitor liable for failing to ask about the extent of the testator's estate, his earlier
wills, and why six of his children were excluded from benefitting under his will.
In *Carr-Glynn v. Frearsons (a Firm)*[41] the solicitor pointed out to the 81-year-old
testatrix that it was not clear whether she was able to leave her share of a house
to her niece, and it was agreed that the testatrix would obtain the deeds so that
the position could be ascertained. The solicitor was negligent in failing to advise
the testatrix to prepare a notice to sever what was in fact a joint tenancy, which
could be done immediately, easily and unilaterally.[42]

Knowledge of the law and attestation. Although there may be exceptions for   **10–222**
obscure points, in general "a lawyer who undertakes to attend a client and
supervise the execution of a will can reasonably be expected to be familiar with
all the comparatively simple provisions of the statute regulating the execution of
wills and setting out the law in relation to gifts to witnesses and to the spouses
of witnesses".[43] Several of the reported cases concern the signing of wills by the
spouses of beneficiaries. For instance, in *Ross v. Caunters*,[44] the defendant
solicitors admitted negligence in failing to warn a testator that the will should not
be witnessed by the spouse of a beneficiary. This happened, with the result that
the gift to the beneficiary was void.[45] In *Esterhuizen v. Allied Dunbar Assurance*

---

[38] [1998] P.N.L.R. 592.
[39] [1998] 2 W.W.R. 522, Saskatchewan QB, upheld on appeal at (2000) 183 D.L.R. (4th) 45.
[40] (1998) 162 D.L.R. (4th) 674.
[41] [1999] Ch. 326.
[42] This conclusion of the Court of Appeal has been criticised by R. Kerridge and A.H.R. Brierley in
"Negligence and conflicts of interest in will-making process" (1999) 115 L.Q.R. 201. They argue that
although it was simple to serve a notice to sever, that could have soured relations between the testatrix
and her nephew, who jointly owned the house. See also *ibid.*, "Will making and the avoidance of
negligence claims [1999] Conv. 399.
[43] *Whittingham v. Crease & Co.* (1978) 88 D.L.R. (3d) 353 at 366, Aitkens J., British Columbia Sup.
Ct.
[44] [1980] 1 Ch. 297. The negligence was admitted, but Megarry V.-C. approved the admission at
304D–F.
[45] See also: *Whittingham v. Crease & Co.* (1978) 88 D.L.R. (3d) 353: the solicitor was negligent in
asking the wife of the beneficiary to witness the will; *Watts v. Public Trustee for Western Australia*
[1980] W.A.R. 97, Sup. Ct Western Australia: the defendant was found to be negligent because he
failed to enquire, on receipt of the signed will witnessed by "Margaret Watts, Housewife", whether
she was married to the beneficiary Norval Watts.

plc[46] Longmore J. held that the defendant will-making company owed a duty to ensure proper attestation, and mere written instructions would not be sufficient; the client should be invited to the office to attest the will, or asked if he would like the solicitor to attend him at home to do so. Contrast *Gray v. Richards Butler (a Firm)*,[47] where Lloyd J. held that written instructions were sufficient, although there was a duty to check the attestation of a will where the solicitor did not personally supervise its execution. However, the minor irregularities apparent on the face of the will, in particular the misplaced signatures of witnesses who gave addresses in different parts of London, were not such as to put him on enquiry that the witnesses were not present at the time of the attestation.

10–223   **Time.** It may be important to act promptly in relation to wills. In *White v. Jones*[48] the solicitors were negligent in failing to complete a new will within two months of being instructed and failing to keep two appointments made with the testator. In *Smith v. Claremont Haynes & Co.*[49] a solicitor had the essence of an intended will made known to him by a testator. The testator had leukaemia, and the solicitor should have realised how ill she was. Despite prompting telephone calls, the solicitor failed to make an appointment to take full instructions for 33 days, by which stage the testator was too ill to give instructions. The solicitor was found to be "well short of the standards reasonably to be expected of a competent solicitor."[50] In *Hooper v. Fynmores (a Firm)*,[51] the solicitors were negligent in cancelling an appointment with an elderly client who was in hospital; this should not happen unless the client was content for the appointment to be missed. In contrast, Neuberger J. held that solicitors were not negligent in *X. v. Woollcombe Younge (a Firm)*[52] when the solicitor took instructions from the testator in hospital, arranging to return next week, before which the client died. A reasonable solicitor could have formed the view that there was no real risk of the testator dying in the next few days, and it was not negligent not to recommend a holding codicil which might be disadvantageous.

10–224   **Other errors.** It is likely that a solicitor will be held to be negligent for clerical errors in the drafting of a will,[53] and it is advisable that the completed will should be checked by the solicitor who drafts it. Gifts to a solicitor must be treated with caution. As a matter of professional conduct, if the gift is of a significant amount, the solicitor must advise the client to be independently advised, and if the client

---

[46] [1998] 2 F.L.R. 668

[47] [2000] W.T.L.R. 143.

[48] [1995] 2 A.C. 207. For the facts see para. 10–048.

[49] *The Times*, September 3, 1991, Judge Barnett Q.C. sitting as a deputy High Court judge. The report is very brief and does not record all the material facts, which are better explained in S. Baughen, "The will that never was: *Ross v. Caunters* extended" (1992) 8 P.N. 99.

[50] Transcript, p. 62. See also *Hawkins v. Clayton* (1988) 78 A.L.R. 69, High Court of Australia: solicitors in possession of a will owed a duty of care to the executor in tort to take reasonable steps to locate the executor. There was a clear breach in failing to take any positive steps for six years. For the facts see para. 10–045.

[51] *The Times*, July 19, 2001, Pumfrey J.

[52] [2001] Lloyd's Rep. P.N. 274. For a commentary on this case see M.A. Jones,: "Third party beneficiaries—disappointed again" (2001) 17 P.N. 113.

[53] For an illustration in a case where the solicitor was not being sued, see *Re Morris* [1971] P. 62. A codicil removed parts of an earlier will to a greater extent than was intended by the testator, due to an error by a typist.

declines to do this he must refuse to act.[54] The solicitor may have to prove that the testator knew and approved of the contents of the will if he wishes to keep the gift,[55] but he might also face an action from the estate for any wasted costs, or from a disappointed beneficiary.

3. DAMAGES

An award of damages or compensation is the principal remedy, and in most cases the only remedy,[56] which the court will grant for breach of duty by a solicitor.[57] Compensation may be awarded for breach of fiduciary duty, and damages for breach of contract or negligence. Where the solicitor's services are valueless to the client as a result of his breach of duty, the solicitor may also be debarred from recovering his costs or ordered to repay any costs which he has received from the client.[58]

10–225

(a) *Breach of fiduciary duty and breach of trust*

Introduction. In *Nocton v. Ashburton*[59] the defendant solicitor advised the plaintiff in connection with a loan he sought. The borrowers were also clients of the defendant and he had a personal interest in the transaction. The security proved insufficient and the plaintiff suffered substantial losses. Neville J. at first instance found that the defendant had given bad advice and "fell far short of the duty which he was under as solicitor", but that he had not been fraudulent. Since the claim was pleaded in fraud, but not in negligence, the plaintiff's claim was dismissed. The House of Lords agreed with Neville J.'s findings, but by a majority held that the plaintiff was entitled to compensation for breach of fiduciary duty. Viscount Haldane L.C. explained that the solicitor's fiduciary duties were separate from his common law duties and that the remedies for breach were in the discretion of the court:

10–226

> "It did not matter that the client would have had a remedy in damages for breach of contract. Courts of Equity had jurisdiction to direct accounts to be taken, and in proper

---

[54] See the Law Society's *Guide to the Professional Conduct of Solicitors*, (8th ed., 1999), p. 318, para. 15.05.

[55] See para 10–017 above.

[56] *e.g. British Mutual Investment Company v. Cobbold* (1875) L.R. 19 Eq. 627: a solicitor acting for clients lending money upon a mortgage failed to spot a defect in the borrower's title to the mortgaged property. Upon the borrower's bankruptcy, the clients filed a bill in equity seeking a declaration that the solicitor was liable to make good the loss which they had sustained and take the property off their hands. Held that the claim was misconceived. The clients' remedy was to claim damages at common law.

[57] But see paras 10–125 to 10–140 above for an alternative remedy where a solicitor misconducts litigation. More diverse remedies are often available in equity, see para. 10–226 below.

[58] This is discussed in para. 10–307, as an instance of recovery by the client of "wasted expenditure". For further discussion of circumstances which may disentitle the solicitor to his fees, see chap. 3 paras 3–006 to 3–009.

[59] [1914] A.C. 932. For a helpful summary of what was decided by *Nocton v. Ashburton*, see *Swindle v. Harrison* [1997] 4 All E.R. 705 at 732 *per* Mummery L.J.

cases to order the solicitor to replace property improperly acquired from the client, or to make compensation if he had lost it by acting in breach of a duty which arose out of his confidential relationship to the man who had trusted him."[60]

Where the solicitor is in breach of fiduciary duty, the remedies are in the discretion of the court, and are not necessarily limited to compensation.[61] Where a solicitor trustee is in breach of duty he may be ordered to indemnify his co-trustees against any resulting liability.[62]

10–227   Claims in particular by lenders against their former solicitors have recenty been framed as breaches of trust in order to attempt to take advantage of the potentially superior remedies afforded by equity. The two main issues to be considered are whether common law rules on remoteness and the like apply, and whether the claimant has to prove that he would have acted differently but for the breach.

10–228   *Brickenden.* In the old case of *Brickenden v. London Loan & Savings*[63] a solicitor acted for the lender, the borrower, and had a personal interest in loan. He failed to disclose the existence of two other mortgages to the lender. The Privy Council held that:

> "When a party, holding a fiduciary relationship, commits a breach of his duty by non-disclosure of material facts, which his constituent is entitled to know in connection with the transaction, he cannot be heard to maintain that disclosure would not have altered the decision to proceed with the transaction, because the constituent's action would be solely determined by some other factors, such as the valuation by another party of the property proposed to be mortgaged. Once the Court has determined that the non-disclosed facts were material, speculation as to what course the constituent on disclosure, would have taken is not relevant".[64]

The case has been applied in a number of commonwealth cases where solicitors have failed to disclose material facts in breach of fiduciary duty.[65] The decision

---

[60] *ibid.* at 956–957. See also the speech of Lord Dunedin at 964–965.

[61] *Nocton v. Ashburton* [1914] A.C. 932. *MacDonald v. Lockhart* (1981) 118 D.L.R. (3d) 397, Nova Scotia CA. For examples of other remedies: where a solicitor has personal dealings with the client in breach of fiduciary duty, the transaction may be set aside, see *e.g. Spector v. Ageda* [1973] Ch. 30, Megarry J.; bribes or secret commissions can be recovered, e.g. *Islamic Republic of Iran v. Denby* [1987] 1 Lloyd's Rep. 367, Leggatt J.

[62] *Re Linsley, Cattley & West* [1904] 2 Ch. 785, Warrington J.: a solicitor was ordered to indemnify a co-trustee against any liability for costs; *Re Partington, Partington v. Allen* (1887) 57 L.T. 654, Stirling J.: a solicitor was primarily liable for the loss sustained by the beneficiaries. However, the solicitor is not liable to indemnify where the co-trustee actively participates in the breach of trust: *Head v. Gould* [1898] 2 Ch. 250, Kekewich J.

[63] [1934] 3 D.L.R. 465. For criticism of the case see Heydon (1994) 110 L.Q.R. 328 at 331–333.

[64] *ibid.* at 469.

[65] *Commerce Capital v. Berk* (1989) 5 R.P.R. (2d) 177 and *Canada Trustco Mortgage Company v. Bartlet & Richards and Gates* (1996) 28 OR 768, both Ontario CA; *Roussel v. Bertrand* (1996) 183 N.B.R. (2d) 81, New Brunswick CA (test interpreted as putting onus on solicitors); *Farrington v. Rowe, McBride & Partners* [1985] 1 NZLR 83, N.Z.C.A.; *Commonwealth Bank of Australia v. Smith* (1992) 102 A.L.R. 453, Federal Court of Australia, General Division, Full Court; *Stewart v. Layton* (1992) 111 A.L.R. 687, Federal Court, General Division, Foster J.; *Unioil International Pty Ltd v. Deloitte Touche Tohmatsu* [1997] 17 W.A.R. 98, HCt of Western Australia (*Brickenden* applied where there was a conflict between duty to client and the solicitor's own interest).

has been doubted in subsequent authority, discussed below. However, the question of its correctness does not arise when the remedy sought is one of recission.[66]

The modern law. In the leading English case of *Target Holdings Ltd v. Redferns*[67] a different view was taken. The solicitors, Redferns, had acted for Target who were mortgagees lending £1,525,000 to a borrower. Redferns obtained the mortgage money, and paid it to the borrowers before the transfers of the property were executed rather than at execution. The money was held by Redferns on a bare trust, which was breached by the early payment. The House of Lords rejected the argument which had persuaded the Court of Appeal that immediately after the moneys were paid away in breach of trust there was an immediate loss and an immediate and continuing right to have the trust fund reconstituted. While common law rules of remoteness of damage and causation do not apply directly in equity, there needs to be a causal connection between the breach of trust and the loss of the estate, which will lead to the same result. Rules applicable to traditional trusts had no application to bare trusts in commercial situations, where the relations were governed by contract. *Target* has been applied in subsequent cases. In *Bristol & West Building Society v. Daniels & Co. (a Firm)*[68] it was held that the defendant solicitors were in breach of fiduciary duty in failing to inform the plaintiff lenders that they also acted for the vendors, but the plaintiff had to prove a causal link with the loss suffered. In contrast, in *Bristol & West Building Society v. May May & Merrimans*,[69] solicitors had received funds in response to a request made on the basis of a report that the solicitor knew or must be taken to have known was misleading. Chadwick J.

10–229

---

[66] See *Maguire v. Makaronis* (1997) 144 A.L.R. 729; [1996] 188 C.L.R. 449: the appellant solicitors loaned moneys to their client, and were in breach of fiduciary duty because they had not obtained fully informed consent to the transaction. The High Court of Australia set the transaction aside, but only on condition that the moneys were repaid. What the respondents would have done had they been informed of the need to obtain independent advice was not relevant, as the issue in the case was setting aside the transaction, and not equitable compensation. For a commentary on the decision , see S. Moriaty, "Fiduciaries and discretion" (1998) 114 L.Q.R. 9.
[67] [1996] 1 A.C. 421. For commentary see R. Fletcher, "Mortgages, markets and the fiduciary principle" (1995) 11 P.N. 137. It should be noted that in some circumstances the trustee may be able to claim relief under s. 61 of the Trustee Act 1925, which was not relied upon by the defendants in *Target*. See also *Tomlinson*, pp. 32–33 and 100–103. The 1991 case of *Alliance & Leicester v. Edgestop* [1999] Lloyd's Rep. P.N. 868, Hoffman J., is probably consistent with the decision in *Target*, where the House of Lords approved but distinguished it. Contrast *Jalmoon Pty Ltd v. Bow* [1997] 2 Qd.R. 62, where the Queensland Court of Appeal found the defendant solicitor liable for breach of trust in paying over moneys received on behalf of the plaintiff company to its 49% shareholder, on his instructions purportedly given on behalf of the plaintiff, and was liable for the amount of the payment made. In "Equity's place in the law of commerce" [1998] L.Q.R. 214 at 223–227, Lord Justice Millett argued that there are two disquieting features about the reasoning in *Target Holdings Limited v. Redferns*. First, there is no sensible distinction to be drawn between traditional family trusts and bare trusts used commercially; trustees of a family settlement could have negligently parted with trust moneys before obtaining an executed mortgage in the same way as Redferns did. Secondly, there is no explanation of why the common law rules on causation apply, which the author explains by an analysis of how equity will take an account of a trustee's dealings with trust property. See also Millett L.J.'s explanation of two different meanings of "constructive trust" in *Paragon Finance v. Thakerar & Co.* [1999] 1 All E.R. 400: constructive trustees may have a trust obligation arising only as a result of an unlawful transaction, and in which case there is no trust or proprietary remedy, the term being only a formula for equitable relief; in contrast in true constructive trusts moneys are held on trust regardless of the conduct of the defendants.
[68] [1997] P.N.L.R. 323, ChD.
[69] [1996] 2 All E.R. 802.

granted summary judgment, following *Brickenden*. However, that case was overruled by the Court of Appeal in *Bristol & West Building Society v. Mothew*,[70] where Millett L.J. made it clear that the breach of fiduciary duty had to be deliberate.

10-230   **Recent commonwealth authority.** Similar conclusions have been reached in the commonwealth. In *Canson Enterprises Ltd v. Boughton*[71] the defendant solicitor acted for the plaintiff in the purchase of property. It was assumed for the purposes of a special case that the solicitor knew that the vendors were making an improper profit, but failed to inform the plaintiff, and that the plaintiff would not have entered the transaction if it had known of the secret profit. The Supreme Court of Canada held that the plaintiff could recover damages for breach of fiduciary duty. A majority held that damages were to be assessed according to common law principles,[72] and a minority held that foreseeability and similar common law limits on damages were not relevant. In *Beach Petroleum NL v. Kennedy*[73] the New South Wales Court of Appeal held that causation had to be established, following *Target Holdings* and distinguishing *Brickenden*. In *Gilbert v. Shanahan*[74] the New Zealand Court of Appeal made it clear that the plaintiff must show that he has suffered loss as a result of the defendant solicitor's breach of fiduciary duty.

10-231   **Measure of compensation.** In the other leading case on this subject, *Swindle v. Harrison*,[75] the plaintiff solicitors loaned monies to their client, the defendant, in order for her to complete the purchase of a hotel. The business failed, and the plaintiffs sought possession of the hotel. The defendant successfully claimed that the plaintiffs were in breach of fiduciary duty as they had not disclosed the profit they were making from the loan. The Court of Appeal held that the defendant was not entitled to equitable compensation as she could not prove that she would not have accepted the loan if the plaintiffs had made full disclosure to her. Evans L.J. also suggested that only if there were equitable fraud would the measure of loss be the same as for common law fraud, otherwise the ordinary common law principles would apply in assessing damages. However, it would appear that Hobhouse and Mummery LL.J. did not make any distinction between fraudulent and non-fraudulent breach of fiduciary duty. According to the interpretation of the case by the Court of Appeal in *Collins v. Brebner*,[76] the majority decided that the principles to be applied to all breaches of fiduciary duty were the same as for fraud at common law, requiring that the fraud induced the transaction and the loss

---

[70] [1997] 1 Ch. 1, see further para. 10–023 above.
[71] (1992) 85 D.L.R. (4th) 129. For the later resolution of the case see *Canson Enterprises Ltd v. Boughton* [1996] 1 W.W.R. 412.
[72] Thus the claimant has to prove causation, see *44246 B.C. Ltd v. 0909 Management Inc.* (2000) 80 B.C.L.R. (3d) 299, BCCA.
[73] (1999) 48 N.S.W.L.R. 1.
[74] [1998] 3 N.Z.L.R. 528, not following *Brickenden*.
[75] [1997] 4 All E.R. 705 . For a commentary, see Tjio and Yeo, "Limited liability for breach of fiduciary duty" (1998) 114 L.Q.R. 181.
[76] [2000] Lloyd's Rep. P.N. 587 at 589. See also *Nationwide Building Society v. Balmer Radmore (a Firm)* [1999] P.N.L.R. 606 at 660F–672C. Blackburne J. exhaustively analysed the authorities, including the Privy Council's decision in *Rama v. Millar* [1996] 1 N.Z.L.R. 257 (where the Court required proof of causation) and concluded that unless the fiduciary had acted dishonestly or in bad faith, the court should assess the actual loss caused by the breach, and the plaintiff has to show in any event that but for the breach of duty he would not have acted in the way which caused his loss.

flowed directly from that transaction, but not that the losses were reasonably foreseeable.

Restitution. Another attempt to obtain a superior remedy than that which existed in contract or tort was made in *Portman Building Society v. Hamlyn Taylor Neck (a firm)*.[77] The defendant solicitors failed to inform the plaintiff lender that the security property was used as a guest house, although the loan was on the basis that the property was to be used as a private residence only. The plaintiff claimed in restitution for money had and received, arguing that it had paid monies over to the defendant solicitors in the mistaken belief that the property would be used as a private residence. The Court of Appeal struck the action out on the grounds that the defendant solicitors were not unjustly enriched by the payment, which it had applied to the purchase of the property, and the transaction was not ineffective. **10–232**

(b) *Remoteness*

The assessment of damages at common law is subject, in every case, to the overriding principle that the damage in respect of which compensation is sought must not be too remote from the solicitor's breach of duty. Broadly speaking, this means that (a) the breach of duty must have "caused" the damage[78] and (b) the damage in question was foreseeable.[79] The law has developed so that we should add a third requirement, which it is convenient if technically wrong to discuss under the heading of remoteness. This is (c) that the loss must be within the scope of the duty.[80] **10–233**

(i) *Causation*

"But for" causation.[81] Whether the claim is brought in contract or tort, it is first necessary to determine whether the solicitor's breach of duty was "the cause" of the alleged damage.[82] The burden of proof is on the claimant to prove causation.[83] Clearly, the breach of duty was not the cause if the damage would **10–234**

---

[77] [1998] 4 All E.R. 202.

[78] As to which see paras 10–234 to 10–239.

[79] As to which see paras 10–240 to 10–243.

[80] As to which see paras 10–244 to 10–248.

[81] In *Bristol & West Building Society v. Mothew* [1998] Ch. 1 the Court of Appeal suggested that where the solicitor negligently gave incorrect advice or information, the plaintiff must only show that he would not have acted as he did if he had not been given such advice, and he does not have to show that he would not have acted as he did if he had been given the proper advice. In that case, misrepresentations were made, and by virtue of the easier test of causation just outlined, the plaintiff lender was able to obtain summary judgment. Millett L.J.'s view of the reliance required for negligent misstatements was based on his interpretation of the Court of Appeal's decision in *Downs v. Chappell* [1997] 1 W.L.R. 426, which Hobhouse L.J. subsequently suggested is wrong, in *Swindle v. Harrison* [1997] 4 All E.R. 705 at 728.

[82] For a statement of the general principles, see *McGregor* (16th ed.), paras 140–191 (in relation to tort) and paras 233–246 (in relation to contract).

[83] See *Wilsher v. East Essex Area Health Authority* [1988] A.C. 1074, which was applied in a solicitor's negligence case by the British Columbia Court of Appeal in *Haag v. Marshall* (1989) 1 C.C.L.T. (2d) 99 with the qualification that "in a situation where it is impossible, as a practical matter, to prove whether the breach of duty caused the loss, it is more in keeping with a common sense approach to causation as a tool of justice to let the liability fall on the defendant". See also paras 10–262 and 10–291. In *Etridge v. Pritchard Englefield* [1999] P.N.L.R. 839 the solicitors were negligent in failing to give the plaintiff any advice about charges she was making on her property to raise money for her husband. The Court of Appeal held that there was no presumption that the client

have occurred in any event.[84] In *Sykes v. Midland Bank Executor & Trustee Co. Ltd*,[85] for example, the Court of Appeal held that the plaintiffs would have entered the underlease in question, even if they had been properly advised by their solicitors. Accordingly, nominal damages only were awarded.[86]

10–235 **Proximity.** Assuming that the claimant overcomes this hurdle, he will still fail if the causal link between the solicitor's breach and the subsequent damage is too tenuous. Thus in *Braid v. W.L. Highway & Sons*,[87] for example, the plaintiff was obliged to sell certain securities in order to meet liabilities which he had incurred to a third party, as a result of his solicitors' negligence. He recovered by way of damages all the sums which he had had to pay to the third party,[88] but he did not recover his stockbroker's fees for selling the securities. Roskill J. stated:

> " . . . it would seem contrary to all principle if this were allowed. What Mr. Braid had to pay was a sum of money. How he raised that money was a very long way from the defendants' breach."

In *Nash v. Phillips*[89] the plaintiffs recovered damages because they were unable to purchase the house of their choice, owing to their solicitors' negligence. One of the matters they complained of was that the house they did purchase ("Chynance") was less convenient that the house they had wished to buy. Foster J. refused to award the plaintiffs damages under this head:

> " . . . in my judgment the inconvenience in this case did not result directly from the solicitor's negligence. The Nashes were not forced to purchase Chynance as a result of his negligence, and all the inconvenience stems from that purchase."

10–236 This distinction was explored in the accountant's negligence case of *Galoo Ltd v. Bright Grahame Murray*,[90] which held that that a distinction must be drawn

---

would have followed the advice which should have been given to her, and the burden remained on the plaintiff to prove on the balance of probabilities that she would have done so.
[84] Unless there are concurrent causes of the damage, as in *Baker v. Willoughby* [1970] A.C. 495. The authors are not aware of any case in which this principle has been applied to a claim against solicitors. The principle was questioned by the House of Lords in *Jobling v. Associated Dairies Ltd* [1982] A.C. 794. See further Hart and Honore, *Causation in the Law* (2nd ed.), pp. 247–248.
[85] [1971] 1 Q.B. 113. For the facts see para. 10–257. This decision has been applied in a number of cases: *G.P. & P. Ltd v. Bulcraig & Davies* (1986) 2 E.G.L.R. 148, although with the opposite result (see para. 10–253); *Stratton Ltd v. Weston, Financial Times* April 11, 1990, ChD.: a solicitor negligently failed to register client's lease; there was no loss as the landlord would have sold free of the lease anyway under a prior equitable mortgage; *Polischuk v. Hagarty* (1983) 149 D.L.R (3d) 65: the solicitor for the purchaser accepted an undertaking from the vendor's solicitor without first consulting his client. At trial the plaintiff recovered nominal damages only, on the basis that (if consulted by the solicitor) he would probably have decided to accept the undertaking. This decision was reversed, however, by the Ontario Court of Appeal, who took a different view of the evidence: (1985) 14 D.L.R. (4th) 446; *Income Trust Co. v. Watson* (1984) 26 B.L.R. 228, Ontario HCt.; *Hanflex Pty Ltd v. N.S. Hope & Associates* [1990] 2 Qd.R. 218, Queensland Full Court.
[86] See, however, paras 10–256 to 10–262 on the differing approach taken in evaluating a chance.
[87] (1964) 191 E.G. 433. See also the New Zealand Court of Appeal case *Inder Lynch Devoy & Co. v. Surbritsky* [1979] 1 N.Z.L.R. 87: because of the delay in receiving the sale price of his former home, the building costs of the plaintiff's proposed new house increased. It was held that the plaintiff was not entitled to recover these additional building costs, because they were too remote.
[88] See para. 10–301.
[89] (1974) 232 E.G. 1219.
[90] [1994] 1 W.L.R. 1360, CA, on which see chap. 15, para. 15–123. See also *Bernasconi v. Nicholas Bennett* [2000] Lloyd's Rep. P.N. 285, discussed in chap. 11 para. 11–053, and *MacMahon v. James Doran & Co.* [2001] P.N.L.R. 857, NIQB, discussed at para 10–248 below.

between a breach which gives the occasion for the loss and one which is the substantial cause of the loss. This rule may encompass the question of the intervening acts of the claimant or a third party which are discussed below. *Galoo* was applied in *Young v. Purdy.*[91] Solicitors wrongfully terminated a retainer to act for the plaintiff in proceedings for ancillary relief. She continued to act for herself, and by remarrying she effectively lost the right to claim relief. The Court of Appeal concluded that the solicitor's negligence was the occasion and not the cause of the loss as the plaintiff acted negligently, and they also held that the loss was not foreseeable. However, in *Aneco Ltd v. Johnson & Higgins Ltd.*[92] Evans L.J. suggested that the search for an effective cause has been replaced by an inquiry into the scope of the duty of care, following *Banque Bruxelles Lambert v. Eagle Star Insurance.*[93]

Intervening act of the claimant. If the immediate cause of the damage in question was some unwise action or inaction on the part of the claimant, then the court will more readily hold that the chain of causation has been broken. A number of cases illustrate this principle.[94] In *Simmons v. Pennington*[95] the plaintiff, on the advice of his solicitors, decided not to re-sell his property, pending the outcome of certain litigation. During this period the property was damaged by fire and, since the insurance policy had lapsed, the plaintiff suffered loss. The Court of Appeal held that it was not necessary to determine whether the solicitor's advice was negligent, since the damages claimed were too remote. The plaintiff's loss was due to his own failure to insure.[96] In *Frank v. Seifert Sedley & Co.*[97] solicitors were acting for the purchaser of a lease. As a result of their negligence the vendor increased the asking price from £7,500 to £9,000. The client agreed to pay the increased price and contracts were exchanged on that basis. The client failed to complete and claimed damages of £1,500 against her solicitors. Melford Stevenson J. held that the plaintiff would have been able to raise the necessary money to pay the increased purchase price, and that her loss flowed from her own failure to complete. He awarded nominal damages. In *Clark v. Kirby-Smith*[98] the plaintiffs lost the opportunity to renew their lease of business premises as a result of their solicitors' negligence. On leaving the premises the plaintiffs were faced with a claim by their landlords for dilapidations, which they settled for £120. Plowman J. held that this loss was not caused by the solicitors' negligence, but by the plaintiffs' own breach of covenant. **10–237**

Intervening act of a third party. The chain of causation may also be broken by the intervening negligence of some third party. However, not every mistake **10–238**

---

[91] [1997] P.N.L.R. 130.

[92] [2000] P.N.L.R. 152 at 161C, an insurers brokers' case, on which see chap. 14 para. 14–120.

[93] [1997] A.C. 191. For the law on scope of duty see paras 10–244 *et seq.* below.

[94] See also *Mallesons Stephen Jaques v. Trenorth Ltd* [1999] 1 V.R. 727, Victoria CA. The defendant solicitors acted for the vendors of commercial premises. They were negligent in failing to include in their draft disclosure statement reference to a supplemental agreement with the tenant giving him a rent-free period. However, there was a break in the chain of causation by the vendor's fraudulent non-disclosure of that agreement to the purchaser.

[95] [1955] 1 W.L.R. 183.

[96] *per* Denning L.J. It was also held that the damage was not foreseeable.

[97] (1964) 108 S.J. 523.

[98] [1964] 1 Ch. 506.

amounts to negligence.[99] In *Cook v. Swinfen*,[1] for example, as a result of the solicitors' breach of duty the client did not defend divorce proceedings brought by her husband. About three months after the decree nisi the solicitors sought counsel's advice in conference on the matter. Counsel advised that they should not move to set aside the decree. Lawton J. held that counsel's advice was wrong, since a motion to set aside the decree nisi would probably have succeeded. However, he went on to hold that counsel's error was not negligent, and that it did not break the chain of causation. Therefore the solicitors were liable for the consequence, namely that there was a decree of divorce against the client. The case subsequently went to the Court of Appeal,[2] but this part of Lawton J.'s judgment was not challenged.[3]

10–239   A different principle was applied in *Connor v. Ritzman*.[4] Solicitors who acted for the purchasers of leasehold property failed to note discrepancies in the leasehold conveyancing documents. The purchasers of the freehold wrongly refused to agree to rectification, but Robert Walker J. held that their intransigence was not a new intervening cause, as solicitors are paid to avoid trouble of this very kind, and the solicitors were liable for their clients' losses. Similarly, in *British Racing Drivers Club v. Hextall Erskine & Co. (a Firm)*[5] the defendant solicitors failed to advise the board of directors that a proposed investment which involved one of the directors needed the approval of a general meeting as a result of section 320 of the Companies Act 1985. It was argued that the subsequent loss was caused by the director's commercial misjudgment, so that the solicitor's negligence was the occasion for the loss rather than the substantial cause of the loss. The judge rejected this argument and held that the purpose of the statutory provision requiring approval of the general meeting was to protect a company against the directors' judgments being distorted by conflicts of interest and loyalties.

(ii) *Foreseeability*

10–240   In order to succeed, the claimant must establish not only that the damage was caused by the solicitor's breach of duty, but also that it was foreseeable. If the claim is brought in contract, then at the time the contract was made the damage must have been "reasonably foreseeable as liable to result from the breach."[6]

---

[99] As discussed in the first two sections of this chapter.

[1] [1966] 1 W.L.R. 635.

[2] [1967] 1 W.L.R. 457.

[3] Another illustration of the same principle is to be found in *Hart & Hodge v. Frame, Son & Co* (1839) 6 C. & F. 193: where an error by magistrates did not break the chain of causation. For the facts see para. 10–310.

[4] (1995) 70 P.&.C.R. D41. See also the New South Wales case of *Barnes v. Hay* (1988) 12 N.S.W.L.R. 337, CA. The solicitors acted for a tenant of a shop, and negligently failed to warn him of the consequences of not taking a formal lease. The tenant was unwarrantably harassed by his lessor in an attempt to obtain vacant possession, which he was not in a position to be able to resist because of his precarious title. The lessor's conduct was not an intervening act which broke the chain of causation, for the solicitors had the duty to advise the tenant in part because he was apt to suffer the very kind of loss that he did, see Mahoney J.A. at 355E–F, and Hope and Priestley JJ.A. at 340F–341A.

[5] [1996] 4 All E.R. 667, Carnwarth J.

[6] *Per* Asquith L.J. in *Victoria Laundry (Windsor) Ltd v. Newman Industries Ltd* [1949] 2 K.B. 528. For a full discussion of the requirement of foreseeability in contract, see *McGregor* (16th ed.), paras 247–281.

This has been interpreted narrowly in *The Heron II*[7]; the event must be "not unlikely", and "a type of damage which was plainly foreseeable as a real possibility but which would only occur in a small minority of cases cannot be regarded as arising in the usual course of events".[8] If the claim is brought in tort, then at the time the breach of duty was committed the damage (or at least the type of damage) must have been reasonably foreseeable as a consequence.[9] For the reasons stated earlier in this chapter,[10] in most of the older solicitors' negligence cases where issues of remoteness have arisen only the contractual rules have been considered. In many cases, of course, foreseeability poses no problem for the claimant, since the solicitor has special knowledge of his client's intentions.[11]

Illustrations. In *Pilkington v. Wood*[12] the plaintiff was not advised by his   **10–241**
solicitor of the defect in title of a house which he bought in Hampshire. The defect only came to light when he needed to move to Lancashire because of a change in his employment. This meant that the plaintiff had difficulty in selling the property. He obtained temporary accommodation in Lancashire during the week and returned to the house in Hampshire, where his wife was still living, at weekends. The plaintiff recovered as damages the diminution in value of the property attributable to the defective title.[13] He did not recover the costs of travel between Hampshire and Lancashire,[14] or the interest payable on his overdraft as a result of the delay in selling the property. Harman J. held that these items were not within the reasonable contemplation of the parties at the time when the solicitor was retained. The decision, at least with respect to the interest payments, must be in doubt given the conclusions in *Hayes v. Dodd*,[15] discussed below.[16]

A similar argument was advanced by the defendant solicitors in *G. & K.*   **10–242**
Ladenbau Ltd v. Crawley & De Reya.[17] As a result of their negligence when acting on the purchase of certain property, rights of common which had been mistakenly registered against it did not come to light until the plaintiffs sought to sell. As a result the sale was delayed and the plaintiffs (i) paid additional interest

---

[7] [1969] 1 A.C. 350.

[8] *ibid. per* Lord Reid at 385–386.

[9] For a full discussion of the requirement of foreseeability in tort, see *McGregor* (16th ed.), paras 192–231.

[10] See paras 10–013 and 10–014.

[11] *e.g. King v. Hawkins & Co., The Times*, January 28, 1982, Mars-Jones J.: solicitors for the purchaser knew that their client intended to extend the property. It was foreseeable that he would incur substantial losses if he did not acquire good title to parts of the land.

[12] [1953] Ch. 770.

[13] See also para. 10–318. For another example see *Matlock Green Garage Ltd v. Potter Brooke-Taylor & Wildgoose (a Firm)* [2000] Lloyd's Rep. P.N. 935, where solicitors who failed to renew the plaintiff's business tenancy could not be expected to foresee the effect this might have on parts of the business carried on at other sites. For the facts see para. 10–265.

[14] For a similar decision on similar facts see *Douglas v. Stuart Wyse Ogilvie Estates Ltd* [2001] S.L.T. 689, OH.

[15] [1990] 2 All E.R. 815, CA.

[16] At para. 10–242. Another case where recovery was not allowed, perhaps surprisingly, is *Piper v. Daybell, Court-Cooper & Co.* (1969) 210 E.G. 1047. The defendant solicitors failed to notice a right of way. The plaintiffs purchased the property, and sold it as a result of the inconvenience caused by the right of way. Nield J. held that this was not foreseeable, and did not allow recovery for professional fees for that transaction.

[17] [1978] 1 W.L.R. 266. For the facts see paras 10–091 and 10–197.

on their mortgage and (ii) lost the interest which they could have earned by investment of the net proceeds of sale. Mocatta J. rejected the argument that these items were too remote, given that the defendants had been told by the plaintiffs that they intended to develop part of the property and sell or let it:

> "the defendants should in my judgment have reasonably contemplated that if they failed to secure an unencumbered title for the plaintiffs without warning them of the defect, the damages the plaintiffs would suffer were "not unlikely" to be the loss of a handsome profit on resale."[18]

It should be noted that the defendants knew that the plaintiffs intended to develop part of the land and let or sell the remainder. In the later Court of Appeal case of *Hayes v. Dodd*[19] the plaintiffs acquired property principally for business purposes where there was no right of way over the only convenient access. It took the plaintiffs five or six years to dispose of the property, and they recovered all the expenses they incurred during those years. There was a dispute over whether rates, insurance, redundancy payments, conveyancing costs and life insurance were too remote. The Court of Appeal decided they were not, although there was little discussion of the matter.[20]

10–243   **Time to consider foreseeability.** One of the problems concerning the contractual rules is that the point of time at which foreseeability must be considered is when the contract was made. This could work injustice to the claimant in solicitors' negligence cases, since much may happen between the date of the retainer and the date when the breach of duty occurs. In *Cook v. Swinfen*,[21] for example, the plaintiff failed to recover damages for anxiety resulting in injury to her health, since this was not reasonably foreseeable when she first instructed the solicitor. In *Malyon v. Lawrance, Messer & Co.*,[22] however, Brabin J. awarded damages for neurosis resulting from the solicitors' negligence, even though this may not have been foreseeable at the time when they were initially retained. The judge refused to accept that the extent of the solicitor's liability was fixed by reference to the situation "which existed at the moment when the plaintiff, as it were, walked into the defendants' office."[23] It may be thought that the contractual rules as to remoteness were somewhat stretched in order to do justice in that case. However, it now seems that there is probably a parallel liability in tort, and the judge's conclusion can be justified on that basis. The problem referred to at the beginning of this paragraph can normally be avoided by applying the tortious rules as to remoteness of damage.

---

[18] *ibid.* at 289E–F.
[19] [1990] 2 All E.R. 815.
[20] *ibid.* at 818B, 824D–E, and 827B. It was unsuccessfully argued that the lessor's harassment was unforeseeable in *Barnes v. Hay* (1988) 12 N.S.W.L.R. 337, CA. The Court applied the tortious rules of foreseeability.
[21] [1967] 1 W.L.R. 457 at 462B, CA. See also *Ekkebus v. Lauinger* (1990) 73 O.R. (2d) 743 HCt. (defendant solicitors failed to ascertain whether hot tub on property being purchased by their clients complied with the appropriate byelaws; plaintiffs liable to visiting child injured by falling into tub; defendants not liable to plaintiffs as loss too remote).
[22] [1968] 2 Lloyd's Rep. 539.
[23] *ibid.* at 550–551.

(iii) *The scope of the duty*[24]

The principle. In *Banque Bruxelles Lambert S.A. v. Eagle Star Insurance Co.*   **10–244**
Ltd[25] the House of Lords held that someone under a duty to advise on what is the
appropriate course of action will be liable for all the foreseeable consequences of
the action taken in reliance, but a person under a duty to take reasonable care to
provide information on which someone relies will generally be regarded as
responsible for the consequences of the information being wrong, and not all the
consequences of the reliance. As a result, negligent valuers sued by mortgage
lenders were held to be liable only for the difference between their valuations and
the correct valuations, and they were not liable for the further loss suffered by the
lenders when the value of the security declined as a result of the fall in the
property market. This principle is of significance in many solicitor's negligence
cases, and most importantly in actions brought by lenders against solicitors who
acted for them in the making of loans.[26] A number of cases involving solicitors
apply the *BBL* principle, which will be discussed below.

Information and advice. It is submitted that solicitors advising in commercial   **10–245**
transactions, like other professional advisers, are generally under a duty to
provide specific information or advice and not to advise on the wisdom of
transactions in general, and thus the loss for which they are responsible will be
limited to the consequences of the specific information or advice being accurate.
Of course the facts of any particular case may show that the solicitor is under a
wider duty to advise on the wisdom of the transaction as a whole. In *Cottingham
v. Attey Bower & Jones (a Firm)*[27] Rimer J. expressly agreed with this statement,
and added that there were no fundamentally different considerations in a domestic conveyancing transaction. In that case solicitors acting for vendors of property
failed to obtain a copy of building regulations consent for substantial renovations
which had never in fact been granted. As the duty was only provide information,
the solicitors were liable for the overpayment due to defects which had not been
noted in the survey report which the claimants had obtained and which assumed
that building regulations had been complied with, but not for all the defects
identified in the property.

Similarly, in *Green v. Turner*[28] it was alleged that the defendant solicitors   **10–246**
negligently advised the plaintiff property developer that the title of property
which he was contemplating purchasing would be registered within four to six
weeks, and that as a result he purchased the property and carried out a limited
scheme of refurbishment, but the sale on was delayed by two months, so that he
incurred a liability of £50,000 to a sub-purchaser. It was held that the alleged loss

---

[24] For a critical view see H. Evans, "The scope of the duty revisited" (2001) 17 P.N. 146; and H.
Evans, *Lawyers' Liabilities*, (2nd ed., 2002), chap. 9.
[25] [1997] A.C. 191, on which see chap. 9 paras 9–113 to 9–118. The case is often referred to under
the name of *South Australia Asset Management Corporation v. York Montague Ltd*, or *SAAMCO*.
[26] This issue is further explored at paras 10–295 and 10–296.
[27] [2000] P.N.L.R. 557.
[28] [1999] P.N.L.R. 28, ChD. For another straightforward example see *Guild (Claims) Ltd v. Eversheds
(a Firm)* [2000] Lloyd's Rep. P.N. 910, Jacobs J., where it was alleged that the solicitors were
negligent in relation to the contents of a circular to the shareholders of Airbreak for the raising of
capital to purchase Sunsail. Airbreak later went into liquidation. The purpose of the advice was to
ensure that the circular was accurate for those who were going to rely on it, which did not include
Airbreak. The solicitor's liability to that company was limited to claims against it brought by third
parties based upon the misleading circular, of which there were none.

was caused by the investment decision, not the decision to purchase. Furthermore, the scope of the duty in any event did not include the alleged loss, as the duty covered the consequences of the information being wrong not the consequences of decisions made in reliance on that information.

10–247 **An exception.** In contrast, in *Carter v. TG Baynes & Sons*[29] the defendant solicitors failed to note that there were restrictive covenants preventing development of the site which the plaintiff intended to purchase, and advised him to go ahead with the transaction. The plaintiff recovered for all foreseeable losses, including those resulting from a fall in the market, as the advice had been to proceed with the works, and it was not limited to giving information.

10–248 **Further cases.**[30] The distinction between information and advice, and the scope of the solicitor's duty, has been explored in cases where lenders have sued the solicitors they instructed, which are summarised below.[31] A number of cases in other areas have also addressed these issues. In *Pearson v. Sanders Witherspoon*[32] the defendant solicitors were negligent in failing to prosecute their client's action timeously against Ferranti, which went into administration. The Court of Appeal held that the loss of opportunity to enforce the judgment obtained was not within the scope of the defendant's duty, which was to act with due expedition, unless expressly assumed by the solicitor, or he was given sufficient notice of the impecuniosity. In *Jenmain v. Steed & Steed*[33] the defendant solicitors acted for the vendors in a contract race. It was held that they were also retained by the claimants, who were some of the proposed purchasers, in a limited capacity which required the solicitors to pass on the fact that they were also dealing with another proposed purchaser. The scope of the duty, based on rule 6A of the Solicitors' Practice Rules 1990, was to avoid wasted costs. The judge found they would have obtained the property if properly advised by the defendants. The Court of Appeal held that they could recover any wasted costs and also the difference between the price they would have paid and the value of the property. However, they could not recover the profits they would have made from the proposed development of the property.

(c) *Measure of damages*

10–249 Whether the claim is brought in contract or tort, the fundamental principle governing the measure of damages is that the claimant should be put, so far as money can do it, and subject to the rules as to remoteness which have just been discussed, in the position he would have occupied if the solicitor had discharged

---

[29] [1998] E.G.C.S. 109, ChD.

[30] For a further example in relation to the loss suffered as a result of a defective will, see *Corbett v. Bond Pearce (a Firm)* [2001] 3 All E.R. 769; [2001] E.W.C.A. Civ. 531 CA, summarised at para. 10–053 above. See also *Trust Co. of Australia v. Perpetual Trustees* (1997) 42 N.S.W.L.R. 237, where McLelland C.J. in Equity applied *BBL* and held that a solicitor who failed to advise the trustee company that a conflict of duty would arise if it acquired property was not responsible for the losses it suffered from an improvident investment which had nothing to do with the solicitor's breaches.

[31] See paras 10–295 and 10–296.

[32] [2000] P.N.L.R. 110. cf. *MacMahon v. James Doran & Co.* [2001] P.N.L.R. 857, NIQB, where the defendant solicitors failed to issue proceedings and were held to be the substantial cause of the plaintiff running up a sizeable overdraft and entering a mortgage to pay it off, as they knew of his financial position and misled him that proceedings would be issued and recovery imminent.

[33] [2000] P.N.L.R. 616.

his duty.[34] Broadly speaking, this may be achieved in one of two ways, depending upon the particular facts of the case: (i) by paying to the claimant the monetary equivalent of any benefits of which he has been deprived[35]; or (ii) by indemnifying the claimant against any expenses or liabilities which he has incurred.[36] In practice, the assessment of damages is subject to a number of rules which are considered below.

(i) *Date of assessment*

The general rule Damages are generally assessed as at the date of breach, **10–250** unless justice requires that some other date should be taken.[37] This principle is illustrated by a number of cases. In *Amerena v. Barling*[38] the defendant solicitor's negligently granted an an option over shares in a company without the plaintiff's authority, which would not have been forthcoming. The Court of Appeal summarised the law as follows: damages will normally fall to be assessed at the date when the cause of action arose[39]; but this principle will not be applied mechanistically in circumstances where assessment at another date may more accurately reflect the overriding compensatory principle.[40] The Court was not satisfied that the taking of an assignment of the option two years later at a cost of £1.75m. was reasonable. They considered that damages should be assessed at the date of breach, when the benefits receivable under the option agreement were not less than the value of the shares over which the plaintiff had granted an option. Only nominal damages were therefore awarded. In *Ricci v. Masons*[41] the diminution in the value of the plaintiff's restaurant business caused by the fact that he had obtained a new lease without statutory protection was assessed at the date of breach, rather than at the date the new lease would have been obtained (where the loss to the plaintiff would have been somewhat less) or at the date of trial. In *Mahoney v. Purnell*[42] the defendant solicitors were negligent in relation to the sale by the plaintiff to his son-in-law of his interest in their jointly owned hotel. May J. assessed damages at the date of sale in 1988, rather than the much higher

---

[34] See: *Livingstone v. Rawyards Coal Co.* (1880) 5 App. Cas. 25 at 39 and *Dodds Properties v. Canterbury City Council* [1980] 1 W.L.R. 433 at 451, 454 and 456 (as to general principles); *Braid v. W.L. Highway & Sons* (1964) 191 E.G. 433, Roskill J., *County Personnel (Employment Agency) Ltd v. Alan R. Pulver & Co.* [1987] 1 W.L.R. 916, at 925C–E, CA, and *Hayes v. Dodd* [1990] 2 All E.R. 815 at 817C and 818F, CA (all in relation to solicitors' negligence). See also *Bartter v. Gambril* (1932) 76 S.J. 868: the enrichment of a third party as a result of solicitor's alleged breach of duty was not relevant to assessment of damages.

[35] See heads of damages (a) to (d), discussed in paras 10–264 to 10–293.

[36] See heads of damage (e) to (j), discussed in paras 10–294 to 10–309.

[37] *Zakrzewski v. Chas. Oldhams & Sons* (1981) 260 E.G. 1125, QBD. For general statements of principle in cases which did not concern solicitors' negligence see *Banque Bruxelles Lambert v. Eagle Star* [1997] A.C. 191 at 220 (Lord Hoffmann) and *Smith New Court Securities Ltd v. Scrimegeour Vickers (Asset Management) Ltd* [1997] A.C. 254 at 266 (Lord Browne-Wilkinson). For a slightly different view see *Reeves v. Thrings & Long* [1996] 1 P.N.L.R. 265 at 278; the facts are summarised at para. 10–269.

[38] (1995) 69 P.&C.R. 252.

[39] see *Miliangos v. George Frank (Textiles) Ltd* [1976] A.C. 443, 468 *per* Lord Wilberforce.

[40] See *County Personnel Ltd v. Alan R. Pulver & Co.* [1987] 1 W.L.R. 916 at 926 *per* Bingham L.J. Followed in *Roker House Investments Ltd v. Saunders* [1997] E.G.C.S. 137, ChD, where the date of assessment was held to be the date the negligence came to light.

[41] [1993] 38 E.G. 154; see para. 10–265 for the facts.

[42] [1996] 3 All E.R. 61.

value of the shares when the hotel was about to be sold in 1989 or the value at the date of trial which was zero.[43]

10–251   **Exceptions.** In a number of cases a date of assessment some time after the breach has been chosen. In *McElroy Milne v. Commercial Electronics Ltd*[44] the plaintiff was developing industrial property and found a tenant, Imagineering. It instructed the defendant solicitors to draft a lease guaranteed by Imagineering's principal shareholder, Studio. In late 1987, the defendant solicitors negligently failed to make Studio party to the lease. Imagineering, which was in financial difficulties, repudiated the lease. The New Zealand Court of Appeal agreed with the assessment by the trial judge: if the lease had been guaranteed, the plaintiff would have been able to sell the development fully let for NZ$5.25m. in January 1989. As a result of the fall in property prices, the plaintiff was instead left with an unsold development at the time of the trial in July 1990 which was worth about NZ$4m. Damages were assessed at NZ$1.25m., relying particularly on *Czarnikow v. Koufos*,[45] subject to a deduction of 25 per cent for contingencies. The Court considered that assessing damages at the date of the breach, although the general rule, was artificial and unjust in this case, and that the fall in the property market was foreseeable.[46] More recently, in *Portman Building Society v. Bevan Ashford (a Firm)*[47] the defendant solicitors negligently failed to reveal information to the plaintiff building society which cast doubt on the reliability of the borrower and his covenant, and in particular that the balance of the purchase price was being raised by a loan secured by a second charge. Immediately after completion, the plaintiff knew of the second charge, and it was argued that the plaintiff could have extracted itself from the transaction at that stage with no loss. The Court of Appeal held that as the plaintiff reasonably did not know of the breach of duty of the defendants, it could recover the full loss it later sustained.

(ii) *Credit for benefits*

10–252   **General principle.** The restitution principle[48] necessarily entails that the claimant should give credit for any incidental or compensating benefits which flow from the solicitor's breach of duty.[49] This factor is not uncommon in cases where, because of a solicitor's negligence, the client's business affairs have taken an altogether different course. For example, in *Port of Sheerness Ltd v. Brachers*[50] the defendant solicitors failed to advise the plaintiffs that dismissing

---

[43] For a further example see *Wapshot v. Davies Donovan & Co.* [1996] 1 P.N.L.R. 361, summarised at para. 10–268 below.
[44] [1993] 1 N.Z.L.R. 39. In *Snipper v. Enever Freeman & Co.* [1991] 2 E.G.L.R. 270 Sheen J. had to assess damages for the loss of enfranchisement rights caused by the defendant solicitor's negligence. If the loss of value at the date of breach in 1983 was taken along with the benefit of an extension to the lease which was obtained in a compromise of proceedings in 1987, that would be unfair to the plaintiff because of inflation between the two dates. The judge assessed the loss as at 1987.
[45] [1969] 1 A.C. 350, HL.
[46] For an example see *Kennedy v. K.B. Van Emden & Co.* [1996] P.N.L.R. 409, summarised at para. 10–275.
[47] [2000] P.N.L.R. 344.
[48] See para. 10–253.
[49] *e.g. Nadreph v. Willmett & Co.* [1978] 1 W.L.R. 1537, Whitford J.: plaintiffs had to pay compensation to their tenants, but got the benefit of vacant possession of the premises.
[50] (1997) I.R.L.R. 214.

dockers would lead to claims for unfair dismissal, and as a result the plaintiffs settled claims at a cost of £2.5m. However, they had to give credit for the fact that the plaintiffs did not have to reinstate or reengage the dockers, enabling them to move straight away to a cheaper system of contracting labour. In accordance with normal principles relating to insurance monies, lenders which sue solicitors for negligence in relation to mortgage transactions do not have to give credit for moneys obtained as a result of taking out a mortgage indemnity guarantee policy.[51]

Further illustrations. The evaluation of the benefit may not be straightfor- **10–253** ward. In *G.P. & P. Ltd v. Bulcraig & Davies*[52] the defendant solicitors were retained in relation to the purchase of new office accommodation for the plaintiff, an advertising agent. The solicitors failed to discover that the premises were in part subject to a conditional planning consent restricting the use of the ground floor premises to the printing trade. The plaintiff took the lease, which was at a very favourable rent, and expended large sums of money improving the premises. After a year and a half of occupation, the plaintiff went into liquidation, and the restrictive user clause was then discovered. The receiver was unable to dispose of the lease, and so surrendered it to the landlord. Damages were assessed on the basis of the expenditure wasted on effecting the improvements. In calculating the recoverable damages, credit was given for the sum received on the surrender of the lease to the landlords, and for the benefit enjoyed in occupying the premises for the period. The judge decided that the beneficial occupation had to be fixed on the basis of a rent taking into account the existence of the planning restriction, because the defendants would be taking advantage of their own wrongdoing in assessing the rent without such a restriction. That decision was not challenged on appeal. The judge also decided that the plaintiff should give credit for the beneficial occupation assessed as the difference between the rental value after the improvements of £118,000 and the rental value before the improvements of £88,000, rather than the difference between the £118,000 and the actual rent paid of £35,000. He did not consider that the plaintiff had to give credit for the favourable bargain it had reached with the landlord. The Court of Appeal came to the opposite conclusion on this issue: but for the defendants' error, there would have been no lease, and thus no favourable bargain with the landlord, and the plaintiff would have had to find premises elsewhere at an open market rent.

A curious problem on evaluating benefits was posed by *Teasdale v. Williams* **10–254** *& Co.*[53] Owing to the negligence of his solicitors the tenant of business premises did not acquire a new lease for five years at a rental of £20,000 per annum. Instead he acquired a seven year lease at a rental of £19,000 for the first two years and £26,500 for the last five years. Leonard J. awarded damages of £17,500, representing the loss of £19,500 in years three to five less the gain of £2,000 in years one and two. He declined to take into account the "gain" in years six and seven (which would arise because there was no rent review at the end of year

---

[51] See *Bristol & West Building Society v. May May & Merrimans (a Firm) (No. 2)* [1998] 1 W.L.R. 336, Chadwick J. (where the solicitors were given the opportunity to join the insurers before any payment was ordered to avoid any risk of double jeopardy), followed by the Court of Appeal in *Portman Building Society v. Bevan Ashford (a Firm)* [2000] P.N.L.R. 344, a solicitors' case, and *Arab Bank plc v. John D. Wood Ltd* [2000] 1 W.L.R. 857, a surveyor's case. See further chap. 9, para. 9–122.

[52] (1986) 2 E.G.L.R. 148, 1st instance; (1988) 1 E.G.L.R. 138, CA.

[53] (1984) 269 E.G. 1040.

five). The Court of Appeal upheld this decision. The "gain" in years six and seven would be offset by the fact that a rent review at the end of year seven would produce a higher figure than a rent review at the end of year five. Forevermore the plaintiff's rent would be reviewed two years later than would have been the case if the solicitors had not be negligent. This approach is surely right. The court will not bring into the assessment of damages a gain which is speculative or remote.

10–255 **Remote or incidental benefits.** Benefits may be too remote or incidental to be taken into account. This is nicely illustrated by *Hayes v. Dodd*.[54] The plaintiffs acquired property for business purposes where there was no right of way over the only convenient access. It took them five or six years to dispose of it, during which the value of the maisonette, which formed part of the property, increased in value. The Court of Appeal decided that credit need not be given for that increase, except to the extent of the interest charges over the maisonette during that period to which the plaintiffs were otherwise entitled.[55] It is submitted that the distinction made is a sensible one, albeit difficult to justify logically. In *Royal Bank of Canada v. Clark*[56] the defendant solicitor negligently advanced the bank's money without obtaining proper security. He was held to be liable to repay the full amount of the advances, even though part of the advances were used by the bank to reduce the borrower's overdraft.

(iii) *Evaluation of a chance*[57]

10–256 In the course of assessing damages, it is frequently necessary to speculate what would have happened if the solicitor had properly discharged his duty. Where the matter is in doubt, an approach sometimes taken by the courts is (i) to assess damages on the basis of a particular hypothesis, and then (ii) to scale down the award according to the probability that the hypothesis is correct.[58] Until relatively recently, it had not been clear when the courts would adopt this approach to the assessment of damages, but it has commonly been used in cases where, as a result of the solicitor's negligence, the client has lost the opportunity to bring or to defend proceedings.[59]

10–257 **What the claimant would have done.** If the question is what the claimant himself would have done, he must prove on the balance of probabilities that he

---

[54] [1990] 2 All E.R. 815. See more generally *Hussey v. Eels* [1990] 2 Q.B. 227, CA, and *Gardner v. Marsh & Parsons* [1996] P.N.L.R. 362. For an application see *Owen v. Fielding* [1998] E.G.C.S. 110, where Steel J. did not give the defendant credit for profits made on the sale of land when the plaintiff had purchased it subject to rights of common due to the defendant solicitor's negligence.
[55] [1990] 2 All E.R. 815 at 818C, 822G, and 826F.
[56] (1978) 88 D.L.R. (3d) 76, aff'd. by the Supreme Court of Canada 105 D.L.R. (3d) 85. See also *Lomond Assured Properties Ltd v. McGregor Donald* [2000] S.L.T. 797, OH, where it was held that developers suing solicitors for obtaining securities which were postponed to other interests over development land did not have to give credit for a settlement from a bank for issuing an unauthorised cheque.
[57] See further: H. Evans *Lawyers' Liabilities* (2nd ed., 2002), chap. 12; *ibid.*, "Damages for solicitors' negligence: (3) damages for the loss of a chance" (1992) 8 P.N. 85; and G. Reid, "The hypothetical outcome in professional negligence claims" (2001) 17 P.N. 129.
[58] The court may have to make a rough and ready assessment accounting for the fact that a range of outcomes are possible, as in *McMorran's Cordova Bay Ltd v. Harman* (1979) 106 D.L.R. 495, British Columbia CA (loss of opportunity to sell property).
[59] See paras. 10–277 *et seq.* below.

would have acted differently. In *Sykes v. Midland Bank Executor & Trustee Co. Ltd*[60] a solicitor going through an underlease with his clients failed to point out to them the effect of a somewhat onerous clause relating to change of user. The plaintiffs were unable to say in evidence whether or not they would have taken the underlease, if they had been correctly advised. The Court of Appeal, reversing the decision of the trial judge, held that "on balance of probabilities" the plaintiffs would have taken the underlease in any event and therefore they were only entitled to nominal damages.

What a third party would have done. If, however, the question is what some   **10–258** third party would have done in the hypothetical scenario following competent advice from the defendant solicitor, then damages are assessed on the basis of the loss of a chance. This has been made clear by the Court of Appeal in *Allied Maples Group Ltd v. Simmons & Simmons.*[61] The plaintiffs wished to acquire some of the assets of Kingsbury Warehouse Limited, a part of the Gillow group of companies. While they had hoped to purchase only some properties, this was not possible because there were conditions against alienation and the like which were personal to Kingsbury. Therefore, the plaintiffs decided to purchase Kingsbury itself and transfer unwanted properties from that company. The defendant solicitors failed to inform them that some properties which had previously been owned by Kingsbury had first tenant liabilities, which might involve claims against Kingsbury if the assignees of those properties defaulted. After the plaintiffs bought Kingsbury, there were such claims. On a preliminary issue, Turner J. found for the plaintiffs, and held that as a result of their solicitors' negligence they had lost the opportunity of negotiating with the Gillow group to obtain protection against potential claims resulting from first tenant liabilities. The Court of Appeal held that provided the plaintiffs could prove on the balance of probabilities that they would have negotiated with the Gillow Group, they could recover substantial damages if there was a significant chance that they might have succeeded in those negotiations. The plaintiffs did not have to prove on the balance of probabilities that they would have succeeded in those negotiations, which would have depended on the hypothetical actions of a third party. Accordingly, the measure of damages was the value of the lost chance. On the facts, the Court held that the plaintiffs had a realistic chance of renegotiating the deal.

---

[60] [1971] 1 Q.B. 113. *cf. Otter v. Church, Adams, Tatham & Co.* [1953] Ch. 280, Upjohn J., where solicitors failed to advise that an airman on active service should execute a disentailing assurance promptly upon attaining 21. Had he done so, the value of his estate on death would have been increased by some £7,000. The court awarded £6,500 to reflect the possibility that the airman may, in any event, have decided not to disentail. The correctness of the case was doubted by Salmon L.J. in *Sykes v. Midland Bank Executor & Trustee Co. Ltd* [1971] 1 Q.B. 113 at 130B; *cf.* Karminski L.J. at 132A–C. In *Hall v. Foong* (1995) 65 S.A.S.R. 281, the Full Court of South Australia followed *Sykes* and held that the plaintiff had not proved what she would have done if the defendant solicitor had not been negligent, and thus awarded her only nominal damages.
[61] [1995] 1 W.L.R. 1602. *cf. Martin Boston & Co. v. Roberts* [1996] 1 P.N.L.R. 45; for facts see para. 10–178 above. The defendant solicitors failed to obtain a charge over a house from a third party in support of her personal guarantee. A majority of the Court of Appeal held, following *Sykes*, that the question of whether the guarantee would have been obtained should be judged on the balance of probabilities. For an earlier example see *Nash v. Phillips* (1974) 232 E.G. 1219, Foster J.: the plaintiffs lost the opportunity to purchase a particular house as a result of their solicitor's negligence. Damages were reduced by 10% to reflect the possibility that they may not in any event have gone ahead with the purchase.

10–259   **Illustrations.** *Allied Maples* was followed by the Court of Appeal in *Stovold v. Barlows.*[62] There, the defendant solicitors were negligent in sending deeds by DX when the purchaser's solicitors were not on the DX, and the plaintiff's sale then failed. The Court of Appeal considered that he had lost a chance of the sale going ahead, which they evaluated on the facts at 50 per cent on an assessment of how long the deeds might have taken to arrive by post and whether the purchaser might still have been tempted by an alternative property. There are now a number of examples of the application of this principle.[63] In *Hartle v. Laceys*[64] the Court of Appeal held that there was a 60 per cent chance of a deal going ahead with the proposed purchaser, but for the defendant solicitors' negligence. In *Inter-Leisure Ltd v. Lamberts*[65] the judge had to evaluate the effect of the defendant solicitors negligently inserting an upwards/downwards rent review clause into a lease instead of an upward only one. He determined that there was a 75 per cent chance that the tenants would have accepted an upwards only rent review clause, and a one-third chance that the tenants would not have exercised a break clause at the end of a third year, so that 25 per cent of the full loss was awarded. In *Abraxas Computer Services Ltd v. Rabin Leacock Lipkan (a Firm)*[66] the defendant solicitors negligently failed to make applications to the court to extend leases under the Landlord and Tenant Act 1954. As a result, the claimant had three months to resolve its accommodation needs, instead of two and a half years. The judge held that the claimant lost the chance of obtaining a better deal on some other property equivalent to that which it did move into, which he assessed as 35 per cent of the difference between what the claimant paid and the offer from an alternative bidder. In *Lloyds Bank plc v. Parker Bullen (a Firm)*[67] the defendant solicitors failed to inform the lender of a covenant against assignment. While the transaction would have gone ahead in any event, there was a prospect of obtaining a more favourable outcome to negotiations with the owner of the borrower. Longmore J. held that there was only a 15 per cent chance of the bank obtaining a more favourable deal, which would have avoided any loss. In *Motor Crown Petroleum Ltd v. S.J. Berwin & Co.*[68] the Court of Appeal upheld a finding by the same judge that the plaintiffs had a 40 per cent chance of obtaining planning permission if the solicitors had challenged in time the local council's designation of the land on which they wished to build a petrol station as open countryside. In contrast, in *Bacon v. Howard Kennedy (a Firm)*,[69] the testator's will, which would have left his estate to the plaintiff, was never concluded due to the defendants' negligence. The court rejected a submission that damages should be reduced because the testator might have made changes to his will, because such a possibility was merely speculative.

10–260   **The limits of the principle.** The courts are still working out all the circumstances in which losses should be considered on the basis of the loss of a chance

---

[62] [1996] 1 P.N.L.R. 91.
[63] See also: *Titanic Investments v. McFarlanes* [1997] N.P.C. 105; *In Rey v. Graham & Oldham (a Firm)* [2000] B.P.I.R. 354, McKinnon J. (failure to apply for adjournment of bankruptcy proceedings, 80% chance of avoiding bankruptcy, damages reduced by 20%).
[64] [1999] Lloyd's Rep. P.N. 315, summarised at para. 10–276 below,
[65] [1997] N.P.C. 49, QBD.
[66] [2000] E.G.C.S. 70; N.P.C. 63, QBD.
[67] [2000] Lloyd's Rep. P.N. 51.
[68] [2000] Lloyd's Rep. P.N. 438. The Court of Appeal rejected a submission that there was no loss, distinguishing *Hotson v. East Berkshire Area Health Authority* [1987] A.C. 750.
[69] [1999] P.N.L.R. 1, H.H. Judge Bromley Q.C., sitting as a Judge of the Chancery Division.

rather than the balance of probabilities. Three particular instances should be noted. *Allied Maples* was applied in the context of the chances of a plaintiff being acquitted of criminal charges if further evidence had been forthcoming in *Acton v. Graham Pearce & Co. (a Firm)*.[70] In contrast, in *Veasey v. Millfeed Co. Ltd*[71] the Court of Appeal assumed without deciding that the question of causation in wasted costs proceedings should be determined on the balance of probabilities, as full discovery and cross-examination did not take place in such an application. In *Cancer Research Campaign v. Ernest Brown & Co.*[72] Harman J. seemed to decide, *obiter*, and it is submitted correctly, that disappointed beneficiaries had to prove only that they lost the chance that they would have received benefits under a putative deed of variation of a will.

The position in the Commonwealth. The High Court of Australia came to an   **10–261** almost identical decision to *Allied Maples in Poseidon Ltd v. Adelaide Petroleum NL*,[73] although in Canada different courts have adopted different views.[74] The New Zealand Court of Appeal upheld a 25 per cent discount to the damages awarded in *McElroy Milne v. Commercial Electronics Ltd*[75] on the basis that even if there had been no breach, the plaintiffs might have had some difficulties.

Burden of proof. As a matter of practice the courts tend to lean in favour of   **10–262** the claimant when considering, hypothetically, what would have happened if the defendant solicitors had performed their duty.[76] A number of cases suggest that on some occasions the burden of proof shifts to the solicitors to show that the alleged benefit would not have materialised in that event,[77] but this must be

---

[70] [1997] 3 All E.R. 908. For the facts of the case see para. 10–218.

[71] [1997] P.N.L.R. 100 (see para. 10–139 for the facts).

[72] [1998] P.N.L.R. 592 at 604. For a contrary view of what the judge found, see J. Murphy, "Probate solicitors, disappointed beneficiaries and the tortious duty to advise on tax avoidance" (1998) 14 P.N.L.R. 107.

[73] (1994) 68 A.L.J.R. 313 (a case which did not concern solicitors); *cf.* the earlier case of *Waribay Pty Ltd v. Minter Ellison* [1991] 2 V.R. 391, Victoria App. Div.

[74] *Bossee v. Clavette* (1984) 56 N.B.R. (2d) 375, New Brunswick CA: solicitors failed to secure release of client's obligations under mortgage; deduction as speculative whether release could have been obtained. *Fraser Park South Estates Ltd v. Lang Michener Lawrence & Shaw* (2001) 3 C.C.L.T. (3d) 270, British Columbia CA: no loss of a substantial chance as a result of solicitor's negligence. *Graybriar Industries Ltd v. Davis & Co.* (1992) 46 B.C.L.R. (2d) 164, affd on damages 72 B.C.L.R. (2d) 190 by the British Columbia CA: plaintiff awarded $60,000 for the loss of the opportunity to continue negotiations which might have led to a more favourable agreement. *Papageorgiou v. Seyl and Parkland Farm Power & Equipment Ltd* (1990) 45 B.C.L.R. (2d) 319, British Columbia CA: plaintiff awarded $15,000 for the loss of a chance to sell his restaurant. *cf. Clarke v. Poje and Kenney* (1989) 38 B.C.L.R. (2d) 110, British Columbia CA: plaintiff could not prove that the defendant solicitor would probably have successfully negotiated a compromise with his bank reducing his liability.

[75] [1993] 1 N.Z.L.R. 39. For the facts see para. 10–251 above. See also *Apatu v. Peach Prescott & Jamieson* [1985] 1 N.Z.L.R. 50, at 69, Eichelbaum J.: loss of opportunity to purchase property, 10% deducted for contingencies.

[76] *e.g. Kitchen v. Royal Air Force Association* [1958] 1 W.L.R. 563, CA, and *Mount v. Barker Austin (a Firm)* [1998] P.N.L.R. 491, discussed at para. 10–291 below.

[77] *e.g. Heywood v. Wellers* [1976] Q.B. 446 at 459: "It was suggested that even if the solicitors had done their duty and taken the man to court he might still have molested her. But I do not think they can excuse themselves on that ground. After all, it was not put to the test: and it was their fault that it was not put to the test. If they had taken him to court as she wished—and as they ought to have done—it might well have been effective to stop him from molesting her any more. We should assume that it would have been effective to protect her, unless they prove that it would not" (*per* Lord Denning M.R.). In *Ferris v. Rusnack* (1984) 9 D.L.R. (4th) 183 the Alberta Court of Queen's Bench applied the same principle, following *Heywood v. Wellers*.

wrong in the light of the House of Lords' decision in *Wilsher v. East Essex Area Health Authority.*[78]

(d) *Heads of damage*

10–263 The losses which may result from breaches of duty by solicitors cover a wide variety of situations. However, certain types of loss are of common occurrence. It is hoped that the classification offered below will be of some assistance.

(i) *Loss of opportunity to acquire or renew an interest in property*

10–264 **Alternative methods of evaluation.** Where, as a result of the solicitor's error, the client is unable to proceed with an intended purchase or renewal, his loss is normally represented by (a) the value of the property he intended to buy less (b) the sum for which he would have bought it.[79] In *Stinchcombe & Cooper Ltd v. Addison, Cooper, Jesson & Co.,*[80] as a result of negligence by the purchasers' solicitors, the vendors were enabled to rescind a contract for the sale of building land. The contract price was £2,250. The value of the land at the time of rescission was £6,500. Damages were assessed at £4,250. An alternative method of quantifying damages was adopted in *Simpson v. Grove Tompkins & Co.*[81] As a result of his solicitors' negligence the plaintiff was unable to purchase certain property in 1978. However, he was able to acquire the property (albeit at an overvalue) in 1979. The Court of Appeal held that the measure of damages was the difference between the market value in 1979 and the price which the plaintiff was originally asked to pay in 1978. By contrast, in *Endhill Pty Ltd v. Grasso Searles & Romano*[82] the defendant solicitors negligently failed to settle a contract for the purchase of land in 1986, as a result of which the plaintiff was unable to obtain the property until 1989. The Queensland Court of Appeal held that the solicitors were not liable for the increased costs of acquiring and building on the land as they were proportionately no greater than inflation in the period of delay.

10–265 **Business tenancies.** Part 2 of the Landlord and Tenant Act 1954, which governs the renewal of business tenancies, gives rise to numerous claims against solicitors. If the tenant's solicitor fails to give notice or to issue proceedings within the specified time limits, the right to a renewal of the tenancy is forfeited. The measure of the tenant's loss in such circumstances is usually the value of the tenancy which would have been obtained (either by order of the court or by

---

[78] [1988] A.C. 1074. See further chap. 12 para. 12–247.
[79] *e.g. Nash v. Phillips* (1974) 232 E.G. 1219, Foster J.: loss of opportunity to purchase house. Value of house £5,250. Agreed purchase price, subject to contract, £4,750. Damages assessed at £500 less notional legal expenses and 10% discount to reflect the possibility that the purchase might not have proceeded. *Jarvis v. T. Richards & Co.* (1980) 124 S.J. 793, Nourse J.: the plaintiff lost the opportunity to have the former matrimonial home conveyed to her. Held that damages should not only include the value of the property when the plaintiff lost it, but also should take account of inflation since that date. See also *Otter v. Church Adams Tatham & Co.* [1953] Ch. 280, Upjohn J. (discussed in para. 10–257) in which the client lost the opportunity, at no cost, to make his interest in entailed property absolute.
[80] (1971) 115 S.J. 368, Brightman J.
[81] *The Times,* May 17, 1982.
[82] [1993] 2 Qd.R. 136.

negotiation with the landlord).[83] In *Clark v. Kirby-Smith*[84] Plowman J. held that the new tenancy would have been at market rent and that there was no evidence as to what its value would have been. He therefore awarded nominal damages only. In *Joliffe v. Charles Coleman & Co.*[85] Browne J. was prepared to speculate in rather more detail. He considered that the county court judge would have been prepared to grant a 14-year lease at a rental of £900 per annum. He also considered that this was worth £200–250 more than the lease which the landlords were prepared to offer after learning of the solicitors' mistake (and which the plaintiffs, in order to mitigate their losses, ought to have accepted).[86] A broadly similar approach was adopted by Leonard J. and the Court of Appeal in *Teasdale v. Williams & Co.*[87] where the tenant accepted a new lease but on less favourable terms. In *Hodge v. Clifford Cowling & Co.*[88] the plaintiff shopkeeper renewed his lease for five years instead of 14 years due to the defendant solicitors negligence, although the rent was not affected. He recovered the difference in value of the business caused by the shorter lease. In *Ricci v. Masons*[89] the defendant solicitors failed to serve a notice under section 25 of the Act. Their client, the plaintiff, was able to negotiate for a new lease. The Judge determined that the plaintiff would have obtained a 10-year term with a six-month redevelopment break clause. The plaintiff was awarded the additional cost of the lease which he had to pay, his costs of abortive proceedings and disbursements, and the diminution in the value of his restaurant business caused by the fact that his lease now had no statutory protection. A different approach was adopted in *Matlock Green Garage Ltd v. Potter Brooke-Taylor & Wildgoose (a Firm)*[90] where the solicitors failed to renew a lease in 1992. But for the negligence, the plaintiff would have obtained leases for a further 10 years, and possibly for longer, rather than the two years which the landlord granted. The plaintiff ceased its garage business in 1994, and was awarded the stream of profits which would reasonably have been expected for the remaining period, capitalised on a conventional multipler/multiplicand basis. The judge did not account for the loss of profits on parts of the business on other sites, as those parts of the business were not bound to close, and the losses were not foreseeable as the defendants could not be assumed to have known about the interrelationship between parts of the business.

Agricultural tenancies. A more conventional result was reached in unusual **10–266** circumstances in *Layzell v. Smith Morton & Long.*[91] The plaintiff's father held an agricultural tenancy. When he died, the defendant solicitors negligently failed to claim a right of succession for the plaintiff pursuant to section 39 of the

---

[83] If the plaintiff moves to alternative premises, he ought to recover the removal costs and incidental expenses as special damages. See para. 10–272. For an example of the loss being the lost opportunity to obtain more favourable terms at another property, see *Abraxas Computer Services Ltd v. Rabin Leacock Lipkan (a Firm)* [2000] E.G.C.S. 70; N.P.C. 63, discussed at para. 10–259 above.

[84] [1964] 1 Ch. 506.

[85] (1964) 219 E.G. 1608.

[86] The total damages awarded were £1,000 because the judge took into account the fact that during the course of the proceedings under the Landlord and Tenant Act 1954 the plaintiffs would have continued to pay the old rent of £108 *per* annum.

[87] (1983) 269 E.G. 1040. See para. 10–254 above.

[88] [1990] 2 E.G.L.R. 89, CA.

[89] [1993] 38 E.G. 154, Mr L. Swift Q.C. sitting as a deputy judge of the Queen's Bench Division.

[90] [2000] Lloyd's Rep. P.N. 935.

[91] [1992] 1 E.G.L.R. 169.

Agricultural Holdings Act 1986. Schiemann J. found that it was all but impossible to obtain a tenancy at the market equivalent to the one the plaintiff had lost as a result of the defendant's negligence. The plaintiff was awarded the cost of the freehold of an equivalent property, less what he could recover from selling the freehold and taking the leasehold on the terms of the one he had lost. The defendant argued that the plaintiff had only lost a source of cheap housing and a higher income than he would otherwise obtain, both of which could be compensated by applying an appropriate multiplier to the yearly loss. The court rejected this approach, which would have resulted in smaller damages; the plaintiff had expected to be a tenant farmer on his family farm, and the court would award damages to put him in the position he would have been but for the defendant's negligence.

10–267   **Difficulties in evaluation.** It is not always possible to evaluate in precise monetary terms what the plaintiff has lost through being unable to remain in occupation of property. *Bryant v. Goodrich*[92] illustrates how the court will treat such a difficulty. A wife gave up possession of the matrimonial home, after the breakdown of marriage, as a result of her solicitor's negligent advice. The court therefore had to assess how much worse off the wife was financially as a result of moving out. Lord Denning M.R. stated that this was "one of those cases, like the loss of a chance, which the court had to deal with as would a judge or jury." Damages were assessed at £600 (including one specific item of £65).

(ii) *Difference in value of property*

10–268   **The normal rule.** Where the purchaser's solicitor errs in his advice he gives or in the investigations which he makes on the client's behalf, the property may prove to be less valuable than was assumed at the time of purchase. The normal measure of damages in such circumstances (as in the cases on surveyors' negligence)[93] is the amount by which the sum paid by the client exceeds the true value of the property at the date of purchase. For instance in *Wapshott v. Davies Donovan & Co.*[94] the Court of Appeal upheld an assessment of damages in relation to defective leases as the difference in value at purchase in 1986, and not when defects first became apparent in March 1988 when the plaintiffs tried to sell the premises. In the majority of cases, the courts are ready to accept that the purchase price represents the value of the property in the condition described by the solicitor. Where, however, the purchase price corresponds with the value of the property in its actual condition, then the purchaser suffers no loss and will be

---

[92] (1966) 110 S.J. 108.
[93] As to which see chap. 9, paras 9–130 to 9–148. *Cf.* the case where there is no valid transaction: see para. 10–304.
[94] [1996] 1 P.N.L.R. 361. The Court held that here were no special circumstances requiring a later date of assessment. For further examples see *Lake v. Bushby* [1949] 2 All E.R. 964, KBD: property less valuable by reason of absence of planning permission for bungalow standing on it. Diminution assessed at £100; *Piper v. Daybell Court-Cooper & Co.* (1969) 210 E.G. 1047, Nield J.: property less valuable by reason of right of way running across it. Diminution assessed at £200.; *Collard v. Saunders* (1972) 221 E.G. 797, Mocatta J.: property less valuable by reason of defects. Diminution assessed at £250; *Trask v. Clark & Sons* [1980] C.L.Y.B. 2588, Talbot J.: footpath ran across plaintiff's property, diminution assessed at £1,500; *Walker v. Giffen Couch & Archer* [1988] E.G.C.S. 64, Peter Gibson J.: diminution in value from public footpath through property assessed at £8,000; *Twidale v. Bradley* [1990] 2 Qd.R. 464, Queensland Sup. Ct: grocery business less valuable without secure title of premises; *Owen v. Fielding* [1998] E.G.C.S. 110, Steel J.: diminution in value assessed at 20% as part of land was subject to rights of common.

entitled to no more than nominal damages.[95] In Scotland there is no such general rule, and each case falls to be considered on its own facts.[96] The difference in value rule applies in Ireland,[97] in Australia,[98] and in Canada.[99]

Exceptions to the rule, general statements. The principle is not an invariable   **10–269**
one. In *County Personnel Ltd v. Alan R. Pulver*[1] Bingham L.J. stated:

> "On the authorities as they stand the diminution in value rule appears almost always, if not always, to be appropriate where property is acquired following negligent advice by surveyors . . . That is not, however, an invariable approach, at least in claims against solicitors, and should not be mechanistically applied in circumstances where it may appear inappropriate."[2]

Two further Court of Appeal cases discuss the general approach to be adopted. In *Reeves v. Thrings & Long*[3] the plaintiff purchased a hotel where access to the hotel car park was by licence only, and he spent some money rectifying this when the problem came to light four years later. The defendant solicitors were not found to be liable. Sir Thomas Bingham M.R., with whom Simon Brown L.J.

---

[95] *Ford v. White* [1964] 1 W.L.R. 885: solicitors advised, incorrectly, that land was not subject to restriction against building. The price paid corresponded with the true value of the land, taking into account the building restriction. Pennycuick J. held that there was no loss. See further chap. 9 para. 9–135. Similarly, the plaintiff was limited to the diminution in value, which was zero, in *Brown v. Cuff Roberts* [1996] C.L.Y. 4499, CA.

[96] This has been stated in: *Haberstich v. McCormick and Nicholson* [1975] S.L.T. 181, IH (solicitor's negligence caused purchaser to obtain property without a wholly good and marketable title; damages assessed at difference in value at later sale of property after it had been improved); and *Di Ciacca v. Archbald Sharp & Sons* [1994] S.L.T. 421, OH (purchaser entered property on payment of deposit, seller later proved to have no title, damages against negligent solicitor could include additional amount required to purchase other property on discovering the defect in title). However, in *Douglas v. Stuart Wyse Ogilvie Estates Ltd* [2001] S.L.T. 689, OH, the diminution in value was said to be the preferred measure, with the cost of repairs as a potentially relevant cross-check.

[97] *Kelly v. Finbarr J. Crowley* [1985] I.R. 212, Murphy J.: diminution in value rule applied; *Doran v. Delaney* [1999] 1 I.L.R.M. 225, Irish HCt: diminution in value as prima facie the measure of damages applied. *Cf. Kehoe v. Louth* [1992] I.L.R.M. 282, Sup. Ct.: the damages awarded for negligently advising that premises were as good as freehold when the plaintiffs purchased the property were the capital value of the annual increase in rates on the revaluation which would be needed under Irish law to enable such a conversion, and the cost of buying out the freeholder less what a reasonable person would think it would cost. The case could be justified as being based on a warranty. No cases were cited by the Court.

[98] *Kyriacou v. Kogarah Municipal Council* (1995) 88 L.G.E.R.A. 110, Sup. Ct NSW, in which *Ford v. White* was cited with approval.

[99] *Messineo v. Beale* (1978) 81 D.L.R. (3d) 713, in which *Ford v. White* was cited with approval, *Toronto Industrial Leaseholds v. Posesorski* (1995) 119 D.L.R. (4th) 193; and *789538 Ontario Ltd Gambin Associates* (1999) 27 R.P.R. (3d) 210, all Ontario CA. *cf. Poolton v. Paci* (1999) 21 R.P.R. (3d) 212 where without referring to authority the Ontario Court of Appeal held that the cost of cure was the primary measure of loss rather than the diminution in value, although in that case there was no evidence that the plaintiff's imperfect title would ever be challenged and minimal damages were awarded.

[1] [1987] 1 W.L.R. 916.

[2] *ibid.* at 925F–G. This dictum was cited by many subsequent cases, *e.g.* Staughton L.J. in *Hayes v. Dodd* [1990] 2 All E.R. 815, at 819B. A very similar approach is followed in Canada, see *Toronto Industrial Leaseholds v. Posesorski* (1995) 119 D.L.R. (4th) 193 at 214, Ontario CA. It has been suggested that a claimant may be able to elect which method to adopt, see Hirst J. at first instance in *Hayes v. Dodd* [1990] 2 All E.R. 815, at 820B. It is plainly implicit in later cases that it is for the court to determine the appropriate measure of damages, not the claimant, on the basis of the parties' pleaded cases and evidence.

[3] [1996] 1 P.N.L.R. 265 at 278.

agreed, considered, *obiter*, three approaches on damages, if it had been established that the plaintiff would not have entered into the transaction. First, damages might be the plaintiff's entire outlay on the purchase and refurbishment of the hotel, which the Judge considered would probably have overcompensated the plaintiff, because whatever he had invested in might have led to loss in the recession at that time. Secondly, it may have been preferable to apply the difference in value test at the date when the problem came to light rather than at the date of breach, although there might be additional claims too. Thirdly, the loss may have been calculated as the costs of rectifying the defect when the problem came to light. The Master of the Rolls concluded that it was undesirable to rule on the proper approach to damages in principle, because assessment of damages is ultimately a factual exercise. He stated that this "is an area in which legal rules may have to bow to the particular facts of the case."[4] In *Oates v. Anthony Pitman & Co.*[5] the Court of Appeal suggested that there were at least three possible approaches to the assessment of damages. First, there was the difference in value rule, which was applied by considering evidence of the value of comparable properties. Secondly, where the property was unusual, or was being purchased for a particular purpose to the knowledge of the solicitor, or there had been a substantial interval before the defect came to light, the estimated cost of correcting the defect might be the most reliable guide to the difference in value. There may be no satisfactory evidence to decide the market value. Thirdly, where the plaintiff has extracted himself from a transaction he would not have entered but for the negligence of the solicitor, damages should be assessed on the basis of the cost of extraction.

10–270   **Illustrations of exceptions.** A number of exceptions appear in the decided cases. Although they may be sensible decisions on their own facts, any general rules extracted from them may be somewhat artificial, and the following classification is tentative.[6]

10–271   **(1) Loss of use of property.** Where an encumbrance or defect in title interferes with the use to which the solicitors know the claimant intends to put the property, his loss may not be limited to the difference in value but may include the loss from such use of the property.[7] This is especially true if the claimant builds on the property before discovering that there is an easement upon which he has encroached.[8]

---

[4] Contrast the case of *Amerena v. Barling,* para. 10–250 above.

[5] [1998] P.N.L.R. 683.

[6] For a different view see H. Evans *Lawyers' Liabilities*, (2nd ed., 2002), chap. 10; and *ibid.*, "Damages for solicitors' negligence: (2) diminution in the value of property" (1992) 8 P.N. 29. See also *CEMP Properties (U.K.) Ltd v. Dentsply Research & Development Corporation* [1989] 2 E.G.L.R. 205, solicitors acting for a vendor who was sued by the purchaser for misrepresentation were ordered to indemnify their clients against the purchaser's claim for wasted expenditure, but not the overpayment the purchaser recovered.

[7] *King v. Hawkins & Co., The Times,* January 28, 1982, Mars-Jones J.

[8] *e.g. Barclay-White v. Guillaume* [1996] E.G.C.S. 123, QBD, where the plaintiff built on land which he did not in fact own due to the negligent of the solicitor in failing to ascertain the correct boundaries, and he recovered his wasted building costs; *Charette v. Provenzano* (1978) 7 C.C.L.T. 23, Ontario HCt.

(2) Costs of extrication. Where the claimants would never have entered the 10–272 transaction at all but for their solicitor's negligence, and have subsequently rid or attempted to rid themselves of the property,[9] it may be appropriate to award as damages the extrication costs.[10] Thus in *County Personnel (Employment Agency) Ltd v. Alan R. Pulver & Co.*[11] the plaintiff entered a lease which had no capital value, and as a result of the negligence of its former solicitors exposed themselves to a longstanding liability. The damages were assessed as the cost actually paid by the plaintiff to extricate itself from the lease. The Court of Appeal considered that an assessment on the basis of the diminution in capital was wholly artificial.[12] In *Hayes v. Dodd* the plaintiffs acquired property where there was no right of way over the only convenient access.[13] It took the plaintiffs five or six years to dispose of the property, and they recovered all the expenses they incurred during those years. Similarly, in *Connor v. Ritzman*[14] the defendants allowed the plaintiff to purchase a lease where there were discrepancies in the conveyancing documents, and the purchasers of the freehold did not consent to rectification. The plaintiff recovered the difference between the sums spent on purchasing and improving the maisonette, the costs of the rectification action, and the mortgage repayments after a failed resale, minus the value of the lease at the date of judgment.

(3) Market value not reflect loss. Although the claimants paid a market rate 10–273 for the property acquired, in some cases the loss may not be nominal but clearly of substance, so that the difference in value rule is inappropriate. Thus in *Murray v. Lloyd*[15] the defendant solicitors negligently advised the plaintiff in 1981 to purchase a residential lease in the name of a company in order to save tax, rather than in her own name. Subsequently in 1986 the plaintiff was unable to have the lease assigned to her, and thus she was unable to obtain a statutory tenancy at the expiry of the lease in 1991. The plaintiff was awarded what it would cost her to acquire what she had lost, which was the cost of purchasing similar rights of occupation on similar terms in similar alternative accommodation. The evidence was that the freehold value of such a house was £460,000, and that a statutory

---

[9] This category could be extended to include attempts by the plaintiffs to rid themselves of the encumbrance, as in *Toronto Industrial Leaseholds Ltd v. Posesorski* (1995) 119 D.L.R. (4th) 193 at 214, Ontario CA. where the costs of unsuccessful litigation to rid property of an option which the solicitor had not noticed were awarded as well as the diminution in value.

[10] Such a measure of loss was not awarded in *Oates v. Pitman* [1998] P.N.L.R. 683 because the plaintiffs did not base their claim on such a basis, and there was insufficient evidence to make the calculations.

[11] [1987] 1 W.L.R. 916. See also *GP&P Ltd v. Bulcraig & Davies* [1986] 2 E.G.L.R. 148 and [1988] 1 E.G.L.R. 138, where a planning restriction was only discovered after the plaintiff had gone into receivership, and the lease was then surrendered. The plaintiff recovered all of its expenditure less what it obtained on surrender.

[12] *ibid.* at 926B and 927H–928A. But see the explanation of Staughton L.J. in *Hayes v. Dodd* [1990] 2 All E.R. 815, at 818–819, and Ralph Gibson L.J. in *Watts v. Morrow* [1991] 1 W.L.R. 1421, cited in chap. 9, para. 9–146.

[13] [1990] 2 All E.R. 815 at 820A.

[14] (1995) 70 P.&.C.R. D41.

[15] [1989] 1 W.L.R. 1060, John Mummery sitting as a High Court judge. This case did not concern advice relating to the value of the property, which was perfectly sound in every way, but to the identity of the purchaser. The difference in value rule may have no application in such circumstances.

tenancy depreciated the value by a quarter. As a result, the plaintiff was awarded £115,000. Similarly, the rule would not apply where the claimants obtained property which was more expensive than property that would suit their needs due to their solicitors' error. In *Computastaff Ltd v. Ingledew Brown Bennison & Garrett*,[16] the defendant solicitors negligently advised the plaintiff that the rateable value of office premises it wished to lease was £3,305 rather than £8,305. The plaintiff would not have entered the lease for that sum. The defendants contended that the plaintiff suffered no loss because it obtained value for what it was paying. The Judge decided that, but for the defendants negligence, the plaintiff would have obtained other offices which were suitable to its needs for the price it wanted to pay.[17]

10–274   **(4) Loss of business profits.** Where premises are acquired for business use, the solicitor's error may affect the profitability of the client's business. In such a case difference in value may not be the measure of the client's loss.[18] In *Simple Simon Catering Ltd v. Binstock Miller & Co.*[19] the plaintiffs took a lease of a restaurant. As a result of their solicitor's negligence, the lease contained a clause permitting the landlords and persons authorised by them to share the use of the kitchen. The trial judge awarded no damages under this head. The Court of Appeal reversed this decision on the grounds that the landlord's right to use the kitchen constituted a serious threat, and remitted the matter for rehearing and reassessment of damages. As to *quantum*, Lord Denning M.R. stated: "It seemed that loss was very much a matter of general assessment, one not to be measured necessarily by the difference in value of the reversion and so forth, but as a matter of general expectation of loss." However, *Oates v. Anthony Pitman & Co.*[20] suggests that loss of profits will not be recoverable. The defendant solicitors failed to advise that there was no grant of planning permission for the use of the property as holiday flats, which is what the plaintiff intended to use it for. The plaintiff did not recover any loss of profits for two reasons: it would appear that such losses would not be recoverable as they would not be attributable to the breach of duty[21]; and the plaintiff could not recover loss of profits from developing a property if he would not have purchased it but for the defendant solicitors' negligence.

10–275   **(5) Radical change in circumstances.** Changes in circumstances after the purchase may make it inappropriate to award the difference in value at the date

---

[16] (1983) 268 E.G. 906, McNeill J.

[17] See also *Carter v. TG Baynes & Sons* [1998] E.G.C.S. 109, ChD. The defendant solicitors failed to note that there were restrictive covenants preventing development of the site which the plaintiff intended to purchase. The plaintiff recovered for his losses sustained as a result of being unable to sell the maisonettes he built, which he could have sold five years earlier but for the covenants, rather than the diminution in value.

[18] *e.g. Braid v. W.L. Highway & Sons* (1964) 191 E.G. 433, Roskill J. See also *Kienzle v. Stringer* (1981) 35 O.R. (2d) 85: owing to the solicitor's negligence, the plaintiff acquired a defective title to a farm. The problem emerged when he sought to sell and the plaintiff incurred substantial costs resolving the situation, and the farm was less profitable. The Ontario Court of Appeal held that damages were not limited to the diminution in value.

[19] (1973) 228 E.G. 527.

[20] [1998] P.N.L.R. 683, CA.

[21] Relying on *Banque Bruxelles Lambert v. Eagle Star* [1997] A.C. 191.

of purchase. In *Kennedy v. K.B. Van Emden & Co.*[22] the plaintiff purchased the underlease of property in 1983 at a premium. The defendant solicitors had failed to advise her that the premium was unlawful. The plaintiff claimed that as a result she would have been unable to assign the underlease at a premium, and she had therefore lost the premium she had paid. However, as a result of statutory changes in 1988 a premium was no longer unlawful. The Court of Appeal declined to award the difference in value at the date of purchase, as that would have given the plaintiff an undeserved windfall.[23] In *Gregory v. Shepherds*[24] the claimant purchased a Spanish holiday flat in 1989, but was unable to sell it in 1991 due to a defect in title. The defect was eventually removed in June 1999, and the flat was sold in January 2000. The Court of Appeal held that it was inappropriate to award the difference in value, and the true measure of loss was the interest over eight years on the capital tied up, less 50 per cent for the personal use of the apartment over that time. The claimant was also awarded the costs of trying to procure the removal of the charge, and an enquiry was ordered into the capital losses sustained from inflation and the difference in exchange rates over the eight years. In *Dent v. Davis Blank Furniss*[25] the defendant solicitors were negligent in 1991 in failing to carry out a search of the commons register in the purchase of a house and garden. The purchasers learned of the problem in 1994, but in 1996 they succeeded in having part of the land de-registered as common land, at a cost of £20,000. Blackburne J. assessed damages in 1996 as the difference between the open market value assuming it to be free from commons registration and the lesser of what the claimants had spent on the property (including acquisition and improvement costs) and its open market value as so improved.

(6) Cost of cure. There have been a few cases in which the plaintiff has been **10–276** awarded the cost of cure.[26] They would appear to share the features that if the defect had been discovered before purchase, it would have been removed, and

---

[22] [1996] P.N.L.R. 409. Contrast *Shaw v. Fraser Southwell (a Firm)* [1999] Lloyd's Rep P.N. 633. The defendants failed to inform purchasers of a lease that an assignment had to be to a limited company. One of the purchasers recovered his diminution in value of £11,500. He sold his share of the flat, which was now the whole of the flat rather than half of it due to his copurchaser's trustee in bankruptcy disclaiming his interest, back to the landlord eight years later. The Court of Appeal held that although the amount he received in excess of the true value of his interest in 1997 cancelled out the diminution in value of his interest in 1989, it was not a sufficiently unusual circumstance to displace the ordinary rule. *Cf.* also *Gardner v. Marsh & Parsons* [1997] P.N.L.R. 362, discussed at chap. 9, para 9–148, and which may not be easy to reconcile with *Kennedy v. Van Emden.*
[23] Contrast the cases of *Amerena v. Barling* (1995) 69 P.&.C.R. 252, see para. 10–250, and *Wapshot v. Davies Donovan & Co.* [1996] 1 P.N.L.R. 361, see para. 10–268.
[24] [2000] P.N.L.R. 769, CA, for the facts see para. 10–200 above.
[25] [2001] Lloyd's Rep. P.N. 534. Followed *obiter* on similar facts in *Patel v. Daybells (a Firm)* [2001] P.N.L.R. 43, Gray J.
[26] See also *Kienzle v. Stringer* (1981) 35 O.R. (2d) 85, Ontario CA.

that subsequently it has been removed.[27] In *Creech v. Mayorcas*[28] the solicitor for the purchaser of a lease failed to obtain the landlord's licence to assign or licence for change of user. It subsequently proved possible to obtain the licences at a cost of £120. The plaintiff recovered this sum by way of damages, together with the amount of rent which he had to pay before the licences were obtained (during which time he could not use the shop) and a small sum in respect of extra wages. In *Braid v. W.L. Highway & Sons*[29] solicitors acting for the purchasers of a hotel business failed to give proper advice concerning the reversion expectant on the term of the lease. The plaintiffs recovered, *inter alia*, the costs of buying out their landlord's interest.

(iii) *Loss of opportunity to bring proceedings*

10–277 **Claimant's claim statute-barred.** Where solicitors fail to issue proceedings within the limitation period, it is not always possible to discover what is the "loss" which the claimant has thereby suffered.[30] The court trying the professional negligence action can only speculate about the outcome of the original proceedings. The intended defendant to the original proceedings is not a party to the professional negligence action, although he may be, and quite commonly is, called as a witness in that action. The correct approach to such cases was considered by the Court of Appeal in *Kitchen v. Royal Air Force Association*.[31] The Court rejected the argument that it should determine on balance of probabilities, whether the plaintiff would have succeeded in the original action. Lord Evershed M.R. (with whom Parker and Sellers L.JJ. agreed) continued:

"If, in this kind of action, it is plain that an action could have been brought, and if it had been brought that it must have succeeded, of course the answer is easy. The damaged plaintiff then would recover the full amount of the damages lost by the failure to bring the action originally. On the other hand, if it be made clear that the plaintiff never had a cause of action, that there was no case which the plaintiff could reasonably ever have formulated, then it is equally plain that the answer is that she can get nothing save nominal damages for the solicitors' negligence. I would add, as was conceded by [counsel for the plaintiff], that in such a case it is not enough for the plaintiff to say: 'Though I had no claim in law, still, I had a nuisance value which I could have so utilized as to extract something from the other side and they would have had to pay something to me in order to persuade me to go away.'

The present case, however, falls into neither one nor the other of the categories which I have mentioned. There may be cases where it would be quite impossible to try 'the

---

[27] But see *Hartle v. Laceys* [1999] Lloyd's Rep. P.N. 315. The plaintiff property developer purchased a plot of land subject to a restrictive covenant in favour of the covenantee which had not been registered and was thus void. The plaintiff purchased an adjoining plot, obtained planning permission to sell both plots, and agreed a sale to a third party. The defendant solicitor, who acted for the plaintiff and did not appreciate that the unregistered covenant was void, informed the covenantee of the proposed sale. The covenantee registered the covenant, and the sale to the third party did not go ahead. The Court of Appeal awarded the plaintiff the difference between the agreed sale price and the amount for which the plots were later sold, plus sums to release the covenants and solicitors' costs, with compound interest, reduced by 40 per cent for the chance of the sale not completing in any event.

[28] (1966) 198 E.G. 1091, Pennycuick J.

[29] (1964) 191 E.G. 433, Roskill J.

[30] If the claim was already statute-barred when the client consulted the solicitor, then he will have suffered no loss from any delay by the solicitor, as in *Coffin v. MacBeath* (1990) 81 Nfld. & P.E.I.R. 333, Newfoundland CA.

[31] [1958] 1 W.L.R. 563.

action within the action' . . . In my judgment, assuming that the plaintiff has established negligence, what the court has to do in such a case as the present is to determine what the plaintiff has lost by that negligence. The question is: Has the plaintiff lost some right of value, some chose in action of reality and substance? In such a case it may be that its value is not easy to determine, but it is the duty of the court to determine that value as best it can."[32]

The defendant solicitors do not step into the shoes of the original defendants. In the ordinary case, the court has to determine the value of the case at the date of a notional trial. This will involve making proper allowance for the probabilities of success and other contingencies. Interest will then be added from that notional trial date. The cases concerning loss of opportunity to sue decided before *Kitchen v. Royal Air Force Association*[33] ought now to be treated with caution, at least in relation to *quantum* of damages.[34] The following paragraphs will illustrate and develop the principles set out in *Kitchen* as they have developed in subsequent case law.[35]

Other jurisdictions and how to determine issues. *Kitchen* has been followed **10–278** in Scotland,[36] Australia,[37] and by most Canadian courts.[38] However, a different approach was taken in *Fisher v. Knibbe*[39] where the Alberta Court of Appeal reversed the trial judge's award of 15 per cent of *quantum* on full liability. The Court considered that the plaintiff would be awarded the value of the lost opportunity, rather than 100 per cent of the lost damages or nominal damages, only where a "trial within a trial" was impossible. In that case, the trial judge had decided that the original defendant was not negligent, and the Court of Appeal considered therefore that only nominal damages should be awarded. In *Hanif v. Middleweeks*[40] the Court of Appeal made it clear that this was not the approach of the English courts. The claimant's counterclaim against his insurers for an indemnity for the loss of his nightclub by fire was struck out. In the professional negligence action the Judge determined that the claimant had only a 25 per cent chance of proving that he had not set fire to the nightclub. The Court of Appeal held that the Judge had and should have determined the chances of proving the

---

[32] *Kitchen v. Royal Air Force Association* [1958] 1 W.L.R. 563 at 574–575.

[33] [1958] 1 W.L.R. 563.

[34] *e.g. Clayton v. Kearsey* (1935) 79 S.J. 180 failure to issue proceedings in respect of road traffic accident. Nominal damages only awarded; *Ashton v. Philip Conway Thomas & Co.* (1939) B.W.C.C. 246: failure to apply for review of an award under the Workmen's Compensation Act 1925. Damages of £133 were awarded, being the amount which would probably have been recovered on the review.

[35] Note also the issue of the burden of proof, which will generally follow the principles set out in relation to actions struck out as a result of the solicitor's negligence, explained in para. 10–291 below.

[36] *Yeoman v. Ferries* [1967] S.C. 255, OH. The case was followed in *Kyle v. P.&J. Stormonth Darling* [1994] S.L.T. 191 and *Siraj-Eldin v. Campbell Middleton Burness & Dickson* [1989] S.L.T. 122, both Inner House of the Court of Session.

[37] See, *Johnson v. Perez* (1989) 82 A.L.R. 587 and *Nikolaou v. Papasavas, Phillips & Co.* (1989) 82 A.L.R. 617, both High Court of Australia.

[38] See, *e.g. Melanson v. Cochrane Sargeant, Nicholson & Paterson* (1968) 68 N.B.R. (2d) 370, New Brunswick CA, and *Rose v. Mitton* (1994) 111 D.L.R. 217, Nova Scotia CA.

[39] (1992) 3 Alta. L.R. (3d) 97.

[40] [2000] Lloyd's Rep. P.N. 920.

claimant's dishonesty in the original action rather than whether the claimant had in fact set fire to his property.[41]

10–279   **Examples of the evaluation.** In *Kitchen* the plaintiff's husband was killed whilst using electrical equipment in the kitchen at home. The plaintiff alleged that the accident was due to a defect in the cooker, for which the electricity company who had connected it were liable. Her solicitors failed to issue proceedings within the time allowed by the Fatal Accidents Acts 1846 to 1908. It was common ground that the maximum sum which would have been recovered in the original action was £3,000. In the professional negligence action the trial judge awarded £2,000 damages. The Court of Appeal upheld the decision, although observing that on the particular facts, the judge's assessment of the plaintiff's prospects was a generous one.[42] Where the original action raised serious issues both on liability and *quantum*, the evaluation of the chance which the claimant has lost becomes more difficult and more speculative. In *Yardley v. Coombes*,[43] for example, the plaintiff, a lorry driver, sustained a fall when the grab handle came away from the cab of his lorry. Subsequently the tuberculosis which had been latent in the plaintiff's right shoulder became serious, and he required an arthrodesis of the joint. Edmund-Davies J. held that on liability the plaintiff had "a fair chance of success". On the question whether the accident had seriously aggravated the tuberculosis, the evidence was more difficult. The judge considered that the plaintiff "was not bound to fail in establishing that the fall was the cause of his tubercular shoulder." In the event of total victory in the original action the plaintiff would have recovered £3,000. Reviewing all the contingencies, Edmund-Davies J. awarded £1,000.

10–280   Three cases in the last decade illustrate the variety of circumstances of the lost action. In *Gascoine v. Ian Sheridan & Co.*[44] the plaintiff alleged that a gynaecologist and radiotherapist negligently gave her irradiation treatment, causing her physical injuries. Her action was struck out for want of prosecution, and her solicitors and barrister admitted liability for that. Mitchell J. heard evidence of a variety of views and approaches from many witnesses. He considered that his task was not to decide whether negligence was proved but to assess in the light of the expert evidence the prospects of success, and he concluded that the plaintiff had lost a 60 per cent chance of successfully establishing negligence in the original action. *Acton v. Graham Pearce & Co. (a Firm)*[45] concerned the lost opportunity of avoiding a criminal conviction. The plaintiff was a solicitor who was convicted and imprisoned for obtaining money from the Law Society by deception by submitting false Green Forms to the Law Society. His appeal succeeded on the basis that memoranda implicating the plaintiff from a former

---

[41] Similarly, the claim should not be denied on public policy grounds as the judge had not found that the claimant had been the arsonist.

[42] See also *Gregory v. Tarlo* (1964) S.J. 219, where McNair J. considered that the plaintiff could have made out a "quite a formidable case" and awarded 75 per cent of the full value of the claim. *Malyon v. Lawrance, Messer & Co.* [1968] 2 Lloyd's Rep. 539 is a more complicated case. The plaintiff was injured in a road traffic accident in Germany, and the negligence of his English solicitors caused him to loss the opportunity to pursue his claim. After hearing evidence from German lawyers, Brabin J. decided that: (i) the plaintiff would have been held 50% to blame for the accident by a German court; (ii) the German courts would have valued his claim on full liability at £550 in respect of personal injuries and £3,500 in respect of loss of profits.

[43] (1963) 107 S.J. 575.

[44] [1994] 5 Med L.R. 437.

[45] [1997] 3 All E.R. 909.

employee were shown by a document examiner to have been typed on dates other than those they bore, and on evidence from the employee's former employer that she was dishonest. The plaintiff successfully sued his solicitors for failing to submit the memoranda to a document analyser or obtain statements from the former employers. Chadwick J. held that the plaintiff would still have had to explain at his criminal trial how he allowed clients to sign Green Forms which had not been completed, or how he thought he could claim costs for work above that allowed in the Green Form scheme. The Judge held that there was a 50 per cent chance that he would not have been convicted, and directed an enquiry into the loss he had suffered as a result.

Harrison v. Bloom Camillin[46] is one of the most detailed lost litigation cases **10–281** to be tried, and it provides a very good illustration of the approach of the courts to evaluating such claims. The defendant solicitors admitted negligence in failing to serve a writ properly in November 1992 in a case where accountants were sued for negligence in relation to a new business venture which turned out disastrously. In relation to the assessment of damages, Neuberger J. held the matters of law should be resolved on the basis of the loss of a chance, as well as matters of fact, but that a court would be more ready to determine that the claimant would have succeeded or failed on a point of law. He also considered that the extent to which a court would be prepared to take a "broad brush" approach depended on the circumstances. In that case, he could form a detailed view on separate issues as there was very substantial evidence, and limited delay from the defendant's negligence. The judge found that there was a better than evens chance of establishing that the accountant's report was negligent, rather less than that in proving that they had made negligent verbal assurances, and there was a small discount in relation to reliance, so that the total discount so far was 35 per cent. There was no discount in relation to contributory negligence, as the Judge was able to come to a firm conclusion that such an allegation would have failed. There was a further 20 per cent discount to reflect the fact that the business might have got into difficulties for reasons unconnected with the accountant's negligence. The total discount of 48 per cent[47] was applied to damages of £101,500 for each claimant for their lost investment, and £20,000 for the loss of earnings of the second claimant. The judge rejected the damages claims for the first claimant's loss of earnings as it was so weak in principle and in fact, and he also dismissed the claim for the increase in value of the claimants' homes because as a matter of law the prospect of its success was so slim. There was a deduction, without discount, for the accountants' fee claim.[48]

The lower threshold. In *Kitchen v. Royal Air Force Association* it was stated **10–282** that there had to be a claim in law, and not merely a nuisance claim.[49] The test has been expressed as the plaintiff having some prospect of success,[50] having anything above a certainty of failure,[51] and whether it would have been open to

---

[46] [2000] Lloyd's Rep. P.N. 89. See para. 10–284 for the judge's views on the claimants's funding difficulties, 10–285 in relation to settlement, 10–287 on notional trial date, and 10–289 on interest.

[47] See the further reasons at [2000] Lloyd's Rep. P.N. 404. The 52% chance of success is calculated as $(100-35) \times (100-20)$.

[48] See the further reasons at [2000] Lloyd's Rep. P.N. 404.

[49] [1958] 1 W.L.R. 563 at 574.

[50] *Buckley v. National Union of General and Municipal Workers* [1967] 3 All E.R. 767, at 774F, Nield J., *Gouzenko v. Harris* (1977) 72 D.L.R. (3d) 293, Ontario HCt.

[51] *Prior v. McNabb* (1977) 78 D.L.R. (3d) 319, Ontario HCt.

a reasonable tribunal to make the plaintiff an award.[52] In a number of cases it has been held that the test was not satisfied and only nominal damages would be awarded.[53] A sum of $1,000, a little more than nominal damages, was awarded in *Appo v. Barker*,[54] $500 being nominal damages in *Melanson v. Cochrane Sargeant, Nicholson & Paterson*.[55] On some occasions the prospects of success are too poor to justify any award of damages. In *Green v. Cunningham John & Co. (a Firm)*[56] the plaintiffs were sued for defective building. The defendant solicitors settled the case without authority and failed to advise their clients to pursue the local authority. The plaintiffs recovered nothing as the settlement was a good one, and an action against the local authority was speculative, expensive and best avoided.

10–283   **The upper threshold: discount for risks of litigation.** At the other extreme, even the best case is not free from risk, and therefore it may be appropriate to make some discount for the hazards of litigation.[57] Thus in *Redman v. Instant Nominees Pty Ltd*[58] the plaintiff lost his right of appeal due to his solicitor's negligence in a case where there was no fresh evidence. The Court of Appeal of Western Australia gave a 10 per cent discount on the basis that the appeal might not have succeed. However, each case must, however, be considered on its own facts, and in some cases no discount may be appropriate.[59] Thus in *Charles v. Hugh James Jones & Jenkins (a Firm)*[60] the Court of Appeal held that there should be no discount in a case where liability had been admitted and there was no evidence to suggest that the plaintiff might have recovered less in settlement or negotiation than the damages assessed by the judge in the professional negligence litigation. In *Dickenson v. James Alexander & Co.*[61] the defendant solicitors acted for the wife in divorce proceedings, and negligently failed to obtain full disclosure from the husband of his assets, with the result that she obtained a disadvantageous settlement. Douglas Brown J. assessed damages on the basis of what a court would have ordered the husband to pay or transfer to her. It was argued on behalf of the defendants that the matter might have been disposed of in negotiation for less than a court might award (presumably in response to a *Calderbank* letter). The judge considered that the husband was not a man who would have compromised the litigation, and therefore there should be no such discount.

---

[52] *Siraj-Eldin v. Campbell Middleton Burness & Dickson* [1989] S.L.T. 122, IH.
[53] *Buckley v. National Union of General and Municipal Workers* [1967] 3 All E.R. 767; *Gouzenko v. Harris* (1977) 72 D.L.R. (3d) 293; *Siraj-Eldin v. Campbell Middleton Burness & Dickson* [1989] S.L.T. 124.
[54] [1981] 50 F.L.R. 198, Sup. Ct Northern Territory.
[55] (1968) 68 N.B.R. (2d) 370, New Brunswick CA.
[56] (1995) 46 Con.L.R. 62, CA. See also *McFarlane v. Wilkinson* [1997] P.N.L.R. 578, where an action brought against two barristers was struck out (*inter alia*) because the breach of statutory duty which it was alleged they should have pleaded would have been bound to fail on the facts.
[57] *e.g.* *McNamara v. Martin Mears & Co.* (1983) S.J. 69, Peter Pain J; *Dolman v. Penrose* (1983) 34 S.A.S.R. 481, South Australian Sup. Ct *in banco*: a case "almost certain of success" was assessed at about 80 per cent of the value on full liability. There may, of course, be some cases where no deduction should be made.
[58] [1987] W.A.R. 277.
[59] *e.g.* in *Johnson v. Perez* (1989) 82 A.L.R. 587 and *Nikolaou v. Papasavas, Phillips & Co.* (1989) 82 A.L.R. 617.
[60] [2000] 1 W.L.R. 1278.
[61] (1990) 6 P.N. 205, at 207.

Funding difficulties and legal aid. Defendants sometimes allege that the   **10–284**
claimant would have been unable to fund the litigation, and thus should be
awarded nothing for their lost opportunity. This issue can be particularly acute in
legal aid or community legal services cases, where funding would not be
forthcoming for an action which had some prospects of success, although those
prospects would have been less than fifty percent. In *Casey v. Hugh James Jones
& Jenkins*[62] the defendant solicitors failed to advise the clients about their rights
of appeal after the withdrawal of legal aid. However, there was no real or
substantial chance of the Legal Aid Board changing its mind if adequate representations had been made. The Court also held that there was no real chance of
the claim succeeding at trial. The plaintiff recovered only nominal damages. In
Harrison v Bloom Camillin[63] a different funding issue arose. It was alleged that
legal aid was obtained dishonestly, as the claimants failed to disclose their
financial circumstances to the Legal Aid Board. Neuberger J. held that, although
funding with legal aid could not be taken into account if acquired dishonestly, the
defendants had not proved that the claimants had been dishonest. Furthermore,
the judge held that if the claimants had lost their legal aid funding after proceedings had been issued, which they would not have done as they would have
refused to accept an income they received from their father, then they would have
been able to and would have funded the action, and the judge was influenced by
the fact that they had been able to fund privately the subsequent proceedings
against their solicitors. It should be noted that the judge did not consider that
these issues should be looked at as the loss of a chance, but on the basis of the
balance of probabilities.

Cost of the original action and settlement. One factor which has received   **10–285**
some attention in the reported decisions is the risk in costs which the claimant
runs in any case where the outcome is uncertain.[64] In *McNamara v. Martin Mears
& Co.*[65] Peter Pain J. gave a discount of a third from the award of £12,000 "for
the costs and hazards of litigation, and for the acceleration of payment." and in
the New Zealand case of *Thompson v. Howley*[66] Somers J. held that the plaintiff
would have won his case, and deducted a sum of $150 for irrecoverable costs,
apparently on the agreement of counsel. In *Corfield v. D.S. Bosher & Co.*[67] the
defendant solicitors failed to appeal an arbitrator's award in time. The judge held
that the plaintiff had a one third chance of persuading a court to set the arbitration
aside, and that in any further arbitration he would probably have obtained
£23,380, of which he was awarded a third. The plaintiff recovered a third of the
costs he had paid to the other side in a failed late appeal to the court. The judge
held that in any arbitration the arbitrator would probably have required each party
to bear their own costs and half of the arbitrator's fee, and so the plaintiff had to
give credit for £6,500, based on agreed figures. In principle, the costs of the

---

[62] [1999] Lloyd's Rep. P.N. 115, Thomas J.
[63] [2000] Lloyd's Rep. P.N. 89; see para. 10–281 for the facts.
[64] See further H. Evans: *Lawyers' Liabilities*, (2nd ed. 2002), chap. 11, and *ibid.*, "Damages for
solicitors' negligence: (1) the loss of litigation (1991) 7 P.N. 201, where further dicta are cited. The
point may develop greater significance in the context of conditional fee agreements.
[65] (1983) S.J. 69.
[66] [1977] 1 N.Z.L.R. 1 at 27.
[67] [1992] 1 E.G.L.R. 163, see esp. 168.

original action should be taken into account in appropriate circumstances. Similarly, account should be taken where appropriate of the chances of settlement.[68] In *MacKenzie v. Middleton Ross & Arnot*[69] the Inner House of the Court of Session held that the pursuers' personal injury claim, which the defendant solicitors negligently failed to issue before the expiry of the limitation period, would have been compromised at approximately £25,000. In *Port of Sheerness Ltd v. Brachers*[70] solicitors gave wrong advice in Industrial Tribunal proceedings which prevented settlement. The chance of settlement was assessed as a near certainty, and Buckley J. awarded the plaintiffs 90 per cent of the costs they incurred. In *Harrison v. Bloom Camillin*[71] Neuberger J. held that the court should take into account the possibility of the lost action settling, but he held that ordinarily the task of establishing the settlement value of a claim was likely to be similar to assessing the value of the lost opportunity of obtaining damages at trial. The issue was of some importance in that case, as the Judge made no deduction to reflect irrecoverable costs in the original action not least because it was likely to settle prior to trial in such a way as to cater for such costs.

10–286   **Means of the original defendant.** One qualification which should be added to the above discussion concerns the means of the original defendant. If he had no assets and no relevant insurance, then a judgment against him may have been valueless. The Western Australian Court of Appeal has held that the plaintiff must prove that the original defendant was able to satisfy any judgment, provided that the defendant has raised the issue in the pleadings.[72] A similar approach has been adopted in Canada, see *Alberta Workers' Compensation Board v. Riggins.*[73] It is submitted that this is right in principle and that an English court would adopt the same approach.

10–287   **The significance of the notional date of trial.** One matter which often has to be determined by the court in assessing damages is the date at which the original action should have come to trial or would have settled, if the defendant solicitors

---

[68] "I think that the possibility of a reasonable compromise must not be forgotten in assessing the value of the lost right to bring an action" *per* Bollen J in *Dolman v. Penrose* (1983) 34 S.A.S.R. 481 at 492, South Australia CA.

[69] [1983] S.L.T. 286.

[70] (1997) I.R.L.R. 214.

[71] [2000] Lloyd's Rep. P.N. 89; see para. 10–281 for the facts.

[72] *Redman v. Instant Nominees Pty Ltd* [1987] W.A.R. 277. See similarly *Perri v. Zaitman* [1984] V.R. 314, Sup. Ct, where the pleadings point was not mentioned.

[73] (1993) 95 D.L.R. (4th) 279, the defendant solicitors settled a personal injury claim at too low a level. After discussing conflicting Canadian decisions, the Alberta Court of Appeal considered that the burden lay on the plaintiff client to prove that he would have recovered the full amount which should have been awarded, but that the defendant solicitor had to place "collectability" in issue first. In that case the issue had not been pleaded and the limited evidence suggested that higher damages would have been collectable. See also the earlier cases of: *Page v. A Solicitor* (1971) 20 D.L.R. 532, New Brunswick CA, aff'd 29 D.L.R. 386: following a road accident, a solicitor failed to sue the deceased driver; damages were assessed at the deceased's insurance cover in the absence of any evidence that he had any funds or property to satisfy any judgment; *Doiron v. Caisse Populaire D'Inkerman Ltee.* (1985) 17 D.L.R. 660, New Brunswick CA; *Aikmac Holdings Ltd v. Loewen* (1993) 86 Man. R. (2d) 56 Manitoba QB: plaintiff failed to discharge onus of proving that she would have recovered her damages; *Buerckert v. Mattison* [1997] 1 W.W.R. 430, Saskatchewan QB: the Court determined that the original defendant would probably have gone bankrupt but would have had to pay half of the plaintiff's notional judgment debt on discharge, which was what the plaintiff was awarded; *Valness v. MacLowich* (1998) 168 Sask.R. 45, Saskatchewan CA: there was sufficient evidence that the original claimant had the ability to satisfy the judgment.

had carried forward the plaintiff's claim with due diligence. In *Johnson v. Perez*[74] the High Court of Australia held that damages crystallised when the action was dismissed for want of prosecution, and in *Nikolaou v. Papasavas, Phillips & Co.*[75] the same Court held that when no action was commenced, damages crystallised when the claim became statute-barred. In both cases the court held that a notional trial date should then be assessed. A court must assess the evidence that would have been available at that time, and the relevant principles of law then governing the assessment of damages.[76] Thus if the plaintiff's claim is in respect of personal injuries, the "tariff" prevailing at that date should be applied, rather than the "tariff" prevailing when the professional negligence action is heard. Furthermore, the plaintiff's prognosis at the time of the notional trial date must be assessed, and what actually happened later should generally be ignored.[77] The same result has been reached in Canada.[78] The question of the date of the notional trial may be important in determining the applicable legal principles in an area of law where there has been significant development. For example, in *Harrison v. Bloom Camillin*[79] the claimants argued that there would have been trial within two and three-quarter years, relying on the length of time the solicitors' negligence trial had taken to come to court, and the defendants suggested nearly six years, relying on statistical evidence. Neuberger J. held that there would have been a hearing in July 1996 and judgment in October 1996. Unusually, the issue was of some importance, as the House of Lords' decision in *Banque Bruxelles Lambert v. Eagle Star*[80] would limit the damages recoverable if it was decided in time for the notional judgment, as the Judge held it was.

The principles discussed above have been qualified by the Court of Appeal in **10–288** *Charles v. Hugh James Jones & Jenkins (a Firm)*.[81] The plaintiff suffered personal injuries in a road accident in 1990, and the defendant solicitors negligently allowed her subsequent action to be struck out. The judge held that the original action would have been tried in January 1996. The Court of Appeal held that a court should consider evidence of the plaintiff's condition which would have been available at the notional trial date, even if the evidence in fact only emerged later. Furthermore, if a condition was of uncertain prognosis at the notional trial date, but became clearer afterwards, it was appropriate to admit later evidence of what in fact happened.[82] The Court tentatively considered that evidence of some entirely new condition which manifested itself only after the notional trial date should not be admitted.

---

[74] (1989) 82 A.L.R. 587.
[75] (1989) 82 A.L.R. 617.
[76] See *Nikolaou v. Papasavas, Phillips & Co.* (1989) 82 A.L.R. 617 at 623 ll. 10–13.
[77] Evidence of what happened later may, in certain cases, assist in determining what a judge at the notional trial date would have done, and what evidence might have been brought then: see *Johnson v. Perez* (1989) 82 A.L.R. 587, at 598–599. For instance, if there were no medical reports prepared at the notional trial date, later medical reports may assist in determining what reports would have said then. The longer the time has passed from the notional trial date, the less material the report will be.
[78] *Rose v. Mitton* (1994) 111 D.L.R. (4th) 217, Nova Scotia CA, expressly following the two Australian cases and para. 4–189 in the 3rd ed. of this book.
[79] [2000] Lloyd's Rep. P.N. 89. However at 116 col. 2 the judge seemed to suggest that if a later authority laid down the law in a way which was not intended to be a departure from the past, that authority should be applied in any event. See para. 10–281 for the facts of the case.
[80] [1997] A.C. 191, discussed at para. 10–244.
[81] [2000] 1 All E.R. 289.
[82] *ibid.* at 1290G, *cf.* 1295D–E.

10–289   **Interest after date of trial.** If the claimant would have recovered damages at a particular date which has been assessed, then those damages would have attracted judgment debt interest thereafter if they had not been paid. The Court of Appeal decided in *Pinnock v. Wilkins & Sons*[83] that such interest is recoverable in an action against solicitors who have lost the plaintiffs' right of action by their negligence. However, in *Harrison v. Bloom Camillin*[84] Neuberger J. held that the appropriate rate of interest was a matter of discretion, and although many cases had awarded judgment rate interest, he considered it just to award the more flexibile short-term investment rate.

10–290   **Deduction of benefits.** One issue which frequently arises, but has not been the subject of any reported decision, is the effect of the deduction of statutory benefits from damages. In personal injury actions, the claimant will often recover significantly less than he is nominally awarded because the defendants are obliged to deduct most statutory benefits from the damages and send that deduction to the Compensation Recovery Unit.[85] The relevant legislation, in summary, only applies to compensation payments made in consequence of an accident by the person liable in respect of the accident.[86] Compensation payable by a solicitor to his client who has lost his personal injury action is therefore not subject to any such deduction. The consequence is that the negligent solicitor will have to pay less to the claimant than he would have been awarded at trial, due to the "CRU clawback" reducing the notional damages that would have been obtained, but the claimant will not lose out twice by having to pay any sum from the damages he recovers from the negligent solicitor to the Compensation Recovery Unit.

10–291   **Claimant's claim dismissed for want of prosecution.** The same approach will be taken where the claimant's claim is dismissed for want of prosecution. Where proceedings are dismissed for want of prosecution, the claimant's solicitors are unlikely, in the majority of cases, to persuade the court that the claim had no value whatsoever. The fact that the defendant solicitors were bringing the action is evidence that they thought it had some prospect of success, so that if they wish to say that the case was hopeless they will need good evidence to rebut the initial factual presumption. In *Mount v. Barker Austin (a Firm)*[87] Simon Brown L.J. considered that the applicable principles were as follows: (1) the legal burden lies on the plaintiff to prove that he has lost something of value, that is a case with real and substantial rather than merely a negligible prospects of success; (2) the evidential burden lies on the defendants to show that despite acting for the plaintiff in the litigation it was in fact of no value to their client; (3) if the court has greater difficulty in discerning the strength of the plaintiff's claim than it would have at the time of the original action, that counts against the defendant solicitors and not the plaintiff; (4) one would expect the court to be generous to the plaintiff in assessing his prospects of success.

---

[83] *The Times*, January 29, 1990. See further on the issue of interest chap. 3, paras 3–019 to 3–024.
[84] [2000] Lloyd's Rep. P.N. 404; see para. 10–281 for the facts.
[85] Note that in a case where the claimant had an X% chance of success, the deduction should be X%, see *Green v. Berry* [2001] 1 Qd.R. 605, Queensland CA.
[86] See s. 1 the Social Security (Recovery of Benefits) Act 1997, which is materially identical to earlier enactments.
[87] [1998] P.N.L.R. 493.

Enforcement proceedings. The principles discussed above apply *mutatis*   **10–292**
mutandis where the claimant loses the opportunity to bring proceedings to
enforce a judgment.[88]

(iv) *Loss of opportunity to defend proceedings*

Where a solicitor fails to put in a defence or to take some other procedural step,   **10–293**
with the result that his client loses the opportunity to contest a claim against him,
the court must consider the merits of the proposed defence. The damages should
represent the value of the opportunity which has been lost, and many of the
principles which have been discussed above will be applicable. In *Godefroy v.
Jay*[89] it was held that the client had no defence and therefore nominal damages
only were awarded. In *Cook v. Swinfen*[90] the solicitor acting for a wife failed to
defend divorce proceedings and allowed the husband to obtain a decree against
her. It was held that, if the solicitors had performed their duty, it was probable
that both parties would have obtained cross-decrees for adultery, but there was an
outside chance that the wife alone would have obtained a decree. Lawton J.
awarded (and the Court of Appeal approved) (i) damages of £200 for loss of the
chance of obtaining a more favourable outcome of the divorce suit; and (ii)
damages of £750 for loss of the chance of obtaining maintenance.[91]

(v) *Losses on loans secured by mortgages*[92]

Basic calculation. The principles to be applied in lender's cases will generally   **10–294**
be the same as those which have been extensively developed by the courts in the
context of negligent surveys carried out for lenders.[93] In *Swingcastle Ltd v.
Alastair Gibson,*[94] a case concerning surveyor's negligence, the House of Lords
held that the usual measure of loss recoverable by a lender is (i) the difference
between the advance and any capital recovered, plus (ii) consequential expenses,
plus (iii) interest to reflect the loss of use of the capital sum advanced, credit
being given for any interest payments made. However, this will be subject to the
type of breach in question which may restrict the damages recoverable.[95] The
interest to be awarded will be at a simple rate only, unless there was evidence of

---

[88] *Harrington v. Binns* (1863) 3 F. & F. 942: measure of damages was the amount which the jury
thought would have been realised if the attorney had issued execution; *Butler v. Knight* (1867) L.R.
2 Ex. 109: judgment for 390 guineas. The plaintiff's attorney agreed to accept 100 guineas in full
satisfaction. The plaintiff claimed the difference (*i.e.* 290 guineas), but there was some doubt as to
what the judgment debtor would have been able to pay. 150 guineas damages awarded.

[89] (1831) 7 Bing. 413. It was also held that the burden of proof rested on the attorney to show that
there was no defence to the original action.

[90] [1967] 1 W.L.R. 457.

[91] See also *Hill v. Finney* (1865) 4 F. & F. 616 in which, as a result of his attorney's advice, the
husband allowed his wife to obtain a decree of judicial separation undefended. In relation to *quantum*,
Cockburn C.J. directed the jury to consider the merits of the proposed defence and to consider what
damage the husband had suffered through not defending. The jury awarded one farthing.

[92] The duties of a solicitor acting for a client lending money were discussed in paras 10–206 to
10–217.

[93] See the discussion in chap. 9, paras 9–150 to 9–174. For earlier cases see: *Wilson v. Rowswell*
(1970) 11 D.L.R. (3d) 737, Sup. Ct Canada; followed in *Collin Hotels Ltd v. Surtees* [1988] 1 W.W.R.
272, Saskatchewan CA ;*Wilson v. Tucker* (1822) 3 Stark. 154; *Donaldson v. Haldane* (1840) 7 C. &
F. 762 and *Ronaldson v. Drummond & Reid* (1991) 8 Rettie 767, Ct Sess.; *Whiteman v. Hawkins*
(1878) 4 C.P.D. 13; *Campbell v. Clason* (1838) 1 Dunlop 270 and (1840) 2 Dunlop 1113, Ct Sess.;
Pretty v. Fowke (1887) 3 T.L.R. 845.

[94] [1991] 2 A.C. 223.

[95] See paras 10–244 *et seq.*, above.

foreseeability within the second limb of *Hadley v. Baxendale*, see *Birmingham Midshires Mortgage Services Ltd v. Phillips*.[96] The losses recoverable will include the cost of in-house lawyers, and estate agency commission where the work was undertaken by a separate legal entity, see *Portman Building Society v. Bevan Ashford (a Firm)*.[97]

10–295 **Scope of duty.** The measures of loss discussed in the previous paragraph will be further subject to the principle in *Banque Bruxelles Lambert SA v. Eagle Star Insurance Co. Ltd*.[98] Someone under a duty to advise on the appropriate course of action will be liable for all the foreseeable consequences of the action taken in reliance, but a person under a duty to take reasonable care to provide information on which someone relies will generally be regarded as responsible for the consequences of the information being wrong, and not all the consequences of the reliance. Thus surveyors sued by lenders were only responsible for the losses sustained up to the difference between the correct valuation and their negligent valuation. In *Bristol & West Building Society v. Mothew*[99] the Court of Appeal applied this principle to a case where the defendant solicitors had misrepresented to the plaintiff lender that the borrower had no other indebtedness. While the plaintiff's loss from the loan was large, the loss within the scope of the broken duty appeared to be modest, as the smallness of the borrower's liability may have a minimal or no effect on their ability to make mortgage repayments to the plaintiff. Determination of the size of the loss was left to the assessment of damages. While a solicitor's duty will be wider than that of a valuer, *Mothew* supports the view that there is no wide duty to advise on the appropriate course of action.[1]

10–296 **An exception: dishonest borrowers.** In *Bristol & West Building Society v. Fancy & Jackson (a Firm)*[2] Chadwick J. considered that the principles in *Banque Bruxelles Lambert* did apply to cases involving solicitors. However, in one of the cases he tried in that managed litigation, *Steggles Palmer*, the consequence of the solicitors' breach was that the plaintiff loaned money to a borrower whom they would not have wanted to lend to as the circumstances of the loan were

---

[96] [1998] P.N.L.R. 468, QBD; *cf. The Mortgage Corporation v. Halifax (S.W.) Ltd* [1999] Lloyd's Rep. P.N. 159, a surveyor's claim.

[97] [2000] P.N.L.R. 344, CA.

[98] [1997] A.C. 191, see para. 10–244 above. For a further explanation of how the principle works in the context of awarding interest, see *Nykredit Mortgage Bank plc v. Edward Erdman Group Ltd (No. 2)* [1997] 1 W.L.R. 1627, considered in chap. 9, para. 9–162. For the effect of contributory negligence on a claim which is subject to a limit from the scope of the duty owed, see *Platform Home Loans Ltd v. Oyston Shipways Ltd* [2000] 2 A.C. 190, considered in chap. 9, paras 9–166 to 9–167.

[99] [1996] 4 All ER 698. See also *The Mortgage Corporation v. Tisdall Nelson Nari & Co.* [1998] P.N.L.R. 81, QBD, which applied *Banque Bruxelles Lambert* to limit damages, and *Halifax Building Society v. Richard Grosse & Co.* [1997] E.G.C.S. 111. For early commentary on how the decision would apply to solicitors, see *Tomlinson*, pp. 94–97; and D. Halpern and T. Rosen Peacocke, "Are solicitors liable for damages resulting from a fall in the market?" (1996) 12 P.N. 77.

[1] *Cf.* the position in Scotland where it was held in *Bristol & West Building Society v. Rollo Steven & Bond* [1988] S.L.T. 9, OH, that the solicitors effectively advised the building society to take a certain course of action and were responsible for the full loss. Similarly in *Leeds & Holbeck Building Society v. Alex Morison & Co. (No. 2)* [2001] P.N.L.R. 13, OH, it was held that if the defenders had been negligent in failing to report that the borrowers intended in due course to use the property for business purposes, then they would have been liable for the full losses as the matter was relevant to the risk of default. See to similar effect *Newcastle Building Society v. Paterson Robertson & Graham* [2001] P.N.L.R. 780, OH.

[2] [1997] 4 All E.R. 582.

suspicious. The defendants were held liable for the full amount of the plaintiff's loss (subject to mitigation and contributory negligence). In contrast, in *Colin Bishop*, the defendants had failed to report back to back sales, and the solicitors were liable only for the amount of the overvaluation of the property. Blackburne J. adopted the same approach in *Nationwide Building Society v. Balmer Radmore (a Firm).*[3] Thus, for instance, *Nationwide Building Society v. A.T.M. Abdullah*[4] was a *Colin Bishop*-type case, whereas in *Nationwide Building Society v. J. R. Jones*[5] the lender recovered the full loss as a report on the back to back nature of the transaction and a direct payment would have meant that the lender would not have wanted to make any loan to this applicant. The approach of these two cases was approved by the Court of Appeal in *Portman Building Society v. Bevan Ashford (a Firm)*[6] where the solicitor failed to report matters relating to the borrower's financial condition. As a result, the plaintiff thought that there was no second charge and that the borrower was paying the balance of the purchase from his own resources, when in fact he had no personal equity and had fraudulently deceived the lender when signing the offer of advance. The plaintiff was entitled to recover its full loss. The Court of Appeal cast the relevant principle in surprisingly wide terms:

> " . . . where a negligent solicitor fails to provide information which shows that the transaction is not viable or which tends to reveal an actual or potential fraud on the part of the borrowers, the lender is entitled to recover the whole of its loss."

This statement of principle has been followed by the Court of Appeal in *Lloyds Bank plc v. Crosse & Crosse.*[7] The defendant solicitors negligently failed to inform the claimant bank in 1989 that the plot of land over which security was taken was subject to restrictive covenants. The Court of Appeal applied *Portman* and limited the recoverable damages to the difference in value in 1989 between the plot without the restrictive covenants and the plot with those covenants.

(vi) *Loss of some other financial advantage*

Losses sustained on the sale of land. If, through the negligence of his **10–297** solicitor, the claimant is obliged to accept a forced sale or to sell his property at less than the full value, then the primary measure of his loss is the difference between the sum which he actually receives and the sum which he would have received in normal circumstances.[8] Alternatively, the solicitor's breach of duty might lead to a delay in the sale of land. In that event the measure of damages might comprise: (i) the amount of any mortgage interest paid during the period of delay, and (ii) the interest which could have been earned by investing the proceeds of sale throughout the period of delay.[9] In order to avoid double

---

[3] [1999] P.N.L.R. 606.
[4] [1999] Lloyd's Rep. P.N. 616.
[5] [1999] Lloyd's Rep. P.N. 414.
[6] [2000] P.N.L.R. 344.
[7] [2001] P.N.L.R. 34;[2001] E.W.C.A. Civ. 366.
[8] *Rumsey v. Owen White & Catlin* (1978) 245 E.G. 225, CA: as a result of the solicitors' negligence the plaintiff agreed to sell certain property with vacant possession, when in fact the tenants had security of tenure. The plaintiff recovered (i) the difference between what he actually received on the sale (£90,000) and what he would have received if he had sold without vacant possession (assessed at £112,000) and (ii) an indemnity against any future liability to the purchaser.
[9] *G. & K. Ladenbau Ltd v. Crawley & De Reya* [1978] 1 W.L.R. 266, Mocatta J.; *Dorey & Dorey v. Romney* (1982) 51 N.S.R. (2d) and 102 A.P.R. 53, Nova Scotia Sup. Ct.

compensation, the "proceeds of sale" under the second head should be taken as the net proceeds after repayment of any mortgage.

10–298　　**Loss of earnings.** Loss of earnings is not a usual consequence of negligence by solicitors. It may arise, for example, where the solicitor advises a client to pursue a course of conduct which results in the client being fairly dismissed. In *Malyon v. Lawrance, Messer & Co.*[10] (in which the plaintiff's claim for damages resulting from a road traffic accident became statute-barred) the plaintiff developed a neurosis which was not expected to clear up until after the conclusion of the litigation. Brabin J. awarded £2,000 compensation for loss of earnings caused thereby, in addition to damages in respect of the value of the original claim.[11]

10–299　　**Loss of life policy.** In *McLellan v Fletcher*,[12] as a result in part of the defendant solicitor's negligence, the plaintiff failed to take out a life insurance policy. The plaintiff was killed shortly afterwards, and his personal representative argued that the deceased has lost the contingent interest in the envisaged life policy. Anthony Lincoln J., apparently giving no reasons for his decision, awarded the deceased the sum insured. This sum was reduced by 75 per cent for contributory negligence, minus the premium which would have been paid. The opposite conclusion was reached in *Lynne v. Gordon Doctors & Walton.*[13] The defendant solicitors acted for a deceased mortgagee, and allegedly failed to ensure that his life was insured as part of the mortgage transaction. On a preliminary issue, Phillips J. decided that no loss was suffered by the deceased, assisted by an earlier Court of Appeal decision.[14] It is submitted that *Lynne v. Gordon Doctors & Walton* should be followed.

10–300　　**Diminution in value of shareholding.** Shareholders and directors sometimes sue their company's solicitors for their own losses. In many cases contractual or tortious duties will be owed to them by the solicitors. Can such claimants recover their losses, which are very often the diminution in value of their shareholdings? The law has recently been reviewed by the House of Lords in *Johnson v. Gore Wood & Co. (a Firm).*[15] While only a company may sue in respect of loss caused by a breach of duty to it, if the company suffers loss but has no cause of action, a shareholder who does have a cause of action may sue even thought the loss is the diminution in value of his shareholding. If the company suffers loss caused by a breach of duty to it, and the shareholder suffers a loss separate and distinct from that suffered by the company as a result of a breach of a duty independently owed to him, both can sue, but neither can recover loss caused to the other by breach of the duty owed to the other. In the latter case, if the shareholder's loss is merely reflective of the loss suffered by the company, the shareholder will have no right of action. Thus in *Johnson* the plaintiff could claim for sums he invested in the company, the cost of personal borrowings, the loss of some of his shareholdings, and his tax liability. As for an alleged diminution in value of his pension and shareholding in the company, the plaintiff could not claim for the enhancement of his pension by payments the company would have made, but he

---

[10] [1968] 2 Lloyd's Rep. 539.
[11] As to which see para. 10–243.
[12] (1987) 3 P.N. 202.
[13] *The Times*, June 17, 1991.
[14] *Griffiths v. Fleming* [1909] 1 K.B. 805 at 820–821.
[15] [2001] 2 W.L.R. 72. For the analogous Canadian position, see *Martin v. Goldfarb* (1999) 41 O.R. (3d) 161.

could for the enhancement of the value of the pension if the payments had been made. Thus, in summary, a shareholder cannot recover loss which is merely a reflection of the company's loss unless the company has no claim, see the Court of Appeal's decision in *Day v. Cook*.[16] As a result, in that case, the claimant could not recover lost investments in property dealings made through his companies, given that the solicitor also owed duties to the companies.[17]

(vii) *Liability to third parties*

One consequence of the solicitor's mistake may be to expose the client to liability to some third party: for example, the liability to pay mesne profits,[18] additional rates[19] or interest.[20] A more dramatic example is afforded by *Hart & Hodge v. Frame Son & Co*.[21] The plaintiffs instructed attorneys to take proceedings against their apprentices for misconduct. The attorneys brought proceedings under the wrong statute. The apprentices were convicted, but the convictions were quashed on appeal. The apprentices then sued the plaintiffs for false imprisonment and recovered damages. The plaintiffs recovered against their attorneys the full amount of their liability to the apprentices. In *Buckley v. Lane Herdman & Co*.[22] solicitors exchanged contracts for the sale of the plaintiffs' house before the plaintiffs had found a house to buy. The plaintiffs were unable to move out on the completion date and therefore faced a claim for specific performance. The plaintiffs ultimately had to pay the purchasers' costs in that action, amounting to £400. They recovered this sum, together with their own costs, from the solicitors. In *Braid v. W.L. Highway & Sons*,[23] as a result of their solicitors' negligence, the plaintiffs faced a claim by their landlord for breach of covenant. They settled this claim on terms amounting to a surrender, but recovered the amount of their liability from the solicitors. **10–301**

Solutions to uncertainty about plaintiff's liability. Often the solicitor is joined as the third party in an action brought against his client. This may be important to avoid the risk of inconsistent findings. It is often convenient in such circumstances to try the third party proceedings immediately after the main action.[24] If, however, at the date of trial, the plaintiff's liability to some third party has yet to be determined, it may not be possible to assess damages against the solicitors. In *Rumsey v. Owen White & Catlin*[25] the plaintiffs were unable to give vacant possession of property which they had sold, as required by the contract. The purchasers' claim for damages had not yet been heard. The Court **10–302**

---

[16] [2001] P.N.L.R. 32; [2001] E.W.C.A. Civ. 592.
[17] The Court of Appeal referred a number of the investments back to the judge for further determination.
[18] As in *Allen v. Clark* (1863) 7 L.T. 781: solicitor acting for purchaser of leasehold property failed to discover that it was mortgaged. The plaintiff recovered, *inter alia*, the mesne profits which he was obliged to pay to the mortgagee.
[19] *Computastaff v. Ingledew Brown Bennison & Garett* (1983) 268 E.G. 906, McNiell J.
[20] As in *Morris v. Duke-Cohan & Co., The Times,* November 22, 1975, Caufield J.: interest was paid to vendor, because the plaintiffs were unable to proceed with purchase.
[21] (1839) 6 C. & F. 193.
[22] [1977] C.L.Y.B. 3143, Judge Faye sitting as an Official Referee
[23] (1964) 191 E.G. 433, Roskill J. See para. 10–235.
[24] *e.g. Cemp Properties (U.K.) Ltd v. Dentsply Research & Development Corporation, Estates Gazette,* August 31, 1991, CA, where, first, the liability of the defendant to the plaintiff was established, secondly the liability was quantified, thirdly the defendant's claim against their former solicitors was tried, and fourthly the solicitors appealed against the second order on *quantum*.
[25] (1978) 245 E.G. 225.

of Appeal therefore gave judgment for the amount of the plaintiffs' loss so far, and ordered that the final assessment of damages should await the outcome of the other action. An alternative course, which was adopted in *Transportation Agency Ltd v. Jenkins*,[26] is to grant a declaration that the solicitors are liable to indemnify the plaintiffs against all sums which they may be held liable to pay to the party in question.

(viii) *Criminal liability*

10–303   The client may find himself in breach of the criminal law, as a result of negligent advice or omissions by his solicitor. The fact of the solicitor's error may constitute excellent mitigation in the criminal proceedings, but will not constitute a defence if (for example) the offence is one of strict liability. The normal measure of damages in such a case[27] is the amount of any fine or penalty imposed together with the costs of legal representation. In *Ashton v. Wainwright*[28] as a result of their solicitors' negligence the plaintiffs committed the offence of supplying drink at an unregistered club. They were convicted before the magistrates' court and fined. In the subsequent action against their solicitors the plaintiffs recovered the amount of fines and costs which they were ordered to pay. Goddard J. dismissed as irrelevant the fact that the fines had been paid out of club funds: "If by the negligence of my solicitor I incur a fine, the fact that a charitable person helps me to pay it so as to enable me to escape imprisonment in default cannot afford him a defence."[29]

(ix) *Wasted expenditure*

10–304   **General rule: wasted expenditure.** Where a solicitor fails to notice that a transaction his client is entering is invalid, the normal measure of loss will be the client's wasted expenditure. Thus in *Clarke v. Milford*[30] a solicitor acting for a purchaser of land failed to notice that the vendor was unable to convey any interest in the property. The client recovered money advanced on the purchase price and taxes he had paid on the property, and not the diminution in value of the property.[31]

10–305   **Wasted expenditure or anticipated gains.** Where as a result of the solicitor's breach of duty a transaction proves to be abortive, the client may recover by way of damages the whole of his expenditure in connection with that transaction. The client cannot at the same time claim the gains which he had anticipated receiving from the transaction, since that would give rise to double compensation. Claims for wasted expenditure and claims for anticipated gains are regarded as alternatives and the client must elect between the two.[32] If the client opts for the wasted expenditure basis, the authority of *Anglia Television v. Reed*[33] allows for

---

[26] (1972) 223 E.G. 1101, Kerr J.
[27] The client will only recover damages under this head in a case where there is no mens rea or culpable negligence on his part: *Osman v. J. Ralph Moss* [1970] 1 Lloyd's Rep. 313, CA. In other cases considerations of public policy preclude the recovery of any damages. For a general discussion of this topic, see *McGregor* (16th ed.), paras 738 to 796.
[28] [1936] 1 All E.R. 805.
[29] *ibid.* at 812.
[30] (1987) 38 D.L.R. (4th) 139, Nova Scotia CA.
[31] For the diminution in value approach see paras 10–268 to 10–276.
[32] For general principles, see *Cullinane v. British "Rema" Manufacturing Co.* [1954] 1 Q.B. 292; *Anglia Television v. Reed* [1972] 1 Q.B. 60.
[33] [1972] 1 Q.B. 60, CA. See *McGregor*, (16th ed.), paras 59 to 65.

the recovery of expenses incurred before contract where the parties contemplate that the expenditure may be wasted upon breach. This may be the case where the solicitor's breach results in the loss of an expected benefit. However, in *G.P. & P. v. Bulcraig & Davis*[34] the defendant solicitors failed to discover that premises to be purchased by the plaintiff were in part subject to a restriction of user clause which rendered them unsuitable. The plaintiff was unable to recover wasted expenditure incurred before the breach, because they would have been incurred even if the defendants had discovered the restrictive user clause (in which case the plaintiff would not have entered the lease).

An illustration. In *Transportation Agency Ltd v. Jenkins*[35] the plaintiffs **10–306** purchased a restaurant business, including the lease of the premises where the business was carried on. Unfortunately, their solicitors failed to notice a number of provisions in the lease which put the venture in jeopardy, principally a covenant prohibiting cooking. By the time that the landlords sought to enforce this covenant the plaintiffs had engaged a manager on terms which gave him a fairly free hand as to the running of the business. The plaintiffs were in no position to stop him cooking. The plaintiffs extricated themselves from the venture as best they could and ultimately the lease was forfeited for non-payment of rent. Kerr J. awarded by way of damages: (i) the total sum which the plaintiffs had paid for the business, plus (ii) the three instalments of rent which they had paid, minus (iii) the total amount which they had received from the manager during the period of operation of the business.

Original solicitors' costs. Where the solicitor's services are valueless as a **10–307** result of his breach of duty, the client is entitled to recover any sum which he has paid to the solicitor by way of costs.[36] This may be regarded either as damages for wasted expenditure or as repayment of a sum for which the consideration has wholly failed.[37] Thus if the solicitor for a claimant sues in the wrong court[38] or commits some other error which renders the whole proceedings useless,[39] he will be debarred from recovering his costs and ordered to repay any costs which he has received. The same principle applies if the client brings a futile action as a result of negligent advice (or negligent lack of advice) by his solicitor.[40] Similarly, if the solicitor for a defendant allows proceedings to go by default, he

---

[34] (1986) 2 E.G.L.R. 148, 152. This point was not in issue on appeal in (1988) 1 E.G.L.R. 138. For the facts see para. 10–253.
[35] (1972) 223 E.G. 1101.
[36] See, *e.g. Heywood v. Wellers* [1976] Q.B. 446 at 458, CA.
[37] One case which does not readily fit into this analysis is *Piper v. Daybell Court-Cooper & Co.* (1969) 210 E.G. 1047, Nield J.: solicitors acting for a purchaser failed to advise their client about a right of way. One item of damages (which was apparently conceded) was the amount of the solicitors' charges. However, it could hardly be said that there was a total failure of consideration or that the solicitors' services were valueless.
[38] *Gill v. Lougher* (1830) 1 Cr. & J. 170; *Long v. Orsi* (1856) 18 C.B. 610; *Cox v. Leech* (1857) 1 C.B. (N.S.) 617.
[39] *Symes v. Nipper* (1840) 12 Ad. & El. 377 n.; *Bracey v. Carter* (1840) 12 Ad. & El. 373; *Saffery v. Wray* (1846) 7 L.T. (O.S.) 183; *Lewis v. Samuel* (1846) 8 Q.B. 685; *Stokes v. Trumper* (1855) 2 K. & J. 232: this case concerned negligence by an attorney acting as advocate. See also *Clarke v. Couchman* (1885) 20 L.J. 318: a solicitor entrusted the conduct of the case to another member of his firm, "through whose want of familiarity with the facts the plaintiff was non-suited." The plaintiff recovered, by way of damages for negligence, the costs which he had incurred. See also *Templer v. McLachlan* (1806) 2 B. & P. (N.R.) 136.
[40] *Hill v. Featherstonhaugh* (1831) 7 Bing. 570.

forfeits his entitlement to remuneration.[41] Where part only of the solicitor's services are rendered valueless by his breach of duty, he may still be entitled to remuneration for the remainder of his services.[42]

10–308 **Later solicitor's costs.** A plaintiff may incur legal costs in litigation commenced to mitigate his loss. In *British Racing Drivers Club v. Hextall Erskine & Co (a Firm)*[43] it was held that the plaintiff could recover costs of proceedings instituted against its former directors from the defendant solicitors on a standard basis only, and not on an indemnity basis.

(x) *Incidental expenses*

10–309 Clearly, any expenses which the claimant incurs as a result of the solicitor's negligence will be recoverable,[44] in addition to the other heads of damage discussed in this section. As illustrations, see *Bailey v. Bullock*[45] or *Buckley v. Lane Herdman & Co.*[46]

(xi) *Physical injury, inconvenience and distress*

10–310 Where as a result of the solicitor's breach of duty the claimant suffers non-pecuniary loss, such as physical injury, inconvenience or (in some cases only) distress, then (subject to the rules as to remoteness) he is entitled to general damages.

10–311 **Inconvenience.** It has long been accepted that physical inconvenience and discomfort resulting from a solicitor's breach of duty sound in damages. For instance in *Wapshott v. Davies Donovan & Co.*[47] the Court of Appeal assessed damages in relation to inconvenience discomfort and distress of £3,000. The

---

[41] *Ferguson v. Lewis* (1879) 14 L.J. 700.

[42] *e.g. Cox v. Leech* (1857) 1 C.B. (N.S.): Attorney sued in the wrong court, but was entitled to recover the costs of sending letters before action. "These letters are distinguishable. They might have produced the desired result." See also *Shaw v. Arden* (1832) 9 Bing. 287.

[43] [1996] 3 All E.R. 667, Carnwath J. For the facts see para. 10–239 above.

[44] Subject to the rules as to remoteness discussed in paras 10–233 to 10–248.

[45] [1950] 2 All E.R. 1167, KBD: owing to solicitors' negligence the plaintiffs were unable to recover possession of their house from tenants for a period. They recovered *inter alia* the costs of storing furniture and garage expenses.

[46] [1977] C.L.Y.B. 3143, Judge Faye sitting as an Official Referee: the plaintiffs recovered the incidental expenses of moving house, which was forced upon them by their solicitors' negligence. *Lomond Assured Properties Ltd v. McGregor Donald* [2000] S.L.T. 797, OH the pursuers recovered for cost of the director's wasted time spent dealing with the problem caused by their solicitors, but not the time spent in the litigation.

[47] [1996] 1 P.N.L.R. 361. For further examples see: *Shilcock v. Passman* (1836) 7 C. & P. 289: plaintiff was awarded £10 damages as compensation for two months which he spent in prison, as a result of the attorney's failure to secure his discharge. *Bailey v. Bullock* [1950] 2 All E.R. 1167, Barry J.: plaintiff instructed the solicitors to recover possession of his house from the tenants. During two years' delay the plaintiff, his wife and child were forced to live with the wife's parents in cramped accommodation. Plaintiff awarded £300 damages for discomfort and inconvenience, but damages for annoyance and mental distress were irrecoverable. *Piper v. Daybell Court-Cooper & Co.* (1969) 210 E.G. 1047, Nield J.: plaintiffs were awarded £50 for the inconvenience and loss of privacy resulting from a right of way running across their land. *Trask v. Clark & Sons* [1980] C.L.Y. 1588, Talbot J.: plaintiff awarded £250 for the inconvenience, anxiety and loss of privacy caused by a public footpath running past his front door. In *Buckley v. Lane Herdman & Co.* [1977] C.L.Y.B. 3143, Judge Faye sitting as an official referee: as a result of premature exchange of contracts by their solicitors, plaintiffs were obliged to leave their home and to move to other unsuitable accommodation for two years at date of trial. They were awarded £750 damages each for inconvenience and distress.

defendant solicitors were retained by two young couples each buying a single bedroom flat, and it was reasonably foreseeable that if the solicitors were negligent then their clients may have to remain in the flats in cramped conditions with young families. As the loss was not too remote, there was no rule of law preventing such damages being awarded.

Distress affecting health. Where the solicitor's breach of duty causes such **10–312** distress as to affect the client's health, then this constitutes a separate head of damages. This is subject to the rules as to remoteness, which will often defeat a claim.[48] In *Malyon v. Lawrence, Messer & Co.*[49] the solicitors' negligence led to an extension of the period for which the plaintiff suffered neurosis, following a road traffic accident. £1,250 was awarded under this head.[50] A claim for distress affecting health means that the whole claim is subject to the three year limitation period appropriate for personal injuries.[51]

Distress not affecting health.[52] It used to be thought that mental distress not **10–313** resulting in injury to health did not sound in damages.[53] However, decisions in other areas of law have established that, in principle, damages for disappointment or distress resulting from breach of contract can be awarded in some circumstances.[54] There are two Court of Appeal cases concerning solicitors which consider this matter, and one from the House of Lords. In *Heywood v. Wellers*[55] the female plaintiff instructed solicitors to bring proceedings against a man to prevent him from molesting her. The clerk handling the matter made a number of errors, as a result of which the proceedings were ineffective. The Court of Appeal held that the plaintiff was entitled to damages in respect of the anxiety, vexation and distress caused by the man's continued molestation. Bridge L.J. emphasised, however, that not all distress resulting from solicitors' negligence sounds in damages, but only that "which is the direct and inevitable consequence of the solicitor's negligent failure to obtain the very relief which it was the sole purpose of the litigation to secure."[56] However, the other members of the Court

---

[48] In *Cook v. Swinfen* [1967] 1 W.L.R. 457 damages for injury to health were refused, on the grounds that such injury was not foreseeable (but see *Heywood v. Wellers* [1976] Q.B. 446, at 459C *per* Lord Denning M.R.). This was distinguished in *Dickinson v. James Alexander & Co.* (1990) P.N. 205 at 212.
[49] [1968] 2 Lloyd's Rep. 539, Brabin J. See also *Wales v. Wales* (1967) 111 S.J. 946.
[50] Similarly, see *Curran v. Docherty* [1995] S.L.T. 716 where the Outer House awarded the pursuer £3,000 with respect to the anxiety and distress caused by the defendant solicitor failing to obtain discharge of a mortgage over her house pursuant to a matrimonial settlement. It appears from the report that the distress did affect the pursuer's health.
[51] See *Bennett v. Greenland Houchen & Co.* [1998] P.N.L.R. 458, CA, *Oates v. Harte Reade & Co.* [1999] P.N.L.R. 763, Singer J., (refusal to allow the personal injury part of the claim to be deleted), *Shade v. the Compton Partnership (a Firm)* [2000] P.N.L.R. 218, CA (allowing the personal injury part of the claim to be deleted). See further chap. 5, para. 5–013.
[52] For a more detailed analysis see H. Evans, 'Lawyers' Liabilities', (2nd ed. 2002), chap.13.
[53] *e.g. Groom v. Crocker* [1939] 1 K.B. 194, CA: *Bailey v. Bullock* [1950] 2 All E.R. 1167, KBD.
[54] *Jarvis v. Swan's Tours* [1973] Q.B. 233; *Jackson v. Horizon Holidays* [1975] 1 W.L.R. 1468 (both cases concerning an unsatisfactory holiday); *Bliss v. South East Thames Regional Health Authority* [1987] I.C.R. 700 (where nothing was awarded because the case did not come within the narrow circumstances where such an award is permitted).
[55] [1976] Q.B. 446.
[56] [1976] Q.B. 446 at 463–464.

of Appeal applied the normal foreseeability test only, which would allow far wider recovery.[57]

10–314   A more restrictive view was adopted in *Hayes v. Dodd*.[58] The plaintiffs decided to purchaser larger premises for their motor repair business. Their solicitors, the defendants, wrongly informed them that a right of way existed over the only proper access to the premises, which was at the rear. The plaintiffs purchased the premises. The owner of adjacent property blocked the rear access, and as a result the business failed. The Court of Appeal did not allow the recovery of damages for anguish and vexation. The Court rejected the application of the foreseeability test alone and followed the classification provided by Dillon L.J. in *Bliss v. South East Thames Regional Health Authority*[59]: that recovery of such damages would be limited to cases " . . . where the contract which has been broken was itself a contract to provide peace of mind or freedom from distress."[60] In *Johnson v. Gore Wood & Co. (a Firm)*[61] the House of Lords struck out a claim by a plaintiff for damages for distress arising out of a commercial conveyancing contract. Their lordships adopted as an authoritative statement of the law the formulation of Bingham L.J. in *Watts v. Morrow*,[62] a surveyor's case, that damages for distress should only be awarded where "the very object of a contract is to provide pleasure, relaxation, peace of mind or freedom from molestation", a test almost identical to *Hayes v. Dodd*. Note that the recovery of damages in tort will be subject to the same rule.[63] However, in *Farley v. Skinner*[63a] a case concerning surveyors, the House of Lords have made it clear that it is sufficient if a major or important part of the contract was to secure pleasure, relaxation or peace of mind.

10–315   **Application of the rule.** *Hayes v. Dodd* concerned the conveyance of commercial property,[64] as did *Johnson v. Gore Wood & Co. (a Firm)*. The Court of Appeal did not allow damages for distress in *Watts & Watts v. Morrow*,[65] a surveyor's negligence case concerning a domestic survey. It is submitted that, by analogy, damages for distress could not normally be recovered from solicitors for the conveyance of residential property.[66] In *McLeish v. Amoo-Gottfried & Co.*[67]

---

[57] Lord Denning M.R. at 459B and James L.J. at 461D–462E. This approach was followed in *Dickinson v. James* Alexander & Co. (1990) 7 P.N. 205 at 212–213, Douglas Brown J., and may be the explanation of the award for anxiety in *Buckley v. Lane Herdman & Co.* [1977] C.L.Y.B. 3143, and *Trask v. Clark & Sons* [1980] C.L.Y. 1588.

[58] [1990] 2 All E.R. 815. The same result was reached in relation to commercial property by the Court of Appeal in *Hartle v. Laceys* [1999] Lloyd's Rep. P.N. 315 In "Anguish, foreseeability and policy" (1989) L.Q.R. 43, K.B. Soh argues that anyone who approaches solicitors for conveyancing is asking for peace of mind.

[59] [1987] I.C.R. 700 at 718.

[60] [1990] 2 All E.R. 815 at 824A–B, *per* Staughton L.J. See also at 818D and 826H–827A.

[61] [2001] 2 W.L.R. 72. For the analogous Canadian position see *Martin v. Goldfarb* (1999) 41 O.R. (3d) 161.

[62] [1991] 1 W.L.R. 1423.

[63] See *Verderame v. Commercial Union* [1992] B.C.L.C. 793 discussed in chap. 14 para. 14–123. Such damages were awarded in *Crossnan v. Ward Bracewell & Co.* (1989) 6 P.N. 103, at 107, Kennedy J., but without any discussion about the principles to be applied.

[63a] October 11, 2001.

[64] Some residential property was also conveyed, but the distress was entirely caused by problems with the commercial property.

[65] [1991] 1 W.L.R. 1421. See chap. 9, para. 9–181.

[66] This was the conclusion of McDermott L.J. in *Smyth v. Huey* [1993] N.I. 236, applying *Watts v. Morrow*.

[67] [1994] 10 P.N. 102. See also *Boudreau v. Benaiah* (2000) 182 D.L.R. (4th) 569, where the Ontario Court of Appeal awarded damages for mental anxiety relating to a forced guilty plea.

Scott Baker J. concluded (without the contrary being argued) that the very essence of a retainer to act for a defendant in a criminal trial was to ensure his peace of mind. There, the solicitors' negligence caused the client to be convicted and fined £450 for assault and possessing an offensive weapon, before the Court of Appeal quashed the conviction over two years later. The client was awarded £6,000, taking into account the distress he was caused by his loss of reputation. Following *McLeish*, in *Rey v. Graham & Oldham (a Firm)*[68] McKinnon J. awarded damages for the distress of being stigmatised as a bankrupt and for being unable to buy a house as a result of bankruptcy caused by the defendant solicitors' negligence. The judge considered that bankruptcy was somewhat akin to a criminal conviction.

(e) *Mitigation of damage*

Examples of failure to mitigate. The claimant in a solicitors' negligence **10–316** action, as in any other action, cannot recover damages in respect of any loss which he ought reasonably to have avoided. Thus in *Joliffe v. Charles Coleman & Co.*,[69] an action arising from the solicitors' failure to apply for a new tenancy under Part 2 of the Landlord and Tenant Act 1954, it was held that the plaintiffs acted unreasonably in refusing the new tenancy which was in fact offered by the landlords. The terms offered were not very much worse than the terms which could have been obtained upon an application under the Act. Damages were therefore assessed on the hypothetical assumption that the landlords' offer had been accepted.

Generous treatment of the claimant. The argument that the claimant has **10–317** failed to mitigate his loss always suffers from the disadvantage that it is advanced by the guilty party. It is put forward as a criticism of the manner in which the innocent party has extricated himself from a situation of the defendant's making. Thus, in the majority of cases,[70] the court tends to lean in favour of the claimant

---

[68] [2000] B.P.I.R. 354.

[69] (1971) 219 E.G. 1608, Browne J. For the facts see para. 10–265. For another example see *Matlock Green Garage Ltd v. Potter Brooke-Taylor & Wildgoose (a Firm)* [2000] Lloyd's Rep. P.N. 935, where solicitors failed to renew the plaintiff's business tenancy, but it was unreasonable of the plaintiffs to close parts of the business carried on at other sites. For the facts see para. 10–265. *cf. Baloch v. Leonard & Kalin* [1996] E.G.C.S. 181, where the Court rejected an allegation of failure to mitigate as the plaintiff had no choice but to accept the landlord's terms. In *Dareway Properties Ltd v. Glovers* [1998] C.L.Y. 4025, QBD, the defendant solicitors failed to ensure that the contract for the purchase of property included a condition that the Charity Commissioners' consent be obtained to develop part of the land. Consent was refused. The plaintiffs refused to enter a similar agreement at no extra cost which would receive consent, as they hoped to unlock extra ransom value from the land. It was held that they had failed to mitigate their loss.

[70] See, *e.g. Dodds Properties v. Canterbury City Council* [1980] 1 W.L.R. 433 at 452C–D, *per* Megaw L.J. *King v. Hawkins & Co., The Times,* January 28, 1982, Mars-Jones J.: the purchaser of property discovered a defect in title owing to his solicitors' negligence. He refused to abandon his plans for improving the property. Held that he was not in breach of his duty to mitigate. *Hayes v. Dodd* [1990] 2 All E.R. 815, CA: the purchaser of two properties discovered that there was no right of way over the only convenient means of access; it was unreasonable to attempt to sell both properties together, which had been done on advice, and caused a four year delay before they were sold. *Barnes v. Hay* (1988) 12 N.S.W.L.R. 337, CA: it was not unreasonable for a tenant to refuse to go out of business when the solicitor's negligence enabled the lessor to harass him causing the business loss, because it was not unreasonable to expect that the position would improve when changes to the shopping complex were complete. For the facts see para. 10–239 above.

on this issue. In *Whiteman v. Hawkins*,[71] for example, a case in which the security for a loan proved to be subject to an equitable charge, the court rejected the argument that the plaintiff should enforce other securities which were available, rather than sue his solicitor.[72] In *Transportation Agency Ltd v. Jenkins*[73] the defendants argued that despite the covenant in the lease against cooking and the other difficulties referred to, the plaintiffs ought not to have simply withdrawn from the transaction. They should have tried to iron out the difficulties with their landlords and to make the business viable. Kerr J. "had no hesitation" in rejecting this submission. In *Gregory v. Shepherds*[74] where the claimants were unable to sell a Spanish holiday apartment for eight years, but they did not have to give credit for the rent he could have obtained during that period as they had not bought the property to let, and any such letting would impinge on the ability to conclude an early sale when they were encouraged to believe that the defect in title would be removed shortly.

10–318   **Fresh litigation: the general rule.**[75] An issue which frequently arises in solicitors' negligence cases is whether the plaintiff ought to embark upon fresh litigation in order to mitigate his loss. In *Pilkington v. Wood*,[76] it was argued that the plaintiff ought to have brought proceedings against the original vendor of his house in respect of the defect in title. This argument was rejected in view of the difficulties which that action would involve. Harman J. stated that the plaintiff's duty to mitigate "does not go so far as to oblige the injured party, even under an indemnity, to embark on a complicated and difficult piece of litigation against a third party."[77] The actual decision in that case is eminently reasonable. The proposed litigation would have involved considerable delay and would have seriously interfered with the plaintiff's domestic arrangements.[78] Subsequent cases have explored how far the claimant must go in pursuing litigation against a third party.[79]

10–319   **Exceptions to the general rule.** In *Western Trust & Savings Ltd v. Clive Travers & Co.*[80] the Court of Appeal held that when a lender sues his solicitors for negligent advice in relation to a mortgage transaction, it should mitigate its loss by obtaining possession and selling the property. This was an ordinary

---

[71] (1878) 4 C.P.D. 13. But *cf.* para 10–319 below.
[72] See also *Westlake v. J.P. Cave* [1998] N.P.C: no obligation to enhance value of land obtained in settlement by applying for planning permission.
[73] (1972) 223 E.G. 1101, Kerr J. For the facts see para. 10–306.
[74] [2000] P.N.L.R. 769, CA, For the facts, see paras 10–200 and 10–275 above.
[75] See H. Evans, "Solicitors and mitigation of loss" (2001) 17 P.N. 93; *ibid.*, *Lawyers' Liabilities* (2nd ed., 2002), chap. 14.
[76] [1953] Ch. 770. See also *Treloar v. Henderson* [1968] N.Z.L.R. 1085, HCt (solicitor's negligence resulted in client being liable under a contract; it was reasonable for the plaintiff not to attempt to avoid the contract, because he would have been sued and probably lost).
[77] *ibid.* at 777.
[78] For the facts see para. 10–241. The plaintiff was not entitled to recover the costs caused by the delay in selling his house.
[79] In *Halifax plc v. Gould & Swayne* [1999] P.N.L.R. 184 Auld L.J. suggested that *Pilkington v. Wood* was not an exhaustive code of the criteria material to assessing whether the plaintiff should reasonably have litigated to mitigate its loss. Buxton L.J. appears to have cautiously agreed.
[80] [1997] P.N.L.R. 295. Contrast *Cottingham v. Attey Bower & Jones (a Firm)* [2000] P.N.L.R. 557, where claimants who had not been advised by solicitors that there was no building regulation consent for what were defective renovation works were not obliged to mitigate their loss by suing the surveyors who had also advised them.

feature of enforcing security, and would have been necessary whether or not there were defects in the security, as there in fact were. The fact that the defendants were not prepared to offer an indemnity was irrelevant. Delays in enforcing security were a failure to mitigate so that the lender was deprived of lost interest and outgoings for the period of delay in *Bristol & West Building Society v. Fancy & Jackson (a Firm)*.[81] In *Dickinson v. James Alexander & Co.*,[82] by reason of the defendant solicitors' negligence, the plaintiff received a very disadvantageous settlement on the divorce from her husband. She failed to apply to vary the original order, despite her growing financial difficulties and her former husband's rising income which were evident in the year or two following the divorce settlement. When she did apply for the order to be varied, six years after the original order, she received a very large increase. Douglas Brown J. decided that the plaintiff had failed to mitigate her loss.

Disappointed beneficiary cases. Two recent Court of Appeal decisions con-   **10–320**
cern cases brought by disappointed beneficiaries.[83] In *Walker v. Medlicott*[84] the plaintiff claimed that the testatrix had informed him and others that she had left property to him, although no reference to such a devise appeared in the defendant solicitors' note of the testatrix's instructions. The Court of Appeal upheld the Judge's finding that negligence had not been proved. The Court also held that in such a case the evidence for a claim in negligence would be the same as that required in an action for rectification, and the plaintiff should have mitigated any loss he sustained by seeking the latter. Contrast *Horsfall v. Haywards*[85] where the defendant solicitors negligently drafted the will leaving the testator's house to his widow rather than merely a life interest to her with a remainder to the plaintiffs. The Court of Appeal held that the plaintiffs had no obligation to sue the widow. The Court cited *Pilkington v. Wood* with approval, and distinguished *Walker v. Medlicott*. The solicitor, who had acted for the estate, had given no advice about rectifying the will or not sending the money to the widow in Canada, so it was reasonable for the plaintiffs to have taken no action before the six months time limit for rectification expired.

Limits of the rule. It is submitted, if the claimant is simply asked to lend his   **10–321**
name to litigation, under a full indemnity as to costs, and the litigation involves no serious hardship for the claimant, it probably would be unreasonable for him to refuse. This situation often arises, where solicitors allow a personal injuries claim to become statute-barred. The solicitors, or their insurers, may wish to make an application to the court, in the claimant's name, to override the time limit under section 33 of the Limitation Act 1980. If the application succeeds, the claimant will be restored to the position he would have occupied if the breach had not occurred (unless the delay has otherwise affected his prospects of success). It seems that, unless the proposed application is plainly hopeless, the claimant would be failing in his duty to mitigate, if he did not allow it to proceed.

---

[81] [1997] 4 All E.R. 582 at 623–62.
[82] (1990) 6 P.N. 205 at 211.
[83] For commentary see B. Rich, "Errors in will-drafting: the limits of a remedy in negligence" (1999) 15 P.N. 211.
[84] [1999] 1 W.L.R. 727. Note that Simon Brown L.J. specifically did not doubt the soundness of the basic rule and correctness of the decision in *Pilkington v. Wood*, although the other two members of the Court of Appeal did not directly address that issue.
[85] [1999] P.N.L.R. 583.

10–322   **Change of solicitor.** The client normally changes solicitors, as soon as it becomes apparent that he might have a claim for negligence against his original solicitors. If thereafter he acts in accordance with the advice of his new solicitors and counsel, he has strong grounds for arguing that he acted reasonably.[86]

4. SHARED RESPONSIBILITY

(a) *Contributory negligence.*[87]

10–323   **The general rule.** Contributory negligence is rarely in issue between an unsophisticated lay client and his solicitor, and it will be unusual for there to be such a finding. For example, in *Manortarn Ltd v. Rose & Bird*[88] the plaintiff, which was a property investment company mostly concerned with residential property, was not contributorily negligent in failing to read the commercial lease of property it was buying and thus failing to notice break clauses. The defendant solicitors were wholly liable for failing to bring them to the plaintiff's attention. Even where the client acts through legally qualified officers, there would ordinarily be no contributory negligence because those officers would be concerned with the business aspects of a transaction and would properly leave the legal aspects of it to the retained solicitors.[89] There are, however, exceptions. In *McLellan v. Fletcher*[90] the defendant solicitor acted for the plaintiff in the purchase of some land. The plaintiff made his own arrangements about an endowment policy. The defendant solicitor was told by the plaintiff that he had arranged to pay premiums for the policy, but was held to be negligent in failing to confirm with the insurers or the building society whether the insurers were on risk. However, Anthony Lincoln J. found the plaintiff 75 per cent contributorily negligent. He had been informed by the insurance company that he had to pay the first premium if the cover was to commence, but believed without grounds that he had done so and informed his solicitor accordingly.

10–324   **Illustrations.** Commonwealth cases provide further illustrations of courts finding claimants contributorily negligent. In *Astley v. Austrust Ltd*[91] the plaintiff

---

[86] See, *e.g. Attard v. Samson* (1966) 110 S.J. 249; *Apatu v. Peach Prescott & Jamieson* [1985] 1 N.Z.L.R. 50, at 72, Eichelbaum J. *cf. Dickinson v. James Alexander & Co.* (1990) 6 P.N. 205, Douglas Brown J. For discussion of an analogous problem in the construction context (first architect negligent, claimant instructs second architect and carries out remedial works in accordance with his advice) see chap. 8, para. 8–296.

[87] The general principles of contributory negligence are referred to in chap. 5, paras 5–113 to 5–119. The issue can normally be raised at the stage of assessment of damages stage after summary judgment has been obtained, depending on what the judgment had decided, see *Maes Finance Ltd v. AL Phillips, The Times*, March 25, 1997, ChD.

[88] [1995] E.G.C.S. 142, QBD.

[89] *Central Trust Co. v. Rafuse* (1986) 31 D.L.R. (4th), Sup. Ct of Canada. For the facts see para. 10–082. Similarly, in *Alberta Workers' Compensation Board v. Riggins* (1993) 95 D.L.R. (4th) 279, Alberta CA, the fact that the plaintiff had a staff of three lawyers was irrelevant once they sought the opinion of outside counsel, and they were not negligent in relying on the advice provided.

[90] (1987) 3 P.N. 202. The case is of limited authority because the principal finding of loss is dubious, see para. 10–299.

[91] [1999] Lloyd's Rep. P.N. 758.

trustee sought advice from the defendant solicitor in relation to its intention of becoming trustee of an existing trading trust. The solicitor negligently failed to advise the trustee about excluding his personal liability if the trust failed. At first instance, the plaintiff was held 50 per cent contributorily negligent in failing properly to assess the financial worth of the proposed venture. The High Court of Australia held that the plaintiff was contributorily negligent even when the very purpose of the duty owed by the defendant was to protect the plaintiff against the loss that happened. However, on the construction of the relevant Australian legislation, contributory negligence did not give rise to an apportionment of the cause of action in contract, even where the contractual duty was concurrent with that in negligence. Contrast the English case of British *Racing Drivers' Club Ltd v. Hextall Erskine & Co.*,[92] where Carnwath J. refused to impute to the company the negligence of its directors, when the negligence of the solicitors was a failure to advise the board that the transaction in question had to be approved by the members. The plaintiff has been found to be contributorily negligent in several Canadian cases,[93] and in New Zealand.[94]

---

[92] [1996] 3 All E.R. 667.

[93] *Bowles v. Johnson* [1988] 4 W.W.R. 242, Manitoba QB: the lawyer acting for the vendors owed a duty of care to the unrepresented purchasers and was negligent in allowing the vendors to continue with a dubious sale at an inflated price; the purchasers were held 50% contributorily negligent in not making suitable enquiries, or determining the value of the land, or obtaining professional advice; *Doiron v. Caisse Populaire D'Inkerman Ltee* (1985) 17 D.L.R. (4th) 660, New Brunswick CA: the defendant solicitors negligently failed to procure personal guarantees as security for a loan made by the plaintiff bank. The bank was 50 per cent contributorily negligent in not giving clear instructions and not inspecting the documents to ascertain that the guarantees were missing; *Earl v. Wilhelm* (2000) 183 D.L.R. (4th) 45, Saskatchewan CA, the defendant solicitor was negligent in failing to ensure that the plaintiff beneficiaries received the land intended by the testator under his will. At first instance there was a 25% deduction for the contributory negligence of the testator in failing to provide full and accurate instructions as to the ownership of the land, but on appeal it was held that the testator's contributory negligence was irrelevant; *Fasken Campbell Godfrey v. Seven-Up Canada Inc* (1997) 142 D.L.R. (4th) 456, Ontario HCt, upheld (2000) 182 D.L.R. (4th) 315: solicitors should have advised a trustee that he required permission from the beneficiaries for a transaction which benefited himself, although no loss was caused thereby. The trustee was a former senior partner of the solicitors, and would have been 80% contributorily negligent; *Klingspon v. Ramsay* [1985] 5 W.W.R. 411, British Columbia Sup. Ct: a solicitor acting for a company negligently created the impression with an investor that her investment in the company was sound; the investor was held 75% contributorily negligent as she failed to pay proper attention to the material about the company which she had seen, or to obtain proper material or advice; *Lawrie v. Gentry Developments Inc.* (1990) 72 O.R. (2d) 512, Ontario High Ct.: solicitors failed to prepare mortgage documents on time; however the client was held to be 25% contributorily negligent for the delay in returning the documents to the solicitor; *Marbel Developments Ltd v. Pirani* (1994) 18 C.C.L.T. (2d) 229, British Columbia Sup. Ct: a solicitor was negligent in failing to warn the plaintiff company that a surveyor's certificate was about to expire, making approval for conversion more difficult. The plaintiff was found to be 50% contributorily negligent, having received some rudimentary education in property law and practice; *MacDonell v. M.& M. Developments Ltd* (1998) 175 N.S.R. (2d) 89, Nova Scotia Sup.Ct: the solicitor failed to review a dealership agreement the client was about to enter and thus failed to explain to him the requirement to notify the automobile manufacturer of an earlier share transfer; the client was 50% contributorily negligent for ignoring the advice of his accountant to notify that manufacturer of the transfer; *Skirzyk v. Crawford* (1990) 64 Man. R. (2d) 220, Manitoba QB, aff'd. Manitoba CA June 11, 1991: the solicitor was found negligent in failing to progress the plaintiff's personal injury litigation. The plaintiff was held 25% contributorily negligent in failing to pursue his claim with diligence.

[94] *Mouat v. Clark Boyce* [1992] 2 N.Z.L.R. 559, NZCA: the plaintiff wished to assist her son by granting a mortgage over her home as security for loans to be made to him, and the defendant solicitors acted for both her and her son. Plaintiff found 50% to blame because she failed to act on the defendants' recommendation that she should take independent legal advice, and she told the defendants that she relied upon and trusted her son. On appeal, the Privy Council reversed the finding that the solicitors were liable, and thus it was not necessary to consider the cross-appeal against the

10–325   **Claims by lenders.** Contributory negligence is frequently an issue in actions brought by mortgage lenders against solicitors; and further guidance can be found in the analogous cases brought against surveyors.[95] Contributory negligence should be deducted only from the total loss, and save in exceptional circumstances not the "capped" loss which is within the scope of the duty.[96] A number of cases against solicitors consider the issue, and there has been a trend towards findings of a high degree of contributory negligence. In *Birmingham Midshires Mortgage Services Ltd v. David Parry*[97] the solicitors were held not to have been negligent, but the plaintiff would have been contributorily negligent in making a non-status loan of 75 per cent of the valuation where the property was expensive, and in failing to apply its own lending criteria. In *Omega Trust Company Ltd v. Wright Son & Pepper (No. 2)*[98] Douglas Brown J. found the plaintiff lender 70 per cent to blame for its losses principally for seven instances of the lender's failure to follow its own criteria, such as failures to obtain relevant up-to-date valuations, to investigate the borrower's financial circumstances, to read the accounts and balance sheets property, to obtain references, or to obtain confirmation that judgment debts had been paid. In *Lloyds Bank plc v. Parker Bullen (a Firm)*[99] solicitors failed to notify the lender of a covenant against alienation, and Longmore J. found the lender 50 per cent contributorily negligent for failing to obtain a valuation of its security leasehold interest. Very high findings of contributory negligence were made in some of the *Nationwide* cases.[1] In *UCB Bank plc v. Hepherd Winstanley & Pugh*,[2] the defendants sought consent

---

finding of contributory negligence (see [1994] 1 A.C. 428 at 438D). In *Gilbert v. Shanahan* [1998] 3 N.Z.L.R. 528, the defendant solicitor negligently failed to advise the plaintiff that he was not legally obliged to sign a guarantee for a lease taken by a company in which he had an interest. The New Zealand Court of Appeal held that the plaintiff was 10% contributorily negligent in failing to draw a preliminary agreement to the notice of the solicitor and enquire whether he was obliged to sign the guarantee as a result.

[95] See chap. 9, paras 9–166 to 9–172. See also H. Evans: "Contributory negligence by lenders" (1998) 14 P.N. 43; *ibid., Lawyers' Liabilities,* (2nd ed. 2002), chap. 8., and T. Dugdale, "Contributory negligence: continuing controversy" (1999) 15 P.N.L.R. 164.

[96] *Platform Home Loans v. Oyston Shipways* [2000] 2 A.C. 190.

[97] [1996] P.N.L.R. 495 upheld on appeal; [1997] N.P.L.C. 153 and [1997] E.G.C.S. 150.

[98] [1998] P.N.L.R. 337.

[99] [2000] Lloyd's Rep. P.N. 61.

[1] *Nationwide Building Society v. Archdeacons* [1999] Lloyd's Rep. P.N. 549 (90% contributory negligence from borrower's known inconsistencies and uncertainties); *Nationwide Building Society v. Balmer Radmore* [1999] Lloyd's Rep. P.N. 558 (75% contributory negligence, if defendants had been liable, for failing to investigate borrower's income, obtain a banker's reference, or heed previous arrears, and making a loan of 90% of the valuation); *Nationwide Building Society v. Goodwin Harte* [1999] Lloyd's Rep. P.N. 338 (breach of fiduciary duty so no deduction, but otherwise 50% from instructing a valuer who was not independent of the applicant, and failing to examine the accounts or obtain proper references); *Nationwide Building Society v. J. R. Jones* [1999] Lloyd's Rep. P.N. 414 (40% contributory negligence from failure to take up bank and credit references, obtain proper accounts, or to enquire why a single man wanted to buy a very large house); *Nationwide Building Society v. Littlestone & Cowan* [1999] Lloyd's Rep. P.N. 625 (66% contributory negligence from in-house over valuation, failure to investigate borrower's ability to pay, and lending in excess of 75% of value); *Nationwide Building Society v. Richard Grosse & Co.* [1999] Lloyd's Rep. P.N. 348 (breach of fiduciary duty so no deduction, but otherwise would have been two-thirds from excessive valuation by employee and flawed assessment of borrower's creditworthiness); *Nationwide Building Society v. Vanderpump & Sykes* [1999] Lloyd's Rep. P.N. 422 (50% reduction as lender made loan of 95% of valuation, had not investigated why there were so many credit searches against the borrower, and had failed to heed valuer's warning that the application might be suspect).

[2] [1999] Lloyd's Rep. P.N. 963.

from the plaintiff to a third charge over the property with a limit to the priority of the plaintiff's charge of £20,000, and were negligent. The plaintiff consented to the third charge, but not specifically to the priority, of which the head office was justifiably ignorant. It was 25 per cent contributorily negligent in failing to appreciate that the only reason for the deed of priority was to limit their security.

Excess LTV. In *Bristol & West Building Society v. Fancy & Jackson (a Firm)*[3]   **10–326** Chadwick J. reduced the damages in two of the cases brought by the plaintiff building society against a number of solicitors because the plaintiff had loaned more than 75 per cent of the value of the security property, without any additional security. He held that the lender should bear all of the loss attributable to making the loan above that percentage. The plaintiff could not rely on the fact that it had prudently obtained a mortgage indemnity guarantee policy because insurance had to be ignored as *res inter alios acta*. Similarly, in *Nationwide Building Society v. A.T.M. Abdullah*[4] Blackburne J. held that the plaintiffs should bear the losses caused by lending more than 75 per cent of the value of the security property.

Circumstances in which contributory negligence cannot be claimed. Any   **10–327** contributory negligence must have a contributory or causative effect on the loss caused by the defendants' negligence.[5] Contributory negligence cannot be raised as a defence against a claim in deceit, see *Alliance & Leicester Building Society v. Edgestop Ltd*.[6] If a claimant can show breach of a contractual provision which does not depend on negligence, such as breach of an express instruction from a mortgagee, then the defendant may not be able to raise a plea of contributory negligence.[7] A solicitor who is in breach of fiduciary duty cannot claim that his client was contributorily negligent or its equitable equivalent, at least where the breach involved a deliberate act or omission, see Blackburne J.'s judgment in *Nationwide Building Society v. Balmer Radmore (a Firm)*.[8] The Judge held that no plea of contributory negligence could be raised against an allegation of breach of fiduciary duty, both on the construction of the Act, and in particular where the defendant's breach was a deliberate wrong. In contrast, the New Zealand Court of Appeal allowed a deduction on the grounds of contributory negligence in relation to a claim for breach of fiduciary duty in *Day v. Mead*.[9] Contributory negligence is not a defence to a claim for breach of warranty of authority.[10]

---

[3] [1997] 4 All E.R. 582.

[4] [1999] Lloyd's Rep. P.N. 616.

[5] *UCB Corporate Services Ltd v. Clyde & Co (a Firm)* [2000] P.N.L.R. 841, CA, where a bank's decision to release a mortgage on the guarantor's house was held to have no causative effect on the loss caused by the solicitors negligence in failing to obtain an enforceable guarantee, which was the opportunity to recover from the guarantors. The bank was also not culpable as it thought it was sufficiently protected by the guarantee.

[6] [1993] 1 W.L.R. 1462, a case brought by a lender principally against a surveyor.

[7] As in *Bristol and West Building Society v. Kramer, The Times,* February 6, 1995. But see para. 10–008 above.

[8] [1999] P.N.L.R. 606 at 672D–677F. See the same Judge's judgment in *Nationwide Building Society v. Thimbleby* [1999] P.N.L.R. 733.

[9] [1987] 2 N.Z.L.R. 433, followed by the Supreme Court of Canada in *Canson Enterprises Ltd v. Broughton & Co* (1992) 85 D.L.R. (4th) 129.

[10] See *Zwebner v. The Mortgage Corporation Ltd* [1997] P.N.L.R. 504, Lloyd J.

(b) *Apportionment of liability*[11]

10–328   Recent developments in the law of tort have led to a growth in the number of claims which are made against more than one professional adviser. Thus the question of apportioning liability under the Civil Liability (Contribution) Act 1978 arises with increasing frequency. In the case of solicitors, three situations commonly give rise to problems of apportionment, usually in the context of settlement negotiations:

(a) Where the client has changed solicitors and both have been negligent.

(b) In a conveyancing-type transaction, where both solicitors and surveyors have been negligent.

(c) Where a financial scheme set up by solicitors and accountants, normally with the aim of reducing tax liability, has gone wrong.

Apportionment may arise in other circumstances.[12]

10–329   **Successive solicitors.** Where different solicitors are sued, it used to be the case under the Solicitors' Indemnity Rules that the same insurers were involved, since both firms were covered by the same insurance policy. The position has now changed.[13] However, even where the same insurance company is involved, the apportionment of liability between solicitors is an important matter, since each firm has its own excess and the damages apportioned to each firm affect that firm's claims record and thus its premium level in future years. Where both firms proceed on the same mistaken basis, for instance that the proper defendant is X, whereas in fact the proper defendant is Y, each firm may be equally culpable; but the negligence of the second firm usually has a much closer causal link with the plaintiff's loss. In this example, the limitation period against Y may expire during the retainer of the second firm. If, of course, the limitation period had expired earlier, the first firm alone would be liable and no question of apportionment would arise. The result is similar where successive solicitors delay prosecuting an action with the result that it is dismissed for want of prosecution. Each firm may be equally culpable, but the negligence of the second firm usually has a much greater causative potency: if that firm had "got a move on" as soon as they were instructed the action would have been saved. If, of course, the action was by then so stale that it would have been struck out as soon as the next move was made, the first firm alone is liable and there is no question of apportionment. Thus where successive solicitors are liable for the same loss, in most cases the firm which acted later will have to pay the larger share of the damages.[14] These observations are, of course, made at a very general level and each case turns upon its own facts. The Australian case *Macpherson & Kelly v. Kevin J. Prunty*

---

[11] The general principles of apportionment are referred to in chap. 4.

[12] See *e.g. Kyriacou v. Kogarah Municipal Council* (1995) 88 L.G.E.R.A. 110, Sup. Ct NSW: council officer advised prospective purchasers that property could be used for wedding receptions, and plaintiff's solicitors failed to advise that this was not so; liability apportioned $\frac{1}{3}$ and $\frac{2}{3}$ respectively.

[13] See para. 10–003 above.

[14] In an extreme case the effect of the first solicitors' negligence may be spent, with the result that the second solicitors alone are liable. See paras 10–238 and 10–239 "Intervening act of a third party."

Associates[15] illustrates a situation in which the first solicitors were principally responsible for the fact that an action was not commenced within the three year limitation period.

Apportionment of liability between solicitors and surveyors.[16] Solicitors and surveyors commonly have to liaise in conveyancing or related matters. For example, in the renewal of business tenancies under Part 2 of the Landlord and Tenant Act 1954, the actual negotiations may take place between surveyors, whilst the respective solicitors take the appropriate procedural steps, such as service of notices and commencement of proceedings. If something goes wrong, possibly through lack of communication between the two firms, liability may well be shared. When considering the relative culpability of the two defendants, which is one factor in the apportionment, the surveyors must be taken to have a basic knowledge of the law relevant to their field of practice.[17] In the situation mentioned above, for example, the surveyors should be familiar with the procedural steps which are required under the Landlord and Tenant Act 1954 and the time limits within which those steps must be taken. Equally a solicitor who deals in property matters must have some idea of market values, the principles upon which rent is assessed and surveying practice.[18] An example of a failure by both professionals in relation to the same point is *Theodore Goddard v. Fletcher King Services Ltd.*[19] The plaintiff solicitors negligently failed to include rent review provisions in two leases which permitted only increases in the rent. They claimed a contribution from surveyors who had acted for the same client and were sent the leases for their approval, and the surveyors were found 20 per cent to blame. **10-330**

The alternative situation in which liability is shared between solicitors and surveyors is where each firm makes a separate mistake, and both mistakes contribute to the same loss.[20] For example, the surveyor overvalues property and the solicitor fails to ascertain that there is an easement over it. In this situation it is even more difficult to formulate any general principles as to apportionment. One factor which is sometimes of assistance is to consider the extent of each firm's involvement in the overall transaction. This is illustrated by *Anglia Hastings & Thanet Building Society v. House & Son*[21]: the plaintiff building society claimed damages against both the valuers and the solicitors who had previously acted for the society when it took a mortgage over two properties. The borrowers defaulted and the two properties proved to be insufficient security. The valuers had produced a valuation which was "wildly wrong", but their overall involvement in the matter had been relatively brief. The solicitors had been **10-331**

---

[15] [1983] V.R. 573, Sup. Ct Victoria, Full Court. The first solicitors failed to institute proceedings for two years and nine months. There was a delay in forwarding their file to the second solicitors, who wrongly assumed that a writ had been issued. The apportionment was 80% to the first solicitors and 20% to the second solicitors.

[16] For an example of a solicitors' nominee company being a third contributorily negligent when suing a valuer, see *Kendall Wilson Securities Ltd v. Barraclough* [1986] N.Z.L.R. 576, NZCA.

[17] See chap. 9, para. 9–056.

[18] See also *Rieger v. Croft & Finlay* (1992) 5 W.W.R. 700, British Columbia Sup. Ct: selling realtor (estate agent) breached contractual duty in failing to advise about rent review provision, as did plaintiff's solicitor. Realtor 60% to blame and solicitors 40%.

[19] (1997) 32 *e.g.* 90.

[20] *e.g. Computastaff Ltd v. Ingledew Brown Bennison & Garrett* (1983) 268 E.G. 906, McNeill J. For the facts of this case see para. 10–273.

[21] (1981) 260 E.G. 1128. See para. 10–207.

involved over several months, and had failed to protect the building society's interests in a number of respects. Bingham J. apportioned liability 30 per cent to the valuers and 70 per cent to the solicitors.[22]

10–332   **Other cases concerning apportionment.** In taxation matters solicitors and accountants often work together closely. Where both solicitors and accountants are responsible for the failure of a "scheme" to reduce tax liability, it is certainly relevant to consider whether the mistake was essentially a "legal" one or a matter of accounting, and it is also necessary to consider who was the client's principal adviser.[23] In wasted costs applications, there may be technical difficulties preventing contribution proceedings and the like.[24] In some cases the wasted costs application is made against both solicitors and counsel, and the Court will normally determine that each will pay a proportion of the costs.[25] *Hanave Pt Ltd v. Lfot Pt Ltd* [26] is an illustration of apportionment between solicitors and the other party to a transaction. The plaintiff had purchased a small shopping complex with a financially weak tenant. There was an equal apportionment between vendors who had misdescribed the tenant as of high quality, and the purchaser's solicitor who had failed to advise his client to investigate the financial standing of the tenants.

---

[22] For further examples see *Bristol & West Building Society v. Christie* [1996] E.G. 53, where liability was apportioned equally, and *Cook v. Power* (1992) 28 R.P.R. (2d) 207, Newfoundland Sup. Ct (solicitors 80% liable for failing to discern potential discrepancies in title, and 25% liable for failing to ascertain the differences in boundaries). See also *Chelsea Building Society v. Goddard & Smith* [1996] E.G.C.S. 157, where surveyors who overvalued a property for a building society were found equally liable with the solicitors who failed to report a back-to-back transaction.

[23] *Mathew v. Maughold Life Assurance Co. Ltd* (1985) 1 P.N. 142 concerned the apportionment between solicitors, accountants and counsel. The case is an illustration only, because on appeal the findings of liability against all parties except the plaintiffs' solicitors were reversed: (1987) 3 P.N. 98. (See further chap. 11, para. 11–047 on this case).

[24] See H. Evans, "The wasted costs jurisdiction" (2001) 64 M.L.R. 51 at 60–62.

[25] *e.g. B v. B (Wasted Costs: Abuse of Process)* [20001] 1 F.L.R. 843, Wall J., where counsel was responsible for 75% of the costs and the solicitor 25%.

[26] (2000) 168 A.L.R. 318, Federal Court of Australia. In a similar Canadian case, *789538 Ontario Ltd v. Gambin Associates* (1999) 27 R.P.R. (3d) 210, the court directed an assignment of the purchaser's cause of action against the vendors to the solicitors. In some cases no recovery would be allowed as the parties would not be responsible for the same damage, as in *Howkins &. Harrison (a Firm) v. Tyler* [2001] P.N.L.R. 27, CA, where surveyors sued by a building society for a negligent valuation were not permitted to recover from the borrowers' directors for that reason, the test being whether payment by the third party would reduce the defendant's liability to the claimant.

CHAPTER 11

BARRISTERS

	PARA.		PARA.
1. General	11–001	(e) Immunity	11–009
(a) The function of a barrister	11–001	(f) Abuse of process	11–025
(b) Duties to clients	11–004	(g) Liability for costs	11–026
(c) Duties to third parties	11–006	2. Liability for breach of duty	11–036
(d) The Standard of Skill	11–008	3. Damages	11–052

1. GENERAL

(a) *The function of a barrister*

It is the function of barristers to appear as advocates before courts and tribunals, **11–001** to give advice and draft documents in connection with litigation, and to do such other advisory or drafting work as may properly be referred to them by solicitors.[1] Barristers no longer have the exclusive rights of audience before the House of Lords, the Court of Appeal, the High Court, and the Crown Court which they used to possess.[2] Barristers are subject to the discipline of the General Council of the Bar.[3] The Bar does now operate within some statutory framework[4]: barristers must be sole practitioners,[5] and it is a professional requirement that all practising barristers insure against claims for professional negligence.[6] In addition to the duties owed by a barrister to his client, which are discussed below, he will also owe duties to the court.[7]

Instructing barristers. Subject to certain recognised exceptions,[8] a barrister **11–002** can only act on the instructions of a solicitor, and is professionally obliged to accept instructions in a field in which he professes to practice.[9] The major exception is that a barrister may, in appropriate circumstances, accept a brief or

---

[1] This chapter is concerned with barristers in independent practice. There are also employed barristers who provide legal services to their employers in government, commerce and industry.

[2] Solicitors may now have full rights of audience, subject to satisfying the rules on experience and qualifications, pursuant to s.27 of the Courts and Legal Services Act 1980 and the Higher Courts Qualification Regulations 1992 made thereunder.

[3] The General Council of the Bar publishes the Code of Conduct of the Bar of England and Wales. The current edition is the sixth, published in 1998.

[4] The Courts and Legal Services Act 1990 has certain provisions that affect the practice of barristers.

[5] See the Code of Conduct of the Bar of England and Wales, 6th ed., para. 207.

[6] *ibid.*, para. 302. Barristers must mutually insure with the Bar Mutual Indemnity Fund.

[7] For a helpful review of such duties, see D. A. Ipp, "Lawyers' duties to the court" (1998) 114 L.Q.R. 62

[8] See the Code of Conduct of the Bar of England and Wales published by the General Council of the Bar, 6th ed. 1998, at paras 102(a)(ii), 210, 306, 901 (for the definition of "professional client"), and Annex E.

[9] The "cab rank" rule; *ibid.*, para. 209.

instructions directly from clients who are members of a professional body that has been approved by the Bar Council. Direct professional access is not allowed for instructions to appear in court (other than a Magistrates' Court) or the Employment Appeals Tribunal.[10]

11–003 **Alternatives to litigation.** A disappointed client now has an alternative remedy to launching proceedings against a barrister. Clients can complain to the Bar Council about inadequate professional service, and may be awarded up to £2,000 compensation, although compensation is limited to the loss which is recoverable at law. If the Bar Council dismisses the complaint, then the client can complain to the Legal Services Ombudsman, who now has the power to award compensation.[11]

(b) Duties to the clients

11–004 **No contractual duties.** In practice, a barrister does not enter a contract either with the solicitor who instructs him, or with the lay client on whose behalf he is instructed. This used to be a rule of law: see *Kennedy v. Broun*[12] and *Rondel v. Worsley*.[13] The rule of law preventing a barrister from entering into a contract for the provision of his services as a barrister was abolished by section 61(1) of the Courts and Legal Services Act 1990.[14] This statutory change does not affect the restrictions imposed by the Bar Council on who may instruct a barrister.[15] Furthermore, the Bar's terms of business include a provision that a barrister does not enter into any contractual relationship when he is instructed by a solicitor, unless the contrary is agreed in writing.[16]

11–005 **Tort and other duties.** A barrister will of course owe duties in tort to his lay client.[17] A barrister will also owe fiduciary duties, including duties of confidence, to the client. For a salutary illustration see *China Light & Power Co. Ltd v. Michael Ford*,[18] where a barrister deliberately used confidential information entrusted to him by his client, which was awarded damages. Barristers are self-employed, and there is no conflict of interest in appearing against or before members of the same chambers; furthermore, the organisation of barristers' chambers should normally prevent any danger of an accidental or improper

---

[10] *ibid.*, Annex E, para. 3.
[11] See Access to Justice Act 1999, s.49.
[12] (1863) 13 C.B. (N.S.) 677.
[13] [1969] 1 A.C. 191.
[14] The section came into force on January 1, 1991.
[15] See s.61(2) of the Act. For the restrictions imposed by the Bar Council, see para. 11–002 above.
[16] See paras 25 and 26 of Annex B of the Code of Conduct of the Bar 1998, as amended.
[17] For confirmation of this obvious principle, see Lord Morris in *Rondel v. Worsley* [1969] 1 A.C. 191 at 244A–B.
[18] [1996] 1 H.K.L.R. 57, CA. See also *Stewart v. Canadian Broadcasting Association* (1997) 150 D.L.R. (4th) 24, Ontario HCt, where a lawyer was held to be in breach of his continuing fiduciary duty by preferring his own financial interests, when he discussed his client's case on television and in part exaggerated his culpability. He was liable for damages for the emotional harm, and for the profits derived from his participation in the programme.

dissemination of confidential information.[19] However, cohabiting counsel should avoid acting on opposite sides in criminal cases.[20]

(c) *Duties to third parties*

Duties to clients' associates. There is limited authority specifically on the duty of barristers to third parties. Duties of care may be owed in some circumstances to associates of the lay client. In *Mathew v. Maughold Life Assurance Co. Ltd* a barrister was instructed on behalf of an insurance company who marketed a tax avoidance scheme.[21] Leonard J. held that the barrister owed a duty to Mr and Mrs Mathew, the clients of the insurance company who were to benefit from the scheme. The point was not considered on appeal. In *Estill v. Cowling*,[22] counsel and solicitors were instructed by E concerning the transfer of shares in her lifetime to her nephews and nieces. The advice was sought on behalf of the trustees of the proposed settlement of the shares. Arden J. held that a duty of care was owed to the trustees, although they had not been appointed yet.   **11–006**

No duty to other side. It is very unlikely that a duty of care is owed to the other side in litigation.[23] In *Connolly-Martin v. Davis*[24] the Court of Appeal struck out an action by the opposing party against a barrister where it was alleged that he had given an undertaking to the other side on his client's behalf without authority and then advised the client that the undertaking was not binding. The Court accepted that, in general, counsel owed no duties to those who were not his client, such as the lay client's adversary. While there would be a duty if there were a voluntary assumption of responsibility on which the other side could reasonably rely, there was no such assumption in that case.   **11–007**

(d) *The standard of skill and care*

A barrister is subject to the same rules as other professional men, and the test as to whether there has been negligence is the standard of the ordinary skilled man exercising and professing to have that special skill.[25] In *Saif Ali v. Sydney Mitchell & Co.*[26] Lord Diplock stressed that not every error made by a barrister (or any other professional man) constitutes negligence, but only such an error "as no reasonably well-informed and competent member of that profession could have made."[27] In *Matrix Securities Ltd v. Theodore Goddard*[28] Lloyd J. rejected   **11–008**

---

[19] *Laker Airways Inc. v. FLS Aerospace Ltd and Burton* [1999] Lloyd's Rep. 45, Rix J. See also *Locabail (U.K.) Ltd v. Bayfield Properties Ltd* [2000] Q.B. 451 for guidance on when a barrister should not act as a judge in a case.
[20] *R. v. Blatt, The Times,* May 30, 1996
[21] (1985) 1 P.N. 142, Leonard J.; (1987) 3 P.N. 98, CA.
[22] [2000] Lloyd's Rep. P.N. 378.
[23] See the remarks of Sir John Donaldson M.R. in *Orchard v. South Eastern Electricity Board* [1987] 1 Q.B. 565 at 571F–G, and Dillon L.J. at 581B-C.
[24] [1999] P.N.L.R. 827.
[25] *Mathew v. Maughold Life Assurance Co. Ltd* (1987) 3 P.N. 98 at 103, CA. *Cf.* para. 11–040.
[26] [1980] A.C. 198 at 218 and 229, For a qualification to Lord Diplock's views see *McManus Development Ltd v. Barbridge Properties Ltd* [1996] P.N.L.R. 431 at 442, CA.
[27] A test adopted by the Court of Appeal in, *e.g. McFarlane v. Wilkinson* [1997] P.N.L.R. 578, an action brought against two barristers, and in the wasted costs cases of *Ridehalgh v. Horsefield* [1994] Ch. 205 and *Re a Barrister (Wasted Costs Order)(No. 9 of 1999)* (2000) 16 P.N. 122.
[28] [1998] P.N.L.R. 290.

allegations that tax counsel had any absolute duties to the client, and adopted the formulation of Lord Diplock in *Saif Ali*.[29] The tax silk's advice was to be judged by that of "the rather small and select group of silks specialising in tax matters." In *Estill v. Cowling*,[30] Arden J. held that the standard of care to be applied to a Chancery barrister who gave advice on a settlement was that of a reasonably competent barrister in general Chancery practice, having experience in tax and trust matters, but not the standard of a barrister who specialised in tax. In *Hall v. Simons*,[31] where the House of Lords abolished immunity, the standard of care for advocacy was expressed by Lord Hope[32] to be that of ordinary professional practice and ordinary skill, and by Lord Hobhouse[33] in identical terms to Lord Diplock in *Saif Ali v. Sydney Mitchell & Co.*

(e) *Immunity*[34]

11–009   **History of immunity.** In *Hall v. Simons*[35] the House of Lords abolished the special immunity of advocates, unanimously in the case of civil actions, and by a majority of four to three in relation to criminal proceedings. Their Lordships considered and rejected the reasons for immunity which were given in two House of Lords cases, *Rondel v. Worsley*[36] and *Saif Ali v. Sidney Mitchell & Co.*[37]

11–010   **Justifications for immunity.** The special immunity of barristers against actions for negligence has been recognised for over 200 years.[38] It was suggested by Lord Campbell in *Purves v. Landell*[39] that the difficulty of a barrister's work was itself a justification for the immunity, but this was rejected in *Saif Ali v. Sidney Mitchell & Co.*[40] A more serious justification for barristers' immunity was based upon the lack of any contract with the client,[41] but as a result of the developments in the law of negligence, this was no longer a tenable basis for barristers' immunity, and it too was rejected in *Rondel v. Worsley*.[42] A third justification, which emerged during the nineteenth century, was the view that the public interest required counsel to be immune: see *Swinfen v. Lord Chelmsford*[43] and *Batchelor v. Pattison and Mackersy*,[44] and this was the foundation of the modern view of immunity.

---

[29] As it was in *Green v. Collyer-Bristow* [1999] Lloyd's Rep. P.N. 799 at 809 *per* Douglas Brown J.

[30] [2000] Lloyd's Rep. P.N. 378,

[31] [2000] 3 W.L.R. 543.

[32] *ibid.*, at 597D–G.

[33] *ibid.*, at 608G–H.

[34] For a more detailed treatment of this topic, see previous editions of this work, in particular the second.

[35] [2000] 3 W.L.R. 543. For commentary see H. Evans, *Lawyers' Liabilities*, (2nd ed., 2002), chap. 5.

[36] [1969] 1 A.C. 191.

[37] [1980] A.C. 198.

[38] See, *e.g. Fell v. Brown* (1791) Peake 131; *Perring v. Rebutter* (1842) 2 M. & Rob. 429.

[39] (1842) 12 C. & F. 91 at 102–103.

[40] [1980] A.C. 198 *per* Lord Wilberforce at 214 F–G. However, in *Rondel v. Worsley* [1969] 1 A.C. 191 at 274 E–F Lord Pearce referred to the difficulties of a barrister's life as one factor which made it reasonable for the bar to enjoy a special immunity.

[41] See *Re Le Brasseur and Oakley* [1896] 2 Ch. 487 at 494 *per* Lindley L.J.

[42] [1969] 1 A.C. 191 at 232 A–C (Lord Reid), 246–247 (Lord Morris) and 271C (Lord Upjohn).

[43] (1860) 5 H. & N. 890.

[44] (1876) 3 R. 914 at 918, Inner House of the Court of Session.

In *Rondel v. Worsley*[45] the House of Lords was called upon to decide whether, **11–011** in 1967, the immunity of the bar could still be upheld on the grounds of public interest. The action arose out of a trial in May 1959, when the appellant was charged with causing grievous bodily harm to one Manning with intent to do so and with assault on Manning occasioning actual bodily harm. The respondent, a barrister, conducted his defence on a "dock brief."[46] The appellant was convicted on the first count and sentenced to 18 months' imprisonment. Some years after his release from prison the appellant issued proceedings against the respondent for professional negligence, alleging that the respondent had failed to put certain questions to witnesses and had failed to call certain witnesses. The House of Lords held unanimously that a barrister was immune from an action for negligence in respect of his conduct and management of a cause in court on the grounds of public policy. The issue next arose in *Saif Ali v. Sidney Mitchell & Co.*,[47] where the argument solely related to its extent. However, Lord Diplock considered that public policy reasons justified the immunity.[48] The other members of the House accepted without question the premise that a barrister was immune in respect of his conduct of cases in court.[49]

The public policy reasons given by the House of Lords in these two cases were **11–012** as follows. They were subjected to considerable academic criticism.[50]

(a) First, the administration of justice required that a barrister should be able to carry out his duty to the court fearlessly and independently, which might be affected if he owed a conflicting duty to his client.[51]

(b) Secondly, actions for negligence against barristers would involve retrying the original actions. This would prolong litigation, and create the risk of inconsistent decisions, which would bring the administration of justice into disrepute.[52]

(c) Thirdly, because of the "cab rank" rule, a barrister was obliged to accept any client, however difficult, who sought his services. It would encourage breaches of this rule if barristers did not have immunity.[53]

---

[45] [1969] 1 A.C. 191.

[46] A procedure, now defunct, where a prisoner could directly instruct any barrister robed in court for a nominal fee.

[47] [1980] A.C. 198. For the facts, see para. 11–013.

[48] *ibid.*, at 223F–H.

[49] See Lord Wilberforce at 213 C–F, Lord Salmon at 227 F–H, Lord Russell at 233B and Lord Keith at 235 B–H.

[50] *e.g.* Zander, *Legal Services for the Community* (M T Smith, 1978), Chap. 4; C. G. Veljanowski, and C. J. Whelan, "Professional negligence and the quality of legal services—an economic perspective" (1983) M.L.R. 700 at 711–718; G. Smith, "Liability for the negligent conduct of litigation: the legacy of *Rondel v. Worsley*" 47 Sask. L.R. 211; J. L. Powell, "Barrister's immunity—time to go" (1995) *Counsel* March/April 11; K. Nicholson "The immunity of barristers from suit in negligence—the Australian experience" (1989) 5 P.N. 124; H. Evans, *Lawyers' Liabilities*, (1st ed. 1996), chap. 4. The opposite view was expressed by R. M. Jackson in "Disappointed litigants and doubtful actions", (1995) *Counsel* May/June.

[51] *Rondel v. Worsley* [1969] 1 A.C. 191 at 227F–228F, 247D–G, 272C–E, 282A–283E, and 290A–C; *cf.* Lord Diplock in *Saif Ali v. Sidney Mitchell & Co.* [1980] A.C. 198 at pp. 219F–220C.

[52] *Rondel v. Worsley* [1969] 1 A.C. 191 at 230B–C and 249F–251D; *Saif Ali v. Sidney Mitchell & Co.* [1980] A.C. 198 at 22D–223D and 235G–236A.

[53] *Rondel v. Worsley* [1969] 1 A.C. 191 at 227D–F, 274G–276D, 281D–G, and 292D–G; *cf. Saif Ali v. Sidney Mitchell & Co.* [1980] A.C. 198 at 221B–F, and 236A–B.

(d) Finally, a barrister's immunity for what he says and does in court is part of the general immunity which attaches to all persons participating in court proceedings: judges, court officials, witnesses, parties and solicitors.[54]

11–013   **Extent of immunity.** In *Rondel v. Worsley*[55] there were a number of comments on the extent of immunity, which were obiter as the action concerned alleged negligence in advocacy. The extent of the barrister's immunity was first addressed in *Saif Ali v. Sidney Mitchell & Co.*,[56] an action that arose out of a road traffic accident in March 1966, which it was alleged was caused wholly or partly by one Mrs S.'s negligence. The barrister settled proceedings against Mrs S.'s husband alone, on the basis that he was the owner of the car and his wife had been driving as his agent, and despite a defence that Mrs S. was not driving as her husband's agent, he later advised that no amendment was necessary. The proceedings against Mr S. were later discontinued. The House of Lords, by a majority of three to two, held that the barrister did not have a defence of immunity. Lords Wilberforce, Diplock and Salmon, who constituted the majority, each adopted the test for determining whether any given piece of work attracted immunity, formulated by McCarthy P. in the New Zealand Court of Appeal case of *Rees v. Sinclair*[57]:

> "I cannot narrow the protection to what is done in court: it must be wider than that and include some pre-trial work. Each piece of before-trial work should, however, be tested against the one rule; that the protection exists only where the particular work is so intimately connected with the conduct of the cause in court that it can fairly be said to be a preliminary decision affecting the way that cause is to be conducted when it comes to a hearing. The protection should not be given any wider application than is absolutely necessary in the interests of the administration of justice, and that is why I should not be prepared to include anything which does not come within the test I have stated."

Lord Wilberforce held[58] that the passage should be "sensibly, and not pedantically, construed." Lord Diplock stated[59] that it would not be wise "to attempt a catalogue of before-trial work which would fall within this limited extension of the immunity." As an illustration, however, he stated that if counsel is instructed to advise on evidence, "his protection from liability for negligence in the conduct of the case at trial is not to be circumvented by charging him with negligence in having previously advised the course of conduct at the hearing that was subsequently carried out." Lord Salmon[60] stated that the immunity might sometimes extend to drafting pleadings and advising on evidence, if the connection between that work and the conduct of the case in court was sufficiently close.

---

[54] *Rondel v. Worsley* [1969] 1 A.C. 191 at 228F–229A and 251E–F; *Saif Ali v. Sidney Mitchell & Co.* [1980] A.C. 198 at 222A–D.

[55] [1969] 1 A.C. 191 at 231G–232A (Lord Reid), 247D–254A (Lord Morris), 285F–286G (Lord Upjohn), 293F–294B (Lord Pearson).

[56] [1980] 1 A.C. 198.

[57] [1974] 1 N.Z.L.R. 180, at 187.

[58] In *Saif Ali v. Sidney Mitchell & Co.* [1980] A.C. 198 at 215 D—E.

[59] *ibid.*, at 224 E–F.

[60] *ibid.*, at 231 F–H.

The issue of the extent of the immunity was revisited in a number of cases. In **11–014**
Landall v. Dennis Faulkner & Alsop[61] Holland J. concluded that it was difficult
to conceive of an activity that is so intimately connected with court proceedings
as advising at the court door. In contrast, failing to carry out a compromise
authorised by a client, and instead agreeing to less advantageous terms which
were announced in court, did not fall within the immunity.[62] Advice given as to
whether to plead guilty or not guilty to a criminal charge did satisfy the test.[63]
Where a barrister was instructed to advise and appear in a negligence action, the
New South Wales Court of Appeal held that the failure to amend to plead interest
was covered by the immunity as well as the failure to ask for interest at the trial.[64]
Similarly, in *McFarlane v. Wilkinson*[65] Rix J. held that advice not to amend
pleadings between the decision on a preliminary issue and its appeal clearly fell
within the test of immunity. In *Kelley v. Corston*[66] the defendant barrister
represented the plaintiff at a hearing for ancillary relief following the dissolution
of her marriage. The proceedings were compromised at court, before the start of
the hearing, and a consent order was made. The plaintiff's claim that the
defendant's advice in relation to the settlement was negligent was struck out by
the Court of Appeal, on the ground that the work was intimately connected with
the conduct of the case in court, and the Court considered that no sensible
distinction could be made between a settlement made at the door of the court and
one made in the course of trial. In *Atwell v. Michael Perry & Co. (a firm)*[67] it was
alleged that counsel had made errors in the assessment of case, which was lost
but later successfully appealed. Sir Richard Scott V.C. held that the advocate's
immunity extended to pre-trial deliberations as to how the case should be
conducted, and he was immune with respect to his "case plan". In *Hall v.
Simons*[68] in the Court of Appeal, it was held that there was no general rule that
a lawyer was or was not immune from liability in advising a client to settle, and
this depended not on when or where such advice was given, but on the advice,
the reasons for it, and the complaint made about it.

***Hall v. Simons* in the House of Lords.** The facts of the three cases which were **11–015**
heard by the House of Lords are summarised elsewhere,[69] and are of little
relevance to the question of immunity which the House had to decide. The Court
of Appeal held that none of the actions should be struck out, as they were neither
an abusive collateral challenge to an earlier judgment of the Court, nor were the
solicitors immune. The House of Lords upheld the result, but came to the more
radical conclusion that the immunity traditionally enjoyed by advocates should

---

[61] [1994] 5 Med. L.R. 268 at 274. Holland J. followed the reasoning of Richardson J. in *Biggar v.
McLeod* [1978] 2 N.Z.L.R. 9, CA, which had reached the same result. The judge also considered that
there could be no immunity from suit for any act or omission reflected in the pleadings, but that there
was for any act or omission after delivery of the brief
[62] *Donellan v. Watson* (1990) 21 N.S.W.L.R. 335, NSWCA.
[63] *Somasundaram v. M. Julius Melchior & Co.* [1988] 1 W.L.R. 1394 at 1403D, CA.
[64] *Keefe v. Marks* (1989) 16 N.S.W.L.R. 713, CA.
[65] [1996] 1 Lloyd's Rep. 406. The whole of the plaintiff's claim was struck out on appeal on different
grounds, see para. 11–050.
[66] [1998] Q.B. 686.
[67] [1998] 4 All E.R. 65. *Cf. Waters v. Maguire* [1999] Lloyd's Rep. P.N. 855, where there was no
immunity on the basis of a "case plan" for a decision in an initial consultation to run one point but
not another, which could have been reconsidered later. The barrister was not in fact negligent.
[68] [1999] 3 W.L.R. 873.
[69] See chap. 10, para. 10–111.

be abolished. The leading speeches were given by Lords Steyn and Hoffmann, with whom Lords Browne-Wilkinson and Millett agreed, adding brief reasons of their own. Lords Hope, Hutton and Hobhouse agreed that immunity should be abolished for civil proceedings, but disagreed in relation to criminal litigation.

11–016   **The starting point.** The House of Lords started from the position that there should be a remedy for a wrong.[70] As Lord Hoffmann put it:

> " . . . my point of departure is that in general English law provides a remedy in damages for a person who has suffered injury as a result of professional negligence. . . . It follows that any exception which denies such a remedy requires a sound justification. Otherwise your Lordships would fail to observe the fundamental principle of justice which requires that people should be treated equally and like cases treated alike."

Their Lordships supported their conclusions with a variety of reasons. For Lord Steyn, the exposure of isolated acts of incompetence would strengthen the legal system, improving advocacy,[71] and he considered that public confidence in the legal system was not enhanced by immunity.[72] Lord Hope emphasised that immunity was a derogation from the fundamental human right of access to the court, which required justification.[73] Lords Hope,[74] Hutton[75] and Hobhouse[76] considered that the difficulty of finding a satisfactory way to define the limits of immunity supported its abolition in the civil sphere.

11–017   **Floodgates.** The House of Lords rejected an argument based on the fear of a flood of litigation.[77] Their Lordships were influenced by a number of considerations: establishing negligence for difficult decisions made in court would not be easy; causation would be hard to prove; under the Civil Procedure Rules it would be easier to strike out bad cases at an early stage; and a vexatious litigant would have difficulty obtaining funding. The House of Lords also rejected the argument that it was for parliament to abolish immunity.[78] In particular, section 62 of the Courts and Legal Services Act 1990 extended the same immunity of a barrister to any advocate, but it did not actually endorse that immunity.

11–018   Their Lordships carefully examined and rejected the four reasons set out above supporting the immunity. While the reasons might have supported immunity 30 years ago, and *Rondel v. Worsley*[79] was or may have been correctly decided at the time,[80] the rule could no longer be justified. Lord Hope suggested[81] that the

---

[70] *ibid.*, at 553E (Lord Steyn), 556B (Lord Browne-Wilkinson), 560E–F (Lord Hoffmann), 581E–582H (Lord Hope), 598D (Lord Hutton),
[71] *ibid.*, at 554C.
[72] *ibid.*, at 554D.
[73] *ibid.*, at 581E–582H. *cf.* Lord Hobhouse at 607E–F, who considered that Human Rights legislation imposed no more rigorous criteria than existing legal principles.
[74] *ibid.*, at 595F–H.
[75] *ibid.*, at 599H–600H. Lord Hutton also considered that the public would not think immunity was just and fair: see at 599D-H.
[76] *ibid.*, at 615H–616B.
[77] *ibid.*, at 553F–554A (Lord Steyn), 562F–563H (Lord Hoffmann).
[78] *ibid.*, at 555A–F (Lord Steyn), 575F–576C (Lord Hoffmann), 607G–608D (Lord Hobhouse).
[79] [1969] 1 A.C. 191.
[80] See [2000] 3 W.L.R. 543 at 554G—H (Lord Steyn), 575E (Lord Hoffmann), 581C–D (Lord Hope), 416H (Lord Hobhouse).
[81] *ibid.*, at 581D.

immunity should only be abolished prospectively, and not retrospectively. While none of the other judges commented on this conclusion, it may be correct,[82] although the fact that the appeals were upheld because immunity was abolished suggests the contrary.

The "cab rank" rule. The first reason was the cab rank rule, without which barristers might not be willing to give their services to clients with a bad reputation or unpopular cause,[83] and which might be undermined without immunity. Lord Steyn[84] considered that the impact of the cab rank rule was not great, as a barrister's clerk may not be enthusiastic for the unwanted brief, and he can raise the fee, within limits. Furthermore, vexatious claims can usually be disposed of summarily. For Lord Hoffmann, this reason also had little substance, and he thought that the fear of a vexatious action was not a prominent consideration in accepting a brief.[85] In contrast, Lord Hobhouse held that the cab rank rule was a legitimate factor to take into account.[86]

11–019

Analogy of other immunities. Secondly, there is an analogy with immunities enjoyed by others participating in court proceedings.[87] Lord Steyn[88] held that such immunities were founded on public policy which sought to encourage freedom of speech in court, and had no weight in relation to the claimed immunity of barristers. Lord Hoffmann, similarly, thought that the basis of the general immunity of witnesses was to encourage freedom of expression, but there was no analogy between a witness who owed no duty of care to anyone, and an advocate who owed a duty of care to his client.[89]

11–020

Relitigation. Thirdly, there is a policy against relitigation, and in particular a concern as to the possibility of conflicting judgments which could bring the administration of justice into dispute. Their Lordships considered that the principle was a sound one, at least in relation to criminal proceedings.[90] However, they recognised that it could not justify barristers' immunity as a separate principle from abuse of process,[91] and their views on abuse of process are discussed under that subject.[92] Lord Hoffmann distinguished two additional strands to the argument, which he rejected: that there would be evidential difficulties in proving what would have happened in earlier proceedings if they had been conducted

11–021

---

[82] The reasons for this conclusion are as follows: *Rondel v. Worsley* was not overruled, but public policy justified a change in the law; the basis of immunity was public policy, which is inherently mutable, and thus there is no departure from the normal principle that the courts declare what the law always has been; and the decisions in the individual cases were identical whether immunity existed or not. *cf.* Hugh Evans, "*Hall v. Simons*" and abuse of process [2001] 17 P.N. 219 at 229–230.

[83] See also Lord Hope at 585F–H.

[84] *ibid.*, at 550F–H.

[85] *ibid.*, at 568C–E.

[86] *ibid.*, at 610F–611A.

[87] See also Lord Hope at 585H–586B.

[88] *ibid.*, at 551A–B.

[89] *ibid.*, at 568F–570A. *cf.* Lord Hobhouse at 611F–612B.

[90] *ibid.*, at 551C–552A (Lord Steyn), 556C–557B (Lord Browne-Wilkinson), 571C, 575C (Lord Hoffmann), 586C–E (Lord Hope).

[91] *ibid.*, at 551C (Lord Steyn), 556H–557A (Lord Browne-Wilkinson), 574G (Lord Hoffmann). *cf.* Lord Hope in relation to criminal proceedings at 593H–595C.

[92] See chap. 10, paras 10–112 to 10–114.

differently, and that it would be invidious to decide what the judge would have decided if a different argument had been advanced.[93]

11–022   **Duty to the court.** Fourthly, there is the duty of a barrister to the court, summarised by Lord Hoffmann as follows[94]:

> "Lawyers conducting litigation owe a divided loyalty. They have a duty to their clients, but they may not win by whatever means. They also owe a duty to the court and the administration of justice. They may not mislead the court or allow the judge to take what they know to be a bad point in their favour. They must cite all relevant law, whether for or against their case. They may not make imputations of dishonesty unless they have been given the information to support them. They should not waste time on irrelevancies even if the client thinks that they are important. So, it was said, the possibility of a claim for negligence might inhibit the lawyer from acting in accordance with his overriding duty to the court. That would be prejudicial to the administration of justice."

In rejecting the argument, Lord Steyn[95] compared the advocate's position to that of a doctor, who may have conflicting ethical duties but no immunity, as did Lord Hoffmann.[96] Lord Steyn[97] also relied on the fact that there was no immunity in the European Union, although he recognised that continental legal systems were different, and he was particularly influenced by the fact that there was no immunity in Canada, without there being any apparent problem. Lord Hoffmann[98] sought to distinguish two strands to the argument. First, that lawyers would be inhibited, consciously or unconsciously, from giving the duty to the court priority to the duty to the client. He considered that most advocates were honest and conscientious, would wish to enjoy a good reputation amongst their peers and the judiciary, and were subject to disciplinary powers already and the possibility of wasted costs orders. He held that an action for negligence would be low on the list of pressures. He was influenced by the fact that where the duties to client and court most acutely came into conflict, which was disclosure of documents, there never had been any immunity.[99] The second strand was that advocates would be exposed to vexatious claims, which Lord Hoffmann rejected as misconceived, as many people who were not immune were vulnerable to vexatious claims when they were doing their best in a difficult job, and also because developments in the civil justice system should reduce the incidence of such claims.

11–023   **Criminal proceedings.** In relation to criminal proceedings, the minority reached a different conclusion. Lord Hope considered that the exposure to actions

---

[93] [2000] 3 W.L.R. 543 at 570B–571B

[94] *ibid.*, at 558C–E. Lord Hobhouse discussed this argument at 608F–610E.

[95] *ibid.*, at 552B–553E.

[96] *ibid.*, at 561H. See also Lord Hutton at 599F–H. Lord Hobhouse rejected the analogy as the conflicting duties were ethical only, see *ibid.*, at 610A–B.

[97] *ibid.*, at 552E–553E. Lord Hoffmann considered that one could not draw any useful conclusions from other legal systems, although he too appeared to be influenced by the Canadian experience, see *ibid.*, at 566F–567C. Lord Hope considered that the antipodean law, supporting immunity, was more relevant, see *ibid.*, at 592B–593E.

[98] *ibid.*, at 560H–567C.

[99] The same point was made by Lord Hobhouse, at 601B–C.

for negligence would tempt advocates in criminal cases to pursue every conceivable point, and this argument justified the immunity.[1] Lord Hutton concluded that there was a risk of an advocate deviating from his duty to the court for fear of being sued by a litigant, and that it was not right that advocates should be vexed by unmeritorious actions from unscrupulous and disreputable persons.[2] Lord Hobhouse thought that abolition of criminal immunity should await another case,[3] he also did not think that abuse of process doctrine was a sufficient answer, in part because he considered that it had very narrow compass,[4] and he feared that the abolition of immunity could prejudice criminal appeals brought on the basis of his lawyers' errors.[5] The majority rejected this reasoning.[6] For Lord Millett, the case for abolishing immunity in civil litigation was stronger than in criminal cases, but it was not easy to draw a line between the two, and such a distinction would not commend itself to the public.

The position in the Commonwealth. Immunity exists in New Zealand.[7] In **11–024** Australia, a bare majority of the High Court of Australia supported immunity in *Giannarelli v. Wraith*,[8] on public policy grounds similar to those previously adopted by the House of Lords. The extent of the immunity there is based on the *Rees v. Sinclair* test.[9] Immunity does not exist in Canada.[10]

(f) *Abuse of process*

If a barrister's client is convicted, the client may not be able to sue him on the **11–025** grounds of abuse of process, on the reasoning of the Court of Appeal in *Somasundaram v. M. Julius Melchior & Co.*[11] The Court of Appeal also considered that the objection could be taken when the original case under attack was a civil one.[12] In *Hall v. Simons*[13] the House of Lords held that the abuse of process principle would ordinarily prevent a claimant suing for a wrongful criminal conviction, as it would be a collateral attack on the verdict of the criminal trial, but that in civil actions that principle will rarely have a place. This difficult issue is discussed in chapter 10 paragraphs 10–108 to 10–115.

---

[1] *ibid.*, at 586H–592A. He also rejected the argument that the Hunter principle was a sufficient alternative protection, see 593F–595C.
[2] *ibid.*, at 601A–605H.
[3] *ibid.*, at 606E.
[4] 613B–614D and 621E–622G.
[5] *ibid.*, at 616C–620E.
[6] For the views of the majority on the minority's reasoning, see *ibid.*, at 551H–552A (Lord Steyn), 567D–568B (Lord Hoffmann), 622H, 623C (Lord Millett).
[7] *Rees v. Sinclair* [1974] 1 N.Z.L.R. 180, CA.
[8] (1988) 91 A.L.R. 417. See the commentary by Nicholson (1989) 5 P.N. 124.
[9] *Giannarelli v. Wraith* (1988) 91 A.L.R. 417, High Court of Australia; *Keefe v. Marks* (1989) 16 N.S.W.L.R. 713, New South Wales CA: *Boland v. Yates Property Corporation Pty Ltd* (2000) 167 A.L.R. 575, High Court of Australia *per* Gleeson C.J. and Callinan J., *cf.* Gaudron J.
[10] *Banks v. Reid* (1977) 81 D.L.R. (3d) 730, Ontario CA. (immunity doubted); *Demarco v. Ungaro* (1979) 95 D.L.R. (3d) 385, Ontario HCt (no immunity for conduct of civil cases in court).
[11] [1988] 1 W.L.R. 1394. See further chap. 10, para. 10–108.
[12] [1988] 1 W.L.R. 1394 at 1402E–1403B. The principle was applied in the context of civil litigation in *Palmer v. Durnford Ford* [1992] 1 Q.B. 483 which has subsequently been doubted in *Walpole v. Partridge & Wilson* [1994] Q.B. 106, CA. See further chap. 10 para. 10–109.
[13] [2000] 3 W.L.R. 543.

(g) *Liability for costs*

11–026   Unlike solicitors, a barrister formerly could not be liable to pay the costs of his lay client or of the opposing side which had been wasted by his defaults, either under the inherent jurisdiction or under the rules of court.[14] The jurisdiction to order the payment of wasted costs was amended by section 4 of the Courts and Legal Services Act 1990 to apply to any "legal or other representative", which is defined by subsection (13) to mean "any person exercising a right of audience or right to conduct litigation", which clearly includes barristers.[15] Since then, a large number of wasted costs applications have been made against barristers.

11–27   **Guidelines.** In *Re a Barrister (Wasted Costs Order) (No. 1 of 1991)*[16] the Court of Appeal laid down guidelines for use in criminal cases. They can be summarised as follows:

(a) First, the wasted costs jurisdiction is draconian, and thus the court must formulate the complaint carefully and concisely.

(b) Secondly, where necessary, a transcript of the part of the proceedings under discussion should be available. A transcript of any wasted costs hearing should be made. (This is required by the 1991 Regulations.)

(c) Thirdly, a defendant should be present if it was in his interests, especially if the matter might affect the course of his trial. Other parties may make representations, and it might be appropriate for counsel for the Crown to be present.

(d) Fourthly, the court recommended a three-stage test:

"(i) Had there been an improper, unreasonable or negligent act or omission? (ii) As a result had any costs been incurred by a party? (iii) If the answers to (i) and (ii) were yes; should the court exercise its discretion to disallow or order the representative to meet the whole or any part of the relevant costs, and if so what specific sum was involved?"

(e) Fifthly, it was inappropriate to propose any deal. The judge should state his complaint, invite comments, and make a ruling.

(f) Sixthly, the judge had to specify the sum to be ordered, or if that was impossible, substitute an alternative procedure.

In *Ridehalgh v. Horsefield*[17] the Court of Appeal gave guidelines on wasted costs orders in civil litigation, which are summarised in chapter 10.[18] A number of decisions concerning barristers illustrate the procedure and application of the wasted costs jurisdiction.

---

[14] *Orchard v. South Eastern Electricity Board* [1987] 1 Q.B. 565 at 571E–F and 581C, CA.; *cf. Kelly v. London Transport Executive* [1982] 1 W.L.R. 1055 at 1065 *per* Lord Denning M.R.; *Fozal v. Gofur, The Times,* July 9, 1993, CA.

[15] The section came into force on October 1, 1991. For the exercise of the jurisdiction, see chap. 10 paras 10–125 to 10–140.

[16] [1993] Q.B. 293.

[17] [1994] Ch. 205.

[18] paras 10–129 to 10–135.

Procedure.[19] In *Filmlab Systems International Ltd v. Pennington*[20] Aldous J.   **11–028**
held that it would rarely be right to apply for a wasted costs order until after the
trial of the action. Contrast *B v. B (Wasted costs: abuse of process)*[21] where Wall
J. held that it was appropriate to hear the application during the course of
proceedings, because the lawyers concerned were no longer instructed in the
litigation, and the issue was not going to be affected by the outcome of the case.
In *Re Freudiana Holdings Ltd*[22] the Court of Appeal held that it was almost
always appropriate for the trial judge to adjudicate on a wasted costs application.
The court considered that unless the wasted costs hearing could take place in
summary form soon after judgment it was unlikely to be appropriate. In that case,
the court held that the judge had been correct to halt proceedings which he had
instigated with an order to show cause when it became clear that there were
numerous matters of fact in issue.[23] In *Royal Institution of Chartered Surveyors
v. Wiseman Marshall*[24] the Court of Appeal stated that it would rarely be
appropriate to grant an adjournment to investigate whether the client was willing
to waive privilege, as that would create complexity and delay. The barrister must
be given the opportunity of considering his ground, taking advice, and obtaining
representation: see *R. v. Luton Family Proceedings Court Justices, ex parte R.*[25]
This is illustrated by *S v. M*,[26] where an application was made near the start of a
hearing after a vital allegation of forgery had been withdrawn, without sufficient
notice, due to lack of expert evidence. The order to show cause was made without
a statement of what the barrister had done wrong, and without satisfying the
requirement that a strong prima facie case had been made out before the
respondent barrister was called upon. In fact there was no prima facie evidence
that she had acted negligently or improperly. Pumfrey J. therefore granted the
appeal against the Master's order to show cause.

Misjudgments as to the strength of a case. It will be relatively rare that **11–029**
misjudgments on the strength of a case, an application, or an argument will lead
to a wasted costs order. In the context of the inherent jurisdiction to make wasted
costs orders, the Privy Council in *Harley v. McDonald*[27] reversed a decision
making a wasted costs order against a barrister for litigating a hopeless case.
There were two important principles behind the decision.

First, applications for wasted costs:

---

[19] See further the detailed guidance given in solicitor's negligence cases, summarised at chap. 10
paras 10–132 and 10–133. On the division of responsibility between solicitor and barrister, see chap.
10 paras 10–106 *et seq.* above.

[20] [1995] 1 W.L.R. 673.

[21] [2001] 1 F.L.R. 843. In that case there was no need to have a hearing to determine whether the
lawyers should be given an opportunity to show cause, as the applicant's prima facie case had been
established at the appeal hearing of which complaint was made. and the lawyers had had a reasonable
opportunity to give reasons why the court should not make the order.

[22] *The Times*, December 4, 1995. To similar effect see *Re P (a Barrister)(Wasted Costs Order), The
Times*, July 23, 2001, CA.

[23] Similarly, one reason why Keen J. dismissed the application for wasted costs in *Chief Constable
of North Yorkshire v. Audsley* [2000] Lloyd's Rep. P.N. 675 was that the costs sought were £168,900,
whereas the likely costs in the wasted costs application were £125–£135,000, and thus the costs in
the application were unjustifiably disproportionate.

[24] [2000] P.N.L.R. 649.

[25] [1998] C.L.Y. 496, CA.

[26] [1998] 3 F.C.R. 665.

[27] [2001] 2 W.L.R. 1749; [2001] U.K.P.C. 18.

"should be confined strictly to questions which are apt for summary disposal by the court. Failures to appear, conduct which leads to an otherwise avoidable step in the proceedings or the prolongation of a hearing by gross repetition or extreme slowness in the presentation of evidence or argument are typical examples. The factual basis for the exercise of the jurisidiction in such circumstances is likely to be found in facts which are within judicial knowledge because the relevant events took place in court of are facts that can easily be verified."[28]

Secondly, fairness to the lawyers requires that notice should be given of allegations relating to issues about the nature or scope of the instructions which the client has given or the advice the lawyers may have tendered.[29] In that case the trial judge had taken account of matters relating to the conduct of the proceedings which took place before the events he observed at trial, and which were not fully tested in the evidence. It is rarely safe to assume that a hopeless case is being litigated on the advice of the lawyers, or that it demonstrates incompetence by the lawyers.

11–030   **Illustrations of no wasted costs order for misjudgments.** In *Filmlab Systems International Ltd v. Pennington*[30] Aldous J. found that counsel's erroneous advice in relation to a discovery application was not an error that no reasonably well-informed and competent member of the Bar could have made, and so he did not make a wasted costs order.

Similarly, in *R. v. Horsham D.C., ex parte Wenman*[31] Brooke J. dismissed a wasted costs application against a barrister and solicitors in relation to judicial review proceedings because there was material on which the district council's decision could be challenged. The judge criticised a number of departures from good practice which took place before the new wasted costs jurisdiction came into force.

In *Sampson v. John Boddy Timber Ltd*[32] the Court of Appeal set aside an order for wasted costs against a barrister who had referred to without-prejudice correspondence in open court. A majority considered that the question of admissibility and privilege was not entirely clear. A legal representative should not be considered to be negligent if he took a point which was fairly arguable.

In *Royal Institution of Chartered Surveyors v. Wiseman Marshall*[33] a wasted costs order was sought, in proceedings brought against the RICS for expelling the claimant from that body, in relation to two allegations which had been pursued. On the first, that the decision to expel the claimant was unreasonable, the Court of Appeal held that counsel's advice that there were reasonable prospects of success was reasonable. In relation to the second, that the RICS had misdirected itself when expelling the claimant, the Court of Appeal refused to infer that counsel had advised that there was more than a 50 per cent chance of success, and they were also able to look at counsel's advice which concluded that there was no prospect of success on that issue. The Court found that the client had instructed counsel to pursue that point, and he was not to be criticised for maintaining it until the end of the oral evidence.

---

[28] *ibid.*, para. 50.
[29] *ibid.*, para. 54.
[30] [1995] 1 W.L.R. 673.
[31] [1995] 1 W.L.R. 681, a case decided before *Ridehalgh*.
[32] *The Independent*, May 17, 1995.
[33] [2000] P.N.L.R. 649.

In *Chief Constable of North Yorkshire v. Audsley*[34] an application was made for wasted costs against a barrister and solicitors in relation to civil litigation against the Chief Constable for malicious prosecution which had been dismissed at the outset of the trial. Keene J. held that this was not hopeless litigation, as there was evidence which could properly form the basis for an allegation that the prosecutor did not have an honest belief in the guilt of the accused, and in any event the court did not know what legal advice was given to the claimant and it was not improper for a lawyer to act for a party whose claim might seem doomed to fail.

Exceptions. Some wasted costs applications against barristers have succeeded **11–031** on these grounds. In *R. v. Secretary of State for the Home Office, ex parte Begum*[35] Harrison J. made a wasted costs order against a barrister where he had advised that documents, which the Treasury Solicitor wished to be put before the court on an *ex parte* application for judicial review, were irrelevant and did not need to be shown to the court. In *Dace v. Redland Aggregates Ltd*[36] Blackburne J. ordered counsel and solicitors to pay the wasted costs of a vexatious application seeking a declaration that a lease had not been determined, which had no chance of success as it was *res judicata*, having being determined in an earlier action. In *B v. B (Wasted costs: abuse of process)*[37] Wall J. made a wasted costs order against solicitors and a barrister who had appealed an order vacating a trial date, as the directions which were given and which were not appealed made it inevitable that the hearing would be postponed.

In *Medcalf v. Mardell*[38] leading and junior counsel signed a draft amended **11–032** notice of appeal which made allegations of dishonesty against the claimant and his legal advisers. In relation to most of the allegations, no evidence was served supporting them. The barristers submitted that there had been no waiver of privilege, that they were aware of their obligation imposed by the Bar's Code of Conduct not to draft any notice of appeal containing allegations of fraud without clear instructions to make them and reasonably credible material before them establishing a *prima facie* case of fraud, and that they would like to put before the court full details of what material was before them but could not do so because of privilege. A majority of the Court of Appeal made a wasted costs order against the barristers, holding that privilege did not avail them as the barristers had to be satisfied that there was reasonable credible material before them in a form which could be put before the court.

Misjudgments on timing. In *Ridehalgh v. Horsefield*[39] one of the appeals, **11–033** *Antonelli v. Wade Gery Farr*, concerned a barrister whose conduct of a trial was impaired because she had accepted the brief at a very late stage. The Court of Appeal held that in accepting the brief, counsel was acting properly in accordance with the "cab rank" rule. The Court rejected each of the specific criticisms of counsel and set aside the wasted costs order made by the judge. In *Re a*

---

[34] [2000] Lloyd's Rep. P.N. 675.
[35] [1995] C.O.D. 176.
[36] [1997] E.G.C.S. 123.
[37] [20001] 1 F.L.R. 843. The Judge was not impressed by the argument that privilege had not been waived, because, even assuming that the appeal was made on the client's instructions, the duty of the lawyers would have been to report to the Legal Services Commission that the client was making them act unreasonably.
[38] [2001] P.N.L.R. 372. The case is currently under appeal to the House of Lords.
[39] [1994] Ch. 205.

Barrister (Wasted Costs Order) (No. 4 of 1993)[40] the barrister had accepted a two-day trial at Derby followed immediately by another in Nottingham. The first trial overran. The Court of Appeal held that the barrister had been over-optimistic in failing to anticipate delays in the first trial, but his conduct was not unreasonable and no wasted costs order should have been made against him.

11–034   In contrast, in *Re a Barrister (Wasted Costs Order) (No. 4 of 1992)*[41] a barrister failed to appear at a trial because he had made no arrangements to ascertain the dates of cases in the relevant list. The Court of Appeal held that he should not have relied wholly on his instructing solicitors to notify him of the dates, but should have liaised with the listing officers, in accordance with normal practice. Similarly, in *R. v. Secretary of State for the Home Department, ex parte-Mahmood*[42] Richards J. made a wasted costs order against a barrister who accepted a case on a day when he had an existing commitment, without making contingency plans for the possibility of being unable to honour the new commitment. In *R. v. Rodney*[43] a barrister did not attend an appeal because he had been erroneously told by his clerk that the appeal was not listed. The Court of Appeal made a wasted costs order against him, as a barrister is vicariously liable for the defaults of his clerk.

11–035   **Other illustrations.** In *Re G (Minors)(Care Proceedings: Wasted Costs)*[44] a local authority applied for care orders in respect of three children, relying on expert medical opinion. The legal representatives failed to provide the first expert with the children's medical records, so that the witness was unable to complete her evidence on the arranged day and had to return another time. Despite assurances that no further problems would occur, a second expert had to be released to read documents. Wall J. held that a barrister instructed for the local authority in care proceedings was responsible for the presentation of the client's case, including ensuring that expert witnesses were aware of new developments and had digested new material. He held that counsel had acted unreasonably and negligently,[45] and a wasted costs order was made in relation to securing the first expert's reattendance, but not in relation to the second expert in respect of whom the Judge was not confident that any costs were in fact wasted. In *Wall v. Lefever*[46] the Court of Appeal held that a barrister was not negligent in misjudging that the principal issue in the case was whether a competent engineer could come to the conclusion that the property in question was stable, when in fact the issue was in failing to report the need for further investigation. In *Re a Barrister (Wasted Costs Order) (No. 9 of 1999)*[47] a barrister acted for a defendant charged with sexual offences. He failed to obtain a record of his client's previous convictions before eliciting from the client in evidence that he had never had an allegation of a sexual nature made against him, which was in fact false. The Court of Appeal held that the barrister had made an error in not obtaining a copy

---

[40] *The Times*, April 21, 1995.
[41] *The Times*, March 15, 1994.
[42] [1999] C.O.D. 119.
[43] [1997] P.N.L.R. 489.
[44] [2000] Fam. 104.
[45] He held that all counsel had acted unreasonably and negligently, but there was no practice direction or the like imposing an obligation on barristers in such non-adversarial litigation to ensure that other parties' experts were properly briefed. Thus a wasted costs order was only made against the local authority's barrister.
[46] [1998] 1 F.C.R. 605.
[47] (2000) 16 P.N. 122.

of his client's record, but it was not an error which no reasonably informed and competent member of the Bar would have made. The barrister had asked for a copy of the record, which was not provided, his client had assured him that he had no previous conviction for sexual offences, and the prosecution counsel had said that he would not refer to previous convictions.

2. LIABILITY FOR BREACH OF DUTY

The respects in which barristers could be held negligent are almost as varied and numerous as those relating to solicitors.[48] In the case of contentious business, the following are among the more common areas of liability: failing to analyse or apply legal principles properly (for instance, failing to keep properly apprised of recent changes in the law); failing to determine the appropriate remedy or procedure; errors in pleading (such as the failure to claim an indemnity from a third party); failing to identify the appropriate parties to litigation; failing to attend to limitation defences; and delays (as a result of which the client loses the chance to bring proceedings or has the proceedings struck out). In the case of non-contentious business, claims have been made for failing to draft documents correctly, leading to adverse tax consequences.

11–036

Knowledge of the law. In *Copeland v. Smith*[49] the Court of Appeal stated that advocates owed a duty to the court to keep themselves up to date with the law. Doubtless the same duty would be owed to a barrister's client. The Court indicated that an advocate should keep up to date with the general law reports, which are the *Weekly Law Reports* and the *All England Law Reports*. The Court expressed no view about the need to keep up to date with specialist law reports, but it is submitted that a barrister practising in a specialist field would be negligent if he failed to do so. *Green v. Collyer-Bristow*[50] is an illustration of a mistake about the law being held to be negligent. Matrimonial counsel advised the plaintiff that she should seek specific enforcement of an agreement with her former husband to transfer real property to her. Counsel failed to notice section 2 of the Law of Property (Miscellaneous Provisions) Act 1989, which imposed more onerous requirements with respect to the need for such an agreement to be in writing than the repealed section 40 of the Law of Property Act 1925, on which he had advised. Although two of the three standard textbooks did not refer to the change in the law, the barrister was held to be liable. In contrast, counsel's advice that the plaintiff should seek to set aside an earlier court order of 1984 was not negligent, although the "better opinion probably" was that such an application would fail.

11–037

Mistakes and mere errors of judgment. As in the case of solicitors,[51] there are usually two stages[52] in determining whether the barrister is liable: (i) Was the

11–038

---

[48] As to which, see chap. 10, section 2.

[49] [2000] 1 W.L.R. 371.

[50] [1999] Lloyd's Rep. P.N. 798

[51] Except where a breach of a specific duty arising under the retainer is alleged: see chap. 10 paras 10–008 to 10–010.

[52] In *Green v. Hancocks* [2001] Lloyd's Rep. P.N. 212 at paras 60–61 Chadwick L.J. considered that where the advice was correct, it may well be irrelevant how the barrister arrived at it, but that each case must be judged on its own circumstances. In that case the allegations made included a failure to address the issues properly as well as the giving of wrong advice.

particular advice or other act or omission complained of "wrong" in the light of the instructions and information placed before him?[53] (ii) If so, did the error amount to negligence?

11–039   **Is there an error?** *Boland v. Yates Property Corporation Pty Ltd*[54] is an example of a barrister's views being found to be correct. The plaintiff was entitled to receive compensation for land which was taken by the Darling Harbour Authority, and it was successfully argued on its behalf that the land had "special value" to it. The plaintiff later sued his lawyers, including counsel, alleging that they negligently failed to propound a theory of "special value" based on the argument that the plaintiff was in a position to develop the land more quickly than any hypothetical purchaser. The High Court of Australia held that there was an insufficient factual basis for such a theory. None of the lawyers were found to be negligent.

11–040   **Mistake or misjudgment?** In relation to the second of these questions, in the case of genuine mistakes, as opposed to misjudgments, there seems to be no reason why the barrister should be treated any more favourably than the solicitor. Indeed, since the barrister holds himself out as a specialist, presumably there are some mistakes which, if committed by a barrister, amount to negligence but, if committed by a solicitor, do not. There are a number of *obiter dicta* of the House of Lords on this subject. Lord Upjohn in *Rondel v. Worsley*[55] expressed the view that counsel would only be guilty of actionable negligence[56] if he committed "some really elementary blunder." This view is difficult to reconcile with the standard of care expected of solicitors.[57] Lord Reid stated that the "the onus of proving professional negligence over and above error of judgment is a heavy one."[58] The point was discussed in *Saif Ali v. Sidney Mitchell & Co.*[59] by each of the three Law Lords who constituted the majority. Lord Wilberforce put the matter in this way[60]:

> "Much if not most of a barrister's work involves exercise of judgment—it is in the realm of art not science. Indeed the solicitor normally goes to counsel precisely at the point where, as between possible courses, a choice can only be made on the basis of judgment, which is fallible and may turn out to be wrong. Thus in the nature of things, an action against a barrister who acts honestly and carefully is very unlikely to succeed."

---

[53] The qualification (contained in the last 11 words) is added, because in the majority of work out of court the barrister is not an investigator of fact, but a processor of facts laid before him. If the barrister gives advice which is correct on the basis of his instructions, it cannot subsequently be said against the barrister that the advice is "wrong", simply because the instructions prove to be mistaken. However, the roles of barrister and solicitor cannot be too rigidly compartmentalised. If the barrister has a conference with the client or expert witness, he may well become an investigator of fact during the conference. Presumably a barrister's failure to elicit information could, in appropriate circumstances, constitute negligence. In addition a barrister may be under a duty to defer advising until further information has been obtained, see para. 11–049.

[54] (2000) 167 A.L.R. 575. For an English example see *Naish v. Thorp Wright & Puxon* [1998] C.L.Y. 4024. Counsel was held not to be negligent in advising that a restraint of trade clause was enforceable, as his advice was correct.

[55] [1969] 1 A.C. 191 at 287 A–B.

[56] Which Lord Upjohn described as "*crassa negligentia*", or "gross negligence".

[57] See chap. 10 paras 10–077, 10–078 and 10–084.

[58] *ibid.*, at 230F.

[59] [1980] A.C. 198.

[60] *ibid.*, at 214F–G.

Lord Diplock stressed[61] that not every error made by a barrister (or any other professional man) constitutes negligence, but only such an error "as no reasonably well-informed and competent member of that profession could have made."[62] He pointed out[63] that the trial judge would be well qualified, without any need of expert evidence, to make allowance for the circumstances in which the allegedly negligent act or omission occurred. Similar observations were made by Lord Salmon[64] as to the nature of a barrister's work and the distinction between errors of judgment and negligence, and also by the House of Lords in *Hall v. Simons*.[65]

Illustrations. A number of cases now illustrate the distinction between errors   **11–041** of judgment and negligence, and in most of them the barrister was found not to be negligent.[66] In *Cook v. S.*[67] the plaintiff consulted the defendant solicitor in connection with divorce proceedings brought against her by her husband. As a result of the defendant's negligence the proceedings were undefended and the husband obtained a decree nisi on the grounds of desertion. Had the proceedings been defended, the probabilities were that both parties would have obtained cross-decrees and the plaintiff's position in regard to maintenance would thereby have been improved. About a month after the decree nisi was pronounced, counsel advised that there was no evidence of adultery against the husband and he could see no point in defending. Lawton J. held that counsel's advice was wrong; that a motion to set aside the decree nisi would probably have succeeded and that this would have been to the plaintiff's advantage. Lawton J. went on to hold, however, that counsel was "not negligent, just mistaken as any lawyer and judge might be."[68] Accordingly, the chain of causation was not broken, and the defendant solicitor was liable for all the consequences of the fact that the husband had obtained an undefended decree.

In *Matrix Securities Ltd v. Theodore Goddard*[69] the claimant promoted a tax   **11–042** avoidance scheme. A tax silk was instructed to advise on a letter sent to the Inland Revenue which sought an assurance that certain capital allowances would be available, which assurance was given. The Inland Revenue later disowned the assurance, and the plaintiff's subsequent litigation with the Inland Revenue was pursued to the House of Lords, where it was held that the allowances were not available, and the Inland Revenue was not bound by the assurances as inadequate disclosure had been made in the letter. Most of the judges who considered the case thought that the letter was inaccurate or misleading, but, the judge trying the negligence action brought against the tax silk considered that counsel's advice on the contents of the letter was not negligent, and that the judgment he made was not one which no reasonably competent tax silk could make. Finally, in *Waters*

---

[61] *ibid.*, at 218D and 220D. For a qualification to Lord Diplock's views, see *McManus Development Ltd v. Barbridge Properties Ltd* [1996] P.N.L.R. 431 at 442, CA. See further para. 11–008 above.
[62] A test adopted in the wasted costs cases of *Ridehalgh v. Horsefield* [1994] Ch. 205 and *Re a Barrister (Wasted Costs Order)(No. 9 of 1999)* (2000) 16 P.N. 122.
[63] [1980] A.C. 198. at pp. 220H–221A.
[64] *ibid.*, at 231C-D.
[65] [2000] 3 W.L.R. 543. See para 11–051 below for an exposition.
[66] See also *Nestle v. Best* [1996] P.N.L.R. 444, where the Court of Appeal struck out an allegation made against solicitors and counsel of allowing an action to continue despite it being hopeless, as it had been supported by expert evidence which was rejected by the judge at trial.
[67] [1966] 1 W.L.R. 635.
[68] *ibid.*, at 641E.
[69] [1998] P.N.L.R. 290.

v. Maguire[70] Garland J. struck out a claim against a barrister who had exercised her judgment not to pursue a claim for direct discrimination based on acts of victimisation, but to pursue only a claim for vicarious liability for a sexual assault of a fellow employee which was in fact bound to fail.

11–043   **Settlement.** Many of the areas upon which a barrister is asked to advise are clearly matters of judgment. One question commonly referred to counsel is whether or not a payment into court or offer of settlement should be accepted.[71] Often there is no "right" or "wrong" answer to this question. Counsel must weigh up subjective matters such as his own assessment of the witnesses, his experience of the trial judge (when known) and the "merits" of the case, as well as purely legal considerations. In the Canadian case of *Karpenko v. Paroian, Courey, Cohen & Houston*[72] Anderson J. expressed the view that only in exceptional cases would a lawyer's advice on such matters amount to negligence:

> "In my view, an important element of public policy is involved. It is in the interests of public policy to discourage suits and encourage settlements. The vast majority of suits are settled. It is the almost universal practice among responsible members of the legal profession to pursue settlement until some circumstance or combination of circumstances leads them to conclude that a particular dispute can only be resolved by a trial. I say nothing of the suits which are settled by reason of sloth, or inexperience, or lack of stomach for the fight. They have nothing to do with this case. What is relevant and material to the public interest is that an industrious and competent practitioner should not be unduly inhibited in making a decision to settle a case by the apprehension that some Judge, viewing the matter subsequently, with all the acuity of vision given by hindsight, and from the calm security of the Bench, may tell him he should have done otherwise. To the decision to settle a lawyer brings all his talents and experience both recollected and existing somewhere below the level of the conscious mind, all his knowledge of the law and its processes. Not least he brings to it his hard-earned knowledge that the trial of a lawsuit is costly, time-consuming and taxing for everyone involved and attended by a host of contingencies, foreseen and unforeseen. Upon all of this he must decide whether he should take what is available by way of settlement, or press on. I can think of few areas where the difficult question of what constitutes negligence, which gives rise to liability, and what constitutes at worst an error in judgment, which does not, is harder to answer. In my view it would be only in the case of some egregious error . . . that negligence would be found."[73]

This dictum was cited with approval in *Chancellor, Masters and Scholars of Oxford University v. John Stedman Design Group*.[74] In *Kelley v. Corston*[75] Judge L.J. suggested, in the context of a consideration of immunity, that no case was bound to succeeed, and it is difficult to underestimate the value of certainty

---

[70] [1999] Lloyd's Rep. P.N. 855. The point is closely allied to the issue of pleading weak points, discussed at para. 11–050 below. Garland J. also held that the barrister, who had no solicitor and was working for the Free Representation Unit, was not negligent in failing to take a more detailed proof or discovering further gender specific acts which could have been pleaded as direct discrimination, as she had a full note from the claimant who provided a different version of events.
[71] This topic has already been discussed in the context of solicitors: see chap. 10, para. 10–190.
[72] (1981) 117 D.L.R. (3d) 383, Ontario HCt.
[73] *ibid.*, at 397–398.
[74] (1991) 7 Const.L.J. 102 at 107, Judge Esyr Lewis Q.C. It was held that the defendants had acted reasonably in entering into a settlement on the advice of counsel, and thus were entitled to pursue contribution proceedings on the basis of that settlement.
[75] [1998] Q.B. 686 at 700E-F.

provided by settlement, factors which should "militate against successful proceedings based on criticism of advice leading to a settlement."

Illustrations. An extreme example of an allegation against counsel of advising an undersettlement can be found in *Hussain v. Cuddy Woods & Cochrane (A Firm)*,[76] where the Court of Appeal upheld an order striking the case out. There was no evidence that the claim was worth more than the £10,000 which the barrister had advised should be accepted in settlement on the third day of trial. Counsel was entitled to take into account the hazards of litigation, the enormous costs for the client if the claim were to fail, or if the payment in were not beaten. No inference could be drawn from the fact that counsel might have a financial interest in the case as his solicitors had not guaranteed payment of all his fees. A less extreme example is *McIlgrom v. Bell Lamb & Joynson*.[77] The claimant was sued as a director of a small company, which had gone into liquidation, for negligently allowing an employee to be exposed to asbestosis. His barrister's advice to accept the settlement proposals of the other side was held by Gibbs J. to be within the range of reasonable views which a well informed barrister could have formed. The factors which he did and was entitled to take into account included: the evidence available as to whether the claimant personally directed or controlled the employees; the law, which included an unreported case on similar facts which had been drawn to his attention; and the fact that the offer to settle for about two-thirds of the value of the claim, with damages and costs being charged on the claimant's property and not to be enforced in his lifetime, meant that the claimant would keep his home.

11–044

An exception. However, in *Griffin v. Kingsmill*,[78] counsel and solicitors were found to be negligent in advising a claimant to accept £50,000 in a personal injury action which would have been worth about £500,000 on full liability. The claimant, who was 12 years old at the time, was a pedestrian hit by a car. There were only two witnesses. The claimant's grandfather said that the claimant was waiting on the side of the road, between the white line and the pavement, and the driver said that she ran alongside the road until she suddenly changed direction and ran into the road. The Court of Appeal held that this was essentially a simple case, and it would take cogent reasons to conclude that the grandfather's evidence was overwhelmingly likely to be rejected, which did not exist. The reasons given by counsel for rejecting the grandfather's evidence were untenable, and he did not properly assess the driver's evidence, which was inconsistent.

11–045

Failures of advice. In *Estill v. Cowling*[79] counsel was instructed in relation to the proposed transfer of shares in a company to the client's nephews and nieces. Arden J. held that counsel was negligent in failing to advise that the proposed gift of shares to a settlement would be an immediately chargeable transfer for the purposes of inheritance tax, and failing to consider an interest in possession trust, which would have been a potentially exempt transfer.[80]

11–046

---

[76] [2001] Lloyd's Rep. P.N. 134.
[77] [2001] P.N.L.R. 28.
[78] [2001] E.W.C.A. Civ. 934.
[79] [2000] Lloyd's Rep. P.N. 378.
[80] This was despite expert evidence from a silk that he was not aware of an interest in possession settlement, which was not mentioned in the predecent book.

11–047   **Giving clear advice.** The question of how comprehensive a barrister's advice must be was considered in *Mathew v. Maughold Life Assurance Co. Ltd.*[81] In March 1974 Mr and Mrs Mathew entered into a scheme in order to minimise liability to estate duty on Mr Mathew's death. In order to achieve the desired result, it was necessary for Mrs Mathew to exercise an option by March 20, 1981, in the event that her husband survived until that date. Unfortunately she did not do so, and in consequence suffered loss. The family solicitor admitted liability, and unsuccessfully attempted to seek contribution from three other professional advisers, including a barrister. The case against the barrister related to advice which he had given orally in conference in 1974 and 1978 and to an opinion which he had written shortly after the 1978 conference. Leonard J. held that the barrister had given adequate advice in 1974, but that his advice in 1978 was inadequate in that he failed to make it clear that the option must be exercised by March 1981. The Court of Appeal reversed that finding and held that the barrister was not liable. At the conference in 1974 the barrister was instructed by the insurance company who had marketed the scheme, and not by Mr or Mrs Mathew. However, Leonard J. held that the barrister owed a duty to them to give an adequate explanation of the scheme to Mr Mathew's solicitor and accountant, who were present at the conference. In relation to the 1974 advice, Leonard J. considered that the barrister was entitled to assume that the solicitor and accountant were following what he said unless they indicated to the contrary and that Mr Mathew's professional advisers would familiarise themselves with the documents before Mr and Mrs Mathew were invited to sign them.[82] The Court of Appeal went further, and considered that even when the barrister was instructed on behalf of Mr Mathew in 1978, he owed no duty to ensure that the lay client fully understood the scheme given the presence of the other professional advisers. He was entitled to assume that his instructing solicitor was familiar with what had been arranged, and had explained it to the client.[83]

11–048   **Advising where not instructed to do so.** One problem which sometimes arises is the extent to which barristers can be held liable for failing to advise on matters which are not specifically raised in their instructions. If the barrister is asked to advise on certain specific points only, it seem unlikely that he will be held liable for failing to advise on other matters. In the Canadian case of *Smith v. McInnis*[84] a solicitor was instructed to pursue claims under fire insurance policies in respect of certain losses by fire. He engaged experienced insurance counsel to advise on the preparation of proofs of loss. The solicitor failed to bring proceedings within the limitation period. In the professional negligence action which followed, the solicitor claimed a contribution from the insurance counsel. The claim failed. It was held by the Supreme Court of Canada that the insurance counsel was not required to give advice about the limitation period. Presumably, however, if it is obvious from the instructions that instructing solicitors are under a misapprehension about some relevant matter on which the barrister's opinion is not specifically sought, or perhaps even that they have overlooked a point of

---

[81] (1985) 1 P.N. 142, Leonard J.; (1987) 3 P.N. 98, CA.
[82] (1985) 1 P.N. 142 at 145 col. 3.
[83] (1987) 3 P.N. 98 at 104.
[84] (1979) 91 D.L.R. (3d) 190. For another example see *Heydon v. NRWA* (2001) 36 A.C.S.R. 462, N.S.W.C.A.

critical importance, he would be held negligent for failing to correct that misapprehension.

Obtaining full instructions. A barrister may be negligent in some circumstance if he settles proceedings or advises on the basis of information or instructions which he ought to realise are inadequate.[85] Thus in medical negligence cases, it is necessary to see copies of the relevant medical notes as well as an expert's report before advising on the merits of a case.[86]

11–049

Pleading weak points. In *McFarlane v. Wilkinson*[87] the plaintiff suffered psychiatric injury as a result of witnessing the catastrophic fire on the Piper Alpha oil-rig from a support vessel. His claim at common law succeeded at first instance, but failed on appeal. He sued his barristers for failing to plead breach of statutory duty. Reversing Rix J., the Court of Appeal held that such a claim was bound to fail. Brooke L.J., with whom the other members of the Court agreed, held that the relevant test was:

11–050

"if a barrister omits to plead a cause of action in a situation where no other reasonably competent barrister, acting with ordinary care, would have failed to plead that cause of action, then he or she will be liable to compensate the client if loss flows foreseeable from that negligence. If on the other hand other reasonably competent barristers holding themselves out as competent to practise in the relevant field and acting with ordinary care might also have decided not to plead that cause of action, then there will be no question of professional negligence."

It was argued by the plaintiff that any properly arguable claim, such as breach of statutory duty in that case, should be pleaded, as it had some settlement value. Brooke L.J. suggested that a client would not thank counsel for taking properly arguable points which were likely to fail if as a consequence the litigation was longer and more expensive. In that case, counsel rightly judged that the plea of breach of statutory duty added nothing to the plea of negligence, and it was "quite absurd to consider that she could be liable in negligence for exercising her judgment in the way she did". The Court of Appeal struck out the claim.

Negligence in court. As a result of the abolition of immunity by the House of Lords in *Hall v. Simons*[88] barristers are vulnerable to being sued for mistakes they make in court. Three of their Lordships made observations about such actions in slightly different terms. In one of the two leadings judgments, Lord Steyn said[89]:

11–051

"when such claims are made courts will take into account the difficult decisions faced daily by barristers working in demanding situations to tight timetables. In this context the observations of Sir Thomas Bingham M.R. in *Ridehalgh v. Horsefield* [1994] Ch.

---

[85] As Richard Fernyhough Q.C. points out at (1997) 13 Cons.L.J. 364, this may not apply in matters of urgency, and statements of case can be settled on the basis of limited information.
[86] See *Locke v. Camberwell Health Authority* (1990) 140 N.L.J. 205 at 206 col. 1. On appeal, further facts came to light. The Court of Appeal stated that the barrister who was criticised by the Judge did not, on the facts of the case, deserve censure, but the Court did not consider the principle discussed: see [1991] 2 Med. L.R. 253.
[87] [1997] 2 Lloyd's Rep. 259.
[88] [2000] 3 W.L.R. 543.
[89] *ibid.*, at 553F–554B. Lord Steyn's speech was agreed by Lord Browne-Wilkinson at 555H and Lord Millett at 622G.

205 are instructive. Dealing with the circumstances in which a wasted costs order against a barrister might be appropriate he observed, at p.236:

'Any judge who is invited to make or contemplates making an order arising out of an advocate's conduct of court proceedings must make full allowance for the fact that an advocate in court, like a commander in battle, often has to make decisions quickly and under pressure, in the fog of war and ignorant of developments on the other side of the hill. Mistakes will inevitably be made, things done which the outcome shows to have been unwise. But advocacy is more an art than a science. It cannot be conducted according to formulae. Individuals differ in their style and approach. It is only when, with all allowances made, an advocate's conduct of court proceedings is quite plainly unjustifiable that it can be appropriate to make a wasted costs order against him.'

For broadly similar reasons it will not be easy to establish negligence against a barrister. The courts can be trusted to differentiate between errors of judgment and true negligence. In any event, a plaintiff who claims that poor advocacy resulted in an unfavourable outcome will face the very great obstacle of showing that a better standard of advocacy would have resulted in a more favourable outcome."

Lord Hope stated that an advocates's

"duty in the conduct of his professional duties is to do that which an advocate of ordinary skill would have done if he had been acting with ordinary care. . . . He must also exercise that judgment with the care which an advocate of ordinary skill would take in the circumstances. It cannot be stressed too strongly that a mere error of judgment on his part will not expose him to liability for negligence."[90]

Finally, Lord Hobhouse indicated that the standard of care to be applied was:

" . . . the same as that applicable to any other skilled professional who has to work in an environment where decisions and exercises of judgment have to be made in often difficult and time constrained circumstances. It requires a plaintiff to show that the error was one which no reasonably competent member of the relevant profession would have made."[91]

3. DAMAGES

11–052   **Remoteness of damage.** Since there is no contract between the barrister and his client, the ordinary rules of remoteness in the law of tort[92] should be applied, in order to determine which losses flowing from the barrister's negligence sound in damages.

11–053   As in solicitors' negligence cases, the loss will have to be within the scope of the defendant's duty, and be proximately caused by it. In *Bernasconi v. Nicholas Bennett*[93] the defendants, a barrister and a firm of solicitors, gave advice to directors on how their company could divest itself of four leases. The company's

---

[90] *ibid.*, at 597D–G.
[91] *ibid.*, at 608F–G.
[92] For the general principles of remoteness in the law of tort, see *McGregor*, 16th ed., paras 192–231.
[93] [2000] Lloyd's Rep. P.N. 285.

liquidator subsequently sued the directors for fraudulent preference. The directors' action against the lawyers, seeking an indemnity, was struck out. The lawyers were not the proximate cause of the loss. It was not alleged that the defendants acted dishonestly or encouraged the directors to act.

Measure of damages. The heads of damage will generally be similar to those **11–054** discussed in relation to solicitors.[94] Where the barrister's negligence has deprived the client of the chance of bringing or defending proceedings, the court must assess the value of the "chance" which has been lost, applying the principles formulated in *Kitchen v. Royal Air Force Association*,[95] as was done in *Gascoine v. Ian Sheridan & Co.*[96] A barrister was one of the defendants whose negligent delay caused the plaintiff's case to be struck out for want of prosecution. In *Griffin v. Kingsmill*[97] counsel negligently advised that a case had no reasonable prospects of success, and as a result a settlement was accepted at about a tenth of the value of the claim on full liability. The Court of Appeal awarded 80 per cent of the full value of the claim, giving a discount for the uncertainties of litigation and the risk of a finding of contributory negligence.

A more difficult question arises if counsel makes a mistake[98] as a result of **11–055** which the case is lost. Does the court have to determine on the balance of probabilities whether, but for that mistake, the case would have been won? And, if so, award the relief which should have been obtained in the earlier action? Alternatively, does the court have to assess the chances of a more favourable outcome, in the absence of the negligent mistake, and then scale down the award of damages accordingly? It would appear from the reasoning of Lord Diplock in *Saif Ali v. Sidney Mitchell & Co.*,[99] and from comments made by Lord Browne-Wilkinson in *Hall v. Simons*[1] in the House of Lords, that the first course is to be preferred. If, therefore, the negligence of counsel transforms an action with a 40 per cent chance of success into an action with no prospect of success, the client would suffered no recoverable loss.[2] However, Lord Diplock's dictum should now be reconsidered in the light of the Court of Appeal's decision in *Allied Maples Group Ltd v. Simmons & Simmons*.[3] It is submitted that his dictum is now unlikely to be followed.

---

[94] See chap. 10, section 3.
[95] [1958] 1 W.L.R. 563, CA.
[96] [1994] 5 Med. L.R. 437. For the facts see chap. 10, para. 10–280.
[97] [2001] E.W.C.A. Civ. 934.
[98] *e.g.* advising wrongly on a period of limitation.
[99] [1980] A.C. 198 at 222 D–E. The reasoning is similar to that of the Court of Appeal in *Sykes v. Midland Bank Executor & Trustee Co.* [1971] 1 Q.B. 113, CA.
[1] [2000] 3 W.L.R. 543 at 556E-F. *Cf.* Lord Hoffmann at 559D.
[2] Since damage is a necessary element in the tort of negligence, the claim would then fail altogether.
[3] [1995] 1 W.L.R. 1602, on which see chap. 10, para. 10–258.

CHAPTER 12

MEDICAL PRACTITIONERS

PARA.
1. General 12–001
   (a) Duties to patient 12–005
       (i) Contractual duties 12–005
       (ii) Statutory duties 12–011
       (iii) Common law duty of
             care 12–015
   (b) Duties to third parties 12–031
   (c) The standard of skill and care 12–067
   (d) General and approved practice 12–090
       (i) Acting in accordance
           with general and
           approved practice 12–092
       (ii) Departing from general
            and approved practice ...12–106
   (e) Expert evidence 12–111
   (f) Res ipsa loquitur 12–117
   (g) Consent to treatment 12–124
       (i) Limits to consent 12–126
       (ii) Voluntary consent 12–128
       (iii) Informed consent 12–130
       (iv) Capacity to consent 12–135
   (h) Allied professions 12–149
   (i) Hospitals and health
       authorities 12–152
   (j) Apportionment of liability 12–164
   (k) Lord Woolf's reforms 12–166
2. Liability for breach of duty 12–167
   (a) Failing to prevent illness 12–169
   (b) Failing to attend or examine a
       patient 12–172

PARA.
   (c) Wrong diagnosis 12–177
   (d) Error in the course of
       treatment 12–186
   (e) Failure of communication
       between hospitals or medical
       practitioners 12–197
   (f) Failing to explain treatment or
       warn 12–201
   (g) Mishandling of mentally
       disturbed patients 12–233
3. Damages 12–241
   (a) Remoteness 12–242
       (i) Causation 12–243
       (ii) Foreseeability 12–282
   (b) Measure of damages 12–287
       (i) Damages for personal
           injury 12–287
       (ii) Aggravated damages 12–288
       (iii) Damages in wrongful
             birth and conception
             claims 12–289
       (iv) Impact of the Human
            Rights Act 1998 12–301
       (v) Claims by unwanted
           disabled child 12–302
       (vi) Negligent report 12–303
       (vii) Scope of liability for
             economic loss 12–304

1. GENERAL

A registered medical practitioner is a person who appears as such in the register **12–001** maintained by the Registrar of the General Medical Council. In order to obtain registration, a practitioner must satisfy the requirements of the Medical Act 1983 (as amended by the Medical Qualifications (Amendment) Act 1991) both as to qualifications and as to experience. Once fully registered, a practitioner is eligible for appointment as a medical officer in any hospital within or outside the National Health Service[1]; he is entitled to practise, and to hold himself out, as a

---

[1] Medical Act 1983, s.47, amended by the Medical (Professional Performance) Act 1995, s.4.

registered medical practitioner[2]; he is also entitled to give medical certificates required by any enactment.[3] Medical practitioners are subject to the discipline of the General Medical Council, whose powers are now derived from the Medical Act 1983 and the Medical (Professional Performance) Act 1995. Medical practitioners (other than consulting surgeons) are commonly given the courtesy title "doctor", whether or not their qualifications include the degree Doctor of Medicine.

12–002   Similarly, a registered dentist is a person who appears as such in the dentists' register maintained by the Registrar of the General Dental Council. In order to obtain registration, a dentist must satisfy the requirements of the Dentists Act 1984.[4] No one may practise dentistry who is not a registered dentist, a visiting EEC practitioner entered in the list of such practitioners or a registered medical practitioner.[5] Dentists are subject to the discipline of the General Dental Council, whose powers are derived from the Dentists Act 1984. Only a registered dentist is entitled to describe himself as "dentist", "dental surgeon" or "dental practitioner".[6]

12–003   Similar arrangements also exist in relation to what are described below[7] as "allied professions".[8]

12–004   **Disciplinary proceedings** Doctors, dentists and each of the allied medical professions referred to above are each subject to the disciplinary jurisdiction of statutory bodies established for that purpose.[9] Although a detailed consideration of the jurisdiction of those bodies is outside the scope of this work, it should be noted that in *McCandless v. General Medical Council*[10] the Privy Council

---

[2] Unqualified persons are not prohibited from practising medicine or surgery. However, they are not permitted to sue for their charges: see Medical Act 1983, s.46. It is a criminal offence if such persons hold themselves out as being registered under the Medical Act 1983: see s.49. This curious compromise has its origin in the Medical Act 1858. It is described by Atiyah as "one of the more interesting and idiosyncratic of the Victorian compromises on the freedom of contract issue, all the more remarkable for having survived to the present day": see *The Rise and Fall of Freedom of Contract*, p. 552.

[3] Medical Act 1983, s.48. For a fuller discussion of the privileges and duties of medical practitioners, see *Halsbury's Laws* (4th ed.), vol. 30, paras 13–18.

[4] See in particular s.15, as amended by the Dental Qualifications (Recognition) Regulations 1996 (S.I. 1996 No. 1496).

[5] Dentists Act 1984, s.38. These provisions are more stringent than the equivalent provisions relating to general medical practice: see n. 2 above.

[6] Dentists Act 1984, s.26.

[7] See paras 12–149 to 12–151 below.

[8] The registration of pharmacists is governed by the Pharmacy Act 1954: see ss. 1–6 for the requirements that must be satisfied. The registration of nurses, midwives and health visitors is governed by the Nurses, Midwives and Health Visitors Act 1997, ss.7–9. The registration of opticians is governed by the Opticians Act 1989, ss.7–9. The registration of osteopaths is governed by the Osteopaths Act 1993, ss.2–4, 6. The registration of chiropodists, dietitians, medical laboratory technicians, occupational therapists, physiotherapists, radiographers, arts therapists, clinical scientists, speech and language therapists, orthoptists, prosthetists and orthotists, and paramedics is governed by the Professions Supplementary to Medicine Act 1960, ss.2–7. Acupuncturists may register with the British Medical Acupuncture Society, and the British Acupuncture Council; registration is voluntary.

[9] For example, doctors are subject to the disciplinary jurisdiction of the General Medical Council, dentists are subject to the disciplinary jurisdiction of the General Dental Council and nurses, midwives and health visitors are subject to the disciplinary jurisdiction of the Central Council for Nursing, Midwifery and Health Visiting.

[10] [1996] 1 W.L.R. 167. In *McCandless* the Privy Council followed its earlier decision in *Doughty v. General Dental Council* [1988] A.C. 164.

rejected an argument to the effect that the conduct of a general practitioner had to be "morally blameworthy" before he or she could be found guilty of "serious professional misconduct" and instead confirmed that "seriously negligent treatment" could support such a charge. In that case the care provided by the practitioner to three patients was found by the Council to have fallen "deplorably short of the standard which patients are entitled to expect from their general practitioners". The practitioner was struck off the Medical Register.

(a) *Duties to Patient*

(i) *Contractual duties*

National Health Service patients. Most medical treatment is undertaken under the National Health Service scheme and there is almost certainly no contract between the patient and those by whom he is treated.[11]   **12–005**

In the fourth edition of this work it was suggested that it might be possible to argue that a contract for services was concluded between a patient and his general practitioner at the time that the patient first enrolled—by permitting his name to be added to that practitioner's list, he increases the remuneration to which the practitioner is entitled thereby providing consideration for the practitioner's services. A similar argument was also suggested in respect of hospital treatment in the National Health Service's "internal market", where funding is intended to "follow the patient". An argument of this nature was accepted in *Pittman Estate v. Bain*.[12] Lang J. found a contract between a patient and the hospital where he was treated under a government funded health-care scheme. The patient gave consideration by submitting himself for treatment, thereby enhancing the reputation of the hospital and increasing the level of government funding to which it became entitled.   **12–006**

The argument was, however, roundly rejected in *Reynolds v. The Health First Medical Group*.[13] The case concerned an allegedly negligent failure on the part of the defendant general practitioners practice to advise the claimant that she was pregnant. She subsequently gave birth to a healthy but unwanted child and sued for, *inter alia*, the cost of bringing up the child. Following the House of Lords' decision in *McFarlane v. Tayside Health Board*,[14] she re-amended her claim to   **12–007**

---

[11] A similar conclusion is reached in Kennedy & Grubb's *Principles of Medical Law* (1998 ed.) at sections 5.012–5.10. In addition, in its Report on Civil Liability and Compensation for Personal Injury, (1978, Cmnd. 7054) the Royal Commission, chaired by Lord Pearson, stated at para. 1313: "Private patients may sue their doctors for a breach of contract . . . under the National Health Service, however there is no contract between patient and doctor and a plaintiff must rely on an action in tort. But the National Health Service patient is in no worse position than the private patient because the same considerations determine if there has been a breach of duty whether the case is brought in contract or tort. In *Hotson v. East Berkshire Area Health Authority* [1987] 1 A.C. 750 at 760B Lord Donaldson M.R was " . . . quite unable to detect any rational basis for a state of the law, if such it be, whereby in identical circumstances, Dr A who treats a patient under the National Health Service, and whose liability therefore falls to be determined in accordance with the law of tort, should be in a different position from Dr B who treats a patient outside the service, and whose liability therefore falls to be determined in accordance with the law of contract, assuming, of course, that the contract is in terms which impose upon him neither more nor less than the tortious duty"; see also *per* Croom-Johnson L.J. at 768F. The decision in *Hotson* concerned causation of loss and was reversed by the House of Lords without comment upon this point.

[12] (1994) 112 D.L.R. (4th) 257, Ontario High Court.

[13] [2000] Lloyd's Rep. Med. 240. For a commentary see [2000] Lloyd's Rep. Med. 244–245.

[14] [2000] 2 A.C. 59, HL considered at para. 12–290 below.

add a claim for breach of a contractual relationship with the defendant. The defendant succeeded in striking out the re-amended parts of the claim. His Honour Judge Simmons declined to follow *Pittman Estate v. Bain*[15] and rejected the argument suggested in paragraph 12–006 above, concluding that there was not "in this instance" a contractual relationship between the claimant and the defendant.[16]

12–008   **Private patients.** Where a medical practitioner is privately engaged, he owes a contractual duty to attend and treat the patient and to exercise reasonable skill and care in so doing.[17] In *Morris v. Winsbury-White*[18] the defendant surgeon agreed to perform an operation on the claimant and to give the case his personal attention. It was argued on behalf of the claimant that this undertaking imposed upon the defendant a greater responsibility than normally fell upon a surgeon. Tucker J. rejected the contention:

> "Mr Winsbury-White did say that he had pledged himself in terms to give this case his personal attention, although he agreed with me that in fact, in his view, that made very little difference as to the nature of his obligations. Of course, in any event his obligation was to perform the operation, and to give the necessary supervision thereafter until the discharge of the patient. I think it is, therefore, involved in that Mr Winsbury-White did expressly or impliedly intimate that the case would have his personal attention. Whether you call it a special contract or not is quite immaterial because, in my view, it merely emphasises, if necessary, or it merely contains, all the necessary ingredients of the ordinary case where a surgeon is retained to perform an operation of this kind. It is necessarily involved that he will perform the operation personally, and I think that it was necessarily involved in such a retainer that he would pay such subsequent visits as were necessary in the ordinary case."[19]

12–009   It has been suggested that there is also an (apparently separate) implied contractual duty "to act at all times in the best interests of the patient".[20] It is submitted that there are difficulties in treating this as one of the usual terms to be

---

[15] n. 12 above.

[16] While Judge Simmonds quite properly restricted his conclusions to the particular facts of *Reynolds* it is submitted that the same result will be reached in virtually every case where services have been provided to a patient under the National Health Services Act 1977. While the Judge accepted that a situation could arise in which there existed a mutual intention on the part of patient and healthcare provider to create contractual relations and so depart from the statutory framework established under the National Health Services Act 1977, it is difficult to envisage such an event in practice. It is therefore submitted that only in truly extraordinary circumstances will a National Health Service patient be able demonstrate the existence of a contractual relationship with those treating him.

[17] See *Shiells and Thorne v. Blackburne* (1789) 1 H.Bl. 158; *Eyre v. Measday* [1986] 1 All E.R. 488; *Thake v. Maurice* [1986] Q.B. 644; Supply of Goods and Services Act 1982, s.13.

[18] [1937] 4 All E.R. 494.

[19] *ibid.* at 500 A-D.

[20] "The relationship between doctor and patient is contractual in origin, the doctor performing services in consideration for fees payable by the patient. The doctor, obedient to the high standards set by the medical profession impliedly contracts to act at all times in the best interests of the patient": *per* Lord Templeman in *Sidaway v. Governors of Bethlem Royal Hospital* [1985] A.C. 871, 904B. The *ratio* of this decision (it is submitted) is contained in the speeches of Lord Diplock and Lord Bridge. The passage here quoted is *obiter*. See also *R. v. Mid Glamorgan Family Health Services Authority, ex p. Martin* [1994] 5 Med. L.R. 383, 394–397 *per* Nourse L.J. (considering whether the common law confers a right of access to medical records).

implied into contracts for medical treatment.[21] If the patient's condition cannot be correctly diagnosed by the exercise of reasonable skill and care, the doctor will not know what action is in the best interests of the patient. If the suggested implied term is qualified to take account of such objections as this, the term would seem to add nothing to the implied contractual duty to exercise reasonable skill and care on the patient's behalf.

Medicine is perhaps the classic example of a profession in which results are   **12–010** not guaranteed and are not expected to be guaranteed.[22] However, it is open to the medical practitioner in any given case to contract or warrant that the proposed treatment will be successful. Indeed, in *Thake v. Maurice*[23] it was held at first instance that the defendant surgeon had done precisely this, albeit unwittingly.[24] The Court of Appeal, by a majority, reversed this part of the decision.[25] In *Worster v. City and Hackney Health Authority*[26] the claimant signed a consent form for a sterilisation operation which included the words "we understand that this means we can have no more children". Garland J. held that this was not a representation that the operation was bound to be successful. It is plain from these authorities that very clear words must be used before a medical practitioner will be held to have undertaken a contractual obligation to achieve success in his treatment.

(ii) *Statutory duties*

Where a contract between a patient and a medical practitioner involves a transfer   **12–011** of goods, there are statutory implied terms as to quality and fitness for purpose.[27] In *Samuels v. Davis*[28] a dentist who agreed to make a denture for his patient was held in breach of an implied warranty as to fitness for purpose when the denture did not fit.

The question whether the statutory warranties are implied where treatment   **12–012** involves the supply of drugs, prosthetics or products of biological origin—such

---

[21] By contrast, it has been suggested that there is a positive duty to withdraw treatment where its continuance is not in the best interests of a patient who is incapable of making decisions about his treatment: see *Airedale N.H.S. Trust v. Bland* [1993] A.C. 789, 819C *per* Butler-Sloss L.J., *obiter*. This suggestion was not adopted by the House of Lords: compare the dicta at 868H *per* Lord Goff, at 877A *per* Lord Lowry and at 884A *per* Lord Browne-Wilkinson. The decision is best understood as dealing with the lawfulness of treatment in the contexts of the law of trespass and the criminal law rather than as defining the scope of duties of care in contract or tort.

[22] See, for example, *Eyre v. Measday* [1986] 1 All E.R. 488: held that the defendant contracted to carry out a sterilisation operation; he did not contract to render the claimant absolutely sterile. Jones J. reached the same conclusion in *Grey v. Webster* (1984) 14 D.L.R. (4th) 706 (New Brunswick).

[23] [1986] Q.B. 644. For the facts see para. 12–228, below.

[24] "I am left in little doubt that the defendant did not intend to enter into a contract which absolutely guaranteed sterility; nor did he use any such word as "guarantee". But the test as to what the contract in fact was does not depend upon what the plaintiffs or the defendant thought it meant, but upon what the court objectively determines that the words used meant. . . . I have been driven . . . to the conclusion that the contract was to make the male plaintiff irreversibly sterile": *ibid*. at 657D and 658C *per* Peter Pain J.

[25] [1986] Q.B. 644. The Court of Appeal applied broadly the same objective test as the trial judge, but on the evidence the majority came to the opposite conclusion. They attached considerable weight to "the common experience of mankind" that the results of medical treatment are uncertain. This reasoning is supported by A. Grubb in a case note: "Failed sterilisation: Is a Claim in Contract or Negligence a Guarantee of Success?" [1986] C.L.J. 196.

[26] *The Times*, June 22, 1987.

[27] Supply of Goods and Services Act 1982, s.4, as amended by the Sale and Supply of Goods Act 1994.

[28] [1943] K.B. 526.

as blood products or donated semen used in artificial insemination procedures—has given rise to a number of cases.[29]

12–013   In the case of *Richardson v. LRC Products Ltd*[30] the claimant became pregnant when a condom failed during sexual intercourse when the teat end became detached. She and her husband already had two children and considered their family to be complete, and she brought an action for damages in respect of the cost of the upbringing of the resulting third child. The claim was brought under the provisions of the Consumer Protection Act 1987 (which came into force on March 1, 1988) on the basis that (1) the failure of the condom had been caused by a weakening of the latex as a result of ozone damage before the condom left the factory, and (2) that the fact of the fracture of the condom indicated the existence of a defect for the purposes of the Act in any event. Ian Kennedy J. found that the claimant had not established that ozone damage to the condom had caused the failure, and that she had not established by the failure of the condom alone that there had been a defect in the condom for which the defendants were liable.

12–014   The case of *A and Others v. The National Blood Authority and Others*[31] explored the defendants' liability for the supply of defective blood products under the Consumer Protection Act 1987 at great length. The claimants had been infected with Hepatitis C from March 1, 1988 to September 1, 1991 through transfusion of blood and blood products supplied by the defendants. Burton J. held that the infected blood was defective within the meaning of the Consumer Protection Act (and the Product Liability Directive 1985/374 by which the extent of the statutory obligation was defined), and that the defendants were liable to the claimants. After detailed analysis of the obligation on the defendants, Burton J. said:

> "I see no difficulty . . . in an analysis which is akin to contract or warranty. Recital 6 [of the Product Liability Directive 1985/374] (" . . . the defectiveness of the product should be determined by reference not to its fitness for use but to the lack of safety which the public at large are entitled to expect") does not in my judgment counter-indicate an approach analogous to contract, but is concerned to emphasise that it is safety which is paramount".[32]

---

[29] Courts in Canada and Australia have considered whether a term of this nature can be implied at common law where medical treatment includes the supply of blood products and donated semen, so as to impose strict contractual liability when those substances are the conduit for infection by the HIV virus. In *ter Neuzen v. Korn* (1995) 127 D.L.R. (4th) 577, Supreme Court of Canada, and *E. v. Australian Red Cross Society* (1991) 105 A.L.R. 53, Aus. Fed. CA; [1991] 2 Med.L.R. 303, the implication was rejected, on the basis that the supply of blood by transfusion was merely an incident of the provision of medical services. A separate contract for the supply of goods could not be identified. The same result was achieved in the Canadian case of *Pittman v. Bain* (1994) 112 D.L.R. (4th) 257. Lang J. held that donated semen administered for the purposes of artificial insemination was not supplied subject to a warranty that it was free from disease. As a biological product (as opposed to manufactured equipment and supplies), the safety of donated semen was difficult to monitor. There are difficulties in applying this argument to blood products, many of which undergo some manufacturing process before use in treatment, and to drugs which are derived from biological sources (*e.g.* some hormones). The question in English law in a consideration of whether or not a warranty of fitness for purpose is to implied into the contract between the patient and the medical practitioner will be whether such products are "goods" within the meaning of the 1982 Act. However it is submitted that there is no good reason why "manufactured" or altered biological products should be treated any differently from other products of non-biological origin, and the effect of the Consumer Protection Act 1987 on the supply of blood products in the U.K. is set out in para. 12–014 below.
[30] [2000] Lloyd's Rep. Med. 280.
[31] [2001] Lloyd's Rep. Med. 187.
[32] *ibid.* at 218, para. 66.

(iii) *Common Law Duty of Care*

It has long been accepted that a medical practitioner owes a duty to exercise **12–015** reasonable skill and care in his treatment of a patient, even where no contract exists between them.[33] In *Gladwell v. Steggall*[34] for example, the claimant, a 10-year-old girl, complained of a pain in her knee. Her father summoned the defendant, a clergyman who "also practised as a medical man". In this instance his treatment had disastrous consequences. Tindal C.J. ruled that the claimant was entitled to succeed despite the absence of any contract between them: "The declaration is not framed as in an action on a contract, but alleges a breach of duty arising out of the employment of the defendant by the plaintiff . . . this is an action *ex delicto*." The medical practitioner assumes a duty of care to the patient, even when he renders his services gratuitously[35] or entirely voluntarily, for example by attending the victim of a road accident.[36] It is submitted that the correct approach in a "rescue" case will always be to analyse precisely what the medical practitioner has taken it upon himself to do. If he has continued to take some responsibility for an accident victim beyond initial first aid he may assume a duty of care which is no longer limited to not making matters worse.

The duty of care in tort is additional to any contractual duties which may be **12–016** owed.[37] Where, therefore, a medical practitioner has been privately engaged by the claimant, it is normal to plead the claim both in contract and tort. Damage is a necessary element of the cause of action in tort. If a claimant shows that a doctor was negligent and in breach of contractual duties that were owed to him, but fails to prove that any loss or injury was caused thereby, then he will be entitled to recover nominal damages in respect of the breach of contract but nothing in respect of his claim in tort—in the latter case he will not be entitled to nominal damages and his claim will be dismissed.[38]

---

[33] *Pippin v. Sheppard* (1822) 11 Price 400; *Pimm v. Roper* (1862) 2 F. & F. 783; *Edgar v. Lamont*, 1914 S.C. 277. In extremely limited circumstances breach of the practitioner's duty might not be actionable. For example, in *Derry v. Ministry of Defence* [1999] P.I.Q.R. P204 the Court of Appeal held that the M.O.D. was entitled to rely upon the statutory immunity from liability in tort conferred by s.10 of the Crown Proceedings Act 1947 to defeat a soldier's claim that a military doctor had negligently failed to diagnose and treat his carcinoma. The case is an oddity: following repeal by the Crown Proceedings (Armed Forces) Act 1987 the provisions of s. 10 of the 1947 act only remained in force in respect of acts or omissions committed before May 15, 1987.

[34] (1839) 5 Bing.(N.C.) 733.

[35] See, *e.g. Goode v. Nash* (1979) 21 S.A.S.R. 419: defendant held liable for negligence, whilst giving his services gratuitously at a public screening for the detection of glaucoma.

[36] The existence of a duty of care in such circumstances was confirmed *obiter* by the Court of Appeal in *Capital & Counties plc v. Hampshire County Council* [1997] Q.B. 1004 at 1035D-E. However in giving the judgment of the Court, Stuart-Smith L.J. remarked that in such circumstances a doctor would be under no general obligation to provide assistance to such a victim and would only owe a duty of care to the victim should he choose to do so. Even then "if he volunteers his assistance his only duty as a matter of law is not to make the victim's condition worse" at 1035D-E.

[37] The relationship between contractual and tortious duties has not generated the same amount of controversy in the case of doctors as it has in respect of other professions, no doubt because the damage caused is normally personal injury. The commencement of the relationship of doctor and private patient will depend upon the time and circumstances of formation of the contract.

[38] See, *e.g. Rich v. Pierpont* (1862) 3 F. & F. 35; *Fish v. Kapur* [1948] 2 All E.R. 176; *Barnett v. Chelsea and Kensington Hospital Management Committee* [1969] 1 Q.B. 428; *Robinson v. Post Office* [1974] 1 W.L.R. 1176. But it is submitted that it would now be surprising to permit a claim to be litigated if nominal damages for breach of contract were all that were realistically being pursued. Unless a claimant could demonstrate that for some reason it was appropriate for such a case to be fought it is likely that it would be struck out under CPR 3.4.

12–017   The duty of care arises out of the relationship of doctor and patient. The relationship and the duty are created when the doctor accepts the patient for treatment.[39] This clearly takes place when a person is accepted onto a general practitioner's list[40] or presents himself at hospital for treatment.[41]

12–018   It is important in light of the House of Lords' decision in *South Australia Asset Management Corp v. York Montague Ltd*[42] to avoid attempting to define the scope of a defendant's duty of care in a vacuum. Lord Hoffman's illustrative example concerned negligence by a doctor: the likelihood is that problems as to the extent of a doctor's duty of care are more likely to arise in cases of advice than in treatment. But an example can be given: in an obstetric case the allegation was that the obstetrician should have diagnosed gestational diabetes in the mother, and that in consequence the baby should have been delivered not later than term. In fact the pregnancy was allowed to continue beyond term, and the baby was injured *in utero* at about 10 days after term by an unforeseen and unforeseeable ischaemic event which was unrelated to the gestational diabetes. The question is whether the doctor (on the assumption that he was negligent in failing to diagnose diabetes) should be liable for the injuries caused to the baby by the unrelated ischaemic event—which would have been avoided if the baby had been delivered at term. It is submitted that such injuries would be outside the scope of the duty breached by the doctor, and that he should not be liable.[43]

12–019   **The doctor as rescuer.** Since there is no obligation to rescue at common law—only an obligation not to make the condition of a victim worse[44]—a doctor might be thought to be under no duty to attend and treat a person who has not hitherto been his patient, even in an emergency.[45] However, in *Lowns v. Woods*[46] the Court of Appeal of New South Wales held that a doctor did owe a duty to attend a person in urgent need of medical care where a direct request had been made for him to do so and there was no reasonable impediment preventing him from attending. The claimant was an 11-year-old boy suffering a prolonged epileptic fit. His 14-year-old sister went on foot to a nearby surgery to summon a doctor. The defendant general practitioner refused to attend, allegedly advising that the child should be brought to his surgery. Applying the test of proximity outlined in *Sutherland Shire Council v. Heyman*[47] the majority in the Court of

[39] *Jones v. Manchester Corporation* [1952] 2 Q.B. 852, 867A *per* Denning L.J.
[40] See the National Health Service (General Medical Services) Regulations 1992 (S.I. 1992 No. 635).
[41] *Barnett v. Chelsea and Kensington Hospital Management Committee* [1969] 1 Q.B. 428, 435D–436B *per* Nield L.J. The time when the relationship commences between a person and a consultant to whom he is referred by his general practitioner is more difficult to identify. It is probably the point at which the consultant decides to accept the referral since the letter of referral may contain information which bears upon whether the patient should be seen urgently or not.
[42] [1997] A.C. 191.
[43] This decision was reached, *obiter*, in the unreported case of *O'Reilly v. Whittington Hospital NHS Trust* by H.H.J. Mackay, sitting as a deputy judge of the QBD, on March 17, 2000. See also *Brown v. Lewisham and North Southwark H.A.* [1999] 4 Lloyd's Rep. Med. 110 at 118.
[44] See n. 37 above.
[45] In *Barnes v. Crabtree, The Times,* November 1 and 2, 1955, it was conceded on behalf of the defendant general practitioner that his duty was to treat any person in an emergency. A general practitioner's contract with a health authority (formerly with a family health services authority, but now see the Health Authorities Act 1995, s.1) requires him on request to visit anyone in his practice area who is involved in an accident or an emergency: see the NHS (General Medical Services) Regulations 1992 (S.I. 1992 No. 635).
[46] (1996) Aust. Tort Reports 63,151, New South Wales CA.
[47] (1985) 157 C.L.R. 424 and see Chap. 2, para. 2–38

Appeal[48] found that there was sufficient proximity between the doctor and the claimant for a duty of care to arise. Relevant to the existence of such duty were (a) his physical proximity to the patient, (b) the "causal proximity" created by the information given to the doctor and his consequent understanding that this was a life-threatening emergency with dire likely consequences if he did not treat, and (c) the "circumstantial proximity". The last was created by the facts, *inter alia*, that the doctor was competent and equipped to treat, he was called upon at his surgery during surgery hours and no personal health or safety risk or existing disability prevented him from responding to the appeal for his professional services. It is doubtful whether *Lowns v. Woods* would be found in England to support a general duty to attend and treat a non-patient in an emergency.[49] Whether any duty arises, and the extent of such a duty, will depend upon detailed consideration of the particular factual circumstances of any case in which it is alleged and the application of ordinary "duty of care" principles.[50] In the context of a rescuing doctor the most important consideration will be the extent (if any) to which he has assumed responsibility for the victim, or is deemed to have done so.

The ambulance service. The case of *Kent v. Griffiths*[51] is worthy of note in this regard. The London Ambulance Service was telephoned by the claimant's general practitioner and asked to send an ambulance to the claimant's home to take the claimant, who had suffered an asthma attack, to hospital "immediately". Despite two further telephone calls being made, and reassurances being given that an ambulance was on its way, no ambulance arrived for 40 minutes. Shortly before she arrived at hospital the claimant suffered a respiratory arrest leading to brain damage. In the claim against the ambulance service Turner J.[52] found that, once four qualifying "conditions" had been satisfied, the ambulance service owed a duty to attend a member of the public within a reasonable time.[53] In finding that those conditions had indeed been satisfied on the facts of the case he also remarked that he:

12–020

" . . . should have found it offensive to and inconsistent with concepts of common humanity if in circumstances such as the present where there had been an unreasonable and unexplained delay in providing the service which [the defendant was] in a position

---

[48] Mahoney J.A., dissenting, considered that any such duty would need extensive qualification and ought to be imposed, if at all, by the legislature.

[49] In this regard see the *obiter* remarks of Stuart-Smith L.J. in *Capital & Counties plc v. Hampshire County Council* [1997] Q.B. 1004 at 1035D-E, at n.37, above. See also L. Haberfield, "*Lowns v. Woods* and the duty to rescue" (1998) 6 Tort L.Rev 56 for a critical analysis of the majority judgments and their failure to reconcile the decisions reached with the established common law principle (and the exceptions to that principle) that there is no duty to rescue, R. Martin, "Further Thoughts on the Liability of Rescuers" (1998) 6 Tort L.Rev. 113 and the commentary on *Lowns v. Woods* at (1998) 6 Med.L.Rev. 126.

[50] See Chap. 2 at paras 2–13–2–53. See S. Smith, "Rights, Remedies and Normal Expectations in Tort and Contract" (1997) 113 L.Q.R. 426 for a further discussion on duties to assist.

[51] [2001] Q.B. 36.

[52] [1999] Lloyd's Rep. Med. 424.

[53] The four qualifying conditions were that (1) there had been an initiating call to the ambulance service, with sufficient information being provided to enable the ambulance service to understand the nature of the request for its services, (2) the ambulance service must have allocated an ambulance to meet the request, (3) the ambulance service must have been informed that time was of the essence, and (4) the ambulance must have failed to arrive at the casualty within a reasonable time: see at 453.

to meet, and had accepted that it would supply an ambulance, the law could not in its turn provide a remedy to the person whose condition was significantly exacerbated in consequence."[54]

12–021　　The ambulance service appealed on the sole ground that it owed no duty of care to members of the public to provide an ambulance within a reasonable time in response to a 999 telephone call. The Court of Appeal dismissed the appeal, rejecting the defendant's argument that as a "rescuer" its only duty when responding to 999 telephone calls was not to add to damage already suffered by a claimant. In the only substantive judgment, Lord Woolf M.R. stated[55]:

> "Here what was being provided was a health service. In the case of health services under the Act of 1977 the conventional situation is that there is a duty of care. Why should the position of an ambulance staff be different from that of doctors or nurses ? . . . The ambulance service is part of the health service. Its care function includes the transporting of patients to and from hospital when the use of an ambulance for this purpose is desirable. It is therefore appropriate to regard [the defendant] as providing services of the category provided by hospitals and not as providing services equivalent to those rendered by the police or fire service.[56]
>
> . . .
>
> The fact that it was a person who foreseeably would suffer further injuries by a delay in providing an ambulance, when there was no reason why it should not be provided, is important in establishing the necessary proximity and thus duty of care in this case. In other words, as there were no circumstances which made it unfair or unreasonable or unjust that liability should exist, there is no reason why there should not be liability if the arrival of the ambulance was delayed for no good reason."

12–022　　**Communication of information.** A doctor will generally be found to owe a duty of care to his patient to avoid physical or psychological injury caused by his advice, treatment or diagnosis.[57] One area where there may still be some uncertainty concerns the communication of bad or distressing news to a claimant. In two recent cases defendant health authorities have conceded that they owed a duty to individuals to whom they were transmitting information to take reasonable care to ensure both that the information was correct and that it was

---

[54] At 453.

[55] [2001] Q. B. 36 at 52G–54B, paras 45 and 49.

[56] The Court of Appeal therefore distinguished its earlier decision in *Capital & Counties plc v. Hampshire County Council* [1997] Q.B. 1004; see para. 12–015, n. 36.

[57] See, for example, *Kralj v. McGrath and St Theresa's Hospital* [1986] 1 All E.R. 54 (damages for psychiatric illness caused by negligent treatment). In *M (a Minor) v. Newham LBC*, reported *sub nom. X (Minors) v. Bedfordshire County Council* [1995] 2 A.C. 633 a mother and child claimed damages for psychiatric illness occasioned by their separation as a result of the alleged negligence of a psychiatrist employed by the defendant authority. The claims were struck out on other grounds but in relation to recoverability for psychiatric injury Sir Thomas Bingham M.R. observed, "It would be little short of absurd if the child were held to be disentitled to claim damages for injury of the very type which the psychiatrist should have been exercising her skill to try and prevent", *ibid.* at 664C. The issue was not mentioned by the House of Lords: *ibid.* In *Page v. Smith* [1996] A.C. 155, a road traffic accident case, a majority in the House of Lords held that where personal injury to the claimant was foreseeable, liability would accrue for psychiatric injury even although physical injury did not occur. The implications of this decision for medical negligence law are discussed at para. 12– 283, below.

communicated in a competent manner.[58] While no doubt justifiable on the peculiar facts of each case, these concessions have been the subject of academic criticism[59] and, it is submitted, were inconsistent with the existing authorities. They should not be taken as necessarily implying that in all cases in which incorrect news is communicated to a patient or in which correct news is communicated to a patient in an improper manner, the communicating authority will be liable for psychological injury suffered by the receiving party. Each case will turn on its own facts and will no doubt depend upon the degree of proximity between the parties, the extent to which psychological harm is a reasonably foreseeable consequence of the authority's actions and whether it is fair, just and reasonable in the circumstances to impose a duty to care to prevent such harm.[60]

An example of a case in which a duty to avoid the risk of psychiatric harm was **12-023** found to exist is *CJD Group B v. The Medical Research Council*.[61] In that case each of the claimants had suffered from dwarfism as a child. For the purposes of a preliminary issue to determine the scope of the defendants' duty of care, it was assumed that each claimant had received injections of human growth hormone after July 1, 1977, despite the defendants being aware by that date that the injections carried a potentially lethal dose of the CJD agent. Each of the claimants had learned subsequently of the devastating and potentially fatal consequences of contracting CJD and, again for the purposes of the preliminary issue, it was assumed that each had a psychiatric injury derived from their awareness that "they may develop" CJD. In concluding that the defendants did owe a duty to the claimants to avoid the risk of psychiatric injury from subsequent discovery of the risks that they faced, Morland J. found that:

> "the defendants . . . could only have concluded that the risk of CJD becoming a reality could occur within a huge time span, that is within a year or two after injection or within many decades after injection . . .
>
> . . . the evidence shows that the defendants not only should have reasonably foreseen the risk of psychiatric injury but did in fact do so."[62]

---

[58] *AB v. Tameside and Glossop Health Authority* [1997] 8 Med. L.R. 91, *Allin v. City & Hackney Health Authority* [1996] 7 Med. L.R. 167. In *AB v. Tameside and Glossop Health Authority* a health worker employed by the defendant authority was diagnosed HIV positive. By letter the authority informed patients and former patients who had received obstetric treatment from the worker that there was a remote risk that they had been infected. Several of the individuals informed in this way claimed to have suffered psychological injury as a result of receiving the news in this way and alleged that the authority had acted negligently in failing to arrange for communication of the information via general practitioners or other health workers qualified to provide appropriate counselling. The authority conceded that it owed a duty to those to take care when communicating news of this nature. In *Allin* the claimant had been told that her newly born baby was dead when in fact it was still alive. She suffered psychiatric harm as a result of this inaccurate news. The defendant authority accepted that it was "under a duty of care in respect of statements of this sort made to the other".

[59] Dziobon and Tettenborn, "When the truth hurts: the incompetent transmission of distressing news" (1997) 13 P.N. 70; M. Jones, "Negligently inflicted psychiatric harm: is the word mightier than the deed?" (1997) 13 P.N. 111. For further comment see (1998) 6 Med. L.Rev. 338.

[60] See also *Bancroft v. Harrogate Health Authority* [1997] 8 Med. L.R. 398, a case in which the claimant sought to recover damages for psychiatric damage resulting, *inter alia*, from the manner in which a consultant had failed adequately to explained her condition to her, and failed adequately to explain to her a plan of treatment in which she could have confidence. The claim failed on the facts, but it seems to have been implicitly accepted that the claim made, if proved, would have justified an award of damages.

[61] [2000] Lloyd's Rep. Med. 161.

[62] *ibid.* at 166.

12–024   **Economic losses.** Whether a duty is owed to take care to avoid causing purely financial loss is also unclear. In *Stevens v. Bermondsey & Southwark Group Hospital Management Committee*[63] the claimant was involved in an accident caused by an employee of the borough council. He was treated at the defendant hospital and, on the strength of what he was told about the seriousness of his condition by the casualty officer, settled his claim against the council for a small sum. Subsequently learning that he had a serious congenital condition which had been activated by the accident, he alleged that, but for the casualty officer's negligence, he would have settled his claim for a larger sum. The action failed. Paull J. held that the doctor's duty was limited to the sphere of medicine and that a doctor was not required to bear in mind possible third party liability to his patient save in special circumstances.[64] The decision might be understood as limiting the scope of a doctor's duty of care to exclude recovery for economic loss which is not consequent upon physical or psychological injury, save where the doctor knows or ought to know that reliance will be placed upon his negligent advice in a way which will directly affect the patient's economic fortunes.[65] In the latter circumstances, it is difficult to see why liability for economic loss caused by negligent advice (or the performance of other medical services) should not now be founded upon the principle in *Hedley Byrne & Co. Ltd v. Heller & Partners Ltd*[66] at least where the claimant is the direct recipient of such advice or services and relies upon them.[67]

12–025   In *Kapfunde v. Abbey National plc and another*[68] the claimant had applied for employment with the first defendant and had completed a medical questionnaire in which she disclosed a history of sickle cell anaemia. The defendant declined to employ the claimant after its part-time occupational health adviser, the second defendant, had assessed the claimant as being unsuitable for employment on the grounds that her medical history made her likely to have an above-average level of absences from work. The claimant alleged that the second defendant's conclusions were negligent and brought an action seeking damages for economic loss. The claim failed. While concluding that "financial loss is clearly foreseeable if a careless error in the doctor's assessment leads to the loss of an opportunity of employment"[69] Millett L.J. (with whom Hutchison L.J. agreed) confirmed that

---

[63] (1963) 107 S.J. 478.

[64] It was found that the claimant's claim against the council severed the chain of causation between the casualty officer's negligence and the loss claimed. See paras 12–303–12–305, below.

[65] See, for example, *McGrath v. Kiely & Powell* [1965] I.R. 497: the claimant recovered the difference between damages awarded to him in a third party action, and those which would have been awarded but for a negligent omission in a medical report prepared for the purposes of the litigation. See also *Kelly v. Lundgard* (1996) 40 Alta.L.R (3d) 234 where Veit J. reached a similar result in the Alberta Queen's Bench Division. However, the author of a medical report prepared for disclosure in the third party action (rather than for the primary purpose of advising as to the merits of the action) will enjoy immunity from suit in respect of its contents: see *Landall v. Dennis, Faulkner & Alsop* [1994] 5 Med.L.R. 268. Cited with approval by the Court of Appeal in *Stanton v. Callaghan* [2000] Q.B. 75, which was followed in *Raiss v. Paimano* [2001] P.N.L.R. 21. Cf. the position of a doctor who provides a report in respect of his patient's injuries for use in negotiations before litigation has begun. Such a doctor will not enjoy immunity from suit as a witness since the report will not be preliminary to his giving evidence as an expert: *Hughes v. Lloyd's Bank plc* [1998] P.I.Q.R. P.98, CA.

[66] [1964] A.C. 465. In *Henderson v. Merrett Syndicates* [1995] 2 A.C. 145, the House of Lords accepted that the principle applies to the performance of professional services generally and is not limited to the provision of advice or information.

[67] See *Goodwill v. British Pregnancy Advisory Service* [1996] 2 All E.R. 161, discussed at para. 12–046 below.

[68] [1999] Lloyd's Rep. Med. 48, CA. *Kapfunde* is considered further at para. 12–305 below.

[69] *ibid.* at 56.

"this is not enough". Such duties that were owed by the defendant's adviser were owed to the defendant alone; the adviser had assumed no responsibility to the claimant to take care to ensure that his conclusions were accurate. In reaching this conclusion the Court of Appeal disapproved the decision of Robert Owen Q.C. in *Baker v. Kaye*,[70] which was to the effect that a doctor who had made a pre-employment assessment of a claimant, which included a physical examination and the taking of blood samples, owed him a duty of care.[71]

The claimant's claim for economic loss also failed in *R. v. Croydon Health*   **12–026**
Authority.[72] In that case the claimant had undergone a pre-employment chest X-ray which ought to have alerted the radiologist to a significant abnormality from which a diagnosis of primary pulmonary hypertension (PPH) would have been made. It was common ground that pregnancy presents a threat to life in a PPH sufferer. The claimant's evidence was that, had she received such a diagnosis and been properly advised, she would at all costs have avoided becoming pregnant. Instead, the radiologist negligently passed the claimant as being fit for work. The claimant was then employed by the defendant Health Authority and subsequently became pregnant and gave birth to a healthy child, although excessive bleeding led to her undergoing a hysterectomy. She sought to recover damages for *inter alia* the costs of raising the child. The Court of Appeal concluded that the scope of the duty owed by the radiologist stopped short of "responsibility for the consequences of the decision, by the plaintiff and her husband, that she should become pregnant".[73]

The most recent consideration of the circumstances in which a duty to avoid   **12–027**
causing financial loss might arise occurred in *Phelps v. Hillingdon LBC*.[74] In that case educational psychologists employed by the defendant had assessed the claimants at school so as to advise the defendant as to the educational needs of each. The defendant had failed to diagnose that three of the claimants suffered from dyslexia. They had therefore received no special schooling. The claimants alleged that such failure had been negligent and had led to them suffering a lack of educational progress with *inter alia* a consequent reduction in their earning potential in later life. The first claimant succeeded in demonstrating that a duty of care was owed to her by the defendant to take reasonable care when carrying out an educational assessment of her needs, and that a reduction in her level of achievement and a loss of employment and wages was a reasonably foreseeable consequence of that duty being breached. The House of Lords expressly rejected the defendant's argument that any duty owed by its educational psychologists could be owed to them alone.[75]

Fiduciary duties. The relationship of doctor and patient is capable of being   **12–028**
characterised as a fiduciary relationship.[76] However, the case of *Bristol & West plc v. Mothew*[77] now makes clear that a claim for breach of a fiduciary duty will not arise merely because a defendant who stands in a fiduciary relationship to a

---

[70] [1997] I.R.L.R. 219, discussed at para. 12–064 below.
[71] *Kapfunde v. Abbey National* [1999] Lloyd's Rep. Med. 48 at 53, CA.
[72] [1998] Lloyd's Rep. Med. 44.
[73] *ibid.* at 60.
[74] [2000] 3 W.L.R. 776.
[75] Lord Slynn at 791C, Lord Nicholls at 803E-G, Lord Clyde at 811H.
[76] *Barclays Bank plc v. O'Brien* [1994] 1 A.C. 180, 189G *per* Lord Browne-Wilkinson.
[77] [1998] Ch. 1, CA.

claimant has breached a duty of care at common law that he owes to the claimant. Such a claim will only arise when the duty breached can truly be characterised as a fiduciary duty.[78]

12–029   It is accepted that a presumption of undue influence may unravel dispositions of property or finance in favour of a doctor who has abused the confidence of his patient.[79] It has been suggested that further development of the concept of fiduciary duties owed by doctors would be a useful complement to the law of negligence, particularly where questions arise as to the extent of the doctor's duty to disclose the risks and implications of proposed treatment, allowing the imposition of more extensive duties than would currently arise in contract or tort.[80] This analysis at one time gained limited support in Canada, where the Supreme Court has founded entitlement to access to medical records upon the fiduciary nature of the doctor–patient relationship[81] and has treated sexual exploitation of a patient by a doctor as breach of fiduciary duty[82] before being rejected in favour of a more traditional approach to fiduciary duty by McLachlin J. in *Smith v. Arndt*.[83] The analysis has been rejected by the High Court of Australia in the context of a claim for access to medical records.[84]

12–030   The nature and extent of a doctor's fiduciary obligations in a range of factual situations has yet to be fully explored in the English courts. The analysis did not find favour in *Sidaway v. Governors of Bethlem Royal Hospital*,[85] a decision concerning the extent of the duty to warn of the risks and implications of proposed treatment. In *R. v. Mid Glamorgan Family Health Services Authority, ex p. Martin*[86] the claimant asserted an entitlement at common law to access to his medical records, which were made before the Access to Health Records Act 1990 came into force.[87] The claimant argued that the health authority owed him a fiduciary duty to disclose to him all the information contained in his medical records. Ruling that there was no common law right to access, Popplewell J.

---

[78] For the facts of *Bristol & West plc v. Mothew* and for further discussion see Chap. 10, para. 10–023 above.

[79] See *Sidaway v. Governors of Bethlem Royal Hospital* [1984] Q.B. 498, 515D-G *per* Dunn L.J. and the authority there cited.

[80] See A. Grubb, "The Doctor as Fiduciary" (1994) C.L.P. 311. *Cf.* "The Fiduciary Relationship— Doctors and Patients" in *Wrongs and Remedies in the Twenty-First Century* (P. Birks, ed., 1996) where Professor Kennedy argues that the fiduciary relationship in this context is a "false dawn". See also P. Bartlett, "Doctors as Fiduciaries: Equitable Regulation of the Doctor–Patient Relationship" (1997) 5 Med. L.Rev. 193.

[81] *McInerney v. MacDonald* (1992) 93 D.L.R. (4th) 415 (and see commentary at (1993) 1 Med. L.Rev. 126). But a duty of disclosure of risks which is wider than that imposed in English law has been accepted in Canada without recourse to the fiduciary analysis: see *Reibl v. Hughes* (1980) 114 D.L.R. (3d) 1. In *Arndt v. Smith* [1996] 7 Med. L.R. 108, British Columbia CA, Lambert J.A. relied on a fiduciary analysis in deciding whether damage was caused by breach of a doctor's duty of disclosure.

[82] *Norberg v. Wynrib* (1992) 92 D.L.R. (4th) 449; *Taylor v. McGillivray* (1993) 110 D.L.R. (4th) 64, New Brunswick Court of Queen's Bench (and commentary at (1995) 3 Med. L.Rev. 108).

[83] (1997) 148 D.L.R. (4th) 48 at 63b-d.

[84] *Breen v. Williams* (1996) 138 ALR. 259, declining to follow *McInerney v. MacDonald* (above). Again, the wide duty to disclose which exists in Australian law rests on common law principles only: see *Rogers v. Whitaker* [1993] 4 Med. L.R. 79, High Court of Australia.

[85] See [1984] Q.B. 493, CA, *per* Browne-Wilkinson L.J. at 518F–519E, Dunn L.J. at 515D-G and [1985] 1 A.C. 871, HL, *per* Lord Scarman at 884B.

[86] [1994] 5 Med. L.R. 383. The decision was upheld on appeal, but without mention of the fiduciary analysis: [1995] 1 W.L.R. 110.

[87] On November 1, 1991. The Act applies only to records made after that date.

specifically rejected the argument that the doctor-patient relationship was to be regarded as giving rise to equitable obligations for these purposes.[88]

(b) *Duties to Third Parties*

The general principles governing liability to third parties are stated above.[89] **12–031**
There is little authority concerning the application of those principles to medical practitioners and no unifying principle emerges therefrom. The circumstances in which a duty of care may be owed to a person to whom it is not apt to apply the description "patient" at any stage[90] are discussed below.

In the ordinary way it will be most unusual for a doctor's negligence to cause **12–032**
personal injury to anyone other than his patient. This did happen, however, in the Canadian case *Urbanski v. Patel*[91]: during an operation the defendant removed the patient's only kidney, believing it to be an ovarian cyst. The patient's father gave one of his kidneys in an unsuccessful attempt to save her life. The defendant was held liable for the injury suffered by the father. It seems likely that an English court would adopt the same approach to this situation. Although it has been questioned whether the donor could recover if he were not related to the patient,[92] there would appear to be no logical reason why this should be the case. Provided that:

(i) there exists the necessary degree of proximity between claimant and defendant;

(ii) harm to the claimant is a reasonably foreseeable consequence of the defendant's actions[93]; and

(iii) it is just and reasonable to impose such a duty of care,

a duty of care is likely to be found to exist. It is submitted that the donor ought to recover, even if he is a stranger. The defendant by his negligence has created a situation in which someone must give up an organ if the patient is not to be left to certain death.

The "nervous shock" cases. In *McLoughlin v. O'Brian*[94] the House of Lords **12–033**
recognised a right of action for psychiatric illness caused to a near relative who

---

[88] [1994] 5 Med. L.R. 383, 391.

[89] See Chap. 2 paras. 2–109–2–115, above. For a detailed discussion of this topic, including a review of the United States authorities, see K. C. de Haan, "My Patient's Keeper? The Liability of Medical Practitioners for Negligent Injury to Third Parties" (1986) 2 P.N. 86. See also paras 12–043 to 12–054 below.

[90] The analysis of the majority in *Lowns v. Woods* (1996) Aust. Tort Reports 63, 151, New South Wales Court of Appeal, discussed at para. 12–019, above, is not easy, but presumably the claimant became a patient as soon as the defendant general practitioner came under a duty to attend and treat him. Likewise, the claimant in *Kent v. Griffiths* [2001] Q.B. 36 became a "patient" as soon as the ambulance service accepted the emergency call.

[91] (1978) 84 D.L.R. (3d) 650.

[92] See G. Robertson, "A New Application of the Rescue Principle" (1980) 96 L.Q.R. 19.

[93] It is not generally necessary in the "rescue" case that the defendant should foresee the identity of the rescuer or even the group of people from which the rescuer is likely to come: see *Charlesworth & Percy*, 9th ed. paras 2–142 to 2–145 and the fourth cumulative supplement.

[94] [1983] 1 A.C. 410. For a full discussion of liability for nervous shock, see *Clerk & Lindsell* (18th ed.), paras 7–62 to 7–83.

witnessed the suffering of family members injured in a violent road accident caused by the defendant's negligence, but did not witness the accident itself. This is the so-called "immediate aftermath" extension to the established principle of liability for foreseeable psychiatric illness suffered by a near relative who witnesses the negligent and traumatic infliction of injury or death.

12–034   The cases of *Alcock v. Chief Constable of South Yorkshire Police*[95] and *Frost v. Chief Constable of South Yorkshire Police*[96] both arose out of the Hillsborough football stadium disaster in 1989, when 95 people died and hundreds were injured as a result of overcrowding on a terrace. In *Alcock* the claimants were relatives of those on the terrace, but none was a spouse or parent. Each of the claimants had been present at the stadium, but remote from the terrace, or had witnessed the event live on television or in later news broadcasts. In *Frost* the claimants were police officers who had tended victims of the tragedy, either at the stadium itself or at a hospital to where bodies had subsequently been taken. Each of the claimants claimed damages against the police for nervous shock.

12–035   The primary issue in *Alcock* was whether liability for nervous shock depended upon foreseeability of shock alone. The House of Lords decided that the ambit of liability to "secondary victims" was circumscribed by requirements of proximity in addition to foreseeability of injury. Each of the claimants was foreseeably injured, but each failed to satisfy the test of proximity in one or more of the three required respects, namely, (i) proximity of familial or analogous tie, and propinquity in (ii) time and (iii) space to the horrifying event or its immediate aftermath. In addition, the requirement that the illness complained of be caused by "shock" remains.[97] This is a term of art, serving to distinguish between violent assault on the mind by sight or sound (but not by communication) of a traumatic event and the gradual attrition of mental health by a series of events or a general state of affairs.[98]

12–036   In *Frost* the issue was once again foreseeability of injury. Once again, each of the claimants was a "secondary victim".[99] They were unable to demonstrate either that they had been at risk of physical injury or that they had reasonably perceived themselves to be at risk of physical injury. They did not satisfy the

---

[95] [1992] 1 A.C. 310, HL.

[96] [1999] 2 A.C. 455, HL.

[97] In *Page v. Smith* [1996] A.C. 155, 189 Lord Lloyd described these restrictions on a right to recover damages for psychiatric injury as "control mechanisms", intended to keep liability within what was regarded as acceptable bounds.

[98] *ibid.* at 401F *per* Lord Ackner and 396G and 398G *per* Lord Keith. The control mechanisms set out in *Alcock* were considered and approved by the New Zealand Court of Appeal in the context of a clinical negligence claim in *van Soest v. Residual Health Management Unit* [2000] 1 N.Z.L.R. 179. The claimants were close relatives of individuals who had died during surgery carried out by the defendant. Each sued *inter alia* for mental suffering caused upon learning of their relatives' deaths. The defendant successfully struck out the claims since, even had the claimants been able to demonstrate that mental suffering had been a reasonably foreseeable consequence of the defendant's negligence towards their relatives, they still needed to demonstrate (i) a physical and temporal proximity to the accident, and (ii) that their mental suffering amounted to a recognisable psychiatric disorder or illness. They failed to show this.

[99] The claimants attempted to distinguish themselves from the bereaved relatives who had witnessed the tragedy at the stadium, and so argue that they were in fact primary victims, on the bases that (i) their attendance at the stadium had been pursuant to contracts of employment with the defendant, and/ or (ii) they ought to be classified as "rescuers" by virtue of their actions. Neither argument met with any success.

conditions necessary to found a claim for psychiatric injury and the claimants therefore failed.[1]

A major difficulty in establishing liability for nervous shock in clinical negli- **12–037** gence cases is the need to show that the claimant's psychiatric damage was caused by shock, that is, the sudden and direct appreciation of the horrifying event to which the breach of duty gives rise, as opposed to the stress, anxiety and grief which naturally attend the terminal illness or death of a loved one, or the gradual or even retrospective realisation of events.[2] As the following four cases demonstrate, each case will turn very much on its own facts, although the suddenness with which the claimant learns of or perceives events, and the nature of the event will always be key factors.[3]

In *Taylor v. Somerset Health Authority*[4] the defendants negligently failed to **12–038** diagnose and treat the claimant's husband's heart condition, with the result that he suffered a fatal heart attack at work. Some 35 minutes after his death, the claimant viewed her husband's body in the hospital mortuary, partly because she refused to believe the doctor who told her that he was dead. Her action for damages for psychiatric injury was dismissed. Auld J. held that there was no traumatic event caused by the health authority's negligence which immediately caused injury to the claimant's husband. The heart attack was merely the final consequence of the gradual deterioration in his condition which the defendant had negligently failed to arrest. If there was no qualifying event, there could be no "immediate aftermath". Further, even were the heart attack to be treated as a qualifying event, the claimant did not see her husband's body soon enough after his death to convey to her the shock of the attack as well as its consequence. Similarly, the body bore no marks which would suggest to her the circumstances of death.

In *Sion v. Hampstead Health Authority*[5] the Court of Appeal struck out as **12–039** disclosing no reasonable cause of action the claim of a father who suffered psychiatric damage as a result of witnessing over some two weeks the deterioration and consequent death (allegedly due to medical negligence) of his adult son, who had been injured in a road accident. The Court held that the claim described causation of illness by the claimant's gradual realisation of the seriousness of his son's condition over the two weeks before death and of the possibility of medical

---

[1] *Alcock v. Chief Constable of South Yorkshire* and *Frost v. Chief Constable of South Yorkshire* were considered and applied in *W v. Essex County Council* [2000] 2 W.L.R. 601, HL. In that case the claimants fostered children placed with them by the defendant. They had received an assurance that none of the children would be known sexual abusers. In fact one of the foster children was a known sexual abuser and, in the period during which he was placed with the claimants, he sexually abused the claimants' own children. The claimants alleged that they had suffered psychiatric illness upon learning that their own children had been abused. The House of Lords allowed the claimants' appeal and refused to strike out the claim, concluding that without a full investigation of the facts it would not be possible to determine (i) whether the claimants were primary or secondary victims, or (ii) the scope of the duty of care that was owed to them by the defendants.

[2] But see *Reilly v. Merseyside Health Authority* [1995] 6 Med. L.R. 246, CA, where claimants who suffered apprehension and fear while trapped in a lift by reason of the health authority's negligence could not recover under this principle. They had suffered "normal human emotions" and not a recognised psychiatric illness.

[3] Psychiatric illness on the part of a claimant resulting from a fear of what might have happened to another, or from what the claimant imagines might have happened to another, will not found a claim: *Palmer v. Tees Health Authority* [1999] Lloyd's Rep. Med. 350. For the facts of *Palmer* see para. 12–050 below.

[4] [1993] 4 Med. L.R. 34.

[5] [1994] 5 Med. L.R. 170.

negligence after the inquest, as well as his natural attendant grief, rather than by any sudden and violent appreciation of events. It is noteworthy that, by contrast with the approach of Auld J. in *Taylor v. Somerset Health Authority*, Peter Gibson L.J. made clear that there need be no external traumatic event in such cases, the requirements of suddenness and violence attaching to the impact of the awareness of what has happened upon the claimant's mind, rather than to the relevant events themselves. He said:

> "I see no reason in logic why a breach of duty causing an incident involving no violence or suddenness, such as where the wrong medicine is negligently given to a hospital patient, could not lead to a claim for damages for nervous shock, for example where the negligence has fatal results and a visiting close relative, wholly unprepared for what has occurred, finds the body and thereby sustains a sudden and unexpected shock to the nervous system."[6]

12–040   In *Tredget v. Bexley Health Authority*[7] both parents of a child who died of the effects of asphyxiation two and a half days after its negligently mismanaged birth suffered a psychiatric grief reaction as a result of their experiences during the delivery, the child's death and its intervening illness. It was found that the delivery itself (at which both parents were present, although the mother's awareness was diminished) was a sufficiently traumatic event to have caused the psychiatric damage suffered by the parents. The judge further held that the course of events from the onset of labour to the child's death, a period of some 48 hours, could not realistically be treated as other than a single qualifying event. *Sion v. Hampstead Health Authority* was distinguished on the facts by the greater degree of involvement in and the immediacy of the parents to the birth of the child in *Tredget*.[8]

12–041   Consideration was also given to this issue in *W v. Essex County Council*.[9] In the judgment of the court Lord Slynn concluded[10] that:

> "While . . . there has to be some temporal and spatial limitation on the persons who can claim to be secondary victims . . . it seems to be that the concept of 'the immediate aftermath' of the incident has to be assessed in the particular factual situation. I am not

---

[6] *ibid.* at 176.

[7] [1994] 5 Med. L.R. 178, Central London County Court.

[8] *ibid.* at 184. A similar result was reached in the case of *Farrell v. Merton Sutton & Wandsworth Health Authority*, unreported, July 31, 2000, E. Steel Q.C. The claimant's son was born seriously disabled as a result of the defendant's negligent handling of the birth. The claimant suffered psychological injury as a result of the trauma of the birth and finding out her son's condition. The defendant's argument that there had been no sufficient "trigger", and that the claimant's injuries had resulted from a gradual realisation of her son's disabilities was rejected. The Judge concluded that "in these particular circumstances her sight of the child . . . was in the immediate aftermath of the birth and she would in any event be compensated as a secondary victim." *Cf. Tan v. East London and the City Health Authority* [1999] Lloyd's Rep. Med. 389, Chelmsford C.C. Shortly prior to the birth, the claimant learned that his son had died *in utero*. The death was due to the defendant's negligence. The claimant witnessed the subsequent birth, held the dead baby at delivery and kept vigil of the baby overnight. The following day he witnessed the baby being placed in a metal box. The claimant subsequently suffered depression. The Judge concluded that the death, the stillbirth, the overnight vigil and removal of the body should not be viewed as a single event; the claimant's illness (which the Judge in any event found fell short of a psychiatric injury or disorder) was not therefore the result of a traumatic event caused by the defendant's negligence.

[9] See para. 12–036, n. 1, above.

[10] [2000] 2 W.L.R. 601, HL at 608B–D.

persuaded that in a situation like the present the parents must come across the abuser or the abused 'immediately' after the sexual incident has terminated."

In *Powell v. Boladz*[11] the defendant failed to diagnose a rare disease in the **12–042** claimant's child, who later died as a result. It was alleged that one of the general practitioners then removed and falsified medical records pertaining to the death. The claimant alleged that this substitution of false documents had caused him to suffer psychiatric illness. The Court of Appeal struck out the claim. No duty of care was owed to the claimant in such circumstances. In any event, psychiatric injury was found not to be a foreseeable consequence of falsifying the records.[12]

Injury through contact with the patient. Where the practitioner is treating a **12–043** patient with an infectious disease at his request, he owes a duty of care to persons whom he should foresee are likely to be infected.[13] Injury may foreseeably be caused to third parties unless the patient is warned to take suitable precautions, in which case a duty may be owed to the third party to advise the patient accordingly. In *Pittman Estate v. Bain*[14] the patient contracted the HIV virus through a blood transfusion. His general practitioner failed to inform him that he had been at risk of infection and did not advise him or his wife to take precautions against transmission of the virus to her through sexual contact. The doctor was held liable to the wife when she established that she had caught the virus from her husband and that, had he been warned, they would have taken precautions which would have protected her from infection. It was assumed that a duty of care was owed to the claimant to warn her husband.

The Court of Appeal of California found a duty of care to warn the patient so **12–044** as to prevent infection of a third party in *Reisner v. Regents of the University of California*.[15] The claimant was infected with the HIV virus following a sexual relationship with JL. JL had been negligently infected with the HIV virus following a blood transfusion carried out by the defendant several years earlier when she was 12 years old. The defendant knew that JL had been infected with the HIV virus but had elected not to divulge the information to her or her family. The California Court of Appeal[16] found little difficulty in concluding that:

(i) the defendant owed a duty of care to warn JL and her family that JL was HIV positive;

(ii) JL and/or her family would in all probability have warned the claimant had they been aware that she was HIV positive; and

---

[11] [1998] Lloyd's Rep. Med. 116.
[12] For criticism of this decision see (1998) 6 Med. L.Rev. 112.
[13] *Evans v. Liverpool Corporation* [1906] 1 K.B. 160 (where the defendants escaped liability not because they owed a duty to no one other than their patients, but because they were not vicariously responsible for the negligence of their visiting physician). See also *X and Y v. Pal* (1991) 23 N.S.W.L.R. 26, [1992] 3 Med. L.R. 195, New South Wales Court of Appeal: negligent exposure of foetus to congenital syphilis in the womb. Held not causative of claimant's disfigurement and mental retardation.
[14] (1994) 112 D.L.R. (4th) 257, Ontario High Court.
[15] 37 Cal. Rptr. 2d 518 (1995). There is a commentary on this case at (1997) 5 Med. L.Rev. 250.
[16] Following *Tarasoff v. Regents of University of California* 551 P. 2d 334 (1976); see para. 12–049 below.

(iii) the claimant was a foreseeable victim of the defendant's negligence even though not readily identifiable at the time of the defendant's negligence.

12–045   By analogy with the infection cases, it is suggested that a duty would be owed to both patient and third parties to warn a patient not to undertake an activity which would be hazardous to third parties by reason of debilitating effects of his condition or treatment. Suppose that the patient is an epileptic of whom it is known that his condition is not reliably controlled by medication and that his occupation involves driving heavy goods vehicles. It might reasonably be expected that his doctor would be found to owe a duty of care to other road users to warn the patient not to drive commercial vehicles.[17] The risk of personal injury or death to other road users in the event that the patient suffered a seizure while driving would be a clearly foreseeable result of failure to advise him in appropriate terms. Provided that the patient should have been regarded as likely to heed such a warning, it is arguable the position of the doctor who fails to warn in such a case is indistinguishable from that of the manufacturer who negligently releases into circulation a car with a defective foot-brake. A duty of care would arise on the principle of *Donoghue v. Stevenson*.[18]

12–046   The defendants in *Goodwill v. British Pregnancy Advisory Service*[19] arranged a vasectomy operation for one M in November 1984 and advised him in April 1985 that since the operation had been successful, he need not use contraception in future. In 1988, M began a sexual relationship with the claimant and no contraception was used. The claimant became pregnant by M and gave birth to a daughter. She brought an action against the defendants for the costs associated with the delivery and upbringing of the child, which costs she alleged were caused by her reliance upon the defendant's negligent representations to M in 1985.[20] The Court of Appeal held that the defendant owed no duty of care to the claimant in advising M, for it was not and could not reasonably be alleged that the defendant knew or ought to have known that their advice to M was likely to be acted upon by the claimant. In 1985, she was one of an indeterminately large class of women who might be a future sexual partner of M. Accordingly, there was insufficient proximity between the parties to justify the imposition of a duty in favour of the claimant. Although the class of non-patients to whom a doctor

---

[17] A duty was found on similar facts to those here suggested in *Spillane v. Wasserman* (1992) 13 C.C.L.T. 267, Ontario High Court: doctors treating an epileptic were held liable to a cyclist who was killed when the patient drove a heavy goods vehicle through a red traffic light during an epileptic fit. The doctors had failed to warn him not to drive and had failed to report his condition to the appropriate licensing authority. But see paras 12–049 to 12–051, below.

[18] [1932] A.C. 562. For the application of the principle to the provision of a defective vehicle, see *Herschthal v. Stewart & Ardern Ltd* [1940] 1 K.B. 155.

[19] [1996] 2 All E.R. 161.

[20] The claimant's claim was advanced as a justifiable increment to existing categories of negligence under the principle in *Hedley Byrne v. Heller* [1965] A.C. 465 but was found wanting when analysed by reference to the criteria for proximity elaborated by Lord Oliver in *Caparo Industries plc v. Dickman* [1990] 2 A.C. 605 at 638. See chap. 2, para. 2–31, above. In addition to the features mentioned in the text, the fact that the claimant had consulted her own doctor about the need for contraception was held to amount to foreseeable independent enquiry which rendered her reliance upon the defendant's advice to M unforeseeable: see at 169E-G *per* Peter Gibson L.J. and at 170E-G *per* Thorpe L.J. The claim was struck out.

advising in these circumstances would owe a duty did not arise for decision in this case, the suggestion was that this was limited to a current sexual partner of the patient of whom the doctor is aware and who is the direct recipient of his advice. Peter Gibson L.J. said:

> "The doctor is concerned only with the man, his patient, and possibly with that man's wife or partner if the doctor intends her to receive and she receives advice from the doctor in relation to the vasectomy and the subsequent tests."[21]

Goodwill bears some similarity to the case of *Reisner v. Regents of the University of California* referred to in para. 12–044, above, and might at first glance suggest that on the facts of *Reisner* a different result might be reached in England to that reached in California. However it is submitted that there are three grounds of distinction. Firstly, the damage suffered in *Goodwill* was primarily economic loss. Secondly, the doctors in *Reisner* actually created the risk of injury to another, while in *Goodwill* they were merely alleged to have failed to give a warning about a pre-existing risk. Thirdly, the claimant in *Goodwill* had taken her own expert advice from a general practitioner and had been given the "all clear". **12–047**

It might be argued that the approach taken by the Court of Appeal in *Goodwill* should be adopted in deciding whether a duty to warn the patient is owed by the treating doctor in the example posed at paragraph 12–045 above. If this is correct, no duty would be found, for there is no group of road users which might sensibly be identified as analogous to current sexual partners. However, the claim in *Goodwill* was, in substance and as pleaded, a claim wholly for financial loss.[22] The imposition of a duty of care to prevent pure economic loss is subject to far more stringent requirements than apply when a duty to guard against the infliction of personal injury is alleged.[23] **12–048**

A related area is the potential liability of psychiatrists to persons foreseeably injured by patients under their care.[24] If a psychiatrist negligently permits the release of a dangerous patient detained under the Mental Health Act 1983 or pursuant to the order of the court, and the patient injures a third party, that third **12–049**

---

[21] *ibid.* at 167G. See also Thorpe L.J. at 170B. Peter Gibson L.J. further suggested that the doctor might owe a duty to the patient's current sexual partner in performing the operation (as opposed to advising in relation to it): see at 167H.

[22] In *Walkin v. South Manchester Health Authority* [1995] 4 All E.R. 132, the Court of Appeal held that an unwanted conception is a species of personal injury within the meaning of s.11 of the Limitation Act 1980. It was not argued that the claim in *Goodwill* should be regarded in this light, however, and that case proceeded on the basis that the claim was for financial loss only. See also paras 12–289 and 12–290, below.

[23] See Chap. 2, paras 2–24–2–25, above.

[24] In the interesting case of *Broadmoor Special Hospital Authority v. Robinson* [2000] Q.B. 775, CA the claimant hospital unsuccessfully sought injunctions to restrain publication of a book written by the defendant, who had been convicted of manslaughter and ordered to be detained in a special hospital. The claimant considered that if the book was published it would be likely to expose the defendant to risk of assault, undermine his mental state and cause distress to other patients and his victim's family. The Court of Appeal determined, by a majority, that it had jurisdiction to grant the injunctions sought but declined to do so as a matter of discretion. The Court held that the hospital authority could not bring proceedings to protect other patients' rights to privacy or confidence or to prevent distress to the victim's family unless the conduct complained of interfered with the performance of the authority's public responsibilities.

party should have a claim.[25] The position is more difficult where a psychiatrist is treating a voluntary patient, and has reason to believe that he might commit a crime.[26] A leading United States authority is *Tarasoff v. The Regents of the University of California*[27]: a university student killed a woman fellow student, having previously informed a psychiatrist of his intention to do so. The psychiatrist informed the police, but not the woman or her parents. The Supreme Court of California held that the psychiatrist owed a duty to take reasonable care to protect foreseeable victims of his patient.[28]

12–050   It is uncertain whether or not a similar action might lie under English law. In *Palmer v. Tees Health Authority*[29] the Court of Appeal struck out a superficially similar claim. The disturbing facts of that case were as follows. The claimant's daughter was abducted, abused and murdered by A. The claimant suffered psychiatric injury upon learning of her daughter's disappearance and subsequent violent death. A had previously been under the defendants' care as a psychiatric patient and (it was alleged) had confessed to having sexual feelings towards children and to an intention to murder a child upon his discharge. It was said by the claimant that the defendants ought to have diagnosed that there was a substantial risk that A would sexually abuse children and treated him accordingly. The claimant commenced proceedings on her own behalf and on behalf of her daughter's estate. The Court of Appeal struck out both claims. The claimant's daughter was not an identifiable victim and there was an insufficient degree of proximity between her and the defendants.[30]

12–051   In the Canadian case of *Wenden v. Trikha*[31] Murray J. suggested that a duty of care might be owed by a hospital or psychiatrist to protect third parties foreseeably injured by a voluntary psychiatric patient who absented himself from hospital and drove a vehicle in a trance state. The requirement of proximity between psychiatrist and third party would require consideration of the particular

---

[25] *Holgate v. Lancashire Mental Hospitals Board, Gill and Robertson* [1937] 4 All E.R. 19; *Dorset Yacht Co. Ltd v. Home Office* [1970] A.C. 1004. See also *Partington v. Wandsworth LBC* [1989] C.L.Y. 2563. In *Reid v. Secretary of State for Scotland* [1999] 2 A.C. 512 Lord Clyde referred at 532B-C to the interests of members of the public who may "reasonably require the assurance that there is no threat to the peaceful enjoyment of their own lives through the release of someone who has been suffering some form of metal disorder."

[26] The public policy objections to an action against the police by a victim of crime, discussed by the House of Lords in *Hill v. Chief Constable of West Yorkshire* [1989] A.C. 53 would seem not to apply.

[27] (1976) 551 P. 2d 334. See also *Garamella v. New York Medical College* [1999] Lloyd's Rep. Med. 3423. A Connecticut District Court refused to strike out the claim by a child patient sexually abused by a psychiatric resident against his college and its senior doctor, to whom the resident had confessed his paedophilia during psychoanalysis which he was required to undergo as part of his training. The decision involved two important findings. First the relationship between the resident and the senior doctor was not a voluntary doctor/patient relationship, with its attendant obligations of patient confidentiality. The senior doctor was required to report to the college upon the resident's suitability for psychiatric qualification. Secondly the senior doctor knew that the resident intended to become a child psychiatrist. As one of the resident's patients during his clinical training rotation, the child was arguably one of a class of identifiable victims to whom the senior doctor owed a duty of care arising from the resident's disclosure.

[28] For discussion of *Tarasoff* and related cases, see K. C. De Haan, "My Patient's Keeper? The liability of medical practitioners for negligent injury to third parties" (1986) 2 P.N. 86 and F. Morris and Dr G. Adshead, "The liability of psychiatrists for the violent acts of their patients" [1997] N.L.J 558.

[29] [1999] Lloyd's Rep. Med. 351, CA.

[30] See Stuart-Smith L.J. at 359. For commentary on *Palmer* see [1999] Lloyd's Rep. Med. 364 and [1999] Med. L.Rev. 331.

[31] (1991) 8 C.C.L.T. (2d) 138, affirmed (1993) 14 C.C.L.T (2d) 225, Alberta CA.

risk posed by the patient, the predictability of his future behaviour and the ability to identify the person or class of persons at risk of harm.[32] On the facts in *Wenden*, unlike those in *Tarasoff*, no individual was identifiable as at particular risk of harm from the patient. The class of persons at risk would include all road users in a wide vicinity of the hospital.[33]

However, despite the decision in *Palmer* it is submitted that there would be **12–052** nothing to prevent a court finding that a duty of care exists in a case where sufficient proximity between defendant and victim existed (for example where the defendant's patient had threatened to harm a particular victim or a victim from an identifiable class), essentially on the basis of *Dorset Yacht Co. Ltd v. Home Office*.[34] Some support for this proposition can be derived from the first instance judgment of Gage J. in *Palmer*, where the Judge stated:

" . . . in holding, as I do, that the defendants owed no duty of care to Rosie, I am not to be taken as holding that health authorities have any general immunity from suit. If the claimant's pleaded case had shown that there existed some distinctive feature or characteristic which demonstrated that Rosie was at some special risk from A other than the general risk to other young female members of the general public, I would have found that the requirement of proximity existed. Subject of course to arguments on fairness, justice and reasonableness in certain circumstances a court might then hold that a duty of care existed."[35]

Irrespective of difficulties in demonstrating a duty of care, establishing negli- **12–053** gence as opposed to mere error of judgment in a difficult area of medicine may however be a formidable task.

Where the class of persons at risk of harm from a patient is suitably small, the **12–054** question may arise whether the doctor's duty is directly to warn those persons. The court was not required to decide whether there was a duty to warn the wife of the patient in either *Pittman Estate v. Bain*[36] or *Goodwill v. British Pregnancy Advisory Service*.[37] In Canada, it has been held[38] that a general practitioner who failed adequately to warn of the risks attached to viral infection of an unborn child did not owe a duty of care directly to advise the father. The father could not be regarded as a patient of the general practitioner for these purposes and the doctor had not in fact advised him. Further, the father's claim was for the cost of

---

[32] (1991) 8 C.C.L.T (2d) 138, 161, citing *Dorset Yacht Co. Ltd v. Home Office* [1970] A.C. 1004, 1070B-E *per* Lord Diplock. But *cf. MacPhail v. Desrosiers* (1998) 166 N.S.R. (2d) 81, (1998) 170 N.S.R. (2d) 145 (M was negligently allowed by the defendants to drive home after undergoing an abortion despite the risk of accident created by her disturbed emotional state. The claimant was a passenger in the car when it crashed. The claimant recovered damages from the defendant).

[33] A similar conclusion was reached by the Manitoba Court of Appeal in *Kines Estate v. Lychuk* (1998) 123 Man. L.R. (2nd) 151. The claimant was killed by L. The claimant's estate alleged that the defendant, under whose care L had been, negligently failed involuntarily to commit L. The claim was struck out. There was an insufficient degree of proximity between the defendant and the claimant for a duty of care to arise.

[34] [1970] A.C. 1004. In *Palmer* Stuart-Smith L.J. remarked *obiter* that the dicta from *Dorset Yacht Co. v. Home Office* were relevant to a consideration of whether it was just, fair and reasonable to impose a duty of care and not to the question of proximity.

[35] [1998] Lloyd's Rep. Med. 447 at 461. For further analysis of *Palmer* see M. Jones, "Liability for psychiatric patients: setting the boundaries" [2000] P.N 3.

[36] (1994) 112 D.L.R. (4th) 257, Ontario High Court.

[37] [1996] 2 All E.R. 161, discussed at para. 12–046, above.

[38] *Arndt v. Smith* (1994) 93 B.C.L.R. (2d) 220, Hutchinson J. The decision was affirmed on appeal without discussion of this point: see [1996] 7 Med. L.R. 108, Court of Appeal of British Columbia.

rearing the child (which, it was alleged, would otherwise have been aborted) and arose from his joint responsibility with the mother for its care. It was therefore derivative of the mother's claim. This reasoning was adopted by the Court of Appeal of Manitoba in *Freeman v. Sutter*.[39] An action brought by the biological father of a child born after a mishandled abortion, but in circumstances where no action was brought by the mother, was struck out.[40]

12-055   **Unborn children.** Where a medical practitioner is treating a pregnant woman, he owes a duty of care to the unborn child. If, as a result of his negligent treatment, the child is born disabled, then, subject to the restrictions set out in section 1 of the Congenital Disabilities (Civil Liability) Act 1976, he may be liable to the child. If negligent treatment of either parent before conception causes a child to the born disabled, then, subject to section 1(4) of the Act, again the doctor may be liable to the child. Section 1A of the Congenital Disabilities (Civil Liability) Act 1976 was added by section 44 of the Human Fertilisation and Embryology Act 1990. This in effect extends the provisions of section 1 to children born as a result of artificial insemination. Subject to restrictions set out, such children can sue for disabilities caused by negligence prior to the artificial insemination. In respect of children born before the 1976 Act came into force, the position is governed by the common law.[41] The medical practitioner owes a "potential" or "contingent" duty of care to the unborn child, which vests at birth. If he negligently damages the embryo in his patient's womb, causing the baby to be born injured, the cause of action in negligence crystallises at birth.[42] In *X and Y v. Pal*[43] the New South Wales Court of Appeal held that an obstetrician and gynaecologist treating a woman owes a duty of care at common law to her future child, which need not have been conceived at the time of the treatment. Doctors consulted by X before and during her pregnancy negligently failed to test her for syphilis, with the result that Y was infected in *utero*.

12-056   **"Wrongful life".** A disabled child has no right of action either under the Act or at common law for "wrongful life": he cannot claim damages on the basis

---

[39] [1996] 4 W.W.R. 748. See, to similar effect, *Koracvich v. Ortho Pharmaceuticals (Canada) Ltd* (1995) 25 C.C.L.T. (2d) 295, Court of Appeal of British Columbia.

[40] Even in *Reisner v. Regents of the University of California* (para. 12–044 above) there was no suggestion that the defendants ought to have taken steps to warn the claimant of JL's infection with the HIV virus.

[41] At (1994) 10 P.N. 94, J. Murphy argues that the meaning of "disability" under the 1976 Act creates a residual role for common law claims for children born after 1976.

[42] At birth, the damage required to complete the cause of action accrues and the child acquires legal personality to sue: *Burton v. Islington Health Authority* [1993] Q.B. 204, CA. The principle has been accepted elsewhere: see *Hamilton v. Fife Health Board* [1993] 4 Med. L.R. 201, Ct of Sess.; *Montreal Tramways v. Leveille* [1933] 4 D.L.R. 337, Supreme Court of Canada. In *Cherry v. Borsman* (1992) 94 D.L.R. (4th) 487, the British Columbia Court of Appeal held that if, in breach of duty to the mother, an abortion is negligently performed and the foetus preserved, the medical practitioner owes a duty of care to the foetus not to injure it. See also *Howarth v. Adey* [1996] 2 V.R. 535, Court of Appeal of Victoria (duty to warn mother of need for Caesarean section in interests of unborn baby). See further A. Whitfield, "Common Law Duties to Unborn Children" (1993) 1 Med. L.Rev. 29.

[43] (1991) 23 N.S.W.L.R. 26, [1992] 3 Med. L.R. 195, (and see commentary at (1993) 1 Med. L.Rev. 119). This part of the claim failed because the injuries complained of were not caused by the syphilis. The difficulties of proving causation in a case where pre-conception injury is alleged are illustrated by *Reay v. British Nuclear Fuels* [1994] 5 Med. L.R. 1, where the claimants failed to prove that paternal pre-conception irradiation was a material contributory cause of their cancers.

that, although his disabilities were unavoidable, the defendant was negligent in failing to ascertain his condition and recommend an abortion.[44]

Medical report on A for the information of B. A further group of cases has **12–057** dealt with the duties of a doctor who is employed by one party to examine and report upon the condition of another. Where a doctor gives a report or certificate on the sanity of someone who is not his patient for the purposes of detention of that person under the Mental Health Act 1983, he probably owes a duty of care to that person.[45] Where the doctor writes a medical report for the benefit of some party other than his patient (for example an insurance company proposing to insure the patient's life) he will owe a duty of care to that other party.[46] Where, however, the doctor is employed by a public authority or by insurers to examine someone who is not his patient, it seems that he owes no general duty of care to that person. In *X (Minors) v. Bedfordshire County Council*[47] a child and its mother alleged psychiatric injury as a result of the removal of the child into local authority care. The decision to take the child into care had taken into account the report of a psychiatrist who was employed or retained by the authority to advise it as to whether the child had been a victim of sexual abuse and, if so, the likely identity of the abuser. A majority in the Court of Appeal[48] held that the psychiatrist owed no duty of care to the claimants when advising the authority for these purposes, and struck out the claim. The appeal to the House of Lords was dismissed. Lord Browne-Wilkinson (with whom Lords Jauncey, Ackner and Lane agreed) held that, by coming into contact with the child in pursuance of a duty owed to the local authority, the psychiatrist did not come under a general professional duty of care to the child:

"The social workers and the psychiatrist were retained by the local authority to advise the local authority, not the claimants. The subject matter of the advice and activities of the professionals is the child. Moreover the tendering of any advice will in many cases involve interviewing, and in the case of doctors, examining the child. But the fact that the carrying out of the retainer involves contact with and relationship with the child cannot alter the extent of the duty owed by the professionals under the retainer from the local authority. The Court of Appeal drew a correct analogy with the doctor instructed by an insurance company to examine an applicant for life insurance. The doctor does not, by examining the applicant, come under any general duty of medical care to the applicant. He is under a duty not to damage the applicant in the course of the examination: but beyond that his duties are owed to the insurance company and not to

---

[44] *McKay v. Essex Area Health Authority* [1982] 1 Q.B. 1166 (see para. 12–302, below). The child's claim for wrongful life was held properly to have been abandoned in *Arndt v. Smith* (1994) 93 B.C.L.R. (2d) 220, British Columbia Supreme Court, following *McKay*. See further C. Stolker, "Wrongful Life and Limits of Liability" (1994) 43 I.C.L.Q. 521.

[45] See para. 12–239, below. See also *Candler v. Crane, Christmas & Co.* [1951] 2 K.B. 164, 180 *per* Denning L.J. quoted in Chap. 2, para. 2–110, above.

[46] See for example the *obiter* comments of Kennedy and Millett L.JJ. in *Kapfunde v. Abbey National plc* [1999] Lloyd's Rep. Med. 48 at 53, 56.

[47] [1995] 2 A.C. 633. In September 1999 the European Commission delivered a unanimous opinion (under the name of *Z and others v. United Kingdom* 28 E.H.R.R. C.D. CD65—CD82) to the effect that the striking out of this claim by the English courts was a breach of Art. 6 of the E.C.H.R. in that its effect was to bestow an immunity on local authorities and deny the claimants a fair hearing by an independent and impartial tribunal. The case is still commented on in detail, although it is submitted that any principle to be extracted from it has to be subject to the decision of the Commission, and the subsequent decision of the House of Lords in the case of *Barrett v. Enfield LBC* [1999] 3 W.L.R. 79, referred to in paras 12–060 to 12–061 below.

[48] Sir Thomas Bingham M.R. dissenting.

the applicant . . . In my judgment in the present cases, the social workers and the psychiatrist did not, by accepting the instructions of the local authority, assume any general professional duty of care to the claimant children. The professionals were employed or retained to advise the local authority in relation to the well-being of the plaintiffs but not to advise or treat the plaintiffs."[49]

12–058   An important part of the reasoning in the House of Lords was that the duty contended for was wider in scope than that owed by the psychiatrist to the local authority under the terms of her retainer by the local authority.[50] As summarised by Lord Browne-Wilkinson,[51] the allegations were that the psychiatrist had failed to investigate the facts of the child's case with proper care and thoroughness and to discuss them with the mother. This would appear to amount in substance to an allegation that the psychiatrist owed a duty of care to the claimants in the performance of her duty to advise the authority. Her advice was intended to be given for the purpose of safeguarding the welfare of the child. It is difficult to see the respects in which conflict or disparity arose between the psychiatrist's existing and alleged duties.

12–059   Lord Browne-Wilkinson went on to say that, even if he were wrong in deciding that there was no duty of care on the grounds summarised above, he did not consider it just and reasonable that a duty should be imposed. The earlier reasoning might therefore be regarded as reaching a conclusion on whether the test of proximity was satisfied. The principal policy grounds which militated against the imposition of a duty were threefold.[52] First, the protection of the child in these circumstances is regulated by an elaborate statutory system which requires participation by a range of bodies and disciplines. It would be unfair to isolate one participant as owing common law duties of care. If potential liability were to be imposed upon all, it would be almost impossible to identify responsibility for a decision which was challenged. Second, such decisions are delicate and difficult and sometimes involve balancing the interests of a child against those of its family. Third, the imposition of liability would encourage both defensive practices by psychiatrists and vexatious and costly litigation. Lord Nolan agreed that these reasons of policy were sufficiently strong to prevent the imposition of a duty of care. Otherwise, he would have upheld the alleged duty of care on the part of the psychiatrist, but, it would appear, he also rejected the argument that a similar duty arose where a doctor conducts an examination for insurance purposes:

"Public policy apart, I am unable to accept that the psychiatrist and the social worker were exempt from a general professional duty of care towards the child. I cannot agree that the relationship was analogous to that which arises in the contractual and commercial context of an examination by an insurance company doctor of an applicant for life insurance."[53]

---

[49] [1995] 2 A.C. 633, 752C–753A, 753E.
[50] On that basis, Lord Browne-Wilkinson distinguished the decisions in *Henderson v. Merrett Syndicates* [1995] 2 A.C. 145 and *White v. Jones* [1995] 2 A.C. 207 in which an underwriting agent and a solicitor respectively were held to owe duties of care to persons affected by their work notwithstanding that they worked under contracts of engagement by others.
[51] *ibid.* at 744B.
[52] And applied equally in relation to the question whether the local authority owed a direct common law duty of care: [1995] 2 A.C. 633, 749G–751B, 754A.
[53] *ibid.* at 771H–772B.

The reasons of policy which were said to prevent the imposition of a duty of **12–060** care upon the local authority's psychiatrist in *X (Minors) v. Bedfordshire County Council* were initially adopted by the Court of Appeal in *Barrett v. Enfield LBC.*[54] The claimant in *Barrett* had been under local authority care from the age of 10 months until he reached majority. During that time he had been moved between different homes on nine occasions. He alleged that this and other failures on the part of the local authority, had caused him to develop a mental illness. His claim was struck out for the policy reasons discussed at paragraph 12–059 above. Evans L.J. concurred in the result but did not agree that the imposition of a duty of care in such circumstances would encourage defensive practices on the part of the local authority professionals. He said:

> "I would agree that what is said to be a 'policy' consideration, namely that imposing a duty of care might lead to defensive conduct on the part of the person concerned and might otherwise require him to spend time or resources on keeping full records or otherwise providing for self-justification, if called upon to do so, should normally be a factor of little, if any, weight. If the conduct in question is of a kind which can be measured against the standard of the reasonable man, placed as the defendant was, then I do not see why the law in the public interest should not require those standards to be observed."[55]

The claimants' appeal was allowed by the House of Lords[56] on the basis that **12–061** the public policy considerations which meant that it would not be fair just or reasonable to impose a common law duty of care on a local authority when deciding whether or not to take action in respect of a case of suspected child abuse did not have the same force once the child was already in local authority care, and that it was therefore arguable that the policy considerations did not apply on the facts of the case; although Lord Slynn (with whom Lord Nolan and Lord Steyn agreed) expressly approved the passage in the judgment of Evans L.J. in the Court of Appeal which is quoted above.[57] The House of Lords distinguished *X v. Bedfordshire County Council* and held that it was inappropriate to decide whether it was fair just and reasonable to impose a duty if care in the abstract and on the basis of assumed hypothetical facts. Concluding that the claimant's case was far from clear, the Court held that he was entitled to have his claim heard and the facts investigated.

Further consideration was given to this matter by the House of Lords in *Phelps* **12–062** *v. Hillingdon LBC.*[58] While finding that a failure on the part of a local authority to comply with the provisions of the Education Acts 1944 and 1981 did not itself sound in damages, Lord Slynn again concluded (as he had done in *Barrett*) that the fact that the acts which the claimant pleaded as negligent had been carried out within the ambit of the local authority's statutory discretion was not of itself a reason to prevent a claim at common law from being brought.[59] Lord Slynn also confirmed that there would remain cases where to recognise a vicarious liability

---

[54] [1998] Q.B. 367.
[55] *ibid.* at 380A-C. Although the claimant's appeal to the House of Lords succeeded on the grounds that it was arguable that the policy considerations in *X (Minors) v. Bedfordshire County Council* did not apply on the facts of *Barrett*, Lord Slynn (with whom Lord Nolan and Lord Steyn agreed) expressly approved this passage: see [1999] 3 W.L.R. 79, 94A-C.
[56] [1999] 3 W.L.R. 79.
[57] [1999] 3 W.L.R. 79, 94A-C.
[58] [2000] 3 W.L.R. 776. For an outline of the facts of *Phelps*, see para. 12–027 above.
[59] *ibid.* at 790B-C.

on the part of a local authority for the failures of its employees or agents would so interfere with the performance of the local authority's duties that it would be wrong to recognise any common law liability on the part of the local authority.[60] However he concluded that on the facts of *Phelps* a duty of care should be found to exist.[61]

12–063　　　The comments of the House of Lords in *X (Minors) v. Bedfordshire County Council*[62] suggested that a doctor who examines a non-patient for insurance purposes will not be liable to the examinee (or his estate) if, for example, he fails to diagnose a cancerous growth (or fails to alert the examinee to it) so that the condition becomes terminal for lack of timely treatment. This result might be thought surprising: personal injury to and the death of the examinee will have been foreseeably caused by the doctor's failure to exercise normal medical skill and care. *A fortiori* the doctor will not be liable when his report inaccurately suggests that the examinee is in poor health and, as a result, the examinee is refused insurance. This result is less surprising: the examinee's claim would be for pure economic loss in circumstances where he cannot claim to have relied upon the report.[63]

12–064　　　A similar conclusion might be expected in relation to a company doctor who examines an applicant for employment but includes a material error in his report, so that the applicant is passed over and the post is filled by someone else.[64] Some doubt was cast on this conclusion by Robert Owen Q.C. in *Baker v. Kaye*,[65] where it was held that a doctor retained by a company to examine a potential employee for his medical fitness to do a particular job did owe a duty of care to the potential employee in carrying out his examination and in interpreting the results of that examination when reporting to the company. Financial loss to the potential employee was clearly foreseeable in the event that a careless error in the examination or report led to loss of the employment opportunity. There was no conflict between the doctor's duties to the company and to the potential employee. However, the finding of a duty of care in *Baker v. Kaye* was expressly disapproved by the Court of Appeal in *Kapfunde v. Abbey National plc.*[66] In that case the Court of Appeal concluded that the defendant doctor owed no duty of care to the claimant who was the subject of his report. Considerable weight appears to have been placed on the fact that there had been no doctor-patient relationship between the parties, the claimant had not entrusted the defendant with conduct of her affairs and the claim was for economic loss. In his judgment Kennedy L.J. remarked:

---

[60] *ibid.* at 790F-G.

[61] Lord Lloyd, Lord Jauncey, Lord Nicholls, Lord Hutton and Lord Millett all gave speeches agreeing with Lord Slynn. Lord Clyde, who also found that a duty of care existed, remarked that the imposition of a duty on the facts of the case ought not to inspire some peculiarly defensive attitude in the performance of the professional responsibilities of the employees of the local authority: see [2000] 3 W.L.R. 776 at 809C.

[62] Lord Browne-Wilkinson at 752H.

[63] But see *Spring v. Guardian Assurance* [1995] 2 A.C. 296, HL, discussed at Chap. 2, para. 2–34 above. That case might be distinguished by the prior relationship between the claimant and the giver of the reference. A doctor who is examining his own patient for insurance purposes is likely to owe him a general duty of care.

[64] A person has a statutory right of access to any medical report prepared about him for insurance or employment purposes: see the Access to Medical Reports Act 1988 s.1.

[65] (1998) 39 B.M.L.R. 12.

[66] [1999] Lloyd's Rep. Med. 48. For the facts of *Kapfunde*, see paras 12–025, above and 12–305, below.

"The only relationship between [the claimant and the defendant] was that between the giver of the advice and the subject of the advice: that is not enough."[67]

It is submitted that a further feature which ought to militate against the **12–065** existence of a duty of care in such situations is the conflict of interest that may well arise on the part of the adviser. He clearly owes a duty of care to the person or entity for whom he is preparing the report. To find that he also owes a duty of care to the subject of the report may well, in many cases, place him in an extremely difficult position and encourage the type of defensive conduct that Lord Browne-Wilkinson was so keen to avoid in *X (Minors) v. Bedfordshire County Council.*[68]

Four further decisions provide strong support for the proposition that a doctor **12–066** will rarely owe a duty of care to a person whom he is not advising or treating as his patient. The first is *R. v. Croydon Health Authority.*[69] The radiologist in that case had been consulted in relation to the claimant's prospects of employment only and his duty did not extend into her private life.[70] The second is *Powell v. Boladz.*[71] In that case the parents' complaint was in relation to the general practitioner (who had falsified records after the death of their child from a rare disease) and not to the treatment of the child. There was therefore insufficient proximity between the claimant and defendants for a duty of care to arise. A doctor treating a child patient owes no duty of care to the parents in administering the treatment, even though such treatment will usually involve giving advice and instructions to the parents.[72] In the same way a doctor who has been treating a child who has died and who tells the relatives what has happened does not thereby enter a doctor/patient relationship with the relatives so as to automatically owe them a duty of care; he will only do so if he is "called up or undertakes to treat them as patients".[73] A doctor owes no "free standing duty of candour" to non-patients. The third decision is *N v. Agrawal.*[74] In that case the defendant was a forensic medical examiner who had examined the claimant after she had complained of rape. He failed to attend the trial of the alleged rapist with the result that the trial collapsed. The claimant alleged that his failure to attend, and

---

[67] *ibid.* at 56.
[68] See para. 12–060 above. For an analysis of *Kapfunde* and *Baker v. Kaye* see D. Allen, "Liability for pre-employment medical assessment?" (1998) 14 P.N. 245.
[69] [1998] Lloyd's Rep. Med. 44. For the facts of *R v. Croydon Health Authority* see para. 12–26 above.
[70] See further para. 12–244 below.
[71] [1998] Lloyd's Med. Rep. 166. For the facts of *Powell* see para. 12–42, above.
[72] See also *Thompson v. Blake-James* [1998] Lloyd's Rep. Med. 187. The claimant's parents consulted the defendant general practitioner on the question of whether the claimant should be vaccinated against measles. At the stage of the consultation the claimant was less than a year old, the normal age for vaccination being two years old. Furthermore, to the knowledge of the defendant, the family was shortly to move to another county so that another general practitioner would be involved in the ultimate decision whether or not to vaccinate the claimant. The claimant was not in fact subsequently vaccinated and approximately four years later contracted measles and developed encephalitis, leading to brain damage. The Court of Appeal rejected the claimant's claim that the defendant had acted negligently in failing to provide proper advice as to vaccination on the grounds that it was not reasonably foreseeable by the defendant that a failure on his part to provide full information to the parents would have any significant bearing on their decision when the claimant reached the appropriate age for vaccination.
[73] *Powell v. Boladz* [1998] Lloyd's Rep. Med. 116 at 123, 124. The decision in *Powell* is criticised at (1998) 6 Med. L.Rev. 112.
[74] [1999] Lloyd's Rep. Med. 257.

the consequent collapse of the trial, exacerbated her psychiatric trauma. The Court of Appeal struck out the claim. The medical examiner was in the same position as the psychiatrist in *X (Minors) v. Bedfordshire County Council*[75] or the passing doctor who went to the assistance of a road traffic accident victim as referred to in *Capital & Counties plc v. Hampshire County Council*.[76] She therefore assumed no duty of care towards the claimant merely be examining her at the behest of the police or CPS, and owed no duty to attend trial as a witness, even though she might reasonably have foreseen that the victim's psychological condition might be exacerbated if the alleged rapist escaped conviction. The final case is *Hillman v. Black*.[77] The defendants had examined the claimant's daughter and reported a belief that she had been sexually abused. The claimant was subsequently accused of being the perpetrator of that abuse. He later sued the defendants, alleging that they had failed to carry out their examinations with due care, causing him to suffer psychiatric illness. The Court struck out the claim on the basis that the only duties owed by the defendants were owed to the child; the defendants owed no duty of care to the claimant.

(c) *The standard of skill and care*

12–067   **The general principle.** Whether he is sued in contract or tort, the medical practitioner is not obliged to achieve success in every case that he treats.[78] His duty, like that of other professional men, is to exercise reasonable skill and care. Perhaps the most well-known formulation of this principle is that used by Tindal C.J. when summing up to the jury in *Lanphier v. Phipos*[79] a medical negligence action tried in 1838:

> "Every person who enters into a learned professional undertakes to bring to the exercise of it a reasonable degree of care and skill. He does not undertake, if he is an attorney, that at all events you shall gain your case, nor does a surgeon undertake that he will perform a cure; nor does he undertake to use the highest possible degree of skill. There may be persons who have higher education and greater advantages than he has, but he undertakes to bring a fair, reasonable and competent degree of skill, and you will say whether, in this case, the injury was occasioned by the want of such skill in the defendant."[80]

12–068   The principle has been eloquently restated on a number of occasions over the last 160 years, of which the following are a selection:

(a) Tindal C.J. in *Hancke v. Hooper*[81]:

> "A surgeon does not become an actual insurer; he is only bound to display sufficient skill and knowledge in his profession. If from some accident, or some variation in the frame of a particular individual, an injury happens, it is not a fault in the medical man."

---

[75] See above at para. 12–057.

[76] See above at para. 12–015 and n. 36.

[77] [1996] 67 S.A.S.R. 490, South Australia Supreme Court.

[78] Except in cases where the medical practitioner undertakes to achieve a specific result: see, for instance, *Thake v. Maurice*, para. 12–010 above.

[79] (1838) 8 C. & P. 475.

[80] *ibid.* at 479.

[81] (1835) 7 C. & P. 81.

(b) Erle C.J. in *Rich v. Pierpont*[82]:

> "A medical man was certainly not answerable merely because some other practitioner might possibly have shown greater skill and knowledge; but he was bound to have that degree of skill which could not be defined, but which, in the opinion of the jury, was a competent degree of skill and knowledge. What that was the jury were to judge. It was not enough to make the defendant liable that some medical men, of far greater experience or ability, might have used a greater degree of skill, nor that even he might possibly have used some greater degree of care."

(c) Lord Hewart C.J. in *R. v. Bateman*[83]:

> "If a person holds himself out as possessing special skill and knowledge and he is consulted, as possessing such skill and knowledge, by or on behalf of a patient, he owes a duty to the patient to use due caution in undertaking the treatment. If he accepts the responsibility and undertakes the treatment and the patient submits to his direction and treatment accordingly, he owes a duty to the patient to use diligence, care, knowledge, skill and caution in administering the treatment . . . . The jury should not exact the highest, or a very high, standard, nor should they be content with a very low standard. The law requires a fair and reasonable standard of care and competence."

(d) Denning L.J. directing the jury in *Hatcher v. Black*[84]:

> "You must not, therefore, find him negligent simply because something happens to go wrong; if, for instance, one of the risks inherent in an operation actually takes place or some complication ensues which lessens or takes away the benefits that were hoped for, or if in a matter of opinion he makes an error of judgment. You should only find him guilty of negligence when he falls short of the standard of a reasonably skilful medical man, in short, when he is deserving of censure—for negligence in a medical man is deserving of censure."

(e) Lord Clyde in Hunter v. Hanley[85]:

> "But where the conduct of a doctor, or indeed of any professional man, is concerned, the circumstances are not so precise and clear cut as in the normal case [of negligence]. In the realm of diagnosis and treatment there is ample scope for genuine difference of opinion and one man clearly is not negligent merely because his conclusion differs from that of other professional men, nor because he has displayed less skill or knowledge than others would have shown. The true test for establishing negligence in diagnosis or treatment on the part of a doctor is whether he has been proved to be guilty of such failure as no doctor of ordinary skill would be guilty of if acting with ordinary care . . . "

---

[82] (1862) 3 F. & F. 35.

[83] (1925) 94 L.J.K.B. 791, 794: this was an appeal by a medical practitioner against his conviction for manslaughter, arising out of the death of a patient. The conviction was quashed because the trial judge's direction to the jury was, in part, more appropriate to a civil claim for damages than a criminal prosecution. The Lord Chief Justice, delivering the judgment of the court, discussed the duties imposed on doctors by both the civil and the criminal law.

[84] *The Times*, July 2, 1954. Part of the summing-up (including the passage quoted) is set out by Lord Denning in *The Discipline of Law* (Butterworths, 1979), pp. 242–244.

[85] 1955 S.C. 200, 204–205. Although this was a Scottish case, Lord Clyde expressly stated that he regarded the standard of care required from doctors to be the same under Scottish law as under English law: see at 205. This passage was cited with approval by Lord Scarman in *Maynard v. West Midlands Regional Health Authority* [1984] 1 W.L.R. 634, 638, subject to the comment that "a doctor who professes to exercise a special skill must exercise the ordinary skill of his speciality."

(f) McNair J. directing the jury in *Bolam v. Friern Hospital Management Committee*[86]:

> "But where you get a situation which involves the use of some special skill or competence, then the test as to whether there has been negligence or not is not the test of the man on the top of a Clapham omnibus, because he has not got this special skill. The test is the standard of the ordinary skilled man exercising and professing to have that special skill. A man need not possess the highest expert skill; it is well established law that it is sufficient if he exercises the ordinary skill of an ordinary competent man exercising that particular art . . . he is not guilty of negligence if he has acted in accordance with a practice accepted as proper by a responsible body of medical men skilled in that particular art . . . Putting it another way round, a man is not negligent if he is acting in accordance with such a practice merely because there is a body of opinion who would take a contrary view."[87]

Further statements of general principle, to the same effect as those quoted above, are to be found in the judgment of Scott L.J. in *Mahon v. Osborne*[88] in the speeches of Lords Edmund-Davies and Fraser in *Whitehouse v. Jordan*[89] and in the speech of Lord Scarman in *Maynard v. West Midlands Regional Health Authority*.[90] A similar standard is applied in other Commonwealth (or former Commonwealth) countries.[91]

12–069   Despite the variety of formulations which have been offered by appellate courts, probably the best known and most often quoted definition of the standard of care required of medical practitioners is McNair J.'s direction to the jury in *Bolam v. Friern Hospital Management Committee*[92] commonly known as "the Bolam test". Indeed the *Bolam* test itself has been the subject of numerous judicial paraphrases and summaries. Lord Scarman in *Sidaway v. Governors of Bethlem Royal Hospital*[93] has reformulated it thus:

> "a doctor is not negligent if he acts in accordance with a practice accepted at the time as proper by a responsible body of medical opinion even though other doctors adopt a different practice."

The *Bolam* test has withstood a series of attacks by determined claimants, sometimes armed with transatlantic authority. In *Whitehouse v. Jordan*[94] the House of Lords held that the *Bolam* test was applicable to medical treatment. In *Maynard v. West Midlands Regional Health Authority*[95] the House of Lords held that the *Bolam* test was applicable to diagnosis. In *Sidaway v. Governors of*

---

[86] [1957] 1 W.L.R. 582, 586. This direction was approved by the Privy Council in *Chin Keow v. Government of Malaysia* [1967] 1 W.L.R. 813, 816, and by Lord Edmund-Davies in *Whitehouse v. Jordan* [1981] 1 W.L.R. 246.
[87] In *Bolitho v. City of Hackney Health Authority* [1998] A.C. 232, 239C Lord Browne-Wilkinson described this direction as the *"locus classicus"* of the test for the standard of care required of a doctor.
[88] [1939] 2 K.B. 14, 31–32.
[89] [1981] 1 W.L.R. 246, 257–258 and 263.
[90] [1984] 1 W.L.R. 634, 638.
[91] See, for example, *Dangerfield v. David* (1911) 17 W.L.R. 249, *Koerber v. Trustees of Kitchener-Waterloo Hospital* (1987) 62 O.R. (2d) 613 (Canada); *Coppen v. Impey* [1916] C.P.D. 309 (South Africa); *F. v. R.* (1983) 33 S.A.S.R. 189 (Australia).
[92] [1957] 1 W.L.R. 582, 5812–587. See para. 12–068, above and para. 12–093, below.
[93] [1985] A.C. 871, 881F.
[94] [1981] 1 W.L.R. 246.
[95] [1984] 1 W.L.R. 634.

Bethlem Royal Hospital[96] the House of Lords held by a majority[97] that the *Bolam* test was applicable to all aspects of a medical practitioner's work and in particular to the extent of the medical practitioner's obligation to inform a patient of the risks of a proposed course of treatment.[98] Lord Diplock stated:

> "The *Bolam* test is far from new, its value is that it brings up to date and re-expresses in the light of modern conditions in which the art of medicine is now practised an ancient rule of common law . . . [99]
>
> In English jurisprudence the doctor's relationship with his patient which gives rise to the normal duty of care to exercise his skill and judgment to improve the patient's health in any particular respect in which the patient has sought his aid, has hitherto been treated as a single comprehensive duty covering all the ways in which a doctor is called upon to exercise his skill and judgment in the improvement of the physical or mental condition of the patient for which his services either as a general practitioner or specialist have been engaged. This general duty is not subject to dissection into a number of component parts to which different criteria of what satisfies the duty of care apply, such as diagnosis, treatment, advice . . . [1]
>
> My Lords, no convincing reason has in my view been advanced before your Lordships that would justify treating the *Bolam* test as doing anything less than laying down a principle of English law that is comprehensive and applicable to every aspect of the duty of care owed by a doctor to his patient in the exercise of his healing functions as respects that patient."[2]

In *Gold v. Haringey Health Authority*[3] the Court of Appeal held that the *Bolam* test applies even to non-therapeutic advice given by a medical practitioner. In *Re F. (Mental Patient: Sterilisation)*[4] the House of Lords held that the Bolam test determined whether medical treatment carried out on a patient unable to consent was lawful. In *Airedale NHS Trust v. Bland*[5] the House of Lords held that the Bolam test applies to the withdrawal of medical treatment from a patient who is incompetent to refuse treatment, even where this will lead to the death of the patient. Finally it seems implicit from the judgment of Kay J. in *Skelton v. Lewisham and North Southwark Health Authority*[6] that the Bolam test applies to an assessment of the standard of note-taking by a doctor.

Nor should the applicable standard of care vary with the circumstances in which medical treatment is rendered to a patient. In *Brooks v. Home Office*[7]   **12–070**

---

[96] [1985] A.C. 871.

[97] Lord Diplock, Lord Bridge and Lord Keith (Lord Templeman and Lord Scarman agreed with the decision of the majority, but on different grounds).

[98] Canada and Australia took a different approach. Instead of considering what the doctors thought the patient should know, the Canadian approach was to consider what a reasonable patient would want to know. The doctor's duty is to give the patient sufficient information to make an informed decision as to their treatment. They must consider with the patient the nature of the illness and the proposed treatment, and they must explain the risks involved with the treatment, they must consider alternative treatments and the consequences of doing nothing. *Reibl v. Hughes* (1980) 114 D.L.R. (3d) 1 Can. Sup. Ct; *Arndt v. Smith* (1997) 148 D.L.R. (4th) 48, Can. Sup. Ct. In *Rogers v. Whitaker* (1992) 109 A.L.R. 625, Aust. HC and [1993] Med. L.R. 79 the Australian High Court also rejected the approach in *Sidaway* and held that the extent of what a patient had to be told depended on a proper assessment of what the patient wanted to be told.

[99] *ibid.* at 892E.

[1] *ibid.* at 893D-E.

[2] *ibid.* at 893H–894A.

[3] [1988] Q.B. 481, 489F-H.

[4] [1990] 2 A.C. 1. See para. 12–138, below.

[5] [1993] A.C. 789.

[6] [1998] Lloyd's Rep. Med. 324, 328.

[7] (1999) 48 B.M.L.R 109.

Garland J. held that, subject to the reasonable constraints of having to be transported and having her freedom restricted, a pregnant woman detained in prison was entitled to expect the same standard of obstetric care and observation as if she were at liberty.

12–071   In the past there has been controversy as to the status and significance of evidence from an expert to the effect that the management complained of by the claimant was approved by a responsible body of medical opinion. It has been thought that a claim of negligence against a doctor can be successfully defended by the defence calling an expert honestly to say that he would have acted in the same way as the defendant. Support for this approach was found in *Maynard v. West Midlands RHA*[8] where Lord Scarman said[9]:

> " . . . a judge's preference for one body of distinguished professional opinion to another also professionally distinguished is not sufficient to establish negligence in a practitioner whose actions have received the seal of approval of those whose opinions, truthfully expressed, honestly held, were not preferred."

And in *Sidaway*[10] Lord Scarman said that "the law imposes the duty of care; but the standard of care is a matter for medical judgment". *Sidaway* is now subject to the decision of the House of Lords in *Bolitho v. City & Hackney H.A.*[11] Patrick Bolitho, aged two, was admitted to hospital suffering from respiratory difficulties; he deteriorated and suffered a cardiac arrest which caused massive brain damage. At one stage a nurse was sufficiently concerned about Patrick's breathing difficulties that she summoned a doctor—but the doctor negligently failed to attend or send a deputy. It was accepted that if the doctor had attended and intubated Patrick, the respiratory failure which caused the cardiac arrest would not have occurred. The case was defended on the question of causation on the basis that even if the doctor had attended she would not have intubated the child, and this aspect is considered below in paragraphs 12–271 to 12–273, below, but the claimants made an assault in the House of Lords on the significance of the defendant's expert evidence. Lord Browne-Wilkinson said in the only speech[12]:

> "[Counsel for the claimant] submitted that the judge had wrongly treated the Bolam test as requiring him to accept the views of one truthful body of expert professional advice even if he was unpersuaded of its logical force. He submitted that the judge was wrong in law in adopting that approach and that ultimately it was for the court, not for medical opinion, to decide what was the standard of care required of a professional in the circumstances of each particular case.
>
> My Lords, I agree with these submissions to the extent that, in my view, the court is not bound to hold that a defendant doctor escapes liability for negligent treatment or diagnosis just because he leads evidence from a number of medical experts who are genuinely of opinion that the defendant's treatment or diagnosis accorded with sound medical practice."

12–072   It is submitted that it now follows that any expert evidence supporting a defendant doctor's approach to treatment, diagnosis or the explanation of risk

---

[8] [1984] 1 W.L.R. 634.
[9] *ibid.* at 639.
[10] [1985] A.C. 871, 881.
[11] [1998] A.C. 232, HL.
[12] *ibid.* at 241.

must be subjected to logical analysis, and (although such cases will obviously be rare) it need not be accepted by the court if the analysis is found wanting.[13]

Standard of skill and care determined by reference to the current state of **12–073** **knowledge.** Advances of medical science or medical knowledge between the date of the alleged negligence and the date of trial should be ignored when determining whether the defendant exercised reasonable skill and care.[14] In *Roe v. Minister of Health*[15] a spinal anaesthetic was kept in glass ampoules stored in phenol solution. The phenol penetrated the ampoules through invisible cracks. In October 1947 the anaesthetic, containing phenol, was injected into two patients, who thereby suffered severe injuries. The risk of such mishaps occurring was first drawn to the attention of the medical profession in 1951 when a book was published on lumbar puncture and spinal anaesthesia. The trial took place in 1953. McNair J. held that Dr G, who was responsible for the anaesthetic, was not negligent in failing to foresee and guard against[16] the risk of invisible cracks. The Court of Appeal affirmed that decision, emphasising that they were judging Dr G by the state of knowledge in 1947.[17] Denning L.J. observed that if the same mistake were made after 1951, it would amount to negligence.[18] The same principle is illustrated by a Canadian case, *McLean v. Weir*[19] in which the claimant suffered quadriplegia as a result of a subclavian angiogram. This was due to the introduction of contrast medium in too great a quantity into the spinal cord. It was held that the second defendant (who performed the procedure) was not negligent when judged by reference to the state of the art at the material time (1973), although he would be negligent if he allowed the same mishap to occur at the date of trial (1977).[20]

---

[13] *Hucks v. Cole* (1968) 112 S.J. 483; [1993] 4 Med. L.R. 393 is an example of this critical approach to expert evidence being applied in 1968; see also recently: *Pearce v. United Bristol Healthcare NHS Trust* [1999] P.I.Q.R. 53, CA; and *Penney v. East Kent H.A.* [2000] Lloyd's Rep. Med. 41, CA. See also the important lecture by Lord Woolf entitled "Are the courts excessively deferential to the Medical Profession?" (2001) 9 Med. L.Rev. 1.

[14] See, *e.g. Chin Keow v. Government of Malaysia* [1967] 1 W.L.R. 813, 817. In the case of claims for ante-natal injury, see s.1(5) of the Congenital Disabilities (Civil Liability) Act 1976.

[15] [1954] 2 Q.B. 66. See also paras 12–122 and 12–286 below.

[16] The risk could have been guarded against quite easily by staining the phenol with a deep dye.

[17] See Somervell L.J., *ibid.* at 77, Denning L.J. at 86 and Morris L.J. at 92.

[18] *ibid.* at 86.

[19] [1980] 4 W.W.R. 609, British Columbia Court of Appeal. The same principle was emphasised in *Koerber v. Trustees of Kitchener-Waterloo Hospital* (1987) 62 O.R. (2d) 613, 617–618, Ontario High Court and *Brown v. University of Alberta Hospital* (1997) 145 DLR (4th) 63 at 107e–f, Alberta Court of Queen's Bench.

[20] For further examples see *Robb v. East London & City Health Authority*, unreported, May 8, 1998, Ebsworth J. (levels of radiotherapy given after surgery for breast cancer not unreasonable in light of practice and perception of the risk of harm at the time of treatment); *Theodorou v. Camden & Islington Health Authority*, unreported, November 3, 1997, P. Goldring Q.C. (failure by consultant paediatrician to refer claimant for neurological opinion not negligent by reference to the standards applicable in 1965); *Rowan v. Steinberg* [1997] 8 Med. L.R. 30, Sc. Ct Sess. (OH) (failure by general practitioner to withdraw patient from tranquillisers not negligent since patient's dependency had occurred long before the existence of such a risk had been recognised generally by the medical profession); *Nawoor v. Barking Havering and Brentwood Health Authority* [1998] Lloyd's Rep. Med. 313, D. Brennan Q.C. (failure by defendant's special care baby unit to adopt an active (as opposed to conservative) treatment regime on discovering a leak in an intravenous line not negligent by reference to the standards applicable at the time of treatment, even though by the date of trial adoption of a conservative regime may well have been negligent); *Pollard v. Crockard*, unreported, January 22, 1997, Holland J. (defendant's surgical technique in carrying out transoral cranio-cervical decompression and posterior cranio-cervical fusion operations not negligent given accepted clinical practice at the time). For a slightly unusual application of the principle see *Skelton v. Lewisham and North*

12–074   The ascertainment of the state of knowledge at the material time is sometimes a central issue at trial. This is determined in part by the recollection of expert witnesses, but largely by reference to the published literature. The question then arises at what point does published material become part of the current knowledge". In order that he not fall behind the development of accepted medical practice, the doctor has an obligation to keep himself informed. In practice, however, a professional person does not read every relevant publication, nor can he remember everything that he reads. Thus in *Crawford v. Board of Governors of Charing Cross Hospital*[21] the Court of Appeal held that an anaesthetist was not negligent in failing to read a particular article in *The Lancet*. In *Gover v. State of South Australia and Perriam*[22] the Supreme Court of South Australia held that an eye surgeon was not negligent by failing to be aware in 1979 of the risk of blindness from an upper lid blepharoplasty:

> "It was a time when the study of the topic was in its early stages, and a considerable amount of the work was being done in another speciality. The matter had not then entered the general corpus of knowledge of which all experts in the defendant's field could reasonably be expected to be aware. It is not enough, on a question like this, simply to discover a few passages on the topic out of a general ophthalmology literature which is, I expect, quite extensive."[23]

Evidence of the current state of knowledge and standard practice in other countries may not be relevant to the standard of care applicable to doctors in this country. In *Whiteford v. Hunter*[24] the defendant's mistaken diagnosis of prostate cancer was not negligent on account of his failure to use an instrument which was routinely used in such circumstances in the United States. In *ter Neuzen v. Korn*,[25] where the claimant alleged that she had been negligently infected with the HIV virus through artificial insemination in British Columbia in January 1985, the evidence was that the risk of infection was not generally known in British Columbia until mid-1985, although it had been appreciated in Australia in 1984. The Supreme Court of Canada held that it was not open to the jury to

---

Southwark Health Authority [1998] Lloyd's Rep. Med. 324 Kay J. (adequacy of defendant's notes assessed by reference to the date on which they were made, not the date of trial).

[21] *The Times*, December 8, 1953.

[22] (1985) 39 S.A.S.R. 543.

[23] *ibid.* at 562. Similarly, in *Gascoine v. Ian Sheridan & Co.* [1994] 5 Med. L.R. 437, Mitchell J. commented that a general gynaecologist and obstetrician had a responsibility to keep himself generally informed on changes in diagnosis, treatment and practice through the mainstream literature such as the leading textbooks and the *Journal of Obstetrics and Gynaecology* but could not reasonably be expected to acquaint himself with the content of more obscure journals: see P. 447. However, in *Shakoor v. Kang Situ* [2001] 1 W.L.R. 410 (see below, para. 12–151) Bernard Livesey Q.C. remarked *obiter* that "An alternative practitioner who prescribes a remedy must take steps to satisfy himself that there has not been any adverse reports in such journals on the remedy which ought to affect the use he makes of it. That is not to say that he must take a range of publications himself. It should be enough if he subscribes to an 'association' which arranges to search the relevant literature and promptly report any material publication to him." The Judge concluded that, even judged by the standards of the reasonably competent general practitioner, the practitioner of Traditional Chinese Herbal Medicine ("TCHM") could not be criticised for failing to have noticed warnings in and letters to the Lancet which potentially impacted on the treatment prescribed by him.

[24] [1950] W.N. 552, HL.

[25] (1995) 127 D.L.R. (4th) 577.

find the Canadian doctors negligent. Their conduct had to be measured by reference to prevailing Canadian standards.[26]

Standard of skill and care determined by reference to the specialisation of   **12–075**
the defendant. In determining whether a medical practitioner has exercised due skill and care, regard must be had to his specialisation or lack of specialisation. Thus in *Hucks v. Cole*[27] Lord Denning M.R. observed that the defendant "was to be judged as a general practitioner with a diploma in obstetrics". In *Langley v. Campbell*[28] the defendant, a general practitioner, failed to diagnose malaria or even to be alerted to the possibility that his patient had contracted some kind of tropical disease. Cusack J. took into account the fact that malaria was not a disease "which normally came in the way of the ordinary general practitioner" and emphasised that he was applying the standard of care of a general practitioner in the defendant's position. However, on the facts he held that the defendant was negligent. Conversely, as the House of Lords has pointed out on three occasions,[29] a practitioner who specialises in any particular area of medicine must be judged by the standard of skill and care of that speciality.[29a] Lord Bridge (with whom Lord Keith agreed) said in *Sidaway v. Governors of Bethlem Royal Hospital*[30]:

> "The language of the *Bolam* test clearly requires a different degree of skill from a specialist in his own special field than from a general practitioner. In the field of neuro-surgery it would be necessary to substitute for Lord President Clyde's phrase, 'no doctor of ordinary skill', the phrase 'no neuro-surgeon of ordinary skill'."[31]

The specialist is required to meet the standards of the ordinarily competent member of his specialism, which need not be those of the most experienced or highly qualified members.[32] Similar principles apply in Canada[33] and Australia.[34]

In *Fleury v. Woolgar*[35] the defendant was the claimant's family (general)   **12–076**
practitioner. She had a special interest in obstetrics and attended and assisted at

---

[26] *ibid.* at 581–582, 589–590.

[27] (1968) 112 S.J. 483; [1993] 4 Med. L.R. 393.

[28] *The Times*, November 6, 1975.

[29] *Whitehouse v. Jordan* [1981] 1 W.L.R. 246, 263B *per* Lord Fraser; *Maynard v. West Midlands Regional Health Authority* [1984] 1 W.L.R. 634, 638H, *per* Lord Scarman (with whom the other four law lords agreed); *Sidaway v. Governors of Bethlem Royal Hospital* [1985] A.C. 871, 892G *per* Lord Diplock, 897C *per* Lord Bridge (with whom Lord Keith agreed).

[29a] In *Poynter v. Hillingdon Health Authority* (1997) 37 B.M.L.R. 192 (for the facts of which, see para. 12–219, below) the authority's heart transplant team was "practising at the very highest level of expertise" and were thus required to meet a correspondingly high standard of care.

[30] [1985] A.C. 871, 897C.

[31] The relevant passage of Lord Clyde's judgment is set out in para. 12–068, above.

[32] "A medical practitioner who holds himself out as being a specialist in a particular field is required to attain the ordinary level of skill amongst those who specialise in the same field. He is not required to attain the highest degree of skill and competence in that particular field": *O'Donovan v. Cork County Council* [1967] I.R. 173, 190 *per* Walsh J., Supreme Court of Ireland.

[33] See *Crits v. Sylvester* (1956) 1 D.L.R. (2d) 502, 508, affirmed (1956) 5 D.L.R. (2d) 601, Supreme Court of Canada; *Koerber v. Trustees of Kitchener-Waterloo Hospital* (1987) 62 O.R. (2d) 613, 617: "Specialists, of course, must be expected to perform at a higher level than general practitioners. They represent themselves as possessing superior skills with additional training", *per* Callaghan A.C.J.H.C; *Brown v. University of Alberta Hospital* (1997) 145 D.L.R. (4th) 63, 107.

[34] See *Rogers v. Whitaker* [1993] 4 Med. L.R. 79, 80, High Court of Australia; *Kite v. Malycha* (1998) 71 S.A.S.R. 321, 336 Supreme Court of South Australia.

[35] (1996) 37 Alta. L.R. (3d) 346, Queen's Bench of Alberta.

the birth of the claimant. In the course of the birth the claimant suffered palsy of the brachial plexus, resulting in permanent disability. The court found that the defendant ought to be judged against the standard of "a family practitioner engaging in a significant practice of obstetrics in a well equipped city hospital." She was not expected to have the same degree of skill as an obstetrician, but she was required to know when an obstetrician should be called.[36] While undoubtedly correct on its particular facts, it is submitted that a court would be likely to reach a different conclusion in the event that a practitioner held himself either as being something that he was not or as being competent in a discipline other than his own. In such a case there would appear to be no logical reason for judging the practitioner by reference to any standard other than that which he held himself out as attaining.[37]

12–077   **Inexperience.** Of necessity, treatment in hospitals is on occasions given by junior doctors of limited experience. The question arises, by what standard should they be judged? In *Junor v. McNicol*[38] it was alleged that M, a house surgeon, was negligent in failing to give the patient a proper course of penicillin injections. M was acquitted of negligence, principally on the ground that she was following the consultant's instructions. In considering the standard of skill and care expected of M, the Lord Chancellor stated: "there was a duty on her to display the care and skill of a prudent qualified house surgeon, it being remembered that such a position was held by a comparative beginner." The standard of care to be expected of junior hospital doctors was the subject of detailed consideration by the Court of Appeal in *Wilsher v. Essex Area Health Authority*.[39] The plaintiff was born prematurely and treated in a special care baby unit, staffed by two consultants, a senior registrar and several junior doctors. Mustill L.J. rejected the submission that a junior doctor should be judged by the standard "required of a person having his formal qualifications and practical experience". He considered that the duty of care related not to the individual but to the post which he occupied:

> "In a case such as the present, the standard is not just that of the averagely competent and well-informed junior houseman (or whatever the position of the doctor) but of such a person who fills a post in a unit offering a highly specialised service."[40]

Sir Nicolas Browne-Wilkinson V.-C. favoured a lower standard:

---

[36] See also *Hucks v. Cole* [1993] 4 Med. L.R. 393.
[37] The case of *Shakoor v. Kang Situ* [2001] 1 W.L.R. 410, Bernard Livesey Q.C., is also of interest in this regard. The defendant was a practitioner of traditional chinese herbal medicine ("TCHM") who prescribed a chinese herbal treatment for the claimant. The claimant subsequently died. The defendant submitted that the standard against which he was to be judged was that of "the reasonably competent practitioner of traditional chinese herbal medicine". That submission was rejected. The judge was influenced by the fact that, as an alternative therapy, TCHM was practised in the West alongside "orthodox" medicine. He concluded that the practitioner of an alternative therapy therefore ought to take account of that fact and should be judged by reference not only to his own branch of medicine, but also by reference to a comparable orthodox branch.
[38] *The Times*, March 26, 1959.
[39] [1987] Q.B. 730. This aspect of the Court of Appeal's decision was not challenged on the appeal to the House of Lords: see [1988] A.C. 1074.
[40] [1987] Q.B. 730, 751B-C.

"In my judgment, if the standard of care required of such a doctor is that he should have the skill required of the post he occupies, the young houseman or the doctor seeking to acquire specialist skill in a special unit would be held liable for shortcomings in the treatment without any personal fault on his part at all."[41]

On this issue Glidewell L.J. preferred the view of Mustill L.J.[42] The view of the majority in *Wilsher* was followed in *Djemal v. Bexley Health Authority*.[43] It was held that the standard of care required in diagnosing the condition of a patient presenting in a hospital accident and emergency department was that of a reasonably competent senior houseman acting as a casualty officer, without any reference to the length of his experience. A doctor with four months' experience in that post was found negligent in failing to elicit a proper history from a patient suffering epiglottitis. As a result, he wrongly diagnosed a viral throat infection and discharged the patient. The patient's condition deteriorated and he suffered brain damage.[44]

Undertaking work beyond one's competence. If a medical practitioner lacks **12–078** the skill and experience to deal with a particular case, he should refer the matter to someone who is competent to deal with it.[45] In *Payne v. St Helier Group Hospital Management Committee*[46] the defendant's casualty officer incorrectly diagnosed the abdominal injuries of a man who had been kicked by a horse. Donovan J. held that the casualty officer was negligent in failing to have the man examined by a doctor of consultant rank. The issue arose in acute form in *Nickolls v. Ministry of Health*[47] in which a distinguished and very courageous

---

[41] *ibid.* at 777E-F.
[42] *ibid.* at 774D-E.
[43] [1995] 6 Med. L.R. 269. See also *Bova v. Spring* [1994] 5 Med. L.R. 120, where the defendant accepted that the standard of care to be expected from her as a trainee general practitioner was not different from that expected of an experienced one.
[44] Failure properly to supervise inexperienced doctors may be a breach of a hospital authority's direct duty of care: see paras 12–155 to 12–161, below.
[45] "It is, no doubt, conceivable that a qualified man may be held liable for recklessly undertaking a case which he knew, or should have known, to be beyond his powers." (*Per* Lord Hewart C.J. in *R. v. Bateman* (1925) 94 L.J.K.B. 791.) For Canadian cases in which a similar principle was applied, see *Fraser v. Vancouver General Hospital* [1951] 3 W.W.R. (N.S.) 337, British Columbia Court of Appeal, affirmed [1952] 3 D.L.R. 785, Supreme Court of Canada (intern held to have been negligent in undertaking to interpret X-ray films, rather than referring them to an expert radiologist) and *Dillon v. Le Roux* [1994] 6 W.W.R. 280, British Columbia Court of Appeal (family physician who was acting as a relief hospital emergency room doctor but had no emergency room training was negligent in failing promptly to call a hospital doctor to assist in diagnosis). See also *Miles v. Judge* (1997) 37 C.C.L.T. 160, Ontario Court of Justice, General Division (surgeon adopted a form of laparoscopic surgery which was an acceptable method of treatment but which he had performed only twice before. Held that his inexperience had led him to perform the procedure negligently, causing damage to major blood vessels); *Brooks v. Home Office*, The Times, February 18, 1999, Garland J. (a woman pregnant with twins who was detained in prison was entitled to expect the same careful standard of obstetric medical care and observation as if she were at liberty that standard was not met because the prison medical service doctor had insufficient obstetrics experience to deal with one twin's lack of growth and failed to seek specialist obstetric advice for five days after the need for it arose, although the breach was not causative of the baby's death); *Marriott v. West Midlands Health Authority* [1999] Lloyd's Rep. Med. 23, CA (negligent failure to refer patient to hospital for full neurological testing where the general practitioner ought to have perceived a risk of intracranial lesion).
[46] [1952] C.L.Y. 2442.
[47] *The Times*, February 4, 1955.

surgeon, who was himself suffering from terminal cancer, continued working until shortly before he died. Eight weeks before his death he operated on the claimant for the removal of a goitre. Both the claimant's laryngeal nerves were damaged during the operation. This issue was whether the surgeon was negligent in undertaking the operation at all. The Court of Appeal observed that surgeons ought not to perform operations unless they were fit to do so. Although the issue was a fine one in that case, the trial judge's decision that the surgeon was not negligent was upheld.

12–079   **Undertaking work in an emergency.** The obligations of the doctor as a rescuer are discussed in paragraph 12–019 above. Subject to the decision in the Australian case of *Lowns v. Woods* and the NHS (General Medical Services) Regulations 1992[48] a doctor is under no obligation to provide a stranger with treatment in an emergency. If he does help, his duty is only not to make the victim's plight worse.[49] The extent of the doctor's duty will depend on the facts of the situation, and what (if anything) the doctor took it upon himself to do. The standard of care to be provided by the doctor will be no more and no less than that which it is reasonable to expect of him in all the circumstances.

12–080   **Misadventure.** A great deal of medical treatment, even if administered with all due skill and care, involves some degree of risk. It is inevitable, therefore, that mishaps will occur for which the patient has no remedy.[50] In *White v. Board of Governors of Westminster Hospital*[51] during an operation on the claimant's right eye the surgeon accidentally cut the retina. Thompson J. acknowledged that the surgeon was operating within a very few millimetres, and held that he had exercised all reasonable skill, care and judgment. The claimant was a victim of mischance. A Canadian decision to the same effect is *Chubey v. Ahsan*[52] where, during an operation to remove a disc, the orthopaedic surgeon inadvertently pierced the aorta and vena cava, causing the patient's death. Solomon J. and the Manitoba Court of Appeal held that this slip was not negligent. The risk of damaging blood vessels was inherent in the operation.[53] Even administering an injection appears to involve some degree of risk. In three reported cases the needle broke during the course of the injection, but it was held that there was no

---

[48] See para. 12–019, above.

[49] See para. 12–015, above.

[50] *Fussell v. Beddard* (1942) 2 B.M.J. 411, affords a striking example: as a result of a misunderstanding between the anaesthetist and the nurse, the claimant was given an excessive quantity of decicaine, from which he died. Lewis J. held that there was no negligence, but an "unfortunate mistake". See generally paras 1331–1332 of the Report of the Royal Commission on Civil Liability and Compensation for Personal Injury, (1978) Cmnd. 7054.

[51] *The Times*, October 26, 1961.

[52] (1977) 71 D.L.R. (3d) 550; see also *Kapur v. Marshall* (1978) 85 D.L.R. (3d) 566, Ontario High Court (a neurosurgeon who pierced an artery whilst removing disc material was held not negligent because the piercing of an artery was a recognised remote risk in this type of operation).

[53] In *Joyce v. Merton, Sutton & Wandsworth Health Authority* [1996] 7 Med. L.R. 1, CA, it was common ground that suturing together the walls of an artery during a routine cardiological procedure was a recognised risk of the procedure, even when carefully performed. But *cf. Barrett v. Swindon Hospital Management Committee* (1973) (cited in *Legal Proceedings Against Doctors and Health Authorities* (Taliscourt Publications, 1980), p. 10) in which a surgeon who jerked a pair of biting forceps one fifth of an inch as a result of an involuntary twitch was held to have been negligent.

negligence by the person administering the injection.[54] In some instances the condition or predisposition of the claimant may itself make the treatment more difficult or more dangerous.[55] For example, in *Williams v. North Liverpool Hospital Management Committee*[56] a doctor injected pentothal into the claimant's tissues rather than her vein. The claimant was exceedingly obese, which made her veins difficult to find. The Court of Appeal (reversing the trial judge)[57] held that the doctor had exercised proper skill and care and could not reasonably have prevented the misfortune. Similarly, in *Ashcroft v. Mersey Regional Health Authority*[58] the defendant (who escaped liability for the failure of a routine operation to remove granulated tissue adhering to the ear drum) relied upon two unusual features of the claimant's ear.[59] The unfortunate claimant in *Jacobs v. Great Yarmouth and Waveney Health Authority*[60] was found to be one of those patients who experience intermittent consciousness, despite the competent administration of general anaesthesia.

On occasions medical treatment involves making a choice between competing risks. This situation commonly arises where a doctor wishes to prescribe a drug which is known to have serious adverse effects. So long as he acts reasonably, he should not be held liable simply because the risks inherent in whichever course he takes materialise or simply because some other doctor (or the judge) feels that he would have taken the opposite course.[61] In *Mahon v. Osborne*[62] Scott L.J. discussed the position of a surgeon in these terms: **12–081**

> "It is not every slip or mistake which imports negligence and, in applying the duty of care to the case of a surgeon, it is peculiarly necessary to have regard to the different

---

[54] *Gerber v. Pines* (1935) 79 S.J. 13 (breaking apparently due to a sudden muscular spasm); *Brazier v. Ministry of Defence* [1965] 1 Lloyd's Rep. 26 (breaking apparently due to a latent defect in the needle); *Galloway v. Hanley* (1956) 1 B.M.J. 580. Compare the Canadian case of *Cardin v. City of Montreal*, at para. 12–83 below, where there was a finding of negligence as a result of a doctor's failure to take an essential precaution.

[55] See also *Smith v. St Helier Group Hospital Management Committee*, *The Times*, May 10, 1956: the claimant (who was an employee rather than a patient in the hospital) sustained dermatitis from contact with Dettol solution to which she was unduly sensitive. Devlin J. held that undue sensitivity to Dettol was not foreseeable and the hospital was not liable.

[56] *The Times*, January 17, 1959.

[57] The trial judge was correct in his statement of the law, which Ormrod L.J. cited with approval: "There are risks inherent in most forms of medical treatment, and anaesthetics is certainly no exception. All one can ask of a practitioner is that he should keep these risks to the minimum to which reasonable skill and reasonable care can reduce them. If he does this, no injury which occurs, however serious, will be actionable."

[58] [1983] 2 All E.R. 245. Affirmed on appeal: [1985] 2 All E.R. 96 (Note).

[59] [1991] 2 Med. L.R. 215; *cf. Ackers v. Wigan Health Authority* [1991] 2 Med. L.R. 232 [1983] 2 All E.R. 245, 247j. See, to similar effect, *Taylor v. Worcester Health Authority* [1991] 2 Med. L.R. 215.

[60] [1995] 6 Med. L.R. 192. See also *Moore v. Worthing District Health Authority* [1992] 3 Med. L.R. 431.

[61] An interesting example of this dilemma is the Australian case, *Battersby v. Tottman* (1984) 35 S.A.S.R. 577: the first defendant prescribed a high dosage of melleril for the claimant (who was suffering from severe mental illness) in the knowledge that this posed a risk to the claimant's eyes. The risk materialised and the claimant suffered serious and permanent eye damage. It was held that the first defendant had acted reasonably in prescribing such a high dosage of melleril. The alternative risk, if the claimant had not been taking melleril, was that she would commit suicide: see *ibid.* at 584.

[62] [1939] 2 K.B. 14.

kinds of circumstances that may present themselves for urgent attention. I will mention a few applicable to a major abdominal operation:

> (1) the multiform difficulties presented by the particular circumstances of the operation;
>
> (2) the condition of the patient and the whole set of problems arising out of the risks to which he is being exposed;
>
> (3) the difficulty of the surgeon's choice between risks;
>
> (4) the paramount need of his discretion being unfettered if he thinks it right to take one risk to avoid greater . . . "[63]

In *Whiteford v. Hunter*[64] the defendant did not verify his diagnosis of cancer by means of a biopsy, because this would have involved serious risk of perforating the bladder wall and consequent ulceration. The House of Lords held (contrary to the trial judge) that the failure to do a biopsy did not amount to negligence.

12–082   In cases involving misadventure in the course of a patient's management, the true consideration of liability will usually depend upon whether the patient has been adequately warned if the misadventure was a known risk, and if inadequate warnings have been given, whether the patient would have decided upon a different course if properly warned.

12–083   **Failure to take precautions.** Where a medical practitioner rejects precautions for no good reason, then any resulting mishap is more likely to be treated as negligent.[65] In *Urry v. Bierer*,[66] for example, during an operation to deliver a child by Caesarian section the defendant did not have tapes attached to the swabs. He relied solely on the swab count by the nurse to ensure that all swabs were removed. One swab was left in the claimant's body. The Court of Appeal held, in the light of evidence as to general practice, that the failure to use tapes did not in itself amount to negligence. However, there was no convincing reason why tapes should not be used. "A surgeon who discarded or disregarded that safeguard could be said to place an additional burden on himself." On the particular facts in this case it was held that the defendant was negligent. The medical practitioner is, of course, only expected to take precaution against risks which he ought reasonably to anticipate. In *Warren v. Greig*[67] a doctor allowed the extraction of all the patient's teeth in a single operation, without first carrying out a blood test to see whether the patient suffered from acute myeloid leukaemia.

---

[63] *ibid.* at 31.
[64] [1950] W.N. 552. See also Wood J.'s description of the comparative risk assessment to be undertaken in deciding whether laparotomy or laparoscopy was the appropriate diagnostic technique to be used on a patient with a history of gynaecological problems: *Darley v. Shale* [1993] 4 Med. L.R. 161 at 168, New South Wales Supreme Court. See further para. 12–125, below.
[65] See, for example, *Cardin v. City of Montreal* (1961) 29 D.L.R. (2d) 492, Supreme Court of Canada: a doctor who continued to inject vaccine into the arm of a struggling child, with the result that the needle broke, was held to have been negligent. Given the serious consequences of a broken needle, immobilisation of the child's arm was an essential precaution. For a slightly different example of failure to take precautions, see *Stokes v. Guest, Keen & Nettlefold* [1968] 1 W.L.R. 1776 (company medical officer failing to protect employees against scrotal cancer). See also *Le Page v. Kingston and Richmond Health Authority* [1997] 8 Med. L.R. 229 (failure to administer prophylactic blood transfusion at the start of a Caesarian section when it was known that the plaintiff was anaemic).
[66] *The Times*, July 15, 1955.
[67] *The Lancet*, February 9, 1935, p. 330.

MacKinnon J. held that, having regard to the rarity of the disease, the doctor was not negligent in omitting this precaution.

Policy considerations. In any given case where a claimant has suffered   **12–084** grievous injuries through no fault of his own, there is a natural desire to see him compensated. Lord Denning was eloquent in pointing out the dangers of raising the standard of skill and care too high, simply in order to compensate deserving claimants in individual cases.[68] In *Whitehouse v. Jordan*[69] he stated:

> "Take heed of what has happened in the United States. 'Medical malpractice' cases there are very worrying, especially as they are tried by juries who have sympathy for the patient and none for the doctor, who is insured. The damages are colossal. The doctors insure but the premiums become very high; and these have to be passed on in fees to the patients. Experienced practitioners are known to have refused to treat patients for fear of being accused of negligence. Young men are even deterred from entering the profession because of the risks involved. In the interests of all, we must avoid such consequences in England. Not only must we avoid excessive damages, we must say, and say firmly, that, in a professional man, an error of judgment is not negligent."

Although upholding the decision in *Whitehouse v. Jordan* the House of Lords[70] criticised the last sentence in the passage quoted above on the basis that an error of judgment may or may not constitute negligence. The two terms were not mutually exclusive. However, the law lords did not discuss, or comment on, the policy considerations to which Lord Denning referred. In *Wilsher v. Essex Area Health Authority*[71] Mustill L.J. voiced similar concerns:

> "The risks which actions for professional negligence bring to the public as a whole, in the shape of an instinct on the part of a professional man to play for safety, are serious and are now well recognised. Nevertheless, the proper response cannot be to temper the wind to the professional man. If he assumes to perform a task, he must bring to it the appropriate care and skill. What the courts can do, however, is to bear constantly in mind that, in those situations which call for the exercise of judgment, the fact that in retrospect the choice actually made can be shown to have turned out badly is not in itself a proof of negligence, and to remember that a duty of care is not a warranty of a perfect result."[72]

---

[68] See *Roe v. Minister of Health* [1954] 2 Q.B. 66, 812–87 (cited with approval in *Koerber v. Trustees of Kitchener-Waterloo Hospital* (1987) 62 O.R. 613, 632); Lord Denning, *The Discipline of Law* (Butterworths, 1979), pp. 241–244. For a powerful reply to Lord Denning's arguments, see the note on *Whitehouse v. Jordan* by G. Robertson, (1981) 44 M.L.R. 457–461.

[69] [1980] 1 All E.R. 650, 658. For the facts, see para. 12–190, below.

[70] [1981] 1 W.L.R. 246, *per* Lords Edmund-Davies, Fraser and Russell.

[71] [1987] Q.B. 730.

[72] *ibid.* at 747B-C. The issues which prompted these observations were not raised in the appeal to the House of Lords: see [1988] A.C. 1074. In *Dowdie v. Camberwell Health Authority* [1997] 8 Med. L.R. 368, the plaintiff suffered permanent damage to the nerves serving his right arm and hand as a result of shoulder dystocia during his birth. In finding that the health authority's obstetric staff had negligently failed to deliver the plaintiff by Caesarean section, Maurice Kay J. nevertheless recognised that: "in this area, even more than in many other areas of medical litigation, a great deal revolves around matters of judgment, that more than one view can coexist within the range of the acceptable and that one must be careful before categorising something as negligent if it was simply an alternative but acceptable judgment which has only become unfortunate with the benefit of hindsight. I am also conscious of the need to make allowances for the pressures within which decisions have to be taken by clinicians."

It seems unlikely, at least in England, that doctors would be deterred altogether from treating particular patients by the fear of negligence actions.[73] However, the risk of doctors practising "defensive medicine" is perhaps a more serious matter.[74] A study undertaken in 1990 revealed that there was a widespread misunderstanding amongst medical practitioners as to the nature of their legal duty to patients; and that there was a tendency to adopt unjustified and defensive medical practices, in order to avoid the risk of being sued.[75] However, if defensive medicine amounts to "adopting procedures which are not for the benefit of the patient but safeguards against the possibility of the patient making a claim for negligence"[76] then such safeguards are misconceived. If a reasonably competent practitioner would regard a procedure as unnecessary, a doctor who fails to carry it out cannot be held negligent and will be more vulnerable to suit if a risk inherent in the procedure materialises. Conversely, a doctor who refrains from carrying out a procedure because he fears litigation will be negligent if a reasonably competent doctor would consider the procedure justified in the interests of the patient.[77]

12–085   Discussion of these important issues is sometimes clouded by an over-simplistic comparison between English and American "malpractice" litigation. Professor Miller noted in 1986 that malpractice claims were brought in the United States nearly 10 times as often as in England, attributing this to a complex combination of factors, including cultural differences, judicial attitudes, differences in the legal system and the rules about costs. She pointed to the deterrent value of malpractice litigation and resented some of the criticisms of the American system expressed by the British judiciary.[78] Interestingly, in 1989 the number of medical negligence claims and the size of medical malpractice

---

[73] This risk was mentioned as long ago as 1927 by McCardie J. in the context of an action for negligently certifying that a person was of unsound mind. See *De Freville v. Dill* (1927) 96 L.J.K.B. 1056: "During the past seven years a number of medical men, who acted in perfect good faith, have been exposed to the most prolonged, harassing and costly litigation upon the allegation that they acted without reasonable care in a matter which is the most difficult, delicate, and indefinite in the whole range of medical practice. It may well be, as was stated at the trial before me, that as a result of past litigation many doctors have refused and will refuse to take any part whatever in the work of certification because of the perils and anxieties of litigation which may follow."

[74] *Whitehouse v. Jordan* itself illustrates the point. At first instance the defendant was held negligent for the manner in which he carried out a trial of forceps (although this finding was reversed on appeal). Shortly afterwards an article appeared in the *British Medical Journal* expressing the fear that the decision might deter obstetricians from undertaking trials of forceps and lead to an increase in Caesarean operations. Such a development would involve greater risks for the patients: see "Negligence and Forceps Delivery" (1979) 1 B.M.J. 763. See generally paras 1319–1324 of the Report of the Royal Commission on Civil Liability and Compensation for Personal Injury, Cmnd. 7054 (1978).

[75] See Tribe and Korgaonkar, "The Impact of Litigation on Patient Care: an enquiry into defensive medical practices" (1991) 7 P.N. 2. These conclusions were based on a questionnaire sent to 400 hospital doctors and general practitioners in Hertfordshire. There was a 56 per cent response rate.

[76] *Whitehouse v. Jordan* [1980] 1 All E.R. 650, 659 *per* Lawton L.J. In *X (Minors) v. Bedfordshire County Council* [1995] 2 A.C. 633, a majority in the Court of Appeal, and the House of Lords considered that the risk of encouraging defensive practices weighed against the imposition of a duty of care on a psychiatrist advising a local authority as to whether a child was being sexually abused.

[77] Support for this proposition can be found in the comments of Evans L.J. in *Barrett v. Enfield Borough Council* [1998] Q.B. 367 at 380A-C, quoted at para. 12–060 above and approved by Lord Slynn (with whom Lord Nolan and Lord Steyn agreed) in the House of Lords: see [1999] 3 W.L.R. 79 at 94A-C.

[78] See Prof. F. Miller, "Medical Malpractice Litigation: Do the British have a Better Remedy?" (1986) *American Journal of Law and Medicine*, Vol. XI, no. 4, p. 433.

insurance premiums started to fall in New York, California and many other states.[79] It is thought that this is due in part to legislation in a number of states limiting medical malpractice claims, and in part to improved patient care as a result of litigation.[80]

In England, the medical profession seems to fare better before the courts than most other professions. The defence of "non-negligent mistake" succeeds more often. It is thought that this is at least in part due to the *Bolam* test (as it has been applied in medical negligence cases[81]) and to the greater degree of deference which the courts traditionally show to expert witnesses in this sphere.[82] The change in the approach to the Bolam test, and to the way that expert witnesses are to be considered following the decision of the House of Lords in *Bolitho v. City & Hackney Health Authority*[83] will make some difference in the future, but it will only be a rare case in which a court will hold that a body of medical opinion is not reasonable or responsible.[84] Since a medical negligence action is almost invariably a claim for personal injuries and since in England (unlike the United States) such claims are assessed by judges according to established tariffs, the medical practitioner's potential liability is kept within predictable bounds. In this respect the medical profession is in a more favourable position than each of the other professions discussed in this work (whose members on occasions face liabilities which go far beyond their available insurance cover). Finally, even when holding a doctor liable, it is not uncommon for the courts to comment that the incident in question ought not to tarnish the defendant's reputation.[85]

12–086

Nonetheless, the United Kingdom has seen a marked increase in the volume of medical negligence litigation since the mid-1970s. In July 1996, it was estimated that there were about 20,000 claims outstanding against the NHS. Of those, some 2,500 had a value in excess of £100,000.[86] The cost to the state of clinical negligence litigation was estimated for the year 1996–1997 to be £300 million[87]; and for the year 1999–2000 the cost was said to be "nearly £400 million".[88] Recent years have also seen a significant change in the way in which such claims are handled. Until 1990, the three principal bodies through whom medical practitioners made insurance arrangements were the Medical Defence Union, the Medical Protection Society and the Medical and Dental Defence Union of Scotland. In January 1990, the Government responded to the growing perception

12–087

---

[79] See D. Henriques, "Just What the Doctor Ordered" (1989) *Barron's*, October 2, 1989.

[80] Although there were variations, the general picture was that there was no dramatic rise in premiums in the course of the 1990s. The cost of medical malpractice in the United States will always be topical: according to the U.S. Congressional Budget Office, medical malpractice insurance premiums amount to less than 1% of health costs—but the sum is still, of course, very large.

[81] See paras 12–093, 12–094 below.

[82] See para. 12–096 below.

[83] [1998] A.C. 232. See paras 12–071 and 12–072, above.

[84] Lord Browne-Wilkinson in *Bolitho* at 243A–C.

[85] See the dissenting judgment of Donaldson L.J. in *Whitehouse v. Jordan* [1980] 1 All E.R. 650, 666C–D; *Clark v. MacLennan* [1983] 1 All E.R. 416, 433F–H; *Thake v. Maurice* [1986] Q.B. 644, 663B–C.

[86] See Lord Woolf's final report on the civil justice system, "Access to Justice" (HMSO, 1996), chap. 15, para. 10 and para. 12–166, below.

[87] Lord Woolf, "Are the courts excessively deferential to the medical profession?" (2001) Med. L. Rev. 1.

[88] According to the press release of July 10, 2001 announcing the setting up of the committee to examine ways of making the system for compensation for clinical negligence "fairer and faster".

of a "medical malpractice crisis" in this country, which was reflected in a marked increase in subscription rates paid by doctors to the medical defence organisations, by the introduction of "NHS indemnity". Since January 1, 1990, health authorities have been obliged to indemnify hospital doctors and dentists against liability for clinical negligence in the course of NHS employment.[89] (Consultants engaged in private work and general practitioners[90] are not included and are indemnified by the medical defence organisations.)[91] The reforms instituted by the NHS and Community Care Act 1990 have led to the transfer of responsibility for many hospitals to autonomous NHS trusts.[92] NHS trust hospitals are not within the financial remit of health authorities but NHS indemnity has been extended to their staff. In November 1995, the NHS Litigation Authority was established. This body administers the Clinical Negligence Scheme for Trusts (CNST), a voluntary scheme which enables NHS trusts to share the costs of medical negligence claims. The scheme covers claims relating to incidents which occurred after April 1, 1995.[93] An important objective is to encourage trusts to introduce systems for effective clinical risk management: part of any claim will still be borne by the relevant trust and there are financial incentives for the adoption of procedures which are designed to reduce the incidence of claims. By July 1996, the vast majority of NHS trusts had joined the scheme,[94] and by July 2001 all but one of the NHS Trusts were members of the scheme.

12–088   One of the questions considered by the Royal Commission on Civil Liability and Compensation for Personal Injury, chaired by Lord Pearson, was whether a system of no-fault compensation should be introduced for medical accidents. Such a system has been introduced in New Zealand[95] and Sweden. The Royal Commission recommended that such a system should not be introduced, at least for the time being, and that the basis of liability in tort for medical injuries should continue to be negligence. They also recommended, however, that a volunteer for

---

[89] See Department of Health Circular H.C. (89) 34 and Health Services Guidelines H.S.G. (96) 48.

[90] Except in respect of work carried out by a general practitioner under a contract with a health authority or NHS Trust.

[91] It is the declared policy of two of these bodies to resist apparently unmeritorious claims, without regard to commercial considerations. On March 5, 1983 the *British Medical Journal* published letters from both, firmly denying that they settled weak claims in order to save costs. "Out of court settlements are entertained only when, on a careful review of all the facts and evidence, the prospect of a successful defence is not good" (*per* the Secretary of the Medical Protection Society). "It is the policy of the union to defend every claim and make out of court settlements only when factual and expert evidence suggest there is a serious risk that the case would not be won in court. The union puts a member's reputation before all other considerations" (*per* the Secretary of the Medical Defence Union). See (1983) 286 B.M.J. 805.

[92] See further paras 12–162 and 12–163, below.

[93] The NHS and Community Care Act 1990, s.21 empowers the Secretary of State to establish schemes whereby NHS Trusts and health authorities may make provision to meet all third party and other liabilities. From April 1, 1996, Trusts and health authorities may also seek reimbursement for payments made in medical negligence claims which relate to incidents which occurred before April 1, 1995. The relevant scheme is the Existing Liabilities Scheme.

[94] In July 1996, the membership of CNST comprised some 384 trusts, amounting to 89.5% of trusts in England. See "Access to Justice" (HMSO, 1996), chap. 15, para. 8.

[95] The New Zealand scheme was introduced in 1974 and covers all cases of "personal injury by accident". Despite reforming legislation in 1992, a satisfactory definition of "medical misadventure" remains elusive: see K. Oliphant, "Defining 'Medical Misadventure': Lessons from New Zealand" (1996) 4 Med. L.Rev. 1.

medical research or clinical trials who suffers severe damage should have a cause of action, based on strict liability, against the appropriate authority.[96]

On July 10, 2001 the Secretary of State announced the creation of a committee **12–089** led by the Chief Medical Officer Liam Donaldson to examine ways of making the system of compensation for clinical negligence "faster and fairer". It is intended that there should be a white paper published in early 2002; and it has been announced that the committee will explore the following four specific ideas: (i) the possibility of no-fault compensation; (ii) the use of structured settlements instead of lump sum payments; (iii) fixed tariff schemes for specific injuries; and (iv) the greater use of mediation for resolving disputes. The white paper is eagerly awaited.

(d) *General and approved practice*

In determining whether a medical practitioner exercised reasonable skill and **12–090** care, the court should (except in obvious cases)[97] have regard to the practice of other practitioners of similar status.[98] This necessarily involves receiving expert evidence.[99] In *Marshall v. Lindsey County Council*[1] Maugham L.J. appeared to consider that evidence as to general practice (if accepted) was binding upon the court:

> "An act cannot, in my opinion, be held to be due to a want of reasonable care if it is in accordance with the general practice of mankind. What is reasonable in a world not wholly composed of wise men and women must depend on what people presumed to be reasonable constantly do. Many illustrations might be given and I will take one from the evidence given in this action. A jury could not, in my opinion, properly hold it to be negligent in a doctor or a midwife to perform his or her duties in a confinement without mask and gloves, even though some experts gave evidence that in their opinion that was a wise precaution. Such an omission may become negligent if, and only if, at some future date it becomes the general custom to take such a precaution among skilled practitioners."[2]

It is suggested that Maugham L.J. somewhat overstated the position in the **12–091** passage quoted above.[3] However, two general principles may be stated with some confidence: (a) if a medical practitioner acts in accordance with the general

---

[96] Report of the Royal Commission on Civil Liability and Compensation for Personal Injury, (1978) Cmnd. 7054. See in particular chap. 24. For further discussion of the policy factors, see Kennedy and Grubb, pp. 535–537.

[97] Where, for example, the wrong limb is amputated. Obvious cases are not normally litigated, except on the question of damages.

[98] In *Albrighton v. Royal Prince Alfred Hospital* [1979] 2 N.S.W.L.R. 165 the Supreme Court of New South Wales held that such evidence was vital to the claimant's claim, and that in the absence of such evidence the case should be withdrawn from the jury.

[99] See, *e.g. Mahon v. Osborne* [1939] 2 K.B. 14: "The proper question as regards Mr Osborne was whether on the night in question he had exercised the reasonable degree of skill and care that a surgeon in his position ought to exercise, whether he had done anything that, exercising such skill and care, he ought not to have done, or left undone anything that, exercising such skill and care, he ought to have done. This question involves matters of fact as to which neither the court nor the jury has knowledge. The facts must be proved by the evidence of experts. . . . Unhappily, the learned judge did not base his question to the jury upon the evidence that was given as to the practice of surgery" (*per* MacKinnon L.J. at 38–39).

[1] [1935] 1 K.B. 516. Decision affirmed by the House of Lords at [1937] A.C. 97.

[2] *ibid.* at 540.

[3] See paras 12–094 to 12–105, below.

and approved practice of the profession, or some responsible part of the profession, he will not be held negligent, save in exceptional circumstances[4]; and (b) if a medical practitioner departs from the general and approved practice for no good reason, and damage results, he is likely to be held negligent.[5]

(i) *Acting in accordance with general and approved practice*

12-092 If a medical practitioner acts in accordance with the general and approved practice of the profession, he will normally have a good defence to a claim for negligence. In *Vancouver General Hospital v. McDaniel*[6] the infant claimant caught smallpox whilst being treated in the defendant hospital for diphtheria. She alleged that the hospital was negligent because (i) smallpox patients were put in rooms on the same floor as herself, and (ii) nurses attended her, who also attended the smallpox patients. A number of expert witnesses expressed approval of the defendant's practice (which was the "unit system" as opposed to the "isolation system" for the treatment of smallpox). It was also established that the defendant's practice conformed with the general practice in other hospitals in Canada and the United States. The Privy Council, reversing the decision of the Court of Appeal of British Columbia, held that the finding of negligence could not be supported:

> "A defendant charged with negligence can clear his feet if he shows that he has acted in accord with general and approved practice. The appellants, in their Lordships' opinion, even if the onus rested on them of doing this, have in this case done so by a weight of evidence that cannot be ignored."[7]

In *Whiteford v. Hunter*[8] it was alleged *inter alia* that the defendant was negligent in failing to verify his diagnosis of cancer by a cytoscopic examination. It appeared from the evidence that it was contrary to approved medical practice in England to use a cytoscope where there was acute urinary retention. The Court of Appeal and House of Lords (reversing the decision of Birkett J.) acquitted the defendant of negligence.

12-093   **Lack of single uniform practice.** In many instances, of course, there is no uniform "general and approved practice". Different schools of thought exist. If a medical practitioner acts in accordance with one respectable school of thought, he is unlikely to be held negligent. In *Bolam v. Friern Hospital Management Committee*[9] the claimant sustained fractures of the acetabula during the course of electro-convulsive therapy. It was alleged that the defendants were negligent *inter alia* in failing to use relaxant drugs and failing to use more than very limited restraint. It appeared from the evidence that relaxant drugs would have eliminated the risk of fractures, but would have involved a small mortality risk. There was a firm body of opinion against relaxants. Some practitioners used them and

---

[4] See paras 12–092 to 12–105, below.
[5] See paras 12–106 to 12–108, below.
[6] (1935) 152 L.T.R. 56.
[7] *ibid.* at 57–58. In the case of *Newbury v. Bath District H.A.* (1998) 47 B.M.L.R. 138 the defendant orthopaedic surgeon used a technique that neither the expert for the claimant nor his own expert would have used. He was held not to have been negligent in using a tried and tested method which was no longer widely used, but which had not been "professionally rejected as wrong".
[8] [1950] W.N. 533. See also para. 12–081, above and para. 12–183, below.
[9] [1957] 1 W.L.R. 582.

some did not. Similarly, there were two schools of thought about manual control. Some practitioners thought that such restraint reduced the risk of fractures (and therefore used it). Some thought that it increased the risk of fractures (and therefore did not use it). McNair J. directed the jury[10] in these terms:

> "[A doctor] is not guilty of negligence if he has acted in accordance with a practice accepted as proper by a responsible body of medical men skilled in that particular art. . . . Putting it the other way round, a man is not negligent, if he is acting in accordance with such a practice, merely because there is a body of opinion who would take a contrary view. At the same time, that does not mean that a medical man can obstinately and pig-headedly carry on with some old technique if it has been proved to be contrary to what is really substantially the whole of informed medical opinion."[11]

The decision of the Court of Appeal in *Hughes v. Waltham Forest Health Authority*[12] affords a recent illustration of the same principle.[13] The decision of two surgeons not to refer the patient for an ERCP examination was endorsed by an eminent surgeon, practising in the same field, as being in accordance with a practice accepted as proper within the profession. The Court of Appeal reversed the trial judge's finding of negligence. The fact that two other surgeons were critical of the decision and that it turned out to be mistaken did not mean that it was negligent.

A rule of law or evidence? The decision of the House of Lords in *Maynard* **12–094** *v. West Midlands Regional Health Authority*[14] is sometimes cited[15] as authority for the proposition that a defendant cannot be found negligent if his actions were in accordance with a general professional practice which is proved by reliable and credible evidence. In that case, R, a consultant physician, and S, a consultant surgeon, decided that the claimant probably had tuberculosis, but that there was a risk of Hodgkin's disease. Hodgkin's disease was fatal unless remedial steps were taken in its early stages. R and S decided to do a mediastinoscopy (an operation to obtain a biopsy) rather than to await the result of a sputum test, which would take several weeks. The biopsy was negative, and it was subsequently confirmed that the claimant had tuberculosis. Unfortunately, however, the mediastinoscopy (although properly performed) caused damage to the claimant's left laryngeal recurrent nerve. At trial the claimant called an expert who said that it was almost certainly a case of tuberculosis from the outset, and that it was wrong and dangerous to undertake the operation. The defendants called distinguished experts who disagreed and who approved the course taken by R and S. Both the Court of Appeal and the House of Lords held that the trial judge

---

[10] Who returned a verdict for the defendants.

[11] *ibid.* at 587.

[12] [1991] 2 Med. L.R. 155. See also *Burgess v. Newcastle Health Authority* [1992] 3 Med. L.R. 224. The claimant suffered injuries following a bilateral shunt operation. It was common ground that there was no single approved technique for carrying out this operation. Turner J. found that the technique which the registrar had adopted was acceptable to a widely respected body of neurosurgeons and accordingly dismissed the allegations of negligence.

[13] For a Canadian illustration of the principle, see *Morrison v. Patel* (1988) 44 C.C.L.T. 264: defendant acted in accordance with the practice of a substantial part of the medical profession in (a) not using peri-operative antibiotics and (b) proceeding by way of open rather than closed reduction of fractured humerus.

[14] [1984] 1 W.L.R. 634.

[15] See, for example, *Gordon v. Wilson*, 1992 S.L.T. 849, 852–853, OH; also reported at [1992] 3 Med. L.R. 401.

was not entitled to make a finding of negligence. Lord Scarman, with whom the other four law lords agreed, stated:

> " . . . a judge's 'preference' for one body of distinguished opinion to another also professionally distinguished is not sufficient to establish negligence in a practitioner whose actions have received the seal of approval of those whose opinions, truthfully expressed, honestly held, were not preferred. If this was the real reason for the judge's finding, he erred in law." [16]

Similarly, in *Sidaway v. Governors of Bethlem Royal Hospital*[17] Lord Scarman said:

> "The *Bolam* principle may be formulated as a rule that a doctor is not negligent if he acts in accordance with a practice accepted at the time as proper by a responsible body of medical opinion even though other doctors adopt a different practice. In short, the law imposes the duty of care; but the standard of care is a matter of medical judgment." [18]

These formulations of the *Bolam* test obscure the distinction between standards or practices which are in fact adopted by the medical profession and those which are acceptable in law. A finding that a body of professional opinion is or is not "responsible" or "respectable" may be a judgment as to the value of the opinion in law or it may be a finding as to the professional esteem in fact accorded to the proponents of a particular practice or standard. The former finding involves evaluation of a doctor's conduct against the legal standard of the reasonably competent doctor: the *Bolam* principle then identifies evidence which may assist the court in carrying out this evaluation but is not conclusive as to the result. The latter finding measures competence solely by reference to the standards in fact set by the medical profession itself: the *Bolam* principle is interpreted as a rule of law which renders the existence of a general practice conclusive. It is submitted that it cannot be right that the court is obliged to give unreserved and universal approval to all the practices of the medical profession (or of some part of the medical profession) whatever those practices may be. Such an extreme proposition would be contrary to principle.[19] In the event that the medical profession adopted some practice which was demonstrably unreasonable (*i.e.* which could be shown to be unreasonable on analysis after argument and after explanation by the experts), it is submitted that the court is entitled to find that a medical

---

[16] [1984] 1 W.L.R. 634, 639G-F. This passage was criticised by Lord Woolf in "Are the courts excessively deferential to the Medical Profession?" (2001) Med. L.Rev. 1, at 7, on the basis that it made no reference to the quality of the honest and truthful opinion.

[17] [1985] A.C. 871, 881F-G. It was because Lord Scarman regarded the *Bolam* test as a rule of law, rather than a rule of evidence, as to the appropriate standard of care in a given case, that he rejected it as appropriate to determine the standard of care in relation to the doctor's duty to warn of risks of treatment. Lord Diplock appeared to support Lord Scarman's interpretation (see *ibid.* at 892B-C) but the majority considered that compliance with practice was not determinative: see para. 12–096, below.

[18] This passage was also referred to by Lord Woolf in "Are the courts excessively deferential to the Medical Profession?" (2001) Med. L.Rev. 1, at 7, in his consideration of the correct analysis of the *Bolam* test.

[19] See, for example, *Cavanagh v. Ulster Weaving Co. Ltd* [1960] A.C. 145. The courts have been willing to review the practices of other professions. For example, in *Edward Wong Finance v. Johnson Stokes & Master* [1984] 1 A.C. 296 the Privy Council upheld a finding that a solicitor was negligent even although she followed a conveyancing procedure which was almost universal in Hong Kong.

practitioner was negligent notwithstanding the fact that he complied with such a practice.[20]

Courts elsewhere have shown themselves willing to question the practices of **12–095** the medical profession. In *Reibl v. Hughes*[21] Brooke J.A. stated in the Ontario Court of Appeal: "The duty to the patient is determined by the court and the evidence of the expert witnesses, if accepted, is relevant to determining whether or not the defendant has discharged that duty." Although the Supreme Court of Canada[22] reversed the decision of the Ontario Court of Appeal, this passage was approved.[23] Laskin C.J.C. stated:

"To allow expert medical evidence to determine what risks are material and, hence, should be disclosed and, correlatively, what risks are not material is to hand over to the medical profession the entire question of the scope of the duty of disclosure, including the question whether there has been a breach of that duty."

Similarly, the Supreme Court of South Australia has rejected the notion that the court is automatically bound by evidence as to the practice of the medical profession. In *F. v. R.*[24] King C.J. said:

"But professions may not adopt unreasonable practices, particularly as to disclosure, not because they serve the interests of the clients, but because they protect the interests or convenience of members of the profession. The court has an obligation to scrutinise professional practices to ensure that they accord with the standard of reasonableness imposed by law."[25]

This view was adopted by the High Court of Australia in *Rogers v. Whitaker*.[26] The central issue in that case was the standard of care required to discharge a doctor's duty to warn his patient of the risks of treatment. However, the court accepted that, in relation to all areas of medical practice, evidence of medical practice was no more than a useful guide. It remained for the court to determine whether the defendant's conduct met the standard of reasonable care required in law.[27] Similarly, in *O'Donovan v. Cork County Council*,[28] Walsh J., giving the judgment of the Supreme Court of Ireland, put it this way:

"If there is a common practice which has inherent defects, which ought to be obvious to any person giving the matter due consideration, the fact that it is shown to have been

---

[20] See paras 12–098 to 12–100, below; and paras 12–71 to 12–072, above.
[21] (1979) 89 D.L.R. (3d) 112. See also, for example, *Chasney v. Anderson* [1950] 4 D.L.R. 223, where it was observed that expert evidence as to general or approved practice was not conclusive on the issue of negligence; especially where the conduct in question did not involve a matter of technical skill and experience, but rather taking proper precautions in regard to something on which an ordinary person was competent to form a view. See also *Brain v. Mador* (1985) 32 C.C.L.T. 157 and the interesting editorial comment.
[22] (1980) 114 D.L.R. (3d) 1.
[23] *ibid.* at 11.
[24] (1983) 33 S.A.S.R. 189, 194; see also *Battersby v. Tottman* (1984) 35 S.A.S.R. 577, 582 (upheld on appeal: see (1985) 37 S.A.S.R. 524).
[25] Bollen J. was critical of some of the English cases, which he considered "concentrated rather too heavily on the practice of the medical profession": *ibid.* at 205.
[26] [1993] 4 Med. L.R. 79.
[27] *ibid.* at 82.
[28] [1967] I.R. 173, Supreme Court of Ireland. The passage quoted is at 193. See also *Dunne v. National Maternity Hospital* [1989] I.R. at 109.

widely and generally adopted over a period of time does not make the practice any the less negligent."

12–096   The extent to which a court may make a finding of negligence despite compliance with a practice approved by a respected body of opinion has also been discussed in England.[29] In *Sidaway v. Governors of Bethlem Royal Hospital*[30] Lord Bridge rejected the contention that the *Bolam* test necessarily involved handing over to the medical profession the entire question of liability:

> "But even in a case where, as here, no expert witness in the relevant medical field condemns the non-disclosure as being in conflict with accepted and responsible medical practice, I am of opinion that the judge might in certain circumstances come to the conclusion that the disclosure of a particular risk was so obviously necessary to an informed choice on the part of the patient that no reasonably prudent medical man would fail to make it."

Lord Bridge was there considering the *Bolam* test in the context of alleged inadequate warning by a medical practitioner. It might be thought that the courts may feel more confident in questioning established medical practice in this area than in the realm of diagnosis or treatment, but the majority of the House of Lords in *Sidaway* saw no reason to distinguish between different areas of medical practice in formulating a test for the appropriate standard of care.[31] It is submitted that there is a residual power to question established medical practice in any area.

12–097   One English case which illustrates this point, although it antedates *Bolam*, is *Clarke v. Adams*.[32] In that case the defendant, a physiotherapist, treated the claimant for a fibrositic condition of the left heel. The instrument which he used was dangerous, because burns caused by it could lead to serious consequences. Before beginning the treatment he warned the claimant in these terms: "When I turn on the machine I want you to experience a comfortable warmth and nothing more; if you do, I want you to tell me." The chief examiner for the Chartered Society of Physiotherapy gave evidence that this warning was an entirely proper one. Slade J. held that the warning was inadequate, even though it was the very warning which the defendant had been taught to give. Accordingly the defendant was liable for the injuries which the claimant suffered as a result of burning.

12–098   There have been further and more recent indications that the courts are willing, in exceptional cases, to find a medical practitioner negligent notwithstanding his compliance with a general professional practice. In *Hucks v. Cole*[33] Sachs L.J. said:

---

[29] In *Hills v. Potter* (Note) [1984] 1 W.L.R. 641, 653C, Hirst J. said: "I do not accept Mr Stone's argument that by adopting the *Bolam* principle, the court in effect abdicates its power of decision to the doctors. In every case the court must be satisfied that the standard contended for on their behalf accords with that upheld by a substantial body of medical opinion, and that this body of medical opinion is both respectable and responsible, and experienced in this particular field of medicine."
[30] [1985] A.C. 871, 900E-F. Lord Keith agreed with Lord Bridge. Lord Templeman appeared to support Lord Bridge's interpretation: *ibid.* at 903E-G. Sir John Donaldson M.R. expressed a similar view in the Court of Appeal: [1984] Q.B. 493, 513–514.
[31] *ibid.* at 893E-H *per* Lord Diplock, at 896G–897D, 900D *per* Lord Bridge, 895G *per* Lord Keith. See also *Gold v. Haringey Health Authority* [1988] Q.B. 481, 490B *per* Lloyd L.J., *cf. Gordon v. Wilson*, 1992 S.L.T. 849, 852–853, Sc., OH, also reported at [1992] 3 Med. L.R. 401.
[32] (1950) 94 S.J. 599.
[33] (1968) 112 S.J. 483; [1993] 4 Med. L.R. 393.

"When the evidence shows that a lacuna in professional practice exists by which risks of grave danger are knowingly taken then however small the risk the court must anxiously examine the lacuna, particularly if the risk can be easily and inexpensively avoided. If the court finds on the analysis of the reasons given for not taking those precautions that in the light of current professional knowledge there is no proper basis for the lacuna and it is definitely not reasonable that those risks should have been taken its function is to state that fact and when necessary to state that it constitutes negligence."

This approach was approved *obiter* by the majority in the Court of Appeal in *Bolitho v. City & Hackney Health Authority*[34] and the decision in the House of Lords in November 1997, affirming the decision of the Court of Appeal needs to be considered in some detail.

Before the decision of the House of Lords in *Bolitho* the Court of Appeal **12–099** returned to this question in *Joyce v. Wandsworth Health Authority*.[35] The claimant suffered from a heart condition. In the course of brachial cardiac catheterisation, a diagnostic procedure, a cardiology registrar mistakenly sutured together the walls of the right brachial artery. The claimant developed vascular complications and, ultimately, a brain stem infarction which caused him to suffer catastrophic injuries. He accepted that the registrar's mistake could have occurred despite the exercise of reasonable care and skill but claimed that his injuries should and would have been avoided if the mistake had been discovered and rectified in time. Judge Overend (sitting as a High Court judge) dismissed the claim. Although disagreeing with his conclusions on certain of the allegations of negligence, the Court of Appeal approved the judge's direction to himself that "a defendant is not guilty of negligence if his acts or omissions were in accordance with accepted clinical practice provided that clinical practice stood up to analysis and was not unreasonable in the light of the state of medical knowledge at the time."[36] Roch L.J. commented that the judge's proviso was very important, because without it, the decision of negligence or no negligence is left in the hands of the doctors, whereas that decision must be one for the courts. Hobhouse L.J. agreed but rejected the suggestion of Dillon L.J. in *Bolitho v. City & Hackney Health Authority*[37] that the concept of *Wednesbury* unreasonableness was of use in assessing whether a generally accepted practice was a practice which met the standard of reasonable care required at law.[38] It is submitted that the approach of Hobhouse L.J. is to be preferred.

As originally formulated by McNair J., the *Bolam* principle required the court **12–100** to decide whether the defendant's conduct was in accordance with or supported by a "responsible" body of opinion. The more interventionist approach approved by the Court of Appeal in *Hucks v. Cole*,[39] *Bolitho v. City & Hackney Health*

---

[34] [1993] 4 Med. L.R. 381 and see commentary at (1993) 1 Med. L.Rev. 241.
[35] [1996] 7 Med. L.R. 1 (and see commentary at (1996) 4 Med. L.Rev. 86). The decision is also important for the approach taken to causation where the complaint is of an omission to procure treatment: see paras 12–271 to 12–273, below.
[36] *ibid.* at 13–14 *per* Roch L.J. Compare also: "[T]he court's only concern will be to be satisfied that the doctor's decision to discontinue is in accordance with a respectable body of medical opinion and that it is reasonable": *Airedale NHS Trust v. Bland* [1993] A.C. 789, *per* Lord Browne-Wilkinson at 884F, *obiter*.
[37] [1993] 4 Med. L.R. 381.
[38] [1996] 7 Med. L.R. 1, at 20.
[39] (1968) 112 S.J. 483; [1993] 4 Med. L.R. 393.

Authority[40] and *Joyce v. Merton, Sutton & Wandsworth Health Authority*[41] recognises that the description of a practice or school of thought as responsible is properly the result of critical evaluation by the court, as the ultimate arbiter of the way in which the reasonably competent doctor would behave.[42] This development goes some way to answer those who have criticised the English courts for applying the *Bolam* principle in a manner regarded as over-protective towards the medical profession.[43] It remains likely, however, that standards and practices which are generally accepted among distinguished members of the medical profession will rarely be held not to be responsible. Where the case does not involve difficult or uncertain questions of medical treatment or complex, scientific or highly technical matters, but turns upon failure to take a simple precaution the need for which is obvious to the ordinary person considering the matter, it is more likely that a practice which neglects that precaution will be held negligent.[44] In *Wiszniewski v. Central Manchester Health Authority*[45] Thomas J. described this approach as follows:

> "In my judgment it is clearly necessary for me to analyse whether the course of treatment put forward by [the defendant's expert witnesses] put the patient unnecessarily at risk and was not one that a competent doctor acting with ordinary skill and care or a responsible body of medical opinion would have followed: see the judgment of Farquarson L.J. in *Bolitho* at p. 386. I reject the submission that such an analysis takes a trial judge into the medical arena; such an analysis of medical evidence given by experts to see if a view put forward is in fact one that a responsible body of medical practitioners could hold about a clinical judgment on an individual patient is no different in this respect to a similar analysis of a judgment by an accountant, underwriter or other professional. A judge has to be conscious of his own lack of medical knowledge and of the fact that clinical decisions are often difficult to make. However where an analysis of the expert evidence on the facts relating to a particular case shows that a decision made by a doctor and supported by experts cannot be justified as one that a responsible medical practitioner would have taken, then a judge should not preclude himself from reaching that conclusion simply because clinical judgment is involved."[46]

Nevertheless, it is likely that the courts will be more ready to challenge established practice when the issue is whether a doctor has adequately warned his patient of the risks and implications of proposed treatment. In *Newell and Newell v. Goldenburg*[47] the defendant vasectomist, in an admitted departure from his own normal practice, had not warned his patient in 1985 of the risk of spontaneous recanalisation. He called expert evidence to support his case that there was a body of medical opinion in 1985 which would not give such a warning. Mantell

---

[40] [1993] 4 Med. L.R. 381.

[41] [1996] 7 Med. L.R. 1.

[42] The decision of the Court of Appeal in *De Freitas v. O'Brien and Connelly* [1995] 6 Med. L.R. 108 is consistent with this analysis. The Court upheld a finding that a very small number of sub-specialists (here, spinal surgeons) constituted a responsible body of opinion: the question is one of the quality, not quantity, of opinion: see *per* Otton L.J. at 115.

[43] See, for example, Professor Giesen (1993) 9 J. of Contemp. Health and Law Policy 273, 291.

[44] See *O'Donovan v. Cork County Council* [1967] I.R. 173, 193.

[45] [1996] 7 Med. L.R. 248. The facts are given at paras 12–181 and 12–284, below.

[46] The judge went on to find that the views espoused by the defendant's medical witnesses were not those which a responsible body of medical opinion would hold in relation to the facts of that case, despite their eminence in the profession.

[47] [1995] 6 Med. L.R. 371. See, to similar effect, *Smith v. Tunbridge Wells Health Authority* [1994] 5 Med. L.R. 334, Morland J.

J. held that such body of opinion was neither reasonable nor responsible, and found the defendant negligent. He also appeared to take the view that a practitioner whose personal standards are higher than those of another section of the profession cannot rely upon the *Bolam* principle to escape liability if he departs from those standards: "The *Bolam* principle provides a defence for those who lag behind the times. It cannot serve those who know better".[48] On the other hand, where the issues are highly complex and technical, and relevant medical knowledge is uncertain or variable, the court is unlikely to condemn as negligent a practitioner who follows prevailing standards.[49]

In *Bolitho v. City & Hackney Health Authority*[50] the claimant argued that **12–101** ultimately it was for the court, not for medical opinion, to decide the standard of care required of a practitioner in the circumstances of each case. The judge had said that, as a layman, he saw the force of the plaintiff's argument that it was unreasonable and illogical not to intubate.[51] The claimant argued that the judge was wrong to treat the *Bolam* principle as requiring him to accept the views of one body of opinion even though he was unpersuaded of its logical force. The appeal was dismissed. Lord Browne-Wilkinson (with whom Lords Slynn, Nolan, Hoffmann and Clyde agreed) said[52]:

> "My Lords, I agree with these submissions to the extent that, in my view, the Court is not bound to hold that a defendant doctor escapes liability for negligent treatment or diagnosis just because he leads evidence from a number of medical experts who are genuinely of the opinion that the defendant's treatment or diagnosis accorded with sound medical practice. In the *Bolam* case itself, McNair J. stated . . . that the defendant had to have acted in accordance with the practice accepted as proper by a 'responsible body of medical men'. Later . . . he referred to 'a standard of practice recognised as proper by a competent reasonable body of opinion.' Again, in the passage which I have cited from Maynard's case, Lord Scarman refers to a 'respectable' body of professional opinion. The use of these adjectives—responsible, reasonable and respectable—all show that the court has to be satisfied that the exponents of the body of opinion relied upon can demonstrate that such opinion has a logical basis. In particular in cases involving, as they so often do, the weighing of risks against benefits, the judge before accepting a body of opinion as being responsible, reasonable or respectable, will need to be satisfied that, in forming their views, the experts have directed their minds to the question of comparative risks and benefits and have reached a defensible conclusion on the matter . . . "

and at 243A–B:

> "These decisions demonstrate that in cases of diagnosis and treatment there are cases where, despite a body of professional opinion sanctioning the defendant's conduct, the defendant can properly be held liable for negligence. (I am not here considering questions of disclosure of risk.) In my judgment that is because, in some cases, it cannot be demonstrated to the judge's satisfaction that the body of opinion relied upon is reasonable or responsible."

---

[48] [1995] 6 Med. L.R. 371 at 374.
[49] See *ter Neuzen v. Korn* (1995) 127 D.L.R. (4th) 577, 595 *per* Sopinka J. (giving the judgment of the Supreme Court of Canada). In "The new Bolam: another false dawn for medical negligence?" (1996) P.N. 120, M. Davies argues that limitations on judicial understanding of medical issues may work to preserve the traditionally deferential approach of the courts to medical experts.
[50] [1998] A.C. 232.
[51] For the facts of this case see para. 12–071, above.
[52] [1998] A.C. 232 (at 241G–242B).

12–102   Lord Browne-Wilkinson expressly excluded from his remarks those cases
where the negligence alleged is a failure to warn a patient of the risks of proposed
treatment. It may be that the decision of the majority in *Sidaway v. Governors of
Royal Bethlem Hospital*[53] was regarded as of similar effect to that of the House
of Lords in *Bolitho*. The majority in *Sidaway* held that, while the *Bolam* principle
applied to such cases, it was open to the court to decide that a general practice
of the profession in relation to warnings was inadequate to meet the needs of a
particular plaintiff: see the passage from the speech of Lord Bridge which is
quoted at para. 12–096, above.

12–103   Lord Browne-Wilkinson emphasised that the court will rarely reject expert
opinion as "indefensible", for two reasons. First, because in the vast majority of
cases the fact that distinguished experts in the field are of a particular opinion
would demonstrate the reasonableness of that opinion. Secondly, because the
assessment of medical risks and benefits is a matter of clinical judgment which
a judge would not normally be able to make without expert evidence. The Court
found that *Bolitho* was not one of those exceptional cases where the judge ought
to have rejected expert testimony. On the evidence, it could not be suggested that
it was illogical for the defendant's expert, a most distinguished practitioner, to
favour running what, in his view, was a small risk of total respiratory collapse
rather than submitting the infant plaintiff to the invasive procedure of intubation.

12–104   The Canadian experience may be instructive in considering when the court
may be expected to reject expert evidence on the grounds explained by Lord
Browne-Wilkinson. In *ter Neuzen v. Korn*,[54] Sopinka J. (for the Supreme Court
of Canada) said:

> "[A]s a general rule, where a procedure involves difficult or uncertain questions of
> medical treatment or complex, scientific or highly technical matters that are beyond the
> ordinary experience and understanding of a judge . . . , it will not be open to find a
> standard medical practice negligent. On the other hand, as an exception to the general
> rule, if a standard practice fails to adopt obvious and reasonable precautions which are
> readily apparent to the ordinary finder of fact, then it is no excuse for a practitioner to
> claim that he or she was merely conforming to such a negligent common practice."

It remains to be seen whether the decision of the House of Lords in *Bolitho* will
be interpreted, similarly, as permitting the rejection of professional practice or
opinion only where a risk obvious to an informed layperson has been ignored.[55]
Early indications are that a more robust interpretation will be adopted in England
and Wales: see, for example, *Marriott v. West Midlands Regional Health Authority*.[56] In that case, the plaintiff was admitted to hospital following a head injury.
He was discharged the next day, but his condition did not improve. Seven days
after discharge, he was attended by his general practitioner, who carried out a
neurological examination but did not refer him back to hospital. Four days later,
he sustained an extradural haematoma which was found to be associated with a
skull fracture which had not been detected earlier. There was expert evidence to

---

[53] [1985] A.C. 871.
[54] (1995) 127 D.L.R. (4th) 577, discussed at para. 12–171, below.
[55] For criticism of this approach see the commentary on *ter Neuzen v. Korn* at (1997) 5 Med. L.Rev.
130.
[56] [1999] Lloyd's Rep. Med. 23.

the effect that there was a body of professional opinion which supported the general practitioner's decision to manage the plaintiff's condition at home. The judge rejected that opinion, holding that since the general practitioner ought to have perceived a risk of intracranial lesion, the only reasonably prudent course was to refer the patient to hospital where proper testing could be carried out. The decision was upheld on appeal. A majority in the Court of Appeal decided that the judge had subjected the expert evidence called on behalf of the general practitioner to analysis in order to see whether it could properly be regarded as reasonable, and had found that it could not. She had been entitled, under *Bolitho*, to do so. This decision suggests that the approach approved in *Bolitho* will not be confined in this jurisdiction to cases where the risk in question would be obvious to a layperson.

In the case of *Glicksman v. Redbridge H.A.*[57] the judge rejected the evidence   **12–105**
of the defendant's expert that an unusual approach (from below) in a hernia repair operation was reasonable. Despite the evidence of the defendant's expert the judge found that "no reasonable body of medical opinion . . . would support this approach". The case of *Calver v. Westwood Veterinary Group*[58] is a case in the field of veterinary medicine of a judge rejecting the evidence of the defendant's expert to the effect that the defendant had acted in accordance with reasonable practice, and being reversed by the Court of Appeal. The claimant's mare had been in foal, and had aborted in a field overnight. The principal surgeon in the defendant group had attended and examined the mare. He concluded that the mare was fit and well and that all of the placenta was present (meaning that none had been retained), and that accordingly no prophylactic antibiotics were either necessary or appropriate. The mare suffered laminitis and had to be destroyed—and the question was whether it was reasonable for the attending vet not to administer antibiotics. One of the associated issues was whether it was possible to be sure that none of the placenta had been retained by the mare. The judge held that the treating vet could not have been sure that none of the placenta had been retained, and could not have been sure that the mare was "fit and well". He held that it was illogical not to administer antibiotics, which were cheap and easy to administer and would have avoided the risk of the metritis which led to the laminitis. Simon Brown L.J. said[59]:

> "I come, therefore, to the critical question arising on the appeal: was the judge entitled to regard this as one of those 'rare case[s]' in which one body of veterinary opinion (represented by Mr Vogel) demonstrated that the other (represented by Mr Hughes and Mr Greenwood) was not capable of withstanding logical analysis, or was it not one of 'the vast majority of cases' where the reasonableness of Mr Hughes' opinion was demonstrated by the fact that it was shared by Mr Greenwood, a distinguished expert in the field?"

In coming to the conclusion that it was not one of those cases which could not withstand logical analysis Simon Brown L.J. was effectively deciding that the judge was not entitled to hold that the treating vet could not be sure that none of

---

[57] Unreported. Decision of H.H.J. Steel on June 29, 2000. 2000 WL 1084378.
[58] [2001] P.I.Q.R. P11. 168, CA.
[59] *ibid.* at 177, para. 31.

the placenta had been retained, nor was he entitled to hold that the treating vet could not reasonably decide that the mare was fit and well in the presence of a raised pulse and raised respiratory rate. The case was determined more on a detailed examination of the evidence,[60] rather than on the basis of interpretation of the principles involved.[61]

(ii) *Departing from general and approved practice*

12–106 If a medical practitioner departs from the general and approved practice for no good cause, and damage results, he is likely to be held negligent.[62] *Clark v. MacLennan*[63] offers an illustration of this principle. The claimant suffered stress incontinence after the birth of her first child. T, the consultant employed by the second defendants, decided that an anterior colporrhaphy should be performed four weeks after the birth. This was a departure from the normal practice, which was to defer such an operation until three months after the birth. Peter Pain J. held that there were no factors to justify this departure from normal practice and that the second defendants were therefore in breach of duty. Lord Clyde analysed the same principle in *Hunter v. Hanley*[64] in these terms:

"It follows from what I have said that in regard to allegations of deviation from ordinary professional practice ... such a deviation is not necessarily evidence of negligence. Indeed it would be disastrous if this were so, for all inducement to progress in medical science would then be destroyed. Even a substantial deviation from normal practice may be warranted by the particular circumstances. To establish liability by a doctor where deviation from normal practice is alleged, three facts require to be established. First of all it must be proved that there is a usual and normal practice; secondly it must be proved that the defender has not adopted that practice; and thirdly (and this is of crucial importance) it must be established that the course the doctor adopted is one which no professional man of ordinary skill would have taken if he had been acting with ordinary care."[65]

---

[60] *ibid.* at 177, para. 32.
[61] See also the case of *Meloche v.Hotel Dieu Grace Hospital* (1999) 179 D.L.R. 77, Ontario CA. In an ophthalmic case primarily concerned with causation, both sides' experts had accepted that it would be speculative to associate a short delay in diagnosis of an ophthalmic ulcer with the subsequent blindness in the eye. The trial judge held that as a matter of "robust common sense" the delay had probably caused the subsequent blindness; but the Court of Appeal held that he was not "filling in a void with common sense pragmatism" but that he was challenging the medical opinions with one of his own. "There was no room for common sense between the two book-ends of medical evidence refuting causation" (at 90).
[62] See, for example, *Chin Keow v. Government of Malaysia* [1967] 1 W.L.R. 813 (doctor departed from normal practice in that he did not inquire into patient's medical history before prescribing penicillin); *Stokes v. Guest, Keen and Nettlefold* [1968] 1 W.L.R. 1776 (company medical officer ignored warning leaflet issued by factory inspectorate); *Robinson v. Post Office* [1974] 1 W.L.R. 1176 (doctor gave claimant a test dose of anti-tetanus serum, waited one minute and then gave the full dose. The normal practice was to wait half-an-hour after the test dose. The doctor only escaped liability because no damage was caused by his negligence); *Ritchie v. Chichester Health Authority* [1994] 5 Med. L.R. 187 (anaesthetic registrar failed to follow a procedure which was prescribed by his consultant and was safe); *Hepworth v. Kerr* [1995] 6 Med. L.R. 139, the facts of which are given at para. 12–109, below. In the case of claims for ante-natal injury, see s.1(5) of the Congenital Disabilities (Civil Liability) Act 1976.
[63] [1983] 1 All E.R. 416.
[64] 1955 S.C. 200.
[65] *ibid.* at 206.

In *Landau v. Werner*[66] the defendant, a psychiatrist, undertook the treatment of **12–107** the claimant, a middle-aged woman in an anxiety state. By July 1949 "transference" had taken place and she had fallen deeply in love with him. Between August 1949 and March 1950 the defendant had a series of social contacts with the claimant, such as taking her out to tea and dinner. This further aroused the claimant's emotional and sexual feelings and her condition deteriorated. The medical evidence was to the effect that social contact between psychiatrist and patient was contrary to normal and approved practice. Barry J. held that the defendant, although acting in good faith, had been negligent. This decision was upheld by the Court of Appeal:

"A doctor might not be negligent if he tried a new technique but if he did he must justify it before the court. If his novel or exceptional treatment had failed disastrously he could not complain if it was held that he went beyond the bounds of due care and skill as recognised generally."[67]

By contrast, in *Holland v. The Devitt & Moore Nautical College Ltd*[68] a school **12–108** medical officer escaped a finding of negligence, even though he had slightly departed from the orthodox method of treatment as described in the textbooks. He was treating a pupil for infective hepatitis. He allowed the boy to get up and then to go home for the mid-term weekend when he showed signs of improvement, even though he had not completely recovered. Streatfeild J. observed:

"Textbook writers, or writers of articles, were writing of a subject generally. They were not writing of a particular patient and it was common ground between all the doctors that something must be left to the judgment of the doctors on the spot, who did not have to treat a case of infective hepatitis only, but had a particular patient, Peter Holland, to treat. . . . It would be a sorry day for the medical profession if it were said that no doctor or surgeon ought to depart one tittle from that which he saw written in the textbooks."

Novel treatment. More substantial departures from general and approved **12–109** practice may occur when the medical practitioner applies a new technique or a new form of treatment. It is clearly in the public interest that new forms of treatment should be developed and any principle of law which stifles such development altogether is manifestly unsatisfactory. This problem was touched upon in the passages quoted above,[69] but it did not receive any detailed analysis in those cases. In *Sidaway v. Governors of Bethlem Royal Hospital*[70] Lord Diplock stressed the importance of permitting the development of medical science:

"Those members of the public who seek medical or surgical aid would be badly served by the adoption of any legal principle that would confine the doctor to some long-established, well-tried method of treatment only, although its past record of success might be small, if he wanted to be confident that he would not run the risk of being held

---

[66] (1961) 105 S.J. 257 and at 1008.
[67] *ibid.* at 1008, *per* Sellers L.J.
[68] *The Times*, March 4, 1960. See also para. 12–187, below.
[69] See paras 12–106 to 12–108, above.
[70] [1985] A.C. 871, 893A–B.

liable in negligence simply because he tried some more modern treatment, and by some unavoidable mischance it failed to heal but did some harm to the patient."[71]

Lord Diplock went on to state that the *Bolam* test itself provided adequate protection for a doctor who made use of some new form of treatment. This is likely once the new form of treatment has won the approval of a responsible body of medical opinion. However, there may be cases where a medical practitioner wishes to use some new form of treatment which has not even attained that degree of acceptance. It is submitted that in those circumstances the question whether the medical practitioner acted reasonably must be determined by reference to all the circumstances of the case, and the mere fact he departed from established practice should not lead automatically to a finding of negligence. Relevant factors would include the information available about the proposed new treatment, the likely effect of the other more established forms of treatment which were available, and the stated wishes of the patient after the relevant facts had been explained to him.[72] Two cases illustrate this approach. In *Waters v. West Sussex Health Authority*[73] a neurosurgeon carried out an operation comprising an unprecedented combination of procedures. There was no established practice either in support of or in opposition to his method. Buxton J. examined the decisions which the defendant had taken individually and in combination in the light of relevant medical literature and expert evidence. He held that the neurosurgeon was not negligent, for his actions were supported by expert witnesses who represented a competent body of professional opinion. The defendant anaesthetist in *Hepworth v. Kerr*[74] deliberately reduced a patient's blood pressure to a dangerously low level in order to provide the surgeon with a blood-free operating field. Although he had used the technique in previous cases, it was both novel and essentially experimental, for it lacked any conventional scientific validation. Further, the surgeon did not in fact require so clean an operating field: thus the anaesthetist had subjected the patient to risks which were both scientifically unwarranted and unnecessary in the particular circumstances of the case. The patient suffered a spinal stroke and the defendant was held liable.

12–110 **Clinical trials.** Yet further difficulties arise when it is desired to use some innovative treatment, not principally for the patient's benefit but for the purpose of gathering information. Clinical trials play an important part in the development of medical science and any principle of law which stifled them altogether

---

[71] In the unreported case of *Linque Pollard v. Hugh Crockard and another*, January 22, 1997 Holland J. the defendant surgeon departed from usual practice in his approach to surgery, and adopted a relatively novel technique. The judge held that it was not negligent of him to have done so because he had established his expertise at the time in respect of this different approach and it was therefore for him an option consistent with accepted clinical practice. Neuro-surgeons without the necessary level of skill would not have been justified in adopting the approach.

[72] The question of explanations and warnings is dealt with in paras 12–124–12–134 and 12–201–12–232, below. Obviously this assumes greater importance where the proposed treatment is innovative. In *Zimmer v. Ringrose* (1981) 16 C.C.L.T. 51 the Alberta Court of Appeal held that the defendant (who used an innovative technique to sterilise the claimant) was negligent in failing to tell the claimant that his technique had not been approved by the medical profession and in failing to give her a comparison between his method and other methods of sterilisation. See also *Coughlin v. Kuntz* [1990] 2 W.W.R. 737, British Columbia Court of Appeal (negligent use of experimental technique for cervical spine discectomy).

[73] [1995] 6 Med. L.R. 362.

[74] [1995] 6 Med. L.R. 139.

would be undesirable.[75] Equally, however, there are sound reasons of policy why anyone who suffers injury as a result of participation in research or clinical trials should recover damages, irrespective of negligence by those who treated him.[76] The principles of law in this area have yet to be worked out.[77] In practice, however, it would seem likely that whether or not a patient who suffered injury as a result of receiving some experimental form of treatment would succeed on liability[78] would depend on the issues of informed consent and causation.[79] Often patients who are offered experimental treatment are faced with the likelihood of a poor outcome if nothing is done. They may agree to the treatment even if all of the uncertainties are properly explained; and it may be alleged that they would have agreed anyway if it can be established that not all of the uncertainties were, in fact, properly explained.

(e) *Expert Evidence*

In assisting the court on the question of liability, the expert witness has two principal functions. First, he has an explanatory or didactic function, in that he explains the technical issues as fully as possible in language comprehensible to laymen. This generally involves explaining the nature of the patient's original condition, the nature of the treatment given, the consequences of the treatment and (where possible) how those consequences flowed from the treatment given. This aspect of the expert evidence may be largely or totally uncontroversial. For example, there may be no dispute that the claimant was suffering from a particular disease, that the defendant prescribed a new type of drug and that the claimant's present complaint is an adverse reaction to that drug. Clearly the court must understand (and resolve any conflicts between) this aspect of the expert reports before it can seriously consider the question of negligence. At this stage of the inquiry the court is largely in the hands of the expert witness. It cannot speculate upon medical matters or come to conclusions or diagnoses which are not supported by at least one of the experts.[80] On the other hand, where there is **12–111**

---

[75] See H. A. F. Dudley, "Informed consent in surgical trials" (1984) 289 B.M.J. 937.

[76] See the Report of the Royal Commission on Civil Liability and Compensation for Personal Injury (1978) Cmnd. 7054, Chap. 24.

[77] For the view that a distinctive regime of liability for harm suffered in the course of research and experimentation is unnecessary, see D. Giesen, "Civil Liability of Physicians for New Methods of Treatment and Experimentation: a comparative examination" (1995) 3 Med. L.Rev. 22.

[78] For discussion of international and national ethical codes applying to research on human subjects, see Kennedy & Grubb, chap. 14.

[79] In the case of *The Creutzfeldt-Jacob Disease Litigation Group B Plaintiffs v. The Medical Research Council* [2000] Lloyd's Rep. Med. 161, the claimants took part in clinical trials to treat their dwarfism. By July 1, 1977 the defendants were aware that the injections used in the experimental treatment included a potentially lethal dose of the CJD agent: Morland J. held that it was negligent to administer the experimental treatment after that date.

[80] *In McLean v. Weir* (1977) 3 C.C.L.T. 87, 101, British Columbia Supreme Court, Gould J. summarised the position in a manner which, it is submitted, is equally applicable in England. "It is true that the court may accept in whole or in part or reject in whole or in part the evidence of any witness on the respective grounds of credibility or plausibility, or a combination of both. But in technical matters, unlike in lay matters within the traditional intellectual competence of the court, it cannot substitute its own medical opinion for that of qualified experts. The court has no status whatsoever to come to a medical conclusion contrary to unanimous medical evidence before it even if it wanted to, which is not the situation in this case. If the medical evidence is equivocal, the court may elect which of the theories advanced it accepts. If only two medical theories are advanced, the court may elect between the two or reject them both; it cannot adopt a third theory of its own, no matter how plausible such might be to the court."

dispute upon an issue of medical fact, the court may prefer the evidence of one party's experts over that of the other's: the *Bolam* test does not apply to opinion evidence on matters of fact.[81]

12–112 The second function of the expert witness is to assist the court in deciding whether the acts or omissions of the defendant constituted negligence.[82] He will recount what was the current state of knowledge at the time the patient was treated,[83] what was the general and approved practice or what were the different schools of thought at that time relating to the patient's condition.[84] He will thereby explain the gravity and foreseeability of the risks attaching to a particular course of treatment or medical procedure and identify any precautions which might have been taken to guard against such risks materialising. He may also state what is the experience and skill usually displayed by medical practitioners with the particular specialisation of the defendant, when they are called upon to diagnose or treat the injury or illness from which the claimant was suffering.[85] Ultimately, however, it is for the court to decide, on the totality of the evidence and applying the *Bolam* test, and the necessary logical analysis, whether the defendant exercised the requisite degree of skill and care. The question whether the defendant was "negligent" is a mixed question of fact and law. The court is not bound in every case by the opinion of the expert witnesses that there was or was not negligence, although in many cases the opinion of expert witnesses on matters within their province, if accepted as representative of a body of responsible professional opinion, leads inevitably to one or other of these conclusions.

12–113 On each of these questions, the court is entitled to, and should, assess the weight of expert testimony using the normal principles of critical evaluation of evidence. The evidence of a particular expert witness may be rejected on grounds

---

[81] See *Loveday v. Renton* [1990] 1 Med. L.R. 117, 182 *per* Stuart-Smith L.J.; *Joyce v. Merton, Sutton & Wandsworth Health Authority* [1996] 7 Med. L.R. 1, 13 *per* Roch L.J. An example is *Corley v. North West Herefordshire Health Authority* [1997] 8 Med. L.R. 45. The plaintiff suffered cerebral palsy as a result of compression of the umbilical cord shortly before his birth. Cresswell J.'s finding that the health authority's obstetric staff had not been negligent in failing to effect a forceps delivery at an earlier stage largely followed from his findings as to the mechanism of cord compression, on which he preferred the evidence of the authority's expert and other witnesses. See, for a further example: *Scott v. Wakefield Area Health Authority* [1997] 8 Med. L.R. 341 (allegation that ophthalmic surgeon should have referred plaintiff for micro-surgery failed on the judge's finding of fact that the cause of deterioration of the plaintiff's eyesight was one which was not amenable to cure by micro-surgery).

[82] In *Scott v. Bloomsbury Health Authority* [1990] 1 Med. L.R. 214, Brooke J. said that it was inappropriate for a complex medical negligence action to be brought, where the only supporting evidence was that given by a consultant who had long retired. Compare *Briffett v. Gander & District Hospital Board* (1996) 29 C.C.L.T. (2d) 251, Newfoundland CA (cardiologists had qualified as general practitioners before specialising and so were qualified to testify as to the standard of care expected of the average general practitioner in a hospital emergency room). In this regard the expert witness plays a crucial role in the trial on liability.

[83] See paras 12–073 to 12–074, above.

[84] See paras 12–090 to 12–109, above. In *Sharpe v. Southend Health Authority* [1997] 8 Med. L.R. 299, Cresswell J. stressed that an expert witness in a medical negligence case should make clear in his initial report (if it be the case) that while he would have adopted a practice or approach different from that which the defendant adopted, he accepts that the defendant's conduct was in accordance with an alternative approach or practice accepted as proper by a responsible body of practitioners in the relevant field. Had the plaintiff's expert done so in that case, the case against one of the defendants would not have begun. In the event, it was withdrawn following the expert's concessions in cross-examination.

[85] See paras 12–075 to 12–078, above.

that the expert has become partial[86] or on grounds that his evidence lacks internal consistency or logic.[87] In *Murphy v. Wirral Health Authority*,[88] Kay J. rejected the evidence of an expert witness for the defence because the witness had lost his objectivity, his views were unsupported by the literature and his argument did not withstand analysis when tested by the views of other expert witnesses. See also the case of *Glicksman v. Redbridge H.A.*[89]

The use of expert evidence in medical negligence cases received specific **12–114** consideration in Lord Woolf's final report on the civil justice system, published in July 1996.[90] Lord Woolf noted that there are significant delays and costs associated with current practice, which normally involves each party instructing its own experts on liability, causation and quantum. He proposed that the parties be required to consider whether a single expert might be jointly instructed to assist the court on issues such as quantum, uncontroversial issues of medical fact, the claimant's condition and prognosis in straightforward cases and on all issues in claims under £10,000.[91] Joint instruction of experts reduces the number of occasions on which expert evidence is rejected because an expert has lost his objectivity and assumed the role of advocate for the party instructing him. But it is rarely agreed outside the area of quantum. The continuing delays in some clinical negligence litigation have been cited as part of the reason for the committee being set up in July 2001 to consider a new clinical compensation scheme for the NHS.[92] In the case of *Stevens v. Gullis*[93] (a building case) the defendant's expert's report failed to comply with the provisions of the CPR, and a subsequent letter failed to correct the deficiencies. The judge made an order debarring him from giving evidence in the third party proceedings, and restricting him to factual evidence only in the main action. This was upheld by Lord Woolf on appeal: he stated that the overriding duty of the expert was owed to the court and not to the party who instructed him; the CPR was intended to focus the mind of the expert on his responsibilities; and where an expert failed to comply with the CPR and showed that he had no conception of his obligations, he should be debarred from giving evidence.

Very often there is no "general and approved practice" or specific school of **12–115** thought by reference to which the defendant's conduct can either be justified or condemned as negligent. The question is simply whether, in all the circumstances of the particular case, the mistake made by the defendant was negligent. In this situation the obvious way that an expert witness can assist the court on the issue of negligence (i.e. the second of the two stages discussed above) is by saying what he would have done in the particular circumstances and/or what he believes other medical practitioners would have done. In *Midland Bank v. Hett, Stubbs & Kemp*[94] (a claim for solicitor's negligence) Oliver J. expressed the view that such

---

[86] See, for example, *Early v. Newham Health Authority* [1994] 5 Med. L.R. 214, 216; *Hepworth v. Kerr* [1995] 6 Med. L.R. 139, 165.
[87] As in *McAllister v. Lewisham and North Southwark Health Authority* [1994] 5 Med. L.R. 343.
[88] [1996] 7 Med. L.R. 99. See also *Robinson v. Jacklin* [1996] 7 Med. L.R. 83 (the evidence of an expert witness called by the defendant was held not to support the existence of a body of competent professional opinion).
[89] See para. 12–105, above.
[90] "Access to Justice" (HMSO, 1996). See further, para. 12–166, below.
[91] *ibid.*, chap. 15, paras 38, 63–77.
[92] See para. 12–089 above.
[93] [2000] P.N.L.R. 229.
[94] [1979] Ch. 384.

evidence is inadmissible.[95] However, in solicitors' negligence cases the court is often able to form its own independent opinion as to the reasonableness or skilfullness of the defendant's conduct on the basis of counsel's submissions alone—a task which is usually impossible in medical negligence cases. It is therefore submitted that the dictum of Oliver J. referred to above should not be applicable in medical negligence cases.[96] Certainly, in practice, evidence from expert witnesses as to what they would have done, or what they believe other medical practitioners would have done, in the particular circumstances is received and acted upon by the court.

12–116   Where the defendant's conduct cannot be defended by evidence that it conformed with a general approved practice, because no general practice or relevant school of thought exists, the decision whether reasonable care and skill were exercised will be informed but not constrained by expert evidence. The facts in *AB v. Tameside and Glossop Health Authority*[97] provide an extreme example. A health worker employed by the defendant authority was diagnosed HIV positive. By letter, the health authority informed patients (and former patients) who had received obstetric treatment from the worker that there was a remote risk that they had been infected. A group of patients claimed to have suffered psychological injury as a result of receiving the news by those means, and alleged that the authority negligently failed to arrange communication via general practitioners or other health workers qualified to provide immediate counselling where necessary. The Court of Appeal reversed French J.'s finding that the authority was in breach of its (admitted) duty of care. Reasserting the established standard of care, the Court rejected the plaintiff's submission that the authority's duty was to employ the best method of communication. It accepted the authority's argument that the *Bolam* principle applied, in theory at least, but held that on the facts of that case the principle offered no practical assistance. The problem had not arisen in comparable circumstances before. Accordingly, there was no evidence of a generally approved practice—there was, in that sense, no adequate well of professional experience upon which the court could usefully draw. Once the authority had decided to provide the information, its duty was simply to take all such steps to implement that decision as were reasonable, having regard to the foreseeable risk that some patients might suffer psychological injury as a result of receiving the information. In deciding the scope of that duty, the Court was assisted by expert opinions offered on behalf of each party but was particularly impressed by the fact that, in guidelines published by the Department of Health's Expert Advisory Group on AIDS some two years after the authority's experience, the Group advised that the authority's approach be followed. The plaintiffs' expert had been in the dissenting minority among the experts in the Group. In *Penney v. East Kent Health Authority*[98] a hospital's pathology laboratory failed to detect abnormal cells when testing the claimant's cervical smear sample. The initial screening process was carried out by biomedical scientists or by cytology screeners. Senior screeners and pathologists then examined any slide which was regarded by the first-stage screeners as showing possible abnormalities. It was common ground that the relevant standard of care was that of the reasonably

---

[95] *ibid.* at 402B-D. See Chap. 10, para. 10–142, above.
[96] See Chap. 10, para. 10–142, above.
[97] [1997] 8 Med. L.R. 91.
[98] [1999] Lloyd's Rep. Med. 123.

competent cytoscreener exercising reasonable care. The unanimous expert evidence was that unless the cytoscreener was satisfied beyond reasonable doubt that a slide was negative, he should pass it up to the next stage for further consideration. H.H. Judge Pepitt Q.C. (sitting as a deputy High Court judge) held that the *Bolam* principle did not apply, for two reasons. First, since the medical expert witnesses agreed that a screener had been wrong not to classify the plaintiff's slide as borderline, and so requiring further checking, no question of acceptable practice arose. Second, the cytoscreeners' task was a mechanical one which did not involve diagnosis. See also *MacPhail v. Desrosiers*[99]: where expert evidence suggested that there was no generally adopted practice on the question whether a patient should be allowed to drive herself home after undergoing an abortion, the court was able to decide what the standard of reasonable skill and care required.

(f) *Res ipsa loquitur*

Medical negligence is the main area of professional negligence in which *res ipsa loquitur* assumes importance. The patient's position is such that he may very well not know, and not be able to establish, what treatment he received and how his injuries were caused. Where he is able to invoke the maxim *res ipsa loquitur*, the defendant cannot escape liability unless he calls evidence to rebut the inference of negligence which arises from the injury itself and its surrounding circumstances. **12–117**

The classic exposition of the maxim is that of Erle C.J. in *Scott v. London & St Katherine Docks*[1]: **12–118**

> "There must be reasonable evidence of negligence. But where *the thing* is shown to be under the management of the defendant or his servants, and the accident is such as in the ordinary course of things does not happen if those who have the management use proper care, it affords reasonable evidence, in the absence of explanation by the defendants, that the accident arose from want of care."[2]

Application of the maxim to medical negligence. If for the words "the thing" (which have been italicised in the above quotation) are substituted the words "the treatment of the claimant", the application of the maxim to medical negligence cases becomes apparent.[3] In *Ratcliffe v. Plymouth and Torbay Health Authority*,[4] the Court of Appeal conducted a review of the authorities in this area. Brooke L.J. summarised the relevant principles (at 172–173). The court considered, in particular, whether a plaintiff is entitled to rely upon the maxim in the absence of expert evidence. In simpler medical situations (for example, a surgeon cuts off the right foot instead of the left, or a swab is left in an operation site) expert evidence will not be necessary. But in most contested cases the plaintiff's evidence will normally be buttressed by expert evidence to the effect that the matter complained of would not ordinarily occur without negligence on the **12–119**

---

[99] (1998) 170 N.S.R. (2d) 145, Nova Scotia CA.
[1] (1865) 3 H. & C. 596: three bags of sugar fell from an upper storey of a warehouse on to the claimant. This raised a presumption of negligence on the part of those in control of the sugar.
[2] *ibid.* at 601. The emphasis has been added.
[3] The argument that the maxim could not apply in medical negligence cases was rejected in *Ritchie v. Chichester Health Authority* [1994] 5 Med. L.R. 187, 205.
[4] [1998] Lloyd's Rep. Med. 162.

defendant's part. Other illustrations are afforded by *Saunders v. Leeds Western Health Authority*[5] and *Coyne v. Wigan Health Authority*.[6] In the former case the claimant suffered a cardiac arrest during the course of an operation. The defendants were unable to rebut the inference of negligence and the claimant succeeded on *res ipsa loquitur*. In the latter case the claimant suffered hypoxia in the recovery ward after a routine operation. The defendants failed to rebut the inference of negligence and the claimant again succeeded on *res ipsa loquitur*. However, not every mishap in the course of treatment raises a presumption of negligence.[7] In *Lock v. Scantlebury*[8] the claimant's lower jaw was dislocated during an operation for the removal of eight teeth. Paull J. stated that it was "by no means proof of negligence" that the jaw became dislocated during such an operation.[9] In *Fish v. Kapur*[10] a dentist left part of the root of a tooth in the claimant's jaw and fractured the jaw. The claimant relied upon *res ipsa loquitur* and the defendant did not give evidence. Lynskey J. held that a fracture of the jaw was not itself prima facie evidence of negligence and the doctrine did not apply.[11] Statistical evidence that the particular operation, although properly performed, fails in a small number of cases may also prevent the application of the maxim.[12] The maxim *res ipsa loquitur* will only apply where the injury suffered by the claimant is not of a kind which might reasonably occur through misadventure in the course of treatment whether attributable to an inherent risk of the procedure even when carefully performed, or to the patient's particular susceptibility to injury.[13]

---

[5] (1985) 129 S.J. 225; [1993] 4 Med. L.R. 355.

[6] [1991] 2 Med. L.R. 301.

[7] See, *e.g.* paras 12–080 to 12–082, above, on misadventure. Thus the maxim did not apply in *O'Malley-Williams v. The Board of Governors of the National Hospital for Nervous Diseases* (1975) 1 B.M.J. 635 (neurological injury following an aortagram), *Hobson v. Munkley* (1977) 74 D.L.R. (3d) 408 (damage to ureter in course of tubal ligation) or *Jacobs v. Great Yarmouth and West Waveney Health Authority* [1995] 6 Med. L.R. 192 (for the facts, see para. 12–123, below).

[8] *The Times*, July 25, 1963.

[9] However, the dentist was held negligent for failing to notice what had occurred. See para. 12–149, below.

[10] [1948] 2 All E.R. 176.

[11] See also *Fletcher v. Bench* (1973) 4 B.M.J. 117 (while dentist was filing away a tooth with a boneburr, the bone-burr broke, leaving part in the jaw. The dentist was unable to find and remove the broken bit of bur. The majority of the Court of Appeal held that *res ipsa loquitur* did not apply).

[12] See, for example, *Considine v. Camp Hill Hospital* (1982) 133 D.L.R. (3d) 11, Nova Scotia Supreme Court (the claimant was incontinent following an operation to remove tissue in the region of the prostate: since the evidence showed that 1–4% of such operations could cause incontinence, it was held that *res ipsa loquitur* did not apply); *Grey v. Webster* (1984) 14 D.L.R. (4th) 706 (*res ipsa loquitur* held not to apply in a case of failure of sterilisation by means of tubal ligation).

[13] "I cannot for my part accept that medical science is such a precise science that there cannot in any particular field be any room for the wholly unexpected result occurring in the human body from the carrying out of a well-recognised procedure": *Delaney v. Southmead Health Authority* [1995] 6 Med. L.R. 355, 360 *per* Dillon L.J. See also the discussion of the application of *res ipsa loquitur* to medical negligence cases by the British Columbia Supreme Court in *Girard v. Royal Columbian Hospital* (1976) 66 D.L.R. (3d) 676: the claimant was given a spinal anaesthetic in preparation for an operation. After the operation he was found to have permanent partial paralysis of both legs. Andrews J. held that the doctrine of *res ipsa loquitur* did not apply: "Although the treatment of the plaintiff was under the control of the defendant doctors it was not under their sole control in the sense that they could see, observe and react to the immediate effects of the external application of such treatment. It was hidden from their view and was subject to the unexplained mysteries of the plaintiff's own physiology . . . medical science has not yet reached the stage where the law ought to presume that a patient must come out of an operation as well or better than he went into it. From my interpretation of the medical evidence the kind of injury suffered by the plaintiff could have occurred without negligence on anyone's part. Since I cannot infer there was negligence on the part of the defendant

In *Mahon v. Osborne*[14] (in which a swab was left in the patient's body after an   **12-120**
operation) a majority[15] of the Court of Appeal considered that the maxim *res ipsa
loquitur* applied. Goddard L.J. put the matter in this way:

> "The surgeon is in command of the operation, it is for him to decide what instruments,
> swabs and the like are to be used, and it is he who uses them. The patient, or, if he dies,
> his representatives, can know nothing about this matter. There can be no possible
> question but that neither swabs nor instruments are ordinarily left in the patient's body,
> and no one would venture to say that it is proper, although in particular circumstances
> it may be excusable, so to leave them. If, therefore, a swab is left in the patient's body,
> it seems to me clear that the surgeon is called on for an explanation, that is, he is called
> on to show not necessarily why he missed it but that he exercised due care to prevent
> it being left there."[16]

Where the treatment of the patient is under the control of several persons, the   **12-121**
maxim cannot apply unless the party sued is responsible for the acts of all those
persons.[17] Thus, when it became established that hospitals were responsible for
the negligence of all their staff, both professional and ministerial,[18] the maxim
received new impetus. In *Cassidy v. Ministry of Health*[19] the claimant was treated
at Walton Hospital, Liverpool for Dupuytren's contraction of the third and fourth
fingers of the left hand. Dr F performed the operation. After the operation (as was
normal) the claimant's left hand and lower arm were kept rigid in a splint. When
released from the splint the claimant's left hand was useless. The third and fourth
fingers were bent and stiff. The two good fingers were also affected. The Court
of Appeal, reversing the trial judge, held that the maxim *res ipsa loquitur*

---

doctors the maxim of *res ipsa loquitur* does not apply." In *Fallows v. Randle* [1997] 8 Med. L.R. 160
in a failed sterilisation case the Court of Appeal held that *res ipsa loquitur* had no application where
the fallope ring on a fallopian tube was found to be missing and pregnancy resulted. The judge had
to decide the most probable explanation for its being missing on the basis of the possible explanations
put forward by the two experts.

[14] [1939] 2 K.B. 14.

[15] Goddard and MacKinnon L.JJ.; Goddard L.J. dissented from the actual decision of the Court.

[16] *ibid.* at 50. Examples of other English cases in which the claimant has succeeded on the basis of
res ipsa loquitur are *Clarke v. Worboys, The Times*, March 18, 1952 (liability for severe burn after pad
placed on claimant's left buttock for the purpose of electro-coagulation) and *Cooper v. Nevill, The
Times*, March 10, 1961 (abdominal pack left in claimant's body after operation). Canadian cases in
which the claimant has succeeded on *res ipsa loquitur* include *Cox v. Saskatoon* [1942] 1 D.L.R. 74
(injury to arm during an operation); *Cavan v. Wilcox* (1973) 44 D.L.R. (3d) 42 (nurse injected bicillin
into claimant's arm: some bicillin entered an artery and caused a blockage and gangrene developed);
Holmes v. Board of Hospital Trustees of City of London (1978) 81 D.L.R. (3d) 67 (tissue emphysema
when oxygen injected at pressure could only occur if needle negligently displaced from trachea);
Feist v. Gordon [1991] 2 Med. L.R. 376 (eyeball pierced during periocular injection).

[17] Thus in *Morris v. Winsbury-White* [1937] 4 All E.R. 494 the doctrine was held not to apply. See
also *McFadyen v. Harvie* [1942] 4 D.L.R. 647. Cf. *Thompson Estates v. Byrne* (1993) 114 N.S.R. (2d)
395, Court of Appeal of Nova Scotia, where a patient under intensive care removed tubes from her
body and suffered brain damage before she was retubated. She was not entitled to rely upon the
maxim: since she was able to disturb her tubation, it was not under the sole management of the
defendant hospital and her pre-existing condition was part of the cause of her injury, which could
therefore have happened without negligence. See also *Elliott v. Bickerstaff* (1999) 48 N.S.W.L.R. 214.
New South Wales Court of Appeal, in which the case concerned an obstetric operation at a private
hospital: the surgeon was sued (but the hospital was not) in respect of a surgical sponge left in the
patient's abdominal cavity at the end of the operation. On the basis that the fault was that of the
theatre nursing staff (for whom the surgeon was not responsible, but the hospital was) *res ipsa
loquitur* did not apply.

[18] As to which, see paras 12–152 to 12–160, below.

[19] [1951] 2 K.B. 343.

applied: "On the basis that the hospital was responsible for all those in whose charge the plaintiff was, the surgeon, the doctor and nurses, the result seems to me to raise a case of *res ipsa loquitur*," *per* Somervell L.J.[20] The defendants did not, on the evidence, succeed in rebutting the inference that there had been some negligence by their staff and accordingly were held liable to the claimant.[21] In *Bull v. Devon Area Health Authority*[22] the majority in the Court of Appeal held that the maxim was properly applied in a case where breach of a health authority's primary duty to provide a safe system of care was alleged. Complications developed at the birth of a second twin in the hospital's maternity unit. As a result of difficulties and delay in tracing a suitably qualified medical practitioner to assist, the baby suffered hypoxia and consequent brain-damage. It was held that the most likely explanation for the delay was either inefficiency in the hospital's system for summoning doctors to obstetric emergencies or negligence by an individual or individuals in the operation of that system. Consequently, the maxim applied and the hospital had the evidential burden of justifying the delays. In *Hay v. Grampian Health Board*,[23] however, the maxim did not apply. The issue in that case was whether a patient's suicide while subject to the hospital's regime of close observation was caused by negligence. There was evidence of the explanation for the event, namely, that a nurse had allowed the patient to go to the bathroom unaccompanied. The question whether it was negligent for the health board's regime to provide such opportunity for self-harm was to be considered on ordinary principles.

12–122   **Inference of negligence rebutted.** Defendants may displace the inference of negligence by adducing evidence to show either that due care was exercised, or that there is an alternative explanation for the claimant's injury which is consistent with the exercise of due care.[24] Cases where evidence of an alternative explanation has been accepted include *Roe v. Minister of Health*,[25] *Brazier v. Ministry of Defence*[26] and *Howard v. Wessex Regional Health Authority*.[27] In *Roe*, two patients suffered permanent paralysis from the waist down after being injected with a spinal anaesthetic at the defendant's hospital. The Court of Appeal held that the maxim *res ipsa loquitur* applied: the facts called for an explanation from the defendants.[28] However, the defendants had given an explanation of the disaster, which was consistent with due care on their part. The

---

[20] *ibid.* at 348. See also Singleton L.J. at 353 and Denning L.J. at 365–366.

[21] "They have busied themselves in saying that this or that member of their staff was not negligent. But they have not called a single person to say that the injuries were consistent with due care on the part of all the members of their staff. They called some of the people who actually treated the man . . . each of whom protested that he was careful in his part; but they did not call any expert at all, to say that this might happen despite all care. They have not therefore displaced the prima facie case against them . . . " *per* Denning L.J., *ibid.* at 366.

[22] [1993] 4 Med. L.R. 117, 131–132 *per* Slade L.J. and 137 *per* Dillon L.J. Mustill L.J. doubted the need to resort to the maxim in this case, since the claimant had proved "inordinate delay": see at 142.

[23] [1995] 6 Med. L.R. 128, Ct of Sess.

[24] See *Delaney v. Southmead Health Authority* [1995] 6 Med. L.R. 355, 359 *per* Stuart-Smith L.J. Since the maxim describes only a prima facie inference of negligence, and the burden of proof remains on the claimant, the defendant need not show that an alternative explanation is more likely than not to be the correct explanation. See also *Browne v. Guys & Lewisham N.H.S. Trust* [1997] 8 Med. L.R. 132; and *Hooper v. Young* [1998] Lloyds' Rep. Med. 61.

[25] [1954] 2 Q.B. 66. See also paras 12–073, above and 12–286, below.

[26] [1965] 1 Lloyd's Rep. 26.

[27] [1994] 5 Med. L.R. 57.

[28] [1954] 2 Q.B. 66. at 80 (*per* Somervell L.J.), 81 (*per* Denning L.J.) and 88 (*per* Morris L.J.).

anaesthetic was kept in glass ampoules, stored in phenol solution. The phenol had penetrated the ampoules through invisible cracks, of which the defendants could not reasonably have been aware. Accordingly, the defendants escaped liability. In *Brazier*, a needle broke in the course of an injection. McNair J. held that *res ipsa loquitur* applied. However, the defendants had established on the balance of probabilities that the mishap was due to a latent defect in the needle. Accordingly, the claimant's claim failed.[29] In *Howard*, the claimant alleged that the tetraplegia which she suffered following maxillo-facial surgery must have been due to a traumatic injury negligently inflicted upon her cervical spine during surgery, relying on the maxim. She failed because the defendant health authority was able to show that there was another possible explanation. The explanation advanced was that the claimant's condition was caused by fibro-cartilaginous embolism (FCE). Notwithstanding that this was an extremely rare occurrence, the defendants were held not liable.[30] By contrast, the defendant's attempt to explain the claimant's condition as caused by extremely remote risks failed in *Glass v. Cambridge Health Authority*.[31] The claimant suffered cardiac arrest while under anaesthetic. The defendant's argument that this was caused by gas embolism resulting from the use of hydrogen peroxide to clean a wound was held to involve a highly unlikely combination of circumstances. As such, it failed to rebut the presumption that due care had not been exercised. In *Browne v. Guys & Lewisham NHS Trust*[32] the defendant established that irritation (which resolved) following a second exploratory operation was not due to lack of care at the first operation, but due to keloid scarring which was removed by the further operation. In *Hopper v. Young*[33] the Court of Appeal allowed an appeal by the defendant on the basis that there had been ample evidence that the kinking of a ureter following an operation could occur without negligence.

In the absence of an explanation for the claimant's condition which is consistent with the exercise of due care, the defendant may succeed if there is evidence that due care was in fact exercised. This is illustrated by cases where the negligence complained of took place during operative procedures carried out under general anaesthetic or on the part of anaesthetists themselves. The maxim is frequently called in aid in such cases, since the claimant's recollection of relevant events is unlikely to be sufficient to enable the precise conduct complained of to be identified. In *Lindsay v. Mid-Western Health Board*,[34] the Irish Supreme Court held that the claimant's failure to return to consciousness after a routine operation required explanation. The claimant was unable to point to any precise instance of negligence but was entitled to rely upon *res ipsa loquitur*. The health board escaped liability by showing that all reasonable care had been taken and was not required to prove an alternative cause of the claimant's condition. *Jacobs v. Great Yarmouth and Waveney Health Authority*[35] and *Delaney v. Southmead Health Authority*[36] are decisions to the same effect. In *Jacobs*, the

12–123

---

[29] *Hajgato v. London Health Association* (1982) 36 O.R. (2d) 669, Ontario High Court is a Canadian decision to the same effect, affirmed: (1983) 44 O.R. (2d) 264.

[30] The judge concluded that there had not been negligent over-extension of the claimant's neck during surgery on the basis of evidence from the operating team that no one had noticed anything untoward.

[31] [1995] 6 Med. L.R. 91.

[32] 1997] 8 Med. L.R. 132.

[33] [1998] Lloyd's Rep. Med. 61.

[34] [1993] I.L.R.M. 550.

[35] [1995] 6 Med. L.R. 192.

[36] [1995] 6 Med. L.R. 355, CA.

claimant complained that she had experienced consciousness before and during an operation because of ineffective anaesthesia. The normal effect of muscle relaxant drugs administered as part of the pre-operative procedure was to paralyse the patient; she was thus unable to signal her awareness to theatre staff so as to obtain corroborative evidence of her complaint. The Court of Appeal upheld the judge's finding that, although the claimant had established a prima facie case of consciousness due to negligence before or during surgery, that case had been answered by the defendant's evidence that all proper steps were taken in administration of the anaesthetic.[37] In *Delaney*, the claimant suffered an injury to the nerves serving his hand during an operation for removal of his gall bladder. He alleged that the only possible explanation was negligent over-rotation of his arm during administration of the general anaesthetic. The allegation failed, and the maxim did not apply, because on the evidence there was no such over-rotation and the defendants had exercised due care. The maxim did not assist the claimant in *Vernon v. Bloomsbury Health Authority*.[38] Injury following administration of gentamicin therapy at a dosage higher than that recommended by the manufacturers or by the pharmaceutical formularies raised an inference of negligence. However, the inference was displaced by evidence that the dosage conformed with the standard set by the responsible body of medical opinion which was represented by the defendant's experts. In *Ratcliffe v. Plymouth and Torbay Health Authority*,[39] the plaintiff suffered a serious and unexpected neurological deficit from the waist down following an operation on his ankle which had involved a spinal anaesthetic. The anaesthetist's evidence as to the manner in which he had carried out the spinal injection was accepted and it was held that he had exercised due care. Since there was ample evidence to support the judge's findings, the plaintiff's appeal failed.

(g) Consent to treatment

12–124　A full discussion of consent to medical treatment is outside the scope of this book.[40] Shortly stated, however, medical treatment which is given without consent constitutes trespass to the person,[41] save in exceptional circumstances.[42] A claim for assault and battery is sometimes pleaded in addition to (or in the

---

[37] This decision highlights the difficulties of proof facing a claimant complaining of ineffective anaesthesia. The Court of Appeal upheld the judge's finding, on the evidence and as "a matter of common sense", that the claimant's memory was unreliable because of the fact that several drugs had been administered to her as part of the operative process.
[38] [1995] 6 Med. L.R. 297.
[39] [1998] Lloyd's Rep. Med. 162.
[40] For a general review of this subject, see Kennedy & Grubb, chaps 3 and 4; Powers & Harris, chap. 5.
[41] See, for example, *Hamilton v. Birmingham Regional Hospital Board* [1969] 2 B.M.J. 456 (sterilisation without consent); *Appleton v. Garrett* [1996] 1 P.I.Q.R. 1 (unnecessary dental treatment without consent); *Schweizer v. Central Hospital* (1974) 53 D.L.R. (3d) 494. "By going into hospital, he does not waive or give up his right of absolute security of the person; he cannot be treated in hospital as a mere specimen, or as an inanimate object which can be used for the purpose of vivisection; he remains a human being, and he retains his rights of control and disposal of his own body; he still has the right to say what operation he will submit to, and, unless his consent to an operation is expressly obtained, any operation performed upon him without his consent is an unlawful interference with his right of security and control of his own body and is a wrong entitling him to damages if he suffers any", *per* Watermeyer J. in *Stoffberg v. Elliott* [1923] C.P.D. 148 (South Africa).
[42] See paras 12–138 to 12–148, below.

alternative to) a claim for negligence, although such claims have greatly diminished following the decision of the House of Lords in *Sidaway v. Governors of Bethlem Royal Hospital*.[43] Proof of consent is a defence to an allegation of trespass to the person.[44] In order to provide an answer to a claim in trespass, it must be shown that the consent given related to the treatment in question, that it was given voluntarily, that the patient was appropriately informed before he consented and that he had capacity in law to consent.[45]

The exercise of reasonable care and skill in treating the patient or in advising **12–125** beforehand as to the risks of proposed treatment is not a defence. This is one of the perceived advantages of framing a case in trespass: evidence as to general and approved practice in disclosure of risks is irrelevant. Another advantage lies in the test for causation. If it is not shown that the patient gave valid consent to the procedure administered, damages will follow for any injury suffered as a direct result of that procedure. Unlike a claim in negligence for failure to warn of the risks of treatment, the claimant need not prove that he would not have consented to the treatment had he been advised beforehand with due care. Further, he will recover damages for injury suffered when a risk inherent in the procedure materialises, notwithstanding that such injury was consistent with the exercise of due care in performance of the procedure. The English courts, however, have been unwilling to encourage actions brought in trespass. This reluctance is illustrated by *Davis v. Barking, Havering and Brentwood Health Authority*.[46] Before undergoing a minor operation, the claimant signed a consent form which authorised the defendant health authority to perform the operation and to administer general, local and such other anaesthetics as were deemed necessary. The anaesthetist administered a general anaesthetic and, during the operation, a caudal block (a type of local epidural anaesthetic). The claimant alleged that she had not consented to the administration of the caudal block because no one had suggested to her before the operation that any anaesthetic other than general would be necessary and a caudal block was not in fact necessary. Dismissing the argument that separate consent was required for each type of anaesthesia used, McCullough J. observed that an approach which required consent for each aspect of treatment (a "sectional" approach) would encourage the bringing of actions in trespass rather than in negligence.[47] The plaintiff in *Williamson v. East London & City Health Authority*[48] claimed damages on the grounds that she had consented to a less serious operation than the defendant's surgeon had performed, but argued that there had been a negligent failure to obtain consent, rather than a trespass. She recovered general damages for *inter alia* her shock upon discovering what had been done, the insult of a non-consensual operation and her loss of certainty that the operation had been necessary, which certainty she would have

---

[43] [1985] A.C. 871. See para. 12–131, below.
[44] The burden of proof is on the defendant: see *Re F (Mental Patient: Sterilisation)* [1990] 2 A.C. 1, 27 *per* Neill L.J.; *Reibl v. Hughes* (1980) 114 D.L.R. (3d) 1, 9, Supreme Court of Canada; *Secretary, Department of Health and Community Services v. J.W.B.* (1992) 106 A.L.R. 385, 453, High Court of Australia; *cf. Freeman v. Home Office* [1984] Q.B. 524.
[45] See paras 12–126 to 12–147, below.
[46] [1993] 4 Med. L.R. 85.
[47] *ibid.* at 90. See also *Hills v. Potter* [1984] 1 W.L.R. 641, 653 *per* Hirst J.; *Sidaway v. Governors of Royal Bethlem Hospital* [1985] 1 A.C. 871, 883E *per* Lord Scarman.
[48] [1998] Lloyd's Rep. Med. 6.

acquired had she been free to obtain further medical opinions. The case of *B v. Leeds Health Authority*[49] was also a case brought in negligence, rather than trespass. The claimant's parents had successfully contended that the defendant had been negligent in the advice given about the infant claimant's treatment for acute lymphoblastic leukaemia. The defendant's appeal was allowed on the basis that in the circumstances, there had been no negligence.

(i) *Limits to consent*

12–126   Just as a practitioner will be liable if the treatment given exceeds the patient's consent, the patient may withdraw consent at any stage in the procedure. Difficulties arise when there are unexpected complications during the course of an operation. It is normally possible to obtain consent before carrying out the further treatment which is necessary; but it is highly inconvenient to take this course, not least for the patient, who may be subjected to two operations where fuller consent would have made the second unnecessary. Three Canadian cases shed light on this situation. In *Marshall v. Curry*[50] the defendant surgeon, in the course of a hernia operation, discovered a seriously diseased testicle, a condition which he could not reasonably have foreseen. He removed the testicle for the protection of the claimant's health and possibly his life. It was held that there was no assault. Similarly, in *Ciarlariello v. Schacter*[51] the patient insisted that an angiogram to which she had previously consented be stopped. The Supreme Court of Canada said that in such circumstances, the practitioner is entitled to continue a procedure only where failure to do so would be life-threatening or cause immediate and serious harm to the health of the patient.[52] It was found on the facts that the claimant had in fact renewed her consent, so that the procedure was lawfully continued. In *Murray v. McMurchy*,[53] however, it was held that a surgeon was not entitled to carry out an unauthorised procedure during the course of an operation merely because it was convenient or desirable to do so.

12–127   This problem is now less likely to arise, because the consent forms signed by patients before undergoing surgery usually refer to the specific operation proposed and then to "such further or alternative operative measures as may be found necessary during the course of such operation". The consent form should be construed in a reasonable manner[54] but the patient's signature is merely evidence of consent. Where the patient is incapable of understanding the form or has not been advised to the extent necessary to give him a broad understanding

---

[49] 2001 E.W.C.A. 51.
[50] [1933] 3 D.L.R. 260.
[51] (1993) 100 D.L.R. (4th) 609.
[52] *ibid.* at 619.
[53] [1949] 2 D.L.R. 442.
[54] See *Davis v. Barking, Havering and Brentwood Health Authority* [1994] 3 Med. L.R. 85, the facts of which are given at para. 12–125 above; *Bruschett v. Cowan* [1991] 2 Med. L.R. 271, Newfoundland CA (consent to muscle biopsy was sufficient to include consent to bone biopsy); *O'Bonswain v. Paradis* [1994] 5 Med. L.R. 399, Ontario High Court (consent to "additional or alternative treatment or operative procedure as in the opinion of [the defendant] are immediately necessary" embraced consent to alternative means of access for dialysis); *cf. Pridham v. Nash* (1986) 33 D.L.R. (4th) 304, where the Ontario High Court held that a consent form in similar terms signed before a laparoscopy (a minor investigative operation) entitled the surgeon to carry out any minor operation found necessary during the laparoscopy; but it would not entitle him to carry out major surgery.

of the nature of the procedures contemplated, his signature on the form will not be conclusive.[55]

(ii) *Voluntary consent*

Consent to medical treatment must be freely given. In other words, such consent **12–128** must not be obtained by imposing unreasonable pressure on the patient. In many situations, of course, it will be reasonable for a doctor to put pressure on a patient to accept treatment which is plainly for his benefit. In prison, however, where the medical officer is also a prison officer, the doctor–patient relationship assumes a different character. In this context the question whether consent to medical treatment was freely given may arise more often. This topic was considered in *Freeman v. Home Office (No. 2)*.[56] In that case McCowan J. rejected the contention that a prisoner could not give valid consent to treatment by the prison medical officer. However, he acknowledged that a prisoner may on occasions be overborne by the medical officer:

> "The right approach, in my judgment, is to say that where, in a prison setting, a doctor has the power to influence a prisoner's situation and prospects a court must be alive to the risk that what may appear, on the face of it, to be a real consent is not in fact so."[57]

The Court of Appeal, in affirming McCowan J.'s judgment, expressly approved this passage.[58]

Consent or refusal to consent may be vitiated by the undue influence of a third **12–129** party. In *Re T (Adult: Refusal of Treatment)*,[59] T, a pregnant woman who had links with Jehovah's Witnesses, was injured in a road traffic accident and taken to hospital. T said that she did not want a blood transfusion. However, she said this at a time when she was under the influence of her mother (a Jehovah's Witness) and when a doctor had advised her that there were other procedures available. On the following day a Caesarian section was performed. The baby was stillborn, T's condition deteriorated and a blood transfusion became essential. The Court of Appeal upheld a declaration that it was not unlawful to administer a blood transfusion to T. The Court held that in the present case T's refusal was not effective, because at the time (a) she was under the undue influence of her mother and (b) she believed that alternative treatments would suffice.

---

[55] " . . . getting the patient to sign a pro forma expressing consent to undergo the operation 'the effect and nature of which have been explained to me' . . . would be no defence to an action based on trespass if no explanation had in fact been given. The consent would have been expressed in form only, not in reality": *Chatterton v. Gerson* [1981] Q.B. 432, 443D-E *per* Bristow J. The same applies to signature of forms of refusal to consent: see *Re T (Adult: Refusal of Treatment)* [1993] Fam. 95, 114G-H *per* Lord Donaldson M.R. See, to similar effect, *Taylor v. Shropshire Health Authority* [1998] Lloyd's Rep. Med. 395. The plaintiff failed to prove that she had not been warned of the risk of failure of a sterilisation operation (although she recovered damages on the basis that the operation had been negligently performed). In so finding, however, Popplewell J. stated that he was not assisted by the defendant's specific consent form for sterilisations, which stated that the plaintiff had been warned of the risk of failure and was signed by her just before the operation. He regarded the form as "pure window dressing" on the facts of that case.
[56] [1984] Q.B. 524.
[57] *ibid.* at 542H–543A.
[58] *ibid.* at 557B-C and 558.
[59] [1993] Fam. 95.

(iii) *Informed consent*

12–130 The doctrine of "informed consent", as developed in certain states in the United States, holds that a patient's consent to medical treatment is vitiated if he is given inadequate information concerning the proposed treatment. Accordingly, he is entitled to claim damages for battery, despite the fact that he apparently consented to the treatment.[60] The Supreme Court of Canada, although imposing a higher duty of disclosure than the English courts,[61] has declined to adopt this doctrine. In *Reibl v. Hughes*[62] Laskin C.J., delivering the judgment of the court, stated:

> "In my opinion, actions of battery in respect of surgical or other medical treatment should be confined to cases where surgery or treatment has been performed or given to which there has been no consent at all or where, emergency situations aside, surgery or treatment has been performed or given beyond that to which there was consent. . . . In situations where the allegation is that attendant risks which should have been disclosed were not communicated to the patient and yet the surgery or other medical treatment carried out was that to which the plaintiff consented . . . I do not understand how it can be said that the consent was vitiated by the failure of disclosure . . . [I]n my view, unless there has been a misrepresentation or fraud to secure consent to the treatment, a failure to disclose the attendant risks, however serious, should go to negligence rather than battery."

12–131 The American doctrine of informed consent has been firmly rejected by the English courts. In *Chatterton v. Gerson*[63] Bristow J. held that negligent failure by a medical practitioner to disclose information would not of itself vitiate the patient's consent to treatment.[64] He then stated:

> "Once the patient is informed in broad terms of the nature of the procedure which is intended, and gives her consent, that consent is real, and the cause of action on which to base a claim for failure to go into risks and implications is negligence, not trespass."[65]

In *Hills v. Potter*[66] Hirst J. followed the approach of Bristow J. in *Chatterton v. Gerson*[67] and deplored reliance on the torts of assault and battery "in medical cases of this kind". Finally, the question was exhaustively reviewed by the Court of Appeal[68] and the House of Lords[69] in *Sidaway v. Governors of Bethlem Royal Hospital*. The Court of Appeal held unanimously that failure to give a patient sufficient information would not vitiate his consent to an operation. In the House of Lords, although the law lords differed as to the extent of the duty of disclosure, they were unanimous in the view that inadequate disclosure of information did

---

[60] *Salgo v. Leland Stanford Jr. University Board of Trustees* 154 Cal App 2d 560; 317 P. 2d 170 (1957); *Canterbury v. Spence* 464 F. 2d 772 (D.C. Cir. 1972); Robertson, G., "Informed consent to Medical Treatment" (1981) 97 L.Q.R. 102.
[61] See paras 12–202 to 12–204, below.
[62] (1980) 114 D.L.R. (3d) 1, 10–11.
[63] [1981] Q.B. 432.
[64] *ibid.* at 442F–G.
[65] *ibid.* at 443A. In reaching his decision Bristow J. took into account the decision of the Ontario Court of Appeal in *Reibl v. Hughes* (1979) 89 D.L.R. (3d) 112, which was then under appeal.
[66] [1984] 1 W.L.R. 641, 653D–E (Note).
[67] [1981] Q.B. 432.
[68] [1984] Q.B. 493.
[69] [1985] A.C. 871.

not vitiate the patient's consent to treatment. Even Lord Scarman, who favoured a more extensive duty of disclosure than his colleagues, agreed with Hirst J.'s comment in *Hills v. Potter*[70] that it would be deplorable to base the law in medical cases of this kind on the torts of assault and battery.[71]

The Canadian case of *Van Mol v. Ashmore*[72] considers the question of who has **12–132** to consent. A 16-year-old girl underwent surgery to remedy narrowing of her aorta; in the course of difficulties in the operation she suffered paraplegia and damage to the laryngeal nerve. The judge held that the operation was not negligently carried out, and that proper consent had been obtained from the parents. The Court of Appeal held, by a majority, that the appeal should be allowed on the basis that the patient herself should have had the appropriate explanation about the risks and advantages of the operation, and that had this happened she would have probably have opted for a more conservative approach.

In *Appleton v. Garrett*,[73] the defendant dentist administered excessive and **12–133** unnecessary dental treatment to his patients on a massive scale. Dyson J. found that he deliberately withheld from his patients the information that their teeth were healthy and that the treatment was unnecessary, so as to secure their consent and his personal gain. The effect of his non-disclosure in bad faith was to vitiate the consents given and entitle the patients to sue in trespass. They were awarded aggravated damages to reflect the outrageous nature of the defendant's conduct. At (1996) 4 Med. L.Rev. 311, the commentator argues that the law of trespass serves a useful purpose in such cases: the prospect of compensation for damage (injury to feelings) which does not sound in negligence should be an important deterrent against cynical conduct by health professionals. But in the cases of *Halkyard v. Mathew*[74] and *R. v. Richardson*[75] in differing circumstances it was held that failures to disclose did not vitiate consent. In *Halkyard* the surgeon failed to disclose to his patient that he suffered from epilepsy: it was held that as long as his medical condition did not affect his capacity to perform the treatment he was under no obligation to disclose it; and in *Richardson* a dentist continued to carry out treatment on patients despite being suspended from practice. She was convicted of assault, but the convictions were overturned on appeal on the basis that fraud only vitiated the consent where the fraud was as to the identity of the person doing the act, or the nature of the act itself.

The question of disclosure of information in the context of a claim for **12–134** negligence is dealt with below.[76] And for a detailed criticism of the current

---

[70] [1984] 1 W.L.R. 641, 653D–E (Note).
[71] [1985] A.C. 871, 883E. See also *Davis v. Barking, Havering and Brentwood H.A.* [1993] 4 Med. L.R. 85, 91 *per* McCullough J; and *Behrens v. Smith* (1997) 153 Sask. R. 294 where Wimmer J. said: "The law imposes upon the medical practitioner a duty to provide sufficient information to enable the patient to reasonably balance the possible risks and benefits and make an informed decision about whether to undergo or forego a recommended treatment. The scope of the duty will vary according to the circumstances of the case and any special considerations affecting the particular patient. That which a patient should be made to understand are the nature, purpose, and likely benefits of the treatment; the recognised risks inherent in it; the availability of alternative treatments; and the possible consequences of leaving the condition untreated".
[72] (1999) 168 D.L.R. (4th) British Columbia CA.
[73] [1997] 8 Med. L.R. 75.
[74] [1999] 67 Alta. L.R. (3d).
[75] [1999] Q.B. 444.
[76] See paras 12–201 to 12–232, below.

position on informed consent under English law see the article "Informed Consent and Other Fairy Stories" by Professor Michael Jones.[77]

(iv) *Capacity to consent*

12–135 Legal capacity to consent depends upon the patient's ability to understand the broad nature of the treatment which he is advised to undergo.[78] The requirement for consent is a recognition of individual autonomy or a right to self-determination. A patient who has capacity in law to give his consent to treatment must also have the right to withhold consent. It follows that he is entitled to refuse consent for any reason whatever or for no reason at all.[79] Where a patient refuses treatment which is recommended for him and does so on grounds which appear to be irrational, there is a danger that he may be regarded as incompetent to give or refuse consent and that his wishes may be overridden. In *Re T (Adult: Refusal of Treatment)*[80] Lord Donaldson M.R. summarised the relevant principles:

> "1. Prima facie every adult has the right and capacity to decide whether or not he will accept medical treatment, even if a refusal may risk permanent injury to his health or even lead to premature death. Furthermore, it matters not whether the reasons for the refusal were rational or irrational, unknown or even non-existent.... However the presumption of capacity to decide, which stems from the fact that the patient is an adult, is rebuttable.
> 2. An adult patient may be deprived of his capacity to decide by long-term mental incapacity....
> 3. If an adult patient did not have the capacity to decide at the time of the purported refusal and still does not have that capacity, it is the duty of the doctors to treat him in whatever way they consider, in the exercise of clinical judgment, to be in his best interests.
> 4. Doctors faced with a refusal of consent have to give very careful and detailed consideration to what was the patient's capacity to decide at the time the decision was made. It may not be a case of capacity or no capacity. It may be a case of reduced capacity. What matters is whether at that time the patient's capacity was reduced below the level needed in the case of a refusal of that importance, for refusals can vary in importance. Some may involve a risk to life or of irreparable damage to health. Others may not."[81]

12–136   These principles were applied in *Re C (Adult: Refusal of Medical Treatment)*.[82] C was a chronic paranoid schizophrenic adult who refused to consent to the amputation of his gangrenous foot. He was granted an injunction against the amputation of his foot without his express written consent. Thorpe J. had to consider whether or not C was competent to give or withhold consent at the time of his refusal. He analysed the process of deciding into three stages: comprehending and retaining treatment information, believing it, and weighing it in order to

---

[77] (1999) 7 Med. L.Rev. 103.
[78] See paras 12–130 to 12–133, above.
[79] See *Sidaway v. Governors of Royal Bethlem Hospital* [1985] A.C. 871, 904F *per* Lord Templeman.
[80] [1993] Fam. 95 at 115–116.
[81] In the case of *R. v. Bournemouth Community and Mental Health NHS Trust, ex parte L.* [1999] 1 A.C. 458 the House of Lords confirmed the basic principle that if a person lacks capacity to take decisions about medical treatment, it is necessary for other appropriately qualified people to take the decisions for him. The principles of necessity may apply (125H–126B).
[82] [1994] 1 W.L.R. 290.

make an informed choice.[83] Applying that test, he found that C's general mental capacity was not so impaired by his schizophrenia that he was incapable of understanding the nature, purpose and effects of the treatment proposed, so that the presumption of competence (his right of self-determination) was not displaced and its expression governed all doctors with notice of it. The injunction merely added the sanction of contempt of court to what under the general law would be an assault. Thorpe J.'s approach to the question whether an adult patient has capacity to consent to or to refuse treatment in *Re C (Adult: Refusal of Treatment)* was approved by the Court of Appeal in *Re MB* [1997] 8 Med. L.R. 217. See also *St George's NHS Trust v. S* [1999] Fam. 26, discussed at para. 12–139, below.

Similarly, a competent adult who refuses treatment because of political or **12–137** religious convictions is entitled to have that refusal honoured. *In Secretary of State for the Home Department v. Robb,*[84] it was held that prison officials and medical staff could lawfully observe and abide by a prisoner's refusal to accept nutrition and hydration and could abstain from forcing them upon him, so long as he retained the mental capacity to refuse. The case of *R. v. Collins and Ashworth Hospital Authority, ex parte Brady*[85] is a case where forcible feeding against the prisoner's will was sanctioned by the court on the basis that Brady had been incapacitated in all his decisions about refusing food by a mental disorder, and that the doctors were legally empowered to supply medical treatment in his best interests in accordance with their clinical judgment.

Medical treatment in the absence of consent may be given in an emergency.[86] **12–138** This is a rule of common law, which is self-evidently necessary. However, the juristic basis of the rule is uncertain. Lord Goff in *Re F (Mental Patient: Sterilisation)*[87] expressed the view that it is founded on the principle of necessity. It is sometimes suggested that the rule is based upon implied consent, although this is somewhat artificial, since the patient has probably never directed his mind to the situation which has arisen.[88] As to the ambit of the rule, it applies when a person is unable to consent (for example, because he is unconscious or mentally handicapped) and treatment is in his best interests.[89] The classic example of a case falling within this rule is the victim of a road accident lying unconscious, who requires a blood transfusion and possibly surgery to save his life. Even in this situation, however, doubt may arise if it is known that the victim is a Jehovah's Witness who would refuse the necessary treatment if he were in a

---

[83] *ibid.* at 292E. The Court of Appeal has doubted whether a patient suffering anorexia nervosa has capacity to refuse food because of the effect of that disorder on the patient's understanding of the consequences of refusal: see *Re W (A Minor) (Medical Treatment)* [1993] Fam. 64; *B v. Croydon Health Authority* [1995] 1 All E.R. 683.

[84] Feeding and hydration have also been regarded as treatment in the case of anorexics: see para. 12–140, below.

[85] [2000] Lloyd's Rep. Med. 355.

[86] See *Re F (Mental Patient: Sterilisation)* [1990] 2 A.C. 1, 55 (*per* Lord Brandon) and 712–78 (*per* Lord Goff).

[87] [1990] 2 A.C. 1.

[88] In *Marshall v. Curry* (1933) 3 D.L.R. 260, Chisolm C.J. rejected the doctrine of implied consent and preferred to base his decision on the surgeon's over-riding duty "to act in order to save the life or preserve the health of the patient". This analysis is valid in the case of an emergency which arises during the course of medical treatment (as happened in *Marshall v. Curry*) because the surgeon or doctor involved has already assumed a duty towards the patient. However, this analysis is more difficult to apply to the doctor who voluntarily treats the unconscious victim of a road accident. He does not act out of legal duty, but the law protects him from any subsequent claim in battery.

[89] *Re F (Mental Patient: Sterilisation)* [1990] 2 A.C. 1, discussed in para. 12–142 below.

position to do so. It has been suggested that in those circumstances a medical practitioner would not be held liable for taking whatever steps were necessary to save the patient's life.[90] However, the Ontario Court of Appeal took a different view in *Malette v. Shulman*.[91] The claimant was seriously injured in a road traffic accident and admitted unconscious to hospital. A Jehovah's Witness card, found in her purse, requested that no blood be administered to her under any circumstances. The defendant doctor administered blood transfusions to her, which he considered necessary to preserve her life. It was held that the Jehovah's Witness card imposed a valid restriction on the emergency treatment which could be given to the claimant, and that the defendant was liable for battery.

12–139   It follows from the above discussion that a patient of full age and capacity can effectively refuse medical treatment, even when it is necessary to save his life. Depending upon its terms, that refusal may include foreseeable future medical treatment even in the event that the patient later becomes incompetent to give or withhold consent.[92] It has been held that a refusal of consent to treatment may be overridden in circumstances where treatment is necessary to save the life of another. In *Re S (Adult: Refusal of Treatment)*[93] Sir Stephen Brown P. granted a declaration that a Caesarean section could be performed on a woman, despite her refusal on religious grounds, in order to save the life of the baby and avoid a serious risk of the mother's death. Urgent decisions in the course of the management of the last stages of pregnancy are the source of some difficult cases. The decision in *Re S*, which was given in circumstances of great urgency, was difficult to reconcile with the mother's right to refuse consent to treatment or with the principle that a foetus does not have legal personality until it is born alive.[94] In *Re MB*[95] following a comprehensive review of the authorities, Butler-Sloss L.J. said, *obiter*, that a woman who has the capacity to decide was entitled to refuse medical intervention, even though the consequence might be the death or serious handicap of the child she carries. It was held that the court did not have jurisdiction to take the interests of the unborn child into consideration in such cases. *Re S (Adult: Refusal of Treatment)*[96] was disapproved. The observations of Butler-Sloss L.J. in *Re MB* were adopted by the Court of Appeal in *St. George's NHS Trust v. S.*[97] S, who was 36 weeks pregnant, was diagnosed with pre-eclampsia and advised that she should be admitted to hospital for an induced delivery. She refused, since she wanted a natural birth. Against her will, she was admitted to a mental hospital for assessment under section 2 of the Mental Health Act 1983 and then transferred to another hospital, which obtained a declaration dispensing with her consent to treatment by Caesarean section. Her appeal, after

---

[90] See "Treatment without Consent: Emergency" (1985) 290 B.M.J. 1505.

[91] [1991] 2 Med. L.R. 162.

[92] See *Re C (Adult: Refusal of Medical Treatment)* [1994] 1 W.L.R. 290. The effect of "advance directives" as to the patient's treatment wishes in the event that he later becomes incapable of making his own treatment decisions was recognised *obiter* in *Airedale NHS Trust v. Bland* [1993] A.C. 789, 864F *per* Lord Goff.

[93] [1993] Fam. 123; see commentary at (1993) 2 Med. L.Rev. 92.

[94] The decision was criticised in Stern, K., "Court-Ordered Caesarian Sections: In Whose Interests?" (1993) 56 M.L.R. 238. The same outcome was achieved in the cases of *Norfolk and Norwich Healthcare NHS Trust v. W* [1996] 2 F.L.R. 613 and *Rochdale Healthcare NHS Trust* [1997] 1 F.C.R. 274 (Johnson J. in both cases) in which neither woman was suffering from a mental disorder, but in one of which there was some doubt as to whether she was capable of understanding and retaining information about the proposed treatment.

[95] [1997] 8 Med. L.R. 217.

[96] [1993] Fam. 123.

[97] [1999] Fam. 26.

the operation, was successful. The Court of Appeal held that an adult of sound mind was entitled to refuse treatment, even when his or her own life depended on receiving such treatment. That right was not diminished by reason of pregnancy merely because the decision to exercise it would result in the death of an unborn child and so might appear morally repugnant. The detention, treatment and transfer of S had been unlawful. At 702H–704J, the Court set out guidelines for use by medical practitioners, hospital authorities and health professionals generally when faced with a patient who refuses surgical or invasive treatment which is regarded as medically necessary.[98]

Mentally disordered patients. Consent is not required for lawful medical   **12–140**
treatment of a patient who is detained under section 3 of the Mental Health Act 1983, provided that the treatment given is for the mental disorder.[99] Such treatment may be given notwithstanding a positive refusal to consent. In *Re KB (Adult) (Mental Patient: Medical Treatment)*,[1] the issue was whether an anorexic patient might lawfully be force-fed under these provisions despite her refusal to eat. It was argued that feeding was not treatment for her psychiatric disorder, but merely relief of the symptoms. Ewbank J. accepted the hospital's argument that relief of the symptoms of the patient's eating disorder was part of the treatment for that disorder, and was necessary in any event for treatment of the underlying disorder to be possible. It was held that forced-feeding of an anorexic patient amounted to "medical treatment given to [the patient] for a medical disorder" under section 63 of the 1983 Act, and so could be administered without consideration of her competence to refuse. That proposition was upheld and extended by the Court of Appeal in *B. v. Croydon Health Authority*.[2] B was detained in hospital under section 3 of the 1983 Act by reason of her borderline personality disorder. Although she was not anorexic, her disorder caused her to refuse food. B was refused an injunction against the hospital to prevent the staff feeding her by tube against her wish. Her appeal was dismissed. Treatment under section 63 had to be considered as a whole. Feeding, being designed to alleviate a symptom of her mental disorder, was ancillary to and a necessary prerequisite of the core treatment administered to deal with that disorder. Hoffman L.J. said:

"Nursing and care concurrent with the core treatment or as a necessary prerequisite to such treatment or to prevent the patient from causing harm to himself or to alleviate the consequences of the disorder are in my view all capable of being ancillary to a treatment calculated to alleviate or prevent a deterioration of the psychopathic disorder. It would seem to me strange if a hospital could, without the patient's consent, give him treatment directed to alleviating a psychopathic disorder showing itself in suicidal tendencies, but not without such consent be able to treat the consequences of a suicide attempt. In my

---

[98] For commentaries on this case, see (1998) 114 L.Q.R. 550 and [1998] C.L.J. 438. For a discussion of the decision in *Re MB*, see S. Michalowski, "Court-Authorised Caesarian Sections—The End of a Trend?" (1999) 62 M.L.R. 115.
[99] Mental Health Act 1983, s.63. See, generally, ss.512–564.
[1] (1994) 19 B.M.L.R. 144; [1994] 2 F.C.R. 1051.
[2] [1995] Fam. 133 (and see commentary at (1995) 3 Med. L.Rev. 191). See also *Riverside Mental Health NHS Trust v. Fox* [1995] 6 Med. L.R. 181, where a declaration that an anorexic woman could lawfully be forced-fed in order to keep her alive was quashed by the Court of Appeal on the grounds that the declaration granted purported to be an interim declaration, a form of relief which does not exist in English law. In "Feeding anorexics who refuse food" (1999) 7 Med. L.Rev. 21, P. Lewis examines the meaning of "best interests" in the context of the force-feeding of anorexic patients.

judgment the term 'medical treatment . . . for the mental disorder' in section 63 includes such ancillary acts."[3]

On that basis, force-feeding of B was held to be treatment under section 63. The decision in *Re C (Adult: Refusal of Medical Treatment)*[4] was distinguished. Although C was a detainee under section 3 on account of his schizophrenia, that mental disorder was wholly unrelated to the gangrenous condition of his foot.[5]

12–141   The approach adopted by the Court of Appeal in *B. v. Croydon Health Authority*[6] was applied by Wall J. in *Tameside and Glossop Acute Services NHS Trust v. CH (a Patient)*.[7] CH was a 41-year-old schizophrenic, detained under the Mental Health Act 1983, who was found to be pregnant. Her obstetrician considered that there was a grave danger that her child would be still-born unless labour was induced and a Caesarian section performed. Her psychiatrist gave evidence that, in his opinion, the birth of a live baby was necessary for treatment of CH's schizophrenia to be effective. Accordingly, it was argued, induction and a Caesarean section were properly regarded as treatment ancillary to the core psychiatric treatment for the mental disorder. Wall J. accepted this reasoning. A declaration was granted that such procedures were lawful, notwithstanding CH's lack of consent to a Caesarean section, which had not even been discussed with her.[8] Wall J. left open the question whether the court has power at common law to authorise the use of reasonable force as a necessary incident of treatment. The question was answered affirmatively in several subsequent decisions at first instance (see *Norfolk and Norwich Healthcare (NHS) Trust v. W*,[9] *Wolverhampton Metropolitan Borough Council v. DB (a Minor)*[10] and *Re C*,[11] and finally by the Court of Appeal in *Re MB*.[12]

12–142   When is it lawful to treat an adult who is not detained under the Mental Health Act 1983, but whose mental disorder means that he or she is incompetent to make treatment decisions? This question first arose for judicial consideration in the controversial area of sterilisation of mentally handicapped women. If a woman is severely mentally handicapped and unable to cope with pregnancy or parent-hood, sterilisation may be thought to be in her best interests. If the problem arises before she attains majority, the necessary consent can be obtained by making her a ward of court and then applying to the court for leave. This was done in *Re B (a Minor)*,[13] a case of a mentally handicapped girl aged 17 living in a council

---

[3] *ibid. per* Hoffman L.J. at 138H–139B. The Court of Appeal also doubted, without deciding, that B had capacity to refuse feeding when she did, by reason of the effect of anorexia nervosa on her understanding of the consequences of refusal. See also to this effect *Re W (A Minor) (Medical Treatment)* [1993] Fam. 64, CA.

[4] [1994] 1 W.L.R. 290, discussed at para. 12–136, above.

[5] [1995] Fam. 133, 138H–139B *per* Hoffman L.J., with whom Henry and Neill L.JJ. agreed.

[6] [1995] Fam. 133.

[7] [1996] 1 F.L.R. 762.

[8] In *Re C (Adult: Refusal of Medical Treatment)* [1994] 1 W.L.R. 290 (discussed at para. 12–136, above), the evidence was that C's chances of survival if his gangrenous foot was not amputated were no more than 15%. On that basis, it might have been argued that, since death was the probable consequence of not amputating, the operation was necessary for effective continued treatment of his schizophrenia. His express and specific refusal to permit amputation would then have been irrele-vant.

[9] (1997) 34 B.M.L.R. 16.

[10] (1997) 37 B.M.L.R. 172.

[11] Unreported, March 5, 1997, Wall J.

[12] [1997] 8 Med. L.R. 217.

[13] [1988] A.C. 199. The case should be contrasted with *Re Eve* (1986) 31 D.L.R. (4th) 1, in which the Canadian Supreme Court refused to authorise sterilisation of a mentally retarded woman.

residential institution. Bush J. granted leave for the sterilisation operation to be carried out and the Court of Appeal and House of Lords upheld the order.[14] Where the woman has attained 18, the wardship jurisdiction is not available. In *T v. T*[15] a 19-year-old girl, who was epileptic and severely mentally handicapped, was found to be pregnant. The doctors treating her considered that she would be unable to cope with pregnancy or parenthood. Wood J. made a declaration that it would not be unlawful, by reason of lack of consent, to carry out an abortion and sterilisation. He considered the case analogous to a situation where treatment is carried out on an unconscious patient, who is unable to consent. The same problem was considered by the House of Lords in *Re F (Mental Patient: Sterilisation)*,[16] where a declaration was upheld to the effect that a proposed sterilisation operation carried out on a 36-year-old mentally handicapped woman without her consent would not be unlawful. It was held that:

(i) the court had no *parens patriae* jurisdiction or jurisdiction under the Mental Health Act 1983 to approve the operation;

(ii) where a person lacks the capacity to consent, medical treatment carried out in his best interests is not unlawful;

(iii) in determining whether particular treatment is, or was, in the best interests of such a person, the *Bolam* test applies[17];

(iv) the court has jurisdiction to make a declaration that a proposed operation is in a patient's best interests. It is good practice to apply for such a declaration before carrying out a sterilisation operation on an adult woman who is unable to consent because of mental incapacity.

In *Re Y (Adult Patient) (Transplant: Bone Marrow)*,[18] the principles enunciated in *Re F* were applied to authorise a bone marrow transplant from the defendant, a mentally disabled adult woman, to her sister. The procedure offered the only

---

[14] For criticism of the decision, see S. Lee, "Sterilisation" (1987) 103 L.Q.R. 331 and M. Brazier, "Sterilisation: Down the Slippery Slope" (1990) 6 P.N. 25. The decision is discussed by A. Grubb and D. Pearl in "Sterilisation and the Courts" [1987] C.L.J. 439. They point out that there is no basic right to reproduce recognised by international law. The only relevant right in English law is the right of control over one's own body. Where a person is incompetent, his right will be valueless unless someone else can exercise it on his behalf.

[15] [1988] 1 All E.R. 613. See also *Re W (A Patient)* [1993] 1 F.L.R. 381; *cf. L. and G.M. v. M.M.: The Director-General, Department of Family Services and Aboriginal and Island Affairs* (1994) F.L.C. 668 (Aus.), where an application by the parents of a 17-year-old physically and intellectually disabled woman for authorisation of her non-therapeutic sterilisation was refused. Warnock J. took the view that to grant the application on grounds of the risk of pregnancy was tantamount to adopting a policy that all such women should be sterilised.

[16] [1990] 2 A.C. 1.

[17] See Lord Bridge at 52D-E, Lord Brandon at 66G–68E and Lord Goff at 78B-C. This approach was followed by Hollis J. in *Re W (an Adult: Mental Patient: Sterilisation)* [1993] 1 F.L.R. 381, authorising the non-therapeutic sterilisation of a 20-year-old mentally disabled woman, notwithstanding that risk of her pregnancy was small. *Cf. Department of Health & Community Services v. JWB and SMB* (1992) 66 A.L.J.R. 300, where the High Court of Australia rejected the application of the *Bolam* test to the decision whether non-therapeutic sterilisation was in the best interests of a mentally disabled girl. For a comparative discussion of the law on sterilisation of mentally handicapped women in England and Australia, see N. Cica, (1993) 1 Med. L.Rev. 186. Cica argues that the *Bolam* principle in this context means that excessive regard will be paid to the opinion of medical practitioners on the social issues which bear upon the lawfulness of a proposed sterilisation. See also D. Giesen, "Comparative legal developments" in *Decision-Making and Problems of Incompetence* (A. Grubb, ed., 1994).

[18] [1997] Fam. 110.

realistic prospect of recovery for the latter. Her interests, however, were irrelevant. Connell J. concluded that the procedure was in the best interests of Y because the continued illness and ultimate death of her sister would reduce the time which their mother was able to spend with Y. The benefits to Y of her relationship with her mother outweighed the extremely low risks to Y's health which were involved in the transplant procedure.[19]

12–143   In *R. v. Bournewood Community and Mental Health NHS Trust*,[20] the House of Lords considered the lawfulness of treatment of an "informal patient". L was an autistic adult who was voluntarily admitted to hospital after becoming agitated at a day centre. Against the will of his carers, he remained in hospital and received treatment for his mental disorder. He lacked capacity to consent to treatment, but did not object to it. He was incapable of making a voluntary decision to leave hospital, but since he did not object, the procedures laid down by the Mental Health Act 1983 were not invoked to detain him or to justify his treatment. It was held that L was to be regarded as admitted under section 131(1) of the 1983 Act, which permits the admission to hospital of patients who lack capacity to consent but do not object. His treatment and care was justified by the common law principle of necessity. An examination of the legislative history of the 1983 Act revealed that its provisions did not exclude the application of the common law doctrine to the treatment of "informal patients" who are not detained under that Act. It was also held (Lords Nolan and Steyn dissenting) that L was not in fact detained, since he was in an open, unlocked ward, even although the hospital would have taken steps to detain him compulsorily under the 1983 Act had he tried to leave.

12–144   In *Re F*[21] the House of Lords referred to a "special category" of medical procedures the performance of which on those incapable of consent would, as a matter of good practice, require court approval. However, very little guidance was given as to the criteria for deciding which procedures fall into this category. In both *Re B*[22] and *Re F* the court rejected a distinction between therapeutic and non-therapeutic treatment as helpful for the purpose of deciding whether treatment was lawful. The distinction has assumed procedural significance, however, as a starting point for determining when the court's approval should be sought in such cases. Thus in *Re GF (Mental Patient Medical Treatment)*[23] the court refused to grant a declaration that the performance of a hysterectomy on a mentally disabled woman for medical (therapeutic) reasons was lawful, even

---

[19] In the case of *Re A (Mental Patient: Sterilisation)* [2000] Lloyd's Rep. Med. 87 the Court of Appeal upheld the judge's decision to refuse permission for a vasectomy on a 28-year-old Down's Syndrome man whose mother (the applicant) was worried that he might begin a sexual relationship when he was moved into local authority care. The Court said that a fresh application could be made if A's freedom was being restricted when he did move into local authority care because of fears that he would have a sexual relationship with another resident. And in the case of *Re SL (Adult Patient: Sterilisations: Patient's Best Interests)* [2000] Lloyd's Rep. Med. 339 the Court of Appeal overruled the judge's decision to allow a hysterectomy on a 29-year-old patient on the grounds that the medical evidence was unanimous that the immediate preferred option was to insert a Mirena contraceptive coil, even though more invasive surgical treatment might become necessary later. It was emphasised that the correct test was not "Is the proposed treatment within the range of acceptable opinion among competent and responsible practitioners?" (*i.e.* the *Bolam* test), but "Is it in the best interests of the patient?"
[20] [1999] 1 A.C. 458.
[21] [1990] 2 A.C. 1.
[22] [1988] A.C. 199.
[23] [1993] 4 Med. L.R. 77. See to similar effect *Re R (a Minor) (Medical Treatment)* [1992] 2 F.L.R. 585.

though its effects would include sterility. The declaration was unnecessary, for the question of whether alleviation of the problems caused to GF by menstruation was a question for clinical judgment.[24] By contrast, approval will almost always be required for non-therapeutic sterilisation of the mentally handicapped.[25]

In *Airedale NHS Trust v. Bland*[26] the House of Lords applied the principles set **12–145** out in *Re F*[27] in deciding whether medical treatment can lawfully be withdrawn from a patient who is permanently insensate. Anthony Bland was in a persistent vegetative state from which he would not recover. The hospital and physicians responsible for attending him sought and were granted declarations that they might lawfully discontinue medical treatment and care designed to keep him alive, including artificial ventilation, nutrition and hydration. It was held (1) that a medical practitioner is under no duty to provide medical treatment and care to a patient who is unable to benefit from it and (2) that the *Bolam* test applies to determine whether treatment and care is beneficial to, or in the best interests of, a patient who is unable to consent to their discontinuance.[28] Since there was a responsible medical opinion that neither life in a persistent vegetative state with no prospect of recovery nor the measures necessary to sustain life in that state were of benefit to Bland, those measures could lawfully be withdrawn. There was no question of balancing Bland's competing interests in continuance and cessation of treatment, respectively, for he had no interest in continuance. This would be so, notwithstanding the existence of a responsible body of medical opinion which supported the view that continuance of treatment was in the patient's interests.[29]

The House of Lords in Bland stated that it is desirable that the approval of the **12–146** court in similar cases be sought as a matter of routine. It was recognised that this requirement is inconsistent with the corollary of the reasoning set out above (namely, that it is not lawful to continue to treat a patient incapable of consent where the continuance of treatment is no longer in the patient's interests) and Lord Goff hoped that it might soon be relaxed.[30] However, in *Frenchay Healthcare NHS Trust v. S*,[31] it was suggested that the court should have a role to play

---

[24] See also *Re H (Mental Patient)* [1993] 4 Med. L.R. 91 (the performance of invasive diagnostic procedures upon an adult schizophrenic); *Re SG (Adult Mental Patient: Abortion)* [1993] 4 Med. L.R. 75 (performance of an abortion upon a mentally handicapped woman did not require authorisation by the court, since adequate safeguards were contained in the provisions of the Abortion Act 1967).

[25] See *Re W (an Adult: Mental Patient: Sterilisation)* [1993] 1 F.L.R. 381. The Official Solicitor's Practice Note [1993] 3 All E.R. 222 seeks (at para. 8) to list the factors which are relevant to the decision whether an incompetent person should be sterilised. And see also *Re A (Mental Patient: Sterilisation)* [2000] Lloyd's Rep. Med. 87, and *Re SL (Adult Patient: Sterilisations: Patient's Best Interests)* [2000] Lloyd's Rep. Med. 339.

[26] [1993] A.C. 789.

[27] [1990] 2 A.C. 1.

[28] *ibid.*, *per* Lord Keith at 362E, *per* Lord Goff at 373D-E, and *per* Lord Browne-Wilkinson at 385F-G. The application of the *Bolam* principle in this context is strongly criticised by J. Finnis in "Bland: Crossing the Rubicon?" (1993) 109 L.Q.R. 329; see also J. Keown, [1993] C.L.J. 209 and D. Robertson "The Withdrawal of Medical Treatment from Patients: Fundamental Legal Issues" (1996) 70 A.L.J. 723. *Airedale* was distinguished in the case of *SL (Adult Patient: Sterilisations: Patient's Best Interests)* [2000] Lloyd's Rep. Med. 339 where the Court of Appeal held in a case involving the possible sterilisation of a patient that the correct test was not the *Bolam* test, but whether or not the proposed treatment was in the best interests of the patient.

[29] Like reasoning has been applied in comparable cases in New Zealand (*Auckland Area Health Authority v. Att.-Gen.* [1993] 1 N.Z.L.R. 235, High Court of New Zealand) and in South Africa (*Clarke v. Hurst* (1992) 4 S.A. 630).

[30] [1993] A.C. 789, 874E.

[31] [1994] 1 W.L.R. 601.

in decisions of such importance, as a matter of law. The Court of Appeal upheld the grant of a declaration that it was lawful to refrain from surgical reinsertion of a feeding tube which had become dislodged from the stomach of a patient. The patient had lain for over two years in a persistent vegetative state following a drugs overdose. Sir Thomas Bingham M.R. said:

> "It is, I think, important that there should not be a belief that what the doctor says is the patient's best interest *is* the patient's best interest. For my part, I would certainly reserve to the court the ultimate power and duty to review the doctor's discretion in the light of all the facts."[32]

12–147   In the case of *NHS Trust A v. Mrs M, and NHS Trust B v. Mrs H*[33] two NHS trusts sought declarations permitting them to discontinue providing nutrition and hydration to the two patients who were both in a persistent vegetative state. This significance of this case was that the Court had to consider the impact of the European Convention on Human Rights, and particularly Article 2, providing the "right to life". The Court approached the case by considering three questions:

1. Is a patient in a PVS alive?

2. Does the withdrawing of artificial nutrition and hydration constitute an "intentional deprivation of life" within the meaning of Article 2(1)? This breaks down into two further questions:

   (a) Is the "intention" of the withdrawal of treatment to bring about the patient's death or shorten his or her life?
   (b) Does an omission to provide life-sustaining treatment constitute "an intentional deprivation"?

3. If the withdrawal does not constitute an intentional deprivation of life, are the circumstances such that Article 2 must be taken to impose a positive obligation to provide life sustaining treatment?

---

[32] *ibid.* at 609C (original emphasis). The Official Solicitor's *Practice Note* [1996] 4 All E.R. 766, which now governs applications to the court in such cases envisages that the discontinuance of life-sustaining treatment (including ventilation, hydration and nutrition by artificial means) will require the prior sanction of a High Court judge "in virtually all cases". See for declarations granted in similar circumstances: *Swindon and Marlborough NHS Trust v. S, The Guardian*, December 10, 1994 (on application of relatives caring for PVS patient at home); *Law Hospital NHS Trust v. Lord Advocate*, 1996 S.C.L.R. 491 and 566, Court of Session (PVS patient); *In the matter of a ward of court* [1995] 2 I.R.L.M. 401, Irish Supreme Court (non-PVS patient); *Re D (Adult: Medical Treatment)* [1998] 1 F.L.R. 411; and *Re H (a Patient)* [1998] 2 F.L.R. 36. (1) The *Practice Note* [1996] 4 All E.R. 766 adopts guidelines for diagnosis of persistent vegetative state published by the Conference of Royal Medical Colleges. For a case where the patient's condition did not fall wholly within those guidelines, see *Re D* (1997) 38 B.M.L.R. 1 and commentary at (1997) 5 Med. L.Rev. 225. (2) *Law Hospital NHS Trust v. Lord Advocate* (1996) S.C.L.R. 491 and 566, Sc Ct Sess, is also reported at (1998) 39 B.M.L.R 166 and a commentary is provided at (1996) 4 Med. L.R. 300. The Scottish court retains a *parens patriae* jurisdiction in respect of incompetent adults. (3) See also *South Buckinghamshire NHS Trust v. R* [1996] 7 Med. L.R. 401 (decision not to resuscitate patient in a "low awareness state" was lawful because in his best interests) *Re D (Medical Treatment: Mentally Disabled Patient)* [1998] 2 F.L.R. 22 (decision to discontinue dialysis was lawful: it was not in D's best interests to continue treatment which had to be administered under general anaesthetic, three or four times a week, because D's mental disability and alcohol and drug abuse problems prevented him from co-operating) and *Shortland v. Northland Health Limited* [1998] N.Z.L.R. 433, NZCA (in patient's best interests to discontinue dialysis, with which he was incapable of co-operating).

[33] [2001] Lloyd's Rep. Med. 28.

The questions were answered as follows:

1. Yes. Patients in PVS are alive, and entitled to protection afforded by the convention;

2. (a) Yes, the whole purpose of stopping the feeding is to bring about the death of the patient;

    (b) No, a responsible decision by the medical team not to provide treatment at the initial stage could not amount to an intentional deprivation of life. The later decision to discontinue treatment no longer in the best interests of the patient is likewise not an intentional deprivation of life;

3. No. There was no obligation in the circumstances to provide the life-sustaining treatment, and the declarations were granted.

Children. If a child has capacity to consent to medical treatment, the same **12–148** principles apply as to an adult. There is a statutory presumption that a child has the same capacity to consent to treatment as an adult from the age of 16.[34] A child under 16 is capable of consenting to medical treatment, provided he or she has sufficient maturity to understand the implications of the proposed treatment[35] and the consequences of refusal of treatment.[36] However, where a child who is "*Gillick* competent" declines to consent to treatment, his parents or the court can do so on his behalf.[37] In the exercise of its wardship jurisdiction, the court may override a parent's wishes for treatment of a child. In *Re O (a Minor) (Medical Treatment)*,[38] the parents of an infant suffering respiratory distress syndrome refused to consent to the transfusion of blood to O on religious grounds. Johnson J. overrode their refusal, authorising a transfusion in the event that O's condition deteriorated to the point where, in the opinion of his doctors, a transfusion was

---

[34] Family Law Reform Act 1969, s.8(1). The presumption may be rebutted.

[35] See *Gillick v. West Norfolk and Wisbech Area Health Authority* [1986] A.C. 112.

[36] See *Re E (a Minor) (Wardship: Medical Treatment)* [1993] 1 F.L.R. 386 (a 15-year-old Jehovah's Witness was not competent to refuse a blood transfusion because although he understood that he would die, he did not realise the full implications of the process of dying: transfusion lawful); on similar facts, *Re S (a Minor) (Consent to Medical Treatment)* [1994] 2 F.L.R. 1065 and *Re E.E. (a Minor) (Wardship: Medical Treatment)* [1994] 5 Med. L.R. 73. See also, on similar facts, the decision authorising transfusion in *Re L (Medical Treatment: Gillick Competency)* [1998] 2 F.L.R. 810. Commentaries on this decision appear at (1999) 62 M.L.R. 585 and at [1999] 7 Med. L.Rev. 58.

[37] See *Re W (a Minor) (Medical Treatment: The Court's Jurisdiction)* [1993] Fam. 64 (authorisation of removal to special hospital and treatment of 16–year-old anorexic), discussed by J. Eekelaar at (1993) 109 L.Q.R. 182 and by M. Mulholland at (1993) 9 P.N. 21. See also, on similar facts, *Re C (A Minor) (Detention: Medical Treatment)* [1997] 2 F.L.R. 180 commentary at (1999) 62 M.L.R. 595.

[38] [1993] 4 Med. L.R. 272. In *Re C (a Minor) (Medical Treatment)* [1998] Lloyd's Rep.Med. 1. The parents of a terminally ill infant refused consent to withdrawal of ventilation from her unless the hospital undertook to restore ventilation should she suffer respiratory arrest. The court granted leave to withdraw ventilation without such undertaking as in the infant's best interests. Neither the court nor parents can insist that treating doctors undertake a course of treatment which they do not consider medically justified. This decision is criticised at (1998) 6 Med. L.Rev. 99. See also *Re C (A Child) (HIV Testing)* [2000] Fam. 48: Wilson J. held that while there might be a rebuttable presumption of law that the united view of a baby's parents was correct in identifying where the welfare of the child lay, on the facts, the overwhelming advantages of testing for HIV a baby born to and breastfed by an HIV-positive woman overrode the wishes of the parents. If the test were to be conducted and was positive, advice could be given (and if necessary enforced by further orders of court) to which the afflicted baby would be entitled.

necessary to avoid damage to his vital organs. By contrast, the Court of Appeal in *Re T (a Minor) Wardship: Medical Treatment*[39] upheld the parents' refusal to consent to a liver transplant operation upon their infant child. The unanimous opinion of the medical experts called was that the surgery was the accepted treatment and gave the child a good chance of an extended and reasonable quality of life, and that without the surgery the child would die at the age of two to two-and-a-half. In the very unusual facts of this case the Court held that in considering the future welfare of the child, it was entitled to take into account wider considerations than the prospects of success of the medical procedure proposed, including the effect on the baby's welfare of the mother's likely ability to cope with the care which the child would require during and after the operation. However, the court will not order that a particular medical procedure be administered where consent to treatment is forthcoming from the child or from those with power to consent upon his behalf. The decision as to the appropriate treatment in the best interests of the patient is then for his attending doctors, and not for the court.[40]

(h) *Allied professions*

12–149 This chapter is principally concerned with doctors and surgeons. The same principles apply, however, to nurses, midwives,[41] dentists and opticians. Any person who professes expertise in any aspect of medical treatment is required to exercise reasonable skill and care, judged by the standards of his own particular profession. Thus in *Lock v. Scantlebury*[42] a dentist who dislocated the patient's jaw during treatment was held negligent for failing to notice what had occurred. He was not negligent, however, in causing the dislocation, since that could happen despite the exercise of reasonable skill and care.[43] In *Parry v. North West Surrey Health Authority*[44] a midwife was held liable for failing properly to

---

[39] [1997] 1 W.L.R. 242. For further discussion of *Re T (a Minor) (Wardship: Medical Treatment)*, see (1996) 4 Med. L.Rev. 315 and (1997) 60 M.L.R. 700.

[40] See *Re J (a Minor) (Child in Care: Medical Treatment)* [1993] Fam. 15 (refusal to order intensive resuscitation of profoundly mentally and physically handicapped child). This applies equally to the withdrawal of treatment: see *R. v. Cambridge & District Health Authority, ex p. B* [1995] 1 W.L.R. 898, Court of Appeal, discussed at para. 12–160, below. See also *R. v. Portsmouth Hospitals NHS Trust, ex p. Glass* [1999] Lloyd's Rep. Med. 367. Over the course of the Trust's treatment of a severely disabled child, disagreements arose between his mother and the Trust. His mother sought judicial review of the doctors' decisions. Scott Baker J. refused to grant a declaration as to the procedural steps which the doctors should take if disagreements arose in future between them and the child's mother as to the treatment to be given to or withheld from the child. There was an almost infinite number of considerations which might arise in the future. If the child's parents, having been fully consulted and fully understanding what doctors proposing to do, disagreed with what was proposed, the matter should be brought before the court for a decision as to what was required in the best interests of the child in the situation then pertaining. The Court of Appeal refused leave to appeal from this decision.

[41] See now the Nurses, Midwives and Health Visitors Act 1997, consolidating previous legislation.

[42] *The Times*, July 25, 1963. See also para. 12–119, above.

[43] See also *Fish v. Kapur* [1948] 2 All E.R. 176; *Fletcher v. Bench* (1973) 4 B.M.J. 117; *Gagnon v. Stortini* [1974] 4 O.R. (2d) 270. Different considerations arise where a dentist agrees to make a set of dentures for a patient. Whether the contract is regarded as one for the sale of goods or as one for work and materials, it is an implied term that the dentures shall be reasonably fit for the purpose intended: *Samuels v. Davis* [1943] K.B. 526.

[44] [1994] 5 Med. L.R. 259. See also *Gaughan v. Bedfordshire Health Authority* [1997] 8 Med. L.R. 182 (midwife negligently applied traction which was excessive in force and duration when it was apparent that the plaintiff's delivery was hindered by shoulder dystocia).

monitor the progress of the claimant's birth, so as to detect that there were difficulties, and for failing promptly to summon a doctor when the claimant's distress became apparent. Nurses occupy a somewhat different position. Traditionally, many of their duties are essentially ministerial. A finding of professional negligence will not be made against a nurse simply because a mishap occurs.[45] Where, however, a nurse makes an error within her area of expertise, she (and her employers) will be liable.[46] In recent years nurses have taken on an increasing number of skilled medical functions. The consequence of these developments must be an extension of nurses' potential liability in negligence.[47]

In the case of *Morera-Lofthouse v. Wray Castle Limited and Blackburn*[48] the **12–150** claimant sued his college of further education, and the GP who acted as the college's medical officer and medical adviser. On the facts of the case the GP was not in breach of his duty of care; the college was, in respect of one short period which was not shown to have caused the claimant's injuries. There was no dispute that the college and the medical officer owed a duty to take reasonable care.

The case of *Shakoor v. Situ*[49] concerned a practitioner in traditional Chinese **12–151** herbal medicine. He gave a course of traditional medicine, prepared with reference to a classic formula, to the claimant's husband for benign lipomata. After taking nine doses of the medicine the patient became seriously ill with liver failure and subsequently died. The experts agreed that the deceased had suffered an "idiosyncratic" reaction to the medicine, which was extremely rare and could not be predicted. The claim failed, but the interest is in the formulation of the duty of care on the practitioner of this alternative medicine. The claimant contended that he should be judged by the standards of a reasonably competent general medical practitioner concerned with skin disorders. The judge held that it was not sufficient to judge the defendant simply by reference to other practitioners in Traditional Chinese Herbal Medicine, but he had also to take account of the fact that he was practising alongside orthodox medicine, and he had to take steps to satisfy himself that there were no adverse reports in orthodox journals which would affect his use of the remedy.

(i) *Hospitals and health authorities*

Vicarious liability. Broadly speaking, a person is liable for the negligence of **12–152** his employees when acting in the course of their employment, but not (save in

---

[45] For example, *Dryden v. Surrey County Council* [1936] 2 All E.R. 535; *Thorne v. Northern Group Hospital Management Committee* (1963) 108 S.J. 115. *Cf. Strangeways-Lesmere v. Clayton* [1936] 2 K.B. 11; *Selfe v. Ilford and District Hospital Management Committee*, *The Times*, November 26, 1970.

[46] *Voller v. Portsmouth Corporation* (1947) 203 L.T.J. 264 (nurses allowed operating equipment to become infected); *Smith v. Brighton and Lewes Hospital Management Committee*, *The Times*, May 2, 1958 (the doctor prescribed a course of 30 streptomycin injections for the claimant. The ward sister allowed 34 injections to be administered with the result that the patient lost her sense of balance).

[47] For example, the Medicinal Products: Prescription by Nurses, etc. Act 1992 enables nurses, midwives and health visitors to prescribe such drugs as may be specified in regulations. The organisation of those three professions is being restructured under the Nurses, Midwives and Health Visitors Act 1992 (discussed by N. Fletcher at (1992) 8 P.N. 94).

[48] [1999] Lloyd's Rep. Med. 159.

[49] [2001] 1 W.L.R. 410.

special circumstances) for the negligence of independent contractors.[50] Thus in *Hancke v. Hooper*[51] a surgeon was held liable for the negligence of his apprentice. However, it was for a long time assumed that hospital authorities were not vicariously responsible for the negligence of their professional staff. The origins of this heresy are to be found in *Evans v. Liverpool Corporation*[52] and *Hillyer v. Governors of St Bartholomew's Hospital*.[53] In the latter case the claimant underwent an operation at a hospital maintained by the defendants. During the operation the claimant's arm came into contact with hot water and was burned. It was held that the defendants were not liable for such negligence as had occurred. The *ratio* of *Hillyer's Case* has been a source of considerable debate amongst legal writers,[54] since Farwell and Kennedy L.JJ. expressed different reasons for their decision and the Master of the Rolls agreed with both judgments. However, the *ratio* of the case appeared to be that hospital authorities were only liable for the performance by their staff of "purely ministerial or administrative duties, such as, for example, attendance of nurses in the wards, the summoning of medical aid in cases of emergency, the supply of proper food and the like".[55] They were not liable for the negligence of professional staff, such as doctors, surgeons and anaesthetists in the performance of their duties.[56] *Hillyer's Case* was followed by Horridge J. in *Strangeways-Lesmere v. Clayton*[57] and by the Court of Appeal in *Marshall v. Lindsey County Council*.[58]

12–153   In *Gold v. Essex County Council*[59] the infant claimant was treated at a hospital maintained by the defendants for warts on her face. Before applying Grenz rays the radiographer failed properly to protect the claimant's face, with the result that she was permanently disfigured. The Court of Appeal held that the defendants were liable for the radiographer's negligence. They held that the authority of *Hillyer's Case* should be restricted to what it actually decided; namely, that when a nurse in an operating theatre did something by the direction of the surgeon which resulted in injury to the patient, the governors were not liable for the act of the nurse. Following *Gold*, the vicarious responsibility of hospital authorities was gradually enlarged.[60] In *Collins v. Hertfordshire County Council*[61] Hilbery J. held that a hospital authority is liable for the acts of a resident junior house

---

[50] For a discussion of vicarious liability, which is beyond the scope of this book, see *Clerk & Lindsell* (18th ed.), chap. 5.
[51] (1835) 7 C. & P. 81.
[52] [1906] 1 K.B. 160. The defendants, acting under the provisions of the Public Health Act 1875, provided a hospital for persons with infectious diseases. As a result of the negligence of a visiting physician to the hospital, a boy was discharged too soon after a mild attack of scarlet fever and infected other members of his family. Walton J. held that the defendants' duty was to provide reasonably skilled and competent medical staff. If they discharged that duty, they were not liable for the negligence of such staff. See also *Hall v. Lees* [1904] 2 K.B. 602 in which a nursing association was held not to be liable for the negligence of the nurses they supplied.
[53] [1909] 2 K.B. 820.
[54] See, *e.g.* Goodhart, A. L., "Hospitals and Trained Nurses" 54 L.Q.R. 553 and Cross, *Precedent in English Law* (3rd ed., Oxford University Press, 1977), pp. 63–64.
[55] *Hillyer v. Governors of St Bartholomew's Hospital* [1909] 2 K.B. 820, 829.
[56] *ibid.* at 825.
[57] [1936] 2 K.B. 11.
[58] [1935] 1 K.B. 516. Decision affirmed by the House of Lords at [1937] A.C. 97.
[59] [1942] 2 K.B. 293.
[60] For similar developments in Scottish law see *MacDonald v. Board of Management for Glasgow Western Hospitals*, 1954 S.C. 453 (hospital authority responsible for any negligence on the part of resident medical officers); *Fox v. Glasgow South Western Hospitals* 1955 S.L.T. 337 (hospital authority liable for alleged negligence of nurse during operation).
[61] [1947] 1 K.B. 598.

surgeon, but not for those of a visiting surgeon. In *Cassidy v. Ministry of Health*[62] the Court of Appeal held that the hospital authority was responsible for all medical staff who had treated the claimant during his operation and afterwards; accordingly the claimant could rely upon the doctrine of *res ipsa loquitur.*[63] In *Razzel v. Snowball*[64] it was held that a part-time surgeon engaged as a specialist under the National Health Service was acting as the agent of the Minister. Accordingly he was entitled to protection under section 21(1) of the Limitation Act 1939 (now repealed).[65] In practice, the effect of the introduction of NHS indemnity in January 1990 is that health authorities and NHS trusts do not argue that consultants (or agency staff) are not employees when engaged on NHS work, since the health authority or NHS trust is obliged to indemnify them against liability for medical negligence.[66]

General practitioners are not employees of health authorities. They will be **12–154** liable for the negligence of nurses employed by them, but it is likely that locum doctors would be regarded as independent contractors.[67] The position may also be different for a private patient. A patient may engage a consultant directly and contract separately with an NHS hospital or a private clinic for nursing and ancillary care. The hospital or clinic will not be vicariously liable for the negligence of the consultant. It may be more difficult in such circumstances to succeed in a claim arising out of injury during an operation. The claimant may be unable to say whether the negligence was that of the surgeon or another member of the theatre staff.

Primary liability. Mishaps may occur not because of the negligence of **12–155** individual doctors or nurses, but because of bad administration or an unsafe system of work. In those circumstances the hospital authority is primarily liable. In *Collins v. Hertfordshire County Council*[68] it was held that the hospital authority was liable by reason of a negligent system in the provision of dangerous drugs. In *Jones v. Manchester Corporation*[69] a house surgeon, who had been qualified for five months, administered the anaesthetic Pentothal too quickly and in excessive quantity with the result that the patient died. The Court of Appeal (Hodson L.J. dissenting) held that the hospital board was negligent in allowing a doctor with such slight experience to administer Pentothal. In *Cassidy v.*

---

[62] [1951] 2 K.B. 343.
[63] The doctrine would not be applicable, unless the defendants were responsible for every person engaged in the treatment of the claimant: see para. 12–121, above. Note that a local authority is not vicariously liable for the negligence of a psychiatrist employed by it in relation to its responsibilities under the Children Act 1989: *X (Minors) v. Bedfordshire County Council* [1995] 2 A.C. 633, discussed at paras 12–057 to 12–062, above.
[64] [1954] 1 W.L.R. 1382. As to the position of a consultant, Denning L.J. observed: " . . . since the National Health Service Act 1946, the term 'consultant' does not denote a particular relationship between a doctor and a hospital. It is simply a title denoting his place in the hierarchy of the hospital staff. He is a senior member of the staff but nevertheless just as much a member of the staff as the house surgeon."
[65] *Higgins v. North West Metropolitan Hospital Board and Bach* [1954] 1 W.L.R. 411 is to the same effect.
[66] See H.C. (89) 34, H.S.G. (96) 48 and para. 12–087, above.
[67] Where general practitioners practise in partnership, they will be jointly liable for the negligence of any one of them: see *Lindley & Banks on Partnership* (1995), paras 12–88 to 12–93.
[68] [1947] 1 K.B. 598.
[69] [1952] 2 Q.B. 852.

Ministry of Health[70] Denning L.J. took a broad view of a hospital authority's primary liability:

> "In my opinion authorities who run a hospital, be they local authorities, government boards, or any other corporation, are in law under the selfsame duty as the humblest doctor; whenever they accept a patient for treatment, they must use reasonable care and skill to cure him of his ailment. The hospital authorities cannot, of course, do it by themselves: they have no ears to listen through the stethoscope, and no hands to hold the surgeon's knife. They must do it by the staff which they employ; and if their staff are negligent in giving the treatment, they are just as liable for that negligence as is anyone else who employs others to do his duties for him. What possible difference in law, I ask, can there be between hospital authorities who accept a patient for treatment, and railway or shipping authorities who accept a passenger for carriage? None whatever."[71]

This view was not shared by the other two members of the court. If correct, it would mean that a health authority would be directly (as opposed to vicariously) liable in tort (i) where hospital staff were negligent; (ii) where through incompetent administration proper treatment was not provided; and (iii) (arguably) where through lack of resources proper treatment was not provided. This issue was considered briefly and obiter by the Court of Appeal in *Wilsher v. Essex Area Health Authority.*[72] Both Sir Nicolas Browne-Wilkinson V.-C. and Glidewell L.J. said that the relevant health authority would be liable if a hospital failed to provide doctors of sufficient skill and experience.[73] That hospitals owe a direct duty of care to their patients was recognised obiter by members of the House of Lords in *X (Minors) v. Bedfordshire County Council,*[74] but without elaboration of the scope of the duty. Lord Browne-Wilkinson said:

> "It is established that those conducting a hospital are under a direct duty of care to those admitted as patients to the hospital (I express no view as to the extent of that duty). They are liable for the negligent acts of a member of the hospital staff which constitute a breach of that duty, whether or not the member of staff is himself in breach of a separate duty of care owed by him to the plaintiff . . . "[75]

12–156   In *Robertson v. Nottingham Health Authority*[76] the Court of Appeal emphatically reaffirmed that a health authority or NHS trust has a non-delegable duty to provide to its patient a proper system of care. The infant plaintiff in that case had suffered catastrophic brain damage of a rare type. Her mother argued that it was caused by hypoxic insult to the foetus during and immediately before labour, which the staff of the defendant authority had failed to prevent by performing a caesarian section hours before they in fact did. The Court of Appeal upheld Otton

---

[70] [1951] 2 K.B. 343.

[71] *ibid.* at 360.

[72] [1987] Q.B. 730. The issue did not arise, even for *obiter* consideration, on the appeal to the House of Lords.

[73] It was alleged in *Hinfey v. Salford Health Authority* [1993] 4 Med. L.R. 143 that the health authority was negligent in allowing a relatively inexperienced obstetrician to manage the claimant's birth without supervision by a consultant or registrar. On the facts in that case, the health authority was not held liable. On levels of staffing, see *Knight v. Home Office* [1990] 3 All E.R. 237, where Pill J. held that it was not negligent of prison authorities to provide a lower level of staff caring for psychiatric patients than would a psychiatric hospital.

[74] [1995] 2 A.C. 633, discussed at paras 12–057 to 12–062, above.

[75] *ibid.*, see 739H–740B. See also 729G *per* Lord Jauncey of Tullichettle.

[76] [1997] 8 Med. L.R. 1.

J.'s finding that negligence had not caused the damage, which was the result of an unknown event which must have happened some days earlier. However, the Court overturned the judge's finding of negligence by the registrar. Instead, Brooke L.J. (for the Court) identified two significant types of breakdown in communications between hospital staff. First, there was no effective communication of information available from CTG traces operated by nurses and midwives to the doctors who were responsible for making the decisions on management of the birth. Secondly, there was a lack of effective communication of the doctors' instructions to the nurses and midwives who were responsible for monitoring the condition of the foetus before labour began. The defendant was in breach of its primary duty of care to the plaintiff in both respects.

Brooke L.J. stated the relevant principles to this effect: **12–157**

(a) a hospital authority owes a non-delegable duty to establish a proper system of care, as it does to engage competent staff and provide proper and safe equipment and premises;

(b) if a hospital authority has put in place effective systems so as to ensure, so far as reasonably practicable, that communication breakdowns do not occur, the hospital is vicariously liable for negligent failure by a staff member to operate such systems effectively;

(c) if no such systems have been put in place, the hospital is directly liable to a patient who suffers injury as a result;

(d) if a patient is injured because of a negligent breakdown in the systems in place for communicating material information to the clinicians responsible for his care, he is not to be denied redress merely because no identifiable person is to blame for the deficiencies in setting up and monitoring the effectiveness of the relevant communication systems.[77]

Hospital authorities have been found to be in breach of a primary duty of care   **12–158**
in several cases. In *Bull v. Devon Area Health Authority*,[78] the health authority
was found negligent in failing to operate an efficient and reliable system for
securing the attendance of experienced doctors to deal with crises arising in the

---

[77] There is a helpful commentary on *Robertson v. Nottingham Health Authority* at (1997) 5 Med. L.Rev. 342. In August 2001 the Secretary of State for Health announced that he was considering the possibility of permitting patients to be treated in other European Community countries where they had excess capacity, and when the patient would be subjected to a long waiting list if required to wait for treatment on the NHS in the United Kingdom. If NHS patients are treated in other European countries the concept of the non-delegable duty owed by a Trust or Health Authority to its patients may become important if there has been negligence in the European hospital, and the patient wishes to sue the NHS hospital which made the referral abroad. If NHS patients are to be treated abroad new issues on liability may arise.

[78] [1993] 4 Med. L.R. 117, followed in *Re R (a Minor)* unreported, July 16, 1996, CA. Brooke L.J., giving the judgment of the Court, said "[I]f a patient is injured by reason of a negligent breakdown in the systems for communicating material information to the clinicians responsible for her care, she is not to be denied redress merely because no identifiable person or persons are to blame for deficiencies in setting up and monitoring the effectiveness of the relevant communication systems." In *AB v. Tameside and Glossop Health Authority* [1997] 8 Med. L.R. 91 (for the facts of which, see para. 12–116, above) the health authority conceded that it owed a duty of care to patients and former patients when informing them that they had been put at a remote risk of HIV infection.

course of childbirth. Similarly, in *Hay v. Grampian Health Board*,[79] the hospital was held to have been negligent in failing to maintain the system of close observation which it operated for depressive patients considered to be at risk of suicide, and which it had instituted in respect of the claimant. The hospital was also held vicariously liable for the negligence of the nurse responsible for the lapse. In *Lybert v. Warrington Health Authority*[80] the health authority was negligent in failing to adopt a proper and effective system for warning patients of the risk of failure of sterilisation operations. Presumably, a health authority's organisation of systems and procedures for treatment will be judged, for the purposes of an allegation of breach of a direct duty, by applying the *Bolam* test. In *Early v. Newham Health Authority*[81] it was held that the procedure which a health authority directed its anaesthetists to follow whenever an attempt to intubate a patient failed was not a procedure that no reasonably competent authority could adopt. There was evidence that other health authorities operated similar drills. The claimant's claim failed. In *Robertson v. Nottingham Health Authority*[82] the Court of Appeal confirmed that the *Bolam* principle applies in deciding the standard of care applicable to the non-delegable duty. Brooke L.J. said (at 13):

> "By reasonable regime of care we mean a regime of a standard that can reasonably be expected of a hospital of the size and type in question—in the present case a large teaching centre of excellence."

The Court of Appeal in *AB v. Tameside and Glossop Health Authority*[83] reached the same conclusion, but on the facts of this case, derived no assistance from the principle in deciding whether the authority was in breach of duty.[84]

12–159   The decisions in *Robertson* and *AB*, taken together with the House of Lords' restatement of the *Bolam* principle in *Bolitho v. City & Hackney Health Authority*[85] appear to allow the development of new arguments on liability in the area of "systems" negligence. For example:

(a) It may no longer be sufficient in all cases to show that the systems in place in a defendant's hospital are in line with those adopted in some other hospitals. The defendant in *Early v. Newham Health Authority*[86] resisted liability because there was evidence that other hospitals directed their

---

[79] [1995] 6 Med. L.R. 128, Ct of Sess.
[80] [1996] 7 Med. L.R. 71, discussed at paras 12–223, 12–230 and 12–279, below.
[81] [1994] 5 Med. L.R. 214. In *Bull v. Devon Health Authority* (1989) [1993] 4 Med. L.R. 117, Slade L.J. considered that an allegation of inadequate staffing levels would have to be considered by reference to prevailing professional standards, applying the *Bolam* test (see at 130), but Mustill L.J. expressed reservations about accepting as a complete defence the argument that an unsatisfactory hospital system was no more unsatisfactory than those available in other hospitals (see at 141). In *A. v. Tameside and Glossop Health Authority* [1997] 8 Med. L.R. 342, the Court of Appeal rejected the *Bolam* test as unhelpful in deciding the standard of care required in relation to the method chosen to inform patients that they had been placed at risk of HIV infection. There was as yet no established practice in this area.
[82] [1997] 8 Med. L.R. 1.
[83] [1997] 8 Med. L.R. 91.
[84] See para. 12–116 above.
[85] [1998] A.C. 232. And see paras 12–099 to 12–104, above.
[86] [1994] 5 Med. L.R. 214.

anaesthetists to follow a similar procedure whenever an attempt to intubate a patient failed. Therefore the procedure could not be said to be one which no reasonably competent authority could adopt. Today, the authority might be called upon specifically to justify that procedure, and it would be subjected to an objective and critical analysis.

(b) Systems failures are often failures to put in place, monitor or maintain systems of administration and non-clinical management, for example, those for effective communication between levels of staff in a department and between staff in different departments. Even where the system concerned is a system for clinical management, the relevant failure may be of an administrative nature, such as the keeping of drug records. In those cases, a judge who might be reluctant to find a logical flaw in a clinical decision might well feel able to find fault with the failures in administration and management which led to the lack of a system, a badly designed system or the breakdown of a good system.

(c) In the light of *Robertson*, a hospital whose systems design is criticised by comparison with other hospitals will have to be prepared to identify its position in the spectrum which extends from "teaching centres of excellence" to cottage hospitals, and to justify its systems (or lack of them) from that point of view. This might prove a difficult and expensive exercise in evidential terms.

(d) The failure to provide appropriately qualified and experienced staff is a systems failure. It is clear law[87] that a treating doctor must meet the standard of care reasonably to be required of someone filling the post that he holds, for example, a senior house officer in an obstetric unit. His personal qualifications and experience are irrelevant. In *Wilsher v. Essex Area Health Authority*[88] both Sir Nicholas Browne-Wilkinson V.-C. and Glidewell L.J. said *obiter* that a hospital authority would be liable if it failed to provide doctors of sufficient skill and experience. A plaintiff might complain that, although the conduct of the senior house officer who treated her cannot be faulted on *Bolam* grounds, she ought to have been treated by a registrar. In the light of *Bolitho*, it may not be sufficient for the defendant to show that other, similar hospitals do not employ more senior staff to administer that sort of treatment.

The question whether and in what circumstances a health authority or a health **12–160** service body (as defined in the National Health Service and Community Care Act 1990) could be liable in tort to an NHS patient for the manner in which it allocates limited resources as between competing demands has not yet been directly addressed by the courts. This raises some fundamental questions, which are beyond the scope of a book on professional negligence. Under section 3 of the National Health Service Act 1977, the Secretary of State has a duty to provide various medical and related services throughout England and Wales. Some of those functions, and corresponding powers, are delegated to health authorities. In

---

[87] See para. 12–077, above.
[88] [1987] Q.B. 730. See para. 12–155, above.

X (Minors) v. Bedfordshire County Council[89] Lord Browne-Wilkinson considered the circumstances in which a local authority might be held to owe a direct duty of care to persons affected by decisions taken in the exercise of its statutory powers under the Children Act 1989. The first requirement is to show that the decision which is challenged is outside the ambit of the statutory discretion. In order to decide whether this requirement is met, it is necessary to examine the factors taken into account by the authority in reaching its decision. If those factors include matters of policy, the decision is not justiciable. If this hurdle is overcome, the imposition of a duty of care is considered on ordinary principles but a duty will not be imposed at common law if it would conflict with the due exercise of statutory duties. It is arguable that decisions as to resource allocation by a hospital or health authority and a fortiori decisions at a higher level as to the budgets allocated to these bodies are non-justiciable matters of policy for the purposes of any claim for damages. The courts are clearly unwilling to adjudicate upon such decisions in the context of public law claims for judicial review. In *R. v. Cambridge District Health Authority, ex parte B*[90] a 10-year-old girl suffered a relapse of her acute myeloid leukaemia, having undergone two courses of chemotherapy and a bone marrow transplant. Her doctors considered that further treatment was not in her best interests, since the chances of a successful outcome were slight and the likely side-effects severe. The cost of further treatment, even if it was performed privately, were significant and the health authority decided not to fund the treatment. It was common ground that, without treatment, B would die. In a decision attended by considerable publicity, Laws J. granted B's father's application for an order of certiorari quashing the decision, on the grounds that the health authority's decision assaulted B's fundamental right to life and that the question whether treatment of this sort was in the patient's best interests was a decision for the patient if an adult, and for B's parents, since she was a child. The health authority's appeal was upheld. The Court of Appeal ruled that the decision whether it was in the best interests of the patient that treatment should be withheld was one for the doctors alone: the courts were not arbiters of the merits of medical decisions, only of their lawfulness. As to the undoubted importance in the case of cost considerations, Sir Thomas Bingham, M.R. said: "[D]ifficult and agonising judgments have to be made as to how a limited budget is best allocated to the maximum advantage of the maximum number of patients. This is not a judgment which the court can make."[91]

---

[89] [1995] 2 A.C. 633, 735F–739E. For the facts of this case, see para. 12–057, above. See also *Ross v. Secretary of State for Scotland* [1990] 1 Med. L.R. 235 and *Danns & Danns v. Department of Health* [1996] P.I.Q.R. P69. *Cf. Re HIV Haemophiliac Litigation* [1996] P.N.L.R. 290, 314A: Ralph Gibson L.J. said that although proof of negligence would be difficult when the defendant was required to exercise discretion as to allocation of public resources, that was insufficient to strike out a claim in negligence. See further Chap. 2, paras 2–79–2–85, above. The appeal in *Danns v. Department of Health* was dismissed: see [1998] P.I.Q.R. P226. *X (Minors) v. Bedfordshire County Council* [1995] 2 A.C. 633 was referred to by the House of Lords in *W v. Essex County Council* [2000] 2 W.L.R. 601, when it reversed the Court of Appeal and refused to strike out a claim that a local authority owed a duty of care to a foster family with which it placed a known sexual abuser.

[90] [1995] 1 W.L.R. 898.

[91] *ibid.* at 906E–F. Applications for judicial review of decisions taken on grounds of lack of resources were refused in *R. v. Secretary of State for Social Services, ex p. Hincks* (1980) 1 B.M.L.R. 93, CA. (decision to postpone expansion of local hospital, further delaying treatment of patients on the waiting list) and *R. v. Central Birmingham Health Authority, ex p. Walker* (1987) 3 B.M.L.R. 32 (decision not to operate on a baby with a heart defect).

It would appear that an allegation of injury through inadequate provision of medication, equipment or staff is more likely to succeed if it can be shown that the deficiency was due to negligence in the organisation of the hospital; where a lack of facilities is attributable to underfunding of the hospital or to decisions within the hospital as to how its limited resources should be allocated, it is unlikely that the court will intervene.[92] For a further example, see *R. v. Sheffield Health Authority*[93]: where financial constraints prevent the supply of assisted fertility services on demand, a health authority is entitled to restrict the availability of those services to groups of patients who are most likely to be successfully treated.

Two further cases should be mentioned on the topic of NHS resources. In the **12–161** case of *R. North and East Devon H.A., ex parte Coughlan*[94] the applicant, who was severely and permanently disabled following a road accident in 1971 had been moved, with other similarly disabled patients, in 1993 from a hospital which the H.A. wished to close into Mardon House, a new purpose-built NHS facility for long-term disabled, which the H.A. assured them would be their home for life. Following the 1996 publication by the H.A. of its criteria for long-term NHS care, it concluded that the applicant and the other residents did not meet those criteria with the result that it considered itself free to transfer the responsibility for providing nursing to the local authority as a social service, with the result that the applicant had to contribute to its cost according to her means. In 1998 the H.A determined to close Mardon House and transfer the care of the applicant to the local authority. The applicant applied for judicial review, and was successful before the judge and the Court of Appeal. It was held that it was lawful for the Secretary of State for Health to take into account available resources , and decide that it was not necessary to provide some nursing services through the NHS, which could then be provided by the local authority in connection with accommodation to a person in need of care and attention under the National Assistance Act 1948. But such nursing could only be of a type which was truly ancillary to the provision of accommodation: the applicant's nursing needs were primarily health care needs, the responsibility for which could not be transferred to the local authority. And it was also held that the H.A. had not established sufficient grounds for breaking their promise to the applicant that Mardon House could be her home for life, and the closure decision constituted an abuse of power. Lord Woolf also said[95] that in the circumstances it could be said that the closure decision was a breach of Article 8 of the European Convention for the Protection of Human Rights.[96] In the case of *R. v. North West Lancashire Health Authority, ex Parte A*[97] the applicants were suffered from gender identity dysphoria; all three of them wanted gender reassignment surgery, two had been diagnosed to have a clinical need for it, the third was awaiting assessment. The H.A. formed a policy in respect of such surgery (which had to be done in London), and refused to refer the applicants to the clinic in London. They successfully applied for judicial review of the H.A.'s decision, and the appeal was unsuccessful. The interest in the case is in the comments made by the Court of Appeal in respect

---

[92] But see *Bull v. Devon Area Health Authority* [1993] 4 Med. L.R. 117, 141 *per* Mustill L.J.
[93] (1994) 25 B.M.L.R 1.
[94] [2001] Q.B. 213.
[95] *ibid.* at 254D–255F.
[96] "Everyone has the right to respect for . . . his home".
[97] [2000] 1 W.L.R. 977.

of the reliance by the applicants on Articles 3 and 8 of the European Convention for the Protection of Human Rights.[98] Buxton L.J. said[99]:

> " . . . I am disturbed by an appeal to Convention and Community authority that has no sensible connexion with the issues in this case; and by the alternative argument that since those systems protect rights that are in some ways related to the rights asserted in this case they can be used as some sort of support for the applicants' primary case. That approach is misconceived. In a case where neither Convention nor Community rights can be asserted, the case either succeeds or fails on domestic law grounds and no other. And with the imminent coming into force of the Human Rights Act 1998 it will be even more important than it is at present to ensure that Convention rights are not asserted in inappropriate circumstances; so that they play their proper, and important, role, but only their proper role, in the protection of the citizen's rights."

12–162   **Structure of National Health Service.** The Secretary of State is under a duty to provide throughout England and Wales, to such extent as he considers necessary to meet all reasonable requirements, hospital and similar accommodation; medical, dental, nursing and ambulance services; and other related facilities for the prevention and treatment of illness.[1] The local administration of these services is now entrusted to health authorities.[2] It is these authorities (rather than the Secretary of State himself) who should be sued in respect of negligence committed by staff at hospitals under their control.[3]

12–163   Under section 5 of the National Health Service and Community Care Act 1990 the Secretary of State is empowered to set up NHS trusts, to own and manage hospitals or other establishments or facilities formerly managed or provided by health authorities. Many NHS trusts have been set up. Under section 4 of the 1990 Act one health service body (*e.g.* a health authority or an NHS trust) may contract to provide goods or services to another health service body. If negligence occurs, the health service body actually providing the treatment will be liable to the patient. It is important to note, however, that liability for clinical negligence accruing before the institution of an NHS trust remains the responsibility of the health authority which the trust succeeds. NHS trusts do not inherit liabilities of this sort. Further, the acquiring authority may be liable if it places a contract which does not provide for an adequate standard of treatment.[4] However, the NHS contract itself does not give rise to any contractual rights or liabilities.[5]

---

[98] Materially, here, the right not to be subjected to inhuman or degrading treatment, and the right to respect for family and private life respectively.

[99] [2000] 1. W.L.R. 977, 1003A–C.

[1] National Health Service Act 1977, s.3.

[2] Regional and district health authorities and family health services authorities were abolished, as from April 1, 1996, by the Health Authorities Act 1995. Health authorities are constituted under the National Health Service Act 1977, s.8, as amended by s.1 of the Health Services Act 1980, s.1 of the National Health Service and Community Care Act 1990 and s.1 of the Health Authorities Act 1995.

[3] See National Health Service Act 1977, Sched. 5, para. 15.

[4] See J. Jacob, "Lawyers go to Hospital" [1991] P.L. 255.

[5] s.4(3). For an analysis of the health care markets introduced into the National Health Service in 1991 and of the response of the medical profession, see F. Miller, "Competition Law and Anti-competitive Professional Behaviour Affecting Health Care" (1992) 55 M.L.R. 453. The possibility that the new structure of the health service will allow the formulation of new species of negligence claims is discussed by C. Newdick in "Rights to N.H.S. resources" (1993) 1 Med. L.Rev. 53. In "N.H.S. contracting: shadows of the law of tort" (1995) 3 Med. L.Rev. 161, K. Barker argues that the publication of standards for the purposes of NHS contracting may result in a higher individual standard of care or at least, an easing of the evidential burden on claimants seeking to allege negligence, by providing evidence of prevailing standards.

(j) *Apportionment of liability*

Apportionment between hospital authorities and doctors. Prior to 1954 it   **12–164**
was common for hospital authorities, when sued for negligence, to bring third
party proceedings against the member of their staff who was alleged to be at
fault. Thus in *Jones v. Manchester Corporation*[6] liability was apportioned, under
section 6 of the Law Reform (Married Women and Tortfeasors) Act 1935, 20 per
cent to the house surgeon and 80 per cent to the hospital board. In *Payne v. St
Helier Group Hospital Management Committee*[7] a hospital casualty officer failed
correctly to diagnose the abdominal injuries of a patient who had been kicked by
a horse. Donovan J. held that the casualty officer was negligent but that the
hospital was not negligent in its system of examination of abdominal injuries. He
granted the hospital authority a full indemnity against the casualty officer. After
1954, however, a private arrangement existed between the hospital authorities
and the bodies representing medical practitioners, as a result of which liability
was apportioned by agreement in individual cases, and third party proceedings or
contribution proceedings were no longer brought.[8] With effect from January 1,
1990, a new arrangement in respect of hospital doctors came into force.[9] Health
authorities are required to give them a full indemnity in respect of liability for
negligence in the course of their NHS employment.[10] However, any private work
undertaken by consultants in a NHS hospital falls outside the scheme,[11] so that
questions of apportionment can still arise in that context.[12]

Apportionment between medical practitioners and pharmacists. A phar-   **12–165**
macist is a skilled professional man. He has a duty to satisfy himself about any
prescription which he makes up and, in case of doubt, to refer back to the
prescribing doctor.[13] In *Dwyer v. Roderick*,[14] where a general practitioner made
a serious error in prescription, liability was apportioned 45 per cent to the
prescribing doctor, 40 per cent to the pharmacist who failed to spot the error and
15 per cent to a partner of the prescribing doctor who failed to spot the error.
Where a prescription is badly written, so that its meaning is unclear, the pharmacist should refer back to the doctor. If the pharmacist goes ahead on his own
interpretation of the prescription and gets it wrong, he is likely to carry the
greater share of responsibility. In *Prendergast v. Sam & Dee Ltd*[15] a general
practitioner, intending to prescribe Amoxil, wrote the prescription to a poor
standard of legibility. The pharmacist read this as Daonil, which for a number of

---

[6] [1952] 2 Q.B. 852. For the facts see para. 12–155, above.
[7] [1952] C.L.Y. 2442.
[8] For more details of the arrangement see C. R. A. Martin, *Law Relating to Medical Practice* (Pitman Medical Publishing Co. Ltd, 1979), pp. 95–96.
[9] Set out in Department of Health Circular H.C. (89) 34 and Health Services Guidelines H.S.G. (96) 48. See para. 12–087, above.
[10] For discussion of the implications of this reform, see J. Jacob, "Lawyers go to Hospital" [1991] P.L. 255, 264–265; M. Brazier, "N.H.S. Indemnity: The Implications for Medical Litigation" (1990) 6 P.N. 88.
[11] Department of Health Circular H.C. (89) 34, para. 5. See further, H.S.G. (96) 48.
[12] As do general practitioners. However, H.C. (89) 34 asks the medical defence organisations and the heath authorities to seek to reach agreement as to their respective liabilities and to co-operate in presenting a defence.
[13] *Prendergast v. Sam & Dee Ltd* [1989] 1 Med. L.R. 36, 37, col. 2.
[14] (1982) 132 New L.J. 176.
[15] [1989] 1 Med. L.R. 36. A reproduction of the prescription form and the medicine label was before the court and appears at page 39 of the report.

reasons was an inappropriate reading of the prescription. The claimant suffered hypoglycaemia and irreversible brain damage as a result of taking Daonil. The Court of Appeal upheld an apportionment of 25 per cent to the doctor and 75 per cent to the pharmacist.

(k) *Lord Woolf's reforms*

12–166 Of the various species of professional negligence litigation which are discussed in this book, medical negligence cases were singled out for specific and detailed consideration by Lord Woolf in "Access to Justice", his 1996 report on the civil justice system in England and Wales.[16] In chapter 15 of his report, Lord Woolf set out and discussed his conclusion that unnecessary litigation and, once litigation is on foot, increased costs and delay are attributable to (i) commonly, a lack of frank communication between aggrieved patients and treating doctors or hospital authorities and (ii) the imbalance of knowledge and expertise between claimant and defendant. Lord Woolf made 12 recommendations for procedural reform which are specific to medical negligence cases. Three are of particular note:

> (i) Health professionals should receive instruction in the legal context of their work, including an indication of what is involved in a claim for negligence, as part of their basic medical training. This, it is hoped, will discourage defensive attitudes on the part of medical practitioners faced with a claim when those attitudes stem from a misunderstanding of their potential liabilities.

> (ii) The General Medical Council and other regulatory bodies should consider whether a rule of professional conduct is required to clarify the responsibility of healthcare professionals to their patients when they discover an act or omission in which they may have been negligent in their care or treatment. Lord Woolf noted that there is no binding authority for a duty to inform the patient in these circumstances.[17]

> (iii) Judges who are likely to try medical negligence cases should receive training in medical issues. This proposal is intended to reduce delays both in hearing cases and in bringing them to trial: a major thrust of Lord Woolf's reforms is the increased involvement of judges in case management.

Further, and of equal importance, were the proposals for reducing the numbers of expert witnesses who need to be called to give evidence in many medical negligence cases which are discussed at paragraph 12–114 above. Following the Woolf Report the Clinical Disputes Forum was set up, which as its first major initiative has produced the pre-action protocol for the resolution of clinical disputes.[18] The progress that has been made has not satisfied the Department of Health. On July 10, 2001 the Secretary of State announced the creation of a committee led by the Chief Medical Officer Liam Donaldson to examine ways of making the system of compensation for clinical negligence "faster and fairer".

---

[16] "Access to Justice", HMSO, 1996.
[17] See para. 12–221, below.
[18] *Civil Procedure* Volume 1 (White Book), C3–001–C3–029.

See paragraph 12–089, above, for more details of the announcement. There may be radical changes in prospect in the field of clinical negligence litigation.

2. LIABILITY FOR BREACH OF DUTY

General. Breach of duty by a medical practitioner is likely to take one of two forms: 12–167

(i) Breach of the implied contractual duty to exercise reasonable skill and care.[19]

(ii) Breach of the duty of care owed by the medical practitioner to his patient, whether or not there is any contract between them.[20]

Both categories involve breaches of the same standard of skill and care and hereafter will be jointly described as "negligence". Where a medical practitioner is privately engaged by the patient, it is possible that he will find himself in breach of some specific contractual duty not involving negligence.[21] In the rare cases where a medical practitioner treats a patient without his consent, he may also be liable for assault.[22]

Instances in which medical practitioners are, or may be, liable for breach of duty are discussed below under seven headings. It is not suggested that this catalogue is exhaustive. The cases serve to illustrate how the principles stated above operate in practice and, in particular, what the courts consider to be the standard of skill and care which may reasonably be expected of medical practitioners.[23] 12–168

(a) *Failing to prevent illness*[24]

Prevention not cure. The object of the medical profession is the promotion of good health and not simply the treatment of illness.[25] Failure to take reasonable steps to prevent illness may in appropriate circumstances amount to negligence. In *Stokes v. Guest, Keen and Nettlefold*,[26] for example, it was held that the defendants' medical officer was negligent in failing to guard against scrotal cancer amongst employees in an engineering factory. Swanwick J. held that the medical officer ought to have instituted six-monthly medical examinations and to 12–169

---

[19] See para. 12–008, above.
[20] See paras 12–015 to 12–023, above.
[21] See para. 12–010, above.
[22] See paras 12–124 to 12–148, above.
[23] For a general discussion of the standard of skill and care, see paras 12–067 to 12–083, above. As to the danger of treating particular cases as precedents, establishing what a medical practitioner ought or ought not to do, see *Mahon v. Osborne* [1939] 2 K.B. 14 (surgeon not necessarily negligent for leaving swabs inside patient; negligence depends on the circumstances of each case).
[24] See paras 12–236 to 12–237, below, for failure to prevent self-inflicted injury or suicide.
[25] This is emphasised by ss.1, 3 of the National Health Service Act 1977 and the NHS (General Medical Services) Regulations 1992 (S.I. 1992 No. 635), Sched. 2, Terms of Service for Doctors in general NHS practice that requires general practitioners to have periodical consultations with their patients, directed to improving their health.
[26] [1968] 1 W.L.R. 1776.

have issued a notice about the risk, describing the symptoms and recommending reference to a doctor.

12–170   **Infectious disease spread.** The medical practitioner must take reasonable care to prevent the spread of infectious diseases.[27] Thus in *Heafield v. Crane*[28] the claimant was admitted to a cottage hospital and put in the same ward as a "gravely suspicious case", which turned out to be puerperal fever. The claimant contracted the disease. Singleton J. held that both the hospital authorities and the doctor in charge were negligent.[29] In *Evans v. Liverpool Corporation*[30] the defendants provided a hospital for persons with infectious diseases. It was argued on the basis of *Rylands v. Fletcher*[31] that the defendants were under an absolute obligation not to discharge patients who might possibly cause contagion to others. Walton J. rejected this contention.

12–171   In *ter Neuzen v. Korn*[32] the Supreme Court of Canada considered whether a doctor responsible for an artificial insemination service was liable to a patient who contracted the HIV virus from contaminated semen. The patient alleged that by January 1985, when she was infected, the defendant ought to have realised the risk of infection by this route and discontinued the service or, at least, warned patients of the risk. The evidence was that the risk was not known in Canada until mid-1985, although it was appreciated elsewhere slightly earlier. The Court held that the doctor was not negligent in this respect.[33] In *Pittman Estate v. Bain*[34] the patient contracted the HIV virus through a blood transfusion. He later died of an AIDS-related disease and his wife discovered that she had contracted the virus. Her husband's general practitioner was negligent in failing to inform her husband that he might be HIV-positive and in failing to advise him or the claimant to take precautions against transmission of the virus to her through sexual contact. In *Re HIV Haemophiliac Litigation*[35] haemophiliacs who had contracted the HIV virus from contaminated imported blood products used in their treatment alleged *inter alia* that the Department of Health had negligently failed to screen donors, heat-treat the blood products so as to inactivate the virus, warn the claimants and achieve NHS self-sufficiency in blood products. The action settled, but the Court of Appeal accepted that the claimants had an arguable claim.[36]

---

[27] In *Vancouver General Hospital v. McDaniel* (1935) 152 L.T.R. 56, the claimant contracted smallpox whilst being treated in the defendants' hospital. It was held that the defendants were not negligent, since they had complied with the general and approved practice as to the containment of smallpox patients. By contrast, it is likely to be difficult to establish liability for transmission of the HIV virus from medical staff to a patient: see M. Mulholland, "AIDS, HIV and the Health Care Worker" (1993) 9 P.N. 79.

[28] *The Times*, July 31, 1937.

[29] *Marshall v. Lindsey County Court* [1935] 1 K.B. 516 is to the same effect: claimant was admitted to a maternity home in which there was a case of puerperal fever; the matron was held to be negligent. Decision affirmed by the House of Lords at [1937] A.C. 97.

[30] [1906] 1 K.B. 160.

[31] (1868) L.R. 3 HL 330.

[32] (1995) 127 D.L.R. (4th) 577.

[33] The doctor had acted in accordance with the general practice of Canadian physicians in circumstances where Canadian medical thinking on a highly technical question was uncertain. It was not open to the jury to find this practice negligent. See *ibid.* at 5912–597.

[34] (1994) 112 D.L.R. (4th) 257, Ontario High Court. See also *X and Y v. Pal* (1991) 23 N.S.W.L.R. 26, [1992] 3 Med. L.R. 195, New South Wales CA: negligent exposure of unborn child to infection by congenital syphilis.

[35] [1996] P.N.L.R. 290.

[36] *ibid.* at 312–315.

(b) *Failing to attend or examine a patient*

If a medical practitioner makes unwarranted assumptions about his patient's   **12–172**
condition without examining him, he is at peril of an action for negligence.

The hospital doctor. In *Barnett v. Chelsea and Kensington Hospital Manage-*   **12–173**
ment Committee[37] the issue arose whether a hospital casualty officer was negligent in failing personally to examine three men who were complaining of
vomiting and abdominal pains. Nield J. held, on the evidence in that case, that the
duty of a casualty officer was in general to see and examine all patients who came
to the hospital casualty department. However, Nield J. recognised that there were
exceptions: for example, where the patient was attending his own doctor and
simply wanted a second opinion; or where the patient had a small cut which the
nurse could perfectly well dress.[38] In *Wisniewski v. Central Manchester Health*
Authority[39] the Court of Appeal held that a senior house officer was negligent for
failing to attend a patient in a maternity ward and for relying on a midwife's
assessment of a CTG trace of a baby's heart rate as the mother went into
labour.[40]

The general practitioner. The general practitioner is entitled and bound to   **12–174**
exercise some discretion in determining whether and when it is necessary to visit
patients who cannot come to his surgery.[41] In *Edler v. Greenwich and Deptford*
Hospital Management Committee[42] a general practitioner decided not to visit a
girl with abdominal pains, because she had previously been seen by the hospital
casualty officer, who thought that there was nothing wrong with her. In fact the
child had a burst appendix. Finnemore J. held that the general practitioner was
not negligent. In *Stockdale v. Nicholls*[43] Otton J. held that it was not negligent of

---

[37] [1969] 1 Q.B. 428.
[38] *ibid.* at 436G–437B.
[39] [1998] Lloyd's Rep. Med. 223.
[40] The trial judge found that the doctor had not been told of the baby's tachycardia, but since both
midwife and doctor were employed by the same defendant, no point was taken on the appeal. The trial
judge also considered whether the doctor had been properly prevented from attending by other events
that night at the hospital but found none had occurred. See *Cummings v. Croydon Health Authority*,
unreported, March 24, 1998, QBD for a case where the claimant failed to show that the defendant
health authority had not responded adequately to her complaints that she was in labour.
[41] A general practitioner's contract with the health authority responsible for local family health
services requires him to make a home visit if in his reasonable opinion it is inappropriate for the
patient to attend normal surgery (or a night or emergency surgery where these are operated): see the
NHS (General Medical Services) Amendment Regulations 1995 (S.I. 1995 No. 80).
[42] *The Times*, March 7, 1953. See also *Stacey v. Chiddy* [1993] 4 Med. L.R. 216, Supreme Court of
New South Wales, the facts of which are given at para. 12–185, n. 89.
[43] [1993] 4 Med. L.R. 191. See also *Morrison v. Forsyth* [1995] 6 Med. L.R. 6, Sc. Ct Sess. (on the
basis of the information given to her, general practitioner not negligent in failing to visit patient or
in failing to ask further questions which might have disclosed the true nature of the patient's
condition). See also *D v. Dr Ahmed*, unreported, March 26, 1998, QBD, David Steel, J.): a toddler
developed a common reaction to the measles vaccine ("mini-measles"). On his father's telephoning
the doctor's surgery, the doctor gave advice over the telephone but did not personally attend on the
claimant. Over the next four days the claimant's condition deteriorated and he was hospitalised and
diagnosed as suffering from haematemesis, hepatitis, pneumonia and possible viral encephalitis. The
claimant alleged that the doctor should have attended him and that if he had done so he would have
been treated with antibiotics, alternatively that he would have been admitted to hospital sooner. The
claimant's case was dismissed, the doctor had quite properly given advice by telephone.

a general practitioner not personally to visit a baby reported to be unwell and having feeding problems. The doctor sent an experienced practice nurse instead. Similarly, in *Durrant v. Burke*,[44] a general practitioner who had given adequate instructions for the care of a sick infant to its mother was not under a duty to visit to ensure that his instructions were followed. In *Kavanagh v. Abrahamson*[45] the patient moved to a new address without notifying his doctor. Subsequently the doctor had occasion to visit him. He went to the old address (which was a flat) and found it empty. He rang the bell of an adjoining flat, but got no answer. He then left to pay other urgent visits, thinking that, if this case was urgent, the patient's wife would contact him again. Fenton Atkinson J. thought that the doctor might have done more than he did after finding that the patient had moved, but the Judge was not prepared to hold that this amounted to negligence.[46] The patient's past medical history and the complaint raised will obviously impact on whether the doctor acted reasonably in not attending or examining that patient.[47]

12–175   Failure to attend and examine in the later stages of treatment may also, of course, constitute negligence. This is illustrated by cases where inadequate arrangements have been made to monitor the patient's recovery or condition. The defendant in *Corder v. Banks*[48] was a plastic surgeon who operated on the claimant for facial disfigurement. The first 48 hours after the operation were crucial in that bleeding might occur and, if it was not attended to properly, irreversible damage might result. The defendant allowed the claimant home, but did not make arrangements for any telephone messages from the claimant to be passed on to him immediately. Bleeding did occur the day after the operation. The claimant's telephone messages to the defendant's surgery did not reach him. Consequently, the defendant did not attend and deal with the bleeding. McNair J. held that the defendant was negligent. In *Joyce v. Merton, Sutton & Wandsworth Health Authority*[49] the patient underwent brachial cardiac catheterisation, a minor surgical procedure designed to assess arterial disease and carried out on a day patient basis. In carrying out the procedure, the registrar sutured together the walls of the patient's brachial artery. This was a non-negligent mishap. However, the registrar and the nurse responsible for the patient's care on the day ward were negligent in discharging him home without impressing upon him that he should contact the hospital if he became concerned about any aspect of his recovery. Roch L.J. pointed out that a doctor must bear in mind that an oral warning may not be understood and remembered by a patient who has reacted

---

[44] [1993] 4 Med. L.R. 258.
[45] (1964) 108 S.J. 320.
[46] Presumably the decision would have been otherwise, if the doctor had (or ought to have) known of the seriousness of the patient's condition. As to a general practitioner's duty to a non-patient requiring emergency treatment, see para. 12–019, above.
[47] See *Sohal v. Brar* [1999] 63 Alta. L.R. (3d) 280, Doctor held to be negligent for failing to immediately re-examine a diabetic patient whose minor foot injury had after three days become swollen and discoloured. Patient subsequently diagnosed with gangrene underwent amputation of part of foot. The claimant failed to show that the doctor's breach and delay had caused or materially contributed to the amputation.
[48] *The Times*, April 9, 1960.
[49] [1996] 7 Med. L.R. 1, CA. The claimant failed on causation: see para. 12–272, below. See also *Cavanagh v. Bristol & Weston Health Authority* [1992] 3 Med. L.R. 49 (failure to monitor patient's condition following eye operation).

badly to a procedure.[50] The result of the negligence was that the suturing error caused vascular complications which were not treated in time to avoid a catastrophic cerebral embolism.

Arranging follow-up. Failure to arrange follow-up or to pursue results of tests **12–176** may be negligent even where no treatment has been given. In *Major v Wilcox*[51] a general practitioner was negligent because he did not advise a patient to contact him if his condition did not improve over the weekend. The claimant had attended his GP twice, complaining of fever and sore throat. The GP diagnosed viraemia and properly concluded that treatment with antibiotics was unnecessary. The claimant was admitted to hospital on the Monday and died a few hours later due to streptococcal septicaemia. The trial judge found no negligence in not treating with antibiotics, but held that the GP had breached his duty of care by not advising the claimant to contact him again if he did not improve, and that the claimant would have attended his GP again if he had been advised to do so. The Court of Appeal upheld the trial judge's findings on the evidence and on the expert opinion that giving such advice to a patient was good practice.[52] In *Judge v. Huntingdon Health Authority*[53] the patient was referred to a consultant surgeon for specialist opinion on a lump in her breast which she had found and her general practitioner had confirmed. The surgeon examined her but failed to find a lump. It was held that he negligently failed to arrange to see the patient again in a different phase of her menstrual cycle. When both the patient and her general practitioner were sure that a lump existed, the surgeon could not exclude the possibility that there was a lump, and it might be malignant. In *C v. A Health Authority*[54] the defendant health authority had breached its duty by failing to offer the claimant an appointment for further tests for foetal defects (which the claimant contended would have resulted in her having a scan at 16 to 20 weeks of pregnancy).[55] Similarly in *Morea-Loftus v. Wray Castle Limited*,[56] it was held that the failure by medical staff at a residential college to make an early morning check on the condition of a student in sickbay was a breach of duty, but the claimant was unable to establish that the breach was causative of his later-diagnosed meningitis. In *Kite v. Malycha*[57] the defendant surgeon was negligent for not pursuing the results of a fine needle aspirate biopsy he had performed on

---

[50] *ibid.* at 12.

[51] Unreported, February 4, 1999, CA, Kennedy, Chadwick and Laws L.JJ.

[52] The *Bolam* test appears to have been applied although there is no express reference to the case in the judgment.

[53] [1995] 6 Med.L.R. 223.

[54] Unreported, November 3, 1998, QBD, Ebsworth J.

[55] The claimant failed on causation to prove that had she attended for such an appointment her consultant would have advised her to have a scan, or that she would have refused to follow his advice and insisted on a scan, or that the scan would have detected her baby's skeletal defects or put the consultant on notice of a need for a further scan. Her consultant's conservative approach was a minority opinion, but nevertheless was reasonable and not negligent, applying the contemporaneous standards of consultant practice. See also *Chissell v. Poole Hospital NHS Trust* [1998] Lloyd's Rep. Med. 357 (health authority not negligent to not conduct a scan or other follow up to operation to terminate pregnancy by suction. Operation failed to remove one of probable pair of twins resulting in continued pregnancy and birth of healthy child).

[56] [1999] Lloyd's Rep. Med. 159.

[57] (1998) 71 S.A.S.R. 325.

the claimant (and for having no follow up system for recording the receipt of such pathology results).[58]

(c) Wrong diagnosis

12-177   **General.** At the date of trial there is often no dispute as to what illness or injury the claimant was in fact suffering from at the time when he consulted the defendant. Thus there is no dispute as to whether the diagnosis made by the defendant was correct or incorrect. If the diagnosis was incorrect, often the sole question is whether the "mistake" was negligent. This issue is seldom resolved by reference to "general and approved practice" or "schools of thought". The question simply is whether, on the symptoms and material presented or available to the defendant, a reasonably careful and skilful medical practitioner might have made the same mistake.

12-178   If a medical practitioner fails to diagnose a relatively common or obvious illness or injury, then he is likely to be held negligent.[59] In *McCormack v. Redpath Brown & Co. Ltd*[60] a casualty officer was held negligent in failing to discover a hole in the claimant's skull of one-quarter to one-half inch in diameter. The claimant was complaining of a blow on the head from a spanner. Paull J. considered that the fracture could not have been missed on any proper physical examination. Other cases in which medical practitioners have been held negligent for failing to diagnose fractures after serious accidents are *Wood v. Thurston*[61] and *Newton v. Newton's Model Laundry Ltd*.[62]

12-179   In determining whether an incorrect diagnosis was negligent, the court must have regard to all the circumstances at the time the diagnosis was made. These include, obviously, the symptoms[63] exhibited by the patient, the information available to the doctor from other sources, the age of the patient and the rarity (or commonness) of the disease from which the patient was suffering. Thus in *Marriott v. West Midlands Regional Health Authority*[64] a general practitioner was

---

[58] The court also held (at 337) that the claimant was entitled to assume that if the pathology report was adverse she would be told about it, and that courts should be wary of founding contributory negligence by a patient who has relied on a competent medical practitioner for advice and treatment.

[59] For example, *Edler v. Greenwich and Deptford Hospital Management Committee*, The Times, March 7, 1953 (hospital casualty officer failed to diagnose appendicitis); *Saumarez v. Medway and Gravesend Hospital Management Committee* (1953) 2 B.M.J. 1109 (failure to diagnose chip fracture of distal phalanx of left middle finger); *Riddett v. D'Arcy* (1960) 2 B.M.J. 1607 (general practitioner examined a baby in the early stages of pneumonia but failed to diagnose the baby's condition, although symptoms of heart failure were present, Southampton County Court); *Gardiner v. Mounfield* [1990] 1 Med. L.R. 205 (failure to diagnose pregnancy). See also *Lock v. Scantlebury*, The Times, July 25, 1963 (dentist failed to notice that the claimant's jaw had become dislocated during extraction of teeth).

[60] The Times, March 24, 1961.

[61] The Times, May 25, 1951 (patient partially run over by a lorry; defendant failed to diagnose a fractured collar bone and 18 fractured ribs).

[62] The Times, November 3, 1959 (claimant fell 12 feet onto concrete; doctor negligent in failing to discover compound fracture of patella of left knee. Not negligent not to diagnose broken wrist, although "many doctors would have spotted it or been suspicious and taken an X-ray").

[63] See, for example, *Serre v. De Tilly* (1975) 8 O.R. (2d) 490, Ontario High Court (brain haemorrhage mistakenly diagnosed as hysteria. Held that the diagnosis was a reasonable one on the basis of the symptoms). Cf. *Wipfli v. Britten* (1982) 28 C.C.L.T. 104, British Columbia Supreme Court (1984) 13 D.L.R. (4th) 169 (failure to diagnose that claimant was carrying twins held negligent, because there were sufficient indicia of the existence of twins).

[64] [1999] Lloyd's Rep. Med. 23, CA.

negligent for failing to give sufficient weight to the patient's complaints and symptoms (of drowsiness and headaches) following a fall and head injury and relying too much on the results of neurological tests (no papilloedema, vomiting or other signs of raised intra-cranial pressure) leading to a missed diagnosis of skull fracture resulting in extradural haematoma and hemiplegia.[65] By contrast in *Sadler v. Henry*[66] Cassels J. held that the defendant was not negligent in failing to diagnose localised meningitis, since there were no signs or symptoms which could reasonably have led him to suspect that condition. In *Hulse v. Wilson*[67] it was held that the defendants were not negligent in failing to diagnose cancer of the penis earlier than they did. Owing to the rarity of such cancer in a young man, the second defendant adhered for some time to the view that the claimant had venereal disease.[68]

Another relevant factor is the time spent and care taken in listening to the   **12–180** patient's history.[69] In *Djemal v. Bexley Health Authority*[70] an inexperienced casualty officer failed to elicit a full history from the patient or the patient's wife and failed to notice the patient's significant inability to swallow. Had he done so, he ought to have realised that advice from an ENT specialist was called for. In fact, the patient had epiglottitis, which, untreated, led to his deterioration to a persistent vegetative state. Sir Haydn Tudor Evans said:

"I find that it is the duty of an examining doctor, and that includes a casualty officer, as an essential preliminary to making a diagnosis, to obtain a proper history and that it is not correct medical practice simply to accept what is related by the patient or the person speaking for him."[71]

---

[65] In *Rampling v. Haringey Health Authority*, unreported, July 30, 1996, Buxton J., the defendants negligently failed to revise their (mistaken) diagnosis of symphysis pubis because they paid too little attention to the patient's complaints of severe pain. As a result, her undisplaced stress fracture was allowed to become displaced during labour.

[66] (1954) 1 B.M.J. 1331. The symptoms which were apparent are set out in some detail in the report. See also *Thornton v. Nicol* [1992] 3 Med. L.R. 41 (failure to diagnose meningitis in baby not negligent: general practitioner's diagnosis of conjunctivitis probably correct and meningitis did not develop until later); *Stockdale v. Nicholls* [1993] 4 Med. L.R. 190 (failure to refer baby to hospital not negligent in the absence of signs of developing septicaemia).

[67] (1953) 2 B.M.J. 890: "The dangers of making a diagnosis too quickly are just as great as making a diagnosis too slowly. I don't think anyone can complain that [the second defendant] did not diagnose cancer straight away. I think the real gravity of the case against [the second defendant] was that he delayed too long satisfying himself beyond doubt that venereal disease was not the cause, and that he should have turned to the only other alternative—cancer. Such a cancer is extremely rare: in a young man of about 30 it is rarer still. Until you get rid of the more likely causes you would not expect it was cancer in a man of this age."

[68] See also *Phillips v. Grampian Health Board* [1991] 3 Med. L.R. 16 (failure to diagnose a relatively uncommon case of testicular cancer was not negligent).

[69] See, for example, *Giurelli v. Girgis* (1980) 24 S.A.S.R. 264, South Australia Supreme Court. White J. stated that listening to the patient's history was as much a part of diagnosis as clinical examination. The fact that the claimant was a difficult patient and tended to exaggerate his complaints of pain did not excuse the defendant's failure properly to listen to and investigate the claimant's complaints. See also *Meyer v. Gordon* (1981) 17 C.C.L.T. 1 (nursing staff held negligent for failing to obtain claimant's obstetric history).

[70] [1995] 6 Med. L.R. 269; see para. 12–077, above.

[71] *ibid.* at 277. See also *Drake v. Pontefract Health Authority* [1998] Lloyd's Rep. Med. 425 (senior house officer negligently failed to diagnose (and accordingly failed to treat) the claimant's agitated depression, resulting in her depressive condition deteriorating until an attempt to commit suicide resulted in serious injury and disablement).

12–181   The amount of time spent by the doctor in examining the patient is also relevant.[72] *Parry v. North West Surrey Health Authority*[73] and *Wiszniewski v. Central Manchester Health Authority*[74] were cases in which a doctor was found to be negligent in failing to attend a patient in the early stages of labour. The result in each case was that the management of the labour was left to the midwife. In *Parry*, this meant that when a crisis developed and the doctor did attend, he lacked adequate first-hand knowledge of the patient to deal with it properly. In *Wiszniewski*, the doctor's neglect left the patient in the sole care of a midwife who was deemed not competent to recognise signs of increasing foetal distress.

12–182   On the other hand, the doctor risks a finding of negligence if he allows the patient's anxiety about a particular diagnostic test to overrule his own better judgment as to the need for it: in *Hutton v East Dyfed Health Authority*,[75] a locum consultant physician did not call for a chest X-ray on a pregnant patient because of her anxiety about possible damage to her unborn child. Any such risk would have been reduced to a level acceptable to her by use of a lead apron, but the physician did not explain this to the patient. A chest X-ray would have revealed that the patient was at real risk of disastrous pulmonary embolism, which would have been prevented by administering heparin, but from which she later died.

12–183   Often, the correct diagnosis of a complaint is (at the material time) a matter of disagreement between practitioners. Where the defendant can call a reputable expert witness to say that on the material available he, too, would have made the same diagnosis, a finding of negligence will be difficult to sustain.[76] It was on this basis that the finding of negligence made by the trial judge in *Maynard v. West Midlands Regional Health Authority*[77] was reversed. The defendant will be in an even stronger position where a number of other doctors actually did make the same mistaken diagnosis as himself.[78] Sometimes the claimant's own condition may make verification of the diagnosis difficult. In *Whiteford v. Hunter*[79] the defendant, while operating on the claimant to remove a prostate gland, saw an

---

[72] In *Parkinson v. West Cumberland Management Committee* (1955) 1 B.M.J. 977 a newly qualified hospital doctor spent an hour examining the patient but failed to diagnose coronary thrombosis. Ashworth J. held that the doctor's mistake did not amount to negligence. *Cf. Seyfert v. Burnaby Hospital Society* (1986) 27 D.L.R. (4th) 96 (claimant came to hospital casualty department with stab wound in left abdomen; the emergency physician negligently discharged claimant after an inadequate period of observation, and failed to discover that the stab wound had penetrated the transverse colon).

[73] [1994] 5 Med. L.R. 259.

[74] [1998] Lloyd's Rep. Med. 223.See also *Judge v. Huntingdon Health Authority* [1995] 6 Med.L.R. 223 (surgeon's failure to use diagnostic aids such as ultrasound scan or fine needle biopsy was not negligent, but their absence made it all the more important that he took proper care in carrying out his manual examination). See para. 12–176, above and para. 12–255, below.

[75] [1998] Lloyd's Rep. Med. 335.

[76] For example, *Crivon v. Barnet Group Hospital Management Committee, The Times,* November 19, 1958 (hospital pathologist wrongly diagnosed a specimen from the claimant's breast as cancer. At the trial Professor S, an acknowledged expert in the field, said that looking at the slide, he too would have diagnosed cancer. "In those circumstances could it be said to be negligence in a pathologist, when he came to a conclusion which a great expert might himself have come to?" (*per* Lord Denning)).

[77] [1984] 1 W.L.R. 634, HL. See para. 12–094, above.

[78] As happened in *Pudney v. Union Castle Mail Steamship Company Ltd* [1953] 1 Lloyd's Law Rep. 73 (claimant suffering from the early stages of osteo-arthritis. Ship's doctor diagnosed mild rheumatic condition. Subsequently other doctors who saw the claimant made the same mistake and diagnosed rheumatic fever. Devlin J. held that the ship's doctor was not negligent in his diagnosis).

[79] [1950] W.N. 553. See also paras 12–074, 12–081 and 12–092, above.

indurated mass, which he wrongly concluded was cancer. He did not do a biopsy, because this would have involved serious risk of perforating the bladder wall. In that event, if the condition were cancerous, an unhealing ulcer would supervene. It was held that the defendant was not negligent in his diagnosis or in failing to verify the diagnosis. In *Abbas v. Kenney*[80] the claimant sought the defendant surgeon's opinion upon a diagnosis of ovarian cancer which had been made in Pakistan. Relying upon a tissue sample which the claimant brought with her, the defendant surgeon formed the view that the diagnosis was correct. He carried out a laparotomy to investigate the extent of the cancer. During the course of the operation, he discovered a mass near to the uterus. Believing it to be a spread of cancer from the right ovary, he carried out a total pelvic clearance. In fact, the claimant did not have cancer: the sample was not hers. The trial judge found that the defendant was not negligent in confirming the diagnosis of cancer or in performing the clearance. He was misled by the tissue sample.

The need to verify or reassess the initial diagnosis was the subject of two **12–184** Canadian decisions,[81] in each of which it was held that an initial erroneous diagnosis was not negligent, but that the subsequent failure to revise that diagnosis was negligent. In *Bergen v. Sturgeon General Hospital*[82] the doctors diagnosed pelvic inflammatory disease when the patient was suffering from appendicitis. They did not take account of the patient's failure to improve after massive doses of antibiotics and took no steps to eliminate the possibility of appendicitis, which was life-threatening. Hope J. held that they were negligent in failing to use the available time and resources to perform routine tests which would have exposed their original error. He stated[83]: "The physician should always reassess the diagnosis. In this case it is my view that the three medical doctors fell into the trap of 'tunnel vision' and either refused or neglected to recognise the seriousness of the original diagnosis that was to be ruled out— namely possible appendicitis. . . . " An English example of liability under this head is *Bova v. Spring*.[84] A general practitioner negligently failed to recognise the uncertainties inherent in his initial (non-negligent) diagnosis of the patient's condition as a pulled muscle in the chest and viral enteritis. As a result, he failed to institute adequate follow-up procedures to guard against the possibility that the true diagnosis was pneumonia, from which the patient died. In *Taylor v. West Kent Health Authority*,[85] delay in diagnosis of the claimant's breast cancer was the result of negligent failure by a registrar to interpret a cytology report and scan, to arrange a biopsy, and to review the claimant earlier than six months after her initial appointment.

Failure to detect more serious condition. In some cases negligence is **12–185** established not on the basis that the defendant should have made a correct diagnosis, but on the basis that he should have been alerted to the risk of

---

[80] [1996] 7 Med. L.R. 47. See also *Ratty v. Haringey Health Authority* [1994] 5 Med. L.R. 413.
[81] *Layden v. Cope* (1984) 28 C.C.L.T. 140, Alberta Court of Queen's Bench; *Bergen v. Sturgeon General Hospital* (1984) 28 C.C.L.T. 155, Alberta Court of Queen's Bench; *Rampling v. Haringey Health Authority*, unreported, July 30, 1996, Buxton J., (failure to revise diagnosis of condition associated with pregnancy when the patient failed to respond to treatment).
[82] (1984) 28 C.C.L.T. 155.
[83] *ibid.* at 174–175.
[84] [1994] 5 Med. L.R. 120. See also *Judge v. Huntingdon Health Authority* [1995] 6 Med. L.R. 223, discussed at para. 12–176, above and para. 12–255, below.
[85] [1997] 8 Med. L.R. 251.

something serious,[86] or that he should have referred the claimant to hospital or to a specialist for assistance sooner.[87] Thus in *Langley v. Campbell*[88] it was held that a general practitioner might not be negligent in failing to diagnose malaria. However, knowing that the patient had just returned from the tropics, he should have been alerted to the possibility that the patient had some kind of tropical disease. If a medical practitioner encounters disturbing symptoms which are outside his experience or his powers of diagnosis, he ought to consult (or refer the patient to) a specialist.[89] In *Dillon v. Le Roux*,[90] the defendant was a general practitioner acting as a relief doctor in a hospital casualty department. He had had no emergency room training. When a patient presented with symptoms which included chest pains, tingling in his hands and feet and difficulty breathing, the defendant ruled out heart attack in favour of a diagnosis of reflux oesophagitis. The Court of Appeal of British Columbia held that he was negligent because (a) a reasonably competent general practitioner would have made a working diagnosis of heart attack and (b) the defendant ought to have realised the limits of his expertise and experience and summoned specialist help. In *Raji Abu Shkara v. Hillingdon Health Authority*[91] the claimant was admitted to the defendant's hospital with a tracheal wound and secondary infection. He suffered repeated episodes of respiratory distress, which were managed by use of oxygen and medication. Finally, he suffered respiratory arrest. He was resuscitated, but brain damage had been caused. The judge held that the nurse and senior house officer on duty the evening of the arrest had failed to suspect that he was suffering a developing hypoxia and had therefore failed to test his blood gases (which would have confirmed that suspicion) and summon appropriate assistance to prevent the arrest. The defendant's appeal succeeded, in part because the trial judge had not found that the claimant's hypoxia had manifested on that evening in a way that

---

[86] See, for example, *R. v. Croydon Health Authority* [1998] Lloyd's Rep. Med. 44 for an example of admittedly negligent failure to recognise an abnormality that required investigation (discussed in paras 12–026 and 12–066 above); *Dale v. Munthali* (1978) 78 D.L.R. (3d) 588 (patient suffering from meningitis; defendant diagnosed flu. Held that the defendant was not negligent in failing to diagnose meningitis, because not all the symptoms were present. But he was negligent in failing to realise this was something more serious than flu. He should have arranged for the patient to be admitted to hospital immediately for further testing). See also *Sabapathi v. Huntley* [1938] 1 W.W.R. 317; *Fraser v. Vancouver General Hospital* [1951] 3 W.W.R.(N.S.) 337; *Bova v. Spring* [1994] 5 Med. L.R. 120 (the facts of which are given at para. 12–184, above).

[87] See, for example, *Sa'ad v. Robinson* [1989] 1 Med. L.R. 40 (18–month-old child sucked hot tea from spout of teapot. General practitioners held negligent for failing promptly to refer the child to hospital and (subsequently) for making inadequate arrangements in respect of the child's admission to hospital).

[88] *The Times*, November 6, 1975.

[89] See, for example, *MacDonald v. York County Hospital* (1973) 1 O.R. (2d) 653, Ontario CA. General surgeon ignored alarming symptoms in claimant's foot after operation. Held that he was negligent in failing to seek the advice or collaboration of a cardiovascular specialist; *Wilson v. Vancouver Hockey Club* (1983) 5 D.L.R. (4th) 282 (doctor suspected that a mole on the claimant's right arm might be cancerous but failed to refer claimant to a specialist or arrange for an immediate biopsy); *Stacey v. Chiddy* [1993] 4 Med. L.R. 216, Supreme Court of New South Wales (general practitioner who failed to examine a palpable breast abnormality was negligent. Such examination would have confirmed or refuted his provisional diagnosis, although possibly via referral to a specialist). In *Djemal v. Bexley Health Authority* [1995] 6 Med. L.R. 269 (discussed at paras 12–077 and 12–180, above), the consequence of the negligent diagnosis was failure to refer the patient for examination by an ENT specialist, who would have diagnosed his condition. Cf. *Richardson v. Kitching* [1995] 6 Med. L.R. 257 (general practitioner not negligent in failing to arrange referral of patient to an ENT specialist).

[90] [1994] W.W.R. 280.

[91] [1997] 8 Med. L.R. 114.

would suggest that it was more serious than on the previous occasions, when distress had not culminated in arrest. Moreover the evidence did not support such a finding.[92]

(d) *Error in the course of treatment*

Mistakes and negligence. Mistakes made in the course of treatment may be **12–186** purely physical (as when the surgeon's hand slips or twitches during an operation), purely intellectual (as when the doctor prescribes the wrong drug) or they may fall somewhere between the two (for example, pulling too hard with a pair of forceps). Whichever form the mistake takes, there are two separate questions to consider, both of which may well be hotly contested: (i) whether the defendant made a "mistake" (judged by the circumstances in which he was acting); (ii) if so, whether the mistake was one which a reasonably careful and skilful medical practitioner would not have made. The claimant must, of course, succeed on both questions in order to establish negligence.[93] The development of laparoscopic ("key-hole") surgery in obstetrics, and extension of the technique to general surgery, has led to claims for damage inadvertently caused by the sharp instruments used to gain access to the opening area.[93a]

The first question. In relation to the first question, the court must consider **12–187** whether the defendant gave the "right" treatment, not whether the treatment "worked". Thus if a doctor summoned to an emergency gives the treatment which is obviously appropriate, but the patient dies, he cannot be said to have made a "mistake". This is so, even if the post mortem and the subsequent investigation of the patient's history reveal that a quite different course of action might have saved his life. A somewhat less extreme case, which nevertheless illustrates this point, is *Holland v. The Devitt & Moore Nautical College Ltd.*[94] A school medical officer was treating a boy for hepatitis. It was common ground

---

[92] Compare with *Fleury v. Woolgar* [1996] 37 Alta. L.R. (3d) 346 (family practitioner who engaged in a significant obstetric practice was not negligent in not calling for assistance in delivering claimant of her baby. The obstetrician who was eventually summoned attempted the delivery by the same traction manoeuvre and this was the likely cause of the baby's fractured arm and brachial plexus injury. The defendant's delay did not contribute to the baby's injuries.)

[93] Examples include: *Gold v. Essex County Council* [1942] 2 K.B. 293 (radiographer covered the claimant's face with a piece of lint only, before treating facial warts with Grenz rays); *Jones v. Manchester Corporation* [1952] 2 Q.B. 852 (house surgeon administered too much Pentothal too quickly); *Bayliss v. Blagg* (1954) 1 B.M.J. 709 (matron of children's hospital failed to heed deterioration in condition of small girl with plaster cast on her leg. The leg, which was infected, remained in plaster and much of the calf muscle was destroyed); *Smith v. Lewisham Group Hospital Management Committee, The Times,* June 21, 1955 and (1955) 2 B.M.J. 64 (claimant aged 86 and suffering from acute cholecystitis. Hospital staff left her on the trolley for a short time, during which she fell and fractured her thigh); *Munro v. United Oxford Hospitals* (1958) 1 B.M.J. 167 (surgeon knocked out four of patient's front teeth during a tonsillectomy); *Hucks v. Cole,* (1968) 112 S.J. 483; [1993] 4 Med. L.R. 393 (general practitioner treating claimant for fulminating septicaemia, failed to prescribe sufficient antibiotics); *Moffat v. Witelson* (1980) 111 D.L.R. (3d) 712 (ophthalmologist failed to heed the serious danger that a penetrating wound of claimant's cornea was causing infection of the anterior chamber of the eye); *White v. Turner* (1981) 120 D.L.R. (3d) 269 and (1983) 5 D.L.R. (4th) 282 (plastic surgeon removed insufficient tissue during mammoplasty); *Kay v. Ayrshire and Arran Health Board* [1987] 2 All E.R. 417; (senior house officer gave greatly excessive dose of penicillin); *Gallant v. Fialkov* (1989) 69 O.R. (2d) 297 (use of sutures to control bleeding after tonsillectomy as a matter of routine); *Bentley v. Bristol and Weston Health Authority (No. 2)* [1991] 3 Med. L.R. 1 (overstretching nerve during hip replacement operation); *Smith v. Salford Health Authority* [1994] 5 Med. L.R. 321 (use of inappropriate aneurism needle in spinal fusion).

[93a] See Powers and Harris, p. 894.

[94] *The Times,* March 4, 1960. See also para.12–108, above.

that the proper treatment was to keep the patient in bed, warm and free from exertion. When the boy was substantially, but not totally, recovered, the medical officer allowed him to get up and go home for the mid-term weekend. This decision proved fatal in that the boy subsequently had a relapse and died. Streatfeild J. considered it the "cruellest misfortune" that despite all indications to the contrary the disease turned out to be more severe than the medical officer believed. The judge held that "not only was there no negligence but that it was not a case in which a mistake had been made at the first stage". Contrast this case with *Le Page v. Kingston and Richmond Health Authority.*[95] During delivery of her child by Caesarean section, the claimant haemorrhaged so seriously that a hysterectomy was required to arrest the bleeding. The authority's obstetric staff were held liable for failing to take precautions against deterioration of her condition to the point where the bleeding became uncontrollable and hysterectomy unavoidable. The judge distinguished between cases where the court was required to review a considered clinical decision and those where, as here, the conduct of medical and nursing staff could only be described as "a catalogue of errors".

12-188   **The right procedure.** The choice of one procedure in preference to another which in the event would have proved more beneficial (or less injurious) to the claimant is not negligent provided that all relevant factors and available evidence and risks bearing on the decision have been properly considered. Thus there are cases where it was not negligent to choose to deliver normally rather than by caesarean section[96] or to operate by laparoscopy and not laparotomy,[97] or to close and reverse a colostomy without undertaking a resection of the colon concerned.[98] In *Smith v. Salford Health Authority*[99] the health authority's failure to properly consider whether surgery, as opposed to conservative treatment, was appropriate for the claimant was not negligent only because due consideration of all relevant factors would not have altered the decision made.[1] The surgeon in *Newbury v Bath District Authority*[2] was "unwise" in his choice of surgical technique but not negligent.[3] However the midwife in *Gaughan v. Bedfordshire*

---

[95] [1997] 8 Med. L.R. 229.
[96] *Hinfey v. Salford Health Authority* [1993] 4 Med. L.R. 143. Compare with *Dowdie v. Camberwell Health Authority* [1997] 8 Med. L.R. 368 (the defendant's obstetric team were not negligent for using traction prior to intravaginal manipulation but were negligent for failing to proceed to delivery by caesarean section as soon as it was known (via the manipulation) that the baby was or was likely to be macrosomic).
[97] *Darley v. Shale* [1993] 4 Med. L.R. 161, Supreme Court of New South Wales. See also *Early v. Newham Health Authority* [1994] 5 Med. L.R. 214 (abandonment of attempt to re-intubate patient for anaesthesia was in accordance with a procedure prescribed by the health authority after proper consideration of the risks).
[98] *McCafferty v. Merton Sutton & Wandsworth Health Authority* [1997] 8 Med. L.R. 387, QBD, in the absence of evidence of a diverticular problem affecting the colon, and considering the risks inherent in a resection operation.
[99] [1994] 5 Med. L.R. 321.
[1] Similarly in *Knight v. Bradley*, unreported, May 13, 1998, QBD, David Foskett Q.C., the surgeon's decision not to suture a tear in the dura (spinal cord covering) was not negligent because this conservative approach had a rational and logical basis supported by expert opinion (although most surgeons would have sutured).
[2] [1998] 47 B.M.L.R. 138, QBD, Ebsworth J.
[3] The claimant sustained cauda equina injury after surgery using Harrington rods, which was the "unwise" choice of technique. Although the selection of technique was not negligent (as it had not been condemned at that date), the defendant had failed to diagnose the claimant's cauda equina lesion and on the balance of probabilities a timeous diagnosis would have led to the removal of the rods, resulting in a better than 50% chance of recovery.

Health Authority[4] was negligent to persist with delivery by traction instead of rotation or suprapubic pressure after realising the delivery was complicated by shoulder dystocia.

The second question. Sometimes the mistake made by the defendant is of such a kind that there is no room for serious argument on the second question. This is so, for example, where the defendant fails to observe a simple, routine procedure,[5] or where he makes a physical error of a kind which does not happen if the treatment is properly carried out.[6] Where the second question does arise, however, the defendant is likely to escape liability if he shows that he complied with a practice accepted as proper by a respectable part of the medical profession.[7] Alternatively, if there was no "practice" applicable to the particular circumstances in which the mistake occurred, he will escape liability if he shows that other reasonably careful and skilful medical practitioners might have made the same mistake.[8] If the defendant was dealing with an emergency, an error of judgment may be easier to justify.[9] **12–189**

Mistakes and errors of judgment. The most important case in this area is, of course, *Whitehouse v. Jordan,*[10] in which the House of Lords held that the *Bolam* test was applicable to actions for negligence in the course of medical treatment.[11] **12–190**

---

[4] [1997] 8 Med. L.R. 182.

[5] For example in *Goode v. Nash* (1979) 21 S.A.S.R. 419, 423, Supreme Court of South Australia, the defendant medical practitioner gave his services gratuitously at a public screening for the detection of glaucoma. The tests were conducted by placing a tonometer on each patient's eye. After each test, the tonometer was sterilised in a flame. The defendant placed the tonometer on the claimant's eye before it had cooled sufficiently, and caused permanent injury. The court rejected the contention that this could be characterised as a mere error of judgment. "There was . . . no exercise of a decision-making process at all, nor the taking of a calculated risk. There was simply a failure, however unintentional and inadvertent, to observe the obvious but critical precaution of ensuring that the instrument was not too hot to place upon the patient's eye" (*ibid.* at 423).

[6] For example, *Gonda v. Kerbel* (1982) 24 C.C.L.T. 222, Ontario Supreme Court: defendant caused a perforation of claimant's bowel, while carrying out a bowel examination using a sigmoidoscope. Compare with *Lavelle v Hammersmith and Queen Charlotte's Special Health Authority*, unreported, January 16, 1998, CA (claimant alleged that a cardiovascular surgeon had mistakenly threaded a balloon catheter into his right middle lobe pulmonary vein during a balloon atrial septostomy operation. This had caused rupture of the vein leading to his severe brain damage. The Court of Appeal did not accept that the experienced doctor concerned had made such a careless mistake and concluded that the vein injury was more likely to have been caused as an attendant risk of the septostomy.

[7] See paras 12–092 to 12–105, above.

[8] See paras 12–067 to 12–077 and 12–093, above. In *Pudney v. Union Castle Mail Steamship Company Ltd* [1953] 1 Lloyd's Law Rep. 73 (see para. 12–183, n. 78, above) it was alleged that the ship's doctor was negligent in the treatment he prescribed, even on the basis of his own diagnosis. It was argued that, having diagnosed a mild rheumatic condition, the doctor was negligent in failing to take precautions against a more serious affliction; he should, for example, have advised immediate rest and prohibited walking. Devlin J. considered that the doctor had exercised reasonable skill and care in treatment and rejected this contention. See also *Spry v. Calman and Camberwell Health Authority*, unreported, April 6, 1998 (radiation treatment eradicated claimant's cancer but damaged small bowel. Claimant alleged that the doses had been excessive. No negligence as defendant was acting consistently with a leading cancer hospital's protocol (actually less radical doses were used), and the doses had to take account of different equipment. The defendant's practice was accepted as proper by a responsible body of clinicians.

[9] See, for example, *Meyer v. Gordon* (1981) 17 C.C.L.T. 1, British Columbia Supreme Court: doctor resuscitating a baby in an emergency situation used certain procedures which were unorthodox and an error of judgment. This did not amount to negligence in the circumstances.

[10] [1981] 1 W.L.R. 246.

[11] See para.12–069, above.

In that case the claimant, who was born with severe brain damage, brought an action for negligence against *inter alia* the senior registrar who attended the birth and the health authority. Bush J. held that the registrar was negligent in that he "pulled too hard and too long" with forceps before delivering the claimant by Caesarean section. The Court of Appeal[12] by a majority held that the judge was wrong in this crucial finding of fact. Lord Denning M.R. and Lawton L.J. added that even if the defendant did make the mistake of pulling too hard and too long, that would not amount to negligence. The House of Lords upheld the Court of Appeal's decision, but solely on the basis that there was no evidence to support the judge's finding of fact (in other words, on the basis that no mistake was made).[13]

12–191   **Adverse reaction to drugs or treatment.** If the claimant suffers an adverse reaction to a drug prescribed or treatment administered by the defendant, this may be because the defendant was taking a calculated and reasonable risk (for example in vaccinating a normal child against whooping cough). If the defendant had failed to familiarise himself with the possible side effects of the drug or if the side effects were disproportionate to the benefit likely to be achieved,[14] a charge of negligence will be more difficult to resist. Where the adverse reactions occur because the defendant is using a new drug or taking part in a clinical trial, different considerations arise.[15] In many cases of "adverse reaction", the decision to prescribe the drug cannot be impugned on the *Bolam*[16] test, and the patient's real complaint is that he was not warned of the side effects or properly consulted before the decision to treat him was made.[17] These cases are discussed below.[18]

12–192   **Injections.** Although the administration of an injection is a purely routine procedure, it does not follow that every mishap in the course of an injection constitutes negligence. This is illustrated by a number of reported cases. In *Caldeira v. Gray*[19] the defendant was held negligent for the manner in which he administered a quinine injection. He travelled beyond the safe area for injection and injured the claimant's sciatic nerve. In *Williams v. North Liverpool Hospital*

---

[12] [1980] 1 All E.R. 650.

[13] See also *Knight v West Kent Health Authority* [1998] Lloyd's Rep. Med. 18, CA (Court of Appeal overturned a finding that an excessive traction force had been used: on the evidence, the amount of force required was a matter of clinical judgment); *Dowdie v Camberwell Health Authority*, see para. 12–84 n. 72 above for facts of this case).

[14] *Graham v. Persyko* (1986) 27 D.L.R. (4th) 699, Ontario Court of Appeal: negligent prescription of prednisone.

[15] See paras 12–109 and 12–110, above.

[16] See para 12–069, above. Examples include *Vernon v. Bloomsbury Health Authority* (1986) [1995] 6 Med. L.R. 297 (gentamicin therapy); *Battersby v. Tottman* (1985) 37 S.A.S.R. 524, discussed at para. 12–081, n. 61, above; *Rowan v Steinberg* [1997] 8 Med L.R. 30, Sc. Ct Sess. (OH): general practitioner not negligent for failing to withdraw claimant from tranquilliser therapy to avoid her dependency on them because the risk of such dependency had occurred in her case before the risk of dependency was generally known to the profession; *Robb v. East London & City Health Authority*, unreported, May 8, 1998 (Ebsworth J.): level of radiotherapy doses prescribed in 1980 was not negligent in the light of what was then perceived to be the risk of harm to the brachial tissues.

[17] In one case the claimant recovered general damages for distress and anxiety, even though, if properly informed at the outset, he would have accepted the drug and suffered the same adverse reaction: *Goorkani v. Tayside Health Board*, 1991 S.L.T. 94 (Note), see para. 12–225 below for facts.

[18] See para. 12–201, below.

[19] [1936] 1 All E.R. 540.

Management Committee[20] a doctor injected Pentothal into the claimant's tissues instead of the vein. On the evidence the claimant's vein was not easy to find and the Court of Appeal reversed the trial judge's finding of negligence.[21] In three cases the needle broke during the administration of the injection without any negligence on the part of the practitioner involved.[22] However, negligence was established in *Strangeways-Lesmere v. Clayton*[23] where nurses injected an excessive quantity[24] of paraldehyde, and in *Smith v. Brighton and Lewes Hospital Management Committee*,[25] where a ward sister allowed an excessive number of injections to be given.[26] Similarly, injection of the wrong drug may be negligent. In *Collins v. Hertfordshire County Council*,[27] a junior house surgeon prepared cocaine instead of procaine as a local anaesthetic, having misunderstood the surgeon's prescription. Hilbery J. held the surgeon liable on the grounds that he was responsible for checking that what he injected was the correct substance. The defendant health authority in *Ritchie v. Chichester Health Authority*[28] had a protocol for the administration of epidural anaesthetic, which required the midwife and the anaesthetist to check that the correct drug had been selected for injection. The trial judge found that the anaesthetist had injected a neurotoxin into the claimant, notwithstanding that this conclusion implied a series of errors on the part of the medical staff.

Operations. The courts have always recognised the dangers which are inher- **12–193** ent in an operation.[29] Mistakes will occur on occasions, despite the exercise of reasonable skill and care, and the patient may suffer grievous injuries in consequence. Even where a routine operation, which has been performed countless times without mishap, fails, it does not necessarily follow that the surgeon was negligent.[30] Where the operation is complex or unusual, any failure is easier to justify.[31] In *White v. Board of Governors of Westminster Hospital*[32] a surgeon

---

[20] *The Times*, January 17, 1959.

[21] See also *Prout v. Crowley* (1956) 1 B.M.J. 580 (the defendant injected ferrivenin partly into the claimant's vein and partly into the surrounding tissue. Held by the Liverpool Court of Passage that there was no negligence); *Muzio v. North West Hertfordshire Health Authority* [1995] 6 Med. L.R. 184 (claimant suffered severe headaches when, as a result of penetration of a spinal membrane by a needle used to administer a spinal anaesthetic, leakage of cerebro-spinal fluid occurred. Her claim failed: the administering anaesthetist had exercised all reasonable care during insertion of the needle).

[22] *Gerber v. Pines* (1935) 79 S.J. 13; *Brazier v. Ministry of Defence* [1965] 1 Lloyd's Rep. 26; *Galloway v. Hanley* (1956) 1 B.M.J. 580. In the first case it was held that the doctor was negligent in failing to inform the patient or her husband what had happened.

[23] [1936] 2 K.B. 11.

[24] The nurses misread their instructions and injected 6 ounces instead of 6 drachms.

[25] *The Times*, May 2, 1958.

[26] The doctor prescribed a course of 30 streptomycin injections. As a result of the ward sister's failure to take proper precautions, 34 injections were administered.

[27] [1947] 1 K.B. 598.

[28] [1994] 5 Med. L.R. 187.

[29] See, for example, *Hajgato v. London Health Association* (1982) 36 O.R. (2d) 669, 681 affirmed (1983) 44 O.R. (2d) 264, Ontario CA (risk of post-operative infection).

[30] *Ashcroft v. Mersey Regional Health Authority* [1983] 2 All E.R. 245 concerned a routine operation for the removal of granulated tissue from the claimant's eardrum. The surgeon damaged the claimant's facial nerve while removing the granulations with the use of forceps. With some hesitation Kilner-Brown J. rejected the contention that the surgeon had used excessive force. Claimant's claim dismissed. This decision was upheld on appeal: see [1985] 2 All E.R. 96 (Note).

[31] See *Lavelle v. Hammersmith and Queen Charlotte Special Health Authority*, para. 12–189, n. 6 above for facts.

[32] *The Times*, October 26, 1961.

accidentally cut the retina during an operation on the claimant's right eye. As a result the eye became useless and had to be removed. Thompson J. acquitted the surgeon of any negligence. He was working within a very few millimetres and exercised due skill, care and judgment.[33] However, where the claimant developed meningitis as a result of some infection in the apparatus used during his operation, it was held that there must have been some negligence by the hospital staff, for which the hospital authority was responsible.[34] Where the operation is a race against time, the court will make greater allowance for mistakes on the part of the surgeon or his assistants.[35] An operation should be carefully planned.[36] The decision to operate, rather than to treat conservatively, may be negligently hasty.[37] Once negligence is established, the claimant should be able to recover damages, even if the ill effects are purely cosmetic.[38]

12–194   **Failure to remove objects.** Many claims arise from the surgeon's failure to remove objects from the patient's body at the end of an operation. In practice such claims are usually settled. Even when they are contested, it is difficult for the defendants to rebut the inference that someone involved in the operation must have been negligent.[39] In *James v. Dunlop*[40] a surgeon failed to remove all the swabs at the end of an operation. The Court of Appeal held that he was not

---

[33] A Canadian decision to the same effect is *Chubey v. Ahsan* (1977) 71 D.L.R. (3d) 550: during an operation to remove a disc the surgeon accidentally pierced the aorta and vena cava. It was held that there was no negligence. Cf. *Hendy v. Milton Keynes Health Authority (No. 2)* [1992] 3 Med. L.R. 119.

[34] *Voller v. Portsmouth Corporation* (1947) 203 L.T.J. 264. The operation was performed in the ward rather than the operating theatre, but Birkett J. did not consider that the doctors were negligent in adopting this course.

[35] "A mistake which would amount to negligence in a 'cold' operation might be no more than misadventure in a 'hot' operation." *Cooper v. Nevill, The Times*, March 10, 1961.

[36] Failure to carry out further assessment by CT scan or myelogram before spinal surgery, so that the surgery was planned on the basis of inadequate information, was held negligent in *Smith v. Salford Health Authority* [1994] 5 Med. L.R. 321, but the claimant failed to show that the breach was causative of his post-operative tetraplegia. See also *Tucker v. Tees Health Authority* [1995] 6 Med. L.R. 54: failure to perform an ultrasound scan to exclude the possibility that the patient was pregnant before conducting a laparotomy to confirm a provisional diagnosis of ovarian cyst was negligent.

[37] See para. 12–196, below.

[38] *MacDonald v. Ross* (1983) 24 C.C.L.T. 242, 247, Nova Scotia Supreme Court: following an operation on claimant's breasts, one breast was appreciably larger than the other and the nipple was misaligned. Surgeon held liable for negligent performance of the operation. "Cosmetic improvement may not be in contemplation where surgery is performed for therapeutic reasons, but it must equally be true that gross and entirely unnecessary, and I stress unnecessary, deformations are not acceptable consequences within the appropriate standard of care in such cases." It is submitted that the English courts would adopt the same approach.

[39] *Dryden v. Surrey County Council* [1936] 2 All E.R. 535 (a wad of gauze was left in the claimant's body during a minor operation. It was held that the doctor who performed the operation was negligent, but the nurses were not); *Hocking v. Bell* [1948] W.N. 21 (the defendant carried out a thyroidectomy on the claimant and temporarily placed a rubber drainage tube in the wound. He left part of the tube *in situ*, negligence established); *Cooper v. Nevill, The Times*, March 10, 1961 (abdominal pack left in the claimant's body. Held that there must have been some negligence on the part of the surgeon or his assistant).

[40] (1931) 1 B.M.J. 730. See also the discussion of this case in *Mahon v. Osborne* [1939] 2 K.B. 14. By contrast in *Elliott v Bickerstaff* (1999) 48 N.S.W.L.R. 214, the Court of Appeal of New South Wales held that even if leaving a sponge in the patient could be taken to indicate negligence by someone, this did not mean that the surgeon was negligent, as the theatre staff could have been negligent (wrongly informing the surgeon that the sponge count indicated all sponges were removed). The claimant was suing her surgeon personally and not the hospital or health authority responsible for employing both the theatre staff.

exonerated simply because the nurse who was counting the swabs for him had made a mistake. A similar point arose in *Mahon v. Osborne*.[41] At the end of an abdominal operation one of the swabs used to pack off adjacent organs was left in the patient's body, with the result that he died three months later. The system used for checking the removal of swabs was as follows: each swab had a tape attached with a Spencer-Wells forceps clipped to the tape, which would hang outside the patient's body as a signal. In addition, the theatre sister counted the swabs used. In the present case the surgeon made a visual search and concluded that all the swabs were removed. He asked the theatre sister if they were all removed and she said "yes". The surgeon did not make a further search by feel before sewing up. The jury found that the surgeon, but not the theatre sister, was negligent. On the surgeon's appeal the Court of Appeal, by a majority, ordered a re-trial on the grounds of the judge's misdirection to the jury. They observed that there was no general rule of law requiring a surgeon in an operation such as this one, after removing all the swabs of which he was aware, to make sure by a separate search by feel that no swabs were left in the patient's body.[42] The question whether the omission by the surgeon to remove a swab constituted failure to exercise reasonable skill and care was to be decided on the evidence given in the particular case. Where the surgeon discards a precaution which is available to ensure the removal of all swabs, he may be judged more harshly.[43]

Post-operative care. The neglect of any reasonable post-operative precaution   **12–195**
may expose a surgeon to liability for a non-negligent mistake which occurred during the course of the operation.[44] The requirement for post-operative aftercare includes dealing with complications and investigating the patient's complaints,[45]

---

[41] [1939] 2 K.B. 14.

[42] In *Elliott v Bickerstaff* , see n. 40 above, the Court of Appeal of New South Wales held (on the evidence in this case) that the surgeon's duty of care to his patient did require him to exercise reasonable skill and care in feeling for sponges in the abdominal cavity as well as asking theatre staff if the sponge count was satisfactory.

[43] See, for example, *Urry v. Bierer*, The Times, July 15, 1955, discussed at para. 12–083, above. For a similar Canadian decision see *Chasney v. Anderson* [1950] 4 D.L.R. 223: surgeon performed tonsil and adenoid operation on child using sponges. He did not use sponges with tapes attached which were available, nor did he have a nurse in attendance to count the sponges. It was held that his failure to remove one of the sponges was negligent. By contrast the surgeon's failure to wear his prescription glasses when performing the claimant's hysterectomy was not negligent in *Stefanyshyn v. Rubin* (1996) 113 Man. R. (2d) 133 because his failure to wear glasses did not cause the suturing error that occurred (a ureter had been tied to the vagina, leading to a fistula and urine leakage), since the ureter was not visible during the surgery.

[44] See, for example, *Lee v. O'Farrell* (1988) 43 C.C.L.T. 269: fracture of femoral head occurred during surgery. Defendant held negligent for failing to detect this by post-operative X-ray (the X-ray taken covered too small a field). See also *Cherekwayo v. Grafton* (1993) 84 Man. R. (2d) 81 (failure to provide suitable post-operative care after breast implantation surgery led to corrective surgery being performed as an emergency); see also *Newbury v Bath District Health Authority* [1998] 47 B.M.L.R. 138, QBD, Ebsworth J. Defendant found liable for failure to test claimant for neurological deficit following spinal surgery and consequent failure to re-operate to remove implants. Held that such removal within 24 hours of surgery would have given claimant more than 50% chance of recovery. This negligence was a material cause of the claimant's damage (although selection of a technique using the offending implants was not negligent).

[45] See para. 12–176, above; *Knight v Bradley*, unreported, May 5, 1998, defendant's negligent delay to dealing with the claimant's post-operative complaints entitled the claimant to damages for the limited consequences of the delay; *Tailleur v. Grande Prairie General & Auxiliary Hospital* [2000] 74 Alta. L.R. (3d) 20, Canadian Court of Appeal (claimant severed Achilles tendon and surgeon sutured tendon and wound and then placed claimant's leg in cast, gas gangrene (rare, infectious

and pursuing the results of tests or undertaking further tests that are indicated or ordered by another clinician.[46]

12–196   **Overintervention.** With the growing panoply of available medical treatments, cases sometimes arise where medical practitioners attempt to treat the incurable or embark on treatment which is worse than the original disability. Thus before considering whether the method of treatment was negligent, it must sometimes be asked whether medical intervention can be justified at all.[47] Whether or not the intervention undertaken can be justified will be determined by the extent of investigation, consideration of other less "invasive" regimes or management, and on expert opinion of the appropriateness of the treatment used. The fact that the patient or his parent has consented is not a defence in circumstances where no reasonably competent medical practitioner would have proceeded at all. In *Doughty v. North Staffordshire Health Authority*[48] the claimant was born with a birthmark on her face. A plastic surgeon employed by the defendants carried out 11 to 13 operations during her childhood. As a result there was a considerable area of scarring on her face and the birthmark remained visible. The defendants were held liable on the basis that no body of reasonably competent medical opinion would have exposed the claimant to that course of plastic surgery. In *De Freitas v. O'Brien and Connelly*[49] the claimant complained that she had been subjected to unnecessary spinal decompression surgery when there was no evidence that her back pain was caused by nerve root compression. The Court of Appeal upheld the conclusions of the trial judge that (a) spinal surgery was a specialism apart from other orthopaedic surgery and neurosurgery which, not-withstanding that it was practised by a very small number of surgeons, repre-sented a respectable body of medical opinion, and (b) a spinal surgeon could reasonably and safely undertake exploratory surgery on the claimant because his

---

disease caused by Clostridia bacteria) developed leading to amputation of the leg. No evidence of negligence by surgeon since no evidence that different type of cast or keeping claimant in hospital without a cast for observation would have led to different result).

[46] See *Taylor v. West Kent Health Authority* [1997] 8 Med. L.R. 251, QBD (claimant's breast lump was aspirated, and cytology report stated: "Blood and groups of mildly atypical epithelial cells possibly from a fibroadenoma or fibrocystic disease. Consider biopsy to confirm." No biopsy undertaken, claimant was reassured at two six-monthly reviews and her carcinoma was only diagnosed when the axillary lymph nodes were involved. Held that no reasonable clinician ought to have taken the cytology report as an exclusion of malignancy, or that no further investigation was necessary. At the very least, failure to seek further clarification of the cytology was negligent. The result was that diagnosis and treatment of the claimant's breast cancer was delayed by over one year. See also *Braun Estate v. Vaughan* (1997) 124 Man. R. (2d) 1, where the doctor failed to follow up the cytology report of a routine PAP smear taken from the claimant's cervix. The report showed evidence of abnormality that required further investigation at the time, but for which there was a 100% probability of recovery with proper treatment. The doctor was held negligent for having no independent system in place to ensure that reports were returned to him, or to ensure that the hospital concerned had such a system in place. The hospital had closed its gynaecological unit and the claimant's records held by the hospital were not forwarded to her general practitioner. The claimant's cervical cancer was undetected for a year, in which time it had become untreatable and the claimant subsequently died from the cancer. The claim for damages succeeded.

[47] In *Atzori v. Dr Chan King Pan* [1999] 3 H.K.L.R.D. 77, the Court of First Instance found that an orthopaedic surgeon: "had set his sights on surgery at a very early stage long before a proper trial of conventional conservative treatment had been conducted and that this accounts in part for the absence of careful neurological testing."

[48] [1992] 3 Med. L.R. 81.

[49] [1995] 6 Med. L.R. 109.

expertise greatly reduced the risk of damage to nerve roots which were not directly involved in the procedure.[50]

(e) *Failure of communication between hospitals or medical practitioners*

It is frequently necessary to transfer the treatment of a patient from one hospital, **12–197** or one hospital department, to another or possibly from a hospital to the patient's own doctor. Plainly, there must be adequate communication between the parties as to the condition diagnosed, the treatment so far given and, possibly, the treatment required. In *Coles v. Reading and District Hospital Management Committee*[51] the hospital authorities were held negligent as a result of the breakdown of communication. The patient's finger was crushed by a large lump of coal. He attended the cottage hospital where nursing staff gave first aid treatment but did not administer an anti-tetanus injection. The sister told him that he should proceed immediately to Battle Hospital at Reading for further treatment. Sachs J. held, however, that the patient was not given to understand the importance of going to Battle Hospital. He also held that the patient should have been given a document to take to Battle Hospital "saying what had been done and what should be done, with particular reference to anti-tetanus injections."[52] Sachs J. stressed the importance of proper communication between different doctors and hospitals within the National Health Service.[53] In this instance the patient did not go to Battle Hospital, but he did subsequently attend his own doctor. He never received an anti-tetanus injection and in consequence died of tetanus. Sachs J. held that both the hospital authorities and the doctor were negligent.

The question of communication also arose in *Chapman v. Rix.*[54] The patient, **12–198** a butcher, stabbed himself in the abdomen while boning a rump of beef. The defendant examined him at the cottage hospital. He realised that the deep fascia had been cut but he concluded wrongly (though not negligently) that the wound had not penetrated the peritoneum. He ordered the wound to be stitched and dressed and then sent the patient home. The defendant told him that he thought it was a surface wound, but he gave emphatic instructions that he should see his own doctor that evening and tell him what had happened and what had been done. Symptoms of pain and nausea developed. The patient saw his own doctor (M) and told him that the hospital had said his wound was superficial. M diagnosed digestive disorder. Five days later the patient died as a result of the wound to his peritoneum. Barry J. held that the defendant was negligent in his failure to communicate directly with M. The Court of Appeal, by a majority, allowed the defendant's appeal. They observed that it might have been better if the defendant had sent a letter to M, but his omission to do so did not constitute

---

[50] Compare with the decision in *Atzori v. Dr Chan King Pan* [1999] 3 H.K.L.R.D. 77.

[51] (1963) 107 S.J. 115; *The Times*, January 30, 1963.

[52] (1963) 107 S.J. 115, 116.

[53] "The National Health Service had been developed on the basis that a patient might well be transferred for treatment from one person to another so that the responsibility for the patient shifted. . . . By proper communication his Lordship meant that which was reasonably necessary for safeguarding a patient's interests. It might not matter if the communication was made to the next person by writing a message or telephoning or whether in the case of a suitable patient it was made direct to the patient. . . . Any system which failed to provide for adequate communication was wrong and negligently wrong." *The Times*, January 30, 1963.

[54] [1994] 5 Med. L.R. 238.

professional negligence. The House of Lords, by a majority of three to two, upheld the Court of Appeal's decision. Lords Goddard, Morton and Hodson considered that the steps taken by the defendant were sufficient to communicate to M that he did not think there was penetration of the peritoneum but there was a degree of risk and the patient needed watching.

12–199   In two Canadian cases,[55] the importance of proper consultation between different doctors treating a patient in the same hospital was emphasised. In *Bergen*, the trial judge condemned the practice of "kerbstone consultations", which occurred when the various doctors happened to meet in the hospital corridors. A hospital authority has a duty to devise and maintain an adequate system for summoning qualified or specialist assistance when required. In *Brown*, an injured child (the claimant) was admitted to the defendant hospital and the treating paediatricians failed to warn the mother of suspected child abuse (based on a CTG scan). The child was discharged and brought back having sustained severe and permanent brain damage. The radioneurologist noticed the suggestive CTG signs of brain haemorrhage due to violent shaking but did not communicate the significance of the finding to the treating paediatricians responsible for the claimant's discharge. The claimant's claim for damages succeeded. The trial judge stated:

> "While I do not conclude that [the radioneurologist] had any obligation to run to the child's side, read the entire history and in effect become the treating physician, it was his duty to advise at least [the paediatric resident] that these subdural bleeds were: (a) likely non-accidental in nature, and (b) because of their age, not consistent with recent trauma. That, in effect, is placing on [the radioneurologist] the obligation to tell [the paediatric resident] that child abuse is suspected."[56]

He continued:

> "Common sense, hospital policy and precise legislation mandate that the medical profession go beyond pure diagnosis and report to the proper authorities circumstances which suggest and especially those that scream child abuse is the likely cause of trauma to the child."[57]

12–200   In *Bull v. Devon Area Health Authority*[58] delay in securing the attendance of an obstetrician at a difficult birth, which resulted in the child suffering pre-birth hypoxia and consequent brain damage, amounted to negligence on the part of the health authority. The delay meant that either the system was inefficient or that some individual working within it had been negligent. In *Robertson v. Notting-ham Health Authority*[59] the Court of Appeal identified two significant types of

---

[55] *Bergen v. Sturgeon General Hospital* (1984) 28 C.C.L.T. 155, 175, Alberta Court of Queen's Bench Division. See also *Brown v University of Alberta Hospital* [1997] 145 D.L.R. (4th) 63, Alberta Court of Queen's Bench. See also *Braun Estate v. Vaughan* (1997) 124 Man. R. (2d) 1, see para. 12–195, n. 46, above.
[56] *per* Marceau J. at p. 114, para. 197.
[57] *per* Marceau J. at p. 114, para. 200.
[58] [1993] 4 Med. L.R. 117, *CA*. See para. 12–158, above. See also *Law Estate v. Simice* (1994) 21 C.C.L.T. (2d) 228 affirmed (1996) 27 C.C.L.T. (2d) 127, British Columbia CA (delays caused by failures of communication between a locum, a general practitioner, a consultant ophthalmologist and a hospital doctor led to patient's death from an undetected aneurism); *Re R (A Minor)*, unreported, July 16, 1996, CA., and the quotation at n. 87 to para. 12–158, above.
[59] [1997] 8 Med. L.R. 1 (for the facts of which see para. 12–156, above).

breakdown in communications between hospital staff. First, there was no effective communication of information available from CTG traces operated by nurses and midwives to the doctors who were responsible for making the decisions on management of the claimant's birth. Secondly, there was a lack of effective communication of the doctor's instructions to the nurses and midwives who were responsible for monitoring the condition of the foetus before labour began. The defendant was in breach of its primary duty of care to the claimant in both respects.[60]

(f) Failing to explain treatment or warn of risks

General principle. The fundamental principle that a patient should be   **12–201**
informed of the treatment which is proposed and warned of any risks which are inherent in that treatment, has long been recognised. It was observed in 1767: "it is reasonable that a patient should be told what is about to be done to him, that he may take courage and put himself in such a situation as to enable him to undergo the operation."[61] The extent of the patient's right to information and of the medical practitioner's correlative duty to inform has been the subject of much judicial discussion in common law countries, leading to different approaches in Canada, England and Wales and Australia.[62] English law applies the *Bolam* test, as modified by Lord Bridge's speech in *Sidaway*.[63] However, the approaches used in other common law jurisdictions are relevant.

Canadian law. Amongst Commonwealth countries, Canada has taken the lead   **12–202**
in developing this area of law. Although there are now important divergences between the law of Canada and English law, the Canadian decisions (especially those of the Supreme Court[64]) are frequently cited in English judgments and have certainly been taken into account by the English courts.[65] In *Hopp v. Lepp*[66] the Supreme Court of Canada postulated an objective duty of disclosure (*i.e.* not one which was solely determined by the customs or practices of the medical profession[67]):

"In summary, the decided cases appear to indicate that, in obtaining the consent of a patient for the performance upon him of a surgical operation, a surgeon, generally,

---

[60] See also *Taylor v. West Kent Health Authority*, para. 12–184 above, for an example of a failure of adequate communication (by report) between clinicians within one hospital where the cytology report by the pathologist who carried out the needle aspiration suggested a benign diagnosis but was not entirely clear. The surgical registrar was negligent to interpret the report as excluding malignancy; at the very least the pathologist should have been asked for clarification.

[61] *Slater v. Baker* (1767) 2 Wils.K.B. 359. See also the Canadian decision *Kenny v. Lockwood* [1932] 1 D.L.R. 507, 525: "the duty cast upon the surgeon was to deal honestly with the patient as to the necessity, character and importance of the operation and its probable consequences and whether success might reasonably be expected to ameliorate or remove the trouble, but that such duty does not extend to warning the patient of the dangers incident to, or possible in, any operation, nor to details calculated to frighten or distress the patient."

[62] As to the American doctrine of informed consent, which has been rejected by the English courts, see paras. 12–130 to 12–134, above. The Australian approach has been adopted in South Africa in preference to the English approach see paras 12–205 to 12–207, below.

[63] See paras 12–208 to 12–213, below.

[64] *Hopp v. Lepp* (1980) 112 D.L.R. (3d) 67; *Reibl v. Hughes* (1980) 114 D.L.R. (3d)1.

[65] For example in *Chatterton v. Gerson* [1981] Q.B. 432.

[66] (1980) 112 D.L.R. (3d) 67, 81.

[67] Effectively the opposite of the *Bolam* test.

should answer any specific questions posed by the patient as to the risks involved and should, without being questioned, disclose to him the nature of the proposed operation, its gravity, any material risks and any special or unusual risks attendant upon the performance of the operation. However, having said that, it should be added that the scope of the duty of disclosure and whether or not it has been breached are matters which must be decided in relation to the circumstances of each particular case."

This statement was adopted by the Canadian Supreme Court in *Reibl v. Hughes*,[68] where further elaboration was given as to the meaning of the crucial phrase "any material risks and any special or unusual risks attendant upon the performance of the operation". It includes any risks which the surgeon knows (or should know) that the patient deems relevant to the decision whether to undergo the operation. A risk which is a mere possibility is not "material", unless its occurrence may result in serious consequences such as paralysis or death.[69] The dangers inherent in any operation, such as the dangers of the anaesthetic or the risks of infection, do not have to be disclosed. The emotional condition of the patient and his fears relating to the operation may in certain cases justify the surgeon in withholding or generalising information. In *Reibl v. Hughes*[70] itself the operation involved a significant risk of stroke. It was held that this was a material risk which ought to have been disclosed. In *Beherns v. Smith*,[71] the trial judge further elucidated the extent of the duty to provide sufficient information to the patient:

"In this regard, the law imposes upon the medical practitioner a duty to provide sufficient information to enable the patient to reasonably balance the possible risks and benefits and make an informed decision whether to undergo or forgo a recommended treatment. The scope of the duty will vary according to the circumstances of the case and any special considerations affecting the particular patient. That which a patient should be made to understand are the nature, purpose, and likely benefits of the treatment; the recognised risks inherent in it; the availability of alternative treatments; and the possible consequences of leaving the condition untreated."[72]

12–203   The Canadian cases since *Reibl v. Hughes*[73] are, essentially, applications of these principles.[74] Medical practitioners have been held in breach of their duty of disclosure (of risk or treatment options) in the following cases: *Casey v. Provan*[75] (small risk of permanent injury to vocal cord); *Considine v. Camp Hill Hospital*[76]

---

[68] (1980) 114 D.L.R. (3d) 1.
[69] See also *White v. Turner* (1981) 31 O.R.(2d) 773, HC at 789 for an explanation of "material" or "special or unusual risks": "In my view, material risks are significant risks that pose a real threat to the patient's life, health or comfort. In considering whether a risk is material or immaterial, one must balance the severity of the potential result and the likelihood of its occurring. Even if there is only a small chance of serious injury or death, the risk may be considered material. On the other hand, if there is a significant chance of slight injury this too may be held to be material. As always in negligence law, what is a material risk will have to depend on the specific facts of the case."
[70] *ibid.*
[71] (1997) 153 Sask.R. 294. The claimant underwent laparoscopic laser removal of abdominal adhesions, during which operation her small bowel was perforated. The court held that the claimant was aware of and understood the general risks of the surgery, and had been provided with sufficient information to make a reasoned decision. The claimant's claim was dismissed.
[72] *ibid.* at 297.
[73] *ibid.*
[74] The Canadian decisions reached before *Hopp v. Lepp*, and *Reibl v. Hughes*, must now be viewed with caution. They can only be relied upon in Canada in so far as the principles upon which they were based are consistent with the decisions of the Supreme Court in those two cases.
[75] (1984) 11 D.L.R. (4th) 708, Ontario High Court.
[76] (1982) 133 D.L.R. (3d) 11, Nova Scotia Supreme Court.

(1 per cent to 4 per cent risk that operation would cause incontinence); *Diack v. Bardsley*[77] (4.4 per cent risk of temporary paraesthesia, 1 per cent risk of permanent paraesthesia); *Mason v. Forgi*[78] (small risk of stroke); *Ferguson v. Hamilton Civic Hospitals*[79] (risk of stroke); *Kitchen v. McMullin*[80] (increased risk of hepatitis from Factor VIII concentrate); *Haughian v. Payne*[81] (risk of paralysis); *Meyer v. Rogers*[82] (diagnostic medical test involving risk of severe allergic reaction in 1 in 2,000 cases); *Arndt v. Smith*[83] (grave but small risk to foetus from maternal chickenpox); *Painter v. Rae*[84] (risk of bowel injury associated with post-partum tubal ligation was a material risk); *Seney v. Crooks*[85] (duty to inform of well-recognised alternative and more invasive treatment); *Ostby v. Bondar*[86] (greater than normal duty to advise of risks of nerve damage to patient who was more susceptible to this risk due to pre-existing conditions); *Semeniuk v. Cox*[87] (failure to advise of three-fold increase of general risks of elective stomach surgery if procedure is a revision surgery).

In the following cases medical practitioners have been held not to be in breach **12–204** of their duty of disclosure: *Bucknam v. Kostuick*[88] (availability of alternative treatment which defendant had rejected as unsuitable); *Gonda v. Kerbel*[89] (risk of bowel perforation); *Hajgato v. London Health Association*[90] (claimant told about risk of infection inherent in operation, but not told about risk that this could destroy hip joint, in view of her emotional condition and apprehension about the operation); *Videto v. Kennedy*[91] (low risk of perforation of bowel and consequences not normally serious); *Mallette v. Hagarty*[92] (remote risk of permanent paraesthesia from dentist's single injection of standard local anaesthetic); *Webster v. Chapman*[93] (general practitioner has no duty to advise of the risk to an unborn child of a drug (Coumadin) prescribed for pelvic thrombosis, where patient assured him that she was using birth control); *Seney v. Crooks*[94] and *Van Mol v. Ashmore*[95] (duty to advise patient about alternative treatments, and the risks and advantages of each); *Halkyard v. Mathew*[96] (surgeon's personal medical

---

[77] (1983) 25 C.C.L.T. 159, British Columbia Supreme Court; (1984) 31 C.C.C.T. 308, British Columbia CA.

[78] (1984) 31 C.C.L.T. 66, Nova Scotia Supreme Court; (1986) 38 C.C.L.T. 171, New Brunswick CA.

[79] (1983) 144 D.L.R. (3d) 214, Ontario High Court; (1985) 18 D.L.R. (4th) 638, Ontario CA.

[80] (1989) 50 C.C.L.T. 215, New Brunswick CA.

[81] (1987) 37 D.L.R. (4th) 624, Saskatchewan CA.

[82] (1991) 78 D.L.R. (4th) 307.

[83] [1996] 7 Med. L.R. 35, at 43, col. 2, British Columbia Supreme Court held that the claimant failed on causation. The claimant's appeal to British Columbia Court of Appeal on causation succeeded, a new trial was ordered, [1996] 7 Med. L.R. 108. On further appeal to the Supreme Court of Canada, the trial judge's decision on causation was upheld, (1997) 148 D.L.R. (4th) 48 (see paras 12–263 and 12–264 below on the "modified objective" approach to causation).

[84] (1998) 127 Man. R. (2d) 133.

[85] (1998) 166 D.L.R. (4th) 337, Alberta CA (upholding decision of trial judge, [1996] 41 Alta. L.R. 192.

[86] [1998] 61 Alta. L.R. 341, Alberta Court of Queen's Bench.

[87] [2000] 70 Alta. L.R. (3d) 30, Alberta Court of Queen's Bench.

[88] (1983) 3 D.L.R. (4th) 99, Ontario High Court.

[89] (1982) 24 C.C.L.T. 222, Ontario High Court.

[90] (1982) 36 O.R. (2d) 669, Ontario High Court; (1983) 44 O.R. (2d) 264, Ontario CA.

[91] (1981) 17 C.C.L.T. 307, Ontario CA.

[92] (1994) 19 Alta.L.R. (2d) 201, Alberta High Court.

[93] [1997] 155 D.L.R. (4th) 82, Manitoba CA.

[94] [1998] 166 D.L.R. (4th) 337, Alberta CA.

[95] [1999] 168 D.L.R.637, British Columbia CA.

[96] [1999] 67 Alta. L.R. (3d) 174, Alberta Court of Queen's Bench.

conditions responding to therapy are not discloseable material risks of treatment). Where problems developed in the course of highly stressful treatment, the Ontario Court of Appeal held that it was a medical decision whether or not to continue; there was no duty on the doctors to inform the claimant of the risks which existed in the new situation.[97]

12–205   **Australian law.** The Supreme Court of South Australia[98] the New South Wales Supreme Court[99] and the New South Wales Court of Appeal[1] rejected the notion that the *Bolam* test determined as a matter of law the appropriate standard of care in cases concerning the provision of advice and information to patients. In *F v. R* King C.J. said:

> "But professions may adopt unreasonable practices, particularly as to disclosure, not because they serve the interests of the clients, but because they protect the interests or convenience of members of the profession. The court has an obligation to scrutinise professional practices to ensure that they accord with the standard of reasonableness imposed by law."[2]

In each of the cases cited above the claimant failed on liability.

12–206   The issue came before the High Court of Australia again in *Rogers v. Whitaker*.[3] The claimant was almost blind in her right eye owing to an injury suffered in childhood. The defendant, an ophthalmic surgeon, offered an operation to remove scar tissue from the right eye. He said that the operation would improve the appearance of the right eye and also, probably, restore some of its vision. Despite the claimant's incessant questioning about possible complications of the operation, the defendant failed to warn the claimant of the very small risk of sympathetic ophthalmia (1 in 14,000—or slightly greater where, as here, there had been an earlier penetrating injury to the eye operated upon) although the defendant was aware of that risk. If warned of the risk, the claimant would not have consented to the operation. The defendant carried out the operation with reasonable skill and care. Unfortunately, the operation did not achieve the intended improvement to the right eye, but did lead to sympathetic ophthalmia in the left eye, leaving the claimant almost totally blind.

12–207   The trial judge, the New South Wales Court of Appeal and the High Court of Australia all held that the defendant was liable for failing to warn the claimant of the risk of sympathetic ophthalmia. It was accepted that the failure to give such warning accorded with a practice accepted as proper by many reputable practitioners, but it was held that the *Bolam* test was inapplicable. In the single judgment given by five of the six judges in the High Court, the reasoning was as follows:

> (i) There is a fundamental difference between (a) diagnosis and treatment and (b) provision of information and advice.

---

[97] *Cliarlariello v. Schacter* (1991) 76 D.L.R. (4th) 449.
[98] In *F v. R* (1984) 33 S.A.S.R. 189, and in *Battersby v. Tottman* (1984) 35 S.A.S.R. 577; (1985) 37 S.A.S.R. 524.
[99] *H. v. Royal Alexandra Hospital for Children* [1990] 1 Med. L.R. 297.
[1] *Albrighton v. Royal Prince Alfred Hospital* [1980] 2 N.S.W.L.R. 542.
[2] (1984) 33 S.A.S.R. 189, 194.
[3] (1992) 109 A.L.R. 625, [1993] 4 Med. L.R. 79.

(ii) In the case of diagnosis and treatment "A responsible professional opinion will have an influential, often a decisive role to play".

(iii) The question whether the patient was given all relevant information does not generally depend upon medical standards or practices.

(iv) A doctor has a duty (subject to the therapeutic privilege) to warn his patient of a material risk inherent in proposed treatment.

(v) "A risk is material if, in the circumstances of the particular case, a reasonable person in the patient's position, if warned of the risk, would be likely to attach significance to it or if the medical practitioner is or should reasonably be aware that the particular patient, if warned of the risk, would be likely to attach significance to it."

(vi) In this case, the claimant had incessantly questioned the defendant as to, amongst other things, possible complications.

(vii) The risk of sympathetic ophthalmia was material because "a reasonable person in the patient's position would be likely to attach significance to the risk, and thus required a warning."[4]

In thus effectively adopting a "prudent patient" test for the standard of care in disclosure cases, the High Court of Australia specifically disapproved *Bolam v. Friern Hospital Management Committee*[5] and *Sidaway v. Governors of Bethlem Royal Hospital.*[6] It is an important divergence from English law, but a case on the same facts might now be decided the same way in England on the basis that the view of a body of expert opinion that it was unnecessary for the patient to be told of this slight risk could not withstand logical analysis in the face of her specific and express desire to be told of just such a risk, in accordance with the analysis of the Court of Appeal in *Pearce v. United Bristol Healthcare NHS Trust* referred to in paragraph 12–213 below.

English law. The first occasion on which the English courts considered the **12–208** developments in Canada was *Chatterton v. Gerson.*[7] In that case the defendant was treating the claimant for pain in the right groin. He told her that he hoped to relieve her pain by interrupting the nerve along which it was signalled to the brain; that this would involve numbness over an area larger than the pain source itself and that it might involve temporary losses of muscle power. The defendant carried out the procedure on the claimant in two operations with an interval of 10

---

[4] See also *Hart v. Chappell* [1994] 5 Med. L.R. 365, Supreme Court of New South Wales, upheld on appeal (on causation) by the defendant to the High Court of Australia [1999] Lloyd's Rep. Med. 223 (a doctor failed to warn his patient that an operation on her throat carried a risk to her voice, even though he was aware that she was a teacher, and she had expressly raised with him the question of possible damage to her voice. Applying the tests set out in *Rogers v. Whitaker*, he was negligent.) *Rogers v. Whitaker* has been adopted in South Africa in preference to the English approach: see *Castell v. De Greef* (1994) (4) S.A. 408. For discussion of the decision in *Rogers v. Whitaker*, see D. Chalmers, and R. Schwartz, "*Rogers v. Whitaker* and Informed Consent in Australia: A Fair Dinkum Duty of Disclosure" (1993) 1 Med. L.Rev. 129; F. A. Trinidade, "Disclosure of Risks in Proposed Medical Treatment" (1993) 109 L.Q.R. 352. In "Malpractice—Medical Negligence in Australia" (1992) Aus.L.J. 67, D. Cassidy reviews the standing of the *Bolam* principle in Australia, and criticises *Rogers* as introducing an anomalous test for breach of a professional duty of care.

[5] [1957] 1 W.L.R. 582.

[6] [1985] A.C. 871.

[7] [1981] Q.B. 432.

months between them. In the event the claimant lost the sensation in her right leg and foot. Bristow J. held that the warning before the first operation was adequate. The condition of the claimant's leg and foot "was not a possibility inherent in the operation of which Dr Gerson should have warned her". There was no need for the defendant before the second operation to repeat the warning which he had previously given. In considering the nature of the defendant's duty of disclosure Bristow J. applied the *Bolam* test:

> "The duty of the doctor is to explain what he intends to do, and its implications, in the way a careful and responsible doctor in similar circumstances would have done: see *Bolam v. Friern Hospital Management Committee*."[8]

After reviewing the expert evidence, Bristow J. continued[9]:

> "In my judgment there is no obligation on the doctor to canvass with the patient anything other than the inherent implications of the particular operation he intends to carry out. He is certainly under no obligation to say that if he operates incompetently he will do damage. The fundamental assumption is that he knows his job and will do it properly. But he ought to warn of what may happen by misfortune however well the operation is done, if there is a real risk of misfortune inherent in the procedure, as there was in the surgery to the carotid artery in the Canadian case of *Reibl v. Hughes* (1978) 89 D.L.R. (3d) 112.[10] In what he says any good doctor has to take into account the personality of the patient, the likelihood of the misfortune, and what in the way of warning is for the particular patient's welfare."

12–209　　In *Hills v. Potter*[11] Hirst J. rejected the submission that he should apply the principles laid down in the two leading Canadian cases[12] and instead applied the *Bolam* test.[13] The claimant in that case suffered spasmodic torticollis (a deformity of the neck) following a cervical anterior rhizotomy (surgery on a nerve root) performed by the first defendant. This operation was not a straightforward one. The evidence was that good results had been achieved in 70–80 per cent of cases, and that in the remaining cases a variety of complications had occurred (such as difficulty in swallowing). The first defendant had given a general warning concerning the risks of a major operation such as this, but had not gone into details. The first defendant's explanation and warning was in line with the practice of all three neuro-surgeons who had given expert evidence.[14] Hirst J., applying "the medical standard", held that he was not in breach of duty.[15]

12–210　　The most recent and the most determined attempt to introduce the American or Canadian principles into this area of the law was made by the claimant in *Sidaway v. Governors of Bethlem Royal Hospital*.[16] This case concerned a spinal operation performed on the claimant by the second defendant for the purpose of

---

[8] *ibid.* at 443E. As to the *Bolam* test, see paras 12–067 to 12–072 and 12–090 to 12–105, above.
[9] *ibid.* at 444D-E.
[10] Ontario CA. *Reibl v. Hughes* had not then reached the Supreme Court.
[11] [1984] 1 W.L.R. 641 (Note).
[12] Namely *Hopp v. Lepp*, *ibid.* and *Reibl v. Hughes*, *ibid.*
[13] [1984] 1 W.L.R. 641, 652–653.
[14] *ibid.* at 645C.
[15] *ibid.* at 653C-D.
[16] [1985] A.C. 871.

relieving pain in her neck, right shoulder and arms. Although the operation was performed with reasonable skill and care, the claimant suffered partial paralysis as a result. Skinner J. found that the second defendant had explained the nature of the operation to the claimant, had mentioned the possibility of disturbing a nerve root and its consequences, but had not mentioned the danger of damage to the spinal cord or the fact that this was an operation of choice rather than necessity. As to the operation, the judge found that the inherent dangers were damage to nerve roots and damage to the spinal cord. The risk of one or other occurring was between 1 and 2 per cent. Damage to the spinal cord was the less likely of the two risks but would lead to the worst consequences. Skinner J. found that the warning given by the second defendant was in accordance with accepted medical practice and, applying the *Bolam* test, dismissed the claim. The claimant appealed unsuccessfully both to the Court of Appeal[17] and to the House of Lords.[18]

The Court of Appeal, in affirming Skinner J.'s decision, unanimously applied the *Bolam* test. In the House of Lords a bare majority, namely Lord Diplock,[19] Lord Bridge[20] and Lord Keith[21] considered that the *Bolam* test was applicable to claims against medical practitioners for inadequate advice.[22] Thus it has now been finally established (albeit by a bare majority) that in negligence actions based upon the omission or inadequacy of any advice, explanation or warning given by the defendant in relation to proposed medical treatment, the *Bolam* test is to be applied. **12–211**

One merit of the *Bolam* test, as Lord Diplock observed,[23] is its flexibility. The duty of disclosure changes as medical knowledge advances and medical practices change. Indeed the duty of disclosure ought to change as public knowledge of medical matters increases,[24] since one factor which a reasonably careful and skilful doctor would take into account is the patient's capacity to understand the **12–212**

---

[17] [1984] Q.B. 493. For discussion of the Court of Appeal's decision, see M. A. Jones, "Doctor Knows Best?" (1984) 100 L.Q.R. 355; I. Kennedy, "The Patient on the Clapham Omnibus" (1984) 47 M.L.R. 454; T. Hodgkinson, "Medical Treatment: Informing Patients of Material Risks" [1984] P.L. 414.

[18] [1985] A.C. 871. For discussion of the House of Lords' decision, see A. Grubb, "Medical law, 'Informed Consent' to Medical Treatment: Who Decides, the Patient or Doctor?" (1985) 44 C.L.J. 199; H. Teff, "Consent to Medical Procedures: Paternalism, Self-Determination or Therapeutic Alliance?" (1985) 101 L.Q.R. 432.

[19] [1985] A.C. 871, 893–895.

[20] *ibid.* at 900.

[21] *Ibid.* at 895.

[22] Lord Templeman defined the duty of disclosure in different terms (at 904G), which may nevertheless lead to the same result as the *Bolam* test in many cases. Lord Scarman considered (at 885–890) that in actions for alleged inadequate warning by medical practitioners, the *Bolam* test should be discarded and that the principles enunciated by the United States Court of Appeals, District of Columbia Circuit in *Canterbury v. Spence* should be applied.

[23] [1985] A.C. 871, 892–893.

[24] The merits of the *Sidaway* decision, as well as the dangers of relying too heavily on the medical standard, were discussed by *The Times* in a leading article on the day after the House of Lords' decision: "Even today, patients are very often far readier to learn about their illness than doctors are ready to recognise; and better able to understand, too. Medical education, as well as habit and pressure of time, all tend to obstruct the development of a relationship of mutual respect and trust. The *Sidaway* case had established that there is no place in English law for a rigid doctrine of informed consent. But it has underwritten a high level of information and consultation as an essential part of good clinical practice today."

information he is given.[25] In the foreseeable future it is most unlikely that the House of Lords will be persuaded to depart from the view of the majority in *Sidaway v. Governors of Bethlem Royal Hospital*.[26]

12–213   The cases decided since *Sidaway* are helpful as illustrations of established principle.[27] The earlier cases[28] are also relevant, since they were generally decided on the *Bolam* test. Where the risks involved are relatively remote, the judgment of Bridge J. in *O'Malley-Williams v. Board of Governors of the National Hospital for Nervous Diseases*[29] is still relevant. Bridge J. stated that there were obvious disadvantages in warning a patient of such risks: "On the one hand you alarm him unnecessarily, on the other hand, you may put him in a position where he feels that he should take the decision, albeit the doctor is obviously much better qualified to weigh up the advantages and the desirability of the proposed operation as against the risks". Where the proposed operation or treatment is purely elective, it is submitted that this consideration carries less weight. If the proposed operation or treatment is not necessary for the patient's welfare (*e.g.* because the patient is being asked to participate in an experiment), it is difficult to conceive of any justification for withholding information concerning the known risks. The decision of the Court of Appeal in *Pearce v. United Bristol Healthcare NHS Trust*[30] is interesting in this context, as an example of the application of *Bolam*, subject to *Bolitho* scrutiny of the expert medical evidence (where the doctor had recommended non-intervention and conservative treatment). The claimant complained that she had not been advised of a risk of stillbirth in the event that her overdue baby was not induced or delivered by Caesarean section. Her doctor recommended that she waited for the delivery to

---

[25] The main criticisms of the use of the *Bolam* test in this area of the law come from those who seek objective rules defining the extent of the information to which a patient is entitled. See for example: M. A. Jones, "Doctor Knows Best?" (1984) 100 L.Q.R. 355. In "Consent to Medical Procedures: Paternalism, Self-Determination or Therapeutic Alliance?" (1985) 101 L.Q.R. 432, H. Teff argues that a greater measure of disclosure than that customarily made by doctors would assist in the formation of a "therapeutic alliance" between doctor and patient and would thus aid the treatment of the patient. For further academic criticism of Sidaway, see Giesen and Hayes, "The Patient's Right to Know—a Comparative View" (1992) An.-Am.L.R. 101; Professor Kennedy argues in "The Patient on the Clapham Omnibus" (1984) 47 M.L.R. 454 that there should be a duty (subject to certain defined exceptions) to disclose "any unusual and material risks inherent in the proposed treatment, and any feasible alternatives" and that the question of materiality should be decided by the court on the basis of the "prudent patient" test. Although academic debate on these questions continues, the direction of the law is probably now fixed (subject, of course, to legislation).

[26] [1985] A.C. 871.

[27] Examples include: *Moyes v. Lothian Health Board* 1990 SLT 444, (applying the *Bolam* test, it was held that the claimant had been adequately warned as to the small risk of stroke); *Gold v. Haringey Health Authority* [1988] Q.B. 481, CA, (the facts of which are discussed in para. 12–229, below); *Blyth v. Bloomsbury Health Authority* [1993] 4 Med. L.R. 151, CA (the facts of which are discussed in para. 12–225, below); *Smith v. Salford Health Authority* [1994] 5 Med. L.R. 321, (the facts of which are discussed at para.12–270, below); *Poynter v. Hillingdon Health Authority*(1997) 37 B.M.L.R. 192 (the *Bolam* test was applied as modified by the remarks of Lord Bridge in *Sidaway*, the facts of this case are discussed at para 12–219, below); *Newbury v. Bath District Health Autority* (1998) 47 B.M.L.R. 138, QBD (applying *Bolam* and *Bolitho*: on the facts and evidence, doctor under no duty to advise patient that his proposed surgical implant technique was unusual, and no duty to advise patient of alternative techniques available); *Williamson v. East London & City Health Authority* [1998] Lloyd's Rep. Med. 6 (damages were awarded for negligent failure to explain to the claimant that a more serious operation was required than that to which she had consented, even though she would have had the same operation in any event, albeit later).

[28] See, for examples, the cases discussed in paras 12–208, 12–209, above, and para. 12–227, below.

[29] (1985) 1 B.M.J. 635.

[30] [1999] P.I.Q.R. P53.

commence naturally. The risk materialised and the baby was stillborn. It was held that the *Bolam* test applies to the giving of advice or failure to give advice as to the risks attaching to both interventionist and conservative treatment but that, in the ordinary event, the patient should be informed of any significant risk which would affect the judgment of a reasonable patient in deciding between treatment options. "Significant risk" is a matter for expert medical evidence (subject to the court's review on *Bolitho* principles). In this case, the risk was regarded by the defendant's medical experts and by the court as of such a low magnitude as to be insignificant. Notwithstanding that the court stated that it was applying *Sidaway* in formulating the requirement of the standard of care, the formula suggested is very close to the "prudent patient" test adopted by the High Court of Australia in *Rogers v. Whittaker*.[31]

Specific considerations affecting what ought to be disclosed by a doctor advising upon treatment options are discussed below.   **12–214**

Explanation or warning curtailed because of the patient's condition or state of mind. It is self-evident that any duty of disclosure or warning must be curtailed where the patient is unfit to receive such disclosure or warning (for example due to the effect of his physical condition on his ability to understand at the time when the information is given, or due to his emotional or mental condition).[32] This is inherent in the *Bolam* test, and it is, in fact, what happened in the *Bolam* case itself.[33] One of the claims made was that the defendants were negligent in failing to warn patients of the dangers of electro-convulsive therapy (ECT) treatment. It was the practice of the doctors involved to say very little and to wait for questions from the patient. McNair J. directed the jury in these terms: "You may well think that when dealing with a mentally sick man and having a strong belief that his only hope of cure is ECT treatment, a doctor cannot be criticised if he does not stress the dangers which he believes to be minimal involved in that treatment."[34] The jury found in favour of the defendants.   **12–215**

In *Smith v. Salford Health Authority*[35] the defendant failed to communicate to the patient the risks of surgery. Potter J. found that even if the defendant had made an attempt to warn of those risks, such warning was not given in terms which were adequate to register with the patient, bearing in mind his condition at the time. He had a headache and was suffering the general ill-effects of a recent myelogram. In an extreme case, where the patient is semi-conscious and in need of urgent treatment to save his life, the most laconic communication may be deemed sufficient. The position is more difficult where the doctor considers it contrary to the patient's best interests to give him an accurate explanation or warning, even though the patient would be capable of understanding it. The Supreme Court of Canada has recognised that the emotional condition of the   **12–216**

---

[31] [1993] 4 Med. L.R. 79, 82–83, and see also paras 12–206 to 12–207, above. The court in *Rogers v. Whittaker*, however, put forward this formulation as an express departure from *Bolam* and *Sidaway*, which it declined to follow. The decision in *Pearce* has attracted considerable academic attention: see the commentary at [1999] 7 Med. L.Rev. 61 and Michael A. Jones, "Informed Consent and Other Fairy Stories" [1999] 7 Med. L.Rev. 103.

[32] See, for example, *Male v. Hopmans* (1967) 64 D.L.R. (2d) 105, Ontario CA.

[33] For the facts, see para. 12–093, above.

[34] [1957] 1 W.L.R. 582 at 590.

[35] [1994] 5 Med. L.R. 321.

patient and his fears relating to the operation may justify a surgeon in with-holding or generalising information.[36] In the New Zealand case *Smith v. Auckland Hospital Board*[37] a similar view was expressed. Woodhouse J. considered that the scope of the duty to advise was governed by the practice of competent and prudent doctors.[38] After reviewing a number of Commonwealth and American authorities, he stated:

> "As it seems to me, the paramount consideration is the welfare of the patient, and given good faith on the part of the doctor, I think the exercise of his discretion in the area of advice must depend upon the patient's overall needs. To be taken into account should be the gravity of the condition to be treated, the importance of the benefits expected to flow from the treatment or procedure, the need to encourage him to accept it, the relative significance of its inherent risks, the intellectual and emotional capacity of the patient to accept the information without such distortion as to prevent any rational decision at all, and the extent to which the patient may seem to have placed himself in his doctor's hands with the invitation that the latter accept on his behalf the responsibility for intricate or technical decisions."[39]

12–217   The medical practitioner may find it necessary on rare occasions not merely to withhold the truth but to tell a positive untruth. This occurred in *Hatcher v. Black*[40]: the second defendant, a surgeon, advised the claimant before an operation that there was no risk to her voice, when he knew that there was some slight risk. He did this for her own good, because it was of vital importance that she should not worry. Denning L.J. directed the jury in strong terms[41] that they should not regard this as negligence. The view has been expressed[42] that *Hatcher v. Black* should be regarded as wrong in the light of *Sidaway v. Governors of Bethlem Royal Hospital*.[43] It is submitted that this is not correct. Lord Diplock commented that, if questioned, "no doubt" the doctor would answer truthfully.[44] However, he did not say that this constituted a legal duty in every case. Lord Bridge said: "when questioned specifically by a patient of apparently sound mind about risks involved in a particular treatment proposed, the doctor's duty must, in my opinion, be to answer truthfully and as fully as the questioner requires."[45] However, this statement was *obiter*. *Hatcher v. Black* was not cited to or considered by the House of Lords in *Sidaway*. Even in this passage Lord Bridge

---

[36] See para. 12–202, above, and *Reibl v. Hughes* (1980) 114 D.L.R. (3d) 1, 13.

[37] [1964] N.Z.L.R. 241. The actual decision was reversed on other grounds (see [1965] N.Z.L.R. 191), but the views of Woodhouse J. on the duty of disclosure are widely cited.

[38] *ibid.* at 248.

[39] *ibid.* at 250.

[40] *The Times*, July 2, 1954. Lord Denning, *The Discipline of the Law* (Butterworths, 1979), pp. 242–244.

[41] "This, however, is not a court of morals but a court of law, and the law leaves this question of morals to the conscience of the doctor himself . . . it does not condemn the doctor when he only does that which many a wise and good doctor so placed would do. No one of the doctors that have been called before you has suggested that Mr. Tuckwell did wrong. All agree that it was a matter for his own judgment. They did not condemn him; nor should we."

[42] K. Williams, "Informed Consent or a Duty to Inform" (1985) 129 S.J. 195.

[43] [1985] A.C. 871.

[44] *ibid.* at 895C–D.

[45] *ibid.* at 898B–C. See now *Poynter v. Hillingdon Health Authority* (1997) 37 B.M.L.R. 192, QBD and *Pearce v. United Bristol Healthcare NHS Trust* [1999] P.I.Q.R. P.53.

accepted that there must be some exceptions to the duty of truthfulness, namely, where the patient is of unsound mind.

Duty to answer patient's questions. Following Lord Woolf M.R.'s judgment in *Pearce v. United Bristol Healthcare NHS Trust*[46] the starting point is that if a patient asks his doctor about a risk, the doctor's duty is to give an honest answer. If the patient is not of sound mind there may be an acceptable reason for not giving an honest answer. In most of the cases relating to inadequate warning or explanation discussed above, the patient himself did not ask specific questions. Where, however, the patient does ask specific questions, generally speaking he is entitled to accurate answers, so far as the doctor is able to give them.[47] **12–218**

In *Poynter v Hillingdon Health Authority*,[48] the claimant underwent a heart transplant at age 15 months. After induction of anaesthesia he suffered a cardiac arrest, which caused severe, permanent brain damage. The operation was otherwise successful. The parents claimed that the surgical team had failed to warn them of the risk of permanent brain damage, and that had they been so warned they would not have consented to the operation. The judge found the actual and foreseeable risk of brain damage was, at the time of the operation, less than 1 per cent. In deciding that the doctors did not owe a duty to the claimant to warn his parents of this risk, he took into account both what the doctors knew of the parents' views on transplants (they considered it unnatural and wrong) and the risks about which the parents had asked before giving their consent. He said that the doctors were entitled to emphasise the benefits of the treatment. He also said *obiter* that it was arguable that the defendant doctors would have been entitled deliberately to withhold information as to a relatively small risk of brain damage attaching to a heart transplant operation, for otherwise the parents' aversion to the operation might have prevented them from making a decision in the best interests of the child. He even considered it arguable that the doctors could have withheld that information in response to a specific question concerning that risk from the parents. However, since the parents had not asked about the specific risk that materialised, this opinion is also *obiter*. The case was decided in the defendant's favour because the judge accepted the defendant's expert evidence that in these circumstances there was a substantial and responsible body of medical opinion that would also not have disclosed the risk. There was nothing in the parents' questions to suggest that disclosure of the risk was so obviously necessary to an informed choice by them that no reasonably prudent doctor could have failed to make it.[49] **12–219**

The duty to advise in relation to the treatment of a minor patient was further considered in *Thompson v. Blake-James*.[50] The Court of Appeal there emphasised that the duty in such circumstances is to the child. Accordingly the doctor's obligation is to take reasonable care to see that the parents are in a position to make an informed decision as to treatment options which is in the patient's best **12–220**

---

[46] [1999] P.I.Q.R. P53 at P54.
[47] See the passages in *Sidaway v. Governors of Bethlem Royal Hospital* referred to at para. 12–217 and n. 41 above, and Lord Woolf M.R.'s judgment in *Pearce v. United Bristol Healthcare NHS Trust* [1999] P.I.Q.R. P53, P54. Contrast with Sir Maurice Drake's *obiter* comments in *Poynter v. Hillingdon Health Authority* (1997) 37 B.M.L.R. 192 (the facts of which are set out at para. 12–219 below).
[48] (1997) 37 B.M.L.R. 192.
[49] Applying Lord Bridge's *Sidaway* modification to the *Bolam* test.
[50] [1998] Lloyd's Rep. Med. 187.

interests. The doctor is not entitled to limit his advice because of the attitude of the parents to the treatment in question.[51]

12–221 However, a general enquiry by a patient about a drug does not impose on hospital staff an obligation to pass on all information available to the hospital about the drug.[52] In *Lee v. South West Thames Regional Health Authority*[53] the Court of Appeal expressed the view, *obiter*, that the duty to answer questions truthfully applied equally after treatment had been given. Thus, if some mishap had occurred, the patient was entitled to be given details.[54] A right to demand recorded information has been conferred by statute.[55] Under the Access to Health Records Act 1990, subject to certain limited exceptions, a person has a right of access to medical records relating to himself. The Act came into force on November 1, 1991. It does not apply to health records prepared before that date, save in so far as it is necessary to make subsequent health records intelligible.

12–222 **Warning required for patient's protection.** Different considerations altogether arise when a warning or explanation is necessary, not to satisfy the patient's curiosity, but to protect him against the inherent risks of the treatment.[56] In *Clarke v. Adams*[57] for example, the defendant, a physiotherapist, was treating the claimant for a fibrositic condition of the left heel. The instrument which he used was dangerous, because burns caused by it could lead to serious consequences. Before applying the treatment the defendant gave the claimant an approved form of warning.[58] Slade J. held that the warning was not adequate to convey to a reasonable person "that his safety depended on his informing the defendant the moment he felt more than a comfortable warmth". Accordingly the defendant was liable for the claimant's injuries. When the patient is being admitted to a hospital or similar institution, failure to inform him of a known risk of infection could also amount to negligence.[59] In some circumstances, it may be

---

[51] This decision was handed down in July 1997, three months after the decision of Sir Maurice Drake in *Poynter*. The Court of Appeal's guidance in *Pearce* and *Blake-James* suggests that the judge's *obiter* comments in *Poynter* were incorrect, and the approach to the withholding of information given to the parents should be limited to the facts of that case.

[52] *Blyth v. Bloomsbury Health Authority* [1989] 4 Med. L.R. 151.

[53] [1985] 1 W.L.R. 845, 850–851. Lord Donaldson M.R. reiterated these views in *Naylor v. Preston Area Health Authority* [1987] 2 All E.R. 353, 360.

[54] Sometimes there is a duty to volunteer such information, whether requested or not. See, for example, *Gerber v. Pines* (1935) S.J. 13: needle broke in the course of an injection. Held that the doctor who administered the injection was negligent in failing to inform the claimant or her husband what had happened on the day of the accident. Damages only 5 guineas.

[55] There is no absolute right of access to medical records at common law: see *R v. Mid Glamorgan Health Authority, ex parte Martin* [1994] 5 Med. L.R. 383, CA for the position in respect of medical records brought into being before November 1, 1991. The procedure for obtaining medical records under the clinical negligence protocol is contained in the CPR at C3–014 White Book, Spring 2001.

[56] See, for example, *Crichton v. Hastings* (1973) 29 D.L.R. (3d) 692 (failure to inform claimant of possible side effect of anti-coagulant drug, in the event of overdose or protracted use); contrast with *Webster v. Chapman* (1997) 155 D.L.R. (4th) 82 (no duty to advise patient of risk to foetus of anti-thrombotic drug, when patient told doctor she was using birth control). See *Major v. Wilcox*, (para. 12–176 above) for a failure to warn patient to seek further assistance if his condition worsened.

[57] (1950) 94 S.J. 599.

[58] As to which see para. 12–097, above.

[59] See, for example, *Marshall v. Lindsey County Court* [1935] 1 K.B. 516, CA; [1937] A.C. 97, H.L.

negligent not to warn a patient to take precautions for the protection of others.[60]

Manner and scope of communication.[61] The manner in which the doctor **12–223** communicates a warning or explanation may itself be critical.[62] In *Lybert v. Warrington Health Authority*[63] the claimant complained that she had not received an adequate warning of the risk of failure of an operation to sterilise her. It was found that a warning had been given but the claimant had not understood it. The Court of Appeal upheld the conclusion of the trial judge that a doctor must take reasonable care to give a warning which is adequate in scope, content and presentation and to take steps to see that his warning is understood. These requirements apply not only to information which the doctor has a duty to provide, but also to any additional information which he volunteers. The warning given to the claimant was given at an inappropriate time and under unsuitable conditions. It lacked sufficient emphasis and clarity, and the doctor had obtained no assurance that it was understood. Both the doctor and the health authority were liable, the latter on the grounds that it failed to institute an effective system to ensure that proper warnings were given in such cases. The case of *Smith v. Tunbridge Wells Health Authority*[64] illustrates that the doctor must bear in mind that his duty to warn is owed to the particular patient. He must take care to see that his explanation is sufficient in the light of the characteristics of that individual, so far as he knows or ought to appreciate them. The 24-year-old claimant was rendered impotent by an operation to repair a rectal prolapse. This was a recognised risk of the operation, but the defendant was liable for failing effectively to communicate the risk to the claimant. Morland J. said[65]:

"When recommending a particular type of surgery or treatment, the doctor, when warning of the risks, must take reasonable care to ensure that his explanation of the risks is intelligible to his particular patient. The doctor should use language, simple but not misleading, which the doctor perceives from what knowledge and acquaintanceship that he may have of the patient (which may be slight), will be understood by the patient so that the patient can make an informed decision as to whether or not to consent to the recommended surgery or treatment."

The doctor will owe no duty to advise about treatment options if he cannot **12–224** reasonably foresee that the patient will rely upon his advice. In *Thompson v. Blake-James*[66] the defendant general practitioner was consulted by the claimant's parents on the question whether she should be vaccinated against measles. The normal age for vaccination was the second year of life. At the time of the consultation, the claimant was less than one year old. Further, the defendant was aware that the claimant's family were shortly to move to another country, so that

---

[60] See para. 12–045, above.

[61] See also para. 12–215, above: Explanation or warning curtailed because of the patient's condition or state of mind.

[62] See *Bancroft v. Harrogate Health Authority* [1997] 8 Med. L.R. 398 (alleged psychiatric damage caused by the manner in which a consultant explained the claimant's condition and his proposed treatment to her: claim failed on the facts).

[63] [1996] 7 Med. L.R. 297.

[64] [1994] 5 Med. L.R. 334.

[65] *ibid.* at 339. See also *McAllister v. Lewisham and North Southwark Health Authority* [1994] 5 Med. L.R. 343 (to leave the claimant with the impression that she had nothing to lose by undergoing surgery was negligent).

[66] [1998] Lloyd's Rep. Med. 187.

another general practitioner would be involved in the ultimate decision whether the claimant should be vaccinated. The Court of Appeal held that, in those circumstances, it was not reasonably foreseeable by the defendant that his failure to inform the parents that an alternative method of vaccination might be suitable for the claimant would have any significant influence on their decision when the claimant reached the appropriate age.

12–225　**Side effects of drugs.** Even where the benefits of a drug outweigh the harmful side effects, it is good medical practice to inform the patient of the side effects, so that he understands the treatment which he is accepting. In *Goorkani v. Tayside Health Board*[67] the claimant, who had lost the sight of one eye, was given the drug chlorambucil to prevent deterioration in the other eye. He became infertile as a result of the drug. The Lord Ordinary held that the defendant was negligent in failing to warn the claimant of the risk of infertility, even though, properly advised, the claimant would have accepted the same treatment.[68] However, a concise statement of the risks and drawbacks is normally sufficient. The patient, especially one in pain or distress, will seldom welcome a medical lecture. In *Blyth v. Bloomsbury Health Authority*[69] the patient was a qualified nurse and made a general enquiry about Depo-Provera, a contraceptive with which she was to be injected. The Court of Appeal held that the hospital staff were not obliged to pass on to her all the information which was available to the hospital about the drug. Accordingly, the claimant's claim failed, even though she suffered from side-effects about which she had not been fully informed.[70] At the other end of the side effect spectrum, in *Shakoor v. Kang Situ*,[71] a practitioner of traditional Chinese herbal medicine was sued for negligence in failing to warn his patient of the risk of injury from ingesting a decoction of herbs which he supplied.[72] The patient died of liver failure following what was described as an "idiosyncratic reaction" to the herbs. Quite apart from the impossibility of predicting such a unique reaction, the judge dismissed the allegation of failure to warn and said:

> "An adverse reaction of the type which occurred is such a rare event that I do not believe that a doctor would be obliged to give a warning and, if a warning were to be given, the risk could legitimately have been presented as being so small that I do not believe that an appropriate warning would have had the effect of dissuading anyone, let alone the deceased, from taking the treatment."[73]

12–226　**Blood products.** Blood products give rise to special problems. They are known carriers of viral infection, but are highly necessary for certain groups of patients, notably haemophiliacs. The degree of risk varies, according to the type of blood product, whether it has been heat treated and so forth. It is good medical practice to inform the patient of the degree of risk involved. The extent of the

---

[67] 1991 S.L.T. 94 (Note).
[68] General damages were awarded for the claimant's distress and anxiety arising from his subsequent discovery of the possibility that he was infertile.
[69] (1987) [1993] 4 Med. L.R. 151.
[70] Contrast with a Canadian case, *Lacroix v. Dominique* (1999) 141 Man. R. (2nd) 1, where a doctor was negligent for not warning his patient of a 10% risk attached to anti-epileptic drugs of causing foetal abnormalities. The claim was dismissed on grounds of limitation.
[71] [2001] 1 W.L.R. 410, QBD, Bernard Livesey Q.C.
[72] Allegations of negligent failure to test liver function prior to treatment and failure to monitor liver function throughout treatment were not pursued at trial, however negligent prescription of the herb decoction was also alleged.
[73] *ibid.* 420F-G.

warning required is, of course, governed by the state of medical knowledge at the material time; and medical knowledge in this area (especially in relation to AIDS) has changed considerably over the last 20 years. In the group hepatitis C action the claimants had all been infected with hepatitis C via blood transfusions. Although the risk of such infection was known, it was impossible to avoid either because the virus had not been discovered or because there was no way of testing for its presence in the blood. The claimants' claims would have been defeated by this "knowledge of the time" defence (so far as they related to infections prior to the date on which detection and prevention of infection measures became available[74]) had they been brought in negligence. In *A and Others v. National Blood Authority*[75] the claimants succeeded on liability by bringing their claims under the Consumer Protection Act 1987 and a Directive[76] that imposed strict liability on the producer, subject to specific defences.[77] In Australia it has been held that the failure to warn a haemophiliac of the AIDS risk in September 1983 was negligent.[78] In Canada (applying the test referred to above[79]) the failure to warn a haemophiliac of the hepatitis risk has been held to be a breach of duty.[80]

Risk of failure of sterilisation. A sterilisation operation differs from most **12–227** other operations in two important respects. First, it is not generally a therapeutic operation. So the justification for not mentioning remote risks given by Bridge J. in *O'Malley-Williams v. Board of Governors of the National Hospital for Nervous Diseases*[81] would seem to have no application. Second, the patient needs to be warned of any risk of failure, not simply in order to decide whether to undergo the operation but also so that the patient and the patient's husband or wife may know how they stand thereafter. If the proposed form of sterilisation has a known risk of failure (whether 1 in 100 or 1 in 1,000), it is difficult to see any good reason why the patient should not be told. Thereafter it would be a matter for the patient and the patient's husband or wife to decide whether they wish to take any further precautions against so unlikely an eventuality. But these are arguments why medical practice might be expected to favour full disclosure. In the light of *Sidaway v. Governors of Bethlem Royal Hospital*[82] these considerations would not lead the courts to override established medical practice—unless it was considered that it could not withstand logical scrutiny.

---

[74] Either March 1, 1989 or March 1, 1990.

[75] [2001] 3 All E.R. 289, QBD.

[76] The Product Liability Directive (85/374/EEC), Art. 6.

[77] The judge held that "avoidability" (of a defect) was not one of the circumstances to be taken into account under Art. 6 since it fell outside the purpose of the Directive, which was intended to eliminate the requirement for proof of fault or negligence. The defence under Art. 7(e) of the Directive did not apply because the existence of the defect was known or should have been known, and it was therefore immaterial that the defect was unavoidable in the product. The purpose of the Directive could not have been to permit a producer, in the face of a known risk, to continue to supply his products without accepting the responsibility for any injuries resulting (by insurance or otherwise) simply because he was unable to identify in which of his products the defect would occur. See also para. 12–014, above.

[78] *H v. Royal Alexandra Hospital* [1990] 1 Med. L.R. 297. The claimant failed on causation.

[79] See paras 12–202 to 12–203, above.

[80] *Kitchen v. McMullin* [1990] 1 Med. L.R. 352.

[81] (1975) 1 B.M.J. 635. See para. 12–213, above.

[82] [1985] A.C. 871.

12–228   The first English decision on the question whether the patient should be warned of this risk is *Waters v. Park*.[83] The defendant carried out an operation for sterilisation on the claimant. Although there was a slight risk that the operation was not effective, Havers J. held that it was not negligent not to advise the claimant of this risk. To do so would cause her anxiety, and there were two schools of thought as to whether the claimant should be warned. In *Thake v. Maurice*[84] the defendant carried out a vasectomy on the first claimant. He told the first claimant and the second claimant (the wife) that the operation was irreversible, but he did not warn them, as was the fact, that there was a small risk of recanalisation. The defendant called no expert evidence as to medical practice[85] but the evidence was that it was his own usual practice to warn of this risk. Peter Pain J. held that the failure to warn the claimants of the risk of recanalisation was "a breach of the contractual duty of care", and the Court of Appeal upheld this part of the decision. The apparent conflict between *Waters v. Park* and *Thake v. Maurice* may be explicable by the lack of expert evidence as to medical practice in the latter case, or it may reflect a change in medical practice.[86]

12–229   In *Gold v. Haringey Health Authority*[87] the claimant underwent a sterilisation operation at the defendant's hospital on the day after her third child was born. She subsequently conceived and bore a further child. Schiemann J. held that the operation had been carried out with reasonable care, but that the defendant had been negligent in failing to warn the claimant about the failure rate of such operations (2 per 1000, or 6 per 1000 if carried out immediately after childbirth). The expert witnesses all said that they personally would have warned about the risk of failure, but that at the relevant time (1979) a substantial body of responsible doctors would not have given any such warning.[88] The judge held that the *Bolam* test only applied to therapeutic advice, and not to non-therapeutic (in this case contraceptive) advice. The judge applied his own judgment about what had been said, and concluded that the defendant ought to have warned the claimant about the failure rate. This decision was reversed on appeal. The Court of Appeal held that the *Bolam* test applies to both therapeutic and non-therapeutic advice.[89] On application of the *Bolam* test, it was held that the defendant was not liable. This decision has been criticised by legal writers,[90] but it would appear to be in line with the House of Lords' decision in *Sidaway v. Governors of Bethlem Royal Hospital*.[91] In Canada, a medical practitioner was held negligent for failing to warn his patient of the risk of failure of a sterilisation operation.[92] However, a special feature of that case was that an alternative method of sterilisation existed, which was more likely to be permanent and which the claimant (if warned about the risks of failure) might have chosen. In *F. v. R.*[93] the Supreme Court of South

---

[83] *The Times*, July 15, 1961.
[84] [1986] Q.B. 644.
[85] He was refused leave to call an expert, having served his report late.
[86] Alternatively, the decision in *Thake v. Maurice* may reflect the apparent "warranty" given by the surgeon concerned.
[87] [1988] Q.B. 481.
[88] *ibid*. at 486B.
[89] *ibid*. at 489F-H.
[90] See S. Lee, "A Reversible Decision on Consent to Sterilisation" (1987) 103 L.Q.R. 515; A. Grubb, "Contraceptive advice and doctors—a law unto themselves" [1988] C.L.J. 12.
[91] [1985] A.C. 871.
[92] *Dendaas v. Yackel* (1980) 109 D.L.R. (3d) 455, Supreme Court of British Columbia. But *cf. Grey v. Webster* (1984) 14 D.L.R. (4th) 706.
[93] (1983) 33 S.A.S.R. 189.

Australia distinguished the Canadian decision and held that the failure of the defendant (a specialist obstetrician and gynaecologist) to warn of a very small risk of failure of a sterilisation operation on the female claimant was not negligent. King C.J. stated:

> "I am of opinion that the better practice, and that which accords best with the rights and interests of the patient, is that adopted by those doctors who do warn of the possibility, however slight, of subsequent pregnancy. But . . . in the totality of the circumstances which I have discussed, and bearing in mind that the appellant was acting in pursuance of a considered judgment as to what was in the best interests of her patient and of a practice followed by a substantial part, probably the greater part, of those medical practitioners practising in this area of medical practice, I consider that her failure to volunteer the information as to the possibility of future pregnancy was not in breach of the legal duty of care."[94]

Recently, however, claimants have succeeded in establishing liability under this head. In *Newell and Newell v. Goldenburg*,[95] Mantell J. held that a vasectomist was negligent in 1985 in failing to warn of the risk of spontaneous recanalisation. It was the vasectomist's own normal practice to warn. He called experts who gave evidence that in 1985 there was a practice not to give such a warning. The defendant argued that, notwithstanding his own usual practice, he had complied with a practice approved by a responsible body of medical opinion. The judge rejected that contention, holding that such a practice was neither responsible nor reasonable. In *Lybert v. Warrington Health Authority*,[96] the Court of Appeal upheld a finding that although something had been said as to the risk of failure of a sterilisation, the doctor's warning had not been sufficiently clear and comprehensible to discharge his duty of care. In the unusual circumstances of that case,[97] the fact that the claimant had behaved as if she had not been warned made it inherently likely that no proper warning had been given.[98] **12–230**

Risk of disability of unborn baby. The development of techniques (such as ultra-sound scans and amniocentesis) for detecting defects in unborn babies has given rise to a new category of claim[99]: namely, that if the defendant had properly advised the claimant as to the condition of the foetus she was carrying, then the claimant would have had an abortion. Thus the defendant's negligence has **12–231**

---

[94] *ibid.* at 196.
[95] [1995] 6 Med. L.R. 371. Further examples of alleged failure to warn of the risk that sterilisation operations would not be successful include: *Eyre v. Measday* [1986] 1 All E.R.; *McLennan v. Newcastle Health Authority* [1992] 3 Med. L.R. 215; *Allan v. Greater Glasgow Health Board* (1993) 17 B.M.L.R. 135; *Stobie v. Central Birmingham Health Authority* (1994) 22 B.M.L.R. 135; *Gowton v. Wolverhampton Health Authority* [1994] 5 Med. L.R. 432.
[96] [1996] 7 Med. L.R. 71.
[97] See para. 12–279, below.
[98] [1996] 7 Med. L.R. 71, 74 *per* Otton L.J.
[99] See, for example, *Gregory v. Pembrokeshire Health Authority* [1989] 1 Med. L.R. 81 (negligent failure to advise that amniocentesis had produced insufficient cultures to allow for testing for Down's syndrome. The claimant failed on causation, because she probably would not have had another amniocentesis anyway); *Rance v. Mid-Downs Health Authority* [1991] Q.B. 587 (referred to in n. 88 at para. 12–278 below) (claimant failed both on negligence and causation); *Arndt v. Smith* [1996] 7 Med. L.R. 35 (first instance) and 108 (British Columbia CA) and [1997] 148 D.L.R. (4th) 48 (Supreme Court of Canada): negligent failure by general practitioner to warn of small but grave risks to foetus from mother's chickenpox held not causative because mother probably would not have had an abortion if warned.

"caused" the claimant to have a handicapped baby.[1] The liability issues in these cases usually are (i) what tests were or should have been done, and (ii) what inferences should have been drawn from the results of such tests. It is normally accepted that full disclosure of any defects discovered in the foetus should be made, since the prime object of the tests is to obtain information for the parents. In practice, therefore, the *Bolam* test in this situation is primarily relevant to the gathering of information, rather than to the extent of disclosure.[2]

12–232 **The evidential problem: what did the doctor say?** A recurrent problem in this kind of case is to establish, as a matter of fact, what explanation, warning or advice the doctor gave. Typically, the doctor himself has no recollection of the conversation in question and the best he can do is tell the court what he usually says in the particular circumstances. The patient, on the other hand, generally does have a recollection of the conversation, because it was an important event in his life and something he often thought about afterwards. Although the opportunity for "reconstruction", even by the most honest of claimants, is present, one would expect that, in evidential terms, the claimant begins with an advantage. A striking feature, however, of the reported cases is that more often than not the court has accepted the defendant's evidence as to his usual practice in preference to the claimant's direct recollection of the particular conversation: see *Chatterton v. Gerson*,[3] *Hills v. Potter*[4] and *Sidaway v. Governors of Bethlem Royal Hospital*.[5] In *Sidaway* Lord Scarman,[6] Lord Diplock,[7] Lord Bridge[8] and Lord Templeman[9] all expressed some surprise that the judge made such detailed findings as to what the second defendant said on the basis of evidence as to his

---

[1] This relatively new category of claim is discussed and criticised by P. R. Glazebrook, in "Capable of Being, But No Right to Be, Born Alive?" [1991] C.L.J. 241. Glazebrook argues that a claim by parents that their handicapped child should have been killed before birth is so offensive that the action should be struck out.

[2] See *Carver v. Hammersmith & Queen Charlotte's Special Health Authority*, unreported, February 25, 2000, QBD: defendant negligently failed to explain to the claimant that Bart's test did not detect one in three Down's syndrome babies and, as such was not diagnostic of Down's syndrome (like amniocentesis). The claimant succeeded on causation that had she known this she would have sought amniocentesis (privately if necessary), and would have terminated the pregnancy (since on the balance of probabilities the amniocentesis would have diagnosed her baby's Down's syndrome); *Rand v. East Dorset Health Authority* [2000] Lloyd's Rep. Med. 181 on similar facts, where a routine pregnancy scan disclosed the likelihood of a Down's syndrome baby, but the parents were not told, thereby depriving them of the opportunity to terminate the pregnancy. Negligence and causation were admitted. Contrast with *Mickle v. Salvation Army Grace Hospital* (1998) 166 D.L.R. (4th) 743, where the claimant parents failed on breach. The baby was born with asymmetrical limb development which was missed on ultrasound scan, but without negligence since no professional guidelines or customary practice required an examination of all of the limbs of a foetus. The claimants also failed on causation (the evidence did not support the parents' claim that they or a reasonable woman in their position would have terminated the pregnancy).

[3] [1981] 1 Q.B. 432, 437–438.

[4] [1984] 1 W.L.R. 641, 644 (Note).

[5] [1985] A.C. 871. See also *Ostby v. Bondar* [1998] 61 Alta. L.R. 341 at 347 where the doctor's evidence as to the warnings he gave as a matter of general practice was preferred (although both his recall and the claimant's was recognised as uncertain) largely due to the existence of his general practice and a note he had made at the time which simply recorded the words "prognosis guarded".

[6] *ibid.* at 877G–H.

[7] *ibid.* at 891D.

[8] *ibid.* at 896C–E.

[9] *ibid.* at 901G–902A.

usual practice. One case which went the other way is *Thake v. Maurice*[10] which concerned an operation for sterilisation. Peter Pain J. accepted the claimants' evidence that they were given no warning (or at least no clear warning) of the risk that the first claimant might become fertile again. The defendant gave evidence that it was his normal practice to give such a warning and the judge was satisfied that all the witnesses were being honest. However, in this case the claimants' evidence was corroborated by their subsequent conduct. The Court of Appeal upheld the judge's finding of fact on this issue. By contrast with solicitors' negligence cases, the Courts are not prepared to infer any causative want of care on the basis of poor note keeping,[11] but in a case concerning brain damage resulting from hypotension during anaesthesia, where the paucity of note taking led the experts to conclude that the anaesthesia record was sub-standard for the time, the Court of Appeal held that the note taking was : "(not) negligent in the legal sense but that it is indicative of an unexplained carelessness, whether in breach of a duty of care or not."[12] In *Taylor v. Shropshire Health Authority*,[13] the claimant failed to prove that she had not been warned of the risk of failure of a sterilisation operation (although she recovered damages on the basis that the operation had been negligently performed). In so finding, however, Popplewell J. was not assisted by the defendant's specific consent form for sterilisations, which stated that the claimant had been warned of the risk of failure and was signed by her. He regarded the form as "pure window dressing" on the facts of the case.

(g) *Mishandling of Mentally Disturbed Patients*

General The medical practitioner is, of course, obliged to exercise reasonable   **12–233** skill and care in the diagnosis and treatment of mental illness.[14] Thus in *Landau v. Werner*[15] a psychiatrist was held liable for unorthodox treatment of a patient in an anxiety state, which led to deterioration of her condition. In *Furber v. Kratter*[16] it was held that the staff of a mental hospital would be liable if they subjected a patient to an unduly harsh regime; indeed, in an extreme case, that might convert the patient's lawful detention under the Mental Health Act 1983 into unlawful imprisonment.[17]

---

[10] [1986] Q.B. 644. See, to similar effect, *Lybert v. Warrington Health Authority* [1996] 7 Med. L.R 71, CA; and a Canadian case: *Joyal v Starreveld* [1996] 37 Alta. L.R. 19, where the claimant's recollection evidence (of receiving no warning of risks associated with reducing anti-epileptic treatment) was preferred over the defendant doctor's evidence of his standard practice of warning.
[11] See *Faithfull v. Wiltshire Health Authority*, unreported, March 29, 2000, QBD, where the judge found that there was no substance to an allegation raised against a midwife of generally poor care based on her admitted poor note keeping.
[12] *Skelton & Lewisham & North Southwark Health Authority* [1998] Lloyd's Rep. Med. 324, the claimant succeeded in his claim against the anaesthetists.
[13] [1998] Lloyd's Rep. Med. 395.
[14] See, for example, *Mahmood v. Siggins* [1996] 7 Med. L.R. 76 and, generally, Powers & Harris, chap. 31.
[15] (1961) 105 S.J. 257 and 1008. See para. 12–107, above.
[16] *The Times*, July 21, 1988.
[17] See *R. v. Bournewood Community and Mental Health NHS Trust, ex p. L* [1999] 1 A.C. 458, HL: patient lacking mental capacity to consent or refuse treatment had not been unlawfully imprisoned. His "detention", such as it was, in an unlocked ward under the Mental Health Act s.131(1), had been justified by the common law doctrine of necessity.

12–234   **The Code of Practice.** Section 118 of the Mental Health Act 1983 requires the Secretary of State to prepare, and lay before Parliament, a code for the guidance of medical practitioners and others in relation to the admission of patients to mental hospitals and nursing homes and in relation to the medical treatment of patients suffering from mental disorder. The code may be altered from time to time, and any alterations must be laid before Parliament. When preparing the code, or any alteration, the Secretary of State is required to consult "such bodies as appear to him to be concerned".[18] The code contains statements of principle and guidance, but is seldom dogmatic. If a medical practitioner departs from the code, this fact could be relied upon as evidence of negligence, but would not in itself be conclusive.[19]

12–235   **Statutory restrictions on proceedings.** Section 139(1) of the Mental Health Act 1983 provides that no person shall be liable for any acts done pursuant to the Act,[20] unless those acts were done "in bad faith or without reasonable care". Since absence of reasonable care is a necessary ingredient of the tort of negligence, this section affords no real protection against claims of the kind discussed above. More substantial protection is derived from section 139(2), which provides that no proceedings shall be brought against any person for acts done pursuant to the Act without the leave of the High Court. However, section 139(2) of the Mental Health Act 1983 differs from its predecessor (section 141(2) of the Mental Health Act 1959) in one important respect. Section 141(2) of the 1959 Act stated that the High Court should not give such leave "unless satisfied that there is substantial ground for the contention that the person to be proceeded against has acted in bad faith or without reasonable care". These words are omitted from section 139(2) of the 1983 Act, but no new criteria for the grant or refusal of leave are stated in their place. The effect of this change in wording was considered by the Court of Appeal in *Winch v. Jones*[21] Sir John Donaldson M.R. said that section 139(2) was intended to strike a balance between the legitimate interest of the applicant to be allowed to pursue a claim which was not frivolous or vexatious, and the equally legitimate interest of the respondent not to be subjected to the undoubtedly exceptional risk of being harassed by baseless claims. The Master of the Rolls said that the issue on an application for leave under section 139(2) was "whether on the material available to the court, including that furnished by the respondent, the applicant's complaint appeared to be such that it deserved the fuller investigation which would be possible if she

---

[18] Mental Health Act 1983, s.118(3). The preparation of the code gave rise to considerable controversy (an account of the negotiations leading up to the adoption of the code is given in P. Fennell, "The Mental Health Act Code of Practice" (1990) 53 M.L.R. 499) and it was not until December 1989 that a draft was laid before Parliament. Neither House passed a resolution requiring it to be withdrawn under s.118(4) and therefore in 1990 the Code of Practice was adopted.

[19] See the discussion of the *Bolam* test in para. 12–068, above.

[20] The ambit of the Mental Health Act 1959, s.141 (the predecessor of the Mental Health Act 1983, s.139) and the nature of the acts to which it applies were considered in *R. v. Bracknell JJ., ex p. Griffiths* [1976] A.C. 314. In *R. v. Runighian* (1977) Crim. L.R. 361, Judge Harrison-Hall held that the section does not apply to proceedings instituted by informal patients (*i.e.* patients admitted under the Mental Health Act 1959, s.5, now the Mental Health Act 1983, s.131), see *R. v. Bournewood Community and Mental Health NHS Trust, ex p. L* [1999] 1 A.C. 458 for an example of proceedings brought by a patient admitted under s. 131.

[21] [1986] Q.B. 296.

was allowed to proceed."[22] In *Furber v. Kratter*[23] Henry J. considered arguments as to the legal validity of the claimant's claim against mental hospital staff in the context of an application under section 139. He decided that, on the facts alleged, the claim was well founded in law, alternatively that it was eminently arguable, and accordingly granted leave.[24]

Prevention of self-inflicted injury and suicide. A particular problem with   **12–236**
mentally disturbed patients is that they may need to be protected against themselves. Defendant health authorities or hospitals may be held liable for failing properly to supervise a suicidal patient, the question is whether or not the defendant exercised reasonable care.[25] It has been accepted that a greater degree of care and supervision is required in relation to patients who were suicide risks. However, not every suicide threat has to be taken seriously. It is for the medical staff to decide in each case whether stricter supervision is called for or whether the threat is merely hysterical and, as such, could be largely or even entirely ignored.[26]

The first case to come before the Court of Appeal concerning attempted   **12–237**
suicide was *Hyde v. Tameside Area Health Authority.*[27] The claimant was not being treated for mental illness in a mental hospital, he was being treated in a general hospital for a physical disability. He became depressed during the course of treatment and jumped out of a window, suffering grave, but not fatal, injuries. On the particular facts, the claim that the hospital staff were negligent in failing to prevent the incident was rejected. Lord Denning M.R. also expressed the view that it should be the policy of the law to discourage medical negligence actions

---

[22] *Winch v. Jones* was distinguished on the facts in *James v. London Borough of Havering* (1992) 15 B.M.L.R. 1, CA. Farquarson L.J. suggested that the question was whether the claimant had made out a prima facie case that the doctor had acted without reasonable care: *ibid.* at 4.

[23] *The Times*, July 21, 1988.

[24] See also *Bailey v. Gallagher* [1996] 2 I.L.R.M. 433, the defendant general medical practitioner certified admission of the claimant to a psychiatric hospital under the Mental Treatment Act 1945 (the equivalent Irish statute). To the defendant's knowledge, the certificate was not activated until some time later. By that time, the statutory period of validity had expired. The Irish Supreme Court held that there was no evidence to suggest that the defendant was guilty of bad faith or want of reasonable care in signing the certificate. However, it was his duty to be alive to the legal consequences of expiry of the certificate's validity and so, since he was aware that the certificate was being activated, he had a duty to ascertain whether it was still in force. His failure to do so amounted to want of reasonable care and the claimant was granted leave to bring an action against him for negligence.

[25] See *Selfe v. Ilford & District Hospital Management Committee, The Times*, November 26, 1970. (The patient was put in a ground floor ward with 26 other patients, three of whom were suicide risks. There was an unlocked window at the back of his bed. The judge considered that supervision by an "absolute minimum" of three nurses was required. There were three nurses on duty at the material time. However, two had left the ward for various reasons and the third was attending to a patient. The claimant slipped out through the window and threw himself from a roof, suffering serious injuries.); see also *Hay v. Grampian Health Board* [1995] 6 Med. L.R. 128 (Scottish Court of Session) (health board held liable to a depressive in-patient who suffered brain damage following a suicide attempt for failing to maintain the system of close observation which it had properly instituted); compare with *Thorne v. Northern Group Hospital Management Committee* (1964) 108 S.J. 115; *The Times*, June 6, 1964, the defendants escaped liability for the suicide of a patient, because they had exercised reasonable care.

[26] See Edmund Davies J. in *Thorne v Northern Group Hospital Management Committee, ibid.* See also *Stadel v. Albertson* [1954] 2 D.L.R. 328 (doctors not put on notice of the patient's suicidal tendencies). *Cf. Mahmood v. Siggins* [1996] 7 Med. L.R. 76 (general practitioner who failed to carry out an adequate mental examination of a manic depressive patient and failed to refer him for specialist assessment was liable for his injuries when he leapt from a third floor window. The doctor had not appreciated the possible significance of the patient's complaint of explosive feelings.)

[27] *The Times*, April 16, 1981; (1986) 2 P.N. 26.

by persons who had attempted unsuccessfully to commit suicide.[28] However, these observations were obiter and were doubted by the Court of Appeal in *Kirkham v. Chief Constable of Greater Manchester Police*.[29] In that case the police were held liable for failing to take reasonable care to prevent a man in custody, of known suicidal tendencies, from committing suicide. The doctrine of *volenti non fit injuria* did not apply, since the deceased was suffering from clinical depression at the time of his suicide. Lloyd L.J held,[30] applying *McGhee v. National Coal Board*,[31] that causation was proved if the claimant showed that the failure to take precautions had materially increased the risk of a suicide attempt. The reasoning of Edmund-Davies J. in *Thorne v. Northern Group Hospital Management Committee* was applied by the Court of Appeal in *Gauntlett v. Northampton Health Authority*.[32] In that case a mental hospital patient, whilst walking unaccompanied to the washroom, set fire to her T-shirt and sustained injuries. The court held that even if an earlier incident involving matches had been recorded, this would probably not have led to the claimant being accompanied by a nurse on every occasion when she went to the washroom. The claimant failed both on negligence and causation. However, where the claimant can show that the defendant failed to diagnose a mental illness (thereby taking a course which no responsible body of medical opinion, in the light of that was known at the time would have taken[33]) resulting in a failure appropriately to treat and a failure to perceive the suicide risk, the claimant will be likely to succeed in a claim for injuries resulting from self-harm.[34]

12–238   **Liability for criminal offences.** It is not open to a mental patient who had committed a serious criminal offence to sue a health authority for negligent failure to treat him so as to prevent the offence, and thereby keep him safe from the consequences of the offence that he has committed. The claimant in *Clunis v. Camden and Islington Health Authority*[35] had a history of mental illness. Three months after he was discharged from hospital into the care of the defendant authority, he killed a man in a sudden and unprovoked attack. He was convicted

---

[28] "Though suicide was no longer a crime, it was still unlawful, and his Lordship felt it was most unfitting that the personal representatives of a suicide should be able to claim damages in respect of his death. An attempted suicide should be in no better position when he did not succeed. . . . The policy of the law should be to discourage such actions. His Lordship would disallow them altogether, at the outset, rather than burden the community with them."

[29] [1990] 2 Q.B. 283, *per* Lloyd L.J. at 289G–290B, Farquharson L.J. at 295E–296D, Sir Denys Buckley at 296E–297C.

[30] *ibid.* at 289E.

[31] [1973] 1 W.L.R. 1.

[32] For further discussion of these issues, see M. Jones, "Saving the Patient from Himself" (1990) 6 P.N. 107. This article reviews the English and Canadian cases on suicide. Jones notes that the philosophical conundrum of attributing responsibility in negligence for self-inflicted harm is touched on only tangentially in the courts' discussion of causation, *ex turpi causa* and *volenti*. The conclusion is that the defendant will not be held liable for the suicide of someone who is wholly sane, but can be held liable where the deceased suffered from some form of mental illness or instability.

[33] Applying the *Bolam* test.

[34] See *Drake v. Pontefract Health Authority* [1998] Lloyd's Rep. Med. 425, QBD. The defendant's psychiatric team failed to diagnose that the claimant's illness included a major depressive element which carried with it a serious risk of suicide. As a consequence of this non-diagnosis, the psychiatric team failed to administer appropriate drug therapy to treat the claimant's agitated depression, and failed adequately to observe the claimant (who left the hospital unattended). The lack of each precaution materially contributed to her attempted suicide, and the defendant health authority was liable for her injuries and damage caused thereby.

[35] [1998] Q.B. 978.

of manslaughter on a plea of diminished responsibility. He alleged that the health authority had negligently failed to arrange for his mental health to be assessed before the incident. The result of an assessment would have been his detention in hospital. He claimed damages for deterioration in his mental health as a result of the incident and for his sentence as a potentially life-long secure mental patient. He also claimed an indemnity against damages which he might be ordered to pay the victim's family. The Court of Appeal struck out the claim, holding that public policy prevented recovery for the consequences of the claimant's own criminal act.[36] His plea of diminished responsibility meant that he must be taken to have known what he was doing and that it was wrong. It was not a plea of insanity—which would have been a plea of "not guilty". The court left open the possibility of recovery where it could be shown that the claimant did not know the nature and quality of his act or that what he had done was wrong—*i.e.* if he had been not guilty by reason of insanity.[37]

Negligent issue of certificates. An application for the compulsory admission   **12–239** of a patient into hospital under Part II of the Mental Health Act 1983 must be supported by the written recommendation of two medical practitioners.[38] It has long been established that in giving any such certificate the medical practitioner owes a duty of care to the person concerned, whether or not that person is his patient. In *Hall v. Semple*[39] Crompton J. directed the jury:

> "If a medical man assumes under this statute the duty of signing such a certificate without making, and by reason of his not making, a due and proper examination, and such enquiries as are necessary, and which a medical man under such circumstances ought to make and is called on to make, not in the exercise of the extremest possible care, but in the exercise of ordinary care, so that he is guilty of culpable negligence, and damage ensue; then ... an action will lie, although there has been no spiteful or improper motive, and though the certificate is not false to his knowledge."[40]

The question of whether or not a duty of care was owed by the doctor in such circumstances was raised in *Everett v. Griffiths*[41] and *Harnett v. Fisher*[42] although in the former case it was held that the doctor was not negligent and in the latter case that the claim was statute-barred. It is noteworthy, however, that Lord

---

[36] The claim was also struck out on the basis that there is no private law cause of action for failure to carry out duties imposed by s.117 of the Mental Health Act 1983 (which section sets out the health authority's obligations concerning aftercare to a discharged mental hospital patient). In reaching this conclusion the Court of Appeal relied on the House of Lords' decision in *X (Minors) v Bedfordshire County Council* [1995] 2 A.C. 633, that exceptionally clear statutory language would be needed to show that Parliament intended to impose a liability in damages for breach of statutory duty in that case. In the light of the the subsequent decisions in *Barrett v. Enfield LBC* [1999] 3 W.L.R. 79 and *Phelps v Hillingdon Borough Council* [2000] 3 W.L.R. 776 that it could not be said that a local authority could never be liable in negligence for damage resulting from failures to fulfill statutory obligations, it may be that this part of the decision is now less authoritative.

[37] For a detailed consideration of this decision see M. A. Jones, "The Violent Mentally Disordered Patient: Who Cares?" (1998) 14 P.N. 99.

[38] Mental Health Act 1983, s.3(3).

[39] (1862) 3 F. & F. 337.

[40] *ibid.* at 355.

[41] [1920] 3 K.B. 163, CA; [1921] 1 A.C. 631, HL.

[42] [1927] A.C. 73. See also *De Freville v. Dill* (1927) 96 L.J.K.B. 1056, where the jury found that the defendant had negligently issued a certificate that the claimant was of unsound mind, with the result that she was detained in a mental hospital overnight.

Browne-Wilkinson in *X (Minors) v. Bedfordshire County Council*[43] and the Court of Appeal in *Clunis v. Camden and Islington Health Authority*[44] considered, *obiter*, that the question had not been decided in *Everett v. Griffiths* and that the question of whether a doctor owes a duty of care to a patient in certifying that the patient is fit to be detained under the Mental Health Acts, remains open for decision.

12–240   In the Canadian case of *Haines v. Bellisimo*[45] the widow of a patient (H) who had committed suicide brought a claim under the Fatal Accidents Act against the psychologist (B) and the psychiatrist (C) who had been responsible for his treatment. Shortly before his death the patient had bought a shotgun. This was reported to the defendants. B then interviewed H for the purpose of making a complete reassessment. He persuaded H to give up the gun and H indicated that he had no present suicide plans. B then decided not to take H into hospital but to continue outpatient treatment. On the particular facts it was held that neither defendant had been negligent. On the question whether B was negligent not to hospitalise H, Griffiths J. acknowledged that there were advantages and disadvantages of each course which had to be weighed up:

> "Obviously, if the therapist feels that there is a real risk of suicide or is in doubt about this, he should opt for hospitalisation. On the other hand, modern psychiatry recognises that close observation, restrictions, and restraint of the patient may be anti-therapeutic and aggravate the feelings of worthlessness which, in themselves, intensify the risk of suicide."[46]

The Ontario Court of Appeal adopted similar reasoning in *Larche v. Ontario*.[47] The claimant, a patient in a minimum security psychiatric hospital, climbed onto the roof of a hospital building in search of a frisbee. He fell and suffered injuries. The hospital was held not liable. The Court considered that, despite the risk, the open setting for a minimum security psychiatric hospital was justified because of the therapeutic benefit of treatment in that setting.

3. DAMAGES

12–241   **General.** An award of damages is the normal remedy sought for breach of duty by a medical practitioner whether the claim is brought in contract or tort. If the medical practitioner is privately retained by the patient and if, as a result of the breach of duty, his services are valueless, he would also be debarred from

---

[43] [1995] 2 A.C. 633 at 753G.
[44] [1998] Q.B. 978 at 993A-B.
[45] (1978) 82 D.L.R. (3d) 215.
[46] *ibid.* at 233. See also *Ganger v. St Paul's Hospital* (1997) 40 B.C.L.R. 116, British Columbia CA. The claimant was unable to show that hospital staff had negligently assessed his mood before allowing him to leave a ward to which he had been transferred for observation after expressing suicidal thoughts. The fact that a treating psychiatrist erred in a risk assessment did not prove negligence. The claimant's claim for damages for injuries suffered in his subsequent suicide attempt failed; *Clinton v. Regina District Health Board and Gellner* (1998) 171 Sask. R. 44, Saskatchewan Court of Queen's Bench. The defendant hospital and doctor were not negligent. On the facts there did not seem to be any risk of imminent suicide, and therefore the patient could not have been apprehended under the Mental Health Services Act.
[47] (1990) 75 D.L.R. (4th) 377. See further Chap. 3, para. 3–06–3–08, above.

recovering his fees or ordered to repay any fees which he has received from the patient.[48]

(a) *Remoteness*

The assessment of damages is subject, in every case, to the overriding principle that the injury in respect of which compensation is sought must be sufficiently proximate to the medical practitioner's breach of duty. Broadly speaking, this means that: **12–242**

(a) the breach of duty must have "caused" the injury[49] and

(b) the injury in question must have been foreseeable.[50]

(i) *Causation*

Whether the claim is brought in contract or tort, it is first necessary to determine whether the medical practitioner's breach of duty was the sole or substantial "cause" of the injury complained of, or that it materially contributed to the injury or damage. The "but for" test is often determinative of causation but it does not invariably yield the right answer. Thus in *Bonnington Castings Ltd v. Wardlaw*[51] Lord Reid stated: **12–243**

> "It would seem obvious in principle that a pursuer or plaintiff must prove not only negligence or breach of duty but also that such fault caused or *materially contributed* to his injury, and there is ample authority for that proposition both in Scotland and in England. . . . What is a material contribution must be a question of degree. A contribution which comes within the exception *de minimis non curat lex* is not material, but I think that any contribution which does not fall within that exception must be material."[52]

If there is a range of possible causes for the injury, and it was merely possible that the injury was caused by the breach of duty, the claimant will fail to prove his case that the breach was the cause of the injury.[53]

The limiting effect of the scope of the duty. In *Rogers v. Whitaker*[54] the New South Wales Court of Appeal suggested the hypothetical example of a patient injured by a crashing aircraft whilst undergoing an operation. If the medical practitioner had negligently advised the operation, it might be said that "but for" such negligent advice, the claimant would not have been injured. Moreover, the type of damage suffered (personal injury) would have been foreseeable. However, the medical practitioner should not be held liable in that situation, since his **12–244**

---

[48] See Chap. 8, para. 8–132, above.
[49] As to which, see paras 12–243 to 12–281, below.
[50] As to which see paras 12–282 to 12–286, below.
[51] [1956] AC 613, HL.
[52] *ibid.* at 620 (emphasis added).
[53] See *Wilsher v. Essex Area Health Authority* [1988] A.C. 1074.
[54] [1992] 3 Med. L.R. 331.

duty does not extend to protecting patients from extraneous or fortuitous accidents.[55] In *R. v. Croydon Health Authority*[56] the Court of Appeal held that, even were the claimant to be regarded as having suffered damage by the conception, birth and upbringing of a healthy and wanted child (which she was not), such damage was outside the scope of the defendant radiologist's duty. He had been consulted in relation to her prospect of employment and his duty did not extend to her private life.[57]

12–245   **Where the damage would have occurred in any event.** If the damage would have occurred in any event,[58] it was not caused by the medical practitioner's breach of duty.[59] In *Barnett v. Chelsea & Kensington Hospital Management Committee*,[60] for example, it was held that a hospital casualty officer was negligent in failing to see and examine a patient who was complaining of vomiting. However, even if the patient had been examined by the casualty officer it appeared on the balance of probabilities that he would still have died. Therefore the defendants' negligence did not cause the patient's death and the claim was dismissed. Similarly, in *Fish v. Kapur*[61] it was held that no loss flowed from the defendant's failure to diagnose a broken jaw, because (even if he had diagnosed it) there was no treatment which he could have given.[62] The same

---

[55] This discussion was *obiter* and was not considered by the High Court (whose decision is summarised in para.12–206, above). See also the mountaineer example given by Lord Hoffman in *Banque Bruxelles Lambert SA v. Eagle Star Insurance Co. Ltd* [1997] A.C. 191 at 213D discussed at Chap. 9, paras 9–113 *et seq.*, above.

[56] [1998] Lloyd's Rep. Med. 44. See para. 12–066, above, for the facts.

[57] See also the unreported case of *O'Reilly v. Whittington Hospital NHS Trust*, H.H.J. Mackay, sitting as a deputy judge of the QBD, March 17, 2000; and *Brown v. Lewisham and North Southwark H.A.* [1999] 4 Lloyd's Rep. Med. 110 at 118, referred to in para. 12–018, n. 43, above.

[58] See, for example, *Kay v. Ayrshire and Arran Health Board* [1987] 2 All E.R. 417, HL: appellant, being treated for meningitis at respondent's hospital, was given a greatly excessive dose of penicillin and subsequently went deaf. Deafness was caused by the meningitis, not the excessive penicillin. See also *Marsden v. Bateman* [1993] 4 Med. L.R. 181 (brain damage in infant caused not by failure to diagnose and treat hypoglycaemia but by defective development at the foetal stage); *De Martell v. Merton and Sutton Health Authority (Liability) (No.2)* [1995] 6 Med. L.R. 234 (cerebral palsy caused by abnormal foetal development and not by midwife's negligent delay in summoning a doctor to a difficult delivery); *Richardson v. Kitching* [1995] 6 Med. L.R. 257 (negligent failure to diagnose an ear tumour not causative because the prospects of success of an earlier operation would not have been significantly different); *Robertson v. Nottingham Health Authority* [1997] 8 Med. L.R. 1 (claimant's brain damage was caused some time before mother's admission to hospital and culpable delay in delivery by Caesarean section did not contribute materially);*Oksuzoglu v. Kay & Another* [1998] 2 All E.R. 361 (amputation of leg for treatment of malignant tumour was not caused by doctor's negligent failure to refer to hospital, amputation was inevitable); Canadian cases: *Egedebo v. Windermere District Hospital* (1993) 78 B.C.L.R. (2d) 63 (paralysis already irreversible before its cause was negligently misdiagnosed and treated); *MacWilliam v. Jeffrey* (1993) 127 N.B.R. (2d) 113 (condition of claimant's mouth was unrelated to dental work performed by the defendant dentist); *Moore v. Castlegar & District Hospital* (1996) 25 B.C.L.R. 188 (RTA caused spinal injury, not care and management at defendant hospital); *Tailleur v Grande Prairie General and Auxiliary Hospital* (1999) 74 Atla. L. R. 20, CA (gangrene infection led to amputation of leg following severed Achilles tendon injury; no evidence that use of a different cast type would have resulted in earlier detection of gangrene, and insufficient evidence that hospitalisation without cast would have led to different result).

[59] See further, Hart and Honore, *Causation in the Law*, second ed., pp. 247–248.

[60] [1969] 1 Q.B. 42. See para. 12–173, above.

[61] [1948] 2 All E.R. 176.

[62] In *Sharpe v. Leicestershire Health Authority* [1994] C.L.Y. 1535 the defendant admitted negligence by failure to treat a fractured finger with the accepted treatment, but denied loss since the claimant made a better recovery that he would have done with the accepted treatment. The claim was settled by acceptance of a payment in.

reasoning was applied by Ashworth J. and approved by the Court of Appeal in *Robinson v. Post Office*[63]: the second defendant decided (quite properly) to give the claimant an injection of anti-tetanus serum (ATS). Where the patient has had a previous dose of ATS (as had the claimant) it is essential that he should first have a test dose. The recognised procedure at the material time was to wait half an hour after the test dose to see if there was any reaction. The second defendant only waited for a minute between giving the test dose and the full dose. It was held that the second defendant was negligent only to wait a minute, but that even if he had waited half an hour no reaction would have appeared. Accordingly, the claim against him was dismissed. In cases where the claimant suffers from cancer, it is often difficult to determine what damage has been caused by late diagnosis, owing to divisions of opinion within the medical profession. In *Sutton v. Population Services Family Planning Programme Ltd*[64] it was held that if the claimant's cancer had been diagnosed at the proper time, its recurrence would have been postponed by four years. She recovered damages for four years' loss of earnings, four years' lost expectation of life and premature onset of the menopause.[65]

Concurrent causes of injury In *Baker v. Willoughby*[66] the effects of the first **12–246** tort which caused injury to the claimant's leg were obliterated by the second tort which resulted in amputation of the leg, but the House of Lords held that the damages flowing from the first tort should not be reduced. The principle was doubted by the House of Lords in *Jobling v. Associated Dairies*.[67] The claimant suffered a back injury at work. Prior to trial he was diagnosed with an unconnected disease which would have prevented his return to work in any event. The latter (non-tortious) event was taken into account to reduce the damages he obtained for his back injury. In *Heil v. Rankin*[68] the Court of Appeal held that the principle that had developed whereby the occurrence of a second tort would be ignored when awarding damages against the first tortfeasor could not be justified on any juridical basis and that there was no general rule that supervening tortious (as compared with non-tortious) acts must be ignored in all circumstances when assessing damages. However, in some circumstances the second act may be ignored for purely pragmatic reasons to ensure just and full compensation is secured for the claimant, alternatively the court can award damages against each defendant that reflect the losses caused by that defendant alone, and apportion the liability for losses caused by both. This was the approach used by the Court of Appeal in *Rahman v Arearose Ltd*.[69] The claimant was violently assaulted at work by two black youths, for which assault his employers, the first defendants, were found liable. He was admitted to the second defendant's hospital and underwent eye surgery. Through the second defendant's (admitted) negligence he lost the sight of this eye. The claimant developed post traumatic stress disorder, a severe depressive disorder of psychotic intensity, a specific phobia of Afro-

---

[63] [1974] 1 W.L.R. 1176.
[64] *The Times*, November 7, 1981.
[65] See also paras 12–251 to 12–258, below.
[66] [1970] A.C. 67.
[67] [1982] A.C. 794.
[68] [2001] Q.B. 272.
[69] [2001] Q.B. 351.

Caribbean people and a personality change. The expert evidence enabled the Court to attribute the PTSD, the depressive disorder (and the personality change) largely to the loss of the eye and the specific phobia to the assault. Since each defendant's acts had caused distinct parts of the claimant's overall psychiatric condition, neither had caused all of it.[70] Whilst the second defendant had caused the claimant's blindness, the claimant's overall suffering had been caused by both defendants, and both should bear the damages claim, 75 per cent by the second defendant, 25 per cent by the first defendant, with some adjustments for specifically attributable heads of damage.

12–247   **Burden of proof.** Since it is a necessary element in his claim, the burden normally rests upon the claimant to show that he would not have suffered the injury or damage complained of if the defendant had not been negligent. Where, however, the defendant's negligence simply had the effect of increasing the risk of that injury or damage occurring, the question whether the defendant's negligence really "caused" the injury or damage becomes highly speculative. By coincidence, this problem was discussed in Canada and England at approximately the same time. Both Hinds J. in *Wipfli v. Britten*[71] and Peter Pain J. in *Clark v. MacLennan*[72] considered that the claimant could rely on the principle of *McGhee v. National Coal Board*[73] in this situation. Applying this principle, Peter Pain J. said: "Where there is a failure to take a precaution, and that very damage occurs against which the precaution is designed to be a protection, then the burden lies on the defendant . . . to show that the damage did not result from his breach of duty."[74] However, this approach was rejected by the House of Lords in *Wilsher v. Essex Area Health Authority*.[75] In that case the claimant was born prematurely and given extra oxygen to enable him to survive. The catheter to monitor oxygen levels was wrongly inserted into the umbilical vein instead of the umbilical artery, with the result that excessive oxygen was given to the claimant during the first 36 hours. The claimant developed retrolental fibroplasia (RLF) which resulted in blindness. RLF could be caused either by prematurity or by excessive oxygen. Peter Pain J. and the Court of Appeal, applying the *McGhee* principle, found in favour of the claimant, but the decision was reversed by the House of Lords. Lord Bridge (with whom Lords Fraser, Lowry, Griffiths and Ackner agreed) reasoned as follows: the burden is on the claimant to prove breach of duty, injury and causation. Lord Wilberforce's reasoning in *McGhee v. National Coal Board*[76] is a minority opinion and is wrong. The actual decision in *McGhee* can be supported on the basis that the claimant had proved causation on balance of probabilities. *McGhee* laid down no new principle. In the instant case the judge had made no finding as to whether the excess oxygen administered

---

[70] The defendant hospital's contention that both defendants had caused the "same damage" within the meaning of the Civil Liability (Contribution) Act 1978 was rejected.

[71] (1982) 22 C.C.L.T. 104, 126, British Columbia Supreme Court. The decision was upheld on appeal, although the British Columbia Court of Appeal was able to determine the issue of causation without relying on *McGhee*: see *Wipfli v. Britten* (1984) 13 D.L.R. (4th) 169, 178.

[72] [1983] 1 All E.R. 416.

[73] [1973] 1 W.L.R. 1.

[74] [1983] 1 All E.R. 416, 427G.

[75] [1988] A.C. 1074.

[76] [1973] 1 W.L.R. 1, 15–7.

to the claimant during the first 36 hours had caused RLF so a retrial was ordered.[77]

In Canada, in *Snell v. Farrell*[78] the Canadian Supreme Court approved and **12-248** followed the House of Lords' approach to causation in *Wilsher.*[79] However in *Webster v. Chapman*[80] the Manitoba Court of Appeal applied the *McGhee* approach and saw no relevant distinction, on the facts of the case, between the statements that continued prescription of a drug materially increased the risk of damage to the claimant and that continued prescription had materially contributed to the damage which occurred. Since there was evidence to support the first statement, the claimant succeeded on causation.

The present position, therefore, is that in a case where negligent medical **12-249** treatment increased the risk of a particular injury occurring and that very injury did occur, there is no short cut for the claimant. He must still prove on balance of probabilities that it was the negligent treatment, rather than some other factor, which caused the injury. For an example of a case where the lack of specific evidence prevented the court making an award for a culpable delay in treatment see *Tahir v. Haringey Health Authority.*[81] The claimant sustained severe neurological damage following surgery for a spinal abscess. He contended that the doctors' delay of 24 hours to diagnosis and treatment had caused a general increment in his injury. At trial, he was only able to establish two to three hours' of negligent delay. The trial judge awarded general damages of £4,000 to reflect the linear proportion of the general damages of £30,000 which would have been

---

[77] The House of Lords' decision is discussed by A. Grubb, in "Causation and Medical Negligence" [1988] C.L.J. 350. Grubb concludes that *McGhee* is consigned to the category of cases decided upon its own unique facts. A contrary view is expressed in A. Boon, "Causation and the Increase of Risk" (1988) 51 M.L.R. 508. See *Hossack v. Ministry of Defence*, unreported, April 18, 2000, CA: claimant's hypothesis for cause of his injury was only one of a number of possibilities, and the causative requirement had not been satisfied.

[78] (1990) 4 C.C.L.T. 229. The Ontario High Court came to a similar conclusion in *Gallant v. Fialkov* (1989) 69 O.R. (2d) 297.

[79] But Sopinka J. observed that "[i]n many malpractice cases, the facts lie particularly within the knowledge of the defendant. In these circumstances, very little affirmative evidence on the part of the claimant will justify the drawing of an inference of causation in the absence of evidence to the contrary", *ibid.* at 300. See *Joyal v. Starreveld* (1996) 37 Alta. L.R. 19 for an example of this approach to causation. The treating clinician failed to warn the claimant not to drive whilst under a reducing regime of anti-epileptic drug therapy. The court held that causation had been proved in the absence of any positive or scientific proof of causation adduced by the claimant and awarded damages because the court held that a seizure was the more likely cause of the claimant's car accident than the alternative causes suggested by the defendant and that if the claimant had received the appropriate warning then he would not have driven, or would not have agreed to the proposed reduction. Compare with *Meloche v. Hotel Dieu Grace Hospital* (1999) 179 DLR (4th) 77, Ontario, CA. The issue in that case was whether negligent delay in diagnosing the claimant's eye infection had caused his subsequent loss of sight. The court of first instance held, following *Snell v. Farrell*, that in the absence of evidence to the contrary adduced by a defendant, an inference of causation may be drawn even though positive or scientific proof is lacking. However, the medical experts for both parties agreed that it would be speculative to associate delay in diagnosis with the claimant's blindness. The Ontario Court of Appeal held that in finding that there was a causal relationship, the judge at first instance had taken the "robust and pragmatic" approach from *Snell v. Farrell* too far. He was not filling a lacuna in the evidence with common sense pragmatism, he was replacing two medical opinions with one of his own and was not entitled to do so. See *Pearce v. United Bristol Healthcare NHS Trust*, [1999] P.I.Q.R. P53, Lord Woolf, for an example of a rare and theoretical instance where the judge might replace medical opinion with his own (as to whether or not non-disclosure of a particular risk was a breach of the duty to adequately advise).

[80] (1998) 155 D.L.R. 82.

[81] [1998] Lloyd's Rep. Med. 104.

awarded had the claimant established 24 hours' negligent delay. The health authority's appeal was upheld. The claimant had failed to prove that some measurable damage was actually caused by the culpable two to three hours' of delay. The claimant's expert evidence was not directed towards proving breach of duty based on a culpable two to three hour delay, but only the main case of twenty four hour delay. The court therefore had no evidential basis for determining what, if any deficit, was caused by the culpable delay and therefore had no real basis for assessing damages. The claimant's award for two to three hours' delay was overturned. A similar finding was made in *Robertson v. Nottingham Health Authority*.[82]

12–250   By contrast the claimant in *Miles v. Redbridge & Waltham Forest Health Authority*[83] succeeded in his claim that the negligent delay in commencing ventilation after his premature delivery caused or materially contributed to his post-delivery brain haemorrhage and his consequent mental difficulties. The defendant doctors had negligently misdiagnosed foetal death during delivery, and given the mother a pethidine injection. The pethidine had depressed the claimant's respiration at birth and inadequate restorative measures were taken, leading to an excess of carbon dioxide in the claimant's blood (hypercarbia). The Court's decision is robust: the causative or contributing factors for the haemorrhage included prematurity itself, the birth process via the birth canal as well as the culpable injection of pethidine to the mother leading to hypercarbia.

12–251   **Loss of a chance.** A claimant may claim that the defendant's negligent failure to give him proper treatment has deprived him of an improvement in his medical condition or has allowed him to deteriorate further. Unless he can show that proper treatment was more likely than not to have produced an improvement or arrested the deterioration, the claimant will be unable to show that the defendant's negligence caused his damage and he will recover nothing. Applying the usual "but for" test of causation produces an "all or nothing" result. Thus, if the chance that proper treatment would have secured the desired result was less than 50 per cent, the claimant cannot prove on the balance of probabilities that the damage would not have occurred in any event. An alternative approach, which would be logically defensible in cases such as *Barnett v. Chelsea & Kensington Hospital Management Committee*,[84] would be to award the claimant compensation for the loss of the chance of recovery, even if that chance is less than 50 per cent.[85] The argument would be that, on the balance of probabilities, the claimant has been deprived of the opportunity to receive treatment. This proof of causation is necessary before proceeding to qualification of loss or the value of the damage suffered using "loss of a chance" discounting. The value of that opportunity, which depends upon the chance that the treatment would have been successful, is a matter for the assessment of damages. This argument was canvassed,

---

[82] [1997] 8 Med. L.R. 1. The Court of Appeal overturned the finding of negligence against the obstetric registrar, in part on the lack of proof that the culpable delay had contributed materially to the damage.
[83] Unreported, February 18, 2000, QBD.
[84] [1969] 1 Q.B. 42. See above, para. 12–245 Where the injury would have occurred in any event.
[85] This approach is commonly adopted in claims against solicitors for the lost chance of gaining some benefit, whether via litigation or not. See Chap. 10, paras 10–256–10–262, above.

unsuccessfully, in the Scottish case *Kenyon v. Bell.*[86] However, it was accepted by the British Columbia Supreme Court in *Seyfert v. Burnaby Hospital Society.*[87]

In England, the former approach and the causation requirement of a "material **12–252** contribution" was applied in *Hotson v. East Berkshire Area Health Authority.*[88] The claimant, a 13–year-old boy, fell from a tree and suffered a fracture of the left femoral epiphysis. He was taken to hospital on the same day but because of the defendants' negligence his injury was not diagnosed or treated for five days. The claimant developed avascular necrosis of the epiphysis. He alleged that the defendant's negligence had caused his disability. At first instance Simon Brown J.[89] held that there was a 75 per cent chance that so many blood vessels had been ruptured by the fall that avascular necrosis was bound to result. He awarded £11,500 (being 25 per cent of the full damages for the injury) for loss of a 25 per cent chance of recovery. This decision was upheld by the Court of Appeal, but reversed by the House of Lords.[90] The House of Lords analysed the case in this manner: it follows from the judge's findings of fact that, on the balance of probabilities, the epiphysis was doomed before the defendants came under a duty to treat the claimant. There was a high probability (75 per cent) that, even with correct diagnosis and treatment, the claimant's disability would have occurred. Therefore the claimant had failed to establish causation (an element of liability) on the balance of probabilities and his claim must fail. Thus the question of whether a claimant who succeeds on causation can recover damages for loss of a chance did not arise directly for decision in this case. The House of Lords were doubtful that such a claim could be maintained, but did not rule it out.[91]

In the majority of clinical negligence cases, the damage has occurred by the **12–253** time of trial. The question then is whether the doctor's conduct did or did not affect the claimant's present condition or prospects. This question can be resolved (on the balance of probabilities) on the basis of the evidence as to the claimant's condition at the time of the negligence. If it is more likely than not that the claimant's condition was then amenable to treatment, then the claimant will recover. If on the balance of probabilities, treatment would have made no difference, he will not. Thus, in *Hotson*, the question of primary fact was whether or not a sufficient number of blood vessels in the claimant's hip had survived his fall to make him one of the 75 out of every 100 patients who would respond to treatment. Since he could not show on the balance of probabilities that a sufficient number of his vessels had survived his original fall, he could not show that he would probably have responded to treatment, so as to establish causation.[92] In effect, he could not show that the damage had not already been done before the defendant's duty arose.

---

[86] 1953 S.C. 125. "If all that the pursuer expected to establish was that there would have been a greater chance of saving the eye if proper care and skill had been exercised, it was impossible to assess in terms of money a matter of pure chance" (*per* Lord Guthrie). Lord Guthrie distinguished the cases cited to him concerning damages for loss of a chance (such as *Chaplin v. Hicks* [1911] 2 K.B. 786) on the basis that they were claims in contract rather than tort.

[87] (1986) 27 D.L.R. (4th) 96: claimant recovered damages for the loss of a 25% chance of avoiding the need for a colostomy.

[88] [1987] A.C. 750.

[89] *sub nom. Hotson v. Fitzgerald* [1985] 1 W.L.R. 1036.

[90] [1987] A.C. 1250.

[91] See Lord Bridge at 782G–783A, Lord Mackay at 786A-G and Lord Ackner at 792H–794A.

[92] See *Richardson v. Kitching* [1995] 6 Med. L.R. 257 for another case where the claimant failed to establish causation.

12–254   In a case where the claimant, if properly treated, would probably but not certainly have recovered, should he receive full damages? Or should damages be discounted to reflect the risk of failure? Such a discount was made in *Clark v. MacLennan*[93] where the basis of the claim was that an operation had been carried out prematurely. The damages were discounted by one-third, to reflect the risk that the operation might not have been successful anyway. But this approach has not usually been adopted,[94] and in *Hotson v. East Berkshire Area Health Authority*[95] Lord Bridge[96] and Lord Ackner[97] stated that it was wrong in principle.

12–255   However, such an award was made in *Judge v. Huntingdon Health Authority*.[98] In *Judge* the claimant was referred to the defendant surgeon by her general practitioner for investigation for a lump in her breast. Negligently, the surgeon failed to detect the lump and failed to arrange to see the claimant again. The lump was cancerous. By the time that this was finally diagnosed, the claimant had a substantially reduced expectation of life. She alleged that, but for the surgeon's negligence, she would have received earlier treatment and had a better expectation of life. The judge found that since the claimant had shown "on a balance of probabilities" that her cancer had not spread to the lymph nodes at the time when the surgeon should have detected it, then she had lost "a very good chance of cure in the sense that she would have had a full expectation of life".[99] He then assessed that chance at 80 per cent. Thus the judge found that the defendant's negligence had caused (on the balance of probabilities) the claimant to lose an 80 per cent chance of a complete cure and directed that damages were to be assessed as 80 per cent of her full life expectation if healthy. The judge took the view that nothing in *Hotson v. East Berkshire Area Health Authority* prevented him from making such an award. It is submitted that this view was correct: in *Hotson* the claimant had failed to prove that his presenting injury had any chance of

---

[93] [1983] 1 All E.R. 416, 432–433. Part of the reasoning elsewhere in the judgment has subsequently been disapproved: see *Wilsher v. Essex Area Health Authority* [1987] Q.B. 730 and [1988] A.C. 1074.

[94] No discount appears to have been made in *Saumarez v. Medway & Gravesend Hospital Management Committee* (1953) 2 B.M.J. 1109, even though the claimant was only deprived of "a good chance" of recovery. See also *Moffat v. Witelson* (1980) 111 D.L.R. (3d) 712. No discount was given in *Straddlers Groups A and C v. Secretary of State for Health* (2000) 54 B.M.L.R. 104, once causation had been proved on the balance of probabilities. In preliminary proceedings it had been established that failure to suspend treatment of new patients with Human Growth Hormone (HGH) after July 1, 1977 was negligent. This action was brought by "straddlers", whose period of treatment straddled this date, and for whom it was assumed that treatment prior to this date had not caused their infection. Thus, to prove negligence the straddlers had to establish, on the balance of probabilities, that they suffered Creutzfeldt-Jakob disease, (CJD) due to the failure to stop treatment at this date. The court was asked to determine whether these patients' treatment would, in fact, have ceased after this date if the Department of Health had informed clinicians of the risk of contracting CJD from HGH treatment. The Secretary of State contended, that the claimants had merely lost a chance of the treatment being stopped, and that discount for this chance should be given. It was held, on the evidence (four endocrinological paediatricians stated that they would have ceased treatment of ongoing patients at this date), that the claimants had proved to the balance of probabilities that their treatment would have stopped, and that accordingly no discount arose for the percentage chance that the treating clinician might not have stopped treatment. See also *Newbury v. Bath District Health Authority* (1998) 47 B.M.L.R. 138, where no discount was applied where the court held on the balance of probabilities that the delay to an operation had lost the claimant a marginally more than 50% chance of recovery.

[95] [1987] A.C. 750.

[96] *ibid* at 783A-C.

[97] *ibid.* at 793F-H.

[98] [1995] 6 Med. L.R. 223.

[99] At 231, col. 2.

successful treatment; in *Judge* the claimant established that her condition was susceptible to treatment, but that treatment might not have achieved a complete cure.

Subsequently, in *Allied Maples Group Ltd v. Simmons & Simmons*,[1] a "loss of a chance" case concerning solicitors negligence, the Court of Appeal[2] emphasised the different approach to be applied to cases where the allegedly negligent act or omission was the direct and actual past cause of the claimed loss, and cases where the court had to consider what the claimant would have done if the negligence had not occurred. In the former cases, once causation of the actual damage suffered was established on the balance of probability, the claimant would in theory recover the loss claimed in full. However, if the extent of the loss depended on a future uncertain event, then quantification of that loss would be discounted to reflect the percentage chance of the uncertain event occurring in the future. If the negligent breach was an omission (for example failure to treat) then the claimant will also have to prove on the balance of probabilities that he or she would have taken the necessary action to obtain the benefit or avoid the risk. In both cases, there would be no discount if the balance only just tipped in favour of the claimant. However, where the quantification of the claimant's loss (after causation is established) depends on future uncertain events (such as the outcome of the course of treatment that was negligently not given due to failure to diagnose the condition), then the chance of the outcome coming to pass or not is not decided on a balance of probabilities, but rather an assessment by the court of the risk materialising. **12–256**

The common thread of analysis in *Allied Maples* and *Judge* is the judgment of Lord Reid in *Davies v. Taylor*[3]: **12–257**

> "When the question is whether a certain thing is or is not true—whether a certain event did or did not happen—then the court must decide one way or the other. There is no question of chance or probability. Either it did happen or it did not happen. But the standard of civil proof is the balance of probabilities. If the evidence shows a balance in favour of it having happened, then it is proved that it did in fact happen . . . You can prove that a past event happened, but you cannot prove that a future event will happen and I do not think that the law is so foolish as to suppose that you can. All you can do is to evaluate the chance. Sometimes it is virtually 100 per cent: sometimes it is virtually nil. But often it is somewhere in between. And if it is somewhere in between I do not see much difference between a probability of 51 per cent and a probability of 49 per cent."

This approach was followed by Andrew Smith J. in the case of *Smith v. NHS Litigation Authority*.[4] Although the application of the *Allied Maples* approach in clinical negligence cases has been criticised in the commentary on *Smith*[5] as being contrary to Lord Bridge's *obiter* comments in *Hotson* at 782G–H, and by

---

[1] [1995] 1 W.L.R. 1602.

[2] See particularly Stuart Smith L.J. at 1609F–1614C-D, with whom Hobhouse L.J. agreed, and with whom Millett L.J. agreed on the analysis of the law and reasoning, but dissented on its application to the facts of the case.

[3] [1974] A.C. 207 at 213. (See *Allied Maples*: Stuart Smith L.J. at 1613H–1614A, Hobhouse L.J. at 1621B-C and Millett L.J. at 1622B—agreement with Stuart Smith L.J.'s analysis of the law) and *Judge per* Deputy Judge Titheridge at 230, col. 2.)

[4] [2001] Lloyd's Rep. Med. 90 at 101, col 2.

[5] *ibid.* at 108.

Adrian Whitfield Q.C. in his commentary on *Chappel v. Hart*.[6] It is submitted that it is consistent with authority, (*Holson* being a case where the Claimant failed to prove causation, so the Court never commenced the quantification of loss process) and in some cases its application will avoid injustice. In the field of delay in diagnosis of cancer, the patient who has lost an estimated 40 per cent chance of successful treatment, but whose condition is now terminal, may justifiably feel aggrieved at the proposition that he or she has lost nothing of value; and the defendants in *Judge* would have been aggrieved at compensating the claimant as if she had lost a certain cure when, as a matter of fact, she had not.

12-258   Lord Bridge's obiter comments in *Hotson*[7] show clear judicial hostility towards the principle of awarding damages for the lost chance of obtaining a better medical outcome of treatment. Nevertheless it does appear that English law allows for recovery of damages for the loss of a chance of a complete or better recovery or outcome due to a negligent act or omission in clinical negligence cases.

12-259   **Canadian law.** In *Lawson v. Laferriere*[8] the Supreme Court of Canada reviewed the issue both in the context of civil law and common law. In March 1971 the patient consulted the defendant, a cancer specialist, about a lump in her right breast. The defendant performed a biopsy, which revealed that the patient had cancer of the breast. The defendant negligently failed to inform the patient of her condition or to follow it up. In 1975 the patient's condition deteriorated and the doctors treating her confirmed the original diagnosis of cancer. The patient died in January 1978. The medical evidence indicated that, whatever treatment the patient had received since 1971, she would probably have died of cancer. The trial judge dismissed a claim by the patient's executor because causation was not established. The Quebec Court of Appeal, by a two to one majority, awarded the executor $50,000 for loss of the chance of a cure. The Supreme Court of Canada, by a majority of six to one, allowed the defendant's appeal in part. The court held that the patient's executor was not entitled to damages for loss of the chance of a cure; but she was entitled to damages for the distress and diminished quality of life which the patient suffered, as a result of the four-year delay in telling her of the diagnosis. Such damages were assessed at $17,500.

12-260   The majority of the court concurred with the judgment of Gonthier J. This judgment reviewed at length the civil law on damages for loss of a chance, surveying the judicial decisions and academic writings on the topic of France, Belgium and Quebec. Gonthier J. also reviewed more briefly the common law on this topic and noted the House of Lords' decision in *Hotson*. He concluded that the "lost chance" approach was inappropriate in all but the exceptional classical cases, such as loss of a lottery ticket. In such cases "the damage can only be understood in probabilistic or statistical terms and . . . it is impossible to evaluate sensibly whether or how the chance would have been realised in that particular case." He considered that such artificial analysis should not be extended to the medical context. Instead the courts should concentrate on what injury had been

---

[6] [1999] Lloyd's Rep. Med. 223 at 254.
[7] At 782G–H.
[8] (1991) 78 D.L.R. (4th) 609, 654.

caused to the individual claimant, such as shorter life or greater pain.[9] *Lawson v. Laferriere* was distinguished (as a civil law case having no application to a common law case of a contract for medical services) by the Canadian Court of Appeal in *de la Giroday v. Brough*[10] where the majority held that there was no basis for loss of a chance in an action based on tort, but that an action in contract for breach of an implied obligation to exercise reasonable care and skill could be decided using a loss of a chance approach.[11] By contrast, in *Brown v. University of Alberta*,[12] the claimant's damages were reduced by 50 per cent to reflect the chances of the very same injury (violent shaking by father leading to brain damage) occurring (without negligence by any doctor) in the future life of the claimant, even if the missed diagnosis of child abuse had been made. The court accepted that contingencies for future events did not need to be proven on the balance of probabilities, thereby apparently accepting the principle of discounting damages for an uncertain future event derived from *Allied Maples, Davies v Taylor* and applied in *Judge*.

Australian law. In *Chappel v. Hart*,[13] the defendant failed to warn the   12–261
claimant that the operation carried a risk of partial loss of her voice. It was found that had she been so warned, the plaintiff would have taken steps to have the surgery performed by an expert and that the risk would then not have materialised. The defendant appealed on the issue of causation, arguing that the claimant's damage was not physical injury but the loss of the chance to have the operation performed by someone else. The defendant further argued that the risk which materialised was a random event and was ever present, no matter who performed the operation. Therefore, it was said, the defendant's failure to warn had not caused the claimant to lose anything of value. The majority in the High Court of Australia rejected this argument. It was wrong to analyse the claimant's damage as the loss of a chance to have the operation performed by another surgeon. On the evidence, had she been properly warned, she would not have undergone the operation when she did. She would not have suffered loss of her voice when she did. The fact that she would have undergone the operation, bearing a risk of the same nature, at a later date did not prevent a finding that the defendant's failure to warn had caused her to suffer the injury of which she

---

[9] See *Sohal v. Brar* (1999) 63 Alta. L.R. (3d) 280 where the applicability of the loss of chance doctrine was rejected. For an application of this approach in the U.K. see: *Sutton v. Population Services Family Planning Programme Ltd, The Times*, November 7, 1981. A different view is expressed by Dr W. Scott in "Causation in Medico-Legal Practice: A Doctor's Approach to the 'Lost Opportunity' Cases" (1992) 55 M.L.R. 521. Scott argues that the "all or none" approach is unsatisfactory because of the practical difficulty in many borderline cases of saying on which side of the 50% line the probabilities fall. In view of the impossibility of precision, he suggests that the courts should deal in fixed bands: 10% chance, 25% chance, 33% chance and so forth. In cases which fall near the 50% borderline, justice to the parties would be much better served by adopting a proportionate approach. A proportionate approach would be workable. From a pragmatic viewpoint, this argument has considerable force. It merits serious consideration in any statutory scheme for compensation for medical accidents.
[10] (1997) 33 C.L.R. (3d) 171.
[11] See *per* Southin J.A. (with whom Newberg J.A. concurred) at para. 42. However, these dicta are all *obiter* and for this reason Finch J.A. (who dissented on the question of breach of duty) declined to consider causation at all.
[12] (1997) 145 D.L.R. (4th) 63, Court of Queen's Bench.
[13] [1999] Lloyd's Rep. Med. 223.

complained, namely the loss of her voice.[14] Strictly speaking the case has no relevance to the debate on recoverability of damages for the loss of a chance, but illustrates the importance of analysis of the nature of the loss claimed.

12–262   **Inadequate warning re proposed treatment.** Where the claimant's case rests on the medical practitioner's failure to give him proper warning of the risks entailed in treatment,[15] it is necessary to prove that (if properly advised) he would not have accepted the treatment.[16] If the claimant fails to establish this hypothetical fact, then no loss flows from the defendant's breach of duty.[17] Where, however, the claimant sues in trespass,[18] this is not a necessary element in his claim.[19]

12–263   In determining what the claimant would have done, if he had been properly advised, there are three possible approaches which could be adopted:

    (i) to consider what a reasonable person would have done in the claimant's position, if properly advised (the objective approach);

    (ii) to consider what this particular claimant would have done, if properly advised, however reasonable or unreasonable that course of action may be (the subjective approach);

    (iii) to consider what a reasonable person having the characteristics or circumstances of the claimant would have done if properly advised (the modified objective approach).

It is implicit in McNair J.'s direction to the jury in *Bolam v. Friern Hospital Management Committee*[20] and in Bristow J.'s judgment in *Chatterton v. Gerson*[21] that in English law the subjective approach is correct. The "missed abortion" cases (discussed below)[22] have also proceeded on this basis. The respective merits of the subjective and objective approaches have not yet been fully debated in the English courts. In practice it appears that evidence of both will weigh with the court, the "modified objective approach". Thus in *Chester v. Afshar*[23] both the subjective and the objective approach to causation were applied, albeit that the objective approach was applied only to confirm that the same outcome was reached using either approach. In *Pearce v. United Bristol Healthcare NHS*

---

[14] The reasoning behind this decision (but not the outcome) has been criticised. See Marc Staunch: "Taking the Consequences for Failure to Warn of Medical Risks," [2000] 63 M.L.R. 261; Peter Cane: "A Warning about Causation" [1999] 115 L.Q.R. 21.

[15] See paras 12–201 to 12–232, above.

[16] *Bolam v. Friern Hospital Management Committee* [1957] 1 W.L.R. 582, 590–591; *Chatterton v. Gerson* [1981] Q.B. 432, 442G–H.

[17] See *Shakoor v. Kang Situ* [2001] 1 W.L.R. 410, 420F–G. The claimant failed on breach and causation; *Newbury v. Bath District Health Authority* [1998] 47 B.M.L.R. 138, QBD. The judge held that there was no negligence in obtaining consent and that in any event, the claimant would have gone ahead with the surgery if she had known of the 1–5% risk of neural damage.

[18] On the grounds that the claimant was not told, even in broad terms, the nature of the treatment proposed. See paras 12–124 to 12–147, above.

[19] *Chatterton v. Gerson* [1981] Q.B. 432, 442H–443A.

[20] [1957] 1 W.L.R. 582, 590–591.

[21] [1981] Q.B. 432, 445B–D.

[22] See para. 12–277, below.

[23] Unreported, 21 December 2000, QBD.

Trust,[24] the Court of Appeal adopted the subjective approach.[25] In *Smith v. Barking, Havering and Brentwood Health Authority*,[26] the defendant health authority admitted negligent failure to warn the claimant of the risk of immediate onset of tetraplegia which attended an operation which she underwent in order to avoid the likely onset of the condition in nine months' time. The claimant's claim was dismissed because it was found that, on the balance of probabilities, she would have had the operation even if properly warned of the risk. While accepting the subjective test as the correct one, Hutchison J. recognised the value of objective considerations in assessing the claimant's evidence on the point. The judge said:

> "Both counsel invited me to accept that in the end the matter must be one for decision on a subjective basis. This must plainly as a matter of principle be right, because the question must be: If this plaintiff had been given the advice that she should have been given, would she have decided to undergo the operation or not? However, there is a particular difficulty involved in this sort of case—not least for the plaintiff herself—in giving, after the adverse outcome of the operation is known, reliable answers as to what she would have decided before the operation had she been given proper advice as to the risks inherent in it. Accordingly, it would, in my judgment, be right in the ordinary case to give particular weight to the objective assessment. If everything points to the fact that a reasonable plaintiff, properly informed, would have assented to the operation, the assertion from the witness box, made after the adverse outcome is known, in a wholly artificial situation and in the knowledge that the outcome of the case depends upon that assertion being maintained, does not carry great weight unless there are extraneous or additional factors to substantiate it. By extraneous or additional factors I mean, and I am not doing more than giving examples, religious or some other firmly-held convictions; particular social or domestic considerations justifying a decision not in accordance with what, objectively, seems the right one; assertions in the immediate aftermath of the operation made in a context other than that of a possible claim for damages; in other words, some particular factor which suggests that the plaintiff had grounds for not doing what a reasonable person in her situation might be expected to have done. Of course, the less confidently the judge reaches the conclusion as to what objectively the reasonable patient might be expected to have decided, the more readily will he be persuaded by her subjective evidence."[27]

The Canadian approach. The matter was considered in *Reibl v. Hughes*[28] by   **12–264**
the Canadian Supreme Court, which decided that the objective approach was correct. However, the court was at pains to point out that this did not put the issue of causation completely in the hands of the medical practitioner. "Merely because medical evidence establishes the reasonableness of a recommended operation does not mean that a reasonable person in the patient's position would necessarily agree to it."[29] The patient's particular circumstances must also be taken into account (thereby modifying the objective approach). In *Reibl v. Hughes*, for example, the court attached importance to the fact that the claimant needed to work another one and a half years in order to earn pension benefits. Naturally he would not want to jeopardise those prospects. In that case it was

---

[24] [1999] E.C.C. 167 (Lord Woolf, with whom L.JJ. Roche and Mummery agreed).
[25] As did Ebsworth J. in *Newbury v. Bath District Health Authority* (1999) 47 B.M.L.R. 138 at 150.
[26] [1994] 5 Med. L.R. 285.
[27] *ibid.* at 288–289. It was common ground in that case that the subjective test was correct.
[28] (1980) 114 D.L.R. (3d) 1.
[29] *ibid.* at 16.

held on balance of probabilities that a reasonable person in the claimant's position, if properly advised, would not have submitted to the treatment in question. As a result of the wide duty of disclosure in Canada[30] coupled with the objective approach to causation, in numerous cases since *Reibl v. Hughes*[31] the claimant has succeeded on breach of duty, but failed to establish causation of loss. In *Arndt v. Smith*,[32] the claimant alleged that, had she been properly warned that the chickenpox which she contracted during pregnancy created certain risks to her unborn child, she would have requested an abortion. The trial judge held that she would not. The Court of Appeal of British Columbia allowed her appeal on the grounds that the judge was not entitled, in applying the objective test, to take into account the claimant's scepticism towards conventional medicine or that the pregnancy was carefully planned and wanted. However, the court recognised that the objective test was inadequate in a case where the hypothetical treatment decision would involve the balancing of overlapping personal, ethical and medical considerations. It would be possible to conclude that some reasonable patients in the position of the claimant would have undergone the treatment, but others, equally reasonable, would not. The court suggested that it was time that the Supreme Court of Canada reconsidered the question of causation in cases where negligence consists in a failure to warn. The majority in the Supreme Court of Canada[33] reversed the decision of the Court of Appeal in British Columbia in *Arndt v. Smith*[34] upholding the finding of the trial judge that, even if warned that her unborn child might be harmed by chicken pox during the pregnancy, the claimant would not have had an abortion.[35] The Supreme Court applied the modified objective test for causation[36]: the question to be asked is: "Would a reasonable patient in the claimant's position have decided to have an abortion?", but in answering that question, the court may take into account the claimant's "reasonable" beliefs, fears, desires and expectations. Thus the claimant cannot rely on proof that she would have reacted unreasonably to the appropriate warning. Under a subjective test she could. As an example of an unreasonable reaction, the majority judgment suggested a patient who would have refused treatment if warned that it carried the risk of causing a temporary

---

[30] See paras 12–202 to 12–204, above.
[31] *Casey v. Provan* (1984) 11 D.L.R. (4th) 708, Ontario High Court; *Considine v. Camp Hill Hospital* (1982) 133 D.L.R. (3d) 11, Nova Scotia Supreme Court; *Diack v. Bardsley* (1983) 25 C.C.L.T. 159, British Columbia Supreme Court; and (1984) 31 C.C.L.T. 308, British Columbia Court of Appeal; *Ferguson v. Hamilton Civic Hospitals* (1983) 144 D.L.R. (3d) 214, Ontario High Court and (1985) 18 D.L.R. (4th) 638, Ontario CA; *Kueper v. McMullin* (1986) 30 D.L.R. (4th) 408, New Brunswick CA; *Haughian v. Paine* (1987) 37 D.L.R. (4th) 624, Saskatchewan CA; *Kitchen v. McMullin* (1989) 50 C.C.L.T. 215, New Brunswick CA; *Meyer v. Rogers* (1991) 78 D.L.R. (4th) 307, Ontario High Court. See also *Layton v. Westcott* (1993) 6 Alta.L.R. 91, Alberta Court of Queen's Bench (reasonable claimant would have agreed to hysterectomy even had she been properly warned of the particular risk in her case); *Hollis v. Birch* (1993) 81 B.C.L.R. (2d) 1, BCCA (surgeon negligent in failing to warn of risk of rupture of proposed breast implantation, case remitted for further evidence of what other women did when so warned, in order to determine what a reasonable woman would have done); *Mickle v. Salvation Army Grace Hospital* [1998] 166 D.L.R. (4th) 743 (where the objective approach was applied but considered in the light of the claimants' circumstances); *cf. Joyal v. Starreveld* , ibid. The claimant succeeded in proving breach and causation.
[32] [1996] 7 Med. L.R. 108, decision reversed by Supreme Court of Canada.
[33] (1997) 148 D.L.R. (4th) 48.
[34] [1996] 7 Med. L.R. 108.
[35] (1997) 148 D.L.R. (4th) 48.
[36] The subjective approach appears to have been preferred by the three dissenting judges (MacLachlin, Sopinka and Iacobucci JJ.)

rash because she believed that the rash would signal the presence of evil spirits in the body.[37]

Australian law. In Australia the subjective approach has been adopted: see **12-265** *Gover v. State of South Australia and Perriam,*[38] *Ellis v. Wallsend District Hospital,*[39] *H. v. Royal Alexandra Hospital for Children*[40] and *Rogers v. Whitaker.*[41]

A recent Australian case has also considered the significance of the fact that a **12-266** patient would have had to have had the same procedure at some stage—even if not at the time of a failure to give a proper warning by a doctor. In *Chappel v. Hart,*[42] the claimant suffered from a progressive condition which sooner or later would require surgery. The defendant ENT surgeon failed to warn her that the operation carried a risk of perforation of the oesophagus, which in turn might lead to infection and partial loss of voice. It was found that had she been so warned, the claimant would not have had the surgery when she did, but would have taken steps to have it performed by "the most experienced [surgeon] with a record and reputation in the field". In fact the surgery was carried out by Dr Chappel, and, without negligence in the course of the operation, the claimant suffered infection and consequential voice loss. The claimant contended that the damage to her throat and voice was caused by the doctor's failure to warn her of the risk of infection; and the doctor contended that there was no causal nexus between the failure to warn and the injury because she would have had to undergo the surgery in any event, and it could not be shown that there would have been a reduced risk of infection if the operation had been carried out by someone else. The High Court of Australia found for the claimant by a majority of three to two. Gaudron J. held[43] that it was established that the risk of infection would have been reduced if she had had the opportunity to retain the most experienced surgeon in the field; Gummow J. considered[44] that the claimant did not have to show that a subsequent operation would have carried less risk; Kirby J. appears to have accepted that there was no evidence to demonstrate that there would have been less risk in the hands of a more experienced surgeon, but believed that it was probably the case as a result of intuition and commonsense. He considered[45] that the doctor had failed to establish that the risks would have been the same in a

---

[37] In "Causation and Disclosure of Medical Risks" L.Q.R. 1998 114 Jan. 52–55, Tony Honore argues that, in cases concerning the duty to disclose the risks of treatment, resort to the modified test for causation suggests that the duty to disclose has been too widely drawn. If the scope of the duty is properly defined, the traditional subjective test for causation does not afford the claimant any undue advantage. In "Causation and the emerging Canadian Doctrine of Informed Consent to Medical Treatment" (1985) 33 C.C.L.T. 131, Philip Osborne advocates the subjective approach. See *Seney v. Crooks* [1998] 166 D.L.R (4th) 337, Alberta CA. The Court of Appeal upheld the trial judge's decision and affirmed the use of the modified objective test of causation in cases concerning failure to advise or warn; see also *Painter v. Rae* [1998] 127 Man. R. (2d) 133, Manitoba Court of Queen's Bench which approves the modified objective test.

[38] (1985) 39 S.A.S.R. 543, 566, Supreme Court of South Australia.

[39] [1990] 2 Med. L.R. 103, New South Wales CA.

[40] [1990] 1 Med. L.R. 297, Supreme Court of New South Wales.

[41] [1992] 3 Med. L.R. 331, New South Wales CA. The issue did not arise for consideration in the High Court of Australia: [1993] 4 Med. L.R. 79. The effect of the wide duty of disclosure imposed by the decision of the High Court, coupled with the subjective test of causation, is highly favourable to claimants. See para. 12–264 above.

[42] [1999] Lloyd's Rep. Med. 223.

[43] *ibid.* at 223.

[44] *ibid.* at 238.

[45] *ibid.* at 247.

postponed operation. In the minority, McHugh J.[46] and Hayne J.[47] considered that there was no or insufficient evidence that the failure to warn exposed the claimant to a greater risk of injury, and that it was therefore caused, not by the negligence, but in consequence of the risk that would have been present whenever the operation was done, and the risk of which she would have accepted.

12–267 It was also unsuccessfully argued by the doctor in *Chappel* that all the claimant had lost was the chance of having the surgery done on a different occasion with substantially the same risk, and that her damages should be discounted on the basis of a loss of a chance accordingly.[48]

12–268 The facts of *Chappel* were certainly unusual, but the result is striking. The evidence in the case showed that the claimant would have had the surgery in any event, and if she had had it on a later occasion, any reduction in the associated risk would have been very small and not in any way measurable. It may be thought surprising that she recovered damages on the basis of the full value of her injuries.[49] It remains to be seen whether, and to what extent, this principle will be followed by English courts.

12–269 **Policy.** There are policy arguments in favour of the objective approach. Subject to the difficulties noted by the Court of Appeal of British Columbia in *Arndt v. Smith*,[50] it is easier to apply. It is less likely to lead to bizarre results. Its main drawback, however, is that if damages are awarded on this basis, they are less directly related to the loss actually suffered by the claimant as a result of the breach of duty. A claimant who was unable to show on the balance of probabilities that he would not have undergone the treatment offered, for example, could nevertheless succeed if a reasonable claimant (or, possibly, a significant number of reasonable claimants[51]) would. Furthermore in England, where the duty of disclosure is less onerous than in Canada,[52] there is less need for a restrictive approach to causation. As English law now stands, however, it is thought that the subjective approach is the correct one.[53]

12–270 In some cases, the nature of the duty breached may increase the difficulty of proving causation. In *Smith v. Salford Health Authority*,[54] the defendant neurosurgeon negligently failed to give the claimant an adequate warning of the risks which attended the operation which he recommended. However, even had he given a proper warning, the likely benefits of the procedure for the claimant were such that the surgeon would have been entitled to emphasise that the risks of adverse effects were remote and to advise strongly that the surgery be undertaken. In those circumstances, Potter J. found that the claimant would probably

---

[46] *ibid.* at 233.
[47] *ibid.* at 253.
[48] See paras 12–251 to 12–258, above on loss of a chance.
[49] See the commentary at [1999] Lloyd's Rep. Med. 223 at 253 where Adrian Whitfield Q.C. argues that the decision of the majority is right, and in accordance with the whole basis of informed consent cases.
[50] [1996] 7 Med. L.R. 108.
[51] *ibid. per* Lambert J.A. at 117.
[52] See paras 12–201 to 12–232, above.
[53] The subjective approach is adopted in the case of solicitors: see *Sykes v. Midland Bank Executor and Trustee Co.* [1971] 1 Q.B. 113, 124–125, 129 and 131–132. The subjective approach is adopted in Hong Kong. In America some states expressly adopt the subjective approach, others purport to adopt the objective approach but import so many subjective factors that the so– called objective test becomes indistinguishable from the subjective test.
[54] [1995] 6 Med. L.R. 321.

have accepted the recommendation.[55] In *Poynter v. Hillingdon Health Authority*[56] the infant claimant failed to prove that doctors responsible for his heart transplant operation were negligent in not disclosing to his parents that the surgery carried a relatively small risk of permanent brain damage. Sir Maurice Drake was of the view, however, that even had such a warning been given, the parents would have consented to the operation. He attached greater weight to the circumstances in which they has actually consented, which involved them setting aside their own strong views against heart transplant so as to secure the claimant's survival, than to their testimony at trial that they would have refused even if told that the relevant risk was tiny in the extreme.[57]

Failure to procure treatment. In some cases, the issue of causation cannot be resolved without considering the way in which a third party would have behaved. The application of the *Bolam* test to questions of causation was considered by the House of Lords in *Bolitho v. City & Hackney Health Authority*.[58] A two-year-old child, hospitalised for breathing difficulties, suffered cardiac arrest. He was revived but had suffered severe brain damage during the arrest. His parents argued that his condition was caused by negligence on the part of the defendant's paediatric registrar in failing to attend and intubate him. Negligence on the part of the doctor in failing to attend was conceded, but it was denied that such failure had caused the child's injuries because, had the registrar attended, she would not have intubated him. She gave evidence to that effect. It was held that in the generality of cases, the *Bolam* test has no part to play in deciding causation. However, in those cases where the breach of duty consisted of an omission to act, a two stage approach to causation was required. The court will ask first, what would have happened had the act been performed? On the facts of *Bolitho*, this question required an enquiry whether, as a matter of fact, the registrar would have intubated the claimant if she had attended him when called. If the answer is that such treatment would have been administered as would have avoided the injuries of which the claimant complains, the claimant has proved causation. Should the claimant fail to show that such treatment would have been administered, he will nonetheless succeed on causation if he can show that it would have been negligent not to administer such treatment. A defendant cannot escape liability by saying that the damage would have occurred in any event because he would have committed some further breach of duty after the initial failure. Lord Browne-Wilkinson (with whom the other four law lords agreed) approved the following passage from the judgment of Hobhouse L.J in the Court of Appeal:

" . . . a plaintiff can discharge the burden of proof on causation by satisfying the court either that the relevant person would in fact have taken the relevant action (although she would not have been at fault if she had not) or that the proper discharge of the relevant person's duty towards the plaintiff required that she take that action."

12–271

---

[55] See also *Pearce v. United Bristol Healthcare NHS Trust* [1999] E.C.C. 167 for an example of the claimant failing to establish that had the proper warning been given by the clinician, the recommendation would not have been accepted by the patient.

[56] (1997) 37 B.M.L.R. 192. See para. 12–219, above, for the facts of this case.

[57] See para. 12–219, above.

[58] [1998] A.C. 232, for Court of Appeal decision see [1993] 4 Med. L.R. 381. See para. 12–098, above.

On the facts, the claimant could not show that the registrar would in fact have intubated. Nor, on the evidence of medical experts, could the claimant show that there was no responsible body of medical opinion in support of the doctor's assertion that, had she attended, she would not have intubated. It was not the case, therefore, that no doctor of ordinary skill would have omitted to intubate the claimant, and accordingly, the claimant failed on causation.[59]

12-272   The majority view of the Court of Appeal[60] in *Bolitho* was followed by the Court of Appeal in *Joyce v. Merton, Sutton & Wandsworth Health Authority*.[61] The claimant underwent a cardiac catheterisation, in the course of which the walls of his brachial artery were (non-negligently) sutured together. He was negligently discharged home without instructions to contact the hospital if he became concerned about any aspect of his recovery. By the time that the suturing error was discovered, it was too late to prevent the claimant suffering cerebral infarct. There appeared to have been a period of 48 hours after the operation when this consequence might have been averted. To establish causation, the claimant had to show that, during that time, his condition in fact deteriorated sufficiently for it to have been brought back to the attention of the cardiologist, that the cardiologist would then have referred him to a vascular surgeon and that the vascular surgeon would have reopened the artery. According to Roch L.J., *Bolitho* established that:

> " . . . in such cases as these . . . the burden of proof that had the doctor not been negligent the child would have been intubated or the artery would have been explored, and that a failure to intubate or a failure to re-explore would have been negligent remains on the plaintiff."[62]

Roch L.J. thus appeared to take the view that it was insufficient for the claimant to show simply that the relevant doctors would have intervened to prevent his injury, it is necessary for him also to show that non-intervention would have been negligent.[63] Hobhouse L.J. took the view that *Bolitho* was authority for the proposition that, in such cases:

> "a plaintiff can discharge the burden of proof on causation by satisfying the court either that the relevant person would in fact have taken the relevant action (although she

---

[59] At the Court of Appeal Simon Brown L.J. dissented. He did not favour the introduction of the *Bolam* test on the issue of causation. He considered that the ordinary tests of factual causation were adequate to deal with the issue. The question was not whether it would have been unreasonable for an attending doctor to intubate the claimant, but whether on the balance of probabilities such a doctor would have intubated. The self-serving evidence of a doctor whose conduct in a hypothetical situation is in issue should be treated with caution, however, and an attending doctor probably would have done whatever she should have done in order to prevent harm to the claimant. Simon Brown L.J. considered that the existence of a responsible body of medical opinion against intubation in these circumstances did not prevent the court finding that, in all the circumstances, the particular claimant probably would have been intubated by an attending doctor.

[60] Which was subsequently upheld by the House of Lords.

[61] [1995] 6 Med. L.R. 60 (and see commentary at (1996) 4 Med. L.Rev. 86). See para. 12-099, above.

[62] *ibid.* at 14.

[63] See *Hunt v. National Health Service Litigation Authority* [2000] W.L. 1480071, QBD (failure to intervene in birth process and perform forceps delivery was negligent).

would not have been at fault if she had not) or that the proper discharge of the relevant person's duty towards the plaintiff required that she take action . . . Properly viewed, therefore, this rule is more favourable to a plaintiff because it gives him two routes by which he may prove his case—either proof that the exercise of proper care would have necessitated the relevant result, or proof that if proper care had been exercised it would in fact have led to the relevant result."[64–65]

Nourse L.J. agreed with both judgments. It appears, therefore, that a claimant who is unable to prove on the balance of probabilities that he would have secured the treatment he required, were it not for the defendant's negligence, will nevertheless succeed if he can show that the failure to provide such treatment would have been a further act of negligence. This approach was adopted by Thomas J. in *Wiszniewski v. Central Manchester Health Authority*,[66] and upheld on appeal by the Court of Appeal.[67]

For an example of the application of this rule on an unusually complicated set   **12–273** of medical facts, see *Brown v. Lewisham & North Southwark Health Authority*.[68] The claimant established breach of duty on the part of one doctor in communicating his history to another, but failed to show that the treatment decision likely to have been taken by the second doctor if given the correct information would have prevented his injury. The decision of the Court of Appeal in *Hallatt v. North West Anglia Health Authority*[69] demonstrates the need for care in seeking to apply the analysis in *Bolitho* to particular allegations of clinical negligence. In that case, the claimant's mother suffered gestational diabetes during her pregnancy. The chain of consequences was as follows: the claimant grew unusually large before birth, his delivery was complicated and delayed by shoulder dystocia, vaginal delivery was eventually abandoned in favour of Caesarean section but he had suffered oxygen deprivation which caused brain damage. It was argued on his behalf that a hospital doctor who saw his mother during the pregnancy negligently decided that a glucose tolerance test (GTT) was unnecessary because he had failed to appreciate that an earlier glucose test was not conclusive evidence of the absence of diabetes. Had he been aware of the limitations of the earlier test, it was alleged, he would have referred the claimant's mother to a consultant who ought to have ordered the test. The Court of Appeal held that there was no room for the application of the *Bolitho* analysis of causation in this case. The claimant's case was a straightforward allegation that the hospital staff failed to order a GTT because they negligently failed to appreciate the limitations of the earlier

---

[64–65] *ibid.* at 20.
[66] [1996] 7 Med. L.R. 248. See para. 12–181, above.
[67] Reported at [1998] Lloyd's Rep. Med. 223. See also *Le Page v. Kingston and Richmond Health Authority* [1997] 8 Med. L.R. 229 (for a summary of the facts of this case see para. 12–187, above), where John Samuels Q.C. (a deputy judge of the High Court) found that had the claimant's uterine haemorrhage been detected by the obstetric staff, as it ought to have been, the registrar would probably have induced a contraction to expel blood which had accumulated in the uterus and administered a drug to control the bleeding. "Would" here clearly meant "would and should", for the judge formulated the test for causation in *Bolam* terms: "Where there is a genuine disagreement as to the probable outcome among the expert witnesses, who have properly taken into account all the material facts relating to the claimant's treatment and condition at all times, the claimant will fail." See also *C v. A Health Authority*, [1999] C.L.Y. 4002, November 3, 1998, QBD, Ebsworth J. See para. 12–176, above for the facts.
[68] [1999] Lloyd's Rep. Med. 110.
[69] [1998] Lloyd's Rep. Med. 197.

test. There was no question, as there had been in *Bolitho*, of a failure to follow correct procedures to procure the appropriate treatment.[70]

12–274   **Novus actus interveniens.** If some extraneous event intervenes between the negligence of the medical practitioner and the loss or injury of which the patient complains, the causal connection may be negatived.[71] In *Stevens v. Bermondsey & Southwark Group Hospital Management Committee*[72] the claimant was injured in an accident caused by an employee of the borough council. The claimant was treated at the defendant's hospital. On the strength of the medical advice he received he settled his claim against the council for £125. He subsequently learnt that he had spondylolisthesis. The claimant claimed that because of the defendant's negligence, he had settled his claim against the council for less than its true value. Paull J. held that this loss was irrecoverable: "His claim against the council was either a *novus actus interveniens* or at least a severing of the direct line of causation stemming from the doctor's negligence."[73] In *Sabri-Tabrizi v. Lothian Health Board*,[74] the claimant had undergone a sterilisation operation but due, she alleged, to the defendant's negligence, she remained fertile. She became pregnant and underwent an abortion. She became pregnant a second time, which pregnancy ended in a stillbirth. The health board applied to strike out her claim for damages in relation to the second pregnancy, arguing that the claimant's

---

[70] For examples of cases where the claimant failed on causation see: *D v. Ahmed, ibid.* Claimant failed on both tests of causation. The defendant doctor had properly advised over the telephone, and if he had attended the claimant he would have given the same advice, which advice was not negligent; *Matthews v. East Suffolk Health Authority*, unreported, February 25, 2000, CA. The claimant failed to prove that the alleged negligence (failure to promptly administer antibiotics). The judge did not accept that the prompt administration would have avoided or quantifiably reduced the claimant's injuries; *Sherlock v. North Birmingham Health Authority* [1997] 40 B.M.L.R. 103, CA. Chadwick L.J. applied the *Bolitho* approach and found that the claimant failed on both tests of causation. The registrar (had he been informed) would not have transferred the claimant to the Intensive Therapy Unit; for a Canadian example see *Clinton v. Regina District Health Board and Gellner* [1998] 171 Sask. R. 44, see para. 12–240, n. 46, above. Only if the allegedly negligent omission (failure to detain a patient in hospital) would have resulted in the detection of the methanol that he had consumed such that his death from methanol poisoning could have been prevented, could causation be proved.

[71] See, generally, *Clerk & Lindsell*, (18th ed.), paras 2–36 to 2–59 and Hart and Honoré, *Causation in the Law*, chap. 6. This is illustrated by *Thompson v. Schmidt* (1891) 8 T.L.R. 120: the defendant gave a written opinion that the claimant was of unsound mind; on the basis of this the relieving officer in the exercise of his discretion under Lunacy Act 1890, s.20, temporarily detained the claimant. The Court of Appeal held, *inter alia*, that the defendant's certificate was not the cause of the detention. "Even though it might possibly be true that the act of the defendant was the *causa sine qua non*, it was not the *causa causans*. In other words, the confinement was not the direct result of the defendant's act, but it was the direct result and the sole result of the act of the relieving officer" (*per* Lord Esher M.R.). See also *Rahman v. Arearose Ltd* [2001] Q.B. 351, the facts of which are discussed at para. 12–246, above, "Concurrent Causes of Injury". See *Joyal v. Starreveld* [1996] 37 Alta. L.R. 19 for a case where failure to advise of the risk of epileptic seizures after reduction of anti-epileptic therapy was the continuing cause of the claimant's road traffic accident (presumed to have been caused by a seizure) and the injuries sustained.

[72] (1963) 107 S.J. 478. See para. 12–024, above.

[73] *cf.* A Canadian case: *Kelly v Lundgard* [1996] 40 Alta. L.R. (3d) 234. The claimant sustained internal injuries in a road traffic accident. In subsequent litigation the defendant (who had treated her by performing life saving surgery) provided a report on her condition including future prognosis. The report omitted to mention the risk of infertility resulting from abdominal adhesions. The claimant settled her claim without taking into account any risk of infertility materialising. Subsequently she discovered she was infertile due to the accident. She successfully claimed against her treating doctors, who should have identified the risk to her or her lawyers in the accident claim. The doctors knew the purpose for which the report was sought. The chain of causation was not broken.

[74] (1998) 43 B.M.L.R. 190.

decision to have sexual intercourse once she knew (because of the first pregnancy) that the sterilisation operation had failed, broke the chain of causation. The Scottish Court of Session (Outer House) accepted the argument and struck out that part of the claimant's claim.[75]

It is a common feature of medical treatment that the patient's care is shared **12–275** between a number of different nurses, doctors and specialists. Where more than one person makes a mistake, it is largely a question of fact and degree whether the earlier error is an effective cause of the patient's injury. Although the citation of authority in this area is of limited value, *Prendergast v. Sam & Dee Ltd*[76] and the Canadian case *Yepremian v. Scarborough General Hospital*[77] do provide helpful illustrations. In *Prendergast* (the facts of which are set out above)[78] it was held that the pharmacist's negligence did not break the chain of causation flowing from the negligence of the prescribing doctor. In *Yepremian* a patient suffered cardiac arrest as the result of the negligence of an internist. It was held that the original failure of a physician and a general practitioner to diagnose the patient's condition (diabetes) was not the effective cause of his injury, and they escaped liability.[79] As to the question of apportionment, where more than one party is liable, see above: "Concurrent causes of injury".[80] In *Thompson v. Blake-James*,[81] advice on options for vaccination of the infant claimant was given successively by two general practitioners. It was foreseeable by the first that the second would advise on that point, and that such advice would be given closer to the time when the decision to vaccinate would normally be made. The second doctor advised in opposite terms to the first. Peter Gibson L.J. was of the view

---

[75] *cf.* with *Emeh v. Kensington & Chelsea & Westminster Area Health Authority* [1985] Q.B. 1012 (the claimant became pregnant following a negligently performed sterilisation operation by the defendant health authority. Her decision not to terminate the pregnancy was rejected by the Court of Appeal (thereby overturning the decision of the judge of first instance), as a *novus actus interveniens* between the health authority's original negligence and the claimant's claimed losses (the cost of bringing up the congenitally deformed child that was born). The Court of Appeal held that the negligent health authority could not expect a woman to terminate a subsequent pregnancy, and held the defendant liable for the claimed losses. See para 12–180 and n. 95 for the effect of *McFarlane* on *Emeh*.

[76] [1989] 1 Med. L.R. 36.

[77] (1980) 110 D.L.R. (3d) 513.

[78] See para. 12–165, above.

[79] *cf. Powell v. Guttman* (1979) 89 D.L.R. (3d) 180: After operating on P's hip, G negligently failed to advise the performance of an arthroplasty operation. This rendered P's femur more susceptible to fracture during any arthroplasty carried out later. Subsequently N carried out an arthoplasty, but in the process caused a fracture to the femur. The Manitoba Court of Appeal held that N's conduct did not amount to a novus actus interveniens. Therefore G was liable for the subsequent fracture. See also: *Law Estate v Simice* [1995] 4 W.W.R. 672, British Columbia CA (claimant's deferring of urgent surgery for brain aneurysm for four days so surgery could be performed in another town did not insulate the doctors who had failed to diagnose the condition thereby causing preceding delay to treatment from liability); *Seney v. Crooks* [1998] 166 D.L.R. (4th) 337, Alberta CA (no contributory negligence by claimant for not telling her surgeon that she wanted a full recovery to her normal state after a fracture injury). See also *Kite v. Malycha* [1998] 71 S.A.S.R. 325, Supreme Court (courts should not be quick to find contributory negligence on the part of a patient who has relied on a competent medical practitioner for advice and treatment—claimant was entitled to assume that if a cytology report was adverse, she would be told about it) and *Hughes v. Cooper* [1998] 41 B.C.L.R. 109 (misdiagnosed as having Crohn's Disease for eight years, found to have colon cancer, onus on defendant doctor to show contributory negligence, patient is entitled to rely on physician's advice and was not contributorily negligent for not seeking additional medical advice).

[80] See para. 12–246, above and Chap. 4, paras 4–01–4–09, above.

[81] [1998] Lloyd's Rep. Med. 187. See para. 12–224, above.

that the advice of the second doctor broke the chain of causation between the parents' decision not to vaccinate and the advice given by the first doctor.

12–276 **Intervening conduct of claimant/contributory negligence.** Successful medical treatment frequently depends upon co-operation by the patient, for example, in taking drugs as and when directed or in notifying his doctor if particular symptoms develop. Lack of co-operation by the patient could constitute contributory negligence or, in a more extreme case, break the chain of causation.[82] In *Crossman v. Stewart*[83] the defendant prescribed a drug for the claimant without warning her that there were risks involved in prolonged use. The claimant continued to use the drug (which she obtained privately from a drug salesman) for a long time after the defendant had stopped prescribing it. The defendant was held negligent for failing to appreciate that the claimant was probably continuing to use the drug. But damages were reduced by two-thirds on account of the claimant's contributory negligence.

12–277 **Inadequate advice re unborn baby.**[84] Where the complaint made is that the defendant failed to detect and advise upon defects in an unborn baby, the issue which arises is what the mother would have done if properly advised. Would she have had any further tests necessary?[85] Once testing was complete, and competent advice given, would she have had an abortion? Has the opportunity to terminate the pregnancy been lost due to the defendant's negligence? In *Gregory v. Pembrokeshire Health Authority*[86] the defendants failed to inform the claimant that an amniocentesis had produced insufficient cultures. It was held that even if the claimant had been informed promptly, in view of the advanced stage of her pregnancy, she probably would not have had another amniocentesis. Her claim therefore failed on causation. By contrast in *Carver v. Hammersmith & Queen Charlotte's Special Health Authority*[87] the claimant was not told that Bart's test was not diagnostic of Down's syndrome, like amniocentesis, but was a screening test that only detected two-thirds of Down's syndrome foetuses. On the facts, the claimant succeeded in proving breach and causation. It was held that had she known the limitations of the test then she would have she would probably have insisted on amniocentesis and terminated the pregnancy.

12–278 One further question to consider is whether the claimant could lawfully have had an abortion at the material time. For the claim to have a realistic prospect of

---

[82] See *Richardson v. LRC Products Ltd* [2000] Lloyd's Rep. Med. 280, QBD: claimant failed to mitigate her loss by not taking morning after pill, which would have been a reasonable step to take after a condom had failed during intercourse. Claim was dismissed.

[83] (1977) 5 C.C.L.T. 45. See also *Brushett v. Cowan* (1990) 69 D.L.R. (4th) 743, Newfoundland Supreme Court, Appeal Division (surgeon held negligent for failing to give claimant proper advice on the use of crutches which he had prescribed; 20 per cent discount for contributory negligence by the claimant). *Cf. Law Estate v. Simice* [1996] W.W.R. 672, British Columbia CA (following a series of delays caused by negligent failures of communication by the defendant doctors, the claimant delayed further before undergoing an operation which, if taken earlier, would have prevented his death; held: claimant's delay was reasonable and did not insulate the doctors from the consequences of their negligence).

[84] See para. 12–231, above.

[85] Assuming that the failure to detect, or the failure to advise was negligent and that the claimant would have sought such tests. See *C v. A Health Authority*, unreported, November 3, 1998, QBD, Ebsworth J. for an example of a case where the failure to advise the mother to attend an appointment for detection of defects was not negligent since attendance at the appointment would not have resulted in her having a scan capable of detecting her child's subsequent defect.

[86] [1989] 1 Med. L.R. 81.

[87] Unreported, February 25, 2000, QBD, Nelson J.

success, it must be shown that the termination of the pregnancy would fall within the scope of section 1(1)(a) to (d) of the Abortion Act 1967 (as amended by section 37(1) to (3) of the Human Fertilisation and Embryology Act 1990). Termination of a pregnancy is now lawful:

" . . . if two registered medical practitioners are of the opinion, formed in good faith—

(a) that the pregnancy has not exceeded its twenty-fourth week and that the continuance of the pregnancy would involve risk, greater than if the pregnancy were terminated, of injury to the physical or mental health of the pregnant woman or any existing children of her family; or

(b) that the termination is necessary to prevent grave permanent injury to the physical or mental health of the pregnant woman; or

(c) that the continuance of the pregnancy would involve risk to the life of the pregnant woman, greater than if the pregnancy were terminated; or

(d) that there is a substantial risk that if the child were born it would suffer from such physical or mental abnormalities as to be seriously handicapped."

Under this section (as amended) in certain circumstances an abortion can be carried out at any stage of the pregnancy. One such circumstance is "that there is a substantial risk that if the child were born it would suffer from such physical or mental abnormalities as to be seriously handicapped".[88]

Causation is also a problem for claimants where the negligence complained of **12–279** is failure to warn of the risk that a sterilisation operation has not been effective or may spontaneously reverse. In *Lybert v. Warrington Health Authority*,[89] the claimant was able to show that, had she been so warned, she would have continued to use contraception and so avoided pregnancy, but only because of her unusual history and circumstances. She had known that a further pregnancy would pose particular risks to her health and she had agreed to a hysterectomy before the sterilisation. The Court of Appeal accepted that, in normal circumstances, it would be intrinsically improbable that contraception would be used after a sterilisation, notwithstanding a proper warning.[90] An important question in such cases is whether the conduct of the mother, in declining to have an abortion when she first discovers the unwanted pregnancy, breaks the chain of causation. This question received detailed consideration in *Emeh v. Kensington and Chelsea and Westminster Area Health Authority*.[91] In that case Park J. held that the claimant's refusal to have an abortion was a novus actus interveniens, because it was so unreasonable as to eclipse the defendants' wrongdoing. Accordingly he held that she could not recover any damages in respect of the period after she had discovered that she was pregnant, save for the costs of a second sterilisation operation. This decision was reversed by the Court of

---

[88] By contrast in *Rance v. Mid-Downs Health Authority* [1991] Q.B. 587, it was held that at the material time the baby was "capable of being born alive" within the meaning of s.1 of the Infant Life (Preservation) Act 1929; therefore any abortion would have been unlawful. Accordingly the claim failed on causation (as well as negligence). The basis of the claim in *Rance* is strongly criticised in P. R. Glazebrook, "Capable of Being, But No Right to Be, Born Alive?" [1991] C.L.J. 241.

[89] [1996] 7 Med. L.R. 71.

[90] *ibid.* at 75. A claimant may succeed in showing that, if properly warned of the risk that a vasectomy would spontaneously reverse, an alternative procedure with a lower failure rate would have been undertaken, such as a female sterilisation. That argument failed in *Newell & Newell v. Goldenburg* [1995] 6 Med. L.R. 371 because sterilisation of the female claimant was contraindicated on medical grounds.

[91] [1985] Q.B. 1012.

Appeal. Waller L.J. based his decision on the particular circumstances of that case.[92] For example, he took into account the fact that the claimant decided not to have an abortion before she decided to sue the defendants. Slade L.J., however, dealt with the matter on a broader basis and concluded: "Save in the most exceptional circumstances, I cannot think it right that the court should ever declare it unreasonable for a woman to decline to have an abortion in a case where there is no evidence that there were any medical or psychiatric grounds for terminating the particular pregnancy."[93] Purchas L.J. tended to agree with Slade L.J., although he indicated that if the claimant's sole motivation in refusing an abortion was to promote an action, it might break the chain of causation.[94]

12–280   It is clear from *Emeh*[95] that in the great majority of cases where the claimant refuses an abortion, such refusal will not break the chain of causation. Even if the prospect of recovering damages is one factor in her decision, she is likely to be influenced by other, more powerful, moral and emotional considerations. However, in the extreme case postulated by Purchas L.J. (where the claimant refuses an abortion purely in order to mount a claim for damages) the question remains open whether the claimant would succeed on causation. If one applies the general principle as formulated by Hart and Honoré in *Causation in the Law*[96] it would seem that the claimant should fail. However, in the situation under discussion this principle is in conflict with a higher principle, namely that it is the policy of the law to preserve life not to destroy it.[97] The mother is in certain circumstances entitled to have an abortion, but she can hardly be under a duty to do so in order to mitigate her loss or in order to reduce the liability of a negligent doctor. It is therefore submitted that of the various approaches adopted by the Court of Appeal in *Emeh v. Kensington and Chelsea and Westminster Area Health Authority*[98] that of Slade L.J. is to be preferred.

12–281   Where the unwanted child results from a failed abortion, rather than a failed sterilisation, different considerations arise. The same objections of principle to the novus actus interveniens defence do not exist. To take an extreme example, if an attempted abortion is unsuccessful and the claimant declines to undergo an identical abortion procedure 24 hours later (with a high prospect of success) solely in order to mount a claim for substantial damages, it is submitted that the claimant's conduct would break the chain of causation from the doctor's initial negligence. In *Fredette v. Wiebe*,[99] where a first attempted abortion failed, the British Columbia Supreme Court held that the claimant's refusal to undergo a second abortion was reasonable. But in that case the failure of the first abortion was not discovered until a late stage and the second abortion procedure would have been more drastic. Thus the decision turned upon the facts of the case,

---

[92] *ibid.* at 1019.
[93] *ibid.* at 1024.
[94] *ibid.* at 1027.
[95] Their Lordships appear to have overruled this decision in *McFarlane*, at least so far as the quantum of damages for a wrongful conception claim is concerned.
[96] "The general principle of the traditional doctrine is that the free, deliberate and informed act or omission of an human being, intended to exploit the situation created by the defendant, negatives causal connection" (p. 136).
[97] See, *e.g. McKay v. Essex Area Health Authority* [1982] 1 Q.B. 1166, 1179–1180 and 1188. See also Art. 2 of the European Convention for the Protection of Human Rights and Fundamental Freedoms. In *Paton v. U.K.* (1980) 3 E.H.R.R. 408 it was left open whether Art. 2 applies to an unborn but viable child.
[98] [1985] Q.B. 1012.
[99] (1986) 29 D.L.R. (4th) 534.

rather than upon any absolute principle. It is suggested that the same approach would be adopted in England.

(ii) *Foreseeability*

In order to succeed the claimant must establish not only that the injury was caused by the medical practitioner's breach of duty but also that it was foreseeable. If the claim is brought in contract, this means that, at the time the contract was made, the injury was "reasonably foreseeable as likely to result from the breach".[1] If the claim is brought in tort, it means that at the time the breach of duty was committed the injury (or at least the type of injury[2]) was reasonably foreseeable as a consequence.[3] An interesting decision on the requirement of forseeability was *Brown v. Lewisham and North Southwark Health Authority*.[4] Following heart surgery, the claimant was discharged from one hospital to another. At the time, he was suffering a chest infection and an undiagnosed deep vein thrombosis (DVT). The DVT was recognised at the second hospital, where the claimant developed a seriously adverse reaction to its treatment with heparin and ultimately lost his leg. The first hospital admitted that it was in breach of duty in discharging the claimant while he had a chest infection. It was held that this admission of breach was not sufficient to permit the claimant to recover against the first hospital in respect of the loss of his leg. The claimant argued that, once he had proved that personal injury of some kind was the forseeable result of the defendant's breach, it was no defence that the injury in fact suffered came about in an unforeseeable way. The argument failed. Beldam L.J. (with whom Morritt and Mantell L.JJ. agreed) said:

> "The public policy of limiting the liability of tortfeasors by the control mechanism of foreseeability seems to me as necessary in cases of medical as in any other type of negligence. I do not see on what policy ground it would be fair or just to hold a doctor to be in breach of duty who failed to diagnose an asymptomatic and undetectable illness merely because he was at fault in the management of a correctly diagnosed but unrelated condition. In short it must be shown that the injury suffered by the patient is within the risk from which it was the doctor's duty to protect him."[5]

[1] *per* Asquith L.J. in *Victoria Laundry (Windsor) Ltd v. Newman Industries Ltd* [1949] 2 K.B. 528. For a full discussion of the requirement of foreseeability in contract, see McGregor, paras 247–281.

[2] See, *e.g. Graham v. Persyko* (1984) 30 C.C.L.T. 84, 96, Ontario High Court: it was foreseeable that the claimant would suffer some side effect from the drug prescribed, although the side effect actually suffered was not reasonably foreseeable. Defendant held liable on the principle of *Hughes v. Lord Advocate* [1963] A.C. 837. The decision was upheld by the Ontario Court of Appeal: (1986) 27 D.L.R. (4th) 699.

[3] For a full discussion of the requirement of foreseeability in tort, see McGregor, 16th ed. paras 192–231.

[4] [1999] Lloyd's Rep. Med. 110.

[5] A slightly unusual point on foreseeability arose in *Kralj v. McGrath and St Theresa's Hospital* [1986] 1 All E.R. 54. As a result of the defendants' negligence one of the claimant's twins died shortly after birth. The claimant already had one child and planned to have a family of three. Thus it was a consequence of the defendant's negligence that the claimant would have to undergo a further pregnancy in order to achieve her planned family. Woolf J. held that this head of damage was not too remote, even though the claimant had never specifically informed the defendants of her desire to have a family of three in any event. See also *R. v. Croydon Health Authority* [1998] Lloyd's Rep. Med. 75 (pregnancy in a married woman of the claimant's age was a foreseeable event, notwithstanding that she had not communicated her desire for a family to the defendant, but no recovery because the claimant's private life was outside the scope of the company doctor's duty).

12–283   Of particular importance for medical practitioners is the decision of the House of Lords in *Page v. Smith*.[6] It was held in that case that if physical injury to the claimant was a foreseeable result of the defendant's negligence, the defendant was liable for any psychiatric injury which occurred as a result of the negligence, even where the claimant did not in fact suffer physical injury and the psychiatric damage was not itself foreseeable. The effect of this decision is that psychiatric injury is to be treated as of the same type as physical injury. Thus where it is foreseeable that the negligence of a doctor will cause the patient to suffer physical injury, liability will follow for any psychiatric injury which results from apprehension of that physical harm, even although it does not materialise. The liability for this psychiatric injury is not limited in time to the period of the breach of duty. In *Creutzfeldt-Jakob Litigation Group B v. Medical Research Council and Secretary of State for Health*[7] the defendants' duty to avoid foreseeable harm included a duty to avoid the risk of psychiatric injury caused to the patient as a consequence of receiving the news and information about the consequences and effects of CJD. Any patient who could prove a genuine psychiatric illness caused by the awareness of the risk of CJD was entitled to compensation.

12–284   In the majority of medical negligence cases, the injury of which the claimant complains is either the continuance of some illness which ought to have been cured or prevented or else the infliction of some new injury in the course of treatment. In practice the injury is normally "foreseeable", whether the contractual or tortious test is applied. Since the defendant is a medical man, he is well placed to foresee the consequences of his own mistakes. The question of foreseeability did arise, however, in *Smith v. Brighton & Lewes Hospital Management Committee*[8]: as a result of the ward sister's negligence 34 streptomycin injections were administered to the claimant, rather than 30, as prescribed by the doctor. Following this treatment the claimant lost her sense of balance. Streatfeild J. held that it was the last injection which probably did the damage. The ward sister ought to have foreseen that some injury might result from giving more injections than the doctor prescribed.[9] It was not necessary that the quality and extent of the damage should be foreseen. Accordingly the claimant recovered damages for the injury she had in fact sustained. In *Hepworth v. Kerr*,[10] the defendant was liable for the consequences of a spinal stroke which the claimant suffered because of his negligent treatment, even though the occurrence of a spinal stroke (as opposed to a cerebral stroke) was not specifically foreseeable in 1979. McKinnon J. held that a spinal stroke was within the general category of risk which was foreseeably caused by the negligence complained of, namely, thrombosis. In *Wiszniewski v. Central Manchester Health Authority*[11] the defendant's negligent mismanagement of the claimant's birth meant that he was deprived of oxygen and suffered from cerebral palsy as a result. The umbilical cord had become knotted around his neck, restricting the foetal blood supply. The health authority argued that this was not a foreseeable consequence of their

---

[6] [1996] A.C. 155. See the commentary on *Page v. Smith* at [1997] C.L.J. 254.
[7] [2000] Lloyd's Rep. Med. 161, QBD.
[8] *The Times*, May 2, 1958.
[9] However, the probability of injury being caused appears to have been small. Streatfield J. considered that if a doctor had prescribed 34 injections rather than 30, that might well not have constituted negligence.
[10] [1995] 6 Med. L.R. 39. The facts are given at para. 12–109, above.
[11] [1996] 7 Med. L.R. 248, upheld in the Court of Appeal [1998] Lloyd's Rep. Med. 223.

negligence in failing to notice and act upon signs of foetal distress. Thomas J. rejected this argument and the Court of Appeal endorsed his decision and reasoning.[12] The foreseeable result of the neglect was that the claimant would be born suffering the effects of pre-birth hypoxia. The precise mechanism by which the foetal blood supply was restricted was irrelevant. In *Thompson v. Blake-James*[13] the defendant general medical practitioner was consulted by the claimant's parents on the question of whether she should be vaccinated against measles. He advised that she should not. She contracted measles and a rare complication left her severely brain damaged. The defendant resisted liability because, on the facts of the case, the Court of Appeal held that it was not reasonably foreseeable that his failure to inform her parents that an alternative method of vaccination might be suitable for the claimant would have had any significant influence upon their decision.

In *Rand v. East Dorset Health Authority*[14] the defendant health authority were **12–285** found liable to the parents of a Down's syndrome child for failing to disclose the results of a routine pregnancy scan that showed the likelihood of a Down's syndrome foetus. The judge held that in the context of the Abortion Act 1967, the scan had been intended to offer a choice whether to terminate a pregnancy or not (where the likelihood was that the pregnancy involved a seriously disabled child). This had established the necessary proximity and foreseeability to make the defendant liable for the consequences of its omission.

In *Roe v. Minister of Health*[15] nupercaine was kept in glass ampoules stored in **12–286** phenol solution. The phenol penetrated the ampoules through invisible cracks and contaminated the nupercaine. The nupercaine was injected into two patients, who suffered permanent paralysis as a result. One of the allegations of negligence was that the nursing staff must have knocked the ampoules together in order to cause the cracking. Denning L.J.[16] held that this was the case. Somervell L.J.[17] and Morris L.J.[18] assumed that this was the case for the purpose of their judgments. The court unanimously held that the injuries in fact caused the patients by this mishap were not foreseeable. "The only consequence which could reasonably be anticipated was the loss of a quantity of nupercaine, but not the paralysis of a patient" (*per* Denning L.J.).[19] "In the case I am assuming, having knocked the ampoules the natural inference is that the nurse would look to see if they were cracked . . . As the judge has found no visible crack and the nursing staff had no reason to foresee invisible cracks, the nurse would reasonably assume no harm had been done" (*per* Somervell L.J.).[20]

(a) *Measure of Damages*

(i) *Damages for Personal injury*

In the vast majority of medical negligence actions, the principal matter of **12–287** complaint is that the defendant has caused, aggravated or failed to cure some

---

[12] *ibid.* 243–245.
[13] [1998] Lloyd's Rep. Med. 187, CA. See para. 12–224, above.
[14] [2000] Lloyd's Rep. Med. 181, QBD, Newman J.
[15] [1954] 2 Q.B. 66. See also paras 12–073 and 12–122, above.
[16] *ibid.* at 84.
[17] *ibid.* at 81.
[18] *ibid.* at 93.
[19] *ibid.* at 86.
[20] *ibid.* at 81.

form of personal injury. The claimant ordinarily claims general damages for pain, suffering and loss of amenity and special damages for financial losses suffered in consequence of the injury (such as loss of earnings or the cost of medical and nursing care). The same principles apply to the assessment of damages for personal injuries and death, whether resulting from medical negligence or from some other form of accident.[21]

(ii) *Aggravated damages*

12–288   In *Kralj v. McGrath and St Theresa's Hospital*[22] a claim for aggravated damages was unsuccessfully advanced in a medical negligence action, on the basis of the allegedly outrageous conduct of the first defendant. This claim was rejected by Woolf J. as wholly inappropriate.[23] In *Appleton v Garrett*[24] the defendant dentist administered excessive dental treatment to his patients on a massive scale. The claimants succeeded in trespass on the basis that their consent to treatment was vitiated by the defendant's deliberate and cynical failure to disclose that the treatment was unnecessary.[25] Dyson J. held that the outrageous nature of the defendant's conduct also informed the appropriate remedy, awarding aggravated damages calculated as 15 per cent of each claimant's award for personal injury.[26] In New Zealand, the Court of Appeal indicated in *Ellison v L*,[27] that awards of exemplary damages should be reserved for cases of truly outrageous conduct (being conduct that was high-handed or in flagrant disregard for the patient's safety and going beyond mere negligence), which cannot be adequately punished in any other way (for example by an award of general damages). It is submitted that a similar approach should be adopted to awards of aggravated or exemplary damages in England and Wales.

---

[21] *Quantum* of damages for personal injuries is too vast a topic for this book and is more than adequately dealt with elsewhere, for example Kemp & Kemp, *The Quantum of Damages*.

[22] [1986] 1 All E.R. 54.

[23] This decision was approved by the Court of Appeal in *AB v. South West Water Services Ltd* [1993] 1 All E.R. 609.

[24] [1997] 8 Med. L.R. 75.

[25] See para. 12–133, above.

[26] In an Australian case, *Backwell v. AAA* [1997] 1 V.R. 182, exemplary (punitive) damages were awarded to the claimant. The claimant was a participant in an artificial insemination programme run by the defendant, by whose negligence, she was artificially inseminated with semen from a donor of an incompatible blood type. She became pregnant and was advised by the defendant to have an abortion and that if she continued the pregnancy and subsequently miscarried, her identity might be revealed and adverse publicity might force the donor insemination programme to close. She was also told that if she did not agree to an abortion, it would be difficult for her to take part in that insemination programme or any other. The defendant admitted that those were false threats. The defendant's false threats had caused distress and placed the claimant in a false dilemma. They were designed to persuade her to act contrary to her religious and moral beliefs. Against her religious beliefs, the claimant underwent an abortion. It was held that it was open to the jury to award modest exemplary damages. The claimant was awarded A$125,000 in exemplary damages, reduced on appeal to A$60,000 (the same as the claimant's award for compensatory damages).

[27] [1998] 1 N.Z.L.R. 416. See also *L v. Robinson* [2000] 3 N.Z.L.R. 499, where the claimant had approached the defendant psychotherapist for treatment following sexual abuse. The defendant engaged in sexual misconduct whilst the claimant was his patient, thereby causing or risking causing further psychological or psychiatric harm to the claimant. The defendant was struck off the medical register, and the court also awarded compensatory and exemplary damages to reflect its condemnation of the defendant's outrageous conduct. Disciplinary action was held to be no bar to such an award.

(iii) *Damages in wrongful birth and wrongful conception claims*

Unwanted pregnancy leading to unwanted but healthy child. Where the **12–289**
medical practitioner was negligent in the performance of a sterilisation or
abortion, the principal "damage" suffered by the claimant is usually not personal
injury, but the arrival of an unplanned baby.[28] Nevertheless, it has been held that
an unwanted conception is a personal injury in the sense that it is an "impairment" of the claimant's bodily condition.[29] The measure of damages for such
damage or injury has been the subject of a number of recent decisions and of
much academic discussion.[30] For claims resulting either from failed sterilisation
or failed termination operations the trend in England and Wales[31] was to permit
recovery under three main heads of damage[32]:

---

[28] Pregnancy itself would not be regarded as personal injury if the claimant throughout wanted to
become pregnant and to bear a child, even though she would not have done so if she had been warned
that her general health made child-bearing dangerous, see *R. v. Croydon Health Authority* [1998]
Lloyd's Rep. Med. 44.

[29] See *Walkin v. South Manchester Health Authority* [1995] 1 W.L.R. 1543, CA. This case concerned
a failed female sterilisation operation that resulted in the birth of a healthy child. The claimant issued
but did not serve her writ within the primary limitation period, and then issued and served a second
writ seeking damages for economic loss arising out of the negligent advice and treatment that led to
the unwanted birth. On a preliminary issue as to whether the shorter limitation period for personal
injuries applied to the apparently economic loss claims in the second writ, the Court of Appeal held
that the economic losses claimed were claims for "damages in respect of personal injuries" within
the meaning of s.11(1) of the Limitation Act 1980, and that such claims for post-natal costs arose out
of the same cause of action as the pre-natal pain and suffering, and that the unwanted pregnancy,
whether caused by negligent advice or surgery, was a personal injury in the sense of an "impairment"
within the meaning of s.38(1). Applied in *Saxby v. Morgan* [1997] P.I.Q.R. P531, another case on
limitation, where the Court of Appeal (Potter and Mummery L.JJ.) described the injury sustained by
the claimant as being the continuation of an unwanted pregnancy. Similarly in *Das v. Ganju* [1999]
Lloyd's Rep. Med. 198, QBD Garland J., also a case on limitation, it was held that the continuation
of pregnancy in circumstances where it would have been terminated but for the alleged negligence,
was "personal injury" for the purposes of s.11 of the Limitation Act 1980. To the extent that the
decision in *Walkin v. South Manchester Health Authority* is contrary to the judgments in *McFarlane
v. Tayside Health Board* [2000] 2 A.C. 59, HL, it has been disapproved by the Court of Appeal (Laws
L.J.) In *Greenfield v. Irwin* [2001] 1 W.L.R. 1279, para. 12–290, below.

[30] See, *e.g.* G. Robertson, "Damages for Failed Abortion" (1981) 44 M.L.R. 215; "Negligence and
the Unborn Child" (1979) 2 B.M.J. 1008; A. Grubb, "Medical law—Failure of Sterilisation—
Damages for Wrongful Conception" (1985) 44 C.L.J. 30; L. Hilliard, "Wrongful Birth: Some Growing
Pains" (1985) 48 M.L.R. 224; Angus Stewart Q.C., "Damages for the Birth of a Child" 40 J.L.S.S. 298.

[31] In Scotland there was a general requirement of reasonableness in the particular circumstances of
the case, see *Anderson v. Forth Valley Health Board* (1997) 44 B.M.L.R. 108; *Allen v. Greater
Glasgow Health Board* (1998) S.L.T. 580. In Canada following *Kealey v. Berezowski* [1996] 136
D.L.R. (4th) 708, the reasons for the sterilisation operation will be considered before the consequences of the failed sterilisation is accepted as a genuine injury or a "blessed event" and before the
claim for healthy child-rearing costs is rejected. Thus, for example, if the birth of the unplanned child
imposed unreasonable financial burdens on an impoverished family, a different outcome might result.
In South Africa the Supreme Court of Appeal held in *Mukheiber v. Raath* (2000) 52 B.M.L.R. 1065,
in a judgment handed down on May 28, 1999 (Pre-*McFarlane*) that the liability of a doctor in a failed
female sterilisation case in negligence and in negligent misrepresentation extended to covering the
costs of the upbringing of the unplanned child, limited only to the parents' means and station in life
and continuing until the child was reasonably able to support itself.

[32] Different considerations prevailed where the claimant did not want a child at all and, because of
the defendant's negligence, had a handicapped child. In those circumstances the normal costs of
upbringing, increased because of the handicap were recovered in: *Robinson v. Salford Health
Authority* [1992] 3 Med. L.R. 270 (failed female sterilisation). In *Fish v. Wilcox* [1994] 5 Med. L.R.
230 (failure to detect foetal abnormalities, loss of opportunity to terminate resulting in disabled child),
the Court of Appeal held that a mother who gave up work to look after a handicapped child which
would not have been born but for the defendant's negligence was not entitled to claim both the value
of her nursing services and her loss of earnings.

1. General damages for the mother's pain and discomfort associated with pregnancy and the birth[33];

2. Special damages for the financial expenditure or loss associated with or consequent upon the pregnancy and birth; and[34]

3. Economic loss caused after the birth of the unwanted child and incurred on the child's upbringing and care.[35]

12-290 Following the decision in *McFarlane v. Tayside Health Board*,[36] the mother's claim for general damages for the physical effects of the pregnancy and birth is recoverable (head (a) above).[37] The claim for special damages arising out of the

---

[33] For cases where such an award was made see: *Scuriaga v. Powell* (1979) 123 S.J. 406 (failed termination); *Udale v. Bloomsbury Area Health Authority* [1983] 1 W.L.R. 1098 (failed female sterilisation); *Thake v. Maurice* [1986] Q.B. 644, (failed male sterilisation), damages for expense of birth and loss of earnings, but no award for pain and distress of labour since the judge held that the joy of the birth offset the pain and distress of the labour; *Allen v. Bloomsbury Health Authority* [1993] 1 All E.R. 651 (failed termination).

[34] For cases where such an award was made see: *Udale v. Bloomsbury Area Health Authority, ibid.*; *Allen v. Bloomsbury Health Authority*; *ibid.*

[35] For cases where such an award was made see: *Emeh v. Kensington and Chelsea and Westminster Area Health Authority* [1985] Q.B. 1012, CA (failed female sterilisation), congenitally deformed child born; *Benarr v. Kettering Health Authority* (1988) 138 N.L.J. 179 (failed male sterilisation), where the damages included a sum for future private education as that was an expectation of this child in this particular family; *Thake v. Maurice, ibid.* the defendant did not appeal against this part of the judgment, although he did appeal on liability. The claimant cross-appealed in relation to damages and recovered an additional £1,500 for pain and suffering during the unwanted pregnancy; *Gold v. Haringey Health Authority* [1988] Q.B. 481 (failed female sterilisation); *Allen v. Bloomsbury Health Authority, ibid.* It appears that no claim was made under this head in *Scuriaga v. Powell* (presumably because a comparable claim for loss of earnings contingent upon the rearing of a child was conceded by the defendant, see *Greenfield v. Irwin* [2001] 1 W.L.R. 1279, CA, *per* Buxton L.J. at 1288). This claim was rejected in *Udale v. Bloomsbury Area Health Authority* on the grounds of public policy. *Cataford v. Moreau* (1981) 114 D.L.R. (3d) 585 is a Canadian decision made at around the same time to the same effect. For a case where the claimant recovered only the additional costs of the handicap see *Salih v Enfield Health Authority* [1991] 3 All E.R. 400 (incorrect diagnosis leading to unwanted handicapped child), the trial judge awarded the whole cost of upbringing of the handicapped child but the Court of Appeal allowed only the additional cost. However, in that case the birth of the handicapped child caused the parents to abandon their intention to have a second child, and this fact was crucial to the Court of Appeal's reasoning. *Cf. McLelland v. Greater Glasgow Health Board* 1999 S.C. 305, Sc. Ct. Sess. (OH). The parents of a Down's syndrome child whose condition was not diagnosed before birth recovered damages for the full cost of rearing the child, notwithstanding that if the pregnancy had been terminated they would have gone on to have another child. Both parents also recovered separately for mental distress (falling short of mental illness) suffered on discovery of the child's condition and during its upbringing. It is submitted that neither award would have been made in England and Wales. The reasoning in *Salih v. Enfield Health Authority* is strongly criticised by P. R. Glazebrook in "Unseemliness Compounded by Injustice" (1992) 51 C.L.J. 226. It was argued that such litigation is morally unacceptable, and that such an action for financial loss is not maintainable in principle, following the House of Lords' decisions in *Governors of the Peabody Donation Fund v. Sir Lindsay Parkinson* [1985] A.C. 210, *Caparo Industries v. Dickman* [1990] 2 A.C. 605 and *Murphy v. Brentwood D.C.* [1991] 1 A.C. 398.

[36] [2000] 2 A.C. 59 (failed male sterilisation). Mrs McFarlane conceived and gave birth to a healthy child as a result of a negligently performed and ineffective vasectomy undergone by Mr McFarlane.

[37] *per* Lord Slynn at 74B–E (on the grounds that it is foreseeable and need not be characterised as "injury"); *per* Lord Steyn at 84C (who characterised the pregnancy as an injury); *per* Lord Hope at 87C–E and 89B–D (who considered that the physical effects of pregnancy and birth did not end with the birth and that losses sustained by the mother after the birth should be recoverable subject to remoteness); *per* Lord Clyde at 102B, 102F–H (who held that the pain, discomfort and inconvenience of the experience did qualify as a potential head of damages); Lord Millett dissenting at 114D–E held

pregnancy and birth is also recoverable.[38] However, the loss claimed under the third head, namely the costs of upbringing of the child is purely economic loss.[39] As such, the simple foreseeability of the loss as the result of the doctor's breach of duty is insufficient to grant recovery of loss at law. For liability for economic loss to lie against a tortfeasor there must be a greater link between the negligent act and the damage than mere foreseeability. There must also be proximity and the imposition of the liability must be fair, just and reasonable.[40] The majority held that this was the position for a claim brought in negligence.[41] Lord Slynn, Lord Steyn and Lord Clyde envisaged that recovery of such costs would or might be permitted if an appropriate contract had been entered into, whereby the outcome was warranted.[42] Their Lordships therefore unanimously rejected the claim for the costs of upbringing of a healthy, unwanted child born as a result of a negligently performed sterilisation operation (a wrongful conception claim). The majority found that in cases concerning an unwanted pregnancy resulting in a healthy child, the scope of the duty of care owed by the doctors did not extend to being liable for the costs of bringing up that healthy child. Their Lordships appeared to reach this conclusion by the application of legal principle for recovery of economic rather than physical loss or loss consequent on physical damage.

However, Lord Justice Buxton in *Greenfield v. Irwin*[43] considered the descrip- **12–291** tion of losses as physical or economic was not significant and that *McFarlane* had been decided by the application of a broad principle. He further considered that their Lordships' decision reached beyond the circumstances of unwanted pregnancy. There was no claim for loss of earnings following the birth (rather than during the pregnancy) in the mother's claim for damages in *McFarlane*[44] but the issue arose in *Greenfield v. Irwin*.[45] The defendant had failed to test for pregnancy before the claimant had received contraceptive injections. The claimant was pregnant and gave birth to a healthy child and claimed damages for the pain and suffering of the pregnancy and birth and loss of earnings caused by the claimant's decision to leave work and rear her child. The claim was rejected on a preliminary issue hearing and the decision upheld by the Court of Appeal. The question for decision was whether or not the general approach of *McFarlane* to remoteness of loss in negligence cases where pregnancies resulted from the negligence applied to the facts of the instant case. The loss of earnings in *McFarlane* was directly related to the pregnancy, and as such it fell within the

---

that the true loss suffered by the McFarlanes was the lost freedom to limit the size of their family. He valued this loss of personal autonomy in this case at not more than £5,000.

[38] *per* Lord Slynn at 74D; *per* Lord Steyn at 84D–E; *per* Lord Hope at 89B; Lord Clyde dissenting at 106D and Lord Millett dissenting at 114G–115A, but noting that such a claim may be possible.

[39] The House was unanimous on the characterisation of the loss as purely economic: see Lord Slynn at 75F; Lord Steyn at 79E–G; Lord Hope at 89D; Lord Clyde at 101G, 105H; Lord Millett at 109A–C.

[40] Applying the "three stage test" from *Caparo Industries plc v. Dickman* [1990] 2 A.C. 605.

[41] *per* Lord Slynn at 75F–76D; Lord Steyn at 83D–84B; Lord Hope at 94B, 95B–C, 96H–97E. Lord Clyde held at 101G–102D that the existence or otherwise of the liability was not the correct approach. He preferred a restitutionary approach with consideration of the extent of liability that the doctors thought they were undertaking and proportionality between the culpable breach and the loss caused.

[42] *per* Lord Slynn at 76C; Lord Steyn at 76H; Lord Clyde at 99E–G.

[43] [2001] 1 W.L.R. 1279, CA.

[44] Although Lord Steyn notes at 84 that the pleaded case also referred to the mother giving up work in the later stages of pregnancy.

[45] *ibid.*

limited recovery of damages arising out of the pregnancy. This claim was different and could not be distinguished from the rejected claim for the costs of maintenance of the child. Both were claims caused by the existence of the child, not the pregnancy, and were not recoverable at law.

12–292   **Unwanted pregnancy leading to unwanted disabled child.** Since the decision in *McFarlane v. Tayside Health* Board, its most controversial effect has been its applicability (or otherwise) to cases where a disabled, unwanted child has been born as a result of either a failed sterilisation or a failure to detect a foetal defect.[46] Any reference in *McFarlane* to the recoverability of damages for the costs of bringing up a disabled child is strictly speaking *obiter*. The only express references were by Lord Clyde,[47] and Lord Steyn[48]:

> "If there is a distinction in cases of wrongful conception between those where the child is healthy and those where the child is unhealthy, or disabled or otherwise imperfect, it has to be noted that in the present case we are dealing with a normal birth and a healthy child." (*Per* Lord Clyde.)

> "Secondly, counsel for the health board was inclined to concede that in the case of an unwanted child who was born seriously disabled the rule may have to be different. There may be force in this concession but it does not arise in the present appeal and it ought to await decision where the focus is on such cases."(*Per* Lord Steyn.)

The scope of application of this decision was also limited by the fact that the claim for costs of upbringing did not include any claim for the cost of care and trouble of bringing up the child (as there almost invariably would be for a disabled child) and Lord Steyn's expressly limiting his speech to the issues that arose in the pleaded case.[49] However, the decision is reported as having overruled *Emeh v. Kensington and Chelsea and Westminster Health Authority*, which did concern a disabled child.[50]

12–293   In *Gail Taylor v. Shropshire Health Authority*[51] judgment was handed down at a *quantum*-only hearing on the same day as the judgment in *McFarlane*. His Honour Judge Nicholl (sitting as a High Court judge) noted that the argument in *McFarlane* had been heard, but wrongly thought that their Lordships had not yet delivered their opinions. Considering himself to be bound by the Court of Appeal

---

[46] See Commentary following *Gail Taylor v. Shropshire Area Health Authority* [2000] Lloyd's Rep. Med. 96, QBD at 107–108.

[47] At 99D–E.

[48] At 84A–B.

[49] *ibid.* at 77B–C.

[50] In the *All England Reports Emeh* is referred to as "considered". The reports also indicate that *Thake v. Maurice* and *Allen v. Bloomsbury Health Authority* have been overruled. In *Rand v. Dorset Health Authority* [2000] Lloyd's Rep. Med. 181, Newman J. noted at 189 that it was unclear from the reports of the decision of the House of Lords in *McFarlane* whether the case of *Emeh* should be considered to be "overruled" as the *Weekly Law Reports* (and subsequently the *Law Reports* state), or "considered" as the All England Reports suggest. However, the judge noted that *Emeh* had proceeded on an erroneous analysis of "injury" and could not be a sound legal basis for the claims made in *Rand*. Henriques J. in *Hardman v. Amin* [2001] P.N.L.R. 303, also noted at 325 that the criticism of *Emeh* was by the same two lords (Lord Steyn and Lord Clyde) who expressly reserved the application of their analysis to a case concerning a disabled child until such a case was brought before them. Accordingly, it appears to be the case that *Emeh* is only criticised in relation to the decision to award the total maintenance costs, rather than the additional cost of disability which did not arise as an alternative measure of damages for consideration in that case.

[51] *ibid.*, (a case where the mother had become pregnant following a negligent sterilisation operation and had given birth to a disabled child).

authority of *Emeh v. Kensington and Chelsea and Westminster Health Authority* and the endorsement therein of the earlier case of *Scuriaga v. Powell*[52] "unless or until the House of Lords repudiates them", the judge held that the reasonable costs of bringing up the unwanted and disabled child of a pregnancy that followed a failed sterilisation were recoverable, subject to offsetting the value of the child's aid and society for the period of the parent's life expectancy.[53] The mother recovered general damages of £15,000 for the physical and psychological effects of pregnancy, and an additional £25,000 for the additional burden and anxiety of bringing up a disabled child, less £2,500, which was an arbitrary sum applied for the joy and comfort derived from the child. Past expenditure on the child was recovered and future expenditure was not to be limited to what the mother could afford. Services, past and present were valued on a scale that was a scaled-down version of the commercial costs of the services.[54]

It seems that the decision in *Taylor* was *per incuriam*.[55] Decisions following *Mc Farlane* indicate that claims for the full cost of maintenance of a disabled child are not maintainable at law, but claims for the extra cost consequences of the child's disability will be recoverable, based on an extended principle of *Hedley Byrne v. Heller*.[56] In *Parkinson v. St James and Seacroft University Hospital NHS Trust*,[57] the Court of Appeal confirmed the principle that damages for the ordinary costs of upbringing were not recoverable even where a negligently performed sterilisation operation had resulted in the birth of an unwanted, disabled child, by applying the economic loss test, and, if required, by the application of principles of distributive justice. Any disability arising from genetic causes or foreseeable events during pregnancy that were not *novus actus interveniens* could found a claim. The degree of disability necessary would be decided on a case-by-case basis. **12–294**

The majority approach of their Lordships in *McFarlane* relied on the application of the three-stage test in *Caparo* for liability for economic loss to limit the scope of the defendant doctor's liability to what the court deemed was reasonable. The requirement for each head of damage claimed to pass a "reasonableness test" led the judge and then the Court of Appeal to reject the claim for the cost of a commercial surrogate pregnancy in *Briody v. St Helen's & Knowsley Health Authority*,[58] where the chances of success were very low. **12–295**

---

[52] *ibid.*

[53] The defendant had conceded that the claimant was entitled to damages for the pain and inconvenience of the pregnancy and further conceded that a claim for compensation for the extra "wear and tear" involved in bringing up a handicapped child where the burden of the additional anxiety and stress was not offset by the benefit and joy of the birth of a child, was recognised in law as a claim for a loss of the mother's amenity, see also *per* Lord MacFadyen in *McLelland v. Greater Glasgow Health Board*, unreported, September 23, 1998.

[54] This award has been considered in *Farrell v. Merton Sutton & Wandsworth Health Authority*, unreported, July 31, 2000, QBD, H.H.J. E. Steel Q.C., to be an adoption and extension of the proposed new head of claim for loss of the freedom to limit the size of one's own family suggested by Lord Millett in his dissenting opinion (and valued by him at not more than £5,000 in straightforward cases). Since the two judgments were handed down on the same day, this is doubtful.

[55] The case is, in any event, *en route* to the Court of Appeal.

[56] See *Rand v. East Dorset Health Authority* [2000] Lloyd's Rep. Med. 181; and *Parkinson v. St James and Seacroft University Hospital NHS Trust* [2001] 3 All ER 97, CA.

[57] *ibid.*

[58] [2000] Lloyd's Rep. Med. 127, QBD, Ebsworth J., a case concerning the loss of a baby and subsequent emergency hysterectomy resulting in loss of fertility.

12-296   **Wanted pregnancy leading to unwanted disabled child.** Where the claimant wanted a child, but would have sought an abortion if she had been advised that the child she was carrying was handicapped, there are, again, two possible measures of damage to consider: (i) the whole cost of bringing up the child, and (ii) the additional cost of bringing up a handicapped child rather than a normal one. In favour of the first measure it can be urged that, if she had received competent ante-natal advice, the whole cost of bringing up that child would have been avoided. On the other hand, the second measure reflects the difference between the cost which she had been led to expect (had the wanted pregnancy resulted in a healthy child) and the cost which she actually incurred (being the increased costs of care of a disabled child). Furthermore if, after the hypothetical abortion, the claimant would have persisted in her attempt to have a normal child, the second measure may reflect her actual loss.

12-297   In *Rand v. East Dorset Health Authority*[59] the claim arose out of a negligent failure by the defendant to inform the claimants of the results of a routine pregnancy scan that had disclosed a likelihood of a Down's syndrome baby. Newman J. noted that following *McFarlane*, the case of *Emeh* was either overruled or erroneous. He considered that there was no distinction to be made between a healthy and a disabled child, and that the claim for costs of maintenance and care was still a claim for economic loss and as such must fail following *McFarlane* as not being maintainable in law. He also came to this conclusion on the grounds that any quantification of such a claim would involve "an invidious and morally offensive valuation" of the benefit to the claimants of their disabled child.[60] He drew a distinction between a wrongful conception case such as *McFarlane* and a wrongful birth case such as *Rand*, and noted that the breached duty in the latter case was not a duty to prevent conception. Nevertheless he held that the fact that a disabled child was born could not extend the duty wider than was permitted in *McFarlane*. However, the judge went on to note that the existence of the Abortion Act 1967 and its presumed purpose of permitting the lawful termination of pregnancies where the foetus was likely to be severely disabled meant that the defendant health authority was liable (based on the extended principle of *Hedley Byrne v. Heller*[61]), for the financial consequences of its omission where that omission resulted in the loss of an opportunity to prevent the birth of a disabled child. He rejected the claims for the full cost of maintenance of the child, apparently on the grounds that this would extend the duty owed by the defendant to a wider extent than was permitted in *McFarlane*, the liability being limited to the consequences flowing from the child's disability only (*i.e.* the extra cost of care over and above the cost of care and maintenance of a healthy child, but limited to the parental means rather than the child's actual needs). The judge also awarded £30,000 to the claimants for the loss of amenity to their life of having to care for their disabled child.

12-298   Given the distinction made by the judge himself between wrongful conception and wrongful birth claims, there may be an argument that the strict application of the measure of damages from *McFarlane* to the latter class of case is not correct

---

[59] [2000] Lloyd's Rep. Med. 181, QBD, Newman J.
[60] This valuation exercise was carried out by Judge Nicholl in *Taylor v. Shropshire Health Authority* [2000] Lloyd's Rep. Med. 96.
[61] [2000] Lloyd's Rep. Med. at 193.

or is not required as a consequence of the *McFarlane* decision unless their Lordships should be taken to have meant their decision to apply to wrongful birth claims and claims concerning disabled children.[62] In the light of the comments of Lord Clyde and Lord Steyn, it is considered doubtful that this should be taken to be their intention; and the Court of Appeal in *N v. Warrington Health Authority*[63] evidently considered that their Lordships had left open the question of liability for the costs of raising a disabled child.[64]

Loss of amenity. In *Farrell v. Merton Sutton & Wandsworth Health Author-* **12–299** *ity*[65] the judge held, relying on the new head of claim referred to by Lord Millett in his dissenting judgment as a claim for "loss of amenity", that the awards made to the parents in *Taylor* and *Rand* were not in respect of economic loss (and therefore presumably not within the ambit of *McFarlane*) but were awards to compensate for the loss of amenity to the lives of the parents of a disabled child, which imposed constraints beyond what would be expected to arise out of the birth of a healthy child. In *Rand* Newman J. expressly stated that the assessment of these general damages should not be calculated by reference to commercial costs or hourly rates for care since it was: "not an award for financial loss under the guise of general damages".[66] However, in *Taylor*, the use of discounted commercial care rates on the basis of the principle from *Housecroft v. Burnett*[67] was expressly approved and used in calculating the enhancement of the general damages award for the physical and psychological effects of pregnancy to take into account the additional burden and anxiety of bringing up a disabled child.

The current approach to each of the claims brought by the mother or parents **12–300** of a disabled child in a wrongful birth claim was demonstrated by the judgment

---

[62] The principle that a claimant could not recover the costs of the upbringing of a healthy child was held by Ian Kennedy J. in *Richardson v. LRC Products Ltd* [2000] Lloyd's Rep. Med. 280, to apply equally to claims brought for breach of statutory duty as to claims brought in negligence.

[63] Unreported, March 9, 2000, CA. The case concerned an application for permission to appeal by the defendant from a finding on a preliminary issue that there was no cut-off of the defendant's potential liability for the costs of care of a disabled child when the child reached 18 years of age. The difficulties arose because in the period between the decision and the appeal, their Lordships' judgments in *McFarlane* was given. Permission to appeal was refused. The case was to be decided on the basis of pre-*McFarlane* law since the parties had entered into a compromise agreement.

[64] The Court of Appeal refused permission to appeal from the decision of Morrison J. whereby he rejected the argument that the defendant health authority should not be required to pay damages for the cost of care of an unwanted child which was born disabled following negligent advice, for any period after that child reached 18 years of age. The defendant argued that the claimants had no legal duty to provide for the child beyond that age and so should not be compensated for doing so. The claimants' award was not limited because Morrison J. held that they were entitled to be restored fully to the position they would have been in but for the negligent advice and it was likely, on the facts, that they would continue to contribute to the cost of care of the child after its 18th birthday. By contrast in *McLelland v. Greater Glasgow Health Board* 1999 S.C. 305, Sc. Ct. Sess. (OH) the parents of a Down's syndrome child whose condition was not diagnosed before birth recovered damages for the full cost of rearing the child until it reached age 18. The court limited the award in that way because it took judicial notice of the fact that the state would provide benefits to keep a disabled adult. In the light of the more recent decisions concerning claims raised under the European Convention on Human Rights, it is submitted that this limiting approach may be incompatible with Art. 8. See para. 12–301 below.

[65] (2001) 57 B.M.L.R. 158, a case concerning the birth of a disabled child following an emergency Caesarean section operation.

[66] [2000] Lloyd's Rep. Med. 181 at 201.

[67] [1986] 1 All E.R. 332, CA.

of Henriques J. in *Hardman v. Amin.*[68] On the preliminary issue of the basis and extent of damages to be awarded and whether or not a claim for past and future care costs following a wrongful birth of a disabled child was barred after *McFarlane,* Henriques J. held that the claim was not precluded by their Lordships' decision and was not limited to the parents' means. The case concerned a child born disabled following the expectant mother's infection with rubella.[69] The defendant general practitioner admitted a failure to warn the claimant of the probable damage to her child. If she had been so warned the claimant would have terminated the pregnancy. Henriques J. held that the mother's claim for loss of earnings was a claim for loss consequential upon the personal injury claim of the suffering and inconvenience of the pregnancy.[70] The claim for past and future care given by the mother fell to be determined in accordance with *Housecroft v. Burnett* (commercial costs of care scaled down by 25 per cent) and could alternatively be awarded as damages for the loss of amenity to private life caused by the anxiety and stress of the care of and obligations to a disabled child. As to the claim for maintenance and upkeep of the extra costs of a disabled child, this was a claim for pure economic loss, and that in circumstances where the claimant relied upon the defendant doctor not only to diagnose her rubella infection, but also to advise her of her lawful entitlement to a termination under the Abortion Act 1967, the extra requirements for establishing liability in addition to foreseeability of the loss (namely proximity and that imposition of such liability was fair just and reasonable) were present.[71] Recovery of the basic maintenance costs was not sought[72] and would, in any event not have been granted, applying both *McFarlane,* and, more particularly the factually similar case of *Salih v. Enfield Health Authority,* where the Court of Appeal took into account the claimants' decision to have no more children instead of continuing to increase their family. The decision has been followed in *Groom v. Selby,*[73] where it was accepted, on behalf of the claimant that the causal proximity between the breach and the damage suffered in the cases of *Rand* and *Hardman* was stronger than in this case. In *Groom v. Selby* the defendant failed to carry out a pregnancy test before sterilising the claimant. The claimant was pregnant but discovered the pregnancy at a late stage when termination was rejected as an option. She gave birth prematurely to a disabled child. The necessary proximity was held to be present to make the defendant liable for the loss properly recoverable under the application of the fair, just and reasonable test from *Caparo* as approved in *McFarlane.* The maintenance costs (comparable to the costs of the upbringing of a healthy

---

[68] [2001] P.N.L.R. 303, QBD. The approach is current at the time of publication, however permission to appeal to the Court of Appeal was granted to the defendant, and Henriques J. suggested that the hearing of this appeal should be listed with the pending appeal in *Taylor v. Shropshire Health Authority.*

[69] Similar facts to *Salih v. Enfield Health Authority* [1991] 3 All E.R. 400.

[70] Citing Lord Clyde's speech in *McFarlane.* In this case the damages for the personal injury were agreed at a modest sum to reflect the fact that the claimant had wanted this pregnancy, and but for the negligence would have gone through a termination and become pregnant again on two further occasions, but had been subjected to a Caesarean section and the shock of realising that her child was born seriously disabled. The claim for loss of earnings was in principle allowed but in practice in this case was reduced to nil by virtue of a set-off of the loss and expense of a future pregnancy and childbirth.

[71] The judge also found that recovery was justified on the grounds of distributive justice and restitution for the wrong done.

[72] Counsel for the claimant reserved the right to raise the claim if the case went to the House of Lords, but recognised that the court of first instance was bound by *Salih.*

[73] [2001] Lloyd's Rep. Med. 39, QBD, Peter Clark J.

child) were again not claimed,[74] but the claim for the additional costs of the child's disability was allowed.[75]

(iv) *Impact of the Human Rights Act 1998*

The more recent cases have included an additional claim under Article 8 of the   **12–301**
European Convention for the Protection of Human Rights and Fundamental Freedoms. Article 8 entitles a person to "respect for his (her) private and family life and his home". It was noted in *Hardman v. Amin*[76] by Henriques J. that although this entitlement had not been a determining factor in his decision, nevertheless his decision reached by the application of the common law was compatible with Article 8. The disabled child's family, was compensated for the additional costs of care, and the family was therefore able to make decisions concerning the child's care independently of the state. The compatibility of the award of damages limited to the additional costs of the disability with Article 8 (and Article 6) was affirmed in *Groom v. Selby*,[77] and was held to be proportionate to the interests of both claimant and defendant,[78] and consistent with the principle of distributive justice referred to by Lord Steyn in *McFarlane*.[79] In *Greenfield v. Irwin*[80] Lord Justice Buxton reviewed the point more comprehensively and came to the conclusion that there was no reason to think that Article 8 imposed any requirements concerning regimes of damages in claims involving unwanted pregnancies or births.

(v) *Claims by unwanted disabled child*

A separate question which arises in such cases is whether the handicapped child   **12–302**
can make his or her own claim to recover damages on the ground that he or she ought not to have been born at all. This was considered in *McKay v. Essex Area Health Authority*.[81] One of the claims advanced in that case was that if the defendants had not been negligent the mother (who had caught German measles while she was pregnant) would have had an abortion. The Court of Appeal held that this part of the child's claim should be struck out on grounds of public policy. This decision was in line with a number of American decisions[82] and it accords with the recommendations of the Royal Commission on Civil Liability and Compensation for Personal Injury.[83]

---

[74] Counsel for the claimant reserved the right to raise the claim if the case went to the House of Lords.

[75] The claims for general and special damages arising out of or consequent upon the suffering and inconvenience of the pregnancy were conceded in principle by the defendant.

[76] [2001] P.N.L.R. 303.

[77] [2001] Lloyd's Rep.Med. 39, Peter Clark J.

[78] Applying the principles of Lord Steyn's judgment in *Frost v. Chief Constable of South Yorkshire Police* [1999] 2 A.C. 455.

[79] And by Lord Hoffman in *Frost, ibid.*

[80] [2001] 1 W.L.R. 1279, [2001] E.W.C.A. Civ. 113, paras 31–37, and para 48.

[81] [1982] 1 Q.B. 1166.

[82] The relevant American decisions are summarised by G. Robertson in an interesting case note on *McKay v. Essex Area Health Authority*: see "Wrongful life" (1982) 45 M.L.R. 697.

[83] Cmnd. 7054 (1978), paras. 1485–1486. In 1997 the supreme administrative court in France (*Conseil d'Etat*), while compensating the parents, rejected a wrongful life claim by the child himself where a negligently performed amniocentesis deprived the mother of the choice of terminating her pregnancy, the English authority of *McKay* being cited with approval in the opinion of the *Commissaire du Gouvernement*. The position of the supreme civil court in France (*Cour de Cassation*) has been less clear. A decision in 1996 appeared to envisage such a claim (Civ 1ere, 26 mars 1996) and in 2000 judgment was given in the notorious *Perruche* case (*Assemblée Plénière*, 17 novembre 2000,

(vi) *Negligent report*

12–303   Where a medical practitioner is negligent in advising or reporting to or for his patient, the claimant may suffer economic loss as opposed to personal injuries. Although there are very few reported cases of this kind,[84] the same principles would seem to apply as in the case of solicitors or accountants.[85] A doctor who provides a report on his patient's injuries for use in negotiations before litigation has begun will not have immunity from suit as a witness, since his report will not be preliminary to his giving evidence as an expert witness *Hughes v. Lloyd's Bank plc.*[86]

(vii) *Scope of liability for economic loss*

12–304   In *Banque Bruxelles Lambert SA v. Eagle Star Insurance Co. Ltd*,[87] a valuer's negligence case, the House of Lords considered the extent to which the author of a negligent overvaluation of property was liable to compensate a lender who relied upon the property as security for a loan. The question becomes acute in circumstances where the value of the property has fallen between the valuation and realisation of the security. Lord Hoffman, giving the judgment of the House of Lords, introduced a distinction between the consequences of (i) negligently providing inaccurate information which is to be relied upon by the recipient in deciding whether to undertake a course of action and (ii) negligently advising upon whether a course of action should be undertaken. The negligent adviser is liable for a wider measure of economic loss than the negligent provider of information. It is possible that the distinction should apply to doctors' liability in the present context. In *R. v. Croydon Health Authority*[88] the defendant health authority admitted negligent failure to warn the claimant to seek medical advice which would have revealed that she was suffering from a condition (PPH) that

---

Bull. No. 9). In that case the mother contracted rubella while pregnant. Negligently she was not advised of the risk to her foetus of being born handicapped and therefore did not seek a termination. The child was born handicapped and the *Cour de Cassation* decided that he could recover damages in respect of his handicapped existence, in effect basing the recovery on the concept of "wrongful life". Inferior courts showed some reluctance in following this decision, which had provoked a storm of public interest, and in July 2001 three appeals in similar cases were heard by the *Cour de Cassation* (*Assemblée Plénière*). The *Avocat Général* (M. Sainte-Rose) in his opinion argued for a rejection of the principle that a "wrongful life" could be compensated. On July 13, 2001 the Court gave its judgment, which accepted the principle that a handicapped child could recover damages for his handicapped existence flowing from his mother being deprived of the choice of terminating the pregnancy, on condition that it was proved that the legal requirements justifying a therapeutic termination had existed in the cases in question. In all three cases the Court held that it had not been proved that those requirements had existed. It seems likely that the effect of these decisions of the *Cour de Cassation* will be overruled by statute to exclude claims for wrongful life.

[84] In *Pimm v. Roper* (1862) 2 F. & F. 783 the claimant failed on liability. In *Stevens v. Bermondsey & Southwark Group Hospital Management Committee* (1963) 107 S.J. 478 the claimant failed on causation: see para. 12–274, above. For an example of a case where the doctors were held to be liable for the losses caused by their negligent misrepresentations in a medico-legal report, see *Kelly v. Lundegard* (1996) 40 Alta. L.R. (3d) 234. The doctors knew the intended purpose for the report and knew the claimant had sustained injuries that might result in infertility. Despite this they failed to raise this in their report, and thereby prevented the claimant from making a claim in respect of this additional effect of the injury.

[85] See, for example, *McGrath v. Kiely & Powell* [1965] I.R. 497: medical report prepared for litigation omitted material fact. Claimant recovered the difference between the damages actually awarded and the damages which should have been awarded in the original action.

[86] [1998] P.I.Q.R. P98, CA. *Cf. Stanton v. Callaghan* [2000] 1 Q.B. 75, CA.

[87] [1997] AC 191, discussed at Chap. 9, paras. 3–113, *et seq.*

[88] [1998] Lloyd's Rep. Med. 44.

meant pregnancy would be life-threatening. Her diagnosis was not eventually made until the final stages of her pregnancy. She claimed damages for the cost of the care of the healthy child that was born, that she alleged would not have been conceived or born, and the pain and suffering of the pregnancy (including the complications caused by the PPH) and her reactive depression. The awards made on all these claims were overturned on appeal to the Court of Appeal. Applying the *McFarlane* measure of damages, no damages were awarded for the cost of the upbringing of the healthy child. However, since the claimant had only consulted the defendant's radiologist as part of her application for employment with the defendant (and the X-ray that disclosed the PPH was only taken for the purposes of the claimant's application for employment), the Court of Appeal held that her domestic life was outside the scope of duty owed by the defendant's radiologist. Applying the principles of remoteness, her only recoverable loss was limited to the consequences of the late diagnosis of PPH, namely the complications in the pregnancy, her subsequent hysterectomy, the additional treatment of PPH that would otherwise have been avoided and exacerbation of her reactive depression.

Duty of care to prevent economic loss. In *Kapfunde v. Abbey National plc*[89]   **12–305** the claimant sought employment with the defendant. Part of the application process involved completing a medical questionnaire. The claimant suffered from and disclosed her history of sickle cell anaemia and chest infection. A doctor, engaged by the defendant as a part-time occupational health adviser, advised that this history was likely to result in more absences from work. The defendant accepted the advice and declined to employ the claimant. The claimant sued the advising doctor and the defendant (as being vicariously liable for the doctor's breach of duty to the claimant) for damages for economic loss. The claimant lost and on appeal to the Court of Appeal, the appeal was dismissed on the grounds that no duty was owed to the claimant by the doctor, applying *X v. Bedfordshire County Council*.[90] The only relationship between the doctor and the claimant was that of giver of advice and subject of that advice. There was no patient–doctor relationship, and certainly no sufficient proximity or special relationship akin to contract. The doctor's duties were owed to the defendant (although in fact there was no vicarious liability as the doctor was engaged under a contract for services). The extra requirements in addition to foreseeability of economic loss were affirmed. It is submitted that even in the light of the House of Lords' decision in *Phelps v. Hillingdon Borough of London*,[91] the approach in this case and these circumstances is correct.

[89] [1999] Lloyd's Rep. Med. 48, CA.
[90] [1995] A.C. 633.
[91] [2000] 3 W.L.R. 776.

CHAPTER 13

FINANCIAL PRACTITIONERS

PARA.
1. General 13–001
   (a) Scope 13–001
   (b) Scheme 13–002
   (c) The financial sector 13–003
   (d) Regulation 13–006
   (e) The 1986 Act 13–010
   (f) FSMA 13–011
       (i) General 13–011
       (ii) The FSA 13–012
       (iii) The general prohibi-
             tion 13–013
       (iv) The financial promotion
             restriction 13–015
       (v) Authorised persons 13–017
       (vi) Approved persons 13–019
       (vii) Exempt persons 13–020
       (viii) Members of profes-
              sions 13–021
   (g) European aspects 13–023
   (h) The continuing relevance of the
       common law 13–024
2. Duties and liabilities 13–026
   (a) Sources 13–026
   (b) Relevant approach 13–027
   (c) Application of the FSMA
       regime 13–028
       (i) Regulated activities 13–029
       (ii) Financial promotion 13–031
       (iii) Investment 13–033
       (iv) Nature of the services ... 13–035
       (v) Status of provider of
            financial services 13–036
       (vi) Status of recipient of
            financial services 13–037
   (d) Duties and liabilities under the
       FSMA 13–038
   (e) Regulatory rules and the FSA
       Handbook 13–039
       (i) General 13–039
       (ii) The principles for
            businesses 13–044
       (iii) Statements of Principle
             and Code of Practice for
             Approved Persons 13–045
       (iv) The "Conduct of
            Business" sourcebook
            ("COB") 13–046
   (f) FSMA imposed regulatory
       liabilities 13–069
       (i) Liabilities related to lack
           of authorisation 13–070

PARA.
       (ii) Liabilities related to
            authorised persons 13–073
       (iii) Liabilities related to
             EEA firms 13–079
       (iv) Liabilities related to
            official listing of
            securities 13–080
   (g) Other statutory liabilities 13–083
       (i) Liability related to
           unlisted securities 13–084
       (ii) The Misrepresentation
            Act 1967 13–085
   (h) Contractual duties 13–089
       (i) Relevant contracts 13–089
       (ii) Regulatory requirements
            as to terms of business
            and customer
            agreements 13–09
       (iii) Incorporation of
             regulatory duties in
             contract 13–091
       (iv) Duty of care and skill ... 13–092
       (v) Appointed
           representatives 13–095
       (i) Tort based duties 13–099
       (j) Fiduciary duties 13–115
3. Breach of duty 13–117
   (a) General 13–117
   (b) Misleading promotion 13–118
4. Defences and relief 13–131
   (a) General 13–131
   (b) Limited immunity of regulators
       from liability in damages 13–132
   (c) Restriction of liability by
       contract 13–133
   (d) Statutory relief 13–135
5. Remedies including damages 13–136
   (a) General 13–136
   (b) Remedies available to
       regulators 13–137
       (i) Grounds for application
           to court 13–138
       (ii) Persons against whom
            orders available 13–141
       (iii) Orders available 13–143
       (iv) The FSA's extra-judicial
            power to require
            restitution 13–148
       (v) The FSA Enforcement
           manual 13–149

PARA.

(c) Remedies available to private litigants 13–150
   (i) Rescission of contract induced by misrepresentation 13–151
   (ii) Recovery of money or property paid under agreements made by or through unauthorised persons 13–152

PARA.

(iii) Damages or compensation 13–157
6. Shared responsibility 13–167
   (a) Contributory negligence 13–167
   (b) Contribution 13–168
7. The process of resolving claims ...13–169
   (a) Ombudsman 13–170
   (b) Compensation scheme 13–190
   (c) Parallel proceedings 13–205

1. General

(a) *Scope*

13–001   This chapter concerns financial practitioners regulated by the Financial Services and Markets Act 2000 ("the FSMA").[1] Some but not all of these were formerly regulated by the Financial Services Act 1986 ("the 1986 Act"). They consist of a very wide range of occupations. Many will fall outside the public perception of a professional. The term "financial practitioner" is used as a neutral generic description in this chapter.

    Negligence, whether contractual or tortious, is inapt to summate the various bases upon which liability may arise in the financial sector. Regulatory duties may be give rise to statutory liability for breach. Fiduciary duties also feature large. Nevertheless, treatment of financial practitioners is now intrinsic to a book on professional negligence, for two main reasons. First, such persons are central to a services-dominated economy. Secondly, despite the importance of statute-imposed regulation, the common law (and professional negligence principles in particular) remain of fundamental relevance. While regulatory duties may provide bases of claim, contractual, tortious and other common law duties do also. Indeed especially in relation to non-private customers, the common law may provide bases of claim in circumstances where regulatory duties do not.

(b) *Scheme*

13–002   The scheme of this chapter is first to provide an overview of the occupations covered and the regulatory regimes established and then to provide an analysis under the major headings identified above. However, it is beyond the scope of this chapter to provide a detailed review of the law relating to regulation of financial services in the United Kingdom. The 1986 Act, the FSMA and related material, including other legislation, subsidiary legislation, rules, codes, European directives and published guidance, are extensive and complex. Reference should be made to specialist works.[2] It is also beyond the scope of this chapter to deal with the law relating to banking, insurance and pensions. The main focus is upon the activities of financial practitioners, principally those relating to

---

[1] This was substantially brought in to force on December 1, 2001.

[2] For the text of such material and detailed commentary, see *Lomnicka and Powell, Encyclopedia of Financial Services Law* (Sweet & Maxwell). This chapter draws considerably on some of that commentary.

investment, as are within the scope of the FSMA regulatory regime, like the 1986 Act regulatory regime before it.

(c) *The financial sector*

A generation ago the financial sector was much less developed and recognisable **13–003** than now. The main players would have been identified as banks, including merchant banks, insurers, stockbrokers, and at the retail level "insurance" agents (*e.g.* "the man from the Pru") and, to the more knowledgeable, some more recondite animals associated with specialist markets, such as discount houses in the gilt market. "The City" served as an embracing halo to identify an otherwise obfuscating cloud. As a generic description it was remarkable less for its precision than its mystique, inexplicable not only to the uninitiated but even to most of those initiated in financial affairs.

A series of events has shaped today's financial sector in the United Kingdom. **13–004** They may be traced through the development of the euro dollar market, the abolition of exchange controls, "Big Bang", privatisation of state enterprises, the shift from occupational pension schemes to private provision for pensions, tax advantaged investment products (*e.g.* PEPs and ISAs) and generally the encouragement of an investment culture. Internationally, currency and capital markets have burgeoned, with a broad trend towards floating exchange rates and free movement of capital. Securities markets have likewise grown, driven by increased mergers and acquisitions activity, privatisation and demutualisation issues and increasing demand from pensions, mutual funds and private sources, as well as technological aids, principally computers and the internet.

These developments have spawned an increasing and constantly evolving **13–005** range of occupations and specialities. Classification is difficult and various. The pantheon of financial activities includes analysis, research, reporting, advice, custody, management, dealing, regulation, compliance and administration. Similarly financial practitioners will include those identified generally as analysts, bankers, brokers, custodians, insurers, investment advisers, journalists, managers, traders, valuers, regulators and compliance officers, as well as more recognisable professions such as accountants, actuaries and lawyers. The difficulty of classification impacts significantly upon the ascertainment and setting of standards.

(d) *Regulation*

Developments in the financial sector have been paralleled by increasing statu- **13–006** tory regulation of the financial sector, dating principally from the 1970s. A series of statutes established regulatory regimes.[3] The main features of relevant regimes are now familiar. Generally, regulated institutions and firms need to be authorised by an appropriate regulator as a condition of carrying on business in a relevant financial sector. Authorisation demands compliance with a range of requirements relating to integrity, competence, avoidance of conflicts of interests, adequate financial resources, accounts and auditing, records and reporting etc. Regulators are given a panoply of powers including powers to take action to seek injunctions

---

[3] *e.g.* Insurance Companies Acts 1974 and 1982, Banking Act 1979 and 1987, Building Societies Act 1986, Financial Services Act 1986, Pensions Act 1995.

and restitution orders, intervention powers and powers to seek winding up and administration orders. These are backed by criminal, civil and disciplinary sanctions. Compensation from an established scheme may also be available.

13–007   Regulation related to general investor protection was a relative latecomer. Investment was formerly generally perceived as synonymous with speculation and the interest of a rich minority. Change the word from "investment" to "savings" or "pensions" and the perspective inevitably changes. This wider perspective resulted in the 1986 Act directed mainly at regulating the conduct of investment business in the United Kingdom. While originally the system of regulation was at least portrayed as statute backed self-regulation, gradually changes were effected so that eventually it could not be mistaken for anything other than a statutory regime of regulation. The FSMA marks further the shift to a fully statutory scheme.

13–008   The imposition and raising of standards are fundamental objectives of the regulatory regimes. Doing so by what is effectively a statutory scheme takes the process of setting standards considerably further than that effected by self-regulation, but necessarily so. Given the past structure and utilisation of the retail investment sector in the United Kingdom, achieving those objectives requires a metamorphosis of culture, from that of salesman to professional adviser. That metamorphosis is far from complete. It is likely to remain incomplete so long as remuneration is contingent on an investment being made, however open (or less opaque) the commission disclosure requirements. Major scandals relating to mis-selling of home income plans, pensions and endowment policies illustrate how far the change in culture has to go. Indeed the Janus faces of representatives of product providers in the investment sector, one of salesman and the other of adviser, portends continuing misunderstanding, misconduct and litigation.

13–009   The FSMA regulatory regime is relevant only to events occurring after it was brought into force.[4] Preceding events are governed by the regulatory regime under the 1986 Act. The latter will remain of relevance for several years in the determination of consequent claims. The main narrative in this chapter generally relates only to the FSMA regime. However, equivalent duties under the FSA regime are identified, largely in footnotes.

(e) *The 1986 Act*

13–010 Until this Act the United Kingdom lacked comprehensive regulation of the financial services industry as it affected investors. Instead it relied on a combination of piecemeal statutory intervention and self regulation. The FSA 1986 was passed after a review of the law on investor protection[5] and extensive further consultation.[6] The institutional structure established was the conferment of regulatory powers on the Secretary of State for Trade and Industry, the powers being (revocably) transferable to a private sector regulatory body, the Securities and Investments Board ("the SIB").[7] In October 1997 the SIB changed its name to

---

[4] On December 1, 2001. See commencement orders.

[5] By Professor L.C.B. Gower: see his Report, *Review of Investor Protection* (Cmnd. 9125).

[6] See the Government's White Paper, Financial Services in the United Kingdom—a new framework for investor protection (Cmnd. 9432).

[7] 1986 Act, s.114. Most of the powers under the 1986 Act initially granted to the Secretary of State (including powers granted under s.114) were transferred to the Treasury by the Transfer of Functions (Financial Services) Order 1992, S.I. 1992 No. 1315.

the Financial Services Authority ("the FSA"). A general regime for regulation of investment business was enacted,[8] including various sub-regimes relating to unsolicited calls,[9] advertisements[10] and collective investment schemes.[11] Key definitions of an "investment"[12] and "investment business"[13] circumscribed the scope of the Act. The regime proceeded from the general prohibition against any person carrying on "investment business" in the United Kingdom unless an authorised or exempted person.[14] Contravention attracted criminal[15] and civil sanctions.[16] Authorisation was obtainable by one of seven routes,[17] including membership of a self-regulating organisation ("SRO")[18] and certification by a recognised professional body ("RPB")[19] as well as (albeit this was discouraged) direct authorisation by SIB.[20] In the conduct of investment business authorised persons were subject to rules and regulations, including those made by SIB and (taking effect by way of contract) rules made by SROs and RPBs.[21] There was a statutory right of action for contravention[22] although this right was later limited so as to be available essentially only to "private investors".[23] There were also disciplinary (but not criminal) sanctions for contravention. Moreover, a range of intervention powers were conferred on SIB.[24]

---

[8] *ibid.*, Part I (ss.1–128C). Substantial amendments were effected by the Companies Act 1989.

[9] *ibid.*, s.56.

[10] *ibid.*, ss.57 and 58.

[11] *ibid.*, Part 1, Chap. VIII (ss.75–95). For recent decisions relating to collective investment schemes, see *Gordon v. J.B. Wheatley & Co (a Firm)* [2000] P.N.L.R. 755; *Secretary of State for Trade and Industry v. Grant*, unreported, September 15, 2000, Neuberger J.; *The Russell-Cooke Trust Company v. Elliott*, unreported, March 23, 2001 and July 16, 2001, Laddie J.

[12] *ibid.*, s.1(1) and Sched. 1, Part I.

[13] *ibid.*, s.1(2) and Sched. 1 Parts II and III.

[14] *ibid.*, s.3.

[15] *ibid.*, s.4.

[16] *ibid.*, ss.5, 6.

[17] *ibid.*, Part 1, Chap. VIII (ss.7–34).

[18] *ibid.*, s.7. Initially there were five SROs. The Securities Association ("TSA") regulated investment business involving securities and bonds and related derivative products, as well as ancillary investment management and advice. The Financial Intermediaries, Managers and Brokers Regulatory Organisation ("FIMBRA") regulated retail investment business by independent investment intermediaries. The Life Assurance and Unit Trust Regulatory Organisation ("LAUTRO") regulated the marketing of life policies and units in regulated collective investment schemes. The Investment Management Regulatory Organisation ("IMRO") regulated fund managers (both independent and those from merchant and other banks). The Association of Futures Brokers and Dealers ("AFBD") covered firms broking and dealing in futures, options and contracts for differences. In April 1991 TSA and AFBD merged to form the Securities and Futures Authority ("SFA"). In July 1994 FIMBRA and LAUTRO merged to form the Personal Investment Authority (PIA). Thereafter three SROs remained: IMRO, SFA and PIA.

[19] *ibid.*, s.15. Prior to the enactment of the FSMA there were nine RPBs: the three Law Societies (of England and Wales, Scotland and Northern Ireland), the three Institutes of Chartered Accountants (in England and Wales, Scotland and Northern Ireland), the Institute of Actuaries and the Association of Certified Accountants. The Insurance Brokers' Registration Council was an RPB, but ceased to be one in 2000.

[20] *ibid.*, s.25.

[21] For the SIB's rule making powers, see *ibid.*, ss.48 to 56. In general, SRO's and RPB's made rules in respect of most matters (*e.g.* conduct of business), but based on the SIB's prototype, which were contractually binding on their members. The contractual mechanism was not appropriate for giving effect to all regulatory requirements. Hence the SIB made cancellation rules (under s.51) and client money regulations (under s.55) which applied directly to SRO members.

[22] *ibid.*, s.62.

[23] *ibid.*, s.62A.

[24] *ibid.*, Part 1, Chap VI (ss.64–71). See also ss.6 and 61.

(f) *FSMA*

(i) *General*

13–011 This Act is much wider in scope than the FSA 1986, regulating not only investment businesses but the banks and mortgage lenders, insurance companies and Lloyd's businesses as well "mutuals" (building societies and friendly societies). Despite its length, the FSMA is distinctly and deliberately skeletal in some areas. Extensive secondary legislative powers are given to the Treasury and the FSA. These powers have been exercised and there is an immense volume of instruments (including regulations, rules and guidance) made by the Treasury and the FSA which contain the body of the regulatory regime. Key terms to the scope of the regulatory regime are "regulated activities", "financial promotion" and "investment", the operative relevant definitions of which are contained in detailed orders made by the Treasury.[25] Rules and guidance made by the FSA are compiled in "The FSA Handbook".[26]

(ii) *The FSA*

13–012 The FSMA confers powers on a single statutory regulator, the FSA.[27] Nevertheless, the Treasury retains overall responsibility for the regulatory regime as a whole and the Bank of England continues to be responsible for the stability of the financial sector. The regulatory capacity of the FSA is remarkably large in terms of scope, powers and discretion. It regulates the whole of the financial sector and concerns itself with both prudential and conduct of business aspects. It has very wide ranging powers of rule-making,[28] authorisation of firms,[29] approval of key personnel,[30] monitoring, investigation, intervention and discipline.[31] It also undertakes the official listing function as the competent authority under E.C. Directives, styling itself as "UKLA" (the "U.K. Listing Authority").[32] The Act requires the FSA to discharge its "general functions" within a framework of four defined "regulatory objectives" and having regard to seven factors, although these operate at a very general level and are not expressed to be applicable to

---

[25] See further paras 13–030 and 13–032 below as to the RAO and FPO.
[26] See further paras 13–039 *et seq.* below.
[27] See its website: www.fsa.gov.uk or www.thefsa.org.uk.
[28] See especially FSMA, Part X (ss.138–177)("Rules and Guidance"). The FSA has power to make rules under many other provisions in the Act.
[29] See *ibid.*, Part IV (ss.40–55) ("Permission to carry on Regulated Activities"). See further para. 13–018 below.
[30] See *ibid.*, ss.59–63 (a new power). See further para. 13–019 below.
[31] The broad nature of FSA's powers is apparent from the titles to the following Parts of the Act which confer various powers upon it: Part V (ss.56–71) ("Performance of Regulated Activities"); Part VII (ss.104–117) ("Control over Business Transfers"); Part VIII (ss.118–131) ("Penalties for Market Abuse"); Part XI (ss.165–176) ("Information Gathering and Investigations"); Part XII (ss.178–192) ("Control over Authorised Persons"); Part XIII (ss.193–204) ("Incoming Firms: Intervention by Authority"); Part XIV (ss.205–211) ("Disciplinary Measures"); Part XVII (ss.235–284) ("Collective Investment Schemes"); Part XVIII (ss.285–301) ("Recognised Investment Exchanges and Clearing Houses"); Part XIX (ss.214–324) ("Lloyd's"); Part XX (ss.325–333) ("Provision of Financial Services by Members of the Professions"); Part XXI (ss.334–339) ("Mutual Societies"); Part XXII ("ss.340–346") ("Auditors and Actuaries"); Part XXIII ("ss.347–354") ("Public Record, Disclosure of Information and Co-operation"); Part XXIV (ss.355–379) ("Insolvency"); Part XXV (ss.380–386) ("Injunctions and Restitution"); Part XXVI (ss.387–396) ("Notices").
[32] FSMA, Part XVI (ss.72–103). The FSA took over as the "competent authority" from The (London) Stock Exchange after it demutualised in May 2000.

specific decisions.[33] The regulatory objectives are: market confidence, public awareness, the protection of consumers and the reduction of financial crime. The Act provides for a compensation scheme[34] and an ombudsman scheme.[35] A tribunal is established, the Financial Services and Markets Tribunal,[36] with powers of control over the FSA in the exercise of its decision-making powers over those persons it regulates. The FSA remains subject to judicial review in the exercise of its functions under the FSMA, as under the 1986 Act.[37] It continues to enjoy limited immunity from liability in damages.[38]

(iii) *The general prohibition*

The regulatory regime under the FSMA proceeds from the general prohibition[39] (specifically so called) against any person carrying on "a regulated activity"[40] in the United Kingdom unless an authorised or exempt person. Contravention of the general prohibition (the "authorisation offence")[41] attracts criminal liability[42] and a range of civil sanctions.[43]   **13–013**

Territorial scope. The general prohibition only relates to the carrying on of a regulated activity *in the United Kingdom*. The wording is apt to cover "inward" activity which affects the United Kingdom market.[44] As regard "outward" activity by persons in the United Kingdom targeting an overseas market, some guidance is given in the FSMA. Thus the natural meaning of "in the United Kingdom" is extended by applying the so-called "home country control" principle of the single market directives whereby the "home state" has responsibility for its firms no matter where within the EEA they operate.[45]   **13–014**

(iv) *The financial promotion restriction*

The FSMA restricts financial promotion[46] by requiring that it is carried out only by or with the approval of an authorised person[47] (the "financial promotion restriction").[48] There are, however, a number of significant exceptions.[49] As in   **13–015**

---

[33] *ibid.*, s.2. For the "regulatory objectives" see s.2(2)) and ss.3–6. For the factors see s.2(3). The factors are called "regulatory principles" by the FSA.

[34] *ibid.*, Part XV (ss.212–224). See paras 13–190 to 13–204 below.

[35] *ibid.*, Part XVI (ss.225–234). See paras 13–170 to 13–189 below.

[36] *ibid.*, Part IX (ss.132–137) and Sched. 13.

[37] For examples of (unsuccessful) applications against the SIB (in the context of the pensions misselling review), see *R. v. Securities and Investments Board, ex p. Independent Financial Advisers Association* [1995] 2 B.C.L.C. 76; *R. v. Securities and Investments Board, ex p. Sun Life Assurance Society plc* [1996] 2 B.C.L.C. 150.

[38] FSMA, s.1(3) and Sched. 1 para. 19; 1986 Act, s.187. See further para. 13–132 below.

[39] *ibid.*, s.19. 1986 Act, s.3.

[40] As to the meaning of this term see paras 13–029 and 13–030 below.

[41] FSMA, ss.417(1), 23(2).

[42] *ibid.*, s.23.

[43] See para. 13–071 below.

[44] There are exclusions in the RAO (as to which see para. 13–030 below) for investment business activity by "overseas persons" (defined in RAO, art. 3), *e.g.* RAO, art.72(1)(2). Where the 1986 Act applies, note s.1(3).

[45] FSMA, s.418. As to the single market directives, see FSMA, Sched. 3 and para. 13–023 below.

[46] For the meaning of financial promotion, see para. 13–031 below.

[47] FSMA, s.21. For equivalent provisions in the 1986 Act, see s.56 (unsolicited calls) and s.57 (advertising).

[48] So called not in the FSMA but in the FPO (see para. 13–032 below).

[49] Contained in the FPO: see para. 13–032 below.

relation to contravention of the general prohibition, contravention of the financial promotion restriction attracts criminal liability[50] and a range of civil sanctions.[51] Authorised persons cannot be in breach of the restriction, but if they act in breach of the FSA's financial promotion rules applicable to them,[52] the usual disciplinary consequences may follow and they may incur statutory liability for damages under section 150 of the FSMA.[53]

13–016   **Territorial scope.** Unlike the general prohibition, the financial promotion restriction is not expressed by reference to promotion "in the United Kingdom". This is unsurprising given modern forms of communication. A distinction needs to be drawn between what may be termed "inward" and "outward" communications, *i.e.* communications originating from outside and inside the United Kingdom respectively. In the case of the former, the restriction only applies if it is "capable of having effect in the United Kingdom".[54] This is hardly a significant limitation. Internet communications even from outside the United Kingdom would be caught by the restriction. As for "outward" communications originating from the United Kingdom, these are all prima facie caught, although the Treasury may by order provide otherwise.[55]

(v) *Authorised persons*

13–017   There are a number of categories of authorised persons[56] (called "firms" in the FSA's Handbook) but there are two main categories. The first consists of domestic concerns authorised by virtue of having obtained a "Part IV permission"[57] from the FSA to carry on one or more regulated activities. The second consists of undertakings authorised in other EEA member states and entitled to exercise their "single European passport" so as to establish branches or provide cross-border services in the United Kingdom. This second category of "incoming firms" is, in accordance with the United Kingdom's E.C. law obligations, granted automatic authorisation for the purposes of FSMA 2000. The latter category comprises two types of such firms, "EEA firms"[58] and "Treaty firms"[59] They are subject to regulation as "authorised persons" by the FSA when they operate in the United Kingdom, but in a manner that is consistent with E.C. law which provides for a division of responsibility between "home" (*i.e.* another EEA Member State) and "host" (United Kingdom) regulators.[60]

---

[50] FSMA, s.25. The 1986 Act imposed criminal liability for contravention of the restrictions on advertising (s. 57(3)), but not for contravention of the restrictions on unsolicited calls (see s.56(2)).

[51] See para. 13–072 below.

[52] Made under the FSMA, s.145. For such rules, see para. 13–050 below.

[53] See paras 13–076 to 13–078 below.

[54] FSMA s.21(3). But note s.21(5).

[55] *ibid.*, s.21(5). See FPO, art. 12. As to the FPO, see para. 13–032 below.

[56] Listed in FSMA, s.31.

[57] See *ibid.*, s.40(4).

[58] Defined in FSMA, s.425(1)(a) and Sched. 3 (essentially firms exercising their "passport" under single market financial services directives, *i.e.* the banking consolidation directive, the insurance directives and the investment services directive (see further FSMA, Sched. 3).

[59] Defined in *ibid.*, s.425(2)(b) and Sched. 4 (essentially firms exercising their rights under the E.U. Treaty).

[60] Similarly, U.K. authorised firms are also able to exercise their single European passport throughout the EEA and special provision is made for this in the FSMA, s.37 and Sched. 3, Part III.

Part IV of the FSMA[61] contains elaborate provisions relating to the grant of **13–018** permission to domestic concerns to carry on regulated activities. The FSA is given a very wide discretion, especially as to the scope and terms of any permission it grants.[62] It may impose limitations[63] and requirements[64] as to how a person is, or is not, to act. The FSA must ensure that the person concerned will satisfy and will continue to satisfy the "threshold conditions" in Schedule 6 in relation to a regulated activity.[65] Of central importance are the requirements that the person concerned has adequate resources and is suitable (*i.e.* fit and proper). The FSA's procedures and policy as to the grant of permission is contained its Authorisation Manual which forms part of the Regulatory Processes block in its Handbook.[66]

(vi) *Approved persons*

The FSMA introduces an additional layer of regulation in the approved person **13–019** regime.[67] Thus key persons within businesses that are authorised (either those with significant managerial control or those dealing with customers or their property) must be approved and regulated by the FSA. Most of the regulators under the 1986 Act (but not the FSA, which did not have the requisite power under the 1986 Act) operated a similar system of regulating key personnel in firms.[68]

(vii) *Exempt persons*

The FSMA makes provision for certain "exempt persons"[69] who are almost **13–020** entirely outside the regulatory regime. Three categories of person are exempt: (1) "appointed representatives" of authorised persons[70]; (2) recognised investment exchanges and recognised clearing houses[71]; and (3) persons specified, or within a class specified, by Treasury order.[72] They do not contravene the general prohibition if they carry on a regulated activity in the United Kingdom as long as they are exempt person in relation to that activity. Unlike authorised person status, exempt person status is generally conferred to a limited extent in relation to certain regulated activities. Thus if exempt persons stray outside such activities they lose exempt person status and thus breach the general prohibition (unless they become authorised in respect of that other activity). Although exempt persons are subject to the financial promotion restriction,[73] the relevant

---

[61] ss.40–55.
[62] FSMA, s.42.
[63] *ibid.*, s.42(7).
[64] *ibid.*, s.43. This may include an "assets requirement" (s.48(4)) entailing the freezing of assets or their transfer to a trustee.
[65] *ibid.*, s.41 and Sched. 6. Note also Financial Services and Markets Act (Variation of Threshold Conditions) Order, S.I. 2001 No. 2507, which varies Sched. 6.
[66] See paras 13–039 *et seq.* below.
[67] See FSMA, ss.59–63.
[68] See n.18 under para. 13–010 above. These regulators included IMRO, the SFA and PIA.
[69] Defined in FSMA, s.417(1). *Cf.* "exempted persons" under the 1986 Act, ss.207(1), 35–46.
[70] FSMA, s.39; the 1986 Act s.44. See further paras 13–095 to 13–098 below.
[71] *ibid.*, s.285; the 1986 Act ss.36–41.
[72] *ibid.*, s.38.
[73] See para. 13–015 above.

Treasury order exempts non-real time and solicited real-time communications made or directed by an exempt person for the purposes of his business in relation to which he is exempt.[74]

(viii) *Members of professions*

13-021   The FSMA[75] replaces those provisions of the 1986 Act[76] which enabled some 15,000 professionals, mainly solicitors and accountants, to become authorised persons by being "certified" by their "recognised professional body" ("RPB"). It replaces the concept of "recognised professional body" with "designated professional body" ("DPB"). All bodies which were RPBs immediately before the FSMA was brought into force,[77] became DPBs.[78] The position under the 1986 Act was that professionals became authorised persons by virtue of their "certification" by their professional body. In contrast the FSMA exempts from the general prohibition the carrying on of certain incidental regulated activities in certain circumstances.[79] Such incidental activities are termed "exempt regulated activities".[80] The role of the FSA in relation to such professionals is limited.[81] The rulebook of a DPB, insofar as it covers "exempt regulated activities" is subject to the approval of the FSA,[82] but otherwise the FSA has very limited rule-making powers. Thus it can make "disclosure rules"[83] and it may issue directions generally limiting the scope of the exemption on investor protection grounds and thus requiring certain activities to be regulated directly by it.[84] As against any professional person, the FSA may issue a "disapplication order" disapplying the exemption from the general prohibition in relation to him if it deems him not "fit and proper".[85] The FSA has a more general power to make a prohibition order prohibiting an individual (including a professional) from performing a "specified function".[86]

13-022   In contrast to the position under the 1986 Act,[86a] professional firms which carry on "mainstream" investment business need to be authorised by the FSA and are subject to all the provisions applicable to authorised persons. These are firms, for example, that give investment advice (such as arranging life assurance

---

[74] The FPO, art. 16. See para. 13–032 below.

[75] Part XX (ss. 325–333).

[76] See 1986 Act, ss. 15–21.

[77] As to these, see n.19 under para. 13–010 above.

[78] The Treasury (not the FSA) is empowered to "designate" professional bodies satisfying certain conditions: FSMA, s.326, and has done so: The Financial Services and Markets Act 2000 (Designated Professional Bodies) Order 2001, S.I. 2001 No. 1225.

[79] See FSMA, s.327.

[80] But members of professions are not "exempt persons" for the purposes of the FSMA.

[81] In order to enable it to exercise its residual regulatory control, it must keep itself informed as to DPBs (s.325(1)) and keep under review the desirability of exercising its Part XX powers (s.325(3)).

[82] FSMA, s.332(5).

[83] *ibid.*, s.332(1)(2): for the purpose of ensuring that their clients are aware that the professionals concerned are not regulated by the FSA.

[84] *ibid.*, s.328, 330.

[85] *ibid.*, s.329. Note the usual procedural safeguards in s.331 of a "warning notice" (see s.387) followed by a "decision notice" (see s.388) and a right of reference to the Financial Services and Markets Tribunal (see Part IX, ss.132–137).

[86] *ibid.*, s.56 (note s.56(8)(b)).

[86a] See the 1986 Act, s.15.

and personal pensions), manage investments on a discretionary basis or undertake major corporate finance advice.

(f) *European aspects*

The financial services sector has long been the subject of European Community   **13–023**
directives. These have been given effect in United Kingdom legislation. Leaving
aside major directives relating to banking and insurance, major directives relate
to promotion of listed securities and other aspects of listing,[87] prospectus requirements for non-listed securities,[88] collective investment schemes,[89] insider dealing,[90] capital adequacy,[91] investment services,[92] and investor compensation
schemes.[93]

(g) *The continuing relevance of the common law*

Despite the impact of financial services legislation, the common law has continu-   **13–024**
ing relevance, particularly the common law relating to contract, tort, trust,
fiduciaries, confidentiality, damages and restitution, as well as other statutes, *e.g.*
the Misrepresentation Act 1967. Investment claims cannot be corralled into a
discrete pen which is the exclusive domain of what may be seen as somewhat
recondite regulatory law. Statute led regulatory law constitutes only another
overlay to other areas of law which impact on investment and the task of the
lawyer is to be acute to the interrelationship and the scope for development.

(h) *Human Rights law*

The influence of the Human Rights Act 1998 ("the HRA")[94] can be clearly be   **13–025**
seen in the FSMA.[95] Nevertheless, it should not automatically be assumed that
the FSMA safeguards all Convention rights and particular provisions should be
examined closely in light of the HRA. The FSA is clearly a public authority for
the purposes of the HRA, at least when it is carrying out functions of a public

---

[87] See the Admissions Directive (Council Directive 79/279 [1979] O.J. L66/21); the Listing Particulars Directive (Council Directive 80/390 [1979] O.J. L100/1) and the Interim Reports Directive
(Council Directive 82/121 [1982] O.J. L48/26). These have been given effect in the U.K. formerly by
Part IV of the 1986 Act and now by Part VI of the FSMA.
[88] The Prospectus Directive (Council Directive 89/298). This has been given effect in the U.K. by the
Public Offers of Securities Regulations 1995 (S.I. 1995 No. 1537) (as amended by S.I. 1999 No. 734
and S.I. 1999 No. 1146), made under the European Communities Act 1982 s.2(2).
[89] The UCITS Directive (Council Directive 85/611 [1985] O.J, L375/3). This has been given effect
in the U.K. formerly by Part 1 Chapter VIII (ss.75–95) of the 1986 Act and now by Part XVII (ss.
235 to 284) of the FSMA and subsidiary rules thereunder.
[90] The Insider Dealing Directive (Council Directive 89/592 [1989] O.J. L334/30).
[91] The Capital Adequacy Directive (Council Directive 93/6 [1993] O.J. L141/1).
[92] The Investment Services Directive (Council Directive 93/22 [1993] O.J. L141/27).
[93] The Investor Compensation Directive (Council Directive 97/9 [1997] O.J. L84/22).
[94] For a detailed consideration of the impact of the Human Rights Act 1998 in the field of financial
services see L.-A. Mulcahy, *Human Rights and Civil Practice* (Sweet & Maxwell, 2001), chap.14.
See also chap. 6 of this book.
[95] Especially in relation to the market abuse regime (FSMA, Part VIII, ss.118–131), disciplinary
powers (FSMA, Part XXVI, ss.387–396) and the Financial Services and Markets Tribunal (Part IX,
ss.132–137). See the sourcebooks in the FSA Handbook (paras 13–039 *et seq.* below) relating to
market conduct, enforcement and decision making.

nature. As such, it is prohibited from acting in a way that is incompatible with a Convention right.[96] The limited immunity from liability in damages conferred upon the FSA by the FSMA, does not extend to an award of damages made against it in relation to an act or omission which is unlawful as a result of section 6(1) of the HRA.[97] Although the primary aim of the HRA is to protect the rights of individuals, the European Court of Human Rights has long recognised that a "company" may be a person for the purposes of the Convention and so have rights capable of protection. In practice, such rights are likely to be far more limited than the rights of an individual. However, rights such as those conferred under Article 6,[98] Article 8,[99] Article 10[1] and Article 1 of Protocol No 1[2] will provide a degree of protection to companies as well as individuals.

2. DUTIES AND LIABILITIES

(a) *Sources*

13–026 The duties of financial advisers and institutions arise from a range of sources: statutes (especially regulatory statutes), the common law and codes of practice. Breach of these duties may (but not invariably) give rise to civil liability. Some liabilities are generally characterised by reference to a duty (*e.g.* breach of contract) others may be characterised by reference to the relevant default (*e.g.* misrepresentation). Whether and, if so, to what extent, liability may arise from one or more such sources will require close analysis of the circumstances and context of each case. Victims of unlawful acts of a public authority may bring proceedings against it.[3]

(b) *Relevant approach*

13–027 In analysing claims from a financial context, the first main issue which needs to be addressed is one of regulatory application. Does any statute-based or other regulatory regime apply? If so, which? What is its impact, taking into account the regulatory classification of both claimant and defendant, the nature of the services provided and relevant contractual arrangements? Does it give rise to any duties and liabilities? To what extent, if at all, does it modify what would otherwise be the position? What is the significance, if any, of the regulatory regime for common law liabilities? The second main issue which needs to be

---

[96] Human Rights Act 1998, s.6(1).
[97] FSMA, s.1(3) and Sched. 1 para. 19 and (as competent authority—see para. 13–012 above) s.102. See further para. 13–132 below. The extent of this immunity of the FSA can itself be challenged in the event that it is shown to be disproportionate to the legitimate needs of society: see for example *Fayed v. United Kingdom* (1994) 18 E.H.R.R 393. The FSMA confers like limited immunity from liability in damages upon operators of the Financial Ombudsman Service and the Financial Services Compensation Scheme: see paras 13–189 and 13–204 below.
[98] The right to a fair trial.
[99] The right to privacy.
[1] The right to freedom of expression.
[2] The right to protection of property.
[3] Human Rights Act 1998, s.7(1) A "victim" is any person who is directly affected by the alleged breach of the Convention. It is not necessary to show detriment: see *e.g. De Jong, Baljet and Van den Brink v. The Netherlands* (1984) 8 E.H.R.R. 20, paras 40–41.

addressed is the relevance of other potential causes of action. These may arise under other relevant statutes such as the Misrepresentation Act 1967. There may be common law causes of action such as breach of contract, tort (especially the torts of deceit and negligence) or breach of fiduciary and confidentiality duties.

(c) *Application of the FSMA regime*

The regulatory regime under the FSMA, like that under the predecessor 1986   **13–028**
Act, contains a range of criteria for its application, graduated to the multifarious range of circumstances to which it relates. Ascertainment of the impact of the relevant regime consequently demands analysis of those criteria and their application to the circumstances of a case. In particular, the impact of the regulatory regime will depend on ascertaining:

  (i) whether or not the services provided involved carrying on a "regulated activity" in the United Kingdom[4];

  (ii) whether or not there was any "financial promotion"[5];

  (iii) whether or not an "investment" was involved and, if so, its type;

  (iv) the nature of the services provided;

  (v) the regulatory status of the provider;

  (vi) the regulatory status of the recipient.

Ascertaining each of these matters is at the forefront of analysis.

(i) *Regulated activities*

The focus of the general prohibition is the carrying on of a "regulated activity"   **13–029**
in the United Kingdom.[6] A regulated activity is an activity which is (1) specified in an order made by the Treasury[7] and (2) carried on by way of business.[8] A regulated activity must fall within one of two categories. The first is a specified activity which relates to an investment also so specified. The second is a specified activity which relates to property of any kind, whether or not an investment.[9]

---

[4] Where the 1986 Act applies, the equivalent question is whether the services involved the carrying on of "investment business" (involving various "investment activities") in the U.K.: see ss. 1, 3 and Sched. 1 Part II, of that Act. As to territorial scope, see para. 13–014 above.
[5] Where the 1986 Act applies, the equivalent question is whether there were any unsolicited ("cold") calls or investment advertising see ss. 56–58 of that Act.
[6] FSMA, s.19. See paras 13–013 and 13–014 above. In relation to the 1986 Act, see the equivalent prohibition in s.3 and the focus on the carrying on of "investment business" in the United Kingdom. "Investment business" involved engaging by way of business in one or more of several defined "investment activities" which were not excluded activities: see s.1(2) and Sched. 1, Parts II and III of the same Act.
[7] The RAO: see para. 13–030 below.
[8] See Lord Diplock's description of the word as an "etymological chameleon" in *Town Investments Ltd v. Department of the Environment* [1978] A.C. 359 at 383C. Note also as to the repetition element connoted, *Smith v. Anderson* [1880] 15 Ch.D. 247 at 277–8. In the context of the meaning of the word in the 1986 Act, s.63 (predecessor to FSMA, s.412), see *Morgan Grenfell & Co. v. Welwyn Hatfield DC* [1995] 1 All E.R. 1.
[9] FSMA, s.22 and Sched. 2.

13–030　　**The RAO.** The relevant order made is the Financial Services and Markets Act 2000 (Regulated Activities) Order 2001 ("the RAO").[10] Activities within the first category presently so specified relate to (1) accepting deposits[11]; (2) effecting and carrying out contracts of insurance[12]; (3) dealing in investments as principal[13]; (4) dealing in investments as agent[14]; (5) arranging deals in investments[15]; (6) managing investments[16]; (7) safeguarding and administering investments[17]; (8) sending dematerialised instructions[18]; (9) establishing etc. a collective investment scheme[19]; (10) establishing etc. a stakeholder pension scheme[20]; (11) advising on investments[21]; (12) advising, managing and arranging activities in relation to Lloyd's[22]; (13) entering as provider into a funeral plan contract[23]; (14) entering into a regulated mortgage contract or administering the same[24] and (15) agreeing to carry on certain specified activities.[25] Each of such activities is defined in more detail and it is essential to have regard to the definitions including any applicable exclusions. Activities within the second category presently so specified relate to (9) and (10).[26] The scheme of the RAO is, broadly, to incorporate under "chapters" a series of articles relating to a "regulated activity", the first article defining the substantive activity and the remainder defining relevant exclusions.[27] There are also some general exclusions in the RAO applying to groups of regulated activities.

(ii) *Financial promotion*

13–031　The term "financial promotion" is not as such defined in the FSMA, but it clearly covers not only advertising but all other forms of promoting certain investment

---

[10] S.I. 2001 No. 544 made under FSMA, s.22(5).

[11] RAO Part II, Chap. II, arts 4, 5–9; *cf.* Banking Act 1987, s.3.

[12] *ibid.*, Chap. III, arts 4, 10–13; *cf.* Insurance Companies Act 1982, s.2.

[13] *ibid.*, Chap. IV, arts 4, 14–20, 66, 68–72; *cf.* 1986 Act, s.1(2), (3) and Sched. 1, Part II (Activities Constituting Investment Business), para. 12 (dealing in investments), Part III (Excluded Activities) (see paras 17–23), Parts IV and Part V (Interpretation).

[14] *ibid.*, Chap. V, arts 4, 21–24, 67–72; *cf.* 1986 Act, s.1(2), (3) and Sched. 1, Part II, para. 12 (dealing in investments), Part III, paras. 19–23, Parts IV and V.

[15] *ibid.*, Chap VI, arts 4, 25–36, 67–72; *cf.* 1986 Act, s.1(2), (3) and Sched. 1, Part II, para. 13 (arranging deals in investments), Part III, paras 18–22, 24, 25B, and Parts IV and V.

[16] *ibid.*, Chap VII, arts 4, 37–39, 66, 68 and 69; *cf.* 1986 Act, s.1(2), (3) and Sched. 1, Part II, para. 14 (managing investments), Part III, paras 18, 19 and 22, Parts IV and V.

[17] *ibid.*, Chap VIII, arts 4, 40–44, 66–69 and 71; *cf.* 1986 Act, s.1(2), (3) and Sched. 1, Part II, para. 13A (custody of investments), Part III, paras 18–22, 24 and 24A, Parts IV and V.

[18] *ibid.*, Chap IX, arts 4, 45–50, 66 and 69; *cf.* 1986 Act, s.1(2), (3) and Sched. 1, Part II, para. 16A (sending dematerialised instructions), Part III, paras 18 and 22, Parts IV and V.

[19] *ibid.*, Chap X, arts 4, 51; *cf.* 1986 Act, s.1(2), (3) and Sched. 1, Part II, para. 16 (establishing etc. collective investment schemes) and Part V.

[20] *ibid.*, Chap XI, arts 4, 52; no 1986 Act equivalent.

[21] *ibid.*, Chap XII, arts 4, 53–55, 67–70 and 72; *cf.* 1986 Act, s.1(2), (3) and Sched. 1, Part II, para. 15 (investment advice), Part III, paras 18, 19, 21, 22, 24, 25 and 25A, Parts IV and V.

[22] *ibid.*, Chap XIII, arts 4, 56–58; no 1986 Act equivalent.

[23] *ibid.*, Chap XIV, arts 4, 59 and 60; no 1986 Act equivalent.

[24] *ibid.*, Chap XV, arts 4, 61–63; no 1986 Act equivalent.

[25] *ibid.*, Chap XVI, arts 4, 64, 65 and 72; In the 1986 Act agreeing to carry on various investment activities was incorporated within the definition of many such activities (see s.1(2), (3) and Sched. 1, Part II, para. 12, 13, 13A, 14, 15 and 16A), subject to like exclusions as the primary activity.

[26] *ibid.*, Chap XI, art. 4(2).

[27] In contrast the scheme under the 1986 Act is, within Sched. 1, to group the substantive definitions of "investment activities" in Part II of that schedule and to group relevant exclusions in Parts III and IV. Apart from schematic layout, there are some substantive differences between what comprises relevant activities (including relevant exclusions) within the 1986 Act and the RAO respectively.

activities. The financial promotion restriction prohibits a person, in the course of business, from communicating an invitation or an inducement to engage in investment activity, unless he is an authorised person or the content of the communication has been approved by an authorised person.[28] The term "engaging in investment activity" is defined by reference to other terms, "controlled activity" and "controlled investment".[29] The definition of these terms along with the circumstances in which the prohibition is disapplied and other matters are left to be detailed by Treasury order.

The FPO. The order made, the Financial Services and Markets Act 2000 **13–032** (Financial Promotion) Order 2001[30] ("the FPO"), is extensive. The definitions of "controlled activities" and "controlled investments" overlap, but do not coincide, with similar definitions of "regulated activities" and "specified investments" in the RAO.[31] There are also definitions relating to different kinds of communications. "Real time communications" are distinguished from "non-real time" communications. There is a wide range of "exemptions" (some qualified) from the promotion prohibition, including by reference to the context of the promotion, the nature of the relevant investments and the categories of persons by whom and to whom the promotion is made. Equivalent provisions in the 1986 Act relating to unsolicited calls and advertising were also subject to similar qualifying regulations or orders.[32]

(iii) *Investment*

Investment is widely defined to include "any asset, right or interest" in the **13–033** context of regulated activities[33] and financial promotion[34] respectively, but detailed definition is left to subordinate legislation.[35] Relevant orders relating to each of those matters contain detailed definitions of the kind of investments to which they relate. In the context of regulated activities,[36] the RAO[37] contains detailed definitions of investments of a "specified kind". In the context of financial promotion,[38] the FPO[39] contains detailed definitions of "controlled investments". The definitions in the two orders generally correspond, but not precisely. There are also some changes from equivalent predecessor legislation.

---

[28] FSMA, s.21. See further paras 13–015 and 13–016 above.

[29] *ibid.*, s.21(8).

[30] S.I. 2001 No. 1335 made under FSMA s.21(15). See also Sched. 2.

[31] See para. 13–030 above.

[32] In relation to unsolicited calls see s.56 and with effect from January 1, 1992, the Common Unsolicited Calls Regulations made by the SIB. In relation to investment advertisements, see ss.57 and 58 and various exemption orders latterly made by the Treasury: S.I. 1996 No. 1586; S.I. 1997 No. 963 and S.I. 1995 No. 1536.

[33] FSMA, s.22(4).

[34] *ibid.*, s.21(14).

[35] *ibid.*, ss. 22(5) and 21(15) and see the RAO and FPO. As to the position under the 1986 Act. An "investment" was generally defined in s.1(1) as "any asset, right or interest falling within any paragraph in Part I of Schedule 1 to this Act". The Secretary of State was enabled (s. 2) to amend that schedule by statutory order. The approach adopted in FSMA allows far more flexibility by enabling alteration of the definition by statutory instrument without the need to amend the main Act.

[36] See *ibid.*, s.22 and Sched. 2, Part II.

[37] See para. 13–030 above.

[38] See FSMA s.21, esp. subss.(9), (10) and (11), and Sched. 2, Part II.

[39] See para. 13–032 above.

The RAO and the FPO contain relevant definitions of the following kinds of investments: (1) deposits,[40] (2) rights under a contract of insurance,[41] (3) shares,[42] (4) instruments creating or acknowledging indebtedness other than those of the next kind[43]; (5) government and public securities[44]; (6) warrants and other instruments entitling the holder to subscribe for any of the last three kinds[45]; (7) certificates representing certain securities[46]; (8) units in a collective investment scheme[47]; (9) rights under a stakeholder pension scheme[48]; (10) options[49]; (11) futures[50]; (12) contracts for differences[51]; (13) Lloyd's syndicate capacity and syndicate membership[52]; (14) funeral plan contracts[53]; and (15) rights or interests in certain other investments.[54] Within the scope of the FPO, but not the RAO, are (16) agreements for qualifying credit.[55] Within the scope of the RAO, but not the FPO, are (17) regulated mortgage contracts.[56]

13–034   The general prohibition and the financial promotion restriction in the FSMA do not only apply if an investment is involved. A regulated activity may relate not only to an investment but also to "property of any kind."[57] The financial promotion restriction is defined by reference to a "controlled activity" which, in turn, is defined in terms of not only an activity related to an investment but also an activity of a "specified kind" or a "specified class of activity".[58] A frequent context for such dispute is alleged collective investment schemes. The fact that the underlying assets of such a scheme may not comprise investments may dupe the unwary into the misconception that no regulated investment is involved. The assets of a collective investment scheme may comprise "property of any description, including money".[59] However, rights to participate to participate in such a scheme are investments. Indeed they are amongst the most heavily regulated kinds of investments. Disputes may also arise as to the appropriate classification of particular investments[60] which in turn will require consideration of relevant Treasury orders.

---

[40] RAO Part III, art. 74; FPO art. 74 and Sched. 1, para. 12; *cf.* Banking Act 1987, s.5; 1986 Act, s.1 and Sched. 1, Part I, para. 2.

[41] *ibid.*, art. 75; FPO art. 4 and Sched. 1, para. 13; *cf.* Insurance Companies Act 1982, s.1 ("insurance business"); 1986 Act, s.1 and Sched. 1, Part I, para. 1.

[42] *ibid.*, art. 76; FPO art. 4 and Sched. 1, para. 14; *cf.* 1986 Act, s.1 and Sched. 1, Part I, para. 1.

[43] *ibid.*, art. 77; FPO art. 4 and Sched. 1, para. 15; *cf.* 1986 Act, s.1 and Sched. 1, Part I, para. 2.

[44] *ibid.*, art. 78; FPO art. 4 and Sched. 1, para. 16; *cf.* 1986 Act, s.1 and Sched. 1, Part I, para. 3.

[45] *ibid.*, art. 79; FPO art. 4 and Sched. 1, para. 17; *cf.* 1986 Act, s.1 and Sched. 1, Part I, para. 4.

[46] *ibid.*, art. 80; FPO art. 4 and Sched. 1, para. 18; *cf.* 1986 Act, s.1 and Sched. 1, Part I, para. 5.

[47] *ibid.*, art. 81; FPO art. 4 and Sched. 1, para. 19; *cf.* 986 Act, s.1 and Sched. 1, Part I, para. 6.

[48] *ibid.*, art. 82. FPO art. 4 and Sched. 1, para. 20. No equivalent under the 1986 Act.

[49] *ibid.*, art. 83; FPO art. 4 and Sched. 1, para. 21; *cf.* the 1986 Act, s.1 and Sched. 1, Part I, para. 7.

[50] *ibid.*, art. 84; FPO art. 4 and Sched. 1, para. 22; *cf.* 1986 Act, s.1 and Sched. 1, Part I, para. 8.

[51] *ibid.*, art. 85; FPO art. 4 and Sched. 1, para. 23; *cf.* 1986 Act, s.1 and Sched. 1, Part I, para. 9.

[52] *ibid.*, art. 86. FPO art. 4 and Sched. 1, para. 24. No equivalent under the 1986 Act.

[53] *ibid.*, art. 87. FPO art. 4 and Sched. 1, para. 25. No equivalent under the 1986 Act.

[54] *ibid.*, art. 89; FPO art. 4 and Sched. 1, para. 27; *cf.* the 1986 Act, s.1 and Sched. 1, Part I, para. 11.

[55] FPO art. 4 and Sched. 1, para. 26. No equivalent under the 1986 Act.

[56] RAO Part III, art. 88. No equivalent under the 1986 Act.

[57] FSMA, s.22(1). See the RAO, arts 4(2), 51 and 52.

[58] FSMA, s.21, esp. s.21(9). See also the RAO, art. 4(1) and Sched. 1, paras 1–11.

[59] FSMA, s.235(1); FSA 1986, s.75(1).

[60] *e.g.* as in *Larussa-Chigi v. CS First Boston Ltd* [1998] C.L.C. 277.

(iv) *Nature of the services*

The duties of a provider of financial services will vary according to the nature of the services provided. Generally, very little will be required where the services are limited to execution only. On the other hand, the duties will be far more extensive if the services are advisory or involve discretionary management of a portfolio of investments. **13-035**

(v) *Status of provider of financial services*

A person may contravene the general prohibition because he is neither an authorised person nor an exempt person. Even if he is authorised, he may contravene his permission requirement by carrying out a regulated activity not covered by his permission. Similarly, an unauthorised person may contravene the financial promotion restriction by communicating an inducement to engage in investment activity without the approval of an authorised person. On the other hand, the particular circumstances in which financial services are provided may be such that their provider does not carry on any regulated or controlled activities by reason of a relevant exclusion in the RAO or FPO. **13-036**

(vi) *Status of recipient of financial services*

This is relevant in a number of respects. In the FPO relevant exclusions are expressed by reference to the status of the recipient, *e.g.* a "certified high net worth individual" and a "certified sophisticated investor". Again the nature and extent of the duties imposed under the Handbook upon a provider of financial services is graduated to the status of the recipient *e.g.*, a "private customer" as defined. The statutory right of action given for contravention of relevant rules by authorised persons is generally limited to a "private person" as defined.[61] **13-037**

(d) *Duties and liabilities under the FSMA*

Integral to the regulatory regime under the FSMA are an array of requirements imposed not only directly by the Act itself but also by delegated powers given to the Treasury and the FSA. In particular the FSA is accorded wide powers to make rules. The FSA is also empowered to give guidance and advice and to issue statements of principle and codes of practice.[62] Contravention of some of statutory and rules may give rise to civil liability under relevant sections of the Act.[63] A similar position prevailed under the 1986 Act and not only in respect of rules made by the FSA (and the SIB before it), but also rules made by SROs.[64] **13-038**

(e) *Regulatory rules and the FSA Handbook*

(i) *General*

The FSMA obliges the FSA to exercise its rule-making powers in writing and also to publish all rule-making instruments in the way appearing to the FSA to **13-039**

---

[61] See para. 13–077 below.
[62] See para. 13–045 below.
[63] See paras 13–069 to 13–082 below.
[64] 1986 Act, ss. 62, 62A.

be best calculated to bring it to the attention of the public.[65] The FSA has undertaken to publish all rule-making instruments in full on its website.[66] The rule-making instruments in force at any particular time are contained in the FSA's Handbook. This is the title given to a continuously updated compendium of such instruments and other material, including published guidance. In ascertaining the requirements under the FSMA apposite to financial advisers and institutions it is vital to examine the relevant version of the Handbook at the relevant time(s). The Handbook is intended to avoid in relation to FSMA regime requirements, a recurrent problem in relation to ascertaining requirements under the FSA regime, namely the absence of a single source for rapidly ascertaining what rules (especially of SROs) and regulations were in force at relevant times in the past.

13–040   As explained in the introductory "Reader's Guide",[67] the Handbook is divided into "sourcebooks" (providing sources of the FSA's requirements and guidance) and manuals (containing the processes to be followed). Each sourcebook in fact comprises the "rule-making instrument" by which the FSA is required to make rules.[68] The general form is a one page formal instrument and an Annex incorporating relevant rules as well as guidance. The contents page of the Handbook reflects its arrangement as follows:

	Sourcebook or manual	Reference Code
	Principles for Businesses	PRIN
High Level Standards	Senior management arrangements, Systems and Controls	SYSC
	Threshold Conditions	COND
	Statements of Principle and Code of Practice for Approved Persons	APER
	The Fit and Proper Test for Approved Persons	FIT
	General provisions	GEN

---

[65] FSMA, s.153.

[66] For the website, see n. 27 under para. 13–012 above. Para. 4 of the Reader's Guide Instrument 2001 identifies this as "the definitive source for determining what the text was at any particular time for legal purposes". Note FSMA, s.154 as to verification of rules.

[67] It has the status of guidance issued under FSMA, s.157(1).

[68] FSMA, s.153(1), (2).

	Sourcebook or manual	Reference Code
	Interim Prudential sourcebooks (5)	IPRU
Business Standards	Conduct of Business	COB
	Market Conduct, including: 　　　Code of market 　　　conduct 　　　Price stabilising 　　　rules 　　　Inter-professional 　　　conduct	MAR
	Training and Competence	TC
	Money Laundering	ML
Regulatory Processes	Authorisation	AUTH
	Supervision	SUP
	Enforcement	ENF
	Decision making	DEC
Redress	Dispute resolution: Complaints	DISP
	Compensation	COMP
	Complaints against the FSA	COAF
	Collective Investment Schemes	CIS
	Credit Unions	CRED
	Professional firms	PROF
	Lloyd's	LLD
	Mortgages	MORT
	Recognised Investment Exchanges an Recognised Clearing Houses	REC
	United Kingdom Listing Authority	UKLA
Special guides		
Schedules		
Transitional provisions		
Summary schedules		
	Record keeping requirements Notification requirements Fees and other required payments Powers exercised in making the handbook Right of action for damages Rules that can be waived Releases	
Glossary of definitions		
Index		

13–041   Each sourcebook follows a similar structure. Each comprises (1) a contents page, (2) a schedule of transitional provisions (if any), (3) the main text, with any annexes or appendices, and (4) six schedules of requirements and supplementary information.[69] Of the schedules to each sourcebook, the fifth is useful in identifying the extent to which rules in the sourcebook attract the right of action granted under the FSMA for contravention of certain rules.[70]

13–042   The main text of each sourcebook or manual is sub-divided into chapters, sections and paragraphs. Each paragraph is accorded a regulatory status:

(i) "R" is used to denote a general or specialised rule made under the FSMA[71] and other powers, other than an evidential rule. The legal effect of such a rule will vary according to the power under which it is made and on the language used in the rule. Contravention may render a firm liable to enforcement action[72] and/or an action for damages.[73]

(ii) "D" is used to indicate a directions or requirement given under various powers conferred by the FSMA.[74] Directions and requirements are binding on the persons or categories of persons to whom they are addressed.

(iii) "P" is used to indicate a statement of principle for approved persons.[75]

(iv) "C" is used to denote a paragraph of the Code of Market Conduct describing behaviour which, in the opinion of the FSMA, does not amount to market abuse.[76] Such descriptions are conclusive for the purposes of the FSMA.[77]

(v) "E" is used to identify an evidential provision.[78] Such a provision does not bind in its own right but instead relates to some other binding rule. Where provided for within the Handbook, compliance with an evidential provision may be relied upon as "tending to establish compliance" with or "tending to establish contravention" of the rule to which it relates. Evidential provisions thus create rebuttable presumptions of compliance with or contravention of the binding rules to which they refer; "E" is also used in relation to provisions of the Code of Practice for Approved Persons[79] and the Code of Market Conduct.[80]

---

[69] The schedules relate to (1) any record-keeping requirements; (2) any notification requirements; (3) fees and other required payments; (4) powers exercised; (5) rights of action for damages and (6) rules that can be waived.

[70] See FSMA, s.150, considered further in paras 13–076 to 13–078 below.

[71] See as to general rules, FSMA s.138 (general rule-making power) and s.139 (ancillary matters) and as to specialised rules, s.140 (managers of authorised unit trust schemes), ss. 141 and 142 (insurance business), s.143 (endorsement of take-over codes), s.144 (price stabilisation), s.145 (financial promotion), s.146 (money laundering) and s.147 (control of information).

[72] See para. 13–012 above.

[73] See paras 13–073 to 13–079 below.

[74] For example, under s.51(3) of the FSMA about the form and content of applications for Part IV permission.

[75] Made under FSMA s.64(1). See further para. 13–045 below. As to approved persons, see para. 13–019 above.

[76] Made under *ibid.*, s.119.

[77] *ibid.*, s.122(1).

[78] Made under *ibid.*, s.149. Contravention of such rules do not give rise to the consequences set out in the Act for other rule breaches.

[79] Made under *ibid.*, s.64(2). See further para. 13–045 below.

[80] Made under *ibid.*, s.119 (in relation to market abuse).

(vi) "G" is used to indicate guidance given by the FSA[81] and for certain other purposes. Guidance may be given for many purposes including to explain the implications of other provisions, to indicate possible means of compliance and to recommend a particular course or arrangement. Guidance is neither binding on those to whom the FSMA or rules made under the FSMA apply, nor does it have 'evidential' effect. It need not be followed to achieve compliance with the relevant rule or other requirement. Nor does it attract disciplinary liability. Significantly (and in contrast to judicial statements in other contexts[82]) the Handbook expressly states that there is no presumption that departing from guidance is indicative of a breach of the relevant rule.[83]

Detailed consideration of the rules, guidance and evidential provisions contained **13–043** within each sourcebook and manual in the Handbook is outside the scope of this chapter. However, of particular relevance to claims against financial services providers are the Principles for Business (referenced "PRIN") and the "Conduct of Business" sourcebook (referenced "COB"). Contravention of certain rules in COB may result in statutory liability in damages.[84] The Compensation sourcebook ("COMP") is discussed later in this chapter.[85]

(ii) *The Principles for Businesses*

In general, these apply to authorised persons with respect to regulated activities. **13–044** They are a general statement of the fundamental obligations of firms under the regulatory system. Although called "principles" they are not foreshadowed as such in the FSMA, unlike equivalent principles made under the 1986 Act[86] and also unlike the Statements of Principle for Approved Persons made under the FSMA.[87] The regulatory status of the Principles for Businesses are in part rules made under rule-making powers in the FSMA[88] and in part guidance.[89] They are made by a rule-making instrument which is incorporated as a sourcebook (referenced "PRIN") within the Handbook. Contravention of such a principle does not of itself attract the right of action under the FSMA for contravention of certain rules, although it may make a firm liable to disciplinary sanctions. Nevertheless conduct which contravenes a principle may amount to a contravention of a rule which does attract that right of action. The 11 principles have some merit in the context of legal advice and forensic presentation as a first point of departure in order to explain the rationale which may be obscured in detailed and complex rules. Hence their quotation in full:

1. **Integrity:** A firm must conduct its business with integrity.

---

[81] Made under *ibid.*, s.157.
[82] See Chap. 8, paras. 8–156 to 8–159 and Chap. 15, para. 15–091.
[83] Reader's Guide, para. 28.
[84] Under FSMA s.150. See paras 13–076 to 13–078 below. Although providing guidance and evidential provisions, none of the High Level Standards sourcebooks (see para. 13–040 above) provide for such statutory liability. Some of those sourcebooks contain no rules (*e.g.* the Fit and Proper Test for Approved Persons) while others (*e.g.* the Principles for Businesses) are specified under s.150(2) of the FSMA as containing provisions giving rise to no such right of action.
[85] See paras 13–190 *et seq.* below.
[86] 1986 Act, s.47A.
[87] FSMA, s.64. See further para. 13–045 below.
[88] FSMA, ss. 138, 145, 146, 150(2) and 156.
[89] Issued under FSMA, s.157.

2. **Skill, care and diligence:** A firm must conduct its business with due skill, care and diligence.

3. **Management and control:** A firm must take reasonable care to organise and control its affairs responsibly and effectively, with adequate risk management systems.

4. **Financial prudence:** A firm must maintain adequate financial resources.

5. **Market conduct:** A firm must observe proper standards of market conduct.

6. **Customers' interests:** A firm must pay due regard to the interests of its customers and treat them fairly.

7. **Communications with clients:** A firm must pay due regard to the information needs of its clients, and communicate information to them in a way which is clear, fair and not misleading.

8. **Conflicts of interest:** A firm must manage conflicts of interest fairly, both between itself and its customers and between a customer and another client.

9. **Customers: relationships of trust:** A firm must take reasonable care to ensure the suitability of its advice and discretionary decisions for any customer who is entitled to rely upon its judgment.

10. **Clients' assets:** A firm must arrange adequate protection for clients' assets when it is responsible for them.

11. **Relations with regulators:** A firm must deal with its regulators in an open and cooperative way, and must disclose to the FSA appropriately anything relating to the firm of which the FSA would reasonably expect notice.[90]

(iii) *Statements of Principle and Code of Practice for Approved Persons*

13–045 These,[91] presently seven in number, are similar in concept to the FSA's Principles for Businesses[92] but are tailored to meet the position of approved persons.[93] While the latter focus on an authorised person's responsibilities when undertaking regulated activities, the Statements of Principle for Approved Persons focus on such persons' responsibilities when undertaking "controlled" functions in the context of regulated activities. By issuing such statements of principle the FSA was required also to issue a code of practice to help determine compliance with them.[94] The code, divided into general and specific matters, has been issued and is incorporated together with the statements of principle as a sourcebook (referenced "APER") in the Handbook. Four statements of principle relate to every approved person. These statements require integrity, due skill and diligence

---

[90] *cf.* the SIB's Statements of Principle issued under the FSA, s.47A on March 15 1990, "the Ten Commandments". Contrasted with the original Ten Commandments, their quality was not divine and their reformulation into eleven under the FSMA may have been intended to avoid that comparison.
[91] Issued under powers conferred under FSMA. s.64.
[92] See para. 13–044 above.
[93] See further para. 13–019 above.
[94] FSMA, s.64(2).

and proper standards of market conduct in carrying out his controlled function and open and cooperative dealings with the FSA and other regulators and disclosure of information of which the FSA would reasonably expect notice. The other three statements of principle relate to an approved person performing a "significant influence position" in relation to his sphere of responsibility in his controlled function insofar as it concerns. They require the taking of reasonable steps to ensure proper organisation, regulatory compliance and the exercise of competence in management. Contravention of a statement of principle does not of itself give rise to any right of action or affect the validity of any transaction[95] but may attract disciplinary sanctions.[96]

(iv) *The "Conduct of Business" sourcebook ("COB")*

In producing this sourcebook the FSA aimed to produce a single set of rules from the existing SRO rulebooks.[97] While total consolidation and harmonisation has not been achieved, COB does now provide for a considerable degree of consistency in relation to the duties and obligations of various categories of financial service providers. COB, in common with other sourcebooks in the Handbook, contains rules, evidential provisions and guidance. **13–046**

Arrangement. COB is divided into 12 chapters. A broad sense of the subject matter of each is derived from their respective titles: 1. Application and general provisions; 2. Rules which apply to all firms[98] conducting designated investment business; 3. Financial promotion; 4. Accepting customers; 5. Advising and selling; 6. Product disclosure and the customer's right to cancel or withdraw; 7. Dealing and managing; 8. Reporting to customers; 9. Client assets; 10. Operators of collective investment schemes; 11. Trustee and depositary activities; 12. Lloyd's. Each chapter is sub-divided into sections and each section follows a similar structure. At the beginning of each chapter the firms and activities to which the various rules, guidance and evidential provisions are directed and the Principles which the provisions of the chapter are intended to amplify are identified. The various rules, evidential provisions and guidance are then set out. Highlighted by italics in the text are terms which are defined in the Glossary to the Handbook. The definitions merit close scrutiny in order to evaluate the scope of the main text. A detailed consideration of COB (and thus of relevant rules and guidance) is beyond the scope of this book. Only some of more relevant matters are briefly dealt with. **13–047**

Scope.[99] COB starts by describing to whom, for what activities and within what territorial limits it applies. Generally, except as otherwise stated, the rules contained in COB apply to every "firm" with respect to the carrying on of all regulated activities[1] and, to the extent specified, non-regulated activities. **13–048**

---

[95] *ibid.*, s.64(8).
[96] *ibid.*, s.66(2)(a).
[97] See the FSA's "Feedback on consultation" on the COB Sourcebook (February 2001).
[98] A "firm" is defined as an authorised person.
[99] See COB, chap 1: Application and General Provisions.
[1] The scope of the regulated activities (see paras 13–029 and 13–030 above) to which the COB applies is determined by the description of the activity as set out in the ROA. A firm will therefore not generally be subject to the COB in relation to any aspect of its business activities which fall within an exclusion found within the ROA.

Although not of direct application to a firm's appointed representatives,[2] a firm will always be responsible for the acts and omissions of its appointed representatives in carrying on business for which the firm has accepted responsibility.[3] Accordingly, anything done or omitted by a firm's appointed representative will be treated as having been done or omitted by the firm.[4]

13–049   **Rules of general application to all firms conducting "designated investment business".**[5] The latter term is defined to cover some but not all categories of regulated activities in the RAO,[6] which are carried on by way of business. Broadly, the categories covered by the term are (true) investment activities (such as were covered by the 1986 Act) as opposed to regulated activities such as accepting deposits and effecting contracts of insurance. A firm carrying on designated investment business is required to communicate information to a "customer"[7] in a way which is clear, fair and not misleading, except in circumstances in which financial promotion requirements apply. The acceptance by such firm of inducements and soft commission is restricted. Rules are also made as to the extent to which such a firm may rely on information provided by others. It will be taken to be in compliance with any of the COB rules that require it to obtain information to the extent that it can show that it was reasonable for it to rely upon information provided to it in writing by another person. A firm will therefore be able to rely upon this provision when carrying out client classifications and obtaining sufficient information in order to satisfy the "know its customer" requirement.[8] Other rules of such general application pertain to Chinese walls and to exclusion of liability.[9]

13–050   **Financial promotion.**[10] A long chapter addresses "financial promotion"[11] and with very limited exceptions, its provisions apply to every firm to which COB applies.[12] The purpose of the chapter is to provide promotion rules and guidance for firms (*i.e.* authorised persons) who wish to communicate and approve a financial promotion. Restrictions on financial promotion by unauthorised persons are imposed by the FSMA itself.[13] However, there are many exemptions to these restrictions as apparent from the FPO.[14] These exemptions have been integrated in the financial promotion rules together with other exemptions.[15] Recognising the extent to which e-mail and the internet are now used, COB expressly provides (albeit in the form of general guidance) that any material meeting the definition

---

[2] See paras 13–095 *et seq.* below.
[3] FSMA, s.39(3).
[4] *ibid.*, s.39(4).
[5] COB, chap. 2.
[6] See paras 13–029 and 13–030 above.
[7] Defined as a "client" who is a "private customer" or an "intermediate customer". The latter terms are also defined in the Glossary.
[8] See para. 13–056 below.
[9] See para. 13–133 below.
[10] COB, chap. 3.
[11] Defined as in accordance with FSMA, s.21(1) as an invitation or inducement to engage in investment activity.
[12] Those exceptions are limited to firms communicating or approving the content of a financial promotion solely for a deposit, a general insurance contract or a pure protection contract. In those cases only limited parts of the chapter apply.
[13] FSMA s.21. See para. 13–015 above.
[14] See para. 13–032 above.
[15] COB, chap. 3, section 3.5.

of a financial promotion, including any video or moving image material incorporated in any site containing a financial promotion, should comply with the financial promotion rules.[16] Other matters addressed in separate sections are territorial scope,[17] confirmation of compliance and approval,[18] records,[19] form and content of financial promotions,[20] "direct offer promotions",[21] "unsolicited real-time financial promotions",[22] unregulated collective investment schemes[23] and financial promotions for an unauthorised person and overseas persons.[24]

Form and content requirements vary as between non-real-time promotions and   **13–051** real-time financial promotions.[25] In respect of the former, the firm must properly identify itself and be able to show that it has taken reasonable steps to ensure that the financial promotion was clear, fair and not misleading. Additional obligations are also imposed (as binding rules) where the financial promotion involves a comparison or contrast, or relates to a specific investment, or gives information about the past performance of an investment or fund or gives a projection. Real-time financial promotions must also be clear, fair and not misleading and further requirements are imposed as to manner of communication. The latter are more stringent if such promotions are unsolicited.[26]

Classification of customers. Any firm intending to conduct, or conducting,   **13–052** designated investment business or ancillary activities relating to designated investment business is required to classify the persons with or for whom it intends to carry on that business or those activities.[27] The purpose of this requirement is to ensure that clients are correctly categorised so that regulatory protections are focussed on those classes of client that need them most, while allowing an appropriately "light-touch" approach for inter-professional business. Firms are obliged to review their classifications of all clients other than private customers at least annually.[28] While the obligation to take reasonable steps to classify a customer is mandatory, it is possible for a firm to classify a client who

---

[16] COB, chap. 3, section 14.
[17] *ibid.*, chap. 3, section 3.8.
[18] *ibid.*, chap. 3, section 3.6.
[19] *ibid.*, chap. 3, section 3.7.
[20] *ibid.*, chap. 3, section 3.8.
[21] *ibid.*, chap. 3, section 3.9.
[22] *i.e.* essentially cold calls. See *ibid.*, chap. 3, section 3.10.
[23] *ibid.*, chap. 3, section 3.10.
[24] *ibid.*, chap. 3, sections 3.12 and 3.13.
[25] *ibid.*, chap. 3, section 3.8. A "real-time financial promotion" is one communicated in the course of a personal visit, telephone conversation or other interactive dialogue. A "non-real-time financial promotion" is a financial promotion that is not a real-time financial promotion and includes a financial promotion communicated by letter, e-mail or included in publications disseminated in paper format, in material displayed on a web-site or in sound or television broadcasts: see the Glossary to the Handbook. In addition, (see COB para. 3.3.4(3) the following are indications that a financial promotion is non real-time: (1) the financial promotion is communicated to more than one person in identical terms, (2) the financial promotion is communicated by way of a system which in the normal course constitutes or creates a record of the communication which is available to the recipient to refer to at a later time, and (3) the communication is made by way of a system which in the normal course does not require the recipient to respond immediately to it. The distinction parallels that between "real time communications" and "non-real-time communications" in the FPO, art. 7.
[26] See COB, chap. 3.10.
[27] *ibid.*, chap. 4, section 1. Note the rule in para. 4.1.4: "Before conducting designated investment business with or for any client, a firm must take reasonable steps to establish whether that client is a private customer, intermediate customer or market counterparty".
[28] *ibid.*, chap 4. para. 4.1.15.

would otherwise be a private customer as an intermediate customer, or to classify a client who would otherwise be an intermediate customer as a market counterparty, if certain conditions are met.[29] However, in each case the firm must advise the client of the regulatory protections that he will lose by being re-classified in this way.

13–053   **Terms of business and customer agreements.**[30] Subject to certain exceptions,[31] every firm conducting or intending to conduct designated investment business with or for a specific customer is required to provide that customer with its "terms of business",[32] setting out the basis on which such business is to be conducted for the customer.[33] Moreover, such terms must be in "adequate detail". Thus generally there must be provisions as to matters itemised in a table of general requirements and, if relevant, a table of requirements pertaining to managing investments on a discretionary basis.[34] A customer agreement is required of a firm intending to conduct any of the following designated investment business with or for a private customer: managing investments on a discretionary basis, a transaction in a contingent liability investment, stock lending activity or underwriting except in respect of a life policy.[35]

13–054   **Advising and selling.**[36] These matters are addressed in another long chapter under eight sections entitled as follows:(1) Polarisation and status disclosure; (2) Know your customer; (3) Suitability; (4) Customers' understanding of risk; (5) Information about the firm; (6) Excessive charges; (7) Disclosure of charges, remuneration and commission; (8) Customers introduced to clearing firms by introducing brokers and overseas introducing brokers.

13–055   **(1) Polarisation and status disclosure.** The "polarisation" principle is given effect in COB, as it was under the 1986 Act regulatory regime.[37] Thus a firm giving advice to a private customer upon packaged products[38] must be within one, but not the other, of two categories. Relevant definitions and requirements imposed on firms reflect this categorisation. The first category is a provider firm,[39] an appointed representative[40] of such firm or a representative (including an employee) of either. These are constrained to advise only on the packaged

---

[29] COB, chap. 4, paras. 4.1.9 and 4.1.12.

[30] *ibid.*, chap. 4, section 2. See further para. 13–090 below.

[31] *ibid.*, chap. 4, paras 4.2.1 and 4.2.8. The latter contains a table listing exceptions, including exceptions relating to "execution-only transactions" and "direct offer financial promotion".

[32] Defined as "a written statement, supplied to a customer, of the terms on which a firm will conduct designated investment business with or for a customer."

[33] COB, chap. 4, para. 4.2.4.

[34] *ibid.*, chap. 4, paras 4.2.9, 4.2.10, 4.2.14 and 4.2.15.

[35] *ibid.*, chap. 4.2.6. There is an exception relating to a private customer habitually resident outside the U.K.

[36] *ibid.*, chap. 5.

[37] The principle is currently under review by the FSA.

[38] A "packaged product" is defined in the Glossary as being: (a) a life policy, (b) a unit in a regulated collective investment scheme, (c) an interest in an investment trust savings scheme or (d) a stakeholder pension scheme. Products (a), (b) or (c) are packaged products whether or not they are held within a PEP or an ISA.

[39] Defined in the Glossary to include a "product provider" or a "marketing group associate". The former is a firm which is (a) a long-term insurer, (b) a friendly society or (c) the operator of a regulated investment scheme or an investment trust savings scheme. The terms "associate" and "marketing group" are also defined.

[40] See paras. 13–095 *et seq.* below.

product issued by that provider firm or by another member of its marketing group.[41] The second category is an independent intermediary[42] or an appointed representative of such intermediary or an employee of either. These must act in the best interests of their customers when advising on packaged products (they are free to recommend such a product issued by any provider). Moreover, they must not enter into commercial arrangements which constrain them in giving such advice on an independent basis.[43] Disclosure requirements are imposed. In relation to packaged products every firm must ensure that private customers are informed of its polarisation status on a timely basis. This obligation entails informing them whether such advice will be (a) independent, (b) restricted to the packaged products of one product provider or marketing group, or (c) given for the purposes of discretionary portfolio management.[44] This rule is mandatory and a firm will be in breach if such advice is not given, whether or not reasonable care was taken to give it.

(2) Know your customer. This requirement pertains to a private customer **13–056** when a firm that (a) gives a personal recommendation concerning a "designated investment", (b) acts as an investment manager, or (c) arranges a pension opt-out or pension transfer from an occupational pension scheme. Before doing so, the firm must take reasonable steps by way of "fact-finding" to ensure that it is in possession of sufficient personal and financial information about the customer relevant for the services that the firm has agreed to provide.[45] Thereafter the firm should keep that information under regular review and, in respect of private customers on whose behalf a firm acts only on an occasional basis, a review should be carried out whenever the customer seeks advice. Moreover, the firm must keep a record of its consequent "fact-find".[46] In addition, the absence of an adequate record makes it far harder for a firm to demonstrate that an adequate enquiry into the customer's circumstances was ever carried out. Such fact-finding is essential in order ensure the suitability of its advice and discretionary decisions.

(3) Suitability. Suitability requirements pertaining to certain advisory, man- **13–057** agement and promotional activities are a core element of the regulatory regime. There are a series of such requirements relating to firms: (a) making a personal recommendation concerning a designated investment to a private customer, (b) acting as an investment manager for a private customer, (c) managing the assets of an OPS or a stakeholder pension scheme, or (d) promoting a personal pension scheme by means of a direct offer financial promotion to a group or employees.[47] There is a general requirement in relation to a private customer that a firm, in the course of designated investment business, must take reasonable steps to ensure that it does not make a personal recommendation to buy or sell a designated investment, or effect a discretionary transaction for a private customer, unless the recommendation or transaction is suitable for the private customer having regard

---

[41] COB, chap. 5, para. 5.1.4. Note also paras 5.1.5 to 5.1.12.
[42] Defined in the Glossary as a firm acting as an intermediary but excluding (a) a firm which is a member of a marketing group (b) a product provider which sells its own packaged products.
[43] *ibid.*, chap. 5, para. 5.1.13.
[44] *ibid.*, chap 5, para. 5.1.14. Note further as to disclosure: paras. 5.1.15 to 5.1.19.
[45] *ibid.*, chap. 5, para. 5.2.5. See guidance in paras 5.2.6 to 5.2.8 and 5.2.11.
[46] *ibid.*, chap. 5, para. 5.2.9. Note also para. 5.2.10.
[47] *ibid.*, chap. 5, section 5.

to the facts disclosed by him and other relevant facts about him of which the firm is or reasonably should be aware.[48] There is a like general requirement when the firm acts as an investment manager.[49] There are other specific suitability requirements. These pertain to packaged products,[50] occupational and stakeholder pension schemes,[51] broker funds,[52] pensions transfers and opt-outs[53] and personal pension schemes.[54] Whether or not a recommendation or transaction is "suitable" will obviously depend upon the facts of each case, although detailed guidance is given as to a range of matters.[55] In many circumstances an explanatory suitability letter is required[56] and guidance is given as to its contents.[57]

13–058   **(4) Customers' understanding of risk.** In relation to a private customer, a firm conducting designated investment business must not: (1) make a personal recommendation of a transaction, (2) act as a discretionary investment manager, (3) arrange a deal in a warrant or derivative, or (4) engage in stock lending activity unless it has first taken reasonable steps to ensure that the customer understands the nature of the risks involved.[58] Once again, the steps that will need to be taken by a firm to satisfy this obligation will vary from customer to customer and from transaction to transaction. Evidential guidance of the types of risk warnings required for various transactions is provided.[59]

13–059   **Product disclosure.**[60] Reflecting Principle 7, which requires a firm to pay due regard to the information needs of its clients, requirements are imposed to provide private customer with information about a product or proposed transaction in a prescribed "key features" format.[61] The design and content of the key features will vary according to product and transaction. Particular requirements govern packaged products, life policies, "schemes",[62] occupational pension schemes, self-invested personal pension schemes, income withdrawals, cash deposit ISAs, traded life policies and stakeholder pension schemes. Projections relating to life policies, schemes and stakeholder pension schemes are subject to separate requirements.[63] With certain defined exceptions, firms are prohibited from providing projections for life policies, schemes or stakeholder pension schemes unless the projection is calculated and presented in accordance with

---

[48] COB chap. 5, para. 5.3.5. Note the qualification in respect of a pooled fund.
[49] *ibid.*
[50] *ibid.*, chap. 5, paras 5.3.6 to 5.3.11. The requirements distinguish between a provider firm and an independent intermediary, reflecting the polarisation principle.
[51] *ibid.*, chap. 5, para. 5.3.12.
[52] *ibid.*, chap. 5, paras 5.3.13(1), 5.3.20.
[53] *ibid.*, chap. 5, paras 5.3.13(2), 5.3.21 to 5.3.27.
[54] *ibid.*, chap. 5, paras 5.3.13(13), 5.3.28.
[55] *ibid.*, chap. 5, paras 5.3.13(4) and 5.3.29 (table).
[56] *ibid.*, chap. 5, paras 5.3.18 to 5.3.19.
[57] *ibid.*, chap. 5, paras 5.3.30 (table).
[58] *ibid.*, chap. 5, paras 5.4.3.
[59] *ibid.*, chap. 5, paras 5.4.4 to 5.4.10.
[60] *ibid.*, chap. 6, section 7.
[61] *ibid.*, chap 6, sections 1 to 5. Note also the information requirements in sections 8 and 9 (relating to insurance contracts and life policy guides) which are not confined to private customers.
[62] Defined for the purposes of COB chap. 6 as (a) a regulated investment trust, (b) an investment trust where relevant shares have been or are to be acquired through an investment trust savings scheme and (c) an investment trust where the relevant shares are to be held within an ISA or PEP which promotes one or more specific investment trust.
[63] *ibid.*, chap. 6, section 6.

relevant rules.[64] In addition, any document containing a projection must include specified statements and warnings.[65] While the rules are numerous and detailed, of particular note are the specific rules that govern both the assumptions that may be made and the information that must be provided in pension projections[66] and the assumptions that are to be made in relation to rates of return for various types of contract.[67] Other sets of rules relate to life and general insurance contracts[68] and with-profit guides.[69]

The customer's right to cancel and withdraw. Rights to cancel and rights to withdraw from certain categories of agreements are given, principally to a customer who is an individual, in specified circumstances.[70] **13–060**

Dealing and managing.[71] Rules and guidance relating to these matters reflect several Principles, especially Principle 6 (fair treatment of customers) and common law duties relating to competence and fiduciaries. They are directed to guard against a range of potential abuses. Relevant provisions are arranged under 15 headings, some of which are dealt with in more detail below: (1) Conflict of interest and material interest; (2) Churning and switching; (3) Dealing ahead; (4) Customer order priority; (5) Best execution; (6) Timely execution; (7) Aggregation and allocation; (8) Realisation of a private customer's assets; (9) Lending to private customers; (10) Margin requirements; (11) Non-exchange traded securities; (12) Customer order execution records; (13) Personal account dealing; (14) Programme trading; and (15) Non-market price transactions. **13–061**

Conflict of interest and material interest.[72] Fair treatment is the critical criterion in this context. So in specified circumstances a firm conducting designated investment business with or for a customer is prohibited from knowingly advising or dealing in the exercise of its discretion unless its takes reasonable steps to ensure fair treatment of the customer. The circumstances are where, in relation to a transaction, the firm has a material interest or a relationship or interest of actual or potential conflict or customers with conflicting interests.[73] While not intended to be a definitive list, a number of reasonable steps are instanced by way of guidance with a view to resolving conflicts. They might include disclosure of the interest to the customer, reliance upon a policy of independence, the establishment and maintenance of Chinese walls.[74] In the event that a firm is unable to manage a conflict of interest using such methods, it should decline to act on behalf of the customer.[75] A specific requirement is imposed on a broker fund adviser when acting for a private customer to obtain from him an acknowledgement of his understanding of the firm's dual role as **13–062**

---

[64] COB, chap. 6, para. 6.6.4.
[65] *ibid.*, chap. 6, paras 6.6.14 to 6.6.18.
[66] *ibid.*, chap. 6, paras 6.6.10 to 6.6.13
[67] *ibid.*, chap. 6, paras 6.6.49 to 6.6.53
[68] *ibid.*, chap. 6, section 8.
[69] *ibid.*, chap. 6, section 9.
[70] *ibid.*, chap. 6, section 7. The provisions are complex.
[71] *ibid.*, chap. 7.
[72] *ibid.*, chap. 7, section 1.
[73] *ibid.*, chap. 7, para. 7.1.3.
[74] *ibid.*, chap. 7, paras 7.1.4 to 7.1.8.
[75] *ibid.*, chap. 7, para. 7.1.9.

both his adviser and that of the life office or operator of the fund in question.[76]

13–063 **Churning and switching.**[77] Restrictions are imposed to guard against a firm entering into transactions for a customer with unnecessary frequency relative to his agreed investment strategy (churning). Thus a firm conducting designated investment business with or for a customers must not in engage discretionary dealing or make personal recommendations in specified circumstances, unless it has reasonable grounds for believing it is in the customer's best interests, both when viewed in isolation and when viewed in the context of earlier transactions. Like restrictions are imposed to guard against switching within or between packaged products unnecessarily relative to what is suitable for a private customer.

13–064 **Dealing ahead.**[78] Restrictions are imposed directed towards postponement of own account transactions by a firm or associate when not in customers' interests. The restrictions apply when a firm or its associate intends to publish a written recommendation or a piece of research or analysis to customers that relates to a designated investment. The firm must not undertake an own account transaction in the relevant or any related designated investment and must take all reasonable steps to ensure that its associates do not do the same until the customers for whom the publication was principally intended have had (or are likely to have had) a reasonable opportunity to act upon it. The restrictions are subject to exceptions.

13–065 **Best and timely execution.** Duties are imposed directed to achieve best execution[79] and timely execution.[80] Every firm that executes a customer order in a designated investment must provide best execution. This has two facets. First, the firm must take reasonable care to ascertain the price which is the best available for the customer order in the relevant market at the time for transactions of the kind and size concerned. Secondly, it must execute the customer order at a price which is no less advantageous to the customer, unless it has taken reasonable steps to ensure that it would be in the customer's best interests not to do so.[81] There are exceptions.[82] As to timely execution, a firm, once it has agreed or decided in its discretion to execute or arrange for the execution of a current customer order in a designated investment, it must do so as soon as reasonably practicable. However, it is not so obliged if it has taken reasonable steps to ensure that postponing execution is in the customer's best interests.[83] Guidance is given as to circumstances when particular care may be needed when assessing the

---

[76] COB, chap. 7, para. 7.1.10.

[77] *ibid.*, chap. 7, section 2.

[78] *ibid.*, chap. 7, section 3.

[79] *ibid.*, chap. 7, section 5.

[80] *ibid.*, chap. 7, section 6.

[81] *ibid.*, chap 7. paras 7.5.1, 7.5.3 and 7.5.5. Note para. 7.5.6 containing evidential provisions as to what is required in order for a firm to take "reasonable care" and the guidance in paras 7.5.7 and 7.5.8.

[82] *ibid.*, chap. 7 para. 7.5.4. These include exceptions relating to life policies, and units in regulated collective investment schemes and circumstances where a firm relies on another person to provide best execution.

[83] *ibid.*, paras 7.6.3 and 7.6.4.

timing of execution of all or part of a customer order and as to when there may be reasonable grounds for postponing execution.[84]

Aggregation and allocation.[85] A series of duties relating to these practices are **13–066** imposed on a firm conducting designated investment claims. A requirement is imposed as to aggregation and allocation only in accordance with standards and procedures which are recorded, consistent and compliant with COB require- ments.[86] Further a firm must have reasonable grounds to believe that aggregation will work to the advantage of the customers concerned and disclose that aggrega- tion may have the effect on some occasions of working to their disadvantage. Other requirements pertain to timing, fairness and pricing of allocation, realloca- tion and record keeping.[87]

Reporting to customers.[88] Requirements are imposed as to written confirma- **13–067** tion of transactions and, in appropriate cases, periodic statements. These reflect Principle 7 relating to communications with clients.

Client assets. Another long chapter[89] contains extensive requirements relating **13–068** to safeguarding and administering investments ("custody rules"), mandates, receipt and holding of client money ("client money rules"), collateral (*i.e.* receipt or holding of assets to secure a the obligation of a client) and distribution ("client money distribution rules").

(f) *FSMA imposed regulatory liabilities*

The 1986 Act imposed civil and sometimes criminal liability for a number of **13–069** contraventions of the regulatory regime. The FSMA does the same and in a wider range of circumstances. The range of remedies available in relation to civil liabilities varies according to whether the claimant is a regulator or private litigant.[90] For purposes of exposition, civil liabilities imposed by FSMA may be classified as follows:

   (i) liabilities related to lack of authorisation;

  (ii) liabilities related to authorised persons;

 (iii) liabilities related to EEA firms;

 (iv) liabilities related to official listing of securities.

(i) *Liabilities related to lack of authorisation*

These comprise the following: **13–070**

  (a) liability for contravention of the general prohibition;

---

[84] COB, chap. 7, paras 7.6.5 and 7.6.6.
[85] *ibid.*, chap. 7, section 7.
[86] *ibid.*, chap. 7, para. 7.7.3.
[87] *ibid.*, chap. 7 paras 7.7.5, 7.7.9. 7.7.11, 7.7.12, 7.7.14, 7.7.16–18.
[88] *ibid.*, chap. 8.
[89] *ibid.*, chap. 9.
[90] See further paras 13–137 to 13–149 (regulator) and 13–152—13–156 (private litigant) below.

(b) liability for contravention of the financial promotion restriction.

13–071 **Liability for contravention of the general prohibition.** Contravention entails civil (and criminal[91]) consequences under the FSMA, as under like provisions of the 1986 Act.[92] Regulators may seek a range of remedies.[93] Moreover, relevant agreements are potentially unenforceable and voidable.[94]

13–072 **Liability for contravention of the financial promotion restrictions.** Contravention entails civil (and criminal[95]) consequences under the FSMA as under like provisions of the 1986 Act.[96] Regulators may seek a range of remedies.[97] Moreover, relevant agreements are potentially unenforceable and voidable.[98]

(ii) *Liabilities related to authorised persons*

13–073 These comprise the following:

(a) liability for acting outside permission;

(b) liability for employment of certain persons;

(c) liability for contravention of FSA rules.

13–074 **Liability for acting outside permission.** In general, persons (unless they have the benefit of automatic authorisation) need to obtain permission in order to undertake any regulated activity.[99] The FSMA provides for liability on an authorised person for carrying on a regulated activity in the United Kingdom otherwise than in accordance with such permission in prescribed cases, at the suit of a person who suffers consequent loss.[1] Under the relevant prescribing regulations,[2] the right of action is limited to a "private person" as therein defined[3] or a person acting in a fiduciary or representative capacity on behalf of a private person and also does not extend to a contravention of a Part IV financial resources requirement.

13–075 **Liability for employment of certain persons.** Authorised persons are required to take reasonable care to ensure that functions in regard to regulated activities are not performed by a person who is the subject of a prohibition order

---

[91] FSMA, s.23.
[92] 1986 Act. ss. 4–6.
[93] See paras 13–137 to 13–148 below.
[94] See paras 13–152 to 13–155 below.
[95] FSMA, s.25.
[96] 1986 Act, ss. 56 (unsolicited calls—but no criminal liability), 57 (restrictions on investment advertising) and 61 (remedies obtainable by FSA).
[97] See paras 13–137 to 13–148 below.
[98] See para. 13–156 below.
[99] As to the grant of permission, see para. 13–018 above.
[1] FSMA, ss. 20 (as to "prescribed", see s.417(1)).
[2] The Financial Services and Markets Act 2000 (Rights of Action) Regulations S.I. 2001 No. 2256, regs 4, 3.
[3] A "private person" is defined in the regulations (reg. 3) as essentially (a) any individual (except in relation to Lloyd's, a Name), unless he suffers the loss in the course of carrying on any regulated activity or an activity which would be such apart from any exclusion in RAO art. 72 (overseas persons) and (b) any person who is not an individual, unless he suffers the loss in the course of carrying on business of any kind. Also excluded from the definition is a government, a local authority (in the U.K. or elsewhere) or an international organisation.

made by the FSA.[4] Similarly they must take reasonable care to ensure that in relation to a "controlled function" they use only a person who has had the requisite FSA approval.[5] The FSMA provides for liability on the part of an authorised person breaching these duties at the suit of a "private person" as prescribed defined by Treasury Order and any other person who suffers consequent loss as prescribed in such an order.[6] Under the relevant prescribing regulations,[7] the right of action is limited to a "private person" as therein defined[8] or a person acting in a fiduciary or representative capacity on behalf of a private person.

Authorised persons' liability for contravention of FSA rules. Section 150 **13–076** of the FSMA renders civilly actionable in certain circumstances, contravention by authorised persons of rules made by the FSA.[9] This statutory liability is akin to a breach of statutory duty action. The FSMA provision follows a like provision in section 62 of the 1986 Act.[10] Such actionability arises only in relation to contravention of a *rule* made by the FSA and then subject to a number of qualifications.[11] The right of action does not arise in the following circumstances. First, rules as to financial resources are excluded.[12] Secondly, the listing rules made by the FSA as "competent authority"[13] are excluded.[14] Thirdly, the FSA may specify that contravention of certain of its rules does not give rise to actionability.[15] Fourthly, the FSA has power to make evidential rules and to provide that contravention of such rules should not be actionable.[16] Moreover, although the FSA's "endorsing rules"[17] endorsing provisions in the Take-over Code[18] and SARs[19] are "rules", the endorsed provisions themselves are not "rules" and so breach of the endorsed provisions in the Take-over Code or SARs are not actionable under the Act.

The section 150 right of action under this section is generally limited to a **13–077** "private person" as prescribed by regulations made by the Treasury,[20] but it is empowered to prescribe that contravention of a rule may be actionable by a wider category of person.[21] The Treasury has made the relevant regulations under the

---

[4] FSMA, s.56(6).

[5] *ibid.*, s.59(1), (2). See para. 13–019 above.

[6] *ibid.*, s.71 (as to "prescribed", see s.417(1)).

[7] The Financial Services and Markets Act 2000 (Rights of Action) Regulations SI 2001 No. 2256, regs 5, 3.

[8] See under para. 13–075 above the definition of a "private person" in the regulations (reg. 3).

[9] FSMA, s.150.

[10] As restricted by 1986 Act, s.62A.

[11] See the definition of "rule" in FSMA, s.417(1).

[12] FSMA, s.150(4)(b). There is little point in giving a right of action for breach of these rules as persons are only likely to suffer loss as a result of breaches if the authorised person becomes insolvent and a right of action would be worthless in such circumstances.

[13] Under FSMA Part VI, s.74(4).

[14] *ibid.*, s.150(4)(a).

[15] *ibid.*, s.150(2) and has done so in its Handbook. Reference should be made to the fifth schedule to each sourcebook. See para. 13–041 above.

[16] *ibid.*, s.149.

[17] FSMA, s.143,

[18] *i.e.* the City Code on Takeovers and Mergers issued by the Panel on Takeovers and Mergers.

[19] *i.e.* the Rules Governing Substantial Acquisitions of Shares issued by the Panel.

[20] FSMA s.150(5) (as to "prescribed", see s.417(1)).

[21] *ibid.*, s.150(3).

FSMA,[22] which both define a "private person"[23] and extend the right of action to a person acting in a fiduciary or representative capacity for a "private person" and other persons for breach of two kinds of rules. The first is a rule prohibiting an authorised person from seeking to make provision excluding or limiting liability.[24] The second is a rule directed at against insider dealing.[25] Thus effectively there is statutory civil liability for insider dealing. Actionability under section 62 of the 1986 Act was also limited (although not initially) to a "private investor" under a provision introduced in response to fears that a wider liability would encourage tactical litigation between professionals.[26] The defendant to a section 150 right of action is the authorised person who is under the relevant obligation imposed by an FSA rule.[27] The right of action is stated to be "subject to the defences and other incidents applying to actions for breaches of statutory duty". Thus the FSA rules are deemed to impose statutory duties for the purposes of liability for their breach. In order to establish a breach, the nature and extent of the duty needs to be determined by interpreting the FSA rule. Moreover the claimant must be within the category of person which the rule, as a matter of interpretation, is intended to protect. He must also must also suffer "loss as a result of the contravention". The normal defences to such actions, *e.g.* contributory negligence,[28] would be applicable. Such issues as limitation would be covered by established case law on breach of statutory duty actions (as "incidents applying to actions for breach of statutory duty").

13–078   As discussed below,[29] contravention of a FSA rule may well give rise to concurrent civil liability in tort or contract and so in practice section 150 liability may not add to the liability already existing at common law. However, being able to point to an explicitly imposed duty, which has been broken with consequent liability under section 150, will often result in a more easily established liability. This is especially the case where the claimant wishes to make a claim under the compensation scheme established under the Part XV of the FSMA.[30] In relation to a claim for compensation under the scheme established under the 1986 Act, the simplest way to establish the liability of an insolvent authorised person for the purposes of such a claim has been to establish a breach of the rulebook. Moreover, breach of the rulebook may have an impact on the extent of common law liability.[31] Breach of a FSA rule does not give rise to any criminal liability.[32] Nor, in contrast to contravention of the general prohibition and the financial

---

[22] The Financial Services and Markets Act 2000 (Rights of Action) Regulations S.I. 2001 No. 2256, regs. 6, 3.

[23] See under para. 13–075 above the definition of a "private person" in the regulations (reg. 3).

[24] See para. 13–133 below.

[25] *i.e.* a "rule directed at ensuring that transactions in any security or contractually based investment [within the meaning of the RAO] are not effect with the benefit of unpublished information that, if made public, would be likely to affect the price of that security or investment."

[26] 1986 Act, s.62A (introduced by the Companies Act 1989, s.193). The limiting regulations made under s.62A, were the Financial Services Act 1986 (Restriction of Right of Action) Regulations 1991, S.I. 1991 No. 489.

[27] The power to make money laundering rules under FSMA s.146 extends (exceptionally) beyond authorised persons (although the rules must be "in connection with the carrying on of regulated activities by authorised persons") but it is only the authorised persons to whom those rules apply that may be sued under s.150 for breach.

[28] See para. 13–167 below.

[29] See paras 13–091 to 13–93 and 13–106 below.

[30] See paras 13–190 to 13–204 below.

[31] See para. 13–091 and 13–092 below.

[32] FSMA, s.151(1).

promotion restriction, does a breach of a rule as such provide a ground for vitiating any transaction.[33] Nevertheless, conduct which is impugnable not only as a breach of a rule but also on other grounds, such as a misrepresentation, may presumably vitiate a transaction. A person is not to be regarded as having contravened a rule if the "rule-making instrument" had not been published sufficiently widely at the time.[34]

(iii) *Liabilities related to EEA firms*

The FSA as "host state" regulator is empowered to impose requirements on "incoming firms".[35] The FSMA imposes liability for contravention of such requirements in prescribed cases, at the suit of any person suffering consequent loss.[36] **13–079**

(iv) *Liabilities related to official listing of securities*

These comprise: **13–080**

(a) liability for misleading listing particulars;

(b) liability for contravention of prospectus requirement.

Liability for misleading listing particulars. Part VI of the FSMA[37] contains the regime for "Official Listing", *i.e.* listing of securities[38] and the publication of "listing particulars".[39] Section 90 imposes liability to pay compensation to a claimant meeting certain criteria if listing particulars or supplementary listing particulars have a defect consisting of an untrue or misleading statement or an omission from them of a matter required to be included by listing rules. This statutory liability is imposed upon persons responsible for the particulars.[40] Such may escape liability if a relevant "exemption" is satisfied.[41] The statutory liability is in addition to any other liability which may be incurred in the same circumstances.[42] For further commentary on this statutory liability, reference should be made to specialist works.[43] However, it is relevant to note that liability is incurred to a plaintiff meeting certain cumulative criteria: (a) he must have acquired some of the securities to which the defective particulars relate; (b) he must have suffered loss; (c) the loss must be in respect of the securities; and (d) the loss must be as a result of the relevant untrue or misleading statement or omission. Acquisition of securities is given an extended meaning to include **13–081**

---

[33] *ibid.*, s.151(2).

[34] *ibid.*, s.153(6), (4), (2). Note also s.154 as to verification of FSA rules in legal proceedings.

[35] See FSMA, Part XIII (ss.193–204). As to incoming firms (comprising EEA firms and Treaty firms), see para. 13–017 above.

[36] FSMA, s.202. See the Financial Services and Markets Act 2000 (Rights of Action) Regulations S.I. 2001 No. 2256, regs 7, 3.

[37] Comprising FSMA, ss. 72 to 103. The FSA is now the "competent authority": see ss. 74, 103(2) and para. 13–012 above.

[38] See FSMA, s.74(5) for definitions of "listing" and a "security".

[39] See *ibid.*, s.79(2).

[40] As defined in Treasury regulations made under s.79(3).

[41] *ibid.*, s.90(2) and Sched. 10.

[42] *ibid.*, s.90(6).

[43] For a commentary on Part VI of FSMA and Part IV of the 1986 Act, see Lomnicka and Powell, *Encyclopedia of Financial Services Law*. For the development of 1986 Act provisions see Powell, *Issues and Offers of Company Securities: The New Regimes* (1988).

circumstances in which the claimant contracted to acquire the securities or an interest in them.[44] Moreover, it is clear that acquisition of securities includes both subscribing for and purchase of securities. A claimant is thus not precluded from making a claim under section 90 by reason of being a purchaser in the market as distinct from a subscriber although he may be precluded from making a claim in tort for negligent misrepresentation on the same facts.[45]

13–082   **Liability for contravention of prospectus requirement.** Listing rules must require the publication of a prospectus before securities are offered to the public in the United Kingdom in advance of their being admitted to the Official List.[46] The FSMA imposes liability for contravention of such requirements at the suit of any person suffering consequent loss.[47]

(g) *Other statutory liabilities*

13–083   Two merit consideration.

(i) *Liability related to unlisted securities*

13–084   In respect of offers of unlisted securities, i.e. securities not on the "Official List",[48] Part IV of the FSMA is parallelled the Public Offers of Securities Regulations 1995.[49] For further commentary on these regulations, reference should be made to specialist works.[50]

(ii) *The Misrepresentation Act 1967*

13–085   **Relevance.** The Misrepresentation Act 1967 is of general application. The Act, in particular section 2(1) (damages for "negligent" misrepresentation) and section 2(2) (damages in lieu of rescission), has particular relevance to claims against financial practitioners. This is because (especially as compared to other professionals and other service providers), there is generally a large element of promotion in their activities. There is frequent scope for invocation of alleged misrepresentations and related liabilities designed to undo consequent investment contracts or relieve their effect. Nevertheless, the 1967 Act is likely to be of significance only in relation claims by persons to whom the statutory right of action under the FSMA (as under the 1986 Act) for contravention of rules (including very prescriptive rules as to financial promotion and advice) is not available.[51] Detailed consideration of the provisions of the 1967 Act is a beyond the scope of this work,[52] but aspects of section 2(1) liability merit comment.

---

[44] FSMA, s.90(7); as to the 1986 Act, s.150(5).

[45] See *Al-Nakib Investments (Jersey) Ltd. v. Longcroft* [1990] 3 All E.R. 321.

[46] FSMA, s.84.

[47] *ibid.*, s.85

[48] See FSMA, s.103(1); *e.g.* securities traded on AIM (the Alternative Investment Market) established by the London Stock Exchange.

[49] S.I. 1995 No. 1537 (as amended by S.I. 1999 Nos 734 and 1146) made under s. 2(2) of the European Communities Act 1972. Reg. 14 provides for liability in respect of untrue or misleading statements and certain omissions in a prospectus.

[50] See Lomnicka & Powell, *op. cit.,* paras 4.499 *et seq.*

[51] See paras 13–076 to 13–078 above.

[52] See generally *Chitty on Contracts* (28th ed.), chap. 6.

Representations as to suitability. The traditional view that, to be actionable, **13–086**
a representation must be a statement of fact rather than one of opinion has been
considerably eroded in recent years.[53] It will provide no obstacle to an investor
whose complaint is to the effect that an investment was misdescribed to him. In
contrast, it may be said that a representation as to "suitability" is more appropriately categorised as a representation of opinion rather than a representation of
fact. Nevertheless, a representor will not escape liability under the 1967 Act
merely because the representation is a statement of opinion or belief, if the
statement carries with it the implication that there are reasonable grounds for
holding that opinion or belief.[54] It is submitted that in almost every case where
a financial practitioner recommends an investment as suitable for an investor, that
recommendation carries with it implicit representations that (1) the nature of the
investment has been carefully considered by the representative, (2) the investor's
needs have been carefully assessed by the representative, and (3) viewed objectively, the investment meets those needs. If one or more of those implicit
representations is false, the fact that the express representation might be one of
opinion rather than of fact will be of no assistance to the maker of the representation.[55]

False in a material respect. No claim will lie under the 1967 Act unless the **13–087**
representation of which complaint is made is false. Difficulty can be encountered
if a statement is literally true, but is nonetheless misleading in certain respects,
or if a statement contains elements which are true and elements which are false.
The test often applied has been to ask whether or not the representation was false
in a 'material respect'.[56] The problem has also been addressed[57] by applying the
test laid down in section 20(4) of the Marine Insurance Act 1906—a statement
will be treated as being true if it is substantially correct and the difference would
not have induced a reasonable person to enter the contract.

Comparison with common law. A claimant who has a cause of action under **13–088**
section 2(1) of the 1967 Act may also have a common law cause of action based
on the tort of negligence. The former statutory cause of action has some relative
advantages. First, there is no need to prove that a duty of care is owed by the
maker of the representation to the recipient. Secondly, provided that the recipient
is able to demonstrate that the representation is false, the burden will fall on the
maker to demonstrate that, despite its falsity, he had reasonable grounds for
believing that it was true. Thirdly, given that the liability in section 2(1) is
expressed by reference to the position prevailing if the misrepresentation had
been made fraudulently, it would seem that the damages recoverable fall to be
assessed by reference to the more favourable measure applicable to the tort of

---

[53] See generally, *Chitty, op. cit.,* paras 6–004 to 6–017.
[54] See *Brown v. Raphael* [1958] Ch. 636
[55] In *ICS Ltd. v. West Bromwich Building Society* [1999] Lloyd's L.Rep. P.N. 496 the defendant
sought to argue that representations made to claimants who had subsequently entered into Home
Income Plans ought to be viewed as nothing more than predictions as to the likely future performance
of the Plans and not as actionable representations. In rejecting this argument Evans Lombe J.
considered that, by making the predictions, the defendant had implicitly stated that it could justify
them on reasonable grounds. Since the defendant could not in fact do so, the representations were
prima facie actionable.
[56] *i.e.* is the respect in which the representation is false "capable of inducing the representee to enter
the contract in question"?: see *Lonrho v. Fayed* [1992] 1 W.L.R. 1.
[57] See *Avon Insurance v. Swire* [2000] 1 All E.R. (Comm.) 573.

deceit rather than that applicable to the tort of negligence.[58] Moreover, for the same reason a defendant will be unable to contend for a reduction in any award on the grounds of the claimant's contributory negligence—unless there is a concurrent claim open to the claimant for negligent misstatement.[59]

(h) *Contractual duties*

(i) *Relevant contracts*

13–089 There will be usually be a contract between the provider and recipient of financial services. Indeed there may be several contracts. A recipient of financial services might well enter into a framework customer agreement at the outset of a relationship and then enter into further separate contracts relating to individual or types of transactions from time to time thereafter. He might have a "services" contract with an independent intermediary and a "product" contract with a product provider. Especially where the facts involve discretionary portfolio management or a contingent liability investment there will usually be several agreements dealing with different aspects of the relationship between the provider and the recipient of the services. Confirmations of transactions and periodic statements will be evidentially relevant in ascertaining the contractual position.[60] Proper analysis of the inter-relationship between the parties will usually require careful consideration of the whole contractual matrix. General principles for analysis, in particular as to interrelationship and effect of relevant documentation and as to incorporation[61] and implication of terms, are no different in investment contexts than in other contractual contexts. However, the regulatory dimension needs to be taken into account.

(ii) *Regulatory requirements as to terms of business and customer agreements*

13–090 As already described,[62] regulatory rules in the COB sourcebook require, subject to exceptions, all firms[63] conducting or intending to conduct designated investment business to provide the customer with terms of business, setting out "in adequate detail" the basis on which such is to be conducted for the customer. In more limited circumstances the rules require a customer agreement. Those documents will ordinarily form the starting point for any analysis of the contractual relationship between the provider and recipient of financial services and their terms will set out the express duties of each party. While providers of financial services are free to design and negotiate their own terms of business, an evidential provision in the COB sourcebook[64] identifies 24 general requirements that ought to be included in terms of business and customer agreements in order for them to meet the requirement for adequate detail. Those general requirements include:

---

[58] See *Smith New Court Securities Ltd v. Scrimgeour Vickers Ltd* [1997] A.C. 254 (wider measure of damages for the tort of deceit than for the tort of negligence).

[59] See *Chitty, op. cit.,* para. 6–074. *Gran Gelato Ltd v. Richcliff (Group) Ltd* [1992] Ch. 560.

[60] See para. 13–067 above as to regulatory reporting requirements.

[61] *e.g.* by reference, as in *Brandeis (Brokers) Ltd v. Herbert Black*, unreported, May 25, 2001, Toulson J. (SFA rules incorporated in contract between LME broker and clients).

[62] See para. 13–053 above.

[63] As to "firm", see under para. 13–047 above.

[64] COB chap. 4, para. 4.2.14. As to the status of an evidential provisions, see para. 13–042 above.

(a) A description of when and how the terms of business are to come into force (GR1).

(b) A statement that the firm is regulated or authorised by the FSA (GR2).

(c) A description of the customer's investment objectives (GR3).

(d) The identification of any restrictions on the type of designated investment in which the customer wishes to invest or the markets on which the customer wishes transactions to be executed (GR4).

(e) The identification of the services that the firm will provide (GR5).

(f) A record of the basis of payment due from the customer for the services provided by the firm (GR6).

(g) A record of whether or not the firm may act as principal in a transaction with the customer (GR11).

(h) A description of the manner in which the firm will ensure fair treatment of the customer in the event that a conflict of interest may or does arise (GR12).

(i) The giving of relevant risk warnings (GR15).

(j) A description of the complaints and compensation arrangements available to customers (GR20 & 21).

(k) A description of the permissible methods of terminating the terms of business and the consequences of termination (GR22 & 23).[65]

Another evidential provision lists additional terms for inclusion in terms of business and customer agreements for discretionary management of investments.[66] The most important of these is a term relating to the extent of the firm's discretion, including any restrictions.

(iii) *Incorporation of regulatory duties in contract*

Regulatory duties such as those imposed by the FSA Handbook or market codes **13–091** of practice or other codes may also be incorporated as contractual duties, whether expressly or implication. Contravention may then be actionable at common law as a breach of contract as well as, in some cases, being actionable by reason of a regulatory statute. Regulatory rules or a code of practice may be incorporated in a contract expressly, including by reference, or by implication. What terms fall to be implied in a contract is a question of law[67] to be determined in accordance with usual principles for implication of terms.[68] These principles were considered in a financial services context in *Clarion Ltd v. National Provident Institution.*[69]

---

[65] Other general requirements pertain to the firm acting as investment manager (GR7); accounting to the customer for transactions executed on his behalf (GR8); the right to withdraw (GR9); unsolicited real-time communications (GR10); the firm acting a broker fund adviser (GR13); use of soft commission agreements (GR14); unregulated collective investment schemes (GR16); underwriting (GR17); stock lending (GR18); any right to realise a private customer's assets (GR19); contracting out of best execution (GR24).

[66] COB chap. 4, paras 4.2.10 and 4.2.15.

[67] *Mosvolds Rederi A/S v. Food Corporation of India* [1986] 2 Lloyd's L.Rep. 68 at 70.

[68] See generally *Chitty on Contracts* (28th ed., 1999) chap. 13–01 to 13–08.

[69] [2000] 1 W.L.R. 1888.

It was alleged that the defendant mutual life office had agreed to grant the claimant investment advisers a special block switching arrangement for their clients' investments. The defendant contended that the SIB Principles were implicitly incorporated as a term of that agreement.[70] Rimer J. rejected the contention. He reasoned, first, since both claimant and defendant were already subject to the SIB Principles at the time that the agreement was made, there was no point in incorporating those principles into the contract. Secondly, a number of the SIB Principles were either irrelevant to or inapplicable to the relationship between claimant and defendant. Thirdly, there was no basis for classifying the agreement between the parties as a generic type which required the implication of the SIB Principles. A contrasting conclusion was reached *obiter* in *Larussa-Chigi v. C.S. First Boston Ltd.*[71] Thomas J. held that relevant agreements between the parties expressly incorporated the London Code of Conduct.[72] He went on to opine that had this not been the case, the code would have been incorporated as an implied term since it was not intended that the foreign exchange transactions in question be unregulated. The implied term to exercise reasonable care and skill[73] may provide another, indirect, route to the incorporation of regulatory rules or code of practice. Thus such rules or code will usually be relevant in ascertaining what is required in order to meet the standard in question.[74]

(iv) *Duty of care and skill*

13–092   **The duty and the standard.** In common with other providers of relevant services acting in the course of business, a provider of financial services will be under an implied if not express contractual duty to exercise reasonable care and skill in carrying out the services required of him.[75] The standard of care and skill will be that to be expected of a like provider engaged to provide the relevant services. Evaluating that standard will generally involve consideration of applicable regulatory requirements. It may also involve considering expert evidence from like practitioners to the defendant as to relevant practices, procedures and safeguards, perhaps in relation to highly specialised investments or markets. The evidence of such practitioners is not determinative. Ultimately the standard is for the court to determine and it may reject even general practice as failing to meet the required standard, as did the Privy Council in 1983 in relation to a conveyancing practice of Hong Kong solicitors.[76] For the court to impose its own higher standard is rare and is more likely in cases where the court is relatively familiar with the practices of the occupation concerned, as in relation to solicitors. Yet as courts become more familiar with claims against financial practitioners, the greater the scrutiny of their practices and the greater the likelihood of a court occasionally imposing its own view of the required standard, as in a recent

---

[70] The defendant contended both that it was a matter of obvious inference that the SIB Principles were incorporated and that the agreement with the claimant was of a particular generic type which required the implication of the SIB Principles.

[71] [1998] CLC 277.

[72] *i.e.* promulgated by the Bank of England and applicable to the defendant as a listed institution under the 1986 Act, s.43. The full title of the code is "A Guide to Accepted Best Practice in the Wholesale Markets in Sterling, Foreign Exchange and Bullion".

[73] See para. 13–092 below.

[74] See *Brandeis (Brokers) Ltd v. Herbert Black*, unreported, May 25, 2001, Toulson J. at para. 20.

[75] See Supply of Goods and Services Act 1982, s.13.

[76] *Edward Wong Finance Co. Ltd v. Johnson, Stokes & Master* [1984] A.C. 296. See Chap. 10, para. 10–085.

pension misselling case, *Loosemore v. Financial Concepts.*[77] The finding of breach of duty was made even though the court appears to have accepted that a reasonable body of financial practitioners would have provided advice of a standard similar to (or even worse than) the advice provided by the defendant:

" . . . in comparison with what many financial advisers and companies were doing at this time—which was to encourage people to opt out and transfer, [the defendant] did well. For he did give some warning. It was not however enough. The Financial Services Act 1986 and the rules made under it by the supervisory agencies brought in radically new standards."[78]

Utility. In many cases the statutory cause of action for breach of a relevant **13–093** regulatory rule may provide a more straightforward basis of claim to a private investor. Reliance also on breach of the contractual duty to exercise reasonable care and skill may then be superfluous. Usually a breach of such rule will also amount to a breach of that contractual duty. On the other hand, the statutory cause of action may not be available to the claimant.[79] The duty of care and skill will then be an important basis of claim, including as an indirect means of invoking breaches of regulatory rules.[80] Moreover, it may not be possible to point to breach of a specific rule. Further, regulatory rules may have limited application or relevance to a claimant, as for example in relation to corporate investors in respect of sophisticated investments such as options, futures and contracts for differences or portfolio management. In such circumstances it will be necessary to fall back on the common law, especially the duty of care and skill.

"Bracket" claims. This an intriguing subject for consideration. In the context **13–094** of valuers, liability for negligent valuation of a property is usually deduced by reference to whether the impugned valuation fell within a "bracket" of "competent valuations" ascertained from expert valuation evidence and often derived from sales of comparable properties. It remains to be seen whether this "bracket" approach will commend itself to the courts in the context of claims against fund managers who have consistently performed well below average. The plethora of performance league tables as well as rating agencies have established a vast information base which can be drawn upon in aid of a "bracket" negligence claims against bad performers. A "bracket" claim is likely to face considerable scepticism in an investment context. Less important than mere demonstration that the impugned investment performance fell outside the alleged bracket of competence will be the reasons why it did so. In the event of a severe market fall it may be possible to show that, in the case of a large fund, relevant protections through put options and other devices, which kept other funds within the bracket, were not in place. Relevant analogies may be drawn from negligence claims by Names against Lloyd's underwriters who failed to take out adequate reinsurance or stop loss insurance.[81]

(v) *Appointed representatives*

General. Persons authorised to carry on regulated activities under the FSMA, **13–095** including provider firms or independent intermediaries, frequently do so through

---

[77] [2001] Lloyd's L.Rep. P.N. 235, Judge Raymond Jack Q.C. For facts, see para. 13–123 below.
[78] *ibid.* at 242.
[79] See paras. 13–076 to 13–078 above as to whom the statutory right of action is available.
[80] See para. 13–091 above.
[81] See Chap. 16, paras. 16–038 to 16–049, 16–052; 16–058 to 16–059.

agents called "appointed representatives". As under the 1986 Act[82] specific provision is made for them under the FSMA.[83] An appointed representative rather than being required to become an authorised person, is accorded exempt person status,[84] but only so long as an authorised person, termed his "principal", takes responsibility, including regulatory responsibility, for him. Thus regulation of appointed representatives is, to some extent, sub-contracted to authorised persons.[85] In contrast to the position under the 1986 Act, the position under the FSMA[86] is that a person cannot simultaneously be both an appointed representative in respect of some activities and an authorised person in relation to others. The principal authorised person's Part IV permission must extend to all of his appointed representatives' activities.[87]

13–096　　**Status requirements.** To be exempt as an appointed representative, a person must fulfil two conditions.[88] First, he must be in a contractual relationship with an authorised person, "his principal", which complies with requirements prescribed by Treasury order and which requires or permits him to carry on business of a kind prescribed in the order. Business so prescribed[89] is generally that which comprises arranging deals in investment, safeguarding and administering investments, advising on investments and agreeing to carry on such activities, as those activities are defined in the RAO.[90] Secondly the principal must accept responsibility in writing for the appointed representative's activities in carrying on that business. An appointed representative is only exempt in relation to those activities for which his principal has accepted responsibility and therefore he ceases to have that status and so potentially breaches the general prohibition[91] if he strays outside the scope of his principal's responsibility.

13–097　　**Liability of principal under the FSMA.** Apart from ordinary common law principles[92] which will apply to render the principal liable for certain activities of his appointed representative, the FSMA makes further provision clarifying the responsibility of the principal.[93] Nevertheless, these provisions only apply in relation to business for which the principal has accepted responsibility.[94] First, whatever the position at common law,[95] the principal is responsible for *anything*

---

[82] 1986 Act, s.44.

[83] FSMA, s.39.

[84] See para. 13–020 above.

[85] See esp. FSMA, s.39(3) and (4); 1986 Act, s.44(6) and (7).

[86] See FSMA s.39(1) (the words in parenthesis).

[87] Similarly a person cannot be both an exempt person by reason of his status as an appointed representative in relation to some activities and an exempt person other than by virtue of such status in relation to other activities: see FSMA, s.38(2).

[88] FSMA, s.39(1). *Cf.* 1986 Act, s.44(2).

[89] See the Financial Services and Markets Act 2000 (Appointed Representatives) Regulations 2001 S.I. 2001 No. 1217 (as amended by S.I. 2001 No. 2508).

[90] RAO, arts 25, 40, 53 and 64. As to the RAO, see para. 13–030 above.

[91] In FSMA s.19 (equivalent to 1986 Act, s.3) . See para. 13–013 above.

[92] Especially in relation to agency (see para. 13–098 below) and, as to criminal law, principles of vicarious liability.

[93] FSMA, s.39, like the 1986 Act, s.44.

[94] Thus in *Emmanuel v. DBS Management plc* [1999] 2 Lloyd's Rep. P.N. 593 (a decision under the 1986 Act s.44), the principal was not liable for activities which were held to be outside the scope of the business for which he had accepted responsibility and for activities undertaken before the agent became an appointed representative.

[95] Which to some extent limits the extent to which a principal is responsible for the activities of his agent.

done or omitted to be done by the appointed representative in carrying out business for which his principal has accepted responsibility "to the same extent as if he had expressly permitted it".[96] Thus the principal will be liable to third parties and accountable to the FSA as his regulator, for the activities of his appointed representative, in so far as this depends on such express permission. In particular, the principal will be liable to third parties on contracts made by his representative without the third party having to prove that the representative was actually (or ostensibly) authorised by the principal to act. And he may be liable as joint tortfeasor with the appointed representative on the basis that he is taken to have expressly permitted any tort the appointed representative engages in. Secondly, special provision is made in relation to determinations whether the principal has complied with a provision contained in or made under the Act (only). Here again anything done (or omitted) by the appointed representative in carrying on the business for which the principal has accepted responsibility is attributed to the principal.[97] Again the wording of this subsection is apt to cover both civil and criminal (and disciplinary) liability but only under the Act. In particular, it enables the FSA to hold the principal responsible for all the activities of the appointed representative but only in deciding if the principal has complied with the regulatory regime. There is no direct attribution (for example, on analogy with the vicarious responsibility of an employer for the torts of his employee) of breaches by the appointed representative to the principal. There is only attribution of the representative's acts and omission for the purposes of deciding if the principal himself has been in breach.

Common law agency principles. An agent has implied authority to do   **13–098** whatever is necessary for, or ordinarily incidental to, the effective execution of his express authority in the usual way.[98] Thus while the terms of an appointed representative's express authority might be limited to providing investment advice to customers in relation to particular products of his principal, conduct that is incidental to the provision of that advice (such as soliciting the customers, identifying the financial and personal circumstances of the particular customer, assisting in any application that the customer might choose to make) will still fall within the actual authority of that representative.[99] Secondly, irrespective of whether or not the agent has actual authority to act on the principal's behalf in the relevant way, a principal will be bound by such acts of an agent if the agent has ostensible or apparent authority to act in that way.[1] Thus if a firm has knowingly or even unwittingly led a customer to believe that an authorised representative is authorised to conduct business on its behalf of a type that he is

---

[96] FSMA, s.39(3); 1986 Act, s.44(6).

[97] FSMA, s.39(4). Also 1986 Act, s.44(7).

[98] See *Bowstead & Reynolds on Agency* (16th ed., 1996) at 117.

[99] See in the context of the 1986 Act, s.44, *Martin v. Britannia Life Ltd* [2000] Lloyd's L.Rep. P.N. 412 at 426–428 *per* Jonathan Parker J. In *Martin* the issue was whether the Defendant was liable for advice given by one of its authorised company representatives in relation to a remortgage as well as other "investments". The representative was authorised only to give advice in relation to "investments" issued by the defendant. A mortgage of real property was not an "investment" for the purposes of the 1986 Act. Nonetheless, it was held that the representative had had actual authority to give such advice since the advice was inherently bound up with and incidental to the advice given by the representative in relation to the other investments.

[1] See generally as to ostensible authority, *Freeman & Lockyer v. Buckhurst Park Properties (Mangal) Ltd* [1964] 2 Q.B. 480 at 503 *per* Diplock L.J. and *Bowstead & Reynolds, op. cit.*

not in fact authorised to conduct, the firm will be bound by the acts and omissions of the representative and will be liable for his defaults.[2]

(i) *Tort-based duties*

(i) *Deceit or fraudulent misrepresentation*

13–099   **General.** The tort of deceit or fraudulent misrepresentation[3] is committed if: (1) the defendant makes a statement of fact; (2) the statement of fact is false; (3) the defendant makes such a statement knowing it to be untrue, or not believing it to be true, or being reckless as to whether or not it is true; (4) the defendant intends that the recipient of the statement should act upon it; and (5) the recipient is in fact influenced to act upon the statement to his detriment.

13–100   There are advantages to a claimant who is able to pursue a claim of fraud against a defendant. First, the damages recoverable in such a claim are likely to be more favourable than in a claim of negligent misstatement.[4] Secondly, a defendant is unable to pursue a plea of contributory negligence against a claimant who has been the victim of fraud.[5] Thirdly time will not begin to run for limitation purposes against the victim of a fraud until the fraud has been discovered or could with reasonable diligence have been discovered.[6] Fourthly, a victim of fraud need not show the same "special relationship" as is necessary to demonstrate a duty of care at common law.

13–101   However, such advantages must be weighed against the increased onus that a plea of fraud places upon a claimant. Any such plea is a "very serious matter" and should only be advanced when there is "reasonably credible material establishing a prima facie case" for such an allegation.[7–8]

13–102   In a retail financial contest, two particular types of fraud are frequently encountered. First, the employee or representative of the provider deliberately or recklessly misrepresents the nature of the proposed investment or some key element in that investment. This type of fraud is often motivated by a desire on the part of the fraudster to maximise the benefit to himself through commission or the like. Secondly, the employee or representative deliberately or recklessly suggests an investment to the investor which he in fact has no authority to suggest. Such investments are frequently ones with which the employee or representative himself has an association or an interest and are often motivated by a simple desire to part the investor from his own money, which is then misappropriated.

---

[2] In *Martin* (above) the representative gave a business card (with which he had been supplied by the defendant) to the customer which bore the defendant's name and logo, the representative's name and the words "Financial Adviser". Jonathan Parker J. held that this was sufficient on the facts of the case to provide the representative with ostensible authority to advise in a far wider capacity than that in which the defendant had expressly authorised him to advise. The defendant was therefore liable for the representative's conduct.

[3] See generally *Clerk & Lindsell on Torts* (18th ed.), paras 15–05 to 15–37

[4] This is particularly so if the scope of the duty of care owed by the defendant at common law is too narrow to enable the entirety of the claimant's loss to be recovered in a claim for negligent misstatement: see *South Australia Asset Management Corporation v. York Montague* [1997] A.C. 191 at 215G–H; *Smith New Court Securities Ltd v. Scrimgeour Vickers Ltd* [1997] A.C. 254

[5] *Standard Chartered Bank v. Pakistan National Shipping Corp. (No. 2)* [2000] 1 Lloyd's L.Rep. 218; *Alliance & Leicester BS v. Edgestop Ltd* [1993] 1 W.L.R. 1462; *Nationwide BS v. Thimbleby* [1999] Lloyd's L.Rep. P.N. 359.

[6] s. 32(1) of the Limitation Act 1980. See further Chap. 5 para. 5–070 above.

[7–8] *Medcalf v. Mardell* [2001] P.N.L.R. 372 at para. 39

In either case, the issue likely to be of primary importance to the victim of the **13–103** fraud will be whether or not he can recover his losses from the principal of the employee or representative *i.e.* whether or not the principal is vicariously liable for the fraud.[9] A principal cannot *per se* avoid responsibility for the conduct of his agent merely because that conduct was fraudulent and, unless the conduct fell outside the scope of the actual or ostensible authority of the representative,[10] the principal will find himself bound by the fraudulent conduct of the representative.[11] Thus a principal may find himself liable for the actions of a representative who knowingly and deliberately either mis-sells a product to a client which, while unsuitable, is nonetheless of a type which the representative is actually authorised by the principal to sell, or mis-sells a product to a client which he is not authorised by his principal to sell but which the victim nonetheless believes that the representative has authority to sell.

In this latter scenario, the liability of the principal will depend to a very great **13–104** extent on the basis for the victim's belief. Only if the victim's erroneous belief as to the authority of the representative has been induced by the words or conduct of the principal will the principal be vicariously liable for the representative's actions. If his belief is based solely on the words or conduct of the fraudulent representative, the principal will not be bound by the representative's actions.[12–13] Equally, if the victim's belief as to the authority of the representative is unreasonable (*i.e.* the victim ought to have appreciated that the representative had no authority to act as he did) then the principal will escape liability for the actions of the representative.[14]

(ii) *Misfeasance in public office*

A regulator may be liable to an individual claimant or class of claimants who **13–105** have lost money as the result of the collapse of an institution for which the regulator was responsible if the claimant is able to demonstrate that the regulator was guilty of the tort of misfeasance in public office.[15] In *Three Rivers D.C. v. Governor and Company of the Bank of England*[16] 6,000 former depositors in the United Kingdom Branch of B.C.C.I. commenced proceedings against the Bank of England on the basis that the Bank of England's decisions (1) to grant B.C.C.I. a licence, and (2) not to revoke that licence when it knew or suspected that B.C.C.I. would probably collapse, amounted to misfeasance in public office. The House of Lords concluded that, as a matter of law, the pleaded claim was not bound to fail. In particular, liability could arise in the event that a public officer exercised his power by acting illegally (or possibly even by omitting to act) in bad faith either: (1) with specific intention to injure the claimant or a class of persons of which the claimant was a member, or (2) with knowledge of, or with

---

[9] The circumstances in which a principal may himself owe a duty of care at common law to such victims to supervise its employees and representatives and/or to prevent them committing such frauds are rare: see para. 13–112 below.
[10] See para. 13–098 above.
[11] See for example *Hambro v. Burnand* [1904] 2 K.B. 10.
[12–13] See generally *Armagas Ltd v. Mundogas Ltd* [1986] A.C. 717. For an example in the field of financial services see *Emmanuel v. DBS Management plc* [1999] Lloyd's L.Rep. P.N. 593
[14] *Houghton & Co v. Nothard Lowe & Wills Ltd.* [1927] 1 K.B. 246 at 260 *per* Bankes L.J. The decision of the Court of Appeal was affirmed by the House of Lords at [1928] A.C. 1.
[15] As to regulators' limited statutory immunity from damages liability, see para. 13–132 below.
[16] [2000] 2 W.L.R. 1220.

reckless indifference to, the probability of causing injury to the claimant or a class of persons of which the claimant was a member.

(iii) *Negligence*

13–106 **Clients.** A financial practitioner will generally owe a duty of care in tort to his client quite apart from any contract that exists between them. As with most professions, that duty will usually be not only concurrent with,[17] but also consistent with,[18] the contractual duty to exercise reasonable care and skill.[19] Consequently, if the parties to a contract have expressly or implicitly agreed a limitation on the scope of the practitioner's duties under the contract, his tortious duty of care will almost certainly be similarly limited. For example, in an execution-only transaction there will be no contractual (nor regulatory) duty to advise on the merits of the transaction. The practitioner's tortious duty of care will be similarly limited, except in very exceptional circumstances.

13–107 **Third parties.** A financial practitioner may owe a tortious duty of care to third parties, *i.e.* a person between whom and the practitioners there is no contractual relationship. Whether such duty arises in particular circumstances falls to be decided in accordance with general tests for the determination of its existence.[20] Nevertheless, in the present, as in other contexts, critical factors will be any statutory context or contractual matrix, the purpose for which any information, advice or other services was provided and the availability of other causes of action or means of redress.

13–108 **Prospectus cases.** Statutory causes of action provide in most circumstances easier bases of claim in respect of misleading statements in prospectuses, as well as listing particulars.[21] Nevertheless, the tortious duty of care may be invoked also, as well as in circumstances where the statutory provisions may not apply. There are two English cases. In *Al-Nakib Investments (Jersey) Ltd v. Longcroft*,[22] CT plc decided to float M Ltd, a subsidiary, on the Unlisted Securities Market and issued a prospectus inviting CT shareholders to subscribe for shares in M and CT under a rights issue. The claimant CT shareholder acquired 400,000 shares by subscription under the rights issue and later acquired further CT and M shares through purchases made through the stock exchange. The claimant alleged that the prospectus contained misrepresentations and that since all of its acquisitions had been made in reliance upon the prospectus, it was entitled to recover the losses sustained from CT and its directors based on breaches of duties of care owed by them. Mervyn Davies J. struck out the claim in respect of the purchase transactions. He held that the prospectus had been addressed to the claimant for a particular purpose (*i.e.* subscription under the rights issue) and not for the purpose of purchasing shares in the market. Accordingly neither CT nor its directors owed any duty of care to the claimant in respect of the purchase

---

[17] See for example *Midland Bank Trust Co. Ltd v. Hett, Stubbs & Kemp (a Firm)* [1979] Ch. 384 and more generally Chap. 2, paras. 2–100 to 2–108.
[18] See *Henderson v. Merrett Syndicates Ltd* [1995] 2 A.C. 145 at 193A–D.
[19] See by way of example *Investors Compensation Scheme Ltd v. West Bromwich Building Society* [1999] Lloyd's L.Rep. P.N. 496 at 504.
[20] See chap. 2, paras 2–109–2–115.
[21] See paras. 13–081 and 13–082 above.
[22] [1990] 3 All E.R. 321.

transactions. The opposite conclusion was reached in *Possfund Custodian Trustee Ltd v. Diamond.*[23] The defendant had issued a prospectus in connection with the flotation of its shares on the unlisted securities market. The prospectus specifically stated that, as part of the same exercise as allotment, the facility would be available for shares to be dealt with subsequently on the unlisted securities market. Two classes of claimant, the first of which had purchased shares at the time of their original placing and the second of which had subsequently bought shares in the unlisted securities market, sought damages from the defendant in deceit and negligence in relation to alleged material representations contained in the prospectus as to the financial position of the defendant which, it was said, had induced them to purchase shares. Lightman J. refused to strike out any part of the claims. An after-market purchaser could sustain a claim in negligence against the issuer of a prospectus if he could establish that he was intended by the issuer to rely upon the prospectus for that purpose, that he had in fact relied upon it for that purpose, and if he could demonstrate the necessary connection between himself and the issuer of the prospectus to render the imposition of a duty of care just, fair and reasonable. On the facts of the case, it was arguable that the prospectus had been worded in such a way as to inform and encourage after-market purchasers in addition to those who had relied on the prospectus when deciding whether to subscribe to the original placing of the shares, and so to give rise to a duty of care to such persons.

Pension beneficiaries. Cases involving these often raise the issue whether, **13–109** expressed generically, a duty of care may be owed by an adviser to a claimant who did not directly rely on his advice or expertise, but who has suffered loss as result of advice provided to another. In *Gorham v. British Telecommunications Plc*[24] G had, prior to 1991, been an employee of Cable & Wireless and thereafter, until his death, of BT. In early 1992, shortly after joining BT and following advice by a representative of Standard Life Assurance Company, G opted to take out a personal pension scheme with that company and to transfer thereto the transferable value of benefits accumulated under the Cable & Wireless scheme. He was eligible to join BT's occupational pension scheme but did not do so, although by October 1992 he believed that he had done so (contrary to his previous belief).[25] BT treated G as having opted out.[26] In November 1992 he ceased paying premiums to Standard Life and there was evidence that he had rang the company's helpline and been advised that the BT scheme was better. The claimant dependants of G (his wife and two children) succeeded in their claim for damages against Standard Life, which was based on breach of an alleged duty of care in tort owed by the company to them in advising G. The recoverable damages related to the capital value of the greater pension rights under the BT occupational pension scheme relative to the personal pension scheme. The claimants failed to recover claimed damages for loss of a lump sum

---

[23] [1996] 2 All E.R. 774.
[24] [2000] 1 W.L.R. 2129, C.A.
[25] G had been told by BT that, unless he positively chose to opt out of its occupational scheme, he would be automatically joined to the scheme and appropriate deductions made from his salary. He did nothing to lead BT to conclude that he had elected to opt out.
[26] Claims against BT and the trustees of the BT pension scheme were dismissed at first instance.

death benefit because there had been a break in the chain of causation consisting of his failure to act upon the helpline advice.[27]

13–110   As to duty, Standard Life accepted that it owed a duty of care in advising G and that it was in breach on the basis that its representative had failed to advise G about the differences between an occupational pension scheme and a personal pension scheme. Consequently, he should have refused to sell the latter to G unless satisfied that G had made an informed choice between the two schemes. Reflecting polarisation requirements,[28] Standard Life was not entitled to advise G as to the merits of the BT scheme. Standard Life disputed that it owed the dependants any duty of care. Nevertheless the Court of Appeal held that it did owe such a duty. It rejected the company's contention that since the dependants did not fall within the category of claimant to which statutory right of action under the 1986 Act[29] extended, there should be no wider duty of care owed at common law.[30] The Court held that a duty of care was owed to the defendants for like reasons to those given by the House of Lords in *White v. Jones*[31]:

> "[G] intended to create a benefit for his wife and children in the event of his predeceasing them . . . It is fundamental to the giving and receiving of advice upon a scheme for pension provision and life insurance that the interests of the customer's dependents will arise for consideration. In my judgment, practical justice requires that the disappointed beneficiaries should have a remedy against an insurance company in circumstances such as the present . . . Advice was expected and was directed not only to the interests of [G] but to the interests of his dependents should he predecease them. The advice was given on the assumption that their interests were involved. Moreover, the provision for them was not merely a windfall in the sense that a legacy may be a windfall; it was central to purpose of the venture into insurance."[32]

In the context of the case the scope of the duty was expressed as "not to give advice to the customer which adversely affects [his dependants'] interest."

13–111   Although the situation did not arise in *Gorham*, Stuart-Smith L.J. doubted whether a duty of care would be owed to beneficiaries such as the claimants in the event that their interests conflicted with the interests of the original recipient of the financial advice.[33] However Pill L.J., with whom Schiemann L.J. agreed, concluded that on a proper analysis of the scope of the duty that was owed by defendants such as Standard Life, no difficulty would in fact arise.[34] The duty owed by Standard Life to the dependants was not one to take care to ensure that they were properly provided for, but rather was a duty not to give negligent advice to the customer which would adversely affect their interests as he intended

---

[27] Sir Murray Stuart-Smith dissented on this point, holding that the causation chain was not broken.

[28] See para. 13–055 above. The term "polarisation" is not referred to as such in the judgments, though its effect is described.

[29] See 1986 Act, ss. 62 and 62A and para. 13–076 above.

[30] [2000] 1 W.L.R. 2129 at 2141.

[31] [1995] 2 A.C. 207.

[32] [2000] 1 W.L.R. 2129 at 2140, 2141–2142.

[33] *ibid.*, at 2147. The example that Schiemann L.J. gave was an investor who wished to enhance his own pension at the expense of his wife's pension.

[34] In carrying out such analysis, Pill L.J. followed the well-known passage from the speech of Lord Bridge in *Caparo* that: "It is never sufficient to ask simply whether A owes B a duty of care. It is always necessary to determine the scope of the duty by reference to the kind of damage from which A must take care to save B harmless" and the similar views expressed by Lord Hoffman in *SAAMCO v. York Montague Ltd* [1997] A.C. 191 at 211.

them to be. In the circumstances (given polarisation requirements) the duty, put at its simplest, was not to sell a Standard Life policy to G.

Principal or employer. Claimants have on a number of occasions attempted **13–112** to fashion a duty of care on the part of financial services providers to take care to protect them against misconduct on the part of appointed representatives or even employees of the provider in circumstances where no other remedy is open to them.[35] In the absence of an express or implied assumption of responsibility for such conduct of the representative or employee, such a duty will be rare.[36]

Employee. There may be occasions in which it is necessary to consider the **13–113** extent to which an employee of a provider of financial services owes a duty of care to the recipient of those services independently to any duty owed by the provider itself.[37] In *Hale v. Guildarch Ltd*[38] the claimants entered into transactions in reliance upon financial advice given to them by the defendants, P and T, both of whom were employees of ADC Group Ltd. By the time the transactions had gone disastrously wrong, ADC was insolvent and uninsured. The judge rejected the claimants' contention that P and T owed them a duty of care.[39] It is submitted that an employee does not owe a duty of care in respect of a task unless at least (1) he clearly and voluntarily intimates that he is undertaking responsibility in a personal capacity and (2) the recipient of the advice is able to demonstrate that he reasonably relied upon that personal acceptance of responsibility for the task.

Regulators. Irrespective of the limited statutory immunity from liability in **13–114** damages granted to regulators and others,[40] regulators do not generally owe a duty of care to investors in the performance of their functions. Considerations decisive to negate a duty of care alleged to have been owed to a third party by

---

[35] For example, if the representative or employee was acting fraudulently, outside the course of his employment and/or actual and ostensible authority

[36] In *Hornsby v. Clark Kenneth Leventhal* [1998] P.N.L.R. the claimant was defrauded by an employee of the defendant firm of accountants who had persuaded him to invest in an "International Fund". The claimant was unable to demonstrate any vicarious liability on the part of the defendant and so contended that the defendant had owed him a duty to supervise and investigate its employees to prevent such frauds being perpetrated. The Court of Appeal held that the defendant owed no such duty to the claimant. Such a duty would arise only if the defendant had actually known of the fraud or been reckless as to its existence. Similarly, in *Emmanuel v. DBS Management Plc* [1999] Lloyd's L.Rep. P.N. 593 the defendant had appointed ITIP to act as its appointed representative under the 1986 Act. ITIP persuaded the claimants to enter into two separate investment transactions neither of which fell within the scope of that for which the defendant had accepted responsibility under the terms of ITIP's appointment. Consequently the claimants were unable to rely upon the provisions of 1986 Act, s.44 (see para. 13–095 above). They attempted to circumvent this difficulty by arguing that the defendant owed them a duty of care at common law to take care to protect them against losses of the type that they suffered at the hands of ITIC. The judge (Jonathan Sumption Q.C.) struck out the claim. There was no basis for holding that the defendant owed a duty of care to the claimant (as a member of the class of persons with whom ITIC had dealt) simply by virtue of having appointed ITIP as its appointed representative in respect of other unrelated transactions.

[37] *e.g.* if the provider is in liquidation and/or uninsured.

[38] [1999] P.N.L.R. 44, Judge Raymond Jack Q.C.

[39] *cf. Merrett v. Babb* [2001] 3 W.L.R. 1, CA: see chap. 9, para. 9–014.

[40] See para. 13–132 below.

statutory, ministerial, administrative, regulatory and complaints-handling bodies[41] have been the availability of alternative bases of redress and regulatory overkill,[42] even though such redress may be of little value to the third party concerned.

(j) *Fiduciary duties*

13–115   **General.** The law relating to fiduciary duties[43] in its application to the financial sector and to the interrelationship of such duties and regulatory duties is still in a relatively immature state of development. Its state motivated the involvement of the Law Commission. Following an earlier Consultation Paper,[44] it published its final report "Fiduciary Duties and Regulatory Rules"[45] in December 1995. In both reports it addresses the law and its application in the financial services sector. A classic statement as to when a person is a fiduciary is that of Professor Finn: "A person will be a fiduciary in his relationships with another when and insofar as that other is entitled to expect that he will act in that other's interest or (as in a partnership) in their joint interest, to the exclusion of their several interests." This statement has the advantage of recognising the feature, important in a financial services context, that a person may be a fiduciary in some but not all aspects of his relationship with another. While fiduciary duties may be variously classified, the Law Commission in both reports formulates four basic rules: the "no conflict" rule,[46] the "no profit" rule,[47] the undivided loyalty rule (which embraces a disclosure requirement)[48] and the duty of confidentiality.[49] The range of services provided by financial conglomerates, the composition of their customer base and the different capacities in which they conduct business are significant factors in generating potential conflicts of interest and duty. Instances include dealing off one's book or buying one's own account, matching orders (agency cross), buying from a customer and selling immediately to another customer (riskless principal transactions), dealing in property in which

---

[41] As to a regulatory context see *Yeun Kun Yeu v. Att.-Gen. of Hong Kong* [1988] A.C. 175, PC; *Minories Finance Ltd. v. Arthur Young.* [1989] 2 All E.R. 105 and *Davis v. Radcliffe* [199] 1 W.L.R. 821, PC, but *cf. Lonrho v. Tebbit* [1992] 4 All E.R. 280, CA; for a ministerial context see *Rowling v Takaro Properties Ltd.* [1988] 1 A.C. 475, PC; and an administrative context, see *Jones v. Department of Employment* [1989] Q.B. 1 CA. See further chap. 2, para. 2–086 above.

[42] See *Rowling v. Takaro Properties Ltd* [1988] 1 A.C. 475, PC at 502.

[43] See generally Finn, "Fiduciary obligations" (1979) and "Commercial Aspects of Trust and Fiduciary Obligations" (McKendrick, ed. 1992). Significant recent English cases are *Kelly v. Cooper* [1993] A.C. 205; *Henderson v. Merrett Syndicates Ltd* [1995] 2 A.C. 145; *Bristol and West B.S. v. Mothew* [1996] 4 All E.R. 698. Fiduciary duties have been subject to close scrutiny in Canada: see especially *Lac Minerals Ltd v. International Corona Resources Ltd* [1990] F.S.R. 441. But Canadian cases must be read subject to the caution that they may be too broadly expressed for entire consumption by an English court.

[44] Law Commission Consultation Paper No. 124 (1992).

[45] Law Commission Paper No. 236.

[46] *i.e.* a fiduciary must not place himself in a position where his own interest conflicts with that of his customer, the beneficiary; there must be "real possibility of conflict".

[47] *i.e.* a fiduciary must not profit from his position at the expense of his customer, the beneficiary.

[48] *i.e.* a fiduciary owes undivided loyalty to his customer, the beneficiary, not to place himself in a position where his duty towards one customer conflicts with a duty that he owes to another customer; a consequence of this duty is that a fiduciary must make available to a customer all the information that is relevant to the customer's affairs.

[49] a fiduciary must only use information obtained in confidence from his customer, the beneficiary, for the benefit of the customer and must not use it for his own advantage, or for the benefit of any other person.

the customer has an interest, preferential or discriminatory treatment in the allocation of investment opportunities and failure to use all the information which the attribution acknowledgment rule deems to be available to a firm. However, the normal incidents of a fiduciary relationship may be modified by any underlying contractual relationship between the parties. Indeed a contractual relationship is usually the source of fiduciary duties in a financial services context. Moreover, the normal incidents of a fiduciary relationship may be modified by regulatory requirements, including as to Chinese walls.[50]

Illustrations. The application of the above principles were recently considered in the context of the rules and practices of the London Metal Exchange by Toulson J. in *Brandeis (Brokers) Ltd v. Herbert Black*.[51] He dismissed a challenge by LME brokers to an arbitral award made against them in favour of their former clients. He endorsed the arbitrators' conclusions that certain rules of the Securities and Futures Authority, the SRO of which the brokers were members, were incorporated in contracts made between the brokers and their clients and also that the brokers owed fiduciary duties to their clients. He concluded that the relationship between the parties was such that the brokers were acting as principal and not as agent for an undisclosed principal, but in all other respects the substance of the relationship was much more closely akin to that of agency than of buyer and seller. Agency was by its nature a form of fiduciary relationship. This impacted on allocation of orders (brokers were required to process the orders of different clients in due turn). Moreover, "front-running" (the placing by a broker of a prior order in advance of placing a clients's order anticipated to move the market) and misuse of confidential information would involve a breach of fiduciary duties. Similarly in *Ata v. American Express Bank Ltd*.[52] it was held that the defendant bank owed a "fiduciary obligation" based on "classic principles" to the plaintiff investor when it performed discretionary management functions for him, but not when performing other functions including execution only functions. **13–116**

3. Breach of Duty

(a) *General*

The object of this section is to provide some case illustrations of breaches of duties in various financial contexts. The section is arranged under various categories, some reflecting titles in the FSA Handbook, but the categories are far from covering the multifarious circumstances in which relevant breaches may arise. In other chapters of this work the main relevant duty for consideration is the practitioner's duty of care, whether arising in contract and/or tort, and the focus of case law is the types of conduct amounting to its breach. The equivalent section in those chapters is arranged around categories reflecting the broad nature of the offending conduct. In contrast, in a financial context the duty of care subsists along with other very specific duties imposed by or under regulatory **13–117**

---

[50] See para. 13–062 above.
[51] Unreported, May 25, 2001. See further para. 13–128 below.
[52] C.A., unreported, June 17, 1998 upholding Rix J., unreported, October 7, 1996. See further, paras 13–134, 13–159 and 13–160 below.

legislation. Many of those duties are expressed by reference to specific kinds of conduct, whether in terms of prescribing good conduct or prohibiting bad conduct. Hence the focus in a financial context on ascertaining the nature and scope of relevant duties which, once properly ascertained, frequently result in an inevitable conclusion on breach.

(b) *Misleading promotion*

(i) *Old prospectus cases*

13–118 There is a large volume of reported cases on misleading statements in a pro- spectus. Most were decided in the half century or so preceding the First World War—the legal flotsam of victims of the heady entrepreneurial optimism of late Empire. These cases must now be approached with some caution and with due regard to the state of the law and to methods and practices for the issue of securities current at the time.[53] However, much of the reasoning remains of enduring relevance. Thus a half truth represented as a whole truth may be tantamount to a false statement.[54] The following observation by Lord Halsbury L.C. merits invocation in many financial promotion contexts:

> "I do not care by what means it is conveyed—by what trick or device of ambiguous language: all those are expedients by which fraudulent people seem to think they can escape from the real substance of the transaction. If by a number of statements you intentionally give a false impression and induce a person to act upon it, it is not the less false if one takes each statement by itself there may be difficulty in shewing that any specific statement is untrue."[55]

(ii) *Present position*

13–119 Prospectus requirements formerly contained in companies legislation relating to a prospectus have now, almost entirely, been superseded by provisions made in or under FSMA relating to listed securities[56] and financial promotion generally,[57] as well as provisions related to other securities in regulations made under the European Communities Act 1972.[58] As previously discussed, both FSMA in relation to listed securities and the regulations in relation to unlisted securities provide for liability in respect of any "untrue or misleading statement" as well as certain omissions.[59] Other rules relating to financial promotion in the FSMA may give rise to section 150 liability in respect of both misleading statements and omissions.[60] Civil liability may also be incurred under the Misrepresentation Act 1967 and at common law for untrue or misleading statements in promotional and reporting documents. Examples of misleading promotion may be found in recent caselaw but apart from being illustrative they are fact specific and do not give rise

---

[53] For an account see Powell, *Issues and Offers of Company Securities: The New Regimes* (1988).
[54] See *Aaron's Reefs v. Twiss* [1896] A.C. 273.
[55] *ibid.* at 281. Note also the observations of Lord Watson at 287.
[56] See para. 13–081 above
[57] See paras 13–050 and 13–051 above.
[58] s.2(2) of that Act. As to the regulations, see para. 13–084 above.
[59] Paras 13–081 and 13–084 above.
[60] See paras 13–076–13–078 above.

to any new principle.[61] Section 397 of the FSMA, provides for criminal liability in respect of misleading etc. statements and practices, as did the equivalent section 47 of the 1986 Act. Neither of these provisions gives rise to a civil claim for damages.[62]

(c) *Failure properly to classify customer*

Under FSMA regime, as under previous regulatory regimes, the nature and scope **13–120** of a financial practitioner's duties are dependant upon his properly classifying his customers.[62a] Failure to do so may result in a consequential failure to perform duties appropriate to the correct classification. Classification was the central issue in *Australia & New Zealand Banking Group Ltd v. Cattan.*[63] The defendant resisted a claim for debts arising from trading losses in the Emerging Market Debt ("EMD") sector on the basis that the claimant had wrongly classified him as a "non-private customer" under IMRO rules. He maintained that but for that classification the claimant would not have permitted him to make relevant trades and he would not have suffered the losses. Morison J. concluded that the defendant had been correctly classified. The judgment made about him by the claimant's representative was both reasonable and right: he had sufficient understanding and experience to waive the protection provided for private customers. Morison J.'s judgment contains a useful analysis of the factors taken into account under the following headings: (1) the source of the defendant's introduction, (2) the knowledge displayed by him, (3) the discussions that took place between the claimant and the defendant which suggested a degree of familiarity with the EMD market "beyond the normal", (4) his background and experience, (5) his familiarity with another EMD trader, and (6) the way he presented himself: "a man who knew his way around the international financial circuit".

(d) *Advising and selling*

There are many and varied requirements in the FSA Handbook relating to **13–121** advising and selling. Like requirements imposed under the predecessor 1986 Act regime have generated several cases, especially requirements relating to "know your customer", customer understanding of risk and suitability.

Martin v. Britannia Life Ltd[64] provides numerous examples of these types of **13–122** failures. In 1991 the claimants contacted the predecessors of the defendant ("LAS") for advice. They met one of LAS's authorised representatives who purported to obtain an overview of the claimants' financial position. LAS subsequently advised the claimants to surrender five life policies, to replace them

---

[61] See for example: *Ball v. Banner* [2000] Lloyd's L.Rep. P.N. 569 (misleading statements in a prospectus for an EZPT); *Re Market Wizard Systems (UK) Ltd* [1988] 2 B.C.L.C. 282 (misleading statements used by the Secretary of State as the basis for an application to wind up the respondent on public interest grounds); *Securities and Investment Board v. Vandersteen Associates NV* [1991] B.C.L.C. 206 (breaches of s. 57 of the 1986 Act resulting from cold-calling by telephone and post); *Secretary of State for Trade and Industry v. Grant,* unreported, September 15, 2000, Neuberger J. (distribution of misleading material relating to collective investment schemes).

[62] See in relation to the 1986 Act, s.47: *Norwich Union Society v. Qureshi* [1998] C.L.C. 1605; *Aldrich v. Norwich Union Life Ins. Co. Ltd* [1998] C.L.C. 1621.

[62a] See para. 13–052 above.

[63] Unreported, August 21, 2001, Morison J .

[64] [2000] Lloyd's L.Rep. P.N. 412, Jonathan Parker J.

with a life policy offered by LAS, to remortgage their house and charge the new life policy as collateral security for the mortgage and to set up a new pension policy with LAS. Although the judge found that the claims brought by the claimants in tort and pursuant to section 62 of the 1986 Act[65] were statute barred, he was extremely critical of LAS.[66] In particular, he found that (1) no adequate steps had been taken to assess the personal and financial circumstances of the claimants—LAS had not "got to know" its customer, (2) the investments that LAS had advised were wholly unsuitable for the claimants,[67] (3) LAS had failed to provide any adequate warning of the risks posed by entering into the investments that were proposed,[68] (4) no adequate advice had been given of the advantages and disadvantages of entering into the package,[69] (5) the advice given to the claimants that it was appropriate to fund a personal pension by means of a remortgage was simply wrong, and (6) the endowment policy advised by LAS was unnecessary and unsuitable since the claimants could have used monies payable under the pension plan as security for the remortgage.

13–123   The extent to which advice should comply with the letter, as well as the spirit, of the 1986 Act and FIMBRA rules were considered in *Loosemore v. Financial Concepts.*[70] The claimant was an NHS employed nurse who in 1988 was considering starting a personal pension plan in order to be independent of the NHS. She was already a member of the NHS occupational pension scheme. She consulted the defendant IFA, who advised that the claimant was "better off" in the NHS scheme while she could remain a member. The claimant ignored the advice, opted out of the NHS scheme and took out a personal pension plan. She subsequently sued the defendant, alleging that the advice that she had received had been negligent and that the defendant had breached section 62 of the FSA. Although the judge found that the defendant's advice in 1988 had been correct, nonetheless he concluded that the advice was deficient in several respects. First, the defendant had failed to establish precisely what benefits the claimant was entitled to under the NHS scheme or to present those benefits to her in order to enable her to consider them. Secondly, he had not compared the amounts that the claimant might expect to receive under the NHS scheme and the personal pension plan. Thirdly, he had failed to take all reasonable steps to ensure that the claimant understood the risk that opting out of the NHS scheme and starting up a personal pension plan might entail. The defendant had therefore breached FIMBRA rules[71] and had been negligent and, despite advising correctly, had deprived the

---

[65] See para. 13–76 to 13–078 above for the equivalent under the FSMA, s.150.

[66] *ibid.* esp. at 429 to 431.

[67] *ibid.* at 429: "I have no doubt that in giving his advice [LAS] was under no illusions that in entering into the package [the claimants] would be extending their commitments well beyond the limits of what they could reasonably afford; but that did not deter [LAS] from his endeavours to procure them to take out policies with LAS".

[68] *ibid.* at 429: "it was plainly [LAS's] duty to advise [the claimants] in the strongest terms that if they entered into the package they would be undertaking very substantial ongoing commitments which they might well find hard to meet ... The adviser's duty is to make sure, so far as he can, that the client's decision is an informed one. In my judgment, [LAS] clearly failed in that duty in this case".

[69] In particular, LAS did not warn that: (1) substantial penalties would be incurred upon early surrender of their existing endowment policies, (2) the premiums under the new policies would increase substantially over time, or (3) the new policies, unlike the old ones, would not qualify for life assurance premium relief.

[70] [2001] Lloyd's L.Rep. P.N. 235, Judge Raymond Jack Q.C.

[71] FIMBRA, rr. 4.1, 4.2 and 4.3. As to FIMBRA, see n. 18 under para. 13–010 above.

claimant of the opportunity to make an informed decision whether to remain in or opt out of the NHS scheme.[72–74]

One of the more striking examples of a financial practitioner's failure to assess **13–124** suitability is to be found in the decision of Longmore J. in *Morgan Stanley UK Group v. Pugilisi Cosentino*.[75] The defendant resisted a claim for substantial losses sustained in a principal exchange rate linked security ("PERLS") investment with the claimant bank. The bank had provided 90 per cent of the funding for the investment by way of a loan to the defendant. In dismissing the bank's claim the judge concluded that the bank had been guilty of a "serious underappreciation of the Financial Services Act".[76] The bank was authorised to carry on investment business under the 1986 Act by virtue of its membership of the Securities Association ("TSA"), then an SRO, and so was bound by its rules. First the transaction was one which necessitated a risk warning being given TSA's rules, but no such warning had in fact been given. Secondly, although the bank had ascertained that the defendant had experience of high-value foreign exchange dealings, it had taken no steps to determine the defendant's wealth or the amount that he was prepared or could afford to lose. Thirdly, the transaction had been structured in such a way that although the borrowing arrangement agreed with the defendant entitled the bank to cease financing the investment at the end of every three- or six-month period (and thus to require the defendant to find money from his own resources to replace the bank's funding at short notice) the investment itself was relatively illiquid and could not be readily realised. Fourthly, the investment was not suitable for the defendant and the bank had no reasonable grounds for believing that it was suitable, contrary to the suitability requirement in TSA's rules. But for the relevant breaches of the rules, the defendant would not have invested in the PERLS transaction. Consequently, the bank was unable to enforce the debt that had been incurred by the defendant on the PERLS investment.

Examples of failures by financial practitioners to ensure an adequate under- **13–125** standing on the part of the customer of the risks associated with a proposed investment can be found in *Australia & New Zealand Banking Group Limited v. Cattan*[77] and *Investors Compensation Scheme Ltd v. West Bromwich Building Society*.[78] The bank in *Cattan* failed to take the defendant through a warning letter, but this occasioned no loss. In contrast, in *ICS v. West Bromwich* the financial practitioner was guilty not only of a wholesale failure to warn investors that the home income plan in which they were proposing to invest created a significant risk of substantial loss but also of positively providing misleading advice to the effect that the home income plan would provide a safe and secure investment for the remainder of the investors' lives. In reality nothing could have been further from the truth. The plan was vulnerable not only to a falling property market but also to one which was static or "only" rising slowly. In normal market conditions it could be expected to last no more than 10 years. It was therefore totally unsuitable for any investor who might have 25 years or more to live.

[72–74] See further para. 13–092 above.
[75] [1998] C.L.C. 481, Longmore J.
[76] At 498C.
[77] Unreported August 2, 2001, Morison J. For the full facts of *Cattan* see para. 13–120 above.
[78] [1999] Lloyd's L.Rep. P.N. 496, Evans Lombe J.

(e) *Dealing and managing*

13–126   Chapter 7 of the COB Sourcebook now sets out the regulatory framework governing these areas.[79] Cases decided under the regime of the 1986 Act may provide assistance for the interpretation of the rules and guidance contained therein.

13–127   Many of the cases decided under the 1986 Act regime concerned perceived conflicts of interest on the part of the financial practitioner. Such conflicts can take many forms. In *Australia & New Zealand Banking Group Ltd v. Cattan*[80] one of the allegations unsuccessfully advanced by the defendant was that the claimant bank had advised him to buy EMD at the same time as it had itself been reducing its own proprietary positions. In rejecting the allegation Morison J. found that the bank had successfully kept its proprietary book entirely separate from its trading desk where its salesmen bought and sold on customers' behalf and that there was no evidence to suggest that its own decision to sell EMD from its proprietary book influenced the advice that it gave to its customers. He concluded:

> "There is nothing wrong or disreputable for a bank to take a different view of the market in relation to its own holdings from the view properly advised to their customers. The reason is obvious: the bank may decide to off-load assets in a particular field for a whole variety of reasons which have nothing to do with an appreciation of how the market is going to respond in the future."[81]

The bank was able to demonstrate that an adequate Chinese wall was in place to prevent any inference being drawn that one department had in any way influenced the other.

13–128   One case in which a financial practitioner was found to have acted in a manner that conflicted with the interests of its clients is *Brandeis (Brokers) Limited v. Black*.[82] The claimant was an LME broker who commenced arbitration proceedings against various of its clients seeking to recover U.S.$12.5 m. in relation to dealings in copper futures. The respondents countered the claim by alleging mispricing,[83] front-running[84] and misuse of confidential information[85] by the

---

[79] See paras 13–061 to 13–066 above.
[80] See para. 13–120 above.
[81] At para. 40.
[82] Unreported, May 25, 2001, Toulson J. See further para. 13–116 above.
[83] Defined and explained by the arbitrators as follows:
"When the broker executing an order in the market on behalf of a client does not give the correct execution to the client, that is to say . . . the broker has executed a transaction at one price but, leaving aside commission, has given a different price."
[84] Defined and explained by the arbitrators as follows:
"Front running occurs where, after a broker has taken an order from a client, the broker goes into the market on its own account (or for the benefit of a discretionary or closely associated client) and carries out a transaction for itself or such other client ahead of the client who has given the order. The broker does this because it believes that the client's order will move the market. The broker wants to deal ahead of the client so as to benefit from the market movement or confer a benefit on others or to avoid a loss on its existing position as a result of the market movement. The client may well suffer loss or damage because the broker's transaction and others which may be triggered by it could move the market against the client."
[85] Which the arbitrators explained as occurring when
"a broker discloses to outside parties or uses for its own purposes confidential information in its possession about a client's positions, transactions or intended transactions. Such information would include information about the client's present own future positions and financial position. Information would not come within this definition if it is in the public domain or merely consists of general gossip or speculation." Front running is a particular form of misuse of confidential information.

claimant. The arbitrators found that the claimant had indeed been guilty of the majority of the transgressions of which it was accused. The claimant's appeal was dismissed by Toulson J.[86]

The nature of criticisms made of financial practitioners within the sphere of **13–129** dealing and managing investments on behalf of a client will frequently depend on the degree of discretion given to the practitioner to deal on the client's behalf. A practitioner who accepts an instruction to act on behalf of a discretionary client will breach the duties of care and skill that he owes to his client if he fails to deal with or manage the client's investment in a way in which a reasonably competent practitioner would have done in the circumstances of the particular transaction. However, no practitioner should to be judged with the benefit of hindsight. It will therefore be necessary in each case to consider whether, on the basis of the information which was available or ought to have been available to the practitioner at the material time, the practitioner has fallen below that standard.[87] The exercise of discretion will, however, entail the financial practitioner owing fiduciary duties to his client, as recognised in *Ata v. American Express Bank Ltd*[88] in a discretionary management context. As observed in the same case "a discretion to trade is precisely that: a discretion and not an obligation" and "it was not obliged to trade had it in its discretion felt it inappropriate to do so, let alone to trade in any particular way". Nevertheless, the defendant bank's fiduciary duty entailed recognising the existence of its discretion and thus a positive obligation to consider the investor's open positions from time to time so as to decide whether or not to trade. While on the facts it was in breach of that duty, the investor failed to establish any consequent loss.

Where a client is an execution-only client, the primary duty on the financial **13–130** practitioner will be to comply with instructions given by the client.[89] The practitioner will have no duty to provide advice about the transaction which the client wishes to undertake and will not be open to criticism should the transaction prove to be disadvantageous to the client.[90] He will however be obliged to comply with instructions within a reasonable time of receipt—if he does not, he will be in breach of his duty of care and skill.[91]

---

[86] The claimant's appeal was on grounds of serious irregularities during the arbitration and errors of law on the part of the arbitrators. The findings of fact made by the arbitrators did not therefore fall to be considered by Toulson J.

[87] In *Stafford and Comstock Ltd v. Conti Commodity Services Ltd* [1981] 1 Lloyd's Rep. 466 the claimant alleged that the claimant commodities broker had negligently failed to "handle" its investments. In rejecting that claim Mocatta J. concluded at 474–475 that:

"a broker cannot always be right in the advice that he gives in relation to so wayward and rapidly changing market as the commodities futures market. An error of judgment, if there be an error of judgment, is not necessarily negligent ... Similarly, losses made on the commodity market do not of themselves, in my judgment, provide evidence of negligence on the part of a broker even if he advised both parts of the particular transaction which produced the loss ... I am satisfied that with the best advice in the world in such an unpredictable market as this it would require exceedingly strong evidence from expert brokers in relation to individual transactions to establish negligence on the part of the defendants."

[88] CA unreported, June 17, 1998, upholding Rix J. unreported, October 7, 1996.

[89] See for example *Bank fur Handel und Effekten v. Davidson* (1975) 55 D.L.R. (3d) 303.

[90] See *e.g. Laskin v. Bache & Co Ltd* (1972) 23 D.L.R. (3d) 385.

[91] See *e.g. Pankhurst v. Garner & Co.* (1960) 25 D.L.R. (2d) 515.

4. DEFENCES AND RELIEF

(a) *General*

13–131 Statutory rights of action granted under the FSMA are expressly subject to "the defences and other incidents applying to actions for breach of statutory duty." Such defences would include, in particular, contributory negligence. Common law causes of action will be subject to defences specific to each particular cause of action.

(b) *Limited immunity of regulators from liability in damages*

13–132 The FSMA[92] confers upon the FSA limited immunity from liability in damages (as did the 1986 Act),[93] including when acting as the U.K. Listing Authority.[94] Thus the FSA is not liable in damages for anything done , or omitted to be done, in the discharge or purported discharge of its functions. The same applies as regards any person who is, or acting as, a member, officer or member of the staff of the FSA. Such immunity is limited in two respects. First, the immunity is lost if the act or omission "is shown to have been in bad faith". Secondly, the immunity does not extend to awards of damages as a result of section 6(1) of the Human Rights Act 1998. Other bodies and persons are accorded like limited immunity.[95] In construing the meaning of "bad faith" it is relevant to have regard to the recent consideration of the concept by the House of Lords in the context of the tort of misfeasance in public office and the limited immunity provision in the Banking Act 1987.[96] The meaning of the term in the context of a like provision in 1986 Act[97] was considered by Lightman J. in *Melton Medes Ltd v. Securities and Investments Board*[98] in striking out an action for damages against the SIB for disclosure of information in contravention of disclosure restrictions in the 1986 Act.[99] He considered that it connoted "either (a) malice in the sense of personal spite or a desire to injure for improper reasons; or (b) knowledge of absence of power to make the decision in question."[1]

---

[92] See FSMA, s.1 and Sched. 1, para. 19.
[93] 1986 Act, s.187.
[94] FSMA, s.102.
[95] *i.e.* the complaints investigator, not any person appointed to conduct an investigation on his behalf (see FSMA, Sched.1, paras 7, 8(8) and 19(2)): the FSA as the U.K. Listing Authority (s.102), the compensation scheme manager (s.222), recognised investment exchanges (RIEs) and recognised clearing houses (RCHs) (s.291) and ombudsmen (Sched.17, para.10). As to the position under the 1986 Act, see s.187. Under that Act the limited immunity did not extend to RIEs and RCHs.
[96] See para. 13–105 above.
[97] In the 1986 Act, s.187.
[98] [1995] Ch. 137
[99] 1986 Act, s.179, a similar provision to the FSMA, s.348.
[1] *ibid.* at 147. He cited Wade, *Administrative Law* (6th ed). at 782 which in turn relied on the discussion of "malice" in *Bourgoin SA v. Ministry of Agriculture* [1986] Q.B. 716. See also *Three Rivers D.C. v. Bank of England (No. 3)* [2000] 1 W.L.R. 1220 (H.L.).

(c) *Restriction of liability by contract*

Save in the case of an authorised unit trust scheme,[2] there is no prohibition in the **13–133** FSMA itself on a financial practitioner seeking to exclude or limit its duties or its liabilities by means of a contractual term. However, every firm which communicates with a "customer"[3] while conducting "designated investment business"[4] is prohibited by the Conduct of Business Rules[5] from seeking in such communications to exclude or restrict or to rely on any exclusion or restriction of any duty or liability it may have to a customer under the FSMA or the regulatory system.[6] Moreover, every such firm is also prohibited from seeking in communications to a "private customer"[7] to exclude or to restrict or to rely on any exclusion or restriction of any other duty or liability that it may have unless it is reasonable for it to do so.[8] Guidance is not given on the factors that might make any such restriction or exclusion reasonable. It is likely that matters similar to those set out in section 11 of and Schedule 2 to the Unfair Contract Terms Act 1977 ("UCTA") will be relevant.

Generally, UCTA has limited relevance. First, sections 2 to 4 of UCTA do not **13–134** apply to any contract of insurance or any contract so far as it relates to the creation or transfer of securities or of any right or interest in securities.[9] This was one of the reasons why it was held that UCTA was not applicable to contracts governing the relationship between an IMRO regulated bank and an investor whereby the bank agreed to effect trading transactions on his behalf relating to emerging market debt.[10] Secondly, it does not apply to any contractual provision authorised or required by the express terms or necessary implication of an enactment.[11] It is submitted that it would thus not apply to contractual provisions authorised or required in the FSA's Handbook.[12] Thirdly, a contract term is to be taken for the purposes of UCTA as satisfying the requirement of reasonableness if it is incorporated or approved by, or incorporated into a contract pursuant to, a decision or ruling of a "competent authority" acting in the exercise of any statutory jurisdiction or function and is not a term of a contract to which the competent authority is itself a party.[13] It is submitted that the FSA is a "competent authority" as defined *qua* a "public authority". Consequently any term incorporated into a contract entered into by a financial practitioner with an

---

[2] FSMA, s.253 of the FSMA provides that "Any provision of the trust deed of an authorised unit trust scheme is void in so far as it would have the effect of exempting the manager or trustee from liability for any failure to exercise due care and diligence in the discharge of his functions in respect of the scheme." This section reflects Arts 9 and 16 of the UCITS Directive.

[3] See under para. 13–049 above.

[4] See para. 13–049 above.

[5] COB, chap. 2, paras 2.5.1 and 2.5.3.

[6] The "regulatory system" is defined as the arrangements for regulating a firm or other person in or under the FSMA, including the threshold conditions, the Principles and other rules, the Statements of Principle, codes and guidance.

[7] See para. 13–052, n. 27 above.

[8] COB, chap 2, paras. 2.5.1 and 2.5.4.

[9] See UCTA, s.1(2) and Sched. para.1(1)(a) and(e) of UCTA. "Securities" is not defined. In *Micklefield v. SAC Technology* [1990] 1 W.L.R. 1002 it was accepted that the word covered shares and that the disapplication provision covered an employment contract which incorporated a share option.

[10] *Australia & New Zealand Banking Group Ltd v. Louis Cattan*, unreported, August 2, 2001, Morison J.

[11] UCTA, s.29(1)(a).

[12] See paras. 13–039 *et seq.* above.

[13] UCTA, s.29(2),(3).

investor by reason of a requirement of the FSA will be deemed to be reasonable. This will include requirements contained within the Handbook.[14] In the emerging market debt case IMRO was taken to be a "competent authority". Since the bank's terms of business reflected IMRO requirements they were to be taken as reasonable.[15]

(d) *Statutory relief*

13–135 A director of a company may seek relief from liability under section 727 of the Companies Act 1985, although it would seem that such relief is available only in respect of a claim against him by or on behalf of or for the benefit of the company.[16] Relief is neither a defence nor a right, but a discretionary power given to the court in proceedings against him for negligence, default, breach of duty or breach of trust, to relieve him wholly or partly from his liability on such terms as the court thinks fit, if certain criteria are satisfied. These are, if in the opinion of the court, the director has acted honestly and reasonably and that, having regard to all the circumstances of the case, including those of his appointment, he ought fairly to be excused.[17] In the context of claims arising from a regulatory context, there is nothing in principle to prevent the grant of such relief but the circumstances in which it is granted are likely to be exceptionally rare given the regulatory responsibilities of directors.[18]

5. REMEDIES INCLUDING DAMAGES

(a) *General*

13–136 The title to this section of the chapter is different from the usual title to the equivalent section in other chapters, which is limited to damages. The explanation is that in relation to financial practitioners the range of remedies frequently sought is wider than damages. There are several reasons for this. First, in the case of other professions the contract of engagement will generally precede the services provided and be the prime basis of claim. Damages for breach of that contract and a concurrent tortious remedy will usually be the only appropriate remedy. In the case of financial practitioners, however, promotion (whether in a prospectus or other advertisement) or investment advice may often precede a

---

[14] In *Australia & New Zealand Banking Group Limited v. Cattan*, unreported, August 2, 2001, Morison J. found that UCTA was of no application in relation to the claimant's terms of business when those terms reflected IMRO's requirements.

[15] *ibid.* Note also *Ata v. American Express Bank Ltd.*, CA. unreported, June 17, 1998, upholding the decision of Rix J., unreported, October 7, 1996: it was assumed that UCTA applied in a discretionary management context but the investor's contention that terms relied upon by the bank did not satisfy the requirement of reasonableness was rejected. For facts, see paras 13–116 above and 13–159 below.

[16] *Customs and Excise Commissioners v. Hedon Alpha Ltd* [1981] 2 All E.R. 697, CA.

[17] This section reflects similar protection given to trustees; see Trustee Act 1925, s.61. In *Re Duomatic* [1969] 2 Ch. 365, the Companies Act 1948, s.448, the predecessor provision to the Companies Act 1985, s.727, was considered in relation to a director. In *Re D'Jan of London Ltd* [1994] 1 B.C.L.C. 561, Hoffman L.J. granted relief under s.727 to a director.

[18] Note in the FSA Handbook the sourcebook, "Senior Management Arrangements, Systems and Controls". As to the Handbook, see paras 13–039 *et seq.* above.

contract (*e.g.* to purchase an investment). The relevant complaint may then be misrepresentation and the remedies sought would be the rescission of that contract and restitution or damages in lieu. Secondly, the impact of regulatory regimes entails that there are statutory causes of action in addition to those at common law. Thirdly, regulatory regimes enable regulators to bring proceedings by way of class recovery for the benefit of investors and to seek a wider range of remedies than those available to private litigants.

(b) *Remedies available to regulators*

The FSMA confers a number of important enforcement powers, more extensive **13-137** than those which existed under the 1986 Act,[19] which enable regulators to act on behalf of investors and obtain various remedies in the events of actual or potential breaches of the regulatory regime. The FSA or the Secretary of State may apply to the court for injunctions, "remedial orders" and "restitution orders" against persons contravening the regulatory regime as well as persons "knowingly concerned in the contravention".[20] The FSA may also so apply against persons engaging in market abuse.[21] Moreover the FSA is empowered to act extra-judicially and obtain "restitution" from authorised persons (only) contravening the regulatory regime[22] and any persons engaging in market abuse.[23]

(i) *Grounds for application to court*

The FSA (only) may apply to the court for relevant orders in relation to a breach **13-138** of two types of "relevant requirements".[24] The first is a "requirement . . . imposed by or under this Act". In essence, this covers any breach of the regulatory regime, including breaches which are criminal offences.[25] The second is a "'requirement . . . imposed by or under any *other* Act" (emphasis added) where the FSA has power under the FSMA to prosecute for its breach.[26] Secondly the Secretary of State may apply in relation to "a requirement . . . imposed by or under this Act" leading to a criminal offence where he has power to prosecute under the FSMA.[27]

---

[19] 1986 Act, ss. 6 and 61. In relation to s.6, see *Securities and Investments Board v. Pantell SA* [1990] Ch. 426 (*Mareva* injunction available) (noted Lomnicka [1989] J.B.L. 509); *Securities and Investments Board v. Pantell SA (No. 2)* [1993] Ch. 256 (noted Lomnicka [1993] J.B.L. 54); *Securities and Investments Board v. Lloyd-Wright* [1993] 4 All E.R. 134 (no undertaking in damages for interlocutory relief); *Securities and Investments Board v. Scandex Capital Management A/S* unreported but noted (1997) Co. Lawyer 217 and affirmed on appeal [1998] 1 W.L.R. 712. Similar powers were conferred on the Bank of England to apply to the court in respect of contraventions of the Banking Act 1987 in ss. 48, 49 and 93 of that Act.
[20] FSMA, ss. 380, 382.
[21] *ibid.*, ss. 381, 383.
[22] *ibid.*, ss. 384(1) and 386.
[23] *ibid.*, ss. 384(2) and 386.
[24] *ibid.*, ss. 380(6)(a), 382(9). As to the meaning of "requirement" in the FSMA, see Lomnicka [2001] J.B.L. 96.
[25] See *ibid.*, s.401(2)(a), for the FSA's prosecuting power, extending to any offence under the FSMA or subordinate legislation thereunder: s.401(1).
[26] *ibid.*, s.402(1) confers on the FSA the power to prosecute for offences of insider dealing under Part V of the Criminal Justice Act 1993 and under prescribed money laundering regulations: see the Money Laundering Regulations 1993, S.I. 1993 No. 1933.
[27] See *ibid.*, s.401(1), (2)(a): same prosecuting power as the FSA.

13–139 **Requirements imposed by or under the FSMA.** Such requirements will include requirements implied in the general prohibition[28] as well as the financial promotion restriction,[29] *i.e.* requirements not to contravene such prohibition and restriction. In relation to authorised persons, such requirements will include those pertaining to acting within the scope of their permission,[30] employment of certain persons[31] and compliance with FSA rules.[32]

13–140 **Requirements imposed by or under any other Act.** Such requirements where the FSA has power under the FSMA to prosecute for breach,[33] pertain to insider dealing[34] and money-laundering.[35]

(ii) *Persons against whom orders available*

13–141 **Contravenors.** Relevant orders may be obtained against any person contravening (or, in the case of an injunction, likely to contravene) a "relevant requirement".[36] Thus the orders are available against authorised persons, exempt persons and any other persons—as long as they are subject to and have beached a "relevant requirement". Most of such requirements are imposed on authorised persons.

13–142 **Persons knowingly concerned.** Relevant orders may also be obtained against "any other person who appears to have been knowingly concerned" in the contravention.[37] The phrase "knowingly concerned" has been transplanted from the 1986 Act,[38] but its precise meaning is unclear.[39] It has two components, one pertaining to the state of mind of the person and one pertaining to their involvement. The case law (under the 1986 Act) is sparse. A person knowingly receiving the proceeds of another's wrongdoing was assumed to be "knowingly concerned" in the wrongdoing in the first of two decisions in the same case.[40] In the second decision[41] it was accepted that solicitors acting for the wrongdoer could also be knowingly concerned and "a person who was the moving light behind a company" was given as another example. In another case it was stated that a director could be someone "knowingly concerned" in the company's breach[42] and that a person could be so concerned "if he merely knew the facts giving rise to the breach, even if he erroneously thought a breach of the law was not

---

[28] See para. 13–013 above.
[29] See para. 13–015 above.
[30] See paras 13–018 and 13–074 above.
[31] See paras 13–019 and 13–075 above.
[32] See the requirements in the FSA Handbook (paras 13–039 *et seq.* above).
[33] FSMA, s.402.
[34] Under Criminal Justice Act 1993, Part V (insider dealing).
[35] Under "prescribed" (see FSMA, s.417(1)) regulations, *i.e.* the Money Laundering Regulations 1993, S.I. 1993 No. 1933, reg. 5.
[36] FSMA, ss. 380(1), (2), (3), 382(1).
[37] *ibid.*, ss. 380(2), (3), 382(1).
[38] 1986 Act ss. 6(2), 61(1).
[39] See Lomnicka, "Knowingly concerned?' Participatory liability to regulators" (2000) 21 Co. Lawyer 120.
[40] *Securities and Investments Board v. Pantell SA* [1990] Ch. 426 (noted Lomnicka [1989] J.B.L. 509).
[41] *Securities and Investments Board v. Pantell SA (No.2)* [1993] Ch. 256 (noted Lomnicka [1993] J.B.L. 54).
[42] *Securities and Investments Board v. Scandex Capital Management A/S* unreported but noted (1997) 18 Co. Lawyer 217, *per* Carnworth J.

occurring".[43] In relation to market abuse, a relevant order may be made against the person concerned, *i.e.* in actual or potential market abuse.[44]

(iii) *Orders available*

These comprise a restraining injunction, a "remedial" order, an asset-freezing order and a restitution order.   **13–143**

Injunction. The court may grant an injunction (or in Scotland, an interdict) restraining contravention of a "relevant requirement".[45] It may do so if satisfied that there is a reasonable likelihood of a contravention or of continuance or repetition of a previous contravention.[46] It may also grant an injunction in relation to market abuse if similarly satisfied.[47]   **13–144**

Remedial order. The court may grant such an order requiring the taking of such steps as it may direct to remedy contravention of a "relevant requirement". The court may make an order if it is satisfied that there has been a contravention and there are steps which could remedy it.[48] It may also grant a remedial order in relation to market abuse if similarly satisfied.[49] The order need not actually require a complete remedy for the contravention but may merely require that the effect of the breach be mitigated.[50] In a case[51] concerning similarly worded provisions of the 1986 Act,[52] the relief available was described as in the nature of "statutory recission of unlawful transactions" in that it enabled the court to unravel transactions.[53] A contrast was drawn[54] with the position under separate restitutionary provisions enabling "disgorgement" and compensation orders to be made.[55] An analogy was drawn with common law rescission. Thus the counterparty to the transaction with the wrongdoer had to be willing to return anything received under the transaction,[56] although on appeal there was disagreement as to what was required of the counterparty in order to achieve this.[57] Moreover, the order had to be directed at specific, identifiable transactions.[58] So-called "class recovery" was only possible under the separate restitution   **13–145**

---

[43] *Securities and Investments Board v. Scandex Capital Management A/S* [1998] 1 W.L.R. 712 CA, following *Burton v. Burton* [1980] Ch. 240 at 246–247.

[44] FSMA, ss. 381, 383.

[45] See further para. 13–146 below.

[46] FSMA, s.380(1), (6).

[47] *ibid.*, s.381(1).

[48] *ibid.*, s.380(2).

[49] *ibid.*, s.381(2).

[50] *ibid.*, s.380(5). The Explanatory Notes to FSMA at para. 665 give the example of an order requiring a correction to be published of a previous misleading advertisement. In relation to market abuse, see s.381(6).

[51] *Securities and Investments Board v. Pantell SA (No. 2)* [1993] Ch. 256 (reporting both Sir Nicolas Browne-Wilkinson V.-C.'s judgment at first instance and the judgments on appeal to the Court of Appeal—Neill, Scott and Steyn L.JJ.).

[52] 1986 Act, s.6(2): order for "restoring the parties to the position in which they were before the transaction [in contravention of s.3] was entered into"; s.61(1): order requiring the taking of steps "to remedy" the relevant contravention.

[53] *ibid.* at 264, 282, 277.

[54] *ibid.* at 265.

[55] 1986 Act, ss. 6(3)(4) and 61(3)(4). Equivalent FSMA provisions are ss. 382 and 383.

[56] *ibid.* at 277, Scott L.J.

[57] *ibid.* at 277–278, Scott L.J. and 283, Steyn L.J.

[58] *ibid.* at 278, 280, Scott L.J.; also at 265.

provisions. The Court of Appeal took a narrow view of the restorative or remedial requirement in the case of contraventions (concerning misrepresentations and misleading advertisements) which did not involve the actual entry into transactions but merely steps preliminary to transactions. It doubted whether it could order the unravelling of the consequent transactions in that the contravention was not the actual making of the transactions but the preliminary steps and therefore the unravelling of the transaction would not remedy the contraventions.[59] Interim payment orders were held to be available under like provisions in the 1986 Act.[60]

13–146   **Asset freezing orders.** In relation to a contravention of a relevant requirement, the court may grant an asset-freezing order (similar to an old style *Mareva* injunction), restraining the disposal or dealing with assets in danger of dissipation.[61] It is enough if there "may have" been a contravention or knowing involvement in one. This contrasts with the *Mareva* jurisdiction, which requires proceedings to have been commenced or be imminent. As regards a person "knowingly concerned", just as the possibility of a breach by the main protagonist is enough, so it would seem that possible involvement in a possible breach is enough. Should proceedings be contemplated or have been commenced, ordinary *Mareva* injunctions may be applied for instead of orders under the FSMA.[62] It would seem that the latter, like *Mareva* injunctions, operate *in personam* against any assets of the defendant and give no security interest in respect of the assets frozen.[63] This is in contrast to an injunction based on a proprietary (*e.g.* tracing claim).[64] Thus it would be advantageous for a person with a separate proprietary claim at common law, not to rely on the FSA acting under the FSMA, but to apply for an injunction freezing specific assets in the hands of the defendant to which he can assert a proprietary claim. In this way he can claim priority over unsecured creditors of the defendant (including the FSA).

13–147   **Restitution orders.** This is the marginal note description of orders which the court may make for contravention of a relevant requirement and also in case of market abuse provided also the court is satisfied that either profits have accrued to the defendant and/or loss or other adverse effect has been caused by the

---

[59] *ibid.* at 279, 286. *Sed quaere.* See Lomnicka [1993] J.B.L. 53 where it is submitted that this was too cautious an interpretation in that the preliminary steps were undertaken in order to induce the transactions and it is difficult to see how the contraventions could be remedied other than by unravelling the transactions they induced. In any event, at common law, misrepresentations may render consequent transactions voidable. FSMA s.380(2) (especially in the light of the new s.380(5)) should be given a broader interpretation.

[60] *Securities and Investments Board v. Scandex Capital Management A/S* unreported but noted (1997) Co. Lawyer 217 and affirmed on appeal [1998] 1 W.L.R. 712 and *FSA v. Lukka*, unreported, April 23, 1999, Ch. D.

[61] FSMA, s.380(3).

[62] See *SIB v. Pantell SA* [1990] Ch. 426: grant of *Mareva* injunction in support of 1986 Act, ss.6 and 61 claims. Noted Lomnicka [1989] J.B.L. 509.

[63] *Cretanor Maritime Co Ltd v. Irish Maritime Management Ltd ("The Cretan Harmony")* [1978] 1 W.L.R. 966 (a *Mareva* case).

[64] For case law on this distinction in the case of *Mareva* injunctions, see *A v. C* [1981] 2 W.L.R. 197 Goff J.; *A.J. Beckhor & Co v. Bilton* [1981] Q.B. 923, Ackner L.J.; *PCW v. Dixon* [1989] 2 Lloyd's Rep. 197, Lloyd J.

contravention or abuse.[65] Thus regulators may obtain financial redress– disgorgement of profits or compensation for loss—on behalf of investors who may not have the resources, inclination or stamina to pursue the wrongdoers. In effect it enables "class recovery" or collective enforcement of their rights.[66] In form it is an order that the persons concerned (whether the main contravenor or a person "knowingly concerned") initially make a payment to the FSA and that the FSA then distribute that award as directed by the court. Thus even if the Secretary of State brings an application as he may in relation to a contravention of certain relevant requirements, it is the FSA that is the initial recipient of the award with the obligation to distribute it. The amount of the award is at the discretion of the court, but the court must have regard to the profits appearing to have accrued and/ or the extent of the loss caused. Thus it would appear that the amount awarded must bear some relation to the profits and/or loss and that the court may not award "punitive" or "exemplary" sums which are, for example, a multiple of the profits made. As an award may not be made against a person in respect of profits accruing unless they have accrued to him, it would seem that in calculating its amount, regard should be had to the same profits. If private proceedings have been or are being taken against the wrongdoer, then no doubt, the court in the exercise of its discretion under this provision, would take any amounts recoverable in those proceedings into account. The order would also direct the FSA as to how the award is to be distributed amongst qualifying persons. These are persons appearing to the court to be person to whom the profits are attributable or who have suffered the loss, as the case may be.

(iv) *The FSA's extra-judicial power to require restitution*

The FSMA confers on the FSA a new power which did not exist under the 1986   **13–148**
Act. It is a power, exercisable extra-judicially, to require authorised persons to make restitution if they make profits or cause loss as a result of breaching the regulatory regime.[67] A like power exists in relation to anyone committing market abuse.[68]

(v) *The FSA Enforcement manual*

The FSA's policy in relation to the exercise of its various enforcement powers is   **13–149**
contained in this manual which forms part of the FSA Handbook.[69]

(c) *Remedies available to private litigants*

There are a range of remedies available to private litigants (persons other than   **13–150**
regulators) in respect of claims arising from a financial context.

---

[65] See FSMA, s.382 as regards contravention of a relevant requirement. Equivalent provisions under the 1986 Act, ss. 6(3)(4) and 61(3)(4), only enabled a restitution order to be made against the main contravenor and not also (as under the FSMA) a person knowingly concerned. See *Securities and Investments Board v. Pantell SA (No. 2)* [1993] Ch. 256 at 285 (no jurisdiction under s.6(3)(4) to make orders against third parties). See FSMA, s.383 as regards market abuse.

[66] As so described in relation to like provisions in the 1986 Act (ss.6(3)(4) and 61(3)(4)) in *Securities and Investments Board v. Pantell SA (No. 2)* [1993] Ch. 256 at 263, 278.

[67] FSMA, s.384.

[68] *ibid.* As to market abuse, see FSMA, ss. 417(1), 118.

[69] See paras 13–039 to 13–043 above.

(i) *Rescission of contract induced by misrepresentation*

13–151   It will be open to a claimant to seek an order for rescission of a contract which he was induced to enter into by a misrepresentation (*e.g.* in an investment advertisement). Usual common law principles for the grant of rescission will apply. The court has power under section 2(2) of the Misrepresentation Act 1967 to award damages in lieu of rescission.

(ii) *Recovery of money or property paid under agreements made by or through unauthorised persons*

13–152   **Contravention of the general prohibition (non-banking).** What may be seen as direct contravention and attributed contravention of the general prohibition[70] may render relevant agreements potentially unenforceable and voidable.[71] Thus an agreement made by a person conducting a regulated activity (other than banking)[72] in breach of the general prohibition (direct contravention) is rendered unenforceable against the other party (the customer) and voidable at the latter's instance.[73] Also rendered unenforceable against the customer and voidable at his instance is an agreement made in the course of a regulated activity (other than banking)[74] by an authorised person not in breach of the general prohibition but in consequence of activity by a third party in breach of the general prohibition (attributed contravention).[75] An example would be an agreement with an authorised person made by a customer on the basis of investment advice by an unauthorised financial adviser. An agreement is rendered unenforceable only if made after the relevant FSMA provision came into force and if its making or performance constituted or was part of the regulated activity.[76] Thus, agreements which are incidental to the regulated activity are not caught. The unenforceability is one-sided and there is nothing to stop the customer from holding the party in breach to the agreement. Moreover, the agreement is not illegal or void to any greater extent.[77]

13–153   **Court's discretion.** The court is given a discretion to uphold the agreement. The discretion arises if the court is satisfied that it is just and equitable to enforce the agreement or to allow retention of the money or property transferred.[78] In making that assessment the court is obliged to have regard to a certain factor (called "the issue") depending on whether the case is one of direct contravention or attributed contravention.[79] In the case of a direct contravention the issue is whether the person in breach of the general prohibition reasonably believed that

---

[70] See para. 13–013 above.
[71] FSMA, ss. 26, 27. As apparent from subs. (3) of each section, it is not retroactive, but note the equivalent provisions in the 1986 Act: ss. 5 (relating to investment business) and 132 (relating to insurance contracts). In relation to EEA firms, see FSMA Sched. 3, paras 16(2) and 17(2): ss. 26 and 27 do not apply in relation to agreements entered into by such firms which have not satisfied the conditions for authorisation under those Schedules.
[72] FSMA, s.26(4). As to banking, see para. 13–155 below.
[73] *ibid.*, ss. 26(1).
[74] *ibid.*, s.27(4). As to banking, see para. 13–155 below.
[75] *ibid.*, ss. 27(1). 1986 Act equivalent: s.5(1)(b). Whereas the latter applied to an agreement by an authorised person or exempt person, FSMA s.27(1) only applies to the latter.
[76] *ibid.*, ss. 26(3), 27(3).
[77] *ibid.*, s.28(9). FSA 1986 s.5(6). See *Lloyd v. Popely* [2001] 1 C.L. 77.
[78] *ibid.*, s.28(3). The onus being on the person seeking to uphold the agreement with the customer.
[79] *ibid.*, s.28(4).

he was not contravening the general prohibition.[80] The test is part subjective and part objective: the person must have both subjectively believed and reasonably believed that he was not in breach. Thus if he was negligent in not seeking authorisation, his agreements cannot be saved by the court. An honest but unreasonable belief is not enough, so ignorance of the provisions of the Act would not constitute reasonable belief. In contrast in the case of an attributed contravention the issue is whether the authorised person knew that the third party was in breach of the general prohibition.[81] The test here is clearly subjective. It is enough to show that the authorised person did not know that the third party was in breach of the general prohibition.

Recovery. In the event that the agreement remains unenforceable the customer is entitled to recover both the money (and any other property) he transferred and also "compensation for any loss" suffered as a result of the breach.[82] Although the statute states that the amount of compensation is that agreed between the parties, or in default of agreement, that determined by the court,[83] no guidance is given as to the calculation of the amount of the compensation. Nevertheless, on electing not to perform the agreement, the other party must also return what he obtained under the agreement by way of any money or property or, if transferred to a third party, its value at the time of transfer.[84] Contravention of the general prohibition does not make an agreement illegal or invalid to any greater extent than provided under the relevant FSMA provisions.[85] **13–154**

Contravention of the general prohibition (banking). Separate and narrower provision is made for contravention of the general prohibition in relation to deposit-taking. Thus a depositor who has parted with deposits to a deposit-taker acting in breach of the general prohibition may apply to the court for an order for the return of his money if he is not otherwise entitled (as under a current account) to recover his money immediately on demand. The court is given a discretion whether or not to make the order.[86] **13–155**

Contravention of the financial promotion restriction. The FSMA provides for similar civil consequences in relation to contravention of the restriction[87] as in relation to a contravention of the general prohibition.[88] Thus it renders unenforceable against the customer and voidable at his instance, certain agreements made and certain obligations undertaken in consequence of a communication in relation to which there has been a contravention of the financial promotion restriction. Also the customer is entitled to recover both any money or other property transferred and also compensation for any loss suffered as a result of the **13–156**

---

[80] *ibid.*, s.28(4),(5).
[81] *ibid.*, s.28(4),(6).
[82] *ibid.*, s.26(2) and s.27(2).
[83] *ibid.*, s.28(2).
[84] *ibid.*, s.28(7), (8).
[85] *ibid.*, s.28(9). Similarly under the 1986 Act, ss. 5(6) and 132(6).
[86] *ibid.*, s.29. See Sched. 3, para. 16(4): Disapplication in relation to EEA firms.
[87] *ibid.*, s.21. See para. 13–015 above.
[88] *ibid.*, s.30. Similarly under the 1986 Act, ss. 56 (unsolicited calls) and 57 (investment advertisements).

transfer.[89] Nevertheless, the court is given a discretion to enforce the agreement or obligation in certain circumstances.[90]

(iii) *Damages or compensation*

13–157   Damages may be claimed on one or more of several bases: statutory liability for damages under the FSMA[91] (or the 1986 Act[92]) breach of contract, tort or damages in lieu of rescission under the Misrepresentation Act 1967. Compensation also may be claimed for defects in listing particulars[93] and a prospectus relating to unlisted securities.[94] Where damages or compensation are claimed, usual general principles for quantification apply.

13–158   **Remoteness.** Although a breach of duty may be established, no loss and damage will be recoverable if too remote. The claimant must establish that, broadly, the loss and damage (a) were caused by the relevant breach of duty and (b) were foreseeable. Moreover, whether or not the starting point for damages assessment is ascertaining the scope of the duty undertaken or imposed,[95] that issue is an important factor in addressing remoteness.

13–159   **Causation illustrations.** That the burden is upon the claimant to prove that the defendant's's default caused loss is apparent from two cases. In *Australia & New Zealand Banking Group Ltd v. Cattan*[96] the clamant was held to have committed "at best technical" breaches of IMRO requirements as to completion of certain formalities before the defendant could be classified as a non-private customer and as such allowed to make certain trades. Nevertheless it was held that such breaches had not caused any loss. Even if he had not been able to enter the relevant trades before the required formalities had been completed, upon their completion he would still have entered the same trades. There was no evidence to indicate that then there would have been any difference in price in the defendant's favour. The effect of there being no loss was fatal to the statutory right of action relied upon, loss being an ingredient of that right of action. Similarly, in *Ata v. American Express Bank Ltd*[97] the plaintiff failed to establish that the defendant bank's breach of fiduciary duty caused him any loss. The judge found as a matter of fact that even if the bank had traded the plaintiff's open positions, that further losses were as likely as any profits. The Court of Appeal rejected the contention that in assessing what the claimant's financial position would have been but for the defendant's default, every presumption should be made against the defendant. It overruled a previous first instance decision to the effect that in assessing damages against a stockbroker who had prematurely sold an investor's shares in breach of contract, the measure of damages was the

---

[89] *ibid.*, s.30(2), (3).
[90] *ibid.*, s.30(4) (8).
[91] *ibid.*, ss. 20 (see para. 13–074 above); s.71 (see para. 13–075 above), s.85 (see para. 13–082 above) and s.150 (see paras 13–076 to 13–078 above).
[92] 1986 Act, ss. 62, 62A (see para. 13–079 above).
[93] FSMA, s.90. Equivalent to 1986 Act, s.150. See para. 13–081 above.
[94] Public Offers of Securities Regulations 1995, reg. 14. See para. 13–084 above.
[95] See *South Australia Asset Mgmt Corp. v. York Montague* [1997] A.C. 191.
[96] Unreported August 2, 2001, Morison J . See other aspects of the case, see paras 13–120 and 13–127 above.
[97] CA, unreported, June 17, 1998 upholding Rix J., unreported, October 7, 1996. As to other aspects of the case, see paras 13–116, 13–134 above and 13–160 below.

highest price at which the shares could have been later sold by the investor.[98] The "chain of causation" from the defendant's relevant failure may be broken by the act or omission of the claimant or some third person. This happened in *Gorham v. British Telecommunications Plc* (summarised above)[99] where the deceased's failure to act on helpline advice indicative of the superiority of the BT occupational scheme precluded his dependants recovering a element of loss consisting of lump sum death benefit.

Evaluation of chance. In other contexts[1] damages are sometimes calculated **13–160** by reference to the value of the chance of which the defendant's default deprived the claimant. However, for this approach to be adopted the claimant must first prove as matter of causation that he has a real or substantial chance as opposed to a speculative one.[2] This would appear to present claimants with an insuperable obstacle to recovery of damages on a lost chance basis in an investment context. It was so held in a commodity trading context in *Bailey v. Balholm Securities*.[3] Kerr J. distinguished cases in which damages had been assessed on a lost chance basis:

> "But those were all cases in which the plaintiff might or might not have obtained some pecuniary advantage or benefit and lost the chance of doing so as the result of the defendant's wrongful act. He therefore lost the chance of being better off than he was, but he was not exposed to the risk of being worse off. In cases like the present, on the other hand, a person who is prevented from speculating in cocoa or sugar futures may have lost the chance of making money or may have been saved from losing money. A cynical view would be that there is an equal chance either way. No doubt experience and skill play a large part, and to this extent there may be said to be a better chance of winning rather than losing. But in my view this is not the kind of situation which the law should recognize as giving a right to damage for the loss of a chance. Even though in law trading in commodity futures does not amount to gambling, the loss of the general opportunity to trade—as opposed to the loss of the particular bargain—is in my view much too speculative to be capable of having any monetary value placed upon it. A wrongful refusal to trade with a person in futures would therefore in my judgment normally only give rise to the recovery if nominal damages."[4]

This reasoning was followed in rejecting a claim for damages based on lost chance in a investment management context in *Ata v. American Express Bank Ltd*.[5]

Measure of damages. The fundamental principle governing the measure of **13–161** damages is that the claimant must be put so far as money can do it in the position he would have occupied if the financial practitioner had properly discharged his duty.[6] Broadly speaking, this can be achieved in one of two ways, depending upon the particular facts of the case (i) by paying to the claimant the monetary

---

[98] *Michael v. Hart* [1901] 2 K.B. 161, Wills J.
[99] [2001] P.N.L.R. 21. For facts see paras 13–109 to 13–111 above.
[1] See *e.g.* chap. 10, para. 10–256 to 10–262.
[2] See *Allied Maple Group v. Simmons & Simmons* [1995] 1 W.L.R. 1602 at 1614.
[3] [1973] 2 Lloyd's Rep. 404, Kerr J.
[4] *ibid.* at 415–6.
[5] CA unreported, June 17, 1998, upholding Rix J., unreported, October 7, 1996. For further aspects of the case, see paras 13–116, 13–134 and 13–159 above.
[6] See *Livingstone v. Rawyards Coal Co.* (1880) 5 App.Cas. 25, 39 and *Dodd Properties (Kent) Ltd v. Canterbury City Council* [1980] 1 W.L.R. 433, 451, 454 and 456 (as to general principles).

equivalent of any benefits of which he has been deprived, or (ii) by indemnifying the claimant against any expenses or liabilities which he has incurred.

13–162   **Benefits received.** Some difficult issues have arisen in the context of the mass of claims arising from misselling of home income plans, pension policies and endowment policies as to as to treatment of certain benefits received in assessing compensation or damages.[7] In *R. v. Investors Compensation Scheme Ltd, ex parte Bowden* the issue was whether in compensating investors for inadequate advice by financial advisers in consequence of which they had taken out home income plans (whereby they raised money on mortgage in order to provide an income), ICS was entitled not to provide compensation for sums received and expended. The context of the proceedings was a judicial review application. Hence the critical question was not whether such sums were compensatable in damages as a matter of common law. Rather the question was whether it was open to ICS as a reasonable public authority to exclude such sums from compensation pursuant to the compensation scheme which it administered. The House of Lords[8] answered that question affirmatively in favour of ICS and declined to resolve the question whether such sums would have been recoverable in a damages claim as a matter of common law. In so doing the House of Lords overruled the Court of Appeal[9] which had ruled against ICS. The Court of Appeal did address the common law position, concluding as follows:

> "Whether dissipated benefit is a recoverable loss must depend on the circumstances. But here the very purpose of the transaction advised by the financial advisers was the achievement of an increase in income. To establish that it is unnecessary to look further than the newspaper advertisement placed by the advisers to which the investor responded. That being so expenditure of money, once it had been paid to the investors, was plainly foreseeable and if that expenditure was on ephemera so that no lasting benefit accrued there was a loss in terms of increased mortgage debt which sounds in undiminished damages against the financial advisers."[10]

13–163   The problem arises again in the context of the misselling of endowment policies. Many house owners who were induced to invest in an endowment policy intended to produce a capital sum sufficient to repay a related mortgage debt, are faced with a funding shortfall and are bringing claims against financial advisers for negligently advising the endowment as opposed to the route of a repayment mortgage. In assessing damages by reference to the capital difference between the value of the endowment policy and the amount which would have been repaid under a repayment route, should credit be given for any lesser outgoings under the endowment route relative to the repayment route, even though such outgoings may have been dissipated on everyday expenditure? The solution apposite to a person on low income who "stretched" to buy and relied on the financial adviser in order to make an informed decision not only as to mortgage type but also as to consequent budgeting, may not be apposite to a person with substantial free assets or high income. Considerations of fair alloca-

---

[7] See *McGregor on Damages* (16th ed.), esp. paras 336 to 356.
[8] [1996] A.C. 261. See further para. 13–200 below.
[9] [1995] Q.B. 107.
[10] *ibid.* at 120G–H.

tion of risk may merit a credit in case of the latter, not least since he can finance a shortfall from future income.[11]

The formulation of a distinguishing principle poses difficulty. Might it be that **13–164** credit or some credit should be given unless the claimant can establish on a balance of probabilities that it is unreasonable to require him to give such credit in his or particular circumstances, having regard to his existing and foreseeable other commitments? Might the credit be rationalised in terms of mitigation? Mitigation rules will not require the impecunious to provide the credit. It may be argued that mitigation does not extend to the expenditure of money. But is not the position different where the expenditure in the form of higher future outgoings reflects the benefit of lower outgoings in the past as a consequence of the claimed default?

In *Needler Financial Services v. Taber*[12] the issue was whether in assessing **13–165** compensation for negligent pension misselling based on the difference between the greater benefits under an occupational pension scheme and a personal pension plan, a credit should be given for benefits received by the investor upon demutualisation of the plan provider. It was held that no credit should be given. Following a review of relevant authorities, the critical question was formulated as "whether the negligence which caused the loss also caused the profit in the sense that the latter was part of a continuous transaction of which the former was the inception." This was a question of fact and was answered in the negative.[13]

Account of profits. This is a well established remedy for breach of fiduciary **13–166** duty as well as for breach of confidence.[14]

6. SHARED RESPONSIBILITY

(a) *Contributory negligence*

In principle, this defence is available to financial practitioners in respect of **13–167** claims made against them to the same extent as it is available to other defendants.[15] In particular, it is available in respect of a claim based on the statutory liability under the FSMA for contravention of regulatory rules,[16] as indeed recognised in relation to like statutory liability under the 1986 Act.[17] Nevertheless, the circumstances in which the defence is successfully invoked in

---

[11] See further Powell [2001] P.N. 206.
[12] Unreported, July 31, 2001.
[13] *Sed quaere.* The decision seems out of accord with the sentiment expressed by Lord Hoffman in *Dimond v. Lovell* [2000] 2 W.L.R. 1121 at 1133A-C. The effect of the compensation payable in such circumstances not being reduced by a credit for demutualisation benefits is to burden the whole community with a cost referable to higher pension contributions.
[14] See *Peter Pan Manufacturing Corp. v. Corsets Silhouette Ltd* [1964] 1 W.L.R. 96; *Att.-Gen. v. Guardian Newspapers Ltd (No. 2)* [1990] 1 A.C. 109. As recognised in a financial services context in *Brandeis (Brokers) Ltd v. Herbert Black*, unreported, May 25, 2001, Toulson J.
[15] But the defence is not available to a claim based on the tort of deceit (see para 13–100 above) and may be limited in respect of a claim based on the Misrepresentation Act 1967, s.2(1) (see para. 13–085 above).
[16] FSMA, s.150. See paras 13–076 to 13–078 above.
[17] 1986 Act, ss. 62, 62A. See *Morgan Stanley UK Group v. Puglisi Cosentino* [1998] C.L.C. 481; *Gorham v. British Telecommunications plc* [2001] P.N.L.R. 21.

relation to claims by claimants in a retail investment context are likely to be relatively rare.

(b) *Contribution*

13–168   Contribution is not a defence but a right conferred by statute[18] upon a defendant, D1, to recover a proportion of the damages for which he is liable to C, from other persons, D2, D3 etc., each of whom is also liable to C in respect of the same damage, based on that other person's share in the responsibility for the damage. While each of D1, D2 and D3 is liable to C, as between themselves the damages are shared as appropriate, *e.g.* a third each. Financial practitioners who advised a claimant successively may make contribution claims as between themselves, as they may where they advised a claimant contemporaneously, whether on the same or different aspects of the transaction complained of.

7. The Process of Resolving Claims

13–169   As in other contexts, many cases are not susceptible to resolution other than by litigation but there are other processes for the resolution of disputes. These include arbitration as well as conciliation and mediation procedures. Specific to the financial services context is a (now) unified Ombudsman scheme.[19] Moreover, in relation to pension misselling, regulators utilised their disciplinary powers to compel authorised firms to carry out a review of relevant previous business. Judicial review applications directed to resist such exceptional use of disciplinary powers were unsuccessful.[20] There is also a compensation scheme.[21]

(a) *Ombudsman*

(i) *Introduction*

13–170   Part XVI[22] and Schedule 17 to the FSMA provide for the establishment of a scheme under which "certain disputes may be resolved quickly and with minimum formality by an independent person".[23] Although called "the ombudsman scheme" in the Act itself, the scheme that was actually established is named the Financial Ombudsman Service ("the FOS").[24] The FOS is operationally independent of the FSA. It is administered by a body corporate as the scheme operator, which must appoint and maintain a panel of suitably qualified persons to act as ombudsmen. One is appointed to act as Chief Ombudsman. However, the FSA retains a number of responsibilities in relation to the FOS. These include appointing the board of the scheme operator, determining the scope of the

---

[18] The Civil Liability (Contribution) Act 1978. See further Chap. 4, paras 4–002 *et seq.*
[19] See paras 13–170 to 13–189 below.
[20] *R. v. Securities and Investments Board, ex p. Independent Financial Advisers Association* [1995] 2 B.C.L.C. 76; *R. v. Securities and Investments Board, ex p. Sun Life Assurance Society plc* [1996] 2 B.C.L.C. 150.
[21] See paras 13–190 to 13–204 below.
[22] FSMA, ss.225–234.
[23] *ibid.*, s.225(1).
[24] Its website is *www.financial-ombudsman.org.uk*

"compulsory jurisdiction",[25] approving the scope of the "voluntary jurisdiction",[26] and setting limits on the awards that can be made under the compulsory jurisdiction.[27]

The FOS replaces eight dispute resolution schemes that previously operated   **13–171**
across the financial services sector.[28] These predecessor schemes were variously organised on a voluntary basis and as a result of statutory and regulatory requirements. Although a single scheme, the FOS creates two separate and non-overlapping jurisdictions: the compulsory jurisdiction and the voluntary jurisdiction. While the broad structure of those schemes is contained in the FSMA itself, details of the operation and procedures of the schemes are to be set out in rules made by the FSA in respect of the compulsory jurisdiction,[29] and by the FOS and approved by the FSA in respect of the voluntary jurisdiction.[30] At the time of writing the FSA and FOS has produced a joint policy statement containing what are described as "Final Rules".[31] It is expected that those "Final Rules" will in due course be confirmed as Compulsory and Voluntary Jurisdiction rules made under Part XVI of the FSMA[32] and for the purposes of this chapter it has been assumed that the rules will reflect the format and wording of the "Final Rules".

(ii) *Compulsory and voluntary jurisdiction*

The compulsory jurisdiction. This is imposed upon all authorised firms[33] and   **13–172**
extends to cover[34] all regulated activities,[35] lending money secured by a charge on land, lending money (other than restricted credit), paying money by a plastic card (other than a store card), and the provision of ancillary banking services.

---

[25] FSMA, s.226. See para. 13–172 below.

[26] *ibid.*, s.227. See para. 13–173 below.

[27] See paras. 13–186 to 13–188 below.

[28] *i.e.* the Office of the Banking Ombudsman ("OBO"), the Office of the Building Societies Ombudsman ("OBSO"), the Office of the Investment Ombudsman ("OIO"—for firms regulated by IMRO), the Insurance Ombudsman ("IOB"), the Personal Insurance Arbitration Service ("PIAS"), the PIA Ombudsman Bureau ("PIAOB"), the SFA Complaints Bureau and Arbitration Service ("SFA CB") and the (voluntary) FSA Direct Regulation Unit and Independent Investigator.

[29] FSMA, s.226(3)(a). Sched. 17 para. 14 provides that the scheme operator is to make rules ("scheme rules") setting out the procedure for reference of complaints and for their investigation, consideration and determination by an ombudsman.

[30] *ibid.*, ss. 227(3)(a) and 227(6). Sched. 17 para. 18 refers to these voluntary jurisdiction rules as "standard terms" for the determination of complaints.

[31] The "Final Rules" are to be found as Annex A to the FSA's and FOS's paper "Complaints handling arrangements: Response on CP49—A joint policy statement" dated December 2000. Minor amendments to those Final Rules were published by the FSA and FOS on 15, June 2001. Both documents are available on the websites of the FSA (www.fsa.gov.uk) and the FOS (www.financial-ombudsman.org.uk). The Rules are divided into four chapters: (1) Complaint Handling Procedures for Firms (DISP 1), (2) Jurisdiction of the FOS (DISP 2), (3) Complaint Handling Procedures of the FOS (DISP 3), and (4) Standard Terms (DISP 4).

[32] Under the Financial Services and Markets Act 2000 (Transitional Provisions) (Ombudsman Scheme and Complaints Scheme) Order 2001, Art. 1(1)(a), the FSA and the FOS have since July 19, 2001 been able to make Rules. They have not yet done so.

[33] See FSMA, s.226(2).

[34] DISP 2.6.1. These activities include any ancillary activities, including advice, provided by the firm in connection with those activities. Complaints about firms which are members of designated professional bodies and which relate to any otherwise exempt regulated activity cannot be handled under the Compulsory Jurisdiction of the FOS.

[35] FSMA, s.226(4) limits the activities which may be covered by the Compulsory Jurisdiction to activities which are "regulated activities or which could be made regulated activities by an order under section 22 [of the FSMA]".

Such services include the provision and operation of cash machines, safe deposit boxes etc.

13–173 **The voluntary jurisdiction.**[36] This is imposed upon "VJ participants". VJ participants are companies, firms, individuals or other businesses which have decided and agreed to participate in the voluntary jurisdiction and to be bound by the standard terms fixed by the scheme operator for VJ participants. The voluntary jurisdiction extends to cover[37] complaints which fall outside the terms of the compulsory jurisdiction but which relate to lending money secured by a charge over land and financial services activities covered by predecessor schemes insofar as the VJ participant was a member of that predecessor scheme in respect of that activity immediately before N2. In practice, the majority of complaints dealt with under the voluntary jurisdiction of the FOS are likely to relate to the activities of unauthorised persons. However, the voluntary jurisdiction is potentially sufficiently broad to cover activities of authorised firms which fall outside the scope of the activities covered by the compulsory jurisdiction.

(iii) *Complaint handling procedures for firms*

13–174 As with its predecessor schemes, the FOS will not accept a complaint for investigation under either the compulsory or voluntary jurisdiction until that complaint has been referred to the firm or VJ participant concerned and investigated. For that reason, every firm and VJ participant is obliged[38] to have in place and operate appropriate and effective internal complaint handling procedures to deal with any expression of dissatisfaction, whether justified or not, from or on behalf of an "eligible complainant" about that firm's provision of or failure to provide a financial services activity.[39] In order to be an "eligible complainant" the complainant must satisfy the criteria set out in the rules.[40] Save in very limited circumstances,[41] there are strict time limits within which a firm or VJ participant must deal with any complaint received by it.[42] Within those limits the

---

[36] See FSMA s.227.

[37] DISP 2.6.8.

[38] DISP Chapter 1. There are exceptions for (1) UCITS qualifiers and (2) firms which do not conduct business with "eligible complainants" and which have no reasonable likelihood of doing so, to the extent that the firm notifies the FSA of this fact: see DISP 1.1.1 and 1.1.5.

[39] DISP 1.2.1. The Guidance given in the remainder in DISP 1.2.4 provides that a firm's procedures should provide for (1) receiving complaints, (2) responding to complaints, (3) the appropriate investigation of complaints, and (4) notifying complainants of their right to go to the FOS where relevant. The precise procedures required will depend upon the size and organisational structure of the firm, the type of business undertaken by the firm, the nature and likely complexity of any complaints it is likely to receive and the likely number of complaints it will receive and have to investigate.

[40] DISP 2.4. See para. 13–175 below.

[41] Where the firm reasonably determines that (1) the complaint has not been made by an eligible complainant, (2) the complaint does not relate to an activity of the firm which comes under the jurisdiction of the FOS, (3) the complaint does not involve an allegation that the complainant has suffered or may suffer financial loss, material distress or material inconvenience, or (4) the complaint has been resolved by close of business on the business day following its receipt: see DISP 1.3.1.

[42] The firm must (1) acknowledge all complaints in writing within five days of receipt (DISP 1.4.1), (2) send a final or holding response within four weeks of receipt (DISP 1.4.4) and (3) (if a final response has not been sent within four weeks of receipt) send a final response or a response which *inter alia* informs the complainant that he may now refer the complaint to the FOS within eight weeks of receipt (DISP 1.4.5). Every final response provided by a firm must also inform the complainant that he may within six months refer the complaint to the FOS if he is dissatisfied with the final response.

complaint must be investigated and the complainant provided with a "final response".[43] If the firm or VJ participant decides that redress is appropriate, the complainant should be provided with fair compensation for any acts or omissions for which the respondent was responsible, and the respondent should comply promptly with any offer of redress which the complainant accepts.[44]

(iv) *Jurisdiction of the FOS*

If a complaint made to a firm is not satisfactorily resolved through the firm's **13–175** internal complaints handling procedures[45] the complainant may be able to refer the complaint to the FOS. If so, it is the duty of the firm to co-operate fully with the FOS in the handling of the complaint.[46] Before the Ombudsman will deal with any complaint, he will need to be satisfied that he has the necessary jurisdiction. In particular, he must be satisfied that[47] the complainant is an eligible complainant[48] and that the respondent to the complaint is subject to either the compulsory jurisdiction or the voluntary jurisdiction.[49] Also he must be satisfied that the activity to which the complaint relates is subject to either the compulsory jurisdiction or the voluntary jurisdiction[50] and that the respondent to the complaint has failed to resolve the complaint to the satisfaction of the complainant within eight weeks of resolving it.[51]

The jurisdiction of the Ombudsman also depends in part upon both the timing **13–176** of the act or omission about which complaint is made and the timing of the complaint. Under the terms of the FSMA the Ombudsman will not be able to deal with a complaint under the compulsory jurisdiction unless (1) the respondent was an authorised person at the time of the relevant act or omission, and (2) the relevant act or omission occurred at a time when compulsory jurisdiction rules were in force in relation to the activity in question.[52]

Equally, under the terms of the FSMA the Ombudsman will not be able to deal **13–177** with a complaint under the voluntary jurisdiction unless three conditions are met. First the respondent was a VJ participant at the time of the act or omission to which the complaint relates.[53] Secondly, the respondent was still a VJ participant at the time that the complaint was referred to the FOS.[54] Thirdly, the relevant act or omission occurred at a time when voluntary jurisdiction rules were in force in

---

[43] A "final response" is one in which the firm (1) accepts the complaint and, where appropriate, offers redress, or (2) offers redress without accepting the complaint, or (3) rejects the complaint and gives reasons for doing so, and contains information about the right to refer the complaint to the FOS.

[44] DISP 1.2.14.

[45] For example, because no Final Response is forthcoming within eight weeks of the complaint being made or because the complainant refuses to accept the contents of the Final Response.

[46] DISP 1.6.1. Such co-operation includes, but is not limited to, producing requested documents, adhering to any specified documents, attending hearings when requested to do so and complying promptly with any settlements or awards.

[47] DISP 2.2.1.

[48] An exhaustive definition of precisely who is an "eligible complainant" is set out in DISP 2.4.3–2.4.12.

[49] *i.e.* the respondent must either be a firm or a VJ participant.

[50] See paras 13–172 and 13–173 above.

[51] This condition exists to maximise the prospects of a complaint being satisfactorily resolved through a firm's own internal complaints handling procedures.

[52] FSMA, s.226(2)(b) and (c).

[53] *ibid.*, s.227(2)(b).

[54] *ibid.*, s.227(2)(c).

relation to the activity in question.[55] The scope of the voluntary jurisdiction has also been expanded by the scheme rules to permit the Ombudsman to consider a complaint even though the relevant act or omission occurred before the VJ participant was participating in the FOS and even though it may have occurred before N2 if (1) the complaint could have been dealt with under a predecessor scheme, or (2) the VJ participant has agreed to such a course.[56]

13–178 The jurisdiction of the FOS has been widened to allow it to determine "relevant existing complaints" and "relevant new complaints".[57] By definition, each of these types of complaint will relate to acts and omissions which occurred before the compulsory or voluntary jurisdiction rules were made. The procedure and scheme rules are modified in relation to relevant existing complaints and relevant new complaints.[58] In particular, the Ombudsman will determine relevant existing complaints by reference to such criteria as would have been applied to determine the complaint by the appropriate Ombudsman under the predecessor scheme.[59] Further, the Ombudsman will, when determining in relation to a relevant new complaint what is fair and reasonable in all the circumstances of the case and what constitutes fair compensation, take into account what determination the appropriate Ombudsman under the predecessor scheme might have been expected to reach.[60]

(v) *Complaints handling procedures of the FOS*

13–179 The procedures adopted by the Ombudsman under the compulsory and voluntary jurisdictions to consider and deal with complaints are very similar.[61] On receipt of a complaint the Ombudsman must consider four matters[62]: first, whether or not he has jurisdiction to deal with the complaint; secondly, whether or not the

---

[55] *ibid.*, s.227(2)(d).

[56] DISP 2.2.1 and 2.6.10.

[57] A "relevant existing complaint" is defined in Art. 2(1) of the Financial Services and Markets Act 2000 (Transitional Provisions) (Ombudsman Scheme and Complaints Scheme) Order 2001 as a complaint which (a) was referred to a predecessor scheme (other than the PIAS) at any time before N2 by a person who was at that time entitled under the terms of the predecessor scheme to refer such a complaint, and (b) was not determined before N2. A "relevant new complaint" is defined in Art. 3(1) of the Financial Services and Markets Act 2000 (Transitional Provisions) (Ombudsman Scheme and Complaints Scheme) Order 2001 as a complaint referred to the FOS which relates to an act or omission occurring *before* N2. The Compulsory Jurisdiction applies to a relevant new complaint only if (1) the respondent was subject to a predecessor scheme prior to N2, (2) the activity about which complaint is made was an activity to which the predecessor scheme applied, and (3) the complainant is eligible and wishes to have the complaint dealt with by the FOS. The FOS is also granted jurisdiction in relation to a limited number of other categories of complaint under the Financial Services and Markets Act 2000 (Transitional Provisions) (Ombudsman Scheme and Complaints Scheme) Order 2001: see Arts 8 to 10.

[58] See Arts 4 and 5 of the Financial Services and Markets Act 2000 (Transitional Provisions) (Ombudsman Scheme and Complaints Scheme) Order 2001.

[59] Art. 6 of the Financial Services and Markets Act 2000 (Transitional Provisions) (Ombudsman Scheme and Complaints Scheme) Order 2001. For a consideration of the principles applied under the various predecessor schemes, see Lomnicka and Powell, *Encyclopedia of Financial Services*.

[60] Art. 7 of the Financial Services and Markets Act 2000 (Transitional Provisions) (Ombudsman Scheme and Complaints Scheme) Order 2001.

[61] DISP 4.2.6 provides that the rules and guidance contained in DISP 3 will apply to VJ participants for the purposes of the voluntary jurisdiction as if they were firms except where the application of DISP 3 to VJ participants is specifically excluded or necessarily inapplicable.

[62] DISP 3.2.1.

complaint is within the relevant time limit[63]; thirdly, whether or not the complainant is an eligible complainant[64]; fourthly, whether or not the complaint is one which should be dismissed without consideration of its merits.[65]

(vi) *The investigation*

If the Ombudsman does not summarily dismiss the complaint, he will proceed to   **13–180** carry out an investigation into the complaint. Each party is given the opportunity to make representations, both in writing and at a hearing.[66] The Ombudsman is also empowered to require a party to provide specified information or documents to assist in his investigation if the information or documents in question are necessary for the determination of the complaint.[67] A failure to comply with a request for information or documents without reasonable excuse can be referred to the court, which may deal with the defaulter as if he were in contempt.[68]

At an appropriate time during his investigation the Ombudsman will send to   **13–181** the parties a provisional assessment, setting out the reasons for that assessment and inviting each party to respond within a specified period.[69] Thereafter the Ombudsman will proceed to determine the complaint. The complaint will be determined by reference to what, in the opinion of the Ombudsman, is fair and reasonable in all of the circumstances of the case. While many of the factors likely to bear upon the decision are those which would be relevant to a determination of legal liability by a court, the Ombudsman is not limited to taking a strictly "legal" approach. Thus matters such as delays in administration, delays in dealing with correspondence, poor quality of service and the manner in which the parties have behaved are all potentially relevant to an assessment of what is "fair and reasonable" in any particular case.

---

[63] The Ombudsman will not entertain a complaint (1) more than six months after the date on which the firm or VJ participant advised the complainant in its final response letter that he could refer his complaint to the FOS (DISP 2.3.1(b)), or (2) more than six years after the event complained of or (if later) more than three years from the date on which the complainant became aware or ought reasonably to have become aware that he had cause for complaint (DISP 2.3.1(c)). The Ombudsman does however have jurisdiction to consider complaints outside these time limits if, in his view, the failure to comply with the time limits has been the result of "exceptional circumstances" (DISP 2.3.2). Examples of exceptional circumstances include the incapacity of the complainant or a failure on the part of the firm or VJ participant to inform the complainant in its final response that any referral to the FOS should take place within six months.

[64] See para. 13–175 above.

[65] DISC 3.3 identifies 17 instances in which the Ombudsman may dismiss a complaint without considering its merits, including (1) if the complainant has suffered no financial loss, material distress or material inconvenience, (3) if the complaint has no reasonable prospect of success, (4) if the firm has already made a fair and reasonable offer of compensation which remains open for acceptance, (6) if the matter has already been considered by the FOS or a predecessor scheme, (8) if the complaint has been the subject of court proceedings in which there has been a decision on the merits, (9) if the complaint is at that time the subject of court proceedings, unless those proceedings have been stayed for the purpose of referring the complaint to the FOS, (13) the complaint is about investment performance, and (17) there is a compelling reason why it is inappropriate for the FOS to deal with the complaint.

[66] The Ombudsman is not fettered by the rules of evidence that would be applied by a court. He is permitted either to exclude evidence that would otherwise be admissible in a court or to include evidence that would not be admissible: DISP 3.5.2.

[67] FSMA, s.231(1).

[68] *ibid.*, s.232(2).

[69] DISP 3.2.10.

13–182   Once the determination becomes final and binding,[70] there is no right of appeal. The only means open to a disgruntled respondent to challenge the determination is by way of judicial review on the basis that the determination was not in fact fair and reasonable. As with predecessor schemes, it is likely that the only determinations potentially susceptible to judicial review will be those made under the compulsory jurisdiction. Determinations made under the voluntary jurisdiction will not be susceptible to judicial review.[71]

(vii) *The award*

13–183   If a complaint dealt with under the scheme is determined in favour of the complainant, the determination may include an award against the respondent of such amount as the ombudsman considers fair compensation for loss or damage[72] suffered by a complainant ("a money award").[73] Also or alternatively it may include a direction a direction that the respondent take such steps in relation to the complainant as the Ombudsman considers just and appropriate.[74]

13–184   The scheme is effectively one-sided since if the complainant accepts the determination, the respondent will be bound by it. The respondent has no option to reject the determination.[75] If the complainant rejects the determination, for whatever reason, he is free to pursue the respondent by other means. Enforcement of the award is available through the courts, both for money awards[76] and for directions to take steps.[77] There is no right of appeal against an accepted determination.

13–185   If a determination is rejected by a complainant who subsequently elects to pursue a claim against the respondent through the courts, the question frequently arises as to what, if anything, can be done with the rejected determination. The short answer is that it will depend upon the facts of each particular case. Clearly the court will not be bound by the determination of the Ombudsman—indeed, the court may decline even to admit that determination in evidence since on one view it is nothing more than a statement of opinion of what is a "fair and reasonable" result in the particular case before the court. However, insofar as the determination contains (for example) an agreed summary of the events which led to the complaint or a statement of assertions made previously by the parties, the determination may become relevant to issues before the court and so become admissible, albeit for limited purposes.

13–186   **Money awards.** The Ombudsman is obliged to assess the amount which would be fair compensation for the loss or damage suffered by the complainant. The approach taken to financial loss is, in general, that adopted by the courts. In addition, the Ombudsman is able to require that "fair compensation" be paid for other heads of loss or damage which would not generally be recoverable through

---

[70] See para. 13–184 below.
[71] See by way of example *R. v. Personal Investment Authority Ombudsman Bureau Limited, ex p. Johannes Mooyer* [2001] E.W.H.C. Admin. 247, unreported, April 5, 2001, Newman J.
[72] Defined in FSMA s.229(3) as financial loss or any other loss or damage of a specified kind.
[73] *ibid.*, s.229(2)(a).
[74] *ibid.*, s.229(2)(b).
[75] *ibid.*, s.228(5). DISP 3.9.13 obliges a firm to comply promptly with any money award or direction made by the Ombudsman.
[76] *ibid.*, s.229(8)(b) and Sched. 17 para. 16.
[77] For example, by injunction to compel required steps to be taken: section 229(9) of the FSMA.

the courts. These heads of loss are pain and suffering, damage to reputation and distress and inconvenience.[78]

13–187 The maximum money award that the Ombudsman may make is £100,000 exclusive of the costs of the complaint.[79] However, in practice the Ombudsman can make determinations the value of which exceed this limit since the limit does not apply to directions to take steps[80] which may well have a monetary value. Interest may be added to the award.[81] Costs may be awarded to a successful complainant.[82] In addition, if the Ombudsman considers that the award necessary to compensate the complainant exceeds the £100,000 limit, he can recommend that the respondent should pay the difference on a voluntary basis. However, that recommendation is not enforceable.

13–188 **Non-money awards.** If the Ombudsman decides that it is just and appropriate to require something other than, or in addition to, a money award he may do so. It does not matter that a court would be unable to order the course of action required by the Ombudsman. Accordingly, the Ombudsman can and frequently does require respondents to reinstate inappropriately surrendered life policies, reissue and back date units in a unit trust scheme and so forth. The one practical limit on the Ombudsman's power is that his direction will operate only as between the parties to the complaint. Accordingly, if the Ombudsman was to determine that a life policy had been surrendered as a result of inappropriate advice given not by the insurance company but by the complainant's own adviser, the Ombudsman could not direct the insurance company to reinstate the policy. The options open to him would be to direct the adviser to seek, at his own expense, the reinstatement of the policy and, if the adviser was unable to achieve that result, to make a money award instead.

(viii) *Immunity*

13–189 The FOS has a limited immunity from action in damages while performing compulsory jurisdiction functions.[83] Similar immunity is provided under the scheme rules in relation to voluntary jurisdiction functions.[84] However, there is no immunity in respect of acts or omissions of the Ombudsman shown to have been in bad faith. An award of damages can be made in respect of acts or omissions which were unlawful as a result of section 6(1) of the Human Rights Act 1998.[85]

---

[78] DISP 3.9.2. Although s.229(4) permits the FSA to specify the maximum amount which may be regarded as fair compensation for pain and suffering, damage to reputation and distress and inconvenience, to date no ceiling has been specified.

[79] FSMA, s.229(4); DISP 3.9.4.

[80] Under FSMA, s.229(2)(b).

[81] Section 229(8)(a) of the FSMA.

[82] See s.230(1) of the FSMA and DISC 3.9.9. A complainant cannot be ordered to pay costs incurred by a respondent in dealing with a complaint: s. 230(3) of the FSMA. s. 230(4) provides for rules to be made permitting the FOS to make an award of costs against a complainant in its favour for the purpose of providing a contribution to resources deployed in dealing with the complaint if, in its opinion, the complainant's conduct was improper or unreasonable or the complainant was responsible for unreasonable delay. To date, there are no such rules, even in draft form.

[83] FSMA, s.1(3), Sched. 17, para. 10.

[84] *ibid.*, s.1(3), Sched. 17, para. 18(5); DISP 4.2.7.

[85] *ibid.*, s.1(3), Sched. 17, para. 10(2); DISP 4.2.7(2). See further para. 13–025 above and Chap. 7, paras 7–005 to 7–012 above for a consideration of the operation of s.6 of the Human Rights Act 1998.

(b) *Compensation scheme*

(i) *Introduction*

13–190   Part XV of the FSMA provides for a compensation scheme. Two main obligations are imposed on the FSA. The first is to establish a body corporate to act as
"scheme manager" for the compensation scheme. This body corporate is the
Financial Services Compensation Scheme Limited ("the FSCS").[86] While the
Chairman and Board of the scheme manager are appointed by, and liable to
removal from office, by the FSA, the actual operation of the compensation
scheme by the FSCS is independent from the FSA.[87] The second is to establish
a scheme for compensating persons in cases where "relevant persons"[88] are
unable or are likely to be unable to satisfy claims made against them.[89] This
scheme is called the Financial Services Compensation Scheme ("the compensation scheme").[90] This single compensation scheme is designed to replace the
numerous and varied compensation schemes which previously existed.[91]

(ii) *Purpose*

13–191   The purpose of the compensation scheme is broadly twofold. First, it is designed
to maintain consumer confidence and to provide a certain level of protection to
consumers in the event of insolvency. Thus the scheme aims to ensure that the
debts due to consumers will still be met to a greater or lesser extent, if the entity
with which consumers have deposited money or taken out an insurance contract
or to which they have provided funds with a view to investment, ceases trading
or is declared insolvent. Secondly, it is designed to provide a degree of consistency and unity within the financial services sector.

(iii) *Structure*

13–192   The broad structure of the compensation scheme is contained in the FSMA itself.
The detail of how the compensation scheme will operate is to be contained in
rules to be made by the FSA.[92] At the time of writing no rules have been made.
However the FSA has produced "Final compensation rules"[93] and it is expected
that these confirm to what will be the actual rules made. For the purposes of this

---

[86] This body took over the management of the Investors Compensation Scheme (under the 1986 Act)
on February 1, 2001.
[87] FSMA, s.212(1)–(5).
[88] See paras 13–196 below
[89] FSMA, s.213(1).
[90] *ibid.*, s.213(2).
[91] These were the Investors Compensation Scheme, the Deposit Protection Scheme, the Building
Societies Investor Protection Scheme, the Policyholders Protection Scheme, the Friendly Societies
Protection Scheme, the compensation arrangements that each of the 8 professional bodies recognised
under the 1986 Act was required to have in place and the various "profession-specific" schemes that
existed.
[92] Under FSMA, s.213(1).
[93] To be found at Annex B of its Policy Statement, "Financial Services Compensation Scheme—
Feedback on CP58 and 'final' text" (September 2001). This document is available on the website of
the FSCS at www.fscs.org.uk. COMP 2.2.1 obliges the FSCS to administer the compensation scheme
in accordance with the rules.

chapter it is therefore assumed that the rules will reflect the format and wording of the "Final compensation rules".[94]

(iv) *Qualifying conditions for compensation*

Once an application for compensation has been received from a claimant, the **13–193** FSCS will proceed to investigate and then, if appropriate, will make an offer of compensation to the claimant. The FSCS is entitled, as part of its investigation, to require "relevant persons" to provide such information or documents as is necessary to enable the fair determination of the claim.[95] It is also entitled to inspect documents held by the liquidator of an insolvent relevant person[96] and by the Official Receiver.[97] Once it has completed its investigation the FSCS may pay compensation[98] to an "eligible claimant" if from its investigations it is satisfied as to the relevant criteria. The first is that an eligible claimant has made an application for compensation.[99] Secondly, the claim must be in respect of a "protected claim" against a "relevant person" who is in default.[1] However, the FSCS has a discretion to reject an application for compensation if the application contains any material inaccuracy or omission, save where it considers that inaccuracy or omission to be wholly unintentional.[2] Moreover, it must reject the application for compensation if the liability of the relevant person to the claimant has been extinguished by operation or law or any civil claim against the relevant person would have been defeated by a defence of limitation at the earlier of two dates: (a) the date the relevant person is determined to be in default; (b) the date the claimant first indicates in writing that he may have a claim against the relevant person.[3]

Eligible claimants. Every person is an "eligible claimant" for the purposes of **13–194** the compensation scheme unless they fall within relevant categories of excluded

---

[94] In addition, the FSA is to produce Funding Rules in relation to the compensation scheme. Once again, at the time of writing no such rules have been made, although the "final text" of the rules is to be found in the FSA's Policy Statement "Financial Services Compensation Scheme Funding Rules—Feedback on CP86 and 'final' text" (September 2001).

[95] FSMA, s.219. If without reasonable excuse the relevant person fails to comply with such a request by the FSCS, the FSCS may refer the matter to the court and the court may deal with the defaulter as if he were in contempt: see, s.221(2).

[96] *ibid.*, s.220.

[97] *ibid.*, s.224. The purposes for which the FSCS may inspect documents held by the Official Receiver are limited to (1) establishing the identity of persons to whom it might be liable to make a payment in accordance with the compensation scheme, and (2) establishing the amount of any payment which it might be liable to make.

[98] COMP 3.2.1. In respect of claims under protected contracts of insurance there is one additional qualifying condition, namely that it is not reasonably practicable or appropriate to take steps to secure continuity of insurance under COMP 3.3.1 and 3.3.4 or to take the measures specified in COMP 3.3.4(2) to provide assistance to an insurance undertaking in financial difficulties. See further para. 13–203 below.

[99] Or, if an application is made by a person on behalf of another, the other on whose behalf the claim is made is an "eligible claimant" who would have been paid compensation by the FSCS had he been able to make the claim himself: COMP 3.2.2. Thus claims may be made under the compensation scheme by personal representatives on behalf of the deceased, by trustees on behalf of beneficiaries and so forth.

[1] COMP 3.2.1.

[2] COMP 8.2.1.

[3] COMP 8.2.3. The FSCS may however disregard a defence of limitation in respect of a claim made in connection with protected investment business if it considers that it would be reasonable to do so.

persons.[4] Even then, such a person can still be an "eligible claimant" if he is able to satisfy one of the several exemptions.[5]

13–195   **Protected claims.** A protected claim[6] is (1) a claim for a protected deposit, (2) a claim under a protected contract of insurance, or (3) a claim in connection with protected investment business[7] as each is defined.

13–196   **Relevant persons.** A relevant person is a person who, at the time that the act or omission which gives rise to the complaint took place, was a participant firm or an appointed representative of a participant firm.[8]

13–197   **Default by relevant persons.** A relevant person is "in default" if the FSCS determines that the relevant person is unable, or is likely to be unable, to satisfy protected claims against it and is satisfied that a protected claim exists and there has been a relevant insolvency related event.[9]

13–198   **Assignment of rights.** As a pre-condition to a payment of compensation, the FSCS may require a claimant to assign the whole or any part of his rights against

---

[4] See: COMP 4.2.2. Persons excluded from the definition of "eligible claimants" are: (1) firms (other than a sole trader firm or a small business whose claim arises out of a regulated activity for which they do not have permission) (2) overseas firms (3) collective investment schemes or operators or trustees of such a scheme (4) pension or retirement funds or trustees of such a fund (other than a trustee of a small self-administered scheme or an occupational scheme of an employer which is not a large company or large partnership) (5) supranational institutions, governments and central administrative authorities (6) provincial, regional, local and municipal authorities (7) directors and managers of the relevant person in default (unless the relevant person in default is a mutual association which is not a large mutual association and the directors and managers do not receive a salary or other remuneration for services performed by them for the relevant person in default) (8) Close relatives of persons excluded by (7), (9) bodies corporate in the same group as the relevant person in default, (10) persons holding 5% or more of the capital of the relevant person in default or of any body corporate in the same group (11) the auditors of the relevant person in default or of any body corporate in the same group as the relevant person in default or the appointed actuary of a friendly society or insurance undertaking in default (12) persons who in the opinion of the FSCS are responsible for or have contributed to the relevant persons's default (13) large companies (14) large partnerships or mutual associations (15) persons whose claim arises from transactions in connection with which they have been convicted of an offence of money laundering, and (16) persons whose claim arises under the Third Parties (Rights against Insurers) Act 1930.

[5] In COMP 4.3. The exemptions vary according to whether the compensation is sought in respect of a protected deposit, a long-term insurance contract, a general insurance contract and a liability subject to compulsory insurance.

[6] "Claim" is defined for the purposes of COMP as "a valid claim made in respect of a civil liability owed by a relevant person to the claimant". This definition is sufficiently broad to include claims for the return of deposits from banks and building societies, claims for actionable breaches under the FSMA and claims for actionable breaches of common law duties of care and skill.

[7] COMP 5.2.1. Note also COMP 14.5.

[8] COMP 6.2.1. A "participant firm" is any firm other than: (1) an incoming EEA firm which is a BCD credit institution or ISD investment firm and whose permission is confined to cross border services; (2) an incoming EEA firm without top up cover which is (a) a BCD credit institution whose permission to carry on regulated activities from a U.K. branch is confined to accepting deposits, or (b) an ISD investment firm (including a credit institution which is an ISD investment firm) whose permission to carry on regulated activities from a U.K. branch is confined to passported activities; (3) a service company; (4) the Society, in respect of activities included in its permission under section 315(2) of the FSMA; (5) a member, in respect of effecting or carrying out Lloyd's policies; (6) an underwriting agent or member's adviser in respect of advising on syndicate participation at Lloyd's or managing the underwriting capacity of a Lloyd's syndicate as a managing agent at Lloyd's; (7) an authorised professional firm that is subject to the rules of the Law Society (England and Wales) or the Law Society of Scotland; (8) an ICVC and (9) a UCITS qualifier.

[9] See COMP 6.3.1–6.3.3. See also COMP 6.3.4.

the relevant person or against any third party to the FSCS on such terms as it thinks fit.[10] Where this is done the FSCS is obliged to make "such recoveries as it reasonably can" through the rights so assigned.[11] It is also obliged to pay any recoveries made through the pursuit of the assigned claim to the claimant, unless equivalent compensation has already been paid by the FSCS to him.[12]

(v) *Compensation*

Offers of compensation. The FSCS is obliged to ensure that a claimant does   **13–199** not suffer any disadvantage by promptly accepting any offer of compensation that might be made to him by the FSCS.[13] The amount of compensation payable to a claimant in respect of any type of protected claim is the amount of his "overall net claim" against the relevant person at the "quantification date".[14] A claimant's overall net claim is the sum of the protected claims of the same category that he has against a relevant person in default, less the amount of any liability which the relevant person may set off against any of those claims.[15] The FSCS will therefore offset against any award of compensation monies to which the relevant person could properly claim to be entitled from the claimant. It will also offset monies that the relevant person (or a third party) has already paid to the claimant, if such payment was connected with the relevant person's liability to the claimant.[16] The quantification date varies according to the type of protected claim in issue.[17]

---

[10] COMP 3.2.1(3), 7.2.1. Where such an assignment is required, there is no obligation on the part of the FSCS to provide the claimant with an indemnity against any liability for costs that might arise in any future proceedings pursued by the FSCS against the relevant body: *R. v. Investors Compensation Scheme Ltd ex p. Bowden* [1994] 1 W.L.R. 17; [1996] A.C. 261.

[11] COMP 7.2.3. An example of one of the compensation scheme's predecessor schemes taking such steps is to be found in *ICS Ltd v. West Bromwich Building Society* [1999] Lloyd's L.Rep. P.N. 496.

[12] COMP 7.2.4. Where the claimant has already received equivalent compensation from the FSCS, any recoveries from the pursuit of the assigned rights will be payable to the FSCS rather than to the Claimant: COMP 7.2.2.

[13] COMP 7.2.5. Suppose A and B each have a protected investment business claim of £60,000 against a relevant person in default. The FSCS offers each claimant £48,000 (the maximum available) as compensation. A accepts the offer of compensation and assigns his rights against the relevant person to the FSCS but B delays accepting the offer. The liquidator of the relevant person in default subsequently makes a payment of 50 pence in the pound to all creditors of the relevant person. A and B are therefore each prima facie entitled to £30,000. If the payment is made after A has accepted the FSCS's offer of compensation but before B does so (1) B would receive £30,000 from the liquidator and could then claim the £30,000 balance of his £60,000 loss from the FSCS, but (2) A would already have assigned his rights against the relevant person in default to the FSCS, who would receive the £30,000 instead of A. In such circumstances, A's prompt acceptance of the FSCS's offer of compensation would have worked to his disadvantage when compared to B, who delayed accepting the offer. The FSCS would almost certainly in such circumstances pass on to A £12,000 of the £30,000 recovered by it from the liquidator.

[14] COMP 12.2.1. In addition, COMP 12.4–12.6 identifies a number of specific matters of which the FSCS must take account when assessing appropriate compensation under particular categories of protected claims.

[15] COMP 12.2.4.

[16] In *R. v. Investors Compensation Scheme, ex p. Bowden* [1996] A.C. 261 investors challenged the decision of the ICS to make deductions from the compensation that was offered to them so that the amount offered fell below the investors' overall net claim. The House of Lords found that the ICS was entitled to exclude elements of a claim which it considered were not essential to provide fair compensation to investors and also to place a reasonable limit on the sums payable to investors in respect of their professional fees. It is doubtful whether the COMP rules would be interpreted so as to permit the FSCS to apply similar deductions or limitations.

[17] See COMP 12.3.1–12.3.6.

13–200 The FSCS may make reduced or interim offers of compensation if the amount of compensation payable is uncertain or if the claimant has reasonable prospects of recovering part of his loss from any other person.[18] Any offer of compensation made by the FSCS must remain open for 90 days unless it appears during that period that no offer should in fact have been made, or the offer is rejected in that period. Upon the expiry of 90 days, the FSCS may withdraw the offer unless its size has been disputed and consideration is being given to making a reduced or interim offer.[19] No offer of compensation will exceed the limits payable by the FSCS for protected claims.[20] For protected deposits, the limit is 100 per cent of the first £2,000 of the claim, 90 per cent of the next £33,000 of the claim and a maximum payment of £31,700. For a protected contract of insurance when the contract is a relevant general insurance contract, the limit is 100 per cent of the claim (to an unlimited maximum) where the claim is in respect of a liability subject to compulsory insurance and 100 per cent of the first £2,000 of the claim and 90 per cent of the remainder of the claim (to an unlimited maximum) in all other cases. For a protected contract of insurance when the contract is a long term insurance contract, the limit is at least 90 per cent of the value of the policy (including future benefits declared before the date the relevant person is determined to be in default) to an unlimited maximum. For protected investment business, the limit is 100 per cent of the first £30,000 of the claim and 90 per cent of the next £20,000 of the claim, to a maximum payment of £48,000.[21]

13–201 These limits apply to the aggregate amount of claims in respect of each category of protected claim that an eligible claimant has against a relevant person. Consequently a claimant who, for example, has a claim against a relevant person for deposits each of £1,500, will not receive 100 per cent compensation on each deposit. He will only receive 100 per cent of £2,000 and 90 per cent of the balance of £1,000, a total of £2,900.

13–202 **Acceptance of offers of compensation.** The FSCS is obliged[22] to pay a claim as soon as reasonably possible after it has satisfied itself that the qualifying conditions for compensation have been met and the amount of compensation due to the claimant has been calculated.[23] With limited exceptions,[24] payment will be made to the claimant or to the order of the claimant unless arrangements have been or are to be made to secure continuity of insurance or the FSCS is taking

---

[18] COMP 8.3.2 and COMP 11.2.4–11.2.5.

[19] COMP 8.3.1. The offer may also be withdrawn if it is rejected.

[20] See in COMP 10.2. Interest, which may be paid on the compensation sum under COMP 11.2.7, is not to be taken into account when applying limits on the compensation sum payable.

[21] COMP 10.2.3.

[22] COMP 9.2.1.

[23] "As soon as reasonably possible" is not defined within the rules, although COMP 9.2.1 provides that all payments must be made within three months unless the FSA has granted the FSCS an extension of time. Even then, appropriate compensation must be paid within four months. COMP 9.2.2 does permit the FSCS in extremely limited circumstances to postpone paying compensation to a claimant.

[24] COMP 11.2.2–11.2.3. These exceptions include (1) claims made in connection with protected investment claims covered by the pensions review (when the FSCS must pay any compensation to the trustee of the occupational pension scheme or the personal pension scheme or other product provider) and (2) claims under a protected contract of insurance against a relevant person that is in provisional liquidation or liquidation (when the FSCS may *inter alia* make payments on behalf of the claimant).

measures to safeguard the claimant in respect of an insurance undertaking in financial difficulty.[25]

Insurance. Insurance, and in particular long-term insurance, can cause diffi- **13–203** culty when the issue of compensation is considered. If, for example, a life policy is payable only upon the death of the policy holder or upon the policy holder reaching a certain age, and he is below that age at the material time, it is not immediately straightforward to see how best to compensate the policy holder. Particular provision is therefore made in the FSMA for the FSCS to make arrangements *not* to make an immediate payment of monetary compensation to such persons. The FSCS may instead secure continuity of insurance for policy holders whose insurer is unable, or appears to be unable, to satisfy claims against it.[26] This may involve either securing or facilitating the transfer of all or part of the long-term insurance business of the relevant person in default to another firm or securing the issue of policies by another firm to eligible claimants in substitution for their existing policies.[27] The FSCS may also take measures to safeguard a policy holder whose insurer encounters financial difficulty.[28] This may involve securing or facilitating the transfer of all or part of the business of the relevant person which consists of carrying out contracts of insurance to another firm. Alternatively it may involve the provision of assistance to the relevant person to enable it to continue to effect or carry out contracts of insurance.[29]

Challenging the FSCS. The FSCS has a limited immunity from action in **13–204** damages while performing functions as scheme manager of the compensation scheme.[30] In addition, the decisions and actions of the FSCS will be susceptible to judicial review.

(c) *Parallel proceedings*

Consideration of claims arising from a financial regulatory context would be **13–205** incomplete without mention of problems arising from parallel proceedings, though detailed consideration is beyond the scope of this book . A scandal from a regulatory context frequently spawns a range of different proceedings and often in different jurisdictions. The problems reflect the different aims of the different proceedings which may be brought. Investigatory (*e.g.* by liquidators, regulatory and professional bodies), criminal, civil and regulatory proceedings all have different aims. There is no obvious hierarchy which may be invoked to prescribe a priority sequence of general application. Different events will merit different sequences. Moreover, much will depend on the will of the various potential initiators of different proceedings. Applications are often made to stay disciplinary proceedings pending the outcome of civil proceedings. The general principle seems now to be clear:

---

[25] See COMP 3.3.3–3.3.6 and 11.2.1.
[26] FSMA, s.216 of the FSMA. The rules governing the circumstances in which the FSCS is obliged to make arrangements to secure continuity of insurance are set out in COMP 3.3.1.
[27] COMP 3.3.2.
[28] FSMA, s.217. The rules governing the circumstances in which the FSCS is obliged to take measures to safeguard eligible claimants where the relevant person about whom complaint is made is an insurance undertaking in financial difficulty are set out in COMP 3.3.3–3.3.6.
[29] COMP 3.3.4.
[30] See FSMA, s.222(1) and para. 13–132 above.

"the court has power to intervene to prevent injustice where the continuation of one set of proceedings may prejudice the fairness of the trial of other proceedings. But it is a power which has to be exercised with great care and only where there is real risk of serious prejudice which may lead to injustice."[31]

13–206   **Disclosure problems.** Regulatory contact and investigatory proceedings generate documents which attract disclosure applications in civil proceedings. These applications are frequently met with claims to various kinds of privilege, *e.g.* public interest immunity, legal professional privilege[32] and privilege against self-incrimination, and invocation of human rights legislation. As to information obtained by regulators pursuant to statutory powers to obtain such information, restrictions are imposed on disclosure *by them* of such information subject to a range of exceptions including in favour of other regulators.[33]

---

[31] *R. v. Panel on Takeovers and Mergers, ex p. Fayed* [1992] B.C.C. 524, CA, *per* Neill L.J. at 531. Compare the (frequently criticised) decision of the Court of Appeal in *R. v. Institute of Chartered Accountants in England and Wales, ex p. Brindle* [1994] B.C.C. 297 in which disciplinary proceedings were stayed with the more orthodox later decision of the Divisional Court in *R. v. Chance, ex p. Smith* [1995] B.C.C. 1095.
[32] See in the context of the 1986 Act, *Kaufmann v. Credit Lyonnais* [1995] C.L.C. 300.
[33] *e.g.* 1986 Act 1986, ss. 179 and 180.

CHAPTER 14

INSURANCE BROKERS

	PARA.
1. General	14–001
(a) Duties to the client	14–010
(i) Contractual duties	14–010
(ii) Duties independent of contract	14–014
(b) Duties to third parties	14–017
(i) Duties to insurers	14–018
(ii) Duties to other third parties	14–025
(c) The standard of skill and care	14–032
2. Liability for breach of duty	14–036
(a) Failing to effect insurance	14–038
(b) Effecting insurance, but not on the terms specified by the client	14–043
(c) Effecting insurance which does not meet the client's requirements	14–046
(d) Failing to exercise discretion reasonably	14–057
(e) Failing to act with reasonable speed	14–059
(f) Failing to disclose material facts to the insurers	14–060

	PARA.
(g) Making a misrepresentation to the insurers	14–069
(h) Failing to keep the client properly informed as to the existence or terms of cover	14–074
(i) Failing to give proper advice	14–081
3. Damages	14–086
(a) Remoteness	14–087
(b) Causation	14–088
(i) Intervening error or omission of the claimant	14–089
(ii) Where the claimant would not have been insured in any event	14–097
(iii) Where the required insurance would not have been granted if the full facts had been known	14–109
(c) Foreseeability	14–113
(i) Measure of damages	14–114
(ii) Contributory negligence	14–126

1. GENERAL

Some insurance contracts are arranged directly between an insurer and an insured. However, the majority of insurance contracts are arranged through intermediaries, most of which fall within one of two categories: insurance agents and insurance brokers. The term "insurance agent" is used to describe persons who normally act as agents of the insurers for the purpose of effecting insurance policies. Insurance agents are commonly employed by particular insurance companies or groups of companies and they do not profess to give disinterested advice about the services which are offered by their competitors.   **14–001**

The term "insurance broker", by contrast, is used to describe persons who normally act as agents of the insured for the purpose of effecting insurance policies. Insurance brokers hold themselves out as experts in insurance generally, or in certain fields of insurance, and offer their services to persons who are seeking the benefit of insurance. Insurance brokers effect policies of insurance or reinsurance on behalf of their clients, give advice in connection with such policies, and, on occasions, assist their clients in making claims against the insurers or reinsurers as the case may be.[1] Although insurance brokers usually draw their remuneration from the insurers (in the form of commission), they are   **14–002**

---

[1] This is not an exhaustive list of the business undertaken by insurance brokers. See, for example, paras. 14–017 to 14–024, below.

expected to act in the best interests of the insured.[2] An intermediary should inform his client whether he is acting as an insurance agent or an insurance broker.[3] This chapter is concerned with claims against insurance brokers.[4]

14–003   As stated above, the insurance broker generally acts as the agent of the insured and not of the insurer.[5] This applies both when he is effecting insurance[6] and when he is handling claims which arise under the policy.[7] There are, however, exceptions to this general rule.[8] The broker may be authorised by particular insurers to effect insurance on their behalf, and when so doing he acts as the agent of those insurers.[9] In non-marine insurance the broker often has implied authority to grant interim insurance (which is normally evidenced by cover notes) and, again, when so doing he acts as agent of the insurers rather than the insured.[10] Even where the broker is acting as agent for the insurers, however, he still owes a duty of care to the insured.[11]

14–004   Regulation of brokers. Prior to the coming into force of the Financial Services and Markets Act 2000 the business of insurance brokers was regulated by the Insurance Brokers (Registration) Act 1977 and the rules and orders made thereunder. The governing body of the profession was the Insurance Brokers

---

[2] See, generally, the Green Paper, Insurance Intermediaries (1977) Cmnd. 6715, which preceded the Insurance Brokers (Registration) Act 1977 (which is to be repealed by the Financial Services and Markets Act 2000). The Code of Conduct drawn up pursuant to the 1977 Act states that it is a fundamental principle that: "Insurance brokers shall do everything possible to satisfy the insurance requirements of their clients and shall ... place the interest of those clients before all other considerations ... " (para. B).

[3] Para. 3.1 of the General Insurance Standards Council Code for Private Customers (2000) states: "We will explain the service we can offer and our relationship with you, including: whether we act for an Insurer or act independently for you as an intermediary; whether we act as an agent of another intermediary or agent; the choice of products and services we can offer you."

[4] Where the usual requirements for the imposition of a duty of care are satisfied (as to which, see chapter 2, para. 2–22 *et seq.* to part 1) insurance agents will be held to owe duties of care to those seeking insurance. See, for example, *Gorham v. British Telecommunications Plc.* [2000] 1 W.L.R. 2129 in which the defendant insurance company conceded that it owed a duty of care to the purchaser of one of its personal pensions. In such cases the same principles relating to breach, causation and loss and damage as set out in this chapter will apply.

[5] In *Searle v. Hales Co.* [1996] Q.B. 68, Adrian Whitfield Q.C. (sitting as a deputy High Court judge) held, allowing the insurer's application to strike out the client's claim, that "prima facie, insurance agents and brokers are agents of the insured and not the insurer ... This relationship is not altered by the fact that a broker's commission may be deducted from the premium": *ibid.* at 71.

[6] *Rozanes v. Bowen* (1928) 32 Ll.L.Rep. 98; *McNealy v. The Pennine Insurance Co. Ltd* [1978] 2 Lloyd's Rep. 18, CA; *Velos v. Harbour Insurance* [1997] 2 Lloyd's Rep. 461 (H.H.J. Hallgarten Q.C.). In New Zealand a broker who receives commission from the insurer is deemed to be the insurer's "representative", so that the insurer is fixed with the broker's knowledge of all matters material to the insurance contract: s.10 of the Insurance Law Reform Act 1977 as applied in *Helicopter Equipment Ltd v. Marine Insurance Co. Ltd* [1986] 1 N.Z.L.R. 448 and *Gold Star Insurance Co. Ltd v. Gaunt* [1998] 3 N.Z.L.R. 80, NZCA. He is not thereby deemed to be the insurer's agent, however. In Australia the Insurance (Agents and Brokers) Act 1984 modifies the role of the broker: see *Manufacturers' Mutual Insurance Ltd v. John H. Boardman Insurance Brokers Pty Ltd* (1994) 68 A.L.J.R. 385.

[7] *Anglo-African Merchants Ltd v. Bayley* [1970] 1 Q.B. 311; *North and South Trust Co. v. Berkeley* [1971] 1 W.L.R. 470; *Callaghan and Hedges v. Thompson* [2000] Lloyd's Rep. I.R. 125, Steel J.

[8] That a broker is agent of the insured is essentially a presumption which can be rebutted: *Winter v. Irish Life Assurance Plc* [1995] 2 Lloyd's Rep. 274 at 282 *per* Sir Peter Webster.

[9] As in *Woolcott v. Excess Insurance Co. Ltd (No. 2)* [1979] 2 Lloyd's Rep. 210; *Excess Life Assurance Co. Ltd v. Firemen's Insurance Co. of Newark, New Jersey* [1982] 2 Lloyd's Rep. 599, 621.

[10] *Stockton v. Mason* [1978] 2 Lloyd's Rep. 430.

[11] *London Borough of Bromley v. Ellis* [1971] 1 Lloyd's Rep. 97, 99. See para. 14–014, below.

Registration Council, established under section 1 of the 1977 Act. Sections 2 and 4 of the Act required the Council to establish and maintain a register of insurance brokers and a list of bodies corporate carrying on business as insurance brokers.[12] It was an offence for individuals who were not registered or for companies which were not enrolled in the list to describe themselves as "insurance brokers"[13]: such parties typically described themselves as "insurance consultants" or "insurance intermediaries".[14] A Code of Conduct for the guidance of insurance brokers was drawn up by the Council, pursuant to section 10 of the Act, and was contained in the Insurance Brokers Registration Council (Code of Conduct) Approval Order 1994.[15]

The Insurance Brokers (Registration) Act 1977 has been repealed by the Financial Services and Markets Act 2000,[16] and the Insurance Brokers Registration Council is to be abolished. In its place is the General Insurance Standards Council (GISC) which is an independent and non-statutory body. The GISC is to be the sole body for the regulation of the general insurance industry, including insurers and independent intermediaries. However, membership of the GISC is voluntary and therefore its true effectiveness remains to be seen. The GISC has produced two Codes of Conduct, one relating to private investors and one for commercial customers.[17] **14–005**

Financial Services & Markets Act 2000. In so far as they carry on a "regulated activity" within the meaning of the Financial Services and Markets Act 2000,[18] insurance brokers are subject to the regime for regulation of such **14–006**

---

[12] The qualifications for registration are set out in s.3 of the Insurance Brokers (Registration) Act 1977. The construction of s.3 is discussed in *Pickles v. Insurance Brokers Registration Council* [1984] 1 W.L.R. 745. The statutory scheme is briefly discussed in *Macmillan v. A.W. Knott Becker Scott Ltd* [1990] 1 Lloyd's Rep. 98.
For a detailed commentary on the regulatory regime established by the 1977 Act, see R.W. Hodgin, *Insurance Intermediaries, Law and Regulation*, chap. 6.
[13] Insurance Brokers Registration Act 1977, s.22. In *Harvest Trucking Co. Ltd v. Davis* [1991] 2 Lloyd's Rep. 638 the defendant was not registered as an insurance broker and described himself as an "insurance intermediary". H.H. Judge Diamond Q.C., sitting in the High Court, stated that although Mr Davis's business was indistinguishable from that of a small insurance broker, "no possible criticism can be made of the fact that Mr Davis carried on business in the way he did".
[14] Many insurance intermediaries who were not members of the Insurance Brokers Registration Council were instead members of the Association of British Insurers. The ABI produced its own Code of Practice to regulate the activities of its members.
[15] S.I. 1994 No. 2569. Before November 21, 1994 the Code of Conduct was contained in the Insurance Brokers Registration Council (Code of Conduct) Approval Order 1978 (S.I. 1978 No. 1394).
[16] At the time of writing the repeal of the Insurance Brokers (Registration) Act 1977 has yet to be implemented.
[17] The two codes are the General Insurance Standards Council Code for Private Customers (2000) and the General Insurance Standards Council Commercial Code. For the full text of these codes, and commentary on them, see R. W. Hodgin, *Insurance Intermediaries, Law and Regulation*, chap. 4. See also the GISC website: www.gisc.co.uk.
[18] Previously, insurance brokers were subject to the regime of the Financial Services Act 1986 in so far as they carried on "investment business" as defined. Under that Act, "long-term insurance contracts" were included among the 11 categories of "investments" defined in the Act. "Long-term insurance contracts" were defined by reference to "long-term business" as defined in the Insurance Companies Act 1982, but the definition was qualified so as, in effect, to embrace policies which were entered into with a view to securing a return in any event and not simply to provide against contingencies. Thus, for example, endowment life insurance were included within the definition but not pure term insurance. In so far as they carried on investment business, insurance brokers needed to be authorised to do so and were thus subject to conduct of business rules, in particular to "know your client" and "best advice" rules. For brokers authorised by the Insurance Brokers Registration

business established under the Act.[19] A full description of that regime as it applies to insurance brokers who carry on a regulated activity is beyond the scope of this book and reference should be made to specialist works.[20]

14-007   The definition of a "regulated activity" is set out in section 22 of the Act, and in the Financial Services and Markets Act 2000 (Regulated Activities) Order 2001.[21] In the Order a distinction is drawn between contracts of general insurance and contracts of long-term insurance (as respectively defined in Parts I and II of Schedule 1 to the Order). Pursuant to article 21 of the Order, buying "contractually based investments" as agent is a specified kind of activity. Similarly, article 53 provides that advising on the merits of buying a "contractually based investment" is a regulated activity. By article 3(1), a "contractually based investment" includes "rights under a qualifying contract of insurance" which (again by article 3(1)) means a contract of long-term insurance which is not (a) a reinsurance contract, nor (b) a limited type of life or health insurance. As a consequence, advising on contracts of general insurance will not usually be a regulated activity, while advising on most contracts of long-term insurance will be.

14-008   An insurance broker or other intermediary may not carry on a "regulated activity" unless he is either an authorised person or an exempt person.[22] An agreement made in breach of this general prohibition is unenforceable by the broker against the innocent party, who is entitled to recover any money paid under the agreement together with compensation.[23] If an insurance broker is authorised, then he will be required to comply with the rules made by the Financial Services Authority which are set out in the Conduct of Business Sourcebook. In particular the broker will be subject to "know your customer", and "suitability" rules.[24] Pursuant to section 150 of the Act, a breach of the rules by an authorised broker may be actionable at the suit of a private person[25] who suffers loss as a result of that breach, subject to the defences and other incidents applying to actions for breach of statutory duty.

14-009   **Lloyd's brokers.** Lloyd's consists of a number of syndicates, each made up of a number of "names", who undertake unlimited liability for their proportion of any given risk. Each syndicate has a number of active underwriters who enter

---

Council, see the Insurance Brokers Registration Council (Conduct of Business) Rules Approval Order 1988 (S.I. 1988 No. 950), Chap. 5, rr. 10(1) and (2). Contravention by authorised persons of conduct of business rules gave rise to civil liability, either under s. 61 of the Financial Services Act 1986 (where the claim was brought by the S.I.B.) or under s. 62 (where the claim was brought by the broker's former clients). Since April 1, 1991 the right to claim under s. 62 of the Act was limited by s. 62A to "private investors" as defined in the Financial Services (Restriction of Right of Action) Regulations 1991 (S.I. 1991 No. 489).

[19] At the time of writing the Act has not yet been brought into force.

[20] Lomnicka and Powell, *Encyclopaedia of Financial Services Law.*

[21] S.I. 2001 No. 544.

[22] See the general prohibition set out in s. 19 of the Financial Services and Markets Act 2000. A breach of the general prohibition is a criminal offence (ss. 23–25).

[23] See ss. 26–28 of the Financial Services and Markets Act 2000. The same remedies were set out in s. 5 of the Financial Services Act 1986.

[24] See Chap. 5 of the *Conduct of Business Sourcebook*, sections 5.2 and 5.3.

[25] The definition of a "private person" for the purposes of s. 150 is set out in reg. 3 of the Financial Services and Markets Act 2000 (Rights of Action) Regulations 2001 (S.I. 2001 No. 2256). The definition includes (a) any individual, unless he suffers the loss in question in the course of carrying on any regulated activity and (b) any person who is not an individual, unless he suffers the loss in question in the course of carrying on business of any kind. Further, governments, local authorities and international organisations are specifically excluded.

contracts on its behalf in "the room" at Lloyd's. Only Lloyd's brokers are allowed to effect contracts of insurance with underwriters in the room.[26] For this privilege Lloyd's brokers are subject to Lloyd's regulations and disciplinary procedures.[27] All Lloyd's brokers must become members of the General Insurance Standards Council.

(a) *Duties to client*

(i) *Contractual duties*

In most cases a contract is made, either expressly or by implication, between **14–010** the insurance broker and his client. Although the client does not normally pay a fee, by placing his insurance through the broker he enables the broker to draw a commission, and this constitutes sufficient consideration. The contract may relate to the insuring of a single risk or class of risks. Alternatively, the brokers may handle all the client's insurance affairs. In any contract between an insurance broker and his client, there is implied by law[28] a term that the broker will exercise reasonable skill and care.[29]

In addition to the implied duty to exercise reasonable skill and care, other **14–011** specific duties are commonly imposed on the broker by his contract with the client.[30] The broker may, for example, agree that he will obtain a particular form of insurance for the client, not merely that he will use reasonable skill and care to do so.[31] Much of the work done by insurance brokers is of a purely routine nature and such that there is no excuse for a failure to carry out the client's instructions.[32] In such cases the client's instructions (once accepted) may be

---

[26] But see *Johns v. Kelly* [1986] 1 Lloyd's Rep. 468, which concerned an "umbrella" agreement whereby a non-Lloyd's broker gained access to the room under the name of a Lloyd's broker. The same arrangement was used in *Velos v. Harbour Insurance* [1997] 2 Lloyd's Rep.461 and *Callaghan and Hedges v. Thompson* [2000] Lloyd's Rep. I.R. 125. Lloyd's syndicates give binding authorities to brokers and others so that it is possible to effect insurance with Lloyd's outside the room: see para. 14–022, below.

[27] Previously those regulations included a Code of Practice which was issued on July 6, 1988 under the Lloyd's Broker Byelaw (No. 5 of 1988). However, this Code has been repealed by the Intermediary Amendment Byelaw (No.10 of 2000). See further chap. 16 below. For a detailed commentary on the regulatory regime established at Lloyd's see R.W. Hodgin, *Insurance Intermediaries, Law and Regulation*, chap. 5.

[28] Unless successfully excluded. See chap. 5, paras 5–01 *et seq.*

[29] The nature of the contract between insurance broker and client was considered at some length by the Australian Supreme Court in *Ogden & Co. Pty Ltd v. Reliance Fire Sprinkler Co. Pty Ltd* [1975] 1 Lloyd's Rep. 52. As in the case of any other contract for professional services, the obligation to exercise reasonable skill and care is implied in order to give business efficacy: see p. 68, col. 1. This common law principle is now embodied in s.13, Supply of Goods and Services Act 1982.

[30] The broker's general duty to exercise reasonable skill and care may be broken down into the performance of specific tasks, but unless there is a clear agreement to the contrary the broker will not be under an absolute obligation to perform those tasks, merely to bring to their performance reasonable skill and care: see *Youell v. Bland Welch & Co. Ltd (No. 2)* [1990] 2 Lloyd's Rep. 431, 458 (the "Superhulls Cover" case) (for the facts of this case see para. 14–021, below.

[31] See para. 14–043, below. Thus in *Texas Homecare Ltd v. Royal Bank of Canada Trust Co (Jersey) Ltd* [1996] C.L.C. 776 (for the facts, see para. 14–030 below) brokers had contracted to place insurance with an insurers of "at least AA status (or equivalent)".

[32] For example, if there is an issue as to whether the broker has obtained insurance which meets his client's instructions or requirements, the issue is not so much whether the broker was negligent as whether the insurers are liable on the policy: if they are not, the broker will have been negligent: see, for example, *Seavision Investment SA v. Evennett, The Tiburon* [1990] 2 Lloyd's Rep. 418, discussed at para. 14–039 below, and *Flying Colours Film Co. Ltd v. Assicurazioni Generali SpA* [1993] 2 Lloyd's Rep. 184 where the argument was solely between the insurers and the brokers, the client standing on the touchline.

regarded as imposing specific contractual obligations, for breach of which the broker would be held liable, without any consideration of the question of negligence.[33]

14–012   It is not normally the function of an insurance broker to decide what kinds of insurance the client should have.[34] However, the broker may by contract assume such a task and then it becomes his duty to investigate the client's activities, in order to identify the risks to be insured. In the Canadian case of *Fine's Flowers Ltd v. General Accident Assurance Co. of Canada*[35] it was held that the brokers had assumed such a duty:

> "But there are other cases, and in my view this is one of them, in which the client gives no such specific instructions but rather relies upon his agent to see that he is protected and, if the agent agrees to do business with him on those terms, then he cannot afterwards, when an insured loss arises, shrug off the responsibility he has assumed. If this requires him to inform himself about his client's business in order to assess the foreseeable risks and insure his client against them, then this he must do. It goes without saying that an agent who does not have the requisite skills to understand the nature of his client's business and assess the risks that should be insured against should not be offering this kind of service."[36]

14–013   **Sub-brokers.** It is not unusual for the broker directly instructed by a client to engage sub-brokers to place the insurance. For example, a non-Lloyd's broker will need to use a Lloyd's broker if a risk is to be brokered in Lloyd's. The question then arises whether a direct contractual relationship exists between the client and the sub-broker. This issue has arisen in two recent decisions. The first is the decision of Rix J. in *Prentis Donegan & Partners Ltd v. Leeds & Leeds*

---

[33] See, for example, the reasoning of Atkin J. in *Dickson & Co. v. Devitt* (1916) 86 L.J.K.B. 315, discussed at para. 14–043, below. By omitting the words "and/or steamers" from one of the insurance slips, the defendant's clerk failed to carry out the plaintiff's instructions. This constituted a specific breach of contract, which was separate from (and additional to) the failure to exercise reasonable skill and care.

[34] For example in *O'Brien v. Hughes-Gibb & Co. Ltd* [1995] L.R.L.R. 90 the owners of a racehorse asked the brokers to arrange cover for "mortality only". Rattee J. held that the brokers had not been in breach of duty for failing to advise the owners to obtain cover against theft or to obtain it for them. Nor is a broker under a duty to advise on the financial wisdom of a transaction: *Moore v. Zerfahs* [1999] Lloyd's Rep. P.N. 144, CA.

[35] (1977) 81 D.L.R. (3d) 139: plaintiff relied on defendant to obtain adequate insurance cover for his horticultural business. Defendant obtained insurance under a policy which did not cover damage to plants by freezing caused by the failure of a water pump (a foreseeable risk). Held that the defendant was liable for breach of contract and negligence. Followed in *McCann v. Western Farmers Mutual Insurance Co.* (1978) 87 D.L.R. (3d) 135 and *Kadaja v. C.A.A.* (1995) 23 O.R. (3d) 275, Ontario Court, General Division.
In Canada this decision has been treated as establishing one of the normal incidents of a broker or insurance agent: see, for example, *Fletcher v. Manitoba Public Insurance Co.* (1990) 74 D.L.R. (4th) 636 (for the facts, see n.49 para. 14–082 below) and *Miller v. Guardian Insurance Co. of Canada* (1995) 127 D.L.R. (4th) 717 (for the facts para. 14–054 n. 54, below). This is not the case in England and Wales: *O'Brien v. Hughes-Gibb & Co. Ltd* [1995] L.R.L.R. 90 (see the preceding footnote). *Fletcher v. Manitoba Public Insurance Co.* (1990) 74 D.L.R. (4th) 636 continues to be followed in Canada (see *e.g. Payer v. Peerless Plating Rack Co.* (1998) 37 O.R. (3d) 781, Ontario Court of Appeal), but evidence that the client relied upon the broker to give such advice is an essential ingredient of a claim on that basis: see *Kalkinis v. Allstate Insurance Company of Canada* (1998) 41 O.R. (3d) 528, Ontario Court of Appeal. Further, the broker's duty to inform and to advise is contingent upon and limited by the insured's description of the nature of his business, see *St. Isidore Asphalte Ltee v. Luminex Signs Ltd* (1996) 176 N.B.R.(2d) 135 (for facts see para. 14–052, n.53, below).

[36] *ibid.* at 149, *per* Wilson J.A. (with whom Blair J.A. agreed).

Co. Inc.[37] who held that usually no direct contract will be made. Only if the client, the broker and the sub-broker all intend that a direct contractual relationship should arise will it do so. Rix J. held that cases where a direct contractual relationship was found (such as *De Bussche v. Alt*[38]) were exceptional. He was concerned with a dispute as to liability for premium and so did not have to consider whether the sub-brokers owed a tortious duty of care to the ultimate client. That issue arose directly in the second case, *Pangood Ltd v. Barclay Brown & Co. Ltd*[39] There, the Court of Appeal held that whether the Lloyd's broker was to be taken as having contracted directly with the insured depended upon the terms upon which he was instructed and that instructions from a broker to obtain a quotation and then to effect insurance in accordance with its terms did not form an adequate basis for holding that the Lloyd's broker had assumed direct contractual responsibility to the insured. Nor was any general duty of care in tort owed: any assumption of responsibility to the insured was confined to obtaining a quotation and communicating it accurately to the other brokers. It did not extend to a duty to draw the attention of the other brokers to a warranty which formed part of the quotation obtained and which was usually included in the sort of policy which was being broked. The Lloyd's brokers were entitled to treat their client, the other brokers, as knowledgeable brokers. The effect of these two decisions is that it is unlikely that Lloyd's brokers will be taken to have contracted directly with an insured when they are instructed through and by other brokers and that the question whether any tortious duty of care was owed will depend upon the terms of the instructions and the nature and extent of the specific duty alleged.

(ii) *Duties independent of contract*

The question of concurrent liability in contract and tort, which has been so **14–014** much discussed in the context of other professions, has provoked little controversy in the case of insurance brokers. The English courts have accepted for some time that the insurance broker owes a duty of care to his client, and may be liable to him in negligence, whether or not there is a contract between the parties.[40] The same view is accepted in Canada,[41] but has been questioned in Australia.[42]

---

[37] [1998] 2 Lloyd's Rep. 326.
[38] (1878) 8 Ch.D. 286.
[39] [1999] Lloyd's Rep.I.R. 405.
[40] See, *e.g. British Citizens Assurance Company v. L. Woolland & Co.* (1921) 8 Ll.L.Rep. 89; *Strong & Pearl v. S. Allison & Co. Ltd* (1926) 25 Ll.L.Rep. 504 (brokers held liable to their clients both in contract and tort); *Coolee Ltd v. Wing, Heath & Co.* (1930) 47 T.L.R. 78; *Sarginson Bros. v. Keith Moulton & Co.* (1942) 73 Ll.L.Rep. 104; *Osman v. J. Ralph Moss Ltd* [1970] 1 Lloyd's Rep. 313; *London Borough of Bromley v. Ellis* [1971] 1 Lloyd's Rep. 97; *Cherry Ltd v. Allied Insurance Brokers Ltd* [1978] 1 Lloyd's Rep. 274; *Mint Security Ltd v. Blair* [1982] 1 Lloyd's Rep. 188; *Dunbar v. A. & B. Painters Ltd* [1985] 2 Lloyd's Rep. 616; *Forsikringsaktieselskapet Vesta v. Butcher* [1989] A.C. 852, C.A., particularly at 860 and 879; *Macmillan v. A.W. Knott Becker Scott Ltd* [1990] 1 Lloyd's Rep. 98; *Youell v. Bland Welch & Co. Ltd (No. 2)* [1990] 2 Lloyd's Rep. 431 (the "Superhulls Cover" case); *Punjab National Bank v. de Boinville* [1992] 1 W.L.R. 1138.
[41] See, *e.g. Myers v. Thompson & London Life Insurance Co.* (1967) 63 D.L.R. (2d) 476 (life insurance agent liable in tort to the insured's estate); *Fine's Flowers Ltd v. General Accident Assurance Co. of Canada* (1978) 81 D.L.R. (3d) 139, (para. 14–012 above); *Wilcox v. Norberg & Wiggins Insurance Agencies Ltd* [1979] 1 W.L.R. 414; *Firestone Canada Inc. v. American Home Assurance Co.* (1989) 67 O.R. (2d) 471.
[42] In *Ogden & Co. Pty Ltd v. Reliance Fire Sprinkler Co. Pty Ltd* [1975] 1 Lloyd's Rep. 52, 73–74, MacFarlan J. tentatively expressed the view that the existence of a contract between the parties

14–015   Where the appointment of an insurance broker is terminated, the client will normally wish to retain his cover whilst making alternative arrangements for insurance. Even after the termination of their appointment, the brokers owe a duty of care to their former client in any transitional arrangements which they make or in any advice which they give as to the continuation of cover. In *Cherry Ltd v. Allied Insurance Brokers Ltd*[43] the defendant brokers, shortly after the termination of their appointment, led the plaintiffs to believe that their original insurance policy against consequential loss would remain in force for another four months and that the sensible thing to do was to cancel the new policy. Two days later the original policy was cancelled but the defendants did not advise the plaintiffs of this fact. As a result the plaintiffs were uninsured against consequential loss when a fire occurred shortly afterwards. Cantley J., applying the principles stated in *Hedley Byrne & Co. Ltd v. Heller & Partners Ltd*,[44] held that the defendants owed a duty of care to the plaintiffs in the advice which they gave and were liable for the breach of that duty.

14–016   Since an insurance broker is the agent of the insured, he is the insured's fiduciary and owes fiduciary duties to the insured.[45] As a result, he may not put himself in a position in which there is a conflict between his own interests and his duty to the insured; he must act honestly, faithfully and loyally in the best interests of the insured; and he may not make a secret profit.[46]

(b) *Duties to third parties*

14–017   Today an insurance broker often performs functions beyond the straightforward effecting of policies of insurance for his client and he may assume responsibilities to others involved in the transaction. The broker's client may not be the only person interested in the policy of insurance or claim which he is handling for his client. In recent years others have claimed that insurance brokers owed them duties and the courts have upheld some of those claims. The cases can usefully be divided between those where the person asserting the duty was an insurer and those concerning other third parties.

(i) *Duties to insurers*

14–018   In a straightforward contract of insurance or reinsurance a broker will be in a contractual relationship with, and be the agent of, the insured. Generally the broker will not be in a contractual relationship with the insured, so that no

---

precluded any liability in negligence. But see *Mitor Investments Pty Ltd v. General Accident Fire and Life Assurance Corporation Ltd* [1984] W.A.R. 365.

[43] [1978] 1 Lloyd's Rep. 274.

[44] [1964] A.C. 465.

[45] See generally Chap. 2, para. 2–125 *et seq.*

[46] Para. 1.1 of the General Insurance Standards Council Code for Private Customers (2000) states: "As Members of the GISC, we promise that we will: avoid conflicts of interest or, if we cannot avoid this, explain the position fully to you." The Core Principles of the General Insurance Standards Council Commercial Code state: "In the course of their General Insurance Activities Members should: seek to avoid conflicts of interest, but where a conflict is unavoidable or does arise, manage it in such a way as to avoid prejudice to any party. Members will not unfairly put their own interests above their duty to any Commercial Customer for whom they act."

contractual duty to exercise skill and care arises.[47] Although the broker is typically paid commission by the insurer, this does not mean that the broker is undertaking to perform any obligation in favour of the insurer.[48] Similarly, the broker will not owe a tortious duty of care to the insurer without more.[49]

Duty to disclose. When seeking to procure insurance for a client the broker   **14–019**
owes an obligation to insurers to disclose all material facts. That obligation is imposed by law, and is owed by the broker personally and not just as the agent of his client.[50] However, the obligation is neither contractual nor tortious, and a breach of it does not sound in damages between the broker and the insurer: the only remedy is avoidance of the insurance contract.[51] Nevertheless, a duty of care in tort may arise, particularly if the broker makes a statement to an insurer. There are few reported examples, not least because any default by a broker while acting as the agent of the insured, whether negligent or not in the case of non-disclosure, usually enables the insurer to avoid liability under the policy of insurance so that he suffers no loss.[52]

Broker giving a signing indication. There are, however, circumstances in   **14–020**
which an insurer may rely on what a broker tells him when entering a contract

---

[47] *Pryke v. Gibbs Hartley Cooper* [1991] 1 Lloyd's Rep. 602, 615 (Waller J.), following *Empress Assurance v. Bowring* (1906) 11 Com. Cas. 107 and *Glasgow Assurance Co. v. Symondson* (1911) 16 Com. Cas. 109. However, a contract may arise if the broker makes a specific promise to the insurer: *General Accident Fire and Life Assurance Corporation v. Tanter, The "Zephyr"* [1985] 2 Lloyd's Rep. 529, 537, CA.

[48] See the reasoning of Waller J. in *Pryke v. Gibbs Hartley Cooper Ltd* [1991] 1 Lloyd's Rep. 602, 614–615.

[49] See *Tai Hing Cotton Mill Ltd v. Liu Chong Hing Bank Ltd* [1986] A.C. 80; *HIH Casualty v. Chase* [2001] 1 Lloyd's Rep.30 (Aikens J). The decisions in *Empress Assurance v. Bowring* (1906) 11 Com. Cas. 107 and *Glasgow Assurance Co. v. Symondson* (1911) 16 Com. Cas. 109 to the effect that no duty of care was owed in tort followed *Le Lievre v. Gould* [1893] 1 Q.B. 491 which was overruled by *Hedley Byrne Co. Ltd v. Heller Partners Ltd* [1964] A.C. 465. They are therefore no longer sound: see *General Accident Fire and Life Assurance Corporation v. Tanter, The "Zephyr"* [1984] 1 Lloyd's Rep. 58, 84 and *Pryke v. Gibbs Hartley Cooper Ltd* [1991] 1 Lloyd's Rep. 602, 618.

[50] s. 19 of the Marine Insurance Act 1906. The position is the same for non-marine insurance: *Pryke v. Gibbs Hartley Cooper Ltd* [1991] 1 Lloyd's Rep. 602.

[51] *Banque Keyser Ullmann SA v. Skandia (U.K.) Insurance Co. Ltd* [1990] 1 Q.B. 665, CA (the decision of the House of Lords [1991] 2 A.C. 249 did not involve this point, although Lord Templeman indicated that he agreed with the Court of Appeal on it); *Bank of Nova Scotia v. Hellenic Mutual War Risks Association (Bermuda) Ltd, The "Good Luck"* [1990] 1 Q.B. 818, CA (overturned on other grounds on appeal [1992] 1 A.C. 233); *PCW Syndicates v. PCW Reinsurers* [1996] 1 Lloyd's Rep. 241 at 255 ("[s. 19] does not, as it seems to me, impose an obligation or duty owed by the agent to the insurer, which could be enforced by an order for specific performance or give rise to a remedy in damages for breach": *per* Staughton L.J). See also *HIH Casualty v. Chase* [2001] 1 Lloyd's Rep. 30 (Aikens J.) in which it was also held that the broker did not owe a common law duty to the insurer "to speak up".

[52] In *Adams-Eden Furniture Ltd v. Kansa General International Insurance Co.* (1996) 113 Man.R.(2d) 142, (Manitoba Court of Appeal), the insurer settled insured's claim, but then sought an indemnity against the broker on the ground the broker had not disclosed all material facts. The insurer's claim for an indemnity was rejected on the basis that the broker owed no duty of care to the insurer. The claim by insurers against their agent failed for a different reason in *Hunt v. Brandie* (1998) 38 O.R. (3d) 154, (Court of Appeal for Ontario): the agent had not followed the correct procedures, but had he done so, insurers would have been obliged to accept the relevant business. They had therefore suffered no loss.

of insurance but will be unable to avoid that contract by reason of the inaccuracy of what he was told. One such situation is where a broker gives a "signing indication" to the underwriters who write lines on his slip. A "signing indication" is a statement by the broker of the extent to which he intends that the slip will be oversubscribed. If, for example, the slip is oversubscribed by 100 per cent, each underwriter only carries half the risk which is shown on the line that he has signed. In this example the slip is "signed down" by 50 per cent. If the broker gives a signing indication of, say, 50 per cent or 30 per cent which is not fulfilled, the underwriters may have legitimate cause for complaint against the broker but they have no conceivable grounds for avoiding the contract of insurance. Each underwriter may then carry a risk which is substantially greater than he expected or intended when writing his line on the slip. In *General Accident Fire and Life Assurance Corporation v. Tanter, The "Zephyr"*[53] the question arose whether a broker who gave a signing indication to an underwriter owed a duty in tort to that underwriter to take reasonable steps to see that the signing down indication was achieved. Hobhouse J. held that the broker did owe such a duty. Although this issue was not directly raised on appeal, the Court of Appeal expressed considerable misgivings as to this part of the decision. Mustill L.J. (with whom Stephen Brown and Oliver L.JJ. agreed) said that a signing indication may in some circumstances give rise to a collateral contract between the broker and the underwriter. But in the absence of such a contract, Mustill L.J. did not see how the broker could owe a tortious duty to achieve the signing down which he had indicated: that entailed a positive obligation to act which would usually only arise in contract.[54] However, Mustill L.J. did say that, had the signing indication been a negligent misrepresentation of existing fact, liability in tort could not have been denied, thus recognising that liability on the basis of *Hedley Byrne & Co. Ltd v. Heller and Partners Ltd*[55] could arise between broker and insurer. The signing indication given was a representation of existing fact, namely that the broker honestly believed it to be accurate on reasonable grounds. In that sense it was accurate so that there was no negligent misstatement. The insurers' complaint was that it had not been acted on subsequently.

14-021 **Misstatement regarding reinsurance.** Another situation in which an insurer may rely upon a statement by a broker when deciding to enter a contract of insurance is where the broker has provisionally arranged reinsurance and makes a representation to the insurer as to the existence or terms of that reinsurance. If it transpires that the reinsurance cover is not as represented the insurer will not be entitled to avoid liability under the policy of insurance. In *Youell v. Bland Welch & Co. Ltd (No. 2)*[56] (the "Superhulls Cover" case), cover was sought

---

[53] [1984] 1 Lloyd's Rep. 58 (Hobhouse J.); [1985] 2 Lloyd's Rep. 529, CA.
[54] It is not clear, however, whether this aspect of Mustill L.J.'s reasoning can survive the recognition by the House of Lords of liability for economic loss caused by negligent omissions: see *Henderson v. Merrett Syndicates Ltd* [1995] 2 A.C. 145 at 180F-G and 181E-F and *White v. Jones* [1995] 2 A.C. 207 at 268H–269A. It is possible that a broker might now be under a tortious duty to exercise reasonable skill, care and diligence in seeking to obtain subscriptions in accordance with the signing indication he has given. He would not, however, warrant that he would actually obtain subscriptions.
[55] [1964] A.C. 465.
[56] [1990] 2 Lloyd's Rep. 431, Phillips J.

against builders' risks during the construction of three LNG ships with a value of U.S.$100 million each. Cover of that size necessarily involved reinsurance. The brokers therefore arranged reinsurance cover before approaching potential insurers. The reinsurance arranged included a clause under which cover of any particular vessel terminated 48 months after the commencement of its construction. There was no such clause in the contract of insurance. When seeking to persuade the insurers to subscribe to the insurance contract the brokers informed them that there was reinsurance available, without mentioning the 48-month clause, so that the reasonable inference was that the reinsurance cover was on the same terms as the insurance policy. The insurers were thereby induced to write larger lines on the insurance policy than they would otherwise have done. Phillips J. found the brokers negligent on various grounds,[57] including a negligent failure to describe the reinsurance properly. That breach occurred before insurers had instructed the brokers to obtain reinsurance for them (and so before any contractual relationship arose), but Phillips J. held that a broker who seeks to persuade an insurer to write a line of original insurance by informing him that specific reinsurance cover is available is in a relationship which gives rise to a duty of care in tort, independent of any contractual relationship.[58]

Coverholders. Contracts of insurance are not always effected between the **14–022** insurer in person and a broker acting for the insured. Insurers give authority to insurance brokers and others to issue insurance policies on their behalf under binding authorities. These will give the holder of the binding authority (often called the coverholder) the authority to make contracts of insurance on the insurer's behalf, subject to restrictions as to class of risk, size of risk and, in some cases, the rate of premium to be paid. For present purposes binding authorities can be divided into two classes: those where the broker is the coverholder and those where the broker acts as an intermediary between the coverholder and the insurer.

Where the broker is the coverholder there is no doubt that he owes a duty to **14–023** the insurer to exercise reasonable skill and care. He is in a direct contractual relationship with the insurer and will also owe a concurrent duty of care.[59] Thus in *Woolcott v. Excess Insurance Co. Ltd*[60] brokers effected household insurance for the plaintiff with the defendant insurers under a binding authority granted to them by the insurers. The brokers knew that the plaintiff had a serious criminal record, but failed to pass this information on to the insurers. The plaintiff's house was subsequently destroyed by fire. The insurers denied liability, on the grounds of non-disclosure of the plaintiff's criminal record. This defence failed because the insurers were fixed with the brokers' knowledge. In third-party proceedings,

---

[57] See paras 14–050, 14–077 and 14–079, below.
[58] When seeking to obtain reinsurance of a risk which he is trying to insure for his immediate client, a broker acts as agent of the potential insurers and not of his immediate client, so that any knowledge he acquires in seeking reinsurance is that of the potential insurers and not of his immediate client: *Société Anonyme d'Intermediaries Luxembourgeois v. Farex* [1995] L.R.L.R. 116. It would appear to follow that the broker owed a duty of care in tort to the potential insurers when seeking reinsurance, but not to his immediate client, the intended insured.
[59] See para. 14–014, above.
[60] [1978] 1 Lloyd's Rep. 633, Caulfield J.; [1979] 1 Lloyd's Rep. 231, CA; [1979] 2 Lloyd's Rep. 210, Cantley J. on retrial.

however, the insurers recovered an indemnity against the brokers on the grounds of the brokers' failure to pass on the information.[61]

14–024   Where the broker is not himself the coverholder, but acts as an intermediary, he is in a contractual relationship with his coverholder who is his client. There is no contract between the broker and the insurer, and therefore the broker owes the insurer no contractual duty to exercise skill and care when acting as intermediary.[62] Nor does a broker owe the insurer a duty of care in tort, without more.[63] However, a broker may come to owe a duty of care to an insurer when acting as an intermediary. In *Pryke v. Gibbs Hartley Cooper Ltd*[64] a coverholder in the United States had been authorised to write fire insurance by a London insurance company and a group of Lloyd's syndicates, the defendant brokers acting as intermediaries. The insurance company and the leading underwriter at Lloyd's learnt that the coverholder might have issued a financial guarantee policy. This would not only have been beyond the coverholder's own authority but was a type of insurance which the Lloyd's underwriters were forbidden to write and which the company did not write as a matter of policy. Upon being contacted by the insurance company and by the leading underwriter the brokers raised the matter with the coverholder and passed his explanation on to the company and leading underwriter. The brokers were about to visit the coverholder and said that they would look into the matter when in the United States. They were held to owe a duty of care in tort to the company, the leading underwriter and to the other syndicates (who knew nothing of the matter at the time) when investigating the matter and reporting back. The duty of care arose because the brokers chose to do more than act as the coverholder's messenger and undertook personal responsibility towards the insurers.

(ii) *Duties to other third parties*

14–025   The broker's client may not be the only person interested in the policy of insurance which the broker is instructed to effect. There may be other persons

---

[61] Other cases where insurers brought claims against coverholders for breach of a duty to exercise reasonable skill and care are: *Gore Mutual Insurance Company v. Barton* (1979) 12 B.C.L.R. 261: failure to advise insurer of material change in risk insured, which would have caused the insurer to refuse to continue insurance. Agent liable; *Canadian General Insurance Company v. Lacey, Stoyles Insurance Services Ltd* (1985) 56 Nfld. & P.E.I.R. 125, Newfoundland District Court: coverholder negligently exceeded its authority by accepting premium under a policy which had been cancelled and negligently reported a subsequent loss without informing the insurer of the cancellation; *Gibraltar General Insurance Company v. L.E. Yingst Co. Ltd* (1990) 89 Sask. R. 93; Saskatchewan Court of Queen's Bench: coverholder failed to include a clause incorporating a statutory one-year limitation period for claims under a policy; *Bos v. Brauer* (1992) 3 Alta.L.R. (3d) 318, where a broker coverholder was found to be in breach of duty in failing to provide accurate information to insurers. However, since there was no evidence that insurers would have acted differently had they received accurate information, they recovered only nominal damages. (The decision of the British Columbia Court of Appeal in *Zanatta Installations Ltd v. Elite Insurance Co.* (1994) 92 B.C.L.R.(2d) 374 is to the same effect.)

[62] *Pryke v. Gibbs Hartley Cooper Ltd* [1991] 1 Lloyd's Rep. 602, 615 following *Empress Assurance Corporation Ltd v. C.T. Bowring & Co. Ltd* (1905) 11 Com.Cas. 107 and *Glasgow Assurance Corporation Ltd v. William Symondson & Co.* (1911) 104 L.T. 254.

[63] *ibid.* The *Empress* and *Glasgow* decisions to the effect that no duty of care was owed in tort followed *Le Lievre v. Gould* [1893] 1 Q.B. 491 which was overruled by *Hedley Byrne Co. Ltd v. Heller Partners Ltd* [1964] A.C. 465. They are therefore no longer sound: see *General Accident Fire and Life Assurance Corporation v. Tanter, The "Zephyr"* [1984] 1 Lloyd's Rep. 58, 84 and *Pryke v. Gibbs Hartley Cooper Ltd* [1991] 1 Lloyd's Rep. 602, 618. See also *Adams-Eden Furniture Ltd v. Kansa General International Insurance Co.* (1996) 113 Man.R.(2d) 142, Manitoba Court of Appeal.

[64] [1991] 1 Lloyd's Rep. 602, Waller J.

who are to directly benefit from the insurance (either by being insured themselves or otherwise) and there may be third parties whose claims against the broker's client will be covered by the proposed insurance. A duty may exist in the former case, but is less likely to do so in the latter. In each case the issue of whether or not the broker owed the third party a duty of care will be resolved in accordance with the usual principles used to determine when a party owes another a duty of care in respect of economic loss.[65]

Potential beneficiaries. One of simplest examples of third parties deriving   **14–026** benefit from another's insurance is the beneficiaries of pension and life insurance policies. In *Gorham v. British Telecommunications*[66] the Court of Appeal considered whether an insurance company which owed a duty of care to one its customers when giving advice in relation to his pension and life insurance cover also owed a duty of care to potential beneficiaries other than himself. The court held that in such a case the position of the customer was analogous to that of a client who seeks his solicitor's advice regarding a will. Applying *White v. Jones*[67] the Court held that a duty was owed to the potential beneficiaries. Pill L.J. described the duty in the following way: "The duty is not one to ensure that the dependants are properly provided for. It is, in the present context, a duty to the dependants not to give negligent advice to the customer which adversely affects their interests as he intends them to be."

Third parties with a known financial interest. A duty of care may also be   **14–027** owed to a third party if, to the broker's knowledge, that third party has a direct financial interest in the insurance being arranged and is actively involved in the arranging of the insurance. In *Punjab National Bank v. De Boinville*[68] the third party was a bank which was providing finance to one of its customers. The bank required its customer to effect insurance to protect the bank's position. The policies were taken out in the name of the customer, which assigned its interest in the policies to the bank soon after they were effected. The Court of Appeal upheld the judge's finding that at times when the bank was not in a contractual relationship with the brokers, it was owed a tortious duty of care by the brokers. Following the approach of Brennan J. in *Sutherland Shire Council v. Heyman*[69] Staughton L.J. (with whom Mann and Dillon L.JJ. agreed) held that it was a justifiable increment to hold that an insurance broker owed a duty of care to the specific person who he knew was to become an assignee of the policy, at all events if, to the broker's knowledge, that person actively participated in giving instructions for the insurance, as was the case.

It is not enough that the third party has a financial interest in the transaction   **14–028** which is the subject of the insurance policy, or is a major creditor of the

---

[65] See generally *Clerk & Lindsell on Torts* (18th ed.), chap. 7.
[66] [2000] 1 W.L.R. 2129.
[67] [1995] 2 A.C. 207. See Chap. 2, para. 2–048, and Chap. 10, paras 10–048 *et seq.*
[68] [1992] 1 W.L.R. 1138.
[69] (1985) 60 A.L.R. 1, 43–44: see Chap. 2, para. 2–38.

insured.[70] In *Punjab National Bank v. De Boinville*[71] Staughton L.J. doubted whether the fact that the broker knew that the bank had some financial interest in the underlying transaction and a right of recourse against the insured, who was the broker's client, would give rise to a duty of care. A more direct interest in the insurance policy is needed. This is illustrated by the decision of Evans J. in *Macmillan v. A.W. Knott Becker Scott Ltd*[72] There, the third parties were former clients of an insolvent professional (a Lloyd's broker). They brought proceedings against the brokers who had negligently failed to ensure that the professional's errors and omissions insurance was effective, with the result that the professional was not insured in relation to their claims against him. The preliminary issue before Evans J. was whether the brokers effecting the errors and omissions insurance owed a duty of care to their professional client's clients and others to whom that professional might be liable for negligence. Evans J. held that loss was foreseeable and that there was sufficient proximity, but that it would not be just and reasonable to impose a duty which would leapfrog the contractual chain. Following the speech of Lord Griffiths in *Smith v. Eric S. Bush*[73] he concluded that brokers could not be deemed to have assumed responsibility towards the plaintiffs.

14–029   The need for the third party to have a direct interest (whether present or future) in the contract of insurance is also shown by the decision of the Court of Appeal in *Verderame v. Commercial Union Assurance Co. Ltd*[74] There the sole directors and shareholders of a limited company were in effect carrying on business through the medium of the company in quasi-partnership. They brought a claim in tort against the company's insurance brokers on the basis that the company had suffered an uninsured loss by reason of the brokers' negligence and that the company had been unable to continue trading as a result, causing loss to them as individuals. The claim was struck out on several grounds, one of them being that the directors were seeking to go behind the corporate status of the company, the brokers' actual client.[75] Their interest was not in the insurance policy, but in the intended insured.

14–030   Even if the third party does have a direct interest in the contract of insurance, which is immediate and known by the broker, this will not necessarily outweigh other factors so as to give rise to a duty of care. Thus in *Texas Homecare Ltd v. Royal Bank of Canada Trust Co. (Jersey) Ltd*[76] the third party was a retailer which contracted with Y that Y would obtain insurance for a "cash-back scheme" with insurers who were "at least AA status or equivalent". The third party was to be the insured. Y then retained the brokers to effect that insurance.

---

[70] In *South Pacific Manufacturing Co. Ltd v. New Zealand Security Consultants & Investigations Ltd* [1992] 2 N.Z.L.R. 282 the New Zealand Court of Appeal considered a claim by the creditors of an insured against a private investigator employed by the insurer to inquire and report on the cause of a fire on the insured's property. The claim was struck out on the basis that even if the investigator owed a duty of care to the insured, such a duty would not extend to persons financially interested in the insured.

[71] [1992] 1 W.L.R. 1138.

[72] [1990] 1 Lloyd's Rep. 98.

[73] [1990] 1 A.C. 831, 862D-E; Chap. 2, para. 2–30 *et seq.*

[74] [1992] B.C.L.C. 793.

[75] Other grounds were that the loss claimed was irrecoverable in law (as to which see paras. 14–121 and 14–123 below), that it would allow directors and shareholders to circumvent the rules governing the winding up of companies, exposing brokers to the risk of having to make double restitution and that the claim advanced was novel and would not be a "justifiable increment" to any existing category.

[76] [1996] C.L.C. 776.

They failed to do so and the insurers with whom they placed the risk became insolvent. The third party claimed in tort directly against the brokers. That claim failed,[77] essentially because it would have cut across the contractual chain by which the parties had chosen to regulate their relationships and which was the origin of the obligation to obtain insurance with an insurer of the required class.[78]

Misstatements to third parties. If a broker choses to give advice or informa-   **14–031**
tion to a third party, without any effective disclaimer of responsibility, in circumstances in which a reasonable person would know that he was being trusted or that his skill or judgment was being relied upon, then he may be found to owe a duty of care to that third person.[79] If the broker fails to exercise reasonable skill and care then he will be found to have breached his duty.[80] For example, in *Baron v. Hartford Fire Insurance Co.*[81] the son of the deceased insured contacted the deceased's broker to ascertain whether his father had any life insurance. The broker incorrectly led the son to believe that no cover was in place and in so doing was found to have owed a duty of care to the son, which he breached in failing to give an accurate answer.

(c) *The Standard of Skill and Care*

Whether he is sued in contract or tort, the insurance broker is required to   **14–032**
exercise reasonable skill and care[82]: in other words that degree of skill and care which is exercised by reasonably competent insurance brokers.[83] In *Chapman v. Walton*,[84] Lord Tindal C.J. described the broker's duty in these terms:

"For the defendant did not contract that he would bring to the performance of his duty, on this occasion, an extraordinary degree of skill, but only a reasonable and ordinary proportion of it; and it appears to us, that it is not only an unobjectionable mode, but the most satisfactory mode of determining this question, to show by evidence whether a majority of skilful and experienced brokers would have come to the same conclusion as the defendant. If nine brokers of experience out of ten would have done the same as the defendant under the same circumstances, or even if as many out of a given number would have been of his opinion as against it, he who only stipulates to bring a

---

[77] The third party's claim against Y in contract succeeded, as did Y's claim against the brokers.
[78] See generally Chap. 2, paras 2–094 *et seq.*
[79] *Hedley Byrne & Co. Ltd v. Heller & Partners Ltd* [1964] A.C. 465. For a discussion of the general principles see Chap. 2, para. 2–024.
[80] *Cherry Ltd v. Allied Insurance Brokers Ltd* [1978] 1 Lloyd's Rep. 274 (for the facts, see para. 14–015 above). See also *London Borough of Bromley v. Ellis* [1971] 1 Lloyd's Rep. 97 (brokers acting as agents for the insurer owed insured a duty of care when they had undertaken to arrange the transfer of insurance to him).
[81] [1998] 1 H.K.L.R.D. 411, Court of First Instance, Seagroatt J. The son's claim ultimately failed because there had been a material misrepresentation to the insurers which entitled them to avoid the policy and the court was not satisfied that the deceased had not colluded in the making of that misrepresentation.
[82] *e.g. Hurrell v. Bullard* (1863) 3 F. & F. 445.
[83] In *Harvest Trucking Co. Ltd v. Davis* [1991] 2 Lloyd's Rep. 638 Judge Diamond Q.C. (sitting as a High Court judge) said: "The liability of an insurance agent to his employer for negligence is comparable to that of any agent. He is bound to exercise reasonable care in the duties which he has undertaken. In no case does the law require an extraordinary degree of skill on the part of the agent but only such a reasonable and ordinary degree as a person of average capacity and ordinary ability in his situation and profession might fairly be expected to exert": *ibid.* at 643.
[84] (1833) 10 Bing. 57. For the facts, see para. 14–057, below.

reasonable degree of skill to the performance of his duty, would be entitled to a verdict in his favour."[85]

14–033   **Specialist markets.** Where a broker undertakes work in a specialist market, he will be required to exercise reasonable skill and care in the context of that market. In *Sharp and Roarer Investments Ltd v. Sphere Drake Insurance plc, The Moonacre*[86] A.D. Colman Q.C., sitting as a deputy judge of the High Court, had to consider the standard of skill required of an insurance broker who undertook to obtain insurance for a yacht when considering whether a broker had been negligent in relation to a particular clause of a marine insurance policy. He referred to *Duchess of Argyll v. Beuselinck*[87] and said:

> "In deciding whether their standard of skill was sufficiently high, it is appropriate . . .
> to require that a non-specialist marine broker should bear no greater skill than that
> which would be expected from a reasonably skilled non-specialist broker. This is not
> the same thing as saying that the standard is that of a marine broker substantially
> inexperienced in the insurance of large yachts. It is rather the standard of a broker who
> has such general knowledge of the yacht insurance market and the cover available in it
> as to be able to advise his client on all matters on which a lay client would in the
> ordinary course of events predictably need advice, in particular in the course of the
> selection of cover and the completion of the proposal."[88]

14–034   **Expert evidence.** Evidence as to the general practice of insurance brokers carries great weight in the determination whether, in any given case, the defendant brokers exercised reasonable skill and care.[89] However, as has been already pointed out,[90] the court cannot abdicate to expert witnesses the responsibility for deciding what does and what does not amount to reasonable skill and care. In exceptional cases the court may consider that the ordinary practice of insurance brokers (as described by expert witnesses) is unduly lax and that the "reasonably competent broker" should do better.[91] Conversely, the ordinary practice of insurance brokers might on occasions be regarded as going beyond their strict legal duty.[92] This was the view taken by McNair J. in *United Mills Agencies Ltd v. R.E. Harvey Bray & Co.*[93]

---

[85] *ibid*. at 63–64. See also *O'Connor v. B.D.B. Kirby & Co.* [1972] 1 Q.B. 90, 101C, quoted at para. 14–072, below.

[86] [1992] 2 Lloyd's Rep. 501; for the facts see para. 14–052, below.

[87] [1972] 2 Lloyd's Rep. 172.

[88] [1992] 2 Lloyd's Rep. 501 at 523, col. 2.

[89] See, *e.g. Fanhaven Pty Ltd v. Bain Dawes Northern Pty Ltd* [1982] 2 N.S.W.L.R. 57, 63.

[90] See chap. 6.

[91] In *Lewis v. Tressider Andrews Associates Pty Ltd* [1987] 2 Qd.R. 533 a broker had received financial details of a new insurance company. There was evidence that the average broker would not have been able to interpret the material and would not have taken any steps to satisfy himself of the solvency and responsibility of the insurer. Connolly J. held that a broker was under a duty to exercise greater skill and care.

[92] Or that the ordinary practice of insurance brokers may not be evidence of or give rise to a duty: *Pryke v. Gibbs Hartley Cooper Ltd* [1991] 1 Lloyd's Rep. 602 (for the facts of which, see para. 14–024, above) where evidence of practice in the Lloyd's market was held not to establish any legal duty.

[93] [1951] 2 Lloyd's Rep. 631; for the facts see para. 14–080, below. When considering whether the defendant brokers were negligent in failing to send the plaintiffs promptly a copy of the cover note, McNair J. disposed of the plaintiffs' contentions in these terms: "It is said that there was, accordingly, failure on the part of the defendants to cause the plaintiffs to be notified promptly of the terms of the cover. On that point evidence was called from an independent broker—and I think, substantially agreed to by Mr Davey—that it is the practice of, at any rate, these two offices of insurance brokers (and I have no doubt the practice of brokers as a whole) that when cover has been placed the clients

Legal knowledge. Since the insurance broker's work revolves around the 14–035
formation of a special kind of legal relationship, some legal knowledge is
essential. Familiarity with the general principles of insurance law and agency
forms part of the "reasonable skill" which the broker is required to possess.[94] If
a legal problem arises which is beyond the broker's competence, he should
advise the client to consult a solicitor.[95] If the broker chooses to give legal advice
himself, then he does so at his peril.[96]

2. LIABILITY FOR BREACH OF DUTY

Broadly speaking, breach of duty by an insurance broker to his client may take 14–036
one of four forms[97]: (i) breach of a specific contractual duty[98]; (ii) breach of the
implied contractual duty to exercise reasonable skill and care[99]; (iii) breach of the
duty of care owed by the insurance broker to his client independently of his
contractual duties[1]; (iv) breach of certain requirements under the Financial
Services and Markets Act 2000 or applicable rules and regulations made thereunder.[2] Negligence is not an essential element of liability under the first head,[3] nor
under the fourth. The second and third heads involve breaches of the same
standard of skill and care, and are jointly referred to in this chapter as "negligence".

Instances in which it has been held that insurance brokers are, or may be, liable 14–037
for breach of duty are discussed below under nine headings. This catalogue is

---

are notified as soon as possible. That seems to me to be good business and prudent office management, but on the evidence I am completely unable to hold that it is part of the duty owed by the broker
to the client so to notify him, in the sense that a failure so to notify him would involve him in legal
liability. No case was spoken to in which any broker had ever been held liable or had ever paid any
client money in respect of such a failure. It seems to me to put quite an intolerable and unreasonable
burden on a broker to say that as a matter of law, apart from prudent practice, he is bound to forward
the cover note as soon as possible. It is no doubt prudent to do so, both to allay the client's anxiety
and possibly to enable the client to check the terms of insurance. That is a very different thing from
saying it is part of his duty." *Ibid.* at 643.
[94] See, *e.g. Park v. Hammond* (1816) 6 Taunt. 495 (insurance broker held negligent for ignorance of
an established rule of law (that an insurance to commence from the loading of goods at a certain point
would not attach on goods previously laden)); *Fanhaven Pty Ltd v. Bain Dawes Northern Pty Ltd*
[1982] 2 N.S.W.L.R. 57, 65. Patent agents are in a similar position: *Lee v. Walker* (1872) L.R. 7 C.P.
121, where the defendant was held negligent as a result of his ignorance of a recent Chancery decision
affecting the procedure for obtaining letters patent.
[95] In *Lewis v. Tressider Andrews Associates Pty Ltd* [1987] 2 Qd.R. 533 a broker had received
financial details of a new insurance company. Connolly J. held that, if the broker could not himself
interpret the documents, he should have gone to his accountant or auditor for advice.
[96] *Sarginson Bros. v. Keith Moulton & Co.* (1942) 73 Ll.L.Rep. 104. See paras. 14–081 to 14–085,
below. See also *Bates v. Barrow Ltd* [1995] 1 Lloyd's Rep. 680 at 690 (for the facts, see n.65
below).
[97] In Canada, negligence by insurance brokers and agents is often held to constitute a breach of
fiduciary duty as well (see, for example, *Fine's Flowers Ltd v. General Accident Assurance Co.*
(1977) 81 D.L.R. (3d) 139). This does not appear to add anything to the claim and cannot survive the
analyses of Lord Browne-Wilkinson in *Henderson v. Merrett Syndicates Ltd* [1995] 2 A.C. 145,
204–206 and of Millett L.J. in *Bristol & West Building Society v. Mothew* [1998] Ch. 1.
[98] See para. 14–010, above.
[99] See para. 14–010, above.
[1] See paras. 14–014 to 14–016, above.
[2] See para. 14–006 to 14–008, above. See also chap. 13.
[3] Although breach of a specific contractual duty is commonly accompanied by, or due to, negligence,
as in *Dickson & Co. v. Devitt* (1916) 86 L.J.K.B. 315.

not, of course, exhaustive.[4] The cases serve to illustrate how the principles stated above operate in practice and, in particular, what the courts consider to be the standard of skill and care which may reasonably be expected of insurance brokers.

(a) *Failing to effect insurance*

14–038   A total failure to effect insurance is the clearest form of breach of duty which the broker could commit.[5] It would only be justified if the broker had done all that was reasonably possible but the required insurance was unobtainable.[6] See, for example, *Smith v. Cologan*[7]: "if a person to whom such orders are sent do what is usual to get the insurance made, that is sufficient, because he is no insurer, and is not obliged to get insurance at all events". Even in those circumstances the broker will still be liable unless he promptly reports the position to his client.[8] Otherwise "he deprives the other of any opportunity of applying elsewhere to procure the insurance".[9] In *Eagle Star Insurance Company Ltd v. National Westminster Finance Australia Ltd*[10] the Privy Council defined the duty of the defendant insurance brokers in these terms:

> "Their duty was to use all reasonable care and skill in seeking to obtain the cover in London which had been sought by their principals, and if for any reason, notwithstanding that they had used that reasonable care and skill, their efforts failed, it was then their further duty to report their failure and, if necessary, to seek further instructions. But they did not undertake that cover would be procured."

14–039   Where a broker purports to effect insurance on behalf of a client, but the insurers successfully deny that they were effectively bound, the broker will

---

[4] Indeed there are other obvious areas in which insurance brokers might incur liability; for example, negligence in the handling of claims (see *Bousfield v. Creswell* (1810) 2 Camp. 545) or fraud in the presentation of claims to underwriters (see *The Litsion Pride* [1985] 1 Lloyd's Rep. 437, in which the broker's duty was discussed in the context of litigation between insured and insurer). There are other cases where brokers have been found negligent which are less obvious: for example: (1) *Johns v. Kelly* [1986] 1 Lloyd's Rep. 468 concerned the negligent supervision by a Lloyd's broker of a non-Lloyd's broker with whom it had an "umbrella arrangement" whereby the non-Lloyd's broker gained access to Lloyd's under the Lloyd's broker's name; (2) *Johnston v. Leslie & Goodwin Financial Services Ltd* [1995] L.R.L.R. 472 concerned the liability of Lloyd's brokers for failing to maintain records of reinsurance obtained for a Lloyd's syndicate so as to enable it to make claims (it is an established custom in the Lloyd's market for brokers to retain such information for underwriters). This was part of a general duty to collect claims when called upon to do so.
[5] *e.g. Transport & Trading Co. Ltd v. Olivier & Co. Ltd* (1925) 21 Ll.L.R. 379. *Cosyns v. Smith* (1983) 146 D.L.R. (3d) 622, Ontario CA: insurance agents instructed by plaintiff to obtain insurance against wind damage to his greenhouses, but failed to do so.
[6] *Avonale Blouse Company Ltd v. Williamson & Geo. Town* (1948) 81 Ll.L.R. 492, where the broker was held to have discharged his duty (for the facts, see para. 14–042, below). In *Markal Investments Ltd v. Morley Shafron Agencies Ltd* (1990) 67 D.L.R. (4th) 422, British Columbia CA the broker was asked to obtain cover against the collapse under the weight of snow of a tent in which the client operated a flea market. The broker approached the insurer among those with whom he regularly dealt who was most likely to accept the risk. The insurer declined and the broker made no further enquiries. He was held liable at first instance (44 D.L.R. (4th) 745), but on appeal the action was dismissed because there was no evidence that any other insurer would have accepted the risk.
[7] (1788) 2 T.R. 188n.
[8] *Smith v. Lascelles* (1788) 2 T.R. 187; *Callander v. Oelrichs* (1838) 5 Bing.N.C. 58. See para. 14–078, below.
[9] *Smith v. Lascelles* (1788) 2 T.R. 187.
[10] (1985) 58 A.L.R. 165, 174 (appeal from Supreme Court of Western Australia).

almost invariably be found to have been negligent. Thus in *Seavision Investment SA v. Evennett, The Tiburon*[11] brokers had purported to obtain war risks cover for a ship owned by a Panamanian company by declaring it under an open cover for ships in German ownership. A loss was suffered and one underwriter denied liability on the basis that the owner was not German so that the risk did not fall within the terms of the open cover. The owner brought proceedings against both the underwriter and the brokers. The brokers conceded at trial that if the underwriter was not liable, they were, a concession which Steyn J. said "anticipated what would have been an inevitable conclusion". He went on to find that the underwriter was not liable and gave judgment against the brokers.[12] The brokers in *Mander v. Commercial Union Assurance Company plc*[13] were held liable on similar grounds: they had purported to reinsure their client's liabilities by making a declaration under an open cover. However, at trial Rix J. held that the declarations were not effective to create a binding contract. In the circumstances the brokers could not and did not dispute that they were in breach of duty.

In exceptional circumstances the broker may bind himself to effect or renew **14-040** insurance in any event. In those circumstances any non-performance by the broker will render him liable for breach of contract,[14] although not necessarily for negligence. It is, however, unusual for a broker to undertake an absolute obligation to procure insurance, since he is generally in no position to compel insurers to accept the risk.[15]

If an insurance broker is retained to effect insurance but does not in fact do so, **14-041** he may nevertheless in the course of his enquiries gain information material to the risk. In these circumstances the broker, possibly, owes no duty to disclose that information to the client for onward transmission to new brokers or insurers.[16]

Amendment or renewal of existing cover. The same principles as those **14-042** stated in the preceding paragraphs apply where the broker is instructed to effect an enlargement, variation or renewal of existing insurance. Thus in *Avonale Blouse Company Ltd v. Williamson & Geo. Town*[17] brokers were instructed to transfer cover from one property to another. They had transferred cover against

---

[11] [1990] 2 Lloyd's Rep. 418.

[12] See also *Block Brothers Industries Ltd v. Westland Insurance Centre Ltd* (1993) 84 B.C.L.R.(2d) 319, where brokers had purported to issue a policy on behalf of an insurer who had not agreed to provide cover on that basis. The brokers were held liable when the insurer successfully resisted a claim by the client on the purported policy.

[13] [1998] Lloyd's Rep. I.R. 93.

[14] *Turpin v. Bilton* (1843) 5 Man. & G. 455; *Hood v. West End Motor Car Packing Co.* [1917] 2 K.B. 38 (in particular at 47); *United Marketing Co. v. Hasham Kara* [1963] 1 Lloyd's Rep. 331. See also the judgment of Hobhouse J. in *General Accident Fire and Life Assurance Corporation v. Tanter, The "Zephyr"* [1984] 1 Lloyd's Rep. 58, at 80, col. 2 to 81, col. 1 (for the facts of the case see para. 14–020, above).

[15] Thus in *T.L. Creda Ltd v. Hay Fielding Ltd*, unreported, October 30, 1984, UB 1568, CA, there was a written agreement between the plaintiffs and the defendant brokers under clause 1 of which the defendants agreed "to obtain a policy document with Lloyd's in accordance with the attached draft policy". The Court of Appeal held that on its true construction this agreement did not impose an absolute obligation on the brokers, but merely an obligation to exercise due diligence and skill in obtaining such a policy, if it was possible.

[16] *Blackburn Low & Co. v. Vigors* (1887) 12 App.Cas. 531, 537, in which it was held that the client was not fixed with knowledge of information gained by his previous brokers.

[17] (1948) 81 Ll.L.R. 492.

fire, but not against burglary, when a loss occurred. They were held not to have been negligent, because it was not possible to transfer cover against burglary until a survey of the new premises had been carried out.[18]

(b) *Effecting insurance, but not on the terms specified by the client*

14–043 Where the client defines the risk against which he wishes to be insured, the broker is expected to carry out these instructions (if it is possible to do so) precisely.[19] In *Dickson & Co. v. Devitt*[20] the plaintiffs instructed the defendant broker to arrange for the insurance of certain machinery to be shipped on the "*Suwa Maru* and/or steamers" against marine and war risks. As a result of an error by the defendant's clerk the words "and/or steamers" were omitted from the slip relating to war risks. The machinery was shipped on a steamer other than the *Suwa Maru* and lost as a result of enemy action. Atkin J. held that the defendant was liable on two grounds: first, failure to carry out the plaintiffs' specific instructions and secondly, (through his clerk) failure to exercise reasonable skill and care. Similarly, it is a breach of duty if a broker, who is instructed to insure goods for their replacement value, only obtains insurance on the basis of actual value.[21] A broker, who is instructed by various companies in the same group to arrange insurance for their respective properties will be in breach of duty to the company which owns a particular property if, despite being informed that that company owns the property, he obtains insurance for that property in the name of a different company.[22] In the context of reinsurance, the broker must usually[23] ensure that the risk reinsured is defined in identical terms to the risk

---

[18] See also *MacDonald v. Charlie Cook Insurance Inc.* (1985) 55 Nfld. & P.E.I.R. 248; 162 A.P.R. 248, Prince Edward Island Supreme Court (brokers who undertook to find an alternative insurer when the existing insurer declined to renew held liable when they failed to do so) and *Galambos v. Kindrachuk Enterprises Ltd* (1988) 63 Sask.R. 229, Saskatchewan Court of Queen's Bench (broker who failed to procure an extension of cover for two new granaries was held to have been negligent).

[19] See, *e.g. Barron v. Fitzgerald* (1840) 6 Bing.N.C. 201: a broker who effected life insurance, but not exactly on the terms specified, was held to be in breach of duty and not entitled to recover the premiums which he had paid. See also *Zulu Airwear Inc. v. Khanna Holdings Ltd* (1998) 55 B.C.L.R. (3d) 136, British Columbia Supreme Court, in which the broker was found liable in both contract and tort for failing to carry out his landlord client's instructions to obtain comprehensive general liability ("CGL") coverage. Instead the broker obtained owners', landlords' and tenants' coverage, which contained an exclusion not found in the CGL policy; and see *Newsome v. Bennie S. Cohen & Son (Qld) Pty Ltd* [1941] Q.S.R. 270.

[20] (1916) 86 L.J.K.B. 315.

[21] *Coyle v. Ray F. Fredericks Insurance Ltd* (1984) 64 N.S.R. (2d) and 143 A.P.R. 93, Nova Scotia Supreme Court. See also *McNicol v. Insurance Unlimited (Calgary) Ltd* (1992) 5 Alta.L.R. (3d) 158: a broker instructed to obtain insurance against ice hazards negligently obtained a policy which excluded cover for damage caused by floods. In *National Insurance and Guarantee Corporation v. Imperio Reinsurance Co (UK) Ltd* [1999] Lloyd's Rep. I.R. 249, Colman J., the brokers were asked to seek confirmation that a policy already obtained included cover for losses represented by self-funding interest. They obtained an endorsement which did not provide the requisite confirmation and were held to have been negligent for having mistakenly formed the view that it did.

[22] *Austcan Investments Pty Ltd v. Sun Alliance Insurance Ltd* (1992) 57 S.A.S.R. 343 at first instance (on appeal, *ibid.*, it was held that the correct company had been insured, but that the broker had been negligent in another respect: see para. 14–080, below).

[23] An insurer may choose not to obtain reinsurance which exactly mirrors the underlying risk: see *Deeny v. Gooda Walker Ltd* [1996] L.R.L.R. 183 at 200–1.

covered by the primary policy of insurance. Any failure to do so is a breach of his express instructions and, almost inevitably, negligent.[24]

Ambiguous instructions. Where the client's instructions are ambiguous, the   **14–044** broker will not be liable if he interprets them in a reasonable manner[25] or in accordance with the usual practice of insurance brokers.[26] In *Vale v. Van Oppen and Co. Ltd*[27] the plaintiffs instructed the defendants (shipping agents) to insure their consignment of goods against "all risks". Contrary to the plaintiffs' intentions, the defendants took the phrase "all risks" to mean "all risks covered by an ordinary marine policy", and effected insurance accordingly. Roche J. held that they had discharged their obligations to the plaintiffs.[28] It is submitted, however, that where an ambiguity is patent, the broker is under a duty to seek clarification from the client before carrying out the instructions.

Specified insurance unavailable. Except in the unusual circumstances men-   **14–045** tioned above,[29] the broker has a good defence if he can show that insurance on the particular terms specified was not available, but he effected insurance on the best terms that he reasonably could.[30] In *Waterkeyn v. Eagle Star & British Dominions Insurance Co. Ltd*[31] the plaintiff claimed damages from the defendant brokers for failing properly to insure his deposit accounts in various Russian banks after the Bolshevik revolution. Greer J. heard evidence "at length" as to the negotiations carried on by the defendants' representative and concluded that he had discharged his duty: " . . . he is not responsible for the fact that this insurance was not as wide as was desired . . . it is all that could have been got from the Underwriters in the circumstances".

(c) *Effecting insurance which does not meet the client's requirements*

An insurance broker is under a duty to ensure, so far as he reasonably can,[32]   **14–046** that he effects insurance which meets the client's requirements.[33] He should

---

[24] *British Citizens Assurance Co. v. L. Woolland & Co.* (1921) 8 Ll.L.Rep. 89 (brokers, arranging reinsurance of a ship, failed to describe it as a sailing vessel). See also *Youell v. Bland Welch & Co. Ltd (No. 2)* [1990] 2 Lloyd's Rep. 431 (the "Superhulls Cover" case) (for the facts, see para. 14–021, above).

[25] *Dixon v. Hovill* (1828) 4 Bing. 665; *Veljkovic v. Vrybergen* [1985] V.R. 419: V, a subcontractor on a building project instructed an insurance agent to obtain insurance. The agent obtained insurance against employers' liability but not against injury to V himself. The Supreme Court of Victoria held that the insurance agent had not been negligent to interpret his instructions in this manner. See also *Ireland v. Livingston* (1872) L.R. 5 H.L. 395.

[26] *Enlayde Ltd v. Roberts* [1917] 1 Ch. 109, 120–121, (*obiter dictum* of Sargant J.).

[27] (1921) 37 T.L.R. 367.

[28] The position is otherwise, however, where someone who is not an insurance broker agrees to effect insurance against all risks: *Yuill & Co. v. Robson* [1908] 1 K.B. 270: *Enlayde Ltd v. Roberts* [1917] 1 Ch. 109.

[29] See para. 14–040, above.

[30] See, *e.g. McIntyre & Co. v. F. J. Krutwig* (1922) 10 Ll.L.R. 430; *King (or Fiehl) v. Chambers & Newman (Insurance Brokers) Ltd* [1963] 2 Lloyd's Rep. 130. As to the duty to notify the client in these circumstances, see para. 14–074, below.

[31] (1920) 4 Ll.L.Rep. 178; 5 Ll.L.Rep. 42.

[32] This obligation is particularly onerous in cases where the broker accepts instructions to arrange insurance for the client against all foreseeable risks. See para. 14–012, above.

[33] Para. 3.2 of the General Insurance Standards Council Code for Private Customers (2000) states: "We will make sure, as far as possible, that the products and services we offer you will match your requirements: We will offer you products and services to meet your needs, and match any requirements you have. If we cannot match your requirements, we will explain the differences in the product

ensure that the risk against which the client wishes to be insured is correctly described in the policy and that the client will be entitled to claim if the need should arise.[34] Thus in an Australian case, brokers who were instructed to obtain insurance against damage by storm, tempest and flood were held negligent for obtaining a policy which excluded "damage caused directly or indirectly by the sea". Having regard to the location of the property, the brokers ought to have appreciated that the only flooding which could occur would be from the sea.[35] Similarly, in *Niagara Frontier Caterers Ltd v. Continental Insurance Co. of Canada*,[36] brokers were held negligent for obtaining an insurance policy subject to a "co-insurance clause" which had the effect of reducing cover under the policy to thirty-five ninetieths of any loss. In *Cee Bee Marine Ltd v. Lombard Insurance Co. Ltd*,[37] cover was arranged in the name of one of two clients. Stock belonging to the other was lost in a fire. The client named on the insurance policy had no insurable interest in the lost stock and so it could not claim under the policy. The other client was not an insured. The broker was held liable. Where the client has specific requirements as to the identity or status of any insurer, the broker should either obtain insurance from an appropriate insurer or advise his client accordingly.[38]

---

or service that we can offer you. If it is not practical to match all your requirements, we will give you enough information so that you can make an informed decision about your insurance." Similarly, para. 11 of the General Insurance Standards Council Commercial Code states: "If members are unable to match Commercial Customer's requirements they will explain the differences in the insurance proposed." Insurance brokers who are subject to the regulatory regime of the Financial Services and Markets Act 2000 (as to which see para. 14–004, above) may incur civil liability to their clients under s.150 of that Act if they effect insurance which does not meet those clients' requirements. For example, they may be in breach of the "Know Your Client" and/or "Suitability" rules.

[34] *e.g. Peter Unruh Construction Company Ltd v. Kelly-Lucy & Cameron Adjusters Ltd* [1976] 4 W.W.R. 419, Alberta Supreme Court, where the agent obtained a policy which excluded cover for loss caused by excavation, although he knew that the insured carried out such work. Held liable for failing to notice this exclusion upon receipt of the policy. See also *McCann v. Western Farmers Mutual Insurance Co.* (1978) 87 D.L.R. (3d) 135 where the defendant arranged insurance of plaintiff's premises, on part of which (as he knew) the plaintiffs carried on business. Held liable for effecting a policy which excluded business use. In *Kadaja v. C.A.A.* (1995) 23 O.R. (3d) 275, Ontario Court General Division, the insured asked his insurer to transfer his car insurance from an old vehicle to a new one and asked for "full coverage". The insurer was found to owe the insured the same duty to advise as that owed by a broker, and was found negligent in failing to advise him of a gap in his cover, namely that the policy which was transferred did not cover him for collision/comprehensive damage. In *All Lift Consultants Ltd v. Adam Crane Service (1980) Ltd* (1988) 88 A.R. 208, Alberta Court of Queen's Bench, the broker obtained and renewed cover which did not extend to a part of the insured's activities of which the broker knew. The broker was held liable. See also *Mitzner v. Miller & Beazley Ltd* (1993) 11 Alta.L.R. (3d) 108: broker held liable for not properly investigating his client's requirements with the result that the policy procured did not cover loss and damage to tools.

[35] *Mitor Investment Pty Ltd v. General Accident Fire & Life Assurance Corporation Ltd* [1984] W.A.R. 365, Supreme Court of Western Australia. In contrast, in *New Forty-Four Mines Ltd v. St. Paul Fire & Marine Insurance Co.* (1987) 78 A.R. 364 the Alberta Court of Appeal held that a broker who offered a warranty to insurers that the insured premises would be watched 24 hours a day was not liable when insurers successfully denied liability for breach of that warranty. The broker had reasonable grounds for believing that the warranty would be complied with.

[36] (1990) 74 O.R. (2d) 191, Ontario High Court. In *GKN Keller Canada Ltd v. Hartford Fire Insurance Co.* (1983) 27 C.C.L.T. 61, Ontario High Court, brokers were held to have been negligent in obtaining an insurance policy with an exemption clause which rendered the cover inadequate for the plaintiffs' needs.

[37] [1990] 2 N.Z.L.R. 1.

[38] *Texas Homecare Ltd v. Royal Bank of Canada Trust Co. Ltd* [1996] C.L.C. 776: for the facts, see para. 14–030 above.

The defendant brokers in *Strong & Pearl v. S. Allison & Co. Ltd*[39] were also **14–047** held liable for failure to obtain a policy on terms appropriate for their client's needs. The plaintiffs instructed the brokers to arrange insurance for their motor yacht while it was laid up for repair. The defendants knew that the plaintiffs proposed to live on board during this period. Nevertheless, they effected a "lying-up policy" in the standard form, which did not cover the yacht while the owners were on board and contained a "no petrol warranty". Subsequently an explosion occurred and the insurers denied liability. Greer J. held that the defendants were negligent and in breach of the implied terms of their employment in failing to obtain insurance which covered the actual circumstances under which the yacht was being laid up.[40]

A further illustration is provided by *Paul Tudor Jones II and Marsh &* **14–048** *McLennan Inc. v. Crowley Colosso Ltd*[41] in which the defendants were English brokers engaged by American brokers to obtain contractor's all risk insurance for a development in the Bahamas. They obtained insurance on terms that cover would not be provided for any part of the works which had been taken over by the employer or for which a certificate of completion had been issued. The development was carried out in phases and the client required and believed that he had obtained cover which would protect his interest in the development until all phases had been completed. The marina had been completed when it suffered substantial damage during a hurricane. The insurers declined to pay. At the time the risk was broked the American brokers, but not the English brokers, had known that there would be certificates of completion for phases of the works. The English brokers had sent the proposed wording to the American brokers for approval. Mance J. held that the English brokers were at fault in failing to draw the attention of the American brokers to the term and the American brokers were at fault in failing to notice it.

Client becoming involved in legal dispute. If the insurance obtained by the **14–049** broker is such that his client becomes involved in a legal dispute then he will be found to be in breach of duty. In *FNCB Ltd v. Barnet Devanney (Harrow) Ltd*[42] the defendant brokers were held liable for failure to obtain a policy on terms appropriate for their client's needs. The brokers were acting for both mortgagor and mortgagee in relation to a composite policy insuring their respective interests in the mortgaged property. They failed to have included a mortgagee protection clause, which insurers would have agreed to at no additional cost. The mortgaged property was damaged by fire and insurers purported to avoid cover because of non-disclosure and misrepresentation by the mortgagor. The mortgagee compromised its claim against insurers and sued the brokers. The Court of Appeal held that the brokers were in breach of duty. The law as to the separate rights of two insured under a composite policy was not clear at the time the risk was broked[43]:

---

[39] (1926) 25 Ll.L.Rep. 504.
[40] The second ground of liability was the defendants' failure to give proper advice to the plaintiffs, as to which see para. 14–081, below.
[41] [1996] 2 Lloyd's Rep. 619.
[42] [1999] Lloyd's Rep. I.R. 459.
[43] It has subsequently been clarified: *New Hampshire Insurance Co. v. MGN Ltd* [1997] L.R.L.R. 24 following *Dixey & Sons v. Parsons* (1964) 192 E.G. 197.

"it is not the function of an insurance broker to take a view on undetermined points of law. The protection to be afforded to the client should, if reasonably possible, be such that the client does not become involved in legal disputes at all. As in the case of a solicitor the insurance broker should protect his client from unnecessary risks including the risk of litigation".

That conclusion was also supported by the absence of evidence that the brokers had acted in accordance with responsible market practice.[44]

14–050　　**Defects in policy wording.** The broker may also be responsible for defects in the wording of the policy of insurance which render it unsatisfactory from his client's point of view. *Thus in Youell v. Bland Welch & Co. Ltd (No. 2)* (the "Superhulls Cover" case),[45] one ground upon which Phillips J. held the brokers liable was their failure to draft the contract of reinsurance with reasonable clarity, obscuring the difference between the cover under the original insurance and that under the reinsurance. In *Firestone Canada Inc. v. American Home Assurance Co.*[46] the brokers arranged a policy to insure against the manufacturers of snow tyres being called upon to honour a weather warranty. As a result of a difference between the clause describing cover and the formula for calculating the premium due, the insured had to pay premium on sales which were not subject to the warranty or to the cover provided. The brokers were found to have been negligent.

14–051　　**Broker's duty to enquire.** The broker is expected to have a basic knowledge of insurance law[47] and, on occasions, to question the client himself so as to elicit relevant information which may not otherwise be volunteered.[48] In *McNealy v.*

---

[44] The decisions set out in this section should be contrasted with *Fomin v. Oswell* in which the defendant brokers were instructed to effect insurance on a vessel bound for Petersburgh. The captain had stated in conversation that he intended to carry simulated papers, although there was no reference to this in the written instructions to insure. The defendants duly effected insurance, but without any clause permitting the vessel to carry simulated papers. It was held that they had discharged their duty. "Notwithstanding the prior conversation, the captain might have resolved not to carry any [simulated papers]" *per* Lord Ellenborough. This decision is a surprising one. It might be thought that the brokers should at least have investigated the matter, before effecting a policy which assumed that no simulated papers would be carried. A possible explanation of the decision is that the plaintiff in this case (unlike the plaintiffs in *Strong & Pearl v. S. Allison & Co. Ltd* and *Sharp and Roarer Investments Ltd v. Sphere Drake Insurance plc, The Moonacre*) was well versed in marine insurance and could be presumed to have given accurate and complete instructions. Alternatively, it may be that a lower standard of skill and care was expected of insurance brokers in the early 19th century and that, had the case arisen more recently, it would have been decided differently.

[45] [1990] 2 Lloyd's Rep. 431 (for the facts see para. 14–017, above).

[46] (1989) 67 O.R. (2d) 471, Ontario High Court.

[47] See *Park v. Hammond* (1816) 6 Taunt. 495, where the defendant through ignorance of an established rule of law, failed properly to define in the terms of cover the risk against which the client was seeking insurance.

[48] Para. 3.2 of the General Insurance Standards Council Code for Private Customers (2000) states: "We will make sure, as far as possible, that the products and services we offer you will match your requirements: If it is practical, we will identify your needs by getting relevant information from you." Para. 7 of the General Insurance Standards Council Commercial Code states: "Members will seek from Commercial Customers such information about their circumstances and objectives as might reasonably be expected to be relevant in enabling them to identify the Commercial Customer's requirements and fulfil their responsibilities to their Commercial Customers."

The Pennine Insurance Co. Ltd[49] the plaintiff, a property repairer and part-time musician, instructed the defendant brokers to effect motor insurance on his behalf. The defendants effected insurance with the Pennine Insurance Company, which offered low rates. Unfortunately a number of categories of persons were excluded from benefiting under the policy, one of which was "whole or part-time musicians". On the occurrence of an accident the plaintiff was unable to claim on the policy. Evidence was given that the brokers had filled in the proposal form on the basis of information given by the plaintiff. When asked what his occupation was, the plaintiff replied "property repairer" and the brokers recorded this answer without further enquiry. The Court of Appeal held that the brokers had failed in their duty. They possessed a leaflet setting out all the categories of excluded persons. They should have gone through the leaflet with the plaintiff, so as to make sure that he did not fall into any of the excluded categories.

A further example is provided by the decision in *Sharp and Roarer Invest-* **14–052** *ments Ltd v. Sphere Drake Insurance plc, The Moonacre.*[50] In that case brokers were held to have been negligent in arranging insurance for a yacht on terms which included an exclusion of cover for any period when the yacht was used as a houseboat. The insured's crew lived on his yacht when it was laid up over winter and this allowed insurers to rely upon the exclusion when a loss occurred. When preparing the proposal form the broker had asked whether the insured or his family would live on the yacht over winter, but failed to ask whether anyone else would. He was therefore held to have been negligent.[51]

There are, however, limits to the scope of a broker's duty to make enquiries. **14–053** A broker will not be found to have acted negligently if he fails to raise questions about the risk to be covered which he had no reason to ask. For example, in *Dallinga v. Sun Alliance Insurance Co.*[52] the owner of goods stored at his son's property arranged contents cover for his son through the defendant broker but did not tell the broker that the goods were his. They were stolen. The son had no insurable interest and the father was not named on the policy, so neither could claim for the loss. The broker had no reason to believe that the goods belonged to the father and the claim against him was dismissed. Obviously if the broker does ask the appropriate questions and the insured withholds essential information from the broker then the broker will not be held responsible for any resulting gap in the insured's cover.[53]

Client giving clear instructions. A broker who receives clear instructions **14–054** from his client as to the insurance to be effected is not under an obligation to

---

[49] [1978] 2 Lloyd's Rep. 18, CA.

[50] [1992] 2 Lloyd's Rep. 501, A.D. Colman q.c., sitting as a deputy judge of the High Court.

[51] The broker was found to have been negligent on other grounds as well see paras 14–062, 14–081 and 14–085, below.

[52] (1993) 10 Alta.L.R. (3d) 59. See also *National Insurance and Guarantee Corporation v. Imperio Reinsurance Co (UK) Ltd* [1999] Lloyd's Rep. I.R. 249, Colman J.: brokers not in breach of duty for failing to realise that the insured wanted excess of loss cover to include loss of interest on the insured's own funds applied as part of the insured scheme.

[53] *St. Isidore Asphalte Ltee v. Luminex Signs Ltd* (1996) 176 N.B.R. (2d) 135, New Brunswick Court of Queen's Bench: insured ran a sign-painting business. A vehicle was stolen from his premises, but his insurance did not extend coverage to vehicles. Broker found not liable because the insured withheld essential information from the broker and thereby failed to adequately describe the nature of the business.

suggest that the client obtain more extensive cover unless he has undertaken to give such advice.[54] Thus in *The Town of Rosetown v. Wilson Agencies Ltd*[55] a town decided to place its insurance business out to tender, specifying the cover it wanted. It failed to seek or obtain excess automobile liability insurance and, on finding itself facing a claim in respect of which it was underinsured, sued both its broker before it went out to tender and the broker whose tender it had accepted. The claim was dismissed. *A fortiori* a client who is adequately informed of possible coverage but decides not to obtain it cannot complain if he then suffers a loss which would have been covered.[56]

14–055   **Appropriate level of cover.** A broker should obtain cover not only against the relevant risks but also at a suitable level to protect his client. This is usually done not by the broker valuing the insured property or interest himself, but by the broker drawing his client's attention to the consequences of underinsurance (which may need checking on each renewal, particularly if the policy covers damage to property on the basis of the cost of reinstatement).

In *JW Bollom & Co. Ltd v. Byas Mosley & Co. Ltd*[57] the insured was under-insured. Moore-Bick J. emphasised that insurance brokers are not valuers and so could not be expected to advise as to the value of a particular piece of property. However, he found that the brokers had acted negligently in failing to advise the insured of the need to obtain cover for the full cost of reinstatement of the property insured and to obtain cover accordingly. Where, however, the broker takes it upon himself to value the property to be insured and negligently underestimates the level of cover needed, he will be in breach of duty. Thus in *Evans v. State Farm Fire and Casualty Co.*[58] brokers who used a computer software program to calculate the reinstatement cost of their client's house, rather than ask questions about the house, were found to have been in breach of duty when their client was underinsured as a result.

---

[54] In Canada such a duty is readily found: see para. 14–012, n. 35, above. For example in *Miller v. Guardian Insurance Co. Ltd* (1995) 127 D.L.R. (4th) 717 the client wanted "full coverage" and the agent was held liable for failing to advise him to obtain the uninsured motorist endorsement. An appeal in *Miller v. Guardian Insurance Co. of Canada* was unsuccessful: (1997) 149 D.L.R. (4th) 375. However, a client who brings such a claim must prove that he relied upon the broker to give such advice and that the broker knew or ought to have known that he would do so: *Kalkinis v. Allstate Insurance Company of Canada* (1998) 41 O.R. (3d) 528, Ontario CA.

[55] (1989) 77 Sask.R. 42, Saskatchewan Court of Queen's Bench. See also *O'Brien v. Hughes-Gibb & Co. Ltd* [1995] L.R.L.R. 90: owners of racehorse requested cover for "mortality only"; brokers held not liable for failing to advise of or obtain cover against theft.

[56] *Davca Building Supplies Ltd v. Wedgewood Insurance Ltd and Clarke* (1992) 99 Nfld. & P.E.I.R. 203. The client was informed of possible cover in respect of liability for damage to trailers towed by his truck but chose not to obtain it. His action against the broker failed. See also *Conway v. Home Securities Ltd* (1996) 108 Man.R. (2d) 58 (client informed of optional sewer back-up coverage, decided not to pay the small additional premium, and then claimed unsuccessfully against broker when he suffered an uninsured loss) and *Madole v. State Farm Mutual Automobile Insurance Co.* (1995) 32 Alta.L.R. (3d) 265 (client informed of possibility of comprehensive cover for existing car, chose not to have it, purchased new car and insured it on same terms as before; his claim against the insurance agent for failing to advise him to obtain comprehensive cover for the new car failed).

[57] [1999] Lloyd's Rep.P.N. 598, Moore-Bick J. See also *Kennedy (B.J.) Agency (1984) Ltd v. Kilgour Bell Ins.* (1999) 139 Man.R.(2d) 276, Manitoba Court of Queen's Bench, in which the broker was negligent in failing to advise his client of the availability of "replacement cost coverage" and the limitations of "actual value" coverage.

[58] (1993) 15 O.R. (3d) 86.

Client with changing requirements. If a broker is aware that his client's **14–056** insurance requirements will change then he should monitor his client's requirements and ensure that those requirements are met. In a Canadian case, *Etter and Hart v. Commercial Union Assurance Co.*,[59] the client purchased a property which included a derelict barn. He advised his broker that he intended to conduct renovations and instructed his broker to arrange the appropriate insurance. The broker arranged insurance, but when the barn was destroyed in a storm the insurer refused liability on the basis that the original barn covered by the policy had been torn down and a new one constructed in its place. The broker was held to have been under a duty to keep himself appraised of his client's renovation plans and activities and to ensure that the client was either insured with the existing coverage or, if not, to advise that other cover was required. The broker had failed to do so and the finding of negligence against him was upheld on appeal.

(d) *Failing to exercise discretion reasonably*

If the client leaves the choice of insurer[60] or the terms of insurance[61] to the **14–057** judgment or discretion of his broker, the latter will not be liable if he acts reasonably and in accordance with the usual practice of insurance brokers. In *Chapman v. Walton*[62] the defendant broker was instructed to effect five policies of insurance on goods being shipped from London to St Thomas, with leave to call at Madeira and Tenerife. Subsequently the client received a letter indicating that the voyage was altered. He took it to the defendant and told the defendant "to do the needful with it". The meaning of the letter was not as clear as it might have been, but the defendant effected such alterations to the policies as he considered appropriate. In the event the ship sank off the Grand Canary Island and, as this was not covered by any of the alterations to the policy, the underwriters refused to pay. At the trial the defendant called "several policy brokers" as witnesses, each of whom expressed the opinion that an insurance broker would have done ample justice to the instructions contained in the letter by procuring the alterations which were in fact made. The jury found for the defendant and a subsequent application to set aside their verdict was dismissed. Lord Tindal C.J. stressed that the issue was not whether the defendant's decision was ultimately proved correct, but whether he exercised reasonable skill, care and judgment.[63]

On the other hand, a broker who chooses an insurer for his client will be liable **14–058** if he fails to exercise sufficient skill and care in making his choice. In *Lewis v. Tressider Andrews Associates Pty Ltd*,[64] the broker chose to place a risk with a new insurer, having received financial details of that insurer. Properly understood, they gave rise to grounds for believing that the insurer was not reliable or

---

[59] (1998) 166 N.S.R. (2d) 299, Nova Scotia CA.
[60] *Moore v. Mourgue* (1776) 2 Cowp. 479; *Comber v. Anderson* (1808) 1 Camp. 523; *Dixon v. Hovill* (1828) 4 Bing. 665 (it is part of the broker's duty to "take reasonable care that the policy [is] underwritten by responsible and solvent persons"); *Hurrell v. Bullard* (1863) 3 F. & F. 445 (*per* Cockburn C.J. at 453).
[61] *Vale v. Van Oppen & Co. Ltd* (1921) 37 T.L.R. 367.
[62] (1833) 10 Bing. 57.
[63] See para. 14–032, above.
[64] [1987] 2 Qd.R. 533.

sound. The broker was held liable when the policy proved worthless.[65] A broker who fails to insert in the policy a clause which is normally inserted,[66] will be liable for any loss thereby caused to the client.[67]

(e) *Failing to act with reasonable speed*

14–059   Any professional man owes a duty to his client to act with reasonable speed. If an insurance broker is guilty of unreasonable delay in effecting or renewing insurance cover and in consequence the client suffers loss for which he is uninsured, then the broker will be liable.[68] What constitutes unreasonable delay is a question of fact.[69] The nature of an insurance broker's business is such that a large part of his work is attended by some degree of urgency. Relevant factors to consider in each case are the nature of the risk to be covered, whether the client is uninsured in the meantime and the availability of the particular insurance required. In *Cock, Russell & Co. v. Bray, Gibb & Co. Ltd*[70] the defendants, marine insurance brokers, were instructed by the plaintiffs on a Friday afternoon to cover the plaintiffs for all risks in a Spanish steamer which was expected shortly. The defendants did nothing that day. On the Saturday they approached various underwriters but without success. On Monday the steamer arrived before the start of business and it transpired that a large part of the cargo was lost. Bailhache J. considered that, having regard to the nature of the risk, the defendants were not guilty of unreasonable delay. On the other hand in *Fraser Valley Mushroom Growers' Co-operative Association v. MacNaughton & Ward Ltd*,[71] brokers were held liable for failure to act with reasonable speed. They were requested to place coverage on goods but had not done so two hours later when the goods were destroyed by fire.[72] *A fortiori*, if a broker receives a request from a client and fails to act on it at all he will be in breach of duty. In *Forsikringsaktieselskapet Vesta v. Butcher*[73] the broker's reinsured client told the

---

[65] Similarly in *Bates v. Barrow Ltd* [1995] 1 Lloyd's Rep. 680 Gatehouse J. would have found brokers who placed stop loss insurance with unauthorised insurance companies liable if he had not held that the policies were enforceable by reason of s. 132 of the Financial Services Act 1986.

[66] As to which the evidence of other insurance brokers is admissible: *Mallough v. Barber* (1815) 4 Camp. 150.

[67] See also *Gibraltar General Insurance Company v. L.E. Yingst Co. Ltd* (1990) 89 Sask.R. 93, discussed in para. 14–023, n.61 above.

[68] *Turpin v. Bilton* (1843) 5 Man. & G. 455; *London Borough of Bromley v. Ellis* [1971] 1 Lloyd's Rep. 97, 99; *Irish Nationwide B.S. v. Malone* (1999) I.L.T.243 (Irish Supreme Court stated that the normal duties of a broker required close attention to the progress of a matter until it had been completed or abandoned).

[69] In *Icarom plc (formerly Insurance Corporation of Ireland plc) v. Peek Puckle (International) Ltd* [1992] 2 Lloyd's Rep. 600 the plaintiff alleged that the defendant broker, having been instructed on January 19, had been negligent in failing to obtain facultative reinsurance cover until January 22, by when a total loss had occurred on the underlying policy. Webster J. held that the brokers had only been instructed on the 22nd, so that the claim failed on its facts. It appears to have been considered to be at least arguable that the brokers would have been negligent had they taken four days to obtain reinsurance cover.

[70] (1920) 3 Ll.L.Rep. 71.

[71] (1982) 37 B.C.L.R. 20, British Columbia Supreme Court.

[72] See also *Labreche Estate v. Harasymiw* (1992) 89 D.L.R. (4th) 95 where an employee of a credit union who assisted a mortgagor in applying for life insurance was held to be in breach of a tortious duty of care in taking three months to complete an application form and generally failing to progress the application.

[73] [1986] 2 All E.R. 488, Hobhouse J. (the brokers did not seek to challenge this finding on appeal: [1989] A.C. 852, CA and HL.)

broker that the insured under the original insurance could not comply with a warranty that the insured property be watched 24 hours a day and asked for confirmation that that was acceptable to reinsurers. The broker failed to act at all and was held by Hobhouse J. to have been in breach of duty.

(f) *Failing to disclose material facts to the insurers*

Insurance contracts are contracts of the utmost good faith and the insured and his agent, the broker, are obliged to disclose all material facts[74] which are or should be within their knowledge, both before the contract is made and on the negotiation of any extension of that contract.[75] If the broker fails to do so, with the result that the insurers subsequently repudiate,[76] he will be liable for the loss sustained.[77] There is a substantial body of case law on what constitutes a "material" fact, but a discussion of these authorities is outside the scope of this work.[78] In brief, however, a fact is material if it was one which would have an effect (not necessarily decisive) on the mind of a prudent underwriter in deciding whether to accept the risk or the premium to be asked.

14-060

In order to avoid the policy for non-disclosure the insurer must also show that he had been induced to enter the contract of insurance on the terms he did by the non-disclosure.[79] In *Container Transport International Inc. v. Oceanus Mutual Underwriting Association (Bermuda) Ltd*[80] (a case in which marine insurers avoided a contract of insurance under section 18(1) of the Marine Insurance Act 1906) Kerr L.J. summarised the broker's duty in these terms:

14-061

" . . . one way of formulating the test as to the duty of disclosure and representation to cases such as the present . . . is simply to ask oneself: 'Having regard to all the

---

[74] The evidence of other insurance brokers as to whether they would have considered the facts material is not admissible: *Campbell v. Rickards* (1833) 5 B. & Ad. 840.

[75] *Bolton v. New Zealand Insurance Co. Ltd* [1995] 1 N.Z.L.R. 224.

[76] There may be a failure to disclose a material fact without negligence: see *Banque Keyser Ullmann SA v. Skandia (U.K.) Insurance Co. Ltd* [1990] 1 Q.B. 665, 781; *Bank of Nova Scotia v. Hellenic Mutual War Risks Association (Bermuda) Ltd, The "Good Luck"* [1990] 1 Q.B. 818. However, a broker will find it difficult to establish that any non-disclosure of information known to him was not negligent: see para. 14–062, below.

[77] *e.g. Maydew v. Forrester* (1814) 5 Taunt. 615. In *W.E. Acres Crabmeal Ltd v. Brien's Insurance Agency Ltd* (1988) 90 N.B.R. (2d) 77 and 228 A.P.R. 77, New Brunswick Court of Queen's Bench, brokers failed to disclose the insured's claims history, entitling insurers to avoid the policy and rendering themselves liable. In *Akedian Co. Ltd v. Royal Insurance Australia Ltd* (1999) 1 V.R. 80, Supreme Court of Victoria, the brokers were found to have breached their duty to the client in failing to disclose to insurers the purchase price of machinery to be insured. In New Zealand, insurers would not be able to repudiate, if, as is customary, the broker receives commission from them, being fixed with the broker's knowledge of all matters material to the contract of insurance by s.10 of the Insurance Law Reform Act 1977: *Helicopter Equipment Ltd v. Marine Insurance Co. Ltd* [1986] 1 N.Z.L.R. 448 and *Gold Star Insurance Co Ltd v. Gaunt* [1998] 3 N.Z.L.R. 80 NZCA. In *Roberts v. Plaisted* [1989] 2 Lloyd's Rep. 341, 345, col. 1, Purchas L.J. expressed dissatisfaction that in English law an insured who has made full disclosure to a broker could nevertheless find himself uninsured because his broker failed to make full disclosure to insurers.

[78] See *MacGillvray on Insurance Law* (9th ed.), paras 17–1 to 17–82 and Clarke, *The Law of Insurance Contracts*, (2nd ed.), pp.583–633.

[79] *Pan Atlantic Insurance Co. Ltd v. Pine Top Insurance Co. Ltd* [1995] 1 A.C. 501.

[80] [1984] 1 Lloyd's Rep. 476, 496–497 (now partly overruled by *Pan Atlantic Insurance Co. Ltd v. Pine Top Insurance Co. Ltd* [1995] 1 A.C. 501).

circumstances known or deemed to be known to the insured and to his broker, and ignoring those which are expressly excepted from the duty of disclosure, was the presentation of the risk in summary form to the underwriter a fair and substantially accurate presentation of the risk proposed for insurance, so that a prudent insurer could form a proper judgment—either on the presentation alone or by asking questions if he was sufficiently put on enquiry and wanted to know further details—whether or not to accept the proposal, and, if so, on what terms?' This is not an onerous duty for brokers to discharge in practice".

In *Pan Atlantic Insurance Co. Ltd v. Pine Top Insurance Co. Ltd*[81] it was held by the trial judge and the Court of Appeal that there was no non-disclosure of a disastrous claims record by a broker who had the statistics with him when broking the risk, but conducted himself so as to reduce the likelihood of the underwriter asking to see them. In the House of Lords Lord Mustill indicated that there might well have been non-disclosure, but that, if there had, the underwriter would have waived it. However a broker who approaches underwriters on that basis acts at his peril. Thus in *Newbury International Ltd v. Reliance National Insurance Co. (U.K.) Ltd*[82] Hobhouse J. rejected a submission that underwriters had had the opportunity to ask further questions, holding that they could only be expected to make such enquiries after a fair presentation of the risk. He held that underwriters were entitled to avoid the policy and, in the circumstances, the brokers conceded that they were in breach of duty.[83]

14-062   Where the broker fails to disclose a material fact which is or should be within his own knowledge, he will almost inevitably be negligent. Thus the fact that the broker has forged his client's signature on the proposal form is a material fact even if the client would have readily signed the form as completed himself. In *Sharp and Roarer Investments Ltd v. Sphere Drake Insurance plc, The Moonacre*,[84] a broker who did so without authority was held liable when insurers avoided cover for non-disclosure.

14-063   In *Coolee Ltd v. Wing Heath & Co.*[85] the plaintiffs were engaged in quarrying sand from pits. They instructed the first defendants, who were insurance brokers but not Lloyd's brokers, to arrange employers' liability insurance for them. The first defendants employed the second defendants, who were Lloyd's brokers, to effect the insurance. The plaintiffs did not originally use explosives in their work

---

[81] [1995] 1 A.C. 501.

[82] [1994] 1 Lloyd's Rep. 83

[83] Potter J. expressed similar views in *Aiken v. Stewart Wrightson Members Agency Ltd* [1995] 1 W.L.R. 1281 at 1315–1316: see Chap. 16, para. 16–017. In *Aneco Reinsurance Underwriting (in liquidation) v. Johnson and Higgins Ltd* [1998] 1 Lloyd's Rep. 565, Cresswell J. stated that it was highly desirable that means be found to record in a form which precluded later dispute what was said between brokers and underwriters when the risk was broked. When documents are presented to underwriters it is good practice to obtain their initial (or "scratch") on them to confirm that they have been seen. In *Mander v. Commercial Union Assurance Company plc* [1998] Lloyd's Rep.I.R. 93 (for the facts see para. 14–039 above) Rix J. indicated that a broker who failed to record adequately his presentation of a risk might be in breach of duty, but that there could be no relevant breach of such a duty unless it were shown that the presentation were faulty.

[84] [1992] 2 Lloyd's Rep. 501: for other grounds upon which the broker was held liable, see paras 14–052, 14–081 and 14–085.

[85] (1930) 47 T.L.R. 78.

and they so stated on the proposal form. When the policy came up for renewal the plaintiffs sent a letter to the first defendants in which they mentioned that they had started using explosives. The first defendants did not appreciate the significance of this point. However, they forwarded a copy of the letter to the second defendants. The second defendants, too, did not notice the point, with the result that the underwriters were never informed. Two workmen were subsequently injured in an explosion, and the underwriters denied liability. Rowlatt J. held that the first defendants were negligent in failing to spot the point and draw it to the attention of the second defendants. On receiving the letter "they ought to have turned up their record of insurance and had the matter adjusted with underwriters". The second defendants were also negligent in failing to notice the point for themselves. Rowlatt J. held that both defendants were liable for the whole of the plaintiffs' loss.

Duty to advise the client. The insurance broker should advise his client of the   **14-064**
duty to disclose all circumstances material to the insurance, and the consequences of failing to do so.[86] The client may not appreciate which facts are "material". It is part of the insurance broker's expertise to recognise matters which ought to be disclosed and he should make sure that they are disclosed to the insurers.[87] In *Akedian Co. Ltd v. Royal Insurance Australia Ltd*,[88] Byrne J. described the broker's duty as follows:

> "The duty of a broker is to disclose material facts known to it and to have a knowledge and understanding of the requirements of the law relating to the duty to disclose and, in particular, as to the materiality of the given fact . . . It is part of the function of a broker to advise its client as to what must be disclosed in this technical area [of Marine Insurance] as well as to communicate the fact or circumstance in question to the insurer so that the policy issued to the insured is not at risk."[89]

If the broker is in doubt as to whether or not a fact is material, the proper and   **14-065**
prudent course is to advise the client that it should be disclosed. If in reality the fact is not material, then its disclosure is most unlikely to prejudice the client in obtaining insurance. If in reality the fact is material but it is not disclosed, then it is no defence for the brokers to say that the question was a borderline one or

---

[86] Para. 3.7 of the General Insurance Standards Council Code for Private Customers (2000) states: "We will explain your duty to give Insurers information before cover begins and during the policy, and what may happen if you do not." Para. 18 of the General Insurance Standards Council Commercial Code states: "Members will explain to Commercial Customers their duty to disclose all circumstances material to the insurance and the consequences of any failure to make such disclosure, both before the insurance commences and during the policy."

[87] For example, in *O & R Jewellers Ltd v. Terry* [1999] Lloyd's Rep.I.R. 436 (Sir Godfrey le Quesne Q.C., sitting as a deputy High Court judge) the brokers conceded that they were under a duty to advise the claimant jewellers to disclose that the managing director of its parent company had convictions for burglary, if they were aware of that fact. The brokers were also found to be in breach of duty in failing to pass on to insurers information as to where the keys to the insured's safes were kept overnight, a failure which also led to avoidance of the policy.

[88] (1999) 1 V.R. 80, Supreme Court of Victoria. The brokers were found negligent in failing to disclose to insurers the purchase price of machinery which was to be insured, as required by s. 24(1) of the Marine Insurance Act 1909.

[89] *ibid.* at 86–87.

one on which the most eminent lawyers might differ in their conclusion[90]: in *Aiken v. Stewart Wrightson Members Agency Ltd*,[91] Potter J., considering the care to be exercised by a reasonably competent Lloyd's managing agent when effecting aggregate excess loss reinsurance for his syndicate, held that the duty "extended to disclosure of facts which were arguably material so as to avoid unnecessary risk of avoidance".[92]

14–066 **Duty to make enquiries.** The broker's duty in this regard is not limited to spotting material facts contained in the information given by his client. There may be other matters that ought to be disclosed, which the client has not thought it necessary to mention. The broker should take reasonable care to elicit such information for himself. Thus in the Australian case *Ogden & Co. Pty Ltd v. Reliance Fire Sprinkler Co. Pty Ltd*,[93] MacFarlan J. held that it was the duty of the brokers "to collect such information regarding the nature of the company's business and its claims history as the underwriters could properly require, and . . . to pass on that information to the underwriters".[94] This duty is particularly important where the client is a private individual with limited experience of insurance matters. In *McNealy v. The Pennine Insurance Co. Ltd*[95] it was a material fact that the plaintiff was a part-time musician. The plaintiff did not appreciate the significance of the fact and did not communicate it to the brokers. The Court of Appeal held that by the exercise of reasonable care the brokers could and should have elicited the matter for themselves.[96]

14–067 There is, however, a limit to the information which a reasonably competent and careful broker can be expected to elicit from the client. To take an extreme example, if an apparently reputable company instructs brokers to arrange insurance of its premises, it can hardly be said that the brokers are negligent if they fail to enquire whether the company's directors have criminal records.[97] In *Lyons v. J.W. Bentley Ltd*[98] brokers effected a householder's comprehensive insurance policy for the plaintiff. The plaintiff did not disclose his or his wife's claims history to the brokers, and consequently this was not passed on to the insurers.

---

[90] In *Chariot Inns Ltd v. Assicurazioni Generali Spa* [1981] I.R. 199 the broker took the view that certain facts did not have to be disclosed and Keane J., taking broadly the same view, held that the insurers were not entitled to repudiate. The Irish Supreme Court took a different view (*viz.* that the facts were material and ought to have been disclosed) and accordingly held the brokers liable in negligence.

[91] [1995] 1 W.L.R. 1281: see Chap. 16, para. 16–017.

[92] *ibid.* at 1313H. In *Akedian Co.Ltd v. Royal Insurance Australia Ltd* (1999) 1 V.R. 80, Supreme Court of Victoria. Byrne J. suggested that "the test of materiality as it affects the broker's duty to advise the client insured to make a disclosure may be more extensive than the same test as it affects the insurer's right to avoid the policy": *ibid.* at 87.

[93] [1975] 1 Lloyd's Rep. 52. See para. 14–073, below.

[94] *ibid.* at 69.

[95] [1978] 2 Lloyd's Rep. 18, CA. For the facts see para. 14–051, above.

[96] See also *Bolton v. New Zealand Insurance Co. Ltd* [1995] 1 N.Z.L.R. 224, where the broker negligently failed to ask his client whether there would be any changes to the crew of the yacht to be insured, although the broker should have realised that the identity of the crew was a material fact.

[97] *Fanhaven Pty Ltd v. Bain Dawes Northern Pty Ltd* [1982] 2 N.S.W.L.R. 57: the New South Wales Court of Appeal held that brokers were not negligent in these circumstances. The Court also held that the brokers were not under a duty to advise the plaintiffs generally as to their duty of disclosure. However, if the broker had notice of some questionable matter the position may be different: *Quinby Enterprises Ltd (in liquidation) v. General Accident Fire and Life Assurance Corporation Public Ltd Co.* [1995] 1 N.Z.L.R. 726, *per* Barker J.

[98] (1944) 77 Ll.L.R. 335.

The insurers later repudiated for non-disclosure. The plaintiff's claim for negligence against the brokers was dismissed.[99]

Reinsurance. Where a broker is placing a reinsurance treaty he should be **14–068** careful to describe fully the nature of the underlying risk which he is seeking to reinsure. Failure to do so will expose his client to a risk that the reinsurance will be avoided for non-disclosure and the broker to a claim for damages. In *Aneco Reinsurance Underwriting (in liquidation) v. Johnson and Higgins Ltd*[1] brokers failed to advise potential reinsurers under a reinsurance treaty that the underlying reinsurance business in respect of which their client wished to obtain cover was limited to a single facultative/obligatory treaty with a number of Lloyd's syndicates, rather than a quota share treaty.[2] The reinsurers had successfully avoided the treaty in arbitration for non-disclosure and in subsequent court proceedings, Cresswell J. held that the brokers were in breach of duty on the same basis. He also held that the brokers were in breach of duty because they had misrepresented the nature of the proposed reinsurance to the lead underwriter and had failed to disclose this to the following market.

(g) *Making a misrepresentation to the insurers*

If the insurance broker makes a representation to the insurers which he knows, **14–069** or should know, may be false, he will be liable for any loss thereby caused to the client.[3] In *Warren v. Henry Sutton & Co.*[4] the plaintiff instructed the defendants to arrange an extension of his motor insurance policy, so that a friend, Mr Wright, with whom he was proposing to go on holiday, would be permitted to drive his car. The defendants enquired about Mr Wright's driving record and the plaintiff may have given some such answer as "no convictions so far as I know". The defendants then informed the insurers (incorrectly) that Mr Wright had no accidents, claims or disabilities. Subsequently an accident occurred and the insurers denied liability on the grounds of misrepresentation. The Court of Appeal by a majority held that the defendants were liable on the grounds that

---

[99] The claim against the brokers also failed in *Gunns v. Par Insurance Brokers* [1997] 1 Lloyd's Rep. 173, Sir Michael Ogden, sitting as a deputy High Court judge. The plaintiff was dyslexic, but this had not prevented him from becoming a successful businessman, and the suggestion that brokers should have done more than they did because of their client's dyslexia was rejected. The Judge stated: "Stupid, illiterate, senile people, and other such persons in similar categories may well call for a broker to take unusual precautions when proposal forms are filled in. In my view in this case there was no call for [the brokers] to do more than they did."

[1] [1998] 1 Lloyd's Rep. 565

[2] Under a facultative/obligatory treaty the reinsured is able to choose which risks are ceded to the reinsurer, who has no choice but to accept them. Under a quota share treaty all risks within the defined parameters must be ceded by the reinsured. Facultative/obligatory treaties are less attractive to reinsurers because they allow the reinsured to select the risks which are reinsured. There is therefore a risk that the reinsured's selection will be unbalanced, producing a concentration of risk (whereas his whole account or defined area of account should be balanced) or that the reinsured will simply choose to reinsure his worst business.

[3] *e.g. Everett v. Hogg Robinson & Gardner Mountain (Insurance) Ltd* [1973] 2 Lloyd's Rep. 217 (broker wrongly stated that no plastics were used by the insured); *Sharp and Roarer Investments Ltd v. Sphere Drake Insurance plc, The Moonacre* [1992] 2 Lloyd's Rep. 501 (broker who forged his client's signature on the proposal form without his client's authority thereby made a misrepresentation to insurers and so was in breach of duty to his client) and *Akedian Co. Ltd v. Royal Insurance Ltd* (1999) 1 V.R. 80, Supreme Court of Victoria (broker knowingly misrepresented the age of machinery which was to be insured).

[4] [1976] 2 Lloyd's Rep. 276.

nothing said by the plaintiff justified the positive representation which they made to the insurers. Lord Denning M.R. dissented on the grounds that the plaintiff was well aware of Mr Wright's bad driving record and the cause of the loss was his own failure to disclose it to the brokers.

14–070   **Approval by the client.** If the client expressly approves or confirms a communication from the brokers to his insurers containing misrepresentations, he cannot thereafter hold the brokers liable for the consequences.[5] In *Bell v. Tinmouth*[6] the client wanted to insure his paintings while on display at M's house. The client referred his broker to M for information about the house and M inaccurately stated that the house was permanently occupied. The paintings were stolen in M's absence and insurers successfully denied cover. The client's claim against the broker failed, the broker reasonably having relied upon the information he received from M and having transmitted it reasonably accurately to insurers.[7]

14–071   The factual basis for a finding that brokers were in breach of duty for making a misrepresentation to insurers will often also support a finding of breach for failing to disclose material facts. Thus, in *Aneco Reinsurance Underwriting (in liquidation) v. Johnson and Higgins Ltd*,[8] Cresswell J. held that the brokers were also in breach of duty for misrepresenting the nature of the underlying business to reinsurers.

14–072   **Completion of the proposal form.** Where new insurance is being arranged for the client, it is quite common for the broker to fill in the proposal form, reading out the questions to the client and recording his answers.[9] The broker's duty in such circumstances was described by Megaw L.J. in *O'Connor v. B.D.B. Kirby & Co.*[10] in these terms:

---

[5] See *Commonwealth Insurance Co. of Vancouver v. Groupe Spinks SA* [1983] 1 Lloyd's Rep. 67, 82, *per* Lloyd J.

[6] (1988) 53 D.L.R. (4th) 731, British Columbia Court of Appeal.

[7] In *Rivard v. Mutual Life Insurance Co. of Canada* (1992) 9 O.R. (3d) 545, Ontario Court (General Division) an insurance agent was held to have been in breach of duty to an intended beneficiary of a policy of life insurance for allowing the person whose life was to be insured to represent falsely that he had never smoked. The misrepresentation was unequivocal and the basis upon which the agent (who had some reason to question what was said) was held negligent is not clear. Yates J. appears to have applied a particularly rigorous standard of care.

[8] [1998] 1 Lloyd's Rep. 565 (discussed in para. 14–068 above). A similar duplication of findings was made in *Sharp and Roarer Investments Ltd v. Sphere Drake Insurance plc, The Moonacre* [1992] 2 Lloyd's Rep. 501 (discussed in paras 14–052, 14–062, 14–081 and 14–085).

[9] Para. 19 of the General Insurance Standards Council Commercial Code states: "Members will make it clear to Commercial Customers that all answers or statements given on a proposal form, claim form, or any other material document, are the Commercial Customer's own responsibility. Commercial Customers should always be asked to check the accuracy of information provided." Para. 20 provides: "If Members believe that any disclosure of material facts by their Commercial Customers is not true, fair or complete, they will request their Commercial Customers to make the necessary true, fair or complete disclosure, and if this is not forthcoming must consider declining to continue acting on their Commercial Customer's behalf."

[10] [1972] 1 Q.B. 90, 101C. See also *Hudson Turner Furs Ltd v. American Insurance Co.* (1964) 43 D.L.R. (2d) 323 (Ontario High Court) where the broker read out and explained the questions on the proposal form to the insured and wrote down the answers. He did not show the completed form to the insured. He was held not to be liable when the insurers avoided liability for breach of a warranty made by answers to those questions. The client's appeal was dismissed (1965) 48 D.L.R. (2d) 508.

"When the broker took it on himself to fill in the proposal form, the duty upon him was to use such care as was reasonable in all the circumstances towards ensuring that the answers recorded to the questions in the proposal form accurately represented the answers given to the broker by the insured. But the duty was not a duty to ensure that every answer was correct."[11]

Different considerations arise where the questions in the proposal form are directed to matters of which the brokers have greater knowledge than their clients, such as details of previous claims which the brokers handled or details of previous insurance which the brokers arranged. The brokers are then under a duty to answer such questions correctly and cannot rely upon their clients.[12]

The broker cannot avoid his responsibility by putting evasive answers in the proposal form. This is illustrated by the Australian case of *Ogden & Co. Pty Ltd v. Reliance Fire Sprinkler Co. Pty Ltd*[13] In that case brokers completed and signed a proposal form for public and products liability insurance on behalf of the F Group of Companies. Questions 1 and 2 of the proposal form, relating to prior claims and cancellations of policies, were bracketed together and answered "not known to brokers". In fact the Group had a record of claims which ought to have been disclosed. MacFarlan J. held that the answer to questions 1 and 2 amounted to misrepresentation. The insurers were entitled to repudiate both for mis-representation and for non-disclosure of material facts. He held that in giving the answer "not known to brokers", the brokers were in breach of their implied contractual duty to exercise reasonable skill and care.[14]   **14–073**

(h) Failing to keep the client properly informed as to the existence or terms of cover

Existence of cover. An insurance broker should keep the client properly informed as to the presence or absence of cover. If the insurance broker is unable   **14–074**

---

[11] See also *Moore v. Zerfahs* [1999] Lloyd's Rep. P.N. 144 in which Stuart-Smith L.J. stated: "It was not the responsibility of the [broker] to advise [the plaintiff] as to the financial wisdom of the loan, merely to complete the application form honestly and carefully." The broker may be absolved from the consequences of negligence in this regard, if the client checks the proposal form and fails to correct the errors: see para. 14–090, below. See also example (20) of the Insurance Brokers Registration Council Code of Conduct (S.I. 1994 No.2569): "In the completion of the proposal form . . . insurance brokers shall make it clear that all answers are the client's own responsibility. The client should always be asked to check the details and told that the inclusion of incorrect information may result, *inter alia*, in a claim being repudiated. On request, a client shall be supplied with a copy of the proposal form . . . at the time of completion."

[12] *Dunbar v. A. & B. Painters Ltd* [1985] 2 Lloyd's Rep. 616: proposal form contained misstatement on matters within the brokers' knowledge. Brokers held liable. This case went to the Court of Appeal, but not on the issue of liability: [1986] 2 Lloyd's Rep. 38. See further para. 14–106, below. See also *Porter v. Prudential of America General Insur. Co.* (1995) 146 N.S.R.(2d) 81, Nova Scotia Supreme Court: proposal form completed by broker. Form silent on client's previous loss of which the broker was aware. Broker held negligent in completing the proposal incorrectly and not in accordance with the information he had been provided with, and in not asking the client all the relevant questions.

[13] [1975] 1 Lloyd's Rep. 52.

[14] *ibid.* at 71: "The answer divorced from the anterior circumstances to which I have already referred was, of course, untrue. Secondly, in its character as an untrue statement it exposed the client, Reliance, and the validity of the policy thereafter to be issued to the risk, as should have been well known to an experienced broker, that the policy would be avoided."

to effect insurance at all[15] or, alternatively, is unable to effect insurance on the specific terms required,[16] he is under a duty to notify the client promptly. Where a broker receives information casting doubt on the reliability or solvency of an insurer of one of his clients, he should pass that information to his client even if he is personally satisfied with the insurer.[17] Where, however, the insurance broker receives instructions from a trade union or association of which the insured is a member, his duties to keep the insured informed are necessarily more restricted.[18]

14-075   **Renewal.** It is the normal practice of insurance brokers to notify their client shortly before a policy falls due for renewal.[19] In a Canadian case *Morash v. Lockhart & Ritchie Ltd*[20] the defendant brokers, who failed to send the plaintiff a renewal form for his fire insurance or to inform him that the policy was expiring, were held liable in negligence.[21] However, in the later Canadian case of *Bijeau v. Pelletier and the Co-operators General Insurance Co.*[22] it was held that there is no duty to renew an insurance policy, or to notify an insured that a policy is about to expire, unless the broker has expressly or (as in *Morash*) impliedly

---

[15] *Smith v. Lascelles* (1788) 2 T.R. 187; *Reardon v. Kings Mutual Insurance Co.* (1981) 120 D.L.R. (3d) 196 and see generally paras. 14–038 to 14–042, above.

[16] *Callander v. Oelrichs* (1838) 5 Bing.N.C. 58 and see paras. 14–046 to 14–048, above. Similarly, if the broker is instructed to obtain insurance cover generally for the client's business, he is under a duty to notify the client if there is any foreseeable risk which is not covered by the policy he effects: *Fine's Flowers Ltd v. General Accident Assurance Co. of Canada* (1977) 81 D.L.R. (3d) 139; *Mitor Investments Pty Ltd v. General Accident Fire and Life Assurance Corporation Ltd* [1984] W.A.R. 365. Thus *Dueck v. Manitoba Mennonite Mutual Insurance Co.* (1993) 83 Man.R.(2d) 291: agent negligently failed to advise clients that new policy was for specific perils rather than for all risks.

[17] *Lewis v. Tressider Andrews Associates Pty Ltd* [1987] 2 Qd.R. 533 (for the earlier facts, see para. 14–058, above). After effecting the insurance the broker received further communications which tended to show that the insurer was not reliable or sound, but failed to pass the information on to his client. He was held to have been negligent.

[18] In *Norwest Refrigeration Services Pty Ltd v. Bain Dawes (W.A.) Pty Ltd* (1984) 55 A.L.R. 509, High Court of Australia, brokers received instructions from a fishermen's co-operative to arrange insurance of the plaintiffs' fishing vessel. The vessel was duly added to the fleet policy which the brokers had previously arranged. Under the policy liability was excluded in the case of a vessel which did not have a current certificate of survey. The plaintiffs were not told of this exclusion and the vessel was lost at a time when it did not have a current certificate of survey. The co-operative were held liable in negligence, but the brokers were held not liable: "we think it was reasonable for Bain Dawes to proceed on the basis that the Co-operative, in the performance of its role of caring for its members, would have made any specific enquiry that was considered necessary in a particular case and that it was sufficient for it simply to act as an intermediary between the Co-operative and the insurer consistently with any specific instructions received from the former". *Ibid.* at 517.

[19] Para. 5.3 of the General Insurance Standards Council Code for Private Customers (2000) states: "We will tell you when you need to renew you policy or, when it will end, in time to allow you to consider and arrange any continuing cover you may need." Similarly para. 32 of the General Insurance Standards Council Commercial Code states: "Members will notify Commercial Customers of the renewal or expiry of their policy in time to allow them to consider and arrange any continuing cover they may need."

[20] (1978) 95 D.L.R. (3d) 647. See also *King v. Sullivan Insurance Inc.* (1993) 109 Nfld. & P.E.I.R. 227, where the broker not only failed to inform his clients that their policy had not been renewed, but led them to believe that it had been.

[21] However, damages were reduced for contributory negligence. The fire did not occur until 18 months after the expiry of the policy. The plaintiff was held contributorily negligent to the extent of 75 per cent for failing to keep himself informed about his insurance cover for so long a period: see para. 14–129, below.

[22] (1996) 176 N.B.R.(2d) 241, New Brunswick CA (claim against insurer's agent dismissed because agent had not given the plaintiff an undertaking to renew the policy).

undertaken to effect renewal. Further, a broker's duty on renewal does not oblige him to renew a policy automatically without his client's instructions.[23]

If, on renewal of the policy, there is any significant variation in the terms, the broker should bring this to the specific attention of his client, who might not otherwise notice the change, even if sent a copy of the policy.[24] Where the terms of insurance are varied on renewal, but there is delay in issuing the new policy, the broker clearly ought to inform his client of the material changes in the terms. Thus in *Mint Security Ltd v. Blair*[25] Lloyd's brokers were held liable for failing to inform the client's principal insurance brokers that upon renewal of a cash in transit policy, the terms of a proposal form completed two-and-a-half years earlier were incorporated. In the intervening two-and-a-half years the clients had varied their procedures from those described in the original proposal form. The insurers escaped liability on this ground, and the plaintiffs recovered against the Lloyd's brokers.[26]

14–076

Where client becomes uninsured. If the client becomes uninsured for any reason, the broker should notify him as a matter of urgency. In *London Borough of Bromley v. Ellis*[27] the brokers were held liable for failing to inform the defendant that his motor insurance policy had been cancelled by the insurers. In *Osman v. J. Ralph Moss Ltd*[28] the defendants arranged motor insurance for the plaintiff with a company which subsequently became insolvent. The defendants then sent a letter to the plaintiff, which was ambiguous in its terms and did not indicate the seriousness of his position. The defendants were held liable for (*inter alia*) failing to warn the plaintiff in clear terms that he was uninsured. In *Youell v. Bland Welch & Co. Ltd (No. 2)* (the "Superhulls Cover" case)[29] a further ground upon which the brokers were held to have been negligent was breach of a duty to ensure that the insurers were warned that reinsurance cover was about to expire because of the 48-month cut-off clause and to exercise reasonable skill and care to make available to the insurers reasonable extensions of cover under the reinsurance contract.[30]

14–077

There are, however, limits to a broker's duties when his client is in danger of becoming uninsured. In *Pacific and General Insurance Co. Ltd*[31] the reinsured

14–078

---

[23] In *Roy v. Edmond Vienneau Assurance Ltee* (1986) 67 N.B.R. (2d) 16 and 172 A.P.R. 16, New Brunswick CA the insured received a renewal notice but failed to act on it. He sued his broker after suffering a loss when uninsured, alleging that the broker owed a duty to renew automatically as a result of a conversation some years before. Even if there had been such a conversation, the brokers had continued to renew only upon receipt of instructions and the claim failed.

[24] *Harvest Trucking Co. Ltd v. Davis* [1991] 2 Lloyd's Rep. 638, (H.H. Judge Diamond Q.C. sitting as a High Court judge): intermediary held liable for failing to draw client's attention to new clause excluding cover for theft from vehicles which were not individually attended, a new and onerous provision. In *Michaels v. Valentine* (1923) 16 Ll.L.Rep. 244, Mayor's and City of London Ct, where the broker sent a copy of the new policy to the client without commenting on one important variation in the terms, it was held that the broker was not in breach of duty. However, this case is only briefly reported and it is doubtful whether it could now be relied upon even as persuasive authority.

[25] [1982] 1 Lloyd's Rep. 188.

[26] *ibid.* at 199–200.

[27] [1971] 1 Lloyd's Rep. 97.

[28] [1970] 1 Lloyd's Rep. 313.

[29] [1990] 2 Lloyd's Rep. 431 (for the facts, see para. 14–021, above).

[30] See also *Grainary Restaurant Ltd v. American Home Insurance Co.* (1987) 81 N.B.R. (2d) 151 and 205 A.P.R. 151, New Brunswick CA: brokers were held liable for failing to inform their client that insurers would not grant further endorsements suspending a condition excluding cover if the premises were unoccupied for more than 30 days and that the existing endorsements had expired.

[31] [1997] L.R.L.R. 65

went into liquidation without putting the broker in funds to pay the premium for its reinsurance. The provisional liquidator made it clear to the brokers that funds would not be forthcoming, but gave them no instructions to cancel the policies. The brokers' accounts at Lloyd's were automatically debited with the premiums, although it was held by Moore-Bick J. that they were not personally liable to the underwriters for the premiums and had had no authority from the reinsured to make the payments. The reinsurers cancelled the policies *ab initio*, on the suggestion of the brokers. The reinsured claimed against the brokers on the ground that they should have advised the provisional liquidator before doing so. Moore-Bick J. dismissed the claim, observing that once the provisional liquidator had decided not to provide funds to pay the premium the brokers were entitled to protect their own interests and that, if the premiums were not paid, there was little if anything the brokers could do to prevent the reinsurers from cancelling them.

14–079   **Terms of cover.** [32] If any onerous term or restriction is included in the policy, this should be notified to the client either before the insurance is effected or as soon as possible thereafter.[33] If necessary the broker should explain to his client the nature and effect of any significant or unusual restrictions or exclusions in the policy.[34]

---

[32] Para. 3.3 of the General Insurance Standards Council Code for Private Customers (2000) states: "We will explain all the main features of the products and services we offer, including: any significant or unusual restrictions or exclusions; any significant conditions or obligations which you must meet." Para. 10 of the General Insurance Standards Council Commercial Code states: "Members will advise Commercial Customers of the key features of the insurance proposed, including the essential cover and benefits, any significant or unusual restrictions, exclusions, conditions or obligations, and the period of cover. In so doing, Members will take into consideration the knowledge held by their Commercial Customers when deciding to what extent it is appropriate for Commercial Customers to have the terms and conditions of a particular insurance explained to them."

[33] See *King (or Fiehl) v. Chambers & Newman (Insurance Brokers) Ltd* [1963] 2 Lloyd's Rep. 130 (client adequately informed; brokers held not liable); *Theriault v. Assurance Levesque et autres* (1995) 162 N.B.R.(2d) 365, New Brunswick Court of Queen's Bench (broker negligent in failing to advise his client that his property was not covered for damages caused by freezing because the property was vacant) . In *Youell v. Bland Welch & Co. Ltd (No. 2)* [1990] 2 Lloyd's Rep. 431 (the "Superhulls Cover" case) (for the facts see para. 14–021, above) Phillips J. held that the brokers were in breach of duty in failing to inform insurers of the 48-month cut-off of cover under the reinsurance after that reinsurance had been obtained for them (this was a separate breach from the failure to advise insurers of the clause when inviting them to enter the insurance contracts). In *J.W. Bollom & Co. Ltd v. Byas Mosley & Co. Ltd* [1999] Lloyd's Rep.P.N. 598 the brokers accepted that their duty extended to taking reasonable steps to ensure that the client is aware of the nature and terms of insurance and, in particular, drawing to his attention and if necessary explaining any terms the breach of which might result in his being uninsured. In *George Barkes (London) Ltd v. LFC (1988) Ltd* [2000] 1 P.N.L.R. 21, H.H.J. Hallgarten Q.C. the plaintiff instructed brokers to renew its contents and property insurance. The brokers procured insurance from a new insurer which provided a lower quotation that the original insurer. Subsequently a theft occurred in circumstances which were excluded under the terms of the new policy (but which would have been covered by the original policy), and the insurers declined to provide any indemnity. The brokers were found to have acted negligently in failing to advise the plaintiff of the restrictions in the new policy.

[34] In *Harvest Trucking Co. Ltd v. Davis* [1991] 2 Lloyd's Rep. 638 Judge Diamond Q.C. (sitting as a High Court judge) said: "If the only insurance which the intermediary is able to obtain contains unusual, limiting or exempting provisions which, if they are not brought to the notice of the assured, may result in the policy not conforming to the client's reasonable and known requirements, the duty falling on the agent, namely, to exercise reasonable care in the duties which he has undertaken, may in those circumstances entail that the intermediary should bring the existence of the limiting or exempting provisions to the express notice of the client, discuss the nature of the problem with him and take reasonable steps either to obtain alternative insurance, if any is available, or alternatively to

If a broker arranges the insurance satisfactorily, whilst it is prudent practice to **14–080**
send the client a copy of the cover note or policy immediately, it seems that the
broker is not generally under a legal duty to do so: *United Mills Agencies Ltd v.
R.E. Harvey Bray & Co.*[35] In that case the plaintiffs instructed the defendants to
effect export cover on their goods, which were at the time in the hands of
packers. The plaintiffs omitted to tell the defendants that there was no existing
insurance to cover the goods whilst they were at the packers. The defendants duly
effected export insurance, but did not insert any clause relating to attachment of
risk while the goods were at the packers. Cover was effected on the Monday
morning. On the Wednesday the defendants sent a copy of the cover note to the
plaintiffs, which was received the following day. On the night of Wednesday/
Thursday a fire occurred at the premises of the packers, in which the plaintiffs'
goods were destroyed. McNair J. held:

(i) The defendants, who were instructed to effect export insurance, were not
negligent in failing to tell the plaintiffs that such insurance did not cover
the goods while at the packers. The defendants were entitled to assume
that the plaintiffs had conducted their business prudently and had
arranged the appropriate form of insurance while the goods were at the
packers.

(ii) The defendants were not negligent in delaying for two days before
sending a copy of the cover note to the plaintiffs.[36]

However, a broker who fails to send a copy of the policy to his client may fall
under a duty to advise the client of any important policy conditions. Thus in the
Australian case of *Austcan Investments Pty Ltd v. Sun Alliance Insurance Ltd*,[37]
brokers were held to have assumed a duty to advise their client of a clause
whereby the policy was avoided if there was a change of use of the insured
premises during the policy period unless agreed by insurers.

(i) *Failing to give proper advice*[38]

Anyone who gives advice on insurance matters in the course of his business **14–081**
owes a duty to exercise reasonable skill and care.[39] In the case of insurance

---

advise the client as to the best way of acting so that his business procedures conform to any
requirements laid down by the policy." *Ibid.* at 643.
[35] [1951] 2 Lloyd's Rep. 631. However, para. 4.3 of the General Insurance Standards Council Code
for Private Customers (2000) states: "We will send you full policy documentation promptly."
Similarly, para. 27 of the General Insurance Standards Council Commercial Code states: "Members
will forward full policy documentation without avoidable delay where this is not included with the
confirmation of cover".
[36] McNair J. accepted that it was the general practice of insurance brokers to notify clients of the
cover as soon as possible, but held that failure to comply with this practice was not negligent. See
para. 14–034, above.
[37] (1992) 57 S.A.S.R. 343.
[38] Insurance brokers who are subject to the regulatory regime of the Financial Services and Markets
Act 2000 (as to which see para. 14–006, above) may incur civil liability to their clients under s.150
of the Act for failure to give proper advice. For example they may be in breach of the "Suitability"
rules.
[39] *M'Neill v. Millen & Co. Ltd* [1907] 2 I.R. 328 (garage owners held liable for wrongly advising
plaintiff that his car was insured); *Gomer v. Pitt & Scott* (1922) 12 Ll.L.Rep. 115; *Random Ford
Mercury Sales Ltd v. Noseworthy* (1992) 95 D.L.R. (4th) 168 (agent negligently advising unpaid
vendor of boat that his interest was covered under insurance arranged for the purchaser; vendor
allowed purchaser to take boat which was lost).

brokers, the giving of advice is one of their most important functions.[40] The insurance broker is expected to have a basic knowledge of insurance law,[41] to understand the insurance policies which he effects and to be reasonably familiar with the insurance market, or at least that part of it in which he practises. In *Osman v. J. Ralph Moss Ltd*[42] the Court of Appeal considered that one respect in which the defendants were negligent[43] was in their initial advice to the plaintiff to insure with a company which was generally known to be in financial difficulties.[44] In *Strong & Pearl v. S. Allison & Co. Ltd*[45] the defendants failed to appreciate that unless and until the insurers agreed to vary the terms, the policy which they had effected would only cover the vessel if it were laid up in one particular boat-yard. Accordingly the second ground upon which the defendants were held liable[46] was that they had incorrectly advised the plaintiffs that the vessel would be covered if it were moved to a different boat-yard. A similar conclusion was reached in *Sharp and Roarer Investments Ltd v. Sphere Drake Insurance plc, The Moonacre*.[47] In *Engel v. Janzen*[48] the insured were going abroad for two months and asked their broker whether they should, cancel their motor insurance policies. The broker advised that they should without pointing out that if they did cancel they would lose insurance cover against personal injury by uninsured or underinsured motorists. The insured acted on the advice and suffered serious injuries at the hands of an impecunious and uninsured motorist. The broker was held liable.[49]

14–082 There are, of course, limitations on a broker's duty to advise. The duty to advise is contingent upon and limited by the insured's description of the nature of his business.[50] A broker will not necessarily be under a duty to advise as to coverage beyond that specifically sought by his client. Nor will a broker be held liable for failing to advise a client that his policy does not provide a certain type of cover if the client is already aware of that and has made his own, informed decision not to obtain the additional cover.[51]

---

[40] The IBRC Code of Conduct provides that brokers shall "provide advice objectively and independently". Code of Conduct, example (1). See also example (11): "Insurance brokers shall explain to the client the differences in, and the relative costs of, the principal types of insurance . . . which in the opinion of the insurance broker, would suit the client's needs . . . "

[41] See para. 14–035, above.

[42] [1979] 1 Lloyd's Rep. 313. For the facts see para. 14–077, above.

[43] In addition to the ground discussed above at para. 14–077.

[44] See also *Lewis v. Tressider Andrews Associates Pty Ltd* [1987] 2 Qd.R. 533, discussed at para. 14–058, above.

[45] (1926) 25 Ll.L.Rep. 504. For the facts see para. 14–047, above.

[46] In addition to the ground discussed above at para. 14–047.

[47] [1992] 2 Lloyd's Rep. 501 (for the facts see para. 14–052 above).

[48] (1990) 65 D.L.R. (4th) 760, British Columbia CA.

[49] See also *Fletcher v. Manitoba Public Insurance Co.* (1990) 74 D.L.R. (4th) 636: public insurance corporation held to be in breach of tortious duty of care in failing to advise insured of availability and importance of underinsured motorist coverage. This decision was followed in *Payer v. Peerless Plating Rack Co. Ltd* (1994) 37 O.R.(3d) 781. In the latter case, brokers were held liable for failing to advise their client of a life insurance policy taken out by his employer, the benefit of which he could have retained when his employment ended. These Canadian decisions followed *Fine's Flowers Ltd v. General Accident Assurance Co. of Canada* (1977) 81 D.L.R. 135 (as to which see para. 14–012 above).

[50] *St. Isidore Asphalte Ltee v. Luminex Signs Ltd* (1996) 176 N.B.R. (2d) 135, New Brunswick Court of Queen's Bench (for facts see para. 14–053 n.53).

[51] *Diamond v. Ranger Unicity Insurance Brokers Ltd* (1997) 119 Man.R. (2d) 99 (clients found to be sophisticated and intelligent people who took a keen interest in their insurance cover; their claim against brokers for failing to advise them to obtain sewer back-up cover failed on the facts). See also *Kalkinis v. Allstate Insurance Company of Canada* (1998) 41 O.R. (3d) 528 where the Court of

Advice on the law. In *Sarginson Bros. v. Keith Moulton & Co.*[52] the plaintiffs   **14–083** (timber merchants and manufacturers) asked the defendants (insurance brokers) whether it was possible to insure their stock of timber against war risks under the Commodity Insurance Scheme. This scheme was contained in the War Risks Insurance Act 1939 and various statutory instruments. The defendants replied, incorrectly, that the timber could not be insured under the scheme. Before giving that advice the only step taken by the defendants was to consult one insurance company. The insurance company told the defendants that a builder's stock of timber did not come within the scheme and showed them certain entries in the list of Board of Trade replies to questions concerning the scheme (which were not directly on point). Hallett J. considered that the defendants had not taken "the steps which a reasonably prudent person would clearly have deemed necessary before that answer could be given with reasonable safety" and accordingly held that the defendants were liable in negligence.

This case raised the question, what standard of skill and competence is   **14–084** expected of the insurance broker when called upon to advise on a matter of law. Hallett J. approached the question, as one of general principle, in this way:

> "In my view, if people occupying a professional position take it upon themselves to give advice upon a matter directly connected with their own profession, then they are responsible for seeing that they are equipped with a reasonable degree of skill and a reasonable stock of information so as to render it reasonably safe for them to give that particular piece of advice. One has a great deal of sympathy, I suppose, with every professional man nowadays, at the way in which his operations are affected by a mass of emergency legislation, emergency regulations and emergency rules and orders. They pour out in unceasing flow, and I can well understand that it is most difficult for those concerned to keep up to date with them. I can well understand that there is always a danger of their being caught out by something. I do not for one moment say they are bound to be acquainted with everything. I think it is open to them always to say: 'Well, this is a difficult matter; I shall have to look this up; I shall have to make enquiries.' They can say, if they like: 'This is a matter for a solicitor, not for me'; and if they went to a solicitor he very likely would say: 'You had better consult Counsel.' No-one is under obligation to give advice on those difficult matters. If they are going to give advice, they can always qualify their advice and make it plain that it is a matter which is doubtful or upon which further investigation is desirable; but if they do take it upon themselves to express a definite and final opinion, knowing, as they must have known in this case, that their clients would act upon that, then I do think they are responsible if they give that information without having taken reasonable care to furnish themselves with such information, of whatever kind it may be, as will render it reasonably safe, in the view of a reasonably prudent man, to express that opinion."[53]

Similar views were expressed more recently by Hutley J.A. in the New South Wales Court of Appeal.[54]

Appeal for Ontario, when allowing an appeal by an insurance agent (who was treated as having similar duties to an insurance broker), stressed the need for a plaintiff to show that he had relied upon the broker to advise as alleged and that the broker knew or ought to have known that he was being relied upon to give such advice.

[52] (1942) 73 Ll.L.Rep. 104.

[53] Ibid. at 107.

[54] *Fanhaven Pty Ltd v. Bain Dawes Northern Pty Ltd* [1982] 2 N.S.W.L.R. 57, 65: "Because law provides the framework of commerce, sometimes a confining and obstructive framework, professional advisers in the field of commerce cannot avoid giving advice on legal topics. Thus, a broker in advising what policies are required by a business is an adviser on legal matters, namely, the types of risk for which the operation of the business may attract liability and the appropriate policies, and

14–085 **Seeking the insurer's advice.** If the client inquires whether his insurance policy covers a particular risk, and there is any doubt about the matter, the broker commonly refers the question to the insurers. In these circumstances the broker's "advisory" function involves little more than acting as a messenger.[55] It is, however, vital that he should accurately transmit the client's queries and the insurers' advice. Any failure in this regard would normally amount to negligence, if the client suffers loss in consequence.[56] If a broker chooses to answer the query without recourse to the insurer, he does so at his peril.[57] Thus in *Sharp and Roarer Investments Ltd v. Sphere Drake Insurance plc, The Moonacre*[58] when finding the broker negligent in relation to the houseboat exclusion clause, A.D. Colman Q.C. said: "If there was any doubt in [the broker's] mind as to the matter it was the duty of the broker to ask the insurers what meaning they attached to the question and the houseboat exclusion."[59]

3. DAMAGES

14–086 An award of damages is the principal remedy which the court will grant for breach of duty by an insurance broker. Since an insurance broker is not normally remunerated by his client, no question of forfeiture or repayment of fees generally arises.[60]

(a) *Remoteness*

14–087 The assessment of damages is subject, in every case, to the overriding principle that the damage in respect of which compensation is sought must be sufficiently proximate to the insurance broker's breach of duty. Broadly speaking, this means that (a) the breach of duty must have "caused" the damage,[61] and (b) the damage in question was foreseeable.[62]

---

if he takes upon himself to so advise and does not do so competently as a broker, he would be liable for loss occasioned by his failure and he could not avoid it by pointing to the fact that his advice involved legal issues."

[55] *e.g. Coles v. Sir Frederick Young (Insurances) Ltd* (1929) 33 Ll.L.Rep. 83.

[56] In *Melik & Co. Ltd v. Norwich Union Fire Insurance Society Ltd* [1980] 1 Lloyd's Rep. 523 the plaintiffs asked their broker, K, whether the insurance of their warehouse premises was still effective, despite a breakdown of the telephones at the premises. After making inadequate inquiries of the insurers, K advised the plaintiffs that they were covered. In the event, Woolf J. held that that advice was correct. If it had not been, however, K would have been liable to the plaintiffs: "it was K's duty to raise the matter much more clearly than he did with the insurers and to get the clear and positive answer [the plaintiffs] required. Instead, he relied upon his own judgment, his own view, that the plaintiffs were insured, and if they were not insured, in my view, he would have been in default in that respect and that would have been sufficient to find liability assuming that there was a loss in respect of that default" (at 534, col. 1.).

[57] In *T. O'Donoghue Ltd v. Harding* [1988] 2 Lloyd's Rep. 281 the brokers answered a query about the extent of cover themselves. Otton J. held that their interpretation of the cover was correct and held the insurers liable. However he went on to say of the broker: "Whether he was wise to give such unequivocal advice to the insured without referring to underwriters is a matter I do not have to decide. Suffice it to say that if I had found the facts marginally different, then Mr Ellis [of the brokers] . . . might well have been shown to be not merely imprudent but even negligent" (at 291, col. 1).

[58] [1992] 2 Lloyd's Rep. 501 (for the relevant facts, see para. 14–052 above).

[59] *ibid*. at 525, col. 2.

[60] Where the client is charged a fee, presumably the same principles would apply to insurance brokers as to other professions. See chap. 3, para. 3–006 *et seq.*

[61] As to which see paras. 14–088 to 14–112, below.

[62] As to which see para. 14–113, below.

(b) *Causation*

Whether the claim is brought in contract or tort, it is first necessary to **14–088** determine whether the insurance broker's breach of duty was "the cause" of the damage of which complaint is made.[63] Arguments as to causation normally take one of three forms: (1) sometimes it is contended that a particular error or omission on the claimant's part was the sole reason why he was uninsured; (2) sometimes it is argued that even if the broker had fully discharged his duty, the claimant would not have been insured against the loss which actually occurred; or (3) sometimes it is argued that if the full facts had been known, the required insurance would not have been obtained. These three topics will be discussed separately.

(i) *Intervening error or omission of the claimant*

Failure to check the documents. In the ordinary way, after the insurance **14–089** broker has effected insurance he sends a copy of the cover note or the policy to the client. Where the insurance has been effected on the wrong terms, it is sometimes suggested that the client alone is responsible for the loss, since he ought to have checked the documents himself. This is not usually an attractive argument. In *Dickson & Co. v. Devitt*[64] Atkin J., rejecting the point, said:

> "It appears to me, however, that the question is whether or not the loss which the plaintiffs have sustained is a reasonable and natural consequence of the defendant's breach of contract. In my opinion, when a broker is employed to effect an insurance, especially when the broker employed is a person of repute and experience, the client is entitled to rely upon the broker carrying out his instructions, and is not bound to examine the documents drawn up in performance of those instructions and see whether his instructions have, in fact, been carried out by the broker. In many cases the principal would not understand the matter, and would not know whether the document did in fact carry out his instructions. Business could not be carried on if, when a person has been employed to use skill and care with regard to a matter, the employer is bound to use his own care and skill to see whether the person employed had done what he was employed to do."[65]

---

[63] For a statement of the general principles, see *McGregor on Damages* (16th ed.), paras 139–191 (in relation to tort) and paras 232–246 (in relation to contract). The damage suffered must be loss in respect of which the broker owed a duty: *Banque Bruxelles Lambert SA v. Eagle Star Insurance Co. Ltd* [1997] A.C. 191. The application of this decision to insurance brokers is discussed further in para. 14–119 below.

[64] (1916) 86 L.J.K.B. 315. For the facts see para. 14–043, above. Followed in *British Citizens Assurance Co. v. L. Woolland & Co.* (1921) 8 Ll.L.Rep. 89.

[65] *ibid.* at 317, 318. In *Youell v. Bland Welch & Co. Ltd (No. 2)* [1990] 2 Lloyd's Rep. 431 (the "Superhulls Cover" case) Phillips J. rejected an argument by counsel for the insurers that *Dickson v. Devitt* and *General Accident Fire & Life Assurance Corporation Ltd v. J.H. Minet & Co. Ltd* (discussed at para. 14–093, below) demonstrated that insurers were entitled not to check a policy of reinsurance effected for them: see para. 14–127, below. There is a Canadian line of authority which suggests that an insured is not required to examine or read his policy: see *Miller v. Guardian Insurance Co. of Canada* (1995) 127 D.L.R. (4th) 717, at 729 (for the facts, see para. 14–054, n.54, above). It is submitted that in an appropriate case an insured will be contributorily negligent for failing to do so: see the next paragraph. An appeal in *Miller v. Guardian Insurance Co. of Canada* was unsuccessful: (1997) 149 D.L.R. 375. The Alberta Court of Appeal held that the insured had no duty to inquire as to the omission of a particular type of cover from his policy in the absence of any knowledge of the availability, importance and effect of the relevant provision.

14–090   **Approval of the proposal form.** Where the broker's breach of duty consists of negligence in completing the proposal form, then the subsequent negligence (or dishonesty) of the client in checking the form may exonerate the broker from liability. In *O'Connor v. B.D.B. Kirby & Co.*[66] the plaintiff instructed the defendant broker to arrange motor insurance on his behalf. The defendant filled in the proposal form on the basis of information given to him by the plaintiff. In answer to one question, however, as a result of a slip or misunderstanding, the broker wrongly stated that the plaintiff's car was kept in a garage. After completing the proposal form the defendant handed it to the plaintiff. The plaintiff glanced at the form, did not notice the mistake and signed it. Some time later, as a result of the misstatement in the proposal form, the insurers repudiated liability. The plaintiff then brought an action against the broker, but his claim was dismissed. The Court of Appeal held that the plaintiff's failure properly to check the proposal form was the sole effective cause of his loss.[67] Davies L.J. conceded that the position would be different if the plaintiff was unable to read or in some degree illiterate.[68] The position is also different where the erroneous answer relates to a matter peculiarly within the broker's knowledge[69] or where (as sometimes unfortunately happens) the client at the broker's invitation signs an uncompleted or partly completed proposal form and leaves it to the broker to answer the remaining questions. In the latter situation the broker deprives the client of the opportunity to check his answers and any error subsequently made by the broker is the immediate cause of the client's loss.[70]

14–091   *O'Connor v. B. D. B. Kirby & Co.* was recently applied by the Court of Appeal in *Ramesh Kumar Kapur v. J. W. Francis & Co.*[71] In that case an earlier claim was not disclosed on the proposal form and as a result the insurers subsequently avoided the policy for non-disclosure. The Court of Appeal found that the plaintiff had noticed the omission of the claim from the proposal and held that this was the sole effective cause of the plaintiff's loss. Therefore, notwithstanding the broker's negligence, the claim failed.

14–092   **Failing to notice a deficiency in the terms of cover.** Failure by a client to notice an error on the face of the policy is most unlikely to be held to have been the sole effective cause of the loss. A finding of contributory negligence is the more probable outcome.[72] Thus in *Youell v. Bland Welch & Co. Ltd (No. 2)* (the

---

[66] [1972] 1 Q.B. 90.
[67] *per* Davies and Karminski L.JJ. The other ground of the decision was that negligence was not established, *per* Davies and Megaw L.JJ.
[68] See also *Gunns v. Par Insurance Brokers* [1977] 1 Lloyd's Rep. 173 (Sir Michael Ogden, sitting as a deputy High Court judge), at para. 14–067, n.99). In *Porter v. Prudential of America General Insur. Co.* (1995) 146 N.S.R.(2d) 81, Nova Scotia Supreme Ct, the broker completed the proposal, knew that the client did not read the proposal before signing it, and it was obvious to him that the client was relying on him to complete the proposal accurately. The broker was held negligent in failing to note on the proposal a previous loss of which he was aware.
[69] *Dunbar v. A. & B. Painters Ltd* [1985] 2 Lloyd's Rep. 616, 620. (The case went to the Court of Appeal, but not in relation to this point: [1986] 2 Lloyd's Rep. 38.)
[70] The broker would also be in breach of the IBRC Code of Conduct, see example (20) of the Insurance Brokers Registration Council Code of Conduct (S.I. 1994 No.2569): "In the completion of the proposal form . . . insurance brokers shall make it clear that all answers are the client's own responsibility. The client should always be asked to check the details and told that the inclusion of incorrect information may result, *inter alia*, in a claim being repudiated . . . "
[71] [1999] Lloyd's Rep. 834.
[72] See paras. 14–126 to 14–131, below.

"Superhulls Cover" case)[73] the brokers sought to argue that the insurers' negligent failure to appreciate that the reinsurance contract contained an exclusion not present in the contract of insurance broke the chain of causation. Phillips J. rejected this argument, but reduced the award of damages by 20 per cent to take account of insurers' negligence. In *Forsikringsaktieselskapet Vesta v. Butcher*[74] the brokers were held liable for failure to act on a request by their client, the reassured, to contact the reinsurers. The reinsured failed to chase up the brokers for several months. Hobhouse J., whose judgment was upheld by the Court of Appeal's,[75] held that the reassured's negligence did not prevent the broker's negligence from being a cause of the loss, although he attributed three-quarters of the blame to the reassured. In *Paul Tudor Jones II and Marsh & McLennan Inc. v. Crowley Colosso Ltd*[76] the English brokers sought to argue that the failure of the American brokers to notice the term as to partial completion broke the chain of causation between their breach and the loss and damage. Mance J. rejected that argument and apportioned the loss equally between the two firms of brokers.

Approval of the policy. Where the client does examine the cover note or **14–093** policy, notices the error or omission and approves what has been done, then the brokers may not be liable for any loss subsequently sustained.[77] In *General Accident Fire & Life Assurance Corporation Ltd v. J.H. Minet & Co. Ltd*[78] the defendants failed to arrange reinsurance for the plaintiffs in accordance with their instructions. The defendants argued, however, that they had delivered a cover note to the plaintiffs, which clearly showed the terms of reinsurance effected and which the plaintiffs had accepted without question. In rejecting this argument the Court of Appeal set out what a broker must show to succeed in such a defence:

> "To succeed on this point the defendants must show that there was a ratification of their action, a ratification, that is, of their having effected a reinsurance different from that which their instructions required. The evidence entirely fails to prove this. Apart from the question whether the plaintiffs were under any duty to read the cover note, I am satisfied that the defendants have not proved that the plaintiffs understood that it did not represent the protection they desired and always desired. Mr. Bunton [of the plaintiffs], who was a marine underwriter, never, I think, understood the position under the original policy, and I am sure never intended anything less than he had instructed Mr. McRobert to obtain."[79]

In *Youell v. Bland Welch & Co. Ltd (No. 2)* (the "Superhulls Cover" case)[80] the **14–094** brokers argued that the insurers were estopped from asserting that the reinsurance was defective, alleging that the failure of the insurers to comment on the terms

---

[73] [1990] 2 Lloyd's Rep. 431 (for the facts see para. 14–021, above).
[74] [1986] 2 All E.R. 488.
[75] [1989] A.C. 852.
[76] [1996] 2 Lloyd's Rep. 619 (for the facts, see 14–048 above).
[77] This was one of the grounds upon which the defendants succeeded in *Smith v. Cologan* (1788) 2 T.R. 188n.
[78] (1942) 74 Ll.L.Rep. 1.
[79] *ibid.* at 9, col. 2.
[80] [1990] 2 Lloyd's Rep. 431 (for the facts, see para. 14–021, above).

of the reinsurance contract when they saw it amounted to a representation that those terms were acceptable to them. The argument failed. Phillips J. held that the insurers had not made an unequivocal representation that they were aware that the reinsurance cover differed from the insurance contract. The brokers, being themselves ignorant of the difference by reason of their own negligence, had not altered their position in reliance on any representation. Phillips J. also held that mere silence by insurers could not be a representation unless the insurers owed the brokers a duty to speak, and following *Dickson v. Devitt*[81] and *General Accident Fire & Life Assurance Corporation Ltd v. J.H. Minet & Co. Ltd*[82] held that the insurers owed no such duty.[83]

14–095   Similar arguments on behalf of negligent brokers were rejected by Colman J. in the more recent case of *National Insurance and Guarantee Corporation v. Imperio Reinsurance Co. (U.K.) Ltd*.[84] In that case the client had received the defective endorsement and had stated to the broker that it seemed to do what the client wanted. The brokers sought to raise defences of waiver, estoppel and ratification. All three failed, the first two for essentially the same reasons as those given by Phillips J., the third because an agent whose principal has indicated that he is prepared to treat a contract made by the agent as binding as between the principal and the other contracting party is not necessarily entitled to assume that the principal is thereby releasing him from all claims and, on the facts, the brokers were not so entitled.

14–096   In practice, therefore, it seems that where as a result of the broker's breach of duty insurance is not effected on the terms required by the client, it will be difficult to establish that the client's subsequent conduct was the sole cause of his loss unless the client actually noticed that the insurance was not as he had required but failed to do anything about it.

(ii) *Where the claimant would not have been insured in any event*

14–097   Typically a claimant in a broker's negligence action will have suffered a loss for which he is not properly insured. His allegation against his broker will be that, but for the broker's negligence, he would have been properly insured and would have received a payment from his insurer. In such cases the broker may be able to establish that, even if he had acted properly, the claimant would not have been insured for the particular loss which he has suffered. This may be for one (or more) of several reasons.

14–098   **Claimant would have chosen not to obtain the required insurance.** If a claimant alleges that owing to his broker's negligence he was not properly insured, it will be a good defence for the broker to show that the claimant would not have purchased the required insurance even if he had been properly advised.

---

[81] (1916) 86 L.J.K.B. 315.

[82] (1942) 74 Ll.L.Rep. 1.

[83] Phillips J. also held that *Dickson v. Devitt* and *General Accident Fire & Life Assurance Corporation Ltd v. J.H. Minet & Co. Ltd* did not establish that insurers could not be contributorily negligent in failing to check the reinsurance policy. He held that on the facts before him insurers were 20% to blame, but that was because they had failed to have proper regard for their own interests as opposed to being in breach of a duty owed to the brokers: see para. 14–127 below.

[84] [1999] Lloyd's Rep I.R. 249 (for the relevant facts see para. 14–043, n. 21 above).

For example,[85] in *Kennedy (B.J.) Agency (1984) Ltd v. Kilgour Bell Ins.*[86] the plaintiff's business was destroyed by fire. However, his insurance covered only a portion of his loss because cover was for "actual value" rather than "replacement cost" coverage. The broker was found to have been negligent in failing to advise the plaintiff of the availability of "replacement cost" coverage. However, the claim failed on causation. The court found that even if the broker had given the proper advice, the plaintiff would not have purchased the "replacement cost" coverage because it was more expensive than the "actual value" cover.

Claimant with no insurable interest. In *Newbury International Ltd v. Reliance National Insurance Co. (U.K.) Ltd*[87] insurers had avoided a policy for non-disclosure by the brokers. The policy was a device for raising money to finance a season of Formula 3 motor racing. Hobhouse J. held that the plaintiffs had no insurable interest in the policy and so would not have been entitled to recover under had it not been avoided. He therefore declined to award substantial damages against the brokers.[88]   **14–099**

Insurer entitled to reject the claim in any event. In many cases there may be more than one basis upon which an insurer is entitled to reject a claim. For example, there may have been a material non-disclosure when the policy was effected, and also a breach of condition when the loss occurred. The insurer may reject the claim on the basis of the non-disclosure or the breach of condition, or both. It is also often the case that the broker is responsible for one, but not both, of the grounds upon which the insurer is entitled to reject the insured's claim. This may provide the broker with a good defence on causation.   **14–100**

Where the insurer rejects liability on the ground for which the broker is not responsible before the other ground is detected then the matter is relatively straightforward. The broker will be able to show (for example) that the material non-disclosure for which he is responsible did not cause the claimant any loss because the insurer had already repudiated liability owing to the claimant's breach of condition in any event. However, the position is more difficult where (as more typically happens) the insurer rejects liability on the ground for which the broker is responsible. For example, if the insurer repudiates liability on the ground of non-disclosure, for which the broker is responsible, the broker will wish to argue that the insurer could and would have exercised its right to reject   **14–101**

---

[85] See also *George Barkes (London) Ltd v. LFC (1988) Ltd* [2000] 1 P.N.L.R. 21 in which the terms of the insured's cover excluded certain types of theft. A theft occurred in circumstances which were excluded. The brokers were found to have acted negligently in failing to advise the claimant of the restrictions in the policy. However, H.H.J. Hallgarten Q.C. found that even if the plaintiff had been properly advised it would still have accepted the policy. Therefore the plaintiffs were entitled to no more than nominal damages.

[86] (1999) 139 Man.R.(2d) 276, Manitoba Court of Queen's Bench.

[87] [1994] 1 Lloyd's Rep. 83.

[88] See also *Fomin v. Oswell* (1813) 3 Camp. 357, 359: "For omitting to include the premiums, the defendants would certainly be liable if the plaintiff had thereby sustained any damage: but the court has decided that he was not entitled to recover upon the policy; and he would not have been in a better situation if the premiums had been included. As to the first complaint [see para. 14–049, n.44 above], there is a loss without an injury; as to the second, there is an injury without a loss. I am therefore of the opinion that on neither ground can the action be maintained" (*per* Lord Ellenborough). Where the broker in breach of a duty owed to the insurer fails to include a customary limitation clause in a policy he issues on the insurer's behalf, there will be no loss if the insurer would have been liable on the policy in any event: *Gibraltar General Insurance Company v. L.E. Yingst Co.* (1990) 89 Sask.R. 93, Saskatchewan Ct of Queen's Bench.

the claim on the basis of the breach of condition, for which the broker was not responsible. The difficulty arises when it is unclear whether or not the insurer would indeed have rejected the claim on the basis of the breach of condition.

14–102   In such a case the brokers must satisfy the court that the insurers would in fact have exercised their rights and declined to meet the claim.[89] Only if this is established can it properly be said that no loss flows from the broker's breach of duty. Such a defence was successful in *Gunns v. Par Insurance Brokers.*[90] There the brokers successfully argued that the claimant would not have recovered under the policy (which had been avoided for non-disclosure) because the insured was in breach of a condition that he should take all reasonable steps to avoid loss and damage and to safeguard the property insured from loss and damage.

14–103   The defence was unsuccessful in *Fraser v. B.N. Furman (Productions) Ltd,*[91] in which an employer instructed its brokers to arrange employers' liability insurance on its behalf. The brokers failed to do so and consequently the employer was uninsured when an employee brought a claim for damages for negligence and breach of statutory duty. It was common ground that if insurance had been effected it would have been with the Eagle Star. The brokers argued that since the employer was in breach of one of the standard conditions of the Eagle Star's employers' liability policies, the insurers would have been entitled to repudiate in any event and therefore no loss flowed from the brokers' breach of duty. The Court of Appeal rejected this argument on two grounds: first, the insurers would not have been entitled to repudiate on the grounds alleged. Secondly (and in the alternative) it was considered "highly improbable" that the Eagle Star would have wished to take the point. In dealing with the second issue Diplock L.J. stated that the court must consider "the chances that an insurance company of the highest standing and reputation, such as Eagle Star, notwithstanding their strict legal rights, would, as a matter of business have paid up under the policy".[92]

14–104   *Fraser v. B.N. Furman (Productions) Ltd* was followed by the New Zealand Court of Appeal in *Cee Bee Marine Ltd v. Lombard Insurance Co. Ltd*[93] In that case stock was lost as a result of the client's negligence. The broker was held to have been negligent in failing to effect insurance covering the stock. He argued that, had insurance been arranged, the insurers would have avoided liability under a clause requiring the insured to take reasonable precautions. The New Zealand Court of Appeal held that when considering whether a clause would have excluded liability the policy should be construed so as to have regard to its commercial objectives. On that basis there was no breach of the term and the broker was liable for the loss. *Fraser v. B.N. Furman (Productions) Ltd* was also followed by the British Columbia Supreme Court in *L.B. Martin Construction Ltd v. Gaglardi.*[94] In that case the brokers admitted liability for having incorrectly

---

[89] In *Everett v. Hogg Robinson and Gardner Mountain (Insurance) Ltd* [1973] 1 Lloyd's Rep. 217 it was held that the burden of proof was on the broker to show that the reinsurers would have repudiated liability in any event (for the facts, see para. 14–107).

[90] [1997] 1 Lloyd's Rep. 173, Sir Michael Ogden, sitting as a deputy High Court judge. Such arguments may not always result in a reduction of damages, however: see the decision of Moore-Bick J. in *JW Bollom & Co. Ltd v. Byas Mosley & Co. Ltd* [1999] Lloyd's Rep.P.N. 598, discussed in para. 14–055 above.

[91] [1967] 1 W.L.R. 898.

[92] *ibid.* at 904E–F.

[93] [1990] 2 N.Z.L.R. 1 (for the facts, see para. 14–046).

[94] (1978) 91 D.L.R. (3d) 393.

informed their client that they had obtained insurance. The insurance which they should have obtained would have contained a relevant exclusion clause, but Taylor J. held that the insurers would have been prepared to compromise a claim under the policy and awarded the clients half their loss.

Where this line of defence is put forward, evidence from the proposed insurers **14–105** (or, if their identity is not known, from any representative insurers) is admissible to show whether or not they would have repudiated on the grounds suggested. In *Fraser v. B.N. Furman (Productions) Ltd* Diplock L.J. indicated that the absence of such evidence was one of the weaknesses of the third party's case.[95]

It may be that, having heard the evidence, the court is uncertain whether the **14–106** insurers would have availed themselves of the opportunity to repudiate. Alternatively, the court may consider that the insurers would have attempted to repudiate, although the outcome of any subsequent litigation is uncertain. In these circumstances the client has suffered some loss as a result of the broker's breach of duty—namely the loss of the chance of recovering a full or partial indemnity from the insurers. The measure of damages is the value of the chance which the client has lost. The correctness of this approach was reaffirmed by the Court of Appeal in *Dunbar v. A. & B. Painters Ltd*[96] although the Court went on to hold (on the facts of that case) that it was certain that the insurers would not have taken advantage of a particular term to avoid liability.

In *Everett v. Hogg Robinson & Gardner Mountain (Insurance) Ltd*[97] the **14–107** defendants effected reinsurance for the plaintiffs, but wrongly (and negligently) told the reinsurers that plastic was not used in the products of the insured. The reinsurers subsequently repudiated. The defendants contended that no loss had been caused, since the reinsurers could and would have repudiated in any event, owing to the plaintiffs' failure to disclose their adverse claims record. Kerr J. found that the reinsurers would, initially, have attempted to repudiate. However,

---

[95] [1967] 1 W.L.R. 898, 909. Diplock L.J. held that the burden was on the brokers to show that the policy would not have covered their client's loss. In *Cee Bee Marine Ltd v. Lombard Insurance Co. Ltd* [1990] 2 N.Z.L.R. 1 the New Zealand Court of Appeal took the same view, but in *Toikan International Insurance Broking Pty Ltd v. Plasteel Windows Australia Pty Ltd* (1988) 15 N.S.W.L.R. 641 the New South Wales Court of Appeal held that the onus was on the client.

[96] [1986] 2 Lloyd's Rep. 38. May L.J., with whom the other members of the court agreed, said at 42, col. 2: "the proper approach for the learned Judge to have adopted in the present case was to have assessed the chances that the insurers would have taken the height point and, having so assessed the chances, tailored his award of damages accordingly". One case which does not at first sight appear to fit into the scheme of the more recent cases is *Thomas Cheshire & Co. v. Vaughan Bros. & Co.* [1920] 3 K.B. 240. In that case the plaintiffs instructed the defendants to effect a PPI policy on a cargo of nitrate which was due to arrive shortly at Liverpool. PPI policies were in common use at the time, and were strictly speaking gaming policies within s. 4(2)(b) of the Marine Insurance Act 1906, and therefore null and void. Nevertheless, it was not the practice of marine insurers to take this point, and evidence was given that they would not have done so in the present case. As a result of the defendants' breach of duty the insurers were entitled to, and did, deny liability because of non-disclosure of a material fact. The Court of Appeal held that since the policy would have been null and void in any event, the plaintiffs were not entitled to recover damages. The Court of Appeal declined to take into account the fact that the insurers would not have relied upon s. 4 of the Marine Insurance Act. It is now thought that this case was decided on grounds of public policy and it has no application to cases where the insurance (or the proposed insurance) is not rendered void or illegal by statute or common law (*e.g. Webster v. De Tastet* (1797) 7 T.R. 157 (failure to insure slaves)). It was on this basis that the Court of Appeal in *Fraser v. B.N. Furman (Productions) Ltd* succeeded in distinguishing the decision. (See the judgment of Diplock L.J. at 908H–909B.)

[97] [1973] 2 Lloyd's Rep. 217.

Kerr J. continued, considering the friendly relations between the plaintiffs and the reinsurers and "the relative minor importance of this difference in terms of money against the background of their business relations as a whole . . . I am convinced that the result would . . . have been . . . a compromise".[98] What the compromise would have been was a matter of guesswork. However, as "a fair and reasonable assessment of the chances in all the circumstances" the plaintiffs were awarded two-thirds of the full value of their claim.[99]

14–108   In the cases discussed above it was clear from the events that actually occurred whether or not the insurer was entitled to repudiate liability irrespective of any negligence on the part of the brokers. However, in some cases it will be open to the brokers to argue that, on the facts as they would hypothetically have been (had the brokers acted properly), the insurers could and would have repudiated liability. Such an argument was raised in *JW Bollom & Co. Ltd v. Byas Mosley & Co. Ltd*[1] in which the brokers were found to have been negligent in failing to draw a condition to the attention of the insured. The brokers argued that this breach was not causative of any loss because, even if the condition had been drawn to the insured's attention, the insured would not have complied with it. Moore-Bick J. accepted that the burden of proof was on the plaintiff to show that, if properly advised, it would have satisfied the condition and was satisfied that this would have been the case. Accordingly, the defence failed.

(iii) *Where the required insurance would not have been granted if the full facts had been known*

14–109   Where the insurer repudiates for non-disclosure or misrepresentation on the part of the broker, any claim by the insured against the broker is based upon the premise that if the true facts had been declared valid insurance would have been obtained. However, the true facts may be so alarming that the client was effectively uninsurable. In these circumstances it may be that no loss was caused by the broker's negligence.[2] Alternatively, it may be that, if the truth had been declared, only limited cover could have been obtained. In this situation the loss

---

[98] *ibid.* at 224. See also *Beattie v. Furness-Houlder Insurance (Northern) Ltd* 1976 S.L.T. (Notes) 60.

[99] In *Pryke v. Gibbs Hartley Cooper Ltd* [1991] 1 Lloyd's Rep. 602 (for the facts of which see para. 14–024, above) one element of the insurer's claim against the brokers was the loss of the chance to sue their American coverholder while it had solvent errors and omissions insurers. The brokers argued that the coverholder's errors and omissions insurers would have relied upon two exclusions in the policy. Waller J. accepted that they would have relied upon both, although they only had a real chance of establishing one, and even that was not certain. He held that given the possibility that neither exclusion would avail them and their exposure to costs and a possible claim for punitive damages in the United States for "bad faith denial of coverage" the errors and omissions insurers would have been prepared to contribute 50% of the sum needed to meet insurers' exposure in the United States as a result of their coverholder's excess of authority, proceeding on the basis of loss of a chance.

[1] [1999] Lloyd's Rep. P.N. 598.

[2] A similar argument was accepted in *Gooderham v. Bank of Novia Scotia* [2000] 47 O.R. 3d 554, Canadian Supreme Court of Justice, in which the defendant bank was found to have acted negligently in failing to forward the plaintiff's application forms to the insurer. On the facts it was found that the bank acted as the agent of the insurer so that a valid contract of insurance existed. However, the court went on to hold that if no such contract had existed, the plaintiff would only have been entitled to nominal damages because he was uninsurable as at the date the insurance application was made.

caused by the broker's negligence is correspondingly reduced but not eliminated.

Arguments of this nature necessarily depend on speculation and are not likely generally to appeal to the court.[3] In *Mint Security Ltd v. Blair*[4] Staughton J. held that if there had been no failure of communication, "some accommodation would have been reached between the plaintiffs and their insurers. Either the procedures would have been improved so far as they could be or a small extra premium would have been charged with the procedures as varied. In the last resort, of course, the plaintiffs need not have carried the cash at all, and then there would have been no loss."[5] **14–110**

In *Cee Bee Marine Ltd v. Lombard Insurance Co. Ltd*[6] the risk which was uninsured by reason of the broker's negligence was a fibreglass boat repair business carried on in a wooden building. This was not a risk likely to appeal to insurers. The New Zealand Court of Appeal held that the measure of damages was the loss of the chance to obtain insurance elsewhere. The award of damages should reflect the value of that chance. The Court was satisfied that the client would not knowingly have carried on its business without insurance, so that the four most obvious possible outcomes were: **14–111**

(i) the client would have obtained insurance with a higher premium;

(ii) the client would have obtained insurance conditional upon a change in the structure of the building;

(iii) the insured would have moved its business elsewhere and obtained insurance;

(iv) it would have ceased to carry on its business so preserving the value of its stock.

The Court discounted the award of damages slightly to take account of these possibilities, including something for the sums which might have had to be expended on the premium and expenses in order to obtain cover. This approach was followed in *O & R Jewllers Ltd v. Terry.*[7] The evidence in that case was that so long as the convicted burglar remained managing director of the plaintiff's parent company, the plaintiff was uninsurable. Even had it been obtained, there

---

[3] Such arguments were rejected by the Privy Council in *Eagle Star Insurance Co. Ltd v. National Westminster Finance Australia Ltd* (1985) 58 A.L.R. 165. In *Youell v. Bland Welch & Co. Ltd (No. 2)* [1990] 2 Lloyd's Rep. 431 (the "Superhulls Cover" case) (for the facts of which, see para. 14–021, above) the insurers admitted on their pleadings the brokers' contention that reinsurance could not have been obtained without the 48-month cut-off clause. As Phillips J. remarked, this may have been a shrewd tactical move on the part of the insurers, rather than a recognition that the broker's contention was correct, because it allowed the insurers to argue that they would not have entered the insurance contracts but for the brokers' negligence, since it was clear that they would not have done so had there been no reinsurance on offer. As explained in para. 14–119 below, the decision of Phillips J. on this point and similar arguments now need to be considered in the light of *Aneco Reinsurance Underwriting (in liquidation) v. Johnson and Higgins Ltd* [2000] Lloyd's Rep. P.N. 1 (for the facts, see para. 14–068 above) and *Banque Bruxelles Lambert SA v. Eagle Star Insurance Co. Ltd* [1997] A.C. 191.
[4] [1982] 1 Lloyd's Rep. 188; for the facts of this case see para. 14–076 above.
[5] *ibid.* at 201.
[6] [1990] 2 N.Z.L.R. 1. For the facts see para. 14–046 above.
[7] [1999] Lloyd's Rep.I.R. 436, Sir Godfrey le Quesne, sitting as a deputy High Court judge (for the facts see para. 14–064, n.87).

were further defences which underwriters could and would have raised, although they might not have succeeded. The judge followed *Cee Bee Marine* and awarded damages on the basis that the plaintiff would have tried to have the dishonest director removed and that, while underwriters would have raised other defences, they might have compromised a claim or lost at trial and, taking the matter broadly, awarded damages representing 30 per cent of full recovery.

14–112   The court in *Cee Bee Marine Ltd v. Lombard Insurance Co. Ltd*[8] followed the dictum of Lord Diplock in *Mallett v. McMonagle*[9] which allows a court when deciding what the chance was that something would have happened (as opposed to deciding what did happen) to decide that the chance was more or less than 50 per cent. and award damages accordingly. In *Markal Investments Ltd v. Morley Shafron Agencies Ltd*[10] the British Columbia Court of Appeal took a different view and held that a client whose broker had failed to obtain insurance had to show on the balance of probabilities that insurance would have been obtained. It is submitted that in the context of claims against brokers for failure to obtain cover, the approach taken in *Cee Bee Marine Ltd v. Lombard Insurance Co. Ltd*[11] is to be preferred. Where the availability of insurance is in doubt, the damage should be characterised as a loss of opportunity.[12]

(c) *Foreseeability*

14–113   Whether the claim is brought in contract or tort, the claimant must establish not only that his loss was caused by the defendant's breach of duty, but also that it was foreseeable. In practice, questions of foreseeability do not generally arise in actions against insurance brokers, because the kinds of loss suffered fall within such a narrow compass.[13] However, where a claimant seeks to recover damages for losses other than the sum which he would have recovered under an insurance

---

[8] *ibid.*

[9] [1970] A.C. 166, 176: "The role of the court in making an assessment of damages which depends upon its view as to what will be and what would have been is to be contrasted with its ordinary function in civil actions of determining what was. In determining what did happen in the past a court decides on the balance of probabilities. Anything that is more probable than not it treats as certain. But in assessing damages which depend upon its view as to what will happen in the future or would have happened in the future if something had not happened in the past, the court must make an estimate as to what are the chances that a particular thing will or would have happened and reflect those chances, whether they are more or less than even, in the amount of damages which it awards."

[10] (1990) 67 D.L.R. (4th) 422 (for the facts see para. 14–038, n.6, above). The court followed *Hotson v. East Berkshire Area Health Authority* [1987] A.C. 750 and *Wilsher v. Essex Area Health Authority* [1988] A.C. 1074. In those cases the House of Lords was concerned with the level of proof needed to establish the cause of an event which had actually occurred. Thus in *Hotson* the claim failed because, on the balance of probabilities, too many blood vessels had been ruptured at the time of the negligent diagnosis.

[11] [1990] 2 N.Z.L.R. 1.

[12] In *Allied Maples Group Ltd v. Simmons & Simmons* [1995] 1 W.L.R. 1602 (a solicitors' case) the Court of Appeal, holding that the plaintiffs' claim was for loss of a chance, proceeded on the basis that the same principles applied to claims against solicitors as insurance brokers and relied upon *Dunbar v. A. & B. Painters Ltd* [1986] 2 Lloyd's Rep. 38 (see para. 14–106, above).

[13] See paras. 14–114 to 14–125, below. The claim against the brokers in *Bates v. Barrow Ltd* [1995] 1 Lloyd's Rep. 680 (for the facts see para. 14–058, n.65 above) would have failed because it was not reasonably foreseeable that an insurer would plead its own breach of the Insurance Companies Acts as a defence to a claim under an illegal policy. However, if it was negligent for the broker to expose his client to that risk, as Gatehouse J. found, it is hard to see how it was not foreseeable that the risk might turn out to be real.

policy, the defendant broker may successfully argue that such losses were not reasonably foreseeable. That argument was successful in *Bolton v. New Zealand Insurance Co. Ltd*[14] The client claimed damages for losses allegedly caused by the need to sell a farm in order to finance repairs of his uninsured yacht, but this head of loss was rejected as being unforeseeable.

(i) *Measure of damages*

The fundamental principle governing the measure of damages is that the **14–114** claimant should be put, so far as money can do so, in the position he would have been in had the defendant discharged his duty.[15] In claims against insurance brokers, the claimant typically alleges that he was uninsured when, but for his broker's negligence, he would have been insured. Therefore the main (and often the only) item of damages claimed is the amount which would have been payable by the insurers (or reinsurers) but for the broker's breach of duty. If there is no doubt that the insurers (or reinsurers) would have satisfied the client's claim, then this loss is plainly recoverable.[16]

The measure of damages is the difference between the sum the claimant should **14–115** have received had his broker acted properly and that which (if anything) he actually received. Therefore if the insurance policy which should have been effected contained a term limiting liability to a sum lower than the claimant's loss, the damages recoverable against the broker will be limited to the same extent.[17] Similarly, where the broker arranges valid but inadequate insurance, the measure of damages will be the difference between the sum recoverable under the policy and the sum which ought to have been recoverable.[18] Where insurers make an *ex gratia* payment, credit should be given for it.[19] In one case, where the insurers paid up under the policy in error but the insured voluntarily reimbursed them, the amount which the insured voluntarily repaid was also recovered in damages.[20]

In some cases it will be open to the defendant broker to argue that, even if he **14–116** had fulfilled his duty, the insurers would not have satisfied the client's claim. This may be for a number of reasons, but typically it is alleged that the insurers would have been entitled to repudiate liability in any event. As discussed above, in such cases damages are assessed on a loss of a chance basis, *i.e.* the court will value the chance the claimant had of recovering a full or partial indemnity from the insurers.[21]

---

[14] [1995] 1 N.Z.L.R. 224; for the facts see para. 14–066, n.96 above.
[15] *Livingstone v. The Rawyards Coal Co.* (1880) 5 App. Cas. 25, 39; *Dodd Properties (Kent) Ltd v. Canterbury City Council* [1980] 1 W.L.R. 433, 451, 454 and 456.
[16] See, *e.g. Smith v. Price* (1862) 2 F. & F. 748; *British Citizens Assurance Company v. L. Woolland & Co.* (1921) 8 Ll.L.Rep. 89; *General Accident Fire & Life Assurance Corporation Ltd v. J.H. Minet & Co. Ltd* (1942) 74 Ll.L.Rep. 1; *London Borough of Bromley v. Ellis* [1971] 1 Lloyd's Rep. 97; *Ramwade Ltd v. W.J. Emson & Co. Ltd* [1987] R.T.R. 72.
[17] *Mint Security Ltd v. Blair* [1982] 1 Lloyd's Rep. 188.
[18] See, *e.g. Coyle v. Ray F. Fredericks Insurance Ltd* (1984) 64 N.S.R. (2d) and 143 A.P.R. 93, Nova Scotia Supreme Court: insurance agents insured boat for actual value, not replacement value as instructed.
[19] *Harvest Trucking Co. Ltd v. Davis* [1991] 2 Lloyd's Rep. 638.
[20] *Maydew v. Forrester* (1814) 5 Taunt. 615.
[21] See paras 14–106 to 14–108 above.

14–117   **Settlement with insurers.** As a result of his broker's breach of duty, an insured may find himself with doubtful or uncertain rights against insurers when he should have had a clear, unequivocal right to indemnity for a loss. If the client enters a reasonable compromise of his claim against the insurers, the measure of loss against the broker is the difference between what he actually recovered from insurers and what he would have recovered had the broker not been negligent.[22] This is illustrated by the decision of the High Court of Australia in *Unity Insurance Brokers Pty Ltd v. Rocco Pezzano Pty Ltd*[23] There the brokers had failed to disclose their client's extensive previous claims record. Section 28 of the Australian Insurance Contracts Act 1984 provides that, save in the case of fraud, insurers are not entitled to avoid for non-disclosure or misrepresentation. They are, however, entitled to reduce the amount payable under the contract to that which would have been payable had there been proper disclosure or the misrepresentation had not been made. The client compromised its claim against the insurers for just over half the full value of the claim. The High Court of Australia held that the brokers were liable for the full shortfall.[24]

14–118   Where a client has compromised his claim against the insurers, it is open to the brokers to claim that the settlement was unreasonably low. The correct approach in such a case was discussed by Rix J. in *Mander v. Commercial Union Assurance Company plc.*[25] Rix J. expressed the view that it was not appropriate to re-litigate the dispute between insured and insurers, but rather to assess the chances of the insured's claim succeeding and then to consider whether the settlement was reasonable or unreasonable in the light of that assessment.[26]

14–119   **Other heads of loss.** The insured may try to claim further losses on the basis that had he realised that his insurance policy was not or might not be effective, he would have acted differently and so not have incurred those further losses. The starting point when considering whether the insured is entitled to recover damages for his additional losses is to establish the extent of the broker's duty in accordance with the principles set out by Lord Hoffmann in *Banque Bruxelles*

---

[22] See, *e.g. Akedian Co. Ltd v. Royal Insurance Australia Ltd* (1999) 1 V.R. 80 (Supreme Court of Victoria) (insurer avoided the plaintiff's policy for non-disclosure and misrepresentation. Plaintiff brought proceedings against the insurer under the policy and against the brokers for negligence. Plaintiff settled its action against the insurer and recovered from the brokers the amount recoverable under the policy less the amount received in the settlement with the insurers); *Bollom v. Byas Mosley* [2000] Lloyd's Rep.I.R.136.

[23] (1998) 154 A.L.R. 361.

[24] See also *FNCB Ltd v. Barnet Devanney (Harrow) Ltd* [1999] Lloyd's Rep I.R. 459 (for the facts see para. 14–049 above). The mortgagee insured had compromised its claim against the insurer, who had relied upon non-disclosure, misrepresentation and breach of condition by the mortgagee, who was also an insured under the composite policy. A subsequent decision of the Court of Appeal (*New Hampshire Insurance Co. v. MGN Ltd* [1997] L.R.L.R.24) held that the non-disclosure, misrepresentation and breach of condition of one insured, the mortgagor, under a composite policy did not affect the claim of another, the mortgagee, but that was too late for the mortgagee. The result of the brokers' negligence was that there was no mortgagee protection clause. The Court of Appeal held that, had there been, the insurers would have settled the mortgagee's claim in full within a reasonable time and that the brokers' breach of duty had caused the lower recovery on settlement. Damages were awarded for the difference between the full claim and the sums recovered on settlement and sale of the mortgaged property.

[25] [1998] Lloyd's Rep.I.R. 93, at 148–9.

[26] For a discussion of the appropriate measure of damages in cases where it is alleged that the insurer would have repudiated liability even if the broker had acted properly, see paras 14–106 to 14–108 above.

Lambert SA v. Eagle Star Insurance Co. Ltd[27] In a straightforward case where the broker negligently fails to disclose a material fact to insurers, the broker's duty (and so the measure of any damages for breach of that duty) will be confined to the policy of insurance which is later avoided. The insured will not be able to recover other losses even if they resulted from his having entered a transaction in reliance on the insurance being in place. However, brokers can undertake a wider role so that the scope of their duty (and so their potential exposure in damages) to their client will be greater. If the brokers undertake to advise their client whether or not a course of action should be taken, then they may be held responsible for all the foreseeable loss which was a consequence of that course of action having been taken.

Broker obtaining insurance and reinsurance. One example is where a **14–120** broker approaches an insurer with a substantial risk which he knows the insurer is only likely to accept if reinsurance is available and the broker offers to obtain that reinsurance. The broker is then acting both for the insured (in seeking to place the insurance contract) and for the insurer/reinsured (in seeking to obtain reinsurance cover). On one view the broker's duty to the insurer/reinsured is limited to the reinsurance contract and does not extend to the underlying contract of insurance. On that basis unreinsured losses suffered on the insurance contract are not within the scope of the broker's duty to the insurer/reinsured and so not recoverable as damages for breach of that duty. However, if the broker has taken an active part in setting up the insurance and reinsurance and has negligently failed to disclose material facts to reinsurers so that they accepted the risk, whereas had the broker made proper disclosure he would have discovered that it was not possible to obtain reinsurance on commercially acceptable terms and would have been under a duty to report accordingly to the insurer/reinsured, then the scope of the broker's duty may be wider. That was the conclusion of the majority of the House of Lords in *Aneco Reinsurance Underwriting (in liquidation) v. Johnson and Higgins Ltd.*[28] The plaintiff in that case had only recovered damages at the first instance to the extent that it would have recovered under the reinsurance treaties which had been avoided. However, the Court of Appeal reversed that finding and held that the client was entitled to recover damages for the whole of the loss which it suffered as a result of having accepted the underlying reinsurance business. The House of Lords upheld the Court of Appeal's decision. In his speech Lord Lloyd stated that "brokers (and others) are liable in contract for the foreseeable consequences of their negligence, including the adverse consequences of entering into a transaction with a third party, provided such a consequence can fairly be held to fall within the scope of the defendant's duty of care." He went on to state that *Banque Bruxelles Lambert S.A. v. Eagle Star Insurance Co. Ltd*[29] was an example of a special class of case where the scope of the defendant's duty is confined to the giving of specific

---

[27] [1997] A.C. 191. See also Chap. 3, paras 3–002 *et seq.*, and Chap 9, paras 9–113 *et seq.*
[28] [2001] UKHL 51 (October 18, 2001) (Lord Millett dissenting), upholding the judgment of the Court of Appeal, [2000] Lloyd's Rep. P.N. 1 (Evans and Ward L.JJ., Aldous L.J. dissenting). The Court of Appeal had reversed the decision of Cresswell J. on the point; (for the facts see para. 14–068 above).
[29] [1997] A.C. 191.

information. If the brokers duty had been confined to the obtaining of reinsurance, then damages would have been limited to the value of the reinsurance which the brokers failed to obtain. However, the scope of the duty owed by the brokers was not so limited since they had undertaken to advise the client as to what course of action to take. Accordingly, the brokers were liable for all the foreseeable consequences of their negligence, namely the full amount of the loss suffered by the client as a result of having entered into the transaction. In reaching this conclusion the House of Lords approved the decision of Phillips J. in *Youell v. Bland Welch & Co. Ltd* ("The Superhulls Cover" Case) (No. 2).[30] Lord Millett dissented on the basis that the proper measure of damages should reflect the fact that the brokers were not liable for all the foreseeable consequences of the client having entered into the transaction, but only for the consequences of it having done so on a false basis, namely that it had effective reinsurance cover.[31]

14-121   **Damages caused by failure to receive insurance moneys.** The client may also seek to claim further damages caused by failure to receive payment under the insurance policy. Thus in *Ramwade Ltd v. W.J. Emson & Co. Ltd*[32] the client's lorry was damaged beyond repair. Owing to the broker's negligence the client was uninsured and so received no payment from the insurers. The client lacked sufficient funds to buy a replacement vehicle and therefore hired a replacement. The client then sought to recover from the brokers the replacement value of the vehicle and the hire charges, on the basis that if the broker's had acted properly it would have received a prompt payment from the insurers and would never have had to incur any hire charges. The Court of Appeal allowed the claim for the replacement value of the lorry but rejected the claim for the hire charges, because the reason why hire charges were incurred was either (i) the client's impecuniosity, in which case damages could not be recovered,[33] or (ii) the failure of the brokers to satisfy their client's claim for damages promptly (*i.e.* the client was seeking to recover damages for non-payment of damages). The first reason may not be an answer to a claim in contract if the client can bring himself under the second limb in *Hadley v. Baxendale*,[34] *i.e.* on the basis that the broker knew when the contract was made that the client would not be able to finance a loss if his insurance failed. The second reason, however, is compelling. *Ramwade Ltd v. W.J. Emson & Co. Ltd* was followed by the Court of Appeal in *Verderame v. Commercial Union Assurance Co. plc*[35] when striking out the claim for consequential losses allegedly caused by failure to recover under the insurance

---

[30] [1990] 2 Lloyd's Rep. 431 (see paras 14–021 and 14–110, n. 3 above).
[31] Lord Millett considered that the concession made by counsel in *Youell v. Bland Welch & Co. Ltd* (No. 2) ("the Superhulls Cover" case) regarding the appropriate measure of loss had been wrongly made.
[32] [1987] R.T.R. 72.
[33] Applying *Owners of Liesbosch Dredger v. Owners of Steamship Edison* [1933] A.C. 449. In relation to a claimant's impecuniosity generally see now *Alcoa Minerals of Jamaica Inc. v. Broderick* [2000] 3 W.L.R. 23, PC.
[34] (1854) 9 Ex. 341: see *McGregor on Damages* (16th ed.), paras 247–264. Thus interest can be awarded at common law as special damages under that head: see *McGregor*, para. 629 and *President of India v. La Pintada Compania Navigacion SA, The "La Pintada"* [1985] A.C. 104, particularly at 125H–127D, *per* Lord Brandon. *Owners of Liesbosch Dredger v. Owners of Steamship Edison* was a tort case.
[35] [1992] B.C.L.C. 793 (for the facts see para. 14–029, above).

policy. A similar claim was rejected by the High Court of New Zealand in *Bolton v. New Zealand Insurance Co. Ltd*[36] on the grounds both of lack of a sufficient causal link and lack of foreseeability.

Litigation costs. Where as a result of the broker's negligence the client finds **14-122** himself uninsured, he may engage in litigation in an attempt to avoid the loss or to obtain reimbursement from some third party. If the client acts reasonably in bringing or defending such proceedings, he will be entitled to recover the cost by way of damages from the broker. The "costs" so recoverable are (a) the taxed costs payable to the other party, and (b) the client's own costs taxed on a solicitor and own client basis.[37] Where the client acts unreasonably in bringing or defending such proceedings, he will not be able to recover the costs against the broker.[38]

Claimant prosecuted. If as a result of the broker's negligence the client is **14-123** prosecuted and convicted of driving whilst uninsured, the amount of the fine and the costs of his own defence are also recoverable as damages against the broker.[39] In the unlikely event that the client is also disqualified (for example under the penalty points system) it is submitted that, subject to questions of causation and foreseeability, he may be entitled to general damages for the actual inconvenience caused by such disqualification. However, where as a result of the broker's negligence the client suffers distress or anxiety, as opposed to inconvenience, he should not usually recover general damages for that distress or anxiety.[40] Such awards should be very rare, because damages for distress are only recoverable if the subject-matter of the contract or tortious duty of care is to provide peace of mind or freedom from distress,[41] whereas insurance brokers are usually retained to obtain monetary protection against contingencies. Thus in *Verderame v. Commercial Assurance Co. plc*[42] the directors claimed damages for anxiety, depression and inconvenience. The Court of Appeal held that such damages would not

---

[36] [1995] 1 N.Z.L.R. 224; for the facts see para. 14–066, n.96 above.
[37] *Strong & Pearl v. S. Allison & Co. Ltd* (1926) 25 Ll.L.Rep. 504, 508. However, in *Seavision Investment SA v. Evennett, The Tiburon* (for the facts of the underlying trial see para. 14–039 above) Steyn J., when considering the basis upon which the brokers should pay the plaintiff's costs of suing the underwriter, said that he derived little assistance from the older cases and awarded costs taxed on the standard basis, rather than on a solicitor and own client or indemnity basis. His judgment on this point is not reported at first instance, but the plaintiff sought to appeal and the relevant part is set out in the judgments of the Court of Appeal: *Seavision Investment SA v. Evennett, The Tiburon* [1992] 2 Lloyd's Rep. 26. The Court of Appeal held that pursuant to s. 18(1)(f) of the Supreme Court Act 1981, it had no jurisdiction to entertain an appeal on the question of costs alone because Steyn J. had refused leave to appeal. However, Parker L.J. expressed "considerable doubt" as to Steyn J.'s decision. It is suggested that he was right to do so.
[38] *Osman v. J. Ralph Moss Ltd* [1970] 1 Lloyd's Rep. 313.
[39] *ibid.* at 316, 318 and 320. But where there is a degree of mens rea or culpable negligence on the part of the client, he cannot recover the fine by way of damages. For a general discussion of this topic, see *McGregor*, paras 748–757.
[40] In *Gaunt v. Gold Star Insurance Co. Ltd* [1991] 2 N.Z.L.R. 341, Gallen J. awarded general damages against a broker for the disruption caused to the plaintiff's life by the insurer's refusal to accept liability. This judgment was confirmed on appeal, although the judgment against the insurer was overruled on other grounds: *Gold Star Insurance Co. Ltd v. Gaunt* [1998] 3 N.Z.L.R. 80.
[41] See *Hayes v. Dodd* [1990] 2 All E.R. 818 and *Watts v. Morrow* [1991] 1 W.L.R. 1421.
[42] [1992] B.C.L.C. 793 (for the facts see para. 14–029, above).

be recoverable against a broker in contract and therefore should not be recoverable in tort.[43]

14–124 **Credit for saved premium.** Where as a result of the broker's breach of duty a cheaper policy or no policy is effected or, alternatively, the policy is avoided *ab initio*, the client makes a small "gain", namely the amount of the premium saved or refunded. The client should give credit against his claim for the amount of this gain,[44] although it is usually relatively modest. In *Bollom v. Byas Mosley*[45] Moore-Bick J. held that the client had to give credit for the additional premium which would have been payable in the year in which the client's loss occurred, but not for premiums payable in earlier years.[46] However, in *Eagle Star Insurance Co. Ltd v. National Westminster Finance Australia Ltd*[47] (where the policy was avoided as a result of the brokers' negligence) the Privy Council rejected the brokers' contention that the plaintiffs should give credit for the amount of premium refunded.[48]

14–125 Where the broker has negligently failed to obtain effective "primary" cover but the client has effective "secondary" cover, the client need not give credit for the latter if any recovery against the brokers diminishes the amount of the claim under the secondary cover, thus precluding the possibility of double recovery.[49]

(ii) *Contributory negligence*

14–126 While the courts are slow to find that the client's own negligence broke the chain of causation between the broker's breach of duty and the client's loss,[50]

---

[43] But damages for "the disruption worry and stress occasioned by the failure to pay out" under the insurance policy were awarded by the New Zealand High Court against the negligent broker in *Bolton v. New Zealand Insurance Co. Ltd* [1995] 1 N.Z.L.R. 224: the English authorities were not referred to in the judgment and it is hard to reconcile this decision with them.

[44] In *Charles v. Altin* (1854) 15 C.B. 46, 63 Jervis C.J. recognised that credit should usually be given for the amount of premium saved. Allowance was made for the saving of premium in *Lewis v. Tressider Andrews Associates Pty Ltd* [1987] 2 Qd.R. 533 and *Cee Bee Marine Ltd v. Lombard Insurance Co. Ltd* [1990] 2 N.Z.L.R. 1. In *Sharp and Roarer Investments Ltd v. Sphere Drake Insurance plc, The Moonacre* [1992] 2 Lloyd's Rep. 501 A.D., Colman Q.C., sitting as a deputy judge of the High Court, appeared to consider it appropriate for credit to be given for returned premium, although he left the point open for further argument.

[45] [2000] Lloyd's Rep.I.R. 136 (for the facts see para. 14–108).

[46] Moore-Bick J. rejected the broker's argument that the client had to give credit for the additional amounts which would have been payable by way of increased premiums throughout the period in which the client would, but for the broker's negligence, have paid higher premiums: "The fallacy in the argument lies in the assumption that [the client's] claim is based on a single continuous breach of duty or on a series of breaches of duty over the years up to and including 1996. It is not. The claim is based on a failure to give proper advice in relation to the renewal of the policy for the 1996/97 year." *Ibid.* at 151.

[47] (1985) 58 A.L.R. 165 (Appeal from Supreme Court of Western Australia).

[48] "Their Lordships . . . do not accept that A.I.B. are entitled to credit for the premiums which the Goldbergs will recover from underwriters. The measure of damages is for the loss which the Goldbergs suffered by not recovering $1,000,000 under the policies. That is $1,000,000." *Ibid.* at 175. In *George Barkes (London) Ltd v. LFC (1988) Ltd* [2000] 1 P.N.L.R. 21 (for the facts see para. 14–079 n. 33 above) H.H.J. Hallgarten Q.C. declined to follow *Eagle Star Insurance Co. Ltd v. National West Finance Australia Ltd*. He held that if the plaintiff was entitled to substantial damages, then the defendants would be entitled to deduct from those the amount of premium the plaintiff had saved as a result of acting on the broker's advice.

[49] *FNCB Ltd v. Barnet Devanney (Harrow) Ltd* [1999] Lloyd's Rep I.R. 459 (for the facts see para. 14–049 above).

[50] See paras. 14–089 to 14–096 above.

they are prepared to reduce an award of damages to reflect want of care on the client's part.[51] Unless the claim is for breach of an absolute contractual obligation,[52] the courts may do this whether the claim is brought in tort or contract or both.[53]

Whether a claimant has been contributorily negligent will depend upon the **14–127** facts of each case rather than upon any fixed rules of law. So in *Youell v. Bland Welch & Co. Ltd (No. 2)* (the "Superhulls Cover" case),[54] the insurers had received a copy of the contract of reinsurance (which did not match the terms of the insurance they had granted) on three occasions. The insurers failed to notice that the reinsurance was not on the same terms as the insurance. The brokers claimed that the insurers were at fault. The insurers cited *Dickson v. Devitt*[55] and *General Accident Fire & Life Assurance Corporation Ltd v. J.H. Minet & Co. Ltd*[56] as authorities for the proposition that they were entitled to rely upon the brokers and were not negligent in failing to compare the wording of the insurance and reinsurance policies and spot the difference between them. Phillips J. rejected that argument and held the insurers 20 per cent to blame.[57] The low percentage may well have owed much to the fact that the brokers had so drafted the reinsurance contract as to make the relevant term difficult to understand[58]: where the wording is straightforward and the person reading it is another broker, a higher percentage may well be justified. Thus in *Paul Tudor Jones II and Marsh & McLennan Inc. v. Crowley Colosso Ltd*[59] Mance J. reduced the damages payable by the English brokers by a third to reflect the negligence of the American brokers in failing to appreciate the effect of the relevant term, which was easy to understand. For similar reasons a reduction of 30 per cent was made by Colman J. in *National Insurance and Guarantee Corporation v. Imperio Reinsurance Co. (U.K.) Ltd*[60] In reaching his decision Colman J. mentioned the

---

[51] In *Cosyns v. Smith* (1983) 146 D.L.R. (3d) 622, however, the Ontario Court of Appeal held that where an insurance agent failed to arrange insurance as instructed, the plaintiff's failure "to check up on the agent" could not in law amount to contributory negligence. The court followed *Becker v. Medd* (1897) 13 T.L.R. 313, CA, a case decided before the passing of the Law Reform (Contributory Negligence) Act 1945. *Cosyns v. Smith* was distinguished in *Firestone Canada Inc. v. American Home Insurance Co.* (1989) 67 O.R. (2d) 471 on the ground that each case turned on its own facts.

[52] See para. 14–010, above.

[53] *Forsikringsaktieselskapet Vesta v. Butcher* [1986] 2 All E.R. 488, Hobhouse J.; [1989] A.C. 852, CA; *Youell v. Bland Welch & Co. Ltd (No. 2)* [1990] 2 Lloyd's Rep. 431 (the "Superhulls Cover" case), Phillips J.

[54] [1990] 2 Lloyd's Rep. 431 (for the facts, see para. 14–043, above).

[55] (1916) 86 L.J.K.B. 315 (see para. 14–093, above).

[56] (1942) 74 Ll.L.Rep. 1 (see para. 14–093, above).

[57] "*Dickson v. Devitt* and *General Accident v. Minet* were cases decided on their own facts and do not lay down some inflexible rule of law as to what a broker's client can properly be expected to do in the exercise of reasonable care to protect his own interests. In the present case those clients were Lloyd's agents. The personnel involved were marine underwriters of great experience. They admitted that they should have read carefully the terms of the cover on the three separate occasions when they received it." [1990] 2 Lloyd's Rep. 431, 460, col. 2. It must be borne in mind that both *Dickson v. Devitt* and *General Accident Fire & Life Assurance Corporation Ltd v. J.H. Minet & Co. Ltd* were decided before the Law Reform (Contributory Negligence) Act 1945.

[58] See para. 14–050, above and *Youell v. Bland Welch & Co. Ltd (No. 2)* [1990] 2 Lloyd's Rep. 423 (the "Superhulls Cover" case) where Phillips J. had to decide what the effect of the clause in the reinsurance policy was (his decision was upheld by the Court of Appeal: [1992] 2 Lloyd's Rep. 127).

[59] [1996] 2 Lloyd's Rep. 619 (for the facts see para. 14–048 above).

[60] [1999] Lloyd's Rep I.R. 249 (for the relevant facts see para. 14–043, n.21, and para. 14–095 above).

desirability of a broadly consistent approach to the application of contributory negligence to claims against brokers.

14–128   **Insurers.** Whilst contributory negligence is not readily found in cases of professional negligence,[61] courts are not slow to hold that insurers, being as knowledgeable about insurance matters as insurance brokers, were contributorily negligent. So in *Forsikringsaktieselskapet Vesta v. Butcher*[62] Hobhouse J. held the insurers 75 per cent to blame for failing to chase up the brokers, who had negligently failed to act on a request to contact the reinsurers about an exclusion clause. This award was upheld on appeal, although it would appear that the Court of Appeal thought that the percentage fixed by Hobhouse J. was at the higher end of the acceptable range.[63] However each case will depend on its facts, and a finding that an insurer was contributorily negligent is not at all inevitable. Thus in *Pryke v. Gibbs Hartley Cooper Ltd*[64] the brokers alleged that the leading underwriter at Lloyd's had been contributorily negligent. He had been given the coverholder's initial explanation, which suggested that the policy issued was not a financial guarantee, and was led to believe by the brokers that their investigations in the United States generally supported that explanation, which suggested that the coverholder had breached the spirit, but not the letter, of his contract. The underwriter had not been shown the copy of the offending policy which the brokers had, nor was he shown a telex from the coverholder which showed that the brokers had a copy of the policy. He did not pursue the matter further. Waller J. held that the underwriter had not been negligent, but indicated that had he seen the documents the position would have been different.[65]

14–129   **Others.** Where the claimant is not an insurer or a person with relevant expertise, the courts are likely to be slower to find contributory negligence. However, they will not be deterred from apportioning a significant part of the blame to the failure of the lay client to have due regard for his own interests if the facts warrant it. Thus in *Morash v. Lockhart & Ritchie Ltd*[66] a client who failed to take any action for 18 months after his existing policy expired was held 75 per cent to blame. In *Firestone Canada Inc. v. American Home Insurance Co.*[67] the client, acting by its advertising manager, was held 50 per cent to blame. The advertising manager had read the clause which was either incomplete or contrary to his understanding of what had been agreed, but did nothing about it. In *Labreche Estate v. Harasymiw*[68] the mortgagor was held to have been 50 per cent negligent for failing to respond in a timely manner to requests from the

---

[61] See generally Chap. 5, paras 5–113 *et seq.*
[62] [1986] 2 All E.R. 388 (see para. 14–059, above).
[63] [1989] A.C. 852. No member of the Court endorsed the apportionment wholeheartedly and Sir Roger Ormrod said he was somewhat surprised (at 879).
[64] [1991] 1 Lloyd's Rep. 602 (see para. 14–024, above).
[65] *ibid.* at 624, col. 2. The claim by the brokers that their client, an underwriter himself, should have realised that the risk to be reinsured was inaccurately described in a material way failed in *Aneco Reinsurance Underwriting (in liquidation) v. Johnson and Higgins Ltd* [1998] 1 Lloyd's Rep. 565 (for the facts see para. 14–068 above). The client did not have sufficient experience of the relevant market to appreciate this (whereas the brokers claimed special expertise) and had no knowledge of what oral presentation of the risk would be made by the brokers.
[66] (1978) D.L.R. (3d) 647 (see para. 14–075, above).
[67] (1989) 67 O.R. (2d) 471 (see para. 14–050, above).
[68] (1992) 89 D.L.R. (4th) 95 (for the facts see para. 14–059, n.72 above).

potential insurers for further information which he should have known they would require before granting cover.

The courts are unlikely to find that a client without any expertise is con- **14–130** tributorily negligent in failing to realise that his broker has not appreciated the purpose or effect of a particular clause. Thus in *Sharp and Roarer Investments Ltd v. Sphere Drake Insurance plc, The Moonacre*[69] the argument that the client should have appreciated the effect of the houseboat exclusion clause was rejected as "entirely misconceived".[70] Similarly in *JW Bollom & Co. Ltd v. Byas Mosley & Co. Ltd*[71] the brokers contended that the insured was negligent in failing to appreciate the need to set the alarm and in not obtaining an adequate level of cover. Moore-Bick J., following a passage from the judgment of Beldam L.J. in *Barclays Bank plc v. Fairclough Building Ltd*[72] rejected those contentions: the insured was entitled to expect the brokers to act with reasonable skill and care so that it was not negligent in failing to guard against the possibility that the broker had failed to do so.

Negligence relating to the insured event. Where the negligence of the client **14–131** causes an accident in respect of which the client would have been insured but for his broker's negligence, it might be thought that no account should be taken of the client's negligence. However, in *Bolton v. New Zealand Insurance Co. Ltd*[73] a finding of 50 per cent contributory negligence was made on the grounds of the client's negligence in causing damage to the uninsured yacht. It is submitted that this is wrong in principle: the purpose of the insurance was to provide indemnity against loss of the yacht, even if the client had been negligent. It was for loss of that indemnity rather than loss of the yacht that the broker was liable and the client did not contribute to that loss.

---

[69] [1992] 2 Lloyd's Rep. 501 (for the relevant facts see para. 14–052, above).
[70] A similar conclusion was reached in *Peter Unruh Construction Company Ltd v. Kelly-Lucy & Cameron Adjusters Ltd* [1976] 4 W.W.R. 419 (for the facts, see para. 14–046, n.34 above).
[71] [1999] Lloyd's Rep.P.N. 598.
[72] [1995] Q.B. 241 at 226G.
[73] [1995] 1 N.Z.L.R. 224 (for the facts see para. 14–066, n.96 above).

CHAPTER 15

ACCOUNTANTS AND AUDITORS

PARA.

1. Introduction 15–001
2. Duties 15–008
   (a) The statutory context 15–009
       (i) Companies legislation:
           the company audit 15–010
       (ii) Regulatory statutes
            relating to the financial
            sector 15–025
       (iii) Whistle-blowing 15–030
   (b) Duties to client 15–031
       (i) Contractual duties 15–031
       (ii) Duty in tort 15–037
       (iii) Fiduciary duties 15–038
   (c) Duties to third parties 15–045
       (i) Overview 15–045
       (ii) *Caparo* 15–053
       (iii) Factors which may be
             relevant 15–062
       (iv) Categories of advisee . 15–073
       (v) Policy considerations:
           duplication of
           remedies 15–087
       (vi) The Contracts (Rights
            against Third Parties)
            Act 1999 15–088
       (vii) The Human Rights Act
             1998 15–089
   (d) The standard of skill and
       care 15–090
       (i) General 15–090
       (ii) Auditing 15–093
   (e) Limitation of liability 15–100
3. Liability for breach of duty 15–102
   (a) Auditing 15–102

PARA.

       (i) Planning, control and
           recording 15–103
       (ii) Accounting and
            internal control
            systems 15–106
       (iii) Evidence 15–108
       (iv) Reporting 15–113
   (b) Other breaches of duty 15–117
4. Damages 15–120
   (a) Remoteness 15–121
       (i) Causation 15–121
       (ii) Foreseeability 15–131
   (b) Measure of damages 15–132
   (c) Heads of damage 15–135
       (i) Lost investment or
           advance 15–136
       (ii) Overpayment 15–137
       (iii) Moneys wrongly paid
             out 15–138
       (iv) Defalcations by
            director or employee ... 15–139
       (v) Costs of fresh audit
           and investigations 15–140
       (vi) Avoidance of double
            recovery 15–141
       (vii) Tax advice and returns 15–143
       (viii) Late notices and
              returns 15–144
       (ix) Negligent advice 15–145
   (d) Contributory negligence and
       contribution 15–146
   (e) Failure to mitigate 15–152
   (f) Statutory relief 15–153

1. INTRODUCTION

The expanding domain. From its origins as a profession concerned primarily   **15–001**
with book-keeping and the preparation and investigation of accounts, accountancy has embraced a wide range of functions. Apart from those original functions, including auditing, the range covers extensive advisory, reporting,
investigatory, regulatory and administrative services. Advice includes most notably taxation matters but also business problems such as organisational structures,
managerial efficiency and take-overs and mergers. Administration includes
administering trusts, receiverships and liquidations, and usually involves a considerable advisory and reporting element. This proliferation of functions has
necessarily resulted in specialisation. While an individual practitioner may be
competent to deal with a wide range of functions commonly performed by

accountants, very rarely will he be sufficiently competent to deal with them all. Indeed the same applies to the smaller-sized firms of accountants. The larger firms will usually be able to offer the whole range of accountancy services through partners or employees. It will be apparent that professional negligence on the part of accountants may arise within very broad contexts. This chapter will be mainly concerned with negligence in the context of the preparation and investigation of accounts and reporting thereon, particularly auditing, and on the part of accountants in private practice. Owing to the substantial amount of specific statutory provisions relevant to the discharge of their duties, consideration of professional negligence on the part of receivers and liquidators belongs more properly to specialist works on receivership and liquidation than to a book on professional negligence covering a number of different professions. Accordingly, professional negligence on the part of receivers and liquidators is not discussed.

The domain of auditors and accountants continues to expand. Their roles are likely to become more extensive and intrusive. Three major propellants of this trend merit specific mention: corporate governance, regulation of the financial sector and privatisation of governmental functions.

15–002   **Corporate governance.** A basically Victorian structure is reflected in current company legislation. A company's constitution is embodied in its memorandum and articles of association. Ownership by the shareholders is separated from management and day-to-day control by the directors. The latter are accountable for the conduct of the company's affairs to the shareholders who may exercise their collective powers to reward, appoint or remove the directors. To that end, shareholders are entitled to an annual report from the directors as to their conduct of the company's affairs. Shareholders are also entitled to a report from independent auditors in order to ensure, so far as possible, that financial information as to the company's affairs prepared by the directors accurately reflects the company's position. Around that basic structure, patchy encrustations of duties have developed through legislation, the common law and regulation in certain sectors—the accumulated product of pragmatic development reflecting the vicissitudes of the moment.

15–003   In the last two decades corporate governance has become a major legal and political issue in the United Kingdom, as elsewhere.[1] The problems attendant upon separation of management from ownership may be encountered in even the most basic company structure. They magnify and proliferate in the case of groups of companies, and especially so in the case of multinationals with a range of subsidiaries incorporated in various jurisdictions, shareholders, directors and managers of different nationalities and sometimes with share listings on more than one investment exchange. Diversity of management and ownership brings diversity of cultures, expectations and standards.

15–004   The subject of corporate governance is very broad. Indeed it has been said that it is in danger of taking over most of traditional company law.[2] The role of auditors is a core issue. Others are the duties of directors, the composition of the

---

[1] For a discussion of the position in Australia, see *Daniels v. Anderson* (1995) 16 A.C.S.R., 607, 644.

[2] Arden J. in a paper presented to the 12th Commonwealth Law Conference, September 1999.

board, the rights of shareholders, the role of institutional investors and information disclosure. Aspiration for better corporate governance has resulted in considerable debate and a kaleidoscope of initiatives, committees, reports, self-regulatory rules and codes as well as piecemeal legislation. In the meantime the courts have done their best to interpret legislation and evolve the common law as best seems appropriate to changing times. The review of company law launched by the Department of Trade and Industry in March 1998 heralds a determination for comprehensive reform which may result in a more rationalised structure based on legislation, rules and codes, including a large element of self regulation.[3]

Regulation in the financial sector. A feature of the 1980s was increasing **15–005** statutory regulation of the financial sector. A series of statutes established regulatory regimes.[4] Both in the statutes themselves and in various rules and regulations made thereunder, there are detailed provisions relating to accounts and monitoring and reporting by accountants, auditors and actuaries. These provisions are designed to achieve regulatory objectives and go considerably further than requirements in company legislation. The most extensive regulatory regime was that established in respect of investment business in the Financial Services Act 1986. This has now been replaced by the far more extensive Financial Services and Markets Act 2000. The regulatory regime established by the 2000 Act extends not only to investment business but also to other financial sectors, principally banking and insurance. Part XXII of the 2000 Act (sections 340 to 346) pertains to auditors and actuaries.

Privatisation of governmental functions. Another feature initiated in the **15–006** 1980s has been the extensive programme of privatisation of state-owned enterprises and (previously perceived) government functions. Privatisation has nevertheless been accompanied by the establishment of varying degrees of regulation, designed to ensure achievement of prescribed objectives, as apparent from implementing legislation. Monitoring and reporting by accountants, auditors and others are generally required. In many cases the implementing legislation provides for a formal regulator.

The structure of the profession. Anybody may call himself an accountant. **15–007** There are currently six main professional bodies for accountants in the United Kingdom: the Institutes of Chartered Accountants in England and Wales, of Scotland and in Ireland, the Association of Chartered Certified Accountants, the Chartered Institute of Management Accountants, and the Chartered Institute of Public Finance and Accountancy. These bodies together comprise the Consultative Committee of Accounting Bodies ("CCAB"). Each body prescribes its own membership requirements, being primarily a combination of examinations and practical training, and regulates its members. The first four are recognised professional bodies under the Financial Services Act 1986 ("the FSA 1986") and so may issue certificates conferring authorised person status on members who so

---

[3] See the Final Report of the Company Law Review Steering Committee, "Modern Company Law for a Competitive Economy" (July 2001).
[4] See further chap. 13, esp. paras 13–006 to 13–009, and paras 15–025 to 15–030 below.

require and qualify. The CCAB is involved in the organisations responsible for setting accounting and auditing standards.[5]

2. DUTIES

15–008   **Overview.** The primary source of an accountant's duties is contractual. In addition the accountant usually assumes a tortious duty of care to his client which typically, but not necessarily, coincides with his contractual duty. He may, in special circumstances, assume a tortious duty of care to third parties. The relationship of accountant and client usually gives rise also to fiduciary duties. Because accountants are often engaged to perform statutory functions such as audit, it is necessary to look at the statutory and regulatory framework; this provides the context in which the contractual, tortious and fiduciary duties arise.

(a) *The statutory context*

15–009   A large number of functions performed by accountants are prescribed and regulated by statute. The prime example is the company audit. Indeed, statutory regulation impinges on the work of this profession more so than that of any other. Accordingly, in assessing most professional negligence claims against accountants, the starting point is the relevant statutory context. Detailed treatment of the various statutory contexts is beyond the scope of this book. However, certain provisions relating to accounts and auditing contained in the Companies Acts of 1985 and 1989 and in regulatory statutes relating to the financial sector merit specific mention.[6]

(i) *Companies legislation: the company audit*

15–010   The relevant provisions are now contained in the Companies Acts of 1985 and 1989. Detailed consideration of these provisions is outside the scope of a book on professional negligence and for such consideration reference should be made to the standard textbooks on company law.[7] A brief outline is given below.

15–011   **Rationale for the company audit.** The approach adopted by the courts[8] is that the management of a company is entrusted to the board of directors which is answerable to the shareholders in general meeting. The auditor's function is to ensure that the financial information prepared by the board is accurate, first to protect the company itself from undetected errors or wrongdoing (*e.g.* declaring dividends out of capital) and secondly to provide shareholders with reliable information for the purpose of enabling them to scrutinise the conduct of the company's affairs and to exercise their collective powers to reward, control or

---

[5] See para. 15–093 below.
[6] See para. 15–025 below.
[7] See *Palmer's Company Law* (25th ed.), Part 9.
[8] *Caparo Industries plc v. Dickman* [1990] 2 A.C. 605, 630 *per* Lord Oliver. See also Bingham L.J.'s judgment in the Court of Appeal in the same case: [1989] Q.B. 653, 676. For the facts see para. 15–056 below.

remove the directors. The Companies Acts do not reflect the wider commercial purpose of enabling those to whom the accounts were addressed or circulated to make informed investment decisions, for example to sell or buy shares.[9] This perception has been the foundation for the rejection of claims in tort by shareholders and parties, other than the company itself, against auditors based on allegedly negligent audit reports.[10]

Appointment of auditors. Part II (comprising sections 24 to 54) of the **15–012** Companies Act 1989 is designed to ensure "that only persons who are properly supervised and appropriately qualified are appointed as company auditors, and that audits by persons so appointed are carried out properly and with integrity and with a proper degree of independence".[11] A person may be appointed as a company auditor only if he is a member of a recognised supervisory body ("RSB") and is eligible for the appointment under its rules.[12] An RSB must maintain and enforce rules as to eligibility for appointment as company auditors and as to the conduct of company audit work.[13] Generally every company must appoint an auditor or auditors.[14] It must do so at the general meeting at which accounts are laid[15] and the appointment then continues from the conclusion of that meeting until the conclusion of the next meeting at which accounts are laid.[16]

Remuneration. The remuneration of auditors appointed by the company in **15–013** general meeting is fixed by the meeting and is required to be stated in the accounts.[17] These rules are designed to ensure that the auditor's independence is safeguarded by proper disclosure.

The preparation of accounts. The directors of a company are under a duty to **15–014** prepare accounts for each financial year, comprising a balance sheet and a profit and loss account.[18] There are specific requirements as to the form and content of

---

[9] *ibid.* at 631. In *Berg Son & Co. Ltd v. Mervyn Hampton Adams* [1993] B.C.L.C. 1045, 1064 Hobhouse J. stressed that the statutory purpose was limited to providing information but not advice. He said that the statutory purpose was simply to furnish the shareholders with accurate information; what the shareholders did with that information fell outside the scope of the purpose.

[10] However, this does not preclude a claim in tort where there are special circumstances: see paras 15–045 *et seq.*, below.

[11] Companies Act 1989 s.24(1). Part II implements the European Council's Eighth Council Directive on company law harmonisation (No. 84/253).

[12] *ibid.* s.25. See paras 15–007 above and 15–093 below.

[13] *ibid.* s.30.

[14] Companies Act 1985 (as modified by the Companies Act 1989 s.119) s.384(1). There are exceptions in favour of dormant companies and certain categories of small companies: s.388A.

[15] *ibid.* s.384(2). There is a modified procedure in the case of a private company which has dispensed with the laying of accounts: see ss. 384(2), 385A and 386.

[16] *ibid.* s.385(2). In default of appointment by the company, the Secretary of State may appoint an auditor: *ibid.* s.387.

[17] *ibid.* s.390A. This requirement extends to expenses and benefits in kind. There are also regulations requiring disclosure in the accounts of remuneration for non-audit work: *ibid.* s.390B and see the Companies Act 1985 (Disclosure of Remuneration for Non-Audit Work) Regulations 1991, S.I. 1991 No. 2128.

[18] *ibid.* s.226. In the case of a group, the directors of the parent company are under a duty to prepare group accounts also: *ibid.* s.227. See further para. 15–080 below.

accounts and as to additional information to be provided by way of notes to the accounts.[19]

15–015   The cornerstone of prudent accounting is that the accounts must give a "true and fair view". This concept is the subject of a number of accounting standards[20] and it is given statutory effect in the Companies Act. Standards are promulgated by the Accounting Standards Board ("ASB"), which is set up under the aegis of the Financial Reporting Council ("FRC"). The FRC comprises the CCAB[21] as well as representatives from Government and industry. Standards issued by the predecessor to the ASB but which have been adopted by the ASB are known as Statements of Standard Accounting Practice ("SSAPs"); standards issued by the ASB are known as Financial Reporting Standards ("FRSs").[22] Although these standards do not directly have the force of law, it was held in 1987 that they are very strong evidence of the proper standard to be applied by the courts.[23] Since that date they have been given added status in two respects.[24] The first is that they are now promulgated by the FRC which represents interests wider than just the accountancy profession. Secondly SSAPs and FRSs have now been given statutory recognition in the Companies Acts.[25] The purpose behind the SSAPs and FRSs is to provide a consistent approach to accounting. It is beyond the scope of this book to examine these standards in detail.[26] Their single most important objective feature is to put flesh on the bare bones of the overriding requirement that the accounts show a true and fair view. Anyone who is concerned with a claim against an accountant should ensure that he looks at the accounting standards which were in force at the date of the alleged breach of duty.

15–016   In almost every case, an accountant who follows accounting standards will be above criticism whilst one who departs from them may expose himself to criticism. Nevertheless, these standards should not be applied slavishly. Prudent accounting should always involve an exercise of judgment. Accounting standards

---

[19] *ibid.* s.226(3) and Sched. 4.

[20] Although the accounting standards are not limited to accounts of companies registered under the Companies Acts, this is the context in which their application most frequently arises. They are therefore discussed at this point in the chapter, but the reader should be aware that accounting standards are also relevant in other contexts.

[21] See para. 15–007 above.

[22] The accounting standards and related documents referred to in this section of the chapter will be found in the volume entitled *Accounting Standards* produced annually by the ICAEW.

[23] *Lloyd Cheyham v. Littlejohn* [1987] B.C.L.C. 303, 313 *per* Woolf J.

[24] See the Opinion of Mary Arden Q.C. (now Arden L.J.) dated April 1993 which is set out as an Appendix to the APB's Forward to Accounting Standards (reproduced in *Palmer's Company Law* (25th ed.), section F.

[25] This is achieved as follows: the Companies Act 1985 s.256 (added by the 1989 Act) makes provision for statements of standard accounting practice to be made by prescribed bodies; the Accounting Standards Board Ltd has been prescribed as a standard setting body (S.I. 1990 No. 1667); the 1985 Act s.226(3) requires accounts to comply with Sched. 4; Sched. 4 para. 36A requires the accounts to state whether they have been prepared in accordance with applicable accounting standards and to give particulars of any material departure from those standards and the reason for such departure.

[26] The objectives of the ASB in issuing accounting standards are set out in the Statement of Principles for Financial Reporting, a document which does not itself have the status of an accounting standard but which provides an overview of the subject. However the reader should exercise caution in relation to Chapter One of that Statement, which says that the objective of financial statements is to provide information that is useful to a wide variety of users for assessing the stewardship of the entity's management and for making economic decisions. This is considerably wider than the scope of the duty recognised in law as being owed to third parties: see paras 15–045 to 15–089 below. Some of the FRSs and SSAPs are considered at paras 15–102 *et seq.* below.

make good servants but bad masters. They represent standards agreed within the profession as being generally appropriate for measuring the financial state of business entities, but the overriding objective is to convey a true and fair view.[27] Standards are constantly being reviewed by the ASB to reflect changes in commerce, but there may be rare cases in which either the standards are out of date or they need modification in order for the accounts to give a true and fair view in a particular case.[28]

The Companies Act requires that the balance sheet and the profit and loss **15–017** account should each give a true and fair view.[29] This is not defined in the Act, which indirectly refers to FRSs and SSAPs.[30] Compliance with this requirement may require additional information to be given[31] and, in special circumstances, may justify departure from prescribed specific requirements.[32] However, many small and medium-sized companies are permitted to deliver abbreviated accounts to the Registrar of Companies[33]; it is recognised that these abbreviated accounts will not give a true and fair view, although there is still a requirement that they be prepared properly in accordance with the relevant provisions.[34]

The auditing of accounts. In theory the directors prepare the accounts first **15–018** and the auditors audit them afterwards. In practice, however, the directors usually involve the auditors at an early stage and discuss the draft accounts with them. This may have important ramifications if a reasonable auditor ought to have given advice at the stage when he is initially consulted and before he gives his audit certificate.[35]

Once appointed, the role of the company's auditors is to make a report to the **15–019** company's members on all annual accounts of the company of which copies are laid before the company in general meeting during their tenure of office.[36] In the report the auditors must state whether in their opinion the annual accounts have been prepared in accordance with the Companies Act 1985 and in particular must state whether "a true and fair view" is given of certain matters. They are:

"(a) in the case of an individual balance sheet, of the state of affairs of the company as at the end of the financial year,

(b) in the case of an individual profit and loss account, of the profit or loss of the company for the financial year,

---

[27] There are exceptional cases in which the accounts are not required to convey a true and fair view: see para. 15–017 below.

[28] *Kripps v. Touche Ross & Co.* (1997) 33 B.C.L.R. (3d) 254, 275, British Columbia CA.

[29] *ibid.* s.226(2).

[30] See para. 15–015, n. 25 above.

[31] Companies Act 1985 s.226(4).

[32] *ibid.* s.226(5).

[33] *ibid.* ss.246–9.

[34] *ibid.* s.247B(2)(b) and see APB Bulletin 1997/1 (The Special Auditors' Report on Abbreviated Accounts in Great Britain) para. 13 (printed in *Auditing and Reporting* published annually by the ICAEW).

[35] *Coulthard v. Neville Russell* [1998] P.N.L.R. 276, CA: for the facts see para. 15–081 below. See also *Pacific Acceptance Corporation Ltd v. Forsyth* [1970] 92 W.N. (N.S.W.) 29, 50 and 59 (for the facts see para. 15–097 below). A different view was taken in *Nelson Guarantee Corporation Ltd v. Nelson* [1958] N.Z.L.R. 609, but it is submitted that *Pacific* is to be preferred.

[36] *ibid.* s.235(1). See *John (Elton) v. Price Waterhouse*, referred to in para. 15–034 below.

(c) in the case of group accounts, of the state of affairs as at the end of the financial year, and the profit and loss for the financial year, of the undertakings included in the consolidation as a whole, so far as concerns the members of the company."[37]

The auditors must also consider whether the information contained in the directors' report for the financial year for which the annual accounts are prepared is consistent with the accounts. If they consider that is not the case, they must state the fact in their report.[38] The auditors' report must contain the name of the auditors and be signed by them.[39]

15–020   In preparing their report the auditors must carry out such investigations as will enable them to form an opinion as to:

"(a) whether proper accounting records have been kept by the company and proper returns adequate for their audit have been received from branches not visited by them; and

(b) whether the company's individual accounts are in agreement with the accounting records and returns."[40]

The auditors must specify in their report if their opinion as to (a) or (b) is adverse and if they fail to obtain all the information and explanations which to the best of their knowledge and belief are needed for the purposes of their audit. Further, if the requirements of Schedule 6, which concerns disclosure of emoluments and other benefits of directors and others, are not complied with in the annual accounts, the auditors must give the relevant particulars in their report, so far as they are able to do so.[41]

15–021   **Rights of auditors.** For the purpose of performing their role, auditors are given certain rights. They have a right of access at all times to the company's books, accounts and vouchers and they may require from the company's officers such information and explanations as they think necessary for the performance of their duties as auditors.[42] An officer who provides misleading information exposes himself to criminal penalties.[43] Auditors also have a right to receive notices and other communications relating to any general meeting, to attend that

---

[37] *ibid.* s.235(2).

[38] *ibid.* s.235(3).

[39] *ibid.* s.236(1). The same applies to the copy sent to the registrar of companies and to every copy laid before the company in general meeting or which is otherwise circulated, published or issued. Contravention of these requirements exposes the company and every officer to a criminal penalty under s.236(4).

[40] *ibid.* s.237(1). For a discussion as to auditing standards, see paras 15–093 *et seq.* below.

[41] *ibid.* s.237. If the auditors consider that the directors were not entitled to take advantage of the exemption from the need to prepare group accounts conferred by s.248, they must state that fact in their report: *ibid.* s.237(4A).

[42] *ibid.* s.389A(1). Requirements are also imposed relating to subsidiary undertakings in order to secure the provision of information to the auditors of any parent company: see s.389A(3) and (4). In *Cuff v. London and County Land and Building Co. Ltd* [1912] 1 Ch. 440, company auditors, threatened with proceedings for negligence against them by the company, were refused a mandatory injunction giving them access to the company's books.

[43] *ibid.* s.389A(2). The requirements relating to subsidiary undertakings (see previous note) are also backed by criminal sanctions: see. s.389A(3), (4) and (5).

meeting and to be heard on any part of the business which concerns them as auditors.[44]

Removal of auditors. An auditor may be removed from office at any time by **15–022** a company by ordinary resolution, notwithstanding anything in any agreement between them.[45] Special notice is required for a resolution at a general meeting of a company for the removal of an auditor before the expiration of his term of office or for the appointment as auditor of a person other than a retiring auditor.[46] The auditor proposed to be removed or the retiring auditor may make representations and provision is made for them to be circulated to members or to be read out at the general meeting, unless the court otherwise directs.[47] Also he must deposit a notice under section 394.[48]

Resignation of auditors. An auditor may resign his office by depositing a **15–023** written resignation notice at the company's registered office; he must simultaneously deposit a statement under section 394, otherwise his resignation notice is not effective.[49] A section 394 notice is required where an auditor ceases to hold office for any reason. It must state either any circumstances connected with the auditor's ceasing to hold office which he considers ought to be brought to the attention of the company's members or creditors or, if he considers that there are no such circumstances, it must state that there are none.[50] In the former case, the company must circulate copies of the statement to every person entitled to be sent copies of the accounts, unless, on the company's application, the court otherwise directs.[51] Moreover, in the same case an auditor proposing to resign may deposit with his resignation notice a signed requisition notice calling on the company's directors forthwith to convene an extraordinary general meeting in order to receive and consider an explanation of the circumstances connected with his resignation, which he wishes to place before the meeting.[52] The auditor may request the company to circulate its members with a statement of the relevant circumstances and, unless the request is received too late, the company must comply, unless the court otherwise directs.[53]

Summary remedy. A claim for professional negligence against an accountant **15–024** will usually be brought by way of action. The cause of action may be breach of contract, the tort of negligence, a statutory cause of action akin to negligence or possibly breach of a constructive trust or a fiduciary duty. As an alternative to proceedings by way of action, section 212 of the Insolvency Act 1986 provides

---

[44] *ibid.* s.390.
[45] *ibid.* s.391. Notice of the passing of such a resolution must be given to the registrar of companies: *ibid.* s.391(2).
[46] *ibid.* s.391A(1).
[47] *ibid.* s.391A(3) to (6).
[48] See the next paragraph.
[49] *ibid.* s.392.
[50] *ibid.* s.394.
[51] *ibid.* s.394(3) to (7). An auditor may incur criminal liability under s.394A for contravention of s.394.
[52] *ibid.* s.392A(2). If the directors do not comply, they may incur criminal liability under s.392A(5). The resigning auditor is entitled to attend and be heard at the meeting convened: s.392A(8).
[53] *ibid.* s.392A(3) to (7).

a summary remedy procedure, formerly known as a misfeasance summons. The section replaces similar provisions under predecessor legislation. Several claims against company auditors discussed in this chapter originated by way of misfeasance summons.[54] A number of points arise in respect of the section[55]:

(1) An auditor is not described as such in this section and he will come within it only if he is an "officer of the company". An auditor is not necessarily an officer of a company.[56] He is an officer, and thus can be proceeded against under the section, if he is duly appointed to the office of auditor by the company.[57] But an auditor appointed *ad hoc* for a limited purpose is not an officer.[58]

(2) This section is procedural only. It does not create any new right or liability but merely provides a summary remedy for enforcing in the liquidation of a company existing rights which might otherwise have been enforced by ordinary action.[59]

(3) There was authority in relation to the predecessor to section 212 that it did not cover claims based exclusively on common-law negligence.[60] However the better view was that the summary procedure did extend to negligence claims, at least against auditors.[61] The current drafting has laid to rest any doubts by referring to "breach of fiduciary or other duty" instead of the narrower wording formerly used ("breach of trust").[62]

---

[54] Predecessor legislation and examples of claims against auditors thereunder are Companies Act 1862 s.165; Companies (Winding-up) Act 1890 s.10, *e.g. Re London and General Bank (No. 2)* [1895] 2 Ch. 673, CA and *Re Kingston Cotton Mill Co. Ltd (No. 2)* [1896] 2 Ch. 279, CA; Companies (Consolidation) Act 1908 s.215, *e.g. Re City Equitable Fire Insurance Co. Ltd* [1925] 1 Ch. 407; Companies Act 1929 s.276; Companies Act 1948 s.333: see *Re Thomas Gerrard & Son Ltd* [1968] Ch. 455; Companies Act 1985 s.631 and the Insolvency Act 1985 s.19. There are equivalent provisions in company statutes of Commonwealth countries.

[55] Only the main points, and only so far as they concern auditors, are here mentioned. For detailed consideration of the section see *Palmer's Company Law* (25th ed.), paras 15.466 *et seq.*, 8.544 *et seq.* (in relation to directors), 9.607 (in relation to auditors).

[56] *Re Western Counties Steam Bakeries and Milling Co.* [1897] 1 Ch. 617, 627, *per* Lindley L.J.

[57] See *Re London and General Bank* [1895] 2 Ch. 166; *Re Kingston Cotton Mill Co. Ltd (No. 2)* [1896] 2 Ch. 279. *cf. Lipschitz v. Wolpert and Abrahams* [1977] 2 S.A.L.R. 732.

[58] *R. v. Shacter* [1960] 2 Q.B. 252, 256; also *Re Western Counties Steam Bakeries and Milling Co.* [1897] 1 Ch. 617 (accountants employed by one of directors of a company to audit its accounts and to prepare a balance sheet but not appointed by the shareholders in general meeting held not to be "officers" of the company for the purposes of Companies (Winding-Up) Act 1890, s.10; proceedings consequently stayed); and *Mutual Reinsurance Co. Ltd v. Peat Marwick Mitchell & Co.* [1997] B.C.L.C. 1, CA (accountant appointed to carry out a specific audit function without being appointed the company's auditor).

[59] *Re Canadian Land Reclaiming and Colonizing Co., Coventry and Dixon's Case* (1880) 14 Ch.D. 660, 670; *Re City Equitable Fire Insurance Co. Ltd* [1925] 1 Ch. 407, 507 and 527; *Re B. Johnson & Co. (Builders) Ltd* [1955] Ch. 634, 648.

[60] *Re B. Johnson & Co. (Builders) Ltd* [1955] Ch. 634, 648; see also *Re Kingston Cotton Mill Co. Ltd (No. 2)* [1986] 2 Ch. 279, 283 and 288.

[61] *per* Kay L.J. in *Re Kingston Cotton Mill Co. Ltd (No. 2)* [1896] 2 Ch. 279, 291.

[62] In making this change Parliament broadly accepted the recommendation of the Jenkins Committee (Cmnd. 1796, para. 503(d)). In *Re D'Jan of London Ltd* [1994] 1 B.C.L.C. 561 Hoffmann J. accepted *sub silentio* that s.212 applied to a claim for common-law negligence against a director. See also *Cohen v. Selby* [2001] 1 B.C.L.C. 176, 183B–G.

(4) Only loss to the company consequent upon the auditor's breach of duty is recoverable under the section.[63] A frequent head of recoverable loss is the amount of dividend paid out of capital as opposed to profits in consequence of audited financial statements incorrectly showing profits instead of losses.[64]

(5) Under the section a discretion is given to the court both as to whether or not to order payment of compensation and as to the amount of compensation ordered.[65]

(ii) *Regulatory statutes relating to the financial sector*

Since the 1970s the financial sector in the United Kingdom has been the **15–025** subject of several statutes imposing regulatory regimes, primarily in relation to insurance, banking, building societies and financial services. The regimes contained extensive provisions relating to accounting and auditing. Where such institutions are companies governed by the Companies Acts, the regimes usually contained provisions which were superimposed on the Companies Acts. The main regulatory statute is now the Financial Services and Markets Act 2000.[66] Part XXII (sections 340–346) relates to auditors and actuaries.

In considering claims arising from a regulatory context it is important to have **15–026** regard to specific provisions in the relevant statute, subordinate legislation and rules,[67] as well as non-statutory rules and guidance issued by regulatory organisations and professional bodies. Regulatory regimes are subject to continuing modification and amendment, frequently effected by delegated legislation.

Deloitte Haskins & Sells v. National Mutual Life Nominees Ltd[68] shows how **15–027** the extent of the duty is moulded by the terms of the relevant legislation. The Securities Regulations in New Zealand required a deposit-taking company to appoint a trustee who would receive periodic reports from the directors and the auditor. Section 50(2) the Securities Act 1978 imposed an express duty on the auditor to send a written report to the company and the trustee upon becoming aware of any matter which in his opinion was relevant to the exercise of the trustee's powers or duties.[69] In March 1986 the auditor became concerned about loans due from associated companies but he failed to submit any report. The company went into liquidation in August 1986. On a claim by the trustee against the auditor, the Privy Council held that section 50(2) created the necessary relationship of proximity between the auditor and the trustee, but the auditor's only duty was to send the report once he had actually formed an opinion. There was no statutory duty, and no basis for superimposing a tortious duty, to form an

---

[63] Thus in *Re Liverpool and Wigan Supply Association Ltd* [1907] Acct. L.R. 4 where creditors sustained loss consequent upon continuing to trade with a company in reliance upon incorrect and misleading balance sheets certified by the company auditor, the liquidator failed to recover such loss upon proceeding by way of a misfeasance summons.

[64] See para. 15–138 below.

[65] The giving of this discretion is somewhat inconsistent with statements that the section is procedural in nature. This discretion is additional to the court's power to grant relief to an auditor under s.727 of the Companies Act 1985: see para. 15–153 below.

[66] See Chap. 13, paras 13–011 *et seq.*

[67] Note also the Accountant's Report Rules made under the Solicitors Act 1974 (*Law Society v. KPMG* [2000] 1 W.L.R. 1921: see para. 15–085 below).

[68] [1993] A.C. 774, PC.

[69] Contrast the English legislation, which imposes a wider duty on the auditor: *ibid.* at 787D. The current English legislation is considered at para. 15–020 above.

opinion. There was therefore no breach of duty before March 1986. There was a breach of duty between March and August 1986, but no loss was caused, since the money would have been lost, even if the breach had been reported in March.

15-028 In a more recent New Zealand case[70] an investor claimed against an auditor who was required by the Securities Regulations to produce a report. The court held that the Regulations contemplated that the report would be relied on by potential investors and that this created a duty of care to investors. The Regulations required a report which gave a true and fair view but they did not require the auditor make any recommendation as to whether or not to invest. Accordingly, in order to succeed, it was not enough for an investor to show that he relied on the fact of there being a report; he had to go further and show that he read the accounts and relied on the certificate which said that the accounts gave a true and fair view.

15-029 Part VI (comprising sections 72 to 103) of the Financial Services and Markets Act 2000[71] contains the regime for "Official Listing of Securities", *i.e.* listing of securities on the London Stock Exchange and provides for the publication of "listing particulars" in respect of the issue of securities as defined.[72] In respect of inaccurate statements in listing particulars an accountant may incur liability under section 90 of the 1986 Act. The provision imposes liability to pay compensation to a claimant meeting certain criteria if listing particulars (including supplementary listing particulars) or a prospectus[73] have a defect consisting of an untrue or misleading statement or an omission from them of a matter required to be included by listing rules. This statutory liability is imposed upon the person or persons responsible for the particulars, as defined in regulations made under section 79(3). Thus an accountant whose report appears in the particulars with his consent will be a person responsible for the particulars to that extent. The latter may escape liability, however, by establishing one of the statutory defences.[74] The statutory liability is in addition to any other liability which may be incurred in the same circumstances. In respect of offers of unlisted securities, *i.e.* securities not on the listed market of the London Stock Exchange,[75] section 150(1) of the Financial Services Act 1986 is now paralleled by regulation 14 of the Public Offers of Securities Regulations 1995.[76] For further commentary on relevant statutes and regulations relating to the listed and unlisted securities regimes, reference should be made to specialist works.[77]

(iii) *Whistle-blowing*

15-030 An important feature of regulatory statutes is the provisions for "whistle-blowing", *i.e.* communication by an auditor or reporting accountant to the

---

[70] *Boyd Knight v. Purdue* [1999] N.Z.L.R. 278.

[71] See previously Part IV (comprising ss.142 to 157) of the Financial Services Act 1986.

[72] See s.142(7).

[73] Financial Services and Markets Act 2000, s.86(1).

[74] *ibid.* s.90(5) and Sched. 10. As to the Financial Services Act 1986, see s.151.

[75] *e.g.* securities traded on AIM (the Alternative Investment Market) established by the London Stock Exchange.

[76] S.I. 1995 No. 1537 made under s.2(2) of the European Communities Act 1972.

[77] See Lomnicka & Powell, *op. cit.,* for detailed commentary on Part IV of the Financial Services Act 1986, Part VI of the Financial Services and Markets Act 2000 and the Public Offers of Securities Regulations 1995. Also *Palmer's Company Law* (25th ed.), Part V "Capital Issues" paras 5.501 *et seq.,* 5.617 *et seq.*

relevant regulatory authority, particularly in the disclosure of fraud.[78] In those statutes no duty to "whistle blow" is directly imposed. Rather the approach generally adopted is to provide that no duty of confidence to which the auditor may be subject should be regarded as contravened by disclosure to the relevant regulator and a power is given to impose a "whistle-blowing" duty by delegated legislation.[79]

The major professional bodies for accountants issued guidance as to communications with regulators under the FSA 1986.[80] However, in the wake of the Bingham Report on the Supervision of B.C.C.I., it was resolved to impose a "whistle-blowing" duty on auditors of institutions across the financial services sphere. Rules imposing such duty have been made under the empowering provisions of the major regulatory statutes.[81] Contravention of such rules gives rise to disciplinary sanctions. Whistle-blowing duties may have causation ramifications in the context of claims against auditors and accountants.[82]

(b) *Duties to client*

(i) *Contractual duties*

The duties of an accountant primarily depend upon the contract between him **15–031** and his client. This regulates the nature and extent of his task and the standard of its performance.[83] It is prudent for an accountant to record his precise instructions in writing to his client. It is particularly important to establish the

---

[78] See the Financial Services and Markets Act 2000, ss.342, 343 superseding: the Banking Act 1987 s.47, the Building Societies Act 1986 s.82, the Financial Services Act 1986 s.109 (to be replaced by the Financial Services and Markets Act 2000 ss. 343 and 344: the Friendly Societies Act 1992 s.79 and the Insurance Companies Act 1982 s.21A (inserted by FSA 1986 s.135). Note the regulations to be made under the 2000 Act and the Financial Institutions (Prudential Supervision) Regulations 1996 (S.I.1996 No 1669) made under the superseded Acts.

[79] This exception to the duty of confidentiality applies only to information acquired by the auditor *qua* auditor. The Financial Services and Markets Act 2000, s.342 creates a further exception where the auditor is auditor both of an authorised person and of another person having "close links" with the authorised person. Relevant statutes do not grapple with the problem of information which is acquired otherwise than *qua* auditor of the relevant company.

[80] See SAS (Statement of Auditing Standard) 620 issued by the Auditing Practices Board (APB): "The auditor's right and duty to report to regulators in the financial sector" (issued March 1994); see also the following APB Practice Notes relating to the auditors' right and duty to report to specific regulators: PN7 relating to the Friendly Societies Commission (issued July 1994); PN15 relating to the Occupational Pensions Regulatory Authority (issued November 1997); and PN21 relating to the Financial Services Authority (issued June 2000). See also PN12 regarding whistle-blowing in relation to money-laundering (issued May 1997). Further guidance is contained in APB Bulletin 1196/2 (The Auditors' Right and Duty to Report to Regulators: Implementation of the Post-BCCI Directive in the UK). (The SAS, the PNs and the Bulletin are all published in *Auditing Standards 2001/2*.) See further paras 15–093 *et seq.* below as to auditing standards.

[81] *e.g.* under s.109 of the Financial Services Act 1986 (to be replaced by ss.342–343 of the Financial Services and Markets Act 2000), the Auditors (Financial Services Act 1986) Rules 1994 (S.I. 1994 No. 526).

[82] See para. 15–127 below.

[83] See, *e.g. International Laboratories Ltd v. Dewar* (1933) 3 D.L.R. 665, Manitoba CA, *per* Robson J.A. at p. 698:
"It cannot be doubted that the measure of the responsibility of auditors depends on the terms of the employment in the particular case. That the relation did exist here is a fact though regard must be had to its exact terms. The defendants were appointed auditors at the shareholders' meeting only on one occasion . . . when the terms of appointment were general. There was discussion during the argument as to whether the audit was to be merely the statutory audit under [the relevant company statute]. I think the Court will have to ascertain the duty and obligation of the defendants from the

nature of the task, for example whether it is an audit or some more limited accountancy function.[84] The extent of investigations required is much greater in the case of the former than in the case of the latter.[85] An accountant who prepares a report for use in connection with an investment circular may be required to assume a responsibility which differs from that of an auditor in the following respects: (i) he may be responsible for the presentation (not merely the auditing) of the information in his report; (ii) he may need to make adjustments to information previously reported so that it gives a true and fair view for the purposes of the investment circular; and (iii) he may be required to comment on financial information which has previously been the subject of an audit.[86]

15–032   **Limiting of liability.** It is now common practice for accountants to include in their letters of engagement clauses limiting their liability. It may be prudent for an accountant to have separate engagement letters where he is providing both auditing and accountancy services, since the responsibilities undertaken in each case are different.[87] An auditor is not permitted to limit his liability in respect of a statutory audit.[88] Even where the broad nature of the accountant's task is not in dispute, it may be difficult to decide the extent of the task and the steps required to perform it. The problem frequently arises where the task is of a limited nature but imprecisely defined.

15–033   **Audit: scope of the contract.** Even where the nature of an engagement is agreed to be an audit, questions may arise as to the scope of the audit contract. As we have seen, a large part of the necessary framework is provided by legislation and regulations. In the case of an audit of a company's accounts, the scope of the contract may also be affected by the company's articles of association.[89] An auditor is expected to agree his terms of engagement in an engagement

---

correspondence by which their work was defined and that the limit of the statutory requirement will not prevail against that understanding."
This passage was cited with approval in *Jamieson, Austin & Mitchell Ltd v. Battrum* [1934] 1 W.W.R. 324. See also *Nelson Guarantee Corp. Ltd v. Hodgson* [1958] N.Z.L.R. 609, 610.

[84] Contrast *The Trustee of the Property of Apfel (a Bankrupt) v. Annan Dexter & Co.* (1926) 70 Acct. L.R. 57 with *Smith v. Sheard* (1906) 34 Acct. L.R. 65. See also *Fox v. Morrish, Grant and Co.* [1918] T.L.R. 126; *Armitage v. Brewer and Knott* (1932) 77 Acct. L.R. 28 (in that case the terms of the auditor's instructions required him to undertake comprehensive checking and vouching and not merely testing); and *Haig v. Bamford* (1976) 72 D.L.R. (3d) 66, 71, S. Ct of Canada. In *Dairy Containers Ltd v. NZI Bank Ltd* [1995] 2 N.Z.L.R. 30, given the terms of his letter to the plaintiff outlining his responsibilities, the Auditor-General was held to have undertaken voluntarily more extensive duties than would ordinarily arise in the case of an audit of a company under the Companies Act. See also *Bloor Italian Gifts Ltd v. Dixon* (2000) 48 O.R. (3d) 760, Ontario CA (see para. 15–103, n. 4).

[85] *McBride's Ltd v. Rooke and Thomas* [1941] 4 D.L.R. 45, 48 (more required by way of examination in the case of a special investigation, as, for example, into the defalcations of a particular employee, than in the case of an audit).

[86] APB Statements of Investment Circular Reporting Standards (published in *Auditing & Reporting 2001/2*).

[87] SAS 140 para. 5.

[88] See para. 15–100 below.

[89] *Re City Equitable Fire Insurance Co. Ltd* [1925] 1 Ch. 407, 520–521 *per* Warrington L.J.:
"I think that that article . . . does in such a case as the present form part of the contract between the company and the auditors, and for the reason that auditors are engaged without any special terms of engagement. When that is the case, then if the articles contain provisions relating to the performance by them of their duties and to the obligations imposed upon them by the acceptance of their office, I think it is quite plain that the articles must be taken to express the terms upon which the auditors accept their position. Of course, if the terms of their employment are expressed as a separate document, then that document must be taken to define the conditions of their

letter.[90] The letter should record acceptance of the audit appointment and sum-marise responsibilities of the directors and the auditors, the scope of the engage-ment and the form of any reports.[91] There are procedural requirements imposed as to regular review and changes in the nature of the engagement.[92] The standard expected of an auditor is to a large extent regulated by Statements of Auditing Standards.[93]

As is apparent from the wording of section 235 of the Companies Act 1985,[94] **15–034** each audit engagement is a separate contract. This may be important if a limitation issue arises. The fact that auditors have negligently performed their duties by failing to report a particular matter in one year does not by itself establish that the absence of a report about the same matter in the next year is negligent. Where what is complained of is an omission to note a particular point the circumstances giving rise to that omission in the year in question need to be examined.[95]

It has been held in Canada in relation to the audit of company's accounts **15–035** required under companies legislation, that although shareholders are entitled by resolution to appoint and remove auditors, that does not give rise to a contract between them (as distinct from the company) and the auditors.[96] It is submitted that the same applies in relation to an audit required under companies legislation in the United Kingdom.

Implied duties. Apart from duties, usually express, defining the nature of a **15–036** particular engagement, an accountant will invariably be under an implied[97] if not express contractual duty to exercise reasonable care and skill.[98] In addition, he will generally be under an implied if not express duty to take reasonable care to keep his client's affairs secret.[99] The implication of particular duties in a contract

---

engagement, and it would not be proper to assume any implied terms either from the provisions of the articles or elsewhere. But in the present case I think it is quite plain that the terms of Art. 150 do, according to their proper construction, whatever that may be, effect a modification in what would prima facie be, but for that article, the obligation and liability of the auditors."
(For the facts see n. 35 to para. 15–112 below). See also *Pacific Acceptance Ltd v. Forsyth* (1970) 92 W.N. (N.S.W.) 29, 51 (set out at para. 15–097 below).
[90] SAS (Statement of Auditing Standards) 140.
[91] SAS 140.4.
[92] SAS 140.2 and 140.3.
[93] See paras 15–093 *et seq.* below.
[94] See para. 15–019 above.
[95] *John (Elton) v. Price Waterhouse* [2001] E.W.H.C. Ch. 438 para. 268 (April 23, 2001, Ferris J.). See also *Midland Bank v. Hett Stubbs & Kemp* [1979] Ch. 384, 403C.
[96] See *Roman Corporation Ltd v. Peat Marwick Thorne (No. 1)* (1992) 8 B.L.R. 43, Ontario Court of Justice, Farley J. See also *Roman Corporation Ltd v. Peat Marwick Thorne (No. 2)* (1993) 12 B.L.R. (2d) 10, Ontario Court of Justice, in which Farley J. struck out an allegation that the company contracted with the auditors as agent for the plaintiffs who constituted a "control block" of share-holders.
[97] See Supply of Goods and Services Act 1982, s.13. See further Chap. 2, paras 2–007, 2–116, *et seq.*, above.
[98] See *e.g. Caparo Industries plc v. Dickman* [1990] 2 A.C. 605, 619, *per* Lord Bridge.
[99] *Weld-Blundell v. Stephens* [1919] 1 K.B. 520, CA; [1920] A.C. 959, HL. In that case an accountant was asked to investigate the affairs of a company. He was given information about two officials which proved to be libellous and he accidentally left the letter at the company's offices. It was held that he was in breach of an implied term to use reasonable care to keep the contents of the letter secret. See also *Fogg v. Gaulter* (1960) 110 L.J. 718 and see para. 15–038 below.

with an accountant will be governed by rules applicable to implication of terms in contracts generally.[1]

(ii) *Duty in tort*

15–037   In common with other professional persons, an accountant generally owes a tortious duty of care to his client quite apart from any contract between them.[2] Although the tortious duty of care is usually co-extensive with the contractual duty, there are cases in which it assumes some practical importance, *e.g.* because the limitation period is different.[3]

(iii) *Fiduciary duties*

15–038   **Fiduciary duties.** An accountant will generally owe fiduciary duties to his client. An accountant's duty has been held to be a duty *uberrimae fidei* and of complete and full disclosure of all facts properly coming within the ambit of the inquiry he was conducting.[4] However, it is submitted that to describe an accountant, or indeed any other person, as a fiduciary without more would be meaningless:

> "To say that a man is a fiduciary only begins analysis; it gives direction to further inquiry. To whom is he a fiduciary? What obligations does he owe as a fiduciary? In what respect has he failed to discharge those obligations? And what are the consequences of his deviation from duty?"[5]

15–039   There are three particular duties or disabilities which are usually labelled "fiduciary",[6] namely: (i) the duty of loyalty, which subsists during the accountant's or auditor's retainer, (ii) the principle of undue influence and (iii) the duty of confidentiality. Cases on breaches of the duty of loyalty, typically involving actual or potential conflicts of interest or secret profits, tend to involve solicitors[7] rather than accountants or auditors. This is no doubt because the relationship of solicitor and client is traditionally seen as a fiduciary relationship in a way that the relationship of accountant or auditor and client is not. Nevertheless there may be cases in which an accountant does assume a duty to act loyally in the best

---

[1] *Investors Compensation Scheme v. West Bromwich Building Society* [1998] 1 W.L.R. 896, 912–913 *per* Lord Hoffmann. For an illustration in relation to auditors see *Simonius Vischer & Co. v. Holt and Thompson* [1979] 2 N.S.W.L.R. 322, in which the auditors sought to imply terms: (a) that the client company would inform them of all and any breaches of authority by its employees of which the auditors were not aware; (b) that the company would take all reasonable steps to avoid suffering loss due to the acts or omissions of its employees; and (c) that the company would inform the auditors of any matters which indicated breaches by its staff of directions which would have a financially disadvantageous effect upon its business. The CA of N.S.W. refused to imply these terms on the ground that they were not required to give business efficacy to the audit contract and were too vague.
[2] See Chap. 2, paras 2–013, *et seq.* A concurrent duty in tort was expressly accepted by Lord Bridge in *Caparo Industries plc v. Dickman* [1990] 2 A.C. 605, 619C and by the S. Ct. of S. Aus. in *Duke Group Ltd v. Pilmer* (1999) 31 A.C.S.R. 213 at 259–269: for the facts see para. 15–151 below.
[3] Thus in *Pech v. Tilgals* (1994) 28 A.T.R. 197 proceedings were commenced more than six years after the date of the audit certificate but within six years of the loss.
[4] *Morton v. Arbuckle (No. 2)* [1919] V.L.R. 487, 491, *per* Irvine C.J.
[5] Quoted by Lord Mustill in *Re Goldcorp Exchange Ltd* [1995] A.C. 74, 98.
[6] This is the classification adopted by Sir Peter Millett (now Lord Millett) in *Equity's Place in the Law of Commerce* [1998] 114 L.Q.R. 214, 219.
[7] *e.g. Bristol & West Building Society v. Mothew* [1998] Ch. 1, 16–22, CA: see Chap. 10, paras 10–023, *et seq.*

interests of the client.[8] Similarly in relation to undue influence: the relationship of accountant and client does not necessarily have the required features of ascendancy on the one side and dependency on the other, but it may be possible to establish a relationship of influence on the facts of a particular case.

In one Canadian case[9] a client retained the defendant accountant for tax- **15–040**
planning and investment advice. The accountant had a financial relationship with the developer of a housing investment, from whom he received fees. The accountant recommended this investment to the client without disclosing the relationship. The client had no previous experience of this type of investment and was heavily reliant on the accountant. The majority of the court held that the defendant was in a fiduciary position towards the plaintiff. La Forest J. distinguished between relationships which were generally regarded as giving rise to a duty of loyalty and those where the relationship was created *ad hoc*. In the latter case it was necessary to look at all the circumstances in order to see whether the relationship was fiduciary. The circumstances included: (i) the scope for the defendant to exercise some discretion or power; (ii) the scope for the defendant to exert undue influence over the plaintiff; (iii) the opportunity for the defendant to exercise his power or discretion unilaterally so as to affect the plaintiff's legal or practical interests; and (iv) the plaintiff's peculiar vulnerability to such exercise of discretion or power. What was required was something more than a simple assumption of responsibility to provide information and execute orders; the extra ingredient was a mutual understanding that the defendant had relinquished his own self-interest and had assumed a duty of loyalty, *i.e.* a duty to act in the best interests of the plaintiff.[10] The court looked at the professional rules in force in British Columbia, which required full disclosure, and said that equity would not hold him to a lower standard.[11] The majority went on to hold that the accountant in that case was in breach of fiduciary duty as well being in breach of contract, and that the plaintiff was entitled to compensation on a restitutionary basis.

Confidentiality. It is the duty of confidentiality which is most relevant in **15–041**
practice to accountants. This duty continues in equity even after the retainer has terminated. Following termination of the retainer the only duty to the former client which survives is a continuing duty to preserve the confidentiality of information imparted during its subsistence. This duty has two consequences in practice. The first is that the accountant may not disclose the information to any third party without the client (or former client)'s consent.[12] This is a strict duty, not merely a duty to use reasonable endeavours to keep the information confidential.[13] However the duty of confidentiality, whether arising in contract or in equity, may be overridden by the statutory or regulatory "whistle-blowing" duty.[14] It has been suggested that a similar "whistle-blowing" duty arises at common law where an auditor suspects fraud on the part of the company's

---

[8] As is shown by *Hodgkinson v. Simms* (see below).
[9] *Hodgkinson v. Simms* (1994) 97 B.C.L.R. (2d) 1, S. Ct. of Canada.
[10] *ibid.* at 21–22.
[11] *ibid.* at 33–34 *per* La Forest J.
[12] In some cases consent may be implied, *e.g.* a report to shareholders in a company audit or disclosure of assets to the Revenue in a tax return completed by an accountant for a client.
[13] *Prince Jefri Bolkiah v. KPMG* [1999] 2 A.C. 222, 235G, HL.
[14] See para. 15–030 above.

management and it may be necessary for him to report directly to a third party without the knowledge of management.[15]

15-042   The second consequence of the duty of confidentiality is that the former client may be entitled to an injunction to restrain the accountant from acting for another client with an adverse interest. The burden of proof is on the first client to show (i) that the accountant is in possession of information which is confidential to him and to the disclosure of which he has not consented and (ii) that the information is or may be relevant to the new matter in which the interest of the other client is or may be adverse to his own.[16]

15-043   The leading case on confidentiality is *Prince Jefri Bolkiah v. KPMG.*[17] The facts were that the plaintiff B had been the chairman of an investment agency, which managed funds for the government of Brunei, and the defendant firm were the auditors to the agency. There was major litigation against B, in relation to which he retained the firm to provide litigation services, including work which could have been done by a solicitor. After that litigation had settled, B ceased to instruct the firm. The government of Brunei then retained the firm to carry out a further investigation. The firm set up an *ad hoc* "Chinese wall" to prevent information acquired whilst acting for B from being used in the enquiry on behalf of the government. The House of Lords held that the issue was one of confidentiality, not conflict of interests, since B was no longer a client of the firm. The Court of Appeal had asked whether there was an appreciable risk of breach of confidentiality and had undertaken a balancing exercise. However, the House of Lords held that the ex-client was entitled to a higher degree of protection: the duty of confidentiality was an unqualified duty, not merely a duty to take reasonable steps. B had to show only that the risk of a breach of confidentiality was more than fanciful: it did not have to be a substantial risk.[18] It was said that Chinese walls needed to be an established part of the organisational structure of the firm and not created *ad hoc*, if they were to be effective.[19] The House of Lords therefore granted B an injunction to restrain the firm from acting for the government.

15-044   The following additional points emerge:

(1) The nature of the retainer: In *Bolkiah* the accountants had undertaken services normally provided by a solicitor. This meant, among other things, that B had the benefit of litigation privilege as well as confidentiality.[20] It will be necessary in every case to look at the precise role undertaken by the accountant in order to see whether it would be a breach of confidence to disclose information. For example, a client who formerly engaged a firm as auditor and not as adviser might find it more difficult to prevent that firm from subsequently acting for a rival.

(2) The position of a partnership: Although notice to one partner is deemed to be notice to the whole firm,[21] for the purpose of breach of confidence the court is concerned only with actual knowledge, not with imputed

---

[15] *Sasea Finance Ltd v. KPMG* [2000] 1 All E.R 676.
[16] *Bolkiah, ibid.* at 235C–F.
[17] [1999] 2 A.C. 222, HL.
[18] *ibid.* at 236H–237F.
[19] *ibid.* at 239D.
[20] *Bolkiah, ibid.* at 234C.
[21] Partnership Act 1890, s.16.

notice. In other words, the court will not deem the knowledge of one partner to be that of another: its only concern is with the risk of the first partner's knowledge actually leaking to the second partner. It may be possible to meet this risk by erecting Chinese Walls.

(3) *Ad hoc* Chinese walls: In *Young v. Robson Rhodes*[22] a firm of accountants was retained to give forensic assistance to members of a Lloyd's syndicate who were suing a second firm of accountants who had audited the syndicate's accounts. The two firms of accountants subsequently decided to merge. The first firm indicated that it could no longer act for the syndicate, who sought to restrain the merger on the basis that the first firm had received confidential information.[23] Laddie J. distinguished *Bolkiah* on the ground that the number of partners and members of staff who had confidential information in the *Young* case was very much smaller than in *Bolkiah*. He concluded that that the remedy of an injunction to prevent the merger would be disproportionate and that an *ad hoc* Chinese Wall would be sufficient, provided that those who had confidential information were physically separated from those who had been involved in defending the litigation. It is submitted that this decision is difficult to reconcile with *Bolkiah*, both because the judge in *Young* permitted an *ad hoc* Chinese wall and because he took proportionality into account. The approach in *Young* has the merit of being more pragmatic and flexible than that in *Bolkiah*, but it cannot be assumed that it is capable of standing with *Bolkiah*, until the matter has been considered again by a higher court.

(c) *Duties to third parties*

(i) *Overview*

The basic rule. Accountants, like other professionals, owe duties of care and   **15–045** skill to their own clients but do not owe them to third parties in the absence of some special factor. The courts recognise that negligent advice or information is capable of causing loss to many more claimants than a negligent product; in order to keep the tort within reasonable bounds, the courts require some extra ingredient beyond mere foreseeability of loss.[24] If there were no extra ingredient, then there would be a risk of imposing "a liability in an indeterminate amount for an indeterminate time to an indeterminate class".[25] This is particularly important in the case of accountants, since the range and number of persons who may suffer loss consequent upon negligent performance of certain engagements by them are very large.[26]

---

[22] [1999] 3 All E.R. 524. A similar approach was taken in *Halewood v. Addleshaw Booth & Co.* [2000] Lloyd's Rep. P.N. 298 (a solicitor's case).
[23] It is submitted that the partners in possession of the confidential information had an actual conflict of interests, in that they stood to gain personally if the claim against the firm were dismissed. However, the case proceeded solely on the basis of confidentiality, not conflict of interests.
[24] *Murphy v. Brentwood District Council* [1991] 1 A.C. 398, 468G *per* Lord Oliver.
[25] *per* Cardozo C.J. in *Ultramares Corporation v. Touche* (1931) 174 N.E. 441, 444, Court of Appeals of New York.
[26] *Caparo Industries plc v. Dickman* [1990] 2 A.C. 605, 632. Various categories of claimant are considered in para. 15–073 below.

15–046 The current state of the law, which we consider in more detail below, may be summarised as follows:

(1) The scope of the duty will depend upon the purpose to be discerned from an analysis of the relevant statute or regulations. In the case of an audit under the Companies Act, the statutory purpose is to provide shareholders with information about the company's financial position so that they are fully informed at the general meeting; the purpose is not to provide the shareholders or anyone else with information so that they may make investment decisions.

(2) Nevertheless, there may be cases where the accountant has undertaken a specific responsibility to a third party or class of third parties. In order to establish this, the claimant must prove:

(a) that the accountant was aware of the nature of the transaction which the claimant had in mind;
(b) that the accountant knew or ought to have known that his statement would be communicated to the claimant, either directly or as a member of a class;
(c) that the accountant knew or ought to have known that the claimant was very likely to rely on the statement in deciding whether or not to proceed with the transaction; and
(d) that the claimant did rely on the statement.

15–047 **The different approaches.** The courts have been searching for at least 40 years for a universal formula which will encapsulate these propositions. So far this search has not met with complete success; indeed some judges have cautioned that it is better to proceed incrementally than to search for a universal formula. The different judicial approaches were reviewed in *Bank of Credit & Commerce International (Overseas) Ltd v. Price Waterhouse (No. 2)*.[27] The plaintiffs in this case were three subsidiaries of BCCI. Two had the same auditor and the third had a different auditor, but all three companies were operated as a single economic unit to the knowledge of both auditors. The liquidators of all three companies sued both firms of auditors for negligence in auditing the accounts. One of the auditors applied to strike out the claim by one of the companies whose accounts had not been audited by that auditor. The Court of Appeal held that, although an auditor did not usually owe a duty to a non-client, in this case this was arguable since the banks and their auditors were in large measure linked in a joint operation.[28] Sir Brian Neill spoke of a barrier to be overcome, but that formulation has subsequently been disapproved.[29]

15–048 Sir Brian Neill said that the courts' search for a test had followed three separate but parallel paths:

(1) The three-fold test: This requires the plaintiff to establish:

---

[27] [1998] P.N.L.R. 564, 583, CA.
[28] For further discussion about the nature of this interdependence, see para. 15–066 below.
[29] *Andrew v. Kounnis Freeman* [2000] Lloyd's Rep. P.N. 263, 269, CA: for the facts see para. 15–084 below.

(i) that it is foreseeable that he will suffer loss by reason of the negligence: this is Lord Atkin's "neighbour" test for negligent acts in *Donoghue v. Stevenson*[30];

(ii) that there is sufficient proximity between the defendant and the plaintiff: this focuses on the closeness and directness of the relationship between the parties; and

(iii) that it is just and reasonable to impose the liability.[31] This test was adopted in *Caparo*[32] although it was observed in that very case that proximity is "no more than a label which embraces not a definable concept but merely a description of circumstances from which, pragmatically, the courts conclude that a duty of care exists".[33] However in *B.C.C.I.* the Court said that the test was useful in focussing attention on the three essential questions of foreseeability, proximity and fairness.

(2) Assumption of responsibility: This requires the plaintiff to establish that the accountant has voluntarily answered a question or tendered skilled advice or services in circumstances where he knows or ought to know that an identified plaintiff will rely on his answers or advice. If the accountant chooses to act or speak in those circumstances, he is said to have assumed responsibility for doing so carefully.[34]

(3) The incremental approach: This approach eschews any attempt to find a universal formula but advocates that the law should proceed incrementally and by analogy with established categories, rather than by a massive extension of a prima facie duty of care restrained only by indefinable limits.[35]

Sir Brian Neill concluded that, at least for the purpose of an application to **15–049** strike out a claim, the court should look at all three tests. He said that it was likely that they all would all lead to the same result, if the facts were properly analysed.[36] We submit that the better approach is to focus on the ingredients which are or are not likely to be sufficient rather than search for a single all-embracing formula. The three critical ingredients are purpose, knowledge and

---

[30] [1932] A.C. 562, 580.

[31] *Smith v. Eric S. Bush* [1990] 1 A.C. 831, 864H *per* Lord Griffiths.

[32] *Caparo Industries plc v. Dickman* [1990] 2 A.C. 605, 616H *per* Lord Bridge.

[33] *ibid.* at 633D *per* Lord Oliver; see also *ibid.* at 617B *per* Lord Bridge. This test was also adopted in *Law Society v. KPMG* [2000] 1 W.L.R. 1921. The courts in Canada have used element (iii) in a different fashion: they have continued to follow the wider pre-*Caparo* test set out in *Anns v. Merton LBC* [1978] A.C. 728, 751–752 but they have refused on policy grounds to allow claims where these would result in indeterminate liability: *Hercules Managements Ltd v. Ernst & Young* [1997] 146 D.L.R. 577, 586 and 597.

[34] *Henderson v. Merrett Syndicates Ltd* [1995] 2 A.C. 145, 180–181 and 192–193 *per* Lord Goff; *White v. Jones* [1995] 2 A.C. 207, 268H and 273G *per* Lords Goff and Browne-Wilkinson. However, in *Caparo* [1990] 2 A.C. 605, 628 and 637, Lords Roskill and Oliver said that it was a convenient label but that it did not tell one anything about the circumstances from which such attribution arose.

[35] *Sutherland Shire Council v. Heyman* (1984) 147 C.L.R. 424, H. Ct. of Aus., quoted with approval in *Caparo, ibid.* at 618 and 633 by Lords Bridge and Oliver.

[36] *Bank of Credit & Commerce International (Overseas) Ltd v. Price Waterhouse (No. 2)* [1998] P.N.L.R. 564, 586F. See also *Merrett v. Babb* [2001] 3 W.L.R. 1, 17F; EWCA Civ. 214 para. 41 of the judgment (a surveyor's case).

reliance, *i.e.* (i) the purpose for which the statement was made and communicated, (ii) the knowledge of the maker of the statement and (iii) reliance by its recipient.[37]

15–050   Whichever general test is applied, it is important to focus on the particular context in which the alleged duty arises. In evaluating a claim against accountants arising from a statutory or regulatory context, it is critical to assess the relevant statute or regulatory scheme. Considerations decisive in such a context to negate a duty of care alleged to have been owed to a third party by statutory, ministerial, administrative, regulatory and complaints-handling bodies have been the availability of alternative bases of redress[38] and regulatory overkill,[39] even though such redress may be of little value to the third party concerned. Like considerations apply in evaluating claims against accountants.

15–051   Most of the reported decisions during the last decade have arisen out of applications to strike out the claim on the ground that no duty of care was owed to the claimant. In general the courts have taken the view that this is a developing area of law and that, provided that something is alleged which might arguably be sufficient to constitute a special factor, the claim should be allowed to proceed to trial.[40] The moral is that, unless it is clear that the claimant's claim must fail, it may be better for the defendant to proceed to trial instead of attempting to strike out. However it remains to be seen whether the current move towards active judicial case-management will bring about a change of climate.

15–052   After considering the basic principle enunciated in *Caparo* we seek to analyse the case law both by reference to factors identified in the cases and by reference to categories of typical advisee. These are no more than guidelines and should not be elevated into rules. A claimant will have made considerable headway in getting his claim off the ground if he can show that his facts are similar to those of a previous decision in which a duty of care was held to exist, at least if the courts adopt the incremental approach. However where a novel set of facts comes before the court, the fact that they do not fit into any established category is not necessarily a reason for holding that there is no duty of care. It is usually necessary to go back to first principles.

(ii) *Caparo*

15–053   **The law prior to *Caparo*.**[41] It used to be thought that there was no liability for a negligent misrepresentation made by one person to another who had acted upon

---

[37] Note in particular the speeches in *Caparo Industries plc v. Dickman, ibid.* of Lord Bridge at 620–621, Lord Oliver at 638 and Lord Jauncey at 659–660 (esp. at 630E "the fundamental question of purpose"). Note also the emphasis on purpose in *James McNaughton Paper Group Ltd v. Hicks Anderson & Co.* [1991] 2 Q.B. 113, 125–127.

[38] As to a statutory context see *Caparo, ibid.*, and *Murphy v. Brentwood* [1991] 1 A.C. 398. As to a regulatory context, see *Yuen Kun Yeu v. Att.-Gen. of Hong Kong* [1988] A.C. 175, PC and *Davies v. Radcliffe* [1990] 1 W.L.R. 821, PC. As to a ministerial context, see *Rowling v. Takaro Properties Ltd* [1988] 1 A.C. 475, PC. As to an administrative context see *Jones v. Department of Employment* [1989] Q.B. 1, CA. For like reasoning in the context of copyright, see *C.B.S. Songs Ltd v. Amstrad Consumer Electronics Plc* [1988] A.C. 1013, 1059–1060, HL, and receivership, see *Downsview Ltd v. First City Corporation Ltd* [1993] A.C. 295, 316, PC.

[39] See *Rowling v. Takaro Properties Ltd* [1988] 1 A.C. 475, 502, PC.

[40] *Coulthard v. Neville Russell* [1998] P.N.L.R. 276, 288–289 (for the facts see para. 15–081 below); *Andrew v. Kounnis Freeman* [2000] Lloyd's Rep. P.N. 263, 272, CA (for the facts see para. 15–084 below); and *Siddell v. Smith Cooper* [1999] P.N.L.R. 511, 520–522 (for the facts see para. 15–067 below).

[41] For a more detailed discussion of the law before *Caparo* see the fourth edition of this work, paras 8–34 to 8–46.

it to his detriment, in the absence of any contractual or fiduciary relationship between the parties or of fraud. It was on this basis that the majority of the Court of Appeal in *Candler v. Crane, Christmas & Co.*[42] dismissed the claim of the plaintiff who had invested money in a company in reliance upon accounts negligently prepared by the defendant accountants and who had lost his investment upon the company's liquidation. Denning L.J., however, in his classic dissenting judgment, took the view that the plaintiff was owed a duty of care by the accountants and was entitled to recover. The majority's decision was overruled and Denning L.J.'s judgment was approved by the House of Lords in *Hedley Byrne & Co. Ltd v. Heller & Partners Ltd.*[43] His judgment was also expressly approved in *Caparo*[44] and there can be little doubt that in the same circumstances as those in *Candler* today, the plaintiff would succeed.

Denning L.J.'s judgment[45] laid the foundations for the modern law in relation **15–054** to claims by third parties against accountants. He considered the types of statements in respect of which professional accountants owe a general duty of care and the persons and transactions to which that duty extends.

(1) Types of statement: he considered that accountants were not liable for (a) casual remarks made in the course of conversation; nor for (b) statements made outside their work; nor for (c) statements not made in their capacity as accountants. But they were "in proper cases", apart from any contract in the matter, under a duty to use reasonable care in the preparation of their accounts and in the making of their reports.

(2) Persons to whom accountants owe a duty of care: he said that the test of proximity in these cases was: Did the accountant know that the accounts were required for submission to the plaintiff and use by him?

(3) Nature of the transactions: he confined liability to transactions for which the accountants knew their accounts were required.[46]

The next milestone was *Hedley Byrne & Co. Ltd v. Heller & Partners Ltd.*[47] **15–055** Although not a claim against accountants, it proved of crucial relevance in the development of the law of accountant's negligence. All their Lordships agreed that in certain circumstances liability could be incurred for a negligent misrepresentation by one person to another even in the absence of any contractual or fiduciary relationship between them or of fraud. They were nevertheless concerned to limit the parameters of such liability. The case is generally regarded as requiring a special relationship to exist for one person to owe another a duty of care in the giving of advice or information. None of their Lordships gave precise criteria for this relationship, all relying upon broad formulations of general principle. Not all these formulations are identical in substance and they differ in

---

[42] [1951] 2 K.B. 164.
[43] [1964] A.C. 465.
[44] [1990] 2 A.C. 605, 623.
[45] [1951] 2 K.B. 164, 174–185.
[46] In this respect the law has developed: the accountant would also be liable today if he *ought* to have known: *Hedley Byrne, ibid.* at 486. On the particular facts in *Candler*, the defendants did actually know of the plaintiff's reliance and it was therefore unnecessary to consider the question whether they ought to have known of it. Note also Denning L.J.'s observation (*ibid.* at 184) that a lawyer is never called upon to express his personal belief in the truth of his client's case, whereas an auditor is always called on to express his opinion that the accounts give a true and fair view.
[47] [1964] A.C. 465.

emphasis. Nevertheless the following passage from a speech of Lord Morris, which Lord Hodson endorsed, broadly reflects the current view of what *Hedley Byrne* established:

> "if in a sphere in which a person is so placed, that others could reasonably rely upon his judgment or his skill or upon his ability to make careful inquiry, a person takes it upon himself to give information or advice to, or allows his information or advice to be passed on to, another person who, as he knows or should know, will place reliance upon it, then a duty of care will arise."[48]

15–056   **The facts of *Caparo Industries plc v. Dickman.*[49]** The claim arose out of the takeover in 1984 of Fidelity plc by Caparo Industries plc, both listed companies, and was brought against two of Fidelity's directors and the auditors of its accounts for the year ended March 31, 1984. In early March 1984 a press release was issued forecasting a significant profits shortfall. Over that month Fidelity's share price fell sharply. In May 1984 the auditors reported upon the accounts giving a clean certificate to the effect that they were properly prepared and gave a true and fair view of relevant matters. The next day Fidelity's directors announced profits well down on predictions. On June 8 Caparo began to buy Fidelity shares. The accounts were sent to the shareholders on June 12, 1984, but Caparo was not registered as a shareholder until later. Nor did it attend Fidelity's annual general meeting on July 4, 1984 when the auditors' report was read and the accounts adopted. Two days later Caparo had acquired 29.9 per cent of Fidelity's issued shares. In September it made a bid for the remaining shares and subsequently acquired them, some compulsorily.

15–057   Caparo maintained that the accounts were inaccurate and misleading, in particular in overvaluing stock and undervaluing after-sales credits, with the result that there was in fact a loss of £400,000 instead of reported profits of £1.3m. It alleged that its share purchases subsequent to the sending of the accounts to shareholders were made in reliance on those accounts and that, if it had known the true position, it would not have bid for them at the price paid or at all. It commenced proceedings against the two directors alleging deceit and against the auditors alleging negligence. It contended that the auditors in carrying out their functions in April and May 1984 owed a duty of care to investors (in the sense of existing shareholders) and potential investors, including Caparo. In support it maintained that the auditors: (1) knew or ought to have known of (a) the press release in early March, (b) the slide in the share price from 143p on March 1 to 75p on April 2, and (c) Fidelity's need for financial assistance; and (2) ought to have foreseen that Fidelity was vulnerable to a takeover bid and that bidders such as Caparo might well rely on the accounts in assessing a bid and suffer loss if the accounts were inaccurate.

15–058   An order was made for the trial of a preliminary issue: whether on the alleged facts the auditors owed a duty of care to Caparo (a) as potential investors in Fidelity or (b) as shareholders in Fidelity as from June 8 and/or 12, 1984, in respect of the audit of the relevant accounts. The judge at first instance, Sir Neil Lawson, held that the auditors owed no duty of care to Caparo in either capacity. On Caparo's appeal, the Court of Appeal by a majority (Bingham and Taylor L.JJ., O'Connor L.J. dissenting in part) allowed the appeal.[50] The Court was

---

[48] *ibid.* at 503, 514.
[49] [1990] 2 A.C. 605.
[50] [1989] Q.B. 653.

unanimously of the view that the requisite relationship of proximity was not established between potential investors in a company and its auditor. Bingham and Taylor L.JJ. concluded that it was established between existing shareholders and the auditor. Thus if an individual shareholder sustained loss by acting in reliance on negligently prepared accounts, whether by selling or retaining his shares or by purchasing additional shares, he was entitled to recover in tort. O'Connor L.J. disagreed and rejected a duty of care in that case also.

The House of Lords took the same view as O'Connor L.J. and the judge at first   **15–059** instance and restored the latter's decision, holding that there was no duty of care owed to Caparo either as an existing shareholder or as a potential investor. The main speeches were delivered by Lords Bridge and Oliver.[51]

Lord Bridge propounded the three-fold test of foreseeability, proximity and fairness, although he warned that these were imprecise terms and he saw the wisdom of following the incremental approach.[52] He distinguished *Smith v. Eric S. Bush*[53] by saying that in that case the defendant knew (i) the nature of the transaction which the plaintiff had in contemplation, (ii) that the information or advice would be communicated to the plaintiff and (iii) that the plaintiff was very likely to rely on it. The defendant could therefore be expected specifically to anticipate (a) that the plaintiff would rely on the advice or information for the very purpose for which he did rely on it and (b) that the plaintiff would reasonably suppose that he was entitled to rely on it. This is to be contrasted with a statement, such as an audit certificate, which is put into general circulation.[54] He concluded:

> "It is never sufficient to ask simply whether A owes B a duty of care. It is always necessary to determine the scope of the duty by reference to the kind of damage from which A must take care to save B harmless."[55]

Lord Oliver took as his starting point the statutory context.[56] He said that it   **15–060** should not be assumed that the purpose of the auditor's certificate was anything other than the fulfilment of the statutory duty of carrying out the annual audit. The statutory purpose of the audit was simply to furnish the shareholders with information.[57] Although it was foreseeable that shareholders and other investors would make investment decisions based on that information, this was not its

---

[51] Lord Roskill gave a short speech agreeing with Lords Bridge and Oliver (*ibid.* at 627F), Lord Ackner (at 629E) agreed with all the speeches, and Lord Jauncey gave a speech which concurred with the main speeches (at 654–663).

[52] See para. 15–048 above.

[53] [1990] 1 A.C. 831. In that case it was held that a surveyor who valued a modestly priced house for a mortgagee but whose fee was paid by the borrower might owe the latter a duty of care. See Chap. 9, paras 9–046, *et seq.* and 9–065, *et seq.*

[54] *ibid.* at 620.

[55] *ibid.* at 627D. The importance of analysing the scope of the duty was emphasised by Lord Hoffmann in *South Australia Asset Management Co. Ltd v. York Montague Ltd* [1997] A.C. 191 (see para. 15–125 below).

[56] This is a reference to the Companies Act: see paras 15–011, *et seq.* above. Lord Jauncey took the same approach: *ibid.* at 658G. Surprisingly, it would appear that no consideration was given to the listing requirements made by the Council of the Stock Exchange and contained in its publication Admission of Securities to Listing ("The Yellow Book") which are now statutory requirements by virtue of Part IV of the Financial Services Act 1986, although they were not at the time of the facts giving rise to the claim in *Caparo*. These include specific requirements relating to publication of financial information, including on a continuing basis. The Stock Exchange is an investment market and potential investors are clearly in contemplation.

[57] See para. 15–011 above.

statutory purpose.[58] He considered the three different tests summarised above[59] and found the greatest assistance in the incremental approach.[60] He then went on to consider the law of negligence and the need for something more than mere foreseeability as a way of controlling the floodgates of liability. A defective bottle of ginger-beer may damage one consumer, but a defective statement may be repeated endlessly and relied on in different ways by different people. He regarded *Smith v. Eric S. Bush* as the high-water mark and distinguished it on the ground that the loss in the present case was strictly unrelated to the intended recipient or to the purpose for which the advice was required. Importantly, he saw no policy reason to extend the law.[61] He said in relation to proximity that:

"it is not a duty to take care in the abstract but a duty to avoid causing to the particular plaintiff damage of the particular kind which he has in fact sustained"[62]

He concluded that:

"The purpose for which the auditors' certificate is made and published is that of providing those entitled to receive the report with information to enable them to exercise in conjunction those powers which their respective proprietary interests confer upon them, and not for the purposes of individual speculation with a view to profit. The same considerations as limit the existence of a duty of care also, in my judgment, limit the scope of the duty."[63]

15–061   The House of Lords in *Caparo* held that the duty was owed to the shareholders as a body and not to individual shareholders. In practice their collective interests are indistinguishable from the interests of the company itself and therefore any loss suffered by the shareholders as a body will be recouped by a claim brought by the company.[64]

(iii) *Factors which may be relevant*

15–062   In *James McNaughton Paper Group Ltd v. Hicks Anderson*[65] the defendant accountants were instructed to prepare accounts for a group of companies in connection with a proposed take-over by the plaintiff. The accounts showed a net loss for the year. At a meeting between the plaintiff and the defendant the defendant said that the group was breaking even or doing marginally worse. The take-over went ahead and the plaintiff later discovered errors in the accounts. The Court of Appeal held that there was insufficient proximity and hence no duty was owed to the plaintiff. Neill L.J. analysed the six factors which were likely to

---

[58] *ibid.* at 631. See also Lord Jauncey *ibid.* at 661G–662B.
[59] see para. 15–048 above.
[60] *ibid.* at 632–638.
[61] *ibid.* at 642F–H. In *Morgan Crucible Co. plc v. Hill Samuel & Co. Ltd* [1991] Ch. 295 Hoffmann J. at first instance justified the distinction between *Smith v. Bush* and *Caparo* in policy terms (*i.e.* differences between the economic relationships of (i) corporate investor and auditor and (ii) house purchaser and valuer respectively and differences between the markets in which the different professionals operated) but the Court of Appeal in that case downgraded the importance of this policy factor. (For the facts of this case, see para. 15–076 below.)
[62] *ibid.* at 651F.
[63] *ibid.* at 654.
[64] *ibid.* at 626C-E (Lord Bridge).
[65] [1991] 2 Q.B. 113.

be relevant in considering proximity.[66] He warned that some of the factors overlapped and that the list was not intended to be comprehensive. It is nevertheless a useful way of analysing the material.

In *Peach Publishing Ltd v. Slater & Co.*[67] the plaintiff said that she would not **15–063** proceed with her proposed purchase of a company unless she received a warranty from the vendor. The vendor would not give the warranty without approval from the defendant, who was his own accountant as well as being the company's auditor. At a meeting the plaintiff pressed the defendant to give his approval, which he did. After the purchase it emerged that the accounts were inaccurate and the purchaser sued the accountant. The Court of Appeal held that the purpose of the assurance had been solely to advise the vendor that he could give the warranty and that the defendant had not assumed a duty to the plaintiff. Sir Brian Neill re-stated in similar terms the factors which he had set out in *B.C.C.I.*[68] We shall now consider his six factors.[69]

The purpose for which the statement was made. Where a statement is made **15–064** for the express purpose of communicating it to the advisee, this is a factor in favour of finding the necessary proximity. Where it is not express, it might in a suitable case be implied from the circumstances. By contrast, where the document is an auditor's certificate in relation to a company audit and there is no indication as to the purpose for which it was made, the court will conclude that it was made merely for the statutory purpose of giving information to the shareholders as a body.[70] In one case[71] it was held that the purpose of the defendant's audit work was limited to the statutory purpose, but that representations made by the auditor at a meeting were made for the purpose of providing the takeover bidder with information upon which he could rely without further enquiry.

The purpose for which the statement was communicated. It is necessary to **15–065** ask whether it was communicated for information only or with a view to some action being taken. Further, if a statement was made for one purpose, it may be unreasonable to impose liability in relation to a different purpose.[72] In one case[73] an accountant was held liable to a third party notwithstanding that he did not intend to proffer information as a means of persuasion; it was sufficient that he knew (or ought to have known) that the information would be relied upon.

---

[66] *ibid.* at 125–127. The test was restated in similar terms by Sir Brian Neill (formerly Neill L.J.) in *B.C.C.I. v. Price Waterhouse (No. 2)* [1998] P.N.L.R. 564, 587.

[67] [1998] B.C.C. 139. Contrast *ADT v. Binder Hamlyn* [1996] B.C.C. 808, where the accountant was aware that the confirmation which the purchaser sought from him was "the final hurdle" to be surmounted before the purchaser agreed to purchase.

[68] In the same case, *ibid.* at 146B, Morritt L.J. put the question as follows: "Whether having regard to all the circumstances of the case and looking at the matter objectively it can be said that [the accountant] undertook responsibility to [the third party] for the substantial accuracy of the management accounts."

[69] Authority for each of these factors may be found in *McNaughton, Peach* and *B.C.C.I.* We have confined ourselves to citing additional authority under each sub-heading.

[70] See para. 15–011 above.

[71] *ADT v. Binder Hamlyn* [1996] B.C.C. 808, May J.

[72] *e.g.* the facts of *Caparo* itself: see paras 15–056 *et seq.* above.

[73] *ADT v. Binder Hamlyn* [1996] B.C.C. 808, May J.; see also *Andrew v. Kounnis Freeman* [2000] Lloyd's Rep. P.N. 263, CA: for the facts see para. 15–084 below.

15–066   **The relationship between the advisee and any relevant third party.** Where the information or advice was initially prepared for someone other than the advisee, it is necessary to consider whether the advisee was likely to look to the third party, and through him to the defendant, for advice or information. Where the statement is communicated through a third party, it is necessary to ask whether such communication was intended or envisaged[74] by the defendant. In *Bank of Credit & Commerce International (Overseas) Ltd v. Price Waterhouse (No. 2)*[75] the Court of Appeal found the necessary proximity in the close relationship between three companies which were operated as a single economic unit and the two firms of auditors who between them audited the accounts of the companies. The Court noted that each auditor relied on information supplied by the other and that the correspondence referred to the interdependence of the companies and the auditors and to the need for close liaison between them.

15–067   In *Siddell v. Smith Cooper*[76] the plaintiffs were shareholders in a private company which borrowed money from a bank on the security of guarantees from the plaintiffs. The defendants were the company auditors and were also its accountants. The company went into receivership as a result of financial irregularities which the defendants had failed to notice. The plaintiffs' guarantee was called upon and the plaintiffs then sought to recover from the defendant. The Court of Appeal refused to strike out the plaintiffs' claim, saying that it was not plain and obvious that the claim would fail. In the first place the defendants were not simply auditors but also accountants providing advice to the company as well as quarterly management accounts. Secondly, the company was a small quasi-partnership, which made it more likely that it would rely on advice from its accountants. The fact that the defendant had a contractual relationship with the company does not necessarily preclude a duty in tort from being owed to the plaintiff.

15–068   **The size of any class to which the advisee belongs.** The larger the class, the harder to establish proximity. The court should look not only at the number of advisees but also at the nature of the class to which they belong.[77]

15–069   **The state of knowledge of the adviser.** The court will ask whether he knew or should reasonably have known: (i) the purpose for which the statement was made or required in the first place, (ii) the purpose for which it was communicated to the advisee[78] and (iii) that the advisee would rely on the statement without obtaining independent advice.[79] Despite dicta to the contrary, the better

---

[74] *Kripps v. Touche Ross & Co* (1997) 33 B.C.L.R. (3d) 254, British Columbia CA: in that case a company which sold certain debentures was required by the local law to file an annual prospectus containing financial statements for the previous year and an unqualified auditors' report. The plaintiff claimed to have purchased debentures in reliance on the defendant auditors' report and sued for negligent misrepresentation. It was held on appeal that, although the auditors did not expressly consent to the inclusion of their report in the prospectus, they knew when they provided their report that its purpose was to facilitate the sale of debentures to the public and they must be taken to have given implicit consent to its inclusion in the prospectus.

[75] [1998] P.N.L.R. 564, 583, CA: for the facts see para. 15–047 above.

[76] [1999] P.N.L.R. 511, CA.

[77] *Siddell v. Smith Cooper, ibid.* at 524: for the facts, see para. 15–067 above.

[78] *Al Saudi Banque v. Clarke Pixley* [1990] Ch. 313 and *Esanda Finance Corporation Ltd v. Peat Marwick Hungerfords* (1997) 71 A.L.J.R. 448 (for the facts of both cases see paras 15–082 *et seq.* below).

[79] See also *Siddell v. Smith Cooper, ibid.* at 525.

view is that liability depends, not on whether the defendant consciously assumed a duty of care, but on whether in all the circumstances it would be reasonable to regard him as having assumed such a duty: "the touchstone of liability is not the state of mind of the defendant".[80] However, reasonableness depends on more than just foreseeability: hence the need to consider all the factors which are put into the melting pot in order to decide whether there is sufficient proximity.[81]

Reliance by the advisee. The court asks: (i) was it reasonable to rely on the statement? and (ii) did the advisee actually rely on it?[82] The cases show that the following have been treated as factors which point towards it being unreasonable to rely on the accountant's statement[83]: that the accounts are labelled "draft" accounts[84]; that if the accounts themselves show that the company is in a poor financial state, this might make it unreasonable to rely on a statement which paints a rosier picture[85]; that the claimant is an experienced businessman who might be expected to seek his own advice[86]; that the defendant's answer was a very general one upon which it was not reasonable for the claimant to rely without further enquiry[87]; and that it is unreasonable to rely on audited accounts beyond a limited period (*i.e.* an audit certificate impliedly has a "sell-by" date).[88]   **15–070**

There is no need to show that the adviser actually intended the advisee to rely, as long as it would be reasonable for the advisee to rely in the circumstances.[89] But it is necessary for the advisee to show that he was aware of the statement[90] and actually relied on it.[91]   **15–071**

Other factors. Other important factors which are not listed in *McNaughton* are: the relationship between the adviser and the advisee (was it a general   **15–072**

---

[80] *Electra Private Equity Partners Ltd v. KPMG Peat Marwick* [1999] Lloyd's Rep. P.N. 670, 682.

[81] In *JEB Fasteners Ltd v. Marks Bloom & Co.* [1981] 3 All E.R. 289 at 296J Woolf J. held an auditor liable to an investor on the ground that it was foreseeable that the investor would rely on the valuation of stock in the accounts. In *Caparo* [1990] 2 A.C. 605, 625 Lord Bridge said that the reasoning in *JEB* was wrong but the decision might be right on its facts, since the auditors did have actual knowledge of the specific purpose for which the accounts were to be relied upon.

[82] For actual reliance, see para. 15–127 below.

[83] In *B.C.C.I. v. Price Waterhouse (No. 2)* [1998] P.N.L.R. 564 the factors making it unreasonable to rely on the statement were held to outweigh the fact that the advice had been given expressly to the plaintiff.

[84] *McNaughton*, [1991] 2 Q.B. 113, 127H and 129E.

[85] *ibid.* at 128B.

[86] *ibid.* at 128C.

[87] *ibid.* at 128D.

[88] *Berg Son & Co. v. Mervyn Hampton Adams* [1993] B.C.L.C. 1045. See also *JEB Fasteners Ltd v. Marks Bloom* [1981] 3 All E.R. 289, 297A (Woolf J.); the case was reversed by CA [1983] 1 All E.R. 583 and was disapproved in *Caparo* [1990] 2 A.C. 605, 625, but not on this point.

[89] *B.C.C.I. v. Price Waterhouse (No. 2) ibid.* at 588; see also *Yue Xiu Finance Co. Ltd v. Dermot Agnew (formerly trading as Deloitte Haskins & Sells)* [1996] 1 H.K.L.R. 137: for the facts see n. 9 to para. 15–077, below.

[90] *Abbott v. Strong* [1998] 2 B.C.L.C. 420, Ferris J.: an accountant, who advised directors on what to include in the prospectus for a rights issue, owed no duty of care to shareholders who were unaware that he was advising.

[91] See para. 15–127 below.

relationship or an ad hoc one?)[92]; whether the adviser had the opportunity to issue a disclaimer[93]; and the terms of the defendant firm's internal manual.[94]

(iv) *Categories of advisee*

15–073   The categories of claimant who most frequently claim to be owed duties of care by accountants are as follows:

(1) Existing shareholders.

(2) Potential investors.

(3) Other companies in the group.

(4) Directors.

(5) Banks and other creditors.

The list is not exhaustive. We shall now consider these and other miscellaneous categories in more detail.

15–074   **Existing shareholders.** The paradigm case is *Caparo*,[95] which established that, unless there are special factors to the contrary, the duty is limited to a duty to the shareholders as a body. In most cases this is identical to the duty owed to the company itself: it is not easy to see what loss the shareholders as a body might suffer independently of the company itself.[96] Indeed, it is submitted that it is wrong both as a matter of principle and as a matter of policy to permit the shareholders as a class to sue independently of the company. It is wrong as a matter of principle, since it conflicts with the general rule that duties are owed only to the client company. It is wrong as a matter of policy because it gives rise to the problems of duplication of remedies.[97] Although the company as a going concern is often identified with its shareholders,[98] this is no longer the case when the company becomes insolvent; at that point the interests of creditors become paramount.[99] In such a case it is submitted that there are strong policy grounds why the claim of the liquidator (effectively acting for the creditors) should prevail over the claim of the shareholders.[1]

15–075   Despite the general rule, there may be a duty to shareholders individually where there is sufficient proximity as discussed above. This would be relevant if

---

[92] *B.C.C.I. v. Price Waterhouse (No. 2)* [1998] P.N.L.R. 564, 587.

[93] *ibid.* at 587.

[94] *ADT Ltd v. Binder Hamlyn* [1996] B.C.C. 808, 837E.

[95] See paras 15–056 *et seq.* above.

[96] *Berg Son & Co. v. Mervyn Hampton Adams* [1993] B.C.L.C. 1045, 1064, Hobhouse J.

[97] See para. 15–087 below.

[98] Hence the principle that the shareholders are entitled to ratify irregular decisions of the board which are not *ultra vires*: *Re Duomatic Ltd* [1969] 2 Ch. 365.

[99] *Winkworth v. Baron* [1986] 1 W.L.R. 1512, 1516E–F, HL (duty owed by directors to the company and its creditors to see that affairs of the company are properly administered and not dissipated); *West Mercia Safetywear Ltd v. Dodd* [1988] B.C.L.C. 250, CA (where company is insolvent, duty to creditors overrides duty to members); *Kinsella v. Russell Kinsella Pty. Limited* [1986] 5 A.C.L.C. 215, CA of Aus. (where company is insolvent, the interests of creditors intrude and they become prospectively entitled, through the mechanism of liquidation, to displace the power of shareholders and directors and to deal with the assets.).

[1] *Duke Group Ltd v. Pilmer* (1999) 31 A.C.S.R. 213, 259 (for the facts see para. 15–151 below); see also *Carr-Glynn v. Frearsons* [1999] Ch. 326, 337–338.

a shareholder sells his shares at an undervalue in reliance on the audit certificate.[2] Thus, where the company's articles of association gave a right of pre-emption to the surviving shareholders to buy back shares at a valuation following death of a shareholder, it was held to be arguable that the accountant owed those shareholders a duty to exercise care in giving a valuation to the company, since he knew or ought to have known that his valuation would affect them.[3]

Potential investors. *Caparo*[4] established that there is no duty of care to investors unless there is sufficient proximity. However, there is usually little difficulty in establishing a duty of care to recipients of takeover circulars and offer documents by an accountant who has consented to the inclusion of information provided by him. Such documents are known to be directed to particular recipients or classes of recipient, who may rely on them for investments purposes.[5] In *Morgan Crucible Co. plc v. Hill Samuel & Co. Ltd*[6] a circular was issued in the course of a contested takeover of a public company. The circular referred to financial statements relating to the target company and made by its auditors; the circular also included a letter from the auditors saying that the forecast had been properly compiled. The plaintiff company increased its offer for the target company and its bid was successful. It then sued various defendants, including the auditors, alleging that it had increased its bid in reliance on their statements. The Court of Appeal considered it arguable that the necessary relationship of proximity could be found on the assumptions that the defendants knew: (i) that the plaintiff would rely on them for the purpose of making an increased bid, (ii) that the defendant intended the plaintiff so to rely, and (iii) that the plaintiff did so rely. On these assumed facts, the representations were made to the plaintiff and not merely to the company. **15–076**

In *Possfund Custodian Trustee Ltd v. Diamond*[7] a prospectus was issued in connection with a flotation of shares in a company. The plaintiffs subscribed for shares and subsequently bought more shares in the aftermarket. The plaintiffs then sued various defendants including the auditors, claiming they had made both purchases in reliance on the prospectus and that the prospectus was inaccurate. The defendants sought to strike out the claim in relation to the aftermarket.[8] Lightman J. held that it was arguable that the duty of care continued in relation to the aftermarket, provided that the representor's intention that the representee should rely could be objectively established. This required the plaintiff to show either (i) that the representor communicated this intention to the representee or (ii) that the representee reasonably assumed that the representor intended him to **15–077**

---

[2] *Morgan Crucible Co. plc v. Hill Samuel & Co. Ltd* [1991] Ch. 295, 305A *per* Hoffmann J. (*obiter*) at first instance.

[3] *Killick v. PriceWaterhouseCoopers* [2001] P.N.L.R. 1, Neuberger J.

[4] See paras 15–056 *et seq.* above.

[5] In addition there may be statutory liability to compensate investors: see para. 15–029 above.

[6] [1991] Ch. 295, CA held that it was arguable on the facts that the accountant knew that the investor would rely on his financial statements and forecast for the purpose of making an increased bid.

[7] [1996] 1 W.L.R. 1351, Lightman J.

[8] The defendants sought to rely on *Peek v. Gurney* (1873) L.R. 6 H.L. 377, in which the House of Lords had held that a prospectus could reasonably be relied on only for the purpose for which it was intended, *i.e.* the subscription of shares in the course of the flotation and not the purchase of shares in the aftermarket.

rely. Proof of such objective intention would arguably be sufficient to establish proximity.[9]

15–078   By contrast, it has been held in New Zealand[10] that it is not sufficient to show that it was foreseeable in a general sort of way that the accounts might be relied on in the course of a takeover; the plaintiff must show that the auditor knew or ought to have known that his report would be relied on by a particular person or class of persons for a specific purpose.[11]

15–079   In addition to liability for information in take-over circulars and offer documents, an accountant might also owe a duty of care in tort in respect of statements made in negotiations on behalf of a client. Whether such a duty arises depends very much on the particular circumstances and the proper analysis of the purpose of the relevant statement and to whom it was directed. For example, in negotiations for the sale of a company an accountant or auditor may be asked to give the prospective purchaser some assurance as to the accuracy of relevant financial statements, including draft statements. He should tread carefully, as the giving of such assurance may result in liability in tort, which may appear hugely disproportionate to the degree of culpability. Relevant case law in this area demonstrates some fine distinctions and differences of analyses.[12]

15–080   **Other companies in the group.** Although an auditor who is instructed to audit the accounts of one company in a group usually owes no duty to other companies in the group, there may be a duty if the facts indicate a sufficiently close

---

[9] For other examples of cases where there was (or was arguably) sufficient proximity see: *ADT v. Binder Hamlyn* [1996] B.C.C. 808 (for the facts see para. 15–064 above); *Yorkshire Enterprises Ltd v. Robson Rhodes*, unreported June 17, 1998, Bell J.; *Haig v. Bamford* (1976) D.L.R. (3d) 68, S. Ct of Can.: (discussed by Bingham L.J. in the CA in *Caparo* [1989] Q.B. 653, 693–694); and *Yue Xiu Finance Co. Ltd v. Dermot Agnew* [1996] 1 H.K.L.R. 137 (accountant instructed to certify valuation of company in circumstances where he knew or ought to have known that vendor would rely on valuation in deciding whether to exercise put option to sell shares in the company. The relationship was as close as it was possible to have, short of contract).

[10] *Scott Group Ltd v. McFarlane* [1978] 1 N.Z.L.R. 553 *per* Richmond P. Although he formed part of the majority which dismissed the appeal of the takeover bidder in that case, the other judge did so on different grounds. Nevertheless, it was this statement by Richmond P. which was approved in *Caparo* [1990] 2 A.C. 605, 624 and 644–645.

[11] For other examples of cases where there was insufficient proximity see: *Al-Nakib Investments (Jersey) Ltd v. Longcroft* [1990] 1 W.L.R. 1390 (doubted in *Possfund*); *James McNaughton Paper Group Ltd v. Hicks Anderson* [1991] 2 Q.B. 113 (for the facts see para. 15–062 above); *Peach Publishing Ltd v. Slater & Co.* [1998] B.C.C. 139 (for the facts see para. 15–063 above); *Dimond Manufacturing Co. Ltd v. Hamilton* [1969] N.Z.L.R. 609, NZCA; and *Boyd Knight v. Purdue* [1999] N.Z.L.R. 278 (for the facts see para. 15–028 above).

[12] *James McNaughton Papers Group Ltd v. Hicks Anderson & Co.* [1991] 2 Q.B. 113, CA (first instance judge held duty owed, but reversed on appeal: very general statement in respect of draft accounts); *ADT Ltd v. BDO Binder Hamlyn* [1996] B.C.C. 808, May J. (duty owed: £65 million damages award settled before appeal); *Downs v. Chappell* [1997] 1 W.L.R. 426, CA (duty owed); *Electra Private Equity Partners v. KPMG Peat Marwick* [1999] Lloyd's Rep. P.N. 670, CA (refusal to strike out claim by purchaser of controlling interest in company against its auditors arising from allegedly incorrect information supplied during acquisition negotiations: reversing Carnwath J. at first instance reported at [1998] P.N.L.R. 135); *Peach Publishing Ltd v. Slater & Co.* [1998] P.N.L.R. 364, CA (held liable by Rimer J. on basis that a duty was owed to the plaintiff third party, but reversed on appeal); *Yorkshire Enterprise Ltd v. Robson Rhodes*, unreported, June 17, 1998, Bell J. (duty owed); *HIT Finance Ltd v. Cohen Arnold* [2000] Lloyd's Rep. P.N. 125, CA (accountants of a guarantor of a company's indebtedness did owe a limited duty of care in respect of financial information provided about the guarantor, but held not in breach; on its true construction the relevant letter merely passed on information provided by the guarantor and did not amount to verification of guarantor's net worth as held by Mantell J. at first instance: [1998] 1 E.G.L.R. 140).

relationship. One example is *Barings plc v. Coopers & Lybrand*.[13] This arose out of the collapse of Barings merchant bank as a result of losses caused to its Singapore subsidiary by the fraudulent trading of its employee Nick Leeson. One of the defendants sued by the parent company was the auditor of the Singapore subsidiary. He objected to service of the writ out of the jurisdiction on the ground that no duty of care was owed by the auditor of the subsidiary company to the parent company, which was in no different a position from the shareholders in *Caparo*. The Court of Appeal held that it was arguable that a duty was owed on the particular facts, namely that the auditor knew that the accounts were required for the preparation of group accounts which showed a true and fair view. Although the loss claimed by the parent company might duplicate the loss claimed by the subsidiary, there was no risk of double jeopardy if all the claims were brought in one action. Another example is *B.C.C.I. v. Price Waterhouse (No. 2)*,[14] where it was held arguable that the auditor of one subsidiary owed a duty of care to another subsidiary in circumstances creating a sufficiently close interdependence.

Directors. In *Coulthard v. Neville Russell*[15] a company carrying on business as   **15–081** a Lloyd's managing agent was taken over by another company, which used money from the managing agent to fund the takeover in breach of section 151 of the Companies Act 1985. The directors were subsequently disqualified from acting as directors and they sued the auditor who had failed to warn of the breach. The Court of Appeal, on an application to strike out, held that it was arguable that the auditor owed a duty of care to the directors. The Court said that Companies Act 1985[16] read in isolation might suggest that the auditors are not instructed until the directors have submitted completed accounts to them. But in practice the directors usually discuss the draft accounts with the auditors before they are approved by the directors. Although it is no part of the auditor's statutory duty to protect the directors personally from the consequences of their mistakes, he may assume such a duty in the course of those discussions. In this case it was arguable that he should have warned the directors that the proposed loan might lead to a qualified auditor's report.

Creditors. There is not usually sufficient proximity between creditors of a   **15–082** company and the auditors but there may be exceptional cases. These tend to involve either guarantors[17] or else banks or other major investors.[18] In *Al Saudi Banque v. Clarke Pixley*[19] a claim was brought by banks which lent money to a company or failed to call in their loan in reliance on unqualified audit certificates. The judge dismissed the claim on a preliminary point. In the case of the banks

---

[13] [1997] P.N.L.R. 179, 186–187, CA.
[14] [1998] P.N.L.R. 564: for the facts see para. 15–047 above. The claim failed for other reasons: see para. 15–070 above.
[15] [1998] P.N.L.R. 276, CA.
[16] See paras 15–014 to 15–020 above.
[17] *Siddell v. Smith Cooper* [1999] P.N.L.R. 511, CA: for the facts see para. 15–067 above; for other examples see *Huxford v. Stoy Hayward & Co* (1989) 5 B.C.C. 421, Popplewell J. and *A.G.C. (Advances) Ltd v. R. Lowe Lippman Figdor & Franck* (1990) 4 A.C.S.R. 337, S. Ct of Vict.; *Craig v. Troy* (1997) 16 W.A.R. 96, S. Ct. of W. Aus. For an example of a case where no duty was owed see *Ikumene Singapore Pte Ltd v. Leon Chee Leng* [1993] 3 S.L.R. 24, CA of Sing.
[18] *e.g. Electra Private Equity Partners v. KPMG Peat Marwick* [1999] Lloyd's P.N. 670.
[19] [1990] Ch. 313, Millett J. This judgment was approved by the House of Lords in *Caparo* [1990] 2 A.C. 605, 623 and 640.

which lent money after the date of the balance sheet, they were in the same position as the potential investors in a company, to whom no duty of care was usually owed. As for the banks which were already creditors at the date of the balance sheet and which allowed their loans to remain outstanding, there was less proximity in their case than there was in the case of existing shareholders of the company. The banks had played no part in appointing the auditors; the auditors had no statutory obligation to report to the banks; the auditors did not supply a copy of their report to the banks, nor did they supply them to the company with the intention or in the knowledge that they would be supplied to the banks. The fact that the banks in question were a small and limited class was insufficient to create the necessary proximity. Further, it was not just and reasonable to impose a duty of care, since this might result in liability in an indeterminate amount if the bank subsequently lent further sums without the auditor's knowledge.

15–083   In an Australian case[20] a financier who made loans to a company in reliance on audited accounts sought to recover damages for negligence from the auditor. Reference was made to the Australian Accounting Standard AAS5, which provided that the test for materiality in financial statements depended on the likely prime users of the statement. The High Court of Australia struck out the claim on the ground that that it was necessary for the plaintiff to prove that the auditor knew or ought to have known that his certificate would be relied on by the plaintiff, either individually or as a member of a class. It was not sufficient for the plaintiff to cite AAS5, as he had done.[21]

15–084   **Bodies which are liable to compensate third parties.** *Andrew v. Kounnis Freeman*[22] concerned the Air Travel Trust, a reserve fund which compensated stranded travellers. In that case an auditor negligently audited the accounts of a travel company which was insolvent. The Civil Aviation Authority ("CAA") had initially refused to renew the company's licence but had agreed following a meeting with the auditor at which the auditor had promised to provide some financial information. The company then continued trading until it collapsed, leaving passengers stranded abroad. The CAA and the Trust, which had to compensate the passengers, made a claim against the auditor. The Court of Appeal refused to strike out the claim. The mere fact that an auditor repeated his statutory report to a third party was not sufficient by itself to amount to an assumption of responsibility to that third party, but it was capable of doing so in the circumstances of this case. Beldam L.J. found the necessary assumption of responsibility in the fact that a reasonable auditor would have realised that the plaintiffs were relying on the certificate and would not be obtaining independent advice and that the defendant did nothing to qualify his liability.[23] Buxton L.J. based his decision on the fact that the auditor, by providing accounts to the plaintiffs in the unusual circumstances of this case, was impliedly giving advice to them and not merely information.[24] The third judge agreed with both judgments.

---

[20] *Esanda Finance Corporation Ltd v. Peat Marwick Hungerfords* (1997) 71 A.L.J.R. 448, H. Ct. of Aus.

[21] The six judges gave five reasoned judgments, each containing different reasons. Brennan C.J. endorsed Lord Oliver's test in *Caparo*, whilst McHugh J. considered a number of policy factors which constituted socio-economic reasons for restricting auditor's liability. The other judgments adopted intermediate positions.

[22] [2000] Lloyd's Rep. P.N. 263, CA.

[23] *ibid.* at 270.

[24] *ibid.* at 271.

Law Society v. KPMG[25] concerned the Accountant's Report Rules made under **15–085** section 34 of the Solicitor's Act 1974. These rules require every solicitor to produce a report from an accountant as a pre-condition to the renewal by the Law Society of his practising certificate. In this case the accountant negligently failed to notice and report on defalcations by partners in a firm of solicitors, as a result of which claims were made by clients of the firm against the Compensation Fund (a fund set up by the Law Society to make payments to victims of fraud by solicitors). The Court of Appeal held that, where a body such as the Law Society has different functions, it was not sufficient to ask whether a duty of care was owed to that body generally; one had to focus on the specific capacity in which the body sued.[26] However in that case there was a duty of care for the following reasons: the body which granted practising certificates was the same legal entity as the body which set up the Fund; it was obvious to a reasonable accountant that his negligence in giving his report might cause the Law Society to make future payments out of the Fund; there was no reason why the accountant should not owe a private law duty to take reasonable care to safeguard the Law Society from exposure to a public law liability to compensate third parties; and there was sufficient proximity and it was fair, just and reasonable to impose a duty of care.[27]

Others. It has been held that there is insufficient proximity arising from the **15–086** mere fact that the claimant is a beneficiary under a trust of which the company is trustee[28] or an employee whose salary was equal to 99 per cent of the profit of the company set up to exploit his talents as a pop star.[29] There may be cases in which an accountant is retained to provide a report for shareholders, but may owe a duty of care to the company itself, which in this situation is not the client.[30]

(v) *Policy considerations: duplication of remedies*

It is submitted that the courts, when considering whether it is just and **15–087** reasonable to impose a duty of care in favour of a third party, should have regard to the following policy issues which arise where the claim overlaps with a claim in contract by the client:

(1) The risk of different defences being available: in some cases there might be a defence of causation or contributory negligence if the client knew or ought to have known of the breaches of duty or did not rely on the

---

[25] [2000] 1 W.L.R. 1921, CA: leave to appeal was refused: [2001] 1 W.L.R. 1122. In New Zealand it has been held that an auditor appointed under the Solicitors Audit Regulations owes duties both to clients whose money was put into the firm's trust account (*Price Waterhouse v. Kwan* [2000] 3 N.Z.L.R. 39, CA) and to innocent partners who are required to make good any loss suffered by clients (*Stringer v. Peat Marwick Mitchell & Co* [2000] 1 N.Z.L.R. 450, Chisholm J.).

[26] *ibid.* at 1928 paras 19–20.

[27] *ibid.* at 1928–1930. The Court suggested *obiter* (at 1930B) that a duty might not be owed to the Solicitors' Indemnity Fund, since this Fund is the solicitor's insurer and since the accountant's report is not prepared for its benefit. For criticism of this decision, see Powell [2001] P.N. 206.

[28] *Anthony v. Wright* [1995] 1 B.C.L.C. 236, 241. (The opposite result has been reached in Australia: *Edwards Karawacki Smith & Co. Pty Ltd v. Jacka Nominees Pty Ltd* (1994) 15 A.C.S.R. 503. See also *Price Waterhouse v. Kwan* [2000] 3 N.Z.L.R. 39, noted at n. 25 to para. 15–085 above.) However the trustee may be the proper claimant: see *Deloitte Haskins & Sells v. National Mutual Life Nominees Ltd* [1993] A.C. 774, PC: for the facts see para. 15–027 above.

[29] *John (Elton) v. Price Waterhouse*, [2001] E.W.H.C. Ch. 438 para. 219 (April 23, 2001, Ferris J.).

[30] *Duke Group Ltd v. Pilmer* (1999) 31 A.C.S.R. 213, 258.

accountant.[31] The English courts have not yet considered the question whether it is just and reasonable to permit this defence to be circumvented by bringing the proceedings in the name of a third party.[32]

(2) The problem of double recovery: there is no problem if the loss claimed by the third party is additional to that suffered by the company.[33] However there are cases where the two are duplicated. The courts have not yet laid down definitive guidelines to deal with this problem, but one practical suggestion[34] has been that both claims should be brought in one set of proceedings, so as to avoid the risk of double recovery.[35]

(3) The "loss of a chance" problem: in cases where the claimant is the *alter ego* of the client (*e.g.* a director or majority shareholder where the company is the client), it is submitted that the client should not be regarded as a third party for the purpose of the "loss of a chance" doctrine.[36]

(vi) *The Contracts (Rights against Third Parties) Act 1999*

15–088   The Contracts (Rights against Third Parties) Act 1999 came into force on November 11, 1999 in relation to contracts made after May 1, 2000. Section 1 permits a contract to be enforced by a third party in two cases: the first is where it expressly so provides; the second is where it purports to create a benefit on him, unless it appears on the true construction of the contract that he was not to benefit.[37]

(vii) *The Human Rights Act 1998*

15–089   In *Osman v. United Kingdom*[38] the European Court of Human Rights held that there was a breach of Article 6 of the European Convention on Human Rights[39] (the right to a fair trial) where an action was struck out because of immunity (in that case, it was police immunity from negligence claims). At one time it was thought that a claimant who established foreseeability and proximity might be able to allege a breach of Article 6 if his claim was struck out on the ground that it was not just and reasonable to impose a duty of care. However, the European

---

[31] See paras 15–121 *et seq.* and 15–146 *et seq.* (esp. 15–148(2)) below.

[32] *e.g.* the facts of *Law Society v. KPMG* [2001] 1 W.L.R. 1921 (see para. 15–085 above).

[33] For a general discussion about duplication between claims by the company and claims by shareholders, see *Johnson v. Gore Wood* [2001] 2 W.L.R. 72; [2000] U.K.H.L. 65, HL a claim against a solicitor which is further discussed in chap. 10. For an illustration of the problems which may arise, see para. 15–074 above.

[34] *Barings plc v. Coopers & Lybrand* [1997] P.N.L.R. 179, 186–187, CA: for the facts see para. 15–080 above.

[35] An analogous issue which has been considered in Australia is the effect of the negligence of the claimant's own employee, which gives rise to a problem as to the interrelationship between contribution and contributory negligence: see para. 15–148(3) below.

[36] *Allied Maples Group Ltd v. Simmons & Simmons* [1995] 1 W.L.R. 1602, 1612C. For a discussion of the "loss of a chance" principle, see para. 15–133 below.

[37] For detailed discussion of this Act, see **Part One** above.

[38] (2000) 29 E.H.R.R. 245. For a fuller discussion, see Chap. 7.

[39] The Convention is now enshrined in the Human Rights Act 1998 and has been directly enforceable in the English courts since October 2000.

Court of Human Rights revisited the question in *Z v. United Kingdom*[40] and did not follow its earlier decision in *Osman*. On this occasion the court said that the "just and reasonable" criterion was a substantive part of the tort and not merely a ground for immunity. In other words, a claimant who failed to persuade the court that it was just and reasonable to impose liability had no grounds for complaint if his claim was struck out; on the contrary it was just that the defendant should be spared the expense of a full trial. However, the court in *Z* went on to hold that there was a breach in that case of Article 13 (the right to an effective remedy). This is a right which arises only where there is an arguable breach of a substantive Convention right. However, it is far from obvious that a claim against an accountant for negligence will involve the breach of any Convention rights. The nearest one comes to it is probably Article 1 of the First Protocol (the right to peaceful enjoyment of possessions), but it is thought unlikely that this will be relevant in a typical claim against an accountant.

(d) *The standard of skill and care*

(i) *General*

In common with other professionals, the standard required of an accountant in carrying out an engagement is that of the reasonable skill and care of an ordinary skilled person carrying out the same engagement.[41] The standard will not be lower for an accountant with limited experience or if a low fee is charged, although the amount of the fee may be some indication of the nature of the engagement.[42] The standard generally remains constant irrespective of the nature of the particular engagement, although what steps will be required to fulfil the standard will vary according to the engagement.[43] The Court should guard against hindsight and only take account of knowledge reasonably available at the time of the alleged breach.[44] **15-090**

Sources of evidence. In *Dairy Containers Ltd v. NZI Bank Ltd*[45] the court listed the following sources of evidence: **15-091**

---

[40] Unreported, May 10, 2001 (see paras 91 to 101 of the majority judgment and see also Arden L.J.'s concurring Opinion).

[41] *Re Kingston Cotton Mill Co. Ltd (No. 2)* [1896] 2 Ch. 279, 288, CA. See also *Calne Gas Co. v. Curtis* (1918) 59 Acct. L.R. 17, 20; and *International Laboratories Ltd v. Dewar* (1933) 3 D.L.R. 665, 692. In *Whiteoak v. Walker* (1988) 4 B.C.C. 122 the judge rejected the plaintiff's argument that the standard was that of a accountant who professed "specialist skills in valuing unquoted shares"; instead he held that the required standard was that of "a reasonably competent chartered accountant in general practice acting as an auditor who has agreed to a request to undertake the valuation task".

[42] Note *Henry Squire, Cash Chemist Ltd v. Ball Baker & Co. (also Mead v. Ball Baker & Co.)* (1912) 106 L.T. 197, 199–200. In discussing the nature of the defendant accountants' duty, Lord Alverstone C.J. attached no importance to their scale of remuneration.

[43] *e.g. ibid.* at 199–200, *per* Lord Alverstone C.J.: "I do not agree that their duty as auditors would be less than their duty in advising a purchaser when he was buying the business." See also *HIT Finance Ltd v. Cohen Arnold* [2000] Lloyd's Rep. P.N. 125 (CA held on the facts of the case that a letter to a lender stating the borrower's net worth was not a warranty but was a statement that the accountant had taken reasonable care in writing the letter based on information from the borrower).

[44] *Re City Equitable Fire Insurance Co. Ltd* [1925] 1 Ch. 407, 505.

[45] [1995] 2 N.Z.L.R. 30.

(1) The standard required as a matter of contract and under the relevant statutes or regulations.[46]

(2) Expert evidence: the court is usually unwilling to find a professional person negligent in the absence of evidence from a professional in the same field.[47] In professional negligence claims it is usually necessary to adduce such evidence, especially if it is alleged that a particular default was the consequence of departure from general practice.[48] But it is not within the province of expert witnesses on the subject of general practice to determine what was the duty of an accountant in a particular case or whether he was in breach of it. That is for the court to determine.[49] In some cases the nature of the negligence may be such as not to require expert evidence to be adduced.[50]

(3) Auditing and accounting standards[51]: in practice these are usually the most important source of evidence. Professional standards, whilst not conclusive, are very strong evidence as to what is a proper standard; third parties reading the accounts are entitled to assume that they have been drawn up in accordance with approved practice unless the accounts state otherwise.[52] However, more recently a Canadian court has emphasised that professional standards do not supplant the degree of care called for by the law: the court had in mind the risk that the profession might set a standard lower than the courts thought reasonable.[53]

(4) The defendant's internal office manuals.[54]

15–092   Older caselaw should be treated with caution since, although the test has always been that of the reasonably competent accountant, the standard to be expected of a reasonably competent practitioner is substantially higher today than it was in the nineteenth century.[55]

---

[46] See paras 15–008 to 15–036 above.

[47] *Sansom v. Metcalfe Hambleton* [1998] P.N.L.R. 542. See also *Pacific Acceptance Corporation Ltd v. Forsyth* (1970) 92 W.N. (N.S.W.) 29, 74–75. In *Sceptre Resources Ltd v. Deloitte Haskins & Sells* (1991) 83 Alta. L.R. (2d) 157 the Supreme Court of Alberta said: "The law allows differing opinions among accountants as it does within the medical and legal professions. Acting in concert with an opinion or practice held by a significant fraction of the profession, is almost always a defence to a suit for malpractice . . . The only exception arises where the practice of the profession is totally unreasonable."

[48] *Henry Squire, Cash Chemist Ltd v. Ball Baker & Co.* (1912) 106 L.T. 197, 202.

[49] *Pacific Acceptance Corporation Ltd v. Forsyth* (1970) 92 W.N. (N.S.W.) 29, 75; *Nelson Guarantee Corp. Ltd v. Hodgson* [1958] N.Z.L.R. 609, 613.

[50] *Murray Bourne Dyck v. F.M.A. Farm Management Associates Ltd* (1996) 3 W.W.R. 509, 512 *per* Wedge J. "If it is found as fact that a filing deadline is missed through the negligence of an accounting professional, then I am satisfied that no expert evidence is required to establish such a common sense standard of competence."

[51] For accounting standards, see paras 15–015 above and 15–112 below.

[52] *Lloyds Cheyham v. Littlejohn* [1987] B.C.L.C. 303, Woolf J.

[53] *Kripps v. Touche Ross & Co.* (1997) 33 B.C.L.R. (3d) 254, British Columbia CA: for the facts see para. 15–066 above.

[54] *ADT Ltd v. Binder Hamlyn* [1996] B.C.C. 808, 837E.

[55] *Re Thomas Gerrard & Son Ltd* [1968] Ch. 455, 475; *Pacific Acceptance Corporation Ltd v. Forsyth* (1970) 92 W.N. (N.S.W.) 29, 73–74.

(ii) *Auditing*

Auditing standards. The Auditing Practices Board ("APB"), established by **15–093**
the CCAB,[56] issues Statements of Auditing Standards ("SASs").[57] Although
SASs do not directly have the force of law, compliance with them is powerful
evidence that the auditor has acted reasonably, whilst failure to comply without
adequate explanation is powerful evidence to the contrary. There are two reasons
why this is so. The first is that the APB is constituted under the aegis of the
CCAB[58] the SASs accordingly represent the agreed view of all the major
professional bodies of accountants as to what constitutes good practice. The
second is that the SASs are given additional status by the Companies Act, in that
every auditor of the accounts of a company registered under the Companies Acts
is required to belong to a RSB,[59] every RSB is required to have auditing
standards and all the professional bodies which make up the CCAB have
undertaken to adopt all the SASs.[60] In practice the standard of skill and care in
any claim against an auditor is more likely to be found in the SASs than in any
caselaw.

It is beyond the scope of this work to examine the SASs in detail, but we shall
summarise the effect of the ones which are most likely to be relevant in a
professional negligence claim against an auditor.[61] We shall focus on the SASs
in force as at October 2001 but anyone concerned with a claim against an auditor
should ensure that he looks at the SASs which were in force at the date of the
alleged breach of duty.

The following basic principles emerge from the SASs and the cases: **15–094**

(1) The responsibility for preparing financial statements belongs to the
directors of the entity. The auditor is responsible for giving an opinion on
those statements.[62] It is no part of the his duty to give advice as to the
prudence or imprudence of the company's business. His duty is to see
that the shareholders receive independent and reliable information
respecting the true financial position of the company at the time of the
audit, so that they can exercise their own judgment.[63]

(2) An audit is not a warranty: in SAS 100,[64] the objective of an audit of
financial statements is described as:

---

[56] See para. 15–007 above.

[57] SASs and other documents referred to in this section are printed in *Auditing & Reporting* published
annually by the ICAEW.

[58] See para. 15–007 above.

[59] See para. 15–012 above.

[60] SAS 010 (The Scope and Authority of APB Pronouncements) para. 10 and see n. 25 to para.
15–015, above.

[61] See paras 15–102 *et seq.* below.

[62] SAS 100 para. 6; and see para. 15–011 above.

[63] *Re London and General Bank (No. 2)* [1895] 2 Ch. 673, 682–683 *per* Lindley L.J.: in that case an
auditor presented a confidential report to directors pointing out the insufficiency and difficulty of
realisation of securities on which loans by the company were advanced. But in his report to the
shareholders he merely made the vacuous comment that the value of the assets was dependent on
realisation. He was held liable upon a misfeasance summons by the liquidator of the company. He had
not reported the true financial position of the company and the shareholders had consequently been
deceived into voting for a dividend which in the event was proved to have been paid from capital and
not from income. This dividend the auditor was required to make good to the liquidator. See also
Duke Group Ltd v. Pilmer (1999) 31 A.C.S.R. 213, 258, S. Ct. of S. Aus.

[64] SAS 100 (issued March 1995) entitled: "Objective and general principles governing an audit of
financial statements". See further para. 15–108 below.

"to enable auditors to give an opinion on those financial statements taken as a whole and thereby to provide reasonable assurance that the financial statements give a true and fair view (where relevant) and have been prepared in accordance with relevant accounting or other requirements."

A degree of imprecision is inevitable because of inherent uncertainties and the need to use judgment in making accounting estimates[65] and selecting appropriate accounting policies. The auditor's duty is to provide *reasonable* assurance.

(3) The auditor should recognise the possibility that fraud or error may materially affect the financial statements.[66]

(4) The auditor's responsibility is a personal one: It is his opinion which must be expressed in his report and not for example that of an in-house accountant employed by the company.[67] It is nevertheless recognised that many engagements including a company audit, are beyond the capacity of a single person to perform and that he may employ others to assist him.[68] But an accountant cannot by delegating abdicate his responsibility, and he will continue to be under a duty to exercise reasonable skill and care although many tasks required by a particular engagement are performed by assistants.[69] The accountant should properly supervise his assistants and be careful not to give them tasks beyond their capacity and experience.[70]

(5) In general it is no answer for an auditor to say that he was working under time constraints. If he needs more time, he should ask the directors to adjourn the general meeting; if they refuse, he should attend and explain the position.[71]

15–095   **The detection of fraud.** One especially important issue in relation to audit work is the question of whether the auditor ought to have detected fraud or defalcations. The classic statements are in *Re London and General Bank (No.*

---

[65] SAS 420 (Audit of Accounting Estimates). "Accounting estimates" means an approximation of the amount of an item in the absence of a precise measurement, *e.g.* allowances to reduce stock and debtors to their estimated realisable value, depreciation, accrued revenue, profits or losses on construction contracts in progress and provision for deferred taxation, for losses from litigation, and for warranty claims. It is inherent in such estimates that they will be less conclusive than other evidence and that more judgment is required in order to decide whether the evidence is sufficient and appropriate (SAS 420 para. 4).

[66] See para. 15–095 below.

[67] *Dominion Freeholders Ltd v. Aird* (1966) 67 S.R. (N.S.W.) 150 at 156–157 *per* Wallace P. and see para. 15–103 below.

[68] *e.g. The Irish Woollen Co. Ltd v. Tyson* (1900) 27 Acct. L.R. 13, Irish CA at 14. This issue is discussed in SAS 240 (Quality Control for Audit Work).

[69] See *Henry Squire, Cash Chemist Ltd v. Ball Baker & Co.* (1912) 106 L.T. 197, 201: "with some slight exceptions, where judgment and discretion come in, the skill of the head clerk must be the same as the skill of the principal. That is to say the principal cannot excuse himself of his clerk's negligence by saying that he [employed a] clerk" *per* Lord Alverstone C.J. (Bracketed words taken from report in 44 Acct. L.R. 25); *Armitage v. Brewer and Knott* (1932) 77 Acct. L.R. 25 (auditors could not get rid of their responsibility by delegating it to junior clerks: *per* Talbot J.).

[70] See *Pacific Acceptance Corp. Ltd v. Forsyth* (1970) 92 W.N. (N.S.W.) 29, 79 and 117–118.

[71] *Re Thomas Gerrard & Son Ltd* [1968] Ch. 455, 477; *Pacific Acceptance, ibid.* at 107.

2)[72] and *Re Kingston Cotton Mill Co. (No. 2)*.[73] In the former case Lindley L.J. stressed that an auditor is not an insurer and does not guarantee the accuracy of the company's books in general or the balance sheet in particular.[74] In the latter case Lopes L.J. said that an auditor is "not bound to be a detective" and that he is "a watchdog but not a bloodhound".[75] The traditional approach was to draw a firm distinction between cases where suspicion was excited, in which case the auditor's duty was to probe to the bottom, and cases where there was nothing to excite suspicion, in which case very little inquiry would usually suffice.[76]

The modern approach[77] is set out in SAS 110.1: "Auditors should plan and **15–096** perform their audit procedures and evaluate and report the results thereof, recognising that fraud or error may materially affect the financial statements." The auditor's responsibility is not to prevent fraud or error but to exercise reasonable care in detecting it. Accordingly failure by an auditor to detect fraud or negligence is not of itself proof of negligence by him; the likelihood of detecting error is greater than that of detecting fraud, since fraud is usually deliberately concealed.[78] When planning the audit he should assess the risk of fraud or error and should design audit procedures which take account of that risk.[79] He should examine "critically and with professional scepticism" the information and explanations provided by the management.[80] If he becomes aware of information indicating that fraud or error may exist, he should obtain an understanding of the circumstances; if he believes that the possible fraud or error might have a material effect on the financial statements, he should perform appropriate procedures; he should document his findings and discuss them with the appropriate level of management; and he should consider the implication of his findings on other aspects of the audit.[81] The auditor is required to approach his task "with an inquiring mind—not suspicious of dishonesty . . . but suspecting that someone may have made a mistake somewhere and that a check must be

---

[72] [1895] 2 Ch. 673, 683, CA: for facts see n. 63 to para. 15–094, above.

[73] [1896] 2 Ch. 279, CA: for the facts see n. 41 to para. 15–112, below.

[74] See also *Calne Gas Co. v. Curtis* (1918) 59 Acct. L.R. 17, 20. In *Re City Equitable Fire Insurance Co.* [1925] 1 Ch. 407, 480, Romer J. said that if in the course of his "long and arduous audit" the auditor concerned had in even one instance fallen short of "the strict duty of an auditor" he could not be excused merely because in general he displayed the highest degree of care and skill. The statement requires qualification. To the extent that it implies that an auditor is strictly liable for any error, it is incorrect, being inconsistent with the standard of reasonable skill and care which allows some degree of error.

[75] By contrast, the detection of fraud was described as one of the main objects of an audit and of primary importance, in the Australian case of *Frankston and Hastings Corporation v. Cohen* (1960) 102 C.L.R. 607, 617; see also *Pacific, ibid.* at 52. *Cf.* Davison and Khan, "Contractual liability of an auditor" [1980] A.B.L.R. 300, 303–304: arguing that the detection of fraud had not been a primary aim of the audit for some considerable time from the profession's viewpoint and to that extent its viewpoint was at variance with the legal interpretation of an audit.

[76] In *Pacific, ibid.* at 62 Moffitt J. cautioned against the traditional approach.

[77] In *Dairy Containers Ltd v. NZI Bank Ltd* [1995] 2 N.Z.L.R. 30, 54, Thomas J. said that metaphors about dogs and detectives tended to obscure the basic duty to plan and carry out the audit cognisant of the possibility of fraud.

[78] SAS 110 paras 18–22; *Pacific, ibid.* at 65. See also *Re Kingston Cotton Mill Co. Ltd (No. 2)* [1896] 2 Ch. 279, 290; *International Laboratories Ltd v. Dewar* (1933) 3 D.L.R. 665, 682 and 693.

[79] SAS 110.2 and 110.3.

[80] SAS 100 para. 11.

[81] SAS 110.4, 110.5 and 110.6. If the auditor comes across irregular or unusual matters, he should not separate them into watertight compartments *Pacific, ibid.* at 62. See also para. 15–030 above ("whistle-blowing" duties).

made to ensure that there has been none"[82] His role is "verification, not detection".[83]

15–097   In the Australian case of *Pacific Acceptance Corporation Ltd v. Forsyth*[84] Moffitt J. in a detailed judgment analysed the function and duties of an auditor having regard to modern audit practice and procedures, particularly auditors' increasing reliance upon a company's internal system of accounting control. The facts were that the auditors of a finance company (Pacific) failed to discover frauds in relation to loans made to T and to entities with which T was connected and gave an unqualified audit report. The loans were intended to be secured. Thereafter Pacific's business relationship with T deepened in several ways. First it entered into a joint venture with T's company through a company named Pavic and it advanced money to Pavic which was lost. Secondly it took over various interests of T. Thirdly Pavic became a wholly owned subsidiary of Pacific and T became a principal shareholder and director of Pacific. Within the framework of the joint venture and takeover T committed further frauds and misappropriation. Fourthly there was a further takeover whereby Pacific acquired almost all T's assets at a time when T's companies were in grave financial difficulties. The court held that Pavic's auditors had qualified their report on Pavic but that the defendant had ignored this qualification.

15–098   Moffitt J. concluded that the contracts being open had imported into them promises to perform the duties prescribed by the relevant Companies Act and also the articles of association of the company.[85] The relevant statute,[86] however, merely required the auditors to report to the shareholders and to give their opinion on certain matters. It did not state what the auditors had to do in order to form their opinions. It was contended for the Pacific auditors that they were required to do no more than report to the shareholders using due care and skill. This contention was rejected:

> "In the absence of express terms the scope of the audit will depend on what is directly or indirectly required or indicated by the particular provisions of the Companies Act and of the articles and any relevant surrounding circumstances. However, whatever the precise content of his audit duty, the auditor promises, first, to conduct an audit of some description and, second, to provide a report of his opinion based on his audit work, which report has to comply with the Companies Act and the articles, and also impliedly

---

[82] *Fomento (Sterling Area) Ltd v. Selsdon Fountain Pen Co. Ltd* [1958] 1 W.L.R. 45, 61: see n. 28 to para. 15–111, below.

[83] *Re City Equitable Fire Insurance Co. Ltd* [1925] Ch. 407, 509.

[84] (1970) 92 W.N. (N.S.W.) 29. The case raises issues relevant to a number of subject headings in this chapter and particular issues will be more fully discussed in their appropriate context. For further statements, see *International Laboratories Ltd v. Dewar* [1933] 3 D.L.R. 665, 670; *McBride's Ltd v. Rooke & Thomas* [1941] 4 D.L.R. 55; *Dimond Manufacturing Co. Ltd v. Hamilton* [1969] N.Z.L.R. 609, 637; and *Scott Group Ltd v. McFarlane* [1978] 1 N.Z.L.R. 553, 580.

[85] See also *Re City Equitable Fire Insurance Co. Ltd* [1925] 1 Ch. 407, 520–521 (n. 89 to para. 15–033, above.)

[86] The Australian Companies Act 1936, s.115. Of the similar Companies (Consolidation) Act 1908, s.113, Warrington L.J. in *Re City Equitable Fire Insurance Co. Ltd* [1925] 1 Ch. 407, 525 observed:

> "It says nothing as to what [the auditors] are to do in order to form that opinion, or to ascertain the truth of the facts to which they are to certify. That is left to be determined by the general rules which, in point of law, are held to govern the duties of the auditors, whether those rules are to be derived from the ordinary law, or from the terms under which the auditors are to be employed."

Cf. now the U.K. Companies Act 1985, s.237(1) (duty to carry out certain investigations: see para. 15–020 above).

agrees to exercise reasonable skill and care in the conduct of the audit and in the making of the report."[87]

The duty to audit carried with it an incidental duty to warn the appropriate **15–099** level of management or the directors, during the course of the audit, of fraud or suspicion of fraud uncovered.[88] Thus if in the course of vouching work the Pacific auditors had uncovered matters which reasonably required them to take further steps which they did not take and which would have uncovered or led them to the uncovering of T's fraudulent and irregular dealings, a breach would have occurred at that time.[89] As for the scope of a statutory audit, Moffitt J. took the view that in planning and carrying out his work an auditor must pay due regard to the possibility of error and fraud.[90] A modern audit of a large company will inevitably rely on the company's own internal systems where possible.[91]

(e) *Limitation of liability*

It is not open to an auditor of a company to seek to exclude or limit his liability **15–100** in relation to the company for negligence or other breach of duty. This is the effect of section 310 of the Companies Act 1985 which declares as void any provision which seeks to do so, whether contained in the articles or a contract with the company or otherwise.[92] The same applies in relation to a provision for an indemnity against such a liability. The company may, however, purchase and maintain insurance against such liability. It may also indemnify the auditor against any liability incurred in defending proceedings against him in which judgement is given in his favour or he is acquitted, or in connection with an application under section 727 of the Companies Act 1985 in which he is granted relief by the court.[93] Section 310 applies only in the context of a company audit.

---

[87] (1970) 92 W.N. (N.S.W.) 29, 51. See also at 50:
   "[A duty to report on the accounts, records required to be kept by statute and the articles and on the balance sheet] would not admit logically of a duty to report to management a discovery of fraud or misappropriation by an employee during the course of the audit year, and it would not admit a right to recover damages arising from a negligent failure to uncover fraud in the course of the audit, as distinct from damage flowing from the falsity in the balance sheet and an opinion negligently given of the shareholders in respect thereof."
   The issues as to what were the relevant duties and when breaches thereof occurred had particular relevance in the case owing to the defence of limitation raised by many of the partners of the Pacific auditors. Moffitt J. derived support for the existence of a duty to audit from the cases of *Frankston and Hastings Corporation v. Cohen* (1960) 102 C.L.R. 607 and *Re Thomas Gerrard & Son Ltd* [1968] 1 Ch. 455, 475 ("basically [the auditor's] duty has always been to audit the company's accounts with reasonable care and skill").
[88] *ibid.* at 45, 50–54. Note also at 54, *per* Moffitt J.:
   "Even if I am wrong and there is no separate duty to audit with an incidental duty to warn, I would not accept, despite the lack of logic that would then appear to exist, that the duty to report in terms of the statute would not include at least at the time of the report a duty to warn somebody at that date; if not the directors, then the shareholders of fraud uncovered."
[89] *ibid.* at 50–54.
[90] *ibid.* at 63.
[91] *ibid* at 55. See para. 15–106 below for discussion about internal control systems.
[92] In *Re City Equitable Fire Insurance Co. Ltd* [1925] 1 Ch. 407 auditors, although held in breach of their duty to the company, were also held not liable on the basis of an article which protected the auditors and other officers from liability for losses not due to their "wilful neglect or default". Such an article would now be void by reason of s.310.
[93] As to s.727, see para. 15–153 below.

15–101   Engagement letters by accountants relating to engagements other than audits are nowadays replete with provisions directed to control or limit liability. They take many forms. It is prudent to describe the nature and parameters of the task to be undertaken and in as precise and unambiguous terms as the circumstances allow. Inherent constraints or limitations are frequently pointed out. Requirements of the client merit mention. There is usually an express statement that the services to be provided are for the benefit of the client only and not any third party. Express disclaimers of responsibility to third parties are common. There may also be provisions seeking to limit liability to clients. These may be variously expressed and by reference to various formulae, *e.g.* a fee multiple. A well drawn limitation of liability clauses should in general survive attack by reference to the Unfair Contract Terms Act 1977[94] or the Unfair Terms in Consumer Contracts Regulations,[95] though much depends on the circumstances of each particular case. Statute apart, a limitation of liability provisions may be challenged on the ground that as a matter of construction it is not effective to exclude or restrict liability[96] or that it has not been incorporated into the relevant contract. The courts have not yet resolved the question whether such a provision is effective against a third party to the contract.[97]

3. LIABILITY FOR BREACH OF DUTY

(a) *Auditing*

15–102   As we have seen,[98] the most relevant material in measuring the standard of skill and care expected of an auditor is to be found in the SASs. The overriding principle is that the auditor is required only to provide reasonable assurance.[99]

---

[94] In *Killick v. PriceWaterhouseCoopers* [2001] P.N.L.R. 1, 8, Neuberger J., in refusing to grant summary judgment on the efficacy of an exclusion clause, listed a number of factors to be taken into account in deciding whether it was reasonable. These included: the way in which the term came into being and was used generally; the strength and bargaining position of the parties relative to each other; whether the client had an opportunity of entering into a similar contract with other persons without having to accept a similar term; how far it would have been practical and convenient to go elsewhere; the reality of the client's consent to the term; the size of the limit compared with other limits and widely used standard terms; the availability of insurance to the accountant; and the possibility of allowing for an option to contract without the limitation clause but with a price increase in lieu.

[95] S.I. 1999 No. 2083, giving effect to Directive 93/13/EEC. The 1999 regulations supersede like regulations made in 1994 (S.I. 1994 No. 3159)

[96] *e.g.* in *Dairy Containers Ltd v. NZI Bank Ltd* [1995] 2 N.Z.L.R. 30, 53, Thomas J., the issue concerned the following provision in the Auditor-General's contract: "The audit examination should not be relied upon to disclose defalcations or other irregularities, but their disclosure, if they exist, may result from the audit tests undertaken." Thomas J. held that the provision did no more than confirm the position relating to detection of such fraud and irregularities, prescribed in relevant professional auditing standards, and was not effective to restrict his liability. See also *Bloor Italian Gifts Ltd v. Dixon* (2000) 48 O.R. (3d) 760, Ontario CA: a clause saying that responsibility for the prevention of defalcations rested with the plaintiff was insufficient to protect an accountant from liability for negligence in failing to notice that the company had (innocently) underpaid tax.

[97] The question was expressly left open by Neuberger J. in *Killick v. PriceWaterhouseCoopers, ibid.* at 9–14.

[98] See para. 15–093 above.

[99] See para. 15–094(2) above.

(i) *Planning, control and recording*

An auditor should plan his work so as to perform the audit effectively. In order **15–103** to do so, he should develop and document an overall audit plan. He should develop and document the nature, timing and extent of planned audit procedures required to implement the overall audit plan and should keep these procedures under review.[1] An important part of his preparatory work is to obtain a knowledge of the business sufficient to enable him to identify and understand the matters which might materially affect the financial statements.[2] An auditor who has audited the company's financial statements in previous years will obviously have more knowledge of the company's affairs than a new auditor; on the one hand he is not expected to remember all the details of previous audits; on the other hand he is not working in a vacuum.[3] Another aspect to be considered at the planning stage is materiality. An error in the financial statements is relevant only if it is "material"; the question whether it is likely to be material is case-sensitive and calls for a exercise of judgment.[4]

Failure to comply with auditing standards at the planning stage is likely to be **15–104** neither necessary nor sufficient to give rise to liability for breach of duty. The issue is more likely to turn on the failure to detect or report on material misstatement in the financial statements. Nevertheless, the source of many failures can be found in the absence of proper planning. The absence of proper planning is likely to be a relevant consideration if the auditor seeks to assert that he could not reasonably have been expected to detect the fraud or error in question.

In *Pacific Acceptance Corporation Ltd v. Forsyth*[5] Moffitt J. recognised that it **15–105** was the usual practice in all but the simplest cases for auditors to lay out a written programme of work which served many purposes. First, it acted as a direction to clerks as to the checks they were required to make. Secondly, it acted as a document against which the reviewing audit manager or partner should check and review the work of those under him. Thirdly, it facilitated, with minimum risk of error, changes in the audit staff during the course of the audit. The preparation or approval of a programme called for the skill and care of a person of sufficient seniority and experience, especially where reliance was placed on the company's internal system of control, since selection of appropriate sampling procedures involved some degree of sophistication. He recognised that there was (in that case) no statutory or contractual obligation to provide or work to a written programme and considered that omissions from the programme in themselves would not be sufficient to make the plaintiff's case. But if there were omissions from the programme and if undiscovered error or fraud occurred in the same area, then failure by the auditors to amend the programme would tend to indicate that the shortcomings were due to negligence. The business of the plaintiff company in that case consisted of lending money on security. On the facts,

---

[1] SAS 200 (Planning).

[2] SAS 210 (Knowledge of Business). See also *Bloor Italian Gifts Ltd v. Dixon* (2000) 48 O.R. (3d) 760, Ontario CA: accountant engaged to prepare financial statements (less than a full audit) was negligent in failing to make intelligent enquiries of management which would have alerted him to the fact that the company paid insufficient retail sales tax.

[3] *Pacific, ibid.* at 62.

[4] SAS 200 (Materiality and the Audit).

[5] (1970) 92 W.N. (N.S.W.) 29, 76–79 and 102 (for the facts see para. 15–097 above). See also *Dairy Containers Ltd v. NZI Bank Ltd* [1995] 2 N.Z.L.R. 30, 59–62, in which the Auditor-General was held negligent in various respects, including lack of planning (for the facts see para. 15–150 below).

Moffitt J. concluded that the omission from the audit programme of procedures to vouch mortgage loan securities was the key to the omissions and deficiencies in the work of the defendant auditors' clerks. In failing to amend the programme to provide for such procedures, the auditors were held negligent. He took a similar view in respect of the employment of inexperienced staff to do work beyond their capacity. If the work was properly done by them, there was no breach of duty by the auditors employing them. But if work was left to audit clerks who were inexperienced and insufficiently supervised and their work was not properly reviewed, then these circumstances would tend to indicate that any shortcomings in the work were due to negligence. He concluded on the facts that the defendant auditors had employed inexperienced staff and failed properly to supervise them.

(ii) *Accounting and internal control systems*

15–106   The company or other entity being audited will have its own accounting and internal control systems. The auditor needs to understand these in order to be able to form the necessary professional judgment as to the audit risk[6] and to design audit procedures which will reduce that risk to an acceptably low level.[7] Audit risk of material financial misstatement is divided into three categories. The first is inherent risk, including the risk that the management might be fraudulent or negligent or that the accounts might contain errors of judgment (*e.g.* in valuing assets or liabilities). The second is control risk, *i.e.* the risk of a failure in the entity's own accounting and internal control systems.[8] The third is detection risk, *i.e.* the risk that the auditor's substantive procedures[9] fail to detect material misstatement. Given the fact that the audit is not expected to involve an examination of every item or class of transactions, that any internal system of accounting and control will be imperfect and that most audit evidence is persuasive rather than conclusive,[10] the auditor is not required to eliminate audit risk but to reduce it to an acceptable level. There are cases in which the auditor may properly decide that the cost of substantive procedures will be disproportionate to their benefit.[11] In other words, before the auditor carries out any substantive procedures,[12] he should make a preliminary assessment of the risks and benefits of these procedures.

15–107   In *Pacific Acceptance Corporation Ltd v. Forsyth*[13] Moffitt J. said:

> "First, there must be a proper inquiry to ascertain the company's system. This would include ascertaining such features as indicate the strength and weaknesses of the system

---

[6] SAS 300 (Accounting and Internal Control Systems and Audit Risk Assessments) contains a detailed analysis of audit risk which is summarised in this paragraph; see also SAS 400.2.

[7] SAS 300.1.

[8] The auditor should beware of relying on an internal system where it is operated by or is within the control of one person: *Irish Woollen Co. Ltd v. Tyson* (1900) 27 Acct. L.R. 13, Irish CA. In general the smaller the company, the fewer the internal controls, or at least the fewer the internal controls upon which an auditor may reasonably rely: SAS 300 para. 26 and see *Guardian Insurance Co. v. Sharp* [1941] 2 D.L.R. 417, 433.

[9] SAS 500 (Considering the Work of Internal Audit): The external auditor has sole responsibility for his audit but it may be reasonable for him to rely to some extent on the work of internal auditors.

[10] SAS 100 para. 10.

[11] SAS 300 para. 25.

[12] Substantive procedures are considered in para. 15–110 below.

[13] (1970) 92 W.N. (N.S.W.) 29, 87–8 and 125 (for the facts see para. 15–097 above). See also *Daniels v. Anderson* (1995) 16 A.C.S.R. 607, 623–628, 642–644 and 651–652 (and the same case in the lower court: (1992) 7 A.C.S.R. 759, 796–802 and at 834–835). For further illustrations, see *Re S.P.*

and hence its reliability. Second, there must be appraisal of it in that a person of sufficient auditing competence should make a decision as to the extent, if any, that the auditors can properly rely upon it. He should decide what procedures should be adopted to check that it is operating as intended and what other conditions should be met before reliance can be placed upon it. Third, there must be testing of its operation. All these essentials may call for revision in the course of the audit. For example, because of the result of testing it might be necessary to make a decision in the course of the testing to extend the testing or even not to rely on the system."

On the facts he held that the defendant auditors had failed in respect of each prerequisite and had not properly addressed themselves to questions of internal control in relation to mortgage loan vouching. He further stressed the importance of independence in the audit approach. The plaintiff's system was unjustifiably absolutely relied upon without any real independent consideration. He further rejected the contention for the auditors that they were justified in not checking documents in that they relied upon the employment of the solicitor seen as part of the company's system of internal control.[14]

(iii) *Evidence*

Sufficient appropriate evidence. SAS 400.1 states that "auditors should   **15–108** obtain *sufficient appropriate* audit evidence to be able to draw *reasonable conclusions* on which to base the audit opinion". Audit evidence is usually persuasive rather than conclusive; auditors therefore need to obtain evidence from a variety of sources. Sufficiency refers to quantity of evidence, appropriateness to quality.[15] As regards quality, although the reliability of audit evidence will vary from case to case, as a general rule it may be said that: external evidence is more reliable than evidence from the entity's own records; evidence from the entity's own records is more reliable where the internal control systems operate effectively; evidence obtained directly by the auditor is more reliable than that obtained by or from the entity; written evidence is more reliable than oral; and original documents are more reliable than copies.[16]

SAS 400 (Audit Evidence) is of critical importance and is likely to form the   **15–109** core of most allegations of breach of duty against auditors. The key is the interrelationship between "sufficient appropriate" evidence and "reasonable conclusions". As we have seen,[17] the auditor seeks to provide reasonable, not absolute assurance. There is inevitably an element of risk, *e.g.* in the fact that he relies on sampling[18] and does not examine every transaction. In considering whether he was negligent in running a risk, one looks at matters such as an

---

Catterson & Sons Ltd (1937) 81 Acct. L.R. 62; *International Laboratories Ltd v. Dewar* [1933] 3 D.L.R. 665, Manitoba CA; *McBride's Ltd v. Rooke & Thomas* [1941] D.L.R. 45, 49 and 53; *Guardian Insurance Co. v. Sharp* [1941] 2 D.L.R. 417; and *Dairy Containers Ltd v. NZI Bank Ltd* [1995] 2 N.Z.L.R. 30, 61.

[14] Note also *Dairy Containers Ltd v. NZI Bank Ltd* [1995] 2 N.Z.L.R. 30, 62–65, in which the Auditor-General was held negligent in various respects, including failure to obtain adequate evidence especially in regard to investments and security documents.

[15] SAS 400 para. 4.

[16] SAS 400 para. 16.

[17] See para. 15–094(2) above.

[18] SAS 430 (Audit Sampling). Care should be taken over the design and selection of the sample, having regard to the specific audit objectives, the nature of the population which the auditor wishes to sample and the sampling and selecting methods. The sample items should be selected so as to be representative. See *Dairy Containers Ltd v. NZI Bank Ltd* [1995] N.Z.L.R. 30, 69.

assessment of the nature and degree of risk of misstatement, the nature of the accounting and internal control systems, the materiality of the item being examined, the auditor's knowledge of the business including experience gained during previous audits, the findings from audit procedures and the source and reliability of information available.[19]

15–110　　　The steps which need to be taken include:

(1) Inspection: reviewing or examining records, documents or tangible assets. An auditor's duty to examine the books in order to satisfy himself that they show the true financial position of the company was given early recognition.[20] If a document under the control of the entity is material to the audit, the auditor should look at it for himself unless there are special circumstances why it is reasonable to make do with something less.[21]

(2) Observation: looking at an operation or procedure being performed by others with a view to determining its manner of performance, *e.g.* stock counting.

(3) Enquiry and confirmation from knowledgeable persons inside or outside the entity.[22] As regards those inside the entity, enquiry should be directed to management or staff at the appropriate level; in deciding that level the interest of the person concerned is a relevant matter. Thus in a matter calling for an explanation concerning the authority of an employee or otherwise reflecting on the performance of his duty, prima facie he is not the person from whom an explanation should be sought or if sought, from

---

[19] SAS 400 paras 5–6.

[20] *Leeds Estate, Building and Investment Co. v. Shepherd* (1887) 36 Ch.D. 787, 802 and *Re London and General Bank (No. 2)* [1895] 2 Ch. 673, 682–683 (for facts see n. 63 to para. 15–094, above). Note the Canadian case of *Revelstoke Credit Union v. Miller* (1984) 28 C.C.L.T. 17, 31 *per* McEachern C.J.S.C.:

"A court must be careful about drawing inferences from the mere recording of facts in voluminous books of record or computer printouts. This is because it is a reality of commercial life that the diffusion of clerical and accounting functions between several members of a department often deprives an organisation such as a credit union of real notice of what is happening, and although a meticulous scrutiny of printouts may tell the whole story, it is useful to remember Mr (Sherlock) Holmes' admonition (to observe what is seen). The crucial question is not whether the facts are recorded and seen but whether they should have been recognised and observed, and, if observed, they should have led to a sceptical or critical train of inquiry in the face of assurances given by trusted persons in authority."

[21] *Pacific Acceptance Corporation Ltd v. Forsyth* (1970) 92 W.N. (N.S.W.) 29, 67–68. It may be argued that Moffitt J. over-emphasises the importance of personal inspection of documents. His view seems over-influenced by the nature of the particular documents not properly inspected on the facts in *Pacific Acceptance*, namely original mortgage and title deeds. It is evident, however, that the courts continue to attach considerable importance to actual inspection of material documents by auditors and their staff. But see *Cork Mutual Benefit Terminable Society v. Atkins Chirnside & Co.* (1905) 45 Acct. L.R. 13 (no duty to examine the pass books of each member of a building society).

[22] *Leeds Estate, Building and Investment Co. v. Shepherd* (1887) 36 Ch.D. 787, 802, Stirling J. In that case an auditor did not acquaint himself with the articles of association of a company and did not carry out appropriate inquiries as required by them. He relied on inaccurate balance sheets prepared by the secretary and manager of the company and relied without further inquiry upon the same person's statement that securities upon which monies were lent were worth more than those monies. He nevertheless certified the accounts in terms indicating that he had carried out proper examination and inquiries. He was held to have been in breach of his duty to the company.

whom it should be accepted without verification.[23] It may be important to consider who should make the enquiry: where it relates to a matter of substance and where the enquiry is to be made of a senior executive, it might require the attention of a person of experience and seniority.[24] Management representations should be recorded in writing. If the representations relate to matters material to the financial statement, the auditor should seek corroborative evidence; if he fails to obtain it, he should consider whether his report needs to be qualified.[25] However, in some circumstances he might reasonably conclude that the cumulative weight of the management representations and the corroborative evidence is sufficient, even though neither would have sufficed without the other.[26]

As regards those outside the entity, one important source of confirma- **15–111** tion is from the entity's bankers. There is now a standard form for requests for information from banks,[27] but the auditor should always consider whether the standard form is appropriate in the circumstances. In appropriate cases the auditor should make enquiries of other persons outside the entity,[28] such as creditors or debtors of the entity, the auditors of a wholly owned subsidiary company[29] or appropriate experts.[30]

(4) Computation: checking arithmetical accuracy or performing independent calculations.

(5) Analytical procedures[31]: analysing the relationships between different items of data or between comparable financial information deriving from different period or different entities, in order to identify consistencies and

---

[23] *Pacific, ibid.* at 71. Note also *W.A. Chip & Pulp Co. Pty Ltd v. Arthur Young & Co.* (1987) 12 A.C.L.R. 25 Pidgeon J., and on appeal, *sub nom. Arthur Young & Co. v. W.A. Chip & Pulp Co. Pty Ltd* (1988) 13 A.C.L.R. 283. *Cf. Short & Compton v. Brackett* (1904) Acct. L.R. 8 (no negligence in failing to notice that clerk had made out wages bills for more than was due) and *Cameron Publications Ltd v. Piers, Conrod & Allen* (1986) 35 B.L.R. 32, Nova Scotia Supreme Court, Appeal Division.

[24] *Pacific* at 72. Moffitt J.'s remarks concerning enquiry were particularly directed towards a branch office audit which in his view was a potential danger point.

[25] SAS 440 (Management Representations). It was formerly held that the auditor was entitled to believe tried servants in whom the entity had placed confidence: *Re Kingston Cotton Mill Co. Ltd (No. 2)* [1896] 2 Ch. 279, 288 (for the facts see n. 41 to para. 15–112, below), but it is submitted that a modern auditor would be expected to show more professional scepticism: *Re City Equitable Fire Insurance Co. Ltd* [1925] 1 Ch. 407, 531; and *Re Thomas Gerrard & Sons Ltd* [1968] Ch. 455. In *ADT v. Binder Hamlyn* [1996] B.C.C. 808, 836B, May J. said that an auditor does not discharge his obligation to express an independent opinion simply by accepting what the directors say; hence management representations are a low grade of audit evidence.

[26] *ADT v. Binder Hamlyn* [1996] B.C.C. 808 at 838.

[27] Practice Note 16 (Bank Reports for Audit Purposes).

[28] *Fomento (Sterling Area) Ltd v. Selsdon Fountain Pen Co. Ltd* [1958] 1 W.L.R. 45, 61, HL *per* Lord Denning: The issue in that case was whether auditors engaged by patent licensors to ascertain the amount of royalties due from licensees were entitled to require production by the licensees of specimens or specifications of particular products in order to establish whether they were patented articles or not.

[29] *Pacific, ibid.* at 107–114. See also SAS 510 (Relationship between Principal Auditors and Other Auditors).

[30] SAS 520 (Using the Work of an Expert); *AWA Ltd v. Daniels t/a Deloitte Haskins & Sells* (1992) 7 A.C.S.R. 759, 775. (The case went to appeal *sub nom. Daniels v. Anderson* (1995) 16 A.C.S.R. 607; and see para. 15–112(8) below.)

[31] SAS 410 (Analytical Procedures).

predicted patterns or significant fluctuations and unexpected relationships.[32]

At the conclusion of the process of gathering evidence the auditor should carry out a review of the financial statements in conjunction with the evidence obtained and should consider whether the information in the financial statements accords with statutory requirements and whether accounting policies accord with accounting standards properly disclosed, consistently applied and appropriate to the entity.[33]

15–112 **Particular items in the accounts.**

(1) Fixed assets: the auditor should consider whether the asset has been valued in accordance with appropriate accounting standards, including depreciation.[34]

(2) Securities and investments: an auditor must take reasonable steps to satisfy himself that the securities exist, are in safe and proper custody and are sufficient. This is particularly important in the case of a finance company the business of which consists of lending money on security. It has been suggested that a company's stockbrokers however respectable or responsible are not proper persons to have the custody of its securities except for short periods of necessity.[35] It has also be said[36] that an auditor is never justified in omitting to make a personal inspection of securities in improper custody whenever such personal inspections are practicable. Failure to inspect supposed securities, mainly first mortgages on freehold property, for loans made by the plaintiff finance company, was the prime default by the defendant auditors in *Pacific Acceptance Corporation Ltd*

---

[32] SAS 400 para. 19–25.

[33] SAS 470.

[34] *e.g.* SSAP 19 (Accounting for Investment Properties); SSAP 21 (Accounting for Leases and Hire Purchase Contracts); FRS 7 (Fair Value in Acquisition Accounting); FRS 10 (Goodwill and Intangible Assets); and FRS 11 (Impairment of Fixed Assets and Goodwill). (For a general discussion about SSAPs and FRSs, see para. 15–015 above.)

[35] *Re City Equitable Fire Insurance Co. Ltd* [1925] 1 Ch. 407, 498 *per* Romer J. at first instance. On appeal Pollock M.R. seemed to concede that during such short periods it might be permissible to accept from stockbrokers a certificate of possession of securities but generally he considered that it was an auditor's duty to take such a certificate only from a person who was not only "respectable" or "trustworthy" but also was within a class of persons who in the ordinary course of their business kept securities for their customers (*ibid.* at 512–513. Sargant L.J. at 530 instanced bankers or safe deposit companies as persons accustomed to keep securities.). In that case there was a large deficiency upon the winding-up of an insurance company, in large part attributable to the managing director's fraud. He was also the senior partner of a firm of stockbrokers through which the company placed investments. It was alleged that the auditors were liable for damage occasioned by the stockbrokers pledging to their customers and losing various securities belonging to the company but in the possession of the stockbrokers. Romer J. at first instance (*ibid.* at 498) and the CA (*ibid. per* Pollock M.R. at 515 and seemingly reluctantly *per* Warrington L.J. at 527; *cf. per* Sargant L.J. at 531) held that the auditors were negligent (i) in accepting a certificate from the stockbrokers that they held large blocks of the company's securities and (ii) in neither insisting upon those securities being put in proper custody nor reporting the matter to the shareholders. However the auditor escaped liability by reason of an exemption clause (see para. 15–100 above).

[36] *ibid. per* Romer J. at 497–498. Note *Re London and General Bank (No. 2)* [1875] 2 Ch. 673, 684 where Lindley L.J. seems to have considered it to be the auditor's duty to see that the bills and securities entered in the books were held by the bank (for facts see n. 63 to para. 15–094, above).

v. Forsyth.[37] The fact that the person whom the duty of attending to the execution and registration of mortgages is a professional man does not place him outside the audit field.[38] It is also the auditor's duty to satisfy himself of the sufficiency of the securities.[39]

(3) Stock-in-trade[40]: it has been held that it is not an auditor's duty to take stock.[41] Nevertheless the exercise of reasonable care may still require reasonable steps to be taken to verify figures concerning stock-in-trade.[42] If the auditor discovers irregularities in documents relating to stock, he may need to go further than an explanation from an employee or director.[43]

(4) Work in progress: it has been held to be the auditor's duty to satisfy himself that nothing is included in the work in progress or the balance

---

[37] (1970) 92 W.N. (N.S.W.) 29, 81: for the facts see para. 15–097 above. In that case the preparation of security documents was entrusted by the company to a solicitor who also acted for the borrowers. It was the practice of the relevant branch office of the company to allow solicitors to hold the security documents. The auditors did not inspect the documents. Had they done so they would have discovered that the company had been duped into making loans, sometimes to fictitious companies, which were unsecured. Moffitt J. considered that at the very least auditors of a finance company should satisfy themselves by some proper means that the securities for each of the material loans during the audit year, or outstanding at the balance date, had as promised been executed and registered. He held that the defendant auditors in neither inspecting the security documents for themselves nor obtaining appropriate certificates from the supposed custodian were negligent.

[38] *Pacific, ibid.* at 86.

[39] *Leeds Estate, Building and Investment Co. v. Shepherd* (1887) 36 Ch.D. 787: for the facts see n. 22 to para. 15–110, above. In that case the auditor of a finance company was held to be negligent in accepting a manager's statement that the securities on which the moneys were lent were not only equal to but worth more than the amount placed against them, without making any proper investigation of the company's accounts. It is submitted, however, that the extent of the inquiry into the sufficiency of securities expected of an auditor is in the absence of special circumstances limited, since this is essentially for the management or the directors of the company and not for its auditors to decide: *Re London and General Bank (No. 2)* [1895] 2 Ch. 673, 682.

[40] See SSAP9 (Stocks and Long Term Contracts) and AG (Auditing Guideline) 405 (Attendance at Stocktaking).

[41] *Re Kingston Cotton Mill Co. Ltd (No. 2)* [1896] 1 Ch. 331 (first instance); [1896] 2 Ch. 275, CA. In that case auditors relied upon certificates as to stock value given by a director of the company which were deliberately overstated. Dividends paid on the basis that the balance sheets were correct were found after discovery of the fraud to have been paid out of capital rather than income. If the auditors had added to the stock-in-trade at the beginning of any of the relevant audit years the purchases of raw material in the same year, and had deducted therefrom their sales, they would have seen that the statement of stock-in-trade at the end of the year was so remarkable as to call for explanation. Lindley and Lopes L.JJ. held that it was not an auditor's duty to take stock and that he was entitled to rely on other people for details of stock-in-trade in the absence of suspicion being aroused. However it is submitted that a higher standard might be imposed today. AG 405 para. 5 says that an auditor should attend at stocktaking where the stocks are material in the financial statements and the auditor is relying on the management's stocktake.

[42] *Henry Squire, Cash Chemist Ltd v. Ball Baker & Co.* (1912) 106 L.T. 197, 201 and 203: it is the duty of an auditor to make a reasonable and proper investigation of stock sheets and if he concludes something was wrong to report the matter. See also *Re Liverpool and Wigan Supply Association Ltd* [1907] Acct. L.R. 4 and *Colmer v. Merrett, Son & Street* (1914) 50 Acct. L.R. 21.

[43] *Re Thomas Gerrard & Son Ltd* [1968] 1 Ch. 455, 476. In that case a company's managing director caused the value of its stock-in-trade to be falsified and overstated. When questioned about altered invoices he gave an explanation which the auditor accepted. Pennycuick J. considered that the auditors should not have contented themselves with the managing director's explanation for the altered invoices but should have examined suppliers' statements and where necessary have communicated with suppliers. Having ascertained the true facts they should then have informed the board. In the circumstances their suspicions ought emphatically to have been aroused. (For discussion of this case see Pennington, 78 *Accountancy*, 694; Baxt [1970] 33 M.L.R. 413.)

sheet which was done after that date and that all expenses or liabilities incurred by the company in connection with the work so valued have been brought into account.[44] If a large proportion of work in progress is subject to reservation of title clauses in favour of suppliers, an auditor should make express reference to this in his report.[45] Moreover in certain circumstances it may be prudent for an auditor to seek legal advice upon the effect of a particular reservation of title clause.

(5) Debtors: the overriding concept is that of prudence.[46] An auditor must take care that he does not bring into his balance sheet at face value a debt that is not a good one.[47] He must make reasonable inquiries as to the provision made for bad debts. If circumstances call for inquiry, the auditor must make proper inquiry.[48] It is nevertheless recognised that in the writing off and the making of provision for bad debts an auditor is dependent upon those who run the audited enterprises since their knowledge of the debtors is generally far greater than his.[49] It is now established practice in the United Kingdom to verify a sample of debtor balances by direct communication with the debtors concerned.[50] On the other hand auditors are not expected to be so astute as to discover whether debts are bad because there is some technical legal defence to their recoverability.[51]

(6) Cash: reasonable steps must be taken to inspect cash records.[52] If an enterprise is large and has many branches it will be impracticable for auditors to check all cash records. Moreover, internal control systems are usually designed to prevent abstraction of money and fabrication of records to conceal the consequent loss. If an auditor has properly relied upon and tested an internal control system[53] it may be difficult to prove him negligent in failing to carry out an inspection of particular documents which would have revealed fraud.[54] On the other hand where the enterprise is small or where there is no internal control system the taking of reasonable steps may require detailed inspection of original cash records such as receipts and bank slips and of cash in hand. Also when

---

[44] *Re Westminster Road Construction & Engineering Co. Ltd* (1932) Acct. L.R. 38 (also referred to as *Smith v. Offer*).
[45] ICAEW Recommendation (Accounting for Goods Sold Subject to Reservation of Title).
[46] *ADT Ltd v. Binder Hamlyn* [1996] B.C.C. 808, 848F.
[47] *Re City Equitable Fire Insurance Co. Ltd* [1925] 1 Ch. 407, 483.
[48] *Arthur E. Green & Co. v. The Central Advance and Discount Corporation Ltd* (1920) 63 Acct. L.R. 1.
[49] See *Scarborough Harbour Commission v. Robinson, Coulson Kirby & Co.* (1934) 78 Acct. L.R. 65, 69; see also *Irish Woollen Co. Ltd v. Tyson* (1900) 27 Acct. L.R. 13, 14 and *Jamieson, Austin & Mitchell Ltd v. Battrum* [1934] 1 W.W.R. 324, 330.
[50] See para. 15–109 above as to audit sampling.
[51] *Frank M. Wright (Construction) Ltd v. Frodoor Ltd* [1967] 1 W.L.R. 506, 523: accountants asked to value shares on the basis of excess of assets over liabilities were not bound when valuing those liabilities to consider whether or not the Moneylenders Acts would apply.
[52] *London Oil Storage Co. Ltd v. Seear, Hasluck and Co.* (1904) 31 Acct. L.R. 1; *Fox v. Morrish, Grant & Co* [1918] T.L.R. 126. see also *Re Kingston Cotton Mill Co. Ltd (No. 2)* [1896] 2 Ch. 279, 287.
[53] See para. 15–106 above.
[54] Compare *Guardian Insurance Co. v. Sharp* [1941] 2 D.L.R. 417 and *McBride's Ltd v. Rooke and Thomas* [1941] 4 D.L.R. 45 in regard to inspection of bank slips when internal control system relied upon.

there is cause for suspicion,[55] detailed inspection will be required. One cause for suspicion may be dishonoured cheques.[56]

(7) Creditors: accounting standards[57] set out the principles of accounting for provisions, contingent liabilities and contingent assets. The objective is to ensure that appropriate recognition criteria and measurement bases are applied and that sufficient information is disclosed in the notes to enable the user to understand their nature, timing and amount. A frequent device resorted to for giving an over-favourable picture of the state of affairs of an enterprise is the suppression of liabilities, frequently by carrying them over from the accounting period subject of an audit to the next. An auditor must take reasonable steps to ascertain liabilities including contingent liabilities, but even the taking of such steps may not lead to discovery of suppressed liabilities.[58] In certain circumstances, such as upon the discovery of the alteration of invoice dates, an auditor should call for statements from creditors and may be held negligent in failing to do so.[59] Specific inquiries concerning liabilities will also be required of an auditor where creditors commonly delay sending invoices and in consequence liabilities incurred cannot be ascertained from invoices received owing to insufficient lapse of time for receipt of all relevant invoices.[60]

(8) Unauthorised transactions: an auditor who comes upon a payment which is *ultra vires* or improper is to inquire into it and, if need be, to disallow it.[61] On the other hand, an auditor of a company is rarely equipped with the knowledge of a lawyer. While he may be liable for failure to discover that a particular transaction is unauthorised owing to the absence of a prerequisite resolution of the directors or shareholders, he will not be liable for failure to ascertain as unauthorised a transaction which only a lawyer would have been likely to recognise as such.[62] But if he ought to realise that there might be a problem, he should make the necessary inquiries[63] and, if appropriate, take expert advice.[64] It has long been recognised as part of the function of an auditor of a local authority to take reasonable steps to check that there are no unauthorised, illegal or

---

[55] *e.g. Hardy Employees' Credit Union Ltd v. Moll Chadwick & Co.* [1980] Qd.R. 362 (failure properly to investigate suspiciously large payments).

[56] *Pacific Acceptance Corporation Ltd v. Forsyth* (1970) 92 W.N. (N.S.W.) 29, 98–99 and 102.

[57] FRS (Financial Reporting Standard) 12 (Provisions, Contingent Liabilities and Contingent Assets).

[58] In *Henry Squire, Cash Chemist Ltd v. Ball Baker & Co.* [1912] L.T. 197, 204 auditors were absolved of negligence in not discovering suppressed liabilities since there was no entry in the books of the audited company which would have revealed them

[59] *Re Thomas Gerrard & Son Ltd* [1968] 1 Ch. 455. See also *Irish Woollen Co. Ltd v. Tyson* (1900) 27 Acct. L.R. 13.

[60] See *Re Westminster Road Construction & Engineering Co. Ltd* (1932) Acct. L.R. 38.

[61] *Fomento (Sterling Area) Ltd v. Selsdon Fountain Pen Co. Ltd* [1958] 1 W.L.R. 45, 61, HL: see n. 18 to para. 15–111 above. See also SAS 120 (Consideration of Law and Regulations).

[62] Note *Trustee of the Property of Blue Band Navigation Co. Ltd v. Price Waterhouse & Co. (No. 2)* [1934] 3 D.L.R. 404, 433, British Columbia CA.

[63] See *AWA Ltd v. Daniels t/a Deloitte Haskins & Sells* (1992) 7 A.C.S.R. 759, 787. On appeal, see *Daniels v. Anderson* (1995) 16 A.C.S.R. 607.

[64] See para. 15–110(3) above.

improper payments and to report to the authority if any are discovered.[65]

(9) Related party transactions: the audit should be planned and performed with the objective of obtaining sufficient audit evidence regarding the adequacy of disclosure of related party transactions.[66]

(10) Post-balance sheet events: the auditor should consider the effect of subsequent events on the financial statements.[67] He should perform procedures devised to obtain sufficient appropriate evidence that all material subsequent events have been identified and properly reflected in the financial statements. Where events happen or are discovered after the date of the auditor's report but before the financial statements are issued, he should consider whether the financial statements need amendment. If the events which happen are discovered after the statements have been issued but before they have been laid before the members, he should consider whether the statements need revision. The important point is that the auditor's duty is not discharged where the audit certificate, although reasonable in the light of facts known at the time, proves to be incorrect before it is relied upon.

(iv) *Reporting*

15–113   The product of an audit is a report by the auditor upon the entity's financial statements. Errors in conducting the audit will usually be reflected in the report. For example, in consequence of inadequate inspection of material documents an unqualified report might be given when, if a proper inspection had been made, the report would need to have been qualified. Various statutes contain provisions making specific requirements concerning the contents of an auditor's report.[68] The Companies Act 1985 requires the report to state that the company's financial statements have not only been properly prepared in accordance with the Act but also give a "true and fair view."[69] Indeed, until recently statutory obligations concerning the audit of an enterprise related exclusively to the audit report rather than both to the audit itself and the consequent report. A prior audit was contemplated, but an auditor's duties incidental and preparatory to making a report were left for the courts to decide. The current Companies Act expressly takes into account the audit itself, by requiring an auditor to carry out such investigations as will enable him to form an opinion on various matters.[70] Nevertheless, the nature of appropriate investigating steps is not defined in the Act but remains within the province of the courts to decide, having regard to the facts of particular cases and the practice of the profession. Indeed somewhat inversely to the statutory approach, the courts' approach to deciding professional

---

[65] *Thomas v. Devonport Corporation* [1900] 1 Q.B. 16, 21, approved in *Roberts v. Hopwood* [1925] A.C. 578, 605 and *Re Risdel, Risdel v. Rawlinson* [1947] 2 All E.R. 312, 315–316; also *Frankston and Hastings Corporation v. Cohen* (1960) 102 C.L.R. 607, 619. *Ultra vires* has always been a particular concern in relation to public authorities; accordingly care needs to be taken in applying these cases to other entities.

[66] SAS 460 (Related Parties); see also FRS 8 (Related Party Disclosures).

[67] SAS 150 (Subsequent Events); see also *Duke Group Ltd v. Pilmer* (1999) 31 A.C.S.R. 213, 273, S. Ct. of S. Aus.

[68] See paras 15–009 *et seq.*, above.

[69] s.235: see para. 15–015 above.

[70] s.237(1): see para. 15–020 above.

negligence cases against auditors is to consider primarily errors in the course of an audit as opposed to errors in the audit report. Moreover, comparative to the number of judicial comments concerned with what should be done in the course of an audit, there are few concerned with the contents or form of the report itself. The point is usually of no great significance, however, since if an auditor has failed to discover a matter in the course of an audit, it goes without saying that he will also have failed to deal with it in his report. Nevertheless, the manner of stating the results of an audit is often crucial.

A Statement of Auditing Standards contains specific requirements as to the **15–114** contents of auditors' reports on financial statements.[71] The primary requirement is that such statements should "contain a clear expression of opinion, based on review and assessment of the conclusions drawn from evidence in the course of the audit". Since the auditor's role is to provide reasonable, not absolute, assurance, it is important that the report indicates the context in which it is given. The SAS states the form which the report should take.[72] The report should contain a clear expression of opinion on the financial statements.[73] Before the auditor can properly express an unqualified opinion, he must be satisfied that the financial statements give a true and fair view and have been prepared in accordance with appropriate accounting policies consistently applied. If there is a limitation on the scope of his examination or if he disagrees with the treatment or disclosure of a matter, he should give a qualified report. If his disagreement is so material or pervasive that he considers the financial statements to be seriously misleading, he should give an adverse opinion. Where the possible effect of a limitation on scope is so material or pervasive that he has been unable to obtain sufficient evidence, he should issue a disclaimer of opinion.[74] Further, he should consider whether the view expressed in the financial statements could be affected by inherent uncertainties which are fundamental; if this is so but the uncertainty is adequately disclosed in the financial statement, he should add an explanatory paragraph to his report but without qualifying his opinion.[75]

In some cases the disclosure of sensitive information might be damaging to the **15–115** company. It is submitted that the correct approach is to look at the scope of the auditor's duty and to consider whether he has discharged his duty to the person or class of persons to whom the duty is owed.[76] A less extensive reporting duty has been recognised in the case of an audit of a company the shareholders of

---

[71] SAS 600. See also APB PN (Practice Note) 8 (Reports by auditors under company legislation in the United Kingdom); APB Bulletin 1997/1 (The Special Auditors' Report on Abbreviated Accounts in Great Britain); APB Bulletin 1999/6 (The Auditors' Report on the Summary Financial Statement); and APB Bulletin 2001/2 (Revisions to the Wording of Auditors' Reports on Financial Statements and the Interim Review Report).

[72] In *Re John Fulton and Co. Ltd* [1932] N.I. 35 an auditor who signed balance sheets "Audited Henry Jenkinson" but who had failed to audit and report on the balance sheets was held to have been in breach of his duty.

[73] *Re London and General Bank (No. 2)* [1895] 2 Ch. 783, CA (for facts see n. 63 to para. 15–094, above). Also note *Shorrock Ltd v. Meggitt plc, The Times*, June 4, 1991, CA.

[74] SAS 600 paras 32–37.

[75] SAS 600.6.

[76] *Pacific Acceptance Corporation Ltd v. Forsyth*. (1970) 92 W.N. (N.S.W.) 29, 58. In *Re London and General Bank (No. 2)* [1895] 2 Ch. 783 (for the facts see n. 63 to para. 15–094, above) Lindley L.J. recognised that the disclosure of certain information in the shape of a printed document circulated among a large body of shareholders might by its consequent publicity be damaging to their interests. In such circumstances he was unwilling to hold an auditor in breach of his duty if instead of publishing his report in such a way as to ensure publicity, he made a confidential report to the shareholders, invited their attention to it and told them where they could see it.

which are also directors than in the case of a company with a large body of shareholders, where an auditor has already communicated material matters to the directors.[77] It is nevertheless submitted that the fact that the shareholders are also directors does not excuse an auditor from performing his statutory duties in making his report.

15–116   In addition to his report to the general meeting, the auditor should consider whether to make a separate report to directors or management on matters coming to his attention during the audit, including material weakness in accounting and internal control systems.[78] This is in addition to, not instead of, a report to the general meeting.[79] It is submitted that, where an auditor discovers wrongdoing within a company and considers that all or some of the management is unaware of the wrongdoing, he may come under a duty to the company to alert the management.[80] If the management is party to the fraud, the auditor may come under "whistle-blowing" duties.[81]

(b) *Other breaches of duty*

15–117   **Valuation.** Accountants are sometimes asked to act as valuers.[82] The articles of association of a private company often have rights of pre-emption requiring a shareholder who wishes to dispose of his shares to offer them to the other shareholders at a price to be determined by the auditor. If the auditor is acting as expert, not arbitrator, he will owe a duty of care to the parties.[83]

15–118   **Preparation of tax returns.** An accountant may be liable if, as a result of his acts or omissions, there is undue delay in submitting a tax return or the tax return is inaccurate.[84] Needless to say, it will be particularly important in this context to consider whether the client has caused or contributed to the loss.[85]

15–119   **Advice.** Accountants frequently give advice on tax or business matters. The principles to be applied are broadly the same as those which apply in the case of solicitors.[86] If the accountant assumes a responsibility for advising the client as

---

[77] *Pendlebury's Ltd v. Ellis Green & Co.* (1936) 80 Acct. L.R. 39; also *International Laboratories Ltd v. Dewar* (1933) 3 D.L.R. 665, 697.

[78] SAS 610; *Daniels v. Anderson* (1995) 16 A.C.S.R. 607, 650, S. Ct. of N.S.W. In *Canadian Woodmen of the World v. Hooper* [1933] 1 D.L.R. 168 auditors of a fraternal order discovered that the order's stockbroker had purchased bonds different from those required by the directors of the order and that this had been concealed from the directors by the order's head clerk. In reliance upon the clerk's and the stockbroker's promises to rectify the matter, the auditors did not report it to the directors until three years later when the promises remained unfulfilled. In failing to report the matter upon original discovery to the directors, the auditors were held negligent.

[79] *Re London and General Bank (No. 2)* [1895] 2 Ch. 783, CA (see n. 63 to para. 15–094, above).

[80] See n. 35 to para. 15–018, above.

[81] See para. 15–030 above.

[82] The reader is referred to the discussion as to accounting standards in para. 15–112 above.

[83] *Arenson v. Casson Beckman, Rutley & Co.* [1977] A.C. 405. As to challenges to the valuation on the ground of mistake, see *Jones v. Sherwood Computer Services plc* [1992] 1 W.L.R. 277. As to the standard of care, see *Whiteoak v. Walker* (1988) B.C.C. 122 (n. 41 to para. 15–090).

[84] *Pech v. Tilgals* (1994) 28 A.T.R. 197.

[85] See paras 15–121 *et seq.* and 15–146 *et seq.* below.

[86] See chap. 10.

to what investment policy he should adopt, he may find that he has crossed the line between "information" and "advice".[87]

4. Damages

The usual remedy for breach of duty by an accountant is an award of damages **15–120** or, if proceedings are brought by way of misfeasance summons against a company auditor under section 212 of the Insolvency Act 1986,[88] compensation. Such compensation is assessed on the same principle as damages are assessed. The section nevertheless gives the court a discretion both as to whether or not to order payment of compensation and as to the amount of compensation ordered.[89]

(a) *Remoteness*

(i) *Causation*

General. An accountant is only liable for such loss as has been caused by his **15–121** breach of duty.[90] In accordance with the usual rule, the burden is on the claimant to establish causation. It is always necessary to consider whether the loss falls

---

[87] *South Australia Asset Management Co. Ltd v. York Montague Ltd* [1997] A.C. 191 (see para. 15–125 below). For an example, see *Craig v. Troy* (1997) 16 W.A.R. 96, S. Ct. of W. Aus., where an accountant was held liable for negligent advice as to the feasibility of a hotel development. In *Aneco Reinsurance Underwriting Ltd v. Johnson & Higgins Ltd*, [2001] U.K.H.L. 51, the House of Lords held by a majority that an insurance broker who wrongly advised an insurer that reinsurance was available was giving advice and not merely information. Although the House of Lords categorised this as an appeal which realised no point of principle, it might be seen as a retreat from *SAAMCO*.

[88] See para. 15–024 above.

[89] A discretion to relieve a company auditor wholly or partly from his liability is also conferred by s.727 of the Companies Act 1985: see para. 15–153 below.

[90] The question of effective cause is considered in para. 15–122 *et seq.* below. For specific illustrations in cases involving accountants see the following: *London Oil Storage Co. Ltd v. Seear, Hasluck & Co.* (1904) 31 Acct. L.R. 93 (Lord Alverstone C.J. directed the jury: "You must not put upon him the loss by reason of theft occurring afterwards or before, but you must put upon him such damages as you consider in your opinion were really caused by his not having fulfilled his duty as Auditor of the company."); *Re City Equitable Fire Insurance Co.* [1925] 1 Ch. 407, 482–483 and 511 (the claim against the auditors for misdescription of certain debts in a balance sheet failed since no one would have been misled by it. Note Romer J. at 482: if proper description of the debts had induced any director or shareholder to make some inquiry as to their nature, the matter would have been different); *JEB Fasteners Ltd v. Marks Bloom & Co.* [1981] 3 All E.R. 289, CA (it was held that the plaintiff would have acted no differently even if it had known the true position as to the accounts); *Canadian Woodmen of the World v. Hooper* [1933] 1 D.L.R. 168, 171 *per* Middleton J.A. (see n. 78 to para. 15–116, above); *Guardian Insurance Co. v. Sharp* [1941] 2 D.L.R. 417 and 426; *West Coast Finance Ltd v. Gunderson, Stokes, Walton and Co.* (1974) 44 D.L.R. (3d) 232 (first instance), (1974) 56 D.L.R. (3d) 468, British Columbia CA; *Toromont Industrial Holdings Ltd v. Thorne, Gunn, Helliwell and Christenson* (1975) 62 D.L.R. (3d) 225 (first instance), (1976) 73 D.L.R. (3d) 122, Ontario CA; *Cambridge Credit Corporation Ltd v. Hutcheson (No. 1)* (1983) 8 A.C.L.R. 123; *(No. 2)* (1983) 8 A.C.L.R. 513; *(No. 3)* (1983) 8 A.C.L.R. 526; *Northumberland Insurance Ltd v. Alexander* (1984) 8 A.C.L.R. 882; (1988) 13 A.C.L.R. 170: *Cambridge Credit Corporation Ltd v. Hutcheson* (1985) 9 A.C.L.R. 545; 9 A.C.L.R. 669 and *Alexander v. Cambridge Credit Corporation Ltd* (1985) 10 A.C.L.R. 42; (1987) 12 A.C.L.R. 202.

within the scope of the accountant's duty.[91] Once it is established that an accountant's negligence was causative of the relevant loss, he remains liable notwithstanding that there may have been other causes of equal efficacy.[92]

15–122 **Effective cause.** In cases involving accountants as in other cases, causation gives rise to difficulties, primarily in the application of principle to the huge variety of circumstances which arise. The perennial problem is to establish whether one or more putative causes provide the required link in law between the duty breached and the loss claimed. The "but for" test is necessary but not sufficient.[93] It is an exclusionary test serving only to filter out non-causal occasions for the loss. Putative causes may survive that test but may still not qualify as "effective causes".[94]

15–123 In seeking the elusive ingredient which is additional to the "but for" test, the Courts have broadly speaking travelled along two routes. The first is to leave it to judicial "common sense" or to speak of "effective cause" without attempting to analyse what makes a cause effective. This was the approach adopted by the Court of Appeal in *Galoo v. Bright Grahame Murray*.[95] In that case a parent company made loans to its subsidiaries and claimed to have done so in reliance on the negligence of the subsidiary's auditor in failing to uncover the subsidiary's insolvency. Glidewell L.J. said that it was necessary to establish whether the negligence was the "effective" or "dominant" cause of the loss and that this was done "by the application of the Court's common sense". The Court held that the negligent audit certificate merely created the *opportunity* for the subsidiaries to incur and continue to incur trading losses, the effective cause of the losses being the unsuccessful trading. In *Smith New Court Securities Ltd v. Scrimgeour Vickers (Asset Management) Ltd*[96] Lord Steyn said that there was no single

---

[91] See para. 15–125 below.

[92] *W.A. Chip & Pulp Co. Pty. Ltd v. Arthur Young & Co.* (1987) 12 A.C.L.R. 25, 42–43; on appeal, *sub nom. Arthur Young & Co. v. W.A. Chip & Pulp Co. Pty Ltd* (1988) 13 A.C.L.R. 283, S. Ct. of W. Aus.; *Duke Group Ltd v. Pilmer* (1994) 27 A.C.S.R. 1, 365 (the case went to appeal at (1999) 31 A.C.S.R. 213).

[93] *Duke Group Ltd v. Pilmer, ibid.*, 282.

[94] In *Downs v. Chappell* [1997] 1 W.L.R. 426, 443D–F, CA, Hobhouse L.J. applied a "but for" test in relation both to a claim for fraudulent misrepresentation against a director and to a claim for negligent misstatement against an accountant. It is submitted that this approach, whilst unexceptionable in relation to fraud, is not the correct test in relation to negligence (the point was expressly left open by Lord Hoffmann in *SAAMCO, ibid.* at 214H). Hobhouse L.J. also applied a cross-check by comparing the contract price with the value which the business would have had, if the representation had been true, but this was disapproved in *Smith New Court Securities Ltd v. Scrimgeour Vickers (Asset Management) Ltd* [1997] A.C. 254, 283. On one reading of Hobhouse L.J.'s judgment, he appeared to apply a different causation test in relation to negligent acts from that which he applied in relation to negligent omissions. That, at least, is how Millett L.J. understood the judgment in *Bristol & West Building Society v. Mothew* [1998] Ch. 1, 11. However Hobhouse L.J. has since made it clear that he was not intending to lay down any such general principle: *Swindle v. Harrison* [1997] 4 All E.R. 705, 727. It is submitted that there is no basis for such a distinction: the duty arises out of an obligation to provide accurate information or advice; it should be immaterial whether the breach of duty occurs because the wrong information was provided or because the right information was not provided (see *White v. Jones* [1995] 2 A.C. 207, 268H *per* Lord Goff).

[95] [1994] 1 W.L.R. 1360, 1374–1375, following the reasoning in *Alexander v. Cambridge Credit Corp. Ltd* (1987) 9 N.S.W.L.R. 310, 333–335.

[96] [1997] A.C. 254, 284–285 (the case was concerned with the measure of damages for fraudulent misrepresentation).

satisfactory theory of causation capable of solving the infinite variety of practical problems confronted by the courts. Judges sometimes applied a pragmatic test of asking whether the condition in question was a substantial factor in producing a result and others asserted "common sense" as the guiding criterion. There was no material difference.

Galoo has been trenchantly criticised in New Zealand.[97] It was said that **15–124** common sense can never provide a test as such, but should simply reflect the approach which any judge will take to a "jury" question. The distinction between the effective cause and the opportunity for the loss was criticised an unhelpful. Instead it was said that the right approach was to treat causation as an issue of fact and to break it down into subsidiary questions. Thus, instead of simply asking whether the negligent audit caused the loss, one should ask: (i) Did the negligent audit lead the company to believe that it was trading profitably? and (ii) Did the company continue trading at a loss in reliance on that belief? If the answer to both questions was "yes", then the auditor was prima facie liable for such loss as was a necessary consequence of continued trading.[98]

Other judges, notably Lord Hoffmann, have analysed in terms of "scope of **15–125** duty" the extra ingredient which goes to make up causation. The starting point is the principle affirmed in *Caparo* that it is always necessary to consider whether the loss falls within the scope of the accountant's duty, and that the scope of the duty is determined by reference to the kind of damage from which the accountant must take care to save the claimant harmless.[99] As stated above,[1] Lord Oliver in *Caparo* held that the statutory purposes of a company auditor's function were limited to (i) protecting the company from the consequences of undetected errors or wrongdoing and (ii) providing its shareholders with reliable information so as to enable them to scrutinise the conduct of the company's affairs and to exercise their collective powers to reward, control or remove the directors. The analysis was taken a step further in *South Australia Asset Management Corporation v. York Montague Ltd*[2] (*"SAAMCO"*), where Lord Hoffmann said that a plaintiff has to prove both that he has suffered loss and that the loss falls within the scope of the duty of care. Lord Hoffmann's thesis is perhaps most clearly expressed in *Environment Agency v. Empress Car Co. (Abertillery) Ltd*,[3] where he said that common-sense answers to questions of causation will differ according to the purpose for which the question is asked. This in turn depends upon the purpose and scope of the rule by which responsibility is being attributed.

---

[97] *Sew Hoy & Sons Ltd v. Coopers & Lybrand* [1996] 1 N.Z.L.R. 392, C.A. of N.Z.; see especially Thomas J. at 408–411.

[98] The Court in *Sew Hoy* treated *Galoo* as a decision on its facts but said that, if *Galoo* laid down a principle of law that losses caused by continued trading could never be recovered, then it was wrongly decided. As regards the measure of damages, it was said in *Sew Hoy* that this was prima facie the difference between (i) the losses attributable to continued trading (but excluding losses arising from any imprudent trading decisions) and (ii) the losses which would have resulted if the company had ceased to trade.

[99] *Caparo Industries plc v. Dickman* [1990] 2 A.C. 605: see paras 15–059 and 15–060 above.

[1] See para. 15–011 above.

[2] [1997] A.C. 191, 218B. Although Lord Hoffmann, *ibid.* at 211A, described the issue in terms of the scope of the duty of care, he has since accepted extra-judicially that it may also be described in terms of causation: "Common sense and causing loss" (Lecture to the Chancery Bar Association, 1999).

[3] [1999] 2 A.C. 22, 29–31.

15–126   *SAAMCO* has been applied in a number of recent cases involving accountants, most notably *Sasea Finance Ltd v. KPMG*,[4] where the Court of Appeal held that it was the auditor's duty was to report to the company's management the fraud of a senior employee as soon as the auditor discovered it or should reasonably have discovered it. *Galoo* was distinguished on the ground that, where the auditor's duty was to draw attention to a fraud, he was responsible for the company continuing to trade fraudulently. The subsequent frauds were the very kind of transactions against the risk of which the auditor had a duty to warn. One potential difficulty arising from *SAAMCO* is the distinction between "information" and "advice"; however the cases to date have accepted that the product of an auditor's work usually falls on the "information" side of the line.[5-6]

15–127   **Reliance.** Where a claim is brought for negligent misstatement, reliance is usually a necessary ingredient of the claim. In such a case the claimant must prove that he relied[7] on the information or advice given by the accountant's certificate.[8] It is necessary for a claimant company to point to at least one natural person within the company who relied, and was misled by, the accountant's negligence.[9] The effects of this case in the context of whistle-blowing duties[10] have yet to be tested. Thus a fraudulently misled company may (*e.g.* by its liquidator) be able to point to a regulator who would not have been misled by the fraud and who would have intervened to prevent further loss, if its auditor or other accountant reporting upon it had "whistle-blown".[11] The fact that all the shareholders and directors of the company may have been fraudulent and were not misled may not then be fatal to the success of the claim. Hence a claimant will be denied recovery of loss which is the product of his own unlawful act even though the accountant was negligent in failing to discover that loss. It is not sufficient for an investor to show merely that he relied on the fact that the accountant had written a report; the claimant has to go further and show that he

---

[4] [2000] 1 All E.R. 676, CA. See also *Yorkshire Enterprises Ltd v. Robson Rhodes*, unreported June 17, 1998, Bell J.; *BCCI v. Price Waterhouse* [1999] B.C.C. 351 (Laddie J. struck out a claim in respect of trading losses allegedly incurred in reliance on a negligent audit certificate on the ground that it was outside the scope of the duty of care; it appears that he would have taken a different view, had the continued trading been a continuation of the fraudulent type of business which the auditor should have discovered). *HIT Finance v. Cohen Arnold* [2000] Lloyd's Rep. P.N. 125 at 129, 141 and 142, CA; *Duke Group Ltd v. Pilmer* (1999) 31 A.C.S.R. 213, 288, S. Ct. of S. Aus.

[5-6] *Boyd Knight v. Purdue* [1999] N.Z.L.R. 278, 292, NZCA: held that an auditor's report required by the Securities Commission gave information not advice, in that it contained no recommendation to potential investors as to whether or not to invest in the company. See also *Berg Son & Co. v. Mervyn Hampton Adams* [1993] B.C.L.C. 1045, 1064, Hobhouse J. (n. 9 to para. 15–011, above). But see para. 15–119 above.

[7] The claimant must also show that it was reasonable to rely on the information or advice: see para. 15–070 above.

[8] *Boyd Knight v. Purdue*, *ibid.* at 292; *Howael Ventures (1984) Inc. v. Arthur Anderson & Co.* [1996] 7 W.W.R. 383.

[9] *Berg Son & Co. v. Mervyn Hampton Adams* [1993] B.C.L.C. 1045, 1065. In *Edwards Karawacki Smith & Co. Pty Ltd v. Jacka Nominees Pty Ltd* (1994) 15 A.C.S.R. 503, the S. Ct. of W. Aus. inclined to the view (i) that the fraud of the director was to be treated as the fraud of the company, but (ii) that this did not relieve the auditor from liability for negligence. It is submitted that this approach has much to commend it, provided of course that there is an innocent victim of the auditor's breach of duty. However it still leaves open the issue of contributory negligence (see para. 15–148(2) below).

[10] See para. 15–030 above.

[11] This is analogous to the position in *Law Society v. KPMG* [2000] 1 W.L.R. 1921 (see para. 15–085 above).

read the accounts and relied on the report which certified that they gave a true and fair view.[12]

It is always necessary to go back to first principles in order to see whether reliance (and, if so, what degree of reliance) is necessary. Where the claim is based on negligent misstatement, it is likely that the causative mechanism will be reliance. Where the negligence consists of a negligent act or omission, it has been suggested that there may be cases in which the necessary causative link may be established without reliance.[13] However it is submitted that, save in exceptional cases, mere foreseeability will not have the necessary causative potency and that a claimant will need to demonstrate reliance, even if it is only general reliance on the defendant's skill and care.[14] **15–128**

Where a negligent misstatement or omission is likely to induce the claimant to act (or refrain from acting) in a particular way and he does in fact act (or refrain from acting) in that way, it is submitted that the court may presume reliance although no direct evidence is called; however this is no more than an inference of fact, not a presumption of law.[15] **15–129**

Intervening act of claimant or third party. The chain of causation may be broken by the act or omission of the claimant or some third person.[16] In order to ascertain whether the chain of causation will be broken, it is necessary to go back to Lord Hoffmann's formulation[17]: where the defendant's duty is to guard against the risk of fraud or mistake by a third party, then any such fraud or mistake on the part of the third party will not constitute an intervening act which breaks the chain of causation.[18] **15–130**

---

[12] *Luscombe v. Roberts and Pascho* (1962) 106 S.J. 373.

[13] *White v. Jones* [1995] 2 A.C. 207, 272D-G *per* Lord Browne-Wilkinson (a solicitor's case: see Chap. 10, para. 10–048 *et seq.*). However care needs to be taken in applying this principle. *White v. Jones* was an exceptional case in which the House of Lords fashioned a remedy in order to avoid injustice (*ibid.* at 260G and 267H–268E *per* Lord Goff). It does not follow that mere foreseeability of loss will usually suffice.

[14] In *Duke Group Ltd v. Pilmer* (1999) 31 A.C.S.R. 213, 284, S. Ct. of S. Aus. (for facts see para. 15–151 below) the Court held that the accountant's breach of duty to the company had caused loss notwithstanding that the directors of the company knew that the statement was inaccurate. The necessary causative link was to be found in the fact that the directors would have been unable to call the necessary shareholders' meeting without a favourable accountant's report and that, if a meeting had been called following an unfavourable report, the shareholders would have been unlikely to vote in favour of the transaction in question.

[15] It is submitted that this represents the law in relation to misrepresentation generally: *Smith v. Chadwick* (1884) 9 App.Cas. 187, 196; however the weight to be given to this presumption is not settled: see *Chitty*, para. 6–034 n. 67. In South Australia this presumption was applied in *Duke Group Ltd v. Pilmer* (1999) 31 A.C.S.R. 213, 282–284, Full Court of S. Ct; however in Western Australia a claim was dismissed in the absence of positive evidence of reliance: *Strategic Minerals Corp. NL v. Basham* (1997) 25 A.C.S.R. 470, Full Court of S. Ct.

[16] See paras 15–146 *et seq.* for contributory negligence and contribution respectively.

[17] See para. 15–125 above.

[18] *Re London and General Bank (No. 2)* [1895] 2 Ch. 673. 688 and 696–697 (for facts see n. 63 to para. 15–094, above); *Re Thomas Gerrard & Son Ltd* [1968] Ch. 455, 477–8 (for facts see n. 43 to para. 15–112, above); *Craig v. Troy* (1997) 16 W.A.R. 96, S. Ct. of W. Aus. (the negligence of the first firm of accountants remained causatively potent notwithstanding the negligence of the second firm); and *Duke Group Ltd v. Pilmer* (1999) 31 A.C.S.R. 213, 287–289 (stock market crash did not break chain of causation because it was foreseeable that the accountant's report would be relied on after the crash). In contrast, in *Weld-Blundell v. Stephens* [1920] A.C. 956 an accountant who was in breach of his duty to take reasonable care to keep secret a libellous document was not liable to indemnify the plaintiff for damages for libel, since the document had been brought to the attention of the person libelled by the intervening act of the person who had shown it to him.

(ii) *Foreseeability*

15–131   In order to succeed the claimant must establish not only that the loss was caused by the breach of duty of the defendant accountant, but also that it was foreseeable. If the claim is brought in contract, this means that, at the time the contract was made, the loss was reasonably foreseeable as likely to result from the breach.[19] If the claim is brought in tort, it means that at the time the breach of duty was committed the damage (or at least the type of damage) was reasonably foreseeable as a consequence.[20] What is foreseeable will depend upon the facts of each case.[21] In practice this issue rarely arises for separate consideration since any loss which falls within the scope of the duty is likely to be foreseeable.[22]

(b) *Measure of damages*

15–132   Whether the claim is brought in contract or tort or by way of misfeasance summons the fundamental principle governing the measure of damages is that the claimant must be put so far as money can do it in the position he would have occupied if the accountant had properly discharged his duty.[23] Broadly speaking, this can be achieved in one of two ways, depending upon the particular facts of the case: either (i) by paying to the claimant the monetary equivalent of any benefits of which he has been deprived, or (ii) by indemnifying him against any expenses or liabilities which he has incurred.

15–133   **Loss of a chance.** In some cases the complaint is that the accountant's breach of duty has prevented the claimant from doing (or not doing) something which might have produced a gain or avoided a loss. He cannot prove that he would actually have done (or refrained from doing) the thing in question, because it is hypothetical. His loss is the loss of the chance of doing (or refraining from doing)

---

[19] *per* Asquith L.J. in *Victoria Laundry (Windsor) Ltd v. Newman Industries Ltd* [1949] 2 K.B. 528. For a full discussion of the requirement of foreseeability in contract, see *McGregor on Damages* (16th ed.), paras 247–281.

[20] For a full discussion of the requirement of foreseeability in tort, see *McGregor*, paras 136–231.

[21] *e.g. Re Kingston Cotton Mill Co. Ltd (No. 2)* [1896] 1 Ch. 331 (for the facts see n. 41 to para. 15–112, above: at first instance Vaughan Williams L.J. held the auditors liable for preference dividends wrongly passed on the basis of the inaccurate balance sheet signed by the auditors, but CA, [1896] 2 Ch. 279 reversed the decision on liability); *Re Thomas Gerrard & Son Ltd* [1968] Ch. 455, 476–477 (for facts see n. 43 to para. 15–112, above: although the defendant was held liable under only one of the three heads of breach alleged, the judge held that it was rightly conceded that the compensation was the same as if breach had been found under all heads, since once put on their guard under any one head the auditors ought to have taken steps which would have led to the detection of the frauds under the other heads); *McBride's Ltd v. Rooke & Thomas* [1941] 4 D.L.R. 45, 55 (it was held that, if in the course of an audit defalcations of an employee are not discovered, it was foreseeable that they would be continued by him); and *Duke Group Ltd v. Pilmer* (1999) 31 A.C.S.R. 213, 288 (stock market crash held to be foreseeable).

[22] Although there is an overlap between the two concepts, foreseeability is concerned with the kind of loss, whilst scope of duty looks at quantification: *Platform Home Loans Ltd v. Oyston Shipways Ltd* [2000] 2 A.C. 190, 209G *per* Lord Hobhouse. In *Law Society v. KPMG* [2000] 1 W.L.R. 1921, 1930, CA left open the possibility of an argument based on foreseeability.

[23] See *Livingstone v. Rawyards Coal Co.* (1880) 5 App.Cas. 25, 39 and *Dodd Properties (Kent) Ltd v. Canterbury City Council* [1980] 1 W.L.R. 433, 451, 454 and 456 (as to general principles). Also see the cases mentioned at n. 90 to para. 15–121, above.

it. The Court of Appeal in *Allied Maples Group Ltd v. Simmons & Simmons*[24] has drawn a distinction between the hypothetical acts or omissions of the plaintiff and those of a third party. In the former case, the issue has to be decided on the balance of probabilities. But where the issue turns on what a third party[25] might hypothetically have done or not done, then the courts assess damages by reference to the value of the chance that the third party would have acted (or refrained from acting) as alleged. This is an exception to the usual principle that issues of fact in a civil case are decided on the balance of probabilities. The "loss of a chance" principle may be categorised under either causation or quantum.[26]

The following principles have emerged in relation to quantifying damages: **15–134**

(1) If the chance of the hypothesis being fulfilled is negligible, it will be treated as nil; conversely, if it is a near certainty, it will be treated as certain.[27]

(2) The legal burden of proof is on the claimant, but in some cases the defendant may have the evidential burden of showing that the chance was no more than negligible.[28]

(3) There is a difference of judicial opinion as to how far the court should delve into the hypothetical question of fact.[29]

(4) Where the outcome depends on two or more hypothetical facts, the courts need to consider their interrelationship. If each is independent of the other, then the right approach is usually to multiply the percentages in order to ascertain the overall chance.[30] But where the hypothetical facts are interdependent, it may be appropriate to take make one single discount.[31]

---

[24] [1995] 1 W.L.R. 1602 (see Chap. 3, para. 3–005 and Chap. 10, para. 10–258). Although this was a case involving solicitors, it is thought that the same principles would apply in relation to accountants. *Allied Maples* has been followed in relation to accountants in *First Interstate Bank of California v. Cohen Arnold* [1996] P.N.L.R. 17, CA; the same principle was applied in *Daniels v. Anderson* (1995) 16 A.C.S.R. 607, 687 *et seq.*

[25] Where the third party is very closely identified with the claimant, the court might treat them as one and the same (*i.e.* apply the balance of probabilities test): *Allied Maples, ibid.* at 1612C *per* Stuart-Smith L.J. (commenting on *Otter v. Church Adams Tatham* [1953] Ch. 280), but see also Millett L.J. in *Allied Maples, ibid.* at 1623H. An example of such a situation would be a claim by a director or shareholder who had control of the company whose accounts were audited by the defendant.

[26] In most cases it will not matter whether it is categorised under causation or quantum, as long as the parties know when it is to be argued if there is a split trial: see the cautionary tale of *Allied Maples, ibid.* at 1609, 1618–1619.

[27] *Allied Maples, ibid.* at 1614C said that the chance had to be "substantial", not "speculative", but in *Mount Barker v. Austin* [1998] P.N.L.R. 493, CA preferred the term "negligible" to "speculative". It is submitted that this is intended to be nothing more than a rough-and-ready way of saving the courts from becoming embroiled in fine-tuning the damages. The courts might take a different view if the alleged loss was (say) a 1% chance of £1 billion.

[28] *Mount Barker v. Austin, ibid.*

[29] Contrast the view of Stuart-Smith L.J. in *Allied Maple, ibid.* at 1614F with that of Millett L.J., *ibid.* at 1623D. A close examination of the evidence on the hypothetical question proved to be decisive in *Pearson v. Sanders Witherspoon* [2000] P.N.L.R. 110, CA (a solicitor's case).

[30] *Harrison v. Bloom Camillin (No. 1) and (No. 2)* [2000] Lloyd's Rep. P.N. 89 and 404, Neuberger J. (a claim against a solicitor for failing to prosecute a claim against accountants for a negligent report which persuaded the claimant to invest in a company).

[31] *Hanif v. Middleweeks*, unreported July 19, 2000, CA (a solicitor's case).

(5) The measure of damages is the amount recoverable if the hypothesis had been fulfilled multiplied by the percentage chance of it being fulfilled. Thus if a claimant has lost a 75 per cent chance of making a gain, or avoiding a loss, of £1 million, the damages would prima facie be £750,0000. If the claimant has lost the chance of being in position X instead of position Y, the measure of damages is prima facie $(X - Y)$ multiplied by the chance (or multiple chances).[32]

(c) *Heads of damage*

15–135   The losses which may result from breach of duty by accountants cover a wide variety. Certain types of losses are of frequent occurrence and are considered below. The discussion is far from definitive of the types of loss for which liability may be incurred and ultimately the appropriate measure of loss and the types of loss depend upon the facts of each case. In particular much will depend upon the nature of the relationship of the claimant to the defendant. In broad terms a distinction may be drawn between losses caused by negligent auditing and losses caused by other negligence of accountants.

(i) *Lost investment or advance*

15–136   Upon the insolvency of an enterprise, a person may fail to recover an investment made originally in reliance upon overstatement of the enterprise's financial position in an offer document or a report upon financial statements, for which an accountant is responsible. Provided entitlement to recovery against the accountant can be demonstrated, the normal measure of damages is the amount of the lost investment.[33] A like position prevails where a loan, as distinct from an equity investment, is made.[34] Credit must be given for any amount recovered upon distribution of any available assets of the enterprise among creditors.[35]

(ii) *Overpayment*

15–137   In consequence of negligent advice by an accountant, an investor may pay more for acquiring shares in a company than he would have done if proper advice or information had been given. In the latter event the usual measure of the damages recoverable against the accountant is the amount of the overpayment. The overpayment is to be calculated by comparing what would have been paid

---

[32] In *First Interstate Bank of California v. Cohen Arnold* [1996] P.N.L.R. 17, CA, the plaintiff bank was held to have lost a two in three chance of being able to sell a property for £3 million; it actually sold the property for £1.4 million. CA assessed damages at £600,000, *i.e.* (£3 million × 66%) less £1.4 million. It is submitted that the amount of damages should have been £1.066 million, *i.e.* (£3 million − £1.4 million) × 66%. The £1.4 million was a certainty: the lost chance related only to the excess of £1.6 million.

[33] *Candler v. Crane Christmas & Co* [1951] 2 K.B. 164 *per* Denning L.J. (discussed at para. 15–053 above); and *Haig v. Bamford* (1972) D.L.R. 68.

[34] See *A.G.C. (Advances) Ltd v. R. Lowe Lippman Figdor & Franck* (1990) 4 A.C.S.R. 337, S. Ct. of Victoria. Vincent J. awarded damages representing increased loans made following date of negligent certification of the relevant accounts by the defendant auditors; a claim in respect of loans made earlier, consisting of alleged recoveries that would have been effected by an earlier receivership of liquidation of the audited company, failed. Note also *Al Saudi Banque v. Clark Pixley* [1990] 1 Ch. 313, 338.

[35] Note *Colmer v. Merrett, Son and Street* (1914) 50 Acct. L.R. 21.

for the shares if proper advice or information had been given, with what was actually paid. Unless it can be shown that in the latter events the value of the shares would have been calculated by simple deduction of the company's liabilities from its assets, that method of calculation is usually not appropriate for assessing the overpayment. A number of contingencies may need to be taken into account, *e.g.* the investor may have been prepared to pay more for the shares than their net asset backing.[36]

(iii) *Moneys wrongly paid out*

Where in consequence of the negligence of the auditors of a company its **15–138** shareholders are induced to vote for dividends which would not have been voted if the auditors had properly discharged their duty, since it would have entailed payment of dividend from capital, the normal measure of damages recoverable by the company from the auditors is the amount of the dividend wrongly paid out.[37] Similarly bonuses to directors, wrongly paid out in consequence of negligently audited accounts falsely showing profits to have been made, have been held to be recoverable from auditors.[38] However, as we have seen,[39] continued trading losses are usually excluded either on causation grounds or on the ground that they fall outside the scope of the duty of care; but they may be recoverable where they are a continuation of the very wrongdoing which the auditor ought to have discovered and reported.

(iv) *Defalcations by director or employee*

Where owing to an accountant (or auditor's) negligence the defalcations of a **15–139** director or employee remain undiscovered for longer than should have been the case, the normal measure of damages recoverable against the accountant is so much of the loss as would have been avoided (whether by prevention of further defalcations or by recovery from the director or employee) given competence on the part of the accountant.[40]

---

[36] *e.g.* see *Dimond Manufacturing Co. Ltd v. Hamilton* [1969] N.Z.L.R. 609, 645; *Scott Group Ltd v. McFarlane* [1978] 1 N.Z.L.R. 553, 576–580 and 582–589. If these facts were to arise today within England and Wales, it is likely that the courts would apply the "loss of a chance" principle: see para. 15–133 above.

[37] See *Leeds Estate Building and Investment Co. v. Shepherd* (1887) 36 Ch.D. 787; *Re London and General Bank (No. 2)* [1985] 2 Ch. 673; *Re Westminster Road Construction and Engineering Co. Ltd* (1932) Acct. L.R. 38; *Re Thomas Gerrard & Son Ltd* [1968] Ch. 455 (in this case the auditors were also held liable for the costs of recovering excessive tax paid but not recovered in respect of the non-existent profits); *Sasea Finance Ltd v. KPMG* [2000] 1 All E.R. 676. See also *Segenhoe Ltd v. Akins* (1990) 1 A.C.S.R. 691, S. Ct. of N.S.W., Giles J., where the above text in a previous edition of this book was referred to (*ibid.* at 701). Note *Galoo Ltd v. Bright Grahame Murray* [1994] 1 W.L.R. 136: the claim for the amount of £500,000 dividend (*ibid.* at 1368) appears to have been overlooked and, it is submitted, wrongly struck out. (This sentence was approved by Collins J. in *Sasea Finance Ltd v. KPMG, The Times*, August 25, 1998; the judgment was reversed but not on this point: [2000] 1 All E.R. 676.)

[38] See *Leeds Estate, Building and Investment Co. v. Shepherd* (1887) 36 Ch.D. 787; *Re Westminster Road Construction and Engineering Co. Ltd* (1932) Acct. L.R. 38

[39] See paras 15–121 *et seq.* above.

[40] See *Fox v. Morrish, Grant and Co.* (1918) T.L.R. 126; *Armitage v. Brewer and Knott* (1932) 77 Acct. L.R. 25; *McBride's Ltd v. Rooke and Thomas* [1941] 4 D.L.R. 45; *Revelstoke Credit Union v. Miller* (1984) 28 C.C.L.T. 17.

(v) *Costs of fresh audit and investigations*

15–140   When consequent upon an auditor's negligence, a fresh audit or an investigation is necessary, the costs thereof together with any incidental but necessary legal expenses may be recovered in damages against the auditor.[41]

(vi) *Avoidance of double recovery*

15–141   The law has been comprehensively reviewed by the House of Lords in *Johnson v. Gore Wood*,[42] from which the following principles emerge:

(1) In many cases the cause of action (if any) will be vested in the company alone and not in its shareholders.[43] There may be other cases in which the cause of action (if any) is vested in the shareholders and not the company[44]: in those cases the shareholders may sue for their own loss, measured by the diminution in value of their shareholding. In neither of these two categories is there any problem of double recovery.

(2) However, there are cases in which duties are owed both to the company and to its shareholders, and in which both suffer loss. In such cases the shareholders are not permitted to sue for diminution in the value of their shares or for loss of dividends, since this merely reflects the loss suffered by the company. Protection of the interests of creditors requires that the company is allowed to recover to the exclusion of the shareholders.

(3) Nevertheless, a shareholder is permitted to sue for any loss which is suffered by him personally if this is additional to any loss suffered by the company, since in such a case there is no problem of double recovery.

15–142   It was held to be arguable (this being an application to strike out) that the following heads of loss were recoverable by the shareholder: sums invested in the company and lost; the cost of personal borrowings (in principle recoverable, provided that this was not a disguised claim for loss of dividend); loss of shares which were transferred to a lender as security for the personal borrowing; and additional tax liability of the shareholder. However a claim to diminution in the value of his pension was struck out, in so far as it related to payments which the company would have made into a pension fund for the shareholder, on the ground that this was merely a reflection of the company's loss.[45] The principles set out

---

[41] See *Toromont Industries Holdings Ltd v. Thorne, Gunn, Helliwell & Christenson* (1976) 73 D.L.R. (3d) 122.

[42] [2001] 2 W.L.R. 72; [2000] U.K.H.L. 65. In this case a solicitor was negligent in acting for a company on exercise of an option; the company sued but compromised its claim, leaving open the possibility of claim by its director, who then sued the solicitor. HL held that the second action was not an abuse of process in the particular circumstances and that in principle the director could sue for any loss which was not merely a reflection of the company's loss. (For a fuller account of this case, see Chap. 10, para. 10–300)

[43] *Caparo Industries plc v. Dickman* [1990] 2 A.C. 605; and see para. 15–074 above.

[44] *e.g.* where the accountant has assumed a responsibility directly towards an investor.

[45] The House of Lords, by a majority, also struck out a claim for damages for mental distress on the ground that such damages were irrecoverable under a commercial contract. This is likely to apply *a fortiori* to a claim against an accountant.

above have been applied to a claim by an employee of a company[46] and ought in principle to apply equally to claims by other third parties.

(vii) *Tax advice and returns*

Negligent tax advice by an accountant may result in a client paying more in tax **15–143** than would have been paid given competent advice. In that event the normal measure of damages is the excess tax paid together with interest thereon.[47] On the other hand, negligence by an accountant may result in tax being paid later than due and the client incurring penalties for late payment. In that event the amount of the penalties are recoverable from the accountant, but credit must be given for the benefit of the use of the amount of the tax due between the time when it was properly payable and when it was in fact paid.[48]

(viii) *Late notices and returns*

A frequent basis of claim against accountants is late filing of notices, elec- **15–144** tions[49] or returns in consequence of which losses are caused to their clients consisting of lost benefits[50] or higher incidence of tax.

(ix) *Negligent advice*

Accountants sometimes give legal or general business advice. Where such **15–145** advice is negligent and the negligence causes loss, damages are quantified in a similar way to claims against solicitors.[51]

(d) *Contributory negligence and contribution proceedings*

General. Contributory negligence is a defence provided by statute[52] which **15–146** enables the court to reduce the damages otherwise due from the defendant, based on the share of the claimant in the responsibility for the damage. The precise

---

[46] *Giles v. Rhind*, unreported July 24, 2001, Blackburne J.

[47] *e.g. Walker v. Hungerfords* (1987) 19 A.T.R. 745, S. Ct of S. Aus., Full Court. Note also the Australian case of *Jindi (Nominees) Ltd v. Dutney* (1993) 26 A.T.R. 206. Owing to the negligence of the defendant accountants in regard to the manner that they acquired shares in company, the plaintiffs were compelled to delay acceptance of a take-over offer for the shares and consequent receipt of the proceeds in order to avoid a liability to tax on the profits from sale of the shares within 12 months of acquisition. Damages were assessed on the basis of interest referable to lost use of the proceeds during the period of delayed receipt, net of tax on the interest.

[48] *e.g.* the Australian case of *Pech v. Tilgals* (1994) 28 A.T.R. 197, esp. at 206–208. See also *Bloor Italian Gifts Ltd v. Dixon* (2000) 48 O.R. (3d) 760, Ontario CA.

[49] *e.g.* a partnership continuation election under s.113(2), Income and Corporation Taxes Act 1988.

[50] *e.g.* in the Canadian case of *Murray Bourne Dyck v. FMA Farm Management Associates Ltd* (1996) 3 W.W.R. 509.

[51] See generally Chap. 10. A recent example is *Punsford v. Gilberts* [1998] P.N.L.R. 763, CA, where an accountant advised a testator on the drafting of a will. It was held that he owed no duty to a beneficiary to advise the testator against making a subsequent gift which caused the bequest to that beneficiary to adeem.

[52] Law Reform (Contributory Negligence) Act 1945. See further, Chap. 4.

reduction will depend on the facts of the particular case. The defence is frequently advanced on behalf of accountants in claims against them.[53] It has been held that the defence is available, not merely where the contributory negligence prevented or hindered an auditor from carrying out his own duties, but also where the claimant failed generally to look after its own interests.[54] As in any professional negligence claim, the standard expected of the claimant will depend upon the factual matrix, in particular the claimant's level of experience and understanding, the accountant's reasonable perception of the same and the scope of the accountant's retainer.[55]

15–147 Contribution is not a defence but a right conferred by statute[56] upon a defendant, D1, to recover a proportion of the damages for which he is liable to C, from other persons, D2, D3 etc., each of whom is also liable to C in respect of the same damage,[57] based on that other person's share in the responsibility for the damage; while each of D1, D2 and D3 is liable to the C, as between themselves the damages are shared as appropriate, *e.g.* a third each. Thus an auditor sued by a company may claim contribution from its directors based on breach of duties owed by the directors to the company.[58]

---

[53] *e.g. De Meza v. Apple* [1975] 1 Lloyd's Rep. 498 (damages reduced by 30%); but see *Henderson v. Merrett Syndicates Ltd* [1996] P.N.L.R. 32, where Cresswell J. held the negligence of the Names' agents was not to be attributed to the Names or, alternatively, that it was not just and equitable that the damages should be reduced having regard to the Names' share in the responsibility for the damage. In the Australian case of *Pech v. Tilgals* (1994) 28 A.T.R. 197, the claim against the defendant accountants for negligent failure to prepare and complete accurate income tax returns was reduced by 20% for contributory negligence on account of the plaintiff's failure to read tax returns before signing them and to check their accuracy. The Australian cases of *Daniels v. Anderson* and *Duke Group Ltd v. Pilmer* and the New Zealand case of *Dairy Containers v. NZI Ltd* are considered in para. 15–149 *et seq.* below; see also *Mirage Entertainment Corp. Ltd v. Arthur Young* (1992) 6 N.Z.C.L.C. 68, 213 (negligence by auditors in valuing assets: wrong accounting methodology; reduction of 40%). See also the following Canadian cases: *West Coast Finance Ltd v. Gunderson, Stokes, Walton & Co.* (1974) 44 D.L.R. (3d) 233 (50% reduction, but finding of liability reversed on appeal: (1975) 56 D.L.R. 461); *H. E. Kane Agencies Ltd v. Coopers & Lybrand* (1983) 23 C.C.L.T. 233, (1985) 17 D.L.R. (4th) 695 (50% reduction); *Revelstoke Credit Union v. Miller* (1984) 28 C.C.L.T. 17, (1984) 2 W.W.R. 297 (15% reduction); and *Bloor Italian Gifts Ltd v. Dixon* (2000) 48 O.R. (3d) 760 (50% reduction).

[54] In other words, the contributory negligence does not need to be causally connected to the Defendant's negligence; it is sufficient that it is a cause of the same damage: *Dairy Containers Ltd v. NZI Bank Ltd* [1995] 2 N.Z.L.R. 30, 74; see also *Platform Home Loans Ltd v. Oyston Shipways Ltd* [2000] 2 A.C. 195, 215 *per* Lord Millett (a valuer's case).

[55] Contrast *De Meza v. Apple* [1975] 1 Lloyd's Rep. 498 (court reduced damages by 30% because client should have noticed an obvious arithmetical error) with *Walker v. Hungerfords* (1987) 44 S.A.S.R. 532, 553–554, Bollen J., upheld on appeal: 19 A.T.R. 745, 747, S. Ct of S. Aus., Full Court (no reduction for arithmetical error made by clerk employed by company, since it was reasonable for him to assume that any errors would be checked by the accountant.) See also *Craig v. Troy* (1997) 16 W.A.R. 96, S. Ct. of W. Aus. (no contributory negligence where accountant informed client of relevant facts but failed to explain their significance).

[56] Civil Liability (Contribution) Act 1978. See further, Chap. 4.

[57] In *Eastgate Group Ltd v. Lindsey Morden Group Inc.*, [2001] EWCA Civ 1446, CA, it was held that a claim against the vendor of shares for breach of warranty was a claim for the "same damage" as a claim against accountants for negligent advice.

[58] An auditor sued by a company may claim contribution from its directors based on breach of (a) a duty of care owed by the directors to him and (b) duties owed by the directors to the company. In an Australian case, *Employers Corporate Investments Pty Ltd v. Cameron* (1977) 3 A.C.L.R. 120 in which auditors were sued by a company for negligence in failing to discover a fraud by the company's employee, the court refused to strike out cross-claims by the auditors against its directors based on (a) alleged breach of duties by the directors to the plaintiff company, *i.e.* a statutory contribution claim and (b) alleged breach of a duty of care owed by the directors to them as auditors. *Cf.* as to (b), *Dominion Freeholders Ltd v. Aird* (1966) 67 S.R. (N.S.W.) 150. In a Canadian case,

Claims against auditors. Three issues merit consideration in relation to **15–148**
claims against auditors for failing to discover or report on fraud by officers of the
company:

(1) Does the auditor's role as watchdog mean that he is responsible for
   detecting the fraud of the company's officers and cannot therefore plead
   that the fraud caused or contributed to the company's loss? One view is
   that the auditor is appointed as a watchdog and that it is his responsibility
   to check on the officers of the company; if he were allowed to avoid or
   reduce his liability on the ground of the fraud of the company through its
   officers, this would negate the very purpose of the audit.[59] The countervailing argument is that, especially given modern corporate structures, it
   is unrealistic to regard auditors as the sole watchdogs. Proper accounting
   is primarily the responsibility of the directors and management of a
   company.[60] It is submitted that the latter argument is to be preferred.
   Indeed, it is arguable that, in relation to claims against auditors, there
   needs to be greater judicial perception of the role and responsibility of
   the directors and senior management of sophisticated corporate organisations, and to corporate governance generally, in avoiding the kind of
   mishaps which are often blamed on auditors. Such a perception may lead
   to substantial reduction of damages awards against company auditors on
   account of contributory negligence.

(2) Is it possible to separate the company from those who control it so as to
   characterise the company as victim rather than wrongdoer? This issue
   arises as a result of the principle that a company is a separate legal
   person. Clearly if the fraud had been committed by an individual client
   he would fail as a matter of causation in his claim against the auditor. By
   the same token, a solvent one-man company controlled by a fraudster
   should not be able to recover damages for the negligence of the auditor
   in failing to spot the controlling director's fraud. But the position is less
   clear-cut where there are innocent shareholders who would otherwise
   suffer for the fraud of the directors, or where the directors and shareholders are all fraudulent but the company is insolvent and there are
   innocent creditors whose only recourse is through a claim by the liquidator. If one took to its logical conclusion the principle that a company

---

Harvey Credit Union Ltd v. G. H. Ward & Partners (1981) 15 B.L.R. 307, the court also refused to
strike out a statutory contribution claim against the plaintiff company's directors based on alleged
breach of duties by the directors to the company.

[59] This was the view of Moffitt J. in *Pacific Acceptance Corporation Ltd v. Forsyth* [1970] 92 W.N.
(N.S.W.) 29, 125. This view was repeated by him in *Simonius Vischer & Co. v. Holt Thompson* [1979]
2 N.S.W.L.R. 322, 329–330 (one of the other judges in that case doubted the availability of the
defence and the third judge left the point open). See also paras 15–126 and 15–130 above.

[60] *Nelson Guarantee Corporation Ltd v. Hodgson* [1958] N.Z.L.R. 609, McCarthy J. (*obiter*); *Daniels
v. Anderson* (1995) 13 A.C.S.R. 607, 721, CA of N.S.W.; and *Dairy Containers Ltd v. NZI Bank Ltd*,
Thomas J. [1995] 2 N.Z.L.R. 30, 74–76. (In this last case Thomas J. took the view that the difficulties
which had motivated other judges to restrict the defence of contributory negligence in other cases
could be readily accommodated in the exercise of apportioning responsibility. He recognised that
balancing the various factors might in many cases result in a nil or negligible assessment of
contributory negligence. In the context of the particular case, however, he considered it "wrong in
principle if the Auditor-General could be sued for failing to report the unauthorised investments and
detect the frauds which occurred and yet not be able to rely upon DCL's own acts which permitted
the unauthorised investments and frauds to occur in the first place.")

is a separate legal entity, it would not be possible to distinguish between these different cases. Fortunately, however, the courts have not shut their eyes to the commercial reality, as distinct from the strict legal position.

(3) If it is proper to take account of the fraud of the company's officers, should this be done by way of contributory negligence or by way of contribution proceedings or both? There is an obvious need to avoid double-counting. In some cases the same acts or omissions of the officer in question might be relied on by the defendant, either to found a defence of contributory negligence against the company or to claim contribution from that officer. In order to prevent double-counting, the Australian court has refused to allow contribution proceedings on the ground that it would not be just and equitable to do so.[61] It has also been held that a defendant is not permitted to elect between the two courses of action. Contributory negligence should logically be considered before contribution proceedings.[62]

Although there is a dearth of English authority, these issues have been considered at length in a number of seminal decisions in Australia and New Zealand.

15–149   In *Daniels v. Anderson*[63] it was held that the question whether an auditor could plead contributory negligence was a matter of construction of the statute, which simply required an inquiry into the fault of the plaintiff and, upon findings that such fault existed and was causative of the damage, a determination of apportionment based on what was just and reasonable. The statute did not exclude apportionment in claims against auditors and there was therefore no basis for a legal rule disentitling them from relying on the statute. Where an employee steals from the company, it may be difficult for the auditor to show contributory negligence by the company, but the auditor's difficulty in that case is one of fact, not law. By contrast, where the officers are at fault and this materially contributes to the loss suffered, the auditor is prima facie entitled to have that fault brought into account. As regards attribution, it was said that the acts of the wrongdoing officers should be attributed to the company in those cases in which the company would be held vicariously liable to a third party for the acts in question: hence the distinction between the case where an employee commits theft outside the scope of his employment and the case where the fraud is perpetrated by the officers within the scope of their employment. The court concluded that the management of the company was negligent in disregarding advice it was given, in failing to set up or implement proper management and control structures and in failing to keep proper records, that the chief executive was negligent in failing to heed warnings he was given about weaknesses in the system and that the board of directors was negligent in failing to lay down a policy to be followed by the management and in failing to set up or implement a proper system of reporting

---

[61] *Daniels v. Anderson* (1995) 16 A.C.S.R. 607, 734–735, approving Glanville Williams' *Joint Torts and Contributory Negligence* at 446.
[62] *Dairy Containers Ltd v. NZI Bank Ltd* [1995] 2 N.Z.L.R. 30, 86. This was based on *Fitzgerald v. Lane* [1989] A.C. 328, 338–9 and 345D–E, HL. See also *Daniels v. Anderson, ibid.* at 735.
[63] (1995) 16 A.C.S.R. 607, 720–733, CA of N.S.W. The relevant statute in New South Wales is modelled on the Law Reform (Contributory Negligence) Act 1945.

by the management to the board. It was held that the negligence should be attributed to the company. Nevertheless the auditor's negligence was of a higher order. He knew that there were no internal controls in existence, that the records were a shambles, and that no steps had been taken to rectify these defects. In the circumstances the court reduced the damages by one third for contributory negligence, but indicated that it would have made a bigger reduction, but for the fact that the auditor had compounded his original negligence by signing an unqualified certificate and by failing at a subsequent board meeting to draw attention to the inadequacies of the system.

In *Dairy Containers Ltd v. NZI Bank Ltd*[64] the plaintiff company was the **15–150** victim of fraudulent diversion of funds by senior executives. The company sued the banks into which the money had been paid and also sued the Auditor-General who audited the company's accounts. The defendants were held liable but were successful in substantially reducing damages for contributory negligence.[65] Thomas J. held that the directors had failed in their primary duty to monitor the business and management of the company. Although they were entitled to delegate to the executives, it was they alone who were ultimately responsible for the management of the company.[66] He held that the directors had abdicated that responsibility and thereby created an environment in which fraud could thrive. Damages payable by the Auditor-General were reduced by 40 per cent for contributory negligence.

In *Duke Group Ltd v. Pilmer*[67] the claim was brought by a company in **15–151** liquidation (formerly known as "KO") against its accountant for negligence arising out of the takeover by KO of another company ("WAL"). The directors of KO were also directors of WAL. The rules of the Australian stock exchange required that a general meeting of KO be held and that a report be circulated from an independent qualified person stating that the proposed price was fair. The report was given by the defendant, who overvalued the shares. The defendant was sued but claimed that the company was contributorily negligent, in that its board of directors knew that the shares were overvalued and knew that the information which it provided to the accountant for the purpose of the valuation was incorrect. The court held that the company, through its directors, was at fault in two respects: firstly in knowingly providing unreliable information to the accountant for the purpose of the valuation, even though it was the expert's duty to check that information, and secondly in accepting a valuation when the directors, being sophisticated businessmen, must have known that it was wrong. The court then considered whether it was right to attribute the knowledge of the directors to the company. The directors should prima facie be considered as the "directing mind and will" of the company for the purpose of the rule relating to

---

[64] [1995] 2 N.Z.L.R. 30.

[65] It was conceded by the Auditor-General that the activities of the fraudster, being patently outside the scope of his employment, should not be attributed to the company, but it was argued that the company through each of the officers was contributorily negligent in failing to report the frauds of the other officers. Thomas J. dismissed this argument as artificial, given that the activities of all the executives in question constituted a programme for fraudulently milking the company (*ibid.* at 77–78). This reasoning has been criticised by Bartlett [1998] 114 L.Q.R. 460, 473–474, as being inconsistent with *Lloyd v. Grace Smith & Co.* [1912] A.C. 716.

[66] *ibid.* at 79–80.

[67] (1999) 31 A.C.S.R. 213, 326–336, S. Ct. of S. Aus., Full Court (see also at first instance: (1994) 27 A.C.S.R. 1, 339).

contributory negligence.[68] However that was not the end of the matter. On the one hand there is a line of authority which suggests that a principal should be insulated from the knowledge of his fraudulent agent where the principal is the victim of the agent's fraud.[69] On the other hand there is also a line of authority which holds that a principal is vicariously liable for the fraud of his agent committed within the course of his employment.[70] The court concluded that the first line of authority was concerned only with attribution of knowledge, whereas the second was concerned with attribution of liability in cases where knowledge was irrelevant. The court applied the second line of authority and held the company contributorily negligent for the acts and omissions of its directors. Damages were reduced by 35 per cent.

(e) *Failure to mitigate*

15–152   The usual principles of mitigation apply to claims against accountants.[71] In particular: the claimant is under a duty to take reasonable steps to mitigate his loss; the burden of proving failure to mitigate lies on the defendant; but the court will not impose a high standard of reasonableness on the claimant. These principles have been applied in relation to auditors in an Australian case[72] in which the company paid out a dividend in reliance on a negligent audit certificate. The Court held that the company's duty to mitigate did not require it to bring uncertain litigation against the shareholders for the recovery of the dividend.

(f) *Statutory relief*

15–153   An auditor may seek relief from liability under section 727 of the Companies Act 1985 although it would seem that such relief is available only in respect of a claim against him by or on behalf of or for the benefit of the company.[73] Relief is neither a defence nor a right, but a discretionary power given to the court in proceedings against the auditor of a company (whether or not also an officer of the company) for negligence, default, breach of duty or breach of trust, to relieve

---

[68] The court based this part of its decision on *Meridian Global Asset Funds Management Asia Ltd v. Securities Commission* [1995] 2 A.C. 500. The issue in that case was whether the defendant company was in breach of a statutory duty to give notice to the Securities Commission of a transaction which its chief investment officer had procured that it enter into without the knowledge of the board. The Privy Council had to consider whether the officer of the company who was responsible for the wrongdoing in question could properly be described as the "directing mind and will" of the company so as to attribute his knowledge to the company. Lord Hoffmann said that the question could not be answered without first considering the context in which it was asked. An officer may be the directing mind and will in relation to a particular transaction for some purposes but not others.
[69] *Belmont Finance Co. v. Williams Furniture Ltd* [1979] Ch. 250, CA.
[70] *Lloyd v. Grace Smith & Co.* [1912] A.C. 716.
[71] See *McGregor on Damages* (16th ed.), paras 282–356.
[72] *Segenhoe Ltd v. Akins* (1990) 1 A.C.S.R. 691, S. Ct of N.S.W. Giles J. considered it to be a matter of doubt whether a company could recover dividends paid out of capital which were innocently received by the shareholders. He therefore applied the principle in *Pilkington v. Wood* [1953] Ch. 770, Harman J., that the duty to mitigate did not require the plaintiff to embark on a complicated and difficult piece of litigation against a third party, even under an indemnity. (It is submitted that that the dictum that the plaintiff is not required to sue even under an indemnity is too widely stated.)
[73] *Customs and Excise Commissioners v. Hedon Alpha Ltd* [1981] 2 All E.R. 697, CA. See also *Dimond Manufacturing Co. Ltd v. Hamilton* [1969] N.Z.L.R. 609, 645, CA of N.Z., and *Jagwar Holdings Ltd v. Julian* (1992) 6 N.Z.C.L.C. 68,041 at 68,070.

him wholly or partly from his liability on such terms as the court thinks fit, if certain criteria are satisfied. These are that, if in the opinion of the court, the auditor has acted honestly and reasonably and that, having regard to all the circumstances of the case, including those of his appointment, he ought fairly to be excused.[74] The requirement of reasonableness means that this defence is unlikely to be available in many cases of professional negligence.[75] It has been held in Australia that the word "reasonably" is not limited in its area of operation to circumstances connected with the discharge of the auditor's duty, but that the court may take into account his conduct after the breach of duty including his conduct in defending the claim against them.[76] There is a difference of opinion in Australia as to whether the negligence of the directors is a relevant factor in relieving the auditor from liability.[77] It is submitted that the question whether the auditor acted honestly and reasonably should be considered by focussing solely on his own acts and omissions, against the background of all the circumstances of the case[78]; however, if the auditor surmounts this hurdle, the court is given a wide discretion in considering whether he ought fairly to be excused. The court is required to consider all the circumstances, which ought surely to include the conduct of the directors.

---

[74] This section reflects similar protection given to trustees; see Trustee Act 1925, s.61. In *Re Duomatic* [1969] 2 Ch. 365, the Companies Act 1948, s.448, the predecessor provision to the Companies Act 1985, s.727, was considered in relation to a director. In *Re D'Jan of London Ltd* [1994] 1 B.C.L.C. 561, Hoffmann L.J. granted relief under s.727 to a director.

[75] *Dimond Manufacturing Co. Ltd v. Hamilton* [1969] N.Z.L.R. 609, NZCA. The Court, while recognising that the section could be invoked even in the case of negligence, considered that there would not be many cases where a negligent auditor could be said to have acted reasonably.

[76] *Pacific Acceptance Corporation Ltd v. Forsyth* (1970) 92 N.S.W. (W.N.) 29, Moffitt J.: for the facts see para. 15–097 above. It is submitted that the better approach is to bring subsequent conduct into account, not in relation to reasonableness, but in considering whether the auditor ought fairly to be excused.

[77] In *Pacific Acceptance, ibid.*, Moffitt J. said that it was irrelevant; however in *AWA Ltd v. Daniels* (1992) 7 A.C.S.R. 759, 854–856 Rogers J. said that the section was an appropriate provision for allocation of fault. He added that, if he were wrong in his view that the defence of contributory negligence was available to the defendant auditors the same facts would enliven the operation of the provisions of the section. (On appeal the C.A. of N.Z. quoted Rogers J.'s view but found it unnecessary to decide the question: *Daniels v. Anderson* (1995) 16 A.C.S.R. 607, 685–686.)

[78] This may include the fact that fraud on the part of the directors is frequently more difficult to detect than negligence: see para. 15–095 above.

CHAPTER 16

MEMBERS' AND MANAGING AGENTS AT LLOYD'S

	PARA.
1. General	16–001
(a) Lloyd's of London	16–001
(i) The old regime	16–004
(ii) The current regime	16–006
(iii) Regulation	16–007
(iv) The LMX spiral in the 1980s	16–009
(b) Duties to client	16–010
(i) Contractual duties	16–010
(ii) Duties independent of contract	16–012
(iii) Fiduciary duties	16–015
(c) Duties to third parties	16–016
2. The standard of care	16–020
3. Liability for breach of duty	16–023
(a) Members' agent—failure to advise adequately as to syndicate participation	16–025
(b) Managing agent—failure to plan properly	16–030
(c) Managing agent—unjustified departure from plan	16–037
(d) Managing agent—failure to obtain adequate reinsurance	16–038
(i) Deciding what reinsurance cover to seek	16–039
(ii) Choosing the reinsurer	16–046
(iii) Maintaining commercial viability	16–050

	PARA.
(iv) Obtaining valid reinsurance	16–052
(e) Managing agent—negligent underwriting of individual risks	16–053
(f) Managing agent—inadequate supervision of active underwriter	16–057
(g) Managing agent—negligence in relation to reinsurance to close	16–058
4. Damages	16–060
(a) Remoteness	16–061
(b) Causation	16–062
(i) Members' agent—consequences of failure to advise adequately as to syndicate participation	16–063
(ii) Losses caused by negligent underwriting	16–067
(c) Foreseeability	16–071
(d) Measure of damages	16–072
(i) Members' agents—consequences of failure to advise adequately as to syndicate participation	16–073
(ii) Losses caused by negligent underwriting	16–077

1. GENERAL

(a) *Lloyd's of London*

The Society of Lloyd's is the cornerstone of the London insurance market. It is established and regulated by the Lloyd's Act 1982 and byelaws made under that Act from time to time.[1] It is also regulated by the Financial Services and Markets Act 2000 and the rules and regulations made by the Financial Services Authority.[2] **16–001**

Lloyd's is not itself an insurer: the insurers in Lloyd's are a multitude of individuals known as Names, each Name writing insurance for himself but not **16–002**

---

[1] See generally *Lloyd's Acts, Byelaws and Regulations*, (Lloyd's of London Press Ltd, 1991).
[2] See further para. 16–007 below, chap. 136 paras 13–011 *et seq.*, and see generally Lomnicka and Powell, *Encyclopaedia of Financial Services Law*.

for the others (so that liability is several and not joint).[3] It would be impossible for each Name to enter each insurance contract and deal with each claim on his own behalf. Save to the extent that they are themselves actively involved in underwriting at Lloyd's, Names act through agents. It is with the duties and liabilities of those agents that this chapter is concerned. Names are members of a number of syndicates. They join for particular years of account, covering all business written in a particular year. After three years a year of account will be closed, if appropriate,[4] usually by reinsuring the liabilities of that year into the next year of account of the same syndicate. The Names making up each syndicate and the size of their lines on each syndicate will vary from year to year.

16–003   The spate of litigation in the early 1990s concerning Lloyd's largely related to events in the 1980s, since when there have been significant changes to the way in which business is conducted at Lloyd's. It is therefore convenient to describe both the regime in the 1980s and the current framework.

(i) *The Old Regime*

16–004   Traditionally Names undertook unlimited personal liability. Upon joining Lloyd's Names who were not themselves underwriting agents had to appoint a members' agent to act for them, either in person or through sub-agents.[5] The relationship between a Name and a members' agent was contractual. Before January 1, 1987 there was no prescribed form of contract, but in practice standard forms of agreement were used.[6] Thereafter agreements had to conform with the Agency Agreements Byelaw (No.1 of 1985).[7] These agreements are considered further below.[8] Members' agents would place Names on one or more syndicates for each year of account.

16–005   Each syndicate had one or more active underwriters, who did the actual underwriting. The active underwriters were employed by an agency which managed the syndicate's affairs.[9] These agencies either concerned themselves solely with the management of underwriting, in which case they were known as managing agents, or acted as members' agents as well, in which case they are known as combined agents. The agreements between Names and members' agents gave the members' agents the power to conduct underwriting on their

---

[3] For a summary of the operation of the Lloyd's market and the structure of Lloyd's, see *Society of Lloyd's v. Clemston* [1997] L.R.L.R. 175 at 188–189, Cresswell J. Lloyd's does not owe syndicate members a contractual or statutory or common law duty to regulate the market with reasonable skill and care, see *Price and Price v. Society of Lloyd's* [2000] Lloyd's Rep.I.R. 453, Colman J.

[4] This is discussed in detail in paras 16–058 and 16–059, below.

[5] The role of a members' agent is discussed in para. 16–010, below.

[6] *Henderson v. Merrett Syndicates Ltd* [1995] 2 A.C. 145 at 171A-C. Some of the provisions are set out in the speech of Lord Goff at 175B-H. The full terms are set out in the appendices to the judgment of Saville J. in *Henderson v. Merrett* at first instance (reported as *The Lloyd's Litigation* [1994] 2 Lloyd's Rep. 193; the agreement appears at 202–210).

[7] Set out at [1994] 2 Lloyd's Rep. 211–226.

[8] See para. 16–010.

[9] A syndicate's core functions are to enter contracts of insurance (including reinsurance), whether directly or through agents, decide upon and implement a reinsurance programme, deal with claims, invest premiums and to consider whether and on what terms the year of account can be reinsured to close. The managing agent is also responsible for maintaining the syndicate's records and preparing its annual audited accounts. See *Society of Lloyd's v. Clemston* [1997] L.R.L.R. 175 at 188–189, Cresswell J.

behalf. This power was either exercised by the members' agents themselves, if they were combined agents, or delegated to managing agents.[10] Where the members' agent was also the managing agent names were known as "direct Names". Where the members' agent entered into a sub-agency agreement with a managing agent they were known as "indirect Names".[11]

(ii) *The current regime*[12]

Since 1990 agreements between Names and members' agents have been governed by Lloyd's byelaw No. 8 of 1988, the Agency Agreements Byelaw, which prescribes new standard forms for use from January 1, 1990. This byelaw removed the distinction between indirect and direct Names. A Name contracts with both his members' agent[13] and directly with the managing agent of each syndicate of which he is a member.[14] His members' agent enters a separate contract with each managing agent.[15] One significant effect of the new contractual arrangements is that the members' agents no longer assume responsibility for underwriting conducted by managing agents pursuant to sub-agency agreements.[16]   **16–006**

(iii) *Regulation*

Lloyd's is regulated by the Lloyd's Act 1982 and the many byelaws made under it by the Council of Lloyd's. It is also regulated by the Financial Services and Markets Act 2000,[17] and the rules and regulations made under it by the Financial Services Authority. The rules made by the FSA are contained within the Lloyd's sourcebook, which is one of the specialist sourcebooks that are part of the FSA's Handbook. The Lloyd's sourcebook contains rules which require the Society to make appropriate byelaws regarding a number of issues.[18]   **16–007**

It is not only the Society that is regulated by the rules and regulations made by the FSA pursuant to the Financial Services and Markets Act 2000. By section 19 of the Act, no person may carry on a "regulated activity" unless he is either an authorised person or an exempt person. The typical activities of members' and   **16–008**

---

[10] A sample sub-agency agreement is appended to the judgment of Saville J. in *The Lloyd's Litigation* [1994] 2 Lloyd's 193 at 208–210.

[11] See *Henderson v. Merrett Syndicates Ltd* [1995] 2 A.C. 145 at 170–171 *per* Lord Goff.

[12] See generally *Lloyd's Acts, Byelaws and Regulations* (Lloyd's of London Press Ltd, 1991).

[13] In the form set out in Sched. 1 to the Agency Agreements Byelaw.

[14] In the form set out in Sched. 3 to the Agency Agreements Byelaw.

[15] In the form set out in Sched. 2 to the Agency Agreements Byelaw.

[16] *The Lloyd's Litigation* [1994] 2 Lloyd's Rep. 193 at 201–202 *per* Saville J. and *Deeny v. Gooda Walker Ltd* [1996] L.R.L.R. 183, at 186 per Phillips J. Both judges were speaking *obiter.*

[17] See Part XIX of the Act (ss. 314–324) which sets out the extent to which the Society of Lloyd's is subject to the general provisions of the Act. By section 315 the Society of Lloyd's is deemed to be an authorised person for the purposes of the Act and is given permission to carry on the regulated activities set out in s.315(2).

[18] For example, r. 4.2.1 requires the Society to make appropriate byelaws governing conduct in the capacity transfer market (*i.e.* any method of transferring capacity in Lloyd's syndicates), and r. 8.2.1 requires the Society to maintain byelaws establishing appropriate arrangements to compensate Names if underwriting agents are unable to satisfy claims made against them by those Names. Breach of the rules contained within the Lloyd's sourcebook does not give rise to a right of action for damages: see Sched. 5 to the Lloyd's sourcebook.

managing agents are regulated activities.[19] Accordingly, members' and managing agents must be authorised and comply with the regulatory regime established under the Act. In particular they must comply with the applicable rules set out in the FSA's Conduct of Business Sourcebook. Chapter 12 of that sourcebook sets out the extent to which the conduct of business rules apply to certain activities at Lloyd's.[20] Pursuant to section 150 of the Act, a breach of the rules may be actionable at the suit of a private person[21] who suffers loss as a result of that breach, subject to the defences and other incidents applying to actions for breach of statutory duty.

(iv) The LMX spiral in the 1980's

16–009   The litigation in the early 1990s concerning Lloyd's largely, if not exclusively, concerned losses suffered as a result of having underwritten London Market excess of loss ("LMX") business in the late 1980s. By excess of loss reinsurance ("XL") insurers seek to limit their exposure to a particularly large risk or to an aggregation of risks which are all exposed to the same event. At the highest levels of such reinsurance cover the insurer is seeking protection from catastrophes. In the London insurance market of the 1980s relatively few insurers wrote XL business. They were therefore highly exposed in the event of any catastrophic event or series of events. This exposure was compounded by "the spiral", which Phillips J. described in these terms in *Deeny v. Gooda Walker Ltd*[22]:

> "Many syndicates which wrote XL cover took out XL cover themselves. Those who reinsured them were thus writing XL on XL. They, in their turn, frequently took out their own XL cover. There thus developed among the syndicates and companies which wrote LMX business a smaller group that was largely responsible for creating a complex intertwining network of mutual reinsurance, which has been described as the spiral. When a catastrophe led to claims being made by primary insurers on their excess of loss covers, this started a process whereby syndicates passed on their liabilities, in excess of their own retentions, under their own excess of loss covers from one to the next, rather like a multiple game of pass the parcel. Those left holding the liability parcels were those who first exhausted their layers of excess of loss reinsurance protection . . .
>
> There were at least two significant ways in which spiral business was written:
>
> *XL on XL*: This described the grant of excess of loss cover in respect of an excess of loss account.
>
> *Whole account*: An underwriter who took out, without exclusion, excess of loss cover in respect of his whole account would thereby obtain excess of loss cover in respect

---

[19] Arts 56–58 of the Financial Services and Markets Act 2000 (Regulated Activities) Order 2001 (S.I.2001 No. 544) provide that the following activities are specified activities for the purposes of s.22 of the Act: art. 56: advising a person to become, or continue or cease to be, a member of a particular Lloyd's syndicate; art. 57: managing the underwriting capacity of a Lloyd's syndicate as a managing agent at Lloyd's; art. 58: the arranging, by the society incorporated by Lloyd's Act 1871 by the name of Lloyd's, of deals in contracts of insurance written at Lloyd's.

[20] The rules are addressed further below at paras 16–022 and 16–029.

[21] The definition of a "private person" for the purposes of s.150 is set out in reg. 3 of the Financial Services and Markets Act 2000 (Rights of Action) Regulations 2001 (S.I.2001 No. 2256). The definition includes (a) any individual, unless he suffers the loss in question in the course of carrying on any regulated activity and (b) any person who is not an individual, unless he suffers the loss in question in the course of carrying on business of any kind. Further, governments, local authorities and international organisations are specifically excluded.

[22] [1996] L.R.L.R. 183 at 190.

of that part of his whole account which itself comprised excess of loss business."[23]

(b) *Duties to Client*

(i) *Contractual duties*

Members' agents. The duties of a members' agent are set out in the written   **16–010** contract between the agent and his Name. Until 1990 a members' agent undertook by contract to act as the underwriting agent for the Name at Lloyd's, both writing risks and settling claims at their sole discretion. A members' agent was entitled to appoint and employ sub-agents to carry on or manage that underwriting. It was an implied term of the contract that the underwriting would be conducted with reasonable skill and care.[24] Unless the members' agent was a combined agent, all underwriting would be delegated to managing agents by sub-agency agreements. The actual and continuing role of a members' agent was set out in these terms by Gatehouse J. in *Brown v. KMR Services Ltd*[25]:

> "(a) to advise the name which syndicates to join and in what amounts, (b) to keep him informed at all times of material factors which may affect his underwriting, (c) to provide him with a balanced portfolio and appropriate spread of risk; a balanced spread of business on syndicates throughout the main markets at Lloyd's, (d) to monitor the syndicates on which it places the name, and to make recommendations whether the name should increase his share on a syndicate, join a new syndicate, reduce his share, or withdraw, (e) to keep regularly in touch with the syndicates to which the name belongs, and (f) to advise and discuss with the name the prospects and past results on which he could be placed."[26]

Members' agents also advise Names of, and if appropriate about, personal stop loss insurance[27] and estate protection policies.[28] It is a term of the contract that

---

[23] See also Robert Kiln, *Reinsurance in Practice*, (3rd ed., 1991), pp. 286–287:

    "In general the underwriting of L.M.X. business requires very special skills, knowledge and nerve. The London market place is one market and all its constituent members tend to write shares in the same business and on the same exposures, for example, oil rigs. Therefore, the accumulation hazard on a book of L.M.X. business can be very large indeed. All such covers tend to be directly additional to each other and the risk of a large proportion of them being involved in the same disaster is very high indeed.

    This is not to say that such a book of business, properly selected, will not be profitable, but it will have a high profitability in loss free years and a high risk of a large accumulating loss when the bad years occur."

    For a further description of the "spiral", see *Society of Lloyd's v. Clemston* [1997] L.R.L.R. 175 at 207–209, Cresswell J.

[24] *Henderson v. Merrett Syndicates Ltd* [1995] 2 A.C. 145 at 176G *per* Lord Goff (see also *The Lloyd's Litigation* [1994] 2 Lloyd's Rep. 193, Saville J., and [1994] 2 Lloyd's 468, CA and *Boobyer v. David Holman & Co. Ltd (No.2)* [1993] 1 Lloyd's Rep. 96, Saville J.).

    A members' agent who was contractually liable for negligent underwriting by a managing agent would usually be entitled to an indemnity against the managing agent: *Wynniatt-Husey v. R.J. Bromley (Underwriting Agencies) plc* [1996] L.R.L.R. 310.

[25] [1994] 4 All E.R. 385 at 390f-h. The facts are set out in para. 16–026, below. For a summary of the relationship between Names and agents see also *Society of Lloyd's v. Clemston* [1997] L.R.L.R. 175 at 199, Cresswell J.

[26] See also *Henderson v. Merrett Syndicates Ltd* [1995] 2 A.C. 145 at 170E *per* Lord Goff.

[27] This is discussed further in para. 16–028, below.

[28] These are policies insuring against liability of Names' estates for years of account left open after a Name's death.

the members' agent will bring reasonable skill and care to the performance of those functions.[29] If a members' agent gives an assurance that he will perform his agency in a particular way, he will be liable for breach of contract if performs his agency in a different way.[30]

16–011   **Managing Agents.** Until 1990 managing agents were only in a direct contractual relationship with direct Names, *i.e.* Names for whom they were acting as members' agents. When acting as combined agents, the contractual duties were those set out in the preceding paragraph.[31] Until 1990 managing agents owed no contractual duties to indirect Names.[32] There was, however, an implied term of the sub-agency agreement between the Name's members' agent and the managing agent that the managing agent would exercise reasonable skill and care.[33] Since 1990 managing agents have been in direct contractual relationships with all Names on the syndicates they manage and owe an express contractual duty to the Names to exercise reasonable skill and care.[34]

(ii) *Duties independent of contract*

16–012   **Members' agents.** Members' agents owe a concurrent tortious duty to their Names.[35] However, where the members' agent was contractually responsible for underwriting, but delegated that task to a managing agent (as was frequently the case before 1990), that tortious duty of care was limited to the tasks actually undertaken by the members' agent.[36] They were allowed to delegate the actual underwriting to the members' agents so that:

> "the common law duty of care is no more than expected and required of a competent members' agent (*qua* members' agent) and therefore that, in respect of the detailed conduct of the underwriting function and the day-to-day management of the Syndicate's affairs in connection with it, the common law duty to be imposed is no more than one of reasonable care in the selection of and liaison with the managing agent coupled with general oversight of the members' interests, it being no part of the members' agent's function (unless put on inquiry as to the competence of the managing agent) to supervise or interfere in managing or controlling the syndicate's affairs. It is the

---

[29] For an example of an express term see *Brown v. KMR Services Ltd* [1995] 4 All E.R. 598 at 625c. Such a term will otherwise be implied by law: s.13, Supply of Goods and Services Act 1982.

Cl. 6.2 (a) of the standard Members' Agent's Agreement (Sched. 1 to the Agency Agreements Byelaw, No.8 of 1988) provides expressly that the members' agent will "use such skill, care and diligence as could reasonably be expected of a members' agent carrying on business at Lloyd's and as is necessary for the proper provision of services, performance of duties and exercise of powers by it under this Agreement."

[30] *Brown v. KMR Services Ltd* [1994] 4 All E.R. 385 at 400b–f.

[31] *Henderson v. Merrett Syndicates Ltd* [1995] 2 A.C. 145 at 194E-F *per* Lord Goff.

[32] *Henderson v. Merrett Syndicates Ltd* [1995] 2 A.C.145 at 202C–203A *per* Lord Goff.

[33] *Henderson v. Merrett Syndicates Ltd* [1997] L.R.L.R. 265, Cresswell J. and *Wynniatt-Husey v. R.J. Bromley (Underwriting Agencies) plc* [1996] L.R.L.R. 310, Langley J. at 338–339. Such a term is to be implied by law: s.13 of the Supply of Goods and Services Act 1982.

[34] Cl. 4.2 (a) of the standard Managing Agent's Agreement (Sched. 3 to the Agency Agreements Byelaw, No.8 of 1988) provides that the managing agent will "use such skill, care and diligence as could reasonably be expected of a managing agent carrying on business at Lloyd's and as is necessary for the proper provision of services, performance of duties and exercise of powers by it under this Agreement."

[35] *Henderson v. Merrett Syndicates Ltd* [1995] 2 A.C. 145: the actual decision concerned the tortious liability of managing agents to direct and indirect names, but it must follow that members' agents owe a duty of care in tort to their names.

[36] *Aiken v. Stewart Wrightson Members Agency Ltd* [1995] 1 W.L.R. 1281, Potter J.

managing agents who are employed for that purpose pursuant to the practice and requirements of the Lloyd's market."[37]

Now that members' agents do not assume contractual liability for underwriting actually carried out by others,[38] their tortious duty of care will be co-extensive with their contractual duty of care.

Managing agents. Under the old regime[39] managing agents owed a tortious **16–013** duty to exercise skill and care to both direct and indirect Names.[40] In the case of direct names, that duty was concurrent with a contractual duty to exercise skill and care. In the case of indirect Names the fact that there was a chain of contracts between Name and members' agent and between members' agent and managing agent (with no direct contract between the Name and the managing agent) did not prevent there being a direct tortious duty owed by the managing agent to the Name. The finding of a tortious duty in such circumstances is most unusual[41] and is because of an assumption of responsibility by the managing agents to indirect Names.[42] Managing agents may also have owed a tortious duty of care to the members' agents with whom they entered sub-agency agreements. Under the new regime[43] the managing agent will owe Names a tortious duty concurrent with his contractual duty.

The individual employed by the managing agent owes a tortious duty of care **16–014** to the Names on whose behalf he acts.[44]

(iii) *Fiduciary Duties*

Both members' and managing agents are subject to the fiduciary obligation not **16–015** to allow their duty to act in the interests of their Names to conflict with their own interests. This is now expressly acknowledged in the prescribed forms of agreement.[45] The question of whether members' or managing agents owed Names any separate fiduciary duty to exercise skill and care was raised in the appeal in *Henderson v. Merrett Syndicates Ltd.*[46] Both Saville J. and the Court of Appeal had not addressed the question, having found that sufficient contractual and

---

[37] *ibid.*, at 1300B-C. See P. Cane, "Contract, tort and the Lloyd's debacle" in *Consensus ad Idem* (F. D. Rose ed., Sweet & Maxwell, 1996) at 100–103.

[38] See para. 16–006, above.

[39] See paras 16–004 and 16–005, above.

[40] *Henderson v. Merrett Syndicates Ltd* [1995] 2 A.C. 145.

[41] *ibid.*, at 195G per Lord Goff: " . . . in many cases in which a contractual chain comparable to that in the present case is constructed it may well prove to be inconsistent with an assumption of responsibility which has the effect of, so to speak, short circuiting the contractual structure so put in place by the parties." It may be that the distinguishing features in *Henderson v. Merrett Syndicates Ltd* were that the function of underwriting was regularly delegated to managing agents and that the managing agent was entering contracts on behalf of indirect Names to which they were immediate parties.

[42] See chap. 2, paras 2–094 *et seq.* See also P. Cane, "Contract, Tort and the Lloyd's Debacle" in *Consensus ad Idem* (F. D. Rose ed., Sweet & Maxwell, 1996) at 111–117.

[43] See para. 16–006, above.

[44] *Wynniatt-Husey v. R.J. Bromley (Underwriting Agencies) plc* [1996] L.R.L.R. 310, Langley J.; *Henderson v. Merrett Syndicates Ltd* [1997] L.R.L.R. 265, Cresswell J.

[45] See cl. 6.2(b), (c) and (d) of the Members' Agent's Agreement (Sched. 1 to the Agency Agreements Byelaw, No.8 of 1988) and cl. 4.2(b), (c) and (d) of the Managing Agent's Agreement (Sched. 3 to the Agency Agreements Byelaw, No.8 of 1988).

[46] [1995] 2 A.C. 145. See P. Cane, "Contract, Tort and the Lloyd's Debacle" in *Consensus ad Idem* (F. D. Rose ed., Sweet & Maxwell, 1996) at 118–119.

tortious duties were owed. In the House of Lords only Lord Browne-Wilkinson considered the point and rejected it as misconceived: while a fiduciary may owe a duty of care, that is "not a separate head of liability but the paradigm of the general duty to act with care imposed by law on those who take it upon themselves to act for or advise others".[47] Moreover, the extent of the fiduciary duties owed, including any duty to exercise skill and care, falls to be determined by reference to the terms of any underlying contract.[48]

(c) *Duties to third parties*

16–016   Apart from the question of duties owed by managing agents to indirect Names,[49] the only area in which the question of the duties owed by members' or managing agents to persons other than the Names with whom a members' or combined agent has contracted has arisen in practice is in the context of reinsurance to close. Reinsurance to close is a contract whereby one year of account of a syndicate is reinsured into another, usually the following year of account of the same syndicate number.[50] The effect is to release Names on the reinsured syndicate from further liability for that year's account (unless and to the extent that they are also Names on the reinsuring syndicate) and to allow them to take any profit. In return for a substantial premium the Names on the reinsuring syndicate will take over the business of the year being closed, which will include the business of all earlier years of account reinsured into that year. They will also enjoy the benefit of all reinsurance obtained for the old years of account (and of any recoveries made) and it is they, rather than the Names on the old years, who will suffer losses should that reinsurance prove to be ineffective because they will have reinsured the liability of the old Names. Where the managing agent is negligent in effecting reinsurance so that the reinsurer avoids the policy several years later, the loss will fall not on the Names at the time the reinsurance was originally effected but in the earliest year of account still open at the date of avoidance.

16–017   In *Aiken v. Stewart Wrightson Members Agency Ltd*[51] the managing agent had arranged aggregate excess of loss reinsurance for all liabilities which the syndicate might incur on its 1975 and earlier years of account. This was for the immediate benefit of the 1979 Names but had obvious possible consequences for Names on future years who would reinsure to close on the basis that the risk of losses above a certain sum on pre-1976 business had been effectively reinsured by others. In 1989 the reinsurer avoided the aggregate excess of loss policy for non-disclosure of material facts. On a trial of preliminary issues Potter J. had to decide whether the managing agent owed a duty of care in tort to Names on following years. He held that it did, not only to the Names on the two years immediately following 1979 (where the identity and interests of the Names were known at the time the reinsurance was made) but also for later years, including 1985 (being the earliest open year when the aggregate excess of loss policy was

---

[47] *ibid.*, at 205F.
[48] See also *Kelly v. Cooper* [1993] A.C. 205. For an alternative view see J. D. Heydon Q.C., (1995) 111 L.Q.R. 1.
[49] See para. 16–013, above.
[50] The Names on the syndicate will vary from year to year as will their individual lines.
[51] [1995] 1 W.L.R. 1281.

avoided), even though their identities and interests were not known at the time the policy had been effected.

Potter J. had no difficulty in finding that a duty was owed to the 1980 and 1981 **16–018** Names on the basis of the evidence of the managing agents as to their intention in effecting the aggregate excess of loss policy at the time.[52] As for later years, he adopted the three-stage test[53] and the incremental approach advocated in *Caparo Industries Ltd v. Dickman*[54] and applied in *Punjab National Bank v. de Boinville*.[55] He held that, in effect, a syndicate at Lloyd's continues from year to year and that, "managing agents are *in reality* concerned to deal on behalf of the Syndicate, protecting its interests without regard to the identity of its Names."[56] While at the time the aggregate excess of loss policy was obtained the managing agents did not know the identities of the Names for future years beyond 1981, they were an identifiable class at any given time and the total liability of the managing agents would not be increased as a result of any changes in the membership of the syndicate.[57]

In *Wynniatt-Husey v. R.J. Bromley (Underwriting Agencies) plc*[58] the Names **16–019** claimed not only against the managing agent at the relevant time, but also against its predecessor. The claim was founded upon an undertaking given to Lloyd's by the predecessor when the management of the syndicate was transferred to the new managing agent. By the undertaking the predecessor promised to provide such support as the successor considered necessary. The claim failed because the Names had not been aware of the undertaking and the undertaking itself did not require the predecessor to supervise its successor, but merely to provide support on request. The successor had not in fact provided any support.

2. THE STANDARD OF CARE

Where the members' or managing agent owes a duty to exercise reasonable skill **16–020** and care, he (or those for whom he is liable) will only be in breach of that duty if he falls below the standards of a reasonably competent members' or managing agent at the relevant time and with the knowledge which such a members' or managing agent had or should have had.[59] In the context of Lloyd's, the standards are those of the Lloyd's market[60] or, if appropriate, the relevant section of the Lloyd's market. However, while expert evidence is of importance in

---

[52] *ibid.*, at 1305H–1306H.

[53] See chap. 2, para. 2–030.

[54] [1990] 2 A.C. 605: see chap. 15, paras 15–056 *et seq.*

[55] [1992] 1 W.L.R. 1138; see chap. 14, para. 14–028, above,

[56] *ibid.*, at 1312G-H; the emphasis is that of Potter J.

[57] However, the brokers employed to effect the reinsurance would not owe a duty of care to later Names: *Deeny v. Walker* [1996] L.R.L.R. 276, Gatehouse J.

[58] [1996] L.R.L.R. 310.

[59] See, for example, *The Lloyd's Litigation* [1994] 2 Lloyd's Rep. 468 at 474, col. 1 *per* Bingham M.R.: " . . . any successful claim against the agent in negligence would, as in any other case, have to show a failure to show the standard of skill and care reasonably to be expected of such an agent at the time and with the knowledge that he had or should have had. His judgment could not be impugned simply because events showed it to be wrong." See also *Brown v. KMR Services Ltd* [1994] 4 All E.R. 385 at 397d-j *per* Gatehouse J. (members' agent) and *Henderson v. Merrett Syndicates Ltd (No.2)* [1996] 1 P.N.L.R. 32, Cresswell J. (managing agent).

[60] In the case of underwriting, the standards are those of a reasonably competent underwriter, whether at Lloyd's or elsewhere.

determining the question, it is ultimately for the court to decide what constitutes reasonable competence. The court is not bound to accept that compliance with a widely followed practice or standard is sufficient and it may be that the approach of a specialised section of the Lloyd's market over a period will not amount to sufficient evidence of what constitutes the exercise of reasonable care. Thus in *Deeny v. Gooda Walker Ltd*[61] Phillips J. addressed the question of the standard of care to be expected of those underwriting excess of loss business in the LMX spiral[62] in these terms:

> " . . . this action is concerned with one area of underwriting, excess of loss reinsurance. At the heart of the action lies one aspect of excess of loss underwriting, the writing of spiral business. That was a business which developed rapidly in the period of the eight years or so that led up to the events with which this action is concerned. Only a relatively small proportion of Lloyd's underwriters specialised in writing spiral business. The London market no longer writes spiral business—at least on the scale and in the manner which developed in the last decade. In these circumstances I do not consider that one can automatically regard the practices of those who wrote spiral business as constituting strong evidence of what constituted the exercise of reasonable skill and care. It is necessary to approach this case with the possibility in mind that, for many involved, a significant involvement in spiral business may not have been compatible with competent underwriting."[63]

Moreover, where Names are being exposed to very great potential liabilities, an appropriate level of skill is to be expected of those who are so exposing them.[64]

16–021   Since 1996 all members' and managing agents have been required to comply with certain core principles.[65] The principles are intended to form a statement of the standards expected of all members' and managing agents. Principle 2 states that: "An agent should act with due skill, care and diligence." Priciple 5 states that: "An agent should seek from members it advises any information about their circumstances and objectives which might reasonably be expected to be relevant in enabling it to fulfil its responsibilities to them. An agent should also take all reasonable steps to give members it advises or for whom it exercises discretion, in a comprehensible and timely way, any information needed to enable them to make balanced and informed decisions."

---

[61] [1996] L.R.L.R. 183.

[62] See para. 16–009 above.

[63] *ibid.*, at 207. See also at 205: "As a broad proposition, any professional who engages in a particular speciality can be expected to demonstrate the level of skill and care appropriate to that speciality."

[64] *ibid.*, at 207–208. But see *Wynniatt-Husey v. R.J. Bromley (Underwriting Agencies) plc* [1996] L.R.L.R. 310 at 313 *per* Langley J.:

"As to the standard of care, that is the standard of a professional underwriter holding himself out as possessing the skill and experience reasonably required to underwrite a marine account which on any view of the evidence, contained a significant proportion of excess of loss ('XL') business. There is no dispute that such business is of a high risk nature. That does not mean in my judgment that some special and stricter standard of care applies in the sense that the standard differs from that of a reasonable underwriter but only that his conduct is to be considered in the context of underwriting an account which included such business."

[65] See the Core Principles Byelaw, No.34 of 1996. The Core Principles are set out in Sched. 2 of the byelaw.

Although a breach of these principles will not necessarily amount to negligence, it is likely to do so.

Where the members' or managing agent's conduct falls within the ambit of the   **16–022**
FSA's Conduct of Business rules[66] then the agent will be required to comply with the requirements of those rules. Additionally, a court is likely to find that those rules set out the standard of skill and care to be expected of an agent, so that a breach of the rules amounts to a failure to act will reasonable skill and care.

3. LIABILITY FOR BREACH OF DUTY

Broadly speaking breach of duty by a members' or managing agent may take one   **16–023**
of four forms:

(i) Breach of a specific contractual duty.

(ii) Breach of an express or implied duty to exercise reasonable skill and care.

(iii) Breach of a tortious duty of care.

(iv) Breach of one or more of the FSA's Conduct of Business rules.[67]

Proof of negligence will not be necessary to establish liability under the first or fourth head, but in order to establish liability under the second and third heads a failure to exercise the same standard of skill and care must be shown. Such a failure is referred to as "negligence" in this chapter.

The principal respects in which members' and managing agents might be held to   **16–024**
have been negligent are discussed below under seven heads, being those which have featured most prominently in the decided cases. However, the catalogue of errors is not closed and this chapter does not attempt to speculate as to other circumstances in which a members' or managing agent might be negligent.

(a) *Members' agent—failure to advise adequately as to syndicate participation*

Advice as to the choice of syndicates which a Name is to join is the most   **16–025**
important task carried out by a members' agent. The extent to which Names will seek or accept such advice will vary: at one extreme they will rely entirely upon their members' agents, while, at the other extreme, "working Names" will be directly involved in Lloyd's and might be as well as or better informed than a competent members' agent. A members' agent is not under a duty to warn of a risk which he knows his Name is aware of,[68] and a working Name who makes his own choice of syndicate without reference to his members' agent may thereby absolve his members' agent from any duty to advise.[69] However, save in those

---

[66] See para. 16–008 and chap. 13, paras 13–046 *et seq.*
[67] This may give rise to liability pursuant to s.150 of the Financial Services and Markets Act 2000 (see para. 16–008 above).
[68] *Brown v. KMR Services Ltd* [1995] 4 All E.R. 598 at 617b *per* Stuart-Smith L.J.
[69] *Berriman (Sir David) v. Rose Thomson Young (Underwriting) Ltd* [1996] L.R.L.R. 426, *per* Morrison J. at 486. Where the members' agent had warranted that the underwriting on those syndicates chosen by the Name would be carried out with reasonable skill and care, he would be liable for breach of contract even if it was the Name and not he who had chosen the syndicates (*ibid.*).

unusual circumstances the duties of a members' agent have been authoritatively summarised in these terms by Hobhouse L.J.:

> "The relevant duties of the members' agent are stated in the express or implicit provisions of the contract between the member and the agent. They are to the same effect: 'to advise the Name which syndicates to join and in what amounts.' This is a duty which has to be performed each year when the decisions have to be made for the following underwriting year. The advice must therefore cover both the selection of the syndicates and the amount of premium to be allocated to each. In selecting the syndicates regard must be had to the classes of business in which the member wishes to become involved, to the quality of the individual syndicates, what business they write and to the sectors of the market to be covered. The agent must make recommendations which are of the appropriate quality, both having regard to the individual syndicates and the composition of the portfolio as a whole. Linked with this must be advice as to the amount of the allocation that the member should make to each syndicate. This must have regard to the same considerations—the character and quality of the syndicate and the need to obtain an appropriate spread and maintain a proper balance.
>
> Such considerations must apply to every member whom the agent is advising. Certain members may need additional advice because of their special need to avoid risk . . . Regard may be had to other information which has been given by the member to the agent about the member's requirements or circumstances . . .
>
> Further, the agent must give the member such information as is necessary for the member to make a reasonably informed decision about the recommendations which the agent is making. The more that the member is himself getting involved in the actual decisions (as opposed to leaving it to the agent), the more it is necessary that the advice given to the member should include the appropriate information . . . The agent need not in the ordinary course repeat the warnings that have already been given. But where a particular syndicate involves some additional risk it is incumbent upon the agent . . . to give an appropriate additional warning coupled with appropriate information."[70]

16–026   The duties owed to Names with very different requirements and attitudes were considered in *Brown v. KMR Services Ltd.*[71] One plaintiff Name, Mr Sword-Daniels, was of relatively modest means, so that he would find losses particularly hard to fund, and wished to adopt a conservative, cautious approach to underwriting. His members' agent placed him on a high proportion of syndicates which were high risk without informing him of the potential liabilities to which he was exposed as a result. Gatehouse J. found the members' agent to have been negligent. The same conclusion was reached in the case of the other plaintiff Name, Mr Brown. Mr Brown was experienced and knowledgeable both as to business and investment matters generally and, by the relevant period, as to the Lloyd's market. He took an active interest in his choice of syndicates (based largely upon their profitability in preceding years) and was aware that some of them involved a higher degree of risk than others. He was nevertheless prepared to participate to a large extent on syndicates which wrote catastrophe excess of loss business. Gatehouse J. held that he was still entitled to receive advice as to the particular risks to which his proposed underwriting would expose him. The Court of Appeal held that the members' agent was under a duty to do more than just warn of the risk. In order to discharge his duty properly in such circumstances the members' agent should have told Mr Brown which of his proposed syndicates were high risk, the nature of the risk, the degree to which the risks on

---

[70] *Brown v. KMR Services Ltd* [1995] 4 All E.R. 598 at 633f–634c.
[71] [1994] 4 All E.R. 385 (*Sword-Daniels and Brown*), Gatehouse J.; [1995] 4 All E.R. 598 (*Brown*), CA.

the proposed syndicates overlapped, the proportion of his total allocation which it was prudent to allocate to such syndicates and the appropriate allocation to make to each of the high risk syndicates.[72]

In assessing the advice which a members' agent should give as to particular syndicates or types of business, he is to be judged by the knowledge which he had or ought to have had. As well as a reasonable understanding of the various classes of business underwritten at Lloyd's, a members' agent should know and understand the underwriting philosophy and the nature of the business underwritten by those syndicates he advises his Names to join. That will include some knowledge of the reinsurance protection which the underwriter proposes to obtain. However, a members' agent is "not required so to question the underwriter of any particular syndicate as to endeavour to second guess the way the risks were written".[73] In *Brown v. KMR Services Ltd*[74] Gatehouse J. held that a combined agency[75] whose underwriters were aware of the inherent risks of writing excess of loss reinsurance was under a duty to communicate that knowledge to those of its employees who advised Names in the capacity of members' agent. On the facts of that case the knowledge in question was such as might be expected to be held by a reasonably competent members' agent in any event. However, in general it would be wrong to require a higher degree of knowledge of a combined agent when acting as a members' agent by reason of the knowledge of its active underwriters: the contractual and tortious expectation of the Name should not depend upon whether his members' agent is also a managing agent. **16–027**

A members' agent may advise a Name to take out personal stop loss insurance as part of his underwriting strategy. Personal stop loss insurance insures Names against losses on their underwriting at Lloyd's in a given year, subject both to a deductible and a limit, the Name retaining the risk of losses falling within the former and above the latter. Although this will provide an element of protection to the Name, a members' agent who has otherwise exposed a Name to risks of which the Name was not but should have been informed will still be in breach of duty.[76] **16–028**

When advising a person to become, or continue or cease to be a member of a particular Lloyd's syndicate, an agent is required to comply with the FSA's Conduct of Business "know your customer" and "suitability" rules.[77] Further, an agent may not advise a potential member who is a private customer to become a member of a particular syndicate unless membership of the Society, as well as of the syndicate, is suitable for that customer having regard to the facts disclosed by him and any other relevant facts about him of which the agent is or reasonably should be aware.[78] **16–029**

---

[72] [1995] 4 All E.R. 598, at 634e-g *per* Hobhouse L.J., with whom the other members of the Court of Appeal agreed on this point.

[73] *Berriman (Sir David) v. Rose Thomson Young (Underwriting) Ltd* [1996] L.R.L.R. 426 at 482 (Morrison J.).

[74] [1994] 4 All E.R. 385.

[75] *i.e.* an agency which acted both as a member's agent and managed one or more syndicates.

[76] *Brown v. KMR Services Ltd* [1994] 4 All E.R. 385 at 394. Gatehouse J. also held that Names need not give credit for sums recovered under personal stop loss policies: see para. 16–074, below.

[77] See r. 12.1.1R(1) and chap. 5 of the Conduct of Business Sourcebook.

[78] r. 12.1.11 of the Conduct of Business rules.

(b) *Managing agent—failure to plan properly*

16-030 Like all insurers, Names risk making losses. Every time an underwriter makes an insurance contract on their behalf he exposes them to the risk of a claim or claims under that policy. Claims can be met from premiums received or by reinsurance. If both are exhausted, then the Names will make a loss. By the exercise of skill and judgment the underwriter should reduce the risk of loss. An underwriter therefore should seek to write a range of business both in terms of class of business and geographical area. This should allow claims on one class of risk written in a particular area (for example property damage caused by a hurricane) to be met by premiums on policies not affected by the underlying event. An underwriter will also wish to reinsure against large claims or aggregations of claims. A proper plan is a vital tool for the underwriter in that regard.[79] The need for and adequacy of such plans has been considered in the context of excess of loss underwriting and, in particular, the LMX market.[80] An underwriter who is writing XL business should formulate and follow a plan as to the extent to which Names are to be exposed to the risk of unreinsured loss.[81] If he does not do so at all, he will be negligent.

16-031 In order to formulate such a plan the underwriter needs to establish the probable maximum loss ("PML") to which the syndicate will be exposed by a single event. The PML is not the same as the aggregate of all the sums payable under the policies to be underwritten, although, if a syndicate writes excess of loss business, its underwriter will need to know the aggregates.[82] Having calculated his aggregates the underwriter should then identify an appropriate event as the source of the PML. The catastrophe chosen should be remote, but nevertheless a practical possibility.[83] If the underwriter chooses one such event rather than another without having any good reason for believing that the PML which might result from the former would be lower than that which might result from the latter, the underwriter will be in breach of duty.[84]

16-032 Having identified an appropriate event, the underwriter should proceed to calculate its potential impact. That involves a difficult exercise of judgment by the

---

[79] Managing agents are now obliged to prepare annual business plans relating to themselves and to each syndicate they manage: para. 57A of the Underwriting Agents Byelaw, No.4 of 1984 as amended.

[80] See para. 16–009, above. The decisions discussed in the following paragraphs all concerned XL business.

[81] *Deeny v. Gooda Walker Ltd* [1996] L.R.L.R. 183 at 198; *Arbuthnott v. Feltrim Underwriting Agencies Ltd* [1995] C.L.C. 437, at 444–445; *Wynniatt-Husey v. R.J. Bromley (Underwriting Agencies) plc* [1996] L.R.L.R. 310, at 320–321.

[82] *Deeny v. Gooda Walker Ltd* [1996] L.R.L.R. 183 at 198; *Wynniatt-Husey v. R.J. Bromley (Underwriting Agencies) plc* [1996] L.R.L.R. 310 at 320.

[83] "An underwriter is not to be criticised for preferring to take one sensible event as opposed to another, or for excluding some events (which might be described as cataclysmic) as being so massive and so destructive as to destroy the world wide insurance market" (Morrison J. in *Berriman (Sir David) v. Rose Thomson Young (Underwriting) Ltd* [1996] L.R.L.R. 426 at 442).

[84] *Arbuthnott v. Feltrim Underwriting Agencies Ltd* [1995] C.L.C. 437 at 476: underwriter decided not to use an earthquake as the relevant catastrophe, because he lacked adequate data to put a realistic figure on the PML which an earthquake might cause. However, his alternative choice of a windstorm was unsatisfactory, because an earthquake was a practical possibility and there was no basis for concluding that its consequences would be less than those of a windstorm. Generally, however, the choice of an appropriate catastrophe should be relatively straightforward: *Wynniatt-Husey v. R.J. Bromley (Underwriting Agencies) plc* [1996] L.R.L.R. 310 at 320.

underwriter. In *Deeny v. Gooda Walker Ltd.*[85] Phillips J. described the task of the underwriter as follows:

"To calculate his exposure to a single event he needs to know how many of the covers that he has written are exposed to the risk of a claim should that event occur. He thus has to divide into different categories the covers that can aggregate. In practice this is normally done by a system of coding the different aggregates. The more carefully the business is recorded under appropriately chosen codes the more confident the underwriter will be able to be as to the limit of his exposure to a single event. As I have already said there will be some categories where it is unlikely, or indeed inconceivable, that a single event will result in a claim on every cover. In respect of those categories the true exposure will be, not the aggregate, but the PML. The estimation of PML has to be made by the application of judgment to the data available."

An underwriter should therefore maintain sufficient data to enable him to make a reasonable estimate of his syndicate's PML. If he fails to do so, he will be in breach of duty.[86]

If an underwriter has sufficient data, he must bring reasonable skill and care to **16–033** the task of assessing it.[87] Thus in *Deeny v. Gooda Walker Ltd*[88] one underwriter claimed to have applied a PML of 15 per cent to whole account reinsurance.[89] Phillips J. held that he had not made any attempt to calculate his syndicate's PML in that way, but that, if he had, he would have been negligent in applying such a low percentage to risks which included a substantial amount of spiral business.[90] Detailed critiques of the assessments of other underwriters have been made in other cases.[91] An underwriter who fails altogether to estimate his syndicate's PML is negligent[92] as is an underwriter who discounts the PML on the basis that it is unlikely to occur.[93]

---

[85] [1996] L.R.L.R. 182 at 198.

[86] *Deeny v. Gooda Walker Ltd* [1996] L.R.L.R. 183 at 218: business coded to assess profitability, not to allow aggregates or PML to be calculated: held to have been negligent. See also *Wynniatt-Husey v. R.J. Bromley (Underwriting Agencies) plc* [1996] L.R.L.R. 310 (where the coding system adopted by the underwriter was defective) and *Berriman (Sir David) v. Rose Thomson Young (Underwriting) Ltd* [1996] L.R.L.R. 426.

[87] "The calculation of the PML amount will involve judgment. And an underwriter is not to be criticised for making a calculation of the PML amount merely because others would or might have made a different calculation." (*per* Morrison J. in *Berriman (Sir David) v. Rose Thomson Young (Underwriting) Ltd* [1996] L.R.L.R. 426 at 442–443).

[88] [1996] L.R.L.R. 182.

[89] *i.e.* excess of loss cover in respect of a whole account. The account so reinsured might include excess of loss business liable to a claim by reason of an event which impacted upon the excess of loss business written directly by the syndicate. A far higher percentage was therefore appropriate.

[90] See para. 16–009 above.

[91] *Arbuthnott v. Feltrim Underwriting Agencies Ltd* [1995] C.L.C. 437 at 476–481, Phillips J. (two out of five allegations of negligence accepted) and 482 (assessment negligent on two grounds); *Berriman (Sir David) v. Rose Thomson Young (Underwriting) Ltd* [1996] L.R.L.R. 426 (failure to include relevant aggregates was negligent; failure to include aggregation for exposure on personal stop loss policies not negligent). See also *Wynniatt-Husey v. R.J. Bromley (Underwriting Agencies) plc* [1996] L.R.L.R. 310, where Langley J. had to decide what factors a reasonably competent underwriter would have applied to the various classes of business, the actual underwriter having failed to do so at all. He held that the underwriter had been negligent for failing to carry out a calculation in accordance with his findings.

[92] *e.g. Deeny v. Gooda Walker Ltd* [1996] L.R.L.R. 183; *Arbuthnott v. Feltrim Underwriting Agencies Ltd* [1995] C.L.C. 437; *Wynniatt-Husey v. R.J. Bromley (Underwriting Agencies) plc* [1996] L.R.L.R. 310.

[93] *Berriman (Sir David) v. Rose Thomson Young (Underwriting) Ltd* [1996] L.R.L.R. 426.

16–034   Having established his syndicate's PML an underwriter can plan how much reinsurance cover he should seek to obtain[94] and what unreinsured risk should remain with the Names. At least in the context of excess of loss underwriting it is not necessarily negligent for an underwriter to plan on the basis that the Names will suffer a substantial loss on some years of account, but make a profit over a number of years. However, an underwriter who adopts such an approach should inform the Names of his decision to do so and of the scale of losses which they will be exposed from time to time.[95] There are also limits to the extent to which a reasonably competent managing agent could decide to expose the Names on its syndicates. To a certain extent that will depend upon the nature of the syndicate, but it has been held that the managing agent of a syndicate which is avowedly high risk could not reasonably decide to leave Names exposed to a loss greater than 100 per cent of stamp capacity.[96] The level of risk to which the Names could reasonably be exposed on any given syndicate is the level of exposure which those Names, properly advised by their members' agents, should have realised they were accepting by participating in that syndicate.[97]

16–035   If an underwriter does warn of the risk of losses in certain circumstances, he will still be in breach of duty if his approach to underwriting in fact exposes his Names to greater risks, either in terms of their financial exposure to a single event or by reference to the type of event or scale of loss which would exhaust the syndicate's reinsurance programme. Thus in *Deeny v. Gooda Walker Ltd*[98] the active underwriter of one syndicate stated in a report to his Names that a loss of 200 per cent of the amount allocated to the syndicate might be suffered. He believed that only the most severe catastrophe would lead to such a loss. That belief was unsound and had he carried out a proper calculation of aggregates and PML he would have known better. Phillips J. held that he had been negligent.

16–036   Assessment of PML, reinsurance cover and exposure to be retained within the syndicate is only part of the plan which a reasonably competent underwriter should make. He should also project the premium which he will receive and the premium he intends to pay for reinsurance.

(c) Managing agent—unjustified departure from plan

16–037   The underwriter should have regard to his plan throughout the year of account and, if circumstances change, consider what changes, if any, should be made to his policy to take account of those changes. For example, if it appears that the target aggregate exposure in a particular area will be exceeded if further business is written, then either the underwriter should cease to accept new business or he

---

[94] As to which see paras 16–040 to 16–045, below.
[95] *Deeny v. Gooda Walker Ltd* [1996] L.R.L.R. 183 at 197; *Arbuthnott v. Feltrim Underwriting Agencies Ltd* [1995] C.L.C. 437 at 484.
[96] *Arbuthnott v. Feltrim Underwriting Agencies Ltd* [1995] C.L.C. 437 at 484–489. Stamp capacity is the amount of net premium which a syndicate is allowed to receive in a year of account.
[97] *Wynniatt-Husey v. R.J. Bromley (Underwriting Agencies) plc* [1996] L.R.L.R. 310, at 332. The syndicate in that case was presented as a medium risk/medium reward syndicate and Langley J. concluded that the greatest level of exposure to which the Names should have been exposed was 50% (*ibid.*, at 336). See also *Berriman (Sir David) v. Rose Thomson Young (Underwriting) Ltd* [1996] L.R.L.R. 426 (40%).
[98] [1996] L.R.L.R. 183.

should obtain an appropriate increase in reinsurance protection.[99] In *Arbuthnott v. Feltrim Underwriting Agencies Ltd*[1] one underwriter departed materially from his planned aggregate exposure. He advanced several possible commercial reasons to justify this departure. Phillips J. rejected them: the effect of the underwriter's decision had been to increase the exposure of the names by some U.S.$28 million, when they were already overexposed.[2]

(iv) *Managing agent—failure to obtain adequate reinsurance*

An adequate programme of reinsurance is an important means of minimising the Names' exposure to loss. Underwriters must exercise reasonable skill and care when deciding what reinsurance to seek and in trying to obtain it. This involves the following: **16–038**

- (i) determining what reinsurance cover to seek to obtain;

- (ii) nominating the reinsurers from whom that reinsurance is to be sought or approving the choice of reinsurers made by brokers for them;

- (iii) ensuring that the rate at which reinsurance is obtained is commercial, so that the syndicate has a reasonable prospect of making a profit;

- (iv) trying to ensure that the reinsurance is valid and not liable to be avoided for non-disclosure or misrepresentation.

Each of those tasks will be considered in turn.

(i) *Deciding what reinsurance cover to seek*

The underwriter must decide what amount of "vertical" and "horizontal" cover should be acquired. The amount of "vertical" protection is the amount of cover for a single loss or aggregation of losses. The amount of "horizontal" protection is the number of losses at a particular level which will be covered, usually the number of times a policy is reinstated after an initial loss. **16–039**

In order to make a reasonable decision as to what vertical cover to seek an underwriter needs to know what his aggregates and PML are.[3] In the absence of that information he will be relying upon luck rather than proper professional judgment. If it transpires that he has thereby exposed his Names to a greater loss than that which he had informed them they would be exposed he will be negligent and liable for any resulting loss.[4] **16–040**

---

[99] *Arbuthnott v. Feltrim Underwriting Agencies Ltd* [1995] C.L.C. 436 at 462 *per* Phillips J. See also *Wynniatt-Husey v. R.J. Bromley (Underwriting Agencies) plc* [1996] L.R.L.R. 310 at 332 *per* Langley J.: "I am quite satisfied on the evidence that a prudent underwriter should have kept under regular review the aggregates he was writing or being asked to write relative to the level of protection he had acquired. By regular review I mean that he should have had in mind *at all times* what his protections and aggregates were and ensured that there was sufficient level of cover to match his PML less only the risk of loss to which it was appropriate to expose his Names."

[1] *ibid.*

[2] *ibid.*, at 480–481.

[3] As to which see paras 16–031 to 16–033, above and *Arbuthnott v. Feltrim Underwriting Agencies Ltd* [1995] C.L.C. 437 at 446 and *Berriman (Sir David) v. Rose Thomson Young (Underwriting) Ltd* [1996] L.R.L.R. 426.

[4] *Deeny v. Gooda Walker Ltd* [1996] L.R.L.R. 183; *Arbuthnott v. Feltrim Underwriting Agencies Ltd* [1995] C.L.C. 437; *Wynniatt-Husey v. R.J. Bromley (Underwriting Agencies) plc* [1996] L.R.L.R. 310 at 321; *Berriman (Sir David) v. Rose Thomson Young (Underwriting) Ltd* [1996] L.R.L.R. 426 at 451.

16–041 An underwriter who makes a reasonable assessment of his syndicate's PML is not required to obtain reinsurance for the entire amount so assessed. He is entitled to decide to retain a degree of net exposure.[5] This may be either above or below the reinsurance he seeks to procure, although in practice he will usually have to accept a level of retention below the reinsurance obtained. However, if he is to proceed on this basis, the underwriter should ensure that the Names are informed of his policy and of the extent of the potential exposure which they face as a result.[6]

16–042 Moreover, an underwriter's decision as to what exposure the Names on his syndicate should risk must be a reasonable one. In *Arbuthnott v. Feltrim Underwriting Agencies Ltd*[7] one underwriter approached the question of exposure not on the basis of the maximum that the syndicate could afford to run, but rather by reference to the amount of reinsurance protection which it could afford to buy. Phillips J. held that his failure to address the matter from the former point of view was negligent.[8] In the same case Phillips J. also had to consider the maximum exposure to which it was reasonable to decide to expose the Names. He held that in view of the need to aim to balance losses with profits over a period of years, the highest level of exposure which a competent managing agent could decide was 100 per cent of the syndicate's stamp capacity.[9]

16–043 The same principles apply to an underwriter's decision as to the amount of horizontal cover to seek. Again the underwriter needs to make a reasonably informed decision and again he is not necessarily obliged to seek to obtain reinsurance which will reinstate as many times as the insurance cover he writes on behalf of his syndicate. For smaller, more frequent claims it would make little sense to try to match reinsurance cover to the underlying business written for the syndicate. However, in the context of catastrophe excess of loss business, where the potential claims are far greater in amount but far less frequent, any failure to match reinstatements must be for some good reason and, in the absence of such a reason an underwriter will be held to have been negligent.[10] A good reason for these purposes might be that an underwriter had to offer a greater number of reinstatements on the business he was writing than he could obtain at a commercial rate on the reinsurance available to him.[11] If an underwriter chooses not to match reinstatements, he will be exposing his Names to risk and should bear this in mind when considering the extent to which the Names are exposed vertically.[12]

16–044 Where joint reinsurance protection is obtained for more than one syndicate, the underwriter should consider carefully the implications of such reinsurance and the adequacy of the joint cover obtained. In *Arbuthnott v. Feltrim Underwriting*

---

[5] *Arbuthnott v. Feltrim Underwriting Agencies Ltd* [1995] C.L.C. 437 at 446.

[6] *Deeny v. Gooda Walker Ltd* [1996] L.R.L.R. 183 at 197–199; *Arbuthnott v. Feltrim Underwriting Agencies Ltd* [1995] C.L.C. 437 at 446.

[7] [1995] C.L.C. 437.

[8] *ibid.*, at 481–482. See also *Wynniatt-Husey v. R.J. Bromley (Underwriting Agencies) plc* [1996] L.R.L.R. 310 and para. 16–051 below.

[9] *ibid.*, at 486–489. See also *Wynniatt-Husey v. R.J. Bromley (Underwriting Agencies) plc* [1996] L.R.L.R. 310, where the syndicate should have been perceived as medium risk/medium reward and Langley J. held that the maximum exposure should have been 50% of stamp capacity.

[10] *Deeny v. Gooda Walker Ltd* [1996] L.R.L.R. 183 at 191–201 and 217–218.

[11] *Berriman (Sir David) v. Rose Thomson Young (Underwriting) Ltd* [1996] L.R.L.R. 426 at 469; but see paras 16–050—16–056, below.

[12] *ibid.*

Agencies Ltd[13] one underwriter obtained a single whole account reinsurance cover for two syndicates, one non-marine and the other marine. If, as was perfectly possible, a single catastrophe produced claims against both syndicates so as to exhaust both syndicates' specific reinsurance programmes, then both would seek to rely upon the same whole-account reinsurance. The underwriter failed to consider and provide properly for this possibility, even though the marine syndicate had written a considerable amount of non-marine business. Phillips J. held that the underwriter should have been aware of this risk and provided against it. He held him to have been negligent for failing to do so.[14]

The underwriter should also seek reinsurance on appropriate terms. In *Arbuthnott* **16–045** *v. Feltrim Underwriting Agencies Ltd*[15] the Names alleged that an underwriter had been negligent for accepting a reinsurance policy which overvalued the U.S. dollar against the pound sterling. Phillips J. rejected this claim, because the underwriter reasonably acted on the basis that the syndicate's dollar exposure was more significant than its exposure in sterling. In the circumstances he was entitled to agree to rates which resulted in a lower sterling excess point and a lower sterling limit of cover.[16]

(ii) *Choosing the reinsurer*

It is not enough to identify the amount of reinsurance which is needed to afford **16–046** reasonable protection to the Names. Unless the reinsurers who agree to provide such reinsurance are solvent when claims come to be made the reinsurance obtained will be worthless. The brokers instructed by the underwriter will themselves owe a duty to exercise skill and care in the choice of reinsurer.[17] They should themselves be reasonably satisfied that the reinsurance security they put before the underwriter is appropriate for the type of risk being reinsured, for example if it is includes a substantial amount of long tail business.[18] However, the brokers will have a less detailed knowledge of the risk to be reinsured than the underwriter. In *Berriman (Sir David) v. Rose Thomson Young (Underwriting) Ltd*[19] Morrison J. described the different roles of broker and underwriter as follows:

> "The list of approved companies prepared by the broker was compiled for general use, although some would be more appropriate than others in some instances. But all the companies on the list would have been approved as sound, in principle. It would be quite inappropriate for a broker to maintain within that list different tiers or levels of soundness. The underwriter, on the other hand, knows better than the broker the nature of the risks which he is writing and the length of tail, if any. He will know how much risk he intends to cede, and he will have been able to evaluate the nature of those risks and the likely impact on them of foreseeable events. The roles of broker and underwriter neatly complement one another: in normal circumstances, an underwriter would be entitled to assume that the broker would only have presented him with a prospective reinsurer which the broker considered to be generally sound, and the broker can assume that a competent underwriter will make a judgment as to the appropriateness of that

---

[13] [1995] C.L.C. 437.
[14] *ibid.*, at 470–474.
[15] [1995] C.L.C. 437.
[16] *ibid.*, at 475.
[17] See chap. 14, para. 14–058 above.
[18] *i.e.* business on which claims can be expected to take a considerable time to be advised or settled.
[19] [1996] L.R.L.R. 426 at 455–466, Morrison J.

security having regard to his particular needs . . . The names on the brokers' list are 'off the peg', whereas the underwriter must tailor the material to meet his own special needs."

16–047 An underwriter should therefore obtain sufficient information about a proposed reinsurer to enable him to judge whether it is suitable security for the risk to be reinsured. Thus an underwriter who has no real information about a reinsurer and decides to accept it because the individual underwriter he meets seems to be "very nice" will be in breach of duty.[20] An underwriter needs to understand properly the information he obtains. It is no good being told a rating if he misinterprets it. In *Berriman (Sir David) v. Rose Thomson Young (Underwriting) Ltd*[21] the brokers made it clear that they took no responsibility for the suitability of one proposed reinsurer and the underwriter misunderstood the rating of that reinsurer. Morrison J. held that he was negligent in accepting that reinsurer as security for 30 per cent of the risk being reinsured. However the underwriter was not negligent for accepting a North Korean company, which depended upon the willingness of the North Korean government to provide funds in bad years. The evidence was that the brokers regarded the company as reasonable security and, in that instance, the underwriter would have been entitled to rely upon their judgment.[22]

16–048 Because Names are members of more than one syndicate, they may find themselves, as members of one syndicate, reinsuring their own liabilities as members of another. In the final analysis they derive no benefit from such reinsurance.[23] To a certain extent that is an inevitable consequence of the structure of Lloyd's, which will depend upon the extent of the overlap between memberships of the reinsured and the reinsuring syndicates. Thus, where both syndicates are managed by the same combined agent who, in his capacity as members' agent, regularly advises Names to join both of the agency's syndicates, there will be a large overlap in membership and any inter-syndicate reinsurance will be of little benefit to the Names. In *Deeny v. Gooda Walker Ltd*[24] the Names alleged that it was negligent for one of the four Gooda Walker syndicates to obtain reinsurance for another, given that the majority of Names on one of the four syndicates were members of at least two of the other three. Phillips J. rejected the allegation that in those circumstances it was negligent without more to obtain inter-syndicate reinsurance, because it depended upon the consequences for the reinsured Names. Given the nature of the spiral,[25] those consequences were very hard to assess. However, he did observe that where there was a high degree of common membership it would usually make sense to avoid inter-syndicate reinsurance and that, in the context of the spiral, the fact that some reinsurance was being provided by the same Names should have reduced the comfort which the underwriter derived from his reinsurance programme.[26]

16–049 A further problem which can arise with the choice of reinsurer is where the reinsurer in turn obtains cover against his liability under the reinsurance which is,

---

[20] *ibid.*, at 456–460.
[21] [1996] L.R.L.R. 426.
[22] *ibid.*, at 466.
[23] Unless their line on the reinsuring syndicate is lower than that on the reinsured syndicate or the reinsured syndicate in turn reinsures part of the risk reinsured.
[24] [1996] L.R.L.R. 183.
[25] As to which see para. 16–009, above.
[26] [1996] L.R.L.R. 183 at 208.

either directly or through reinsurance, provided by the reinsured. The underwriters in *Deeny v. Gooda Walker Ltd*[27] were alleged to have been negligent for obtaining and providing reinsurance to the same syndicates or companies. Phillips J. refused to hold that such reciprocal reinsurance was negligent in itself.[28]

(iii) *Maintaining commercial viability*

The cost of reinsurance is met by the syndicate from the premium received in **16–050** relation to the underlying business. A reasonably competent underwriter should therefore ensure that the relationship between the premiums received by the syndicate for accepting the risks and the premiums paid for reinsuring against claims on those risks is such that there is a reasonable prospect of making a profit. If the cost of reinsurance is so high that a profit is unlikely to be made, then he should consider whether the rates at which he is accepting business are appropriate[29] and whether he should be continuing to write business of the relevant class.[30] Thus in *Deeny v. Gooda Walker Ltd*[31] one active underwriter sought to increase his syndicate's reinsurance cover following the Piper Alpha disaster. The cost was such that the excess of loss business he continued to write at low rates was "doomed to be loss making" and Phillips J. held that the losses so suffered were the result of the underwriters' incompetence.[32]

An underwriter whose reinsurance programme is based essentially upon the **16–051** cost of obtaining reinsurance rather than upon a proper assessment of the vertical and horizontal cover needed to obtain appropriate protection will be in breach of duty. Thus in *Arbuthnott v. Feltrim Underwriting Agencies Ltd*[33] one underwriter's reinsurance programme involved obtaining as much cover as possible by spending approximately half the syndicate's gross premium income. This approach was condemned by Phillips J. as unacceptable.[34]

(iv) *Obtaining Valid Reinsurance*

As stated above,[35] the underwriter will know more about the risk to be reinsured **16–052** than the broker instructed to obtain the reinsurance. Underwriters should also be aware of the duty of an insured or reinsured to make full disclosure of all material

---

[27] [1996] L.R.L.R. 183.

[28] *ibid.*, at 208–209. See also *Berriman (Sir David) v. Rose Thomson Young (Underwriting) Ltd* [1996] L.R.L.R. 426 at 457, where Morrison J. criticised the underwriter for his mistaken view that by obtaining reinsurance with a company outside the London market he would reduce the effects of the spiral: the underwriter should have realised that the reinsurer would in turn obtain cover in the London market.

[29] See paras 16–053 to 16–056, below.

[30] *Wynniatt-Husey v. R.J. Bromley (Underwriting Agencies) plc* [1996] L.R.L.R. 310 at 321.

[31] [1996] L.R.L.R. 183.

[32] *ibid.*, at 217.

[33] [1995] C.L.C. 437.

[34] *ibid.*, at 468F-H: "I do not find it negligent *per se* that Mr Fagan budgeted to spend not more than 50 per cent of his premium income on reinsurance. On the contrary, any competent underwriter would need to decide the maximum that he could afford to spend if the account were to remain viable. What is not satisfactory is Mr Fagan's statement that his programme was based on buying as much cover as he could for the money that he could afford to spend. The correct approach should have been to work out, on the basis of PML calculations, how much reinsurance he needed and then to calculate whether he could afford to buy it. If he could not, he should have concluded that his programme was not viable and attempted to redesign it accordingly." See also para. 16–040 above.

[35] para. 16–038.

facts and not to make any misrepresentation to the reinsurer.[36] They should therefore take care that the broker is informed of all material facts and that the information they provide to the broker for presentation to the proposed reinsurers is full and accurate. In *Aiken v. Stewart Wrightson Members Agency Ltd*[37] the managing agent made an unintentional but material misrepresentation to the reinsurers. They also failed to disclose their own reserves for asbestosis and diethylstilboestrol ("DES") claims, both of which were material. Potter J. held that they had thereby been negligent. He described the duty of the managing agent, Pulbrook, in these terms:

" . . . it was the duty of Pulbrook as prudent managing agents seeking unlimited protection in respect of the whole of the account for the years up to 1979 to consider with care what required to be disclosed to a prospective reinsurer. This duty applied especially to the matters which were giving Pulbrook concern and were arguably, if not obviously, material to the prudent reinsurer, in particular the mounting claims for asbestosis and DES which were the reason why the reinsurance was being sought in the first place. Further, that duty extended to disclosure of facts which were arguably material, *so as to avoid unnecessary risk of avoidance.*"[38]

If there are "grey areas" which might require disclosure the managing agent should apply his mind to them or, if he wishes to rely upon the broker for advice, he should provide the broker with the information to enable the broker to resolve the question.[39]

(e) *Managing agent—negligent underwriting of individual risks*

16–053 Insurance allows the risk of loss to be shared: a number of insureds pay premiums to insurers to reflect the risk of loss and the insurers use the premiums of all to meet the losses of few. The insurers should be left with sufficient to meet their expenses and to make a profit. That should be the case if the premiums required by insurers are properly rated. The decision whether to accept a risk and at what premium is a matter of professional judgment for the underwriter. In order to exercise that judgment with reasonable competence he needs:

(i) to form a reasonably informed view of the nature of the risk which he is being asked to accept on behalf of his syndicate, and

(ii) to determine and require a premium which adequately reflects that risk.

16–054 Particular difficulties arise when the proposed risk is a "run-off" contract. Run-off contracts involve the reinsurance of another syndicate's or insurer's portfolio of business, so that, subject to the solvency of the reinsurer and any deductible, the reinsured is relieved of any further liability on that portfolio. The premium paid is almost invariably very substantial. However, where the underlying business contains a significant amount of long tail business,[40] particular care is needed because "no one knows the length of the tail, and tails have a habit of

---

[36] See chap. 14, paras 14–060 and 14–069.

[37] [1995] 1 W.L.R. 1281; for the facts see para. 16–17, above.

[38] *ibid.*, at 1313G-H; the emphasis is Potter J.'s. See also chap. 14, para. 14–065 above.

[39] *ibid.*, at 1314A-E.

[40] *i.e.* business on which claims can be expected to take a considerable time to be advised or settled.

wagging for a very long time and wagging very vigorously".[41] The dangers inherent in underwriting such risks were the subject of the decision of Cresswell J. in *Henderson v. Merrett Syndicates Ltd.*[42] That case concerned the writing of 11 run-off contracts in the late 1970s and early 1980s, a time of increasing perception of the losses which were arising and which might arise from claims relating to asbestos (both personal injury and property damage) and pollution. In respect of nine of the 11 contracts the underwriter was held to have been negligent, mainly because each "contract exposed the plaintiffs to potentially huge liabilities, unlimited in time or amount, which were not capable of reasonable quantification on the material before [the underwriter]. There was insufficient placing or other information available at the time the risk was considered to enable a reliable assessment to be made with a reasonable degree of confidence of [the syndicate's] ultimate net retained potential liability under the contract."[43] If such contracts were to be written at all, then full details of the IBNR[44] loss reserves for both asbestos and non-asbestos related claims and of the methodology used to calculate those reserves should have been required. Underwriting involves an acceptance of risk, but the underwriter should have a reasonable perception of what that risk is, particularly where the potential liability is unlimited in time or amount.

Having obtained a reasonable understanding of the risk which is being broked **16–055** to him, the underwriter's next task is to consider the adequacy of the premium offered. In *Deeny v. Gooda Walker Ltd*[45] Phillips J. summarised the correct approach to rating in these terms:

> " . . . it is a fundamental principle applying to all insurance business that the underwriter must satisfy himself that the premium received is commensurate with the risk assumed. If not so satisfied he should not write the risk. This basic principle is subject to pragmatic exceptions. Sometimes it will be politic to accept an unattractive risk as a loss leader to a broker who has more attractive business in his gift. The majority of business written tends to be renewal business. Such business, once rejected will find another home and not return. This again may justify the short term expedient of accepting a risk at an unattractive rate."[46]

Four elements make up an adequate premium: the basic risk premium, a loading for random fluctuations, a loading for administrative expenses and brokerage and a loading for profit. Generally an underwriter can and should rely upon past experience of the market in general and of his own syndicate in particular.[47]

That task is more difficult when the risk being insured is catastrophe excess of **16–056** loss business. It is in the nature of such cover that losses will usually be infrequent and irregular. Moreover, the degree of risk will depend upon the nature of the insured's exposure to loss from a single event or aggregation of events. Historic experience is therefore not a useful guide. The correct approach is for

---

[41] Robert Kiln, *Reinsurance in Practice* (3rd ed.), p. 384.
[42] [1997] L.R.L.R. 265.
[43] *ibid.*, at 324.
[44] "Incurred but not reported", *i.e.* losses which have been suffered but not advised to the insurer.
[45] [1996] L.R.L.R. 183.
[46] *ibid.*, at 201. See also *Arbuthnott v. Feltrim Underwriting Agencies Ltd* [1995] C.L.C. 437 at 444B-E, *per* Phillips J. for a discussion of the particular problems of rating excess of loss business at Lloyd's.
[47] *ibid.*, at 201.

the underwriter to consider the type and level of event which would result in a claim on such cover and the likelihood of such an event. That would involve a high degree of judgment rather than mathematical precision, but if not attempted at all the underwriter would have no proper basis at all for agreeing a premium and so be negligent.[48] The information which the underwriter needs is essentially the same as that required for a proper calculation of PML.[49] An underwriter who underwrites high layers of excess of loss business at low rates on the basis that no claims will be made will be negligent: he should derive no comfort from the claims history of such business and ignores the fact that protection is being sought by those he is reinsuring.[50] Nor should a reasonably competent underwriter accept such business at whatever rate was offered simply on the basis of recent claims history.[51]

(f) *Managing agent—inadequate supervision of active underwriter*

16-057   While the acts and omissions of the active underwriter are inevitably the primary source of findings of liability against managing agents, it is the managing agents and not the underwriters who contract to carry out the underwriting. The active underwriters are their employees, but they are not just entitled to leave them to run their syndicates on their own. While an allegation of lack of supervision of the active underwriter will generally cause no loss unless the underwriter himself has also been negligent,[52] the board of a managing agency has a separate duty to consider and approve the active underwriter's underwriting policy and to monitor its implementation.[53] That requires the board to obtain and analyse sufficient data to check that the underwriter has drawn up a reasonable plan and to monitor his implementation of it. It is not sufficient for them to rely upon the underwriter's assurance that all is well.[54] The board should therefore possess sufficient expertise to analyse and question the approach of the active underwriter.[55]

(g) *Managing agent—negligence in relation to reinsurance to close*

16-058   The decision as to whether to effect reinsurance to close[56] and on what terms, is one of the most important functions of a managing agent. Once effected it is final and there is no means of adjusting the rights between the parties.[57] If the managing agent also manages the reinsuring syndicate he must act equitably between the Names on the syndicate which is to be closed and the Names on that which is to reinsure them. The managing agent should therefore only effect reinsurance to close between succeeding years of the same syndicate if he is in

---

[48] *Deeny v. Gooda Walker Ltd* [1996] L.R.L.R. 183 at 202.
[49] See paras 16–031 to 16–033 above.
[50] *Deeny v. Gooda Walker Ltd* [1996] L.R.L.R. 183 at 212.
[51] *ibid.*, at 215–216. However, it is extremely hard to show that an underwriter should have decided to cease to write business at all: *ibid.*, at 216.
[52] *Deeny v. Gooda Walker Ltd* [1996] L.R.L.R. 183 at 186–190; *Wynniatt-Husey v. R.J. Bromley (Underwriting Agencies) plc* [1996] L.R.L.R. 310 at 319.
[53] *Arbuthnott v. Feltrim Underwriting Agencies Ltd* [1995] C.L.C. 437 at 483; *Berriman (Sir David) v. Rose Thomson Young (Underwriting) Ltd* [1996] L.R.L.R. 426 at 454–455.
[54] *ibid.*, at 483–484.
[55] *Wynniatt-Husey v. R.J. Bromley (Underwriting Agencies) plc* [1996] L.R.L.R. 310 at 319.
[56] See para. 16–016 above.
[57] *Henderson v. Merrett Syndicates Ltd* [1997] L.R.L.R. 265, Cresswell J.

a position to form a reasonable judgment as to the liabilities which are to be reinsured. That involves considering the likely level of claims, because that is a critical ingredient of the premium. For these purposes there are two classes of claim: those known to be outstanding and those incurred[58] but not reported. Assessment of the latter can never be certain and requires the exercise of judgment by the underwriter. A reasonable projection can usually be made on the basis of past experience and the knowledge of the underlying business to be reinsured. However, if the underwriter is unable to arrive at a reasonably accurate assessment of the appropriate premium, he should leave the year open.

In *Henderson v. Merrett Syndicates Ltd*[59] the portfolios of the relevant syndi- **16–059** cates contained not only a large account of business which was likely to give rise to asbestos and pollution-related claims but also 11 run-off contracts which also included significant amounts of such business.[60] The underwriter effected rein- surance to close over a period of years when it was increasingly known that the level of such claims was likely to be substantial, but when it was not clear how high it might be. He was sued on the basis that he should not have effected such reinsurance at all.[61] Cresswell J. rejected that allegation in respect of the first three years in question. However in later years there were significant areas of uncertainty, as more of the eleven run-off contracts formed part of the underlying portfolio and as the potential scale of asbestos and pollution claims became clearer. By the fourth year there were fundamental uncertainties as to the future development of asbestos claims (both personal injury and property damage) and pollution claims. Those uncertainties were compounded by the run-off contracts. The underwriter failed to make sufficient enquiries as to the likely exposure, either on the syndicate's own direct business or under the run-off contracts. He was therefore held to have been negligent.

4. Damages

An award of damages is the usual ultimate remedy against members' and **16–060** managing agents. However, because of the uncertain and continuing extent of the liabilities to which Names may become exposed as a result of breaches of duty by their members' and managing agents, declarations that the Names are entitled to be indemnified against certain types of loss in the future may also be obtained in appropriate cases.[62] The scope of any such indemnity should, however, be the same as that of any award of damages made after the true extent of the relevant liabilities had become known. The question of abatement of the members' or managing agents' fees to reflect their defective discharge of their duties[63] has not been the subject of significant judicial decision.

---

[58] *i.e.* claims to be made on policies already written.
[59] [1997] L.R.L.R. 265, Cresswell J.
[60] As to which see para. 16–054, above.
[61] An allegation that the premium should have been higher would have been of little use to the plaintiffs, given the enormous scale of the losses eventually suffered.
[62] The courts have also awarded damages on an interim basis.
[63] See chap. 3, paras 3–006 *et seq.*

(a) *Remoteness*

16–061   It is not enough for a Name to show that his members' or managing agent was negligent and that he suffered losses in the relevant year of account of the syndicate in question. He must show that the losses of which he complains were sufficiently related to the breach of duty which he has proved. To do so he must show that (a) the losses were "caused" by that breach of duty,[64] and (b) the loss and damage was reasonably foreseeable.[65]

(b) *Causation*

16–062   In order to recover damages for a particular loss, a Name must show that there was a sufficient causal link between that loss and the breach of duty (whether contractual or tortious) which he has established. This has proved to be a fruitful area for arguments both by Names and on behalf of members' and managing agents. In response the courts have adopted a pragmatic approach rather than embarking upon any overly technical and precise exercise, which would have increased costs but not produced a materially different result.

(i) *Members' agents—consequences of failure to advise adequately as to syndicate participation*

16–063   As a result of the shortcomings of his members' agent, a Name may receive inadequate advice as to which syndicates he should join and as to the extent to which he should participate in them. Those syndicates may then suffer losses in the relevant years and the Name may seek damages to the extent that they do. The following arguments have arisen in that context:

> (i) The Name would have joined the same syndicates even if properly advised.
>
> (ii) The Name would have joined other syndicates which would have made losses.
>
> (iii) There was an insufficient causal link between the losses which the Name suffered on the syndicate and the inadequate advice given by the members' agent.

It is for the Name to show that he would have acted differently, but for the members' agent to show that he would have joined other, loss-making syndicates or that the losses were caused by some intervening event.

16–064   The Name must show that he would have acted differently had he received correct advice and that, had he so acted, he would have avoided or reduced his losses. The question as to what difference proper advice would have been made is to be approached on the basis that the Name should have received all that advice which a reasonably competent members' agent would have given. Thus if

---

[64] As to which see paras 16–062 to 16–070, below.
[65] As to which see para. 16–071, below.

a Name appreciates that certain types of syndicate are higher risk than others and shows a predilection for membership of such syndicates, he is nevertheless entitled to advice as to the proper balance of his portfolio. If he does not receive such advice and is able to satisfy the court that he would have acted upon it, at least to a certain extent, then he will be entitled to damages accordingly.[66]

On the other hand, a Name who should not have been placed on a high risk **16–065** syndicate should not give credit for the average loss suffered by Lloyd's syndicates in the relevant year of account. That average would include high risk syndicates and it would be hard to show that the Name would have suffered a loss, albeit smaller, because he would have joined some other, unspecified syndicate had he been correctly advised.[67] It might be different if a specific alternative syndicate had been considered at the time the Name was being advised.

In *Brown v. KMR Services Ltd*[68] the members' agent sought to argue that the **16–066** breach of duty which resulted in Mr Sword-Daniels being on certain syndicates was the occasion for the loss rather than the effective cause of the loss.[69] This argument was rejected on the facts: Mr Sword-Daniels had been placed on high risk syndicates, *i.e.* syndicates with a high risk of high losses. The members' agent had not argued that the managing agents of those syndicates had conducted the underwriting negligently and that that negligence broke the chain of causation. Such a plea would not have been of avail, because the members' agent was contractually liable for any want of care by the managing agent.[70]

(ii) *Losses caused by negligent underwriting*

Where underwriting has been carried out negligently, it does not follow that the **16–067** Names are entitled to recover all losses suffered as members of the syndicate for the relevant year of account. They are entitled only to recover damages for the losses which were actually caused by the negligent acts or omissions of the underwriter. If, for example, the underwriter was at fault as to the amount of "vertical" reinsurance he obtained,[71] the Names could not recover all their losses, some of which would relate to business underwritten in earlier years or arise from lack of "horizontal" reinsurance cover.[72] Moreover, proof of negligent underwriting in one respect will not lead to the drawing of the inference that the underwriter was negligent in other respects so as to circumvent the need to show a sufficient causal link.[73] Nor is it possible simply to compare the losses suffered by the syndicate in question with the results of a hypothetical syndicate writing

---

[66] *Brown v. KMR Services Ltd* [1995] 4 All E.R. 598, CA; varying [1994] 4 All E.R. 385 (*Brown's Case*).

[67] *Brown v. KMR Services Ltd* [1994] 4 All E.R. 385 at 399g–400a *per* Gatehouse J. (*Sword-Daniels' Case*, which was not the subject of appeal).

[68] [1994] 4 All E.R. 385 (*Sword-Daniel's Case*, which was not subject to appeal); for the facts see para. 16–026, above.

[69] The argument relied upon, *inter alia*, *Galoo Ltd v. Bright Grahame Murray (a Firm)* [1994] 1 W.L.R. 1360, as to which see chap. 15, paras 15–123 *et seq.*

[70] [1994] 4 All E.R. 385 at 398a-g and [1995] 4 All E.R. 598 at 643g. Under the present regime the members' agent may well be in a better position: see para. 16–006.

[71] See para. 16–039, above.

[72] *Deeny v. Gooda Walker Ltd* [1996] L.R.L.R. 183 at 224–225.

[73] *ibid.*, at 227–228.

similar business in a competent manner: that would be an "artificial and unrealistic exercise".[74]

16–068   The fact that the consequences of negligent underwriting of catastrophe business have been exacerbated by a concatenation of catastrophes does not give rise to a defence of causation. There is nothing in the occurrence of catastrophes to break the chain of causation, because they are by their nature random events.[75] However, if they are such as to have caused losses to syndicates whose underwriters had not been negligent, then an appropriate reduction in damages should be made.[76]

16–069   Different considerations apply where an underwriter has negligently obtained reinsurance with reinsurers who are unlikely to be good security for the risk reinsured and, on the strength of that reinsurance, has underwritten business upon which losses have subsequently been suffered. In those circumstances there is no sufficient link between the total losses on the loss-making business underwritten and the inadequate reinsurance. The Names are entitled to damages only for that part of their total losses which was ineffectively reinsured with inappropriate reinsurers.[77]

16–070   Where the negligence consists of failure to make full disclosure to reinsurers or in making a misrepresentation to reinsurers,[78] it might be argued that, had the potential reinsurers been given full and accurate information no reinsurance could have been obtained. Similar issues have arisen in the context of claims against insurance brokers.[79] Save in extreme cases the courts are unlikely to adopt an "all or nothing" approach. Rather, they are likely to approach the question on the basis of loss of a chance or, if there is sufficiently clear evidence, to hold that reinsurance would have been obtained, either at the same or a higher premium.[80]

(c) Foreseeability

16–071   In cases against members' agents for negligent advice and against both members' agents and managing agents for negligent underwriting defendants have sought to argue that losses caused by one or more catastrophes were not reasonably foreseeable. In the context of catastrophe XL business[81] such a plea is unsustainable: the risk being underwritten is loss caused by one or more catastrophes and if negligent advice or underwriting exposes a Name unduly to the risk of such losses, those who so exposed him cannot be heard to say that the losses were not reasonably foreseeable.[82] As against members' agents who negligently place their Names on syndicates writing catastrophe XL business, loss caused by catastrophes should have been foreseeable, even if its extent was not.[83]

---

[74] *ibid.*, at 228.

[75] *Wynniatt-Husey v. R.J. Bromley (Underwriting Agencies) plc* [1996] L.R.L.R. 310 at 314.

[76] *Deeny v. Gooda Walker Ltd* [1996] L.R.L.R. 183 at 225–227.

[77] *Berriman (Sir David) v. Rose Thomson Young (Underwriting) Ltd* [1996] L.R.L.R. 426 at 485.

[78] See para. 16–052, above.

[79] See chap. 14, at para. 14–109.

[80] *Aiken v. Stewart Wrightson Members Agency Ltd* [1995] 1 W.L.R. 1281, reported in summary only on this point. See also Chap. 14, paras 14–109 to 14–112.

[81] See para. 16–009, above.

[82] *Arbuthnott v. Feltrim Underwriting Agencies Ltd* [1995] C.L.C. 437 at 491H–492B.

[83] *Brown v. KMR Services Ltd* [1994] 4 All E.R. 385 at 398j–299a, Gatehouse J.; [1995] 4 All E.R. 598 at 630f–621j; Stuart-Smith L.J. and 641j–643h, Hobhouse L.J.

(d) *Measure of damages*

In both contract and tort, damages are awarded to compensate the injured party 16–072
for the wrong he has suffered. The award of damages is calculated so far as
possible to put him in the position in which he would have been had his legal
right not been invaded.[84] The principle is easily stated. Its strict application
would present serious practical difficulties in claims against members' and
managing agents and has led the courts to adopt a pragmatic approach to the
calculation of some losses.

(i) *Members' agents—consequences of failure to advise adequately as to syndicate participation*

Subject to questions of causation[85] a Name who suffers losses on a syndicate 16–073
which he would not have joined had he been properly advised, is entitled to
damages equivalent to his losses on that syndicate.[86]

The Name may have been advised by his members' agent to take out stop-loss 16–074
insurance as part of his overall underwriting philosophy. If he did so and thereby
mitigated his losses it might be thought that, as against the members' agent who
advised him to obtain that insurance, the Name should give credit for sums so
recovered. However, in *Brown v. KMR Services Ltd*[87] that argument was rejected.
Gatehouse J. followed a well-established line of authority that a contract of
insurance was to be regarded as *res inter alios acta* and so disregarded for the
purposes of assessing damages.[88] Although a Name is bound to account to his
stop loss insurers if he recovers damages for losses caused by negligent underwriting for which he has already been compensated by those insurers,[89] so that
credit should not be given where the breach of duty relates to negligent underwriting,[90] it is hard to see why a members' agent sued for negligent advice as to
a Name's underwriting philosophy should not be entitled to a credit for recoveries which were made as a result of that same advice.

A Name may participate in a syndicate for a number of years as a result of 16–075
negligent advice from his members' agent. He may make a profit on some years
followed by a loss on others. However, the Name need not give credit for those
earlier profits when claiming damages for the later losses: he was entitled to
proper advice in respect of each year and had a separate cause of action for each
year.[91]

A Name who makes an underwriting loss will be able to claim tax relief for 16–076
that loss. However, no credit should be given by reason of such relief. This is
because the damages recovered by the Name will themselves be subject to
tax.[92]

---

[84] *The Albazero* [1977] A.C. 744 at 841 *per* Lord Diplock, cited in *Deeny v. Gooda Walker Ltd* [1996] L.R.L.R. 183 by Phillips J. at 229.
[85] See para. 16–062, above.
[86] *Brown v. KMR Services Ltd* [1994] 4 All E.R. 385, Gatehouse J.; [1995] 4 All E.R. 598, CA. For the facts see para. 16–026, above.
[87] [1994] 4 All E.R. 385 (not subject to appeal on this point).
[88] *Bradburn v. Great Western Railway Co.* (1874) L.R. 10 Exch. 1; *Parry v. Cleaver* [1970] A.C. 1.
[89] *Napier and Ettrick (Lord) v. Hunter* [1993] A.C. 713.
[90] See para. 16–081, below.
[91] *Brown v. KMR Services Ltd* [1995] 4 All E.R. 585 at 640c–641j *per* Hobhouse L.J., with whom Peter Gibson L.J. agreed.
[92] *Deeny v. Gooda Walker Ltd (No.2)* [1996] 1 W.L.R. 426, HL.

(ii) *Losses caused by negligent underwriting*

16–077   Where the underwriter negligently fails to obtain adequate "vertical" reinsurance[93] and his Names suffer serious losses as a result of one or more catastrophes, the correct measure of loss may be difficult to establish in practice. Difficult questions as to the effect of catastrophic and other less serious losses on the complicated reinsurance programmes which Lloyd's syndicates have and as to the problems in practice which the underwriter would have had in obtaining sufficient reinsurance cover might arise. It is not practicable to seek to unravel or to rewrite an entire year's business. The courts have adopted a pragmatic, but broadly just, approach.

16–078   The starting point is to establish the PML.[94] The next stage is to establish the extent to which a reasonably competent underwriter could have decided to expose his Names to the risk of loss in the event of the PML. That will depend upon the information as to the syndicate's approach to underwriting which the Names should have known, either directly or through their members' agent.[95] The next stage is to compare the vertical reinsurance cover actually obtained with that which should have been obtained (on the assumption that it could have been obtained). That reinsurance should have left the Names' exposed to the permitted extent only when it was exhausted and not at any lower level. Then the cost of such reinsurance should be estimated and credit given for it.[96] Finally the unreinsured losses which would have been reinsured need to be established.[97] Those losses, subject to credit for the notional reinsurance premiums, represent the basic measure of loss.[98]

16–079   That general approach has been refined in a number of respects, some of them extremely technical.[99] To the extent that Names fail to establish that it was incompetent deliberately to choose to retain exposure at low layers, losses resulting from that decision are not recoverable.[1] Where the underwriter instructed brokers to seek reinsurance but they were unable to obtain it, then the Names cannot complain of the underwriter's acts or recover damages for the lack of such reinsurance against those liable for him.[2] Where no allegation of negligence leading to any lack of "horizontal" reinsurance cover is established, damages should be reduced to allow for the reduction of the reinsurance cover which should have been obtained by a series of minor losses.[3] On the other hand, the allowance for deliberate exposure should be treated as being above the

---

[93] See para. 16–039, above.
[94] See para. 16–031, above.
[95] See para. 16–034, above.
[96] This may be an essentially theoretical exercise, if such reinsurance would have been hard or impossible to obtain. However, the alternative approach (on the basis that the underwriter should have ceased to accept risks in the absence of adequate reinsurance) involves a complex and impracticable exercise which should lead to the same result: see the comments of Phillips J. in *Deeny v. Gooda Walker Ltd* [1996] L.R.L.R. 183 at 230.
[97] Thus damages will not be recoverable for losses which exceed a competently calculated PML.
[98] See *Deeny v. Deeny Walker* [1996] L.R.L.R. 183; *Arbuthnott v. Feltrim Underwriting Agencies Ltd* [1995] C.L.C. 437, *Arbuthnott v. Feltrim Underwriting Agencies Ltd (No.2)* [1995] C.L.C. 1550; *Arbuthnott v. Feltrim Underwriting Agencies Ltd (No.3)* [1996] C.L.C. 714; *Berriman (Sir David) v. Rose Thomson Young (Underwriting) Ltd* [1996] L.R.L.R. 426.
[99] See, for example, *Arbuthnott v. Feltrim Underwriting Agencies Ltd (No.3)* [1996] C.L.C. 714, where Longmore J. had to decide a sequence of detailed issues as to the assessment of damages.
[1] *Deeny v. Gooda Walker Ltd* [1996] L.R.L.R. 183 at 230.
[2] *ibid.* Unless they could show that the underwriter was negligent to continue to accept business given the unavailability of the reinsurance he had sought to obtain.
[3] *ibid.*

reinsurance cover which should have been obtained, not below it or in the middle of it.[4] Unless and to the extent that it is shown that the reinsurance strategy of the underwriter was negligent, the additional notional cover should be on the same basis as that actually obtained, both as to type of cover and as to any co-insurance[5] reasonably made by the underwriter. Credit should be given for the the losses which would have been retained as a consequence of that strategy.[6] Where, as a result of the underwriter's reasonable decision to obtain reinsurance cover which undervalued one currency[7] as opposed to another, the Names are entitled to recover damages in the undervalued currency on the basis of the reinsurance obtained and not at some other rate.[8]

Where reinsurance cover is successfully avoided or fails to respond to claims **16–80** as a result of the underwriter's negligence then the basic measure of loss is the sum which would have been recovered from such reinsurance.[9] If the court concludes that reinsurers would have required a higher premium had they been fully informed, then credit should be given for the additional premium.[10]

As in claims against members' agents for failure to give proper advice, credit **16–081** need not be given for recoveries made by Names on stop loss insurance,[11] for profits on earlier years,[12] or for tax relief on losses.[13]

Apart from the basic measures of loss set out above, Names may also be able **16–082** to recover consequential losses. For example, where a syndicate goes into run-off[14] as a result of losses caused by the underwriter's negligence, each Name on that syndicate will incur a share of the costs of that run-off which otherwise would have been borne by the syndicate into which the open year was reinsured to close. Such costs are recoverable.[15] If a Name's personal expenses at Lloyd's are increased as a result, damages may be recovered for the increase.[16] The same is true of losses caused by the effect of movements of exchange rates on losses caused by the underwriter's negligence.[17]

---

[4] *Arbuthnott v. Feltrim Underwriting Agencies Ltd (No.2)* [1995] C.L.C. 1550, at 1551–1552 *per* Phillips J.

[5] *i.e.* a retention of a percentage of the risk reinsured.

[6] *Arbuthnott v. Feltrim Underwriting Agencies Ltd (No.2)* [1995] C.L.C. 1550 at 1552–1553 *per* Phillips J.

[7] See para. 16–045, above.

[8] *Arbuthnott v. Feltrim Underwriting Agencies Ltd (No.3)* [1996] C.L.C. 714, 717 *per* Longmore J.

[9] Unless the court proceeds on the basis of "loss of a chance", as to which see para. 16–070, above.

[10] *Aiken v. Stewart Wrightson Members Agency Ltd* [1995] 1 W.L.R. 1281.

[11] See para. 16–074, above and *Deeny v. Gooda Walker Ltd* [1996] L.R.L.R. 183 at 231; *Arbuthnott v. Feltrim Underwriting Agencies Ltd* [1995] C.L.C. 437 at 492. It follows that Names who failed to take out stop loss insurance are not precluded from recovering damages for losses which would have been recovered from such insurance.

[12] See para. 16–075, above and *Arbuthnott v. Feltrim Underwriting Agencies Ltd* [1995] C.L.C. 437 at 492.

[13] See para. 16–076, above.

[14] *i.e.* where there is no reinsurance to close so that the syndicate is left open.

[15] *Deeny v. Gooda Walker Ltd* [1996] L.R.L.R. 183 at 231.

[16] *ibid.*

[17] *ibid.*

CHAPTER 17

INFORMATION TECHNOLOGY PROFESSIONALS

	PARA.
17. Information Technology Professionals	
1. General	17–001
(a) Standard software	17–002
(b) Bespoke and modified standard software	17–004
(c) The nature of software	17–005
(d) Software as goods	17–007
(d) Services or goods?	17–008
(e) Nature of the service	17–010
(f) Implied warranties at common law	17–013
2. Duties	17–014
(a) Duties to client	17–014
(i) Bespoke software	17–014
(ii) Modified standard software	17–023
(iii) Communication of client's purpose	17–031
(iv) Implementation and testing	17–036
(v) The importance of co-operation between the parties	17–038
(vi) Duties of support	17–044
(vii) Staff training	17–023
(viii) User's operation manual	17–046
(ix) Implied terms of reasonable skill and care	17–047
(x) Common law duty of care	17–051
(xi) Supply of standard/modified standard software: consultant or supplier?	17–052
(xii) Negligent misstatements	17–055
(xiii) Collateral contract	17–056
(xiv) Advice on computer systems	17–057

	PARA.
(xv) Grant of quiet possession: "time-bombs"	17–059
(b) Duties other than to client	17–061
(i) Common law liability to third parties	17–061
(ii) The Consumer Protection Act 1987	17–072
(iii) "Safety-critical" information	17–078
3. Standard of care and breach	17–079
(a) Standard of care	17–079
i. Contracts for services	17–079
ii. Contracts for sale/supply of goods	17–082
(b) "Bugs" and "bedding in"—inevitable defects and software	17–085
(c) The time when the obligation of fitness for purposes arises	17–090
(d) The time when the obligation ceases	17–092
(e) "State of the art" defence	17–094
4. Causation	17–095
5. Remedies	17–098
(a) Contract	17–099
(b) Repudiation: when possible?	17–100
(c) Acceptance: when deemed?	17–101
(d) Time of the essence?	17–102
(e) "Reliance loss" and "expectation loss": election neccessary?	17–106
(f) Quantum: difficulties in calculation	17–112
(g) Tort	17–116
6. Exclusion and limitation of liability	17–118
7. Duty to mitigate	17–124
8. Contributory negligence	17–126
9. Limitation	17–131

1. GENERAL

This chapter considers the professional liability of providers of information **17–001** technology services.[1] The principal services considered are the supply, develop-

---

[1] Much of the chapter concerns the supply of software, which may be the subject of copyright and/or duties of confidentiality. Liability arising from breaches of copyright and/or confidence are however beyond the scope of this book, and the reader is referred to Toulson and Phipps, *Confidentiality*, and *Copinger and James on Copyright*.

ment and maintenance of computer systems and software. No professional body has yet been established in respect of consultants and others who provide services in these fields.[2] As yet, therefore, there is no code of conduct, regulatory framework or any other guidelines which governs the appointment or work of such consultants. However this makes information technology professionals no less suitable for inclusion in this book than (for example) architects or engineers. The development of the legal principles governing the liability of the latter professionals is rarely influenced (at least expressly) by the fact or nature of such self-regulation. In any event, as will be seen below, in practice the absence (to date) of a recognised professional body and/or self-regulation has not deterred or hindered the courts in their adaptation of the common law to provide principles governing the duties owed by information technology professionals to their clients.

(a) Standard software

17–002   Only brief mention is made here of the supply of standard ("off the shelf") software, since it is unlikely ever to be categorised as a supply of services,[3] and therefore falls outside the scope of this chapter.[4] When a standard software package is sold this is invariably on a medium such as a disk,[5] in which case the agreement to supply the disk is a contract for the sale (or, depending on its terms, the hire) of goods. Whether the goods can be regarded as also including the software on the disk, so that the statutory implied warranties of satisfactory quality and fitness for purpose apply not only to the disk itself but also to the software, is a separate (and difficult) question. However in England and Wales the answer to this question is probably yes.[6] As yet the question has only arisen directly in Scotland, where the Scottish Court of Session determined that such a contract should be treated as *sui generis*: *Beta Computers (Europe) Ltd v. Adobe Systems (Europe) Ltd* [1996] F.S.R. 387.[7]

---

[2] A kitemark offering acccreditation and training was however launched by the British Government in 1999.

[3] Many of the reasons for this are discussed in paras 17–004 onwards, and apply here *a fortiori*.

[4] For a discussion of the legal issues arising from the supply of standard software, see D. Rowland and E. Macdonald, *Information Technology Law*, esp. pp. 106–116.

[5] It may however be electronically transmitted by downloading or e-mail, for example. If so, the question of whether the transfer can amount to a sale of goods is a still more difficult one, raising similar issues to those considered below at paras 17–005 to 17–007.

[6] This is the view expressed (*obiter*) by the Court of Appeal in *St Albans City and District Council v. International Computers Ltd*: see paras 17–018 to 17–022 below. It also accords with common sense. "Most consumers would be surprised, and rightly so, at the suggestion that the retailer from whom their software was bought guaranteed only the floppy disc and the system documentation (the handbook)—not the performance and quality of the programs recorded on it": Napier, "The future of information technology law" [1992] C.L.J. 46 at 56.

[7] The case concerned the supply of a "shrink-wrapped" software package, *i.e.* software packaged so as to indicate that the software (the copyright of which belonged to a third party, I) was subject to a strict end-user licence. The pursuers sought to recover payment for the supply of the software. The defenders contended that there was an absolute right to reject the package until it was opened. Lord Penrose reasoned (at 375) that what the defenders sought to have supplied was access to I's intellectual property in a medium which they could use and from which they could copy the software onto their own hardware, in order to use it for business purposes. The subject of the contract was thus a complex product, comprising the medium (*i.e.* the disk) and the manifestation on it of particular intellectual property. Lord Penrose considered that there were no true analogies to this type of product, and that the only acceptable view is that the supply of proprietary software for a price is a contract "*sui generis*".

Standard software of this kind is usually sold on the basis that the purchaser   **17–003**
is granted a conditional licence to use the software by the copyright owner,
usually a "shrink wrap" licence, in which the customer agrees to licence conditions by opening the packaging to the software. However, since the owner of the
copyright is invariably a third party to the contract of sale, and the packaging is
generally only opened after that contract (*i.e.* the purchase) has been concluded,
it is doubtful that in such circumstances the licence conditions are validly
incorporated into the contract of sale.[8]

(b) *Bespoke and modified standard software*

This chapter is instead concerned with the position where information technology   **17–004**
professionals contract to supply either tailor-made ("bespoke") software (*i.e.*
software which is written for the client from scratch), or *modified* standard
software. In such cases two difficult and interrelated questions arise:

(i) does such software (*i.e.* the program itself) represent "goods", so that a
contract for its supply is capable of being treated as a traditional nominate
contract for the sale of goods[9]; and

(ii) even if software is goods, is the contract for the supply of the software in
fact one for the supply of goods, or instead a contract for the supply of
services.

These questions are potentially important because, ordinarily, the law applies a
different regime of warranties depending on whether a particular contract is for
the supply of goods, or the supply of services, namely, fault-based warranties of
reasonable skill and care if the contract is for the supply of services, or strict
liability warranties (of satisfactory quality and fitness for purpose) if the contract
is for the supply of goods.

(c) *The nature of software*

The difficulties in answering these questions stem partly from the nature of   **17–005**
software itself. The term software is probably synonymous (at least for the
purposes of this chapter) with "computer program", a convenient definition for
which appears in the United States Copyright Act, at section 101: "a set of
statements or instructions to be used directly or indirectly in a computer in order
to bring about a particular result". On this basis, programs and software are a
form of information. However it is well established that, in general, information
is not property at all.[10] For this reason it has been said[11] that software, of itself,
does not fall within the conventional legal definition of goods, namely the
definition contained in section 61 of the Sale of Goods Act 1979, which defines

---

[8] Arguably, by opening the packaging the user enters into a separate contract with the copyright
owner.
[9] This first question arises equally in the case of standard software: see para. 17–002 above.
[10] *Boardman v. Phipps* [1967] 2 A.C. 46, *per* Lord Upjohn at 127F.
[11] *St Albans City and District Council v. International Computers Ltd* [1996] 4 All E.R. 481; [1997]
1 F.S.R. 251.

goods as "including all personal chattels other than things in action and money".[12]

17–006   The difficulty is compounded by the fact that, in the case of a contract for the supply of bespoke (or modified standard) software, the subject matter of the contract, *i.e.* the software itself, does not exist (at least not in the form in which it is required) at the time the contract is made.

(d) *Software as goods*

17–007   The question whether software constitutes goods has not arisen directly for decision in the English courts.[13] The U.S. courts have however been prepared to treat software as falling within the definition of goods contained in the Uniform Commercial Code,[14] which is comparable to the definition contained in section 61 of the Sale of Goods Act 1979, even where it is transmitted independently of any tangible medium such as a disk.[15] In reaching this conclusion, the U.S. courts appear to have been much influenced by commercial and policy considerations, including the importance of software in the commercial world, and the desirability of its supply being subject to regulation specifically devised for commercial transactions (namely, in the United States, the Uniform Commercial Code).[16] These considerations appear to apply equally in this country. Accordingly, and given that even information other than software has now become an established form of merchandise,[17] the time may well have come to recognise software as at least being capable of representing goods and therefore subject to the whole of the Sale of Goods Act 1979.

(e) *Services or goods?*

17–008   Traditionally, the legal categorisation of a contract as one for the supply of services or for the supply of goods is performed by applying the "substance of the contract" test: is the substance of the contract the skill and expertise to be exercised by the contractor, or its end product? If, as the Court of Appeal has suggested,[18] the end product (*i.e.* the software) is no more than information, and therefore not capable of amounting to goods in the legally recognised sense, then on one view the contract must be one for the supply of services. This reasoning becomes unattractive, however, once it is recognised that software is very often supplied to the client on disk, in which case (as appears now to be relatively

---

[12] For a more detailed analysis of whether software represents goods, see A. Scott, "Software as goods: nullum simile est idem" [1987] Comp. Law & Practice 133.

[13] See further paras 17–008 to 17–009 below. The Court of Appeal has however expressed the view, *obiter*, that software *per se* is not goods: *St Albans City and District Council v. International Computers Ltd* (1996) 4 All E.R. 481; [1997] 1 F.S.R. 251. Nevertheless warranties corresponding to those imposed by statute will generally be imposed by the common law: see para. 17–013 below.

[14] Art. 2–105 of the Uniform Commercial Code defines goods as "all things (including specifically manufactured goods) which are movable at the time of identification to the contract for sale other than the money in which the price is to be paid, investment securities and things in action."

[15] *Schroders Incorporated v. Hogan Systems Inc.* 522 NYS 2d 404; *Communications Groups Inc. v. Warner Communications* Misc. 2d 80.

[16] *Advent Systems Ltd v. Unisys Corp.* 925 F 2d 670, U.S. Court of Appeal, Weis J.

[17] Customer data bases are frequently sold for mail-shot purposes, for example.

[18] *St Albans City and District Council v. International Computers Ltd* (1996) 4 All E.R. 481; [1997] 1 F.S.R. 251.

uncontroversial[19]) the disk and software together do represent goods. If A agrees to write bespoke software for B and to supply it to him on disk, in circumstances where the substance of the contract is clearly the provision of the software itself, rather than the service of writing it, then the contract is one for the supply of goods. It would be absurd if the law required that it be treated as a contract for the supply of services merely because A had in fact agreed to provide the software by email. The particular mode of supply of the software would appear to be entirely irrelevant to the categorisation of the contract as one either for the supply of goods or the supply of services.

Similarly, if an application of the "substance of the contract" test suggests that the essence of the contract is the supply of the end product, *i.e.* the software, rather than the service of writing it, then the fact that software does not fall within the traditional definition of goods does not appear to be a sound reason for denying the client the warranties of satisfactory quality and fitness for purpose which he would otherwise enjoy. **17–009**

(f) *Nature of the service*

In *Robinson v. Graves* [1935] 1 K.B. 584 at 587 Greer L.J. (in considering the statutory wording in section 4 of the Sale of Goods Act 1893) thought that there would be nothing more surprising to the parties to a contract for the commissioning of a portrait than to be told that they were making a bargain about the sale of goods. Rather, the bargain or "substance" was the undertaking by the artist commissioned by the client to use such skill as he possessed in producing the portrait requested. In such a case it can readily be seen that a warranty of skill and care from the contractor (*i.e.* the artist) is all important to the client, and probably more important, and indeed more appropriate, than a warranty of fitness for purpose. The circumstances are not dissimilar when an architect is retained to carry out design work. It is the proper carrying out of the service which is of primary concern to the client.[20] Accordingly, the client will usually satisfy him or herself of the aptitude and suitability of the particular architectural practice, and will rely on them to ensure that the work is carried out by suitably skilled and experienced individuals with the appropriate level of skill and care.[21] **17–010**

The same is probably not true in the case of a contract for the supply of bespoke software. The identity, qualifications and experience of the individuals who carry out the work, *i.e.* who write the program, may well be matters of complete indifference to the client.[22] The client's principal concern is in the satisfactory operation of the finished product, the software itself. This is likely to be reflected in the way that the client goes about selecting a supplier, namely by **17–011**

---

[19] See para. 17–002, n. 5 above.
[20] The same is not necessarily true when the client appoints a design and build contractor to produce a building, or even only a structure within an existing building such as a new staircase. The staircase can hardly be said to be only "ancillary" to the design work. It forms the (or a) substantive part of the contract. Hence the recognition (in general) of a "fitness for purpose" obligation in such contracts, though not where the client retains an architect to carry out the design work separately. There is probably also a policy justification for the absence of strict liability in the latter case.
[21] Hence in *Munken Bank and Marshall v. Kensington Hotel* (1999) 15 Const. L.J. 231, it was held that it was wrong to use the term "architect" in respect of staff who had architectural qualifications but who were not registered architects
[22] Indeed, the client may well recognise that a particularly gifted recent graduate (for example) may be an extremely able program-writer despite having no relevant experience.

drafting a specification sheet and inviting tenders, often without reviewing portfolios as is the norm in the selection of architects, for example.

17–012   Moreover, the client's concern that the software to be supplied should operate satisfactorily probably represents a reasonable expectation on his part. It has been said that, in commissioning an architect, the client will usually expect the exercise of reasonable care in the carrying out of the architect's service, but, given "the uncertainties of their art"[23] it is not reasonable for the client to expect more, such as a warranty of fitness for purpose. This may or may not be true in relation to all architectural work today, but the client of a software house probably cannot be criticised as unreasonable for expecting the finished software to operate reasonably satisfactorily and to fulfil its intended purpose. The situation is more analogous, in the construction industry, to a composite contract for the design and construction of a building or structure, where fitness for purpose warranties are commonplace (though often expressly excluded), than to a "design only" contract as is necessarily the case in the appointment of an architect.[24]

(g) *Implied warranties at common law*

17–013   These considerations appear to have been recognised in *St Albans City and District Council v. International Computers Ltd*,[25] in which *obiter dicta* of the Court of Appeal suggest that the supply of bespoke software by transmission rather than on disk, although not a sale of goods within the scope of the 1979 Act, will be subject to implied terms of quality and fitness for purpose imposed by the common law.[26] However, and perhaps importantly, any apparent harshness in imposing strict liability on computer consultants in this way has been mitigated by the courts in granting latitude to computer consultants in determining what is reasonably fit for the client's purpose,[27] in allowing consultants ample opportunity to rectify errors emerging in their software[28] and by requiring co-operation on the part of the client.[29]

2. Duties

(a) *Duties to client*

(i) *Bespoke software: warranties of satisfactory quality and fitness for purpose*

17–014   Where a software contractor (or "software house" as they are also known) contracts for the supply not only of software but also the hardware on which it is to be used, the contract will generally be regarded as one for the provision of

---

[23] *per* the Supreme Court of Minnesota in *City of Mounds View v. Walijarva* (1978) 263 N.W. (2d) 420.
[24] See para. 17–010, n. 20 above.
[25] [1996] 4 All E.R. 481; [1997] 1 F.S.R. 251.
[26] See further paras 17–018 to 17–022 below.
[27] See paras 17–028 to 17–029, below.
[28] See paras 17–036 to 17–037, below.
[29] See paras 17–038 to 17–043, below.

an entire computer system, and thus for the sale of goods.[30] Warranties of satisfactory quality and reasonable fitness for purpose will therefore apply to the whole system, *i.e.* to the operation of both the hardware and software.[31]

This situation arose in the Australian case of *Toby Construction Products Ltd*   **17–015**
v. Computer Bar Sales Pty Ltd.[32] The defendant agreed to supply the claimant, by way of purchase, "the following computer hardware and software collectively referred to as 'the Equipment' ". The claimant alleged that the Equipment was deficient and brought a claim for lost profits, relying on implied conditions and warranties said to arise in the contract of purchase pursuant to statute.[33] The statutes only applied if the Equipment was "goods" within the meaning of the statutes.[34] Rogers J. determined the preliminary issue of whether the statute applied to the contract by applying the "substance of the contract" test.[35] He concluded that the substance of the contract was the sale of a total computer system, *i.e.* hardware and software, which, "whilst representing the fruits of much research and work, was in current jargon off the shelf, in a sense mass produced. There can be no comparison with a one off painting. Rather is the comparison with a mass produced print of a painting."[36]

In *Toby Construction Products Ltd v. Computer Bar Sales Pty Ltd*[37] Rogers J.   **17–016**
specifically left open the question whether software by itself represents "goods". This issue arose in the English case of *Eurodynamic Systems v. General Automation Ltd*.[38] ED specialised in the design and development of bespoke business/technical and accounting software. GA was a computer manufacturer. In 1980 ED entered into negotiations with GA to become one of its franchisees, with a view to marketing complete computer systems. ED used a programming language known as Cobol. GA primarily used Fortran, but indicated that their systems could also be used in Cobol. In 1981 ED agreed to purchase a "Boss 2" computer system from GA and entered into a franchise agreement with it. Under the franchise agreement GA was obliged to provide, maintain and update the Boss 2 system software, such support being free for 12 months. During the first year of use of the computer system ED complained that the system software, and the technical support offered by GA, were inadequate, principally because of the limited availability of facilities in Cobol language. ED alleged that these failures represented breaches by GA of implied terms of the franchise agreement that the Boss 2 computer system would be fit for purpose and of merchantable quality. GA denied that the franchise agreement was subject to these implied terms, since (1) there was no sale of the system software, only a licence to use it and to transfer it to customers, and (2) software does not constitute goods.

---

[30] See *Toby Construction Products Ltd v. Computer Bar Sales Pty Ltd*, discussed at paras 17–015 and 17–016 below, and, for an example of the same approach being taken in Canada, *Lalese Enterprises Inc. v. Arete Technologies Inc.* (1994) 59 C.P.R. 3d 438, British Columbia Supreme Court. However this will not necessarily be so in every case. See further *Gretton & Starkey (trading as Open Systems Design) v. British Millerain Co. Ltd*, unreported, July 29, 1998, H.H.J. Thornton Q.C., discussed at paras 17–027 to 17–028 below. The judge's reasoning might, in appropriate cases, apply as much to a contract for the supply of hardware and bespoke software as to hardware and standard software.
[31] Pursuant to ss.14(2) and 14(3) of the Sale of Goods Act 1979.
[32] [1983] 2 N.S.W.L.R. 48.
[33] The Sale of Goods Act 1923 and/or the Trade Practices Act 1974.
[34] The statutes each defined "goods" as "including" various specific items not relevant to the facts of the case.
[35] *Robinson v. Graves* [1935] 1 K.B. 579; para. 17–010 above.
[36] At 51G.
[37] [1983] 2 N.S.W.L.R. 48.
[38] Unreported, QBD, September 6, 1988, Steyn J.

17–017   Steyn J. rejected the first of these contentions, since the licence provision in the franchise agreement could not on its own take the transaction outside the scope of the Sale of Goods Act: "Although the ideas and concepts in the software remained GA's intellectual property, the reality of the transaction is that there has been a transfer of a product."[39] However he found the second contention to be "far more formidable".[40] Steyn J. considered that the materials placed before him[41] indicated that the problem was far more complex than realised during oral argument, and was not prepared to decide such "important issues of legal principle" without further argument. He was however prepared to proceed on the assumption that the implied terms were established.[42] He went on to find that although there had been no breach of any such implied terms, GA had repudiated the contract by unequivocally refusing to deal with ED's complaints regarding the system, which repudiation had been validly accepted by ED.[43] Judgment was therefore given for ED.

17–018   The issue of whether the supply of bespoke software alone is a supply of goods or of services came before the Court of Appeal in *St Albans City and District Council v International Computers Ltd.*[44] The claimant local authority engaged the defendant (ICL) to supply a computer system to be used in administering its collection of the community charge. The claimant used the system to determine the population in its area. An error in the software resulted in the figure being overstated by some 3,000. The claimant set its community charge based on that figure, and suffered significant losses as a result, which it sought to recover from ICL in an action for breach of express, alternatively implied, terms of the contract. The Court of Appeal held that ICL was in breach of an express term that it would supply software which enabled the authority accurately to determine the population in its area.[45] It was further held that, even in the absence of an express term, a contract of the kind in this case (*i.e.* "a contract for the transfer into a computer of a program intended by both parties to instruct or enable the computer to achieve specified functions")[46] would in any event be subject to implied terms of quality and fitness for purpose arising at common law[47] which were to the same effect.

17–019   The reasoning of the Court of Appeal, which is contained in the judgment of Sir Iain Glidewell,[48] began with consideration of the commonly arising situation

---

[39] p. 20 of transcript. Steyn J.'s reasoning is supported in an article by Mr Graham Smith in *Reed: Computer Law* (2nd ed.) at p. 44.

[40] p. 20.

[41] He appears to have been particularly influenced by Mr Andrew Scott's article "Software as goods: nullum simile est idem" (1987) Computer Law and Practice, 133.

[42] Steyn J. went on to hold (at p. 22) that even if the implied terms existed ED had not established breaches of them. However he was satisfied that GA had repudiated the contract by an unequivocal refusal to deal with the complaints raised by ED regarding the operating software.

[43] p. 22/3 of transcript.

[44] (1996) 4 All E.R. 481; [1997] F.S.R. 251.

[45] At 487h. One of the central issues in the case was as to the measure of loss suffered by the authority, which had recouped its loss by increasing subsequent community charges. On this issue the Court of Appeal reduced the level of damages awarded by Scott Baker J. at first instance.

[46] At 494c.

[47] Applying the dictum of Lord Pearson in *Trollope & Colls Ltd v North West Metropolitan Regional Hospital Board* [1973] 1 W.L.R. 601 at 609: "An unexpected term can be implied if and only if the courts find that the parties must have intended that term to form part of their contract; it is not enough for the court to find that such a term would have been adopted by the parties as reasonable men if it had been suggested to them; it must have been a term that went without saying, a term which, though tacit, formed part of the contract which the parties made for themselves".

[48] At 492, Nourse and Hirst L.JJ. agreed (at 487h and 492c).

in which a computer program is transferred to the client on disk. In such a case, in Sir Iain Glidewell's view, the disk is within the statutory definition of goods, but the program itself is not. However, if the program is defective, then the seller or hirer of the disk is in breach of the statutory implied terms of quality and/or fitness for purpose. This followed, according to the Sir Iain Glidewell, from an analogy with the position of the seller of a vehicle instruction manual, and the following reasoning. Such a manual, including the instructions, would be goods. If the manual contains erroneous instructions likely to cause users to damage their vehicles the defect in the instructions would constitute a breach of the statutory implied terms. There is no logical reason why this should not also be correct in relation to a computer disk containing a defective program or instruction.

The second part of the Court's reasoning[49] recognised that on the particular **17–020** facts of the case the relevant programs were not supplied on disk, but were transferred directly onto the authority's computer by ICL employees. According to the Court of Appeal, the transfer of a program in this way does not constitute a transfer of goods. There is therefore no statutory implication of terms as to quality/fitness for purpose. Nevertheless, in "a contract for the transfer into a computer of a program intended by both parties to instruct or enable the computer to achieve specified functions", a term requiring fitness for purpose can and should be implied as a matter of common law, since the parties must have intended such a term to form part of the contract, and such a term "went without saying".[50]

Since the contract in this case was found to contain corresponding express **17–021** terms, the whole of the reasoning was *obiter*. The first part of the reasoning (at paragraph 17–019 above) is doubly so, since (as the Court recognised at the second stage) the software in question was not in fact supplied on disk. This part of the reasoning, and the analogy on which it is based (a vehicle instruction manual), are not without difficulty, however. There are significant differences between a computer program and an instruction manual, including their purpose and mode of use. Printed material is used directly and independently by reading for enjoyment or interest, whereas software generally has to be copied for use, and can only be used by interaction with hardware.[51] Moreover, on established principles it may well be that the writing of an instruction manual should give rise to an obligation only to exercise reasonable skill and care, not a warranty of fitness for purpose. If, for example, an accountant gives general tax advice to his clients orally, only a warranty of reasonable skill and care is provided. If he reproduces his advice in a publication which he sells to interested clients, it

---

[49] At 493h onwards.

[50] Applying the above mentioned (n. 47) dictum of Lord Pearson in *Trollope & Colls Ltd v. North West Metropolitan Regional Hospital Board* at 609.

[51] In an interesting case comment on the *St Albans City and District Council v. International Computers Ltd* decision ((1995) 58 M.L.R. 585), Elizabeth Macdonald points out that "software is not simply a set of instructions, like some sort of manual, telling an individual what to do. In contrast with the manual, the software interacts directly with the hardware. If there is a defect in it, there may well not be any point at which an individual has an opportunity to assess what is occurring and intervene to prevent some unexpected and unwanted result. Software may be information but it is not pure information." Since, however, the manual's instructions are normally beyond the reader's knowledge and expertise, this opportunity (and the ground of distinction) may be little more than theoretical. In the Scottish case of *Beta Computers (Europe) Ltd v. Adobe Systems (Europe) Ltd* [1996] F.S.R. 366, Lord Penrose rejected the analogy with printed material (at 376) and identified a number of further potential grounds of distinction between printed material and software on disk.

would be surprising if the contents of the publication were subject to a warranty of fitness for purpose. The same may well be true, at least in some cases, with an instruction manual. On the other hand, it has been suggested[52] that the conclusion is supported by the approach which has been taken in criminal law to the problem of computer hacking, in which the physical form which a program takes on the disk is emphasised.[53]

17–022   In any event, the second part of the Court of Appeal's reasoning (at paragraph 17–020 above) is, it is submitted, clearly sound.[54] Moreover that reasoning would appear to apply as much to a contract for the supply of software on disk as to a contract for the "transfer of a program into a computer", provided always that both parties intend the program "to instruct or enable the computer to achieve specified functions".[55] Whether this qualification is satisfied is of course unlikely to depend on the mode of supply of the software. Indeed, the qualification is surely satisfied in all contracts for the supply of software, however transmitted. Accordingly, even if the reasoning in the first part of the passage is susceptible to criticism, the latter reasoning appears to justify the imposition of strict liability implied terms (*i.e.* of satisfactory quality and fitness for purpose) in all, or virtually all, cases of software supply.

(ii) *Modified standard software*

17–023 Where a software house is appointed not to write software from scratch but to supply and modify, or "tailor", an existing software package (whether produced by that software house or a third party), the contract might be categorised as either:

(a) the supply of goods (*i.e.* the standard software) together with associated services (the tailoring); or

(b) the supply of goods alone, namely the end product of the modification process: the tailored software.

In any particular case the modification process envisaged by the parties might be only very limited, so that the finished product remains in substantially the same form as the original standard product, or so extensive as to render the finished product more in the nature of bespoke software, and the original software simply part of the fabric of construction. The former case would appear to fall into category (a) and the latter into category (b). The distinction is potentially important because in category (a) the contract is likely to be subject to statutory

---

[52] D. Rowland and E. Macdonald, *Information Technology Law*, p. 106, and Elizaberth Macdonald 58 M.L.R. 585 at 590.

[53] In *R. v. Whiteley* (1991) 33 Cr. Rep. 25 the Court of Appeal (Criminal Division) had to determine whether the alteration or deletion of files on computer disks represented criminal damage within s.1(1) of the Criminal Damage Act 1971. In answering this question in the affirmative, Lord Lane C.J. stated: "There can be no doubt that the magnetic particles upon the metal disc were part of the discs and if the appellant was proved to have intentionally and without lawful excuse altered the particles in such a way as to cause an impairment of the value or usefulness of the disc to the owner, there would be damage within the meaning of s.1. The fact that the alteration could only be perceived by operating the computer did not make the alteration any less real . . . ".

[54] See further paras 17–008 to 17–012 above.

[55] The need for consistency of approach irrespective of the mode of transfer has been emphasised both in court and in published articles: see *e.g.* Lord Penrose in *Beta v. Adobe* [1996] F.S.R. 366 at 376.

implied terms as to fitness for purpose and satisfactory quality only in relation to the standard software, and terms requiring reasonable skill and care for the tailoring process, whereas in category (b), applying the *St Albans* case, the tailored software would be subject to the stricter warranty of fitness for purpose and satisfactory quality.

An illustration of a case which clearly falls into category (a) is provided by the recent decision of the Technology and Construction Court in *Jonathon Wren & Co. Ltd v. Microdec plc.*[56] W was a recruitment company and M a producer of specialist software for use by staff recruitment agencies. Between 1983 and 1996 M developed a number of different versions of the software, known as Profile versions 3 to 7. In April 1996 M offered W a demonstration of Profile version 7, also known as "Profile 2000," which was then a new product. W was impressed with the demonstration and in May 1996 entered a contract with M (which made reference to M's standard terms and conditions) for the purchase of Profile 2000,[57] together with the following associated services, namely installation, maintenance and a specified number of days of staff training. W alleged that the package was defective and that as a result its business failed and it ceased trading. **17–024**

In a trial of preliminary issues as to the terms of this agreement, H.H.J. Bowsher Q.C. held that M's standard terms and conditions had not been validly incorporated into the contract. However the agreement was subject to implied terms that (i) the application software and services would fulfil W's objective of fully computerising its recruitment process, (ii) the application software, Profile 2000, would be of reasonably satisfactory quality and reasonably fit for the purposes of W, (iii) the associated services to be provided by M, including the installation of the software on W's existing computer system, would be performed by M with reasonable skill and care, and (iv) those services (including in particular the installation of the software) would be performed within a reasonable time.[58] There was no discussion of the basis on which these terms were implied. **17–025**

In *Jonathon Wren v. Microdec* any tailoring process was limited indeed; effectively it comprised no more than implementation of the standard software on the client's own computer system. However it provides a useful illustration of the implied terms likely to arise in contracts for the supply of standard software with relatively limited tailoring services. Another decision of the Technology and Construction Court which is closer to the border between categories (a) and (b) referred to in paragraph 17–023 above, but ultimately found to lie within category (a), is *Gretton & Starkey (trading as Open Systems Design) v. British Millerain Co. Ltd.*[59] **17–026**

In *Gretton & Starkey,* BM was a fabric dyeing and coating company. OSD was a small software house which worked predominantly with clients in the textile industry. Its principal asset was a software package called TEXpro, which provided accounting, stock control and management facilities. TEXpro could be tailored to the individual requirements of each customer. BM entered into negotiations directly with OSD in which, as the Judge found, OSD described the functions and attributes of the systems it offered and BM decided whether these **17–027**

---

[56] [1999] 65 Con. L.R. 157.
[57] It is not clear from the judgment whether the software package was delivered on disk or installed onto W's computer network by M's employees, but the latter seems more likely.
[58] At 171, 172.
[59] Unreported, July 29, 1998, H.H.J. Thornton Q.C.

met their general requirements. OSD did not provide a detailed list of its requirements, indeed BM was not even clear as to what it wanted. The intention was that the software would be tailored to meet BM's reasonable requirements when those were communicated to OSD, though this was to be only after the contract was entered into. The contract ultimately executed was for the supply of specified hardware and software, together with associated services including software support, staff training, on-site implementation and consultancy. The software comprised a number of modules of the TEXpro package, which were to be delivered in phases, together with a Global 2000 accounting package. The services were to include an unusually "high degree of post-contract tailoring", not least because BM's requirements were largely to be identified as the contract was being performed.[60]

17–028   In determining what terms were to be implied into the contract as to merchantability,[61] fitness for purpose and the exercise of reasonable skill and care the Judge referred to the reasoning of Sir Iain Glidewell in the *St Albans* case[62] as offering the clearest statement of principle.[63] He considered that in the case before him, however, the contract in question was in truth three contracts in one: (i) a contract for the supply of hardware and disks or other software media; (ii) a contract for the supply of software modules and (iii) a contract for the provision of specialised services, namely the tailoring of the modules to achieve the functions appropriate to BM's needs.[64] The hardware and disks were not the subject of criticism in the case. As to (ii) and (iii), the Judge asked himself what implied terms arose at common law by applying the dictum of Lord Pearson in *Trollope & Colls Ltd v. North West Metropolitan Regional Hospital Board*.[65] He concluded that (a) the modules, in their untailored forms, were required to be fit for their purpose for use in textile manufacturing stock control and monitoring systems and suitable to be tailored for a use reasonably associated with such a purpose; (b) the tailoring, training, help facilities, report writing and after-sales services to be provided by OSD had to be provided with the exercise of reasonable skill and care.[66]

17–029   The Judge's reasoning was that it went without saying that *some* quality standard was to be imported into the contract, and that the appropriate standard was that which mirrored similar terms as to quality in similar contracts. Accordingly, since the contract in this case comprised three "sub-agreements", the appropriate implied term in sub-agreement (ii) was the term at (a) above, since sub-agreement (ii) was analogous to the transfer of computer programs in the *St Albans* case itself. In the case of (iii), the appropriate term was (b) on the basis that "[a]ny contract which consists entirely of the supply of professional services has implied into it a term as to the exercise of reasonable skill and care".[67]

17–030   Although it is not entirely clear from the judgment, it does not appear to have been argued in *Gretton & Starkey* that the contract was subject to an implied term that the *tailored* software would be of merchantable quality and/or fit for its

---

[60] Para. 24 of judgment.
[61] The contract was entered into prior to the Sale of Goods Act 1994, which replaced this term with "satisfactory quality"
[62] Paras 17–019 to 17–022 above.
[63] Para. 45 of judgment.
[64] Para. 46 of judgment.
[65] See para. 17–018, n. 47 above.
[66] The Judge went on to find that BM had failed to establish that any of its 411 complaints against OSD represented breaches of these contractual terms.
[67] p. 12 of judgment.

purpose. In other words, that this was a case which fell within category (b) in paragraph 17–023 above.[68] Applying the Judge's own reasoning, *i.e.* that "the appropriate standard was that which mirrored similar terms as to quality in similar contracts", if the contract had been described not as three sub-agreements but as a single one for the provision of tailored software, then by analogy with the provision of bespoke software in the *St Albans* case the appropriate warranty would have been that the *tailored* software would be of merchantable quality and/ or fit for its purpose. However, this conclusion was effectively ruled out by the particular (and somewhat unusual) facts of the case. Had OSD specified its requirements at the outset, and BM agreed to provide TEXpro software duly tailored to meet those needs, the case might well have fallen within category (b).

(iii) *Communication of client's purpose*

The implied obligation on the software supplier to provide software which is "fit **17–031** for purpose" does not extend to all of the client's purposes, whatever they may be, even if not communicated to the supplier. Only those purposes which are within the supplier's (objective) knowledge are included in the scope of the warranty. This point arose in *Saphena Computing Ltd v. Allied Collection Agencies Ltd.*[69] The claimant, SCL, was a software supplier and the defendant, ACA, a debt-collecting agency. In January 1985 SCL agreed to supply batch software to ACA. This was supplied in February 1985, and a number of initial defects were rectified by SCL. Later, in about May 1985, ACA instructed SCL to supply on-line software. This also suffered numerous defects, and caused fresh defects in the batch software. SCL was in the process of rectifying the various defects when, in February 1986, the parties agreed to terminate their relationship. ACA alleged (by counterclaim) that SCL had breached implied terms that the software would be fit for its purpose. Mr Recorder Havery Q.C. (as he then was) held that both supply contracts were subject to the following implied term of fitness for purpose:

> "In my judgment it was an implied term of each contract for the supply of software that the software would be reasonably fit for any purpose which had been communicated to the plaintiffs before the contract was made and for any further purpose subsequently communicated, provided in the latter case that the plaintiffs accepted the defendants' instructions to make the relevant modification. The making of the modification constitutes or implies acceptance of the instructions".[70]

The counterclaim for breach of this implied term in each of the software contracts failed since, by entering into the termination agreement in February 1986, ACA agreed to accept the software in its then condition, and deprived SCL of further opportunity to rectify the defects.

The latter part of the passage extracted above from the judgment of Mr **17–032** Recorder Havery Q.C. appears simply to confirm that the parties are free to vary the terms of the contract by mutual consent at any time after it is executed. If the

---

[68] This may well be because, as already indicated above, BM had not identified its precise requirements at the time of the contract. See however the decision in *Saphena* below.

[69] [1995] F.S.R. 616. An appeal to the Court of Appeal (at [1995] F.S.R. 646), which was dismissed, did not disturb any of the Recorder's findings. The decision of the Court of Appeal is discussed further below at paras 17–036 to 17–037.

[70] At 644.

client does give instructions to make modifications, however, the circumstances (and in particular the terms of the original contract) will have to be considered carefully to determine whether an acceptance by the supplier (in making the modifications) is unconditional or in consideration of (reasonable) payment by the client. The continuing duties of the supplier are considered further below,[71] and if the making of the modifications fall within their scope then no further payment will be due. This was the position in *Gretton & Starkey*,[72] where the original contract contemplated that the supplier would carry out significant modifications to the software after installation in order to meet the needs of the client as identified post-contract. Otherwise, the circumstances will usually be such that the supplier will be entitled to reasonable remuneration for the work involved in carrying out the modification.

17–033   Since the supplier's obligation to provide software fit for its purpose is potentially the client's principal safeguard in ensuring proper performance by the supplier, it is obviously of critical importance that the client takes care to identify, and communicate, all of its objectives and requirements to the supplier. For this reason it is now common practice for clients to appoint computer consultants specifically for this purpose, whose task is to prepare and develop, in consultation with the client, a detailed functional specification for the proposed computer software or system.

17–034   The importance to the client of clearly communicating its requirements to the supplier is illustrated by *Micron Computer Systems Ltd v. Wang (UK) Ltd.*[73] In that case Micron claimed that a computer system comprising hardware and software supplied to it by Wang suffered from a number of faults, including (principally) an inability to perform "transaction logging". The express terms of the contract of supply included a warranty by Wang that the software would conform substantially with Micron's functional specification for a period of 90 days. In addition Micron relied on implied terms that the system would be fit for the purpose for which it was sold and of merchantable quality. In dismissing Micron's claim for alleged breaches of contract by Wang in this (and all other) respects, Steyn J. said[74]:

> "The acknowledged absence of a transaction logging facility is not in reality a fault in the system which was sold. Micron can only complain about its absence if Micron can establish a contractual term, express or implied, or an actionable representation, to the effect that the system included such a facility. In order to make good its case on transaction logging, Micron must therefore establish that they made known to Wang that they required such a facility."

The Judge found that Micron did not in fact communicate to Wang that it required transaction logging. Its functional specification did not refer to transaction logging, and at best Micron only referred to transaction logging in vague phrases ("simultaneous background back-up") which were insufficient to alert Wang to what they intended to convey.[75] Accordingly there was no "fault" in the system in this (or any other) respect, and Wang were not in breach of the express or implied terms of the contract.

---

[71] At paras 17–036 and 17–044.
[72] Unreported, July 29, 1998, H.H.J. Thornton Q.C.; paras 17–027 to 17–030 above.
[73] Unreported, May 9, 1990, QBD, Steyn J.
[74] p. 9 of transcript.
[75] p. 10 of transcript.

It is clearly not the case, however, that only purposes which are specifically **17–035** and expressly communicated by the client to the supplier will become the subject of the implied (or any express) term requiring fitness for purpose. It might be implicit from the client's instructions, from earlier dealings between the parties or from normal trade practice that the client has a particular purpose for the software (or system) ordered from the supplier. *Jonathon Wren v. Microdec*,[76] the facts of which are set out above in paragraph 17–024, provides an example. In that case it was held that a contract for the supply of software was subject to implied terms requiring the software to be of reasonably satisfactory quality and reasonably fit for the purposes of the client (W). The Judge went on to identify what those purposes were.[77] The first was the overall objective of the client (which was communicated to the supplier, M) to fully computerise its recruitment process. In addition, however, the Judge found that the purposes for which the software was to be fit included six specific requirements identified in the client's statement of case.[78] Four of these functions (such as a rapid search facility) had not been communicated to M, but had simply been extracted from M's sales literature as to the software's alleged capabilities.[79] The requirements were nonetheless included by the Judge in the list of warranted purposes, apparently on the basis that the supplier "would have understood [them] as the common aim"[80] of W and/or because they were promised in the sales literature[81] which was provided to the client before it ordered the software. In other words, these requirements were implicit in the client's instructions, and the circumstances of the transaction.

(iv) *Implementation and testing*

In a contract for the provision of bespoke or modified standard software there **17–036** will invariably be an express provision dealing with the implementation and testing to be carried out by the supplier. This will include the process of debugging. In the absence of express provision, a corresponding obligation will normally arise by necessary implication at common law. Unless specified otherwise, the supplier will ordinarily be obliged to complete these processes within a reasonable time. These propositions follow from the decision of the Court of Appeal in *Saphena Computing Ltd v. Allied Collection Agencies Ltd*,[82] the facts of which are set out above in paragraph 17–031.[83] The judgment of Staughton L.J. contains the following important passage[84]:

---

[76] [1999] 65 Con. L.R. 157.
[77] At 172, para. 58.
[78] Namely those at para. 8 of the statement of case, which is extracted both at pp. 163 and 172 of the judgment.
[79] At 163, 172.
[80] At 163.
[81] At 172.
[82] [1995] F.S.R. 616, Mr Recorder Havery Q.C.; *ibid.*, 646, CA.
[83] See further the decision in *Eurodynamic Systems Plc v. General Automation Ltd* discussed in para. 17–016 above. At p. 17 of the judgment Steyn J. stated that, according to the expert evidence in the case, it is acceptable and normal practice to supply software which contains bugs and errors. He added that the basis of that practice was that "pursuant to the supplier's support obligation (free or chargeable as the case may be) the supplier will correct errors or bugs that prevent the product from being properly used." Hence on the particular facts in that case the supplier was not in breach of any obligation to supply software which was fit for purpose and of merchantable quality (the existence of which Steyn J. was prepared to assume) even though there were minor errors requiring correction.
[84] At 652.

"It was, we are told, common ground that the law governing these contracts was precisely the same whether they were contracts for the sale of goods or for the supply of services.[85] It is therefore unnecessary to consider into which category they might come. But it is important to remember that software is not necessarily a commodity which is handed over or delivered once and for all at one time. It may well have to be tested and modified as necessary. It would not be a breach of contract at all to deliver software in the first instance with a defect in it . . .

[Delivery of the software] will necessarily be accompanied by a degree of testing and modification. Naturally it could be expected that the supplier will carry out those tasks. He should have both the right and the duty to do so . . . No doubt there was a time limit for that purpose—a reasonable time is that which the law would ordinarily supply."[86]

17–037 In *Saphena Computing Ltd v. Allied Collection Agencies Ltd* this process of testing and modification was still continuing on February 11, 1986, more than six months after even the second contract had been entered into. Nevertheless a reasonable time was not found to have elapsed by then. On that date the parties terminated their relationship. Accordingly SCL were not obliged, or entitled, to do any more work on the software, and therefore were not liable for any defects which had not been remedied as at that date.

(v) *The importance of co-operation between the parties*

17–038 In any contract for the supply of software, or an entire computer system, success is usually heavily dependent on a high level of co-operation between the parties at all stages of the contract, but particularly at the stage of implementation and testing. The law therefore generally implies mutual contractual obligations of co-operation accordingly. The relevant principles were recently considered in the Technology and Construction Court in relation to a contract for the supply of a "standard" computer system in *Anglo Group plc v. Winther Brown & Co.*[87] WB (a distributor of decorative mouldings) purchased a computer system from BML comprising both hardware and a standard software package ("Charisma"). The principal agreement was entered into on December 21, 1995, on BML's standard form. Delivery was to take place in February/March 1996 and the system was to go live by July 1996. The system did go live on July 1, 1996, but WB raised a number of complaints regarding its performance. BML sought to deal with these, but by April 1997 WB was so dissatisfied with the system that it purported to repudiate the agreement and claimed damages from BML for (*inter alia*) breaches of the agreement. In an important section of the judgment[88] entitled "The contract: Parties' Duty of Co-operation", Judge Toulmin stated:

"126. It is important to understand the nature of the contracts between WB and BML. It is well understood that the design and installation of a computer system requires the

---

[85] The "common ground" referred to in passing by the learned Lord Justice has been described by the editors of the *Encyclopaedia of Information Technology Law* as a "remarkable statement". Since different statutory regimes apply depending on whether the supply was of goods or services the statement certainly seems to be doubtful. It may be that the parties agreed no more than that even if the contract was one for the supply of services it was nonetheless subject to an implied term of fitness for purpose by operation of the common law, so that the law governing the contract was "precisely the same" for the purposes of that case.

[86] These views were based on a passage contained in one of the expert reports in the case, but appear to be of general application.

[87] Unreported, March 1, 2000, QBD (TCC), H.H.J. Toulmin C.M.G., Q.C.

[88] paras 125 to 129.

active co-operation of both parties. Frequently a client employs a consultant to assist it in the process . . . WB did not do that in relation to Charisma. Instead it invited proposals from selected hardware and software suppliers and developed its requirements in discussions with potential suppliers.[89] It is clear that WB was always interested only in a package system and was not prepared to spend money on bespoke software which could adapt the computer system to WB's particular working practices. It was almost inevitable in these circumstances that while Charisma (or any other standard system) could be expected to provide an 80% fit or better with WB's existing procedures, it was unlikely to provide a 100% fit. This meant that it was inevitable that there would be some procedures of WB which WB would have to adapt to Charisma . . .

127. The duty of co-operation in my view extends to the customer accepting where possible reasonable solutions to problems that have arisen. In the case of unimportant or relatively unimportant items that have been promised and cannot be supplied each party must act reasonably, consistent, of course, with its rights.

128. In relation to a contract for the supply of a standard computer system it is an implied term that:

(a) the purchaser communicates clearly any special needs to the supplier;
(b) the purchaser takes reasonable steps to ensure that the supplier understands those needs;
(c) the supplier communicates to the purchaser whether or not those precise needs can be met and if so how they can be met. If they cannot be met precisely the appropriate options should be set out by the supplier;
(d) the supplier takes reasonable steps to ensure that the purchaser is trained in how to use the system;
(e) the purchaser devotes reasonable time and patience to understanding how to operate the system;
(f) the purchaser and supplier work together to resolve the problems which will almost certainly occur. This requires active co-operation from both parties. If such co-operation is not present it is likely that the purchaser will not achieve the desired results from the system."

Judge Toulmin then considered whether, in the light of these obligations, the **17–039** numerous alleged defects constituted breaches of the agreement, and if so whether there was such a fundamental breach as to entitle WB to repudiate the agreement. The Judge rejected virtually all of WB's complaints, largely on the basis that BML had put forward reasonable solutions to the various problems, and/or WB had unreasonably refused to adopt those solutions. Judge Toulmin rejected the claim for repudiation, therefore, stating that, while a failure by a computer company to deliver individual requirements (and particularly those which constitute expected enhancements in a replacement computer system) can, in principle, amount to a fundamental breach leading to a repudiation, this had not happened in the present case. Most of WB's complaints had been rejected. Those few complaints which were not rejected either had been or could, given reasonable co-operation by WB, have been remedied before April 1997. Taken as a whole they did not amount to a fundamental breach of contract giving rise to a right of repudiation by WB.[90] As to the minority of complaints which did represent breaches of the agreement by BML, such as delay in resolving various bugs, Judge Toulmin found that WB had failed to prove any associated loss.

---

[89] Judge Toulim considered that where, as in this case, the client of a computer company has limited computer knowledge and nevertheless chose not to employ its own computer consultant, the need for active co-operation between the parties *throughout the project* was "of crucial importance" (para. 126 of judgment).
[90] Para. 232 of judgment.

17–040   In *Anglo Group plc v. Winther Brown & Co.* the implied terms requiring co-operation on the part of the customer were said to be based on the fact that (i) standard not bespoke software was ordered, rendering it "inevitable" that post-installation adaptation would be required, and (ii) the client (WB) lacked computer knowledge and chose not to employ a computer consultant. However, as has already been seen,[91] in all or virtually all instances of the supply of computer software or systems it is implicit that some level of testing and modification will be required. In *Saphena Computing Ltd v. Allied Collection Agencies Ltd*, which concerned bespoke software, the Court of Appeal stated that the supplier is not only under a duty to carry out the processes of testing and modification but that he should have the "right" to do so. It is clearly inherent in such a right that the supplier should be given reasonable opportunity to carry out testing and modification, and therefore that he should be given appropriate level of co-operation in order to achieve this.

17–041   *Anglo Group plc v. Winther Brown & Co.* illustrates that the extent of the obligation of co-operation probably differs in every case depending on precisely what was (or ought to have been) envisaged by the parties at the outset as to the level of "fit" of the software or system at the time of delivery. Where (as in *Anglo Group*) (i) the customer has chosen not to have software specifically written for him, and (ii) has not spelt out his requirements in detail in advance, there is a heavy onus on that customer to assist the supplier in the process of adaptation following delivery.[92] If, on the other hand, the contract is to supply bespoke software, and a clear and comprehensive specification has been provided by the customer at the outset, it will usually be incumbent on the supplier, at the time of delivery, to supply software which has already been written with those particular requirements in mind. Ordinarily, therefore, it would not be open to the supplier at that stage to require the customer to co-operate in a modification process necessitated by a requirement which could and should have already been taken into account (though not necessarily met)[93] by that stage.[94]

17–042   Following delivery of the software or system the process of implementation will often lead to reappraisal of the specification by the customer. If the customer reasonably revises his requirements during the process, the duty of co-operation will oblige the supplier to respond accordingly. In particular, if the contract is for modified standard software and the revision is simply the result of the "inevitable" inability of the software in its original standard form to meet all of the customer's requirements, and is a reasonable step towards achieving the overall objective, the supplier will be obliged to meet the revised specification without

---

[91] Para. 39 and *Saphena Computing Ltd v. Allied Collection Agencies Ltd*, above.

[92] *Gretton & Starkey*, discussed in para. 17–027 above, is another example of a case in which the points at (i) and (ii) were present. As in *Anglo Group*, the customer had onerous post-delivery obligations, all the more so in Gretton & Starkey, since not only was there a limited specification of requirements in advance (*i.e.* point (ii)), but it was specifically envisaged that there would be a high level of input by the customer as the contract was being performed, *i.e.* in actually bringing the software into operation: see para. 24 of judgment.

[93] It is unlikely that a supplier could ever reasonably be expected to have met a particular requirement of software at the very time of delivery: see paras 17–091 to 17–092 below.

[94] This proposition also derives support from a passage in the judgment of Nourse L.J. in *St Albans City and District Council v. ICL* [1996] 4 All E.R. 481: "Parties who respectively agree to supply and acquire a system recognising that it is still in the course of development cannot be taken, merely by virtue of that recognition, to intend that the supplier shall be at liberty to supply software which cannot perform the function expected of it at the stage of development at which it is supplied."

further payment.[95] If, on the other hand, the revision is independent of the implementation process the supplier will usually be entitled to reasonable remuneration for the further work involved. Where no detailed list of the customer's requirements is prepared in advance of the contract, it will often be difficult to draw this distinction in practice.

The duty of co-operation in a contract for the supply of software was also **17–043** recognised by the Court of Appeal in *Systems Team Plusmark Ltd v. Kingswood Fluid Power Group plc.*[96] This was a claim by a computer and software supplier (STP) for damages for breach of a contract with KFP for the supply of computer equipment and tailored software. STP relied on implied terms of the contract that KFP would (i) co-operate with STP so as to enable STP to perform the contract, (ii) ensure that the representative of KFP appointed to supervise the project would perform his duties in a proper manner, and (iii) ensure that instructions, information and details required by STP were given or made available in reasonable time so as not to impede STP in performance of the contract. The case came before the Court of Appeal on an appeal by KFP as to whether judgment entered against it in default of its service of a defence ought to be set aside. KFP had to establish an arguable defence with a real prospect of success. In the course of argument the existence of the implied terms was neither challenged by KFP nor doubted by the Court. Interestingly, Hutchison L.J. noted that the particular contract in this case was "in many ways similar to a standard building contract",[97] particularly in that the whole of the work was subject to supervision by KFP's project manager. There was also a 16-week contract programme, in relation to which the parties had proceeded as if party to a building contract: STP had requested an extension of time arising from (*inter alia*) late information and alleged repudiation by KPF for its refusal to provide these. In its reasoning the Court did not need to draw upon principles applicable to construction law contracts in order to determine that KFP did indeed have a meritorious defence, but the case appears to leave open such a course in any future similar case.

(vi) *Duties of support*

When implementation and "acceptance testing" have been successfully effected **17–044** in respect of all of the components of the software or system supplied, the customer's right to reject the system is lost. However even at this stage it is perfectly normal, and acceptable, for bugs to appear in the software or system from time to time. The process of testing will rarely result in a program being totally bug free. Rather, the expression "bug free" has to be seen as meaning "acceptably free from bugs". As Ian J. Lloyd points out[98]: "It is impossible to test even the simplest program in an exhaustive fashion. This is because of the myriad possibilities for interaction (whether desired or not) between the various elements of the program." For this reason contracts for the supply of software or a computer system invariably require the supplier to provide support facilities following implementation. Often this is free during the first year or other specified period ("the warranty period") and then at an agreed cost thereafter. In the absence of express provision an implied term will usually arise for the provision of such a warranty period requiring correction of bugs. The duration of

---

[95] This follows from the sixth of the implied terms listed in the *Anglo Group* case.
[96] Unreported, April 30, 1996, CA.
[97] p. 1 of judgment.
[98] *Information Technology Law* (2nd ed., Butterworths) p. 409.

that period will be a reasonable length of time having regard to the expectation of the parties and the circumstances of the contract. In the absence of express agreement, however, it will usually be difficult to imply a further obligation of continuing (paid) support facilities.

(vii) *Staff training*

17–045 The supplier's obligation to provide a computer system or software which is fit for the customer's purpose will carry with it an obligation to ensure that it is fit for use by the customer's own staff. If the staff are already computer literate and versed in the use of the kind of system or software which is to be provided then no problem will arise, provided of course that use of the system/software is indeed within their capabilities. If, on the other hand, complete retraining of the staff is required, which was not agreed with or envisaged by the customer at the outset, this may constitute a breach of the implied obligation of fitness for purpose, giving rise to a liability in damages for the associated disruption to the customer. Between these two extremes lies the usual case, in which the parties envision (and the contract therefore impliedly provides) that use of the software or system will be within the reasonable capabilities of the customer's staff following appropriate training by the supplier, which the supplier is therefore usually duty bound to provide.

(viii) *User's operation manual*

17–046 Usually a computer or software supply contract will also be subject to an implied term that both a system specification (detailing the technical specification and capabilities of the system, and demonstrating how it meets the functional requirements) and a user manual will be supplied to the customer. Moreover the user manual should be in a form which the intended users will understand. British Standard BS 7649 "Guide to design and preparation of documentation for users of application software" contains recommendations for the preparation and content of user manuals and provides helpful guidance as to the likely extent of this obligation.

(ix) *Implied terms of reasonable skill and care*

17–047 We have already seen that a contract for the supply of software is likely to be subject to an implied (and often an express) term requiring the software to be of satisfactory quality and (reasonably) fit for its purpose. In most circumstances the latter obligation is likely to be more onerous than an obligation to exercise reasonable skill and care. However there may nevertheless be circumstances in which the client of a software house will wish to assert and rely on an obligation that the supplier will exercise reasonable skill and care in performing the services it is required to provide under the contract. This might be, for example, (i) where the installation of the software has not (yet) been completed (so that a requirement of fitness for purpose is of limited assistance)[99] and the client is dissatisfied with the supplier's performance to date, or (ii) where installation of bespoke or modified standard software has been completed, and the software is (or might be) technically fit for its purpose, but the performance of the software is not such as is reasonably to be expected from a software house exercising the appropriate

---

[99] But see below at para. 17–089 for the continuing and evolving nature of the fitness for purpose obligation.

level of skill and care in and about writing or modifying the particular software.

An example of the first situation arose in *Salvage Association v. CAP Finan-* **17–048** *cial Services Ltd.*[1] SA was a marine surveying company which required computer accounting software. CAP was a computer software house. CAP entered into two contracts with SA: in March 1987, to carry out an analysis of SA's requirements and to specify how these were to be achieved, and in September 1987 to develop the appropriate software for SA. Pursuant to the first contract, in July 1987 a "System Specification" and "User Requirement Specification" were produced by CAP and approved by SA. Pursuant to the second contract, system software was developed and delivered by CAP to SA in September 1988. However the software suffered from numerous faults. These were still not resolved by July 1989. As a result SA terminated the second contract and claimed damages from CAP for breach.

SA did not allege that the second contract was subject to an implied term of **17–049** fitness for purpose, only that, pursuant to section 13 of the Sale of Goods and Services Act 1982, it was subject to an implied term as to reasonable care and skill.[2] The Judge accepted that the contract was one for the supply of a service to which this part of the Act applied, and that the term was not negatived by any of the express provisions of the second contract. He held that SA had been entitled to terminate the contract since CAP were in repudiatory breach, in that they had delivered a system which, after two-and-a-half years, was still unusable because of significant deficiencies in CAP's performance.[3] Moreover SA were entitled to terminate the contract, *i.e.* accept CAP's repudiation, since there was no prospect of CAP completing the system within a reasonable time.[4] CAP's liability for damages is considered further below.[5]

In *Salvage Association v. CAP* the court had no difficulty in finding an implied **17–050** term to exercise reasonable skill and care in a contract which was subject to an express term requiring fitness for purpose. The question arises as to whether a contractual obligation to exercise reasonable skill and care can and should be implied in a contract which is not subject to an express term requiring fitness for purpose but only an implied one. If the contract is one for the supply of software on disk then, according to the *St Albans* case, an implied term requiring fitness for purpose will be imposed by statute.[6] In such a case there seems to be no reason in logic or principle why an implied term requiring the supplier to exercise reasonable skill and care in and about carrying out the services required of it (writing or modifying the software, or implementing it, for example) should not

---

[1] [1995] F.S.R. 654, H.H.J. Thayne Forbes Q.C.: judgment delivered October 21, 1992.
[2] It should be noted, however, that the second contract contained an express term that CAP would provide the System to SA as described in the User Requirement Specification, by July 1988: [1995] F.S.R. 654 at 660.
[3] The Judge considered that the fundamental problems with the system were "the inevitable result of a significant lack of knowledge, experience and expertise . . . on the part of those assigned to the project by CAP. In addition . . . the project had throughout been mismanaged by CAP at all levels": [1995] F.S.R. 654 at 679.
[4] The Judge found that "SA were fully justified in coming to the conclusion that CAP had failed to deliver a useable system and that there was no prospect that it either would or could do so by January 1, 1990 or within a reasonable timescale thereafter. In all the circumstances of this case, I have every sympathy with SA's loss of confidence both in the sysem itself and in CAP's ability to complete it satisfactorily." [1995] F.S.R. 654 at 680.
[5] See para. 17–106, below.
[6] [1996] 4 All E.R. 481 at 493h.

also apply, whether pursuant to section 13 of the Sale of Goods and Services Act 1982 or at common law. Moreover, there is again no reason to treat a contract for the provision of bespoke or modified standard software other than on disk (which, according to the *St Albans* case, will ordinarily be subject to a common law implied term requiring fitness for purpose) any differently. It follows that all contracts for the supply of bespoke or modified standard software are probably subject not only to implied terms requiring that the software be fit for its purpose, but also implied terms requiring the supplier to exercise reasonable skill and care in and about performing the services it is contractually obliged to provide.

(x) *Common law duty of care*

17–051 In any event, the supplier of bespoke software will usually owe a common law duty of care to its client to exercise reasonable skill and care in and about performing the services of writing the relevant software, on the basis that, in the ordinary case, there will almost certainly have been an assumption of responsibility towards the client.[7] Moreover (i) economic loss[8] would almost certainly be a foreseeable consequence of any negligence on the part of the supplier, (ii) the relationship would usually be one of sufficient proximity (given the supplier's special knowledge and the client's likely reliance) and it would appear to be fair, just and reasonable to impose such a duty.[9] The duty will extend not only to the writing and/or modification of the software, but also to the associated services of implementation, testing and staff training, for example. *DSL Group Ltd v. Unisys International Services Ltd*[10] (which is discussed further below at paragraph 17–055) provides an example of a case in which a software house was found to owe a *Hedley Byrne v. Heller* type duty of care not only in respect of pre-contract statements but also in relation to advice given after the contract was entered into as to the design of the software database.[11]

(xi) *Supply of standard/modified standard software: consultant or supplier?*

17–052 A more difficult question is whether a particular supplier of either standard or modified standard software, or of a computer system including such software, assumed the position of a professional consultant, or was merely acting as a supplier. Only in the former case will the supplier owe a duty of care to the client to advise on the suitability of what is being supplied. The distinction is often very difficult to draw. In *Jonas & Erickson Software v. Fitz-Wright Co Ltd*,[12] for example, FW contracted with JE (a software house) for the supply of a computer

---

[7] *Henderson v. Merrett Syndicates Ltd* [1995] 2 A.C. 145.

[8] Needless to say, if the software is intended for "safety-critical" application, such as in a medical or emergency service computer system, the case for a duty of care would be even stronger, and probably irresistible.

[9] Applying the test for the existence of a *Hedley Byrne v. Heller* type duty stipulated by the House of Lords in *Caparo v. Dickman* [1990] 2 A.C. 605. The fact that the tortious duty may be wider than any corresponding one does not appear to be a ground of objection: *Holt v. Payne Skillington* [1996] P.N.L.R. 179, CA.

[10] October 19, 1994, reported at [1995] Masons C.L.R. 5, discussed in para. 17–041 below.

[11] The availability of a remedy in negligence not only in tort but also in contract is not merely of academic interest. The client may prefer to bring his claim in tort rather than in contract in order to take advantage of a more favourable limitation period, for example. (The cause of action in tort only accrues, and the limitation period commences, on proof of loss, which may be later than the date of breach, which triggers accrual of the contractual claim.)

[12] Unreported, October 5, 1990, Supreme Court of British Columbia, Selbie J.

system to integrate its production and accounting. The system was to include software in standard form (known as "TABS") but which could be customised to meet FW's needs, together with ongoing support services. In a claim by FW for (*inter alia*) negligent misstatement, JE contended that it was no more than a supplier selling software and hardware. However, the judge found that FW were "essentially computer illiterate", had no separate consultant assisting them and were relying on JE to act as consultants on their behalf. Moreover JE were aware of all of the foregoing, and, the Judge found, had held themselves as consultants for FW. For all of these reasons JE owed FW a duty of care to ensure that the product they sold FW was adequate for their needs and capable of fulfilling them.[13]

By contrast, the supplier of hardware, software and associated services was   **17–053**
held not to owe a duty of care in *Comyn Ching Ltd v. Linkirk Hardware Ltd.*[14] In that case SWEL were architectural ironmongery wholesalers who, in about 1988, wished to computerise their operations. ABT supplied computers and software to three of SWEL's sites. There was no formal written contract. In 1994 SWEL brought proceedings against ABT for negligent misstatement, misrepresentation and breach of contract and collateral contract, claiming damages in excess of £3 million. The duty of care alleged against ABT was not a general duty to take reasonable skill and care but a specific one, either to take proper steps to ascertain the user's requirements or to warn SWEL that they had not taken such steps. It was significant, however, that at the outset SWEL had deliberately decided not to employ a consultant, even though they had limited knowledge of computers. ABT had offered to investigate their requirements but that offer was rejected. For this reason, H.H.J. Bowsher Q.C. held, the case was distinguishable from *Jonas & Erickson Software v. Fitz-Wright Co. Ltd*, and ABT owed no duty of care to SWEL.

This last decision illustrates that, in order for a duty of care to arise, there must   **17–054**
be not only (foreseeable) reliance by the client on the supplier as a consultant, but that reliance must be reasonable. Where the client has, without good reason, declined either to appoint his own consultant or to accept an offer by the supplier himself to provide consultancy, there can be little difficulty in concluding that he has acted unreasonably in this regard and/or that it would not be fair, just and reasonable to impose a duty of care on the supplier to provide appropriate consultancy *gratis*.

(xii) *Negligent misstatements*

It is clear that statements made by any computer supplier or software house   **17–055**
(whether acting as a consultant or otherwise) during the course of pre-contractual negotiations can give rise to a *Hedley Byrne v. Heller*-type duty of care and a liability for negligent misstatement. In *DSL Group Ltd v. Unisys International Services Ltd*,[15] for example, DSL, a software house, obtained a computer and operating software from another computer/software supplier, U. These were for onward supply to one of DSL's clients, TR. Disenchanted with the software's capabilities, TR terminated its contract with DSL and sued DSL for damages. That action was settled. DSL in turn sued U, claiming *inter alia* that U was guilty of negligent misstatement (and deceit) in relation to the software's capabilities.

---

[13] p. 2 of judgment.
[14] Unreported, April 1997, QBD, Official Referees, H.H.J. Bowsher Q.C.
[15] October 19, 1994, reported at [1995] Masons C.L.R. 5.

H.H.J. Hicks Q.C. considered that U owed DSL a duty of care in relation to these pre-contract statements because *inter alia*: (i) the purpose of the statements had been to induce DSL (and its client) to contract with U; (ii) DSL relied on U for guidance in relation to the subject matter of the statements; and (iii) U were aware of DSL's reliance. In addition, U owed a duty of care and were guilty of negligent misstatement (and deceit) in relation to one of the statements made by them to DSL after the contract was entered into, which was to the effect that DSL's approach to the design of the system was adequate.

(xiii) *Collateral contract*

17–056   It should also be noted that pre-contract statements can, as in any commercial context, be such as to give rise to a collateral warranty on the principles in *Esso Petroleum Company Limited v. Mardon*.[16] In *Mackenzie Patten & Co. v. British Olivetti Ltd*, for example, pre-contractual representations made by a computer supplier to a firm of solicitors regarding the capabilities of the computer were found to give rise to a collateral contract.[17]

(xiv) *Advice on computer systems*

17–057   The liability of computer consultants employed to advise in connection with the acquisition of a computer system was considered in *Stephenson Blake (Holdings) Limited v. Streets Heaver Limited*.[18] SBH employed SH to advise it on a new computerised accounting system. On SH's recommendation, SBH placed a purchase order with a company, O, for such a system, but was dissatisfied with it. SBH alleged that SH was negligent in recommending O's system. In an action for damages brought before the (then) Official Referees of the Queen's Bench Division, Hicks J. held that the contract was subject to the following implied terms:

(1) where the client has put forward a specification, the consultant is under a duty of reasonable care and skill to ensure that the recommended system conformed to the description;

(2) the consultant must warn the client in plain terms when budgetary constraints or other difficulties mean that the requirements of the client cannot be met;

(3) if the consultant has any concerns about the ability of the client's staff to cope with the changes acquired by the new system it must communicate those concerns to the client;

(4) the consultant is under an independent duty to ensure that the hardware and software are compatible with the specification—it cannot rely on the assurances of the supplier who has a vested interest;

(5) the consultant has a duty to ensure that the suppliers recommended had the requisite skilled staff to provide maintenance and support;

---

[16] [1976] Q.B. 801.
[17] Unreported, January 11, 1984, QBD.
[18] [1994] Masons C.L.R. 17; [1998] Masons C.L.R. Rep. 25.

(6) if the requirements of the client changed then the consultant has a duty to warn of any incompatibility between the system and any changes.

Further the consultant must air any concerns he has at an early stage during the **17–058** currency of the project. The Court found that most of the elements of the system recommended by SH were either incomplete or "not well proven" in commercial use, that the system was unaccpetably deficient in its capacity to carry out the functions required of it and that it contained an excessive number of faults. The hardware was also seriously inadequate. In relation to some of the software defects the Court was not satisfied that SBH had shown that SH should have carried out more exhaustive testing to discover them. However as to the hardware it was clear that SH had advised calamitously without any independent testing or calculation of their own, on the recommendation of a supplier who had an obvious incentive to under-supply. Accordingly SH were in breach of the above implied terms and liable for damages which were to be assessed.

(xv) *Grant of quiet possession: "time-bombs"*

Licensors of standard software sometimes include in the software supplied to **17–059** their customers a device commonly known as a "time bomb" which enables the licensor to deactivate the software if, for example, the licensor discovers that the licensee is in breach of the licence provisions. The legality of such devices was considered by the Court of Appeal in the recent case of *Rubicon Computer Systems Ltd v. United Paints Ltd.*[19] R sold a computer system to UP to replace its ageing system. UP withheld about 15 per cent of the purchase price as a result of a dispute over whether R was obliged to transfer data from the old system to the new one. R still had access to the system and put a time lock device in it which, if activated, prevented the system working. R then activated the device, which rendered the system useless. The Court of Appeal held that section 12(2)(b) of the Sale of Goods Act 1979 applied to the contract and introduced into it an implied term that the buyer "will enjoy quiet possession of the goods except so far as it may be disturbed by the owner or other person entitled to the benefit of any charge or encumbrance so disclosed or known." On ordinary principles, wrongful interference with the goods (the hardware and software system) by the seller after property in the goods had passed constituted a breach of that implied term. Moreover, the breach was repudiatory in nature, notwithstanding that the device was easily removed.

Applying the reasoning of the Court of Appeal in the *St Albans*[20] case, it would **17–060** appear that such a term ought to be implied at common law even where the Act does not itself apply, for example where software alone is supplied other than on disk. It has been suggested, however,[21] that the decision in *Rubicon* extends the meaning of "quiet possession" to an unacceptable degree since, ordinarily, the statutory implied term is only invoked where the buyer is deprived of physical possession by someone claiming title or a right to possession of the goods. However any such extension would appear to be justified given the need for an effective remedy in these circumstances, and is certainly consistent with the interpretation placed on "quiet possession" in landlord and tenant cases.

---

[19] [2000] Masons C.L.R. 3, CA.
[20] [1996] 4 All E.R. 481.
[21] Case Commentary of Mr Richard Stephens, [2000] Masons C.L.R. 3 at 4.

(b) *Duties other than to client*

(i) *Common law liability to third parties*

17–061   As in the case of all professionals, the question of whether a software house or computer supplier owes a common law duty of care to a person other than its client depends upon the type of loss suffered by that third party.[22]

17–062   **Personal injury/damage to other property.** It is now commonplace for software or computer systems to be supplied in circumstances in which the foreseeable consequence of negligence on the part of the supplier, leading to an error or defect in the software or system, is personal injury or damage to other property. Examples include software or computer systems for safety critical applications such as in aircraft and hospital equipment, or for the operation of industrial machinery.

17–063   In the case of the supply of an entire system for such applications, such as the control unit for an industrial laser, it is clear that such a system represents goods,[23] and therefore a product, to which the principles established in *Donoghue v. Stephenson*[24] apply. Accordingly, provided that personal injury or property damage is indeed a foreseeable consequence of negligence on the part of the supplier, the necessary proximity for a duty of care to arise will almost inevitably be established,[25] so that a duty of care will exist in favour of all persons who suffer such injury or damage. This would appear to be so even if the product is one which provides factual information for the user, such as an aircraft altimeter.[26]

17–064   If the supply is of software alone, and the software is supplied on disk or some other medium, then (as already seen in the last section) the law treats this as the supply of goods.[27] There seems to be no reason why, in the present context, such a supply should not also be treated as the supply of a product and therefore one in relation to which a duty of care is owed by the supplier to eventual users (or persons affected) who ultimately suffer foreseeable personal injury or property damage. The same is true where software is provided other than on disk, by downloading or by telephone line, for example. It would clearly be illogical to apply different legal principles to such forms of supply.

17–065   However, in some circumstances the supply of a computer system or software depends upon input from professionals who are required to exercise judgment and express opinions which become incorporated into the software itself. Often the very essence of such a system or software is that it provides recommendations or advice to the user. Examples include the supply of medical equipment (or associated software) which provides diagnoses of medical conditions, or software which provides management or accounting guidance. In such cases,

---

[22] See *South Australia Asset Management Corp. v. York Montague Ltd* [1996] 3 W.L.R. 87.
[23] *Toby Construction Products Ltd v. Computer Bar Sales Pty Ltd* [1983] 2 N.S.W.L.R. 48.
[24] [1932] A.C. 562, HL.
[25] The position has now been reached where foreseeability of phyiscal damage will in itself give rise to a sufficient relationship of proximity for a duty of care to arise in respect of such damage: see Chap. 1. Such a duty would therefore only be displaced if, for public policy reasons, it would not be fair, just and reasonable for such a duty to be imposed. It is difficult to imagine a situation in which this would be the case, at least where the relevant loss is personal injury.
[26] A different view is however expressed in the *Encyclopaedia of Information Technnology Law* at para. 7.34.
[27] *St Albans City and District Council v. International Computers Ltd* [1996] 4 All E.R. 481.

although a particular recommendation is supplied to the user through a computer program or equipment, there seems to be no reason why the liability of the person responsible for the recommendation or opinion ought to be determined any differently from how it would be had the recommendation been provided in writing or orally. Such liability would be determined in accordance with the principles stated by the House of Lords in *Caparo v. Dickman.*[28] Again, where physical damage has been suffered, the requirements for establishing a duty of care will almost inevitably be made out on the basis of physical damage alone.

If the particular professional who is the author of the recommendation is **17–066** someone other than the actual supplier of the software or computer, then it would appear that no liability in common law negligence attaches to the supplier, provided that the professional was chosen with due care.[29] However liability would arise on the part of the professional who made the recommendation, provided that the three–stage test established in *Caparo v. Dickman* is satisfied.

"Other property". The criteria considered above apply to negligence claims **17–067** in respect of personal injury or damage to property other than the computer system or software which is itself being supplied. Where the complaint is that the very system or software supplied is defective, the claim is one for economic loss. The principles relevant to such a claim are discussed further below. If software alone has been supplied and, when it is loaded onto hardware, it causes damage to that hardware, then such damage is clearly physical damage recoverable under *Donoghue v. Stephenson* principles. A more difficult question arises where the software destroys or damages particular files or other software on that hardware. Should this be categorised as damage to "other property"? Although there is no direct authority on the point, the decision of the Court of Appeal (Criminal Division) in *R. v. Whiteley,*[30] which has already been considered above,[31] suggests that the answer is yes. If files or software other than that supplied are erased or corrupted (for example), this represents an impairment of the usefulness of the disk on which the files or software are stored (*i.e.* the hardware, or conceivably a disk), which constitutes physical damage for the purpose of the Criminal Damage Act 1971. Arguably precisely the same approach should apply in determining whether the owner of the hardware (or disks) on which the damaged files or software are stored has a civil right to compensation under the tort of negligence.[32]

However, if the same reasoning is applied to the case of the supply of a **17–068** complete computer system, the corruption or erasure of files stored on that system would represent damage to the system itself, and therefore, on the face of it, irrecoverable economic loss. On the other hand it would be recoverable property damage if the erasure or corruption was to files stored on a floppy disk or other medium separate from the original system supplied. The distinction appears to be arbitrary and irrelevant to the question of whether damages ought to be recoverable in respect of the loss of or damage to the particular file.

---

[28] [1990] 2 A.C. 605.
[29] *Taylor v. Rover Co. Ltd* [1966] 1 W.L.R. 1491.
[30] [1993] F.S.R. 168, CA.
[31] At para. 17–021, n. 53.
[32] This is the view expressed by the authors of the *Encyclopaedia of Information Technology Law*, at para. 7.79.

17–069   Two alternative approaches are: (i) to treat damage to computer files as no more than economic loss, or (ii) to treat damage to files stored in the system itself as property damage, *i.e.* damage to property other than the system as originally supplied. The first proposition is unattractive since it would lead to the conclusion that where an item of package software on disk is rendered useless by a defective computer system even this would not give rise to an action for damages under *Donoghue v. Stephenson* principles. Some support for the proposition at (ii) might be drawn from some of the *obiter dicta* in the decision of the House of Lords in *D & F Estates Ltd v. Church Commissioners*.[33] In that case Lord Bridge considered that it may well be arguable that in the case of complex structures or chattels one element of the structure or chattel should be regarded as distinct from another for the purpose of determining whether damage is to "other property". If so, then if any one component of the structure or chattel malfunctions and causes damage to another of the components the supplier of the defective component, if he was negligent, ought to be liable for that damage provided that the two components are sufficiently distinct for the second component to be properly regarded as "other property". This proviso might be satisfied, for example, if the defect in the system is in a physical component which is distinct from the hard disk on which the corrupted or erased file was stored. If, on the other hand, the defect in the system is in fact a defect in software which is stored on the same hard disk as the affected files then the complex structure argument still leads to the conclusion that the loss is purely economic. It may well be that, arbitrary as this distinction appears to be, it is the inevitable conclusion of the application of the established common law principles.

17–070   **Economic loss.** If the loss of which a third party complains is based upon (i) a defect or error in the very system or software supplied or recommended, or (ii) the financial consequences of such a defect or error, then the loss is properly categorised as economic loss. Since economic detriment of this kind is clearly the most likely form of loss to be occasioned to third parties by the negligence of IT professionals, this area could form the backdrop to a renewed challenge of the restrictive rules of recovery in respect of economic losses in English law. As the law currently stands, third parties can only recover damages for pure economic loss where the loss is the result of a negligent misstatement by the tortfeasor upon which they reasonably relied, or where the tortfeasor has assumed responsibility for the task from which the loss flows.[34] In relation to information technology, it is more likely that consultants will fall within the former category,[35] whilst suppliers could only usually be potentially liable within the latter.

17–071   In the context of information technology, in which the level of expertise and understanding of IT products and systems of those outside the industry is often limited, it will often be difficult for an IT supplier or consultant to argue either that their client did not rely on them, or that they did not assume responsibility for the task in question. However with more sophisticated clients such defences might conceivably be available.[36]

---

[33] (1988) 41 B.L.R. 1.
[34] See chap. 3, above.
[35] Provided the requirements laid down by the House of Lords in *Caparo Industries v. Dickman* are met—see chap. 15, paras 15–056 *et seq.*, above.
[36] The level of expertise of the client also has ramifications for any allegations of contributory negligence: see below at paras 17–125 *et seq.*

(ii) *The Consumer Protection Act 1987*

Given the proliferation of computer technology in purely private, non-commercial applications, the potential liability of producers and importers of computer products under the Consumer Protection Act 1987 should not be ignored. Under this Act, the producer (or, in certain circumstances, importer) of a product is liable for any personal injury or damage to (non-commercial) property resulting from a defect in that product, providing that the product was produced during the course of a business.   **17–072**

Liability under the Act is strict,[37] but attaches only to "products". It is clear that any defect in hardware comes within the terms of the Act, but it remains open to doubt whether software could properly be classified as a "product" under the statute. Section 1(2) provides that " 'product' means any goods or electricity and . . . includes a product which is comprised in another product, whether by virtue of being a component part or raw material or otherwise." The interpretations of "goods" and "substances" in the interpretation section of the Act (s.45) do not assist: the former being a non-exhaustive list of examples of things that can be goods, the latter an unhelpful definition of elemental substances.   **17–073**

Software as a "product". It seems clear (for the reasons given above in the discussion as to whether software constitutes "goods" or "services") that software provided by physical medium (*e.g.* by disk) would fall within the definition of "product" in the Act. However real doubt remains as to whether software which is downloaded directly, or provided in some other non-tangible way, would constitute a "product" for the purposes of the Act.   **17–074**

The courts have not yet addressed this matter. However it would be a surprising, and arbitrary, state of affairs if the manner in which the software is downloaded were to be determinative of the liability of its producer for defects within it. The definition of product within the Act is, it is submitted, drafted sufficiently widely to allow a court to find that software in itself constitutes a product, and therefore to avoid such a state of affairs. It should be noted, however, that the preponderance of academic opinion is that software transmitted in an "intangible" form would *not* be a "product" for the purposes of the Act.[38]   **17–075**

Defences. By section 3(1) of the Act, a product is defective if it is not as safe as those using it are entitled to expect. Thus the producer may have a defence in relation to the use to which the product was being put at the time of the alleged malfunction, for example that the use was not one which was reasonably envisaged or provided for by the producer.[39]   **17–076**

There is also the possibility that a producer could utilise a "state of the art" defence in accordance with section 4(1)(e). Under this section it is a defence to show "that the state of scientific and technical knowledge at the relevant time was not such that a producer of products of the same description as the product in question might be expected to have discovered the defect if it had existed in his products while they were under his control."   **17–077**

---

[37] Subject to the limited defences discussed below at paras 17–076 to 17–077.
[38] See *e.g.* Lloyd, *Information Technology Law* (2nd ed.), p. 446; and Reed, *Computer Law* (3rd ed.), p. 89.
[39] See s.3(2).

(iii) *"Safety-critical" information*

17–078   It is not difficult to imagine the courts imposing a relatively strict duty upon the suppliers of and consultants for computer equipment and software which generate information critical to the physical safety of others. Items falling within this category include the hardware and software in systems regulating the passage of trains on a rail network, or air traffic control, for example. Provided that the proximity aspect of the duty of care test is present, there is no reason why the providers of equipment and systems which generate such information ought not to be liable for foreseeable personal injury which results from their negligence. It is anticipated that the standard of care to be attained by people voluntarily dealing in such critical equipment would be a stringent one.

3. Standard of Care and Breach

(a) *Standard of Care*

(i) *Contracts for services*

17–079   As already discussed, in many cases involving the recommendation and/or provision of software and hardware, there is likely to be a term implied into the relevant contract of retainer that the equipment or software will be of satisfactory quality and reasonably fit for its purpose. This standard is explored further below. However there will remain cases in which the contract is clearly for the provision of services alone, or is construed by the court as comprising both a goods *and* a services aspect, and in those circumstances the usual professional duty of care attaches to the services part of the performance, *i.e.* a duty to act with all the skill, diligence and care to be expected of a reasonably competent member of the profession.

17–080   Since there is, as yet, no professional body regulating the IT industry,[40] there is no obvious point of reference for determining an industry wide level of acceptable practice in areas of IT consultancy practice. However there is a number of project management and development methodologies which are widely used, and which give some guidance as to good practice in the provision of consultancy services.[41] Nevertheless a failure to adopt such methodologies will not necessarily be evidence of negligence. Whether there has been a breach of duty will be a matter of fact in each case, and close regard must of course be had to express terms of the retainer and communicated requirements of the client.

17–081   As set out in paragraphs 17–085 to 17–087 below, it is accepted as an idiosyncrasy of the IT industry that no software or system can be expected to be entirely free of bugs and errors. Thus it is clear that any professional who has recommended or provided a modified system which does not operate perfectly is not necessarily negligent or in breach of contract. It is a matter of fact and degree on the particular facts of each case as to what constitutes an unacceptable operating standard for the software or system recommended or provided. The

---

[40] See further para. 17–001 above.
[41] Included in this category are PRINCE ("Projects in Controlled Environments"), DSDM ("Dynamic Systems Development Method"), and SSADM ("Structural Systems Analysis and Design Method").

further question then arises as to whether the consultant or modifier was in breach of contract/duty in recommending or providing such a system. As discussed below (at paragraph 17–094), it is anticipated that a "state of the art" or "frontiers of knowledge" defence will rarely be available: IT consultants and software modifiers are expected to be circumspect in their assessments of what can be achieved, and to make such assessments and recommendations to clients in the light of the current state of knowledge within the industry.

(ii) *Contracts for sale/supply of goods*

What is satisfactory quality/reasonably fit for purpose? Where the contract **17–082** between the parties is for the provision of goods (hardware or bespoke software), there is implied by statute (or by common law, where the software is provided by a non-physical medium: the *St Albans* case, above) there is normally a requirement that the goods will be of "satisfactory quality" and "fit for their purpose". Section 14 of the Sale of Goods Act 1979 provides, materially, as follows:

"**14—2)** . . . Where the seller sells goods in the course of a business, there is an implied term that the goods supplied under the contract are of satisfactory quality.
(2A) For the purposes of this Act, goods are of satisfactory quality if they meet the standard that a reasonable person would regard as satisfactory, taking account of any description of the goods, the price (if relevant) and all the other relevant circumstances.
(2B) For the purposes of this Act, the quality of goods includes their state and condition and the following (among others) are in appropriate cases aspects of the quality of goods—

(a) fitness for all the purposes for which goods of the kind in question are commonly supplied,
(b) appearance and finish,
(c) freedom from minor defects,
(d) safety, and
(e) durability.

(2C) The term implied by subsection (2) above does not extend to any matter making the quality of the goods unsatisfactory—

(a) which is specifically drawn to the buyer's attention before the contract is made,
(b) where the buyer examines the goods before the contract is made, which that examination ought to reveal . . .

(3) Where the seller sells goods in the course of a business and the buyer, expressly or by implication, makes known . . . any particular purpose for which the goods are being bought, there is an implied term that the goods supplied under the contract are reasonably fit for that purpose . . . except where the circumstances show that the buyer does not rely, or that it is unreasonable for him to rely, on the skill or judgment of the seller . . . "

The Supply of Goods and Services Act 1982 applies to "contracts for the **17–083** transfer of goods", defined by section 1 of that Act as "a contract under which one person transfers or agrees to transfer to another the property in goods . . . " The relevant parts of section 4 of the Act are identical to subsections 14(2) and 14(3) of the Sale of Goods Act 1979 (above), and imply terms of satisfactory quality and fitness for purpose.

In cases in which there is no physical medium transferred between the parties, **17–084** and to which the judgment of the Court of Appeal in *St Albans City and District*

Council v. International Computers Ltd applies, the term requiring fitness for purpose and satisfactory quality to be implied by the common law is probably to be given the same meaning as has been given to those terms when construed by the courts in a statutory context.[42]

(b) *"Bugs" and "bedding in"—inevitable defects and software*

17–085   As can be seen from the above definitions, there is an objective element to the test of both fitness and satisfactory quality. However the objectively reasonable view to be taken of fitness and quality must relate to the *specific* goods in question. Hence the determination of what constitutes "satisfactory quality" or a product "reasonably fit for its purpose" is subject to the idiosyncracies of the IT industry. For example, in *Eurodynamic Systems v. General Automation Ltd*,[43] a case in which the High Court was concerned with a dispute as to the quality of an operating system for a computer, Steyn J. observed that:

> "The expert evidence convincingly showed that it is regarded as acceptable practice to supply computer programmes [*sic*] (including system software) that contains errors and bugs. The basis of the practice is that, pursuant to his support obligation (free or chargeable as the case may be), the supplier will correct errors and bugs that prevent the product from being properly used. Not every bug or error in a computer programme can therefore be categorised as a breach of contract."

17–086   Note should also be taken of the (*obiter*) observation of Staughton L.J. in *Saphena* that (emphasis added): *"Just as no software developer can reasonably expect a buyer to tell him what is required without a process of feedback and reassessment, so no buyer should expect a supplier to get his programs right first time"*[44]

17–087   In *Micron Computer Systems Ltd v. Wang*[45] the claimant purchased a computer system consisting of both hardware and software from the defendant. Discussing the problems experienced by the claimant with the running of the software, Steyn J. noted that: "Some of the problems were plainly only the teething problems which are commonplace in the installation of any such computer system",[46] and that "It was simply teething problems in the installation process which is perfectly normal in the computer industry".[47]

17–088   It is apparent from these passages that the expectation in the IT industry is that software will not be free from error upon delivery or activation, but that some period of "bedding in" or "debugging" is to be expected.[48] It is a matter of

---

[42] The judgment of Sir Iain Glidewell does not elaborate upon the content of the term to be implied. In relation to contracts for the transfer of software alone, he states that "such a contract is subject to an implied term that the program will be reasonably fit for, *i.e.* reasonably capable of achieving, the intended purpose." [1996] 4 All E.R. 481 at 494d. Immediately preceding this passage the learned judge discusses the relevant terms implied elsewhere by the Sale of Goods Act 1979 and the Supply of Goods and Services Act 1982, and he can only have had a term identical to those in mind.

[43] Unreported, September 6, 1988, QBD.

[44] See also the observations of Staughton L.J. in the same case, in the passage reproduced at para. 17–036, above.

[45] Unreported, May 9, 1990, QBD. See further paragraph 17–034 above.

[46] p. 7 of the transcript.

[47] p. 12 of transcript.

[48] It is doubtful that the courts would be so lenient in relation to faults in hardware. It is also doubtful whether standard (*i.e.* non-bespoke) software would be accorded the same degree of indulgence. Again it is a matter of fact and degree in each case.

degree in each case as to how many faults or errors are acceptable, and the timescale within which the provider ought to have the system running acceptably bug free. This has ramifications for the compliance of the buyer with its duty of co-operation[48a] (*i.e.* in relation to the period over which this duty is in operation), with the implied term that the seller or provider has a right to test and modify the system and with its obligation to mitigate any losses it suffers.[48b]

Particular problems arise in relation to the meaning of fitness for purpose   **17–089** where the purpose in question is communicated to the supplier late, or in gradual stages. In some computer contracts, the buyer collaborates with the seller/ supplier in the design process for bespoke software by working out its require- ments during the currency and progression of the contract. In such cases the buyer is under a duty to sufficiently and timeously communicate its require- ments.[48c] However, assuming that this duty is complied with, the fact that the obligation was an evolving one will not absolve the supplier from liability if the final product does not comply with the specification as ultimately agreed. As Nourse L.J. said in *St Albans City and District Council v. ICL*[49]:

> "Parties who respectively agree to supply and acquire a system recognising that it is still in the course of development cannot be taken, merely by virtue of that recognition, to intend that the supplier shall be at liberty to supply software which cannot perform the function expected of it at the stage of development at which it is supplied."

(c) *The time when the obligation of fitness for purposes arises*

In sale of goods law the obligation to provide goods which are of satisfactory   **17–090** quality and fit for their purpose arises, in the absence of anything to the contrary in the relevant contract, at the time the property in the goods passes. On the basis of the authorities referred to above,[49a] it would appear that in cases involving bespoke (or in some circumstances modified) computer software the relevant obligation only arises at a later stage, at a point when reasonable testing, refinement and adjustment have allowed the system to run in an acceptably bug- free manner, and to perform the functions for which it was acquired.

Although the issue has not been put directly in this way in the reported cases,   **17–091** it would appear that this conclusion is based on the existence of an implied term to this effect. This is consistent with the passages cited above, and any departure from the usual point in time at which the obligation arises (*i.e.* as laid down by the relevant statutes) offers the advantage that it is equally applicable to cases in which software is downloaded or transferred without any physical medium, to which the statutory provisions do not strictly relate by virtue of the absence of a transfer of property.

(d) *The time when the obligation ceases*

Whilst, in general, the supplier's obligation to test and modify the system or   **17–092** software ends when the system becomes of satisfactory quality or fit for its

---

[48a] See above, paragraph 17–038.
[48b] See discussion below, paragraphs 17–124 to 17–125.
[48c] See discussion above, paragraphs 17–031 to 17–035.
[49] [1996] 4 All E.R. 481.
[49a] See paragraphs 17–085 to 17–087.

purpose, the parties can of course vary the contract and thereby end the obligation sooner. In *Saphena v. Allied Collection Agencies*[50] the parties (the supplier and purchaser of on-line software) agreed to end their relationship *before* the bugs had been satisfactorily worked out of the system. Mr Recorder Havery Q.C. held[51] that this was a consensual variation of the contract such that the supplier would not be liable to the purchaser for the system's failure to be fit for its purpose as the contract work had not been completed.

17–093   Another way in which the obligation to test and modify can be brought to an end is by the purchaser accepting the goods. Whilst the nature of software again makes the precise application of the Sale of Goods Act provisions problematic,[52] in relation to acceptance it is submitted that the buyer can clearly indicate acceptance of the goods at any time. The clearest indication of such acceptance might be by means of systems acceptance tests, especially so if such tests are specified in the contract.[53]

(e) *"State of the art" defence*

17–094   Given the rapidly evolving nature of information technology, it may be that defendants will attempt to argue that the system or software they contracted to provide could not in fact have been provided by any party, and that, as a result, and given the state of knowledge in the industry at the time, it cannot be said that they were negligent in contracting to provide it. In support of this, it might be argued that to condemn as negligent those who attempt to push back the boundaries of technology would be unduly restrictive and would hinder progress in the industry. Such an argument was advanced on behalf of the defendants in the building case of *IBA v. EMI and BICC*.[54] In that case the House of Lords found that negligence could properly be found even where the defendant's work could be said to be at the "cutting edge", if the party in question had not approached the project with sufficient circumspection. A similar approach can probably be expected by the courts in the area of Information Technology.[55]

4. CAUSATION

17–095   The related facts that no IT system can be bug- or error-free, and that there appears to be an implied term in IT contracts that the consultant/supplier is entitled to a reasonable period of time to correct errors and ensure that the system is running in an acceptable manner, may present difficulties for claimants in

---

[50] [1995] F.S.R. 616. See further paragraph 17–031 above.

[51] *ibid.*, at 640.

[52] s.35(1) of that Act deems the buyer to have accepted goods "when he intimates to the seller that he has accepted them; or when the goods have been delivered to him and he does any act in relation to them inconsistent with the ownership of the seller." The latter of these is problematic in relation to software, but the former ought to present no difficulties provided the acceptance is clearly and unequivocally communicated.

[53] See further Rowland and MacDonald, *Information Technology Law*, p. 87.

[54] (1980) 14 B.L.R. 1.

[55] See the observations of Nourse L.J. in *St Albans District Council v. International Computers Ltd* [1996] 4 All E.R. 481 at 487c, and of Hirst L.J. in *Professional Reprographic Services v. DPS Typecraft*, unreported, February 15, 1993, CA, approving the comments of the trial judge on this issue.

establishing causation of loss. In borderline cases in which, for example, a system is found to have only marginally more bugs than is acceptable; or in which the problems are reduced to an acceptable level but outside the timescale in which this result would have been reasonably expected, it may be difficult for a claimant to establish which part or parts of its loss are causally attributable to the default of the defendant, and which parts are attributable to the "acceptable" initial errors in the system.

Questions of causation may also arise in situations in which software is **17–096** subsequently modified by a different party, and then becomes inoperative. There may be difficult causation issues as to whether the more recent modification was the operative cause of the defect, or whether the original program was defectively designed. Such cases would turn upon the expressed requirements of the client in the original contract (*i.e.* in relation to future modification), and in all probability upon expert evidence.

There are also difficulties in IT cases in proving exactly what losses have **17–097** flowed from the defects in hardware or software of which complaint is made. These problems result largely from the fact that contracts for the provision of software and computer systems are aspirational in nature: they are entered into as a means of improving the efficiency and profitability of businesses, and measuring the expected results is often problematic. These difficulties are discussed further in the context of remedies, below.

5. REMEDIES

The remedies available in respect of a breach of contract and/or duty by an IT **17–098** professional are no different from those available under the general law of contract and tort. The issue of quantification of damages for pecuniary loss, and the related question of election between "reliance" and "expectation" loss, presently represent the main area of interest in IT contract disputes. This area is examined at paragraphs 17–106 to 17–111, below.

(a) *Contract*

The provision of hardware, and of software conveyed by physical medium, **17–099** constitutes a sale of goods in accordance with the Sale of Goods Act 1979. The terms implied by that Act as to satisfactory quality and fitness for purpose are, by virtue of section 14(6), deemed to be conditions of the contract. Accordingly breach of these conditions gives the buyer a right to repudiate the contract.

(b) *Repudiation: when possible?*

As has already been discussed (at paragraph 17–090), there appears to be an **17–100** implied term in contracts for the provision of software that the time for compliance with these conditions is *not* the point at which property in the goods passes (as in general sale of goods law), but is some later point in time at which it is reasonably to be expected that the system will be operating in an acceptably bug-free manner.[56] In these circumstances it is not always clear exactly when the

---

[56] As mentioned above, there appears to be no such concession in relation to defects in hardware.

buyer is entitled to repudiate the contract. Advising on this point may therefore prove to be a very delicate exercise. Buyers must be careful that a severance of their relationship with the supplier is not construed as a variation of contract as opposed to a repudiation.[57]

(c) *Acceptance: when deemed?*

17–101   Where there is a continuing relationship between supplier and buyer after delivery it is often difficult to establish when the buyer can be deemed to have "accepted" the goods[58] and thereby lost his right of repudiation. In the absence of a contractual provision for defined acceptance tests, it may be difficult to advise upon when "acceptance" has taken place, and a careful review of all the circumstances will be required.

(d) *Time of the essence?*

17–102   Of course the parties may oust or modify the implied term as to continued relationship after supply of software by including a contractual term as to the date upon which the system must be operating satisfactorily. It will be a matter of construction in each case as to whether a provision as to the time for completion has been made a condition or "of the essence" of the contract.[59]

17–103   Where the defendant is not the supplier of the goods (or non-physically delivered software) but the consultant who recommended the items or system in question, the claimant will not generally be able to sue upon a condition of quality or fitness for purpose, and the contractual measure of damages will reflect what would have happened had the consultant's advice been to the standard required (*i.e.* non-negligent). In most circumstances the *quantum* of loss will be the same in relation to claims against consultants as those against suppliers, *i.e.* the amount required to put the claimant in the position he would have been in had the advice been correct and had the system delivered the required functionality.

17–104   **Damages.** The normal measure of contractual damages applies, namely the amount to put the claimant in the position he would have been in had the contract been properly performed. In contracts for the supply of computer equipment and software (and contracts for advice on which equipment or software to obtain) this is often very difficult to calculate. The reason why people and businesses usually install and upgrade computer equipment is to improve the efficiency of, and often to expand, their business. As His Honour Judge Hicks Q.C. stated in *Stephenson Blake (Holdings) Ltd v. Streets Heaver Ltd,*[60] the assessment of what would have

---

[57] See in this respect the *Saphena* case (para. 17–037, above), in which an agreement between supplier and buyer to sever relations before the bugs had been satisfactorily removed from a system was held to be a consensual variation of contract which terminated the supplier's obligation to make right the defect.

[58] See s.35 of the Sale of Goods Act 1979 and the discussion of this point at para. 17–093, above.

[59] Examples of time being "of the essence" in IT contracts can be found in the *South West Water* case, and in *Salvage Association v. CAP.*

[60] Unreported, March 2, 1994, ORB; case note at [1994] Masons C.L.R. 17.

happened had the hardware or system worked properly is "necessarily hypothetical".[61] These hypothetical losses will often include a claim for lost profits, for which cogent evidence is required.

Given this uncertainty in the calculation of what is generally described as **17–105** "expectation loss", a claimant in an IT case will often seek to include in its claim a measure of the "reliance loss" suffered, for example the costs incurred in preparing to implement the systems and equipment contracted for, which have subsequently been wasted.[62] Whether this is a sustainable head of loss depends of course on the facts of the case, but in situations where there is at least a prima facie case for recovery under this head, the issue arises as to whether the claimant must make an election between reliance and expectation loss, or whether elements of both are recoverable.

(e) *"Reliance loss" and "expectation loss": election necessary?*

Since Lord Denning's pronouncement in *Anglia TV v. Reed*[63] the traditional **17–106** position has been that such an election must be made, so that the claimant does not obtain double recovery by being awarded both the costs of setting up a business opportunity *and* the lost profits that such an opportunity or venture would have generated. This was the position adopted by H.H.J. Thayne Forbes in *Salvage Association v. CAP Financial Services*,[64] in which Lord Denning's dictum in *Anglia TV* was applied.

However, this position was recently examined in the IT case of *Kwik Fit* **17–107** *Insurance Services Ltd v. Bull Information Systems Ltd*.[65] In that case, KFIS had retained Bull as prime contractor to design, develop, deliver, install and implement an enterprise wide computer system. Various breaches of contract were alleged against Bull and it was contended that the result of these breaches was that the system was never operational. KFIS claimed losses under heads including: restitution of the moneys paid to Bull under the agreement; costs and expenses directly incurred by KFIS in contemplation of and pursuant to the agreement between the parties, to the extent that such costs and expenses would be wasted if an alternative solution was implemented by another supplier; and "indirect" or consequential losses (*i.e.* "expectation losses") consisting mainly of projected losses of revenue.

The case came before Mr Colin Reese Q.C., sitting as a deputy in the Technol- **17–108** ogy and Construction Court, for the hearing of certain preliminary issues and applications. One of the applications made by Bull was that KFIS should be compelled to make an election at an early stage before trial as to whether they were going to pursue "reliance losses" (which came to around £1.4m.) or "expectation losses" (which came to over £25m. and would take much time, effort and expense to investigate). It was submitted on behalf of KFIS that the terms "expectation loss" and "reliance loss" were not terms of art, and indeed were not used in the *Anglia TV* case itself. All that was established was that a claimant could not "have his cake and eat it" by claiming the cost of setting up

---

[61] para. 158 of judgment.
[62] In certain circumstances this can include even pre-contractual expenditure—see *Anglia TV v. Reed* [1972] Q.B. 60.
[63] [1972] Q.B. 60 at 64.
[64] [1995] F.S.R. 654.
[65] Unreported, June 23, 2000, TCC.

a business venture and the gross profits that would have been generated from it. The set-up costs and the generated profits were not alternative measures of loss but different ways of approaching the same loss, and whilst the claimant might choose at some stage to limit his claim to the costs incurred, this was not a true "election". There was no necessary inconsistency between a claim for expenses incurred in reliance on the contract and a claim for loss of profit, provided there was no double-counting.

17–109   In support of this proposition KFIS cited paragraph 27–063 of *Chitty on Contract* (28th ed.):

> "Claiming for wasted expenditure in addition to net loss of expected profit. In principle the claimant should be entitled to claim damages both for his wasted expenditure incurred up to the date of his terminating the contract and also for the net loss of profit which he would have made but for the breach. There can be no valid objection to this, provided the calculations show that there is no overlapping in the claimant's recovery, *viz.* his net loss of profits is calculated by deducting from his expected gross return both the cost of his performance and reliance expenditure to the date of termination and the cost of the further expenditure which he would have incurred after that date if he had completed his performance. However the Court of Appeal (in *Cullinane v. British 'Rema' Manufacturing Co. Ltd*[66]) has ruled that the claimant must choose between claiming for his wasted reliance expenditure and claiming for his loss of expected profits, holding that he is not entitled to recover both. This position is correct if it is interpreted to mean that the claimant should not recover both his gross return or profits expected under the contract (or from the activity in question) and also the (now wasted expenditure) incurred in reliance on the contract which he had intended to meet from that gross return. But it is submitted that the ruling against a 'split' claim cannot be justified if the claimant can show that there is no overlapping between the two claims."

17–110   Similar passages in *Treitel on Contract* (10th ed.) were also cited. The deputy Judge accepted these propositions and ruled that KFIS did not have to make any such "election".[67]

17–111   It is submitted that the approach outlined above and endorsed in *Kwik Fit Insurance Services Ltd v. Bull Information Systems Ltd* is sound in principle, and should be borne firmly in mind by claimants when calculating and pleading losses for breach of IT contracts.[68]

(f) *Quantum: difficulties in calculation*

17–112   There are numerous addition difficulties to calculating the *quantum* of a claim in this area. One example of this is where a defective system corrupts or destroys data already held by the claimant. It is submitted that, by analogy to the approach taken in the criminal case of *R. v. Whiteley*,[69] this would represent (recoverable) damage to property. However the quantification of such a loss is often difficult. Such cases can only be dealt with on their individual facts, and it is anticipated

---

[66] [1954] 1 Q.B. 292.
[67] See para. 80 of judgment.
[68] The normal contractual rules of remoteness apply to IT contracts, and lost profits can accordingly only be recovered in accordance with the rule in *Hadley v. Baxendale*.
[69] [1993] F.S.R. 168, see discussion at para. 17–067, above.

that cogent (possibly expert) evidence will be required to establish the value to a claimant of raw data.[70]

Restitution. Restitution of the moneys paid to the defendant under an IT   **17–113** contract has been sought in a number of cases where the systems provided ultimately transpired to be useless, on the basis of a total failure of consideration. In both *Stephenson Blake (Holdings) Ltd v Streets Heaver Ltd*[71] and the *Salvage Association* case[72] such claims failed, in the latter case H.H.J. Thayne Forbes commenting that it is "well nigh impossible to prove a total failure of consideration unless no part of the service contracted is provided for".[73]

This is in line with the general approach in the law of restitution. However, a   **17–114** different view was taken by H.H.J. Toulmin Q.C. in *South West Water Services Ltd v. International Computers Ltd*[74] in which the claimant did obtain restitution of the contract price. The contracted for computer system was never received, the judge holding that "SWW did not contract in a vacuum to receive management know-how. They contracted to receive management services to enable the computer system to be delivered and not as an end in itself . . . The buyer did not get any part of that for which they paid the purchase money."

It is suggested that this view is not in line with the general law of restitution,[75]   **17–115** and is unlikely to be followed. It will be rare that restitution of the contract price is ordered in situations in which the defendant has clearly gone some way towards performing its obligations under the contract.

(g) *Tort*

It will be relatively rare for claimants to have to rely upon a claim in tort, as there   **17–116** is almost invariably a contractual relationship between the party seeking to acquire or upgrade IT equipment or software and those who supply or advise upon such products. The situations in which a tortious claim might arise have already been discussed above,[75a] for example where the ultimate user of software has no direct relationship with supplier or manufacturer. In situations in which a duty can be established, the measure of loss is the usual tortious one, *i.e.* the amount to put the claimant into the situation he would have been in had the tort not occurred. This can include pure economic loss,[75b] and where the relevant

---

[70] See for example the case of *Logical Computer Ltd v. Euro Carparks Ltd* (unreported, June 19, 2001, QB), in which two grossly incompetent repair operatives damaged the defendant's hard disk and erased data from the payroll, the nominal ledger, the suppliers database and the sales ledger. The claimant sued for its fees for this and other work. The defendant's counterclaim included a claim for the value of lost data. The Court found that the lost data would never in fact be reinputted, and for this reason a claim for the cost of so doing was disproportionate to the benefit to be obtained and should therefore, in accordance with *Ruxley Electronics v. Forsyth* [1996] 1 A.C. 344, should not be allowed. H.H.J. Fernyhough Q.C. held that the correct way of dealing with this particular claim was as a diminution in value of the system as a whole, relying on *Chaplin v. Hicks* [1911] 1 K.B. 786 as the justification of such an award of general damages. The judge assessed the diminution in value of the system without the lost data at £15,000. The claim for the cost of reinputting the data had been just over £45,000.
[71] Unreported, March 2, 1994.
[72] [1995] F.S.R. 654.
[73] [1995] F.S.R. 654 at 682.
[74] Unreported, June 29, 1999, TCC; case note at [1999] Masons C.L.R. 400.
[75] See *Chitty on Contracts,* paras 30–048 *et seq.*
[75a] Paragraphs 17–061 to 17–071.
[75b] See above, paragraph 17–070.

relationship is established, the tortfeasor will be liable for losses in relation to which he had a duty to keep the claimant harmless.[76]

17–117   A potentially interesting problem in relation to recovery in tort presents itself when the loss claimed is for damage to software not 'attached' to any physical medium. It is well established that for liability in tort to attach the victim must have property in the damaged item at the time damage occurs—*Leigh & Sillivan Ltd v. Aliakmon Shipping Co. Ltd*[77]—which would technically mean that damage to software alone would not be susceptible to a claim in tort, unless a court was willing to find that software could represent "property" for this purpose.

6. Exclusion and Limitation of Liability

17–118   There are no special rules applicable to the IT industry in relation to exclusion and limitation clauses. However such clauses are invariably used in IT contracts. This is perhaps understandable given the potentially substantial liability that can arise as a result of a defect in modern IT systems. Accordingly the construction and/or application of exclusion clauses arises as an issue in many of the reported IT cases, but to date they have not given rise to any new statements of principle. The following brief summary of the issues that have arisen to date may be of assistance, however, should future disputes arise involving similar facts and/or similar or related clauses in the industry.

17–119   **Contracting on the other party's standard terms.** In *Salvage Association v. CAP Financial Services*[78] it was held that, although the parties had negotiated some important points in their first contract, there had been no negotiation or alteration of the general terms or conditions, and accordingly the parties had contracted on the defendant's standard terms. The exclusion clauses in the contract therefore had to pass the test of reasonableness laid down in section 11 of the Unfair Contract Terms Act 1977. In relation to the second contract between them, the claimant had considered and received advice on each term of the contract, and where it had sought changes these had generally been agreed. Accordingly the parties had been of equal bargaining power and the UCTA requirement of reasonableness did not apply to the exclusion clauses contained in this contract.[79]

17–120   Many of the cases to date deal with the issue of whether one of the party's standard terms were incorporated into the contract, which is usually decided on (and specific to) the facts of the individual case. In *St Albans DC v. ICL*[80] the

---

[76] See *South Australia Asset Management Corporation v. York Montague Ltd* [1997] A.C. 191, and discussion thereof in chap. 15, para. 15–125, above. As far as a claim in tort ever needs to be relied upon against an IT consultant, it is worth noting that such consultants will very rarely be retained to provide bare information. They almost always give positive advice on a course of action, and under *SAAMCO* principles they would accordingly be liable for all the consequences of that advice being wrong.

[77] [1986] A.C. 785.

[78] [1995] F.S.R. 654.

[79] It should be noted, however, that both contracts imposed duties on the defendant, breach of which would have constituted negligence. Accordingly the exclusion clauses attempted to exclude liability for negligence and thereby fell foul of s.2 of UCTA, meaning that they in fact had to comply with the requirements of reasonableness in s.11. It is submitted that this will often be the case, and practitioners should be alert to the operation of UCTA in this manner.

[80] [1996] 4 All E.R. 481 at 491.

Court of Appeal discussed the decision of Thayne Forbes Q.C. in *Salvage Association v. CAP*, and held that dealing on standard terms was not dependent upon the absence of negotiations. Even if there had been negotiations over the terms in question the learned judge would still have found that the parties had contracted on the defendant's standard terms.

Reasonableness of term. In the *St Albans* case, the Court of Appeal upheld   **17–121** the trial judge's decision that the term in question, which purported to limit ICL's liability for breach of contract to the price of the equipment or service in question or £100,000, whichever was the lesser, and to exclude liability entirely for "any direct or consequential loss or loss of business profits sustained by the customer", was unreasonable.[81]

In the *Salvage Association* case, the Court held that a clause which purported   **17–122** to limit the defendant's liability for any failure of their warranty to repair defects in the system provided within a reasonable period of time to the lesser of the price of the repair or £25,000, was unreasonable. In reaching this decision the judge emphasised the fact that the claimant was unable to insure effectively against the risk of non-performance by the defendant, whereas the defendant had considerable insurance cover and, in recent similar contracts, had adopted the policy of raising the limitation to £1,000,000.

In *South West Water v. ICL*,[82] clauses which purported to exclude the defen-   **17–123** dant's liability for fraudulent misrepresentation prior to the contract, and to limit its liability to £250,000 if the system did not make it to the stage of acceptance testing, were both found to be manifestly unreasonable.

7. DUTY TO MITIGATE

The duty of mitigation is the same in contract and tort, namely that the claimant   **17–124** should take all reasonable steps to mitigate its losses.[83] This can present problems in IT disputes where there is an express or implied term that the supplier is to be allowed a reasonable amount of time to ensure that the system or software runs satisfactorily and free from bugs. Where this is the case, it is difficult for a claimant to know the point at which he ought to start taking steps of his own to remedy the situation. If he starts too soon, he will be in breach of his obligation to allow the supplier reasonable time and any expense he incurs may not be deemed reasonable; if he waits too long he may well face the argument that he failed to reasonably mitigate his losses.

Other arguments which may succeed in the IT sphere include the contention   **17–125** that the claimant ought not to have replaced the defective system with an entirely new one. There are occasions where the claimant can be shown to have replaced hardware as well as software unnecessarily, since different software could have fulfilled the claimant's purposes whilst using the same hardware.[84]

---

[81] [1996] 4 All E.R. 481 at 492b.
[82] [1999] Masons C.L.R. 400.
[83] See, for example, *McGregor on Damages* (16th ed.), paras 282 *et seq.*
[84] An argument along these lines was partially successful for the defendant in *Stephenson Blake (Holdings) Ltd v. Streets Heaver Ltd*, unreported, March 2, 1994, QB.

8. Contributory Negligence

17–126   A defence of contributory negligence is not of course available in relation to breaches of contract, save where the contractual term imposes no more than a duty to take reasonable care alongside an attendant obligation in tort.[85] Consequently no defence of contributory negligence will be available for a defendant who is in breach of the contractual terms of satisfactory quality and/or fit for their purpose.

17–127   Accordingly contributory negligence will usually only be available as a defence to consultants who do not supply the goods themselves. As indicated earlier, in a specialist field such as IT, where lay knowledge is generally very limited, a defendant will have significant difficulties in establishing contributory negligence on the part of the claimant. The defendant in *Stephenson Blake v. Streets Heaver*[86] argued that its client, the claimant, had negligently contributed to its own loss in a number of ways (including a failure to carry out adequate systems testing, and going "live" with the system too early). All of the allegations failed, primarily on the basis that the defendant had been kept informed of the intended actions of the claimant and yet said nothing to prevent the actions being taken. The claimant did not know enough about computer systems to realise that what it was doing was likely to cause or contribute towards their loss. It is to be expected that this will normally be the correct analysis.[87]

17–128   However, there will be cases in which the alleged contributory negligence relates to a matter so basic and obvious that even a claimant with no specific technical knowledge will be held to have been negligent. Such a situation arose in *Logical Computer Ltd v. Euro Carparks Ltd.*[88] In that case the negligence of the claimant's operatives had caused the defendant's system to crash, destroying a quantity of crucial data on the defendant's hard disk. The claimant sued for its fees and the defendant counterclaimed for its losses attendant upon the disruption to its business. In relation to the counterclaim, the claimant contended that the defendant had been negligent in failing to ensure that their system was regularly backed up.

17–129   The judge held that the claimant had indeed been negligent, in three respects: ordering the wrong backup tapes and failing to check that they were the correct type; failing to check at any time that the backup system was working satisfactorily; and in failing to detect the error message that had been shown on the server. The judge observed that:

> "In my judgment, in this day and age, these were serious shortcomings. The Defendant's business was heavily dependant upon the proper functioning of its computer systems and this was well understood. They also knew that the backup system was a vital defence against computer malfunction which is, unfortunately, far from rare. It is therefore vital that this line of defence is regularly checked to see that it is functioning

---

[85] *Forsikringsaktieselskapet Vesta v. Butcher* [1989] A.C. 852.
[86] See n. 84, above.
[87] It should not be forgotten that the client is under an obligation to co-operate with his IT supplier—see *Anglo Group plc v. Winther Brown,* unreported, March 1, 2000—and where such co-operation is not forthcoming and the breach in question is not related to a term for satisfactory quality or fitness for purpose, it is submitted that this would be likely to be construed as either a failure to mitigate or contributory negligence on the client's part, depending upon exactly how they had failed to co-operate.
[88] Unreported, June 19, 2001, QB.

properly for, if not, the consequences can be disastrous. It should be common practice in every business which uses computers for the backup system to be regularly checked for malfunction. I do not consider this a matter of special expertise or knowledge possessed only by the qualified few. To my mind it is a matter of business common sense and risk management. If the Defendant did not have sufficiently qualified or experienced personnel to understand and take steps to avoid this risk, then they could have employed outside assistance and advice for this purpose. But to place this line of defence in the hands of an employee who did not understand how it worked or, more importantly, how to verify that it was working satisfactorily was, in my judgment, a major error."

The learned judge reduced the damages on the counterclaim by 50 per cent for **17–130** contributory negligence. Accordingly practitioners should always be astute as to whether the claimant can justifiably be criticised for not doing enough to guard against computer failure.

9. Limitation

There are no special rules of limitation in this area. However, the reasonable **17–131** period which suppliers and advisers appear to have to put right defects in installed software and systems[89] may present difficulties in pinning down the precise date upon which the contract was breached, and accordingly in determining the date upon which the contractual limitation period began to run.

The limitation period in tort will in most cases only be relevant where the **17–132** damage accrues some considerable time after the installation of the relevant hardware/system, and there is a problem with contractual limitation. For example, a defective system that destroys crucial data and files some years after its installation. Where the loss suffered is pure economic loss, questions will arise as to when the limitation period starts running, *i.e.* date of "damage" or date of discoverability, an area less than clear in English law.[90]

---

[89] See above, paras 17–090 to 17–091.
[90] See chap. 15, paras 15–016 *et seq.*, above.

CHAPTER 18

PATENT AGENTS AND TRADE MARK ATTORNEYS

		PARA.			PARA.
1.	General	18–001		(e) The standard of skill	18–010
	(a) The function of a patent agent	18–002		(f) Immunity	18–012
	(b) The function of a trade mark			(g) Liability for costs	18–013
	attorney	18–006		(h) Privilege	18–014
	(c) Duties to clients	18–008	2.	Liability for breach of duty	18–015
	(d) Duties to third parties	18–009	3.	Damages	18–020

1. GENERAL

There are very few reported cases against patent agents or trade mark attorneys.[1] **18–001**
Reference should therefore be made to the general principles to be applied to
professionals, set out in the first part of this work, and, given the analogous
nature of much of their work, to the chapters on solicitors and barristers.[2]

(a) *The function of a patent agent*[3]

Patent agents deal with matters related to patents. Their functions can broadly be **18–002**
divided into two: applying for and obtaining patents on their client's behalf,[4] and
advising on intellectual property rights, including questions of validity and
infringement. A patent agent's work includes clerical tasks such as filing forms
at the Patent Office and paying renewal fees, but also matters requiring technical
and legal skill such as drafting patent specifications and advising on validity and
infringement.

Court proceedings. Patent agents may conduct proceedings relating to patents **18–003**
before the Comptroller.[5] They can do anything in connection with proceedings
before the patents county court which a solicitor may do,[6] which will include
appearing as an advocate. They may also appear on behalf of any party to an
appeal from the Comptroller to the Patents Court.[7] The Chartered Institute of

---

[1] In part this is due to the small size of the profession. There are about 1,400 registered patent agents
and 900 registered trade mark attorneys, with about 600 of these being dually qualified.

[2] See chaps 10 and 11.

[3] For a general exposition of the law relating to patents, see *Terrell on the Law of Patents* (15th ed.,
2000). For the statutory framework relating to patent agents, see *Halsbury's Laws of England* (4th ed.,
reissue), vol. 35, paras 692 to 713.

[4] A patent agent in the United Kingdom will normally himself deal with patents in the United
Kingdom and with European patents. Given the necessity for international protection, a patent agent
will often also apply for patents in other jurisdictions, normally through a foreign agent.

[5] Copyright, Designs and Patents Act 1988, s.274(1). The Comptroller General of Patents, Designs
and Trade Marks controls the Patents Office, see Patents and Designs Act 1907, s.62. Any person may
appear in person or as a representative before the Comptroller, see the Patents Act 1977, s.102A.

[6] Save for preparing a deed. See Copyright, Designs and Patents Act 1988, s.292.

[7] Patents Act 1977, s.102A.

Patent Agents is an appropriate body under the Courts and Legal Services Act,[8] and thus Patent Agents have a right to conduct litigation and appear as an advocate in relation to a wider range of proceedings,[9] subject to certain restrictions.[10] European patent agents may appear before the European Patent Office. Patent agents may instruct counsel directly.[11]

18–004   **Regulation.** While anyone may practice before the Patent Office, only registered patent agents may call themselves patent agents or patent attorneys,[12] and in practice almost all practitioners are registered. The register of patent agents is maintained by the Chartered Institute of Patent Agents,[13] which for most practical purposes is the professional regulatory body.[14] Registered patent agents must pass qualifying examinations and complete a period of practice under the supervision of a patent agent or suitably qualified lawyer for two years.[15] Only someone on the European list may call himself a European patent agent or attorney.[16]

18–005   **Alternatives to litigation.** A disappointed client now has an alternative remedy to launching proceedings. The Chartered Institute of Patent Agents can issue a reprimand or exclude or suspend a member for breach of the Rules of Professional Conduct, but it also has the power to require a member to pay compensation to a client, forgo fees, or pay a fine, where the client has not received the service expected of a patent agent.

(b) *The function of a trade mark attorney*[17]

18–006   It is the function of a trade mark attorney to advise on trade mark law, including protection and infringement of trade marks, and to act for clients to obtain registration of a trade mark. His work includes clerical tasks such as filing forms at the Trade Mark Registry and paying renewal fees, but also matters requiring technical and legal skill such as selecting new marks and advice on infringement. Trade mark attorneys have no rights of audience in the High Court or county

---

[8] ss.27 and 28. See the Chartered Institute of Patents Order, S.I. 1999 No. 3137.

[9] Essentially conducting litigation in respect of intellectual property in the county court, the Chancery Division and appeals therefrom.

[10] The patent agent must hold a certificate permitting him to conduct litigation issued by the Chartered Institute, which has (*inter alia*) training and experience requirements.

[11] In Part IV para. 401(a) of the Code of Conduct of the Bar of England and Wales, a barrister in independent practice may only supply services to a professional client, a BarDIRECT client or if appointed by the court. In the definitions of Part X para. 1001, "professional client" includes a patent agent and trade mark agent.

[12] Copyright, Designs and Patents Act 1988, s.276.

[13] Pursuant to the Register of Patent Agents Rules 1990, S.I. 1990 No. 1457, which are made under the Copyright, Designs and Patents Act 1988, s.275.

[14] However only the Secretary of State for Trade and Industry can remove someone from the register for misconduct.

[15] In theory it is possible to qualify by passing the examinations and carrying out unsupervised practice for four years, although it would not appear that this route is ever followed.

[16] Copyright, Designs and Patents Act 1988, s.277.

[17] For the law relating to trademarks, see *Kerly's Law of Trade Marks and Tradenames* (13th ed., 2001). Chap. 22 of that work sets out the statutory framework relating to trade mark attorneys.

court, but along with any other agent, they may appear before the registrar or on appeal before the appointed person.[18] They may instruct counsel directly.[19]

Regulation. While any person may carry out any procedure relating to a trade **18–007** mark,[20] only a registered trade mark agent can describe himself as such.[21] Registration is undertaken by the Institute of Trade Mark Attorneys, which determines the necessary examination qualification.

(c) *Duties to the clients*

In accordance with normal principles, a patent agent or trade mark attorney will **18–008** owe contractual duties to the client, and also concurrent duties in tort.[22] Equitable duties will be owed, in particular not to breach the confidence of the client.[23]

(d) *Duties to third parties*

In appropriate circumstances, duties may be owed to third parties, although there **18–009** are no reported cases of such third parties suing patent agents or trade mark attorneys. As with solicitors, it will in general be very rare that duties of care will be owed to third parties who are in conflict with the client, particularly if there are proceedings between the third party and the client.[24]

(e) *The standard of skill*

General. Patent agents and trade mark attorneys are required to exercise **18–010** reasonable care and skill.[25] The test of what is required is an objective one. In *Andrew Master Hones Ltd v. Cruikshank and Fairweather*[26] Graham J. held:

> "The degree of knowledge and care to be expected is thus seen to be that degree possessed by a notional duly qualified person practising that profession. The test is, therefore . . . an objective test referable to the notional member of the profession, and not a subjective test referable to the particular professional man employed."

Codes of conduct. Both the Chartered Institute of Patents Agents and the **18–011** Institute of Trade Mark Attorneys have produced codes of practice.[27] Such codes of conduct do not determine the law, but in practice the courts are very ready to

---

[18] See the Trade Marks Act 1994, s.82. Appeals to the appointed person are pursuant to s.76 of the Act.
[19] See para. 18–003, n. 11 above.
[20] Trade Marks Act 1994, s.82.
[21] *ibid.*, s.84.
[22] See *Henderson v. Merrett Syndicates Ltd* [1995] 2 A.C. 145 and chap. 2 paras 2–100 *et seq.*
[23] This is particularly important as an invention can only be patented if it is new, see Patents Act 1977, ss.1 and 2. See also the Chartered Institute of Patents Agents' Rules of Professional Conduct r. 4 dealing with conflicts of interest, and the corresponding guidance in the Guidelines Concerning the Observance of the Rules of Professional Conduct
[24] See chap 10 paras 10–055 to 10–074.
[25] s.13, Supply of Goods and Services Act 1982. This provision simply restates the common law.
[26] [1980] R.P.C. 16 at 18. This was not an issue on appeal. For the facts of the case see para. 18–017 below.
[27] The Chartered Institute of Patents Agents has promulgated both Rules of Professional Conduct, and Guidelines Concerning the Observance of the Rules of Professional Conduct.

follow them as establishing the duties and common practice of a profession.[28] The Code of Practice of the Institute of Trade Mark Attorneys is likely to be of limited assistance in any professional negligence litigation, being largely concerned with publicity, relations between trade mark attorneys and change of agents. The Chartered Institute of Patents Agents' Rules of Professional Conduct, and Guidelines Concerning the Observance of the Rules of Professional Conduct, may be of more assistance.[29]

(f) *Immunity*

18–012 Although there was no direct judicial authority for the proposition, it appeared clear that a patent agent or trade mark attorney acting as an advocate had the same immunity as a barrister,[30] but such immunity has now been abolished.[31]

(g) *Liability for costs*

18–013 When undertaking litigation, patent agents may be made liable for wasted costs in the same way as a solicitor or barrister may be,[32] in relation to proceedings before the Court of Appeal, High Court and county court.[33] It would appear that a wasted costs order may be made by the Trade Mark Registry against a trade mark attorney.[34]

(h) *Privilege*

18–014 Communications between a patent agent or European patent attorney and his client relating to intellectual property are privileged in the same way as those between a solicitor and his client.[35] There is a similar privilege with respect to communications beween a trade mark agent and his client.[36] It should follow that a former client suing a patent agent or trade mark attorney will waive privilege, within certain limits, in the same way as if he sued his solicitor.[37]

---

[28] See chap. 10 paras 10–091 and 10–092.
[29] See in particular the Rules of Professional Conduct for Patent Agents Holding and Acting within the Scope of Litigation Right Certificates.
[30] See in particular the Supply of Services (Exclusion of Implied Terms) Order 1982, S.I. 1982 No. 1771, which provided that s.13 of the 1982 Supply of Goods and Services Act does not apply to "the services of an advocate in court or before any tribunal, inquiry or arbitrator and in carrying out preliminary work directly affecting the conduct of the hearing."
[31] *Hall v. Simons* [200] 3 W.L.R 543. See generally chap. 11 paras 11–009 to 11–024.
[32] On which see chap. 10 paras 10–125 to 10–140 and chap. 11 paras 11–026 to 11–035.
[33] The Supreme Court Act 1981, s.51(6) permits a court to make a wasted costs order against a "legal or other representative." The Civil Procedure Rules Part 48.7 refers to "legal representative", which is defined in r. 2.3 as including "other authorised litigator (as defined in the Courts and Legal Services Act 1990)", on which see para. 18–003 above.
[34] See *Sun Microsystems Inc.'s Trade Mark Application* [2001] R.P.C. 461, where such an application failed.
[35] Copyright, Designs and Patents Act 1988, s.280. By the Patents Act 1977, s.103, legal professional privilege will extend to communications between a solicitor and his client relating to pending or contemplated proceedings before the Comptroller or courts under certain conventions. Thus this privilege will extend to communications between a patent agent and his client.
[36] Trade Marks Act 1994, s.87.
[37] See further Chap. 10.

2. LIABILITY FOR BREACH OF DUTY

General. Given the paucity of reported cases, there are few illustrations of the **18–015** type of circumstances in which patent agents or trade mark attorney may be found to be negligent. While this book does not speculate as to other areas in which liability is likely to be established, it is appropriate to mention that if an agent or attorney misses a deadline, it must be highly unlikely that there will be many circumstances in which he would not be found to be negligent.

Ignorance of the law. A patent agent or trade mark attorney must have **18–016** adequate knowledge of the law and practice of intellectual property. This is illustrated by the old case of *Lee v. Walker*.[38] The plaintiffs retained the defendant patent-agent to obtain a patent for a "new automaton vase or depot for holding coals", and he filed a provisional specification on April 30, 1870. In accordance with ordinary practice, he intended to wait until the expiration of four months before giving notice of intention to proceed with the patent, and then to wait two more months before filing the complete specification and obtaining the patent. In the meantime, on June 15, 1870 one Perman filed for a provisional specification for "improvements in coal vases", which turned out to be substantially the same as the plaintiffs' invention, and on September 10, 1870 he obtained a grant of patent for it. The Attorney-General rejected the plaintiffs' application on the authority of a case decided in May 1869, *ex parte Bates*,[39] which decided that the second application for provisional protection was entitled to have his letters-patent sealed, in the absence of fraud. Brett and Grove JJ. affirmed the decision of Lush J. that the patent agent was negligent. Grove J. hesitated to impute negligence on the basis of delay in giving notice of intention to proceed with the patent until the end of the prescribed notice, or on the basis of the defendant's ignorance of the fact that Perman's invention, of which the defendant had notice, was in substance the same. However, the judges agreed that the defendant was negligent in failing to know of *ex parte Bates*. According to Brett J.:

" . . . an agent of this kind is not bound to be accurately acquainted with the whole law of patents: but I think he is bound to know the law as to the practice of obtaining patents; and, as this was a most important decision with respect to the sealing of patents, the very practice the conduct of which he undertook for reward, I think he was bound to know it. Since that decision, patent-agents are not entitled to carry on their business as they had done before."[40]

The case is, of course, of some antiquity. The relevant law has changed greatly, and the knowledge of the law and practice of intellectual property required of patent agents and trade mark attorneys will probably have increased since then.[41]

---

[38] (1872) L.R. 7 C.P. 121
[39] L.R. 4. Ch. 577.
[40] (1872) L.R. 7 C.P. 121 at 126, and see the similar comments of Grove J.
[41] For another example, in the context of trade mark attorneys, see *Halifax Building Society v. Urquart-Dykes and Lord* [1997] R.P.C. 55 at 77, ll. 20–25, where the defendant was held to be negligent in an "elementary failure" to understand the procedure adopted by the registrar on separate applications by different persons of marks that are identical or nearly resemble each other pursuant to s.12(3) of the Trade Marks (Amendment) Act 1984, which was set out in the registrar's Work Manual. For the facts of the case see para. 18–018 below.

18–017 **Taking proper instructions.**[42] It is essential that a patent agent takes full and proper instructions from the client about his invention if there is a question of an earlier similar patent or "prior art".[43] This is illustrated by *Andrew Master Hones Ltd v. Cruikshank and Fairweather.*[44] The plaintiff had developed a device for reconditioning *in situ* marine crankshafts, which were large and could not realistically be removed from ships. The machine was an inverted lathe consisting of rings, encircling the crankshaft, connected by bars, one of which held a cutting tool, with the whole cage driven by a pair of belts so that it rotated around the shaft. The plaintiff instructed the defendant patent agents, who filed a provisional[45] specification, but an objection was raised by the examiner, based on two earlier patents. The defendants informed the plaintiff that as a result it would be unable to obtain a valid patent, and on receiving no further instructions they took no further steps. The defendants were found to be negligent as they failed to ascertain from the plaintiff what were the features of the invention which distinguished it from the prior art and which resulted in success in practice. They were also liable in three other respects: they took a superficial and incorrect view of one of the earlier patents; they failed to explain that the client might still obtain a valid patent despite their views[46]; and they should not have assumed that the client had decided to take their advice and abandon the application.

18–018 **Giving proper advice, including commercial advice.**[47] While a patent agent or trade mark attorney will generally owe no duty to give commercial advice, giving sufficient legal advice may entail suggesting that the client considers the commercial consequences. In *Halifax Building Society v. Urquart-Dykes and Lord*[48] Jacob J. explained what was required:

> "I think that where a trade mark agent undertakes to pursue a trade mark application for a client then his duties to that client extends to advising in relation to all legal pitfalls reasonably connected with the application. The trade mark agent is not under a duty to give commercial advice as such, but he is under a duty to keep his client informed of the legal problems which may arise and his duty extends to warning his client to consider any commercial problems which may arise as a result of the legal problems which he, as trade mark agent, should reasonably discern."

---

[42] For another example, in the context of trade mark attorneys, see *Halifax Building Society v. Urquart-Dykes and Lord* [1997] R.P.C. 55 at 67, ll. 22 to 25, where Jacob J. stated that the duty "extends to informing his client of any matter in relation to which he needs instructions on the facts to give proper advice . . . the client may not have the expertise to know what facts matter and what do not. The client is entitled to expect his agent to ask for the information necessary to give proper advice", and at 76, ll. 9–10: "A trade mark agent's job in making or pursuing an application normally involves finding out just what his clients do."

[43] Similarly, it will be important to obtain detailed instructions in drafting an application so it is properly defined.

[44] [1980] R.P.C. 16. The issue of negligence was not canvassed on appeal on the defendants' concession, on the assumption that the plaintiff's specification was sufficiently different from the two earlier patents, that they were negligent in failing to bring to the plaintiff's attention that the application would become void unless it was put in order by April 7, 1970, and that if it had been put in order it would have been accepted by the Patent Office, see [1981] R.P.C. 389 at 396.

[45] Abolished by the Patents Act 1977, s.15.

[46] But compare the position of solicitors, where the law is uncertain as to whether a solicitor has to explain that his view of the law may not be correct, see chap. 10, para. 10–152.

[47] See also chap. 10 paras 10–169 to 10–172 in relation to giving commercial advice.

[48] [1997] R.P.C. 55 at 67, ll. 11–20.

In that case, the plaintiff instructed the defendant trade mark agents to make a series of applications involving the word "Halifax", which it did on September 30, 1986. The next day, Provident Financial Group plc applied to register the same name for motor insurance services, which they had carried out through a subsidiary, Halifax Insurance Company Limited, from 1966. The registry cited Provident's application, and sent the defendants Provident's evidence of prior use. The plaintiff was dilatory in providing evidence of its prior use, and in a letter dated February 5, 1990 the defendants correctly informed their client that the registry had indicated that it would allow Provident's application to proceed to registration unless the plaintiff could provide evidence in respect of motor insurance before 1966. However, the defendants were negligent in failing to explain in detail how the system of applications would work and what the plaintiff should do, in particular that if it failed to provide evidence to rebut the priority claim, its application would be suspended. Most importantly, the defendants failed to inform their client that it was open to them to resolve the conflict with Provident by agreement to the satisfaction of the registrar, and that a failure to reach agreement would be likely to lead to cross-oppositions.[49]

Instruction of foreign agents. In *Arbiter Group plc v. Gill Jennings and Every*   **18–019**
(a firm)[50] the claimants sought advice from the defendant patent agents as to whether their new kind of jukebox might infringe an existing U.S. patent, as they had been warned at a fair where they had exhibited the jukebox that it infringed two U.S. patents. The patent agents instructed U.S. patent searchers to carry out a search to check this, who reported erroneously that the patent was still in force, when it had in fact lapsed through non-payment of annual renewal fees, which the defendants passed on to the claimant. The claimant alleged that by the time they discovered that the advice was erroneous, three years later, it was too late to sell the jukebox successfully in the United States, and they sued the defendant patent attorneys.[51] Swinton Thomas L.J. held:

> "A professional man in appropriate circumstances is entitled to delegate tasks. Whether he is entitled to delegate a particular task will depend on the nature of the task. He is entitled to delegate some tasks to others but is not entitled to delegate others. It all depends on the nature of the task involved. If he does delegate he must delegate to a suitably qualified and experienced person."[52]

The court recognised that there was a risk that the person to whom the task is delegated may make a mistake, and the question to be considered was the degree of risk and whether it was appropriate that the delegator should take it. In that case, the defendants were entitled to delegate the search to U.S. patent searchers, and they were entitled to rely on the results and not carry out further inquiries themselves.[53]

---

[49] *ibid.* at 71, l. 33 to 72, l. 13 and 81, ll. 1–3.The defendants were also negligent in other respects, see para. 18–016, n. 41 and para. 18–017, n. 42, and in failing later, when told that the plaintiff intended to offer motor insurance in addition to their other services to advise that this required serious and in depth consideration as Provident would obtain registration, see [1997] R.P.C. 55 at 78, ll. 18–25. In fact, no loss was caused by the negligence, see paras 18–021 and 18–022 below.
[50] [2000] P.N.L.R. 680.
[51] The American patent agent searchers were second defendants, but they had gone out of business.
[52] *ibid.* at 686.
[53] The claimant further relied on *Edward Wong Finance Co. Ltd v. Johnson Stokes & Master* [1984] A.C. 296, which was distinguished, see chap. 10, para. 10–088 above.

3. Damages

18–020   **Causation and loss of a chance.** Consonant with the general law,[54] a claimant will have to prove on the balance of probabilities that he would have acted differently if properly advised, for instance in prosecuting a patent application. This is a question of causation, but quantification of damages only has to satisfy an easier test: the claimant will recover substantial damages if there was a significant chance (for instance) that it might have obtained a valuable patent. This may involve considering whether the patent would have been granted, whether revocation proceedings might have been brought[55] and what the results of those proceedings would have been, and whether a competitor could easily have avoided infringing such claims.[56]

18–021   *Halifax Building Society v. Urquart-Dykes and Lord*[57] is a salutary example of a plaintiff failing to produce sufficient evidence to prove its case. The trade mark attorneys essentially failed in 1990 to advise their client to negotiate with Provident, which was attempting to register the name "Halifax" for motor insurance services. Eventually, proceedings were commenced by Provident, and in 1993 Halifax negotiated an assignment of all Provident's registrations and applications, with Provident ceasing to use the name, for £2m. The plaintiff failed to produce as witnesses any of their commercial men to prove that it would have negotiated with Provident earlier if properly advised, and the claim failed on causation. Jacobs J. also held that it was entirely speculative that the plaintiffs missed a valuable chance of obtaining a better deal from Provident if it had negotiated in 1990 rather than 1993, and the £2m. price was a good one at either time.

18–022   **Remoteness and scope of duty.** In the normal way, a plaintiff will have to establish that his loss is not too remote, and that it was within the scope of the duty the defendant owed. Jacobs J. addressed both of these issues in *Halifax Building Society v. Urquart-Dykes and Lord.*[58] He considered that the loss within the scope of the duty was the foreseeable loss, which was the chance of the plaintiff acting in accordance with the advice which should have been given.[59] The plaintiff claimed, *inter alia*, for the litigation and administrative costs of the proceedings brought by Provident. Jacobs J. rejected this claim. The defendants had advised the plaintiff not to proceed with motor insurance, which advice it

---

[54] See *Allied Maples v. Simmons & Simmons* [1995] 1 W.L.R. 1602, CA.
[55] Pursuant to the Patents Act 1977, s.72. Compare *Alexander Turnbull & Co. Ltd v. Cruickshank and Fairweather* (1905) 22 R.P.C. 521, where the Inner House of the Court of Session struck out a plea in a patent agent's negligence case that the patent was invalid for want of novelty, a decision which would probably not be followed now.
[56] Some indication of the factors that may have to be taken into account are given by Buckley L.J. in *Andrew Master Hones Ltd v. Cruikshank and Fairweather* [1981] R.P.C. 389 at 403, ll. 29–38.
[57] [1997] R.P.C. 55 at 83 to 87. See para. 18–018 above for the facts. While Jacobs J. did not cite the case of *Allied Maples v. Simmons & Simmons* [1995] 1 W.L.R. 1602, he correctly applied the law which it lays down.
[58] [1997] R.P.C. 55 at 83 to 87. See paras 18–018 and 18–021 above for the facts.
[59] Applying *Banque Bruxelles Lambert v. Eagle Star Insurance* [1997] A.C. 191, on which see chap. 3 paras 3–02 to 3–04, and chap. 9 paras 9–113 to 9–118. Essentially it would appear that this principle would not prevent recovery of the claimed loss of profits on motor insurance during the period of the injunction, the legal costs of defending the action, the internal costs, and the loss of a chance of obtaining a better settlement with Provident. The claim failed on other grounds.

ignored, and they were not responsible for the plaintiff when it "wilfully sailed into the eye of the storm".[60]

Valuation of lost patent. In *Andrew Master Hones Ltd v. Cruikshank and*   **18–023**
Fairweather[61] the defendants had failed to advise the plaintiff fully on a patent application, which was not pursued. The Court of Appeal held that the plaintiff company lost whatever benefits might have accrued to the company if the application had been accepted by the Patent Office.[62] The Court held that the logical method of assessing damages may be to quantify the price at which the plaintiff could have disposed its right to pursue is application on the open market on the assumption that it had been accepted by the Patent Office,[63] which would involve a potential purchaser forming a view on matters such as the potential success of revocation proceedings, and the potential profitability of any patent which might be obtained. In that case, an enquiry was directed as to damages.

---

[60] [1997] R.P.C. 55 at 87, applying *Galoo Ltd v. Bright Grahame Murray* [1994] 1 W.L.R. 1360, on which see chap. 15 paras 15–123 to 15–126.
[61] [1981] R.P.C. 389, esp. at 403. For the facts see para. 18–017 above.
[62] Presumably discounted by the chances of the Patent Office not accepting the patent, which was plainly very large on the facts, see *ibid.*, at 403, l. 35.
[63] In principle, if this assumption is made, then the resulting valuation should be reduced to account for the contingency of the patent not being accepted, see the previous paragraph.

INDEX

ABATEMENT OF FEES
  construction professionals, and, 8–316
ABUSE OF PROCESS
  barristers, and, 11–025
  solicitors, and
    civil cases, 10–114
    criminal cases, 10–113
    Hall v. Simons, 10–111—10–112
    leading cases, 10–108—10–109
    other types, 10–115
    subsidiary cases, 10–110
    wasted costs order, 10–137
ACCESS TO COURT, RIGHT OF
  human rights, and, 7–010
ACCOUNT OF PROFITS
  financial practitioners, and, 13–166
ACCOUNTANTS
  accounts
    audit of, 15–018—15–020
    preparation of, 15–014—15–017
  alternative remedy, 15–024
  audit
    financial sector businesses,
      15–025—15–031
    generally, 15–018—15–020
    introduction, 15–010
    liability for breach of duty,
      15–102—15–116
    preparation of accounts,
      15–014—15–017
    rationale, 15–011
  auditors
    appointment, 15–012
    audit function, 15–014—15–020
    removal, 15–022
    remuneration, 15–013
    resignation, 15–023
    rights, 15–021
  business advice, 15–119
  causation
    effective cause, 15–122—15–126
    generally, 15–121
    intervening acts, 15–130
    reliance, 15–127—15–129
  confidentiality, 15–041—15–044
  contractual duties
    implied, 15–036
    introduction, 15–031
    limitation of liability, 15–032
    statutory requirements,
      15–033—15–035

ACCOUNTANTS—*cont.*
  contribution
    claims against auditors,
      15–148—15–151
    generally, 15–147
  contributory negligence
    claims against auditors,
      15–148—15–151
    generally, 15–146
  corporate governance, 15–002—15–004
  damages
    causation, 15–121—15–130
    foreseeability, 15–131
    heads of damage, 15–135—15–145
    introduction, 15–120
    measure, 15–132—15–134
    mitigation, 15–152
    remoteness, 15–121—15–130
    statutory relief, 15–153
  duties
    client, to, 15–031—15–037
    fiduciary, 15–038—15–044
    overview, 15–008
    statute, under, 15–009—15–030
    third parties, to, 15–045—15–090
  duties to client
    contract, under, 15–031—15–036
    tort, in, 15–037
  duties to third parties
    Caparo, 15–053—15–061
    categories of advisee,
      15–073—15–086
    Contracts (Rights against Third
      Parties) Act 1999, 15–088
    Human Rights Act 1998, 15–089
    overview, 15–045—15–052
    policy considerations, 15–087
    relevant factors, 15–062—15–072
  duties under statute
    companies legislation,
      15–010—15–024
    financial sector legislation,
      15–025—15–031
    introduction, 15–009
    whistle-blowing, 15–030
  fiduciary duties
    confidentiality, 15–041—15–044
    generally, 15–038—15–040
  financial services, 15–005
  foreseeability, 15–131

ACCOUNTANTS—*cont.*
heads of damage
defalcation by director, 15–139
double recovery, 15–141—15–142
fresh audit cost, 15–140
introduction, 15–135
investigation cost, 15–140
lost advance, 15–136
lost investment, 15–136
monies wrongly paid out, 15–138
negligent advice, 15–145
overpayment, 15–137
tax advice, 15–143
tax returns, 15–143—15–144
introduction, 15–001
liability for breach of duty
auditing, 15–102—15–116
business advice, 15–119
tax advice, 15–119
tax returns, 15–118
valuation, 15–117
limitation of liability, 15–100—15–101
loss of a chance, 15–133—15–134
measure of damages
introduction, 15–132
loss of a chance, 15–133—15–134
misfeasance summons, 15–024
mitigation, 15–152
privatisation, 15–006
regulation, 15–007
remoteness
causation, 15–121—15–130
foreseeability, 15–131
standard of skill and care
auditing, 15–093—15–099
generally, 15–090—15–092
tax advice, 15–119
tax returns, 15–118
tort, duties in, 15–037
valuation, 15–117
whistle-blowing, 15–030
ACQUIESCENCE
generally, 5–109—5–112
ACTING BEYOND COMPETENCE
solicitors, and, 10–099
ACTING FOR BOTH PARTIES TO
TRANSACTION
borrower and lender, 10–102
generally, 10–100
group litigation, 10–103
informed consent, 10–101
ACTING ON CLIENT'S INSTRUCTIONS
exceptions to general rule, 10–124
general rule, 10–123

ACTING ON COUNSEL'S ADVICE
background, 10–116
client's position, 10–122
development of law, 10–117
examples of failure of defence, 10–119
examples of success of defence,
10–120
further limits, 10–121
summary of law, 10–118
ADDITIONAL PAYMENTS
construction professionals, and,
8–233—8–235
ADJUDICATION OF CONSTRUCTION DISPUTES
applicable contracts, 8–334
applicable operations, 8–335
challenging decisions
generally, 8–338
human rights, and, 8–342
jurisdiction of adjudicator, 8–340
natural justice, on grounds of, 8–341
enforcement of decisions
generally, 8–337
impecuniosity, 8–343
generally, 8–332—8–333
introduction, 8–011
jurisdiction of adjudicator
challenges to, 8–340
generally, 8–339
time limits, 8–336
ADVERSARY OF CLIENT
barrister's duty, and, 11–007
solicitor's duty, and
contentious business,
10–062—10–064
generally, 10–055
non-contentious business,
10–056—10–061
ADVERSARY IN CONTENTIOUS BUSINESS
barrister's duty, and, 11–007
solicitor's duty, and
criminal cases, 10–064
exceptions to general rule,
10–063—10–064
general rule, 10–062
ADVERSARY IN NON-CONTENTIOUS BUSINESS
barrister's duty, and, 11–007
solicitor's duty, and
Commonwealth cases, 10–061
exceptions to general rule,
10–058—10–060
general rule, 10–056—10–057
reliance on solicitor's
representations,
10–058—10–059
ADVERSE REACTION TO TREATMENT
medical practitioners, and, 12–191

ADVICE, FAILURE TO GIVE
barristers, and
clarity, 11–047
generally, 11–046
when not so instructed, 11–048
construction professionals, and
advice to claimant, 8–271
advice to third party, 8–272
patent agents, and, 18–018
solicitors, and
attendance notes, and, 10–174
confirmatory letters, and, 10–174
costs information, as to, 10–157
general business matters, as to,
10–169—10–172
introduction, 10–154
legal documents, on,
10–166—10–167
matters coming to notice, as to,
10–158—10–159
matters not asked to advise upon, as
to, 10–160—10–163
obvious risks, as to, 10–165
progress of matter, as to, 10–156
recipient of advice, 10–155
reminder of advice, and, 10–168
solicitor's own negligence, as to,
10–164
unequal transactions, in, 10–173
trade mark attorney, and, 18–018
ADVICE, FAILURE TO GIVE (SOLICITORS)
attendance notes, and, 10–174
business matters, as to,
10–169—10–172
confirmatory letters, and, 10–174
costs information, as to, 10–157
introduction, 10–154
legal documents, on, 10–166—10–167
matters coming to notice, as to,
10–158—10–159
matters not asked to advise upon, as to
generally, 10–160—10–161
statements of principle,
10–162—10–163
obvious risks, as to, 10–165
progress of matter, as to, 10–156
recipient of advice, 10–155
reminder of advice, and, 10–168
solicitor's own negligence, as to,
10–164
unequal transactions, in, 10–173
ADVICE ON APPEAL
solicitors, and, 10–184
ADVICE ON SETTLEMENT BY BARRISTER
examples, 11–044—11–045
introduction, 11–043

ADVISING AND SELLING
breach of duty, 13–121—13–125
introduction, 13–054
know your customer, 13–056
polarisation, 13–055
status disclosure, 13–055
suitability, 13–057
understanding of risk, 13–058
ADVOCATES
barristers
and see BARRISTERS
abuse of process, 11–025
damages for breach,
11–052—11–055
duties to client, 11–004—11–005
duties to third parties,
11–006—11–007
function, 11–001
immunity to suit, 11–009—11–024
inadequate professional service,
11–003
instructions, 11–002
liability for breach of duty,
11–036—11–051
liability for costs, 11–026—11–035
standard of skill and care, 11–008
human rights, and
confidentiality of communications,
7–033—7–035
introduction, 7–031
wasted costs orders, 7–032
immunity from suit, and
generally, 2–097
human rights, and, 7–030
solicitors
and see SOLICITORS
apportionment of liability,
10–323—10–332
damages, 10–225—10–322
defences to claim for breach,
10–106—10–124
duties to client, 10–004—10–039
duties to third parties,
10–040—10–076
exclusion of liability, 10–141
function, 10–001—10–002
liability for breach of duty,
10–146—10–224
liability for costs, 10–125—10–140
practice and procedure,
10–142—10–145
regulation, 10–003
standard of skill and care,
10–077—10–105
AGGRAVATED DAMAGES
medical practitioners, and, 12–288

AGGREGATION AND ALLOCATION
  financial practitioners, and, 13–066
ALLIED MEDICAL PROFESSIONS
  and see MEDICAL PRACTITIONERS
  disciplinary proceedings, 12–004
  registration, 12–003
ANSWERING PATIENT'S QUESTIONS
  medical practitioners, and,
    12–218—12–221
ANTICIPATED GAINS
  heads of damage, and, 10–305
APPOINTED REPRESENTATIVES
  authority at common law, 13–098
  introduction, 13–095
  liability of principal, 13–097
  status requirements, 13–096
APPORTIONMENT OF LIABILITY
  co-defendants, between
    and see CONTRIBUTION
    basis of assessment, 4–012—4–014
    basis of liability 4–006—4–009
    defences, 4–010— 4–011
    entitlement to contribution, 4–002
    introduction, 4–001
    liability of claimant, 4–003—4–005
    time for starting claim, 4–015
  construction professionals, and
    amount of contribution, 8–325
    discretion, 8–328—8–32
    distinct causes of damage, 8–324
    distinct types of damage, 8–323
    final certificate, 8–321
    joint insurance, 8–322
    introduction, 8–317—8–318
    "same damage", 8–319—8–320
    settlement, and, 8–326—8–327
  medical practitioners, and
    hospital authorities and doctors,
      12–164
    practitioners and pharmacists,
      12–165
  solicitors, and
    introduction, 10–328
    other cases, 10–332
    successive solicitors, 10–329
  surveyors and solicitors, between,
    10–330—10–331
APPRAISAL AND VALUATION MANUAL
  effect, 9–024—9–025
  generally, 9–023
APPROVAL OF DESIGN
  construction professionals, and,
    8–204—8–205
APPROVED PERSONS
  Code of Practice, 13–045
  introduction, 13–019

ARCHITECTS
  and see CONSTRUCTION PROFESSIONALS
  adjudication, 8–332—8–344
  apportionment of liability,
    8–317—8–329
  causation, 8–270—8–279
  contributory negligence, 8–330—8–331
  damages for breach of duty,
    8–264—8–315
  date of cause of action, and
    Bank of East Asia, 5–028—5–029
    date of damage, 5–030—5–033
    degree of damage, 5–022
    "doomed from start", 5–020—5–021
    Murphy, 5–024—5–027
    Pirelli, 5–017—5–019
    successive owners, 5–023
    uncertainty, 5–034
  duties, 8–019—8–181
  expert witness, as, 8–263
  foreseeability, 8–280—8–284
  functions, 8–004
  immunity from suit, and, 2–097
  liability for breach of duty,
    8–182—8–262
  pre-action protocols, 8–009
  remoteness, 8–265—8–284
  surveyors' functions, and, 9–001
ASSESSMENT OF DAMAGES
  Banques Bruxelles Lambert case,
    3–002—3–004
  hypothetical basis, on, 3–005
  introduction, 3–001
ASSET FREEZING ORDERS
  contravenors, against, 13–141
  generally, 13–146
  grounds of application,
    13–138—13–140
  introduction, 13–137
  knowingly concerned persons, against,
    13–142
ASSOCIATES OF LAY CLIENT
  barristers' duties, and, 11–006
  solicitor's duty, and, 10–042
ASSUMPTION OF RESPONSIBILITY
  directors and employees, 2–090
  generally, 2–078
ATTENDANCE NOTES
  solicitors, and, 10–174
ATTESTATION
  solicitors, and, 10–222
ATTRIBUTION
  contributory negligence, and, 5–119
AUDITING
  and see ACCOUNTANTS

AUDITING—*cont.*
 liability for breach of duty, and
  evidence, 15–108—15–112
  internal control systems,
   15–106—15–107
  introduction, 15–102
  planning, 15–103—15–105
  reporting, 15–113—15–116
 standard care and skill, and
  fraud detection, 15–095—15–099
  standards, 15–093—15–094
AUDITORS
 and see ACCOUNTANTS
 appointment, 15–012
 audit function, 15–014—15–020
 removal, 15–022
 remuneration, 15–013
 resignation, 15–023
 rights, 15–021
AUSTRALIA
 duty of care, and, 2–063—2–065
 immunity from suit for barristers, and,
  11–024
 solicitor's confidentiality, and, 10–031
AUTHORISED CONVEYANCING
  PRACTITIONERS BOARD
 generally, 10–002
AUTHORISED PERSONS
 acting outside permission, 13–074
 contravention of FSA rules,
  13–076—13–078
 employment of certain persons, 13–075
 introduction, 13–017—13–018
 regulatory liabilities, 13–073—13–078

"BALL-PARK" FIGURES
 surveyors, and, 9–038
BAR COUNCIL
 generally, 11–001
BARRISTERS
 abuse of process, 11–025
 advice on settlement
  examples, 11–044—11–045
  introduction, 11–043
 cab-rank rule, 11–019
 clarity of advice, 11–047
 confidentiality, and, 11–005
 damages for breach
  measure, 11–054—11–055
  remoteness, 11–052—11–053
 direct professional access, 11–002
 duties
  client, to, 11–004—11–005
  third parties, to, 11–006—11–007

BARRISTERS—*cont.*
 duties to client
  contract, in, 11–004
  tort, in, 11–005
 duties to third parties
  adversary of lay client, 11–007
  associates of lay client, 11–006
 errors of judgment
  examples, 11–041—11–042
  existence of error, 11–038
  introduction, 11–039
  nature of error, 11–040
  settlement advice, 11–043—11–045
 failure of advice
  clarity, 11–047
  generally, 11–046
  when not so instructed, 11–048
  failure to obtain full instructions,
   11–049
 fiduciary duty, and, 11–005
 function, 11–001
 human rights, and
  confidentiality of communications,
   7–033—7–035
  introduction, 7–031
  wasted costs orders, 7–032
 immunity from suit, and
  and see below
  background, 11–009
  extent, 11–013—11–024
  human rights issues, 7–030
  introduction, 2–097
  justification, 11–010—11–012
 inadequate professional service, 11–003
 instructions, 11–002
 liability for breach of duty
  clarity of advice, 11–047
  errors of judgment, 11–038—11–045
  failure of advice, 11–046—11–048
  failure to obtain full instructions,
   11–049
  introduction, 11–036
  knowledge of law, 11–037
  mistakes, 11–038—11–045
  mistakes in court, 11–051
  pleading weak points, 11–050
 liability for costs
  and see WASTED COSTS ORDER
  guidelines, 11–027
  introduction, 11–026
  misjudgements, 11–029—11–030
  procedure, 11–028

BARRISTERS—*cont.*
measure of damages, 11–054—11–055
mistakes
examples, 11–041—11–042
existence of error, 11–038
introduction, 11–039
nature of error, 11–040
settlement advice, 11–043—11–045
mistakes in court, 11–051
pleading weak points, 11–050
remoteness, 11–052—11–053
rights of audience, 11–001
settlement, advice on
examples, 11–044—11–045
introduction, 11–043
standard of skill and care, 11–008
wasted costs
and see WASTED COSTS ORDER
guidelines, 11–027
introduction, 11–026
misjudgements, 11–029—11–030
procedure, 11–028
BARRISTERS, IMMUNITY OF
background, 11–009
extent
Commonwealth position, 11–024
Hall v. Simons, 11–015—11–0
introduction, 11–013—11–014
Hall v. Simons, decision in
analogy to other immunities, 11–020
cab-rank rule, 11–019
criminal proceedings, 11–023
duty to court, 11–022
flood of litigation fear,
11–017—11–018
introduction 11–015
re-litigation, 11–021
starting point, 11–016
human rights issues, 7–030
introduction, 2–097
justification
academic criticism, 11–012
generally, 11–010
public interest, 11–011
BASIS OF LIABILITY
surveyors, and
Building Societies Ombudsman
scheme, under, 9–017—9–018
concurrent liability, 9–010
contributory negligence, 9–011
defective premises, 9–012
Financial Services Act, under, 9–016
individuals, of, 9–014
introduction, 9–007—9–008

BASIS OF LIABILITY—*cont.*
surveyors, and—*cont.*
limitation, 9–009
listing particulars, for, 9–015
misdescription of property, 9–013
BEDDING IN OF SOFTWARE
IT professionals, and, 17–085—17–089
BENEFICIARIES, DUTY OF CARE TO
generally, 2–114
insurance brokers, and, 14–026
solicitors, and
background, 10–047—10–048
conflict of interest, 10–051
double recovery, 10–052
identity of beneficiary, 10–050
non-will cases, 10–053
other jurisdictions, in, 10–054
scope of principle, 10–049
BEST AND TIMELY EXECUTION
financial practitioners, and, 13–065
BETTERMENT
construction professionals, and,
8–297—8–299
BILLS OF QUANTITIES, PREPARATION OF
construction professionals, and, 8–221
BLOOD PRODUCTS, SUPPLY OF
medical practitioners, and, 12–012,
12–226
BODY OF OPINION TEST
construction professionals, and,
8–145—8–150
expert evidence, and, 6–009
human rights, and, 7–047—7–049
medical practitioners, and
different schools of thought,
12–093—12–094
generally, 12–068—12–069
BOLAM TEST
construction professionals, and,
8–145—8–150
expert evidence, and, 6–009
human rights, and, 7–047—7–049
medical practitioners, and
different schools of thought,
12–093—12–094
generally, 12–068—12–069
BORROWER'S FINANCIAL STATUS
mortgage lenders' claims by,
10–211—10–212
"BRACKET" CLAIMS
financial practitioners, and, 13–094
BREACH OF COMMON LAW DUTY
introduction, 2–083
regulatory bodies, 2–086
scope, 2–084
supervisory bodies, 2–086

BREACH OF COMMON LAW DUTY—*cont.*
vicarious liability, 2–085
BREACH OF DUTY OF CARE
negligence, and, 2–015
BREACH OF FIDUCIARY DUTY, DAMAGES FOR
background, 10–228
Commonwealth cases, 10–230
introduction, 10–226—10–227
measure, 10–231
modern law, 10–229
restitution, and, 10–232
BREACH OF STATUTORY DUTY
negligence, and, 2–082
BRIBES
solicitors, and, 10–022
BUDGETS
construction professionals, and,
8–193—8–199
BUGS IN SOFTWARE
IT professionals, and, 17–085—17–089
BUILDABILITY
construction professionals, and, 8–216
BUILDING SOCIETIES, DUTIES OF SURVEYOR
TO
generally, 9–029—9–031
surveys for lenders, 9–030—9–031
BUILDING SOCIETIES OMBUDSMAN SCHEME
surveyors, and, 9–017—9–018
BUILDING SURVEYORS
and see CONSTRUCTION PROFESSIONALS
adjudication, 8–332—8–344
apportionment of liability,
8–317—8–329
causation, 8–270—8–279
contributory negligence, 8–330—8–331
damages for breach of duty,
8–264—8–315
date of cause of action, and
Bank of East Asia, 5–028—5–029
date of damage, 5–030—5–033
degree of damage, 5–022
"doomed from start", 5–020—5–021
Murphy, 5–024—5–027
Pirelli, 5–017—5–019
successive owners, 5–023
uncertainty, 5–034
duties, 8–019—8–181
expert witness, as, 8–263
foreseeability, 8–280—8–284
functions, 8–007
immunity from suit, and, 2–097
liability for breach of duty,
8–182—8–262
pre-action protocols, 8–009
remoteness, 8–265—8–284

BUSINESS ADVICE
accountants, and, 15–119
solicitors, and, 10–169—10–172

CAB-RANK RULE
barristers, and, 11–019
CAMOUFLAGED DEFECTS
surveyors, and, 9–095
CANADA
duty of care, and
directors and employees,
2–089—2–090
general approach, 2–058—2–062
immunity from suit for barristers, and,
11–024
solicitor's confidentiality, and, 10–031
CANCELLATION RIGHTS
financial practitioners, and, 13–060
CARE AND SKILL, STANDARD OF
accountants, and
and see below
auditing, 15–093—15–099
generally, 15–090—15–092
advances in knowledge, 2–124
barristers, and, 11–008
construction professionals, and
Bolam test, 8–145—8–150
Codes of Practice, 8–158—8–161
delegation to specialists,
8–177—8–181
errors, 8–165—8–167
evidence, 8–151—8–155
experience of client, 8–135—8–137
general practice, 8–145—8–150
knowledge, 8–144
knowledge of law, 8–162—8–164
ordinary competent and skilled
practitioner, 8–133—8–143
res ipsa loquitur, 8–156—8–157
special steps required,
8–170—8–176
specialism, 8–168—8–169
time of assessment, 8–139
contractual liability, and, 2–007
experience, 2–118—2–119
formulation of
individuals, 2–120
organisation, 2–121
person undertaking work of other
profession, 2–122
generally, 2–116—2–117
introduction, 2–002
IT professionals, and
bedding in, 17–085—17–089
bugs, 17–085—17–089

CARE AND SKILL, STANDARD OF—*cont.*
  IT professionals, and—*cont.*
    contract for services,
      17–079—17–081
    contract for sale/supply of goods,
      17–082—17–094
    fitness for purpose, 17–082—17–094
    satisfactory quality, 17–082—17–094
    "state of the art" defence, 17–094
  Lloyds' agents, and 16–020—16–022
  medical practitioners, and
    and see below
    Bolam test, 12–086
    consent to treatment, and,
      12–124—12–148
    current state of knowledge,
      12–073—12–074
    emergency situation, 12–080
    expert evidence as to,
      12–111—12–116
    failure to take precautions, 12–083
    general and approved practice,
      12–090—12–110
    generally, 12–067—12–072
    inexperience, 12–077
    misadventure, 12–080—12–082
    policy issues, 12–084—12–089
    res ipsa loquitur, and,
      12–117—12–123
    specialisation, 12–075—12–076
    working beyond one's competence,
      12–078
  new techniques, 2–123
  qualifications, 2–118—2–119
  solicitors, and
    and see below
    aggravating factors,
      10–098—10–103
    censure, 10–105
    general practice, 10–084—10–092
    mitigating factors, 10–096—10–097
    seriousness of claim, 10–104
    specialists, 10–093—10–095
    standard of reasonableness,
      10–077—10–083
  surveyors, and
    general practice and knowledge,
      9–054—9–057
    keeping up to date, 9–056
    margin of error, 9–058—9–061
    new developments, 9–056
    onus of proof, 9–062
    "reasonably skilled", 9–052—9–053
    relevance of the "bracket",
      9–059—9–061
    relevance of type of service, 9–057

CARE AND SKILL, STANDARD OF
    (ACCOUNTANTS)
  auditing
    fraud detection, 15–095—15–099
    standards, 15–093—15–094
  generally, 15–090
  sources of evidence, 15–091—15–092
CARE AND SKILL, STANDARD OF (MEDICAL
    PRACTITIONERS)
  Bolam test
    different schools of thought,
      12–093—12–094
    generally, 12–068—12–069
  clinical trials, 12–110
  consent to treatment
    capacity to, 12–135—12–139
    children, by, 12–148
    informed, 12–130—12–134
    introduction, 12–124—12–125
    limits on, 12–126—12–127
    mentally disordered patients, by,
      12–140—12–147
    voluntary, 12–128—12–129
  current state of knowledge,
    12–073—12–074
  different schools of thought,
    12–093—12–105
  emergency situation, 12–080
  expert evidence as to, 12–111—12–116
  failure to take precautions, 12–083
  general and approved practice
    acts in accordance, 12–092—12–105
    departures from, 12–106—12–110
    different schools of thought,
      12–093—12–105
    introduction, 12–090—12–091
  generally, 12–067—12–072
  inexperience, 12–077
  misadventure, 12–080—12–082
  novel treatment, 12–109
  policy issues, 12–084—12–089
  res ipsa loquitur, and
    application to medical negligence,
      12–119—12–121
    introduction, 12–117—12–118
    rebuttal of inference,
      12–122—12–123
  specialisation, 12–075—12–076
  working beyond one's competence,
    12–078
CARE AND SKILL, STANDARD OF
    (SOLICITORS)
  acting beyond competence, 10–099
  acting for both parties to transaction
    borrower and lender, 10–102
    generally, 10–100

CARE AND SKILL, STANDARD OF
(SOLICITORS)—*cont.*
acting for both parties to
transaction—*cont.*
group litigation, 10–103
informed consent, 10–101
aggravating factors
acting beyond competence, 10–099
acting for both parties to transaction,
10–100—10–103
unnecessary risks, 10–098
censure, 10–105
Client Care Code
example, 10–092
generally, 10–091
errors, 10–096
general practice as evidence
differing practices, 10–090
exception to general rule,
10–085—10–088
general rule, 10–084
taking instructions, 10–092
uniformity, 10–091
unsafe common practice, 10–089
hindsight, 10–083
ignorance, 10–082
inexperienced practitioners,
10–093—10–095
judgment, 10–080
knowledge of law, 10–081—10–082
lack of time, 10–097
mitigating factors
errors, 10–096
lack of time, 10–097
seriousness of claim, 10–104
specialists, 10–093—10–095
standard of reasonableness
general obligations, 10–079
generally, 10–077
hindsight, 10–083
ignorance of solicitor, 10–082
judgment of solicitor, 10–080
knowledge of law, 10–081—10–082
reasonably competent solicitor,
10–078
unnecessary risks, 10–098
unsafe common practice, 10–089
CARELESS PERFORMANCE OF PUBLIC DUTY
duty of care, and, 2–081
CARRY OUT INSTRUCTIONS, FAILURE TO
surveyors, and, 9–077—9–078
CAUSATION
accountants, and
effective cause, 15–122—15–126
generally, 15–121
intervening acts, 15–130

CAUSATION—*cont.*
accountants, and—*cont.*
reliance, 15–127—15–129
construction professionals, and
advice to claimant, 8–271
advice to third party, 8–272
concurrent causes, 8–273—8–276
intervening acts, 8–277—8–279
introduction, 8–270
financial practitioners, and
evaluation of a chance, 13–160
examples, 13–159
insurance brokers, and
intervening error or omission,
14–089—14–096
introduction, 14–088
no insurance if facts been known,
14–109—14–112
not likely been insured in any event,
14–097—14–108
IT professionals, and, 17–095—17–097
Lloyd's agents, and
failure to advise on participation,
16–063—16–066
introduction, 16–062
negligent underwriting,
16–067—16–070
medical practitioners, and
contributory negligence, 12–276
failure to procure treatment,
12–271—12–273
inadequate advice concerning unborn
baby, 12–277—12–281
inadequate warning of treatment,
12–262—12–270
intervening conduct, 12–276
introduction, 12–243—12–250
loss of a chance, 12–251—12–261
novus actus interveniens,
12–274—12–275
patent agents, and, 18–020—18–021
solicitors, and
"but for", 10–234
intervening acts, 10–237—10–239
proximity, 10–235—10–236
wasted costs order, 10–134
surveyors, and
generally, 9–120
mortgage indemnity guarantees,
9–122
novus actus interveniens,
9–123—9–124
reliance, 9–121
trade mark attorney, and,
18–020—18–021

CEASING TO ACT
solicitors, and, 10–191
CENSURE
solicitors, and, 10–105
CHARTERED SURVEYORS
and see SURVEYORS
basis of liability, 9–007—9–018
damages for breach, 9–110—9–194
duties to client, 9–019—9–032
duties to third parties, 9–033—9–051
liability for breach of duty,
9–075—9–109
limitation of liability, 9–063—9–072
mutual valuer, 9–074
qualifications, 9–003
standard of care and skill,
9–052—9–062
CHILD PROTECTION
human rights, and, 7–026
CHILDREN
consent to treatment, and, 12–148
CHIROPODISTS
and see MEDICAL PRACTITIONERS
disciplinary proceedings, 12–004
registration, 12–003
CHOICE OF CONTRACT, ADVICE ON
construction professionals, and,
8–225—8–227
CHOICE OF MATERIALS
construction professionals, and, 8–215
CHURNING
financial practitioners, and, 13–063
CLAIMS PROCEDURE
financial practitioners, and
compensation scheme,
13–190—13–204
introduction, 13–169
Ombudsman, 13–170—13–189
parallel proceedings,
13–205—13–206
group actions, and
costs, 6–005
generally, 6–003—6–004
CLARITY OF ADVICE
barristers, and, 11–047
mortgage lenders' claims by, and,
10–216
CLERK OF WORKS, ROLE OF
construction works, and, 8–246—8–247
CLIENT CARE CODE
example, 10–092
generally, 10–091
CLINICAL NEGLIGENCE
human rights, and, 7–026
CLINICAL TRIALS
medical practitioners, and, 12–110

CODES OF CONDUCT
patent agents, and, 18–011
CODES OF PRACTICE
construction professionals, and,
8–158—8–161
COLLATERAL CONTRACTS
IT professionals, and, 17–056
COLLATERAL WARRANTIES
construction professionals, and,
8–064—8–065
COMMERCIAL ADVICE
patent agents, and, 18–018
COMMUNICATION OF DISTRESSING
INFORMATION
medical practitioners, and,
12–022—12–023
COMPANY DOCTOR, REPORT BY
duty to third parties, and, 12–057
COMPANY PARTICULARS
surveyors, and, 9–015
COMPENSATION
confidence, for breach of,
3–015—3–016
defective listing particulars, for,
13–157
fiduciary duty, for breach of,
3–011—3–014
COMPENSATION SCHEME (FINANCIAL
SERVICES)
assignment of rights, 13–198
default by relevant provider, 13–197
eligible claimants, 13–194
immunity from suit, 13–204
insurance, and, 13–203
introduction, 13–190
offers
acceptance, 13–202
amount, 13–199—13–201
protected claims, 13–195
purpose, 13–191
qualifying conditions, 13–193
relevant provider, 13–196
structure, 13–192
COMPLAINTS PROCEDURES
human rights, and, 7–065
CONCEALMENT, LIMITATION PERIOD FOR
date when time restarts, 5–073—5–074
deliberate commission of breach,
5–075—5–076
effect of concealment after breach,
5–071
generally, 5–070
relevant facts, 5–072
unlikely to be discovered, 5–078
CONCURRENT DUTIES
surveyors, and, 9–032

CONCURRENT LIABILITIES
case law, 2–102—2–105
competing considerations, 2–101
introduction, 2–100
extent of tortious duty, 2–107—2–108
scope of concurrent duty, 2–106
surveyors, and
generally, 9–037
introduction, 9–010
CONDITIONS OF ENGAGEMENT
construction professionals, and
generally, 8–019—8–020
limitation of liability, 8–021—8–025
surveyors, and
generally, 9–026
limitation of liability, 9–027—9–028
CONDUCT OF BUSINESS SOURCEBOOK
advising and selling, 13–054—13–058
arrangement, 13–047
cancellation, 13–060
client assets, 13–068
customer agreements, 13–053
customer classification, 13–052
dealing and managing,
13–061—13–066
designated investment business, 13–049
financial promotion, 13–050—13–051
introduction, 13–046
product disclosure, 13–059
reporting to customers, 13–067
scope, 13–048
terms of business, 13–053
withdrawal, 13–060
CONFIDENCE, DUTY OF
accountants, and, 15–041—15–044
barristers, and, 11–005
case law origin
contractual duties, 2–153
equitable duties, 2–154
existence of proprietary right,
2–151—2–152
introduction, 2–148—2–149
theoretical basis, 2–150
compensation for breach,
3–015—3–016
confidentiality of information, 2–156
continuation of
case law, 2–165—2–166
considerations, 2–167
generally, 2–163—2–164
detriment, 2–162
disclosure of information
public interest, in, 2–160
required by law, 2–161

CONFIDENCE, DUTY OF—cont.
elements of claim fro breach
circumstances in which information
imparted, 2–157
confidentiality of information, 2–156
detriment, 2–162
introduction, 2–155
misuse of information,
2–158—2–161
generally, 2–006
human rights, and
access to, 7–060
disclosure of, 7–061
medical records, 7–062—7–063
introduction, 2–147
justified use of information
disclosure in public interest, 2–160
disclosure required by law, 2–161
introduction, 2–159
misuse of information
exceptions, 2–159—2–161
introduction, 2–158
solicitors, and
Commonwealth position, 10–031
confidentiality of information,
10–029
examples, 10–027—10–028
generally, 10–026
overriding circumstances, 10–032
sufficiency of barriers, 10–030
CONFIDENTIAL INFORMATION
human rights, and
access to, 7–060
disclosure of, 7–061
medical records, 7–062—7–063
mortgage lenders' claims, and, 10–217
solicitors, and
Commonwealth position, 10–031
confidentiality of information,
10–029
examples, 10–027—10–028
generally, 10–026
overriding circumstances, 10–032
sufficiency of barriers, 10–030
CONFIRMATORY LETTERS
solicitors, and, 10–174
CONFLICT OF INTEREST
financial practitioners, and, 13–062
solicitors, and
borrower and lender, 10–102
generally, 10–100
group litigation, 10–103
informed consent, 10–101
CONSENT TO TREATMENT
capacity to, 12–135—12–139
children, by, 12–148

CONSENT TO TREATMENT—*cont.*
human rights, and, 7–059
informed, 12–130—12–134
introduction, 12–124—12–125
limits on, 12–126—12–127
mentally disordered patients, by,
    12–140—12–147
voluntary, 12–128—12–129
CONSEQUENTIAL LOSS
construction professionals, and,
    8–305—8–306
CONSTRUCTION PROFESSIONS
architects, 8–004
building surveyors, 8–007
engineers, 8–005
introduction, 8–003
project managers, 8–008
quantity surveyors, 8–006
CONSTRUCTION PROFESSIONALS
adjudication of disputes
    applicable contracts, 8–334
    applicable operations, 8–335
    challenging decisions, 8–338—8–343
    enforcement of decisions, 8–337
    generally, 8–332—8–333
    introduction, 8–011
    jurisdiction of adjudicator,
        8–339—8–340
    time limits, 8–336
apportionment of liability
    amount of contribution, 8–325
    discretion, 8–328—8–32
    distinct causes of damage, 8–324
    distinct types of damage, 8–323
    final certificate, 8–321
    joint insurance, 8–322
    introduction, 8–317—8–318
    "same damage", 8–319—8–320
    settlement, and, 8–326—8–327
causation
    advice to claimant, 8–271
    advice to third party, 8–272
    concurrent causes, 8–273—8–276
    intervening acts, 8–277—8–279
    introduction, 8–270
contract, types of
    design and build, 8–016—8–017
    introduction, 8–012
    management, 8–018
    traditional, 8–013—8–015
    turnkey, 8–016—8–017
contributory negligence, 8–330—8–331
damages for breach of duty
    abatement of fees, 8–316
    heads, 8–289—8–312
    introduction, 8–264

CONSTRUCTION PROFESSIONALS—*cont.*
damages for breach of duty—*cont.*
    measure, 8–285—8–287
    mitigation of loss, 8–313—8–315
    remoteness, 8–269—8–284
    scope of duty, 8–265—8–268
duties
    client, to, 8–019—8–063
    other, 8–132
    standard of care and skill,
        8–133—8–181
    third parties, to, 8–064—8–131
duties to client
    contract, under, 8–019—8–039
    tort, in, 8–040—8–063
duties to third parties
    collateral warranties, 8–064—8–065
    common law, at, 8–069—8–131
    statute, under, 8–066—8–068
expert witness, as, 8–263
foreseeability
    date of assessment of loss,
        8–283—8–284
    introduction, 8–280—8–281
    type of loss, 8–282
heads of damage
    consequential loss, 8–305—8–306
    diminution in value, 8–300—8–301
    distress, 8–309—8–311
    excess expenditure, 8–303
    inconvenience, 8–309—8–311
    introduction, 8–289
    loss of amenity, 8–312
    personal injury, 8–308
    rectification costs, 8–290—8–299
    third party, liability to, 8–307
    underpayment, 8–304
    wasted expenditure, 8–302
inducing breach of contract, 8–132
introduction
    claims, 8–009—8–011
    construction professions,
        8–003—8–008
    contract types, 8–012—8–018
liability for breach of duty
    administration of contract,
        8–228—8–237
    bills of quantities, 8–221
    certification, 8–252—8–258
    choice of contract, 8–225—8–227
    compliance with legal requirements,
        8–200—8–202
    costs estimates, 8–193—8–199
    design and specification,
        8–203—8–220
    inspection of works, 8–238—8–251

CONSTRUCTION PROFESSIONALS—*cont.*
liability for breach of duty—*cont.*
introduction, 8–182
investigation of defects, 8–262
selection of contractor,
8–222—8–224
site examination, 8–183—8–184
specialist survey, 8–259—8–261
supervision of works, 8–238—8–251
tender process, 8–222—8–224
measure of damages
introduction, 8–285—8–286
loss of a chance, 8–287—8–288
pre-action protocols, 8–009
relevant professions
architects, 8–004
building surveyors, 8–007
engineers, 8–005
introduction, 8–003
project managers, 8–008
quantity surveyors, 8–006
remoteness
causation, 8–270—8–279
foreseeability, 8–280—8–284
introduction, 8–269
scope of duty, 8–265—8–267
shared responsibility
apportionment of liability,
8–317—8–329
contributory negligence,
8–330—8–331
standard of care and skill
Bolam test, 8–145—8–150
Codes of Practice, 8–158—8–161
delegation to specialists,
8–177—8–181
errors, 8–165—8–167
evidence, 8–151—8–155
experience of client, 8–135—8–137
general practice, 8–145—8–150
knowledge, 8–144
knowledge of law, 8–162—8–164
ordinary competent and skilled
practitioner, 8–133—8–143
res ipsa loquitur, 8–156—8–157
special steps required,
8–170—8–176
specialism, 8–168—8–169
time of assessment, 8–139
Technology and Construction Court,
8–010
wrongful interference with contract,
8–132
CONSTRUCTIVE TRUSTS
solicitors, and, 10–036

CONSTRUCTIVE TRUSTS, ACTIONS
CONCERNING
limitation in equity, and,
5–082—5–088
CONSUMER
duty of care, and, 2–022—2–023
CONSTRUCTION (DESIGN & MANAGEMENT)
REGULATIONS 1994
construction professionals, and, 8–048
CONSUMER PROTECTION ACT 1987,
LIABILITY UNDER
defences, 17–076—17–077
generally, 17–072—17–073
relevant product, 17–074—17–075
"safety-critical" information, 17–078
CONSTRUCTIVE TRUSTS
solicitors, and, 10–036
contractual duties
continuing obligations, 10–012
express instructions,
10–008—10–010
nature, 10–007
retainer, 10–004—10–006
termination of retainer, 10–011
contributory negligence
examples, 10–324
generally, 10–323
mortgage lenders' claims,
10–325—10–327
costs information, 10–157
CONTRACT, LIMITATION IN
and see LIMITATION IN CONTRACT
concealment, 5–070—5–078
date of cause of action, 5–014—5–015
fraud, 5–070—5–078
latent damage, and, 5–049—5–055
period of limitation, 5–010—5–013
personal injuries and death,
5–056—5–069
CONTRACTOR, SELECTION OF
construction professionals, and,
8–222—8–224
CONTRACTORS
construction professionals, and,
8–105—8–111
CONTRACTS (RIGHTS OF THIRD PARTIES)
ACT 1999
accountants, and, 15–088
construction professionals, and,
8–067—8–068
CONTRACTUAL DUTIES
accountants, and
implied, 15–036
introduction, 15–031
limitation of liability, 15–032

CONTRACTUAL DUTIES—*cont.*
  accountants, and—*cont.*
    statutory requirements,
      15–033—15–035
  barristers, and, 11–004
  construction professionals, and
    express terms, 8–019—8–020
    implied terms, 8–026—8–028
    limitation of liability, 8–021—8–025
    scope, 8–029—8–038
  financial practitioners, and
    appointed representatives,
      13–095—13–098
    duty of care and skill,
      13–092—13–094
    incorporation of regulatory duties,
      13–091
    relevant contracts, 13–089
    terms of business, 13–090
  insurance brokers, and
    introduction, 14–010—14–012
    sub-brokers, of, 14–013
  IT professionals, and
    and see below
    collateral contracts, 17–056
    common law, at, 17–051
    consultant/supplier dichotomy,
      17–052—17–054
    co-operation, 17–038—17–043
    fitness for purpose, 17–014—17–035
    implementation, 17–036—17–037
    installation, 17–047—17–050
    negligent misstatements, 17–055
    operation manual, 17–046
    satisfactory quality, 17–014—17–035
    support, 17–044
    systems advice, 17–057—17–058
    testing, 17–036—17–037
    "time-bombs", 17–059—17–060
    training of staff, 17–045
    user operation manual, 17–046
  Lloyd's agents, and, 16–010—16–011
  medical practitioners, and
    NHS patients, 12–005—12–007
    private patients, 12–008—12–010
  solicitors
    continuing obligations, 10–012
    express instructions,
      10–008—10–010
    nature, 10–007
    retainer, 10–004—10–006
    termination of retainer, 10–011
  surveyors, and
    Appraisal and Valuation Manual,
      9–023—9–025
    building societies, to, 9–029—9–031

CONTRACTUAL DUTIES—*cont.*
  surveyors, and—*cont.*
    conditions of engagement, 9–026
    introduction, 9–019—9–020
    Practice Statements, 9–022—9–025
    reasonable expectations test, 9–021
    unfair terms, 9–027—9–028
CONTRACTUAL (IT PROFESSIONALS)
  collateral contracts, 17–056
  common law, at, 17–051
  consultant/supplier dichotomy,
    17–052—17–054
  co-operation, 17–038—17–043
  fitness for purpose
    bespoke software, 17–014—17–022
    communication by client of,
      17–031—17–035
    modified standard software,
      17–023—17–030
  implementation
    common law duty, 17–051
    generally, 17–036—17–037
  installation, 17–047—17–050
  modification of software
    common law duty, 17–051
    generally, 17–023—17–030
  negligent misstatements, 17–055
  operation manual, 17–046
  satisfactory quality
    bespoke software, 17–014—17–022
    modified standard software,
      17–023—17–030
  staff training
    common law duty, 17–051
    generally, 17–045
  support, 17–044
  systems advice, 17–057—17–058
  testing
    common law duty, 17–051
    generally, 17–036—17–037
  "time-bombs", 17–059—17–060
  training of staff, 17–045
    common law duty, 17–051
    generally, 17–045
  user operation manual, 17–046
  writing of software
    common law duty, 17–051
    generally, 17–014—17–022
CONTRACTUAL LIABILITY
  exception to rule, 2–012
  fiduciary obligations, and, 2–128
  general rule, 2–007—2–011
  reasonable care and skill,
    2–116—2–124

CONTRIBUTION BETWEEN DEFENDANTS
accountants, and
claims against auditors,
15–148—15–151
generally, 15–147
basis of assessment, 4–012—4–014
basis of liability
generally, 4–006
"same damage", 4–007—4–009
construction professionals, and, 8–056
defences
excluded issues, 4–010
included issues, 4–011
entitlement, 4–002
financial practitioners, and, 13–168
introduction, 4–001
liability of claimant, 4–003—4–005
surveyors, and, 9–173
time for starting claim, 4–015
CONTRIBUTORY NEGLIGENCE
accountants, and
claims against auditors,
15–148—15–151
generally, 15–146
attribution, 5–119
construction professionals, and
generally, 8–330—8–331
introduction, 8–055
contract, and, 5–115
financial practitioners, and
generally, 13–167
introduction, 13–131
generally, 5–113—5–114
insurance brokers, and
generally, 14–126—14–127
insurers, 14–128
lay clients, 14–129—14–130
uninsured indemnity cover, and,
14–131
IT professionals, and, 17–126—17–130
lenders, by
evaluation, 9–168—9–172
generally, 9–166—9–167
introduction, 9–011
medical practitioners, and, 12–276
mitigation of claim, 5–118
professional negligence, and,
5–116—5–117
solicitors, and
examples, 10–324
generally, 10–323
mortgage lenders' claims,
10–325—10–327
surveyors, and
evaluation, 9–168—9–172

CONTRIBUTORY NEGLIGENCE—cont.
surveyors, and—cont.
generally, 9–166—9–167
introduction, 9–011
CONVEYANCING, MISCONDUCT OF
enquiries before contract, 10–201
handing over purchase monies, 10–200
matters coming to notice, 10–199
National protocol, 10–204
non-registration of interests, 10–198
remote contingencies, 10–197
searches, 10–193—10–194
standard of care, 10–196
suspicious circumstances, 10–195
time limits, 10–202
undue influence, 10–205
width of duty, 10–203
CO-OPERATION
IT professionals, and, 17–038—17–043
CO-ORDINATION OF DESIGN
construction professionals, and, 8–218
CORPORATE GOVERNANCE
accountants, and, 15–002—15–004
CORRESPONDENCE, RIGHT TO RESPECT FOR
generally, 7–013
introduction, 7–004
COSTS
group actions, and, 6–005
COSTS ESTIMATE
construction professionals, and,
8–193—8–199
COSTS INFORMATION
solicitors, and, 10–15
COURT PROCEDURE
expert evidence
admissibility, 6–011
appropriateness, 6–013
court rules, 6–010
excluded cases, 6–008—6–009
functions of expert, 6– 006—6–007
impartiality of expert, 6–015—6–017
instruction, 6–012
presentation, 6–012
qualification of expert, 6–014
relevance, 6–011
group actions, and
costs, 6–005
generally, 6–003—6–004
COVERHOLDERS
insurance brokers, and,
14–022—14–024
CRACKS
surveyors, and, 9–093—9–094
CREDIT FOR BENEFITS
examples, 10–253—10–254
general principle, 10–252

CREDIT FOR BENEFITS—*cont.*
incidental benefits, 10–255
CREDIT FOR COST OF PROPER DESIGN
construction professionals, and, 8–294
CREDIT FOR SAVED PREMIUM
insurance brokers, and,
14–124—14–125
CURRENT STATE OF KNOWLEDGE
medical practitioners, and,
12–073—12–074
CUSTOMER AGREEMENTS
general requirements, 13–090
introduction, 13–053
CUSTOMER CLASSIFICATION
breach of duty, 13–120
generally, 13–052

DAMAGE
negligence, and, 2–016
DAMAGES
accountants, and
and see below
causation, 15–121—15–130
foreseeability, 15–131
heads of damage, 15–135—15–145
introduction, 15–120
measure, 15–132—15–134
mitigation, 15–152
remoteness, 15–121—15–130
statutory relief, 15–153
allocation of risk, 3–003
assessment of
Banques Bruxelles Lambert case,
3–002—3–004
hypothetical basis, on, 3–005
introduction, 3–001
barristers, and
measure, 11–054—11–055
remoteness, 11–052—11–053
construction professionals, and
and see below
abatement of fees, 8–316
heads, 8–289—8–312
introduction, 8–264
measure, 8–285—8–287
mitigation of loss, 8–313—8–315
remoteness, 8–269—8–284
scope of duty, 8–265—8–268
financial practitioners, and
and see below
causation, 13–158—13–160
foreseeability, 13–158
introduction, 13–157
measure of, 13–161—13–165
remoteness, 13–158—13–160

DAMAGES—*cont.*
insurance brokers, and
and see below
causation, 14–088—14–112
foreseeability, 14–113
introduction, 14–086
measure, 14–114—14–125
remoteness, 14–087—14–113
introduction, 3–001
IT professionals, and
generally, 17–104—17–112
mitigation of loss, 17–124—17–125
Lloyd's agents, and
and see below
causation, 16–062—16–070
foreseeability, 16–071
introduction, 16–060
measure, 16–072—16–082
remoteness, 16–061—16–071
medical practitioners, and
and see below
causation, 12–243—12–281
foreseeability, 12–282—12–286
introduction, 12–241
measure of, 12–287—12–305
remoteness, 12–242—12–286
patent agents, and
causation, 18–020—18–021
remoteness, 18–022
valuation of lost patent, 18–023
solicitors, and
and see below
breach of fiduciary duty, for,
10–226—10–232
causation, 10–234—10–239
foreseeability, 10–240—10–248
heads of damage, 10–263—10–315
introduction, 10–225
measure, 10–249—10–262
mitigation, 10–316—10–322
remoteness, 10–233—10–243
surveyors, and
and see below
causation, 9–120—9–124
establishment of loss, 9–112
foreseeability, 9–125—9–127
introduction, 9–110—9–111
loss within scope of duty,
9–113—9–118
measure, 9–128—9–194
remoteness, 9–119—9–127
trade mark attorney, and
causation, 18–020—18–021
remoteness, 18–022
valuation of lost patent, 18–023

DAMAGES (ACCOUNTANTS)
causation
  effective cause, 15–122—15–126
  generally, 15–121
  intervening acts, 15–130
  reliance, 15–127—15–129
foreseeability, 15–131
heads of damage
  defalcation by director, 15–139
  double recovery, 15–141—15–142
  fresh audit cost, 15–140
  introduction, 15–135
  investigation cost, 15–140
  lost advance, 15–136
  lost investment, 15–136
  monies wrongly paid out, 15–138
  negligent advice, 15–145
  overpayment, 15–137
  tax advice, 15–143
  tax returns, 15–143—15–144
introduction, 15–120
measure of damages
  introduction, 15–132
  loss of a chance, 15–133—15–134
mitigation, 15–152
remoteness
  causation, 15–121—15–130
  foreseeability, 15–131
statutory relief, 15–153
DAMAGES (CONSTRUCTION PROFESSIONALS)
abatement of fees, 8–316
causation
  advice to claimant, 8–271
  advice to third party, 8–272
  concurrent causes, 8–273—8–276
  intervening acts, 8–277—8–279
  introduction, 8–270
consequential loss, 8–305—8–306
diminution in value, 8–300—8–301
distress, 8–309—8–311
excess expenditure, 8–303
foreseeability
  date of assessment of loss,
    8–283—8–284
  introduction, 8–280—8–281
  type of loss, 8–282
inconvenience, 8–309—8–311
introduction, 8–264
heads of damage
  consequential loss, 8–305—8–306
  diminution in value, 8–300—8–301
  distress, 8–309—8–311
  excess expenditure, 8–303
  inconvenience, 8–309—8–311
  introduction, 8–289
  loss of amenity, 8–312

DAMAGES (CONSTRUCTION
  PROFESSIONALS)—cont.
heads of damage—cont.
  personal injury, 8–308
  rectification costs, 8–290—8–299
  third party, liability to, 8–307
  underpayment, 8–304
  wasted expenditure, 8–302
loss of amenity, 8–312
measure of damages
  introduction, 8–285—8–286
  loss of a chance, 8–287—8–288
mitigation of loss, 8–313—8–315
personal injury, 8–308
third party, liability to, 8–307
rectification costs
  betterment, 8–297—8–299
  credit for cost of proper design,
    8–294
  date of assessment, 8–295
  failure to review a design, 8–296
  introduction, 8–290—8–293
remoteness
  causation, 8–270—8–279
  foreseeability, 8–280—8–284
  introduction, 8–269
scope of duty, 8–265—8–268
underpayment, 8–304
wasted expenditure, 8–302
DAMAGES (INSURANCE BROKERS)
causation
  evaluation of a chance, 13–160
  examples, 13–159
foreseeability, 13–158
introduction, 13–157
measure of damages
  benefits received, 13–162—13–165
  introduction, 13–161
remoteness
  causation, 13–158—13–160
  foreseeability, 13–158
  introduction, 13–158
DAMAGES (INSURANCE BROKERS)
causation
  intervening error or omission,
    14–089—14–096
  introduction, 14–088
  no insurance if facts been known,
    14–109—14–112
  not likely been insured in any event,
    14–097—14–108
foreseeability, 14–113
introduction, 14–086
measure
  additional losses, 14–119

DAMAGES (INSURANCE BROKERS)—*cont.*
measure—*cont.*
credit for saved premium,
14–124—14–125
fines and costs, 14–123
introduction, 14–114—14–116
litigation costs, 14–122
non-receipt of insurance proceeds,
14–121
settlement with insurers,
14–117—14–118
unreinsured losses, 14–120
remoteness
causation, 14–088—14–112
foreseeability, 14–113
introduction, 14–087
DAMAGES (LLOYD'S AGENTS)
causation
failure to advise on participation,
16–063—16–066
introduction, 16–062
negligent underwriting,
16–067—16–070
foreseeability, 16–071
introduction, 16–060
measure of damages
failure to advise on participation,
16–073—16–076
introduction, 16–072
negligent underwriting,
16–077—16–082
remoteness
causation, 16–062—16–070
introduction, 16–061
foreseeability, 16–071
DAMAGES (MEDICAL PRACTITIONERS)
causation
contributory negligence, 12–276
failure to procure treatment,
12–271—12–273
inadequate advice concerning unborn
baby, 12–277—12–281
inadequate warning of treatment,
12–262—12–270
intervening conduct, 12–276
introduction, 12–243—12–250
loss of a chance, 12–251—12–261
novus actus interveniens,
12–274—12–275
contributory negligence, 12–276
failure to procure treatment,
12–271—12–273
foreseeability, 12–282—12–286
inadequate advice concerning unborn
baby, 12–277—12–281

DAMAGES (MEDICAL
PRACTITIONERS)—*cont.*
inadequate warning of treatment
Australian law, 12–265—12–268
Canadian law, 12–264
introduction, 12–262—12–263
policy issues, 12–269—12–270
intervening conduct, 12–276
introduction, 12–241
loss of a chance
Australian law, 12–261
Canadian law, 12–259—12–260
introduction, 12–251—12–258
measure of
aggravated damages, 12–288
personal injury, 12–287
wrongful birth claims,
12–289—12–305
novus actus interveniens,
12–274—12–275
remoteness
causation, 12–243—12–281
foreseeability, 12–282—12–286
introduction, 12–242
DAMAGES (SOLICITORS)
anticipated gains, 10–305
breach of fiduciary duty, for
background, 10–228
Commonwealth cases, 10–230
introduction, 10–226—10–227
measure, 10–231
modern law, 10–229
causation
"but for", 10–234
intervening acts, 10–237—10–239
proximity, 10–235—10–236
credit for benefits
examples, 10–253—10–254
general principle, 10–252
incidental benefits, 10–255
date of assessment
exception to general rule, 10–251
general rule, 10–250
difference in value in property
cure costs, 10–276
exceptions to general rule,
10–269—10–270
extrication costs, 10–272
general rule, 10–268
loss of business profits, 10–274
loss of use of property, 10–271
market value not reflect loss, 10–273
radical change in circumstances,
10–275
distress
affecting health, 10–312

DAMAGES (SOLICITORS)—*cont.*
distress—*cont.*
not affecting health,
10–313—10–315
diminution in value of shareholding,
10–300
evaluation of a chance
burden of proof, 10–262
Commonwealth cases, 10–261
examples, 10–259
generally, 10–256
likely act of claimant, 10–257
likely act of third party, 10–258
limits of principle, 10–260
foreseeability
examples, 10–241—10–242
introduction, 10–240
time for consideration, 10–243
heads of damage
criminal liability, 10–303
difference in value in property,
10–268—10–276
distress, 10–312—10–315
incidental expenditure, 10–309
inconvenience, 10–311
introduction, 10–263
loss of financial advantage,
10–297—10–300
loss of opportunity to acquire
interest in property,
10–264—10–267
loss of opportunity to bring
proceedings, 10–277—10–292
loss of opportunity to defend
proceedings, 10–293
loss on secured loans,
10–294—10–297
physical injury, 10–310
third party liability, 10–301—10–302
wasted expenditure,
10–304—10–308
incidental expenditure, 10–309
inconvenience, 10–311
introduction, 10–225
loss of earnings, 10–298
loss of life policy, 10–299
loss of opportunity to acquire interest
in property
agricultural tenancies, 10–266
business tenancies, 10–265
evaluation difficulties, 10–267
generally, 10–264
loss of opportunity to bring
proceedings
Commonwealth cases, 10–278
costs risk, 10–285

DAMAGES (SOLICITORS)—*cont.*
loss of opportunity to bring
proceedings—*cont.*
deduction of benefits, 10–290
enforcement proceedings, and,
10–292
examples, 10–279—10–281
extent of claim, 10–282
generally, 10–277
interest after trial, 10–289
legal aid, 10–284
means of defendant, 10–286
notional date of trial,
10–287—10–288
risks of litigation , 10–283
want of prosecution, and, 10–291
loss of opportunity to defend
proceedings, 10–293
loss on sale of land, 10–297
loss on secured loans
dishonest borrowers, 10–296
generally, 10–294—10–295
measure
credit for benefits, 10–252—10–255
date of assessment, 10–250—10–251
evaluation of a chance,
10–256—10–262
introduction, 10–249
mitigation
change of solicitor, 10–322
disappointed beneficiary cases,
10–320
fresh litigation, 10–318—10–319
generous treatment of claimant,
10–317
introduction, 10–316
limits of rule, 10–321
physical injury, 10–310
remoteness
causation, 10–234—10–239
foreseeability, 10–240—10–243
introduction, 10–233
scope of duty, 10–244—10–248
third party, liability to,
10–301—10–302
wasted expenditure
examples, 10–306
general rule, 10–304—10–305
later solicitors' costs, 10–308
original solicitors' costs, 10–307
DAMAGES (SURVEYORS)
causation
generally, 9–120
mortgage indemnity guarantees,
9–122

DAMAGES (SURVEYORS)—*cont.*
causation—*cont.*
novus actus interveniens,
9–123—9–124
reliance, 9–121
discomfort, damages for
examples, 9–189
generally, 9–181—9–185
injury to health, 9–186—9–187
quantum, 9–188
establishment of loss, 9–112
foreseeability, 9–125—9–127
incidental expenses, 9–190—9–194
inconvenience, damages for
examples, 9–189
generally, 9–181—9–185
injury to health, 9–186—9–187
quantum, 9–188
introduction, 9–110—9–111
loss within scope of duty,
9–113—9–118
measure of damages
discomfort, 9–181—9–189
incidental expenses, 9–190—9–194
inconvenient, 9–181—9–189
introduction, 9–128—9–129
negligent survey for lender,
9–150—9–174
negligent survey for purchaser who
completes, 9–130—9–148
negligent survey for purchaser who
withdraws, 9–149
overvaluation for vendor, 9–175
rent review, 9–179—9–180
undervaluation for vendor,
9–176—9–177
warranty of valuation, 9–178
negligent survey for lender
assessment of total loss,
9–151—9–154
"cap" theory, 9–159—9–160
contribution from defaulting
borrower, 9–173
contributory negligence,
9–166—9–172
interest on damages, 9–162
introduction, 9–150
joint responsibility, 9–173—9–174
loss within scope of duty,
9–155—9–161
"measurable, relevant loss", 9–161
mortgagor's covenants to repay,
9–163—9–165
"no transaction/successful
transaction" cases,
9–157—9–158

DAMAGES (SURVEYORS)—*cont.*
negligent survey for purchaser who
completes
collateral benefits, 9–148
cost of repairs, 9–141—9–145
extraction costs, 9–146—9–147
formulation of measure,
9–135—9–137
generally, 9–130—9–134
nature of loss, 9–138—9–139
other decisions, 9–140
repair cost, 9–141—9–145
negligent survey for purchaser who
withdraws, 9–149
overvaluation for vendor, 9–175
remoteness of damage
causation, 9–120—9–124
foreseeability, 9–125—9–127
introduction, 9–119
rent review, 9–179—9–180
undervaluation for vendor,
9–176—9–177
warranty of valuation, 9–178
DATE OF CAUSE OF ACTION (CONTRACT)
generally, 5–014—5–015
DATE OF CAUSE OF ACTION (TORT)
architects, claims against
Bank of East Asia, 5–028—5–029
date of damage, 5–030—5–033
degree of damage, 5–022
"doomed from start", 5–020—5–021
Murphy, 5–024—5–027
Pirelli, 5–017—5–019
successive owners, 5–023
uncertainty, 5–034
engineers, claims against
Bank of East Asia, 5–028—5–029
date of damage, 5–030—5–033
degree of damage, 5–022
"doomed from start", 5–020—5–021
Murphy, 5–024—5–027
Pirelli, 5–017—5–019
successive owners, 5–023
uncertainty, 5–034
financial advisers, claims against,
5–048
insurance brokers, claims against,
5–046—5–047
introduction, 5–016
solicitors, claims against
action dismissed for want of
prosecution, 5–043
client acquires less valuable rights,
5–040—5–042
client incurs obligation,
5–037—5–039

DATE OF CAUSE OF ACTION (TORT)—*cont.*
  solicitors, claims against—*cont.*
    omissions capable of remedy, 5–045
    purchase of property, 5–044
  surveyors, claims against
    mortgagees, by, 5–036
    purchasers, by, 5–035
DATE OF KNOWLEDGE
  construction professionals, and, 8–054
  death, 5–063
  latent damage, 5–054—5–055
  medical negligence actions,
    5–058—5–062
  personal injuries, 5–056—5–062
  surveyors, and, 9–009
DEALING AHEAD
  financial practitioners, and, 13–064
DEALING AND MANAGING
  aggregation and allocation, 13–066
  best and timely execution, 13–065
  breach of duty, 13–126—13–130
  churning, 13–063
  conflict of interest, 13–062
  dealing ahead, 13–064
  introduction, 13–061
  material interest, 13–062
  switching 13–063
DEATH CLAIMS, LIMITATION PERIOD FOR
  date of knowledge, 5–063
  discretionary exclusion of time limit
    introduction, 5–064
    manner of exercise, 5–065—5–066
    relevance of fault, 5–067—5–069
  generally, 5–063
  introduction, 5–012
DECEIT
  financial practitioners, and,
    13–099—13–104
DEFALCATION BY DIRECTOR
  accountants, and, 15–139
DEFECTIVE PREMISES ACT
  construction professionals, and,
    8–041—8–047
  surveyors, and, 9–012
DEFENCES
  and see under individual headings
  acquiescence, 5–109—5–112
  contribution between defendants, and
    excluded issues, 4–010
    included issues, 4–011
  contributory negligence
    attribution, 5–119
    contract, and, 5–115
    generally, 5–113—5–114
    mitigation of claim, 5–118

DEFENCES—*cont.*
  contributory negligence—*cont.*
    professional negligence, and,
      5–116—5–117
  exclusion of liability
    incorporation of clause, 5–006
    introduction, 5–001—5–002
    statutory framework, 5–003—5–005
    third parties, to, 5–007—5–009
  financial practitioners, and
    introduction, 13–131
    limitation of liability,
      13–133—13–134
    regulators' limited immunity, 13–132
    statute, under, 13–135
  laches
    introduction, 5–098—5–102
    limitation, and, 5–108
    prejudice, 5–106—5–107
    unreasonable delay, 5–103—5–105
  limitation in contract
    concealment, 5–070—5–078
    date of cause of action,
      5–014—5–015
    fraud, 5–070—5–078
    latent damage, and, 5–049—5–055
    period of limitation, 5–010—5–013
    personal injuries and death,
      5–056—5–069
  limitation in equity
    analogous application of statute,
      5–089—5–095
    express application of statute,
      5–082—5–088
    introduction, 5–079—5–081
    no limitation, 5–096—5–097
  limitation in tort
    concealment, 5–070—5–078
    date of cause of action,
      5–016—5–048
    fraud, 5–070—5–078
    latent damage, and, 5–049—5–055
    period of limitation, 5–010—5–013
    personal injuries and death,
      5–056—5–069
  restriction of liability
    incorporation of clause, 5–006
    introduction, 5–001—5–002
    statutory framework, 5–003—5–005
    third parties, to, 5–007—5–009
  solicitors, and
    and see below
    abuse of process, 10–108—10–115
    acting on client's instructions,
      10–123—10–124

DEFENCES—*cont.*
solicitors, and—*cont.*
acting on counsel's advice,
10–116—10–122
immunity from suit,
10–106—10–107
DEFENCES (SOLICITORS)
abuse of process
civil cases, 10–114
criminal cases, 10–113
Hall v. Simons, 10–111—10–112
leading cases, 10–108—10–109
other types, 10–115
subsidiary cases, 10–110
wasted costs order, 10–137
acting on client's instructions
exceptions to general rule, 10–124
general rule, 10–123
acting on counsel's advice
background, 10–116
client's position, 10–122
development of law, 10–117
examples of failure of defence,
10–119
examples of success of defence,
10–120
further limits, 10–121
summary of law, 10–118
immunity from suit
background, 10–106
generally, 10–107
DEFINITION OF EXTENT OF SERVICE
surveyors, and, 9–073
DEGRADING TREATMENT, PROHIBITION
AGAINST
medical practitioners, and, 7–042
DELAY
laches, and, 5–103—5–105
misconduct in litigation by solicitors,
and
defending proceedings, 10–186
issuing proceedings, 10–185
progressing proceedings,
10–187—10–188
undertakings by solicitor, and, 10–071
DELEGATION
construction professionals, and,
8–177—8–181
patent agents, and, 18–019
solicitors, and, 10–148
trade mark attorney, and, 18–019
DELIBERATE COMMISSION OF BREACH
fraud, and, 5–075—5–076
DENTISTS
and see MEDICAL PRACTITIONERS
disciplinary proceedings, 12–004

DENTISTS—*cont.*
generally, 12–149—12–151
registration, 12–002
DENTURE, SUPPLY OF
medical practitioners, and, 12–011
DESIGN AND BUILD CONTRACTS
construction works, and, 8–016—8–017
DESIGN AND SPECIFICATION
approvals, 8–204—8–205
buildability, 8–216
change instructed by client, 8–219
choice of materials, 8–215
compliance with brief, 8–206
co-ordination of design, 8–218
generally, 8–203
integration of design , 8–217
level of detail, 8–214
novel design, 8–207—8–209
over-design, 8–220
published standards, 8–213
risk assessment, 8–210—8–212
supervisability, 8–216
DESIGNATED INVESTMENT BUSINESS
financial practitioners, and, 13–049
DESIGNATED PROFESSIONAL BODIES
financial practitioners, and,
13–021—13–022
DETRIMENT
confidentiality, and, 2–162
DIFFERENCE IN VALUE IN PROPERTY
cure costs, 10–276
exceptions to general rule,
10–269—10–270
extrication costs, 10–272
general rule, 10–268
loss of business profits, 10–274
loss of use of property, 10–271
market value not reflect loss, 10–273
radical change in circumstances,
10–275
DIFFERENT SCHOOLS OF THOUGHT
medical practitioners, and,
12–093—12–105
DIMINUTION IN VALUE
construction professionals, and,
8–300—8–301
solicitors, and, 10–300
DIMINUTION IN VALUE OF SHAREHOLDING
solicitors, and, 10–300
DIRECT PROFESSIONAL ACCESS
barristers, and, 11–002
DIRECTORS' DUTY OF CARE
Canadian case law, 2–089—2–090
generally, 2–088
introduction, 2–087

DISABLED CHILD, BIRTH OF
medical practitioners, and, 12–056,
12–231
DISAPPOINTED BENEFICIARY CASES
generally, 2–048
mitigation, 10–320
DISCIPLINARY PROCEEDINGS
human rights, and
generally, 7–065—7–066
procedural guarantees, 7–067
medical practitioners, and, 12–004
DISCLOSURE OF CONFIDENTIAL
INFORMATION
public interest, in, 2–160
required by law, 2–161
DISCOMFORT, DAMAGES FOR
examples, 9–189
generally, 9–181—9–185
injury to health, 9–186—9–187
quantum, 9–188
DISCRETION
apportionment of liability, and,
8–328—8–32
undertakings by solicitor, and, 10–070
DISPUTE RESOLUTION
construction professionals, and
applicable contracts, 8–334
applicable operations, 8–335
challenging decisions, 8–338—8–343
enforcement of decisions, 8–337
generally, 8–332—8–333
introduction, 8–011
jurisdiction of adjudicator,
8–339—8–340
time limits, 8–336
financial practitioners, and
compensation scheme,
13–190—13–204
introduction, 13–169
Ombudsman, 13–170—13–189
parallel proceedings,
13–205—13–206
DISTRESS, DAMAGES FOR
construction professionals, and,
8–309—8–311
solicitors, and
affecting health, 10–312
not affecting health,
10–313—10–315
DIVERSION OF OPPORTUNITIES
fiduciary obligations, and, 2–141
DOCTOR/PATIENT RELATIONSHIP
undue influence, and, 2–144
DOCTORS
and see MEDICAL PRACTITIONERS
apportionment of liability, 12–164

DOCTORS—cont.
disciplinary proceedings, 12–004
registration, 12–001
DONOGHUE V. STEVENSON PRINCIPLE
duty of care, and, 2–022—2–023
DOUBLE JEOPARDY
surveyors, and, 9–051
DOUBLE RECOVERY
generally, 15–087
heads of damage, 15–141—15–142
DRY ROT
surveyors, and, 9–091
DUTIES TO CLIENT
accountants, and
contract, under, 15–031—15–036
fiduciary duties, 15–038—15–044
tort, in, 15–037
barristers, and
contract, in, 11–004
tort, in, 11–005
construction professionals, and
contract, under, 8–019—8–038
tort, in, 8–039—8–063
contractual
and see CONTRACTUAL DUTIES
accountants, 15–031—15–036
barristers, 11–004
construction professionals,
8–019—8–039
insurance brokers, 14–010—14–013
Lloyd's agents, 16–010—16–011
solicitors, 10–004—10–012
surveyors, 9–019—9–031
fiduciary
and see FIDUCIARY OBLIGATIONS
accountants, 15–038—15–044
barristers, 11–005
construction professionals, 8–063
Lloyd's agents, 16–015
solicitors, 10–016—10–033
insurance brokers, and
contract, under, 14–010—14–013
tort, in, 14–014—14–016
IT professionals, and
and see below
collateral contracts, 17–056
common law, at, 17–051
consultant/supplier dichotomy,
17–052—17–054
co-operation, 17–038—17–043
fitness for purpose, 17–014—17–035
implementation, 17–036—17–037
installation, 17–047—17–050
negligent misstatements, 17–055
operation manual, 17–046
satisfactory quality, 17–014—17–035

DUTIES TO CLIENT—*cont.*
IT professionals, and—*cont.*
support, 17–044
systems advice, 17–057—17–058
testing, 17–036—17–037
"time-bombs", 17–059—17–060
training of staff, 17–045
user operation manual, 17–046
Lloyd's agents, and
contract, under, 16–010—16–011
fiduciary, 16–015
tort, in, 16–012—16–014
medical practitioners, and
and see DUTIES TO PATIENT
common law, at, 12–015—12–030
contract, under, 12–005—12–010
fiduciary, 12–028—12–030
statute, under, 12–011—12–014
tort, in, 12–015—12–030
patent agents, and, 18–008
solicitors, and
contract, under, 10–004—10–012
fiduciary, 10–016—10–033
tort, in, 10–013—10–015
trust, 10–034—10–039
surveyors, and
contract, under, 9–019—9–031
tort, in, 9–032
tort, in
and see TORT, DUTIES IN
accountants, 15–037
barristers, 11–005
construction professionals,
8–040—8–063
insurance brokers, 14–014—14–016
Lloyd's agents, 16–012—16–014
solicitors, 10–013—10–015
surveyors, 9–032
trade mark attorney, and, 18–008
DUTIES TO CLIENT (IT PROFESSIONALS)
collateral contracts, 17–056
common law, at, 17–051
consultant/supplier dichotomy,
17–052—17–054
co-operation, 17–038—17–043
fitness for purpose
bespoke software, 17–014—17–022
communication by client of,
17–031—17–035
modified standard software,
17–023—17–030
implementation
common law duty, 17–051
generally, 17–036—17–037
installation, 17–047—17–050

DUTIES TO CLIENT (IT
PROFESSIONALS)—*cont.*
modification of software
common law duty, 17–051
generally, 17–023—17–030
negligent misstatements, 17–055
operation manual, 17–046
satisfactory quality
bespoke software, 17–014—17–022
modified standard software,
17–023—17–030
staff training
common law duty, 17–051
generally, 17–045
support, 17–044
systems advice, 17–057—17–058
testing
common law duty, 17–051
generally, 17–036—17–037
"time-bombs", 17–059—17–060
training of staff, 17–045
common law duty, 17–051
generally, 17–045
user operation manual, 17–046
writing of software
common law duty, 17–051
generally, 17–014—17–022
DUTIES TO INSURERS BY BROKERS
coverholders, 14–022—14–024
disclosure, of, 14–019
introduction, 14–018
misstatement concerning reinsurance,
14–021
signing indication, under, 14–020
DUTIES TO PATIENT
common law, at
communication of distressing
information, 12–022—12–023
economic loss, 12–024—12–027
introduction, 12–015—12–018
rescuer cases, 12–019—12–021
contract, under
NHS patients, 12–005—12–007
private patients, 12–008—12–010
fiduciary
introduction, 12–028
nature and extent, 12–030
undue influence, 12–029
statute, under, 12–011—12–014
tort, in
communication of distressing
information, 12–022—12–023
economic loss, 12–024—12–027
introduction, 12–015—12–018
rescuer cases, 12–019—12–021

DUTIES TO PURCHASER OF PROPERTY BY
    SURVEYORS
  Smith v. Bush, 9–046—9–051
  Yianni, 9–043—9–045
DUTIES TO THIRD PARTIES
  accountants, and
    and see below
    Caparo, 15–053—15–061
    categories of advisee,
      15–073—15–086
    Contracts (Rights against Third
      Parties) Act 1999, 15–088
    Human Rights Act 1998, 15–089
    overview, 15–045—15–052
    policy considerations, 15–087
    relevant factors, 15–062—15–072
  barristers, and
    adversary of lay client, 11–007
    associates of lay client, 11–006
  construction professionals, and
    and see below
    collateral warranties, 8–064—8–065
    common law, at, 8–069—8–131
    statute, under, 8–066—8–068
  insurance brokers, and
    beneficiaries, 14–026
    financially interested persons,
      14–027—14–030
    insurers, 14–018—14–024
    introduction, 14–017
    misstatements, 14–031
    other parties, 14–025
    potential beneficiaries, 14–026
  IT professionals, and
    economic loss, 17–070—17–071
    introduction, 17–061
    personal injury, 17–062—17–066
    product liability, 17–072—17–077
    property damage, 17–067—17–069
  Lloyd's agents, and, 16–016—16–019
  medical practitioners, and
    disabled children, 12–056
    generally, 12–031—12–032
    infection from contact with patient,
      12–043—12–054
    medical report for insurer, etc.,
      12–057—12–066
    nervous shock cases,
      12–033—12–042
    unborn children, 12–055
    "wrongful life" cases, 12–056
  patent agents, and, 18–009
  solicitors, and
    and see below
    adversary in litigation,
      10–055—10–064

DUTIES TO THIRD PARTIES—*cont.*
  solicitors, and—*cont.*
    beneficiaries without reliance,
      10–047—10–054
    fraud, 10–076
    generally, 10–040—10–046
    undertakings, 10–065—10–074
    warranty of authority, 10–075
  surveyors, and
    general principles, 9–033
    Hedley Byrne, 9–034—9–038
    knowledge of reliance,
      9–039—9–042
    purchaser of property, 9–043—9–051
  trade mark attorney, and, 18–009
DUTIES TO THIRD PARTIES (ACCOUNTANTS)
  advisee
    categories, 15–073—15–086
    knowledge, 15–069
    relationship with third party,
      15–066—15–067
    reliance, 15–070—15–071
    size of class, 15–068
  Caparo
    background, 15–053—15–055
    facts of case, 15–056—15–061
  categories of advisee
    bodies liable to compensate,
      15–084—15–085
    creditors, 15–082—15–083
    directors, 15–081
    existing shareholders,
      15–074—15–075
    group companies, 15–080
    introduction, 15–073
    others, 15–086
    potential investors, 15–076—15–079
  Contracts (Rights against Third Parties)
    Act 1999, under, 15–088
  double recovery, 15–087
  Human Rights Act 1998, under,
    15–089
  loss of a chance, 15–087
  overview
    basic rule, 15–045—15–046
    different approaches,
      15–047—15–52
  policy considerations, 15–087
  relevant factors
    advisee/third party relationship,
      15–066—15–067
    generally, 15–062—15–063
    knowledge of adviser, 15–069
    purpose for which statement
      communicated, 15–065

DUTIES TO THIRD PARTIES
(ACCOUNTANTS)—*cont.*
relevant factors—*cont.*
purpose for which statement made,
15–064
reliance by advisee,
15–070—15–071
size of class of advisees, 15–068
DUTIES TO THIRD PARTIES (CONSTRUCTION
PROFESSIONALS)
collateral warranties, 8–064—8–065
common law, at
Commonwealth cases,
8–112—8–124
definition of type of loss,
8–070—8–079
economic loss, 8–086—8–111
introduction, 8–069
personal injury, 8–080—8–081
property damage, 8–082—8–085
scope of duty, 8–125—8–131
Commonwealth cases
Australia, 8–119—8–121
Canada, 8–112—8–118
Hong Kong, 8–124
New Zealand, 8–122—8–123
contractors, 8–105—8–111
Contracts (Rights of Third Parties) Act
1999, under, 8–067—8–068
economic loss
complex structure theory,
8–091—8–096
contractors, 8–105—8–111
exceptions to general rule,
8–090—8–111
expenditure necessary to avoid
liability, 8–097
general rule, 8–086—8–089
Hedley Byrne principle,
8–098—8–103
subsequent purchasers, 8–104
statute, under, 8–066—8–068
subsequent purchasers, 8–104
DUTIES TO THIRD PARTIES (SOLICITORS)
adversary
contentious business,
10–062—10–064
generally, 10–055
non-contentious business,
10–056—10–061
adversary in contentious business
criminal cases, 10–064
exceptions to general rule,
10–063—10–064
general rule, 10–062
adversary in non-contentious business

DUTIES TO THIRD PARTIES
(SOLICITORS)—*cont.*
adversary in non-contentious
business—*cont.*
Commonwealth cases, 10–061
exceptions to general rule,
10–058—10–060
general rule, 10–056—10–057
reliance on solicitor's
representations,
10–058—10–059
associate of client, 10–042
beneficiaries without reliance
background, 10–047—10–048
conflict of interest, 10–051
double recovery, 10–052
identity of beneficiary, 10–050
non-will cases, 10–053
other jurisdictions, in, 10–054
scope of principle, 10–049
fraud, 10–076
generally, 10–040—10–046
no reliance, where
Commonwealth cases, 10–045
generally, 10–044
solicitor as officer of court, 10–046
reliance
non-client establishing duty, by,
10–042
non-client without duty, by, 10–043
without retainer, 10–041
undertakings
and see UNDERTAKINGS
construction, 10–068
enforcement, 10–069—10–074
examples, 10–067
generally, 10–066
introduction, 10–065
warranty of authority, 10–075
DUTY OF CARE
advocates, and, 2–097
analysis of issues
assumption of responsibility, 2–078
correct analysis of authority, 2–070
introduction, 2–066
just and reasonable, 2–076—2–078
need for guiding principles, 2–09
proximity, 2–075
role of authority, 2–068
role of general principle, 2–067
underlying principles, 2–071—2–074
applicable situations
elements, 2–019—2–021
examples, 2–018
introduction, 2–017

DUTY OF CARE—*cont.*
approaches
  co-existence of, 2–050—2–053
  exclusive, 2–036—2–037
  extensions to *Hedley Byrne*,
    2–045—2–049
  inclusive, 2–026—2–030
  incremental, 2–038—2–044
  Lord Atkin's, 2–022—2–025
  threefold test, 2–030—2–035
architects, and, 2–097
assumption of responsibility
  directors and employees, 2–090
  generally, 2–078
Australia, in, 2–063—2–065
beneficiaries, to, 2–114
breach of, 2–015
breach of common law duty,
  introduction, 2–083
  regulatory bodies, 2–086
  scope, 2–084
  supervisory bodies, 2–086
  vicarious liability, 2–085
breach of statutory duty, 2–082
Canada, in
  directors and employees,
    2–089—2–090
  general approach, 2–058—2–062
careless performance of public duty,
  2–081
case law
  Anns v. Merton, 2–027—2–028
  Caparo, 2–031—2–033, 2–037
  Donoghue v. Stevenson,
    2–022—2–023
  Hedley Byrne, 2–024—2–025
Commonwealth approaches
  Australia, 2–063—2–065
  Canada, 2–058—2–062
  New Zealand, 2–054—2–057
concurrent liability, and
  case law, 2–102—2–105
  competing considerations, 2–101
  introduction, 2–100
  extent of tortious duty,
    2–107—2–108
  scope of concurrent duty, 2–106
consumer, to, 2–022—2–023
directors, by
  Canadian case law, 2–089—2–090
  generally, 2–088
  introduction, 2–087
economic loss, and, 2–024—2–025
employees, by
  firms, 2–091—2–093
  introduction, 2–087

DUTY OF CARE—*cont.*
employees, by—*cont.*
  limited liability companies,
    2–088—2–090
exclusive approach, 2–036—2–037
expert witnesses, and, 2–097
firms, by
  introduction, 2–091
  Merrett v. Babb, 2–092—2–093
"foreseeability" test, 2–035
Hedley Byrne approach
  co-existence with different
    approaches, 2–050—2–053
  extensions to, 2–045—2–049
  introduction, 2–024—2–025
human rights, and
  effective remedy, 7–024—7–025
  framing of claims, 7–026—7–029
  interlocutory striking out, 7–023
  introduction, 7–019—7–020
  Z. v. United Kingdom,
    7–021—7–022
immunity from suit, and,
  2–097—2–099
inclusive approach
  introduction, 2–026
  two-stage test, 2–027—2–028
incremental approach
  adoption by House of Lords,
    2–039—2–040
  criticisms of, 2–043—2–044
  Hedley Byrne approach, and,
    2–050—2–053
  introduction, 2–038—2–038
  three-fold test, and, 2–041—2–042
injury to neighbour, 2–022—2–023
intended beneficiaries, to, 2–114
introduction, 2–014
"just and reasonable" test
  analysis of problems, 2–076—2–078
  introduction, 2–035
liability to third parties
  background, 2–110
  intended beneficiaries, 2–114
  introduction, 2–109
  persons under duty, 2–111
  third parties entitled to benefit,
    2–112
  transactions subject to duty, 2–113
limited liability companies, by
  Canadian case law, 2–089—2–090
  introduction, 2–088
line of reasoning, 2–019—2–020
local authorities, by
  breach of common law duty,
    2–083—2–086

DUTY OF CARE—*cont.*
local authorities, by—*cont.*
breach of statutory duty, 2–082
careless performance of public duty,
2–081
classification of claims, 2–080
introduction, 2–079
mutual valuers, and, 2–097
New Zealand, in, 2–054—2–057
particular situations
directors and employees,
2–087—2–093
immunity, 2–097—2–099
public authorities, 2–079—2–086
sub-contractors, 2–094—2–096
"proximity" test
analysis of problems, 2–075
introduction, 2–035
public authorities, by
breach of duty arising from
performance of statutory duty,
2–083—2–086
breach of statutory duty, 2–082
careless performance of public duty,
2–081
classification of claims, 2–080
introduction, 2–079
"reasonably foreseeable" test,
2–035
regulatory bodies, by, 2–086
sub-contractors, by
competing considerations, 2–096
generally, 2–094—2–095
supervisory bodies, by, 2–086
three-fold test
continued application, 2–042
generally, 2–030—2–034
Hedley Byrne approach, and,
2–050—2–053
incremental approach, and,
2–041
summary, 2–035
two-stage test
introduction, 2–027
subsequent use, 2–028—2–029
vicarious liability, 2–085

EEA FIRMS
financial practitioners, and, 13–079
ECONOMIC LOSS
construction professionals, and
common law, at, 8–086—8–111
statute, under, 8–049

ECONOMIC LOSS—*cont.*
construction professionals (common
law), and
Commonwealth cases,
8–112—8–124
complex structure theory,
8–091—8–096
contractors, 8–105—8–111
exceptions to general rule,
8–090—8–111
expenditure necessary to avoid
liability, 8–097
general rule, 8–086—8–089
Hedley Byrne principle,
8–098—8–103
subsequent purchasers, 8–104
generally, 2–024—2–025
IT professionals, and
contractual duties, and, 17–051
generally, 17–116—17–117
tortious duties, 17–070—17–071
medical practitioners, and
generally, 12–024—12–027
wrongful birth/conception claims,
12–303—12–305
surveyors, and, 9–034—9–035
ECONOMIC RIGHTS
human rights, and, 7–016
EFFECTING INSURANCE ON TERMS NOT
AGREED
ambiguous instructions, 14–044
introduction, 14–043
lack of availability, 14–045
EFFECTING INSURANCE ON TERMS NOT MEET
REQUIREMENTS
change of requirements, 14–056
clarity of instructions, 14–054
defective policy wording, 14–050
enquiries by broker, 14–051—14–053
introduction, 14–046—14–049
level of cover, 14–055
EFFECTIVE REMEDY, RIGHT TO
generally, 7–024—7–025
EMERGENCY SITUATION
medical practitioners, and, 12–080
EMPLOYEES, DUTY OF CARE OF
firms, and, 2–091—2–093
introduction, 2–087
limited liability companies, and,
2–088—2–090
EMPLOYEE, LIABILITY OF
financial practitioners, and, 13–113
EMPLOYER, LIABILITY OF
financial practitioners, and, 13–112
ENGINEERS, CLAIMS AGAINST
and see CONSTRUCTION PROFESSIONALS

ENGINEERS, CLAIMS AGAINST—*cont.*
adjudication, 8–332—8–344
apportionment of liability,
   8–317—8–329
causation, 8–270—8–279
contributory negligence, 8–330—8–331
damages for breach of duty,
   8–264—8–315
date of cause of action, and
   Bank of East Asia, 5–028—5–029
   date of damage, 5–030—5–033
   degree of damage, 5–022
   "doomed from start", 5–020—5–021
   Murphy, 5–024—5–027
   Pirelli, 5–017—5–019
   successive owners, 5–023
   uncertainty, 5–034
duties, 8–019—8–181
expert witness, as, 8–263
foreseeability, 8–280—8–284
functions, 8–005
immunity from suit, and, 2–097
liability for breach of duty,
   8–182—8–262
pre-action protocols, 8–009
remoteness, 8–265—8–284
ENQUIRIES BEFORE CONTRACT
solicitors, and, 10–201
EQUALITY OF ARMS, RIGHT TO
human rights, and, 7–011
EQUITABLE REMEDIES
account of profits, 3–017
compensation
   breach of confidence, 3–015—3–016
   breach of fiduciary duty,
      3–011—3–014
injunction, 3–018
rescission, 3–009—3–010
EQUITY, LIMITATION IN
analogous application of statute,
   5–089—5–095
express application of statute,
   5–082—5–088
introduction, 5–079—5–081
no limitation, 5–096—5–097
obedience to statute, 5–081
ERRORS IN COURSE OF TREATMENT
adverse reaction to treatment, 12–191
failure to remove objects, 12–194
generally, 12–186—12–196
injections, 12–192
operations, 12–193
over-intervention, 12–196
post-operative care, 12–195
right procedure, 12–188
right treatment, 12–187

ERRORS OF JUDGMENT
barristers, and
   examples, 11–041—11–042
   existence of error, 11–038
   introduction, 11–039
   nature of error, 11–040
   settlement advice, 11–043—11–045
construction professionals, and,
   8–165—8–167
ESTIMATED REALISATION PRICE
surveyors, and, 9–023
EUROPEAN CONVENTION ON HUMAN
   RIGHTS
and see HUMAN RIGHTS
introduction, 7–001
EVALUATION OF A CHANCE
financial practitioners, and, 13–160
solicitors, and
   burden of proof, 10–262
   Commonwealth cases, 10–261
   examples, 10–259
   generally, 10–256
   likely act of claimant, 10–257
   likely act of third party, 10–258
   limits of principle, 10–260
EVIDENCE
experts, from
   admissibility, 6–011
   appropriateness, 6–013
   court rules, 6–010
   excluded cases, 6–008—6–009
   functions of expert, 6–006—6–007
   impartiality of expert, 6–015—6–017
   instruction, 6–012
   presentation, 6–012
   qualification of expert, 6–014
   relevance, 6–011
medical practitioners, and, 12–232
misconduct in litigation by solicitors,
   and, 10–180—10–182
EXAMINATION OF CONSTRUCTION SITE
effect of proposed works, 8–191
generally, 8–183
ground investigations, 8–185—8–189
measurement, 8–184
non-physical restraints, 8–192
EXCESS EXPENDITURE
construction professionals, and, 8–303
EXCLUSION OF LIABILITY
accountants, and, 15–100—15–101
financial practitioners, and,
   13–133—13–134
incorporation of clause, 5–006
introduction, 5–001—5–002
IT professionals, and
   introduction, 17–118

EXCLUSION OF LIABILITY—*cont.*
IT professionals, and—*cont.*
other party's standard terms,
17–119—17–120
reasonableness of term,
17–121—17–123
solicitors, and, 10–141
statutory framework
UCTA 1977, 5–003—5–004
UTCCR 1999, 5–005
surveyors, and
commercial property, 9–071
definition of extent of service, and,
9–073
introduction, 9–063
residential property, 9–064—9–070
Scotland, in, 9–072
third parties, to
comment, 5–009
introduction, 5–007
mortgage applications, in, 5–008
EXPERT EVIDENCE OF STANDARD OF SKILL
AND CARE
accountants, and, 15–091
admissibility, 6–011
appropriateness, 6–013
construction professionals, and,
8–151—8–155
court rules, 6–010
excluded cases
Bolam test doesn't apply, 6–009
solicitors' negligence, 6–008
functions of expert, 6–006—6–007
impartiality of expert, 6–015—6–017
instruction, 6–012
insurance brokers, and, 14–034
medical practitioners, and,
12–111—12–116
presentation, 6–012
qualifications of expert, 6–014
relevance, 6–011
EXPERT WITNESSES
construction professionals as, 8–263
experience, 6–014
functions, 6–006—6–007
impartiality, 6–015—6–017
immunity from suit, and, 2–097
qualifications, 6–014
solicitors as, 10–142
surveyors as, 9–006
EXTENSIONS OF TIME
construction professionals, and,
8–233—8–235
EXTRICATION, COSTS OF
heads of damage, and, 10–272

FAILURE PROPERLY TO CLASSIFY CUSTOMER
financial practitioners, and, 13–120
FAILURE TO ACT WITH REASONABLE SPEED
insurance brokers, and, 14–059
FAILURE OF ADVICE BY BARRISTERS
clarity, 11–047
generally, 11–046
when not so instructed, 11–048
FAILURE TO ADVISE ON SYNDICATE
PARTICIPATION
causation, 16–063—16–066
generally, 16–025—16–029
measure of damages, 16–073—16–076
FAILURE TO ARRANGE FOLLOW-UP
medical practitioners, and, 12–176
FAILURE TO ATTEND PATIENT
GP, 12–174—12–175
hospital doctors, 12–173
introduction, 12–172
FAILURE TO CARRY OUT INSTRUCTIONS
surveyors, and, 9–077—9–078
FAILURE TO COMMUNICATE
medical practitioners, and,
12–197—12–200
FAILURE TO DIAGNOSE ILLNESS
generally, 12–177—12–184
more serious condition, 12–185
FAILURE TO DIAGNOSE SPECIAL NEEDS
human rights, and, 7–026
expert witnesses, as, 10–142
FAILURE TO DISCLOSE MATERIAL FACTS TO
INSURER
advice to client of duty to disclose,
14–064—14–065
description of reinsurance risk, 14–068
enquiry of client, 14–066—14–067
generally, 14–060—14–063
FAILURE TO EFFECT INSURANCE
existing cover, in respect of, 14–042
generally, 14–038—14–041
FAILURE TO EXAMINE PATIENT
GP, 12–174—12–175
hospital doctors, 12–173
introduction, 12–172
FAILURE TO EXERCISE DISCRETION
REASONABLY
insurance brokers, and,
14–057—14–058
FAILURE TO EXPLAIN TREATMENT
answering patient's questions,
12–218—12–221
Australian law, 12–205—12–207
blood products, 12–226
Canadian law, 12–202—12–204
curtailment by reason of patient's
condition, 12–215—12–217

FAILURE TO EXPLAIN TREATMENT—*cont.*
  disability of unborn baby, 12–231
  English law, 12–208—12–214
  evidence, and, 12–232
  general principle, 12–201
  manner of communication,
      12–223—12–224
  side effects of drugs, 12–225
  sterilisation, 12–227—12–230
  warning for patient's protection,
      12–222
FAILURE TO EXPLAIN LEGAL DOCUMENTS
  solicitors, and, 10–166—10–167
FAILURE TO GIVE ADVICE
  barristers, and
    clarity, 11–047
    generally, 11–046
    when not so instructed, 11–048
  construction professionals, and
    advice to claimant, 8–271
    advice to third party, 8–272
  Lloyd's agents, and
    causation, 16–063—16–066
    generally, 16–025—16–029
    measure of damages,
        16–073—16–076
  patent agents, and, 18–018
  solicitors, and
    attendance notes, and, 10–174
    confirmatory letters, and, 10–174
    costs information, as to, 10–157
    general business matters, as to,
        10–169—10–172
    introduction, 10–154
    legal documents, on,
        10–166—10–167
    matters coming to notice, as to,
        10–158—10–159
    matters not asked to advise upon, as
        to, 10–160—10–163
    obvious risks, as to, 10–165
    progress of matter, as to, 10–156
    recipient of advice, 10–155
    reminder of advice, and, 10–168
    solicitor's own negligence, as to,
        10–164
    unequal transactions, in, 10–173
  trade mark attorney, and, 18–018
FAILURE TO GIVE ADVICE (SOLICITORS)
  attendance notes, and, 10–174
  business matters, as to,
      10–169—10–172
  confirmatory letters, and, 10–174
  costs information, as to, 10–157
  introduction, 10–154
  legal documents, on, 10–166—10–167

FAILURE TO GIVE ADVICE
    (SOLICITORS)—*cont.*
  matters coming to notice, as to,
      10–158—10–159
  matters not asked to advise upon, as to
    generally, 10–160—10–161
    statements of principle,
        10–162—10–163
  obvious risks, as to, 10–165
  progress of matter, as to, 10–156
  recipient of advice, 10–155
  reminder of advice, and, 10–168
  solicitor's own negligence, as to,
      10–164
  unequal transactions, in, 10–173
FAILURE TO GIVE PROPER ADVICE
  introduction, 14–081—14–082
  law, on, 14–083—14–085
FAILURE TO INSPECT PROPERLY
  introduction, 9–082
  limited survey, 9–097
  observation, 9–090—9–096
  particular parts, 9–083
  relevance of type of survey,
      9–097—9–09
  uncovering and opening up,
      9–084—9–089
FAILURE TO KEEP CLIENT INFORMED
  existence of cover, as to, 14–074
  renewal of cover, of need for,
      14–075—14–076
  terms of cover, of, 14–079—14–080
  uninsured, of becoming,
      14–077—14–078
FAILURE TO MAKE PROPER APPRAISAL
  surveyors, and, 9–104—9–106
FAILURE TO MAKE SUFFICIENT INQUIRIES
    (SURVEYORS)
  generally, 9–100—9–101
  hearsay information, 9–102—9–103
FAILURE TO OBSERVE (SURVEYORS)
  camouflaged defects, 9–095
  cracks, 9–093—9–094
  dry rot, 9–091
  introduction, 9–090
  roof, 9–092
  subsidence, 9–093—9–094
  totality of unnoticed defects, 9–096
  woodworm, 9–091
FAILURE TO OBTAIN ADEQUATE
    REINSURANCE
  amount of reinsurance sought,
      16–039—16–045
  choice of reinsurer, 16–046—16–049
  commercial viability, 16–050—16–051

FAILURE TO OBTAIN ADEQUATE
  REINSURANCE—*cont.*
introduction, 16–038
validity of reinsurance, 16–052
FAILURE TO OBTAIN FULL INSTRUCTIONS
barristers, and, 11–049
FAILURE TO OPEN UP
surveyors, and, 9–084—9–089
FAILURE TO PLAN PROPERLY
Lloyd's agents, and, 16–030—16–036
FAILURE TO PREVENT ILLNESS
introduction, 12–169
spread of infectious disease,
  12–170—12–171
FAILURE TO PROCURE TREATMENT
medical practitioners, and,
  12–271—12–273
FAILURE TO RECOGNISE DEFECT
surveyors, and, 9–099
FAILURE TO REMOVE OBJECTS
medical practitioners, and, 12–194
FAILURE TO REVIEW A DESIGN
construction professionals, and, 8–296
FAILURE TO TAKE PRECAUTIONS
medical practitioners, and, 12–083
FAILURE TO UNCOVER
surveyors, and, 9–084—9–089
FAILURE TO WARN OF DEFECT
surveyors, and, 9–108—9–109
FAILURE TO WARN OF RISKS
medical practitioners, and,
  12–201—12–232
FAIR DEALING
fiduciary's interest, 2–140
full advice and disclosure,
  2–137—2–138
full value, 2–139
generally, 2–136
introduction, 2–134
FAIR TRIAL, RIGHT TO
applicable proceedings, 7–012
"civil rights and obligations", 7–006
"criminal charge", 7–008
"determination", 7–007
express rights, 7–009
generally, 7–005
implied rights, 7–010—7–011
introduction, 7–004
medical practitioners, 7–043
FAMILY LIFE, RIGHT TO RESPECT FOR
generally, 7–013
introduction, 7–004
medical practitioners, 7–044
FIDUCIARY OBLIGATIONS
accountants, and
  confidentiality, 15–041—15–044

FIDUCIARY OBLIGATIONS—*cont.*
accountants, and—*cont.*
  generally, 15–038—15–040
barristers, and, 11–005
compensation for breach,
  3–011—3–014
construction professionals, and, 8–063
contractual liability, and, 2–128
dealings with principal
  fair dealing, 2–136
  fiduciary's interest, 2–140
  full advice and disclosure,
    2–137—2–138
  full value, 2–139
  introduction, 2–134
  self-dealing, 2–135
diversion of opportunities, 2–141
effect, 2–128
excluded obligations, 2–126—2–127
fair dealing
  fiduciary's interest, 2–140
  full advice and disclosure,
    2–137—2–138
  full value, 2–139
  generally, 2–136
  introduction, 2–134
financial practitioners, and
  examples, 13–116
  generally, 13–115
generally, 2–006
introduction, 2–125
Lloyd's agents, and, 16–015
medical practitioners, and
  introduction, 12–028
  nature and extent, 12–030
  undue influence, 12–029
nature, 2–129—2–130
retainer, and, 2–131—2–133
self dealing
  fiduciary's interest, 2–140
  full advice and disclosure,
    2–137—2–138
  full value, 2–139
  generally, 2–135
  introduction, 2–134
solicitors, and
  and see below
  bribes, 10–022
  confidentiality, 10–026—10–033
  generally, 10–016
  inconsistent engagements,
    10–023—10–025
  obtaining personal benefit, 10–030
  personal dealings with client,
    10–018—10–019
  personal profit, 10–021

FIDUCIARY OBLIGATIONS—*cont.*
solicitors, and—*cont.*
secret commissions, 10–022
undue influence, 10–017
tortious liability, and, 2–128
unauthorised profits, 2–141
undue influence
classification, 2–142—2–145
rebutting the presumption, 2–146
FIDUCIARY OBLIGATIONS (SOLICITORS)
bribes, 10–022
confidentiality
Commonwealth position, 10–031
confidentiality of information,
10–029
examples, 10–027—10–028
generally, 10–026
overriding circumstances, 10–032
sufficiency of barriers, 10–030
inconsistent engagements
Canadian position, 10–025
generally, 10–023—10–024
obtaining personal benefit, 10–030
personal dealings with client,
10–018—10–019
personal profit, 10–021
secret commissions, 10–022
undue influence, 10–017
FINANCIAL OMBUDSMAN SERVICE (FOS)
award, 13–183—13–188
complaints handling procedure, 13–179
immunity from suit, 13–189
internal complaints handling,
13–172—13–174
introduction, 13–170—13–171
investigation procedure,
13–180—13–182
jurisdiction, 13–175—13–178
money awards, 13–186—13–187
non-money awards, 13–188
FINANCIAL PRACTITIONERS
account of profits, 13–166
advising and selling
breach of duty, 13–121—13–125
introduction, 13–054
know your customer, 13–056
polarisation, 13–055
status disclosure, 13–055
suitability, 13–057
understanding of risk, 13–058
aggregation and allocation, 13–066
application of FSMA regime
advising and selling,
13–054—13–058
financial promotion,
13–031—13–032

FINANCIAL PRACTITIONERS—*cont.*
application of FSMA regime—*cont.*
introduction, 13–028
investment, 13–033—13–034
nature of services, 13–035
provider of financial services,
13–036
recipient of financial services,
13–037
regulated activities, 13–029—13–030
appointed representatives
authority at common law, 13–098
introduction, 13–095
liability of principal, 13–097
status requirements, 13–096
approved persons
Code of Practice, 13–045
introduction, 13–019
asset freezing orders
contravenors, against, 13–141
generally, 13–146
grounds of application,
13–138—13–140
introduction, 13–137
knowingly concerned persons,
against, 13–142
authorised persons
acting outside permission, 13–074
contravention of FSA rules,
13–076—13–078
employment of certain persons,
13–075
introduction, 13–017—13–018
regulatory liabilities,
13–073—13–078
best and timely execution, 13–065
"bracket" claims, 13–094
cancellation, 13–060
causation
evaluation of a chance, 13–160
examples, 13–159
churning, 13–063
claim resolution
compensation scheme,
13–190—13–204
introduction, 13–169
Ombudsman, 13–170—13–189
parallel proceedings,
13–205—13–206
client assets, 13–068
common law, and, 13–024
compensation, 13–157
compensation scheme
acceptance of offer, 13–202
amount, 13–199—13–201
assignment of rights, 13–198

FINANCIAL PRACTITIONERS—*cont.*
  compensation scheme—*cont.*
    default by relevant provider, 13–197
    eligible claimants, 13–194
    immunity from suit, 13–204
    insurance, and, 13–203
    introduction, 13–190
    offers, 13–199—13–201
    protected claims, 13–195
    purpose, 13–191
    qualifying conditions, 13–193
    relevant provider, 13–196
    structure, 13–192
  Conduct of Business sourcebook
    advising and selling,
      13–054—13–058
    arrangement, 13–047
    cancellation, 13–060
    client assets, 13–068
    customer agreements, 13–053
    customer classification, 13–052
    dealing and managing,
      13–061—13–066
    designated investment business,
      13–049
    financial promotion,
      13–050—13–051
    introduction, 13–046
    product disclosure, 13–059
    reporting to customers, 13–067
    scope, 13–048
    terms of business, 13–053
    withdrawal, 13–060
  conflict of interest, 13–062
  contractual duties
    appointed representatives,
      13–095—13–098
    duty of care and skill,
      13–092—13–094
    incorporation of regulatory duties,
      13–091
    relevant contracts, 13–089
    terms of business, 13–090
  contribution, 13–168
  contributory negligence
    generally, 13–167
    introduction, 13–131
  customer agreements
    general requirements, 13–090
    introduction, 13–053
  customer classification
    breach of duty, 13–120
    generally, 13–052
  damages
    causation, 13–158—13–160
    foreseeability, 13–158

FINANCIAL PRACTITIONERS—*cont.*
  damages—*cont.*
    introduction, 13–157
    measure of, 13–161—13–165
    remoteness, 13–158—13–160
  date of cause of action, and, 5–048
  dealing ahead, 13–064
  dealing and managing
    aggregation and allocation, 13–066
    best and timely execution, 13–065
    breach of duty, 13–126—13–130
    churning, 13–063
    conflict of interest, 13–062
    dealing ahead, 13–064
    introduction, 13–061
    material interest, 13–062
    switching 13–063
  deceit, 13–099—13–104
  defences
    introduction, 13–131
    limitation of liability,
      13–133—13–134
    regulators' limited immunity, 13–132
    statute, under, 13–135
  designated investment business, 13–049
  designated professional bodies,
    13–021—13–022
  development of sector,
    13–003—13–005
  dispute resolution
    compensation scheme,
      13–190—13–204
    introduction, 13–169
    Ombudsman, 13–170—13–189
    parallel proceedings,
      13–205—13–206
  duties
    contract, under, 13–089—13–098
    fiduciary, 13–115—13–116
    relevant approach, 13–027
    sources, 13–026
    statute, under, 13–028—13–088
    tort, in, 13–099—13–114
  EEA firms, 13–079
  employee, liability of, 13–113
  employer, liability of, 13–112
  European issues, 13–023
  evaluation of a chance, 13–160
  exclusion of liability, 13–133—13–134
  exempt persons, 13–020
  failure properly to classify customer,
    13–120
  fiduciary duties
    examples, 13–116
    generally, 13–115

FINANCIAL PRACTITIONERS—*cont.*
Financial Ombudsman Service
award, 13–183—13–188
complaints handling procedure,
13–179
immunity from suit, 13–189
internal complaints handling,
13–172—13–174
introduction, 13–170—13–171
investigation procedure,
13–180—13–182
jurisdiction, 13–175—13–178
money awards, 13–186—13–187
non-money awards, 13–188
financial promotion
generally, 13–031—13–032
misleading, 13–118—13–119
restrictions, 13–015—13–016
financial promotion restrictions
generally, 13–015
liability, 13–072
recovery of monies paid, 13–156
territorial scope, 13–016
foreseeability, 13–158
fraudulent misrepresentation,
13–099—13–104
general prohibition
generally, 13–013
liability, 13–071
recovery of monies paid,
13–152—13–155
territorial scope, 13–014
human rights, and, 13–025
injunctions
contravenors, against, 13–141
generally, 13–144
grounds of application,
13–138—13–140
introduction, 13–137
knowingly concerned persons,
against, 13–142
internal complaints procedure
complaints handling, 13–174
compulsory jurisdiction, 13–172
voluntary jurisdiction, 13–173
know your customer, 13–056
lack of authorisation
financial promotion restriction,
13–072
general prohibition, 13–071
introduction, 13–070
liability for breach of duty
advising and selling,
13–121—13–125
dealing and managing,
13–126—13–130

FINANCIAL PRACTITIONERS—*cont.*
liability for breach of duty—*cont.*
failure properly to classify customer,
13–120
introduction, 13–117
misleading promotion,
13–118—13–119
limitation of liability, 13–133—13–134
listing of securities liabilities
introduction, 13–080
misleading particulars, 13–081
prospectus requirements, 13–082
material interest, 13–062
measure of damages
benefits received, 13–162—13–165
introduction, 13–161
misfeasance in public office, 13–105
misleading promotion,
13–118—13–119
misrepresentation
common law position, and, 13–088
false in material respect, 13–087
introduction, 13–085
suitability, 13–086
negligence, 13–106—13–107
Ombudsman scheme
award, 13–183—13–188
complaints handling procedure,
13–179
immunity from suit, 13–189
internal complaints handling,
13–172—13–174
introduction, 13–170—13–171
investigation procedure,
13–180—13–182
jurisdiction, 13–175—13–178
money awards, 13–186—13–187
non-money awards, 13–188
overview, 13–002
parallel proceedings
disclosure issues, 13–206
generally, 13–205
pension beneficiaries, 13–109—13–111
polarisation, 13–055
principal, liability of, 13–112
product disclosure, 13–059
prospectus cases, 13–108
recovery of monies paid
contravention of financial promotion
restriction, 13–156
contravention of general prohibition,
13–152—13–155
regulation
background, 13–006—13–009
FSA 1986, 13–010
FSMA 2000, 13–011

FINANCIAL PRACTITIONERS—*cont.*
  regulation—*cont.*
    introduction, 13–001
  regulation under FSMA 2000
    approved persons, 13–019
    authorised persons, 13–017—13–018
    designated professional bodies,
      13–021—13–022
    exempt persons, 13–020
    financial promotion restriction,
      13–015—13–016
    Financial Services Authority, 13–012
    general prohibition, 13–013—13–014
    generally, 13–011
  regulators, liability of
    generally, 13–114
    limited immunity, 13–132
  regulatory liabilities
    authorised persons, 13–073—13–078
    EEA firms, 13–079
    lack of authorisation,
      13–070—13–072
    introduction, 13–069
    listing of securities,
      13–080—13–082
  regulatory rules
    Conduct of Business sourcebook,
      13–046—13–068
    generally, 13–039—13–043
    principles, 13–044
    statements of principle, 13–045
  remedial orders
    contravenors, against, 13–141
    generally, 13–145
    grounds of application,
      13–138—13–140
    introduction, 13–137
    knowingly concerned persons,
      against, 13–142
  remedies
    introduction, 13–136
    private litigants, for,
      13–150—13–166
    regulators, for, 13–137—13–149
  remedies for private litigants
    account of profits, 13–166
    compensation, 13–157
    damages, 13–157—13–165
    introduction, 13–150
    recovery of monies paid,
      13–152—13–156
    rescission, 13–151
  remedies for regulators
    asset freezing orders, 13–146
    contravenors, against, 13–141
    FSA restitution order, 13–148

FINANCIAL PRACTITIONERS—*cont.*
  remedies for regulators—*cont.*
    grounds of application,
      13–138—13–140
    injunctions, 13–144
    introduction, 13–137
    knowingly concerned persons,
      against, 13–142
    remedial orders, 13–145
    restitution orders, 13–147—13–148
  remoteness
    causation, 13–158—13–160
    foreseeability, 13–158
    introduction, 13–158
  reporting to customers, 13–067
  rescission, 13–151
  restitution orders
    contravenors, against, 13–141
    FSA, by, 13–148
    generally, 13–147—13–148
    grounds of application,
      13–138—13–140
    introduction, 13–137
    knowingly concerned persons,
      against, 13–142
  restriction of liability, 13–133—13–134
  shared responsibility
    contribution, 13–168
    contributory negligence, 13–167
  standard of care and skill
    "bracket" claims, 13–094
    generally, 13–093
    introduction, 13–092
  status disclosure, 13–055
  statutory duties
    application of FSMA regime,
      13–028—13–037
    generally, 13–038
    misrepresentation, 13–085—13–088
    regulatory liabilities,
      13–069—13–082
    regulatory rules, 13–039—13–068
    unlisted securities, 13–084
  suitability, 13–057
  switching 13–063
  terms of business
    general requirements, 13–090
    introduction, 13–053
  tort, duties in
    deceit, 13–099—13–104
    employee, of, 13–113
    employer, of, 13–112
    fraudulent misrepresentation,
      13–099—13–104
    misfeasance in public office, 13–105
    negligence, 13–106—13–107

FINANCIAL PRACTITIONERS—*cont.*
tort, duties in—*cont.*
pension beneficiaries,
13–109—13–111
principal, of, 13–112
prospectus cases, 13–108
regulators, of, 13–114
understanding of risk, 13–058
unlisted securities, 13–084
withdrawal, 13–060
FINANCIAL PROMOTION
generally, 13–031—13–032
misleading, 13–118—13–119
restrictions
generally, 13–015
liability, 13–072
recovery of monies paid, 13–156
territorial scope, 13–016
FINANCIAL SERVICES ACT 1986
financial practitioners, and, 13–010
surveyors, and, 9–016
FINANCIAL SERVICES AUTHORITY (FSA)
generally, 13–012
FINES AND COSTS
insurance brokers, and, 14–123
FIRMS, DUTY OF CARE OF
introduction, 2–091
Merrett v. Babb, 2–092—2–093
FITNESS FOR PURPOSE
computer software, and
bespoke software, 17–014—17–022
communication by client of,
17–031—17–035
modified standard software,
17–023—17–030
standard of care, and,
17–082—17–094
contractual liability, and, 2–012
medical practitioners, and,
12–011—12–014
FORESEEABILITY OF DAMAGE
accountants, and, 15–131
construction professionals, and
date of assessment of loss,
8–283—8–284
introduction, 8–280—8–281
type of loss, 8–282
financial practitioners, and, 13–158
introduction, 2–035
Lloyd's agents, and, 16–071
medical practitioners, and,
12–282—12–286
solicitors, and
examples, 10–241—10–242
introduction, 10–240
time for consideration, 10–243

FORESEEABILITY OF DAMAGE—*cont.*
surveyors, and, 9–125—9–127
FRAUD
limitation period for
date when time restarts,
5–073—5–074
deliberate commission of breach,
5–075—5–076
effect of concealment after breach,
5–071
generally, 5–070
relevant facts, 5–072
unlikely to be discovered, 5–078
solicitor's duty, and, 10–076
surveyors, and, 9–033
FRAUDULENT MISREPRESENTATION
financial practitioners, and,
13–099—13–104
FREEDOM OF THOUGHT, CONSCIENCE AND
RELIGION, RIGHT TO
generally, 7–045
FRESH AUDIT COST
accountants, and, 15–140
FRESH LITIGATION
mitigation of damage, and,
10–318—10–319
FULL ADVICE AND DISCLOSURE
fiduciary obligations, and,
2–137—2–138
FULL VALUE
fiduciary obligations, and, 2–139

GENERAL INSURANCE STANDARDS COUNCIL
generally, 14–005
GENEROUS TREATMENT OF CLAIMANT
mitigation of damage, and, 10–317
GEO-TECHNICAL ENGINEERS
surveyors' functions, and, 9–001
GIVING OF ADVICE
patent agents, and, 18–018
solicitors, and
law, 10–151—10–152
practical issues, 10–153
wills, 10–220
trade mark attorney, and, 18–018
GROUND INVESTIGATIONS
construction professionals, and,
8–185—8–189
GROUP ACTIONS
costs, 6–005
introduction, 6–001
procedure, 6–003—6–004
professional negligence, and, 6–002
GUARDAIN/WARD RELATIONSHIP
undue influence, and, 2–144

HEADS OF DAMAGE (ACCOUNTANTS)
  defalcation by director, 15–139
  double recovery, 15–141—15–142
  fresh audit cost, 15–140
  introduction, 15–135
  investigation cost, 15–140
  lost advance, 15–136
  lost investment, 15–136
  monies wrongly paid out, 15–138
  negligent advice, 15–145
  overpayment, 15–137
  tax advice, 15–143
  tax returns, 15–143—15–144
HEADS OF DAMAGE (CONSTRUCTION
    PROFESSIONALS)
  consequential loss, 8–305—8–306
  diminution in value, 8–300—8–301
  distress, 8–309—8–311
  excess expenditure, 8–303
  inconvenience, 8–309—8–311
  introduction, 8–289
  loss of amenity, 8–312
  personal injury, 8–308
  rectification costs
    betterment, 8–297—8–299
    credit for cost of proper design,
      8–294
    date of assessment, 8–295
    failure to review a design, 8–296
    introduction, 8–290—8–293
  third party, liability to, 8–307
  underpayment, 8–304
  wasted expenditure, 8–302
HEADS OF DAMAGE (INSURANCE BROKERS)
  additional losses, 14–119
  credit for saved premium,
    14–124—14–125
  fines and costs, 14–123
  introduction, 14–114—14–116
  litigation costs, 14–122
  non-receipt of insurance proceeds,
    14–121
  settlement with insurers,
    14–117—14–118
  unreinsured losses, 14–120
HEADS OF DAMAGE (SOLICITORS)
  anticipated gains, 10–305
  criminal liability, 10–303
  difference in value in property
    cure costs, 10–276
    exceptions to general rule,
      10–269—10–270
    extrication costs, 10–272
    general rule, 10–268
    loss of business profits, 10–274
    loss of use of property, 10–271

HEADS OF DAMAGE (SOLICITORS)—cont.
  difference in value in property—cont.
    market value not reflect loss, 10–273
    radical change in circumstances,
      10–275
  distress
    affecting health, 10–312
    not affecting health,
      10–313—10–315
  diminution in value of shareholding,
    10–300
  incidental expenditure, 10–309
  inconvenience, 10–311
  introduction, 10–263
  loss of earnings, 10–298
  loss of life policy, 10–299
  loss of opportunity to acquire interest
    in property
    agricultural tenancies, 10–266
    business tenancies, 10–265
    evaluation difficulties, 10–267
    generally, 10–264
  loss of opportunity to bring
    proceedings
    Commonwealth cases, 10–278
    costs risk, 10–285
    deduction of benefits, 10–290
    enforcement proceedings, and,
      10–292
    examples, 10–279—10–281
    extent of claim, 10–282
    generally, 10–277
    interest after trial, 10–289
    legal aid, 10–284
    means of defendant, 10–286
    notional date of trial,
      10–287—10–288
    risks of litigation , 10–283
    want of prosecution, and, 10–291
  loss of opportunity to defend
    proceedings, 10–293
  loss on sale of land, 10–297
  loss on secured loans
    dishonest borrowers, 10–296
    generally, 10–294—10–295
  physical injury, 10–310
  third party, liability to,
    10–301—10–302
  wasted expenditure
    examples, 10–306
    general rule, 10–304—10–305
    later solicitors' costs, 10–308
    original solicitors' costs, 10–307
HEALTH AUTHORITIES
  and see MEDICAL PRACTITIONERS
  apportionment of liability, 12–164

HEALTH AUTHORITIES—*cont.*
   primary liability, 12–155—12–161
   structure of NHS, 12–162—12–163
   vicarious liability, 12–152—12–154
HEALTH VISITORS
   and see MEDICAL PRACTITIONERS
   disciplinary proceedings, 12–004
   registration, 12–003
HEDLEY BYRNE PRINCIPLE
   extensions to
      contractual parties, 2–046—2–047
      disappointed beneficiary, 2–048
      introduction, 2–045
      practical application, 2–049
   incremental approach, and,
      2–050—2–053
   introduction, 2–024—2–025
   surveyors, and, 9–034—9–038
   threefold test, and, 2–050—2–053
HINDSIGHT
   solicitors, and, 10–083
HOME, RIGHT TO RESPECT FOR
   generally, 7–013
   introduction, 7–004
HOPELESS LITIGATION
   wasted costs order, and,
      10–135—10–136
HOSPITAL WAITING LISTS
   human rights, and, 7–054
HOSPITALS
   and see MEDICAL PRACTITIONERS
   apportionment of liability, 12–164
   primary liability, 12–155—12–161
   structure of NHS, 12–162—12–163
   vicarious liability, 12–152—12–154
HUMAN RIGHTS
   access to court, right of, 7–010
   accountants, and, 15–089
      loss of a chance, 15–087
   advocates, and, 7–030
   child protection, and, 7–026
   clinical negligence, and, 7–026
   complaints procedures, and, 7–065
   confidential information
      access to, 7–060
      disclosure of, 7–061
      medical records, 7–062—7–063
   consent to treatment, and, 7–059
   Convention rights, 7–004—7–018
   correspondence, right to respect for
      generally, 7–013
      introduction, 7–004
   degrading treatment, prohibition
      against, 7–042
   disciplinary proceedings
      generally, 7–065—7–066

HUMAN RIGHTS—*cont.*
   disciplinary proceedings—*cont.*
      procedural guarantees, 7–067
   duty of care, and
      effective remedy, 7–024—7–025
      framing of claims, 7–026—7–029
      interlocutory striking out, 7–023
      introduction, 7–019—7–020
      Z. v. United Kingdom,
         7–021—7–022
   economic rights, 7–016
   effective remedy, right to,
      7–024—7–025
   equality of arms, right to, 7–011
   failure to diagnose special needs, and,
      7–026
   fair trial, right to
      applicable proceedings, 7–012
      "civil rights and obligations", 7–006
      "criminal charge", 7–008
      "determination", 7–007
      express rights, 7–009
      generally, 7–005
      implied rights, 7–010—7–011
      introduction, 7–004
      medical practitioners, 7–043
   family life, right to respect for
      generally, 7–013
      introduction, 7–004
      medical practitioners, 7–044
   freedom of thought, right to, 7–045
   home, right to respect for
      generally, 7–013
      introduction, 7–004
   hospital waiting lists, and, 7–054
   immunity from suit, and
      introduction, 7–030
      lawyers, 7–031—7–035
      medical practitioners, 7–036—7–064
   inhuman treatment, prohibition against,
      7–042
   innocence, presumption of, 7–012
   introduction, 7–001—7–003
   lawyers
      confidentiality of communications,
         7–033—7–035
      introduction, 7–031
      wasted costs orders, 7–032
   life, right to
      clinical negligence, and, 7–026
      introduction, 7–018
      medical practitioners, 7–039—7–041
      police, actions against, 7–026
   limitation period, 7–027
   marry, right to, 7–046

HUMAN RIGHTS—*cont.*
medical care, right to
  allocation of resources,
    7–051—7–052
  blanket bans, 7–053
  hospital waiting lists, 7–054
  introduction, 7–050
medical information, access to
  disclosure, 7–061
  introduction, 7–060
  records, 7–062—7–063
medical practitioners
  access to medical information,
    7–060—7–063
  clinical negligence, 7–047—7–049
  complaints procedures, 7–065
  consent to treatment, 7–059
  degrading treatment, prohibition
    against, 7–042
  fair trial, right to, 7–043
  family life, right to respect for,
    7–044
  freedom of thought, right to, 7–045
  inhuman treatment, prohibition
    against, 7–042
  introduction, 7–036—7–037
  life, right to, 7–039—7–041
  marry, right to, 7–046
  medical care, right to, 7–050—7–054
  private life, right to respect for,
    7–044
  relevant rights, 7–038
  withdrawal of treatment,
    7–055—7–058
  wrongful birth/conception claims,
    12–301
nature of charge, right to know, 7–013
peaceful enjoyment of possessions,
  right to
  economic rights, 7–016
  fair balance test, 7–017
  generally, 7–014
  introduction, 7–004
  principles, 7–015
police, actions against, 7–026
presumption of innocence, 7–012
private life, right to respect for
  child protection, and, 7–026
  failure to diagnose special needs,
    and, 7–026
  generally, 7–013
  introduction, 7–004
  lawyer/client confidentiality,
    7–033—7–035
  medical practitioners, 7–044

HUMAN RIGHTS—*cont.*
professional disciplinary proceedings
  generally, 7–065—7–066
  procedural guarantees, 7–067
public authorities, and, 7–001
relevant rights, 7–004—7–018
self-incrimination, right against, 7–012
striking out, and
  interlocutory, 7–023
  introduction, 7–019—7–020
  Z. v. United Kingdom,
    7–021—7–022
treatment, right to
  allocation of resources,
    7–051—7–052
  blanket bans, 7–053
  hospital waiting lists, 7–054
  introduction, 7–050
  withdrawal of treatment,
    7–055—7–058
  wrongful birth/conception claims,
    12–301

IGNORANCE OF LAW
  construction professionals, and,
    8–162—8–164
  patent agents, and, 18–016
  trade mark attorney, and, 18–016
  solicitors, and
    generally, 10–081—10–082
    wills, 10–222
  trade mark attorney, and, 18–016
IMMUNITY FROM SUIT
  barristers, and
    and see below
    background, 11–009
    extent, 11–013—11–024
    human rights issues, 7–030
    introduction, 2–097
    justification, 11–010—11–012
  duty of care, and, 2–097—2–099
  financial practitioners, and
    compensation scheme, 13–204
  human rights, and
    introduction, 7–030
    lawyers, 7–031—7–035
    medical practitioners, 7–036—7–064
  patent agents, and, 18–012
  solicitors, and
    background, 10–106
    generally, 10–107
  trade mark attorney, and, 18–012
IMMUNITY FROM SUIT (BARRISTERS)
  background, 11–009

IMMUNITY FROM SUIT (BARRISTERS)—*cont.*
extent
  Commonwealth position, 11–024
  Hall v. Simons, 11–015—11–0
  introduction, 11–013—11–014
Hall v. Simons, decision in
  analogy to other immunities, 11–020
  cab-rank rule, 11–019
  criminal proceedings, 11–023
  duty to court, 11–022
  flood of litigation fear,
    11–017—11–018
  introduction 11–015
  re-litigation, 11–021
  starting point, 11–016
human rights issues, 7–030
introduction, 2–097
justification
  academic criticism, 11–012
  generally, 11–010
  public interest, 11–011
IMPLEMENTATION OF SOFTWARE
  common law duty, 17–051
  generally, 17–036—17–037
IMPOSSIBILITY
  undertakings by solicitor, and, 10–072
IMPROPER, UNREASONABLE OR NEGLIGENT
  wasted costs order, and, 10–130
INADEQUATE ADVICE CONCERNING UNBORN
  BABY
  medical practitioners, and,
    12–277—12–281
INADEQUATE PROFESSIONAL SERVICE
  barristers, and, 11–003
INADEQUATE SUPERVISION OF ACTIVE
  UNDERWRITER
  Lloyd's agents, and, 16–057
INADEQUATE SURVEYORS REPORT
  failure to warn of defect,
    9–108—9–109
  generally, 9–107
INADEQUATE WARNING OF TREATMENT
  Australian law, 12–265—12–268
  Canadian law, 12–264
  introduction, 12–262—12–263
  policy issues, 12–269—12–270
INCIDENTAL EXPENSES
  solicitors, and, 10–309
  surveyors, and, 9–190—9–194
INCONSISTENT ENGAGEMENTS
  Canadian position, 10–025
  generally, 10–023—10–024
INCONVENIENCE, DAMAGES FOR
  construction professionals, and,
    8–309—8–311
  solicitors, and, 10–311

INCONVENIENCE, DAMAGES FOR—*cont.*
surveyors, and
  examples, 9–189
  generally, 9–181—9–185
  injury to health, 9–186—9–187
  quantum, 9–188
INCORPORATED SOCIETY OF VALUERS AND
  AUCTIONEERS (ISVA)
  generally, 9–002
INCORPORATION OF CLAUSES
  exclusion of liability, and, 5–006
INDUCING BREACH OF CONTRACT
  construction professionals, and, 8–132
INEXPERIENCE
  medical practitioners, and, 12–077
  solicitors, and, 10–093—10–095
INFECTION FROM CONTACT WITH PATIENT
  medical practitioners, and,
    12–043—12–054
INFORMATION TECHNOLOGY PROFESSIONALS
  causation, 17–095—17–097
  collateral contracts, 17–056
  Consumer Protection Act 1987,
    liability under
    defences, 17–076—17–077
    generally, 17–072—17–073
    relevant product, 17–074—17–075
    "safety-critical" information, 17–078
  contributory negligence,
    17–126—17–130
  co-operation, 17–038—17–043
  duties
    client, to, 17–014—17–060
    third parties, to, 17–061—17–078
  duties to client
    collateral contracts, 17–056
    common law, at, 17–051
    consultant/supplier dichotomy,
      17–052—17–054
    co-operation, 17–038—17–043
    fitness for purpose, 17–014—17–035
    implementation, 17–036—17–037
    installation, 17–047—17–050
    negligent misstatements, 17–055
    operation manual, 17–046
    satisfactory quality, 17–014—17–035
    support, 17–044
    systems advice, 17–057—17–058
    testing, 17–036—17–037
    "time-bombs", 17–059—17–060
    training of staff, 17–045
    user operation manual, 17–046
  duties to third parties
    Consumer Protection Act 1987,
      under, 17–072—17–077
    economic loss, 17–070—17–071

INFORMATION TECHNOLOGY
PROFESSIONALS—*cont.*
duties to third parties—*cont.*
introduction, 17–061
personal injury, 17–062—17–066
property damage, 17–067—17–069
economic loss
contractual duties, and, 17–051
generally, 17–116—17–117
tortious duties, 17–070—17–071
exclusion of liability
introduction, 17–118
other party's standard terms,
17–119—17–120
reasonableness of term,
17–121—17–123
fitness for purpose
bespoke software, 17–014—17–022
communication by client of,
17–031—17–035
modified standard software,
17–023—17–030
implementation
common law duty, 17–051
generally, 17–036—17–037
installation, 17–047—17–050
introduction, 17–001
limitation, 17–131—17–132
mitigation of loss, 17–124—17–125
modification of software
common law duty, 17–051
generally, 17–023—17–030
nature of software, 17–005—17–006
negligent misstatements, 17–055
operation manual, 17–046
product liability
defences, 17–076—17–077
generally, 17–072—17–073
relevant product, 17–074—17–075
"safety-critical" information, 17–078
remedies for breach of duty
damages, 17–104—17–112
economic loss, 17–116—17–117
exclusion of liability,
17–118—17–123
introduction, 17–098
mitigation of loss, 17–124—17–125
repudiation, 17–099—17–103
restitution, 17–113—17–115
restriction of liability
introduction, 17–118
other party's standard terms,
17–119—17–120
reasonableness of term,
17–121—17–123
"safety-critical" information, 17–078

INFORMATION TECHNOLOGY
PROFESSIONALS—*cont.*
satisfactory quality
bespoke software, 17–014—17–022
modified standard software,
17–023—17–030
staff training
common law duty, 17–051
generally, 17–045
standard of care
bedding in, 17–085—17–089
bugs, 17–085—17–089
contract for services,
17–079—17–081
contract for sale/supply of goods,
17–082—17–094
fitness for purpose, 17–082—17–094
satisfactory quality, 17–082—17–094
"state of the art" defence, 17–094
support, 17–044
supply of software
bespoke, 17–004
goods, as, 17–007—17–009
implied warranties, 17–013
modified standard, 17–004
off-the-shelf, 17–002—17–003
services, as, 17–008—17–012
systems advice, 17–057—17–058
testing
common law duty, 17–051
generally, 17–036—17–037
"time-bombs", 17–059—17–060
training of staff
common law duty, 17–051
generally, 17–045
user operation manual, 17–046
writing of software
common law duty, 17–051
generally, 17–014—17–022
INFORMED CONSENT
consent to treatment, and,
12–130—12–134
INHUMAN TREATMENT, PROHIBITION
AGAINST
generally, 7–042
INJECTIONS
medical practitioners, and, 12–192
INJUNCTIONS
financial practitioners, and
contravenors, against, 13–141
generally, 13–144
grounds of application,
13–138—13–140
introduction, 13–137
knowingly concerned persons,
against, 13–142

INJUNCTIONS—*cont.*
  generally, 3–018
INJURY TO NEIGHBOUR
  duty of care, and, 2–022—2–023
INNOCENCE, PRESUMPTION OF
  human rights, and, 7–012
INSPECTION OF CONSTRUCTION WORKS
  clerk of works, role of, 8–246—8–247
  confidence in contractor, 8–244
  design and specification, and, 8–216
  intentional defects, 8–245
  introduction, 8–238—8–239
  scope of duty, 8–240—8–241
  stages of work, at, 8–242—8–243
  working methods, 8–248—8–251
INSTALLATION OF SOFTWARE
  IT professionals, and, 17–047—17–050
INSTRUCTIONS
  barristers, and, 11–002
INSTRUCTIONS TO FOREIGN AGENTS
  construction professionals, and,
    8–177—8–181
  patent agents, and, 18–019
  trade mark attorney, and, 18–019
INSUFFICIENT KNOWLEDGE OR EXPERIENCE
  surveyors, and, 9–079—9–081
INSURANCE
  construction professionals, and, 8–236
INSURANCE AGENTS
  meaning, 14–001
INSURANCE BROKERS
  causation
    intervening error or omission,
      14–089—14–096
    introduction, 14–088
    no insurance if facts been known,
      14–109—14–112
    not likely been insured in any event,
      14–097—14–108
  contractual duties
    introduction, 14–010—14–012
    sub-brokers, of, 14–013
  contributory negligence
    generally, 14–126—14–127
    insurers, 14–128
    lay clients, 14–129—14–130
    uninsured indemnity cover, and,
      14–131
  coverholders, and, 14–022—14–024
  damages
    causation, 14–088—14–112
    foreseeability, 14–113
    introduction, 14–086
    measure, 14–114—14–
    remoteness, 14–087—14–113

INSURANCE BROKERS—*cont.*
  date of cause of action, and,
    5–046—5–047
  duties
    client, to, 14–010—14–016
    third parties, to, 14–017—14–032
  duties to client
    contract, under , 14–010—14–013
    tort, in, 14–014—14–016
  duties to insurers
    coverholders, 14–022—14–024
    disclosure, of, 14–019
    introduction, 14–018
    misstatement concerning reinsurance,
      14–021
    signing indication, under, 14–020
  duties to third parties
    beneficiaries, 14–026
    financially interested persons,
      14–027—14–030
    insurers, 14–018—14–024
    introduction, 14–017
    misstatements, 14–031
    other parties, 14–025
    potential beneficiaries, 14–026
  effecting insurance on terms not agreed
    ambiguous instructions, 14–044
    introduction, 14–043
    lack of availability, 14–045
  effecting insurance on terms not meet
      requirements
    change of requirements, 14–056
    clarity of instructions, 14–054
    defective policy wording, 14–050
    enquiries by broker,
      14–051—14–053
    introduction, 14–046—14–049
    level of cover, 14–055
  expert evidence of duty of care,
    14–034
  failure to act with reasonable speed,
    14–059
  failure to disclose material facts
    advice to client of duty to disclose,
      14–064—14–065
    description of reinsurance risk,
      14–068
    enquiry of client, 14–066—14–067
    generally, 14–060—14–063
  failure to effect insurance
    existing cover, in respect of, 14–042
    generally, 14–038—14–041
  failure to exercise discretion
    reasonably, 14–057—14–058
  failure to give proper advice
    introduction, 14–081—14–082

INSURANCE BROKERS—*cont.*
 failure to give proper advice—*cont.*
  law, on, 14–083—14–085
 failure to keep client informed
  existence of cover, as to, 14–074
  renewal of cover, of need for,
   14–075—14–076
  terms of cover, of, 14–079—14–080
  uninsured, of becoming,
   14–077—14–078
 foreseeability, 14–113
 function, 14–002—14–003
 introduction, 14–001
 liability for breach of duty
  effecting insurance on terms not
   agreed, 14–043—14–045
  effecting insurance on terms not
   meet requirements,
   14–046—14–056
  failure to act with reasonable speed,
   14–059
  failure to disclose material facts,
   14–060—14–068
  failure to effect insurance,
   14–038—14–042
  failure to exercise discretion
   reasonably, 14–057—14–058
  failure to give proper advice,
   14–081—14–085
  failure to keep client informed,
   14–074—14–080
  introduction, 14–036—14–037
  misrepresentation to insurer,
   14–069—14–073
 Lloyd's brokers, and, 14–009
 meaning, 14–002
 measure of damages
  additional losses, 14–119
  credit for saved premium,
   14–124—14–125
  fines and costs, 14–123
  introduction, 14–114—14–116
  litigation costs, 14–122
  non-receipt of insurance proceeds,
   14–121
  settlement with insurers,
   14–117—14–118
  unreinsured losses, 14–120
 misrepresentation to insurer
  approval by client, 14–070—14–071
  completion of proposal,
   14–072—14–073
  introduction, 14–069
 misstatements
  reinsurance, as to, 14–021
  third parties, to, 14–031

INSURANCE BROKERS—*cont.*
 regulation
  FSMA 2000, under,
   14–006—14–008
  IB(R)A 1977, under,
   14–004—14–005
 remoteness
  causation, 14–088—14–112
  foreseeability, 14–113
  introduction, 14–087
 signing indication, and, 14–020
 standard of skill and care
  expert evidence, 14–034
  generally, 14–032
  legal knowledge, 14–035
  specialist markets, 14–033
 sub-brokers, role of, 14–013
 tort, duties in, 14–014—14–016
INSURANCE BROKERS REGISTRATION
  COUNCIL
 abolition, 14–005
 generally, 14–004
INTEGRATION OF DESIGN
 construction professionals, and, 8–217
INTENDED BENEFICIARIES
 duty of care, and, 2–114
INTEREST
 court rules, under, 3–023
 equity, in, 3–024
 statute, under
  discomfort claims, 3–021
  generally, 3–019
  inconvenience claims, 3–021
  nature of transaction, 3–022
  personal injury claims, 3–020
INTERVENING ACTS
 construction professionals, and
  claimant, by, 8–279
  third party, by, 8–277—8–278
 insurance brokers, and,
   14–089—14–096
 medical practitioners, and, 12–276
 solicitor, and
  claimant, by, 10–237
  third party, by, 10–238—10–239
INVESTIGATION, COSTS OF
 accountants, and, 15–140
INVESTIGATION OF DEFECTS
 construction professionals, and, 8–262
ISSUE OF INSTRUCTIONS
 construction professionals, and,
   8–229—8–232
ISSUE OF PROCEEDINGS BY SOLICITORS
 delay, 10–185
 generally, 10–176

JUDGMENT
  solicitors, and, 10–080
"JUST AND REASONABLE" TEST
  and see DUTY OF CARE
  analysis of problems, 2–076—2–078
  introduction, 2–035
JUSTIFIED USE OF INFORMATION
  disclosure in public interest, 2–160
  disclosure required by law, 2–161
  introduction, 2–159

KNOW YOUR CUSTOMER
  financial practitioners, and, 13–056
KNOWING ASSISTANCE
  solicitors, and, 10–038
KNOWING RECEIPTS
  solicitors, and, 10–037
KNOWLEDGE OF LAW
  construction professionals, and,
    8–162—8–164
  insurance brokers, and, 14–035
  patent agents, and, 18–016
  solicitors, and
    generally, 10–081—10–082
    wills, 10–222
  trade mark attorney, and, 18–016
KNOWLEDGE OF RELIANCE
  surveyors, and, 9–039—9–042

LACHES
  introduction, 5–098—5–102
  limitation, and, 5–108
  prejudice, 5–106—5–107
  unreasonable delay, 5–103—5–105
LACK OF AUTHORISATION
  financial promotion restriction, 13–072
  general prohibition, 13–071
  introduction, 13–070
LACK OF TIME
  solicitors, and, 10–097
LATENT DAMAGE
  construction professionals, and, 8–054
  date of knowledge, 5–054—5–055
  15-year long stop, 5–051
  generally, 5–049—5–050
  introduction, 5–011
  negligence, 5–053
  successive owners of property, 5–052
LAW, KNOWLEDGE OF THE
  construction professionals, and,
    8–162—8–164
  insurance brokers, and, 14–035
  patent agents, and, 18–016

LAW, KNOWLEDGE OF THE—cont.
  solicitors, and
    generally, 10–081—10–082
    wills, 10–222
  trade mark attorney, and, 18–016
LAWYERS
  barristers
    and see BARRISTERS
    abuse of process, 11–025
    damages for breach,
      11–052—11–055
    duties to client, 11–004—11–005
    duties to third parties,
      11–006—11–007
    function, 11–001
    immunity to suit, 11–009—11–024
    inadequate professional service,
      11–003
    instructions, 11–002
    liability for breach of duty,
      11–036—11–051
    liability for costs, 11–026—11–035
    standard of skill and care, 11–008
  human rights, and
    confidentiality of communications,
      7–033—7–035
    introduction, 7–031
    wasted costs orders, 7–032
  immunity from suit, and
    generally, 2–097
    human rights, and, 7–030
  solicitors
    and see SOLICITORS
    apportionment of liability,
      10–323—10–332
    damages, 10–225—10–322
    defences to claim for breach,
      10–106—10–124
    duties to client, 10–004—10–039
    duties to third parties,
      10–040—10–076
    exclusion of liability, 10–141
    function, 10–001—10–002
    liability for breach of duty,
      10–146—10–224
    liability for costs, 10–125—10–140
    practice and procedure,
      10–142—10–145
    regulation, 10–003
    standard of skill and care,
      10–077—10–105
LEGAL AID
  wasted costs order, and, 10–138
LEGAL DOCUMENTS, EXPLANATION OF
  solicitors, and, 10–166—10–167

LEGAL SERVICES OMBUDSMAN
complaints against barristers, and,
11–003
LIABILITY
contractual
and see CONTRACTUAL LIABILITY
generally, 2–007—2–012
exclusion of
and see EXCLUSION OF LIABILITY
introduction, 5–001—5–002
statutory framework, 5–003—5–006
third parties, to, 5–007—5–009
professional
and see PROFESSIONAL LIABILITY
positive duties, 2–001—2–004
restrictions and inhibitions,
2–005—2–006
restriction of
and see RESTRICTION OF LIABILITY
introduction, 5–001—5–002
statutory framework, 5–003—5–006
third parties, to, 5–007—5–009
surveyors, and
basis, 9–007—9–018
breach of duty, for, 9–075
individuals, of, 9–014
third parties, to
background, 2–110
intended beneficiaries, 2–114
introduction, 2–109
persons under duty, 2–111
third parties entitled to benefit,
2–112
transactions subject to duty, 2–113
tortious
and see TORTIOUS LIABILITY
duty of care, 2–022—2–078
generally, 2–013—2–021
particular situations, 2–079—2–115
LIABILITY FOR BREACH OF DUTY
accountants, and
and see below
auditing, 15–102—15–116
business advice, 15–119
tax advice, 15–119
tax returns, 15–118
valuation, 15–117
barristers, and
and see below
clarity of advice, 11–047
errors of judgment, 11–038—11–045
failure of advice, 11–046—11–048
failure to obtain full instructions,
11–049
introduction, 11–036
knowledge of law, 11–037

LIABILITY FOR BREACH OF DUTY—*cont.*
barristers, and—*cont.*
mistakes, 11–038—11–045
mistakes in court, 11–051
pleading weak points, 11–050
construction professionals, and
and see below
administration of contract,
8–228—8–237
bills of quantities, 8–221
certification, 8–252—8–258
choice of contract, 8–225—8–227
compliance with legal requirements,
8–200—8–202
costs estimates, 8–193—8–199
design and specification,
8–203—8–220
inspection of works, 8–238—8–251
introduction, 8–182
investigation of defects, 8–262
selection of contractor,
8–222—8–224
site examination, 8–183—8–184
specialist survey, 8–259—8–261
supervision of works, 8–238—8–251
tender process, 8–222—8–224
financial practitioners, and
advising and selling,
13–121—13–125
dealing and managing,
13–126—13–130
failure properly to classify customer,
13–120
introduction, 13–117
misleading promotion,
13–118—13–119
insurance brokers, and
and see below
effecting insurance on terms not
agreed, 14–043—14–045
effecting insurance on terms not
meet requirements,
14–046—14–056
failure to act with reasonable speed,
14–059
failure to disclose material facts,
14–060—14–068
failure to effect insurance,
14–038—14–042
failure to exercise discretion
reasonably, 14–057—14–058
failure to give proper advice,
14–081—14–085
failure to keep client informed,
14–074—14–080
introduction, 14–036—14–037

LIABILITY FOR BREACH OF DUTY—*cont.*
insurance brokers, and—*cont.*
misrepresentation to insurer,
14–069—14–073
Lloyd's agents, and
and see below
failure to advise adequately on
syndicate participation,
16–025—16–029
failure to obtain adequate
reinsurance, 16–038—16–052
failure to plan properly,
16–030—16–036
inadequate supervision of active
underwriter, 16–057
introduction, 16–023—16–024
negligent reinsurance to close,
16–058—16–059
negligent underwriting of risks,
16–053—16–056
unjustified departure from plan,
16–037
medical practitioners, and
and see below
error in course of treatment,
12–186—12–196
failure to attend patient,
12–172—12–176
failure to communicate,
12–197—12–200
failure to examine patient,
12–172—12–176
failure to explain treatment,
12–201—12–232
failure to prevent illness,
12–169—12–171
failure to warn of risks,
12–201—12–232
introduction, 12–167—12–168
mishandling mentally disturbed
patients, 12–233—12–240
wrong diagnosis, 12–177—12–185
patent agents, and
business advice, 18–018
generally, 18–015
giving of advice, 18–018
instruction of foreign agents, 18–019
knowledge of law, 18–016
taking instructions, 18–017
solicitors, and
and see below
classification of breaches, 10–149
delegation, and, 10–148
failure to give advice,
10–154—10–174
generally, 10–146—10–147

LIABILITY FOR BREACH OF DUTY—*cont.*
solicitors, and—*cont.*
giving wrong advice,
10–151—10–153
misconduct of litigation,
10–175—10–191
misconduct of non-contentious
business, 10–192—10–224
surveyors, and
and see below
failure to carry out instructions,
9–077—9–078
failure to inspect properly,
9–082—9–098
failure to make proper appraisal,
9–104—9–106
failure to make sufficient inquiries,
9–100—9–103
failure to recognise, 9–099
inadequate report, 9–107—9–109
insufficient knowledge or experience,
9–079—9–081
introduction, 9–075—9–076
trade mark attorney, and
business advice, 18–018
generally, 18–015
giving of advice, 18–018
instruction of foreign agents, 18–019
knowledge of law, 18–016
taking instructions, 18–017
LIABILITY FOR BREACH OF DUTY
(ACCOUNTANTS)
auditing
evidence, 15–108—15–112
internal control systems,
15–106—15–107
introduction, 15–102
planning, 15–103—15–105
reporting, 15–113—15–116
business advice, 15–119
tax advice, 15–119
tax returns, 15–118
valuation, 15–117
LIABILITY FOR BREACH OF DUTY
(BARRISTERS)
clarity of advice, 11–047
errors of judgment
examples, 11–041—11–042
existence of error, 11–038
introduction, 11–039
nature of error, 11–040
settlement advice, 11–043—11–045
failure of advice
clarity, 11–047
generally, 11–046
when not so instructed, 11–048

LIABILITY FOR BREACH OF DUTY
(BARRISTERS)—*cont.*
failure of advice—*cont.*
failure to obtain full instructions,
11–049
failure to obtain full instructions,
11–049
introduction, 11–036
knowledge of law, 11–037
mistakes
examples, 11–041—11–042
existence of error, 11–038
introduction, 11–039
nature of error, 11–040
settlement advice, 11–043—11–045
mistakes in court, 11–051
pleading weak points, 11–050
mistakes in court, 11–051
pleading weak points, 11–050
LIABILITY FOR BREACH OF DUTY
(CONSTRUCTION PROFESSIONALS)
additional payments, 8–233—8–235
administration of contract
additional payments, 8–233—8–235
extensions of time, 8–233—8–235
insurance, 8–236
introduction, 8–228
issue of instructions, 8–229—8–232
notice of non-performance, 8–237
performance bonds, 8–236
approval of design, 8–204—8–205
bills of quantities, preparation of,
8–221
budgets, 8–193—8–199
buildability, 8–216
certification procedure
contractor's duty, 8–258
duty to client, 8–253
final certificates, 8–255
interim certificates, 8–254
introduction, 8–252
other certificates, 8–256—8–257
practical completion, 8–256
choice of contract, advice on,
8–225—8–227
choice of materials, 8–215
compliance with legal requirements,
8–200—8–202
contractor, selection of, 8–222—8–224
co-ordination of design, 8–218
costs estimates, 8–193—8–199
design and specification
approvals, 8–204—8–205
buildability, 8–216
change instructed by client, 8–219
choice of materials, 8–215

LIABILITY FOR BREACH OF DUTY
(CONSTRUCTION
PROFESSIONALS)—*cont.*
design and specification—*cont.*
compliance with brief, 8–206
co-ordination of design, 8–218
generally, 8–203
integration of design , 8–217
level of detail, 8–214
novel design, 8–207—8–209
over-design, 8–220
published standards, 8–213
risk assessment, 8–210—8–212
supervisability, 8–216
examination of site
effect of proposed works, 8–191
generally, 8–183
ground investigations, 8–185—8–189
measurement, 8–184
non-physical restraints, 8–192
extensions of time, 8–233—8–235
ground investigations, 8–185—8–189
inspection of works
clerk of works, role of,
8–246—8–247
confidence in contractor, 8–244
design and specification, and, 8–216
intentional defects, 8–245
introduction, 8–238—8–239
scope of duty, 8–240—8–241
stages of work, at, 8–242—8–243
working methods, 8–248—8–251
insurance, 8–236
integration of design , 8–217
introduction, 8–182
investigation of defects, 8–262
issue of instructions, 8–229—8–232
notice of non-performance, 8–237
novel design, 8–207—8–209
over-design, 8–220
performance bonds, 8–236
planning requirements, 8–200—8–202
practical completion, 8–256
risk assessment, 8–210—8–212
selection of contractor, 8–222—8–224
site examination
effect of proposed works, 8–191
generally, 8–183
ground investigations, 8–185—8–189
measurement, 8–184
non-physical restraints, 8–192
specialist survey, 8–259—8–261
specification and design
approvals, 8–204—8–205
buildability, 8–216
change instructed by client, 8–219

LIABILITY FOR BREACH OF DUTY
(CONSTRUCTION
PROFESSIONALS)—cont.
specification and design—cont.
choice of materials, 8–215
compliance with brief, 8–206
co-ordination of design, 8–218
generally, 8–203
integration of design , 8–217
level of detail, 8–214
novel design, 8–207—8–209
over-design, 8–220
published standards, 8–213
risk assessment, 8–210—8–212
supervisability, 8–216
supervision of works
clerk of works, role of,
8–246—8–247
confidence in contractor, 8–244
design and specification, 8–216
intentional defects, 8–245
introduction, 8–238—8–239
scope of duty, 8–240—8–241
stages of work, at, 8–242—8–243
working methods, 8–248—8–251
tender process, 8–222—8–224
terms of contract, advice on,
8–225—8–227
LIABILITY FOR BREACH OF DUTY
(INSURANCE BROKER)
effecting insurance on terms not agreed
ambiguous instructions, 14–044
introduction, 14–043
lack of availability, 14–045
effecting insurance on terms not meet
requirements
change of requirements, 14–056
clarity of instructions, 14–054
defective policy wording, 14–050
enquiries by broker,
14–051—14–053
introduction, 14–046—14–049
level of cover, 14–055
failure to act with reasonable speed,
14–059
failure to disclose material facts
advice to client of duty to disclose,
14–064—14–065
description of reinsurance risk,
14–068
enquiry of client, 14–066—14–067
generally, 14–060—14–063
failure to effect insurance
existing cover, in respect of, 14–042
generally, 14–038—14–041

LIABILITY FOR BREACH OF DUTY
(INSURANCE BROKER)—cont.
failure to exercise discretion
reasonably, 14–057—14–058
failure to give proper advice
introduction, 14–081—14–082
law, on, 14–083—14–085
failure to keep client informed
existence of cover, as to, 14–074
renewal of cover, of need for,
14–075—14–076
terms of cover, of, 14–079—14–080
uninsured, of becoming,
14–077—14–078
introduction, 14–036—14–037
misrepresentation to insurer
approval by client, 14–070—14–071
completion of proposal,
14–072—14–073
introduction, 14–069
LIABILITY FOR BREACH OF DUTY (LLOYD'S
AGENTS)
failure to advise adequately on
syndicate participation,
16–025—16–029
failure to obtain adequate reinsurance
amount of reinsurance sought,
16–039—16–045
choice of reinsurer, 16–046—16–049
commercial viability,
16–050—16–051
introduction, 16–038
validity of reinsurance, 16–052
failure to plan properly,
16–030—16–036
inadequate supervision of active
underwriter, 16–057
introduction, 16–023—16–024
negligent reinsurance to close,
16–058—16–059
negligent underwriting of risks,
16–053—16–056
unjustified departure from plan, 16–037
LIABILITY FOR BREACH OF DUTY (MEDICAL
PRACTITIONERS)
error in course of treatment
adverse reaction to treatment,
12–191
failure to remove objects, 12–194
generally, 12–186—12–196
injections, 12–192
operations, 12–193
over-intervention, 12–196
post-operative care, 12–195
right procedure, 12–188
right treatment, 12–187

LIABILITY FOR BREACH OF DUTY (MEDICAL
    PRACTITIONERS)—*cont.*
  failure to arrange follow-up, 12–176
  failure to attend patient
    GP, 12–174—12–175
    hospital doctors, 12–173
    introduction, 12–172
  failure to communicate,
      12–197—12–200
  failure to diagnose
    generally, 12–177—12–184
    more serious condition, 12–185
  failure to examine patient
    GP, 12–174—12–175
    hospital doctors, 12–173
    introduction, 12–172
  failure to explain treatment
    answering patient's questions,
        12–218—12–221
    Australian law, 12–205—12–207
    blood products, 12–226
    Canadian law, 12–202—12–204
    curtailment by reason of patient's
        condition, 12–215—12–217
    disability of unborn baby, 12–231
    English law, 12–208—12–214
    evidence, and, 12–232
    general principle, 12–201
    manner of communication,
        12–223—12–224
    side effects of drugs, 12–225
    sterilisation, 12–227—12–230
    warning for patient's protection,
        12–222
  failure to prevent illness
    introduction, 12–169
    spread of infectious disease,
        12–170—12–171
  failure to warn of risks,
      12–201—12–232
  introduction, 12–167—12–168
  mishandling mentally disturbed patients
    Code of Practice, 12–234
    generally, 12–233
    issue of certificates,
        12–239—12–240
    self-inflicted injury, 12–236—12–237
    statutory restrictions, 12–235
    suicide, 12–236—12–237
  wrong diagnosis
    generally, 12–177—12–184
    more serious condition, 12–185
LIABILITY FOR BREACH OF DUTY
    (SOLICITORS)
  classification of breaches, 10–149
  delegation, and, 10–148

LIABILITY FOR BREACH OF DUTY
    (SOLICITORS)—*cont.*
  failure to explain legal documents,
      10–166—10–167
  failure to give advice
    attendance notes, and, 10–174
    confirmatory letters, and, 10–174
    costs information, as to, 10–157
    general business matters, as to,
        10–169—10–172
    introduction, 10–154
    legal documents, on,
        10–166—10–167
    matters coming to notice, as to,
        10–158—10–159
    matters not asked to advise upon, as
        to, 10–160—10–163
    obvious risks, as to, 10–165
    progress of matter, as to, 10–156
    recipient of advice, 10–155
    reminder of advice, and, 10–168
    solicitor's own negligence, as to,
        10–164
    unequal transactions, in, 10–173
  generally, 10–146—10–147
  giving wrong advice
    law, 10–151—10–152
    practical issues, 10–153
  misconduct of conveyancing
    enquiries before contract, 10–201
    handing over purchase monies,
        10–200
    matters coming to notice, 10–199
    National protocol, 10–204
    non-registration of interests, 10–198
    remote contingencies, 10–197
    searches, 10–193—10–194
    standard of care, 10–196
    suspicious circumstances, 10–195
    time limits, 10–202
    undue influence, 10–205
    width of duty, 10–203
  misconduct of litigation
    advice on appeal, 10–184
    ceasing to act, 10–191
    delay, 10–185—10–188
    evidence, 10–180—10–182
    hearing, at, 10–183
    introduction, 10–175
    issuing proceedings, 10–176
    pursuit of obvious remedy, 10–178
    pursuit of unmeritorious claims,
        10–179
    settlements, 10–189—10–190
    statements of case, 10–177

LIABILITY FOR BREACH OF DUTY
(SOLICITORS)—*cont.*
misconduct of non-contentious business
conveyancing, 10–193—10–205
introduction, 10–192
mortgage lenders, claims by,
10–206—10–217
wills, 10–218—10–224
mortgage lenders, claims by
background, 10–207
borrower's financial status,
10–211—10–212
Bowerman duty, 10–208—10–210
clarity of communications, 10–216
confidential information, 10–217
contributory negligence,
10–325—10–327
direct payments of price,
10–213—10–214
introduction, 10–206
other matters, 10–215
trusts, and, 10–035
wills, preparation of
attestation, 10–222
giving advice, 10–220
introduction, 10–218
knowledge of law, 10–222
other errors, 10–224
prompt actions, 10–223
scope of duty, 10–221
taking instructions, 10–219
LIABILITY FOR BREACH OF DUTY
(SURVEYORS)
failure to carry out instructions,
9–077—9–078
failure to inspect properly
introduction, 9–082
limited survey, 9–097
observation, 9–090—9–096
particular parts, 9–083
relevance of type of survey,
9–097—9–09
uncovering and opening up,
9–084—9–089
failure to make proper appraisal,
9–104—9–106
failure to make sufficient inquiries
generally, 9–100—9–101
hearsay information, 9–102—9–103
failure to observe
camouflaged defects, 9–095
cracks, 9–093—9–094
dry rot, 9–091
introduction, 9–090
roof, 9–092
subsidence, 9–093—9–094

LIABILITY FOR BREACH OF DUTY
(SURVEYORS)—*cont.*
failure to observe—*cont.*
totality of unnoticed defects, 9–096
woodworm, 9–091
failure to open up, 9–084—9–089
failure to recognise defect, 9–099
failure to uncover, 9–084—9–089
failure to warn of defect,
9–108—9–109
inadequate report
failure to warn of defect,
9–108—9–109
generally, 9–107
insufficient knowledge or experience,
9–079—9–081
introduction, 9–075—9–076
LIABILITY FOR COSTS
and see WASTED COSTS ORDER
barristers, and
guidelines, 11–027
introduction, 11–026
misjudgements, 11–029—11–030
procedure, 11–028
patent agents, and, 18–013
solicitors
abuse of process, 10–137
background, 10–126
causation, 10–134
guidelines, 10–129
hopeless litigation, 10–135—10–136
improper, unreasonable or negligent,
10–130
introduction, 10–125
lawyer's position, 10–131
legal aid, and, 10–138
other errors, 10–140
present rule, 10–127
practice and procedure,
10–132—10–133
procedural errors, 10–139
recipient, 10–128
trade mark attorney, and, 18–013
LIABILITY TO THIRD PARTIES
background, 2–110
exclusion of liability, and
comment, 5–009
introduction, 5–007
mortgage applications, in, 5–008
intended beneficiaries, 2–114
introduction, 2–109
persons under duty, 2–111
third parties entitled to benefit, 2–112
transactions subject to duty, 2–113
LICENSED CONVEYANCERS
generally, 10–002

LIFE, RIGHT TO
clinical negligence, and, 7–026
introduction, 7–018
medical practitioners, 7–039—7–041
police, actions against, 7–026
LIKIERMAN REPORT (1989)
restriction of liability, and, 5–002
LIMITATION
contract, in
and see below
concealment, 5–070—5–078
date of cause of action,
5–014—5–015
fraud, 5–070—5–078
latent damage, and, 5–049—5–055
period of limitation, 5–010—5–013
personal injuries and death,
5–056—5–069
equity, in
and see below
analogous application of statute,
5–089—5–095
express application of statute,
5–082—5–088
introduction, 5–079—5–081
no limitation, 5–096—5–097
human rights-related claims, and,
7–027
IT professionals, and, 17–131—17–132
surveyors, and
generally, 9–009
misdescription of property, 9–013
tort, in
and see below
concealment, 5–070—5–078
date of cause of action,
5–016—5–048
fraud, 5–070—5–078
latent damage, and, 5–049—5–055
period of limitation, 5–010—5–013
personal injuries and death,
5–056—5–069
LIMITATION IN CONTRACT
concealment
date when time restarts,
5–073—5–074
deliberate commission of breach,
5–075—5–076
effect of concealment after breach,
5–071
generally, 5–070
relevant facts, 5–072
unlikely to be discovered, 5–078
date of cause of action, 5–014—5–015
date of knowledge
death, 5–063

LIMITATION IN CONTRACT—*cont.*
date of knowledge—*cont.*
latent damage, 5–054—5–055
personal injuries, 5–056—5–062
death
discretionary exclusion of time limit,
5–064—5–069
primary limitation period, 5–063
introduction, 5–012
fraud
date when time restarts,
5–073—5–074
deliberate commission of breach,
5–075—5–076
generally, 5–070
relevant facts, 5–072
subsequent decisions, 5–077
unlikely to be discovered, 5–078
latent damage, and
date of knowledge, 5–054—5–055
15-year long stop, 5–051
generally, 5–049—5–050
introduction, 5–011
negligence, 5–053
successive owners of property,
5–052
period of limitation
characterisation of claim, 5–013
generally, 5–010
latent damage, 5–011
personal injuries and death, 5–012
personal injuries
discretionary exclusion of time limit,
5–064—5–069
primary limitation period,
5–056—5–062
introduction, 5–012
persons under disability, 5–010
primary limitation period
death, 5–063
generally, 5–010
personal injuries, 5–056—5–062
LIMITATION IN EQUITY
analogous application of statute,
5–089—5–095
express application of statute,
5–082—5–088
introduction, 5–079—5–081
no limitation, 5–096—5–097
obedience to statute, 5–081
LIMITATION IN TORT
architects, claims against
Bank of East Asia, 5–028—5–029
date of damage, 5–030—5–033
degree of damage, 5–022
"doomed from start", 5–020—5–021

LIMITATION IN TORT—*cont.*
architects, claims against—*cont.*
Murphy, 5–024—5–027
Pirelli, 5–017—5–019
successive owners, 5–023
uncertainty, 5–034
concealment
date when time restarts,
5–073—5–074
deliberate commission of breach,
5–075—5–076
effect of concealment after breach,
5–071
generally, 5–070
relevant facts, 5–072
unlikely to be discovered, 5–078
construction professionals, and, 8–054
date of cause of action
architects, against, 5–017—5–034
engineers, against, 5–017—5–034
financial advisers, against, 5–048
insurance brokers, against,
5–046—5–047
introduction, 5–016
solicitors, against, 5–037—5–045
surveyors, against, 5–035—5–036
date of knowledge
death, 5–063
latent damage, 5–054—5–055
personal injuries, 5–056—5–062
death
discretionary exclusion of time limit,
5–064—5–069
primary limitation period, 5–063
introduction, 5–012
engineers, claims against
Bank of East Asia, 5–028—5–029
date of damage, 5–030—5–033
degree of damage, 5–022
"doomed from start", 5–020—5–021
Murphy, 5–024—5–027
Pirelli, 5–017—5–019
successive owners, 5–023
uncertainty, 5–034
financial advisers, claims against,
5–048
fraud
date when time restarts,
5–073—5–074
deliberate commission of breach,
5–075—5–076
generally, 5–070
relevant facts, 5–072
subsequent decisions, 5–077
unlikely to be discovered, 5–078

LIMITATION IN TORT—*cont.*
insurance brokers, claims against,
5–046—5–047
latent damage, and
date of knowledge, 5–054—5–055
15-year long stop, 5–051
generally, 5–049—5–050
introduction, 5–011
negligence, 5–053
successive owners of property,
5–052
period of limitation
characterisation of claim, 5–013
generally, 5–010
latent damage, 5–011
personal injuries and death, 5–012
personal injuries
discretionary exclusion of time limit,
5–064—5–069
primary limitation period,
5–056—5–062
introduction, 5–012
persons under disability, 5–010
primary limitation period
death, 5–063
generally, 5–010
personal injuries, 5–056—5–062
solicitors, claims against
action dismissed for want of
prosecution, 5–043
client acquires less valuable rights,
5–040—5–042
client incurs obligation,
5–037—5–039
omissions capable of remedy, 5–045
purchase of property, 5–044
surveyors, claims against
mortgagees, by, 5–036
purchasers, by, 5–035
LIMITATION OF LIABILITY
accountants, and, 15–100—15–101
construction professionals, and
conditions of engagement,
8–021—8–025
financial practitioners, and,
13–133—13–134
incorporation of clause, 5–006
introduction, 5–001—5–002
IT professionals, and
introduction, 17–118
other party's standard terms,
17–119—17–120
reasonableness of term,
17–121—17–123
solicitors, and, 10–141

LIMITATION OF LIABILITY—*cont.*
  statutory framework
    UCTA 1977, 5–003—5–004
    UTCCR 1999, 5–005
  surveyors, and
    commercial property, 9–071
    conditions of engagement,
      9–027—9–028
    definition of extent of service, and,
      9–073
    introduction, 9–063
    residential property, 9–064—9–070
    Scotland, in, 9–072
  third parties, to
    comment, 5–009
    introduction, 5–007
    mortgage applications, in, 5–008
LIMITED LIABILITY COMPANIES
  duty of care, and
    Canadian case law, 2–089—2–090
    introduction, 2–088
LINE OF REASONING
  duty of care, and, 2–019—2–020
LISTING OF SECURITIES
  introduction, 13–080
  misleading particulars, 13–081
  prospectus requirements, 13–082
LISTING PARTICULARS
  surveyors, and, 9–015
LITIGATION COSTS
  insurance brokers, and, 14–122
LLOYD'S BROKERS
  and see INSURANCE BROKERS
  generally, 14–009
LLOYD'S MEMBERS' AND MANAGING
    AGENTS
  causation
    failure to advise on participation,
      16–063—16–066
    introduction, 16–062
    negligent underwriting,
      16–067—16–070
  contractual duties, 16–010—16–011
  damages for breach
    causation, 16–062—16–070
    foreseeability, 16–071
    introduction, 16–060
    measure, 16–072—16–082
    remoteness, 16–061—16–0
  duties
    client, to, 16–010—16–015
    third parties, to, 16–016—16–019
  duties to client
    contract, under, 16–010—16–011
    fiduciary, 16–015
    tort, in, 16–012—16–014

LLOYD'S MEMBERS' AND MANAGING
    AGENTS—*cont.*
  duties to third parties, 16–016—16–019
  failure to advise on participation
    causation, 16–063—16–066
    generally, 16–025—16–029
    measure of damages,
      16–073—16–076
  failure to obtain adequate reinsurance
    amount of reinsurance sought,
      16–039—16–045
    choice of reinsurer, 16–046—16–049
    commercial viability,
      16–050—16–051
    introduction, 16–038
    validity of reinsurance, 16–052
  failure to plan properly,
    16–030—16–03671
  foreseeability, 16–071
  inadequate supervision of active
    underwriter, 16–057
  fiduciary duties, 16–015
  inadequate supervision of active
    underwriter, 16–057
  introduction, 16–001—16–003
  liability between agents and names
    current regime, 16–006
    old regime, 16–004—16–005
  liability for breach of duty
    failure to advise adequately on
      syndicate participation,
      16–025—16–029
    failure to obtain adequate
      reinsurance, 16–038—16–052
    failure to plan properly,
      16–030—16–036
    inadequate supervision of active
      underwriter, 16–057
    introduction, 16–023—16–024
    negligent reinsurance to close,
      16–058—16–059
    negligent underwriting of risks,
      16–053—16–056
    unjustified departure from plan,
      16–037
  LMX spiral, 16–009
  measure of damages
    failure to advise on participation,
      16–073—16–076
    introduction, 16–072
    negligent underwriting,
      16–077—16–082
  negligent reinsurance to close,
    16–058—16–059
  negligent underwriting of risks
    causation, 16–067—16–070

LLOYD'S MEMBERS' AND MANAGING
    AGENTS—*cont.*
  negligent underwriting of risks—*cont.*
    generally, 16–053—16–056
    measure of damages,
        16–077—16–082
  regulation, 16–007—16–008
  reinsurance to close
    duties to third parties,
        16–016—16–019
    negligence, 16–058—16–059
  remoteness
    causation, 16–062—16–070
    introduction, 16–061
    foreseeability, 16–071
  run-off contracts, 16–053—16–056
  standard of care, 16–020—16–022
  tort, duties in, 16–012—16–014
  unjustified departure from plan, 16–037
LOCAL AUTHORITIES, DUTY OF CARE BY
  breach of common law duty,
      2–083—2–086
  breach of statutory duty, 2–082
  careless performance of public duty,
      2–081
  classification of claims, 2–080
  introduction, 2–079
LOSS OF A CHANCE
  accountants, and
    generally, 15–087
    measure of damages,
        15–133—15–134
  construction professionals, and,
      8–287—8–288
  medical practitioners, and
    Australian law, 12–261
    Canadian law, 12–259—12–260
    introduction, 12–251—12–258
  patent agents, and, 18–030—18–021
  trade mark attorney, and,
      18–030—18–021
LOSS OF AMENITY
  construction professionals, and, 8–312
  medical practitioners, and,
      12–299—12–300
LOSS OF BUSINESS PROFITS
  heads of damage, and, 10–274
LOSS OF EARNINGS
  heads of damage, and, 10–298
LOSS OF LIFE POLICY
  heads of damage, and, 10–299
LOSS OF OPPORTUNITY
  acquire interest in property, to
    agricultural tenancies, 10–266
    business tenancies, 10–265
    evaluation difficulties, 10–267

LOSS OF OPPORTUNITY—*cont.*
  acquire interest in property, to—*cont.*
    generally, 10–264
  bring proceedings, to
    Commonwealth cases, 10–278
    costs risk, 10–285
    deduction of benefits, 10–290
    enforcement proceedings, and,
        10–292
    examples, 10–279—10–281
    extent of claim, 10–282
    generally, 10–277
    interest after trial, 10–289
    legal aid, 10–284
    means of defendant, 10–286
    notional date of trial,
        10–287—10–288
    risks of litigation , 10–283
    want of prosecution, and, 10–291
  defend proceedings, to, 10–293
LOSS OF USE OF PROPERTY
  heads of damage, and, 10–271
LOSS ON SALE OF LAND
  heads of damage, and, 10–297
LOSS ON SECURED LOANS
  dishonest borrowers, 10–296
  generally, 10–294—10–295
LOST ADVANCE
  accountants, and, 15–136
LOST INVESTMENT
  accountants, and, 15–136

MANAGEMENT CONTRACTS
  construction works, and, 8–018
MARKET VALUE
  surveyors, and, 9–023
MARRY, RIGHT TO
  generally, 7–046
MATTERS COMING TO NOTICE
  solicitors, and, 10–158—10–159
MATTERS NOT ASKED TO ADVISE UPON,
    ADVICE ON
  generally, 10–160—10–161
  statements of principle,
      10–162—10–163
MEASURE OF DAMAGES
  accountants, and
    introduction, 15–132
    loss of a chance, 15–133—15–134
  barristers, and, 11–054—11–055
  construction professionals, and
    introduction, 8–285—8–286
    loss of a chance, 8–287—8–288
  financial practitioners, and
    benefits received, 13–162—13–165

MEASURE OF DAMAGES—*cont.*
  financial practitioners, and—*cont.*
    introduction, 13–161
  Lloyd's agents, and
    failure to advise on participation,
      16–073—16–076
    introduction, 16–072
    negligent underwriting,
      16–077—16–082
  medical practitioners, and
    and see below
    aggravated damages, 12–288
    personal injury, 12–287
    wrongful birth claims,
      12–289—12–305
  solicitors, and
    and see below
    credit for benefits, 10–252—10–255
    date of assessment, 10–250—10–251
    evaluation of a chance,
      10–256—10–262
    introduction, 10–249
  surveyors, and
    and see below
    discomfort, 9–181—9–189
    incidental expenses, 9–190—9–194
    inconvenient, 9–181—9–189
    introduction, 9–128—9–129
    negligent survey for lender,
      9–150—9–174
    negligent survey for purchaser who
      completes, 9–130—9–148
    negligent survey for purchaser who
      withdraws, 9–149
    overvaluation for vendor, 9–175
    rent review, 9–179—9–180
    undervaluation for vendor,
      9–176—9–177
    warranty of valuation, 9–178
MEASURE OF DAMAGES (MEDICAL
  PRACTITIONERS)
  aggravated damages, 12–288
  personal injury, 12–287
  unwanted, disabled child
    claims by, 12–302
  unwanted pregnancy
    unwanted, disabled child,
      12–292—12–294
    unwanted, healthy child,
      12–289—12–291
  wanted pregnancy
    unwanted, disabled child,
      12–296—12–298
  wrongful birth claims
    economic loss, 12–303—12–305
    human rights, 12–301

MEASURE OF DAMAGES (MEDICAL
  PRACTITIONERS)—*cont.*
  wrongful birth claims—*cont.*
    loss of amenity, 12–299—12–300
    unwanted pregnancy,
      12–289—12–294
    wanted pregnancy, 12–296—12–298
MEASURE OF DAMAGES (SOLICITORS)
  credit for benefits
    examples, 10–253—10–254
    general principle, 10–252
    incidental benefits, 10–255
  date of assessment
    exception to general rule, 10–251
    general rule, 10–250
  evaluation of a chance
    burden of proof, 10–262
    Commonwealth cases, 10–261
    examples, 10–259
    generally, 10–256
    likely act of claimant, 10–257
    likely act of third party, 10–258
    limits of principle, 10–260
    introduction, 10–249
MEASURE OF DAMAGES (SURVEYORS)
  discomfort, damages for
    examples, 9–189
    generally, 9–181—9–185
    injury to health, 9–186—9–187
    quantum, 9–188
  incidental expenses, 9–190—9–194
  inconvenience, damages for
    examples, 9–189
    generally, 9–181—9–185
    injury to health, 9–186—9–187
    quantum, 9–188
  introduction, 9–128—9–129
  negligent survey for lender
    assessment of total loss,
      9–151—9–154
    "cap" theory, 9–159—9–160
    contribution from defaulting
      borrower, 9–173
    contributory negligence,
      9–166—9–172
    interest on damages, 9–162
    introduction, 9–150
    joint responsibility, 9–173—9–174
    loss within scope of duty,
      9–155—9–161
    "measurable, relevant loss", 9–161
    mortgagor's covenants to repay,
      9–163—9–165
    "no transaction/successful
      transaction" cases,
      9–157—9–158

MEASURE OF DAMAGES
(SURVEYORS)—*cont.*
negligent survey for purchaser who
completes
collateral benefits, 9–148
cost of repairs, 9–141—9–145
extraction costs, 9–146—9–147
formulation of measure,
9–135—9–137
generally, 9–130—9–134
nature of loss, 9–138—9–139
other decisions, 9–140
repair cost, 9–141—9–145
negligent survey for purchaser who
withdraws, 9–149
overvaluation for vendor, 9–175
remoteness of damage
causation, 9–120—9–124
foreseeability, 9–125—9–127
introduction, 9–119
rent review, 9–179—9–180
undervaluation for vendor,
9–176—9–177
warranty of valuation, 9–178
MEDICAL CARE, RIGHT TO
allocation of resources, 7–051—7–052
blanket bans, 7–053
hospital waiting lists, 7–054
introduction, 7–050
MEDICAL INFORMATION, ACCESS TO
disclosure, 7–061
introduction, 7–060
records, 7–062—7–063
MEDICAL NEGLIGENCE ACTIONS
date of knowledge, and, 5–058—5–062
expectation, and, 2–003
MEDICAL PRACTITIONERS
apportionment of liability
hospital authorities and doctors,
12–164
practitioners and pharmacists,
12–165
causation
contributory negligence, 12–276
failure to procure treatment,
12–271—12–273
inadequate advice concerning unborn
baby, 12–277—12–281
inadequate warning of treatment,
12–262—12–270
intervening conduct, 12–276
introduction, 12–243—12–250
loss of a chance, 12–251—12–261
novus actus interveniens,
12–274—12–275

MEDICAL PRACTITIONERS—*cont.*
common law duty
communication of distressing
information, 12–022—12–023
economic loss, 12–024—12–027
introduction, 12–015—12–018
rescuer cases, 12–019—12–021
company doctor, report by, 12–057
consent to treatment
capacity to, 12–135—12–139
children, by, 12–148
informed, 12–130—12–134
introduction, 12–124—12–125
limits on, 12–126—12–127
mentally disordered patients, by,
12–140—12–147
voluntary, 12–128—12–129
contractual duties
NHS patients, 12–005—12–007
private patients, 12–008—12–010
contributory negligence, 12–276
damages
causation, 12–243—12–281
foreseeability, 12–282—12–286
introduction, 12–241
measure of, 12–287—12–305
remoteness, 12–242—12–286
disabled children, 12–056
disciplinary proceedings, 12–004
duties
patient, to, 12–005—12–030
third parties, to, 12–031—12–066
duties to patient
common law, at, 12–015—12–030
contract, under, 12–005—12–010
fiduciary, 12–028—12–030
statute, under, 12–011—12–014
tort, in, 12–015—12–030
duties to third parties
disabled children, 12–056
generally, 12–031—12–032
infection from contact with patient,
12–043—12–054
medical report for insurer, etc.,
12–057—12–066
nervous shock cases,
12–033—12–042
unborn children, 12–055
"wrongful life" cases, 12–056
economic loss, 12–024—12–027
error in course of treatment
adverse reaction to treatment,
12–191
failure to remove objects, 12–194
generally, 12–186—12–196
injections, 12–192

MEDICAL PRACTITIONERS—*cont.*
error in course of treatment—*cont.*
operations, 12–193
over-intervention, 12–196
post-operative care, 12–195
right procedure, 12–188
right treatment, 12–187
failure to arrange follow-up, 12–176
failure to attend patient
GP, 12–174—12–175
hospital doctors, 12–173
introduction, 12–172
failure to communicate,
12–197—12–200
failure to diagnose
generally, 12–177—12–184
more serious condition, 12–185
failure to examine patient
GP, 12–174—12–175
hospital doctors, 12–173
introduction, 12–172
failure to explain treatment
answering patient's questions,
12–218—12–221
Australian law, 12–205—12–207
blood products, 12–226
Canadian law, 12–202—12–204
curtailment by reason of patient's
condition, 12–215—12–217
disability of unborn baby, 12–231
English law, 12–208—12–214
evidence, and, 12–232
general principle, 12–201
manner of communication,
12–223—12–224
side effects of drugs, 12–225
sterilisation, 12–227—12–230
warning for patient's protection,
12–222
failure to prevent illness
introduction, 12–169
spread of infectious disease,
12–170—12–171
failure to procure treatment,
12–271—12–273
failure to warn of risks,
12–201—12–232
fiduciary duties
introduction, 12–028
nature and extent, 12–030
undue influence, 12–029
foreseeability, 12–282—12–286
human rights, and
access to medical information,
7–060—7–063
clinical negligence, 7–047—7–049

MEDICAL PRACTITIONERS—*cont.*
human rights, and—*cont.*
complaints procedures, 7–065
consent to treatment, 7–059
degrading treatment, prohibition
against, 7–042
fair trial, right to, 7–043
family life, right to respect for,
7–044
freedom of thought, right to, 7–045
inhuman treatment, prohibition
against, 7–042
introduction, 7–036—7–037
life, right to, 7–039—7–041
marry, right to, 7–046
medical care, right to, 7–050—7–054
private life, right to respect for,
7–044
relevant rights, 7–038
withdrawal of treatment,
7–055—7–058
inadequate advice concerning unborn
baby, 12–277—12–281
inadequate warning of treatment
Australian law, 12–265—12–268
Canadian law, 12–264
introduction, 12–262—12–263
policy issues, 12–269—12–270
infection from contact with patient,
12–043—12–054
intervening conduct, 12–276
introduction, 12–001—12–003
liability for breach of duty
error in course of treatment,
12–186—12–196
failure to attend patient,
12–172—12–176
failure to communicate,
12–197—12–200
failure to examine patient,
12–172—12–176
failure to explain treatment,
12–201—12–232
failure to prevent illness,
12–169—12–171
failure to warn of risks,
12–201—12–232
introduction, 12–167—12–168
mishandling mentally disturbed
patients, 12–233—12–240
wrong diagnosis, 12–177—12–185
loss of a chance
Australian law, 12–261
Canadian law, 12–259—12–260
introduction, 12–251—12–258

MEDICAL PRACTITIONERS—*cont.*
measure of damages
aggravated damages, 12–288
personal injury, 12–287
wrongful birth claims,
12–289—12–305
mishandling mentally disturbed patients
Code of Practice, 12–234
generally, 12–233
issue of certificates,
12–239—12–240
self-inflicted injury, 12–236—12–237
statutory restrictions, 12–235
suicide, 12–236—12–237
nervous shock cases, 12–033—12–042
novus actus interveniens,
12–274—12–275
remoteness
causation, 12–243—12–281
foreseeability, 12–282—12–286
introduction, 12–242
res ipsa loquitur
application to medical negligence,
12–119—12–121
introduction, 12–117—12–118
rebuttal of inference,
12–122—12–123
rescuer cases
ambulance service, 12–020—12–021
doctors, 12–019
standard of skill and care
Bolam test, 12–086
consent to treatment, and,
12–124—12–148
current state of knowledge,
12–073—12–074
emergency situation, 12–080
expert evidence as to,
12–111—12–116
failure to take precautions, 12–083
general and approved practice,
12–090—12–110
generally, 12–067—12–072
inexperience, 12–077
misadventure, 12–080—12–082
policy issues, 12–084—12–089
res ipsa loquitur, and,
12–117—12–123
specialisation, 12–075—12–076
working beyond one's competence,
12–078
statutory duties, 12–011—12–014
tort, duties in
communication of distressing
information, 12–022—12–023
economic loss, 12–024—12–027

MEDICAL PRACTITIONERS—*cont.*
tort, duties in—*cont.*
introduction, 12–015—12–018
rescuer cases, 12–019—12–021
unborn children, 12–055
undue influence, 12–029
Woolf's reforms, 12–166
wrong diagnosis
generally, 12–177—12–184
more serious condition, 12–185
"wrongful life" cases, 12–056
MEDICAL REPORT FOR INSURER, ETC.
medical practitioners, and,
12–057—12–066
MENTALLY DISORDERED PATIENTS
consent to treatment, and,
12–140—12–147
MIDWIVES
and see MEDICAL PRACTITIONERS
disciplinary proceedings, 12–004
generally, 12–149—12–151
registration, 12–003
MINERALS SURVEYOR
surveyors' functions, and, 9–001
MISADVENTURE
medical practitioners, and,
12–080—12–082
MISCONDUCT OF LITIGATION (SOLICITORS)
advice on appeal, 10–184
ceasing to act, 10–191
delay
defending proceedings, 10–186
issuing proceedings, 10–185
progressing proceedings,
10–187—10–188
evidence, 10–180—10–182
hearing, at, 10–183
introduction, 10–175
issuing proceedings, 10–176
pursuit of obvious remedy, 10–178
pursuit of unmeritorious claims,
10–179
settlements, 10–189—10–190
statements of case, 10–177
MISCONDUCT OF NON-CONTENTIOUS
BUSINESS
conveyancing
enquiries before contract, 10–201
handing over purchase monies,
10–200
matters coming to notice, 10–199
National protocol, 10–204
non-registration of interests, 10–198
remote contingencies, 10–197
searches, 10–193—10–194
standard of care, 10–196

MISCONDUCT OF NON-CONTENTIOUS
  BUSINESS—*cont.*
  conveyancing—*cont.*
    suspicious circumstances, 10–195
    time limits, 10–202
    undue influence, 10–205
    width of duty, 10–203
    introduction, 10–192
  mortgage lenders, claims by
    background, 10–207
    borrower's financial status,
      10–211—10–212
    Bowerman duty, 10–208—10–210
    clarity of communications, 10–216
    confidential information, 10–217
    contributory negligence,
      10–325—10–327
    direct payments of price,
      10–213—10–214
    introduction, 10–206
    other matters, 10–215
    trusts, and, 10–035
  wills, preparation of
    attestation, 10–222
    giving advice, 10–220
    introduction, 10–218
    knowledge of law, 10–222
    other errors, 10–224
    prompt actions, 10–223
    scope of duty, 10–221
    taking instructions, 10–219
MISDESCRIPTION OF PROPERTY
  surveyors, and, 9–013
MISFEASANCE IN PUBLIC OFFICE
  financial practitioners, and, 13–105
  generally, 2–080
MISFEASANCE SUMMONS
  accountants, and, 15–024
MISHANDLING MENTALLY DISTURBED
  PATIENTS
  Code of Practice, 12–234
  generally, 12–233
  issue of certificates, 12–239—12–240
  self-inflicted injury, 12–236—12–237
  statutory restrictions, 12–235
  suicide, 12–236—12–237
MISLEADING PROMOTION
  financial practitioners, and,
    13–118—13–119
MISREPRESENTATION
  financial practitioners, and
    common law position, and, 13–088
    false in material respect, 13–087
    introduction, 13–085
    suitability, 13–086

MISREPRESENTATION—*cont.*
  insurance brokers, and
    approval by client, 14–070—14–071
    completion of proposal,
      14–072—14–073
    introduction, 14–069
MISTAKES BY BARRISTERS
  examples, 11–041—11–042
  existence of error, 11–038
  introduction, 11–039
  nature of error, 11–040
  settlement advice, 11–043—11–045
MISTAKES IN COURT
  barristers, and, 11–051
MISSTATEMENTS BY INSURANCE BROKERS
  reinsurance, as to, 14–021
  third parties, to, 14–031
MISUSE OF INFORMATION
  exceptions
    disclosure in public interest, 2–160
    disclosure required by law, 2–161
    introduction, 2–159
  introduction, 2–158
MITIGATION OF DAMAGE/LOSS
  accountants, and, 15–152
  construction professionals, and,
    8–313—8–315
  IT professionals, and, 17–124—17–125
  solicitors, and
    change of solicitor, 10–322
    disappointed beneficiary cases,
      10–320
    errors, 10–096
    fresh litigation, 10–318—10–319
    generous treatment of claimant,
      10–317
    introduction, 10–316
    lack of time, 10–097
    limits of rule, 10–321
MODIFICATION OF SOFTWARE
  common law duty, 17–051
  generally, 17–023—17–030
MONIES WRONGLY PAID OUT
  accountants, and, 15–138
MORTGAGE APPLICATIONS
  exclusion of liability, and, 5–008
MORTGAGE FRAUDS
  surveyors, and, 9–007
MORTGAGE INDEMNITY GUARANTEES
  surveyors, and, 9–122
MORTGAGE LENDERS, CLAIMS BY
  contributory negligence, and
    excess LTV, 10–326
    excluded cases, 10–327
    generally, 10–325

MORTGAGE LENDERS, CLAIMS BY—*cont.*
  solicitors, against
    background, 10–207
    borrower's financial status,
      10–211—10–212
    Bowerman duty, 10–208—10–210
    clarity of communications, 10–216
    confidential information, 10–217
    contributory negligence,
      10–325—10–327
    direct payments of price,
      10–213—10–214
    introduction, 10–206
    other matters, 10–215
    trusts, and, 10–035
  surveyors, against, 5–035
MULTI-PARTY ACTIONS
  costs, 6–005
  introduction, 6–001
  procedure, 6–003—6–004
  professional negligence, and, 6–002
MUTUAL VALUERS
  duty of care, and, 2–097
  surveyors, and, 9–074

NATIONAL HEALTH SERVICE (NHS)
  and see MEDICAL PRACTITIONERS
  structure, 12–162—12–163
NATURE OF CHARGE, RIGHT TO KNOW
  human rights, and, 7–013
NEGLIGENCE
  applicable situations
    elements, 2–019—2–021
    examples, 2–018
    introduction, 2–017
  breach of duty of care, 2–015
  conditions
    breach of duty of care, 2–015
    damage suffered by claimant, 2–016
    duty of care, 2–014
    introduction, 2–013
  damage suffered by claimant, 2–016
  duty of care
    and see DUTY OF CARE
    applicable situations, 2–017—2–021
    concurrent liability, 2–100—2–108
    introduction, 2–014
    liability to third parties,
      2–109—2–115
    particular situations, 2–079—2–099
    theoretical basis, 2–022—2–078
  line of reasoning, 2–019—2–020
  reasonable care and skill,
    2–116—2–124
  surveyors, and, 9–007

NEGLIGENT MISREPRESENTATION
  surveyors, and, 9–007
NEGLIGENT MISSTATEMENTS
  IT professionals, and, 17–055
NEGLIGENT REINSURANCE TO CLOSE
  Lloyd's agents, and, 16–058—16–059
NEGLIGENT SURVEYS
  lender, for
    assessment of total loss,
      9–151—9–154
    "cap" theory, 9–159—9–160
    contribution from defaulting
      borrower, 9–173
    contributory negligence,
      9–166—9–172
    interest on damages, 9–162
    introduction, 9–150
    joint responsibility, 9–173—9–174
    loss within scope of duty,
      9–155—9–161
    "measurable, relevant loss", 9–161
    mortgagor's covenants to repay,
      9–163—9–165
    "no transaction/successful
      transaction" cases,
      9–157—9–158
  purchaser who completes, for
    collateral benefits, 9–148
    cost of repairs, 9–141—9–145
    extraction costs, 9–146—9–147
    formulation of measure,
      9–135—9–137
    generally, 9–130—9–134
    nature of loss, 9–138—9–139
    other decisions, 9–140
    repair cost, 9–141—9–145
  purchaser who withdraws, for, 9–149
NEGLIGENT UNDERWRITING OF INSURANCE
  RISKS
  causation, 16–067—16–070
  generally, 16–053—16–056
  measure of damages, 16–077—16–082
NERVOUS SHOCK CASES
  medical practitioners, and,
    12–033—12–042
NEW ZEALAND
  duty of care, and, 2–054—2–057
  immunity from suit for barristers, and,
    11–024
  solicitor's confidentiality, and, 10–031
NHS PATIENTS
  medical practitioners, and,
    12–005—12–007
NON-CONTENTIOUS LEGAL WORK
  expectation, and, 2–003

NON-RECEIPT OF INSURANCE PROCEEDS
insurance brokers, and, 14–121
NOTICE OF NON-PERFORMANCE
construction professionals, and, 8–237
NOVEL DESIGN
construction professionals, and,
8–207—8–209
NOVEL TREATMENT
medical practitioners, and, 12–109
NOVUS ACTUS INTERVENIENS
medical practitioners, and,
12–274—12–275
surveyors, and, 9–123—9–124
NURSES
and see MEDICAL PRACTITIONERS
disciplinary proceedings, 12–004
generally, 12–149—12–151
registration, 12–003

OBSERVE, FAILURE TO (SURVEYORS)
camouflaged defects, 9–095
cracks, 9–093—9–094
dry rot, 9–091
introduction, 9–090
roof, 9–092
subsidence, 9–093—9–094
totality of unnoticed defects, 9–096
woodworm, 9–091
OBTAINING PERSONAL BENEFIT
solicitors, and, 10–030
OBVIOUS RISKS, ADVICE AS TO
solicitors, and, 10–165
OMBUDSMAN SERVICE, FINANCIAL (FOS)
award, 13–183—13–188
complaints handling procedure, 13–179
immunity from suit, 13–189
internal complaints handling,
13–172—13–174
introduction, 13–170—13–171
investigation procedure,
13–180—13–182
jurisdiction, 13–175—13–178
money awards, 13–186—13–187
non-money awards, 13–188
OPEN MARKET VALUE
surveyors, and, 9–023
OPEN UP, FAILURE TO
surveyors, and, 9–084—9–089
OPERATION MANUAL
IT professionals, and, 17–046
OPERATIONS
medical practitioners, and, 12–193
OPTICIANS
and see MEDICAL PRACTITIONERS
disciplinary proceedings, 12–004

OPTICIANS—cont.
generally, 12–149—12–151
registration, 12–003
OSTEOPATHS
and see MEDICAL PRACTITIONERS
disciplinary proceedings, 12–004
registration, 12–003
OVER-DESIGN
construction professionals, and, 8–220
OVER-INTERVENTION
medical practitioners, and, 12–196
OVERPAYMENT
accountants, and, 15–137
OVERVALUATION FOR VENDOR
surveyors, and, 9–175

PARALLEL PROCEEDINGS
disclosure issues, 13–206
generally, 13–205
PARENT/CHILD RELATIONSHIP
undue influence, and, 2–144
PATENT AGENTS
alternative remedies, 18–005
causation, 18–020—18–021
Codes of Conduct, 18–011
damages
causation, 18–020—18–021
remoteness, 18–022
valuation of lost patent, 18–023
duties
client, to, 18–008
third parties, to, 18–009
function
conduct of proceedings, 18–003
generally, 18–002
immunity from suit, 18–012
introduction, 18–001
liability for breach of duty
business advice, 18–018
generally, 18–015
giving of advice, 18–018
instruction of foreign agents, 18–019
knowledge of law, 18–016
taking instructions, 18–017
liability for costs, 18–013
loss of a chance, 18–030—18–021
privilege, 18–014
regulation
exclusion, 18–005
generally, 18–004
suspension, 18–005
remoteness, 18–022
standard of skill and care
Codes of Conduct, 18–011
generally, 18–010

PATENT AGENTS—*cont.*
valuation of lost patent, 18–023
wasted costs order, 18–013
PATIENTS
consent to treatment, and,
12–140—12–147
PEACEFUL ENJOYMENT OF POSSESSIONS,
RIGHT TO
economic rights, 7–016
fair balance test, 7–017
generally, 7–014
introduction, 7–004
principles, 7–015
PENSION BENEFICIARIES
financial practitioners, and,
13–109—13–111
PERFORMANCE BONDS
construction professionals, and, 8–236
PERSONAL DEALINGS WITH CLIENT
solicitors, and, 10–018—10–019
PERSONAL ESTATE OF DECEASED PERSON,
ACTIONS CONCERNING
limitation in equity, and,
5–082—5–088
PERSONAL INJURIES, DAMAGES FOR
construction professionals, and,
8–080—8–081
IT professionals, and, 17–062—17–066
medical practitioners, and, 12–287
PERSONAL INJURY CLAIMS, LIMITATION
PERIOD FOR
date of knowledge, 5–056—5–062
discretionary exclusion of time limit
introduction, 5–064
manner of exercise, 5–065—5–066
relevance of fault, 5–067—5–069
generally, 5–056
introduction, 5–012
PERSONAL PROFIT
solicitors, and, 10–021
PERSONS UNDER DISABILITY
limitation period, and, 5–010
PHARMACISTS
and see MEDICAL PRACTITIONERS
apportionment of liability, 12–165
disciplinary proceedings, 12–004
registration, 12–003
PHYSICAL INJURY, DAMAGES FOR
construction professionals, and, 8–308
solicitors, and, 10–310
PLANNING LAW
construction professionals, and,
8–200—8–202
PLEADING WEAK POINTS
barristers, and, 11–050

POLARISATION
financial practitioners, and, 13–055
POLICE, ACTIONS AGAINST
human rights, and, 7–026
POST-OPERATIVE CARE
medical practitioners, and, 12–195
PRACTICAL COMPLETION
construction professionals, and, 8–256
PRACTICE STATEMENTS (RICS)
effect, 9–024—9–025
generally, 9–022
PRE-ACTION PROTOCOLS
construction professionals, and, 8–009
PREJUDICE
laches, and, 5–106—5–107
PRESUMPTION OF INNOCENCE
human rights, and, 7–012
PRIMARY LIMITATION PERIOD
death, 5–063
generally, 5–010
personal injuries, 5–056
surveyors, and, 9–009
PRIVATE LIFE, RIGHT TO RESPECT FOR
child protection, and, 7–026
failure to diagnose special needs, and,
7–026
generally, 7–013
introduction, 7–004
lawyer/client confidentiality,
7–033—7–035
medical practitioners, 7–044
PRIVATE PATIENTS
medical practitioners, and,
12–008—12–010
PRIVATISATION
accountants, and, 15–006
PRIVILEGE
patent agents, and, 18–014
solicitors, and
between clients, 10–145
waiver, 10–144
trade mark attorney, and, 18–014
PROCEDURAL ERROR
wasted costs order, and, 10–139
PRODUCT DISCLOSURE
financial practitioners, and, 13–059
PRODUCT LIABILITY OF SOFTWARE
defences, 17–076—17–077
generally, 17–072—17–073
relevant product, 17–074—17–075
"safety-critical" information, 17–078
PROFESSION
characteristics
collective organisation, 1–004
morality, 1–003
nature of work, 1–002

PROFESSION—*cont.*
  characteristics—*cont.*
    status, 1–005—1–006
  definition, 1–001
  nature, 1–007—1–008
PROFESSIONAL DISCIPLINARY PROCEEDINGS
  human rights, and, 7–026
  generally, 7–065—7–066
  procedural guarantees, 7–067
  medical practitioners, and, 12–004
PROFESSIONAL LIABILITY
  positive duties, 2–001—2–004
  restrictions and inhibitions,
    2–005—2–006
PROGRESS OF MATTER, ADVICE AS TO
  solicitors, and, 10–156
PROJECT MANAGERS
  and see CONSTRUCTION PROFESSIONALS
  adjudication, 8–332—8–344
  apportionment of liability,
    8–317—8–329
  causation, 8–270—8–279
  contributory negligence, 8–330—8–331
  damages for breach of duty,
    8–264—8–315
  date of cause of action, and
    Bank of East Asia, 5–028—5–029
    date of damage, 5–030—5–033
    degree of damage, 5–022
    "doomed from start", 5–020—5–021
    Murphy, 5–024—5–027
    Pirelli, 5–017—5–019
    successive owners, 5–023
    uncertainty, 5–034
  duties, 8–019—8–181
  expert witness, as, 8–263
  foreseeability, 8–280—8–284
  functions, 8–008
  immunity from suit, and, 2–097
  liability for breach of duty,
    8–182—8–262
  pre-action protocols, 8–009
  remoteness, 8–265—8–284
PROMPT ACTION
  wills, and, 10–223
PROPER INSPECTION, FAILURE BY SURVEYOR
    TO MAKE
  introduction, 9–082
  limited survey, 9–097
  observation
    camouflaged defects, 9–095
    cracks, 9–093—9–094
    dry rot, 9–091
    introduction, 9–090
    roof, 9–092
    subsidence, 9–093—9–094

PROPER INSPECTION, FAILURE BY SURVEYOR
    TO MAKE—*cont.*
  observation—*cont.*
    totality of unnoticed defects, 9–096
    woodworm, 9–091
  particular parts, 9–083
  relevance of type of survey,
    9–097—9–099
  uncovering and opening up,
    9–084—9–089
PROSPECTUS CASES
  financial practitioners, and, 13–108
PROSTHETICS, SUPPLY OF
  medical practitioners, and, 12–012
"PROXIMITY" TEST
  and see DUTY OF CARE
  analysis of problems, 2–075
  introduction, 2–035
PUBLIC AUTHORITIES
  duty of care, and
    breach of duty arising from
      performance of statutory duty,
      2–083—2–086
    breach of statutory duty, 2–082
    careless performance of public duty,
      2–081
    classification of claims, 2–080
    introduction, 2–079
  human rights, and, 7–001
PUBLIC INTEREST, DISCLOSURE IN
  confidentiality, and, 2–161

QUANTITY SURVEYORS
  and see CONSTRUCTION PROFESSIONALS
  adjudication, 8–332—8–344
  apportionment of liability,
    8–317—8–329
  causation, 8–270—8–279
  contributory negligence, 8–330—8–331
  damages for breach of duty,
    8–264—8–315
  date of cause of action, and
    Bank of East Asia, 5–028—5–029
    date of damage, 5–030—5–033
    degree of damage, 5–022
    "doomed from start", 5–020—5–021
    Murphy, 5–024—5–027
    Pirelli, 5–017—5–019
    successive owners, 5–023
    uncertainty, 5–034
  duties, 8–019—8–181
  expert witness, as, 8–263
  foreseeability, 8–280—8–284
  functions, 8–006, 9–004
  immunity from suit, and, 2–097

QUANTITY SURVEYORS—*cont.*
liability for breach of duty,
8–182—8–262
pre-action protocols, 8–009
remoteness, 8–265—8–284

RADICAL CHANGE IN CIRCUMSTANCES
heads of damage, and, 10–275
REASONABLE CARE AND SKILL, STANDARD
OF
advances in knowledge, 2–124
contractual liability, and, 2–007
experience, 2–118—2–119
formulation of
individuals, 2–120
organisation, 2–121
person undertaking work of other
profession, 2–122
generally, 2–116—2–117
introduction, 2–002
new techniques, 2–123
qualifications, 2–118—2–119
"REASONABLY FORESEEABLE" TEST
and see DUTY OF CARE
introduction, 2–035
RECOGNISE DEFECT, FAILURE TO
surveyors, and, 9–099
RECOVERY OF LAND, ACTIONS CONCERNING
limitation in equity, and,
5–082—5–088
RECOVERY OF MONIES PAID
financial promotion restriction,
contravention of, 13–156
general prohibition, contravention of,
13–152—13–155
RECTIFICATION OF CONSTRUCTION, COSTS
OF
betterment, 8–297—8–299
credit for cost of proper design, 8–294
date of assessment, 8–295
failure to review a design, 8–296
introduction, 8–290—8–293
REDEMPTION OF MORTGAGED LAND,
ACTIONS CONCERNING
limitation in equity, and,
5–082—5–088
REGULATORY BODIES
duty of care, and, 2–086
REINSURANCE TO CLOSE
duties to third parties, 16–016—16–019
negligence, 16–058—16–059
RELIANCE ON SOLICITOR AS OFFICER OF
COURT
generally, 10–046

RELIANCE ON SOLICITOR'S ADVICE
beneficiaries, by
background, 10–047—10–048
conflict of interest, 10–051
double recovery, 10–052
identity of beneficiary, 10–050
non-will cases, 10–053
other jurisdictions, in, 10–054
scope of principle, 10–049
non-client establishing duty, by, 10–042
non-client without duty, by, 10–043
without retainer, 10–041
RELIGIOUS ADVISER/DISCIPLE RELATIONSHIP
undue influence, and, 2–144
REMEDIAL ORDERS
contravenors, against, 13–141
generally, 13–145
grounds of application,
13–138—13–140
introduction, 13–137
knowingly concerned persons, against,
13–142
REMINDER OF ADVICE
solicitors, and, 10–168
REMOTE CONTINGENCIES
solicitors, and, 10–197
REMOTENESS OF DAMAGE
and see CAUSATION
and see FORESEEABILITY
accountants, and
causation, 15–121—15–130
foreseeability, 15–131
barristers, and, 11–052—11–053
construction professionals, and
causation, 8–270—8–279
foreseeability, 8–280—8–284
introduction, 8–269
PROSPECTUS CASES
financial practitioners, and
causation, 13–158—13–160
foreseeability, 13–158
introduction, 13–158
insurance brokers, and
causation, 14–088—14–112
foreseeability, 14–113
introduction, 14–087
Lloyd's agents, and
causation, 16–062—16–070
introduction, 16–061
foreseeability, 16–071
medical practitioners, and
causation, 12–243—12–281
foreseeability, 12–282—12–286
introduction, 12–242
patent agents, and, 18–022

PROSPECTUS CASES—*cont.*
solicitors, and
causation, 10–234—10–239
foreseeability, 10–240—10–243
introduction, 10–233
scope of duty, 10–244—10–248
surveyors, and
causation, 9–120—9–124
foreseeability, 9–125—9–127
introduction, 9–119
trade mark attorney, and, 18–022
REMUNERATION, LOSS OF
introduction, 3–006—3–007
RENT REVIEW
surveyors, and, 9–179—9–180
REPORTING TO CUSTOMERS
financial practitioners, and, 13–067
REPUDIATION
IT professionals, and, 17–099—17–103
RES IPSA LOQUITUR
construction professionals, and,
8–156—8–157
medical practitioners, and
application to medical negligence,
12–119—12–121
introduction, 12–117—12–118
rebuttal of inference,
12–122—12–123
RESCISSION
financial practitioners, and, 13–151
generally, 3–009—3–010
RESCUER CASES
ambulance service, 12–020—12–021
doctors, 12–019
RESPECTABLE BODY OF OPINION TEST
construction professionals, and,
8–145—8–150
expert evidence, and, 6–009
human rights, and, 7–047—7–049
medical practitioners, and
different schools of thought,
12–093—12–094
generally, 12–068—12–069
RESTITUTION
financial practitioners, and
contravenors, against, 13–141
FSA, by, 13–148
generally, 13–147—13–148
grounds of application,
13–138—13–140
introduction, 13–137
knowingly concerned persons,
against, 13–142
IT professionals, and, 17–113—17–115
solicitors, for, 10–232

RESTRICTION OF LIABILITY
accountants, and, 15–100—15–101
financial practitioners, and,
13–133—13–134
incorporation of clause, 5–006
introduction, 5–001—5–002
IT professionals, and
introduction, 17–118
other party's standard terms,
17–119—17–120
reasonableness of term,
17–121—17–123
solicitors, and, 10–141
statutory framework
UCTA 1977, 5–003—5–004
UTCCR 1999, 5–005
surveyors, and
commercial property, 9–071
definition of extent of service, and,
9–073
introduction, 9–063
residential property, 9–064—9–070
Scotland, in, 9–072
third parties, to
comment, 5–009
introduction, 5–007
mortgage applications, in, 5–008
RETAINER
fiduciary obligations, and,
2–131—2–133
RETAINER, SOLICITOR'S
continuing obligations, 10–011
express
construction, 10–009—10–010
formation, 10–004
generally, 10–008
formation
inferred by conduct, 10–005
introduction, 10–004
writing, in, 10–006
implied, 10–005
nature of
express instructions, 10–008
introduction, 10–007
oral, 10–006
termination, 10–011
RIGHTS OF AUDIENCE
barristers, and, 11–001
RISK ASSESSMENT
construction professionals, and,
8–210—8–212
ROOF, INSPECTION OF
surveyors, and, 9–092
ROYAL INSTITUTION OF CHARTERED
SURVEYORS (RICS)
generally, 9–002

RUN-OFF CONTRACTS
Lloyd's agents, and, 16–053—16–056

"SAFETY-CRITICAL" INFORMATION
IT professionals, and, 17–078
SATISFACTORY QUALITY OF SOFTWARE
bespoke software, 17–014—17–022
modified standard software,
17–023—17–030
standard of care, and, 17–082—17–094
SEARCHES
solicitors, and, 10–193—10–194
SECRET COMMISSIONS
solicitors, and, 10–022
SELECTION OF CONTRACTOR
construction professionals, and,
8–222—8–224
SELF DEALING
fiduciary's interest, 2–140
full advice and disclosure,
2–137—2–138
full value, 2–139
generally, 2–135
introduction, 2–134
SELF-INCRIMINATION, RIGHT AGAINST
human rights, and, 7–012
SELF-INFLICTED INJURY
medical practitioners, and,
12–236—12–237
SETTLEMENT, ADVICE ON
barristers, and
examples, 11–044—11–045
introduction, 11–043
solicitors, and, 10–189—10–190
SETTLEMENTS
construction professionals, and,
8–326—8–327
insurance brokers, and,
14–117—14–118
SHARED RESPONSIBILITY
construction professionals, and
apportionment of liability,
8–317—8–329
contributory negligence,
8–330—8–331
financial practitioners, and
contribution, 13–168
contributory negligence, 13–167
solicitors, and
apportionment of liability,
10–328—10–332
contributory negligence,
10–323—10–327
SIDE EFFECTS OF DRUGS
medical practitioners, and, 12–225

SIGNING INDICATION
insurance brokers, and 14–020
SINGLE JOINT EXPERT
experience, 6–016
SITE EXAMINATION
effect of proposed works, 8–191
generally, 8–183
ground investigations, 8–185—8–189
measurement, 8–184
non-physical restraints, 8–192
SKILL AND CARE, STANDARD OF
accountants, and
and see below
auditing, 15–093—15–099
generally, 15–090—15–092
advances in knowledge, 2–124
barristers, and, 11–008
construction professionals, and
Bolam test, 8–145—8–150
Codes of Practice, 8–158—8–161
delegation to specialists,
8–177—8–181
errors, 8–165—8–167
evidence, 8–151—8–155
experience of client, 8–135—8–137
general practice, 8–145—8–150
knowledge, 8–144
knowledge of law, 8–162—8–164
ordinary competent and skilled
practitioner, 8–133—8–143
res ipsa loquitur, 8–156—8–157
special steps required,
8–170—8–176
specialism, 8–168—8–169
time of assessment, 8–139
contractual liability, and, 2–007
experience, 2–118—2–119
financial practitioners, and
"bracket" claims, 13–094
generally, 13–093
introduction, 13–092
formulation of
individuals, 2–120
organisation, 2–121
person undertaking work of other
profession, 2–122
generally, 2–116—2–117
insurance brokers, and
expert evidence, 14–034
generally, 14–032
legal knowledge, 14–035
specialist markets, 14–033
introduction, 2–002
IT professionals, and
bedding in, 17–085—17–089
bugs, 17–085—17–089

SKILL AND CARE, STANDARD OF—*cont.*
IT professionals, and—*cont.*
contract for services,
17–079—17–081
contract for sale/supply of goods,
17–082—17–094
fitness for purpose, 17–082—17–094
satisfactory quality, 17–082—17–094
"state of the art" defence, 17–094
Lloyds' agents, and 16–020—16–022
medical practitioners, and
and see below
Bolam test, 12–086
consent to treatment, and,
12–124—12–148
current state of knowledge,
12–073—12–074
emergency situation, 12–080
expert evidence as to,
12–111—12–116
failure to take precautions, 12–083
general and approved practice,
12–090—12–110
generally, 12–067—12–072
inexperience, 12–077
misadventure, 12–080—12–082
policy issues, 12–084—12–089
res ipsa loquitur, and,
12–117—12–123
specialisation, 12–075—12–076
working beyond one's competence,
12–078
new techniques, 2–123
patent agents, and
Codes of Conduct, 18–011
generally, 18–010
qualifications, 2–118—2–119
solicitors, and
and see below
aggravating factors,
10–098—10–103
censure, 10–105
general practice, 10–084—10–092
mitigating factors, 10–096—10–097
seriousness of claim, 10–104
specialists, 10–093—10–095
standard of reasonableness,
10–077—10–083
surveyors, and
general practice and knowledge,
9–054—9–057
keeping up to date, 9–056
margin of error, 9–058—9–061
new developments, 9–056
onus of proof, 9–062
"reasonably skilled", 9–052—9–053

SKILL AND CARE, STANDARD OF—*cont.*
surveyors, and—*cont.*
relevance of the "bracket",
9–059—9–061
relevance of type of service, 9–057
trade mark attorney, and
Codes of Conduct, 18–011
generally, 18–010
SKILL AND CARE, STANDARD OF
(ACCOUNTANTS)
auditing
fraud detection, 15–095—15–099
standards, 15–093—15–094
generally, 15–090
sources of evidence, 15–091—15–092
SKILL AND CARE, STANDARD OF (MEDICAL
PRACTITIONERS)
medical practitioners, and, 12–110
Bolam test
different schools of thought,
12–093—12–094
generally, 12–068—12–069
clinical trials, 12–110
consent to treatment
capacity to, 12–135—12–139
children, by, 12–148
informed, 12–130—12–134
introduction, 12–124—12–125
limits on, 12–126—12–127
mentally disordered patients, by,
12–140—12–147
voluntary, 12–128—12–129
current state of knowledge,
12–073—12–074
different schools of thought,
12–093—12–105
emergency situation, 12–080
expert evidence as to, 12–111—12–116
failure to take precautions, 12–083
general and approved practice
acts in accordance, 12–092—12–105
departures from, 12–106—12–110
different schools of thought,
12–093—12–105
introduction, 12–090—12–091
generally, 12–067—12–072
inexperience, 12–077
misadventure, 12–080—12–082
novel treatment, 12–109
policy issues, 12–084—12–089
res ipsa loquitur, and
application to medical negligence,
12–119—12–121
introduction, 12–117—12–118
rebuttal of inference,
12–122—12–123

SKILL AND CARE, STANDARD OF (MEDICAL
PRACTITIONERS)—*cont.*
specialisation, 12–075—12–076
working beyond one's competence,
12–078
SKILL AND CARE, STANDARD OF
(SOLICITORS)
acting beyond competence, 10–099
acting for both parties to transaction
borrower and lender, 10–102
generally, 10–100
group litigation, 10–103
informed consent, 10–101
aggravating factors
acting beyond competence, 10–099
acting for both parties to transaction,
10–100—10–103
unnecessary risks, 10–098
censure, 10–105
Client Care Code
example, 10–092
generally, 10–091
errors, 10–096
general practice as evidence
differing practices, 10–090
exception to general rule,
10–085—10–088
general rule, 10–084
taking instructions, 10–092
uniformity, 10–091
unsafe common practice, 10–089
hindsight, 10–083
ignorance, 10–082
inexperienced practitioners,
10–093—10–095
IT professionals, and
bedding in, 17–085—17–089
bugs, 17–085—17–089
contract for services,
17–079—17–081
contract for sale/supply of goods,
17–082—17–094
fitness for purpose, 17–082—17–094
satisfactory quality, 17–082—17–094
"state of the art" defence, 17–094
judgment, 10–080
knowledge of law, 10–081—10–082
lack of time, 10–097
mitigating factors
errors, 10–096
lack of time, 10–097
seriousness of claim, 10–104
specialists, 10–093—10–095
standard of reasonableness
general obligations, 10–079
generally, 10–077

SKILL AND CARE, STANDARD OF
(SOLICITORS)—*cont.*
standard of reasonableness—*cont.*
hindsight, 10–083
ignorance of solicitor, 10–082
judgment of solicitor, 10–080
knowledge of law, 10–081—10–082
reasonably competent solicitor,
10–078
unnecessary risks, 10–098
unsafe common practice, 10–089
SOLICITOR/CLIENT RELATIONSHIP
undue influence, and, 2–144
SOLICITORS
abuse of process
civil cases, 10–114
criminal cases, 10–113
Hall v. Simons, 10–111—10–112
leading cases, 10–108—10–109
other types, 10–115
subsidiary cases, 10–110
wasted costs order, 10–137
acting on client's instructions
exceptions to general rule, 10–124
general rule, 10–123
acting on counsel's advice
background, 10–116
client's position, 10–122
development of law, 10–117
examples of failure of defence,
10–119
examples of success of defence,
10–120
further limits, 10–121
summary of law, 10–118
apportionment of liability
introduction, 10–328
other cases, 10–332
solicitors and surveyors, between,
10–330—10–331
successive solicitors, 10–329
attendance notes, 10–174
bribes, 10–022
causation
"but for", 10–234
intervening acts, 10–237—10–239
proximity, 10–235—10–236
confidence, duty of
Commonwealth position, 10–031
confidentiality of information,
10–029
examples, 10–027—10–028
generally, 10–026
overriding circumstances, 10–032
sufficiency of barriers, 10–030
confirmatory letters, 10–174

SOLICITORS—*cont.*
conflict of interest
Canadian position, 10–025
generally, 10–023—10–024
constructive trusts, 10–036
contractual duties
continuing obligations, 10–012
express instructions,
10–008—10–010
nature, 10–007
retainer, 10–004—10–006
termination of retainer, 10–011
contributory negligence
examples, 10–324
generally, 10–323
mortgage lenders' claims,
10–325—10–327
costs information, 10–157
damages
breach of fiduciary duty, for,
10–226—10–232
causation, 10–234—10–239
foreseeability, 10–240—10–248
heads of damage, 10–263—10–315
introduction, 10–225
measure, 10–249—10–262
mitigation, 10–316—10–322
remoteness, 10–233—10–243
date of cause of action, and
action dismissed for want of
prosecution, 5–043
client acquires less valuable rights,
5–040—5–042
client incurs obligation,
5–037—5–039
omissions capable of remedy, 5–045
purchase of property, 5–044
defences to claim for breach
abuse of process, 10–108—10–115
acting on client's instructions,
10–123—10–124
acting on counsel's advice,
10–116—10–122
immunity from suit,
10–106—10–107
delegation, 10–148
dishonesty, 10–039
duties
client, to, 10–004—10–039
third parties, to, 10–040—10–076
duties to client
contract, under, 10–004—10–012
fiduciary, 10–016—10–033
tort, in, 10–013—10–015
trust, 10–034—10–039

SOLICITORS—*cont.*
duties to third parties
adversary in litigation,
10–055—10–064
beneficiaries without reliance,
10–047—10–054
fraud, 10–076
generally, 10–040—10–046
undertakings, 10–065—10–074
warranty of authority, 10–075
exclusion of liability, 10–141
expert witnesses, as, 10–142
failure to explain legal documents,
10–166—10–167
failure to give advice
attendance notes, and, 10–174
confirmatory letters, and, 10–174
costs information, as to, 10–157
general business matters, as to,
10–169—10–172
introduction, 10–154
legal documents, on,
10–166—10–167
matters coming to notice, as to,
10–158—10–159
matters not asked to advise upon, as
to, 10–160—10–163
obvious risks, as to, 10–165
progress of matter, as to, 10–156
recipient of advice, 10–155
reminder of advice, and, 10–168
solicitor's own negligence, as to,
10–164
unequal transactions, in, 10–173
fiduciary duties
bribes, 10–022
confidentiality, 10–026—10–033
generally, 10–016
inconsistent engagements,
10–023—10–025
obtaining personal benefit, 10–030
personal dealings with client,
10–018—10–019
personal profit, 10–021
secret commissions, 10–022
undue influence, 10–017
foreseeability
examples, 10–241—10–242
introduction, 10–240
time for consideration, 10–243
function, 10–001—10–002
giving wrong advice
law, 10–151—10–152
practical issues, 10–153
heads of damage
criminal liability, 10–303

SOLICITORS—*cont.*
 heads of damage—*cont.*
  difference in value in property,
   10–268—10–276
  distress, 10–312—10–315
  incidental expenditure, 10–309
  inconvenience, 10–311
  introduction, 10–263
  loss of financial advantage,
   10–297—10–300
  loss of opportunity to acquire
   interest in property,
   10–264—10–267
  loss of opportunity to bring
   proceedings, 10–277—10–292
  loss of opportunity to defend
   proceedings, 10–293
  loss on secured loans,
   10–294—10–297
  physical injury, 10–310
  third party liability, 10–301—10–302
  wasted expenditure,
   10–304—10–308
 immunity from suit
  background, 10–106
  generally, 10–107
 inconsistent engagements
  Canadian position, 10–025
  generally, 10–023—10–024
 knowing assistance, 10–038
 knowing receipts, 10–037
 liability for breach of duty
  classification of breaches, 10–149
  delegation, and, 10–148
  failure to give advice,
   10–154—10–174
  generally, 10–146—10–147
  giving wrong advice,
   10–151—10–153
  misconduct of litigation,
   10–175—10–191
  misconduct of non-contentious
   business, 10–192—10–224
 liability for costs
  abuse of process, 10–137
  background, 10–126
  causation, 10–134
  guidelines, 10–129
  hopeless litigation, 10–135—10–136
  improper, unreasonable or negligent,
   10–130
  introduction, 10–125
  lawyer's position, 10–131
  legal aid, and, 10–138
  other errors, 10–140
  present rule, 10–127

SOLICITORS—*cont.*
 liability for costs—*cont.*
  practice and procedure,
   10–132—10–133
  procedural errors, 10–139
  recipient, 10–128
 limitation of liability, 10–141
 measure of damages
  credit for benefits, 10–252—10–255
  date of assessment, 10–250—10–251
  evaluation of a chance,
   10–256—10–262
  introduction, 10–249
 misconduct of conveyancing
  enquiries before contract, 10–201
  handing over purchase monies,
   10–200
  matters coming to notice, 10–199
  National protocol, 10–204
  non-registration of interests, 10–198
  remote contingencies, 10–197
  searches, 10–193—10–194
  standard of care, 10–196
  suspicious circumstances, 10–195
  time limits, 10–202
  undue influence, 10–205
  width of duty, 10–203
 misconduct of litigation
  advice on appeal, 10–184
  ceasing to act, 10–191
  delay, 10–185—10–188
  evidence, 10–180—10–182
  hearing, at, 10–183
  introduction, 10–175
  issuing proceedings, 10–176
  pursuit of obvious remedy, 10–178
  pursuit of unmeritorious claims,
   10–179
  settlements, 10–189—10–190
  statements of case, 10–177
 misconduct of non-contentious business
  conveyancing, 10–193—10–205
  introduction, 10–192
  investment of monies,
   10–206—10–217
  wills, 10–218—10–224
 mortgage lenders, claims by
  background, 10–207
  borrower's financial status,
   10–211—10–212
  Bowerman duty, 10–208—10–210
  clarity of communications, 10–216
  confidential information, 10–217
  contributory negligence,
   10–325—10–327

SOLICITORS—*cont.*
mortgage lenders, claims by—*cont.*
direct payments of price,
10–213—10–214
introduction, 10–206
other matters, 10–215
trusts, and, 10–035
obtaining personal benefit, 10–030
personal dealings with client,
10–018—10–019
personal profit, 10–021
practice and procedure
expert evidence, 10–142—10–143
foreign practice, 10–143
privilege, 10–144—10–145
privilege
between clients, 10–145
waiver, 10–144
regulation, 10–003
remoteness
causation, 10–234—10–239
foreseeability, 10–240—10–243
introduction, 10–233
scope of duty, 10–244—10–248
restriction of liability, 10–141
retainer
formation, 10–004
implication, by, 10–005
termination, 10–011
writing, in, 10–006
secret commissions, 10–022
shared responsibility
apportionment of liability,
10–328—10–332
contributory negligence,
10–323—10–327
standard of skill and care
aggravating factors,
10–098—10–103
censure, 10–105
general practice, 10–084—10–092
mitigating factors, 10–096—10–097
seriousness of claim, 10–104
specialists, 10–093—10–095
standard of reasonableness,
10–077—10–083
tort, duties in
background, 10–013
Commonwealth position, 10–015
generally, 10–014
trust duties
constructive trusts, 10–036
dishonesty, 10–039
express trusts, 10–034
implied trusts, 10–034
knowing assistance, 10–038

SOLICITORS—*cont.*
trust duties—*cont.*
knowing receipts, 10–037
mortgage lenders, 10–035
undue influence, 10–017
vicarious liability, 10–146—10–147
wasted costs order
abuse of process, 10–137
background, 10–126
causation, 10–134
guidelines, 10–129
hopeless litigation, 10–135—10–136
improper, unreasonable or negligent,
10–130
introduction, 10–125
lawyer's position, 10–131
legal aid, and, 10–138
other errors, 10–140
present rule, 10–127
practice and procedure,
10–132—10–133
procedural errors, 10–139
recipient, 10–128
wills, preparation of
attestation, 10–222
giving advice, 10–220
introduction, 10–218
knowledge of law, 10–222
other errors, 10–224
prompt actions, 10–223
scope of duty, 10–221
taking instructions, 10–219
SPECIALISATION
construction professionals, and,
8–168—8–169
insurance brokers, and, 14–033
medical practitioners, and,
12–075—12–076
solicitors, and, 10–093—10–095
SPECIALIST SURVEY
construction professionals, and,
8–259—8–261
SPECIFICATION AND DESIGN
approvals, 8–204—8–205
buildability, 8–216
change instructed by client, 8–219
choice of materials, 8–215
compliance with brief, 8–206
co-ordination of design, 8–218
generally, 8–203
integration of design , 8–217
level of detail, 8–214
novel design, 8–207—8–209
over-design, 8–220
published standards, 8–213
risk assessment, 8–210—8–212

SPECIFICATION AND DESIGN—*cont.*
supervisability, 8–216
SPREAD OF INFECTIOUS DISEASE
medical practitioners, and ,
12–170—12–171
STAFF COMPUTER TRAINING
common law duty, 17–051
generally, 17–045
STANDARD CONDITIONS OF ENGAGEMENT
construction professionals, and
generally, 8–019—8–020
limitation of liability, 8–021—8–025
surveyors, and
generally, 9–026
limitation of liability, 9–027—9–028
STANDARD OF CARE AND SKILL
accountants, and
and see below
auditing, 15–093—15–099
generally, 15–090—15–092
advances in knowledge, 2–124
barristers, and, 11–008
construction professionals, and
Bolam test, 8–145—8–150
Codes of Practice, 8–158—8–161
delegation to specialists,
8–177—8–181
errors, 8–165—8–167
evidence, 8–151—8–155
experience of client, 8–135—8–137
general practice, 8–145—8–150
knowledge, 8–144
knowledge of law, 8–162—8–164
ordinary competent and skilled
practitioner, 8–133—8–143
res ipsa loquitur, 8–156—8–157
special steps required,
8–170—8–176
specialism, 8–168—8–169
time of assessment, 8–139
contractual liability, and, 2–007
experience, 2–118—2–119
financial practitioners, and
"bracket" claims, 13–094
generally, 13–093
introduction, 13–092
formulation of
individuals, 2–120
organisation, 2–121
person undertaking work of other
profession, 2–122
generally, 2–116—2–117
introduction, 2–002
insurance brokers, and
expert evidence, 14–034
generally, 14–032

STANDARD OF CARE AND SKILL—*cont.*
insurance brokers, and—*cont.*
legal knowledge, 14–035
specialist markets, 14–033
IT professionals, and
bedding in, 17–085—17–089
bugs, 17–085—17–089
contract for services,
17–079—17–081
contract for sale/supply of goods,
17–082—17–094
fitness for purpose, 17–082—17–094
satisfactory quality, 17–082—17–094
"state of the art" defence, 17–094
Lloyds' agents, and 16–020—16–022
medical practitioners, and
and see below
Bolam test, 12–086
consent to treatment, and,
12–124—12–148
current state of knowledge,
12–073—12–074
emergency situation, 12–080
expert evidence as to,
12–111—12–116
failure to take precautions, 12–083
general and approved practice,
12–090—12–110
generally, 12–067—12–072
inexperience, 12–077
misadventure, 12–080—12–082
policy issues, 12–084—12–089
res ipsa loquitur, and,
12–117—12–123
specialisation, 12–075—12–076
working beyond one's competence,
12–078
new techniques, 2–123
patent agents, and
Codes of Conduct, 18–011
generally, 18–010
qualifications, 2–118—2–119
software supply, and
bedding in, 17–085—17–089
bugs, 17–085—17–089
contract for services,
17–079—17–081
contract for sale/supply of goods,
17–082—17–094
fitness for purpose, 17–082—17–094
satisfactory quality, 17–082—17–094
"state of the art" defence, 17–094
solicitors, and
and see below
aggravating factors,
10–098—10–103

STANDARD OF CARE AND SKILL—*cont.*
  solicitors, and—*cont.*
    censure, 10–105
    general practice, 10–084—10–092
    mitigating factors, 10–096—10–097
    seriousness of claim, 10–104
    specialists, 10–093—10–095
    standard of reasonableness,
      10–077—10–083
  surveyors, and
    general practice and knowledge,
      9–054—9–057
    keeping up to date, 9–056
    margin of error, 9–058—9–061
    new developments, 9–056
    onus of proof, 9–062
    "reasonably skilled", 9–052—9–053
    relevance of the "bracket",
      9–059—9–061
    relevance of type of service, 9–057
  trade mark attorney, and
    Codes of Conduct, 18–011
    generally, 18–010
STANDARD OF CARE AND SKILL
  (ACCOUNTANTS)
  auditing
    fraud detection, 15–095—15–099
    standards, 15–093—15–094
  generally, 15–090
  sources of evidence, 15–091—15–092
STANDARD OF CARE AND SKILL (MEDICAL
  PRACTITIONERS)
  medical practitioners, and, 12–110
  Bolam test
    different schools of thought,
      12–093—12–094
    generally, 12–068—12–069
  clinical trials, 12–110
  consent to treatment
    capacity to, 12–135—12–139
    children, by, 12–148
    informed, 12–130—12–134
    introduction, 12–124—12–125
    limits on, 12–126—12–127
    mentally disordered patients, by,
      12–140—12–147
    voluntary, 12–128—12–129
  current state of knowledge,
    12–073—12–074
  different schools of thought,
    12–093—12–105
  emergency situation, 12–080
  expert evidence as to, 12–111—12–116
  failure to take precautions, 12–083
  general and approved practice
    acts in accordance, 12–092—12–105

STANDARD OF CARE AND SKILL (MEDICAL
  PRACTITIONERS)—*cont.*
  general and approved practice—*cont.*
    departures from, 12–106—12–110
    different schools of thought,
      12–093—12–105
    introduction, 12–090—12–091
    generally, 12–067—12–072
    inexperience, 12–077
    misadventure, 12–080—12–082
    novel treatment, 12–109
    policy issues, 12–084—12–089
    res ipsa loquitur, and
      application to medical negligence,
        12–119—12–121
      introduction, 12–117—12–118
      rebuttal of inference,
        12–122—12–123
    specialisation, 12–075—12–076
    working beyond one's competence,
      12–078
STANDARD OF CARE AND SKILL
  (SOLICITORS)
  acting beyond competence, 10–099
  acting for both parties to transaction
    borrower and lender, 10–102
    generally, 10–100
    group litigation, 10–103
    informed consent, 10–101
  aggravating factors
    acting beyond competence, 10–099
    acting for both parties to transaction,
      10–100—10–103
    unnecessary risks, 10–098
  censure, 10–105
  Client Care Code
    example, 10–092
    generally, 10–091
  errors, 10–096
  general practice as evidence
    differing practices, 10–090
    exception to general rule,
      10–085—10–088
    general rule, 10–084
    taking instructions, 10–092
    uniformity, 10–091
    unsafe common practice, 10–089
  hindsight, 10–083
  ignorance, 10–082
  inexperienced practitioners,
    10–093—10–095
  judgment, 10–080
  knowledge of law, 10–081—10–082
  lack of time, 10–097
  mitigating factors
    errors, 10–096

STANDARD OF CARE AND SKILL
(SOLICITORS)—*cont.*
mitigating factors—*cont.*
lack of time, 10–097
seriousness of claim, 10–104
specialists, 10–093—10–095
standard of reasonableness
general obligations, 10–079
generally, 10–077
hindsight, 10–083
ignorance of solicitor, 10–082
judgment of solicitor, 10–080
knowledge of law, 10–081—10–082
reasonably competent solicitor,
10–078
unnecessary risks, 10–098
unsafe common practice, 10–089
"STATE OF THE ART" DEFENCE
IT professionals, and, 17–094
STATEMENTS OF CASE
misconduct in litigation by solicitors,
and, 10–177
STATUTORY DUTIES
accountants, and
and see below
companies legislation,
15–010—15–024
financial sector legislation,
15–025—15–031
introduction, 15–009
whistle-blowing, 15–030
financial practitioners, and
application of FSMA regime,
13–028—13–037
generally, 13–038
misrepresentation, 13–085—13–088
regulatory liabilities,
13–069—13–082
regulatory rules, 13–039—13–068
unlisted securities, 13–084
medical practitioners, and,
12–011—12–014
STATUTORY DUTIES (ACCOUNTANTS)
audit
financial sector businesses,
15–025—15–031
generally, 15–018—15–020
introduction, 15–010
preparation of accounts,
15–014—15–017
rationale, 15–011
auditors
appointment, 15–012
audit function, 15–014—15–020
removal, 15–022
remuneration, 15–013

STATUTORY DUTIES (ACCOUNTANTS)—*cont.*
auditors—*cont.*
resignation, 15–023
rights, 15–021
introduction, 15–009
whistle-blowing, 15–030
STERILISATION
medical practitioners, and,
12–227—12–230
STRIKING OUT
interlocutory, 7–023
introduction, 7–019—7–020
Z. v. United Kingdom, 7–021—7–022
STRUCTURAL ENGINEERS
surveyors' functions, and, 9–001
SUB-BROKERS
insurance brokers, and, 14–013
SUB-CONTRACTORS, DUTY OF CARE OF
competing considerations, 2–096
generally, 2–094—2–095
SUBSIDENCE
surveyors, and, 9–093—9–094
SUBSTANTIAL BODY OF OPINION TEST
construction professionals, and,
8–145—8–150
expert evidence, and, 6–009
human rights, and, 7–047—7–049
medical practitioners, and
different schools of thought,
12–093—12–094
generally, 12–068—12–069
SUCCESSIVE OWNERS
claims against architects, and, 5–023
latent damage, and, 5–052
SUFFICIENT INQUIRIES ABOUT PROPERTY,
FAILURE TO MAKE
generally, 9–100—9–101
hearsay information, 9–102—9–103
SUICIDE
medical practitioners, and,
12–236—12–237
SUITABILITY
financial practitioners, and, 13–057
SUPERVISION OF CONSTRUCTION WORKS
clerk of works, role of, 8–246—8–247
confidence in contractor, 8–244
design and specification, 8–216
intentional defects, 8–245
introduction, 8–238—8–239
scope of duty, 8–240—8–241
stages of work, at, 8–242—8–243
working methods, 8–248—8–251
SUPERVISORY BODIES
duty of care, and, 2–086
SUPPORT OF SOFTWARE
IT professionals, and, 17–044

SUPPLY OF SOFTWARE
    bespoke, 17–004
    goods, as, 17–007—17–009
    implied warranties, 17–013
    modified standard, 17–004
    off-the-shelf, 17–002—17–003
    services, as, 17–008—17–012
SURVEYS FOR LENDERS
    generally, 9–030—9–031
SURVEYORS
    and see CONSTRUCTION PROFESSIONALS
    Appraisal and Valuation Manual
        effect, 9–024—9–025
        generally, 9–023
    "ball-park" figures, 9–038
    basis of liability
        Building Societies Ombudsman
            scheme, under, 9–017—9–018
        concurrent liability, 9–010
        contributory negligence, 9–011
        defective premises, 9–012
        Financial Services Act, under, 9–016
        individuals, of, 9–014
        introduction, 9–007—9–008
        limitation, 9–009
        listing particulars, for, 9–015
        misdescription of property, 9–013
    building societies, duties to
        generally, 9–029—9–031
        surveys for lenders, 9–030—9–031
    Building Societies Ombudsman
        scheme, 9–017—9–018
    camouflaged defects, 9–095
    carry out instructions, failure to,
        9–077—9–078
    causation
        generally, 9–120
        mortgage indemnity guarantees,
            9–122
        novus actus interveniens,
            9–123—9–124
        reliance, 9–121
    company particulars, and, 9–015
    concurrent duties, 9–032
    concurrent liability
        generally, 9–037
        introduction, 9–010
    conditions of engagement
        generally, 9–026
        unfair terms, 9–027—9–028
    contractual duties
        Appraisal and Valuation Manual,
            9–023—9–025
        building societies, to, 9–029—9–031
        conditions of engagement, 9–026
        introduction, 9–019—9–020

SURVEYORS—cont.
    contractual duties—cont.
        Practice Statements, 9–022—9–025
        reasonable expectations test, 9–021
        unfair terms, 9–027—9–028
    contributory negligence by lender
        evaluation, 9–168—9–172
        generally, 9–166—9–167
        introduction, 9–011
    cracks, 9–093—9–094
    damages
        causation, 9–120—9–124
        establishment of loss, 9–112
        foreseeability, 9–125—9–127
        introduction, 9–110—9–111
        loss within scope of duty,
            9–113—9–118
        measure, 9–128—9–194
        remoteness, 9–119—9–127
    date of cause of action, and
        mortgagees, by, 5–036
        purchasers, by, 5–035
    defective premises, 9–012
    definition of extent of service, 9–073
    discomfort, damages for
        examples, 9–189
        generally, 9–181—9–185
        injury to health, 9–186—9–187
        quantum, 9–188
    double jeopardy, and, 9–051
    dry rot, 9–091
    duties
        client, to, 9–019—9–0
        scope, 9–008
        third parties, to, 9–033
    duties to client
        contract, under, 9–019—9–031
        tort, in, 9–032
    duties to purchaser of property
        Smith v. Bush, 9–046—9–051
        Yianni, 9–043—9–045
    duties to third parties
        general principles, 9–033
        Hedley Byrne, 9–034—9–038
        knowledge of reliance,
            9–039—9–042
        purchaser of property, 9–043—9–051
    economic loss, 9–034—9–035
    estimated realisation price, 9–023
    exclusion of liability
        commercial property, 9–071
        definition of extent of service, and,
            9–073
        introduction, 9–063
        residential property, 9–064—9–070
        Scotland, in, 9–072

SURVEYORS—*cont.*
 expert witnesses, as, 9–006
 failure to carry out instructions,
  9–077—9–078
 failure to inspect properly
  introduction, 9–082
  limited survey, 9–097
  observation, 9–090—9–096
  particular parts, 9–083
  relevance of type of survey,
   9–097—9–09
  uncovering and opening up,
   9–084—9–089
 failure to make proper appraisal,
  9–104—9–106
 failure to make sufficient inquiries
  generally, 9–100—9–101
  hearsay information, 9–102—9–103
 failure to observe
  camouflaged defects, 9–095
  cracks, 9–093—9–094
  dry rot, 9–091
  introduction, 9–090
  roof, 9–092
  subsidence, 9–093—9–094
  totality of unnoticed defects, 9–096
  woodworm, 9–091
 failure to open up, 9–084—9–089
 failure to recognise defect, 9–099
 failure to uncover, 9–084—9–089
 failure to warn of defect,
  9–108—9–109
 Financial Services Act, and, 9–016
 foreseeability of damage,
  9–125—9–127
 fraud, 9–033
 functions, 9–004—9–005
 inadequate report
  failure to warn of defect,
   9–108—9–109
  generally, 9–107
 incidental expenses, 9–190—9–194
 inconvenience, damages for
  examples, 9–189
  generally, 9–181—9–185
  injury to health, 9–186—9–187
  quantum, 9–188
 insufficient knowledge or experience,
  9–079—9–081
 introduction, 9–001
 knowledge of reliance, 9–039—9–042
 liability
  basis, 9–007—9–018
  breach of duty, for, 9–075
  individuals, of, 9–014

SURVEYORS—*cont.*
 liability for breach of duty
  failure to carry out instructions,
   9–077—9–078
  failure to inspect properly,
   9–082—9–098
  failure to make proper appraisal,
   9–104—9–106
  failure to make sufficient inquiries,
   9–100—9–103
  failure to recognise, 9–099
  inadequate report, 9–107—9–109
  insufficient knowledge or experience,
   9–079—9–081
  introduction, 9–075—9–076
 limitation of liability
  commercial property, 9–071
  definition of extent of service, and,
   9–073
  introduction, 9–063
  residential property, 9–064—9–070
  Scotland, in, 9–072
 limitation period
  generally, 9–009
  misdescription of property, 9–013
 listing particulars, 9–015
 market value, 9–023
 measure of damages
  discomfort, 9–181—9–189
  incidental expenses, 9–190—9–194
  inconvenient, 9–181—9–189
  introduction, 9–128—9–129
  negligent survey for lender,
   9–150—9–174
  negligent survey for purchaser who
   completes, 9–130—9–148
  negligent survey for purchaser who
   withdraws, 9–149
  overvaluation for vendor, 9–175
  rent review, 9–179—9–180
  undervaluation for vendor,
   9–176—9–177
  warranty of valuation, 9–178
 misdescription of property, 9–013
 mortgage indemnity guarantees, 9–122
 mutual valuer, 9–074
 negligent survey for lender
  assessment of total loss,
   9–151—9–154
  "cap" theory, 9–159—9–160
  contribution from defaulting
   borrower, 9–173
  contributory negligence,
   9–166—9–172
  interest on damages, 9–162
  introduction, 9–150

SURVEYORS—*cont.*
  negligent survey for lender—*cont.*
    joint responsibility, 9–173—9–174
    loss within scope of duty,
      9–155—9–161
    "measurable, relevant loss", 9–161
    mortgagor's covenants to repay,
      9–163—9–165
    "no transaction/successful
      transaction" cases,
      9–157—9–158
  negligent survey for purchaser who
    completes
    collateral benefits, 9–148
    cost of repairs, 9–141—9–145
    extraction costs, 9–146—9–147
    formulation of measure,
      9–135—9–137
    generally, 9–130—9–134
    nature of loss, 9–138—9–139
    other decisions, 9–140
    repair cost, 9–141—9–145
  negligent survey for purchaser who
    withdraws, 9–149
  novus actus interveniens,
    9–123—9–124
  observe, failure to
    camouflaged defects, 9–095
    cracks, 9–093—9–094
    dry rot, 9–091
    introduction, 9–090
    roof, 9–092
    subsidence, 9–093—9–094
    totality of unnoticed defects, 9–096
    woodworm, 9–091
  open market value, 9–023
  open up, failure to, 9–084—9–089
  overvaluation for vendor, 9–175
  Practice Statements
    effect, 9–024—9–025
    generally, 9–022
  proper inspection, failure to make
    introduction, 9–082
    limited survey, 9–097
    observation, 9–090—9–096
    particular parts, 9–083
    relevance of type of survey,
      9–097—9–09
    uncovering and opening up,
      9–084—9–089
  qualifications, 9–003
  quantity surveyors
    and see QUANTITY SURVEYORS
    functions, 9–004
  recognise defect, failure to, 9–099
  regulation, 9–002

SURVEYORS—*cont.*
  remoteness of damage
    causation, 9–120—9–124
    foreseeability, 9–125—9–127
    introduction, 9–119
  rent review, 9–179—9–180
  restriction of liability
    commercial property, 9–071
    definition of extent of service, and,
      9–073
    introduction, 9–063
    residential property, 9–064—9–070
    Scotland, in, 9–072
  roof, 9–092
  standard conditions of engagement
    generally, 9–026
    unfair terms, 9–027—9–028
  standard of care and skill
    general practice and knowledge,
      9–054—9–057
    keeping up to date, 9–056
    margin of error, 9–058—9–061
    new developments, 9–056
    onus of proof, 9–062
    "reasonably skilled", 9–052—9–053
    relevance of the "bracket",
      9–059—9–061
    relevance of type of service, 9–057
  subsidence, 9–093—9–094
  sufficient inquiries, failure to make
    generally, 9–100—9–101
    hearsay information, 9–102—9–103
  surveys for lenders, 9–030—9–031
  uncover, failure to, 9–084—9–089
  undervaluation for vendor,
    9–176—9–177
  unfair terms, 9–027—9–028
  warn of defect, failure to,
    9–108—9–109
  warranty of valuation, 9–178
  woodworm, 9–091
SUSPICIOUS CIRCUMSTANCES
  solicitors, and, 10–195
SWITCHING
  financial practitioners, and, 13–063
SYSTEMS ADVICE
  IT professionals, and, 17–057—17–058

TAX ADVICE BY ACCOUNTANTS
  generally, 15–119
  heads of damage, 15–143
TAX RETURNS BY ACCOUNTANTS
  generally, 15–118
  heads of damage, 15–143—15–144

TECHNOLOGY AND CONSTRUCTION COURT
construction professionals, and, 8–010
TENDER PROCESS
construction professionals, and,
8–222—8–224
TERMS OF CONTRACT, ADVICE ON
construction professionals, an,
8–225—8–227
TESTING OF SOFTWARE
common law duty, 17–051
generally, 17–036—17–037
THIRD PARTIES, DUTIES TO
accountants, and
and see below
Caparo, 15–053—15–061
categories of advisee,
15–073—15–086
Contracts (Rights against Third
Parties) Act 1999, 15–088
Human Rights Act 1998, 15–089
overview, 15–045—15–052
policy considerations, 15–087
relevant factors, 15–062—15–072
barristers, and
adversary of lay client, 11–007
associates of lay client, 11–006
construction professionals, and
and see below
collateral warranties, 8–064—8–065
common law, at, 8–069—8–131
statute, under, 8–066—8–068
IT professionals, and
economic loss, 17–070—17–071
introduction, 17–061
personal injury, 17–062—17–066
product liability, 17–072—17–077
property damage, 17–067—17–069
Lloyd's agents, and, 16–016—16–019
patent agents, and, 18–009
solicitors, and
and see below
adversary in litigation,
10–055—10–064
beneficiaries without reliance,
10–047—10–054
fraud, 10–076
generally, 10–040—10–046
undertakings, 10–065—10–074
warranty of authority, 10–075
surveyors, and
general principles, 9–033
Hedley Byrne, 9–034—9–038
knowledge of reliance,
9–039—9–042
purchaser of property, 9–043—9–051
trade mark attorney, and, 18–009

THIRD PARTIES, DUTIES TO (ACCOUNTANTS)
advisee
categories, 15–073—15–086
knowledge, 15–069
relationship with third party,
15–066—15–067
reliance, 15–070—15–071
size of class, 15–068
Caparo
background, 15–053—15–055
facts of case, 15–056—15–061
categories of advisee
bodies liable to compensate,
15–084—15–085
creditors, 15–082—15–083
directors, 15–081
existing shareholders,
15–074—15–075
group companies, 15–080
introduction, 15–073
others, 15–086
potential investors, 15–076—15–079
Contracts (Rights against Third Parties)
Act 1999, under, 15–088
double recovery, 15–087
Human Rights Act 1998, under,
15–089
loss of a chance, 15–087
overview
basic rule, 15–045—15–046
different approaches,
15–047—15–52
policy considerations, 15–087
relevant factors
advisee/third party relationship,
15–066—15–067
generally, 15–062—15–063
knowledge of adviser, 15–069
purpose for which statement
communicated, 15–065
purpose for which statement made,
15–064
reliance by advisee,
15–070—15–071
size of class of advisees, 15–068
THIRD PARTIES, DUTIES TO (CONSTRUCTION
PROFESSIONALS)
collateral warranties, 8–064—8–065
common law, at
Commonwealth cases,
8–112—8–124
definition of type of loss,
8–070—8–079
economic loss, 8–086—8–111
introduction, 8–069
personal injury, 8–080—8–081

THIRD PARTIES, DUTIES TO (CONSTRUCTION
   PROFESSIONALS)—*cont.*
common law, at—*cont.*
   property damage, 8–082—8–085
   scope of duty, 8–125—8–131
Commonwealth cases
   Australia, 8–119—8–121
   Canada, 8–112—8–118
   Hong Kong, 8–124
   New Zealand, 8–122—8–123
contractors, 8–105—8–111
Contracts (Rights of Third Parties) Act
   1999, under, 8–067—8–068
economic loss
   complex structure theory,
      8–091—8–096
   contractors, 8–105—8–111
   exceptions to general rule,
      8–090—8–111
   expenditure necessary to avoid
      liability, 8–097
   general rule, 8–086—8–089
   Hedley Byrne principle,
      8–098—8–103
   subsequent purchasers, 8–104
   statute, under, 8–066—8–068
   subsequent purchasers, 8–104
THIRD PARTIES, DUTIES TO (SOLICITORS)
adversary
   contentious business,
      10–062—10–064
   generally, 10–055
   non-contentious business,
      10–056—10–061
adversary in contentious business
   criminal cases, 10–064
   exceptions to general rule,
      10–063—10–064
   general rule, 10–062
adversary in non-contentious business
   Commonwealth cases, 10–061
   exceptions to general rule,
      10–058—10–060
   general rule, 10–056—10–057
   reliance on solicitor's
      representations,
      10–058—10–059
associate of client, 10–042
beneficiaries without reliance
   background, 10–047—10–048
   conflict of interest, 10–051
   double recovery, 10–052
   identity of beneficiary, 10–050
   non-will cases, 10–053
   other jurisdictions, in, 10–054
   scope of principle, 10–049

THIRD PARTIES, DUTIES TO
   (SOLICITORS)—*cont.*
fraud, 10–076
generally, 10–040—10–046
no reliance, where
   Commonwealth cases, 10–045
   generally, 10–044
   solicitor as officer of court, 10–046
reliance
   non-client establishing duty, by,
      10–042
   non-client without duty, by, 10–043
   without retainer, 10–041
undertakings
   and see UNDERTAKINGS
   construction, 10–068
   enforcement, 10–069—10–074
   examples, 10–067
   generally, 10–066
   introduction, 10–065
   warranty of authority, 10–075
THIRD PARTIES, LIABILITY TO
background, 2–110
exclusion of liability, and
   comment, 5–009
   introduction, 5–007
   mortgage applications, in, 5–008
heads of damage, and
   construction professionals, 8–307
   solicitor, 10–301—10–302
intended beneficiaries, 2–114
introduction, 2–109
persons under duty, 2–111
third parties entitled to benefit, 2–112
transactions subject to duty, 2–113
"TIME-BOMBS"
IT professionals, and, 17–059—17–060
TORT, DUTIES IN
accountants, and, 15–037
barristers, and, 11–005
construction professionals, and
   and see below
   common law, at, 8–049—8–063
   introduction, 8–039
   statute, under, 8–040—8–048
financial practitioners, and
   deceit, 13–099—13–104
   employee, of, 13–113
   employer, of, 13–112
   fraudulent misrepresentation,
      13–099—13–104
   misfeasance in public office, 13–105
   negligence, 13–106—13–107
   pension beneficiaries,
      13–109—13–111
   principal, of, 13–112

TORT, DUTIES IN—*cont.*
  financial practitioners, and—*cont.*
    prospectus cases, 13–108
    regulators, of, 13–114
  insurance brokers, and,
      14–014—14–016
  IT professionals, and
    and see below
    Consumer Protection Act 1987,
        under, 17–072—17–077
    economic loss, 17–070—17–071
    introduction, 17–061
    personal injury, 17–062—17–066
    property damage, 17–067—17–069
  Lloyd's agents, and, 16–012—16–014
  medical practitioners, and
    communication of distressing
        information, 12–022—12–023
    economic loss, 12–024—12–027
    introduction, 12–015—12–018
    rescuer cases, 12–019—12–021
  solicitors, and
    background, 10–013
    Commonwealth position, 10–015
    generally, 10–014
  surveyors, and, 9–032
TORT, DUTIES IN (CONSTRUCTION
    PROFESSIONALS)
  common law, at
    concurrent duty of care,
        8–057—8–062
    concurrent liability, 8–054
    contribution, 8–056
    contributory negligence, 8–055
    fiduciary duty, 8–063
    introduction, 8–049—8–053
  Construction (Design & Management)
      Regulations 1994, under, 8–048
  contribution, and, 8–056
  contributory negligence, and, 8–055
  date of knowledge, and, 8–054
  Defective Premises Act, under,
      8–041—8–047
  economic loss, and, 8–049
  introduction, 8–039
  latent damage, and, 8–054
  limitation period, and, 8–054
  statute, under, 8–040
TORT, DUTIES IN (IT PROFESSIONALS)
  Consumer Protection Act 1987, under
    defences, 17–076—17–077
    generally, 17–072—17–073
    relevant product, 17–074—17–075
    "safety-critical" information, 17–078
  economic loss, 17–070—17–071
  introduction, 17–061

TORT, DUTIES IN (IT
    PROFESSIONALS)—*cont.*
  personal injury, 17–062—17–066
  property damage, 17–067—17–069
TORT, LIMITATION IN
  and see LIMITATION IN TORT
  concealment, 5–070—5–078
  date of cause of action, 5–016—5–048
  fraud, 5–070—5–078
  latent damage, and, 5–049—5–055
  period of limitation, 5–010—5–013
  personal injuries and death,
      5–056—5–069
TORTIOUS LIABILITY
  applicable situations
    elements, 2–019—2–021
    examples, 2–018
    introduction, 2–017
  breach of duty of care, 2–015
  conditions
    breach of duty of care, 2–015
    damage suffered by claimant, 2–016
    duty of care, 2–014
    introduction, 2–013
  damage suffered by claimant, 2–016
  duty of care
    and see DUTY OF CARE
    applicable situations, 2–017—2–021
    concurrent liability, 2–100—2–108
    introduction, 2–014
    liability to third parties,
        2–109—2–115
    particular situations, 2–079—2–099
    theoretical basis, 2–022—2–078
  fiduciary obligations, and, 2–128
  line of reasoning, 2–019—2–020
  reasonable care and skill,
      2–116—2–124
  wasted costs order, 18–013
TRADE MARK ATTORNEY
  causation, 18–020—18–021
  Codes of Conduct, 18–011
  damages
    causation, 18–020—18–021
    remoteness, 18–022
  duties
    client, to, 18–008
    third parties, to, 18–009
  function, 18–006
  immunity from suit, 18–012
  introduction, 18–001
  liability for breach of duty
    business advice, 18–018
    generally, 18–015
    giving of advice, 18–018
    instruction of foreign agents, 18–019

TRADE MARK ATTORNEY—*cont.*
liability for breach of duty—*cont.*
knowledge of law, 18–016
taking instructions, 18–017
liability for costs, 18–013
loss of a chance, 18–030—18–021
privilege, 18–014
regulation, 18–007
remoteness, 18–022
standard of skill and care
Codes of Conduct, 18–011
generally, 18–010
wasted costs order, 18–013
TRAINING OF STAFF ON COMPUTERS
common law duty, 17–051
generally, 17–045
TREATMENT, CONSENT TO
capacity to, 12–135—12–139
children, by, 12–148
human rights, and, 7–059
informed, 12–130—12–134
introduction, 12–124—12–125
limits on, 12–126—12–127
mentally disordered patients, by,
12–140—12–147
voluntary, 12–128—12–129
TREATMENT, RIGHT TO
allocation of resources, 7–051—7–052
blanket bans, 7–053
hospital waiting lists, 7–054
introduction, 7–050
TRUST AND CONFIDENCE
undue influence, and, 2–145
TRUST DUTIES
solicitors, and
constructive trusts, 10–036
dishonesty, 10–039
express trusts, 10–034
implied trusts, 10–034
knowing assistance, 10–038
knowing receipts, 10–037
mortgage lenders, 10–035
TRUST PROPERTY, ACTIONS CONCERNING
limitation in equity, and,
5–082—5–088
TURNKEY CONTRACTS
construction works, and, 8–016—8–017

UNAUTHORISED PROFITS
fiduciary obligations, and 2–141
UNBORN CHILDREN
medical practitioners, and, 12–055
UNCOVER, FAILURE TO
surveyors, and, 9–084—9–089

UNDERPAYMENT
construction professionals, and, 8–304
UNDERSTANDING OF RISK
financial practitioners, and, 13–058
UNDERTAKINGS BY SOLICITOR
construction, 10–068
enforcement
delay, and, 10–071
discretion, 10–070
generally, 10–069
impossibility, and, 10–072
methods, 10–074
practice, 10–073
examples, 10–067
generally, 10–066
introduction, 10–065
UNDERVALUATION FOR VENDOR
surveyors, and, 9–176—9–177
UNDUE INFLUENCE
classification
actual undue influence, 2–143
introduction, 2–142
relationships involving trust and
confidence, 2–145
relationships presumed to give rise,
2–144
introduction, 2–006
medical practitioners, and, 12–029
rebutting the presumption, 2–146
solicitors, and
conveyancing, 10–205
generally, 10–017
UNEQUAL TRANSACTIONS
solicitors, and, 10–173
UNFAIR TERMS
and see EXCLUSION OF LIABILITY
generally, 5–003—5–005
surveyors, and, 9–027—9–028
UNJUSTIFIED DEPARTURE FROM PLAN
Lloyd's agents, and, 16–037
UNLISTED SECURITIES
financial practitioners, and, 13–084
UNMERITORIOUS CLAIMS
solicitors, and, 10–179
UNNECESSARY RISKS
solicitors, and, 10–098
UNREASONABLE DELAY
laches, and, 5–103—5–105
UNREINSURED LOSSES
insurance brokers, and, 14–120
UNSAFE COMMON PRACTICE
solicitors, and, 10–089
UNWANTED DISABLED CHILD, CLAIMS IN
RESPECT OF
economic loss, 12–303—12–305

Unwanted disabled child, claims in
    respect of—*cont.*
  general damages
    unwanted pregnancy,
      12–292—12–294
    wanted pregnancy, 12–296—12–298
  human rights, 12–301
  loss of amenity, 12–299—12–300
User operation manual
  IT professionals, and, 17–046

Valuation of businesses
  accountants, and, 15–117
Valuation of land
  surveyors, and, 9–001
Valuation of lost patent
  patent agents, and, 18–023
Vicarious liability
  duty of care, and, 2–085
  hospitals, and, 12–152—12–154
  solicitors, and, 10–146—10–147
Voluntary consent
  consent to treatment, and,
    12–128—12–129

Want of prosecution, action dismissed
    for
  claims against solicitor, and, 5–043
Warn of defect, failure to
  surveyors, and, 9–108—9–109
Warning for patient's protection
  medical practitioners, and, 12–222
Warranty of authority
  solicitor's duty, and, 10–075
Warranty of valuation
  surveyors, and, 9–178
Wasted costs order
  barristers, and
    and see below
    guidelines, 11–027
    introduction, 11–026
    misjudgements, 11–029—11–030
    procedure, 11–028
  patent agents, and, 18–013
  solicitors, and
    background, 10–126
    guidelines, 10–129—10–140
    introduction, 10–125
    lawyer's position, 10–131
    present rule, 10–127
    recipient, 10–128
  trade mark attorney, and, 18–013
Wasted costs order (barristers)
  guidelines, 11–027

Wasted costs order (barristers)—*cont.*
  introduction, 11–026
  misjudgements as to strength of case
    examples of grant of order,
      11–031—11–032
    examples of refusal of order, 11–030
    introduction, 11–029
  misjudgements on timing,
    11–033—11–034
  other examples, 11–035
  procedure, 11–028
Wasted costs order (solicitors)
  background, 10–126
  causation, 10–134
  guidelines
    abuse of process, 10–137
    causal link, 10–134
    improper, unreasonable or negligent,
      10–130
    introduction, 10–129
    hopeless litigation, 10–135—10–136
    legal aid lawyers, 10–138
    other errors, 10–140
    procedural error, 10–139
  introduction, 10–125
  lawyer's position, 10–131
  present rule, 10–127
  practice and procedure,
    10–132—10–133
  recipient, 10–128
Wasted expenditure
  construction professionals, and, 8–302
  solicitors, and
    examples, 10–306
    general rule, 10–304—10–305
    later solicitors' costs, 10–308
    original solicitors' costs, 10–307
Whistle-blowing
  accountants, and, 15–030
Wills, preparation of
  attestation, 10–222
  giving advice, 10–220
  introduction, 10–218
  knowledge of law, 10–222
  other errors, 10–224
  prompt actions, 10–223
  scope of duty, 10–221
  taking instructions, 10–219
Withdrawal of treatment
  human rights, and, 7–055—7–058
Woodworm
  surveyors, and, 9–091
Working beyond one's competence
  medical practitioners, and, 12–078
Writing of software
  common law duty, 17–051

WRITING OF SOFTWARE—*cont.*
generally, 17–014—17–022
WRONG DIAGNOSIS
generally, 12–177—12–184
more serious condition, 12–185
WRONGFUL BIRTH/CONCEPTION, CLAIMS IN
RESPECT OF
economic loss, 12–303—12–305
general damages
unwanted pregnancy,
12–292—12–294

WRONGFUL BIRTH/CONCEPTION, CLAIMS IN
RESPECT OF—*cont.*
general damages—*cont.*
wanted pregnancy, 12–296—12–298
human rights, 12–301
loss of amenity, 12–299—12–300
WRONGFUL INTERFERENCE WITH CONTRACT
construction professionals, and, 8–132
"WRONGFUL LIFE" CASES
medical practitioners, and, 12–056